Hoover's Handbook of

World
Business
2021

10 9 8 7 6 5 4 3 2 1

Publishers Cataloging-in-Publication Data

Hoover's Handbook of World Business 2021

    Includes indexes.

    ISBN 978-1-64972-057-3

    ISSN 1055-7199

    1. Business enterprises — Directories. 2. Corporations — Directories.

HF3010 338.7

U.S. AND WORLD BOOK SALES

Mergent Inc.

580 Kingsley Park Drive
Fort Mill, SC
29715
Phone: 704-559-6961
e-mail: skardon@ftserussell.com
Web: www.mergentbusinesspress.com

Mergent Inc.

Executive Managing Director: John Pedernales

Publisher and Managing Director of Print Products: Thomas Wecera

Director of Print Products: Charlot Volny

Quality Assurance Editor: Wayne Arnold

Production Research Assistant: Davie Christna

Data Manager: Jason Horvat

MERGENT CUSTOMER SERVICE-PRINT
Support and Fulfillment Manager: Thomas Wecera 212-413-7726

ABOUT MERGENT, INC.

For over 100 years, Mergent, Inc. has been a leading provider of business and financial information on public and private companies globally. Mergent is known to be a trusted partner to corporate and financial institutions, as well as to academic and public libraries. Today we continue to build on a century of experience by transforming data into knowledge and combining our expertise with the latest technology to create new global data and analytical solutions for our clients. With advanced data collection services, cloud-based applications, desktop analytics and print products, Mergent and its subsidiaries provide solutions from top down economic and demographic information, to detailed equity and debt fundamental analysis. We incorporate value added tools such as quantitative Smart Beta equity research and tools for portfolio building and measurement. Based in the U.S., Mergent maintains a strong global presence, with offices in New York, Charlotte, San Diego, London, Tokyo, Kuching and Melbourne. Mergent, Inc. is a member of the London Stock Exchange plc group of companies. The Mergent business forms part of LSEG's Information Services Division, which includes FTSE Russell, a global leader in indexes.

Abbreviations

AB – Aktiebolag (Swedish)*
ADR – American Depositary Receipts
AG – Aktiengesellschaft (German)*
AFL-CIO – American Federation of Labor and Congress of Industrial Organizations
AMEX – American Stock Exchange
A/S – Aktieselskab (Danish)*
ASA – Allmenne Aksjeselskaper (Norwegian)*
ATM – asynchronous transfer mode; automated teller machine
CAD/CAM – computer-aided design/computer-aided manufacturing
CASE – computer-aided software engineering
CD-ROM – compact disc – read-only memory
CEO – chief executive officer
CFO – chief financial officer
CMOS – complementary metal-oxide semiconductor
COMECON – Council for Mutual Economic Assistance
COO – chief operating officer
DAT – digital audio tape
DOD – Department of Defense
DOE – Department of Energy
DOT – Department of Transportation
DRAM – dynamic random-access memory
DVD – digital versatile disc/digital video disc
EC – European Community
EPA – Environmental Protection Agency
EPS – earnings per share
EU – European Union
EVP – executive vice president
FCC – Federal Communications Commission

FDA – Food and Drug Administration
FDIC – Federal Deposit Insurance Corporation
FTC – Federal Trade Commission
GATT – General Agreement on Tariffs and Trade
GmbH – Gesellschaft mit beschränkter Haftung (German)*
GNP – gross national product
HDTV – high-definition television
HMO – health maintenance organization
HR – human resources
HTML – hypertext markup language
ICC – Interstate Commerce Commission
IMF – International Monetary Fund
IPO – initial public offering
IRS – Internal Revenue Service
KGaA – Kommanditgesellschaft auf Aktien (German)*
LAN – local-area network
LBO – leveraged buyout
LNG – liquefied natural gas
LP – limited partnership
Ltd. – Limited
MFN – Most Favored Nation
MITI – Ministry of International Trade and Industry (Japan)
NAFTA – North American Free Trade Agreement
Nasdaq – National Association of Securities Dealers Automated Quotations
NATO – North Atlantic Treaty Organization
NV – Naamlose Vennootschap (Dutch)*
NYSE – New York Stock Exchange
OAO – open joint stock company (Russian)

OAS – Organization of American States
OECD – Organization for Economic Cooperation and Development
OEM – original equipment manufacturer
OOO – limited liability company (Russian)
OPEC – Organization of Petroleum Exporting Countries
OS – operating system
OTC – over-the-counter
P/E – price-to-earnings ratio
PLC – public limited company (UK)*
RAM – random-access memory
R&D – research and development
RISC – reduced instruction set computer
ROA – return on assets
ROI – return on investment
SA – Société Anonyme (French)*; Sociedad(e) Anónima (Spanish and Portuguese)*
SA de CV – Sociedad Anónima de Capital Variable (Spanish)*
SEC – Securities and Exchange Commission
SEVP – senior executive vice president
SIC – Standard Industrial Classification
SpA – Società per Azioni (Italian)*
SPARC – scalable processor architecture
SVP – senior vice president
VAR – value-added reseller
VAT – value-added tax
VC – venture capitalist
VP – vice president
WAN – wide-area network
WWW – World Wide Web
ZAO – closed joint stock company (Russian)

* These abbreviations are used in companies' names to convey that the companies are limited liability enterprises; the meanings are usually the equivalent of *corporation* or *incorporated*.

Contents

List of Lists

HOOVER'S RANKINGS

Companies Profiled

Companies Profiled

Companies Profiled

Companies Profiled (continued)

About Hoover's Handbook of World Business 2021

This edition of *Hoover's Handbook of World Business* is focused on its mission of providing you with premier coverage of the global business scene. Featuring 300 of the world's most influential companies based outside of the United States, this book is one of the most complete sources of in-depth information on large, non-US-based business enterprises available anywhere.

Hoover's Handbook of World Business is one of our four-title series of handbooks that covers, literally, the world of business. The series is available as an indexed set, and also includes *Hoover's Handbook of American Business*, *Hoover's Handbook of Private Companies*, and *Hoover's Handbook of Emerging Companies*. This series brings you information on the biggest, fastest-growing, and most influential enterprises in the world.

HOOVER'S ONLINE FOR BUSINESS NEEDS

In addition to Hoover's widely used MasterList and Handbooks series, comprehensive coverage of more than 40,000 business enterprises is available in electronic format on our Web site at www.hoovers.com. Our goal is to provide our customers the fastest path to business with insight and actionable information about companies, industries, and key decision makers, along with the powerful tools to find and connect to the right people to get business done. Hoover's has partnered with other prestigious business information and service providers to bring you all the right business information, services, and links in one place.

We welcome the recognition we have received as the premier provider of high-quality company information — online, electronically, and in print — and continue to look for ways to make our products more available and more useful to you.

We believe that anyone who buys from, sells to, invests in, lends to, competes with, interviews with, or works for a company should know all there is to know about that enterprise. Taken together, this book and the other Hoover's products and resources represent the most complete source of basic corporate information readily available to the general public.

HOW TO USE THIS BOOK

This book has four sections:

1. "Using Hoover's Handbooks" describes the contents of our profiles and explains the ways in which we gather and compile our data.

2. "A List-Lover's Compendium" contains lists of the largest, fastest-growing, and most valuable companies of global importance.

3. The company profiles section makes up the largest and most important part of the book — 300 profiles of major business enterprises, arranged alphabetically.

4. Three indexes complete the book. The first sorts companies by industry groups, the second by headquarters location. The third index is a list of all the executives found in the Executives section of each company profile.

Using Hoover's Handbooks

SELECTION OF THE COMPANIES PROFILED

The 300 profiles in this book include a variety of international enterprises, ranging from some of the largest publicly traded companies in the world — Daimler AG, for example — to Malaysia's largest and oldest conglomerate, Sime Darby Berhad. It also includes many private businesses, such as Bertelsmann AG and LEGO, as well as a selection of government-owned entities, such as Mexico's Petróleos Mexicanos. The companies selected represent a cross-section of the largest, most influential, and most interesting companies based outside the United States.

In selecting these companies, we followed several basic criteria. We started with the global giants, including Toyota and Royal Dutch Shell, and then looked at companies with substantial activity in the US, such as Vivendi and Diageo. We also included companies that dominate their industries (e.g., AB Electrolux, the world's #1 producer of household appliances), as well as representative companies from around the world (an Indian conglomerate, Tata; two firms from Finland, Nokia and Stora Enso Oyj; and two companies from Russia, OAO Gazprom and OAO LUKOIL). Companies that weren't necessarily global powerhouses but that had a high profile with consumers (e.g., IKEA) or had interesting stories (Virgin Group) were included. Finally, because of their truly global reach, we added the Big Four accounting firms (even though they are headquartered or co-headquartered in the US).

ORGANIZATION

The profiles are presented in alphabetical order. You will find the commonly used name of the enterprise at the beginning of the profile; the full, legal name is found in the Locations section. For some companies, primarily Japanese, the commonly translated English name differs from the actual legal name of the company, so both are provided. (The legal name of Nippon Steel Corporation is Shin Nippon Seitetsu Kabushiki Kaisha.) If a company name starts with a person's first name (e.g., George Weston Limited), it is alphabetized under the first name. We've also tried to alphabetize companies where you would expect to find them — for example, Deutsche Lufthansa is in the L's and Grupo Televisa can be found under T.

The annual financial information contained in the profiles is current through fiscal year-ends occurring as late as June 2016. We have included certain nonfinancial developments, such as officer changes, through September 2016.

OVERVIEW

In the first section of the profile, we have tried to give a thumbnail description of the company and what it does. The description will usually include information on the company's strategy, reputation, and ownership. We recommend that you read this section first.

HISTORY

This extended section, which is present for most companies, reflects our belief that every enterprise is the sum of its history and that you have to know where you came from in order to know where you are going. While some companies have limited historical awareness, we think the vast majority of the enterprises in this book have colorful backgrounds. We have tried to focus on the people who made the enterprises what they are today. We have found these histories to be full of twists and ironies; they make fascinating reading.

EXECUTIVES

Here we list the names of the people who run the company, insofar as space allows. We have shown age and pay information where available, although most non-US companies are not required to report the level of detail revealed in the US.

Although companies are free to structure their management titles any way they please, most modern corporations follow standard practices. The ultimate power in any corporation lies with the shareholders, who elect a board of directors, usually including officers or "insiders," as well as individuals from outside the company. The chief officer, the person on whose desk the buck stops, is usually called the chief executive officer (CEO) in the US. In other countries, practices vary widely. In the UK, traditionally, the Managing Director performs the functions of the CEO without the title, although the use of the term

CEO is on the rise there. In Germany it is customary to have two boards of directors: a managing board populated by the top executives of the company and a higher-level supervisory board consisting of outsiders.

As corporate management has become more complex, it is common for the CEO to have a "right-hand person" who oversees the day-to-day operations of the company, allowing the CEO plenty of time to focus on strategy and long-term issues. This right-hand person is usually designated the chief operating officer (COO) and is often the president of the company. In other cases one person is both chairman and president.

We have tried to list each company's most important officers, including the chief financial officer (CFO) and the chief legal officer. For companies with US operations, we have included the names of the US CEO, CFO, and top human resources executive, where available.

The people named in the Executives section are indexed at the back of the book.

The Executives section also includes the name of the company's auditing (accounting) firm, where available.

LOCATIONS

Here we include the company's full legal name and its headquarters, street address, telephone and fax numbers, and Web site, as available. We also list the same information for the US office for each company, if one exists. Telephone numbers of foreign offices are shown using the standardized conventions of international dialing. The back of the book includes an index of companies by headquarters location.

In some cases we have also included information on the geographic distribution of the company's business, including sales and profit data. Note that these profit numbers, like those in the Products/Operations section below, are usually operating or pretax profits rather than net profits. Operating profits are generally those before financing costs (interest income and payments) and before taxes, which are considered costs attributable to the whole company rather than to one division or part of the world. For this reason the net income figures (in the Historical Financials section) are usually much lower, since they are after interest and taxes. Pretax profits are after interest but before taxes.

PRODUCTS/OPERATIONS

This section lists as many of the company's products, services, brand names, divisions, subsidiaries, and joint ventures as we could fit. We have tried to include all its major lines and all familiar brand names. The nature of this section varies by company and the amount of information available. If the company publishes sales and profit information by type of business, we have included it (in US dollars).

COMPETITORS

In this section we have listed enterprises that compete with the profiled company. This feature is included as a quick way to locate similar companies and compare them. Because of the difficulty in identifying companies that only compete in foreign markets, the list of competitors is still weighted to large international companies with a strong US presence.

HISTORICAL FINANCIALS

Here we have tried to present as much data about each enterprise's financial performance as we could compile in the allocated space. Financial data for all companies is presented in US dollars, using the appropriate exchange rate at fiscal year-end.

While the information presented varies somewhat from industry to industry, it is less complete in the case of private companies that do not release data (although we have always tried to provide annual sales and employment). The following information is generally present.

A five-year table, with relevant annualized compound growth rates, covers:

- Sales — fiscal year sales (year-end assets for most financial companies)
- Net income — fiscal year net income (before accounting changes)
- Net profit margin — fiscal year net income as a percent of sales (as a percent of assets for most financial firms)
- Employees — fiscal year-end or average number of employees
- Stock price — the fiscal year close
- P/E — high and low price/earnings ratio
- Earnings per share — fiscal year earnings per share (EPS)
- Dividends per share — fiscal year dividends per share

The information on the number of employees is intended to aid the reader interested in knowing whether a company has a long-term trend of increasing or decreasing employment. As far as we know, we are the only company that publishes this information in print format.

The numbers on the left in each row of the Historical Financials section give the month and the year in which the company's fiscal year actually ends. Thus, a company with a September 30, 2018, year-end is shown as 9/18.

In addition, we have provided in graph form a stock price history for companies that trade on the major US exchanges. The graphs, covering up to five years, show the range of trading between the high and the low price, as well as the closing price for each fiscal year. For public companies that trade on the OTC or Pink Sheets or that do not trade on US exchanges, we graph net income. Generally, for private companies, we have graphed net income, or, if that is unavailable, sales.

Key year-end statistics in this section generally show the financial strength of the enterprise, including:

- Debt ratio (long-term debt as a percent of shareholders' equity)
- Return on equity (net income divided by the average of beginning and ending common shareholders' equity)
- Cash and cash equivalents
- Current ratio (ratio of current assets to current liabilities)
- Total long-term debt (including capital lease obligations)
- Number of shares of common stock outstanding
- Dividend yield (fiscal year dividends per share divided by the fiscal year-end closing stock price)
- Dividend payout (fiscal year dividends divided by fiscal year EPS)
- Market value at fiscal year-end (fiscal year-end closing stock price multiplied by fiscal year-end number of shares outstanding)
- Fiscal year sales for financial institutions.

Per share data has been adjusted for stock splits. The data for public companies with sponsored American Depositary Receipts has been provided to us by Morningstar, Inc. Other public company information was compiled by Hoover's, which takes full responsibility for the content of this section.

In the case of private companies that do not publicly disclose financial information, we usually did not have access to such standardized data. We have gathered estimates of sales and other statistics from numerous sources.

Hoover's Handbook of

World Business

A List-Lover's Compendium

The 100 Largest Global Public Companies by Sales in Hoover's Handbook of World Business 2021

Rank	Company	Sales ($ mil)	Rank	Company	Sales ($ mil)	Rank	Company	Sales ($ mil)
1	Walmart Inc	$523,964	40	Ford Motor Co. (DE)	$127,144	79	Deutsche Telekom AG	$90,417
2	China Petroleum & Chemical C	$426,286	41	PJSC Lukoil	$125,991	80	Enel SpA	$90,188
3	Amazon.com Inc	$386,064	42	Banco Santander SA	$125,750	81	Hitachi, Ltd.	$88,398
4	PetroChina Co Ltd	$358,163	43	Itau Unibanco Holding S.A.	$125,516	82	Legal & General Group PLC (U	$88,195
5	Royal Dutch Shell Plc	$352,106	44	Marathon Petroleum Corp.	$124,813	83	BNP Paribas (France)	$87,744
6	Volkswagen AG	$283,647	45	Prudential Plc	$124,308	84	Facebook Inc	$85,965
7	BP PLC	$282,423	46	PJSC Gazprom	$122,672	85	Reliance Industries Ltd	$85,217
8	Toyota Motor Corp	$275,725	47	Kroger Co (The)	$122,286	86	LVMH Moet Hennessy Louis Vuit	$84,499
9	Apple Inc	$274,515	48	China Railway Group Ltd	$122,285	87	Tesco PLC	$83,354
10	Exxon Mobil Corp	$264,938	49	Stellantis NV	$121,469	88	Carrefour S.A.	$83,244
11	Cementos Bio-Bio S.A. (Chile)	$263,182	50	SAIC Motor Corp Ltd	$121,198	89	JD.com, Inc.	$82,907
12	CVS Health Corp	$256,776	51	Fannie Mae	$120,304	90	Johnson & Johnson	$82,059
13	Berkshire Hathaway Inc	$254,616	52	China Railway Construction Cor	$119,348	91	Manulife Financial Corp	$80,573
14	UnitedHealth Group Inc	$242,155	53	Allianz SE	$118,041	92	ENI S.p.A.	$79,762
15	McKesson Corp	$231,051	54	Bayerische Motoren Werke AG	$117,003	93	China Communicat C Group Ltd	$79,732
16	Glencore PLC	$215,111	55	Bank of America Corp	$113,589	94	Aeon Co Ltd	$79,146
17	Samsung Electronics Co Ltd	$199,548	56	Electricite de France	$112,224	95	Airbus SE	$79,130
18	Daimler AG	$193,952	57	Home Depot Inc	$110,225	96	Grupo Financiero Galicia SA	$79,061
19	AmerisourceBergen Corp.	$189,894	58	Japan Post Holdings Co Ltd	$110,089	97	Target Corp	$78,112
20	Industrial and Commercial Ba	$184,033	59	Nippon Telegraph & Telephone	$109,621	98	Intel Corp	$77,867
21	Alphabet Inc	$182,527	60	Phillips 66	$109,559	99	International Business Machines	$77,147
22	AT&T Inc	$181,193	61	Valero Energy Corp	$108,324	100	Raytheon Technologies Corp	$77,046
23	Hon Hai Precision Industry C	$178,459	62	China Mobile Limited	$107,199			
24	Total SE	$176,249	63	Credit Agricole SA	$105,429			
25	Costco Wholesale Corp	$166,761	64	Anthem Inc	$104,213			
26	Exor NV	$161,403	65	Assicurazioni Generali S.p.A	$104,204			
27	China Construction Bank Corp	$157,301	66	Wells Fargo & Co (New)	$103,915			
28	Cigna Corp (New)	$153,566	67	Federal Reserve System	$103,846			
29	Cardinal Health, Inc.	$152,922	68	Comcast Corp	$103,564			
30	Honda Motor Co Ltd	$150,546	69	Citigroup Inc	$103,449			
31	Mitsubishi Corp	$149,021	70	ITOCHU Corp (Japan)	$101,179			
32	Chevron Corporation	$146,516	71	HSBC Holdings Plc	$101,027			
33	Microsoft Corporation	$143,015	72	Nestle SA	$96,064			
34	JPMorgan Chase & Co	$142,422	73	General Electric Co	$95,214			
35	AXA SA	$140,272	74	CITIC Ltd	$94,189			
36	Walgreens Boots Alliance Inc	$139,537	75	Eneos Holdings Inc	$92,232			
37	Rosneft Oil Co OJSC (Moscow)	$139,403	76	Dell Technologies Inc	$92,154			
38	General Motors Co	$137,237	77	Hyundai Motor Co., Ltd.	$91,586			
39	Verizon Communications Inc	$131,868	78	Nissan Motor Co., Ltd.	$91,007			

SOURCE: MERGENT INC., DATABASE, JANUARY 2021

The 100 Largest Global Public Companies by Income
Hoover's Handbook of World Business 2021

Rank	Company	Net Income ($ mil)	Rank	Company	Net Income ($ mil)	Rank	Company	Net Income ($ mil)
11	Berkshire Hathaway Inc	$81,417	36	Cementos Bio-Bio S.A. (Chile)	$13,104	71	Electricite de France	$8,112
2	Apple Inc	$57,411	37	Nestle SA	$13,043	72	Novartis AG Basel	$8,072
3	Industrial and Commercial Ba	$44,871	38	Procter & Gamble Co (The)	$13,027	73	Rio Tinto Ltd	$8,010
4	Microsoft Corporation	$44,281	39	Taiwan Semiconductor Manufac	$11,822	74	BHP Group Plc	$7,956
5	Alphabet Inc	$40,269	40	Liberty Global plc	$11,521	75	BHP Group Ltd	$7,956
6	China Construction Bank Corp	$37,764	41	Rosneft Oil Co OJSC (Moscow)	$11,376	76	AbbVie Inc	$7,882
7	JPMorgan Chase & Co	$36,431	42	LVMH Moet Hennessy Louis Vuitton	$11,284	77	Nippon Telegraph & Teleph)	$7,879
8	Facebook Inc	$29,146	43	Total SE	$11,267	78	Amgen Inc	$7,842
9	Bank of America Corp	$27,430	44	Home Depot Inc	$11,242	79	British American Tobacco Plc	$7,532
10	Amazon.com Inc	$21,331	45	Cisco Systems Inc	$11,214	80	Grupo Financiero Galicia SA	$7,498
11	Alibaba Group Holding Ltd	$21,266	46	Investor AB	$10,882	81	Stellantis NV	$7,435
12	Ping An Insurance (Group) Co	$21,262	47	Visa Inc	$10,866	82	PepsiCo Inc	$7,314
13	Intel Corp	$20,899	48	Comcast Corp	$10,534	83	HSBC Holdings Plc	$7,293
14	Wells Fargo & Co (New)	$19,549	49	PJSC Lukoil	$10,286	84	Freddie Mac	$7,214
15	Citigroup Inc	$19,401	50	Banco Santander SA	$10,252	85	ConocoPhillips	$7,189
16	PJSC Gazprom	$19,328	51	Petroleo Brasileiro SA	$10,151	86	Philip Morris International Inc	$7,185
17	Verizon Communications Inc	$19,265	52	Oracle Corp	$10,135	87	Novo-Nordisk AS	$6,951
18	Toyota Motor Corp	$19,126	53	Merck & Co Inc	$9,843	88	CITIC Ltd	$6,922
19	Samsung Electronics Co Ltd	$18,625	54	RWE AG	$9,541	89	U.S. Bancorp (DE)	$6,914
20	Pfizer Inc	$16,273	55	BASF SE	$9,455	90	Lockheed Martin Corp	$6,833
21	Itau Unibanco Holding S.A.	$16,250	56	International Business Mach	$9,431	91	American Express Co.	$6,759
22	Royal Dutch Shell Plc	$15,842	57	GlaxoSmithKline Plc	$9,283	92	General Motors Co	$6,732
23	China Mobile Limited	$15,326	58	BNP Paribas (France)	$9,176	93	AIA Group Ltd.	$6,648
24	Johnson & Johnson	$15,119	59	Anheuser Busch InBev SA/NV	$9,171	94	CVS Health Corp	$6,634
25	Volkswagen AG	$14,984	60	Morgan Stanley	$9,042	95	Commonwealth Bank of Austral	$6,602
26	Walmart Inc	$14,881	61	Coca-Cola Co (The)	$8,920	96	PetroChina Co Ltd	$6,500
27	Exxon Mobil Corp	$14,340	62	Allianz SE	$8,886	97	HDFC Bank Ltd	$6,483
28	Fannie Mae	$14,160	63	Cnooc Ltd.	$8,773	98	KDDI Corp	$6,451
29	Roche Holding AG	$13,962	64	Toronto Dominion Bank	$8,741	99	Gazprom Neft PJSC	$6,430
30	Novatek Joint Stock Co	$13,906	65	Royal Bank of Canada (Montre	$8,594	100	VMware Inc	$6,412
31	AT&T Inc	$13,903	66	Goldman Sachs Group Inc	$8,466			
32	UnitedHealth Group Inc	$13,839	67	China Life Insurance Co Ltd	$8,377			
33	Sberbank Russia	$13,576	68	Eli Lilly & Co	$8,318			
34	Tencent Holdings Ltd.	$13,410	69	China Petroleum & Chemical C	$8,277			
35	Hongkong And Shanghai Bankin	$13,382	70	Mastercard Inc	$8,118			

SOURCE: MERGENT INC., DATABASE, JANUARY 2021

The 100 Largest Global Public Employers
Hoover's Handbook of World Business 2021

Rank	Company	Employees	Rank	Company	Employees	Rank	Company	Employees
1	Walmart Inc	2,200,000	35	Rosneft Oil Co OJSC (Moscow)	334,600	69	FedEx Corp	245,000
2	Amazon.com Inc	1,298,000	36	Teleperformance SA	331,065	70	Raytheon Technologies Corp	243,200
3	Randstad NV	687,280	37	Walgreens Boots Alliance Inc	331,000	71	Infosys Ltd.	242,371
4	Volkswagen AG	671,200	38	UnitedHealth Group Inc	325,000	72	JBS S.A.	242,000
5	G4S Plc	551,748	39	Carrefour S.A.	321,383	73	Continental AG (Germany, Fed	241,458
6	Compass Group PLC (United Ki	548,143	40	Sumitomo Electric Industries	320,975	74	Jabil Inc	240,000
7	Deutsche Post AG	546,924	41	Lowe's Companies Inc	320,000	75	Wal-Mart de Mexico S.A.B. de	238,972
8	Accenture plc	506,000	42	Fomento Economico Mexicano,	314,656	76	HSBC Holdings Plc	235,351
9	United Parcel Service Inc	495,000	43	X5 Retail Group NV	307,444	77	Dairy Farm International Hol	230,000
10	PJSC Gazprom	473,800	44	Hitachi, Ltd.	301,056	78	JD.com, Inc.	227,730
11	ISS	471,056	45	CK Hutchison Holdings Ltd	300,000	79	P.T. Astra International TBK	226,105
12	Sodexo	470,237	46	Daimler AG	298,655	80	Yamato Holdings Co., Ltd.	224,945
13	China Mobile Limited	464,656	47	Fresenius SE & Co KGaA	294,134	81	Accor SA	223,370
14	Jardine Matheson Holdings Lt	464,000	48	Cognizant Technology Solutio	292,500	82	Vinci SA	222,397
15	Yum China Holdings Inc	450,000	49	Nestle SA	291,000	83	Capgemini SE	219,314
16	Kelly Services, Inc.	446,700	50	CVS Health Corp	290,000	84	Honda Motor Co Ltd	218,674
17	Industrial and Commercial Ba	445,106	51	CITIC Ltd	287,910	85	Woolworths Group Ltd	215,000
18	Kroger Co (The)	435,000	52	TJX Companies, Inc.	286,000	86	Deutsche Telekom AG	210,533
19	Tesco PLC	423,092	53	Sberbank Russia	281,300	87	Casino Guichard Perrachon S.	209,696
20	Aeon Co Ltd	420,165	54	China Telecom Corp Ltd	281,215	88	Bank of America Corp	208,000
21	Home Depot Inc	415,700	55	HCA Healthcare Inc	280,000	89	Publix Super Markets, Inc.	207,000
22	China Petroleum & Chemical C	402,206	56	SYNNEX Corp	277,900	90	General Electric Co	205,000
23	Japan Post Holdings Co Ltd	400,001	57	Costco Wholesale Corp	273,000	91	McDonald's Corp	205,000
24	Berkshire Hathaway Inc	391,500	58	Albertsons Companies Inc	270,000	92	Disney (Walt) Co. (The)	203,000
25	International Business Mac Corp.	383,800	59	PepsiCo Inc	267,000	93	Denso Corp. (Japan)	202,363
26	Koninklijke Ahold Delhaize N	380,000	60	Wells Fargo & Co (New)	260,000	94	Fareast Islami Life Insuranc	200,288
27	Nippon Telegraph & Telepho)	370,826	61	Panasonic Corp	259,385	95	Citigroup Inc	200,000
28	Securitas AB	370,000	62	JPMorgan Chase & Co	256,981	96	BNP Paribas (France)	198,816
29	Target Corp	368,000	63	China Unicom (Hong Kong) Ltd	256,385	97	Banco Santander SA	196,419
30	Siemens AG (Germany)	363,000	64	Jardine Cycle & Carriage Ltd	250,000	98	ACS Actividades de Construcc	194,036
31	Toyota Motor Corp	359,542	65	Concentrix Corp	250,000	99	George Weston Ltd	194,000
32	Starbucks Corp.	349,000	66	State Bank Of India	249,448	100	Loblaw Companies Ltd	194,000
33	China Construction Bank Corp	347,156	67	Aramark	247,900			
34	Yue Yuen Industrial (Holding	347,100	68	AT&T Inc	246,000			

SOURCE: MERGENT, INC., DATABASE, JANUARY 2021

Hoover's Handbook of

World Business

The Companies

77 Bank, Ltd. (The) (Japan)

EXECUTIVES

President, HIDEFUMI KOBAYASHI
Managing Director, KOICHI SUZUKI
Managing Director, ATSUSHI SHITO
Managing Director, YOSHIKAZU ONODERA
Managing Director, TAKUJI TABATA
Auditors: Deloitte Touche Tohmatsu LLC

LOCATIONS

HQ: 77 Bank, Ltd. (The) (Japan)
 3-3-20 Chuo, Aoba-ku, Sendai, Miyagi 980-8777
Phone: (81) 22 267 1111
Web: www.77bank.co.jp

COMPETITORS

Fukuoka Financial
 Group
Gunma Bank

Ito-Yokado
Japan Post
Sumitomo Mitsui

HISTORICAL FINANCIALS

Company Type: Public

Income Statement				FYE: March 31
	ASSETS ($ mil.)	NET INCOME ($ mil.)	INCOME AS % OF ASSETS	EMPLOYEES
03/20	80,792	168	0.2%	4,244
03/19	77,905	159	0.2%	4,296
03/18	82,101	172	0.2%	4,442
03/17	77,360	144	0.2%	4,436
03/16	76,570	141	0.2%	4,420
Annual Growth	1.4%	4.5%	—	(1.0%)

2020 Year-End Financials

Return on assets: 0.2%
Return on equity: 3.8%
Long-term debt ($ mil.): —
No. of shares (mil.): 74
Sales ($ mil): 1,077

Dividends
 Yield: —
 Payout: —
Market value ($ mil.): —

A.P. Moller - Maersk A/S

Oceangoing containers mean big money for A.P. Moller - Maersk. Operating in about 130 countries the conglomerate specializes in global container shipping and related services. It operates through Maersk Line which transports cargo via a fleet of more than 700 containerships Damco which provides freight forwarding and supply chain management services and APM Terminals a major container terminal operator. Other activities include marine towing and salvage through Svitzer and refrigerated containers manufactured by Maersk Container Industry. In keeping with its core container shipping and logistics services business it is in the process of selling off its energy business which includes oil drilling and tankers.

Operations

A.P. Moller - Maersk has four segments: Ocean Logistics & Services Terminals & Towage and Manufacturing & Others.

Ocean segment which consist of approximately 70% of company's revenue Ocean includes the ocean activities of Maersk Liner Business (Maersk Line Safmarine and Sealand - A Maersk Company) together with the Hamburg S d brands (Hamburg S d and Alian §a) as well as strategic transhipment hubs under the APM Terminals brand (Rotterdam Maasvlakte II Algeciras Tangier Tangier-Med II Port Said and the joint ventures Salalah Tanjung Pelepas and Bremerhaven).

Logistics & Services was supported by growth in most of the strategic areas including margin optimisation in intermodal and effects from new warehousing facilities partially offset by lower margins in sea and air freight forwarding and inland services. It consist of approximately 15% of total revenue.

Terminals & Towage includes gateway terminals involving landside activities (being port activities where the customers are mainly the carriers) and towage services under the Svitzer brand. It consists of approximately 10% of revenue.

Manufacturing & others represent the remaining in the company's revenue. It includes the activities of Maersk Container Industry with the production and sale of reefer containers at the factory in China following the announcement in January 2019 to exit the dry container business altogether.

Geographic Reach

Denmark-based company A.P. Moller - Maersk operates in nearly 350 ports in more than 120 countries worldwide. It operates in USA Australia France Nigeria China and Hong Kong UK Germany India Netherlands Brazil Singapore etc. USA is the leading country which consist of more than 15% of total revenue.

Financial Performance

Revenues for A.P. Moller - Maersk has been fluctuating in the last five years. It has an overall decline of 4% between 2015 and 2019.

Revenue was on par with 2018. The increase of less than 1% in Ocean was due to less than 1% higher average freight rates and higher other revenue but with a decrease in volumes. The increase in Terminals & Towage of 3% was due to higher volumes in Terminals while revenue declined by 2% in Logistics & Services because of the very high volume in Q4 2018. The decrease of 22% in Manufacturing & Others was due to exiting the dry container business and divesting the bulk activities both in January.

The company suffered a loss of $44 million in 2019 compared to a profit of $3 billion in 2018.

Cash at the end of fiscal 2019 was $4.8 billion a $2 billion increase from 2018. Cash from operations contributed $5.9 billion investing activities generated $874 million. Financing activities used another $4.8 billion for dividends to shareholders.

Strategy

A.P. Moller's strategy is to accelerate its contribution to container logistics by reducing complexity and waste along the global containerized supply chains. A.P. Moller has designed the strategy around its customers' needs and pain points hereby creating a market opportunity that will deliver value to customers as well as profitable growth and improved performance for A.P. Moller.

The first phase of strategy execution focused on improving the customer experience and the financial performance of the Ocean business to create a strong foundation for the next phases of the strategy.

The next phase in the strategy is about growing the business by innovating existing products combined with selling landside logistics products to A.P. Moller's existing customers - as well as growth in its Terminals & Towage business.

Mergers and Acquisitions

In 2020 A.P. Moller - Maersk reached an agreement with Bridgepoint Development Capital to acquire KGH Customs Services (KGH) a Sweden-based specialist in trade and customs management services in Europe. This will further enhance Maersk's capabilities as an integrated container logistics company offering end-to-end supply chain solutions to its customers. Maersk will acquire KGH for a consideration of SEK 2.6B (US$ 279 million).

In early 2020 A.P. Moller - Maersk completes acquisition of Performance Team a US-based warehousing and distribution company to further strengthen its capabilities as an integrated container logistics company offering end-to-end supply chain solutions to its customers. The transaction has been valued at US$ 545 million.

Company Background

Founded by Peter M¡rsk M ller and his son Arnold Peter M ller A.P. M ller - M¡rsk styles the company and family name as "M¡rsk" but uses "Maersk" for the names of most of its subsidiaries. A.P. M ller - M¡rsk's main shareholder is The A.P. M ller and Chastine Mc-Kinney M ller Foundation which was established by company founder A.P. M ller in 1953.

EXECUTIVES

Group Vice CEO; CEO Energy Division, Claus V. Hemmingsen, age 58
CEO Maersk Oil, Gretchen H. Watkins
CEO Maersk Container Industry, Stig Hoffmeyer
Group CFO, Jakob Stausholm, age 52
CEO Damco, Klaus R. Sejling, age 43
CEO APM Terminals, Morten H. Engelstoft, age 52
CEO Svitzer, Henriette H. Thygesen
Group CEO; CEO Transport and Logistics Division, Soren Skou, age 57
CEO Maersk Tankers, Christian M. Ingerslev
CEO Maersk Drilling, J rn Madsen
CEO Maersk Supply Service, Steen S. Karstensen
Chairman, Jim Hagemann Snabe, age 55
Auditors: PricewaterhouseCoopers Statsautoriseret Revisionsaktieselskab

LOCATIONS

HQ: A.P. Moller - Maersk A/S
 Esplanaden 50, Copenhagen K DK-1098
Phone: (45) 33 63 33 63
Web: www.maersk.com

2017 Sales

	% of total
USA	16
China and Hong Kong	6
United Kingdom	4
Germany	3
India	3
Netherlands	3
Brazil	2
Turkey	2
Denmark	1
Singapore	1
Other countries	59
Total	**100**

PRODUCTS/OPERATIONS

2017 Sales

	$ mil.	% of total
Maersk Line	24,299	74
APM Terminals	4,138	13
Damco	2	8
Maersk Container Industry	1,016	3
Svitzer	659	2
Other businesses unallocated and eliminations	(1835)	-
Total	**30,945**	**100**

Selected Business Areas

Container shipping & related
 Damco (freight forwarding and supply chain management services)
 Maersk Container Industry (manufacturing of dry and refrigerated containers)
 Maersk Line (global container shipping)

MCC Transport (intra-Asia container shipping)
Safmarine (Africa Middle East and Indian
subcontinent container shipping)
Seago Line
SeaLand
Svitzer (specialized marine services including towing
salvage and emergency response)
Terminal activities
APM Terminals (port operations inland transportation
and container repair)

COMPETITORS

CMA CGM
COSCO Group
China Shipping
DP World
Evergreen Marine
Hanjin Shipping
Hapag-Lloyd
Hutchison Port Holdings
Hyundai Merchant Marine
INTERNATIONAL CONTAINER TERMINAL SERVICES
 INC.
John Swire & Sons
Kawasaki Kisen
Mediterranean Shipping Company
Mitsui O.S.K. Lines
NYK Line
Neptune Orient
Orient Overseas
PSA International
SSA Marine
Saltchuk
Shanghai International Port
Singamas

HISTORICAL FINANCIALS

Company Type: Public

Income Statement   FYE: December 31

	REVENUE ($ mil.)	NET INCOME ($ mil.)	NET PROFIT MARGIN	EMPLOYEES
12/19	38,890	(84)	—	86,279
12/18	39,019	3,169	8.1%	80,220
12/17	30,945	(1,205)	—	85,667
12/16	35,464	(1,939)	—	87,736
12/15	5,883	115	2.0%	88,355
Annual Growth	60.3%	—	—	(0.6%)

2019 Year-End Financials

Debt ratio: 30.2%
Return on equity: (-0.2%)
Cash ($ mil.): 4,768
Current ratio: 1.19
Long-term debt ($ mil.): 14,750

No. of shares (mil.): 20
Dividends
 Yield: 11.3%
 Payout: —
Market value ($ mil.): 144

	STOCK PRICE ($) FY Close	P/E High/Low		PER SHARE ($) Earnings	Dividends	Book Value
12/19	7.18	—	—	(4.00)	0.82	1,398
12/18	6.24	0	0	152.00	0.08	1,571
12/17	8.69	—	—	(58.00)	0.07	1,474
12/16	8.00	—	—	(93.00)	0.15	1,507
12/15	6.51	0	0	5.40	1.05	242
Annual Growth	2.5%	—	—	—	(6.0%)	55%

AB Electrolux (Sweden)

AB Electrolux knows how to run a household. The firm a top maker of household appliances worldwide sells about 60 million products annually. Electrolux cranks out washing machines stoves refrigerators and freezers under the AEG Elec-

trolux Frigidaire Westinghouse and Zanussi names. Electrolux makes foodservice and laundry equipment under the Electrolux and Zanussi labels for the mass market. Electrolux largest market is the US accounting for nearly one-third of its revenue. AB Electrolux was founded in 1919 by Axel Wenner-Gren.

Operations
AB Electrolux produces appliances for the consumer market and products comprise mainly of refrigerators freezers cookers dryers washing machines dishwashers microwave ovens vacuum cleaner and other small appliances.

Geographic Reach
Stockholm-based AB Electrolux boasts a global reach as its products are sold in more than 120 markets. The US is the company's biggest single market representing 30% of sales followed by Brazil with more than 10% of sales and after that no other country accounts for more than 10% of sales suggesting enviable geographic diversification.

By region the company split into four segment: Europe (about 40% of revenue); North America (about 35%); Latin America (more than 15%); Asia-Pacific Middle East and Africa (about 15%).

Financial Performance
Note: Growth rates may differ after conversion to US Dollars.

The company's net sales in 2019 were SEK119.0 million. Net sales for continuing operations increased by 3.0% in 2019. Product-mix improvements and price increases explain the growth in Europe. The sales growth in Latin America was mainly driven by Brazil and increased volumes mix improvements and price increases also contributed positively. Asia-Pacific Middle East and Africa reported a sales decline.

Cash held by the company at the end of 2019 decreased to SEK 11.5 million. Cash provided by operating was SEK8.4 million. Cash used for financing and investing activities were SEK 1.6 million and SEK 7.7 million respectively. Main cash uses for 2019 were for capital expenditures amortization of long-term borrowings and dividends paid.

Strategy
Electrolux has a clear strategy to deliver profitable growth and create shareholder value. At the heart of the strategy is a strong consumer focus. In 2019 Electrolux continued executing on the path to profitable growth. Product mix improved through continued focus on product portfolios with strong consumer benefits.

To accelerate profitable growth the business was reorganized into four regional consumer-focused business areas ensuring a unified approach to each market. This meant that the Home Care & SDA business area was combined with the four major appliances business areas. A new global consumer experience organization responsible for functions such as marketing design and digital consumer solutions was established to support the business areas. The investments in modularized products in automated production continued. These are important to further increase competitiveness in order to drive growth through more innovative products as well as lowering costs. The re-engineering program totaling SEK8 billion continued in 2019. The freezer and refrigerator production in US was consolidated to a new factory in Anderson. The cost savings from this program and the streamlining measures above are expected to be approximately SEK3.5 billion annually with full effect from 2024.

Mergers and Acquisitions
In early 2019 Electrolux acquired France-based UNIC S.A.S a manufacturer of professional espresso machines for an undisclosed amount. The acquisition complements the Electrolux offering

of products for beverage service and further develops its position as a leader in complete solutions for the hospitality industry.

EXECUTIVES

EVP and Head of Major Appliances North America, G. Alan Shaw
CEO, Jonas Samuelson, age 52
EVP and Head Professional Products, Alberto Zanata, age 60
COO, Jan Brockmann, age 55
CFO, Anna Ohlsson-Leijon, age 52
EVP and Head of Small Appliances, Ola Nilsson, age 51
CEO Middle East and Africa Region (MEA), Lorenzo Milani
VP Information Systems, JP Iversen
EVP and Head of Major Appliances Europe Middle East and Africa (EMEA), Daniel (Dan) Arler, age 51
Interim Head of Major Appliances Latin America, Ricardo Cons, age 53
EVP and Head of Major Appliances Asia/Pacific, Kenneth L. Ng, age 58
SVP Marketing and Brands, Lars Hygrell
Deputy Chairman, Ronnie Leten, age 64
Auditors: Deloitte AB

LOCATIONS

HQ: AB Electrolux (Sweden)
S:t Goransgatan 143, Stockholm SE-105 45
Phone: (46) 8 738 60 00   **Fax:** (46) 8 738 74 61
Web: www.electroluxgroup.com

2018 Sales

	% of total
USA	31
Brazil	10
Germany	5
Australia	4
Sweden	5
Switzerland	2
Canada	2
United Kingdom	3
France	4
Italy	4
Other	30
Total	**100**

PRODUCTS/OPERATIONS

2018 Sales

	% of total
Major Appliances North America	31
Major Appliances Europe Middle East and Africa	35
Latin America	14
Asia/Pacific	7
Homecare and Small Domestic Appliances	6
Professional Products	7
Total	**100**

Selected Products and Brands

Consumer durables
 Core A
 Floorcare products
Professional products
 Foodservice equipment
 Laundry equipment

COMPETITORS

Ali SpA
BISSELL
BSH Bosch und Siemens
 Hausger ote
Fisher & Paykel
 Appliances Holdings
Franke Group
GE Appliances &
 Lighting
Gree Electrical
 Appliances

Haier Group
Hobart Corp.
Indesit
LG Electronics
Miele
Philips Electronics
Royal Appliance
SEB
Samsung Group
Whirlpool
WinWholesale

HISTORICAL FINANCIALS

Company Type: Public

Income Statement
FYE: December 31

	REVENUE ($ mil.)	NET INCOME ($ mil.)	NET PROFIT MARGIN	EMPLOYEES
12/19	19,910	419	2.1%	48,652
12/18	20,772	636	3.1%	54,419
12/17	20,426	961	4.7%	55,692
12/16	20,264	752	3.7%	55,400
12/15	20,669	262	1.3%	58,265
Annual Growth	(0.9%)	12.5%	—	(4.4%)

2019 Year-End Financials

Debt ratio: 1.8%
Return on equity: 11.3%
Cash ($ mil.): 1,808
Current ratio: 0.98
Long-term debt ($ mil.): 1,378

No. of shares (mil.): 287
Dividends
Yield: 3.6%
Payout: 122.6%
Market value ($ mil.): 14,071

	STOCK PRICE ($) FY Close	P/E High/Low		PER SHARE ($) Earnings	Dividends	Book Value
12/19	48.96	6	5	1.45	1.78	13.14
12/18	42.37	5	3	2.20	1.91	12.66
12/17	64.65	4	2	3.33	1.76	11.98
12/16	49.66	4	3	2.60	1.60	10.31
12/15	48.20	12	8	0.91	1.47	8.72
Annual Growth	0.4%	—	—	12.5%	4.9%	10.8%

AB SKF

AB SKF is on a roll ... or at least its bearings are. One of the world's leading makers of roller and ball bearings SKF produces a variety of bearings and units as well as seals mechatronics (electromechanical tools and systems) and lubrication systems and related products and services. SKF's business is divided by customer segment into three divisions: Industrial (consisting of seven business units; catering to industrial OEMs) Automotive (OEMs and aftermarket) and Specialty Business (includes Kaydon and General Bearing among others). It operates in about 130 countries worldwide and has around 15000 distributor locations.

Operations
SKF's divided into two sales division; Industrial & Automotive.
Industrial generates about 70% and Automotive around 30% of its total sales in 2019.

Geographic Reach
SKF has 130 sites in 28 countries and 15 technical centers around the globe. The company has 103 manufacturing units in 29 countries.

Sales and Marketing
The company markets its products to the specific segments of Industrial Distribution (about 35% of net sales); Industry General (around 15%); Industry Heavy and Special (nearly 10%); and Cars and Light Trucks (some 10%).

Financial Performance
In 2019 net sales amounted to SEK 86013 million (SEK 85713 million in 2018) corresponding to an increase of 0.4% compared to 2018. The change of the Swedish krona towards other currencies had a positive impact in 2019 of 5%.

Net debt amounted to SEK 22176 million at the end of 2019. The increase was mainly attributable to the accounting for leases according to IFRS 16 and provisions for post-employment benefits.

Cash held by the company at the end of 2019 decreased by SEK 3960 million to SEK 6430 million. Cash provided by operations was SEK 9410 million while cash used for investing and financing activities were SEK 4457 million and SEK 8997 million respectively. Main use for cash was investments in financial assets.

Strategy
SKF's strategy is centered around the rotating shaft and the two value propositions - Product and Rotating Equipment Performance. SKF has also identified six strategic focus areas that are central to realize the vision and the mission. The company's strategic focuses are digital sales; new business models; innovation; world-class manufacturing; future workforce; and cleantech.

SKF's strategy is the foundation from which the company works towards its vision of "a world of reliable rotation" and its mission of becoming "the undisputed leader in the bearing business." Sustainability is embedded in SKF's business.

HISTORY

SKF began as the brainchild of Sven Wingquist a maintenance engineer at the Swedish textile company Gamlestadens Fabriker. Displeased with imported bearings used in Gamlestadens Fabriker's factories Wingquist (with resources allotted by Fabriker) founded Svenska Kullagerfabriken (SKF) in 1907 and produced bearings from his own workshop. In 1910 SKF had one factory in Sweden; the following year the company established another in the UK.

SKF reaped the financial benefits of being based in a neutral country during WWI selling its products to both the Allied and Central powers. In 1914 subsidiaries were established in Belgium the Netherlands and Russia. Two years later SKF bought a steel works company in Sweden to supply the company with steel. Also in 1916 SKF opened a plant in the US. By 1918 the company had 12 factories and its sales force spanned 100 countries. An economic slump sagged the company's sales in the early 1920s. SKF's Volvo subsidiary entered the automobile manufacturing industry in 1926 and acted as SKF's testing unit until it was spun off in 1935.

The onset of the Great Depression allowed SKF to purchase some of its German competitors. In 1929 SKF's stock began trading internationally and the company purchased Swedish machine toolmaker Lidkopings Mekaniska Verkstad. In the thick of the Depression SKF concentrated its efforts on R&D and in 1932 it patented two spherical rolling-bearing products.

The company enjoyed a few prosperous years after the Depression but WWII and harder times were lurking. During the war the Allies bombed SKF's Schweinfurt and Canstatt factories. The company's reconstruction efforts included building manufacturing plants in Spain Canada and the Netherlands followed by expansion into Brazil and India. By 1950 the company boasted 18 factories with 65% of its workforce operating outside Sweden. In 1957 the company added a new ball and roller factory (one of its biggest buildings) to its ranks. SKF built a research center in the US in 1963. In 1969 astronaut Neil Armstrong took photos of the historic moon landing with a camera fitted with SKF bearings.

EXECUTIVES

President Industrial Division, Alrik Danielson, age 59
SVP and CFO, Christian Johansson, age 57
President SKF USA Inc., Poul Jeppesen, age 68
President Automotive and Areospace, Stephane Le-Mounier, age 56

President Industrial Sales Asia, Patrick Tong, age 59
SVP Group Technology Development, Bernd Stephan
President Industrial Sales Americas, John Schmidt, age 52
President Industrial Sales Europe and Middle East and Africa (MEA), Erik Nelander, age 58
President Business and Product Development, Victoria van Camp, age 55
President Bearing Operations, Luc Graux, age 58
Chairman, Leif –stling
Auditors: PricewaterhouseCoopers AB

LOCATIONS

HQ: AB SKF
Hornsgatan 1, Gothenburg SE-415 50
Phone: (46) 31 337 10 00   **Fax:** (46) 31 337 28 32
Web: www.skf.com

PRODUCTS/OPERATIONS

2016 Sales by Division

	% of total
Industrial Market	70
Automotive Market	30
Total	**100**

2016 Sales

	% of total
Europe excl. Sweden	38
North America (incl. Mexico)	25
Asia-Pacific	26
Latin America	6
Middle East/Africa	3
Sweden	2
Total	**100**

Selected Products
Bearing housings
Bearing units
Composite dry sliding bearings & FW bushings
Coupling systems
High-precision bearings
Hydraulic seals
Industrial shaft seals
Rolling bearings
Spherical plain bearings & rod ends

Selected Markets
Aerospace
Agriculture
Bicycle
Cars
Compressors
Construction
Drive-by-wire
Electric motors & generators
Electric motors for consumer goods
Electric power tools
Food & beverage
Home appliance
HPI oil & gas
Industrial fans
Industrial pumps
Industrial transmission
Machine tool
Marine
Material handling
Medical & healthcare
Metals industry
Mining mineral processing & cement
Plastic & rubber
Printing machines
Pulp & paper
Racing
Railways
Skates
Traditional electric power generation
Trucks trailers & buses
Two wheelers
Wind energy

Selected Services

Asset management services
Condition monitoring
Energy & sustainability management
Mechanical maintenance
Operator driven reliability (ODR)
Remanufacturing services
SKF certified electric motor rebuilder
SKF certified maintenance partners
SKF distributor network
SKF engineering consultancy services
SKF logistics services
Training

COMPETITORS

Applied Industrial Technologies
Freudenberg
GE
Ingersoll-Rand Industrial Technologies
JTEKT
Kaydon
Lincoln Industrial
NSK
NTN
Nippon Bearing
Parker-Hannifin
Rheinmetall
Schaeffler
Timken

HISTORICAL FINANCIALS

Company Type: Public

Income Statement

FYE: December 31

	REVENUE ($ mil.)	NET INCOME ($ mil.)	NET PROFIT MARGIN	EMPLOYEES
12/19	14,393	929	6.5%	43,360
12/18	14,343	1,219	8.5%	44,428
12/17	13,042	916	7.0%	45,678
12/16	12,180	666	5.5%	44,868
12/15	12,717	649	5.1%	46,635
Annual Growth	3.1%	9.4%	—	(1.8%)

2019 Year-End Financials

Debt ratio: 2.8%
Return on equity: 16.1%
Cash ($ mil.): 1,076
Current ratio: 2.07
Long-term debt ($ mil.): 2,107

No. of shares (mil.): 455
Dividends
Yield: 3.2%
Payout: 31.6%
Market value ($ mil.): 9,184

	STOCK PRICE ($) FY Close	P/E High/Low	PER SHARE ($) Earnings	Dividends	Book Value
12/19	20.17	2 1	2.04	0.65	13.05
12/18	15.13	2 1	2.67	0.65	12.32
12/17	22.15	2 1	2.01	0.61	10.30
12/16	18.35	2 2	1.46	0.68	9.57
12/15	16.09	3 2	1.43	0.63	9.12
Annual Growth	5.8%	— —	9.4%	0.5%	9.4%

ABB Ltd

ABB is a European industrial electrical equipment company making products used in electrical grids and transmission industrial automation robotics & discrete automation motion and power grids serving customers in utilities industry and transport & infrastructure globally. Its product lines are diverse and serve customers in a wide range of sectors including OEMs process industries such as pulp and paper oil and gas and metals and mining companies hybrid and batch manufacturers such as food and beverage companies transportation equipment manufacturers discrete manufacturing companies logistics utilities as well as customers in the automotive industry. Its new ABB Ability division develops "Industrial Internet of Things" solutions and counts Shell Oil BASF Volvo and BMW as customers to name a few. Operating for more than 130 years Zurich Switzerland-based ABB has facilities in upwards of 100 countries worldwide. It is in the process of selling a majority stake in its Power Grids business which makes transformers and long-distance power transmission systems to Hitachi.

Operations

ABB operates through four segments: Electrification Products Robotics & Discrete Automation Motion Industrial Automation and Corporate and Other.

Electrification Products generates nearly 45% of ABB's sales and manufactures products and services such as electric vehicle charging infrastructure solar power solutions modular substation packages distribution automation products switchboard and panelboards switchgear UPS solutions circuit breakers measuring and sensing devices control products wiring accessories enclosures and cabling systems and intelligent home and building solutions designed to integrate and automate lighting heating ventilation security and data communication networks.

Motion segment produce about 25% of sales and manufactures and sells motors generators drives wind converters mechanical power transmissions complete electrical powertrain systems and related services and digital solutions for a wide range of applications in industry transportation infrastructure and utilities.

Industrial Automation accounts for more than 20% of sales and develops integrated automation and electrification systems and solutions as well as services such as remote monitoring preventive maintenance and cybersecurity services.

The Robotics & Discrete Automation division sells robotics controllers software function packages cells programmable logic controllers (PLC) industrial PCs (IPC) servo motion engineered manufacturing solutions turn-key solutions and collaborative robot solutions for a wide range of applications. It pulls in around 10% of sales.

The ABB Ability digital solutions appear within all divisions that produce technical solutions for performance and energy optimization asset health condition monitoring and cybersecurity.

Geographic Reach

Zurich Switzerland-based ABB's operations extend to more than 100 countries across Europe (more than 35% of sales) the Asia Middle East and Africa (AMEA) region (a third of sales) and the Americas (over 30%).

ABB has properties in the US China Germany Italy Finland Sweden Switzerland Canada Czech Republic and India.

Sales and Marketing

The Business delivers products to customers through a global network of channel partners and end-customers. Most of the Business's revenue is derived from sales through channel partners like distributors original equipment manufacturers (OEMs) engineering procurement construction (EPC) contracting companies system integrators utilities and panel builders. The company also sells directly to end-users utilities and other ABB subsidiaries. Its diverse customer base covers industries such as software and digital solutions EV charging robotics and machine factory automation data centers food and beverage rail building marine oil and gas chemicals and other discrete markets as well as in printing pulp and paper and the metal industry among others. Customers include Shell Oil CenterPoint Energy Con Edison BASF Royal Caribbean Cargill Volvo and BMW.

Financial Performance

Note: Growth rates may differ after conversion to US Dollars.

ABB's sales have a modest increase in 2019. It grew by 1% to $28 billion that year. Revenues were higher in the Electrification and Motion Businesses while revenues decreased in the Industrial Automation and Robotics & Discrete Automation Businesses.

Net income attributable to ABB decreased by $734 million to $1.4 billion in 2019 compared to 2018 due to lower income coming from continuing operation.

ABB's cash position increased by $99 million during fiscal 2019 ending the year at $3.5 billion. The company's operating activities generated cash of $2.3 billion while its investing activities used $815 million and its financing activities used $1.4 billion. ABB's primary cash uses were for purchases of investments and debt repayments.

Strategy

ABB announced itsnew strategy to focus simplify and lead the digital transformation of industries for enhanced customer value and shareholder returns. To deliver on its ambitions it is introducing a new operating model ABB Operating System (ABB-OS). ABB-OS provides a common framework across the Group governing management processes such as market validation budgeting and portfolio management in order to facilitate clear decision making and a balanced approach to value creation. Its new simplified operating model also positions the Businesses to be the single interface to customers maximizing proximity and speed. Each Business is intended to have full entrepreneurial ownership of operations functions research and development and territories. Significant amounts of company resources and management effort were dedicated to both of these areas in 2019.

The company is targeting to achieve the following targets using this strategy: 3-6 percent annual comparable revenue growth; Operational EBITA margin of 13-16 percent; Return on Capital Employed (ROCE) of 15-20 percent; Cash conversion to net income of approximately 100 percent; and Basic EPS growth above revenue growth.

Mergers and Acquisitions

In late-2019 ABB has completed its acquisition of a majority stake in Chargedot Shanghai New Energy Technology Co. Ltd. ("Chargedot"). The acquisition is expected to further strengthen ABB's relationship with leading Chinese electric vehicle manufacturers and broaden the company's e-mobility portfolio with hardware and software developed specifically for local requirements as well as service offerings.

EXECUTIVES

President Region Americas and Head of Group Service Business Integration, Greg Scheu, age 59
President Region Asia Middle East and Africa (AMEA), Frank Duggan, age 61
President Region Europe and Chairman of Divisional Transformation Team, Bernhard Jucker, age 66, $886,327 total compensation
CEO, Ulrich Spiesshofer, age 56, $703,285 total compensation
President Process Automation Division, Peter Terwiesch, age 54
CFO, Timo Ihamuotila, age 54
President Discrete Automation and Motion (DM) Division, Sami Atiya
President Power Grids Division, Claudio Facchin, age 55
President Electrification Products Division, Tarak Mehta, age 54

Managing Director ABB Finland, Pekka Tiitinen, age 54
Managing Director ABB India, Bazmi Husain
Vice Chairman, Jacob Wallenberg, age 64
Chairman, Peter R. Voser, age 62
Auditors: KPMG AG

LOCATIONS

HQ: ABB Ltd
Affolternstrasse 44, P.O. Box 8131, Zurich CH-8050
Phone: (41) 43 317 7111 **Fax:** (41) 43 317 7958
Web: www.abb.com

2018 Sales

	$ mil.	% of total
Asia Middle East and Africa	9,491	34
Europe	10,129	37
The Americas	8,042	29
Total	**27,662**	**100**

PRODUCTS/OPERATIONS

2018 Sales

	$ mil.	% of total
Electrification Products	11,686	41
Robotics and Motion	9,147	32
Industrial Automation	7,394	26
Corporate and Other	273	1
Inter-segment elimination	-838	-
Total	**27,662**	**100**

Selected Products

Electrification Products
  Modular substation packages
  Distribution automation
  Measuring and sensing devices
  Circuit breakers
  Control products
  Wiring accessories
  Cabling systems
  KNX systems
Robotics and Motion
  Robots
  Robot automation solutions
  Controllers
  Electrical motors and generators
  Mechanical power transmission products
  Low- and medium-voltage drive
Industrial Automation
  Performance optimization
  Automation solutions
  System 800xA
  PLC Automation
  Decathlon Software
  Turbochargers

COMPETITORS

ALSTOM	KUKA
Atlas Copco	Legrand
BAE Systems Inc.	Leviton
CNH Industrial	Rittal Corp.
Crompton Greaves	Rockwell Automation
Danaher	Schneider Electric
Eaton	Siemens AG
Emerson Electric	ThyssenKrupp
FANUC	Technologies
Honeywell	Voith
International	WEG Ind strias
Hubbell	Yaskawa Electric
Hyosung	Yokogawa Electric
Hyundai Corporation	

HISTORICAL FINANCIALS

Company Type: Public

Income Statement
FYE: December 31

	REVENUE ($ mil.)	NET INCOME ($ mil.)	NET PROFIT MARGIN	EMPLOYEES
12/19	27,978	1,439	5.1%	144,400
12/18	27,662	2,173	7.9%	146,600
12/17	34,312	2,213	6.4%	134,800
12/16	33,828	1,899	5.6%	132,300
12/15	35,481	1,933	5.4%	135,800
Annual Growth	(5.8%)	(7.1%)	—	1.5%

2019 Year-End Financials

Debt ratio: 19.6%
Return on equity: 10.4%
Cash ($ mil.): 4,110
Current ratio: 1.31
Long-term debt ($ mil.): 6,772

No. of shares (mil.): 2,133
Dividends
  Yield: 3.2%
  Payout: 117.3%
Market value ($ mil.): 51,396

	STOCK PRICE ($) FY Close	P/E High/Low	PER SHARE ($) Earnings	Dividends	Book Value
12/19	24.09	36 27	0.67	0.79	6.34
12/18	19.01	28 18	1.02	0.81	6.54
12/17	26.82	26 20	1.03	0.76	6.93
12/16	21.07	26 18	0.88	0.73	6.26
12/15	17.73	27 20	0.87	0.75	6.61
Annual Growth	8.0%	— —	(6.3%)	1.3%	(1.0%)

Absa Group Ltd (New)

EXECUTIVES

Group Chief Executive and Director, Maria Ramos, age 61
Deputy CEO, David W. P. Hodnett, age 50
Financial Director, Jason Quinn
Group Chairman, Wendy E. Lucas-Bull, age 68
Auditors: Ernst & Young Inc.

LOCATIONS

HQ: Absa Group Ltd (New)
7th Floor, Barclays Towers West, 15 Troye Street, Johannesburg 2001
Phone: (27) 11 350 4000
Web: www.absa.africa

PRODUCTS/OPERATIONS

2016 Sales

	% of total
RBB	71
CIB	22
WIMI	7
Total	**100**

2016 Sales

	% of total
Interest income	58
Non-interest income	42
Total	**100**

COMPETITORS

FirstRand	Standard Bank Group
Nedcor	Standard Chartered
Sanlam	

HISTORICAL FINANCIALS

Company Type: Public

Income Statement
FYE: December 31

	ASSETS ($ mil.)	NET INCOME ($ mil.)	INCOME AS % OF ASSETS	EMPLOYEES
12/19	99,627	1,015	1.0%	38,472
12/18	89,627	967	1.1%	40,856
12/17	94,710	1,122	1.2%	41,073
12/16	80,168	1,070	1.3%	41,241
12/15	73,403	919	1.3%	41,772
Annual Growth	7.9%	2.5%	—	(2.0%)

2019 Year-End Financials

Return on assets: 1.0%
Return on equity: 12.8%
Long-term debt ($ mil.): —
No. of shares (mil.): 828
Sales ($ mil): 9,980

Dividends
  Yield: 5.8%
  Payout: 100.9%
Market value ($ mil.): 17,086

	STOCK PRICE ($) FY Close	P/E High/Low	PER SHARE ($) Earnings	Dividends	Book Value
12/19	20.62	2 1	1.22	1.21	9.73
12/18	21.99	2 1	1.16	1.27	9.20
12/17	29.44	2 1	1.35	1.30	10.57
12/16	25.00	1 1	1.26	1.21	8.00
12/15	18.50	2 1	1.08	1.26	6.77
Annual Growth	2.7%	— —	3.0%	(0.9%)	9.5%

Abu Dhabi Commercial Bank

Auditors: Deloitte & Touche (M.E.)

LOCATIONS

HQ: Abu Dhabi Commercial Bank
Sheikh Zayed Bin Sultan Street, Plot C-33, Sector E-11, P.O. Box 939, Abu Dhabi
Phone: (971) 2 696 2222
Web: www.adcb.com

HISTORICAL FINANCIALS

Company Type: Public

Income Statement
FYE: December 31

	ASSETS ($ mil.)	NET INCOME ($ mil.)	INCOME AS % OF ASSETS	EMPLOYEES
12/19	110,315	1,304	1.2%	0
12/18	76,196	1,317	1.7%	0
12/17	72,158	1,164	1.6%	0
12/16	70,318	1,129	1.6%	0
12/15	62,148	1,340	2.2%	0
Annual Growth	15.4%	(0.7%)	—	

2019 Year-End Financials

Return on assets: 1.4%
Return on equity: 10.8%
Long-term debt ($ mil.): —
No. of shares (mil.): —
Sales ($ mil): 5,383

Dividends
  Yield: —
  Payout: 53.5%
Market value ($ mil.): —

Abu Dhabi Islamic Bank

Auditors: Deloitte & Touche (M.E.)

LOCATIONS

HQ: Abu Dhabi Islamic Bank
  P.O. Box 313, Abu Dhabi
Phone:
Web: www.adib.co.ae

HISTORICAL FINANCIALS

Company Type: Public

Income Statement				FYE: December 31
	ASSETS ($ mil.)	NET INCOME ($ mil.)	INCOME AS % OF ASSETS	EMPLOYEES
12/19	34,305	707	2.1%	0
12/18	34,089	680	2.0%	0
12/17	33,567	625	1.9%	0
12/16	33,292	531	1.6%	0
12/15	32,229	525	1.6%	0
Annual Growth	1.6%	7.7%	—	—

2019 Year-End Financials

Return on assets: 2.0%
Return on equity: 14.1%
Long-term debt ($ mil.): —
No. of shares (mil.): —
Sales ($ mil): 1,832

Dividends
  Yield: —
  Payout: 43.3%
Market value ($ mil.): —

Accenture plc

Accenture one of the world's largest consulting firms offers a portfolio of management consulting strategy digital technology interactive and business operations services to some of the top companies and government organizations in the world. The company's corporate clients span a broad spectrum of more than 40 industries — from retail to communications. Clients use Accenture's services to improve decision-making; mitigating risk and enhancing security; implementing modern change management programs; shaping and delivering value from largescale cloud migrations; building more resilient supply chains; and reinventing manufacturing and operations with smart connected products and platforms. Accenture has its North America head office in New York and gets over 65% outside Europe.

Operations

Accenture's business is divided into five operating groups based on client industries: Products (consumer goods retail travel life sciences); Financial Services; Communications Media & Technology; Health & Public Service (private and public health organizations educational institutions); and Resources (chemicals energy forestry mining and metals). Revenue contributions are evenly dispersed between the five with the largest Products accounting for about 30% of sales Communications Media and Technology Health and Public Service and Financial Services with approximately 20% of sales each and the smallest Resources accounting for some 15% each. Cutting across the five segments are five further Services and Solutions offerings namely Accenture Strategy Accenture Consulting Accenture Digital Accenture Technology and Accenture Operations.

In addition to reporting revenues by geographic markets the company also reports revenues by two types of work: consulting (some 55% of sales) and outsourcing (around 45%).

Geographic Reach

Dublin-based Accenture serves clients in more than 200 cities spanning about 50 countries. The company makes over 45% of sales from North America nearly 35% from Europe and the remainder from its growth markets of the Middle East the Asia/Pacific region and Latin America.

To get close to the action Accenture has major offices in the world's leading business centers including in the US (Boston Chicago New York and San Francisco) Europe (Dublin Frankfurt London Madrid Milan Paris Rome) and the Asia/Pacific region (Bangalore Beijing Manila Mumbai Sao Paolo Shanghai Singapore Sydney and Tokyo) among others.

Sales and Marketing

Accenture derives its revenue primarily from Forbes Global 2000 governments and government agencies and other enterprises.

It has partnerships with leading players in the tech industry including SAP Microsoft Oracle Salesforce and Workday.

The company's advertising costs for the years 2020 2019 and 2018 were $57.7 million $85.5 million and $78.5 million respectively.

Financial Performance

The company's revenue in 2020 increased to $44.3 billion. North America revenues increased 5% in local currency led by growth in Public Service Life Sciences Software & Platforms Health and Banking & Capital Markets. These increases were partially offset by declines in Chemicals & Natural Resources and High Tech. Revenue growth was driven by the United States.

Net income for 2020 increased to $5.1 billion compare from the prior year with $4.8 billion.

Cash held by the company at the end of 2020 increased to $8.4 billion compared from the prior year with $6.1 billion. Cash provided by operations was $8.2 billion while cash used for investing and financing activities were $1.9 billion and $4.0 million respectively. Main uses for cash were purchases of businesses and investments; and purchases of shares.

Strategy

Accenture growth strategy begins with a focus on what its clients need. Regardless of industry the company's clients must transform every aspect of their business to meet the needs of today's digital world. Accenture are helping its clients use technology to build their digital core to drive enterprise-wide transformation such as moving them to the cloud and embedding security across the enterprise by transforming their operations such as replatforming their ERP systems and through its Operations services and Industry X and by accelerating their growth?such as through creating omni-channel experiences through Interactive.

The company are uniquely able to deliver this transformation because of its ability to bring applied innovation and deliver 360-degree value for its clients. Accenture define 360-degree value as delivering the financial business case and unique value a client may be seeking and striving where possible to partner with its clients to achieve greater progress on inclusion and diversity with its diverse teams reskill its clients' employees help its clients achieve their sustainability goals and create meaningful experiences both with Accenture and for the customers and employees of its clients.

Mergers and Acquisitions

Accenture is in a period of intense acquisition activity as it continues its pivot to digital cloud and security.

In early 2021 Accenture has acquired Wolox a leading Argentinean cloud native and agile development company that provides digital solutions to help clients achieve successful business outcomes.

The addition of the Wolox team enhances the global capabilities of Accenture Cloud First a multi-service group providing a full stack of cloud services to help clients across every industry accelerate their digital transformation innovate faster and create differentiated sustainable value. Terms were not disclosed.

In 2021 Accenture has acquired Real Protect a privately held Brazil-based provider of managed security and cyber defense services (MSS) extending its cybersecurity presence and capabilities in Latin America. Financial terms were not disclosed. Real Protect's approximately 90 cybersecurity professionals who serve a variety of clients in the healthcare energy oil & gas and financial services industries will join Accenture Security's global workforce of nearly 7000 professionals.

In 2020 Accenture has completed its acquisition of Sentelis an independent data consulting and engineering company headquartered in France which specializes in designing and scaling data and artificial intelligence (AI) capabilities. Sentelis would join Accenture Applied Intelligence and complement its focus on helping clients build the right data strategy and foundation to industrialize AI across their businesses.

In 2020 Accenture in Italy has completed the acquisition of Turin-based boutique systems integrator PLM Systems. The acquisition will expand Accenture's capabilities to help clients improve how they generate manage and benefit from product data in design engineering and manufacturing.

In 2020 Accenture has acquired NIKE Group an Italian consulting firm that provides regulatory technology (RegTech) services and solutions to financial services firms. Accenture announced its intent to acquire the business on April 14 2020. Financial terms of the transaction were not disclosed. The team at NIKE Group will join Accenture's Italian Financial Services practice. The acquisition enhances Accenture's RegTech and compliance capabilities for clients in Italy and across Europe.

EXECUTIVES

Group Chief Executive Accenture Strategy, Mark A. Knickrehm, age 55
Group Chief Executive Financial Services, Richard A. Lumb, age 59, $972,812 total compensation
Chairman and CEO, Pierre Nanterme, age 61, $957,585 total compensation
CFO, David P. Rowland, age 59, $1,136,125 total compensation
Group Chief Executive Growth Markets, Gianfranco Casati, age 61, $967,329 total compensation
COO, Johan G. (Jo) Deblaere, age 58
Group Chief Executive Resources, Jean-Marc Ollagnier, age 59
Group Chief Executive Products, Alexander M. (Sander) van't Noordende, $1,136,125 total compensation
Group Chief Executive Communications Media and Technology, Robert E. (Bob) Sell
Group Chief Executive Health and Public Service, Daniel T. (Dan) London, age 55
Chief Technology and Innovation Officer, Paul Daugherty
Group Chief Executive Accenture Digital, Michael R. (Mike) Sutcliff
Group CEO North America, Julie Sweet, age 52, $1,136,125 total compensation
Group Chief Executive Accenture Operations, Debra A. Polishook
Federal CIO Advisory Director Accenture Federal Services (AFS), Dave McClure
Auditors: KPMG LLP

LOCATIONS

HQ: Accenture plc
  1 Grand Canal Square, Grand Canal Harbour, Dublin 2
Phone: (353) 1 646 2000
Web: www.accenture.com

2018 Sales

	% of total
North America	45
Europe	33
Growth Markets	19
Total	**100**

PRODUCTS/OPERATIONS

2018 sales

	% of total
CommunicationsMedia & Technology	19
Financial Services	20
Health & Public Service	16
Products	26
Resources	14
Reimbursement	5
Total	**100**

2018 sales

	% of total
Consulting	52
Outsourcing	43
Reimbursement	5
Total	**100**

Selected Practice Areas

Communications and high technology
  Communications
  Electronics and high technology
  Media and entertainment
Products
  Automotive
  Consumer goods and services
  Health and life sciences
  Industrial equipment
  Retail
  Transportation and travel services
Financial services
  Banking
  Capital markets
  Insurance
Resources
  Chemicals
  Energy
  Natural resources
  Utilities
Government

Selected Services

Customer relationship management
Finance and performance management
Human performance
Strategy
Supply chain management
Outsourcing
  Application outsourcing
  Business process outsourcing (BPO)
  Customer contact
  Finance and accounting
  Human resources
  Learning
  Procurement
  Infrastructure outsourcing
Systems integration and technology
  Enterprise architecture
  Information management
  Infrastructure consulting
  Intellectual property
Research and developmen

COMPETITORS

Bain & Company	Computer Sciences
Booz Allen	Corp.
Boston Consulting	Deloitte Consulting
Capgemini	HP Enterprise Services
Capgemini North	IBM
America	McKinsey & Company
Charteris	Unisys

HISTORICAL FINANCIALS

Company Type: Public

Income Statement

	REVENUE ($ mil.)	NET INCOME ($ mil.)	NET PROFIT MARGIN	EMPLOYEES
08/20	44,327	5,107	11.5%	506,000
08/19	43,215	4,779	11.1%	492,000
08/18	41,603	4,059	9.8%	459,000
08/17	36,765	3,445	9.4%	425,000
08/16	34,797	4,111	11.8%	384,000
Annual Growth	**6.2%**	**5.6%**	**—**	**7.1%**

FYE: August 31

2020 Year-End Financials

Debt ratio: 0.1%
Return on equity: 32.4%
Cash ($ mil.): 8,415
Current ratio: 1.40
Long-term debt ($ mil.): 54
No. of shares (mil.): 634
Dividends
  Yield: 1.3%
  Payout: 40.5%
Market value ($ mil.): —

ACS Actividades de Construccion y Servicios, S.A.

Turning the rains (and the wind) on the plains of Spain into electricity provides the current for growth at ACS Actividades de Construcci n y Servicios one of Spain's largest construction and infrastructure groups. ACS Group operates in three primary business areas: construction environment and industrial services. The company's activities include civil engineering installation and maintenance of energy facilities transport services and highway management. ACS has grown by investing in such firms as former construction rival Dragados and Germany-based infrastructure giant HOCHTIEF. The group is active in more than 60 countries mainly in Europe and Latin America. ACS is run by Florentino Perez who is best known as the president of Real Madrid the world's most successful soccer team.

Operations

ACS divides its business into three segments: Construction Industrial Services and Services.

ACS's construction business which generates nearly 80% of the company's revenue consists of three independent multinational construction companies: Dragados HOCHTIEF and Iridium. The companies operate in a diverse range of sectors including public works (highways railways ports and airports) social value (residential buildings social facilities and installations) infrastructure services (transport communications energy resources and defense) and mining.

The Industrial Services segment brings in nearly 20% of ACS' revenue and develops constructs maintains and operates energy industrial and mobility infrastructure. Its activities are grouped into two business lines Industry Support Services and EPC Projects.

The Services segment which generates the remaining 5% or so of revenue and does business as Clece provides services across some 30 social-focused activities. These include education services sustainability and assistance for at-risk groups.

Geographic Reach

ACS is active in more than 60 countries; its largest markets are the US (accounting for nearly 40% of all sales) Australia Spain Hong Kong Canada Mexico and Germany.

Financial Performance

Note: Growth rates may differ after conversion to US dollars.

ACS' revenue had been on a steady decline since 2012 until 2017 when its revenue ticked up 9% to ?34.9 billion. The large Construction segment grew 12% thanks to a recovery in the CIMIC its Australian construction arm and positive growth in HOCHTIEF and Dragados. Growth in the Industrial Services business was materially flat as a slowdown in Mexico was offset by an improvement in Spain and higher activity in Asia and South Africa. A 6% fall in sales in the Services business was a result of its wind-down of logistics services.

Aside from 2012 when it incurred a stinging loss ACS' net income has held remarkable steady in the mid-?700 million range. In 2017 it inched past the ?800-million mark for the first time a 17% increase on 2016. The improved profits mostly stemmed from the strong Construction performance and lower debt levels.

The company achieved its goal of reducing net debt to near-zero in 2017 funneling its operating cash of ?1.7 billion into paying down its debt by more than ?1 billion. It ended the year with net debt of ?153 million — a relatively trivial figure for a company the size of ACS and an all-time low.

Strategy

In 2017 ACS completed a six-year quest to strengthen its balance sheet by reducing its net debt. Standing at ?9.3 billion in 2011 progressive use of operating cash to pay down debt reduced the company's net debt levels to just ?153 million at the end of 2017. The debt reduction helped lift ACS' credit rating to BBB (investment grade) and with lower interest payments to make each year the company's profits will rise.

The company is pursuing opportunities in the public-private partnership (PPP) sector. It has identified more than 150 projects worth upwards of a combined ?200 billion mostly in the US Canada Australia and Europe. It views these markets as showing a favorable infrastructure investment climate.

HISTORY

In war-torn Europe in 1942 the Spanish construction company Obras y Construcciones Industriales (Ocisa) was born. The company soon began a 50-year association with Spain's hydroelectric industry marked by the completion of the dam and reservoir project Presa de Bachimana in 1950. The company built nine more dam and reservoir projects in Spain (including Presa de la Llosa completed in 1997).

As the demand for public works projects decreased and competition increased Spanish constructors began working abroad especially in Latin America where Ocisa was contracted in 1975 to create an irrigation tunnel in Venezuela's Andes.

A six-year economic expansion measured by the success of Spain's "Big Seven" construction companies including #5 Ocisa reached its end in 1992 when the Spanish government the country's biggest builder was forced to cut spending on infrastructure. This triggered consolidation in Spain's construction industry including Ocisa's 1993 acquisition of Construcciones Padros in which Ocisa held a 25% stake. Adopting the new name OCP Construcciones it also absorbed the assets of its installation and assembly subsidiary Compania de la Distribucion de Electricidad (Grupo Cobra).

The slowdown in public works projects continued and companies sought additional pooling of resources and diversification of activities at home and abroad. In 1996 OCP bought a 40% stake in the state-owned construction firm Auxini increased to 100% a year later. Also in 1997 the OCP group led by its president Florentino Perez acquired Gines Navarro Construcciones controlled (79%) by the powerful investment group led by brothers Carlos and Juan March. The two companies combined to create Spain's third-largest construction group Actividades de Construcciones y Servicios or Grupo ACS.

EXECUTIVES

Chairman President and CEO, Florentino Pérez Rodr guez, age 73
Chairman and CEO Industrial Services, Eugenio Llorente G mez
Chairman and CEO Turner Construction, Peter J. Davoren, age 65
Chairman and CEO Flatiron, John A. DiCiurcio, age 65
CEO Dragados, Ignacio Segura Suriñach
Corporate General Manager, Angel Manuel Garcia Altozano
Chairman and CEO HOCHTIEF AG and CEO Leighton Holdings, Marcelino Fern ndez Verdes
CEO Environment, José Mar a L pez-Piñol
CEO HOCHTIEF Solutions, Nikolaus Graf von Matuschka, age 57
CEO Iridium, Juan Santamaria Cases
Vice Chairman, Pablo Vallbona Vadell
Executive Vice Chairman, Antonio Garc a Ferrer, age 75
Auditors: KPMG Auditores, S.L.

LOCATIONS

HQ: ACS Actividades de Construccion y Servicios, S.A. Avenida de Pio XII, 102, Madrid 28036
Phone: (34) 91 343 9200   **Fax:** (34) 91 343 9456
Web: www.grupoacs.com

2017 Sales

	% of total
North America	45
Asia/Pacific	29
Spain	13
Rest of Europe	7
South Africa	5
Africa	1
Total	**100**

PRODUCTS/OPERATIONS

2017 Sales

	% of total
Construction	78
Industrial Services	18
Environment	4
Total	**100**

Selected Subsidiaries
Concessions
  Concesiones Viarias Chile S.A. (infrastructures)
  Iridium Concesiones de Infraestructuras S.A.
Construction
  Acainsa S.A. (real estate development)
  Ave Lalin
  Consorcio Tecdra S.A.
  Constructora Norte Sur S.A. (48% Chile)
  Desaladora Barcelona (28%)
  Guadarrama Iv (33%)
  Inmobiliaria Alabega S.A. (real estate development)
  Isla Verde Ute (35%)
  Soterram. Basurto Ute Tecsa-Necso (50%)
  Terminal Aeropuerto (70%)
Environment
  Consenur S.A. (management and treatment of hospital waste)
  Empordanesa de Neteja S.A. (urban solid waste management and street cleaning)
  Mapide S.A. (interior cleaning)
  Publimedia Sistemas Publicitarios S.L. (advertising services)
  RetraOil S.L. (treatment of oils and marpoles)
  Servicios Generales de Jaé;n S.A. (75% water)

  Somasur S.A. (intermediary company Morocco)
  Urbaser de Mé;jico S.A. (collection of urban solid waste and street cleaning)
  Urbaser Valencia C.A. (collection of urban solid waste and street cleaning)
  Ute Ecoparc V (20% USW treatment)
  Vertederos de Residuos S.A. (84% VERTRESA collection of urban solid waste and street cleaning)
Industrial Services
  ACS industrial Services LLC (energy production US)
  Actividades de Servicios e Instalaciones Cobra S.A. (auxiliary energy and communications distribution Guatemala)
  Andasol 1 S.A. (energy production)
  API Movilidad S.A. (road maintenance)
  BTOB Construccion Ventures S.L. (administrative management)
  Central Té;rmica de Mejillones S.A. (engineering supply and construction Chile)
  Cobra Ingenierí;a de Montajes S.A. (installations and assembly)
  Cobra Perù S.A. (auxiliary energy and communications distribution)
  Coinsal Instalaciones y Servicios S.A. de C.V. (installations and assembly El Salvador)
  Cymi Holding S.A. (securities holding company Brazil)
  Dragados Gulf Construction Ltd. (Saudi Arabia)
  Emurtel S.A. (50% electrical installations)
  Enq S.L. (electrical installations)
  Etra Catalu Â Â a S.A. (electrical installations)
  Extresol-1 S.L. (energy production)
  Gerovitae La Guancha S.A. (senior social and health center operations)
  Humiclima Est S.A. (air conditioning)
  Incro S.A. (50% engineering)
  Infraest. Energé;ticas Medioambi. Extreme Â Â as S.L. (services)
  Instalaciones y Servicios Codeven C.A. (air conditioning)
  Mantenimiento y Montajes Industriales S.A. (industrial maintenance and assemblies)
  Mexsemi S.A. de C.V. (99.7% assemblies Mexico)
  Opade Organizac. y Promoc de Actividades Deportivas S.A. (athletic activities organization and promotion)
  Parque Eólico Marmellar S.L. (70% energy production)
  Portumasa S.A. (manufacture and sale of electical equipment Portugal)
  Semi Maroc S.A. (99.7% assemblies)
  Serveis Catalans Serveica S.A. (electrical installations)
  SICE LLC. (design construction installation and maintenance of traffic and trade)
  Sistemas Radiantes F. Moyano S.A. (telecommunications)
  Tecnotel de Canarias S.A. (air conditioning)
  Ute C.T. Andasol 1 (80% fossil fuel plant)
  Venezolana de Limpiezas Indust. C.A. (83% VENELIN Venezuela)
Services
  Valdemingomez 2000 S.A. (34% Valdemingómez degasification)

COMPETITORS

Abengoa	Ferrovial
Acciona	Grupo San José
Aker Solutions	Hyundai Engineering
Andrade Gutierrez	and Construction
Balfour Beatty	Kellogg Brown & Root
Bechtel	UK
Bilfinger	OHL
Black & Veatch	Odebrecht
Brisa	Salini Impregilo
Cintra	Skanska
DP World	TECNOCOM
FCC Barcelona	VINCI

HISTORICAL FINANCIALS
Company Type: Public

Income Statement

	REVENUE ($ mil.)	NET INCOME ($ mil.)	NET PROFIT MARGIN	FYE: December 31 EMPLOYEES
12/19	44,210	1,080	2.4%	194,036
12/18	42,243	1,047	2.5%	191,823
12/17	42,201	961	2.3%	181,527
12/16	34,242	792	2.3%	169,766
12/15	38,506	790	2.1%	200,516
Annual Growth	**3.5%**	**8.1%**	—	**(0.8%)**

2019 Year-End Financials

Debt ratio: 26.6%
Return on equity: 21.8%
Cash ($ mil.): 9,082
Current ratio: 1.01
Long-term debt ($ mil.): 7,043

No. of shares (mil.): 314
Dividends
  Yield: 0.2%
  Payout: 60.7%
Market value ($ mil.): 2,489

	STOCK PRICE ($) FY Close	P/E High/Low		PER SHARE ($) Earnings	Dividends	Book Value
12/19	7.91	3	2	3.51	2.13	15.76
12/18	7.70	3	2	3.32	1.59	15.74
12/17	7.79	4	3	2.97	0.00	13.73
12/16	6.32	3	2	2.42	0.00	11.30
12/15	8.25	—	—	2.37	0.00	10.97
Annual Growth	**(1.0%)**	—	—	**10.3%**	—	**9.5%**

Adecco Group AG

Any way you stack it Adecco is the world's largest employment agency serving more than 100000 clients from more than 5000 offices worldwide. The bulk of Adecco's business is providing temporary staffing permanent placement and outsourcing under the brands Adecco and Adia. The company also operates several professional staffing businesses including Badenoch + Clark Modis Spring Professional Vettery and Yoss which source IT engineering and technical finance and legal and medical and science staff. Adecco does most of its business in Europe particularly France but it has operations globally. Pontoon General Assembly and LHH is Adecco's HR outsourcing business fulfilling an organization's staffing needs. Adecco traces its roots to 1957 and has a history of growing through mergers and acquisitions.

Operations
Adecco provides staffing services under four categories: temporary staffing permanent placement career transition and other solutions.

Temporary staffing is by far the company's largest operation at more than 85% of sales focuses on deploying associates to organizations on a temporary basis. Permanent placement services account for 2% of sales provide employers recruitment process of talents for permanent roles and Career Transition supports organizations and their employees through changes that require individuals to transition out of their existing roles underpinned by expert coaching and training.

Other solutions accounted for 10% of sales focuses on HR solutions such as outsourcing managed Service and recruitment process outsourcing.

By industry sector Adecco's Workforce Solutions business sources staff for general office and industrial settings under the brands Adecco and Adia. Adia provides on-demand staff mainly for the hospitality and events industry. Workforce Solutions generates more than 70% of sales.

Professional Staffing & Solutions fills vacancies in the IT Engineering Finance Legal and Medical & Science sectors. It trades under five brands: Badenoch + Clark (generalist) Modis (IT and engineering) Spring (IT) Vettery (tech sales and finance) and Yoss (tech).

Geographic Reach

Zurich Switzerland-based Adecco operates in 60 countries. France is its largest market accounting for about 25% total sales while North America generates nearly 20% of sales. Adecco also trades in most countries in Western Central Northern and Eastern Europe as well as Japan India the MENA region and Australasia which account for about 10% of sales.

Sales and Marketing

Adecco Group provides temporary staffing permanent placement career transitioning outsourcing talent development and other services to more than 100000 clients from more than 5000 offices worldwide.

Adecco Group uses marketing automation tools such as their digital AI chatbots and client portal Mon Agence en Ligne.

Marketing expenses totaled EUR 105 EUR 101 and EUR 85 in 2019 2018 and 2017 respectively.

Financial Performance

Note: Growth rates may differ after conversion to US Dollars.

Adecco's has enjoyed a consistent revenue growth over the years. Between 2015 and 2019 it has an increase of 6%. However due to the weakening demand in some European markets and North America it had a slight decline of revenue in 2019.

The company's revenue for 2019 is ?23.4 billion a decrease of 2% compared to ?23.9 in 2018.This was driven by the weakening demand in most European markets and North America. Another reason is the decline of 4% in Temporary Staffing comprising a 7% decline in temp hours sold partially offset by a 3% increase in the average bill rate. General Staffing's revenue also declined by 4% with Industrial down by 6% and 1% of Office.

Adecco posted a net income of ?728 million in 2019 a 58% increase compared to the prior year. This was driven by the ?239 million increase in operating income.

Adecco's cash position increased by ?698 million during 2019 ending the year at ?1.4 billion. It generated ?880 million from its operations while investing activities provided another ?324 million and its financing activities used ?524 million. The company's main cash uses were capital expenditures long-term debt repayments and dividend payouts.

Strategy

The Adecco Group launched Modis Academy in 2019 an alliance between Modis and General Assembly as a digital talent incubator and skills accelerator. Modis Academy offers candidates the opportunity to upskill themselves and be matched with potential employers. Modis Academy enrolls high-potential individuals to be trained for real-life roles through either a virtual "Remote Flex" programme or the full-time "Immersive" experience. This talent incubation model enables Modis to support clients in finding talent.

In 2019 Adecco hired approximately 10000 new colleagues across the 60 countries they operate. They launched a career portal leveraging new technology to differentiate the candidate journey and colleague experience. By redefining their recruitment processes Adecco believes they are driving efficiencies and business growth. The company is establishing ways of working to reflect the needs and wants of next-gen workforces. One example is their "portfolio careers" which enable more flexible working solutions such as project participation job shadowing and role sharing.

Addeco's GrowTogether programme continues to expand in terms of breadth and depth; embedding a culture of customer-centricity and continuous process improvement while re-applying and leveraging proven digital tools. This programme increase effectiveness in sales recruiting and middle and back-office activities. The company have digitalized many of their middle-office processes including the majority of timesheet capture and a significant proportion of timesheet interpretation. They are also focusing on driving candidate and client acquisition through digital channels such as our chatbots online portals and mobile apps.

EXECUTIVES

Regional Head North America, Robert P. (Bob) Crouch, age 52

Regional Head of Asia Pacific, Christophe Duchatellier, age 58

Regional Head of UK and Ireland, John L. Marshall

Regional Head of Italy Eastern Europe & MENA and India, Sergio Picarelli, age 54, $187,500 total compensation

CEO, Alain Dehaze, age 56, $145,227 total compensation

Regional Head Iberia and South America, Enrique Sanchez, age 54, $161,296 total compensation

CFO, Hans P. van Amstel

Regional Head of France, Christophe Catoir, age 48

Regional Head of Northern Europe, Mark De Smedt

Regional Head of Germany Austria and Switzerland (DACH), Franz-Josef Sch rmann, age 51

Vice Chairman, Thomas C. (Tom) O'Neill, age 75

Chairman, Rolf Dorig, age 63

Auditors: Ernst & Young Ltd.

LOCATIONS

HQ: Adecco Group AG
  Bellerivestrasse 30, Zurich 8008
Phone: (41) 44 878 88 88   **Fax:** (41) 44 829 88 88
Web: www.adeccogroup.com

2018 sales

	% of total
France	24
North America & UK&I General Staffing	13
North America & UK&I Professional Staffing	14
Germany Austria Switzerland	9
Benelux & Nordics	9
Italy	8
Japan	5
Iberia	5
Rest of the World	11
Career Transition & Talent Development	2
Total	**100**

PRODUCTS/OPERATIONS

2018 sales

	% of total
General Staffing	
Office	23
Industrial	53
Professional Staffing	
IT	11
Engineering & Technical	4
Finance & Legal	4
Medical & Science	2
Solutions	
Career Transition & Talent Development	2
BPO	1
Total	**100**

Selected Brands

Adecco
Badenoch & Clark
Modis
Spring Professional

Selected Services

Career Transition
Outsourcing Talent Development and other services
Permanent Placement
Temporary Staffing

COMPETITORS

Insperity	Synergie
Kelly Services	Technical Aid
ManpowerGroup	Corporation
Randstad Holding	Volt Information
Robert Half	

HISTORICAL FINANCIALS

Company Type: Public

Income Statement   FYE: December 31

	REVENUE ($ mil.)	NET INCOME ($ mil.)	NET PROFIT MARGIN	EMPLOYEES
12/19	26,303	816	3.1%	34,662
12/18	27,332	524	1.9%	34,774
12/17	28,362	944	3.3%	33,787
12/16	23,977	763	3.2%	33,391
12/15	23,973	8	0.0%	32,000
Annual Growth	2.3%	211.1%	—	2.0%

2019 Year-End Financials

Debt ratio: 18.5%	No. of shares (mil.): 162
Return on equity: 19.3%	Dividends
Cash ($ mil.): 1,516	Yield: 2.3%
Current ratio: 1.33	Payout: 14.8%
Long-term debt ($ mil.): 1,770	Market value ($ mil.): 5,127

	STOCK PRICE ($) FY Close	P/E High/Low		PER SHARE ($) Earnings	Dividends	Book Value
12/19	31.64	7	5	5.02	0.74	27.29
12/18	23.50	14	8	3.17	1.23	25.07
12/17	38.33	9	8	5.59	0.96	25.83
12/16	32.65	8	5	4.48	0.91	23.03
12/15	34.17	874603		0.05	1.08	21.36
Annual Growth	(1.9%)	—	—209.8%		(8.9%)	6.3%

Adidas AG

From famous athletes to school kids adidas wants to help everyone get in the game. The German sportswear company sells sports shoes apparel and equipment sporting its iconic three-stripe logo in more than 160 countries. One of the top sporting goods manufacturers worldwide (along with NIKE and Under Armour) adidas focuses on football soccer basketball running and training gear and apparel as well as lifestyle goods. Its other major brand Reebok sells fitness and gym apparel. All in adidas sells adidas and Reebok-branded products through more than 2500 owned stores as well as a franchise network and via a wholesale channel. Founder Adi Dassler brother of PUMA creator Rudi began making shoes in Germany in the early 1920s.

Operations

adidas-branded goods account for 90% of the company's sales and span performance sportswear and casual fashion. adidas makes shoes apparel and equipment for soccer running football basketball rugby and more. Its sports-fashion product lines include adidas Originals and adidas Neo.

Reebok is a fitness brand catering to runners gym-goers and other fitness fanatics. Its Reebok

Classics range serves casual fashion for customers outside the gym.

With just two brands adidas may have limited scope for brand positioning compared to arch-rival Nike which makes products under the NIKE Jordan Hurley and Converse brands.

By product category footwear is adidas' biggest and fastest-growing product category. It generates around 60% of total sales and includes the top-of-the-line Boost range. Apparel accounts for around 35% of sales with the remainder chalked up to hardware (balls bags and fitness equipment).

The Runtastic business is a social network platform that allows for the gamification of sports and includes software hardware and services.

Geographic Reach

Based in Bavaria Germany adidas has legions of customers across the globe's major regions. It sells adidas and Reebok-branded clothing through 2300 stores worldwide and extends its reach further via a franchise network of 14000 mono-branded stores and a wholesale function that supplies around 150000 third-party retailers. Its e-commerce operation reaches customers in 40 countries worldwide via adidas.com Reebok.com and its app.

The Asia/Pacific region is the company's biggest territory accounting for one-third of sales. Europe accounts more than a quarter North America for more than 20% and Latin America for more than 5%. Russia/CIS region and other markets accounts for the remainder.

Western Europe remains its biggest territory at around 30% of total sales while fast-growing North America and Greater China account for around 20% each. The Middle East Africa and Other Asia (excl Japan) generates around 15% Latin America some 10% and Japan around 5%.

adidas outsources nearly all its manufacturing. Its 130 independent manufacturing suppliers are located in more than 55 countries but 70% are in Asia. Vietnam accounts for more than 40% of its footwear manufacturing while apparel manufacturing its more evenly dispersed led by Cambodia at a quarter of production. China no longer the cheapest destination for manufacturing outsourcing accounts for less than 20% of production.

Sales and Marketing

Sophisticated product positioning in its footwear category in particular grants the adidas brand high value in the functional sportswear and premium casual fashion market segments. The Yeezy 350 casual sneaker for instance designed in partnership with Kanye West goes for hundreds of dollars a pair but equally the company can sell budget $20 trainers without degrading its three-stripe brand equity.

adidas spends half its marketing budget on sponsorship deals which range widely across sports teams events and sportspeople. Soccer is adidas' most extensive category and includes sponsorships of the soccer World Cup the German national soccer team club teams Bayern Munich and Manchester United as well as hundreds of leading players across the world including Lionel Messi Paul Pogba and Gareth Bale. It also has sponsorship arrangements in basketball tennis rugby boxing and a large number of Olympic sports.

The majority of adidas' sales come from newly launched products and adidas faces a constant test to maintain a deep and innovative product pipeline.

Financial PerformanceNote: Growth rates may differ after conversion to US Dollars.

Over the last ten years adidas has grown strongly and trails only Nike in revenue and profitability.

In fiscal 2018 revenue growth slowed to 3% (from 15% in 2017) but net revenue of ?21.9 billion was nevertheless a company record. Growth was led by the Asia/Pacific region up 12% and

North America up 10%. Performance was weaker elsewhere with Russia Latin America and Emerging Markets recording double-digit falls while Europe declined a marginal 1%. The divestiture of a number of non-core business such as Rockport and TaylorMade also weighed on sales (they contributed ?667 million to sales in 2017).

By product category footwear growth slowed sharply growing 3% compared to 23% in 2017. Apparel grew 6% while hardware most impacted by the divestitures fell 13%.

Net income jumped 55% to ?1.7 billion as the company successfully grew its top line without adding to cost of sales; margin increased 1.1 pp to 10.8%. That was possible due mainly to the absence of the divested loss-making subsidiaries in addition to efficiency gains and better pricing channel and product mix.

adidas' coffers swelled in 2018 ending the year ?1.0 billion higher at ?2.6 billion. It generated ?2.6 billion in cash from its operations and used ?636 million in its investing activities and ?951 million in its financing activities. The company's cash use consisted primarily of property plant and equipment purchases and ?1.0 billion in treasury share repurchases.

Strategy

With the sale of its loss-making golf business adidas' margins have increased giving the company more cash to invest in its adidas and Reebok brands.

The Reebok brand strategy is based on its transformation to a general sports apparel retailer to focusing entirely on sports fitness — running gym and combat sports. For the latter two Reebok has sponsorship arrangements with CrossFit a popular branded workout/fitness company and UFC the world's leading mixed-martial arts company. Such tie-ins are key to revitalizing the Reebok brand and lifting flat revenue growth in North America in particular. To up its focus on the market adidas created a US-specific Reebok team and moved its regional HQ to Boston. Additionally Reebok is cutting roughly half its brick-and-mortar stores and will lean on online channels for sales growth. It is also rationalizing its wholesale strategy to cover only those retailers that boost Reebok's brand equity.

On the marketing front adidas will continue to increase marketing spend in absolute terms but withdraw to a degree from sponsorships the costs of which are increasingly subject to intense bidding wars between adidas and its rivals. It will reduce sponsorship spend from 50% of its marketing budget to around 45% and concurrently increase its budget for digital advertising point-of-sale and grassroots activations (pick-up sports leagues etc) It is also developing its non-sport partnerships particularly with musicians Kanye West and Pharrell Williams and fashion designers Yohji Yamamoto Stella McCartney and Alexander Wang.

Company Background

adidas was founded in 1924 by Adi Dassler (hence "adi-das") in the small German town of Herzogenaurach. It found fame early on when US sprinter Jesse Owens won four gold medals at the 1936 Olympics in Berlin while wearing adidas running spikes. Adi's brother Rudolf left the company in acrimonious circumstances in 1947 and formed Puma also in Herzogenaurach; the two companies entered into an intense rivalry (later eclipsed by the adidas-NIKE rivalry). adidas became a public company in 1995 and in 2006 acquired Reebok which as of 2019 is the only non-adidas apparel brand used by the company.

HISTORY

adidas grew out of an infamous rift between German brothers Adi and Rudi Dassler who cre-

ated athletic shoe giants adidas and Puma. As WWI was winding down Adi scavenged for tires rucksacks and other refuse to create slippers gymnastics shoes and soccer cleats at home. His sister cut patterns out of canvas. By 1926 the shoes' success allowed the Dasslers to build a factory. At the 1928 Amsterdam Olympics German athletes first showcased Dassler shoes to the world. In 1936 American Jesse Owens sprinted to Olympic gold in Dassler's double-striped shoes.

Business boomed until the Nazis commandeered the Dassler factory to make boots for soldiers. Although both Rudi and Adi were reportedly members of the Nazi party only Rudi was called to service. Adi remained at home to run the factory. When Allied troops occupied the area Adi made friends with American soldiers — even creating shoes for a soldier who wore them at the 1946 Olympics. Rudi came home from an American prison camp and joined his brother; together they scavenged the war-torn landscape for tank materials and tents to make shoes.

Soon a dispute between the brothers split the business. Rumors circulated that Rudi resented that Adi had failed to use his American connections to help spring him from prison camp. Rudi set up his own factory facing Adi across the River Aurach. The brothers never spoke to each other again except in court. Rudi's company was named Puma and Adi's became adidas. Adi added a third stripe to the Dassler's trademark shoe while Rudi chose a cat's paw in motion. Thus began one of the most intense rivalries in Europe. The children of Puma and adidas employees attended separate elementary schools and the employees even distinguished themselves by drinking different beers.

With Adi's innovations throughout the late 1940s and 1950s (such as the replaceable-cleat soccer shoe) adidas came to dominate the world's athletic shoe market. In the late 1950s it capitalized on the booming US market overtaking the canvas sneakers made by P.F. Flyers and Stride Rite (Keds). The company also initiated the practice of putting logos on sports bags and clothing.

adidas continued to expand globally in the 1960s and 1970s to maintain its dominant position. However a flood of new competitors following the 1972 Munich Olympics and the death of Adi in 1978 signaled the end of an era. As NIKE and Reebok captured the North American market during the 1980s adidas made one of its biggest missteps — it turned down a sneaker endorsement offer from a young Michael Jordan in 1984.

French politician and entrepreneur Bernard Tapie bought the struggling company in 1989 but he stepped down in 1992 amid personal political and business scandals. The next year Robert Louis-Dreyfus became CEO. He shifted production to Asia pumped up the advertising budget and brought in former NIKE marketing geniuses to re-establish the company's identity.

adidas became adidas-Salomon in 1997 with its $1.4 billion purchase of Salomon a French maker of skis and other sporting goods. The company also opened its first high-profile store in Portland Oregon that year. In a 1998 reorganization Louis-Dreyfus sacked Jean-Francois Gautier as Salomon's president in the wake of disappointing sales particularly from TaylorMade Golf Salomon's golf subsidiary.

Amid a 10% slide in revenue several key executives decided to leave the company in 2000 including adidas America CEO Steve Wynne. Citing poor health Louis-Dreyfus soon followed (but remained as chairman); he was replaced by the new CEO of adidas America Ross McMullin who soon after was diagnosed with cancer. Later that year the company announced it would consolidate its apparel under the Heritage label to reinforce its position in the burgeoning casual wear market.

In 2001 Louis-Dreyfus retired as chairman and in March COO Herbert Hainer became chief executive. That year adidas-Salomon opened adidas Originals retail stores in Tokyo and Berlin; that was followed with a New York City store in 2002. Despite slumping sales in the US amid deep discounting by competitors adidas announced in 2003 that it would not offer discounts and still intended to capture 20% of the country's shoe market.

Britain's Barclays Bank PLC became adidas' largest shareholder in 2004 raising its stake to 5.4%. The company changed its name in 2006 to adidas AG.

In May 2008 adidas AG won a $305 million award from a federal jury in Oregon for trademark violation of its three-stripe design by Collective Brands the operator of the Payless and Stride Rite shoe-store chains.

In November 2011 adidas acquired outdoor specialist Five Ten a leading brand in the technical outdoor markets and outdoor action sports community for $25 million.

EXECUTIVES

President and CEO TaylorMade-adidas Golf, Mark King
Member Executive Board Finance, Robin J. Stalker, age 63
Global Operations, Glenn Bennett, age 58
CEO and Director, Kasper B. Rorsted, age 57
Global Brands, Eric Liedtke
CEO TaylorMade-adidas Golf, Ben Sharpe
Chairman, Igor Landau, age 76
Deputy Chairwoman, Sabine Bauer, age 57
Deputy Chairman, Willi Schwerdtle, age 67
Auditors: KPMG AG Wirtschaftsprüfungsgesellschaft

LOCATIONS

HQ: Adidas AG
Adi-Dassler-Strasse 1, Herzogenaurach D-91074
Phone: (49) 91 32 84 0   **Fax:** (49) 91 32 84 2241
Web: www.adidas-group.com

2018 Sales

	% of total
Asia/Pacific	33
Europe	27
North America	21
Latin America	7
Emerging Markets	5
Russia/CIS	3
Other Businesses	4
Total	**100**

PRODUCTS/OPERATIONS

2018 Sales by Product

	% of total
Footwear	58
Apparel	38
Hardware	4
Total	**100**

2018 Sales by Brand

	% of total
adidas	92
Reebok	8
Total	**100**

COMPETITORS

ASICS	K-Swiss
Amer Sports	Mizuno
Benetton	NIKE
Columbia Sportswear	New Balance
Converse	PUMA SE
Deckers Outdoor	Quiksilver
FUBU	Saucony
Fila Korea	Skechers U.S.A.
Fila USA	Under Armour
Head N.V.	VF Corporation

HISTORICAL FINANCIALS
Company Type: Public

Income Statement   FYE: December 31

	REVENUE ($ mil.)	NET INCOME ($ mil.)	NET PROFIT MARGIN	EMPLOYEES
12/19	26,542	2,218	8.4%	59,533
12/18	25,096	1,949	7.8%	57,016
12/17	25,435	1,315	5.2%	56,888
12/16	20,369	1,073	5.3%	57,876
12/15	18,424	690	3.7%	55,555
Annual Growth	9.6%	33.9%	—	1.7%

2019 Year-End Financials

Debt ratio: 12.8%	No. of shares (mil.): 195
Return on equity: 30.0%	Dividends
Cash ($ mil.): 2,492	Yield: 0.8%
Current ratio: 1.25	Payout: 11.9%
Long-term debt ($ mil.): 1,790	Market value ($ mil.): 31,904

	STOCK PRICE ($) FY Close	P/E High/Low		PER SHARE ($) Earnings	Dividends	Book Value
12/19	162.80	17	10	11.23	1.34	38.94
12/18	104.34	15	11	9.64	1.12	36.67
12/17	99.82	22	16	6.45	0.88	37.93
12/16	78.55	17	9	5.27	0.60	33.91
12/15	48.51	16	9	3.43	0.60	30.82
Annual Growth	35.3%	—	—	34.5%	22.2%	6.0%

Adient Plc

Auditors: PricewaterhouseCoopers LLP

LOCATIONS

HQ: Adient Plc
25-28 North Wall Quay, IFSC, Dublin 1 D01 H104
Phone: (354) 734 254 5000
Web: www.adient.com

HISTORICAL FINANCIALS
Company Type: Public

Income Statement   FYE: September 30

	REVENUE ($ mil.)	NET INCOME ($ mil.)	NET PROFIT MARGIN	EMPLOYEES
09/20	12,670	(547)	—	77,000
09/19	16,526	(491)	—	83,000
09/18	17,439	(1,685)	—	85,000
09/17	16,213	877	5.4%	85,000
09/16	16,837	(1,533)	—	75,000
Annual Growth	(6.9%)	—	—	0.7%

2020 Year-End Financials

Debt ratio: 41.9%	No. of shares (mil.): 93
Return on equity: (-35.6%)	Dividends
Cash ($ mil.): 1,692	Yield: —
Current ratio: 1.17	Payout: —
Long-term debt ($ mil.): 4,097	Market value ($ mil.): —

AEGON NV

Dutch life insurance giant Aegon serves nearly 30 million customers worldwide. Its subsidiaries which include Transamerica and Scottish Equitable plc operate primarily in the US the Netherlands and the UK offering personal and commercial life insurance annuities and accident and supplemental health insurance as well as retirement and savings advice and management services. Aegon has insurance operations in more than 20 countries in the Americas Europe and Asia as well in the Netherlands. In 2019 Aegon has changed its grouping of the operating segments. From the previously separate Spain & Portugal segments and Central & Eastern Europe it is now combined under Southern & Eastern Europe segments.

Operations
Aegon divides its operations along geographic lines. The Americas is its biggest market representing about 45% of revenue and more than 55% of earnings. It covers business units in United States Brazil and Mexico.

In Asia (around 5% of total revenue) Aegon operates partnerships in China India and Japan and also serves high-net-worth individuals in Singapore and Hong Kong. The Europe segment covers the operations in UK (nearly 30% of sales) the Netherlands (around 15%) and Southern & Eastern Europe (around 5%).

Aegon Asset Management is a global active investment manager serving institutional and private investors. It offers fixed income equities real estate absolute return liability-driven and multi-asset solutions. The division trades under the Aegon name in most of the world except the UK where it does business as Kames Capital and the Netherlands where is operates as TKP Investments. The segment accounts for less than 5% of total revenue.

Geographic Reach
The Americas and Europe are by far Aegon's largest markets together bringing in some 95% of total revenue. Europe generates nearly 50% of revenue. The UK gets most of its revenue from insurance products while the Netherlands is a bigger source in investment income. The Americas accounts for around 45% of revenue but is more profitable more than 55% of earnings.

Aegon is based in The Hague in the Netherlands.

Sales and Marketing
Aegon primarily sells its products and services through brokers agents independent financial advisors employee benefit consultants and banks. It also does some direct selling. Aegon's partnership with Banco Santander allows Aegon to sell products through the Spanish banking giant's branch network.

Aegon Asset Management uses several sales and distribution channels including affiliated companies direct to institutional clients independent investment advisors investment consultants joint ventures and third-party investment platforms.

Financial Performance
Note: Growth rates may differ after conversion to US Dollars.

Aegon's revenues have generally declined in the last five years. It fell 17% between 2015 and 2019 struggling to return to its peak of ?33.9 billion in 2015. Net income has seen a similar trend despite surpassing its net loss of ?523 million in 2015; overall it rose 392% over the same period.

Aegon's revenues in 2019 fell 2% to ?28.2 billion from ?28.9 billion in the year prior due to declines in premium and fee and commission income despite a slight increase in its investment income.

Net income in 2019 rose considerably to ?1.5 billion as underlying earnings before tax of ?1.9 billion were partly offset by fair value losses other charges net impairments and income taxes.

Aegon's cash balance rose ?3.5 billion to ?12.3 billion during 2019. Operating activities generated ?7.3 billion while investing activities used ?86 million and financing used ?3.7 billion. Aegon's main cash uses in 2019 were repayment of trust pass-through securities perpetual repayments and treasury share purchases.

Strategy

Aegon has embarked on its next three-year plan which runs from 2019-2021. Its focus is on capital generation and shareholder returns and sustainable growth. In 2019 it sold its stake in the partnership with Sony Life in Japan which allows Aegon to fully focus on its most promising businesses customer segments and opportunities in Asia.

Going further Aegon announced in late 2019 that it will scrap the Kames Capital and TKP Investment asset management brands in the UK and Netherlands in favor of combining them with its US business. The newly formed ?300 million global asset manager will trade under the Aegon name. The move aims to leverage Aegon's greater brand recognition globally and to make it more responsive to changing market conditions.

Aegon has also made further strides in transferring the administration of its Transamerica brand's life and annuity business to a third-party TCS as well as the transfer of the administration and claims management for the long-term care insurance business line.

The company also continued to make investments intended to make it a more data-driven innovative customer-centric and agile company. It invested in training programs to ensure its employees are developing to become knowledgeable analysts and skilled stewards of Aegon's data. It has also ramped up the Aegon Analytical Academy and is inspiring its leaders of the future with the PULSE program.

HISTORY

AEGON traces its roots to 1844 when former civil servant and funeral society agent J. Oosterhoff founded Algemeene Friesche a burial society for low-income workers. The next year a similar organization Groot-Noordhollandsche was founded. These companies later became insurers and expanded nationwide. Meanwhile Olveh a civil servants' aid group was founded in 1877. The three companies merged in 1968 to form mutual insurer AGO.

AEGON's other operations came from different traditions. Vennootschap Nederland was founded in 1858 as a tontine (essentially a death pool with the survivors taking the pot) by Count A. Langrand-Dumonceau an ex-French Foreign Legionnaire from Belgium. In 1913 the company merged with Eerste Nederlandsche whose accident and health division had been previously spun off as Nieuwe Eerste Nederlandsche.

A year after Vennootschap was founded C. F. W. Wiggers van Kerchem founded a similar scheme Nillmij in the Dutch East Indies. The government promoted Nillmij to colonial civil servants and military people and for a while the company enjoyed a monopoly in the colony. Nillmij's Indonesian operations were nationalized after independence in 1957 but its Dutch subsidiaries continued to operate. All insurers were hit by fast-growing postwar government social programs. As a result industry consolidation came early to the Netherlands. In 1969 Eerste Nederlandsche Nieuwe Eerste Nederlandsche and Nillmij merged to form Ennia.

AGO demutualized in 1978 and became AGO Holding N.V. which was owned by Vereniging AGO. Meanwhile the shrinking Dutch insurance market forced companies to look overseas. AGO moved into the US in 1979 by buying Life Investors; by 1982 half of its sales came from outside the Netherlands. Ennia meanwhile expanded in Europe (it entered Spain in 1980) and the US (buying Arkansas-based National Old Line Insurance in 1981).

AGO and Ennia merged in 1983 to form AEGON. Vereniging AGO became Vereniging AEGON and received a 49% stake in the combined entity. (This stake was later reduced.) The company made more purchases at home and abroad and spent much of the rest of the decade assimilating operations.

AEGON's US units accounted for about 40% of sales in the mid-1980s and the firm increased that figure with acquisitions. In 1986 it bought Baltimore-based Monumental Corp. (life and health insurance) and expanded the company's US penetration.

This left AEGON underrepresented in Europe as deregulation paved the way for economic union and social service cutbacks spurred opportunities in private financial planning in the region. So in the 1990s AEGON began buying European companies including Regency Life (UK 1991) and Allami Biztosito (Hungary 1992). It formed an alliance with Mexico's Grupo Financiero Banamex in 1994. This reduced its reliance on US sales. It continued buying specialty operations in the US particularly asset management lines.

In 1997 AEGON began to concentrate on life insurance and financial services and shed its other operations. It bought the insurance business of Providian (now part of Washington Mutual) and sold noncore lines such as auto coverage. The next year it sold FGH Bank (mortgages) to Germany's Bayerische Vereinsbank (now Bayerische Hypotheken und Vereinsbank) and in 1999 sold auto insurer Worldwide Insurance.

That year AEGON expanded further in the US with the $9.7 billion purchase of Transamerica and bought the life and pensions businesses of the UK's Guardian Royal Exchange. In 2000 the company sold Labouchere N.V. a Dutch banking subsidiary to Dexia. Also in 2000 AEGON acquired UK-based third-party administrator HS Administrative Services.

Following the Transamerica acquisition the company divested several assets to focus on life insurance and pensions. In 2003 and 2004 diverse parts of Transamerica Finance (including its real estate tax unit and trailer leasing business) were sold to various companies including First American GE Commercial Finance and a joint venture held by Goldman Sachs and Cerberus Capital Management.

EXECUTIVES

CEO AEGON Continental Europe, Marco Keim, age 59

CEO, Alexander R. (Alex) Wynaendts, age 61, $1,253,040 total compensation

CEO Americas and Member Management Board Aegon N.V., Mark W. Mullin, age 58

CEO AGEON Asset Management, Sarah A. C. Russell, age 58

CFO, Matthew J. (Matt) Rider, age 57

CEO Aegon UK Member Management Board Aegis N.V., Adrian Grace, age 57

Chief Risk Officer, Allegra van H ¶vell-Patrizi, age 46

Global CTO, Mark Bloom, age 55

Chairman, Robert J. Routs, age 74

Vice Chairman, Corien M. Wortmann-Kool, age 61

Auditors: PricewaterhouseCoopers Accountants N.V.

LOCATIONS

HQ: AEGON NV
Aegonplein 50, P.O. Box 85, The Hague 2501 CB
Phone: (31) 70 344 32 10
Web: www.aegon.com

2018 sales

		% of total
Europe	49	
Americas	45	
Asia	4	
Asset Management	2	
Total	**100**	

PRODUCTS/OPERATIONS

2018 Sales

	% of total
Premiums	67
Investment income	24
Fees & commissions	9
Other	
Total	**100**

COMPETITORS

AXA	Lloyds Banking Group
Achmea	MassMutual
Allianz	MetLife
Allstate	Mutual of Omaha
American General	New York Life
Ameriprise	Old Mutual
Aviva	Principal Financial
FMR	Prudential
Franklin Templeton	Prudential plc
ING	Rabobank Group
Jackson National Life	SNS REAAL
John Hancock Financial Services	Standard Life Aberdeen
Legal & General Group	Symetra
Lincoln Financial Group	The Vanguard Group
	Zurich Insurance Group

HISTORICAL FINANCIALS

Company Type: Public

Income Statement				FYE: December 31
	ASSETS ($ mil.)	NET INCOME ($ mil.)	INCOME AS % OF ASSETS	EMPLOYEES
12/19	494,407	1,391	0.3%	23,757
12/18	449,641	813	0.2%	26,543
12/17	474,614	2,959	0.6%	28,318
12/16	449,199	461	0.1%	29,380
12/15	454,391	774	0.2%	31,530
Annual Growth	2.1%	15.8%	—	(6.8%)

2019 Year-End Financials

Return on assets: 0.3%
Return on equity: 5.2%
Long-term debt ($ mil.): —
No. of shares (mil.): —
Sales ($ mil): 69,135
Dividends
Yield: 7.3%
Payout: 53.6%
Market value ($ mil.): —

	STOCK PRICE ($) FY Close	P/E High/Low		PER SHARE ($) Earnings	Dividends	Book Value
12/19	4.53	10	7	0.63	0.33	10.55
12/18	4.65	24	16	0.33	0.33	9.91
12/17	6.30	6	5	1.37	0.31	11.04
12/16	5.53	39	22	0.16	0.27	9.90
12/15	5.67	31	20	0.29	0.27	11.19
Annual Growth	(5.5%)	—	—	20.9%	5.7%	(1.4%)

Aeon Co Ltd

Retail holding company AEON has about 300 subsidiaries and more than 25 affiliated companies. It is the Japanese leader in supermarkets (more than 2200 stores under the Maxvalu name and others) and general merchandise (more than 600 stores under various AEON banners). The company also operates drugstores and pharmacies and clothing and other specialty stores. Beyond retail stores AEON offers credit and money card banking insurance and other financial services and develops and operates malls and shopping centers. It operates solely in Asia with Japan its largest market.

Operations

AEON's business is divided into seven primary categories. The company generates about 70% of its revenue from about 2200 supermarkets (community discount and convenience stores under the Maxvalu name and others) and nearly 600 general merchandise stores operating primarily under various AEON names.

Its drugstore and specialty chains — operated under such names as Welcia and AEON Pharmacy and GFoot and Talbots Japan respectively — account for about 20% of sales combined. The rest of revenue is brought in by international stores (locations in China and Southeast Asian countries) as well as financial services and the development and operation of more than 300 malls and shopping centers (about 15% combined).

Geographic Reach

AEON operates in more than a dozen countries across Asia. It relies very heavily on Japan by far its largest market accounting for more than 90% of revenue. China and Southeast Asian countries such as Cambodia Thailand and Vietnam contribute the rest (about 10% combined).

Financial Performance

AEON's revenue has been rising consistently for the last five years. Except the decline in 2018 its profits followed a similar pattern in the same period.

For the fiscal year ended February 29 2020 AEON posted record-high consolidated operating revenue. Consolidated operating revenue was 8604207 million yen (up 1%). Ordinary profit was 205828 million yen (down 4%).

Cash at the end of fiscal 2019 was 814.5 billion yen a decrease of 326.7 billion yen. Cash from operations contributed 469.9 billion yen to the coffers while investing activities used 662.4 billion yen. Financing activities added 143.8 billion yen.

Strategy

AEON has established a goal of 10 trillion yen in revenue by the end of fiscal 2020. To help it achieve that goal the company is focused on four "shifts" — the shift to regional markets the shift to digital markets the shift to Asian markets and underlying the first three the shift to transformative investment. In recent years customer preferences and needs have increasingly diversified in ways including health orientation low-price orientation and growing interest in ethical consumption that takes into consideration the global environment and local communities. Also the market presence of companies that principally engage in e-commerce businesses is further strengthening and competition is intensifying. In this environment to rapidly respond to customer changes as a corporate group with an everlasting innovative spirit Aeon will implement a shift in direction toward regional digital and Asia markets and a shift in investments to support this change of direction as set forth as the direction for innovation and will continue innovation with the aim of becoming the number-one company in each region and business field.

Company Background

AEON's predecessor company Jusco was established in 1969 through a joint venture of three other entities. It launched its retail development business that year and five years later introduced AEON's first private-brand product J-Cup.

In 1976 Jusco was listed on the Tokyo Osaka and Nagoya Stock Exchanges. The company expanded into financial services and specialty retail in the 1980s and opened its first store outside Japan (in Malaysia). By the end of the decade Jusco Group was renamed AEON Group (Jusco Co. took the AEON Co. name in 2001).

AEON became a holding company in 2008.

EXECUTIVES

President, Motoya Okada, age 68
Group COO, Yoshiki Mori, age 70
VP; President AEON Mall, Soichi Okazaki
EVP, Shouhei Murai
EVP, Masaaki Toyoshima
VP IT Innovation, Hidenori Osano
CFO, Akinori Yamashita
Chairman, Hiroshi Yokoo
Auditors: Deloitte Touche Tohmatsu LLC

LOCATIONS

HQ: Aeon Co Ltd
1-5-1 Nakase, Mihama-ku, Chiba 261-8515
Phone: (81) 43 212 6042
Web: www.aeon.info

2018 Sales

	% of total
Japan	92
ASEAN	4
China	3
Other	1
Total	**100**

PRODUCTS/OPERATIONS

2018 Sales

	% of total
General Merchandise Stores	34
Supermarkets	36
Services and Specialty Stores	9
Health and Wellness Stores	8
Shopping Center Development	4
Financial Services	4
International Business	5
Total	**100**

Selected Store Names

Abilities Jusco (CDs DVDs and books)
Asbee (shoe stores)
Blue Grass (apparel for teenage girls)
Claire's Nippon (women's clothing)
Cox (family casual clothing)
HapYcom (drugstores)
Home Wide Corp. (home centers)
JUSCO (apparel food and household item superstores)
JUS-Photo (film developing)
Laura Ashley Japan (clothing and home furnishings)
Maxvalu (supermarkets)
Mega Sports (Sports Authority stores)
MINISTOP (convenience stores)
MYCAL Corporation (supermarkets)
My Basket (small-scale supermarkets)
Nustep (family footwear stores)
Petcity (pets & pet supplies)
Sports Authority (sporting goods)

COMPETITORS

A.S. Watson	Ito-Yokado
Carrefour	METRO AG
Costco Wholesale	Rakuten
Dairy Farm	Seiyu
International	Seven & i
Fast Retailing	Takashimaya
Heiwado	Tesco
Isetan Mitsukoshi	The Gap

HISTORICAL FINANCIALS

Company Type: Public

Income Statement

FYE: February 29

	REVENUE ($ mil.)	NET INCOME ($ mil.)	NET PROFIT MARGIN	EMPLOYEES
02/20	79,146	246	0.3%	420,165
02/19	76,884	213	0.3%	419,912
02/18	78,334	228	0.3%	411,104
02/17	73,139	100	0.1%	406,146
02/16	72,383	53	0.1%	396,414
Annual Growth	2.3%	46.8%	—	1.5%

2020 Year-End Financials

Debt ratio: 0.2%
Return on equity: 2.4%
Cash ($ mil.): 11,240
Long-term debt ($ mil.): 16,743

No. of shares (mil.): 847
Dividends
  Yield: 0.0%
  Payout: 110.0%
Market value ($ mil.): 15,394

	STOCK PRICE ($) FY Close	P/E High/Low		PER SHARE ($) Earnings	Dividends	Book Value
02/20	18.17	1	1	0.29	0.32	11.57
02/19	21.33	1	1	0.25	0.29	11.75
02/18	16.75	1	1	0.27	0.28	12.79
02/17	14.76	1	1	0.12	0.26	11.99
02/16	13.22	2	2	0.06	0.25	12.03
Annual Growth	8.3%	—	—	47.3%	6.5%	(1.0%)

AGC Inc

Auditors: KPMG AZSA LLC

LOCATIONS

HQ: AGC Inc
1-5-1 Marunouchi, Chiyoda-ku, Tokyo 100-8405
Phone: (81) 3 3218 5603
Web: www.agc.com

HISTORICAL FINANCIALS

Company Type: Public

Income Statement

FYE: December 31

	REVENUE ($ mil.)	NET INCOME ($ mil.)	NET PROFIT MARGIN	EMPLOYEES
12/19	13,982	409	2.9%	59,834
12/18	13,848	814	5.9%	58,853
12/17	13,007	615	4.7%	58,171
12/16	10,965	405	3.7%	55,555
12/15	11,017	356	3.2%	55,546
Annual Growth	6.1%	3.5%	—	1.9%

2019 Year-End Financials

Debt ratio: 0.2%
Return on equity: 3.8%
Cash ($ mil.): 1,048
Current ratio: 1.54
Long-term debt ($ mil.): 3,692

No. of shares (mil.): 221
Dividends
  Yield: 3.1%
  Payout: 12.1%
Market value ($ mil.): 1,575

	STOCK PRICE ($) FY Close	P/E High/Low		PER SHARE ($) Earnings	Dividends	Book Value
12/19	7.11	0	0	1.84	0.22	48.10
12/18	6.56	0	0	3.62	0.20	46.69
12/17	8.70	0	0	2.67	0.17	46.57
12/16	6.77	0	0	1.75	0.15	40.50
12/15	5.67	0	0	1.54	0.15	39.32
Annual Growth	5.8%	—	—	4.6%	10.1%	5.2%

Ageas NV

Auditors: PwC Reviseurs d'Entreprises SRL / PwC Bedrijfsrevisoren BV

LOCATIONS

HQ: Ageas NV
Rue du Marquis 1, Brussels 1000
Phone: (32) 2 557 57 11   **Fax:** (32) 2 557 57 50
Web: www.ageas.com

HISTORICAL FINANCIALS
Company Type: Public

Income Statement   FYE: December 31

	ASSETS ($ mil.)	NET INCOME ($ mil.)	INCOME AS % OF ASSETS	EMPLOYEES
12/19	172,228	1,540	0.9%	10,741
12/18	160,013	1,273	0.8%	11,009
12/17	162,617	980	0.6%	11,260
12/16	164,116	42	0.0%	12,080
12/15	164,418	1,211	0.7%	11,919
Annual Growth	1.2%	6.2%	—	(2.6%)

2019 Year-End Financials

Return on assets: 0.9%
Return on equity: 9.4%
Long-term debt ($ mil.): —
No. of shares (mil.): 190
Sales ($ mil): 23,760

Dividends
  Yield: 2.8%
  Payout: 21.4%
Market value ($ mil.): 11,295

	STOCK PRICE ($) FY Close	P/E High/Low		PER SHARE ($) Earnings	Dividends	Book Value
12/19	59.28	12	9	7.99	1.71	92.67
12/18	44.71	13	11	6.47	1.70	76.20
12/17	48.81	16	12	4.86	1.65	76.00
12/16	39.57	354	246	0.20	1.37	73.26
12/15	46.38	13	9	5.62	1.30	84.33
Annual Growth	6.3%	—	—	9.2%	7.1%	2.4%

Ahli United Bank

EXECUTIVES

Deputy Chairman, Mohammed Jassim Al-Marzouq
Auditors: Ernst & Young

LOCATIONS

HQ: Ahli United Bank
Building 2495, Road 2832, Al-Seef District, P. O. Box 2424, Manama
Phone: (973) 17 585 858   **Fax:** (973) 17 580 569
Web: www.ahliunited.com

COMPETITORS

ABC International Bank	Dallah Albaraka Group
Al Rajhi Banking	Gulf International
Arab Bank	Bank
Arab Banking Corp.	NBK
Arab National Bank	Riyad Bank
Banque Saudi Fransi	Saudi British Bank
British Arab Commercial Bank	

HISTORICAL FINANCIALS
Company Type: Public

Income Statement   FYE: December 31

	ASSETS ($ mil.)	NET INCOME ($ mil.)	INCOME AS % OF ASSETS	EMPLOYEES
12/19	40,280	730	1.8%	0
12/18	35,507	697	2.0%	0
12/17	33,241	618	1.9%	0
12/16	31,322	570	1.8%	0
12/15	33,965	537	1.6%	0
Annual Growth	4.4%	8.0%	—	—

2019 Year-End Financials

Return on assets: 1.9%
Return on equity: 15.5%
Long-term debt ($ mil.): —
No. of shares (mil.): —
Sales ($ mil): 2,127

Dividends
  Yield: —
  Payout: 63.2%
Market value ($ mil.): —

AIA Group Ltd.

Asian giant AIA Group is the second-largest life insurance company in the world by market value. The life insurance and wealth management company operates in some 20 markets across the Asia/Pacific region. It offers life insurance credit insurance employee benefits and pension services to its corporate clients. For individuals the company provides basic life insurance along with savings investment and retirement products. Other offerings include medical insurance critical illness protection accident coverage and disability coverage.

Operations

AIA's reportable segments are Hong Kong (including Macau) Thailand China Singapore (including Brunei) Malaysia Other Markets and Group Corporate Centre. Except for the latter segment they all provide life accident and health insurance and distribute savings plans and related financial services.

The Hong Kong segment brings in more than 40% of total revenue followed by Thailand and China which bring in some 15% of revenue each.

Geographic Reach

AIA has operations in nearly 20 countries in the Asia/Pacific region with the notable exception of Japan. ( ) It owns branches and subsidiaries in Australia Brunei Cambodia China Hong Kong Indonesia Korea Macau Malaysia New Zealand the Philippines Singapore Sri Lanka Taiwan Thailand and Vietnam; it also owns a 49% stake in Indian joint venture Tata AIA Life and has a representative office in Myanmar.

Sales and Marketing

AIA primarily markets its products through agents; it also works with distribution partners such as banks financial advisors specialist advisors and brokers throughout the region.

Through its extensive network of agents partners and employees across the region AIA serves more than 36 million individual policyholders and more than 16 million participating members of group insurance schemes.

Financial Performance

The company's revenue increased by 46% to $47.2 billion in 2019. The increase was primarily due to higher premiums and fee income and an investment returns of about $14.4 billion.

Net income fell 151% to $6.7 billion in 2019 due to higher revenues.

The company ended 2019 with $3.8 billion in net cash about $1.6 billion more than it had at the end of fiscal 2018. Operating activities provided $3.3 billion in cash while investing activities used $245 million and financing activities used another $1.5 billion. AIA's main cash uses in 2019 were for dividends paid and payments for intangible assets.

Strategy

An important strategic priority for AIA is to further enhance the professionalism and quality of its market-leading proprietary agency force through the use of technology. The company continue to invest in digital technology that provides simple and effective support for its agents and agency leaders across all of its key activities including sales servicing and recruitment. AIA applies a comprehensive digital roadmap for its agency applications and management tools that uses a human-centric design approach to ensure the best possible user experience.

For example AIA is currently rolling out new digital recruitment platforms across the group with content and features tailored to each market's unique programmes and customer propositions. These platforms are now live in Hong Kong Malaysia and Mainland China and will be expanded to other markets in the near future. The company also rolled out an innovative interactive Financial Health Check tool in Hong Kong that provides agents with a detailed customer needs and insurance gap analysis and continued driving the adoption of Master Planner in Mainland China which enables a systematic and structured approach to sales activity management for agency leaders. AIA have also continued to embed new propensity models into its leads generation platforms that enable its agents to target and meet specific customer needs. Over 95% of total policies submitted by agency distribution in 2019 were submitted through its interactive Point of Sales (iPoS) platform.

Mergers and Acquisitions

In 2019 AIA Group Limited a joint execution cooperation agreement with between AIA Australia Limited and Commonwealth Bank of Australia under the alternative completion structure and arrangements for the purchase of CBA's life insurance business (known as "CommInsure Life") The Colonial Mutual Life Assurance Society Limited ("CMLA") and certain affiliated companies which was announced on 23 August 2019.

The Joint Cooperation Agreement allows for an agreed management and oversight structure to be implemented enabling AIA to exercise an appropriate level of direct management control and oversight of both the AIA Australia and CMLA businesses while awaiting the final completion through either a share sale as originally contemplated or an asset transfer mechanism.

Company Background

Founded in Shanghai in 1919 by Cornelius Vander Starr AIA was the original business that would later grow to become American International Group (AIG) and was a cornerstone of that company's Asia-based operations. However in 2010 AIG spun off the business through a public offering.

EXECUTIVES

Group CFO, Garth Jones
Regional Chief Executive Hong Kong Australia the Philippines Vietnam New Zealand and Macau, Gordon Watson
Group Chief Executive and President, Ng Keng Hooi
Group COO, Simeon Preston

Regional Chief Executive Malaysia Korea Sri Lanka India and Cambodia, William Lisle, age 55
Group Chief Risk Officer, Cheong Jin Keat, age 54
Group Chief Investment Officer, Mark Konyn
Chairman, Edmund S.W. Tse, age 82
Auditors: PricewaterhouseCoopers

LOCATIONS

HQ: AIA Group Ltd.
35/F, AIA Central, No. 1 Connaught Road Central,
Phone: (852) 2832 1800   **Fax:** (852) 2834 1753
Web: www.aia.com

2018 Sales by Segment

	% of total
Hong Kong	41
Thailand	14
China	13
Singapore	11
Malaysia	6
Other Markets	14
Group Corporate Centre	1
Total	**100**

PRODUCTS/OPERATIONS

2018 Sales

	$ mil.	% of total
Net premiums & fee income	31,913	88
Investment return	4,077	11
Other	30	1
Total	**36,297**	**100**

COMPETITORS

AXA Asia Pacific	Dah Sing Financial
China Insurance	Holdings Limited
China Life Insurance	MetLife
China Pacific	Ping An Insurance
Insurance	Sun Life

HISTORICAL FINANCIALS

Company Type: Public

Income Statement FYE: December 31

	ASSETS ($ mil.)	NET INCOME ($ mil.)	INCOME AS % OF ASSETS	EMPLOYEES
12/19	284,132	6,648	2.3%	23,000
12/18*	229,806	3,163	1.4%	22,000
11/17	215,691	6,120	2.8%	20,000
11/16	185,074	4,164	2.2%	20,000
11/15	167,622	2,691	1.6%	20,000
Annual Growth	14.1%	25.4%	—	3.6%

*Fiscal year change

2019 Year-End Financials

Return on assets: 2.5%	Dividends
Return on equity: 13.7%	Yield: 1.5%
Long-term debt ($ mil.): —	Payout: 114.6%
No. of shares (mil.): —	Market value ($ mil.): —
Sales ($ mil): 47,234	

	STOCK PRICE ($) FY Close	P/E High/Low	PER SHARE ($) Earnings	Dividends	Book Value
12/19	42.09	82 57	0.55	0.63	4.76
12/18*	32.88	146 114	0.26	0.48	3.23
11/17	32.76	69 44	0.51	0.41	3.48
11/16	24.41	80 56	0.35	0.34	2.90
11/15	24.12	130 93	0.22	0.24	2.44
Annual Growth	14.9%	— —	25.7%	27.3%	18.2%

*Fiscal year change

AIB Group PLC

Allied Irish Banks (AIB) one of Ireland's largest banks and private employers is looking beyond the Emerald Isle for its proverbial pot o' gold. The company offers retail and commercial accounts and loans life insurance financing leasing pension and trust services through a network of 200 branches 74 EBS Limited offices 10 business centers and 755 ATMs. The company's capital markets division offers commercial treasury services corporate finance and investment banking services. In the US AIB specializes in financial services for the not-for-profit sector.

Operations

Over the years AIB has reorganized into a more simplified structure in which its divisions were integrated and its AIB and First Trust operations were more closely aligned. To attract additional customers the bank also introduced mobile banking services to its offerings.

Auditors: Deloitte Ireland LLP

LOCATIONS

HQ: AIB Group PLC
Bankcentre, P.O. Box 452, Ballsbridge, Dublin 4
Phone: (353) 1 660 0311   **Fax:** 212 515-6710
Web: www.aibgroup.com

PRODUCTS/OPERATIONS

2013 Sales

	% of total
Interest and similar income	86
Fee and commission income	11
Others	3
Total	**100**

COMPETITORS

Bank Millennium	HSBC
Bank of America	Irish Bank Resolution
Bank of Ireland	Lloyds Banking Group
Barclays	Royal Bank of Scotland
Citigroup	Ulster Bank

HISTORICAL FINANCIALS

Company Type: Public

Income Statement FYE: December 31

	ASSETS ($ mil.)	NET INCOME ($ mil.)	INCOME AS % OF ASSETS	EMPLOYEES
12/19	110,662	367	0.3%	9,520
12/18	104,826	1,250	1.2%	9,831
12/17	107,962	1,335	1.2%	9,720
12/16	100,965	1,431	1.4%	10,376
12/15	112,321	1,503	1.3%	10,204
Annual Growth	(0.4%)	(29.7%)	—	(1.7%)

2019 Year-End Financials

Return on assets: 0.3%	Dividends
Return on equity: 2.3%	Yield: —
Long-term debt ($ mil.): —	Payout: 66.1%
No. of shares (mil.): —	Market value ($ mil.): —
Sales ($ mil): 3,436	

Air Canada Inc

As the country's leading airline Air Canada serves more than 215 destinations on six continents primarily in Canada and the US. The carrier operates a fleet of nearly 190 aircrafts from hubs in Calgary Montreal Toronto and Vancouver. It extends its network as part of the Star Alliance global marketing group which is led by United Airlines and Lufthansa. Besides its passenger business which generates the majority of sales with around 90% Air Canada also hauls cargo and offers ground handling and travel arrangement services. Air Canada serves more than 51 million customers. About 30% of its revenue comes from its domestic operations.

Operations

Passenger revenue (about 90% of the company's total revenue) is recognized when transportation is provided it also includes revenue fees and surcharges from passenger-related services such as excess baggage and seat selection.

The company is also Canada's largest provider of Air Cargo (nearly 5%) provides direct cargo services to more than 150 Canadian US transborder and international destinations and has sales representation in more 45 countries.

Other revenue (more than 5%) is comprised of revenues from the sale of the ground portion of vacation packages ground handling services onboard sales and loyalty programs.

Geographic Reach

Headquartered in Montreal Air Canada has concierge assistance at nearly 50 airports globally.

Air Canada generates some 30% of its revenue in its domestic operations.

Financial Performance

Note: Growth rates may differ after conversion to US Dollars. Note: Growth rates may differ after conversion to US Dollars.

Air Canada had operating revenues of $19.1 billion in 2019 compared to operating revenues of $18 billion in 2018 an increase of $1.1 billion or 6% on a yield improvement of 5% and traffic increase of 2%. The yield improvement year-over-year included additional revenue from Aeroplan flight redemptions and other revenues subsequent to the Aeroplan acquisition on January 10 2019.

The company had a net income of $1.5 billion in 2019 versus a net income of $37 million in 2018.

The company's cash for the year ended 2019 was C$2.1 billion. Operating activities generated C$5.7 billion while investing activities used C$2.8 billion primarily for additions to property equipment and intangible assets. Financing activities used another C$1.4 billion mainly for reduction of long-term debt and lease liabilities.

Strategy

Air Canada enhances its domestic and transborder network through capacity purchase agreements ("CPAs") with regional airlines operating flights on behalf of Air Canada. These regional carriers operating under the banner of Air Canada Express form an integral part of the airline's international network strategy providing valuable traffic feed to Air Canada and Air Canada Rouge routes. During 2019 the Air Canada Express fleet was comprised of 48 Bombardier regional jets 73 Bombardier Dash-8 turboprop aircraft and 25 Embraer 175 aircraft for a total of 146 aircraft. During 2019 a total of five 18-passenger Beech 1900 aircraft were also operated by regional airlines on behalf of Air Canada.

Mergers and Acquisitions

In late 2020 Air Canada agreed to acquire Montreal- based Transat for approximately $190 million. The combination will provides stability for Transat's operations and its stakeholders and will position Air Canada and indeed the Canadian aviation industry to emerge more strongly as it enters the post-COVID-19 world.

In 2019 Air Canada completed its purchase from Aimia Inc. ("Aimia") of Aeroplan owner and operator of the Aeroplan loyalty business. The aggregate purchase price for the acquisition consisted of $450 million in cash plus $67 million in cash for closing adjustments (total purchase consideration of $517 million). The acquisition also included the assumption of the Aeroplan Miles liability. Air Canada plans to launch an enhanced Aeroplan Program in the third quarter of 2020. Air Canada believes that the new program will enable the airline to further strengthen customer relationships to offer members more flexible rewards with better value and to deliver a more consistent end-to-end customer experience

EXECUTIVES

President and CEO, Calin Rovinescu, age 65, $1,308,860 total compensation

EVP and CFO, Michael S. (Mike) Rousseau, $492,692 total compensation

President Passenger Airlines, Benjamin (Ben) Smith, $444,077 total compensation

VP Air Canada Maintenance and Engineering, Richard Steer

EVP and Chief Commercial Officer, Lucie Guillemette

VP Cargo, Lise-Marie Turpin

VP Flight Operations, Ed Doyle

VP In-Flight Service, Renee Smith-Valade

VP Airports North America, Mark D. Southern

Chairman, Vagn S ,rensen, age 61

Auditors: PricewaterhouseCoopers LLP

LOCATIONS

HQ: Air Canada Inc
7373 Cote-Vertu Boulevard West, Saint-Laurent, Quebec H4S 1Z3
Phone: 514 422-5000   **Fax:** 514 422-0296
Web: www.aircanada.com

2018 Sales

	% of total
Canada	30
U.S. transborder	22
Atlantic	26
Pacific	15
Other	7
Total	**100**

PRODUCTS/OPERATIONS

2018 Sales

	% of total
Passenger	90
Cargo	4
Other	6
Total	**100**

COMPETITORS

Air France-KLM	China Eastern Airlines
Alaska Air	Delta Air Lines
American Airlines Group	Hawaiian Holdings
British Airways	Japan Airlines
CanJet	Korean Air
Cathay Pacific	WestJet

HISTORICAL FINANCIALS

Company Type: Public

Income Statement

FYE: December 31

	REVENUE ($ mil.)	NET INCOME ($ mil.)	NET PROFIT MARGIN	EMPLOYEES
12/19	14,691	1,133	7.7%	32,903
12/18	13,265	122	0.9%	29,900
12/17	12,964	1,625	12.5%	27,823
12/16	10,890	650	6.0%	0
12/15	9,984	218	2.2%	24,863
Annual Growth	**10.1%**	**51.0%**	**—**	**7.3%**

2019 Year-End Financials

Debt ratio: 16.0%	No. of shares (mil.): 263
Return on equity: 35.0%	Dividends
Cash ($ mil.): 1,604	Yield: —
Current ratio: 0.97	Payout: —
Long-term debt ($ mil.): 3,505	Market value ($ mil.): 9,853

	STOCK PRICE ($) FY Close	P/E High/Low		PER SHARE ($) Earnings	Dividends	Book Value
12/19	37.35	7	4	4.18	0.00	12.81
12/18	19.00	35	25	0.44	0.00	10.94
12/17	20.57	3	1	5.86	0.00	9.87
12/16	10.18	3	2	2.30	0.00	3.31
12/15	7.34	10	7	0.74	0.00	0.03
Annual Growth	**50.2%**	**—**	**—**	**54.1%**	**—**	**343.5%**

Air France-KLM

Air France-KLM is a holding company made up of two national airlines. Together Air France-KLM is the fourth-largest airline in Europe after Ryanair Group Deutsche Lufthansa and IAG and one of the largest in the world. The company flies over 100 million customers and 1.1 million tons of cargo each year to around 390 destinations in nearly 160 countries. It has some 555 aircraft. Air France and KLM fly independently out of the company's hubs in Paris and Amsterdam. The group also operates transatlantic joint ventures with partners Delta Air Lines and Virgin Atlantic and is a member of the SkyTeam alliance with about 20 other airlines including Korean Air AeroMexico China Airlines and Kenya Airways. About a third of revenue comes from France.

Operations

Air France-KLM offers passenger transportation cargo transportation and aircraft maintenance services and transports over 100 million passengers and 1.1 million tons of cargo annually. It has a fleet of around 555 aircraft in operation. Some 80% of its total cargo tonnage is carried in the bellies of its passenger aircraft and around 20% in the full - freighter fleet.

The company's single operating segment consists of four businesses. Its Network business is its primary passenger and cargo business that operates under the brands Air France and KLM and domestic operators Air France HOP and KLM Cityhopper. It generates more than 85% of sales.

Its low-cost Transavia airline accounts for more than 5% of sales and flies customers in the Netherlands and France to some 130 Middle Eastern European and North African destinations. Transavia has a fleet of nearly 75 primarily B737-800 aircraft. Air France-KLM's Maintenance unit also generates nearly 10% of total revenue and serves both Air France-KLM and third parties with maintenance repair and overhaul services. Its three main areas or service are airframe maintenance engine main-

tenance and component support (electronic mechanical pneumatic and hydraulic).

Geographic Reach

The Air France-KLM network is organized around its hubs at Paris-Charles de Gaulle and Amsterdam-Schiphol airports. With these two major hubs the company links Europe to the rest of the world spanning more than 310 destinations across around 115 countries.

About 30% of its revenue comes from France and the remaining 70% comes from international operations.

Financial PerformanceNote: Growth rates may differ after conversion to US Dollars.

Revenues stood at ?27.2 billion up by 4% versus 2018 restated notably thanks to the strong revenue growth in the low - cost and maintenance businesses.

The company's net income in 2019 decreased by ?130 million to ?290 million from ?420 million in the prior year. The decrease was primarily due to the increase on their external expenses and salaries and related costs.

Cash at the end of fiscal 2019 was ?3.7 billion an increase of ?131 million from the prior year. Cash from operations contributed ?3.9 billion to the coffers while investing activities used ?3.3 billion mainly for purchases of property plant and equipment. Financing activities used another ?447 million for payments on debts and leases.

Strategy

Five orientations have been identified to achieve the Air France???KLM Group's goals and build on the important 2019 achievements in terms of brand fleet and product simplification.

The optimization of the Air France???KLM model will enable a reduction in operating costs and increased efficiency taking full advantage of the Group's assets. Increasing commercial and fleet flexibility is a Group priority allowed by continuous and trustful social discussions. A number of changes have already been approved and launched enabling fleet product and cabin optimization and offering growth opportunities for Transavia France.

Simplifying and renewing the fleet is an important part of these changes implemented by the Group. By reducing the number of aircraft types and adjusting cabin layouts the Group will gain greater operational flexibility (operations marketing catering maintenance) and economies of scale.

The formation of the Air France???KLM Group offers the opportunity to capitalize on the international reach of each airline while continuing to build synergies. Leveraging this potential will be key in the coming years. Much has already been accomplished and has proven to be to the benefit of all our airlines. The synergies have concerned sales revenue management strategic alliances IT cargo and maintenance. Some areas can be further built on and will constitute the next focus such as Fleet & network Human Resources Commercial & Alliances Purchasing & Procurement Digital & Data Management.

Company Background

KLM was established in 1919 as Koninklijke Luchtvaartmaatschappij with service in the Netherlands and colonies. In 1920 it operated its first flight between London and Amsterdam and later introduced new regular routes serving Amsterdam Rotterdam Brussels Paris and London then expanded to Bremen Copenhagen and Malm ¶. KLM's fleet then consisted of the Fokker aircraft.

Air France dates back to 1933 with the merger of the five French airlines Air Union Air Orient Société Générale de Transport Aérien (SGTA) CIDNA and Aéropostale.

The two companies merged in 2004 creating what is now Air France-KLM a holding company made up of two national airlines.

EXECUTIVES

CFO, Frédéric Gagey, age 65

EVP Human Resources and Corporate Secretary, Jer´me Nanty, age 60

CEO Air France, Franck Terner, age 60

EVP Commercial Sales and Alliances, Patrick Alexandre, age 65

EVP Commercial Strategy, Pieter Bootsma, age 51

President and CEO KLM Royal Dutch Airlines, Pieter Elbers, age 50

EVP Information Technology, Jean-Christophe Lalanne, age 56

Chairman and CEO Air France-KLM and Chairman Air France, Jean-Marc Janaillac, age 67

COO KLM, René de Groot, age 52

EVP Air France-KLM Cargo, Marcel de Nooijer, age 51

EVP Air France-KLM Engineering and Maintenance, Anne Brachet

Vice Chairman, Leni Boeren

Auditors: Deloitte et Associes

LOCATIONS

HQ: Air France-KLM
2, rue Robert Esnault-Pelterie, Paris 75007
Phone: (33) 1 41 56 78 00   **Fax:** (33) 1 41 56 56 00
Web: www.airfranceklm.com

2017 Sales

	% of total
Metropolitan France	32
Benelux	15
Other Europe	19
Africa	5
Middle-Eastern Gulf and India	2
Asia-Pacific	8
North America	13
West Indies Caribbean Guyana Indian Ocean and South America	6
Total	**100**

PRODUCTS/OPERATIONS

2018 Sales

	% of total
Network	87
Transavia	6
Maintenance	7
Other	-
Total	**100**

COMPETITORS

Aer Lingus	Ryanair
Air Berlin	SAS
American Airlines	SNCF
Group	United Continental
Austrian Airlines	Virgin Atlantic
Brussels Airlines	Airways
IAG	easyJet
Lufthansa	

HISTORICAL FINANCIALS

Company Type: Public

Income Statement				FYE: December 31
	REVENUE ($ mil.)	NET INCOME ($ mil.)	NET PROFIT MARGIN	EMPLOYEES
12/19	30,526	325	1.1%	90,386
12/18	30,364	468	1.5%	88,888
12/17	30,908	(328)	—	87,312
12/16	26,234	836	3.2%	82,175
12/15	28,387	128	0.5%	96,417
Annual Growth	1.8%	26.2%	—	(1.6%)

2019 Year-End Financials

Debt ratio: 26.0%
Return on equity: 14.0%
Cash ($ mil.): 4,171
Current ratio: 0.68
Long-term debt ($ mil.): 7,040

No. of shares (mil.): 427
Dividends
Yield: —
Payout: —
Market value ($ mil.): 4,710

	STOCK PRICE ($) FY Close	P/E High/Low		PER SHARE ($) Earnings	Dividends	Book Value
12/19	11.02	23	13	0.68	0.00	6.00
12/18	10.88	19	9	1.00	0.00	4.96
12/17	16.25	—	—	(0.97)	0.00	8.42
12/16	5.36	4	2	2.38	0.00	3.65
12/15	7.52	27	18	0.37	0.00	0.83
Annual Growth	10.0%	—	—	16.6%	—	64.1%

Airbus SE

Airbus SE (formerly European Aeronautic Defence and Space Company or EADS) is busy in the commercial and military aerospace and related markets. Europe's largest supplier it rivals Boeing in the competitive skies. The company's commercial aircraft division is the world's largest manufacturer of large commercial aircraft (seating 100-plus passengers) while its military division manufactures transport tankers and mission aircraft. Other segments include Airbus Helicopters (civil and military helicopters) and Airbus Defence and Space (satellites and launcher systems combat aircraft missile systems radar defense electronics and unmanned aerial systems).

Operations

Airbus has three operating divisions: Airbus Airbus Defence and Space and Airbus Helicopters.

The Airbus segment more than 75% of the company's revenue and manufactures passenger airliners ranging in capacity from 100 to more than 600 seats.

The Airbus Defence and Space segment (15% of revenue) is Europe's number one defense and space enterprise and among the world's top ten space businesses. Its four core business groups are Military Aircraft Space Systems Communications Intelligence & Security (CIS) and Unmanned Aerial Systems (UAS). It develops products for governments institutions and commercial customers.

Airbus Helicopters (almost 10%) is a global leader in the civil and military rotorcraft market. Its product range includes light single-engine light twin-engine medium and medium-heavy rotorcraft which are adaptable to all kinds of mission types based on customer needs.

Geographic Reach

Airbus is headquartered in the Netherlands but has its main operational base in Toulouse France. The company operates worldwide. The Commercial Aircraft division has operations in France Germany Spain and the UK as well as subsidiaries in the US China Japan India and the Middle East. Airbus Helicopters conducts its activities in four primary locations - two in France one in Germany and one in Spain. The Defence and Space division is headquartered in Ottobrunn near in Munich Germany with main production facilities in France Germany Spain and the UK and also has engineering centers and offices in more than 80 countries.

Airbus' customer base is geographically diversified with customers in the Asia/Pacific region accounting for more than 30% of total sales Europe more than30% North America more than 15% Middle East for about 10% and Latin America and other countries accounts the remainder.

Sales and Marketing

Airbus' customers are mostly airline companies include Avolon Jetblue Airways Moxy Vietjet Air

and Scandinavian Airlines. Airbus Helicopters' principal military clients are Ministries of Defence (MoDs) in Europe Asia the US and Latin America.

Financial Performance

Consolidated revenues increased to - 70.5 billion (2018: - 63.7 billion) mainly driven by the higher commercial aircraft deliveries and a favourable mix at Airbus and to a lesser extent the favourable exchange rate development.

Net loss was ?1.4 billion a 56% change (?1.7 billion) from ?3.1 billion net income in 2018.

Airbus' cash balance weakened during 2019 ending the year ?114 million lower at ?9.3 billion. Its operations generated ?3.8 billion while it used ?2.9 billion in its investing activities and ?958 million in its financing activities. Airbus' main cash uses in 2019 were capital expenditures borrowing repayments and divide.

Strategy

As part of its business strategy the Company may acquire or divest businesses and/or form joint ventures or strategic alliances. Executing acquisitions and divestments can be difficult and costly due to the complexities inherent in integrating or carving out people operations technologies and products. There can be no assurance that any of the businesses that the Company intends to acquire or divest can be integrated or carved out successfully as timely as originally planned or that they will perform well and deliver the expected synergies or cost savings once integrated or separated. In addition regulatory administrative or other contractual conditions can prevent transactions from being finalized. The Company's business results of operations and financial condition may be materially affected if these transactions will not be successfully completed or do not produce the expected benefits.

Mergers and Acquisitions

In late 2019 Airbus acquires Seattle's-areas MTM an industrial automation company for an undisclosed sum. It is located in Mukilteo Washington near Seattle. The move deepens Airbus' commitment to expanding advanced robotics capabilities within its manufacturing processes. MTM perfectly fits Airbus' ambition for engineering and innovative manufacturing solutions while maintaining agility.

Company Background

Airbus dates back to the formation of Airbus Industry GIE (later Airbus SAS) in 1970 a European effort to establish a civil aviation company capable of competing with the US hegemony of Boeing Lockheed and McDonnell Douglas. It launched the A300 in 1974 and after a big win when Eastern Air Lines bought its aircraft by 1980 Airbus trailed only Boeing among the world's commercial jet makers. The European Aeronautic Defence and Space Company NV was established in the Netherlands in 2000 to consolidate various European aviation businesses including Eurocopter Group a leader helicopter manufacturer. It changed its name to Airbus in 2014 in respect of its main subsidiary.

HISTORY

The growth of the European Aeronautic Defence and Space Company — EADS — is overshadowed by the long history of its components and by the obstacles overcome to cement the deal: The French and the Germans historically aren't overly fond of each other so how did it come to pass that Germany's DaimlerChrysler Aerospace AG (DASA) and France's Aerospatiale Matra put aside their differences to band together with Spain's Construcciones Aeron uticas SA (CASA)?

The US aerospace sector in the 1990s saw many companies consolidate scrambling to make their way in the post-Cold War era. Boeing the largest aerospace company in the world got that way by acquiring a number of operations including Rockwell International's aerospace and defense operations (1995) and most importantly McDonnell Douglas in a $16 billion deal (1997). In the same era defense giant Lockheed merged with Martin Marietta (1995) and acquired Loral (1997). These US companies had it relatively easy — they all paid taxes to Uncle Sam but acquisition deals in Europe were stymied by concerns over national security and privatization because much of Europe's defense industry was government-owned.

Spurred into action by their US rivals DASA and British Aerospace (now BAE SYSTEMS) — partners in Airbus — began merger talks in 1997. Fearful of being left out in the cold France's government-owned Aerospatiale — another Airbus partner — began talks to merge with Matra a French defense company controlled by Lagard re. Weeks after the Aerospatiale-Matra deal was announced in 1998 the chairman of DASA's parent company J rgen Schrempp met with Lagard re's CEO Jean-Luc Lagard re and proposed a three-way deal. It never occurred and in 1999 the BAE SYSTEMS and DASA deal fell through as well.

Later that year Schrempp and Lagard re met again and laid the groundwork for a merger between DASA and Aerospatiale Matra. Less than three weeks after the Aerospatiale-Matra merger was completed Lagard re found itself pitching the DASA/Aerospatiale Matra merger idea to a stunned French government (which still held a 48% stake in Aerospatiale Matra). Marathon negotiations ensued. Late in the year Spain's Construcciones Aeron uticas SA (CASA) agreed to become part of EADS.

In 2000 EADS went public and Airbus announced that it would abandon its consortium structure in favor of incorporation. The next year EADS began pushing for a consolidation of army and naval equipment manufacturing among EU countries similar to the aerospace consolidation that created EADS. For Airbus the long-sought switch from consortium to corporation finally occurred in July 2001 when Airbus S.A.S. was incorporated.

EADS bought out BAE SYSTEMS' 25% share in their Astrium joint venture in 2003. In October 2004 EADS agreed to acquire US defense electronics maker Racal Instruments as part of its plan to increase defense sales in the US. Rumors surfaced the next month that EADS was discussing a merger deal with French defense company Thales.

In December 2004 EADS and BAE SYSTEMS gave Airbus the green-light to build the superjumbo twin-deck A380 a plane that competes directly with Boeing's upcoming 787 Dreamliner. A few months later in early 2005 EADS was given preferred bidder status for the UK's Royal Air Force aerial refueling tanker contract. The program was valued at approximately $25 billion.

Claiming victory at last in 2006 Airbus beat Boeing on deliveries (434 vs. 398) but Boeing racked up a record 1004 plane orders while Airbus notched only 790. Moreover EADS' shares took a pounding in 2006 on Airbus' announcement that deliveries of the A380 would be delayed by six or seven months due to manufacturing glitches. A group of EADS shareholders cried foul and filed suit when it was revealed that co-CEO No 1 Forgeard and five other EADS directors exercised stock options weeks before an internal investigation into the delays was launched. Two weeks later Forgeard fell on his sword and resigned. Louis Gallois former chairman of Soci t Nationale des Chemins de Fer Fran ais (SNCF) France's state railway company was named to replace him. The same fate befell Airbus boss Gustav Humbert who was replaced by Christian Streiff a former executive at French building materials concern Compagnie de Saint-Gobain.

The production logjams at Airbus also prompted some of the company's airline customers to seek compensation in lieu of taking their business elsewhere (Boeing). EADS forecast that the production delays at Airbus would be a $2.5 billion drain on profits over four years. In the wake of the additional delivery delays Airbus CEO Christian Streiff was sent packing after only three months on the job. EADS Co-CEO Louis Gallois was named as his replacement.

In 2006 Daimler announced plans to gradually reduce its stake in EADS from about 30% to half that amount. Later that year EADS acquired Sofrelog of France (a maker of maritime monitoring systems). Russian bank Vneshtorgbank (100% controlled by the Russian government) also purchased a 5% stake in EADS for about $1.17 billion. The stake did not entitle Vneshtorgbank to a board seat but the move was expected to strengthen cooperation between EADS and the re-emerging Russian aerospace industry.

After long negotiations EADS shifted in 2007 to a new management structure aimed at cutting down on the damaging political bickering between its German and French management and shareholder factions. Politicians like German Chancellor Angela Merkel and French President Nicolas Sarkozy touted the compromise as a success. Others namely labor forces were more skeptical — calling the latest management shake-up just another round of musical chairs that leaves the power struggles between Paris and Munich largely unresolved.

EADS continued to expand into emerging markets especially regions including Asia the Middle East and North and South America. Deliveries included the company's (long-delayed) A380 model launched with Singapore Airlines in late 2008. Adding to Airbus's standing the all-new A350-XWB (made for the most part of lighter-weight composite materials) sliced into about two-thirds of jet demand in the Middle East. It also forged alliances and won contracts in Brazil China Japan and North America.

Airbus launched a cost-cutting initiative in 2008 that slashed some 10000 jobs. Dubbed Power8 the plan marched out cost-saving measures that aimed to reduce development cycles by two years and boost overall productivity by 20%. Central to Power8 was the spinoff of some of Airbus's manufacturing facilities to new partners. Partner funding of planes like the A350-XWB (spurred by assurances of subcontract work) plus plant sales risked an ongoing row between Airbus and unions as well as factory owners — stakeholders who feared plant divestitures and more job cuts. That year EADS captured its first big US military contract when Airbus North America was given the opportunity to make US Army light utility helicopters.

The company was awarded a contract to replace outdated KC-135 refueling tankers in conjunction with Northrop Grumman for the US Air Force — an upset protested by rival bidder Boeing. Soon after the Government Accountability Office (GAO) announced its findings of flaws in the bidding process. EADS and Northrop Grumman dropped out of the bidding in early 2010 with EADS vowing not to submit a proposal unless it was assured that it had a fair chance to win. By late summer — after US president Obama assured French president Nicolas Sarkozy that the Pentagon tanker bidding process would be fair — EADS announced that it would consider once again to enter into the bidding war. The contract to build the US tanker valued at approximately $35 billion went to Boeing in early 2011.

In September 2012 EADS (now the Airbus Group) announced it was considering a merger with UK-based BAE Systems a global provider of sensors flight controls and aircraft. However the proposed $45 billion merger — which would have created the largest global aerospace and defense player on the planet both in total sales and market value — was called off weeks later after it failed to pass European governmental and regulatory hurdles.

Preparing to capitalize on demand Airbus Group hammered out its Vision 2020 goals under which it pursues the world's #1 position in air and space platforms systems and services. Services are targeted to achieve a 25% share of the business in less than 10 years. To this end Airbus Group has been scouting deals in the services sector. In August 2011 it agreed to purchase Vizada a global satellite-based mobile communication services provider from French private-equity Apax France. The whopping ?673 million ($969 million) deal bolsters Airbus Group's subsidiary Astrium a top contractor of space-technology wares in Europe and furthers opportunities beyond Europe with maritime aerospace as well as land media and other commercial customers. Hard on its heels Airbus Group took over more than 98% of Canada-based Vector Aerospace for C$625 million (about $341 million). Vector joins Eurocopter as a stand-alone business adding a multi-platform aviation repair and overhaul business.

EXECUTIVES

EVP Space Systems; CEO Airbus Defence and Space France, Fran §ois Auque, age 62
CEO, Thomas (Tom) Enders, age 59
CTO, Jean J. Botti, age 61
CEO Airbus Helicopters, Guillaume Faury, age 51
CFO Airbus Group and Airbus, Harald Wilhelm, age 52
EVP Military Aircraft Airbus Defence and Space, Domingo Urena-Raso, age 60
CEO Airbus, Fabrice Bregier, age 57
COO, Gunter Butschek, age 57
Chief Human Resources Officer Airbus Group and Airbus, Thierry Baril, age 53
CEO Airbus Defence and Space, Bernhard Gerwert, age 65
CEO Airbus Group North America, Allan McArtor, age 77
Vice Chairman, Josep Pique i Camps, age 65
Chairman, Denis Ranque, age 68
Auditors: Ernst & Young Accountants LLP

LOCATIONS

HQ: Airbus SE
Mendelweg 30, Leiden 2333 CS
Phone: (31) 71 5245 600   **Fax:** (31) 71 5232 807
Web: www.airbusgroup.com

2018 Sales

	% of total
Asia Pacific	37
Europe	28
North America	17
Middle East	10
Latin America	2
Other countries	6
Total	**100**

PRODUCTS/OPERATIONS

2018 Sales

	% of total
Airbus	74
Airbus Defence and Space	17
Airbus Helicopters	9
Other HQ / Consolidation	-
Total	**100**

Selected Products

Commercial Aircraft
A series passenger aircraft
ACJ series corporate jets
Beluga cargo planes
Helicopters
H series helicopters
ACH corporate helicopters
Tiger attack helicopter
NH90 military helicopter
Hforce weapons system
Defence and Space
A400M airlifter aircraft
A330 MRTT tanker/transport aircraft
Eurofighter Typhoon fighter jet
Zephyr High Altitude Pseudo-Satellite (HAPS)
Unmanned aircraft systems
Earth observation
Ariane rocket launchers
Orion human spacecraft
Bartolomeo space platform

COMPETITORS

AVIC Aircraft Co. Ltd.	Kawasaki Heavy
Aerojet Rocketdyne	Industries
Antonov	Leonardo
BAE SYSTEMS	Lockheed Martin
BAE Systems Inc.	Northrop Grumman
Bell Helicopter	Raytheon
Boeing	Saab AB
Bombardier	Sikorsky
Dassault Aviation	Space Exploration
E'Prime Aerospace	Technologies
Embraer	Thales

HISTORICAL FINANCIALS

Company Type: Public

Income Statement   FYE: December 31

	REVENUE ($ mil.)	NET INCOME ($ mil.)	NET PROFIT MARGIN	EMPLOYEES
12/19	79,130	(1,529)	—	134,931
12/18	72,956	3,497	4.8%	133,671
12/17	80,037	3,444	4.3%	129,442
12/16	70,301	1,050	1.5%	133,782
12/15	70,199	2,936	4.2%	136,574
Annual Growth	3.0%	—	—	(0.3%)

2019 Year-End Financials

Debt ratio: 9.9%
Return on equity: (-17.3%)
Cash ($ mil.): 10,457
Current ratio: 0.91
Long-term debt ($ mil.): 9,194

No. of shares (mil.): 782
Dividends
Yield: 0.9%
Payout: —
Market value ($ mil.): 28,750

	STOCK PRICE ($) FY Close	P/E High/Low		PER SHARE ($) Earnings	Dividends	Book Value
12/19	36.75	—	—	(1.96)	0.35	8.58
12/18	23.78	8	6	4.49	0.35	14.36
12/17	24.78	7	5	4.44	1.92	20.66
12/16	16.42	13	10	1.36	1.63	5.00
12/15	16.84	5	3	3.73	0.25	8.29
Annual Growth	21.6%	—	—	—	8.4%	0.8%

Aisin Seiki Co Ltd

The AISIN Group (Aisin Seiki Co. Ltd.) claims it supplies up to 15000 out of the 30000 parts that make up a car. The company's main business offers automotive-related products such as transmissions brakes and engine and car navigation systems. Its energy and home business offers items for more comfortable living with products that include heating and cooling systems and shower toilets with jet sprays. The company has approximately 215 consolidated subsidiaries and companies worldwide. Separate business segments include Aisin Seiki Group Aisin AW Group ADVICS Group and Aisin Takaoka Group. The company generates almost 55% of its revenue from its powertrain products.

Operations

AISIN operates through some 215 subsidiaries that are spread throughout four main segments.

Aisin Seiki Group is its largest segment (around 40% of total sales) and sells automotive parts as well as life and energy products. Aisin AW Group (about 40%) makes automatic transmissions and car navigation systems. The ADVICS Group (nearly 15%) is responsible for making brake components while Aisin Takaoka Group (more than 5%) manufactures the cart-iron parts for engines and brakes.

Overall the company generates almost 55% of sales from powertrain products some 20% from chassis & vehicle safety systems almost 20% from body business (power sliding door system and sunroof) and nearly 5% from the energy and home products business. The remainder of sales comes from ICT and electronics (car navigation systems and sensors) business.

Geographic Reach

Based in Japan AISIN Group has operations all over the globe. It operates almost 80 subsidiaries in Japan and over 135 internationally. The company's 13 core companies have about 20 development sites and nearly 15 advanced research facilities in Asia Europe and North America along with three test courses.

Sales and Marketing

AISIN Group's major customers for automotive products include Toyota Motor Nissan Motor Mazda General Motors and Volvo. Lifestyle-related products' customers include Toyota Housing Corp LIXIL Corp and Janis Ltd. Top customers who purchase the company's energy-related products include Tokyo Gas Saibu Gas Daikin Industries and Toho Gas.

Financial Performance

Note: Growth rates may differ after conversion to US Dollars.

The Group's revenue in 2020 decreased by 6% to Å 3.8 trillion compared to the prior year with Å 4.0 trillion.

Profit for fiscal 2020 decreased by 81% to Å 29.5 billion due to lower revenues while having almost the same operating expenses.

Cash held by the Group at the end of 2020 increased by Å 318 billion to Å 675.2 billion. Cash provided by operations and financing activities were Å 354.9 billion and Å 13.2 billion respectively. Cash used for investing activities was Å 414.5 million primarily for purchase of property plant and equipment.

Strategy

Since its establishment AISIN Group has adhered to the basic principle of "Quality First" and has sought to offer appealing products that meet customers' needs. Upholding the company's corporate principles of "Contributing to the advancement of society" and "Harmony with society and nature" the group promotes corporate behavior that helps create a sustainable society. The values and initiatives dovetail neatly with the Sustainable Development Goals (SDGs) and AISIN Group is working to contribute to the accomplishment of the SDGs through its business activities.

Mergers and Acquisitions

In early 2020 AISIN Group acquired all shares of Aisin AW Co Ltd (AW) held by Toyota Motor Corporation for Å 300 billion in preparation for the merger between Aisin Seiki Group and AW.

Company Background

Aisin Seiki traces its roots to 1943 when Tokai Hikoki was founded to produce airplane engines for the Japanese war effort. After the war the company switched to manufacturing sewing machines and auto parts. Aisin Seiki took its present name in 1965 after Tokai Hikoki merged with Shinkawa Kogyo.

EXECUTIVES

Managing Officer, Naofumi Fujie
EVP, Makoto Mitsuya
EVP, Hitoshi Okabe
President, Yasumori Ihara
Chairman, Kanshiro Toyoda, age 78
Auditors: PricewaterhouseCoopers Aarata LLC

LOCATIONS

HQ: Aisin Seiki Co Ltd
2-1 Asahi-machi, Kariya, Aichi 448-8650
Phone: (81) 566 24 8265
Web: www.aisin.co.jp

PRODUCTS/OPERATIONS

2019 Sales

	% of total
Aisin Seiki Group	39
Aisin AW Group	36
Advics Group	13
Aisin Takaoka Group	7
Other	5
Total	**100**

Selected Products

Automotive
Chassis and vehicle safety systems
Body products
ICT and electronics
Energy System
GHP
Cogeneration system
Life and Amenity
Bed furniture and fabric (ASLEEP)
House remodeling service (Livelan)
Home-use sewing machine
Cogeneration system
Shower-toilet seat
Audio equipment

COMPETITORS

APM Automotive	Hitachi America
BorgWarner	Magna International
Calsonic Kansei	Meritor
DENSO	Robert Bosch
DURA Automotive	Sumitomo Electric
Dana	Tenneco
Delphi Automotive	Visteon
Systems	ZF Friedrichshafen

HISTORICAL FINANCIALS

Company Type: Public

Income Statement   FYE: March 31

	REVENUE ($ mil.)	NET INCOME ($ mil.)	NET PROFIT MARGIN	EMPLOYEES
03/20	34,864	221	0.6%	144,334
03/19	36,508	994	2.7%	148,359
03/18	36,811	1,267	3.4%	141,615
03/17	31,864	1,132	3.6%	135,094
03/16	28,880	863	3.0%	120,976
Annual Growth	4.8%	(28.8%)	—	4.5%

2020 Year-End Financials

Debt ratio: 0.2%	No. of shares (mil.): 269
Return on equity: 1.8%	Dividends
Cash ($ mil.): 5,655	Yield: 5.6%
Current ratio: 1.74	Payout: 166.9%
Long-term debt ($ mil.): 7,823	Market value ($ mil.): 6,527

	STOCK PRICE ($) FY Close	P/E High/Low		PER SHARE ($) Earnings	Dividends	Book Value
03/20	24.22	0	0	0.82	1.38	43.76
03/19	35.78	0	0	3.69	1.35	45.13
03/18	55.52	0	0	4.62	1.30	45.78
03/17	49.73	0	0	3.97	0.89	39.59
03/16	37.49	0	0	3.04	0.88	34.69
Annual Growth	(10.3%)	—	—	(27.9%)	11.8%	6.0%

AKBANK

The vaults at Akbank have enough room for Turkish lira and the euro. The bank provides banking services in Turkey through nearly 1000 branches about 4300 ATMs and more than 360000 point-of-sale terminals. Internationally Akbank operates branches in Germany and in Malta; it also has subsidiary banks in the Netherlands and in Dubai. Akbank which is Turkey's second-largest publicly traded bank after Is Bankasi also provides private bank and international trade finance services. Subsidiaries provide non-banking financial capital-market and investment services. The Sabanci family and its companies control 55% of Akbank.

Operations

Akbank operates five main business segments: Retail Banking which serves consumers; the Corporate Banking Commercial Banking and SME Banking division which provides financial and banking services to large medium and small corporate and commercial customers; The Treasury Unit which trades a variety of treasury bond foreign currency and derivative trading securities on behalf the bank; Private Banking which provides banking and investment management services for affluent individuals; and International Banking which provides foreign currency financing foreign currency and TL clearances and money transfers through agent financial institutions.

Akbank generated 81% of its total revenue from interest income on loans in 2014 while 16% of the bank's revenue came from fee and commission income. Its loan portfolio was comprised of corporate loans (32% of loan assets) SME loans (37%) and consumer loans (31%).

Akbank's overseas subsidiaries include its German bank Akbank AG; Akbank Dubai Limited while its non-banking subsidiaries include AkInvestment AKAsset Management and Aklease.

Geographic Reach

Akbank boasts more than 990 branches across Turkey and has an additional branch in Malta. It also operates overseas through subsidiary banks in Frankfurt Germany and in Dubai UAE.

Sales and Marketing

Akbank serves a wide variety of industries including the energy infrastructure petrochemicals real estate telecommunications and transportation industries.

Financial Performance

Note: Growth rates may differ after conversion to US dollars.

Akbank has struggled to sustain revenue or profit growth in recent years though its business has remained stable. The bank had a breakout year in 2014 however with revenue jumping by 22% to TL$18.1 billion (around $7.7 billion). Most of the rise was driven by strong interest income growth from both the Retail Banking and the Corporate Banking Commercial banking and SME Banking divisions as the bank successfully grew its consumer loans (excluding credit card loans) by nearly 12% its general purpose loans by 21% and its mortgage loans by nearly 4% during the year. Akbank's fee and commission income also grew by 12% during the year further padding its top line.

Higher revenue and foreign exchange gains in 2014 drove the bank's net income higher by 7% to TL$3.3 billion (roughly $1.4 billion). Akbank's operating cash however declined by 30% to TL$1.4 billion for the year as the bank collected less cash from deposits during the year.

Strategy

As the second-largest bank in Turkey Akbank reiterated in 2015 that it's mid to long-term growth plans include being the leader of the country's banking industry while also looking toward international growth in markets where its clients enjoy high business volumes. It's also been working to manage its costs effectively executing more than 60 effective cost management actions in 2014 alone for an estimated TL$26 million (about $11 million) in sustainable savings.

Domestically Akbank has been moving toward digital banking channels that are quickly taking the industry by storm allowing the bank to slow expensive branch-expansion plans and cut operating costs significantly while giving customers faster access to banking services. In 2014 the bank launched new versions of its Akbank Direkt platform for mobile and internet banking differentiating user experiences for its variety of customer groups. Its Direkt Business was introduced for micro business segment customers while its Akbank Direkt Plus was unveiled for higher-income clients. Meanwhile its Mobile Banking platform was updated with iBeacon technology which allowed customers to make card-free cash withdrawal transactions from ATMs; while its cash management e-Invoice system allowed bank customers to send and receive e-invoices to and from business partners and suppliers.

Toward gaining more international exposure in growing regions Akbank sometimes partners with prominent banks in based in other regions. In 2014 for example the bank secured a cooperation agreement with Barclays Africa Group to provide banking services for Turkish companies that do business or invest in sub-Saharan countries in Africa via Barclays Africa branches. The deal also included joint financing opportunities for Turkish companies looking to grow in Africa as well as co-operation in trade and letters of guarantee transactions between Turkey and African countries.

EXECUTIVES

EVP Treasury, Kerim Rota
EVP Information Technology, Turgut G ney
EVP Consumer Banking, A. Galip T ¶zge
CEO and Board Member, Hakan Binbasgil
EVP International Banking, H lya Kefeli
EVP Payment Systems and Corporate Communication, Mehmet Sindel
EVP Commercial Banking, Kaan G r
EVP Credits, Ahmet Fuat Ayla
EVP Corporate Banking, Alper Hakan Y ksel
EVP Direct Banking, Orkun Oguz
EVP SME Banking, B lent Oguz
EVP and CFO, K.Atil zus
EVP Private Banking, Saltik Galatali
EVP Operation, zlen Sanibelli

EVP Human Resources and Strategy, Burcu Civelek Y ce
Vice Chairman, Hayri Culhaci
Chairman, Suzan Sabanci Din şer
Auditors: PwC Bagimsiz Denetim ve Serbest Muhasebeci Mali Musavirlik A.S.

LOCATIONS

HQ: AKBANK
Sabanci Center 4, Istanbul, Levent 34330
Phone: (90) 212 385 55 55   **Fax:** (90) 212 319 52 52
Web: www.akbank.com.tr

PRODUCTS/OPERATIONS

2014 Sales

	% of total
Interest income	81
Fee and commission received	16
Dividend income	-
Other operating income	3
Total	**100**

Selected Businesses

AKAssetmanagement
AKLease
AKInvestment
AKbank AG
Akbank Dubai Limited

COMPETITORS

Citi Turkey	Ko §
Finansbank	T rk Ekonomi Bankasi
GarantiBank	Yapi Kredi
Isbank	

HISTORICAL FINANCIALS

Company Type: Public

Income Statement

FYE: December 31

	ASSETS ($ mil.)	NET INCOME ($ mil.)	INCOME AS % OF ASSETS	EMPLOYEES
12/19	305,518	4,239	1.4%	13,136
12/18	279,776	4,503	1.6%	13,367
12/17	269,465	4,748	1.8%	14,253
12/16	232,305	3,829	1.6%	14,218
12/15	197,607	2,648	1.3%	16,543
Annual Growth	11.5%	12.5%	—	(5.6%)

2019 Year-End Financials

Return on assets: 1.4%	Dividends
Return on equity: 10.9%	Yield: 17.2%
Long-term debt ($ mil.): —	Payout: —
No. of shares (mil.): —	Market value ($ mil.): —
Sales ($ mil.): 32,708	

	STOCK PRICE ($) FY Close	P/E High/Low	PER SHARE ($) Earnings	Dividends	Book Value
12/19	2.71	290161	0.01	0.47	0.08
12/18	2.48	419123	0.01	0.15	0.09
12/17	5.16	406259	0.01	0.09	0.08
12/16	4.36	504345	0.01	0.08	0.06
12/15	4.61	970494	0.01	0.08	0.06
Annual Growth	(12.4%)	— —	6.3%	56.6%	10.0%

ALFA SAB de CV

ALFA is the alpha dog of business diversification. This Mexico-based multinational is the holding company for five leading businesses - Sigma (perishable refrigeration); Alpek (polyester & polypropylene); Nemak (aluminum); Axtel (IT & Communication); and Newpek (Oil & Gas). ALFA has presence primarily in the Americas and Europe followed by India China Turkey and Russia. Primary industries served by ALFA includes food and beverage automotive government communications and energy. More than 30% of the company's total revenue comes from Mexico.

Operations
Sigma is the leading revenue earner for ALFA bringing in more than 35% of annual sales. It manages the production marketing and distribution of refrigerated food in Mexico Europe the US and Latin America.

Alpek (approximately 35% of revenue) is a top polyester producer with a dominant position in the Mexican market for polypropylene expandable polystyrene and caprolactam.

Nemak manufactures lightweight aluminum products for automotive industries like trains and electric vehicles. It brings in about 25% of revenue for the parent company.

Axtel (nearly 5% sales) serves the Mexican government and public with IT services while Newpek has limited oil & gas exploration in US and Mexico.

Geographic Reach
Mexico-based Alfa markets its products in over 45 countries. Mexico is largest market accounting for about a third of the total sales followed by South Central America and the US which contribute over a quarter each the remaining revenue is from Canada Europe and other countries.

Sales and Marketing
Alfa's businesses provide its products into different markets; Sigma (food); Alpek (containers for beverages food and consumer products packaging for electronics and appliances textiles construction and automotive); Nemak (automotive); Axtel (Enterprise Government and Mass market) Newpek (Energy oil and gas). Advertising expenses were $2562 and $2782 for fiscal years 2019 and 2018 respectively.

Financial Performance
AFLA's revenue decreased 8% to $337.8 billion compared to $366.4 billion in 2018. Alpek ($119.7) Sigma ($124.5) and Nemak ($77.4) were the main contributors of revenue in 2019.

Net income was $5.8 billion 66% less than $13.1 billion in 2018.

Cash and cash equivalents at the end of the year were $25.2 billion $1.2 billion less than the previous year. Cash generated from operating activities was $30.6 billion. Investing activities generated $861 million primarily from the sale of businesses while financing activities used $31.4 billion primarily for payments of debt.

Strategy
Alpek acquired an integrated PTA-PET site in Ipojuca Pernambuco Brazil with a capacity of 640000 and 450000 tons per year of PTA and PET respectively. Citepe also operates a textured polyester filament plant with a capacity of 90000 tons per year. The operation was carried out due to Alpek's strategy of making continuous and selected investments in integration efficiency and expansion projects in order to achieve sustainable growth.

Company Background
In 1974 a group of businessmen led by Roberto Garza Sada founded ALFA to manage the group's interests in various businesses. A year after the company acquires Polioles (polystyrene urethanes and glycols) and Nylon de México (nylon).

EXECUTIVES

President, lvaro Fern ndez Garza

President Alpek, Jose de Jes s V ldez Simancas
President Nemak, Armando T mez Mart nez
President Sigma, Mario H. P ez Gonz lez
President Axtel, Rolando Zubir n Shelter
CFO, Ram n A. Leal Chapa
SVP Development and Director, Armando Garza Sada, age 63
Auditors: Deloitte LLP

LOCATIONS

HQ: ALFA SAB de CV
Avenida Gomez Morin 1111 Sur, Col. Carrizalejo, San Pedro Garza Garcia, Nuevo Leon 66254
Phone: (52) 81 8748 2521
Web: www.alfa.com.mx

2015 Sales

	% of total
North America	68
South Central America	5
Other Countries	27
Total	**100**

PRODUCTS/OPERATIONS

2015 Sales

	% of total
Alpek	32
Sigma	36
Nemak	28
Alestra	2
Newpek	1
Others	1
Total	**100**

Selected Operations
Alpek
  Akra Polyester
  DAK Americas
  Indelpro (51% polypropylene)
  Polioles (expandable polystyrene glycol and solvents urethanes)
  Univex (caprolactam and ammonium sulphate)
Nemak (aluminum engine blocks and heads)
Sigma
  Sigma Alimentos (processed meats yogurt cheese prepared meals)
Alestra (telecommunications)
Newpek (Natural gas and oil fields)

COMPETITORS

Akzo Nobel	SANLUIS
ConAgra	Schreiber Foods
Cydsa	Shaw Industries
Danone	Telmex
Iusacell	Tyson Fresh Meats
Mitsui Chemicals	Unifi

HISTORICAL FINANCIALS
Company Type: Public

Income Statement				FYE: December 31
	REVENUE ($ mil.)	NET INCOME ($ mil.)	NET PROFIT MARGIN	EMPLOYEES
12/19	17,851	306	1.7%	83,000
12/18	18,634	668	3.6%	83,701
12/17	16,123	(104)	—	86,200
12/16	14,198	112	0.8%	81,000
12/15	14,868	217	1.5%	72,800
Annual Growth	4.7%	9.0%	—	3.3%

2019 Year-End Financials

Debt ratio: 2.2%	No. of shares (mil.): —
Return on equity: 8.0%	Dividends
Cash ($ mil.): 1,331	Yield: —
Current ratio: 1.29	Payout: 68.7%
Long-term debt ($ mil.): 7,216	Market value ($ mil.): —

Alfresa Holdings Corp Tokyo

Alfresa Holdings distributes prescription drugs medical tests and devices and over-the-counter (OTC) supplements on a wholesale basis in the Japanese market. The firm is Japan's largest pharmaceuticals wholesaler holding as the third largest in the world. It also has an overseas business development arm which targets other Asian markets for growth. Its offerings also include OTC drugs diagnostic reagents and health foods. Its manufacturing division researches develops manufactures and markets these items as well as active pharmaceutical ingredients (APIs) used by other firms to make drugs.

Operations
Alfresa operates in four primary segments: Ethical Pharmaceuticals Wholesaling Self-Medication Products Wholesaling Manufacturing and Medical-Related (dispensing pharmacies).

The group's Ethical Pharmaceuticals Wholesaling segment contributes more than 85% of the group's total revenue. In addition to selling prescription drugs tests medical devices and other products it provides services to hospitals clinics pharmacies and other customers.

The Self-Medication Products Wholesaling segment provides OTC drugs health foods supplements and other items to drugstores and pharmacies. It brings in some 10% of the group's revenue.

The smallest segments are Manufacturing and Medical-Related. Manufacturing develops and manufactures drugs APIs tests medical devices and other products while Medical-Related provides dispensing pharmacy services. Each segment provides the remainder of Alfresa's total revenue.

Geographic Reach
Alfresa is headquartered in Tokyo and is ranked three as the largest pharmaceutical market in the world. The company seeks to expand in other parts of Asia particularly in China and Vietnam. In China the Group established joint venture REMEJE PHARMACEUTICALS (CHINA) CO. LTD. in 2005 as a representative office for pharmaceuticals and healthcare-related products. In Vietnam the Group established joint venture Alfresa Codupha Healthcare Vietnam Co. Ltd. (Alcopha) in 2013 to conduct import and sales mainly of medical devices and materials and diagnostic reagents and is gradually setting up a stable management foundation. There are more than 200 warehouse in Japan and in overseas.

Sales and Marketing
Alfresa's customers include hospitals medical care facilities drugstores and pharmacies. Company's products and services offer to over 100000 customers throughout Japan.

Financial Performance
The Group's net sales increased 1% due to growth in sales volumes for hepatitis C therapeutic agents and anticancer drugs.

The company's net income increased by Å 9.7 billion to Å 61.2 billion compared to Å 51.6 billion from the prior year. The increase was primarily due to the 68% increase on their other income.

Cash held by the company in 2019 increased by Å 9.5 billion to Å 205.1 billion compared to Å 195.6 billion in the prior year. Cash from operations was Å 46.9 billion while cash used for investing and financing activities were Å 12.9 billion and Å 24.9 billion respectively.

Strategy
Alfresa's basic approach to financial and capital strategy under the 19?21 Mid-term Management

Plan is to raise corporate value by pursuing the optimal balance of financial soundness capital efficiency and shareholder returns. In particular the company will press forward even further with investments and measures to promote growth based on issues identified in the previous plan.

The Alfresa Group uses capital cost as a management indicator measuring and updating provisional figures each year while referring to information from multiple external professional organizations. In addition to monitoring the profitability of existing businesses they also refer to the latest cost of capital when making investment decisions and evaluating businesses or investment securities.

Company Background

Alfresa was created in 2003 from the combination of wholesalers Azwell and Fukujin.

EXECUTIVES

President, Taizo Kubo
Deputy President, Shunichi Miyake
Chairman, Denroku Ishiguro, age 69
Deputy President, Hiroyuki Kanome
Auditors: KPMG AZSA LLC

LOCATIONS

HQ: Alfresa Holdings Corp Tokyo
1-1-3 Otemachi, Chiyoda-ku, Tokyo 100-0004
Phone: (81) 3 5219 5100
Web: www.alfresa.com

PRODUCTS/OPERATIONS

2018 Sales by Segment

	% of total
Ethical Pharmaceuticals Wholesaling	88
Self-Medication Products Wholesaling	10
Pharmaceutical Manufacturing	1
Medical-Related	1
Total	**100**

COMPETITORS

Astellas	Takeda Pharmaceutical
Medipal	Toho Pharmaceutical
Suzuken	

HISTORICAL FINANCIALS

Company Type: Public

Income Statement				FYE: March 31
	REVENUE ($ mil.)	NET INCOME ($ mil.)	NET PROFIT MARGIN	EMPLOYEES
03/20	24,859	371	1.5%	14,562
03/19	23,843	376	1.6%	14,718
03/18	24,512	335	1.4%	14,629
03/17	22,824	276	1.2%	14,609
03/16	22,942	311	1.4%	14,556
Annual Growth	2.0%	4.5%	—	0.0%

2020 Year-End Financials

Debt ratio: 0.0%	No. of shares (mil.): 211
Return on equity: 8.7%	Dividends
Cash ($ mil.): 1,939	Yield: —
Current ratio: 1.24	Payout: —
Long-term debt ($ mil.): 5	Market value ($ mil.): —

Alibaba Group Holding Ltd

Auditors: PricewaterhouseCoopers

LOCATIONS

HQ: Alibaba Group Holding Ltd
c/o Alibaba Group Services Limited, 26/F Tower One, Times Square, 1 Matheson Street, Causeway Bay,
Phone:
Web: www.alibabagroup.com

HISTORICAL FINANCIALS

Company Type: Public

Income Statement				FYE: March 31
	REVENUE ($ mil.)	NET INCOME ($ mil.)	NET PROFIT MARGIN	EMPLOYEES
03/20	72,536	21,265	29.3%	117,600
03/19	53,628	12,506	23.3%	101,958
03/18	35,614	9,120	25.6%	66,421
03/17	22,523	6,215	27.6%	50,097
03/16	14,393	10,169	70.7%	36,446
Annual Growth	49.8%	20.3%	—	34.0%

2020 Year-End Financials

Debt ratio: 1.3%	No. of shares (mil.): —
Return on equity: 23.5%	Dividends
Cash ($ mil.): 47,033	Yield: —
Current ratio: 1.91	Payout: —
Long-term debt ($ mil.): 17,116	Market value ($ mil.): —

	STOCK PRICE ($) FY Close	P/E High/Low		PER SHARE ($) Earnings	Dividends	Book Value
03/20	194.48	32	21	0.99	0.00	5.06
03/19	182.45	50	31	0.59	0.00	3.43
03/18	183.54	66	34	0.44	0.00	2.55
03/17	107.83	50	34	0.30	0.00	1.98
03/16	79.03	26	16	0.50	0.00	1.56
Annual Growth	25.2%	—	—	19.0%	—	34.2%

Alimentation Couche-Tard Inc

Alimentation Couche-Tard is the name of the company but you might know it through its brands like Circle K and Corner Store in the US and Statoil in Europe. The company is the second-largest convenience store operator in North America (behind 7-Eleven Inc.) and the leader in Canada where it operates under Couche-Tard banner. While most of its sales are rung up in the US it operates in Europe as well as about 15 countries in other parts of the world through license agreements. Most of the company's revenue comes from sales of fuel (it pumps about 14 billion gallons a year). Alimentation Couche-Tard which is French for "food for those who go to bed late" has expanded through acquisitions around the world.

Operations

In Couche-Tard's global operations Circle K Statoil Couche-Tard and Mac's have been its key brands.

Fuel accounts for about three-quarters of the company's revenue with merchandise and services

supplying about a quarter of sales. The company also operates commercial fuel.

The company's reliance on fuel makes it sensitive to fuel prices that can fluctuate wildly. While accounting for some 72% of sales fuel supplies 46% of gross profit.

Tobacco products account for nearly 40% of the merchandise and service revenue. Couche-Tard also sells brands of cigarettes made for the company which could expose it to legal action.

Geographic Reach

Couche-Tard operates and licenses about 16000 global sites with more than 9000 convenience stores in North America more than 2700 in Europe and 2000 around the world. The company has operations throughout the US (not including Hawaii and Alaska) in Scandinavia the Baltic states Ireland Russia and Poland. In Scandinavia Couche-Tard operates automated fuel-only sites under the Ingo brand. The company classifies as international operations its licensed stores in Asia Indonesia Central America and the Middle East.

United States generates approximately 70% of company's revenue. Europe is almost 20% and the remainder comprised of Canada's revenue.

Sales and Marketing

The company launched its Easy Pay loyalty program in all U.S. markets providing everyday fuel discounts to its most loyal customer. Couche-Tard recognizes sales of merchandise and goods to certain independent operators and franchisees made from the company's distribution centers and sales of road transportation fuel upon delivery to its customers.

Financial Performance

The company's revenue decreased by $5.0 billion to $54.2 billion due to the decrease on their road transportation fuel revenues and other revenues. The decrease was primarily due to the decrease on their operations at U.S. and Europe.

Net earnings amounted to $2.4 billion for fiscal 2020 compared with $1.8 billion for fiscal 2019. The results for fiscal 2020 were affected by a pretax net gain of $61.5 million on the disposal of their interests in CrossAmerica Partners LP a pretax net gain of $41.0 million on the disposal of a portion of their U.S. wholesale fuel business as part of an asset exchange with CAPL a positive impact on income tax of $33.6 million from an adjustment to deferred tax assets pre-tax foreign exchange gain of $33.5 million acquisition costs of $6.7 million pre-tax restructuring costs of $4.5 million and an income tax expense of $2.7 million following the asset exchange transactions with CAPL.

Cash held by the company at the end of 2020 increased by $2.9 billion to $3.6 billion compared to $706.4 million in the prior year. Cash provided by operations and financing activities were $3.7 billion and $480.7 million respectively. Cash used for investing activities was $1.2 billion primarily for purchase of property and equipment intangible assets and other assets.

Strategy

Couche-Tard's five-year strategy to double again requires that they grow market share in the U.S. and expand to new growth markets and industries. Maintaining financial discipline allows them to take advantage of opportunities as they arise.

Coming into fiscal 2020 the company accelerated the pace of new store construction after a significant effort to develop their project pipelines. Couche-Tard had good momentum with the new builds until the pandemic triggered a pause in many of these projects. The company also introduced new design for their North American sites that mirrors the Holiday stores format and improves the customer journey.

The company continued to roll out their new store concept in Europe which is now at more than 300 sites with enhanced food fuel charging WIFI washrooms and parking. These stores provide a welcoming ambiance and comfortable seating area high-quality food displayed in an attractive way and improved merchandising in the rest of the store. Couche-Tard instituted learning from their initial pilots which led to improved profitability.

Mergers and Acquisitions

In early 2020 Couche-Tard acquired 17 stores from a franchise operator. These convenience stores operate under the Holiday banner in South Dakota and Minnesota within the United States.

Couche-Tard also acquired 13 company operated stores through distinct transactions. The company owns the land and building for the remaining 6 sites.

In early 2019 company acquired six company-operated stores and two commission operated retail sites through distinct transactions. The company owns the land and building for three sites and leases the land and the building for the remaining three sites. It was settled for a total cash consideration of $13.1.

EXECUTIVES

CEO, Brian P. Hannasch, $286,000 total compensation

SVP Operations and President CST Brands Inc., Darrell Davis

CFO, Claude Tessier

Group President European Operations, Jacob Schram

Group President Global Fuels and Operations North-East, Jean Bernier

EVP Scandinavia, Hans-Olav H idahl

EVP Central and Eastern Europe, J rn Madsen

Chairman, Alain Bouchard

Auditors: PricewaterhouseCoopers LLP

LOCATIONS

HQ: Alimentation Couche-Tard Inc
4204 Industriel Boulevard, Laval, Quebec H7L 0E3
Phone: 450 662-6632   **Fax:** 450 662-6633
Web: www.couche-tard.com

2018 Sales

	$ mil.	% of total
US	34,178	67
Europe	10,315	20
Canada	6,901	13
Total	**51,394**	**100**

PRODUCTS/OPERATIONS

2018 Sales

	$ mil.	% of total
Road Transportation Fuel	37,116	72
Merchandise and Services	12,976	25
Other	1,302	3
Total	**51,394**	**100**

COMPETITORS

7-Eleven	Pilot Flying J
Casey's General Stores	QuikTrip
Chevron	Racetrac Petroleum
Exxon Mobil	Royal Dutch Shell
Gate Petroleum	Sheetz
Kum & Go	Sobeys
Loblaw	TravelCenters of
Marathon Oil	America

HISTORICAL FINANCIALS

Company Type: Public

Income Statement

FYE: April 26

	REVENUE ($ mil.)	NET INCOME ($ mil.)	NET PROFIT MARGIN	EMPLOYEES
04/20	54,132	2,353	4.3%	131,000
04/19	59,117	1,833	3.1%	109,000
04/18	51,394	1,673	3.3%	0
04/17	37,904	1,208	3.2%	105,000
04/16	34,144	1,193	3.5%	0
Annual Growth	**12.2%**	**18.5%**	—	—

2020 Year-End Financials

Debt ratio: 30.1%
Return on equity: 24.8%
Cash ($ mil.): 3,641
Current ratio: 1.72
Long-term debt ($ mil.): 7,515

No. of shares (mil.): 1,112
Dividends
 Yield: 0.0%
 Payout: 12.4%
Market value ($ mil.): 31,704

	STOCK PRICE ($) FY Close	P/E High/Low	PER SHARE ($) Earnings	Dividends	Book Value
04/20	28.49	31 10	2.09	0.26	9.05
04/19	58.81	38 25	1.63	0.22	7.90
04/18	44.19	37 28	1.48	0.18	6.70
04/17	46.02	50 38	1.06	0.17	5.29
04/16	43.00	45 36	1.05	0.12	4.44
Annual Growth	**(9.8%)**	—	**18.8%**	**20.4%**	**19.5%**

Allianz SE

One of the world's biggest insurers Allianz SE offers a range of insurance products and services — including life health and property/casualty coverage for individuals and businesses — through subsidiaries ventures and affiliates operating all over the globe (Allianz SE and its subsidiaries are collectively known as the Allianz Group). Based in Munich Germany the company serves more than 100 million customers in such key markets as France Germany Italy and the US. In addition to selling insurance Allianz provides retail and institutional asset management services through Allianz Asset Management private equity investment through Allianz Capital Partners and banking services through Allianz Bank.

Operations

Allianz operates through four business segments — Property/Casualty Life/Health Asset Management and Corporate and Other — which are further divided primarily by geography into 11 reportable segments. The company is one of the world's largest property/casualty insurers offering auto property accident general liability and travel insurance among others. The Life/Health business segment offers savings and investment products in addition to life and health policies. Allianz gets generates about 55% of its revenue from its Life/Health segment; the Property/Casualty segment accounts for more than 40% of revenue. These two segments do most of their business in France Germany Italy and the US.

The Asset Management segment that generates roughly 5% of revenue has two primary investment management businesses — PIMCO and Allianz Global Investors (AllianzGI). Combined these units have nearly ?1.7 trillion in third-party assets under management making Allianz one of the world's largest active asset managers. They offer a variety of stock bond and alternative investment products

and chiefly operate in France Germany Italy the UK the US and the Asia/Pacific region.

Geographic Reach

Headquartered in Munich Germany Allianz operates in more than 70 countries with most of its operations in Europe. It also operates in the Asia/Pacific region Africa and the Americas.

Sales and Marketing

Allianz has sponsorship arrangements with a collection of leading sports stadia including those occupied by Bayern Munich Juventus OGC Nice Rapid Wein Palmeiras and Minnesota United FC (soccer) as well as Saracens FC (rugby).

Financial Performance

Note: Growth rates may differ after conversion to US Dollars.

Allianz's revenue hasn't changed that much over the last five years shifting up or down a few percent each year. Overall revenue grew 14% between 2015 and 2019. Net income however has grown consistently over the same period rising by about 19%.

In 2019 revenues grew 6% to ?142.4 billion compared to ?132.3 billion in 2018. Allianz's Life/Health business segment recorded a strong sales increase for single premium capital-efficient products in Germany as well as higher sales of non-traditional variable annuity products in the US. Its Property-Casualty business segment and Asset Management business segment have also driven revenues higher.

Net income rose 8% to ?8.3 billion in 2019 as a result of the growth in its operating profit and non-operating result by ?11.9 billion and ?335 million respectively. A slightly lower tax rate by 25% also contributed to the rise.

Allianz's cash balance ended fiscal 2019 rose by ?3.8 billion to ?21.1 billion. The company's operations generated ?36.4 billion while its investing activities used ?27.7 billion and its financing activities ?4.9 billion. Allianz's main cash uses in 2019 were investments loans and advancements repayments of liabilities and dividends paid to shareholders.

Strategy

Allianz has outlined its objectives for its medium-term strategy with the motto "Simplicity wins": outperform by moving ahead of its competitors both traditional business and disruptors; transform by becoming simpler and deeply digital; and rebalance by building market-leading positions in large profitable and fast-growing geographies as well as in new areas of business.

To implement these strategic objectives Allianz has defined a number of strategic priorities and are implementing initiatives and programs to address the five dimensions of its Renewal Agenda. These five dimensions being true customer centricity digital by default technical excellence growth engines and inclusive meritocracy.

It has also made several investments and acquisitions to further its business capabilities. Among these recent acquisitions and investments are automobile and other property/casualty business SulAmérica a strategic partnership with Virtus Investment Partners in the US retail market a bancassurance joint venture with Banco Bilbao Vizcaya Argentaria a life insurance joint venture with AEON Financial Service and an investment in ControlExpert to improve claims through artificial intelligence and automation.

Additionally under Allianz Global Corporate & Specialty a new comprehensive transformation program named "New AGCS" was launched. The program aims to regain profitability and market leadership in the corporate and specialty insurance segment. AGCS will also simplify its regional organization reducing the number of regional units from seven to six and moving from a country-centric to a more global set-up with regional delivery.

Mergers and Acquisitions

In mid-2020 Allianz acquired the automobile and other property & casualty business from SulAmérica in Brazil for 3.2 billion Brazilian real (US$595 million). This completion of the transaction positions the company as the number two carrier in motor insurance and makes it one of the top three insurers in property-casualty insurance in Brazil.

In mid-2020 Allianz acquired Aldi logistics in Australia for A$648 million. The acquisition is a 50-50 joint venture between Charter Hall Group and Allianz Real Estate with the latter acting on behalf of several Allianz companies. "This transaction is in line with our strategy of aligning our investments to secular mega trends in the Asia Pacific region" said Rushabh Desai chief executive for Asia Pacific at Allianz Real Estate.

In 2019 Allianz's UK subsidiary acquire Legal & General Insurance Limited the general insurance business of Legal & General Group Plc for Å 242 million. It also bought out the remaining 51% stake in LV General Insurance Group for to Å 578 million from Liverpool Victoria Friendly Society.

In mid-2019 Allianz X the digital investment unit of the Allianz Group agreed to acquire Berlin-based Finanzen.de a European B2B online marketplace for high-value consumer traffic in the insurance and financial services sectors. Transaction were not disclosed.

Company Background

In 1890 Allianz is founded in Munich Germany by insurance specialist Carl Thieme and banker Wilhelm Finck. In 1893 Allianz opened its office in London for international operations headed by Carl Schreiner. By the year 1938 the employee strength reached to a number of 24000. The Munich headquarters of Allianz was destroyed by bombs during the World War II. The expansions went through with the establishment of more branches in many countries of the world like Spain Brazil the Netherlands.

HISTORY

Carl Thieme founded Allianz in Germany in 1890. That year the company took part in the creation of the Calamity Association of Accident Insurance Companies a consortium of German Austrian Swiss and Russian firms to insure international commerce.

By 1898 Thieme had established offices in the UK Switzerland and the Netherlands. His successor Paul von der Nahmer expanded Allianz into the Balkans France Italy Scandinavia and the US. After a hiatus during WWI Allianz returned to foreign markets.

In WWII Allianz insured Auschwitz Dachau and other death camps. Company documents show Allianz wasn't worried about risk at the SS troop-guarded camps. After the German defeat the victors seized Allianz's foreign holdings except for a stake in Spain's Plus Ultra. In the 1950s Allianz repurchased confiscated holdings in Italian and Austrian companies.

Allianz saturated the German market and began a full-scale international drive in the late 1950s and 1960s. It became Europe's largest insurer through a series of acquisitions beginning in 1973. Allianz formed Los Angeles-based Allianz Insurance in 1977.

In 1981 Allianz launched a takeover (which turned hostile) of the UK's Eagle Star insurance company. After a 1983 bidding joust with Britain's B.A.T Industries (now part of Zurich Financial Services) Allianz withdrew.

The firm consoled itself by shopping. In 1984 it won control of Riunione Adriatica di Sicurt (Ras) Italy's second-largest insurance company. Two years later the firm bought Cornhill (now Allianz

Insurance plc) on its third try. As the Iron Curtain crumbled Allianz in 1989 acquired 49% of Hungaria Biztosito. Its drang nach Osten continued the next year after national reunification when it gained control of Deutsche Versicherungs AG East Germany's insurance monopoly. Allianz that year became the first German insurer licensed in Japan; it also bought the US's Fireman's Fund Insurance.

Natural disasters led to large claims and set the company back in 1992 the first time in 20 years it lost money from its German operations. Allianz restructured operations that year; profits surged in 1993 mostly from international business.

Allianz expanded in Mexico in 1995 forming a life and health insurance joint venture with Grupo Financiero BanCrecer (now owned by Grupo Financiero Banorte). The company set up an asset management arm in Hong Kong in 1996 with an eye to further Asian expansion getting a license in China the next year. In 1997 after Holocaust survivors sued Allianz and other insurers for failing to pay on life policies after WWII Allianz agreed to participate in a repayment fund.

In 1998 Allianz bought control of Assurances Générales de France; it was the white knight that prevented Assicurazioni Generali from taking the company. In 1999 Allianz said it would restructure some of its insurance operations including spinning off its marine and aviation lines to better compete in the multinational market. That year US subsidiary Allianz Life bought Life USA Holding. In 2000 Allianz bought 70% of PIMCO Advisors Holdings to strengthen its asset management operations. That year the company continued its push into Asia buying a 12% stake in Hana Bank of South Korea and planning to boost its ownership of Malaysia British Assurance Life. Also in 2000 Allianz acquired Dutch insurer Zwolsche Algemeene.

Allianz remained acquisitive in 2001 buying US investment manager Nicholas-Applegate and taking a majority stake in ROSNO one of Russia's largest insurers. Also that year it bought a nearly 96% stake in German banking giant Dresdner and acquired the remainder the following year.

Allianz paid out claims of some $1.3 billion relating to the terrorist attacks on the World Trade Center. The company set up a terrorism insurance unit offering coverage primarily for companies within the European Union.

EXECUTIVES

CEO Allianz Worldwide Care, Ida Luka-Lognoné, age 58
Member Management Board and Chairman and CEO, Oliver B ¤te, age 55, $700,000 total compensation
Management Board Member and COO, Christof Mascher, age 60, $309,571 total compensation
Management Board Member and CFO, Dieter Wemmer, age 64
Management Board Member Investments, Maximilian Zimmerer, age 62
Management Board Member Global Insurance Lines and Anglo Markets, Axel Theis, age 63
CEO TIO, Daryl Madden
Chief Market Manager, Paul Kernaghan
Vice Chairman, Wulf H. Bernotat, age 72
Auditors: PricewaterhouseCoopers GmbH Wirtschaftspruefungsgesellschaft

LOCATIONS

HQ: Allianz SE
Koeniginstrasse 28, Munich D-80802
Phone: (49) 89 38 00 0   **Fax:** (49) 89 38 00 3425
Web: www.allianz.com

2018 sales

	% of total
Western & Southern Europe	32
US	11
Germany	27
Specialty insurance	16
Growth markets	9
Broker markets	4
Total	**100**

PRODUCTS/OPERATIONS

2018 sales

	% of total
Life/Health	54
Property/Casualty	41
Asset Management	5
Total	**100**

Selected Operations and Brands

Allianz
Allianz Global Corporate and Specialty
Allianz Global Investors
Allianz Worldwide Care
Euler Hermes
PIMCO

COMPETITORS

AEGON	MetLife
AXA	New York Life
Allstate	Old Mutual
Aviva	Prudential
Berkshire Hathaway	Prudential plc
CNP Assurances	RSA Insurance
ERGO	State Farm
Generali	Talanx
Generali Deutschland	The Hartford
Groupama	Zurich Insurance Group
ING	ageas SA/NV
Legal & General Group	

HISTORICAL FINANCIALS

Company Type: Public

Income Statement

FYE: December 31

	ASSETS ($ mil.)	NET INCOME ($ mil.)	INCOME AS % OF ASSETS	EMPLOYEES
12/19	1,135,324	8,885	0.8%	147,268
12/18	1,027,889	8,545	0.8%	142,460
12/17	1,080,437	8,155	0.8%	140,553
12/16	933,199	7,267	0.8%	140,253
12/15	924,676	7,206	0.8%	142,459
Annual Growth	5.3%	5.4%	—	0.8%

2019 Year-End Financials

Return on assets: 0.8%	Dividends
Return on equity: 11.7%	Yield: —
Long-term debt ($ mil.): —	Payout: 50.9%
No. of shares (mil.): 416	Market value ($ mil.): —
Sales ($ mil): 118,040	

Alpha Bank SA

EXECUTIVES

General Manager and COO, Spyros N. Filaretos, age 62
Managing Director and CEO, Demetrios P. Mantzounis, age 73
Deputy CEO, George C. Aronis, age 64
General Manager and Chief Risk Officer, Spiros A. Andronikakis, age 60

Manager Loans Division Retail, Periklis M. Kitrilakis
Deputy CEO, Artemios Ch. Theodoridis
Deputy CEO, Vassillios E. Psaltis
Executive General Manager, Efstathios A. Kakogiannis
Executive General Manager, Penelope E. Konidari
Executive General Managers, Lazaros A. Papagaryfallou
Executive General Manager, Constantinos R. Dorkofikis
Executive General Manager, Ioannis M. Emiris
Executive General Managers, Theodoros I. Athanassopoulos
Executive General Managers, Athanasios I. Athanasopoulos
Executive General Managers, Isidore S. Passas
Executive General Managers, Georgios V. Michalopoulos
Executive General Manager, Damianos I. Charalampidis
Director, Evangelos J. Kaloussis, age 78
Chairman, Vasileios T. Rapanos
Auditors: Deloitte Certified Public Accountants S.A.

LOCATIONS
HQ: Alpha Bank SA
40 Stadiou Street, Athens GR-102 52
Phone: (30) 210 326 0000   **Fax:** (30) 210 326 5438
Web: www.alpha.gr

2015 Sales

	% of total
Greece	84
Other countries	16
Total	**100**

PRODUCTS/OPERATIONS

2015 Gross Sales

	% of total
Retail banking	47
Corporate banking	36
South Eastern Europe	14
Asset management and insurance	3
Total	**100**

2015 Sales

	% of total
Interest and similar income	87
Fee and commission income	11
Other income	2
Total	**100**

Selected Services
Bancassurance
Business Banking
Cards
Consumer Loans
Deposit Accounts
Housing Loans
Investment Products
Private Banking

COMPETITORS

Bank of Cyprus	National Bank of
Citigroup	Greece
EFG Eurobank Ergasias	Piraeus Bank S.A.
HSBC	

HISTORICAL FINANCIALS
Company Type: Public

Income Statement   FYE: December 31

	ASSETS ($ mil.)	NET INCOME ($ mil.)	INCOME AS % OF ASSETS	EMPLOYEES
12/19	71,248	108	0.2%	10,530
12/18	69,864	60	0.1%	11,314
12/17	72,899	25	0.0%	11,727
12/16	68,497	44	0.1%	12,699
12/15	75,478	(1,494)	—	14,779
Annual Growth	(1.4%)	—	—	(8.1%)

2019 Year-End Financials

Return on assets: 0.1%	Dividends
Return on equity: 1.1%	Yield: —
Long-term debt ($ mil.): —	Payout: —
No. of shares (mil.): 1,543	Market value ($ mil.): 857
Sales ($ mil): 3,230	

	STOCK PRICE ($) FY Close	P/E High/Low		PER SHARE ($) Earnings	Dividends	Book Value
12/19	0.56	9	4	0.07	0.00	6.14
12/18	0.29	21	9	0.03	0.00	6.02
12/17	0.57	73	44	0.01	0.00	7.45
12/16	0.50	25	10	0.03	0.00	6.25
12/15	0.68	—	—	(3.88)	0.00	6.40
Annual Growth	(5.0%)	—	—	—	—	(1.0%)

Aluminum Corp of China Ltd.

Auditors: Ernst & Young Hua Ming LLP

LOCATIONS
HQ: Aluminum Corp of China Ltd.
No. 62, North Xizhimen Street, Haidian District, Beijing 100082
Phone: (86) 10 8229 8560   **Fax:** (86) 10 8229 8158
Web: www.chalco.com.cn

HISTORICAL FINANCIALS
Company Type: Public

Income Statement   FYE: December 31

	REVENUE ($ mil.)	NET INCOME ($ mil.)	NET PROFIT MARGIN	EMPLOYEES
12/19	27,316	122	0.4%	0
12/18	26,204	126	0.5%	65,211
12/17	27	211	765.5%	64,794
12/16	20,746	57	0.3%	65,755
12/15	19,007	31	0.2%	70,368
Annual Growth	9.5%	40.1%	—	—

2019 Year-End Financials

Debt ratio: 5.5%	No. of shares (mil.): —
Return on equity: 1.5%	Dividends
Cash ($ mil.): 1,302	Yield: —
Current ratio: 0.70	Payout: —
Long-term debt ($ mil.): 7,506	Market value ($ mil.): —

	STOCK PRICE ($) FY Close	P/E High/Low		PER SHARE ($) Earnings	Dividends	Book Value
12/19	8.69	290	193	0.01	0.00	(0.00)
12/18	7.82	415	171	0.01	0.00	(0.00)
12/17	17.93	266	123	0.01	0.00	(0.00)
12/16	10.21	583	330	0.00	0.00	(0.00)
12/15	8.24	1660	703	0.00	0.00	401.27
Annual Growth	1.3%	—	—	36.3%	—	—

Ambev SA

Auditors: PricewaterhouseCoopers Auditores Independentes

LOCATIONS
HQ: Ambev SA
Rua Dr. Renato Paes de Barros, 1017, 3rd floor, Sao Paulo 04530-001
Phone: (55) 11 2122 1200   **Fax:** (55) 11 2122 1526
Web: www.ambev.com.br

HISTORICAL FINANCIALS
Company Type: Public

Income Statement   FYE: December 31

	REVENUE ($ mil.)	NET INCOME ($ mil.)	NET PROFIT MARGIN	EMPLOYEES
12/19	13,085	2,930	22.4%	51,352
12/18	12,942	2,840	21.9%	49,617
12/17	14,459	2,213	15.3%	51,432
12/16	14,011	3,854	27.5%	53,250
12/15	11,796	3,136	26.6%	52,738
Annual Growth	2.6%	(1.7%)	—	(0.7%)

2019 Year-End Financials

Debt ratio: 0.7%	No. of shares (mil.): —
Return on equity: 20.0%	Dividends
Cash ($ mil.): 2,960	Yield: 2.2%
Current ratio: 1.10	Payout: 56.3%
Long-term debt ($ mil.): 599	Market value ($ mil.): —

	STOCK PRICE ($) FY Close	P/E High/Low		PER SHARE ($) Earnings	Dividends	Book Value
12/19	4.66	7	5	0.18	0.10	0.97
12/18	3.92	9	5	0.18	0.13	0.92
12/17	6.46	14	10	0.14	0.15	0.88
12/16	4.91	8	6	0.24	0.18	0.88
12/15	4.46	7	5	0.20	0.12	0.78
Annual Growth	1.1%	—	—	(1.6%)	(3.7%)	5.7%

America Movil SAB de CV

América Móvil offers wireless phone service from the Rio Grande to Tierra del Fuego and beyond. The company is Latin America's top mobile carrier with more than 275 million subscribers in 25 countries. In Mexico the company has about 77 million subscribers to its Telcel and Telmex brands. Its second largest market is Brazil where it has about 55 million subscribers through Claro. América Móvil also provides fixed-line service in Central America and the Caribbean. While the company's operations are centered in Latin America it also offers service in the US through TracFone and Eastern Europe through A1. The company also offers broadband Pay TV and IT services. Billionaire Carlos Slim Helú owns most of América Móvil. Nearly a third of its revenue is generated in Mexico.

Operations

About 85% of América Móvil's revenue comes from it wireless and fixed telephone and other services while equipment sales account for more than 15% of revenue.

Wireless voice and data are the big money makers for América M vil providing more than half of its revenue. Service revenue is generated by monthly subscriptions use charges billed to customers and use charges billed to other service providers for calls completed on the company's network.

Equipment sales include handsets and accessories as well as office equipment household appliances and electronics.

The company also provides pay TV through cable and satellite services information technology services and streaming video.

Geographic Reach

Considering its nearly worldwide reach América M vil could be called Mundo M vil. The company has operations in throughout the western hemisphere (not including Canada) as well as Europe. More than 30% of revenue comes from Mexico with Brazil accounting for more than 15% and the US generates roughly 15% of revenue.

The company's other markets are the Southern Cone (Argentina Chile Paraguay and Uruguay) and Europe (Austria Belarus Bulgaria Croatia Macedonia Serbia and Slovenia). Those regions combine for approximately 15% combined of revenue. The remaining revenue (more than 20% combined revenues) comes from Colombia the Andean Region (Ecuador and Peru) Central America (Costa Rica El Salvador Guatemala Honduras Nicaragua and Panama) and the Caribbean (the Dominican Republic and Puerto Rico).

Sales and Marketing

América M vil reaches customers through a network of retailers and service centers for retail customers and a dedicated sales force for corporate customers. The company counts more than 490000 points of sale and about 2900 customer service centers. America Movil's subsidiaries also sell their services and products online.

For the years ended December 31 2017 2018 and 2019 advertising expenses were Ps. 28.7 million Ps. 26.3 million and Ps. 22.8 million respectively.

Financial Performance

After increasing continuously since 2015 América M vil's revenue declined by 3% in 2019.

In 2019 revenue declined 3% to about 1 trillion pesos from 2018. Services revenue dipped about 3%.

América M vil's net income leaped about 29% higher to 67.7 billion pesos in 2019 from 2018.

The company had 19.7 billion pesos in cash and equivalents in 2019 compared to 21.7 billion pesos in 2018. In 2019 operating activities generated 234.3 billion pesos while investing activities used 163.1 billion pesos and financing activities used 71.3 billion pesos.

Strategy

America Movil intends to build on its position as leaders in integrated telecommunications services in Latin America and the Caribbean and to grow in other parts of the world by continuing to expand its subscriber base through the development of existing businesses and strategic acquisitions when opportunities arise. The company has developed world-class integrated telecommunications platforms to offer customers new services and enhanced communications solutions with higher data speed transmissions at lower prices. The company continues investing in its networks to increase coverage and implement new technologies to optimize network capabilities.

Mergers and Acquisitions

America Movil in 2019 said it would buy Nextel's Brazil operations for $905 million and merge the acquired business with Claro its existing service in Brazil. The deal serves to add heft to America Movil Brazil operations in competing with the other large operators in the country Telefonica Telecom

Italia and Oi. The deal follows America Movil's purchases of Telefonica's assets in Guatemala and El Salvador respectively for a total of about $648 million also in 2019.

Company Background

América M vil was formed in 2000 from a spin-off from Telmex which was at the time Mexico's largest local and long-distance phone service provider. In late 2006 América M vil acquired majority owner América Telecom in a move to streamline the structure of the company and to free up assets for share buybacks or dividends.

EXECUTIVES

CEO Telmex, Héctor Slim Seade, age 57
CFO, Carlos José Garc a Moreno Elizondo
CEO Peru, Humberto Ch ´vez L pez
CEO Central America, Juan Antonio Aguilar
CEO Dominican Republic, Oscar Peña Chac n
CEO Argentina Uruguay and Paraguay, Julio Carlos Porras
CEO and Director, Daniel Hajj Aboumrad, age 54
CEO Panama, Oscar Borda
CEO Puerto Rico, Enrique Ortiz de Montellano Rangel
CEO Telekom Austria, Alejandro Plater, age 53
Executive Director Fixed Line Operations, Oscar Von Hauske Sol s
Executive Director Mobile Operations, ngel Alija Guerrero
COO Telcel, Patricia Raquel Hevia Coto
CEO Columbia, Carlos Hern n Zenteno de los Santos
CEO Ecuador, Alfredo Escobar San Lucas
CEO Corporate Market Unit Brazil, José Formoso Mart nez
CEO Residential Market Unit Brazil, Daniel Feldmann Barros
President Brazil, José Ant nio Guaraldi Félix
CEO Chile, Mauricio Escobedo V zquez
CFO and Acting CEO United States, Gustavo Blanco Villanueva
Chairman, Carlos Slim Domit, age 53
Vice Chairman, Patrick Slim Domit, age 51
Auditors: Mancera, S.C. (member of Ernst & Young Global)

LOCATIONS

HQ: America Movil SAB de CV
Lago Zurich 245, Plaza Carso/Edificio Telcel, Colonia Ampliacion Granada, Mexico City, Miguel Hidalgo 11529
Phone: (52) 55 2581 4449   **Fax:** (52) 55 2581 4422
Web: www.americamovil.com

2015 Sales

	% of total
Mexico wireless	22
Brazil	19
US	12
Mexico fixed	11
Southern cone	8
Europe	8
Colombia	7
Andean region	6
Central America	4
Caribbean	3
Total	**100**

PRODUCTS/OPERATIONS

2018 Sales

	% of total
Mexico Wireless	21
Brazil	18
US	14
Southern Cone	10
Europe	9
Telmex	9
Colombia	7
Andean Region	5
Central America	4
Caribbean	3
Total	**100**

2018 Sales

	% of total
Services	83
Equipment	17
Total	**0**

Selected Operations

Amé;rica Móvil Peru (8.3 million subscribers)
AM Wireless Uruguay (800000 subscribers)
AMX Argentina (17 million subscribers)
AMX Paraguay (500000 subscribers)
Claro Chile (3.6 million subscribers)
Claro Panama (100000 subscribers)
Codetel (Dominican Republic 4.8 million subscribers)
Comcel (Colombia 27.7 million subscribers)
Conecel (Ecuador 9.4 million subscribers)
CTE (El Salvador 800000 subscribers)
ENITEL (Nicaragua 2.2 million subscribers)
Oceanic (Jamaica 400000 subscribers)
Sercom Honduras (1.4 million subscribers)
TELPRI (Puerto Rico 1.6 million subscribers)
TracFone (US 14.4 million subscribers)
Telgua (Guatemala 1.2 million subscribers)

COMPETITORS

AT&T	TIM Participa § µes
Alfa SA	Telecom Argentina
Axtel	Telef nica
Brasil Telecom	Telef nica de
Iusacell	Argentina
Millicom	Telef nica Brasil
NII Holdings	Telemig Celular
Sprint Communications	Vivo Participa § µes

HISTORICAL FINANCIALS

Company Type: Public

Income Statement

FYE: December 31

	REVENUE ($ mil.)	NET INCOME ($ mil.)	NET PROFIT MARGIN	EMPLOYEES
12/19	53,243	3,579	6.7%	191,523
12/18	52,797	2,673	5.1%	194,431
12/17	51,859	1,488	2.9%	191,851
12/16	47,140	418	0.9%	194,193
12/15	51,473	2,017	3.9%	195,475
Annual Growth	0.8%	15.4%	—	(0.5%)

2019 Year-End Financials

Debt ratio: 2.1%	No. of shares (mil.): —
Return on equity: 36.2%	Dividends
Cash ($ mil.): 1,043	Yield: 2.3%
Current ratio: 0.63	Payout: 682.7%
Long-term debt ($ mil.): 26,167	Market value ($ mil.): —

	STOCK PRICE ($) FY Close	P/E High/Low	PER SHARE ($) Earnings	Dividends	Book Value
12/19	16.00	16 13	0.05	0.37	0.14
12/18	14.25	23 16	0.04	0.33	0.14
12/17	17.15	42 28	0.02	0.31	0.15
12/16	12.57	102 80	0.01	0.70	0.15
12/15	14.06	38 27	0.03	0.67	0.07
Annual Growth	3.3%	— —	16.1%	(14.0%)	20.5%

AMMB Holdings BHD

Auditors: Ernst & Young PLT

LOCATIONS

HQ: AMMB Holdings BHD
Level 22, Bangunan AmBank Group, No. 55, Jalan Raja Chulan, Kuala Lumpur 50200
Phone: (60) 3 2036 2633   **Fax:** (60) 3 2032 1914
Web: www.ambankgroup.com

COMPETITORS

Al Rajhi Banking	Insurance Australia
Bank Muamalat	Macquarie Group
Bank of Baroda	Maybank
Bank of China	Mitsui Sumitomo
Bank of East Asia	Insurance
CIMB Group	OCBC Bank
DBS Group Holdings	Public Bank
Dallah Albaraka Group	RHB Capital
HSBC	Standard Chartered
Hong Leong Bank	United Overseas Bank

HISTORICAL FINANCIALS

Company Type: Public

Income Statement				FYE: March 31
	ASSETS ($ mil.)	NET INCOME ($ mil.)	INCOME AS % OF ASSETS	EMPLOYEES
03/20	39,184	310	0.8%	0
03/19	38,908	368	0.9%	0
03/18	35,679	292	0.8%	10,000
03/17	30,438	299	1.0%	10,672
03/16	34,555	336	1.0%	10,842
Annual Growth	3.2%	(2.0%)	—	—

2020 Year-End Financials

Return on assets: 0.8%
Return on equity: 7.3%
Long-term debt ($ mil.): —
No. of shares (mil.): —
Sales ($ mil): 1,824

Dividends
Yield: —
Payout: 29.7%
Market value ($ mil.): —

AMP Ltd.

EXECUTIVES

Director Product Manufacturing AMP Financial Services, Craig Meller, age 57
CEO AMP Capital, Adam Tindall
Group Executive Operations, Wendy Thorpe
CFO, Gordon Lefevre
CIO, Craig Ryman
Group Executive Advice and New Zealand, Jack Regan
Group Executive Wealth Solutions and Customer, Paul Sainsbury
Group Executive AMP Bank, Sally Bruce
Group Executive Insurance, Megan Beer
Chief Risk Officer, Saskia Goedhart
Chairman, Catherine Brenner, age 50
Auditors: Ernst & Young

LOCATIONS

HQ: AMP Ltd.
33 Alfred Street, Sydney, New South Wales 2000
Phone: (61) 2 9257 5000   **Fax:** (61) 2 9257 7178
Web: www.amp.com.au

PRODUCTS/OPERATIONS

2015 Sales

	% of total
Investment gains	61
Fee revenue	21
Life insurance premiums & related revenue	17
Other	1
Total	**100**

Selected Services

Business Banking
Insurance Products
Investment Products
Loans
Personal Banking
Retirement Products
Superannuation

COMPETITORS

AXA Asia Pacific	National Australia
Australia and New	Bank
Zealand Banking	QBE
Aviva	RSA Insurance
Commonwealth Bank of	St. Andrew's Australia
Australia	Suncorp-Metway
Macquarie Group	ageas SA/NV

HISTORICAL FINANCIALS

Company Type: Public

Income Statement				FYE: December 31
	ASSETS ($ mil.)	NET INCOME ($ mil.)	INCOME AS % OF ASSETS	EMPLOYEES
12/19	103,581	(1,730)	—	0
12/18	102,537	19	0.0%	6,100
12/17	115,804	663	0.6%	5,600
12/16	101,198	(248)	—	5,400
12/15	102,159	710	0.7%	5,400
Annual Growth	0.3%	—	—	—

2019 Year-End Financials

Return on assets: (-1.6%)
Return on equity: (-42.7%)
Long-term debt ($ mil.): —
No. of shares (mil.): —
Sales ($ mil): 4,127

Dividends
Yield: —
Payout: —
Market value ($ mil.): —

Ampol Ltd

An industrial wonder in the Land Down Under Caltex Australia is the island continent's top oil refining and marketing company with about a 30% share of the retail fuel market. It is engaged in the refining distribution and marketing of fuels and lubricants across the country and oversees a network of 2000 Caltex and Ampol branded gas stations. Caltex Australia's two refineries have a combined capacity of 35 million liters per day. The company also owns and operates 11 coastal storage terminals lubricant blending plants a petroleum products pipeline and a fleet of fuel trucks. In early 2015 Chevron sold its 50% stake in Caltex Australia.

Operations

It sources the supply of both crude oil and refined products on the international market and refines crude oil into gasoline diesel jet fuel base oil for lubricants and many specialty products such as petroleum gas and bitumen.

Caltex Australia's two refinery complexes are Kurnell (located on the southern shore of Botany Bay near Sydney) and Lytton (at the mouth of the Brisbane River near Brisbane). The combined annual production at the Kurnell and Lytton refineries breaks down as 50% gasoline 30% diesel and 15% jet fuel. The remainder of the production consists of fuel oil waxes and lubricants bitumen sulfur LPG and other gasses.

The company's marketing activities ranges from retail service stations operations to equity and non-equity resellers and direct sales to corporate customers. Caltex Australia supplies products via a network of pipelines terminals depots and the company-owned and contracted transport fleet.

In 2015 Caltex Australia had 496 Star convenience stores 795 Service stations 81 depots 42 rail cars and 252 road tankers.

Petrol (gasoline) accounted for 30% the company's total revenues in 2014; diesel 30%; and jet fuel 10%.

Geographic Reach
The company operates in Australia and Singapore.

Sales and Marketing

Caltex Australia sources the supply of both crude oil and refined products on the international market and refines crude oil into gasoline diesel jet fuel along with small amounts of fuel oil and specialty products liquid gas petroleum and other gases. The company buys and sells products and schedules product movements to meet marketing sales and the company's broad distribution capabilities encompass pipelines terminals depots and both a company and contracted transportation fleet.

The Marketing segment promotes and sells Caltex Australia fuels lubricants specialty products and convenience store goods through a national network of Caltex Caltex Woolworths and Ampol branded service stations as well as through company owned and non-equity resellers and direct sales to corporate customers. Caltex Star Mart StarCard StarCash Vortex Premium Bio E10 Unleaded Havoline and Delo are leading sub-brands each with significant and growing market shares in their respective product categories.

Financial Performance
In fiscal 2014 Caltex Australia's net revenues decreased by 20% due to lower fuel sales volumes and the decline in crude prices which resulted in lower sales revenues.

Total refinery production in 2014 of all products was 10.2 billion liters compared with 11.4 billion liters in 2013 reflecting the closure of the Kurnell refinery and its conversion to terminal operations in October 2014 which impacted revenues.

Caltex Australia's overall transport fuel sales volumes grew 3%. Retail diesel margins have continued to grow strongly driven by the premium diesel product Vortex Diesel and as a result of growth in the diesel vehicle market. Diesel fuel volumes increased approximately 6% driven by premium fuels growth which increased approximately 49%.

Overall petrol volumes decreased approximately 1% in line with the market. However premium petrol sales volumes continue to grow with Vortex Premium Unleaded sales volumes increasing by 4%. Jet fuel volumes grew by 3%.

Specialty products fell in 2014 mainly driven by the sale of the bitumen business in 2013. Lubricants volumes and margins also declined in a competitive market.

In 2014 Caltex Australia's net income decreased by 96% due to the loss from inventory driven by the significant decline in crude oil prices and net finance cost increased due to higher unwinding of discount on long term provisions as the result of changes in the predicted spending and pattern and a decrease in the government bond rate.

Cash inflow increased by 9% due to higher fuel margins and sales volumes in 2014.

Strategy
The company intends to accelerate strategic growth initiatives in order to deliver on its target of delivering top quartile total shareholder returns. Caltex Australia's focus for the short term is to remain the outright leader in transport fuels in Australia. In support of this short term priorities include the optimization of the entire value chain from product sourcing to customer underpinned by the growth of its product sourcing requirements via Ampol Singapore.

Lytton refinery will continue to focus on capturing further operational and margin improvements. (A major maintenance program required the refinery to shut down for seven weeks in 2015.)

It will also continue to expand its retail network leveraging core capabilities of retailing supply chain management and infrastructure services.

Upgrading its infrastructure in 2014 the company shut down of the last of Kurnell refinery's process units and opend the new Kurnell terminal now Australia's largest transport fuels terminal.

Mergers and Acquisitions

In late 2016 the company agreed to purchase Gull New Zealand for NZ$340 million.

In 2014 Caltex Australia acquired Scott's Fuel Divisions for $86.5 million plus incidental acquisition costs. The acquisition complements Caltex's Australia's existing national network.

Company Background

Growing its business to keep up with demand in 2011 Caltex Australia dissolved the Vitalgas Pty Ltd joint venture agreement by acquiring the stake held by Origin Energy Holdings for $4.1 million. The unit then became Calgas Pty Ltd.

It also bought Graham Bailey Pty Ltd for $19.1 million. Bailey is Australia's leading provider of marine fuel remote infrastructure and related services with operations in all major Australian ports and a network of 16 sites from the south of Western Australia through to Darwin in the Northern Territories.

EXECUTIVES

Managing Director and CEO, Julian Segal
CFO, Simon Hepworth, $293,510 total compensation
General Manager Refining & Supply, Gary Smith
Chairman, Elizabeth Bryan, age 73
Auditors: KPMG

LOCATIONS

HQ: Ampol Ltd
Level 24, 2 Market Street, Sydney, New South Wales 2000
Phone: (61) 2 9250 5000 **Fax:** (61) 2 9250 5742
Web: www.caltex.com.au

PRODUCTS/OPERATIONS

2011 Sales

	% of total
Refining & supply	53
Marketing	47
Total	**100**

Major Subsidiaries

Caltex Australia Petroleum Pty Ltd
Caltex Lubricating Oil Refinery Pty Ltd
Caltex Petroleum Distributors Pty Ltd
Caltex Refineries (NSW) Pty Ltd
Caltex Refineries (Qld) Pty Ltd

COMPETITORS

BP	Royal Dutch Shell
Continental Energy	Wesfarmers
Exxon Mobil	

HISTORICAL FINANCIALS

Company Type: Public

Income Statement				FYE: December 31
	REVENUE ($ mil.)	NET INCOME ($ mil.)	NET PROFIT MARGIN	EMPLOYEES
12/19	15,645	268	1.7%	7,644
12/18	15,338	395	2.6%	6,629
12/17	16,733	484	2.9%	4,724
12/16	12,957	440	3.4%	3,045
12/15	14,644	381	2.6%	3,078
Annual Growth	**1.7%**	**(8.4%)**	**—**	**25.5%**

ANA Holdings Inc

ANA Holdings is the parent of All Nippon Airways one of Japan's leading carriers along with Japan Airlines. With a fleet of more than 305 aircraft ANA services around 100 airports worldwide. . It extends its network through code-sharing with members of the Star Alliance an airline marketing partnership that includes such carriers as United Continental's United Airlines and Continental and Lufthansa. (Code-sharing enables airlines to sell tickets on one another's flights.) Besides passenger service ANA's air transportation operations include cargo and mail hauling and aircraft maintenance and ground support. The company also sells travel packages and operates hotels. The company generates majority of sales from its home country Japan.

Operations

ANA's reportable segments are Air Transportation (about 75% of total sales) Airline Related (nearly 15%) Travel Services (around 5%) and Trade and Retail (some 5%).

Air Transportation conducts domestic and International passenger operations cargo and mail operations and other transportation services. Airline Related offers airport passenger and ground handling services and maintenance services.

Travel Services specializes in the development and sales of travel plans and also conducts planning and sales of branded travel packages using air transportation. Trade and Retail mainly imports and exports goods related to air transportation and is involved in in-store and non-store retailing.

Geographic Reach

ANA is headquartered in Tokyo Japan and generates about 85% of total sales domestically. The remaining sales are from Americas Europe China and other Asia. The company serves nearly 55 domestic airports and about 50 international.

Sales and Marketing

ANA served almost 60 million passengers and has around 35 million ANA Mileage Club Members in 2019. The company's advertising expenses were Å 11.8 million in 2020 and Å 12.8 million in 2019.

Financial Performance

Fiscal 2019 consolidated operating revenues amounted to Å 2.0 trillion an Å 84.0 billion (4%) decrease year on year. This decrease was mainly due to reduced revenues in the company's mainstay Air Transportation Business.

The preceding factors combined to decrease income before income taxes by Å 102.5 billion (67%) year on year to Å 51.5 billion. After income taxes municipal taxes business taxes and other adjustments net income attributable to owners of the parent decreased Å 83.1 billion (75.0%) to Å 27.6 billion.

Cash and cash equivalents decreased Å 75.9 billion from the beginning of the fiscal year amounting to Å 135.9 billion at the end of the fiscal year. Cash provided by operations and financing activities were Å 130.1 billion and Å 23.8 billion respectively. Cash used for investing activities was Å 230.2 billion mainly for purchases of property and equipment.

Strategy

The ANA Group has been pursuing growth strategies mainly through the International Business in line with the company's FY2018?2022 ANA Group Corporate Strategy which we formulated in February 2018. During fiscal 2019 All Nippon Airways Co. Ltd. (ANA) introduced new routes from Narita to Perth Chennai and Vladivostok. The company also put ultra-wide body aircraft into service as part of a Hawaii Strategy. The Cargo Business adopted wide-body freighters for Shanghai and Chicago routes to strengthen its ability to capture demand for not only special items including oversize cargo but also trilateral cargo. The merger of Peach Aviation Limited and Vanilla Air Inc. in its LCC Business has resulted in a more efficient business structure to confront tough global competition in the future. To further enhance basic quality for greater competitiveness ANA has been persistent in addressing the engine component issues related to the Boeing 787 while at the same time it made up-front investments in safety quality and services as well as human resources including the active recruitment of employees who will lead us into the future. As a result of these activities the company continued to generate record-high operating revenues on a consolidated basis through the third quarter of fiscal 2019.

Mergers and Acquisitions

In early 2019 ANA acquired a 9.5% stake of PAL Holdings Inc. for an undisclosed amount. PAL Holdings is the parent of Philippine Airlines Inc. (PAL) the Philippine flag carrier and the largest airline in the Philippines. ANA acquires the shares from Trustmark Holdings Corporation which is owned by the Lucio Tan family and is the largest shareholder of PAL Holdings. The purchase underscores ANA's belief in the dynamism of the Asian region and the great potential of the Philippines' multi-awarded flag carrier and its confidence that the Philippine air travel market continues to serve as an economic leader for the ASEAN region.

Company Background

Two domestic Japanese air carriers that started in 1952 — Nippon Helicopter and Aeroplane Transport and Far East Airlines — consolidated operations in 1957 as All Nippon Airways (ANA).

EXECUTIVES

SEVP Government and Industrial Affairs Strategic Planning-Asia Pacific Airport and Facilities Planning, Shigeyuki Takemura
EVP; Chairman CSR Promotion Committee Public Relations Executive Secretariat Legal and Insurance General Administration and CSR Promotion, Yoshinori Maruyama
EVP Finance Accounting and Investor Relations, Kiyoshi Tonomoto
President and CEO, Yuji Hirako
Chairman, Shinichiro Ito
Vice Chairman, Osamu Shinobe
Auditors: Deloitte Touche Tohmatsu LLC

LOCATIONS

HQ: ANA Holdings Inc
1-5-2 Higashi-Shimbashi, Minato-ku, Tokyo 105-7140
Phone: (81) 3 6735 1001
Web: www.anahd.co.jp

2014 Sales

	% of total
Japan	86
Overseas	14
Total	**100**

PRODUCTS/OPERATIONS

2014 Sales

	% of total
Air transportation	73
Airline related	11
Travel services	8
Trade and Retail	6
Other businesses	2
Total	**100**

COMPETITORS

Accor	Delta Air Lines
Air France-KLM	EVA Air
American Airlines	East Japan Railway
Group	Hyatt
American Express	Japan Airlines
British Airways	Kintetsu
Carlson Wagonlit	Korean Air
Cathay Pacific	Qantas
Central Japan Railway	Singapore Airlines
China Airlines	Virgin Atlantic
China Eastern Airlines	Airways
China Southern	West Japan Railway
Airlines	

HISTORICAL FINANCIALS

Company Type: Public

Income Statement   FYE: March 31

	REVENUE ($ mil.)	NET INCOME ($ mil.)	NET PROFIT MARGIN	EMPLOYEES
03/20	19,905	278	1.4%	49,448
03/19	20,753	1,116	5.4%	47,074
03/18	19,881	1,450	7.3%	45,878
03/17	17,798	996	5.6%	43,274
03/16	18,060	788	4.4%	40,040
Annual Growth	2.5%	(22.9%)	—	5.4%

2020 Year-End Financials

Debt ratio: 0.3%
Return on equity: 2.5%
Cash ($ mil.): 1,103
Current ratio: 1.08
Long-term debt ($ mil.): 7,278

No. of shares (mil.): 334
Dividends
  Yield: 2.7%
  Payout: —
Market value ($ mil.): 1,693

	STOCK PRICE ($) FY Close	P/E High/Low		PER SHARE ($) Earnings	Dividends	Book Value
03/20	5.06	0	0	0.83	0.14	31.95
03/19	7.42	0	0	3.34	0.11	33.10
03/18	7.66	0	0	4.21	0.11	29.77
03/17	6.30	0	0	2.85	0.10	26.39
03/16	5.71	0	0	2.25	0.07	22.68
Annual Growth	(3.0%)	—		(22.0%)	20.9%	8.9%

Angang Steel Co Ltd

EXECUTIVES

Chairman, Yidong Wang
Auditors: Ruihua Certified Public Accountants (Special General Partnership)

LOCATIONS

HQ: Angang Steel Co Ltd
Production Area of Angang Steel, Tie Xi District, Anshan City, Liaoning Province 114021
Phone: (86) 412 8417273   **Fax:** (86) 412 6727772
Web: www.ansteel.com.cn

2013 Sales

	% of total
Domestic Sales	
Northeast China	36
East China	24
South China	20
North China	8
Central South China	1
Northwest China	1
Southwest China	1
Export Sales	9
Total	**100**

PRODUCTS/OPERATIONS

Selected Products

Cold-rolled products
Cold-rolled silicon steel products
Color coated products
Galvanized products
Hot-rolled products
Plate products
Seamless steel pipe products
Wire products

COMPETITORS

Baosteel	Lung Kee
Hunan Valin Iron &	Tangshan Iron and
Steel	Steel
Jiangsu Shagang	Wuhan Iron & Steel

HISTORICAL FINANCIALS

Company Type: Public

Income Statement   FYE: December 31

	REVENUE ($ mil.)	NET INCOME ($ mil.)	NET PROFIT MARGIN	EMPLOYEES
12/19	15,174	256	1.7%	0
12/18	15,288	1,156	7.6%	0
12/17	12,955	861	6.6%	0
12/16	8,335	232	2.8%	37,363
12/15	8,123	(707)	—	37,821
Annual Growth	16.9%	—	—	—

2019 Year-End Financials

Debt ratio: 3.4%
Return on equity: 3.4%
Cash ($ mil.): 671
Current ratio: 0.80
Long-term debt ($ mil.): 704

No. of shares (mil.): —
Dividends
  Yield: —
  Payout: —
Market value ($ mil.): —

Anglo American Plc (United Kingdom)

From a lump of coal to a piece of diamond Anglo American mines and sells it all. The UK-based owner of De Beers Anglo American is a top global mining company with assets producing bulk commodities and minerals like coal iron ore and nickel platinum diamonds and copper. Annually it produces some 40.7 million tons (Mt) of coal from over 10 mines around 42.4 Mt of iron ore from three mines about 640 kt of copper from three mines and some 30.8 Mcts of diamond from eight mines. Though present in five continents Anglo American has a major presence in Asia where it generates most of the sales. De Beers produces a third of the world's rough diamonds.

Operations

The company's segments include Platinum Group Metals (more than 20% of sales) Iron Ore (over 20%) Coal Copper (nearly 20%) De Beers (about 20%) and Nickel and Manganese (some 5%).

Segments predominantly derive revenue as follows ?platinum group metals and nickel; iron ore; metallurgical coal and thermal coal; copper; rough and polished diamonds; nickel manganese ore and alloys. Iron ore generates the most sales (about 20%) among the other products.

Geographic Reach

The company's most significant presence is in Asia accounting to about 70% of sales where China generates some 30%. Its other productive assets can be found in South Africa Australia Botswana Brazil Canada Chile Colombia Namibia Peru and Zimbabwe. Anglo America is headquartered in London UK and has corporate offices in the UK Finland Shanghai and Singapore.

Sales and Marketing

The company's customers operate in some of the world's most critical and diverse industries - from automotive to steelmaking from technology and jewelry to energy production. It engages with customers through business and industry forums.

Financial Performance

Compared to the revenue in 2018 the company's revenue rose 5% to $31.8 billion in 2019. This was primarily due to a higher sales volume in the company's iron ore and platinum segments.

Profit attributable to equity shareholders was $3.5 billion.

The company's cash for the year ended 2019 was $6.3 billion. Operating activities $7.7 million while investing activities used $4.7 billion mainly for capital expenditures. Financing activities used another $3.1 billion primarily for payment of dividends.

Strategy

The company focuses on securing and continuously improving assets that offer the most attractive long term value-creation potential as measured by sustainable cash flow and returns.

Where appropriate the company aims to seek partners for the development of major greenfield projects at the right time and for value and are likely to not commit to the full development of more than one such project at any given time. The company will continue to maintain optionality to progress with value accretive projects.

Additionally the partnerships the company builds locally and globally are central to maintaining its regulatory and social licenses to operate and its sustained commercial success.

EXECUTIVES

CEO Base Metals and Group Director Strategy and Business Development, Duncan Wanblad
CEO De Beers, Bruce Cleaver
Chief Executive, Mark Cutifani, $1,469,080 total compensation
Group Director People and Organization, Didier Charreton
Deputy Chairman Anglo American South Africa, Norman B. Mbazima
CEO Platinum, Chris Griffith
Finance Director, Stephen Pearce
CEO Bulk Commodities, Seamus French
CEO Marketing, Peter Whitcutt
Technical Director, Tony OÁ'Neill
Chairman, Stuart Chambers
Auditors: Deloitte LLP

LOCATIONS

HQ: Anglo American Plc (United Kingdom)
20 Carlton House Terrace, London SW1Y 5AN
Phone: (44) 20 7968 8888   **Fax:** (44) 20 7968 8500
Web: www.angloamerican.com

PRODUCTS/OPERATIONS

2018 sales

	% of total
Coal	26
De Beers	20
Platinum Group Metals	19
Copper	17
Iron Ore	12
Nickel and Manganese	6
Corporate and other	-
Total	**100**

Selected Subsidiaries

Platinum
 Anglo Platinum Corporation Limited (75% South
 Africa)
Base Metals
Anglo American Sur (75% copper mines Chile)
 Empresa Minera de Mantos Blancos SA (copper Chile)
 Minera Loma de Ní;quel CA (91% nickel Venezuela)
 Minera Quellaveco SA (80% copper Peru)
 Minera Sur Andes Limitada (copper Chile)
Coal
Anglo Coal (South Africa)
 Anglo Coal (Callide) Pty Limited (Australia)
Ferrous Metals and Industries
 Kumba Resources Limited (65%; coal iron ore heavy
 minerals; South Africa)
Industrial Minerals
 Copebras Limitada (phosphate products Brazil)
Diamonds
 De Beers S.A. (45%)

COMPETITORS

BHP Billiton	Peñoles
Freeport-McMoRan	Rio Tinto Limited
Glencore	Teck
Impala Platinum	Vale
Norilsk Nickel	Vedanta Resources

HISTORICAL FINANCIALS
Company Type: Public

Income Statement				FYE: December 31
	REVENUE ($ mil.)	NET INCOME ($ mil.)	NET PROFIT MARGIN	EMPLOYEES
12/19	29,870	3,547	11.9%	63,000
12/18	27,610	3,549	12.9%	64,000
12/17	26,243	3,166	12.1%	69,000
12/16	21,378	1,594	7.5%	80,000
12/15	20,455	(5,624)	—	91,000
Annual Growth	9.9%	—	—	(8.8%)

2019 Year-End Financials

Debt ratio: 19.1%
Return on equity: 14.6%
Cash ($ mil.): 6,345
Current ratio: 1.92
Long-term debt ($ mil.): 9,744

No. of shares (mil.): 1,371
Dividends
 Yield: 3.6%
 Payout: 19.2%
Market value ($ mil.): 19,815

	STOCK PRICE ($) FY Close	P/E High	Low	PER SHARE ($) Earnings	Dividends	Book Value
12/19	14.45	5	4	2.76	0.53	18.08
12/18	11.04	5	3	2.74	0.48	16.80
12/17	10.35	4	2	2.45	0.22	16.35
12/16	7.05	6	1	1.23	0.00	13.56
12/15	2.19	—	—	(4.36)	0.00	11.82
Annual Growth	60.4%	—	—	—	—	11.2%

Anheuser-Busch InBev SA/NV

Auditors: DELOITTE Bedrijfsrevisoren / Reviseurs
d'Entreprises

LOCATIONS

HQ: Anheuser-Busch InBev SA/NV
 Brouwerijplein 1, Leuven 3000
Phone: (32) 16 27 6111   **Fax:** (32) 16 50 6111
Web: www.ab-inbev.com

HISTORICAL FINANCIALS
Company Type: Public

Income Statement				FYE: December 31
	REVENUE ($ mil.)	NET INCOME ($ mil.)	NET PROFIT MARGIN	EMPLOYEES
12/19	52,329	9,171	17.5%	170,000
12/18	54,619	4,368	8.0%	172,603
12/17	56,444	7,996	14.2%	182,915
12/16	45,517	1,241	2.7%	206,633
12/15	43,604	8,273	19.0%	152,321
Annual Growth	4.7%	2.6%	—	2.8%

2019 Year-End Financials

Debt ratio: 43.5%
Return on equity: 13.0%
Cash ($ mil.): 7,238
Current ratio: 0.83
Long-term debt ($ mil.): 97,564

No. of shares (mil.): 1,959
Dividends
 Yield: 2.4%
 Payout: 44.3%
Market value ($ mil.): 160,747

	STOCK PRICE ($) FY Close	P/E High	Low	PER SHARE ($) Earnings	Dividends	Book Value
12/19	82.04	22	14	4.53	2.01	38.65
12/18	65.81	52	30	2.17	3.30	32.96
12/17	111.56	31	26	3.98	4.08	37.54
12/16	105.44	185	139	0.71	1.70	44.37
12/15	125.00	26	21	4.96	0.00	26.23
Annual Growth	(10.0%)	—	—	(2.2%)	—	10.2%

Anhui Conch Cement Co Ltd

EXECUTIVES

Chairman, Gao Dengbang
Auditors: KPMG Huazhen LLP

LOCATIONS

HQ: Anhui Conch Cement Co Ltd
 39 Wenhua Road, Wuhu City, Anhui Province 241000
Phone: (86) 553 8398976   **Fax:** (86) 553 8398931
Web: www.conch.cn

2015 Sales by Region

	% of total
Central China	31
East China	27
South China	20
West China	21
Overseas	1
Total	**100**

PRODUCTS/OPERATIONS

2015 Sales by Principal Activities

	% of total
Cliker and cement products	98
Materials and other products	1
Service income	1
Total	**100**

COMPETITORS

Boral	HeidelbergCement
CEMEX	LafargeHolcim
CK Hutchison	Taiheiyo Cement
Cementir	

HISTORICAL FINANCIALS
Company Type: Public

Income Statement				FYE: December 31
	REVENUE ($ mil.)	NET INCOME ($ mil.)	NET PROFIT MARGIN	EMPLOYEES
12/19	22,567	4,827	21.4%	0
12/18	18,667	4,334	23.2%	0
12/17	11,573	2,436	21.1%	0
12/16	8,054	1,234	15.3%	44,859
12/15	7,849	1,160	14.8%	47,832
Annual Growth	30.2%	42.8%	—	—

2019 Year-End Financials

Debt ratio: 0.9%
Return on equity: 26.8%
Cash ($ mil.): 7,901
Current ratio: 3.54
Long-term debt ($ mil.): 1,124

No. of shares (mil.): —
Dividends
 Yield: 2.9%
 Payout: 115.3%
Market value ($ mil.): —

	STOCK PRICE ($) FY Close	P/E High	Low	PER SHARE ($) Earnings	Dividends	Book Value
12/19	36.51	6	4	0.91	1.06	(0.00)
12/18	23.99	6	4	0.82	0.80	(0.00)
12/17	23.50	8	5	0.46	0.30	(0.00)
12/16	14.01	9	5	0.23	0.25	2.07
12/15	13.32	14	9	0.22	0.43	2.04
Annual Growth	28.7%	—	—	42.9%	25.4%	—

AntarChile S.A. (Chile)

EXECUTIVES

CEO, Jorge Andueza Fouque
Finance and Administration Manager, Patricio
Tapia Costa
Vice Chairman, José Tom ́s Guzm ́n Dumas
Chairman, Roberto Angelini Rossi
Auditors: PricewaterhouseCoopers

LOCATIONS

HQ: AntarChile S.A. (Chile)
 Avenida El Golf 150, Piso 21, Santiago, Las Condes
Phone: (56) 2 461 7710   **Fax:** (56) 2 461 7717
Web: www.antarchile.cl

COMPETITORS

Endesa S.A.	Repsol
Enersis	Royal Dutch Shell
Falabella	Walmart Chile
International Paper	
Petrobras	
Distribuidora	

HISTORICAL FINANCIALS

Company Type: Public

Income Statement
FYE: December 31

	REVENUE ($ mil.)	NET INCOME ($ mil.)	NET PROFIT MARGIN	EMPLOYEES
12/19	23,716	126	0.5%	0
12/18	23,970	671	2.8%	0
12/17	20,353	399	2.0%	0
12/16	16,699	325	2.0%	31,720
12/15	18,160	316	1.7%	26,702
Annual Growth	6.9%	(20.4%)	—	—

2019 Year-End Financials

Debt ratio: 36.9%
Return on equity: 1.8%
Cash ($ mil.): 2,252
Current ratio: 2.25
Long-term debt ($ mil.): 8,470

No. of shares (mil.): 456
Dividends
  Yield: —
  Payout: —
  Market value ($ mil.): —

Aozora Bank Ltd

EXECUTIVES

President, Shinsuke Baba
Deputy President, Masaki Tanabe
Managing Executive Officer, Jorge A. Leon
Senior Managing Executive Officer, Takeo Saito
Managing Executive Officer, Clark D. Graninger
Managing Executive Officer, Katsuya Hosono
Senior Managing Executive Officer, Masatatsu Ozeki
Managing Executive Officer, Kei Tanikawa
Managing Executive Officer, Yukio Sekizawa
Managing Executive Officer, Koji Yamakoshi
Managing Executive Officers, Hideaki Kuraishi
Managing Executive Officer, Masaaki Harada
Chairman, Makoto Fukuda
Auditors: Deloitte Touche Tohmatsu LLC

LOCATIONS

HQ: Aozora Bank Ltd
  6-1-1 Kojimachi, Chiyoda-ku, Tokyo 102-8660
Phone: (81) 3 6752 1111   **Fax:** 212 314-3124
Web: www.aozorabank.co.jp

PRODUCTS/OPERATIONS

Selected affiliates
ABN Advisors
Aozora Asia Pacific Finance Limited
Aozora Europe Limited
Aozora Investments Management
Aozora Loan Services
Aozora Real Estate Investment Advisors
Aozora Regional Consulting Co. Ltd.
Aozora Securities
Aozora Trust Bank
AZB Funding
AZB Funding 2
AZB Funding 3
AZB Funding 4 Limited

COMPETITORS

Mitsubishi UFJ Financial Group	Resona
	Shinsei Bank
Mizuho Financial	Sumitomo Mitsui
Mizuho Trust & Banking Ltd	Sumitomo Mitsui Trust Holdings
Norinchukin Bank	Tokyo Tomin Bank

HISTORICAL FINANCIALS

Company Type: Public

Income Statement
FYE: March 31

	ASSETS ($ mil.)	NET INCOME ($ mil.)	INCOME AS % OF ASSETS	EMPLOYEES
03/20	48,823	259	0.5%	2,433
03/19	47,452	326	0.7%	2,390
03/18	46,265	405	0.9%	2,291
03/17	41,017	392	1.0%	2,191
03/16	40,899	387	0.9%	2,124
Annual Growth	4.5%	(9.6%)	—	3.5%

2020 Year-End Financials

Return on assets: 0.5%
Return on equity: 6.4%
Long-term debt ($ mil.): —
No. of shares (mil.): 116
Sales ($ mil): 1,698

Dividends
  Yield: 7.4%
  Payout: 15.7%
  Market value ($ mil.): 547

	STOCK PRICE ($) FY Close	P/E High/Low		PER SHARE ($) Earnings	Dividends	Book Value
03/20	4.69	0	0	2.22	0.35	33.75
03/19	6.13	0	0	2.79	0.39	34.74
03/18	10.18	0	0	3.47	0.44	35.20
03/17	74.11	0	0	3.36	0.41	32.10
03/16	69.30	0	0	3.06	0.29	30.90
Annual Growth	(49.0%)	—	—	(7.7%)	5.0%	2.2%

Aptiv PLC

Cars these days are more computer than machine and for that you've got Aptiv to thank. The company's main business is designing and assembling a car's electrical architecture including its wiring assemblies cabling and safety distribution. Aptiv also makes advanced electrical systems and software such as those involved in autonomous driving and vehicle connectivity. Domiciled in Jersey for tax reasons Aptiv has operations across the globe and counts the 25 largest auto manufacturers as customers. Aptiv formerly known as Delphi Automotive spun off its powertrain business in 2017 and renamed itself Aptiv.

Change in Company Type

Aptiv spun off its Powertrain Systems segment in 2017 forming an independent company named Delphi Technologies. Its continuing operations Electrical/Electronic Architecture Electronics and Safety have been renamed Aptiv. Aptiv's new focus on the future of the driving industry by accelerating its position within the self-driving and connected vehicles market.

Operations

Delphi's business is organized into two divisions: Signal and Power Solutions and Advanced Safety and User Experience.

The Signal and Power Solutions segment generates more than 70% of sales and designs manufactures and assembles electrical architecture for automobiles including engineered component products connectors wiring assemblies and harnesses cable management electrical centers and hybrid high voltage and safety distribution systems. Aptiv electrical systems are designed to meet the higher demands of modern computerized vehicles with integrated entertainment nagivation and other connectivity systems.

The Advanced Safety and User Experience accounts for the other 30% of sales and provides hardware and software to fit out a vehicle with body controls infotainment and connectivity systems active and passive safety electronics autonomous driving software and technologies and systems integration.

Geographic Reach

Domiciled in Jersey UK Aptiv has operations in around 45 countries. It has more than 125 manufacturing facilities and some 15 major technical centers (eight in North America give in the Asia/Pacific region and two in EMEA). The company's revenue is well diversified: the US generates more than 35% of revenue; the EMEA region brings in around 35% and the Asia-Pacific region more than 25%. Latin America accounts for the remainder.

Aptiv's regional model is set up to serve its major markets in a cost-efficient way. It serves the US from Mexico South America from Brazil Europe from Eastern Europe and the Asia/Pacific region from China.

Sales and Marketing

Aptiv's customer base includes all 25 of the largest automotive OEMs in the world; GM and VW are Aptiv's two biggest customers and account for roughly 20% of the company's sales each year. Other customers include Ford Fiat-Chrysler Daimler Groupe PSA (Peugeot Citroen) Toyota and Renault-Nissan. On the flipside Aptiv only serves one market and is thus exposed to the fortunes of the auto industry. The high cost of a car makes the auto industry vulnerable to economic downturns as customers shy away from big-ticket purchases; the growth of other modes of transport particularly trains also presents a threat to the auto industry.

Financial Performance

Note: Aptiv restated its historical revenue after the powertrain spin-off. This analysis uses Aptiv's revenue on a continuing basis.

In 2018 Aptiv's sales grew 12% to $14.4 billion despite a 1% decrease in global auto production. The higher revenue was a result of higher demand across all major regions as well as revenue contributions from two acquired businesses (KUM and Winchester). Currency movements particularly relating to the euro and yuan had beneficial effects.

Net income dipped somewhat in 2018 falling 22% to $1.1 billion as a higher cost of sales eroded margin. Higher cost of sales reflected investment in advanced technology higher commodity costs and increased depreciation.

Aptiv's cash position reduced by $1.0 billion during 2018 ending the year at $568 million. It generated $1.6 billion from operations and used $2.0 billion and $555 million in its investing and financing activities respectively. Its investing cash use was mainly in acquisitions and cap ex while financing cash use was in share repurchases and dividends.

Strategy

Aptiv's strategy is a bet on the rapidly growing mobility solutions industry a technology-led car-as-a-service business. To focus on mobility Aptiv divested its businesses that fell outside this core mission: the powertrain business (sold in 2017) and the thermal systems unit (sold in 2015). The company's development going forward focuses on three megatrends it has identified as stimulating growth in the mobility industry "safe" "green" and "connected" which it will serve by developing and buying in new technologies. These devices and systems include emergency braking anti-distraction and collision avoidance; electric vehicle charging and power distribution; and vehicle-to-vehicle and vehicle-to-infrastructure communication and over-the-air data transfer.

From a geographic standpoint Aptiv expects its growth driver to be the Asia/Pacific region. The company will (continue to) invest in partnerships and joint ventures manufacturing operations technical centers R&D facilities and other infrastructure in support of its Asia growth strategy.

Mergers and Acquisitions

In 2018 Aptiv made two acquisitions of companies active in harsh-environment connectivity. First it acquired KUM a maker of connectors and cable management solutions; and secondly it acquired Winchester Interconnect a maker of interconnectivity solutions for harsh environments. It paid Snow Phipps Group around $650 million for Winchester which will operate independently within Aptiv's Signal & Power Solutions segment.

In 2017 Delphi acquired Massachusetts-based nuTonomy a company specializing in autonomous car technology for $400 million.

Company Background

The company's return to the public markets and eventual profitability hasn't been easy. Delphi has struggled financially for years; it was only sporadically profitable for after being spun off in 1999. Delphi filed for bankruptcy in 2005 and emerged four years later as a heavily indebted private company owned by its investors Elliot Management GM and Silver Point Capital. By that time it had laid off more than 75000 workers closed more than 70 sites reduced its products lines from 119 to 33 exited 11 businesses and had its pension (primarily for UAW workers) frozen and taken over by federal Pension Benefit Guaranty Corporation (PBGC). (In the end the union workers' pension was kept afloat by taxpayers as part of the 2009 auto industry bailout).

In 2011 Delphi was finally able to pay off GM for its $3.8 billion stake and PBGC for the $594 million it owed. The two transactions were funded with cash and $2.5 billion of new bank debt as part of a $3 billion credit facility from by investment bank J.P. Morgan Securities. The company makes about half of what it made five years ago and plans the use the proceeds from its IPO to fund operations buy equipment and repay more debt.

Paying off GM helped pave the way for the company's return to health and a new business strategy to show investors doesn't hurt either. Admittedly Delphi has much leaner operations after its restructuring and moved the bulk of its operations outside the US to emerging markets where overall costs especially labor costs are lower. Delphi no longer has any UAW employees on its payroll; outside the US it relies on non-salary and temporary workers to manage a flexible workforce.

EXECUTIVES

President CEO and Director, Kevin P. Clark, age 58
SVP and CFO, Joseph R. Massaro, age 50
SVP Marketing and Communications, J. Christopher (Chris) Preuss
SVP and President Powertrain Systems and Delphi Product & Service Solutions, Liam Butterworth
President Delphi Product and Service Solutions, Keith D. Stipp
SVP and President Electronics and Safety, Jugal K. Vijayvargiya
SVP and President Delphi Electrical/Electronic Architecture; President Delphi Asia Pacific, Majdi B. Abulaban
VP Sales and President Delphi Europe Middle East Africa and Russia, Michael Gassen
SVP Global Supply Management, Sidney Johnson
SVP and CIO, Matthew Peterson
SVP and CTO, Glen De Vos
VP Global Operations and President Delphi Mexico, William H. Guggina
SVP and President Electronics and Safety (E&S), David Paja
Chairman, Rajiv L. (Raj) Gupta, age 74
Auditors: Ernst & Young LLP

LOCATIONS

HQ: Aptiv PLC
5 Hanover Quay, Grand Canal Dock, Dublin D02 VY79
Phone: (353) 1 259 7013
Web: www.delphi.com

2018 Sales

	$ mil.	% of total
United States	5,390	37
Europe Middle East & Africa	4,689	33
Asia/Pacific	3,916	27
South America	2,700	2
Total	**14,335**	**100**

PRODUCTS/OPERATIONS

2018 Sales by Segment

	$ mil.	% of total
Signal and Power Solutions	10,402	72
Advanced Safety and User Experience	4,078	28
Total	**14,435**	**100**

Selected Products

Automotive Industry
Connection Systems
Driver Interface
Electrical/Electronic Architecture
Hybrid & Electric Vehicle Products
Infotainment
Safety Electronics
Sensors

COMPETITORS

Aisin Seiki	Magna International
Autoliv	Magneti Marelli
BorgWarner	Molex
Continental AG	Motorola Solutions
DENSO	Robert Bosch
Dana	Sanden
Federal-Mogul	Sumitomo Electric
Johnson Controls Power Solutions	TE Connectivity
	Valeo
LEONI	Visteon
Lear Corp	Yazaki

HISTORICAL FINANCIALS

Company Type: Public

Income Statement				FYE: December 31
	REVENUE ($ mil.)	NET INCOME ($ mil.)	NET PROFIT MARGIN	EMPLOYEES
12/19	14,357	990	6.9%	141,000
12/18	14,435	1,067	7.4%	143,000
12/17	12,884	1,355	10.5%	129,000
12/16	16,661	1,257	7.5%	145,000
12/15	15,165	1,450	9.6%	139,000
Annual Growth	(1.4%)	(9.1%)	—	0.4%

2019 Year-End Financials

Debt ratio: 32.4%
Return on equity: 27.2%
Cash ($ mil.): 412
Current ratio: 1.31
Long-term debt ($ mil.): 3,971
No. of shares (mil.): 255
Dividends
  Yield: 0.9%
  Payout: 22.6%
Market value ($ mil.): —

Arab Banking Corporation (B.S.C.) (Bahrain)

Auditors: Ernst & Young

LOCATIONS

HQ: Arab Banking Corporation (B.S.C.) (Bahrain)
ABC Tower, Diplomatic Area, P.O. Box 5698, Manama
Phone: (973) 17 543 000   **Fax:** (973) 17 533 163
Web: www.bank-abc.com

COMPETITORS

Ahli United Bank	Dallah Albaraka Group
Al Rajhi Banking	Gulf International
Arab Bank	Bank
Arab National Bank	NBK
Banque Audi	Saudi British Bank
British Arab Commercial Bank	

HISTORICAL FINANCIALS

Company Type: Public

Income Statement				FYE: December 31
	ASSETS ($ mil.)	NET INCOME ($ mil.)	INCOME AS % OF ASSETS	EMPLOYEES
12/19	30,068	194	0.6%	436
12/18	29,549	202	0.7%	394
12/17	29,499	193	0.7%	358
12/16	30,141	183	0.6%	344
12/15	28,195	180	0.6%	344
Annual Growth	1.6%	1.9%	—	6.1%

2019 Year-End Financials

Return on assets: 0.6%
Return on equity: 4.9%
Long-term debt ($ mil.): —
No. of shares (mil.): —
Sales ($ mil): 1,679
Dividends
  Yield: —
  Payout: 50.0%
Market value ($ mil.): —

Arab National Bank

EXECUTIVES

Chairman, Salah Rashed Al Rashed
Deputy Chairman, Ahmad Abdullah Al Aqil
Auditors: Ernst & Young & Co.

LOCATIONS

HQ: Arab National Bank
P.O. Box 56921, Riyadh 11564
Phone: (966) 1 402 9000   **Fax:** (966) 1 402 7747
Web: www.anb.com.sa

COMPETITORS

Ahli United Bank	NBK
Al Rajhi Banking	Saudi British Bank
Arab Banking Corp.	Standard Chartered
Dallah Albaraka Group	
Gulf International Bank	

HISTORICAL FINANCIALS

Company Type: Public

Income Statement				FYE: December 31
	ASSETS ($ mil.)	NET INCOME ($ mil.)	INCOME AS % OF ASSETS	EMPLOYEES
12/19	48,917	806	1.6%	4,170
12/18	47,544	882	1.9%	4,132
12/17	45,787	807	1.8%	4,170
12/16	45,329	760	1.7%	4,403
12/15	45,393	789	1.7%	4,846
Annual Growth	1.9%	0.5%	—	(3.7%)

2019 Year-End Financials

Return on assets: 1.6%	Dividends
Return on equity: 11.0%	Yield: —
Long-term debt ($ mil.): —	Payout: 49.5%
No. of shares (mil.): 1,500	Market value ($ mil.): —
Sales ($ mil): 2,521	

ArcelorMittal SA

Few metal makers have the mettle of Arcelor-Mittal. The company is easily the largest steel-making entity in the world producing nearly 90 million metric tons of crude steel annually about 5% of the world steel output. Operating in over 60 countries ArcelorMittal manufactures the full range of steel products: slabs and coil coated steel and tin-plate wire rod and rebar and billets and blooms as well as all manner of electrical steel products. ArcelorMittal is also a major iron ore mining company; its nearly 15 mines supply more than half the company's iron ore needs. CEO and founder Lakshmi Mittal controls more than 35% of Arcelor-Mittal.

Operations

ArcelorMittal reports five reportable segments: Europe; NAFTA; Brazil; ACIS (Africa and CIS); and Mining.

Europe is ArcelorMittal's leading segment bringing in approximately 50% of all company revenue. This segment is the largest flat-steel producer in Europe with operations from Spain to Romania. It makes flat long and tubular products sold to customers in the automotive general industry and packaging industries. The segment includes a downstream steel distribution segment providing value-added and customized steel services through further processing.

The NAFTA segment generates nearly 25% of sales and produces flat long and tubular products in Canada the US and Mexico. Flat products include slabs hot-rolled coil cold-rolled coil coated steel products and plate. Customers include automotive energy construction packaging appliance industries and via distributors and processors.

Brazil (more than 10% of sales) makes flat (slabs hot-rolled coil cold-rolled coil and coated steel) as well as long and tubular products.

ACIS bring in less than 10% of ArcelorMittal's sales. ACIS produces a combination of flat long and tubular products. It has six flat and long production facilities in three countries.

ArcelorMittal also carries out high quality and low-cost iron ore and coal reserves through mining (which accounts for the remaining sales). It also sells limited amounts of mineral products to third parties. The company has mines in North and South America Europe the CIS and Africa. Its contribution to final sales is negligible and mostly serves the company's other segments. It supplies more than 50% of ArcelorMittal's iron ore needs more than 10% of its PCI (pulverized coal injection) and coal requirements and approximately 95% of its coke needs.

Geographic Reach

Headquartered in Luxembourg City ArcelorMittal has steel-making operations in nearly 20 countries on four continents including some 45 integrated and mini-mill steel-making facilities.

ArcelorMittal operates through subsidiaries in Europe Africa Asia and the Americas (including ArcelorMittal Brasil). It's the largest producer of steel in North and South America and Africa the fifth-largest steel producer in the Commonwealth of Independent States region and has a growing presence in Asia.

The company has iron ore mines in Brazil Bosnia Canada Kazakhstan Liberia Mexico Ukraine and the US with coal mining in Kazakhstan and the US.

Overall approximately 50% of its steel is produced in Europe and close to 40% in the Americas.

ArcelorMittal's logistics network includes some 15 owned or partially owned deep-water ports and linked railway sidings.

Sales and Marketing

ArcelorMittal's markets are all those that consume steel as an input including the automotive appliance engineering construction energy and machinery markets. It sells its steel products primarily in local markets and through its centralized marketing organization to a diverse range of customers in approximately 160 countries. It prefers to export through its international network of sales agencies for maximum cost-efficiency.

Financial Performance

ArcelorMittal had sales of $70.6 billion for the year ended December 31 2019 representing a 7% decrease from sales of $76.0 billion for the year ended December 31 2018 primarily due to a 10% decrease in average steel selling prices partially offset by less than 1% increase in steel shipments and higher marketable iron ore selling prices.

In 2019 the company's net income fell by about $7.7 billion resulting to a loss of $2.4 billion due to the decrease on their sales while their cost of sales increase.

The company's cash at the end of 2019 increased for about $2.7 billion to $4.9 billion from $2.2 billion from the prior year. Cash from operations and financing activities provided $6.0 billion and $2.7 billion respectively. Cash used for investing activities was $3.8 billion.

Strategy

ArcelorMittal's strategy is to leverage four distinctive attributes that will enable it to capture leading positions in the most attractive areas of the steel industry value chain from mining at one end to distribution and first-stage processing at the other: Global scale and scope; Unmatched technical capabilities; Diverse portfolio of steel and related businesses particularly mining; and Financial capability.

ArcelorMittal looks to expand its leadership role in attractive markets and segments by leveraging the Company's technical capabilities and its global scale and scope. These are critical differentiators for sophisticated customers that value the distinctive technical and service capabilities the Company offers.

ArcelorMittal is working to continue to create value from its world-class mining business. Mining forms part of the steel value chain but typically enjoys a number of structural advantages such as a steeper cost curve. The Company's strategy is to create value from its most significant assets through selective expansion/de-bottlenecking by controlling cost and capital expenditure and by supplying products that are highly valued by steel producers.

ArcelorMittal strives to achieve best-in-class competitiveness. Operational excellence including health and safety the number one priority is at the core of the Company's strategy in both steel and mining. The Company steadily optimizes its asset base to ensure it is achieving high operating rates at its best assets. Its technical capabilities and the diversity of its portfolio of businesses underpin a strong commitment to institutional learning and continuous improvement through measures such as benchmarking and best-practice sharing. Innovation in products and processes also plays an important role while supporting overall competitiveness.

Critical to implementing this strategy are five key enablers: a clear license to operate; a strong balance sheet; a decentralized organizational structure; active portfolio management; and the best talent.

HISTORY

ArcelorMittal is the product of decades of steel-making by India's Mittal family. In 1967 patriarch Mohan Mittal unsuccessfully tried to open a steel mill in Egypt. He and his four younger brothers then set up a steel company in India but squabbles pushed Mohan to chart his own course eventually giving rise to an empire that flourished under the Ispat name. Mohan's son Lakshmi began working part-time at the family steel mill while in school; he started full-time at 21 after graduating in 1971.

Mohan set up an operation in Indonesia in 1975 (Ispat Indo) and put Lakshmi in charge. The next year fueled by ambitions and held back by government regulations in India Lakshmi formed Ispat International in Jakarta Indonesia to focus on expansion through acquisitions. He spent the next decade strengthening the Indonesian operations and perfecting the minimill process using direct-reduced iron (DRI).

Ispat took advantage of the recessionary late 1980s and early 1990s by making a string of acquisitions. In 1988 it took over the management of Trinidad and Tobago's state steel companies (bought in 1994; renamed Caribbean Ispat).

In 1992 Ispat bought Mexico's third-largest (albeit bankrupt) steel and DRI producer. Two years later it acquired Canada's Sidbec-Dosco steelmaker. Also that year Lakshmi took exclusive control of international operations leaving his brothers Pramod and Vinod to control the Indian divisions.

The mid-1990s brought more acquisitions: In 1995 Ispat bought Germany's Hamburger Stahlwerks and a mill in Kazakhstan. The next year it purchased Ireland's only steelmaker Irish Steel. Lakshmi moved to London in 1996 and purchased a home on Bishops Avenue known as "millionaire's row." (Saudi Arabia's King Fahd was a neighbor.)

In 1997 the company bought the long-product (wire rod) division of Germany's Thyssen AG (renamed Ispat Stahlwerk Ruhrort and Ispat Walzdraht Hochfeld). It also completed a $776 million IPO.

Ispat acquired Chicago-based Inland Steel in 1998 (and renamed it Ispat Inland) including the steel-finishing operations of I/N Tek (60% Inland-owned joint venture with Nippon Steel) and I/N Kote (50% Inland-owned joint venture with NSC).

In 1999 Ispat formed a joint venture with Mexican steelmaker Grupo Imsa to make flat-rolled steel to sell throughout most of the Americas. It also paid $96 million for France-based Usinor's Unim tal Tr fileurope and Soci t M tallurgique de R vigny subsidiaries which specialize in carbon long products. That year Ispat Inland became the target of a US federal criminal grand jury investigation and a related civil lawsuit for allegedly defrauding the Louisiana Highway Department. (The case was settled for $30 million with the cost split between Ispat Inland and Contech Construction Products Inc. of Ohio.)

In 2000 the company responded to a downturn in the steel industry by starting a Web-based joint venture with Commerce One to connect buyers and sellers in the worldwide metals market. It also offered to buy VSZ Slovakia's #1 steelworks but was outbid by U.S. Steel.

After struggling with heavy debt high labor and energy costs new environmental regulations and EU steel quotas in 2001 Ispat closed down its subsidiary Irish Ispat which accounted for about 2% of the parent company's steel production.

In 2002 the company's 51%-owned pipe making subsidiary Productura Mexicana de Tuberia sold almost all of its production assets.

The present ArcelorMittal was forged in 2004 when Ispat International (of which the Mittal family owned 70%) purchased LNM Holdings (wholly owned by the Mittals) for $13 billion. In 2006 the former Mittal Steel agreed to buy rival Arcelor for about $34 billion to create ArcelorMittal.

Mittal Steel had established its hold on the world steel market through its 2005 purchase of the US-based International Steel Group (ISG) for $4.5 billion. The purchase made the company the largest steel producer (ahead of U.S. Steel and Nucor) in the US a market that had long been a targeted area for expansion for CEO Mittal. Once the deal closed the company combined ISG's operations with those of subsidiary Ispat Inland to form a single North American entity Mittal Steel USA (now ArcelorMittal USA).

Also in 2005 Mittal Steel acquired a 93% stake in Ukrainian state-run steel company KryvorizhStal with the winning $4.84 billion bid in an auction held by the Ukrainian government. The price was high but Mittal was anxious to gain a stronger foothold in the region — and to keep its rivals away from KryvorizhStal. (This fact incidentally went a long way to convincing Mittal it needed to combine with Arcelor; the competition for acquisitions was driving prices dramatically upward.)

The company also began to broaden its portfolio outside the steel industry dipping its toe into the energy business. In mid-2005 Mittal formed two joint ventures with India's government-controlled Oil & Natural Gas Corporation: one to buy stakes in foreign oil and gas projects the other involved in oil and gas trading and shipping. The ventures began to look for business in places like Indonesia Kazakhstan Angola and Trinidad and Tobago.

After consolidating his family's various steel interests in the early part of this decade Mittal began work on the steel industry as a whole and was soon the world's largest steel producer.

By 2006 Mittal Steel no longer was content to be merely the world's largest steel producer; it wanted to dominate the market. The company announced an offer to the shareholders of Arcelor then the industry's #2 player to buy that company and in the process create the world's first 100-million-ton steel producer. Arcelor and seemingly half the governments of Western Europe initially fought the attempt.

Mittal improved its proposed price however and Arcelor's board finally approved the offer when Mittal also made ownership/corporate governance concessions. The combined company is 43% owned by the Mittal family. After a few months of a transitional management team arrangement Lakshmi Mittal took over as CEO of the combined company toward the end of 2006.

In 2009 ArcelorMittal completed its acquisition of the laser-welding steel activities of Noble International a leader in the niche industry. It also acquired Mexican steel producer Sicarsta for nearly $1.5 billion an acquisition that combined with its

Lazaro Cardenas created Mexico's largest steel company.

In 2011 the company spun off its stainless and specialty steels steel operations into Aperam which immediately became the world's sixth-largest stainless steel producer. ArcelorMittal made the decision in 2010 to spin off its stainless steel units in Europe and Brazil after determining that they were underperforming and would better thrive as a separate business.

After spinning its wheels in an escalating bidding war in 2011 ArcelorMittal joined rival Nunavut Iron Ore in making a joint acquisition of Canada-based Baffinland Iron Mines for $594 million. Both companies sought access to Baffinland's Mary River Project an undeveloped deposit of iron ore on sparsely populated North Baffin Island located inside the Arctic Circle as a source of raw materials. The venture faces stiff challenges including building an infrastructure around the mine's formidable location and shipping the ore out to Europe and other production sites.

Also that year the company bought a 40% stake in G Steel Public Company greatly expanding its presence in Asia. G Steel produces about 2.5 million ton of steel annually at its two slab-rolling plants in Thailand. The deal was part of ArcelorMittal's strategy of establishing a presence in emerging markets with with the potential for future growth.

In 2012 ArcelorMittal expanded its presence in China by increasing its stake in a joint venture with Valin Group known as Valin ArcelorMittal Automotive (VAMA) from 33% to 49%. VAMA is trying to enhance its position in China as a supplier of high-strength steels and products for the automotive market. The joint venture scheduled to become operational in 2014 will increase its planned capacity from 1.2 million tons to 1.5 million tons.

That year it sold New Jersey-based Skyline Steel a North American steel foundation and piling products distributor and specialty steel plate and bar producer Astralloy to US-based Nucor for $605 million.

EXECUTIVES

CFO; CEO ArcelorMittal Europe, Aditya Mittal, age 44
CEO, Wim de Klerk
CEO ArcelorMittal USA, John L. Brett
CEO ArcelorMittal USA, Andy Harshaw
VP Commercial Flat Carbon South America, Benjamin M. Baptista Filho
EVP and CTO, Robrecht Himpe, age 62
VP Global Automotive and Commercial Coordination, Brian Aranha
CEO ArcelorMittal Mining, Simon Wandke
CEO ArcelorMittal Nafta Flat Rolled, Jim Baske
CEO ArcelorMittal Africa and CIS Algeria Kazakhstan South Africa and Ukraine, Davinder Chugh
CEO South America Long, Jefferson de Paula
Chairman, Lakshmi N. Mittal, age 69
Auditors: Deloitte Audit S.a.r.l.

LOCATIONS

HQ: ArcelorMittal SA
24-26, Boulevard dAvranches, Luxembourg L-1160
Phone: (352) 4792 1   **Fax:** (352) 4792 2235
Web: www.arcelormittal.com

2018 Sales

	$ mil.	% of total
Europe	38,263	50
Americas	29	38
Asia & Africa	8,702	12
Total	**76,033**	**100**

PRODUCTS/OPERATIONS

2018 Sales

	% of total
NAFTA	25
Europe	49
Brazil	11
ACIS	10
Mining	5
Others and eliminations	-
Total	**100**

2018 sales

Sales by type of products	% of total
Flat products	61
Long products	21
Tubular products	3
Mining products	1
Others	14
Total	**100**

Segments and Selected Products
Flat Carbon Europe
  Coated products
  Coil
  Cold-rolled
  Hot-rolled
  Plate
  Slab
  Tin plate
Flat Carbon Americas
  Coated products
  Steel
  Plate
  Coil
  Cold-rolled
  Hot-rolled
  Slabs
Long Carbon Americas & Europe
  Billets
  Blooms
  Rebar
  Sections
  Wire rod
Asia Africa & Comonwealth of Independent States
  Flat products
  Long products
  Pipes
  Tubes
ArcelorMittal Steel Solutions & Services (in-house trading and distribution arm)

COMPETITORS

AK Steel Holding Corporation
BHP Billiton
Baosteel
BlueScope Steel
China Steel
Evraz
Gerdau
JFE Holdings
Mechel OAO
Nippon Steel & Sumitomo Metal Corporation
Nucor
POSCO
Severstal
Shougang Corp.
Tata Steel
Ternium
ThyssenKrupp
United States Steel

HISTORICAL FINANCIALS

Company Type: Public

Income Statement				FYE: December 31
	REVENUE ($ mil.)	NET INCOME ($ mil.)	NET PROFIT MARGIN	EMPLOYEES
12/19	70,615	(2,391)	—	191,248
12/18	76,033	5,149	6.8%	208,583
12/17	68,679	4,568	6.7%	197,108
12/16	56,791	1,779	3.1%	198,517
12/15	63,578	(7,946)	—	209,404
Annual Growth	**2.7%**	**—**	**—**	**(2.2%)**

2019 Year-End Financials

Debt ratio: 16.3%	No. of shares (mil.): 1,012
Return on equity: (-5.9%)	Dividends
Cash ($ mil.): 4,867	Yield: 0.9%
Current ratio: 1.34	Payout: —
Long-term debt ($ mil.): 11,471	Market value ($ mil.): 17,752

	STOCK PRICE ($) FY Close	P/E High/Low		PER SHARE ($) Earnings	Dividends	Book Value
12/19	17.54	—	—	(2.42)	0.17	38.06
12/18	20.67	7	4	5.04	0.09	41.52
12/17	32.31	7	2	4.46	0.00	38.03
12/16	7.30	5	2	1.86	0.00	29.56
12/15	4.22	—	—	(13.29)	0.00	45.76
Annual Growth	42.8%	—	—	—	—	(4.5%)

Arch Capital Group Ltd

EXECUTIVES

Chief Executive Officer, Marc Grandisson
Executive Vice President, Francois Morin
Chairman Of The Board, Constantine Iordanou
Auditors: PricewaterhouseCoopers LLP

LOCATIONS

HQ: Arch Capital Group Ltd
Waterloo House, Ground Floor, 100 Pitts Bay Road,
Pembroke HM 08
Phone: (1) 441 278 9250   **Fax:** (1) 441 278 9255
Web: www.archcapgroup.com

COMPETITORS

AXIS Capital Holdings	PartnerRe
Allied World Assurance	RenaissanceRe
Berkshire Hathaway	Sompo International
Chubb Limited	Swiss Re
Everest Re	The Hartford
HCC Insurance	Transatlantic Holdings
Hannover Re	Travelers Companies
Lloyd's	W. R. Berkley
Munich Re Group	XL Group plc
National Mortgage Insurance	Zurich Insurance Group

HISTORICAL FINANCIALS

Company Type: Public

Income Statement				FYE: December 31
	ASSETS ($ mil.)	NET INCOME ($ mil.)	INCOME AS % OF ASSETS	EMPLOYEES
12/19	37,885	1,636	4.3%	4,300
12/18	32,218	757	2.4%	3,642
12/17	32,051	619	1.9%	3,140
12/16	29,372	692	2.4%	3,250
12/15	23,177	537	2.3%	2,030
Annual Growth	13.1%	32.1%	—	20.6%

2019 Year-End Financials

Return on assets: 4.6%	Dividends
Return on equity: 15.6%	Yield: —
Long-term debt ($ mil.): —	Payout: —
No. of shares (mil.): 405	Market value ($ mil.): —
Sales ($ mil.): 6,928	

Asahi Group Holdings Ltd.

Auditors: KPMG AZSA LLC

LOCATIONS

HQ: Asahi Group Holdings Ltd.
1-23-1 Azumabashi, Sumida-ku, Tokyo 130-8602
Phone: (81) 3 5608 5116
Web: www.asahigroup-holdings.com

HISTORICAL FINANCIALS

Company Type: Public

Income Statement			FYE: December 31
	REVENUE ($ mil.)	NET INCOME ($ mil.)	NET PROFIT MARGIN	EMPLOYEES
12/19	19,241	1,309	6.8%	35,996
12/18	19,280	1,373	7.1%	34,663
12/17	18,529	1,253	6.8%	38,319
12/16	14,593	762	5.2%	31,142
12/15	14,034	629	4.5%	30,604
Annual Growth	8.2%	20.1%	—	4.1%

2019 Year-End Financials

Debt ratio: 0.4%	No. of shares (mil.): 458
Return on equity: 11.8%	Dividends
Cash ($ mil.): 446	Yield: 2.1%
Current ratio: 0.68	Payout: 32.2%
Long-term debt ($ mil.): 4,927	Market value ($ mil.): —

Asahi Kasei Corp

Auditors: PricewaterhouseCoopers Aarata LLC

LOCATIONS

HQ: Asahi Kasei Corp
1-1-2 Yuraku-cho, Chiyoda-ku, Tokyo 100-8440
Phone: (81) 3 6699 3030
Web: www.asahi-kasei.co.jp

HISTORICAL FINANCIALS

Company Type: Public

Income Statement			FYE: March 31
	REVENUE ($ mil.)	NET INCOME ($ mil.)	NET PROFIT MARGIN	EMPLOYEES
03/20	19,821	957	4.8%	40,689
03/19	19,598	1,332	6.8%	39,283
03/18	19,232	1,603	8.3%	34,670
03/17	16,841	1,028	6.1%	33,720
03/16	17,283	817	4.7%	32,821
Annual Growth	3.5%	4.0%	—	5.5%

2020 Year-End Financials

Debt ratio: 0.2%	No. of shares (mil.): 1,387
Return on equity: 7.5%	Dividends
Cash ($ mil.): 1,915	Yield: 4.6%
Current ratio: 1.31	Payout: —
Long-term debt ($ mil.): 2,696	Market value ($ mil.): 19,472

	STOCK PRICE ($) FY Close	P/E High/Low		PER SHARE ($) Earnings	Dividends	Book Value
03/20	14.03	0	0	0.69	0.64	9.02
03/19	20.72	0	0	0.95	0.67	8.93
03/18	26.80	0	0	1.15	0.53	8.68
03/17	19.53	0	0	0.74	0.36	7.37
03/16	13.44	0	0	0.58	0.32	6.65
Annual Growth	1.1%	—	—	4.2%	18.9%	7.9%

ASE Technology Holding Co Ltd

Advanced Semiconductor Engineering (ASE) helps chip makers wrap up production. The company is one of the world's leading providers of semiconductor packaging services; it also designs and manufactures interconnect materials and provides front-end and final chip testing services through its subsidiary ASE Test. The company provides electronic manufacturing services through Universal Scientific Industrial (USI) and it owns ISE Labs an engineering test services provider in Silicon Valley. Customers in the US account for about 65% of ASE's sales. The company has more than 240 customers around the world; some of the largest include Broadcom Microsoft NVIDIA and STMicroelectronics.

EXECUTIVES

Chairman and CEO, Jason C. S. Chang, age 76
Vice Chairman and President, Richard H. P. Chang, age 73
CFO, Joseph Tung, age 61
COO, Tien Wu, age 62
General Manager China Region, Rutherford Chang
Auditors: Deloitte & Touche

LOCATIONS

HQ: ASE Technology Holding Co Ltd
26 Chin Third Road, Nantze Export Processing Zone,
Nantze, Kaohsiung
Phone: (886) 2 6636 5678   **Fax:** (886) 2 2757 6121
Web: www.aseglobal.com

2016 Sales

	% of total
US	68
Taiwan	14
Asia	9
Europe	8
Others	1
Total	**100**

PRODUCTS/OPERATIONS

2017 Sales

	% of total
EMS	46
Packaging	43
Testing	9
Other	2

2017 Sales

	% of total
IC Wire Bonding	49
Bumping Flip Chip WLP and SiP	30
Discrete and Other	11
Total	**100**

ASML Holding NV

ASML Holding is one of the world's largest makers of semiconductor manufacturing equipment specializing in photolithography systems used to imprint circuitry patterns onto silicon wafers. ASML's products include EUV (extreme ultraviolet) lithography systems DUV (deep ultraviolet) lithography systems refurbished systems and metrology and inspection systems. Headquartered in Veldhoven the Netherlands ASML staffs some 60 offices in more than 15 countries. More than 70% of its revenue comes from chip manufacturers in Asia and its customers include the world's biggest chipmakers. The company was founded in 1984 and has produced versions of its flagship TWINSCAN systems since 2001.

Financial Performance

ASML has turned in steady robust growth over the past five years with revenue increasing at an average annual rate of about 17%.

In 2018 sales jumped 22% to ?10.6 billion up about ?1.7 billion in 2017 driven by a 28% rise in system sales. The company sold more systems and more high-end systems in 2018. Revenue from China was 100% higher in 2018 over 2017 as chipmakers outfitted new factories in the country.

ASML's profit advanced to about ?2.6 billion in 2018 from about ?2 billion in 2017 lifted by the stronger revenue especially the higher margins on the high-end equipment.

The company had ?3.1 billion in cash in 2018 compared to ?2.2 billion the year before. In 2018 operating activities provided ?3 billion while investing activities used ?491 million and financing activities used ?1.7 billion.

Strategy

ASML's DUV systems have been the workhorse of the company's product line providing a strong base of installed systems. And the systems are still going strong. The company sold about 190 DUV systems in 2018 a 17% increase from 2017.

ASML's more advanced EUV systems which can lay down more intricate designs on smaller pieces of silicon are just getting off the ground. ASML sold 18 EUV systems in 2018 and it expects to ship 30 in 2019. To accelerate the pace of adoption the company raised its research and development spending devoted to EUV equipment. Further the company bought about 25% of indirect interest in Carl Zeiss SMT GmbH a manufacturer of optical devices in Germany to aid continued development of EUV systems.

ASML is riding a wave of chip manufacturers moving to new processes for patterning intricate features that can only be produced economically with EUV equipment. The need for advanced chips for 5G communications networks contributes a rising demand for logic chips made with EUV systems.

ASML's sales in China doubled in 2018 from 2017 increasing the country's share of ASML sales to nearly 20%. While not substantially affected by trade tensions between China and the US in 2018 ASML could experience fallout if US-China trade tensions continue. In particular US restrictions on what technology can be sold to Chinese customers could have an impact of ASML's sales which has some operations in the US.

EXECUTIVES

President and CEO, Peter Wennink, age 63, $638,820 total compensation
EVP and Chief Program Officer, Frits van Hout, age 60
EVP and CFO, Wolfgang U. Nickl, age 51

EVP and COO, Frederic Schneider-Maunoury
President and CTO, Martin van den Brink
Chairman Supervisory Board, Arthur P. M. van der Poel, age 72
Vice Chairman, Douglas A. (Doug) Grose
Chairman, Gerard J. Kleisterlee, age 72
Auditors: KPMG Accountants N.V.

LOCATIONS

HQ: ASML Holding NV
  De Run 6501, Veldhoven 5504 DR
Phone: (31) 40 268 3000
Web: www.asml.com

2018 Sales

	% of total
Korea	34
Taiwan	18
United States	18
China	17
EMEA	6
Japan	5
Singapore	2
Total	100

PRODUCTS/OPERATIONS

2018 Sales

	% of total
Net system sales	75
Net service and field option sales	25
Total	100

COMPETITORS

Advantest	KLA-Tencor
Amtech Systems	MAPPER Lithography
Applied Materials	Nikon
Canon	PDF Solutions
Canon Nanotechnologies	Suss MicroTec
JEOL	Synopsys
JMAR Technologies	Ultratech

HISTORICAL FINANCIALS

Company Type: Public

Income Statement   FYE: December 31

	REVENUE ($ mil.)	NET INCOME ($ mil.)	NET PROFIT MARGIN	EMPLOYEES
12/19	13,271	2,910	21.9%	24,900
12/18	12,533	2,967	23.7%	16,647
12/17	10,852	2,539	23.4%	19,216
12/16	7,174	1,554	21.7%	16,647
12/15	6,848	1,510	22.1%	14,681
Annual Growth	18.0%	17.8%	—	14.1%

2019 Year-End Financials

Debt ratio: 15.4%
Return on equity: 21.3%
Cash ($ mil.): 3,965
Current ratio: 2.58
Long-term debt ($ mil.): 3,489

No. of shares (mil.): 419
Dividends
  Yield: 1.0%
  Payout: 51.1%
Market value ($ mil.): —

Assicurazioni Generali S.p.A.

Italy's largest insurance company (and one of the largest in Europe) Assicurazioni Generali writes insurance for risks as varied as pensions and car insurance. Present in almost 50 countries

Generali's core businesses are involved in both life and property/casualty insurance (including accident health motor and home). The company targets individuals and SMEs and counts around 61 million customers across Europe the Asia/Pacific region and Latin America; it's native Italy represents a third of sales. Generali has been in business since 1831.

Operations

Generali comprises more than 400 companies in total which offer various types of insurance in a plurality of geographies. The company divides these into two operating segments: Life and Property & Casualty.

The Life segment accounts for 60% of Generali's gross premiums written and offers savings and protection policies health coverage and supplementary pension policies. The Property & Casualty segment provides coverage under three categories: insurance against damage to property specifically covering the destruction loss and deterioration of assets; insurance against personal injury including the loss of capacity to generate income; and insurance against public liability for damage to third-parties and their property. The segment accounts for about 40% of gross premiums written.

Generali provides additional financial services including Banca Generali which offers such services as wealth management and bank insurance products.

Geographic Reach

Based in Trieste Italy Generali divides its operations into five core geographic regions. Italy accounts for about 30% of sales Germany and France generate 15% each the ACEER (Austria Central & Eastern Europe and Russia) segment represents 15% of revenue and other international countries (including Spain Switzerland Americas Southern Europe Asia and the Europ Assistance unit) bring in 15%.

Sales and Marketing

Generali serves some 61 million customers around the world. It sells through channels including its own global network of agents as well as financial advisors and brokers. It also sells by telephone and online.

Financial Performance

Note: Growth rates may differ after conversion to US Dollars.

Assicurazioni Generali's revenue has been on a gradual decline for the last five years but profits have been inching upward.

In 2019 the insurer's revenue fell 7% to ?63.1 billion due to a net loss from its investment activities of ?7.1 billion compared to a net gain of ?4.6 billion in the prior year. Gross written premiums grew 5% thanks to gains in the Life segment's savings policies particularly in Italy Asia and France; and in Property & Casualty thanks to growth motor insurance.

Net income grew 14% to ?2.7 billion mostly thanks to gains from disposals of Generali's Germany Belgian and Guernsey business for ?173 million and an Irish business for ?49 million. Profits from continuing operations were down 2%.

Generali's cash balance grew ?177 million to ?6.8 billion during 2019. Operating activities generated ?20 billion while investing activities used ?16.4 billion and financing used ?3.7 billion.

Strategy

At the end of 2018 Generali concluded its 2016-18 strategic plan and entered into a new strategic phase that runs from 2019 to 2021. Generali's goal is to become a life partner for its customers offering customized insurance and increased convenience by digitizing internal and customer-facing operations. The company has about ?1 billion earmarked for internal initiatives.

From a financial perspective Generali is targeting ?10.5 billion in cumulative capital generation a 35% increase in cash retained and a ?1.5-2.0 billion reduction in total debt. To improve its financial performance Generali is exiting markets where it's less strong to free up capital for deployment in more promising markets. Since 2017 the company has divested entities in Belgium Colombia Germany Guatemala Guernsey Ireland Panama and the Netherlands.

Mergers and Acquisitions

In 2020 Generali finalized the acquisition of Seguradoras Unidas and the service company AdvanceCare from Calm Eagle Holdings S.ó r.l. and Calm Eagle Parent Holdings II S.ó r.l. entities majority owned by investment funds managed by certain affiliates of Apollo Global Management Inc.

In 2019 Generali made three acquisitions. It acquired Union Investment TFI from the German group Union Asset Management Holding AG. Union Investment TFI boasts a client base of about 135000 retail investors and 550 institutional investors and offers funds spanning equities fixed income and absolute return.

Also in 2019 Generali acquired Adriatic Slovenica and KD Funds from KD Group in Slovenia. Adriatic Slovenic will be integrated into Generali's Central and Eastern Europe division.

Lastly in 2019 Generali's Europ Assistance subsidiary acquired Trip Mate from Arthur J. Gallagher. Trip Mate is active in the tour operator travel insurance market in the United States and its acquisition strengthens Europ Assistance's position as one of the top-three travel insurance providers in the US.

HISTORY

Assicurazioni Generali was founded as Assicurazioni Generali Austro-Italiche in 1831 by a group of merchants led by Giuseppe Morpurgo in the Austro-Hungarian port of Trieste. Formed to provide insurance to the city's bustling trade industry the company offered life marine fire flood and shipping coverage. That year Morpurgo established what he intended to be Generali's headquarters in Venice. (While the company maintained offices in both cities Trieste ultimately won out.)

By 1835 Generali had opened 25 offices in Central and Western Europe; it had also expelled Morpurgo. The firm moved into Africa and Asia in the 1880s. In 1900 Generali began selling injury and theft insurance. In 1907 Generali's Prague office provided the young experimental writer Franz Kafka his first job. (He found it disagreeable and quit after a few months.)

During WWI the firm's Venice office pledged allegiance to Italy while the office in Trieste (still part of Austria-Hungary) stayed loyal to the Hapsburgs. After the war Trieste was absorbed by the new Italian republic. Under Edgardo Morpurgo Generali expanded further in the 1920s managing 30 subsidiaries and operating in 17 countries. As fascist Italy aligned itself with Germany in the 1930s adoption of anti-Semitic laws caused Morpurgo and a number of other high-ranking Jewish employees to flee the country. In 1938 Generali moved its headquarters to Rome (but moved them back to Trieste after war's end).

The firm maintained steady business both before and during Nazi occupation in WWII; in 1945 however the Soviets seized all Italian properties in Eastern Europe including 14 Generali subsidiaries. In 1950 Generali invaded the US market offering shipping and fire insurance and reinsurance. Generali established a cooperative agreement with Aetna Life and Casualty (now Aetna Inc.) in 1966 further cementing its US connections.

In 1988 Generali tried to acquire French insurer Compagnie du Midi. Foreshadowing Generali's later dealings with Istituto Nazionale delle Assicurazioni (INA) Midi escaped Generali's grasp through a merger with AXA. As the Iron Curtain frayed in 1989 Generali formed AB Generali Budapest through a joint venture with a Hungarian insurer. In 1990 the firm opened an office in Tokyo through an agreement with Taisho Marine and Fire Insurance (which became Mitsui Marine & Fire Insurance and is now Mitsui Sumitomo Insurance). By 1993 Generali had become Italy's largest insurer.

In 1997 the firm was accused along with other major European insurers of not paying on policies of Holocaust victims. (It moved to settle claims in 1999.)

EXECUTIVES

Managing Director and Group CEO, Philippe Donnet, age 60
Group Compliance Officer, Maurizio Basso
CEO Generali CEE Holding B.V., Luciano Cirin , age 56
CEO Generali France, Eric Lombard
Group Chief Risk Officer, Sandro Panizza, age 62
CEO Generali Deutschland Holding and Country Manager Germany, Giovanni Liverani
Group Chief Information & Digital Officer, Bruce M. Hodges, age 53
Group Chief Insurance Officer, Valter Trevisani
Group CFO, Luigi Lubelli
CEO Global Business Lines and International, Frédéric de Courtois
Group Chief Investment Officer, Tjmothy (Tim) Ryan, age 52
CEO Generali Italia and Country Manager Italy, Marco Sesana, age 47
Vice Chairman, Francesco G. Caltagirone, age 77
Chairman, Gabriele Galateri di Genola, age 74
Vice Chairman, Clemente Rebecchini, age 56
Auditors: E&Y S.p.A.

LOCATIONS

HQ: Assicurazioni Generali S.p.A.
Piazza Duca degli Abruzzi 2, P.O. Box 538, Trieste 34132
Phone: (39) 40 6711   **Fax:** (39) 40 671 600
Web: www.generali.com

2018 Sales

	% of total
Italy	3
Germany	15
France	13
Austria CEE & Russia	14
International	
Spain	5
Switzerland	5
Americas and Southern Europe	2
Asia	1
Europ Assistance	2
Investments Asset & Wealth Management	10
Total	**100**

PRODUCTS/OPERATIONS

2018 Sales by Segment

	% of total
Life	57
Property/casualty	37
Holding & other	6
Total	**100**

COMPETITORS

AIG	ING
AXA	Milano Assicurazioni
Achmea	Swiss Re
Allianz	Unipol
Allianz France	UnipolSai
Aviva	Zurich Insurance Group
ERGO	ageas SA/NV

Company Type: Public

Income Statement				FYE: December 31
	ASSETS ($ mil.)	NET INCOME ($ mil.)	INCOME AS % OF ASSETS	EMPLOYEES
12/19	577,746	2,997	0.5%	71,936
12/18	590,722	2,644	0.4%	70,734
12/17	643,826	2,529	0.4%	71,327
12/16	550,309	2,197	0.4%	73,727
12/15	545,203	2,211	0.4%	76,191
Annual Growth	1.5%	7.9%	—	(1.4%)

2019 Year-End Financials

Return on assets: 0.5%
Return on equity: 10.2%
Long-term debt ($ mil.): —
No. of shares (mil.): 1,569
Sales ($ mil): 104,203

Dividends
Yield: 3.1%
Payout: 57.1%
Market value ($ mil.): —

Associated British Foods Plc

They say man cannot live on bread alone so foodstuffs producer Associated British Foods (ABF) also sells tea sugar cereals and clothes. ABF's bread-baking operation is its oldest function but it makes the biggest chunk of its money from clothes - the company owns low-cost high-street fashion chain Primark. ABF also makes and markets grocery products sugar ingredients and agricultural products. Its grocery lines include household staples Allinson Tip Top Karo syrup Argo corn starch Kingsmill bread Silver Spoon sugar and Twinings tea. In the US it owns Fleischmanns Yeast and ingredient and spice maker ACH. Other divisions churn out sugar specialty oils and animal feed. ABF's activities span nearly 48 countries worldwide.

Operations

ABF's business is divided up into Groceries Agriculture Sugar Ingredients and Retail. Several of the segments are customers of each other — for instance part of the Sugar division's output is sold under the Groceries segment as Silver Spoon.

The Groceries segment responsible for around 25% of sales manufactures products such as hot beverages sugar oils and baked goods. Its brands include hot beverages Twinings (tea) and Ovaltine (hot chocolate) Silver Spoon and Billington's (sugar) Jordans and Dorset Cereals (breakfast cereals) Mazola (corn oil) and others.

The Agriculture and Ingredients segments both generate around 10% of sales and manufacture animal feed and bakery ingredients respectively. Food-related activities comprise 60% of total revenue.

However despite its focus on food ABF's largest segment by revenue is Retail. The segment owns low-cost high-street chain Primark which pulls in about half of total sales and has sites in the UK Republic of Ireland Spain Portugal Germany the Netherlands Belgium Austria and France and the US.

Geographic Reach

Based in the UK ABF racks up sales in more than 100 countries worldwide. It has direct operations in around 50 countries across Europe southern Africa the Americas the Asia/Pacific region and Australia. ABF generates close to 40%

of its annual sales in the UK and another nearly 40% in countries in Europe and Africa. The Asia/Pacific region accounts for around 15% of sales and the Americas the remaining 10% (note: the percentages don't sum tidily to 100% due to rounding).

The Sugar business operates factories in the UK (1 million tons capacity) Spain (400000 tons) six African countries (1.7 billion tons combined) and north east China (two factories with 180000 tons capacity together). ABF's Ingredients operations has more than 50 plants in 25 countries.

Primark operates 360 stores in 11 countries around half of which are in the UK. Spain Ireland and Germany are its next biggest markets.

Sales and Marketing

ABF's branded products are sold through supermarkets and other retail outlets and via wholesale channels. To keep expenses down Primark neither sells online nor operates any significant marketing function. It relies on word-of-mouth for brand awareness.

Financial Performance

Note: Growth rates may differ after conversion to US Dollars.

ABF's sales have grown every year since 2015 albeit unevenly. In fiscal 2018 (ended 15 September) the company grew its sales just 1% to £15.6 billion. Revenue drivers were Primark which defied prevailing trends in the UK retail sector to grow 6% thanks to three store openings and the Agriculture business which grew 15% aided by a large beet crop. On the downside revenue in the Sugar segment fell 15% due lower prices in the EU and the Ingredients business fell 2% on the back of weakness in Latin America and unfavorable shifts in exchange rates.

Net income fell 16% to £1.0 billion in 2018 as the previous year benefited from a £293 million gain on the sale of certain businesses partially offset by a 50% (£151 million) reduction in tax on overseas activities. Profits were supported by Primark which accounts for a massive +80% of net income; by contrast the struggling sugar division's profits fell by 80% to £80 million.

ABF's cash position reduced by £103 million 2018 ending the financial year at £1.3 billion. Lower net income impacted on operating cash while net cash use in financing activities increased.

Strategy

In recent years Primark has been ABF's most successful segment by a distance and as a result is the focus of investment activities. ABF adds around 1 million sq. ft. of store space each year (across roughly 15 stores) — a fairly conservative rate of growth it has to be said. It opened 15 in 2018 of which 5 were in Germany and in 2019 it will open another 15 concentrated in Germany France Spain and the UK while entering Slovenia for the first time.

The Grocery businesses various brands are given leeway to operate independently. For instance Ryvita's growth strategy is to focus on growth in core markets while Jordans Dorset and AB World Foods are looking to move into new markets and expand in developing ones.

Mergers and Acquisitions

In 2017 ABF's Grocery segment acquired Acetum a balsamic vinegar producer based in Modena Italy for £284 million. In the Agriculture segment it acquired a small aerial survey and informatics company and as part of UK Ingredients business the company acquired Holgran a supplier of malted grains and Fleming Howden and Edinburgh-based blender and distributor of bakery ingredients.

Also in 2017 the company acquired UK sports nutrition businesses H5 and Reflex Nurition. High5

makes a hydration and energy brand popular with endurance athletes and Reflex manufactures a range of premium protein- based recovery products.

EXECUTIVES

Finance Director, John G. Bason, age 63, $984,225 total compensation
Chief Executive, George G. Weston, age 56, $1,427,426 total compensation
Auditors: Ernst & Young LLP Chartered Accountants

LOCATIONS

HQ: Associated British Foods Plc
Weston Centre, 10 Grosvenor Street, London W1K 4QY
Phone: (44) 20 7399 6500   **Fax:** (44) 20 7399 6580
Web: www.abf.co.uk

2018 Sales

	% of total
UK	38
Europe & Africa	38
Asia/Pacific	14
The Americas	10
Total	**100**

PRODUCTS/OPERATIONS

2018 Sales

	% of total
Retail	48
Grocery	22
Sugar	12
Ingredients	9
Agriculture	9
Total	**100**

Selected Products and Brands

Agriculture
  Animal feeds (AB Agri)
Grocery
  Bread baked goods and cereal
  Allinson breads
  Burgen breads
  Jordans cereals
  Kingsmill breads
  Ryvita rye crispbread
  Speedibake bakery products
  Sunblest bread snacks and rolls
  Tip Top bread and baked goods (Australia)
  Herbs and spices
  Durkee (US)
  Gravies
  Sauces
  Seasonings
  Soup bases
  Spices
  Spice Islands (US)
  Seasonings
  Spices
  Tone's spices (US)
  Hot beverages sugar and sweeteners
  Billington's cane sugars
  Jacksons of Picadilly teas
  Karo corn syrup
  Ovaltine
  Silver Spoon sugar (UK)
  La Tisaniere teas and infusions (France)
  Twinings teas
  Meat
  Don Deligoods (Australia)
  KRC (Australia)
  Vegetable oils
  Capullo canola oil (Mexico)
  Mazola corn oil (US)
  World foods
  Blue Dragon (Asian)
  Patak's (Indian)
  Other
  Askeys ice cream and dessert accompaniments
  Baking Mad
  Baking advice
  Recipes

Tips
    Crusha milkshake mix
Ingredients
    Specialty ingredients
    Enzymes
    Specialty proteins and lipids
    Yeast extracts
    Yeast and bakery ingredients
    Argo corn starch
Retail clothing
    Primark
    Accessories
    Childrenswear
    Footwear
    Homeware
    Hosiery
    Lingerie
    Menswear
    Womenswear
Sugar
    Beet sugar

COMPETITORS

ADM	Mondelez International
ALDI	Morrisons
ASDA	Nestlé
Armani	Nine West
Bahlsen	Nordzucker
Bakkavor	NutraSweet
Bill Blass	Oscar Mayer Limited
Burberry	PVH
Carrefour	Perry Ellis
Celestial Seasonings	International
Chr. Hansen A/S	Premier Foods
Cosun	Pura Foods
Cumberland Packing	R.C. Bigelow
Danisco A/S	Ralph Lauren
Donna Karan	Renshawnapier
Gap UK	Republic of Tea
General Mills	St. John Knits
Greencore	Stash Tea
Gucci	Sucri ˮre de
Harrods	Pithiviers
Heinz	S dzucker
Hwa Hong	T.K. Maxx
Iconix Brand Group	Tata Global Beverages
Imperial Sugar	Tate & Lyle
Ingredion	Tereos
J Sainsbury	Tesco
Kenneth Cole	Unilever UK Foods
Kerry Group	United Biscuits
Marks & Spencer	Waitrose
McCormick & Company	Wal-Mart
Merisant	Warburtons

HISTORICAL FINANCIALS

Company Type: Public

Income Statement   FYE: September 12

	REVENUE ($ mil.)	NET INCOME ($ mil.)	NET PROFIT MARGIN	EMPLOYEES
09/20	17,875	583	3.3%	133,425
09/19	19,704	1,093	5.5%	138,097
09/18	20,391	1,318	6.5%	137,014
09/17	20,839	1,625	7.8%	132,590
09/16	17,652	1,077	6.1%	129,916
Annual Growth	0.3%	(14.2%)	—	0.7%

2020 Year-End Financials

Debt ratio: 3.6%
Return on equity: 4.8%
Cash ($ mil.): 2,560
Current ratio: 1.82
Long-term debt ($ mil.): 407

No. of shares (mil.): 791
Dividends
    Yield: 0.0%
    Payout: 53.0%
Market value ($ mil.): 19,659

	STOCK PRICE ($) FY Close	P/E High/Low		PER SHARE ($) Earnings	Dividends	Book Value
09/20	24.83	60	35	0.74	0.39	15.16
09/19	29.35	30	23	1.38	0.50	14.87
09/18	29.35	35	23	1.67	0.49	15.23
09/17	42.96	30	21	2.06	0.44	14.29
09/16	35.94	46	31	1.36	0.39	11.74
Annual Growth	(8.8%)	—	—	(14.2%)	0.0%	6.6%

Astellas Pharma Inc

Auditors: Ernst & Young ShinNihon LLC

LOCATIONS

HQ: Astellas Pharma Inc
    2-5-1 Nihonbashi-Honcho, Chuo-Ku, Tokyo 103-8411
Phone: (81) 3 3244 3000
Web: www.astellas.com

HISTORICAL FINANCIALS

Company Type: Public

Income Statement   FYE: March 31

	REVENUE ($ mil.)	NET INCOME ($ mil.)	NET PROFIT MARGIN	EMPLOYEES
03/20	13,116	1,970	15.0%	15,883
03/19	13,171	2,241	17.0%	16,243
03/18	13,110	1,660	12.7%	16,617
03/17	13,225	2,205	16.7%	17,202
03/16	13,840	1,952	14.1%	17,217
Annual Growth	(1.3%)	0.2%	—	(2.0%)

2020 Year-End Financials

Debt ratio: 0.1%
Return on equity: 15.3%
Cash ($ mil.): 3,157
Current ratio: 1.09
Long-term debt ($ mil.): —

No. of shares (mil.): 1,860
Dividends
    Yield: 2.3%
    Payout: 34.2%
Market value ($ mil.): 28,354

	STOCK PRICE ($) FY Close	P/E High/Low		PER SHARE ($) Earnings	Dividends	Book Value
03/20	15.24	0	0	1.05	0.36	6.99
03/19	14.97	0	0	1.16	0.33	6.72
03/18	15.28	0	0	0.82	0.31	6.47
03/17	13.18	0	0	1.04	0.30	6.21
03/16	13.29	0	0	0.90	0.26	5.97
Annual Growth	3.5%	—	—	3.8%	8.4%	4.0%

AstraZeneca Plc

AstraZeneca's products run the gamut from A (blood pressure drug Atacand) to Z (prostate and breast cancer drug Zoladex). One of the world's major pharmaceutical firms AstraZeneca specializes in drugs for cardiovascular metabolic neurological gastrointestinal respiratory oncology and infection therapy areas. The firm's biggest sellers include cholesterol reducer Crestor cardiovascular drug Brilinta acid reflux remedy Nexium and Symbicort for asthma. AstraZeneca also markets drugs that aim to treat high cholesterol diabetes pain viral diseases and various cancers. The company has more than 30 factories globally and R&D centers in the UK US Sweden and China and its products are sold in more than 100 countries.

Operations

AstraZeneca operates as a single operating segment that researches develops manufactures and commercializes biopharmaceuticals. Its research focuses on four therapy areas: Cardiovascular Renal & Metabolism; Respiratory; Oncology; and Other.

Oncology brings in more than 35% of total sales. Its major products include Faslodex for breast cancer and Zoladex for breast and prostate cancers.

The Cardiovascular & Metabolic Diseases group is brings in about 30% of total sales. Its major products include Crestor for high cholesterol and Brilinta for the treatment of coronary syndromes and prevention of further coronary events. Other drugs include Farxiga Onglyza Bydureon and Byetta (for type-2 diabetes); Symlin (diabetes); Seloken/Toptol-XL and Atacand (hypertension heart failure and angina).

The Respiratory unit brings in more than 20% of total sales largely from the sales of asthma drug Symbicort (the company's single biggest earner).

The Other segment brings in more than 10% of total sales produces drugs in the areas of autoimmunity infection neuroscience and gastroenterology. Its leading drugs include acid reflux medication Nexium and schizophrenia treatment Seroquel.

Geographic Reach

Cambridge UK-based AstraZeneca has operations in Europe North America Central America South America the Middle East Africa and the Asia/Pacific region. It manufactures products from more than 30 sites in more than 15 countries. The company has R&D centers in the US the UK Sweden Japan and China.

The Americas is AstraZeneca's most lucrative region accounting for about 40% of sales. The Asia/Pacific region Africa and Australasia together represent more than 35% of sales Continental Europe more than 15% and the company's native UK generate about 10% of sales.

Sales and Marketing

AstraZeneca markets its products to physicians through sales and marketing teams who are active in more than 100 countries. It typically sells through local marketing companies which it owns as well as through distributors and local representative offices.

Financial Performance

Total Revenue for the year was up 10% (CER: 13%) to $24.4 million comprising Product Sales of $23.6 million up 12% (CER: 15%) and Collaboration Revenue of $819 million; a decrease of 21% (CER: 20%).

The company's profit decreased by 40% to $1.2 billion in 2019. The fall was primarily due to higher selling general and administrative costs and lower other operating income and expense.

Cash held by the company at the end of 2019 increased by $547 million to $5.2 billion from $4.7 billion in the prior year. Cash provided by operations was $3.0 billion while cash used for investing and financing activities were $657 million and $1.8 billion respectively. AstraZeneca's main cash uses in 2019 were capital expenditures and paid dividends.

Strategy

AstraZeneca's strategic priorities are focused on delivering value to patients and society.

Delivering growth and therapy area leadership by supplying medicines that can transform care and ensuring that it reach patients who need them. Accelerating innovative science in search of solutions that prevent treat and even cure some of the world's most serious health challenges. Being a great place to work by living its values and behaviors delivering as an enterprise team and leading in sustainability.

The company's return to Product Sales growth also re-ects its success in responding to a changing world. It is a world of economic growth and increasing wealth of a growing and ageing global population and challenged by an increasing burden of chronic and non-communicable diseases.

HISTORY

AstraZeneca forerunner Imperial Chemical Industries (ICI) was created from the 1926 merger of four British chemical companies — Nobel Industries; Brunner Mond and Company; United Alkali; and British Dyestuffs — in reaction to the German amalgamation that created I. G. Farben. ICI plunged into research recruiting chemists engineers and managers and forming alliances with universities. Between 1933 and 1935 at least 87 new products were created including polyethylene.

Fortunes declined as competition increased after WWII. In 1980 ICI posted losses and cut its dividend for the first time. In 1982 turnaround artist John Harvey-Jones shifted ICI from bulk chemicals to high-margin specialty chemicals such as pharmaceuticals and pesticides. That business became Zeneca which ICI spun off in 1993.

The takeover specter loomed large over the company during its first year. Zeneca had several drugs in its pipeline but it also had expiring patents on others making them fair game for competitors. Bankrolled by its agrochemical business Zeneca forged alliances with other pharmaceutical firms. In 1994 it entered a marketing alliance with Amersham International (now Amersham) to sell Metastron a nuclear-medicine cancer agent. The next year Zeneca formed a joint venture with Chinese companies Advanced Chemicals and Tianli to make textile-coating chemicals.

In 1995 Glaxo was forced to sell a migraine drug candidate to complete its merger with Wellcome. Zeneca's gamble in buying the then-unproven drug (Zomig) paid off when the product gained US FDA approval two years later.

By 1997 Zeneca completed its gradual acquisition of Salick Health Care formed to create more humane cancer treatment programs. The purchase followed a trend of large drug firms moving into managed care which raised concerns that centers might be pressured to use their parent companies' drugs but Zeneca maintained that Salick would remain independent except to the extent that it offered an opportunity to evaluate treatments.

In 1998 Zeneca got the FDA's OK to sell its brand of tamoxifen (Nolvadex) to women at high risk of contracting breast cancer. In 1999 it sued Eli Lilly to protect Nolvadex against Lilly's marketing claim that its osteoporosis treatment Evista reduced breast cancer risk a use for which it was not approved.

In 1999 Zeneca completed its purchase of Sweden's Astra to form AstraZeneca. That year the firm sold its specialty chemicals unit Zeneca Specialties to Cinven Group and Investcorp. With its agricultural business stagnated due to crippled markets in Asia and Europe AstraZeneca announced plans to merge the unit with the agrochemicals business of Novartis and spun it off as Syngenta.

In 2013 AstraZeneca sold its only non-pharma business Aptium Oncology an operator of cancer treatment centers in the US. This came on the heels of selling its other non-core units Astra Tech (medical devices) and Dentsply Sirona (dental implant systems).

EXECUTIVES

EVP Oncology, Jamie Freedman
CEO and Director, Pascal Soriot, age 59
EVP MedImmune, Bahija Jallal
CFO nd Director, Marc Dunoyer
EVP Global Product and Portfolio Strategy (GPPS) Global Medical Affairs (GMA) and Corporate Affairs (CA), Mark Mallon
EVP IMED Biotech Unit and Global Head of Business Development, Menelas (Mene) Pangalos
EVP Europe, Ruud Dobber
EVP Global Product and Portfolio Strategy, Luke Miels
EVP Human Resources, Fiona Cicconi
EVP Operations and Information Technology, Pam Cheng
EVP Global Medicines Development and Chief Medical Officer, Sean Bohen
EVP International, Leon Wang
EVP Europe, Iskra Reic
Chairman, Leif Johansson, age 69
Auditors: PricewaterhouseCoopers LLP

LOCATIONS

HQ: AstraZeneca Plc
1 Francis Crick Avenue, Cambridge Biomedical Campus, Cambridge CB2 0AA
Phone: (44) 20 3749 5000 **Fax:** (44) 1223 352 858
Web: www.astrazeneca.com

2018 sales

	$ mil.	% of total
The Americas	8,529	39
Asia Africa and Australasia	7,351	33
Continental Europe	3,820	17
UK	2,390	11
Total	**22,090**	**100**

PRODUCTS/OPERATIONS

2018 Sales

	$ mil.	% of total
Products		
Cardiovascular Renal & Metabolism	6,710	30
Respiratory	4,911	22
Oncology	46,028	27
Other	3,400	16
Externalization	1,041	10
Total	**22,090**	**100**

Selected Products

Cardiovascular
  Atacand (angiotensin II antagonist for hypertension and heart failure)
  Brilinta (acute coronary syndromes and events in high-risk post myocardial infarction)
  Crestor (statin for cholesterol-lowering drug)
  Onglyza (type 2 diabetes)
  Plendil (calcium antagonist for hypertension and angina)
  Seloken/Toprol-XL (beta-blocker for blood pressure heart failure angina)
  Zestril (ACE inhibitor for hypertension other)
Gastrointestinal
  Losec/Prilosec (acid reflux disease)
  Nexium (acid reflux disease)
Infection and Other Products
  FluMist (intranasal flu vaccine)
  Merrem/Meronem (intraveneous antibiotic for serious hospital infections)
  Synagis (for respiratory syncytial virus or RSV in infants)
Neuroscience
  Diprivan (general anesthetic)
  Local anesthetics (Carbocaine Citanest Naropin Xylocaine)
  Seroquel (anti-psychotic for schizophrenia and bipolar)
  Zomig (migraines)
Oncology
  Arimidex (aromatase inhibitor for breast cancer)
  Casodex (anti-androgen for prostate cancer)
  Faslodex (oestrogen receptor antagonist for breast cancer)
  Iressa (kinase inhibitor for non-small cell lung cancer)
  Nolvadex (breast cancer)
  Zoladex (LHRH agonist for prostate and breast cancer)
Respiratory & Inflammation
  Oxis (beta-agonist for asthma and chronic obstructive pulmonary disease)
  Pulmicort (anti-inflammatory for asthma)
  Rhinocort (topical nasal anti-inflammatory)
  Symbicort (anti-inflammatory and bronchodilator in one inhaler for asthma and chronic obstructive pulmonary disease)

Selected Subsidiaries

AstraZeneca AB (Sweden)
AstraZeneca BV (The Netherlands)
AstraZeneca Canada Inc.
AstraZeneca do Brasil Limitada
AstraZeneca Farmaceutica Spain SA
AstraZeneca GmbH (Germany)
AstraZeneca KK (Japan)
AstraZeneca LP (US)
AstraZeneca Pharmaceuticals Co. Limited (China)
AstraZeneca Pharmaceuticals LP (US)
AstraZeneca Pty Limited (Australia)
AstraZeneca SAS (France)
AstraZeneca SpA (Italy)
AstraZeneca UK Limited
IPR Pharmaceuticals Inc. (Puerto Rico)
MedImmune L.L.C. (US)
Novexel SA (France)
NV AstraZeneca SA (Belgium)
Zeneca Holdings Inc. (US)

COMPETITORS

Amgen	Novartis
Bayer AG	Pfizer
Bristol-Myers Squibb	Regeneron
Eli Lilly	Pharmaceuticals
Gilead Sciences	Roche Holding
GlaxoSmithKline	Sanofi
Johnson & Johnson	Teva
Merck	

HISTORICAL FINANCIALS

Company Type: Public

Income Statement

FYE: December 31

	REVENUE ($ mil.)	NET INCOME ($ mil.)	NET PROFIT MARGIN	EMPLOYEES
12/19	24,384	1,335	5.5%	70,600
12/18	22,090	2,155	9.8%	64,400
12/17	22,465	3,001	13.4%	61,100
12/16	23,002	3,499	15.2%	59,700
12/15	24,708	2,825	11.4%	61,500
Annual Growth	(0.3%)	(17.1%)	—	3.5%

2019 Year-End Financials

Debt ratio: 28.6%	No. of shares (mil.): 1,312
Return on equity: 10.4%	Dividends
Cash ($ mil.): 5,369	Yield: 2.7%
Current ratio: 0.86	Payout: 133.0%
Long-term debt ($ mil.): 15,730	Market value ($ mil.): 65,423

	STOCK PRICE ($) FY Close	P/E High/Low		PER SHARE ($) Earnings	Dividends	Book Value
12/19	49.86	49	34	1.03	1.37	10.00
12/18	37.98	24	19	1.70	1.37	9.84
12/17	34.70	15	11	2.37	1.37	11.81
12/16	27.32	12	9	2.76	1.37	11.74
12/15	33.95	33	14	2.23	1.38	14.63
Annual Growth	10.1%		—	(17.6%)	(0.2%)	(9.1%)

Athene Holding Ltd

Auditors: PricewaterhouseCoopers LLP

LOCATIONS

HQ: Athene Holding Ltd
96 Pitts Bay Road, Pembroke HM 08
Phone: (1) 441 279 8400
Web: www.athene.com

HISTORICAL FINANCIALS

Company Type: Public

Income Statement

	ASSETS ($ mil.)	NET INCOME ($ mil.)	INCOME AS % OF ASSETS	EMPLOYEES
12/19	146,875	2,172	1.5%	1,325
12/18	125,505	1,053	0.8%	1,275
12/17	99,747	1,448	1.5%	1,125
12/16	86,720	805	0.9%	1,125
12/15	80,854	562	0.7%	1,360
Annual Growth	16.1%	40.2%	—	(0.6%)

FYE: December 31

2019 Year-End Financials

Return on assets: 1.5%
Return on equity: 20.0%
Long-term debt ($ mil.): —
No. of shares (mil.): 177
Sales ($ mil): 16,258

Dividends
Yield: —
Payout: —
Market value ($ mil.): —

Atlantia SPA

Holding company Atlantia (formerly Autostrade) has taken a toll on Italy's motorways. Through its main subsidiary Autostrade per l'Italia the company oversees more than 3400 km (2100 miles) of highways in Italy and it built one of the major roads that leads to Rome the Autostrada del Sole. The company's roads account for more than 60% of Italy's toll road network. It also has invested in tollway projects outside of Italy. The holding company changed its name from Autostrade to Atlantia in 2007. An investment group led by a Benetton family holding company (which controls the clothing maker by the same name) is Atlantia's largest shareholder with a 40% stake.

EXECUTIVES

CEO Atlantia and Autostrade Italy, Giovanni Castellucci, age 61
CFO, Giancarlo Guenzi, age 64
President, Fabio Cerchiai, age 76
Auditors: Deloitte & Touche S.p.A.

LOCATIONS

HQ: Atlantia SPA
Via Antonio Nibby, 20, Rome 00161
Phone: (39) 06 44172652   **Fax:** (39) 06 44172696
Web: www.atlantia.it

2015

	% of total
Italy	87
Brazil	6
Chile	5
United States	1
Poland	1
Total	**100**

PRODUCTS/OPERATIONS

2015 Sales

	% of total
Italian motorways	71
Italian airport	15
Overseas motorways	10
Atlantia and Other Activities	4
Total	**100**

COMPETITORS

ASTM	Cintra
Abertis	EIFFAGE
Autoroutes du Sud de la France	VINCI

HISTORICAL FINANCIALS

Company Type: Public

Income Statement

	REVENUE ($ mil.)	NET INCOME ($ mil.)	NET PROFIT MARGIN	EMPLOYEES
12/19	14,163	152	1.1%	30,633
12/18	8,505	936	11.0%	30,903
12/17	7,651	1,404	18.4%	15,394
12/16	6,525	1,184	18.2%	14,584
12/15	6,557	928	14.2%	14,406
Annual Growth	21.2%	(36.3%)	—	20.8%

FYE: December 31

2019 Year-End Financials

Debt ratio: 63.1%
Return on equity: 1.7%
Cash ($ mil.): 6,360
Current ratio: 0.96
Long-term debt ($ mil.): 46,967

No. of shares (mil.): 818
Dividends
Yield: 2.8%
Payout: 172.4%
Market value ($ mil.): 9,554

	STOCK PRICE ($) FY Close	P/E High/Low	PER SHARE ($) Earnings	Dividends	Book Value
12/19	11.68	82 60	0.19	0.33	10.17
12/18	10.41	16 10	1.15	0.47	11.82
12/17	15.77	12 9	1.71	0.43	12.86
12/16	11.64	10 7	1.44	0.31	9.30
12/15	13.20	13 10	1.13	0.30	8.99
Annual Growth	(3.0%)	—	(35.9%)	2.5%	3.1%

Atlas Copco AB (Sweden)

Atlas Copco has the globe covered with products and services that enhance industrial productivity. Serving all major continents the group is one of the world's largest manufacturer of air compressors. It also sells and rents such equipment as expanders and air treatment systems vacuum systems used in semiconductor manufacturing drilling and rock excavation equipment construction and demolition tools and power tools and assembly systems. Its products are used by a wide range of industries from aerospace and automotive to infrastructure and oil and gas. Based in Stockholm Sweden Atlas Copco has customers in 100 countries and generates revenue evenly across the globe.

Operations

Atlas Copco is organized into four business segments: Compressor Technique Vacuum Technique Industrial Technique and Power Technique.

Compressor Technique is the largest at 45% of sales. It provides stationary and large gas and process compressors for use in the food pharmaceutical electronics and textile industries. Its compressors also power industrial tools with a wide range of applications. It also makes blowers which provide consistent low-pressure air for applications such as wastewater treatment and conveying.

The Vacuum Technique segment makes systems that provide low-pressure air serving the semiconductor manufacture industrial vacuum and scientific vacuum markets. Atlas Copco generates nearly a quarter of sales from vacuum products.

Industrial Technique (a fifth of sales) manufactures industrial power tools assembly systems quality assurance products and software and service. The auto industry represents more than half of segment sales. The fourth segment Power Technique represents around 10% of sales. It provides air power and flow solutions such as compressors pumps light towers and generators.

Overall sales of services account for about 35% of sales and equipment 65%.

Geographic Reach

Atlas Copco's global reach spans more than 180 markets in North America South America Europe the Middle East Africa and Asia/Pacific.

The group has an extensive manufacturing footprint spanning 20 countries though its factories are concentrated in Sweden Belgium France Germany Italy Czechia the UK US China India South Korea and Japan. Its distribution centers located in Europe and the US handle outbound logistics.

Sales and Marketing

Atlas Copco's products are sold and rented under different brands through a worldwide sales and service network. The company has its own sales operations (customer centers) in about 70 countries while in other countries its offerings are marketed through independent distributors and service networks.

Atlas Copco's biggest customer industries are general manufacturing process industry electronics motor vehicles and service which together account for nearly 90% of sales.

Financial Performance

Note: Growth rates may differ after conversion to US Dollars.

Atlas Copco's sales and profits are growing but not particularly dynamically.

In 2018 the company's sales grew 11% to SEK95.4 billion ($11 billion) thanks to revenue uplift in all segments. The Compressor Technique segment grew strongly thanks to increased demand in Europe and Asia particularly in China.

Net income jumped from SEK1.9 billion to SEK12.2 billion due to a gain on the sale of its mining and rock excavation business. Underlying profits were higher in line with revenue growth.

Atlas Copco's cash on hand fell SEK9.1 billion during 2018 ending the year at SEK16.4 billion. The company's operations generated SEK16.8 billion offset by the SEK4.3 billion used in its investing activities and SEK21.6 billion used in financing. Atlas Copco's main cash uses in 2018 were capital expenditures acquisitions dividends and share repurchases.

Strategy

Atlas Copco's strategy is four-fold: organically increasing its presence in growth markets (this includes making select acquisitions that support organic growth); strengthening its aftermarket business (which includes consumables parts service maintenance and training); developing new and improved products through research and development; and maintaining operational efficiency. The aftermarket business in particular provides a steady revenue stream that helps the company stay resilient in difficult economic times.

New products in recent times have included a new medical dryer oil-free screw compressors a flexible vacuum for industrial use a new type of test bench a quality assurance platform and fuel efficient generators. Atlas Copco also tightened its focus on industrial customers with the sale of its Mining and Rock Excavation business which was publicly floated and changed its name to Epiroc.

An established player in Europe Atlas Copco is trying to match that market presence particularly in Asia and North America. In China and the US for instance the company is growing through a combination of organic initiatives (new office and production facility openings) and acquisitions of smaller companies that round out its product portfolio in each of its four business areas. Atlas Copco isn't neglecting Europe however as it continues to make select acquisitions in markets like Belgium France Spain Sweden and Switzerland. In other territories Atlas Copco is winning large contract orders for equipment in South and Central America.

On the product development side Atlas Copco is launching a slate of energy-efficient products such as oil-free screw blowers large oil-injected screw compressors centrifugal compressors and a medical air vacuum system. It also unveiled various air products with a selection of dryers and a high-capacity filter.

Mergers and Acquisitions

Atlas Copco typically makes smaller "bolt-on" acquisitions of manufacturers and distributors around the world to support the three stages of its growth strategy: extending its core business building new businesses related to the core; and adding new technologies and markets.

In 2019 the company acquired the cryogenic business of Brooks Automation Inc. for $675 million. The deal includes cryo pump operations in Chelmsford Massachusetts and Monterrey Mexico a worldwide network of sales and service centers and Brooks Automation's 50% share of Ulvac Cryogenics Inc. It extends Atlas Copco's product line and geographic reach. The acquired business became part of the Semiconductor and Semiconductor Service divisions within Atlas Copco's Vacuum Technique business area.

In 2018 the company made five bolt-on acquisitions with combined revenue of SEK530 million and one disposal.

EXECUTIVES

SVP Controlling and Finance, Hans Ola Meyer, age 66

President Portable Air, Geert Follens, age 61

President CEO and Director, Mats Rahmstr ¶m, age 55

SEVP and President Construction Technique, Andrew Walker, age 59

President U.S. Division, Scott Carnell

SEVP and President Mining and Rock Excavation Technique, Helena Hedblom, age 48

SEVP and President Industrial Technique, Henrik Elmin, age 50

President Compressor Technique, Vagner Rego

Chairman, Hans Str berg, age 63

Auditors: Deloitte AB

LOCATIONS

HQ: Atlas Copco AB (Sweden)
Sickla Industrivag 19, Stockholm 105 23
Phone: (46) 8 743 80 00   **Fax:** (46) 8 643 37 18
Web: www.atlascopco.com

2018 Sales

	% of total
Europe	31
Asia & Australia	35
North America	24
Africa & Middle East	6
South America	4
Total	**100**

PRODUCTS/OPERATIONS

2018 Sales

	% of total
Compressor Technique	46
Vacuum Technique	23
Industrial Technique	19
Power Technique	12
Total	**100**

Selected Products

Compressor Technique
  Air dryers coolers filters
  Air treatment and gas purification equipment
  Air management systems
  Compressors (gas and process)
  Compressors (oil-free and oil-injected stationary)
  Compressors (portable)
  Electric power generators
  Specialty rental services
  Turbo expanders
Construction and Mining Technique
  Construction and demolition tools
  Drilling equipment (surface)
  Drilling tools (rock)
  Exploration drilling
  Loading equipment
  Mobile crushers and screeners
  Raiseboring equipment
  Rigs (underground rock drilling)
  Rigs (surface drilling)
  Road construction equipment
  Rock reinforcement and bolting
  Tunneling and mining equipment
  Water well gas coal bed methane
Industrial Technique
  Aftermarket products software and service
  Air motors
  Air assembly tools
  Drills
  Electrical assembly tools
  Fixtured applications
  Grinding
  Hoist and trolleys
  Pneumatic power tools and systems
  Power tools (industrial)

COMPETITORS

Apex Tool Group	Neff
Boart Longyear	Nordson
Cameron Compression	Parker-Hannifin
Caterpillar	Robert Bosch Tool
Doosan Infracore	Sany Heavy Industry
Ebara Technologies	Siemens AG
Gardner Denver	Stanley Black and
Graco	Decker
Hitachi	Sullair
Ingersoll-Rand	Wacker Neuson
MAN	

HISTORICAL FINANCIALS

Company Type: Public

Income Statement				FYE: December 31
	REVENUE ($ mil.)	NET INCOME ($ mil.)	NET PROFIT MARGIN	EMPLOYEES
12/19	17,363	2,764	15.9%	38,774
12/18	15,958	17,766	111.3%	36,862
12/17	19,482	2,789	14.3%	47,599
12/16	16,961	1,996	11.8%	44,695
12/15	17,096	1,960	11.5%	43,588
Annual Growth	0.4%	9.0%	—	(2.9%)

2019 Year-End Financials

Debt ratio: 3.1%
Return on equity: 34.5%
Cash ($ mil.): 2,511
Current ratio: 1.77
Long-term debt ($ mil.): 2,967
No. of shares (mil.): 1,217
Dividends
  Yield: 1.6%
  Payout: 28.8%
Market value ($ mil.): 48,864

	STOCK PRICE ($) FY Close	P/E High/Low		PER SHARE ($) Earnings	Dividends	Book Value
12/19	40.15	3	2	2.27	0.66	7.32
12/18	23.93	1	0	14.62	11.90	5.85
12/17	43.10	3	2	2.28	0.79	8.36
12/16	30.54	3	2	1.64	0.74	7.32
12/15	24.42	4	2	1.60	1.44	6.41
Annual Growth	13.2%	—	—	9.1%	(17.9%)	3.4%

Atos Origin

Auditors: Deloitte & Associés

LOCATIONS

HQ: Atos Origin
  River Ouest, 80, Quai Voltaire, Bezons 95870
Phone: (33) 1 73 26 00 00
Web: www.atos.net

HISTORICAL FINANCIALS

Company Type: Public

Income Statement				FYE: December 31
	REVENUE ($ mil.)	NET INCOME ($ mil.)	NET PROFIT MARGIN	EMPLOYEES
12/19	13,173	3,816	29.0%	108,317
12/18	14,227	721	5.1%	122,110
12/17	15,358	720	4.7%	97,267
12/16	12,459	611	4.9%	97,337
12/15	11,737	442	3.8%	91,322
Annual Growth	2.9%	71.4%	—	4.4%

2019 Year-End Financials

Debt ratio: 24.9%
Return on equity: 51.7%
Cash ($ mil.): 2,709
Current ratio: 1.09
Long-term debt ($ mil.): 2,976
No. of shares (mil.): 108
Dividends
  Yield: 31.5%
  Payout: 14.9%
Market value ($ mil.): 1,817

	STOCK PRICE ($) FY Close	P/E High/Low		PER SHARE ($) Earnings	Dividends	Book Value
12/19	16.73	1	0	35.43	5.28	73.12
12/18	16.26	5	3	6.81	0.39	65.11
12/17	29.15	6	4	6.83	0.38	53.17
12/16	21.07	4	2	5.86	0.23	43.52
12/15	16.90	4	4	4.34	0.18	40.71
Annual Growth	(0.3%)	—	—	69.1%	133.2%	15.8%

AUDI AG

Auditors: PricewaterhouseCoopers GmbH

LOCATIONS

HQ: AUDI AG
  Auto-Union-Strasse 1, Ingolstadt D-85045
Phone: (49) 841 89 0   **Fax:** (49) 841 89 325 24
Web: www.audi.com

HISTORICAL FINANCIALS
Company Type: Public

Income Statement
FYE: December 31

	REVENUE ($ mil.)	NET INCOME ($ mil.)	NET PROFIT MARGIN	EMPLOYEES
12/19	62,515	4,322	6.9%	90,640
12/18	67,850	3,873	5.7%	91,674
12/17	72,078	4,261	5.9%	90,402
12/16	62,631	2,095	3.3%	87,112
12/15	63,631	4,579	7.2%	82,838
Annual Growth	(0.4%)	(1.4%)	—	2.3%

2019 Year-End Financials
Debt ratio: 1.7%
Return on equity: 13.5%
Cash ($ mil.): 13,171
Current ratio: 1.46
Long-term debt ($ mil.): 908

No. of shares (mil.): 43
Dividends
  Yield: —
  Payout: —
Market value ($ mil.): —

Australia & New Zealand Banking Group Ltd

Auditors: KPMG

LOCATIONS
HQ: Australia & New Zealand Banking Group Ltd
ANZ Centre Melbourne, Level 9, 833 Collins Street,
Docklands, Victoria 3008
Phone: (61) 3 9273 5555   **Fax:** (61) 3 8542 5252
Web: www.anz.com

HISTORICAL FINANCIALS
Company Type: Public

Income Statement
FYE: September 30

	ASSETS ($ mil.)	NET INCOME ($ mil.)	INCOME AS % OF ASSETS	EMPLOYEES
09/20	741,812	2,545	0.3%	38,579
09/19	662,905	4,022	0.6%	39,060
09/18	679,851	4,615	0.7%	39,924
09/17	703,341	5,021	0.7%	44,896
09/16	696,998	4,349	0.6%	46,554
Annual Growth	1.6%	(12.5%)	—	(4.6%)

2020 Year-End Financials
Return on assets: 0.3%
Return on equity: 5.8%
Long-term debt ($ mil.): —
No. of shares (mil.): —
Sales ($ mil): 19,938

Dividends
  Yield: 5.6%
  Payout: 85.7%
Market value ($ mil.): —

	STOCK PRICE ($) FY Close	P/E High/Low		PER SHARE ($) Earnings	Dividends	Book Value
09/20	12.46	16	8	0.84	0.71	15.36
09/19	19.21	9	7	1.36	1.11	14.49
09/18	20.20	10	9	1.53	1.12	14.87
09/17	23.36	12	9	1.65	1.22	15.73
09/16	21.25	11	9	1.44	1.26	15.10
Annual Growth	(12.5%)	—	—	(12.6%)	(13.5%)	0.4%

Awa Bank, Ltd.

When it comes to serving customers in the Tokushima Prefecture few financial institutions go "way back" like Awa Bank. Established in 1896 the bank serves both private and corporate customers offering the typical array of banking products such as savings foreign and domestic exchanges credit cards and ATM maintenance. Its lending operations includes loans for houses cars and education while its leasing segment provides equipment leasing services to small and midsized businesses. Awa Bank operates through a network of more than 90 branches and four subsidiaries.

Operations
The Bank has two business segments. Its Banking segment is engaged in deposit loan securities investment and domestic exchange and foreign exchange businesses as well as the sale of public bond investment trust and insurance products. The Leasing segment offers leasing services.
Auditors: KPMG AZSA LLC

LOCATIONS
HQ: Awa Bank, Ltd.
2-24-1 Nishi-Sembacho, Tokushima 770-8601
Phone: (81) 88 623 3131
Web: www.awabank.co.jp

COMPETITORS
Chugoku Bank   Shikoku Bank
Hyakujushi Bank
Mitsubishi UFJ
  Financial Group

HISTORICAL FINANCIALS
Company Type: Public

Income Statement
FYE: March 31

	ASSETS ($ mil.)	NET INCOME ($ mil.)	INCOME AS % OF ASSETS	EMPLOYEES
03/20	31,102	102	0.3%	1,874
03/19	30,076	98	0.3%	1,880
03/18	30,932	111	0.4%	1,890
03/17	28,673	111	0.4%	1,909
03/16	27,749	115	0.4%	1,925
Annual Growth	2.9%	(2.9%)	—	(0.7%)

2020 Year-End Financials
Return on assets: 0.3%
Return on equity: 4.2%
Long-term debt ($ mil.): —
No. of shares (mil.): 42
Sales ($ mil): 613

Dividends
  Yield: —
  Payout: —
Market value ($ mil.): —

AXA SA

Auditors: Mazars

LOCATIONS
HQ: AXA SA
25, Avenue Matignon, Paris 75008
Phone: (33) 1 40 75 48 43
Web: www.axa.com

HISTORICAL FINANCIALS
Company Type: Public

Income Statement
FYE: December 31

	ASSETS ($ mil.)	NET INCOME ($ mil.)	INCOME AS % OF ASSETS	EMPLOYEES
12/19	876,743	4,330	0.5%	120,869
12/18	1,065,827	2,450	0.2%	104,065
12/17	1,043,069	7,443	0.7%	95,728
12/16	942,674	6,154	0.7%	97,707
12/15	966,206	6,118	0.6%	98,279
Annual Growth	(2.4%)	(8.3%)	—	5.3%

2019 Year-End Financials
Return on assets: 0.4%
Return on equity: 5.8%
Long-term debt ($ mil.): —
No. of shares (mil.): —
Sales ($ mil): 140,271

Dividends
  Yield: 5.3%
  Payout: 88.3%
Market value ($ mil.): —

	STOCK PRICE ($) FY Close	P/E High/Low		PER SHARE ($) Earnings	Dividends	Book Value
12/19	28.15	19	14	1.70	1.50	32.89
12/18	21.39	40	27	0.90	1.50	30.00
12/17	29.67	13	11	2.98	2.78	35.01
12/16	25.20	11	8	2.43	2.30	30.81
12/15	27.32	13	9	2.37	1.07	30.76
Annual Growth	0.8%	—	—	(8.1%)	8.9%	1.7%

BAE Systems Plc

BAE Systems helped win the Battle of Britain in 1940 with its Spitfire and Mosquito fighters; today it is one of the leading military contractors and major foreign players in the US defense market. BAE's main products and services provide land air and sea combat and support vehicles; weapons systems; cyber defense; and electronic sensors and systems. Based in the UK BAE has close ties with the UK Government but its biggest market is the US which it supplies through BAE Systems Inc one of the biggest suppliers to the US Department of Defense. BAE's fighter aircraft include the Hawk Tornado and the next-generation Eurofighter Typhoon.

Operations
BAE Systems operates through five primary segments: Electronic Systems Cyber & Intelligence Platforms & Services (US) Air and Maritime.

Air is the largest segment bringing in more than 35% of sales. It designs upgrade and builds fixed-wing military and training aircraft and provides training support and information services to the Royal Air Force and other customers worldwide. Its primary airframes are the Eurofighter Typhoon the Hawk Advanced Jet Trainer and the Tornado.

Electronic Systems generates over 20% of sales and produces commercial and defense electronics for flight and engine control electronic warfare systems electro-optical sensors precision guidance and seeker solutions persistent surveillance capabilities communication systems and hybrid-electric drive systems.

Platforms and Services (US) accounts for more than 15% of sales and carries out the production and service support of armored combat and tactical vehicles military and commercial ships major and minor caliber naval guns and missile launchers canisters artillery systems intelligent munitions and armor systems.

Maritime generates about 15% of sales and designs and manufactures naval ships and submarines and compatible combat systems and equipment. The segment also provides an array of associated services including training maintenance and modernization programs to support ships and equipment.

Cyber & Intelligence accounts nearly 10% of sales and covers the company's cyber security secure government and commercial financial security activities.

Overall BAE generates about 40% of sales from Military and technical services support nearly 35% from Platforms more than 20% from Electronic Systems and about 5% from Cyber.

Geographic Reach

UK-based BAE Systems has major operations in the UK US Australia and Saudi Arabia.

The US generates about 45% of sales Other International Markets more than 20% the UK almost 20% Saudi Arabia close to 15% and Australia nearly 5%.

Sales and Marketing

BAE's largest customers are the US UK and Saudi Arabia governments. As well as governments BAE also sells to large prime contractors and commercial businesses.

The company engages third parties to assist sales and marketing activities of BAE.

Financial Performance

BAE's sales grew 9% from Å 16.8 billion in 2018 to Å 18.3 billion in 2019. The growth is due to the increase in sales on all of the company's segments.

2019's net income grew 48% to Å 1.5 billion compared to Å 1 billion in 2018.

BAE Systems cash at the end of 2019 was Å 2.6 billion. Operating activities generated Å 1.6 billion. Investing activities used Å 232 million with another Å 2 billion used in financing activities.

Strategy

BAE's strategy is comprised of five key long-term areas of focus that will help the company to achieve its vision and mission. It is centered on maintaining and growing our core franchises and securing growth opportunities through advancing our three strategic priorities and demonstrating the Company behaviors.

The five key long-term areas consists of maintaining and growing the company's defense business; Continuing to grow business in adjacent markets; developing and expanding international business; inspiring and developing a diverse workforce to drive success; and Enhancing financial performance and deliver sustainable growth in shareholder value.

Mergers and Acquisitions

In mid-2020 BAE Systems acquired Raytheon's Airborne Tactical Radios for $275 million. Raytheon based in Massachusetts US is one of the industry's leading providers of battle-tested products and capabilities that will expand the company's Electronic Systems Portfolio.

In early 2020 BAE Systems entered into an agreement to acquire Collins Aerospace's Military Global Positioning System for $1.9 billion. Collins Aerospace based in Florida US is one of the leading providers of mission critical military GPS receiver solutions. The acquisition will also contribute to the company's Electronic Systems Portfolio.

In late 2019 BAE Systems acquired Prismatic Ltd. UK-based company Prismatic Ltd. designs and demonstrates novel high value aerospace systems. The acquisition will help the company to develop a revolutionary solar powered aircraft.

In mid-2019 BAe Systems acquirew Riptide Autonomous Solutions (Riptide). Riptide is based in Massachusetts U.S. and a provider of innovative affordable unmanned underwater vehicle (UUV) technology and solutions. The acquisition will enable the company to address rapidly expanding maritime mission requirements.

Company Background

Post-Wright brothers and pre-WWII a host of aviation companies sprang up to serve the British Empire — too many to survive after the war when the empire contracted. Parliament took steps in 1960 to save the industry by merging companies to form larger stronger entities — Hawker-Siddeley Aviation and British Aircraft Corporation (BAC).

Hawker-Siddeley made up of aircraft and missiles divisions was created by combining A.V. Roe Gloster Aircraft Hawker Aircraft Armstrong Whitworth and Folland Aircraft. It attained fame in the 1960s for developing the Harrier "jump jet."

BAC was formed from the merger of Bristol Aeroplane English Electric and Vicker-Armstrong. In 1962 it joined France's Aerospatiale to build the supersonic Concorde and became a partner in ventures to develop the Tornado and Jaguar fighters. The cost of these ventures plus the commercial failure of the Concorde was more than the company could bear. Realizing British aviation was again in trouble the British government nationalized BAC and Hawker-Siddeley in 1976 and merged them in 1977 with Scottish Aviation to form British Aerospace (BAe).

HISTORY

Post-Wright brothers and pre-WWII a host of aviation companies sprang up to serve the British Empire — too many to survive after the war when the empire contracted. Parliament took steps in 1960 to save the industry by merging companies to form larger stronger entities — Hawker-Siddeley Aviation and British Aircraft Corporation (BAC).

Hawker-Siddeley made up of aircraft and missiles divisions was created by combining A.V. Roe Gloster Aircraft Hawker Aircraft Armstrong Whitworth and Folland Aircraft. It attained fame in the 1960s for developing the Harrier "jump jet."

BAC was formed from the merger of Bristol Aeroplane English Electric and Vicker-Armstrong. In 1962 it joined France's Aerospatiale to build the supersonic Concorde and became a partner in ventures to develop the Tornado and Jaguar fighters. The cost of these ventures plus the commercial failure of the Concorde was more than the company could bear. Realizing British aviation was again in trouble the British government nationalized BAC and Hawker-Siddeley in 1976 and merged them in 1977 with Scottish Aviation to form British Aerospace (BAe).

EXECUTIVES

Group Managing Director Programmes and Support, Nigel Whitehead
COO BAE Systems Inc. and President Electronic Systems, Tom Arseneault
Managing Director BAE Systems Applied Intelligence, Kevin Taylor
CEO, Charles Woodburn, age 48
Group Managing Director International, Guy Griffiths
Group Finance Director, Peter Lynas
President and CEO BAE Systems Inc., Jerry Demuro
Chairman, Roger Carr
Auditors: Deloitte LLP

LOCATIONS

HQ: BAE Systems Plc
  6 Carlton Gardens, London SW1Y 5AD
Phone: (44) 1252 373232
Web: www.baesystems.com

2018 Sales

	% of total
US	46
UK	22
Saudi Arabia	15
Rest of Europe	7
Rest of Middle East	4
Australia	3
Canada	3
Rest of Asia and Pacific	-
Total	**100**

PRODUCTS/OPERATIONS

2018 Sales

	% of total
Air	33
Electronic Systems	23
Maritime	17
Platforms & Services (US)	17
Cyber & Intelligence	10
Total	**100**

COMPETITORS

Aerojet Rocketdyne	ITT Corp.
Airbus Group	L3 Technologies
Astronautics	Leonardo
Boeing	Lockheed Martin
Bombardier	Meggitt-USA
DRS Technologies	Navistar International
Fabbrica D'Armi Pietro	Northrop Grumman
Beretta	RUAG Holding
General Dynamics	Rockwell Collins
Honeywell	Sotera Defense
International	Thales
Horstman Defence	Ultra Electronics
Systems	United Technologies

HISTORICAL FINANCIALS

Company Type: Public

Income Statement				FYE: December 31
	REVENUE ($ mil.)	NET INCOME ($ mil.)	NET PROFIT MARGIN	EMPLOYEES
12/19	24,172	1,949	8.1%	87,800
12/18	21,476	1,276	5.9%	78,000
12/17	24,747	1,153	4.7%	76,000
12/16	21,884	1,123	5.1%	76,000
12/15	24,877	1,360	5.5%	75,000
Annual Growth	(0.7%)	9.4%	—	4.0%

2019 Year-End Financials

Debt ratio: 17.5%
Return on equity: 26.9%
Cash ($ mil.): 3,416
Current ratio: 1.01
Long-term debt ($ mil.): 3,988

No. of shares (mil.): —
Dividends
  Yield: 3.6%
  Payout: 186.4%
Market value ($ mil.): —

	STOCK PRICE ($) FY Close	P/E High/Low	PER SHARE ($) Earnings	Dividends	Book Value
12/19	30.28	67 50	0.61	1.11	2.23
12/18	23.42	112 73	0.40	1.11	2.22
12/17	31.18	138 110	0.36	1.13	2.01
12/16	29.03	106 79	0.35	1.01	1.33
12/15	29.46	114 87	0.43	1.21	1.40
Annual Growth	0.7%	—	9.2%	(2.1%)	12.3%

Baidu Inc

Auditors: Ernst & Young Hua Ming LLP

LOCATIONS

HQ: Baidu Inc
Baidu Campus, No. 10 Shangdi 10th Street, Haidian
District, Beijing 100085
Phone: (86) 10 5992 8888   **Fax:** (86) 10 5992 0000
Web: www.baidu.com

HISTORICAL FINANCIALS

Company Type: Public

Income Statement   FYE: December 31

	REVENUE ($ mil.)	NET INCOME ($ mil.)	NET PROFIT MARGIN	EMPLOYEES
12/19	15,285	292	1.9%	37,779
12/18	14,554	3,923	27.0%	45,887
12/17	12,069	2,604	21.6%	39,343
12/16	10,039	1,655	16.5%	45,887
12/15	9,446	4,790	50.7%	41,467
Annual Growth	12.8%	(50.3%)	—	(2.3%)

2019 Year-End Financials

Debt ratio: 3.1%	No. of shares (mil.): 34
Return on equity: 1.2%	Dividends
Cash ($ mil.): 4,759	Yield: —
Current ratio: 2.89	Payout: —
Long-term debt ($ mil.): 8,281	Market value ($ mil.): 4,371

	STOCK PRICE ($) FY Close	P/E High/Low		PER SHARE ($) Earnings	Dividends	Book Value
12/19	126.40	3	2	7.96	0.00	673.21
12/18	158.60	0	0	111.04	0.00	663.56
12/17	234.21	1	0	74.58	0.00	471.47
12/16	164.41	1	0	45.34	0.00	378.13
12/15	189.04	0	0	135.40	0.00	330.03
Annual Growth	(9.6%)	—	—	(50.8%)	—	19.5%

Baloise Holding AG

Founded in 1863 as a fire insurance company B loise-Holding today is a general insurer that sells such standardized products as group and individual life policies and accident property and health insurance to small firms and individuals. The company is one of the leading insurers in Switzerland operating primarily there and in Germany; together the countries account for over 65% of its sales. Through subsidiaries it also operates in other nearby countries including Belgium and Luxembourg. B loise also provides banking pension plans and other financial services through its B loise Bank SoBa. The company uses its own sales force as well as partner distributors and independent brokers to sell its wares.

Operations

B loise operates through four segments: Non-Life Life Banking (including asset management) and Other Activities. Its Non-Life segment offers accident and health coverage as well as liability motor property and marine products which are primarily targeted towards retail clients. Life provides individuals and companies with endowment policies term insurance investment-linked products and private placement life insurance. B loise's Banking segment includes subsidiaries B loise

Bank SoBa in Switzerland while the group's Other Activities segment comprises investment companies real estate companies and financing firms. Life insurance accounts for nearly 45% of revenue while another more than 35% accounts in non life insurance and the remaining accounts the rest.

Geographic Reach

Switzerland accounts for more than 50% of B loise's revenues while the remaining accounts in Germany Belgium and Luxembourg. The group also has operations in Germany (including the regional branch of Basler versicherungs). In Luxembourg the company operates B loise Assurance.

Its head office is located in Basel.

Sales and Marketing

The company sells its products through its own sales department as well as partners and outside brokers. It serves private and corporate end customers at all Baloise locations.

Financial Performance

Baloise has reported increasing revenue from 2015 to 2017 a fall in revenue in 2018 and a rise again in 2019. Revenue increased by 24% for the past five years. Net income followed a similar trend reporting a 36% increase for the past five years.

Revenue increased from CHF 7.3 billion in 2018 to CHF 11 billion in 2019. Revenue increase resulted from an increase in premiums earned and policy fees realized gains and losses on investments and premiums earned and policy fees offset by a decrease in investment income and income from services rendered.

Net income was CHF 689.5 million a 32% increase from the previous year.

Strategy

Last year Baloise sharpened its strategic focus. It used its insights from the first three years of the Simply Safe strategic phase to set priorities for its digital initiatives. Baloise had initially experimented in various different areas gaining invaluable experience but is now concentrating on the 'Home' and 'Mobility' ecosystems. This is where it sees the greatest opportunities for building on its robust core business by expanding the portfolio of services for its customers.

Baloise also made huge progress with strengthening optimizing and diversifying its core business. In the life business it is continuing to improve the business mix by focusing on risk and unit-linked products. The company also capitalized on the opportunities for growth in Switzerland presented by the withdrawal of a competitor. The strategic reallocation of the non-life portfolio in Germany is having a positive impact. The German business's turnaround is reflected in a considerable increase in new customers.

The 2019 results for the Luxembourg business unit were also robust. Baloise unlocked opportunities and possibilities in Belgium's attractive non-life insurance market when it acquired insurance company Fidea NV in the first half of the year. The announced acquisition of Athora's non-life insurance portfolio will also markedly strengthen the market position of the Belgian business. These two acquisitions will underpin Belgium's role as a second key pillar within the Baloise Group alongside the Swiss business. They will also help to diversify the business. The Athora portfolio will significantly strengthen Baloise's position in the Wallonia region of Belgium.

Mergers and Acquisitions

In 2020 As part of a strategic partnership Baloise Asset Management is acquiring a stake in Zurich-based asset manager Tolomeo Capital AG. With this transaction Baloise Asset Management will further strengthen its position as one of Switzerland's leading rule-based asset managers. In addition it will exploit synergies and complementary capabilities in areas such as automated

investment solutions and alternative investments. Terms were not disclosed.

In 2020 Baloise has acquired two plots of land as part of the Giessen development in D bendorf. Plans for the approximately 35000 square metre site include the construction of 500 new homes as well as commercial units and green spaces by 2026. The acquisition of the land and the planned development expands Baloise's investment portfolio of rented property in highly attractive locations. Terms were not disclosed.

In 2019 As part of its Simply Safe strategy Baloise Asset Management part of the Baloise Group has acquired a stake in business start-up Brainalyzed a specialist in machine learning and artificial intelligence (AI). Following a two-year partnership and its first experiences with swarm-based artificial intelligence Baloise has decided to invest in the company. Brainalyzed's innovative approach to AI will help Baloise Asset Management to successfully expand its third-party asset management business.

Company Background

The Basler Versicherungs-Gesellschaft gegen Feuerschaden (Baloise Insurance Company for Fire Damage) is founded in 1863. Today it is known as the Baloise Group and operates in four countries under the umbrella of B loise Holding Ltd. At the time of its greatest geographical expansion around 1938 it had offices in about 50 countries worldwide.

HISTORY

In 1863 15 business leaders in Basel Switzerland formed the B loise Fire Insurance Company. This was followed in 1864 by the formation of the Baloise transportation and life insurance companies.

B loise-Holding was created in 1962 as a holding company for the previously independent insurance entities. In 1971 it merged all of its non-life companies into the Baloise Insurance Group.

Under its then-new chairman and president Rolf Sch uble B loise-Holding began in 1993 to reorganize its operations as it implemented a new corporate strategy. Key components of the strategy included a focus on the company's core European markets and a pattern of discarding less-profitable businesses. In 1998 B loise-Holding sold off its US operations.

Strengthening its position as a full-fledged financial services company in 2000 B loise acquired Swiss bank Solothurner (now B loise Bank SoBa).

The same year it purchased Belgian bank HBK-Spaarbank Belgian insurer Amazon Insurance N.V. and Swiss regional bank Solothurner Bank SoBa.

EXECUTIVES

Head Asset Management, Martin Wenk, age 63
CFO, German Egloff, age 62
Head Corporate Center, Thomas Sieber
CEO Basler Germany, Jan De Meulder
CEO Basler Switzerland, Michael Mueller
Group CEO, Gert De Winter
Auditors: Ernst & Young Ltd.

LOCATIONS

HQ: Baloise Holding AG
Aeschengraben 21, Basel CH-4002
Phone: (41) 58 285 89 42   **Fax:** (41) 58 285 70 70
Web: www.baloise.com

2014 Sales

	% of total
Switzerland	48
Germany	18
Belgium	17
Luxembourg	16
Other	1
Total	**100**

PRODUCTS/OPERATIONS

2014 Sales

	% of total
Non-life insurance	47
Life	53
Total	**100**

Selected Subsidiaries

Austria
Basler Versicherungen (insurance and pension products for private and business clients)
Belgium
Mercator Verzekeringen (personal and property insurance for individuals and small to mid-sized businesses)
Germany
Basler Versicherungen (personal and property insurance for individuals small and mid-sized enterprises and selected industrial clients)
Deutscher Ring (insurance and pension products for individuals)
Luxembourg
Bâloise Assurances (life personal and property insurance for private and business clients)
Switzerland
Bâloise Bank SoBa (banking products and services)
Basler Versicherungen (insurance and pension products for individuals and small to mid-sized enterprises)

COMPETITORS

AEGON	Helvetia Group
AIG	ING
AXA	Ita sa
AXA Versicherungen	Munich Re Group
Achmea	Prudential plc
Allianz	Swiss Life
Hannover Re	Zurich Insurance Group

HISTORICAL FINANCIALS
Company Type: Public

Income Statement
FYE: December 31

	ASSETS ($ mil.)	NET INCOME ($ mil.)	INCOME AS % OF ASSETS	EMPLOYEES
12/19	90,015	718	0.8%	7,646
12/18	82,193	531	0.6%	7,203
12/17	86,605	561	0.6%	7,286
12/16	79,196	525	0.7%	7,270
12/15	79,331	515	0.7%	7,387
Annual Growth	3.2%	8.6%	—	0.9%

2019 Year-End Financials
Return on assets: 0.8%
Return on equity: 10.9%
Long-term debt ($ mil.): —
No. of shares (mil.): 45
Sales ($ mil): 11,281
Dividends
Yield: 0.0%
Payout: 2.2%
Market value ($ mil.): 826

	STOCK PRICE ($) FY Close	P/E High/Low		PER SHARE ($) Earnings	Dividends	Book Value
12/19	18.13	1	1	15.51	0.36	152.44
12/18	14.92	1	1	11.30	0.32	130.30
12/17	15.24	1	1	11.76	0.31	136.98
12/16	12.48	1	1	11.02	0.28	118.74
12/15	12.70	1	1	10.72	0.29	117.44
Annual Growth	9.3%	—	—	9.7%	4.9%	6.7%

Banco BBVA Argentina SA

EXECUTIVES

President, Mar a Isabel Goiri
Vice President, Jorge Delfin Luna
Vice President, Alfredo Castillo
Auditors: KPMG

LOCATIONS

HQ: Banco BBVA Argentina SA
111 Cordoba Av, Buenos Aires C1054
Phone: (54) 11 4346 4286   **Fax:** (54) 11 4346 4000
Web: www.bancofrances.com.ar

COMPETITORS

Banco Bradesco	Banco do Brasil
Banco Galicia	Ita Unibanco
Banco Macro	Santander R o
Banco de Chile	
Banco de la Naci n Argentina	

HISTORICAL FINANCIALS
Company Type: Public

Income Statement
FYE: December 31

	ASSETS ($ mil.)	NET INCOME ($ mil.)	INCOME AS % OF ASSETS	EMPLOYEES
12/19	143,631	5,068	3.5%	6,302
12/18	114,337	(471)	—	6,089
12/17	100,815	602	0.6%	6,082
12/16	47,991	1,152	2.4%	6,253
12/15	35,020	1,196	3.4%	5,784
Annual Growth	42.3%	43.5%		2.2%

2019 Year-End Financials
Return on assets: 3.9%
Return on equity: 24.9%
Long-term debt ($ mil.): —
No. of shares (mil.): 612
Sales ($ mil): 51,581
Dividends
Yield: 4.6%
Payout: 235.1%
Market value ($ mil.): 3,413

	STOCK PRICE ($) FY Close	P/E High/Low		PER SHARE ($) Earnings	Dividends	Book Value
12/19	5.57	1	0	8.27	0.26	42.72
12/18	11.33	—	—	(0.77)	0.46	23.49
12/17	25.20	8	5	1.06	0.25	25.33
12/16	17.43	—	—	2.15	0.00	9.70
12/15	19.08	—	—	2.23	0.00	8.08
Annual Growth	(26.5%)	—	—	38.8%	—	51.6%

Banco Bilbao Vizcaya Argentaria SA (BBVA)

Auditors: KPMG Auditores, S.L.

LOCATIONS

HQ: Banco Bilbao Vizcaya Argentaria SA (BBVA)
Plaza San Nicolas 4, Bilbao
Phone: (34) 91 537 7000   **Fax:** (34) 91 537 6766
Web: www.bbva.com

HISTORICAL FINANCIALS
Company Type: Public

Income Statement
FYE: December 31

	ASSETS ($ mil.)	NET INCOME ($ mil.)	INCOME AS % OF ASSETS	EMPLOYEES
12/19	1,099,458	5,526	0.5%	126,973
12/18	1,064,838	8,377	0.8%	125,627
12/17	1,085,877	5,537	0.5%	131,856
12/16	1,151,648	5,468	0.5%	134,792
12/15	1,180,323	4,157	0.4%	137,968
Annual Growth	(1.8%)	7.4%	—	(2.1%)

2019 Year-End Financials
Return on assets: 0.5%
Return on equity: 7.3%
Long-term debt ($ mil.): —
No. of shares (mil.): —
Sales ($ mil): 68,712
Dividends
Yield: 5.2%
Payout: 39.2%
Market value ($ mil.): —

	STOCK PRICE ($) FY Close	P/E High/Low		PER SHARE ($) Earnings	Dividends	Book Value
12/19	5.58	14	10	0.74	0.29	11.52
12/18	5.29	13	7	1.20	0.30	11.20
12/17	8.50	19	13	0.76	0.33	10.96
12/16	6.77	15	11	0.79	0.41	11.36
12/15	7.33	27	19	0.61	0.41	11.76
Annual Growth	(6.6%)	—	—	4.8%	(8.2%)	(0.5%)

Banco Bradesco SA

Auditors: KPMG Auditores Independentes

LOCATIONS

HQ: Banco Bradesco SA
Cidade de Deus S/N, Vila Yara, Sao Paulo, Osasco
06029-900
Phone: (55) 11 3684 4011   **Fax:** (55) 11 3684 3213
Web: www.bradesco.com.br

HISTORICAL FINANCIALS
Company Type: Public

Income Statement
FYE: December 31

	ASSETS ($ mil.)	NET INCOME ($ mil.)	INCOME AS % OF ASSETS	EMPLOYEES
12/19	342,942	5,229	1.5%	97,329
12/18	336,383	4,272	1.3%	98,605
12/17	369,587	5,158	1.4%	98,808
12/16	366,250	5,498	1.5%	108,793
12/15	259,228	4,578	1.8%	0
Annual Growth	7.2%	3.4%		

2019 Year-End Financials
Return on assets: 1.5%
Return on equity: 16.2%
Long-term debt ($ mil.): —
No. of shares (mil.): —
Sales ($ mil): 39,580
Dividends
Yield: 5.3%
Payout: 65.9%
Market value ($ mil.): —

	STOCK PRICE ($) FY Close	P/E High/Low		PER SHARE ($) Earnings	Dividends	Book Value
12/19	8.95	5	3	0.62	0.44	4.18
12/18	9.89	5	3	0.51	0.19	3.99
12/17	10.24	5	3	0.67	0.21	4.85
12/16	8.71	5	2	0.65	0.21	4.03
12/15	4.81	5	2	0.54	0.19	2.85
Annual Growth	16.8%	—	—	3.4%	22.7%	10.0%

Banco BTG Pactual S.A.

LOCATIONS

HQ: Banco BTG Pactual S.A.
Av. Brigadeiro Faria Lima, 3477, Sao Paulo
Phone: (55) 11 3383 2159   **Fax:** (55) 11 3383 2001
Web: www.btgpactual.com

HISTORICAL FINANCIALS

Company Type: Public

Income Statement   FYE: December 31

	ASSETS ($ mil.)	NET INCOME ($ mil.)	INCOME AS % OF ASSETS	EMPLOYEES
12/19	41,382	1,000	2.4%	0
12/18	34,008	624	1.8%	0
12/17	35,460	719	2.0%	0
12/16	34,229	1,454	4.2%	0
12/15	61,353	186	0.3%	0
Annual Growth	(9.4%)	52.3%	—	—

2019 Year-End Financials

Return on assets: 2.7%
Return on equity: 19.8%
Long-term debt ($ mil.): —
No. of shares (mil.): 1,731
Sales ($ mil): 3,899

Dividends
 Yield: —
 Payout: —
 Market value ($ mil.): —

Banco Comercial Portugues SA

Auditors: Deloitte & Associados, SROC S.A.

LOCATIONS

HQ: Banco Comercial Portugues SA
Praca D. Joao I, 28, Porto 4000-295
Phone: (351) 21 321 1081   **Fax:** (351) 21 321 1079
Web: www.millenniumbcp.pt

HISTORICAL FINANCIALS

Company Type: Public

Income Statement   FYE: December 31

	ASSETS ($ mil.)	NET INCOME ($ mil.)	INCOME AS % OF ASSETS	EMPLOYEES
12/19	91,666	339	0.4%	18,585
12/18	86,946	344	0.4%	15,929
12/17	86,237	223	0.3%	15,727
12/16	75,247	25	0.0%	15,807
12/15	81,565	256	0.3%	17,252
Annual Growth	3.0%	7.2%	—	1.9%

2019 Year-End Financials

Return on assets: 0.3%
Return on equity: 5.0%
Long-term debt ($ mil.): —
No. of shares (mil.): —
Sales ($ mil): 3,303

Dividends
 Yield: —
 Payout: —
 Market value ($ mil.): —

Banco de Chile

Banco de Chile proffers a place for pesos. Chile's second-largest bank after Banco Santander Chile it has some 300 branches and 1400 ATMs in its home country as well as operations in Argentina Brazil China Mexico and the US. In addition to corporate and retail banking the company offers (through subsidiaries) mutual funds brokerage insurance financial planning factoring and other services. The Luksic family through such entities as Quiñenco and Sociedad Matriz Banco de Chile controls a majority of the bank. In 2008 Citigroup bought a 10% stake in the bank (with an option to acquire more) from Quiñenco and merged its Chilean operations into Banco de Chile.

EXECUTIVES

President of the Board, Pablo Granifo Lavin
First Vice President, Andr nico Luksic Craig
Second Vice President, Alvaro Jaramillo Escallon
Auditors: Ernst & Young Audit SpA

LOCATIONS

HQ: Banco de Chile
 Paseo Ahumada 251, Santiago
Phone: (56) 2 637 1111   **Fax:** (56) 2 653 5156
Web: www.bancochile.cl

COMPETITORS

BBVA Chile	Banco de Crédito e
BBVA Provida	Inversiones
Banco Santander Chile	CORPBANCA

HISTORICAL FINANCIALS

Company Type: Public

Income Statement   FYE: December 31

	ASSETS ($ mil.)	NET INCOME ($ mil.)	INCOME AS % OF ASSETS	EMPLOYEES
12/19	55,648	819	1.5%	13,562
12/18	51,320	869	1.7%	13,831
12/17	52,945	930	1.8%	14,023
12/16	47,026	862	1.8%	14,611
12/15	43,826	860	2.0%	14,973
Annual Growth	6.2%	(1.2%)	—	(2.4%)

2019 Year-End Financials

Return on assets: 1.5%
Return on equity: 15.9%
Long-term debt ($ mil.): —
No. of shares (mil): —
Sales ($ mil): 3,465

Dividends
 Yield: 3.7%
 Payout: 9,914.2%
 Market value ($ mil.): —

	STOCK PRICE ($) FY Close	P/E High/Low		PER SHARE ($) Earnings	Dividends	Book Value
12/19	20.99	5	4	0.01	0.79	0.05
12/18	28.60	15	5	0.01	0.77	0.05
12/17	96.53	17	13	0.01	0.75	0.06
12/16	70.45	13	11	0.01	0.76	0.05
12/15	59.41	11	10	0.01	0.80	0.04
Annual Growth	(22.9%)	—	—	(0.7%)	(0.3%)	4.8%

Banco De Sabadell SA

Banco de Sabadell (also known as BancoSabadell) is one of the top banking groups in Spain offering corporate commercial and private banking through more than 2400 branches mostly in Spain as well as in France Morocco the UK and the US. The company operates under five banking brands: SabadellAtl ntico and SabadellHerrero for business banking; SabadellSolbank which specializes in providing banking services for tourists and the tourism industry; ActivoBank for online banking; and SabadellUrquijo for private banking. BancoSabadell also offers insurance products through bancassurance along with asset management and securities brokerage services.

Operations

BancoSabadell operates four main business segments: Commercial Banking; Corporate Banking and Global Businesses; Markets and Private Banking; and Asset Management.The Commercial Banking division generates more than 80% of BancoSabadell's total revenue and provides traditional banking products and services to large and medium-sized businesses SMEs retailers and sole proprietors mostly under its SabadellAtl ntico brand in Spain as well as under a number of regional brand names. The division also operates bancassurance which provides insurance products.

Corporate Banking and Global Businesses (10% of overall revenue) provides corporate banking structured and corporate finance development capital consumer finance and national trade services serving mostly large corporations and financial institutions in Spain and overseas. The Markets and Private Banking segment (4% of overall revenue) provides savings and investment management services including securities market trading wealth management and custody services. The division comprises the group's SabadellUrquijo Private Banking business; Investment Products and Research unit; Treasury and Capital Markets unit; and Securities Trading and Custody Services unit.The Asset Management division (3% of overall revenue) manages real estate as well as non-performing assets through real estate asset manager Solvia. Solvia boasts a retail sales unit and sales teams that specializes in consolidating portfolio assets for sale to institutional buyers. It also liquidates assets with special or unusual features.The bank's foreign country affiliates include BS America (in Florida); and BancSabadell d'Andorra (in the Principality of Andorra) in which Banco Sabadell holds a nearly 51% controlling stake.

Geographic Reach

Most of the bank's 2400-plus branches are located in Spain though it also has branches in France Morocco the UK and the US (in Miami Florida). Additionally it has representative offices in Algeri Brazil China Dominican Republic India Mexico Poland Singapore Turkey Venezuela United Arab Emirates and the US.

Financial Performance

Note: Growth rates may differ after conversion to US dollars.

BancoSabadell's revenues and profits have been trending higher over the past few years thanks to growing fee income from the sale of managed investment products coupled with declining loan loss provisions as the bank has worked to de-risk its loan portfolio by selling off non-performing assets.

The bank's net interest income jumped by 25% to ?2.26 billion ($2.74 billion) in 2014 as the bank paid less in interest expense on deposits while net fee income and net trading income also grew by double-digits due to higher sales of managed investment products and services and higher capital gains respectively. Higher revenue in 2014 also pushed BancoSabadell's profit higher by a whopping 154% to ?371.68 million ($451.77 million) for the year.

Strategy

Banco Sabadell reiterated in 2015 its strategy toward improving profitability domestically which included three main priorities: to grow its existing domestic business by cross-selling its wide variety of services to existing customers and by leveraging its large scale to boost profit margins; continue to de-risk its loan portfolio and strengthen its balance sheet; and increase overall productivity across its operations without sacrificing service quality. These initiatives the company insists will help support future plans to expand internationally.

As part of its global expansion plans the bank announced in late 2015 that it would begin operations in Mexico for the first time and begin to introduce its business banking services before launching its banking services for individuals. Earlier during the year the bank acquired TSB Bank expanding its reach significantly in the UK market.

Toward its long-term balance sheet transformation strategy which spanned from 2014 through 2016 Banco Sabadell regularly sells its non-performing loan assets to de-risk its loan portfolio. To this end in 2014 for example the company sold a fully-provisioned loan portfolio (worth ?554 million or roughly $673 million) to international investor Aiqon Capital reducing the bank's exposure to non-strategic assets.

The company is not opposed to selling off underperforming parts of its business either to free up resources. In mid-2014 it sold its unpaid debt management and collection business to Lindorff Spain for a capital gain amounting to ?162 million (about $197 million).

Mergers and Acquisitions

In April 2014 the group purchased Britain-based TSB Banking Group plc from Lloyds Banking Group for Å 1.7 billion ($2.5 billion) as part of its global expansion plans. The deal meant that 22% of Sabadell's assets would be located outside of Spain compared with just 5% at present.

In 2014 Banco Sabadell purchased JGB Bank from GNB Holdings for some $49.6 million. Following the acquisition JGB Bank was folded into Sabadell United Bank (SUB) the group's Florida-based subsidiary.

In 2013 the bank purchased Lloyds Banking Group España from Lloyds TSB Bank Plc which included 28 branches and ?1.71 million in assets as well as Spanish subsidiaries Lloyds Bank International S.A.U. and Lloyds Investment España.

Company Background

Previously BancoSabadell acquired Miami-based Mellon United National Bank (which it rebranded Sabadell United Bank) and its 15 branches from The Bank of New York Mellon in 2010. The following year it acquired the assets and branches of the failed Lydian Private Bank further adding to its operations in the region. In 2007 the company acquired TransAtlantic Bank and BBVA's private banking business also both based in Miami.

Closer to home BancoSabadell acquired smaller rival Banco Guipuzcoano in 2010. The following year it acquired savings bank Caja de Ahorros del Mediterraneo (CAM) which had been seized by the government for a symbolic ?1. That deal brought some 5 million additional customers to the bank increased its assets by around 75% and upped its branch numbers by more than 900. CAM is now SabadellCAM.

EXECUTIVES

Managing Director, Jaime Guardiola Romojaro

General Manager, Tomas Varela Muina
General Manager, Miguel Montes Guell
Director-General Manager, Jose Luis Negro Rodriguez
Chairman, Jose Oliu Creus
Auditors: PricewaterhouseCoopers Auditores, S.L.

LOCATIONS

HQ: Banco De Sabadell SA
Avenida Oscar Espla, 37, Alicante 03007
Phone: (34) 93 902 323 000
Web: www.bancsabadell.com

PRODUCTS/OPERATIONS

2013 Sales

	% of total
Net interest income	44
Income from trading and exchange differences	38
Fee and Commission income	18
Total	**100**

2014 Sales

	%
Commercial Banking	83
Corporate Banking	10
Sabadell Urquijo Banking	2
Investment Managment	2
Real Estate Asset Management	3
Total	**100**

COMPETITORS

BBVA	Banco Popular Español
Banco Pastor	Grupo Santander

HISTORICAL FINANCIALS

Company Type: Public

Income Statement   FYE: December 31

	ASSETS ($ mil.)	NET INCOME ($ mil.)	INCOME AS % OF ASSETS	EMPLOYEES
12/19	251,222	862	0.3%	25,349
12/18	254,602	8	0.0%	15,319
12/17	265,342	4	0.0%	15,374
12/16	224,383	5	0.0%	26,022
12/15	227,239	4	0.0%	21,879
Annual Growth	2.5%	279.8%	—	3.7%

2019 Year-End Financials

Return on assets: 0.3%	Dividends
Return on equity: 6.1%	Yield: 0.0%
Long-term debt ($ mil.): —	Payout: 10.8%
No. of shares (mil.): —	Market value ($ mil.): —
Sales ($ mil): 7,905	

	STOCK PRICE ($) FY Close	P/E High/Low	PER SHARE ($) Earnings	Dividends	Book Value
12/19	2.42	20 12	0.15	0.02	2.57
12/18	2.44	87 47	0.06	0.11	2.42
12/17	4.10	31 24	0.17	0.08	2.76
12/16	3.01	27 18	0.14	0.03	2.41
12/15	3.35	59 25	0.14	0.42	2.41
Annual Growth	(7.8%)	— —	0.3%	(56.1%)	1.7%

Banco Santander Brasil SA

If you're looking for a place to park a "brazillion" dollars Banco Santander (Brasil) is there. The bank part of Spain's Banco Santander provides financial services through 3566 branches primarily in Brazil's south and southeast with a major presence in the states of S o Paulo and Rio Grande do Sul. Santander Brasil also offers wholesale banking to large corporations. Additional services include asset management private banking and insurance. In 2013 it launched a new category of specialized financial services (61 Santander Select branches with 400 relationship managers). The company accounts for about a quarter of its parent's revenues. Banco Santander owns more than 80% of Santander Brasil.

Company Background

The parent company listed approximately 15% of its shares of its Brazilian unit on the New York Stock Exchange in a 2009 IPO. It turned out to be the world's largest IPO that year raising some R$13 billion ($8 billion). The proceeds from the offering have been used to drive growth by funding new branches and lending. It is also growing its insurance and credit card businesses; the company recently began offering its Santander-Ferrari credit card.

In late 2010 Santander rebranded its Brazilian brands — Banco Real and Santander Brasil — under the same name and platform. (It completed similar restructuring efforts in the UK and Mexico.) The parent company has high hopes for its Latin American operations especially in the high-growth markets of Brazil and Mexico. As such Santander is committed to investing in those units as it solidifies its position as a leading global bank.

Santander Brasil is the result of the 2006 merger of Banco Santander banks Banco Santander Brasil Banco Santander Meridional and Banco do Estado de S o Paulo. The company added to its Brazilian bank empire when it acquired Banco Real in 2008. At the time Banco Real was the fourth largest non governmentowned Brazilian bank. The acquisition boosted Santander Brasil into the top three of banks in Brazil (along with Banco Bradesco and Ita Unibanco)

Brazil is a promising region of the world for banking. The country was a resilient market during the economic downturn. Employment levels rose and a new middle class emerged. As the Brazilian economy expands Santander Brasil expects lending and overall demand for banking services to grow.

EXECUTIVES

CEO, Claudio Melandri
Director Risk, Franco Rizza
General Counsel, Cristian Florence
CFO, Emiliano Muratore
Director Human Resources, Maria Eugenia de la Fuente
Director Technology and Operations, Ricardo Bartel
Vice Chairman, Oscar E. Von Chrismar, age 66
Chairman, Vittorio Corbo Lioi
Vice Chairman, Roberto Mendez Torres
Auditors: PricewaterhouseCoopers Auditores Independentes

LOCATIONS

HQ: Banco Santander Brasil SA
Avenida Presidente Juscelino Kubitschek, 2041 and 2235 Bloco A, Vila Olimpia, Sao Paulo 04543-011
Phone: (55) 11 3174 8589 **Fax:** (55) 11 3174 6751
Web: www.santander.com.br

PRODUCTS/OPERATIONS

2013 Sales

	% of total
Interest and similar income	82
Fee and commission income	17
Gains on financial transactons	1
Total	**100**

COMPETITORS

Banco Bradesco	Credicorp
Banco do Brasil	Ita Unibanco
Caixa Econ mica	
Federal	

HISTORICAL FINANCIALS

Company Type: Public

Income Statement				FYE: December 31
	REVENUE ($ mil.)	NET INCOME ($ mil.)	NET PROFIT MARGIN	EMPLOYEES
12/19	22,842	4,081	17.9%	47,819
12/18	21,023	3,241	15.4%	48,012
12/17	26,630	2,693	10.1%	47,404
12/16	30,085	2,253	7.5%	0
12/15	18,384	2,470	13.4%	0
Annual Growth	5.6%	13.4%	—	—

2019 Year-End Financials

Debt ratio: —	No. of shares (mil.): —
Return on equity: 17.4%	Dividends
Cash ($ mil.): 5,007	Yield: 3.8%
Current ratio: —	Payout: 1.5%
Long-term debt ($ mil.): —	Market value ($ mil.): —

	STOCK PRICE ($) FY Close	P/E High/Low		PER SHARE ($) Earnings	Dividends	Book Value
12/19	12.13	1	0	5.21	0.47	6.32
12/18	11.13	1	0	4.13	0.46	6.16
12/17	9.67	1	1	3.42	0.44	6.86
12/16	8.89	1	0	2.85	0.24	6.75
12/15	3.89	4	2	0.31	0.27	5.23
Annual Growth	32.9%	—	—	102.2%	14.8%	4.8%

Banco Santander Chile

A majority-owned indirect subsidiary of Spanish financial services giant Grupo Santander Banco Santander Chile is the largest bank in its home country. From more thanÂ 460 branches throughout Chile (including about 100 Banafe bank locations catering to middle-income clients) the bank offers consumer banking residential mortgage financing credit cards auto loans and investment management services for approximately 2.3 million customers. The bank also hasÂ about 40Â payment centers operating as Santander SuperCaja. Corporate banking services include commercial lending and leasing trade financing financial advisory services and cash management.

EXECUTIVES

President of the Board, Vittorio Corbo Lioi
First Vice President, Oscar Von Chrismar Carvajal
Second Vice President, Roberto Mendez Torres
Auditors: PricewaterhouseCoopers Consultores, Auditores SpA

LOCATIONS

HQ: Banco Santander Chile
Bandera 140, 20th Floor, Santiago
Phone: (11) 562 320 2000
Web: www.santander.cl

COMPETITORS

BBVA Chile	Banco de Crédito e
BBVA Provida	Inversiones
Banco de Chile	Scotiabank

HISTORICAL FINANCIALS

Company Type: Public

Income Statement				FYE: December 31
	ASSETS ($ mil.)	NET INCOME ($ mil.)	INCOME AS % OF ASSETS	EMPLOYEES
12/19	108,065	1,322	1.2%	11,200
12/18	83,616	1,272	1.5%	11,305
12/17	76,546	1,202	1.6%	11,068
12/16	79,123	1,017	1.3%	11,354
12/15	74,012	958	1.3%	11,723
Annual Growth	9.9%	8.4%	—	(1.1%)

2019 Year-End Financials

Return on assets: 1.3%	Dividends
Return on equity: 18.7%	Yield: 3.6%
Long-term debt ($ mil.): —	Payout: 20,808.5%
No. of shares (mil.): —	Market value ($ mil.): —
Sales ($ mil): 5,796	

	STOCK PRICE ($) FY Close	P/E High/Low		PER SHARE ($) Earnings	Dividends	Book Value
12/19	23.07	10	6	0.01	0.83	0.04
12/18	29.90	11	9	0.01	1.12	0.04
12/17	31.27	11	7	0.01	0.85	0.04
12/16	21.87	9	6	0.01	0.86	0.03
12/15	17.64	10	7	0.01	0.90	0.03
Annual Growth	6.9%	—	—	8.4%	(2.0%)	5.2%

Banco Santander Mexico SA, Institucion de Banca Multiple, Grupo Financiero Santander Mexico

EXECUTIVES

Executive President CEO and Director, Marcos Alejandro Mart nez Gavica
VP Administration and Finance and Director, Pedro José Moreno Cantalejo

VP Retail Banking, Juan Sebasti n Moreno Blanco, age 56
Chairman, Carlos G mez y G mez
Auditors: PricewaterhouseCoopers, S.C.

LOCATIONS

HQ: Banco Santander Mexico SA, Institucion de Banca Multiple, Grupo Financiero Santander Mexico
Avenida Prolongacion Paseo de la Reforma 500, Col. Lomas de Santa Fe, Delegacion Alvaro Obregon, Mexico City 01219
Phone: (52) 55 5257 8000 **Fax:** (52) 55 5269 2701
Web: www.santander.com.mx

PRODUCTS/OPERATIONS

2014 Sales

	% of total
Retail Banking	85
Global Wholesale Banking	13
Corporate Activities	2
Total	**100**

2014 Sales

	% of total
Interest income and similar income	75
Fee and commission income	21
Gains/(losses) on financial assets and liabilities (net)	3
Other operating income	1
Total	**100**

COMPETITORS

BBVA Bancomer	HSBC Fianzas
Banamex	Inbursa
Banco Compartamos	Scotiabank
Banorte	

HISTORICAL FINANCIALS

Company Type: Public

Income Statement				FYE: December 31
	ASSETS ($ mil.)	NET INCOME ($ mil.)	INCOME AS % OF ASSETS	EMPLOYEES
12/19	77,567	1,077	1.4%	15,857
12/18	71,639	984	1.4%	16,016
12/17	67,471	948	1.4%	15,116
12/16	65,291	797	1.2%	16,976
12/15	67,695	806	1.2%	17,208
Annual Growth	3.5%	7.5%	—	(2.0%)

2019 Year-End Financials

Return on assets: 1.4%	Dividends
Return on equity: 15.8%	Yield: 4.9%
Long-term debt ($ mil.): —	Payout: 210.8%
No. of shares (mil.): —	Market value ($ mil.): —
Sales ($ mil): 8,096	

	STOCK PRICE ($) FY Close	P/E High/Low		PER SHARE ($) Earnings	Dividends	Book Value
12/19	6.78	3	2	0.16	0.33	1.05
12/18	6.16	3	2	0.14	0.29	0.92
12/17	7.31	4	3	0.14	0.00	0.86
12/16	7.19	4	3	0.12	0.00	0.76
12/15	8.67	5	3	0.12	0.00	0.93
Annual Growth	(6.0%)	—	—	7.5%	—	3.1%

Banco Santander SA (Spain)

Spain's Banco Santander is one of the largest banks in the world. Beyond Spain it offers retail banking and consumer finance in Portugal the UK and other parts of Europe as well as the US. Subsidiaries such as Banco Santander Chile Banco Santander (Brasil) Santander R o in Argentina and Grupo Financiero Santander (Mexico) make it a top banking group in Latin America (generating nearly 45% of the group's revenue). Other units offer asset management private banking corporate and investment banking and insurance. All told the company has some ?1.5 trillion in assets about 144 million customers and more than 13000 branch locations.

Operations

Banco Santander has operations in retail banking and consumer finance commercial and wholesale banking private banking asset management and insurance.

The bank is organized principally along geographic lines where its primary geographies constitute separate segments: Continental Europe the UK Latin America and the US.

Banco Santander then divides its business along four further operational lines that are global in scope: Retail Santander Corporate & Investment Banking and Wealth Management in addition to Real estate activity Spain. Retail Banking covers all Santander's customer banking businesses; Santander Corporate & Investment Banking houses global corporate banking investment banking and equities activities; Wealth Management includes Santander Asset Management Private Banking's corporate unit and International Private Banking in Miami and Switzerland. The Real estate activity Spain business provides loans and advances to customer and foreclosed assets of customers

Net interest income accounts for around 70% of total revenue.

Geographic Reach

Madrid-based Banco Santander is well diversified between mature economies and emerging markets making financial results more predictable. Its main geographies are Brazil (generating more than 25% of profits) Spain (more than 15%) and the UK (15%) and Mexico (roughly 10%). Its other main territories are Chile Argentina the US Portugal and Poland which account for around 5% of sales each give or take a few percent. Santander Consumer Finance generates around 15% of profits.

There are around 200 million people in Latin America who don't have a bank presenting Santander ample opportunity to grow its customer base.

Sales and Marketing

In 2018 Banco Santander became the official sponsor of the UEFA Champions League Europe's premier club soccer tournament for three seasons from 2018.

Santander has 144 million customers and nearly 20 million of what it terms 'loyal customers' i.e. customers it has deeper relationships with either via online or multiple accounts.

Financial PerformanceNote: Growth rates may differ after conversion to US Dollars.

After a fruitful 2017 in which Banco Santander's revenue grew 10% the company's top line growth ground to a halt a year later. The ?48.4 billion total income reported in 2018 was materially unchanged from the prior year. Net interest income net fee and commission income and gains/losses on financial assets were all more or less the same. Growth of 3% in interest-earning assets thanks to the acquisition of Banco Popular in 2017 was offset by currency headwinds.

A positive trend of five consecutive years of net income growth continued in 2018 with Banco Santander's net income rising 18% to ?7.8 billion. The strong performance was a result of underlying profit growth in seven of Santander's ten core units with five showing double-digit growth. The bank registered a rise in loyal and digital customers which are typically more profitable for the company. Santander is a remarkably profitable bank overall boasting a top-tier efficiency ratio (47%) and ranks among the highest European banks in terms of return on equity.

Banco Santander's cash balance grew ?2.7 billion to ?113.7 billion during 2018. Operating activities generated ?3.4 billion investing activities generated ?3.1 billion and financing activities used ?3.3 billion.

Strategy

Santander's short-term focus is on integrating Banco Popular a failing Spanish bank that it bought for a token one euro in 2017. The bank will raise ?7 billion in capital to rebuild Popular's balance sheet which contains ?37 billion in non-performing real estate loans. While costly the Popular acquisition made Santander Spain's biggest bank and strengthened its presence in the SMEs market. As part of the acquisition it sold off 51% of Popular's property assets worth ?30 billion and sold Totalbank to Chile's Banco de Crédito e Inversiones for $528 million. It also reached an agreement to sell its Puerto Rico business to First-Bank Puerto Rico raising $1.1 billion. It will take until 2020 to fully integrate Popular.

Growth in loyal customers who buy multiple services and who stick with the bank for a long time and digital customers who are cheaper to serve are key to boosting Santander's profit. The bank continues to work hard to swell the ranks of both customer types and loyal customers have grown from 13.8 million in 2015 to 19.9 million in 2018 and digital customers have surged from 16.6 million in 2015 to 32.0 million in 2018.

Mergers and Acquisitions

In 2019 Banco Santander agreed to buy out joint venture partner Allianz's 60% stake in Allianz Popular for ?936.5 billion. The deal marks the termination of an agreement for the exclusive distribution of certain non-life insurance products through the Banco Popular network. It also acquired a majority stake in Ebury a UK-based currency transfer platform for Å 350 million.

Company Background

In 2017 Banco Santander acquired failing Spanish bank Banco Popular for one euro. While Santander has quite the mess to sort out — Popular is saddled with ?37 billion in toxic real estate loans — the purchase made Santander the #1 bank in Spain and Portugal and has the potential to make a solid contribution to profits. The acquisition included various asset sales including a ?30 billion property sale — the largest in Spanish history.

HISTORY

In 1857 a group of Basque businessmen had formed Banco Santander to finance Latin American trade. The emergence of Cantabria as a leading province after WWI helped the bank expand first regionally and then nationally.

The Bot n family has been closely identified with the bank for decades. Emilio Bot n served first as a board member and then for a few years as chairman before his death in 1923. The post was held by his son Emilio Bot n-Sanz de Sautuola from 1950 to 1986 when his son Emilio Bot n Sanz de Sautuola y Garc a de los R os (known as Don Emilio) took over.

Spanish banks were spared the worst of the Great Depression (thanks to their isolation and the country's shunning the gold standard) but Spain's civil war was draining. In the early 1940s Santander expanded into Madrid and other major Spanish cities and merged with a few rivals. In the 1950s and 1960s as interest rates were controlled and mergers halted banks competed by building branch networks and investing overseas particularly in Latin America. In 1965 Santander joined with Bank of America to form Bankinter (it divested most of its stake by the mid-1990s).

Tight economic controls were relaxed in the 1970s after Franco's death. Despite global recession Santander continued to invest in Latin America through the mid-1980s.

In the late 1980s Santander prepared to compete in a deregulated Spain and Europe forming alliances with Royal Bank of Scotland Kemper (now part of Zurich Financial Services) and Metropolitan Life Insurance. In 1989 the bank jump-started competition by introducing Spain's first high-interest account.

Santander focused on home in the 1990s. Spurned by Banco Hispano Americano (BHA) Santander acquired a 60% stake in the ailing Banco Español de Crédito (Banesto) which became wholly owned in 1998. The bank took a hit when Latin America plunged into an economic crisis that year. With profit margins falling the bank merged with BCH in 1999.

BCH was formed by the 1991 merger of Banco Central and BHA. BHA had been established in 1900 by investors in Latin America; Central had been founded in 1919. The mixed banks offered both commercial and investment banking; they funded industrialization and investment in Latin America and became two of Spain's largest banks before the civil war.

After the war BHA sold its Latin American assets when the currency dried up while Central used mergers and acquisitions to expand across Spain. Isolated from WWII by Franco the two banks used their dual strategies to fund overseas investment and domestic-branch growth.

After Franco's death the banks faced increased competition at home and abroad. Central bought BHA in 1991 to remain competitive as Spain entered the European Economic Community (now the EU) in 1992.

Following the merger BCH trimmed 20% of its branches fired some 10000 employees and sold unprofitable holdings. Focused on Latin America the bank took small stakes in small banks. Losing its edge BCH merged with Santander in 1999.

In 2000 the newly merged BSCH focused on expanding in Europe and Latin America. Among its European moves was its alliance with Société Générale to buy investment-fund management firms particularly in the US. In Latin America the bank bought Brazil's Banco Meridional Banco do Estado de S o Paulo (Banespa) and Grupo Financiero Serfin Mexico's #3 bank. Critics questioned the $5 billion price tag BSCH paid for Banespa charging that the formerly state-run bank was overvalued in 2001. Executive in-fighting saw ex-Santander chairman Emilio Bot n triumph over ex-BCH chairman José Mar a Amus tegui for control of BSCH's helm. Soon after the bank started doing business as simply Santander Central Hispano. The following year the bank sold off its shares of Germany's Commerzbank and France's Société Générale.

In one of Europe's largest cross-border bank mergers ever Santander paid more than ?12 billion ($15 billion) for British bank Abbey National in 2004. It solidified its UK operations through the approximately ?1.25 billion ($2.6 billion) purchase of Alliance & Leicester. Abbey then acquired the retail deposit business of Bradford & Bingley after it was nationalized in 2008.

Another acquisition helped Santander grow in South America. In 2007 the company along with Royal Bank of Scotland and Fortis acquired the Netherlands-based ABN AMRO (the international retail banking giant with more than 4350 branches) for around ?71 billion ($87 billion). As part of the bid Banco Santander took ABN AMRO's Brazilian operations doubling its market share in Brazil. Also a part of the ABN AMRO deal Santander became the largest non-government-owned bank in Uruguay.

In 2009 the Venezuelan government took over Banco Santander subsidiary Banco de Venezuela the third-largest bank in the country. The government paid some ?755 million ($1 billion) to nationalize the bank.

Also that year Santander acquired the approximately three-quarters of Sovereign it didn't already own. Santander then purchased a more than ?3 billion ($4 billion) US car loan portfolio and a loan servicing platform from HSBC.

In 2010 Santander took full control of its Mexico unit by acquiring Bank of America's 25% stake in Grupo Financiero Santander for ?2 billion ($2.5 billion) as well as the rest of Puerto Rican unit Santander BanCorp it didn't already own. It then acquired GE Capital's $2 billion consumer mortgage business in Mexico for $162 million plus the assumption of debt. The company has also been opening new branches in the region. While the financial downturn and the European sovereign debt crisis has been rough for Spain and Portugal Mexico holds promise for growth. Hoping to cash in on some of that growth Banco Santander spun off nearly 25% of Grupo Financiero Santander in a public offering worth more than $4 billion.

Banco Santander also made a big move into Eastern Europe. In 2011 it paid ?4 billion (nearly $6 billion) for Poland's Bank Zachodni. The acquisition may signal more acquisitions for Santander in neighboring Eastern European countries.

In 2010 Santander bought a ?2.5 billion ($3 billion) auto loan portfolio from Citigroup.

Banco Santander also operates Santander UK the result of the 2010 merger of Abbey National Bradford & Bingley and the former Alliance & Leicester (all of which were acquired by Santander). Santander's acquisitions in the UK helped bump up profits from the region in 2009 and 2010 but in 2011 profits slipped as a result of remediation charges related to mis-sold payment protection insurance.

EXECUTIVES

CEO Banco Santander USA, Scott E. Powell, age 57
CEO, Jose Antonio Alvarez
CFO, Jose Garcia Cantera
Head Technology and Operations, Andreu Plaza Lopez
President Brazil, Sergio Rial
First Vice Chairman, Bruce N. Carnegie-Brown, age 61
Vice Chairman, Rodrigo Echenique Gorillo
Chairman, Ana P. Bot n, age 60
Auditors: PricewaterhouseCoopers Auditores, S.L.

LOCATIONS

HQ: Banco Santander SA (Spain)
Santander Group City, Av. Cantabria s/n, Madrid, Boadilla del Monte 28660
Phone: (34) 91 259 65 20
Web: www.santander.com

2018 sales

	% of total
Continental Europe	32
United Kingdom	11
Latin America	43
United States	14
Eliminations -	
Total	**100**

PRODUCTS/OPERATIONS

2018 sales

	% of total
Retail Banking	87
Corporate & Investment Banking	10
Wealth Management	3
Eliminations -	
Total	**100**

2018 sales

	% of total
Net interest income	70
Net fee and commission income	24
Other	6
Total	**100**

COMPETITORS

BBVA	Citigroup
Banco Comercial	Deutsche Bank
Portugu s	Esp rito Santo
Banco do Brasil	HSBC
Bank of America	JPMorgan Chase
Barclays	

HISTORICAL FINANCIALS

Company Type: Public

Income Statement

FYE: December 31

	ASSETS ($ mil.)	NET INCOME ($ mil.)	INCOME AS % OF ASSETS	EMPLOYEES
12/19	2,396,113	10,252	0.4%	196,419
12/18	2,296,309	12,289	0.5%	202,713
12/17	2,272,759	10,415	0.5%	202,251
12/16	2,107,247	9,762	0.5%	191,635
12/15	2,109,033	9,388	0.4%	189,464
Annual Growth	**3.2%**	**2.2%**	**—**	**0.9%**

2019 Year-End Financials

Return on assets: 0.4%
Return on equity: 6.6%
Long-term debt ($ mil.): —
No. of shares (mil.): —
Sales ($ mil): 125,749

Dividends
Yield: 4.6%
Payout: 97.4%
Market value ($ mil.): —

	STOCK PRICE ($) FY Close	P/E High/Low	PER SHARE ($) Earnings	Dividends	Book Value
12/19	4.14	14 10	0.57	0.19	9.48
12/18	4.48	17 10	0.70	0.20	9.35
12/17	6.54	17 13	0.63	0.62	9.21
12/16	5.18	13 9	0.65	0.49	9.81
12/15	4.87	21 12	0.63	0.34	9.60
Annual Growth (0.3%)	**(4.0%)**		**— —**	**(2.5%)**	**(13.6%)**

BanColombia SA

EXECUTIVES

President, JUAN CARLOS MORA URIBE
Auditors: PricewaterhouseCoopers Ltda.

LOCATIONS

HQ: BanColombia SA
Carrera 48 # 26-85, Avenida Los Industriales, Medellin
Phone: (57) 4 404 1837   **Fax:** (57) 4 404 5146
Web: www.grupobancolombia.com

PRODUCTS/OPERATIONS

2013 Sales

	% of total
Interest income	
Loans	65
Financial leases	9
Investment sercurities	5
Fees and other service income	
Credit and debit card fees	7
Commissions from banking services	4
Collections and payment fees	3
Trust activities	2
Checking fees	1
Others	4
Total	**100**

Selected Subsidiaries

Banca de Inversion Bancolombia S.A. (investment banking)
Bancolombia (Panamá;) S.A.
Bancolombia Puerto Rico
Factoring Bancolombia S.A. (99.97%)
Fiduciaria Bancolombia S.A. (trust services 98.8%)
Inversiones Financieras Banco Agricola S.A. (investments 98.4%)
Leasing Bancolombia S.A.
Patrimonio Autonomo CV Sufinanciamiento (loan management)
Valores Bancolombia S.A. (securities brokerage)

COMPETITORS

BBVA	Bicsa Panama
Banco Latinoamericano	Citigroup
de Comercio Exterior	Credicorp
Banco de Crédito e	
Inversiones	

HISTORICAL FINANCIALS

Company Type: Public

Income Statement

FYE: December 31

	ASSETS ($ mil.)	NET INCOME ($ mil.)	INCOME AS % OF ASSETS	EMPLOYEES
12/19	130,023	1,716	1.3%	31,075
12/18	121,225	1,464	1.2%	31,040
12/17	112,300	1,440	1.3%	31,061
12/16	108,088	1,578	1.5%	31,598
12/15	106,277	1,387	1.3%	34,390
Annual Growth	**5.2%**	**5.5%**	**—**	**(2.5%)**

2019 Year-End Financials

Return on assets: 1.3%
Return on equity: 12.0%
Long-term debt ($ mil.): —
No. of shares (mil.): 509
Sales ($ mil): 13,149

Dividends
Yield: 2.2%
Payout: 67.1%
Market value ($ mil.): 27,927

	STOCK PRICE ($) FY Close	P/E High/Low		PER SHARE ($) Earnings	Dividends	Book Value
12/19	54.79	0	0	1.82	1.24	29.05
12/18	38.10	0	0	1.56	1.35	26.85
12/17	39.66	0	0	1.53	1.27	24.97
12/16	36.68	0	0	1.67	1.18	22.98
12/15	26.75	0	0	1.48	1.17	20.83
Annual Growth	19.6%	—	—	5.3%	1.4%	8.7%

Bangkok Bank Public Co., Ltd. (Thailand)

EXECUTIVES

President, Chartsiri Sophonpanich
Auditors: Deloitte Touche Tohmatsu Jaiyos Audit Co., Ltd.

LOCATIONS

HQ: Bangkok Bank Public Co., Ltd. (Thailand)
333 Silom Road, Bangrak, Bangkok 10500
Phone: (66) 0 2231 4333   **Fax:** (66) 0 2231 4890
Web: www.bangkokbank.com

COMPETITORS

Bank of Ayudhya	Siam Commercial
CIMB Group	Standard Chartered
DBS Group Holdings	TMB Bank
KASIKORNBANK	Thanachart Capital
Krung Thai	United Overseas Bank

HISTORICAL FINANCIALS

Company Type: Public

Income Statement				FYE: December 31
	ASSETS ($ mil.)	NET INCOME ($ mil.)	INCOME AS % OF ASSETS	EMPLOYEES
12/19	107,988	1,202	1.1%	0
12/18	96,345	1,092	1.1%	25,287
12/17	94,428	1,013	1.1%	0
12/16	82,252	888	1.1%	0
12/15	78,707	948	1.2%	0
Annual Growth	8.2%	6.1%	—	—

2019 Year-End Financials

Return on assets: 1.1%
Return on equity: 8.5%
Long-term debt ($ mil.): —
No. of shares (mil.): 1,908
Sales ($ mil): 6,244

Dividends
Yield: 0.0%
Payout: —
Market value ($ mil.): 52,493

	STOCK PRICE ($) FY Close	P/E High/Low		PER SHARE ($) Earnings	Dividends	Book Value
12/19	27.50	2	1	0.63	0.90	7.52
12/18	32.00	2	2	0.57	0.81	6.69
12/17	33.14	2	1	0.53	0.81	6.46
12/16	22.25	2	1	0.47	0.73	5.55
12/15	22.78	2	1	0.50	0.71	5.26
Annual Growth	4.8%	—	—	6.1%	6.0%	9.4%

Bank Audi SAL

Auditors: BDO, Semaan, Gholam & Co.

LOCATIONS

HQ: Bank Audi SAL
Bank Audi Plaza, Omar Daouk Street, Bab Idriss, Beirut
Phone: (961) 1 994000   **Fax:** (961) 1 990555
Web: www.bankaudigroup.com

HISTORICAL FINANCIALS

Company Type: Public

Income Statement				FYE: December 31
	ASSETS ($ mil.)	NET INCOME ($ mil.)	INCOME AS % OF ASSETS	EMPLOYEES
12/19	39,535	(605)	—	6,288
12/18	47,201	499	1.1%	6,306
12/17	43,751	538	1.2%	6,541
12/16	44,249	445	1.0%	7,017
12/15	42,253	389	0.9%	6,891
Annual Growth	(1.6%)	—	—	(2.3%)

2019 Year-End Financials

Return on assets: (-1.4%)
Return on equity: (-18.3%)
Long-term debt ($ mil.): —
No. of shares (mil.): 278
Sales ($ mil): 3,525

Dividends
Yield: —
Payout: —
Market value ($ mil.): —

Bank Hapoalim B.M. (Israel)

The largest bank in Israel Bank Hapoalim caters to individual commercial and corporate clients at home and abroad. Within Israel the Bank Hapoalim Group hasÂ more than 270 full-service branches and business centers. Another 30 express branches are in the works. Overseas it has about 45 branchesÂ correspondent offices and financial subsidiaries in Asia Australia Europe Latin America and North America; its international focus is on private banking and the corporate sector. Bank Hapoalim provides investment banking servicesÂ including theÂ underwriting of and investment in companies; it also provides trust services to individuals and businesses.

EXECUTIVES

deputy managing director, Avraham Kohava
deputy managing director, Dan Koler Alexander
deputy managing director, Eti Ben Zeev
deputy managing director, Ofer Levy
deputy managing director, Ran Oz
deputy managing director, Shimon Gal
deputy managing director, Yael Almog
deputy managing director, Zachi Cohen
deputy managing director, Zeev Hayu
Auditors: Ziv Haft

LOCATIONS

HQ: Bank Hapoalim B.M. (Israel)
50 Rothschild Blvd., Tel-Aviv 66883
Phone: (972) 3 567 3333   **Fax:** (972) 3 560 7028
Web: www.bankhapoalim.com

COMPETITORS

Bank Leumi le-Israel	Israel Discount Bank
First International	Mizrahi Tefahot
Bank of Israel	UBS

HISTORICAL FINANCIALS

Company Type: Public

Income Statement				FYE: December 31
	ASSETS ($ mil.)	NET INCOME ($ mil.)	INCOME AS % OF ASSETS	EMPLOYEES
12/19	134,203	520	0.4%	8,964
12/18	122,844	691	0.6%	9,427
12/17	130,908	766	0.6%	11,173
12/16	116,667	684	0.6%	11,628
12/15	110,354	787	0.7%	11,804
Annual Growth	5.0%	(9.8%)	—	(6.6%)

2019 Year-End Financials

Return on assets: 0.3%
Return on equity: 4.7%
Long-term debt ($ mil.): —
No. of shares (mil.): 1,335
Sales ($ mil): 4,578

Dividends
Yield: —
Payout: 55.4%
Market value ($ mil.): —

Bank Leumi Le-Israel B.M.

Bank Leumi le-Israel looms large as one of Israel's largest financial institutions. The company whose name translates as National Bank of IsraelÂ offersÂ retail banking (for consumers and small businesses) commercial banking (middle-market businesses) corporate banking (large companies) and private banking (wealthy clients) through deposits mortgagesÂ and other loansÂ credit cards trust services and investments.Â It hasÂ about 235Â branches in Israel and more than 80Â locations (including branches agencies and representative offices) in some 20 countries including the US. Subsidiary LeumiÂ Partners provides corporate investment banking services and makes direct investments in nonbanking businesses.

EXECUTIVES

chief executive, Hanan Friedman
vice-president, Arbel Shmulik
vice-president, Eran Zik
vice-president, Hana Ben Zvi Bosmat
vice-president, Irit Irit
vice-president, Michael Goldfarb Shlomo
vice-president, Michal Carmi Dana
vice-president, Sharon Gur
chairman, Samer Haj Yihye
Auditors: Kost Forer Gabbay & Kasierer

LOCATIONS

HQ: Bank Leumi Le-Israel B.M.
34 Yehuda Halevi Street, Tel-Aviv 65546
Phone: (972) 3 514 8111   **Fax:** (972) 3 566 1872
Web: www.bankleumi.com

COMPETITORS

Bank Hapoalim	HSBC
Bank of America	Israel Discount Bank
Citigroup	Mizrahi Tefahot
First International	Standard Chartered
Bank of Israel	UniCredit

HISTORICAL FINANCIALS
Company Type: Public

Income Statement				FYE: December 31
	ASSETS ($ mil.)	NET INCOME ($ mil.)	INCOME AS % OF ASSETS	EMPLOYEES
12/19	135,779	1,019	0.8%	9,239
12/18	122,772	868	0.7%	9,740
12/17	129,875	913	0.7%	11,201
12/16	114,193	726	0.6%	11,636
12/15	106,484	724	0.7%	12,528
Annual Growth	6.3%	8.9%	—	(7.3%)

2019 Year-End Financials

Return on assets: 0.7%	Dividends
Return on equity: 9.9%	Yield: —
Long-term debt ($ mil.): —	Payout: 40.2%
No. of shares (mil.): 1,524	Market value ($ mil.): —
Sales ($ mil): 4,780	

Bank Muscat S.A.O.G

EXECUTIVES

Director & Chairman, Sheikh Khalid bin Mustahail Al Mashani
Auditors: PricewaterhouseCoopers LLC

LOCATIONS

HQ: Bank Muscat S.A.O.G
 Building No. 120/4, Block No. 311, Street No. 62,
 Airport Heights, Seeb PC 112
Phone: (968) 24 795555   **Fax:** (968) 2470 7806
Web: www.bankmuscat.com

HISTORICAL FINANCIALS
Company Type: Public

Income Statement				FYE: December 31
	ASSETS ($ mil.)	NET INCOME ($ mil.)	INCOME AS % OF ASSETS	EMPLOYEES
12/19	31,965	482	1.5%	3,818
12/18	31,958	467	1.5%	3,779
12/17	28,996	459	1.6%	3,712
12/16	28,100	458	1.6%	3,747
12/15	32,578	455	1.4%	3,712
Annual Growth	(0.5%)	1.4%	—	0.7%

2019 Year-End Financials

Return on assets: 1.5%	Dividends
Return on equity: 9.4%	Yield: —
Long-term debt ($ mil.): —	Payout: 187.4%
No. of shares (mil.): —	Market value ($ mil.): —
Sales ($ mil): 1,751	

Bank of Ayudhya Public Co Ltd

EXECUTIVES

President and Chief Executive, Seiichiro Akita
Vice Chairman, Noriaki Goto
Auditors: Deloitte Touche Tohmatsu Jaiyos Audit Co., Ltd.

LOCATIONS

HQ: Bank of Ayudhya Public Co Ltd
 1222 Rama III Road, Bang Phongphang Subdistrict,
 Yannawa District, Bangkok 10120
Phone: (66) 2 296 2000   **Fax:** (66) 2 683 1304
Web: www.krungsri.com

COMPETITORS

BNP Paribas Bangkok	Krung Thai
Bangkok Bank	Siam Commercial
Citigroup	Thanachart Capital

HISTORICAL FINANCIALS
Company Type: Public

Income Statement				FYE: December 31
	ASSETS ($ mil.)	NET INCOME ($ mil.)	INCOME AS % OF ASSETS	EMPLOYEES
12/19	79,213	1,099	1.4%	0
12/18	67,191	767	1.1%	0
12/17	64,115	712	1.1%	0
12/16	52,610	597	1.1%	0
12/15	47,335	517	1.1%	0
Annual Growth	13.7%	20.7%		—

2019 Year-End Financials

Return on assets: 1.4%	Dividends
Return on equity: 12.7%	Yield: —
Long-term debt ($ mil.): —	Payout: —
No. of shares (mil.): —	Market value ($ mil.): —
Sales ($ mil): 5,489	

Bank of Canada (Ottawa)

Whether you say "bank" or "banque" the Bank of Canada is the country's central bank. It is responsible for setting monetary policy (by setting interest rates) issuing and safeguarding currency from counterfeiting managing the Canadian banking system and managing funds for the government and other clients. The Bank of Canada works through six regional offices including one in New York City. A governor senior deputy governor 12 outside directors and the Deputy Minister of Finance oversee the bank which averages a $1.8 billion profit annually. The funds are contributed to the government.

Operations

The Bank of Canada has eight set dates throughout the year when it announces whether or not it will adjust interest rates. Bank directors are appointed by the Minister of Finance for a three-year term. Appointees are subject to approval by Canada's Cabinet the Governor in Council.

Geographic Reach

The company is headquartered in Ontario Canada and has regional offices in Halifax (Atlantic Provinces) Montreal (Quebec) Toronto (Ontario) Calgary (Prairies Nunavut and the Northwest Territories) and Vancouver (British Columbia and the Yukon). The company also has an office in New York.

Financial Performance

The bank's revenues decreased 3% from 2014 to 2015 due to lower interest earned on investments. The decline in interest revenue was fueled by lower yields on newly acquired bonds compared with yields on investments that have matured. Net income however increased 4% from 2014 to 2015 due to lower interest expenses on deposits premises costs and bank note research production and processing expenses.

Company Background

The Bank of Canada was formed in 1934 as a private entity; it became part of the government four years later.

EXECUTIVES

Chairman and Governor, Stephen S. Poloz
Deputy Governor, Lawrence L. Schembri
Deputy Governor, Timothy Lane
Chief Internal Auditor, Carmen P. Vierula
COO, Filipe Dinis
Senior Deputy Governor, Carolyn Wilkins
Deputy Governor, Lynn K. Patterson
Chief Information Technology Services and CIO, Sylvain Chalut
Chief Corporate Services, Dinah Maclean
Chief of the International Economic Analysis Department (INT), Césaire Meh
Chief of Economic and Financial Research, Rhys R. Mendes
Chief of the Bank of CanadaÂ's Financial Stability Department, Ron Morrow
Chief of the BankÂ's Canadian Economic Analysis Department (CEA), Eric Santor
Chief of the Currency Department, Richard Wall
Auditors: KPMG LLP

LOCATIONS

HQ: Bank of Canada (Ottawa)
 234 Wellington Street, Ottawa, Ontario K1A 0G9
Phone: 800 303 1282   **Fax:** 613 782-7713
Web: www.bankofcanada.ca

HISTORICAL FINANCIALS
Company Type: Public

Income Statement				FYE: December 31
	ASSETS ($ mil.)	NET INCOME ($ mil.)	INCOME AS % OF ASSETS	EMPLOYEES
12/19	121,150	1,318	1.1%	1,800
12/18	117,517	1,138	1.0%	1,750
12/17	112,500	988	0.9%	1,700
12/16	107,443	1,078	1.0%	1,700
12/15	102,421	1,190	1.2%	1,600
Annual Growth	4.3%	2.6%	—	3.0%

2019 Year-End Financials

Return on assets: 1.1%	Dividends
Return on equity: 246.6%	Yield: —
Long-term debt ($ mil.): —	Payout: —
No. of shares (mil.): 0	Market value ($ mil.): —
Sales ($ mil): 2,316	

Bank of East Asia Ltd.

Bank of East Asia provides retail and commercial banking services in Hong Kong and mainland China. Its offerings include deposit accounts consumer loans mortgages business loans credit cards private banking and investment management. Bank of East Asia has some 130 locations in Hong Kong and more than 60 in mainland China; internationally it has about 30 offices in the British Virgin Islands Malaysia Singapore the UK and Vietnam. The bank's subsidiaries include online securities and futures brokerage provider East Asia Securities Blue Cross (Asia-Pacific) Insurance and Tricor which performs outsourced business services.

EXECUTIVES

Chairman and CEO, David K. P. Li, age 82
Chief Investment Officer, Samson K. C. Li, age 60
Deputy Chief Executive, Adrian David M. K. Li, age 47
Deputy Chief Executive, Brian David M. B. Li, age 46
COO, Tong Hon-shing, age 61
Deputy Chairman, Allan C. Y. Wong, age 69
Deputy Chairman, Arthur K. C. Li, age 75
Auditors: KPMG

LOCATIONS

HQ: Bank of East Asia Ltd.
10 Des Voeux Road Central,
Phone: (852) 3608 3608   **Fax:** (852) 3608 6000
Web: www.hkbea.com

PRODUCTS/OPERATIONS

2014 Sales

	% of total
Interest income	83
Non-interest income	17
Total	**100**

COMPETITORS

Bank of China (Hong Kong)	Dah Sing Banking
Bank of Communications	Dah Sing Financial Holdings Limited
CITIC International Financial	Hang Seng Bank
China Development Bank	Public Financial Holdings
China Minsheng Banking	Shanghai Pudong Development Bank
Chong Hing Bank	

HISTORICAL FINANCIALS

Company Type: Public

Income Statement				FYE: December 31
	ASSETS ($ mil.)	NET INCOME ($ mil.)	INCOME AS % OF ASSETS	EMPLOYEES
12/19	111,110	418	0.4%	9,846
12/18	107,180	831	0.8%	9,796
12/17	103,508	1,196	1.2%	9,978
12/16	98,742	480	0.5%	10,389
12/15	100,808	712	0.7%	13,653
Annual Growth	2.5%	(12.4%)	—	(7.8%)

2019 Year-End Financials

Return on assets: 0.3%
Return on equity: 3.1%
Long-term debt ($ mil.): —
No. of shares (mil.): —
Sales ($ mil): 4,532
Dividends
Yield: 0.0%
Payout: 86.1%
Market value ($ mil.): —

	STOCK PRICE ($) FY Close	P/E High/Low		PER SHARE ($) Earnings	Dividends	Book Value
12/19	2.18	4	2	0.11	0.10	4.83
12/18	3.18	2	1	0.26	0.12	4.52
12/17	4.22	1	1	0.41	0.11	4.55
12/16	3.80	4	2	0.16	0.09	3.98
12/15	3.63	2	2	0.25	0.12	4.03
Annual Growth	(11.9%)	—	—	(17.9%)	(4.9%)	4.6%

Bank of Ireland Group plc

EXECUTIVES

Director, MICHAEL SWEENEY
Auditors: KPMG

LOCATIONS

HQ: Bank of Ireland Group plc
40 Mespil Road, Dublin 4
Phone:
Web: www.bankofireland.com

HISTORICAL FINANCIALS

Company Type: Public

Income Statement				FYE: December 31
	ASSETS ($ mil.)	NET INCOME ($ mil.)	INCOME AS % OF ASSETS	EMPLOYEES
12/19	148,073	433	0.3%	10,440
12/18	141,625	710	0.5%	10,367
12/17	146,912	795	0.5%	10,892
12/16	130,009	837	0.6%	11,208
12/15	142,643	1,023	0.7%	11,145
Annual Growth	0.9%	(19.3%)	—	(1.6%)

2019 Year-End Financials

Return on assets: 0.3%
Return on equity: 4.0%
Long-term debt ($ mil.): —
No. of shares (mil.): 1,069
Sales ($ mil): 6,958
Dividends
Yield: 3.3%
Payout: 31.6%
Market value ($ mil.): 5,773

	STOCK PRICE ($) FY Close	P/E High/Low		PER SHARE ($) Earnings	Dividends	Book Value
12/19	5.40	19	10	0.40	0.18	10.11
12/18	5.62	17	9	0.66	0.13	9.84
Annual Growth	(3.9%)	—	—	(11.6%)	7.6%	0.7%

Bank of Iwate, Ltd. (The) (Japan)

EXECUTIVES

President, SACHIO TAGUCHI
Managing Director, Osamu Sakamoto

Managing Director, Keiji Iwata
Auditors: KPMG AZSA LLC

LOCATIONS

HQ: Bank of Iwate, Ltd. (The) (Japan)
1-2-3 Chuodori, Morioka, Iwate 020-8688
Phone: (81) 19 623 1111   **Fax:** (81) 19 652 6751
Web: www.iwatebank.co.jp

COMPETITORS

77 Bank	Norinchukin Bank
Citigroup	Resona
Ito-Yokado	Shinsei Bank
Japan Post	Sumitomo Mitsui
Mitsubishi UFJ Financial Group	Sumitomo Mitsui Trust Holdings
Mizuho Financial	

HISTORICAL FINANCIALS

Company Type: Public

Income Statement				FYE: March 31
	ASSETS ($ mil.)	NET INCOME ($ mil.)	INCOME AS % OF ASSETS	EMPLOYEES
03/20	32,109	34	0.1%	1,994
03/19	31,689	37	0.1%	2,057
03/18	33,495	52	0.2%	2,116
03/17	31,773	90	0.3%	2,128
03/16	31,295	63	0.2%	1,992
Annual Growth	0.6%	(13.9%)	—	0.0%

2020 Year-End Financials

Return on assets: 0.1%
Return on equity: 1.9%
Long-term debt ($ mil.): —
No. of shares (mil.): 17
Sales ($ mil): 417
Dividends
Yield: —
Payout: 33.0%
Market value ($ mil.): —

Bank of Japan

Founded in 1882 as Japan's central bank the Bank of Japan primarily issues banknotes and acts as a treasurer for the government. It operates 30-plus branches more than a dozen local offices and a handful of overseas offices. The bank is responsible for implementing lending rate changes as well as maintaining fluctuations in reserve requirements. It also compiles data and performs research and analysis pertaining to the overall economy. The bank's policy board meets more than a dozen times each year to make decisions on monetary policies. The policies are carried out by the Bank of Japan's providing and absorbing funds into the market. The Bank of Japan's first banknotes were issued in 1885.

Geographic Reach

Tokyo-based Bank of Japan boasts 32 branches and 14 local offices in Japan plus 7 representative offices abroad.

Strategy

As the central bank for the land of the rising sun the Bank of Japan is in charge of monetary policy and the sustainability of the country's currency with the goal of keeping inflation low while ensuring the highest rate of employment by preventing deflation. It also is the sole issuer of the country's currency the Bank of Japan notes employing a range of measures to prevent counterfeiting including watermarks special inks and micro-lettering.

The bank stands by a handful of organizational principles to keep the public's trust and confidence. These principles are: to promote the public interest by fulfilling the core purposes outlined in the Bank of Japan Act demonstrate accountability of policies and operations via its various external networks; ensure excellence in central banking services and respond to changes in environment; ensure integrity and high standards of morality through every officer and employee of the organization; and make effective and efficient use of management resources when it comes to operations and organizational management.

Company Background

The Bank of Japan's first banknotes were issued in 1885 with konnyaku powder being mixed with the paper in order to discourage counterfeiting. One minor glitch however was that the konnyaku powder attracted rats; consequently the initial banknotes were removed from circulation in 1899.

EXECUTIVES

Executive Director, Atsushi Miyanoya
Director General Information System Services, Tomohisa Takeda
Governor, Haruhiko Kuroda
Executive Director, Masayoshi Amamiya
Director-General Personnel and Corporate Affairs, Nobuyasu Yoshioka
Executive Director, Kimihiro Etoh
Director-General Payment and Settlement Systems, Hiromi Yamaoka
Executive Director, Eiji Maeda
Director-General Administration, Takeshi Nakamura
Director-General Monetary Affairs, Takeshi Kato
Director-General International, Shigeto Nagai
Executive Director, Shigehiro Kuwabara
Director-General Financial System and Bank Examination, Yasuhiro Yamada
Director-General Financial Markets, Seiichi Shimizu
Director-General Research and Statistics, Toshitaka Sekine
Director-General Currency issue, Yutaka Okada
Director-General Operations, Mitsuru Nomura
Director-General Information System Services, Masayuki Mizuno
Director-General Public Relations, Seiichi Tsurumi
Director-General Institute for Monetary and Economic Studies, Shigenori Shiratsuka
Deputy Governor, Kikuo Iwata
Deputy Governor, Hiroshi Nakaso
Auditors: Ryuichi Shogan; Toshihiko Fujita; Ryota Yanagihara

LOCATIONS

HQ: Bank of Japan
  2-1-1 Nihonbashi Hongoku-cho, Chuo-ku, Tokyo 103-0021
Phone: (81) 3 3279 1111
Web: www.boj.or.jp

HISTORICAL FINANCIALS

Company Type: Public

Income Statement				FYE: March 31
	REVENUE ($ mil.)	NET INCOME ($ mil.)	NET PROFIT MARGIN	EMPLOYEES
03/19	21,612	5,300	24.5%	4,636
03/18	17,312	7,202	41.6%	4,653
03/17	14,707	4,531	30.8%	4,646
03/16	14,222	3,660	25.7%	4,646
03/15	17,321	8,409	48.6%	4,900
Annual Growth	5.7%	(10.9%)	—	(1.4%)

Bank of Kyoto Ltd (Japan)

For financial services in Kyoto proper protocol might involve a visit to The Bank of Kyoto. The regional bank serves Kyoto and neighboring prefectures through some 165 branch offices. The bank serves businesses particularly small and medium-sized local companies as well as individual consumers. In addition to traditional deposit banking and lending The Bank of Kyoto and its subsidiaries offer credit cards leasing stock brokerage and business consulting services. The bank has worked to expand its operations beyond its home base and has opened branches to the north in the Kinki Region. Founded in 1941 the bank has about $81 billion in assets and ranks as Kyoto Prefecture's largest retail bank.

Geographic Reach

The Bank of Kyoto operates 110 branches in Kyoto Prefecture 28 in Osaka Prefecture a dozen in Shiga eight in Hyogo and seven branches in Nara.

Strategy

The Bank of Kyoto is aggressively opening branches to expand its reach beyond Kyoto Prefecture. Since opening its first branch at Kusatsu in Shiga Prefecture in 2000 the bank has opened branches in five neighboring prefectures (Kyoto Osaka Shiga Nara and Hyogo).

EXECUTIVES

President, NOBUHIRO DOI
Auditors: Deloitte Touche Tohmatsu LLC

LOCATIONS

HQ: Bank of Kyoto Ltd (Japan)
  700 Yakushimae-cho, Karasuma-dori Matsubara-Agaru, Shimogyo-ku, Kyoto 600-8652
Phone: (81) 75 361 2211   **Fax:** (81) 75 343 1276
Web: www.kyotobank.co.jp

COMPETITORS

Mitsubishi UFJ Financial Group	Resona
Mizuho Financial	Sumitomo Mitsui

HISTORICAL FINANCIALS

Company Type: Public

Income Statement				FYE: March 31
	ASSETS ($ mil.)	NET INCOME ($ mil.)	INCOME AS % OF ASSETS	EMPLOYEES
03/20	92,846	187	0.2%	3,969
03/19	87,274	286	0.3%	4,092
03/18	89,263	181	0.2%	4,154
03/17	79,596	166	0.2%	4,099
03/16	72,614	189	0.3%	4,052
Annual Growth	6.3%	(0.3%)	—	(0.5%)

Bank of Montreal (Quebec)

Auditors: KPMG LLP

LOCATIONS

HQ: Bank of Montreal (Quebec)
  129 rue Saint Jacques, Montreal, Quebec H2Y 1L6
Phone: 416 867-6785   **Fax:** 416 867-6793
Web: www.bmo.com

HISTORICAL FINANCIALS

Company Type: Public

Income Statement				FYE: October 31
	ASSETS ($ mil.)	NET INCOME ($ mil.)	INCOME AS % OF ASSETS	EMPLOYEES
10/20	713,601	3,645	0.5%	43,360
10/19	646,973	4,211	0.7%	45,513
10/18	589,502	4,150	0.7%	45,454
10/17	552,342	4,162	0.8%	45,200
10/16	514,211	3,454	0.7%	45,000
Annual Growth	8.5%	1.4%	—	(0.9%)

	STOCK PRICE ($) FY Close	P/E High/Low		PER SHARE ($) Earnings	Dividends	Book Value
10/20	59.47	10	6	5.68	3.19	65.87
10/19	73.99	9	7	6.57	3.07	60.66
10/18	74.74	10	9	6.22	2.95	54.47
10/17	76.61	10	8	6.16	2.74	53.30
10/16	63.60	9	8	5.17	2.56	48.97
Annual Growth	(1.7%)	—	—	2.3%	5.7%	7.7%

Bank of Nagoya, Ltd.

Auditors: KPMG AZSA LLC

LOCATIONS

HQ: Bank of Nagoya, Ltd.
  3-19-17 Nishiki, Naka-ku, Nagoya, Aichi 460-0003
Phone: (81) 52 951 5911   **Fax:** (81) 52 961 6605
Web: www.meigin.com

COMPETITORS

Bank of Kyoto	Resona
Bank of Yokohama	Shizuoka Bank

Chiba Bank
Mitsubishi UFJ
  Financial Group
Mizuho Trust & Banking
  Ltd

Sumitomo Mitsui
Sumitomo Mitsui Trust
  Holdings

HISTORICAL FINANCIALS
Company Type: Public

Income Statement   FYE: March 31

	ASSETS ($ mil.)	NET INCOME ($ mil.)	INCOME AS % OF ASSETS	EMPLOYEES
03/20	36,250	42	0.1%	2,396
03/19	35,191	55	0.2%	2,445
03/18	36,103	54	0.2%	2,486
03/17	32,802	53	0.2%	2,534
03/16	31,651	62	0.2%	2,535
Annual Growth	3.5%	(9.0%)	—	(1.4%)

2020 Year-End Financials
Return on assets: 0.1%
Return on equity: 2.0%
Long-term debt ($ mil.): —
No. of shares (mil.): 18
Sales ($ mil): 617

Dividends
Yield: —
Payout: 28.4%
Market value ($ mil.): —

Bank of Nova Scotia
Halifax

The Bank of Nova Scotia provides retail corporate and investment banking services primarily in Canada and Latin America. The Bank of Nova Scotia serves customers through its network of approximately 950 branches more than 3650 automated banking machines (ABMs) and the internet mobile telephone banking and specialized sales teams. Canadian Banking also provides an alternative self-directed banking solution to over 2 million Tangerine Bank customers Its retail banking focuses on its home country and several key Latin & Central American countries. The Global Banking & Markets segment extends the bank's reach to dozens of other countries including the United States Latin America Europe and Asia-Pacific. Bank services include deposit accounts loans insurance brokerage asset management wealth management foreign exchange services equity underwriting and trust services. The bank was founded in 1832.

Operations
The Bank of Nova Scotia operates three segments: Canadian Banking International Banking and Global Banking & Markets.

Canadian Banking serves more than 11 million retail small business commercial banking and wealth management clients. It interacts with its customers through a network of almost 1000 physical branches and more than 3600 ATMs along with mobile and digital banking platforms. The segment provides financial advice and solutions such as debit & credit cards checking accounts home mortgages and insurance products. It also sells wealth management services and products to help clients achieve investment and retirement objectives. The unit generates about 45% of all revenue and earnings.

The International Banking business (about 40% of the revenue) provides products and services similar to the Canadian Banking segment but to more than 11 million Retail Corporate and Com-

mercial customers. The customers are served by a network of more than 1900 branches 5500 ATMs and contact centers.

Global Banking and Markets (GBM) (about 15%) provides corporate clients with lending and transaction services investment banking advice and access to capital markets.

Geographic Reach
Toronto Canada-based Bank of Nova Scotia generates roughly half of its revenue from Canada with its home province of Ontario representing about half of all Canadian revenue. Its southern neighbor the US accounts for about 5% of revenue while its major South American markets such as Mexico Peru Chile Brazil and Colombia combine to bring in some 15%. Asia Pacific's share of revenue is growing in recent years and has surpassed the 20% mark.

It also has operations in Europe and the Caribbean with a relatively large presence in Panama Dominican Republic and Costa Rica. Within Asia it runs its business in China India Hong Kong Japan South Korea Malaysia and others.

Sales and Marketing
The Bank of Nova Scotia serves about 65% of its loans to personal customers and the remaining 35% to commercial and corporate enterprises. It markets its products and services through its website printed material available in bank branches and other methods. Its business clients operate in several industries including real estate & construction financial services wholesale & retail energy automotive healthcare technology media agriculture and others.

Advertising and business development costs were $625 million for 2019 and $581 for both 2018 and 2017.

The company also partnered with charities such as United Way Greater Toronto Big Brothers Big Sisters and FC Barcelona and the FC Barcelona Foundation to support its customers and communities.

Financial Performance
Note: Financial results are denoted in the company's home currency the Canadian Dollar denoted CAD$.

The Bank of Nova Scotia has produced steady financial growth year after year. Net interest income increased from 2015 -2019 and the same goes for non-interest income.

In FY2019 (ended October 31 2019) the firm earned CAD$17.1 billion in net interest income and CAD$13.8 billion in non-interest income. The total revenue of CAD$31.0 billion was almost 10% higher than the prior year's result due to growth in retail and commercial lending.

Net income for the year was CAD$8.8 billion an increase of one percent compared to FY2018. Global Banking & Markets lodged a stellar year with a 17% earnings.

Cash at the end of FY2019 was CAD$10.9 billion. Financing activities used CAD$1.3 billion mostly as a disbursement of dividends to shareholders. Investing activities gained the coffers by CAD$15.2 billion due to interest-bearing deposits with other financial institutions. Operating activities used CAD$12.0 billion because of loans asset and interest paid.

Strategy
The geographic aspect of the Bank's strategic repositioning program is substantially complete. The Bank's sharpened footprint has positioned it as a leading Bank in the Americas and allows it to connect with the customers in other parts of the world. The business model is predicated on a high degree of strategic diversification. This strategy enables the company to expand its network in different continents.

The company also embraces and executes a secure Cloud-first technology strategy. Cloud computing is the on-demand delivery of computing power database storage and applications on a pay-as-you-go basis. Moving to the Cloud brings down costs improves the speed of innovation enables analytics and helps deliver enhanced digital solutions to the clients.

In terms of its customers the Canadian Bank will build stronger relationships with its customers in order to drive increased loyalty and higher engagement. This will be driven by ongoing efforts to build a high-quality team comprised of diverse and highly engaged employees In addition leadership enterprise productivity digital transformation business mix alignment and strong risk culture are prioritiies and part of the strategy.

Mergers and Acquisitions
In 2019 the Bank acquired 51% of the voting shares of Banco Cencosud Peru in exchange for a total consideration of $133 million in cash. The Bank and Banco Cencosud will jointly manage the credit card operations and offer other products and services to customers in partnership for 15 years.

In 2019 the Bank acquired 97.44% of the voting shares of Banco Dominicano del Progreso a bank with operations in the Dominican Republic in exchange for a total consideration of $440 million in cash.

EXECUTIVES
EVP and Co-Head Information Technology Enterprise Technology, Michael Zerbs
EVP and General Counsel, Deborah M. Alexander
President and CEO, Brian J. Porter, $450,000 total compensation
EVP Latin America, Dieter W. Jentsch
Group Head and CFO, Sean McGuckin
Chief Risk Officer, Stephen P. Hart
EVP and Chief Administrative Officer International Banking, Marianne Hasold-Schilter
EVP Canadian Banking, James McPhedran
EVP Global Financial Institutions and Transaction Banking, Marian Lawson
EVP and Group Treasurer, Andrew Branion
EVP and Chief Credit Officer, Terry Fryett
Group Head Canadian Banking, James O'Sullivan
Group Head International Banking and Digital Transformation, Ignacio (Nacho) Deschamps
EVP and Chief Marketing Officer, John Doig
EVP Retail Payments Deposits and Unsecured Lending, Mike Henry
EVP and Co-Head Information Technology Business Systems, Kyle McNamara
EVP International Corporate and Commercial Banking, James Neate
EVP Operations, Dan Rees
EVP Canadian Commercial Banking, Gillian Riley
EVP Digital Banking, Shawn Rose
EVP Retail Distribution Canadian Banking, Maria Theofilaktidis
Auditors: KPMG LLP

LOCATIONS
HQ: Bank of Nova Scotia Halifax
  1709 Hollis Street, Halifax, Nova Scotia B3J 3B7
Phone: 416 866-3672   **Fax:** 416 866-7767
Web: www.scotiabank.com

PRODUCTS/OPERATIONS

FY2017 Revenue

	% of total
Interest	
Loans	62
Securities & Deposits with financial institutions	5
Non-interest	
Banking	11
Wealth management	9
Trading	4
Underwriting and other advisory	2
Non-trading foreign exchange	2
Net gain on sale of investment securities	2
Insurance underwriting income net of claims	2
Net income from investments in associated corporations	1
Others	3
Total	**100**

FY2017 Revenue

	% of total
Canadian Banking	46
International Banking	37
Global Banking and Markets	17
Total	**100**

Selected Canadian Subsidiaries

BNS Capital Trust
BNS Investment Inc.
  Montreal Trust Company of Canada
  Scotia Merchant Capital Corporation
Dundee Bank of Canada
Maple Trust Company
National Trustco Inc.
  The Bank of Nova Scotia Trust Company
  National Trust Company
RoyNat Inc.
Scotia Capital Inc.
  1548489 Ontario Limited
  Scotia iTrade Corp.
Scotia Asset Management L.P.
Scotia Capital Inc.
Scotia Dealer Advantage Inc.
Scotia Insurance Agency Inc.
Scotia Life Insurance Company
Scotia Mortgage Corporation
Scotia Securities Inc.
Scotiabank Capital Trust
Scotiabank Subordinated Notes Trust.
Scotiabank Tier 1 Trust

Selected International Subsidiaries

The Bank of Nova Scotia Berhad (Malaysia)
The Bank of Nova Scotia International Limited
  (Bahamas)
    The Bank of Nova Scotia Asia Limited (Singapore)
    The Bank of Nova Scotia Trust Company (Bahamas)
    Ltd.
  Scotiabank & Trust (Cayman) Ltd. (Cayman Islands)
BNS (Colombia) Holdings Limited
Grupo BNS de Costa Rica S.A.
Scotia Insurance (Barbados) Limited
Scotiabank (Bahamas) Limited
Scotiabank (British Virgin Islands) Limited
Scotiabank Caribbean Treasury Limited (Bahamas)
Scotiabank (Hong Kong) Limited
Scotiabank (Ireland) Limited
Scotia Group Jamaica Limited (72%)
  The Bank of Nova Scotia Jamaica Limited
  Scotia DBG Investments Limited (77% Jamaica)
Grupo Financiero Scotiabank Inverlat S.A. de C.V. (97%
  Mexico)
Nova Scotia Inversiones Limitada (Chile)
  Scotiabank Chile S.A.
Scotia Capital (USA) Inc.
Scotia Holdings (US) Inc.
  The Bank of Nova Scotia Trust Company of New York
  Scotiabanc Inc. (US)
Scotia International Limited (Bahamas)
  Scotiabank Anguilla Limited
Scotiabank de Puerto Rico
Scotiabank El Salvador S.A.
Scotiabank Europe plc (UK)
Scotiabank Peru S.A.A.
Scotiabank Trinidad and Tobago Limited

COMPETITORS

BMO Financial Group   HSBC Bank Canada

Banamex	JPMorgan Chase
Banco Santander Chile	National Bank of
Bank of America	Canada
Bicsa Panama	RBC Financial Group
CIBC	TD Bank
Citigroup	

HISTORICAL FINANCIALS
Company Type: Public

Income Statement
FYE: October 31

	ASSETS ($ mil.)	NET INCOME ($ mil.)	INCOME AS % OF ASSETS	EMPLOYEES
10/20	854,331	4,947	0.6%	92,001
10/19	824,596	6,231	0.8%	101,813
10/18	760,435	6,367	0.8%	97,629
10/17	712,455	6,130	0.9%	55,645
10/16	669,932	5,222	0.8%	88,901
Annual Growth	6.3%	(1.3%)	—	0.9%

2020 Year-End Financials

Return on assets: 0.5%
Return on equity: 9.6%
Long-term debt ($ mil.): —
No. of shares (mil.): 1,211
Sales ($ mil): 32,872
Dividends
Yield: 0.0%
Payout: 67.9%
Market value ($ mil.): 50,349

	STOCK PRICE ($) FY Close	P/E High/Low		PER SHARE ($) Earnings	Dividends	Book Value
10/20	41.56	11	6	3.98	2.71	42.27
10/19	57.33	9	7	5.07	2.62	42.15
10/18	53.71	9	8	5.19	2.55	40.49
10/17	64.52	10	8	5.05	2.33	38.97
10/16	53.76	9	7	4.31	2.17	34.81
Annual Growth	(6.2%)	—	—	(2.0%)	5.6%	5.0%

Bank of Queensland Ltd

EXECUTIVES

Director, NEIL SUMMERSON
Auditors: KPMG

LOCATIONS

HQ: Bank of Queensland Ltd
Level 6, 100 Skyring Terrace, Newstead, Queensland
4006
Phone: (61) 7 3212 3333   **Fax:** (61) 7 3212 3399
Web: www.boq.com.au

HISTORICAL FINANCIALS
Company Type: Public

Income Statement
FYE: August 31

	ASSETS ($ mil.)	NET INCOME ($ mil.)	INCOME AS % OF ASSETS	EMPLOYEES
08/19	37,412	200	0.5%	2,098
08/18	38,260	242	0.6%	2,039
08/17	40,704	277	0.7%	2,031
08/16	38,228	254	0.7%	1,959
08/15	34,209	226	0.7%	1,991
Annual Growth	2.3%	(3.0%)	—	1.3%

2019 Year-End Financials

Return on assets: 0.5%
Return on equity: 7.7%
Long-term debt ($ mil.): —
No. of shares (mil.): 405
Sales ($ mil): 1,508
Dividends
Yield: 0.0%
Payout: 187.2%
Market value ($ mil.): 4,987

	STOCK PRICE ($) FY Close	P/E High/Low		PER SHARE ($) Earnings	Dividends	Book Value
08/19	12.31	20	16	0.47	0.87	6.41
08/18	16.01	23	16	0.59	1.16	7.02
08/17	20.10	23	17	0.69	1.02	7.63
08/16	15.78	24	17	0.64	0.99	7.09
08/15	18.27	24	19	0.59	1.27	6.67
Annual Growth	(9.4%)	—	—	(5.7%)	(9.0%)	(1.0%)

Bank of the Philippine Islands

EXECUTIVES

President and Chief Executive, Cezar Consing
Chairman, Jaime Augusto Zobel De Ayala
Vice Chairman, Fernando Zobel De Ayala
Auditors: Isla Lipana & Co.

LOCATIONS

HQ: Bank of the Philippine Islands
Ayala North Exchange Tower 1, Ayala Ave. Corner
Salcedo St., Legaspi Village, Makati City 1229
Phone: (63) 2 246 5902
Web: www.bpi.com.ph

COMPETITORS

DBS Group Holdings	Pag-IBIG Fund
Maybank	United Overseas Bank
Metropolitan Bank and	
Trust	

HISTORICAL FINANCIALS
Company Type: Public

Income Statement
FYE: December 31

	ASSETS ($ mil.)	NET INCOME ($ mil.)	INCOME AS % OF ASSETS	EMPLOYEES
12/19	43,546	568	1.3%	21,429
12/18	39,703	439	1.1%	18,911
12/17	38,220	449	1.2%	17,047
12/16	34,853	445	1.3%	15,201
12/15	32,365	389	1.2%	14,647
Annual Growth	7.7%	10.0%	—	10.0%

2019 Year-End Financials

Return on assets: 1.3%
Return on equity: 11.1%
Long-term debt ($ mil.): —
No. of shares (mil.): —
Sales ($ mil): 2,566
Dividends
Yield: 0.0%
Payout: 523.1%
Market value ($ mil.): —

	STOCK PRICE ($) FY Close	P/E High/Low		PER SHARE ($) Earnings	Dividends	Book Value
12/19	39.86	6	5	0.13	0.66	1.18
12/18	37.89	—	—	0.10	0.21	1.05
12/17	37.89	7	6	0.11	0.44	0.92
12/16	39.70	7	7	0.11	0.67	0.85
12/15	41.21	—	—	0.10	0.47	0.82
Annual Growth	(0.8%)	—	—	6.2%	9.1%	9.7%

Bank Polska Kasa Opieki SA

EXECUTIVES

Supervisory Board Member, Malgorzata Barbara Sadurska
Board of Directors Vice President, Leszek Marcin Skiba
Supervisory Board Member, Sabina Bigos Jaworowska
Supervisory Board Member, Marian Majcher
Supervisory Board Member, Beata Kozlowska Chyla
Supervisory Board Member, Stanislaw Ryszard Kaczoruk
Supervisory Board Member, Michal Rafal Kaszynski
Board of Directors Vice President, Marek Grzegorz Lusztyn
Board of Directors Vice President, Tomasz Kubiak
Auditors: KPMG Audyt Spolka z ograniczona odpowiedzialnoscia sp. k.

LOCATIONS

HQ: Bank Polska Kasa Opieki SA
  53/57 Grzybowska Street, Warsaw 00-950
Phone: (48) 22 656 00 00   **Fax:** (48) 22 656 00 04
Web: www.pekao.com.pl

COMPETITORS

AIB	Nordea Bank
Bank BPH	PKO Bank Polski SA
Bank Millennium	Provident Financial
Citi Handlowy	

HISTORICAL FINANCIALS
Company Type: Public

Income Statement				FYE: December 31
	ASSETS ($ mil.)	NET INCOME ($ mil.)	INCOME AS % OF ASSETS	EMPLOYEES
12/19	53,593	570	1.1%	15,678
12/18	50,910	609	1.2%	16,714
12/17	53,251	710	1.3%	17,339
12/16	41,650	544	1.3%	17,757
12/15	43,122	585	1.4%	18,327
Annual Growth	5.6%	(0.6%)	—	(3.8%)

2019 Year-End Financials

Return on assets: 1.1%
Return on equity: 9.3%
Long-term debt ($ mil.): —
No. of shares (mil.): 262
Sales ($ mil): 2,594

Dividends
  Yield: —
  Payout: 63.0%
Market value ($ mil.): —

Bank Sarasin & Co

EXECUTIVES

Managing Director, Edmond Michaan
Chairman of the Board, J rg Haller
Vice Chairman Of The Board, Pierre-Alain Bracher
Board Member, Enid Ying Lai Choi
Board Member, Philippe Dupont
Board Member, Jorge Alberto Kininsberg
Board Member, Jacob Safra
Auditors: Deloitte AG

LOCATIONS

HQ: Bank Sarasin & Co
  Elisabethenstrasse 62, Basel, Postfach 4002
Phone: (41) 58 317 44 44   **Fax:** (41) 58 317 44 00
Web: www.jsafrasarasin.com

COMPETITORS

Credit Suisse	UBS
HSBC	

HISTORICAL FINANCIALS
Company Type: Public

Income Statement				FYE: December 31
	ASSETS ($ mil.)	NET INCOME ($ mil.)	INCOME AS % OF ASSETS	EMPLOYEES
12/19	37,889	393	1.0%	2,178
12/18	35,814	353	1.0%	2,151
12/17	36,036	323	0.9%	2,155
12/16	21,433	118	0.6%	0
12/15	21,644	136	0.6%	0
Annual Growth	15.0%	30.3%	—	—

2019 Year-End Financials

Return on assets: 1.0%
Return on equity: 9.0%
Long-term debt ($ mil.): —
No. of shares (mil.): 0
Sales ($ mil): 1,634

Dividends
  Yield: —
  Payout: —
Market value ($ mil.): —

Bankia S A

Auditors: Ernst & Young, S.L.

LOCATIONS

HQ: Bankia S A
  Paseo de la Castellana 189, Madrid, Las Rozas 28046
Phone: (34) 91 787 7575   **Fax:** (34) 91 791 1600
Web: www.bankia.com

HISTORICAL FINANCIALS
Company Type: Public

Income Statement				FYE: December 31
	ASSETS ($ mil.)	NET INCOME ($ mil.)	INCOME AS % OF ASSETS	EMPLOYEES
12/19	234,061	607	0.3%	16,035
12/18	235,020	805	0.3%	15,924
12/17	256,451	604	0.2%	17,757
12/16	200,794	849	0.4%	13,505
12/15	225,433	1,132	0.5%	13,571
Annual Growth	0.9%	(14.4%)	—	4.3%

2019 Year-End Financials

Return on assets: 0.2%
Return on equity: 4.0%
Long-term debt ($ mil.): —
No. of shares (mil.): —
Sales ($ mil): 4,375

Dividends
  Yield: 6.2%
  Payout: 72.3%
Market value ($ mil.): —

Bankinter, S.A.

EXECUTIVES

CEO, Mar a D. Dancausa Treviño
Chairman, Pedro Guerrero Guerrero, age 68
Auditors: PricewaterhouseCoopers Auditores, S.L.

LOCATIONS

HQ: Bankinter, S.A.
  Paseo de la Castellana, 29, Madrid 28046
Phone: (34) 91 339 75 00   **Fax:** (34) 91 339 83 23
Web: www.bankinter.com

PRODUCTS/OPERATIONS

2014 Sales

	% of total
Interest and similar income	54
Fee and commission income	14
Other revenues	32
Total	100

Selected Subsidiaries

Aircraft S.A.
Bankinter Consultoria Asesoramiento y Atencion Telefonica S.A.
Bankinter Gestion de Seguros S.A.
Bankinter International B.V. (Netherlands)
Bankinter Seguros de Vida S.A.
Gesbankinter S.A.
Hispamarket S.A.
Intergestora S.A.
Intergestora Nuevas Tecnologias S.C.R. S.A.
Intermobiliaria S.A.

COMPETITORS

AEGON	Banco de Sabadell
BBVA	Deutsche Bank
Banco Español de Crédito	Esp rito Santo
Banco Popular Español	Grupo Santander
	La Caixa

HISTORICAL FINANCIALS
Company Type: Public

Income Statement				FYE: December 31
	ASSETS ($ mil.)	NET INCOME ($ mil.)	INCOME AS % OF ASSETS	EMPLOYEES
12/19	94,011	618	0.7%	8,531
12/18	87,609	602	0.7%	5,605
12/17	85,510	593	0.7%	5,578
12/16	70,936	517	0.7%	5,486
12/15	63,892	409	0.6%	4,205
Annual Growth	10.1%	10.9%	—	19.3%

2019 Year-End Financials

Return on assets: 0.6%
Return on equity: 11.8%
Long-term debt ($ mil.): —
No. of shares (mil.): 898
Sales ($ mil): 3,468

Dividends
  Yield: —
  Payout: 48.3%
Market value ($ mil.): —

Banque Cantonale Vaudoise

EXECUTIVES

Managing Director, Pascal Kiener
Chairman Of The Board, Jacques de Watteville
Vice Chairman Of The Board, Jean-Fran ßois Schwarz

Board Member, Eftychia Fischer
Board Member, George Clemons
Board Member, Ingrid Deltenre
Board Member, Fabienne Freymond Cantone
Board Member, Peter Ochsner
Auditors: KPMG SA

LOCATIONS

HQ: Banque Cantonale Vaudoise
  Place Saint-Francois 14, P.O. Box 300, Lausanne 1001
Phone: (41) 21 212 10 10   **Fax:** (41) 21 212 12 22
Web: www.bcv.ch

COMPETITORS

Bank Sarasin	Swiss Post
Credit Suisse	UBS
HSBC Private Bank	
Merrill Lynch Bank	
(Suisse)	

HISTORICAL FINANCIALS

Company Type: Public

Income Statement   FYE: December 31

	ASSETS ($ mil.)	NET INCOME ($ mil.)	INCOME AS % OF ASSETS	EMPLOYEES
12/19	50,017	375	0.8%	1,921
12/18	48,655	355	0.7%	1,896
12/17	46,533	328	0.7%	1,922
12/16	43,309	304	0.7%	1,943
12/15	43,719	338	0.8%	1,947
Annual Growth	3.4%	2.6%	—	(0.3%)

2019 Year-End Financials

Return on assets: 0.7%	Dividends
Return on equity: 10.2%	Yield: —
Long-term debt ($ mil.): —	Payout: —
No. of shares (mil.): 8	Market value ($ mil.): —
Sales ($ mil.): 1,187	

Baoshan Iron & Steel Co Ltd

Auditors: Deloitte Touche Tohmatsu Certified Public
  Accountants Limited

LOCATIONS

HQ: Baoshan Iron & Steel Co Ltd
  Baosteel Command Center, No. 885, Fujin Road,
  Baoshan District, Shanghai 201900
Phone: (86) 21 26647000   **Fax:** (86) 21 26646999
Web: www.baosteel.com/plc/

HISTORICAL FINANCIALS

Company Type: Public

Income Statement   FYE: December 31

	REVENUE ($ mil.)	NET INCOME ($ mil.)	NET PROFIT MARGIN	EMPLOYEES
12/19	41,972	1,785	4.3%	0
12/18	44,372	3,135	7.1%	0
12/17	44,487	2,945	6.6%	0
12/16	26,743	1,291	4.8%	0
12/15	25,270	155	0.6%	0
Annual Growth	13.5%	83.9%	—	—

2019 Year-End Financials

Debt ratio: 1.1%	No. of shares (mil.): —
Return on equity: 7.0%	Dividends
Cash ($ mil.): 1,931	Yield: —
Current ratio: 0.98	Payout: —
Long-term debt ($ mil.): 1,581	Market value ($ mil.): —

Barclays PLC

Raising the bar for global finance Barclays PLC owns one of Europe's largest banks a top market-making investment bank the top UK credit card and a British universal bank Its flagship Barclays Bank UK has nearly 965 branches in the UK reaching around 10 million digitally-active customers and some 8.5 million active mobile banking users. Barclays International has retail operations throughout Europe UK and the Americas as well as extensive investment banking and wealth management activities. Barclays provides consumer lending and payment processing services.

Operations

Barclays operates two businesses: Barclays International and Barclays UK.

Barclays International generates around two thirds of revenue and consists of its corporate and investment bank; and consumer cards and payments. Barclays International's diversified business portfolio provides balance resilience and exciting growth opportunities. The division has strong global market positions and continues to invest in people and technology in order to deliver sustainable improved returns. Barclays International offers customers and clients a range of products and services spanning consumer and wholesale banking.

Barclays UK (accounts for around a third of revenue) a ring fenced bank comprised largely of UK Personal and Business Banking and Barclaycard Consumer UK businesses. UK Personal Banking offers retail solutions to help customers with their day-to-day banking needs. UK Business Banking serves business clients from high growth start-ups to small and medium-sized enterprises with specialist advice for their business banking needs. Barclaycard Consumer UK is a leading credit card provider offering flexible borrowing and payment solutions while delivering a leading customer experience.

Geographic Reach

Barclays serves customers in around 25 countries. In the UK it has nearly 965 retail banking branches. The UK accounts for some 55% of Barclays' net revenue the Americas nearly 35% and Europe nearly 10%. It also generates a small amount in the Asia-Pacific region and Africa and the Middle East.

Barclays' head office is located in London United Kingdom.

Sales and Marketing

Barclays UK's customers and clients consists of high growth and small and medium-sized companies. Barclays International's customers and clients consists of consumers; corporates; financial institutions; and money managers and institutional investors.

Barclays spent some Â 425 million on marketing advertising and sponsorship in 2019 from some Â 495 million and nearly Â 435 million in 2018 and 2017.

Financial Performance

Note: Growth rates may differ after conversion to US Dollars.Barclays' financial performance has been underwhelming during the last five years.

Net interest income and non-interest income have both fluctuated over the period causing total revenue to be similarly uneven.

In 2019 Barclays' revenue increased 2% to Â 21.6 billion.

Barclays had an increase of 54% in profits from Â 1.6 billion in 2018 to Â 2.5 billion in 2019 primarily due to a larger profit after tax in respect of continuing operations.

The bank's cash balance grew during 2019 ending the year Â 27.8 billion lower at Â 183.4 billion. Barclay's operations used cash of Â 12.3 billion. Its investing activities used Â 12.8 billion while financing activities generated Â 690 million. The bank's primary cash uses were capital expenditures debt repayments and share repurchases.

Strategy

As a purpose-driven organization Barclays aspires to create opportunities to rise for all of its stakeholders. Its strategy has been developed to balance the needs of customers and clients colleagues investors and wider society. Barclays has transformed over the last four years responding to changes in the economic and regulatory environment and to the changing needs of customers and clients.

Barclays' four strategic pillars consists of: focusing on customers and clients; becoming more digital; protecting and strengthening its culture; and maintaining and increasing its diversification.

The company's strategy builds on its strengths and will steer it through those challenges.

Company Background

Legal troubles have caused headwinds for Barclays's bottom line in recent years. In mid-2012 the company admitted to manipulating the London Interbank Offered Rate (LIBOR) a benchmark for daily global short-term interest rates. The bank repeatedly manipulated the LIBOR in order to make its funding position look stronger than it actually was; the rigging also helped the bank make money on credit derivatives. Chairman Martin Agius and CEO Bob Diamond both resigned as a result of the developments and the company paid US and UK regulators some Â 290 million ($453 million) in settlement fines. Shortly after the LIBOR scandal the UK's Serious Fraud Office launched an inquiry into payments Barclays made to sovereign investor Qatar Holding in 2008. At the behest of regulators Barclays ringfenced its UK consumer bank from its riskier investment banking assets in 2018.

HISTORY

Barclays first spread its wings in 1736 when James Barclay united his family's goldsmithing and banking businesses. As other family members joined the London enterprise it became known as Barclays Bevan & Tritton (1782).

Banking first became regulated in the 19th century. To ward off takeovers 20 banks combined with Barclays in 1896. The new firm Barclay & Co. began preying on other banks. Within 20 years it bought 17 including the Colonial Bank chartered in 1836 to serve the West Indies and British Guiana (now Guyana). The company renamed Barclays Bank Ltd. in 1917 weathered the Depression as the UK's #2 bank.

Barclays began expanding again after WWII and by the late 1950s it had become the UK's top bank. It had a computer network by 1959 and in 1966 it introduced the Barclaycard in conjunction with Bank of America's BankAmericard (now Visa).

In 1968 the UK's Monopolies Commission barred Barclays' merger with two other big London banks but had no objections to a two-way merger so Barclays bought competitor Martins.

Barclays moved into the US consumer finance market in 1980 when it bought American Credit

138 former Beneficial Finance offices and Bankers Trust's branch network.

During the 1980s London banks faced competition from invading overseas banks local building societies and other financial firms. Banking reform in 1984 led to formation of a holding company for Barclays Bank PLC.

To prepare for British financial deregulation in 1986 Barclays formed Barclays de Zoete Wedd (BZW) by merging its merchant bank with two other London financial firms. Faced with sagging profits Barclays sold its California bank in 1988 and its US consumer finance business in 1989.

In 1990 Barclays bought private German bank Merck Finck & Co. and Paris bank L'Européenne de Banque. The company countered 1992's bad-loan-induced losses by accelerating a cost-cutting program begun in 1989. To appease stockholders chairman and CEO Andrew Buxton (a descendant of one of the bank's founding families) gave up his CEO title hiring Martin Taylor (previously CEO of textile firm Courtaulds) for the post.

The company sold its Australian retail banking business in 1994 then began trimming other operations including French corporate banking and US mortgage operations. However it bought the Wells Fargo Nikko Investment Company to boost Asian operations.

Barclays' piecemeal sale of BZW signaled its failure to become a global investment banking powerhouse. In 1997 it sold BZW's European investment banking business to Credit Suisse First Boston retaining the fixed-income and foreign exchange business. (Credit Suisse bought Barclays' Asian investment banking operations in 1998.)

Losses in Russia and a $250 million bailout of US hedge fund Long-Term Capital Management hit Barclays Capital in 1998. Taylor resigned that year in part because of his radical plans for the bank. Sir Peter Middleton stepped in as acting CEO; Barclays later tapped Canadian banker Matthew Barrett for the post. (Middleton also became chairman upon Buxton's retirement.)

Barclays in 1999 started a move toward online banking at the expense of traditional branches. The company announced free lifetime Internet access for new bank customers.

In 2000 the bank ruffled feathers when it announced the closure of about 170 mostly rural UK branches. Also in 2000 the company sold its Dial auto leasing unit to ABN AMRO and bought Woolwich plc. The following year Barclay's closed its own life insurance division opting instead to sell the life insurance and pension products of London-based Legal & General Group.

In 2004 chief executive Barrett was named Barclays' chairman succeeding Peter Middleton who became chairman of Centre for Effective Dispute Resolution (CEDR) and later chancellor of the University of Sheffield.

After exiting the South African market in 1987 over apartheid concerns Barclays returned in a big way in 2005 buying a majority stake (about 57%) in the Absa Group one of the country's largest retail banks. The deal also represented the largest-ever direct foreign investment there. The next year Barclays sold its South African businesses including corporate international retail and commercial operations to Absa.

The company entered the US credit card market when it bought Juniper Financial (now Barclays Bank Delaware) from Canadian Imperial Bank of Commerce (CIBC) in 2004. In a previous hook-up with CIBC Barclays merged its Caribbean banking business with CIBC's to create an 85-branch regional bank FirstCaribbean International Bank with each company owning 44%; Barclays sold its stake to CIBC in 2006.

In 2005 the bank sold its vendor finance businesses in the UK and Germany to CIT Group. Bar-

clays said that the sale will allow it to focus on its commercial leasing business.

The bank moved to assimilate its Woolwich acquisition in 2006 when it closed 200 branches and consolidated Woolwich branches into existing Barclays locations. It retained the Woolwich mortgage brand but switched account holders to Barclays accounts.

The company and HSBC formed a joint venture that manages their cash handling operations in the UK. Named Vaultex the joint venture acquired Loomis Cash Management in 2007.

Marcus Agius succeeded the retiring Matthew Barrett as chairman in 2007.

Although the company withdrew its bid for Dutch banking giant ABN AMRO (narrowly escaping that troubled deal) in 2008 it bought Russian bank Expobank from Petropavlovsk Finance. Expobank was one of the largest ATM networks in Russia and part of the booming consumer banking industry there. Also that year Barclays sold noncore business Barclays Life and its portfolio of some 760000 life and pension policies to Swiss Re for Å 753 million ($1.5 billion).

The group chose not to participate in the UK's bank bailouts as the global financial crisis intensified in late 2008 but pursued its own capital-raising plan. Through the deal sovereign investment fund Qatar Investment Authority became the bank's largest shareholder with a 5% stake.

In 2009 it shut down US-based subprime mortgage lender EquiFirst which it had purchased from Regions Financial before it fell victim to the mortgage bust.

Later that year it sold a majority of Barclays Global Investors to American money manager BlackRock for Å 9.5 billion ($15 billion). In exchange it gained a 20% stake in the new Black-Rock with some $3 trillion under management for institutional clients around the world. The deal provided the bank with much-needed cash and cleared the way for a commercial partnership with BlackRock.

Another major transaction was the Å 1 billion ($1.8 billion) acquisition of Lehman Brothers' North American operations a deal which made Barclays Capital one of the world's largest investment banks.

EXECUTIVES

Chairman Barclays UK and Director, Ian Cheshire, age 61

Group CEO and Director, James E. (Jes) Staley, age 63

CEO Barclays Bank Ireland, Kevin Wall
Interim CEO Markets Division, Tim Throsby
Group Finance Director, Tushar Morzaria
Group COO, Paul Compton
Group Chief Risk Officer, C.S. Venkatakrishnan
Executive Chairman, John McFarlane, age 73
Deputy Chairman, Gerry Grimstone
Auditors: KPMG LLP

LOCATIONS

HQ: Barclays PLC
1 Churchill Place, London E14 5HP
Phone: (44) 20 7116 3170
Web: www.barclays.com

2018 Sales

	% of total
UK	52
Americas	36
Europe	8
Africa and Middle East	3
Asia	1
Total	**100**

PRODUCTS/OPERATIONS

2018 Sales

	% of total
Barclays International	66
Barclays UK	34
Head Office	-
Total	**100**

COMPETITORS

AXA UK	Lloyds Banking Group
Bank of New York	Mitsubishi UFJ
Mellon	Financial Group
CIBC	Mizuho Financial
Citigroup	RBC Financial Group
Deutsche Bank	Royal Bank of Scotland
Grupo Santander	Standard Chartered
HSBC	The Vanguard Group
Invesco	UBS
JPMorgan Chase	

HISTORICAL FINANCIALS

Company Type: Public

Income Statement				FYE: December 31
	ASSETS ($ mil.)	NET INCOME ($ mil.)	INCOME AS % OF ASSETS	EMPLOYEES
12/19	1,505,743	4,323	0.3%	80,800
12/18	1,446,931	2,739	0.2%	83,500
12/17	1,530,666	(1,732)	—	79,900
12/16	1,492,316	2,558	0.2%	119,300
12/15	1,659,796	(72)	—	129,400
Annual Growth	(2.4%)	—	—	(11.1%)

2019 Year-End Financials

Return on assets: 0.2%	Dividends
Return on equity: 5.1%	Yield: 3.6%
Long-term debt ($ mil.): —	Payout: 193.0%
No. of shares (mil.): —	Market value ($ mil.): —
Sales ($ mil): 39,767	

	STOCK PRICE ($) FY Close	P/E High/Low	PER SHARE ($) Earnings	Dividends	Book Value
12/19	9.52	70 50	0.19	0.35	4.91
12/18	7.54	119 78	0.12	0.24	4.66
12/17	10.90	— —	(0.14)	0.16	5.06
12/16	11.00	112 63	0.13	0.22	4.70
12/15	12.96	— —	(0.03)	0.38	5.27
Annual Growth	(7.4%)	— —	—	(2.3%)	(1.8%)

BASF SE

BASF is one of the world's biggest chemicals companies. Its portfolio is divided into the Chemicals Materials Industrial Solutions Surface Technologies Nutrition & Care and Agricultural Solutions segments and serves nearly all sectors.. Based in Germany BASF's manufacturing footprint spans more than 90 countries and around 360 production sites worldwide. The company's market dominance is impressive holding a top-three market position in around 70% of its business areas while its broad product portfolio — from basic chemicals to high value-added products and system solutions — serves around 100000 customers globally.

Operations

BASF restructured its segments in 2019. The company operates through 11 divisions grouped into six segments: Surface Technologies (Catalysts and Coatings) Materials (Performance Materials and Monomers) Chemicals (Petrochemicals and Intermediates) Industrial Solutions (Dispersions & Pigments and Performance Chemicals) Agricultural Solutions Nutrition & Care (Care Chemicals and Nutrition & Health) and Others.

The Surface Technologies segment products includes catalysts and battery materials for the automotive and chemical industries surface treatments colors and coatings. This segment accounts for over 20% of the total revenue. The Materials segment (generates some 20%) offers advanced materials and its precursors for new applications and systems. Its product portfolio includes isocyanates and polyamides as well as inorganic basic products and specialties for plastics and plastics processing. The Chemicals segment brings in around 15% of sales and makes basic chemicals and intermediates contributing to the organic growth of key value chains. Alongside internal transfers customers include the chemical and plastics industries.

The Industrial Solutions segment develops and markets ingredients and additives for industrial applications such as polymer dispersions pigments resins electronic materials antioxidants and additives. The segment represents around 15% of total sales.

Agricultural Solutions (nearly 15% of revenue) provides fungicides herbicides insecticides and biological crop protection and seed treatment.. It offers farmers innovative solutions including those based on digital technologies combined with practical advice.

BASF's "Verbund" (meaning composite or combined) manufacturing strategy is a highly efficient manufacturing technique that uses the by-products of one process as the input for a second.

Geographic Reach
BASF is based in the industrial city of Ludwigshafen Germany and has operations in more than 90 countries. It manages its vast activities through around 10 operating divisions which are further divided into some 75 strategic business units.

Six of BASF's manufacturing sites are highly efficient "Verbund" sites including its Ludwigshafen sitewhich is the world's largest chemicals plant. BASF's total production footprint totals around 360 sites worldwide.

BASF's R&D activities focus on three key sites in Europe Asia and North America: Process Research & Chemical Engineering (Ludwigshafen Germany); Advanced Materials & Systems Research (Shanghai China); and Bioscience Research (Research Triangle Park North Carolina).

Germany is BASF's largest single market at roughly 25% of total sales the rest of the Europe were 20%. North America accounts for nearly 30% and Asia over 20% of sales.

Sales and Marketing
BASF boasts a global base of around 100000 customers ranging from major global customers and medium-sized businesses to end consumers.

BASF established its four global service units.. The four global units are Global Procurement which makes purchasing even more effective Global Engineering Services and Global Digital Services which offer services for individual sites globally for the divisions or other units of the BASF Group and newly established Global Business Services unit will be a global flexible and demand-driven service unit that strengthens the competitiveness of the divisions and provides services in areas such as finance human resources environmental protection health and safety intellectual property communications supply chain and consulting.

Financial Performance
Note: Growth rates may differ after conversion to US Dollars. The world economy saw much weaker growth in 2019 than in 2018. Growth in global industrial production and in the global chemical industry (excluding pharmaceuticals) was also significantly below the prior-year level. In this market BASF's business did not perform as well as it expected: sales were down slightly from the prior-year figure and earnings declined considerably. Sales declined by ?904 million to ?59.3 billion in 2019 due to lower volumes and prices. The Chemicals and Materials segments in particular recorded lower sales volumes. By contrast prices rose significantly in the Surface Technologies segment. Offsetting effects came from the acquisition of significant businesses and assets from Bayer in the Agricultural Solutions segment and positive currency effects. Net income amounted to ?8.4 billion considerably higher than the prior-year figure of ?4.7 billion due to a book gain of ?5.7 billion from the deconsolidation of the Wintershall companies following the merger of the oil and gas activities of Wintershall and DEA on May 2019. BASF's cash position weakened in 2019 ending the year ?64 million lower at ?2.4 billion. The company's operations produced a cash inflow of ?7.5 billion ?465 million below the 2018 figure. Investing activities used ?1.2 billion for payments made for intangible assets and property plant and equipment which amounted to ?3.8 billion. Financing activities used ?6.4 billion largely due to the ?1.7 billion reduction in U.S. dollar commercial paper and the repayment of bonds in the amount of ?2.0 billion.

Strategy
BASF is passionate about chemistry and its customers. To be the world's leading chemical company for its customers BASF will grow profitably and create value for society. Thanks to its expertise its innovative and entrepreneurial spirit and the power of its Verbund integration it makes a decisive contribution to changing the world for the better. Creating chemistry for a sustainable future is what drives BASF and what it does best.

Its aspiration is to be the world's leading chemical company and achieve profitable growth. It aims to primarily grow organically and thus is strengthening its customer focus. Its growth strategy is based on investment in strategic growth markets and innovation-driven sectors. The Asian market continues to play a key role. With a share of more than 40% China is already the world's largest chemical market and drives the growth of global chemical production. By 2030 China's share will increase to nearly 50% - and BASF wants to participate in this growth.

To further its growth in this dynamic market BASF plans to build an integrated Verbund site in Zhanjiang in the southern Chinese province of Guangdong. It also wants to expand its existing joint venture with Sinopec at the Verbund site in Nanjing.

Mergers and Acquisitions
In 2020 BASF closed the acquisition of Solvay's polyamide business headquartered in Belgium. The transaction broadens BASF's polyamide capabilities with innovative and well-known products such as Technyl. This will allow BASF to support its customers with even better engineering plastics solutions e.g. for autonomous driving and e-mobility. The transaction also enhances the company's access to growth markets in Asia as well as in North and South America. Through the backward integration into the key raw material adiponitrile (ADN) BASF will now be present along the entire value chain for polyamide 6.6 and improve its supply reliability. The purchase price for the polyamide business acquired by BASF on a cash and debt-free basis amounts to ?1.3 billion

In 2019 BASF Acquires 3D Printing Service Provider Sculpteo to expand its position as a leading service provider in the additive manufacturing sector. The acquisition of the French 3D printing specialist based in Paris and San Francisco will enable BASF 3D Printing Solutions GmbH a wholly-owned subsidiary of BASF New Business GmbH to market and establish new industrial 3D printing materials more quickly. Terms were not disclosed.

Also in 2019 ASF acquired a majority share of the internet platform UBench with offices in Turnhout and Geel Belgium. Both companies have agreed not to disclose financial details of the transaction. The transaction includes UBench International NV CarRoll BVBA and DLight BVBA.

BASF merged its wet-end paper and water chemicals business in early 2019 with Solenis a global producer of chemicals for water-intensive industries including pulp paper oil and gas chemical processing mining biorefining power and municipal markets. The combined entity in which BASF will hold a 49% stake will retain the Solenis brand.

Company Background
Originally named Badische Anilin & Soda-Fabrik BASF AG was founded in Mannheim Germany by jeweler Frederick Englehorn in 1861. Unable to find enough land for expansion in Mannheim BASF moved to nearby Ludwigshafen in 1865. The company was a pioneer in coal tar dyes and it developed a synthetic indigo in 1897. Its synthetic dyes rapidly replaced more expensive organic dyes.

BASF scientist Fritz Haber synthesized ammonia in 1909 giving BASF access to the market for nitrogenous fertilizer (1913). Haber received a Nobel Prize in 1918 but was later charged with war crimes for his work with poison gases. Managed by Carl Bosch another Nobel Prize winner BASF joined the I.G. Farben cartel with Bayer Hoechst and others in 1925 to create a German chemical colossus. Within the cartel BASF developed polystyrene PVC and magnetic tape. Part of the Nazi war machine I.G. Farben made synthetic rubber and used labor from the Auschwitz concentration camp during WWII.

After the war I.G. Farben was dismantled. BASF regained its independence in 1952 and rebuilt its war-ravaged factories. Strong postwar domestic demand for basic chemicals aided its recovery and in 1958 BASF launched a US joint venture with Dow Chemical. (BASF bought out Dow's half in 1978.) The company moved into petrochemicals and became a leading manufacturer of plastic and synthetic fiber.

EXECUTIVES

Member Executive Board and CFO, Hans-Ulrich Engel, age 62, $764 total compensation

Chairman of the Board of Executive Directors, Kurt W. Bock, age 63, $1,651 total compensation

Member Executive Board and Head of Construction Chemicals Crop Protection and Bioscience Research and Region Europe, Harald Schwager, age 61

Group VP Agricultural Products Global Marketing, Michael Heinz, age 56

Member Executive Board and Head of Engineering and Maintenance Environment Health and Safety European Site and Verbund Management Human Resources Industrial Relations Director and Site Director Ludwigshafen, Margret Suckale, age 64

Vice Chairman of the Board of Executive Directors and CTO, Martin Brudermuller, age 59, $1,098 total compensation

Head Greater China Asia Pacific ASEAN South and East Asia; Member Board of Executive Directors, Sanjeev Gandhi, age 54

Chairman and CEO BASF Corporation, Wayne T. Smith, age 60

SVP Regional Business Unit Amines Europe,
 Christoph Wegner
President Petrochemicals, Hartwig Michels, age 56
President Regional Division Europe, Markus
 Kramer, age 55
President Nutrition and Health, Melanie Maas-
 Brunner, age 51
President Coatings, Dirk Bremm
Vice Chairman, Michael Diekmann, age 66
Chairman, J rgen Hambrecht, age 74
Vice Chairman, Robert Oswald, age 65
Auditors: KPMG AG Wirtschaftspruefungsgesellschaft

LOCATIONS

HQ: BASF SE
 Carl-Bosch-Strasse 38, Ludwigshafen D-67056
Phone: (49) 621 60 0   **Fax:** (49) 621 602525
Web: www.basf.com

2018 Sales

	% of total
Europe	
Germany	29
Other Countries	16
North America	27
Asia Pacific	22
South America Africa Middle East	6
Total	**100**

PRODUCTS/OPERATIONS

2018 Sales

	% of total
Functional Materials & Solutions	34
Performance Products	25
Chemicals	26
Agricultural Solutions	10
Other	5
Total	**100**

Selected Products

Chemicals
 Inorganics
 Ammonia
 Formaldehyde
 Melamine
 Sulfuric acid
 Urea
 Intermediates
 Performance chemicals
 Water-based resins
 Petrochemicals
 Feedstocks
 Industrial gases
 Plasticizers
 Specialty chemicals
Plastics
 Engineering plastics
 Foams
 Polyamides and intermediates
 Polyurethanes
 Styrenics
Functional Solutions
 Catalysts
 Battery materials
 Chemical catalysts
 Coatings
 Automotive coatings
 Decorative paints
 Industrial coatings
 Pigments
 Construction chemicals
Performance Products
 Automotive fluids
 Care chemicals
 Paper chemicals
 Pharma ingredients
 Textile chemicals
Agricultural Solutions
 Crop protection
 Fungicides
 Herbicides
 Insecticides

COMPETITORS

3M	Evonik Degussa
Air Products	Exxon Mobil
Akzo Nobel	FMC
Albemarle	Formosa Plastics
Ashland	Henkel
BP	LANXESS
Bayer AG	LG Group
Cargill	Royal Dutch Shell
DSM	SABIC
Dow Chemical	TOTAL
Eastman Chemical	Taminco

HISTORICAL FINANCIALS

Company Type: Public

Income Statement   FYE: December 31

	REVENUE ($ mil.)	NET INCOME ($ mil.)	NET PROFIT MARGIN	EMPLOYEES
12/19	66,597	9,454	14.2%	117,628
12/18	71,775	5,390	7.5%	118,371
12/17	77,289	7,286	9.4%	114,333
12/16	60,766	4,282	7.0%	111,975
12/15	76,733	4,342	5.7%	113,249
Annual Growth	(3.5%)	21.5%	—	1.0%

2019 Year-End Financials

Debt ratio: 26.3%	No. of shares (mil.): 918
Return on equity: 22.0%	Dividends
Cash ($ mil.): 2,724	Yield: 3.4%
Current ratio: 1.87	Payout: 6.2%
Long-term debt ($ mil.): 18,081	Market value ($ mil.): 17,189

	STOCK PRICE ($) FY Close	P/E High/Low		PER SHARE ($) Earnings	Dividends	Book Value
12/19	18.72	2	2	10.27	0.64	50.73
12/18	17.59	5	3	5.85	0.66	43.71
12/17	27.47	17	4	7.92	0.66	44.16
12/16	92.57	21	14	4.66	0.57	36.57
12/15	76.02	24	17	4.72	0.56	36.66
Annual Growth	(29.6%)	—	—	21.5%	3.2%	8.5%

BAWAG Group AG

EXECUTIVES

Gesch ftsf hrer, Alexander Wolfgring
Gesch ftsf hrer, Martina Tommasini
Auditors: KPMG Austria Wirtschaftspruefungs- und
 Steuerberatungsgesellschaft

LOCATIONS

HQ: BAWAG Group AG
 Wiedner Gurtel 11, Vienna A-1100
Phone: (43) 5 99 05 0
Web: www.bawaggroup.com

COMPETITORS

Bank Austria	Oberbank AG
Erste Bank	RZB Group
Investkredit	

HISTORICAL FINANCIALS

Company Type: Public

Income Statement   FYE: December 31

	ASSETS ($ mil.)	NET INCOME ($ mil.)	INCOME AS % OF ASSETS	EMPLOYEES
12/19	51,267	515	1.0%	3,696
12/18	51,187	499	1.0%	3,474
12/17	55,227	559	1.0%	3,437
12/16	41,963	510	1.2%	2,951
12/15	38,893	429	1.1%	3,072
Annual Growth	7.1%	4.7%	—	4.7%

2019 Year-End Financials

Return on assets: 1.0%	Dividends
Return on equity: 11.7%	Yield: —
Long-term debt ($ mil.): —	Payout: 57.6%
No. of shares (mil.): 87	Market value ($ mil.): —
Sales ($ mil): 1,930	

Bayer AG

You could get a headache trying to name all of Bayer's products. The company which created aspirin in 1897 makes prescription products and works in oncology and radiology through its Pharmaceuticals division; OTC products like Claritin and Canesten via its Consumer Health division; and crop protection and pest control via its Crop Science division. Its top selling pharmaceuticals include oral anticoagulent Xarelto and eye disease medicine Eylea. Also known as Bayer Group the firm has over 390 operating subsidiaries worldwide and operates in the US through Bayer Corporation. More than 30% of the company's revenue is generated from the US.

Operations

Bayer operates in three reportable segments: Crop Science Pharmaceuticals and Consumer Health.

The Crop Science segment does business in seeds crop protection and non-agricultural pest control and accounts for around 45%% of Bayer's revenue.

It generates over 40% of its total revenue from its Pharmaceuticals operation which manufactures prescription products especially for women's health care and cardiology and specialty therapeutics in the areas of oncology hematology and ophthalmology.

The Consumer Health business includes consumer care and medical care and makes primarily non-prescription and OTC medicines supplements and dermatology products such as Aspirin (for which it owns the trademark in more than 50 countries) Berocca and Aleve. The segment brings in nearly 15% of sales.

Geographic Reach

Bayer headquartered in Leverkusen Germany generates around 35% of sales from North America its largest geographical segment. It also generates significant revenue in Europe the Middle East and Africa (around 30%) and the Asia/Pacific region (roughly 20%). Latin America brings in approximately 15% of sales. The US is Bayer's single largest geography at over 30% of sales.

Most of Bayer's core manufacturing facilities are in Germany and the US. The company also has operations Latin America Africa and the Middle East. Overall Bayer comprises more than 390 consolidated companies operating in over 85 countries around the world.

Sales and Marketing

Bayer's Pharmaceuticals products are distributed primarily through wholesalers hospitals and pharmacy chains while Crop Science products are sold through wholesalers and regional distributors. The Consumer Health division's well-known and established brands are sold through major supermarket chains and pharmacies.

Financial Performance

Note: Growth rates may differ after conversion to US Dollars.

Total reported net sales in 2019 posted year-on-year growth of ?6.8 billion or 19% to ?43.5 billion. Sales were derived primarily from product deliveries and licenses.

After income tax expense income from discontinued operations after taxes and noncontrolling interest net income in 2019 came to ?4.1 billion.

Bayer's coffers declined by ?867 billion in 2019 ending the year at ?3.2 billion. Operating activities generated ?8.2 billion while investing and financing activities used ?671 million and ?8.4 billion respectively.

Strategy

Bayer focuses on four strategic levers to deliver attractive returns for its shareholders while also making a positive contribution to society and for the environment:

As a global leader in health and nutrition Bayer continues to develop its business. It creates value with strategy-based resource allocation focused on profitable growth. The company is active in regulated and highly profitable sectors that are driven by innovation and in which Bayer can achieve above-average growth rates.

Bayer develops innovations and leverage cutting-edge research to solve major challenges in health and nutrition. As part of these endeavors the company is expanding its access to innovation by collaborating with third parties. At the same time it is advancing the digital transformation of its value creation chain and working on the co-creation of disruptive technologies aided for example by the latest Leaps by Bayer initiatives.

Sustainability is an integral part of its business strategy. As a corporate objective it is afforded the same status as the company's financial indicators. In 2019 Bayer advanced its approach to make a positive contribution to society and for the environment. Its targets for 2030 are aligned with the United Nations' Sustainable Development Goals and the Paris Agreement climate targets.

The company is strengthening the operational performance of its business through measures such as the Bayer 2022 synergy and efficiency program.

On September 20 2019 Bayer raised its stake in the joint venture BlueRock Therapeutics L.P. Cambridge Massachusetts United States from 40.8% to 100%. Bayer made an upfront payment of ?201 million for the remaining stake. Further amounts totaling up to ?325 million are payable upon the achievement of pre-defined research-based milestones.

Mergers and Acquisitions

In late 2019 Bayer acquired BlueRock Therapeutics a US biotech firm for ?201 million (plus up to ?325 million in performance-related bonuses). BlueRock focuses on engineering cell therapies in the fields of neurology cardiology and immunology on a proprietary pluripotent stem cell technology. The acquisition will build Bayer's cell therapy pipeline based in BlueRock Therapeutics' iPSC platform.

In mid-2019 Bayer acquired 28% of stakes of Century Therapeutics LLC for ?129 million. Century Therapeutics is based in US that develops allogeneic immune cell therapies for cancer. The transaction brought Bayer a total of 36% of stake in Century Therapeutics and will help the company

to advance multiple programs for hematologic and solid malignancies into clinical testing.

EXECUTIVES

Chairman Board of Management, Werner Baumann, age 58

Member Board of Management Human Resources Technology and Sustainability, Hartmut Klusik

Member Board of Management Innovation and Latin America, Kemal Malik, age 58

Member Board of Management and Head of the Crop Science Division, Liam Condon

Member Board of Management and Head of the Consumer Health Division, Erica L. Mann

Chairman of the Executive Board Bayer Business Services, Daniel Hartert

President Bayer North American Animal Health, Joyce Lee

Member Board of Management and Head of the Pharmaceuticals Division, Dieter Weinand, age 60

President and CEO Bayer Crop Science LP, James Blome

CFO and Asia Pacific, Johannes Dietsch, age 59

President Pharmaceuticals Americas, Carsten Brunn

Chairman Supervisory Board, Werner Wenning, age 74

Vice Chairman Supervisory Board, Oliver Z hlke, age 52

Auditors: Deloitte GmbH

LOCATIONS

HQ: Bayer AG
Kaiser-Wilhelm-Allee 1, Leverkusen 51368
Phone: (49) 214 30 1   **Fax:** (49) 214 30 71985
Web: www.bayer.com

2017 Sales

	% of total
Europe/Middle East/Africa	38
North America	29
Asia/Pacific	22
Latin America	11
Total	**100**

2017 Sales

	% of total
United States	24
Germany	10
China	7
Brazil	5
Other	54
Total	**100**

PRODUCTS/OPERATIONS

2017 Sales

	% of total
Pharmaceuticals	50
Crop Science	28
Consumer Health	17
Animal Health	5
Total	**100**

Selected Operations and Products

HealthCare
Animal health products
Diabetes care products
Consumer care products (over-the-counter drugs)
Pharmaceuticals
CropScience
BioScience (biotechnology and seeds)
Crop protection (insecticides and herbicides)
Environmental science (lawn care and non-agricultural pesticides)

Selected Brands

HealthCare
Adalat (cardiovascular medication)
Advantage (animal health)
Aleve/Flanax (analgesic)
Alka-Seltzer (analgesic and antacid)

Aspirin (analgesic)
Aspirin Cardio (cardiovascular)
Avalox/Avelox (antibiotic)
Bepanthen/Bepanthol (skin care treatment)
Betaferon/Betaseron (multiple sclerosis medication)
Baytril (animal health infections)
Breeze/Contour (diabetes care glucose meters)
Canesten (antifungal)
Cipro/Ciprobay (antibiotic)
Glucobay (diabetes treatment)
Iopamiron (diagnostic imaging)
Kogenate (hematology/cardiology)
Levitra (impotence drug)
Magnevist (diagnostic imaging)
Mirena (contraceptive)
Nexavar (oncology)
One-A-Day (vitamins)
Supradyn (multivitamin)
Ultravist (diagnostic imaging)
Yasmin/Yasminelle/YAZ (contraceptive)
CropScience
Confidor/Gaucho/Admire/Merit (insecticides/seed treatment)
Flint/Stratego/Sphere/Nativo (fungicides)
Poncho (seed treatment)
Ficam/Maxforce/Esplanade/K-Othrine (Environmental Science)

COMPETITORS

3M	Evonik Degussa
Abbott Labs	GE Healthcare
Akzo Nobel	GlaxoSmithKline
Allergan plc	Johnson & Johnson
AstraZeneca	Merck
BASF SE	Merck KGaA
Baxter International	Mitsubishi Chemical
Boehringer Ingelheim	Holdings
Boston Scientific	Novartis
Bristol-Myers Squibb	Pfizer
Celanese	Rhodia
DSM	Roche Holding
Dow Chemical	Sanofi
Eastman Chemical	Syngenta
Eli Lilly	Teva

HISTORICAL FINANCIALS

Company Type: Public

Income Statement				FYE: December 31
	REVENUE ($ mil.)	NET INCOME ($ mil.)	NET PROFIT MARGIN	EMPLOYEES
12/19	48,890	4,593	9.4%	107,435
12/18	45,333	1,941	4.3%	110,838
12/17	41,974	8,794	21.0%	99,762
12/16	49,382	4,784	9.7%	115,688
12/15	50,456	4,476	8.9%	117,330
Annual Growth	**(0.8%)**	**0.6%**	**—**	**(2.2%)**

2019 Year-End Financials

Debt ratio: 33.4%	No. of shares (mil.): 982
Return on equity: 8.7%	Dividends
Cash ($ mil.): 3,576	Yield: 7.4%
Current ratio: 1.40	Payout: 11.7%
Long-term debt ($ mil.): 39,800	Market value ($ mil.): 19,924

	STOCK PRICE ($) FY Close	P/E High/Low		PER SHARE ($) Earnings	Dividends	Book Value
12/19	20.28	5	4	4.68	1.51	54.10
12/18	17.57	18	10	2.06	0.96	56.46
12/17	31.09	18	4	10.08	0.59	53.35
12/16	104.28	22	17	5.74	0.49	38.73
12/15	124.84	32	24	5.41	0.45	31.96
Annual Growth	**(36.5%)**	**—**	**—**	**(3.6%)**	**35.5%**	**14.1%**

Bayerische Motoren Werke AG

Bayerische Motoren Werke better known as BMW is among the top 10 automakers in the world and first in premium automotive sales. It manufactures and sells over 2.5 million premium-brand cars and off-road vehicles each year under the BMW MINI and Rolls-Royce names. Spare parts and accessories are also offered. Its vehicles and products are sold worldwide through company branches independent dealers subsidiaries and importers. In addition the company also offers car leasing and credit financing for both retail and corporate fleet customers as well as dealer financing and insurance. BMW also makes motorcycles. BMW generates majority of sales internationally.

Operations

The BMW Group comprises three main segments: Automotive Motorcycles and Financial Services. An "Other Entities" segment consists of holding companies and group financing companies.

The Automotive segment contributes nearly 75% of total group revenue and sells BMW-branded cars MINI-branded cars and the 100-year-old luxury Rolls-Royce line. Motorcycles (less than 5%% of sales) are geared toward premium markets with models in the sport tour roadster heritage adventure and urban mobility categories.

Financial Services which account for about 25%of sales offers financing and leasing to retail customers through nearly 60 entities as well as through co-operation agreements with local financial services providers and importers.

Geographic Reach

Based in Munich Germany BMW operates 30-plus production and assembly plants in about 15 countries and racks up sales in more than 140 countries. The company also operates almost 45 dedicated sales subsidiaries and financial services locations and nearly 15 R&D centers worldwide.

BMW's cars are popular worldwide pulling in billions in sales from Europe North America Asia and other major markets. It generates nearly 45% of its revenue in Europe and over 30% in Asia (primarily in China). The US contributes almost 25% of revenues. The MINI brand is particularly popular in its spiritual home of the UK where the majority of MINIs are manufactured.

Sales and Marketing

BMW sells more than 2.5 million cars for fiscal year 2019. Its sales network comprises around 3500 BMW 1600 MINI and some 150 Rolls-Royce dealerships. In Germany cars are sold through BMW branches and independent dealerships. Outside Germany vehicles are distributed through subsidiaries and independent importers. Motorcycles are sold by more than 1200 dealerships and importers.

Financial Performance

Note: Growth rates may differ after conversion to US Dollars.

The company's revenue increased by 8% to ?104.2 billion compared to ?96.9 billion in the prior year. The rise was primarily due to the increase on sales in their automotive and financial services division.

Net income fell 29% to ?5.0 billion due to higher cost of sales and other operating expenses.

BMW's cash position improved during 2019 ending the year ?1.1 billion higher at ?12.0 billion representing a healthy level of cash reserves. Its operating activities produced ?3.7 billion and its financing activities provided ?4.8 billion while investing activities used ?7.3 billion.

Strategy

The BMW Group has combined its wealth of experience in the field of e-mobility with its wide-ranging knowledge of battery cells to form a new competence centre in Munich. It is tasked with continuing to develop battery cell technology and master the processes required for cell production. Based on current technology the aim is to significantly increase the energy density of battery cells and thus also the range for customers.

The further development of battery cell technology is a key success factor in the BMW Group's electric offensive strategy enabling it to have a direct impact on both the performance and the cost of the battery. This holistic approach ensures that the BMW Group is always at the cutting edge of technology while simultaneously covering the entire value chain including research and development assembly and design of battery cells. Swift decision-making and comprehensive collaboration are making it possible to develop battery cells in a complete transparent and sustainable manner. Moreover it is crucial to take recycling into account from the very beginning.

HISTORY

BMW's logo speaks to its origin: a propeller in blue and white the colors of Bavaria. In 1913 Karl Rapp opened an aircraft-engine design shop near Munich. He named it Bayerische Motoren Werke (BMW) in 1917. The end of WWI brought German aircraft production to a halt and BMW shifted to making railway brakes until the 1930s. BMW debuted its first motorcycle the R32 in 1923 and the company began making automobiles in 1928 after buying small-car company Fahrzeugwerke Eisenach.

In 1933 BMW launched a line of larger cars. The company built aircraft engines for Hitler's Luftwaffe in the 1930s and stopped all auto and motorcycle production in 1941. BMW chief Josef Popp resisted and was ousted. Under the Nazis the company operated in occupied countries built rockets and developed the world's first production jet engine.

With its factories dismantled after WWII BMW survived by making kitchen and garden equipment. In 1948 it introduced a one-cylinder motorcycle which sold well as cheap transportation in postwar Germany. BMW autos in the 1950s were large and expensive and sold poorly. When motorcycle sales dropped the company escaped demise in the mid-1950s by launching the Isetta a seven-foot three-wheeled "bubble car."

In the 1970s BMW's European exports soared and the company set up a distribution subsidiary in the US. The company also produced larger cars that put BMW on par with Mercedes-Benz.

EXECUTIVES

Member Management Board Sales and Brand BMW Aftersales BMW Group, Pieter Nota, age 56
Chairman of the Management Board, Harald Kr ger, age 56, $601,944 total compensation
Board of Management Member Finance, Nicolas Peter
Deputy Chairman Supervisory Board, Manfred Schoch
Member Supervisory Board, Karl-Ludwig Kley, age 69
Deputy Chairman Supervisory Board, Stefan Quandt
Chairman of the Supervisory Board, Norbert Reithofer, age 65
Deputy Chairman Supervisory Board, Stefan Schmid
Auditors: PricewaterhouseCoopers GmbH

LOCATIONS

HQ: Bayerische Motoren Werke AG
  Aktiengesellschaft, Munich 80788
Phone: (49) 89 3 82 0   **Fax:** (49) 89 3895 5858
Web: www.bmwgroup.com

2018 Sales

	% of total
Europe	
Germany	14
Rest of Europe	32
Americas	
US	17
Rest of Americas	4
Asia	
China	19
Rest of Asia	11
Other Regions	3
Total	**100**

PRODUCTS/OPERATIONS

2018 Sales

	% of total
Automotive	74
Financial services	24
Motorcycles	2
Elimination	-
Total	**100**

Selected Products

Automobiles
  BMW
  1 Series
  3 Series
  5 Series
  6 Series
  7 Series
  X3 X5 X6 sports utility vehicles
  M Models
  Z4
  MINI Electric
  MINI Cooper
  MIMI Hatch
  MIMI Clubman
  Rolls-Royce Phantom
  Rolls-Royce Wraith
  Rolls-Royce Dawn
Motorcycles
  BMW

COMPETITORS

Daimler	Mitsubishi Motors
Ducati	Nissan
FCA US	Porsche
Fiat Chrysler	Renault
Ford Motor	Suzuki Motor
General Motors	Toyota
Harley-Davidson	Ultra Motorcycle
Honda	Volkswagen
Kawasaki Heavy	Yamaha
Industries	Yamaha Motor
Mazda	

HISTORICAL FINANCIALS

Company Type: Public

Income Statement

FYE: December 31

	REVENUE ($ mil.)	NET INCOME ($ mil.)	NET PROFIT MARGIN	EMPLOYEES
12/19	117,003	5,518	4.7%	133,778
12/18	111,633	8,150	7.3%	134,682
12/17	118,290	10,333	8.7%	129,932
12/16	99,425	7,246	7.3%	124,729
12/15	100,398	6,937	6.9%	122,244
Annual Growth	3.9%	(5.6%)	—	2.3%

2019 Year-End Financials

Debt ratio: 37.5%	No. of shares (mil.): 602
Return on equity: 8.4%	Dividends
Cash ($ mil.): 13,513	Yield: 3.4%
Current ratio: 1.10	Payout: 11.1%
Long-term debt ($ mil.): 57,958	Market value ($ mil.): 16,326

	STOCK PRICE ($) FY Close	P/E High/Low		PER SHARE ($) Earnings	Dividends	Book Value
12/19	27.12	4	3	8.39	0.93	110.64
12/18	26.97	3	2	12.39	1.13	109.50
12/17	34.67	3	2	15.73	1.01	107.75
12/16	31.01	3	2	11.03	0.00	82.63
Annual Growth	(4.4%)	—	—	(6.6%)	—	7.6%

BAYWA Bayerische Warenvermittlung Landwirtschaftlicher Genossenschaften AG

BayWa sells wholegrain wholesale. The Germany commodities trader (pronounced bay-vah) deals in agricultural produce (grain and oilseed fertilizers feed seed fresh fruit production) agricultural equipment building materials (building components and equipment) renewable energy products and services (wind solar) and energy (gas heating oil lubricants mineral oils). BayWa's trades mainly in New Zealand Asia and South America but it has operations in around 45 countries in total including the US. The company was founded as Bavarian Trading Co. in 1923. Germany generates most of BayWa's sales.

Operations

BayWa operates three principal segments: Agriculture Energy and Building Materials.

The Agriculture segment generates around 65% of total sales and consists of four businesses: Agri Supply & Trade "BAST" (grain and oilseeds trading); Agricultural Trade & Services (grain and oilseed marketing); Global Produce (fresh fruit and vegetable trading); and Agricultural Equipment (buys and sells machinery equipment and systems for agriculture).

The Energy segment generates more than 25% of annual sales and consists of a Conventional Energy (sale of oils fuels lubricants wood pellets) and Renewable Energies (development and project planning of wind solar and biomass systems). BayWa is one of Europe's largest renewable energy plant manufacturers and one of the top-ten solar developers worldwide.

Building Materials generates some 10% of sales and consists of building materials trading of the company.

BayWa also operates a nascent Innovation & Digitalization segment that employs technology to bring down costs for agricultural producers.

Geographic Reach

Based in Munich Germany BayWa has operations in about 45 countries mostly in Europe but also in the US Germany accounts for about 45% of total sales followed by Austria which gives in roughly 15% Netherlands generate about 10% of total sales and rest comes from other countries.

The company's Building Materials division trades materials in Germany and Austria. It operates about 130 locations in Germany and more than 30 in Austria.

Sales and Marketing

BayWa's customers include producers of starch and feedstuffs malt houses breweries and biofuel manufactures as well as agriculture and forestry local government and industrial customers.

The company's advertising costs were ?55.9 in 2019 and ?51.2 in 2018.

Financial Performance

Note: Growth rates may differ after conversion to US Dollars.

BayWa has achieved year-over-year revenue growth for the past five years. Revenue increased by 14% from 2015 to 2019.

Revenue in 2019 amounted to ?17.1 billion a 3% increase from the previous year. The slight increase in revenue resulted from a slight increase in revenues of Energy and Agriculture segments offset by a significant decrease in revenues of Building Materials Innovation and Digitization and Other Activities segments.

Net income was ?36.7 million ?4.4 million more than the previous year.

Cash and cash equivalents at the end of the year were ?229.7 million 90% more than the previous year. Cash provided by operating activities used by operating activities was ?212 million. Investing activities used ?149.4 million primarily for investments in intangible assets and property plant and equipment. Financing activities generated ?469.6 million primarily from incoming payments from borrowing of loans.

Strategy

BayWa is taking two market-driven approaches regarding its further strategic development: ensuring business continuity by enhancing competitive strength as well as growth in new business areas by developing innovative customer-focused business models. The group's growth ambitions focus on Renewable Energies BAST and Global Produce business units.

The objective in the Energy segment is to further advance the global expansion of renewable energies. Another focus is on the scale continued internationalization and expanding the service business as well as on the provision of integrated energy solutions. Examples include the combination of installations for generating renewable energy with efficient energy storage systems as well as the cross-segment development of innovative products and services.

The Conventional Energy business unit continuously promotes the expansion of mobility solutions in the fields of charging infrastructure for e-mobility LNG filling stations and digital mobility. Furthermore BayWa also offers e-mobility solutions created based on comprehensive fleet analysis and targeted at fleet operators.

In the Agriculture segment BayWa aims to deepen existing customer ties and attract new customers by seizing opportunities to export to international markets expanding agricultural products range through the addition of specialties.

Mergers and Acquisitions

In late 2020 BayWa r.e. a subsidiary of BayWa AG acquired Enable Energy Inc. (EEI) a US-based commercial and industrial (C&I) solar and energy storage solutions provider with extensive skills in engineering procurement and construction (EPC) and operations and maintenance (O&M) support. The acquisition represents the latest move in BayWa r.e.'s growth and expansion strategy in the Americas.

In late 2019 BayWa r.e. acquires Toronto-based software house PowerHub for an undisclosed amount. PowerHub's state-of-the-art software is today providing asset intelligence to clients in 20

countries around the world. The new addition to the BayWa r.e. offers a leading cloud-based asset intelligence software solution and extends BayWa r.e.'s scope of digital technology services in the field of renewable energy operations and further expands its globally successful services business.

In mid-2019 BayWa r.e. acquired Canadian solar distributor and service provider National Solar Distributors Inc. The acquired company serves all of Canada's provinces and territories as a wholesaler of equipment for the residential and commercial grid-tie markets as well as for industrial and small off-grid applications. The acquisition is part of BayWa r.e.'s expansion in North America.

EXECUTIVES

Management Board MemberBayWa Agri Services, Roland Schuler, age 64
Chairman Board of Management and CEO, Klaus J. Lutz, age 61
Deputy Chairman and Chairman General Works Council, Gunnar Metz
CFO, Andreas Helber
Member Board of Management renewable energy GmbH, Matthias Taft, age 53
Member Board of Management RWA Raiffeisen Ware Austria AG, Reinhard Wolf, age 60
Auditors: Deloitte GmbH Wirtschaftspruefungsgesellschaft

LOCATIONS

HQ: BAYWA Bayerische Warenvermittlung Landwirtschaftlicher Genossenschaften AG Arabellastrasse 4, Munich D-81925
Phone: (49) 89 9222 3887   **Fax:** (49) 89 9212 3887
Web: www.baywa.de

Sales 2018

	% of total
Germany	43
Austria	14
Netherlands	10
Other International	33
Total	**100**

PRODUCTS/OPERATIONS

2018 Sales

	% of total
Agriculture	66
Energy	24
Building materials	10
Innovation & Digitalisation	-
Other activities	-
Total	**100**

COMPETITORS

ADM	Italmobiliare
BASF SE	METRO AG
BP	Mitsubishi Corp.
Cargill	Origin Enterprises
Chevron	REWE
Deere	Royal Dutch Shell
Dole Food	SMA Solar Technology
Dow Chemical	Saint-Gobain
Exxon Mobil	Toyota
Ford Motor	Vestas Wind Systems
Franz Haniel	Wal-Mart
General Motors	ZF Friedrichshafen
Hanson Limited	

HISTORICAL FINANCIALS

Company Type: Public

Income Statement   FYE: December 31

	REVENUE ($ mil.)	NET INCOME ($ mil.)	NET PROFIT MARGIN	EMPLOYEES
12/19	19,419	41	0.2%	19,193
12/18	19,300	36	0.2%	17,864
12/17	19,134	47	0.2%	17,323
12/16	16,349	32	0.2%	16,711
12/15	16,358	52	0.3%	16,229
Annual Growth	4.4%	(5.9%)	—	4.3%

2019 Year-End Financials

Debt ratio: 55.6%
Return on equity: 3.4%
Cash ($ mil.): 257
Current ratio: 1.28
Long-term debt ($ mil.): 2,263

No. of shares (mil.): 35
Dividends
  Yield: —
  Payout: 139.7%
Market value ($ mil.): —

BBMG Corp

EXECUTIVES

Chairman, Weiping Jiang
Auditors: Ernst & Young Hua Ming LLP

LOCATIONS

HQ: BBMG Corp
Tower D, Global Trade Center, No. 36, North Third
Ring East Road, Dongcheng District, Beijing 100013
Phone: (86) 10 66411587   **Fax:** (86) 10 66412086
Web: www.bbmg.com.cn

HISTORICAL FINANCIALS

Company Type: Public

Income Statement   FYE: December 31

	REVENUE ($ mil.)	NET INCOME ($ mil.)	NET PROFIT MARGIN	EMPLOYEES
12/19	13,197	530	4.0%	0
12/18	12,083	474	3.9%	0
12/17	9,785	435	4.5%	0
12/16	6,874	386	5.6%	49,721
12/15	6,301	310	4.9%	28,619
Annual Growth	20.3%	14.3%	—	—

2019 Year-End Financials

Debt ratio: 6.1%
Return on equity: 6.2%
Cash ($ mil.): 3,064
Current ratio: 1.37
Long-term debt ($ mil.): 9,089

No. of shares (mil.): —
Dividends
  Yield: —
  Payout: —
Market value ($ mil.): —

BCE Inc

BCE is Canada's largest provider of telecommunications services. The company (formerly Bell Canada Enterprises) owns Bell Canada the incumbent provider of long-distance and local telephone access in Ontario and Quebec as well as the Atlantic provinces with more than 33 million subscribers. It also provides broadband internet access to about 3.9 million subscribers and TV subscriptions to more than 2.9 million viewers. BCE's mobile holdings include wireless carrier Bell Mobility and subsidiary Virgin Mobile Canada. The company's brands include Bell Fibe (internet protocol TV) AlarmForce (home security) TSN (sports network) and CraveTV.

Operations

Bell Wireline which generates more than half of BCE's sales provides data internet access TV and local and long distance telephone as well as well as other communications services and products. It serves Bell's residential small and medium-sized business and enterprise customers in Ontario's and Quebec's metro areas.

Bell Wireless accounts for more than a third of BCE's revenue with wireless voice and data communication products and services to Bell's residential small and medium-sized business and large enterprise customers across Canada.

Bell Media brings in about an eighth of BCE's revenue. The segment encompasses 30 conventional TV stations; 30 specialty TV channels including TSN Space Discovery and RDS; four national pay-TV services including The Movie Network (TMN); and more than 100 licensed radio stations in 54 markets across Canada. The unit also offers out-of-home advertising with billboards and digital formats.

Geographic Reach

BCE provides local access network in Ontario Québec the Atlantic provinces and Manitoba as well as in Canada's Northern Territories.

The company's broadband fiber network consists of fiber-to-the-node (FTTN) and fiber-to-the-premise (FTTP) locations covers 9.5 million homes and businesses in Ontario Québec the Atlantic provinces and Manitoba.

Sales and Marketing

BCE has an extensive retail network with more than 2360 retail locations across Canada including 1360 Bell-branded stores and The Source stores and Glentel-operated stores. It also sells through third-party dealers and retailers.

Financial Performance

(Figures are in Canadian dollars and might differ from other sources due to exchange rates).

BCE's revenue has risen for seven years in a row reaching a company high in 2018.

The company's sales hit $23.4 billion in 2018 a 3% increase from 2017 driven by BCE revenues increased by 3.1% in 2018 compared to last year driven by growth in its three segments. Service revenue rose about 2% and product revenue was about 14% higher in 2018 compared to 2017. The MTS acquisition also contributed to the revenue gain.

BCE's earnings dipped 2.5% to $2.9 billion due to higher expenses including impairment charges of $200 million related to the Bell Media segment higher depreciation and amortization expense and higher finance costs.

The company's coffers held $3.3 billion in cash and equivalents in 2018 compared to $4.8 billion in 2017. In 2018 BCE had $5.7 billion generated from operations while investing and financing activities used $3.4 billion and $2.5 billion respectively.

Strategy

Just because BCE is the biggest telecom company in Canada doesn't mean it can't get bigger. In 2018 the company began new services to attract new customers and hold on to current customers.

In phone service BCE rolled out a prepaid wireless service called Lucky. The company said the service should keep its postpaid customers who want to change to a prepaid plan. Lucky's rate plan of $20 give BCE a service to pitch to price-conscious consumers. The plan helped drive 480000 net wireless subscribers a 44% increase year-to-year.

Also in 2018 BCE started an over-the-top (OTT) service that offers premium channels from the US that include HBO Showtime Starz and Hulu to help it to keep cord-cutters as customers and attract non-pay-TV subscribers. Additionally BCE started an OTT version of its TSN sports network.

BCE expanded its wireless capabilities setting the goal of it wireless-to-the-home program to reach 1.2 million homes up from 800000 homes. The increase was driven by a Canadian government program which allows for an acceleration of the company's capital cost allowance.

The company continues to lose customers of its traditional residential lines. The number of subscribers fell to 2.9 million in 2018 from 3.2 million in 2017 a 7.5% decrease.

Mergers and Acquisitions

In 2018 BCE acquired Axia NetMedia Corp. the Calgary-based operator of SuperNet. The broadband network in Alberta provides service to provincial and municipal offices Indigenous communities schools libraries healthcare institutions businesses and internet service providers.

In 2018 BCE bought AlarmForce Industries the second biggest home security company in Canada for $166 million. The deal positions BCE in the smart home automation market and extends its reach deeper into the home.

BCE acquired Manitoba Telecom Services (MTS) for $3.1 billion) in 2017. The deal expanded BCE's operations in the west of Canada adding around 490000 Manitoba Telecom subscribers. BCE intends to invest in building out wireless and internet networks in Manitoba.

Company Background

Alexander Graham Bell experimented with the telephone in his native Canada before moving to the US in the mid-1870s. His father sold his Canadian patent rights to National Bell Telephone which combined with Canada's Hamilton District Telegraph to form Bell Telephone Company of Canada. Known as Bell Canada it received a charter in 1880 and settled in Montreal. By 1882 it had 40 exchanges. AT&T owned 48% of the company in 1890 but by 1925 Canadians owned 95% of Bell Canada. (AT&T severed all ties in 1975.)

EXECUTIVES

Chief Brand Officer Bell Canada; President Bell Mobility, Wade Oosterman
President and CEO BCE and Bell Canada, George A. Cope, age 59, $900,000 total compensation
EVP and CFO, Siim A. Vanaselja, $526,667 total compensation
President The Source, Charles Brown
EVP and CIO, Michael Cole
President Bell Media, Mary Ann Turcke
President Bell Business Markets, Tom Little
EVP Customer Operations, John Watson
EVP and CTO, Stephen Howe
EVP and Chief Legal and Regulatory Officer, Mirko Bibic
EVP Corporate Services, Bernard le Duc
Auditors: Deloitte LLP

LOCATIONS

HQ: BCE Inc
1, Carrefour Alexander-Graham-Bell, Verdun, Quebec H3E 3B3
Phone: 514 870-8777   **Fax:** 514 786-3970
Web: www.bce.ca

PRODUCTS/OPERATIONS

2018 Sales

	% of total
Bell Wireline	52
Bell Wireless	35
Bell Media	13
Total	**100**

2018 Sales

	% of total
Services:	
Data	32
Wireless	27
Voice	14
Media	11
Other services	1
Products:	
Wireless	9
Data	2
Wireless	2
Total	**100**

COMPETITORS

Allstream	Shaw Broadcast
Amazon.com	Services
COGECO	Shaw Communications
Hulu	Sprint Communications
Netflix	TELUS
Quebecor	Vonage
Rogers Communications	YouTube

HISTORICAL FINANCIALS

Company Type: Public

Income Statement · FYE: December 31

	REVENUE ($ mil.)	NET INCOME ($ mil.)	NET PROFIT MARGIN	EMPLOYEES
12/19	18,402	2,334	12.7%	52,100
12/18	17,233	2,045	11.9%	52,790
12/17	18,122	2,222	12.3%	51,679
12/16	16,116	2,147	13.3%	48,090
12/15	15,489	1,818	11.7%	49,968
Annual Growth	**4.4%**	**6.4%**	**—**	**1.1%**

2019 Year-End Financials

Debt ratio: 33.5%	No. of shares (mil.): 903
Return on equity: 14.6%	Dividends
Cash ($ mil.): 111	Yield: 5.1%
Current ratio: 0.56	Payout: 94.0%
Long-term debt ($ mil.): 17,213	Market value ($ mil.): 41,896

	STOCK PRICE ($) FY Close	P/E High/Low	Earnings	PER SHARE ($) Dividends	Book Value
12/19	46.35	15 12	2.59	2.39	17.90
12/18	39.53	14 12	2.28	2.31	16.65
12/17	48.01	16 15	2.48	2.29	16.96
12/16	43.24	14 12	2.47	2,03	14.95
12/15	38.62	14 12	2.15	2.01	14.16
Annual Growth	**4.7%**	**— —**	**4.8%**	**4.5%**	**6.0%**

BDO Unibank Inc.

EXECUTIVES

President & Chief Executive Officer, Nestor Tan
Chairman, Teresita Sy
Auditors: Punongbayan & Araullo

LOCATIONS

HQ: BDO Unibank Inc.
  BDO Corporate Center,, 7899 Makati Avenue, Makati
  City 0726
Phone: (63) 2 840 7000
Web: www.bdo.com.ph

COMPETITORS

Bank of the Philippine Islands	Philippine National Bank
Citibank	
Metropolitan Bank and Trust	

HISTORICAL FINANCIALS

Company Type: Public

Income Statement · FYE: December 31

	ASSETS ($ mil.)	NET INCOME ($ mil.)	INCOME AS % OF ASSETS	EMPLOYEES
12/19	62,975	872	1.4%	38,510
12/18	57,545	622	1.1%	36,387
12/17	53,560	563	1.1%	33,747
12/16	46,956	526	1.1%	31,443
12/15	43,356	533	1.2%	28,217
Annual Growth	**9.8%**	**13.1%**	**—**	**8.1%**

2019 Year-End Financials

Return on assets: 1.4%	Dividends
Return on equity: 12.6%	Yield: 0.4%
Long-term debt ($ mil.): —	Payout: 68.5%
No. of shares (mil.): —	Market value ($ mil.): —
Sales ($ mil): 4,368	

	STOCK PRICE ($) FY Close	P/E High/Low	Earnings	PER SHARE ($) Dividends	Book Value
12/19	32.08	3 2	0.20	0.13	1.66
12/18	25.32	4 3	0.14	0.13	1.43
12/17	31.78	5 4	0.13	0.13	1.37
12/16	20.33	3 3	0.14	0.14	1.20
12/15	22.55	4 3	0.15	0.23	1.17
Annual Growth	**9.2%**	**— —**	**7.9%**	**(12.5%)**	**9.3%**

BHP Group Ltd

At its core BHP is a miner of copper and iron ore?they make enough in a year to build tracks to the moon and back! This Melbourne-based dual-listed company (parent BHP Billiton Limited; BHP Billiton Plc) is well-known as one of the world's top producers of key commodities. Beyond iron ore its activities include exploration and development of untapped resources extraction and processing of commodities as well as rehabilitation and closure of operational sites primarily in Australia and the Americas. With some $46.2 billion in economic contribution BHP has significant annual productions of iron ore (more than 235 Mt) petroleum (some 120 MMBoe) coal (about 70 Mt) and copper (about 1.7 Mt).

Operations

BHP has two major product groups?minerals and petroleum and some related marketing and supply activities.

BHP has four reportable segments Petroleum Copper Iron Ore and Coal. Iron ore accounts for about 40% of company's revenue and involves in activity of mining ores. Copper accounts for about 25% and involves in mining of copper zinc silver molybdenum uranium and gold. Coal activities are mining metallurgical coals and energy coals and account for about 20%. Petroleum involves in exploration development and production of oil and gas. This segment accounts for about 15%.

In Australia its operated mineral assets include Western Australia Iron Ore Queensland Coal (BMA and BMC) New South Wales Energy Coal Olympic Dam and Nickel West. Olympic Dam is one of the world's largest ore bodies. In the Americas its operated mineral assets are comprised of Escondida Pampa Norte and Jansen along with non-operated assets Antamina Cerrej "n and Samarco. BHP also has petroleum operated assets like Shenzi Angostura Pyrenees and Macedon. Ad-

ditionally it has non-operated assets of Atlantis Mad Dog Bass Strait and North West Shelf.

Geographic Reach

Melbourne-based BHP has presence in Chile Peru Brazil Colombia and Canada the US Australia Trinidad and Tobago the UK and Algeria. Asia Pacific generates the majority of company's revenue which accounts for a total of about 90% while Europe North America South America and the rest of the world generates the remaining revenue.

Sales and Marketing

With a strong market position and brand name BHP is one of the world's leading producers of copper and iron ore. It operates the largest single copper mine (Escondida in Chile) and is the largest supplier of seaborne metallurgical coal in the world.

The company sells its commodities to China US Japan India and in Europe.

Its principal offices are in Australia Canada Chile Malaysia Singapore the UK and the US.

Financial Performance

After a decrease in revenue in 2016 the company bounced back the following year and continued its revenue growth trend until 2019. Net income for the same five-year period fluctuated.

In 2019 revenue increased by 3% to $44.3 billion. The hike primarily came from higher average realized prices for iron ore petroleum and metallurgical coal and higher sales volume as a result of record production at Jimblebar and the expiry of Wheelara Joint Venture.

More impressively the company recorded a profit of $8.3 billion up from $3.7 billion the previous year despite being offset by an exceptional loss of US$842 million related to the Samarco dam failure.

Cash at the end of fiscal 2019 was $15.6 billion. Operations provided $17.9 billion and investing activities generated another $2.6 billion. Financing activities used $20.5 billion mainly for payment of dividends.

Strategy

BHP's main strategy is to have the best capabilities best commodities and best assets to create long-term value and high returns.

The Company has a simple and diverse portfolio of tier one assets. They are long life low cost and expandable. To extract the most value and the highest returns from its assets BHP apply its values and culture operate them safely and productively and deploy technology. This has worked for shareholders. Since 2016 the Company have strengthened its balance sheet through a US$17 billion reduction in net debt reinvested US$27 billion in development options and more importantly returned more than US$29 billion to shareholders.

To maintain this track record it must make the most of its portfolio and develop options that secure success. Future success depends not only on BHP's commitment to capital discipline but also social value which is its contribution to its people the environment and communities. It informs the way in which it provides resources achieve commercial success and make the workplace safe. BHP have a responsibility to produce strong commercial sustainable and social outcomes for its shareholders communities and society. This inspired the company to refresh its purpose to acknowledge people as the driving force behind its achievements and reflect on its broader contribution.

Company Background

From two small mining companies founded in the mid-1800s to the eventual merger of Broken Hill Proprietary and Billiton in 2001 today BHP is a leader in the resources industry. BHP began as a silver lead and zinc mining company in Broken Hill Australia in 1885. Billiton goes back further to 1851 as a tin mining company in the island of Belitung in Indonesia. Over the next century it expanded into businesses like oil & gas nickel diamond mining and marketing and potash businesses with varying success stories. In 2015 BHP decided to simplify its vast portfolio by spinning off some of its metals and mining businesses into a global company South32.

HISTORY

In 1883 Charles Rasp a boundary rider for the Mt. Gipps sheep station believed valuable ore lay in the Broken Hill outcrop in New South Wales Australia. He gathered a few young speculators and The Broken Hill Proprietary Company (BHP) was incorporated in 1885. BHP immediately found a massive lode of silver lead and zinc. None of the founders knew how to run a mine so they recruited US engineers William Patton and Herman Schlapp. From the beginning labor and management clashed. The founding directors set up the head office in Melbourne far from the mine and gambled with gold sovereigns in the boardroom. But the miners worked in dangerous conditions. An 1892 labor strike was the first of BHP's bitter strikes.

In 1902 the new general manager Guillaume Delprat invented a flotation process that recovered valuable metals from iron ore waste. Delprat also foresaw a future in steel although Australia had no steel industry. BHP commissioned the Newcastle steelworks in 1915 and soon became the country's largest steel producer. BHP's 1935 purchase of Australian Iron and Steel its only competitor gave it a virtual steel monopoly while high tariffs protected it from outside competition. Its exhausted Broken Hill mine was closed that year.

In the 1960s BHP got into oil when it partnered with Esso Standard the Australian subsidiary of Standard Oil of New Jersey for offshore exploration. In 1967 the partners found oil in the Bass Strait which soon supplied 70% of Australia's petroleum. In the 1960s and 1970s BHP began expanding its iron ore manganese and coal interests. Meanwhile public opposition mounted to BHP's market power and labor practices and in 1972 the government took steps to limit BHP's power removing some subsidies and tax breaks.

The weak steel market of the 1970s and 1980s caused BHP to lay off almost a third of its steelworkers in 1983 but with government intervention BHP radically improved its steel productivity. In 1984 BHP bought Utah International's mining assets from General Electric (including Chile's rich Escondida copper mine). In 1986 corporate raider Robert Holmes à Court took a run at BHP; BHP decided to become an international mining company to prevent further raids. Its acquisitions in the late 1980s included ERG Inc. and Monsanto Oil (combined into BHP Americas) Aquila Steel and Pacific Refining in Hawaii.

A peace deal with Holmes à Court gave BHP about 37% of Foster's Brewing but in 1992 BHP took a $700 million write-down after Foster's stock declined. BHP also bought Arizona-based Magma Copper in 1996 but plunging world copper prices forced a $420 million write-down.

With new worries over Asia's economic troubles BHP soon was struggling. In 1997 BHP sold most of its stake in Foster's and three senior executives resigned. In 1998 the company unloaded Pacific Refining which was acquired by Tesoro Petroleum for about $275 million.

As BHP's woes continued CEO John Prescott resigned; Paul Anderson was recruited from Duke Energy to succeed Prescott. In 1999 D. R. Argus took over as chairman replacing Jeremy Ellis. In a restructuring move the company sold its engineering power insurance and information technology businesses in 1999 and 2000. BHP began to sell $2 billion worth of steel operations (including its long product unit OneSteel which was later re-

named Arrium). In 2000 the company shortened its official name to BHP Limited.

BHP acquired Billiton in 2001 forming BHP Billiton Ltd. and BHP Billiton plc. The combined BHP Billiton had sales of almost $20 billion and a market capitalization approaching $30 billion. In addition BHP paid $436 million for Dia Met Minerals which owned 29% of Canada's only producing diamond mine Ekati.

Also in 2001 BHP Billiton and Alcoa combined their North American metals distribution businesses as joint venture Integris Metals (subsequently sold and integrated into Ryerson). In order to focus on its minerals and oil and gas operations in 2002 BHP Billiton spun off its steel business as BHP Steel (now called Bluescope Steel).

In 2005 BHP Billiton acquired metals and minerals company WMC Resources which had been the subject of much takeover speculation and the target of the Swiss mining heavyweight Xstrata (since renamed Glencore). Its offer of $7.3 billion surpassed Xstrata's and was accepted and endorsed by the WMC board which had turned down the two earlier proposals by Xstrata. The addition of WMC added significantly to BHP Billiton's copper nickel and uranium operations.

In 2008 BHP Billiton Mitsubishi Alliance (BMA) spent $2.4 billion to buy the Saraji East metallurgical coal project from New Hope Corporation. Each of BMA's owners paid $1.2 billion to New Hope for the project which lies adjacent to one of BMA's coal mines.

Though the global recession of 2008-2009 certainly pushed the company's fortunes down BHP Billiton experienced eyebrow-raising growth thanks in part to generally high commodity prices and the emerging Asian economies. China for example represented 20% of the company's total sales in 2007 doubling its share from just three years prior. The continent as a whole accounted for more than half of sales.

Due to the strong demand BHP Billiton increased production of iron ore coking coal and manganese. The shifting nature of the market though changed the company's highest-grossing segments. In 2009 high coal prices helped that business immensely while conversely the Base Metals business of copper lead zinc and precious metals mining suffered from low prices driving down the unit's revenues. On the petroleum side the company continued to acquire oil and gas exploration leases in the Gulf of Mexico.

Two failed deals by BHP Billiton occurred in 2010: a $39 billion takeover of Potash Corporation of Saskatchewan and a proposed joint venture with Rio Tinto Ltd. BHP Billiton's offer for Potash Corporation was first rejected by that company's board as inadequate and then by Canadian regulators who ruled the offer to be anticompetitive. After a $150 billion bid to buy Rio Tinto fell through due to the global economic meltdown the companies proposed a joint iron ore venture in Western Australia which also failed because of opposition from European regulatory authorities.

In 2010 BHP Billiton acquired Athabasca Potash Inc. (API) for about $320 million. API's projects are located in Saskatchewan close to BHP Billiton's own potash operations.

In 2011 BHP acquired Chesapeake Energy's Fayetteville shale gas holdings in Arkansas for $4.75 billion. That year it also acquired Petrohawk Energy another US-based gas producer with projects in the Eagle Ford and Haynesville shale plays for $15.1 billion. In 2012 natural gas prices began to plummet. Although the company defended the long-term growth outlook for the shale assets it did not rule out a possible writedown later that year for those investments.

Following the Petrohawk announcement in 2011 BHP acquired three subsidiaries of HWE

Mining a company owned by Leighton Holdings for $735 million. The HWE Mining subsidiaries provide contract iron ore mining services in Western Australia to BHP and the acquisition allows the company to both own and operate the mines.

In 2012 it sold its 51% stake in the Chidliak diamond exploration project in Canada's Baffin Island to the project operator Peregrine Diamonds giving it full ownership. The sale follows BHP's review of its diamond businesses to determine whether they fit in its strategy. The company also owns an 80% stake in Canada's EKATI diamond mine which is still under review. The company could receive less than $500 million for the sale of the mine.

EXECUTIVES

CEO, Andrew Mackenzie
Director Marketing Petroleum and Freight, Mike Henry
President HSE Marketing and Technology, Dean Della Valle
President Copper, Daniel Malchuk
CFO, Peter Beaven
President Corporate Affairs, Tony Cudmore
Interim President Copper, Edgar Basto
President Human Resources, Mike Fraser
President Petroleum Operations, Steve Pastor
Chairman, Jacques A. (Jac) Nasser, age 71
Auditors: Ernst & Young

LOCATIONS

HQ: BHP Group Ltd
171 Collins Street, Melbourne, Victoria 3000
Phone: (61) 3 9609 3333   **Fax:** (61) 3 9609 3015
Web: www.bhpbilliton.com

2015 Sales

	% of total
Asia Pacific	
China	36
Japan	11
South Korea	6
Australia	5
India	4
Rest of Asia	11
Europe	
United Kingdom	1
Rest of Europe	5
North America	17
South America	3
Rest of the world	1
Total	**100**

PRODUCTS/OPERATIONS

2015 Sales

	% of total
Iron ore	33
Petroleum and Potash	26
Copper	26
Coal	13
Group and unallocated items	2
Total	**100**

Selected Divisions

Coal
  Metallurgical
  Energy
Iron ore
Petroleum
  Crude oil
  Ethane
  LPG
  Natural gas
Base metals
  Copper
  Gold
  Lead
  Silver
  Zinc
Aluminum

Alumina
Aluminum
Bauxite
Manganese
Stainless steel materials
Cobalt
Ferrochrome
Nickel
Diamonds and specialty products
Diamonds
Potash
Titanium minerals

COMPETITORS

Anglo American
ArcelorMittal
Arconic
BP
Chevron
Chinalco
Codelco
ConocoPhillips
Exxon Mobil
Fortescue Metals
Freeport-McMoRan
Koch Industries Inc.
Kumba Iron Ore
Marathon Oil
Newmont Mining
Nippon Steel & Sumitomo Metal Corporation
Norsk Hydro ASA
Repsol
Rio Tinto Limited
Royal Dutch Shell
TOTAL
Tata Europe
Teck
Vale

HISTORICAL FINANCIALS

Company Type: Public

Income Statement				FYE: June 30
	REVENUE ($ mil.)	NET INCOME ($ mil.)	NET PROFIT MARGIN	EMPLOYEES
06/20	42,931	7,956	18.5%	31,589
06/19	44,288	8,306	18.8%	28,926
06/18	43,638	3,705	8.5%	27,161
06/17	38,285	5,890	15.4%	26,146
06/16	30,912	(6,385)	—	26,827
Annual Growth	8.6%	—	—	4.2%

2020 Year-End Financials

Debt ratio: 22.5%
Return on equity: 16.6%
Cash ($ mil.): 13,426
Current ratio: 1.45
Long-term debt ($ mil.): 19,446
No. of shares (mil.): —
Dividends
Yield: 5.7%
Payout: 273.2%
Market value ($ mil.): —

	STOCK PRICE ($) FY Close	P/E High/Low	PER SHARE ($) Earnings	Dividends	Book Value
06/20	49.73	37 20	1.57	2.86	9.48
06/19	58.11	36 27	1.60	6.60	9.34
06/18	50.01	75 52	0.69	2.94	10.44
06/17	35.59	38 25	1.10	1.08	10.76
06/16	28.56	— —	(1.20)	1.56	10.20
Annual Growth	14.9%	— —	—	16.4%	(1.8%)

BHP Group Plc

BHP Group (formerly BHP Billiton) mines copper and iron ore by the ton. The UK half of dual-listed Anglo-Australian BHP is among the world's biggest mining companies (BHP Billiton Limited is Australia-listed). Beyond iron ore its activities include exploration and development of untapped resources extraction and electrowinning processing of commodities as well as rehabilitation and closure of operational sites primarily in Australia and the Americas. BHP has significant annual productions of iron ore (about 250 Mt) petroleum (some 110 MMBoe) coal (around 40 Mt) and copper (about 1724 Kt). The company's largest market is China with over 60% of total sales.

Operations

BHP has four reportable segments? Iron Ore (about 50% of sales) Copper (some 25%) Coal (around 15%) and Petroleum (nearly 10% The Iron Ore segment's principal activity is mining of iron ore. The Copper segment includes mining of copper silver zinc molybdenum uranium and gold. The Coal segment's principal activity is mining of metallurgical coal and energy coal. The Petroleum segment includes exploration development and production of oil and gas.

Geographic Reach

Headquartered in London BHP has presence in Chile Peru Brazil Colombia and Canada the US Australia Trinidad and Tobago the UK and Algeria. China is the company's largest market with over 60% of total sales followed by Japan with about 10%.

In Australia its operated mineral assets include Western Australia Iron Ore Queensland Coal (BMA and BMC) New South Wales Energy Coal Olympic Dam and Nickel West. Olympic Dam is one of the world's largest ore bodies. In the Americas its operated mineral assets are comprised of Escondida Pampa Norte and Jansen along with non-operated assets Antamina Cerrej "n and Samarco. BHP also has petroleum operated assets like Shenzi Angostura Pyrenees and Macedon. Additionally it has non-operated assets of Atlantis Mad Dog Bass Strait and North West Shelf.

Sales and Marketing

The company has over 9000 suppliers around the world.

Financial Performance

BHP's revenue (year ended June 2020) decreased 3% to $42.9 billion in 2020. This decrease was primarily attributable to lower average realized prices for coal petroleum and copper and lower volumes due to natural field decline at Petroleum and lower grade at Escondida and Spence combined with planned maintenance across a number of its assets. This was partially offset by higher average realized prices for iron ore record production at WAIO record average concentrator throughput at Escondida and improved operational stability.

Profit of the company for the year was $8 billion lower by 4% compared to profit the year prior. Lower revenue and high expenses contributed to the decrease in profit.

Cash and cash equivalents at end of the year were $13.4 billion. Operations provided $15.7 billion in 2020 while investing activities used $7.6 billion and financing activities used another $9.8 billion. The main cash uses for the year were for purchases of property and equipment and dividends payment.

Strategy

BHP's strategy is to have the best capabilities best commodities and best assets to create long-term value and high returns. Its strategy is underpinned by its disciplined approach to capital allocation and risk management and its overriding commitment to generating social value for its stakeholders. Social value is at the core of its approach and purpose - to bring people and resources together to build a better world. It underpins its decisions and actions from the positive contribution it makes to the environment and society to support the needs of its workforce partners customers economies and communities. The longevity of BHP's assets means it must think and plan in decades. The long-term health of its business is dependent on the long-term health of its society and a sustainable natural environment.

As it looks to the future BHP and its products will play an essential role as the world's population continues to grow improved living standards are pursued and momentum towards decarbonization increases.

It has secured and will continue to grow options in copper and nickel where increasing demand and its capability gives it competitive opportunities. It is moving to concentrate its coal portfolio on higher-quality coking coals with greatest potential upside for quality premiums as steelmakers seek to improve blast furnace utilization and reduce emissions intensity and will pursue options to divest its interests in BMC New South Wales Energy Coal (NSWEC) and Cerrej n. In oil and gas it will continue to invest in opportunities that are resilient under a range of price scenarios and which are aligned to its strengths. It will seek to divest oil and gas assets that are mature or which are likely to realize greater value under different ownership. This approach to actively managing its portfolio for value risk and returns over multiple time horizons will yield superior returns for its investors and greater value for its partners and communities.

Mergers and Acquisitions

In late 2020 BHP has completed the transaction to acquire an additional 28% working interest in Shenzi a six-lease development in the deepwater Gulf of Mexico from Hess Corporation (Hess) for US$505 million. The transaction brings BHP's working interest to 72% and adds approximately 11000 barrels of oil equivalent per day of production (90% oil).

In mid-2020 BHP has agreed to acquire the Honeymoon Well Nickel Project comprising the Honeymoon Well development project and a 50% interest in the Albion Downs North and Jericho exploration joint ventures from MPI Nickel Pty Ltd a wholly owned subsidiary of Norilsk Nickel Australian Holdings BV. The combined tenement package is located in the northern Goldfields region of Western Australia. Terms were not disclosed.

Company Background

From two small mining companies founded in the mid-1800s to the eventual merger of Broken Hill Proprietary and Billiton in 2001 today BHP is a leader in the resources industry. BHP began as a silver lead and zinc mining company in Broken Hill Australia in 1885. Billiton goes back further to 1851 as a tin mining company in the island of Belitung in Indonesia. Over the next century it expanded into businesses like oil & gas nickel diamond mining and marketing and potash businesses with varying success stories. In 2015 BHP decided to simplify its vast portfolio by spinning off some of its metals and mining businesses into a global company South32.

EXECUTIVES

CEO, Andrew Mackenzie, $1,120,620 total compensation
President Governance and Group Company Secretary, Jane F. McAloon, age 56
CFO, Peter Beaven
President Petroleum, Timothy J. (Tim) Cutt, age 61
President Iron Ore, Jimmy Wilson
President Coal., Mike Henry
President Copper, Daniel Malchuk
President HSE Marketing and Technology and Chief Commercial Officer, Dean Della Valle
President Aluminium Manganese & Nickel, Daniel MalchukBE
President Corporate Affairs, Tony Cudmore
Chairman, Jac Nasser
Auditors: KPMG LLP

LOCATIONS

HQ: BHP Group Plc
Nova South, 160 Victoria Street, London SW1E 5LB
Phone: (44) 20 7802 4000   **Fax:** (44) 20 7802 4111
Web: www.bhp.com

2015 Sales

	% of total
Australia	5
United Kingdom	1
Rest of Europe	5
China	36
Japan	11
Rest of Asia	11
North America	17
South America	3
Southern Africa	
Rest of world	1
India	4
South Korea	6
Total	**100**

PRODUCTS/OPERATIONS

2015 Sales

	% of total
Iron Ore	33
Petroleum and Potash	26
Copper	26
Coal	13
Group and unallocated items	2
Total	**100**

COMPETITORS

Anglo American	Norilsk Nickel
Arconic	Norsk Hydro ASA
BP	Rio Tinto plc
Chevron	Vale
Newmont Mining	

HISTORICAL FINANCIALS

Company Type: Public

Income Statement				FYE: June 30
	REVENUE ($ mil.)	NET INCOME ($ mil.)	NET PROFIT MARGIN	EMPLOYEES
06/20	42,931	7,956	18.5%	31,589
06/19	44,288	8,306	18.8%	28,926
06/18	43,638	3,705	8.5%	27,161
06/17	38,285	5,890	15.4%	26,146
06/16	30,912	(6,385)	—	26,827
Annual Growth	**8.6%**	**—**		**4.2%**

2020 Year-End Financials

Debt ratio: 25.8%
Return on equity: 16.6%
Cash ($ mil.): 13,426
Current ratio: 1.45
Long-term debt ($ mil.): 22,036

No. of shares (mil.): —
Dividends
  Yield: 6.9%
  Payout: 182.1%
Market value ($ mil.): —

	STOCK PRICE ($) FY Close	P/E High/Low	PER SHARE ($) Earnings	PER SHARE ($) Dividends	PER SHARE ($) Book Value
06/20	41.15	33 16	1.57	2.86	9.48
06/19	51.11	32 24	1.60	4.40	9.34
06/18	44.95	69 45	0.69	1.96	10.44
06/17	30.76	34 22	1.10	1.08	10.76
06/16	25.38	— —	(1.20)	1.56	10.20
Annual Growth	**12.8%**	**— —**	**—**	**16.4%**	**(1.8%)**

Bid Corp Ltd

Auditors: PricewaterhouseCoopers Inc.

LOCATIONS

HQ: Bid Corp Ltd
2nd floor, North Wing, 90 Rivonia Road, Postnet Suite 136, Sandton 2196
Phone: (27) 10 592 2150
Web: www.bidcorpgroup.com

HISTORICAL FINANCIALS

Company Type: Public

Income Statement				FYE: June 30
	REVENUE ($ mil.)	NET INCOME ($ mil.)	NET PROFIT MARGIN	EMPLOYEES
06/20	15,009	150	1.0%	23,427
06/19	16,017	508	3.2%	25,858
06/18	14,791	439	3.0%	26,448
06/17	16,224	496	3.1%	25,613
06/16	16,796	406	2.4%	24,064
Annual Growth	**(2.8%)**	**(22.0%)**	**—**	**(0.7%)**

2020 Year-End Financials

Debt ratio: 2.1%
Return on equity: 4.3%
Cash ($ mil.): 870
Current ratio: 1.07
Long-term debt ($ mil.): 565

No. of shares (mil.): 334
Dividends
  Yield: —
  Payout: 90.7%
Market value ($ mil.): —

BNP Paribas (France)

Ask this company "Où est la banque?" and the answer is virtually everywhere. One of Europe's largest banks BNP Paribas and its many subsidiaries offer a wide range of retail and corporate and investment banking services across Europe North America Africa and the Asia/Pacific region. Additional services include corporate vehicle leasing digital banking and investment services and private banking and wealth management. BNP Paribas operates in Italy through BNL banca commerciale and in Belgium via BNP Paribas Fortis. In the US the company owns BancWest. BNP Paribas earns roughly 75% of its revenue from customers in Europe (mainly in France Belgium Italy and Luxembourg). BNP has more than ?2 trillion in assets.

Operations

BNP Paribas operates two core businesses: Retail Banking & Services and Corporate & Institutional Banking.

Retail Banking & Services operates more than 7000 branches in more than 70 countries and accounts for around 75% of the bank's total revenue. The segment consists of its domestic retail banking networks in France Italy (BNL bc) Belgium (BNP Paribas Fortis) and Luxembourg (BGL BNP Paribas) as well as certain specialized retail banking divisions (Personal Investors Leasing Solutions Arval and New Digital Businesses). BNP Paribas is the leading private bank in France and #1 for cash management and professional equipment financing in Europe. BNL bc holds a residential mortgage market share of around 7% in Italy and a 4% household current account market share.

International Financial Services consists of all BNP Paribas Group's retail banking businesses outside the euro zone split between Europe-Mediterranean and BancWest in the United States. It also includes personal finance insurance and wealth and asset management activities.

Corporate and Institutional Banking generates the remaining 25% of revenue. It consists of three divisions. Corporate Banking provides services in Europe the Middle East Africa the Asia/Pacific region and Americas as well as corporate finance activities. Global Markets offers fixed income currency and commodities and equity and prime services. Securities Services caters to management companies financial institutions and other corporations.

Broadly speaking the company makes more than 45% of its net revenue from interest (after interest expense). Net commission income brings in more than 20% and the rest arises from gains on financial instruments and available-for-sale financial assets insurance and other activities that generate more than 30% of revenues combined.

Geographic Reach

While it caters to more than 70 countries Paris-based BNP focuses mainly on four domestic markets where it holds leading positions: Belgium France Italy and Luxembourg. Europe is the bank's largest market accounting for more than 75% of revenue. North America contributed more than 10% while the Asia/Pacific and Africa region and other countries each contributed more than 5%.

In France BNP Paribas' retail network consists of more than 1800 branches and more than 5000 ATMs. Its private banking network consists of numerous centers throughout France 2 wealth management offices more than 20 general business centers approximately 80 SME centers and more than 60 We Are Innovation (WAI) start-up support locations.

In Italy through BNL banca commerciale BNP Paribas operates more than 720 branches 1800 ATMs more than 35 private banking centers 45 small business centers around 45 branches dealing with SMEs large corporates local authorities and public sector organizations and a few trade centers for cross-border activities and investment desks that assist local and international companies with direct investments in Italy.

BNP Paribas' Belgium unit operates around 600 branches more than 2700 ATMs around 20 small business centers 270 Fintro franchises around 660 retail outlets in partnership with Bpost Bank.

In Luxembourg it supports its 183000 customers via more than 40 branches about 130 ATMs and five private banking centers.

BancWest is active in some 25 Western and Mid-Western US states. It operates around 535 branches.

The Europe-Mediterranean segment operates a network in more than 1910 branches across 14 countries including Turkey Poland Ukraine Morocco Tunisia Algeria and seven countries in Sub-Saharan Africa.

Sales and Marketing

BNP Paribas has a deep sponsorship relationship with tennis. Led by its long-term sponsorship of the Roland Garros French Open tennis tournament held each summer in Paris the company also sponsors the Davis Cup the Fed Cup the BNP Paribas Masters and more. The company also has a number of cultural sponsorships across music theater film and dance.

Financial Performance

Note: Growth rates may differ after conversion to US dollars.

BNP Paribas has recorded sluggish revenue growth in the past five years due to a lackluster interest rate and market environment. Meanwhile net income has trended slowly but consistently upwards and BNP's profit margins are among the highest out of Europe's leading commercial banks.

In 2019 BNP Paribas' revenue rose 5% to ?44.6 billion. Revenues in the operating divisions rose by 6% with an increase in all the divisions: a 1% increase in Domestic Markets 7% in International Financial Services and 12% in CIB which posted strong revenue growth with very good performance by Global Markets and Corporate Banking.

The Group's net income attributable to equity holders came at ?8.2 billion up 9% compared to ?7.5 billion in the prior year. Operating income rose by 10% to ?10.1 billion mostly from the increase in its operating divisions.

BNP's cash balance weakened during 2019 ending the year ?30.3 billion lower at ?152.2 billion. The bank's operations used ?50.8 billion while investing activities used another ?323 million. Financing activities generated ?20.1 billion. Operating activities were net cash negative due to a ?75.6 billion net decrease in cash related to operating assets and liabilities.

Strategy

BNP Paribas' 'Road to 2020' plan rests on four pillars: grow the business provide a new customer experience accelerate digitization and improve operating efficiency. BNP Paribas is investing ?3 billion to make better use of data implement new customer journeys adapt information systems and upgrade its operational model. The shift to digital also includes the closure of hundreds of its traditional (and more expensive) branches; in total the bank expects the initiative to produce cost savings of ?3.4 billion.

The exceptional transformation costs under the 2020 plan totalled ?2.7 billion in three years. The Group will no longer have transformation costs in 2020 which will enable it to reduce spending by ?7 million in 2020 compared to 2019. The recurring savings generated by the plan at the end of 2019 totalled ?1.8 billion in line with the objectives. The Group expects to generate an additional ?1.5 billion in additional recurring savings in 2020 thereby attaining the target of ?3.3 billion in cumulative recurring cost savings.

In 2020 the Group anticipates continuing to grow business in all the operating divisions by leveraging a strong business drive and the contribution of the diversified and integrated model. The reinforcement of the franchises within the integrated model should continue in particular for CIB with the ongoing development of its businesses and the strengthening of its businesses and the strengthening of its European leadership.

Mergers and Acquisitions

In early 2020 BNP Paribas acquired the depository unit of Spain-based Banco Sabadell for 115 million euros. Soledad Lecube head of BNP Paribas Securities Services Spain commented: "The acquisition of Sabadell's depositary banking business consolidates our position as a leading asset servicing provider in Spain where we are the first depositary bank for independent asset managers."

HISTORY

BNP Paribas Group's predecessor Banque Nationale de Paris (BNP) is the progeny of two state banks with parallel histories; each was set up to jump-start the economy after a revolution in 1848.

For a century Paris-based Comptoir National d'Escompte de Paris (CNEP) bounced between private and public status depending on government whim. It was the #3 bank in France from the late 19th century through the 1950s.

Banque National pour le Commerce et l'Industrie (BNCI) started in Alsace a region that was part of Germany from the Franco-Prussian War until WWI. BNCI served as an economic bridge between Germany and France which had to give the bank governmental resuscitation during the Depression. By the 1960s BNCI had passed CNEP in size.

French leader Charles de Gaulle expected banking to drive post-WWII reconstruction and in 1945 CNEP and BNCI were nationalized. In 1966 France's finance minister merged them and they became BNP. That year the company started an association with Dresdner Bank of Germany under which the two still operate joint ventures primarily in Eastern Europe.

By 1993 privatization was again in vogue and BNP was cut loose by the government. It expanded outside France to ameliorate the influences of the French economy and government. Even before it was privatized BNP was involved in such politically charged actions as the bailout of OPEC money repository Banque Arabe and the extension of credit to Algeria's state oil company Sonatrach.

The privatized BNP looked overseas in the late 1990s. In 1997 alone it won the right to operate in New Zealand bought Laurentian Bank and Trust of the Bahamas took control of its joint venture with Egypt's Banque du Caire and opened a subsidiary in Brazil.

BNP bought failed Peregrine Investment's Chinese operations in 1998. That year the bank also expanded in Peru opened an office in Algeria opened a representative office in Uzbekistan set up an investment banking subsidiary in India and bought Australian stock brokerage operations from Prudential.

After a decade of globe-trotting BNP brought it on home in 1999 and set off a year of tumult in French banking. As France's other two large banks (Société Générale and Paribas) made plans to merge BNP decided it would absorb both banks as a means to get a bigger chunk of the to-be-privatized Crédit Lyonnais and to protect France from Euro-megabank penetration by creating the globe's largest bank.

Executives at Société Générale (SG) had other ideas forming a cartel called "Action Against the BNP Raid." Meanwhile BNP tried to boost to controlling stakes its holdings in the two banks. (In Europe's cross-ownership tradition the target banks also owned part of BNP.) France's central bank tried unsuccessfully to negotiate a deal (the government supported the triumvirate merger). A war of words was played out in the media and finally shareholders had to vote on the proposals. In the end BNP won control of Paribas but not SG. As BNP prepared to integrate a reluctant Paribas into its operations regulators ordered BNP to relinquish its stake in SG. The newly merged company was dubbed BNP Paribas Group.

In 2000 BNP Paribas and Avis Group launched a fleet-management joint venture. BNP also bought 150 shopping centers from French retailer Carrefour and the 40% of merchant bank Cobepa that it didn't already own. In 2001 BNP Paribas took full control of US-based BancWest. The company bought United California Bank from UFJ Holdings (now part of Mitsubishi UFJ Financial Group) the following year.

The bank opened up a second "home market" when it bought Italy's Banca Nazionale del Lavoro (BNL) for $11 billion in 2006.

Two of the French bank's most transformative acquisitions included the deal to buy Italian bank Banca Nazionale del Lavoro in 2006 and the 75% purchase of Fortis Bank (which also included a 25% stake in Fortis Insurance). Both deals boosted BNP Paribas' retail banking business across Europe. Retail banking is now responsible for more than 60% of BNP Paribas' revenues.

In addition to the Fortis and BNL acquisitions BNP Paribas looked to grow in new markets. BNP Paribas acquired Sahara Bank in Libya and a 51% stake in UkrSibbank one of Ukraine's leading banks.

In 2008 as the world's economies struggled to stay afloat the French government agreed to inject ?10.5 billion ($14 billion) into the nation's top six banks including BNP Paribas. The government didn't receive shares in the banks it assisted; rather the capital injections were meant to help reenergize lending activities in France. A year after receiving the cash BNP Paribas announced plans to repay the government's aid.

In 2009 after a couple of false starts and a seven-month saga BNP Paribas acquired control of Fortis Banque (also known as Fortis Bank). Fortis' Dutch operations were excluded from the transaction. The deal further cemented BNP Paribas as a top European bank. Fortis Bank was nationalized in October 2008 to prevent its collapse and the takeover by BNP Paribas was delayed and revised to satisfy Fortis shareholders and other interested parties. Upon the closing of the deal BNP Paribas became the market leader in Belgium and Luxembourg. The Belgian government gained more than 10% of BNP Paribas in the transaction.

BNP Paribas complimented its 2009 acquisition of Fortis with the purchase of private bank Insinger de Beaufort.

In 2011 BNP Paribas continued its strategy of expanding in high growth markets and acquired a majority of South Africa's Cadiz Securities. BNP Paribas also owns Banque Internationale pour le Commerce et l'Industrie which is active in six African nations and a majority of T rk Ekonomi Bankasi in Turkey. BNP Paribas has been expanding in China Egypt Israel and Russia as well.

In 2012 the company sold the bulk of its controlling stake in real estate firm Klépierre to US mall owner Simon for some ?1.5 billion (around $2 billion) to further raise its capital levels.

EXECUTIVES

Deputy COO, Michel Konczaty
Head of Group Development and Finance, Philippe Bordenave, age 66
Chairman and CEO BNP Paribas Fortis, Maxime (Max) Jadot, age 64
Deputy COO and Head International Financial Services, Jacques d'Estais, age 61
Deputy COO and Group General Manager North America; Head Corporate and Institutional Banking, Alain Papiasse, age 61
Head International Retail Banking, Stefaan Decraene, age 55
CEO and General Manager BNL, Andrea Munari, age 57
Head of Group Human Resources, Yves Martrenchar, age 63
CEO and Director, Jean-Laurent Bonnafé, age 59
Head French Retail Banking, Marie-Claire Capobianco
Head Compliance, Eric Martin
Head Corporate and Investment Banking, Yann Gérardin
Deputy COO and Head Domestic Markets, Thierry Laborde
CEO BNP Paribas Personal Finance, Laurent David
CEO BNP Paribas Cardif, Renaud Dumora
CEO BNP Paribas UK, Jean-Michel Boyer
Chief Investment Officer, Ritesh Jain
CEO Cardif Iberia, Cecilia Boned
CEO LÂ'Atelier BNP Paribas, Alessandro Promutico
Chairman, Jean Lemierre, age 71
Auditors: Deloitte & Associés

LOCATIONS

HQ: BNP Paribas (France)
16, Boulevard des Italiens, Paris 75009
Phone: (33) 1 40 14 45 46   **Fax:** (33) 1 42 98 21 22
Web: www.bnpparibas.com

2018 Sales

	% of total
Europe	75
North America	11
Asia & Pacific	7
Others	7
Total	**100**

PRODUCTS/OPERATIONS

2018 Sales

	% of total
Retail Banking & Services:	
Domestic Markets	
French Retail Banking	14
Belgian Retail Banking	8
BNL banca commerciale	7
Other Domestic Markets activities	7
International Financial Services	
Personal Finance	13
International Retail Banking	
BancWest	6
Wealth and Asset Management	6
EuropeMediterranean	8
Insurance	6
Corporate & Institutional Banking:	
Global Markets	11
Corporate Banking	9
Securities Services	5
Other Activities:	—
Total	**100**

2018 Sales

	% of total
Net interest income	49
Net commission income	22
Net gain on financial instruments at fair value through profit or loss	14
Net gain on available-for-sale financial assets and other financial assets not measured at fair value	1
Net income from insurance activities	10
Net income from other activities	4
Total	**100**

COMPETITORS

ABN AMRO Group	HSBC
BBVA	JPMorgan Chase
Banco Popular Español	Natixis
Bank of America	Société Générale
Barclays	U.S. Bancorp
Citigroup	UBS
Crédit Agricole	Wells Fargo
Deutsche Bank	

HISTORICAL FINANCIALS

Company Type: Public

Income Statement				FYE: December 31
	ASSETS ($ mil.)	NET INCOME ($ mil.)	INCOME AS % OF ASSETS	EMPLOYEES
12/19	2,430,466	9,176	0.4%	198,816
12/18	2,337,155	8,618	0.4%	202,625
12/17	2,349,860	9,301	0.4%	196,128
12/16	2,193,026	8,132	0.4%	192,418
12/15	2,172,096	7,291	0.3%	189,077
Annual Growth	2.8%	5.9%	—	1.3%

2019 Year-End Financials

Return on assets: 0.3%
Return on equity: 7.8%
Long-term debt ($ mil.): —
No. of shares (mil.): 1,249
Sales ($ mil): 87,744

Dividends
Yield: 5.6%
Payout: 24.2%
Market value ($ mil.): 37,085

STOCK PRICE ($)		P/E		PER SHARE ($)		
FY Close		High/Low		Earnings	Dividends	Book Value
12/19	29.69	5	4	6.97	1.68	96.59
12/18	22.54	7	4	6.56	1.76	93.03
12/17	37.35	7	5	7.25	1.62	97.95
12/16	31.85	5	3	6.34	1.24	85.29
12/15	28.26	6	5	5.59	0.83	84.24
Annual Growth	1.2%	—	—	5.7%	19.5%	3.5%

Boc Hong Kong Holdings Ltd

BOC Hong Kong (Holdings) is the parent of Bank of China (Hong Kong) which has more than 190 branches 280 automated banking centers and over 1000 self-service machines in Hong Kong. The bank serves retail customers small entrepreneurs and corporate customers providing loans trade related products and other credit facilities investment and insurance products. It also operates banknote printing business. Bank of China which is controlled by the Chinese government owns about two-thirds of BOC Hong Kong.

Operations
BOC Hong Kong (Holdings) operates under four operating segments: Personal Banking Corporate Banking Treasury and Insurance.

Both Corporate Banking (about 40% of revenue) and Personal Banking (about 30% of revenue) provide general banking services including various deposit products overdrafts loans and other credit facilities investment and insurance products and foreign currency and derivative products. Corporate Banking serves corporate clients while Personal Banking serves retail customers.

Treasury (about 30% of revenue) manages the funding and liquidity interest rate and foreign exchange positions of the bank in addition to proprietary trades. The Insurance segment represents the business mainly relating to life insurance products including individual life insurance and group life insurance products.

Overall BOC Hong Kong (Holdings) generates more than 50% of its revenue from interest income followed by insurance premiums for about 25% of revenue and commissions about for 15%.

Geographic Reach
Hong Kong-based BOC Hong Kong (Holdings) has operations in the US Singapore and China. It also has branches in Thailand Malaysia Vietnam the Philippines Indonesia Cambodia Laos and Brunei.

Sales and Marketing
BOC Hong Kong (Holdings)'s five largest customers accounted less than 30% of total interest income and other operating income of the bank in 2019.

Financial Performance
In 2019 BOCHK's annual profit hit a new high of HK$34.1 billion representing a growth of 4% year-on-year.

Cash held by the company at the end of 2019 decreased to HK$331.7 billion compared to HK$626.1 billion in the prior year. Cash used for operations investing activities and financing activities were HK$268.7 billion HK$3.3 billion and HK$18.5 billion respectively.

Strategy
BOCHK's strategic goal is to "Build a Top-class Full-service and Internationalised Regional Bank". Capitalising on its advantages as a major commercial banking group in Hong Kong BOCHK aims to increase local market penetration and actively expand its business in the Southeast Asian region. The company strive to provide customers with comprehensive professional and high-quality services. As one of the three note-issuing banks and the sole clearing bank for Renminbi ("RMB") business in Hong Kong BOCHK has strong market positions in all major businesses. Its strong RMB franchise has made the company the first choice for customers in RMB business.

EXECUTIVES

Vice Chairman and CEO, Yue Yi, age 63
CFO, Sui Yang, age 45
COO, Zhong Xiangqun
Deputy Chief Executive Corporate Banking Financial Institutions and Product Management Corporate Credit Management Centre and China Business, Lin Jingzhen, age 55
Deputy Chief Executive Personal Banking and Product Management Channel Management Private Banking and BOCCC, Kung Yeung (Ann) Yun Chi, age 57
Vice Chairman, Chen Siqing, age 59
Chairman, Guoli Tian, age 58
Auditors: Ernst & Young

LOCATIONS

HQ: Boc Hong Kong Holdings Ltd
53th Floor, Bank of China Tower, 1 Garden Road,
Phone: (852) 2846 2700   **Fax:** (852) 2810 5830
Web: www.bochk.com

PRODUCTS/OPERATIONS

2014 Sales

	% of total
Interest income	58
Fee and commission income	17
Gross earned premiums	20
Net trading gain	3
Others	2
Total	**100**

COMPETITORS

AXA Asia Pacific	Citigroup
Bank of Communications	Dah Sing Financial
Bank of East Asia	Holdings Limited
CITIC International	HSBC
Financial	Hang Seng Bank
Chong Hing Bank	Standard Chartered

HISTORICAL FINANCIALS

Company Type: Public

Income Statement				FYE: December 31
	ASSETS ($ mil.)	NET INCOME ($ mil.)	INCOME AS % OF ASSETS	EMPLOYEES
12/19	388,613	4,133	1.1%	14,668
12/18	377,025	4,085	1.1%	14,046
12/17	338,538	3,975	1.2%	13,050
12/16	300,182	7,157	2.4%	12,836
12/15	305,493	3,457	1.1%	15,000
Annual Growth	6.2%	4.6%	—	(0.6%)

2019 Year-End Financials

Return on assets: 1.0%
Return on equity: 11.0%
Long-term debt ($ mil.): —
No. of shares (mil.): —
Sales ($ mil.): 14,307

Dividends
Yield: 5.3%
Payout: 954.8%
Market value ($ mil.): —

	STOCK PRICE ($)	P/E	PER SHARE ($)		
	FY Close	High/Low	Earnings	Dividends	Book Value
12/19	69.18	30 21	0.39	3.70	3.67
12/18	73.94	35 24	0.39	3.28	3.39
12/17	101.57	35 24	0.38	3.22	2.94
12/16	71.55	15 9	0.68	4.95	2.74
12/15	60.72	34 23	0.33	2.85	2.35
Annual Growth	3.3%	— —	4.6%	6.8%	11.8%

BOE Technology Group Co Ltd

Whether you are looking at a laptop computer or a flat-screen billboard you could be looking at BOE Technology Group. The company makes semiconductor display panels used in notebooks computer monitors TVs navigation systems and handheld devices. BOE specializes in thin-film transistor liquid-crystal display (TFT-LCD) panels which appear brighter and sharper than traditional LCD displays. It also makes light-emitting diode (LED) and high-brightness LCD modules and LED backlights. BOE Technology's products are sold to global OEMs such as AU Optronics and TPV Technology.

Operations
The Display Devices business accounts for some 80% of BOE's revenue.

The Intelligent Systems business 16% of revenue develops the company's products for Internet of Things applications for mobile health products opto-electronics vehicles and display network.

The other 4% of revenue comes from the Health Services business and the company's "other" category.

Geographic Reach
BOE customers in China generate 43% of revenue and customers in other Asian account for another 44%. The company has eight manufacturing plants located across China. Europe and the Americas are responsible for about equal shares of the remaining revenue.

The company makes its displays in eight plants in China.

Sales and Marketing
The company's five biggest customers generate about 36% of its revenue.

Financial Performance
Rising sales in all product and geographic markets boosted revenue 33% in 2015 from 2014. Profit fell 36% as higher general and administrative costs cut into the higher revenue. Cash flow for 2015 was 30% higher than n 2014.

Company Background
Founded as Beijing Orient Electronics Group in 1993 the company changed its name to BOE Technology in 2001.

EXECUTIVES

Chairman and CEO, Wang Dongsheng
Vice Chairman and President, Chen Yanshun
EVP and COO, Liu Xiaodong
EVP and CHRO, Song Ying
EVP and Co-COO, Wang Jiaheng
EVP, Wang Yanjun
SVP and CFO, Sun Yun
EVP and CTO, Dong Youmei
VP and Chief Strategy Officer, Yao Xiangjun

VP and Chief Risk Officer, Xie Zhongdong
Auditors: KPMG Huazhen LLP

LOCATIONS
HQ: BOE Technology Group Co Ltd
12 Xihuan Middle Road, Beijing Economic-Technological Development Area, Beijing 100176
Phone: (86) 10 64318888   **Fax:** (86) 10 64366264
Web: www.boe.com

2013 Sales
	% of total
PRC	54
Other Asian Regions	39
America	5
Europe	2
Total	**100**

PRODUCTS/OPERATIONS

2013 Sales
	% of total
TFT-LCDs	79
Display System	11
Backlight Products	5
Others	5
Total	**100**

Products and Services
Display Device
For Mobile
For TPC
For NB
For MNT
For TV
For DID
Electronic Material
Smart System Product
Display System
Environment Lighting
Photovoltaic System
ODM/OEM
Smart Healthcare Service

COMPETITORS

AU Optronics	LG Display
Chimei Innolux	NEC Display Solutions
Dalian Daxian	SVA Group
HannStar Display	Samsung Electronics
IRICO	Sharp Electronics

HISTORICAL FINANCIALS
Company Type: Public

Income Statement   FYE: December 31

	REVENUE ($ mil.)	NET INCOME ($ mil.)	NET PROFIT MARGIN	EMPLOYEES
12/19	16,679	275	1.7%	0
12/18	14,118	499	3.5%	0
12/17	14,414	1,162	8.1%	0
12/16	9,921	271	2.7%	49,151
12/15	7,486	251	3.4%	42,837
Annual Growth	22.2%	2.3%	—	—

2019 Year-End Financials
Debt ratio: 5.6%
Return on equity: 2.1%
Cash ($ mil.): 8,187
Current ratio: 1.33
Long-term debt ($ mil.): 15,538
No. of shares (mil.): —
Dividends
Yield: —
Payout: —
Market value ($ mil.): —

Bombardier Inc.

Bombardier is a leading manufacturer of both planes and trains. It makes and sells business aircraft including its iconic Learjet and Challenger and its transportation division manufactures a variety of rail vehicles including people movers such as metro trains monorail systems and high-speed trains. The company also provides aftermarket parts as well as engineering services at its worldwide network of service centers. Most of Bombardier's business is generated in Europe and North America. In 2019 Bombardier agreed to sell its CRJ Series commercial regional jet program to Mitsubishi Heavy Industries for $550 million and sell its Aerostructures business to Spirit AeroSystems Holding in a deal valued at about $700 million.

Operations
Bombardier divides itself into two main segments: Transportation and Aviation. The Transportation segment makes and sells rail vehicles such as automated people movers monorails advanced rapid transit trains and high-speed trains and locomotives. It also offers fleet maintenance and signaling solutions for mass transit.

The Aviation segment includes Business Aircraft Commercial Aircraft and Aerostructures and Engineering Services. These include the Learjet Challenger and Global aircraft families. The Aerostructures and Engineering Services division provides aircraft structures component repair aircraft parts and aftermarket technical support.

In 2018 and 2019 Bombardier made some major moves to focus on its core Business Jet and Transportation businesses. In 2018 it formed a partnership with Airbus which gave Airbus a majority stake in Bombardier's C Series commercial aircraft program which has since been rebranded the Airbus A220. Bombardier holds a 34% stake in the partnership.

In 2019 Bombardier exited its business aircraft training and Q Series aircraft businesses and agreed to sell its CRJ regional jet operations to Mitsubishi Heavy Industries. The completion of the CRJ Series deal will mark Bombardier's exit from the commercial aircraft market. Bombardier has also announced it would sell its Aerostructures business to Spirit AeroSystems Holding.

Geographic Reach
Headquartered in Montreal Canada Bombardier does business in North America Europe and Asia-Pacific.

Financial Performance
Bombardier's revenue improved in 2018 after several years of heading in the wrong direction. Sales fell nearly 20% between 2015 and 2018.

Sales in 2018 increased less than 1% to C$16.23 billion compared to C$16.2 billion in 2017. Growth in 2018 was fueled by the Transportation Business Jet and Aerostructures and Engineering Services segments.

Net income in 2018 was C$232 million compared to a C$494 million loss in 2019. The improvement was primarily due to cost savings resulting from Airbus taking over operations of Bombardier's C Series commercial aircraft program (now the Airbus A220).

Cash at the end of 2018 was $C3.19 billion an increase of C$130 million from the prior year. Cash from operations contributed C$597 million to the coffers while investing activities used C$701 million mainly for capital expenditures. Financing activities brought in C$221 million primarily from the issuance of Class B shares.

Strategy

Bombardier is still working its way through a business transformation which began in 2015. The company is focusing on its core Transportation and Business Jet operations. In 2018 Bombardier achieved two major milestones in its transformation. Its Global 7500 business jet entered service and the lengthy development and investment process will start reaping financial benefits. Bombardier also finalized its Airbus partnership which gave the aerospace giant a controlling interest in Bombardier's C Series commercial aircraft program (the C Series has since been rebranded as the Airbus A220). The deal frees Bombardier from the high costs associated with playing in the commercial aircraft space while leveraging Airbus' procurement sales and marketing resources for greater reach and scale. Bombardier holds a 35% stake in the partnership.

The company further tightened its focus in 2019 with a slew of deals. Early that year it sold its flight and technical training business to Canada-based flight simulator company CAE for net proceeds of about C$500 million. Later that year Bombardier sold the assets of its Q Series turboprop aircraft business to De Havilland Aircraft of Canada an affiliate of Longview Aviation Capital Corp. for about C$300 million.

Also in 2019 Bombardier agreed to sell its CRJ Series commercial regional jet program to Mitsubishi Heavy Industries for about C$550 million essentially marking the end of Bombardier's foray into the commercial aircraft market. Later that year the company agreed to sell its Aerostructures business to Spirit AeroSystems Holding in a deal valued at about C$700 million.

Paring down its noncore aerospace holdings gives Bombardier room to concentrate on its Transportation segment which at the end of 2018 enjoyed a project backlog of more than $35 billion while improving the mix of service and signaling contracts. Bombardier is well positioned to take advantage of the trend of urbanization and strong demand for efficient and environmentally friendly public transportation.

Company Background

Bombardier got its start in the 1920s when mechanic Joseph-Armand Bombardier began converting old cars into snowmobiles. He founded L'Auto-Neige Bombardier Limited in 1942 to make commercial snow vehicles. In 1959 Bombardier introduced the first personal snowmobile the Ski-Doo. Bombardier went public in 1969.

The company won its first mass transit contract to build Montreal subway cars.

During the 1980s Bombardier continued to diversify. The company entered the European railcar market in 1986 the same year it acquired Canadair Canada's largest aerospace company from the national government.

Bombardier began development of a commuter aircraft the Canadian Regional Jet in 1989. In 1990 the company bought US-based Learjet and two years later it acquired a stake in de Havilland a regional aircraft maker.

Bombardier doubled the size of its European operations in 1998 by buying German railcar maker Deutsche Waggonbau. In 2001 Bombardier acquired DaimlerChrysler's Adtranz rail systems unit. Bombardier divested its Recreational Products unit (snowmobiles and personal watercraft) in 2003.

In 2007 the company launched its plan to enter the commercial jet business with the C Series line of planes.

EXECUTIVES

President and CEO, Alain M. Bellemare, age 58

CIO, Jeff Hutchinson
President Bombardier Commercial Aircraft, Fred S. Cromer
President Division Western Europe Middle East and Africa Transportation, Laurent Troger
President Bombardier Business Aircraft, David M. Coleal
SVP and CFO, John Di Bert
President Bombardier China, Jianwei Zhang
President Aerostructures and Engineering Services, Michael Ryan
Vice Chairman, Jean-Louis Fontaine, age 80
Vice Chairman, J. R. André Bombardier, age 77
President and CEO, Pierre Beaudoin, age 57
Auditors: Ernst & Young LLP

LOCATIONS

HQ: Bombardier Inc.
800 Rene-Levesque Boulevard West, Montreal, Quebec H3B 1Y8
Phone: (1) 514 861-9481   **Fax:** (1) 514 861-2420
Web: www.bombardier.com

2017 Sales

	% of total
North America	35
Europe	36
Asia-Pacific	13
Rest of World	6
Total	**100**

PRODUCTS/OPERATIONS

2017 Sales

	% of total
Transportation	49
Aerospace	
Business Aircraft	29
Commercial Aircraft	14
Aerostructures and Engineering	8
Corporate and Eliminations	-
Total	**100**

Selected Operations

Aerospace
  Business aircraft
  Challenger
  Global
  Learjet
  Commercial aircraft
  CRJ Series
  CSeries
  Q-Series
  Specialized aircraft modified for special missions
  Training and aircraft services
  Maintenance
  Parts
  Technical support
  Training
Transportation
  INNOVIA automated people mover (APM)
  INNOVIA Monorail 300
  FLEXITY trams and light rail vehicles
  Customized transportation systems
  Propulsion and controls
  Rail control systems
  Other rail vehicles
  Commuter/regional trains
  Intercity/high-speed trains
  Locomotives
  Metros
  Rapid transit
  Services
  Fleet maintenance
  Material management
  Operations and maintenance
  Vehicle refurbishment and modernization

COMPETITORS

ALSTOM	Harsco
AeroCentury	Kawasaki Rail Car
Airbus Group	Leonardo
Blue Star Jets	Mitsubishi Heavy
Boeing	Industries

COMAC
Dassault Aviation
Embraer
Flight Options
Greenbrier Companies
Gulfstream Aerospace
NetJets
Piper Aircraft
Siemens AG
Thales
XOJET

HISTORICAL FINANCIALS

Company Type: Public

Income Statement

	REVENUE ($ mil.)	NET INCOME ($ mil.)	NET PROFIT MARGIN	FYE: December 31 EMPLOYEES
12/19	15,757	(1,797)	—	60,400
12/18	16,236	232	1.4%	68,000
12/17	16,218	(516)	—	69,500
12/16	16,339	(1,022)	—	66,000
12/15	18,172	(5,347)	—	70,900
Annual Growth	**(3.5%)**	**—**		**(3.9%)**

2019 Year-End Financials

Debt ratio: 37.3%	No. of shares (mil.): —
Return on equity: —	Dividends
Cash ($ mil.): 2,578	Yield: —
Current ratio: 0.88	Payout: —
Long-term debt ($ mil.): 9,325	Market value ($ mil.): —

	STOCK PRICE ($) FY Close	P/E High/Low	PER SHARE ($) Earnings	Dividends	Book Value
12/19	1.47	— —	(0.76)	0.00	(3.20)
12/18	1.47	41 13	0.09	0.00	(2.34)
12/17	2.40	— —	(0.25)	0.00	(2.60)
12/16	1.61	— —	(0.48)	0.00	(2.39)
12/15	0.96	— —	(2.58)	0.00	(1.83)
Annual Growth	**11.4%**	**— —**	**—**	**—**	**—**

Bouygues S.A.

If all roads lead to Bouygues that's because the company built them. Bouygues (pronounced "bweeg") operates in three primary business areas: construction telecommunications and media. Its road buildings and property development contracting services operate through Bouygues Construction road builder Colas and property developer Bouygues Immobilier. The group also owns around 90% stake in Bouygues Telecom (France's #3 mobile phone carrier) almost 454% of TF1 (France's leading TV channel) and nearly 15% of industrial group ALSTOM. All three of its primary businesses are among the leading lights in their respective fields. Bouygues' principal owners are brothers Martin and Oliver Bouygues and the company's employees. Bouygues generates majority of sales from France.

Operations

Bouygues SA is a diversified industrial group with five main business segments: Bouygues Construction Bouygues Immobilier Colas Bouygues Telecom and TF1.

Colas generates the biggest sale accounting for more than 35%. Its three main activities are: roads construction materials and railways. It also includes transport of water and energy in France. Colas has significant additional construction materials production and recycling activities which it operates via a network of quarries as well as emulsion asphalt and ready-mix concrete plants.

Bouygues Construction which accounts for almost 35% of sales is a benchmark player in sustainable construction through the construction of many eco-neighborhoods low-carbon buildings and structures certified against the best world eco-standards as well as through rehabilitation of sites to reach positive-energy status.

Bouygues Telecom accounts for more than 15% of sales and boasts more than 95 million SIM card sales excluding MtoM including nearly 18 million mobile customers of which around 10 million are on high-speed 4G plans. Of its nearly 4 million fixed line customers over 1 million are high-speed FTTH (fiber-to-the-home) customers.

Bouygues Immobilier produces more than 5% of sales and is one of France's leading property developers developing residential commercial and office buildings.

TF1 which generates over 5% of sales offers unique range if unencrypted and pay-TV content and services that responds to the people's new ways of consuming media.

The French conglomerate also has nearly 15% stake in Alstom (making it the largest shareholder) which builds trains metros trams and e-buses.

Geographic Reach

Paris-based Bouygues' largest market is France which accounts for nearly 60% of its total sales. Europe excluding France contributes almost 20%% of total sales and North America more than 10%. The firm is also active in Africa the Asia/Pacific region Central America and the Middle East. While the company does business in more than 90 countries worldwide it is mainly active in developed nations.

In the Construction segment Bouygues carries out almost 60% of its business outside France. The Colas roads business operates in 50 countries worldwide.

Financial Performance

Note: Growth rates may differ after conversion to US dollars.

The TF1 group posted consolidated sales of ?2.3 billion in 2019 up ?49 million or up 2% versus 2018 due to: a ?10 million year-on-year increase in sales in the Broadcasting sector resulting from additional revenue sources alongside advertising. Advertising sales decreased slightly reflecting a tough comparison base for the TF1 TV channel offset in part by growth in MYTF1 advertising sales; a ?19 million decrease in sales in the Studios and Entertainment sector attributable to the deconsolidation of Téléshopping. Excluding the impact of this disposal the sector posted growth on the strength of good performances by Newen and the TF1 Entertainment music business and; the digital division (Unify) which benefited for the first year from the full effects of its consolidation.

Net profit attributable to the Group amounted to ?1.2 billion in 2019 versus ?1.3 billion in 2018 a decrease of ?124 million. This reflects a ?133 million year-on-year decrease in operating profit to ?1.7 billion which in 2019 included only ?20 million of net non-current income versus ?265 million in the previous year (mainly at Bouygues Telecom).

Cash held by the company at the end of 2019 increased by ?664 million to ?3.4 billion compared to ?2.7 billion in the prior year. Cash provided by operations was ?3.4 billion while cash used for investing and financing activities were ?602 million and ?2.2 billion respectively.

Strategy

Bouygues' main shareholders are Martin and Oliver Bouygues (more than 20% through holding company SCDM) and its employees (nearly 20%) which together have a controlling share. This ownership structure lessens shareholder volatility and gives the company greater scope to pursue a long-term strategic vision.

Bouygues' current preoccupation is to find ways to enhance its traditionally analog businesses with technology. It has a digital strategy that permeates through the company's entire fabric from employee and customer to product and services and to the more abstract concept of Bouygues' business model. Examples are diverse and include dynamic road markings and LED-based street lighting (SoWATT); robo-valeting parking technology; and Bbox fibre modem that gives similar speed to fibre. .Bouygues Construction's geographic strategy is increasing its presence in those countries where it has a long-term presence particularly via acquisitions. In 2018 it expanded in Australia and Switzerland and entered Germany. The segment's backlog decreased 3% to ?21.6 billion in 2019.

The Bouygues group's aim is to create value over the long term and share it with its stakeholders. In order to do this it draws on a stable ownership structure and has defined a strategic framework within which its five business segments (Bouygues Construction Bouygues Immobilier Colas TF1 and Bouygues Telecom) roll out their operational strategies to fulfil the Bouygues group's mission. Its business segments provide growth over the long term since they all satisfy constantly evolving and essential needs such as housing transportation communication information and entertainment. Their diversity helps to cushion the impact of the difficulties that some may experience from time to time.

Mergers and Acquisitions

Bouygues makes frequent acquisitions particularly in the Construction business.

In mid-2020 Bouygues under Bouygues Telecom acquired Euro Information for ?530 million. Euro Information is based in Strasbourg France and a fintech company of Credit Mutuel group that manages IT systems of 16 federations. The acquisition is fully in line with the company's growth strategy that will strengthen its customer base and expand its distribution network.

In early 2020 Bouygues acquired Granite Contracting LLC through Colas in the US. Granite Contracting is North Carolina-based company specializing in asphalt mix production and paving. The transaction expands the growing market of the company in North and South Carolina.

Colas a Bouygues subsidiary acquired Asfalcura in mid-2019. Asfalcura is a company based in Chile that specializes in road construction. The acquisition is part of the company's development strategy in South America.

In early 2019 Bouygues acquires Skanska's asphalt assets in Poland through its subsidiary Colas for ?29 million. Skanska based in Stockholm Sweden is one of the leading project development and construction groups. The transaction will expand the company's foothold in Poland.

Bouygues Telecom a Bouygues subsidiary acquired Nerim SAS. Nerim provides support to customer's key issues such as connect communicate host and develop business applications and is headquartered in Paris France. The acquisition is fully in line with the company's strategy of accelerating its expansion to market of miro-businesses SMEs and intermediate-sized businesses.

HISTORY

With the equivalent of $1700 in borrowed money Francis Bouygues son of a Paris engineer started Entreprise Francis Bouygues in 1952 as an industrial works and construction firm in the Paris region of France. Within four years his firm had expanded into property development.

By the mid-1960s Bouygues had entered the civil engineering and public works sectors and developed regional construction units across France. In 1970 it was listed on the Paris stock exchange. Four years later the company established Bouygues Offshore to build oil platforms.

In 1978 the firm built Terminal 2 of Paris' Charles de Gaulle airport. Three years later it won the contract to construct the University of Riyadh in Saudi Arabia (then the world's largest building project at 3.2 million sq. ft.) which was completed in 1984. That year Bouygues acquired France's #3 water supply company Saur and power transmission and supply firm ETDE.

Expansion continued in 1986 with the purchase of the Screg Group which included Colas France's top highway contractor. The next year the company led a consortium to buy 50% of newly privatized network Société Télévision Fran Şaise 1 (TF1). Bouygues became the largest shareholder with a 25% stake (increased to 40% by 1999). In 1988 the company began building the Channel Tunnel (completed 1994) and moved into its new ultramodern headquarters dubbed Challenger in Saint-Quentin-en-Yvelines outside Paris.

After rumors of failing health Francis Bouygues resigned as chairman in 1989. His son Martin took over as chairman and CEO although the patriarch called France's "Emperor of Concrete" remained on the board until his death in 1993.

Despite fears that the group would suffer without its founder's leadership Bouygues continued to grow with the 1989 acquisition of a majority interest in Grands Moulins de Paris France's largest flour milling firm (sold 1998). In 1990 it purchased Swiss construction group Losinger.

The company entered the telecom industry in 1993 with a national paging network and added a mobile phone license a year later. In 1996 the group listed 40% of Bouygues Offshore's shares on the New York and Paris stock exchanges. Also that year it launched mobile phone operator Bouygues Telecom and entered a partnership with Telecom Italia.

By 1999 Bouygues Telecom had reached 2 million customers and Bouygues bought back a 20% share held by the UK's Cable and Wireless to increase its stake to nearly 54%. That year Bouygues Offshore bought Norwegian engineering firm Kvaerner and the group spun off its construction sector creating Bouygues Construction.

After word circulated that Deutsche Telekom wanted to acquire the group's telecom unit Bouygues became the target of takeover rumors. Francois Pinault France's richest businessman became Bouygues' largest non-family shareholder when he increased his stake to 14% (later reduced to about 2%). Pinault's biggest rival Bernard Arnault upped his stake to more than 9% of the group fueling speculation of a battle over control of the board.

In 2001 the company pulled out of France's auction for a third-generation wireless license and remained the only European incumbent mobile carrier without a major domestic investment in 3G technology (until 2009). The next year the company agreed to buy Telecom Italia's stake in Bouygues Telecom increasing Bouygues' ownership in the mobile operator from 54% to more than 65%. In 2002 the company sold its 51% stake in oil field platform construction unit Bouygues Offshore to Italian oil services group Saipem which announced plans to bid for the remaining shares.

However talks with German utility giant E.ON over the sale of Bouygues' Saur subsidiary failed that year after E.ON decided to focus instead on its electricity and gas operations.

In 2005 Bouygues was more successful when it sought to sell Saur piecemeal. It sold several divisions of the subsidiary (Coved Saur France Saur International and Stereau) to French private equity firm PAI Partners but retained the African and Italian (Sigesa-Crea) divisions of the firm.

Bouygues bought the French government's 21% stake in ALSTOM for $2.5 billion in 2006. The deal was approved on the condition that it not try to control the company for at least three years. Bouygues did build up its holding after the acquisition though eventually holding 29% of the shares.

In 2008 property developer Bouygues Immobilier expanded with the acquisition of Urbis a French rival. That year Colas bought the Gouyer Group of companies (distribution of construction materials) in Martinique and Guadeloupe while Bouygues Telecom acquired a fixed-line network that allowed it to launch the Bbox broadband router and Internet services that include VoIP e-mail Internet access and television; the telecom unit also gained the previously denied right to offer the iPhone 3G.

EXECUTIVES

Deputy CEO, Olivier Bouygues, age 70, $920,000 total compensation

Chairman and CEO, Martin Bouygues, age 68, $920,000 total compensation

Chairman and CEO TF1, Nonce Paolini, age 71

Chairman and CEO Bouygues Construction, Yves Gabriel, age 70, $850,000 total compensation

Chairman and CEO Bouygues Telecom, Olivier Roussat, age 56

CFO, Philippe Marien, age 64

Chairman and CEO Bouygues Immobilier; Director, Francois Bertiere, age 70

Chairman and CEO Colas; Director, Herve Le Bouc, age 69

Auditors: Mazars

LOCATIONS

HQ: Bouygues S.A.
32 avenue Hoche, Paris, Cedex 08 F-75378
Phone: (33) 1 44 20 10 00
Web: www.bouygues.com

2018 Sales

	% of total
Europe	
France	61
European Union	11
Other countries	5
North America	11
Asia-Pacific	5
Africa	3
Central and South America	1
Middle East	1
Oceania	3
Total	**100**

PRODUCTS/OPERATIONS

2018 Sales

	% of total
Colas	37
Bouygues Construction	34
Bouygues Telecom	15
Bouygues Immobilier	8
TF1	6
Total	**100**

Selected Subsidiaries and Affiliates

Construction
Autoroute de liaison Seine-Sarthe SA (33%)
Bouygues Bâtiment Ile-de-France SA (99.9%)
Bati-Ré;nov SA (99.3%)
Bouygues Bâtiment International SA (99.9%)
Bouygues Thaï Ltd (49%)
DTP Singapour Pte Ltd (99.9%)
Kohler Investment SA (Luxembourg 99.9%)
Bouygues Construction SA (99.9%)
ETDE SA (99.9%)
Exprimm IT (99.9%)
Icel Maidstone Ltd (UK 99.9%)
Quille SA (99.9%)
Westminster Local Education Partnership Ltd (UK 80%)
Media
Mé;tro France Publications (15%)
Té;lé;vision Française 1 SA (TF1 43%)

TF1 Vidé;o (43%)
TV Breizh (43%)
Property
Bouygues Immobilier
Parque Empresearial Cristalia SL
SNC Bouygues Immobilier Entreprises Île-de-France
Roads
Cofiroute (16%)
Colas Guadeloupe (97%)
Colas Hungaria (97%)
Colas Polska (97%)
Colas SA (96%)
Spac (97%)
Telecommunications
Bouygues Telecom SA (90%)

COMPETITORS

Alarko	Fluor
Amec Foster Wheeler	Groupe SNEF
Anglian Water Group	HOCHTIEF
Atlantia	Hyundai Engineering
Balfour Beatty	and Construction
Bechtel	MWH Global
Bilfinger	Orange
CANAL+	Orange Switzerland
CSCEC	SUEZ Environnement
Dragados	Severn Trent
EIFFAGE	Skanska
Engie	VINCI
FCC Barcelona	

HISTORICAL FINANCIALS

Company Type: Public

Income Statement — FYE: December 31

	REVENUE ($ mil.)	NET INCOME ($ mil.)	NET PROFIT MARGIN	EMPLOYEES
12/19	42,676	1,329	3.1%	130,450
12/18	40,929	1,501	3.7%	129,275
12/17	39,623	1,300	3.3%	119,836
12/16	33,682	772	2.3%	122,615
12/15	35,421	438	1.2%	120,254
Annual Growth	**4.8%**	**31.9%**	**—**	**2.1%**

2019 Year-End Financials

Debt ratio: 16.4%
Return on equity: 11.7%
Cash ($ mil.): 4,012
Current ratio: 0.98
Long-term debt ($ mil.): 4,756
No. of shares (mil.): 379
Dividends
  Yield: 2.7%
  Payout: 82.0%
Market value ($ mil.): —

BP PLC

BP is one of the largest oil and gas companies in the world. With proven reserves of approximately 20 million barrels of oil and oil equivalents BP explores produces and sells oil and gas fuels lubricants wind power and biofuels. With presence in some 80 countries it sells 12 million tons of petrochemical products annually through contracts or via 18900 retail sites. BP's main brands include the eponymous BP brand which appears on rigs offices and gas stations gas station-specific brands Amoco (US) and Aral (Germany) lubricant brand Castrol and gas station convenience store brands ampm and Wild Bean Café.

Operations

BP has two major operating segments: Downstream and Upstream. A third segment Rosneft is also reported.

The downstream segment is BP's primary earner bringing in some 80% of total sales. BP manages the refining manufacturing marketing transportation and supply and trading of crude oil petroleum petrochemicals products lubricants and related services to wholesale and retail customers.

Upstream activities (about 20% of revenue) include oil and natural gas exploration field development and production transportation storage and processing. BP also markets and trades LNG and natural gas liquids.

BP's interest in Rosneft is accounted for using the equity method the biggest oil producer in Russia and although reported as a separate operating segment it does not contribute to sales.

Other businesses and corporate comprises the biofuels and wind businesses the group's shipping and treasury functions and corporate activities worldwide.

Geographic Reach

BP is headquartered in London. Its upstream business' principal areas of production are Angola Argentina Australia Azerbaijan Egypt Oman Trinidad the UAE the UK and the US. In the US BP has upstream activities in Alaska Arkansas Colorado New Mexico Oklahoma Texas and Wyoming.

Downstream BP has major refineries in the US North West (Cherry Point) Rockies (Whiting and Toledo) as well as refineries in Germany Netherlands Spain South Africa New Zealand and Australia.

BP is not particularly dependent on any one market about 30% of its revenue coming from the US and the rest being spread across the world.

Sales and Marketing

BP primarily sells oil and gas through pipelines and by ship truck and rail serving 10 million retail customer every day. It has more than 60000 suppliers helping it sell about 12 million tons of petrochemical products annually through contracts or via 18900 retail sites.

Major company brands include eponymous BP as well as AMOCO ampm Aral and Castrol. With more than 2.5 million customers visit an Aral service station Aral is one of the most recognized brands in Germany while BP and Castrol are leading brands of motor oil and lubricants. US retail brand ampm has more than 950 locations throughout the US west coast.

Financial Performance

BP's revenue is closely tied to the price of crude oil. The company's revenue has been continuously increasing in the past two years since it plummeted in 2016. However in 2019 its revenue slightly declined again. Between 2015 and 2019 the company's sales increased by 25%.

In 2019 the company's revenue fell to $278.4 billion or about 7% lower than the prior year to $298.8 billion.

Net income decreased to $4.0 billion in 2019 a 57% lower compared to $9.4 billion in 2018.

BP's cash at the end 2019 fiscal year was $22.5 billion a $4 million lower than the previous year. Operating activities provided $25.8 billion while investing activities used $17 billion mainly from capital expenditures. Financing activities used another $8.8 billion mainly for repayments of long-term financing repurchase of shares and lease liability payments.

Strategy

BP's strategy allows the company to be competitive flexible and resilient while also responding to a rapidly changing energy landscape with growing expectations for the company to adapt to changing demands from stakeholders.

The company remains committed to managing its portfolio for value and investing with discipline in flexible and resilient options which together support its pursuit of a strategy which BP believes it is consistent with the goals of the Paris Agreement.

Growing advantage oil and gas in the Upstream. Invest in oil and gas producing both with increasing efficiency (lower cost higher margin and close to markets) with a focus on carbon. Market-led growth in the Downstream. Innovate with advanced products and strategic partnerships building competitively advantaged businesses that deliver profitable marketing growth. Venturing and low carbon across multiple fronts. Pursue new opportunities to meet evolving technology consumer and policy trends. Modernizing the whole group. Simplify the company's processes and enhance its productivity through digital solutions.

Company Background

BP's history dates back to efforts of British companies to capitalize on discoveries of rich oil deposits in Middle East in the late 19th and early 20th Centuries. These included the Anglo-Persian Oil Company (later the Anglo-Iranian Oil Company) in which the British Government took a majority share in 1914. It became British Petroleum in 1954 and following a number of other acquisitions became BP in 2000. BP's modern history is marked by the 2010 Deepwater Horizon disaster a massive spill in the Gulf of Mexico that resulted in the highest fines and penalties in the history of the US.

EXECUTIVES

Group Chief Executive, Robert W. (Bob) Dudley, $1,194,450 total compensation
Chief Executive Alternative Energy and EVP Regions, Dev Sanyal
CEO US Lower 48 Onshore, David C. Lawler
Deputy Group Chief Executive, H. Lamar McKay
Group Operating Officer Strategy and Regions Upstream, Andy Hopwood
EVP Safety and Operational Risk, Bob Fryar
Chief Executive Upstream, Bernard Looney
EVP and Group Human Resources Director, Helmut Schuster
CFO, Brian Gilvary
President Russia, David Campbell
President Oman, Yousuf al Ojaili
Chief Executive Downstream, Tufan Erginbilgic
Chief Executive BP Integrated Supply and Trading (IST), Alan Haywood
Regional President Azerbaijan Georgia and Turkey (AGT), Gary Jones
Chairman, Carl-Henric Svanberg
Auditors: Deloitte LLP

LOCATIONS

HQ: BP PLC
1 St. James's Square, London SW1Y 4PD
Phone: (44) 20 7496 5311   **Fax:** (44) 20 7496 4573
Web: www.bp.com

2018 Sales

	% of total
US	33
Other countries	67
Total	**100**

PRODUCTS/OPERATIONS

2018 Sales

	% of total
Downstream	91
Upstream	9
Other businesses and corporate	-
Total	**100**

Major Operations
Refining and marketing
 Marketing
 Refining
 Supply and trading
 Transportation and shipping
Exploration and production

Field development
 Gas processing and marketing
 Oil and gas exploration
 Pipelines and transportation
Gas and power
 Natural gas marketing and trading
 Natural gas liquids
Chemicals
 Chemical intermediates
 Feedstock
 Performance products
 Polymers
Other
 Coal mining
 Solar power

Selected Subsidiaries

Atlantic Richfield Co
BP America Inc. (US)
BP Amoco Chemcal Company (US)
BP Oil Australia
BP Exploration Operating Company
BP Espa Â Â a (Spain)
BP International
BP Norge (Norway)
BP Oil New Zealand
BP Shipping
BP Southern Africa (South Africa)
Burmah Castrol
The Standard Oil Company (US)

COMPETITORS

Apache	Marathon Oil
Ashland	Norsk Hydro ASA
BASF SE	Occidental Petroleum
BG Group	PEMEX
BHP Billiton	PETROBRAS
Chevron	Petr leos de
ConocoPhillips	Venezuela
Dow Chemical	Repsol
Eni	Royal Dutch Shell
Exxon Mobil	Sinclair Oil
Hess Corporation	Sunoco
Huntsman International	TOTAL
Imperial Oil	Valero Energy
Koch Industries Inc.	

HISTORICAL FINANCIALS

Company Type: Public

Income Statement

FYE: December 31

	REVENUE ($ mil.)	NET INCOME ($ mil.)	NET PROFIT MARGIN	EMPLOYEES
12/19	282,423	4,026	1.4%	70,100
12/18	303,282	9,383	3.1%	73,000
12/17	243,372	3,389	1.4%	74,000
12/16	185,474	115	0.1%	74,500
12/15	225,316	(6,482)	—	79,800
Annual Growth	**5.8%**	**—**	**—**	**(3.2%)**

2019 Year-End Financials

Debt ratio: 22.9%
Return on equity: 4.0%
Cash ($ mil.): 22,472
Current ratio: 1.12
Long-term debt ($ mil.): 57,237
No. of shares (mil.): —
Dividends
 Yield: 6.4%
 Payout: 1,238.5%
Market value ($ mil.): —

	STOCK PRICE ($) FY Close	P/E High/Low	PER SHARE ($) Earnings	Dividends	Book Value
12/19	37.74	228182	0.20	2.44	4.86
12/18	37.92	102 78	0.47	2.41	4.95
12/17	42.03	244194	0.17	2.38	4.97
12/16	37.38	61314531	0.01	2.38	4.90
12/15	31.26	— —	(0.35)	2.39	5.30
Annual Growth	**4.8%**	**— —**	**—**	**0.6%**	**(2.1%)**

Braskem S A

Much like the Amazon Braskem is a South American giant the continent's largest petrochemical company. The company produces thermoplastic resins (Polyethylene Polypropylene and Polyvinyl Chloride). Braskem also makes aromatics like benzene ethylene propylene and butadiene. It has some 40 industrial units installed in four countries (Brazil United States Mexico and Germany). Brazil accounts for the majority of sales.

Operations

Braskem has a broad and diversified portfolio of chemical and petrochemical products. The company has an annual production capacity of more than 8 million tons of thermoplastic resins (Polyethylene Polypropylene and Polyvinyl Chloride) and more than 10 million tons of basic chemicals (Ethylene Propylene Butadiene Benzene among others).

Geographic Reach

The company operates some 40 industrial units installed in in Brazil US Mexico and Germany. Brazil accounted for about 55% of 2019 sales while other major markets and other countries (including US and Mexico) accounted for around 45%. The company also has around 15 sales offices and serves customers in 100 countries.

The company is based in Sao Paulo.

Sales and Marketing

The company serves customers in markets and sectors including food packaging construction industrial retail automotive personal care and cleaning agribusiness health among others Some of its customers include Pic Plast Let's Talk Packaging and Wecycle.

Financial Performance

Braskem's revenue decreased by 13% to R$60 billion compared to R$68.9 billion in 2018. Brazil's revenue accounted for more than half of the company's revenue in 2019. The decrease in total revenue was caused by a slight decrease among all geographical markets' revenue except exports.

The company reported a net income of R$2.8 billion as opposed to a net income of R$2.9 billion in the previous year.

Strategy

With a focus on further strengthening Braskem's initiatives for sustainable development it has made public its position concerning the Circular Economy a document where the company defined priority actions to expand and promote recycling and the reuse of plastic waste. This commitment also covers further investments in new resins from renewable sources a goal intended to expand the portfolio that today includes green plastic I'm green and to support new technologies business models development of the recycling chain and consumer engagement actions.

EXECUTIVES

Executive Director People and Organization Information Technology and Procurement, Marcelo Arantes de Carvalho
Executive Officer Polyolefins COMPERJ and Renewable Chemicals, Luciano N. Guidolin
Executive Officer Basic Petrochemicals, Marcelo de Oliveira Cerqueira
CEO, Fernando Musa
CFO, Pedro v. L. Teixeira de Freitas
Chairman, Newton S. de Souza

LOCATIONS

HQ: Braskem S A
  Rua Eteno, 1561, Polo Petroquimico de Camacari,
  Camacari, Bahia 42810-000
Phone: (55) 11 3576 9000   **Fax:** (55) 11 3576 9532
Web: www.braskem.com.br

2014 Sales

	% of total
Brazil	57
United States	20
Other countries	23
Total	**100**

PRODUCTS/OPERATIONS

2014 Sales

	% of total
Basic Petrochemicals	45
Polyolefins	33
USA and Europe	14
Vinyls	5
Chemical Distribution and others	3
Total	**100**

Selected Products

Basic Petrochemicals
  Benzene
  Butadiene
  Butene-1
  Ethylene
  Isoprene
  Mixed xylene
  Ortho-xylene
  Para-xylene
  Propylene
  Toluene
  Methyl tertiary-butyl ether (MTBE)
Polyolefins
  Polyethylene
  Polyethylene terephthalate (PET)
  Polyvinyl chloride (PVC)

COMPETITORS

BASF SE	ExxonMobil Chemical
Chevron Phillips	Petroqu mica Triunfo
Chemical	YPF

HISTORICAL FINANCIALS

Company Type: Public

Income Statement				FYE: December 31
	REVENUE ($ mil.)	NET INCOME ($ mil.)	NET PROFIT MARGIN	EMPLOYEES
12/19	13,016	(632)	—	7,940
12/18	14,944	728	4.9%	8,008
12/17	14,869	1,166	7.8%	7,713
12/16	14,644	(126)	—	7,657
12/15	11,938	792	6.6%	7,995
Annual Growth	2.2%	—	—	(0.2%)

2019 Year-End Financials

Debt ratio: 14.3%
Return on equity: (-44.5%)
Cash ($ mil.): 1,692
Current ratio: 1.44
Long-term debt ($ mil.): 9,380

No. of shares (mil.): 795
Dividends
  Yield: 2.4%
  Payout: —
Market value ($ mil.): 11,781

	STOCK PRICE ($) FY Close	P/E High/Low		PER SHARE ($) Earnings	Dividends	Book Value
12/19	14.80	—	—	(0.79)	0.37	1.53
12/18	24.46	9	6	0.92	1.77	2.11
12/17	26.26	7	4	1.47	0.75	2.39
12/16	21.21	—	—	(0.16)	1.51	1.06
12/15	13.54	4	1	1.00	0.36	0.64
Annual Growth	2.2%	—	—	—	0.3%	24.3%

Brenntag AG, Muehleim/Ruhr

EXECUTIVES

Vorstandsvorsitzender, Stefan Zuschke
Auditors: PricewaterhouseCoopers GmbH
  Wirtschaftsprüfungsgesellschaft

LOCATIONS

HQ: Brenntag AG, Muehleim/Ruhr
  Messeallee 11, Essen 45131
Phone: (49) 201 6496 1141   **Fax:** (49) 201 6496 2003
Web: www.brenntag.de

HISTORICAL FINANCIALS

Company Type: Public

Income Statement				FYE: December 31
	REVENUE ($ mil.)	NET INCOME ($ mil.)	NET PROFIT MARGIN	EMPLOYEES
12/19	14,395	524	3.6%	17,492
12/18	14,372	527	3.7%	16,616
12/17	14,077	432	3.1%	15,416
12/16	11,085	380	3.4%	14,826
12/15	11,269	397	3.5%	14,459
Annual Growth	6.3%	7.1%	—	4.9%

2019 Year-End Financials

Debt ratio: 28.3%
Return on equity: 13.7%
Cash ($ mil.): 584
Current ratio: 1.82
Long-term debt ($ mil.): 2,174

No. of shares (mil.): 154
Dividends
  Yield: 1.6%
  Payout: 5.1%
Market value ($ mil.): 1,669

	STOCK PRICE ($) FY Close	P/E High/Low		PER SHARE ($) Earnings	Dividends	Book Value
12/19	10.80	4	3	3.39	0.17	25.55
12/18	8.71	4	3	3.41	0.17	24.29
12/17	12.60	6	4	2.81	0.16	23.07
12/16	11.10	5	4	2.46	0.14	20.16
12/15	11.46	5	5	2.57	0.13	18.66
Annual Growth	(1.5%)	—	—	7.2%	8.1%	8.2%

Bridgestone Corp (Japan)

Auditors: Deloitte Touche Tohmatsu LLC

LOCATIONS

HQ: Bridgestone Corp (Japan)
  3-1-1 Kyobashi, Chuo-ku, Tokyo 104-8340
Phone: (81) 3 6836 3162   **Fax:** 615 937-3621
Web: www.bridgestone.co.jp

HISTORICAL FINANCIALS

Company Type: Public

Income Statement				FYE: December 31
	REVENUE ($ mil.)	NET INCOME ($ mil.)	NET PROFIT MARGIN	EMPLOYEES
12/19	32,473	2,695	8.3%	143,589
12/18	33,192	2,652	8.0%	143,509
12/17	32,380	2,562	7.9%	142,669
12/16	28,531	2,270	8.0%	143,616
12/15	31,485	2,361	7.5%	144,303
Annual Growth	0.8%	3.4%	—	(0.1%)

2019 Year-End Financials

Debt ratio: 0.1%
Return on equity: 12.5%
Cash ($ mil.): 4,064
Current ratio: 2.23
Long-term debt ($ mil.): 3,539

No. of shares (mil.): 704
Dividends
  Yield: 4.0%
  Payout: 20.0%
Market value ($ mil.): 13,018

	STOCK PRICE ($) FY Close	P/E High/Low		PER SHARE ($) Earnings	Dividends	Book Value
12/19	18.49	0	0	3.72	0.74	29.98
12/18	19.19	0	0	3.52	0.74	28.81
12/17	23.24	0	0	3.33	0.62	27.73
12/16	18.05	0	0	2.89	0.58	24.96
12/15	17.09	0	0	3.01	0.50	23.46
Annual Growth	2.0%	—	—	5.5%	10.4%	6.3%

British American Tobacco Plc (United Kingdom)

British American Tobacco (BAT) is the world's second-largest publicly-traded tobacco company by market share (after Philip Morris International). The company rolls more than 5300 billion cigarettes a year sold in over 200 markets across 50-plus countries. BAT sells five global cigarette brands (including Dunhill Kent Rothmans Lucky Strike and Pall Mall). Other combustible brands include Benson & Hedges and Kool. The company is pivoting to reduced-risk tobacco/nicotine delivery products such as vapor heated tobacco snus and moist snuff. Additionally BAT owns Reynolds American the #2 cigarette maker in the US and about 30% of India's ITC. Most of BAT's revenue comes from the US.

Operations

British American Tobacco (BAT) divides its business into three units: Strategic Combustible New categories and Strategic Traditional Oral products.

The Strategic Combustible segment makes cigarette brands Kent Dunhill Lucky Strike Pall Mall Rothmans Newport Camel and Natural American Spirit. It accounts for about 90% of company's sales.

New Categories generate roughly 5% of sales. It comprises of Tobacco Heating Products Vapour products and Modern Oral products and the rest of the company's revenue comes from Traditional Oral products.

BAT sources tobacco from some 90000 tobacco farmers worldwide.

Geographic Reach

Based in London UK BAT operates some 45 factories in about 45 countries. The US is its largest market accounting for some 40% of sales followed by Europe and North Africa at about a quarter of sales Asia/Pacific and Middle East at a fifth of sales and Americas and Sub-Saharan Africa at more than 15% of sales.

Sales and Marketing

BAT sells its products through some 11 million retail outlets worldwide.

Financial Performance

Note: Growth rates may differ after conversion to US dollars.

In 2019 revenue grew 6% to Å 25.9 billion (2018: Å 24.5 million up 25% on 2017). The higher revenue in 2019 was due to pricing across the cigarettes portfolio (with price mix of 9%) and an increase in revenue from Traditional Oral (up 15% 2018 up 127%) and New Categories (up 37% 2018 up 138%) which more than offset a 5% decline in cigarette volume (2018: increase of 3%).

Cash held by the company at the end of 2019 decreased by Å 293 million to Å 2.0 billion compared to Å 2.3 billion in the prior year. Cash provided by operations was Å 9.0 billion while cash used for investing activities was Å 639 million. Cash used for Å 8.6 billion primarily for reductions in and repayments of borrowings.

Strategy

Consequently the company has evolved its strategy to put a sharper focus on delivering a step change in New Categories performance fuelled by investment from the continued delivery of its combustible business.

The company's Diversity and Inclusion Strategy which is built on the three pillars of: driving ownership and accountability; building diverse talent pools; and creating enablers; all of which are underpinned by an inclusive culture.

Mergers and Acquisitions

In mid-2019 BAT acquired South Africa-based Twisp Proprietary Limited a leading South African vaping products company for Å 25 million. The acquisition allows BAT to expand its geographical presence in South Africa with the help of Twisp's nearly 70 dedicated stores.

Company Background

In fall 2011 it purchased Colombia's second-largest cigarette maker Productora Tabacalera de Colombia (Protabaco) for $452 million. Protabaco's brands include Mustang (the country's #2 selling cigarette) Premier and President. The deal elevates BAT from third place to second in Colombia's cigarette market.

HISTORY

After a year of vicious price-cutting between Imperial Tobacco (UK) and James Buchanan Duke's American Tobacco in the UK Imperial counterattacked in the US. To end the cigarette price war in the UK the firms created British American Tobacco (BAT) in 1902. The truce granted Imperial the British market American the US market and they jointly owned BAT in the rest of the world.

With Duke in control BAT expanded into new markets. In China it was selling 25 billion cigarettes a year by 1920. When the Communist revolution ended BAT's operations in China the company lost more than 25% of its sales (although China later reemerged as a major export market for the company's cigarettes).

A 1911 US antitrust action forced American to sell its interest in BAT and opened the US market to the company. BAT purchased US cigarette manufacturer Brown & Williamson in 1927 and continued to grow through geographic expansion until the 1960s. In 1973 BAT and Imperial each regained control of its own brands in the UK and

Continental Europe. Imperial sold the last of its stake in BAT in 1980.

Fearing that mounting public concern over smoking would limit the cigarette market BAT acquired nontobacco businesses; it changed its name to B.A.T Industries in 1976. The acquisitions of retailers Saks (1973) Argos (UK 1979) Marshall Field (1982) and later insurance firms diversified the company's sales base. After a 1989 hostile takeover bid from Sir James Goldsmith it sold its retail operations and retained its tobacco and financial services.

In 1994 B.A.T acquired the former American Tobacco for $1 billion. In 1997 the company acquired Cigarrera de Moderna (with 50% of Mexico's cigarette sales) and formed a joint venture with the Turkish tobacco state enterprise Tekel.

B.A.T's tobacco operations were spun off in 1998 as British American Tobacco (BAT). The financial services operations were merged with Zurich Insurance in a transaction that created two holding companies: Allied Zurich (UK) and Zurich Allied (Switzerland). With the changes Martin Broughton became chairman of BAT.

The company in 1999 paid $8.2 billion to buy Dutch cigarette company Rothmans International (Rothmans Dunhill) from Switzerland's Compagnie Financiere Richemont and South Africa's Rembrandt Group — both controlled by Anton Rupert. With the purchase BAT received a controlling stake in Canada's Rothmans Benson & Hedges (RBH).

In early 2000 BAT bought the 58% of Canada's Imasco it didn't already own. Imasco sold off its financial services and BAT received Imasco's Imperial Tobacco unit (not related to the UK's Imperial Brands) in the deal. (Formerly called Imperial Tobacco Company of Canada Imasco was created in 1908 with help from BAT.) BAT also unloaded its share of RBH via a public offering.

In 2001 BAT bought the 40.5% of its BAT Australasia subsidiary (formed in 1999 through the Rothmans merger) it didn't already own. Broughton announced that year that the Chinese government had approved development plans that would allow the company to build a factory in China. The company also announced it would build the first foreign-owned cigarette factory in South Korea at that time the world's #8 tobacco market.

Increasing its Latin American regional presence BAT purchased a controlling stake in Peru's top tobacco company Tabacalera Nacional and several of its suppliers in 2003. However two months later BAT said it would not make the million-dollar investment in the company. The announcement came soon after Peru raised taxes on cigarettes. By the end of the year BAT had purchased tobacco manufacturer Ente Tabacchi Italiani S.p.A. from the Italian government. BAT sold the distribution end of its Italian business to Compañ a de Distribuci n Integral Logista in 2004 the same year that Broughton retired; the company named Jan du Plessis as chairman and Paul Adams as CEO.

In June 2009 the company acquired an 85% stake in Indonesia's fourth largest cigarette maker PT Bentoel Internasional Investama Tbk for Å 303 million ($494 million) from Rajawali Group. Later that year Richard Burrows became chairman; he replaced du Plessis who had become chairman of Rio Tinto. Replacing Adams Nicandro Durante became CEO in early 2011. BAT in fall 2011 acquired Colombia's second-largest cigarette maker Productora Tabacalera de Colombia (Protabaco) for $452 million.

EXECUTIVES

Chief Executive, Nicandro Durante, age 63, $516,791 total compensation
Finance Director, Ben Stevens, age 60, $528,901 total compensation
Director Special Projects, Jean-Marc Lévy
COO International, Jack Bowles, age 56
Managing Director Next Generation Products, Des Naughton, age 53
Regional Director Western Europe, Naresh Sethi
Director Operations, Alan Davy
Regional Director Americas and Sub-Saharan Africa, Ricardo Oberlander
Regional Director Asia-Pacific and Middle East, Johan Vandermeulen
Chairman, Richard Burrows, age 75
Auditors: KPMG LLP

LOCATIONS

HQ: British American Tobacco Plc (United Kingdom)
Globe House, 4 Temple Place, London WC2R 2PG
Phone: (44) 20 7845 1000   **Fax:** (44) 20 7240 0555
Web: www.bat.com

2018 sales

	%
US	39
Europe and North Africa	24
Asia/Pacific and Middle East	20
Americas	17
Total	**100**

PRODUCTS/OPERATIONS

2018 sales

	% of total
Combustible Portfolio	63
Potentially Risk-Reduced Products	
Vapor	1
THP	2
Modern Oral -	
Traditional Oral	4
Other	30
Total	**100**

Selected Brands

Benson & Hedges
Camel Snus
Craven 'A'
Dunhill
glo
Granit
Grizzly
John Player Gold Leaf
Kent
Kool
Lucky Strike
Lyft
Kodiak
Mocca
Pall Mall
Peter Stuyvesant
Player's Gold Lead
Rothmans
State Express 555
Viceroy
VIP
Vogue
Vuse
Vype

COMPETITORS

Altria	Santa Fe Natural
Imperial Brands	Tobacco
Japan Tobacco	Swedish Match
Philip Morris	Swisher International
International	Universal Corporation
Reemtsma	Vector Group
Cigarettenfabriken	

Income Statement   FYE: December 31

	REVENUE ($ mil.)	NET INCOME ($ mil.)	NET PROFIT MARGIN	EMPLOYEES
12/19	34,172	7,532	22.0%	94,846
12/18	31,270	7,701	24.6%	95,239
12/17	27,408	50,695	185.0%	91,402
12/16	18,145	5,717	31.5%	85,335
12/15	19,419	6,357	32.7%	87,577
Annual Growth	15.2%	4.3%	—	2.0%

2019 Year-End Financials

Debt ratio: 42.4%
Return on equity: 8.8%
Cash ($ mil.): 3,335
Current ratio: 0.71
Long-term debt ($ mil.): 49,922

No. of shares (mil.): —
Dividends
Yield: 6.0%
Payout: 80.6%
Market value ($ mil.): —

	STOCK PRICE ($) FY Close	P/E High/Low	PER SHARE ($) Earnings	Dividends	Book Value
12/19	42.46	17 13	3.29	2.58	36.92
12/18	31.86	25 12	3.36	2.52	36.43
12/17	66.99	7 3	24.72	3.07	35.81
12/16	112.67	49 35	3.07	1.94	4.97
12/15	110.45	50 42	3.41	2.27	3.58
Annual Growth	(21.3%)	— —	(0.9%)	3.3%	79.2%

Brookfield Asset Management Inc

Brookfield Asset Management sees the money flowing in from a wide variety of sources. The company has over $540 billion in assets under management including real estate renewable power infrastructure and private equity. It owns a global portfolio of commercial retail residential and development properties. Brookfield is also one of the world's largest investors in renewable power owning more than 5200 power-generating facilities including wind and solar plants with a total of approximately 20000 megawatts of generating capacity. The company's private equity business invests in high-quality companies with high barriers to entry. Most of the company's revenue were generated from the UK with more than 30% of sales.

Operations

Brookfield Asset Management has seven core business segments: Private Equity Real Estate Infrastructure Renewable Power Residential Development Asset Management and Corporate Activities.

The Private Equity segment invests in a broad range of industries with a focus on business services infrastructure services and industrial operations. It accounts for around 65% of total revenue.

The Real Estate segment develops owns and operates the group's retail office core retail LP investments and other properties. Its holdings include 450 million sq. ft. of space around the world. The segment brings in some 15% of total revenue.

The Infrastructure segment develops owns and operates the group's infrastructure assets including utility transport energy data infrastructure and sustainable resource holdings. It accounts for some 10% of revenue.

Renewable Power assets include wind solar water storage and other power-generation facilities in the Americas and Europe. It brings in more than 5% of revenue.

Residential Development is engaged in land condominium and home development in North America and Brazil. It also accounts for less than 5% of revenue.

The Corporate Activities segment manages investment of cash and financial assets as well as the management of corporate leverage including corporate borrowings and preferred equity.

The Asset Management operations include managing listed partnerships private funds and public securities on behalf of the company's investors as well as share of the asset management activities of Oaktree.

Overall revenues from contracts with customers accounted more than 85% of the company's total sales while other revenues account for the rest.

Geographic Reach

Toronto-based Brookfield Asset Management has a wide variety of holdings around the world with operations in the Asia/Pacific region Europe the Middle East North America and South America. More than 30% of its revenue comes from its business in the UK. Its next-largest markets are the US (some 25% of revenue) Canada and Europe (about 10% each) Australia (about 10%) Brazil (more than 5%) Asia (less than 5%) and Columbia (less than 5%).

Sales and Marketing

Brookfield Asset Management's investors include sovereign wealth funds and other institutional investors and individuals.

Financial Performance

Brookfield Asset Management has seen substantial revenue growth in recent years. Its annual revenue has risen more than 240% since 2015. Net income has also seen growth over the same period though not as much rising by 20% between 2015 and 2019.

Revenue increased to $67.8 billion in 2019 an approximately 19% increase from the year prior. The increase was driven by acquisitions of new businesses and assets and same-store growth across businesses partially offset by lower revenue from its road fuel distribution business and the absence of $2 billion of revenues from businesses sold in the current and prior year.

Net income was $2.8 billion in 2019 a decrease of $777 million from $3.6 billion the year prior. This was due to an increase in interest expense by $2.4 billion fair value losses of $831 million compared to gains of $1.8 billion in the prior year depreciation and amortization expense by $1.8 billion and a tax expense of $495 million compared to an income tax recovery of $248 million in the prior year.

Cash provided by operating activities was $6.3 billion in 2019 while investing activities used $36.7 billion mainly for acquisitions. Financing activities provided another $28.7 billion. The company ended fiscal 2019 with $6.8 billion in cash and cash equivalents.

Strategy

Brookfield Asset Management raises private and public capital from the world's largest institutional investors sovereign wealth funds and individuals with a focus on generating attractive investment returns that will allow its investors and their stakeholders to meet their goals and protect their financial future. It operates in more than 30 countries and has more than $540 billion in assets under management.

The group is always on the lookout for acquisition opportunities and other ways to invest in out-of-favor promising markets with high barriers to entry as well as opportunities to sell assets to raise more capital. Among the larger purchases by

Brookfield and its affiliates in 2019 were a majority stake in US-based alternative investment manager Oaktree Capital for around $4.8 billion private Australian hospital operator Healthscope for about $4.1 billion and leading Brazilian heavy equipment and light vehicle fleet management company Ouro Verde.

Brookfield aims to invest in assets that address such environmental and social priorities as climate change and the workplace. For example in 2019 it reduced its Scope 1 and 2 emissions by 20% and its global gross carbon intensity continues to be one of the lowest among comparable power companies. Brookfield Renewable's portfolio of green energy generation also helped to avoid approximately 27 million metric tons of carbon dioxide equivalent emissions on a net basis.

Mergers and Acquisitions

In 2019 Brookfield Asset Management partnered with New Zealand-based infrastructure investor Infratil to purchase the New Zealand business of British multinational telecommunications conglomerate Vodafone Group for about $2.2 billion. An affiliate of Brookfield Asset Management agreed to buy railroad company Genesee & Wyoming for about $6.3 billion in 2019 expanding its worldwide portfolio of rail companies.

Brookfield also agreed to acquire four hotels in India from Hotel Leela Venture in 2019 for about $575 million. The hotels are in Bengaluru Chennai Delhi and Udaipur.

In 2019 Brookfield Asset Management agreed to acquire a majority stake in US-based alternative investment manager Oaktree Capital for around $4.8 billion. The deal aids Brookfield in its push to rival Blackstone in size. That same year Brookfield Business Partners the publicly traded business services and industrials company of Brookfield Asset Management agreed to acquire Healthscope in 2019 for about $4.1 billion. The company is the second-largest private hospital operator in Australia and the largest pathology services provider in New Zealand.

Company Background

Brookfield Asset Management was established in 1899 as the S o Paulo Railway Light and Power Company. In the 1950s the company began investing in real assets and in the 1990s it scooped up major commercial properties in New York and Boston. It also invested in renewable energy holdings. The group established its first third-party fund in 2001 launching its asset management operations.

In 2017 Brookfield Renewable Partners partnered with other investors to acquire 51% of TerraForm Power a portfolio of solar and wind power assets for a total commitment of $656 million. Later that year the investors acquired all of TerraForm Global another renewable power portfolio with assets in Brazil China and India for a total of $750 million. Also in 2017 the company acquired a portfolio of manufactured housing communities in the US for $768 million.

EXECUTIVES

Chief Executive Officer Director, J. Bruce Flatt, age 54, $485,450 total compensation
Managing Partner CEO Infrastructure, Samuel J. B. (Sam) Pollock, $755,788 total compensation
Managing Partner and CFO, Brian D. Lawson, age 61, $485,450 total compensation
Vice Chair of Brookfield Property Group and Brookfield Property Partners, Richard B. (Ric) Clark, age 61
Managing Partner Real Estate, Brett M. Fox
Senior Vice Chair Private Equity, Joseph S. (Joe) Freedman

Vice Chair Infrastructure and Renewable Power, Harry A. Goldgut

Vice Chair Renewable Power, Richard Legault

Managing Partner COO, Lori Pearson

Managing Partner CEO Private Equity, Cyrus Madon

Managing Partner Private Funds Group, Leo van den Thillart

Managing Partner Infrastructure, Jeff Kendrew

Executive Chair Latin America, Luiz Ildefonso Sim ṃes Lopes

Managing Partner CEO Real Estate, Brian Kingston

Managing Partner and COO Real Estate, William Powell

Managing Partner and COO Infrastructure, Ben Vaughan

Managing Partner Infrastructure & Chief Executive Officer Brookfield Agriculture Group, Renato Cavalini

Managing Director Private Funds, Julian Schiller

Managing Director Private Funds, Grant Berlin

Managing Director Real Estate, Matt Smith

Managing Partner Private Equity, David Levenson

CFO Brookfield Brazil, Sergio L. Campos

Chair Brookfield Asset Management Inc. and Deputy Chair TD Bank Group, Frank J. McKenna, age 72

Vice Chair, Jeffrey M. (Jeff) Blidner

Vice Chair, Barry Blattman

Auditors: Deloitte LLP

LOCATIONS

HQ: Brookfield Asset Management Inc
Suite 300, Brookfield Place, 181 Bay Street, Toronto, Ontario M5J 2T3
Phone: 416 363-9491   **Fax:** 416 365-2856
Web: www.brookfield.com

2017 Sales

	$ mil.	% of total
UK	15,106	37
US	8,284	20
Canada	5,883	14
Australia	4,405	11
Brazil	3,206	8
Other	3,902	10
Total	**40,786**	**100**

PRODUCTS/OPERATIONS

2017 Sales by Segment

	$ mil.	% of total
Private Equity	24,220	60
Real Estate	6,824	17
Infrastructure	3,859	10
Renewable Power	2,788	7
Residential Development	2,447	6
Corporate Activities	362	-
Asset Management	286	-
Total	**40,786**	**100**

Selected Subsidiaries

Brookfield Infrastructure Partners L.P. (70%)
Brookfield Office Properties Inc. (32%)
Brookfield Renewable Partners L.P. (40%)
Brookfield Residential Properties (31%)
Norbord Inc. (40%)

COMPETITORS

Berkshire Hathaway	Equity Office
Blackstone Group	Pinetree Capital
CBRE Group	RREEF Funds
Dundee Corp.	
Equity Group Investments	

HISTORICAL FINANCIALS

Company Type: Public

Income Statement
FYE: December 31

	REVENUE ($ mil.)	NET INCOME ($ mil.)	NET PROFIT MARGIN	EMPLOYEES
12/19	67,826	2,807	4.1%	151,000
12/18	56,771	3,584	6.3%	100,000
12/17	40,786	1,462	3.6%	80,750
12/16	24,411	1,651	6.8%	55,700
12/15	19,913	2,341	11.8%	55,700
Annual Growth	**35.9%**	**4.6%**	**—**	**28.3%**

2019 Year-End Financials

Debt ratio: 44.2%
Return on equity: 8.6%
Cash ($ mil.): 6,778
Current ratio: —
Long-term debt ($ mil.): 143,375

No. of shares (mil.): 1,509
Dividends
  Yield: 1.1%
  Payout: 24.6%
Market value ($ mil.): 87,237

	STOCK PRICE ($) FY Close	P/E High/Low		PER SHARE ($) Earnings	Dividends	Book Value
12/19	57.80	33	21	1.73	0.43	23.20
12/18	38.35	19	16	2.27	0.40	20.81
12/17	43.54	48	36	0.89	0.37	19.64
12/16	33.01	34	26	1.03	0.35	18.41
12/15	31.53	37	19	1.51	0.32	17.55
Annual Growth	**16.4%**	**—**	**—**	**3.6%**	**7.8%**	**7.2%**

Brookfield Business Partners LP

Auditors: Deloitte LLP

LOCATIONS

HQ: Brookfield Business Partners LP
73 Front Street, 5th Floor, Hamilton HM 12
Phone: (441) 294 3309
Web: www.brookfield.com

HISTORICAL FINANCIALS

Company Type: Public

Income Statement
FYE: December 31

	REVENUE ($ mil.)	NET INCOME ($ mil.)	NET PROFIT MARGIN	EMPLOYEES
12/19	43,032	43	0.1%	67,030
12/18	37,168	74	0.2%	46,651
12/17	22,823	(58)	—	26,900
12/16	7,960	(32)	—	20,400
12/15	6,753	208	3.1%	19,100
Annual Growth	**58.9%**	**(32.6%)**	**—**	**36.9%**

2019 Year-End Financials

Debt ratio: 43.7%
Return on equity: 2.3%
Cash ($ mil.): 1,986
Current ratio: 1.16
Long-term debt ($ mil.): 21,256

No. of shares (mil.): 150
Dividends
  Yield: 0.6%
  Payout: 40.3%
Market value ($ mil.): —

BT Group Plc

The history of BT Group is the history of telecommunications. The company formerly known as British Telecom and tracing its lineage back to the earliest days of the telegraph provides phone internet and other data and IT services to customers in the UK and abroad. BT operates through several divisions: Corporate clients are served through its BT Global Services unit BT Enterprise provides communications and IT services in the UK and the Republic of Ireland and BT Consumer offers consumer fixed-voice and broadband services in the UK. BT's Openreach division is dedicated to building and operating the UK's telecom infrastructure which it offers to other carriers on a neutral basis. BT generates majority of revenue from its home country.

Operations

BT divides its operations into four segments: Consumer Enterprise Global and Openreach.

The BT Consumer segment generates around 45% of sales and offers provides broadband TV sports channels and mobile services through the brands BT EE and Plusnet. The BT brand combines home phone broadband BT TV BT Sport and Mobile offerings. EE is the UK's largest mobile carrier offering 4G and 5G to millions of UK customers. It operates over 600 retail stores.

The Enterprise segment serves small and medium-sized enterprises (SMEs) in fixed-voice and data mobility and IT services.

BT Enterprise accounts for over 25% of BT Group's revenue. BT Global Services the group's enterprise telecommunications division accounts for about 20% of sales. It provides voice and data communications as well as managed network and IT services to corporate and public sector customers in around 180 countries. Openreach is the group's smallest segment with roughly 10% of sales.

Openreach owns and manages the UK's physical telecommunications infrastructure which it is legally bound to allow rival telecoms operators to access for both retail and wholesale offerings.

Overall BT generates around 40% of sales from its Fixed-Access Subscriptions followed by its Mobile subscriptions for more than 20% of sales. ICT & Managed Networks and Equipment and Other services account for almost 40% of sales combined.

Geographic Reach

Based in London BT Group generates around 85% of its revenue at home in the UK. Internationally it has staff in almost 60 countries worldwide and has customers in around 180 which together account for the remaining of sales. The firm also has a presence in high-growth regions in Asia Pacific Latin America the Middle East and Africa.

Sales and Marketing

BT Group's customers are UK individuals; households; small medium and large businesses; public sector organizations; and companies around the world. Some of its customers are also its competitors such as the major telecoms companies that pay to use its Openreach infrastructure. All told BT Group serves more than 30 million consumers over 1 million businesses and around 4000 multinational corporations.

BT has a sponsorship deal with the Football Association meaning England's men's women's agegroup and disability national soccer teams will sport its logo until 2024.

Financial Performance

Reported revenue was Â 22.9billion down 2% and adjusted revenue was Â 22.8billionn down 3%. This mainly reflects the impact of regulation declines in legacy products strategic reductions of low margin business and divestments.

Net income fell 20% to Å 1.7 billion in fiscal 2020 This was impacted by the higher upfront interest expense associated with IFRS 16 lease liabilities recognised on 1 April 2019.

BT Group's cash on hand fell Å 186 million during fiscal 2020 ending the year at Å 1.4 billion. The company's operations generated Å 6.5 billion partially offset by its financing which used Å 807 million and Å 5.7 billion used in its investing activities.

Strategy

At the core of their strategy is the convergence of BT's leading network capabilities to provide unrivalled customer experiences. For large and global customers work is already underway on a truly differentiated software-driven solution to deliver the modular highly automated services required for success in today's digital economy.

BT have already progressed the sale of non-core parts of their business such as BT Fleet Solutions and their IT business for the legal profession Tikit. Internationally as the company sharpen their customer focus on the leading transnational organizations they are divesting some infrastructure no longer needed to deliver global services in the digital economy.

Company Background

BT Group dates back to the 1840s and the early days of the telegraph. The UK government took control of the multitude of companies that sprang up and housed them under the Post Office government branch — then a major department of government. The Post Office telecommunications activities were renamed British Telecom (BT) in 1980 and separated out from the Post Office — by that point a nationalized industry rather than government department — in 1981. BT was privatized in 1984 and the telecom market was opened to competition. British Telecom became BT in 1991. In 2005 Ofcom the regulator ordered the creation of Openreach a BT Group company tasked with the management of the UK's telecom infrastructure and allowing unbiased access for rival telecom companies. The company acquired EE in 2016 and became the UK's biggest mobile network.

EXECUTIVES

Group Finance Director, Simon Lowth, age 59
CEO, Gavin Patterson, age 53
CIO, J. Howard Watson, age 58
CEO Openreach, Clive Selley
CEO - BT Global Services, Luis Alvarez
Chairman, Jan P. du Plessis, age 65
Auditors: PricewaterhouseCoopers LLP

LOCATIONS

HQ: BT Group Plc
BT Centre, 81 Newgate Street, London EC1A 7AJ
Phone: (44) 20 7356 5000 **Fax:** (44) 20 7356 5520
Web: www.btplc.com

2018 Sales

	% of total
Europe Middle East & Africa (ecxl. UK)	11
UK	83
Americas	4
Asia Pacific	2
Total	**100**

PRODUCTS/OPERATIONS

2019 Sales

	% of total
Consumer	45
Enterprise	25
Global Services	20
Openreach	10
Total	**100**

2019 Sales by Market

	% of total
Fixed-Access Subscriptions	39
Mobile Subscriptions	23
Equipment and Other Services	17
ICT & Managed Networks	21
Total	**100**

Selected Subsidiaries and Affiliates

Basilica Computing Limited (IT services)
British Telecommunications plc (telecommunication related services and products)
BT Americas Inc. (telecommunication related services and products US)
BT Australasia Pty Limited (telecommunication related services and products Australia)
BT Centre Nominee 2 Limited (property holding company)
BT Communications Ireland Limited (telecommunications services)
BT Conferencing Inc. (Audio video and Web conferencing services US)
BT Convergent Solutions Limited (communications related services and products)
BT ESPAÑA Compa Å Å í;a de Servicios Globales de Telecomunicaciones S.A. (telecommunication related services and products Spain)
BT Fleet Limited (fleet management)
BT France SA (telecommunication related services and products)
BT Frontline Pte Ltd (communications related services and products Singapore)
BT (Germany) GmbH & Co. oHG (telecommunication related services and products)
BT Global Services Limited (international telecommunications network systems)
BT Holdings Limited (investment holding company)
BT Hong Kong Limited (telecommunication related services and products)
BT Infrastructures Critiques (IT systems and network services France)
BT INS Inc (Information telecommunication consulting and software US)
BT Italia SpA (telecommunications related services and products Italy 97%)
BT Limited (international telecommunication network systems provider)
BT Nederland NV (telecommunication related services and products The Netherlands)
BT US Investments Limited (investments holding company US)
Communications Global Network Services Limited (telecommunication related services and products Bermuda)
Communication Networking Services (UK) (telecommunication related services and products)
Infonet Services Corporation (global managed network services provider US)
Infonet USA Corporation (global managed network services provider US)
Radianz Americas Inc. (global managed network services provider US)

COMPETITORS

Accenture	THUS Ltd.
COLT Group	TalkTalk
Cable & Wireless	Telecom Italia
Capgemini	Telecom plus
Deutsche Telekom	Telef nica
Easynet	Telenor
IBM Global Services	TeliaSonera
KCOM Group	Verizon Enterprise
KPN	Solutions
Orange	Virgin Media
Orange Business	Virgin Media Finance
Services	PLC
Sky plc	Vodafone

HISTORICAL FINANCIALS

Company Type: Public

Income Statement

FYE: March 31

	REVENUE ($ mil.)	NET INCOME ($ mil.)	NET PROFIT MARGIN	EMPLOYEES
03/20	28,296	2,142	7.6%	0
03/18	30,690	2,828	9.2%	106,700
03/18	33,335	2,855	8.6%	105,800
03/17	30,040	2,382	7.9%	106,400
03/16	27,409	3,725	13.6%	102,500
Annual Growth	**0.8%**	**(12.9%)**	**—**	

2020 Year-End Financials

Debt ratio: 45.0%	No. of shares (mil.): —
Return on equity: 13.8%	Dividends
Cash ($ mil.): 1,913	Yield: —
Current ratio: 1.09	Payout: 26.5%
Long-term debt ($ mil.): 20,373	Market value ($ mil.): —

Bupa Finance plc

Auditors: KPMG LLP

LOCATIONS

HQ: Bupa Finance plc
1 Angel Court, London EC2R 7HJ
Phone:

HISTORICAL FINANCIALS

Company Type: Public

Income Statement

FYE: December 31

	REVENUE ($ mil.)	NET INCOME ($ mil.)	NET PROFIT MARGIN	EMPLOYEES
12/19	16,264	(159)	—	79,986
12/18	15,141	506	3.3%	77,706
12/17	16,544	765	4.6%	62,412
12/16	13,590	579	4.3%	64,980
12/15	14,565	517	3.6%	61,951
Annual Growth	**2.8%**	**—**	**—**	**6.6%**

2019 Year-End Financials

Debt ratio: —	No. of shares (mil.): 200
Return on equity: (-1.7%)	Dividends
Cash ($ mil.): 1,629	Yield: —
Current ratio: —	Payout: —
Long-term debt ($ mil.): —	Market value ($ mil.): —

BYD Co Ltd

Battery manufacturer BYD has seen its sales go vroom after it entered the automobile business. BYD was once the second-largest rechargeable battery producer in the world after Energizer. But now the company gets juiced from selling its line of midsize gas and hybrid vehicles in China. BYD manufactures about a dozen models including a handful of sedans a couple of minivans an SUV and a convertible coupe. With its background in batteries BYD is also on track to produce its first plug-in all-electric car the E6. The company still manufactures electronic components for mobile phones nickel batteries and lithium- ion batteries.

Berkshire Hathaway subsidiary MidAmerican Energy Holdings owns a 10% stake in BYD.

EXECUTIVES

Chairman, Chuanfu Wang
Vice Chairman, Xiangyang Lv
Auditors: Ernst & Young Hua Ming (LLP)

LOCATIONS

HQ: BYD Co Ltd
Unit 1712, 17th Floor, Tower 2, Grand Central Plaza, No. 138 Shatin Rural Commmittee Road, New Territories,
Phone:
Web: www.byd.com.cn

2014 Sales

	% of total
China	86
USA	4
Europe	3
India	1
Other	6
Total	**100**

PRODUCTS/OPERATIONS

Product Selected
Automobiles Photovoltaic
Handset and Assembly Services
Rechargeable Battery

2014 Sales

	% of total
Automobiles and related products	47
Handset components & assembly services	44
Rechargeable batteries & photovoltaic business	9
Total	**100**

COMPETITORS

Brilliance China	Highpower
Chang'an Automobile	International
Changan Ford Mazda	LG Chem
Automobile	National Electric
Chery Automobile	Vehicle Sweden
China BAK	Procter & Gamble
China FAW	SAIC Motor
Dongfeng Motor	SANYO
Dongfeng Peugeot	Samsung SDI
Edgewell Personal Care	Shanghai Automotive
Geely Automobile	Spectrum Brands

HISTORICAL FINANCIALS
Company Type: Public

Income Statement   FYE: December 31

	REVENUE ($ mil.)	NET INCOME ($ mil.)	NET PROFIT MARGIN	EMPLOYEES
12/19	18,357	232	1.3%	0
12/18	18,908	404	2.1%	0
12/17	16,275	624	3.8%	0
12/16	14,430	727	5.0%	194,000
12/15	11,950	434	3.6%	200,000
Annual Growth	**11.3%**	**(14.5%)**	—	—

2019 Year-End Financials

Debt ratio: 5.2%
Return on equity: 2.8%
Cash ($ mil.): 1,818
Current ratio: 0.99
Long-term debt ($ mil.): 3,149
No. of shares (mil.): —
Dividends
  Yield: 0.4%
  Payout: —
Market value ($ mil.): —

C.P. All Public Co Ltd

EXECUTIVES

Chairman, Dhanin Chearavanont
Auditors: KPMG Phoomchai Audit Ltd.

LOCATIONS

HQ: C.P. All Public Co Ltd
313 C.P. Tower, 24th Floor, Silom Road, Kwang Silom, Khet Bangrak, Bangkok 10500
Phone: (66) 2 677 9000 **Fax:** (66) 2 679 0050
Web: www.cpall.co.th

HISTORICAL FINANCIALS
Company Type: Public

Income Statement   FYE: December 31

	REVENUE ($ mil.)	NET INCOME ($ mil.)	NET PROFIT MARGIN	EMPLOYEES
12/19	19,172	750	3.9%	0
12/18	16,317	646	4.0%	0
12/17	15,022	611	4.1%	0
12/16	12,625	465	3.7%	0
12/15	11,265	379	3.4%	0
Annual Growth	**14.2%**	**18.6%**	—	—

2019 Year-End Financials

Debt ratio: 1.3%
Return on equity: 25.0%
Cash ($ mil.): 1,002
Current ratio: 0.64
Long-term debt ($ mil.): 4,355
No. of shares (mil.): —
Dividends
  Yield: 1.2%
  Payout: —
Market value ($ mil.): —

	STOCK PRICE ($) FY Close	P/E High/Low		PER SHARE ($) Earnings	Dividends	Book Value
12/19	23.75	14	7	0.08	0.30	0.35
12/18	12.62	—	—	0.07	0.04	0.29
12/17	12.62	—	—	0.07	0.03	0.26
12/16	12.62	—	—	0.05	0.00	0.17
12/15	12.62	—	—	0.04	0.00	0.12
Annual Growth	**17.1%**	—	—	**17.3%**	—	**32.0%**

Canadian Imperial Bank Of Commerce (Toronto, Ontario)

Now more than 150 years old Canadian Imperial Bank of Commerce (CIBC) has assets worth more than $400 billion and is one of Canada's "Big 5" banks. It serves more than 11 million clients in Canada the US and around the world. Through four strategic business units CIBC provides a range of financial products and services to individuals small businesses and commercial corporate and institutional customers.

Operations

CIBC organizes its operations into four main business segments. The largest Canadian Personal and Small Business Banking generates more than half of the company's total revenues and provides financial advice products and services through a team of advisors to personal and small business clients.

The Canadian Commercial Banking and Wealth Management division (more than 20% of revenues) and U.S. Commercial Banking and Wealth Management (5%) both offer relationship-oriented commercial and private banking and wealth management services to middle-market companies entrepreneurs and high-net-worth individuals and families.

Capital Markets (about 20%) sells integrated global markets products and services investment banking advice corporate banking and research to corporate government and institutional clients globally.

In addition the Corporate and Other segment covers internal administrative groups as well as Client Connectivity and Innovation and CIBC's operations at FirstCaribbean International Bank Limited (CIBC FirstCaribbean).

Geographic Reach

CIBC does almost 85% of its business in Canada (plans are in the works for a new global headquarters CIBC Square to be built in Toronto Ontario).

Although working to increase its footprint in the US US operations currently represent not even 10% of sales. The company also does business in the Caribbean (close to 10% of total revenues). It generates less than 2% of sales in other countries.

Sales and Marketing

CIBC provides financial products and services to 11 million individual small business commercial corporate and institutional clients from Canada and around the world.

The bank has been increasing its advertising spend over the past few years for strategic initiatives and for developing its enhanced travel rewards program. It spent C$282 million toward advertising and business development in fiscal 2017 up 5% from its spend in 2016.

Financial Performance

Note: Growth rates may differ after conversion to US dollars.

CIBC has enjoyed steady top-line growth over the past few years thanks to higher fee- and commission-based income from its banking insurance and investment-related products and services. Revenue grew by 8% to C$16.2 billion in fiscal 2017 (ended October) aided by the acquisition of CIBC Bank USA in 2017.

Net income increased almost 10% to C$4.7 billion in 2017 (the CIBC Bank USA acquisition contributed almost C$1 billion) the third consecutive year of healthy profit growth.

Cash flow from operations was down significantly in 2017 primarily due to C$10.5 billion spent in securities purchased under resale agreements.

Strategy

To grow its business CIBC is continuing its client-oriented focus and simplifying its banking operations; investing in technology for online and mobile banking solutions; and expanding into US markets under the CIBC name with targeted acquisitions.

The company has remodeled more than 100 of its banking centers in Canada creating a more open concept which encourages clients to have advice-based conversations with bank staff. CIBC is targeting affluent clients and business owners and building relationships emphasizing financial planning and advice.

It has also invested in technology and digital platforms such as online and mobile banking solutions; its CIBC Global Money Transfer product allows customers to send money to more than 50 countries and CIBC is the first bank in Canada to offer three mobile wallet services and free mobile credit scores. In 2017 it launched a new direct banking brand through Simplii Financial a low-cost banking service offered by phone online or through a mobile device.

Its acquisitions of US-based PrivateBank and Geneva Advisors in 2017 represent CIBC's move to expand into more US markets under the CIBC name particularly in the wealth management space.

Mergers and Acquisitions

CIBC completed the US$5 billion acquisition of Chicago-based PrivateBancorp Inc. and its subsidiary The PrivateBank in June 2017. The purchase establishes the company in the US and allows it to serve a broader range of clients under the CIBC brand.

Later in 2017 the company continued with another Chicago-based acquisition - Geneva Advisors a private wealth management firm. The US$200 million purchase is aimed at growing this business in the US.

HISTORY

In 1858 Bank of Canada was chartered; Toronto financier William McMaster bought the charter in 1866 when investors failed to raise enough money to open it and changed the name to Canadian Bank of Commerce.

The firm opened in 1867 bought the Gore Bank of Hamilton (1870) and expanded within seven years to 24 branches in Ontario as well as Montreal and New York. Led by Edmund Walker the bank spread west of the Great Lakes with the opening of a Winnipeg Manitoba branch in 1893 and joined the Gold Rush with branches in Dawson City Yukon Territory and Skagway Alaska in 1898.

As the new century began the bank's purchases spanned the breadth of Canada from the Bank of British Columbia (1901) to Halifax Banking (1903) and the Merchants Bank of Prince Edward Island (1906). More buys followed in the 1920s; the bank's assets peaked in 1929 and then plunged during the Depression. It recovered during WWII.

In 1961 Canadian Bank of Commerce merged with Imperial Bank of Canada to become Canadian Imperial Bank of Commerce (CIBC). Imperial Bank was founded in 1875 by Henry Howland; it went west to Calgary and Edmonton and became known as "The Mining Bank." It bought Barclays Bank (Canada) in 1956.

As the energy and agriculture sectors declined in the early 1980s two of CIBC's largest borrowers Dome Petroleum and tractor maker Massey-Ferguson defaulted on their loans. Deregulation opened investment banking to CIBC which in 1988 bought a majority share of Wood Gundy one of Canada's largest investment dealers; CIBC also purchased Merrill Lynch Canada's retail brokerage business.

In 1992 CIBC added substantially to its loss reserves (resulting in an earnings drop of 98%) to cover real estate losses from developer Olympia & York and others. This launched more cost-cutting as the company reorganized by operating segments.

Deregulation allowed CIBC to begin selling insurance in 1993; the company built a collection of life credit personal property/casualty and nonmedical health companies.

In 1996 the bank formed Intria a processing and technical support subsidiary. The next year CIBC Wood Gundy became CIBC World Markets and CIBC bought securities firm Oppenheimer & Co. and added its stock underwriting and brokerage abilities to CIBC World Markets.

In 1998 increasing foreign competition prompted CIBC and Toronto-Dominion to plan a merger (as did Royal Bank of Canada and Bank of Montreal); the government halted both plans citing Canada's already highly concentrated banking industry.

Spurned the bank overhauled its operations to spark growth in the late 1990s. To cut costs it eliminated some 4000 jobs and sold its more than $1-billion real estate portfolio. It teamed with the Winn-Dixie (1999) and Safeway (2000) supermarket chains to operate electronic branches in the US. The firm scaled back its disappointing international operations and began selling its insurance units.

In 2000 CIBC created Amicus as a holding company for CIBC World Markets' retail electronic banking business. The following year the bank sold its merchant card services business to US-based Global Payments.

In 2002 the company snagged US-based Merrill Lynch's Canadian retail brokerage asset management and securities operations renaming it CIBC Asset Management Inc. That same year CIBC merged its Caribbean banking business with that of UK-based Barclays to create FirstCaribbean Bank.

The next year CIBC sold the Oppenheimer private client and asset-management divisions to Fahnestock Viner (now Oppenheimer Holdings). It sold Juniper Financial a Delaware-based credit card issuer to Barclays for some $293 million in 2004.

In 2004 and again in 2006 CIBC was sued by creditors of Internet telecommunications company Global Crossing stating that the bank had engaged in insider trading to the tune of $2 billion. Creditors demanded a return of the proceeds. CIBC denied the claims but in 2006 two units of the bank agreed to pay $17.4 million to investors in the ill-fated telecom.

More trouble came in 2005 when CIBC agreed to pay some $2.4 billion in an investor class-action suit to resolve claims that the company helped notorious energy trader Enron to conceal losses.

EXECUTIVES

EVP and General Counsel Legal and Regulatory Compliance, Michael G. Capatides
President CIBC Asset Management, Stephen (Steve) Geist
EVP Brand Corporate and Client Relationships, Stephen J. Forbes
President and CEO Wealth Management, Victor Dodig
Managing Director and Head Cash Equities CIBC World Markets, Rik Parkhill
Managing Director and Group Co-Head Wholesale Banking, Harry Culham
SVP and Chief Auditor, Kevin J. Patterson
EVP Retail Distribution and Channel Strategy, Christina Kramer
SEVP and Group Head Retail and Business Banking, J. David Williamson, age 60, $285,933 total compensation
SEVP and Chief Risk Officer, Laura Dottori-Attanasio
EVP Human Resources, Jacqueline C. Moss
Managing Director and Head Equity Markets, Roman Dubczak
EVP Finance Shared Services, Kevin Glass
Managing Director and Global Head Investment Banking CIBC World Markets, Geoffrey (Geoff) Belsher
Managing Director and Head U.S. Region/Risk CIBC World Markets; President and CEO CIBC World Markets, Gary W. Brown
Managing Director and Head Capital Markets Trading, Christian Exshaw
EVP Products and Payments, Jenny Fagg
Managing Director and Head CIBC Wood Gundy, Monique Gravel
EVP Human Resources, Sandy Sharman
Chairman and CEO Atlantic Trust, Jack Markwalter
Senior Executive Vice-President Managing Director, Richard E. Venn

Chairman, Charles Sirois, age 66
Auditors: Ernst & Young LLP

LOCATIONS

HQ: Canadian Imperial Bank Of Commerce (Toronto, Ontario)
Commerce Court, Toronto, Ontario M5L 1A2
Phone: 416 980 2211
Web: www.cibc.com

2017 Sales

	% of total
Canada	83
Caribbean	8
US	7
Other Countries	2
Total	**100**

PRODUCTS/OPERATIONS

2017 Sales

	% of total
Canadian Personal and Small Business Banking	52
Canadian Commercial Banking and Wealth Management	22
Capital Markets	17
US Commercial Banking and Wealth Management	5
Corporate and other	4
Total	**100**

PRODUCT CATEGORIES
Financial advice
Mobile banking
Online banking
Mobile investment consulting
Mobile wallets
Business Plus credit cards
Digital cart
Simplii Financial
Wealth management services
CIBC Integrated Payments service
CIBC Active Global Currency Pool
Commercial banking services
CIBC Global Money Transfer service
International Student Pay

COMPETITORS

BMO Financial Group	JPMorgan Chase
Barclays	National Bank of
Caisses centrale	Canada
Desjardins	RBC Financial Group
Citigroup	Scotiabank
Goldman Sachs	TD Bank

HISTORICAL FINANCIALS

Company Type: Public

Income Statement				FYE: October 31
	ASSETS ($ mil.)	NET INCOME ($ mil.)	INCOME AS % OF ASSETS	EMPLOYEES
10/20	578,505	2,849	0.5%	43,853
10/19	494,687	3,868	0.8%	45,157
10/18	454,740	4,011	0.9%	44,220
10/17	440,006	3,657	0.8%	44,928
10/16	374,749	3,195	0.9%	43,213
Annual Growth	11.5%	(2.8%)	—	0.4%

2020 Year-End Financials

Return on assets: 0.5%
Return on equity: 9.5%
Long-term debt ($ mil.): —
No. of shares (mil.): 446
Sales ($ mil): 18,958
Dividends
Yield: 0.0%
Payout: 70.8%
Market value ($ mil.): 33,350

	STOCK PRICE ($) FY Close	P/E High/Low		PER SHARE ($) Earnings	Dividends	Book Value
10/20	74.62	11	6	6.18	4.38	69.22
10/19	85.26	8	7	8.50	5.67	65.45
10/18	86.32	8	7	8.87	5.39	60.10
10/17	88.05	8	7	8.75	5.14	54.99
10/16	74.96	7	6	8.00	4.81	44.19
Annual Growth	(0.1%)	—	—	(6.2%)	(2.3%)	11.9%

Canadian National Railway Co

Canadian National Railway (CN) is Canada's #1 railroad and one of the largest in North America. It operates a network of about 20000 route miles of track spanning Canada and the US connecting the Atlantic the Pacific and the Gulf of Mexico. Crossing the continent north-south and east-west CN hauls such freight as coal forest products petroleum and chemicals and grain and fertilizers. It operates about 20 intermodal terminals which transfer freight between truck and train and 80 warehousing and distribution facilities. Other transportation services include international freight forwarding. CN's revenues are fairly balanced among Canadian traffic US traffic transborder traffic and overseas traffic.

Financial Performance

In 2010 CN began seeing recovery in many markets in line with a strengthening overall economy. Thanks in part to government stimulus programs North American industrial production picked up as did automotive production. There was also modest improvement in housing and construction.

CN's 2011 revenues increased by 9% and profits jumped 17% over the prior year as a result of higher freight volumes a higher fuel surcharge and freight rate increases. It also collected additional revenue on the sale of indirect subsidiary IC Rail-Marine Terminal Company ($60 million) and the sale of its Kingston subdivision known as the Lakeshore East ($288 million).

Strategy

CN's rail and transportation services are backed by co-production arrangements marketing alliances and interline agreements. Its freight revenues are derived from main commodity groups representing a diversified and balanced portfolio of goods transported between a wide range of origins and destinations. This product and geographic diversity better positions it to face economic fluctuations.

A key part of CN's business plan is to grow at low incremental cost. It seeks to achieve this by making service improvements for customers especially at origin and destination points. It's also investing in capital programs to maintain a safe and fluid railway while improving productivity. Train productivity is being improved through the acquisition of new locomotives. In 2012 CN announced it had ordered 2200 freight cars in addition to 1300 containers. Previously in 2012 CN acquired 600 box cars used to haul forest products and metals.

In late 2011 the company merged three of its US subsidiaries Duluth Missabe and Iron Range Railway Company (DMIR) Duluth Winnipeg and Pacific Railway Company (DWP) and Wisconsin Central Ltd. into a single company which will operate under the name Wisconsin Central Ltd. The merger increased operational efficiency and improved service in the region extending from Duluth Minnesota to Superior Wisconsin.

EXECUTIVES

VP and CIO, Serge Leduc
EVP Corporate Services and Chief Legal Officer, Sean Finn, $522,341 total compensation
EVP and Chief Marketing Officer, Jean-Jacques (JJ) Ruest
EVP and CFO, Ghislain Houle, age 56
CEO, Luc Jobin, age 61, $337,095 total compensation
EVP and COO, Mike Cory
President and CEO CN Investment Division, Russell J. Hiscock
Chairman, Robert L. Pace, age 65
Auditors: KPMG LLP

LOCATIONS

HQ: Canadian National Railway Co
935 de La Gauchetiere Street West, Montreal, Quebec
H3B 2M9
Phone: 888 888-5909
Web: www.cn.ca

2016 sales

	% of total
Canada	66
U.S.	34
Total	**100**

PRODUCTS/OPERATIONS

2016 sales

	% of total
Rail freight revenues	94
Other revenues	6
Total	**100**

COMPETITORS

Burlington Northern Santa Fe	Kansas City Southern
CSX	Norfolk Southern
Canadian Pacific Railway	OmniTRAX
	Pioneer Railcorp
Genesee & Wyoming	Schneider National
J.B. Hunt	Union Pacific

HISTORICAL FINANCIALS

Company Type: Public

Income Statement — FYE: December 31

	REVENUE ($ mil.)	NET INCOME ($ mil.)	NET PROFIT MARGIN	EMPLOYEES
12/19	15,105	4,269	28.3%	25,975
12/18	14,501	4,382	30.2%	25,720
12/17	13,205	5,553	42.1%	23,945
12/16	12,188	3,685	30.2%	22,249
12/15	12,769	3,582	28.1%	23,172
Annual Growth	4.3%	4.5%	—	2.9%

2019 Year-End Financials

Debt ratio: 31.9%
Return on equity: 23.6%
Cash ($ mil.): 64
Current ratio: 0.66
Long-term debt ($ mil.): 12,015
No. of shares (mil.): 712
Dividends
  Yield: 1.7%
  Payout: 48.0%
Market value ($ mil.): 64,428

	STOCK PRICE ($) FY Close	P/E High/Low		PER SHARE ($) Earnings	Dividends	Book Value
12/19	90.45	16	13	5.90	1.62	25.65
12/18	74.11	16	12	5.94	1.39	24.63
12/17	82.50	12	9	7.33	1.67	22.71
12/16	67.40	15	10	4.73	1.52	19.72
12/15	55.88	16	12	4.45	0.97	19.23
Annual Growth	12.8%	—	—	7.3%	13.7%	7.5%

Canadian Natural Resources Ltd

Canadian Natural Resources has exploited Canada's resources to become one of the country's largest natural gas producers. The company has large oil holdings (light medium and heavy crude assets) in British Columbia and Alberta as well as in Saskatchewan. It also has holdings in the North Sea and offshore Africa. In addition the company has major interests in oil sands production in Canada. Canadian Natural Resources has reported proved reserves of more than 10 billion barrels of oil bitumen and natural gas liquids (including about 6.5 billion barrels of synthetic crude oil) and approximately 6.5 trillion cu. ft. of natural gas and produced an average of nearly 1 million barrels of oil equivalent per day. The company was founded in 1989.

Operations

Canadian Natural Resources generates more than half of its revenue through three geographic segment activities. These include the exploration development production and marketing of crude oil natural gas liquids and natural gas. Its Oil Sands Mining and Upgrading activities account for over 45% of revenue are reported in a separate segment from exploration and production activities. Midstream and Refining activities include the company's pipeline operations an electricity co-generation system and Redwater Partnership.

Geographic Reach

Canadian Natural Resources' exploration and production activities are conducted in three geographic segments: North America (accounts for about 45% of total revenue); North Sea (around 5%); and Offshore Africa (less than 5%).

The company is headquartered in Calgary Alberta with about 15 domestic operating locations. It also has nearly 5 international offices in Central Africa the UK and West Africa.

Sales and Marketing

Canadian Natural Resources customers are mainly in the crude oil and natural gas industry.

Financial Performance

Note: Growth rates may differ after conversion to US Dollars.

Revenue rose 9% to $24.4 billion in 2019 from $22.3 billion the year prior. The increase was primarily due to higher realized crude oil and NGLs pricing in North America together with increased crude oil and NGLs sales volumes in the North America Exploration and Production segment following the acquisition of thermal and heavy oil assets from Devon offsetting the impact of a proactive piping replacement in one of the hydrogen units at Horizon together with the unplanned maintenance at the non-operated Scotford Upgrader and at Horizon in the first half of the year.

The company reported net earnings of $5.4 billion in 2019 compared with $2.6 billion for 2018. The increase in net earnings and adjusted net earnings from operations for 2019 was primarily due to higher crude oil and NGLs sales volumes and netbacks in the Exploration and Production segments and higher realized foreign exchange gains partially offset by lower SCO sales volumes in the Oil Sands Mining and Upgrading segment lower natural gas netbacks in the Exploration and Production segments and higher realized risk management losses.

Canadian Natural Resources' cash position strengthened by $38 million ending the year with $139 million in cash. Operating activities generated $8.8 billion in 2019 while financing and investing activities used $1.5 billion and $7.3 billion respectively. The company's main cash uses in 2019 were dividends expenditures on property plant and equipment and the acquisition of Devon assets.

Strategy

Canadian Natural Resources' objectives are to increase crude oil and natural gas production reserves cash flow and net asset value on a per common share basis through the economic and sustainable development of its existing crude oil and natural gas properties and through the discovery and/or acquisition of new reserves. The company strives to meet these objectives in a sustainable and responsible way maintaining a commitment to environmental stewardship and safety excellence.

The company's three-phase crude oil marketing strategy includes: blending various crude oil streams with diluents to create more attractive feedstock; supporting and participating in pipeline expansions and/or new additions; and supporting and participating in projects that will increase the downstream conversion capacity for heavy crude oil and bitumen (thermal oil).

Strategic accretive acquisitions are a key component of the company's strategy. The company has used a combination of internally generated cash flows and debt and equity financing to selectively acquire properties generating future cash flows in its core areas. The company's financial discipline commitment to a strong balance sheet and capacity to internally generate cash flows provides the means to responsibly and sustainability grow in the long term.

Mergers and Acquisitions

In late 2020 Canadian Natural Resources completed the acquisition of all the issued and outstanding common shares of Painted Pony Energy Ltd. Painted Pony has Northeast British Columbia and Calgary head office. The company will also assume Painted Pony's total debt of approximately $350 million. This acquisition further strengthens Canadian Natural's natural gas assets and production base in key operating areas and complements the company's diversified portfolio. This transaction also allows to further insulate against natural gas costs in oils sands operations and has minimal impact on the low overall corporate decline rate.

In mid-2019 the company completed the acquisition of all of the assets of Devon Canada Corporation (Devon). Devon's high quality land and production are located in Western Canada and are within Canadian Natural's core areas. The asset base consists of 100% operated long life low decline thermal in situ production as well as 95% operated conventional primary heavy crude oil production both adjacent to existing Canadian Natural assets. Canadian Natural Resources acquires Devon for a cash purchase price of C$3.775 billion.

Company Background

The company was founded in 1989.

EXECUTIVES

EVP Canadian Conventional, Lyle G. Stevens, age 66
COO, Tim S. McKay, age 59, $208,548 total compensation
President, Steve W. Laut, age 63, $223,996 total compensation
EVP, Douglas A. (Doug) Proll, age 70
SVP Exploration, Kendall W. (Ken) Stagg, age 59
VP Mining, Philip A. Keele, age 61
SVP Production Development Operations, Bill R. Peterson, age 54
Director Investor Relations, Corey B. Bieber, age 57
SVP North America Operations, Scott G. Stauth, age 63
VP Technology Development, Joy P. Romero, age 63
SVP Exploitation, Darren M. Fichter
VP Drilling and Completions, Kevin B. Kowbel
VP Information and Corporate Services, Steve C. Suche
SVP Horizon Projects, Réal J.H. Doucet
VP Thermal Projects, S. John Parr
VP Bitumen Production, Casey D. McWhan
VP Infrastructure Logistics and Project Controls, Jay E. Froc
Chairman, N. Murray Edwards
Auditors: PricewaterhouseCoopers LLP

LOCATIONS

HQ: Canadian Natural Resources Ltd
2100, 855 - 2 Street S.W., Calgary, Alberta T2P 4J8
Phone: 403 514-7777
Web: www.cnrl.com

2015 Sales

	% of total
Exploration and Production	
North America	68
North Sea	5
offshore Africa	4
Oil sands mining and upgrading	22
Midstream	1
Total	**100**

COMPETITORS

BP	Husky Energy
Barnwell Industries	Imperial Oil
Devon Energy	Murphy Oil
Dominion Energy	Shell Canada
Encana	Suncor
Exxon Mobil	Syncrude

HISTORICAL FINANCIALS

Company Type: Public

Income Statement   FYE: December 31

	REVENUE ($ mil.)	NET INCOME ($ mil.)	NET PROFIT MARGIN	EMPLOYEES
12/19	17,563	4,159	23.7%	10,180
12/18	15,440	1,902	12.3%	9,709
12/17	13,282	1,912	14.4%	9,973
12/16	7,808	(151)	—	7,270
12/15	8,901	(458)	—	7,568
Annual Growth	**18.5%**	—	—	**7.7%**

2019 Year-End Financials

Debt ratio: 20.6%	No. of shares (mil.): 1,186
Return on equity: 16.1%	Dividends
Cash ($ mil.): 106	Yield: 3.4%
Current ratio: 0.68	Payout: 43.0%
Long-term debt ($ mil.): 14,276	Market value ($ mil.): 38,395

	STOCK PRICE ($) FY Close	P/E High/Low		PER SHARE ($) Earnings	Dividends	Book Value
12/19	32.35	7	5	3.49	1.13	22.64
12/18	24.13	17	10	1.56	1.02	19.54
12/17	35.72	18	14	1.62	0.88	20.65
12/16	31.88	—	—	(0.14)	0.70	17.54
12/15	21.83	—	—	(0.42)	0.71	18.01
Annual Growth	**10.3%**			—	**12.2%**	**5.9%**

Canadian Tire Corp Ltd

Don't be fooled by its name: Canadian Tire sells much more than tires. About 490 Canadian Tire general merchandise stores run by a network of associate dealers across Canada sell automotive home and sports and leisure products including bicycles. The company's 90-plus PartSource auto parts stores cater to automotive do-it-yourselfers and professionals while its roughly 385-location Mark's Work Wearhouse chain offers work and casual apparel and footwear for men and women. Its Canadian Tire Petroleum subsidiary runs 300 gas bar locations making it one of the country's largest independent gasoline retailers. Established in 1922 Canadian Tire also owns Canada's largest sporting goods retailer FGL Sports.

Operations

Canadian Tire operates three business segments: Retail CT REIT and Financial Services.

The Retail segment (which made up 89% of Canadian Tire's total revenue in fiscal 2015 ended January) includes the business from its Canadian Tire PartSource Canadian Tire Petroleum (CTP) Mark's and various FGL Sports stores. Its Canadian Tire stores make up about half of its total revenue and are operated by independent business owner dealers. Its CTP stores sell fuel and related products from about 300 agent operated gas bars that boast 296 convenience stores and over 80 car wash stations. The company's 415 FGL Sports stores sell sports-related footwear apparel and equipment under the Sport Chek Hockey Experts Sports Experts National Sports Intersport Pro Hockey Life and Atmosphere banners.

The Financial Services segment (8% of revenue) markets a range of Canadian Tire-branded credit cards through its subsidiary Canadian Tire Financial Services (CTFS). (One in five Canadian households had a Canadian Tire credit card in 2014.) CTFS's subsidiary Canadian Tire Bank offers personal loans and lines of credit; high-interest and tax-free savings accounts; insurance plans; and warranty products. Scotiabank acquired a 20% stake in the company's financial services business in October 2014 which raised nearly $477 million in net proceeds for Canadian Tire.

The CT REIT segment (3% of revenue) owned 273 properties spanning 20 million square feet of gross leasable area across all provinces and two territories in Canada as of early 2015. Its property portfolio included Canadian Tire stores retail centers anchored by Canadian Tire stores company distribution centers a mixed-use commercial property and devleopment lands where future Canadian Tire stores could be built.

Geographic Reach

Canadian Tire's retail outlets blanket the country with a store network that served about 90% of Canada's population in 2014. The company has representative offices in the Pacific Rim related to product sourcing logistics and vendor management. Its four distribution facilities are in Brampton Ontario; Calgary Alberta; and Montreal Quebec.

Sales and Marketing
Canadian Tire's supply chain partners include common carrier trucking companies third-party logistics companies ocean carriers and railways.

Financial Performance
Note: Growth rates may differ after conversion to US dollars. This analysis uses financials from the company's annual report.

Canadian Tire's annual revenues and profits have been trending higher since 2009 with a growing total store base and rising same-store sales.

The company's revenue climbed 6% to C$12.5 billion ($10.7 billion) in fiscal 2015 (ended January 3 2015) mostly thanks to a combination of 6% Retail sales growth from strong performance from its Canadian Tire and FGL Sports stores; and 5% Financial Services business growth as credit card sales and balances grew. Its Retail business grew for a variety of factors: its Canadian Tire's retail sales improved with enhanced assortments and new products; its automotive business posted strong results through the year; its FGL Sports sales grew thanks to strong same-store sales at its Sport Chek locations and new store openings; and Mark's sales grew thanks to new marketing campaigns that promoted new assortments and national brands in men's casual wear and footwear.

Revenue growth in FY2015 drove Canadian Tire's net income up 13% to C$639.3 million ($548 million) for the year. The company's operating cash levels fell 36% to C$574.8 million ($492.5 million) despite higher earnings due to unfavorable working capital changes mostly related to merchandise inventories.

Strategy
Canadian Tires' President and CEO laid out a handful of priorities in late 2015 as the company's strategy for growth. These included: continuing to strengthen the company's brands; growing its relationships with its independently-owned Canadian Tire Dealers; embracing the new world of retail by utilizing in-store digital and digital marketing practices and building its e-commerce channel; becoming more productive and efficient; and continuing to look for inorganic growth opportunities building upon its successful acquisitions of the Forzani Group (now FGL Sports) and Mark's Work Wearhouse it made in the past.

Some of the company's other priorities outlined in 2015 included: renovating its Canadian Tire stores with expanded Living categories and better store design; building Mark's market share in the overall casual apparel and casual footwear market with a specific focus on menswear in the jeans outwear and casual footwear categories; and expanding its FGL Sports' Sport Check store network — especially adding new large urban flagship concept stores — while closing over 100 other retail locations by 2017.

To boost traffic and customer retention within its existing stores Canadian Tires has been pushing its "My Canadian Tire Money" card and mobile app loyalty program. The program launched in October 2014 not only gives customers reward points for shopping at the Canadian Tire-affiliated stores but also provides allows the company to leverage customer shopping data to build new retail strategies and personalized relationships over the long term.

HISTORY

In 1922 brothers John and Alfred Billes bought Hamilton Tire and Garage in Toronto a city with 40000 cars at the time. In addition to the usual repair parts tires and batteries the brothers also provided a homemade brand of antifreeze. They fired up earnings even more by renting spaces in their heated garage so drivers in that cold land wouldn't have trouble starting their cars in the morning.

Five years after buying the garage the Billes brothers incorporated as Canadian Tire. Aptly named the company began fielding requests for auto parts from across the country. In 1928 Canadian Tire published a French-English bilingual catalog that is still distributed to 9 million homes.

The Great Depression had little effect on the company as more Canadians sought to hold on to their cars (numbering a million in 1930) rather than buy new ones. For these many do-it-yourself auto mechanics Canadian Tire introduced the super-lastic tire guarantee the first time in the country a tire was guaranteed for other than the manufacturers' defects. Also in the 1930s the company opened its first associate store in Hamilton Ontario forming the pattern for many such stores to come.

The 1950s saw Canadian Tire roll out a chain of gas stations and introduce a cash bonus coupon called Canadian Tire Money that gas-buying customers could redeem on store merchandise. In the early 1960s customers could earn Tire Money at retail stores as well as gas stations.

Tiring of its core product the company began diversifying its line selling small appliances and other housewares. In the early 1970s tires and other auto supplies accounted for half of Canadian Tire's sales; by 1978 those products accounted for about 35%.

In the next decade the company found itself going south. In 1982 it bought the Texas-based White Stores chain. After disappointing results however Canadian Tire had sold all its US stores by 1986.

In 1994 Canadian Tire introduced its Next Generation stores with expanded offerings and a more customer-friendly format. In another innovation five years later the company announced plans to launch a chain of 200 PartSource stores aimed at garage professionals and advanced do-it-yourselfers. In 2000 Canadian Tire launched an e-commerce site that now markets 15000 products.

In order to focus on its own credit card the company sold its credit card management operations to Citigroup-owned Associates Financial Services of Canada in 2001. Also that year Canadian Tire acquired the Mark's Work Wearhouse apparel chain.

In 2002 the company built and opened 20 stores; in 2003 19 stores were opened.

Tom Gauld formerly president of Canadian Tire Financial Services succeeded Wayne Sales and president and CEO of Canadian Tire in April 2006. Sales remained on the board of directors as vice chairman.

In September 2008 Canadian Tire sold 11 of its retail properties to two commercial real estate firms for a combined $164 million and change. The sale is part of the company's plan to sell and lease back a dozen of its properties for $174 million.

In January 2009 Gauld retired and was succeeded as CEO by director Stephen Wetmore.

In August 2011 Canadian Tire acquired Canada's largest sporting goods retailer The Forzani Group for C$771 million (nearly US$800 million). Forzani which owns the Sport Chek and Athletes World chains among others will operate as a separate business unit as part of the acquisition.

The 2011 acquisition of the Forzani Group — the first major purchase by CEO Stephen Wetmore — was designed to shore up the retailer's position in sporting goods and apparel and give it more competitive heft as it prepared for the 2013 arrival of the US's #2 discounter Target Corp in Canada.

EXECUTIVES

President & Board Member, Greg Hicks
Executive Vice President, Gregory Craig
Executive Vice President, Mahes Wickramasinghe
Executive Vice President, Iain Kennedy
Vice President, John Pershing
Executive Vice President, Jim Christie
Senior Vice President, John Koryl
Senior Vice President, Robyn Collver
Senior Vice President, Susan O'Brien
Senior Vice President, Lisa Greatrix
Auditors: Deloitte LLP

LOCATIONS

HQ: Canadian Tire Corp Ltd
2180 Yonge Street, Toronto, Ontario M4P 2V8
Phone: 416 480-8725   **Fax:** 416 480-8763
Web: www.investors.canadiantire.ca

PRODUCTS/OPERATIONS

2015 Stores

	No.
Canadian Tire Stores	493
FGL Sports	436
Mark's Work Wearhouse	383
Gas bars	297
PartSource	91
Total	**1,700**

2015 Revenue

	% of total
Canadian Tire Retail	89
Financial services	8
CT Reit	3
Eliminations	-
Total	**100**

Selected Products

Automotive
  Batteries and accessories
  Car radio and video systems and parts
  Car security systems
  Emergency road kits
  Lighting and electrical products
  Test and tune supplies and equipment
  Tires
  Truck and trailer accessories
  Wiper blades
Garden and patio
  Barbecues and accessories
  Fertilizers
  Garden tools
  Garden wear
  Patio furniture
  Pest control supplies
  Sheds
  Wheelbarrows and carts
Home products
  Bathroom cabinets and other supplies
  Batteries
  Cleaning supplies
  Electrical
  Electronics
  Home dé;cor
  Kitchen products
  Laundry products
  Lighting products
  Mailboxes
  Pet supplies
  Plumbing supplies
  Safety and security products
  Storage and organization products
Sports and recreation
  Baseball
  Bicycles
  Camping equipment and supplies
  Curling
  Fishing equipment and supplies
  Golf equipment and supplies
  Skateboard and scooters
  Snowshoeing
  Sport and duffel bags
Workshop
  Carpentry tools

Electrical products
Generators
Power tool accessories
Shop vacuums
Welding and soldering equipment and supplies

COMPETITORS

Ace Hardware	Loblaw
BP	Midas
CARQUEST	RONA
Chevron	Sears Canada
Costco Wholesale	Sobeys
Canada	Sports Authority
Couche-Tard	True Value
Exxon Mobil	Uni-Select
Foot Locker	Wal-Mart Canada
Home Depot Canada	West Fraser Timber
Hudson's Bay	

HISTORICAL FINANCIALS

Company Type: Public

Income Statement   FYE: December 28

	REVENUE ($ mil.)	NET INCOME ($ mil.)	NET PROFIT MARGIN	EMPLOYEES
12/19	14,717	788	5.4%	31,574
12/18	14,235	700	4.9%	31,686
12/17	13,604	744	5.5%	29,710
12/16*	12,840	677	5.3%	29,220
01/16	12,434	667	5.4%	27,772
Annual Growth	4.3%	4.2%	—	3.3%

*Fiscal year change

2019 Year-End Financials

Debt ratio: 40.5%
Return on equity: 18.2%
Cash ($ mil.): 208
Current ratio: 1.66
Long-term debt ($ mil.): 5,671

No. of shares (mil.): 61
Dividends
 Yield: 0.0%
 Payout: 32.9%
Market value ($ mil.): 6,495

	STOCK PRICE ($) FY Close	P/E High/Low		PER SHARE ($) Earnings	Dividends	Book Value
12/19	105.57	9	8	12.74	4.20	68.98
12/18	102.57	13	9	10.77	3.65	70.29
12/17	128.95	12	10	10.80	2.63	72.35
12/16*	103.53	12	8	9.34	2.33	70.69
01/16	85.23	13	9	8.72	2.13	68.28
Annual Growth	5.5%	—	—	9.9%	18.6%	0.3%

*Fiscal year change

Canadian Western Bank

Auditors: KPMG LLP

LOCATIONS

HQ: Canadian Western Bank
 Suite 3000, 10303 Jasper Avenue NW, Canadian
 Western Bank Place, Edmonton, Alberta T5J 3X6
Phone: 780 423 8888   **Fax:** 780 423 8897
Web: www.cwb.com

HISTORICAL FINANCIALS

Company Type: Public

Income Statement   FYE: October 31

	ASSETS ($ mil.)	NET INCOME ($ mil.)	INCOME AS % OF ASSETS	EMPLOYEES
10/20	34,365	273	0.8%	2,505
10/19	31,820	290	0.9%	2,278
10/18	29,387	266	0.9%	2,178
10/17	26,780	231	0.9%	2,174
10/16	25,540	190	0.7%	2,100
Annual Growth	7.7%	9.5%	—	4.5%

2020 Year-End Financials

Return on assets: 0.8%
Return on equity: 8.6%
Long-term debt ($ mil.): —
No. of shares (mil.): 87
Sales ($ mil): 1,485

Dividends
 Yield: 0.0%
 Payout: 40.2%
Market value ($ mil.): 1,599

	STOCK PRICE ($) FY Close	P/E High/Low		PER SHARE ($) Earnings	Dividends	Book Value
10/20	18.36	9	4	2.90	1.16	38.73
10/19	25.67	8	6	3.08	0.81	34.19
10/18	23.51	12	8	2.83	0.77	29.44
10/17	26.63	11	7	2.45	0.94	28.16
10/16	18.86	11	7	2.16	0.69	26.92
Annual Growth	(0.7%)	—	—	7.6%	13.9%	9.5%

Canon Inc

Auditors: Ernst & Young ShinNihon LLC

LOCATIONS

HQ: Canon Inc
 30-2, Shimomaruko 3-chome, Ohta-ku, Tokyo 146-8501
Phone: (81) 3 3758 2111   **Fax:** (81) 3 5482 9680
Web: www.global.canon/ja/

HISTORICAL FINANCIALS

Company Type: Public

Income Statement   FYE: December 31

	REVENUE ($ mil.)	NET INCOME ($ mil.)	NET PROFIT MARGIN	EMPLOYEES
12/19	36,230	1,261	3.5%	187,041
12/18	39,846	2,548	6.4%	195,056
12/17	41,137	2,439	5.9%	197,776
12/16	34,296	1,518	4.4%	197,673
12/15	38,317	2,220	5.8%	189,571
Annual Growth	(1.4%)	(13.2%)	—	(0.3%)

2019 Year-End Financials

Debt ratio: 0.0%
Return on equity: 4.5%
Cash ($ mil.): 4,162
Current ratio: 1.92
Long-term debt ($ mil.): 3,602

No. of shares (mil.): 1,063
Dividends
 Yield: 5.3%
 Payout: 125.0%
Market value ($ mil.): 29,096

	STOCK PRICE ($) FY Close	P/E High/Low		PER SHARE ($) Earnings	Dividends	Book Value
12/19	27.35	0	0	1.18	1.47	25.52
12/18	27.60	0	0	2.36	1.52	26.40
12/17	37.40	0	0	2.25	1.36	26.81
12/16	28.14	0	0	1.39	1.41	25.70
12/15	30.13	0	0	2.03	1.34	27.39
Annual Growth	(2.4%)	—	—	(12.7%)	2.5%	(1.8%)

Capgemini SE

Auditors: KPMG S.A.

LOCATIONS

HQ: Capgemini SE
 Place de l'Etoile 11 rue de, Paris, Tilsitt 75017
Phone: (33) 1 47 54 50 00   **Fax:** (33) 1 47 54 50 25
Web: www.capgemini.com

HISTORICAL FINANCIALS

Company Type: Public

Income Statement   FYE: December 31

	REVENUE ($ mil.)	NET INCOME ($ mil.)	NET PROFIT MARGIN	EMPLOYEES
12/19	15,859	961	6.1%	219,314
12/18	15,113	835	5.5%	211,313
12/17	15,334	982	6.4%	199,698
12/16	13,239	972	7.3%	193,077
12/15	12,977	1,224	9.4%	180,639
Annual Growth	5.1%	(5.9%)	—	5.0%

2019 Year-End Financials

Debt ratio: 20.3%
Return on equity: 10.7%
Cash ($ mil.): 2,763
Current ratio: 1.28
Long-term debt ($ mil.): 2,878

No. of shares (mil.): 169
Dividends
 Yield: 1.5%
 Payout: 6.8%
Market value ($ mil.): 4,119

	STOCK PRICE ($) FY Close	P/E High/Low		PER SHARE ($) Earnings	Dividends	Book Value
12/19	24.36	5	3	5.61	0.38	55.93
12/18	19.53	6	4	4.87	0.40	51.33
12/17	23.74	5	4	5.71	0.75	49.70
12/16	16.82	9	3	5.54	0.29	44.76
12/15	46.32	7	5	6.89	0.27	43.57
Annual Growth	(14.8%)	—	—	(5.0%)	9.7%	6.4%

Carrefour S.A.

Carrefour (which means "crossroads" in French) is a retailer and operates in approximately 12225 stores under various banners including hypermarkets (Carrefour) supermarkets (Carrefour Market) convenience stores (including City Contact and Express) and cash-and-carry outlets (Promocash) in 30 countries in Europe Latin America Africa-Middle-East and Asia. Besides France Carrefour's core markets are Belgium Italy Poland Romania and Spain. Nearly half of the company's total sales is generated from France.

Operations

Carrefour's store network consists of around 1200 hypermarkets an assortment of 20000 to 80000 product references for a sales area ranging from 2400 to 23000m2. With surfaces of between 1000 and 3500m2 the Carrefour Market banner offers a wide choice of fresh and local products as well as an assortment of non-food products adapted to its customers. The company's convenience stores sales areas ranging from 200 to 900m2 Proxi Carrefour Bio Carrefour Contact Carrefour Express and Carrefour City are the company's daily living brands. Nearly 415 cash and carry outlets and it is developing particularly in Brazil under the Atacadao brand and in France under the Promocash brand. The cash & carry format offers traders restaurateurs and professionals a wide range of food and non-food products presented on pallets individually or in multipack at wholesale prices.

In addition the company has strongly developed local services around e-commerce: click & collect drive home delivery - including delivery in one hour.

Geographic Reach

France (including its overseas territories) is Carrefour's largest market accounting for 50% of sales. As well as its mainline Carrefour-branded hypermarkets and supermarkets its convenience store network consists of the Carrefour City Carrefour Contact Carrefour Express and Carrefour Bio banners. Its cash and carry businesses operate as Promocash.

The rest of Europe particularly Belgium Poland Italy Spain and Romania generates more than 30% of sales and has around 4300 stores Carrefour is also present in other European countries via partnerships including in Turkey via Sabanci which operates more than 640 stores in the country.

Latin America accounts for around 20% of total sales. Carrefour is the leading retailer in both Brazil and Argentina. In the Asia/Pacific region (less than 5% of sales) Carrefour is active in China. Taiwan as well as Indonesia via franchising. It has 475 stores in the region.

Carrefour also has around 460 stores spread across Africa the Middle East and the Dominican Republic.

Carrefour has separate retail websites in each of its geographies.

Sales and Marketing

In France Carrefour has improved its price positioning. Strengthening loyalty schemes with the new "Market Loyalty Premium" launched in early 2020 in supermarkets (approximately 10% discount every day on fresh products such as fruits and vegetables butcher fishmonger flowers and plants; approximately 15% discount for Pass cardholders).

The company is outperforming the market in food e-commerce. Sizeable investments in digital are again reflected in an increase of more than 30% in food e-commerce sales in 2019.

Financial Performance Note: Growth rates may differ after conversion to US Dollars.

Carrefour's sales have been on a general upward track for the last five years but the company's profits have declined steeply in the past years with consecutive losses in 2017 and 2018 before recovering in 2019.

In 2019 revenue fell ?24 million to ?74.1 billion due to changes in exchange rates which reduced net sales by ?2.4 billion almost exclusively attributable to the Latin America region.

Net income was ?1.3 billion a vast improvement from the ?344 million loss of the prior year. The company sold 80% of its equity interest in Carrefour China to Chinese group Suning.com which took effect in September of 2019 at ?615 million. A disposal gain of around ?1.1 billion was recognized from discontinued operations.

Carrefour's cash on hand grew ?166 million during 2019 ending the year at ?4.5 billion. The company's operations generated ?3.2 billion. Its financing activities used ?1.9 billion and its investing activities used another ?1 billion. Carrefour's main cash uses in 2019 were acquisitions while the company issued bonds to support liquidity.

Strategy

The company's "Carrefour 2022" strategy is wide-ranging and touches most if not all parts of its business. Launched in 2018 Carrefour 2022 has four main pillars the company is focused on: deploying a simplified and open organization gaining in productivity to reinforce its attractiveness

creating an omni-channel universe of reference and making "eating better" accessible to everyone.

Carrefour is investing ?2.8 billion in e-commerce with the goal of generating ?5 billion from online by 2022. The company overhauled all of its interfaces and applications to offer a comprehensive range of services accessible from a single site in each country which includes drive-up walk-up click and collect next-day delivery and express delivery. It also plans on opening 3000 convenience stores by 2022 in addition to the opening of 200 drive pick-up points in 2018.

It has also established a partnership with Spanish start-up Glovo which enables Carrefour to offer home delivery services in only 30 minutes in France Spain Italy and Argentina. Carrefour Brazil has also posted strong growth in e-commerce sales from its successful collaboration with the Rappi delivery application among others. The aim is to roll out home delivery of Carrefour products in all French cities with more than 10000 inhabitants by 2022.

Additionally Carrefour is forming partnerships to boost its competitiveness and operational efficiency. Carrefour was chosen by Google to be its first global food partner in 2019 applying artificial intelligence and machine learning techniques by applying these to concrete cases such as anticipating stock shortages. In an effort to combat waste and address environmental challenges Carrefour has collaborated with the Too Good To Go application which helps its customers identify unsold food at low prices.

Mergers and Acquisitions

n mid-2020 Carrefour Italy inaugurated a new Carrefour Express Via Fumagalli in Milan. The endpoint of a major challenge consisted of integrating 25 Conad points of sale into the Carrefour network 21 under the Express banner and 4 Market stores. This operation strengthens Carrefour's presence in Italy in a highly strategic region and segment.

Also in the same year Carrefour has entered into an agreement with Dairy Farm to acquire Wellcome Taiwan consolidating its position as the leading multi-format food retailer in that market. The transaction's enterprise value is 97 million euros1. Wellcome Taiwan posted net sales of around 390 million euros in 2019.

EXECUTIVES

Executive Director Assets Development and New Ventures, Jacques Ehrmann, age 60
Executive Director Italy, Eric Uzan, age 59
Executive Director China and Taiwan, Thierry Garnier, age 53
Chairman and CEO, Alexandre Bompard, age 48
Executive Director Spain, No «l Prioux, age 60
Executive Director Northern Europe, Gérard Lavinay
Executive Director Poland, Guillaume de Colonges
Executive Director Brazil, Charles Desmartis
Deputy Chief Executive Officer and CFO, Pierre-Jean Sivignon
Executive Director Spain, Pascal Clouzard
Executive Director Argentina, Daniel Fernandez
Executive Director Belgium, Fran §ois Melchior de Polignac
Executive Director International Partnerships, Stéphane Thouin
Deputy Chief Executive Officer and General Secretary, Jér ´me Bédier
Executive Director Romania, Jean-Baptiste Dernoncourt
Executive Director Ta wan, Rami Baitieh
Executive Communications Director, Marie-No «lle Brouaux
Vice Chairman, Georges Ralli, age 72
Auditors: Mazars

LOCATIONS

HQ: Carrefour S.A.
33, avenue Emile-Zola, TSA 55555, Boulogne-Billancourt 92100
Phone: (33) 1 41 04 26 00   **Fax:** (22) 1 41 04 26 01
Web: www.carrefour.com

2018 Sales

	% of total
France	47
Europe	28
Latin America	18
Asia	7
Total	**100**

PRODUCTS/OPERATIONS

2018 Stores

	No.
Convenience	7,029
Supermarkets	3,319
Hypermarkets	1,384
Cash & Carry	379
Total	**12,111**

Selected Operations and Banners

Hypermarkets
  Carrefour
Supermarkets
  Champion
  GB
  Globi
  GS
  Marinopoulos
  Norte
  Super GB
  Super GS
  Unic
Hard discount stores
  Ed
  Minipreco
Other stores
  Cash-and-carry stores
  Docks Market
  Promocash
  Puntocash
Convenience stores
  8 à Huit
  Di per Di
  GB Express
  Marché; Plus
  Proxi
  Shopi
Other Operations
Carfuel (petroleum products)
Comptoirs Modernes (supermarkets)
Costco UK (20% warehouse club)
Erteco (hard-discount stores)
Financiera Pryca (46% consumer credit Spain)
Fourcar B.V. (investments The Netherlands)
GlobalNetXchange (Internet-based supply exchange joint venture)
Ooshop (online shopping)
Prodirest (catering)
Providange (auto centers)
S2P (60% consumer credit)

COMPETITORS

AEON	La Rinascente
ALDI	Lianhua Supermarket
Ahold Delhaize	Lidl
Auchan	Lotteshopping
Brasileira de	METRO AG
Distribui § o	Marui Group
Casino Guichard	Migros
China Nepstar	REWE
Dairy Farm	Rallye
International	SHV Holdings
E.Leclerc	Super Indo
Edeka Zentrale	Tengelmann
Eroski	Tesco
Falabella	Viavarejo
Galeries Lafayette	Wal-Mart
H&M	WuMart
ITM Entreprises	Zara

HISTORICAL FINANCIALS

Company Type: Public

Income Statement
FYE: December 31

	REVENUE ($ mil.)	NET INCOME ($ mil.)	NET PROFIT MARGIN	EMPLOYEES
12/19	83,244	1,267	1.5%	321,383
12/18	89,230	(642)	—	363,862
12/17	97,069	(636)	—	378,923
12/16	83,176	787	0.9%	372,330
12/15	85,891	1,067	1.2%	380,920
Annual Growth	(0.8%)	4.4%	—	(4.2%)

2019 Year-End Financials

Debt ratio: 28.3%
Return on equity: 11.8%
Cash ($ mil.): 5,014
Current ratio: 0.82
Long-term debt ($ mil.): 9,116

No. of shares (mil.): 807
Dividends
 Yield: 3.1%
 Payout: 6.4%
Market value ($ mil.): 2,658

	STOCK PRICE ($) FY Close	P/E High/Low		PER SHARE ($) Earnings	Dividends	Book Value
12/19	3.29	3	2	1.59	0.10	13.82
12/18	3.32	—	—	(0.84)	0.11	13.47
12/17	4.34	—	—	(0.84)	0.17	15.80
12/16	4.84	—	—	1.07	0.00	14.74
12/15	5.72	5	4	1.47	0.09	14.42
Annual Growth	(12.9%)	—	—	2.0%	3.0%	(1.1%)

Casino Guichard Perrachon S.A.

You're unlikely to hit the jackpot at Casino Guichard-Perrachon but odds are you'll go home with the groceries. One of the world's leading food retailers Casino Group owns and operates more than 15300 stores including hypermarkets (mostly Géant) supermarkets (Casino and Monoprix to name a few) restaurants (Casino Cafétéria) and discount stores (Leader Price). It is the third-largest food retailer (behind Carrefour and Auchan) and the #1 convenience store operator in France (primarily as Petit Casino but other banners include Franprix Vival and Spar). Most of its stores are in France but it has outlets in 8 countries in Asia and South America including Brazil Colombia and Thailand.

Operations

Its retail operations bring in the bulk of revenue at around 73% but it also earns significant revenue from electronics and through e-commerce.

Of its 10627 stores 6917 are convenience stores 867 Franprix 810 Leader Price 698 Monoprix 441 Casino supermarkets 146 Indian Ocean and 128 Casino hypermarkets. It also operates 621 stores in other activities.

Geographic Reach

Casino is headquartered in France. It has more than 250 affiliated stores in 45 countries including France Belgium Colombia Brazil Argentina Uruguay Thailand Senegal Cote d'Ivoire Cameroon Madagascar and Mauritius.

Sales and Marketing

Casino deals in physical retail and e-commerce.

Financial Performance

Note: Growth rates may differ after conversion to US Dollars.

Sales fell 5% to ?46.1 billion primarily due to a decrease in revenue from Latin American electronics sales.

Strategy

Casino Group is pursuing a strategy of geographic diversification with a particular focus on Latin America. It combined its Latam operations into a single structure under the xito subsidiary. In Asia the Group continued to expand across all formats during the year supporting the development of modern retailing in the region.

Casino is working hard to ramp up its digitalization capabilities. In late 2017 it signed a deal with UK online grocer Ocado to use its technology platform to expand its online offering. Ocado's sophisticated robotics online technology and delivery software make it arguably the world leader.

Casino has been selling off assets to raise cash to pay down debts. In 2019 it identified ?2 billion in real estate assets to sell off coming on top of a ?1.5 billion asset sale in 2018 and ?3.1 billion in disposals in 2016.

Mergers and Acquisitions

In 2018 Casino agreed to acquire Sarenza an online footwear specialist. The acquisition plays into Casino's digital strategy and Sarenza will be part of its Monoprix subsidiary.

Company Background

Casino is controlled by Euris which is controlled by Jean-Charles Naouri Casino's chairman and CEO.

EXECUTIVES

Finance Director, Antoine Giscard d'Estaing
Chairman Chief Executive Officer, Jean-Charles Naouri, age 71
Auditors: ERNST & YOUNG et Autres

LOCATIONS

HQ: Casino Guichard Perrachon S.A.
 1, Cours Antoine Guichard, Saint-Etienne, Cedex 1 42008
Phone: (33) 4 77 45 31 31   **Fax:** (33) 4 77 45 38 38
Web: www.groupe-casino.fr

PRODUCTS/OPERATIONS

2015 Stores

	No.
France	10,627
International	
Argentina	27
Uruguay	65
Brazil	2,181
Colombia	1,668
Thailand	734
Vietnam	42
Total	15,344

2015 type of Stores (France)

	No.
Casino hypermarket	128
Supermarkets	441
Monoprix	698
Franprix	867
Leader price	810
Convenience stores	6,916
Indian ocean	146
Other Activities	621
Total	10,627

2015 Sales

	% of Total
France Retail	41
Latam Retail	32
Latam Electronics	11
Asia	9
E-Commerce	7
Total	100

Selected Operations

Banque du Groupe Casino (60% financial services)
Big C (36% Thailand)
Casino Enterprise (non-food operations)
Cativen (66% Venezuela)
Cdiscount.com (67% e-commerce)
Companhia Brasileira de Distribuição (34% Brazil)
Devoto (97% supermarkets Uruguay)
Exito Colombia SA (55% supermarkets)
Franprix (supermarkets)
Gé;ant (hypermarkets)
Imagica (photo and digital imaging processing)
Leader Price (supermarkets)
Libertad (hypermarkets Argentina)
Vindé;mia (supermarkets; Madagascar Mauritius Ré;union)

COMPETITORS

ALDI	ITM Entreprises
Auchan	Kingfisher
Carrefour	METRO AG
E.Leclerc	Migros
Groupe Flo	Tesco
Guyenne et Gascogne	Wal-Mart Brazil
IGA	

HISTORICAL FINANCIALS

Company Type: Public

Income Statement
FYE: December 31

	REVENUE ($ mil.)	NET INCOME ($ mil.)	NET PROFIT MARGIN	EMPLOYEES
12/19	39,644	(1,607)	—	209,696
12/18	42,527	(61)	—	214,458
12/17	45,339	143	0.3%	226,606
12/16	38,043	2,828	7.4%	227,842
12/15	50,261	(46)	—	325,820
Annual Growth	(5.8%)	—	—	(10.4%)

2019 Year-End Financials

Debt ratio: 31.0%
Return on equity: (-24.9%)
Cash ($ mil.): 4,010
Current ratio: 0.96
Long-term debt ($ mil.): 9,084

No. of shares (mil.): 107
Dividends
 Yield: —
 Payout: —
Market value ($ mil.): —

Cathay Financial Holding Co

EXECUTIVES

Director; Chairman Cathay Insurance (China), Fa-Te Chang
EVP Cathay Life Insurance, Ming-Ho Hsiung
Chairman Cathay Financial Holdings and Cathay Life Insurance, Hong-Tu Tsai
Vice Chairman; Chairman Cathay United Bank, Gregory K.H. Wang
President and Director, Chang-Ken Lee
CFO and First Deputy Spokesperson, Grace Chen
Director; Managing Director Cathay Life Insurance, Cheng-Ta Tsai

Director; Chairman Cathay Century Insurance, Cheng-Chiu Tsai

Director; Vice Chairman Cathay United Bank, Tsu-Pei Chen

Director; President Cathay Century Insurance, J. H. Hsu

EVP and Director; Chairman Cathay Securities Corporation, David P. Sun

EVP and Spokesperson, Alan Lee

Auditors: Deloitte & Touche

LOCATIONS

HQ: Cathay Financial Holding Co
296, Jen Ai Road, Sec. 4, Taipei
Phone: (886) 2 2708 7698   **Fax:** (886) 2 2325 2488
Web: www.cathayholdings.com

COMPETITORS

Bank of China	Hua Nan Financial
Chang Hwa Bank	Mega Financial
Chinatrust Financial	Shin Kong
E.Sun	SinoPac Holdings
First Financial	Taishin
Holding	Taiwan Business Bank

HISTORICAL FINANCIALS

Company Type: Public

Income Statement   FYE: December 31

	ASSETS ($ mil.)	NET INCOME ($ mil.)	INCOME AS % OF ASSETS	EMPLOYEES
12/19	336,204	2,096	0.6%	0
12/18	301,604	1,682	0.6%	0
12/17	298,176	1,898	0.6%	0
12/16	251,457	1,471	0.6%	0
12/15	230,339	1,750	0.8%	46,633
Annual Growth	9.9%	4.6%	—	—

2019 Year-End Financials

Return on assets: 0.6%   Dividends
Return on equity: 9.7%   Yield: —
Long-term debt ($ mil.): —   Payout: —
No. of shares (mil.): —   Market value ($ mil.): —
Sales ($ mil): 10,518

Cathay Pacific Airways Ltd.

Auditors: KPMG

LOCATIONS

HQ: Cathay Pacific Airways Ltd.
33rd Floor, One Pacific Place, 88 Queensway,
Phone: (852) 2747 5210   **Fax:** (852) 2810 6563
Web: www.cathaypacific.com

HISTORICAL FINANCIALS

Company Type: Public

Income Statement   FYE: December 31

	REVENUE ($ mil.)	NET INCOME ($ mil.)	NET PROFIT MARGIN	EMPLOYEES
12/19	13,737	217	1.6%	34,200
12/18	14,180	299	2.1%	32,400
12/17	12,448	(161)	—	32,700
12/16	11,960	(74)	—	33,800
12/15	13,203	774	5.9%	26,833
Annual Growth	1.0%	(27.2%)	—	6.3%

2019 Year-End Financials

Debt ratio: 5.8%   No. of shares (mil.): —
Return on equity: 2.6%   Dividends
Cash ($ mil.): 1,908   Yield: 2.9%
Current ratio: 0.48   Payout: 388.8%
Long-term debt ($ mil.): 9,825   Market value ($ mil.): —

	STOCK PRICE ($) FY Close	P/E High/Low		PER SHARE ($) Earnings	Dividends	Book Value
12/19	7.23	21	14	0.06	0.21	2.05
12/18	7.01	16	10	0.08	0.08	2.08
12/17	7.83	—	—	(0.04)	0.01	1.99
12/16	6.53	—	—	(0.02)	0.18	1.81
12/15	8.62	9	5	0.20	0.30	1.57
Annual Growth	(4.3%)	—	—	(27.2%)	(7.8%)	6.9%

Ceconomy AG

Ceconomy (formerly Metro) is Europe's leading consumer electronics retailer. Through the retail brands Media Markt and Saturn Ceconomy sells thousands of electronic items such as gaming household appliances smart home telecommunications computer photo as well as an option to rent rather than buy appliances for more than 1000 stores in around 15 European countries including its home market of Germany. Its other businesses includes digital advertising company Retail Media Group and Deutsche Technikberatung which offers installation assistance connection and troubleshooting of electronic devices at home. Ceconomy separated out Metro its grocery retail business as a standalone entity in 2017. Ceconomy holds some 25% stake in Fnac Darty France's largest electronics retailer.

Operations

Subsidiary MediaMarktkt Saturn Retail Group holds Ceconomy's main interests Media Market Saturn Media Markt is Ceconomy's biggest business operating more than 850 stores in some 15 countries. In addition to physical and online retail Media Markt offers after-sales services such as delivery assembly and installation and repairs. It also offers appliance rental. Saturn operates more than 170 stores in three European countries. Most of its stores are host to "SmartBars" which offer repair and other services.

Subsidiary Retail Media Group develops advertising campaigns based on impersonal visitor and purchase statistics. Lastly Deutsche Technikberatung offers professional assistance with home installation networking and troubleshooting of electronic appliances.

The company generates approximately 13% of total sales from online.

Geographic Reach

Germany is home to more than 430 of Dusseldorf-based Ceconomy's total base of some 1050 stores. Its second biggest presence is in Italy with over 115 stores while its remaining stores are relatively well diversified across some 15 other countries in Western/Southern Europe Eastern Europe and Central Europe as well as Turkey.

Ceconomy reports sales under three regions: DACH (Germany Austria Switzerland and Hungary) which accounts for nearly 60% of the sales; Western Europe (more than 30%); and Eastern Europe and other countries (the rest).

Sales and Marketing

Ceconomy operates two customer loyalty programs Media Markt Club and Saturn Card. The special feature is that customers can work their way up the levels of the customer card by collecting "bits" which allows them to claim certain advantages.

Financial Performance

After dropping in 2016 Ceconomy's revenue has been declining gradually with the exception of 2019. Its net income has been fluctuating in the same period.

In the past financial year 2018/19 CECONOMY's Group sales increased slightly by 0.2 per cent compared with the prior-year period to ?21.5 billion.

The company's net income resurfaced from a loss of ?212 million in 2018 to a profit of ?122 million in 2019.

Ceconomy's cash position rose during 2019 ending the year at ?1.1 billion. The company's operating activities generated ?86 million and its financing activities used ?178 million while investing activities generated ?118 million.

Strategy

Ceconomy's strategic approach consists of:

Customer orientation. With its omnichannel business model CECONOMY is guided by customers' expectations and requirements. The full customer focus allows customers to shop wherever whenever and however they want. In addition we continuously and systematically measure our customers' satisfaction using the net promoter score (NPS) in order to permanently enhance our service quality.

Sustainability. Sustainability and climate awareness are of enormous and increasing importance both for CECONOMY and for customers. For this reason measures to increase sustainability are very important. For example there is now a pilot project enabling customers to recycle old mobile phones by depositing them in innovative recycling machines in selected stores. The customers are paid back the residual value of the phones in the form of a voucher.

Centralization. Ceconomy's development is closely tied to lean efficient and effective structures and processes that are being incrementally established throughout the Group. The Group is therefore also defining what Group-wide cooperation will look like in the future: more centralized and with clear responsibilities at all levels.

Digitalization. One of Ceconomy's main strengths is to set digital trends systematically adjust the portfolio on that basis and promote innovation. The areas in which digital trends can be used are diverse and constantly provide new opportunities to make the shopping experience even more enjoyable.

Services. Ceconomy does more than merely sell products: the Group delivers solutions in the digital world and is constantly expanding its range of services. In recent financial years for example the service portfolio of Deutsche Technikberatung has been expanded and SmartBars rolled out to all stores.

HISTORY

Otto Beisheim founded METRO SB-Grossmarkte in the German town of Mulheim in 1964. A wholesale business serving commercial customers it operated under the name METRO Cash

& Carry. Three years later Beisheim received backing from the owners of Franz Haniel & Cie (an industrial company founded in 1756) and members of the Schmidt-Ruthenbeck family (also in wholesaling). This allowed METRO to expand rapidly in Germany and in 1968 into the Netherlands under the name Makro Cash & Carry via a partnership with Steenkolen Handelsvereeniging (SHV). During the 1970s the company expanded its wholesaling operations within Europe and moved into retailing.

METRO's foray into retailing was aided during the next decade by the acquisition of department store chain Kaufhof AG. By the 1980s the rise of specialty stores had many department stores on the defensive and Kaufhof's owners sold it to METRO and its investment partner Union Bank of Switzerland.

As METRO's ownership interest in Kaufhof rose above 50% the chain began converting some of its stores from department stores into fashion and sporting goods sellers. Kaufhof began acquiring a stake in computer manufacturer and retailer Vobis in 1989. In 1993 METRO now operating as METRO Holding AG acquired a majority interest in supermarket company Asko Deutsche Kaufhaus which owned the Praktiker building materials chain. The reclusive Beisheim retired from active management the following year.

To cut costs and prepare for expansion into Asia in 1996 METRO Holding merged its German retail holdings — Kaufhof; Asko; another grocery operation Deutsche SB Kauf; and its German cash-and-carry operations — into one holding company METRO AG.

EXECUTIVES

Chairman, Olaf Koch, age 50
CFO, Mark Frese, age 56
Vice Chairman, Werner Klockhaus, age 60
Chairman, Franz M. Haniel, age 65
Auditors: KPMG AG Wirtschaftsprüfungsgesellschaft

LOCATIONS

HQ: Ceconomy AG
  Benrather Strasse 18-20, Duesseldorf D-40213
Phone: (49) 211 6886 0   **Fax:** (49) 211 68 86 20 00
Web: www.ceconomy.de

2018 Sales

	% of total
DACH (Germany Austria Switzerland Hungary)	58
Western/Southern Europe	32
Eastern Europe	8
Others	2
Total	**100**

2018 stores

	Number
Germany	432
Austria	52
Switzerland	27
Hungary	29
Belgium	28
Greece	12
Italy	115
Luxembourg	2
Netherlands	49
Portugal	10
Spain	86
Poland	86
Turkey	71
Sweden	28
Others	28
Total	**1,022**

PRODUCTS/OPERATIONS

Selected Operations
Consumer Electronics
  Media Markt
  Saturn
Other OperationsiBoodJukeRetail Media GroupDeutsche Teknikberatung

COMPETITORS

Amazon.com	Best Buy
Apple Inc.	Samsung Group

HISTORICAL FINANCIALS
Company Type: Public

Income Statement

	REVENUE ($ mil.)	NET INCOME ($ mil.)	NET PROFIT MARGIN	EMPLOYEES
09/19	23,404	133	0.6%	55,259
09/18	24,807	(245)	—	61,827
09/17	26,175	1,301	5.0%	68,804
09/16	65,211	668	1.0%	226,053
09/15	66,393	753	1.1%	233,962
Annual Growth	(22.9%)	(35.2%)	—	(30.3%)

FYE: September 30

2019 Year-End Financials
Debt ratio: 4.0%
Return on equity: 16.8%
Cash ($ mil.): 1,234
Current ratio: 0.94
Long-term debt ($ mil.): 318
No. of shares (mil.): 356
Dividends
  Yield: —
  Payout: —
Market value ($ mil.): —

Cementos Bio-Bio S.A. (Chile)

Auditors: Ernst & Young Chile

LOCATIONS

HQ: Cementos Bio-Bio S.A. (Chile)
  Calle Alfredo Barros Errazuriz 1968, Piso 9, Santiago, Providencia
Phone: (56) 2 560 7000   **Fax:** (56) 2 560 7051
Web: www.cbb.cl

HISTORICAL FINANCIALS
Company Type: Public

Income Statement

	REVENUE ($ mil.)	NET INCOME ($ mil.)	NET PROFIT MARGIN	EMPLOYEES
12/19	263,182	13,103	5.0%	2,846
12/18	262,569	19,773	7.5%	2,901
12/17	266,556	23,858	9.0%	3,048
12/16	289,959	17,898	6.2%	3,345
12/15	296,137	21,141	7.1%	3,337
Annual Growth	(2.9%)	(11.3%)	—	(3.9%)

FYE: December 31

2019 Year-End Financials
Debt ratio: 22.4%
Return on equity: 5.6%
Cash ($ mil.): 21,336
Current ratio: 1.76
Long-term debt ($ mil.): 98,554
No. of shares (mil.): 264
Dividends
  Yield: —
  Payout: —
Market value ($ mil.): —

Cemex S.A.B. de C.V.

You certainly couldn't accuse CEMEX of being stuck in the mud. The building materials company is the number two cement maker in the world (after LafargeHolcim). The majority of its sales come from cement; the company has about 55 cement plants and an annual production capacity of about 95 million tons. It also produces markets and distributes ready-mix concrete aggregates and clinker (an intermediate product used to make cement). CEMEX operates in North America (through CEMEX Inc.) as well as in Africa Asia Europe the Middle East and South America. The US Mexico and Europe each account for a quarter of sales.

Operations
Cemex has nearly 95 million tons of installed cement capacity. It also produces 55 million cu. meters of ready-mix concrete and 150 million tons of aggregates each year. It produces concrete using both the dry and wet process but nearly all its plants use the dry process. Vertically integrated Cemex owns around 180 quarries.

Cemex generates 45% of sales from cement 40% from ready-mix and 15% from aggregates.

Geographic Reach
Based in Monterrey Mexico Cemex has around 55 production facilities in 20 countries around the globe. Its biggest producers in terms of installed cement capacity are Mexico the US Spain Egypt the Philippines and Colombia.

Cemex's revenue is well diversified geographically with the US Europe and Mexico each accounting for around a quarter of sales. The South Central America and the Caribbean region pulls in 15% of sales and the other 10% is accounted for by the Asia Middle East and Africa region.

Financial Performance
Note: Growth rates may differ after conversion to US Dollars.

Cemex's sales have grown in each of the last five years. In 2018 the company's sales grew 8% to Mex$276.9 billion (around $14.2 billion) thanks to higher cement and ready-mix volume and currency tailwinds.

Net income dipped 31% to Mex$10.5 billion in 2018 due to a sharp increase in tax expense and a sharp decrease in financial income partially offset by higher sales.

Cemex's cash on hand fell Mex$8.7 billion during 2018 ending the year at Mex$6.1 billion. The company's operations generated Mex$26.5 billion offset by the Mex$15.7 billion used in its investing activities and Mex$15.7 billion used in its financing. Cemex's main cash uses in 2018 were capital expenditures debt repayments and other financial obligations.

Strategy
Cemex enters new markets and refigures its productive portfolio through acquisitions and disposals. Its recent history has been characterized by divestitures having made around 12 full or partial sales spin-offs or flotations since 2015 partly balanced by a couple of acquisitions.

Another of Cemex's preoccupations is adding value by introducing a digital suite Cemex Go which went live in 2017. Cemex Go offers order placement live tracking and invoice and payment management. After an initial rollout in Mexico and the US Cemex Go is now live in more than 20 countries mostly in the Americas and Europe.

EXECUTIVES

EVP Legal and Secretary Board of Directors, Ramiro Villarreal
President CEMEX Mexico, Juan Romero Torres, age 61

President CEMEX Asia Middle East and Africa, Joaqu n M. Estrada Su ˜rez, age 57

President CEMEX Europe, Jaime G. Elizondo Chapa, age 57

President CEMEX South Central America and the Caribbean, Jaime Muguiro Dom nguez

EVP Strategic Planning and New Business Development, Juan P. San Agust n

EVP Administration and Organization, Luis Hern ˜ndez

CEO, Fernando A. Gonz ˜lez Olivieri

EVP Corporate Affairs and Enterprise Risk Management, Mauricio Doehner

EVP Finance and CFO, José A. Gonz ˜lez

President CEMEX USA, Ignacio Madridejos Fern ˜ndez

President Cemex Dominican Republic, Alejandro Ramirez Cantu

EVP Sustainability and Operations Development, Jes s V. Gonz ˜lez Herrera

President CEMEX UK, Michel Andre

VP Strategic Planning CEMEX Mexico, Ignacio A. Mijares Elizondo

President CEMEX Egypt, Carlos E. Gonz ˜lez Gallegos

Chairman, Rogelio Zambrano Lozano

Auditors: KPMG Cardenas Dosal S.C. (member of KPMG International)

LOCATIONS

HQ: Cemex S.A.B. de C.V.
Avenida Ricardo Margain Zozaya 325, Colonia Valle del Campestre, San Pedro Garza Garcia, Nuevo Leon 66265
Phone: (52) 81 8888 8888   **Fax:** (52) 81 8888 4417
Web: www.cemex.com

2018 Sales

	% of total
United States	26
Europe	26
Mexico	24
South Central America & Caribbean	14
Asia Middle East and Africa	10
Total	**100**

PRODUCTS/OPERATIONS

2018 Sales

	% of total
Cement	45
Ready mix	39
Aggregates	16
Total	**100**

Selected Subsidiaries

CEMEX Mé;xico S. A. de C.V.
 CEMEX Espa Â Â a S.A. (Spain)
 Assiut Cement Company (Egypt)
 Cement Bayano S.A. (Panama)
 CEMEX Asia Holdings Ltd. (Singapore)
 APO Cement Corporation (Philippines)
 CEMEX (Thailand) Co. Ltd.
 Solid Cement Corporation (Philippines)
 CEMEX Colombia S.A.
 CEMEX (Costa Rica) S.A.
 CEMEX de Puerto Rico Inc
 CEMEX Dominicana S.A. (Dominican Republic)
 CEMEX France Gestion (S.A.S.)
 CEMEX Corp. (US)
 CEMEX Venezuela S.A.C.A.
CEMEX U.K.
 CEMEX Austria AG
 CEMEX Czech Republic s.r.o.
 CEMEX Deutschland AG. (Germany)
 CEMEX Holdings (Israel) Limited
 CEMEX Investments Limited (UK)
 CEMEX Polska sp. Z.o.o. (Poland)
 CEMEX SIA (Latvia)
 Readymix plc (Ireland)

COMPETITORS

Aggregate Industries	Martin Marietta
Ash Grove Cement	Materials
Buzzi Unicem USA	Siam Cement
CRH	Sumitomo Osaka Cement
Cementos Portland	TXI
Valderrivas	Taiheiyo Cement
Eagle Materials	Tarmac
Essroc	Trinity Industries
HeidelbergCement	U.S. Concrete
Italcementi	Ube-Mitsubishi Cement
Italmobiliare	Vulcan Materials
LafargeHolcim	

HISTORICAL FINANCIALS

Company Type: Public

Income Statement

	REVENUE ($ mil.)	NET INCOME ($ mil.)	NET PROFIT MARGIN	EMPLOYEES
12/19	13,130	143	1.1%	40,640
12/18	14,079	532	3.8%	42,024
12/17	13,103	772	5.9%	40,878
12/16	12,126	678	5.6%	41,853
12/15	12,994	69	0.5%	43,117
Annual Growth	0.3%	19.9%	—	(1.5%)

FYE: December 31

2019 Year-End Financials

Debt ratio: 40.1%	No. of shares (mil.): —
Return on equity: 0.1%	Dividends
Cash ($ mil.): 788	Yield: 2.6%
Current ratio: 0.85	Payout: 3,210.0%
Long-term debt ($ mil.): 10,347	Market value ($ mil.): —

	STOCK PRICE ($) FY Close	P/E High/Low	PER SHARE ($) Earnings	Dividends	Book Value
12/19	3.78	1797932	0.00	0.10	0.21
12/18	4.82	36 22	0.01	0.00	0.21
12/17	7.50	30 20	0.02	0.00	0.20
12/16	8.03	27 11	0.02	0.00	0.19
12/15	5.57	322174	0.00	0.00	0.20
Annual Growth	(9.2%)	— —	16.9%	—	1.1%

Cencosud SA

Cencosud feeds and outfits its customers in Argentina Brazil Chile Colombia and Peru. One of Latin America's largest and most acquisitive retailers the multi-format retailer operates 760-plus supermarkets under the Santa Isabel banner in Chile Disco and Vea names in Argentina GBarbosa brand in Brazil and Wong banner in Peru. It also runs more than 35 hypermarkets in Chile and Argentina under the Jumbo banner. Fast-growing Cencosud's other retail activities include convenience and home improvement stores and some 40 Paris department stores located in Chile. Other activities include shopping centers travel agencies and banking. Cencosud is expanding rapidly in Brazil Latin America's largest economy.

EXECUTIVES

Financial Retail Managing Director, Patricio Rivas, age 57

Corporate Risk Managing Director, Marcelo Reyes, age 53

CEO, Jaime Soler Bottinelli, age 48

CFO, Rodrigo Larrain, age 48

Managing Director Regional Shopping Centers, Carlos Madina, age 53

Home Improvement Stores Managing Director, Antonio Ureta, age 46

Department Stores Managing Director, Ricardo Bennett, age 45

CIO, Andrés Artigas, age 54

Chairman, Horst Paulmann Kemna, age 84

Auditors: PricewaterhouseCoopers

LOCATIONS

HQ: Cencosud SA
Avenida Kennedy 9001, Piso 6, Santiago, Las Condes 4144
Phone: (56) 22 959 0545   **Fax:** (56) 22 959 0368
Web: www.cencosud.com

2016 Sales

	% of total
Chile	42
Argentina	24
Brazil	15
Peru	10
Colombia	9
Total	**100**

2016 Store locations

	Nos
Chile	384
Argentina	356
Brazil	211
Peru	105
Colombia	115
Total	**1,171**

PRODUCTS/OPERATIONS

2016 Sales

	% of total
Supermarkets	72
Home Improvement	13
Department Stores	11
Shopping Centers	2
Financial Services	2
Total	**100**

COMPETITORS

Brasileira de	Falabella
Distribui § o	Hipermarc
Carrefour España	Lojas Americanas
Casino Guichard	Wal-Mart

HISTORICAL FINANCIALS

Company Type: Public

Income Statement

	REVENUE ($ mil.)	NET INCOME ($ mil.)	NET PROFIT MARGIN	EMPLOYEES
12/19	12,955	154	1.2%	125,269
12/18	13,898	275	2.0%	133,846
12/17	17,003	715	4.2%	135,821
12/16	15,496	581	3.8%	139,093
12/15	15,510	327	2.1%	143,813
Annual Growth	(4.4%)	(17.1%)	—	(3.4%)

FYE: December 31

2019 Year-End Financials

Debt ratio: 0.0%	No. of shares (mil.): —
Return on equity: 2.6%	Dividends
Cash ($ mil.): 1,448	Yield: —
Current ratio: 1.27	Payout: —
Long-term debt ($ mil.): 4,206	Market value ($ mil.): —

Cenovus Energy Inc

Cenovus Energy reserves the right to recover and refine oil in the US and Canada. With major operations in the oil sands plays of Alberta and Saskatchewan the company has proved and probable reserves of 3.7 billion barrels of oil and 1.1 trillion cu.ft. of natural gas. It also owns stakes in two refineries in Illinois and Texas capable of processing heavy oil that were part of a 50/50 joint venture with ConocoPhillips. That venture provides integration of Cenovus' upstream oil production with downstream refining of such consumer products as diesel gasoline and jet fuel. Its Foster Creek and Christina Lake oil sands projects had a capacity of 288000 gross barrels of oil equivalent per day in 2014. Cenovus purchased ConocoPhillips' Western Canadian assets in 2017.

Operations

The company's segments are Oil Sands (bitumen assets at Foster Creek Christina Lake and Narrows Lake; Conventional (crude oil NGLs and natural gas in Alberta and Saskatchewan including the heavy oil assets at Pelican Lake); and Refining and Marketing (the transporting selling and refining crude oil into petroleum and chemical products).

Cenovus is a 50% partner in the Narrows Lake oil sands project and owns 100% of the Grand Rapids and Telephone Lake oil sands projects. In 2014 the company average crude oil and NGLs production was 203500 barrels per day and natural gas production was 488 million cu. ft. of natural gas equivalent per day.

Geographic Reach

Cenovus' reserves and production are located in Canada (52% in 2014) primarily within Alberta and Saskatchewan and the US (48%).

Financial Performance

The company's revenues have been increasing over the last few years. Net revenues increased by 5% in 2014 due to higher upstream revenues as a result of an increase in blended crude oil sales volumes and rising sales prices for blended crude oil and natural gas partially offset by higher royalties.

Cenovus' net income increased by 12% in 2014 due to higher net revenues and a gain on the sale of non-core assets.

Cash flow decreased by 0.4% due to a decline in operating cash flow from Refining and Marketing as a result of a decrease in average market crack spreads higher heavy crude oil feedstock costs increased operating expenses an inventory write-down and lower refined product output.

Strategy

Cenovus' strategy is to create long-term value through the development of its vast oil sands assets including boost the capacity of its Foster Creek and Christina Lake oil sands projects to 620000 gross barrels per day (from 288000 in 2014).

To raise cash to pay down debt in 2013 the company sold its Shaunavon tight oil asset (producing 3600 barrels of oil per day) in southern Saskatchewan to Surge Energy for $240 million.

Company Background

Cenovus Energy was formed in late 2009 as a spinoff from major Canada-based oil and gas player EnCana.

The split allowed EnCana to focus almost exclusively on natural gas exploration and development in North America while Cenovus took on responsibilities as an integrated oil company with the intent of boosting its production and refining capacities. An expansion at the Wood River refinery in Illinois is placed Cenovus among the leading heavy oil refiners in the US. The coker and refinery upgrade (completed in late 2011) increased its crude oil refining capacity and more than doubled its heavy crude oil refining capacity.

In 2010 Cenovus reported an improvement in revenues and income as the result of global economy bouncing back from a recession which produced higher commodity prices and demand driving up sales of the company's products.

EXECUTIVES

EVP and CTO, Harbir S. Chhina
EVP Environment Corporate Affairs Legal and General Counsel, Al Reid
EVP and CFO, Ivor M. Ruste, age 64, $429,975 total compensation
EVP Safety and Chief Digital Officer, Judy Fairburn
EVP Strategic Planning and President Downstream, Robert Pease
EVP and President Upstream Oil & Gas, Kieron McFadyen
EVP Deep Basin, Drew Zieglgansberger
President CEO and Director, Alex Pourbaix
Chair, Patrick D. Daniel, age 73
Auditors: PricewaterhouseCoopers LLP

LOCATIONS

HQ: Cenovus Energy Inc
4100, 225 6 Avenue S.W., Calgary, Alberta T2P 1N2
Phone: 403 766-3770
Web: www.cenovus.com

PRODUCTS/OPERATIONS

2014 Sales

	% of total
Refining & marketing	62
Upstream	
Oil sands	23
Conventional	15
Total	**100**

2014 Sales

	% of total
Canada	52
United States	48
Total	**100**

COMPETITORS

Baytex Energy	Shell Canada
Canadian Natural	Suncor
Husky Energy	Syncrude
Imperial Oil	

HISTORICAL FINANCIALS

Company Type: Public

Income Statement   FYE: December 31

	REVENUE ($ mil.)	NET INCOME ($ mil.)	NET PROFIT MARGIN	EMPLOYEES
12/19	15,497	1,684	10.9%	2,361
12/18	15,306	(1,959)	—	2,264
12/17	13,594	2,685	19.8%	2,882
12/16	9,003	(404)	—	2,775
12/15	9,405	444	4.7%	3,005
Annual Growth	**13.3%**	**39.5%**	**—**	**(5.9%)**

2019 Year-End Financials

Debt ratio: 14.4%
Return on equity: 11.9%
Cash ($ mil.): 142
Current ratio: 1.30
Long-term debt ($ mil.): 5,144

No. of shares (mil.): 1,228
Dividends
　Yield: 2.1%
　Payout: 15.5%
Market value ($ mil.): 12,473

	STOCK PRICE ($) FY Close	P/E High/Low		PER SHARE ($) Earnings	Dividends	Book Value
12/19	10.15	6	4	1.37	0.22	12.00
12/18	7.03	—	—	(1.59)	0.20	10.44
12/17	9.13	5	2	2.43	0.16	12.97
12/16	15.13	—	—	(0.48)	0.15	10.32
12/15	12.62	25	15	0.54	0.86	10.71
Annual Growth	**(5.3%)**	—	—	**26.1%**	**(29.3%)**	**2.9%**

Central Japan Railway Co.

Central Japan Railway known as JR Central provides passenger transportation throughout a network of some 1970 km (1221 miles) of track and about 405 stations. The company's shinkansen (high-speed) lines connect the metropolitan areas of Tokyo Nagoya and Osaka. In addition JR Central operates a dozen conventional rail lines mainly in the Nagoya and Shizuoka areas and provides bus services. The company also earns revenue from department store and hotel operations; food and beverage sales; leasing real estate near its train stations; and travel agency services. JR Central was one of seven companies formed in the 1987 privatization of Japanese National Railways.

Operations

JR Central's operations are divided across four main segments: Transportation (more than 75%) Merchandise and Other (nearly 15%) Real Estate (some 5%) and Other (more than 5%).

Geographic Reach

The company has its head office in Nagoya and Tokyo. Branch offices reside in Shizuoka and regional offices are located in Mie; Iida; Kansai; Shinkansen; Osaka; Washington DC; London; and Sydney.

Financial Performance

JR Central's 2020 revenues decreased 2% to Å 1.8 trillion which was mainly due to Å 30.1 billion decrease in transportation revenue.

Net income for the year was Å 397.8 billion a 9% decrease from 2019. The decrease was due to lower revenue and higher operating expenses.

Cash and cash equivalents at the end of the year were Å 761.3 billion. Cash provided by operations was Å 595.2 billion while investing and financing activities each used Å 552.4 billion and Å 32.9 billion respectively. Main cash uses were for capital expenditures and purchases of property plant and equipment.

Strategy

In early 2020 JR Central launched its online reservation service allowing overseas travelers to purchase before coming to Japan and from all over the world tickets to the Tokaido Sanyo Shinkansen (bullet train) which runs through Japan's "golden route" connecting Tokyo Mt. Fuji Nagoya Kyoto Osaka Hiroshima Hakata and other destinations.

This new service makes it easy and simple to book and buys tickets from countries outside of Japan. Moreover travelers may change their bookings as many times as they like without any additional charge.

EXECUTIVES

President, Yoshiomi Yamada
EVP, Tsutomu Morimura
Senior Corporate Executive Officer, Masaki Seki
Senior Corporate Executive Officer, Sumio Kudo
Senior Corporate Executive Officer, Noriyuki
  Shirakuni
Senior Corporate Executive Officer, Yutaka Osada
EVP, Koei Tsuge
EVP, Shin Kaneko
EVP, Naotoshi Yoshikawa
Senior Corporate Executive Officer, Katsumi
  Miyazawa
Chairman, Yoshiyuki Kasai
Auditors: Deloitte Touche Tohmatsu LLC

LOCATIONS

HQ: Central Japan Railway Co.
  1-1-4 Meieki, Nakamura-ku, Nagoya, Aichi 450-6101
Phone: (81) 52 564 2620
Web: www.jr-central.co.jp

PRODUCTS/OPERATIONS

2014 Sales

	% of total
Transportation	70
Merchandise & other	12
Real Estate	4
Other	14
Total	**100**

COMPETITORS

East Japan Railway
Keihin Electric
  Express Railway
Keio Corporation
Keisei Electric
  Railway

Nagoya Railroad
Odakyu Electric
  Railway
Tobu Railway
West Japan Railway

HISTORICAL FINANCIALS

Company Type: Public

Income Statement   FYE: March 31

	REVENUE ($ mil.)	NET INCOME ($ mil.)	NET PROFIT MARGIN	EMPLOYEES
03/20	16,993	3,665	21.6%	38,715
03/19	16,959	3,961	23.4%	37,927
03/18	17,158	3,724	21.7%	37,361
03/17	15,714	3,514	22.4%	36,868
03/16	15,480	3,004	19.4%	36,758
Annual Growth	2.4%	5.1%	—	1.3%

2020 Year-End Financials

Debt ratio: 0.4%
Return on equity: 10.8%
Cash ($ mil.): 3,743
Current ratio: 5.41
Long-term debt ($ mil.): 38,939

No. of shares (mil.): 197
Dividends
  Yield: 0.8%
  Payout: —
Market value ($ mil.): 3,211

	STOCK PRICE ($) FY Close	P/E High/Low		PER SHARE ($) Earnings	Dividends	Book Value
03/20	16.30	0	0	18.68	0.14	179.19
03/19	23.25	0	0	20.22	0.13	159.11
03/18	19.13	0	0	18.98	0.13	146.06
03/17	16.33	0	0	17.86	0.12	122.24
03/16	17.66	0	0	15.27	0.10	104.71
Annual Growth	(2.0%)	—	—	5.2%	9.4%	14.4%

Centrica Plc

Centrica is centered on supplying the energy needs of its more than 25 million customer accounts mainly in the UK Ireland and North America via five major brands? British Gas Bord G is Energy Centrica Energy Centrica Storage and Direct Energy. It is one of the largest electricity and gas supplier in the UK with an increasing presence in the US. It also offers related installation repair and maintenance services digital smart technologies (the Hive) and energy hedging and optimization strategies (Neas). The company holds a 69% interest in Spirit Energy an exploration and production company that is a joint venture with Bayerngas Norge which the company intends to exit by the end of 2020.

Operations

Centrica reports three business segments?Centrica Consumer Centrica Business and Upstream.

Bringing in more than 50% % of yearly sales Centrica Business segment consists of its Direct Energy business (electricity natural gas and energy services in North America) and the Energy Marketing & Trading business through Neas (risk management hedging and optimization). This segment also supplies gas & electricity to corporate and industrial clients in the UK under the British Gas brand.

The Centrica Consumer segment (almost 45% of annual revenue) primarily supplies gas and electricity to residential customers in the UK North America and Ireland. It also provides end-to-end design installation repair and maintenance and service solutions including optimization. Additionally through its Connected Home business Centrica markets its Hive home devices software and services globally.

Upstream division generates about 5% of revenue and consists of Nuclear and Exploration & Production (focused on development of new oil fields in the UK and Europe) Spirit Energy and Centrica Storage (produces of cushion gas in the UK).

Geographic Reach

The company is headquartered in Windsor UK and operates globally in almost 35 countries among others U.S. Canada France Italy Ireland Norway and Germany.

Centrica's UK market is the largest contributor to the company's revenues; it generates more than 45% of sales. It is followed by US market that accounts for almost 40% of sales. The remaining revenues are from: Canada (more than 5%) Republic of Ireland (almost 5%) Norway (less than 5%) and Rest of the world (over 5%).

Sales and Marketing

Centrica supplies gas and electricity to residential customers in the UK (through brands like British Gas Local Heroes and Dyno) Ireland (through Bord G is) and North America (under the Direct Energy brand).

Financial Performance

Centrica's revenue has been fluctuating in the last five years. It has an overall change of 4%.

Centrica revenue decreased 3% in 2019 to Å 22.7 billion.

Centrica had a net loss of over Å 1 billion in 2019.

Cash holdings decreased to Å 794 million at the end of 2019. Operations generated Å 1.3 billion and investments used Å 503 million with an additional Å 1.1 billion spent in financing activities.

Strategy

Centrica's medium-term strategic objectives are as follows: Demonstrating customer-led gross margin growth; Driving cost efficiency towards being

'most efficient price setter'; Improving organizational effectiveness Securing the capabilities it needs for 2020 and beyond; and Maintaining capital discipline and balance sheet strength.

For long-term growth its focus areas are energy supply; in-home servicing; home solutions; energy optimization; and business services & solutions.

Additionally Centrica has developed capabilities to help customers reduce their emissions. The company will also be exiting hydrocarbon production creating a leading international energy services and solutions provider.

Mergers and Acquisitions

In mid-2019 Centrica announced the agreement to purchase SmartWatt Energy Inc. for $37 million. SmartWatt is headquartered in New York US and one of the leading energy services and solutions company in the US. The acquisition will expand Centrica's operation throughout the US and is expected to close in July 2019.

Company Background

Centrica traces its roots back to British Gas which is one of the oldest companies in the world with a history stretching back over 200 years. However the company as it stands today only dates back to 1986 when the gas industry was privatized and British Gas Plc was formed with a "tell Sid" campaign encouraging customers to buy shares in the company.

In 1997 Centrica was founded when British Gas was split into two separate companies.

HISTORY

William Murdock invented gas lighting in 1792. In 1812 the Gas Light and Coke Company of London was formed as the world's first gas supplier to the public and by 1829 the UK had 200 gas companies.

In the second half of the 19th century the gas industry began looking for new uses for the fuel. Gas stoves were introduced in 1851 the geyser water heater was invented in 1868 and in 1880 the first gas units to heat individual rooms were developed.

Gas companies countered the emerging electricity industry by renting gas stoves at low prices and installing gas fittings (stove pipe and lights) in poor homes with no installation charges or deposits. By 1914 the UK had 1500 gas suppliers.

The electricity industry soon made major strikes against the gas industry's dominance. In 1926 the government began reorganizing the fragmented electricity supply industry building a national power grid and establishing the Central Electricity Generating Board to oversee it.

The gas industry was nationalized in 1949 and 1050 gas suppliers were brought under the control of the British Gas Council. Still the gas industry was losing. Supplying gas was more expensive than generating electricity: Gas was seen as a power supply of the past. The Gas Council sought to change that image through an aggressive marketing campaign in the 1960s touting gas as a modern clean fuel. Other factors played a part in its re-emergence: The Clean Air Act of 1956 steadily reduced the use of coal for home heating liquefied natural gas was discovered in the North Sea and OPEC raised oil prices in the 1970s. When natural gas was introduced most of the old gasworks were demolished and the British Gas Council (which became the British Gas Corp. in 1973) set about converting free of charge every gas appliance in the UK to natural gas.

As Margaret Thatcher's government began privatizing state industries the British Gas Corp. was taken public in 1986. Freed from government control British Gas expanded its international exploration and production activities. When the US gas industry began deregulating British Gas formed joint venture Accord Energy in 1994 with US gas trader Natural Gas Clearinghouse (now NGC) to sell gas on the wholesale market.

With the opening of the UK gas-supply market (which began regionally in 1996 and went nationwide in 1998) British Gas split into two public companies to avoid a conflict of interest between its supply business and its monopoly transportation business. In 1997 it spun off Centrica the retail operations and BG (now BG Group) which received the transportation business and the international exploration and production operations.

The UK electricity supply market began opening up to competition in 1998 and Centrica won 750000 UK electricity customers most of them also gas customers. In 1999 it bought The Automobile Association which it sold to venture capitalists in 2004. In 2000 Centrica began offering telecom services in the UK.

Centrica moved into North America in 2000 by purchasing two Canadian companies: natural gas retailer Direct Energy Marketing and gas production company Avalanche Energy. It gained a 28% stake in US marketing firm Energy America through the Direct Energy transaction and purchased the remaining 72% from US firm Sempra Energy the next year. Continuing its non-domestic strategy Centrica bought a 50% interest in Belgium energy supplier Luminus.

The firm purchased 60% of the 1260-MW Humber Power station in 2001 its first domestic power plant interest. It also acquired the UK operations of Australia's One.Tel and it bought Enron's European retail supply business Enron Direct for $137 million.

In 2002 Centrica purchased the retail energy services business of Canadian pipeline company Enbridge for $637 million; it also agreed to acquire another Enron-controlled company US retail energy supplier NewPower Holdings for $130 million. But Centrica withdrew its offer to buy NewPower a month after the deal was announced because of concerns about NewPower's potential Enron-related liabilities. Later that year Centrica acquired 200000 retail customer accounts in Ohio and Pennsylvania from NewPower.

In 2004 the company brought all its UK upstream activities together under Centrica Energy.

In 2005 Centrica acquired Oxxio the Netherlands #4 energy supplier.

To pursue green energy options in 2007 British Gas launched British Gas New Energy.

In 2007 Centrica acquired Newfield Exploration's North Sea assets for $486 million and in 2008 it acquired its first gas and oil assets in the Norwegian North Sea for $375 million (from Marathon Oil).

Growing it retail business in 2008 Centrica acquired Electricity Direct a UK commercial retail supplier serving nearly 1 million customers.

In 2008 Centrica's British Gas unit acquired 40000 small and mid-sized business customers from UK retail energy provider BizzEnergy in the wake of the latter's sudden financial collapse.

Centrica began in 2012 a program to save Å 500 million ($788 million) in costs over the next two years by identifying efficiencies. Although the company plans to continue investing for further growth it has already started cutting 2300 positions company-wide as well as implementing a pay freeze across much of the group. It set out to develop a better relationship with its customers by simplifying the purchase of gas and electricity. It also decided to make the cost of delivery more transparent by giving its customers a breakdown on their bill of the actual costs of providing the energy.

Through its aggressive acquisition strategy in North America the company has gained more than 6 million retail power and gas supply customers in

less than a decade as part of its Direct Energy operations. Building on its portfolio of offerings in 2011 it acquired Illinois-based Home Warranty of America (HWA) for Å 30 million ($48 million). HWA provides whole home warranty plans to more than 70000 customers through a network of 4000 contractors.

Direct Energy also made three acquisitions in 2011 for its residential energy supply business in North America: Gateway Energy Services First Choice Power and Vectren Retail. The deals part of the company's strategy of acquiring smaller suppliers and buying in deregulated markets added more than 750000 customers.

In a major move to grow its upstream business and its Norwegian operations Centrica completed a Å 936 million ($1.5 billion) deal in 2012 to acquire Norwegian assets from Statoil and ConocoPhillips. Combined the new assets will increase the company's reserves by almost 40% and its production by more than 30%. The acquisition includes proved and probable reserves of 117 million barrels of oil equivalent and production of 34000 barrels of oil evalent per day. The buy also makes Centrica one of Norway's fastest growing companies with a third of its gas and oil production originating from that region. The company's upstream operations also have a presence in Trinidad and the Netherlands.

In spite of the growth of Centrica's gas assets the company decided to raise its gas and electricity prices by 17% in late 2011 to cover the rising wholesale commodity prices in the first half of the year. Mild weather that year led to a decline per household averaging 21% less in gas and 4% less in electricity consumption. With lower residential demand customer bills were 4% lower on average in 2011. Consumer complaints over higher prices for heating homes in the UK led to protests at the offices of utility companies and at town halls early in 2012.

EXECUTIVES

Interim Managing Director British Gas, Ian Peters
CEO, Iain C. Conn
Managing Director International Upstream, Mark Hanafin
CFO, Jeff Bell
Chairman, Richard (Rick) Haythornthwaite
Auditors: Deloitte LLP

LOCATIONS

HQ: Centrica Plc
  Millstream, Maidenhead Road, Windsor, Berkshire SL4 5GD
Phone:
Web: www.centrica.com

PRODUCTS/OPERATIONS

2017 Sales by Geography

	% of total
UK	48
US	34
Rest of Europe	12
Others	6
Total	**100**

2017 Sales by Segment

	% of total
Centrica Business	54
Centrica Consumer	43
Exploration & Production	2
Centrica Storage	1
Total	**0**

COMPETITORS

Community Energy	RWE npower
Constellation Energy	STASCO
Group	Scottish and Southern
Dominion Energy	Energy
E.ON UK	Southern Company
EDF Energy	Southern Company Gas
Electrabel	United Utilities
Gasunie	Viridian Group
Green Mountain Energy	Western Power
IBERDROLA	Distribution

HISTORICAL FINANCIALS

Company Type: Public

Income Statement				FYE: December 31
	REVENUE ($ mil.)	NET INCOME ($ mil.)	NET PROFIT MARGIN	EMPLOYEES
12/19	29,942	(1,350)	—	29,147
12/18	37,901	233	0.6%	31,780
12/17	37,850	449	1.2%	34,901
12/16	33,339	2,056	6.2%	38,278
12/15	41,451	(1,107)	—	38,848
Annual Growth	**(7.8%)**	—	—	**(6.9%)**

2019 Year-End Financials

Debt ratio: 38.8%	No. of shares (mil.): —
Return on equity: (-46.9%)	Dividends
Cash ($ mil.): 1,772	Yield: 9.8%
Current ratio: 0.93	Payout: —
Long-term debt ($ mil.): 5,924	Market value ($ mil.): —

	STOCK PRICE ($) FY Close	P/E High/Low	PER SHARE ($)		
			Earnings	Dividends	Book Value
12/19	4.86	— —	(0.24)	0.48	0.28
12/18	6.87	257197	0.04	0.60	0.71
12/17	7.43	214123	0.08	0.63	0.65
12/16	11.53	38 29	0.38	0.58	0.60
12/15	12.75	— —	(0.22)	0.72	0.34
Annual Growth	**(21.4%)**	— —	—	**(9.6%)**	**(5.4%)**

Charoen Pokphand Foods Public Co., Ltd. (Thailand)

Fish fowl or human Charoen Pokphand Foods Public Company (CPF) feeds them all. The company Thailand's largest food conglomerate makes animal feed; raises pigs ducks and chickens; and sells their meat via its livestock division. The aquaculture unit of the company which includes Seafoods Enterprise and Thai Prawn Culture Center produces and processes shrimp prawns and some finfish. CPF also sells eggs sausage and other value-added food products. The company has some 75 subsidiaries including chicken farms in Turkey; feed production and aquaculture operations in China Laos Malaysia and Russia; and a fast-food restaurant in Shanghai. Parent Charoen Pokphand Group owns about 40% of CPF.

Mergers and Acquisitions

Charoen Pokphand Foods agreed to buy Paulsen Foods a German meat supplier for about $13.6 million. The deal would raise CPF's profile in Europe. Paulsen can import 6100 tons of poultry meat from Thailand into the European Union a quota which CPF can fill with its poultry products.

In 2016 CPF agreed to acquire frozen meal maker Bellisio Foods from current owner Centre Partners. The deal valued at more than $1 billion will enable the Bangkok-based company to expand its international holdings and marks its first acquisition of a US-based company.

EXECUTIVES

Vice Chairman President CEO and Acting COO Food Business, Adirek Sripratak
COO Aquaculture Business, Pong Visedpaitoon, age 73
EVP General Administration Unit, Voravit Janthanakul, age 71
COO Livestock Business, Teerasak Urunanon, age 69
EVP Aquatic Feed Unit, Vitit Pootanasap, age 64
CFO, Paisan Chirakitcharern, age 59
COO Domestic Trading, Virachai Ratanabanchuen
EVP Livestock Farming Unit, Anek Boonnoon
EVP Poultry Breeding and Farming Research and Development Unit, Prajit Udnoon
EVP Swine Breeding and Farming Research and Development Unit, Somkuan Choowatanapakorn
COO Overseas Trading, Pisit Ohmpornnuwat
EVP Information Technology and Application Unit, Praderm Chotsuparach
EVP Livestock Feed Unit, Rewat Hathaisattayapong
EVP Aquatic Farming Unit and Aquatic Breeding and Farming Research and Development Unit, DVM Sujint Thammasart
EVP Poultry Processing Unit, Siripong Arunratana
EVP Pork and Egg Processing Unit, Prapoj Choakpichitchai
EVP Aquatic Food Processing Unit, Songphol Srirongmuang
EVP Ready Meal Unit and Corporate Food Research and Development Unit, Sukhawat Dansermsuk
EVP Food Corporate Quality Assurance Unit, Sommai Tachasirinugune
EVP Domestic Trading Unit, Prasit Boondoungprasert
EVP Five Star and Restaurant Business Unit, Sathit Sangkanarubordee
EVP Marketing Unit, Vittavat Tantivess
EVP Aquatic Product Trading Strategy Unit, Viboon Supakarapongkul
EVP Human Resources Unit, Sumeth Vongbunyong
Chairman, Dhanin Chearavanont, age 80
Vice Chairman, Prasert Poongkumarn
Vice Chairman, Min Tieanworn, age 84
Vice Chairman, Chingchai Lohawatanakul
Auditors: KPMG Phoomchai Audit Ltd.

LOCATIONS

HQ: Charoen Pokphand Foods Public Co., Ltd. (Thailand)
313 C.P. Tower, Silom Road, Silom, Bangrak, Bangkok 10500
Phone: (66) 2 766 8000   **Fax:** (66) 2 638 2139
Web: www.cpfworldwide.com

2015 sales

	% of total
Asia	57
Thailand	33
Europe	8
America	1
Other	1
Total	**100**

PRODUCTS/OPERATIONS

Selected Brands
Livestock feed products
CP
Hi-Gro
Hogtonal
Hyprovite
Anvipro
Star Feed
Novo
Safe Feed
Erawan
Aquatic Animal Feed
Star Feed
Hi-Grade
Blanca
Stargate
Safe Fish
Safe Fo

2015 Sales

	% of total
Livestock business	85
Aquaculture business	15
Total	**100**

Selected Products
Swine feed
Chicken feed
Duck feed
Shrimp feed
Fish feed
Farming Products
Swine
Broilers
Layers
Ducks
Shrimps
Fish

COMPETITORS

COFCO	Nissin Food Products
China Huaren Organic Products	PPB Group
	People's Food Holdings
Indofood	S.K. Foods
NH Foods	Thai Agri Foods
Nisshin Seifun Group	Thai Union

HISTORICAL FINANCIALS
Company Type: Public

Income Statement				FYE: December 31
	REVENUE ($ mil.)	NET INCOME ($ mil.)	NET PROFIT MARGIN	EMPLOYEES
12/19	17,878	619	3.5%	0
12/18	16,752	480	2.9%	0
12/17	15,393	468	3.0%	0
12/16	12,975	410	3.2%	0
12/15	11,694	306	2.6%	0
Annual Growth	**11.2%**	**19.2%**	**—**	**—**

2019 Year-End Financials

Debt ratio: 1.7%
Return on equity: 11.0%
Cash ($ mil.): 1,106
Current ratio: 0.90
Long-term debt ($ mil.): 6,596

No. of shares (mil.): —
Dividends
Yield: —
Payout: —
Market value ($ mil.): —

Chiba Bank, Ltd

Auditors: Ernst & Young ShinNihon LLC

LOCATIONS

HQ: Chiba Bank, Ltd
1-2 Chiba-Minato, Chuo-ku, Chiba 260-8720
Phone: (81) 43 245 1111
Web: www.chibabank.co.jp

HISTORICAL FINANCIALS
Company Type: Public

Income Statement				FYE: March 31
	ASSETS ($ mil.)	NET INCOME ($ mil.)	INCOME AS % OF ASSETS	EMPLOYEES
03/20	143,803	442	0.3%	6,884
03/19	135,123	455	0.3%	6,942
03/18	135,438	506	0.4%	7,090
03/17	126,072	471	0.4%	7,122
03/16	118,737	493	0.4%	7,040
Annual Growth	**4.9%**	**(2.7%)**	**—**	**(0.6%)**

2020 Year-End Financials

Return on assets: 0.3%
Return on equity: 5.0%
Long-term debt ($ mil.): —
No. of shares (mil.): 742
Sales ($ mil): 2,238

Dividends
Yield: —
Payout: 28.1%
Market value ($ mil.): —

China Aviation Oil Singapore Corp Ltd

EXECUTIVES

CEO and Executive Director, Meng Fanqiu, age 51
CFO, Wang Chunyan
COO, Jean Teo
Deputy Chairman and Lead Independent Director, Wang Kai Yuen
Chairman, Lin Wanli
Auditors: Deloitte & Touche LLP

LOCATIONS

HQ: China Aviation Oil Singapore Corp Ltd
8 Temasek Boulevard, #31-02 Suntec Tower Three, 038988
Phone: (65) 6334 8979   **Fax:** (65) 6333 5283
Web: www.caosco.com

2016 Sales

	$ mil.	% of total
People's Republic of China	5,981	51
Singapore	1,780	15
USA	976	8
Hong Kong	934	8
Japan	285	3
Philippines	373	3
The Republic of China	272	2
South Korea	71	1
Other countries	1,028	9
Total	**11,703**	**100**

PRODUCTS/OPERATIONS

2016 Sales

	$ mil.	% of total
Middle distillates	7,754	66
Other oil products	3,949	34
Total	**11,703**	**100**

COMPETITORS

MercFuel
Royal Dutch Shell
World Fuel Services

HISTORICAL FINANCIALS

Company Type: Public

Income Statement				FYE: December 31
	REVENUE ($ mil.)	NET INCOME ($ mil.)	NET PROFIT MARGIN	EMPLOYEES
12/19	20,343	99	0.5%	0
12/18	20,611	93	0.5%	0
12/17	16,267	85	0.5%	0
12/16	11,703	88	0.8%	0
12/15	8,987	61	0.7%	0
Annual Growth	22.7%	13.0%	—	—

2019 Year-End Financials

Debt ratio: —
Return on equity: 12.4%
Cash ($ mil.): 378
Current ratio: 1.45
Long-term debt ($ mil.): —
No. of shares (mil.): 860
Dividends
  Yield: —
  Payout: 40.4%
Market value ($ mil.): —

China Coal Energy Co Ltd

EXECUTIVES

Chairman and Executive Director, Wang An
President, Yang Lieke
CFO, Weng Qing'an
Vice Chairman, Li Yanjiang
Auditors: PricewaterhouseCoopers

LOCATIONS

HQ: China Coal Energy Co Ltd
No. 1, Huangsidajie, Chaoyang District, Beijing 100120
Phone: (86) 10 82236028   **Fax:** (86) 10 82256479
Web: www.chinacoalenergy.com

2014 Sales

	% of total
Domestic markets	99
Asia Pacific markets	1
Total	**100**

PRODUCTS/OPERATIONS

2014 Sales

	% of total
Coal operations	82
Coal mining equipment operations	8
Coal chemicals operations	6
Other operations	4
Total	**100**

Main Business

Coal Production Sales
And Trading
Coal-based Chemicals
Coal Mining Equipment
Manufacturing
Power Generation
Subsidiaries
China Coal Pingshuo Industry Coal Limited Liability Corporation
Shanghai Datun Energy Resources Co. Ltd.
China Coal & Coke Holdings Ltd.
China National Coal Mining Equipment Co. Ltd.
Xi an Engineering Design Co. Ltd. China Coal
China Coal Handan Design Engineering Co.，Ltd.
China National Coal Development Co. Ltd.
China Coal Tendering Co.，Ltd.
China National Coal Industry Qinhuangdao Imp. & Exp. Co. Ltd.
Shanghai ChinaCoal East China Co. Ltd.
China Coal Energy Shandong Co. Ltd.
  China Nati
Huajin Coking Coal Co. Ltd.
Chinacoal Energy(Heilongjiang) Company Limited
Zhongtian Synergetic Energy Company Limited
China Coal Energy Company Limited Xinjiang Branch
Sunfield Resources Co. Ltd.

COMPETITORS

BHP Billiton
Shenhua
U.S. China Mining
  Group
Yanzhou Coal

HISTORICAL FINANCIALS

Company Type: Public

Income Statement				FYE: December 31
	REVENUE ($ mil.)	NET INCOME ($ mil.)	NET PROFIT MARGIN	EMPLOYEES
12/19	18,581	808	4.4%	0
12/18	15,140	499	3.3%	0
12/17	12,466	371	3.0%	0
12/16	8,731	246	2.8%	47,113
12/15	9,126	(503)	—	52,648
Annual Growth	19.5%	—	—	—

2019 Year-End Financials

Debt ratio: 4.9%
Return on equity: 5.9%
Cash ($ mil.): 3,679
Current ratio: 0.66
Long-term debt ($ mil.): 8,073
No. of shares (mil.): —
Dividends
  Yield: —
  Payout: —
Market value ($ mil.): —

China Communications Constructions Group Ltd

EXECUTIVES

Chairman, Yusheng Chen
Auditors: PricewaterhouseCoopers Zhong Tian LLP

LOCATIONS

HQ: China Communications Constructions Group Ltd
85 De Sheng Men Wai Street, Xicheng District, Beijing 100088
Phone: (86) 10 8201 6562   **Fax:** (86) 10 8201 6524
Web: www.ccccltd.cn

HISTORICAL FINANCIALS

Company Type: Public

Income Statement				FYE: December 31
	REVENUE ($ mil.)	NET INCOME ($ mil.)	NET PROFIT MARGIN	EMPLOYEES
12/19	79,731	2,889	3.6%	0
12/18	71,365	2,861	4.0%	0
12/17	74,192	3,162	4.3%	0
12/16	62,174	2,411	3.9%	0
12/15	62,146	2,437	3.9%	115,179
Annual Growth	6.4%	4.4%	—	—

2019 Year-End Financials

Debt ratio: 4.4%
Return on equity: 9.4%
Cash ($ mil.): 18,027
Current ratio: 1.01
Long-term debt ($ mil.): 37,798
No. of shares (mil.): —
Dividends
  Yield: 0.0%
  Payout: 336.2%
Market value ($ mil.): —

	STOCK PRICE ($)	P/E		PER SHARE ($)		
	FY Close	High/Low	Earnings	Dividends	Book Value	
12/19	15.99	18 13	0.17	0.56	(0.00)	
12/18	19.12	20 15	0.17	0.61	(0.00)	
12/17	21.89	26 18	0.19	0.48	(0.00)	
12/16	22.65	25 15	0.14	0.45	(0.00)	
12/15	20.21	41 21	0.15	0.43		
1,401.63						
Annual Growth	(5.7%)	—	—	3.1%	6.6%	

China Construction Bank Corp

Auditors: Ernst & Young

LOCATIONS

HQ: China Construction Bank Corp
No. 25, Financial Street, Xicheng District, Beijing 100033
Phone: (86) 10 6621 5533   **Fax:** (86) 10 6621 8888
Web: www.ccb.com

HISTORICAL FINANCIALS

Company Type: Public

Income Statement				FYE: December 31
	ASSETS ($ mil.)	NET INCOME ($ mil.)	INCOME AS % OF ASSETS	EMPLOYEES
12/19	3,655,564	37,764	1.0%	347,156
12/18	3,376,230	36,450	1.1%	345,971
12/17	3,399,862	37,068	1.1%	352,621
12/16	3,018,937	33,332	1.1%	362,482
12/15	2,825,371	35,128	1.2%	369,183
Annual Growth	6.7%	1.8%	—	(1.5%)

2019 Year-End Financials

Return on assets: 1.0%
Return on equity: 12.5%
Long-term debt ($ mil.): —
No. of shares (mil.): —
Sales ($ mil): 157,300
Dividends
  Yield: 5.1%
  Payout: 490.6%
Market value ($ mil.): —

	STOCK PRICE ($)	P/E	PER SHARE ($)		
	FY Close	High/Low	Earnings	Dividends	Book Value
12/19	17.30	17 14	0.15	0.04	1.27
12/18	16.30	21 15	0.15	0.04	1.15
12/17	18.45	19 16	0.15	0.72	1.09
12/16	15.17	16 11	0.13	0.66	0.91
12/15	13.61	22 14	0.14	0.05	0.88
Annual Growth	6.2%	— —	1.9%	(2.4%)	9.6%

China Eastern Airlines Corp., Ltd.

One of China's three largest airline companies (along with Air China and China Southern Airlines) China Eastern Airlines (CEA) transports passengers and cargo to about 150 destinations in China and foreign cities in more than 20 countries. The carrier operates a fleet of about 250 aircraft including Airbus and Boeing models. CEA's primary hub is in Shanghai; the company also maintains bases in northwestern and southwestern China. CEA Holding a company owned by the Chinese government owns a controlling stake in the airline. In late 2009 the company acquired smaller rival Shanghai Airlines in a deal worth $1.3 billion.

EXECUTIVES

President and Director, Ma Xulun, age 56
VP and CFO, Wu Yongliang, age 57
VP and President Shanghai Airlines, Tian Liuwen
VP Chief Engineer and Chief Security Officer, Feng Liang
Chairman, Liu Shaoyong, age 63
Auditors: Ernst & Young Hua Ming LLP

LOCATIONS

HQ: China Eastern Airlines Corp., Ltd.
  No. 92, Kong Gang San Road, Shanghai 200335
Phone: (86) 21 6268 6268 **Fax:** (86) 21 6268 6116
Web: www.ceair.com

2015 Sales

	% of total
China	65
Hong Kong Macau & Taiwan	4
International	31
Total	100

PRODUCTS/OPERATIONS

2015 Sales

	% of total
Traffic revenues:	
Passenger	83
Cargo & mail	7
Tour operations income	4
Ground service income	3
Cargo handling & processing income	1
Other	2
Total	100

COMPETITORS

ANA Holdings	Delta Air Lines
Aeroflot	Dragonair
Air Canada	Hainan Airlines
Air China	Japan Airlines
Air France-KLM	Korean Air

American Airlines Group	Lufthansa
Asiana Airlines	Qantas
British Airways	Singapore Airlines
Cathay Pacific	Thai Airways
China Airlines	United Continental
China Southern Airlines	

HISTORICAL FINANCIALS
Company Type: Public

Income Statement
FYE: December 31

	REVENUE ($ mil.)	NET INCOME ($ mil.)	NET PROFIT MARGIN	EMPLOYEES
12/19	17,369	459	2.6%	0
12/18	16,709	393	2.4%	0
12/17	15,631	976	6.2%	0
12/16	14,193	649	4.6%	0
12/15	14,468	698	4.8%	710,330
Annual Growth	4.7%	(10.0%)	—	

2019 Year-End Financials

Debt ratio: 2.5%
Return on equity: 5.2%
Cash ($ mil.): 194
Current ratio: 0.25
Long-term debt ($ mil.): 3,823
No. of shares (mil.): —
Dividends
  Yield: —
  Payout: —
Market value ($ mil.): —

	STOCK PRICE ($)	P/E	PER SHARE ($)		
	FY Close	High/Low	Earnings	Dividends	Book Value
12/19	27.37	192 112	0.03	0.00	(0.00)
12/18	27.38	217 136	0.03	0.36	(0.00)
12/17	36.14	82 56	0.07	0.34	(0.00)
12/16	22.35	88 61	0.05	0.33	(0.00)
12/15	28.14	135 61	0.05	0.00	411.73
Annual Growth	(0.7%)	— —	(13.5%)		

China Evergrande Group

EXECUTIVES

VP and Chairman Evergrande Cultural Industry Group, Tao Huang
VP and Director Combating Bureaucracy, Yuzhi Liu
EVP and Chairman EvergrandeFinance Group, Huofa Qin
CFO, Darong Pan
VP and Chairman HengTen NetworksGroup, Xiaohua Zhang
EVP, Weikang Liang
VP and Chairman EvergrandeHotel Management Group, Chuan Wang
EVP, Zhaohui Tan
VP and Director Poverty Alleviation Office, Dong Yao
EVP and Chairman Evergrande Tourism Group, Shawn Siu
Chairman, Ka Yan Hui
Vice Chairman, Haijun Xia
Auditors: PricewaterhouseCoopers

LOCATIONS

HQ: China Evergrande Group
  No. 1126 Haide 3rd Road, Nanshan District, Shenzhen, Guangdong Province 518054
Phone: (852) 2287 9226
Web: www.evergrande.com

COMPETITORS

China Vanke	New World China Land
Citychamp Dartong	Shanghai Forte Land
Gree Group	Xiamen C&D
Guangzhou R&F Properties	Xinyuan
	Yanlord Land

HISTORICAL FINANCIALS
Company Type: Public

Income Statement
FYE: December 31

	REVENUE ($ mil.)	NET INCOME ($ mil.)	NET PROFIT MARGIN	EMPLOYEES
12/19	68,632	2,483	3.6%	133,123
12/18	67,777	5,435	8.0%	131,694
12/17	47,794	3,745	7.8%	125,526
12/16	30,449	733	2.4%	89,250
12/15	20,498	1,610	7.9%	83,372
Annual Growth	35.3%	11.4%	—	12.4%

2019 Year-End Financials

Debt ratio: 5.2%
Return on equity: 12.4%
Cash ($ mil.): 21,565
Current ratio: 1.37
Long-term debt ($ mil.): 61,470
No. of shares (mil.): —
Dividends
  Yield: —
  Payout: 50.0%
Market value ($ mil.): —

China Fortune Land Development Co Ltd

EXECUTIVES

Legal Representative, Wenxue Wang
Auditors: Zhejiang Pan-China Certified Public Accountants Co., Ltd.

LOCATIONS

HQ: China Fortune Land Development Co Ltd
  Zhongtang, Baiguan Town, Shangyu, Zhejiang Province 312300
Phone: (86) 575 2158191 **Fax:** (86) 575 2151888
Web: www.ekingair.com

HISTORICAL FINANCIALS
Company Type: Public

Income Statement
FYE: December 31

	REVENUE ($ mil.)	NET INCOME ($ mil.)	NET PROFIT MARGIN	EMPLOYEES
12/19	15,120	2,099	13.9%	0
12/18	12,183	1,707	14.0%	0
12/17	9,164	1,349	14.7%	0
12/16	7,750	934	12.1%	0
12/15	5,902	739	12.5%	0
Annual Growth	26.5%	29.8%	—	—

2019 Year-End Financials

Debt ratio: 4.5%
Return on equity: 31.1%
Cash ($ mil.): 6,174
Current ratio: 1.58
Long-term debt ($ mil.): 16,851

No. of shares (mil.): —
Dividends
  Yield: —
  Payout: —
Market value ($ mil.): —

China Gezhouba Group Co., Ltd.

EXECUTIVES

Chairman, Yanzhang Ding
Auditors: Daxin Certified Public Accountants

LOCATIONS

HQ: China Gezhouba Group Co., Ltd.
  7/F., Block B, Gezhouba Hotel, No. 558, Jiefang
  Avenue, Wuhan, Hubei Province 430033
Phone: (86) 27 83790455   **Fax:** (86) 27 83790755
Web: www.cggc.cn

HISTORICAL FINANCIALS

Company Type: Public

Income Statement				FYE: December 31
	REVENUE ($ mil.)	NET INCOME ($ mil.)	NET PROFIT MARGIN	EMPLOYEES
12/19	15,800	782	4.9%	0
12/18	14,629	677	4.6%	0
12/17	16,413	719	4.4%	0
12/16	14,437	488	3.4%	0
12/15	12,668	413	3.3%	0
Annual Growth	5.7%	17.3%	—	—

2019 Year-End Financials

Debt ratio: 4.5%
Return on equity: 11.4%
Cash ($ mil.): 3,173
Current ratio: 1.19
Long-term debt ($ mil.): 7,427

No. of shares (mil.): —
Dividends
  Yield: —
  Payout: —
Market value ($ mil.): —

China Grand Automotive Services Co Ltd

Auditors: Zon Zun Certified Public Accountants Office Ltd.

LOCATIONS

HQ: China Grand Automotive Services Co Ltd
  No. 18, Qixianling Jingxian Street, High-Tech Zone,
  Dalian, Liaoning Province 116025
Phone: (86) 411 84820297   **Fax:** (86) 411 84820297
Web: www.merro.com.cn

HISTORICAL FINANCIALS

Company Type: Public

Income Statement				FYE: December 31
	REVENUE ($ mil.)	NET INCOME ($ mil.)	NET PROFIT MARGIN	EMPLOYEES
12/19	24,497	373	1.5%	0
12/18	24,159	473	2.0%	0
12/17	24,696	596	2.4%	0
12/16	19,501	403	2.1%	0
12/15	14,427	306	2.1%	0
Annual Growth	14.2%	5.1%	—	—

2019 Year-End Financials

Debt ratio: 5.4%
Return on equity: 6.9%
Cash ($ mil.): 3,602
Current ratio: 1.08
Long-term debt ($ mil.): 2,038

No. of shares (mil.): —
Dividends
  Yield: —
  Payout: —
Market value ($ mil.): —

China Life Insurance Co Ltd

China Life Insurance Company also known as China Life provides long-term individual and group life insurance policies annuity contracts and long-term health insurance policies in force. It also provides both individual and group accident and short-term health insurance policies and services. It has more than 300 million individual and group policies in force. China Life sells its individual products primarily through its own network comprised of exclusive agents direct sales representatives and dedicated and non-dedicated agencies. In addition to life insurance the company provides asset management services and health and accident insurance. The company is a life insurance company established in Beijing China on 30 June 2003.

Operations

China Life operates in four primary segments: Life Insurance (more than 80% of total revenue) Health Insurance (around 15% of revenue) Accident Insurance and Other (less than 5% combined).

Life Insurance business relates primarily to the sale of life insurance policies including those life insurance policies without significant insurance risk transferred.

The Health Insurance business relates primarily to the sale of health insurance policies including those health insurance policies without significant insurance risk transferred.

Accident Insurance business relates primarily to the sale of accident insurance policies.

China Life also controls China Life Asset Management Company making it one of the largest insurance asset managers in the nation.

Geographic Reach

Based in Beijing China Life has branches in nearly all of China's geographic regions.

Sales and Marketing

China Life has an extension distribution network of exclusive agents direct sales representatives and dedicated and non-dedicated agencies. Sales are also conducted through individual business bank and phone sales channels.

The company kept in close contact with investors by various means such as phone and internet corresponded with them through more than 1700 emails answered more than 350 calls and emails and recorded a click-through rate of 40000 viewers for the internet broadcast of results briefings and open days.

Financial Performance

Except in 2018 China Life's total revenue has been on an upward trend for the last five years while its net income has fluctuated.

The company's total revenue rose 16% from RMB 627.4 billion in 2018 to RMB 729.5 billion in 2019.

Net income skyrocketed from RMB 11.4 billion in 2018 to RMB 58.3 billion in 2019.

China Life's cash at the end of 2019 totaled RMB 53.3 billion. Operating activities provided RMB 286 billion while investing and financing activities used RMB 247.5 billion and RMB 36.1 billion respectively.

Strategy

In 2019 despite the complicated situation of increased risks and challenges at home and abroad China Life concentrated on the strategic goal of "China Life Revitalization" with "Dual Centers and Dual Focuses" as its strategic core adhered to the overall keynote of making steady progress and upheld the operational guideline of "prioritizing business value strengthening sales force achieving stable growth upgrading technology optimizing services and guarding against risks."

The company accelerated the establishment of a development system of "Yi Ti Duo Yuan" with strengthened individual agent channel in coordination with other channels as well as a market-oriented investment management system strengthened technological empowerment focused on the transformation of sales and the development of protection-oriented business reformed its sales models investment and services systems constantly improved the efficiency of risk prevention and control and achieved the coordinated growth of business scale and value.

Company Background

China Life's history goes back to 1949 when its predecessor People's Insurance Company of China (PICC) was established. The unified national insurer was created just 20 days after the founding of new China. In 2003 PICC was dissolved and replaced by four state-owned firms including China Life. The company went public that year listing on the Hong Kong Stock Exchange and the New York Stock Exchange. It listed on the Shanghai Stock Exchange in 2007.

EXECUTIVES

Chairman and Executive Director, Yang Mingsheng, age 64
CFO, Zhao Lijun
Auditors: Ernst & Young Hua Ming LLP

LOCATIONS

HQ: China Life Insurance Co Ltd
  16 Financial Street, Xicheng District, Beijing 100033
Phone: (86) 10 63631191   **Fax:** (86) 10 66575112
Web: www.e-chinalife.com

PRODUCTS/OPERATIONS

2017 Sales by Segment

	% of total
Life Insurance	86
Health Insurance	11
Accident Insurance	2
Other	1
Total	100

COMPETITORS

AEGON	Generali
Aviva	ING
Bank of China	Manulife Financial
CIGNA	MetLife
China Pacific	PICC Property
Insurance	Ping An Insurance

HISTORICAL FINANCIALS

Company Type: Public

Income Statement
FYE: December 31

	ASSETS ($ mil.)	NET INCOME ($ mil.)	INCOME AS % OF ASSETS	EMPLOYEES
12/19	535,586	8,376	1.6%	0
12/18	473,141	1,656	0.4%	102,817
12/17	445,273	4,956	1.1%	102,297
12/16	388,382	2,754	0.7%	99,739
12/15	376,980	5,342	1.4%	98,823
Annual Growth	**9.2%**	**11.9%**	—	—

2019 Year-End Financials

Return on assets: 1.6%
Return on equity: 16.1%
Long-term debt ($ mil.): —
No. of shares (mil.): —
Sales ($ mil) 23,385

Dividends
Yield: 0.6%
Payout: 31.2%
Market value ($ mil.): —

	STOCK PRICE ($) FY Close	P/E High/Low		PER SHARE ($) Earnings	Dividends	Book Value
12/19	13.83	7	5	0.27	0.08	(0.00)
12/18	10.49	41	26	0.06	0.26	(0.00)
12/17	15.61	16	13	0.17	0.14	(0.00)
12/16	12.87	23	15	0.10	0.25	1.55
12/15	15.99	62	12	0.19	0.32	1.76
Annual Growth	**(3.6%)**	—	—	**9.4%**	**(28.4%)**	

China Merchants Shekou Industrial Zone Holdings Co Ltd

EXECUTIVES

Chairman, Shaobin Lin
Auditors: Shinewing Certified Public Accountants (Special General Partnership)

LOCATIONS

HQ: China Merchants Shekou Industrial Zone Holdings Co Ltd
3rd Building, Nanhai E Cool, No. 6, Xinghua Road, Shekou, Nanshan District, Shenzhen, Guangdong Province 518067
Phone: (86) 755 26819600   **Fax:** (86) 755 26818666
Web: www.cmsk1979.com

HISTORICAL FINANCIALS

Company Type: Public

Income Statement
FYE: December 31

	REVENUE ($ mil.)	NET INCOME ($ mil.)	NET PROFIT MARGIN	EMPLOYEES
12/19	14,036	2,304	16.4%	0
12/18	12,834	2,215	17.3%	0
12/17	11,595	1,877	16.2%	0
12/16	9,154	1,379	15.1%	0
12/15	7,579	746	9.9%	19,813
Annual Growth	**16.7%**	**32.5%**	—	—

2019 Year-End Financials

Debt ratio: 3.3%
Return on equity: 18.7%
Cash ($ mil.): 10,825
Current ratio: 1.62
Long-term debt ($ mil.): 12,519

No. of shares (mil.): —
Dividends
Yield: —
Payout: —
Market value ($ mil.): —

China Mobile Limited

China Mobile Limited sees unlimited potential. The company is one of China's largest wireless operator by subscribers which total some 1 billion. China Mobile currently puts in an all-out effort to drive the "5G+" plan forward to pursue and promote 5G+4G coordinated development. In general the company provides mobile telecommunications related services such as data and voice services. In addition to its flagship postpaid GoTone brand the company targets the youth and budget-conscious markets with M-Zone and Easy Own prepaid services. State-controlled China Mobile Communications Corporation (CMCC) indirectly holds a majority stake of less than 75% through intermediary subsidiary China Mobile (Hong Kong) Group Limited. The company was founded in 1997.

Operations

China Mobile provides telecommunications services (such as voice and data services) telecommunication related products (such as handsets) customer point rewards and/or other promotional goods/services.

In terms of the company's sales telecommunications services accounts for more than 90% while sales of products and others account for almost 10%.

China Mobile's Telecommunications service is divided in voice services which accounts for over 12% of total sales and data services which is further divided in: wireless data traffic (more than 50% of total sales); applications and information services (some 10%); wireline broadband (almost 10%); and SMS & MMS.

The company has three popular brands: "GoTone" "M-zone" and "Easy Own". In addition it works further on the integrated development of "network+ cloud+ DICT" for its business line.

The company also accelerated the implementation of "5G+" by formulating well-coordinated development of 5G and 4G. It constructed and began operating more than 50000 5G base stations and launched 5G commercial services in 50 cities.

Geographic Reach

Hong Kong based China Mobile has its presence in approximately 50 cities in China.

Sales and Marketing

The majority of China Mobile operating revenue is from contracts with the customers. In general the company serves individual and corporate customers. Its five largest customers generates less than 30% of total revenue.

Financial Performance

China Mobile recorded operating revenue of RMB745.9 billion for the 2019 financial year up by 1% compared to last year. Of this telecommunications services revenue amounted to RMB674.4 billion or a growth of 1% year-on-year.

Cash held by the company at the end of 2019 increased by RMB 118.6 billion to RMB 175.9 billion compared from the previous year with RMB 57.3 billion. Cash provided by operations was RMB 247.6 billion while cash used for investing and financing activities were RMB 64.2 billion and RMB 64.9 billion respectively. Main uses for cash was payment for property plant and equipment.

Strategy

Coupled with this was the impact of government policies including the continued implementation of the "speed upgrade and tariff reduction". Against this backdrop China Mobile joined together to overcome these hurdles and work towards its ultimate goal of becoming a world-class enterprise by building a dynamic "Powerhouse". This was centered on the key strategy of high-quality development supported by a value-driven operating system that leverages its advantages of scale to drive further convergence integration and digitization across the board. China Mobile structured its organization to enable effective and synergetic capability building and collaborative growth while nurturing internal vitality. In addition the company further implemented its "5G+" plan to spearhead the development of "four growth engines" comprising the "customer" "home" "business" and "new" markets. These measures have helped China Mobile obtain positive momentum in overall operating results which was a hard-earned achievement for it in a tough year.

Company Background

China Mobile Limited was incorporated in Hong Kong on 3 September 1997. The Company was listed on the New York Stock Exchange ("NYSE") and The Stock Exchange of Hong Kong Limited ("HKEX" or the "Stock Exchange") on 22 October 1997 and 23 October 1997 respectively.

EXECUTIVES

CEO, Li Yue, age 60
VP and CFO, Xue Taohai, age 63
VP and Executive Director, Sha Yuejia, age 62
VP and Executive Director, Liu Aili, age 57
Chairman, Shang Bing, age 64
Auditors: PricewaterhouseCoopers Zhong Tian LLP

LOCATIONS

HQ: China Mobile Limited
60/F, The Center, 99 Queens Road Central,
Phone: (852) 3121 8888   **Fax:** (852) 3121 8809
Web: www.chinamobileltd.com

PRODUCTS/OPERATIONS

2015 Sales

	% of total
Telecommunication Services	
Voice Services	56
Data Services	33
Other	5
Other products & services	6
Total	**100**

2015 Sales

	% of total
Revenue from telecommunications services	87
Revenue from sales of products and others	13
Total	**100**

COMPETITORS

China Telecom
  Corporation Limited
China Unicom
City Telecom

Hutchison
  Telecommunications
PCCW Ltd.
Vodafone

HISTORICAL FINANCIALS

Company Type: Public

Income Statement   FYE: December 31

	REVENUE ($ mil.)	NET INCOME ($ mil.)	NET PROFIT MARGIN	EMPLOYEES
12/19	107,199	15,325	14.3%	464,656
12/18	107,122	17,123	16.0%	459,152
12/17	113,795	17,561	15.4%	464,656
12/16	102,018	15,659	15.3%	460,647
12/15	102,907	16,712	16.2%	438,645
Annual Growth	1.0%	(2.1%)	—	1.5%

2019 Year-End Financials

Debt ratio: —
Return on equity: 9.8%
Cash ($ mil.): 25,284
Current ratio: 1.15
Long-term debt ($ mil.): —

No. of shares (mil.): —
Dividends
  Yield: 0.0%
  Payout: 228.1%
Market value ($ mil.): —

	STOCK PRICE ($) FY Close	P/E High/Low		PER SHARE ($) Earnings	Dividends	Book Value
12/19	42.27	10	7	0.74	1.70	7.75
12/18	48.00	9	7	0.84	1.89	7.47
12/17	50.54	11	9	0.86	3.57	7.40
12/16	52.43	11	9	0.76	1.49	6.89
12/15	56.33	14	10	0.82	1.63	6.90
Annual Growth	(6.9%)	—	—	(2.3%)	1.0%	2.9%

China Overseas Land & Investment Ltd

China Overseas Land & Investment (COLI) builds upon its bricks-and-mortar aspirations both in Hong Kong and mainland China. The company specializes in property development and commercial property management operation. Other businesses include construction design and property management. The company targets its investment and development efforts in about 50 major cities including Beijing Guangzhou Hong Kong and Shanghai. Hua Dong Region accounts for its largest geographic market which accounts for more than 25% of total revenue.

Operations

Known as China Overseas Property in mainland China the company operates through three primary segments: Property Development Property Investments and Other Operations (revenue from hotel operation provision of construction and building design consultancy services). The largest segment Property Development accounts for more than 95% of total revenue and the remaining accounts the rest.

Geographic Reach

COLI has a strong presence in the Hua Dong and Hua Bei regions which brought in more than 25% and more than 20% of revenues respectively. To a lesser extent it also operates in the Northern Region Hua Bei Region Western Region Macau and Hong Kong.

Its head office is located in Hong Kong.

Sales and Marketing

The five largest customers of the Group accounted for less than 30% of the Group's revenue while the five largest suppliers of the Group accounted for less than 30% of the Group's total purchases.

Financial Performance

NOTE: Growth rates may differ after conversion to US dollars.

During the year the revenue of the company increased to RMB163.7 billion (2018: RMB144.0 billion) representing an increase of 14% as compared to last year.

Profit attributable to equity shareholders of the company amounted to RMB41.6 billion (2018: RMB37.7 billion) representing an increase of 10%.

Cash held by the company at the end of 2019 increased to RMB 92.9 billion compared to RMB 84.0 billion in the prior year. Cash provided by operations and financing activities were RMB 9.9 billion and RMB 1.5 billion respectively. Cash used for investing activities was RMB 2.6 billion mainly for capital contributions to joint ventures.

Strategy

In 2019 the company maintained its prudent investment strategy targeting the efficient replenishment of high-quality land reserves. Through strategies of "going smart" and industrialization the company strengthened research and development and application of smart communities smart homes and green technologies to rapidly transform it into product advantages for the company and boost customer satisfaction.

Company Background

COLI was incorporated in Hong Kong in 1979.

EXECUTIVES

VP Chief Architect and Director, Luo Liang, age 55
Chairman and CEO, Yan Jianguo, age 53
CFO and Director, Nip Yun Wing, age 65
Auditors: PricewaterhouseCoopers

LOCATIONS

HQ: China Overseas Land & Investment Ltd
  10/F., Three Pacific Place, 1 Queens Road East,
Phone: (852) 2988 0666   **Fax:** (852) 2865 7517
Web: www.coli.com.hk

PRODUCTS/OPERATIONS

2014 Sales

	% of total
Property development	97
Property investment	1
Other operations	2
Total	**100**

Operations
Property development
Property investment
Property-related business
  Construction design
  Property management

COMPETITORS

China Vanke
Chinese Estates
Hang Lung Group
Hongkong Land
Kowloon Development
  Company

New World Development
Orient Overseas
Sun Hung Kai
  Properties

HISTORICAL FINANCIALS

Company Type: Public

Income Statement   FYE: December 31

	REVENUE ($ mil.)	NET INCOME ($ mil.)	NET PROFIT MARGIN	EMPLOYEES
12/19	23,519	5,981	25.4%	6,200
12/18	21,892	5,732	26.2%	5,900
12/17	21,246	5,216	24.6%	5,600
12/16	21,157	4,774	22.6%	5,500
12/15	19,104	4,297	22.5%	5,300
Annual Growth	5.3%	8.6%	—	4.0%

2019 Year-End Financials

Debt ratio: 3.7%
Return on equity: 14.7%
Cash ($ mil.): 13,717
Current ratio: 2.17
Long-term debt ($ mil.): 22,690

No. of shares (mil.): —
Dividends
  Yield: 2.6%
  Payout: 94.0%
Market value ($ mil.): —

	STOCK PRICE ($) FY Close	P/E High/Low		PER SHARE ($) Earnings	Dividends	Book Value
12/19	19.50	5	4	0.55	0.51	3.68
12/18	16.87	29	3	0.52	0.46	3.30
12/17	92.25	31	21	0.48	0.48	3.40
12/16	79.10	30	21	0.47	0.47	2.62
12/15	103.27	35	22	0.47	0.52	2.51
Annual Growth	(34.1%)	—	—	—	4.1%	(0.4%) 10.1%

China Pacific Insurance (Group) Co., Ltd.

Auditors: PricewaterhouseCoopers

LOCATIONS

HQ: China Pacific Insurance (Group) Co., Ltd.
  1 South Zhongshan Road, Huangpu, Shanghai 200010
Phone: (86) 21 58767282   **Fax:** (86) 21 68870791
Web: www.cpic.com.cn

HISTORICAL FINANCIALS

Company Type: Public

Income Statement   FYE: December 31

	REVENUE ($ mil.)	NET INCOME ($ mil.)	NET PROFIT MARGIN	EMPLOYEES
12/19	54,997	3,986	7.2%	111,247
12/18	51,335	2,619	5.1%	107,741
12/17	49,083	2,253	4.6%	101,887
12/16	38,317	1,736	4.5%	0
12/15	29,159	2,729	9.4%	0
Annual Growth	17.2%	9.9%	—	—

2019 Year-End Financials

Debt ratio: —
Return on equity: 16.9%
Cash ($ mil.): 2,137
Current ratio: —
Long-term debt ($ mil.): —

No. of shares (mil.): —
Dividends
  Yield: —
  Payout: 32.6%
Market value ($ mil.): —

China Petroleum & Chemical Corp

China Petroleum and Chemical Corporation (Sinopec Corp.) is China's largest producer and supplier of refined oil products and its second-largest crude oil producer. It is also China's largest petrochemicals producer and distributor and the world's fourth-largest ethylene producer. Operations include oil and gas exploration and production; crude oil processing; oil products trading transportation distribution and marketing; and petrochemicals manufacturing. In 2010 it reported proved reserves of 2.9 billion barrels of oil and 6.5 trillion cu. ft. of natural gas; it also owns more than 29600 gas stations and 34 refineries. China's government controls about 76% of the company through Sinopec Group.

EXECUTIVES

Vice Chairman and President, Dai Houliang, age 57, $105,482 total compensation
Chairman, Wang Yupu
Auditors: PricewaterhouseCoopers Zhong Tian LLP

LOCATIONS

HQ: China Petroleum & Chemical Corp
No. 22 Chaoyangmen North Street, Chaoyang District, Beijing 100728
Phone: (86) 10 5996 0028   **Fax:** (86) 10 5996 0386
Web: www.sinopec.com

2015 Sales

	% of total
Mainland China	78
Others	22
Total	**100**

PRODUCTS/OPERATIONS

2015 Sales

	% of total
Marketing and distribution	34
Refining	28
Chemicals	10
Exploration and production	4
Corporate and others	24
Total	**100**

COMPETITORS

BASF SE	Chevron
BP	Exxon Mobil
Bangchak Petroleum	Furmanite
Public	PetroChina
CNOOC	Royal Dutch Shell
CPC	TOTAL

HISTORICAL FINANCIALS

Company Type: Public

Income Statement				FYE: December 31
	REVENUE ($ mil.)	NET INCOME ($ mil.)	NET PROFIT MARGIN	EMPLOYEES
12/19	426,285	8,276	1.9%	402,206
12/18	420,333	9,172	2.2%	423,543
12/17	362,691	7,855	2.2%	446,225
12/16	278,066	6,721	2.4%	451,611
12/15	310,858	4,994	1.6%	351,019
Annual Growth	**8.2%**	**13.5%**	**—**	**3.5%**

2019 Year-End Financials

Debt ratio: 0.7%	No. of shares (mil.): —
Return on equity: 7.9%	Dividends
Cash ($ mil.): 18,384	Yield: 8.2%
Current ratio: 0.77	Payout: 7,305.2%
Long-term debt ($ mil.): 8,447	Market value ($ mil.): —

	STOCK PRICE ($) FY Close	P/E High/Low	PER SHARE ($) Earnings	Dividends	Book Value
12/19	60.15	176117	0.07	4.99	0.88
12/18	70.60	196134	0.08	7.72	0.86
12/17	73.37	212168	0.06	3.66	0.92
12/16	71.02	194123	0.06	1.78	0.85
12/15	59.98	341205	0.04	2.85	0.86
Annual Growth	**0.1%**	**— —**	**13.3%**	**15.0%**	**0.6%**

China Railway Construction Corp Ltd

Auditors: Ernst & Young Hua Ming LLP

LOCATIONS

HQ: China Railway Construction Corp Ltd
East, No. 40 Fuxing Road, Haidian District, Beijing 100855
Phone: (86) 10 5268 8600   **Fax:** (86) 10 5268 8302
Web: www.crcc.cn

HISTORICAL FINANCIALS

Company Type: Public

Income Statement				FYE: December 31
	REVENUE ($ mil.)	NET INCOME ($ mil.)	NET PROFIT MARGIN	EMPLOYEES
12/19	119,348	2,902	2.4%	0
12/18	106,148	2,607	2.5%	0
12/17	104,646	2,467	2.4%	0
12/16	90,628	2,016	2.2%	0
12/15	92,468	1,947	2.1%	254,366
Annual Growth	**6.6%**	**10.5%**	**—**	**—**

2019 Year-End Financials

Debt ratio: 2.0%	No. of shares (mil.): —
Return on equity: 10.6%	Dividends
Cash ($ mil.): 22,547	Yield: 0.0%
Current ratio: 1.10	Payout: 125.8%
Long-term debt ($ mil.): 16,394	Market value ($ mil.): —

	STOCK PRICE ($) FY Close	P/E High/Low	PER SHARE ($) Earnings	Dividends	Book Value
12/19	10.93	10 7	0.19	0.24	(0.00)
12/18	13.54	11 7	0.18	0.22	(0.00)
12/17	11.56	14 10	0.17	0.19	(0.00)
12/16	13.01	14 8	0.15	0.17	(0.00)
12/15	12.31	21 10	0.15	0.18	1.27
Annual Growth	**(2.9%)**	**— —**	**6.1%**	**7.6%**	**—**

China Railway Group Ltd

China Railway Group keeps its infrastructure construction projects on the right track. A subsidiary of state-owned China Railway Engineering Corporation the company designs and constructs railways roads bridges tunnels subways and other structures. It also offers related consulting and engineering services as well as property development and construction services for commercial and residential buildings and other projects. In addition to its core transportation-related projects the company pursues projects from municipal and energy entities in China and abroad. Some of those projects have included hydroelectricity facilities ports and docks.

Operations

China Railway Group operates through five main segments. Its Infrastructure Construction segment generated 82% of its total sales in 2014 and works on railways highways bridges railways irrigation works dams docks airports and municipal works among other projects. Its Property Development segment (5% of revenue) is its next largest and sells or manages residential and commercial properties. The other segments include Survey Design and Consulting Services (2%); Engineering Equipment and Component Manufacturing (2%); and other (9%).

Geographic Reach

Beyond China the group has worked on construction projects in the Americas Europe Africa and the Asia Pacific. Still the group generated 96% of its total revenue from China in 2014.

Sales and Marketing

China Railway Group's largest customer is the China Railway Corporation which accounted for 32% of its total revenue in 2014. Its four next largest customers combined made up another 2.5% of its total revenue.

Financial Performance

Note: Growth rates may differ after conversion to US dollars. This analysis uses financials from the company's annual report.

China Railway Group's annual revenues and profits have grown more than 30% since 2011 thanks mostly to increased demand for infrastructure construction in China with the growing economy.

The group's revenue climbed 9% to RMB$590.2 billion ($95.9 billion) during 2014 mostly driven by double-digit growth in its infrastructure construction business with more demand for railways highways building construction and urban rail work. The group's Survey Design and Consulting Services business grew 12% due to a rise in infrastructure project activity while its manufacturing and property development businesses each grew by 6% during the year.

Strong revenue growth in 2014 drove China Railway Group's net income higher by 9% to RMB$10.26 billion ($1.67 billion). The group's operating cash levels more than doubled to RMB$19.4 billion ($3.16 billion) in FY2014 mostly as it was able to collect more of its trade receivables with stronger management initiatives.

Strategy

Buoyed by an influx of infrastructure funds from the Chinese government's "One Belt and One Road" policy the group in 2015 planned to build a new China brand for high speed rail and expand its construction projects globally (through its "Go Global" campaign) in new infrastructure markets such as Russia and Israel. The group also planned to invest more in Research Development and Technological Achievements creating some 957 new research projects during 2014 with support from national funds amounting to nearly RMB$29 million.

Despite a strategy to expand internationally most of China Railway Group' work still originates in China. Recent projects include new light rail systems and highways in some of China's larger cities. Ultimately a state-owned company China Railway Group receives much of its funding for projects from the Chinese government which has been pushing to expand the country's public transportation infrastructure.

Company Background

China Railway Group traces its roots back to the 1950s. It has completed hundreds of infrastructure projects in more than 50 countries since the 1970s.

EXECUTIVES

President and Director, Zhang Zongyan
Chairman and Executive Director, Shi Dahua
Auditors: Deloitte Touche Tohmatsu CPA LLP

LOCATIONS

HQ: China Railway Group Ltd.
918, Block 1, No. 128 South 4th Ring Road West, Fengtai District, Beijing 100070
Phone:
Web: www.crec.cn

PRODUCTS/OPERATIONS

2015 Sales

	% of total
Infrastructure Construction	85
Property Development	5
Survey Design and Consulting Services	2
Engineering Equipment and Component Manufacturing	2
Other Businesses	6
Total	**100**

COMPETITORS

Bechtel	CSCEC
Beijing Urban Construction	Hyundai Engineering and Construction
Bouygues	Shimizu
CCCC	Zhejiang Expressway

HISTORICAL FINANCIALS

Company Type: Public

Income Statement				FYE: December 31
	REVENUE ($ mil.)	NET INCOME ($ mil.)	NET PROFIT MARGIN	EMPLOYEES
12/19	122,284	3,402	2.8%	0
12/18	107,648	2,500	2.3%	0
12/17	106,549	2,469	2.3%	0
12/16	92,648	1,801	1.9%	0
12/15	92,376	1,797	1.9%	291,149
Annual Growth	**7.3%**	**17.3%**	—	—

2019 Year-End Financials

Debt ratio: 3.0%	No. of shares (mil.): —
Return on equity: 11.4%	Dividends
Cash ($ mil.): 22,729	Yield: —
Current ratio: 1.05	Payout: —
Long-term debt ($ mil.): 16,291	Market value ($ mil.): —

China Resources Land Ltd

China Resources Land does more than dabble in property development investment and management. The company which is part of China Resources (Holdings) Company primarily develops properties in urban areas of China such as Beijing Shanghai Shenzhen and Chengdu. It specializes in mid-range and upscale residential and commercial properties. China Resources Land also also offers property management services. Other divisions are involved in interior design and furniture manufacturing. The company owns major properties in the country including the Beijing China Resources Building China Resources Times Square and Shenzhen City Crossing.

Operations

The company operates in four segments: sale of developed properties property investments and management hotel operations and construction and decoration services.

Geographic Reach

In 2013 China Resources Land's geographic reach expanded to 42 cities with over 70 projects under development.

EXECUTIVES

Executive Director SVP and CFO, Yu Jian, age 48
Executive Director and Vice Chairman, Tang Yong, age 48
Auditors: Ernst & Young

LOCATIONS

HQ: China Resources Land Ltd
46th Floor, China Resources Building, 26 Harbour Road, Wanchai,
Phone: (852) 2877 2330   **Fax:** (852) 2877 9068
Web: www.crland.com.hk

PRODUCTS/OPERATIONS

2015 sales

	% of total
Sales of developed properties	90
Property investment & management	6
Hotel operations	1
Construction decoration services & others	3
Total	**100**

COMPETITORS

China Vanke	Hopson Development
Guangzhou R&F Properties	New World China Land
	Shanghai Forte Land

HISTORICAL FINANCIALS

Company Type: Public

Income Statement				FYE: December 31
	REVENUE ($ mil.)	NET INCOME ($ mil.)	NET PROFIT MARGIN	EMPLOYEES
12/19	21,231	4,120	19.4%	51,976
12/18	17,619	3,523	20.0%	46,518
12/17	15,173	2,945	19.4%	38,087
12/16	14,098	2,514	17.8%	33,524
12/15	13,339	2,261	17.0%	31,481
Annual Growth	**12.3%**	**16.2%**	—	**13.4%**

2019 Year-End Financials

Debt ratio: 2.5%	No. of shares (mil.): —
Return on equity: 17.5%	Dividends
Cash ($ mil.): 9,154	Yield: 0.0%
Current ratio: 1.33	Payout: —
Long-term debt ($ mil.): 16,268	Market value ($ mil.): —

	STOCK PRICE ($) FY Close	P/E High/Low		PER SHARE ($) Earnings	Dividends	Book Value
12/19	48.40	12	9	0.59	1.54	3.70
12/18	37.51	11	8	0.51	1.13	3.01
12/17	29.69	10	7	0.42	0.84	2.64
12/16	21.98	11	8	0.36	0.58	2.17
12/15	28.77	13	9	0.33	0.58	2.14
Annual Growth	**13.9%**	—	—	**15.4%**	**27.7%**	**14.7%**

China Resources Pharmaceutical Group Ltd

Auditors: Ernst & Young

LOCATIONS

HQ: China Resources Pharmaceutical Group Ltd
Room 4104-05, 41/F, China Resources Building, 26 Harbour Road, Wanchai,
Phone:
Web: www.crpharm.com

HISTORICAL FINANCIALS

Company Type: Public

Income Statement				FYE: December 31
	REVENUE ($ mil.)	NET INCOME ($ mil.)	NET PROFIT MARGIN	EMPLOYEES
12/19	26,256	422	1.6%	67,000
12/18	24,219	515	2.1%	62,000
12/17	22,076	445	2.0%	56,000
Annual Growth	**9.1%**	**(2.7%)**	—	**9.4%**

2019 Year-End Financials

Debt ratio: 2.6%	No. of shares (mil.): —
Return on equity: 8.2%	Dividends
Cash ($ mil.): 1,608	Yield: —
Current ratio: 1.25	Payout: 21.1%
Long-term debt ($ mil.): 1,187	Market value ($ mil.): —

	STOCK PRICE ($) FY Close	P/E High/Low		PER SHARE ($) Earnings	Dividends	Book Value
12/19	0.00	—	—	0.07	0.01	0.83
12/18	0.00	—	—	0.08	0.02	0.80
Annual Growth	—	—	—	**(9.6%)**	**(7.7%)**	**2.0%**

China Shenhua Energy Co., Ltd.

EXECUTIVES

CFO, Zhang Kehui, age 54
Executive Director and President, Han Jianguo
Chairman, Zhang Yuzhuo, age 58
Vice chairman and Executive director, Ling Wen, age 57
Auditors: Deloitte Touche Tohmatsu Certified Public Accountants LLP

LOCATIONS

HQ: China Shenhua Energy Co., Ltd.
  22 Andingmen Xibinhe Road, Dongcheng District, Beijing 100011
Phone: (86) 10 5813 3399   **Fax:** (86) 10 5813 1804
Web: www.csec.com

2008 Sales

	% of total
China	91
Other countries	9
Total	**100**

COMPETITORS

China Yangtze Power	Yankuang
Peabody Energy	Yanzhou Coal
Rio Tinto Limited	
U.S. China Mining Group	

HISTORICAL FINANCIALS

Company Type: Public

Income Statement

	REVENUE ($ mil.)	NET INCOME ($ mil.)	NET PROFIT MARGIN	EMPLOYEES
				FYE: December 31
12/19	34,760	6,215	17.9%	0
12/18	38,396	6,377	16.6%	0
12/17	38,224	6,920	18.1%	0
12/16	26,371	3,270	12.4%	0
12/15	27,264	2,717	10.0%	95,498
Annual Growth	**6.3%**	**23.0%**	—	—

2019 Year-End Financials

Debt ratio: 1.0%
Return on equity: 12.7%
Cash ($ mil.): 7,398
Current ratio: 1.68
Long-term debt ($ mil.): 5,806

No. of shares (mil.): —
Dividends
  Yield: 5.0%
  Payout: 133.8%
Market value ($ mil.): —

	STOCK PRICE ($) FY Close	P/E High/Low		PER SHARE ($) Earnings	Dividends	Book Value
12/19	8.33	5	3	0.31	0.42	(0.00)
12/18	8.64	5	4	0.32	0.47	(0.00)
12/17	10.38	5	4	0.35	1.64	(0.00)
12/16	7.39	8	4	0.16	0.14	(0.00)
12/15	6.23	13	6	0.14	0.87	
	2,266.63					
Annual Growth	**7.5%**			—	— 23.0%	(16.4%) —

China Southern Airlines Co Ltd

One of China's top three airline companies along with China Eastern Airlines and Air China China Southern Airlines operates a fleet of about 860 passenger and cargo transport aircraft including Boeing models 787777 757& 737 and Airbus models A380 330 321 320 319 from its hub in Guangzhou and about 15 branches regional bases. China Southern Airlines has about 3000 daily flights to around 245 destinations in nearly 45 countries and regions across the world primarily in the Asia/Pacific region. The company generates most of its sales domestically.

Operations

China Southern Airlines' scope of business includes: provision of services of domestic regional and international scheduled and unscheduled air transportation of passenger cargo mail and baggage; provision of services of general aviation; provision of services of aircraft maintenance; acting as an agency of domestic and foreign airlines; offering airlines catering services (operated by branch office only); and conducting other aviation and relevant businesses among others.

The company generates vast majority of sales from traffic activities. The remaining is from other operating activities including commission general aviation and hotel and tour operations.

Geographic Reach

China Southern Airlines headquarters is located in Guangzhou. It has about 15 branches in Beijing Shenzhen and other cities and around 10 holding aviation subsidiaries including Xiamen Airlines. The company has set up SAGA in Zhuhai and has set up nearly 25 domestic offices in Hangzhou Qingdao and other places and approximately 55 overseas offices in Sydney New York and other places. It generates more than 70% of total sales from domestic operations over 25% from international and less than five percent from Hong Kong Macau & Taiwan.

Sales and Marketing

To expand its global reach China Southern Airlines has joined the SkyTeam marketing and code-sharing alliance which along with Delta and KLM includes such carriers as Air France and Korean Air Lines. (Code-sharing allows airlines to sell tickets on one another's flights and thus offer potential passengers more destinations.)

The company has almost 3235 major customers which account for about 15% of the company's total revenue.

Financial Performance

China Southern Airlines' revenue has been climbing for the last five years with an overall growth of 38% or RMB 42.7 billion between 2015 and 2019.

The company's revenue for 2019 was RMB 154.3 billion a 7% growth from the previous year. The company's domestic and international business were the primary contributors to this growth.

Profit for 2019 totaled RMB 3.1 billion an 8% decline from the previous year. The higher sales for the year was offset by an even higher operating expense.

The company's cash at the end of 2019 was RMB 1.8 billion a 73% decline from the previous year. Operating activities generated RMB 31.2 billion while investing activities used RMB 14.4 billion mainly for capital expenditures. Financing activities used another RMB 21.8 billion primarily for repayment of bank borrowings.

Strategy

During 2019 the company's strategy which was unchanged from 2018 was to maintain a debt ratio at a range of levels to support the operations and development of its business in the long run. In order to maintain or adjust the debt ratio the company may adjust the amount of dividends paid to shareholders issue new shares return capital to shareholders raise new debt financing or sell assets to reduce debt.

Mergers and Acquisitions

In late 2019 China Southern Airlines acquired 100% equity interests in Pearl Aviation Services at a consideration of RMB 9 million. Pearl Aviation Services is headquartered in Australia. The acquisition enables the company to engage in hotel management services business.

In early 2019 China Southern Airlines acquired about 20% equity interest in Shenyang Aircraft Maintenance a former joint venture of the company at a cash consideration of RMB 14 million. The acquisition of Shenyang Aircraft Maintenance enables the company to engage in comprehensive maintenance service.

EXECUTIVES

EVP, Liu Qian, age 55
Vice Chairman and President, Tan Wan Geng, age 57, $74,091 total compensation
EVP and Director, Zhang Zi Fang, age 63
EVP and Senior Engineer, Ren Ji Dong, age 56
CFO, Xiao Li Xin, age 53
EVP and Chief Pilot and Chairman Zhuhai Airlines Company Limited, Wang Zhi Xue
COO Marketing and Sales, Guo Zhi Qiang, age 56
COO Flight Safety, Feng Hua Nan, age 57
Chairman, Wang Changshun, age 60
Auditors: PricewaterhouseCoopers Zhong Tian LLP

LOCATIONS

HQ: China Southern Airlines Co Ltd
  278 Ji Chang Road, Guangzhou, Guangdong Province 510405
Phone: (86) 20 8612 4462   **Fax:** (86) 20 8665 9040
Web: www.csair.com

2014 Sales

	% of total
Domestic	77
International	21
Hong Kong Macau & Taiwan	2
Total	**100**

PRODUCTS/OPERATIONS

2014 Sales

	% of total
Traffic revenue	96
Other	4
Total	**100**

Selected Services

Excess baggage
Carry-on baggage
Delayed/damaged/lost baggage
Checked Baggage
Restrictions on baggage transportation
Special baggage

COMPETITORS

ANA Holdings	Guangshen Railway
Air China	Hainan Airlines
Air India	Korean Air
Air Philippines	Lufthansa
American Airlines Group	Lung Cheong
Cathay Pacific	Malaysian Airlines
China Airlines	Qantas
China Eastern Airlines	Singapore Airlines
	Swire Pacific

Dragonair   Thai Airways
EVA Air   United Continental

HISTORICAL FINANCIALS
Company Type: Public

Income Statement   FYE: December 31

	REVENUE ($ mil.)	NET INCOME ($ mil.)	NET PROFIT MARGIN	EMPLOYEES
12/19	22,178	380	1.7%	0
12/18	20,880	433	2.1%	0
12/17	19,591	908	4.6%	0
12/16	16,530	727	4.4%	0
12/15	17,191	575	3.3%	87,202
Annual Growth	6.6%	(9.8%)	—	—

2019 Year-End Financials
Debt ratio: 2.2%   No. of shares (mil.): —
Return on equity: 4.1%   Dividends
Cash ($ mil.): 286   Yield: 0.9%
Current ratio: 0.18   Payout: 962.2%
Long-term debt ($ mil.): 1,959   Market value ($ mil.): —

	STOCK PRICE ($) FY Close	P/E High/Low		PER SHARE ($) Earnings	Dividends	Book Value
12/19	33.60	226	128	0.03	0.31	(0.00)
12/18	30.36	231	93	0.04	0.68	(0.00)
12/17	51.82	91	47	0.09	0.67	(0.00)
12/16	25.71	70	47	0.07	0.50	(0.00)
12/15	38.15	159	57	0.06	0.27	0.61
Annual Growth	(3.1%)	—	—	(14.3%)	3.0%	

China Taiping Insurance Holding Co., Ltd.

EXECUTIVES
Chairman, Fan Lin
Auditors: PricewaterhouseCoopers

LOCATIONS
HQ: China Taiping Insurance Holding Co., Ltd.
25/F., 18 King Wah Road, North Point,
Phone: (852) 2854 6100   **Fax:** (852) 2544 5269
Web: www.ctih.cntaiping.com

HISTORICAL FINANCIALS
Company Type: Public

Income Statement   FYE: December 31

	ASSETS ($ mil.)	NET INCOME ($ mil.)	INCOME AS % OF ASSETS	EMPLOYEES
12/19	118,074	1,156	1.0%	65,957
12/18	96,028	878	0.9%	75,341
12/17	85,279	785	0.9%	77,472
12/16	65,175	615	0.9%	60,270
12/15	62,964	818	1.3%	53,682
Annual Growth	17.0%	9.0%	—	5.3%

2019 Year-End Financials
Return on assets: 1.0%   Dividends
Return on equity: 12.6%   Yield: —
Long-term debt ($ mil.): —   Payout: 12.2%
No. of shares (mil.): —   Market value ($ mil.): —
Sales ($ mil): 31,628

China Telecom Corp Ltd

LOCATIONS
HQ: China Telecom Corp Ltd
31 Jinrong Street, Xicheng District, Beijing 100033
Phone: (86) 10 6642 8166   **Fax:** (86) 10 6601 0728
Web: www.chinatelecom-h.com

HISTORICAL FINANCIALS
Company Type: Public

Income Statement   FYE: December 31

	REVENUE ($ mil.)	NET INCOME ($ mil.)	NET PROFIT MARGIN	EMPLOYEES
12/19	53,998	2,948	5.5%	281,215
12/18	54,828	3,083	5.6%	280,747
12/17	56,278	2,860	5.1%	284,206
12/16	50,731	2,592	5.1%	287,076
12/15	50,996	3,087	6.1%	291,526
Annual Growth	1.4%	(1.1%)	—	(0.9%)

2019 Year-End Financials
Debt ratio: 2.4%   No. of shares (mil.): —
Return on equity: 5.9%   Dividends
Cash ($ mil.): 2,987   Yield: 0.0%
Current ratio: 0.28   Payout: —
Long-term debt ($ mil.): 9,000   Market value ($ mil.): —

	STOCK PRICE ($) FY Close	P/E High/Low		PER SHARE ($) Earnings	Dividends	Book Value
12/19	41.19	220	152	0.04	1.43	0.63
12/18	50.73	210	146	0.04	1.23	0.62
12/17	47.47	236	206	0.04	1.28	0.62
12/16	46.13	236	185	0.03	1.05	0.56
12/15	46.45	299	174	0.04	1.05	0.58
Annual Growth	(3.0%)	—	—	(1.7%)	7.9%	2.0%

China Unicom (Hong Kong) Ltd

EXECUTIVES
Chairman and CEO, Chang Xiaobing, age 63
Executive Director and President, Lu Yimin, age 56
Executive Director and CFO, Li Fushen, age 57
Auditors: KPMG Huazhen LLP

LOCATIONS
HQ: China Unicom (Hong Kong) Ltd
75th Floor, The Center, 99 Queen's Road Central,
Phone: (852) 2121 3220   **Fax:** (852) 2121 3232
Web: www.chinaunicom.com.hk

PRODUCTS/OPERATIONS

2013 Sales	% of total
Mobile	51
Fixed-line	30
Telecommunication products	19
Total	100

COMPETITORS
Beijing Mobile	China Tietong
China Mobile	Hunan Telecom
China Mobile Communications	Pacnet
China Telecom Corporation Limited	Shanghai Mobile

HISTORICAL FINANCIALS
Company Type: Public

Income Statement   FYE: December 31

	REVENUE ($ mil.)	NET INCOME ($ mil.)	NET PROFIT MARGIN	EMPLOYEES
12/19	41,751	1,628	3.9%	256,385
12/18	42,289	1,482	3.5%	260,964
12/17	42,233	280	0.7%	267,590
12/16	39,486	90	0.2%	270,484
12/15	42,658	1,626	3.8%	268,887
Annual Growth	(0.5%)	0.0%	—	(1.2%)

2019 Year-End Financials
Debt ratio: 0.6%   No. of shares (mil.): —
Return on equity: 3.5%   Dividends
Cash ($ mil.): 5,022   Yield: 1.9%
Current ratio: 0.41   Payout: 332.7%
Long-term debt ($ mil.): 986   Market value ($ mil.): —

	STOCK PRICE ($) FY Close	P/E High/Low		PER SHARE ($) Earnings	Dividends	Book Value
12/19	9.36	35	23	0.05	0.18	1.50
12/18	10.66	42	32	0.05	0.07	1.49
12/17	13.53	240	170	0.01	0.01	1.53
12/16	11.55	416	319	0.00	0.22	1.37
12/15	12.06	43	26	0.07	0.29	1.49
Annual Growth	(6.1%)	—	—	(5.9%)	(11.7%)	0.3%

China United Network Communications Ltd

Auditors: PricewaterhouseCoopers Zhongtian Certified Public Accountants Co., Ltd.

LOCATIONS
HQ: China United Network Communications Ltd
29th Floor, No. 1033, Changning Road, Changning District, Shanghai 200050
Phone: (86) 21 52732228   **Fax:** (86) 21 52732220
Web: www.chinaunicom-a.com

HISTORICAL FINANCIALS

Company Type: Public

Income Statement
FYE: December 31

	REVENUE ($ mil.)	NET INCOME ($ mil.)	NET PROFIT MARGIN	EMPLOYEES
12/19	41,751	716	1.7%	0
12/18	42,289	593	1.4%	0
12/17	42,233	65	0.2%	0
12/16	39,486	22	0.1%	0
12/15	42,658	534	1.3%	0
Annual Growth	(0.5%)	7.6%	—	—

2019 Year-End Financials

Debt ratio: 0.6%	No. of shares (mil.): —
Return on equity: 3.5%	Dividends
Cash ($ mil.): 5,556	Yield: —
Current ratio: 0.40	Payout: —
Long-term debt ($ mil.): 986	Market value ($ mil.): —

China Vanke Co Ltd

EXECUTIVES

Deputy Chairman, Lin Song, age 58
Chairman, Shi Wang, age 69
Auditors: KPMG Huazhen Certified Public Accountants

LOCATIONS

HQ: China Vanke Co Ltd
Vanke Center, No. 33, Huanmei Road, Dameisha, Yantian District, Shenzhen, Guangdong Province 518083
Phone: (86) 755 25606666   **Fax:** (86) 755 25531696
Web: www.vanke.com

PRODUCTS/OPERATIONS

2015 Sales

	% of total
Property development	97
Property service	2
Other	1
Total	**100**

COMPETITORS

CapitaLand	New World China Land
China Overseas Land & Investment	New World Development
China Resources Land	SRE Group
Chinese Estates	Shanghai Forte Land
Evergrande Real Estate Group	Singapore Land
	Xinyuan
	Yanlord Land

HISTORICAL FINANCIALS

Company Type: Public

Income Statement
FYE: December 31

	REVENUE ($ mil.)	NET INCOME ($ mil.)	NET PROFIT MARGIN	EMPLOYEES
12/19	52,871	5,586	10.6%	0
12/18	43,278	4,910	11.3%	0
12/17	37,326	4,310	11.5%	0
12/16	34,630	3,027	8.7%	0
12/15	30,109	2,789	9.3%	0
Annual Growth	15.1%	19.0%	—	—

2019 Year-End Financials

Debt ratio: 2.1%	No. of shares (mil.): —
Return on equity: 22.6%	Dividends
Cash ($ mil.): 23,884	Yield: —
Current ratio: 1.13	Payout: —
Long-term debt ($ mil.): 23,564	Market value ($ mil.): —

Chubb Ltd

Chubb Limited sells property/casualty insurance life insurance and reinsurance through subsidiaries around the globe. The world's largest publicly traded property/casualty insurer Chubb primarily provides those lines of insurance to commercial and personal customers in some 55 nations and territories. Policies offered include general liability homeowners auto accident workers' compensation and specialty crop and marine coverage. It also offers services such as risk management loss control and complex claims management programs. The company's Chubb Tempest Re businesses provide reinsurance to property/casualty insurers in North America and Europe. Chubb holds total assets of around $170 billion.

Operations

Chubb operates through six primary business segments: North America Commercial P&C Insurance Overseas General Insurance North America Personal P&C (property and casualty) Insurance Life Insurance North America Agricultural Insurance and Global Reinsurance.

The largest segments are North America Commercial P&C Insurance (more than 40% of net premiums earned) and Overseas General Insurance (some 30% of net premiums earned).

North America Commercial P&C Insurance serves large institutional customers corporations and small and mid-sized companies in the US Canada and Bermuda. It also includes the group's Westchester and Chubb Bermuda wholesale and specialty units.

Overseas General Insurance is composed of Chubb International and Chubb Global Markets the group's international specialty and excess and surplus business. Chubb International operates in Europe the Asia/Pacific region Eurasia and Africa and Latin America. It offers property/casualty accident and health specialty and personal lines products. Chubb Global Markets offers specialty insurance and includes Chubb's Lloyd's of London Syndicate 2488.

North America Personal P&C Insurance (15% of net premiums) provides affluent and high-net-worth consumers in the US and Canada with property liability travel and recreational marine coverage.

The Life Insurance segment (5% of net premiums) operates through Chubb Life Chubb Tempest Life re and other units. It offers individual life and group benefit insurance primarily in developing markets.

North America Agricultural Insurance also active in the US and Canada provides crop multi-peril crop crop-hail farm and ranch and specialty commercial insurance products. It accounts for about 5% of net premiums.

Global Reinsurance is the group's smallest segment bringing in some 2% of net earned premiums. It includes Chubb Tempest Re Bermuda Chubb Tempest Re USA Chubb Tempest Re International and Chubb Tempest Re Canada.

Geographic Reach

Chubb has offices around the world including North America (Philadelphia Pennsylvania Delaware New Jersey and Connecticut) Europe (including it headquarters in Switzerland) Bermuda Latin America Asia/Pacific and the Far East. It generates around 60% of net premiums from North America. Chubb Global Markets operates out of Lloyd's of London the world-renowned specialty insurance market.

The geographic spread of Chubb's business mitigates the impact of weakness in a single or group of markets. Markets elsewhere would most likely be up.

Sales and Marketing

Chubb's customers range from individuals (including wealthy individuals) and small businesses to multi-national corporations and other insurance companies. Most of the company's business is conducted through company agents or third-party insurance brokers or agents.

Chubb employs 4000 agents on its Chubb Marketplace quoting platform that quote issue and service clients.

Chubb has counted most of the Fortune 1000 as clients for many years.

Financial Performance

Chubb's revenue has been growing in the low single-digits in the years following the 2015 merger with ACE that added $11 billion to its top line. Similarly Chubb has been struggling to sustain meaningful growth in its bottom line.

In fiscal 2018 the company's sales grew 3% to $27.8 billion led by higher net premiums in the North America Commercial P&C Insurance segment a result of rate increases new business written and strong renewals. The Overseas General Insurance business also grew strongly amid growth in most regions and lines of business. The other segments grew more modestly except the small Global Reinsurance unit which fell 3%.

Net income grew 3% to $4.0 billion in 2018 although underlying performance was better as the 2017 figure was inflated by a $450 million bump from the 2017 US Tax Cuts and Jobs Act. A less-damaging hurricane season contributed to lower loss expenses while net investment income increased as well.

Chubb's cash balance grew $489 million during 2018 ending the year at $1.3 billion. The company generated $5.5 billion from its operations while it used $2.9 billion in its investing activities and $2.0 billion in its financing activities. Chubb's main cash uses during the year were net purchases of maturities held for sale long-term debt repayments and dividends.

Strategy

Chubb has built up a portfolio of insurance businesses whose scale and business model is hard to replicate raising a high barrier to entry. It holds leading positions in the US commercial insurance market and the casualty products and risk management services market for corporations; the fourth-largest commercial insurer serving SMEs; the third-biggest excess and surplus lines writer; and the largest personal lines coverage for affluent families and individuals by a distance.

As with every major company the world over Chubb is finding new ways to do business by developing its digital capabilities. Investments in internal and external data analytics machine learning and web scraping have helped Chubb with its risk selection and pricing models. Rather than replacing jobs robotics and automation have helped Chubb's underwriters spend more time on higher value activities and its claims handlers on the time-sensitive complex claims. The automation of low-value activities should save the company big bucks over the coming five years.

Company Background

In early 2016 the former ACE Limited acquired the US's Chubb Corporation for $28 billion and took the Chubb name.

EXECUTIVES

VP and Division President North America Agriculture, Michael J. Coleman, age 76

SVP and Division President Westchester, Bruce L. Kessler

EVP Global Underwriting, Jacques Q. Bonneau

EVP and Chief Investment Officer, Timothy A. Boroughs, age 70

Chairman and CEO, Evan G. Greenberg, age 65, $1,400,000 total compensation

EVP and CFO, Philip V. Bancroft, age 61, $768,750 total compensation

EVP and President North America Commercial and Personal Insurance, Paul J. Krump, age 60, $840,000 total compensation

EVP Global Accident and Health and Life, Edward (Ed) Clancy

SVP and Chief Claims Officer, Frank Lattal

Vice Chairman Chubb Group and President North America Major Accounts and Specialty Insurance, John J. Lupica, age 54, $793,519 total compensation

EVP Chief Digital Officer and Chief Risk Officer Chubb Group, Sean Ringsted, age 56, $575,000 total compensation

SVP Chubb Group and President Chubb Life, Russell G. Bundschuh

SVP and President European Group, Andrew Kendrick

VP and Division President Bermuda and Global Accounts, Joseph S. (Joe) Clabby

SVP and President Chubb Tempest Re Group, James E. Wixtead

Vice Chairman and COO; Chairman Insurance Overseas General, John W. Keogh, age 56, $896,111 total compensation

EVP and President Overseas General Insurance, Juan C. Andrade, age 54

SVP; Regional President ACE Latin America, Jorge L. Cazar

EVP and Global Corporate Development Officer Chubb Group, Rainer Kirchgaessner

SVP; President Combined Insurance, Brad Bennett

SVP and Division President North America Commercial Insurance, Steven R. Pozzi, age 63

VP and Division President Commercial Property and Casualty Overseas General Insurance, David Furby

VP and CIO, Kevin Shearan

SVP Chubb and Group Regional President Asia Pacific, Paul McNamee

SVP Chubb Group and Division President Field Operations North America Insurance, Gerard Butler

VP and Division President Personal Insurance Overseas General Insurance, Darryl Page

EVP and General Counsel, Joseph F. Wayland, age 62

SVP and Division President North America Major Accounts, Christopher A. (Chris) Maleno

SVP and Chief Actuary Chubb Group, Paul OÀ'Connell

SVP and Division President North America Personal Risk Services, Frances D. O'Brien

SVP and Regional President Asia Pacific, Juan Luis Ortega

VP and Chief Reinsurance Officer, Michael Kessler

VP and Division President North America Small Commercial Insurance, James Williamson

SVP Chubb Group and Division President North America Commercial Insurance, C. Scott Gunter

Auditors: PricewaterhouseCoopers LLP

LOCATIONS

HQ: Chubb Ltd
Baerengasse 32, Zurich CH-8001
Phone: (41) 43 456 7600
Web: www.acegroup.com

PRODUCTS/OPERATIONS

2018 Sales by Segment

	$ mil.	% of total
Net premiums earned		
North America Commercial P&C Insurance	12,402	37
Overseas General Insurance	8,612	26
North America Personal P&C Insurance	4,593	14
Life Insurance	2,218	6
North America Agricultural Insurance	1,569	5
Global Reinsurance	670	2
Net investment income	3,305	10
Net realized gains	(652)	
Total	**32,717**	**100**

COMPETITORS

AEGON	ING
AIG	Liberty Mutual
AXA	MetLife
Allianz	Munich Re Group
Allstate	Old Republic
American Financial Group	OneBeacon
Berkshire Hathaway	Swiss Re
CNA Financial	The Hartford
Fairfax Financial Holdings	Travelers Companies
Hannover Re	W. R. Berkley
	XL Group plc

HISTORICAL FINANCIALS

Company Type: Public

Income Statement				FYE: December 31
	ASSETS ($ mil.)	NET INCOME ($ mil.)	INCOME AS % OF ASSETS	EMPLOYEES
12/19	176,943	4,454	2.5%	33,000
12/18	167,771	3,962	2.4%	32,700
12/17	167,022	3,861	2.3%	31,000
12/16	159,786	4,135	2.6%	31,000
12/15	102,366	2,834	2.8%	22,000
Annual Growth	14.7%	12.0%	—	10.7%

2019 Year-End Financials

Return on assets: 2.5%	Dividends
Return on equity: 8.4%	Yield: 1.9%
Long-term debt ($ mil.): —	Payout: 37.6%
No. of shares (mil.): 451	Market value ($ mil.): —
Sales ($ mil): 34,186	

Chubu Electric Power Co Inc

Chubu Electric Power is Japan's an electric utility. The company supplies power to about 16 million people in central Japan's Chubu region a manufacturing region in Japan that includes Nagoya. The company has biomass hydroelectric nuclear wind and solar power generating facilities and it has a capacity of more than 33400 MW. In addition the company offers services utilizing renewable energy that align with customer needs towards the realization of a low-carbon society including the CO2-free menu service. In response to deregulation Chubu Electric Power has moved into newer industries including IT natural gas supply real estate management and overseas consulting.

Operations

The company operate its business into three reportable segment: Customer Service & Sales Power Network and JERA.

Customer Service & Sales focuses on expansion of total energy services centered on gas & electric power. Power Network is focus on provision of power network services and JERA focuses on fuel upstream and procurement to power generation and wholesale of electricity and gas.

Electricity (90% of total revenue) has about 210 power generation facilities in Japan a transmission line that runs more than 12200 kilometers a distribution line that runs more than 133300 kilometers and nearly 930 transformer substations.

Other (15%) provides energy services such as the sale of gas and liquefied natural gas (LNG) and the provision of co-generation systems.

Geographic Reach

The company's headquarter is located in Higashi-shincho Higashi-ku Nagoya.

In addition to Japan the company has offices in Australia Mexico UAE The Netherlands India Canada Indonesia Philippines Mexico Oman Thailand Taiwan Qatar Vietnam and the US.

Sales and Marketing

The company supplies electricity to residential commercial and industrial customers via transmission and distribution lines.

Moreover the company created new forms of community which are connected home service Korekara Denki (energy services based on customer participation) smart pole service and regional information bank.

Financial Performance

Note: Growth rates may differ after conversion to US Dollars.

In 2019 consolidated operating revenue increased by 1% from the previous consolidated fiscal year to 3.1 trillion yen mainly due to an increase in fuel cost adjustment charge and increase in surcharge and grant based on Act on Special Measures Concerning Procurement of Electricity from Renewable Energy Sources by Electric Utilities.

The company's net income in 2019 fell by 3.9 billion yen to 62.2 billion yen from 66 billion yen in the prior year.

Cash held by the company at the end of 2019 decreased by 402.5 billion yen to 147.6 billion yen compared to 550.1 billion yen in the prior year. Cash provided by operations was 255.9 billion while cash used for investing and financing activities were 647.6 billion yen and 5.9 billion yen respectively.

Strategy

In April 2020 the Chubu Electric Power Group split off their power transmission and distribution business. At the same time the company split off their sales business and put into practice business model that separates power generation from sales. With each of their businesses dealing with customers and society and developing independently they are more certain to deliver good-quality environmentally friendly energy that is essential for their daily lives and business in a safer more affordable and more stable manner.

Building on this foundation along with energy the company will provide new services that exceed the expectations of their customers and society while utilizing digital technology through the creation of community support infrastructure. Through these activities they will contribute to the resolution of social issues including the achievement of a low-carbon society which is an urgent issue worldwide.

Mergers and Acquisitions

In 2019 Mitsubishi Corporation and Chubu Electric Power Co. Inc. were selected as the preferred buyers in a bid for the Dutch Energy Company "Eneco".

Both MC and Chubu have since been completing the acquisition procedures. The total value of this acquisition is 4.1 billion euros (500 billion yen).

Eneco is an integrated energy company that is actively engaged in renewable power generation projects.

EXECUTIVES

President, Akihisa Mizuno
EVP, Tomohiko Ohno
EVP, Masatoshi Sakaguchi
EVP, Kazuhiro Matsubara
EVP, Satoru Katsuno
Senior Managing Executive Officer, Ryosuke Mizutani
Senior Managing Executive Officer, Yutaka Watanabe
Senior Managing Executive Officer, Satoshi Onoda
Senior Managing Executive Officer, Masanori Matsuura
Chairman, Toshio Mita
Auditors: KPMG AZSA LLC

LOCATIONS

HQ: Chubu Electric Power Co Inc
1 Higashi-Shincho, Higashi-ku, Nagoya, Aichi 461-8680
Phone: (81) 52 951 8211
Web: www.chuden.co.jp

PRODUCTS/OPERATIONS

2016 Sales

	% of total
Electric power	90
Energy	3
Other	7
Total	**100**

COMPETITORS

Chugoku Electric Power	Kyushu Electric Power
Hokkaido Electric Power	Osaka Gas
	Shikoku Electric
Hokuriku Electric Power	Tohoku Electric Power
	Tokyo Electric
KEPCO	Tokyo Gas

HISTORICAL FINANCIALS

Company Type: Public

Income Statement				FYE: March 31
	REVENUE ($ mil.)	NET INCOME ($ mil.)	NET PROFIT MARGIN	EMPLOYEES
03/20	28,244	1,505	5.3%	28,448
03/19	27,406	717	2.6%	30,321
03/18	26,870	700	2.6%	30,554
03/17	23,286	1,025	4.4%	30,635
03/16	25,415	1,511	5.9%	30,659
Annual Growth	**2.7%**	**(0.1%)**	**—**	**(1.9%)**

2020 Year-End Financials

Debt ratio: 0.4%
Return on equity: 8.8%
Cash ($ mil.): 1,368
Current ratio: 0.53
Long-term debt ($ mil.): 16,204

No. of shares (mil.): 756
Dividends
  Yield: —
  Payout: —
  Market value ($ mil.): —

Chugoku Bank, Ltd. (The)

EXECUTIVES

President, SADANORI KATO
Managing Director, SHINICHI TANIGUCHI
Managing Director, TATSUO HIRAMOTO
Managing Director, HIROYUKI OHARA
Managing Director, HIROMICHI KATO
Chairman, MASATO MIYANAGA
Auditors: KPMG AZSA LLC

LOCATIONS

HQ: Chugoku Bank, Ltd. (The)
1-15-20 Marunouchi, Kita-ku, Okayama 700-8628
Phone: (81) 86 223 3111   **Fax:** 212 371-7173
Web: www.chugin.co.jp

PRODUCTS/OPERATIONS

Selected Subsidiaries

CBS Company Limited
Chugin Asset Management Company Limited
Chugin Securities Co. Ltd.
The Chugin Card Company Limited
The Chugin Credit Guarantee Co. Limited
The Chugin Lease Company Limited
The Chugin Operation Center Co. Limited

COMPETITORS

Awa Bank	Mizuho Financial
Hiroshima Bank	Norinchukin Bank
Hyakujushi Bank	Resona
Mitsubishi UFJ Financial Group	Sumitomo Mitsui

HISTORICAL FINANCIALS

Company Type: Public

Income Statement				FYE: March 31
	ASSETS ($ mil.)	NET INCOME ($ mil.)	INCOME AS % OF ASSETS	EMPLOYEES
03/20	75,056	109	0.1%	4,885
03/19	74,530	146	0.2%	4,933
03/18	79,739	200	0.3%	5,012
03/17	74,092	181	0.2%	5,132
03/16	69,459	242	0.3%	5,134
Annual Growth	**2.0%**	**(18.0%)**	**—**	**(1.2%)**

2020 Year-End Financials

Return on assets: 0.1%
Return on equity: 2.2%
Long-term debt ($ mil.): —
No. of shares (mil.): 188
Sales ($ mil): 1,172

Dividends
  Yield: —
  Payout: 34.7%
  Market value ($ mil.): —

CIMB Group Holdings Bhd

CIMB Group is the second-largest financial services firm in Malaysia behind Maybank. It is the holding company for CIMB Bank CIMB Investment Bank and CIMB Islamic which provide retail and commercial banking and financial services to 13 million customers throughout Southeast Asia. While it has a presence in 17 countries (including a CIMB Securities office in New York City) the bank's main markets are Malaysia Indonesia Singapore Thailand and Cambodia. Altogether the group has more than 1050 branches. CIMB Group's offerings include corporate and consumer banking investment banking Islamic banking stock brokerage asset management and insurance. It was established in 1924 as Bian Chiang Bank.

Mergers and Acquisitions

CIMB Investment Bank became one of the largest investment banking franchises in Asia in 2012 with the acquisition of most of the Asian investment banking business of the Royal Bank of Scotland. The acquisition gave CIMB a presence in Taiwan and Australia and expanded its operations in Hong Kong India and China. RBS kept its business in South Korea.

Auditors: PricewaterhouseCoopers

LOCATIONS

HQ: CIMB Group Holdings Bhd
Level 13, Menara CIMB, Jalan Stesen Sentral 2, Kuala Lumpur Sentral, Kuala Lumpur 50470
Phone: (60) 3 2261 0085   **Fax:** (60) 3 2261 0099
Web: www.cimb.com

COMPETITORS

AmBank Group	Hong Leong Bank
Bank Muamalat	Malaysian Industrial
Bank Negara	Development Finance
Bank Pembangunan	Maybank
DBS Group Holdings	Public Bank
Edaran Otomobil	RHB Bank Berhad
Guoco	RHB Capital

HISTORICAL FINANCIALS

Company Type: Public

Income Statement				FYE: December 31
	ASSETS ($ mil.)	NET INCOME ($ mil.)	INCOME AS % OF ASSETS	EMPLOYEES
12/19	140,118	1,114	0.8%	35,265
12/18	129,222	1,350	1.0%	36,104
12/17	124,778	1,102	0.9%	37,597
12/16	108,285	794	0.7%	38,945
12/15	107,219	661	0.6%	40,545
Annual Growth	**6.9%**	**13.9%**	**—**	**(3.4%)**

2019 Year-End Financials

Return on assets: 0.8%
Return on equity: 8.4%
Long-term debt ($ mil.): —
No. of shares (mil.): —
Sales ($ mil): 7,024

Dividends
  Yield: —
  Payout: —
  Market value ($ mil.): —

CITIC Ltd

CITIC Limited has investments in steel real estate energy aviation and communications. With stakes in steel plants with an annual capacity of more than 7 million tons CITIC is China's largest producer of specialty steel (heat-resistant anti-corrosion and other enhanced steel). CITIC also owns stakes in facilities that produce raw materials needed in steel production including iron ore mines and coking coal plants. Property developments include office and residential towers and the group owns several land banks in and around Shanghai. State-owned CITIC Group owns more than half of CITIC Limited.

Operations

CITIC's primary businesses are specialty steel manufacturing iron ore mining and property development in mainland China. These three businesses constituted over 70% of total assets at the end of 2012.

Geographic Reach

The company's headquarters are located in Hong Kong. It performs operations in different parts of China including Beijing Chongqing Guangzhou Hainan Hong Kong Shanghai and Tianjin.

Financial Performance

The company's total annual revenue has been strong in recent fiscal years. After claiming a little more than $9 billion in revenue during fiscal 2010 its revenue spiked to $12.8 billion in fiscal 2011 and leveled off at about $12.0 billion in fiscal 2012.

EXECUTIVES

Vice Chairman and President, Wang Jiong, age 60
Executive Director, Li Qingping
Executive Director, Jian Pu
Chairman, Chang Zhenming, age 63
Auditors: PricewaterhouseCoopers

LOCATIONS

HQ: CITIC Ltd
   32nd Floor, CITIC Tower, 1 Tim Mei Avenue, Central,
Phone: (852) 2820 2111   **Fax:** (852) 2877 2771
Web: www.citic.com

2015 Sales

	% of total
Mainland China	87
Hong Kong and Macau	6
Overseas	7
Total	**100**

PRODUCTS/OPERATIONS

2015 Sales

	% of total
Financial Services	49
Manufacturing	14
Resources and energy	11
Real estate	7
Engineering contracting	4
Others	15
Total	**100**

COMPETITORS

CK Hutchison	Shanghai Industrial
Guangdong Investment	Sino Land
Henderson Investment	Sun Hung Kai
Jardine Matheson	Properties
New World Development	Wing Tai

HISTORICAL FINANCIALS

Company Type: Public

Income Statement				FYE: December 31
	REVENUE ($ mil.)	NET INCOME ($ mil.)	NET PROFIT MARGIN	EMPLOYEES
12/19	94,188	6,922	7.3%	287,910
12/18	88,459	6,414	7.3%	273,344
12/17	76,207	5,617	7.4%	243,036
12/16	65,760	5,560	8.5%	127,610
12/15	71,937	5,394	7.5%	133,526
Annual Growth	**7.0%**	**6.4%**	**—**	**21.2%**

2019 Year-End Financials

Debt ratio: —
Return on equity: 9.3%
Cash ($ mil.): 95,088
Current ratio: —
Long-term debt ($ mil.): —

No. of shares (mil.): —
Dividends
  Yield: —
  Payout: 25.1%
Market value ($ mil.): —

CK Hutchison Holdings Ltd

Auditors: PricewaterhouseCoopers

LOCATIONS

HQ: CK Hutchison Holdings Ltd
   48th Floor, Cheung Kong Center, 2 Queen's Road Central,
Phone: (852) 2128 1188   **Fax:** (852) 2128 1705
Web: www.ckh.com.hk

HISTORICAL FINANCIALS

Company Type: Public

Income Statement				FYE: December 31
	REVENUE ($ mil.)	NET INCOME ($ mil.)	NET PROFIT MARGIN	EMPLOYEES
12/19	38,400	5,115	13.3%	300,000
12/18	35,383	4,979	14.1%	300,000
12/17	31,798	4,491	14.1%	300,000
12/16	33,508	4,256	12.7%	290,000
12/15	21,514	15,297	71.1%	270,000
Annual Growth	**15.6%**	**(24.0%)**	**—**	**2.7%**

2019 Year-End Financials

Debt ratio: 3.6%
Return on equity: 8.5%
Cash ($ mil.): 17,610
Current ratio: 1.36
Long-term debt ($ mil.): 39,206

No. of shares (mil.): —
Dividends
  Yield: 3.7%
  Payout: —
Market value ($ mil.): —

	STOCK PRICE ($) FY Close	P/E High/Low		PER SHARE ($) Earnings	Dividends	Book Value
12/19	9.53	1	1	1.33	0.35	15.88
12/18	9.48	1	1	1.29	0.33	15.18
12/17	12.56	2	1	1.16	0.30	15.24
12/16	11.35	2	1	1.10	0.29	14.20
12/15	13.44	1	0	4.76	8.92	14.33
Annual Growth	**(8.2%)**	**—**	**—**	**(27.3%)**	**(55.3%)**	**2.6%**

Clydesdale Bank PLC (United Kingdom)

Clydesdale Bank won't horse around with your money. Founded in 1838 the full-service Scotland-based financial institution is owned by National Australia Bank. Along with standard personal and commercial services such as deposit accounts lending credit cards and financial advice the bank also dabbles in agribusiness and private banking. Clydesdale Bank has some 140 retail branches in Scotland and England. It is one of the only banks in Scotland that issues its own notes. Sister firm Yorkshire Bank also operates as a National Australia Bank brand in the UK.

Operations

Clydesdale Bank reports under National Australia Bank's retail and commercial "UK Banking" business. UK Banking consists of banking and wealth management activities operating under the "Clydesdale Bank" and " Yorkshire Bank" brands. Together the two UK brands offer services through a network of retail branches direct banking business and private banking centers and broker channels.

The UK Banking business operates under two main segments: Business & Private Banking and Retail Banking.

The Retail Banking segment generates nearly 60% of the UK Banking revenues. It provides products and services to personal customers including savings and deposit accounts mortgages overdraft lines of credit personal loans insurance and financial planning.

The remaining 40% of revenues come from the Business & Private Banking business which includes business banking centers small business and private banking customers and offers loans wealth management international services treasury solutions and day to day banking services.

Geographic Reach

Clydesdale Bank operates 140 retail branches and a network of business and private banking centers in Scotland and across the UK. The bank added two new UK branches in mid-2014 in Princes Square and in Perth.

Financial Performance

The UK Banking group (which reports the combined results of Clydesdale Bank and Yorkshire Bank) grew its revenue — defined as net interest income plus non-interest income — by 2% to Å 963 million in fiscal 2014. This is mostly from a 2% increase in net interest income thanks to a combination of higher interest margins increased mortgage business from the Retail segment and low rates of deposit paid to its customers. Non-interest income also grew by 4% in 2014 primarily thanks to gains in the fair value of the bank's investment holdings and hedging ineffectiveness.

Despite revenue growth the UK Banking group's profits continued to be hindered by "legacy conduct" expenses in 2014 as the bank had to set aside millions for customers that were allegedly mislead by the firm's sales payment protection insurance and interest rate hedging products. Because the UK Banking group had Å 433 million more in such expenses than in 2013 the group suffered a net loss of Å 178 million — more than four times what it lost in 2013.

Cash from operations also suffered with a net outflow of Å 629 million in 2014 compared to a net inflow of Å 3.8 billion the year before. While the Å 162 million drop in before-tax net income played a role the bank also used Å 1.19 billion toward operating assets in 2014 as it lent out significantly more for mortgage loans. By comparison in 2013 operating assets provided Å 6.13 billion in cash as the bank sold off many of its assets held for sale.

Strategy

The UK Banking group which includes Clydesdale Bank and Yorkshire Bank is dedicated to being a strong customer focused bank for the communities it serves. With this in mind and for the sake of turning around two years of losses the group will continue to follow a few key strategic objectives.

It's first objective is customer and cost oriented and involves the reshaping of the group's Retail Branch network. In March 2014 the group announced that it would close 28 unsustainable branches and relocate three of them to more targeted locations. The group also announced that it would invest in six new flagship branches in heartland locations that would provide access to new in-house facilities services and technology. To that end in mid-2014 Clydesdale Bank opened two new branches (in Perth and Princes Square) that will highlight the bank's new technology and register customers for internet and mobile banking assist with product discussions and collect customer feedback.

In addition the group plans to control its lending risk by creating a better framework for its management teams and intends to grow its credit portfolio with sustainable types of loans such as mortgages. The group has already seen lower risk and higher returns from its Retail Banking segment in 2014 as mortgage lending and interest margins on loans provided Â 23 million more net interest income compared the prior year. In December 2014 to further this initiative the group announced an aggressive Â 1000 cash back mortgage offer to new home-buying customers.

EXECUTIVES

COO, Debbie Crosbie
CEO and Director, David Duffy, age 58
CFO, Ian Smith
Chairman, James (Jim) Pettigrew, age 60
Auditors: Ernst & Young LLP

LOCATIONS

HQ: Clydesdale Bank PLC (United Kingdom)
   30 St. Vincent Place, Glasgow, Scotland G1 2HL
Phone: (44) 0141 248 7070   **Fax:** (44) 0141 204 0828
Web: www.cbonline.co.uk

COMPETITORS

AIB	Nationwide Building
Barclays	Society
Co-operative Bank	Royal Bank of Scotland
HSBC	Santander UK
Lloyds Banking Group	

HISTORICAL FINANCIALS

Company Type: Public

Income Statement   FYE: September 30

	ASSETS ($ mil.)	NET INCOME ($ mil.)	INCOME AS % OF ASSETS	EMPLOYEES
09/19	112,156	(262)	—	8,703
09/18	56,841	(311)	—	5,769
09/17	58,002	(393)	—	6,040
09/16	51,777	(722)	—	6,718
09/15	58,740	(377)	—	4,616
Annual Growth	17.5%	—	—	17.2%

2019 Year-End Financials

Return on assets: (-0.3%)
Return on equity: (-5.0%)
Long-term debt ($ mil.): —
No. of shares (mil.): —
Sales ($ mil): 3,311
Dividends
   Yield: —
   Payout: —
Market value ($ mil.): —

CNH Industrial NV

Auditors: Ernst & Young LLP

LOCATIONS

HQ: CNH Industrial NV
   25 St. James's Street, London SW1A 1HA
Phone: (44) 1268 533000
Web: www.cnhindustrial.com

Cnooc Ltd.

CNOOC Limited manages China's offshore oil and gas exploration and production activities in partnership with international oil and gas firms. Under Chinese government-regulated production sharing contracts CNOOC Limited has the sole right to acquire up to 51% of any successful discovery offshore China made by foreign partners. CNOOC LimitedÂ has 2.6 billion barrels of oil equivalent in estimated proved reserves primarily in the South China Sea. CNOOC LimitedÂ is also engaged in oil refining natural gas processing and refined products marketing. The oil producer has a net production of 469.4 barrels of oil equivalent per day. To grow it global assets in 2012 the company agreed to buy Nexen for $15 billion.

EXECUTIVES

EVP General Counsel and Compliance Officer, Chen Wei, age 62
CEO and Director, Yuan Guangyu, age 62
SVP and General Manager CNOOC China Limited Shanghai Branch, Zhang Guohua, age 61
CFO and Joint Company Secretary, Zhong Hua, age 60
EVP and General Manager Tianjin Branch CNOOC (China) Limited, Li Yong, age 57
President and Director, Xu Keqiang
EVP Chief Geologist and General Manager Exploration, Xie Yuhong, age 59
Chairman, Yang Hua, age 59
Vice Chairman, Liu Jian, age 62
Auditors: Deloitte Touch Tohmatsu

LOCATIONS

HQ: Cnooc Ltd.
   65/F, Bank of China Tower, 1 Garden Road,
Phone: (852) 2213 2500   **Fax:** (852) 2525 9322
Web: www.cnoocltd.com

2007 Sales

	% of total
China	86
Other countries	14
Total	**100**

HISTORICAL FINANCIALS

Company Type: Public

Income Statement   FYE: December 31

	REVENUE ($ mil.)	NET INCOME ($ mil.)	NET PROFIT MARGIN	EMPLOYEES
12/19	28,079	1,422	5.1%	63,499
12/18	29,706	1,068	3.6%	64,625
12/17	27,361	295	1.1%	63,356
12/16	24,872	(252)	—	62,828
12/15	25,912	253	1.0%	64,391
Annual Growth	2.0%	54.0%	—	(0.3%)

2019 Year-End Financials

Debt ratio: 52.4%
Return on equity: 25.5%
Cash ($ mil.): 5,773
Current ratio: 5.81
Long-term debt ($ mil.): 24,854
No. of shares (mil.): 1,350
Dividends
   Yield: 1.8%
   Payout: 15.6%
Market value ($ mil.): —

PRODUCTS/OPERATIONS

2015 Sales

	% of total
Exploration and Production	87
Trading business	13
Total	**100**

2015 Sales

	% of Total
Oil and gas sales	86
Marketing revenues	12
Other income	2
Total	**100**

Selected Subsidiaries

CNOOC China Limited (China)
CNOOC Finance (2002) Limited (British Virgin Islands)
CNOOC Finance (2003) Limited (British Virgin Islands)
CNOOC International Limited (British Virgin Islands)
CNOOC Offshore Oil (Singapore) Pte. Ltd.

COMPETITORS

Anadarko Petroleum	Exxon Mobil
Apache	PetroChina
BP	Royal Dutch Shell
Chevron	Sinopec Corp.

HISTORICAL FINANCIALS

Company Type: Public

Income Statement   FYE: December 31

	REVENUE ($ mil.)	NET INCOME ($ mil.)	NET PROFIT MARGIN	EMPLOYEES
12/19	33,514	8,773	26.2%	18,703
12/18	32,997	7,660	23.2%	18,312
12/17	28,642	3,792	13.2%	19,030
12/16	21,095	91	0.4%	19,718
12/15	26,397	3,117	11.8%	20,585
Annual Growth	6.1%	29.5%	—	(2.4%)

2019 Year-End Financials

Debt ratio: 2.8%
Return on equity: 14.1%
Cash ($ mil.): 7,262
Current ratio: 2.26
Long-term debt ($ mil.): 19,567
No. of shares (mil.): —
Dividends
   Yield: 5.0%
   Payout: 4,267.8%
Market value ($ mil.): —

	STOCK PRICE ($) FY Close	P/E High/Low	PER SHARE ($) Earnings	Dividends	Book Value
12/19	166.67	136105	0.20	8.35	1.44
12/18	152.45	170109	0.17	6.84	1.36
12/17	143.56	266205	0.08	5.04	1.31
12/16	123.96	135488088	0.00	4.04	1.23
12/15	104.38	372215	0.07	6.62	1.33
Annual Growth	12.4%	—	29.8%	6.0%	2.0%

Co-operative Bank plc

EXECUTIVES

CEO, Liam Coleman
CIO, Steve Friedlos
CFO, John Worth
HR Director, Tracey Kneller
Director Retail and Business Banking, Heather Lauder
General Counsel and Secretariat, Brona McKeown
Chief Risk Officer, Steven Pickering

Director Product and Communications, Matthew
 Carter
Chairman, Dennis Holt
Auditors: Ernst & Young LLP

LOCATIONS

HQ: Co-operative Bank plc
 P.O. Box 101, 1 Balloon Street, Manchester M60 4EP
Phone: (44) 161 832 3456   **Fax:** (44) 161 829 4475
Web: www.co-operativebank.co.uk

PRODUCTS/OPERATIONS

2016 Sales

	% of total
Interest receivable and similar income	86
Fee and commission income	14
Total	**100**

COMPETITORS

Bank of England	Royal Bank of Scotland
Barclays	Santander UK
HSBC	Standard Life Bank
Lloyds Banking Group	
Nationwide Building	
Society	

HISTORICAL FINANCIALS

Company Type: Public

Income Statement				FYE: December 31
	ASSETS ($ mil.)	NET INCOME ($ mil.)	INCOME AS % OF ASSETS	EMPLOYEES
12/19	30,948	(202)	—	3,357
12/18	29,496	(87)	—	3,547
12/17	33,078	314	1.0%	3,965
12/16	33,937	(515)	—	4,766
12/15	43,018	(923)	—	5,714
Annual Growth	(7.9%)	—	—	(12.5%)

2019 Year-End Financials

Return on assets: (-0.6%)	Dividends
Return on equity: (-9.1%)	Yield: —
Long-term debt ($ mil.): —	Payout: —
No. of shares (mil.): —	Market value ($ mil.): —
Sales ($ mil) 801	

Co-Operative Group (CWS) Ltd.

The Co-operative Group feels a duty of care to its customers from cradle to grave. The assortment of businesses run by Britain's largest cooperative society include principally grocery retail insurance and funeralcare alongside other businesses such as financial and legal advice and electrical goods retail. The company is one of the UK's largest grocery retailers with about 2775 food stores and is Britain's largest funeral service provider with over 1000 funeral homes. Established in 1863 the Co-op is owned by its 4 million members. Anyone can become a member of the Group granting the member cashback voting rights and a share of profits by subscribing for Å 1.

Operations

The Co-operative Group operates five businesses: Food Funeralcare Insurance Electrical and Legal Services. Food generates around 75% of sales each year while Funeralcare and Insurance generate less than 5% each. The majority of the remainder around 15% is brought in by joint-buying activities operated by the Co-operative for itself and other independent co-operative societies.

The Food segment sells groceries at 2775 stores up and down the UK. It also sells fuel at certain sites.

Funeralcare offers pre-need and at-need funerals (meaning planning ahead and after-the-fact funerals) through 1000 funeral homes across the UK. Insurance offers car young driver breakdown home travel pet business and van insurance. The Legal Services business offers will services family law personal injury employment solicitors and conveyancing. The Electrical segment sells a range of dishwashers fridges freezers ovens small appliances vacuum cleaners and more from big name brands such as Indesit Dyson Sony and Samsung.

Geographic Reach

Manchester-based Co-operative Group's reach covers much of the UK.

Financial PerformanceNote: Growth rates may differ after conversion to US Dollars.

Co-operative Group nearly collapsed in 2013 due to the frenzied competitive environment in the UK food retail sector particularly from discounters like Aldi and Lidl (Aldi overtook Co-op Food as the UK's fifth largest grocery retailer in 2017) as well as pressure from the advance of e-commerce. Since then thanks to an aggressive sell off strategy that saw the company dispose its banking farming travel and pharmacy businesses the company has paid down debt and returned its core Food business to growth.

In fiscal 2016 revenue increased 2% to Å 9.5 billion thanks to growth in food and insurance. Food was up despite weakness at the pump which had a negative effect on revenue of around Å 200 million thanks to its store opening program. Most of Co-op's revenue growth came from the 112 store openings in the year while the 155 refitted stores also had a positive impact. The Insurance segment grew 28% to Å 439 million due to improvements in pricing and distribution capabilities. Funeralcare was able to grow revenue around Å 8 million despite a lower death rate during the year thanks to an expansion of its services particularly into a lower price point.

The company lost Å 134 million during the year as higher operating profit was offset by an increase in finance costs and losses in joint ventures.

Cash from operations fell 13% to Å 247 million due mostly to an increase in receivables.

Strategy

After its near-collapse in 2013 Co-operative Group has been selling off a number of its businesses to raise cash and give it space to invest in its main businesses of Food Funeralcare and Insurance. In 2014 the company sold its Pharmacy business to Bestway Group for Å 620 million its Farms business to the Wellcome Trust its Sunwin Services Group business to Cardtronics for Å 41.5m and Co-operative Estates sold the former Co-operative Food regional distribution center at Halesowen to Dawn Meats.It also sold its Motor business in 2015 its Travel business in 2016 and in 2017 it completed the sale of its entire banking operations.

With its finances stabilized in 2016 Co-operative Group began investing in its businesses once more. It has been opening new convenience stores at a rate of knots (in 2016 it opened 112) and has been refurbishing many more (155 in 2016). The company's strategy is based on owning the convenience market where prices are of less importance than convenience and which offers protection against the likes of Aldi and Lidl who have less of a hold in the market.

It also penned a deal in 2018 to become the exclusive wholesale supplier of Costcutter's 2200 stores and will acquire co-operative-like organization Nisa which has revenue of around Å 1.2 billion.

Mergers and Acquisitions

In 2017 Co-operative Group agreed to acquire Nisa a brand and buying group of independent retailers and wholesalers active in the UK. The company fought off Sainsbury's for the company's signature and the deal will add some Å 1.25 billion to Co-operative Group's annual revenue.

HISTORY

Co-operative Group originally was known as the North of England Co-operative Society with 300 members located mostly in Lancashire and Yorkshire. The society used its collective strength to buy goods in bulk at favorable prices reflecting the retail consumer co-operative movement sweeping across Europe in the mid-1800s. Social responsibility profit sharing and honesty about products were guiding principles.

The North of England Co-operative Society changed its name to the Co-operative Wholesale Society (CWS) in 1872 and started diversifying into financial services. The Co-operative Bank was created as an arm of CWS as was Co-operative Insurance Society.

John Mitchell was elected chairman in 1874 and led an expansion into manufacturing to provide more control over the goods required by customers. Boots soap and biscuits were made in CWS factories. Tea was imported from India where CWS owned plantations and brought to Britain in the co-op's ships.

By 1904 CWS owned a convalescent home for sick members and the Co-operative Insurance Society started offering death benefits. Within weeks of the outbreak of WWI in 1914 CWS was turning out 10000 uniforms a day for the army. In WWII CWS officials served on advisory boards for food and nonfood goods.

CWS moved into the era of the modern supermarket in 1942 when a member of the London Co-operative Society adopted the American idea of taking away the shop counter and letting customers select their own goods.

CWS merged with the Scottish Co-operative Wholesale Society in 1973.

Chief executive Graham Melmoth took the helm in 1996 after rising through CWS over 22 years. He spearheaded the merger with Co-operative Retail Services in 2000 and the name change to Co-operative Group the next year. In 2001 Co-operative Group began a major reorganization and revamped its membership rules to meet the competition from leading retailers such as Tesco.

Melmoth retired in September 2002 and was succeeded by board member Martin Beaumont. In October 2002 the Co-operative Group acquired rival convenience store operator Alldays for Å 131 million. In 2002 the co-op switched all of its private-label chocolate to the Fairtrade label. (The Co-op pioneered Fairtrade in the UK with bananas.)

In 2003 Co-operative Group acquired the Balfour chain of convenience stores and newsstands for Å 31 million. The travel group bought Sunshare Vacations.

In May 2004 Co-operative Group acquired 64 convenience stores under the Spar and Local Plus banners in southwest England from Conveco further reinforcing its position as the UK's largest convenience store operator. That month chairman Keith Darwin retired and was succeeded by Bob Burlton a board member for 11 years. In August the co-op sold its dairy business Associated Co-operative Creameries (ACC) to now defunct Dairy

Farmers of Britain for Å 75 million. Falling profits at the co-op's supermarkets and convenience stores led to the resignation in September of Malcolm Hepworth head of the Food Retail Group after seven years with the company.

In 2005 the Co-operative Group sold its Priority Motors Group to Reg Vardy to concentrate on its core financial and food retailing businesses. Later in the year the co-op announced plans to sell or shut down its loss-making department store unit selling off what it can and then closing whatever is left by February 2007.

In July 2007 Co-operative Group merged with its smaller rival United Co-operatives to create a group with about 4500 outlets including 2300 food stores nationwide. The tie-up formed the world's largest cooperative retailer. Following the merger Beaumont retired as chief executive allowing Peter Marks the chief executive of United to run the combined business. In September the co-op sold its retail shoe business Shoefayre to the Shoe Zone Group for an undisclosed sum.

In 2008 the Co-op remodeled 700 of its food stores as part of a Å 200 million refurbishment program.

In March 2009 the Co-operative Group acquired Somerfield Group for about Å 1.5 billion ($3 billion). The purchase increased its grocery store count to some 3000 shops with about 8% of the UK grocery market.

In 2010 the Co-op acquired funeral provider Plymouth and South West Co-operative Society (PSW) the operator of 30-plus funeral homes.

In 2012 it grew its food retailing business with the addition of 83 convenience stores opened or acquired including the purchase of Scottish chain David Sands. It also opened 27 new funeral homes refurbished a crematorium and invested in new vehicles. Also in 2012 the Co-op disposed of some of its auto dealerships and its clothing business.

Meanwhile the Co-op's big name in travel retailing has diminished as tough economic times hammer the travel and tourism market. In a move to reduce its exposure the Co-op in 2011 merged its retail travel business which boasts 400-plus outlets across the UK with travel service scion Thomas Cook and independent retailer Midlands Co-operative Society. The deal created the largest retail travel operation in the UK with more than 1200 outlets. (However Thomas Cook is expected to shutter as many as 200 locations post merger.) The merged entity is 66.5%-owned by Thomas Cook 30%-owned by the Co-op with the remainder owned by Midlands.

In a major expansion in 2012 it reached a deal with Lloyds to acquire more than 630 Cheltenham and Gloucester and Lloyds TSB branches (an estimated 4.8 million Lloyds customers). The European Commission has ruled that Lloyds sell part of itself by the end of 2013 in order to increase competition in the banking sector.

EXECUTIVES

Chief Executive The Co-Operative Bank, Niall S. K. Booker, age 61
Group CEO, Richard Pennycook, age 57
Executive Director External Affairs, Nick Folland, age 55
Group CFO, Ian Ellis
Managing Director Co-Operative Insurance, Mark Summerfield, age 58
CEO Consumer Services, Rod Bulmer, age 49
COO, Pippa Wicks
Chief Executive Retail, Steve Murrells
Managing Director Electrical, James Holland
Managing Director Co-Operative Legal Services, Matt Howells
President, Nick Crofts

Chairman, Allan L. Leighton, age 67
Auditors: Ernst & Young LLP

LOCATIONS

HQ: Co-Operative Group (CWS) Ltd.
  1 Angel Square, Manchester M60 0AG
Phone:
Web: www.co-operative.coop

PRODUCTS/OPERATIONS

2016 Sales

	% of total
Food	75
federal	17
funeral	3
Insurance	4
Other	1
Total	**100**

2016 Stores

	No.
Food stores	2,774
Funeral homes	1,026
Total	**3,800**

COMPETITORS

ALDI	John Lewis
ASDA	Lidl
American Express	Lloyds Banking Group
Barclays Bank	Lloyds Pharmacy
Bongrain	Marks & Spencer
Booker Group	Superdrug
Carlson Wagonlit	TUI
FrieslandCampina	Tesco
Fromageries Bel	Waitrose
HSBC	Wessanen
Iceland Foods	Wm Morrison
J Sainsbury	Supermarkets

HISTORICAL FINANCIALS

Company Type: Public

Income Statement				FYE: January 5
	REVENUE ($ mil.)	NET INCOME ($ mil.)	NET PROFIT MARGIN	EMPLOYEES
01/19	12,759	(195)	—	62,786
01/18*	12,828	94	0.7%	65,887
12/16	11,651	(164)	—	70,399
01/16	13,730	22	0.2%	69,078
01/15	14,562	333	2.3%	80,957
Annual Growth	**(3.3%)**	**—**		**(6.2%)**

*Fiscal year change

2019 Year-End Financials

Debt ratio: 13.8%
Return on equity: (-5.0%)
Cash ($ mil.): 354
Current ratio: 0.98
Long-term debt ($ mil.): 1,260

No. of shares (mil.): —
Dividends
  Yield: —
  Payout: —
Market value ($ mil.): —

Coca-Cola European Partners plc

Auditors: Ernst & Young LLP

LOCATIONS

HQ: Coca-Cola European Partners plc
  Bakers Road, Uxbridge UB8 1EZ
Phone: (44) 1895 231 313
Web: www.ccep.com

HISTORICAL FINANCIALS

Company Type: Public

Income Statement				FYE: December 31
	REVENUE ($ mil.)	NET INCOME ($ mil.)	NET PROFIT MARGIN	EMPLOYEES
12/19	13,492	1,223	9.1%	17,498
12/18	13,190	1,040	7.9%	23,500
12/17	13,260	824	6.2%	23,500
12/16	9,643	579	6.0%	19,100
12/15	3,180	208	6.5%	25,600
Annual Growth	**43.5%**	**55.7%**	**—**	**(9.1%)**

2019 Year-End Financials

Debt ratio: 38.5%
Return on equity: 17.1%
Cash ($ mil.): 354
Current ratio: 0.75
Long-term debt ($ mil.): 6,312

No. of shares (mil.): 456
Dividends
  Yield: 1.3%
  Payout: —
Market value ($ mil.): —

Colas SA Boulogne

Colas paves the way for drivers worldwide. The global road construction group was founded on and named after the creation of a revolutionary technical process — cold asphalt. Colas provides construction and maintenance services for infrastructure projects (roads airports ports railroads) urban redevelopment projects and recreation facilities around the world. In addition to its work on roads and related projects the company produces construction materials including concrete and aggregates from an international network of quarries gravel pits and asphalt plants. Colas also provides complementary services including design and engineering concessions and soil treatment. Colas is a division of French construction giant Bouygues to which it contributes around a third of total revenue.

Operations

Colas' two primary businesses are Roads its core business and complementary Specialized Activities which include Railways. The company completes around 80000 projects annually.

The Roads division generates 80% of sales and consists of the construction and maintenance activities and the production and sales of road construction materials.

Specialized Activities account for 20% of sales and comprises four categories. Colas Rail designs and engineers large-scale railway projects and renews and maintains conventional and high-speed lines trams and metro systems. The Waterproofing business (Smac) produces and sells waterproofing membranes and cladding for buildings. The Road

Safety and Signalling unit (Aximum) manufactures installs and maintains road safety equipment signs and access control equipment. The Networks business (Spac) installs pipes for carrying fluids (oil gas and water) and dry networking (electricity heating and telecommunications).

Geographic Reach

Colas operates in more than 50 countries worldwide. The company's materials production and recycling is carried out via a dense network of 740 quarries 125 emulsion plants 570 asphalt plants 170 ready-mix concrete plants and one bitumen plant in France and abroad.

Financial Performance

Note: Growth rates may differ after conversion to US Dollars.

In fiscal 2017 Colas' sales grew 6% to €11.7 billion driven by an upturn in the French roads market as well as new road and motorway projects in central Europe. Good performances were recorded in Mainland France Europe North America and the Rest of the World. Revenue from Specialized Activities was up slightly on the previous year as two major gas pipeline projects in France offset a 3% fall in the Railways business.

Net income fell 8% to €328 million due largely to a €74 million capital gain recorded in 2016 partially offset by a decrease in tax relating to the 2017 US Tax Cuts and Jobs Act. Operating profit was up €33 million.

Strategy

Colas' growth strategy rests on enhancing the range of products and services offered; sharing worldwide expertise in key sectors such as quarrying and bitumen products; doing more to control the availability and quality of its two key resources (aggregates and bitumen); and strengthening and extending its network of local profit centers.

Mergers and Acquisitions

In 2018 Colas acquired British company Allied Infrastructure Management Ltd a leader in airport services and maintenance in the UK. In the same year it also acquired Topcoat Asphalt Contractors an Adelaide Australia-based specialist in bitumen products manufacturing.

EXECUTIVES

Managing Director International, Thierry Genestar
Chairman and CEO, Hervé Le Bouc, age 69
Managing Director North America, Louis Gabanna, age 64
Group Human Resources Manager, Philippe Tournier
Auditors: Mazars

LOCATIONS

HQ: Colas SA Boulogne
1 rue du Colonel Pierre Avia, Paris, Cedex 75730
Phone: (33) 1 47 61 75 00   **Fax:** (33) 1 47 61 76 00
Web: www.colas.com

2017 Sales

	% of total
France	52
North America	22
Europe (excluding France)	17
Rest of the world	9
Total	**100**

PRODUCTS/OPERATIONS

2017 Sales

	% of total
Roads Mainland France	37
Roads Europe	14
Roads North America	22
Roads Rest of the World	10
Specialized Activities	17
Total	**100**

COMPETITORS

CEMEX	LafargeHolcim
EIFFAGE	Peter Kiewit Sons'
FCC Barcelona	Skanska
Ferrovial	Tarmac
Italcementi	VINCI

HISTORICAL FINANCIALS

Company Type: Public

Income Statement

FYE: December 31

	REVENUE ($ mil.)	NET INCOME ($ mil.)	NET PROFIT MARGIN	EMPLOYEES
12/19	15,385	293	1.9%	59,853
12/18	15,121	258	1.7%	57,997
12/17	14,049	393	2.8%	58,273
12/16	11,632	374	3.2%	58,803
12/15	13,041	254	2.0%	56,901
Annual Growth	**4.2%**	**3.6%**	**—**	**1.3%**

2019 Year-End Financials

Debt ratio: 9.6%
Return on equity: 9.2%
Cash ($ mil.): 547
Current ratio: 1.00
Long-term debt ($ mil.): 483

No. of shares (mil.): 32
Dividends
  Yield: —
  Payout: 80.1%
Market value ($ mil.): —

Coles Group Ltd (New)

Auditors: Ernst & Young

LOCATIONS

HQ: Coles Group Ltd (New)
800-838 Toorak Road, Hawthorn East, Victoria 3123
Phone: (61) 03 9829 5111
Web: www.colesgroup.com.au

HISTORICAL FINANCIALS

Company Type: Public

Income Statement

FYE: June 30

	REVENUE ($ mil.)	NET INCOME ($ mil.)	NET PROFIT MARGIN	EMPLOYEES
06/19	26,949	1,005	3.7%	0
06/18	28,904	1,165	4.0%	0
Annual Growth	**(6.8%)**	**(13.8%)**	**—**	**—**

2019 Year-End Financials

Debt ratio: 10.4%
Return on equity: 43.4%
Cash ($ mil.): 658
Current ratio: 0.79
Long-term debt ($ mil.): 1,022

No. of shares (mil.): 1,333
Dividends
  Yield: —
  Payout: 32.9%
Market value ($ mil.): —

	STOCK PRICE ($) FY Close	P/E High/Low	PER SHARE ($) Earnings	Dividends	Book Value
06/19	0.00	— —	0.75	0.25	1.76
06/18	0.00	— —	0.87	0.00	2.00
/0.00	—	—(0.00)	0.00	(0.00)	
Annual Growth	**—**		**—**	**—**	**—**

Commercial Bank of Qatar

EXECUTIVES

Chairman, Abdullah Bin Khalifa Al Attiyah
Auditors: Ernst & Young

LOCATIONS

HQ: Commercial Bank of Qatar
P.O. Box 3232, Doha
Phone: (974) 4449 0000   **Fax:** (974) 4449 0070
Web: www.cbq.com.qa

HISTORICAL FINANCIALS

Company Type: Public

Income Statement

FYE: December 31

	ASSETS ($ mil.)	NET INCOME ($ mil.)	INCOME AS % OF ASSETS	EMPLOYEES
12/19	40,545	555	1.4%	0
12/18	37,120	457	1.2%	0
12/17	38,048	165	0.4%	0
12/16	35,831	137	0.4%	2,138
12/15	33,926	391	1.2%	2,286
Annual Growth	**4.6%**	**9.1%**	**—**	**—**

2019 Year-End Financials

Return on assets: 1.4%
Return on equity: 9.6%
Long-term debt ($ mil.): —
No. of shares (mil.): —
Sales ($ mil): 2,348

Dividends
  Yield: —
  Payout: 5.4%
Market value ($ mil.): —

Commerzbank AG

Auditors: Ernst & Young GmbH
Wirtschaftspruefungsgesellschaft

LOCATIONS

HQ: Commerzbank AG
Kaiserplatz, Frankfurt am Main 60261
Phone: (49) 69 136 20   **Fax:** (49) 69 28 53 89
Web: www.commerzbank.com

HISTORICAL FINANCIALS

Company Type: Public

Income Statement

FYE: December 31

	ASSETS ($ mil.)	NET INCOME ($ mil.)	INCOME AS % OF ASSETS	EMPLOYEES
12/19	520,554	723	0.1%	48,512
12/18	529,502	990	0.2%	49,410
12/17	542,427	187	0.0%	49,417
12/16	507,299	294	0.1%	49,941
12/15	580,158	1,156	0.2%	51,305
Annual Growth	**(2.7%)**	**(11.1%)**	**—**	**(1.4%)**

2019 Year-End Financials

Return on assets: 0.1%
Return on equity: 2.2%
Long-term debt ($ mil.): —
No. of shares (mil.): 1,252
Sales ($ mil): 13,386

Dividends
  Yield: 2.3%
  Payout: 25.5%
Market value ($ mil.): 7,602

| STOCK PRICE ($) | P/E | PER SHARE ($) | | |
FY Close	High/Low	Earnings	Dividends	Book Value
12/19 6.07	18 10	0.57	0.14	26.33
12/18 6.66	23 9	0.79	0.23	25.80
12/17 14.93	128 71	0.14	0.00	27.64
12/16 7.65	46 25	0.23	0.19	24.12
12/15 10.35	16 11	0.96	0.22	25.57
Annual Growth(12.5%)	—	—(12.1%)	(9.7%)	0.7%

Commonwealth Bank of Australia

Commonwealth Bank of Australia (CBA) one of Australia's Four banks offers retail private business and institutional banking services funds management insurance and investment services. CBA's brands include Bankwest Colonial First State online brokerage CommSec and ASB Bank which provides banking investment and financial services. CBA serves its some 17.4 million customers via more than 1170 branch offices and nearly 4000 ATMs in Australia and online. In addition CBA operates in Australia New Zealand United Kingdom the United States China Japan Europe Singapore Hong Kong and Indonesia. CBA offers life insurance and a provider of home loans in Australia. It has total assets of A$976 billion.

Operations

Broadly speaking Commonwealth Bank of Australia (CBA) generates around 85% of its revenue from interest income from its various banking divisions and New Zealand operations. Other banking income provides more than 10% of total revenue. Income from fund management and insurance income account for the remainder.

CBA operates seven divisions. Its Retail Banking unit which generates some 70% of its revenue provides deposit home loan and consumer loan products to retail customers and small businesses. The Business and Private Banking division (less than five percent of revenue) provides personalized banking services to Agribusiness customers and high-net-worth individuals as well as margin lending through CommSec and retail banking products and servicing to non-relationship managed small business customers.

Institutional Banking and Markets (about 15% of revenue) provides debt and equity capital raising financial and commodities price risk management and transactional banking services to corporate institutional and government clients. Its Wealth Management division provides superannuation investment retirement and insurance products and services including financial planning. The rest of its revenue comes from its operations in New Zealand (almost 15% of revenue) and IFS incorporates the Indonesian retail and business banking operations and associate investments in China and Vietnam (less than 5% of revenue).

Geographic Reach

Commonwealth Bank of Australia generates around 85% of its revenue from customers in Australia and more than 10% in New Zealand. The bank operates retail banks in New Zealand (ASB) and Indonesia (Commonwealth Bank of Indonesia). It has minority investments in China and Vietnam. It also has banking branch offices in London New York Japan Singapore Malta Hong Kong New Zealand Beijing and Shanghai.

Sales and Marketing

Commonwealth Bank of Australia provides financial education to school children in Australia through its Start Smart program which has reached more than three million pupils since its inception. It also funds the Commonwealth Bank Teaching Awards and Evidence For Learning. It invested $13.1 million in education programs.

CBA has 7.0 million active digital customers. CBA uses CommBank app and the Customer Engagement Engine which uses artificial intelligence to analyze data and serve customers with the information and services that are most relevant to them.

Advertising marketing and loyalty costs were A$453 million A$496 million and A$462 million for the years 2019 2018 and 2017 respectively.

Financial Performance

Note: Growth rates may differ after conversion to US dollars.

Commonwealth Bank of Australia (CBA) has steadily grown its revenue in recent years as it grows its interest-earning assets. In fiscal 2017 CBA's revenue grew 5% to A$25.9 billion due to higher home loans. The bank also recorded higher other income relating to gains on the sale of its investment in Visa.

Net income grew 8% to A$9.9 billion due to higher revenue lower impairment charges and changes in hedging and IFRS volatility.

CBA used A$18.1 billion in operating activities in 2019

Net cash provided by investing activities was A$983 million. Net cash used in financing activities was A$25.7 billion and cash at the end of the year was A$17.0 billion. It decreased by more than 25% compared to 2018.

Strategy

CBA's strategy is to become a simpler better bank that delivers balanced and sustainable outcomes for the customers community people and shareholders. CBA is becoming a simpler bank by focusing on the core banking businesses and simplifying the organization to reduce costs and create the capacity to invest while also reducing risk and making it easier for the customers and people to get things done. Becoming a better bank is about being more capable and reliable acting transparently and doing the right thing and consistently delivering better outcomes for the stakeholders. The set three execution priorities: simplify the business; lead in retail and commercial banking; and best in digital.

To support the implementation of its strategy CBA is investing in four critical capabilities: operational risk and compliance cost reduction data and analytics and innovation.

In 2020 CBA is making a new feature to assist and aid customers during this pandemic. This tool or feature will enable customers to locate manage and plan their finances effectively. The Corona Virus money plan feature will make actions and suggestions based on the customer's situation and degree of impact during this pandemic.

HISTORY

The Commonwealth Bank Act of 1911 allowed banks to conduct both savings bank and central bank functions and paved the way for the founding of the Commonwealth Bank of Australia the next year. The bank initially operated through a single main office and in nearly 500 post offices in Victoria; it spread out through the entire country over the next few years.

The young bank was drafted during WWI to help the federal government organize war loans and a merchant shipping fleet. In 1919 the bank took over responsibility for issuing notes from the Federal Treasury. In 1928 it created the Commonwealth Savings Bank from its savings department.

Australia — heavily indebted to British lenders — was devastated by the Great Depression. As banks failed the Commonwealth Bank picked up several other institutions including the state banks in Western Australia and New South Wales. During those years Commonwealth took on more and more of the functions of a central bank.

During WWII the bank again came to the aid of its country acting as an agent for the federal government. After the war when the Australian economy stabilized the bank began offering home loans.

After years of controversy in 1959 two bank acts formally separated the Commonwealth Bank's central bank and savings functions. The Reserve Bank of Australia took over the central bank functions in 1960 and the trading and savings operations were taken over by the new Commonwealth Development Bank later renamed the Commonwealth Banking Corporation (a subsidiary of Commonwealth Bank of Australia).

The bank concentrated on expansion and diversification in the 1970s establishing travel home insurance and financing (CBFC 1978); it set its sights on technology in the 1980s expanding its credit card offerings and introducing electronic banking.

The US's 1987 stock market crash again affected Australia's banks which spent almost a decade recovering. Luckily for Commonwealth Bank it wasn't the hardest hit.

In 1988 Commonwealth Bank moved into life insurance and investment services forming subsidiaries Commonwealth Life and Commonwealth Management Services (now together known as CBA Financial Services). In 1989 the bank bought 75% of New Zealand-based ASB Bank.

Commonwealth faced a bevy of challenges including banking deregulation that began in 1982 foreign competition and 1990's banking-law amendments allowing banks to be publicly traded. All of these factors influenced Commonwealth's decision to reorganize. The government sold approximately 30% of its stake in 1991 in part to help Commonwealth fund its acquisition of the State Bank of Victoria. The government sold the rest of its stake in 1996.

That year the company's push into electronic banking bore fruit — some 60% of all its banking transactions were online; that figure later rose to 80%. The company moved into e-commerce in 1999 putting out a call for an overseas partner; Commonwealth's stated goal was to generate one-quarter of its income outside Australia. Also that year Commonwealth and a division of The Bank of Nova Scotia joined forces to form a commodities trading group specializing in metals. In 2000 the company bought Australian financial services firm Colonial Limited.

In late 2008 the company acquired Australia-based BankWest from British bank HBOS (now part of Lloyds Banking Group). The US$1.5 billion deal included insurer and asset manager St. Andrew's (which was later sold) and bolstered CBA's presence in western Australia. Its 2008 acquisitions of BankWestfrom HBOS bolstered its position in western Australia.

In 2010 CBA entered the Chinese insurance market with the launch of a joint venture with Bank of Communications.

In 2011 the bank opened branches in China India and Indonesia and bought a 20% sake in Vietnam International Bank. Also that year the bank continued to strengthen its ties to China signing a referral agreement with Agricultural Bank of China to capture potential customers.

EXECUTIVES

Group Chief Risk Officer, David Cohen
**Group Executive Chief Executive and Managing
  Director ASB,** Barbara Chapman
Managing Director and CEO, Ian Narev, age 52
Group Executive Financial Services and CFO, Rob
  Jesudason
Group Executive Wealth Management, Annabel F.
  Spring
Group Executive Retail Banking Services, Matt
  Comyn
Group Executive Human Resources, Melanie Laing
**Group Executive Institutional Banking and
  Markets,** Kelly Bayer Rosmarin
Group Executive Marketing and Strategy, Vittoria
  Shortt
Group Executive International Financial Services,
  Coenraad (Coen) Jonker
Group Executive Business and Private Banking,
  Adam Bennett
**Group General Counsel and Group Executive
  Group Corporate Affairs,** Anna Lenahan
Chairman, Catherine B. Livingstone, age 65
Auditors: PricewaterhouseCoopers

LOCATIONS

HQ: Commonwealth Bank of Australia
  Ground Floor, Tower 1, 201 Sussex Street, Sydney,
  New South Wales 2000
Phone: (61) 2 9378 2000   **Fax:** (61) 2 9118 7192
Web: www.commbank.com.au

2017

		% of total
Australia	83	
New Zealand	11	
Other locations	5	
Total	**100**	

PRODUCTS/OPERATIONS

2017

	% of total
Interest income	60
Other banking income	19
Premiums from insurance contracts	10
Funds management income	8
Investment revenue (funds management	2
Investment revenue (insurance	1
Total	**100**

2017 Sales by Segment

	% of total
Retail banking services	43
Business & private banking	16
Institutional banking & markets	12
Wealth Management	10
New Zealand	9
Bankwest	8
IFS and Other Divisions	4
Total	**100**

Selected Brands

ASB (New Zealand)
Bankwest
Colonial First State
CommInsure
CommSec
FirstChoice
Sovereign

COMPETITORS

AMP Limited	Macquarie Group
AXA Asia Pacific	National Australia
Asteron	Bank
Australia and New	QBE
Zealand Banking	Suncorp-Metway
HSBC	Westpac Banking
Lloyds Banking Group	

HISTORICAL FINANCIALS

Company Type: Public

Income Statement
FYE: June 30

	ASSETS ($ mil.)	NET INCOME ($ mil.)	INCOME AS % OF ASSETS	EMPLOYEES
06/20	694,916	6,602	1.0%	48,167
06/19	684,170	6,005	0.9%	48,238
06/18	720,056	6,888	1.0%	45,753
06/17	750,192	7,628	1.0%	45,614
06/16	694,231	6,865	1.0%	45,129
Annual Growth	**0.0%**	**(1.0%)**	**—**	**1.6%**

2020 Year-End Financials

Return on assets: 0.9%
Return on equity: 13.5%
Long-term debt ($ mil.): —
No. of shares (mil.): 1,768
Sales ($ mil): 24,312

Dividends
  Yield: 5.6%
  Payout: 78.0%
Market value ($ mil.): 85,101

	STOCK PRICE ($) FY Close	P/E High/Low		PER SHARE ($) Earnings	Dividends	Book Value
06/20	48.13	11	7	3.59	2.74	27.91
06/19	58.19	12	9	3.28	2.97	27.58
06/18	54.13	12	9	3.82	3.08	28.29
06/17	63.77	12	9	4.30	3.16	28.12
06/16	55.85	12	10	3.94	3.22	26.18
Annual Growth	**(3.7%)**	**—**	**—**	**(2.3%)**	**(4.0%)**	**1.6%**

Compagnie de Saint-Gobain

Auditors: KPMG Audit

LOCATIONS

HQ: Compagnie de Saint-Gobain
  Les Miroirs, 18, avenue d'Alsace, Courbevoie 92400
Phone: (33) 1 47 62 30 00
Web: www.saint-gobain.com

HISTORICAL FINANCIALS

Company Type: Public

Income Statement
FYE: December 31

	REVENUE ($ mil.)	NET INCOME ($ mil.)	NET PROFIT MARGIN	EMPLOYEES
12/19	47,826	1,578	3.3%	170,643
12/18	47,873	480	1.0%	181,001
12/17	48,960	1,877	3.8%	179,149
12/16	41,310	1,384	3.4%	172,063
12/15	43,204	1,410	3.3%	168,114
Annual Growth	**2.6%**	**2.9%**	**—**	**0.4%**

2019 Year-End Financials

Debt ratio: 27.5%
Return on equity: 7.5%
Cash ($ mil.): 5,599
Current ratio: 1.35
Long-term debt ($ mil.): 11,548

No. of shares (mil.): 542
Dividends
  Yield: 3.6%
  Payout: 10.3%
Market value ($ mil.): 4,429

	STOCK PRICE ($) FY Close	P/E High/Low		PER SHARE ($) Earnings	Dividends	Book Value
12/19	8.17	3	2	2.90	0.30	40.21
12/18	6.59	14	8	0.87	0.31	37.76
12/17	11.01	4	4	3.37	0.30	40.15
12/16	9.22	4	3	2.48	0.27	35.76
12/15	8.65	4	3	2.49	0.27	36.96
Annual Growth	**(1.4%)**	**—**	**—**	**3.8%**	**2.5%**	**2.1%**

Compagnie Financiere Richemont SA

Compagnie Financière Richemont sells
the stuff of suave. It markets Cartier jewelry Piaget
and Baume & Mercier watches Alfred Dunhill
leather goods Montblanc pens and Chloé
haute coture. Richemont the world's second-
largest luxury goods firm behind French rival
LVMH Moët Hennessy Louis Vuitton also
owns jeweler Van Cleef & Arpels. Customers can
get their hands on Richemont's finery at its 1120
boutiques scattered across five continents as well
as online. Each of Richemont's "maisons" are operated independently supported by central support
services (market research manufacturing logistics
HR) and regional support platforms (distribution
centers IT finance after-sales). Richemont was
founded in Switzerland by South African Johann
Rupert.

Operations

By product Richemont generates 40% of its
sales each from jewelry and watches. Pens clothing
and leather goods account for around 5% each.
Other items such as Purdey firearms bring in the
remainder.

Richemont's maisons are supported by regional
and central service organizations which provide
legal logistics IT HR real estate and finance services. The approach expands the maisons' margins
while allowing them to focus on customer-facing
activities of product design sales and marketing.

Geographic Reach

Richemont generates 40% of its sales from the
Asia/Pacific region its biggest geography. Europe
accounts for around 25% the Americas 15% and
Japan and the Middle East and Africa less than
10% each.

Sales and Marketing

Richemont generates around 65% of sales
through its retail channel (boutiques and online)
and the rest from its wholesale channel.

Financial Performance

Note: Growth rates may differ after conversion
to US Dollars.

Over the last five years Richemont's sales have
been trending upwards albeit unevenly and relatively slowly.

In fiscal 2018 sales grew 3% to €11.0 billion due to a poor comparison year and strong
performances in jewelry. Richemont's specialist
watchmaker maisons declined. Geographically the
bright spots were China Hong Kong South Korea
and Macau while sales in Europe fell 3%.

Net income was materially unchanged in 2018
at €1.2 billion as top-line growth and a lower
cost of sales were eroded by higher finance costs
higher taxation and a bump in selling and administrative expenses.

Richemont's cash position improved markedly in 2018 thanks to stronger operating cash flow and €4.0 billion in proceeds from borrowings.

Strategy

Richemont's general growth strategy is based on utilizing its central and regional support hubs to deepen market penetration in fast growing markets such as the Asia/Pacific region while making targeted acquisitions. In particular the acquisition of Yoox Net-A-Porter Group in 2018 beefed up its e-commerce business.

Mergers and Acquisitions

In 2019 Richemont agreed to acquire Italian jewelry brand Buccellati from a Chinese investment group. Buccellati will slot in alongside Cartier and Van Cleef & Arpels.

In 2018 Richemont acquired the remaing share it did not own of Yoox Net-A-Porter Group a Milan-based online fashion retailer for ?2.8 billion. Yoox Net-A-Porter owns umbrella brand Yoox and British online retailers Mr Porter Net-A-Porter and the Outnet. The acquisition advances Richemont's pursuit of growth in the online space.

EXECUTIVES

Co-CEO, Richard Lepeu, age 68
Co-CEO, Bernard Fornas, age 73
CEO Cartier, Stanislas de Quercize
CFO and Board Member, Gary Saage, age 60
Group Operations Director, Hans-Peter Bichelmeier
CEO IWC Schaffhausen, Georges Kern
CEO Montblanc, Jér 'me Lambert
CEO Piaget, Philippe Léopold-Metzger
Chairman, J P Rupert, age 70
Auditors: PricewaterhouseCoopers SA

LOCATIONS

HQ: Compagnie Financiere Richemont SA
50 chemin de la Chenaie, CP 30, Geneva, Bellevue Ch-1293
Phone: (41) 22 721 3500   **Fax:** (41) 22 721 3550
Web: www.richemont.com

2018 Sales

	% of total
Asia-Pacific	40
Europe	27
Americas	16
Middle East and Africa	8
Japan	9
Total	**100**

PRODUCTS/OPERATIONS

2018 Sales

	% of total
Jewelry Maisons	59
Specialist Watchmakers	25
Other businesses (apparel & leather & accessories)	17
Total	**100**

2018 Sales

	% of total
Retail	63
Wholesale	37
Total	**100**

2018 Sales

	% of total
Jewelry	41
Watches	40
Leather goods	7
Clothing	4
Writing instruments	4
Other	4
Total	**100**

Major Brands

A. Lange & Söhne (watches)
Alaia
Alfred Dunhill (menswear and accessories)
Baume & Mercier (watches)
Cartier (jewelry and watches)
Chloé; (womenswear jewelry fragrances and accessories)
Dunhill
Giampiero Bodino (jewelry)
IWC (watches)
Jaeger-LeCoultre (watches)
Lancel (leather goods)
Montblanc (writing instruments)
Officine Panerai (watches)
Peter Millar
Piaget (watches)
Purdey (firearms)
Roger Dubuis (watches)
Vacheron Constantin (watches)
Van Cleef & Arpels (jewelry and watches)

COMPETITORS

Armani	Movado Group
Chanel	Prada
Douglas Holding	Ralph Lauren
Gucci	Rolex
Harry Winston	Swatch
Herm ¨s	Tiffany & Co.
LVMH	

HISTORICAL FINANCIALS

Company Type: Public

Income Statement				FYE: March 31
	REVENUE ($ mil.)	NET INCOME ($ mil.)	NET PROFIT MARGIN	EMPLOYEES
03/20	15,598	1,022	6.6%	35,657
03/19	15,710	3,129	19.9%	35,640
03/18	13,534	1,505	11.1%	28,740
03/17	11,375	1,292	11.4%	28,580
03/16	12,614	1,922	15.2%	28,810
Annual Growth	**5.5%**	**(14.6%)**	**—**	**5.5%**

2020 Year-End Financials

Debt ratio: 23.1%
Return on equity: 5.4%
Cash ($ mil.): 4,888
Current ratio: 2.86
Long-term debt ($ mil.): 4,328

No. of shares (mil.): 512
Dividends
  Yield: 2.1%
  Payout: 6.3%
Market value ($ mil.): 2,754

	STOCK PRICE ($) FY Close	P/E High/Low		PER SHARE ($) Earnings	Dividends	Book Value
03/20	5.37	5	3	1.80	0.12	36.60
03/19	7.26	2	1	5.53	0.11	37.14
03/18	8.95	5	4	2.66	0.11	35.20
03/17	7.86	4	2	2.29	0.10	32.36
03/16	6.60	2	2	4.48	0.09	33.45
Annual Growth	**(5.0%)**	**—**		**(20.4%)**	**5.3%**	**2.3%**

Compagnie Generale des Etablissements Michelin SCA

LOCATIONS

HQ: Compagnie Generale des Etablissements Michelin SCA
23, place des Carmes-Dechaux, Clermont-Ferrand 63000
Phone: (33) 4 73 32 20 00
Web: www.michelin.com

HISTORICAL FINANCIALS

Company Type: Public

Income Statement				FYE: December 31
	REVENUE ($ mil.)	NET INCOME ($ mil.)	NET PROFIT MARGIN	EMPLOYEES
12/19	27,097	1,965	7.3%	127,187
12/18	25,226	1,920	7.6%	117,393
12/17	26,324	2,037	7.7%	114,069
12/16	22,075	1,769	8.0%	111,708
12/15	23,090	1,272	5.5%	111,700
Annual Growth	**4.1%**	**11.5%**	**—**	**3.3%**

2019 Year-End Financials

Debt ratio: 21.9%
Return on equity: 13.8%
Cash ($ mil.): 1,645
Current ratio: 1.57
Long-term debt ($ mil.): 5,643

No. of shares (mil.): 178
Dividends
  Yield: 3.3%
  Payout: 7.6%
Market value ($ mil.): 4,367

	STOCK PRICE ($) FY Close	P/E High/Low		PER SHARE ($) Earnings	Dividends	Book Value
12/19	24.45	3	2	10.85	0.83	83.13
12/18	19.60	3	2	10.59	0.83	77.33
12/17	28.62	3	3	11.20	0.78	74.96
12/16	22.21	2	2	9.53	0.59	62.15
12/15	19.07	4	2	6.74	0.54	56.82
Annual Growth	**6.4%**	**—**		**12.6%**	**11.0%**	**10.0%**

Compal Electronics Inc

EXECUTIVES

SVP and CFO, Gary Lu
Auditors: KPMG

LOCATIONS

HQ: Compal Electronics Inc
No. 581 & 581-1, Ruiguang Road, Neihu District, Taipei 11492
Phone: (886) 2 8797 8588   **Fax:** (886) 2 2659 1566
Web: www.compal.com

2017 Sales

	% of total
United States	38
Mainland China	13
Netherlands	11
Germany	4
UK	4
Others	30
Total	**100**

PRODUCTS/OPERATIONS

2017 Sales

	% of total
IT Product Segment	98
Strategically Integrated Product Segment	2
Total	**100**

2017 Sales

	% of total
5C Electronic Products	100
Others	-
Total	**100**

COMPETITORS

ASUSTeK
BenQ
Celestica
China Techfaith
First International
  Computer
Flextronics
Hon Hai

Inventec
Jabil
MiTAC
Pegatron
Quanta Computer
Sanmina
Tatung
Wistron

HISTORICAL FINANCIALS

Company Type: Public

Income Statement

FYE: December 31

	REVENUE ($ mil.)	NET INCOME ($ mil.)	NET PROFIT MARGIN	EMPLOYEES
12/19	32,748	232	0.7%	0
12/18	31,640	291	0.9%	0
12/17	29,935	193	0.6%	0
12/16	23,702	251	1.1%	0
12/15	25,785	264	1.0%	0
Annual Growth	6.2%	(3.2%)	—	—

2019 Year-End Financials

Debt ratio: 0.7%
Return on equity: 6.5%
Cash ($ mil.): 2,223
Current ratio: 1.34
Long-term debt ($ mil.): 284

No. of shares (mil.): —
Dividends
  Yield: —
  Payout: 75.9%
Market value ($ mil.): —

Companhia Brasileira de Distribuicao

What began as a S o Paulo pastry shop is now Brazil's #1 retailer: Companhia Brasileira de Distribui § o (CBD). The company operates more than 1600 stores including: supermarkets under the P o de A § car Sendas and Extra banners; Extra hypermarkets and convenience stores; Ponto Frio electronics and appliance shops; Casas Bahia household appliance and furniture shops; and numerous e-commerce sites. CBD's strategy of operating diversified businesses and acquiring regional chains has enabled it to claim the title of Brazil's leading merchant. The founding Diniz family and French food retailer Casino Guichard-Perrachon own about two-thirds of CBD and share control of the company.

EXECUTIVES

CEO, Ronaldo Iabrudi dos Santos Pereira
Auditors: ERNST & YOUNG Auditores Independentes S.S.

LOCATIONS

HQ: Companhia Brasileira de Distribuicao
Avenida Brigadeiro Luis Antonio 3142, Sao Paulo 01402-901
Phone: (55) 11 3886 0421 **Fax:** (55) 11 3884 2677
Web: www.gpari.com.br

PRODUCTS/OPERATIONS

2016 Sales

	% of total
Food Retail	65
Cash & Carry	35
Total	**100**

2016 Sales

	% of total
Extra	40
Assaí;	35
Pão de Açucar	16
Proximidade	3
Other business	6
Total	**100**

COMPETITORS

Carrefour
Lojas Americanas
Makro Atacadista

Rallye
Wal-Mart Brazil

HISTORICAL FINANCIALS

Company Type: Public

Income Statement

FYE: December 31

	REVENUE ($ mil.)	NET INCOME ($ mil.)	NET PROFIT MARGIN	EMPLOYEES
12/19	14,089	121	0.9%	145,506
12/18	12,725	323	2.5%	94,119
12/17	13,473	186	1.4%	91,106
12/16	12,736	(148)	—	93,658
12/15	17,477	66	0.4%	0
Annual Growth	(5.2%)	16.1%		

2019 Year-End Financials

Debt ratio: 6.1%
Return on equity: 4.4%
Cash ($ mil.): 1,978
Current ratio: 0.86
Long-term debt ($ mil.): 2,663

No. of shares (mil.): 99
Dividends
  Yield: —
  Payout: —
Market value ($ mil.): —

Compass Group PLC (United Kingdom)

Look in almost any direction and you'll likely see a foodservice operation run by this company. Compass Group is the world's largest contract foodservices provider with operations in more than 50 countries at more than 50000 client locations including its largest market the US. It provides hospitality and foodservice for a variety of businesses and such public-sector clients as cultural institutions hospitals and schools. The company also provides operations in sporting and leisure venues exhibit centers visitor attractions and major events as well as support services to major companies in the oil gas mining and construction industries. Its foodservice brands include Chartwells Crothall and Levy Restaurants.

Operations

Compass Group trades under some 15 brands. These include Eurest Restaurant Associates Flik Canteen and Bon Appetit (business and industry); medirest morrison and crothall (healthcare and seniors); Chartwells Flik and Bon Appetit (education); Levy (sports and leisure); and ESS (defense offshore and remote).

Business & Industry accounts for nearly 40% of sales provides nutritious foods while healthcare and seniors generates about 25% of sales provides public and private sectors with quality assurance of food and some support services.

Education (about 20% of sales) provides dining solutions and support in academic fields from kindergarten to college.

Other segment includes Sports & Leisure (about 15% of sales) operates at some sporting and leisure venues exhibition centres visitor attractions and major events. Defense Offshore and Remote (about 10% of sales) provides food and somesupport services to major companies in the oil gas mining and construction industries.

Geographic Reach

UK-Based Compass Group operates primarily in North America Europe and other regions worldwide. North America is the company's biggest territory accounting for some 60% of sales. Europe (Western Europe Scandinavia and Russia and Turkey) generates 25% of sales. Other countries which stretch from most of South America to Africa South Asia and China bring in the remaining 15% of sales. The company also has a very strong presence in Australia and Japan while China and India have strong long-term growth potential being the high growth economies of emerging markets.

Sales and Marketing

Compass Group operates in five sectors: business & industry (around 40% of sales) healthcare & seniors (more than 20%) education (nearly 20%) sports & leisure (more than 10%) and defense offshore & remote (less than 10%).

Compass Group has a roughly 10% share of the global foodservice market.

Financial Performance

Note: Growth rates may differ after conversion to US Dollars.

Compass Group has delivered five consecutive years of revenue growth. In fiscal 2018 (ended September 30) the company grew its sales 2% to Å 23.2 billion as good performances in North America and Europe were partially offset by falling sales in the rest of the world.

Net income fell 3% to Å 1.1 billion due to lower operating margins as higher headcount expenses and commissions and fees paid to clients push up operating costs.

Compass Group's cash position strengthened in 2018 ending the year Å 602 million higher at Å 969 million. It generated Å 1.9 billion from its operations while investing activities used Å 1.1 billion and its financing activities Å 135 million. The company's primary cash uses in 2018 were acquisitions capital expenditures borrowing repayments and dividend payouts.

Strategy

While the company makes the occasional bolt-on acquisition Compass Group's priority is driving organic revenue growth. The company is intent on expanding its 10% global share of the food services market believing that as economic conditions and regulatory burdens put pressure on organizations' budgets the benefits of food service outsourcing will become more apparent. Compass Group's scale allows the company to operate more efficiently providing a competitive advantage. In the Defence Offshore & Remote market segment the company's approach is to build lasting strategic relationships with large local and international operators.

Mergers and Acquisitions

In 2019 Compass Group PLC acquired Fazer Group for an enterprise value of approximately ?475 million. Fazer Food Services is a renowned food catering business in the Nordic region with operations in Finland Sweden Norway and Denmark across several sectors including Business & Industry Education Healthcare Seniors and Defence. This acquisition will further strengthen Compass Group's existing offer and will enable Compass to create more compelling and innovative solutions for its clients and consumers.

EXECUTIVES

Group Chief Executive, Richard J. Cousins, age 61, $313,000 total compensation
Group COO North America, Gary R. Green, age 63
COO Europe, Dominic Blakemore, age 50
Finance Director, Johnny Thompson
Chairman, Paul S. Walsh, age 65
Auditors: KPMG LLP

LOCATIONS

HQ: Compass Group PLC (United Kingdom)
Compass House, Guildford Street, Chertsey, Surrey
KT16 9BQ
Phone: (44) 1932 573 000
Web: www.compass-group.com

20187 sales

	% of total
North America	59
Europe	25
Rest of the World	16
Total	**100**

PRODUCTS/OPERATIONS

2018 sales

	% of total
Business & Industry	39
Healthcare & Seniors	24
Education	18
Sports & Leisure	12
Defence Offshore and Remote	7
Total	**100**

Selected Operating Units

All Leisure (sports and leisure venues)
Bon Appé;tit Management Company (on-site dining services)
Canteen (vending services)
Chartwells (education foodservices)
Crothall (health care facilities management)
ESS (offshore and remote foodservices)
Eurest (corporate foodservice)
FLIK (upscale foodservices)
Levy Restaurants (fine dining sports and leisure events)
Medirest (health care services)
Morrison Management Specialists (health care foodservice)
Restaurant Associates Managed Services (corporate dining and sporting and leisure events)
Scolarest (education foodservices)

COMPETITORS

ARAMARK	Healthcare Services
Autogrill	Legion Group
Centerplate	Reliance Security
Delaware North	Sodexo
Elior	
Farsight Security Services	

HISTORICAL FINANCIALS

Company Type: Public

Income Statement — FYE: September 30

	REVENUE ($ mil.)	NET INCOME ($ mil.)	NET PROFIT MARGIN	EMPLOYEES
09/20	39,847	265	0.7%	548,143
09/19	49,715	2,218	4.5%	596,452
09/18	45,891	2,248	4.9%	595,841
09/17	45,099	2,320	5.1%	588,112
09/16	39,178	1,982	5.1%	527,180
Annual Growth	**0.4%**	**(39.5%)**	**—**	**1.0%**

2020 Year-End Financials

Debt ratio: 51.2%
Return on equity: 3.2%
Cash ($ mil.): 2,965
Current ratio: 0.94
Long-term debt ($ mil.): 7,340

No. of shares (mil.): 1,785
Dividends
  Yield: 3.1%
  Payout: 204.5%
Market value ($ mil.): 26,942

Stock Price

	STOCK PRICE ($) FY Close	P/E High/Low	PER SHARE ($) Earnings	Dividends	Book Value
09/20	15.09	335 141	0.16	0.47	5.36
09/19	25.75	37 28	1.40	0.46	4.19
09/18	22.62	32 28	1.42	0.44	3.29
09/17	21.62	31 23	1.42	0.67	2.64
09/16	19.41	33 26	1.21	0.63	3.03
Annual Growth	**(6.1%)**	**— —**	**(39.6%)**	**(7.1%)**	**15.4%**

Continental AG (Germany, Fed. Rep.)

Continental AG keeps rolling along as one of Europe's largest manufacturers of tires for cars trucks motorcycles agricultural and construction vehicles. Its Automotive Group is Continental's largest segment manufacturing brake and traction control systems passive safety products sensors and chassis and powertrain products. The Rubber Group comprises its Tires division (sold under brands including Continental Uniroyal and General) as well as its ContiTech division which produces vibration control and power transmission systems as well as conveyor belts and fluid systems. Germany is the largest single market accounting for about 20% of total revenue.

Operations

Continental's Automotive Group generates about 60% of total sales each year while its Rubber Group hauls in the remaining 40%. Automotive comprises the Chassis and Safety division which manufactures intelligent systems for driving safety and vehicle dynamics; the Powertrain division which develops system solutions and powertrains; and the Interior division. The Interior division specializes in information management and produces network solutions for cars and commercial vehicles.

The Rubber Group comprises two divisions - Tire and ContiTech. The Tire division manufactures tires for a multitude of vehicles and sports equipment. ContiTech makes parts intelligent components and systems made of rubber plastic metal and fabric for machine and plant engineering mining agriculture and the automotive industry.

Geographic Reach

With nearly 600 locations in about 60 countries Continental does half of its business in Europe (about 20% in Germany) with the other half divided between North America and Asia. The company also has operations in South America Africa and Australia.

Continental AG is headquartered in Hanover Germany.

Sales and Marketing

The automotive manufacturing business is the largest group accounting for about 70% total sales.

Financial Performance

For the five-year period beginning in 2015 revenue steadily climbed and posted a 13% growth in that span.

In 2019 there have been a 0.2% increase in sales to ?44.5 billion. The Rubber group was able to achieve a slight increase in sales which was almost offset by sales decrease in Automotive group.

Net income suffered a loss of ?1.2 billion. The primary reasons for this were the weaker operating performance and the negative impact of special effects which mainly comprised impairment and re-

structuring expenses in the third and fourth quarters of 2019.

Cash at the end of fiscal 2019 was ?3.3 billion a ?580 million increase from 2018. Operating activities provided ?4.4 billion in cash and investing activities used ?3.7 billion for capital expenditures. Financing activities used another ?220 million for debt payments.

Strategy

Continental's seven strategic dimensions have not changed since its implementation:

Value creation- by enhancing the value of the corporation on a long-term basis.

Regional sales balance- aim to gradually increase share of consolidated sales in Asian markets to 30% and 25% in North and South America.

Top market position- by maintaining its position among the three leading suppliers in all relevant markets.

In the market for the market- by aiming for at least eight out of 10 application development to be carried out locally.

Balanced customer portfolio- by reducing its dependence on the automotive industry.

Technological balance- by managing and structuring its product and technology portfolio with the goal of being represented and competitive in all phases of the respective life cycles.

Great people culture- by promoting a culture of trust and personal responsibility.

Mergers and Acquisitions

In 2019 Continental announced the successful completion of the acquisition of Kathrein Automotive GmbH after antitrust authorities officially cleared the transaction. Incorporating the automotive division of Rosenheim-based antenna and satellite technology manufacturer Kathrein is a move that will give Continental an important key segment to add to its wealth of expertise. Intelligent vehicle antennas are the starting point for future-proof connectivity concepts in the vehicle interior and beyond. Terms were not disclosed.

HISTORY

A group of financiers and industrialists with interests in the rubber industry founded Continental-Caoutchouc und Gutta-Percha Compagnie in Hanover Germany in 1871. The company's products included solid tires for carriages and bicycles rubberized fabrics and various consumer items.

In 1892 Continental was the first German maker of pneumatic bicycle tires. During this period the budding automobile and motorcycle industries created fresh demand for solid tires. Continental began producing pneumatic tires for automobiles in 1898. By 1904 Continental was first to develop a treaded tire. Between 1905 and 1913 Continental expanded into Australia Denmark Italy Norway Romania Sweden and the UK by forming marketing subsidiaries. However the onset of WWI caused a shift to military production and the overseas sales network dissolved.

Poor overall economic conditions atrophied postwar tire industry growth and by the late 1920s the company merged several German rubber firms to create a much larger and stronger Continental. In 1929 the company changed its name to Continental Gummi-Werke AG.

EXECUTIVES

Chairman Executive Board, Elmar Degenhart, age 62
Executive Board Member Human Resources and Personnel, Heinz-Gerhard Wente, age 69
Member Executive Board Chassis and Safety, Ralf Cramer, age 54

Member Executive Board Interior, Helmut Matschi, age 57

Member Executive Board Tire Division, Nikolai Setzer, age 49

Member Executive Board Finance Controlling Compliance Law and IT, Wolfgang Sch ¤fer, age 61

Member Executive Board Powertrain Division, José A. Avila, age 65

Chairman Supervisory Board, Wolfgang H. Reitzle, age 71

Deputy Chairman Supervisory Board, Werner Bischoff, age 73

Auditors: KPMG AG

LOCATIONS

HQ: Continental AG (Germany, Fed. Rep.)
Vahrenwalder Strasse 9, Hanover D-30165
Phone: (49) 511 938 01   **Fax:** (49) 511 938 81 770
Web: www.continental-corporation.com

2017 Sales

	% of total
Europe	
Germany	20
Europe excluding Germany	29
North America	25
Asia	22
Other cegions	4
Total	**100**

PRODUCTS/OPERATIONS

2017 Sales

	% of total
Automotive Group	
Chassis & safety	22
Interior	21
Powertrain	17
Rubber Group	
Tires (passenger & light truck)	26
ContiTech	14
Total	**100**

Selected Automotive Group Products

Chassis and Safety
　Chassis components
　Electronic brake systems
　Hydraulic brake systems
　Passive safety and ADAS
　Sensors
Interior
　Body and security
　Commercial vehicles and aftermarket
　Connectivity
　Instrumentation and displays
　Interior modules
　Multimedia
Powertrain
　Engine systems
　Fuel supply
　Hybrid electric vehicle
　Sensors and actuators
　Transmissions

Selected Rubber Group Products

ContiTech
　Air spring systems
　Benecke-Kaliko group
　Conveyor belt group
　Elastomer coatings
　Fluid technology
　Power transmission group
　Vibration control
Tires
　Commercial vehicles
　Off-road vehicles
　Passenger and light truck
　Motorcycles
　Bicycles

COMPETITORS

AirBoss of America	McLaren Performance
Bridgestone	Meritor
China Enterprises	Michelin
Cooper Tire & Rubber	Nokian Tyres
DENSO	Pirelli
Dana	Robert Bosch
Delphi Automotive Systems	Standard Motor Products
Gates Corp.	Sumitomo Rubber
Goodyear Tire & Rubber	Toyo Tire & Rubber
Hankook Tire	Trelleborg
Kumho Tire	Valeo
Lear Corp	Visteon
Magna International	Yokohama Rubber

HISTORICAL FINANCIALS

Company Type: Public

Income Statement				FYE: December 31
	REVENUE ($ mil.)	NET INCOME ($ mil.)	NET PROFIT MARGIN	EMPLOYEES
12/19	49,938	(1,375)	—	241,458
12/18	50,851	3,317	6.5%	243,226
12/17	52,756	3,577	6.8%	230,656
12/16	42,815	2,959	6.9%	216,019
12/15	42,731	2,970	7.0%	207,899
Annual Growth	**4.0%**	**—**	**—**	**3.8%**

2019 Year-End Financials

Debt ratio: 18.8%
Return on equity: (-7.3%)
Cash ($ mil.): 3,752
Current ratio: 1.06
Long-term debt ($ mil.): 3,789

No. of shares (mil.): 200
Dividends
　Yield: 2.9%
　Payout: —
Market value ($ mil.): 2,565

	STOCK PRICE ($) FY Close	P/E High/Low		PER SHARE ($) Earnings	Dividends	Book Value
12/19	12.83	—	—	(6.88)	0.37	86.42
12/18	13.78	4	1	16.59	0.77	102.21
12/17	53.88	4	3	17.89	0.37	94.87
12/16	38.50	3	2	14.79	0.29	75.34
12/15	48.11	4	3	14.86	0.52	69.63
Annual Growth	**(28.1%)**	**—**	**—**	**—**	**(8.2%)**	**5.5%**

COSCO Shipping Holdings Co Ltd

EXECUTIVES

Legal Representative, Jiafu Wei
Auditors: Ruihua Certified Public Accountants, LLP

LOCATIONS

HQ: COSCO Shipping Holdings Co Ltd
2nd Floor, 12 Yuanhang Business Centre, Central Boulevard and East Seven Road Junction, Tianjin Port Free Trade Zone, Tianjin 300461
Phone: (86) 22 66270898   **Fax:** (86) 22 66270899
Web: www.chinacosco.com

HISTORICAL FINANCIALS

Company Type: Public

Income Statement				FYE: December 31
	REVENUE ($ mil.)	NET INCOME ($ mil.)	NET PROFIT MARGIN	EMPLOYEES
12/19	21,709	972	4.5%	0
12/18	17,566	178	1.0%	0
12/17	13,901	409	2.9%	0
12/16	10,247	(1,426)	—	0
12/15	8,838	43	0.5%	34,913
Annual Growth	**25.2%**	**117.3%**	**—**	**—**

2019 Year-End Financials

Debt ratio: 6.1%
Return on equity: 23.2%
Cash ($ mil.): 7,233
Current ratio: 1.03
Long-term debt ($ mil.): 11,425

No. of shares (mil.): —
Dividends
　Yield: —
　Payout: —
Market value ($ mil.): —

Cosmo Energy Holdings Co Ltd

LOCATIONS

HQ: Cosmo Energy Holdings Co Ltd
1-1-1 Shibaura, Minato-ku, Tokyo 105-8302
Phone: (81) 3 3798 3128
Web: ceh.cosmo-oil.co.jp

HISTORICAL FINANCIALS

Company Type: Public

Income Statement				FYE: March 31
	REVENUE ($ mil.)	NET INCOME ($ mil.)	NET PROFIT MARGIN	EMPLOYEES
03/20	25,223	(259)	—	10,155
03/19	25,015	479	1.9%	9,700
03/18	23,761	685	2.9%	9,842
03/17	20,502	476	2.3%	9,880
03/16	19,985	(447)	—	10,285
Annual Growth	**6.0%**	**—**	**—**	**(0.3%)**

2020 Year-End Financials

Debt ratio: 0.3%
Return on equity: (-10.7%)
Cash ($ mil.): 488
Current ratio: 0.81
Long-term debt ($ mil.): 4,000

No. of shares (mil.): 84
Dividends
　Yield: —
　Payout: —
Market value ($ mil.): —

Country Garden Holdings Co Ltd

EXECUTIVES

Chairman and CEO, Yeung Kwok Keung, age 66
President and Executive Director, Mo Bin, age 54
Associate President and Executive Director, Zhu Rongbin
CFO, Wu Bijun, age 47
Vice Chairman, Yang Huiyan, age 39
Auditors: PricewaterhouseCoopers

LOCATIONS

HQ: Country Garden Holdings Co Ltd
Suite 1702, 17/F., Dina House, Ruttonjee Centre, 11 Duddell Street, Central,
Phone:
Web: www.countrygarden.com.cn

PRODUCTS/OPERATIONS

2016 Sales

	% of total
Property development	97
Construction fitting & decoration	1
Property management	1
Hotel operation	1
Total	**100**

2016 Sales

	% of total
Guangdong	29
Jiangsu	17
Anhui	7
Zhejiang	5
Hubei	4
Hebei	4
Hunan	4
Fujian	3
Henan	3
Others	24
Total	**100**

Selected Projects

Country Garden - Galaxy Palace
Country Garden - Grand Garden
Country Garden - Springs City
Country Garden - Ten Miles Coast
Country Garden City Garden
Country Garden Grand Lake
Country Garden Phoenix City
Dalang Country Garden
Heshan Country Garden
Holiday Island
Malaysia Project
Tianjin Country Garden

COMPETITORS

China Overseas Land & Investment
China Vanke
Evergrande Real Estate Group
Guangzhou R&F Properties
Shanghai Forte Land
Sino Land
Xinyuan
Yanlord Land

HISTORICAL FINANCIALS

Company Type: Public

Income Statement — FYE: December 31

	REVENUE ($ mil.)	NET INCOME ($ mil.)	NET PROFIT MARGIN	EMPLOYEES
12/19	69,832	5,683	8.1%	101,784
12/18	55,112	5,032	9.1%	131,387
12/17	34,867	4,005	11.5%	124,837
12/16	22,045	1,658	7.5%	94,450
12/15	17,433	1,428	8.2%	68,150
Annual Growth	**41.5%**	**41.2%**	**—**	**10.5%**

2019 Year-End Financials

Debt ratio: 2.7%
Return on equity: 28.9%
Cash ($ mil.): 35,782
Current ratio: 1.17
Long-term debt ($ mil.): 36,407
No. of shares (mil.): —
Dividends
  Yield: —
  Payout: 31.9%
Market value ($ mil.): —

Covestro AG

Auditors: KPMG AG

LOCATIONS

HQ: Covestro AG
Building K12, Kaiser-Wilhelm-Allee 60, Leverkusen D-51373
Phone: (49) 214 6009 2000   **Fax:** (49) 214 6009 3000
Web: www.covestro.com

HISTORICAL FINANCIALS

Company Type: Public

Income Statement — FYE: December 31

	REVENUE ($ mil.)	NET INCOME ($ mil.)	NET PROFIT MARGIN	EMPLOYEES
12/19	13,935	619	4.4%	17,201
12/18	16,738	2,087	12.5%	16,770
12/17	16,947	2,408	14.2%	16,176
12/16	12,569	839	6.7%	15,579
Annual Growth	**3.5%**	**(9.6%)**	**—**	**3.4%**

2019 Year-End Financials

Debt ratio: —
Return on equity: 10.4%
Cash ($ mil.): 839
Current ratio: 2.21
Long-term debt ($ mil.): —
No. of shares (mil.): 182
Dividends
  Yield: 4.2%
  Payout: 28.6%
Market value ($ mil.): 4,165

	STOCK PRICE ($) FY Close	P/E High/Low		PER SHARE ($) Earnings	Dividends	Book Value
12/19	22.77	10	7	3.39	0.98	31.97
12/18	25.00	6	3	10.83	0.98	33.48
12/17	51.90	5	4	11.90	0.58	31.84
12/16	34.70	9	8	4.15	1.43	21.84
/0.00	—	—	(0.00)	0.00	(0.00)	
Annual Growth	**—**		**—**	**—**	**—**	

CPFL Energia SA

EXECUTIVES

Chief Financial and Investor Relations Officer, Gustavo Estrella, age 46
CEO, Andre Dorf
Chairman, Murilo C. Lemos dos Santos Passos, age 73
Vice Chairman, Décio Bottechia, age 55
Auditors: KPMG Auditores Independentes

LOCATIONS

HQ: CPFL Energia SA
Rua Jorge de Figueiredo Correa, No. 1,632, Jardim Professora Tarcilia, Campinas, Sao Paulo 13087-397
Phone: (55) 19 3756 8704
Web: www.cpfl.com.br

PRODUCTS/OPERATIONS

2014 Sales

	% of total
Distribution	79
Generation conventional source	4
Generation Renewable source	6
Commercialization	10
Services	1
Others	
Total	**100**

Selected Subsidiaries

Companhia Paulista de Força e Luz (CPFL Paulista)
Companhia Piratininga de Força e Luz (CPFL Piratininga)
Rio Grande Energia
CPFL Brasil
CPFL Geração de Energia S.A. (CPFL Generation)

COMPETITORS

AES
CESP
COPEL
Duke Energy
ELETROBR S
Enersis
Light Servicos de Eletricidade

HISTORICAL FINANCIALS

Company Type: Public

Income Statement — FYE: December 31

	REVENUE ($ mil.)	NET INCOME ($ mil.)	NET PROFIT MARGIN	EMPLOYEES
12/19	17,939	1,619	9.0%	13,302
12/18	16,863	1,233	7.3%	13,467
12/17	16,029	707	4.4%	13,344
12/16	11,454	539	4.7%	13,217
12/15	12,110	518	4.3%	9,584
Annual Growth	**10.3%**	**33.0%**	**—**	**8.5%**

2019 Year-End Financials

Debt ratio: 25.7%
Return on equity: 23.2%
Cash ($ mil.): 1,161
Current ratio: 1.03
Long-term debt ($ mil.): 9,260
No. of shares (mil.): 1,152
Dividends
  Yield: —
  Payout: 22.6%
Market value ($ mil.): —

CrediCorp Ltd.

Auditors: Gaveglio, Aparicio y Asociados S.C.R.L

LOCATIONS

HQ: CrediCorp Ltd.
Clarendon House, Church Street, Hamilton HM 11
Phone:
Web: www.credicorpnet.com

HISTORICAL FINANCIALS

Company Type: Public

Income Statement — FYE: December 31

	ASSETS ($ mil.)	NET INCOME ($ mil.)	INCOME AS % OF ASSETS	EMPLOYEES
12/19	56,649	1,286	2.3%	35,828
12/18	52,450	1,178	2.2%	34,024
12/17	52,606	1,262	2.4%	33,636
12/16	46,578	1,046	2.2%	33,282
12/15	45,668	908	2.0%	33,658
Annual Growth	**5.5%**	**9.1%**	**—**	**1.6%**

2019 Year-End Financials

Return on assets: 2.3%
Return on equity: 17.0%
Long-term debt ($ mil.): —
No. of shares (mil.): 79
Sales ($ mil): 5,939
Dividends
  Yield: 3.9%
  Payout: 56.0%
Market value ($ mil.): —

Credit Agricole SA

Auditors: ERNST & YOUNG et Autres

HQ: Credit Agricole SA
12 place des Etat-Unis, Montrouge, Cedex 92127
Phone: (33) 1 43 23 52 02
Web: www.credit-agricole.com

HISTORICAL FINANCIALS

Company Type: Public

Income Statement				FYE: December 31
	ASSETS ($ mil.)	NET INCOME ($ mil.)	INCOME AS % OF ASSETS	EMPLOYEES
12/19	1,984,649	5,438	0.3%	75,423
12/18	1,860,248	5,038	0.3%	73,346
12/17	1,858,408	4,374	0.2%	73,707
12/16	1,609,410	3,737	0.2%	137,871
12/15	1,665,723	3,829	0.2%	71,495
Annual Growth	4.5%	9.2%	—	1.3%

2019 Year-End Financials

Return on assets: 0.2%
Return on equity: 7.9%
Long-term debt ($ mil.): —
No. of shares (mil.): —
Sales ($ mil): 105,428

Dividends
Yield: 5.3%
Payout: 23.3%
Market value ($ mil.): —

	STOCK PRICE ($) FY Close	P/E High/Low		PER SHARE ($) Earnings	Dividends	Book Value
12/19	7.23	5	3	1.66	0.39	24.49
12/18	5.33	6	4	1.59	0.37	23.53
12/17	8.22	8	6	1.35	0.36	24.47
12/16	6.14	6	3	1.18	0.32	21.64
12/15	5.86	6	4	1.32	0.20	22.24
Annual Growth	5.4%	—	—	6.0%	18.5%	2.4%

Credit Suisse Group AG

Credit Suisse is one of Switzerland's top financial services firms though a distant second to behemoth rival UBS. The group provides investment management and advice private banking and asset management services to clients worldwide. Its investment banking offerings include debt and equity underwriting of public securities offerings and private placements. The group also provides wealth management services and asset management services to individual institutional and government clients. With around 145 retail branches in Switzerland it operates in about 50 countries.

Operations

Credit Suisse operates three divisions with a regional focus: Swiss Universal Bank International Wealth Management and Asia Pacific. The three are supported by two other divisions with specialist investment banking capabilities Global Markets and Investment Banking & Capital Markets.

Swiss Universal Bank offers financial advice and solutions to private corporate and institutional clients primarily in Switzerland. The Private Clients business serves high- and ultra-high-net-worth individuals (UHNWIs). Corporate & Institutional Clients serves large businesses SMEs institutional clients external asset managers and financial institutions. It generates more than 25% of sales.

Through its Private Banking business the International Wealth Management segment offers comprehensive advisory services and tailored investment and financing solutions to rich people in Europe the Middle East Africa and Latin America. It serves pension funds governments foundations and endowments corporations and individuals. It generates around 25% of total sales.

Global Markets offers financial products and services and also provides support to Credit Suisse's global wealth management businesses. It offers global securities sales trading and execution prime brokerage and investment research. It brings in around 25% of sales.

The Asia Pacific segment combines wealth management financing and underwriting and advice to offer integrated advisory services to UHNWIs and entrepreneur and corporate clients. It accounts for more than 15% of sales.

Investment Banking & Capital Markets offers advice on mergers and acquisitions divestitures takeovers restructuring and spin-offs. It accounts for the remaining less than 10% of revenue.

Credit Suisse generates some 50% of revenue from fee and commission income around 30% from net interest income and the rest from trading and other revenue streams.

Geographic Reach

Zurich Switzerland-based Credit Suisse has operations in about 50 countries. It generates more than 40% of sales from the Americas while more than 35% comes from Switzerland itself. The Asia/Pacific region accounts for nearly 15% of sales and the remaining around 10% or so comes from Europe the Middle East and Africa (EMEA).

Sales and Marketing

Credit Suisse serves global corporates SMEs rich people governments institutions institutional investors such as pensions and hedge funds and private individuals.

Financial Performance

Credit Suisse's revenue in 2019 was CHF 22.5 billion up 8% compared to the previous year driven by increase in trading and other revenues.

Net income attributable to shareholders was CHF 3.4 billion in 2019 up 69% compared to the previous year. The 2019 results included certain significant gains from the transfer of the InvestLab fund platform to Allfunds Group of CHF 327 million and the revaluation of our equity investment in SIX Group AG of CHF 498 million.

Cash at the end of the year was CHF 101.9 billion CHF 1.8 billion higher compared to CHF100 billion in 2018. The company's operations produced CHF 18.4 billion. Investing activities used CHF 1.3 billion primarily due to originating loans to be held to maturity other receivables and the investment securities portfolio while financing activities used CHF 22.2 billion primarily due to issuance of debt and receipt of customer deposits.

Strategy

Credit Suisse successfully completed its three-year restructuring plan at the end of 2018 and the discipline that has been shown in 2018 continued in 2019. In 2020 the company aims to maintain its momentum mainly by growing revenues in wealth management increasing profitability in its investment banking business maintaining cost discipline and optimizing its operating model.

To grow revenues in wealth management Credit Suisse focused on growing revenue streams across net income and recurring commissions and fees which accounted for the majority of its Wealth Management-related revenues as of the end of 2019.

As part of the strategy to increase profitability in its investment banking businesses the company continued to drive closer collaboration with wealth management and global connectivity through ITS. To replicate the success of ITS in Asia Pacific ATS was established.

To optimize its operating model the company continued to focus on its control functions with the belief that this will be key to its success as its businesses grow. Since 2015 significant investments were made to strengthen the company's risk management and compliance functions. Control efforts also include all of its other corporate functions and front office businesses. Front-to-back technology advancements and tools are leveraged across the bank to further strengthen the operating model.

Company Background

The bank has been plagued by litigation charges in recent years. In 2012 Credit Suisse handed over information to the US government as part of an investigation into hidden Swiss bank accounts that are used by wealthy Americans to evade taxes. Credit Suisse was among other Swiss banks that were being investigated. Swiss privacy laws have typically protected wealthy individuals who funnel money through offshore accounts.

HISTORY

In 1856 shortly after the creation of the Swiss federation Alfred Escher opened Credit Suisse (CS) in Zurich. Primarily a venture capital firm CS helped fund Swiss railroads and other industries. It later opened offices in Italy and helped establish the Swiss Bank Corporation.

CS shifted its focus to commercial banking in 1867 and sold most of its stock holdings. By 1871 it was Switzerland's largest bank buoyed by the nation's swift industrialization. In 1895 CS helped create the predecessor of Swiss utility Electrowatt. Foreign activity grew in the 1920s. A run on banks in the Depression forced CS to sell assets at a loss and dip into reserves of unreported retained profits.

Trade declined in WWII but neutrality left Switzerland's institutions intact and made it a major banking center partly due to CS's role as a conduit for the Nazis' plundered gold. Foreign exchange and gold trading became important activities for CS after WWII. Mortgage and consumer credit acquisitions fueled domestic growth in the 1970s.

In 1978 the bank took a stake in US investment bank First Boston and with it formed London-based Credit Suisse-First Boston (CSFB). CS created 44%-owned holding company Credit Suisse First Boston to own First Boston CSFB and Tokyo-based CS First Boston Pacific.

The stock market crash of 1987 led a damaged First Boston to merge with CSFB the next year. In 1990 CS (renamed CS Holding) injected $300 million into CSFB and shifted $470 million in bad loans from its books becoming the first foreign owner of a major Wall Street investment bank.

In the early 1990s CS Holding strengthened its insurance business with a Winterthur Insurance alliance. In 1993 and 1994 acquisitions helped it gain share in its overbanked home market.

In 1996 CS Holding reorganized as Credit Suisse Group and grew internationally including further merging the daredevil US investment banking operations into Credit Suisse's more staid and relationship-oriented corporate banking. It bought Winterthur (Switzerland's #2 insurer) in 1997 as well as Barclays' European investment banking business.

Credit Suisse and other Swiss banks came under fire in 1996 for refusing to relinquish assets from Jewish bank accounts from the Holocaust era and for gold trading with the Nazi regime. In 1997 the banks agreed to establish a humanitarian fund for Holocaust victims. A stream of lawsuits by American heirs and boycott threats from US states and cities led in 1998 to a tentative $1.25 billion settlement (unpopular in Switzerland) with Credit Suisse on the hook for about a third of that.

CS in 1998 expanded its investment banking by buying Brazil's Banco de Investimentos Garantia; it also moved to expand US money management operations by allying with New York-based

Warburg Pincus Asset Management. By 1999 that joint venture — which was to give the investment firm access to CS's mutual fund distribution channels in Europe and Asia — had morphed into CS's $650 million purchase of Warburg Pincus Asset Management.

Japan revoked the license of the company's financial products unit for obstructing an investigation (the harshest penalty ever given to a foreign firm at the time); it also accused the company of helping 60 others hide losses and cover up evidence.

In 2000 the company started a mortgage and home-buying Web site and decided to allow searches of Holocaust-era accounts. The next year as a part of its European expansion Credit Suisse acquired Spanish broker and asset manager General de Valores y Cambios.

Under former chairman and CEO Lukas M hlemann the company expanded Credit Suisse First Boston when it bought US investment firm Donaldson Lufkin & Jenrette in 2000 and renamed it Credit Suisse First Boston (USA).

The collapse of Credit Suisse's share price along with what proved to be an over-ambitious acquisition strategy brought about the downfall of M hlemann who was pressured out by shareholders in 2002.

In 2005 Credit Suisse merged with its Credit Suisse First Boston subsidiary creating a global Credit Suisse brand and in 2006 reorganized into three distinct operating segments — investment banking private banking and asset management along with insurance.

Credit Suisse sold insurance subsidiary Winterthur to AXA in 2006 for nearly $10 billion. A Winterthur sale had been on Credit Suisse's agenda for a while as a plan to divest noncore operations. Also that year Credit Suisse and General Electric jointly acquired a 50% stake in London City Airport which serves about 2 million travelers a year. The following year as a cost-saving measure Credit Suisse combined four private banks and one securities dealer into Clariden Leu.

The company named Brady Dougan CEO in 2007. Dugan was the first non-German speaker to hold the position.

Globally the investment banking industry was hit hard by the US subprime mortgage crisis and Credit Suisse was no exception. The company reported a net loss of ?5.4 billion in 2008 the worst in its history. Credit Suisse turned down a bailout offer from the Swiss government in 2008 but it did receive a capital injection of CHF10 billion ($8.7 billion) from private investors. However the capital infusion couldn't prevent losses as global credit markets froze and consumer and shareholder confidence fell.

The company cut more than 5000 jobs or some 11% of its workforce mostly from its investment banking unit. It also reviewed its results for 2007 and among its findings discovered rogue traders in its ranks la the beleaguered Soci t G n rale. Credit Suisse reduced its results accordingly.

In 2008 it bought an 80% stake in US firm Asset Management Finance Corporation a division of National Bank of Canada. Also in 2008 it expanded its Middle East franchise when it bought majority ownership in joint venture Saudi Swiss Securities which it renamed Credit Suisse Saudi Arabia. It has added Shariah-compliant banking for Islamic clients and has expanded in other markets including Brazil Kazakhstan and Turkey.

The following year Credit Suisse sold certain fund management assets and businesses to Aberdeen Asset Management in exchange for about 25% of Aberdeen's shares.

EXECUTIVES

President and CEO Credit Suisse Holdings (USA) Inc., Eric Varvel, age 57
CEO, Tidjane C. Thiam, age 58
CFO, David Mathers, age 56
CEO Asia Pacific, Helman Sitohang
COO, Pierre-Olivier Bouée
CEO Investment Banking and Capital Markets, James L. Amine
Chief Risk Officer, Joachim Oechslin, age 49
CEO Swiss Universal Bank, Thomas P. Gottstein
CEO International Wealth Management, Iqbal Khan
Co-Head of Credit, Brian Chin
Head of Integration; Executive Vice Chairman Credit Suisse (USA), Richard E. Thornburgh, age 69
Chairman, Urs Rohner, age 61
Vice Chair and Lead Independent Director, Noreen Doyle, age 71
Auditors: KPMG AG

LOCATIONS

HQ: Credit Suisse Group AG
Paradeplatz 8, Zurich CH 8001
Phone: (41) 44 333 6607   **Fax:** (41) 44 333 1790
Web: www.credit-suisse.com

2018 sales

	% of total
Switzerland	36
Americas	42
Asia Pacific	14
EMEA	8
Total	**100**

PRODUCTS/OPERATIONS

2018 sales

	% of total
Commissions & fees	57
Net interest income	33
Trading revenues	3
Other	7
Total	**100**

2018 sales

	% of total
Swiss Universal Bank	26
International Wealth Management	25
Global Markets	23
Asia Pacific	16
Investment Banking & Capital Markets	10
Strategic Resolution Unit	-
Corporate Center	-
Total	**100**

COMPETITORS

AEGON	JPMorgan Chase
Barclays	Mitsubishi UFJ
Citigroup	Financial Group
Deutsche Bank	Mizuho Financial
Goldman Sachs	Morgan Stanley
Grupo Santander	Nomura Securities
HSBC	TD Bank
ING	UBS

HISTORICAL FINANCIALS

Company Type: Public

Income Statement

FYE: December 31

	ASSETS ($ mil.)	NET INCOME ($ mil.)	INCOME AS % OF ASSETS	EMPLOYEES
12/19	814,416	3,536	0.4%	47,860
12/18	781,647	2,057	0.3%	45,680
12/17	815,899	(1,007)	—	46,840
12/16	805,441	(2,662)	—	47,170
12/15	826,505	(2,964)	—	48,200
Annual Growth	(0.4%)	—	—	(0.2%)

2019 Year-End Financials

Return on assets: 0.4%
Return on equity: 7.8%
Long-term debt ($ mil.): —
No. of shares (mil.): —
Sales ($ mil): 23,258
Dividends
Yield: 1.9%
Payout: 19.8%
Market value ($ mil.): —

	STOCK PRICE ($) FY Close	P/E High/Low		PER SHARE ($) Earnings	Dividends	Book Value
12/19	13.45	11	8	1.37	0.26	18.53
12/18	10.86	24	13	0.78	0.74	17.51
12/17	17.85	—	—	(0.42)	1.21	16.84
12/16	14.31	—	—	(1.30)	0.69	19.69
12/15	21.69	—	—	(1.74)	1.20	22.90
Annual Growth	(11.3%)	—	—	—	(32.0%)	(5.2%)

Credito Emiliano Spa Credem Reggio Emilia

EXECUTIVES

President Titolare, LUCIO IGINO ZANON DI VALGIURATA
Vice Presidente, FRANCO TERRACHINI
Vice Presidente, ENRICO CORRADI
Vice Presidente, LUIGI MARAMOTTI
Consigliere, BENEDETTO GIOVANNI MARIA RENDA
Consigliere, PAOLA GINA MARIA SCHWIZER
Consigliere, RICCARDO BRUNO
Consigliere, CLAUDIA ALFIERI
Consigliere, ERNESTINA MORSTOFOLINI
Auditors: Ernst & Young S.p.A.

LOCATIONS

HQ: Credito Emiliano Spa Credem Reggio Emilia
Via Emilia San Pietro 4, Reggio Emilia 42100
Phone: (39) 522 5821   **Fax:** (39) 522 433969
Web: www.credem.it

2008 Sales

	% of total
Italy	
North-central	63
Southern & islands	35
Other countries	2
Total	**100**

PRODUCTS/OPERATIONS

2008 Sales

	% of total
Retail banking	59
Corporate loans	16
Investment banking	
Wealth management	5
Other	20
Total	**100**

COMPETITORS

Antonveneta	Intesa Sanpaolo
BPER-Emilia Romagna	Mediobanca
Banca Popolare di	Monte dei Paschi di
Milano	Siena
Interbanca	UniCredit

HISTORICAL FINANCIALS

Company Type: Public

Income Statement   FYE: December 31

	ASSETS ($ mil.)	NET INCOME ($ mil.)	INCOME AS % OF ASSETS	EMPLOYEES
12/19	53,477	226	0.4%	6,201
12/18	49,435	213	0.4%	6,195
12/17	49,849	223	0.4%	6,140
12/16	41,780	139	0.3%	6,068
12/15	40,796	180	0.4%	5,516
Annual Growth	7.0%	5.7%	—	3.0%

2019 Year-End Financials

Return on assets: 0.4%	Dividends
Return on equity: 3.0%	Yield: —
Long-term debt ($ mil.): —	Payout: —
No. of shares (mil.): 330	Market value ($ mil.): —
Sales ($ mil): 2,038	

Cresud SA Comercial Industrial Financiera Y Agropecuaria Cres

EXECUTIVES

President, Eduardo Sergio Elsztain
Vice President, Sa l Zang
Vice President, Alejandro Gustavo Elsztain
Auditors: Price Waterhouse & Co. S.R.L.

LOCATIONS

HQ: Cresud SA Comercial Industrial Financiera Y Agropecuaria Cres
Moreno, 877, 23rd floor, Buenos Aires C1091AAQ
Phone: (54) 11 4344 4600   **Fax:** (54) 11 4344 4611
Web: www.cresud.com.ar

PRODUCTS/OPERATIONS

Selected Subsidiaries

Agro Uranga S.A. (36% dairy farming)
Agropecuaria Cervera S.A. (99% agricultural cattle-breeding and forestry property development)
BrasilAgro Companhia Brasileira de Propiedades Agrí;colas (14% sugar cane grain cotton forestry livestock Brazil)
Cactus Argentina S.A. (24% joint venture with Cactus Feeders Inc. and Tyson Foods Inc. feed lot production)
Futuros y Opciones.Com S.A. (68% agricultural Web site)
FyO Trading S.A. (69% agricultural production and commerce)
Inversiones Ganaderas S.A. (99% farming)
IRSA Inversiones y Representaciones Sociedad Anónima (42% real estate development and management)

COMPETITORS

ADM	Friona Industries

Ag Processing Inc.	JBS
Alico Inc.	King Ranch
Bartlett and Company	Koch Industries Inc.
Brasil Foods	Lykes Bros.
Bunge Limited	Sadia
Cargill	Tyson Foods
DeWied International	Tyson Fresh Meats
Eleva	

HISTORICAL FINANCIALS

Company Type: Public

Income Statement   FYE: June 30

	REVENUE ($ mil.)	NET INCOME ($ mil.)	NET PROFIT MARGIN	EMPLOYEES
06/20	39,449	1,242	3.1%	3,185
06/19	26,643	(5,929)	—	3,370
06/18	12,754	1,705	13.4%	0
06/17	25,306	477	1.9%	2,635
06/16	11,780	(443)	—	0
Annual Growth	35.3%	—	—	—

2020 Year-End Financials

Debt ratio: 19.2%	No. of shares (mil.): 501
Return on equity: 18.6%	Dividends
Cash ($ mil.): 31,917	Yield: —
Current ratio: 1.34	Payout: —
Long-term debt ($ mil.): 101,332	Market value ($ mil.): 1,485

	STOCK PRICE ($) FY Close	P/E High/Low		Earnings	PER SHARE ($) Dividends	Book Value
06/20	2.96	—	—	(2.41)	0.00	15.86
06/19	10.48	—	—	(11.81)	0.00	10.33
06/18	14.82	2	1	3.08	0.40	12.32
06/17	19.45	8	5	0.89	0.00	9.66
06/16	14.13	—	—	(0.84)	0.00	0.60
Annual Growth	(32.3%) 126.6%	—	—	—	—	—

CRH Plc

CRH has built its business upon building materials. Through subsidiaries (including Oldcastle in North America) the Ireland-based international company makes and distributes cement concrete aggregate glass and asphalt for commercial residential and infrastructure projects across the globe. CRH has over 3100 operating locations and a presence in around 30 countries CRH has become the top supplier of building materials in North America and the largest heavyside materials business in Europe. It operates as Tarmac in the UK. The largest Irish company CRH was formed in 1970 and has grown quickly in recent years thanks to a relentless acquisition program.

Operations

CRH operates in three operating segments: Americas materials (around 40% of revenue) Europe materials (about 35%) and Building products (25%).

Americas Materials Division is a vertical integrated supplier of building materials used widely in construction projects throughout North America. Typically these materials are resource-backed in mineral deposits found within their extensive network of quarry locations where they are processed for supply as aggregates asphalt cement and readymixed concrete.

Europe Materials Division manufactures and supplies a broad range of materials for use in construction projects including aggregates cement lime asphalt readymixed concrete and cement products. With an extensive in the strong and stable markets of Western Europe a strong footprint in growing Eastern European markets and an attractive position in Asia the Division is geographically balanced and has broad exposure to residential non-residential and infrastructure sectors.

Building products is a new division established by CRH in 2019 as part of their strategy to create a more simplified and focused business which is better positioned to exploit opportunities presented by economic development changing demographics sustainability and other evolving trends in construction markets globally. The Division brings together related products businesses in Europe North America and Asia Pacific across four strategic product groups for growth: Architectural Products Building Envelope Infrastructure Products and Construction Accessories.

Geographic Reach

Ireland-based CRH operates in more than 30 countries. The United States was the company's largest market with around 55% of revenue followed by the United Kingdom with approximately 15% and Ireland with less than 5% of revenue.

CRH operates from around 1450 locations in the Americas (around 45 US states six Canadian provinces and three Brazil states) and over 1160 across Europe.

Sales and Marketing

CRH serves three primary sectors residential non-residential and infrastructure drawing comparable sales from each.

Financial Performance

Note: Growth rates may differ after conversion to US dollars.

In 2019 revenue from continuing and discontinued operations increased by 6% to ?28.3 billion driven by positive underlying construction demand and a favorable pricing environment in their core markets in Europe and North America.

Net income fell by 24% to ?1.9 billion reflecting a further year of progress for the Company given the prior year included an after-tax gain of ?1.1 billion on certain divestment activity.

In the end of fiscal year 2019 the company's cash held increased by 60% to ?3.8 billion from ?2.3 billion from the prior year. Cash from operations provided ?3.5 billion cash from investing activities provided ?195 million and cash used for financing activities were ?2.3 billion.

Strategy

CRH's strategy is to grow and improve their business in a sustainable and responsible way through a relentless focus on performance improvement focused growth and value creation for the benefit of all their stakeholders. The company's strategy is underpinned by four strategic objectives: including: Continuous Improvement; Focused Growth; Benefits of Scale and Integrations; and Developing Leaders.

In 2019 their UK Cement & Lime business undertook a Supply Chain Excellence review covering six areas: customer service offering network optimization order taking and scheduling model distribution road fleet strategy value-adding technology and organizational design.

In 2019 the company continued to actively divest business which were no longer a strategic fit for the Group including their Europe Distribution business their Shutters & Awnings and Perimeter Protection businesses in Europe and their cement joint venture in India.

CRH procures ?14 billion in products and services annually in key areas such as raw materials energy logistics production services consumable and mobile plant.

The company also broadened their development offering to include critical experiences such as stretch assignments global collaboration projects and exposure one-to-one coaching as well as strengthening inclusion and diversity training across their leadership programmes and senior leadership teams.

Company Background

The Group resulted from the merger in 1970 of two leading Irish public companies Cement Limited (established in 1936) and Roadstone Limited (incorporated in 1949). Cement Limited manufactured and supplied cement while Roadstone Limited was primarily involved in the manufacture and supply of aggregates readymixed concrete mortar coated macadam asphalt and contract surfacing to the Irish construction industry.

EXECUTIVES

Finance Director, Maeve Carton, age 61
CEO, Albert Manifold, age 57
Chairman, Nicky Hartery, age 68
Auditors: Ernst & Young

LOCATIONS

HQ: CRH Plc
Belgard Castle, Clondalkin, Dublin 22
Phone: (353) 1 404 1000   **Fax:** (353) 1 404 1007
Web: www.crh.com

2018 sales

	% of total
United States	45
Rest of Europe	25
UK	12
Benelux	9
Ireland	2
Rest of the World	7
Total	**100**

2018 Sales

	% of total
Europe	
Heavyside	28
Distribution	14
Lightside	6
Americas	
Materials	33
Distribution	9
Asia	2
Total	**100**

PRODUCTS/OPERATIONS

2018 sales

	% of total
Cement lime and cement products	12
Aggregates asphalt and readymixed products	27
Construction contract activities	21
Construction accessories	2
Perimeter protection shutters & awnings and network access products	2
Architectural and precast products	17
Architectural glass and glazing systems and wholesale hardware distribution	6
General Builders Merchants DIY and Sanitary Heating & Plumbing	14
Total	**100**

Selected Activities and Products

Materials
  Aggregates
  Agricultural and chemical lime
  Asphalt
  Cement
  Concrete products
  Ready-mixed concrete
Products
  Architectural concrete
  Building products
  Building envelope products
  Construction accessories
  Clay facing bricks pavers and blocks
  Structural concrete
Distribution
  Builders merchants
  DIY stores

COMPETITORS

BUZZI UNICEM	Italcementi
Boral	Kingspan
CEMEX	Marshalls
CIMPOR	Martin Marietta
Cementos de Chihuahua	Materials
Dyckerhoff	Saint-Gobain
Grafton Group	Titan Cement
HeidelbergCement	Travis Perkins
Home Depot	Vulcan Materials
Imerys	Wienerberger

HISTORICAL FINANCIALS

Company Type: Public

Income Statement

	REVENUE ($ mil.)	NET INCOME ($ mil.)	NET PROFIT MARGIN	EMPLOYEES
				FYE: December 31
12/19	28,213	2,165	7.7%	86,951
12/18	30,679	2,882	9.4%	89,831
12/17	30,232	2,271	7.5%	89,213
12/16	28,618	1,312	4.6%	86,778
12/15	25,743	788	3.1%	78,106
Annual Growth	**2.3%**	**28.7%**	**—**	**2.7%**

2019 Year-End Financials

Debt ratio: 27.1%
Return on equity: 11.7%
Cash ($ mil.): 4,215
Current ratio: 1.61
Long-term debt ($ mil.): 9,205
No. of shares (mil.): 799
Dividends
  Yield: 1.9%
  Payout: 29.9%
Market value ($ mil.): 32,249

	STOCK PRICE ($) FY Close	P/E High/Low	Earnings	PER SHARE ($) Dividends	Book Value
12/19	40.33	17 11	2.68	0.80	23.79
12/18	26.35	12 8	3.45	0.81	22.51
12/17	36.09	18 15	2.70	0.80	20.72
12/16	34.38	23 15	1.57	0.68	17.61
12/15	28.82	34 23	0.97	0.69	17.22
Annual Growth	**8.8%**	**— —**	**29.1%**	**3.9%**	**8.4%**

CRRC Corp Ltd

Auditors: Deloitte Touche Tohmatsu Certified Public Accountants LLP

LOCATIONS

HQ: CRRC Corp Ltd
No. 16 Central West Fourth Ring Road, Haidian District, Beijing 100036
Phone: (86) 10 5186 2188   **Fax:** (86) 10 6398 4785
Web: www.crrcgc.cc

HISTORICAL FINANCIALS

Company Type: Public

Income Statement

	REVENUE ($ mil.)	NET INCOME ($ mil.)	NET PROFIT MARGIN	EMPLOYEES
				FYE: December 31
12/19	32,912	1,695	5.2%	0
12/18	31,851	1,643	5.2%	0
12/17	32,426	1,659	5.1%	0
/	0	0	—	0
Annual Growth	**—**	**—**		**—**

2019 Year-End Financials

Debt ratio: 0.8%
Return on equity: 8.9%
Cash ($ mil.): 6,453
Current ratio: 1.26
Long-term debt ($ mil.): 1,023
No. of shares (mil.): —
Dividends
  Yield: —
  Payout: —
Market value ($ mil.): —

	STOCK PRICE ($) FY Close	P/E High/Low	Earnings	PER SHARE ($) Dividends	Book Value
12/19	0.00	— —	0.06	0.00	(0.00)
Annual Growth	**—**		**—**	**—**	**—**

Dah Sing Banking Group Ltd

Auditors: PricewaterhouseCoopers

LOCATIONS

HQ: Dah Sing Banking Group Ltd
36th Floor, Everbright Centre, 108 Gloucester Road, Wanchai,
Phone: (852) 2507 8866   **Fax:** (852) 2598 5052
Web: www.dahsing.com

COMPETITORS

Bank of China	Chong Hing Bank
Bank of China (Hong Kong)	Hang Seng Bank
Bank of Communications	Public Financial Holdings
Bank of East Asia	Shanghai Pudong
China Construction Bank	Development Bank
China Development Bank	Wing Hang Bank
China Minsheng Banking	Wing Lung Bank

HISTORICAL FINANCIALS

Company Type: Public

Income Statement

	ASSETS ($ mil.)	NET INCOME ($ mil.)	INCOME AS % OF ASSETS	EMPLOYEES
				FYE: December 31
12/19	31,258	287	0.9%	2,970
12/18	29,401	316	1.1%	2,899
12/17	28,053	279	1.0%	2,825
12/16	26,463	276	1.0%	2,751
12/15	25,291	283	1.1%	2,619
Annual Growth	**5.4%**	**0.3%**	**—**	**3.2%**

2019 Year-End Financials

Return on assets: 0.9%
Return on equity: 8.2%
Long-term debt ($ mil.): —
No. of shares (mil.): 1,405
Sales ($ mil): 1,255
Dividends
  Yield: —
  Payout: 30.1%
Market value ($ mil.): —

Dah Sing Financial Holdings Ltd.

Auditors: PricewaterhouseCoopers

LOCATIONS

HQ: Dah Sing Financial Holdings Ltd.
36th Floor, Everbright Centre, 108 Gloucester Road,
Wanchai,
Phone: (852) 2507 8866   **Fax:** (852) 2598 5052
Web: www.dahsing.com

COMPETITORS

Bank of China	Chong Hing Bank
Bank of Communications	Hang Seng Bank
Bank of East Asia	Shanghai Pudong
China Construction	Development Bank
Bank	Wing Hang Bank
China Minsheng Banking	Wing Lung Bank

HISTORICAL FINANCIALS

Company Type: Public

Income Statement   FYE: December 31

	ASSETS ($ mil.)	NET INCOME ($ mil.)	INCOME AS % OF ASSETS	EMPLOYEES
12/19	32,145	219	0.7%	3,097
12/18	30,298	244	0.8%	3,027
12/17	28,858	691	2.4%	2,949
12/16	28,788	243	0.8%	2,999
12/15	27,453	251	0.9%	2,830
Annual Growth	4.0%	(3.3%)	—	2.3%

2019 Year-End Financials

Return on assets: 0.7%
Return on equity: 6.5%
Long-term debt ($ mil.): —
No. of shares (mil.): 319
Sales ($ mil): 1,317
Dividends
 Yield: —
 Payout: 27.8%
Market value ($ mil.): —

Dai Nippon Printing Co Ltd

A leading commercial printer Dai Nippon Printing (DNP) has diversified beyond the business of spreading ink on paper. The global firm still produces books and magazines dictionaries catalogs and business forms and it has addedÂ items such as CD-ROMs hologramsÂ andÂ smart cards to the mix while subsidiary CHI Group sells e-books. Its Lifestyle and Industrial Supplies segmentÂ makes decorative materials for use in fixtures and furniture along withÂ packaging for consumer products.Â Its Electronics segment's productsÂ includeÂ photomasks used in the manufacture of integrated circuits and color filters for LCD panels. DNP also has a Beverage unit through which it owns a majorityÂ of Hokkaido Coca-Cola Bottling.

EXECUTIVES

EVP, Koichi Takanami
EVP, Masayoshi Yamada

President, Yoshitoshi Kitajima
EVP, Yoshinari Kitajima
Senior Managing Director, Masahiko Wada
Senior Managing Director, Tetsuji Morino
Senior Executive Corporate Officer, Kouichi
 Hashimoto
Senior Managing Director, Tokuji Kanda
Senior Executive Corporate Officer, Sakae Hikita
Auditors: ARK LLC

LOCATIONS

HQ: Dai Nippon Printing Co Ltd
1-1-1 Ichigaya-Kagacho, Shinjuku-ku, Tokyo 162-8001
Phone: (81) 3 6735 0129
Web: www.dnp.co.jp

2016 Sales

	% of total
Japan	84
Asia	10
Other countries	6
Total	**100**

PRODUCTS/OPERATIONS

2016 Sales

	% of total
Information Communication	56
Lifestyle & Industrial Supplies	26
Electronics	14
Beverages	4
Total	**100**

Selected Products and Services

Information Communication
 Bank notes
 Books
 Business forms
 Catalogs
 CD-ROMs and DVDs
 Direct mail
 Magazines
 Plastic cards
 Promotional publications
Lifestyle and Industrial Supplies
 Decorative materials
 Packaging
Electronics
 Color filters for liquid crystal displays
 Photomasks
 Projection TV screens
 Shadowmasks for color TVs
Beverages

COMPETITORS

3M	R.R. Donnelley
Asahi Breweries	Sapporo
Graphic Packaging	Siemens AG
Holding	Suntory Holdings
Hitachi	TSMC
LG Display	Toppan Printing
Photronics	Vesuvius
Quad/Graphics	

HISTORICAL FINANCIALS

Company Type: Public

Income Statement   FYE: March 31

	REVENUE ($ mil.)	NET INCOME ($ mil.)	NET PROFIT MARGIN	EMPLOYEES
03/20	12,914	640	5.0%	48,192
03/19	12,655	(322)	—	47,449
03/18	13,299	258	1.9%	46,523
03/17	12,612	225	1.8%	45,836
03/16	12,964	299	2.3%	45,662
Annual Growth	(0.1%)	21.0%	—	1.4%

2020 Year-End Financials

Debt ratio: 0.1%
Return on equity: 7.2%
Cash ($ mil.): 3,436
Current ratio: 1.84
Long-term debt ($ mil.): 1,041
No. of shares (mil.): 280
Dividends
 Yield: 2.8%
 Payout: 13.7%
Market value ($ mil.): 2,944

	STOCK PRICE ($) FY Close	P/E High/Low		PER SHARE ($) Earnings	Dividends	Book Value
03/20	10.48	0	0	2.17	0.30	30.03
03/19	11.97	—	—	(1.07)	0.29	29.80
03/18	10.47	0	0	0.85	0.30	32.87
03/17	10.88	0	0	0.73	0.29	30.04
03/16	8.81	0	0	0.95	0.26	28.85
Annual Growth	4.4%	—	—	23.0%	3.1%	1.0%

Dai-ichi Life Holdings Inc

Auditors: KPMG AZSA LLC

LOCATIONS

HQ: Dai-ichi Life Holdings Inc
1-13-1 Yuraku-cho, Chiyoda-ku, Tokyo 100-8411
Phone: (81) 3 3216 1222
Web: www.dai-ichi-life-hd.com

HISTORICAL FINANCIALS

Company Type: Public

Income Statement   FYE: March 31

	REVENUE ($ mil.)	NET INCOME ($ mil.)	NET PROFIT MARGIN	EMPLOYEES
03/20	57,965	298	0.5%	63,719
03/19	59,981	2,032	3.4%	62,938
03/18	61,108	3,427	5.6%	62,943
03/17	54,689	2,068	3.8%	62,606
03/16	60,642	1,589	2.6%	61,446
Annual Growth	(1.1%)	(34.2%)	—	0.9%

2020 Year-End Financials

Debt ratio: —
Return on equity: 0.8%
Cash ($ mil.): 20,677
Current ratio: —
Long-term debt ($ mil.): —
No. of shares (mil.): 1,133
Dividends
 Yield: —
 Payout: 217.4%
Market value ($ mil.): —

Daikin Industries Ltd

Founded in 1924 Daikin Industries is the #1 air conditioning company in the world. Daikin makes air conditioning and refrigeration products for residential and industrial use. Residential products include air cleaners dehumidifiers and air conditioners; industrial products range from infrared ceramic space heaters to marine vessel air conditioners. Daikin also sells chemicals (fluorocarbons surfactants and mold-release agents) oil hydraulics for machinery and products such as aircraft parts for defense organizations. The US and Japan are its largest markets each generating about 25% of net sales.

Operations

Daikin operates in three reportable business segments?Air Conditioning Chemicals and Others.

Daikin's Air Conditioning business accounts for almost 90% of total revenue and offers a wide range of air conditioning products such as room air conditioning systems air purifiers heat pump hot water and room heating systems water chillers and industrial dust collectors to name a few.

The Chemicals business offers fluorine compounds with distinctive characteristics such as fluoropolymers fluoroelastomers and fluorocarbon gas which are developed to support a variety of industries including the semiconductor and automotive markets. This segment accounts for almost 10% of total revenue.

The Others segment includes four divisions and generates less than 5% of total revenue. The filter business represents the sale of air filters for air conditioning systems. The oil hydraulics business comprises the manufacture of equipment that facilitates the smooth movement of various types of machinery such as industrial and construction machinery and vehicles. Its defense systems business manufactures artillery shells warheads and fuses as well as aircraft parts; processing technologies for these products are also used for home-use oxygen therapy equipment such as respiration synchronizers and oxygen concentrators. The electronics systems business includes database systems and product development.

Geographic Reach

The company's corporate headquarters is located in Osaka Japan. Daikin utilizes a market-centered local production strategy that places its manufacturing facilities close to its target markets. The number of production bases totals more than 90 global locations. The US and Japan each account for almost 25% of net sales followed by China Asia and Oceania and Europe each generating around 15% of total revenue.

Sales and Marketing

The company advertises through its website as well as in the Japanese financial publication the Nikkei Shimbun.

Financial Performance

Note: Growth rates may differ after conversion to US Dollars.

Daikin's net sales as well as profits have increased steadily over the past several consecutive years. Revenue in fiscal 2018 (ended March 31) was Å 2290 billion a 12% increase from Å 2044 billion in 2017 primarily due to robust expansion in the global economy and increases in personal consumption and private capital investment.

Despite higher raw material costs net income saw a 23% increase to Å 189.1 billion in 2018 due in part to decreased taxes paid in the US as a result of corporate income tax law revisions (the Tax Cuts and Jobs Act.)

Cash at the end of fiscal 2018 was Å 357.0 billion an increase of Å 12.9 billion from the prior year. Cash from operations contributed Å 223.7 billion to the coffers while investing activities used Å 127.5 billion mainly for property and equipment purchases as well as for investment securities. Financing activities used another Å 73.5 billion for loan payments and dividends to stockholders.

Strategy

The Daikin Group is currently in the second half of its five-year strategic management plan FUSION 20 which includes expanding its air conditioning business through Internet of Things (IoT) and artificial intelligence (AI) technologies and strengthening its environmental technologies. It also plans to increase production capacity in the US and Asia and expand its sales and service network through acquisitions in each country. Daikin is targeting its product development capabilities and identifying cost reductions to increase profit margins.

Daikin is highly dependent on its main air conditioning products business which generates almost 90% of its sales. It is therefore aiming to expand its heating and water heater business as well as its commercial refrigeration business. It is building digital factories and using AI technology for data analysis to create networked air-conditioning systems for entire buildings. It is also offering design and engineering services for commercial customers as well as maintenance repair and troubleshooting support.

The company is investing about Å 600 billion in R&D activities (conducted at its Technology and Innovation Center (TIC) in Osaka) over the next three years. It is promoting the adoption of R32 refrigerants and further developing its refrigerant technologies aimed at reducing COÅ emissions to zero.

Some of Daikin's cost-cutting initiatives include improving inventory optimization and creating standardization in its financial operations with IT integration activities.

Mergers and Acquisitions

In late 2018 Daikin Industries agreed to acquire Austria-based AHT Group a manufacturer of commercial plug-in refrigeration and freezing systems for supermarkets discount chains and ice cream and beverage manufacturers. The acquisition valued at ?881 million fits into Daikin's strategy to expand in the commercial refrigeration market in Europe. With the addition of AHT's products for food retailers to its own air conditioning and refrigeration products Daikin believes it is well positioned to expand further into the US and Asia.

Company Background

Daikin Industries traces its roots back to 1924. Founded in Osaka Japan as Osaka Kinzolu Kogyosho Limited Partnership the company began as a town factory with no more than 15 employees making radiator tubes for aircraft. In 1933 the company began doing research on flourine refrigerants and later began manufacturing a methyl chloride type refrigerator dubbed the Mifujirator. With the successful development of fluorocarbon gas the company began mass-producing the Mifujirator starting in 1942. It introduced Japan's first packaged air conditioner for commercial use and began marketing the first residential window air conditioner in 1958. The company was renamed Daikin Kogyo Co. Ltd. in 1963 and later to the current Daikin Industries Ltd. in 1982.

EXECUTIVES

Senior Executive Officer Air Conditioning Business Director and Chairman Daikin Fluorochemicals (China) Co. Ltd, Ken Tayano, age 74

President and COO, Masanori Togawa, age 72

Senior Executive Officer Leader of the GRT Project and Director, Takashi Matsuzaki, age 62

Senior Executive Officer Air Conditioning Europe Africa and Middle East (EMEA) and Director, Masatsugu Minaka, age 67

Senior Executive Officer IT Development and Director, Koichi Takahashi, age 64

Senior Executive Officer Leader of ATT Project and Leader of SSJ Project and Director, Jiro Tomita, age 71

Chairman, Noriyuki Inoue, age 85

Auditors: Deloitte Touche Tohmatsu LLC

LOCATIONS

HQ: Daikin Industries Ltd
Umeda Center Bldg., 2-4-12 Nakazaki-Nishi, Kita-ku, Osaka 530-8323
Phone: (81) 6 6373 4356
Web: www.daikin.co.jp

2018 sales

	% of total
Japan	24
USA	24
China	17
Asia and Oceania	15
Europe	14
Other regions	6
Total	**100**

PRODUCTS/OPERATIONS

2018 Sales

	% of total
Air conditioning	89
Chemicals	9
Other	2
Total	**100**

Selected Products and Operations

Air Conditioning and Refrigerator Division
  Split/multi-split type air conditioners
  Unitary (ducted split)
  Air to water heat pump systems
  Heating systems
  Air purifiers
  Medium/low temperature refrigeration
  Sky/air (packaged air conditioners for shops and small offices)
  Ventilation products
  Control systems
  Commercial air cleaners
  Commercial air conditioners
  Container refrigeration
  Large-scale refrigerators
  Marine vessel air conditioners and refrigerators
  Marine-type container refrigeration units
  Room air cleaners
  Room air conditioners
Chemical Division
  Equipment and systems
  Fluorocarbon gas
  Synthesized products
Oil Hydraulics Division
  Centralized lubrication units and systems
  Oil hydraulic products for industrial machinery
  Oil hydraulic products for mobile equipment
Defense Systems Division
  Aircraft components
  Ammunition
  Warheads for aerial torpedoes

COMPETITORS

Brooks Automation	Paloma Group
Dyneon	Pribuss Engineering
Ingersoll-Rand Climate	Tecumseh Products
Solutions	Trane Inc.
Lennox	UTC Climate Controls &
Lockheed Martin	Security

HISTORICAL FINANCIALS

Company Type: Public

Income Statement   FYE: March 31

	REVENUE ($ mil.)	NET INCOME ($ mil.)	NET PROFIT MARGIN	EMPLOYEES
03/20	23,494	1,572	6.7%	89,957
03/19	22,404	1,707	7.6%	86,472
03/18	21,571	1,780	8.3%	78,837
03/17	18,281	1,376	7.5%	75,543
03/16	18,199	1,219	6.7%	68,598
Annual Growth	6.6%	6.6%	—	7.0%

2020 Year-End Financials

Debt ratio: 0.1%	No. of shares (mil.): 292
Return on equity: 11.9%	Dividends
Cash ($ mil.): 3,415	Yield: 1.3%
Current ratio: 1.88	Payout: 2.9%
Long-term debt ($ mil.): 2,977	Market value ($ mil.): 3,505

	STOCK PRICE ($)	P/E		PER SHARE ($)		
	FY Close	High/Low		Earnings	Dividends	Book Value
03/20	11.98	0	0	5.37	0.16	45.24
03/19	11.69	0	0	5.83	0.13	43.77
03/18	11.07	0	0	6.08	0.13	41.80
03/17	201.72	0	0	4.71	0.12	34.04
03/16	149.14	0	0	4.18	0.09	30.97
Annual Growth	(46.8%)	—	—	6.5%	13.9%	9.9%

Daimler AG

Daimler's cars may stop on a dime but they cost a little more than that. Daimler's passenger car business Mercedes-Benz is number one in the premium vehicle category worldwide and includes luxury brands Mercedes-AMG and Mercedes-Maybach as well as its compact Smart brand and the new EQ electric car. It's also the world's biggest manufacturer of commercial vehicles: Its Daimler Trucks Daimler Buses and Mercedes-Benz Vans divisions sell vehicle brands like Freightliner Western Star Fuso and BharatBenz. The company's product portfolio is rounded out by a range of customized financial services and mobility services. Daimler sells its vehicles worldwide but North America represents more than 35% of its net sales.

Operations

Daimler operates through five business segments: Mercedes-Benz Cars (more than 50% of net sales) Daimler Trucks (more than 20%) Daimler Mobility (some 15%) Mercedes-Benz Vans (about 10%) and Daimler Buses (nearly 5%).

The Mercedes-Benz Cars division comprises several premium automobiles including its Mercedes AMG high-performance brand the Mercedes-Maybach luxury brand E-Class and S-Class luxury sedans the smart electric car and its new EQ electric car which includes all Mercedes' electric mobility features. This division also offers the Mercedes me digital connectivity platform.

Daimler Trucks division includes Mercedes-Benz trucks as well as Western Star Freightliner FUSO BharatBenz (manufactured locally for the Indian market) and Thomas Built Buses.

Daimler Mobility offers financing leasing fleet management investments credit card and insurance brokerage as well as innovative mobility services.

Daimler Buses division is a full-line bus supplier with Mercedes-Benz Setra and BharatBenz brands covering every segment in the global bus market.

Geographic Reach

Based in Stuttgart Germany Daimler has customers in almost every country in the world. Its manufacturing footprint spans dozens of facilities worldwide. The company has van factories in Germany Spain the US Argentina China and Russia.

Its Daimler Trucks division develops and produces vehicles in a global network under the brands Mercedes Benz Freightliner Western Star FUSO and BharatBenz. The division's around 30 production facilities are located in the NAFTA region Europe Asia and South America.

North America is its biggest market with more than 35% of sales followed by Europe with nearly 35% and the Asia/Pacific with about 25% of sales.

Sales and Marketing

Daimler's digital mobility solutions offers maximum flexibility. Carsharing allows customer to rent cars per minute. SHARE NOW is one of the world's largest car-sharing services with over 20000 vehicles in over 30 cities. FREE NOW is a Ride-Hailing and an optimal supplement for all who want to be chauffeured by taxi through a foreign city. The company's offer reaches up to the Micro-Mobility solution of an E-Scooter. Daimler's multimodal platform REACH NOW they bundle mobility solutions with the local public transport of cities.

Financial Performance

Note: Growth rates may differ after conversion to US Dollars.

In the year 2019 Daimler's revenue of ?172.7 billion (2018: ?167.4 billion) was slightly above the prior-year level. The development of revenue was positively affected primarily by stronger pricing for new vehicles at Daimler Trucks and growth in contract volume at Daimler Mobility.

Net income fell 64% to ?2.7 billion in 2019 compared to ?7.6 billion in the prior year.

Daimler's cash on hand grew ?3.0 billion during 2019 ending the year at ?18.9 billion. The company's operations generated ?7.9 billion and its financial yielded ?5.6 billion partially offset by the ?10.6 billion used in its investing activities. Daimler's main cash uses in 2019 were capital expenditures while it drew on its long-term financing to add to liquidity.

Strategy

The company firmly believe that individual mobility will be a basic human need in the coming decade as well and that the market for sustainable automobiles in the luxury segment will continue to grow. Demand for goods transport services remains a key pillar of the economy and its prosperity and this demand can be expected to increase even further around the globe for years to come. The markets for financial services and the demand for fleet management services and digital mobility solutions are also likely to develop positively in the future. Daimler AG are committed to the principles of sustainability and in particular of climate protection and are therefore setting its course for CO_2- neutral mobility.

Daimler's goal is to safeguard and expand the leading positions that its divisions occupy in its respective segments. Individual and self-determined mobility is likely to remain its primary business model for the car segment over the coming decade. Although flexible forms of use will continue to spread the company's experience at present shows that such use will augment rather than replace the use of privately owned passenger cars. Volumes in the premium and luxury segments in particular should increase further. Growth here is likely to be driven primarily by China and other Asian markets although the more established markets in Europe and the United States will contribute to this growth as well. The company plans to exploit this potential in particular with its range of high-quality models such as the G-Class as well as through its Mercedes-AMG and Mercedes-Maybach sub-brands.

Mergers and Acquisitions

In 2019 Daimler Trucks acquired Torc Robotics a specialist in self-driving software and sensors for commercial industrial and military use as well as consumer vehicles. Daimler hopes Torc will accelerate its development of highly automated trucks.

HISTORY

Daimler-Benz was formed by the merger of two German motor companies — Daimler and Benz — in 1926. Daimler-Benz bought Auto Union (Audi) in 1958 (sold to Volkswagen in 1966). The company's Mercedes cars gained international fame and sales expanded worldwide in the 1970s.

Daimler-Benz diversified in the 1980s buying aerospace heavy truck (Freightliner) and consumer and industrial electrical companies. Although diversification continued sales slowed. Losses at its aerospace unit forced Daimler-Benz into the red in 1995. Also that year the company and ABB Asea Brown Boveri (now ABB) formed joint venture Adtranz the #1 train maker in the world and J rgen Schrempp became chairman of the management board (CEO).

In 1998 Daimler-Benz acquired Chrysler and introduced a subcompact car the smart in Europe. The newly formed DaimlerChrysler rolled both companies' financial services units into Daimler-Chrysler Interservices (DEBIS) in 1999.

EXECUTIVES

Chairman Management Board ND Head Mercedes-Benz Cars Division, Dieter Zetsche, age 67, $2,192,796 total compensation

Member Management Board Finance and Controlling Daimler Financial Services, Bodo Uebber, age 60, $945,912 total compensation

EVP; Head Mercedes-Benz Transporter, Wilfried Porth, age 61, $547,482 total compensation

Head Daimler Global Truck and Buses, Martin Daum, age 60

Member Management Board; Head Greater China, Hubertus Troska

Head of Group Research and Mercedes-Benz Cars Development, Ola K llenius, age 51

Head of Daimler AG. Integrity and Legal Affairs, Renata Jungo Br ngger

Head of Mercedes-Benz Cars Marketing and Sales, Britta Seeger

Chairman Supervisory Board, Manfred Bischoff, age 78

Auditors: KPMG AG, Wirtschaftsprüfungsgesellschaft

LOCATIONS

HQ: Daimler AG
  Mercedesstrasse 120, Stuttgart 70327
Phone: (49) 711 17 97875   **Fax:** (49) 711 17 94075
Web: www.daimler.com

2018 Sales

	% of total
Europe	36
North America (NAFTA)	25
Asia	23
Other markets	6
Other revenue	10
Total	**100**

PRODUCTS/OPERATIONS

2018 Sales

	% of Sales
Mercedes-Benz Cars	53
Daimler Trucks	22
Daimler Financial Services	14
Mercedes-Benz Vans	8
Daimler Buses	2
Total	**100**

Selected Divisions and Brands

Mercedes-Benz Cars
  Mercedes-AMG
  Mercedes-Maybach
  Mercedes me
  smart
  EQ
Daimler Trucks
  Freightliner
  FUSO
  Mercedez-Benz
  Western Star
  BharatBenz
Mercedes-Benz Vans
  Mercedez-Benz
  Freightliner
Daimler Buses
  Mercedes-Benz
  Setra

BharatBenz
Daimler Financial Services
  Mercedes-Benz Bank
  Daimler Truck Financial
  moovel
  Car2Go
  mytaxi

COMPETITORS

AUDI	Nissan
BMW	PACCAR
Fiat Chrysler	PROTON Holdings
Ford Motor	Peugeot
General Motors	Porsche Holding
Honda	Renault
Hyundai Motor	Scania
Isuzu	Subaru
Kia Motors	Suzuki Motor
MAN	Tesla Motors
Mazda	Toyota
Mitsubishi Motors	Volkswagen
Navistar International	Volvo

HISTORICAL FINANCIALS

Company Type: Public

Income Statement				FYE: December 31
	REVENUE ($ mil.)	NET INCOME ($ mil.)	NET PROFIT MARGIN	EMPLOYEES
12/19	193,952	2,668	1.4%	298,655
12/18	191,662	8,301	4.3%	298,683
12/17	196,991	12,616	6.4%	289,321
12/16	161,825	9,002	5.6%	282,488
12/15	162,801	9,175	5.6%	248,015
Annual Growth	4.5%	(26.6%)	—	4.8%

2019 Year-End Financials

Debt ratio: 48.4%
Return on equity: 3.7%
Cash ($ mil.): 21,201
Current ratio: 1.21
Long-term debt ($ mil.): 95,676

No. of shares (mil.): 1,069
Dividends
  Yield: 4.5%
  Payout: 25.0%
Market value ($ mil.): 14,528

	STOCK PRICE ($) FY Close	P/E High/Low		PER SHARE ($) Earnings	Dividends	Book Value
12/19	13.58	7	5	2.49	0.62	64.38
12/18	13.11	13	2	7.76	0.81	69.22
12/17	84.64	9	7	11.80	0.70	71.74
Annual Growth	(59.9%)	—	—	(32.2%)	(3.2%)	(2.7%)

Daito Trust Construction Co., Ltd.

EXECUTIVES

VP, Hitoshi Kadouchi
President and CEO, Naomi Kumakiri, age 62
Managing Director, Katsuma Kobayashi
Senior Executive Officer, Shoji Yamada
Managing Director, Shuji Kawai
Senior Executive Officer, Takuya Ishii
Auditors: Deloitte Touche Tohmatsu LLC

LOCATIONS

HQ: Daito Trust Construction Co., Ltd.
  2-16-1 Konan, Minato-ku, Tokyo 108-8211
Phone: (81) 3 6718 9111
Web: www.kentaku.co.jp

COMPETITORS

Daiwa House Industry	Shimizu
HASEKO	Tobishima
Mitsui Fudosan	Tokyu Construction
Sekisui House	

HISTORICAL FINANCIALS

Company Type: Public

Income Statement				FYE: March 31
	REVENUE ($ mil.)	NET INCOME ($ mil.)	NET PROFIT MARGIN	EMPLOYEES
03/20	14,613	832	5.7%	21,916
03/19	14,368	812	5.7%	21,754
03/18	14,662	827	5.6%	20,834
03/17	13,390	734	5.5%	19,556
03/16	12,570	599	4.8%	19,144
Annual Growth	3.8%	8.6%	—	3.4%

2020 Year-End Financials

Debt ratio: 0.0%
Return on equity: 30.9%
Cash ($ mil.): 1,602
Current ratio: 1.54
Long-term debt ($ mil.): 562

No. of shares (mil.): 68
Dividends
  Yield: 6.1%
  Payout: 11.8%
Market value ($ mil.): 1,580

	STOCK PRICE ($) FY Close	P/E High/Low		PER SHARE ($) Earnings	Dividends	Book Value
03/20	23.02	0	0	12.03	1.43	37.99
03/19	34.93	0	0	10.94	1.36	37.16
03/18	42.75	0	0	10.97	1.36	36.82
03/17	34.89	0	0	9.59	0.78	31.93
03/16	35.60	0	0	7.68	0.62	28.23
Annual Growth	(10.3%)	—	—	11.9%	23.2%	7.7%

Daiwa House Industry Co Ltd

More than a half-century ago Daiwa House Industry called its first prefabricated homes "Pipe Houses" because they were made from steel pipes. Today the group's seven businesses build lease sell and manage rental properties single-family houses condominiums and commercial buildings. Daiwa's other businesses include energy efficiency and construction support services as well as operation of hotels and sports clubs. Daiwa has around 80 offices throughout Japan other Asian countries and Mexico; the company also owns about 10 factories and manages autonomous group companies in some 20 countries.

Operations

Daiwa House Industry's revenue is diversified across seven business segments.

Through its Rental Housing segment (more 25% of net sales) Daiwa manages more than 540000 (mostly Japanese) housing units.

The company designs and builds constructions in Japan ranging from medical buildings and elderly welfare and housing facilities to food processing facilities and offices under its Logistics Business and Corporate Facilities segment (about 20%).

Daiwa's Other Businesses division (around 15%) includes operations in construction and construction materials logistics interior design home products energy efficiency services hotels sports clubs and parking lots.

Daiwa's Commercial Facilities business (roughly 15%) constructs commercial buildings including retail properties hotels and residential facilities that include retail stores. Retail construction accounts for about 40% of the segment's contracts.

In its Single-Family Houses division (about 10%) Daiwa has constructed and sold more than 610000 single-family homes. The company also builds entire housing subdivisions.

Via its Condominiums segment (more than 5%) Daiwa has sold around 200000 condominium units and manages some 350000 in Japan.

The company conducts renovations principally for single-family houses condominiums and rental housing through its Existing Homes business (less than 5%).

Daiwa also divides its business into three broad areas: Housing (which generates over 45% of net sales) includes single-family house rental housing and condominium construction and renovation services; Business (nearly 40%) constructs and operates commercial and business logistics medical and nursing care facilities; and Life (almost 15%) operates home goods stores hotels and other constructions.

Geographic Reach

Headquartered in Osaka Japan Daiwa House Industry has around 35 offices in Japan about 45 branches some 10 factories and research and training centers in Nara Osaka and Tokyo. The company also has international offices in China Taiwan Indonesia Philippines Vietnam Myanmar and Mexico.

Sales and Marketing

Daiwa House Industry is focusing its marketing on promotion of its xevo? series of single-family houses and condominium features including interconnected smart appliances that utilize AI. The company is also emphasizing constructions that ameliorate societal needs in Japan including nursing homes environmentally friendly housing and medical buildings.

Financial Performance

Note: Growth rates may differ after conversion to US dollars.

Daiwa House Industry has grown every year since fiscal 2014 expanding net sales by more than 40% in that time thanks to consistent improvements in the Japanese economy. Despite a net loss in 2015 caused by a change in the discount rate for Daiwa's employee retirement plan benefit obligation the company doubled its net income over the last five years. Cash added about 65% as the company nearly tripled its debt.

Daiwa's net sales increased 8% to ¥3.8 trillion in 2017 owing mostly to growth in its Other Businesses segment through which the company opened three new home goods stores three logistics facilities a fitness facility and a city hotel. Daiwa's Commercial Facilities and Rental Housing businesses also posted solid gains. The company opened a shopping mall introduced new housing products and services and increased its three-story and medium- to high-rise rentals.

Daiwa's net income increased 17% to ¥236.4 billion in 2017 on the strength of its net sales growth.

The company ended 2017 with ¥326.1 billion in cash up ¥112.8 billion from the previous year. Operations provided ¥382.4 billion; Daiwa used ¥313.7 billion on investments (primarily for purchase of property manufacturing plants equipment and intangible assets) and added ¥41.8 billion through financings (mostly from corporate bond issuances).

Strategy

In fiscal 2016 Daiwa House Industry launched a medium-term management plan that includes objectives for each of its business segments.

For its Rental Housing business the company is growing its urban and family properties and expanding its products to include medium- to high-rise rental housing multifunction rental housing dorms and company buildings.

Daiwa is expanding its Commercial Facilities offerings beyond storefronts to include hotels and facilities that address social problems including nursing homes daycares and logistics centers. In 2017 the company opened a shopping mall that incorporates residences.

In Logistics Business and Corporate Facilities Daiwa is increasing development of build-to-suit and multitenant properties and partnering with other companies to develop a logistics platform that includes warehouse and vehicle management systems and fulfillment support. The company began construction of 19 new logistics facilities in 2017.

Japan's aging and shrinking population is negatively impacting Daiwa's Single-Family Houses segment. The company is aiming to up sales of its higher-margin xevo? series of houses which provide earthquake resistance external wall thermal insulation and high ceilings. The proportion of home orders comprised of xevo? has grown from some 30% to about 40% since 2015.

Daiwa is expanding its Condominiums business beyond Tokyo. The company opened a condominium and began selling homes in a condominium development attached to a shopping mall outside of Tokyo in 2017.

In 2017 Daiwa began renovating homes for resale in its Existing Homes segment.

Mergers and Acquisitions

Daiwa House Industry is strengthening its international presence through acquisitions. In 2018 the company acquired the single-family houses business of FD Communities which provided Daiwa with real estate assets in 12 locations and equity interests in six joint ventures in Georgia and South Carolina. That year the company also purchased Rawson Group an Australian single-family home construction and land development company.

Company Background

Founded in 1955 by Nobuo Ishibashi Daiwa House Industry first developed homes that could be quickly built using steel pipe frameworks to withstand natural disasters. The technique was first used for warehouses depots and offices primarily for the Japanese National Railways and the Japanese government. The company went on to develop study rooms that that could be built in three hours larger prefabricated houses targeting newlyweds and eventually large-scale residential complexes.

EXECUTIVES

EVP and CFO, Tetsuji Ogawa, age 79
President Nihon Jyutaku Ryutu, Minoru Fujita
President and COO, Naotake Ohno, age 72
Chairman and CEO, Takeo Higuchi, age 82
Senior Managing Executive Officer, Takuya Ishibashi, age 67
Senior Managing Executive Officer, Tatsushi Nishimura, age 71
President Daiwa Royal, Ken Harada
Senior Managing Executive Officer, Shigeru Numata, age 71
President Daiwa Logistics, Isamu Ogata, age 72
Senior Managing Executive Officer, Katsutomo Kawai, age 73
President Daiwa Lease, Shunsaku Morita
President Daiwa Odakyu Construction, Atsushi Kanakubo
President Daiwa Royal Golf, Seishu Umaoka
President Daiwa House Reform, Junichi Sugiura

President Daiwa House Life Support, Toshinori Inaguchi
President Osaka Marubiru, Haruyuki Yoshimoto
President Eneserve, Yoshio Kinoshita
President Higashi-Fuji, Masamichi Yagita
President Daiwa Energy, Hidekazu Matsushima
President Daiwa House Insurance, Shigeru Sasashita
President Fujita, Takuji Ueda
President Daiwa House Asset Management, Yuji Yamada
EVP, Tamio Ishibashi, age 65
President Daiwa Living Management, Masaru Akashi
President Daiwa Rakuda Industry, Masato Shima
President Daiwa Service, Tomoyuki Kido
President Global Community, Takashi Yamada
President Daiwa LifeNext, Yoshinori Watanabe
President Cosmos Initia, Yoshiyuki Takagi
President Daiwa Homes Online, Norio Togashi
President Daiwa Core Factory, Syuji Oda
President Daiwa Lantec, Kazuo Shimoe
President Daiwa Information Service, Katsuyuki Fujita
President Daiwa House REIT Management, Hirotaka Najima
President Media Tech, Mitsuo Adachi
President Daiyoshi Trust, Yoshihiro Oho
President Frameworx, Junichi Akiba
President Daiwa House Financial, Hiroshi Osada
President Royal Home Center, Masaaki Nakayama
President Daiwa Resort, Seiji Kushida
President Sports Club NAS, Yoshinari Shibayama
President Nishiwaki Royal Hotel, Hideaki Tomiyama
President Shinwa Agency, Nobuyuki Otsuji
President Daiwa House California, Takeshi Wakita
Auditors: Deloitte Touche Tohmatsu LLC

LOCATIONS

HQ: Daiwa House Industry Co Ltd
3-3-5 Umeda, Kita-ku, Osaka 530-8241
Phone: (81) 6 6225 7804   **Fax:** (81) 6 6342 1399
Web: www.daiwahouse.co.jp

PRODUCTS/OPERATIONS

2017 Sales

	% of total
Rental housing	26
Logistics Business and Corporate Facilities	22
Commercial Facilities	16
Single-Family Housing	10
Condominiums	7
Existing Homes	3
Other Businesses	16
Total	**100**

COMPETITORS

Daikyo	Sumitomo Mitsui
Daito Trust	Construction
Construction	Sumitomo Realty
HASEKO	Taisei
Nishimatsu	Takenaka
Construction	Toda
Sekisui House	Tokyu Construction
Shimizu	

HISTORICAL FINANCIALS

Company Type: Public

Income Statement

FYE: March 31

	REVENUE ($ mil.)	NET INCOME ($ mil.)	NET PROFIT MARGIN	EMPLOYEES
03/20	40,351	2,152	5.3%	70,344
03/19	37,415	2,144	5.7%	67,174
03/18	35,748	2,225	6.2%	64,402
03/17	31,419	1,804	5.7%	60,539
03/16	28,432	922	3.2%	57,095
Annual Growth	**9.1%**	**23.6%**	**—**	**5.4%**

2020 Year-End Financials

Debt ratio: 0.2%	No. of shares (mil.): 664
Return on equity: 14.0%	Dividends
Cash ($ mil.): 2,592	Yield: 4.4%
Current ratio: 1.62	Payout: 33.8%
Long-term debt ($ mil.): 6,915	Market value ($ mil.): 16,351

	STOCK PRICE ($) FY Close	P/E High/Low		PER SHARE ($) Earnings	Dividends	Book Value
03/20	24.62	0	0	3.24	1.10	23.96
03/19	31.82	0	0	3.22	1.02	21.71
03/18	38.59	0	0	3.35	0.91	20.85
03/17	28.83	0	0	2.72	0.79	17.57
03/16	28.12	0	0	1.39	0.57	15.70
Annual Growth	**(3.3%)**		**—**	**23.6%**	**17.9%**	**11.1%**

Danone

Danone is one of the largest dairy food and water producers in the world. The company is organized around three core activities: Essential Dairy and Plant Based Waters and Specialized Nutrition. The #1 maker of fresh dairy products worldwide Danone sells dozens of global and regional yogurt brands including top-sellers Dannon and Activia functional brands like Actimel and Danonino and Greek yogurt brands Oikos and Danio. The company's evian Volvic Aqua water brands (among others) make it #3 worldwide in bottled water and Danone is also the world's #2 baby nutrition company. Its medical nutrition products are #1 in Europe. It also owns US organic food company WhiteWave Foods. The company generates more than half of its revenue in Europe and NORAM region.

Operations

Danone has three principal product categories: Essential Dairy and Plant-Based (EDP) Waters and Specialized Nutrition.

EDP carries out the production and distribution of fresh fermented dairy products and other dairy specialties; plant-based products and drinks (from soy almond hazelnut rice oat and coconut); and coffee creamers. Its main brands in the segment are Activia Actimel Alpro Danonino Oikos and Prostokvashino. Danone generates more than 50% of total sales from EDP.

Specialized Nutrition comprises two units Early Life Nutrition and Medical Nutrition. Early Life produces and distributes specialized nutrition for babies and young children particularly infant milk formula products but also "weaning foods". Global brands include Aptamil and Nutrilion while market-specific products include Cow&Gate Blédina Bebelac Malyutka and Dumex. Advanced Medical Nutrition produces specialized nutrition for those with certain illnesses or weakened by age under the umbrella brand of Nutricia. The two businesses together account for around 30% of sales.

The Waters business bottles and sells natural flavored and vitamin-enhanced waters under the global brands Evian and Volvic and local brands such as Aqua Mizone Bonafont and Villavicencio. It generates around 20% of sales.

Geographic Reach

Paris-based Groupe Danone is a force in dairy water and nutrition products in more than 120 countries worldwide. Overall Groupe Danone rings up around 55% of sales in the combined Europe and Noram (North America — the US and Canada) region. The remaining sales about 45% are spread across the globe and is led by China Russia Indonesia Mexico and Brazil. In the Asia/Pacific region Danone is active mainly in the Waters and Early Life Nutrition businesses and in Africa and the Middle East its main businesses are Waters and Essential Dairy and Plant-Based.

The company's policy of focusing on high market shares in the countries in which it operates has been successful: It holds #1 positions worldwide in Fresh Dairy and Plant-Based products.

Danone operates about 190 production plants worldwide.

Sales and Marketing

Danone approaches the market through distribution aimed at major retail chains and commercial sales points. In emerging markets Danone makes most of its sales through a small-scale point-of-sale network where in-house sales teams sign exclusivity agreements with wholesalers. In Latin America a significant portion of the Waters business comes from direct-to-customer sales such as home and office delivery. Its Specialized Nutrition products are also sold through specialized distribution channels such as hospitals and pharmacies.

Danone's e-commerce presence is based on traditional brick-and-mortar retailers setting up their own e-commerce operation through which they sell Danone products. It also has relationship with online pureplay companies and makes direct-to-customer sales via its own Danone website.

Danone's top ten customers (five being French) account for roughly 20% of sales and the top five account for nearly 15%.

Financial Performance

Note: Growth rates may differ after conversion to US Dollars.

Danone has been struggling to achieve sustained like-for-like revenue growth over the last five years. Revenue grew 13% between 2015 and 2019 while net income rose 50% in the same period.

In 2019 Danone's sales rose 3% to ?25.3 billion which included a negative scope effect mainly reflecting the deconsolidation of Earthbound Farm a positive impact of currencies as well as an organic contribution of Argentina to growth.

Danone's net income fell down 18% to ?1.9 billion due to ?609 million operating expenses from the disposal of Earthbound Farm the strategic restructuring of the EDP and Waters Reporting Entities the transformation of the organization the impairment of two brands in the EDP and one brand in the Specialized Nutrition Reporting Entity and costs associated with the integration of White-Wave.

Danone's cash balance weakened during 2019 ending the year ?195 million lower at ?644 million. The company's operations generated ?3.4 billion. Investing activities used ?1 billion mainly for capital expenditures and purchases of subsidiaries. Financing activities used another ?2.4 billion mostly for bonds repaid and transactions with non-controlling interests.

Strategy

Danone has set a goal it hopes to accomplish by 2030. In line with its 'One Planet One Health' vision and to adequately respond to the challenges and opportunities of the ongoing food revolution the company has defined its Danone 2030 Goals. The integrated set of nine long-term goals embeds Danone's business model brand and trust models.

Danone is also working towards B Corp status - a designation for companies that meet high standards of sustainability with a dual economic and social agenda. Danone's ambition to obtain this certification is an expression of its long-time commitment to sustainable business and to Danone's dual project of economic success and social progress. For the company the certification means a significant step toward making sustainable business mainstream?and which it believes to be the future.

In terms of incorporating technology into its business Danone has also made considerable progress. Danone's leading organic baby food brand Happy Family Organics' success in e-commerce further strengthens the company's 2020 e-commerce ambition. This ambition pertains to doubling its e-business size and reaching ?2 billion online sales by 2020.

Danone has also partnered with Microsoft For the AI Factory for AgriFood. Start-ups applying will benefit from the joint support of Microsoft and Danone as well as Danone's 'One Planet One Health' vision and access to real cases under demanding conditions of quality and performance.

EXECUTIVES

Vice Chairman and Co-COO, Jacques Vincent, age 73, $2,192,509 total compensation
EVP Fresh Dairy Products, Thomas Kunz, age 63
CEO, Emmanuel Faber, age 57, $1,968,672 total compensation
Chairman President and CEO Stonyfield Farm, Gary Hirshberg
Deputy General Manager and Co-COO; Director, Bernard Hours, age 64, $4,104,140 total compensation
General Manager Medical Nutrition, Flemming Morgan, age 64
EVP Research and Development, Jean-Philippe Paré, age 62
Exec. VP Baby Nutrition; Member of the Executive Committee, Felix Garcia
EVP of Research & Development; Member of the Executive Committee, Jean-Philippe Pare
CFO and Member the Executive Committee, Pierre-Andre Terisse
General Manager South-Eastern Europe, Adrian Pascu
Chairman, Franck Riboud, age 64
Auditors: PricewaterhouseCoopers Audit

LOCATIONS

HQ: Danone
17, Boulevard Haussmann, Paris 75009
Phone: (33) 1 44 35 20 20   **Fax:** (33) 1 44 35 26 95
Web: www.danone.com

2018 Sales

	% of total
Asia-Pacific Latin America Middle East Africa & CIS	45
Europe and NORAM	55
Total	**100**

PRODUCTS/OPERATIONS

2018 sales

	% of total
Essential Dairy & Plant-Based (North America)	20
Essential Dairy & Plant-Based (International)	33
Specialized Nutrition	29
Waters	18
Total	**100**

COMPETITORS

Abbott Nutrition	Granarolo
Ajinomoto	HP Hood
Arla Foods	Heinz
Associated British	Kellogg
Foods	Kerry Group
Beech-Nut	Lactalis
Blue Bell	Leche Pascual
China Mengniu Dairy	Mead Johnson
Coca-Cola	Metagenics
Dairy Crest	Nestlé
Dairy Farm	Novartis
International	Ornua
Dairygold	Parmalat
Dean Foods	PepsiCo
Dr Pepper Snapple	Pfizer
Group	Shanghai Bright Dairy
Dreyer's	& Food
Feihe	Sodiaal
Fonterra	Unilever NV
FrieslandCampina	Wells' Dairy
General Mills	Wessanen
Gerber Products	Wimm-Bill-Dann
Glanbia plc	Yili Group

HISTORICAL FINANCIALS

Company Type: Public

Income Statement

FYE: December 31

	REVENUE ($ mil.)	NET INCOME ($ mil.)	NET PROFIT MARGIN	EMPLOYEES
12/19	28,391	2,165	7.6%	102,449
12/18	28,230	2,690	9.5%	105,783
12/17	29,581	2,940	9.9%	104,843
12/16	23,170	1,816	7.8%	99,187
12/15	24,411	1,396	5.7%	99,781
Annual Growth	**3.8%**	**11.6%**	**—**	**0.7%**

2019 Year-End Financials

Debt ratio: 41.7%	No. of shares (mil.): 648
Return on equity: 11.4%	Dividends
Cash ($ mil.): 723	Yield: 2.6%
Current ratio: 0.90	Payout: 13.2%
Long-term debt ($ mil.): 14,455	Market value ($ mil.): 10,700

	STOCK PRICE ($) FY Close	P/E High/Low		PER SHARE ($) Earnings	Dividends	Book Value
12/19	16.49	6	5	3.31	0.43	29.83
12/18	13.98	5	4	4.16	0.44	28.92
12/17	16.77	4	4	4.69	0.42	27.49
12/16	12.58	5	4	2.95	0.33	22.43
12/15	13.61	7	5	2.29	0.34	22.32
Annual Growth	**4.9%**	**—**		**9.7%**	**6.6%**	**7.5%**

Danske Bank A/S

When you're the largest bank in Denmark there's nowhere to grow but out. Danske Bank serves 2.7 million consumers and 211000 SMEs and 2000 corporate and institutional clients across its four core markets of Denmark Sweden Norway and Finland in addition to 12 other countries. The bank offers business banking home finance and savings trading asset management day-to-day banking and leasing. Founded in 1871 Danske Bank has grown over the years by merging with other local and regional banks. It is growing its position in the Nordics and further afield.

Operations

Danske Bank operates five primary segments Personal Banking Business Baking Corporate &

Institutions Wealth Management and Northern Ireland. It also has a general Other Activities segment.

Personal Banking generates 25% of sales and serves personal and private banking customers with traditional banking services and financial advice to high-net worth clients respectively.

Business Banking accounts for around 25% of sales and provides financing investing cash management and risk management services to small and medium-sized businesses through the bank's network of finance centers branches contact centers and online channels.

Corporate & Institutions brings in around 25% of sales. It provides wholesale banking services to the largest institutional and corporate customers in the Nordic region. The segment's products and services include cash management services; trade finance solutions; custody services; equity bond foreign exchange and derivatives products; corporate finance; and acquisition finance.

Wealth Management generates some 15% of sales and includes the Danica Pension Asset Management and insurance businesses.

Danske Bank's Northern Ireland business offers personal business and private banking in Northern Ireland. It accounts for less than 5%.

Other Activites also bring in 5%.

Geographic Reach

Denmark accounts for 55% of Copenhagen-based Danske Bank's total revenue. Sweden brings in around 15% Norway more than 10% Finland 10% and the UK (principally Northern Ireland) 5%.

As well as the four Nordic countries and Northern Ireland Danske operates in Ireland the UK Estonia Latvia Lithuania Luxembourg Russia Germany Poland the US and India.

Financial Performance

Note: Growth rates may differ after conversion to US dollars.

Danske Bank's revenue has been growing thanks to acquisition-fueled international expansion efforts.

In fiscal 2017 Danske's total income increased a marginal 1% to DKK50.6 billion (roughly $7.9 billion) as strength in business banking home finance and savings and trading was mostly offset by weakness in day-to-day banking life insurance and other items. Geographically revenue in its home market declined while Sweden and Norway recorded postitive growth; revenue from Finland and the UK was comparable with the prior year.

Net income rose 5% to DKK 20.9 billion (some $3.5 billion). The bottom line was boosted by a reversal in loan impairment charges worth DKK 873 million driven by higher credit quality and higher property prices.

Strategy

Danske Bank continues to grow its market share in Sweden Norway and Finland. Its focus on customer satisfaction risk and profitability helped it attract new business in the business banking category whlie a shift to a customer-driven business model in fixed income currency and commodities bore fruit in a low-valiatility environment. In personal banking Danske formed strategic partnerships with Akademikerne Saco and TCO; the TCO partnership consists of 14 trade unions with 1.3 million members. In Finland the company merged its Danske Bank Plc and Danske Bank A/S subsidiaries renamed Danske Bank A/S Finland Branch to simplify the organizational structure and improve efficiency.

Like many banks worldwide Danske is digitalizing many of its services. Digitalization has the twin advantages of significantly improving ease of access for customers while allowing Danske to operate in a more capital-light way and reduce its branch-count. The majority of its new customers arrive via online. Other initiatives in the online space include MobilePay a mobile payment platform and GateTu a business-to-business solution developed in partnership with A.P. Moller-Maersk Danske's biggest shareholder.

Mergers and Acquisitions

Danske Bank's Danica Pension business acquired SEB Pension Danmark in 2017. The acquisition adds to Danica's asset base and will help drive economies of scale improving its competitive position.

HISTORY

Leathersmith-turned-stock trader Gottlieb Gedalia founded Den Danske Landmandsbank Hypothek- og Vexelbank i Kj benhavn (The Danish Farmer's Bank Mortgage and Exchange Bank of Copenhagen. It would change its name four times before finally settling on the less-verbose Danske Bank.

Even in its early years Danske Bank never restricted itself to purely agricultural concerns preferring to offer a wide range of banking services that appealed to farmers merchants and businessmen alike. Isak Gl ckstadt who managed the bank from 1872 until his death in 1910 guided the bank to prominence in Copenhagen's corporate landscape where it became a leading commercial bank. Gl ckstadt's son Emil succeeded his father as managing director in 1910. Despite his best efforts Danske Bank could not cope with the strains of WWI and the Depression; the Danish government had to rescue the firm from bankruptcy. But the bank survived German occupation during WWII mostly unscathed.

During the 1960s and 1970s Denmark's government encouraged Danish banks to expand internationally. Danske Bank pounced on the opportunity by forming consortium banks with such Nordic neighbors as Skandinaviska Enskilda Banken (aka S-E-Banken). Danske Bank stayed ahead of its competitors through acquisitions including the purchase of two large Danish banks in 1990 making it Denmark's largest bank.

By 1990 the bank also had made its presence felt worldwide but Asian economic crises in the early 1990s caused the bank's international subsidiaries to fall short of expectations. After restructuring its international business the bank focused more energy on its Nordic customers. It bought Sweden's −stg ¶ta Enskilda in 1998 and Norway's Fokus Bank in 1999. In 2000 Danske bought fellow Danish Bank BG Bank. Danske also added a Finnish asset management company and a majority interest in Pol-Can Bank of Poland in the same year. In 2001 Danske and BG trimmed down redundant branches.

Danske Bank bought the banking operations of Finnish insurer Sampo for more than $5 billion in 2007. The acquisition brought in more than 150 branches in Finland Estonia Latvia and Lithuania. It followed Danske Bank's 2005 acquisitions of National Irish Bank and Northern Bank from National Australia Bank for some $1.8 billion.

EXECUTIVES

Managing Director Fokus Bank, Thomas F. Borgen, age 56

Head Personal Banking, Tonny Thierry Andersen, age 56

Head Business Banking, Lars Stensgaard M rch, age 48

Head Corporates and Institutions, Glenn Soderholm, age 56

COO, Jim Ditmore, age 60

CFO, Jacob Aarup-Andersen, age 43

Vice Chairman, Trond . Westlie, age 59

Chairman, Ole G. Andersen, age 64
Auditors: Deloitte Statsautoriseret Revisionspartnerselskab

LOCATIONS

HQ: Danske Bank A/S
  Holmens Kanal 2-12, Copenhagen K DK-1092
Phone: (45) 33 44 00 00   **Fax:** 212 370-9564
Web: www.danskebank.com

PRODUCTS/OPERATIONS

2017 Sales

	% of total
Net interest income	49
Net fee income	32
Net trading income	16
Other income	3
Total	**100**

2017 Sales by Segment

	% of total
Personal Banking	25
Business Banking	23
Corporate & Institutions	23
Wealth Management	17
Northern Ireland	4
Other Activities	5
Eliminations (2)	
Reclassification	3
Total	**100**

COMPETITORS

ABN AMRO Group	ING
Citigroup	Jyske
Credit Suisse	Nordea Bank
Crédit Agricole	SEB AB
Deutsche Bank	Svenska Handelsbanken
DnB NOR	UniCredit Bank AG

HISTORICAL FINANCIALS

Company Type: Public

Income Statement				FYE: December 31
	ASSETS ($ mil.)	NET INCOME ($ mil.)	INCOME AS % OF ASSETS	EMPLOYEES
12/19	793,360	3,013	0.4%	22,006
12/18	754,846	2,933	0.4%	20,683
12/17	746,632	4,242	0.6%	19,768
12/16	734,849	4,049	0.6%	19,303
12/15	694,603	2,640	0.4%	19,049
Annual Growth	**3.4%**	**3.4%**	**—**	**3.7%**

2019 Year-End Financials

Return on assets: 0.3%	Dividends
Return on equity: 8.5%	Yield: 5.3%
Long-term debt ($ mil.): —	Payout: 12.2%
No. of shares (mil.): 853	Market value ($ mil.): 6,868
Sales ($ mil): 32,532	

	STOCK PRICE ($) FY Close	P/E High/Low		PER SHARE ($) Earnings	Dividends	Book Value
12/19	8.05	1	0	3.52	0.43	42.13
12/18	9.99	1	1	3.48	0.56	40.29
12/17	19.55	1	1	4.66	0.44	39.70
12/16	15.18	1	1	4.26	0.40	37.58
Annual Growth	**(19.1%)**	**—**	**—**	**(4.6%)**	**2.0%**	**2.9%**

Datang International Power Generation Co Ltd

EXECUTIVES

Vice Chairman and President, Wu Jing, age 63
Chairman, Chen Jinhang, age 64
Auditors: ShineWing (HK) CPA Limited

LOCATIONS

HQ: Datang International Power Generation Co Ltd
No. 9 Guangningbo Street, Xicheng District, Beijing
100033
Phone: (86) 10 88008800   **Fax:** (86) 10 88008111
Web: www.dtpower.com

PRODUCTS/OPERATIONS

2015 Sales

	% of total
Sales of electricity	90
Sales of chemical products	3
Heat supply	2
Sales of coal	-
Others	5
Total	**100**

2015 Sales

	% of total
Power generation Segment	93
Chemical segment	3
Coal segment	-
Other segments	4
Total	**100**

COMPETITORS

AES	China Resources Power
CLP Holdings	Huadian Power
China Power	Huaneng Power

HISTORICAL FINANCIALS

Company Type: Public

Income Statement

	REVENUE ($ mil.)	NET INCOME ($ mil.)	NET PROFIT MARGIN	EMPLOYEES
12/19	13,718	153	1.1%	0
12/18	13,577	179	1.3%	33,483
12/17	12,936	229	1.8%	0
12/16	8,250	(396)	—	22,966
12/15	9,529	429	4.5%	24,704
Annual Growth	**9.5%**	**(22.7%)**	**—**	**—**

2019 Year-End Financials

Debt ratio: 8.2%
Return on equity: 1.8%
Cash ($ mil.): 1,169
Current ratio: 0.42
Long-term debt ($ mil.): 15,587

No. of shares (mil.): —
Dividends
  Yield: 0.0%
  Payout: 6,530.4%
Market value ($ mil.): —

	STOCK PRICE ($) FY Close	P/E High/Low	PER SHARE ($) Earnings	Dividends	Book Value
12/19	3.69	205 146	0.00	0.24	(0.00)
12/18	4.69	87 60	0.01	0.01	0.40
12/17	5.59	68 49	0.02	0.01	0.60
12/16	5.08	— —	(0.03)	0.42	0.43
12/15	6.20	58 28	0.03	0.35	0.52
Annual Growth	**(12.2%)**	**—**	**(42.0%)**	**(9.0%)**	**—**

DBS Group Holdings Ltd.

DBS Group is the holding company for DBS Bank the largest bank in Singapore and a significant presence throughout Southeast Asia. DBS Bank offers personal and private banking in addition to commercial banking services to small and midsized companies through some 80 branches in its home country. The company also has around 50 locations in Hong Kong plus operations in China India Indonesia Malaysia The Philippines Taiwan and Thailand. DBS Group owns a 20% stake in the Bank of the Philippine Islands (that country's second-largest bank) as well. Other activities include capital markets brokerage fund management private equity and equipment and trade finance.

EXECUTIVES

Chief Administrative Officer, Jeanette Wong
CFO, Chng Sok Hui
Chief Risk Officer, Elbert Pattijn
CEO, Piyush Gupta, age 60
Managing Director and Head Group Technology and Operations, David Gledhill
Managing Director and Group Head Consumer Banking and Wealth Management, Tan Su Shan, age 52
President Director DBS Indonesia, Paulus Sutisna
Group Executive Singapore Country Head DBS Bank, Sim S Lim
CEO DBS Bank (Hong Kong) Limited, Sebastian Paredes
CEO DBS India, Surojit Shome
Chief Investment Officer Consumer Banking & Wealth Management, Hou Wey Fook
Chairman, Peter Seah Lim Huat, age 73
Auditors: PricewaterhouseCoopers LLP

LOCATIONS

HQ: DBS Group Holdings Ltd.
12 Marina Boulevard, Marina Bay Financial Centre Tower 3, 018982
Phone: (65) 6878 8888   **Fax:** 213 627-0228
Web: www.dbs.com

2016 Sales

	% of total
Singapore	66
Hong Kong	18
Rest of the greater China	7
South and Southeast Asia	6
Rest of the world	3
Total	**100**

PRODUCTS/OPERATIONS

2016 Sales

	% of total
Institutional Banking	45
Consumer Banking/wealth management	37
Treasury	10
Others	8
Total	**100**

2016 Sales

	% of total
Interest income	64
Net fee and commission income	20
Net Trading income	12
Net income from investment securities	3
Other income	1
Total	**100**

Selected Subsidiaries

DBS Bank
  Bank of the Philippines Islands (20.3%)
  Cholamandalam DBS Finance Limited (37.4%)
  DBS Asia Capital Limited
  DBS Asset Management Ltd
  DBS Diamond Holdings Ltd
  DBS Bank (Hong Kong) Limited
  Hutchison DBS Card Ltd (50%)
  DBSN Services Pte. Ltd.
  DBS Vickers Securities (Singapore) Pte Ltd
  The Islamic Bank of Asia Limited (50%)
  PT Bank DBS Indonesia (99%)

COMPETITORS

AmBank Group	Hong Leong Finance
Amara	Maybank
Bangkok Bank	Maybank Kim Eng
Bank Central Asia	Metropolitan Bank and
Bank Mandiri	Trust
Bank Rakyat	OCBC Bank
Bank of China	Standard Chartered
HSBC	United Overseas Bank

HISTORICAL FINANCIALS

Company Type: Public

Income Statement

FYE: December 31

	ASSETS ($ mil.)	NET INCOME ($ mil.)	INCOME AS % OF ASSETS	EMPLOYEES
12/19	430,307	4,750	1.1%	28,000
12/18	404,457	4,095	1.0%	0
12/17	387,534	3,271	0.8%	24,174
12/16	333,271	2,932	0.9%	22,194
12/15	323,906	3,151	1.0%	22,000
Annual Growth	**7.4%**	**10.8%**	**—**	**6.2%**

2019 Year-End Financials

Return on assets: 1.1%
Return on equity: 12.7%
Long-term debt ($ mil.): —
No. of shares (mil.): —
Sales ($ mil): 15,245

Dividends
  Yield: 5.3%
  Payout: 231.1%
Market value ($ mil.): —

	STOCK PRICE ($) FY Close	P/E High/Low	PER SHARE ($) Earnings	Dividends	Book Value
12/19	77.16	34 28	1.83	4.16	14.84
12/18	69.73	42 31	1.58	4.98	14.12
12/17	74.66	45 31	1.27	1.79	13.89
12/16	47.75	31 22	1.15	1.56	12.17
12/15	46.70	34 26	1.25	1.71	11.43
Annual Growth	**13.4%**	**—**	**9.9%**	**24.9%**	**6.8%**

DCC Plc

DCC offers international sales marketing and support services across four divisions: Liquid Petroleum Gas (LPG) Retail & Oil Technology and Healthcare. It distributes to end users or resellers in 20 countries sourcing product wholesale from refineries and manufacturers. DCC operates through dozens of subsidiaries including Butagaz Exertis Certas and Flogas. It also trades under the Esso brand under license in Norway. Most revenue comes from the UK. DCC was founded in 1976 as a venture capital company before expanding into commodity distribution.

Operations

DCC operates under four reportable segments: DCC Retail & Oil DCC Technology. DCC LPG and DCC Healthcare.

Retail & Oil generate about 60% of revenue. The group is the leading operator of retail petrol stations in Europe and is the leading reseller of fuel cards in Britain and leading oil distributor in Europe.

Technology brings up more than 25% of revenue. It is a leading route-to-market and supply chain partner for global technology brands and customers.

LPG gives in more than 10% of revenue. The group markets its LPG in Europe North America and Asia. It also involves in retailing of natural gas and electricity as well as the sales and distribution of industrial gases including refrigerants.

Healthcare generate about 5% of revenue. It provides products and services to healthcare providers and health and beauty brand owners.

Geographic Reach
Dublin-based DCC generate more than 45% of its revenue from Europe followed France which gives in about 20% Ireland brings up more than 5% and the rest comes from other countries.

Financial Performance
Note: Growth rates may differ after conversion to US Dollars.

Overall the company's revenue decreased by 3% to Â 14.8 billion primarily driven by the lower oil price that prevailed during 2019.

The company's profit decreased by 1% to Â 254.2 million compared from Â 271.1 million in the prior year. The decrease was due to lower revenue while having a higher finance cost.

Cash held by the company at the end of 2019 increased by Â 218.7 million to Â 1.7 billion compared to the prior year with Â 1.5 billion. Cash provided by operations and financing activities were Â 529.1 million and Â 427.0 million respectively. Cash used for investing activities was Â 319.5 million primarily for acquisition of subsidiaries and purchase of property plant and equipment.

Strategy
In September 2019 DCC Healthcare completed the disposal of DCC Vital's UK generic pharma activities and related manufacturing facility in Ireland (Kent Pharma and Athlone Laboratories). The disposal sharpens the strategic focus of DCC Vital allowing it to concentrate on those areas where it has market-leading positions and sustainable competitive advantage in particular in the sales marketing and distribution of medical products in Britain and Ireland. Whilst part of the DCC cash flows generated by the disposed business more than recovered its acquisition cost however the transaction resulted in a loss on disposal of Â 34.7 million principally representing a non-cash impairment of the goodwill recognized on the initial acquisition of the business.

DCC Healthcare made considerable strategic progress during the year in generating very good profit growth significantly expanding its presence in the US nutrition market with two substantial acquisitions and strengthening its position in the primary and secondary healthcare sectors in Britain with a number of small bolt-on acquisitions.

Company Background
In early 2020 DCC Healthcare acquired Minnesota based Amerilab Technologies Inc. a specialist provider of contract manufacturing and related services in effervescent nutritional products for $85 million. The acquisition is part of the company's step to build a business of scale in the world's largest health supplements and nutritional products market.

In late 2019 DCC Healthcare acquired Florida-based Ion Labs Inc. a contract manufacturer of nutritional products for $60 million. This acquisition represented a significant step in DCC Health & Beauty Solutions' strategy to build a material

presence in the attractive US health supplements and nutritional products market.

EXECUTIVES

Chief Executive, Donal Murphy, age 55
Managing Director DCC Corporate Finance, Michael Scholefield
CIO, Peter Quinn
Finance and Development Director SerCom, Niall Ennis, age 49
Managing Director DCC Healthcare, Conor Costigan, age 48
Managing Director DCC Retail and Oil, Eddie O'Brien
CFO, Fergal O'Dwyer, age 60
Managing Director DCC LPG, Henry Cubbon
Chairman, John J. Moloney, age 65
Auditors: KPMG

LOCATIONS

HQ: DCC Plc
DCC House, Leopardstown Road, Foxrock, Dublin 18
Phone: (353) 1 279 9400   **Fax:** (353) 1 283 1017
Web: www.dcc.ie

2018 sales

	$ mil.	% of total
United Kingdom	7,741	54
France	2,712	19
Ireland	927	6
Other	2,884	21
Total	**14,264**	**100**

PRODUCTS/OPERATIONS

2018 Sales

	% of total
Retail & Oil	65
Technology	22
LPG	10
Healthcare	4
Total	**100**

COMPETITORS

BP	Shamrock Foods Limited
Biffa	Shell Oil
CEVA Logistics UK	Sitel UK
Cardinal Health	TOTAL
Central Foods	UDG Healthcare
Computacenter	Waste Recycling
Ingram Micro UK	Wincanton

HISTORICAL FINANCIALS

Company Type: Public

Income Statement   FYE: March 31

	REVENUE ($ mil.)	NET INCOME ($ mil.)	NET PROFIT MARGIN	EMPLOYEES
03/20	18,228	303	1.7%	12,773
03/19	19,946	343	1.7%	12,418
03/18	20,044	367	1.8%	10,430
03/17	15,318	269	1.8%	10,848
03/16	15,259	256	1.7%	10,540
Annual Growth	**4.5%**	**4.3%**	**—**	**4.9%**

2020 Year-End Financials

Debt ratio: 32.5%	No. of shares (mil.): 98
Return on equity: 10.0%	Dividends
Cash ($ mil.): 2,216	Yield: 2.0%
Current ratio: 1.50	Payout: 20.2%
Long-term debt ($ mil.): 2,292	Market value ($ mil.): 3,164

	STOCK PRICE ($) FY Close	P/E High/Low	PER SHARE ($)		
			Earnings	Dividends	Book Value
03/20	32.15	— —	3.08	0.64	31.22
03/19	41.92	— —	3.66	0.57	31.87
03/18	41.92	— —	4.11	0.57	25.87
03/17	41.92	23 14	3.02	0.25	20.78
03/16	48.40	24 19	2.89	0.45	21.46
Annual Growth	**(9.7%)**	**— —**	**1.6%**	**9.3%**	**9.8%**

Denso Corp. (Japan)

DENSO Corporation is the number 2 global automotive parts manufacturer (behind Bosch). The Japan-based company supplies OEM and aftermarket components and systems for most of the world's carmakers (Toyota Motor accounts for roughly half of DENSO's total revenue). DENSO products include powertrain systems vehicle electronics electrification systems and cockpit systems as well as advanced safety and automated driving technologies. The company has expanded recently into industrial and consumer products such as bar code readers industrial robots and home energy management systems. About half of its sales are generated in Japan.

Operations
DENSO is divided into five product groups: thermal systems powertrain systems mobility electronics electrification systems and sensor & semiconductor (less than 5%).

The thermal systems business (about 25% of sales) provides air conditioning systems for cars and buses truck refrigeration units radiators and cooling systems. It also develops products for interior thermal management that monitor the driver's physical condition and adjust for temperature humidity and even fragrance.

Powertrain systems (nearly 25%) manufactures engine-related products such as variable cam timing (VCT) systems exhaust gas sensors and products for drive systems such as oil pressure control valves.

Mobility electronics (more than 20%) encompasses DENSO's connected car offerings for advanced safety and automated driving systems.

The electrification systems segment (more than 15%) is focused on products that provide more energy-efficient powertrains and moreeco-friendly technologies. This segment makes hybrid and electric car drive systems steering and braking control products and power supply and starting system products.

Other Automotive which is more than 5% of total revenue supplies automotive parts and service tools.

Geographic Reach
Based in Japan DENSO operates in about 35 countries and regions. Approximately 45% of the company's revenue is generated in Japan and more than 20% in other Asian countries. The company does more than 20% of its business in North America (with minor operations through subsidiaries in South America) and about 10% in Europe.

Sales and Marketing
Sales to original equipment manufacturers (OEMs) account for about 90% of DENSO's sales with the remaining revenue coming from aftermarket and non-automotive activities. Its largest customer Toyota Motor Group accounts for roughly half of sales.

Financial Performance

Note: Growth rates may differ after conversion to US Dollars.

DENSO's revenue has been increasing steadily over the past five years except for 2020.

Although sales volume remained flat until the third quarter revenue of the Group decreased by Å 209.3 billion or 4% to Å 5.2 billion for the year ended March 31 2020 due to a significant market contraction caused by the COVID-19 pandemic in the fourth quarter and exchange rate fluctuations.

Profit attributable to owners of the parent company decreased by Å 186.4 billion or 73% to Å 68.1 billion. Primarily due to a provision for quality costs in the second half of the fiscal year and reduction in production volume reflecting lower sales.

Cash at the end of fiscal 2020 was Å 597.8 billion a decrease of Å 113.8 billion from the prior year. Cash from operations contributed Å 595.3 billion to the coffers while investing activities used Å 447.4 billion mainly for purchases of property and equipment. Financing activities used another Å 240.9 billion for loan payments dividends to stockholders and the company's stock repurchase program.

Strategy

DENSO aims to achieve sustainable growth in a changing environment by remaining alert to the needs of society. The company have identified four priority areas: electric vehicles advanced safety/autonomous vehicles connectivity and factory automation/agriculture. They will continue to create new value by using their accumulated technology and experience to drive further progress in new mobility-related fields by contributing to the advancement of manufacturing through their factory automation business and by applying DENSO technology to their agriculture business.

DENSO has been developing mass-production process technologies to their plants around the worlds to achieve the same high "Monozukuri (manufacturing)" level globally. Hirose Plant has been establish development and mass-production process as Electrification Global Mother with EIC. They will developing good mass-production line to all over the global production plants.

Mergers and Acquisitions

In 2019 DENSO purchased a stake in Infineon Technologies one of the top manufacturers of in-vehicle semiconductor products. DENSO will combine Infineon Technologies' advanced semiconductor technologies with its own in-vehicle technologies and expertise to accelerate the development of new and emerging mobility solutions.

Company Background

Originally the in-house parts supplier for Toyota Nippondenso Co. (the predecessor to DENSO) was spun off by Toyota in 1949. Nippondenso remained dependent upon Toyota for sales as it still does today.

In 1966 Nippondenso established sales offices in the US then turned to Europe establishing a branch office Germany in 1970. It later went on to establish subsidiaries in the US Canada Europe and Asia. In 1984 Nippondenso joined with Allen Bradley Co. (US) to develop factory automation equipment. The company changed its name to DENSO CORPORATION in 1996. In 2001 the company merged its industrial equipment subsidiaries (bar code scanners and factory automation robots) and spun them off as majority-owned subsidiary DENSO Wave (now part of the company's non-automotive business segment). In 2006 DENSO added four new Chinese production facilities that make navigation systems air conditioner compressors instrument panels and oil filters. It has also established technical centers in China and Thailand.

Over the years DENSO has partnered with rival parts suppliers Bosch and Aisin Seiki and carmaker Toyota Motor forming joint ventures and alliances to collaborate on the development of emerging technologies such as advanced safety features and automated driving.

EXECUTIVES

EVP, Masahiko Miyaki
EVP, Haruya Maruyama
EVP, Yasushi Yamanaka
President and CEO, Koji Arima
CEO North America Thermal Systems Center, Steve Milam
President DENSO Manufacturing Canada, Rich van Oorschot
Vice Chairman, Koji Kobayashi
Senior Managing Director Corporate Center and Electric Systems Business Group, Nobuaki Katoh
Auditors: Deloitte Touche Tohmatsu LLC

LOCATIONS

HQ: Denso Corp. (Japan)
1-1 Showa-cho, Kariya, Aichi 448-8661
Phone: (81) 566 61 7910   **Fax:** (81) 566 25 4913
Web: www.denso.co.jp

2019 Sales

	% of total
Japan	43
Asia	23
North America	22
Europe	11
Others	1
Total	**100**

PRODUCTS/OPERATIONS

2019 Sales

	% of total
Thermal Systems	26
Powertrain Systems	24
Mobility Systems	17
Electrification Systems	15
Electronic Systems	12
Other Automotive	2
FA-New Business	4
Total	**100**

Products & Services

Electronics
Powertrain ECU (electronic control unit) designSemiconductor sensorPower cardsAcoustic vehicle alerting systemsBody control computers
Powertrain
VCTCommon rail systemsSpark plugExhaust gas sensorHigh pressure pumps
Thermal
CondensersRadiatorsBus air-conditionersRefrigeration unitsWater cooled intercoolers
Mobility
Milimeter-wave radarIntegrated cockpit systems

COMPETITORS

APM Automotive	JTEKT
Adept Technology	Magna International
Aisin Seiki	Robert Bosch
Continental AG	Valeo
Delphi Automotive Systems	Visteon
Faurecia	Yazaki
Hyundai Mobis	ZF Friedrichshafen

HISTORICAL FINANCIALS

Company Type: Public

Income Statement

FYE: March 31

	REVENUE ($ mil.)	NET INCOME ($ mil.)	NET PROFIT MARGIN	EMPLOYEES
03/20	51,961	686	1.3%	202,363
03/19	54,071	2,566	4.7%	206,521
03/18	51,505	3,232	6.3%	204,314
03/17	45,646	2,597	5.7%	185,134
03/16	45,619	2,462	5.4%	182,229
Annual Growth	**3.3%**	**(27.3%)**	**—**	**2.7%**

2020 Year-End Financials

Debt ratio: 0.0%	No. of shares (mil.): 774
Return on equity: 1.9%	Dividends
Cash ($ mil.): 6,027	Yield: 4.0%
Current ratio: 1.65	Payout: —
Long-term debt ($ mil.): 3,558	Market value ($ mil.): 12,290

	STOCK PRICE ($) FY Close	P/E High/Low		PER SHARE ($) Earnings	Dividends	Book Value
03/20	15.86	0	0	0.89	0.64	44.20
03/19	19.52	0	0	3.29	0.61	46.79
03/18	27.71	0	0	4.14	0.56	46.53
03/17	22.08	0	0	3.29	0.54	42.50
03/16	19.91	0	0	3.10	0.50	39.73
Annual Growth	**(5.5%)**	**—**	**—**	**(26.9%)**	**6.4%**	**2.7%**

Desjardins Group

Auditors: PricewaterhouseCoopers LLP/s.r.l./s.e.n.c.r.l.

LOCATIONS

HQ: Desjardins Group
Federation des caisses Desjardins du Quebec, 100 Des Commandeurs Street, Levis, Quebec G6V 7N5
Phone: 418 835-8444   **Fax:** 418 833-5873
Web: www.desjardins.com

HISTORICAL FINANCIALS

Company Type: Public

Income Statement

FYE: December 31

	REVENUE ($ mil.)	NET INCOME ($ mil.)	NET PROFIT MARGIN	EMPLOYEES
12/19	18,177	1,781	9.8%	47,849
12/18	14,493	1,542	10.6%	46,200
12/17	15,109	1,563	10.3%	45,547
12/16	12,598	1,180	9.4%	47,655
12/15	12,297	1,205	9.8%	47,654
Annual Growth	**10.3%**	**10.3%**	**—**	**0.1%**

2019 Year-End Financials

Debt ratio: 0.3%	No. of shares (mil.): —
Return on equity: 9.0%	Dividends
Cash ($ mil.): 2,848	Yield: —
Current ratio: —	Payout: —
Long-term debt ($ mil.): 1,073	Market value ($ mil.): —

Deutsche Bank AG

Deutsche Bank AG is one of the financial groups in the world and in Germany. In its home country it operates more than 1930 retail branch locations in some 60 countries across five continents.

Deutsche Bank serves private individuals corporate customers and institutional clients with a wide variety of investment financial and related products and services. The bank's asset management business holds some ?768 billion in assets under management. All in Deutsche has around ?1.3 trillion in assets under management. Deutsche Bank generates most of its revenue from outside of Germany.

Operations

In accordance with Deutsche Bank strategy announcement in mid-2019 their business operations were reorganized in the third quarter of 2019 under the divisional structure comprising the following segments: Corporate Bank (CB) Investment Bank (IB) Private Bank (PB) Asset Management (AM) Capital Release Unit (CRU) and Corporate & Other (C&O).

PB is Deutsche's largest business accounting 35% of net revenue. It serves private customers in Germany. The Private and Commercial Business International serves private and small business clients as well as commercial and corporate clients in Italy Spain Belgium and India. In addition the Private Bank covers Wealth Management clients globally.

IB previously part of the former Corporate & Investment Bank includes Deutsche Bank's Origination & Advisory businesses generates 30% of sales. It also includes Fixed Income Currency (FIC) Sales & Trading which includes their Global Credit Trading Foreign Exchange Rates and Emerging Markets Debt businesses.

CB made about 25% of total revenue includes the Global Transaction Bank which was previously part of the former Corporate & Investment Bank as well as the German Commercial Clients division formerly part of the Private & Commercial Business (Germany).

The Asset Management operates under the DWS brand. It is unchanged from Deutsche Bank's previous segmentation and provides investment solutions to individual investors and institutions with a diversified range of Active Passive and Alternative Asset Management products and services. It generates 10% of net sales.

CRU and C&O contributes less than 5% each for the company's revenue. New Capital Release Unit (CRU) includes substantially all of their Equities Sales & Trading business lower yielding fixed income positions particularly in Rates their former CIB Non-Strategic portfolio as well as the exited businesses from their Private & Commercial Bank which include their retail operations in Portugal and Poland. While Corporate & Other includes revenues costs and resources held centrally that are not allocated to the individual business segments.

Overall net interest income accounts for more 70% of Deutsche's total net revenue. Net fee and commission income represents about 25% of sales.

Geographic Reach

Headquartered in Frankfurt the financial capital of Germany (and continental Europe) Deutsche is active in around 60 countries worldwide. It derives around 40% of sales from its home market of Germany while its other major markets are the US (more than 20%) and the Rest of Europe Middle East and Africa and Asia/Pacific (around 15%).

Private & Commercial Clients (PCC) Germany and Postbank offer cash services at more than 10000 cash points. Postbank offers financial services at around 4500 Deutsche Post DHL partner retail outlets. PCC International is present in Italy Spain Belgium Portugal Poland and India.

Sales and Marketing

The global coverage function in the Corporate Bank brings together the Corporate Banking Coverage unit focusing on international Large Corporate clients Global Subsidiary Coverage covering subsidiaries of multinational clients and Finance Solutions Group providing treasury solutions.

Coverage of the IB's clients is provided by the Institutional Client Group which houses their debt sales team and works in conjunction with Finance Solutions Group in the Corporate Bank covering capital markets and Treasury solutions.

Private Bank Germany business and Private & Commercial Business International have similar distribution channels. Those include branch network supported by customer call centers and self-service terminals; advisory centers of the Deutsche Bank brand in Germany Italy and Spain which connects branch network with digital offerings; online and mobile banking including Digital Platform through which they provide a transaction platform for banking brokerage and self-services combined with a multi-mobile offering for smartphones and tablets; and lastly financial advisors as an additional service channel in collaboration with self-employed financial advisors as well as sales and cooperation partners.

Financial Performance

Note: Growth rates may differ after conversion to US dollars.

Deutsche Bank has implemented significant strategic transformations to improve its long term profitability and returns. With this the bank's operations comprising of its corporate investment and private banks asset management capital release unit and corporate and other were reorganized.

In 2019 Deutsche Bank's revenue fell another 2% to ?23.2 billion with the non-recurrence of revenues associated with discontinued business activities negative mark-to-market impacts as well as hedging and de-risking costs in its Capital Release Unit. The rest of the bank's operating segments have reported either flat or with further decline. The only units to report higher revenue were the Asset Management unit which increased 7% and Corporate & Other with ?155 million compared to negative ?120 million in the prior year.

The bank's transformation has also driven it to a net loss of ?5.3 billion in 2019 compared to a profit of ?341 million in 2018. In line with the transformation it absorbed the transformation charges goodwill impairments and restructuring and severance expenses.

Deutsche Bank's cash balances weakened during 2019 ending the year ?52 billion lower at ?28.9 billion. The bank's operations used ?40.4 billion and its financing activities used ?2.8 billion while investing activities used another ?10.3 billion. Deutsche's main cash uses in 2019 were purchases of financial assets and treasury shares and repayments of securities and long-term debt.

Strategy

Deutsche Bank's dream of being a global investment bank to compete with the Wall St. top dogs lies in tatters. The bank's directors' new priorities are re-establishing it as a sturdier more conventional bank while scaling down its investment bank's horizons. In mid-2019 DB's CEO swung the ax on 18000 staff — representing one-fifth of its workforce — mostly in Europe and the US and including its entire global equities business. By 2022 the bank estimates a 74000 employee reduction. The restructuring which includes the establishment of a "bad bank" to hold ?74 billion in unwanted assets will cost ?7.4 billion and push Deutsche back into the red after it briefly (and barely) emerged from successive net losses in the 2018 financial year.

Deutsche's investment bank's reduced focus will be on its financing capital markets advisory services and sales and trading businesses.

In accordance with its strategic transformations it reorganized its business segments in the third quarter of 2019 into the following: Corporate Bank Investment Bank Private Bank Asset Management Capital Release Unit and Corporate & Other.

In terms of its IT strategy Deutsche will continue to invest about ?13 billion until 2022 as part of improving its cloud capabilities and upgrading important legacy infrastructure.

Company Background

Deutsche Bank was founded in 1870 in Berlin by Adelbert Delbr ck a private banker and Ludwig Bamberger a politician and currency expert. Shortly after it opened its first international branches in China (Shanghai and Yokohama) and the UK (London). In its first century of activity significant events included financing steel company Krupp (which became ThyssenKrupp) the Northern Pacific Railroad and film company UFA (which made films including Fritz Lang's Metropolis). Deutsche dipped its toe into investment banking in the late 1980s and by the late 1990s the bank was dead-set on taking on global leaders in investment banking such as JPMorgan and Goldman Sachs. Deutsche responded slowly to the 2008 financial crisis stumbling from net loss to net loss before CEO Christian Sewing in 2019 cut a fifth of its workforce and retrenched the bank with downwardly revised investment banking ambitions.

HISTORY

Georg von Siemens opened Deutsche Bank in Berlin in 1870. Three years later the firm opened an office in London and was soon buying other German banks. In the late 1800s Deutsche Bank helped finance Germany's electrification (carried out by Siemens AG) and railroad construction in the US and the Ottoman Empire. Von Siemens ran the bank until his death in 1901.

The bank survived post-WWI financial chaos by merging with Disconto-Gesellschaft and later helped finance the Nazi war machine. After the war the Allies split the company into 10 banks; it became extinct in Soviet-controlled East Germany.

The bank was reassembled in 1957 and primarily engaged in commercial banking often taking direct interests in its customers. It added retail services in the 1960s. In 1975 to prevent the Shah of Iran from gaining a stake in Daimler-Benz (now Daimler) the bank bought 29% of that company.

The firm opened an investment banking office in the US in 1971 and a branch office in 1978. In the 1980s it expanded geographically buying Bank of America's Italian subsidiary (1986) and UK merchant bank Morgan Grenfell (1989); it also moved into insurance creating life insurer DB Leben (1989).

Terrorists killed chairman Alfred Herrhausen a symbol of German big business in 1989. After German reunification in 1990 successor Hilmar Kopper oversaw the bank's reestablishment in eastern Germany.

In 1994 Deutsche Bank bought most of ITT's commercial finance unit. That year the company suffered scandal when real estate developer Jurgen Schneider borrowed more than DM1 billion and disappeared; he was later found and returned to Germany.

The company grew its global investment banking operations in 1995 under its Morgan Grenfell subsidiary. Corporate culture clashes prompted Deutsche Bank to take greater control of the unit and restructure it in 1998.

Deutsche Bank's global aspirations suffered a setback in 1998 when losses on investments in Russia trimmed its bottom line. Still trying to put WWII behind it the bank accepted responsibility for its wartime dealing in gold seized from Jews but has rejected liability to compensate victims of Nazi forced labor who toiled in industrial companies in which it holds stakes.

In 1999 the bank acquired Bankers Trust. Despite a decision to divest its industrial portfolio that year the company bought Tele Columbus the #2 cable network in Germany and Piaggio the Italian maker of the famed Vespa motor scooter. On the banking front Deutsche Bank bought Chase Manhattan's Dutch auction business and sought a foothold in Japan through alliances with Nippon Life Insurance and Sakura Bank (now part of Sumitomo Mitsui Banking).

In 2000 the company agreed to merge with Dresdner Bank (after which they would spin off their retail banking businesses) but the merger collapsed in part over the fate of investment banking subsidiary Dresdner Kleinwort Benson. German mega-insurer Allianz bought Dresdner in 2001. Deutsche Bank's reorganization plans the same year saw the bank eliminate 2600 jobs worldwide and realign its businesses into two divisions. Deutsche Bank also bought Banque Worms from French insurer AXA.

Looking for a steady supply of cash in 2001 Deutsche Bank's Morgan Grenfall Private Equity bought 3000 English pubs owned by UK-based conglomerate Whitbread plc. In 2002 more shuffling of the executive board members allowed Deutsche Bank to grow in the international Anglo-American style rather than as a domestic player.

In 2004 Deutsche Bank acquired Berkshire Mortgage (now Deutsche Bank Berkshire Mortgage) one of the top multifamily residential lenders in the US. The next year it bought Russian financial services company United Financial Group and combined its depositary business with its own.

The year 2006 was a bad year for the company from a public relations standpoint. Fallout from former chairman Rolf Breuer's remarks regarding the financial stability of banking client Kirch Holding led to a shake-up in the executive suite and the board that year. Later UK financial regulators charged the bank an $11.1 million fine for market misconduct related to trading activity in 2004. In the US the IRS investigated the bank for alleged abusive tax shelters.

The bank also took a public relations hit when its CEO Josef Ackermann went on trial for illegal bonuses during his tenure at Mannesmann.

To boost its lending operations in the US the company bought MortgageIT a real estate investment trust for some ?285 million ($430 million) in 2007. The timing wasn't great: the subsidiary suffered a major loss a victim of the US subprime mortgage crisis. Also that year Deutsche Bank acquired Abbey Life from Lloyds Banking Group for some ?1 billion ($2 billion.) This acquisition fared better than MortgageIT finishing out the year in the black.

Deutsche Bank's expansion was slowed in 2008 when its proposed acquisition of some of ABN AMRO's assets — including corporate and commercial units parts of Hollandische Bank Unie and a factoring company — from Fortis was canceled.

On the heels of a global expansion which began in earnest in 2002 Deutsche Bank was hit hard by the worldwide financial crisis. The company reported a fourth-quarter loss of ?4.8 billion in 2008 largely due to declines in its trading and asset management businesses. Its Americas business primarily the US operations was hit the hardest by far.

But in 2009 Deutsche Bank's growth seemed to pick back up again as it acquired Dresdner Bank's global agency securities lending business from Commerzbank. The business was merged with Deutsche's trust and securities services unit. The deal expanded Deutsche Bank's custody platform.

EXECUTIVES

Head of Global Banking Division and Global Transaction Banking, J rgen Fitschen, age 72, $600,000 total compensation
CFO, Marcus Schenck, age 55
Co-CEO, John Cryan, age 60
CIO and Head of Operations Corporate and Investment Banking, Pascal Boillat
Chief Risk Officer, Stuart Lewis
COO, Kim Hammonds
Global Head Equities Trading; Head Equities EMEA, Rick Saunders
COO Global Equities Trading, Leonie Ryan
Head Global Markets, Garth Ritchie
CEO Deutsche Securities Saudi Arabia, Jamal Al Kishi
Chairman, Paul Achleitner, age 64
Deputy Chairman, Alfred Herling, age 67
Auditors: KPMG AG Wirtschaftspruefungsgesellschaft

LOCATIONS

HQ: Deutsche Bank AG
Taunusanlage 12, Frankfurt am Main D-60262
Phone: (49) 69 910 00   **Fax:** (49) 69 910 34 225
Web: www.deutsche-bank.com

2018 Sales

	% of total
Germany	38
Americas	22
UK	14
Rest of Europe Middle East and Africa	13
Asia/Pacific	13
Other	-
Total	**100**

PRODUCTS/OPERATIONS

2018 Sales

	% of total
Corporate & Investment Bank	51
Private & Commercial Bank	40
Asset Management	9
Other	-
Total	**100**

COMPETITORS

BNP Paribas	KfW
Barclays	Landesbank Berlin
Citigroup	Merrill Lynch
Citigroup Global	Mizuho Financial
Markets	Morgan Stanley
Commerzbank	National Australia
Cortal Consors	Bank
Credit Suisse	Rabobank Group
Goldman Sachs	Société Générale
Grupo Santander	TD Bank
HSBC	UBS
JPMorgan Chase	UniCredit Bank AG

HISTORICAL FINANCIALS

Company Type: Public

Income Statement				FYE: December 31
	ASSETS ($ mil.)	NET INCOME ($ mil.)	INCOME AS % OF ASSETS	EMPLOYEES
12/19	1,456,984	(6,051)	—	87,597
12/18	1,543,879	305	0.0%	91,737
12/17	1,767,841	(900)	—	97,733
12/16	1,679,430	(1,480)	—	99,744
12/15	1,774,466	(7,400)	—	101,104
Annual Growth	**(4.8%)**	—	—	**(3.5%)**

2019 Year-End Financials

Return on assets: (-0.4%)	Dividends
Return on equity: (-8.4%)	Yield: 1.5%
Long-term debt ($ mil.): —	Payout: —
No. of shares (mil.): 2,066	Market value ($ mil.): —
Sales ($ mil): 38,806	

Deutsche Lufthansa AG (Germany, Fed. Rep.)

Germany's air ambassador Deutsche Lufthansa rivals the world's largest airlines. Operating in about 580 subsidiaries and affiliated companies the global aviation group runs Europe's largest passenger airline. Lufthansa Passenger Airlines operates a global route network of more than 315 destinations in over 100countries with a fleet of almost 765 aircrafts. The company's logistics is also a market leader in international airfreight transportation through Lufthansa Cargo. Lufthansa is also comprised of AirPlus Lufthansa Aviation Training and offers IT services through Lufthansa Systems. The majority of Lufthansa's sales come from Europe.

Operations

Lufthansa operates five business segments Network Airlines MRO (maintenance repair and overhaul) Eurowings Logistics and Catering.

Network airlines segment consists of Lufthansa's multi-hub airlines Lufthansa Germany Airlines SWISS and Austrian Airlines. It offers premium and high-quality products and services comprehensive route networks combined with highest level of travel flexibility. The segment generates more than 60% of sales.

The Eurowings segment (over 10% of sales) holds Lufthansa's budget airline operations providing low-cost direct services under the Eurowings Germanwings and Eurowings Europe banners. It also includes Brussels Air and Lufthansa's equity investment in SunExpress. Doing business as Lufthansa Technik the MRO segment is one of the leading global providers of maintenance repair and overhaul services for civilian commercial aircraft. It accounts for more than 10% of sales.

Catering provides in-flight food from locations at more than 200 airports primarily under the LSG Sky Chefs brand. It accounts for over 5% of sales.

Logistics generates more than 5% of Lufthansa's revenue. It consists of Lufthansa's 15-plus owned freight aircraft in addition to cargo marketing services that sells hull capacity of its own planes chartered craft and extra belly capacity of Lufthansa's passenger aircraft fleet.

Overall Traffic generates more than 75% of Lufthansa's Revenue.

Geographic Reach

Cologne Germany-based Lufthansa's largest market is Europe which generates more than 65% of total revenue. North America generates over 150% and the Asia/Pacific region more than 10%. Lufthansa also generates revenue in Central and South America the Middle East and Africa.

Sales and Marketing

The Lufthansa Group sells flight tickets and related ancillary services primarily via agents websites or other airlines in the course of interlining. It carries more than 140 million passengers each year.

Financial PerformanceNote: Growth rates may differ after conversion to US Dollars.

Lufthansa's sales have been fluctuating over the last five years.

In 2019 the airline grew its sales 2% to ?36.4 billion. This was due to the growth in both traffic and other revenue.

Net income fell 44% from ?2.2 billion in to ?1.2 billion in 2019.

Lufthansa's cash position decreased in 2019 ending the year ?3 million lower at ?1.4 billion. Lufthansa's operating activities produced cash of ?4.0 billion while its investing activities used ?3.4

billion and its financing activities used ?161 million. The company's main cash uses in 2018 were investments and additions to repairable spare parts and purchases of securities.

Strategy

Lufthansa Group's strategy consists of: strengthening its position as leading European airline group; profitable expansion of market leadership in home markets; as well as strengthening of core business among others.

The financial strategy of the Lufthansa Group seeks to increase its Company value in a sustainable manner. It will concentrate on three dimensions: improving profitability focusing capital allocation and maintaining financial stability.

HISTORY

The Weimar government created Deutsche Luft Hansa (DLH) in 1926 by merging private German airlines Deutscher Aero Lloyd (founded 1919) and Junkers Luftverkehr (formed in 1921 by aircraft manufacturer Junkers Flugzeugwerke). DLH built what would become Europe's most comprehensive air route network by 1931. It served the USSR through Deruluft (formed 1921; dissolved 1941) an airline jointly owned by DLH and the Soviet government. In 1930 DLH and the Chinese government formed Eurasia Aviation Corporation to develop air transport in China.

DLH established the world's first trans-Atlantic airmail service from Berlin to Buenos Aires in 1934 and went on to develop air transport throughout South America. The outbreak of WWII ended operations in Europe and the Chinese government seized Eurasia Aviation in 1941. Klaus Bonhoeffer head of DLH's legal department led an unsuccessful coup against the Nazi leadership and was executed in 1945. Soon afterward all DLH operations ceased.

In 1954 the Allies allowed the recapitalization of Deutsche Lufthansa. The airline started with domestic routes returned to London and Paris (1955) and then re-entered South America (1956). In 1958 it made its first nonstop flight between Germany and New York and initiated service to Tokyo and Cairo. Meanwhile it started a charter airline with several partners in 1955. Lufthansa bought out its partners in 1959 and renamed the unit Condor two years later.

The carrier resumed service behind the Iron Curtain in 1966 with flights to Prague. The stable West German economy helped Lufthansa maintain profitability through most of the 1970s. The reunification of Germany in 1990 ended Allied control over Berlin airspace allowing Lufthansa which had bought Pan Am's Berlin routes to fly there under its own colors for the first time since the end of WWII.

EXECUTIVES

Chief Network and Distribution Officer Swiss International Air Lines, Harry Hohmeister, age 56
Chairman and CEO, Carsten Spohr, age 54
CEO Eurowings and Aviation Services, Karl U. Garnadt, age 64
CIO, Roland Sch tz, age 52
CFO, Simone Menne, age 61
CEO Austrian Airlines, Kay Kratky, age 62
Auditors: PricewaterhouseCoopers GmbH

LOCATIONS

HQ: Deutsche Lufthansa AG (Germany, Fed. Rep.) Lufthansa Aviation Center (LAC), Airportring, Frankfurt D-60546
Phone: (49) 69 696 0   **Fax:** (49) 69 696 33022
Web: www.lufthansagroup.com

2018 Sales

	% of total
Europe	62
North America	18
Asia/Pacific	13
Central and South America	3
Middle East	2
Africa	2
Total	**100**

PRODUCTS/OPERATIONS

2018 Sales

	% of total
Network Airlines	57
Eurowings	11
MRO	15
Catering	8
Logistics	7
Other	2
Total	**100**

COMPETITORS

AAR Corp.	ITA Software
Aer Lingus	Iberia
Air Berlin	Japan Airlines
Air France-KLM	Jeppesen Sanderson
Alitalia	Korean Air
American Airlines Group	Qantas
Aviall	Ryanair
British Airways	SR Technics
Delta Air Lines	TIMCO Aviation
Deutsche Bahn	Virgin Atlantic Airways
Gate Gourmet	easyJet
IAG	

HISTORICAL FINANCIALS

Company Type: Public

Income Statement   FYE: December 31

	REVENUE ($ mil.)	NET INCOME ($ mil.)	NET PROFIT MARGIN	EMPLOYEES
12/19	41,664	1,361	3.3%	138,353
12/18	41,656	2,477	5.9%	135,534
12/17	42,777	2,833	6.6%	129,424
12/16	33,529	1,875	5.6%	124,306
12/15	35,136	1,849	5.3%	120,652
Annual Growth	**4.4%**	**(7.4%)**	**—**	**3.5%**

2019 Year-End Financials

Debt ratio: 26.4%   No. of shares (mil.): 478
Return on equity: 12.3%   Dividends
Cash ($ mil.): 1,588   Yield: 3.5%
Current ratio: 0.71   Payout: 22.4%
Long-term debt ($ mil.): 9,426   Market value ($ mil.): 8,679

	STOCK PRICE ($) FY Close	P/E High/Low		PER SHARE ($) Earnings	Dividends	Book Value
12/19	18.15	10	6	2.86	0.64	23.82
12/18	22.95	8	4	5.24	0.67	22.80
12/17	36.80	7	3	6.03	0.43	24.15
12/16	12.90	4	3	4.02	0.37	15.90
12/15	15.71	5	3	4.00	0.00	13.52
Annual Growth	**3.7%**	**—**	**—**	**(8.0%)**	**—**	**15.2%**

Deutsche Post AG

Deutsche Post AG (operating as Deutsche Post DHL Group) has outgrown its mailbox origins. While it's still Europe's largest postal service the company is also one of the world's leading providers of express delivery freight transport supply chain management and e-commerce solutions. The company does business in Europe (its largest market) the Americas and Asia Pacific. In Germany its Post and Parcel Germany division delivers more than 55 million letters and around 5.2 million packages per day. Deutsche Post can trace its lineage back to the earliest days of centralized post in Germany when Maximilian I established reliable postal links across the Holy Roman Empire.

Operations

Deutsche Post operates through five divisions: Express; Post and Parcel Germany; Global Forwarding Freight; Supply Chain and e-Commerce solutions.

The Express division (about 25% of sales) delivers urgent documents through its core product Time Definite International (TDI) which offers pre-defined delivery times.

Post and Parcel Germany contributes about 25% of total revenues and represents the company's mail and package delivery services primarily in Germany where it owns more than 60% of the market. Deutsche Post's Global Forwarding and Freight division (about 25%) brokers transport services between customers and freight carriers by air ocean and ground transportation.

The Supply Chain segment (about 20%) offers warehousing and logistics services such as planning sourcing and production activities primarily to the automotive technology and life sciences and healthcare sectors.

Lastly the eCommerce solutions generating nearly 5% of the total revenue geared towards providing high-quality solutions particularly to customers in the rapid growing e-commerce sector. Its core activities include national last-mile parcel delivery in selected countries. It also supplies cross-border non-TDI services.

Deutsche Post trades under two brand names Deutsche Post and DHL.

Geographic Reach

Based in Bonn Germany Deutsche Post delivers to almost everywhere in the world. Germany accounts for about 30% of total sales; wider Europe contributes a similar amount again. The rest arises mainly from the Americas and the Asia Pacific region.

Sales and Marketing

The company's products and services are targeted towards both private and business customers and range from physical and hybrid letters to special products for merchandise delivery and include additional services as registered mail cash on delivery and insured items. The company markets through retail outlets post boxes mail centers paketshops salespoints letter and parcel delivery parcel centers packstations.

Expenses for advertising and public relations was ?371 million in 2019 and ?374 in 2018 respectively

Financial Performance

Note: Growth rates may differ after conversion to US Dollars.

Except in 2016 when it declined Deutsche Post's revenue has been increasing yearly. It has an overall growth of 7% between 2015 and 2019. Its net income has fluctuated during the same five-year period.

In financial year 2019 consolidated revenue rose by ?1.8 billion to ?63.3 billion for reasons including positive currency effects of ?746 million. The proportion of revenue generated abroad increased from 69.5% to 69.9%.

Net income grew 26% from ?2.1 billion in 2018 to ?2.6 billion in 2019. This was primarily due to higher revenues.

The company had a cash and cash equivalents of ?2.9 billion at the end of 2019. Operating activities provided ?6 billion while investing activities used ?2.1 billion. Financing activities used another ?4.1 billion. Main cash uses in 2019 were for capital expenditures and dividends paid.

Strategy

Deutsche Post's Strategy 2025 provides a foundation for continuing its profitable growth trajectory going forwards. The four trends of globalization e-commerce digitalization and sustainability will remain important drivers of growth for the logistics sector and are reflected in the company's corporate strategy.

The company's divisions form the core of the group. Since all five divisions have distinct profiles and service offerings Deutsche Post's group strategy is structured along multi-divisional lines. The company focuses upon the specific growth drivers that will strengthen the profitable core of the company's business units with the goal of achieving industry-leading margins in all segments.

Deutsche Post sees systematic digitalization throughout the group as a key lever in driving forwards its business. This is why the company is investing in initiatives designed to enhance both the customer experience and the employee experience as well as to improve operational excellence. The company is modernizing its IT systems and integrating new technologies with the aim of steadily improving its performance processes and standards. Between now and 2025 spending on digitalization is expected to reach around ?2 billion. This is projected to contribute at least ?1.5 billion annually to earnings by 2025.

HISTORY

The German postal system was established in the 1490s when German emperor Maximilian I ordered a reliable and regular messenger service to be set up between Austria (Innsbruck where the emperor had his court) and the farther reaches of his Holy Roman Empire: the Netherlands France and Rome. The von Tassis (later renamed Taxis) family of Italy was responsible for running the network. Family members settled in major cities across Europe to expand the postal business.

Although the family operated what was officially an exclusively royal mail service by the early 1500s the company was also delivering messages for private patrons. In 1600 a family member who served as general postmaster was authorized to collect fees for private mail deliveries. By the early 19th century Thurn und Taxis as the company was then called was the leading postal service in the Holy Roman Empire serving more than 11 million people.

The dissolution of the Holy Roman Empire prompted by Napoleon's military adventures led to the creation of a federation of 39 independent German states. Thurn und Taxis had to make agreements with members of the separate states including Austria and Prussia. After Austria's defeat in 1866 by Prussia the confederation was dissolved and all Thurn und Taxis postal systems were absorbed by Prussia. When Bismarck's Prussian-led German Reich was established in 1870 the new postal administration (Reichspostverwaltung) began issuing postage stamps valid across Germany.

After Germany was defeated in WWII and split into two nations in 1949 two postal systems were established: Deutsche Post (East Germany) and Deutsche Bundespost (West Germany). The fall of the Berlin Wall in 1989 preceded a reunion of the two German states in 1990. That year Deutsche Post led by chairman Klaus Zumwinkel was integrated into Deutsche Bundespost.

EXECUTIVES

CEO, Frank Appel, age 59, $867,167 total compensation
CEO DHL Express, Ken Allen, age 65
CEO Post eCommerce Parcel, J rgen Gerdes, age 56, $357,500 total compensation
CEO DHL Supply Chain Williams Lea, John Gilbert
CFO, Melanie Kreis
Chair Supervisory Board, Wulf von Schimmelmann
Auditors: PricewaterhouseCoopers GmbH

LOCATIONS

HQ: Deutsche Post AG
Zentrale - Investor Relations, Bonn 53250
Phone: (49) 228 182 6 3636   **Fax:** (49) 228 182 6 3199
Web: www.dpdhl.de

2018 Sales

	% of total
Europe	
Germany	30
Europe (excluding Germany)	30
Americas	18
Asia/Pacific	18
Other regions	4
Total	**100**

PRODUCTS/OPERATIONS

2018 Sales

	% of total
PeP	29
Express	25
Global Forwarding Freight	23
Supply Chain	21
Corporate Center/Other	2
Total	**100**

Selected Services

Mail and package delivery
Dialogue marketing services
Time Definite International (TDI) express delivery
Air freight
Freight forwarding services
Contract logistics
Ocean freight
Outsourcing and system solutions for the mail business

COMPETITORS

CEVA Logistics	Panalpina
DB Schenker Rail AG	Panalpina World
Expeditors	Transport (UK)
FedEx	PostNL
Geodis	Poste Italiane
HITACHI TRANSPORT	Royal Mail
SYSTEM LTD.	Ryder System
Kuehne + Nagel	TNT Express
International	UPS
La Poste	US Postal Service
Neovia	XPO logistics
Nippon Express	

HISTORICAL FINANCIALS

Company Type: Public

Income Statement   FYE: December 31

	REVENUE ($ mil.)	NET INCOME ($ mil.)	NET PROFIT MARGIN	EMPLOYEES
12/19	71,117	2,945	4.1%	546,924
12/18	70,486	2,376	3.4%	547,459
12/17	72,457	3,252	4.5%	513,338
12/16	60,538	2,786	4.6%	498,459
12/15	64,513	1,677	2.6%	497,745
Annual Growth	**2.5%**	**15.1%**	**—**	**2.4%**

Debt ratio: 12.0%	No. of shares (mil.): 1,235
Return on equity: 18.9%	Dividends
Cash ($ mil.): 3,213	Yield: 3.2%
Current ratio: 0.89	Payout: 53.0%
Long-term debt ($ mil.): 6,276	Market value ($ mil.): 46,727

	STOCK PRICE ($) FY Close	P/E High/Low	PER SHARE ($) Earnings	Dividends	Book Value
12/19	37.82	18 12	2.35	1.24	12.83
12/18	27.33	28 16	1.90	1.37	12.62
12/17	47.59	22 16	2.58	1.23	12.37
12/16	32.74	15 10	2.22	0.87	9.66
12/15	27.78	27 20	1.33	0.91	9.92
Annual Growth	**8.0%**	**— —**	**15.3%**	**8.1%**	**6.6%**

Deutsche Telekom AG

Operating the autobahn on the global information superhighway Deutsche Telekom (DT) is a leading telecom company in Europe and one of the largest carriers in the world. Operating as T-Mobile in the US and in certain other European countries the company's core business is serving its over 230 million customers with fixed-network and mobile communications services and products as well as for enterprise information and communication technology (ICT). Germany's one of the leading fixed-line telephone operator it provides domestic and international long-distance voice services. It is a leading ISP offering other data and multimedia services such as its Entertain-branded internet television. DT's T-Systems International delivers ICT services for businesses. DT generates majority of sales in North America.

Operations

Deutsche Telekom is divided into five segments: three geographic-based segments (Germany Europe and the US) Systems Solutions segment and Group Development.

Deutsche Telekom's Germany segment operates fixed-network and mobile telecoms infrastructure for businesses and consumers in the country. It accounts for around 25% of the company's total sales. The Europe segment consists of similar activities in Central and Eastern Europe and generates nearly 15% of sales.

In the US Deutsche Telekom operates in the mobile communications market as T-Mobile US and is the third-largest provider in the country. T-Mobile US is Deutsche Telekom's biggest business accounting for over 45% of total sales.

The Systems Solutions segment which accounts for almost 10% of sales offers more complex solutions for business customers including data centers and cloud networking in the areas of IT telecoms digital and security. The remaining sales are from Group Development and Group Headquarters & Group services.

Overall DT generates more than 90% of sales from Telecommunications and nearly 10% from ICT solutions.

Geographic Reach

Deutsche Telekom (DT) headquartered in Bonn Germany operates in more than 50 countries worldwide. The company gets nearly 70% of its revenue from outside Germany mostly in the US but also in Central and Eastern Europe (Greece Romania Hungary Poland the Czech Republic Croatia Slovakia Austria Albania Macedonia and Montenegro).

Sales and Marketing

Deutsche Telekom is known for its recognizable hot pink corporate color scheme. The company sponsors a number of high-profile venues and organizations particularly within sports such as the Seattle Mariners baseball field and a multi-purpose indoor venue in Las Vegas. Deutsche Telekom also sponsors Bayern Munich Germany's most successful soccer team.

Financial Performance

Note: Growth rates may differ after conversion to US Dollars.

In 2019 The company generated net revenue of EUR 80.5 billion which was 6% or EUR 4.9 billion up on the prior-year. The increase was primarily due to United States operating segment contributed to the positive revenue trend with an increase of 11% due primarily to higher service revenues from the rise in the average branded customer base triggered in particular by the continued growth in existing and greenfield markets and the growing success in new customer segments and rate plans. Net profit increased by EUR 1.7 billion to EUR 3.9 billion.

The company's loss from financial activities decreased by EUR 0.7 billion to EUR 2.2 billion. Positive measurement effects from embedded derivatives at T?Mobile US were offset by increased finance costs resulting from the application of IFRS 16.

Deutsche Telekom's cash on hand increased 205% to ?2.1 billion. Cash provided by operations was $17.8 billion while investing and financing activities were $14.5 billion and $1.8 billion respectively.

Strategy

Deutsche Telekom's basic strategy is essentially more of the same. The company's next three-year plan touches on similar topics: more entertainment content delivered digitally; further convergence of its fixed-mobile offering MagentaEins; and more investment in fixed fiber networks. Deutsche Telekom included in the joint Gigabit Project wants to be in a position to offer 90% of German households companies in business parks schools and educational institutions optical fiber connections that will offer speeds of up to 1Gbit/s. In the 5G mobile connectivity the network is transmitting data in almost 10 German cities: Berlin Darmstadt Munich Cologne Frankfurt Bonn Hamburg and Leipzig. By the end of 2020 the company intends to cover the 20 largest German cities.

And it's Deutsche Telekom's 5G ambitions that are the driving factor behind the landmark 2018 deal to merge its T-Mobile US subsidiary with rival carrier Sprint. The $26 billion deal will bring Deutsche Telekom sufficient muscle to roll out a 5G network which requires the set-up of hundreds of thousands of antennas on even footing with rivals AT&T and Verizon. The tie-up would also provide cost synergies by allowing the combined company to reduce redundant cell sites. It's a trick the company is also repeating in the Netherlands where it bought out a smaller rival to better challenge the current duopoly held by KPN and VodafoneZiggo.

Mergers and Acquisitions

In early 2020 Deutsche Telecom completed the merging of T-Mobile US with US telecom carrier Sprint (the third- and fourth-largest carriers in the US). The combined company would boast around 125 million subscribers closing the gap to rivals AT&T (141 million) and Verizon (150 million). The deal is worth $26 billion.

In a move with similar motives to the Sprint deal Deutsche Telekom's T-Mobile Netherlands subsidiary acquired Tele2 in a cash-plus shares deal in early 2019. The combination will help Deutsche Telekom compete more effectively with leading players KPN and VodafoneZiggo.

EXECUTIVES

CTO, Bruno Jacobfeuerborn
Member Management Board Technology and Innovation, Claudia Nemat, age 52
CEO, Timotheus Hottges, age 59
Member Board of Management; T-Systems, Reinhard Clemens, age 61
Member Board of Management; Managing Director Telekom Deutschland GmbH, Niek Jan Van Damme, age 60
Member Board of Management; CFO, Thomas Dannenfeldt
Member Board of Management; Data Privacy Legal Affairs and Compliance Acting Chief Human Resources Officer, Thomas Kremer, age 63
Auditors: PricewaterhouseCoopers GmbHWirtschaftsprüfungsgesellschaft

LOCATIONS

HQ: Deutsche Telekom AG
Friedrich-Ebert-Allee 140, Bonn D-53113
Phone: (49) 228 181 49494   **Fax:** (49) 228 181 94004
Web: www.telekom.com

2017 Sales

	% of total
US	48
Europe	
Germany	28
Other European countries	15
System Solutions	7
Group Development	2
Total	**100**

PRODUCTS/OPERATIONS

2017 Sales

	% of total
Telecommunications	90
ICT solutions	9
Other	1
Total	**100**

COMPETITORS

AT&T	Tele Columbus
BT	Tele2
COLT Group	Telecom Italia
Cable & Wireless	Telef nica
Freenet	Telef nica O2 Germany
HP Enterprise Services	Telekom Austria
Invitel	Telenor
KPN	TeliaSonera
Orange	United Internet
Proximus	Verizon
QSC	Versatel
Swisscom	Vodafone
TDC	Vodafone GmbH

HISTORICAL FINANCIALS

Company Type: Public

Income Statement				FYE: December 31
	REVENUE ($ mil.)	NET INCOME ($ mil.)	NET PROFIT MARGIN	EMPLOYEES
12/19	90,417	4,341	4.8%	210,533
12/18	86,640	2,480	2.9%	215,675
12/17	89,843	4,148	4.6%	217,349
12/16	77,179	2,824	3.7%	218,341
12/15	75,403	3,544	4.7%	225,243
Annual Growth	4.6%	5.2%	—	(1.7%)

2019 Year-End Financials

Debt ratio: 45.5%
Return on equity: 12.3%
Cash ($ mil.): 6,055
Current ratio: 0.75
Long-term debt ($ mil.): 61,624

No. of shares (mil.): —
Dividends
  Yield: 9.1%
  Payout: 81.8%
Market value ($ mil.): —

	STOCK PRICE ($) FY Close	P/E High/Low		PER SHARE ($) Earnings	Dividends	Book Value
12/19	16.29	22	19	0.92	1.49	7.48
12/18	16.98	39	32	0.53	0.74	7.43
12/17	17.66	29	24	0.89	0.70	7.74
12/16	17.10	30	26	0.61	0.56	6.62
12/15	17.88	27	19	0.77	0.53	6.98
Annual Growth	(2.3%)	—	—	4.5%	29.3%	1.7%

Dexia SA

Auditors: DELOITTE Bedrijfsrevisoren CVBA / Reviseurs d'Entreprises SCRL

LOCATIONS

HQ: Dexia SA
Place du Champ de Mars, 5, Brussels B-1050
Phone: (32) 2 213 50 81
Web: www.dexia.com

HISTORICAL FINANCIALS

Company Type: Public

Income Statement				FYE: December 31
	ASSETS ($ mil.)	NET INCOME ($ mil.)	INCOME AS % OF ASSETS	EMPLOYEES
12/19	135,097	(1,008)	—	606
12/18	181,861	(541)	—	773
12/17	216,900	(553)	—	996
12/16	224,661	372	0.2%	1,148
12/15	250,824	177	0.1%	1,203
Annual Growth	(14.3%)	—	—	(15.8%)

2019 Year-End Financials

Return on assets: (-0.6%)
Return on equity: (-12.1%)
Long-term debt ($ mil.): —
No. of shares (mil.): 420
Sales ($ mil): 7,489

Dividends
  Yield: —
  Payout: —
Market value ($ mil.): —

	STOCK PRICE ($) FY Close	P/E High/Low		PER SHARE ($) Earnings	Dividends	Book Value
12/19	0.00	—	—	(0.00)	0.00	19.51
12/18	1.58	—	—	(1.29)	0.00	20.45
12/17	1.58	—	—	(18.74)	0.00	
	3,070.41					
12/16	1.58	0	0	12.07	0.00	
	2,246.68					
Annual Growth		—	—	—	—	—
(69.5%)						

Diageo Plc

Diageo is the first name on the guest list for many a party. The UK-based company is a global leader in spirits and liqueurs boasting a portfolio of world-renowned brands such as Smirnoff vodka Captain Morgan rum Johnnie Walker whisky Baileys Irish cream and Tanqueray gin. It also makes beer including Guinness and wine. With more than 200 global local and luxury brands it owns some two dozen of the world's top 100 premium spirits labels. Diageo rings up sales in virtually every country in the world and has 150-plus production sites globally. North America is its largest market accounting for more than a third of total sales.

Operations

Diageo groups its products into three main alcohol types: spirits beer and ready-to-drink. Spirits comprise most of the company's revenue generating some 70%. Beer accounts for about 15% of sales and ready-to-drink products (such as premixed gin and tonic) generate about 5%. Other products including wine bring in the remaining sales.

Breaking it down further scotch accounts for about 25% of sales followed by beer (about 15%) and vodka (more than 10%).

Its brands are also split into categories such as Global (brands available in most of the world such as Smirnoff and Johnnie Walker) Local Stars (individual to one market and providing a platform for growth) and Reserve (luxury exclusive brands at the above-premium price point such as Ciroc and Casamigos).

Geographic Reach

Diageo divides its operations along geographic lines to more easily cater to variations in consumer tastes through location-specific brand strategy accounts marketing and corporate functions.

The company generates about 35% of sales in North America with Europe & Turkey and the Asia/Pacific region each adding another 20%-25%. Diageo generates more than 10% of sales in Africa and nearly 10% in Latin America and the Caribbean.

Diageo has offices and production facilities in North America Latin America and Caribbean Europe Africa and the Asia/Pacific region. It sells products in more than 180 markets in these regions. The company's broad geographic footprint protects it from instability in one or multiple of its operating environments.

Financial Performance

Note: Growth rates may differ after conversion to US Dollars.

Over the last five years Diageo's revenue and profits have been on the rise bar a small slump in 2016 fueled by acquisitions and organic growth. Overall revenue is up about 20% since fiscal 2015 (ended June) and net income is up a third.

In fiscal 2019 the company reported revenue of Å 12.9 billion up 6% from the prior year. Growth was almost entirely organic led primarily by increases in North America (volume growth of 2%) and the Asia-Pacific region (volume growth of 5%).

Net income grew 5% to Å 3.2 billion that year driven by revenue growth and finance income among other items.

Cash at the end of fiscal 2018 was Å 721 million an increase of Å 54 million from the prior year. Cash from operations contributed Å 3.2 billion to the coffers while investing activities used Å 270 million mainly for capital expenditures. Financing activities used another Å 2.9 billion for dividends to stockholders and stock repurchase.

Strategy

Like many of its peers in the alcohol industry Diageo is pursuing a policy of premiumization in its mature and emerging markets. In mature markets the company leverages its premium core and reserve brands which position customers to trade up into luxury categories. In emerging markets Diageo's approach is to use accessible price points to introduce customers and potential customers to the world of higher-priced premium spirits. Globally the company is betting on some 750 million new customers being able to afford international premium spirits over the next ten years.

Diageo continues to invest in its giant brands to build them for the future. It has announced Å 150 million in Scotch whisky tourism including a new

Johnnie Walker Experience in Edinburgh and $130 million for expansion of the Bulleit distillery in Kentucky. In addition Diageo increased its stake in Sichuan Shuijingfang Co. its super-premium baijiu business in China to 63%.

From a product standpoint the company is focused on attracting new customers (more than 50% of product innovations in fiscal 2019 were focused on new customers compared to about 30% four years ago). Recent launches that illustrate that point include White Walker by Johnnie Walker a limited-edition whisky introduced in collaboration with HBO's behemoth Game of Thrones and Ketel One Botanical spirit drink infused with real fruit.

Mergers and Acquisitions

Following its premiumization strategy in 2018 Diageo acquired Belsazar a premium German aperitif and Pierde Almas an ultra-premium mezcal.

Company Background

Diageo was created by Guinness and GrandMet's 1997 merger.

Guinness began business in 1759 when Arthur Guinness leased a small brewery in Dublin Ireland. Guinness began specializing in porters in 1799. Managed by the third generation of Guinnesses the company went public as a London-based firm in 1886.

GrandMet was established by Maxwell Joseph. In 1931 he began acquiring properties for resale but WWII slowed his progress. He started buying hotels in 1946 and by 1961 GrandMet had gone public.

EXECUTIVES

President Latin America and Caribbean, Alberto Gavazzi
CEO, Ivan M. Menezes, age 59, $2,360,864 total compensation
President Diageo Greater China and Asia, Sam Fischer
CFO, Kathryn A. Mikells, age 54
President Diageo Africa and Asia/Pacific, Nicholas B. (Nick) Blazquez, age 59
CEO United Spirits Limited, Anand Kripalu, age 61
President Diageo North America, Deirdre A. Mahlan, age 58, $1,096,559 total compensation
President Diageo Europe Russia and Turkey, John Kennedy
President Africa, John O'Keeffe
President Global Supply and Procurement, David Cutter
Chairman, Javier Ferr ̃n, age 64
Auditors: PricewaterhouseCoopers LLP

LOCATIONS

HQ: Diageo Plc
Lakeside Drive, Park Royal, London NW10 7HQ
Phone: (44) 20 8978 6000
Web: www.diageo.com

2019 Sales

	% of total
North America	35
Europe & Turkey	23
Asia-Pacific	21
Africa	12
Latin America & Caribbean	9
Total	**100**

PRODUCTS/OPERATIONS

2019 Sales

	% of total
Spirits	69
Beer	16
Ready-to-drink	6
Other	9
Total	**100**

Selected Brands

Strategic brands
 Baileys Original Irish Cream liqueur
 Buchanan's De Luxe Scotch whiskey
 Captain Morgan rum
 Cîroc vodka
 Crown Royal Canadian whisky
 Don Julio
 Guinness stout
 J&B Scotch whiskey
 Johnnie Walker Scotch whisky
 Ketel One vodka
 Smirnoff vodka
 Tanqueray London Dry and Tanqueray No. TEN gin
 Windsor Premier Scotch whisky

COMPETITORS

Anheuser-Busch InBev	Carlsberg A/S
Asahi Breweries	Constellation Brands
Asia Pacific Breweries	E. & J. Gallo
Bacardi	Heineken
Beam Suntory	Molson Coors
Brown-Forman	Pernod Ricard
Campari	

HISTORICAL FINANCIALS

Company Type: Public

Income Statement   FYE: June 30

	REVENUE ($ mil.)	NET INCOME ($ mil.)	NET PROFIT MARGIN	EMPLOYEES
06/20	23,485	2,815	12.0%	27,775
06/19	25,713	6,314	24.6%	28,420
06/18	24,306	6,039	24.8%	29,917
06/17	24,080	5,319	22.1%	30,433
06/16	20,953	4,484	21.4%	32,078
Annual Growth	2.9%	(11.0%)	—	(3.5%)

2020 Year-End Financials

Debt ratio: 100.7%	No. of shares (mil.): —
Return on equity: 18.5%	Dividends
Cash ($ mil.): 6,640	Yield: 2.5%
Current ratio: 1.77	Payout: 286.6%
Long-term debt ($ mil.): 29,556	Market value ($ mil.): —

	STOCK PRICE ($) FY Close	P/E High/Low	PER SHARE ($) Earnings	Dividends	Book Value
06/20	134.39	293171	1.20	3.43	5.28
06/19	172.32	134101	2.60	3.45	7.05
06/18	144.01	122 97	2.42	3.40	7.38
06/17	119.83	116 94	2.11	3.02	7.48
06/16	112.88	136113	1.78	3.41	6.79
Annual Growth	4.5%	— —	(9.5%)	0.2%	(6.1%)

Dixons Carphone PLC

Auditors: Deloitte LLP

LOCATIONS

HQ: Dixons Carphone PLC
 1 Portal Way, London W3 6RS
Phone: (44) 203 110 3251
Web: www.dixonscarphone.com

HISTORICAL FINANCIALS

Company Type: Public

Income Statement

FYE: May 2

	REVENUE ($ mil.)	NET INCOME ($ mil.)	NET PROFIT MARGIN	EMPLOYEES
05/20*	12,746	(204)	—	42,209
04/19	13,458	(412)	—	42,990
04/18	14,493	228	1.6%	43,760
04/17	13,699	381	2.8%	45,461
04/16	14,231	235	1.7%	41,847
Annual Growth	(2.7%)	—	—	0.2%

*Fiscal year change

2020 Year-End Financials

Debt ratio: 14.0%
Return on equity: (-6.5%)
Cash ($ mil.): 827
Current ratio: 0.82
Long-term debt ($ mil.): 350

No. of shares (mil.): 1,162
Dividends
  Yield: —
  Payout: —
Market value ($ mil.): —

DNB ASA

Financial services 'n real estate are what DnB NOR is for. One of the largest banks in Norway the company serves retail and corporate clients at more than 150 locations in 20 countries operating under the DnB NOR Bank Nordlandsbanken and Postbanken banners. In addition to traditional banking services such as deposits and loans it also provides life and pension insurance (through its Vital subsidiary) credit cards (through Cresco) and mutual funds and institutional asset management in Norway and Sweden (through DnB NOR Asset Management) as well as real estate brokerage and capital markets services. The Norwegian government owns about a third of DnB Nor.

EXECUTIVES

EVP DNB Markets, Ottar Ertzeid, age 55, $295,360 total compensation
EVP Finance, Bj rn Erik N ss, age 66
EVP Wealth Management, Tom Rathke, age 63, $2,604,000 total compensation
EVP IT and Operations, Liv Fiksdahl, age 56, $298,129 total compensation
EVP Products, Kari Olrud Moen, age 52
Group EVP Corporate Communications, Trond Bentestuen, age 51
EVP Large Corporates and International, Harald Serck-Hanssen
EVP Corporate Banking Norway, Kjerstin Braathen, age 51
EVP HR, Solveig Hellebust
EVP Risk Management, Terje Turnes
EVP Corporate Communications, Thomas Midteide
Chairman, Anne Carine Tanum, age 67
Vice Chairman, Tore Olaf Rimmereid, age 61
Auditors: Ernst & Young AS

LOCATIONS

HQ: DNB ASA
  Dronning Eufemias gate 30, Oslo 0191
Phone: (47) 915 03000
Web: www.dnb.no/en

2013 Sales

	% of total
Norway	80
Other international operations	15
Baltics and Poland	5
Total	**100**

PRODUCTS/OPERATIONS

2013 Sales

	% of total
Large corporate and international customers	36
Personal customers	37
Small and medium-sized enterprises	16
Trading	6
Traditional pension products	5
Total	**100**

COMPETITORS

ABN AMRO Group	HSBC
BNP Paribas	Nordea Bank
Credit Suisse	SEB AB
Danske Bank	Svenska Handelsbanken
Deutsche Bank	UBS
Grupo Santander	

HISTORICAL FINANCIALS

Company Type: Public

Income Statement

FYE: December 31

	ASSETS ($ mil.)	NET INCOME ($ mil.)	INCOME AS % OF ASSETS	EMPLOYEES
12/19	317,848	2,799	0.9%	9,336
12/18	303,559	2,686	0.9%	9,638
12/17	329,086	2,544	0.8%	9,561
12/16	308,372	2,168	0.7%	11,459
12/15	294,845	2,767	0.9%	11,840
Annual Growth	1.9%	0.3%	—	(5.8%)

2019 Year-End Financials

Return on assets: 0.9%
Return on equity: 10.5%
Long-term debt ($ mil.): —
No. of shares (mil.): 1,580
Sales ($ mil): 9,786

Dividends
  Yield: 5.0%
  Payout: 52.7%
Market value ($ mil.): 29,450

	STOCK PRICE ($) FY Close	P/E High/Low		PER SHARE ($) Earnings	Dividends	Book Value
12/19	18.64	1	1	1.77	0.94	17.44
12/18	15.99	1	1	1.68	0.88	16.08
12/17	18.57	14	1	1.57	0.69	16.24
12/16	148.80	14	9	1.33	0.53	14.73
12/15	123.63	11	8	1.70	0.51	13.24
Annual Growth	(37.7%)	—	—	1.0%	16.8%	7.1%

Doosan Heavy Industries & Construction Co Ltd

Doosan Heavy Industries & Construction quenches the world's thirst for power and water. The engineering procurement and construction contractor provides the equipment for nuclear coal-fired and combined-cycle power plant projects worldwide. Doosan Heavy also provides water treatment facility technology for power plants and wastewater plants. Through various other divisions it also supplies casting and forging products and materials handling equipment. Founded in 1962 Doosan Heavy is partially owned by the Doosan Corporation and is headquartered in Changwon South Korea.

Operations

Doosan Heavy manufactures an expansive selection of heavy industrial products. It builds a range of thermal and nuclear power generation equipment including boilers turbines and generators. The company manufactures earthmoving equipment such as bulldozers and bobcats constructs high-speed rail lines creates crankshafts for large ships and builds wind turbine generators. It also engages in engineering procurement and construction of thermal power plants including nuclear coal-fired and combined-cycle project. Doosan Heavy also provides water treatment facility technology for power plants seawater desalination facilities urban drinking water and wastewater plants.

Its business segments include Power Generation Water Industrial Plants Castings & Forgings and Construction among others. It is part owner of other affiliated Doosan Corporation subsidiaries the most notable being Doosan Infracore. The Power Generation segment and Doosan Infracore together account for roughly 80% of Doosan Heavy's revenue.

Geographic Reach

Changwon South Korea-headquartered Doosan Heavy is a global conglomerate with operations in every major region in the world. Its primary location in South Korea is along the country's southeastern coast where sea transport for incoming and outgoing shipments is facilitated.

It operates six European subsidiaries: Doosan Power Systems Doosan Babcock Doosan Skoda Power Doosan Lentjes Doosan Enpure and Doosan IMGB.

The company has five subsidiaries in Asia and the Middle East: Doosan Power Systems India Doosan Vina DCS Vina Doosan Heavy Industries Japan and Doosan Power Systems Arabia.

In the Americas Doosan Heavy operates subsidiaries Doosan Hydro Technology Doosan HF Controls Doosan Heavy Industries America Doosan GridTech and Doosan Power Services America.

Financial Performance

Note: Financial results are denominated in the company's home currency the Korean Won (?).

In 2016 Doosan Heavy generated ?13.9 trillion (roughly US$ 13 billion) 4% less than the previous year mostly due to a decrease in sales in its affiliated Doosan Infracore business segment.

It had a ?215 billion loss compared to a ?1.7 trillion loss in 2015. Despite lower revenue in 2016 the company reduced its cost of sales (as a percentage of revenue) and drastically lowered selling and administrative expenses allowing more of its top-line sales to flow down to the earnings bottom line.

Strategy

Doosan Heavy anticipates continued growth in the build out of power plants with specific emphasis on coal power in emerging markets. It expects mature energy markets to look for ways to get more efficiency out of existing plants and as a result the company launched its Service Business Group to address this growing need. The market for its water treatment products & services continues its slow upward trend with an expected increase of over 7% between 2017 and 2021.

Its affiliated Doosan Infracore business which saw a downturn in sales in 2016 sees brighter times ahead as it completed the restructuring of its business and addressed malaise in its Bobcat division. Additionally Infracore shed assets in recent years so it could repurpose the obtained funds to pay down debt which in turn reduced its recurring debt interest payment burden.

EXECUTIVES

Chairman and CEO, Park Gee-won, age 55
CEO Doosan Power Systems, Ryu Myong-Dong
CEO Doosan Babcock, Andy Hunt
CEO Doosan Skoda Power, Jiri Smondrk
CEO Doosan Lentjes GmbH, Thomas Wehrheim
President and CEO Doosan IMGB, Daerak Son
General Director Doosan Vina, Ryu Hang Ha
CEO Doosan Hydro Technology, Kim Jinwan
Auditors: KPMG Samjong Accounting Corp.

LOCATIONS

HQ: Doosan Heavy Industries & Construction Co Ltd
22, Doosanvolvo-ro Seongsan-gu, Changwon-si,
Gyeongsangnam-do 51711
Phone: (82) 55 278 6114   **Fax:** (82) 55 264 5551
Web: www.doosanheavy.com

PRODUCTS/OPERATIONS

2016 Sales by Segment (incl. Intersegment)

	% of total
Power generation	79
Water	6
Industrial Plants	1
Castings & Forgings	7
Construction	7
Wholesale & Retail	-
Total	**100**

Selected Subsidiaries

America
  Doosan GridTech
  Doosan Heavy Industries America
  Doosan HF Controls
  Doosan Hydro Technology
  Doosan Power Services Americas
Asia
  Doosan Power Systems India
  Doosan Heavy Industries Japan
  Doosan Power Systems Arabia
  Doosan VINA
  Doosan DCS VINA
Europe
  Doosan Babcock
  Doosan Enpure
  Doosan Lentjes
  Doosan IMGB
  Doosan Power Systems
  Doosan Skoda Power

COMPETITORS

Bechtel
Bouygues
Caterpillar
Hyflux
Hyundai Heavy
  Industries
Kawasaki Heavy
  Industries
MCFA
Mitsubishi Heavy
  Industries

Samsung Heavy
  Industries
Sany Heavy Industry
Skanska
Sumitomo Heavy
  Industries
Volvo Construction
  Equipment

HISTORICAL FINANCIALS

Company Type: Public

Income Statement

FYE: December 31

	REVENUE ($ mil.)	NET INCOME ($ mil.)	NET PROFIT MARGIN	EMPLOYEES
12/19	13,562	(342)	—	0
12/18	13,239	(469)	—	7,294
12/17	13,622	(273)	—	7,609
12/16	11,564	(142)	—	7,728
12/15	13,772	(882)	—	7,771
Annual Growth	(0.4%)	—	—	—

DSV Panalpina AS

EXECUTIVES

Acting Managing Director, Jens Bj .rn Andersen
Auditors: PricewaterhouseCoopers Statsautoriseret
Revisionsaktieselskab

LOCATIONS

HQ: DSV Panalpina AS
  Hovedgaden 630, Hedehusene 2640
Phone: (45) 43 20 30 40
Web: www.dsv.com

HISTORICAL FINANCIALS

Company Type: Public

Income Statement

FYE: December 31

	REVENUE ($ mil.)	NET INCOME ($ mil.)	NET PROFIT MARGIN	EMPLOYEES
12/19	14,231	556	3.9%	61,216
12/18	12,123	613	5.1%	47,394
12/17	12,060	479	4.0%	45,636
12/16	9,622	236	2.5%	44,779
12/15	7,424	300	4.0%	22,783
Annual Growth	17.7%	16.7%	—	28.0%

2019 Year-End Financials

Debt ratio: 1.4%
Return on equity: 11.5%
Cash ($ mil.): 307
Current ratio: 0.96
Long-term debt ($ mil.): 1,189

No. of shares (mil.): 228
Dividends
  Yield: 0.1%
  Payout: 40.6%
Market value ($ mil.): 13,235

	STOCK PRICE ($) FY Close	P/E High/Low		PER SHARE ($)		
				Earnings	Dividends	Book Value
12/19	57.83	3	2	2.77	0.11	32.46
12/18	32.95	2	1	3.31	0.11	12.54
12/17	39.47	3	2	2.54	0.96	12.98
12/16	22.13	3	2	1.27	0.80	10.27
12/15	20.30	2	1	1.74	0.78	9.37
Annual Growth	29.9%	—	—	12.2%	(38.6%)	36.4%

Dubai Islamic Bank Ltd

EXECUTIVES

Chief Executive Officer Group, Adnan
  Abdusshakoor Chilwan
Chief Executive Officer, Mohamed Abdulla Al Nahdi
Chairman, H E Mohammad Ibrahim Abdulrahm Al
  Shaibani
Auditors: KPMG Lower Gulf Limited

LOCATIONS

HQ: Dubai Islamic Bank Ltd
  P.O. Box 1080, Dubai
Phone: (971) 4 295 3000   **Fax:** (971) 4 295 4111
Web: www.alislami.ae

HISTORICAL FINANCIALS

Company Type: Public

Income Statement

FYE: December 31

	ASSETS ($ mil.)	NET INCOME ($ mil.)	INCOME AS % OF ASSETS	EMPLOYEES
12/19	63,116	1,365	2.2%	0
12/18	60,907	1,338	2.2%	0
12/17	56,456	1,176	2.1%	0
12/16	47,635	979	2.1%	0
12/15	40,811	968	2.4%	0
Annual Growth	11.5%	9.0%	—	—

2019 Year-End Financials

Return on assets: 2.2%
Return on equity: 15.8%
Long-term debt ($ mil.): —
No. of shares (mil.): —
Sales ($ mil): 3,726

Dividends
  Yield: —
  Payout: —
Market value ($ mil.): —

E.ON SE

E.ON is a German-based international privately-owned clean energy company focuses on building cutting-edge distributed energy systems across Europe. The company's operations are energy networks customer solutions innogy and renewables. Its non-strategic operations are reported under non-core Business. These include power and gas distribution customer service sales and farms. With customers in Germany Denmark Sweden Italy the UK Czech Republic Hungary Romania Slovakia and Turkey E.ON boasts not more than 4100 GWh per commodity 351000 kilometers of energy networks in Germany and about 6 million connection points for power.

Operations

E.ON has four core businesses - Customer Solutions innogy Energy Networks and Renewables.

Customer solutions brings in almost half of the annual net sales. It serves municipal public industrial commercial and residential customers through a portfolio of products and services that focus on distributed generation and storage and sustainable mobility solutions. Its turn-key distributed-energy solutions is also part of this segment.

innogy (nearly 25% of sales) segment consists particularly of the network and sales businesses as well as the corporate functions and internal services of the innogy Group. innogy operates its network business primarily in Germany Poland Hungary and Croatia.

Energy Networks (about 20% of annual sales) consist of the company's distribution grids that supply renewable energy to its European customers. Its power and gas networks safely and reliably carrying out any necessary maintenance and repairs and expanding its power and gas networks which frequently involves adding customer connections. It is subdivided into three regional markets: Germany Sweden and East-Central Europe including Turkey Czech Republic Hungary Romania and Slovakia.

E.ON's Renewables business (accounts for about 5% of sales) builds operates and manages onshore and offshore wind solar and other carbon-neutral technologies.

The company's nuclear power business in Germany managed by PreussenElektra of Hanover will be phased out and dismantled as per German laws.

Geographic Reach
E. ON's Corporate Headquarters is in Essen Germany. E.ON's main presence is in Germany the United Kingdom Sweden Italy the Czech Republic Hungary and Romania. It has employees in Netherlands and Poland as well.

Sales and Marketing
E.ON has major customers in Germany Sweden Italy the UK Czech Republic Hungary Romania Slovakia and Turkey.

The company's customers are across all categories: residential small and medium-sized enterprises large commercial and industrial and public entities. E.ON's Renewables products are marketed into renewable incentive programs wholesale markets and long-term contracts.

The integration of innogy will give the new E.ON a customer base of 40 million (including 19 million innogy customers) making it one of Europe's biggest end-customer suppliers.

Advertising and marketing expenses in the amount of ?131 million in 2019 and ?176 million in 2018.

Financial Performance
Note: Growth rates may differ after conversion to US Dollars.

E.ON's revenue and net income has shifted in the past five years. Revenue declined by 4% between 2015 and 2019 while net income declined by 122% over the same period.

E.ON sales grew 38% to ?41.5 billion in 2019 from ?30.1 billion in 2019. The increase is primarily attributed to the acquisition of the innogy Group in September 2019. In addition the IFRS Interpretations Committee clarified the accounting treatment of commodity futures transactions that are settled with physical delivery that cannot be classified as own-use contracts pursuant to IFRS 9 and that are accounted for as derivatives which E.ON has applied from the start of the 2019 financial year.

In 2019 net income fell by over 50% to ?1.6 billion compared to ?3.2 billion the prior year. E.ON's discontinued operations as well as higher restructuring expenses for expenditures in the acquisition of innogy for the restructuring measures in Germany and at npower innogy's U.K. sales business contributed to the loss.

Cash at the end of 2019 was ?1.9 billion a decrease of ?2.1 billion from the prior year. Cash from operations contributed ?2.9 billion to the coffers while investing activities used ?5.8 billion mainly in purchases of investments in property plant and equipment as well as equity investments. Financing activities contributed ?792 million from proceeds of financial liabilities.

Strategy
E.ON's objective is to systematically focus the company on the new energy world of increasingly empowered and proactive customers. It will create new markets for its customers by providing them with new products services and technologies. The company's efforts will be guided by its principles of integration focus efficiency and growth.

The company began integrating its innogy SE last year and after the squeeze-out and acquisition of its remaining stock will accelerate this process in the current year. Its focus is on combining the respective organizational entities in line with its Target Operating Model. After the transaction is completed the new E.ON will be the first European player to focus exclusively on municipal commercial and residential customers and will generate a large part of its EBIT with regulated business.

In addition to strengthening its core businesses the innogy takeover will enable it to leverage sub-

stantial synergies of about ?740 million by 2022 thereby making important progress toward its efficiency targets. It expects the systematic optimization and digitization of its business processes to deliver additional efficiency gains.

As its growth strategy calls for extensive investments in both business segments the main focus will be on Energy Networks in which it will invest about ?3.2 billion in 2020. It also plans to invest about ?0.9 billion in Customer Solutions.

Mergers and Acquisitions
In late 2019 E.ON closes the purchase of innogy shares from RWE. E.ON now owns a majority stake in innogy shortly after the EU Commission cleared the transaction.

In mid-2019 E.ON concluded the 100% acquisition of Coromatic a leading Sweden-based provider of facility-critical services. Headquartered in Stockholm the company has more than 5000 customers in Scandinavia in a wide variety of sectors such as data centers healthcare the public sector transportation manufacturing telecommunications finance and retail. The parties agreed not to disclose the purchase price.

EXECUTIVES

CEO Customer Solutions and Country Chairman E.ON Sweden, Marc Hoffmann
Chairman Board of Management and CEO, Johannes Teyssen
Member Management Board and COO Networks and Renewables, Ing. Leonhard Birnbaum, age 53
CEO E.ON UK, Michael Lewis
CEO E.ON Climate and Renewables, Anja Dotzenrath
Member Board of Management and CFO, Marc Spieker, age 45
Member Board of Management and COO Commercial, Karsten Wildberger, age 51
Deputy Chairman Supervisory Board, Ulrich Lehner, age 74
Chairman Supervisory Board, Karl-Ludwig Kley
Auditors: PricewaterhouseCoopers GmbH Wirtschaftpruefungsgesellschaft

LOCATIONS

HQ: E.ON SE
Bruesseler Platz 1, Essen D-45131
Phone: (49) 211 184 00   **Fax:** (49) 211 45 79 5 01
Web: www.eon.com

2016 Sales

	% of total
Germany	57
United Kingdom	20
Europe (other)	16
Sweden	6
Other	1
Total	**100**

PRODUCTS/OPERATIONS

2016 Sales

	% of total
Customer Solutions	53
Energy Networks	38
Renewables	3
Non-Core Business	3
Corporate Functions/Other	3
Total	**100**

2016 Sales

	% of total
Electricity	78
Gas	17
Other	5
Total	**100**

COMPETITORS

BASF SE	Endesa S.A.
Bayer AG	Enel
Business Group Benelux	Engie
Deutsche Telekom	Eni
Dow Chemical	Orange
EVN	RWE
Electricité de France	Vattenfall
EnBW	

HISTORICAL FINANCIALS
Company Type: Public

Income Statement   FYE: December 31

	REVENUE ($ mil.)	NET INCOME ($ mil.)	NET PROFIT MARGIN	EMPLOYEES
12/19	46,443	1,758	3.8%	78,948
12/18	34,327	3,690	10.8%	43,302
12/17	46,143	4,705	10.2%	42,699
12/16	40,873	(8,922)	—	43,138
12/15	127,118	(7,623)	—	56,490
Annual Growth	**(22.3%)**	—	—	**8.7%**

2019 Year-End Financials

Debt ratio: 36.3%	No. of shares (mil.): —
Return on equity: —	Dividends
Cash ($ mil.): 4,044	Yield: 3.3%
Current ratio: 0.85	Payout: 46.4%
Long-term debt ($ mil.): 31,465	Market value ($ mil.): —

	STOCK PRICE ($) FY Close	P/E High/Low		PER SHARE ($) Earnings	Dividends	Book Value
12/19	10.67	17	13	0.76	0.35	3.91
12/18	9.87	8	6	1.71	0.26	3.04
12/17	10.88	7	4	2.21	0.19	2.22
12/16	7.05	—	—	(4.57)	1.43	(0.57)
12/15	9.52	—	—	(3.92)	0.41	9.17
Annual Growth (19.2%)	**2.9%**	—	—	—	**(3.5%)**	

East Japan Railway Co.

If you want to ride the rails into Tokyo you could find yourself cruising at 168 mph aboard a bullet train operated by East Japan Railway better known as JR East. The company serves more than 15 million people daily and carries passengers on more than 7400 km of track in the eastern half of the Japanese mainland including the Tokyo area. JR East's Shinkansen (bullet-train) lines connect metropolitan Tokyo with other major cities. Besides its transportation-related operations JR East generates revenue from leasing restaurant and retail space in its stations and from managing shopping centers and office buildings on property that has been developed near its stations.

Operations
East Japan Railway has four operating segments: Transportation Retail & Services Real Estate & Hotels and Other.

The Transportation segment includes passenger transportation operations which are centered on railway operations as well as travel agency services cleaning services station operations facilities maintenance operations and railcar manufacturing and maintenance. The segment accounts for almost 70% of the company's total revenue.

The Retail & Services segment consists of JR East's life-style service business that includes retail sales and restaurant operations wholesale businesses a truck transportation business and advertising and publicity. The segment accounts for more than 15% of revenue.

The Real Estate & Hotels segment encompasses JR East's life-style service business that includes shopping center operations leasing of office buildings and other properties and hotel operations. This segment accounts for more than 10% of total revenue.

JR East's Other segment consists of IT & Suica which includes credit cards and information processing among other businesses. The segment accounts for nearly 5% of total revenue.

Geographic Reach

The railway business of JR East spans the eastern half of the Hons Shinkansen network which connects Tokyo with regional cities in five directions.

The company is headquartered in Tokyo Japan. It also has offices internationally located in New York Paris London and Singapore.

Sales and Marketing

JR East major customers was omitted as no single outside customer contributes about 10% or more to company's total sales.

The average number of passengers per day is about 17 million.

Financial Performance

Note: Growth rates may differ after conversion to US Dollars.

As a result of the company's initiatives during the fiscal year under review operating revenues increased 2% year on year to Â 3.0 trillion ($27.0 billion).

JR East profit attributable to owners of parent increased 2% to Â 295.2 billion ($2660 million) mainly due to higher income before income taxes.

In fiscal 2019 net cash provided by operating activities totaled Â 663.8 billion ($6.0 billion) Â 40.4 billion less than in the previous fiscal year. This result was mainly due to an increase in major receivables. Net cash used in investing activities amounted to Â 594.4 billion ($5.3 billion) Â 52.6 billion more than in the previous fiscal year. This result was mainly due to an increase in payments for purchases of fixed assets. Net cash used in financing activities came to Â 120.7 billion ($1.1 billion) Â 14.4 billion less than in the previous fiscal year. This result was mainly due to an increase in proceeds from procurement of interest-bearing debt.

Strategy

In July 2018 the company announced the Group Management Vision "Move Up 2027" and entered the second year.

The goal of "Move Up 2027" is to create a service that integrates transportation services lifestyle services and IT/Suica starting from "people". This is a service that only JR East has because it has a multi-layered "real" network that supports the living infrastructure. The group will build an ecosystem centered on "people" who continue to create new value by fusing technological innovation and big data.

"Move Up2027" will finally enter the full-scale execution phase. Following the lifestyle service business growth vision "NEXT10" formulated in 2017 in 2018 the company started "Medium-term Vision for Service Quality Reforms 2020" and "Group Safety Plan 2023" and newly established "Technology Innovation Promotion Division". JR East have steadily laid the foundation for the strong promotion of "Reform 2027". In the future based on these JR East will put the transition from the "railway infrastructure starting point" to the "human starting point" on track. To realize the future depicted in "Move Up 2027" it will concretely accelerate measures in line with the three focus points of "safety" "life" and "happiness of employees and their families."

EXECUTIVES

President and CEO, Tetsuro Tomita
Vice Chairman Technology and Overseas Related Affairs, Masaki Ogata
EVP, Yuji Fukasawa
EVP, Naomichi Yagishita
Executive Director Public Relations Finance and Administration and CFO, Satoshi Seino
Auditors: KPMG AZSA LLC

LOCATIONS

HQ: East Japan Railway Co.
2-2-2 Yoyogi, Shibuya-ku, Tokyo 151-8578
Phone: (81) 3 5334 1111   **Fax:** (81) 3 5334 1320
Web: www.jreast.co.jp

PRODUCTS/OPERATIONS

2017 Sales

	% of total
Transportation	64
Retail & Services	18
Real Estate & Hotels	11
Other	7
Total	**100**

COMPETITORS

FedEx	Kintetsu
Keihin Electric	Odakyu Electric
Express Railway	Railway
Keio Corporation	UPS
Keisei Electric	
Railway	

HISTORICAL FINANCIALS

Company Type: Public

Income Statement				FYE: March 31
	REVENUE ($ mil.)	NET INCOME ($ mil.)	NET PROFIT MARGIN	EMPLOYEES
03/20	29,710	2,000	6.7%	98,415
03/19	30,268	2,976	9.8%	99,034
03/18	29,745	2,913	9.8%	99,584
03/17	29,046	2,802	9.6%	98,544
03/16	28,909	2,473	8.6%	99,200
Annual Growth	0.7%	(5.2%)	—	(0.2%)

2020 Year-End Financials

Debt ratio: 0.3%
Return on equity: 6.3%
Cash ($ mil.): 1,552
Current ratio: 0.55
Long-term debt ($ mil.): 26,222

No. of shares (mil.): 377
Dividends
Yield: 1.9%
Payout: —
Market value ($ mil.): 4,762

	STOCK PRICE ($) FY Close	P/E High/Low		PER SHARE ($) Earnings	Dividends	Book Value
03/20	12.61	0	0	5.29	0.24	84.01
03/19	16.05	0	0	7.80	0.22	81.06
03/18	15.64	0	0	7.55	0.20	74.82
03/17	14.52	0	0	7.20	0.20	68.76
03/16	14.31	0	0	6.31	0.17	62.79
Annual Growth	(3.1%)	—	—	(4.3%)	9.5%	7.6%

Eaton Corp plc

Auditors: Ernst & Young LLP

LOCATIONS

HQ: Eaton Corp plc
Eaton House, 30 Pembroke Road, Dublin 4 44114-2584
Phone: (353) 1 637 2900
Web: www.eaton.com

HISTORICAL FINANCIALS

Company Type: Public

Income Statement				FYE: December 31
	REVENUE ($ mil.)	NET INCOME ($ mil.)	NET PROFIT MARGIN	EMPLOYEES
12/19	21,390	2,211	10.3%	101,000
12/18	21,609	2,145	9.9%	99,000
12/17	20,404	2,985	14.6%	96,000
12/16	19,747	1,922	9.7%	95,000
12/15	20,855	1,979	9.5%	97,000
Annual Growth	0.6%	2.8%	—	1.0%

2019 Year-End Financials

Debt ratio: 25.3%
Return on equity: 13.7%
Cash ($ mil.): 370
Current ratio: 1.70
Long-term debt ($ mil.): 7,819

No. of shares (mil.): 413
Dividends
Yield: 3.0%
Payout: 50.4%
Market value ($ mil.): —

Ecopetrol SA

Ecopetrol performs crude oil and natural gas exploration production refining and transportation. The largest company in Colombia (where it accounts for 60% of national production and is one of the world's 40 largest oil companies) Ecopetrol has two large refineries (Barrancabermeja and Cartagena) strategically located to supply the domestic market and to export oil and oil products to the southern US. Ecopetrol explores for oil and gas across Colombia and is expanding internationally through exploration partnerships in Brazil Peru and the US Gulf of Mexico. In 2013 the company reported proved reserves of more than 1.4 billion barrels of oil equivalent.

Geographic Reach

Headquartered in Bogota Colombia the company has exploration and production activities in Brazil Peru and the US (Gulf of Mexico). In 2013 it derived almost 40% of its revenues from Colombia and nearly 30% from the US.

Sales and Marketing

The company's crude oil export sales are made both in the spot market and through long-term contracts primarily to refiners in the US Gulf Coast Far East Europe and the U. West Coast. It sell natural gas to distribution companies through take-or-pay or swing contracts.

Strategy

The company has ambitious expansion plans including the doubling of refining capacity and the emergence of Ecopetrol as a leader in biofuels production. The company's goal is to produce 1 million barrels of oil equivalent per day by 2015 and 1.3 million of oil equivalent per day in 2020.

Ecopetrol's strategy is focused on supplying the local market and exporting crude oil refined products petrochemical products and natural gas to end-users including refineries and wholesalers in order to improve its margins. It also intends to increase its market participation in crude oil and refined products in Asia and Europe.

In an effort to enhance the strategic and logistical framework of Colombia's oil industry in response to the increase in hydrocarbon production and higher sales of crudes and refined products both within Colombia and on the international markets in 2012 the company established Cenit as a wholly-owned subsidiary specializing in logistics and transportation of hydrocarbons within Colombia.

During 2012 the company acquired 23908 kilometers of additional seismic equivalent which includes 13908 kilometers in the US Gulf Coast and 10000 kilometers in Brazil. During the first quarter of 2013 it drilled five stratigraphic wells out of which two exhibited evidence of hydrocarbons (Segua 1 and Circe 1).

EXECUTIVES

VP Development and Production, Héctor Manosalva Rojas
President, Felipe Bay n Pardo
VP Engineering and Projects, Jurguen Loeber
VP Exploration, Max Torres
VP Technic, Rafael Guzman
VP Refining and Industrial Processes, Tom s Hernandez
VP Transportation and Logistics, Rafael Espinosa
President Cenit Transporte y Log stica de Hidrocarburos SAS, Luisa Fernanda Lafaurie Rivera
VP Commercial and Marketing, Patricia Zuluaga
CFO, Mar a Fernanda Suarez
President Board of Directors, Carlos Cure
Auditors: Ernst & Young Audit S.A.S.

LOCATIONS

HQ: Ecopetrol SA
Carrera 13 No. 36-24, Bogota
Phone: (57) 1 234 4000   **Fax:** (57) 1 234 5628
Web: www.ecopetrol.com.co

2013 Sales

	% of total
Colombia	38
US	29
Asia	16
Europe	7
Central America and Caribbean	5
South America	3
Others	2
Total	**100**

PRODUCTS/OPERATIONS

2013 Sales

	% of total
Exploration & production	59
Refining activities	34
Transportation & logistics	7
Total	**100**

COMPETITORS

BP	Hunt Oil
Exxon Mobil	Nexen
Gran Tierra Energy	Pacific Exploration
HKN	Repsol Oil & Gas
Houston American Energy	Royal Dutch Shell

HISTORICAL FINANCIALS
Company Type: Public

Income Statement

	REVENUE ($ mil.)	NET INCOME ($ mil.)	NET PROFIT MARGIN	EMPLOYEES
12/19	21,765	4,184	19.2%	15,157
12/18	21,131	3,505	16.6%	12,228
12/17	18,749	2,405	12.8%	11,682
12/16	16,151	815	5.0%	10,920
12/15	16,518	(2,270)	—	10,765
Annual Growth	**7.1%**	**—**	**—**	**8.9%**

FYE: December 31

2019 Year-End Financials

Debt ratio: 0.0%	No. of shares (mil.): —
Return on equity: 25.0%	Dividends
Cash ($ mil.): 2,154	Yield: 8.9%
Current ratio: 1.07	Payout: 1,703.3%
Long-term debt ($ mil.): 10,116	Market value ($ mil.): —

	STOCK PRICE ($) FY Close	P/E High/Low		Earnings	PER SHARE ($) Dividends	Book Value
12/19	19.96	0	0	0.10	1.78	0.40
12/18	15.88	0	0	0.09	0.61	0.41
12/17	14.63	0	0	0.06	0.15	0.38
12/16	9.05	0	0	0.02	0.01	0.34
12/15	7.01	—	—	(0.06)	1.04	0.32
Annual Growth	**29.9%**	**—**	**—**	**—**	**14.4%**	**6.2%**

EDP Energias de Portugal S.A.

If you live in Portugal or Brazil you can plug into EDP - Energias de Portugal a state-controlled holding company for utilities that generate transmit distribute and supply electricity. EDP serves about 10 million electric customers. Other operations include a majority stake in Spanish utility HC Energ a. EDP (a major wind energy player) has a combined generating capacity of more than 25 GW (around 26680 MW) from its domestic hydroelectric coal and wind-powered plants. Majority of its sales were generated in Portugal.

Operations
EDP is a multinational vertically integrated company which is present throughout the electricity value chain and in the gas commercialization activity. The company operates through three segments: Client Solutions & Energy Management (about 60% of sales) Networks (around 30%) and Renewables (some 10%).

The Client Solutions & Energy Management segment includes activities such as generation of electricity from non-renewable sources mainly coal and gas; electricity and gas supply and related energy solutions services to clients; and energy management businesses responsible for management of purchases and sales of energy in iberian and brazilian markets and also for the related hedging transactions. This operates under subsidiaries such as EDP - Comercializa § o e Servi §os de Energia Ltda. and EDP - Gest o da Produ § o de Energia S.A. among others.

The Networks segment corresponds to the activities of electricity distribution and transmission including last resort suppliers. This segment includes but not limited to EDP G s Servi §o Uni-

versal S.A. and EDP S o Paulo Distribui § o de Energia S.A.

The Renewables segment corresponds to the activity of generation of electricity from renewable sources mainly hydro wind and solar which operates under EDP - Gest o da Produ § o de Energia S.A. among others.

Overall about 85% of the company's sales were generated by its electricity and network access.

Geographic Reach
Headquartered in Lisbon the company has facilities in about 20 countries in four continents including Portugal Spain France Belgium Italy Brazil Poland Mexico the US Canada the UK China and Nigeria among others. Portugal accounts for around 45% of EDP's sales while Spain Brazil US and other countries account for the rest.

Sales and Marketing
The company distributes some 80 TWh of electricity through overhead and underground lines to nearly 10 million electricity customers of which more than 5 million customers are in liberalized market and about 5 million customers are in last resort. It also serves nearly 1.5 million gas customers.

Financial Performance
Note: Growth rates may differ after conversion to US Dollars.

EDP's revenue fell 6% to ?14.3 billion in 2019 from ?15.3 billion the year prior. Sales from electricity and network access and other declined in 2019 partly offset by the increase in gas and network access and revenue from assets assigned to concessions.

Net income also fell 1% to ?511.8 million in 2019 from ?519.2 million in 2018 mainly due to the decline in revenue and an increased amortization and impairment that year.

Cash and cash equivalents at the end of the year were ?1.5 billion a ?258.5 million decrease from the year prior. Operating activities generated ?2.2 billion in 2019 while investing activities used ?1.6 billion mainly for property plant and equipment and intangible assets. Financing activities used another $834.4 million mostly for payments to financial debt dividends paid and interest and similar costs of financial debt.

Strategy
At the beginning of 2019 EDP presented an update of its strategic plan up to 2022. In it EDP conveyed its vision the strategic pillars as well as the repositioning of its business segments. It has also presented its key strategic initiatives and the goals for the 2019-22 period.

EDP's vision is to assume the leadership of the energetic transition ensuring the creating of superior value. With the strategic architecture that has been followed it is already well positioned to lead the energy transition: it counts with 2.5 times more renewable installed capacity than the average of the other integrated players; its asset base is 'young' having an average residual life of 25 years which allows it to have visibility over the coming years. The vision shapes the company up to 2030 and will guide the company through: decarbonization digitalization and decentralization.

To achieve this ambitious vision EDP defined five strategic pillars: accelerated and focused growth; continuous portfolio optimization; solid balance and low risk profile; efficient and digitally enabled; and attractive shareholder remuneration.

This ambitious strategic plan also involves a transformation in the way it looks and organizes the company. A simpler and more focused structure allows the sharing of best practices and enhances efficiency throughout the organization. Thus in order to enable the organization to deliver on the commitments made in the strategic plan and respond more effectively to the energy transition EDP presented its three operating platforms:

Renewables; Networks; and Client Solutions and Energy Management.

HISTORY

EDP - Energias de Portugal has its roots in the several power enterprises that sprouted throughout the country during the infancy of electricity. The first recorded event in Portugal's electrification was the import of six voltaic arc lamps in 1878. The nation's first large-scale project saw the light in 1893 when the city of Braga was illuminated by the Sociedade de Electricidade do Norte de Portugal.

Electricity grew throughout the 1900s in the form of municipal concession contracts for distribution and government-licensed power plants. Large-scale power stations were not in effect in Portugal until after 1947 when Companhia Nacional de Electricidade was formed to interconnect the small generating systems dotting the nation. From the 1950s to mid-1970s new companies were formed to bring electricity to various parts of Portugal.

The original Electricidade de Portugal was founded in the wake of a leftist revolution during the 1970s in Portugal. In what became known as the Captain's Revolution military officers overthrew the Portuguese government which had been a dictatorship since 1933. The new government dominated by Marxists nationalized Portugal's industries including its generation transmission and distribution companies in 1975. The next year the Portuguese government created Electricidade de Portugal to unify the recently nationalized companies.

A new Social Democrat government came to power in 1987 and decided to denationalize Portuguese industry including EDP. The company reorganized into four major sectors in 1994: production (headed by its CPPE subsidiary) transmission distribution and services (led by its REN subsidiary which operated the national grid four regional utilities and 10 services units). EDP was the holding company.

Seeking opportunities opened up by the privatization of Brazil's state-owned electricity distributor EDP joined a consortium with Spain's Endesa and Chile's Chilectra to buy 70% of Rio de Janeiro distributor CERJ in 1996. The next year EDP gained a license to help build a hydro plant in Brazil. By 1998 the Endesa-led consortium had gained control of another Brazilian distributor Coelce.

The Portuguese government floated 30% of EDP in 1997 raising $1.76 billion. In a joint venture with the UK's PowerGen and Germany's Siemens EDP formed Turbog´s to operate a power plant that would produce 20% of Portugal's electricity.

In 1998 EDP forged an alliance with Spain's Iberdrola and bought 80% of Guatemalan utility EEGSA. That year EDP and S o Paulo utility CPFL gained control of S o Paulo distributor Bandeirante. In 1999 EDP acquired stakes in two other Brazilian distributors. It also joined the UK's Thames Water to develop projects in Portugal Chile and Brazil and bought 45% of Chilean water and sewage company Essel. (EDP exchanged its stake in Essel for Thames Water's interest in the Portuguese joint venture in 2002.) The Portuguese state reduced its stake in EDP to about 50% in 1999.

Stepping up its telecommunications activities in 2000 EDP made its telecom unit Onitelecom (ONI) fully operational and agreed to share a fiber-optic network on the Iberian Peninsula with Spain's Iberdrola. (In 2006 however the company sold its stake in ONI.) Also in 2000 the Portuguese government acquired a majority stake in EDP's REN unit and

EDP combined its four power distribution utilities into one unit (EDP Distribui § o).

In 2001 EDP and Spanish savings bank Cajastur jointly bid to buy Hidrocant´brico one of Spain's leading utilities. EDP won control of 20% of Hidrocant´brico while German utility Energie Baden-W rttemberg (EnBW) won control of 60%. The following year after a fierce bidding war the two companies agreed that EDP would control the majority share (40%) while EnBW would own only 35%.

The company changed its name from EDP - Electricidade de Portugal to EDP - Energias de Portugal in 2004.

Since 2007 the company has sold much of its holdings in other firms to pay down debt. Divestment deals include a 30% stake in Portugal's national transmission grid operator Rede Eléctrica Nacional (REN); a 40% stake in TURBOG S - Produtora Energética the company behind the construction of gas power station Tapada do Outeiro; and a 27% stake in PORTUGEN - Energia which is in charge of operating Tapada do Outeiro. In 2011 it sold a 7.7% stake in Brazil's Ampla Energia to a subsidiary of Spain's Endesa for ?85 million ($121 million).

EXECUTIVES

Executive Director and CFO, Nuno M. Pestana de Almeida Alves, age 62
CEO, Ant nio Lu s Guerra Nunes Mexia, age 60
Executive Director, Jo o Manuel Manso Neto, age 62
Executive Director, Ant nio Manuel Barreto Pita de Abreu
Executive Director, Ant nio Fernando Melo Martins da Costa, age 66
Executive Director, Jo o Manuel Ver ssimo Marques da Cruz, age 59
Executive Director, Miguel Stilwell de Andrade
Auditors: PriceWaterHouseCoopers & Associados, SROC, Lda.

LOCATIONS

HQ: EDP Energias de Portugal S.A.
  Avenida 24 de Julho, 12, Lisbon, Poente 1249-300
Phone: (351) 21 001 25 00   **Fax:** (351) 21 001 28 99
Web: www.edp.pt

2014 Sales

	% of total
Portugal	51
Spain	27
Brazil	18
US	2
Other	2
Total	**100**

PRODUCTS/OPERATIONS

2014 Sales

	% of total
Electricity and Network access	87
Gas and Network access	10
Revenue from assets assigned to concessions	3
Sales of CO2 licences	0
Other	0
Total	**100**

COMPETITORS

AES	Endesa S.A.
Cemig	Enel
E.ON	IBERDROLA
ELETROBR S	Jazztel
Electrabel	RWE
Electricité de France	

HISTORICAL FINANCIALS

Company Type: Public

Income Statement				FYE: December 31
	REVENUE ($ mil.)	NET INCOME ($ mil.)	NET PROFIT MARGIN	EMPLOYEES
12/19	16,092	574	3.6%	11,660
12/18	17,496	594	3.4%	11,631
12/17	18,875	1,334	7.1%	11,657
12/16	15,410	1,014	6.6%	11,992
12/15	16,901	994	5.9%	12,084
Annual Growth	(1.2%)	(12.8%)	—	(0.9%)

2019 Year-End Financials

Debt ratio: 43.9%	No. of shares (mil.): —
Return on equity: 5.7%	Dividends
Cash ($ mil.): 1,732	Yield: 4.9%
Current ratio: 0.95	Payout: 1,353.6%
Long-term debt ($ mil.): 14,735	Market value ($ mil.): —

	STOCK PRICE ($) FY Close	P/E High/Low	PER SHARE ($)		
			Earnings	Dividends	Book Value
12/19	43.08	314239	0.16	2.13	2.74
12/18	34.85	291217	0.16	2.27	2.83
12/17	34.66	131103	0.37	2.34	3.15
12/16	30.65	135105	0.27	1.24	2.73
12/15	36.16	163129	0.27	1.37	2.60
Annual Growth	4.5%	—	(12.8%)	11.6%	1.3%

Eiffage SA

French construction firm Eiffage is responsible for some of France's biggest and most recognizable landmarks including the Channel Tunnel the Louvre pyramid and through an ancestor company the Eiffel Tower from which Eiffage takes its name. Today the company operates through dozens of subsidiaries that build infrastructure and commercial projects primarily in Western Europe. Active in around 50 countries and almost every construction vertical the group consists of four business lines: Concessions Construction Energy Systems and Infrastructures. One of Europe's largest construction firms completes some 100000 projects annually split between private and public sector contracts. France accounts for the vast majority of Eiffage's business.

Operations

Eiffage's participation in infrastructure projects accounts for some 30% of its annual revenue. It consists of a road and motorway construction business a metal-based construction arm (structures shells and facades) and Eiffage Génie Civil a general constructor covering a large range of projects and works including viaducts and tunnels.

The Construction and Energy Systems businesses both bring in some 25% of sales. Construction is active in urban and property development construction maintenance and works and services. Energy Systems designs builds and operates electrical industrial HVAC and energy equipment and systems.

Operating mostly under public-private partnership models the Concessions business brings in 20% of total sales and operates toll roads and builds and manages public facilities (such as prisons sports stadia schools power plants and high-speed rail lines.

Geographic Reach

Eiffage drums up business in around 50 countries worldwide mostly in Europe. France is Eiffage's single largest market accounting for 80% of total revenue. The rest of Europe accounts for nearly 20% of sales while a few percent comes from outside Europe.

Sales and Marketing
Eiffage often works under a public-private partnership arrangement usually with the French government. To pay down debt Eiffage has since 2011 sold off €1.5 billion in PPP contracts.

Financial Performance
Note: Growth rates may differ after conversion to US Dollars.

In fiscal 2017 Eiffage's revenue increased 7% or around €1 billion to €15.3 billion. The company grew both its contracting and concessions revenue while non-France revenue grew a strong 15%. An increase in light and heavy goods vehicle traffic helped motorway concession revenue grow 4% while the Energy Systems business rose 9% on the back of growth internationally in addition to contributions from acquisitions.

Net income also grew 7% thanks to higher revenue and lower debt payments. The company has been selling off public-private partnership (PPP) contracts and using the proceeds to pay off debt. Between 2011 and 2017 the company realized €1.5 billion in PPP proceeds.

Eiffage's cash position was largely unchanged on prior year as stronger cash generation from operations and lower investment expenditure were offset by higher debt repayments as the company continued its deleveraging program.

Strategy
Eiffage partnered with Carillion and Kier on a number of significant rail infrastructure projects in the UK including the HS2 London-Birmingham link and the Cross Rail lines. Carillion went bust in 2018 and to keep the under-pressure projects from stalling Eiffage took the decision to partner 50:50 with Kier and offer laid-off Carillion workers employment.

The company has also been deleveraging by selling off public-private partnership contracts and using the proceeds to pay off debt.

Mergers and Acquisitions
In 2018 advanced its European expansion strategy through a number of acquisitions. Eiffage agreed to acquired Kropman a Netherlands-based specialist in electrical and mechanical engineering contamination control and measurement. It also acquire Priora a Swiss-based construction firm for €340 million and Spanish construction firm Ingenieria y Montajes for €25 million.

In 2017 Eiffage acquired Saipem's maritime works business which is active mainly in Kuwait Congo and Panama.

EXECUTIVES
CEO, Max Roche
Interim Chairman, Jean-Fran §ois Roverato
Auditors: KPMG Audit IS

LOCATIONS
HQ: Eiffage SA
Campus Pierre Berger, 3-7, place de l'Europe, Velizy-Villacoublay 78140
Phone: (33) 1 34 65 89 89
Web: www.eiffage.com

2013 Sales
	% of total
France	84
Rest of Europe	14
Other countries	2
Total	**100**

PRODUCTS/OPERATIONS

2017 Sales
	% of total
Infrastructures	31
Energy	25
Construction	25
Concessions	20
Metal	-
Property development (2)	
Total	**100**

Major Subsidiaries
Clemessy
Eiffage Concessions (highway and other infrastructure operations)
Eiffage Construction (building industry and property development)
Eiffage Energie
Eiffage Travaux Publics (road and railway construction civil engineering and earthworks)
Eiffel (metallic construction and glass facades)
Forclum (electrical contracting and facilities management)

COMPETITORS
Ballast Nedam NV	Hyundai Engineering
Bechtel	and Construction
Bilfinger	STRABAG SE
Bouygues	Sacyr Vallehermoso
Colas	Schneider Electric
Fluor	Skanska
HOCHTIEF	VINCI

HISTORICAL FINANCIALS
Company Type: Public

Income Statement				FYE: December 31
	REVENUE ($ mil.)	NET INCOME ($ mil.)	NET PROFIT MARGIN	EMPLOYEES
12/19	20,990	814	3.9%	51,252
12/18	19,348	720	3.7%	50,051
12/17	18,302	653	3.6%	49,203
12/16	15,109	501	3.3%	49,439
12/15	15,320	339	2.2%	50,854
Annual Growth	8.2%	24.4%	—	0.2%

2019 Year-End Financials
Debt ratio: 51.3%	No. of shares (mil.): 97
Return on equity: 14.4%	Dividends
Cash ($ mil.): 4,962	Yield: —
Current ratio: 0.94	Payout: 37.8%
Long-term debt ($ mil.): 12,011	Market value ($ mil.): —

Electricite de France

State-owned Electricité de France (EDF) has been quick to expand into global deregulated markets. One of the world's top electric utilities (as well as one of the last major state-controlled energy giants in Europe) EDF has a generating capacity of nearly 560 TWh (primarily from nuclear sources) and provides power to nearly 30 million French customers and over 10 million customers in other countries. EDF generates majority of its total sales from France.

Operations
EDF operates in nine segments: France - Generation and Supply France - Regulated Activities Framatome United Kingdom Italy Other International EDF Renewables Dalkia and Other activities.

France - Generation and Supply Activities segment generates more than 35% of total sales. The segment includes EDF's energy production and sales activities commodity trading and other activities.

France - Regulated Activities which accounts for over 20% of total sales consists of distribution transmission EDF's island activities and the activities of Electricité de Strasbourg.

The UK Italy Dalkia and Framatone segments include entities of its subgroups. The segments generate about 35% of sales combined.

The remaining sales are from Other International EDF Renewables and Other Activities.

The Generation/Supply brings in around 60% of EDF's annual sales and generates and delivers electricity to industry local authorities small businesses and residential customers it also includes EDF trading.

The Distribution generates around 40% of sales and manages France's low and medium-voltage public distribution network.

Geographic Reach
EDF operates power plants in Europe Africa the Americas Asia and the Middle East.

In the UK EDF's units include EDF Energy UK Ltd EDF Energy Holdings Limited and EDF Development Company Ltd. In Italy operations are led by the Edison subgroup TdE and Edison SpA.

EDF International and the other gas and electricity entities are located in continental Europe the US Latin America and Asia.

EDF is headquartered in Paris France which also generates about 60% of the company's sales.

Sales and Marketing
EDF's Generation and Supply provides energy generation and energy sales to industry local authorities small businesses and residential consumers. This segment also includes EDF Trading. Distribution focuses on management of the low and medium-voltage public electricity distribution networks. Other activities focuses on services and production of equipment and fuel for reactors energy services (district heating thermal energy services) for industry and local authorities and new businesses mainly aimed at boosting electricity generation through cogeneration and renewable energy sources (e.g. wind turbines photovoltaic panels etc.).

Financial Performance
Note: Growth rates may differ after conversion to US Dollars. IFRS 15 a new set of accounting rules meant EDF restated its 2017 revenue figures ?4.7 billion lower (operating profits were unaffected).

The company's revenue increased by 4% to ?71.3 billion in 2019 compared to ?68.5 billion in the prior year. The rise was primarily due to the increase on their operations in France and international activities.

Net income by the end of 2019 increased by 335% to ?5.2 billion compared to ?1.2 billion in the prior year primarily due to the higher Other financial income and expenses.

Cash held by the company at the end of 2019 increased by ?595 million to ?3.9 billion from ?3.3 billion in the prior year. Cash provided by operations and financing activities were ?14.0 billion and ?2.2 billion respectively. Cash used for investing was ?15.7 billion.

Strategy
EDF's currently adopted strategy with regards to the fuel cycle in agreement with the French State is to process spent fuel and to recycle the separated plutonium in the form of MOX fuel (Mixed OXide of plutonium and uranium). The quantities processed by Orano at the request of EDF totalling approximately 1100 tonnes per year are determined based on the quantity of recyclable

plutonium in the reactors that are authorised to load MOX fuel.

Strategic safety spare parts for generation facilities are treated as property plant and equipment and depreciated over the residual useful life of the installations. The costs of operations that are necessary for generation assets to remain in service and are undertaken at the time of scheduled shutdowns particularly during major inspections are capitalised and amortised over a period corresponding to the time elapsing between two inspections.

Mergers and Acquisitions

n the early 2020 EDF acquired Pod Point one of the UK's largest electric vehicle (EV) charging company. The acquisition is the largest investment of EDF in the EV market in line with its plan to become the leading energy company for electric mobility in France the UK Italy and Belgium.

In late 2019 Pivot Power was acquired by EDF. Pivot Power is based in the UK and specializes in battery storage and infrastructure for EV charging. The transaction is in line with EDF's Electric mobility plan.

EDF subsidiary EDF renewable acquired LUXEL Group in the early 2019. LUXEL is an independent solar energy player based in France. The acquisition will contribute to EDF Renewable's growth in solar energy and will take part to EDF's Solar Plan which aims to establish EDF as a leader in photovoltaic energy.

HISTORY

The French government nationalized hundreds of regional private firms to form Electricit de France (EDF) in 1946 as part of an effort to rebuild the nation's badly shaken post-war economy. This was a marked difference from the notoriously complex and inefficient pre-war electrical industry.

By the 1950s EDF had taken advantage of the centralized control and developed massive hydroelectric projects. Hydroelectric power would account for more than 70% of EDF's power.

But in France as elsewhere hydro wasn't enough to keep up with the growing demand for electricity and fossil fuels became an increasingly important power source. Then came the oil shortages of the 1970s and France — with limited domestic supplies of oil and gas — began searching for alternatives to fossil-fueled plants. Nuclear power was determined to be the answer.

The government moved to invest billions of dollars in developing its relatively small nuclear power production facilities. Muddled with Malthusian predictions of power shortages and a preoccupation with having enough energy to be self-reliant France found its nuclear operations left the government with more energy than it could use and more debt than it wanted. The company began to build a cable connecting the Continent to the UK in 1981. With the power grids of the two countries connected in 1986 EDF was finally able to start exporting its power to the Brits.

The 1990s brought with them deregulation. EDF fought to keep the UK-France grid closed to other energy sellers. After the government forbade the utility from diversifying into areas other than electricity in 1995 the company turned its attention to foreign investment especially in Latin America.

The company faced increasing deregulatory pressures from without in the late 1990s. The newly formed European Union required open competition from member states. Begrudgingly and behind schedule EDF opened about 30% of its market to competition in 2000.

Other members of the EU complained that EDF was trying to play it both ways: It was making aggressive acquisitions in the UK liberalized market (it bought London Electricity in 1999) while resisting a competition-enabling breakup or even al-

lowing a foreign competitor to buy a stake in the French market.

EDF in 2001 expanded its stake in Italy's Montedison a conglomerate with substantial energy holdings by forming a consortium (Italenergia) with Italian automaker Fiat and some Italian banks to wrest control of Montedison from Italian bank MEDIOBANCA. Although the consortium owns 94% of Montedison EDF has only 2% of voting rights. (Montedison changed its name to Edison in 2002.)

EDF also purchased a 35% interest in German utility Energie Baden-W rttemberg in 2001 and it merged its energy services unit with Dalkia a unit of Vivendi Environnement (now Veolia Environnement) taking a 34% stake in Dalkia (which will eventually be increased to 50%). EDF subsidiary London Electricity agreed to buy $2.4 billion in UK assets from TXU Europe that year including a 2000 MW power plant TXU's Eastern Electricity distribution unit and its interest in TXU/EDF joint venture 24seven; the deals were completed in 2001 and 2002.

In 2002 EDF increased its stake in Brazilian utility Light Servi os de Eletricidade to 88% by swapping Light's interest in S o Paulo utility Eletropaulo for AES's 24% interest in Light. Later that year EDF purchased UK electric and gas utility SEEBOARD (1.9 million customers) from US utility AEP in a $2.2 billion deal.

Deregulation of 70% of the French market took effect in July 2004. Between 2000 and 2004 only 30% of the market was deregulated just more than the percentage required by European Union (EU) rulings.

EDF acquired Edison SpA (Italy's second-largest power group) in partnership with Italian utility company AEM SpA in 2005 for an estimated $15.4 billion.

Expanding its presence and its position as a nuclear power provider in the US in 2009 EDF unit EDF Development acquired 49.99% of Constellation Energy's Constellation Energy Nuclear Group LLC for $4.5 billion. (However another joint venture between these two parties aimed at developing new nuclear power plants in the US was terminated in 2010 after strategic disagreements between the principals).

In a move to boost its position as both a major energy and a nuclear power player in Europe in 2009 EDF acquired British Energy with its 1.1 million customer accounts for about $18 billion.

In 2010 EDF signed two new agreements with China National Nuclear Corporation and China Guangdong Nuclear Power Holding Company solidifying its role as a long term partner in China's nuclear development program. (The company has worked in China for 25 years).

To help pay down debt to pay for its expansion in 2010 Hong Kong's Cheung Kong Infrastructure and Hongkong Electric both controlled by Hong Kong-based billionaire Li Ka-shing acquired EDF's three UK distribution UK grids in a deal valued at about $9 billion. In 2011 EDF sold its 45% stake in German power utility Energie Baden-W rttemberg for $6.1 billion.

In 2012 EDF acquired the Italy-based energy group Edison by purchasing Delmi's entire investment (50%) in Transalpina Di Energia for a total of ?784 million. Following this acquisition the Group held 78.96% of the capital and 80.64% of the voting rights in Edison.

Not to be left out in the competitive renewable energy market EDF is seeking to boost its wind and solar energy output from a few hundred MW in 2008 to 4000 MW (in 2012) and higher in 2013.

The company is working on a ?6 billion Flamanville EPR construction project in France. In early 2013 the civil engineering work was 94%

complete and 39% of the electro-mechanical equipment was in place. Its other projects included French offshore projects at Saint-Nazaire Courseulles-sur-Mer and F camp.

EXECUTIVES

Director Upstream-Downstream Optimisation and Trading Division, Philippe Torrion
SEVP HR, Marianne Laigneau
Chairman and CEO, Jean-Bernard Lévy, age 64
Chief Executive EDF Energies Nouvelles, Antoine Cahuzac
SEVP Commerce Optimisation and Trading and Island Energy Systems, Henri Lafontaine
SEVP Gas and Southern Europe; Chief Executive Edison, Bruno Lescoeur
Chief Executive EDF Energy, Vincent de Rivaz
Director Hydraulic Production and Engineering Division, Xavier Ursat
Interim CFO, Xavier Girre
Auditors: KPMG S.A

LOCATIONS

HQ: Electricite de France
22/30 avenue Wagram, Paris, Cedex 08 75382
Phone: (33) 1 40 42 22 22   **Fax:** (33) 1 40 42 32 17
Web: www.edf.com

PRODUCTS/OPERATIONS

2018 Sales

	% of total
France-Regulated Activities	22
France-Generation and Supply Activities	35
UK	12
Italy	12
Dalkia	6
Framatone	4
International	3
EDF Renewables	2
Other Activities	4
Total	**100**

COMPETITORS

Business Group Benelux	Hydro-Québec
Centrica	IBERDROLA
E.ON	International Power
ELETROBR S	RWE
Endesa S.A.	Scottish and Southern
Enel	Energy
Energias de Portugal	Vattenfall
Engie	Veolia Environnement

HISTORICAL FINANCIALS

Company Type: Public

Income Statement   FYE: December 31

	REVENUE ($ mil.)	NET INCOME ($ mil.)	NET PROFIT MARGIN	EMPLOYEES
12/19	112,224	8,111	7.2%	161,552
12/18	108,540	1,852	1.7%	162,208
12/17	109,572	4,993	4.6%	152,033
12/16	112,045	4,486	4.0%	154,845
12/15	118,029	1,867	1.6%	159,112
Annual Growth	(1.3%)	44.4%	—	0.4%

2019 Year-End Financials

Debt ratio: 34.9%	No. of shares (mil.): —
Return on equity: 11.3%	Dividends
Cash ($ mil.): 6,190	Yield: 3.1%
Current ratio: 1.30	Payout: 2.9%
Long-term debt ($ mil.): 88,603	Market value ($ mil.): —

	STOCK PRICE ($)	P/E		PER SHARE ($)		
	FY Close	High/Low	Earnings	Dividends	Book Value
12/19	2.17	2 1	2.36	0.07	23.60
12/18	3.02	18 12	0.31	0.11	23.27
12/17	2.44	3 2	1.54	0.21	22.26
12/16	1.98	2 2	1.81	0.23	25.73
12/15	2.94	17 8	0.50	0.41	28.51
Annual Growth	(7.3%)	—	47.1%	(36.1%)	(4.6%)

Empire Co Ltd

Empire Company Limited (Empire) comprises an empire of supermarkets food distribution and real estate investments. The company operates through wholly-owned subsidiary Sobeys a chain of more than 1500 food and drug stores across Canada under names such as Sobeys Safeway FreshCo and IGA as well as more than 350 retail fuel locations. Additionally the company distributes food to its own stores and other retailers. Empire invests in commercial real estate through stakes in real estate investment trust Crombie REIT and residential property developer Genstar. Empire and its subsidiaries franchisees and affiliates employ approximately 127000 people.

Operations

Empire's business is organized in two reportable segments?Food Retailing and Investments and Other Operations.

Empire's Food Retailing business consists of wholly-owned subsidiary Sobeys Inc. Banners include Foodland Thrifty Foods and Lawton's Drug. The segment consists of company-owned franchised and affiliated stores and locations. Virtually all of Empire's revenue is generated by this segment.

The Investments and Other Operations segment (less than 1% of sales) principally consists of real estate investments and various other corporate operations. It includes a more than 40% stake in both Crombie REIT and Genstar.

Geographic Reach

Headquartered in Stellarton Nova Scotia Empire operates retail stores and fuel locations in every province in Canada. Its stake in real estate investment trust Crombie REIT allows the company to profit from income-producing properties such as shopping centers freestanding stores and mixed-use developments in urban and suburban markets in Canada. Its Genstar California-based hasoperations in Ontario Western Canada and the US.

Sales and Marketing

The company has AIR MILES loyalty program for its customers. AIR MILES are earned by Sobeys customers based on purchases in stores. The company pays a per point fee under the terms of the agreement with AIR MILES.

Financial Performance

Empire Company's revenue for the last five years was in the $23 billion to $26 billion range. Revenue increased by 12% for the last five years. Net income has increased steadily for the last five years with the company suffering a net loss only in 2016.

Revenue in 2020 amounted to $26.6 billion a 6% increase from the previous year which resulted from an increase in sales across all formats except for fuel. Fuel sales for the quarter decreased by approximately 40% due to a combination of lower demand and a sharp decrease in fuel prices.

Net income increased 51% to $583.5 million compared to $387.3 million in 2019.

Cash and cash equivalents at the end of the year were $1 billion 82% higher than the previous year. Cash provided by operating activities was $2.1 billion. Investing activities used $376.3 million while financing activities used $1.3 billion. Main cash uses were purchases of property and equipment advances on credit facilities and payments of lease liabilities.

Strategy

Empire has invested in people to create a more diverse and inclusive workforce that enables the company to build healthy communities through programs such as the Community Action Fund and the Strengthening Our Inclusive Leadership program. As a result the company received 5 industry leading inclusion awards.

The company has reduced its environmental impact and enhanced resilience to climate change to protect the planet for future generations.

The company has also put its focus on sustainable sourcing of products which won the company a Business Innovator of the Year award.

Company Background

J. W. Sobey started a butcher shop and meat delivery business in Nova Scotia in 1907 later expanding to a full-service grocery operation in 1924. By 1939 Sobeys had six grocery stores in Nova Scotia and continue to grow by promising low prices and introducing new products and concepts into the Sobey grocery business. On a trip through the US in the 1940s Sobey executives witnessed first-hand the operation of a new type of grocery store?the supermarket. Sobeys introduced the first supermarket in Nova Scotia in 1947.

While continuing to build its grocery operation Sobeys began investing in real estate carried out as the Empire Company. Empire went public on the Toronto Stock Exchange in 1983. At the same time the Sobeys chain was folded into Empire. In 1987 Sobeys opened its first store in Ontario; by the early 1990s Sobeys had expanded in Ontario and into Quebec.

The 1998 acquisition of The Oshawa Group (owner of the IGA and Price Chopper grocery chains) tripled the size of Sobeys and made its food service distributorship the largest in Canada. Later that year Empire took Sobeys public again retaining a majority stake in the grocery business. In 2000 Empire sold its 25% stake in US-based grocery retailer Hannaford Bros. Co. to Delhaize America for more than $800 million in cash and stock.

In 2013 Sobeys bought more than 200 Safeway stores in Western Canada for a whopping $5.8 billion. An anti-competition ruling against the company in 2014 prompted Sobeys to sell off its one remaining Price Chopper store to the North West Company.

EXECUTIVES

EVP and CFO Empire Company and Sobeys, Michael H. Vels
President and CEO Empire Company and Sobeys, Michael B. Medline
EVP, Fran §ois Vimard
EVP Technology and Lead of Transformation Office, Clinton Keay
Chairman, James M. (Jim) Dickson
Auditors: PricewaterhouseCoopers LLP

LOCATIONS

HQ: Empire Co Ltd
115 King Street, Stellarton, Nova Scotia B0K 1S0
Phone: 902 752-8371   **Fax:** 902 238-7124
Web: www.empireco.ca

PRODUCTS/OPERATIONS

Related Businesses
Pharmacy
Wholesale
Fuel/Convenience
Liquor
Private Label Brands
Loyalty Reward Programs
Real Estate

COMPETITORS

Costco Wholesale Canada	Loblaw
	METRO
Couche-Tard	Shoppers Drug Mart
Golub	Wal-Mart Canada
Jim Pattison Group	Whole Foods
Katz Group	

HISTORICAL FINANCIALS
Company Type: Public

Income Statement				FYE: May 2
	REVENUE ($ mil.)	NET INCOME ($ mil.)	NET PROFIT MARGIN	EMPLOYEES
05/20	27,066	590	2.2%	63,000
05/19	25,617	392	1.5%	60,000
05/18	24,657	161	0.7%	120,000
05/17	24,233	160	0.7%	62,000
05/16	25,005	(2,157)	—	65,000
Annual Growth	2.0%	—	—	(0.8%)

2020 Year-End Financials
Debt ratio: 11.5%
Return on equity: 14.7%
Cash ($ mil.): 1,021
Current ratio: 0.80
Long-term debt ($ mil.): 1,119
No. of shares (mil.): 268
Dividends
Yield: 0.0%
Payout: 22.3%
Market value ($ mil.): 5,808

	STOCK PRICE ($)	P/E		PER SHARE ($)		
	FY Close	High/Low	Earnings	Dividends	Book Value
05/20	21.60	13 8	2.18	0.49	14.78
05/19	22.21	17 12	1.44	0.45	14.93
05/18	19.48	35 25	0.60	0.43	13.82
05/17	15.70	30 19	0.59	0.42	13.61
05/16	16.38	— —	(7.88)	0.41	13.50
Annual Growth	7.2%	— —	—	4.7%	2.3%

Empresa Distribuidora y Comercializadora Norte SA Edenor

EXECUTIVES

President, Ricardo Alejandro Torres
Vice President, Gustavo Mariani
Auditors: Price Waterhouse & Co. S.R.L.

LOCATIONS

HQ: Empresa Distribuidora y Comercializadora Norte SA Edenor
Av. del Libertador 6363, 12th Floor, Buenos Aires C1428ARG
Phone: (54) 11 4346 5000   **Fax:** (54) 11 4346 5324
Web: www.edenor.com

COMPETITORS

AES	Enersis
Electroandina	

HISTORICAL FINANCIALS

Company Type: Public

Income Statement

FYE: December 31

	REVENUE ($ mil.)	NET INCOME ($ mil.)	NET PROFIT MARGIN	EMPLOYEES
12/19	28,444	3,837	13.5%	4,777
12/18	17,695	1,359	7.7%	4,878
12/17	7,697	215	2.8%	4,789
12/16	4,136	(375)	—	4,746
12/15	1,202	361	30.0%	4,696
Annual Growth	120.5%	80.5%	—	0.4%

2019 Year-End Financials

Debt ratio: 2.6%
Return on equity: 26.9%
Cash ($ mil.): 129
Current ratio: 0.73
Long-term debt ($ mil.): 2,592

No. of shares (mil.): 875
Dividends
  Yield: —
  Payout: —
Market value ($ mil.): 5,478

	STOCK PRICE ($) FY Close	P/E High/Low		PER SHARE ($) Earnings	Dividends	Book Value
12/19	6.26	2	0	4.38	0.00	21.38
12/18	27.06	13	4	1.53	0.00	11.09
12/17	49.70	68	38	0.24	0.00	0.37
12/16	27.85	—	—	(0.42)	0.00	0.13
12/15	17.53	16	7	0.40	0.00	0.54
Annual Growth	(22.7%) 151.1%	—	—	81.7%	—	—

Empresas COPEC SA

EXECUTIVES

CEO Corpesca, Arturo Natho Gamboa
CEO Copec S.A., Lorenzo Gazmuri Schleyer
CFO, Rodrigo Huidobro Alvarado
CEO Sonacol, Roberto Hetz Vorpahl
CEO, Eduardo Navarro Beltr˜n
EVP Celulosa Arauco y Constituci˜ln, Mat as Domeyko Cassel
CEO Abastible, Joaqu n Cruz Sanfiel
CEO Metrogas, V ctor Turpaud Fern˜ndez
CEO Orizon, Rigoberto Rojo Rojas
CEO Alxar Miner a, Erwin Kaufmann Salinas
CEO Mina Invierno, Sebasti˜n Gil Clasen
Chairman, Roberto Angelini Rossi
Auditors: PricewaterhouseCoopers

LOCATIONS

HQ: Empresas COPEC SA
  Avenida El Golf 150, Piso 17, Santiago, Las Condes 6500586
Phone: (56) 2 461 7000   **Fax:** (56) 2 461 7070
Web: www.copec.cl

PRODUCTS/OPERATIONS

2007 Sales

	% of total
Fuels	73
Forestry	26
Fisheries	1
Total	**100**

COMPETITORS

Endesa S.A.	Petrobras
Enersis	Distribuidora
Falabella	Repsol
International Paper	Walmart Chile

HISTORICAL FINANCIALS

Company Type: Public

Income Statement

FYE: December 31

	REVENUE ($ mil.)	NET INCOME ($ mil.)	NET PROFIT MARGIN	EMPLOYEES
12/19	23,716	172	0.7%	0
12/18	23,970	1,070	4.5%	36,166
12/17	20,353	639	3.1%	0
12/16	16,699	554	3.3%	31,714
12/15	18,160	539	3.0%	26,694
Annual Growth	6.9%	(24.8%)	—	—

2019 Year-End Financials

Debt ratio: 33.1%
Return on equity: 1.6%
Cash ($ mil.): 2,214
Current ratio: 2.27
Long-term debt ($ mil.): 8,347

No. of shares (mil.): 1,299
Dividends
  Yield: —
  Payout: —
Market value ($ mil.): —

Enbridge Inc

Canada-based Enbridge is one of the biggest pipeline operators in North America. Its over 17000 miles of crude pipeline straddles Canada and the US and carries more than 65% of all US-bound Canadian oil exports and about 20% of all natural gas consumed in the US. Enbridge's regulated business supplies gas to some 3.8 million customers in Ontario Quebec. As well as fossil fuels the company also invests in renewable energy with investments in North American and European renewable energy totaling 1750 MW of installed capacity. In all the US accounts for 60% of Enbridge's revenue.

Operations

Enbridge divides its operations into five reportable segments: Energy Services Liquids Pipelines Gas Transmission and Midstream Gas Distribution and Storage and Renewable Power Generation.

Energy Services provides energy supply and marketing services to North American refiners producers and other customers. The segment represents about 60% of Enbridge's sales.

Liquids Pipelines generates the second-most revenue (around 20%). The segment consists of pipelines and related terminals in Canada and the United States that transport various grades of crude oil and other liquid hydrocarbons. It includes Canadian Mainline the Lakehead System Regional Oil Sands System Bakken System and other feeder pipelines.

Gas Transmission and Midstream maintains natural gas pipelines and gathering and processing facilities including US Gas Transmission Canadian Gas TransmissionUS Midstream and other assets. The segment brings in over 10% of revenue.

Gas Distribution and Storage consists of natural gas utility operations the core of which is Enbridge Gas Inc. which serves residential commercial and industrial customers throughout Ontario and maintains natural gas distribution business in Quebec and New Brunswick. This business segment also includes natural gas distribution activities in

Québec and an investment in Noverco Inc. (Noverco). It represents around 10% of sales.

Renewable Power Generation (around a percent of revenue) consists primarily of investments in wind and solar assets as well as geothermal waste heat recovery and transmission assets. The segment includes the Montana-Alberta Tie-Line (MATL) a 300 MW transmission line which runs from Great Falls Montana to Lethbridge Alberta. The segment's investments represent approximately 1991 MW of net generation capacity.

Overall commodity revenue generates almost 60% followed by transportation and others which generates around a third of revenue while the remainder comes from gas distribution.

Geographic Reach

Headquartered in Calgary Alberta Canada Enbridge has over 17100 miles of active crude pipeline across North Americóincluding over 8600 miles of active pipe in the United States and 8500 miles of active pipe in Canada. Its gas transmission and midstream pipelines cover about 23900 miles in 30 US states five Canadian provinces and offshore in the Gulf of Mexico.

Additionally subsidiary Enbridge Gas Inc.'s network currently consists of over 48600 miles of gas distribution mainlines 41500 miles of gas distribution service lines and 3400 miles of gas transmission lines.

Financial Performance

Enbridge's revenue has been rising over the last five years with an overall growth of 48%. The company's net income has been following a similar trend with an overall growth of almost 2200%.

In 2019 Enbridge grew its sales 8% to C$50.1 billion.

Net income almost doubled from C$2.9 billion in 2018 to C$5.7 billion in 2019.

Enbridge's cash balance grew from C$39 million to C$676 million during 2019. Operating activities generated C$9.4 billion while investing activities used C$4.7 billion with C$4.7 billion for financing activities.

Strategy

Following a successful merger with Spectra Enbridge is now well balanced between oil and natural gas assets that includes its vast natural gas transmission franchise liquids pipeline business and natural gas utility business. The company's key strategic priorities are summarized below:

Commitment to Safety and Operational Reliability - Enbridge's commitment to safety and operational reliability means achieving and maintaining industry leadership in safety (process public and personal) and ensuring the reliability and integrity of the systems the company operates in order to generate transport and deliver energy while protecting people and the environment.

Optimize Core Businesses - Examples include throughput enhancements on liquids system from the application of drag-reducing agents and improvements in scheduling logistics at the company's terminals revenue optimization through negotiated toll settlements or rate cases ongoing synergy capture following recent utility merger and more generally creating sustainable cost savings across the organization through process improvement and/or system enhancements.

Execute and Extend Growth - Enbridge's ongoing objective is to deliver its slate of secured projects at the lowest practical cost while maintaining the highest standards for safety quality customer satisfaction and environmental and regulatory compliance.

Company Background

Enbridge is an early pioneer in the development of oil production in Western Canada. The company was born in 1949 when crude oil was discovered in Leduc No. 1. Starting life as the Interprovincial

Pipe Line Company it was conceived as a pipeline that will carry Alberta crude to refineries in Regina.

In 1950 it sold some 3 million barrels of oil. By 2018 the company will sell close to that volume every day.

Enbridge merged with Spectra in early 2017 to create one of the largest energy infrastructure company in North America with an enterprise value of approximately US $126 billion.

EXECUTIVES

EVP Corporate Development, J. Richard Bird, age 71, $514,566 total compensation
President Gas Pipelines and Processing, C. Gregory (Greg) Harper, age 56
EVP and CFO, John K. Whelen
President CEO and Director, Al Monaco, age 61, $416,893 total compensation
EVP People and Partners, Karen L. Radford, age 51
EVP and Chief Legal Officer, David T. Robottom
President Liquids Pipelines, Guy Jarvis
COO, Leon Zupan
President Enbridge Gas Distribution, Glenn Beaumont
Chairman, David A. Arledge, age 76
Auditors: PricewaterhouseCoopers LLP

LOCATIONS

HQ: Enbridge Inc
  200, 425 - 1st Street S.W., Calgary, Alberta T2P 3L8
Phone: 403 231-3900
Web: www.enbridge.com

2018 Sales

	% of total
US	59
Canada	41
Total	**100**

PRODUCTS/OPERATIONS

2018 Sales

	% of total
Commodity sales	60
Transportation and other services	31
Gas distribution	9
Total	**100**

Selected Subsidiaries and Affiliates

Gas Pipelines Processing and Energy Services
  Aux Sable Liquids Products Inc. (43%)
  Alliance Pipeline Limited Partnership (50%)
  Tlbury Solar Project
  Vector Pipeline Limited Partnership (60%)
Gas Distribution
  Enbridge Gas Distribution
  Enbridge Gas New Brunswick (63%)
  Gazifère Inc.
  Niagara Gas Transmission Limited
Liquids Pipelines
  Chicap Pipe Line Company (44%)
  Enbridge Energy Partners L.P. (13%)
  Enbridge Pipelines (Athabasca) Inc.
  Enbridge Pipelines (North Dakota) Inc.
  Enbridge Pipelines (NW) Inc.
  Enbridge Pipelines (Toledo) Inc.
  Enbridge Pipelines Inc.
  Frontier Pipeline Company (78%)
  Mustang Pipe Line Partners (30%)
  Olympic Pipe Line (85%)
Sponsored Investments
  Enbridge Income Fund (72%)
  Enbridge Energy Partners L.P. (25.5%)
Corporate
  Noverco Inc. (39%)
  Gaz Mé;tropolitain and Company Limited Partnership (71%)
  Vermont Gas Systems Inc.

COMPETITORS

Con Edison	ONEOK Partners
Hydro One	TransCanada
Koch Industries Inc.	Williams Companies
National Fuel Gas	
New York Power Authority	

HISTORICAL FINANCIALS

Company Type: Public

Income Statement

FYE: December 31

	REVENUE ($ mil.)	NET INCOME ($ mil.)	NET PROFIT MARGIN	EMPLOYEES
12/19	38,449	4,381	11.4%	11,300
12/18	34,056	2,116	6.2%	12,000
12/17	35,399	2,280	6.4%	12,700
12/16	25,644	1,535	6.0%	7,733
12/15	24,331	180	0.7%	8,652
Annual Growth	**12.1%**	**121.9%**	**—**	**6.9%**

2019 Year-End Financials

Debt ratio: 30.5%	No. of shares (mil.): 2,025
Return on equity: 8.4%	Dividends
Cash ($ mil.): 519	Yield: 5.5%
Current ratio: 0.55	Payout: 146.1%
Long-term debt ($ mil.): 45,815	Market value ($ mil.): 80,534

	STOCK PRICE ($) FY Close	P/E High/Low		PER SHARE ($)		
				Earnings	Dividends	Book Value
12/19	39.77	15	13	2.02	2.22	25.05
12/18	31.08	26	19	1.07	2.08	25.23
12/17	39.11	28	21	1.32	1.92	27.36
12/16	42.12	22	16	1.43	1.57	16.83
12/15	33.19	—	—	(0.03)	1.46	15.68
Annual Growth	**4.6%**	**—**	**—**	**—**	**10.9%**	**12.4%**

Endesa S.A.

EXECUTIVES

CFO, Paolo Bondi
CEO, Jose D. Bogas Galvez
Chairman, Borja Prado Eulate, age 64
Auditors: Ernst & Young, S.L.

LOCATIONS

HQ: Endesa S.A.
  Calle Ribera Del Loira 60, Madrid 28042
Phone: (34) 91 213 10 00   **Fax:** (34) 91 563 81 81
Web: www.endesa.es

2009 Sales

	% of total
Europe	
Spain & Portugal	68
Latin America	32
Total	**100**

COMPETITORS

AES	International Power
Business Group Benelux	PPL Corporation
E.ON	RWE
Edison	Red Eléctrica de España
Electricité de France	
Energias de Portugal	Sempra Energy
Gas Natural SDG	Telef nica
HC Energ a	Vattenfall
IBERDROLA	

HISTORICAL FINANCIALS

Company Type: Public

Income Statement

FYE: December 31

	REVENUE ($ mil.)	NET INCOME ($ mil.)	NET PROFIT MARGIN	EMPLOYEES
12/19	22,632	191	0.8%	9,952
12/18	23,127	1,622	7.0%	9,763
12/17	24,043	1,753	7.3%	9,706
12/16	20,039	1,489	7.4%	9,694
12/15	22,109	1,182	5.4%	10,000
Annual Growth	**0.6%**	**(36.5%)**	**—**	**(0.1%)**

2019 Year-End Financials

Debt ratio: 23.2%	No. of shares (mil.): 1,058
Return on equity: 2.0%	Dividends
Cash ($ mil.): 250	Yield: 0.0%
Current ratio: 0.72	Payout: 316.2%
Long-term debt ($ mil.): 6,345	Market value ($ mil.): 14,674

	STOCK PRICE ($) FY Close	P/E High/Low		PER SHARE ($)		
				Earnings	Dividends	Book Value
12/19	13.86	89	75	0.18	0.57	8.15
12/18	11.62	9	8	1.53	0.56	9.77
12/17	11.66	11	8	1.65	0.57	10.30
12/16	11.07	10	6	1.40	0.50	8.93
12/15	14.99	15	9	1.12	0.30	9.30
Annual Growth	**(1.9%)**	**—**	**—**	**(36.7%)**	**17.5%**	**(3.2%)**

Enel Americas SA

EXECUTIVES

General Manager, Luca D'Agnese
Deputy General Manager, Daniel Fern ndez
Administration Finance and Control Officer, Javier Gal n
Procurement Officer, Antonio Barreda Toledo
Chairman, Francisco de Borja Acha Besga
Vice Chairman, Francesco Starace
Auditors: Ernst & Young Audit SpA

LOCATIONS

HQ: Enel Americas SA
  Avenida Santa Rosa 76, Piso 16, Santiago
Phone: (56) 2 353 4639   **Fax:** (56) 2 378 4790
Web: www.enersis.cl

PRODUCTS/OPERATIONS

2016 Sales

	% of total
Distribution	67
Generation and Transmission	33
Total	**100**

2016 Sales

	% of total
Brazil	36
Colombia	30
Peru	17
Argentina	17
Total	**100**

Selected Subsidiaries

Ampla Energ;a e Serviços (distribution generation and transmission Brazil)
Centrais Elé;tricas Cachoeira Dourada (distribution generation and transmission Brazil)
Chilectra (distribution)
Compa Â Â í;a Americana de Multiservicios (CAM electricity support services and engineering)

Edelnor (distribution Peru)
Edesur (distribution Argentina)
Endesa Brasil Consolidated (distribution generation and transmission Brazil)
Endesa Chile (generation)
Endesa Fortaleza (distribution generation and transmission Brazil)
Inmobiliaria Manso de Velasco (IMV real estate)
Synapsis (information and telecommunications)

COMPETITORS

AES	ELETROBR S
AntarChile	Enron
CESP	Escelsa
COPEC	Hydro-Québec
COPEL	IBERDROLA
CPFL Energia	Light Servicos de
CPFL Paulista	Eletricidade
Cemig	Pampa Energia
Duke Energy	Petrobras Argentina

HISTORICAL FINANCIALS

Company Type: Public

Income Statement

FYE: December 31

	REVENUE ($ mil.)	NET INCOME ($ mil.)	NET PROFIT MARGIN	EMPLOYEES
12/19	14,314	1,614	11.3%	17,295
12/18	13,184	1,201	9.1%	18,364
12/17	10,540	709	6.7%	11,393
12/16	7,794	574	7.4%	10,324
12/15	7,481	933	12.5%	12,348
Annual Growth	17.6%	14.7%	—	8.8%

2019 Year-End Financials

Debt ratio: 16.4%
Return on equity: 19.3%
Cash ($ mil.): 1,939
Current ratio: 0.98
Long-term debt ($ mil.): 4,890

No. of shares (mil.): —
Dividends
Yield: 3.4%
Payout: 1,787.3%
Market value ($ mil.): —

	STOCK PRICE ($) FY Close	P/E High/Low	PER SHARE ($) Earnings	Dividends	Book Value
12/19	10.98	447312	0.02	0.38	0.13
12/18	8.92	573338	0.02	0.29	0.12
12/17	11.17	905650	0.01	0.22	0.11
12/16	8.21	2 1	0.01	0.31	0.11
12/15	12.15	1 1	0.02	0.42	0.17
Annual Growth	(2.5%)	— —	6.7%	(2.6%)	(6.7%)

Enel Societa Per Azioni

Arrivederci monopolio! Buongiorno diversified energy player. Italy based Enel is one of Europe's top integrated energy companies that sells gas and electricity to more than 70 million end users in about 50 countries in across approximately five continents. With installed energy generation capacity of about 45 GW and more than 3.8 million kilometers of distribution networks Enel's portfolio of power stations includes hydroelectric wind geothermal solar thermoelectric and other renewables. About 60% of its energy generation is hydroelectric.

Operations

Enel reports six business segments three of which are its leading revenue earners? Thermal generation and trading (more than 30% of annual sales) End-user markets (nearly 35%) Infrastructure and Networks (more than 20%) and Enel Green Power (about 10%). The two other seg-

ments Enel X and Services bring in a combined less than 5% of revenue.

Hydroelectric generates the 60% of electric generation followed by wind (nearly 30%) and geothermal and solar bring in a combined about 10% of revenue.

Geographic Reach

Enel is primarily present across Europe and Americas with some presence in Africa and Asia.

The company produces energy in all corners of the world from Morocco and South Africa to Russia Chile India and Canada.

Enel finds its largest customers in Europe bringing in nearly 45% of annual sales followed by Italy (35% of sales) and Americas (more than 20%).

Its corporate office is located in Italy.

Sales and Marketing

Enel generates around 230 TWh of electricity annually and further distributes some 505 TWh through its own grids along with selling about 105 million m3 of gas every year.

Other than Italy and Iberia the company has significant customer concentrations in Brazil The Netherlands Chile Germany Colombia Argentina France Peru Russia and Romania.

Financial Performance

The company's revenue increased by 6% to ?80.3 billion in 2019 compared to ?75.6 billion in the prior year. The additional increase in revenue is attributable to the positive performance of Infrastructure and Networks in particular in Latin America mainly due to the contribution of Enel Distribui § o S o Paulo in Brazil and the settlement of outstanding regulatory items in Argentina and to Thermal Generation and Trading in Italy reflecting in particular an increase in trading activities.

Group net income for 2019 amounted to ?2.2 billion compared with ?4.8 billion the previous year. The decrease was primarily due to higher depreciation amortization and impairment losses.

Cash holdings of the company increased from ?6.7 billion in 2018 to ?9.1 billion in 2019. Operations generated ?11.3 billion offset by ?9.1 billion in investments and ?2.4 billion provided by financing activities. CAPEX was approximately ?9.9 billion.

Strategy

The world of utilities is experiencing an era of profound transformation mainly driven by the challenge of decarbonizing the energy sector. The progressive shift of generation from fossil fuels to renewable sources together with the acceleration in the electrification of final consumption will be the main trends in the energy transition. Energy infrastructures and digital platforms will be key factors in enabling this transition and achieving the United Nations' Sustainable Development Goals. The sustainable strategy and the integrated business model developed in recent years have allowed the group to constantly create value and will allow us to benefit from the opportunities emerging from this transition while limiting the related risks.

Thanks to a development model based on the organic build-out of renewable generation assets that gives us great flexibility in the use of capital the group is capable of responding swiftly to any unexpected scenario changes that could be triggered by the pandemic that has been spreading around the world in these last few months. In November 2019 Enel presented the 2020-2022 Strategic Plan which while confirming the strategic direction already set explicitly integrates the SDG objectives into its financial strategy

Mergers and Acquisitions

In 2019 Enel S.p.A. ("Enel") acting through its renewable subsidiary Enel Green Power North America Inc. ("EGPNA") finalised the acquisition of 100% of seven fully operational renewable plants totalling about 650 MW from Enel Green

Power North America Renewable Energy Partners LLC ("EGPNA REP") an equally owned joint venture between EGPNA and GE Capital's Energy Financial Services the energy investing arm of General Electric. The overall consideration paid for the transaction amounts to approximately $256 million for an enterprise value equal to around $900 million.

HISTORY

Italy's energy consumption doubled in the 1950s as the country experienced a period of rapid industrialization and urbanization. A tight-knit oligopoly controlled the electric power industry and included Edison SADE La Centale SME and Finelettrica. The economic boom pushed into the 1960s and the Italian government created Enel (Ente Nazionale per l'Energia Elettrica) in 1962 to nationalize the power industry. In 1963 Enel began gradually buying some 1250 electric utilities. About 160 municipal utilities and the larger independents such as Edison were left out of the takeover.

The company spent the late 1960s and early 1970s connecting Italy's unwieldy transmission network and building new power plants including the La Spezia thermoelectric plant (600 MW). Construction costs coupled with the high prices Enel was required to pay for its takeover targets caused the utility to become steeped in debt. The Arab oil embargoes of the early 1970s made matters worse and the Italian government helped Enel with an endowment in 1973.

The energy crisis also prompted Enel to build its first nuclear power plant Caorso which came on line in 1980. However nuclear power was short-lived in Italy: After the 1986 Chernobyl accident a national referendum forced Enel to deactivate its nukes in 1987. The firm also stepped up its development of renewable energy sources in the 1980s.

Meanwhile Enel opened its Centro Nazionale de Controllo (CNC) in Rome in 1985 to supervise Italy's power grid. The next year the company turned its first profit.

To begin disassembling Enel's monopoly the Italian government in 1992 opened the power generation market to outside producers and converted Enel into a joint stock company (with the state holding all of the shares). Following the European Union's 1997 directive to deregulate Europe's power industry Enel unbundled its utility activities and began trimming its staff.

Italy's Bersani Decree (passed in 1999) outlined the restructuring process: Enel was ordered to divest 25% of its capacity (15000 MW) and turn over a portion of its municipal distribution networks to local governments to enhance competition in the country's power market. Accordingly it transferred management of the national transmission grid to an independent government-owned operator Gestore della Rete di Trasmissione Nazionale (GRTN) and reduced its customer count by approximately 1 million through municipal distribution asset sales.

Enel had already begun to diversify. It started Wind Telecomunicazioni a joint venture with France Telecom — later renamed Orange— and Deutsche Telekom in 1998. (Deutsche Telekom sold its stake to the other partners in 2000.) Wind first offered fixed-line and mobile telecom services to corporations; it extended the services to residential users in 1999. In addition Enel began building water infrastructure to serve local distributors and purchased three water operations in southern Italy.

Also in 1999 the government floated 32% of Enel in one of the world's largest IPOs at the time. The next year the company bought Colombo Gas (a northern Italian gas distributor with about

75000 customers) and it transferred control of its transmission network to Gestore della Rete di Trasmissione Nazionale (an independent government-owned operator) while retaining ownership of the assets.

Enel bought fixed-line telephone company Infostrada from Vodafone in 2001 acquired two more Italian gas distributors and sold its 5400-MW Elettrogen generation unit to Spain's Endesa for $2.3 billion. That year Enel put its 7000-MW Eurogen generation unit on the auction block. The high bidder with a $2.6 billion offer was a consortium backed by Fiat and lectricité de France; the sale was completed in 2002.

Also in 2002 Enel merged Infostrada into Wind Telecomunicazioni to create one of Italy's top telecom companies it purchased Camuzzi Gazometri's gas distribution business (Italy's second-largest) for $870 million from Mill Hill Investments and it bought Endesa's Viesgo unit (2400 MW of generating capacity and 500000 power customers) for about $1.8 billion.

Enel sold its final generation divestment company Interpower (2600 MW) to a consortium of utilities (including Belgian utility Electrabel and Italian utility ACEA) for about $880 million in 2003.

That year Enel purchased France Telecom's 27% stake in Wind for $1.4 billion making the unit a wholly owned subsidiary. (Enel had flirted with the idea of taking Wind public but instead sold the unit in 2006 to the Egypt-based Weather Investments consortium which had the backing of Orascom Telecom's chairman and CEO Naguib Sawiris.)

The Italian government began the second round of Enel's privatization process in 2003 by selling a 7% stake to Morgan Stanley for more than $2.3 billion. In 2004 the government further reduced its stake by nearly 20% through a public offering of shares.

In 2005 it acquired power distribution and sales businesses in Romania and in 2006 in Slovakia.

With Italian regulators requiring that Enel divest 80% of its Terna subsidiary (which holds the company's power transmission assets) by 2007 Enel spun off 50% of the unit in an IPO in 2004. The following year it divested another 44% and the company reduced its holding to about 5% by January 2006. Grid management and operational functions were also transferred from GRTN back to Terna.

In 2008 the company set Enel Green Power to develop wind solar geothermal and biomass projects. By 2009 it was operating alternative energy plants worldwide with a generating capacity of 4700 MW. In 2010 Enel Green Power acquired Pagoda Wind Power which is developing 4000 MW of wind projects in California.

In what could have been a large cross-border deal Enel considered making a bid for France's SUEZ (now GDF SUEZ) utility company. Perhaps in reaction to the news of Enel's interest France's Gaz de France made a bid for SUEZ (consummated in 2008) a move that Italy called protectionist.

Unperturbed by its failure to secure SUEZ the company took control of Spain's power giant Endesa in 2007 increasing its market share as a European power player. Hoping to pay down what had become a heavy debt load the company in 2009 sold an 80% stake in gas distributor Enel Rete Gas for $666 million.

In 2012 Enel Green Power consolidated its position in the Greek renewable industry through the launching of two new plants - a wind farm and a photovoltaic plant - both located in the Peloponnese region.

EXECUTIVES

Head of Country Iberia CEO Endesa and Chairman Elcogas S.A., José Dami n Bogas G lvez
Head of Country Italy, Carlo Tamburi, age 61
Head of Global Thermal Generation, Enrico Viale
Head of Global Trading, Claudio Machetti, age 62
CEO and General Manager, Francesco Starace, age 65
Head of Global Infrastructure and Networks, Livio Gallo
Head of Human Resources and Organization, Francesca Di Carlo, age 57
Head of Legal and Corporate Affairs, Giulio Fazio, age 49
CFO, Alberto De Paoli, age 55
Head of Europe and North Africa, Roberto Deambrogio, age 45
Head of Global E-Solutions, Francesco Venturini, age 52
Head of Global Procurement, Francesco Buresti
Head of Global Information and Communications Technology, Carlo Bozzoli, age 58
Head of South America, Luca D'Agnese
Head of North and Central America Sub-Saharian Africa and Asia, Antonio Cammisecra, age 60
Chairman, Patrizia Grieco
Auditors: EY S.p.A.

LOCATIONS

HQ: Enel Societa Per Azioni
  Viale Regina Margherita, 137, Rome 00198
Phone: (39) 6 8509 3184   **Fax:** (39) 6 8509 5810
Web: www.enel.com

2018 sales

	% of total
Italy	50
Iberia	26
South America	19
Europe and Euro-Mediterranean Affairs	3
North and Central America	2
Africa Asia and Oceania	-
Total	**100**

PRODUCTS/OPERATIONS

2018 Sales

	% of total
Thermal Generation and Trading	41
End-user markets	35
Infrastructure and Networks	16
Enel Green Power	4
Enel X	1
Services	3
Total	**100**

2018 sales

	% of total
Sale of electricity	57
Transport of Electricity	14
Fees from network operators	1
Transfers from institutional market operators	2
Sales of gas	6
Transport of gas	1
Sale of fuel	11
Other	8
Total	**100**

COMPETITORS

A2A	Eni
ABB	HC Energ a
ACEA	IBERDROLA
Acque Potabili	International Power
E.ON	Italgas
ERG S.p.A.	RWE
Edison	Risanamento
Electricité de France	

HISTORICAL FINANCIALS

Company Type: Public

Income Statement   FYE: December 31

	REVENUE ($ mil.)	NET INCOME ($ mil.)	NET PROFIT MARGIN	EMPLOYEES
12/19	90,188	2,440	2.7%	68,253
12/18	86,659	-5,484	6.3%	69,272
12/17	89,473	4,530	5.1%	62,900
12/16	74,536	2,713	3.6%	62,080
12/15	82,407	2,391	2.9%	67,914
Annual Growth	**2.3%**	**0.5%**	**—**	**0.1%**

2019 Year-End Financials

Debt ratio: 40.2%
Return on equity: 7.0%
Cash ($ mil.): 10,137
Current ratio: 0.91
Long-term debt ($ mil.): 60,824

No. of shares (mil.): —
Dividends
  Yield: 2.2%
  Payout: 74.5%
Market value ($ mil.): —

	STOCK PRICE ($) FY Close	P/E High/Low	PER SHARE ($) Earnings	Dividends	Book Value
12/19	7.85	38 27	0.24	0.18	3.36
12/18	5.81	13 10	0.54	0.16	3.57
12/17	6.11	18 12	0.44	0.12	4.10
12/16	4.37	17 14	0.27	0.10	3.61
12/15	4.14	21 16	0.25	0.09	3.75
Annual Growth	**17.3%**	**—**	**(1.5%)**	**19.9%**	**(2.7%)**

Eneos Holdings Inc

ENEOS (formerly JXTG) is an integrated energy holding company that combines the businesses of two of Nippon Oil and Nippon Mining Holdings in petroleum refining and marketing oil and natural gas exploration and production and metals. In addition the company supplies electricity and hydrogen. ENEOS produces 105000 barrels of oil equivalent from its exploration and production asserts. Its refineries have the capacity to process roughly 1.7 million barrels of crude oil per day representing more than a quarter of the total amount of crude oil processed per day in Japan. In 2019 the company decided to change its name to ENEOS Holdings.

Operations

ENEOS operates through three major segments: Energy Oil and Natural Gas E&P and Metals.

The company's Energy business accounted for about 85% of total revenues. This segment focus on petroleum refining & marketing lubricants basic chemical products specialty & performance chemical products gas coal electricity and new energy.

Its Metals segment (about 10%) includes non-ferrous metal resources development and mining copper gold silver sulfuric acid copper foils materials for rolling and processing thin film materials non-ferrous metal recycling and industrial waste treatment transportation by ships non-ferrous metal products titanium and electric wires.

Its Oil and Natural Gas E&P business (less than 5% of revenue) offer oil and natural gas exploration development and production.

Other businesses include asphalt paving civil engineering work construction work electric wires land transportation real estate leasing business and common JX Group activities including fund procurement.

JX Holdings has a nearly 40% market share in Japan of both fuel oil marketing and lubricating oil marketing.

Geographic Reach

Based in Tokyo Japan ENEOS markets refined products across Japan; is engaged in exploration development and production of oil and gas in more than 15 countries around the world; and has stake in a copper mine in Chile.

Financial Performance

Note: Growth rates may differ after conversion to US Dollars.

ENEOS had a fluctuating revenue trend for the last five years. Still it has an overall growth of 33% in that period. Net income was also sporadic starting at a loss in 2015 resurfacing and climbing for the next few years then ultimately became a loss at 2019.

As a result of losses recorded due to inventory valuation of crude oil and products arising from the significant decline in the crude oil price and the recording of impairment loss in the Oil and Natural Gas E&P business the consolidated business results for this fiscal year which is the final year for the First Medium-Term Management Plan revenue decreased 10% from the previous fiscal year to Å 10 trillion and operating loss was Å 113.1 billion (profit of Å 537.1 billion in the previous fiscal year).

The cash and cash equivalents at the end of this fiscal year amounted to Å 393.3 billion an increase of Å 14.4 billion from the beginning of the fiscal year. Operating activities generated Å 510.7 billion while investing and financing activities used Å 371.3 billion and Å 119.8 billion respectively.

Strategy

JX Holdings allocates profits and cash reserves from its Japan-based petroleum refining and marketing operations and from other existing businesses to the development of petroleum natural gas and mineral resources as well as new energy businesses. In the near future it plans to formulate a new long-term vision for 2030.

In the meantime JX Holdings is working to strengthen its sales network by opening new service stations and converting others to self-service. It is also reevaluating its card strategy and expanding the number of service stations that offer the Dr. Drive car care service. The group is aiming to increase its production volume of 200000 barrels per day.

In Malaysia the installation work for the floating production storage and offloading (FPSO) system was completed in the Layang oil and gas field which had been producing natural gas since May 2017 in the SK10 mining area and the crude oil production was commenced in the field in December 2019.

In the United Kingdom North Sea the long-term development work such as the excavation of the production well installation of the production platform and laying of the pipelines was completed 5 in the Mariner oil field for which the development plan was approved in 2013 and the Culzean gas field for which the development plan was approved in 2015; the production of natural gas was commenced in the Culzean gas field in June 2019 and the production of crude oil was commenced in the Mariner oil field in August 2019. The development work under the development and production projects in the Culzean gas field and the Mariner oil field had been pushed forward in cooperation with operators and other business partners as large-scale projects in the United Kingdom North Sea in recent years and the projects are positioned as important ones which support the production of crude oil and natural gas by JXTG Group and contribute to the generation of cash flows in the future over the long term.

Company Background

The merger of Nippon Oil and Nippon Mining in 2010 was spurred on by changes in the Japanese oil industry including excess refining capacity due to the continued decline in domestic demand for refined petroleum products a growing consumer awareness of environmental issues and alternative energy options and a sluggish Japanese economy. Such trends prompted the two to consider restructuring and integrating their businesses to strengthen competitiveness. Following the merger JX Nippon set up upstream oil business JX Nippon Oil & Gas Exploration and metals unit JX Nippon Mining and Metals as operating subsidiaries.

Petroleum refining and marketing will continue to be a core segment that JX Holdings plans to expand further throughout Asia and arpund the world. However it may also look for future opportunities to engage in new energy markets such as fuel cells and photovoltaic power generation to keep up with the growing green trend.

In 2012 the company's wholly owned subsidiary JX Nippon Exploration and Production (U.K.) Limited signed sale and purchase agreements to acquire an extensive portfolio of non-operated oil and gas assets in the UK Continental Shelf from ENI. The assets give JX a substantial long-term oil and gas production base in the UK.

EXECUTIVES

President, Isao Matsushita, age 73
Executive Officer, Yuji Nakajima
Executive Officer, Satoru Uchida
Executive Officer, Susumu Hara
Executive Officer, Ichiro Yamamoto
Chairman, Yasushi Kimura, age 73
Auditors: Ernst & Young ShinNihon LLC

LOCATIONS

HQ: Eneos Holdings Inc
  1-1-2 Otemachi, Chiyoda-ku, Tokyo 100-8162
Phone: (81) 3 6257 7075
Web: www.hd.eneos.co.jp

2014 Sales

	% of total
Japan	74
China	19
Other countries	7
Total	**100**

PRODUCTS/OPERATIONS

2014 Sales

	% of total
Energy	87
Metals	8
Oil & natural gas exploration & production	2
Other	3
Total	**100**

COMPETITORS

Cosmo Oil	Mitsui Mining and
Exxon Mobil	Smelting
Honeywell	SK Innovation
International	Showa Shell Sekiyu
Idemitsu Kosan	Singapore Petroleum
Mitsubishi Electric	Sumitomo Metal Mining

HISTORICAL FINANCIALS

Company Type: Public

Income Statement				FYE: March 31
	REVENUE ($ mil.)	NET INCOME ($ mil.)	NET PROFIT MARGIN	EMPLOYEES
03/20	92,231	(1,731)	—	55,359
03/19	100,498	2,910	2.9%	54,978
03/18	97,008	3,408	3.5%	54,956
03/17	62,832	1,341	2.1%	47,777
03/16	77,810	(2,480)	—	37,860
Annual Growth	**4.3%**	**—**		**10.0%**

2020 Year-End Financials

Debt ratio: 0.2%	No. of shares (mil.): —
Return on equity: (-7.4%)	Dividends
Cash ($ mil.): 3,671	Yield: 5.6%
Current ratio: 1.06	Payout: —
Long-term debt ($ mil.): 12,768	Market value ($ mil.): —

	STOCK PRICE ($) FY Close	P/E High/Low		PER SHARE ($)		
				Earnings	Dividends	Book Value
03/20	7.21	—	—	(0.53)	0.41	6.61
03/19	9.00	0	0	0.86	0.36	7.36
03/18	11.80	0	0	1.00	0.32	6.99
03/17	9.82	0	0	0.54	0.30	6.13
03/16	7.73	—	—	(1.00)	0.28	5.36
Annual Growth	**(1.7%)**	**—**	**—**	**—**	**9.6%**	**5.4%**

Engie SA

Engie channels its energy into being Europe's top power gas and infrastructure player. It is engaged in the purchasing production and marketing of natural gas and electricity; the development and maintenance of major natural gas and electricity infrastructures; and the creation and marketing of energy and environmental services. With operations in about 70 countries power producer Engie has approximately 100 GW of installed capacity spanning natural gas nuclear coal solar onshore and offshore wind biomass and geothermal. Engie serves some 24 million customers. The company was formed when Gaz de France absorbed SUEZ in 2008.

Operations

Engie operates three core business Electricity Gas and Energy Services.

Engie's electricity-generation footprint spans nuclear solar hydroelectric offshore and onshore wind biomass geothermal and biogas. It professes nearly 100GW of installed capacity and around nearly 25GW being renewable. Engie's gas business carries out the transmission storage distribution and trade of natural gas and liquefied natural gas. It boasts Europe's biggest distribution network Europe's second largest storage capacity (and third globally) and operates around 130 biogas projects. Engie Energy Services provides engineering heating and cooling mechanics robotics. and other energy-efficiency services for municipalities companies and individuals.

To work efficiently Engie operates through nearly 25 business units about ten in France (including Elengy France BtoB and France Renewable Energy) about 15 in Europe and worldwide (including UK Benelux and North America) and global units (Global Energy Management Hydrogen GTT and Tractebel).France generates majority of the revenue (more than 30%) rest of Europe generates for more than 25% and the remaining revenues come from Latin America USA Canada and others.

Geographic ReachEngie has activities in about 70 countries power plants and natural gas terminals and storage facilities in about 5 continents and about 320 urban heating and cooling networks in almost 20 countries. Europe accounts for about 35% of sales with France alone accounting for about 40%. North America South America Asia Middle East and Africa accounts for the remaining of sales. Its headquarters is located in France.

Sales and Marketing

Engie serves about 24 million electric natural gas/LNG and energy services customers. It serves individuals cities and municipalities and corporations. Engie is among the world's largest electricity producers.

Engie records relatively light R&D spend at nearly ?190 million in 2019.

Financial Performance

The company's revenue increased by 5% to ?60.1 billion in 2019 compared to ?57.0 billion in the prior year. The increase was driven by scope effects including various acquisitions in Client Solutions (primarily in the United States with Conti France and Latin America with CAM) and in BtoB Supply in the US partially offset by the disposals of ENGIE's stake in Glow in Thailand in March 2019 and of BtoB Supply activities in Germany at the end of 2018.

Net income for the year 2019 increased by 1% maintaining the ?1.6 billion mark. The increase was primarily due to the increase on their revenue while losing their income on their discontinued operations.

Cash held by the company at the end of 2019 was ?1.8 billion higher (?10.5 billion) than the prior year with ?8.7 billion. Cash provided by operations and financing activities were ?8.2 billion and ?212 million respectively. Cash used by investing activities was ?7.2 billion.

Strategy

ENGIE continued to pursue its strategic focus (Client Solutions Networks Renewables Thermal and Nuclear) on the energy transition in 2019.

In Client Solutions ENGIE and its partners won commercial contracts for the University of Iowa (United States) government buildings in Ottawa (Canada) a "smart region" around Angers (France) and industrial buildings in Singapore. ENGIE Impact was created to bring large customers with solutions to build their sustainability roadmap and accelerate their energy transition.

In Networks ENGIE announced on June 13 2019 that the consortium in which it holds a majority stake completed the acquisition of a 90% shareholding in TAG the largest gas transmission network owner in Brazil. TAG has a portfolio of long-term contracts providing an attractive earnings stream and improves diversification of ENGIE's geographic footprint in Networks activities. In January 2020 ENGIE also further strengthened its position in Brazil by announcing the acquisition of a project of a 1800 km power transmission line.

In Renewables 3.0 GW of renewable capacity was commissioned and the 9 GW commissioning target over 2019-21 is now fully secured. The new joint-venture in Mexico with Tokyo Gas and the strategic partnership signed with Edelweiss Infrastructures Yield in India at the beginning of 2020 demonstrate ENGIE's ability to deploy the DBSO model and attract partners for the development of its portfolio.

In Thermal ENGIE continued to execute its carbon footprint reduction strategy with coal now approximately 4% of global power generation capacity following the disposal of its 69.1% stake in

Glow in Thailand and Laos (3.2 GW of generation capacity of which 1.0 GW is coal) ending its participation in coal in the Asia-Pacific region and the disposal of its German and Dutch coal assets (capacity of 2.3 GW).

In Nuclear an arrangement on Belgian nuclear provisions was reached reducing uncertainty for all parties regarding the level of provisions and their funding.

Mergers and Acquisitions

In 2019 Engie in partnership with Canadian investment firm CDPQ agreed to acquire the TAG (Transportada Associada de Gas) natural gas pipeline company from Brazilian oil major Petrobras. The about $8.6 billion deal plays into Engie's push into natural gas and low-emission energy and includes about 2800 miles of pipeline spanning ten states in the north of Brazil.

In 2019 Engie acquired Vol-V Biomasse a vertically integrated biomass company based in France. The acquisition makes Engie France's leading biomethane producer growing its portfolio to nearly 80 projects and helping it in its quest to produce about 5 TWh/year of biomethane by 2030. Terms were not disclosed.

EXECUTIVES

Executive Vice-President Energy Service, Jér´me Tolot, age 69

EVP Global Gas and LNG Business Line, Jean-Marie Dauger, age 68

Executive Vice-President Communications Marketing and Sustainable Development, Valérie Bernis, age 62

Chairman and CEO; Chairman SUEZ-TRACTEBEL GDF SUEZ Energy Services and SUEZ Environnement, Gérard Mestrallet, age 71

Executive Vice-President Energy International Business, Dirk Beeuwsaert, age 73

Chairman and CEO ONDEO-Degrémont, Jean-Louis Chaussade, age 69

Vice Chairman and President, Jean-Fran Şois Cirelli, age 62

EVP and COO, Isabelle Kocher, age 53

CEO of GDF SUEZ Energy International, Willem van Twembeke, age 55

Head Energy France, Henri Ducré, age 64

Group CIO, Yves Le Gélard

Executive Vice-President Infrastructures, Jean-Claude Depail, age 72

Director of Group Purchasing, Claire Brabec-Lagrange

Director of the Group Sales and Marketing, Jean-Louis Blanc

CEO Elengy, Martin Lestang

EVP and CFO, Judith Hartmann

Auditors: ERNST & YOUNG et Autres

LOCATIONS

HQ: Engie SA
1, Place Samuel de Champlain, Courbevoie 92400
Phone: (33) 1 44 22 00 00
Web: www.engie.com

2018 Sales

	% of total
Europe	
France	41
Belgium	10
Other EU countries	26
Other European countries	1
Asia Middle East and Oceania	8
North America	6
South America	7
Africa	1
Total	**100**

COMPETITORS

BG Group	Eni
Bouygues	Gas Natural SDG
CANAL+	Gasunie
Centrica	Gazprom
Covanta	Italgas
Dragados	National Grid
E.ON	RWE
Electricité de France	SABESP
Electricité de Strasbourg	United Utilities
	Vattenfall
Enel	Veolia Environnement

HISTORICAL FINANCIALS

Company Type: Public

Income Statement   FYE: December 31

	REVENUE ($ mil.)	NET INCOME ($ mil.)	NET PROFIT MARGIN	EMPLOYEES
12/19	67,431	1,104	1.6%	171,103
12/18	69,394	1,182	1.7%	249,795
12/17	77,953	1,705	2.2%	155,128
12/16	70,363	(438)	—	153,090
12/15	76,117	(5,028)	—	154,935
Annual Growth	(3.0%)	—	—	2.5%

2019 Year-End Financials

Debt ratio: 27.0%	No. of shares (mil.): —
Return on equity: 2.8%	Dividends
Cash ($ mil.): 11,810	Yield: 7.8%
Current ratio: 1.05	Payout: 220.4%
Long-term debt ($ mil.): 33,685	Market value ($ mil.): —

	STOCK PRICE ($) FY Close	P/E High/Low	Earnings	Dividends	Book Value
12/19	16.17	50 41	0.38	1.26	15.39
12/18	14.32	46 35	0.42	0.84	16.88
12/17	17.17	35 25	0.54	1.03	18.39
12/16	12.74	— —	(0.24)	1.04	17.43
12/15	17.60	— —	(2.17)	1.12	19.58
Annual Growth	(2.1%)	— —	—	3.1%	(5.8%)

ENI S.p.A.

Eni is one of the world's major oil and gas suppliers engaging in exploration development production and trading activities worldwide. Downstream its portfolio of refineries transmission networks and power generation plants sell fuels/biofuels chemical products lubricants and gas & power. Outside its home country of Italy Eni is active Africa Europe and North America as well as other productive gas regions such as Kazakhstan and Venezuela. Europe which accounts for most of Eni's sales is home to more than 5400 service stations. The company has 4.7 GW of installed energy generation capacity and more than 7 billion barrels of oil equivalent proved hydrocarbon reserves.

Operations

Eni has four reporting segments: Gas & Power; Exploration & Production; Refining & Marketing and Chemicals; and Corporate and Other activities.

Gas & Power generates more than 50% of Eni's total sales. The segment consists of Eni's supply and marketing of natural gas and LNG and the supply production and marketing of power. Natural gas and power reach wholesale and retail customers while LNG is sold to businesses/other entities only.

The Refining & Marketing and Chemicals segment accounts for around 25% of sales and comprises Eni's manufacturing supply and distribution and marketing activities of oil and chemical products.

Exploration & Production generates about 25% of sales. Explores for develops and produces crude oil LNG and natural gas including the construction and operations of liquefaction plants.

Corporate and other activities generates more than 1% of sales. It provide services to the operating subsidiaries comprising holding financing and treasury IT HR real estate legal assistance captive insurance as well as the results of the Group environmental.

Taking an Upstream-Downstream view of Eni the company's Upstream units have onshore and offshore projects that pick oil exploration blocks drill wells and manage the whole hydrocarbon production operations. In the Midstream and Downstream sectors Eni manages the transportation and storage of hydrocarbons as well as the refining marketing and distribution of oil products.

Geographic Reach

Based in Rome Italy Eni is active in more than 65 countries worldwide across Europe (Italy Norway and the UK) Africa (Algeria Angola Congo Egypt Ghana Libya Mozambique Nigeria) the US Venezuela and Kazakhstan. Of Eni's 5400 service stations in Europe about 4200 are in Italy.

Europe accounts for nearly 70% of annual sales Africa generates about 15% of sales Asia more than 10% of sales and the Americas gives in roughly 5% of sales.

Sales and Marketing

Eni spent ?176 million ?161 million and ?102 million in marketing expense for fiscal years 2019 2018 and 2017 respectively.

Financial Performance

Note: Growth rates may differ after conversion to US Dollars.

Total revenues amounted to ?71.0 billion reporting a decrease of 8%. Sales from operations in the full year of 2019 (?70.0 billion) decreased by ?5.9 billion or down by 8% from 2018.

In the full year 2019 the group reported net profit attributable to Eni's shareholders of ?148 million (?4.1 billion in the full year 2018). The reported operating profit was ?6.4 billion approximately 36% lower than in 2018 down by ?3.6 billion; approximately 80% of the decline is related to the E&P segment.

Eni's cash on hand fell during 2019 ending the year ?4.9 billion higher at ?6.0 billion. The company's operations generated ?12.4 billion while its investing activities used ?11.4 billion and its financing used ?5.8 billion. Its biggest cash uses were investments in tangible assets long-term debt repayments and dividends.

Strategy

Eni's business model is focused on creating value for its stakeholders and shareholders through a strong presence along the whole value chain.

Firstly Eni's business is constantly focused on the operational excellence. A continuous commitment to the valorization of people and in HSE to the safeguard of health and safety and environmental protection; the efficiency and resilience of operations thanks to which Eni has accelerated projects' time-to-market reducing its break-even; a solid financial discipline; and the maximum attention to the integrity and respect for human rights.

Secondly Eni's business model envisages a path to decarbonization with the ambition to lead the company to become carbon neutral in the long-term.

Lastly Eni's value creation will leverage on the alliances for the promotion of local development in its countries of operation. Eni is not only committed to address the valorization of resources of producing countries allocating its unity initiatives - from diversification of local economies to health projects education access to water and hygiene. This distinctive approach called Dual Flag is based on collaborations with institutions cooperation agencies and local stakeholders in order to identify certain necessary actions to meet the needs of communities in line with the National Development Plans and the 2030 UN Agenda.

EXECUTIVES

Chief Midstream Gas and Power Officer and Chairman Eni Trading & Shipping S.p.A., Massimo Mantovani, age 58
EVP Integrated Compliance, Luca Franceschini, age 54
CEO, Claudio Descalzi, age 66
CFO, Massimo Mondazzi, age 57
SEVP Corporate Affairs and Governance, Roberto Ulissi, age 58
SEVP Internal Audit, Marco Petracchini, age 56
EVP External Communication Department, Marco Bardazzi, age 54
Chief Retail Market Gas and Power Officer, Alberto Chiarini, age 57
Chief Exploration Officer, Luca Bertelli, age 62
SEVP Legal Affairs, Marco Bollini
Chief Development Operations & Technology Officer, Roberto Casula, age 58
EVP Energy Solutions, Luca Cosentino
EVP International Affairs, Lapo Pistelli, age 56
EVP Integrated Risk Management, Jadran Trevisan, age 59
Chief Upstream Officer, Antonio Vella, age 63
Chairman, Emma Marcegaglia, age 56
Auditors: PricewaterhouseCoopers SpA

LOCATIONS

HQ: ENI S.p.A.
   Piazzale Enrico Mattei 1, Rome 00144
Phone: (39) 2 52041730   **Fax:** (39) 2 52041765
Web: www.eni.com

2018 Sales

	% of total
Europe	
Italy	33
Other EU countries	27
Other countries	9
Asia	13
Africa	11
Americas	7
Total	**100**

PRODUCTS/OPERATIONS

2018 Sales

	% of total
Gas & power	57
Refining & marketing and chemicals	30
Exploration & production	13
Corporate & other activities	-
Total	**100**

Selected Subsidiaries and Affiliates

Distrigas NV (gas Belgium)
EniPower SpA (power generation)
Italgas SpA (natural gas supply)
Saipem SpA (42.9% oil field services)
Snam Rete Gas SpA (52.5% gas pipeline)
Snamprogetti SpA (contracting and engineering)

COMPETITORS

A2A	Hellenic Petroleum
Ashland	Marathon Oil
BASF SE	Occidental Petroleum
BG Group	PEMEX
BP	PETROBRAS
Chevron	Petr leos de
ConocoPhillips	Venezuela
ERG S.p.A.	Royal Dutch Shell
Edison	Sunoco
Exxon Mobil	TOTAL

HISTORICAL FINANCIALS

Company Type: Public

Income Statement				FYE: December 31
	REVENUE ($ mil.)	NET INCOME ($ mil.)	NET PROFIT MARGIN	EMPLOYEES
12/19	79,762	166	0.2%	32,053
12/18	88,109	4,725	5.4%	31,701
12/17	85,083	4,044	4.8%	32,934
12/16	59,861	(1,545)	—	33,536
12/15	75,095	(9,566)	—	29,053
Annual Growth	**1.5%**	**—**	**—**	**2.5%**

2019 Year-End Financials

Debt ratio: 27.4%   No. of shares (mil.): —
Return on equity: 0.3%   Dividends
Cash ($ mil.): 6,729   Yield: 4.3%
Current ratio: 1.18   Payout: 3,010.2%
Long-term debt ($ mil.): 26,574   Market value ($ mil.): —

	STOCK PRICE ($) FY Close	P/E High/Low	PER SHARE ($) Earnings	Dividends	Book Value
12/19	30.96	895726	0.04	1.33	15.03
12/18	31.50	33 26	1.32	1.37	16.22
12/17	33.19	40 33	1.13	1.39	15.99
12/16	32.24	— —	(0.43)	1.21	15.55
12/15	29.80	— —	(2.66)	1.53	15.65
Annual Growth	**1.0%**	**— —**	**—**	**(3.4%)**	**(1.0%)**

Equinor ASA

EXECUTIVES

Chairman Of The Board, Lars Johannes Nordli
Auditors: Ernst & Young AS

LOCATIONS

HQ: Equinor ASA
   Forusbeen 50, Stavanger N-4035
Phone: (47) 51 99 00 00   **Fax:** (47) 51 99 00 50
Web: www.statoil.com

HISTORICAL FINANCIALS

Company Type: Public

Income Statement				FYE: December 31
	REVENUE ($ mil.)	NET INCOME ($ mil.)	NET PROFIT MARGIN	EMPLOYEES
12/19	64,358	1,843	2.9%	21,412
12/18	79,593	7,535	9.5%	20,525
12/17	61,187	4,590	7.5%	20,245
12/16	45,873	(2,922)	—	20,539
12/15	54,781	(4,254)	—	21,581
Annual Growth	**4.1%**	**—**	**—**	**(0.2%)**

2019 Year-End Financials

Debt ratio: 24.5%
Return on equity: 4.3%
Cash ($ mil.): 5,177
Current ratio: 1.27
Long-term debt ($ mil.): 24,945

No. of shares (mil.): —
Dividends
  Yield: 5.0%
  Payout: 180.3%
Market value ($ mil.): —

	STOCK PRICE ($) FY Close	P/E High/Low		PER SHARE ($) Earnings	Dividends	Book Value
12/19	19.91	43	29	0.56	1.01	12.36
12/18	21.17	13	9	2.27	0.91	12.91
12/17	21.42	15	12	1.40	0.76	12.04
12/16	18.24	—	—	(0.91)	0.69	10.85
12/15	13.96	—	—	(1.34)	0.85	12.67
Annual Growth	9.3%	—	—	—	4.5%	(0.6%)

Ericsson

Auditors: PricewaterhouseCoopers AB

LOCATIONS

HQ: Ericsson
  Torshamnsgatan 21, Kista, Stockholm SE-164 83
Phone: (46) 10 719 0000
Web: www.ericsson.com

HISTORICAL FINANCIALS

Company Type: Public

Income Statement   FYE: December 31

	REVENUE ($ mil.)	NET INCOME ($ mil.)	NET PROFIT MARGIN	EMPLOYEES
12/19	38,023	372	1.0%	99,417
12/18	35,282	(1,092)	—	95,359
12/17	33,687	(5,891)	—	100,735
12/16	37,252	287	0.8%	111,464
12/15	41,320	2,267	5.5%	116,281
Annual Growth	(2.1%)	(36.4%)	—	(3.8%)

2019 Year-End Financials

Debt ratio: 2.2%
Return on equity: 2.6%
Cash ($ mil.): 7,543
Current ratio: 1.32
Long-term debt ($ mil.): 4,728

No. of shares (mil.): —
Dividends
  Yield: 1.2%
  Payout: 96.2%
Market value ($ mil.): —

	STOCK PRICE ($) FY Close	P/E High/Low		PER SHARE ($) Earnings	Dividends	Book Value
12/19	8.78	16	11	0.11	0.11	4.17
12/18	8.87	—	—	(0.33)	0.13	4.41
12/17	6.68	—	—	(1.80)	0.07	5.07
12/16	5.83	19	9	0.09	0.30	7.16
12/15	9.61	3	2	0.69	0.25	7.42
Annual Growth	(2.2%) (13.4%)	—	—	(36.5%)	(19.3%)	

Erste Group Bank AG

First there was Erste. Erste Group Bank is the holding company of Erste Bank Austria's first savings bank founded in 1819. However the company has grown beyond its home country to number some 2500 branches throughout Central and East-ern European that serve some 16.4 million customers. The company has operating subsidiaries in Austria Croatia the Czech Republic Hungary Slovakia Serbia and Romania as well as an indirect presence in four other countries in the region. Erste Group banks provide financial services such as savings and lending to individuals and small to medium-size businesses. It also has a private banking arm. Erste Bank is Austria's largest lender.

Operations

Erste Group operates through six segments Retail Corporates Group Markets Asset/Liability Management Savings Banks and a group corporate center. Retail Corporates and Savings Bank generate around 90% of sales.

The Retail segment serves private individuals micro businesses and freelance professionals through the local bank network together with leasing and asset management subsidiaries. It offers mortgages consumer loans investment products current accounts and savings products as well as cross-selling products such as leasing insurance and building society products. The segment brings in half of Erste's total sales.

Corporates serves businesses ranging from SMEs to large companies as well as commercial real estate and public sector businesses. The Savings Bank segment consists of the banks that are part of the Austrian Haftungsverbund cross-guarantee savings bank sector.

Geographic Reach

Erste Bank's home country of Austria is home to some 920 branches the most of any country. The Czech Republic has 520 Erste branches Romania 510 Slovakia 270 Croatia 155 Hungary 115 and Serbia 85.

Strategy

Erste is investing heavily in its digital capabilities to remain competitive in the long-term. In 2017 digital investments totaled one quarter of the bank's entire general administrative expense. The company is setting up a company-wide database which will act as a foundation for improved data quality and a simplified product portfolio as well as advancing group-wide process standardization.

Relatedly Erste has high hopes for its digital banking platform called George which it hopes to establish as the first pan-European banking platform in its seven core markets. The flexibility and customization of George's architecture supports third-party co-operation.

EXECUTIVES

Chairman, Andreas Treichl, $1,642,528 total compensation
Management Board Member Controlling and Information Management, Gernot Mittendorfer, age 56
Management Board Member Enterprise wide Risk Management, Andreas Gottschling, age 53
Management Board Member Investment Banking and Steering and Operating Office Corporates, Jozef Sikela
First Vice Chairman, Georg Winckler, age 77
Chairman, Friedrich R –DLER, age 70
Second Vice Chairman, Jan Homan, age 73
Auditors: Sparkassen-Prufungsverband (Prufungsstelle)

LOCATIONS

HQ: Erste Group Bank AG
  Am Belvedere 1, Vienna A-1100
Phone: (43) 5 0100 10100
Web: www.erstegroup.com

PRODUCTS/OPERATIONS

2017 Sales

	% of total
Net interest income	67
Net fee & commission income	36
Net trading result	1
Total	**100**

Selected Subsidiaries

Banca Comerciala Romana S.A. (BCR)
Ceská; Sporitelna (Czech Republic)
Erste Bank a.d. Novi Sad (Serbia)
Erste Bank Croatia (Erste & Steiermärkische Bank d.d.)
Erste Bank der oesterreichen Sparkassen AG
  Autoleasing EBV
  Sparkasse Salzburg
  Wohnbaubank
Erst Bank Hungary Nyrt.
Erste Bank Ukraine (formerly Bank Prestige)
Slovenská; sporitelna a.s. (Slovakia)

COMPETITORS

BAWAG
Banca Comerciala Romana
Bank Austria
Credit Suisse
Deutsche Bank
Deutsche Post
Deutsche Postbank
Erste & Steierm ɔrkische Bank
Investkredit
OTP Bank
Oberbank AG
RZB Group
UBS
UniCredit Bank AG

HISTORICAL FINANCIALS

Company Type: Public

Income Statement   FYE: December 31

	ASSETS ($ mil.)	NET INCOME ($ mil.)	INCOME AS % OF ASSETS	EMPLOYEES
12/19	275,855	1,650	0.6%	47,284
12/18	271,172	2,053	0.8%	47,397
12/17	264,516	1,577	0.6%	47,702
12/16	219,863	1,335	0.6%	47,034
12/15	217,562	1,054	0.5%	46,467
Annual Growth	6.1%	11.9%	—	0.4%

2019 Year-End Financials

Return on assets: 0.6%
Return on equity: 9.8%
Long-term debt ($ mil.): —
No. of shares (mil.): 408
Sales ($ mil): 11,302

Dividends
  Yield: 4.0%
  Payout: 21.1%
Market value ($ mil.): 7,656

	STOCK PRICE ($) FY Close	P/E High/Low		PER SHARE ($) Earnings	Dividends	Book Value
12/19	18.76	7	5	3.63	0.76	42.97
12/18	16.53	6	4	4.60	0.68	40.29
12/17	21.80	8	6	3.52	0.57	40.64
12/16	14.62	5	3	3.09	0.25	32.13
12/15	15.73	7	4	2.47	0.00	29.20
Annual Growth	4.5%	—	—	10.0%	—	10.1%

Essity Aktiebolag (Publ)

Auditors: Ernst & Young AB

LOCATIONS

HQ: Essity Aktiebolag (Publ)
P.O. Box 200, Stockholm SE-101 23
Phone: (46) 8 788 51 00
Web: www.essity.com

HISTORICAL FINANCIALS
Company Type: Public

Income Statement   FYE: December 31

	REVENUE ($ mil.)	NET INCOME ($ mil.)	NET PROFIT MARGIN	EMPLOYEES
12/19	13,864	990	7.1%	45,980
12/18	13,238	880	6.7%	47,000
12/17	13,317	989	7.4%	47,700
12/16	11,168	419	3.8%	0
12/15	11,686	727	6.2%	0
Annual Growth	4.4%	8.0%	—	—

2019 Year-End Financials

Debt ratio: 2.6%
Return on equity: 18.2%
Cash ($ mil.): 314
Current ratio: 0.97
Long-term debt ($ mil.): 4,295

No. of shares (mil.): 702
Dividends
  Yield: 1.9%
  Payout: 43.9%
Market value ($ mil.): 22,658

	STOCK PRICE ($) FY Close	P/E High/Low		PER SHARE ($) Earnings	Dividends	Book Value
12/19	32.26	3	2	1.41	0.62	8.28
12/18	24.50	2	2	1.25	0.68	7.50
12/17	28.52	3	2	1.41	0.70	7.34
Annual Growth	6.4%	—	—	0.0%	(3.0%)	3.1%

Eurobank Ergasias Services & Holdings SA

EXECUTIVES

chief executive, Fokion Christos Karavias
chairman, George Panagiotis Zanias
vice-chairman, George Konstantinos Chryssikos
Auditors: KPMG Certified Auditors S.A.

LOCATIONS

HQ: Eurobank Ergasias Services & Holdings SA
8 Othonos Street, Athens 105 57
Phone: (30) 210 333 7000   **Fax:** (30) 210 323 3866
Web: www.eurobank.gr

COMPETITORS

Alpha Bank
Emporiki Bank
National Bank of
  Greece

Piraeus Bank S.A.

Exor NV

LOCATIONS

HQ: Exor NV
Gustav Mahlerplein 25, Amsterdam, North Holland
1082 MS
Phone: (31) 20 240 2 222   **Fax:** (31) 20 240 2 738
Web: www.exor.com

HISTORICAL FINANCIALS
Company Type: Public

Income Statement   FYE: December 31

	REVENUE ($ mil.)	NET INCOME ($ mil.)	NET PROFIT MARGIN	EMPLOYEES
12/19	161,403	3,427	2.1%	23
12/18	164,099	1,542	0.9%	22
12/17	171,937	1,668	1.0%	21
12/16	147,895	621	0.4%	0
Annual Growth	3.0%	76.6%	—	—

2019 Year-End Financials

Debt ratio: —
Return on equity: 22.4%
Cash ($ mil.): 25,750
Current ratio: —
Long-term debt ($ mil.): —

No. of shares (mil.): 231
Dividends
  Yield: —
  Payout: 3.2%
Market value ($ mil.): —

	STOCK PRICE ($) FY Close	P/E High/Low		PER SHARE ($) Earnings	Dividends	Book Value
12/19	0.00	—	—	14.73	0.48	72.84
Annual Growth	—	—	—	—	—	—

Fairfax Financial Holdings Ltd

Fairfax Financial Holdings provides insurance reinsurance and other financial services around the globe. Its subsidiaries including Odyssey Group

HISTORICAL FINANCIALS
Company Type: Public

Income Statement   FYE: December 31

	ASSETS ($ mil.)	NET INCOME ($ mil.)	INCOME AS % OF ASSETS	EMPLOYEES
12/19	72,711	142	0.2%	13,456
12/18	66,403	104	0.2%	13,162
12/17	71,960	124	0.2%	15,816
12/16	70,103	242	0.3%	16,285
12/15	80,114	(1,286)	—	17,521
Annual Growth	(2.4%)	—	—	(6.4%)

2019 Year-End Financials

Return on assets: 0.2%
Return on equity: 2.1%
Long-term debt ($ mil.): —
No. of shares (mil.): —
Sales ($ mil): 3,047

Dividends
  Yield: —
  Payout: —
Market value ($ mil.): —

Allied World and Crum & Forster focus on property/casualty coverage and associated investment management. The company also offers reinsurance and specialty insurance policies. Its operations span countries in Southeast Asia Eastern Europe Middle East and Brazil. Chairman and CEO Prem Watsa's unorthodox business strategies have been compared to those of Warren Buffett; he controls more than 40% of the voting rights of Fairfax Financial. Majority of its sales were generated in the US.

Operations

Fairfax Financial's operating segments are largely represented by its subsidiaries: Odyssey Group (formerly OdysseyRe) Allied World Crum & Forster Brit Northbridge Zenith National Fairfax Asia Runoff Other Insurance and Reinsurance and Other (non-insurance operations).

US-based Odyssey Group accounting for about 25% of sales underwrites property/casualty reinsurance worldwide. It also underwrites specialty insurance primarily in the US and the UK including through the Lloyd's of London market.

Allied World (more than 15% of sales) provides property/casualty and specialty insurance and reinsurance worldwide (including on the Lloyd's exchange) while Crum & Forster (more than 15% of sales) provides commercial and specialty insurance in the US market.

Subsidiaries Brit (Lloyd's specialty insurance and reinsurance) Northbridge (commercial coverage in Canada) and Zenith National (US workers' compensation) each represent between 5% and 10% of sales.

Fairfax Asia includes the Falcon Pacific Insurance AMAG Insurance and Fairfirst Insurance subsidiaries and other assets. The Runoff segment includes discontinued activities in Europe and the US.

Non-insurance operations include stakes in restaurants and retail companies such as Recipe Pickle Barrel Toys R Us Canada Golf Town and William Ashley. It also has some freight energy financial technology and real estate investments.

About 55% of sales came from casualty insurance while property accounts for about 35% and specialty accounts for about 10%.

Geographic Reach

The company corporate office is located in Ontario Canada. It also has operations in the US in which the US accounts for about 60% of sales while international accounts for about 20% and the remaining accounts for Canada and Asia.

Sales and Marketing

The company uses brokers to distribute its business and in some instances will distribute through agents or directly to customers. The company may also conduct business through third parties such as managing general agents where it is cost effective to do so and where the company can control the underwriting process to ensure its risk management criteria are met. Each of these channels has its own distinct distribution characteristics and customers.

Financial Performance

The increase in income to $21.5 billion in 2019 from $17.8 billion in 2018 principally reflected increased net gains on investments higher net premiums earned increased other revenue and interest and dividends partially offset by decreased share of profit of associates.

Cash held by the company at the end of 2019 decreased by $686 million to $3.9 billion. Cash provided by operations was $1.4 billion while cash used for investing and financing activities were $1.2 billion and $0.8 billion respectively. Main uses for cash were purchases of investments in associates and repayments.

Strategy

The company's risk management strategy for debt instruments is to invest primarily in those of high credit quality issuers and to limit the amount of credit exposure to any one corporate issuer. Management considers high quality debt instruments to be those with an S&P or Moody's issuer credit rating of BBB/Baa or higher. While the company reviews third party credit ratings it also performs its own analysis and does not delegate the credit decision to rating agencies. The company endeavors to limit credit exposure by monitoring fixed income portfolio limits on individual corporate issuers and credit quality and may from time to time initiate positions in certain types of derivatives to further mitigate credit risk exposure.

Mergers and Acquisitions

In 2020 Fairfax Financial Holdings Limited announces that Prem Watsa its Chair and CEO has advised that over the last few days he has purchased in the market about 482600 subordinate voting shares of Fairfax for an aggregate purchase cost of approximately US$148.95 million.

In 2019 Fairfax Financial Holdings Limited announces that it has acquired an additional 256200 equity shares of Quess Corp Limited. Upon completion of the acquisition of these additional Quess shares and the previously announced spinout of Quess shares by Thomas Cook (India) Limited the parent of Quess and a subsidiary of Fairfax to its shareholders Fairfax will own more than 30% of Quess.

Company Background

Fairfax was founded in 1985 by Chairman and CEO V. Prem Watsa.

EXECUTIVES

VP International Operations, Jean Cloutier
President, Paul C. Rivett, age 52
Vice President and Chief Risk Officer, Peter Clarke
VP and CFO, David Bonham
Chairman and CEO, V.Prem Watsa
Auditors: PricewaterhouseCoopers LLP

LOCATIONS

HQ: Fairfax Financial Holdings Ltd
95 Wellington Street West, Suite 800, Toronto, Ontario M5J 2N7
Phone: 416 367-4941   **Fax:** 416 367-4946
Web: www.fairfax.ca

Sales 2016

	% of total
United States	62
Canada	13
Asia	11
International	14
Total	**100**

PRODUCTS/OPERATIONS

2016 Sales

	% of total
Casualty	56
Property	32
Specialty	12
Total	**100**

2016 Sales

	% of total
OdysseyRe	24
Crum & Forster	21
Brit	20
Northbridge	11
Zenith National	8
Fairfax Asia	7
Runoff	2
Other	7
Total	**100**

Selected Subsidiaries

Insurance
  Asian Insurance
  Falcon Insurance Company (Hong Kong) Ltd.
  First Capital Insurance Limited (Singapore)
  Canadian Insurance
  Northbridge Financial Corporation
  Commonwealth Insurance Company
  Federated Holdings of Canada Limited
  Lombard General Insurance Company of Canada
  Markel Insurance Company of Canada
  U.S. Insurance
  Crum & Forster Holdings Corporation
Reinsurance
  CRC (Bermuda) Reinsurance Limited
  Odyssey Re Holdings Corp.
  Polish Re (Poland)
  Wentworth Insurance Company Ltd. (Barbados)
Runoff
  nSpire Re Limited
  RiverStone Group LLC
  RiverStone Holdings Limited
  TRG Holding Corporation

COMPETITORS

AIG	Everest Re
Aviva	General Re
Baldwin & Lyons	ING
Berkshire Hathaway	Manulife Financial
Chubb Limited	Nationwide
Co-operators General	RenaissanceRe
Insurance	Sun Life
Economical Insurance	Travelers Companies
Group	Wawanesa Mutual

HISTORICAL FINANCIALS

Company Type: Public

Income Statement   FYE: December 31

	ASSETS ($ mil.)	NET INCOME ($ mil.)	INCOME AS % OF ASSETS	EMPLOYEES
12/19	70,508	2,004	2.8%	44,043
12/18	64,372	376	0.6%	39,043
12/17	64,090	1,740	2.7%	38,040
12/16	43,384	(512)	—	31,134
12/15	41,529	567	1.4%	23,576
Annual Growth	**14.1%**	**37.1%**	**—**	**16.9%**

2019 Year-End Financials

Return on assets: 2.9%	Dividends
Return on equity: 14.5%	Yield: 0.0%
Long-term debt ($ mil.): —	Payout: 14.3%
No. of shares (mil.): 27	Market value ($ mil.): 12,962
Sales ($ mil): 21,532	

	STOCK PRICE ($) FY Close	P/E High/Low	Earnings	PER SHARE ($) Dividends	Book Value
12/19	469.11	7 6	69.79	10.00	520.37
12/18	440.08	49 35	11.65	10.00	467.76
12/17	530.34	8 6	64.98	10.00	483.75
12/16	486.70	— —	(24.18)	10.00	411.01
12/15	471.00	25 18	23.15	10.00	447.02
Annual Growth	**(0.1%)**	**— —**	**31.8%**	**(0.0%)**	**3.9%**

Far East Horizon Ltd.

Auditors: Ernst & Young

LOCATIONS

HQ: Far East Horizon Ltd.
Suite 6305, 63/F, Central Plaza, 18 Harbour Road, Wanchai,
Phone: (852) 2588 8688   **Fax:** (852) 2511 8660
Web: www.fehorizon.com

HISTORICAL FINANCIALS

Company Type: Public

Income Statement   FYE: December 31

	ASSETS ($ mil.)	NET INCOME ($ mil.)	INCOME AS % OF ASSETS	EMPLOYEES
12/19	37,447	623	1.7%	17,903
12/18	38,668	571	1.5%	12,813
12/17	34,952	496	1.4%	11,558
12/16	23,986	415	1.7%	8,184
12/15	21,450	385	1.8%	6,084
Annual Growth	**14.9%**	**12.8%**	**—**	**31.0%**

2019 Year-End Financials

Return on assets: 1.6%	Dividends
Return on equity: 11.1%	Yield: —
Long-term debt ($ mil.): —	Payout: 28.9%
No. of shares (mil.): —	Market value ($ mil.): —
Sales ($ mil): 4,012	

Fast Retailing Co., Ltd.

Fast Retailing is the world's third-largest apparel retailer behind Inditex (owner of the ZARA brand) and H&M. Since 1963 the company has been working to fill the gap in Japan's casual wear market. Through its UNIQLO brand (a combination of the words unique and clothing) the company operates more than 2000 stores in Japan and in foreign markets including Greater China Southeast Asia and Oceania Europe and the US and Canada. Fast Retailing along with its subsidiaries markets functional basics for men women and children under the LifeWear concept of everyday comfort. The company's GU and Global Brands retail divisions also operate almost 1400 other stores selling products under the GU Theory Comptoir des Cotonniers J Brand and Princesse tam.tam brand names. .

Operations

The company operates in four business segments: UNIQLO Japan UNIQLO International GU and Global Brands.

UNIQLO is Fast Retailing's mainstay brand offering basic casualwear at reasonable prices. UNIQLO Japan operates about 830 stores and contributes more than 40% of the company's total revenue. UNIQLO International (more than 40%) operates about 1250 stores.

GU is considered to be the company's more low-priced "fun" fashion brand and generates about 10% of sales through almost 400 stores. Its Global Brands business (more than 5%) operates through close to 1000 stores and features clothing under the Theory Comptoir des Cotonniers Princesse tam.tam and J Brand names.

Fast Retailing is a specialty store retailer of private label apparel (SPA) using a business model where the company controls the entire process from design through manufacture and retail sales.

Geographic Reach
Based in Tokyo Japan Fast Retailing operates through about 3400 stores in Japan Greater China Southeast Asia and Oceania the US and Canada Europe and Russia. Its product development centers are located in the cities of Tokyo New York London Paris Shanghai and Los Angeles.

Sales and Marketing
Fast Retailing's UNIQLO divisions sell products via stores and e-commerce channels and market core products via TV commercials promotional flyers and through email and social media. Online sales in the US account for about 20% of UNIQLO's overall revenue and in China about 15%. In Japan more than 7% of UNIQLO's business is conducted online; the company is hoping to increase online sales in Japan by allowing customers to collect online purchases from nearby UNIQLO stores.

Financial Performance
Fast Retailing has seen an upward trend in revenue over the last five years with double-digit growth in 2018. Sales increased by 14% to Å 2130 billion in 2018 (ended August) compared with Å 1812 million the previous year.

Along with higher sales net income also increased by 30% to Å 154.8 billion in 2018. Athough improving UNIQLO North America posted a profit loss in 2018 with brand visibility still low in the US and Canada.

Cash at the end of fiscal 2018 was Å 69.4 billion an increase of Å 9.6 billion from the prior year. Cash from operations contributed Å 176.4 billion to the coffers while investing activities used Å 57.2 billion mainly for purchases of property and equipment related to building out store networks. Accounting for dividends to stockholders financing activities provided Å 198.2 billion primarily from the inflow from a corporate bond issue.

Strategy
Already Asia's largest apparel retailer Fast Retailing seeks no less than to become #1 in the world by 2020. To succeed it plans to leverage its successful model of combining quality and aggressive pricing of its private-label apparel with the international expansion of its UNIQLO chain. It is also looking to integrate its physical stores and e-commerce operations to give customers a seamless experience.

The company is focused on producing reasonably-priced yet high-quality clothing designed for relaxed everyday comfort?a concept it calls LifeWear. To increase sales the company has recently developed several new products including its cold-weather HEATTECH innerwear Ultra Light Down and its 3D Knit fabric that uses technology to produce a whole garment seamlessly.

Fast Retailing aims to change the entire consumer retail industry by transforming its supply chain with an information-driven digital approach to managing and integrating design planning production distribution and retail sales. Dubbed the Ariake Project the company is working to build a supply chain that uses advanced information technology to create links between the company's partner factories warehouses and stores worldwide. It's using a new partnership with Google and its own vast amounts of information to analyze big data such as colors and design features popular with consumers. Fast Retailing is also using technology such as artificial intelligence and advanced algorithms to more accurately predict fluctuating production volumes. The company has incorporated RFID tags on all products and working with logistics partner Daifuku Co. Ltd. opened its first fully automated warehouse dedicated to online sales in 2018.

In 2018 UNIQLO International surpassed UNIQLO Japan in sales for the first time. The company has seen rapid growth in Greater China Southeast Asia South Korea and India. It plans to open more large-format stores in prime urban locations (and promote its GU brand) in Asian markets in the future. Plans are underway to expand in Europe as well; its first store opened in Sweden in 2018. To become profitable in the US Fast Retail also is planning new large-format stores in prime locations versus smaller stores in declining American shopping malls.

EXECUTIVES

Chairman President and CEO, Tadashi Yanai, age 71
Group EVP, Shuichi Nakajima
Group EVP, Ning Pan
Group EVP, Takeshi Okazaki
Group EVP, Osamu Yunoki
Group EVP and Head Production Dept., Yoshihiro Kunii
Group EVP, Takahiro Wakabayashi
President Global Creative, John C. Jay
Group EVP, Takao Kuwahara
Group EVP, Taku Morikawa
Auditors: Deloitte Touche Tohmatsu LLC

LOCATIONS

HQ: Fast Retailing Co., Ltd.
Midtown Tower, 9-7-1 Akasaka, Minato-ku, Tokyo 107-6231
Phone: (81) 3 6865 0050
Web: www.fastretailing.com

PRODUCTS/OPERATIONS

2018 sales

	% of total
UNIQLO International	42
UNIQLO Japan	41
GU	10
Global Brands	7
Total	**100**

COMPETITORS

AEON	L.L. Bean
Benetton	Marui Group
Bloomingdale's	Mitsukoshi
Daiei	Otto Group
Daimaru	Seiyu
H&M	Takashimaya
Inditex	The Gap
Isetan	Tokyu Department Store
Isetan Mitsukoshi	Wal-Mart
Ito-Yokado	

HISTORICAL FINANCIALS
Company Type: Public

Income Statement | | | | FYE: August 31

	REVENUE ($ mil.)	NET INCOME ($ mil.)	NET PROFIT MARGIN	EMPLOYEES
08/20	20,254	911	4.5%	128,492
08/19	23,095	1,639	7.1%	137,281
08/18	21,476	1,560	7.3%	124,679
08/17	18,773	1,202	6.4%	76,143
08/16	18,012	484	2.7%	69,921
Annual Growth	**3.0%**	**17.1%**	**—**	**16.4%**

2020 Year-End Financials

Debt ratio: —	No. of shares (mil.): 102
Return on equity: 9.5%	Dividends
Cash ($ mil.): 11,025	Yield: 0.7%
Current ratio: 2.56	Payout: 4.9%
Long-term debt ($ mil.): —	Market value ($ mil.): 6,113

	STOCK PRICE ($)	P/E		PER SHARE ($)		
	FY Close	High/Low		Earnings	Dividends	Book Value
08/20	59.87	0	0	8.91	0.44	94.46
08/19	58.49	0	0	16.04	0.43	92.73
08/18	46.58	0	0	15.28	0.34	85.29
08/17	28.65	0	0	11.78	0.31	72.35
08/16	35.18	0	0	4.75	0.31	56.81
Annual Growth	**14.2%**	**—**	**—**	**17.1%**	**9.1%**	**13.6%**

Faurecia SA (France)

Take a seat — Faurecia is one of the world's largest automotive seat makers. In addition to car seats it also manufactures emission control systems vehicle interiors and doors and front-end systems. Although Europe accounts for over 50% of sales it supplies most major carmakers including GM Ford and Volkswagen. Faurecia also deals in precious metals and ceramics for use in its catalytic converter businesses though Faurecia Exhaust Systems which together with EMCON Technologies makes emission control technologies in the US. Bertrand Faure and ECIA a Peugeot S.A. subsidiary merged in 1999 to create Faurecia. Faurecia has struggled to keep its CEO seat filled going through three executives in less than five years.

Operations
Faurecia operates four business units. Emission Control Technologies the largest segment accounting for around 36% of sales designs and manufactures exhaust systems; Automotive Seating representing 28% of sales designs and assembles vehicle seats seating frames and adjustable mechanisms; Interior Systems (25% of sales) makes instrument panels door panels and modules and acoustic components; and Automotive Exteriors (11%) designs and manufactures front ends and safety modules.

Geographic Reach
Faurecia has 330 sites including 30 R&D centers in 34 countries around the world. Europe is the company's largest market at some 55% of sales.

Sales and Marketing
Faurecia works with some of the biggest names in the automotive industry. Its five main customers represent 72% of sales. VW leads the way with 22.7% followed by Ford (15.9%) PSA (Peugeot Citroen 13.3%) GM (7.6%) and Daimler (7.1%).

Financial Performance
Note: Growth rates may differ after conversion to US Dollars.

In fiscal 2015 sales climbed 9% to ?20.7 billion. Product sales (parts and components) were up 6.0% while sales of tooling R&D prototypes and other services were down 15.6%. Catalytic converter monolith sales (precious metals and ceramics used in emission control systems) were up 12.4%.

Net income was up 123% to ?371.8 million due to higher margins in Europe and an upturn in product sales in North America partially offset by lower sales in South America as a result of the region's difficult economic climate and lower sales in Asia (despite reduced costs). The company's cash position strengthened markedly due mostly to the sale of the Automotive Exteriors business up to ?1.25 billion from a low base.

Strategy
Faurecia signed a definitive agreement to sell its Automotive Exteriors business which had revenue of around ?2.0 billion in fiscal 2015 to Plastic

Omnium for ?665 million. The deal does not include Faurecia's composites business its Smart plant in France or two joint ventures in Brazil and China. The sale of the business is to reduce debt which it will do almost entirely.

Faurecia has high hopes for its composites business as the automotive industry looks increasingly towards lightweighting in search of greater fuel efficiency.

In 2015 Faurecia formed a joint venture with Beijing WKW Automotive Parts in order to strengthen its position in China.

EXECUTIVES

EVP Faurecia China, Jean-Michel Vallin, age 65
EVP Faurecia North America, Mark Stidham
EVP Faurecia Emissions Control Technologies, Christophe Schmitt
EVP Faurecia Group Human Resources, Jean-Pierre Sounillac
CEO, Patrick Koller
EVP Faurecia and Group CFO, Michel Favre
EVP Faurecia Interior Systems, Jean-Michel Renaudie
EVP Faurecia Group Strategy, Hervé Guyot
EVP Faurecia Group Communications, Kate Philipps
EVP Faurecia Automotive Seating, Hagen Wiesner, age 59
EVP Group Operations, Eelco Spoelder, age 48
Chairman, Yann Delabriere
Auditors: Mazars

LOCATIONS

HQ: Faurecia SA (France)
23-27, avenue des Champs-Pierreux, Nanterre 92000
Phone: (33) 1 72 36 70 00   **Fax:** (33) 1 72 36 70 07
Web: www.faurecia.com

2016 Sales

	% of total
Europe	52
North America	28
Asia	16
South America	3
Rest of the World	1
Total	**100**

PRODUCTS/OPERATIONS

2016 Sales

	% of total
Clean Mobility	39
Automotive Seating	35
Interior Systems	26
Total	**100**

2016 Sales by Customer

	% of total
VW Group	15
Ford group	14
Renault-Nissan	12
Peugeot S.A.	11
GM	8
Daimler	6
BMW	4
Others	30
Total	**100**

COMPETITORS

Benteler Group	Magna International
DURA Automotive	Magneti Marelli
IAC Group	Meritor
Kongsberg Automotive	Tenneco
Lear Corp	Visteon

HISTORICAL FINANCIALS

Company Type: Public

Income Statement

FYE: December 31

	REVENUE ($ mil.)	NET INCOME ($ mil.)	NET PROFIT MARGIN	EMPLOYEES
12/19	19,949	662	3.3%	115,496
12/18	20,069	802	4.0%	114,693
12/17	24,192	731	3.0%	109,275
12/16	19,756	673	3.4%	98,608
12/15	20,444	404	2.0%	102,869
Annual Growth	(0.6%)	13.1%	—	2.9%

2019 Year-End Financials

Debt ratio: 25.7%
Return on equity: 15.0%
Cash ($ mil.): 2,604
Current ratio: 0.92
Long-term debt ($ mil.): 3,472

No. of shares (mil.): 136
Dividends
  Yield: —
  Payout: 30.3%
Market value ($ mil.): —

Ferguson PLC (New)

Ferguson PLC is one of the world's largest distributors of heating and plumbing supplies to professional contractors. The company distributes heating and cooling equipment plumbing supplies pipes valves safety equipment and fire protection products as well as building materials in North America and Europe. Key customers include building contractors plumbing and heating engineers and industrial and mechanical contractors. In 2019 the company announced it was spinning off its Wolseley subsidiary as a separate public company. Wolseley will focus on the UK market while Ferguson will concentrate solely on customers in the UK.

EXECUTIVES

Chief Executive Officer, Frank Roach
Chief Executive Officer, Ian Meakins
Chairman, Gareth Davis
Auditors: Deloitte LLP

LOCATIONS

HQ: Ferguson PLC (New)
1020 Eskdale Road, Winnersh Triangle, Wokingham RG41 5TS
Phone: (44) 0118 927 3800   **Fax:** (44) 118 929 8701
Web: www.fergusonplc.com

2011 Sales

	% of total
North America	
US	40
Canada	6
UK	18
Nordic region	16
France	14
Central Europe	6
Total	**100**

PRODUCTS/OPERATIONS

2011 Sales by Market

	% of total
Residential repair maintenance & improvement	36
Non-residential repair maintenance & improvement	21
Residential new construction	20
Non-residential new construction	16
Civil infrastructure	7
Total	**100**

2011 Sales by Product

	% of total
Plumbing heating & air conditioning	40
Building materials	30
Civil/waterworks commercial & industrial	28
Other	2
Total	**100**

Selected Products

Building materials
  Beams and trusses
  Bricks blocks and aggregates
  Cement
  Doors and frames
  Glass
  Insulation
  Plaster and plasterboard
  Roofing materials
  Tiles and flooring
  Timber products
Civil/waterworks industrial and commercial
  Carbon and stainless steel pipes valves and fittings
  Drainage pipes
  Underground pressure pipes
Plumbing heating and air conditioning
  Air conditioning equipment
  Baths and showers
  Boilers and burners
  Brassware
  Control equipment
  Copper tubing
  Heat pumps
  Hot water cylinders
  Plastic pipes and fittings
  Radiators and valves
  Sanitaryware
  Solar equipment
  Ventilation equipment
Other
  Electrical cables
  Lighting
  Wiring
  Services
  Customer inventory management
  Installation
  Maintenance

Selected Subsidiaries

CFM
  Heating appliances Luxembourg
DT Group
  Building materials Denmark
Ferguson Enterprises Inc.
  Wholesale distribution of plumbing heating and piping products US
Manzardo SpA
  Heating and plumbing equipment Italy
OAG AG
  Heating and plumbing products Austria
PB&M
  Building materials and wood distribution France
Tobler
  Heating and plumbing products Switzerland
Wasco Holding BV
  Heating equipment The Netherlands
Wolseley Canada
  Wholesale distribution of plumbing heating and ventilation products Canada
Wolseley France
  Building materials plumbing and heating products France
Wolseley UK Limited
  Construction products UK
Woodcote Group
  Construction materials Czech Republic

COMPETITORS

84 Lumber	MPS Builders and
B&Q	Merchants
Castorama Dubois	MSC Industrial Direct
Emco Corporation	Noland
Grafton Group	SIG plc
HD Supply	Saint-Gobain Building
HSS Hire	Distribution
Hewden Stuart	Speedy Hire
Interline Brands	Thermador Groupe
Jewson	Travis Perkins
Kingfisher	Waxman
Lowe's	

HISTORICAL FINANCIALS
Company Type: Public

Income Statement				FYE: July 31
	REVENUE ($ mil.)	NET INCOME ($ mil.)	NET PROFIT MARGIN	EMPLOYEES
07/19	26,798	1,349	5.0%	35,939
07/18	27,308	1,667	6.1%	34,056
07/17	19,971	1,027	5.1%	33,511
07/16	19,017	868	4.6%	39,717
07/15	20,761	331	1.6%	40,375
Annual Growth	6.6%	42.0%	—	(2.9%)

2019 Year-End Financials
Debt ratio: 25.1%	No. of shares (mil.): 230
Return on equity: 26.3%	Dividends
Cash ($ mil.): 1,379	Yield: 0.3%
Current ratio: 1.72	Payout: 43.5%
Long-term debt ($ mil.): 2,795	Market value ($ mil.): 1,717

	STOCK PRICE ($) FY Close	P/E High/Low		PER SHARE ($)		
				Earnings	Dividends	Book Value
07/19	7.46	2	1	5.82	2.53	23.01
07/18	7.90	2	1	6.74	2.49	23.03
07/17	6.01	2	2	4.28	1.52	18.80
07/16	5.58	2	2	3.54	1.39	16.00
07/15	6.71	8	5	1.35	1.49	16.47
Annual Growth	2.7%	—	—	44.2%	14.2%	8.7%

FIH Mobile Ltd

Auditors: Deloitte Touche Tohmatsu

LOCATIONS
HQ: FIH Mobile Ltd
No. 369 Jianshe South Road, Anci District, Langfang City, Hebei Province
Phone:
Web: www.fihmb.com

HISTORICAL FINANCIALS
Company Type: Public

Income Statement				FYE: December 31
	REVENUE ($ mil.)	NET INCOME ($ mil.)	NET PROFIT MARGIN	EMPLOYEES
12/19	14,378	(12)	—	85,729
12/18	14,929	(857)	—	97,484
12/17	12,080	(525)	—	92,779
12/16	6,233	138	2.2%	74,652
12/15	7,450	229	3.1%	81,013
Annual Growth	17.9%	—	—	1.4%

2019 Year-End Financials
Debt ratio: 8.6%	No. of shares (mil.): —
Return on equity: (-0.5%)	Dividends
Cash ($ mil.): 1,545	Yield: —
Current ratio: 1.18	Payout: —
Long-term debt ($ mil.): —	Market value ($ mil.): —

Financiere De L Odet SA (France)

EXECUTIVES
Chairman and CEO, Vincent Bolloré, age 68
Auditors: Constantin Associés

LOCATIONS
HQ: Financiere De L Odet SA (France)
Odet, Ergue-Gaberic 29500
Phone: (33) 1 46 96 44 33   **Fax:** (33) 1 46 96 44 22
Web: www.financiere-odet.com

2016 Sales
	% of total
France and overseas departments and territories	39
Africa	22
Europe excluding France	17
Americas	13
Asia/Pacific	9
Total	**100**

PRODUCTS/OPERATIONS

2016 Sales
	% of total
Transportation and logistics	54
Communications	23
Oil logistics	19
Electricity storage and solutions	3
Other activities	1
Total	**100**

2016 Sales
	% of total
Provision of services	77
Sale of goods	21
Income from associated activities	2
Total	**100**

COMPETITORS
Anglo-Eastern Plantations	Geodis
	New Britain Palm
DHL	SIPH
DP World	

HISTORICAL FINANCIALS
Company Type: Public

Income Statement				FYE: December 31
	REVENUE ($ mil.)	NET INCOME ($ mil.)	NET PROFIT MARGIN	EMPLOYEES
12/19	27,918	136	0.5%	83,801
12/18	26,393	139	0.5%	81,003
12/17	22,148	442	2.0%	74,828
12/16	10,682	241	2.3%	58,023
12/15	11,813	323	2.7%	55,383
Annual Growth	24.0%	(19.4%)	—	10.9%

2019 Year-End Financials
Debt ratio: 23.7%	No. of shares (mil.): 4
Return on equity: 3.2%	Dividends
Cash ($ mil.): 3,304	Yield: —
Current ratio: 0.82	Payout: 3.4%
Long-term debt ($ mil.): 10,585	Market value ($ mil.): —

First Abu Dhabi Bank PJSC

Auditors: KPMG Lower Gulf Limited

LOCATIONS
HQ: First Abu Dhabi Bank PJSC
FAB Building, Khalifa Business Park 1 Al Qurum, P. O. Box 6316, Abu Dhabi
Phone:
Web: www.bankfab.com

HISTORICAL FINANCIALS
Company Type: Public

Income Statement				FYE: December 31
	ASSETS ($ mil.)	NET INCOME ($ mil.)	INCOME AS % OF ASSETS	EMPLOYEES
12/19	223,817	3,409	1.5%	5,451
12/18	202,620	3,270	1.6%	0
12/17	182,156	2,486	1.4%	0
12/16	114,537	1,441	1.3%	0
12/15	110,691	1,424	1.3%	0
Annual Growth	19.2%	24.4%	—	—

2019 Year-End Financials
Return on assets: 1.6%	Dividends
Return on equity: 11.9%	Yield: —
Long-term debt ($ mil.): —	Payout: 67.2%
No. of shares (mil.): —	Market value ($ mil.): —
Sales ($ mil): 9,095	

Flex Ltd

Flex Ltd. a top contract manufacturer offers solutions that span from initial design through ramp-up and volume manufacturing as well as through end of life and circularity offerings. Flex's services range from design engineering to manufacturing and assembly to logistics to innovation services and power modules. It makes and assembles printed circuit board assembly and assembly of systems and subsystems that incorporate printed circuit boards and complex electromechanical components. Its customer roster includes Abbott Philips Johnson & Johnson Ford Nexteer Fiat Chrysler Teradyne Dyson Xerox Cisco Nokia Ericssons Lenovo/Motorola HP and Bose. Flex covers a lot of ground around the world operating more than 100 locations in approximately 30 countries. Majority of the company's revenue are generated from international markets.

Operations

Flex divides its business into four segments: Industrial & emerging industries Communications & enterprise compute Consumer technologies group and High reliability solutions.

Operations under the Industrial & Emerging Industries segment around 30% of revenue include semiconductor and capital equipment office solutions industrial automation and kiosks household industrial and lifestyle.

The Communications & Enterprise Compute segment almost 30% of revenue makes equipment that includes radio access base stations remote radio heads and small cells for wireless infrastructure; optical routing and switching products for the data and video networks; server and storage platforms for both enterprise and cloud based deployments; storage and security appliance products; and rack-level solutions converged infrastructure and software-defined product solutions.

The Consumer Technologies Group over 20% of revenue includes our consumer-related businesses in IoT enabled devices audio and consumer power electronics mobile devices; and various supply chain solutions for consumer computing and printing devices.

The High Reliability Solutions group some 20% of revenue makes products for medical application including urgical equipment drug delivery diagnostics telemedicine disposable devices imaging and monitoring patient mobility and ophthalmology; and our automotive business including vehicle electrification connectivity autonomous and smart technologies.

Geographic Reach

Flex operates a network of more than 100 facilities in approximately 30 countries across five continents. Its extensive network of innovation labs design centers manufacturing and services sites in the world's major consumer and enterprise products markets are located in Asia the Americas and Europe.

The company's headquarters is located in Changi South Lane Singapore and its headquarters in U.S. is located in San Jose California.

Customers in China account for about 25% of sales with customers in Mexico generating nearly 20% of sales and US customers supplying some 15%.

Sales and Marketing

Flex delivers technology innovation supply chain and manufacturing solutions to various industries such as automotive and healthcare. Among the company's customers are Abbott Philips and Johnson & Johnson Ford Nexteer Fiat Chrysler Teradyne Dyson Xerox Cisco Nokia Ericsson Lenovo/Motorola HP and Bose.

Financial Performance

Flex had uneven revenue for the past five years. Net sales for fiscal year 2020 decreased 8% or $2.0 billion to $24.2 billion from the prior year. With the exception of Flex's IEI segment whose net sales increased $1.1 billion net sales for all of its remaining segments declined from the previous year.

Net income totaled $88 million representing a decrease of $6 million or 6% compared to fiscal year 2019.

Flex held about $1.9 billion in cash in 2020 compared to about $1.7 billion the year before. In 2020 the company had a negative cash flow of $1.5 billion while investing activities provided $2.3 billion and financing activities used $508.5 billion.

Strategy

Flex helps customers responsibly build products that create value and improve people's lives. It does this by providing its customers with product development lifecycle services from innovation design and engineering to manufacturing supply chain solutions logistics and circularity offerings. Its strategy is to enable and scale innovation for customers maintain its leadership in its capabilities and build extended offerings in high-growth industries and markets.

Talent. To maintain the company's competitiveness and world-class capabilities Flex focuses on hiring and retaining the world's best talent. It has taken steps to attract the best engineering functional and operational leaders and have accelerated efforts to develop the future leaders of the company.

Customer Focus. Flex believes that building strong partnerships with customers and delivering on its commitments strengthens trust and customer retention. Its customers come first and it has a relentless focus on delivering distinctive

products and services in a cost-effective manner with fast time to market. Flex is highly collaborative and leverages its global system and processes to operate with speed and responsiveness to provide customers with a reliant supply chain partner.

Market Focus. Flex focuses on companies that are leaders in their industry and value the company's superior capabilities in design manufacturing and supply chain services. It focuses on high-growth industries and markets where it has distinctive competence and compelling value propositions. Examples include its investments in specific technologies and industries including healthcare automotive industrial markets and energy. Flex's market-focused approach to managing business increases customers' competitiveness by leveraging its deep vertical industry and cross-industry expertise as well as global scale regional presence and agility to respond to changes in market dynamics.

Global Operations Capabilities. The company continues to invest in maintaining the leadership of its world-class manufacturing and services capabilities including automation new product introduction and large-scale manufacturing.

EXECUTIVES

CEO, Michael M. (Mike) McNamara, age 63, $1,250,000 total compensation

President Automotive, Christopher J. Obey

President Innovation and New Ventures, Jeannine P. Sargent, age 55

CFO, Christopher E. (Chris) Collier, age 52, $700,000 total compensation

President Industrial and Emerging Industries, Douglas (Doug) Britt, age 55

President Global Operations and Components, Fran §ois Barbier, age 61, $710,000 total compensation

EVP and General Counsel, D. Scott Offer, age 55, $316,955 total compensation

President Flex Ide8, Fei Liu

President High Reliability Solutions, Paul J. Humphries, age 65, $710,000 total compensation

President Consumer Technologies Group, Mike Dennison

President Communications and Enterprise Compute, Caroline Dowling

President Strategic Partnerships, Ruvi Shaibel

President Multek, Franck Lize

President Manufacturing Operations, Tzahi Rodrig

SVP Information Technology/Systems (IT/IS) and CIO, Gus Shahin

Chairman, Michael D. Capellas, age 65

Auditors: DELOITTE & TOUCHE LLP

LOCATIONS

HQ: Flex Ltd
2 Changi South Lane, 486123
Phone: (65) 6876 9899
Web: www.flex.com

2018 Sales

	$ mil.	% of total
China	6,649	25
Mexico	4,539	17
US	3,106	12
Brazil	2,181	8
Malaysia	1,996	8
India	1,805	7
Other countries	5,935	23
Total	**26,211**	**100**

PRODUCTS/OPERATIONS

2018 Sales

	$ mil.	% of total
Communications & Enterprise Compute	8,336	32
Consumer Technologies Group	6,836	26
Industrial & emerging industries	6,813	24
High reliability solutions	4,829	18
Total	**26,211**	**100**

Selected Services

Assembly and manufacturing
　Box build (complete systems)
　Complex electromechanical components
　Printed circuit boards (PCBs)
　Subsystems (including those that incorporate PCBs)
Engineering
　Design
　Prototyping
　Test development
Materials procurement and management
　Planning
　Purchasing
　Warehousing
Network support
　Installation and maintenance of telecommunications systems and corporate networks
Packaging
Plastic and metal components
Product distribution
Recycling and refurbishment
Testing of PCBs subsystems and systems
Warranty repair

COMPETITORS

ASUSTeK	Plexus
Benchmark Electronics	Quanta Computer
Cal-Comp Electronics	SYNNEX
Celestica	Sanmina
Compal Electronics	TTM Technologies
Hon Hai	Venture Corp.
Jabil	Wistron
Pegatron	

HISTORICAL FINANCIALS

Company Type: Public

Income Statement

FYE: March 31

	REVENUE ($ mil.)	NET INCOME ($ mil.)	NET PROFIT MARGIN	EMPLOYEES
03/20	24,209	87	0.4%	160,000
03/19	26,210	93	0.4%	200,000
03/18	25,441	428	1.7%	200,000
03/17	23,862	319	1.3%	200,000
03/16	24,418	444	1.8%	200,000
Annual Growth	(0.2%)	(33.4%)	—	(5.4%)

2020 Year-End Financials

Debt ratio: 20.7%　　　　　　No. of shares (mil.): 497
Return on equity: 3.0%　　　Dividends
Cash ($ mil.): 1,922　　　　　Yield: —
Current ratio: 1.26　　　　　 Payout: —
Long-term debt ($ mil.): 2,689　Market value ($ mil.): —

Fomento Economico Mexicano, S.A.B. de C.V.

From soda pop to shops FEMSA is quenching Mexico's thirsty throats. Fomento Econ mico Mexicano or FEMSA is a top soft drink bottler and convenience store operator in Latin America. Its Coca-Cola FEMSA subsidiary is the world's largest

Coca-Cola bottler. FEMSA bottles Coca-Cola Sprite other soft drinks juices and water in twelve Latin American countries. FEMSA also owns more than 19000 OXXO convenience stores in Colombia Chile and Peru primarily in the northern part of the country through its FEMSA Comercio subsidiary. Over 70% of FEMSA's revenue comes from Mexico and Central America.

Operations

FEMSA holds (15%) stake in Heineken. In addition to its beverage operations and retail holdings (The OXXO chain is the largest and fastest-growing in the Americas.) it provides logistics refrigeration services and plastics to internal and external customers.The company's business units include Coca-Cola FEMSA (more than 35% of sales) and FEMSA Comerico which is divided to Proximity division (approximately 35% of sales) Health division (around 10%) and Fuel division (about 10%). Other business unit accounts for the rest.

Geographic Reach

Headquartered in Nuevo Le n Mexico FEMSA operates in Argentina Brazil Colombia Costa Rica Guatemala Mexico Nicaragua Panama and Ecuador. Subsidiary Coca-Cola FEMSA operates in Argentina Brazil Central America Colombia Mexico and Venezuela.

Mexico and Central America provided most of the company's revenues more than 70%.

Sales and Marketing

FEMSA advertised its products through product promotions and image advertising campaigns.

Financial Performance

FEMSA's revenue increased 8% from M$469.7 million in 2018 to M$506.7 million in 2019. Coca-Cola FEMSA's total revenues increased 6.7% driven by price increases aligned with inflation volume growth in key territories the consolidation of its acquisitions in Guatemala and Uruguay partially offset by the depreciation of the Argentine peso the Brazilian real and the Colombian peso in each case as compared to the Mexican peso.

The company's net income was M$20.7 million an 8% decrease from the previous year. The higher gross profit was offset by an even higher expense.

The company's cash at the end of 2019 totaled M$65.6 million. Operating activities generated M$61.6 million while investing activities used M$14.1 million mainly for capital expenditures. Financing activities used another M$38.4 million mainly for bank loans payments.

Strategy

FEMSA understands the importance of connecting with its end consumers by interpreting their needs and ultimately delivering the right products to them for the right occasions and the optimal value proposition. The company strives to achieve this by developing brand value expanding its significant distribution capabilities and improving the efficiency of its operations while aiming to reach its full potential. FEMSA continues to improve its information gathering and processing systems in order to better know and understand what consumers want and need and it is improving its production and distribution by more efficiently leveraging its asset base.

Mergers and Acquisitions

In late 2019 Fomento Econ mico Mexicano S.A.B. de C.V. announced that Solistica FEMSA's logistics subsidiary has successfully completed the acquisition of AGV a leader in value-added warehousing and distribution in Brazil. This transaction represents an important new building block for Solistica's strategy in Brazil. Solistica will now become the first fully integrated Third Party Logistics (3PL) solution provider in the Brazilian market building a key differentiating factor among the leading players in the industry. Terms were not disclosed.

Also in 2019 Fomento Econ mico Mexicano S.A.B. de C.V. announced that FEMSA Comercio through its majority-owned subsidiary Socofar has successfully completed the acquisition of Corporaraci n GPF a leading drugstore operator based in Quito Ecuador for an undisclosed terms. This transaction represents a new building block of FEMSA Comercio's drugstore strategy in South America.

EXECUTIVES

CEO Coca-Cola FEMSA, Carlos Salazar Lomel n, age 69

VP Corporate Development, Federico Reyes Garc a, age 75

CFO, Eduardo Padilla Silva, age 63

VP Administration and Corporate Control, José Gonz lez Ornelas, age 69

CEO FEMSA Empaques, Alfonso Garza Garza, age 58

CEO FEMSA Comercio, Daniel Rodr guez Cofré

Chairman and CEO, José Antonio Fern ndez Carbajal

Auditors: Mancera, S.C. (member of Ernst & Young Global)

LOCATIONS

HQ: Fomento Economico Mexicano, S.A.B. de C.V. General Anaya 601 Poniente, Colonia Bella Vista, Monterrey, Nuevo Leon 64410
Phone: (52) 81 8328 6000   **Fax:** (52) 81 8328 6080
Web: www.femsa.com

2014

	Geography mil (pesos)	%
Mexico and Central America	186,736	71
South America	69,172	26
Venezuela	8,835	3
Consolidation adjustments	(1294)	-
Total	**263,449**	**100**

PRODUCTS/OPERATIONS

2014

	Business Unit mil (pesos)	%
Coca-Cola FEMSA	147,298	53
FEMSA Comercio	109,624	40
Other	20,069	7
Consolidation Adjustments	(13542)	-
Total	**263,449**	**100**

COMPETITORS

Andina	Empresas Polar
Arca Continental	Nestlé Waters
Danone Water	Organizaci n Cultiba
Dr Pepper Snapple Group	Pepsi Amercias Beverages

HISTORICAL FINANCIALS

Company Type: Public

Income Statement				FYE: December 31
	REVENUE ($ mil.)	NET INCOME ($ mil.)	NET PROFIT MARGIN	EMPLOYEES
12/19	26,782	1,094	4.1%	314,656
12/18	23,888	1,219	5.1%	297,073
12/17	23,373	2,152	9.2%	295,097
12/16	19,307	1,021	5.3%	266,144
12/15	17,935	1,017	5.7%	246,158
Annual Growth	**10.5%**	**1.8%**	**—**	**6.3%**

2019 Year-End Financials

Debt ratio: 1.0%	No. of shares (mil.): —
Return on equity: 8.1%	Dividends
Cash ($ mil.): 3,465	Yield: 1.5%
Current ratio: 1.26	Payout: 2,758.8%
Long-term debt ($ mil.): 5,377	Market value ($ mil.): —

	STOCK PRICE ($) FY Close	P/E High/Low	PER SHARE ($) Earnings	Dividends	Book Value
12/19	94.51	98 85	0.05	1.48	0.74
12/18	86.05	80 68	0.06	1.39	0.73
12/17	93.90	44 37	0.11	1.29	0.71
12/16	76.21	84 70	0.05	1.17	0.57
12/15	92.35	110 80	0.05	1.37	0.58
Annual Growth	**0.6%**	**— —**	**1.8%**	**2.0%**	**6.3%**

Fonterra Co-Operative Group Ltd

Green lush and overflowing with cows New Zealand makes more milk than its citizens can drink. Fonterra Co-operative Group sells the excess and value-added dairy products to some 140 markets around the world (China is its largest single market). The co-op is the world's largest dairy exporter providing industrial dairy ingredients as well as fluid milk yogurt cheese and ice cream for consumers. Its well-known brands include Anchor Anmum Anlene NZMP and Farm Source. Fonterra operates more than 30 manufacturing sites across New Zealand which process some 16 billion liters of milk annually. The co-op is owned by its 10000 farmer shareholders.

Financial Performance

Fonterra's revenue has been trending up since fiscal 2016 (ended July) but overall is still down 8% since fiscal 2014. Net income had been growing strongly until fiscal 2017 when it fell slightly; it plummeted into the red in fiscal 2018.

In fiscal 2018 the company reported revenue of NZ$20.4 billion up 6% from the prior year. Growth was powered by Asia which offset a steep decline in the US and flat performance in other areas. Fonterra had less volume to sell because of low opening inventories and lower milk collections but was able to overcome that by shifting more of its volume to higher-value products.

Net income fell dramatically that year from NZ$734 million in fiscal 2017 to a loss of NZ$221 million. The results were impacted by two one-off items: a payment related to the 2013 recall of three batches of Whey Protein Concentrate because of a potential food safety issue as well as an impairment loss from the company's investment in China-based Beingmate Baby & Child Food Co.

Cash at the end of fiscal 2018 was NZ$285 million a decrease of NZ$97 million from the prior year. Cash from operations contributed NZ$1.5 billion to the coffers while investing activities used NZ$948 million mainly for capital expenditures. Financing activities used another NZ$725 million for dividends to stockholders and interest paid.

Strategy

Fonterra's primary strategy is moving more of its milk into higher-value products. Since fiscal 2016 it has invested in more than half a dozen plants and lines to turn more milk into cheese cream butter and other value-added items. The company's fiscal 2019 plans call for a new cream cheese plant at Darfield a third mozzarella line at Clandeboye and a new butter line at Edgecumbe.

It is also focused on cost control and evaluation of its major assets partnerships and holdings particularly in light of its net loss in fiscal 2018. Fonterra is specifically looking at its nearly 20% stake in Beingmate the Chinese foodservice company which has not met expectations.

EXECUTIVES

CEO, Theo C. A. Spierings
COO NZMP, Kelvin Wickham
COO Global Consumer and Foodservice, Lukas Paravicini
Managing Director Global Operations, Robert Spurway
Global CIO, Gerben Otter
COO Velocity and Innovation, Judith Swales
COO Farm Source, Miles Hurrell
Acting CFO, Paul Washer
Chairman, John Wilson
Auditors: KPMG

LOCATIONS

HQ: Fonterra Co-Operative Group Ltd
   Private Bag 92032, Auckland 1142
Phone: (64) 9 374 9000   **Fax:** (64) 9 374 9001
Web: www.fonterra.com

2018 Sales

	% of total
China	20
Other Asia	28
Latin America	11
New Zealand	10
Australia	9
US	4
Europe	3
Rest of World	15
Total	**100**

PRODUCTS/OPERATIONS

2018 Sales

	% of total
Ingredients	69
Consumer and Food Service	30
China Farms	1
Total	**100**

COMPETITORS

Arla Foods	Land O'Lakes
Burns Philp	Megmilk Snow Brand
Dairy Farmers of America	Meiji Co.
	Mondelez International
Danone	Murray Goulburn Co-op
Emmi	Nestlé
FrieslandCampina	Saputo
Glanbia plc	Tate & Lyle
Goodman Fielder	Terrena
Lactalis	Wesfarmers

HISTORICAL FINANCIALS

Company Type: Public

Income Statement

FYE: July 31

	REVENUE ($ mil.)	NET INCOME ($ mil.)	NET PROFIT MARGIN	EMPLOYEES
07/20	13,511	456	3.4%	0
07/19	13,291	(368)	—	0
07/18	13,934	(150)	—	0
07/17	14,402	549	3.8%	21,400
07/16	12,237	576	4.7%	21,300
Annual Growth	**2.5%**	**(5.6%)**	**—**	**—**

2020 Year-End Financials

Debt ratio: 22.5%
Return on equity: 10.9%
Cash ($ mil.): 524
Current ratio: 1.43
Long-term debt ($ mil.): 3,515
No. of shares (mil.): 1,612
Dividends
   Yield: —
   Payout: —
Market value ($ mil.): —

Fortescue Metals Group Ltd

Iron may be a bit dull to your point of view but Fortescue Metals Group thinks it shines as brightly as any gold. The company Australia's third-largest miner (behind Rio Tinto and BHP Billiton) has more than 1 billion tons of iron ore reserves; it began production in 2008 and produced about 165 million tons in fiscal 2015. It shipments has already been sold to steel producers around the world including Chinese steel producers such as Baosteel. As the infrastructure in the region wouldn't support mining operations the company built a rail line and two ports to make its operations commercially viable.

Operations

Fortescue Metals has discovered and developed significant iron ore deposits and constructed some of the largest mines in the world.

The Chichester Hub which includes the Cloudbreak and Christmas Creek mines is located in the Chichester Ranges and produces more than 90 million tonnes per annum of iron ore and an additional six mtpa from Fortescue's joint venture with BC Iron.

The Solomon Hub is located in the Hamersley Ranges and includes the Firetail and Kings Valley mines which produce in excess of 70 million tons per year. The company has constructed world class facilities at its five-berth Herb Elliott Port in Port Hedland and operates the fastest heavy haul railway in the world with up to 42 ton axle load capacity over 620 km of track including 12 bridges.

Fortescue Metals has a large tenement portfolio in the Pilbara Western Australia. The exploration drilling program is focused primarily on identifying and defining new targets for bedded mineralization in and around the existing Chichester and Solomon Hubs. It also manages a joint venture covering 320 sq. km. near Orange in central New South Wales in an area prospective for copper.

Fortescue Metals wholly owns its purpose-designed rail and port facilities constructed to support the production and sale of iron ore from its mines in the remote areas of Pilbara.

Geographic Reach

Based in Australia Fortescue Metals' primary market is China which in fiscal 2015 (June year end) accounted for 94% of the company's total sales.

Financial Performance

After experiencing stable revenue growth since fiscal 2010 the company's revenues decreased by 27% to $8.6 billion compared to $11.8 million in fiscal 2015 due to a decline revenue from sales of iron ore. Revenues from the sale of iron ore decreased by 28% reflecting the impact of lower realized price of $7.2 billion offset by a $4 billion increase generated from higher shipments.

Fortescue Metals net income has been on the same trend at its revenues. In fiscal 2015 the company's net income decreased by 88% due to a decline in revenues.

In fiscal 2015 the company's operating cash inflow decreased by 67% primarily due to a decline in net income and a change in working capital items.

Strategy

The company continues to evaluate opportunities that afford low cost entry to exploration potential in a range of commodities including green technology. For instance the company is investing on making transportation of hydrogen economically viable. In 2019 Fortescue Metals agreed to fund Commonwealth Scientific and Industrial Research Organisation's (CSIRO) metal membrane technology hoping to transform hydrogen into a low-emission fuel.

Company Background

Fortescue Metals was formed in 2003 after its majority shareholder The Metal Group purchased Allied Mining & Processing.

EXECUTIVES

CEO, Neville (Nev) Power
Director Operations, Greg Lilleyman
CFO, Elizabeth Gaines
Director Sales and Marketing, David Liu
Chairman, Andrew (Twiggy) Forrest, age 58
Auditors: PricewaterhouseCoopers

LOCATIONS

HQ: Fortescue Metals Group Ltd
   Level 2, 87 Adelaide Terrace, East Perth, Western Australia 6004
Phone: (61) 8 6218 8888   **Fax:** (61) 8 6218 8880
Web: www.fmgl.com.au

2015 Sales

	% of total
China	94
Others	6
Total	**100**

PRODUCTS/OPERATIONS

2015 Sales

	% of total
Sales of iron ore	97
Sales of joint venture ore	1
Other revenue	2
Total	**100**

COMPETITORS

BHP Billiton	Rio Tinto Limited
International Ferro Metals	Vale

HISTORICAL FINANCIALS

Company Type: Public

Income Statement

FYE: June 30

	REVENUE ($ mil.)	NET INCOME ($ mil.)	NET PROFIT MARGIN	EMPLOYEES
06/20	12,820	4,735	36.9%	0
06/19	9,965	3,187	32.0%	0
06/18	6,887	879	12.8%	0
06/17	8,447	2,093	24.8%	0
06/16	7,083	984	13.9%	3,890
Annual Growth	**16.0%**	**48.1%**	**—**	**—**

2020 Year-End Financials

Debt ratio: 18.1%
Return on equity: 39.6%
Cash ($ mil.): 4,855
Current ratio: 2.25
Long-term debt ($ mil.): 4,193
No. of shares (mil.): —
Dividends
   Yield: 10.4%
   Payout: 78.5%
Market value ($ mil.): —

	STOCK PRICE ($) FY Close	P/E High/Low		PER SHARE ($) Earnings	Dividends	Book Value
06/20	19.21	14	6	1.53	2.01	4.30
06/19	12.70	12	5	1.03	1.39	3.44
06/18	6.53	34	23	0.28	0.52	3.12
06/17	8.03	17	8	0.67	0.44	3.12
06/16	5.28	17	6	0.32	0.06	2.70
Annual Growth	**38.1%**			**— 48.4%**	**142.0%**	**12.4%**

Fosun International Ltd

EXECUTIVES

Director, Yongyi Zhou
Auditors: Ernst & Young

LOCATIONS

HQ: Fosun International Ltd
  Room 808, ICBC Tower, 3 Garden Road, Central,
Phone: (852) 2509 3228   **Fax:** (852) 2509 9028
Web: www.fosun.com

HISTORICAL FINANCIALS

Company Type: Public

Income Statement				FYE: December 31
	REVENUE ($ mil.)	NET INCOME ($ mil.)	NET PROFIT MARGIN	EMPLOYEES
12/19	20,548	2,127	10.4%	71,000
12/18	15,898	1,949	12.3%	70,000
12/17	13,526	2,022	15.0%	63,000
12/16	10,651	1,478	13.9%	53,000
12/15	12,132	1,237	10.2%	55,800
Annual Growth	14.1%	14.5%	—	6.2%

2019 Year-End Financials

Debt ratio: 4.1%	No. of shares (mil.): —
Return on equity: 12.8%	Dividends
Cash ($ mil.): 13,458	Yield: —
Current ratio: 1.04	Payout: 23.1%
Long-term debt ($ mil.): 18,043	Market value ($ mil.): —

Fresenius Medical Care AG & Co KGaA

Fresenius Medical Care is one of the largest dialysis providers in the world. Its staff treats approximately 340000 patients at some 4000 dialysis clinics worldwide about half of which are based in the US. In addition to performing dialysis Fresenius Medical Care is a leading manufacturer of dialysis machines dialyzers and other supplies that are sold to hospitals and clinics through internal sales efforts and independent distributors. It also offers dialysis support services including laboratory testing and care coordination programs. Fresenius SE owns about 30% of Fresenius Medical Care.

Operations

Dialysis care services account for a majority (80%) of annual revenue. The company provides hemodialysis treatments through its global network of 4000 dialysis clinics as well as on an as-needed basis for contracted hospitals. Related offerings include laboratory diagnostic and medication administration services as well as the provision of equipment and support for home dialysis patients. Care coordination offerings include renal pharmacy and health plan management services and operation of vascular access urgent care and specialist physician practices.

Dialysis products accounting for about 20% of sales include hemodialysis machines dialyzers peritoneal dialysis cyclers hemodialysis concentrates bloodlines and water treatment systems. It also makes renal pharmaceuticals apheresis (blood cleansing) products liver support therapies and acute cardiopulmonary products.

Geographic Reach

With a majority of its operations in the US (North America accounts for about 70% of sales) Fresenius Medical Care is increasing its presence in other regions including Europe Latin America and the Middle East. The company has dialysis clinic operations in about 50 countries while its dialysis products segment serves customers in 150 countries.

Fresenius Medical Care?s corporate headquarters is in Bad Homburg Germany. The North America operations are based in Waltham Massachusetts while the Asia-Pacific headquarters is located in Hong Kong and the Latin America headquarters is in Rio de Janeiro.

Sales and Marketing

Fresenius Medical Care's core dialysis care segment relies heavily on Medicare reimbursement; Medicare's end stage renal disease (ESRD) program accounts for about 45% of patient service revenue. Private and alternative payers including Medicaid account for the remainder of sales. Products are sold to dialysis clinics (including its own clinics) hospitals and specialty care facilities.

The company markets its dialysis products through local sales forces independent distributors dealers and sales agents. Products are shipped from central and regional warehouse facilities to dialysis centers and patients' homes.

Financial Performance

Note: Growth rates may differ after conversion to US Dollars.

The company reported strong sales growth each year from 2014 to 2017 but revenues declined slightly in 2018 due to divestitures. Overall sales increased more than 25% over the five-year period. Net income increased each year between 2014 and 2018.

Revenue in 2018 decreased 7% to some ?16.5 billion in 2018 due to the divestiture of the Sound Physicians operations.

Net income attributable to Fresenius Medical Care shareholders rose by about 55% to nearly ?2 billion in 2018 due to lower sales and administrative expenses cost of revenues and interest expense.

The company ended 2018 with ?2.1 billion in cash up ?1.2 billion from 2017. Operating activities contributed ?2.1 billion while investing activities used ?245 million (mostly on property equipment and acquisitions minus divestiture proceeds) and financing activities used ?681.7 million via debt payments dividends and distributions.

Strategy

Fresenius Medical Care has been a leading consolidator of dialysis treatment (renal care) operations particularly in the US. It typically grows by opening or acquiring singular or small groups of dialysis locations in targeted regions. The firm is working to expand in emerging markets; it added its first dialysis centers in China in 2018.

The company is also looking to grow by offering new dialysis products and technologies including upgrades on its existing equipment lines. In 2019 it introduced the 4008A dialysis machine which caters to customers in emerging markets by minimizing costs.

To further broaden its operations Fresenius Medical Care is expanding into additional areas beyond patient care and dialysis products such as dialysis medication (drugs regulating patient mineral and blood levels) and home therapies. It has formed partnerships with several drugmakers and is pursuing additional acquisitions and partnerships in those fields. It acquired home dialysis equipment maker NxStage Medical in 2019 and it formed a partnership with biotech research firm Humacyte in 2018.

The company has also entered several outpatient care markets outside of renal care such as urgent care ambulatory surgery and cardiovascular and endovascular care centers. In 2018 however Fresenius Medical Care sold its majority stake in Sound Physicians a hospital physician management group to streamline its care coordination offerings.

Mergers and Acquisitions

In early 2019 Fresenius Medical Care acquired NxStage Medical for about $2 billion. The deal expanded the company's presence in the US (a key target market) and provided it with NxStage's portfolio of portable dialysis machines. The company is focused on growing its home therapy operations as pressure mounts on health providers to lower operating costs.

Company Background

Fresenius Medical Care was formed in 1996 by the merger of Fresenius AG's dialysis systems division with chemical maker W. R. Grace's National Medical Care (NMC) dialysis services division. Fresenius traces its roots back to the 1462 founding of Hirsch Pharmacy in Frankfurt (acquired by the Fresenius family in the 18th century) and its 1966 entry into the dialysis equipment market. NMC was founded in 1968 by Constantine Hampers who opened his first dialysis clinic in Boston in 1971.

In 1998 Fresenius Medical Care expanded its clinics through the purchase of NEOMEDICA and expanded its laboratory services by buying Spectra Laboratories. Subsequent acquisitions expanded international operations.

In 2005 the company transformed its structure from a corporation to a share-limited partnership; the restructuring included a name change from Fresenius Medical Care AG to Fresenius Medical Care AG & Co. KGaA.

The company acquired US rival Renal Care Group which had 460 locations in 2006. Later acquisitions added dialysis medications and dialysis filter cartridges.

In 2017 Fresenius Medical Care acquired day-hospital operator Cura Group to further expand in Australia's dialysis market.

EXECUTIVES

Chairman Management Board and CEO, Rice Powell, age 64, $700,000 total compensation
CFO, Michael Brosnan, age 64
CEO Global Research and Development, Olaf Schermeier, age 46
CEO Global Manufacturing Operations, Kent Wanzek, age 59
CEO Europe Middle East and Africa (EMEA), Dominik Wehner, age 50
CEO North America, William (Bill) Valle, age 60
CEO Asia-Pacific, Harry de Wit, age 57
Chairman Supervisory Board, Gerd Krick, age 82
Vice Chairman, Dieter Schenk, age 68
Auditors: KPMG AG Wirtschaftsprüfungsgesellschaf

LOCATIONS

HQ: Fresenius Medical Care AG & Co KGaA
  Else-Kroener-Strasse 1, Bad Homburg 61352
Phone: (49) 6172 608 2522   **Fax:** (49) 6172 609 2301
Web: www.fmc-ag.com

2011 Sales

	% of total
North America	
Dialysis care	57
Dialysis products	6
International	
Dialysis products	19
Dialysis care	17
Total	**100**

PRODUCTS/OPERATIONS

2011 Payer Breakdown

	% of total
Medicare ESRD program	46
Private/alternative payers	43
Medicaid & other government sources	6
Hospitals	5
Total	**100**

Selected Acquisitions

COMPETITORS

Amgen	MEDIVATORS
Asahi Kasei	Nephros
B. Braun Melsungen	NxStage
Baxter International	Quest Diagnostics
DaVita	Rockwell Medical
Dialysis Clinic Inc	Terumo
Gambro AB	Tivity Health
LabCorp	Toray Industries

HISTORICAL FINANCIALS

Company Type: Public

Income Statement

FYE: December 31

	REVENUE ($ mil.)	NET INCOME ($ mil.)	NET PROFIT MARGIN	EMPLOYEES
12/19	19,622	1,346	6.9%	120,659
12/18	18,949	2,269	12.0%	112,658
12/17	21,318	1,534	7.2%	114,000
12/16	17,910	1,243	6.9%	109,319
12/15	16,737	1,029	6.2%	104,033
Annual Growth	4.1%	7.0%	—	3.8%

2019 Year-End Financials

Debt ratio: 46.9%	No. of shares (mil.): 298
Return on equity: 10.1%	Dividends
Cash ($ mil.): 1,131	Yield: 1.2%
Current ratio: 1.02	Payout: 10.1%
Long-term debt ($ mil.): 11,816	Market value ($ mil.): 10,987

	STOCK PRICE ($) FY Close	P/E High/Low		PER SHARE ($) Earnings	Dividends	Book Value
12/19	36.83	11	8	4.45	0.45	45.00
12/18	32.39	8	5	7.39	0.43	43.88
12/17	52.55	13	11	4.99	0.41	38.41
12/16	42.21	12	9	4.06	0.31	35.30
12/15	41.84	14	11	3.38	0.30	32.38
Annual Growth	(3.1%)	—	—	7.1%	10.9%	8.6%

Fresenius SE & Co KGaA

Fresenius offers a wide range of dialysis and infusion products and services through its four core business segments which operate as legally independent entitites: Fresenius Medical Care Fresenius Kabi Fresenius Helios and Fresenius Vamed. The company's Medical Care division specializes in treating chronic kidney failure in almost 4000 dialysis clinics worldwide. Fresenius Kabi provides nutrition infusion and IV therapies and related equipment. Fresenius Helios operates private hospitals in Germany while Fresenius Vamed offers facility management project development and other services to hospitals and health facilities. Fresenius has operations in more than 100 countries and the Europe is its biggest market.

Operations

Of its four segments Medical Care is Fresenius' largest at around half the company's annual sales. Helios brings in around a quarter Kabi a fifth and Vamed is the remainder or so.

Medical Care serves almost 350000 patients via a network of upwards of around 4000 clinics. Its production sites found on every continent provide dialysis products (machines dialyzers and disposables).

Fresenius Helios runs some 110 hospitals (including about 90 acute-care facilities and seven maximum-care hospitals) with more than 35000 beds in Germany.

Fresenius Kabi produces IV drips and other infusion and nutrition devices.

Fresenius Vamed provides project development planning technical and operation management and turnkey construction services to hospitals and other health care facilities around the world.

Geographic Reach

Headquartered in Bad Homburg near Frankfurt in Germany. North America is Fresenius' largest market at more than 40% of total sales. Europe follows with almost 45% while the Asia/Pacific region (more than 10%) Latin America (5%) and Africa account for the remainder.

The company's 90 or so production sites are located in the US China Japan Germany and Sweden. The company also has production facilities in other European countries and in Latin America and South Africa.

Sales and Marketing

Fresenius offers its products and services to hospitals and other health care organizations. Their sales and marketing network is divided among their markets. In around 65 sales and marketing organizations worldwide their employees are committed to improving the patients' quality of life each day.

Financial Performance

Note: Growth rates may differ after conversion to US Dollars.

The company's revenue increased by 8% to ?35.5 billion compared to ?33.0 billion in the prior year. The rise was due to the increase of every business segment of the company.

Fresenius' net income in 2019 rise to ?1.9 billion a ?43 million increase compared to ?1.87 billion in 2018. The increase was due to the increase on their revenue and decrease on their noncontrolling interest in profit.

Fresenius' cash ending the year 2019 at ?1.7 billion a ?1.1 billion decrease. Cash provided by operations was ?4.3 billion while cash used for investing and financing activities were ?4.9 billion and ?484 million respectively.

Strategy

Fresenius invests in and manages a diversified portfolio of healthcare businesses that create value. With their four business segments they focus on a defined number of health care areas. The company continuously develop those business areas and strive to assume leading positions in the respective healthcare areas. Fresenius has a defined strategic priorities to pursue its goal to strengthen the position of the company as a leading global provider of products and therapies for critically and chronically ill patients: Profit from megatrends: gearing businesses towards the megatrends health and demographics; Create value: long-term value creation by allocating capital to profitable growth areas; Act responsibly: commitment to responsible management and ethical business principles; and Collaborate: fostering intragroup cooperation to leverage synergies.

Mergers and Acquisitions

In mid-2020 Fresenius acquires Malteser Hospital ("MKHB") in the western German city of Bonn. MKHB offers a wide range of medical services with specialties in general surgery pulmonology and oncology including palliative care. The acquisition will greatly strengthen our Helios team in North Rhine-Westphalia.

Fresenius Helios acquires Centro Médico Imbanaco (CMI) in Cali further expanding the company's presence in Colombia's attractive private hospital market.

In late 2019 Fresenius Helios acquires has acquired CediMed a leading medical diagnostics group in Colombia for ?40. The acquisition will be another step in strengthening the company's presence in Latin America's growing and consolidating healthcare services markets.

In 2019 Fresenius Medical Care acquired Nxstage Medical a US-based medical technology and services company with annual sales of around $366 million. The $2 billion deal will strengthen Fresenius' dialysis business.

HISTORY

Fresenius was founded as the Hirsch Pharmacy in 1462. The Fresenius family took over its ownership in the 18th century and converted it into a pharmaceutical manufacturing entity in 1912.

Fresenius entered the dialysis equipment market in 1966. The company formed its Fresenius Medical Care unit in 1996 when it merged its dialysis systems division with National Medical Care (NMC).

In 1999 Fresenius formed its Fresenius Kabi division by combining its infusion pharmaceutical operations with the former infusion solution business of drugmaker Pharmacia & Upjohn which it acquired the previous year.

The company conducted a number of expansion efforts within the Kabi division in the following decade including the 2007 purchase of IV drug manufacturing firms Labesfal (Portugal) and Filaxis (Argentina) as well as German medical device maker Clinico. Also that year the company bought the artificial colloid product business of Kyorin to build up a presence in the Tokyo market.

It then purchased Indian oncology drug manufacturer Dabur Pharma in 2008. Also that year the unit expanded its reach in the US market for injectable drugs by acquiring US generics maker APP Pharmaceuticals for $3.7 billion plus debt.

Following the acquisition of German private clinic operator Helios Kliniken Fresenius refreshed its acute care operations by separating its hospital division (Fresenius ProServe) into two business segments Fresenius Helios and Fresenius Vamed in 2008.

EXECUTIVES

CEO Fresenius Medical Care, Rice Powell, age 64
CEO, Stephan Sturm, age 57
CEO Fresenius Kabi AG, Mats Henriksson, age 53
CEO Fresenius Helios, Francesco De Meo, age 56
CEO Fresenius Vamed, Ernst Wastler, age 61
Deputy Chairman, Gerhard Rupprecht, age 72
Chairman, Gerd Krick, age 82
Auditors: KPMG AG

LOCATIONS

HQ: Fresenius SE & Co KGaA
Else-Kroener-Strasse 1, Bad Homburg D-61352
Phone: (49) 6172 608 0   **Fax:** (49) 6172 608 2488
Web: www.fresenius.com

2017 Sales

	% of total
North America	45
Europe	41
Asia Pacific	9
Latin America & other regions	4
Africa	1
Total	**100**

PRODUCTS/OPERATIONS

2017 Sales

	% of total
Fresenius Medical Care	52
Fresenius Kabi	19
Fresenius Helios	26
Fresenius Vamed	3
Corporate/Other (-)	
Total	**100**

Selected Services

Fresenius Medical Care
  Dialysis facility operation
  Disease management
  Disposable dialysis supplies
  Hemodialysis equipment
  Peritoneal dialysis equipment
Fresenius Kabi
  Blood volume replacement
  Enteral nutrition
  Infusion and IV devices
  Infusion therapies
  IV generic drugs
  Parenteral nutrition
  Tranfusion products
Fresenius Helios
  HELIOS Kliniken Group (61 private hospitals Germany)
Fresenius Vamed
  Construction management
  Facility planning
  Maintenance services
  Operational management
  Project development
  Staff recruitment and training

COMPETITORS

Asahi Kasei	Haemonetics
B. Braun Melsungen	Hospira
Baxter International	Johnson & Johnson
Becton Dickinson	Pfizer
Bio-Reference Labs	Terumo
DaVita	Teva
Dialysis Clinic Inc	

HISTORICAL FINANCIALS

Company Type: Public

Income Statement

FYE: December 31

	REVENUE ($ mil.)	NET INCOME ($ mil.)	NET PROFIT MARGIN	EMPLOYEES
12/19	39,756	2,114	5.3%	294,134
12/18	38,398	2,321	6.0%	276,750
12/17	40,620	2,174	5.4%	273,249
12/16	31,117	1,647	5.3%	228,968
12/15	30,090	1,479	4.9%	222,305
Annual Growth	7.2%	9.3%	—	7.3%

2019 Year-End Financials

Debt ratio: 34.8%
Return on equity: 11.7%
Cash ($ mil.): 1,857
Current ratio: 1.10
Long-term debt ($ mil.): 18,081

No. of shares (mil.): 557
Dividends
  Yield: 1.0%
  Payout: 3.9%
Market value ($ mil.): 7,781

	STOCK PRICE ($) FY Close	P/E High/Low		PER SHARE ($) Earnings	Dividends	Book Value
12/19	13.96	4	3	3.79	0.15	33.80
12/18	12.15	6	3	4.16	0.15	31.73
12/17	19.43	7	6	3.90	0.12	29.93
12/16	19.48	7	5	2.99	0.09	24.44
12/15	17.85	8	5	2.70	0.08	21.83
Annual Growth	(6.0%)	—	—	8.9%	17.0%	11.6%

FUJIFILM Holdings Corp

Fujifilm's main businesses over 85% of revenue together are document operations and healthcare and materials. The document business sells printers and office products and provides manage prints services. The Healthcare & Material Solutions business's products include diagnostic instruments such as X-ray and ultrasound machines as well as pharmaceuticals. The company's imaging unit which makes photographic films and papers digital cameras and photofinishing equipment is its smallest. Customers overseas account for over 55% sales. Founded in 1934 the company's first product was film for motion pictures.

Operations

Fujifilm's document solutions business generates about 45% of revenue. Besides printers and office equipment the segment has a commercial printer business that provides high-speed digital printing systems and printing workflow tools.

The Healthcare & Materials segment about 45% of revenue has businesses in medical systems pharmaceuticals bio CDMO regenerative medicine and life sciences as well as display materials industrial products electronic materials and fine chemicals.

The Imaging Solutions business about 15% of revenue makes photographic equipment as the Instax instant camera digital cameras and optical devices such as lenses.

As of March 2020 the company has over 315 consolidated subsidiaries.

Geographic Reach

The company is headquartered in Tokyo Japan.

Financial Performance

In FY2019 FUJIFILM recorded Â 2.3 trillion in consolidated revenue a 5% decrease compared to the previous year. This is caused by factors such as a sales decrease in the photo imaging business optical device and electronic imaging business and document business although sales increased in the medical systems business bio CDMO business regenerative medicine business and electronic materials business.

Net income attributable to FUJIFILM Holdings was Â 125 billion a 10% decrease from the previous year.

The company's cash for FY 2019 was Â 396.1 billion. Operating activities generated Â 255.7 billion while investing activities used Â 244.9 billion mainly for acquisitions of businesses. Financing activities used another Â 250.9 billion mainly for equity transactions.

Strategy

The company promotes its growth strategy by consistently anticipating the future and centering on a variety of technologies such as optics chemicals and electronics.

EXECUTIVES

Chairman and CEO, Shigetaka Komori
President and COO, Kenji Sukeno
President and COO, Shigehiro Nakajima
Auditors: KPMG AZSA LLC

LOCATIONS

HQ: FUJIFILM Holdings Corp
  9-7-3 Akasaka, Minato-ku, Tokyo 107-0052
Phone: (81) 3 6271 1111
Web: www.fujifilmholdings.com

2018 Sales

	% of total
Japan	41
Asia	27
Americas	19
Europe	13
Total	**100**

PRODUCTS/OPERATIONS

2018 Sales

	% of total
Document Solutions	43
Healthcare & Material Solutions	41
Imaging Solutions	16
Total	**100**

2018 Sales

	% of total
Sales	86
Rentals	14
Total	**100**

Selected Products

Document
  Color/Monochrome digital multifunction devices
  DocuWorks docyument handlingn software
  On-demand publishing systems
  Computer publishing systems
Imaging
  Color photo printing paper and chemicals
  Digital cameras and accessories
  Instant films
  Digital minilabs/dry minilabs
  Motion picture films
  Photo lab equipment
  Photographic films
Healthcare and Material Solutions
  Digital mammography systems
  Synapse medical-use picture archiving and communications systems
  X-ray films
  Digital endoscopes
  Low-molecular pharmaceuticals
  functional cosmetics

COMPETITORS

Agfa	Lexmark
Bayer AG	NEC
Brother Industries	Nikon
Canon	Novartis
Eastman Kodak	Olympus
GlaxoSmithKline	Pfizer
HP	Philips Electronics
Hitachi	Ricoh Company
Konica Minolta	Samsung Electronics
Kyocera	Sony
Kyocera Document Solutions	Xerox

HISTORICAL FINANCIALS

Company Type: Public

Income Statement

FYE: March 31

	REVENUE ($ mil.)	NET INCOME ($ mil.)	NET PROFIT MARGIN	EMPLOYEES
03/20	21,327	1,151	5.4%	83,987
03/19	21,955	1,247	5.7%	82,841
03/18	22,915	1,324	5.8%	88,392
03/17	20,769	1,176	5.7%	88,690
03/16	22,187	1,098	4.9%	88,009
Annual Growth	(1.0%)	1.2%	—	(1.2%)

2020 Year-End Financials

Debt ratio: 0.1%
Return on equity: 6.2%
Cash ($ mil.): 3,648
Current ratio: 2.26
Long-term debt ($ mil.): 4,635

No. of shares (mil.): 399
Dividends
  Yield: 1.6%
  Payout: 28.7%
Market value ($ mil.): 19,994

	STOCK PRICE ($) FY Close	P/E High/Low		PER SHARE ($) Earnings	Dividends	Book Value
03/20	50.02	0	0	2.81	0.80	45.02
03/19	45.55	0	0	2.94	0.70	44.94
03/18	40.11	0	0	3.03	0.68	45.51
03/17	39.16	0	0	2.64	0.62	41.75
03/16	39.40	0	0	2.35	0.55	40.61
Annual Growth	6.1%	—	—	4.6%	10.1%	2.6%

Fujitsu Ltd

Auditors: Ernst & Young ShinNihon LLC

LOCATIONS

HQ: Fujitsu Ltd
Shiodome City Center, 1-5-2 Higashi-Shinbashi,
Minato-ku, Tokyo 105-7123
Phone: (81) 3 6252 2220
Web: www.fujitsu.com

HISTORICAL FINANCIALS
Company Type: Public

Income Statement   FYE: March 31

	REVENUE ($ mil.)	NET INCOME ($ mil.)	NET PROFIT MARGIN	EMPLOYEES
03/20	38,897	1,613	4.1%	141,947
03/19	39,851	1,054	2.6%	145,845
03/18	41,323	1,707	4.1%	156,471
03/17	45,470	892	2.0%	171,753
03/16	47,785	874	1.8%	173,722
Annual Growth	(5.0%)	16.5%	—	(4.9%)

2020 Year-End Financials

Debt ratio: 0.0%
Return on equity: 13.4%
Cash ($ mil.): 4,555
Current ratio: 1.38
Long-term debt ($ mil.): 883

No. of shares (mil.): 200
Dividends
 Yield: 1.6%
 Payout: 3.7%
Market value ($ mil.): 3,566

	STOCK PRICE ($) FY Close	P/E High/Low		PER SHARE ($) Earnings	Dividends	Book Value
03/20	17.81	0	0	7.97	0.29	62.48
03/19	14.43	0	0	5.17	0.23	56.32
03/18	30.37	0	0	8.32	0.18	53.28
03/17	30.97	0	0	4.32	0.36	43.34
03/16	18.53	0	0	4.23	0.13	38.15
Annual Growth	(1.0%)	—	—	17.2%	22.9%	13.1%

G4S Plc

Auditors: PricewaterhouseCoopers LLP

LOCATIONS

HQ: G4S Plc
5th Floor, Southside, 105 Victoria Street, London
SW1E 6QT
Phone: (44) 207 963 3100
Web: www.g4s.com

HISTORICAL FINANCIALS
Company Type: Public

Income Statement   FYE: December 31

	REVENUE ($ mil.)	NET INCOME ($ mil.)	NET PROFIT MARGIN	EMPLOYEES
12/19	15,503	(181)	—	551,748
12/18	15,011	163	1.1%	559,880
12/17	15,643	471	3.0%	573,671
12/16	15,167	395	2.6%	592,897
12/15	13,714	15	0.1%	611,366
Annual Growth	3.1%	—	—	(2.5%)

2019 Year-End Financials

Debt ratio: 98.1%
Return on equity: (-17.5%)
Cash ($ mil.): 1,488
Current ratio: 1.48
Long-term debt ($ mil.): 4,374

No. of shares (mil.): 1,545
Dividends
 Yield: 3.6%
 Payout: —
Market value ($ mil.): —

Galp Energia, SGPS, SA

EXECUTIVES

Vice Chairman and CEO, Carlos Nuno Gomes da Silva
CCO Corporate Service and New Energies, Carlos Costa Pina
CFO, Filipe Cris stomo Silva
COO, Thore E. Kristiansen
CCO and Head Supply Refining and Planning, José Carlos da Silva Costa
CCO and Head Gas and Power, Pedro Carmona de Oliveira Ricardo
CCO and Head Iberian and International Oil Marketing, Tiago C mara Pestana
Vice Chairman, Miguel Athayde Marques, age 65
Chairwoman, Paula Amorim
Auditors: Ernst & Young Audit & Associados - SROC, S.A.

LOCATIONS

HQ: Galp Energia, SGPS, SA
Rua Tomas de Fonseca, Torre C, Lisbon 1600-209
Phone: (351) 217 240 866   **Fax:** (351) 217 242 965
Web: www.galp.com

PRODUCTS/OPERATIONS

2013 Sales

	% of total
Refining & marketing	83
Gas & power	17
Total	**100**

Selected Subsidiaries

Galp Power (electricity generation and sales)
Galpgeste (management and operation of service stations)
GDP Gá;s de Portugal
Petróleos de Portugal (Petrogal; exploration and production refining transport distribution and sales of oil products)
Sacor Maritima (marine transport)
Sopor (51% distribution and sale of oil products)
Transgá;s Armazenagem (natural gas underground storage)

COMPETITORS

BP	Repsol
Endesa S.A.	Royal Dutch Shell
Exxon Mobil	TOTAL

HISTORICAL FINANCIALS
Company Type: Public

Income Statement   FYE: December 31

	REVENUE ($ mil.)	NET INCOME ($ mil.)	NET PROFIT MARGIN	EMPLOYEES
12/19	19,017	436	2.3%	6,386
12/18	19,837	848	4.3%	6,360
12/17	18,352	736	4.0%	6,389
12/16	13,980	189	1.4%	6,475
12/15	17,009	133	0.8%	6,792
Annual Growth	2.8%	34.5%	—	(1.5%)

2019 Year-End Financials

Debt ratio: 33.5%
Return on equity: 8.6%
Cash ($ mil.): 1,639
Current ratio: 1.60
Long-term debt ($ mil.): 4,108

No. of shares (mil.): 829
Dividends
 Yield: 4.4%
 Payout: 71.8%
Market value ($ mil.): 6,933

	STOCK PRICE ($) FY Close	P/E High/Low		PER SHARE ($) Earnings	Dividends	Book Value
12/19	8.36	18	15	0.53	0.37	5.98
12/18	7.76	12	8	1.02	0.34	6.33
12/17	9.17	13	10	0.89	0.30	6.68
12/16	7.51	34	22	0.23	0.24	6.34
12/15	5.83	45	29	0.16	0.17	6.27
Annual Growth	9.4%	—	—	34.1%	21.6%	(1.2%)

Gazprom Neft PJSC

EXECUTIVES

Chairman and CEO, Alexander V. Dyukov, age 53
Deputy chairman and Deputy CEO for Logistics Processing and Sales, Anatoly Cherner, age 67
Deputy CEO Foreign Asset Management, Kirill Kravchenko, age 44
Deputy Chairman and First Deputy CEO, Vadim Yakovlev, age 50
Deputy Chairman and Deputy CEO Administration, Vitaliy Baranov
Deputy CEO International Business Development, Vladislav Baryshnikov
Deputy CEO Economics and Finance, Alexei Yankevich
Auditors: AO PricewaterhouseCoopers Audit

LOCATIONS

HQ: Gazprom Neft PJSC
3-5 Pochtamtskaya St., St. Petersburg 190000
Phone: (7) 812 363 31 52   **Fax:** (7) 812 363 31 51
Web: www.gazprom-neft.ru

2018 Sales

	% of total
Russian Federation	51
Commonwealth of Independent States	1
Export & international operations	44
Total	**100**

PRODUCTS/OPERATIONS

2018 Sales

	% of total
Petroleum products	67
Crude oil	29
Gas	1
Other	3
Total	**100**

2018 Sales by Segment

	% of total
Downstream	33
Upstream	67
Total	**100**

COMPETITORS

BP	Occidental Petroleum
Bashneft JOSC	Rosneft
Devon Energy	Royal Dutch Shell
Exxon Mobil	Surgutneftegas
JX Nippon Oil & Energy	TOTAL
LUKOIL	Tatneft
Mitsui	Transneft

HISTORICAL FINANCIALS

Company Type: Public

Income Statement   FYE: December 31

	REVENUE ($ mil.)	NET INCOME ($ mil.)	NET PROFIT MARGIN	EMPLOYEES
12/19	39,933	6,430	16.1%	78,800
12/18	35,716	5,404	15.1%	66,500
12/17	32,136	4,380	13.6%	67,882
12/16	25,241	3,269	13.0%	0
12/15	19,878	1,485	7.5%	0
Annual Growth	19.1%	44.3%	—	—

2019 Year-End Financials

Debt ratio: 0.3%	No. of shares (mil.): —
Return on equity: 20.5%	Dividends
Cash ($ mil.): 3,252	Yield: 10.8%
Current ratio: 1.50	Payout: 210.6%
Long-term debt ($ mil.): 11,006	Market value ($ mil.): —

	STOCK PRICE ($) FY Close	P/E High/Low		PER SHARE ($) Earnings	Dividends	Book Value
12/19	34.30	0	0	1.36	3.72	7.01
12/18	25.38	0	0	1.15	2.05	5.60
12/17	20.88	0	0	0.93	2.00	5.69
12/16	17.52	0	0	0.69	0.06	4.71
12/15	10.61	1	0	0.31	0.63	3.32
Annual Growth	34.1%	—	—	44.3%	55.7%	20.5%

GD Power Development Co, Ltd.

EXECUTIVES

Chairman, Yongpeng Zhu
Auditors: RSM China Certified Public Accountants

LOCATIONS

HQ: GD Power Development Co, Ltd.
No. 19, Anyuan, Anhui Beili, Chaoyang District, Beijing 100101
Phone: (86) 10 58682200   **Fax:** (86) 10 64829900
Web: www.600795.com.cn

HISTORICAL FINANCIALS

Company Type: Public

Income Statement   FYE: December 31

	REVENUE ($ mil.)	NET INCOME ($ mil.)	NET PROFIT MARGIN	EMPLOYEES
12/19	16,757	268	1.6%	0
12/18	9,521	199	2.1%	0
12/17	9,194	341	3.7%	0
12/16	8,412	680	8.1%	0
12/15	8,404	671	8.0%	0
Annual Growth	18.8%	(20.5%)	—	—

2019 Year-End Financials

Debt ratio: 7.2%	No. of shares (mil.): —
Return on equity: 3.5%	Dividends
Cash ($ mil.): 1,497	Yield: —
Current ratio: 0.39	Payout: —
Long-term debt ($ mil.): 18,565	Market value ($ mil.): —

Geely Automobile Holdings Ltd

Auditors: Grant Thornton Hong Kong Limited

LOCATIONS

HQ: Geely Automobile Holdings Ltd
Room 2301, 23rd Floor, Great Eagle Centre, 23 Harbour Road, Wan Chai,
Phone: (852) 2598 3333   **Fax:** (852) 2598 3399
Web: www.geelyauto.com.hk

PRODUCTS/OPERATIONS

Selected Subsidiaries
Centurion Industries Limited
DSI Holdings Pty Limited
Jinan Geely Automobile Parts and Components
  Company Limited
Linkstate Overseas Limited
Luckview Group Limited
Value Century Group Limited
Zhejiang Geely Gearbox Limited

COMPETITORS

Anhui Jianghuai Automobile Co. Ltd.	Dongfeng Motor
	FAW CAR CO.Ltd.
BYD	Guangzhou Automobile
Beiqi Foton Motor	Group Co. Ltd.
Brilliance China	SAIC Motor
Changan Ford Mazda	Shanghai Automotive
Automobile	Shanghai General
Chery Automobile	Motors
Daihatsu	Xiamen King Long Motor
Denway Motors	Group Co. Ltd.

HISTORICAL FINANCIALS

Company Type: Public

Income Statement   FYE: December 31

	REVENUE ($ mil.)	NET INCOME ($ mil.)	NET PROFIT MARGIN	EMPLOYEES
12/19	13,997	1,176	8.4%	43,000
12/18	15,497	1,825	11.8%	52,400
12/17	14,254	1,634	11.5%	41,600
12/16	7,736	736	9.5%	35,100
12/15	4,640	348	7.5%	18,700
Annual Growth	31.8%	35.6%	—	23.1%

2019 Year-End Financials

Debt ratio: 0.5%	No. of shares (mil.): —
Return on equity: 16.4%	Dividends
Cash ($ mil.): 2,770	Yield: 2.2%
Current ratio: 1.03	Payout: 28.0%
Long-term debt ($ mil.): 596	Market value ($ mil.): —

GlaxoSmithKline Plc

GlaxoSmithKline (GSK) gives anxiety asthma and other ailments the ax. One of the top five pharmaceutical firms in the world GSK's bestsellers include respiratory neurological cardiovascular and dermatology drugs as well as vaccines and antivirals and consumer healthcare products. It boasts four billion-dollar drugs: Advair/Seretide its stalwart asthma medication; Relvar/Breo Ellipta a chronic obstructive pulmonary disease treatment; and two HIV medications Triumeq and Tivicay. In the consumer healthcare business GSK racks up big sales from its Sensodyne toothpaste brand joint-pain relief medicine Voltaren and fever relief medicine Panadol. Based in the UK GSK has customers across the globe.

Operations

GSK operates through three primary segments: Pharmaceuticals Consumer Healthcare and Vaccines. Pharmaceuticals is the largest by far pulling more than half of revenue.

The Pharmaceuticals division develops and manufactures drugs for a wide variety of purposes but with a specialism in drugs that treat respiratory disease and HIV. Asthma medication Advair has been GSK's primary money spinner for many years although it faces intensifying competition from biosimilars and generics. HIV drugs Trimueq and Tivicay are GSK's next biggest while other respiratory drugs include Relvar/Breo Ellipta Ventolin and Flixotide. The division's R&D activity focuses on respiratory HIV/infectious illnesses oncology and immuno-inflammation medicine.

GSK's Consumer Healthcare segment generates more than 25% of sales and produces products in the oral health wellness nutrition and skin health categories. Its major brands include Advil Voltaren Centrum Caltrate and Otrivin. In 2019 GSK combined its Consumer Healthcare segment with the consumer health division of Pfizer to create an over-the-counter giant adding brands such as Advil Centrum and Robitussin.

The Vaccines segment has around 40 pediatric adolescent adult and travel vaccines on the market in more than 160 countries. Meningitis vaccines Bexsero and Menveo are its biggest earner followed by flu vaccine Fluarix and Shingles vaccine Shingrix. Sales of vaccines account for around 20% of GSK's annual sales.

Geographic Reach

Headquartered in London GSK has an extensive network of manufacturing sites and R&D centres in about 35 countries and major R&D centers are located in the UK the US Belgium and China. It has presence in approximately 150 countries.

The US is GSK's largest market at some 40% of sales. Europe generates a quarter.

Sales and Marketing

GSK sells its products through a small number of wholesalers in addition to hospitals pharmacies physicians and other groups. Sales to the three largest wholesalers amounted to approximately 80% of the sales of the US Pharmaceuticals and Vaccines business.

Financial Performance

Note: Growth rates may differ after conversion to US dollars.

GSK's revenue has been rising in the last five years with an overall growth of 41% between 2015 and 2019. Its net income after a colossal drop in 2016 redeemed itself yearly. 2019's net income is 45% lower compared to 2018's. Group turnover for the year increased 10% from $33.8 billion in 2018 to Å 33.8 billion in 2019 with growth delivered by Vaccines and Consumer Healthcare and Pharmaceuticals flat at CER. Pro-forma turnover growth for the Group was 4% CER. The company's net income was Å 4.6 billion in 2019 a 28% increase from the previous year. This was primarily due to the larger turnover and a positive operating income compared to the operating loss in the previous year.

GSK's cash and bank overdrafts at end of 2019 totaled Å 4.8 billion a Å 744 million increase from 2018. Operating activities generated Å 8 billion while investing activities used 5.4 billion. Financing activities used another Å 1.8 billion. GSK's main cash uses in 2019 were for capital expenditures and dividends paid.

Strategy

GSK's strategy is to bring differentiated high-quality and needed healthcare products to as many people as possible with our three global businesses scientific and technical know-how and talented people. The company also works with world-leading experts and form strategic partnerships to complement its existing capabilities.

GSK prepares for the future by investing in R&D and new products. Since announcing its new approach to R&D in 2018 the company has made significant progress to strengthen its pipeline particularly in oncology. It now has 39 medicines and 15 vaccines in the pipeline and in 2019 it had three major approvals eight regulatory submissions six positive read-outs from pivotal studies and has progressed four new assets into pivotal studies. During 2019 GSK also completed transactions with Tesaro and with Merck KGaA further strengthening its position in oncology and initiated alliances to build out platform technologies in genomics with the University of California and in cell therapy with Lyell Immunopharma.

In early 2020 consistent with its strategic priorities and previous announcements GSK started a two-year programme to prepare itself for separation into two new leading companies: New GSK a biopharma company with an R&D approach focused on science related to the immune system use of genetics and new technologies; and a new Consumer Healthcare company with category-leading power brands and innovation based on science and consumer insights.

Mergers and Acquisitions

In early 2019 GlaxoSmithKline acquired US-based oncology pharma company Tesaro in a Å 4 billion deal. That deal brought the company Tesaro's newly launched PARP inhibitor Zejula for the treatment of ovarian cancer. PARP inhibitors have shown promise in treating certain cancers in combination with other drugs.

HISTORY

Englishman Joseph Nathan started an import-export business in New Zealand in 1873. He obtained the rights to a process for drying milk and began making powdered milk in New Zealand selling it as baby food Glaxo.

Nathan's son Alec dispatched to London to oversee baby food sales in Britain increased Glaxo's name recognition by publishing the Glaxo Baby Book a guide to child care. After WWI the company began distribution in India and South America.

In the 1920s Glaxo launched vitamin D-fortified formulations. It entered the pharmaceutical business with its 1927 introduction of Ostelin a liquid vitamin D concentrate and continued to grow globally in the 1930s introducing Ostermilk (vitamin-fortified milk).

Glaxo began making penicillin and anesthetics during WWII; it went public in 1947. A steep drop in antibiotic prices in the mid-1950s led Glaxo to diversify; it bought veterinary medical instrument and drug distribution firms.

In the 1970s the British Monopolies Commission quashed both a hostile takeover attempt by Beecham and a proposed merger with retailer and drugmaker Boots. Glaxo launched US operations in 1978.

Glaxo shed nondrug operations in the 1980s to concentrate on pharmaceuticals. A 1981 marketing blitz launched antiulcer drug Zantac (to vie with SmithKline's Tagamet) in the US where Glaxo's sales had been small. The company boosted outreach by contracting to use Hoffmann-La Roche's sales staff. The Zantac sales assault gave Glaxo leadership in US antiulcer drug sales.

Under CEO Sir Richard Sykes Glaxo in 1995 made a surprise bid for UK rival Wellcome. Founded in 1880 by Americans Silas Burroughs and Henry Wellcome to sell McKesson-Robbins' products outside the US Burroughs Wellcome and Co. began making its own products two years later. By the 1990s the company which fostered Nobel Prize-winning researchers led the world in antiviral medicines. Its primary drug products were Zovirax (launched 1981) and Retrovir (1987).

Though an earlier bid by Glaxo had been rejected Sykes won the takeover with backing from Wellcome Trust Wellcome's largest shareholder.

In 1997 the company formed a new genetics division buying Spectra Biomedical and its gene variation technology. That year the company pulled diabetes drug Romozin (Rezulin in the US) from the UK market over concerns that it caused liver damage.

Glaxo in 1998 ended its joint venture with Warner-Lambert (begun 1993) selling its former partner the Canadian and US marketing rights to acid blocker Zantac 75.

In 1999 Glaxo trimmed its product line pulling hepatitis treatment Wellferon because of slow sales and selling the US rights to several anesthesia products. It also cut some 3400 jobs (half from the UK). Also that year Glaxo threatened to leave the UK after the National Health Service opted not to cover antiflu inhalant Relenza claiming the drug is not cost-effective.

The FDA in 2000 approved Glaxo's Lotronex for irritable bowel syndrome but several hospitalizations linked to the drug prompted the FDA to ask the company to withdraw it from the US market. Later that year Glaxo completed its merger with former UK rival SmithKline Beecham to create GlaxoSmithKline (GSK).

In 2015 GSK bought Novartis' Vaccines and Consumer Health business and sold its cancer drugs business to the same company.

EXECUTIVES

CEO, Emma Walmsley
President Pharmaceuticals R&D, Patrick Vallance
CFO, Simon Dingemans, $1,152,511 total compensation
President Global Affairs, Phil Thomson
President Global Manufacturing & Supply, Roger Connor
President Global Pharmaceuticals, Luke Miels
CEO Viiv Healthcare JV, Deborah Waterhouse
President Global Vaccines, Luc Debruyne
CEO GSK Consumer Healthcare, Brian McNamara

Chairman, Philip Hampton, age 67
Auditors: Deloitte LLP

LOCATIONS

HQ: GlaxoSmithKline Plc
  980 Great West Road, Brentford, Middlesex TW8 9GS
Phone: (44) 20 8047 5000   **Fax:** (44) 20 8047 7807
Web: www.gsk.com

2017 Sales

	% of total
US	37
International	36
Europe	27
Total	**100**

PRODUCTS/OPERATIONS

2017 Sales

	% of total
Pharmaceuticals	57
Consumer healthcare	26
Vaccines	17
Total	**100**

Selected Products

Pharmaceuticals
  Respiratory
    Beconase (allergies)
    Becotide/Beclovent (asthma and chronic obstructive pulmonary disease)
    Flixonase/Flonase (allergies)
    Flixotide/Flovent (asthma and chronic obstructive pulmonary disease)
    Seretide/Advair (asthma and chronic obstructive pulmonary disease)
    Serevent (asthma and chronic obstructive pulmonary disease)
    Ventolin (asthma and chronic obstructive pulmonary disease)
    Veramyst/Avamys (rhinitis)
  Cardiovascular and urogenital
    Arixtra (deep vein thrombosis and pulmonary embolism)
    Avodart (prostatic hyperplasia)
    Benlysta (systemic lupus erychematosus with HGS)
    Coreg CR (heart failure and hypertension)
    Fraxiparine (deep vein thrombosis and pulmonary embolism)
    Levitra (erectile dysfunction with Bayer)
    Lovaza (coronary heart disease)
    Vesicare (overactive bladder)
    Volibris (pulmonary hypertension)
  Central nervous system disorders
    Horizant (post-herpetic neuralgia or restless leg syndrome)
    Imigran/Imitrex (migraines)
    Lamictal (epilepsy and bipolar disorder)
    Potiga/Trobalt (epilepsy and partial seizures)
    Requip (Parkinson's disease)
    Seroxat/Paxil (depression)
    Treximet (migraine)
    Wellbutrin SR (depression)
    ViiV Healthcare (HIV with Pfizer)
    Combivir/Biovir (reverse transcriptase inhibitor for HIV/AIDS)
    Epivir/3TC (reverse transcriptase inhibitor for HIV/AIDS)
    Epizicom/Kivexa (combination of Epivir and Ziagen for HIV/AIDS)
    Lexiva/Telzir (protease inhibitor for HIV/AIDS)
    Selzentry (HIV)
    Trizivir (three reverse transcriptase inhibitors for HIV/AIDS)
  Antibacterials
    Amoxil and Augmentin (antibiotics non-US only)
  Dermatology
    Bactroban (skin infections)
    Duac (acne vulgaris)
    Zovirax (herpes infections shingles chicken pox and cold sores)
  Antivirals
    Relenza (influenza)
    Hepsera (hepatitis B)
    Valtrex/Zelitrex (shingles and genital herpes)
    Zeffix/Septavir/Heptodin/Epivir HBV (hepatitis B)
  Vaccines

Cervarix (human papilloma virus)
Fluarix (influenza)
FluLaval (influenza)
Infanrix/Pediarix (diphtheria tetanus pertussis polio and hepatitis B)
Rotarix (rotavirus)
Synflorix (pneumonia)
Twinrix (hepatitis A and hepatitis B)
Metabolic
Avandia Avandamet (type 2 diabetes)
Boniva/Bonviva (osteoporosis with Roche)
Consumer products
Over-the-counter medicines
Abreva (cold sores)
alli (weight loss)
Breathe Right (nasal strips)
Citrucel (laxative)
Commit (smoking-cessation)
Contac (respiratory product)
Nicabate/NicoDerm/NiQuitin CQ (smoking-cessation)
Nicorette (smoking-cessation)
Panadol (analgesic)
Tums (antacid)
Oral care
Aquafresh (toothpaste and toothbrushes)
Corega (denture care)
Dr Best (toothbrushes)
Macleans (toothpaste)
Odol (toothpaste)
Polident (denture cleaner)
Poli-Grip (denture adhesive)
Sensodyne (toothpaste)
Nutritional health care
Horlicks (milk-based malted food and chocolate drinks)
Lucozade (glucose energy drink)
Ribena (line of juice drinks rich in vitamin C)

COMPETITORS

Abbott Labs	Mylan
Amgen	Novartis
AstraZeneca	Novo Nordisk
Bayer AG	Pfizer
Biogen	Procter & Gamble
Bristol-Myers Squibb	Reckitt Benckiser
Colgate-Palmolive	Roche Holding
Dr. Reddy's	Sanofi
Eli Lilly	Takeda Pharmaceutical
Gilead Sciences	Teva
Johnson & Johnson	UCB
Merck	

HISTORICAL FINANCIALS

Company Type: Public

Income Statement — FYE: December 31

	REVENUE ($ mil.)	NET INCOME ($ mil.)	NET PROFIT MARGIN	EMPLOYEES
12/19	67,453	9,282	13.8%	99,437
12/18	61,592	7,240	11.8%	95,490
12/17	60,323	3,061	5.1%	98,462
12/16	55,733	1,822	3.3%	99,300
12/15	47,807	16,830	35.2%	101,255
Annual Growth	9.0%	(13.8%)	—	(0.5%)

2019 Year-End Financials

Debt ratio: 73.3%	No. of shares (mil.): —
Return on equity: 58.9%	Dividends
Cash ($ mil.): 9,406	Yield: 4.2%
Current ratio: 0.81	Payout: 194.4%
Long-term debt ($ mil.): 45,123	Market value ($ mil.): —

	STOCK PRICE ($) FY Close	P/E High/Low	PER SHARE ($) Earnings	Dividends	Book Value
12/19	46.99	50 40	1.85	2.00	4.57
12/18	38.21	57 48	1.46	2.11	1.76
12/17	35.47	141 110	0.62	2.06	(0.03)
12/16	38.51	242 199	0.37	2.64	0.46
12/15	40.35	28 22	3.44	2.39	2.10
Annual Growth	3.9%	—	— (14.4%)	(4.4%)	21.5%

Glencore PLC

One of the world's largest energy metals and agricultural products companies (and indeed one of the world's largest companies overall) Glencore is active at every stage of commodity supply chain. With presence in approximately 35 countries and a diversified portfolio of upwards of 90 commodities its operations span some 150 sites and facilities from crude oil production and coal mining to custom metallurgical products biofuels and storage and handling of grains. Customers include the automotive steel power generation oil and food processing industries. Glencore was founded in 1974 and is headquarted in Switzerland.

Operations

Glencore is organized and operates on a worldwide basis in two core business segments - Marketing activities and Industrial activities.

Marketing activities which generates almost 85% of company's revenue use their scale and capabilities to extract additional margin throughout their business model and provide a high quality service to their customers and a reliable supply of quality product.

Industrial activities which generates the remaining 15% of total revenue provide a consistent source of volumes for their marketing operations which are supplemented by third party production.

Metals and minerals which are more than 60% of revenue are copper cobalt zinc nickel and ferroalloys - and also market aluminum/alumina and iron ore from third parties.

Energy products which are almost 40% of total revenue is a major producer and marketer of coal with mines in Australia Africa and South America - while their oil business is one of the leading marketers of crude oil refined products and natural gas.

Geographic Reach

Glencore headquartered in Switzerland and has operations around the world. The company operates approximately in 35 countries has 150 sites and more than 30 offices around the world.

Asia is the largest market which generates almost 40%. Second is Europe which generates approximately 35%. Americas generates almost 20% and Oceania and Africa generates the remainder.

Financial Performance

The company's revenue decreased by $5.4 billion to $215.1 billion in 2019 compared to $220.5 in the prior year.

Net loss attributable to equity holders was $404 million in 2019 compared to a net income of $3408 million in 2018 driven largely by lower commodity prices compared to prior year and various impairments charges across our portfolio mainly relating to our Colombian coal Chad oil and African copper portfolios owing to a lower forecast Atlantic steam coal price environment the expiration of certain oil exploration licenses and revisions to Mutanda's mine plan.

Cash held by the company at the end of 2019 decreased by $134 million to $1.9 billion compared to $2.0 billion in 2018. Cash generated from operations was $8.7 billion while cash used for investing and financing activities were $3.7 billion and $5.1 billion respectively.

Strategy

The company's strategic priorities were: Integration of sustainability throughout their business; Maintain a robust and flexible balance sheet; and Focus on cost control and operational efficiencies. Glencore believe that by being a responsible operator with a reputation for doing things the right way they will be seen by their stakeholders as a partner of choice.

The company are achieving this through continuous improvement. This approach is delivered through their health and safety programmes advancing their environmental performance respecting human rights and by developing maintaining and strengthening their relationships with all of their stakeholders.

Mergers and Acquisitions

In 2019 Glencore concluded the acquisition (via a rights issue) of an additional 42.9% interest in Polymet Mining Corp ("Polymet") a company in the early stages of developing the NorthMet polymetallic (copper nickel and precious metals) deposit in Minnesota for a total consideration of $243 million.

In early 2019 Glencore completed the acquisition of an additional 10% of Ulan and 2.7% of Hail Creek for a net consideration of $124 million and $39 million respectively increasing Glencore's interest in Ulan and Hail Creek to 100% and 84.7% respectively.

EXECUTIVES

CEO, Ivan Glasenberg, age 63
CFO, Steven Kalmin
Chairman, Anthony B. (Tony) Hayward, age 63
Auditors: Deloitte LLP

LOCATIONS

HQ: Glencore PLC
Baarermattstrasse 3, P.O. Box 1363, Baar CH-6341
Phone: (41) 41 709 2000   **Fax:** (41) 41 709 3000
Web: www.glencore.com

2018 Sales

	% of total
Asia	43
Europe	35
The Americas	17
Oceania	3
Africa	2
Total	**100**

PRODUCTS/OPERATIONS

2018 Sales

	% of total
Energy products	63
Metals and minerals	37
Corporate and other	-
Total	**100**

Selected Operations

Agricultural Products
  Barley
  Corn
  Meals
  Rice
  Sugar
  Wheat
Energy Products
  Coal
  Oil
Metals and Minerals
  Copper
  Ferroalloys
  Lead
  Nickel
  Zinc
Viterra ($6.2 billion; Canada; grain merchant)

COMPETITORS

ADM	Noble Group
Anglo American	Norsk Hydro ASA
BHP Billiton	Rio Tinto Limited

HISTORICAL FINANCIALS
Company Type: Public

Income Statement				FYE: December 31
	REVENUE ($ mil.)	NET INCOME ($ mil.)	NET PROFIT MARGIN	EMPLOYEES
12/19	215,111	(404)	—	160,000
12/18	219,754	3,408	1.6%	158,000
12/17	205,476	5,777	2.8%	145,977
12/16	152,948	1,379	0.9%	154,832
12/15	170,497	(4,964)	—	156,468
Annual Growth	6.0%	—	—	0.6%

2019 Year-End Financials

Debt ratio: 29.8%
Return on equity: (-0.9%)
Cash ($ mil.): 1,899
Current ratio: 1.06
Long-term debt ($ mil.): 29,067

No. of shares (mil.): —
Dividends
 Yield: 5.5%
 Payout: —
Market value ($ mil.): —

	STOCK PRICE ($) FY Close	P/E High/Low		PER SHARE ($)		
			Earnings	Dividends	Book Value	
12/19	6.18	— —	(0.03)	0.34	3.05	
12/18	7.24	49 29	0.24	0.34	3.31	
12/17	10.41	25 17	0.40	0.18	3.49	
12/16	6.74	76 20	0.10	0.00	3.11	
12/15	2.63	— —	(0.37)	0.36	2.90	
Annual Growth	23.9%	— —	—	(1.3%)	1.3%	

Gold Corp Holdings (Australia)

Auditors: Caroline Spencer

LOCATIONS

HQ: Gold Corp Holdings (Australia)
 Perth Mint Buildings, 310 Hay Street, East Perth,
 Western Australia 6004
Phone: (61) 8 9421 7222 **Fax:** (61) 8 9221 2258
Web: www.perthmint.com

HISTORICAL FINANCIALS
Company Type: Public

Income Statement				FYE: June 30
	REVENUE ($ mil.)	NET INCOME ($ mil.)	NET PROFIT MARGIN	EMPLOYEES
06/19	12,660	5	0.0%	397
06/18	13,921	4	0.0%	413
06/17	6,226	13	0.2%	454
06/16	6,701	21	0.3%	441
06/15	5,076	10	0.2%	410
Annual Growth	25.7%	(15.3%)	—	(0.8%)

2019 Year-End Financials

Debt ratio: 65.5%
Return on equity: 6.2%
Cash ($ mil.): 86
Current ratio: 1.02
Long-term debt ($ mil.): —

No. of shares (mil.): 31
Dividends
 Yield: —
 Payout: —
Market value ($ mil.): —

Great Eastern Holdings Ltd (Singapore)

EXECUTIVES

Chief Executive Officer, Khor
Chief Financial Officer, Tony Cheong
Managing Director Operations, Ho
Managing Director Human Resources, Chiang
Chairman, Norman Ka Cheung Ip
Auditors: Ernst & Young LLP

LOCATIONS

HQ: Great Eastern Holdings Ltd (Singapore)
 1 Pickering Street, #16-01 Great Eastern Centre,
 048659
Phone: (65) 6248 2000 **Fax:** (65) 6438 3889
Web: www.greateasternlife.com

COMPETITORS

China Life Insurance	Guoco
China Pacific	Ping An Insurance
Insurance	Prudential plc
Edaran Otomobil	

HISTORICAL FINANCIALS
Company Type: Public

Income Statement				FYE: December 31
	ASSETS ($ mil.)	NET INCOME ($ mil.)	INCOME AS % OF ASSETS	EMPLOYEES
12/19	71,729	746	1.0%	4,595
12/18	62,452	543	0.9%	4,255
12/17	63,298	865	1.4%	4,779
12/16	49,220	407	0.8%	4,614
12/15	46,566	555	1.2%	0
Annual Growth	11.4%	7.6%	—	—

2019 Year-End Financials

Return on assets: 1.1%
Return on equity: 12.5%
Long-term debt ($ mil.): —
No. of shares (mil.): 473
Sales ($ mil): 13,822

Dividends
 Yield: —
 Payout: 28.3%
Market value ($ mil.): —

Great Wall Motor Co Ltd

EXECUTIVES

Vice Chairman, Fengying Wang
Auditors: Deloitte Touche Tohmatsu Certified Public
 Accountants LLP

LOCATIONS

HQ: Great Wall Motor Co Ltd
 No. 2266 Chao Yang Road South, Baoding, Hebei
 Province 071000
Phone: (86) 312 2197813 **Fax:** (86) 312 2197812
Web: www.gwm.com.cn

COMPETITORS

BYD	Dongfeng Motor
Chang'an Automobile	Geely Automobile
Chery Automobile	Shanghai Automotive
China FAW	

HISTORICAL FINANCIALS
Company Type: Public

Income Statement				FYE: December 31
	REVENUE ($ mil.)	NET INCOME ($ mil.)	NET PROFIT MARGIN	EMPLOYEES
12/19	13,826	646	4.7%	0
12/18	14,426	757	5.2%	0
12/17	15,546	772	5.0%	0
12/16	14,201	1,519	10.7%	0
12/15	11,707	1,240	10.6%	68,999
Annual Growth	4.2%	(15.0%)	—	—

2019 Year-End Financials

Debt ratio: 0.3%
Return on equity: 8.4%
Cash ($ mil.): 1,397
Current ratio: 1.25
Long-term debt ($ mil.): 173

No. of shares (mil.): —
Dividends
 Yield: 5.8%
 Payout: —
Market value ($ mil.): —

Great-West Lifeco Inc

Holding company Great-West Lifeco majority-owned by Power Financial is one of Canada's largest insurance organizations. Through subsidiaries (including Great-West Life Assurance in Canada) the company offers a range of individual and group life and health insurance retirement savings and investment products reinsurance and services to financial institutions. Great-West Life Assurance's two major subsidiaries Canada Life and London Life Insurance provide individual insurance and wealth-management products in Canada Germany Ireland and the UK. Great-West Lifeco also has retirement and asset management operations in the US.

Strategy

In 2019 Great-West Lifeco sold substantially all of the individual life and annuity insurance operations of its US-based Great-West Life & Annuity Insurance (GWL&A) subsidiary to Protective Life for $1.2 billion. The company retained GWL&A's US retirement and investment management divisions Empower Retirement and Great-West Investments. GWL&A also retained a small block of life insurance policies that will be administered by Protective Life.

Mergers and Acquisitions

In 2017 Great-West subsidiary Great-West Life Assurance acquired Financial Horizons Group a leading Managing General Agency (MGA) from investment firm Genstar Capital. An acquisitive firm Financial Horizons has 30 offices across Canada with a network of some 6600 advisors.

Irish Life bought Irish health insurer Aviva Health and acquired the 49% of GloHealth it didn't already own in 2016. The unit then combined Aviva Health and GloHealth to create Irish Life Health; the moves provided the group with entry into that nation's health insurance market.

EXECUTIVES

President and CEO U.S., Robert L. Reynolds, age 68
EVP General Counsel and Compliance, Andrew D. Brands
President and CEO, Paul A. Mahon
EVP and CFO, Garry MacNicholas
President and COO Canada, J. Dave Johnston
EVP and Chief Investment Officer, S. Mark Corbett

EVP and Chief Human Resources Officer, Grace Palombo
President and COO Canada, Dave Johnston
Auditors: Deloitte LLP

LOCATIONS

HQ: Great-West Lifeco Inc
100 Osborne Street North, Winnipeg, Manitoba R3C 1V3
Phone: 204 946-1190   **Fax:** 204 946-4139
Web: www.greatwestlifeco.com

2012 Sales

	$ mil.	% of total
US		
Asset management	23	40
Financial services	6	10
Canada		
Wealth management	9	16
Group insurance	7	12
Individual insurance	3	7
Europe		
Insurance & annuities	5	8
Reinsurance	4	7
Total	**59**	**100**

PRODUCTS/OPERATIONS

Selected Subsidiaries & Affiliates

The Great-West Life Assurance Company
  Canada Life Financial Corporation
  The Canada Life Assurance Company
  Canada Life Capital Corporation Inc.
  The Canada Life Group (U.K.) Limited
  Canada Life International Re Limited
  Canada Life Irish Holding Company Limited
  Crown Life Insurance Company
  Laketon Investment Management Ltd.
  London Insurance Group
  London Life Insurance Company
  London Reinsurance Group Inc.
  GWL&A Financial Inc. (US)
  Great-West Life & Annuity Insurance Company
  Advised Assets Group LLC
  FASCore LLC

COMPETITORS

AXA Financial
CIBC
Industrial Alliance Insurance and Financial Servic
John Hancock Financial Services
Liberty Mutual
Manulife Financial
Nationwide Financial
Prudential
RBC Financial Group
RBC Insurance
Sun Life

HISTORICAL FINANCIALS

Company Type: Public

Income Statement
FYE: December 31

	ASSETS ($ mil.)	NET INCOME ($ mil.)	INCOME AS % OF ASSETS	EMPLOYEES
12/19	346,468	1,913	0.6%	24,000
12/18	314,064	2,272	0.7%	24,200
12/17	334,899	1,817	0.5%	23,300
12/16	296,746	2,050	0.7%	0
12/15	287,948	2,079	0.7%	0
Annual Growth	**4.7%**	**(2.1%)**	**—**	**—**

2019 Year-End Financials

Return on assets: 0.5%
Return on equity: 10.5%
Long-term debt ($ mil.): —
No. of shares (mil.): 927
Sales ($ mil): 34,325

Dividends
  Yield: 0.0%
  Payout: 66.2%
Market value ($ mil.): 23,794

	STOCK PRICE ($) FY Close	P/E High/Low		PER SHARE ($) Earnings	Dividends	Book Value
12/19	25.66	11	8	1.91	1.27	18.78
12/18	20.60	9	6	2.20	1.14	18.23
12/17	27.89	14	12	1.73	1.17	18.23
12/16	26.03	10	9	1.98	1.03	16.55
12/15	24.90	10	8	1.99	0.94	16.27
Annual Growth	**0.8%**	**—**	**—**	**(1.0%)**	**7.8%**	**3.6%**

Gree Electric Appliances Inc Of Zhuhai

Gree Electric Appliances finds it agreeable to keep things cool. The world's #1 maker of household air conditioners manufactures and distributes about a dozen different types of air conditioners — from small window units to large commercial systems. Gree Electric Appliances has manufacturing facilities in China Brazil and Pakistan capable of producing 10 million air conditioning units per year. The firm has been expanding its manufacturing facilities for several years and continues to explore new areas. Its appliances are sold in more than 180 countries. Company president Mingszhu Dong regularly makes Fortune magazine's list of the 50 most powerful women in business. Gree Group owns Gree Electric Appliances.

Operations

Gree Electric Appliances is an international air conditioning enterprise with integrated R&D manufacturing marketing and service. It has three brands — GREE TOSOT and KINGHOME — with a wide product range which includes residential air conditioners central air conditioners air source water heaters smart phones home appliances refrigerators etc.

Geographic Reach

The company has about 10 production bases around the world seven in China (Zhuhai Chongqing Hefei Zhengzhou Wuhan Shijiazhuang and Wuhu) as well as in Brazil and Pakistan.

Sales and Marketing

The company uses e-commerce to sell its products.

Financial Performance

In fiscal 2015 Gree Electric Appliances' net sales decreased by RMB 40 billion due to lower sales from household appliance manufacturing. Sale of air conditioners saw a decrease of about RMB 35 billion.

Net income dropped by RMB 1.6 billion due to decreased sales and lower income from investments.

In fiscal 2015 net cash provided by the operating activities increased by 31% due to a change in refund of tax and levies.

Strategy

Gree Electric Appliances' is focused on increasing its investment in R&D sustaining innovation in products and improving product quality and competitiveness.

Mergers and Acquisitions

In 2016 Gree Electric Appliances suspended its planned acquisition of electric vehicle maker Zhuhai Yinlong New Energy Co. Zhuhai Yinlong's shareholders declined to sell the company. The acquisition would have established Gree Electric's entry into the electric vehicle market.

EXECUTIVES

President, Mingzhu Dong
Auditors: China Audit Asia Pacific Certified Public Accountants Co., Ltd.

LOCATIONS

HQ: Gree Electric Appliances Inc Of Zhuhai
Jinji West Road, Qianshan, Zhuhai, Guangdong Province 519070
Phone: (86) 756 8669232   **Fax:** (86) 756 8622581
Web: www.gree.com.cn

2015 Sales

	% of total
Domestic	85
Overseas	15
Total	**100**

PRODUCTS/OPERATIONS

2015 Sales

	% of total
Household appliance manufacturing	90
Other businesses	10
Total	**100**

2015 Sales

	% of total
Air conditioners	85
Home appliances	2
Others	3
Other businesses	10
Total	**100**

COMPETITORS

Electrolux	Haier Group
Electrolux Home Appliances China	Samsung Group
GuangDong Midea	Whirlpool

HISTORICAL FINANCIALS

Company Type: Public

Income Statement
FYE: December 31

	REVENUE ($ mil.)	NET INCOME ($ mil.)	NET PROFIT MARGIN	EMPLOYEES
12/19	28,816	3,549	12.3%	0
12/18	29,080	3,809	13.1%	0
12/17	23,053	3,442	14.9%	0
12/16	15,857	2,220	14.0%	0
12/15	15,484	1,929	12.5%	0
Annual Growth	**16.8%**	**16.5%**		

2019 Year-End Financials

Debt ratio: 0.8%
Return on equity: 24.5%
Cash ($ mil.): 18,021
Current ratio: 1.26
Long-term debt ($ mil.): 6

No. of shares (mil.): —
Dividends
  Yield: —
  Payout: —
Market value ($ mil.): —

Grupo Aval Acciones Y Valores SA

EXECUTIVES

Presidente, LUIS CARLOS SARMIENTO GUTIERREZ
Auditors: KPMG S.A.S.

HQ: Grupo Aval Acciones Y Valores SA
  Carrera 13 No. 26A-47, Bogota
Phone: (57) 1 241 9700   **Fax:** (57) 1 287 1565
Web: www.grupoaval.com.co

HISTORICAL FINANCIALS

Company Type: Public

Income Statement				FYE: December 31
	REVENUE ($ mil.)	NET INCOME ($ mil.)	NET PROFIT MARGIN	EMPLOYEES
12/19	14,118	1,671	11.8%	111,192
12/18	13,113	1,604	12.2%	91,191
12/17	13,186	1,080	8.2%	80,565
12/16	12,350	1,178	9.5%	77,050
12/15	10,111	1,124	11.1%	76,095
Annual Growth	8.7%	10.4%	—	9.9%

2019 Year-End Financials

Debt ratio: —	No. of shares (mil.): —
Return on equity: 16.1%	Dividends
Cash ($ mil.): 16,586	Yield: 4.0%
Current ratio: —	Payout: 469.8%
Long-term debt ($ mil.): —	Market value ($ mil.): —

	STOCK PRICE ($) FY Close	P/E High/Low		PER SHARE ($) Earnings	Dividends	Book Value
12/19	8.72	0	0	0.08	0.35	0.49
12/18	5.90	0	0	0.07	0.34	0.44
12/17	8.50	0	0	0.05	0.40	0.40
12/16	7.94	0	0	0.05	0.38	0.39
12/15	6.52	0	0	0.05	0.70	0.36
Annual Growth	7.5%	—	—	10.4%	(15.9%)	8.0%

Grupo Bimbo SAB de CV (Mexico)

Bread isn't the only thing rising at Grupo Bimbo. The company is the largest commercial baking operation in Mexico where pan Bimbo is synonymous with soft white sandwich bread. It is one of the top bakers in the world as well. Offering more than 13000-plus products under some 100-plus umbrella brands Grupo Bimbo produces bread cookies and tortillas under the T a Rosa Bimbo Wonder and Marinela brands. Not content with dominating the Latin American bread markets the company also owns major operations in the US including Texas-based Mrs. Baird's and Bimbo Bakeries USA.

Operations

Grupo Bimbo makes snacks which include sliced bread buns & rolls pastries cakes cookies english muffins and tortillas though its 1700 sales centers.

Geographic Reach

Mexico-based Grupo Bimbo operates about 195 facilities in more than 30 countries Mexico generate about 50% of company's revenue followed by North America with about 35% and both Latin America and EAA countries brings about 10% of revenee.

Sales and Marketing

Grupo Bimbo spent $11 million $11.5 million and $10.4 million in advertising and promotional expense for years 2019 2018 and 2017 respec-

tively. Its largest customer accounts for more than 10% of its net sales.

Financial Performance

Net sales during 2019 grew 3% excluding the FX effect as a result of organic growth in Mexico and EAA coupled with strategic bolt-on acquisitions completed during the period; including the FX effect net sales increased 1%.

Cash held by the company at the end of 2019 increased by $1.3 billion to $6.3 billion compared from $7.6 billion in the prior year. Cash provided by operations was $28.5 billion while cash used for investing and financing activities were $12.9 billion and $16.6 billion respectively. Main use for cash was loans paid and purchase of property plant and equipment.

Strategy

In early 2020 Grupo Bimbo through its subsidiary Bimbo QSR announced a joint venture with Food Town the exclusive buns supplier and franchisee of McDonald's in Kazakhstan. This joint venture in which Grupo Bimbo holds 51% of share strengthens the manufacturing footprint of Bimbo QSR and aligns its relationship with the Quick Service Restaurants ("QSR") clients in Central Asia. This operation broadens Grupo Bimbo's global presence to 33 countries and strengthens its leadership in the QSR industry which is expected to have a compounded annual growth rate of 8.9% by 2023 in Asia..

EXECUTIVES

Chairman and CEO, Daniel Javier Servitje Montull, age 61
President Bimbo Bakeries USA, Alfred F. (Fred) Penny, age 66
CFO, Diego Gaxiola Cuevas, age 49
President Barcel, Ricardo Padilla Anguiano
SEVP, Javier Augusto Gonz lez Franco
President Bimbo S.A. de S.V., Miguel ngel Espinoza Ram rez
SEVP, Gabino Miguel G mez Carbajal
Auditors: Mancera, S.C. (Ernst & Young Global)

LOCATIONS

HQ: Grupo Bimbo SAB de CV (Mexico)
  Prolongacion Paseo de la Reforma No. 1000, Colonia Pena Blanca Santa Fe, Delegacion Alvaro Obregon, Mexico City 01210
Phone: (52) 55 5268 6600   **Fax:** (525) 55 5268 6697
Web: www.grupobimbo.com

2014 Plants

	No.
US & Canada	85
Latin America	32
Mexico	39
Europe	10
Asia	1
Total	167

2014 Sales

	% of total
US & Canada	47
Mexico	38
Other countries	15
Total	100

PRODUCTS/OPERATIONS

Selected Brands

Asia
  Bimbo
Latin America
  Mexico
  Barcel
  Bimbo
  Clever
  Coronado
  Del Hogar

El Globo
La Corona
Lonchibon
Marinela
Milpa Real
Ricolino
Suandy
Tí;a Rosa
Vero
Other countries
Bimbo Centroamé;rica
Breddy
Coronado Centroamé;rica
Ideal
La Mejor
Lido
Marinela
Monarca
Pix
Schmidt
Tulipan
Europe
Bimbo
Eagle
US
Arnold
Bimbo USA
Boboli
Brownberry
Earthgrains
Entenmann's
Francisco
Frenchbakery
Heiner's
Holsum
Home Maid Bread
Marinela USA
Master
Mickey
Mrs. Baird's
Old Country
Old Home
Orowea
Rainbo
Sara Lee
Stroehmann
Taystee
Thomas'
Tia Rosa USA

COMPETITORS

Aunt Millie's Bakeries	Lewis Bakeries
Azteca Foods	Mars Incorporated
Chattanooga Bakery	McKee Foods
Chupa Chups	Minsa
Flowers Foods	Mondelez International
Frito-Lay	Otis Spunkmeyer
George Weston	Pepperidge Farm
Glisten	Procter & Gamble
Gonnella Baking	Roman Meal
Greyston Bakery	Rubschlager Baking
Gruma	Schwebel Baking
Grupo Corvi	Snyder's-Lance
HARIBO	Spangler Candy
Haribo of America	Stroehmann Bakeries
Hershey	L.C.
Jelly Belly Candy	Tootsie Roll
King's Hawaiian	United States Bakery
Klosterman Baking	Yamazaki Baking
La Tortilla Factory	

HISTORICAL FINANCIALS

Company Type: Public

Income Statement				FYE: December 31
	REVENUE ($ mil.)	NET INCOME ($ mil.)	NET PROFIT MARGIN	EMPLOYEES
12/19	15,429	333	2.2%	148,638
12/18	14,659	295	2.0%	138,432
12/17	13,579	234	1.7%	138,171
12/16	12,185	285	2.3%	130,913
12/15	12,616	297	2.4%	127,152
Annual Growth	5.2%	2.9%	—	4.0%

Debt ratio: 1.6%
Return on equity: 8.2%
Cash ($ mil.): 330
Current ratio: 0.81
Long-term debt ($ mil.): 4,295

No. of shares (mil.): —
Dividends
  Yield: —
  Payout: —
Market value ($ mil.): —

Grupo Financiero Banorte S.A. BDE C V

EXECUTIVES

Director General, Alejandro Valenzuela
Auditors: Galaz, Yamazaki, Ruiz Urquiza, S.C.
  (member of Deloitte & Touche Tohmatsu)

LOCATIONS

HQ: Grupo Financiero Banorte S.A. BDE C V
  Avenida Prolongacion Reforma 1230, 14 piso, Col.
  Cruz Manca Santa Fe, Delegacion Cuajimalpa, Mexico
  City 05349
Phone: (52) 55 1670 2256
Web: www.banorte.com

HISTORICAL FINANCIALS

Company Type: Public

Income Statement   FYE: December 31

	ASSETS ($ mil.)	NET INCOME ($ mil.)	INCOME AS % OF ASSETS	EMPLOYEES
12/19	147,615	3,412	2.3%	0
12/18	151,395	2,985	2.0%	30,548
12/17	126,513	2,233	1.8%	29,915
12/16	118,476	1,803	1.5%	27,929
12/15	111,969	1,598	1.4%	27,594
Annual Growth	7.2%	20.9%	—	—

2019 Year-End Financials

Return on assets: 2.2%
Return on equity: 19.9%
Long-term debt ($ mil.): —
No. of shares (mil.): —
Sales ($ mil): 20,402

Dividends
  Yield: 5.1%
  Payout: 119.9%
Market value ($ mil.): —

	STOCK PRICE ($) FY Close	P/E High/Low		PER SHARE ($) Earnings	Dividends	Book Value
12/19	27.88	3	2	1.19	1.42	6.31
12/18	24.50	3	2	1.04	0.82	5.63
12/17	27.36	—	—	0.81	0.00	4.95
12/16	24.86	—	—	0.65	0.00	4.78
12/15	27.34			0.58	0.28	4.59
Annual Growth	0.5%	—	—	19.8%	50.2%	8.3%

Grupo Financiero Galicia SA (Argentina)

EXECUTIVES

President, Eduardo José Escasany
Vice President, Pablo Gutiérrez
Auditors: Price Waterhouse & Co. S.R.L.

LOCATIONS

HQ: Grupo Financiero Galicia SA (Argentina)
  Tte. Gral. Juan D. Peron 430, Piso 25, Buenos Aires
  C1038
Phone: (54) 11 4343 7528   **Fax:** (54) 11 4331 9183
Web: www.gfgsa.com

PRODUCTS/OPERATIONS

Selected subsidiaries
Banco de Galicia y Buenos Aires S.A
Galicia Administradora de Fondos S.A.
Galicia Warrants S.A.
Net Investment S.A.
Sudamericana Holding S.A.

COMPETITORS

Banco Francés   Citigroup
Banco Macro   Santander R o
Banco de la Naci n
  Argentina

HISTORICAL FINANCIALS

Company Type: Public

Income Statement   FYE: December 31

	ASSETS ($ mil.)	NET INCOME ($ mil.)	INCOME AS % OF ASSETS	EMPLOYEES
12/19	216,795	7,497	3.5%	9,718
12/18	180,165	(1,096)	—	10,209
12/17	154,849	2,148	1.4%	11,649
12/16	76,611	1,903	2.5%	11,956
12/15	51,152	1,372	2.7%	12,058
Annual Growth	43.5%	52.9%	—	(5.3%)

2019 Year-End Financials

Return on assets: 3.7%
Return on equity: 27.2%
Long-term debt ($ mil.): —
No. of shares (mil.): 1,426
Sales ($ mil): 79,060

Dividends
  Yield: 1.8%
  Payout: 5.7%
Market value ($ mil.): 23,156

	STOCK PRICE ($) FY Close	P/E High/Low		PER SHARE ($) Earnings	Dividends	Book Value
12/19	16.23	2	1	5.26	0.30	25.26
12/18	27.57	—	—	(0.77)	0.36	13.33
12/17	65.85	13	5	1.61	0.11	14.30
12/16	26.92	—	—	1.46	0.00	4.95
12/15	27.08	—	—	1.06	0.02	3.52
Annual Growth	(12.0%)	—	—	49.4%	88.4%	63.6%

Gunma Bank Ltd (The)

EXECUTIVES

President, AKIHIKO FUKAI
Managing Director, Takaya Kimura
Executive Vice President, Tetsuo Igarashi
Chairman, Takuji Tsuchikane
Auditors: Ernst & Young ShinNihon LLC

LOCATIONS

HQ: Gunma Bank Ltd (The)
  194 Motosoja-machi, Maebashi, Gunma 371-8611
Phone: (81) 27 252 1111
Web: www.gunmabank.co.jp

COMPETITORS

77 Bank   Ito-Yokado
Hachijuni Bank   Japan Post

HISTORICAL FINANCIALS

Company Type: Public

Income Statement   FYE: March 31

	ASSETS ($ mil.)	NET INCOME ($ mil.)	INCOME AS % OF ASSETS	EMPLOYEES
03/20	77,538	205	0.3%	4,730
03/19	73,504	210	0.3%	4,743
03/18	75,383	267	0.4%	4,737
03/17	71,432	235	0.3%	4,724
03/16	67,958	254	0.4%	4,671
Annual Growth	3.4%	(5.3%)	—	0.3%

2020 Year-End Financials

Return on assets: 0.2%
Return on equity: 4.3%
Long-term debt ($ mil.): —
No. of shares (mil.): 419
Sales ($ mil): 1,317

Dividends
  Yield: —
  Payout: 24.6%
Market value ($ mil.): —

Hachijuni Bank, Ltd. (Japan)

Auditors: Deloitte Touche Tohmatsu LLC

LOCATIONS

HQ: Hachijuni Bank, Ltd. (Japan)
  178-8 Aza Okada, Oaza Nakagosho, Nagano 380-8682
Phone: (81) 26 227 1182
Web: www.82bank.co.jp

HISTORICAL FINANCIALS

Company Type: Public

Income Statement   FYE: March 31

	ASSETS ($ mil.)	NET INCOME ($ mil.)	INCOME AS % OF ASSETS	EMPLOYEES
03/20	96,458	203	0.2%	5,101
03/19	94,375	203	0.2%	5,301
03/18	87,666	243	0.3%	5,484
03/17	77,847	235	0.3%	5,449
03/16	72,775	268	0.4%	5,482
Annual Growth	7.3%	(6.7%)	—	(1.8%)

2020 Year-End Financials

Return on assets: 0.2%
Return on equity: 2.9%
Long-term debt ($ mil.): —
No. of shares (mil.): 489
Sales ($ mil): 1,521

Dividends
  Yield: —
  Payout: 31.3%
Market value ($ mil.): —

Haci Omer Sabanci Holding AS

EXECUTIVES

President Cement, Mehmet Hacikamiloglu
CEO, Mehmet G ¶ §men, age 64
CFO, Baris Oran
President Insurance, Haluk Din şer, age 58
President Retail, Ata Koseoglu
President Human Resources, Meral E. Kurdas
President Industry, Cenk Alper
Vice Chairman, Erol Sabanci, age 82
Chairman, Guler Sabanci
Auditors: PwC Bagimsiz Denetim ve Serbest
Muhasebeci Mali Musavirlik A.S.

LOCATIONS

HQ: Haci Omer Sabanci Holding AS
Sabanci Center 4, Levent, Istanbul 34330
Phone: (90) 212 385 80 80   **Fax:** (90) 212 385 88 88
Web: www.sabanci.com

PRODUCTS/OPERATIONS

2016 sales

	% of total
Domestic sales	88
Foreign sales	12
Total	**100**

2016 sales

	% of total
Turkey	92
EU Countries	8
Total	**100**

2016 sales

	% of total
Financial instutions	27
Manufacturing	18
Public sector	17
Individual	15
Wholesale and retail trade	9
Other	14
Total	**100**

Selected Investments

Cement
  Akçansa
  Çimsa
Energy
  Enerjisa
Financial services
  Akbank
  Aksigorta
Retail
  Carrefoursa
  Teknosa
Industrial
  Brisa
  Kordsa Global
  Temsa
  Sasa
  Yunsa
Other
  Bimsa
  Philip Morrissa
  Philsa
  Tursa

COMPETITORS

Alarko	Global Yatirim
Alfa Group	Ko §
Berkshire Hathaway	Yazicilar
Dogan Holding	

HISTORICAL FINANCIALS

Company Type: Public

Income Statement   FYE: December 31

	ASSETS ($ mil.)	NET INCOME ($ mil.)	INCOME AS % OF ASSETS	EMPLOYEES
12/19	68,286	635	0.9%	62,051
12/18	70,249	723	1.0%	64,294
12/17	93,633	920	1.0%	63,152
12/16	87,371	753	0.9%	62,312
12/15	90,896	765	0.8%	63,281
Annual Growth	(6.9%)	(4.6%)	—	(0.5%)

2019 Year-End Financials

Return on assets: 0.9%
Return on equity: 12.0%
Long-term debt ($ mil.): —
No. of shares (mil.): —
Sales ($ mil): 10,240

Dividends
  Yield: —
  Payout: 264.6%
  Market value ($ mil.): —

	STOCK PRICE ($) FY Close	P/E High/Low		PER SHARE ($) Earnings	Dividends	Book Value
12/19	0.00	—	—	0.00	0.01	0.03
12/18	0.00	—	—	0.00	0.01	0.03
12/17	0.72	40	23	0.00	0.02	0.03
Annual Growth		—	—	(8.9%)	(14.0%)	

(5.6%)

Haier Smart Home Co Ltd

Auditors: Shandong Huide CPA Co., Ltd.

LOCATIONS

HQ: Haier Smart Home Co Ltd
Haier Industrial Park, Laoshan District, Qingdao,
Shandong Province 266101
Phone: (86) 532 88931670   **Fax:** (86) 532 88931689
Web: www.haier.net/cn/

HISTORICAL FINANCIALS

Company Type: Public

Income Statement   FYE: December 31

	REVENUE ($ mil.)	NET INCOME ($ mil.)	NET PROFIT MARGIN	EMPLOYEES
12/19	28,852	1,179	4.1%	0
12/18	26,651	1,081	4.1%	0
12/17	24,472	1,064	4.3%	0
12/16	17,146	725	4.2%	0
12/15	13,819	662	4.8%	0
Annual Growth	20.2%	15.5%	—	—

2019 Year-End Financials

Debt ratio: 2.7%
Return on equity: 18.8%
Cash ($ mil.): 5,199
Current ratio: 1.05
Long-term debt ($ mil.): 2,914

No. of shares (mil.): —
Dividends
  Yield: —
  Payout: —
  Market value ($ mil.): —

Hakuhodo Dy Holdings Inc

EXECUTIVES

President and CEO, Hirokazu Toda
EVP and CFO, Kunihiko Sawada
Senior Executive Corporate Officer, Michael Birkin, age 62
Senior Executive Corporate Officer, Mitsumasa Matsuzaki
Chairman, Junji Narita, age 94
Auditors: KPMG AZSA LLC

LOCATIONS

HQ: Hakuhodo Dy Holdings Inc
5-3-1 Akasaka, Minato-ku, Tokyo 107-6320
Phone: (81) 3 6441 6247
Web: www.hakuhodody-holdings.co.jp

COMPETITORS

Asatsu-DK	Omnicom
Dentsu	Publicis Groupe
Grey Group	Video Research
Havas	WPP
Interpublic Group	

HISTORICAL FINANCIALS

Company Type: Public

Income Statement   FYE: March 31

	REVENUE ($ mil.)	NET INCOME ($ mil.)	NET PROFIT MARGIN	EMPLOYEES
03/20	13,507	413	3.1%	34,081
03/19	13,053	428	3.3%	31,392
03/18	12,572	280	2.2%	27,719
03/17	11,228	231	2.1%	24,384
03/16	10,821	254	2.3%	22,135
Annual Growth	5.7%	13.0%	—	11.4%

2020 Year-End Financials

Debt ratio: 0.1%
Return on equity: 15.6%
Cash ($ mil.): 1,534
Current ratio: 1.50
Long-term debt ($ mil.): 978

No. of shares (mil.): 373
Dividends
  Yield: 0.0%
  Payout: 48.3%
  Market value ($ mil.): 11,641

	STOCK PRICE ($) FY Close	P/E High/Low		PER SHARE ($) Earnings	Dividends	Book Value
03/20	31.19	0	0	1.11	0.54	7.14
03/19	32.65	0	0	1.15	0.49	6.84
03/18	28.43	0	0	0.75	0.47	8.68
03/17	25.00	0	0	0.62	0.39	7.32
03/16	21.83	0	0	0.68	0.29	6.53
Annual Growth	9.3%	—	—	13.0%	16.4%	2.3%

Hang Seng Bank Ltd.

Auditors: PricewaterhouseCoopers

LOCATIONS

HQ: Hang Seng Bank Ltd.
83 Des Voeux Road Central,
Phone: (852) 2198 1111   **Fax:** (852) 2868 4047
Web: www.hangseng.com

HISTORICAL FINANCIALS

Company Type: Public

Income Statement				FYE: December 31
	ASSETS ($ mil.)	NET INCOME ($ mil.)	INCOME AS % OF ASSETS	EMPLOYEES
12/19	215,363	3,190	1.5%	10,331
12/18	200,622	3,091	1.5%	10,298
12/17	189,171	2,561	1.4%	9,980
12/16	177,604	2,090	1.2%	9,708
12/15	172,163	3,547	2.1%	10,141
Annual Growth	5.8%	(2.6%)	—	0.5%

2019 Year-End Financials

Return on assets: 1.5%
Return on equity: 14.5%
Long-term debt ($ mil.): —
No. of shares (mil.): 1,911
Sales ($ mil): 10,029

Dividends
Yield: 4.4%
Payout: 56.5%
Market value ($ mil.): 39,422

	STOCK PRICE ($) FY Close	P/E High/Low		PER SHARE ($) Earnings	Dividends	Book Value
12/19	20.62	2	2	1.64	0.92	12.01
12/18	22.38	2	2	1.59	0.81	10.82
12/17	24.75	2	2	1.32	0.74	10.18
12/16	18.55	2	2	1.07	1.07	9.49
12/15	19.11	145	114	0.02	0.65	9.58
Annual Growth	1.9%		—	—207.5%	9.0%	5.8%

Hannover Rueckversicherung SE

Who insures insurance companies over and over? Hannover! Hannover R ck (Hannover Re) is the second-largest German reinsurance company (Munich Re is #1) and the fourth-largest such company in the world. Through more than 100 subsidiaries the company provides property and casualty (Hannover Re's largest segment) financial life and health reinsurance products in about 150 countries worldwide. Financial reinsurance is provided through Hannover Re Advanced Solutions a Dublin-based consortium managed jointly with HDI Reinsurance (Ireland); both Hannover Re and HDI Reinsurance (Ireland) are subsidiaries of HDI Haftpflichtverband der Deutschen Industrie.

EXECUTIVES

Executive Board Member Property and Casualty Target Markets, Michael Pickel, age 60
CFO, Roland Vogel
Executive Board Member Life and Health, Klaus Miller, age 60
Executive Board Member Property and Casualty Specialty Lines Worldwide, Sven Althoff
Executive Board Member Life and Health, Claude Ch¨vre
Executive Board Member Property and Casualty Coordination and Global Reinsurance, J rgen Gr ber
Deputy Chairman, Klaus Sturany, age 74
Executive Board Member Non-Life, Ulrich Wallin, age 59
Chairman, Herbert K. Haas
Auditors: PricewaterhouseCoopers GmbH Wirtschaftpruefungsgesellschaft

LOCATIONS

HQ: Hannover Rueckversicherung SE
Karl-Wiechert-Allee 50, Hannover D-30625
Phone: (49) 511 5604 0   **Fax:** (49) 511 5604 1188
Web: www.hannover-re.com

2013 Premiums Written

	% of total
Europe	
Germany	9
UK	19
France	4
Other countries	12
North America	
US	24
Other countries	5
Asia	12
Australia	6
Africa	3
Other regions	6
Total	**100**

COMPETITORS

Everest Re	Reinsurance Group of
General Re	America
Lloyd's	SCOR
Munich Re Group	Swiss Re
PartnerRe	XL Group plc

HISTORICAL FINANCIALS

Company Type: Public

Income Statement				FYE: December 31
	ASSETS ($ mil.)	NET INCOME ($ mil.)	INCOME AS % OF ASSETS	EMPLOYEES
12/19	80,116	1,441	1.8%	3,083
12/18	73,874	1,213	1.6%	3,317
12/17	73,359	1,149	1.6%	3,251
12/16	67,078	1,236	1.8%	2,893
12/15	68,854	1,253	1.8%	2,762
Annual Growth	3.9%	3.6%	—	2.8%

2019 Year-End Financials

Return on assets: 1.8%
Return on equity: 13.3%
Long-term debt ($ mil.): —
No. of shares (mil.): 120
Sales ($ mil): 24,046

Dividends
Yield: 2.2%
Payout: 67.3%
Market value ($ mil.): 11,788

	STOCK PRICE ($) FY Close	P/E High/Low		PER SHARE ($) Earnings	Dividends	Book Value
12/19	97.75	9	6	11.96	2.15	98.02
12/18	67.66	8	7	10.07	2.19	83.34
12/17	62.92	9	7	9.53	8.26	84.77
12/16	54.20	6	5	10.25	6.86	78.77
12/15	57.35	6	4	10.39	1.75	72.87
Annual Growth	14.3%		—	— 3.6%	5.3%	7.7%

Hanwa Co Ltd (Japan)

Auditors: KPMG AZSA LLC

LOCATIONS

HQ: Hanwa Co Ltd (Japan)
1-13-1 Tsukiji, Chuo-ku, Tokyo 104-8429
Phone: (81) 3 3544 2202   **Fax:** (81) 3 3544 2351
Web: www.hanwa.co.jp

HISTORICAL FINANCIALS

Company Type: Public

Income Statement				FYE: March 31
	REVENUE ($ mil.)	NET INCOME ($ mil.)	NET PROFIT MARGIN	EMPLOYEES
03/20	17,572	(125)	—	5,455
03/19	18,733	125	0.7%	4,733
03/18	16,867	163	1.0%	4,211
03/17	13,541	146	1.1%	3,774
03/16	13,462	226	1.7%	3,631
Annual Growth	6.9%	—	—	10.7%

2020 Year-End Financials

Debt ratio: 0.3%
Return on equity: (-7.7%)
Cash ($ mil.): 619
Current ratio: 1.72
Long-term debt ($ mil.): 2,325

No. of shares (mil.): 40
Dividends
Yield: —
Payout: —
Market value ($ mil.): —

HDFC Bank Ltd

Auditors: KPMG Assurance and Consulting Services LLP

LOCATIONS

HQ: HDFC Bank Ltd
HDFC Bank House, Senapati Bapat Marg, Lower Parel, Mumbai 400 013
Phone: (91) 22 6652 1099   **Fax:** (91) 22 2496 0737
Web: www.hdfcbank.com

HISTORICAL FINANCIALS

Company Type: Public

Income Statement				FYE: March 31
	ASSETS ($ mil.)	NET INCOME ($ mil.)	INCOME AS % OF ASSETS	EMPLOYEES
03/20	397,605	6,483	1.6%	116,971
03/19	330,802	5,482	1.7%	98,061
03/18	283,156	4,446	1.6%	88,253
03/17	225,855	3,500	1.5%	84,325
03/16	192,719	2,937	1.5%	87,555
Annual Growth	19.8%	21.9%	—	7.5%

2020 Year-End Financials

Return on assets: 1.7%
Return on equity: 14.7%
Long-term debt ($ mil.): —
No. of shares (mil.): —
Sales ($ mil): 35,127

Dividends
Yield: 1.0%
Payout: 34.9%
Market value ($ mil.): —

	STOCK PRICE ($) FY Close	P/E High/Low		PER SHARE ($) Earnings	Dividends	Book Value
03/20	38.46	3	1	1.18	0.41	8.60
03/19	115.91	3	2	1.01	0.27	7.47
03/18	98.77	3	2	0.85	0.25	5.64
03/17	75.22	3	2	0.68	0.20	4.99
03/16	61.63	3	2	0.58	0.18	4.28
Annual Growth	(11.1%)		—	— 19.5%	23.4%	19.0%

Hebei Iron & Steel Co Ltd

Hesteel (formerly the Hebei Iron and Steel or the HBIS Group) has a steely presence in China as its second largest (and longest established) iron & steel company producing around 45 million metric tons annually. The company is #4 in the world by steel output behind ArcelorMittal Baosteel and Nippon Steel. It smelts processes and distributes some 200-different iron and steel products. Products include plates rods wires and profiles primarily serving the automobile manufacturing and construction industries. Almost all its sales come from the domestic Chinese market.

Operations

Hesteel reports four business segments.

Iron & Steel is the core business segment producing around 200 products almost everything except seamless tube. The company's cold-rolled sheet ultra-strength rebar heavy plate steel pipe and special steel bars are the dominant products. This segment also has its own regional marketing and R&D divisions catering to customers globally.

Hesteel's Overseas business manages four steel companies and two mines spreading across three continents.

The Non-Steel sector is a budding segment within the company that aims to focus on the expansion of Hesteel's activities from mining resources to modern logistics equipment manufacturing steel trade processing resource utilization technology medical health and even providing social services.

Centered on integration of production and finance Hesteel's Finance segment is geared towards efficient capital operations and providing leases securities and supply chain financial services like factoring.

Geographic Reach

Though majority of Hesteel's iron and steel products serves the domestic Chinese market the company claims that its products are present in more than 100 countries. Additionally the company has direct ownership or shares in approximately 70 companies including the US the UK Australia South Africa Canada Singapore Switzerland and Hong Kong. A clear majority of the company's sales (more than 70%) is concentrated in North China region.

Sales and Marketing

Hesteel's leading products include coils (hot & cold rolled pickling and galvanized) heavy plates rebars wire rods sections and strips serving a wide range of industries including construction manufacturing shipping and energy. More than 70% of the company's sales comprised of specialized products sold to automakers including BMW Mercedes-Benz Volkswagen and Toyota as well as producers of appliances.

Strategy

Hesteel's domestic sales has been boosted by the Belt and Road Initiative a development strategy adopted by the Chinese government to build road and maritime infrastructure. However with increasing global competition and a continued weak demand in the industry due to oversupply Hesteel is trying to expand its steel business globally by boosting the number of international assets and global marketing service platforms.

The company acquired the Smederevo mill in Serbia back in 2016 to increase its presence in Europe's high-end manufacturing business which saw significant production and profitability increases the following year. In 2017 Hesteel ac-quired Palabora Mining the largest copper producer in South Africa. A few years earlier the company's 51% stake in Switzerland-based Duferco the world's largest steel products marketing service provider indicated its desire to boost global steel sales. Hesteel also claims to be investing in mineral resources financial services modern logistics steel trading and social services including setting up of specialized subsidiaries like HBIS Energy HBIS Chemical and HBIS New Material. However almost all its revenue continues to come from iron & steel sales in North China.

Though an excess supply of steel products in the Chinese market dampened demand for 2017 Hesteel aims to produce 2% more steel for 2018 (some 27 million tons). Stronger demand from the construction of the new city of Xiongan infrastructure projects in the Beijing-Tianjin-Hebei region plus the continued construction of the Belts & Roads projects has resulted in a slightly improved forecast. One indication is the company's incremental raising of domestic steel prices three times between August 2017 and September 2018.

However domestic output restrictions may lower output while stringent environmental standards may raise production costs. For instance Hesteel is looking to set up new plants away from its home province of Hebei as tight regulations over steel producers in the area are expected to be maintained in the near future due to smog pollution.

Mergers and Acquisitions

Hesteel acquired 98 properties of Serbia's steel mill Zelezara Smederevo in July 2016 for a total of €46 million with an aim to increases its global sales of steel products with a special eye on Europe's high-end manufacturing business.

In 2017 the company along with other investors also acquired Palabora Copper a South African copper mining company. It operates a mine with an annual capacity of 45000 tons and a smelter comples in Limpopo.

EXECUTIVES

Chairman, Yong Yu
Vice Chairman, Zhaofeng Peng
Auditors: Zhongxing Caiguanghua CPA Office Co., Ltd.

LOCATIONS

HQ: Hebei Iron & Steel Co Ltd
No. 40, Yuhua West Road, Qiaoxi District, Shijiazhuang, Hebei Province 050000
Phone: (86) 311 66770709   **Fax:** (86) 311 66778711
Web: www.hebgtgf.com

COMPETITORS

Anshan Iron and Steel
Baosteel
China Steel
Jiangsu Shagang
Maanshan Iron & Steel
Mitsubishi Steel Mfg.
Nippon Steel & Sumitomo Metal Corporation
Shougang Corp.
Wuhan Iron & Steel
Xinxing Ductile Iron Pipes

HISTORICAL FINANCIALS

Company Type: Public

Income Statement   FYE: December 31

	REVENUE ($ mil.)	NET INCOME ($ mil.)	NET PROFIT MARGIN	EMPLOYEES
12/19	17,460	367	2.1%	0
12/18	17,585	527	3.0%	0
12/17	16,747	279	1.7%	0
12/16	10,735	224	2.1%	0
12/15	11,256	88	0.8%	0
Annual Growth	11.6%	42.9%	—	—

2019 Year-End Financials

Debt ratio: 5.1%	No. of shares (mil.): —
Return on equity: 4.5%	Dividends
Cash ($ mil.): 3,531	Yield: —
Current ratio: 0.52	Payout: —
Long-term debt ($ mil.): 1,641	Market value ($ mil.): —

HeidelbergCement AG

HeidelbergCement believes in concrete results. One of the world's largest building materials companies HeidelbergCement sells cement concrete sand and gravel. It is No.1 worldwide in aggregates production and ready-mixed concrete and No. 2 in cement. Together the three product categories account for about 85% of sales. (Aggregates are the main component in concrete and asphalt but are also used as base courses in the construction of infrastructure such as roads.) HeidelbergCement also offers services such as worldwide trading in cement and coal by sea. The company has around 600 mining sites and over 3000 plants worldwide. All total it has some 2700 locations across five continents.

Operations

HeidelbergCement extracts raw materials produces building materials conducts marketing and distributes materials to customers. Specific activities include geological exploration of raw material deposits purchasing or leasing the land where the deposits are located obtaining mining concessions and environmental certifications constructing manufacturing facilities in cooperation with external service providers extracting raw materials and facilities maintenance.

The company sold nearly 126 million metric tons of cement some 308 million metric tons of aggregates roughly 50 million cubic meters of ready-mixed concrete and about 11 million metric tons of asphalt. It operates about 135 cement plants (plus 20 as part of joint ventures) around 600 quarries and aggregate pits and over 1460 ready-mixed concrete production sites worldwide.

Cement contributes more than 40% to total sales ready-mixed concrete-asphalt some 25% and aggregates about 20%. Other service-based joint ventures account for the remainder.

Geographic Reach

Headquartered in Germany HeidelbergCement has operations in more than 50 countries. The company is divided into five geographic regions: Western and Southern Europe (more than 25% of total sales) North America (slightly less than 25%) Asia/Pacific (about 20%) Northern and Eastern Europe-Central Asia (about 15%) and Africa-Eastern Mediterranean Basin (about 10%). Trading subsidiary HTC accounts for the remaining revenue. HCT supplies customers in about 90 countries from about 45 supplier countries. The majority of deliveries go to Africa Asia and North America. Key supplier countries include Saudi Arabia Turkey Vietnam and Indonesia.The US is the company's largest market by country at around 20% of sales. Other major markets include the UK Germany Australia and France.

Sales and Marketing

HeidelbergCement's products are used for the construction of houses traffic routes infrastructure and commercial and industrial facilities.

Financial Performance

Note: Growth rates may differ after conversion to US Dollars.

The company's revenue has been rising in the last five years with an overall growth of 40% between 2015 and 2019.

Group revenue rose by 4% in comparison with the previous year to ?18.9 billion (previous year: ?18.1 billion). Excluding consolidation and exchange rate effects Group revenue grew by 2%. Changes to the scope of consolidation of ?71 million and exchange rate effects of ?326 million had a positive impact on revenue.

The company's profit for the year ended 2019 was ?1.1 billion a 5% decrease compared to the previous year.

The company's cash for the year ended 2019 totaled ?3.5 billion. Operating activities generated ?2.7 billion while investing activities used ?905.8 million mainly for capital expenditures. Financing activities used another ?873.4 million mainly for repayment of bonds loans and lease liabilities.

Strategy

HeidelbergCement's target is to increase the value of the group in the long term through sustainable and result-oriented growth. Earning the cost of capital is the necessary prerequisite to guarantee the company's permanent entrepreneurial ability to act and invest continuously in innovation and growth as well as in the development of its personnel and the company.

The four pillars of our business strategy are as follows:

Operational excellence and digitalization. A key objective is to make sure that the productivity enhancement in input factors such as working time capital and energy at least offsets inflation-related cost increases;

Sustainability. The sustainability strategy has six action areas: Driving profitability and innovation; Achieving excellence in occupational health and safety; Reducing the company's ecological footprint; Enabling the circular economy; Being a good neighbor; and ensuring compliance and creating transparency;

Profitable growth and vertical integration. The creation development and maintenance of vertically integrated market positions in the cement aggregates ready-mixed concrete and asphalt business lines is the core of the growth strategy of HeidelbergCement. The company's goal are strong positions in markets with long-term potential. It strives to avoid markets with unjustifiable high political economic or compliance risks and to retain key market positions regardless of economic cycles; and

Financial performance. The company aims to achieve a balance between short-term profitability and long-term value creation. Investment decisions are taken based on their market strategic financial and technical attractiveness.

Mergers and Acquisitions

To strengthen its market position in Bangladesh HeidelbergCement completed the purchase of a 100% shareholding in both Emirates Cement Bangladesh Limited and Emirates Power Company Limited Munshiganj in late 2019. The purchase price of ?19.7 million was paid in cash

In 2019 HeidelbergCement finalized the acquisition of the aggregates and ready-mixed concrete activities of Cemex in central France. By purchasing 100% of the shares in Cemex Bétons Centre

et Ouest S.A.S. Rungis as well as production sites and distribution facilities for aggregates HeidelbergCement has acquired 28 ready-mixed concrete plants and seven aggregates quarries and has strengthened its vertically integrated market position in central France. The purchase price of ?28.0 million was paid in cash.

Company Background

HeidelbergCement traces its roots back to 1872 when Johann Philipp Schifferdecker a wealthy brewer went to Heidelberg Germany where his son was studying chemistry. Once there he bought a bankrupt cement plant located on the Neckar River near Heidelberg.

EXECUTIVES

Member of the Managing Board Regional Responsibility for Central Europe East, Daniel Gauthier, age 64

Member Managing Board Asia-Oceania and Heidelberg Technology Center, Albert Scheuer, age 62

Chairman, Bernd Scheifele, age 62

Member of the Managing Board Central Europe Central Asia Sales and Marketing and worldwide coordination of secondary cementitious materials., Andreas Kern, age 62

CFO, Lorenz N ¤ger

Deputy Chairman, Dominik von Achten, age 55

Auditors: Ernst & Young GmbH

LOCATIONS

HQ: HeidelbergCement AG
Berliner Strasse 6, Heidelberg D-69120
Phone: (49) 6221 481 13227 **Fax:** (49) 6221 481 13217
Web: www.heidelbergcement.com

2015 sales

	% of total
Western and Northern Europe	30
North America	27
Asia-Pacific	20
Eastern Europe-Central Asia	8
Africa-Mediterranean Basin	7
Group Services	8
Total	**100**

PRODUCTS/OPERATIONS

2015 sales

	% of total
Cement	40
Aggregates	20
Ready-mixed concrete-asphalt	27
Service-joint ventures other	13
Total	**100**

Selected Products

Cement
  Binders for geotechnology environmental technology and road construction
  Decorative concrete
  Fast-hardening cement
  Masonry cement
  Specialty cements for hydraulic engineering sewage works construction soil injection and masonry repair and waste dump sealing
Concrete
  Light heavy and aerated concrete building blocks
  Pavers
  Prefab ceilings walls cellar units and sewage works units
Building Materials
  Building chemicals
  Dry mortar
  Environmental technology
  Expanded clay
  Limestone and lime products
  Sand-lime bricks
  Special gypsums
Aggregates
Other
  Plaster

Self-compacting concrete
Steel-fiber concrete

COMPETITORS

Aggregate Industries	Tarmac
BUZZI UNICEM	Titan Cement
CEMEX	U.S. Concrete
CRH	USG
Eagle Materials	Vicat
FLSmidth	Vulcan Materials
Franz Haniel	Wienerberger
LafargeHolcim	

HISTORICAL FINANCIALS

Company Type: Public

Income Statement   FYE: December 31

	REVENUE ($ mil.)	NET INCOME ($ mil.)	NET PROFIT MARGIN	EMPLOYEES
12/19	21,264	1,224	5.8%	55,047
12/18	20,787	1,308	6.3%	57,939
12/17	20,755	1,100	5.3%	59,054
12/16	15,973	745	4.7%	60,424
12/15	14,700	871	5.9%	45,453
Annual Growth	9.7%	8.9%	—	4.9%

2019 Year-End Financials

Debt ratio: 34.8%	No. of shares (mil.): 198
Return on equity: 3.3%	Dividends
Cash ($ mil.): 3,976	Yield: 2.1%
Current ratio: 1.12	Payout: —
Long-term debt ($ mil.): 10,640	Market value ($ mil.): 2,871

	STOCK PRICE ($) FY Close	P/E High/Low		PER SHARE ($) Earnings	Dividends	Book Value
12/19	14.47	4	2	6.18	0.30	96.12
12/18	12.22	4	2	6.60	0.29	89.06
12/17	21.58	5	4	5.54	0.25	87.95
12/16	18.62	5	3	3.86	0.18	85.64
12/15	16.65	4	3	4.64	0.11	86.45
Annual Growth	(3.4%)	—	—	7.4%	29.4%	2.7%

Heineken Holding NV (Netherlands)

Auditors: Deloitte Accountants B.V.

LOCATIONS

HQ: Heineken Holding NV (Netherlands)
Tweede Weteringplantsoen 5, Amsterdam 1017 ZD
Phone: (31) 20 622 11 52   **Fax:** (31) 20 625 22 13
Web: www.heinekenholding.com

HISTORICAL FINANCIALS

Company Type: Public

Income Statement   FYE: December 31

	REVENUE ($ mil.)	NET INCOME ($ mil.)	NET PROFIT MARGIN	EMPLOYEES
12/19	26,911	1,220	4.5%	85,853
12/18	25,733	1,100	4.3%	85,610
12/17	26,238	1,171	4.5%	80,425
12/16	21,953	822	3.7%	73,525
12/15	22,340	1,042	4.7%	73,767
Annual Growth	4.8%	4.0%		3.9%

2019 Year-End Financials

Debt ratio: 41.1%
Return on equity: 14.3%
Cash ($ mil.): 2,044
Current ratio: 0.68
Long-term debt ($ mil.): 15,006

No. of shares (mil.): 288
Dividends
 Yield: 1.5%
 Payout: 17.7%
Market value ($ mil.): 14,041

	STOCK PRICE ($) FY Close	P/E High/Low	PER SHARE ($) Earnings	Dividends	Book Value
12/19	48.75	14 11	4.23	0.75	31.16
12/18	43.15	15 12	3.82	0.72	28.46
12/17	49.45	15 11	4.06	0.66	27.61
12/16	34.95	15 12	2.85	0.59	24.19
12/15	39.41	12 8	3.62	0.52	25.53
Annual Growth	5.5%	— —	4.0%	9.2%	5.1%

Heineken NV (Netherlands)

EXECUTIVES

Director, Marcus Goumans
Auditors: Deloitte Accountants B.V.

LOCATIONS

HQ: Heineken NV (Netherlands)
 Tweede Weteringplantsoen 21, Amsterdam 1017 ZD
Phone: (31) 20 523 92 39   **Fax:** (31) 20 626 35 03
Web: www.theheinekencompany.com

HISTORICAL FINANCIALS

Company Type: Public

Income Statement				FYE: December 31
	REVENUE ($ mil.)	NET INCOME ($ mil.)	NET PROFIT MARGIN	EMPLOYEES
12/19	26,911	2,431	9.0%	85,853
12/18	25,733	2,179	8.5%	85,610
12/17	26,238	2,319	8.8%	80,425
12/16	21,953	1,626	7.4%	73,525
12/15	22,340	2,060	9.2%	73,767
Annual Growth	4.8%	4.2%	—	3.9%

2019 Year-End Financials

Debt ratio: 38.7%
Return on equity: 14.2%
Cash ($ mil.): 2,044
Current ratio: 0.68
Long-term debt ($ mil.): 13,880

No. of shares (mil.): 575
Dividends
 Yield: 1.4%
 Payout: 17.7%
Market value ($ mil.): 30,739

	STOCK PRICE ($) FY Close	P/E High/Low	PER SHARE ($) Earnings	Dividends	Book Value
12/19	53.43	15 11	4.23	0.75	31.51
12/18	43.97	16 13	3.82	0.72	28.84
12/17	52.12	16 12	4.06	0.66	28.01
12/16	37.41	17 13	2.85	0.59	24.54
12/15	42.75	14 9	3.59	0.53	25.88
Annual Growth	5.7%	— —	4.2%	9.1%	5.0%

Hengli Petrochemical Co Ltd

EXECUTIVES

Chairman, Luo Shaoning
Auditors: Dalian Hualian Certified Public Accountants Co., Ltd.

LOCATIONS

HQ: Hengli Petrochemical Co Ltd
 No. 1, Zhoushuizi Square, Ganjingzi District, Dalian, Liaoning Province 116033
Phone: (86) 411 86641861   **Fax:** (86) 411 86641645
Web: www.dlrpm.com

HISTORICAL FINANCIALS

Company Type: Public

Income Statement			FYE: December 31
	REVENUE ($ mil.)	NET INCOME ($ mil.)	NET PROFIT MARGIN	EMPLOYEES
12/19	14,483	1,440	9.9%	0
12/18	8,732	483	5.5%	0
12/17	3,425	264	7.7%	0
12/16	2,770	169	6.1%	0
12/15	129	(37)	—	0
Annual Growth	225.2%	—	—	—

2019 Year-End Financials

Debt ratio: 8.4%
Return on equity: 31.3%
Cash ($ mil.): 2,372
Current ratio: 0.65
Long-term debt ($ mil.): 7,512

No. of shares (mil.): —
Dividends
 Yield: —
 Payout: —
Market value ($ mil.): —

Henkel AG & Co KGAA

Home and hearth are at the heart of Henkel. The company makes branded products for laundry and homecare (Persil All Pril) cosmetics and toiletries (Schwarzkopf Dial Syoss) and many adhesives (Loctite Pritt UniBond). Henkel's business is centered in Europe with a growing presence in developing economies such as Asia Africa the Middle East and Latin America. Henkel owns subsidiaries in about 80 countries including Henkel North American Consumer Goods in the US with offices located nearly everywhere. Started in 1876 the company is owned by descendants of the founding Henkel family.

Operations

Henkel divides its business into three units. Adhesive technologies accounts for more than 45% of sales which includes industrial adhesives as well as those for consumers craftsmen and building. Laundry & Home Care accounts for about one-third of sales; and Beauty Care accounts for about 20%.

Geographic Reach

Laundry & Homecare and Beauty Care products are primarily sold in Europe and North America as well as certain developing regions. The company's adhesive products have a worldwide presence. Emerging markets (Eastern Europe Africa/Middle East Latin America and Asia excluding Japan) generate more than 40% of Henkel's sales. Henkel's business in Europe and North America is highly mature so it relies on its emerging markets for organic growth.

Henkel has around 185 manufacturing facilities that dot around 55 countries. Its largest plants are located in D sseldorf Germany (its headquarters) and in Bowling Green Kentucky US and make detergents and household cleaning products as well as adhesives. The company's cosmetics and toiletries are produced at about 10 plants.Henkel's regional centers are located in Mexico Brazil Austria UAE China and US (Connecticut).

Sales and Marketing

Each of Henkel's three units claims a large share of their market through established brands. In Beauty Care 90% of sales are driven by the business unit's top-10 brands; in Laundry and Homecare around 65%; and in Adhesive Technologies more than 80%.

Henkel's customer base of around 130000 industry and retail clients is managed primarily by its own sales teams. Henkel's retail customers service the needs of private users craftsmen and smaller industrial customers.

Financial Performance

Note: Growth rates may differ after conversion to US Dollars.

Henkel's last five years have been characterized by consistent revenue and profit growth although it slipped back in both regards in 2018.

In fiscal 2018 the company's sales fell by less than 1% to ?19.9 billion as a fall in the Laundry and Home Care segment was partially offset by marginal gains in the Adhesive and Beauty segments. The fall in the Laundry and Home Care segment was largely a result of unfavorable exchange rate movements while on a like-for-like basis sales grew 2% thanks to pricing increases.

Geographically Henkel's emerging markets grew strongly overall particularly Africa and the Middle East Eastern Europe and Latin America while sales in Asia fell below prior year. Sales in North America fell due to delivery difficulties and intense competition while sales in Europe were flat.

Net income fell 8% in 2018 to ?2.3 billion adversely affected by the 2017 US Tax Cuts and Jobs Act which pushed up the effective tax rate from 15% to nearly 24%. Income before tax was more or less the same in 2017 and 2018.

Henkel's cash position weakened slightly during 2018 falling ?470 million to ?919 million by year-end. It generated ?2.5 billion from operations while Henkel's investing activities used a similar amount. Financing activities absorbed ?412 million.

Strategy

Henkel maintains a robust investment program. In 2018 its capital expenditure amounted to ?853 million which mainly went towards increasing production capacity new products and improving business processes. More specifically its 2018 projects included supply chain optimizations and enhancing IT system architecture; acquiring new technologies; expanding detergent capsule production capacity at its Salt Lake City and Bowling Green facilities; building a new adhesive factory in Spain and a new adhesives and metal pretreatment factory in India. Henkel spreads its investments evenly across its three business units and from a geographic standpoint focuses its investment program on Western Europe Eastern Europe and North America.

Mergers and Acquisitions

Henkel is an acquisitive firm buying up companies to build out its presence in certain markets and boost its product portfolio. Henkel made three acquisitions in 2018. In early 2018 it acquired Uni n Técnico Comercial based in Lima Peru strengthening Henkel's presence in the maintenance repair and overhaul adhesives market in Latin America. Later in 2018 Henkel acquired

Canada-based JemPak Corporation strengthening the existing Laundry & Home Care portfolio in North America. Towards the end of the year Henkel acquired Chile-based Aislantes Nacionales strengthening its presence in the Chilean tile adhesives and building materials market.

In 2017 Henkel made acquisitions in its adhesive technologies and beauty care businesses including Darex Packaging in the US and Sonderhoff in Germany. Professional hair care in the US has been a particular focus of the company with the late 2017 purchases of Zotos International for about $485 million and Nattura for an undisclosed amount. (In 2014 it picked up three US-based professional hair care product companies - Sexy Hair Alterna and Kenra.)

Company Background

In 1876 Fritz Henkel and his two partners founded Henkel & Cie in Aachen Germany. The company launched a laundry detergent based on sodium silicate which they named "Universal-Washmittel". Henkel's first branded product was launched in 1878. In 1913 Henkel founded a subsidiary in Switzerland. Fritz passed in 1930 and was succeeded by his capable sons Fritz Jr. and Hugo. Henkel became a limited company in 1975 and in 1985 it went public. Major product launches have included Persil (1907) and the Pritt stick (1969); it acquired Loctite in 1997. The company was renamed Henkel AG & Co in 2008.

EXECUTIVES

SVP Information Technology, Peter Wroblowski
CEO, Hans Van Bylen, age 59
SVP Adhesive Technologies; President Asia-Pacific, Jan-Dirk Auris, age 52
EVP Finance and Purchasing and Integrated Business Solutions, Carsten Knobel, age 52
EVP Laundry and Home Care, Bruno Piacenza, age 55
EVP Human Resources and Infrastructure Services, Kathrin Menges, age 56
EVP Beauty Care, Pascal Houdayer, age 51
Vice Chairman Supervisory Board, Winfried Zander, age 66
Member Supervisory Board, Simone Bagel-Trah, age 52
Auditors: KPMG AG

LOCATIONS

HQ: Henkel AG & Co KGAA
Henkelstrasse 67, Duesseldorf D-40191
Phone: (49) 211 797 0   **Fax:** (49) 211 798 4040
Web: www.henkel.com

2018 Sales

	% of total
Western Europe	31
North America	25
Asia Pacific	17
Eastern Europe	14
Africa/Middle East	6
Latin America	6
Corporate	1
Total	**100**

PRODUCTS/OPERATIONS

2018 Sales

	% of total
Adhesive Technologies	50
Industrial Business	38
Consumers Craftsmen and Building	9
Laundry & Home Care	32
Beauty Care	20
Corporate	1
Total	**100**

Selected Brands

Adhesives technologies
Ariasana
Ceresit
LePage
Loctite
Metylan
Pattex
Ponal
Pritt
Rubson
Sellotape
Sista
Solvite
Tangit
Technomelt
Teroson
UniBond
Cosmetics and toiletries
Aok
Barnängen
Clynol viton
Denivit
Diadermine
Dial
Dry Idea
Fa
La Toja
Licor del Polo
Neutromed
Right Guard
Schwarzkopf
Smooth 'N Shine
Syoss
Theramed
Tone
Vademecum
Laundry and homecare
Bref
Dixan
Mir
Persil
Perwoll
Pril
Pur
Purex
Soft Scrub
Somat
Spee
Vernel

COMPETITORS

3M	Estée Lauder
Alticor	H.B. Fuller
Avon	Johnson & Johnson
BASF SE	Kimberly-Clark
Bayer AG	L'Oréal
Beiersdorf	Procter & Gamble
Church & Dwight	Reckitt Benckiser
Clorox	S.C. Johnson
Colgate-Palmolive	Shiseido
Dow Chemical	Unilever PLC

HISTORICAL FINANCIALS

Company Type: Public

Income Statement				FYE: December 31
	REVENUE ($ mil.)	NET INCOME ($ mil.)	NET PROFIT MARGIN	EMPLOYEES
12/19	22,583	2,340	10.4%	52,450
12/18	22,788	2,646	11.6%	53,000
12/17	24,009	3,019	12.6%	53,700
12/16	19,759	2,167	11.0%	51,350
12/15	19,702	2,092	10.6%	49,850
Annual Growth	**3.5%**	**2.8%**	**—**	**1.3%**

2019 Year-End Financials

Debt ratio: 14.1%	No. of shares (mil.): 259
Return on equity: 11.7%	Dividends
Cash ($ mil.): 1,641	Yield: 1.5%
Current ratio: 1.07	Payout: 6.6%
Long-term debt ($ mil.): 2,169	Market value ($ mil.): 6,123

	STOCK PRICE ($)	P/E		PER SHARE ($)		
	FY Close	High/Low		Earnings	Dividends	Book Value
12/19	23.57	21	4	5.38	0.36	80.05
12/18	98.36	23	18	6.08	0.40	75.01
12/17	120.16	23	20	6.94	0.35	71.87
12/16	105.00	24	17	4.98	0.28	61.15
12/15	95.80	24	19	4.81	0.25	57.27
Annual Growth	**(29.6%)**	**—**	**—**	**2.8%**	**10.0%**	**8.7%**

Hennes & Mauritz AB

Auditors: Ernst & Young AB

LOCATIONS

HQ: Hennes & Mauritz AB
Master Samuelsgatan 46A, Stockholm SE-106 38
Phone: (46) 8 796 55 00   **Fax:** (46) 8 24 80 78
Web: www.hm.com

HISTORICAL FINANCIALS

Company Type: Public

Income Statement				FYE: November 30
	REVENUE ($ mil.)	NET INCOME ($ mil.)	NET PROFIT MARGIN	EMPLOYEES
11/19	38,950	2,249	5.8%	126,376
11/18	35,209	2,117	6.0%	123,283
11/17	33,469	2,708	8.1%	123,178
11/16	32,175	3,118	9.7%	114,586
11/15	30,266	3,497	11.6%	104,634
Annual Growth	**6.5%**	**(10.4%)**	**—**	**4.8%**

2019 Year-End Financials

Debt ratio: 2.4%	No. of shares (mil.): 1,655
Return on equity: 23.2%	Dividends
Cash ($ mil.): 2,060	Yield: 0.0%
Current ratio: 1.30	Payout: 14.9%
Long-term debt ($ mil.): 1,781	Market value ($ mil.): 6,306

	STOCK PRICE ($)	P/E		PER SHARE ($)		
	FY Close	High/Low		Earnings	Dividends	Book Value
11/19	3.81	1	0	1.36	0.20	5.77
11/18	3.63	1	0	1.28	0.22	5.92
11/17	4.64	1	0	1.64	0.23	6.04
11/16	5.77	1	0	1.88	0.24	6.19
11/15	7.36	1	1	2.11	0.24	5.87
Annual Growth	**(15.2%)**	**—**	**—**	**(10.5%)**	**(3.8%)**	**(0.4%)**

Hino Motors, Ltd.

Hino Motors introduced Japan's first truck in 1918 long before Godzilla was throwing vehicles all over Tokyo. These days the company not only manufactures medium- and heavy-duty diesel trucks but it also makes buses special-purpose vehicles and industrial diesel engines. Hino Motors dominates Japan's domestic truck market beating out such competitors as Mitsubishi Motors and Isuzu Motors and manufactures 150000 Hino-brand trucks and buses each year. Toyota Motor owns more than 50% of the company.

Geographic Reach

In Japan Hino Motors produces vehicles engines and components at four plants. Its manufacturing operations in other nations include plants for producing trucks buses and components in Thailand Indonesia Vietnam China Pakistan Colombia and the US. It generates nearly 65% of its total sales from Japan and 27% from other countries in Asia.

Sales and Marketing

Manufacturing vehicles and service parts for Toyota Motor represents more than 26% of the company's sales

Financial Performance

The company's revenue increased by 17% in 2013 primarily due to additional sales derived from Japan Asia and as well from other countries. The demand in the truck (heavy light and medium-duty) and bus market in Japan was healthy due to reconstruction demand and an eco-car tax reduction/subsidy measure which increased the overall sales in Japan.

As for overseas markets Hino Motors experienced favorable sales in the Asian countries of Indonesia and Thailand. The company was also aided by the 2012 launch of the small model Hino 300 Series which increased the sales volume of trucks and buses outside Japan in 2013.

Strategy

The company has a strong brand in Southeast Asia and it has strengthened its presence in the region by dividing the sales and production functions at its Thailand and Indonesian operations into separate companies. Meanwhile it has grown its presence in Africa which it expects will become an important Hino market along with Southeast Asia Oceania and Latin America.

EXECUTIVES

President, Yasuhiko Ichihashi, age 68
EVP, Koichi Ojima
EVP, Hiroshi Kokaji
EVP, Kenji Suzuki
President Canada, Yumiko Kawamura
Chairman, Masakazu Ichikawa
Auditors: PricewaterhouseCoopers Aarata LLC

LOCATIONS

HQ: Hino Motors, Ltd.
3-1-1 Hinodai, Hino, Tokyo 191-8660
Phone: (81) 42 586 5111   **Fax:** 248 699-9310
Web: www.hino.co.jp

2016 Sales

	% of total
Japan	66
Asia	21
Other	13
Total	**100**

PRODUCTS/OPERATIONS

2016 Sales

	% of total
Trucks and buses	53
Total	**20**
Service parts	6
Other	21
Total	**100**

Selected Overseas Subsidiaries and Affiliates

Hino Motor Sales Australia Pty. Ltd.
Hino Motor Sales U.S.A. Inc.
Hino Motors (Malaysia) Sdn. Bhd.
Hino Motors Sales (Thailand) Ltd.
Hinopak Motors Ltd. (Pakistan)
Shenyang Shenfei Hino Automobile Manufacturing Co. Ltd. (China)

COMPETITORS

Ashok Leyland	Navistar International
China Yuchai	PACCAR
Cummins	Renault
Daimler	Scania
General Motors	UD Trucks
Isuzu	Volvo
Mitsubishi Fuso Truck & Bus	

HISTORICAL FINANCIALS

Company Type: Public

Income Statement				FYE: March 31
	REVENUE ($ mil.)	NET INCOME ($ mil.)	NET PROFIT MARGIN	EMPLOYEES
03/20	16,725	289	1.7%	44,188
03/19	17,891	495	2.8%	45,442
03/18	17,308	483	2.8%	44,629
03/17	15,059	441	2.9%	42,775
03/16	15,543	579	3.7%	41,725
Annual Growth	**1.8%**	**(15.9%)**	**—**	**1.4%**

2020 Year-End Financials

Debt ratio: 0.1%
Return on equity: 5.7%
Cash ($ mil.): 374
Current ratio: 1.16
Long-term debt ($ mil.): 182

No. of shares (mil.): 574
Dividends
  Yield: 4.9%
  Payout: 510.2%
Market value ($ mil.): 29,908

	STOCK PRICE ($) FY Close	P/E High/Low		PER SHARE ($) Earnings	Dividends	Book Value
03/20	52.09	2	1	0.51	2.57	8.70
03/19	84.58	1	1	0.86	2.60	8.54
03/18	128.44	2	1	0.84	2.67	8.24
03/17	124.29	1	1	0.77	2.65	7.25
03/16	109.82	1	1	1.01	3.67	6.67
Annual Growth	**(17.0%)**	**—**	**—**	**(15.9%)**	**(8.5%)**	**6.9%**

Hirogin Holdings Inc

EXECUTIVES

President, TOSHIO HEYA
Auditors: KPMG AZSA LLC

LOCATIONS

HQ: Hirogin Holdings Inc
1-1-7 Nishikaniya, Minami-ku, Hiroshima 732-0804
Phone: (81) 82 247 5151
Web: www.hirogin.co.jp

COMPETITORS

Aozora Bank	Miyazaki Bank
Chugoku Bank	Shizuoka Bank
Higo Bank	
Mitsubishi UFJ Financial Group	

HISTORICAL FINANCIALS

Company Type: Public

Income Statement				FYE: March 31
	ASSETS ($ mil.)	NET INCOME ($ mil.)	INCOME AS % OF ASSETS	EMPLOYEES
03/20	86,951	223	0.3%	4,729
03/19	80,841	230	0.3%	4,767
03/18	85,247	243	0.3%	4,792
03/17	79,362	279	0.4%	4,520
03/16	73,028	279	0.4%	4,517
Annual Growth	**4.5%**	**(5.4%)**	**—**	**1.2%**

2020 Year-End Financials

Return on assets: 0.2%
Return on equity: 4.9%
Long-term debt ($ mil.): —
No. of shares (mil.): 312
Sales ($ mil): 1,171

Dividends
  Yield: —
  Payout: 28.8%
Market value ($ mil.): —

Hitachi, Ltd.

Auditors: Ernst & Young ShinNihon LLC

LOCATIONS

HQ: Hitachi, Ltd.
1-6-6 Marunouchi, Chiyoda-ku, Tokyo 100-8280
Phone: (81) 3 3258 1111   **Fax:** 650 244-7037
Web: www.hitachi.co.jp

HISTORICAL FINANCIALS

Company Type: Public

Income Statement				FYE: March 31
	REVENUE ($ mil.)	NET INCOME ($ mil.)	NET PROFIT MARGIN	EMPLOYEES
03/20	88,398	883	1.0%	301,056
03/19	95,590	2,243	2.3%	295,941
03/18	94,461	3,659	3.9%	307,275
03/17	92,381	2,331	2.5%	309,887
03/16	101,173	1,735	1.7%	380,355
Annual Growth	**(3.3%)**	**(15.5%)**	**—**	**(5.7%)**

2020 Year-End Financials

Debt ratio: 0.1%
Return on equity: 2.7%
Cash ($ mil.): 8,190
Current ratio: 1.40
Long-term debt ($ mil.): 7,982

No. of shares (mil.): 966
Dividends
  Yield: 3.0%
  Payout: 190.4%
Market value ($ mil.): 55,512

	STOCK PRICE ($) FY Close	P/E High/Low		PER SHARE ($) Earnings	Dividends	Book Value
03/20	57.45	1	1	0.91	1.74	32.97
03/19	64.87	0	0	2.32	1.44	34.07
03/18	73.09	0	0	3.79	1.26	34.23
03/17	54.33	0	0	2.41	1.08	30.98
03/16	46.88	0	0	1.80	0.97	28.56
Annual Growth	**5.2%**	**—**	**—**	**(15.5%)**	**15.8%**	**3.7%**

Hokkoku Bank, Ltd. (The) (Japan)

EXECUTIVES

President, SHUJI TSUEMURA
Managing Director, Hideaki Hamasaki
Managing Director, Akira Nakanishi
Chairman, Hanbei Kometani
Auditors: Ernst & Young ShinNihon LLC

LOCATIONS

HQ: Hokkoku Bank, Ltd. (The) (Japan)
2-12-6 Hirooka, Kanazawa, Ishikawa 920-8670
Phone: (81) 76 263 1111
Web: www.hokkokubank.co.jp

PRODUCTS/OPERATIONS

Selected Subsidiaries
The Hokkoku General Leasing Co. Ltd.
The Hokkoku Credit Service Co. Ltd.
The Hokkoku Credit Guarantee Co. Ltd.
The Hokkoku Management Ltd.
The Hokkoku Servicer Ltd.

COMPETITORS

Aomori Bank	Miyazaki Bank
Bank of the Ryukyus	Mizuho Financial
Fukui Bank	Musashino Bank
Hokuhoku Financial	Resona
Group	Shinsei Bank
Mitsubishi UFJ	Sumitomo Mitsui
Financial Group	

HISTORICAL FINANCIALS

Company Type: Public

Income Statement				FYE: March 31
	ASSETS ($ mil.)	NET INCOME ($ mil.)	INCOME AS % OF ASSETS	EMPLOYEES
03/20	46,957	67	0.1%	2,278
03/19	45,413	77	0.2%	2,309
03/18	44,948	95	0.2%	2,338
03/17	38,641	97	0.3%	2,327
03/16	34,765	85	0.2%	2,348
Annual Growth	7.8%	(5.7%)	—	(0.8%)

2020 Year-End Financials

Return on assets: 0.1%
Return on equity: 2.9%
Long-term debt ($ mil.): —
No. of shares (mil.): 28
Sales ($ mil): 688

Dividends
  Yield: —
  Payout: —
  Market value ($ mil.): —

Hokuhoku Financial Group Inc

EXECUTIVES

President, EISHIN IHORI
Auditors: Deloitte Touche Tohmatsu LLC

LOCATIONS

HQ: Hokuhoku Financial Group Inc
1-2-26 Tsutsumicho-dori, Toyama 930-8637
Phone: (81) 76 423 7331
Web: www.hokuhoku-fg.co.jp

PRODUCTS/OPERATIONS

Selected Subsidiaries and Affiliated Companies
Hokugin Lease Co. Ltd.
Hokugin Software Co. Ltd.
Hokuriku Capital Co. Ltd.
Hokuriku Card Co. Ltd.
Hokuriku Hosho Services Co. Ltd.
Nihonkai Services Co. Ltd.
The Hokkaido Bank Ltd.
  Dogin Business Service Ltd.
  Dogin Card Co. Ltd.
The Hokuriku Bank Ltd.
  Hokugin Business Services Co. Ltd.
  Hokugin Corporate Co. Ltd.
  Hokugin Office Services Co. Ltd.
  Hokugin Real Estate Services Co. Ltd.
  Hokugin Shisankanri Co. Ltd.
  Hokuriku International Cayman Limited

COMPETITORS

Bank of Nagoya	Mitsubishi UFJ
Hachijuni Bank	Financial Group
Hokkoku Bank	Sapporo Hokuyo
Hyakujushi Bank	

HISTORICAL FINANCIALS

Company Type: Public

Income Statement				FYE: March 31
	ASSETS ($ mil.)	NET INCOME ($ mil.)	INCOME AS % OF ASSETS	EMPLOYEES
03/20	125,700	186	0.1%	7,983
03/19	119,067	219	0.2%	8,412
03/18	122,390	199	0.2%	8,751
03/17	111,168	251	0.2%	8,808
03/16	103,567	256	0.2%	8,755
Annual Growth	5.0%	(7.7%)	—	(2.3%)

2020 Year-End Financials

Return on assets: 0.1%
Return on equity: 3.3%
Long-term debt ($ mil.): —
No. of shares (mil.): 131
Sales ($ mil): 1,683

Dividends
  Yield: —
  Payout: 28.1%
  Market value ($ mil.): —

Hon Hai Precision Industry Co Ltd

Hon Hai Precision Industry Co. also known by its trade name Foxconn is the world's largest contract electronics manufacturer. It makes mobile phones computers servers and TVs. Other products include components such as connectors cable assemblies enclosures flat-panel displays game consoles and motherboards. Hon Hai also provides design engineering and mechanical tooling services. Expanding beyond manufacturing Hon Hai conducts research into nanotechnology and other advanced areas. The global company's customers include Apple Cisco Dell and Amazon. Chairman Terry Gou founded Hon Hai in 1974 to make plastic switches for TVs. About 35% of the company's total sales is generated from the US.

Operations

The company capitalizes on its expertise in Cloud Computing Mobile Devices IoT Big Data AI Smart Networks and Robotics / Automation. The company has expanded not only its capabilities into the development of electric vehicles digital health and robotics but also three key technologies - AI semiconductors and new-generation communications technology. These technologies are keys to driving its long-term growth strategy and the four core product pillars: consumer products (includes consumer electronics such as smartphone devices feature phones wearable devices and smart entertainment devices like television sets game consoles set-top boxes and audio systems) enterprise products (includes network communication and cloud equipment and systems used by businesses general consumers and also includes devices used by general consumers such as routers servers edge computing data centers and satellite communications) computing products (includes electronic computing equipment needed for work and daily life such as desktop computers laptops tablets multi-function devices and printers used in the office) and components (includes key components for the supply chain such as connectors and optical components electronic components semiconductor products automotive equipment and related services) and others.

With a focus on research and development the company owns more than 83500 patents.

Geographic Reach

Taipei-based Hon Hai's has more than 5 factory complexes in four cities in China and other manufacturing facilities in Mexico Brazil the Czech Republic Hungary Slovakia Vietnam India and the US.

The US supply about 35% of Hon Hai's revenue Ireland generates more than 25% of revenue China and Singapore account for about 10% each and others generate the remaining sales.

Sales and Marketing

Hon Hai biggest customer is Apple (Customer E) which accounts for approximately 50% of total revenue.

Financial Performance

Note: Growth rates may differ after conversion to US Dollars.

Hon Hai posted steadily increasing sales in the last five years. Revenue grew 19% between 2015 and 2019 with a NT$5.3 trillion in 2019. Profits have continued to fall in the same period by 21% from NT$146.9 billion in 2015 to NT$115.3 billion in 2019.

In 2019 revenue grew less than 1% to NT$5.3 trillion from NT$5.2 trillion in 2018. Revenue from its operating segments fell to NT$5.4 trillion in 2019 from NT$5.7 trillion the prior year.

Hon Hai's net income fell 11% from NT$129.1 billion in 2018 to NT$115.3 billion in 2019 due to an increase of NT$5.1 billion in operating expenses.

Hon Hai held about NT$29.9 billion in cash and cash equivalents in 2019 compared to NT$82.9 billion in 2018. Cash from operations was a negative NT$90.4 billion. Financing activities used NT$94.2 billion mainly for repayments of corporate bonds cash dividends and repayment of leasing principals. Investing activities provided NT$131.2 billion from dividend received and in receivables from purchase of raw materials.

Strategy

Hon Hai pursues continued excellence in operational management and cost control and provides a "One-Stop Shop" solution for global leading brands. Its commitment is to maintain the high quality of service and related added-value services enable computing communication consumer electronics (3C) to enrich lives of the world population. In order to provide its customers with more timely services the company has actively established related manufacturing bases design centers service centers in Europe the Americas and Asia to satisfy its clients' global design manufacturing and assembly needs.

In terms of Hon Hai's long-term business development plan it is focusing on innovation and research and development efforts. The company's global R&D center in Dingpu is fitted with precision machinery precision molds and nontechnology research facilities. Leveraging the leadership of the R&D center this enables the company to better integrate towards technology including forays into new territories or applying new technologies to traditional manufacturing methods to increase quality reduce wasted resources and increase global standards.

The company has also expanded beyond the Greater china region actively searching for investments and collaborations across US Japan Korea Germany India and South East Asian countries established Foxconn Institute for Research in Science and Technology and attracting advanced R&D talents.

Company Background

Hon Hai Precision Industry Co. Ltd. or also knew to their business as Foxconn Technology Group or better known as Foxconn is a Taiwanese multinational electronics contract manufacturer headquartered in Tucheng New Taipei City Taiwan. It was founded in 1974 as Hon Hai Plastics Corporation by Terry Gou and later renamed as Hon Hai Precision Industry Co. Ltd. in 1982.

EXECUTIVES

Chairman and CEO, Terry T.M. Gou
Director and President, Lu Fang-ming
Director and President, Chien Yi-bin
Auditors: PricewaterhouseCoopers Taiwan

LOCATIONS

HQ: Hon Hai Precision Industry Co Ltd
No. 2, Zihyou Street, Tucheng District, New Taipei 236
Phone: (886) 2 2268 3466
Web: www.foxconn.com

PRODUCTS/OPERATIONS

2017 Sales

	% of total
Ireland	30
US	29
China	9
Singapore	8
Japan	3
Taiwan	2
Others	19
Total	**100**

Selected Products

Cable assemblies
CD-ROMs
Connectors
E-book readers
Enclosures
Flat-panel displays
Game consoles
Handsets
Keyboards
LCD (liquid-crystal display) TVs
Mobile phones
Motherboards
Personal computers
Servers
Smartphones
Switches
Tablets
Thermal products

COMPETITORS

ASUSTeK	Inventec
Amphenol	Jabil
BenQ	MiTAC
Cal-Comp Electronics	Quanta Computer
Celestica	Sanmina
First International	TPV Technology
Computer	Universal Scientific
Flextronics	Venture Corp.

HISTORICAL FINANCIALS

Company Type: Public

Income Statement — FYE: December 31

	REVENUE ($ mil.)	NET INCOME ($ mil.)	NET PROFIT MARGIN	EMPLOYEES
12/19	178,459	3,851	2.2%	0
12/18	173,086	4,219	2.4%	0
12/17	158,732	4,678	2.9%	0
12/16	134,728	4,595	3.4%	0
12/15	136,401	4,469	3.3%	830,174
Annual Growth	**6.9%**	**(3.7%)**	**—**	**—**

2019 Year-End Financials

Debt ratio: 0.6%
Return on equity: 9.4%
Cash ($ mil.): 28,654
Current ratio: 1.55
Long-term debt ($ mil.): 7,250

No. of shares (mil.): —
Dividends
Yield: 2.9%
Payout: 68.2%
Market value ($ mil.): —

	STOCK PRICE ($) FY Close	P/E High/Low		PER SHARE ($) Earnings	Dividends	Book Value
12/19	6.12	1	1	0.28	0.18	2.99
12/18	4.75	1	1	0.26	0.00	2.86
12/17	6.20	1	1	0.27	0.00	2.11
12/16	5.05	1	1	0.26	0.00	1.92
12/15	4.96	1	1	0.26	0.03	1.78
Annual Growth	**5.4%**	**—**	**—**	**1.7%**	**56.2%**	**13.8%**

Honda Motor Co Ltd

Honda Motor Company is Japan's #2 automaker (after #1 Toyota) and the world's largest motorcycle producer. The company's global car models include the Accord CR-V Civic Fit and its new Clarity Fuel Cell model. Honda's line of motorcycles includes everything from scooters to superbikes. The company's power products division makes commercial and residential machinery (lawn mowers snow blowers and tillers); portable generators; an outboard motors. Its Honda Aero subsidiary also manufactures jet and turboprop engines. More than half of Honda's sales comes from North America.

Operations

Four reporting segments comprise Honda Motor's operations: the Automobile business Financial Services business Motorcycle business and Life Creation and other businesses.

Automobile business generates more than 65% of total sales. It offers vehicles that use gasoline engines of three four or six-cylinder configurations diesel engines gasoline-electric hybrid systems and gasoline-electric plug-in hybrid systems.

Financial Services generates more than 15% of total sales. It offers retail lending leasing to customers and other financial services such as wholesale financing to dealers through finance subsidiaries.

Motorcycle Business generates about 15% of total sales. Honda produces a wide range of motorcycles with engine displacement ranging from the 50cc class to the 1800cc class. Honda's motorcycle lineup uses internal combustion engine of air- or water-cooled and in single two four or six-cylinder configurations. Honda also has electric vehicles in its lineup. Honda's motorcycle lineup consists of sports business and commuter models.

Life Creation and Other Businesses generates more than 1% of total sales. Honda manufactured

a variety of power products including general purpose engines generators water pumps lawn mowers riding mowers robotic mowers brush cutters tillers snow blowers outboard marine engines walking assist devices and portable battery inverter power sources.

Geographic Reach

Headquartered in Tokyo Honda's major geographic areas are concentrated in North America (the US Canada and Mexico); Asia (Thailand Indonesia China India Pakistan and Vietnam); Japan; and Europe (the UK Germany Italy Belgium France). North America generates roughly 55% of net sales while Asia brings in more than 20% of sales. Japan accounts about 15% and Europe and other regions generates about 10% of sales combined. The Financial Services business provides financing and leasing through its subsidiaries in Japan the US Canada the UK Germany Brazil and Thailand.

Sales and Marketing

Most of Honda's products are distributed under the Honda trademarks in Japan and/or in overseas markets. In Japan Honda produces and sells motorcycles automobiles and power products through its domestic sales subsidiaries and independent retail dealers.

Financial Performance

Honda's consolidated sales revenue for the fiscal year 2020 (ended March) decreased by Å 957.6 billion or 6.0% to Å 14.9 trillion from the fiscal year 2019 (ended March) due mainly to decreased sales revenue in the Automobile business as well as negative foreign currency translation effects which was partially offset by increased sales revenue in the Financial services business.

Profit for the year decreased by Å 166.3 billion or 25% to Å 509.9 billion from the previous fiscal year.

Consolidated cash and cash equivalents on 2020 (ended March) increased by Å 178.2 billion from 2019 (ended March) to Å 2.7 trillion. Net cash provided by operating activities amounted to Å 979.4 billion of cash inflows while net cash used in investing activities amounted to Å 619.4 billion and net cash used in financing activities amounted to Å 87.4 billion.

Strategy

Honda engages in business operations through alliances and joint ventures with other companies in expectation of synergy effects and increased efficiency or to meet the requirements of the countries in which business development is being undertaken.

As Honda advances its mid- and long-term initiatives toward further electrification more widespread use and evolution of driver-assistive technologies and further provision of mobility services the utilization of alliances and other forms of partnership are gaining importance.

Going forward trends in the negotiations regarding trade agreements particularly those related to the United States could have adverse effects on Honda's business and operating results. Honda will continue to monitor the status of negotiations and take action in consideration of the impact on Honda.

Especially noteworthy is the fact that the United States-Mexico-Canada Agreement (USMCA) is expected to enter into force in July 2020. The revision of various rules such as the rules of country of origin for automobiles sold within the regions covered in USMCA may adversely affect Honda's business in North America.

Mergers and Acquisitions

In late 2019 Honda R&D Co. Ltd. a subsidiary of the Japanese automaker has announced the acquisition of all the outstanding shares of California-based Drivemode Inc. a company that develops smartphone apps for drivers for an undisclosed amount. Honda claims this move will further strengthen the automaker's new value creation in the areas of digital and connected mobility products.

HISTORY

Soichiro Honda spent six years as an apprentice at Tokyo service station Art Shokai before opening his own branch of the repair shop in Hamamatsu in 1928. He also raced cars and in 1931 received a patent for metal spokes that replaced wood in wheels.

Honda started a piston ring company in 1937. During WWII the company produced metal propellers for Japanese bombers. When bombs and an earthquake destroyed most of his factory Honda sold it to Toyota in 1945.

In 1946 Honda began motorizing bicycles with war-surplus engines. When this proved popular Honda began making engines. The company was renamed Honda Motor Co. in 1948 and began producing motorcycles. Soichiro Honda hired Takeo Fujisawa in 1949 to manage the company so Honda could focus on engineering. Honda's innovative overhead valve design made its early 1950s Dream model a runaway success. In 1952 the smaller Cub sold through bicycle dealers accounted for 70% of Japan's motorcycle production.

Funded by a 1954 public offering and Mitsubishi Bank Honda expanded capacity and began exporting. American Honda Motor Company was formed in Los Angeles in 1959 accompanied by the slogan "You meet the nicest people on a Honda" in a campaign crafted to counter the stereotypical biker image. Honda added overseas factories in the 1960s and began producing lightweight trucks sports cars and minicars.

The company began selling its tiny 600 model in the US in 1970 but it was the Civic introduced in 1973 that first scored with the US car market. Three years later Honda introduced the Accord which featured an innovative frame adaptable for many models. In 1982 Accord production started at the company's Ohio plant.

EXECUTIVES

Senior Managing Officer and Director President Chief Executive Officer and Representative Director Honda R&D Co. Ltd., Yoshiyuki Matsumoto

EVP Executive Officer and Representative Director Risk Management Officer and Corporate Brand Officer, Seiji Kuraishi, age 62

Senior Managing Officer COO Regional Operations (North America) President and Director Honda North America Inc. and President and Chief Executive Officer American Honda Motor Co. Inc., Toshiaki Mikoshiba

Senior Managing Officer and Director and COO Production Operations, Yoshi Yamane

Managing Officer President and Director Honda Aircraft Company LLC, Michimasa Fujino

Managing Officer and SEVP and Director Honda North America Inc., Soichiro Takizawa

Operating Officer; COO Motorcycle Operations, Shinji Aoyama

President and CEO, Takahiro Hachigo, age 61

President and CEO Honda Motorcycle & Scooter India (HMSI), Minoru Kato

Managing Officer and President Chief Executive Officer and Representative Director Honda Engineering Co. Ltd., Toshihiko Nonaka

Senior Managing Officer and Director CFO and Chief Officer Driving Safety Promotion Center, Kohei Takeuchi

Operating Officer COO Regional Operations (Europe Region) and President and Director Honda Motor Europe Ltd., Katsushi Inoue
Auditors: KPMG AZSA LLC

LOCATIONS

HQ: Honda Motor Co Ltd
1-1, Minami-Aoyama 2-chome, Minato-ku, Tokyo 107-8556
Phone: (81) 3 3423 1111
Web: www.honda.co.jp

2017 Sales

	% of total
North America	56
Asia	19
Japan	14
Europe	5
Other regions	6
Total	**100**

PRODUCTS/OPERATIONS

2017 Sales

	% of total
Automobiles	72
Financial Services	13
Motorcycles	12
Power products & other businesses	3
Total	**100**

Selected Acura Models

ILX sedan
TLX sedan
RLX sedan
RDX SUV
MDX SUV
NSX Supercar

Selected Honda Car and Truck ModelsPassenger cars

Gold Wing
CB1100
CBR1000RR
CB1000R
VFR800F
Rebel
CB250R/CB300R
CB125R
CRF1000L Africa Twin
X-ADV
CRF250 Rally
PCX
SuperCub
Monkey

Selected ATVs

Utility ATVs
  TRX250X ATV sport
  TRX90X sport
  FourTrax Rincon
  FourTrax Foreman Rubicon 4x4
  FourTrax Rancher
  FourTrax Recon
  Pioner SxS
  Forza scooter
  PCX150 scooter
  Ruckus scooter
  Metropolitan scooter

Selected Power Products

Lawn mowers
Miimo robotic lawnmower
Marine motors
Portable generators
LiB-AID E500 portable power source
Pumps
Snowblowers
Tillers

COMPETITORS

BMW	Mahindra Renault
Briggs & Stratton	Mazda
Brunswick Corp.	Mitsubishi Motors
Caterpillar	Nissan

Daihatsu	Peugeot
Daimler	Renault
Exmark Manufacturing	Subaru
FCA US	Suzuki Motor
Fiat Chrysler	Tata Motors
Ford Motor	Textron
General Motors	Toro Company
Harley-Davidson	Toyota
Hyundai Motor	Triumph Motorcycles
Indian Motorcycle	Viper Motorcycle
Isuzu	Volkswagen
Kawasaki Heavy	Volvo
Industries	Yamaha Motor
Kia Motors	

HISTORICAL FINANCIALS

Company Type: Public

Income Statement   FYE: March 31

	REVENUE ($ mil.)	NET INCOME ($ mil.)	NET PROFIT MARGIN	EMPLOYEES
03/20	150,545	4,595	3.1%	218,674
03/19	160,201	6,153	3.8%	219,722
03/18	154,882	10,681	6.9%	215,638
03/17	141,150	6,216	4.4%	211,915
03/16	147,220	3,473	2.4%	208,399
Annual Growth	**0.6%**	**7.2%**	**—**	**1.2%**

2020 Year-End Financials

Debt ratio: —   No. of shares (mil.): 1,726
Return on equity: 5.5%   Dividends
Cash ($ mil.): 26,944   Yield: 4.6%
Current ratio: 1.26   Payout: 41.8%
Long-term debt ($ mil.): —   Market value ($ mil.): 38,780

	STOCK PRICE ($) FY Close	P/E High/Low		PER SHARE ($) Earnings	Dividends	Book Value
03/20	22.46	0	0	2.62	1.04	46.79
03/19	27.17	0	0	3.49	0.99	47.38
03/18	34.73	0	0	5.96	0.88	44.98
03/17	30.26	0	0	3.45	0.84	40.81
03/16	27.34	0	0	1.93	0.73	37.83
Annual Growth	**(4.8%)**	**—**	**—**	**8.0%**	**9.1%**	**5.5%**

Hong Leong Bank Berhad

Auditors: PricewaterhouseCoopers PLT

LOCATIONS

HQ: Hong Leong Bank Berhad
Level 30, Menara Hong Leong, No. 6, Jalan Damanlela, Bukit Damansara, Kuala Lumpur 50490
Phone: (60) 3 2080 9888   **Fax:** (60) 3 2080 9801
Web: www.hlb.com.my

COMPETITORS

AmBank Group	Edaran Otomobil
Bank Muamalat	Hang Seng Bank
Bank of China	Maybank
Berjaya Group	Norinchukin Bank
CIMB Group	Sime Darby

HISTORICAL FINANCIALS
Company Type: Public

Income Statement FYE: June 30

	ASSETS ($ mil.)	NET INCOME ($ mil.)	INCOME AS % OF ASSETS	EMPLOYEES
06/20	51,637	582	1.1%	8,090
06/19	50,153	644	1.3%	7,958
06/18	50,238	653	1.3%	8,045
06/17	45,556	499	1.1%	8,212
06/16	47,604	477	1.0%	0
Annual Growth	2.1%	5.1%	—	—

2020 Year-End Financials

Return on assets: 1.1%	Dividends
Return on equity: 9.4%	Yield: —
Long-term debt ($ mil.): —	Payout: 29.5%
No. of shares (mil.): 2,086	Market value ($ mil.): —
Sales ($ mil): 2,062	

Hongkong & Shanghai Banking Corp Ltd

LOCATIONS
HQ: Hongkong & Shanghai Banking Corp Ltd
HSBC Main Building, 1 Queen's Road Central,
Phone: (852) 2822 1111 **Fax:** (852) 2810 1112
Web: www.hsbc.com.hk

HISTORICAL FINANCIALS
Company Type: Public

Income Statement FYE: December 31

	REVENUE ($ mil.)	NET INCOME ($ mil.)	NET PROFIT MARGIN	EMPLOYEES
12/19	45,691	13,381	29.3%	0
12/18	39,830	13,152	33.0%	0
12/17	36,787	11,327	30.8%	0
12/16	32,847	10,141	30.9%	0
12/15	33,732	11,551	34.2%	67,552
Annual Growth	7.9%	3.7%	—	—

2019 Year-End Financials

Debt ratio: —	No. of shares (mil.): —
Return on equity: 13.3%	Dividends
Cash ($ mil.): 28,751	Yield: —
Current ratio: —	Payout: —
Long-term debt ($ mil.): —	Market value ($ mil.): —

HSBC Bank Canada

Boasting around $70 billion in assets HSBC Bank Canada is one of the largest foreign-owned banks in Canada. Through more than 150 bank branches across the country it provides a range of commercial and retail financial services including deposit accounts loans and mortgages import and export financing equipment leasing and investment capital financing. Through subsidiaries the bank also offers brokerage services insurance mutual funds merchant banking trust services and portfolio management and investment counseling. HSBC Bank Canada is controlled by one of the largest banks on the planet UK-based financial services heavyweight HSBC Holdings.

Operations
HSBC Bank Canada operates three business segments: Retail banking and Wealth management which offers banking services to 800000 retail and high-net-worth clients; Commercial Banking which serves small and mid-sized businesses and multi-national companies; and Global Banking and Markets which consists of its markets capital financing and investment banking divisions.

The bank made 68% of its total revenue from interest income during 2015 with 80% of that being loan interest. Another 30% came from fee income with about half of that coming from credit facilities and funds under management fees and the rest coming from various service fees involving account services credit card corporate finance remittance brokerage commissions insurance and trustee fees among others.

Geographic Reach
The Vancouver-based bank operates branches across Canada.

Financial Performance
Note: Growth rates may differ after conversion to US dollars. This analysis uses financials from the company's annual report.

HSBC Bank Canada's annual revenues and profits have been in decline in recent years mostly as it's struggled to grow its loan business and as interest margins have been shrinking in the low-interest environment.

The bank's revenue slipped 9% to C$2.5 billion ($1.8 billion) during 2015 with all three segments reporting lower revenue due to the tough Canadian economy and the sharp decline in oil prices.

Revenue declines low interest margins and higher loan loss provisions stemming from more non-performing energy loans in 2015 caused HSBC Bank Canada's net income to fall more than 30% to C$447 million ($322.4 million). The bank's operating cash levels climbed sharply to C$3.65 billion ($2.63 billion) for the year (operations used C$546 million in 2014) despite the drop in earnings mostly thanks to favorable working capital changes related to changes in operating liabilities.

Strategy
HSBC Canada continued to follow its four strategic initiatives in early 2016 which included: leveraging its distinct geographic network which connects developed and fast-growing regions; connecting its clients to global growth opportunities; continuing to leverage its wide variety of financial products to benefit from global trends; and boost collaboration with other global businesses to better serve international clients.

Company Background
In 2012 as part of parent HSBC's restructuring efforts to create a leaner group HSBC Bank Canada announced plans to wind down the Consumer Finance segment which provided products including mortgages loans specialty insurance and credit cards through subsidiary HSBC Financial. The closure followed the 2011 sale of the full-service investment advisory business of HSBC Securities (Canada) to National Bank of Canada. Both divestitures reflected the group's strategy to focus on commercial banking retail banking and wealth management.

EXECUTIVES
EVP Commercial Banking; Regional President Central and Eastern Canada, Linda Seymour
EVP Personal Financial Services and Wealth Management, Margaret Willis
Co-Head Global Markets, Jason Henderson
CFO, Jacques Fleurant
President and CEO, Sandra Stuart
Chairman, Samuel (Sam) Minzberg
Auditors: PricewaterCoopers LLP

LOCATIONS
HQ: HSBC Bank Canada
300-885 West Georgia Street, Vancouver, British Columbia V6C 3E9
Phone: 604 685-1000 **Fax:** 604 641-3098
Web: www.hsbc.ca

PRODUCTS/OPERATIONS

2015 sales

	% of total
Interest income	66
Fee income	25
Net trading income	5
Gains less losses from financial investments	2
Other operating income	2
Total	100

Selected Products
Banking
Chequing accounts
Credit cards
eSwitch
Foreign currency accounts
Savings accounts
Tax-Free Savings Accounts (TFSA)
Travel insurance

Selected Subsidiaries
Household Trust Company
HSBC Capital (Canada) Inc.
HSBC Financial Corporation Limited
HSBC Global Asset Management (Canada) Limited
HSBC Investment Funds (Canada) Inc.
HSBC Loan Corporation (Canada)
HSBC Mortgage Corporation (Canada)
HSBC Securities (Canada) Inc.
HSBC South Point Investments (Barbados) LLP
HSBC Trust Company (Canada)

COMPETITORS
BMO Financial Group	National Bank of
CIBC	Canada
Canadian Western Bank	RBC Financial Group
IGM Financial	Scotiabank
Laurentian Bank	TD Bank

HISTORICAL FINANCIALS
Company Type: Public

Income Statement FYE: December 31

	ASSETS ($ mil.)	NET INCOME ($ mil.)	INCOME AS % OF ASSETS	EMPLOYEES
12/19	81,839	426	0.5%	5,688
12/18	75,934	500	0.7%	5,779
12/17	76,880	502	0.7%	5,681
12/16	70,238	360	0.5%	5,870
12/15	67,696	298	0.4%	6,060
Annual Growth	4.9%	9.4%	—	(1.6%)

2019 Year-End Financials

Return on assets: 0.5%	Dividends
Return on equity: 9.4%	Yield: —
Long-term debt ($ mil.): —	Payout: 77.6%
No. of shares (mil.): 498	Market value ($ mil.): —
Sales ($ mil): 2,921	

	STOCK PRICE ($) FY Close	P/E High/Low	PER SHARE ($)		
			Earnings	Dividends	Book Value
12/19	0.00	— —	0.85	0.66	9.41
12/18	0.00	— —	1.00	0.00	8.22
Annual Growth	—	— —	(3.9%)	—	3.4%

HSBC Bank Plc (United Kingdom)

EXECUTIVES

Director, Jonathan Symonds
Auditors: PricewaterhouseCoopers LLP

LOCATIONS

HQ: HSBC Bank Plc (United Kingdom)
8 Canada Square, London E14 5HQ
Phone: (44) 20 7991 8888
Web: www.hsbc.co.uk

HISTORICAL FINANCIALS

Company Type: Public

Income Statement				FYE: December 31
	ASSETS ($ mil.)	NET INCOME ($ mil.)	INCOME AS % OF ASSETS	EMPLOYEES
12/19	840,525	(1,337)	—	17,754
12/18	772,386	1,922	0.2%	30,437
12/17	1,106,036	2,443	0.2%	45,342
12/16	1,004,814	(260)	—	55,346
12/15	1,078,768	2,877	0.3%	67,290
Annual Growth	(6.0%)	—	—	(28.3%)

2019 Year-End Financials

Return on assets: (-0.1%)
Return on equity: (-4.0%)
Long-term debt ($ mil.): —
No. of shares (mil.): 796
Sales ($ mil): 19,368

Dividends
Yield: —
Payout: —
Market value ($ mil.): —

HSBC Holdings Plc

HSBC would be a real alphabet soup if the company's name reflected its geographic diversity. The international bank is one of the world's largest banking groups and the largest in Europe by assets under management (at around $2,7 trillion). Alongside its home markets of Hong Kong and the UK HSBC has subsidiaries throughout Europe the wider Asia/Pacific region the Middle East Africa and the Americas. All told the company serves more than 40 million customers in about 65 countries. Its activities include personal banking and wealth management services commercial banking credit cards private banking investment banking and lending. HSBC was founded by the Scot Sir Thomas Sutherland in Hong Kong then a British colony in 1865 as was incorporated in the UK in 1991.

Operations

HSBC operates four core business segments: Retail Banking and Wealth Management (RBWM) Commercial Banking (CBM) Global Banking and Markets (GB&M) and Global Private Banking (GPB).

RBWM accounts for around 40% of the firm's total revenue and provides personal banking and wealth management products and services to individual customers. It also offers current and savings account mortgages and personal loans credit cards debit cards and local and international payment services insurance investment products and global asset management as well as financial planning services.

CMB generates more than 25% of total revenue each year. It provides commercial customers including companies ranging in size from SMEs to corporations credit and lending liquidity international trade and receivables finance commercial insurance and investments and treasury and cash management-related services. CMB also offers its customers access to products and services offered by other global businesses such as GB&M which include foreign exchange products raising capital on debt and equity markets and advisory services.

The GB&M division accounts for over 25% of HSBC's total revenue. It offers financing advisory and transaction services for major government corporate and institutional clients and private investors around the globe.

GPB accounts for less than 5% of sales and provides investment and wealth management services to high-net-worth individuals and families. A Corporate Center function accounts for the remainder.

The bank has always had a bent toward international expansion even from its inception. HSBC owns all or parts of HSBC Bank plc in the UK The Hongkong and Shanghai Banking Corporation HSBC France The Saudi British Bank and Hong Kong's Hang Seng Bank. The company was also one of the first foreign banks to receive regulatory approval to incorporate in Mainland China where it owns about 20% of Bank of Communications one of the largest commercial banks in the country.

Geographic Reach

London-based HSBC operates in around 65 countries. It generates about 50% its revenue from the Asia/Pacific region (including Hong Kong) and around 30% from Europe (including the UK). North America brings in more than 10% of sales Latin America around 5% and the Middle East and North Africa around 5% as well.

Sales and Marketing

HSBC serves about 40 million customers ranging from individuals to large corporations and everything in between.

Financial Performance

HSBC's revenue has been rising in the last three years. During the same period profit attributable to the ordinary shareholders of the parent company has fluctuated.

HSBC's revenue grew 4% in 2019 compared to 2018. Net income declined 33% in the same period.

Cash and Cash equivalents at the end of the year totaled $293.7 billion. Operating activities generated $29.7 billion. Investing and financing activities used $35.3 billion and $14.8 billion respectively.

Strategy

In accordance to the company's introduction of its 2020 business update HSBC is adjusting its plan in order to upgrade the return profile of risk-weighted assets ('RWAs') reduce cost base and streamline its organization. This aims to position the Group to increase returns for investors create the capacity to invest in the future and build a sustainable platform for growth.

The business update also consists of its plan to remodel its Europe business to focus on its strengths reducing European RWAs by around 35% and lowering costs. To achieve this HSBC will focus its client coverage on key international European clients and connecting them to Asia and the Middle East.

The Group will continue to invest in its growth opportunities its customer experience and delivering value to all of oits stakeholders. It intends to reinvest the RWAs saved as a consequence of restructuring in its high-returning Asia and Middle East businesses HSBC UK its market-leading transaction banking franchise and the international wealth opportunity.

Additionally the company's remodelling plans will be accompanied by a substantial cost reduction program and a number of steps to simplify HSBC. These aim to reduce its overall cost base and to accelerate the pace of change.

Mergers and Acquisitions

In 2020 HSBC Insurance (Asia) Limited an indirect wholly-owned subsidiary of HSBC Holdings plc has entered into an agreement to acquire the remaining 50% equity interest in HSBC Life Insurance Company Limited its life insurance joint venture in China from The National Trust Limited. The transaction will be structured as a transfer of equity interest and is subject to regulatory approvals including from the China Banking and Insurance Regulatory Commission. Terms were not disclosed.

Company Background

In Asia HSBC sold its private banking operations in Japan to Credit Suisse in 2012. It also shut down its retail banking operations in Japan though it continues to offer corporate banking there. HSBC sold its US credit card portfolio worth some $30 billion to Capital One in 2012 and sold 195 US bank branches mainly in upstate New York to First Niagara Financial Group for Â 613 million ($1 billion).

HISTORY

Scotsman Thomas Sutherland and other businessmen in 1865 opened the doors to Hongkong & Shanghai Bank financing and promoting British imperial trade in opium silk and tea in East Asia. It soon established a London office and created an international branch network emphasizing China and East Asia. It claims to have been the first bank in Thailand (1888).

War repeatedly disrupted but never demolished the bank's operations. During WWII the headquarters were temporarily moved to London. (They moved back on a permanent basis in 1991.) The bank's chief prewar manager Sir Vandeleur Grayborn died in a Japanese POW camp. After the Communists took power in China in 1949 the bank gradually withdrew; by 1955 only its Shanghai office remained and it was later closed. The bank played a key role in Hong Kong's postwar growth by financing industrialists who fled there from China.

In the late 1950s Hongkong & Shanghai Bank's acquisitions included the British Bank of the Middle East (founded 1889; now The Saudi British Bank) and Mercantile Bank (with offices in India and Southeast Asia). In 1965 the company bought 62% of Hang Seng Hong Kong's #2 bank. It also added new subsidiaries including Wayfoong (mortgage and small-business finance 1960) and Wardley (investment banking Hong Kong 1972).

In the late 1970s and into the 1980s China began opening to foreign business. The bank added operations in North America to capitalize on business between China and the US and Canada. Acquisitions included Marine Midland Bank (US 1980) Hongkong Bank of Canada (1981) 51% of treasury securities dealer Carroll McEntee & McGinley (US 1983) most of the assets and liabilities of the Bank of British Columbia (1986) and Lloyds Bank Canada (1990).

Following the 1984 agreement to return Hong Kong to China Hongkong & Shanghai Bank began beefing up in the UK buying London securities dealer James Capel & Co. (1986) and the UK's #3 bank Midland plc (1992). In 1993 the company formed London-based HSBC Holdings and divested assets most notably its interest in Hong Kong-based Cathay Pacific Airways.

HSBC then began expanding in Asia again particularly in Malaysia where its Hongkong Bank Malaysia became the country's first locally incorporated foreign bank. The company returned to China with offices in Beijing and Guangzhou. It also added new European branches.

Latin American banks acquired in 1997 were among the non-Asian operations that cushioned HSBC from the worst of 1998's economic crises. Nonetheless The Hong Kong Monetary Authority took a stake in the bank to shore up the stock exchange and foil short-sellers.

In 1999 China's government made HSBC a loan for mainland expansion. That year the company was foiled in its attempt to buy South Korea's government-owned Seoulbank but did buy the late Edmond Safra's Republic New York Corporation and his international bank holding company Safra Republic Holdings (it negotiated a $450 million discount on the $10 billion deal after a Japanese probe of Republic's securities division caused delays).

The company unveiled several online initiatives in 2000 including Internet ventures with CK Hutchison Holdings and Merrill Lynch and bought CCF (then called Cr dit Commercial de France now HSBC France). However HSBC's plans to buy a controlling stake in Bangkok Metropolitan Bank fell through before the year's end.

In 2001 HSBC agreed to pick up Barclays Bank's fund management operations in Greece. Later in response to the slowing economy it froze the salaries of 14000 employees. Argentina's 2001 peso devaluation cost the company half a billion dollars in currency conversion losses alone. Total charges pertaining to Argentina equaled more than $1 billion that year.

HSBC expanded its consumer finance operations with the purchase of US-based Household International (now HSBC Finance) in 2003.

The next year HSBC acquired The Bank of Bermuda as well as Marks and Spencer Financial Services (aka M&S Money) one of the UK's leading credit card issuers. It bought US credit card company Metris the following year.

HSBC's Latin American operations at this point were primarily in Argentina Brazil and Mexico. The company expanded its presence in Central America and the Caribbean with the 2006 purchase of Panama-based Banistmo a banking group with offices in the Bahamas Colombia Costa Rica El Salvador Honduras and Nicaragua.

HSBC sold its regional banking operations in France to Banque Populaire in 2008. The deal included eight banks with around 400 branches. Also that year the company canceled its proposed $6 billion acquisition of Lone Star's 51% stake in Korea Exchange Bank a deal that had been held up for months by an investigation by the South Korean government. HSBC cited weakened asset values in the global financial markets for the cancellation.

Beset by mortgage defaults the group closed its Decision One US-based wholesale subprime lending unit in 2007. In 2009 it shuttered its North American consumer lending business placing related portfolios (excluding credit cards) in run-off. To further reduce its exposure to consumer credit it sold a $4 billion car loan portfolio and servicing platform to an affiliate of Santander USA.

The company acquired a majority stake in Indonesian lender Bank Ekonomi in 2009 doubling its presence in the nation.

In 2010 HSBC sold HSBC Insurance Brokers to Marsh & McLennan in a Â 135 million ($218 million) cash-and-stock deal. As part of the transaction the companies entered into a strategic partnership under which Marsh markets insurance and risk management services to HSBC's corporate and private clients ahead of other providers.

In late 2011 the Financial Services Authority (the UK regulator of financial services providers) fined HSBC Â 10.3 million after it was found that salespeople at its NHFA Limited subsidiary had sold inappropriate and unsuitable five-year bonds to nearly 3000 elderly customers. HSBC which had alerted the FSA once it was made aware of the issue closed NHFA to new business that year.

EXECUTIVES

President and CEO HSBC North America Holdings Inc., Patrick J. (Pat) Burke, age 58
Group Chief Executive, Stuart T. Gulliver, age 60, $1,237,440 total compensation
Chief Executive Global Banking and Markets, Samir Assaf, age 60
Deputy Chairman and Chief ExecutiveThe Hong Kong and Shanghai Banking Corporation, Peter T. S. Wong, age 69
Chief Executive Global Private Banking, Peter W. Boyles, age 64
Group Director Finance, Iain J. Mackay, age 58
Chief Executive Retail Banking and Wealth Management, John Flint, age 51
Group COO, Andy Maguire, age 53
Chief Executive HSBC Latin America and Executive Chairman HSBC Mexico, Paulo Maia, age 61
CEO HSBC Bank plc, Antonio Simoes, age 44
Chief Executive Global Commercial Banking, Noel Quinn
CEO HSBC Singapore, Tony Cripps
Group Managing Director and Chief Legal Officer, Stuart Levy
Group Chairman, Mark E. Tucker, age 62
Auditors: PricewaterhouseCoopers LLP

LOCATIONS

HQ: HSBC Holdings Plc
8 Canada Square, London E14 5HQ
Phone: (44) 20 7991 8888   **Fax:** (44) 20 7992 4880
Web: www.hsbc.com

2018 income

	% of total
Asia	49
Europe	30
North America	11
Latin America	5
MENA	5
Total	**100**

PRODUCTS/OPERATIONS

2018 Sales by Segment

	% of total
Retail banking & wealth management	40
Global banking & markets	29
Commercial banking	28
Global private banking	3
Total	**100**

Selected Subsidiaries

Hang Seng Bank Limited (62% Hong Kong)
The Hong Kong and Shanghai Banking Corporation Limited
HSBC Asset Finance (UK) Ltd.
HSBC Bank Argentina S.A. (99.9%)
HSBC Bank A.S. (Turkey)
HSBC Bank Australia Limited
HSBC Bank Bermuda Limited
HSBC Bank Brasil S.A. - Banco Mùltiplo
HSBC Bank Canada
HSBC Bank (China) Company Limited
HSBC Bank Egypt S.A.E. (95%)
HSBC Bank International Limited (Jersey)
HSBC Bank Malaysia Berhad
HSBC Bank Malta p.l.c. (70%)
HSBC Bank Middle East Limited
HSBC Bank (Panama) S.A.
HSBC Bank plc
HSBC Bank USA N.A.
HSBC Finance Corporation (US)
HSBC France
HSBC Mexico S.A. Institución de Banca Mùltiplo Grupo Financiero HSBC (99.9%)
HSBC Private Banking Holdings (Suisse) S.A. (Switzerland)
HSBC Securities (USA) Inc.
HSBC Trinkaus & Burkhardt AG (80% Germany)
Marks and Spencer Retail Financial Services Holdings Limited

COMPETITORS

BBVA	Lloyds Banking Group
Bank of America	Mitsubishi UFJ
Bank of China	Financial Group
Barclays	Mizuho Financial
CIBC	Prudential plc
Citigroup	RBC Financial Group
Credit Suisse	Royal Bank of Scotland
Deutsche Bank	Standard Chartered
Intesa Sanpaolo	UBS
JPMorgan Chase	

HISTORICAL FINANCIALS

Company Type: Public

Income Statement			FYE: December 31
	ASSETS ($ mil.)	**NET INCOME** ($ mil.)	**INCOME AS % OF ASSETS**	**EMPLOYEES**

	ASSETS ($ mil.)	**NET INCOME** ($ mil.)	**INCOME AS % OF ASSETS**	**EMPLOYEES**
12/19	2,715,152	7,293	0.3%	235,351
12/18	2,558,124	13,637	0.5%	235,217
12/17	2,521,771	10,798	0.4%	228,687
12/16	2,374,986	2,479	0.1%	241,000
12/15	2,409,656	13,522	0.6%	264,000
Annual Growth	3.0%	(14.3%)	—	(2.8%)

2019 Year-End Financials

Return on assets: 0.2%	Dividends
Return on equity: 3.9%	Yield: 6.5%
Long-term debt ($ mil.): —	Payout: 848.3%
No. of shares (mil.): —	Market value ($ mil.): —
Sales ($ mil): 101,027	

	STOCK PRICE ($) FY Close	**P/E** High/Low	**PER SHARE ($)** Earnings	Dividends	Book Value
12/19	39.09	149 118	0.30	2.55	9.06
12/18	41.11	88 61	0.63	2.55	9.30
12/17	51.64	108 83	0.48	2.55	9.51
12/16	40.18	614 418	0.07	2.55	8.83
12/15	39.47	77 57	0.64	2.50	9.57
Annual Growth	(0.2%)	— —	(17.3%)	0.4%	(1.4%)

Huadian Power International Corp., Ltd.

EXECUTIVES

Deputy General Manager and Chairman Huadian Qudong Power Generation Co Tianjin Huadian Fuyuan Thermal Power Co. Hangzhou Huadian Xiasha Thermal Power Co. Huadian Zibo Thermal Power Co. Huadian Laizhou Power Generation Co. and Huadian International Shandon, Xing Shibang, age 60
CFO, Chen Cunlai, age 58
Deputy General Manager and Director, Geng Yuanzhu, age 56

Deputy General Manager and Executive Director Sichuan Huadian Luding Hydropower Company Limited, Luo Xiaoqian, age 58
Deputy General Manager and Chairman Anhui Wenhui New Products Promotion Company Limited and Anhui Hualin International Energy Company Limited, Peng Guoquan, age 54
Deputy General Manager and Chairman Shanxi Maohua Energy Investment Company Limited, Wang Huiming, age 58
Deputy General Manager Chief Engineer and Executive Director Huadian Zhejiang Longyou Thermal Power Co. and Huadian International Shandong Project Co. and Chairman Anhui Huadian Lu'an Power Generation Co. Tianjin Huadian Nanjiang Thermal Power Co., Xie Yun, age 57
Chairman, Li Qingkui, age 64
Vice Chairman and General Manager, Chen Jianhua, age 60
Vice chairman, Chen Dianlu, age 66
Auditors: Deloitte Touche Tohmatsu Certified Public Accountants LLP

LOCATIONS

HQ: Huadian Power International Corp., Ltd.
No. 2 Xuanwumennei Street, Xicheng District, Beijing 100031
Phone: (86) 10 8356 7888   **Fax:** (86) 10 8356 7963
Web: www.hdpi.com.cn

PRODUCTS/OPERATIONS

2013 Sales

	% of total
PRC power Segment	88
Singapore Segment	11
All other Segment	1
Total	**100**

2013 Sales

	% of total
Sales of power & heat	97
Port service	1
Transportation service	1
Others	1
Total	**100**

COMPETITORS

A-Power Energy	China Yangtze Power
AES	Datang Power
CLP Holdings	Huaneng Power
China Power	Power Assets
China Resources Power	

HISTORICAL FINANCIALS
Company Type: Public

Income Statement				FYE: December 31
	REVENUE ($ mil.)	NET INCOME ($ mil.)	NET PROFIT MARGIN	EMPLOYEES
12/19	13,459	489	3.6%	0
12/18	12,846	246	1.9%	0
12/17	12,141	66	0.5%	0
12/16	9,122	481	5.3%	0
12/15	10,283	1,128	11.0%	24,968
Annual Growth	7.0%	(18.8%)	—	—

2019 Year-End Financials
Debt ratio: 7.0%
Return on equity: 6.0%
Cash ($ mil.): 946
Current ratio: 0.40
Long-term debt ($ mil.): 10,794
No. of shares (mil.): —
Dividends
  Yield: 0.0%
  Payout: —
Market value ($ mil.): —

	STOCK PRICE ($) FY Close	P/E High/Low	PER SHARE ($) Earnings	Dividends	Book Value
12/19	14.25	49 49	0.04	0.22	(0.00)
12/18	14.25	—	0.02	0.00	(0.00)
Annual Growth	(0.0%)	—	16.2%	—	

Huaneng Power International Inc

EXECUTIVES

Chairman, Peixi Cao, age 65
President, Guoyue Liu, age 57
Chief Engineer, Yong He
VP and Chief Accountant, Hui Zhou, age 57
Vice Chairman, Guo Junming, age 55
Chaiman, Xiangdong Ye, age 53
Auditors: KPMG Huazhen LLP

LOCATIONS

HQ: Huaneng Power International Inc
Huaneng Building, 6 Fuxingmennei Street, Xicheng District, Beijing 100031
Phone: (86) 10 6322 6999   **Fax:** (86) 10 6322 6888
Web: www.hpi.com.cn

2013 Sales

	% of total
PRC power	89
Singapore	11
Total	**100**

COMPETITORS

AES	Hong Kong and China
CLP Holdings	Gas
China Power	Huadian Power
China Resources Power	Korea Electric Power
Datang Power	Power Assets

HISTORICAL FINANCIALS
Company Type: Public

Income Statement				FYE: December 31
	REVENUE ($ mil.)	NET INCOME ($ mil.)	NET PROFIT MARGIN	EMPLOYEES
12/19	24,932	242	1.0%	0
12/18	24,695	209	0.8%	57,960
12/17	23,428	275	1.2%	53,962
12/16	16,390	1,269	7.7%	42,210
12/15	19,848	2,102	10.6%	42,039
Annual Growth	5.9%	(41.7%)	—	—

2019 Year-End Financials
Debt ratio: 8.0%
Return on equity: 1.8%
Cash ($ mil.): 1,912
Current ratio: 0.43
Long-term debt ($ mil.): 20,673
No. of shares (mil.): —
Dividends
  Yield: 2.5%
  Payout: 5,965.0%
Market value ($ mil.): —

	STOCK PRICE ($) FY Close	P/E High/Low	PER SHARE ($) Earnings	Dividends	Book Value
12/19	20.09	435 305	0.01	0.52	(0.00)
12/18	25.01	437 298	0.01	2.02	(0.00)
12/17	25.00	303 227	0.02	1.56	(0.00)
12/16	26.04	61 38	0.08	2.47	(0.00)
12/15	34.30	62 35	0.14	2.20	804.39
Annual Growth	(12.5%)	—	(50.6%)	(30.4%)	—

Huayu Automotive Systems Company Ltd

Auditors: Deloitte Touche Tohmatsu CPA Ltd.

LOCATIONS

HQ: Huayu Automotive Systems Company Ltd
No. 489, Weihai Road, Shanghai 200041
Phone: (86) 21 22011701   **Fax:** (86) 21 22011790

HISTORICAL FINANCIALS
Company Type: Public

Income Statement				FYE: December 31
	REVENUE ($ mil.)	NET INCOME ($ mil.)	NET PROFIT MARGIN	EMPLOYEES
12/19	20,698	928	4.5%	0
12/18	22,850	1,167	5.1%	0
12/17	21,588	1,007	4.7%	0
12/16	17,899	874	4.9%	0
12/15	14,030	736	5.2%	0
Annual Growth	10.2%	6.0%	—	—

2019 Year-End Financials
Debt ratio: 1.1%
Return on equity: 13.6%
Cash ($ mil.): 4,719
Current ratio: 1.20
Long-term debt ($ mil.): 548
No. of shares (mil.): —
Dividends
  Yield: —
  Payout: —
Market value ($ mil.): —

Hunan Valin Steel Co Ltd

EXECUTIVES

Chairman, Huiquan Cao
Auditors: KPMG Huazhen

LOCATIONS

HQ: Hunan Valin Steel Co Ltd
20th Floor Valin Plaza, Main Building, Valin Park, No. 222, Xiangfu West Road, Changsha, Hunan Province 410014
Phone: (86) 731 89952818   **Fax:** (86) 731 82245196
Web: www.valin.cn

HISTORICAL FINANCIALS
Company Type: Public

Income Statement
FYE: December 31

	REVENUE ($ mil.)	NET INCOME ($ mil.)	NET PROFIT MARGIN	EMPLOYEES
12/19	15,423	631	4.1%	0
12/18	13,283	985	7.4%	0
12/17	11,779	633	5.4%	0
12/16	7,193	(151)	—	0
12/15	6,389	(455)	—	0
Annual Growth	24.6%	—	—	—

2019 Year-End Financials
Debt ratio: 3.8%	No. of shares (mil.): —
Return on equity: 19.2%	Dividends
Cash ($ mil.): 960	Yield: —
Current ratio: 0.69	Payout: —
Long-term debt ($ mil.): 290	Market value ($ mil.): —

Hyakugo Bank Ltd. (Japan)

EXECUTIVES

President, TOSHIYASU ITO
Executive Vice President, Yoshihiko Watanabe
Managing Director, Tetsuya Yamamoto
Managing Director, Masakazu Sugiura
Auditors: KPMG AZSA LLC

LOCATIONS

HQ: Hyakugo Bank Ltd. (Japan)
21-27 Iwata, Tsu, Mie 514-8666
Phone: (81) 59 227 2151
Web: www.hyakugo.co.jp

COMPETITORS

Aozora Bank	Mitsubishi UFJ
Iyo Bank	Financial Group
Mie Bank	Shizuoka Bank

HISTORICAL FINANCIALS
Company Type: Public

Income Statement
FYE: March 31

	ASSETS ($ mil.)	NET INCOME ($ mil.)	INCOME AS % OF ASSETS	EMPLOYEES
03/20	59,303	105	0.2%	4,194
03/19	56,574	97	0.2%	4,238
03/18	54,072	110	0.2%	4,231
03/17	49,525	80	0.2%	4,229
03/16	47,505	121	0.3%	4,282
Annual Growth	5.7%	(3.5%)	—	(0.5%)

2020 Year-End Financials
Return on assets: 0.1%	Dividends
Return on equity: 3.3%	Yield: —
Long-term debt ($ mil.): —	Payout: 20.0%
No. of shares (mil.): 253	Market value ($ mil.): —
Sales ($ mil): 863	

Hyakujushi Bank, Ltd.

Auditors: Ernst & Young ShinNihon LLC

LOCATIONS

HQ: Hyakujushi Bank, Ltd.
5-1 Kamei-cho, Takamatsu, Kagawa 760-8574
Phone: (81) 87 831 0114
Web: www.114bank.co.jp

COMPETITORS

Awa Bank	Mizuho Financial
Chugoku Bank	Norinchukin Bank
Hiroshima Bank	Resona
Mitsubishi UFJ Financial Group	Sumitomo Mitsui

HISTORICAL FINANCIALS
Company Type: Public

Income Statement
FYE: March 31

	ASSETS ($ mil.)	NET INCOME ($ mil.)	INCOME AS % OF ASSETS	EMPLOYEES
03/20	45,637	71	0.2%	2,978
03/19	44,206	50	0.1%	3,050
03/18	44,987	96	0.2%	3,164
03/17	44,063	86	0.2%	3,216
03/16	42,028	103	0.2%	3,242
Annual Growth	2.1%	(9.0%)	—	(2.1%)

2020 Year-End Financials
Return on assets: 0.1%	Dividends
Return on equity: 2.8%	Yield: —
Long-term debt ($ mil.): —	Payout: 30.6%
No. of shares (mil.): 29	Market value ($ mil.): —
Sales ($ mil): 708	

Hyundai Motor Co., Ltd.

Hyundai vehicles run the gamut from budget cars to luxury sedans to commercial trucks. South Korea's leading carmaker Hyundai Motor produces compact and luxury cars SUVs minivans trucks buses and other commercial vehicles. Its cars are sold in 200 countries through some 6000 dealerships. Hyundai generates more than one-third of its sales in South Korea but its vehicles are also popular in emerging markets such as China and India. The company operates a dozen manufacturing plants in Brazil China the Czech Republic India Russia Turkey and the US. It sells roughly 4.5 million cars each year with most of it comes from South Korea. Hyundai also owns more than a third stake in Kia Motors.

Operations

Hyundai Motor Company operates under three segments; Vehicle; Finance; and Other Segments.

The Vehicle Segment generate about 85% of total sales. It is engaged in the manufacturing and sale of motor vehicles.

The Finance segment gives more than 10% of total sales. It operates vehicle financing credit card processing and other financing activities.

Others segment generate more than 5% of total sales. Includes the R&D train manufacturing and other activities.

Geographic Reach

Headquartered in Seoul South Korea. Hyundai's geographic areas are in Asia (excluding South Korea) North America and Europe. South Korea generates about 40% of total sales while North America brings in nearly 30% of total sales Europe gives about 25% of total sales and Asia and other countries generates about 10% of total sales combined. Hyundai have manufacturing plants in India Indonesia the Czech Republic Russia Turkey Singapore and Brazil.

Financial Performance

Sales of the company increased by ?8.9 trillion to ?105.7 trillion in 2019 primarily due to higher sales of goods.

Profit for the year increased by 94% to ?3.2 trillion due to higher revenues. Cash held by the company at the end of 2019 decreased by ?431.7 billion to ?8.7 trillion.

Cash provided by operations and financing activities were ?419.8 billion and ?4.9 trillion respectively. Cash used for investing activities was ?5.9 trillion mainly for acquisitions of property plant and equipment.

Strategy

Hyundai Motor Company ponders the sustainable future of society and seeks to create social value together with stakeholders in addition to economic value creation which is its fundamental corporate role.

To this end the company have defined its strategic goal as "smart mobility-based customer experience innovation" based on its "new "Strategy 2025" while also setting goals for environmental and social change across the entire value chain including business sites and suppliers by focusing on "pursuing eco-friendly value throughout the entire value chain" "creating a sustainable supply chain" and "building a healthy corporate culture".

In addition "for contributing to the development of local communities" Hyundai will continue its creative innovation drive based on the strategy of creating shared value (CSV) thereby generating social value for more global community members and ushering in a sustainable future.

EXECUTIVES

President Ulsan Plant, Yoon Gap Han
President and CEO, Lee Won Hee
Chairman, Chung Mong-Koo, age 72
Vice Chairman, Chung Eui-Sun, age 49
Auditors: KPMG Samjong Accounting Corp.

LOCATIONS

HQ: Hyundai Motor Co., Ltd.
12, Heolleung-ro Seocho-gu, Seoul 06797
Phone: (82) 2 3464 1114   **Fax:** (82) 2 3463 3484
Web: www.hyundai-motor.com

2018 Sales

	% of total
South Korea	16
Overseas	84
Total	**100**

PRODUCTS/OPERATIONS

Selected Models
Commercial vehicles
Aero (large city bus)
Aero Town (medium bus)
County (small bus)
e-Mighty (light commercial truck)
Super Aero City (bus)
Universe (large coach bus)
Passenger cars
Accent (compact coupe)
Atos Prime (subcompact)
Avante XD

Azera (sedan)
Elantra (sedan)
Entourage (minivan)
Equus/Centennial (premium sedan)
Genesis (premium coupe)
Getz (compact sedan)
Santa Fe (SUV)
Sonata (sedan)
Tiburon (coupe)
Tucson (SUV)
Trajet (SUV)
Veracruz (SUV)

COMPETITORS

BYD	Honda
Chery Automobile	Isuzu
Daihatsu	Maruti Suzuki
Daimler	Mazda
Dongfeng Motor	Nissan
FCA US	Peugeot
Fiat Chrysler	Renault
Ford Motor	Ssangyong Motor
GM Korea	Tata Motors
General Motors	Toyota
Hindustan Motors	Volkswagen

HISTORICAL FINANCIALS

Company Type: Public

Income Statement				FYE: December 31
	REVENUE ($ mil.)	NET INCOME ($ mil.)	NET PROFIT MARGIN	EMPLOYEES
12/19	91,585	2,580	2.8%	0
12/18	86,836	1,352	1.6%	0
12/17	90,399	3,782	4.2%	68,590
12/16	77,952	4,500	5.8%	67,517
12/15	78,160	5,454	7.0%	66,404
Annual Growth	4.0%	(17.1%)	—	—

2019 Year-End Financials

Debt ratio: 0.0%	No. of shares (mil.): 201
Return on equity: 4.3%	Dividends
Cash ($ mil.): 7,519	Yield: —
Current ratio: 1.43	Payout: 35.3%
Long-term debt ($ mil.): 45,922	Market value ($ mil.): —

IA Financial Corp Inc

Industrial Alliance Insurance and Financial Services (iA Financial Group) covers all of Canada with its individual and group insurance savings and retirement products. The company sells life health and disability insurance as well as retirement savings plans and annuities to individuals and employers across the country. To a much lesser extent it offers life insurance products in parts of the US. The group manages mutual funds through its IA Clarington unit and it brokers securities and funds through Investia FundEX Investments and iA Securities. iA Financial Group also sells auto and homeowners insurance. Its products are distributed by more than 3000 advisors.

Operations

iA Financial Group operates through four primary lines of business: Individual Wealth Management (nearly half of all premiums and deposits) Individual Insurance Group Insurance and Group Savings and Retirement.

Personal insurance products include life critical illness disability and travel coverage while wealth management offerings include mutual funds annuities and private wealth management services.

The Group Insurance line is divided into three divisions: Employee Plans (including life health and dental) Dealer Services (creditor insurance car loans and replacement insurance) and Special Markets Solutions (including critical illness accidental death and dismemberment and travel medical). Group Savings and Retirement offers insured annuities and capital accumulation products.

The group also offers general insurance in Quebec through iA Auto and Home.

Sales and Marketing

iA Financial Group distributes its retail insurance products in Canada through its own team of agent affiliates managing general agents and independent advisors. In the US these products are sold through independent marketing organizations and car dealerships.

The group distributes its commercial products through specialized advisors consulting firms and car dealerships.

General insurance is distributed through direct sales referrals and partners.

Financial Performance

Because it straddles both general insurance and financial services iA Financial Group measures growth both in its premium revenues and the assets it has under administration. Both measurements have generally reflected positive growth.

Total revenue rose 21% to $11.3 billion in 2017 thanks to increases in net premiums (which grew 11%) and investment income (which grew 62%). Premium income growth was driven by group insurance and segregated fund activities.

However iA Financial's rapid growth led policy benefits and expenses (such as commissions) to increase in 2017 causing net income to fall 4% to $515.5 million. Cash flow from operations totaled $645 million versus a cash outflow of $96 million in 2016 due to an increase in insurance contract liabilities a decrease in reinsurance assets and other factors.

Strategy

iA Financial Group works to diversify its distribution network product offerings and geographical presence and it's been largely successful on all three fronts through acquisitions and organic growth. Historically limited to the Quebec market the firm has expanded its services into every Canadian province and is now making more than 60% of its sales outside of Quebec.

It has also augmented its financial services and wealth management offerings through acquisitions and it has moved into new insurance coverage niches. Through acquisitions it entered the individual disability and health insurance markets. Used car insurance is a non-glamorous niche that IA has snuggled into through the acquisition of National Warranties MRVW and three Quebec-based specialty insurers that offer creditor insurance and replacement warranty products to car dealers.

In 2018 iA Financial introduced a new critical illness product for younger adults. The product named TRANSITION boasts a quick and easy application process as well as more affordable rates.

While the US contributes only a small fraction (less than 5%) to iA Financial Group's revenues the company is intent on establishing a solid base to the south. Through careful acquisitions of firms such as Dealers Assurance Company and Southwest Reinsure it has built up its operations in the US.

iA Financial is in the middle of a digital transformation initiative with a focus on modernizing its administration distribution and marketing activities. For example in 2017 it launched the new EVO platform through which about half of all individual insurance applications can be processed in mere minutes. And in 2018 it made individual insurance claims services available online.

Mergers and Acquisitions

To further grow its financial services offerings iA Financial Group acquired wealth management firm HollisWealth from Scotiabank in 2017. Thanks largely to that purchase iA Financial ended the year with some $170 billion in assets under management and administration (a 34% increase over the prior year's total). Further building its brokerage distribution capabilities the acquired Canadian insurance managing general agent PPI Management in 2018. That company provides life insurance expertise to independent advisors through 15 offices across the country; its advisory division focuses on ultra-wealthy clients.

Also in 2018 the company bought Dealers Assurance Company and Southwest Reinsure thereby expanding its car dealership business to the US. The US$135 million deal also more than doubled its vehicle warranty business.

Company Background

Founded in 1892 iA Financial Group converted from a mutual to a public company in 2000.

EXECUTIVES

EVP and Assistant to the President, Normand Pépin

President iA Securities Inc., Richard Legault

EVP Individual Insurance and Annuities, Denis Ricard

EVP Group Benefits and Retirement Solutions, Renée Laflamme

EVP U.S. Development, Michael L. Stickney

SVP Information Systems, Guy Daneau

President and CEO, Yvon Charest

President Investia Financial Services Inc., Louis H. DeConinck

EVP CFO and Chief Actuary, René Chabot

EVP and Chief Investments Officer, Michel Tremblay

EVP Wealth Management, Carl Mustos

President American-Amicable Group of Companies, Joe W. Dunlap

President and General Manager MRA, Daniel Riopel

President iA Private Wealth Management, Mark Arthur

President FundEX Investments Inc., David Chapman

President and COO iA Auto and Home Insurance Inc., Michael Laurin

President CTL Corp., Sean O'Brien

Chairman, Jocelyne Bourgon

Auditors: Deloitte LLP

LOCATIONS

HQ: IA Financial Corp Inc
1080, Grande Allee West, P.O. 1907 Station Terminus, Quebec City, Quebec G1K 7M3
Phone: 418 684-5000   **Fax:** 418 684-5185
Web: www.ia.ca

PRODUCTS/OPERATIONS

2017 Sales by Segment

	% of total
Individual Insurance	36
Individual Wealth Management	30
Group Savings and Retirement	16
Group Insurance	15
Other	3
Total	**100**

Selected Subsidiaries

FundEX Investments Inc. (mutual fund broker)
IA American Life Insurance Company (US)
IA Clarington Investments Inc. (mutual fund management and promotion)
Investia Financial Services Inc. (mutual fund broker)
Solicour Inc. (financial services brokerage)
The Excellence Life Insurance Company (life and health insurance)

COMPETITORS

CPP Investment Board	Manulife Financial
Canada Life	Power Financial
Desjardins Financial	RBC Insurance
Security	Standard Life Aberdeen
E-L Financial	Sun Life
Great-West Lifeco	Wawanesa Mutual
ING	

HISTORICAL FINANCIALS

Company Type: Public

Income Statement

FYE: December 31

	ASSETS ($ mil.)	NET INCOME ($ mil.)	INCOME AS % OF ASSETS	EMPLOYEES
12/19	74,069	717	1.0%	6,800
12/18	64,340	641	1.0%	0
12/17	62,686	537	0.9%	6,115
12/16	57,769	560	1.0%	5,350
12/15	53,605	390	0.7%	5,148
Annual Growth	8.4%	16.4%	—	7.2%

2019 Year-End Financials

Return on assets: 1.0%
Return on equity: 11.9%
Long-term debt ($ mil.): —
No. of shares (mil.): 106
Sales ($ mil): 15,457

Dividends
 Yield: 0.0%
 Payout: 27.5%
Market value ($ mil.): 3,424

	STOCK PRICE ($) FY Close	P/E High/Low		PER SHARE ($) Earnings	Dividends	Book Value
12/19	32.01	5	5	6.48	1.79	58.03
12/18	31.50	9	6	5.66	1.61	53.33
12/17	47.22	10	9	4.87	1.45	48.72
12/16	38.21	7	5	5.26	1.28	45.43
12/15	32.33	10	9	3.62	1.17	41.36
Annual Growth	(0.2%)	—	—	15.7%	11.1%	8.8%

Iberdrola SA

EXECUTIVES

Authorised Signing Officer, Fernando Julio Arias Coterillo
Auditors: KPMG Auditores, S.L.

LOCATIONS

HQ: Iberdrola SA
 Plaza Euskadi, 5, Bilbao 48009
Phone: (34) 944 151 411   **Fax:** (34) 944 663 194
Web: www.iberdrola.com

HISTORICAL FINANCIALS

Company Type: Public

Income Statement

FYE: December 31

	REVENUE ($ mil.)	NET INCOME ($ mil.)	NET PROFIT MARGIN	EMPLOYEES
12/19	40,911	3,824	9.3%	34,306
12/18	40,168	3,451	8.6%	34,078
12/17	37,476	3,361	9.0%	28,750
12/16	30,848	2,856	9.3%	28,389
12/15	34,221	2,637	7.7%	27,169
Annual Growth	4.6%	9.7%	—	6.0%

2019 Year-End Financials

Debt ratio: 36.5%
Return on equity: 8.9%
Cash ($ mil.): 2,372
Current ratio: 0.71
Long-term debt ($ mil.): 34,353

No. of shares (mil.): —
Dividends
 Yield: 2.9%
 Payout: 208.3%
Market value ($ mil.): —

	STOCK PRICE ($) FY Close	P/E High/Low		PER SHARE ($) Earnings	Dividends	Book Value
12/19	41.31	82	59	0.59	1.23	6.65
12/18	32.09	69	56	0.53	1.22	6.86
12/17	30.94	80	63	0.53	1.20	7.03
12/16	26.23	66	54	0.44	0.91	6.18
12/15	28.32	76	63	0.41	0.96	6.48
Annual Growth	9.9%	—	—	9.1%	6.6%	0.6%

ICICI Bank Ltd (India)

You see ICICI Bank is India's #2 bank (after State Bank of India) and its largest private bank boasting over 13 trillion rupees in assets. The bank has more than 5300 branches nationwide. Its Retail banking group offers a range of products from savings investments protection and retirement plan while Wholesale Banking does the same for top business houses large private sector companies financial institutions and public sector. The rural and SME banking unit offers financial products and services to individuals households and small businesses. Its International Banking unit deals with the bank's foreign operations and international trade finance-related service. The bank also offers life and property/casualty insurance through subsidiaries.

Operations

ICICI operates three core business segments: Retail Banking (more than 40% of revenue); Treasury (roughly 35% of revenue) which manages the bank's investment portfolio and includes the Proprietary Trading Group Markets Group and Asset Liability Management Group; and Wholesale Banking (about 25% of revenue) which serves corporate customers in India and overseas in providing working capital finance export finance trade transaction and commercial banking and foreign currency term loans; and

The Bank's key subsidiaries include ICICI Prudential Life Insurance (one of the largest private sector life insurers in the country) ICICI Lombard General Insurance (property/casualty coverage) ICICI Prudential Asset Management (mutual funds) ICICI Securities (investment banking and brokerage) and ICICI Venture Funds Management (venture capital).

Geographic Reach

Mumbai-based ICICI generates more than 95% of its total revenue in its home country. The bank has an international presence through its ICICI Bank UK and ICICI Bank Canada subsidiaries in the UK and Canada respectively. It also has branches in the US China Singapore Hong Kong Dubai Sri Lanka Bahrain and South Africa.

Sales and Marketing

ICICI's customers can execute their trade finance and foreign exchange transactions through the Trade Online and FXOnline.

Financial Performance

Note: Growth rates may differ after conversion to US dollars. This analysis uses the company-provided financials from its 2020 Annual Report.

Revenue for the year ended 2020 was ?1.8 trillion. All of the Bank's segments had a hand in the 18% growth for the year.

The Bank had a net profit of ?79.3 billion a 136% growth from the previous year.

The Bank's cash for the year ended 2020 was ?1.2 trillion. Operating activities generated ?784.5 billion while investing activities used ?371.1 billion mainly for held-to-maturity securities. Financing activities used another ?26.4 billion primarily for repayment of long-term borrowings.

Strategy

ICICI Bank is focused on building and nurturing a leading future ready organization with the customer at the core.

The strategic focus of the Bank during fiscal 2020 was to continue to grow its core operating profits in a risk-calibrated and granular manner. This was driven by the objective of 'One Bank One ROE' that enabled synergies across businesses. Further the principle of 'Fair to Customer Fair to Bank' emphasizing the need to deliver fair value to customers while creating value for shareholders guides the Bank's operations. The underlying pillars of leveraging digital a customer centric and service-oriented approach simplification of processes and enhancing customer experience were factors that were common across all businesses.

Efforts aimed at delivering maximum value to customers were further strengthened during the year. A strategic focus in this regard was to extensively leverage data analytics and market intelligence to create strategies and unique value propositions across market segments. It also facilitated better targeting resourcing channel and product alignment capability building and marketing and alliances. The Bank enhanced its focus on exploring customer ecosystems that offered the opportunity to provide a wide range of products and services.

EXECUTIVES

Managing Director and CEO, Chanda D. Kochhar, age 59
Executive Director, N. S. Kannan, age 55
Executive Director, Krishnaswamy Ramkumar, age 59
President, Zarin Daruwala
Executive Director, Rajiv Sabharwal
President, Vijay Chandok
CFO, Rakesh Jha
Chairman, Mahendra Kumar Sharma, age 73
Auditors: KPMG Assurance and Consulting Services LLP

LOCATIONS

HQ: ICICI Bank Ltd (India)
 ICICI Bank Towers, Bandra-Kurla Complex, Mumbai 400051
Phone: (91) 22 33667777   **Fax:** (91) 22 26531122
Web: www.icicibank.com

PRODUCTS/OPERATIONS

2015 Sales by Segment

	% of total
Treasury	39
Wholesale Banking	30
Retail Banking	30
Other Banking	1
Total	**100**

COMPETITORS

BNP Paribas	ING
Bank of Baroda	Industrial Development
Bank of India	Bank of India

Canara Bank   Punjab National Bank
Citigroup   Standard Chartered
GE Money India   State Bank of India
HDFC Bank   UCO Bank
HSBC

HISTORICAL FINANCIALS

Company Type: Public

Income Statement   FYE: March 31

	ASSETS ($ mil.)	NET INCOME ($ mil.)	INCOME AS % OF ASSETS	EMPLOYEES
03/20	343,079	2,382	0.7%	131,232
03/19	308,579	1,059	0.3%	117,340
03/18	280,055	1,921	0.7%	112,360
03/17	245,620	2,537	1.0%	107,971
03/16	228,859	2,535	1.1%	97,132
Annual Growth	10.7%	(1.5%)	—	7.8%

2020 Year-End Financials

Return on assets: 0.7%	Dividends
Return on equity: 8.0%	Yield: 0.8%
Long-term debt ($ mil.): —	Payout: 7.7%
No. of shares (mil.): —	Market value ($ mil.): —
Sales ($ mil): 37,311	

	STOCK PRICE ($) FY Close	P/E High/Low		PER SHARE ($) Earnings	Dividends	Book Value
03/20	8.50	1	0	0.36	0.07	4.73
03/19	11.46	2	1	0.16	0.04	4.42
03/18	8.85	1	1	0.30	0.07	4.29
03/17	8.60	1	0	0.43	0.14	4.47
03/16	7.16	1	0	0.43	0.28	4.03
Annual Growth	4.4%	—	—	(4.4%)	(29.4%)	4.1%

Idemitsu Kosan Co Ltd

As long as Japanese drive Toyotas there will be a role for Idemitsu Kosan. The company is the #2 oil refiner in Japan (behind Nippon Oil). At its four refineries in Japan (processing 640000 barrels per day) Idemitsu Kosan produces petroleum products such as gasoline and other fuels kerosene and lubricants. It markets its fuel products through a network of 4600 service stations. Idemitsu Kosan sells heavy oil and jet fuels to industries and kerosene and liquefied petroleum gas to the residential sector. The company also has interests in oil exploration and production as well as coal and uranium. In 2016 it agreed to buy a 31.3% stake in Showa Shell Sekiyu from Royal Dutch Shell for $1.35 billion.

Operations

Idemitsu Kosan has three reportable segments: Its petroleum products business includes fuel oil and petrochemical products. Its petrochemical products operations consist of the basic chemicals business which jointly operates an ethylene complex with Mitsui Chemicals and the functional materials business which develops functional flexible polypropylene. The company's resources businesses is engaged in exploration activities to expand its oil reserves.

In addition to its oil and gas businesses the company has a number of New Growth activities including agro-business (pesticides) and green energy (wind solar and geothermal). Idemitsu Kosan is also developing electronic materials (organic light-emitting diode luminous materials with Sony Corporation) and lithium battery development.

Geographic Reach

Idemitsu Kosan has offices in Africa Asia (East South East and South West) Australia Europe (including Russia) the Middle East and North and South America.

Financial Performance

In 2012 the company's revenues increased by 18% due to increases in the prices of crude oil and naphtha significant rises in coal prices and an increase in the volume of products sold. Japan accounted for 84% of the company's revenues that year.

Net income increased by 6% in 2012 thanks to higher revenues and the result of progress in streamlining activities in production sales and distribution as well as improved product margins for petrochemical products despite a contraction of margins for petroleum products.

Strategy

To meet increased demand Idemitsu Kosan is enhancing its petroleum products business in the growing overseas markets centered on the Pacific Rim. As part of this process in 2012 it acquired Freedom an independent Australian petroleum products distributor that sells petroleum products wholesale and operates about 40 gas stations on Australia's east coast.

That year it also opened an office in China formed a joint venture in Taiwan and set up a lubricant manufacturing and sales company in Vietnam.

Idemitsu Kosan unified its ethylene production with Mitsui Chemicals in 2010 to promote efficiency.

Company Background

Pooling their LPG resources and expertise in 2006 Idemitsu Kosan merged its LPG operations with those of Mitsubishi to form Astomos Energy.

EXECUTIVES

CEO, Takashi Tsukioka
EVP, Yoshihisa Matsumoto
EVP, Daisuke Seki
EVP, Hiroshi Seki
Auditors: Deloitte Touche Tohmatsu LLC

LOCATIONS

HQ: Idemitsu Kosan Co Ltd
3-1-1 Marunouchi, Chiyoda-ku, Tokyo 100-8321
Phone: (81) 3 3213 3150
Web: www.idss.co.jp

2016 Sales

	% of total
Japan	75
Asia and Oceania	16
North America	6
Europe	2
Other	1
Total	**100**

PRODUCTS/OPERATIONS

2016 Sales

	% of total
Petroleum products	77
Petrochemical products	15
Resources	6
Others	2
Total	**100**

Products & Services
Agri-Bio
Electronic Materials
Lubricants
Packing Materials Logistics Plastics
Petrochemicals
Petroleum Transportation
Refinery & Plant
Renewable Energy
Research & Development

Resource Development

SUBSIDIARIES
AltaGas Idemitsu Joint Venture Limited Partnership
Apolloretailing Co.Ltd.
Astomos Energy Corp.
Formosa Idemitsu Petrochemicals Corporation
Idemitsu Apollo Corporation
Idemitsu Australia Resources Pty Ltd
Idemitsu Canada Corporation
Idemitsu Canada Resouces Ltd.
Idemitsu Credit Co. Ltd.
Idemitsu Engineering Co. Ltd.
Idemitsu Insurance Service Co.Ltd.
Idemitsu International (Asia) Pte.Ltd.
Idemitsu Oita Geothermal Co.Ltd.
Idemitsu Petroleum Norge AS
Idemitsu Petroleum UK Ltd.
Idemitsu Retail Marketing Co. Ltd.
Idemitsu SM (Malaysia) Sdn.Bhd.
Idemitsu Tanker Co. Ltd.
Idemitsu Unitech Co. Ltd.
Nghi Son Refinery and Petrochemical LLC
Prime Polymer Co. Ltd.
PS Japan Corp.
SDS Biotech K.K.

COMPETITORS

Cosmo Oil	JXTG Holdings
JX Nippon Mining & Metals	SK Innovation
JX Nippon Oil & Energy	Showa Shell Sekiyu

HISTORICAL FINANCIALS

Company Type: Public

Income Statement   FYE: March 31

	REVENUE ($ mil.)	NET INCOME ($ mil.)	NET PROFIT MARGIN	EMPLOYEES
03/20	55,696	(211)		18,273
03/19	39,958	735	1.8%	13,398
03/18	35,133	1,528	4.4%	12,657
03/17	28,534	788	2.8%	12,655
03/16	31,792	(320)	—	9,203
Annual Growth	15.0%	—	—	18.7%

2020 Year-End Financials

Debt ratio: 0.3%	No. of shares (mil.): 297
Return on equity: (-2.3%)	Dividends
Cash ($ mil.): 1,218	Yield: 0.0%
Current ratio: 0.94	Payout: —
Long-term debt ($ mil.): 5,970	Market value ($ mil.): 3,547

	STOCK PRICE ($) FY Close	P/E High/Low		PER SHARE ($) Earnings	Dividends	Book Value
03/20	11.91	—	—	(0.70)	0.60	35.57
03/19	19.05	0	0	3.63	0.41	38.50
03/18	19.38	0	0	7.96	0.31	39.34
03/17	15.99	0	0	4.93	0.22	32.64
03/16	8.55	—	—	(2.00)	0.22	27.87
Annual Growth	8.6%	—	—	—	28.5%	6.3%

IHI Corp

Auditors: Ernst & Young ShinNihon LLC

LOCATIONS

HQ: IHI Corp
3-1-1 Toyosu, Koto-ku, Tokyo 135-8710
Phone: (81) 3 6204 7065   **Fax:** (81) 3 6204 8800
Web: www.ihi.co.jp

HISTORICAL FINANCIALS

Company Type: Public

Income Statement
FYE: March 31

	REVENUE ($ mil.)	NET INCOME ($ mil.)	NET PROFIT MARGIN	EMPLOYEES
03/20	12,772	118	0.9%	28,964
03/19	13,395	360	2.7%	29,286
03/18	14,976	78	0.5%	29,706
03/17	13,293	46	0.4%	29,659
03/16	13,708	13	0.1%	29,494
Annual Growth	(1.8%)	71.6%	—	(0.5%)

2020 Year-End Financials

Debt ratio: 0.2%
Return on equity: 3.7%
Cash ($ mil.): 1,356
Current ratio: 1.18
Long-term debt ($ mil.): 2,130

No. of shares (mil.): 149
Dividends
Yield: 0.0%
Payout: 20.9%
Market value ($ mil.): 939

	STOCK PRICE ($) FY Close	P/E High/Low		PER SHARE ($) Earnings	Dividends	Book Value
03/20	6.30	0	0	0.78	0.16	20.21
03/19	6.00	0	0	2.33	0.14	20.45
03/18	7.84	0	0	0.51	0.07	19.84
03/17	11.25	0	0	0.30	0.00	18.48
03/16	7.96	2	1	0.09	0.13	18.40
Annual Growth	(5.7%)	—	—	72.2%	5.3%	2.4%

Iida Group Holdings Co., Ltd.

EXECUTIVES

President, Masashi Kanei
Auditors: Ernst & Young ShinNihon LLC

LOCATIONS

HQ: Iida Group Holdings Co., Ltd.
  1-2-11 Nishikubo, Musashino, Tokyo 180-0013
Phone: (81) 422 60 8888
Web: www.ighd.co.jp

HISTORICAL FINANCIALS

Company Type: Public

Income Statement
FYE: March 31

	REVENUE ($ mil.)	NET INCOME ($ mil.)	NET PROFIT MARGIN	EMPLOYEES
03/20	12,915	495	3.8%	9,693
03/19	12,145	591	4.9%	8,561
03/18	12,575	654	5.2%	7,736
03/17	11,023	686	6.2%	7,041
03/16	10,116	578	5.7%	6,386
Annual Growth	6.3%	(3.8%)	—	11.0%

2020 Year-End Financials

Debt ratio: 0.3%
Return on equity: 6.9%
Cash ($ mil.): 3,565
Current ratio: 2.30
Long-term debt ($ mil.): 1,864

No. of shares (mil.): 288
Dividends
Yield: —
Payout: —
Market value ($ mil.): —

Imperial Brands PLC

Auditors: Ernst & Young LLP

LOCATIONS

HQ: Imperial Brands PLC
  121 Winterstoke Road, Bristol BS3 2LL
Phone: (44) 117 963 6636
Web: www.imperialbrandsplc.com

HISTORICAL FINANCIALS

Company Type: Public

Income Statement
FYE: September 30

	REVENUE ($ mil.)	NET INCOME ($ mil.)	NET PROFIT MARGIN	EMPLOYEES
09/20	65,071	2,987	4.6%	32,500
09/19	63,137	2,018	3.2%	32,700
09/18	60,998	2,733	4.5%	33,300
09/17	60,445	2,815	4.7%	33,800
09/16	55,223	1,260	2.3%	33,900
Annual Growth	4.2%	24.1%		(1.0%)

2020 Year-End Financials

Debt ratio: 72.0%
Return on equity: 30.4%
Cash ($ mil.): 3,249
Current ratio: 0.78
Long-term debt ($ mil.): 20,403

No. of shares (mil.): 946
Dividends
Yield: 13.2%
Payout: 74.3%
Market value ($ mil.): 16,751

	STOCK PRICE ($) FY Close	P/E High/Low		PER SHARE ($) Earnings	Dividends	Book Value
09/20	17.70	17	9	3.16	2.35	10.29
09/19	22.60	34	21	2.11	2.45	10.37
09/18	34.71	31	23	2.86	2.37	12.09
09/17	43.27	35	28	2.94	2.01	11.89
09/16	51.47	168	77	1.32	1.39	11.07
Annual Growth	(23.4%)	—	—	24.4%	14.1%	(1.8%)

Imperial Oil Ltd

Imperial Oil Canada's fifth-largest oil integrated company behind Canadian Natural Resources holds sway over a vast empire of oil and gas resources. Imperial is one of Canada's top natural gas producers a leading refiner and marketer of petroleum products and a major supplier of petrochemicals. It sells petroleum products including gasoline heating oil and diesel fuel under the Esso name and other brand names. The company reported proved reserves in 2019 of about 3.5 billion barrels of oil-equivalent including nearly 40 million barrels of liquids about 580 billion cu. ft. of natural gas approximately 415 million barrels of synthetic oil and roughly 3 billion barrels of bitumen. Exxon Mobil owns about 70% of Imperial.

Operations

Imperial has three main segments: Downstream Upstream and Chemical.

Downstream operations (almost 70%) consist of the transportation and refining of crude oil blending of refined products and the distribution and marketing of those products. Its Upstream operations (almost 30%) include the exploration for and production of crude oil natural gas synthetic oil and bitumen. The company's Chemical operations consist of the manufacturing and marketing of various petrochemicals such as ethylene benzene aromatic and aliphatic solvents plasticizer intermediates and polyethylene resin.

In addition to its conventional upstream operations Imperial owns 25% of Syncrude Canada which operates the world's largest oil sands development with synthetic oil and bitumen/heavy oil end products.

The Downstream segment owns and operates three refineries. The Strathcona and Sarnia refineries process Canadian crude oil and the Nanticoke refinery processes a combination of Canadian and foreign crude oil. The Strathcona refinery operates lubricating oil production facilities. The company maintains a nationwide distribution system to handle bulk and packaged petroleum products moving from refineries to market by pipeline tanker rail and road transport It also owns and operates natural gas liquids and products pipelines in Alberta Manitoba and Ontario and has interests in the capital stock of one crude oil and two products pipeline companies.

Geographic Reach

Most of the company's production comes from fields in Alberta and the Northwest Territories. The company operates its business in Canada.

Sales and Marketing

The company sells gasoline to motorists at more than 2300 primarily Esso-branded gas stations across Canada.

It markets almost 500 petroleum products throughout Canada to all types of customers. It also serves the Canadian agriculture residential heating and small commercial markets and sells petroleum products to large industrial and commercial accounts as well as to other refiners and marketers.

Financial Performance

Net income in 2019 was C$2.2 billion compared to net income of C$2.3 million in 2018. The 2019 results include a favorable impact largely non-cash of C$662 million associated with the Alberta corporate income tax rate decrease. In June 2019 the Alberta government enacted a 4% decrease in the provincial tax rate from 12% to 8% by 2022.

Cash held by the company at the end of 2019 increased by C$730 million to C$1.7 billion. Cash provided by operations was C$4.4 billion while cash used for investing and financing activities were C$1.7 billion and C$2.0 billion respectively. Cash usage was primarily for additions to property plant and equipment and common shares purchased.

Strategy

Imperial's Upstream business strategies guide the company's exploration development production research and gas marketing activities. These strategies include maximizing asset reliability accelerating development and application of high impact technologies maximizing value by capturing new business opportunities and managing the existing portfolio as well as pursuing sustainable improvements in organizational efficiency and effectiveness. These strategies are underpinned by a relentless focus on operations integrity commitment to innovative technologies disciplined approach to investing and cost management development of employees and investment in the communities within which the company operates.

Imperial's Downstream business strategies competitively position the company across a range of market conditions. These strategies include targeting industry leading performance in reliability safety and operations integrity as well as maximizing value from advanced technologies capitalizing on integration across Imperial's businesses selectively investing for resilient and advantaged returns operating efficiently and effectively and providing quality valued and differentiated products and services to customers.

EXECUTIVES

Chairman President and CEO, R. M. (Rich) Kruger, $4,837,802 total compensation
SVP Finance and Administration and Treasurer, Paul J. Masschelin, age 66, $499,694 total compensation
SVP Upstream, B.P. (Bart) Cahir
VP and General Counsel, W.J. (Bill) Hartnett, $434,333 total compensation
Treasurer, David Bailey
VP Fuels Lubricants and Specialties Marketing, B.G. Merkel, $424,333 total compensation
Auditors: PricewaterhouseCoopers LLP

LOCATIONS

HQ: Imperial Oil Ltd
505 Quarry Park Boulevard S.E., Calgary, Alberta T2C 5N1
Phone: 587 476-3740   **Fax:** 587 476-1166
Web: www.imperialoil.ca

PRODUCTS/OPERATIONS

2016 Sales

	% of total
Downstream	74
Upstream	22
Chemical	4
Total	**100**

COMPETITORS

Abraxas Petroleum	Marathon Oil
Ashland	Murphy Oil
BHP Billiton	Occidental Petroleum
BP	PEMEX
Barnwell Industries	PETROBRAS
Canadian Natural	Petr leos de
ConocoPhillips	Venezuela
Devon Energy	Pioneer Natural
Dominion Energy	Resources
Encana	Repsol Oil & Gas
Eni	Royal Dutch Shell
Hunting	Suncor
Husky Energy	Sunoco
Koch Industries Inc.	TOTAL

HISTORICAL FINANCIALS

Company Type: Public

Income Statement — FYE: December 31

	REVENUE ($ mil.)	NET INCOME ($ mil.)	NET PROFIT MARGIN	EMPLOYEES
12/19	34,530	2,227	6.5%	6,000
12/18	35,541	2,343	6.6%	5,700
12/17	29,794	496	1.7%	5,400
12/16	27,698	2,192	7.9%	5,600
12/15	27,226	1,136	4.2%	5,700
Annual Growth	6.1%	18.3%	—	1.3%

2019 Year-End Financials

Debt ratio: 12.4%
Return on equity: 9.0%
Cash ($ mil.): 1,739
Current ratio: 1.38
Long-term debt ($ mil.): 5,023

No. of shares (mil.): 743
Dividends
Yield: 2.4%
Payout: 38.4%
Market value ($ mil.): 19,691

	STOCK PRICE ($) FY Close	P/E High/Low		PER SHARE ($) Earnings	Dividends	Book Value
12/19	26.47	10	8	2.92	0.64	33.04
12/18	25.32	12	9	2.90	0.56	31.69
12/17	31.19	61	48	0.59	0.64	29.77
12/16	34.76	14	10	2.58	0.60	29.89
12/15	32.52	34	22	1.34	0.42	27.99
Annual Growth	(5.0%)		—	21.5%	11.1%	4.2%

Industria De Diseno Textil (Inditex) SA

Industria de Diseño Textil (Inditex) makes disposable chic fashions that are here today and gone tomorrow. The Spanish designer-cum-retailer uses technology and an armada of designers to master cheap chic. Inditex sells on a global scale with more than 7475 shops in upwards of 75 countries under eight different banners: Zara Oysho Massimo Dutti Pull&Bear Bershka Stradivarius Zara Home and Uterq e. The firm's stores answer to popular trends by feeding back to designers in Spain what customers are asking for locally. Inditex responds in about two weeks with new designs. Amancio Ortega Gaona one of the world's wealthiest men founded Zara in 1975 and later created Inditex as a holding company.

Operations

Inditex's eight brands — Zara Oysho Massimo Dutti Pull&Bear Bershka Stradivarius Zara Home and Uterq e — have brick-and-mortar and online stores. A leader in fast fashion Inditex produces 65000 new designs each year.

Zara is Inditex's primary brand and brings in around 65% of the company's revenue. It makes trendy clothing for men and women across all age groups at a mid price point. With an army of 700 designers pumping out 20000 pieces a year Zara is both a supplier (of itself) and retailer enabling it to respond with great speed to changes in taste and fashion. It has 2250 stores around the world.

Bershka is Inditex's second-biggest earner bringing in around 10% of revenue. It targets a younger demographic at a lower price point.

Its other brands Massimo Dutti (upscale fashion) Oysho (lingerie and undergarments) Pull&Bear (urban youth 14-28) Uterque (high-end women's fashion) and Stradivarius account for the remaining 25% of revenue combined.

Inditex rings up a bit more than 10% of its sales online which lags behind a number of its rivals.

Geographic Reach

Based in North West Spain Inditex has a store base of 7475 owned stores and franchises. In Spain and Europe its stores are almost all owned stores while in the Americas and the Rest of the World it has a larger concentration of franchises. Europe (excluding Spain) is host to around 45% of Inditex's total store count while Spain accounts for 20%. The Rest of the World also has around 20% and the Americas hosts the remainder.

By revenue Europe (excl. Spain) generates 45% of sales Spain brings in more than 15% the Americas another 15% and the Asia/Pacific region and rest of the world accounts for nearly 25%.

Much of Inditex's manufacturing is located close to Spain (such as in Portugal Morocco Turkey and Spain itself) giving it an advantage over rivals such as H&M that source almost all their products from the Asia/Pacific region.

Sales and Marketing

Inditex records minimal marketing spending relying on word-of-mouth to promote Zara.

The company's store and online function are fully integrated and draw from the same stock pool. It carries out twice-weekly stock distributions to all its stores worldwide and can fulfill orders to stores and online customers in 2-48 hours. It offers same day delivery in metropolitan areas and next-day delivery as a global standard.

Financial Performance Note: Growth rates may differ after conversion to US Dollars.

Inditex has grown its revenue consistently for more than a decade.

In fiscal 2017 sales increased 9% to ?25.3 billion thanks to further growth in its store base in the Americas and the Rest of the World in particular. Like-for-like sales were up in all geographies and across all brands. Online sales grew 41% to 10% of net sales and the company began selling online for the first time in Singapore Malaysia Thailand Vietnam and India. Inditex closed 341 stores mostly in Europe during 2017 as part of its continual store optimization process which represents a notable increase on previous years.

Net income increased 7% to ?3.4 billion as revenue growth outpaced rises in cost of sales. It also made a ?356 million gain on the sale of 15 properties during the year.

Cash from operations fell slightly down 4% to ?4.0 billion mostly due to a higher income tax expense.

Strategy

Driven by its best-in-class logistics and supply chain system Inditex continues to expand rapidly. In 2017 the company opened 183 net new stores (consisting of 524 openings and 341 'absorptions' (the company's term for closures)). It concentrates its store opening program on the less developed markets in the Asia/Pacific region as well as the US. In 2018 Inditex will places greater attention on Australia and New Zealand; in March it opened a dedicated online store in Australia.

Other initiatives Inditex will complete in 2018 include the roll-out of RFID (Radio Frequency Identification or the electronic tagging of products to speed up their journey to stores) an upgrade of its HQ and logistics and lower capital intensity growth.

EXECUTIVES

Chairman and CEO, Pablo Isla
Auditors: DELOITTE, S.L.

LOCATIONS

HQ: Industria De Diseno Textil (Inditex) SA
Avda. de la Diputacion s/n, Edificio INDITEX, La Coruna, Arteixo 15142
Phone: (34) 98 118 5400
Web: www.inditex.es

2010 Sales

	% of total
Europe	
Spain	32
Other countries	46
America	10
Asia & other regions	12
Total	**100**

2010 Stores

	No.
Europe	
Spain	1,916
Other countries	2,006
Americas	390
Asia & other regions	595
Total	**4,907**

PRODUCTS/OPERATIONS

2015 Stores

	No.
Zara	2,162
Bershka	1,044
Pull & Bear	936
Stradivarius	950
Massimo Dutti	740
Oysho	607
Zara Home	502
Uterqüe	72
Total	**7,013**

2015 Sales

	% of total
Zara	65
Bershka	9
Massimo Dutti	7
Pull & Bear	7
Stradivarius	6
Zara Home	3
Oysho	2
Uterqüe	1
Total	**100**

COMPETITORS

ASOS	French Connection
Adolfo Dom nguez	H&M
Arcadia	Kering
Benetton	L Brands
Carrefour	LVMH
Cortefiel	NEXT plc
Diesel SpA	Prada
El Corte Inglés	Selfridges
Fast Retailing	The Gap

HISTORICAL FINANCIALS

Company Type: Public

Income Statement

FYE: January 31

	REVENUE ($ mil.)	NET INCOME ($ mil.)	NET PROFIT MARGIN	EMPLOYEES
01/20	31,222	4,016	12.9%	176,611
01/19	30,036	3,956	13.2%	174,386
01/18	31,553	4,194	13.3%	171,839
01/17	25,053	3,392	13.5%	162,450
01/16	22,821	3,138	13.8%	152,854
Annual Growth	**8.2%**	**6.4%**	**—**	**3.7%**

2020 Year-End Financials

Debt ratio: 0.1%	No. of shares (mil.): —
Return on equity: 24.6%	Dividends
Cash ($ mil.): 5,276	Yield: 2.0%
Current ratio: 1.56	Payout: 26.8%
Long-term debt ($ mil.): 6	Market value ($ mil.): —

	STOCK PRICE ($) FY Close	P/E High/Low	PER SHARE ($) Earnings	Dividends	Book Value
01/20	16.82	15 11	1.29	0.35	5.28
01/19	14.00	16 11	1.27	0.31	5.40
01/18	17.88	21 16	1.35	0.27	5.39
01/17	16.54	18 14	1.09	0.24	4.38
01/16	16.42	20 15	1.01	0.20	4.00
Annual Growth	**0.6%**	**—**	**6.3%**	**14.7%**	**7.2%**

Industrial and Commercial Bank of China Ltd

Boasting assets of roughly RMB$30 trillion Industrial and Commercial Bank of China (ICBC) provides corporate retail and investment banking as well as asset management pensions financial leasing insurance and other financial services to 8.1 million corporate customers and 650 million personal customers across China through about 16200 branches and nearly 430 overseas institutions in about nearly 50 countries and regions. ICBC provides its products and services to corporations government agencies financial institutions individual customers and other transactions. The Chinese government controls about 70% of ICBC. Industrial and Commercial Bank of China was founded on1984.

Operations

Industrial and Commercial Bank of China (ICBC) operates three business segments. Corporate banking?which brings in roughly 50% of the bank's total operating income?provides traditional banking products loans trade financing deposit-taking activities corporate wealth management services custody activities and various other financial services to corporations government agencies and financial institutions. Its personal banking division makes up more than 35% of the bank's operating income and provides deposit loan products as well as private banking services card business personal wealth management services and various types of personal intermediary services to individuals. Its treasury operations?which provide about 15% of total revenues?manage the bank's money market foreign exchange and investment securities.

In addition to these divisions the bank also provides wealth management asset custody and pension services and has a precious metals franchise treasury and asset securitization businesses.

Altogether the bank makes around 80% of its operating income from net interest (mostly from loans and advances followed by investment interest) while around 20% comes from net fee and commission income.

Geographic Reach

Industrial and Commercial Bank of China (ICBC) is based in Beijing and generates more than 90% of its operating income from China while the remainder comes from about 50 other countries and regions.

ICBC has subsidiaries and approximately 430 branches overseas. It has operations in Asia Pacific Americas Europe and Middle East.

Sales and Marketing

Industrial and Commercial Bank of China (ICBC) offers its services through its e-banking network the internet telephone and self-service banking centers. It has about 16000 branches more than 26000 self-service centers and greater than 82000 ATMs throughout China as well as roughly 430 overseas branches in about 50 countries and regions.

ICBC also caters to institutional customers in the fields of medical care education labor union religion public resources land and resources housing and construction.

The number of ICBC Mobile customers reached 361 million.

Financial Performance

Note: Growth rates may differ after conversion to US dollars.

ICBC's operating income rose for almost 10% to RMB$776.0 billion in 2019 driven mostly by increased net interest income as the bank increased its interest-generating assets and margins.

Net income rose with operating income gaining five percent to RMB$312.2 million.

ICBC's cash stores lost RMB$59.1 billion in 2019 to end the year at RMB$1.4 trillion. Operations provided RMB$618.5 billion. Investments used RMB$875.9 billion?mostly for financial investments and financing activities gained RMB$112.9 billion?primarily for issuance of other equity instruments.

Strategy

The Bank explored the new growth model of corporate deposits and accelerated the pilot promotion of innovative products to meet the customized financial needs of corporate customers. New technologies such as big data and visualization were innovated and adopted to build a fund transfer map and promote the research and implementation of closed-loop management of corporate deposit funds.

The Bank strengthened the application and promotion of advantageous platforms and continued to consolidate its leading advantages in the field of corporate payment. It promoted its global cash management platform and deepened its global business by virtue of the Bank's international strategy to build a global cash management business system.

In terms of personal banking the bank promoted the online service of "ICBC e-Wallet" and provided customers with financial services such as settlement wealth management and financing in cooperation with JD and Vanke. It also improved the intelligent services of offline outlets to boost their intelligent transformation.

Moreover the Bank proposed a strategy of building the "No.1 Personal Bank" in 2019 pointing out the direction for the future development of personal banking business. Adhering to "customer-centric" the strategy strives to achieve the overall improvement of personal banking business in terms of market competitiveness value contribution risk control and customer satisfaction and leads the market on a comprehensive sustainable and high quality basis.

The Bank sought for a strategic transformation toward a smart bank by incorporating ICBC Information and Technology Co. Ltd. and FinTech Research Institute and putting in place a new FinTech framework. This transformation will result to a faster and overhauling/optimizing service and a top-level design.

Company Background

Industrial and Commercial Bank of China (ICBC) was established in 1984 and went public in 2006. The bank ventured into the US broker-dealer business in 2010 when it acquired the Prime Dealer Services unit of Fortis Securities from BNP Paribas.

EXECUTIVES

Chief Risk Officer, Wei Guoxiong, age 65
SEVP, Zhang Hongli
Chairman Board of Supervisors, Qian Wenhui
SEVP, Wang Xiquan
SEVP, Zheng Wanchun, age 56
SEVP, Gu Shu
SEVP, Wang Jingdong
CIO, Lin Xiaoxuan
Chairman and Executive Director, Yi Huiman, age 56
Auditors: KPMG Huazhen LLP

LOCATIONS

HQ: Industrial and Commercial Bank of China Ltd
No. 55 Fuxingmennei Avenue, Xicheng District, Beijing 100140
Phone: (86) 10 66106114   **Fax:** (86) 10 66107571
Web: www.icbc.com.cn

2018 Sales

	% of total
Mainland China	92
Overseas and other	8
Total	**100**

PRODUCTS/OPERATIONS

2018 Sales

	% of total
Interest	85
Non-interest	
Fees and commissions	15
Other	
Total	**100**

2018 Sales by Segment

	% of total
Corporate banking	48
Personal banking	38
Treasury operations	13
Other	1
Total	**100**

Selected Services

Corporate banking services
Corporate Deposits and Loans
Institutional Banking
Investment Banking
Small and medium-sized enterprise business
Settlement and cash management
International settlement and trade finance
E-finance
ICBC Mobile
ICBC Mall
ICBC Link
Financing product line
Payment product line
Investment and wealth management product line
Personal banking services
Personal Finance
E-banking
Bank Card
Precious Metals
Private Banking
Global Market
Financial Asset Services
Wealth Management business
Asset Custody services
Pension services
Precious metal
Agency Treasury business
Asset securitization business
Agency sales
Treasury operations
Money Market activities
Investment
Financing
Channel and Development and Service Enhancement
Service enhancement
Consumer protection

COMPETITORS

Agricultural Bank of China	China Development Bank
Bank of China	China Everbright Bank
Bank of Communications	China Eximbank
CITIC International Financial	China Merchants Bank
China CITIC Bank	HSBC
China Construction Bank	Hua Xia Bank
	Shenzhen Development Bank

HISTORICAL FINANCIALS

Company Type: Public

Income Statement
FYE: December 31

	ASSETS ($ mil.)	NET INCOME ($ mil.)	INCOME AS % OF ASSETS	EMPLOYEES
12/19	4,327,168	44,871	1.0%	445,106
12/18	4,027,096	43,277	1.1%	449,296
12/17	4,008,806	43,957	1.1%	453,048
12/16	3,475,954	40,070	1.2%	461,749
12/15	3,419,761	42,671	1.2%	466,346
Annual Growth	**6.1%**	**1.3%**	**—**	**(1.2%)**

2019 Year-End Financials

Return on assets: 1.0%
Return on equity: 12.4%
Long-term debt ($ mil.): —
No. of shares (mil.): —
Sales ($ mil): 184,033

Dividends
Yield: 0.0%
Payout: 484.7%
Market value ($ mil.): —

	STOCK PRICE ($) FY Close	P/E High/Low	PER SHARE ($) Earnings	Dividends	Book Value
12/19	15.37	18 14	0.12	0.60	1.08
12/18	14.16	21 16	0.12	0.59	0.95
12/17	16.11	21 16	0.12	0.59	0.92
12/16	11.84	16 12	0.11	0.56	0.80
12/15	11.96	22 14	0.12	0.67	0.77
Annual Growth	**6.5%**	**— —**	**1.0%**	**(2.8%)**	**8.7%**

Infineon Technologies AG

Infineon Technologies makes semiconductors microcontrollers sensors switches and other devices that manage power energy security and other functions in cars phone appliances and machinery. The company's products are No. 1 or 2 in their markets for automotive industrial power control power management and digital security applications. Automotive is Infineon's biggest market accounting for about 45% of sales. Customers include Bosch Bombardier Gemalto and Osram. Geographically Greater China and Europe each account for about a third of the Germany-based company's sales. In 2019 Infineon agreed to buy US-based Cypress Semiconductor for $10.1 billion (?9 billion).

Financial Performance

Infineon's revenue has steadily climbed rising an average 11% a year from 2014-2018 while net income posted annual advances of about 5% before jumping nearly 50% in 2018 from 2017.

In 2018 (ended September) the company's sales grew 8% to ?7.6 billion up ?536 million from 2017. The company's automotive products accounted for about 55% of the revenue growth while demand also increased for semiconductors used in industrial power supply RF and sensor applications. Digital Security revenue slipped 6% because of lower sales of SIM cards used in mobile phones.

Net income jumped 36% to about ?1.1 billion in 2018 from 2017 on the stronger sales and ?270 million received from the sale of the RF power components business to Cree Inc.

Infineon had ?871 million in cash in 2018 compared to ?948 million the previous year. Its operations generated ?1.8 billion while investing and financing activities used ?1.4 billion and ?645 million respectively.

Strategy

Infineon zeroes in on markets with rising demand for technology focusing on the fastest-growing roles for semiconductors: making autos safer more efficient and autonomous; reducing energy use in objects from washing machines to locomotives; and keeping mobile phones connected.

By relying on its extensive manufacturing operations Infineon keeps control over the quality and costs of its products. The company is building a ?1.6 billion 300-mm fabrication plant in Austria to augment its 300-mm plant in Germany which is reaching production capacity.

Infineon would add a range of microcontrollers and memory products to its portfolio with the acquisition of Cypress Semiconductor announced in 2019. With Cypress's product line Infineon would expand its lineup and have opportunities to increase sales to the automotive industrial and Internet of Things markets. The exta bulk of Cy-

press's products and $2.5 billion revenue could fortify Infineon to compete in the consolidating semiconductor industry. Infineon agreed to pay ?9 billion ($10.1 billion) for Cypress. The deal was expected to close in late 2019 or early 2020.

The company's dependence on the China market (about one-third of revenue) could have an impact on Infineon's sales if worldwide trade tensions ratchet higher. It also could be affected by trade restrictions between the European Union and the US.

EXECUTIVES

CEO, Reinhard Ploss, age 65, $501,620 total compensation
Head Group Controlling, Dominik Asam, age 51
Member Management Board Operations, Jochen Hanebeck
Member Management Board Strategy Development Sales and Marketing and Regions, Helmut Gassel
Chairman Supervisory Board, Wolfgang Mayrhuber, age 73
Auditors: KPMG AG

LOCATIONS

HQ: Infineon Technologies AG
Am Campeon 1-15, Neubiberg D-85579
Phone: (49) 89 234 0   **Fax:** (49) 89 234 9552987
Web: www.infineon.com

2018 sales

	% of total
Germany	15
Greater China	34
Europe Middle East Africa	17
Americas	12
Asia-Pacific	15
Japan	7
Total	**100**

PRODUCTS/OPERATIONS

2018 sales

	% of total
Automotive	43
Power Management & Multi-market	31
Industrial Power Control	17
Digital Security Solutions	9
Other Operating Segments	
Total	**100**

COMPETITORS

AMD	ON Semiconductor
Atmel	Oki Semiconductor
Fairchild Semiconductor	STMicroelectronics
Fujitsu Semiconductor	Texas Instruments
Mitsubishi Electric	Toshiba Semiconductor & Storage Products
NXP Semiconductors	Vishay Intertechnology

HISTORICAL FINANCIALS

Company Type: Public

Income Statement
FYE: September 30

	REVENUE ($ mil.)	NET INCOME ($ mil.)	NET PROFIT MARGIN	EMPLOYEES
09/19	12,634	1,369	10.8%	41,418
09/18	11,957	1,691	14.1%	40,098
09/17	11,114	1,243	11.2%	37,479
09/16	10,185	1,170	11.5%	36,299
09/15	9,119	994	10.9%	35,424
Annual Growth	**8.5%**	**8.3%**	**—**	**4.0%**

2019 Year-End Financials

Debt ratio: 18.2%
Return on equity: 11.5%
Cash ($ mil.): 1,606
Current ratio: 3.58
Long-term debt ($ mil.): 2,413

No. of shares (mil.): 1,244
Dividends
Yield: 1.1%
Payout: 17.8%
Market value ($ mil.): 22,417

	STOCK PRICE ($) FY Close	P/E High/Low	PER SHARE ($) Earnings	Dividends	Book Value
09/19	18.01	32 21	1.18	0.21	10.91
09/18	22.72	33 23	1.49	0.29	8.97
09/17	25.22	36 23	1.10	0.22	7.85
09/16	17.78	27 17	1.04	0.21	7.02
09/15	11.31	24 16	0.88	0.19	6.53
Annual Growth	12.3%	— —	7.6%	2.6%	13.7%

Infosys Ltd.

Infosys Technologies is one of India's leading technology services firms mainly providing software development and engineering to corporations around the worldwide. The company also provides digital marketing artificial intelligence automation analytics engineering services and Internet of Things services among others Its US-based consulting arm provides IT and professional consulting services while subsidiary Infosys BPM provides business process outsourcing services. Infosys makes almost all of its sales overseas with North America accounting for 60% of the total. Key industries served by the company are financial services insurance manufacturing telecom retail and consumer goods.

Financial Performance

Infosys' revenue grew at a steady 7% a year from 2015-2019 (ended March) while net income fluctuated between $2 billion and $2.5 billon.

In 2019 Infosys reported about $11.8 billion in revenue an 8% increase from 2018 driven by higher volumes across most of its businesses and highlighted by strong growth in its digital businesses. The company's software services accounted for about 95% of revenue with the rest generated by products and platforms.

Net income fell to $2.2 billion in 2019 from $2.5 billion in 2018 due to investments in sales and marketing localization strategy investments in agile digital and worker retraining. The company also had higher costs for technical sub-contractors and currency fluctuations.

Infosys had about $2.8 billion in cash in 2019 compared to about $3 billion in 2018. Operations generated $2.2 billion in 2019 while investing activities used $225 million and financing activities used $2 billion.

Strategy

Infosys has shifted its focus and resources to help customers digitize their businesses. To do so the company has increased its own digital efforts. It has invested in its agile digital methods infused its core services with intelligent automation and retrained workers with relevant skills. Revenue from its digital-related services for customers rose about 34% in 2019 from 2018 and accounted for about a third of total revenue.

Infosys put other strategic initiatives into practice in the US its biggest market. To address a lack of technically skilled workers the company went beyond computer science and related disciplines to recruit liberal arts and design students. It also looked for workers from community colleges as well as those who had lost previous jobs. Infosys

has teamed up with local schools to provide training for recruits and built its own education center in Indianapolis Indiana.

The company depends on a small cadre of customers for a significant portion of its revenue. Its 10 largest customers accounted for about 20% of revenue in 2019. The loss of one of those customers could have an impact on Infosys' revenue.

As an Indian company that gets 60% of revenue from the US Infosys is subject to currency exchange rate fluctuations. In 2019 every percentage point depreciation or appreciation in the exchange rate between the Indian rupee and the US dollar affected the company's incremental operating margins by about 0.47%. The rupee depreciated 8.7% against the US dollar in 2019.

Mergers and Acquisitions

In 2018 Infosys agreed to acquire Fluido a provider of cloud consulting implementation and training services. Fluido based in Espoo Finland offers consulting for Salesforce.com implementations. The deal is to strengthen Infosys' position as a provider of Salesforce enterprise cloud services in the Nordic region. Infosys expects the deal to close in the quarter than ends in March 2019.

Infosys completed two acquisitions in 2015. One was of Panaya Inc. a provider of automation technology for large scale enterprise software management. This acquisition strengthens the competitiveness of its current service lines by leveraging automation machine learning and artificial intelligence. The other was of Kallidus Inc. also known as Skava and its affiliate a provider of digital experience including mobile commerce and in-store shopping experiences to large retail clients. The acquisition of Skava is part of the company's strategy to help clients bring new digital experiences to customers.

HISTORY

After receiving a master's degree in electrical engineering from one of India's highly regarded Institutes of Technology (Kanpur) in the 1960s Narayana Murthy left for France and a job developing software for the air traffic control system at Paris' Charles de Gaulle airport.

During college Murthy had developed the belief that communism was the answer to his country's problems with poverty and corruption a stance that was fortified during his time spent with Paris leftists in the 1970s. But while hitchhiking back to India in 1974 Murthy's Marxist sympathies eroded quickly after he was jailed in Hungary for allegedly disclosing state secrets while talking with Austrian tourists on a train. Murthy became a socialist at heart but capitalist in practice setting out on a mission to create wealth rather than redistribute it.

That mission officially began in 1981 when Murthy convinced six fellow software engineers to start their own company. Infosys was founded that year with $250 in capital (mostly borrowed from their wives) and no idea of what it would sell.

From the beginning Murthy looked for business outside India where he was able to sell customizable inexpensive software to multinational corporations such as Reebok and Nordstrom. But a lack of reputation and government regulations made business difficult for Infosys during the 1980s — it took nine months just to get the company's first telephone line and three years to import new computers. Infosys opened its first US office in 1987.

Many of the government regulations that had kept India's economy stagnant were lifted when reform swept the country in 1991. But this also opened the door for companies such as IBM (which had been asked to leave in 1977) and Digital Equipment (later acquired by Compaq) to enter India and lure away its best engineers. While no Indian company had ever done this before Murthy

initiated a stock option plan and other perks to retain his employees. Infosys went public in 1993. Morgan Stanley swooped in to salvage the undersubscribed IPO in a move that would later reap millions when Infosys' stock began to soar.

EXECUTIVES

EVP and Head Talent Fulfilment and Technology Operations, Binod Hampapur Rangadore, $32,577 total compensation
Interim CEO and Managing Director, U. B. Pravin Rao
CEO Edgeverve, Pervinder Johar, age 54
EVP and Global Head Infosys Consulting, Sanjay Purohit, age 54
EVP and Head Strategic Sales Programs, Anup Uppadhayay, age 48
EVP and Head Global Services Â– Application Development and Maintenance Independent Validation Services and Business Intelligence, Srikantan (Tan) Moorthy
EVP and Head Infrastructure Facilities Administration Security and Sustainability, Ramadas Kamath U.
President and Chief Delivery Officer, Ravi Kumar S.
EVP and Group Head Human Resource Development, Krishnamurthy Shankar
EVP and Head of Financial Services Infosys Brazil and Infosys Mexico, Mohit Joshi
EVP Head Healthcare Insurance and Life Sciences and Head High-Tech, Manish Tandon
EVP and CFO, Ranganath D. Mavinakere
EVP and Head of Retail CPG and Logistics; Head of Americas, Sandeep Dadlani
President Energy Utilities Resources Telecommunications and Services; Head Europe; Head Consulting, Rajesh Krishnamurthy
EVP General Counsel and Chief Compliance Officer, David D. Kennedy
CEO BPO Business, Anantha Radhakrishnan
CEO and Managing Director, Vishal Sikka
Auditors: Deloitte Haskins & Sells LLP

LOCATIONS

HQ: Infosys Ltd.
Electronics City, Hosur Road, Bangalore, Karnataka 560 100
Phone: (91) 80 2852 0261   **Fax:** (91) 80 2852 0362
Web: www.infosys.com

2019 Sales

	% of total
North America	61
Europe	24
India	2
Rest of the World	13
Total	**100**

PRODUCTS/OPERATIONS

2019 Sales

	% of total
Software services	95
Software products	5
Total	**100**

2019 Sales by Market

	% of total
Financial services & insurance	32
Retail	16
Communication	13
Manufacturing	10
Life Sciences	6
All Other Segments	3
Total	**100**

Selected Services

Business process management
Custom application development

Engineering
Information technology consulting
Infrastructure management
Maintenance and production support
Management consulting
Operations and business process consulting
Package evaluation and implementation
Software re-engineering
Systems integration
Testing

COMPETITORS

3i Infotech	Deloitte Consulting
Accenture	Genpact
Amdocs	HCL Technologies
Atos	HP Enterprise Group
Capgemini	IBM Global Services
Cognizant Tech	NTT Data
Solutions	Tata Consultancy
Computer Sciences	Wipro
Corp.	

HISTORICAL FINANCIALS

Company Type: Public

Income Statement   FYE: March 31

	REVENUE ($ mil.)	NET INCOME ($ mil.)	NET PROFIT MARGIN	EMPLOYEES
03/20	12,780	2,331	18.2%	242,371
03/19	11,799	2,199	18.6%	228,123
03/18	10,939	2,486	22.7%	204,107
03/17	10,208	2,140	21.0%	200,364
03/16	9,501	2,052	21.6%	194,044
Annual Growth	7.7%	3.2%	—	5.7%

2020 Year-End Financials

Debt ratio: —	No. of shares (mil.): —
Return on equity: 25.7%	Dividends
Cash ($ mil.): 2,465	Yield: 3.6%
Current ratio: 2.62	Payout: 128.0%
Long-term debt ($ mil.): —	Market value ($ mil.): —

	STOCK PRICE ($) FY Close	P/E High/Low		PER SHARE ($) Earnings	Dividends	Book Value
03/20	8.21	22	13	0.55	0.30	2.04
03/19	10.93	41	18	0.51	1.40	2.17
03/18	17.85	34	26	0.55	0.19	2.29
03/17	15.80	43	29	0.47	0.17	2.33
03/16	19.02	81	34	0.45	0.18	2.04
Annual Growth	(18.9%)	—	—	5.1%	14.0%	(0.0%)

ING Groep NV

ING Groep is one of the world's largest banking and financial services companies boasting operations in more than 40 countries. Based in the Netherlands ING's main focus is its home Benelux market as well as the rest of Europe; it also has operations in the Americas Australia and Asia. It offers a full range of banking products and services including payments savings insurance investments and secured and unsecured lending as well as wholesale banking. ING Groep has a total assets of ?892 billion. About 70% of its total sales comes from outside of Netherlands.

Operations

ING operates through six primary banking segments: Wholesale Banking (around 305) Retail Netherlands (roughly 25%) Retail Other (about 20%) Retail Belgium (nearly 15%) Retail Germany (some 10%) and Corporate Line Banking.

ING's Retail Banking maintain a high-level of system availability of online payment channels with its system availability for retail customers was almost 100%. Revenue arises from retail and private banking activities including the SME and mid-corporate segments. Products include payments savings insurance investments and secured and unsecured lending.

The Wholesale Banking business provides specialized lending tailored corporate finance debt and equity markets solutions and working capital.

Geographic Reach

ING operates in more than 40 countries in Europe North America Latin America Australia and the Asia region. Its revenue base is diversified with the Netherlands its largest single market accounting for about 30% of its total underlying banking income followed by Belgium (more than 15%) and Germany (nearly 15%). Other important countries are Australia Austria Czech Republic France Germany Italy and Spain.

The ING is headquartered in Amsterdam in the Netherlands.

Sales and Marketing

ING serves 40 million clients ranging from large companies to multinational corporations and financial institutions. Marketing and sales method include mobile banking.

Financial Performance

Note: Growth rates may differ after conversion to US Dollars.

ING's total income has been growing over the past five years. In 2019 the bank's total income grew ?130 million to ?18.3 billion thanks to modest increases in net interest income net fee and commission income and investment and other income. Gains were found mainly in its Challenger and Growth Markets and Retail Belgium largely offset by a decline in Retail Netherlands due to lower net interest income on savings and current accounts.

Net income rose 2% to ?4.8 billion from ?4.7 billion in 2018. Commercial performance was robust in 2019 further evidenced by an increase in the number of primary retail customers of more than 830000 to 13.3 million.

ING's cash rose 14% in 2019 ending the year ?54 billion. The bank's operations generated ?13.1 billion its investing activities used ?2.5 billion and its financing activities used another ?4.2 billion. The strong growth resulted from an increase in the balance of debt securities and disposals and redemptions of securities and financial assets.

Strategy

ING Groep's immediate priority is improving in the area of "Know Your Customer" an innocent-sounding bit of corporate jargon that hints at the rather more serious matter of hundreds of millions of euros being laundered over many years through ING's accounts. ING has continued to focus on this program in 2019. It now has 4000 FTEs working in KYC-related activities. It is also working on tools that use machine learning and artificial intelligence to increase the effectiveness of its KYC operations.

More broadly ING's core business strategy is to continue developing online touchpoints that customers rely on to access ING's services. The bank is rolling out functionality such as digital advisors and forecasting tools and is joining forces with fintech startups such as Countingup a mobile banking app for freelancers and the self-employed as well as a partnership with Minna Technologies that provides a new subscription service to its customers.

Company Background

Prior to the economic meltdown ING took aim at becoming a financial services player in all four corners of the world and made acquisitions accordingly. Along with much of the insurance industry it shifted its base from traditional life insurance products to investment-backed products

which favor companies that can sell through banks. ING utilized its owns banks to distribute such products. The company also targeted expansion in growing economies such as South Korea Turkey and Thailand to meet anticipated consumer demand for new banking and retirement options. In more mature markets like North America and Europe the company had the aging population in its sights and placed retirement planning and pensions as sources of future growth.

HISTORY

ING Groep's roots go back to 1845 when its earliest predecessor the Netherlands Insurance Co. was founded. The firm began expanding geographically; in 1903 it added life insurance. In 1963 it merged with the century-old Nationale Life Insurance Bank to form Nationale-Nederland (NN). Over the next three decades the company grew primarily through acquisitions in Europe North America and Australia. In 1986 NN became the first European life insurance company to be licensed in Japan.

Another predecessor the Rijkspostspaarbank was founded in 1881 to provide Dutch citizens with simple post office savings accounts. In 1918 the Postcheque-en Girondienst (giro) system was established to allow people to use vouchers drawn on their savings accounts to pay bills. This system became the main method of settling accounts (instead of bank checking accounts).

Rijkspostspaarbank and Postcheque merged in 1986 to become Postbank. Postbank merged in 1989 with the Nederlandse Middenstandsbank (founded 1927) to become NMB Postbank. The vast amounts of cash tied up in the post office savings and giro systems fueled NMB's business.

In 1991 as the European economic union became a reality and barriers between banking and insurance began to fall NN merged with NMB Postbank to form Internationale Nederland Groep (ING). ING began cutting costs shedding redundant offices and unprofitable operations in both its segments. In the US where insurance and banking were legally divided the company "debanked" itself in order to keep its more lucrative insurance operations (but retained the right to provide banking services to those operations).

ING sought to increase its investment banking and finance operations in the 1990s. In 1995 it took over UK-based Barings Bank (personal banker to the Queen of England) after Nicholas Leeson a trader in Barings' Singapore office lost huge sums of money in derivatives trading. The acquisition gave the firm a higher profile but cost more than anticipated and left it embroiled in lingering legal actions.

In 1996 ING bought Poland's Bank Slaski (the company had first entered Poland in 1994). The next year it expanded its securities business by acquiring investment bank Furman Selz doubled its US life insurance operations by purchasing Equitable of Iowa and listed on the NYSE. In 1998 ING's acquisition strategy again involved Europe and North America: It bought Belgium's Banque Bruxelles Lambert and Canadian life insurer Guardian Insurance Co. (from Guardian Royal Exchange now part of AXA UK).

ING turned eastward in 1999 kicking off asset management operations in India and buying a minority stake in South Korea's HC&B (formerly Housing & Commercial Bank). In 2000 the company bulked up its North American operations with the purchase of 40% of Savia SA a Mexican insurance concern. It also bought US firm ReliaStar Financial in a $6 billion deal and Charterhouse Securities from CCF (then called Crédit Commercial de France).

In 2004 ING realigned its management structure dividing the company's operations into six business lines: Insurance Americas Insurance Europe Insurance Asia-Pacific Wholesale Banking Retail Banking and ING Direct. ING boosted its North American insurance operations with the acquisition of Allianz's Canadian property and casualty operations.

The company struggled with investment banking arm ING Barings. The unit was reorganized and streamlined for cost-savings purposes but ultimately was put on the block. Its Asian equities operations were sold to Macquarie Bank in 2004. Barings Private Equity Partners unit was sold to its management. The Barings investment management operations were sold as well.

The company struggled with investment banking arm ING Barings. The unit was reorganized and streamlined for cost-savings purposes but ultimately was put on the block. Its Asian equities operations were sold to Macquarie Bank in 2004. Barings Private Equity Partners unit was sold to its management. The Barings investment management operations were sold to MassMutual in 2005 while Northern Trust bought up its fund administration trust and custody operations.

ING sold most of ING BHF-Bank to Sal. Oppenheim during 2004. The next year ING turned over its US life reinsurance operations to Scottish Re and sold subsidiary Life Insurance Company of Georgia to Jackson National Life.

During 2005 ING acquired a 20% stake in the Bank of Beijing as part of a strategic alliance. In 2006 the company sold off its UK brokerage business Williams de Bro to The Evolution Group.

In 2008 the company acquired CitiStreet a leading US administrator of defined-contribution retirement savings pension health and other plans; it paid about $900 million for the firm.

After the global financial crisis hit in 2008 ING accepted a ?10 billion (more than $13 billion) bailout loan from the Dutch government. The bailout was intended to shore up the company's capital position and reassure wary investors. Strategic measures to further offset losses and repay debt were enacted in 2009 including layoffs and asset sales. CEO Michael Tilmant stepped down and was replaced by former chairman Jan Hommen. By the end of 2009 job cuts totaled about 10% of its workforce. The company also outlined plans to split the company in half by separating its insurance and banking operations.

Prior to the bailout ING has already been working to simplify and streamline its operations through a "Back to Basics" strategy. Restructuring measures under the strategy include the refocusing of ING's banking operations on (mostly Central) Europe and the reduction of the company's US financial product offerings.

In early 2009 the company sold its ING Canada property/casualty business which was then renamed Intact Financial. ING sold its life insurance joint venture stake in Australia and New Zealand to partner ANZ and offloaded its noncore annuity and mortgage businesses in Chile to life insurer Corp Group Vida Chile in late 2009. The company also sold its Taiwanese life insurance business to Fubon Financial Holding in a deal worth ?447 million ($600 million) in mid-2009. ING gained a 5% stake in Fubon through the deal which it sold the following year for another ?395 million ($522 million).

In early 2010 ING completed sales of the company's Swiss Private Banking unit to Julius Baer for $506 million and its Asian Private Banking unit (operating in Hong Kong the Philippines and Singapore) to OCBC Bank for nearly $1.5 billion. In addition the company sold its North American reinsurance operations to RGA and most of its US insurance brokerage operations to Lightyear Capital in early 2010. ING has also agreed to sell its stake in one of its Chinese life insurance ventures

(Pacific Antai with China Pacific Insurance) to China Construction Bank.

In 2011 ING sold its Asian and European real estate investment management (REIM) operations as well as select US REIM assets for about $940 million to broker CBRE Group (formerly CB Richard Ellis Group). The firm sold its remaining US REIM assets to Lightyear Capital for some $100 million. Also that year the firm agreed to sell its Australian investment management business to UBS for an undisclosed sum.

Farther south in 2011 the company sold its Latin American insurance operations to Columbian insurer GrupoSura for $3.7 billion. The sale included insurance savings and investment management operations in Chile Colombia Mexico Uruguay and Peru. It also sold ING Car Least to BMW.

In 2016 the group exited the insurance business to focus on the European banking market.

EXECUTIVES

Chairman Executive Board and CEO, Ralph A. J. G. Hamers, age 55
CFO, Koos Timmermans
Chief Risk Officer, S.J.A. (Steven) van Rijswijk
Vice Chairman Supervisory Board, Hermann-Josef M. Lamberti, age 64
Chairman Supervisory Board, Jeroen van der Veer, age 74
Auditors: KPMG Accountants N.V.

LOCATIONS

HQ: ING Groep NV
Bijlmerplein 888, Amsterdam 1102 MG
Phone: (31) 20 563 6710
Web: www.ing.com

2018 sales

	% of total
Netherlands	32
Belgium	17
Germany	14
Other Challengers	10
Growth Markets	13
Wholesale Banking Rest of the World	13
Other	1
Total	**100**

PRODUCTS/OPERATIONS

2018 Sales

	% of total
Net interest income	76
Net fee and commission income	15
Valuation results & net trading income	6
Investment income	1
Share of results from associates and joint ventures	1
Other	1
Total	**100**

2018 sales

	%
Retail Banking	67
Wholesale Banking	32
Corporate Line Banking	1
Total	**100**

COMPETITORS

ABN AMRO Group	HSBC
Barclays	KBC
Citigroup	Rabobank Group
Deutsche Bank	UBS

HISTORICAL FINANCIALS

Company Type: Public

Income Statement

FYE: December 31

	ASSETS ($ mil.)	NET INCOME ($ mil.)	INCOME AS % OF ASSETS	EMPLOYEES
12/19	997,600	4,382	0.4%	53,431
12/18	1,013,043	5,452	0.5%	52,233
12/17	1,011,602	6,549	0.6%	51,504
12/16	889,281	5,253	0.6%	51,943
12/15	912,600	5,365	0.6%	57,553
Annual Growth	2.3%	(4.9%)	—	(1.8%)

2019 Year-End Financials

Return on assets: 0.4%
Return on equity: 7.8%
Long-term debt ($ mil.): —
No. of shares (mil.): —
Sales ($ mil): 31,778

Dividends
Yield: 5.1%
Payout: 55.2%
Market value ($ mil.): —

	STOCK PRICE ($) FY Close	P/E High/Low		PER SHARE ($) Earnings	Dividends	Book Value
12/19	12.05	14	9	1.12	0.62	14.70
12/18	10.66	16	9	1.40	0.64	14.44
12/17	18.46	14	11	1.69	0.65	14.94
12/16	14.10	11	7	1.35	0.56	12.87
12/15	13.46	14	9	1.38	0.35	12.66
Annual Growth	(2.7%)	—		(5.1%)	15.4%	3.8%

Inner Mongolia Yili Industrial Group Co., Ltd.

Auditors: Da Hua Certified Public Accountants (Special General Partnership)

LOCATIONS

HQ: Inner Mongolia Yili Industrial Group Co., Ltd.
No. 1, Jinshan Road, Jinshan Development Zone, Hohhot, Inner Mongolia Autonomous Region 010110
Phone: (86) 471 3350092   **Fax:** (86) 471 3601621
Web: www.yili.com

HISTORICAL FINANCIALS

Company Type: Public

Income Statement

FYE: December 31

	REVENUE ($ mil.)	NET INCOME ($ mil.)	NET PROFIT MARGIN	EMPLOYEES
12/19	12,966	996	7.7%	0
12/18	11,565	936	8.1%	0
12/17	10,458	922	8.8%	0
12/16	8,728	815	9.3%	54,983
12/15	9,293	713	7.7%	0
Annual Growth	8.7%	8.7%	—	—

2019 Year-End Financials

Debt ratio: 1.2%
Return on equity: 25.6%
Cash ($ mil.): 1,627
Current ratio: 0.82
Long-term debt ($ mil.): 67

No. of shares (mil.): —
Dividends
Yield: —
Payout: —
Market value ($ mil.): —

innogy SE

Auditors: PricewaterhouseCoopers GmbH Wirtschaftpruefungsgesellschaft

LOCATIONS

HQ: innogy SE
Opernplatz 1, Essen 45128
Phone: (49) 201 12 02
Web: www.innogy.com

HISTORICAL FINANCIALS

Company Type: Public

Income Statement

FYE: December 31

	REVENUE ($ mil.)	NET INCOME ($ mil.)	NET PROFIT MARGIN	EMPLOYEES
12/19	37,651	433	1.2%	34,523
12/18	40,153	(747)	—	42,904
12/17	49,291	932	1.9%	42,393
Annual Growth	(12.6%)	(31.8%)	—	(9.8%)

2019 Year-End Financials

Debt ratio: —
Return on equity: 5.0%
Cash ($ mil.): 637
Current ratio: 1.16
Long-term debt ($ mil.): —

No. of shares (mil.): 555
Dividends
Yield: —
Payout: —
Market value ($ mil.): —

	STOCK PRICE ($) FY Close	P/E High/Low	PER SHARE ($) Earnings	Dividends	Book Value
12/19	0.00	— —	0.79	0.00	15.01
12/18	0.00	— —	(1.35)	0.00	16.28
Annual Growth	—	— —	—	—	(4.0%)

Intact Financial Corp

Intact Financial is active in Canada's and US' property/casualty marketplaces providing automobile property and liability insurance to both individual and small to midsized commercial clients. Intact distributes insurance under the Intact Insurance brand through a wide network of brokers including its wholly-owned subsidiary BrokerLink and directly to consumers through belairdirect. The company's Jevco sells non-standard auto policies in Ontario. Intact Financial began in 1809 as The Halifax Fire Insurance Association.

Operations

Personal insurance business accounts for nearly 60% of direct premiums written by Intact Financial while commercial insurance makes up the balance. Personal auto coverage alone contributes more than 35% of all direct premiums written.

The company has two reportable segments: Canada and US in which more than 85% of sales came to Canada and the remaining accounts in US. The company products are available through its brands including belairdirect BrokerLink Frank Cowan and intact insurance specialty solutions.

Geographic Reach

Intact Financial operates across Canada and the US. Its corporate office is located in Toronto Ontario.

Sales and Marketing

The company distributes its products thru independent agencies brokers wholesalers subsidiaries and managing general agencies.

Financial Performance

Total revenues for 2019 was C$11.2 billion a 7% increase from the previous year. The company had higher net premiums for the year.

Net income attributable to shareholders totaled C$754 million a 7% growth from the previous year.

The company's cash at the end of 2019 was C$936 million. Operating activities generated C$1.3 million while investing activities used C$842 million mainly for purchases of investments. Financing activities generated another C$57 million.

Strategy

While there may be some short-term adjustments the company's strategic roadmap for the next decade is largely in place. It will be focused on four big ideas: strengthening its leadership position in Canada; building a leading North American Specialty insurer; transforming its competitive advantages and; investing in people to sustain the company's strong culture and engaged workforce.

Mergers and Acquisitions

In 2019 Intact Financial Corporation announced that it has entered into a definitive agreement with Princeton Holdings Limited to acquire The Guarantee Company of North America a specialty lines insurer in Canada and the U.S. and Frank Cowan Company Limited a managing general agent focused on specialty insurance for a cash consideration of approximately $1 billion. The transaction is expected to close in the fourth quarter of 2019 subject to regulatory approvals.

In 2019 Intact Financial Corporation completed the acquisition of On Side Restoration one of the nation's leading Canadian-owned restoration companies with 35 branches from Victoria BC to St. John's Newfoundland. They are joining forces to strengthen repair and restoration services for personal and commercial property claims customers across Canada. With this acquisition IFC will deepen its claims expertise and strengthen its supply chain network. Terms were not disclosed.

Company Background

As ING Canada the company went public in 2004 and used a portion of the proceeds from the IPO to acquire the Canadian operations of Allianz Group. After the IPO Dutch insurance giant ING Groep held 70% of the company. It sold its holdings in 2008 to help offset losses elsewhere. Half of its holdings were sold to the public while the other half went to institutional investors. Following the separation the company changed its name to Intact Financial in 2009.

EXECUTIVES

CEO, Charles Brindamour
EVP Governance and Capital Management, Mark A. Tullis
SVP Ontario, Debbie Coull-Cicchini
President Service and Distribution, Louis Gagnon
SVP Atlantic Canada, Alan Blair
SVP Personal Lines, Martin Beaulieu
President BrokerLink, Peter (Pete) Weightman
SVP Claims, Mathieu Lamy
SVP Finance and CFO, Louis Marcotte
SVP Commercial Lines, Alain Lessard
SVP Western Canada, Jennie Moushos
President Intact Insurance, Jean-Francois Blais
SVP Claims, Patrick Barbeau
SVP Specialty Solutions and Surety, Joe DÃ'Annunzio
SVP Quebec, Jean-Fran Şois Desautels
SVP Personal Lines, Darren Godfrey
SVP International and Ventures, Karim Hirji

SVP and Managing Director Intact Investment Management, Werner Muehlemann
EVP Investment Management Corporate Legal Corporate Development Audit and Finance, Don Fox
President CEO and Director, Claude Dussault
Auditors: Ernst & Young LLP

LOCATIONS

HQ: Intact Financial Corp
700 University Avenue, Toronto, Ontario M5G 0A1
Phone: 902 420-1732 **Fax:** 902 420-2856
Web: www.intactfc.com

2015 Premiums

	% of total
Ontario	41
Quebec	27
Alberta	18
British Columbia	6
Rest of Canada	8
Total	**100**

PRODUCTS/OPERATIONS

2015 Premiums

	% of total
Personal auto	45
Commercial property & casualty	23
Personal property	23
Commercial auto	9
Total	**100**

COMPETITORS

Allstate	Gore Mutual
Aviva	ICBC
Co-operators General Insurance	Kingsway
	Optimum General
Economical Insurance Group	Quebec Assurance
	State Farm
Fairfax Financial Holdings	TD Bank
	Wawanesa Mutual

HISTORICAL FINANCIALS

Company Type: Public

Income Statement

FYE: December 31

	ASSETS ($ mil.)	NET INCOME ($ mil.)	INCOME AS % OF ASSETS	EMPLOYEES
12/19	32,699	763	2.3%	0
12/18	28,819	715	2.5%	14,000
12/17	28,280	801	2.8%	0
12/16	23,280	547	2.4%	0
12/15	21,503	714	3.3%	0
Annual Growth	11.0%	1.7%	—	—

2019 Year-End Financials

Return on assets: 2.4%
Return on equity: 9.1%
Long-term debt ($ mil.): —
No. of shares (mil.): 143
Sales ($ mil): 11,523

Dividends
Yield: 0.0%
Payout: 59.8%
Market value ($ mil.): 15,363

	STOCK PRICE ($) FY Close	P/E High/Low	PER SHARE ($) Earnings	Dividends	Book Value
12/19	107.42	21 14	5.14	3.08	61.93
12/18	71.89	18 15	4.85	2.84	56.82
12/17	83.39	15 12	5.82	2.59	54.29
12/16	71.49	19 15	4.02	2.35	47.04
12/15	64.16	15 12	5.27	2.15	44.09
Annual Growth	13.8%	— —	(0.6%)	9.4%	8.9%

Inter RAO UES PJSC

EXECUTIVES

Chairman, Igor Ivanovich Sechin
Auditors: Ernst & Young LLC (member of Ernst & Young Global Limited)

LOCATIONS

HQ: Inter RAO UES PJSC
Bolshaya Pirogovskaya Street, Building 27-2, Moscow 119435
Phone: (7) 495 664 88 40 **Fax:** (7) 495 664 88 41
Web: www.interrao.ru

HISTORICAL FINANCIALS
Company Type: Public

Income Statement				FYE: December 31
	REVENUE ($ mil.)	NET INCOME ($ mil.)	NET PROFIT MARGIN	EMPLOYEES
12/19	16,583	1,311	7.9%	0
12/18	13,811	1,015	7.4%	0
12/17	15,862	931	5.9%	0
12/16	14,178	992	7.0%	48,945
12/15	10,905	307	2.8%	50,797
Annual Growth	11.0%	43.7%	—	—

2019 Year-End Financials

Debt ratio: 0.0%	No. of shares (mil.): —
Return on equity: 15.7%	Dividends
Cash ($ mil.): 1,541	Yield: —
Current ratio: 2.99	Payout: 1,580.4%
Long-term debt ($ mil.): 7	Market value ($ mil.): —

International Consolidated Airlines Group SA

Auditors: Ernst & Young, S.L.

LOCATIONS

HQ: International Consolidated Airlines Group SA
El Caserio, Iberia Zona Industrial No. 2, Camino de La Munoza s/n, Madrid 28042
Phone: (44) 20 8564 2800
Web: www.iairgroup.com

HISTORICAL FINANCIALS
Company Type: Public

Income Statement				FYE: December 31
	REVENUE ($ mil.)	NET INCOME ($ mil.)	NET PROFIT MARGIN	EMPLOYEES
12/19	28,637	1,925	6.7%	64,642
12/18	27,949	3,303	11.8%	63,531
12/17	27,537	2,398	8.7%	63,422
12/16	23,828	2,038	8.6%	63,387
12/15	24,897	1,628	6.5%	60,862
Annual Growth	3.6%	4.3%	—	1.5%

2019 Year-End Financials

Debt ratio: 44.8%	No. of shares (mil.): 1,984
Return on equity: 25.3%	Dividends
Cash ($ mil.): 7,503	Yield: 8.0%
Current ratio: 0.89	Payout: 140.3%
Long-term debt ($ mil.): 13,934	Market value ($ mil.): 32,841

	STOCK PRICE ($) FY Close	P/E High/Low	PER SHARE ($) Earnings	Dividends	Book Value
12/19	16.55	21 12	0.95	1.33	3.86
12/18	15.58	13 10	1.57	0.51	3.86
12/17	17.52	19 13	1.11	0.45	4.13
12/16	10.79	48 10	0.93	0.37	2.65
12/15	44.75	65 44	0.77	0.18	2.79
Annual Growth	(22.0%)	— —	5.4%	66.0%	8.5%

Intesa Sanpaolo S.P.A.

Intesa Sanpaolo vies with UniCredit for banking supremacy in Italy. Its Banca dei Territori specialized in offering insurance pension and personal and asset protection services from approximately 3500 branches throughout Italy with retail banking for consumers and small businesses. The bank also provides investment banking international subsidiary banks asset management private banking and insurance. Through Fideuram Vita and other subsidiaries Intesa Sanpaolo offers life property and casualty insurance. Asset management is handled by Eurizon Capital while Banca Fideuram arm provides financial planning services.

Operations

Intesa Sanpaolo operates through six segments: Banca dei Territori Corporate and Investment Banking International Subsidiary Banks Private Banking Insurance and Asset Management. It also operates a corporate center and a capital-light bank.

Banca dei Territori oversees the traditional lending and deposit collecting activities and related financial services in Italy. The bank also offers industrial credit factoring and leasing via Mediocredito Italiano and instant banking with Banca 5. Banca dei Territori generates around 45% of Intesa Sanpaolo's revenue.

ntesa Sanpaolo's corporate banking division serves corporate and public customers via more than 25 branches. It has corporate banking subsidiaries in Ireland Brazil Luxembourg and Russia. It accounts for more than 20% of total sales.

The International Subsidiary Banks carry out similar activities to Banca dei Territori but in Intesa Sanpaolo's international markets through commercial banking subsidiaries and associates. Together they generate around 10% of the company's total revenue.

The Private Banking division operates around 230 branches that serve around 92000 private clients and High Net Worth Individuals. Its subsidiaries include Fideuram Intesa Sanpaolo Private Banking and Sirefid. Private Banking generates another 10% of total company sales.

The Insurance business (some 5% of sales) provides insurance and pension products under Fideuram Vita Intesa Sanpaolo Assicura and Intesa Sanpaolo Vita.

Asset Management has more than ?122 billion in assets under management held primarily by subsidiary Eurizon. It brings in around 5% of revenue.

Geographic Reach

All told Intesa Sanpaolo has approximately 3500 branches including retail and business branches.

It has over 990 branches in more than 10 countries in Central and South-Eastern Europe and Commonwealth of Independent States & South Mediterranean. It also has an international cross-border support network in some 25 countries.

Italy accounts for around 80% of Intesa Sanpaolo's revenue. Europe brings in about 15% and the rest of the world 5%.

Intesa Sanpaolo is headquartered in Torino Italy.

Sales and Marketing

Intesa Sanpaolo group serves individuals (including households in financial difficulty) small to mid-size enterprises (SMEs) startup and large businesses consumer associations public entities and industrial associations.

Financial Performance

Intesa Sanpaolo's financial performance has been volatile in recent years as the bank has been grappling with recession in Italy and has been working to de-risk its portfolio from the toxic assets accumulated during the financial crisis.

In fiscal 2019 (ended March 21) Intesa Sanpaolo's operating income grew 2% to ?17.9 billion thanks to increases in insurance income and higher profits in financial assets. Net interest income and net fee and commission income were flat.

Net income increased 3.3% to ?4.2 billion in 2019. The change was driven by a rise in operating income a fall in operating costs and lower adjustments for credit risk. The amount of levies and charges for the banking system was still significant although slightly lower than in 2018.

Intesa Sanpaolo's cash position decreased during fiscal 2019 ending the year ?605 million lower at ?9.7 billion. The bank's operations provided ?4.4 billion while it used ?1.3 billion in its investing activities and ?3.8 billion in its financing activities. The main cash uses during 2019 were asset purchases and dividends.

Strategy

Intesa Sanpaolo's 2018-21 strategy is three pronged: carry out de-risking reduce costs via simplification of its operating model and grow revenue.

First de-risking is the first pillar through which the group aims to reduce the level of gross non-performing loans as a proportion of total loans at no cost to shareholders. Over the plan period a 49% reduction in the stock of gross non-performing loans is envisaged with respect to the figure at the beginning of 2018 as well as a 50% reduction in the cost of credit with a target of 41 basis points in 2021 and the achievement of a gross NPL ratio of 6.0%.

Second to reduce operating costs the company will cut its workforce deploy flexible work contracts and close bank branches in conjunction with expanding its capital light Banca 5. It will also set up a new HQ in Milan consolidating some of its corporate functions.

The third pillar of the business plan seeks to increase operating income by capturing significant business opportunities in all the divisions. It aims to be in the top-four private and commercial insurance companies and the first in retail non-motor. It will also strengthen Eurizon Capital and develop a presence in the Chinese wealth management market. Its goals will be supported by personnel development and digitization.

Mergers and Acquisitions

In 2019 Intesa Sanpaolo acquires a portfolio of performing residential mortgages for 900 million euro from the Italian branch of Barclays Bank Ireland PLC. The mortgages which are mainly for the purchase of first homes were granted to Italian customers and are backed by residential properties located in Italy.

Company Background

Intesa Sanpaolo is the result of the 2007 mega-merger between Banca Intesa and Sanpaolo IMI. After the merger the company reshuffled its assets and sold off some branches in order to comply with antitrust orders and raise capital.

HISTORY

In Italy charity begins at home and often heads to the financial institutions. In 1563 Turin citizens founded Compagnia di San Paolo a foundation that provided education and dowries to orphaned girls and aid to impoverished nobility. In 1579 the organization began a pawn shop the Monte di Pieta or Mountain of Mercy (founded in 1519 and reopened by the Compagnia). The foundation grew over the next 200 years fattened by bequests and inheritances from wealthy Piedmontese families.

The French Republican government in Piedmonte gradually took control of the foundation's operations and closed it in 1802. The Monte di Pieta was reopened in 1804 and under the French influence became more bank-like. In 1848 the charitable and financial operations were formally divided.

Industrialization came slowly to Italy after its unification in the 1860s (the country remained largely agricultural until after WWII) and the organization survived a banking crisis from 1887 to 1894 by operating conservatively. It contributed to the WWI effort by purchasing government bonds. In 1928 the foundation separated Monte di Pieta's credit and pawn operations and adopted the name Istituto di San Paolo di Torino - Beneficenza e Credito (San Paolo).

Specialized institutions were founded in the 1920s to finance utilities and transportation; one of them La Centrale Societa per il Finanziamento di Imprese Elettriche e Telefoniche was formed in 1925 to help finance Italy's energy and telecommunications industries. In 1965 this entity enlarged its focus and changed its name to La Centrale Finanziaria Generale a forerunner of Banca Intesa.

La Centrale's interests in energy were transferred to ENEL the state holding company in 1985 leaving it with banking finance and insurance holdings. That year the bank merged with Nuovo Banco Ambrosiano formerly Banco Ambrosiano.

Banco Ambrosiano was founded in 1896 by Guiseppi Tovino whose good works and sturdy faith made him a saint (he was beatified in 1998). Betraying his legacy in 1981 chairman Roberto Calvi was found hanging under the Blackfriars Bridge in London. Calvi called "God's Banker" for his connections to the Vatican left behind a tangle of debt phony holding companies and fraud that implicated the Catholic Church brought down an archbishop and involved a secretive Masonic lodge. Banco Ambrosiano was taken over by a group of creditor banks and its name was changed to Nuovo Banco Ambrosiano.

In 1989 Nuovo Banco Ambrosiano merged with its subsidiary Banco Cattolica del Veneto and became known as Banco Ambroveneto. It bought La Cassa di Risparmio delle Provincie Lombarde (Cariplo) Italy's biggest savings bank in 1997; they merged to form Banca Intesa the following year. Cariplo was founded by the Austro-Hungarian government in 1823 when the region was still recovering from Napoleon's depredations. Count Giovanni Pietro Porro wanted to allow artisans and day laborers to set aside money and the company remained true to that mission throughout Italy's unification and two world wars.

Italy began its race toward privatization in 1990 to counter the growing interest of foreign banks in the Italian market and help the nation meet the criteria for joining the European Union. In 1992

San Paolo was one of the first banks to sell a 20% stake in itself (it sold another 20% in 1997). The bank bought several regional and national banks over the next few years and in 1998 merged with investment bank Istituto Mobiliare Italiano or IMI (founded 1931) to form Sanpaolo IMI.

Banca Intesa was the product of a combination of the staid Cassa di Risparmio delle Provincie Lombarde (Cariplo) and the somewhat more colorful Banco Ambroveneto whose history helped inspire the plot of The Godfather Part III . It took over Banca Commerciale Italiana (BCI or Comit) in 2000 creating one of Italy's largest banks. Banca Intesa integrated BCI to form IntesaBci the following year and then in late 2002 rebranded as Banca Intesa.

Banca Intesa and Sanpaolo IMI merged in 2007. After the deal antitrust authorities ordred the company to sell some 200 branches to France-based Crédit Agricole. In late 2008 the Italian banking group sold 36 branches to Veneto Banca for ?274 million ($401 million).

A good portion of its branches were acquired in 2007 when Intesa Sanpaolo increased its stake in Banca CR Firenze to some 60% in preparation for taking over the bank outright. Banca CR Firenze added about 550 locations in Tuscany and surrounding regions to Intesa Sanpaolo's network.

The next year the bank upped its stake in Cassa dei Risparmi di Forli e della Romagna to about 70% increasing its influence in northern Italy. During more reshuffling of assets Intesa Sanpaolo sold a 30% stake in Cassa di Risparmio di Fano to Credito Valtellinese in 2009.

EXECUTIVES

Chief Risk Officer, Bruno Picca, age 71
Head of Planning and Control, Carlo Messina, age 59
Head of Italian and International Subsidiary Banks Divisions, Giovanni Boccolini, age 67
Chief Economist, Gregorio de Felice
Chief Lending Officer, Eugenio Rossetti, age 65
CFO, Stefano Del Punta
Head Corporate and Investment Banking Division, Gaetano Micciche
COO, Eliano Omar Lodesani
Chairman Management Board; President Intesa Sanpaolo Bank, Gian Maria Gros-Pietro
Chairman Supervisory Board, Giovanni Bazoli, age 88
Deputy Chairman Supervisory Board, Mario Bertolissi, age 72
Senior Deputy Chairman Management Board, Marcello Sala
Auditors: KPMG S.p.A.

LOCATIONS

HQ: Intesa Sanpaolo S.P.A.
   Piazza San Carlo, 156, Torino 10121
Phone: (39) 11 5551
Web: www.group.intesasanpaolo.com

2018 Sales

	% of total
Italy	80
Europe	16
Rest of the world	4
Total	**100**

PRODUCTS/OPERATIONS

2018 Sales

	% of total
Net interest income	41
Net fee and commission income	44
Profits on tradings	6
Income from insurance business	9
Total	**100**

2018 sales

	% of total
Banca del Territorio	50
Corporate and Investment Banking	20
International Subsidiary Banking	10
Private Banking	10
Asset Management	4
Insurance	6
Total	**100**

Selected Subsidiaries

Banca CR Firenze
Banca dell'Adriatico
Banca di Credito Sardo
Banca di Trento e Bolzano
Banca Fideuram
Banca IMI
Banca Intesa
Banca Intesa Beograd
Banca Monte Parma
Banca Prossima
Banco di Napoli
Bank of Alexandria
Banka Koper
Cassa dei Risparmi di Forlì e della Romagna
Cassa di Risparmio del Friuli Venezia Giulia
Cassa di Risparmio del Veneto
Cassa di Risparmio della Provincia di Viterbo (CARIVIT)
Cassa di Risparmio di Civitavecchia
Cassa di Risparmio di Pistoia e della Lucchesia
Cassa di Risparmio di Rieti (CARIRI)
Cassa di Risparmio di Venezia
Cassa di Risparmio in Bologna
Casse di Risparmio dell'Umbria
CIB Bank
Epsilon Associati SGR
Equiter
Eurizon A.I. SGR
Eurizon Capital
IMI Fondi Chiusi SGR
IMI Investimenti
Infogroup

COMPETITORS

BBVA	Dexia
BNL bc	Mediobanca
Banca Popolare di Milano	Monte dei Paschi di Siena
Banco Popolare	UniCredit

HISTORICAL FINANCIALS

Company Type: Public

Income Statement

	ASSETS ($ mil.)	NET INCOME ($ mil.)	INCOME AS % OF ASSETS	EMPLOYEES
12/19	916,291	4,695	0.5%	59,998
12/18	902,094	4,638	0.5%	92,117
12/17	955,240	8,770	0.9%	1
12/16	765,620	3,284	0.4%	89,126
12/15	736,846	2,983	0.4%	90,807
Annual Growth	5.6%	12.0%	—	(9.8%)

FYE: December 31

2019 Year-End Financials

Return on assets: 0.5%	Dividends
Return on equity: 7.6%	Yield: 8.3%
Long-term debt ($ mil.): —	Payout: 80.0%
No. of shares (mil.): —	Market value ($ mil.): —
Sales ($ mil): 40,653	

Investec Ltd

Auditors: Ernst & Young Inc.

LOCATIONS

HQ: Investec Ltd
  100 Grayston Drive, Sandown, Sandton 2196
Phone: (27) 11 286 7000   **Fax:** (27) 11 286 7777
Web: www.investec.com

HISTORICAL FINANCIALS

Company Type: Public

Income Statement   FYE: March 31

	ASSETS ($ mil.)	NET INCOME ($ mil.)	INCOME AS % OF ASSETS	EMPLOYEES
03/20	32,143	542	1.7%	5,784
03/19	45,516	424	0.9%	5,284
03/18	80,962	710	0.9%	0
03/17	66,835	552	0.8%	9,716
03/16	65,280	530	0.8%	8,966
Annual Growth	(16.2%)	0.6%	—	(10.4%)

2020 Year-End Financials

Return on assets: 1.5%   Dividends
Return on equity: 21.9%   Yield: —
Long-term debt ($ mil.): —   Payout: —
No. of shares (mil.): 267   Market value ($ mil.): —
Sales ($ mil): 2,456

Investec plc

Investec plc is one half of a dual-listed financial services firm providing private banking asset management brokerage and investment banking primarily to wealthy clients and financial institutions. (Partner Investec Limited is based in South Africa.) Investec plc delivers solutions for its clients in three core areas: Asset Management Wealth and Investment and Specialist Banking. It makes half of its operating income through its various Specialty Banking services and the rest comes from its Asset Management and Wealth & Investment services. Investec plc's top markets are in the UK Europe and Australia.

Operations

Investec plc operates three business segments: Specialist Banking Asset Management and Wealth & Investment.

Specialist Banking generates about 40% of the company's overall revenue. It manages principal investments which provide capital to entrepreneurs and existing commercial enterprises and via property investment and property fund management. It also offers corporate and institutional banking activities such as treasury and trading services specialized lending (including funds & debt) and institutional research. This segment also makes available private banking services like foreign exchange lending deposits and investments. Specialist Banking serves entrepreneurs business of all sizes institutions private equity managers and high net worth investors.

Asset Management makes money for its clients by allocating their investment funds to various financial instruments including physical property equities bonds and the like. It hosts nearly 200 investment professionals operates through five geographically-defined departments all supported by

the company's global operations platform. It accounts for roughly 35% of revenue.

Wealth & Investment tends to the investment needs of charities pension schemes and private individuals. It's Investec Wealth & Investment subsidiary manages services for UK clients while other units (such as Investec Bank Switzerland Investec Wealth & Investment Ireland and Investec Capital Asia Limited) cares for non-UK customers. In general the segment provides investments and savings vehicles pensions and retirement schemes and financial planning.

Broadly speaking Investec plc generates 60% of total revenue from fee and commission income about 20% from interest income and the rest from trading and other income sources. Investec plc manages some Â 95 billion in assets.

Geographic Reach

London-based Investec plc has a scattered worldwide presence. In Europe it has a well-established brand and operations particularly in the UK Switzerland the Republic of Ireland and Guernsey. It also conducts business via offices in Canada Hong Kong Singapore Australia and India.

Financial Performance

Investec plc interest income rose about 3% in FY2017 (ended 31 March 2017) to Â 563 million and fee income jumped nearly 15% to Â 932 million. Investment income was Â 60 million and trading income rose about 40% to $130 million. In total the firm earned Â 1.7 billion. Operating income for the year rose 18% to Â 1.2 billion.

Earnings for FY2017 were Â 160 million up more than 30% compared to the prior year. Investec plc continued to lower its impairment charges by managing down the quality-challenged assets contained in its legacy UK loan portfolio.

Cash at the end of the year was Â 3.7 billion up Â 257 million from the prior year. Operating activities contributed Â 375 million while investing and financing activities combined used about Â 125 million.

Strategy

Following the 2015 divestitures businesses Investec Bank (Australia) Ltd Kensington Group plc (UK) and Start Mortgage Holdings Ltd (Republic of Ireland) the firm's operations and financial results stabilized. In 2017 it appears poised to pursue growth opportunities. It brought on board additional personnel in part to help build out its suite of UK private offerings. It spent money to improve its IT infrastructure and even funded upgrades to its UK office space.

Although former businesses were shed in years past some leftover financial headwinds still require attention. The company continues to actively manage down the UK legacy portfolio in which are held a number of asset experiencing credit quality issues. Since the peak in 2012 when it held some Â 200 million of legacy impairments Investec plc has steadily reduced such assets to a 2017 mark of some Â 50 million. The lower amount reduces overall risk to the company and lowers the amount of loan loss allowance is must put aside in anticipation of loan defaults.

One of its strengths is its international reach which allows clients to invest deposit obtain financing and move money between countries where its customers live work and holiday. Operating from its UK base it can assist customers located in countries linked to past and present British ties including Australia Republic of Ireland Canada and into South Africa where its corporate affiliate calls home.

Investec plc must be doing something right as the amount of funds under management grew nearly 20% in 2017 to Â 97 billion. Customer deposits ticked up 2% to Â 11 billion.

According to reports Investec entered talks in 2019 to sell its private client stockbroking business

in Ireland for up to $68 million to either Brewin Dolphin Holdings Allied Irish Banks or Rathbone Brothers.

Company Background

With its beginnings as a South African leasing company Investec expanded into the UK in 2002. In 2010 it acquired UK asset manager Rensburg Sheppards (now Investec Wealth & Investment) boosting its funds under management by about half.

EXECUTIVES

Managing Director, Bernard Kantor, age 70
Group Risk and Finance Director, Glynn R. Burger, age 63
CEO Investec Asset Management, Hendrik Toit
CEO, Stephen Koseff
Joint Chairman, Fani Titi, age 55
Joint Chairman, David J. Prosser
Auditors: Ernst & Young LLP

LOCATIONS

HQ: Investec plc
  30 Gresham Street, London EC2V 7QP
Phone: (44) 20 7597 4000   **Fax:** (44) 20 7597 4491
Web: www.investec.com

PRODUCTS/OPERATIONS

FY2017 Operating Income

	% of total
Net Interest income	20
Fee and commission income	65
Trading income	10
Investment income	4
Others	1
Total	**100**

FY2017 Operating Income

	% of total
Speciality Banking	52
Wealth & Investment	22
Asset Management	26
Total	**100**

Selected Segments

Asset Management
Wealth & Investment
Specialist Banking

COMPETITORS

Barclays	ING
Citigroup	Invesco Perpetual
Fleming Family & Partners	Lloyds Banking Group Northern Trust
Grupo Santander	Prudential plc
HSBC	Royal Bank of Scotland

HISTORICAL FINANCIALS

Company Type: Public

Income Statement   FYE: March 31

	ASSETS ($ mil.)	NET INCOME ($ mil.)	INCOME AS % OF ASSETS	EMPLOYEES
03/20	30,791	797	2.6%	0
03/19	29,653	247	0.8%	0
03/18	28,963	190	0.7%	0
03/17	23,456	199	0.9%	9,716
03/16	26,998	176	0.7%	8,966
Annual Growth	3.3%	45.8%	—	—

2020 Year-End Financials

Return on assets: 2.7%   Dividends
Return on equity: 27.6%   Yield: 0.0%
Long-term debt ($ mil.): —   Payout: —
No. of shares (mil.): 664   Market value ($ mil.): 3,021
Sales ($ mil): 1,666

	STOCK PRICE ($)	P/E	PER SHARE ($)		
	FY Close	High/Low	Earnings	Dividends	Book Value
03/20	4.55	— —	(0.00)	0.54	4.44
03/19	12.65	— —	(0.00)	0.00	4.51
Annual Growth	(64.1%)	— —	—	—	(0.4%)

Investor AB

EXECUTIVES

President Patricia Industries, B ¶rje E. Ekholm, age 57, $678,240 total compensation
President and CEO, Johan Forsell, age 50
CFO, Helena Saxon
Chairman, Jacob Wallenberg, age 64
Vice Chairman, Marcus Wallenberg, age 64
Auditors: Deloitte AB

LOCATIONS

HQ: Investor AB
  Arsenalsgatan 8C, Stockholm SE-103 32
Phone: (46) 8 614 20 00   **Fax:** (46) 8 614 21 50
Web: www.investorab.com

COMPETITORS

Berkshire Hathaway	KBC
Cobepa	Onex
EXOR	

HISTORICAL FINANCIALS

Company Type: Public

Income Statement				FYE: December 31
	REVENUE ($ mil.)	NET INCOME ($ mil.)	NET PROFIT MARGIN	EMPLOYEES
12/19	15,528	10,881	70.1%	15,560
12/18	4,506	(251)	—	21,162
12/17	9,658	5,401	55.9%	20,054
12/16	6,917	3,713	53.7%	19,292
12/15	4,998	2,067	41.4%	16,702
Annual Growth	32.8%	51.5%	—	(1.8%)

2019 Year-End Financials

Debt ratio: 1.5%
Return on equity: 27.0%
Cash ($ mil.): 2,067
Current ratio: 3.45
Long-term debt ($ mil.): 7,814
No. of shares (mil.): 765
Dividends
  Yield: —
  Payout: 10.5%
Market value ($ mil.): —

Israel Discount Bank Ltd.

Who doesn't love a discount? Israel Discount Bank the third-largest bank in Israel has about 150 locations across the country. The bank offers standard consumer services like deposits loans and credit cards in addition to private banking international trade and commercial banking activities. Israel Discount Bank oversees four subsidiaries — Discount Mortgage Bank Mercantile Discount Bank (which has about 75 branches) Israel Discount Bank of New York and IDB (Swiss) Bank Ltd. It also owns a 26% stake in First International Bank of Israel the country's fifth-largest bank. In 2015 IDB sold Uruguay-based subsidiary Discount Bank Latin America to Bank of Nova Scotia in a deal worth $65 million.

Company Background

In 2010 Israel Discount Bank announced it was selling off Tachlit Investment House its portfolio management subsidiary that has about $3 billion in assets under management.

EXECUTIVES

vice-president, Arik Frishman
vice-president, Asaf Pasternak
vice-president, Avi Levy
vice-president, Avraham Levy
vice-president, Esther Deutsch
vice-president, Nir Abel
vice-president, Ran Oz
vice-president, Yaki Zano
chairman, Uri Levin
Auditors: Ziv Haft

LOCATIONS

HQ: Israel Discount Bank Ltd.
  23 Yehuda Halevi Street, Tel-Aviv 65136
Phone: (972) 3 514 5555   **Fax:** (972) 3 514 5346
Web: www.discountbank.co.il

COMPETITORS

Bank Hapoalim	Mizrahi Tefahot
Bank Leumi le-Israel	
First International Bank of Israel	

HISTORICAL FINANCIALS

Company Type: Public

Income Statement				FYE: December 31
	ASSETS ($ mil.)	NET INCOME ($ mil.)	INCOME AS % OF ASSETS	EMPLOYEES
12/19	75,199	492	0.7%	9,472
12/18	63,744	401	0.6%	9,407
12/17	63,728	362	0.6%	9,374
12/16	57,168	235	0.4%	9,401
12/15	52,477	191	0.4%	9,710
Annual Growth	9.4%	26.6%	—	(0.6%)

2019 Year-End Financials

Return on assets: 0.6%
Return on equity: 9.5%
Long-term debt ($ mil.): —
No. of shares (mil.): 116
Sales ($ mil): 3,281
Dividends
  Yield: 0.8%
  Payout: 98.2%
Market value ($ mil.): 5,471

	STOCK PRICE ($)	P/E	PER SHARE ($)		
	FY Close	High/Low	Earnings	Dividends	Book Value
12/19	47.00	32 23	0.42	0.41	46.44
12/18	30.23	28 20	0.34	0.18	39.27
12/17	29.97	27 22	0.31	0.00	38.59
12/16	19.03	22 19	0.22	0.00	33.37
12/15	16.50	26 21	0.18	0.00	32.24
Annual Growth	29.9%	— —	23.5%	—	9.6%

Isuzu Motors, Ltd. (Japan)

Isuzu Motors has been trucking along since 1916 as one of Japan's first automobile makers. The company is one of the world's top commercial truck manufacturers boasting heavy- medium- and light-duty models. Isuzu is also a leading diesel engine maker for such companies as Adam Opel and GM; its engines are used in automotive as well as industrial and marine applications. Other vehicle products include sightseeing and private buses passenger pickup trucks and SUVs. Its D-MAX pickup is particularly popular in Thailand and South America. Isuzu Motors which sells its products in more than 100 countries through a worldwide distributor network has stopped selling passenger vehicles in the US.

EXECUTIVES

Senior Executive Officer and Director, Masanori Katayama, age 65
Managing Executive Officer and Director, Kazuhiko Ito
Managing Executive Officer and Director, Yoshifumi Komura
Managing Executive Officer and Director, Makoto Kawahara
Managing Executive Officer Director and Chairman Isuzu Motors India (IMI), Hiroshi Nakagawa, age 66
EVP and Director, Takao Shiomi
Managing Executive Officer and Director, Kuniharu Nakagawa
Managing Executive Officer, Toru Nakata
Senior Executive Officer Sales Division Isuzu Motors Japan and Chairman Isuzu Motors South Africa, Haruyasu Tanishige
Chairman, Susumu Hosoi
Auditors: Ernst & Young ShinNihon LLC

LOCATIONS

HQ: Isuzu Motors, Ltd. (Japan)
  6-26-1 Minami-Oi, Shinagawa-ku, Tokyo 140-8722
Phone: (81) 3 5471 1169
Web: www.isuzu.co.jp

2016 Sales

	% of total
Japan	36
Thailand	18
Other	46
Total	**100**

PRODUCTS/OPERATIONS

2016 Sales

	% of total
Vehicles	72
Engines & components	5
Parts of overseas production	4
Other	19
Total	**0**

Selected Vehicles and Brands

Buses
  Erga heavy-duty bus
  Erga Mio medium-duty bus
Commercial vehicles
  C&E Series heavy-duty trucks & tractors
  F Series medium-duty trucks
  N Series light-duty trucks
Diesel engines
  Automotive
  Industrial
  Marine

Pickup trucks & SUVs
  D-MAX
  MU-7 (Thailand)
  Panther (Indonesia)

Selected Subsidiaries and Affiliates
Anadolu Isuzu Otomotiv Sanayi Ve Ticaret AS (Turkey)
DMAX Ltd. (US)
Isuzu Australia Limited
Isuzu Motors Europe N.V. (Belgium)
Isuzu (China) Holding Co. Ltd.
Isuzu Commercial Truck of America Inc.
Isuzu Commercial Truck of Canada Inc.
Isuzu Motors America LLC
Isuzu Motors Asia Ltd. (Singapore)
Isuzu Motors Co. (Thailand) Ltd.
Isuzu Motors Germany GmbH
Isuzu Motors Polska Sp. zo. o. (Poland)
Isuzu Philippines Corporation
Isuzu Truck (UK) Ltd.
P.T. Isuzu Astra Motor Indonesia
Qingling Motors Co. Ltd. (China)

COMPETITORS

Ashok Leyland	MAN
China Yuchai	Mitsubishi Fuso
Cummins	Navistar International
Daimler	PACCAR
Daimler Trucks North	Renault
America	Scania
Ford Motor	UD Trucks
General Motors	Volkswagen
Hino Motors	Volvo

HISTORICAL FINANCIALS

Company Type: Public

Income Statement   FYE: March 31

	REVENUE ($ mil.)	NET INCOME ($ mil.)	NET PROFIT MARGIN	EMPLOYEES
03/20	19,161	748	3.9%	46,925
03/19	19,406	1,024	5.3%	47,255
03/18	19,497	995	5.1%	44,532
03/17	17,469	839	4.8%	42,610
03/16	17,159	1,021	6.0%	42,049
Annual Growth	2.8%	(7.5%)	—	2.8%

2020 Year-End Financials

Debt ratio: 0.1%	No. of shares (mil.): 738
Return on equity: 8.6%	Dividends
Cash ($ mil.): 2,961	Yield: 5.4%
Current ratio: 1.86	Payout: —
Long-term debt ($ mil.): 2,161	Market value ($ mil.): 4,770

	STOCK PRICE ($) FY Close	P/E High/Low		PER SHARE ($) Earnings	Dividends	Book Value
03/20	6.46	0	0	1.01	0.35	11.89
03/19	13.14	0	0	1.36	0.32	11.37
03/18	15.44	0	0	1.26	0.30	10.98
03/17	13.23	0	0	1.07	0.30	9.28
03/16	10.28	0	0	1.23	0.26	8.49
Annual Growth	(11.0%)	—	—	(4.8%)	7.7%	8.8%

Itau CorpBanca

EXECUTIVES

Chairman Of The Board, Jorge Andres Saieh Guzman
Vice Chairman Of The Board, Ricardo Villela Marino
Auditors: PricewaterhouseCoopers Consultores Auditores SpA

LOCATIONS

HQ: Itau CorpBanca
  Rosario Norte 660, Santiago, Las Condes
Phone: (56) 2 660 2240   **Fax:** (56) 2 660 2206
Web: www.itau.cl

PRODUCTS/OPERATIONS

Selected Subsidiaries
Corp Legal S.A.
CorpBanca Administradores General de Fondos S.A.
CorpBanca Agencia de Valores S.A.
CorpBanca Asesorí;as Financieras S.A.
CorpBanca Corredores de Seguros S.A.
CorpBanka Corredores de Bolsa S.A.
SMU Corp S.A.

COMPETITORS

BBVA Chile	Banco de Crédito e
Banco Latinoamericano	Inversiones
de Comercio Exterior	Citibank
Banco Santander Chile	Scotiabank
Banco de Chile	

HISTORICAL FINANCIALS

Company Type: Public

Income Statement   FYE: December 31

	ASSETS ($ mil.)	NET INCOME ($ mil.)	INCOME AS % OF ASSETS	EMPLOYEES
12/19	45,602	154	0.3%	8,987
12/18	42,251	246	0.6%	9,179
12/17	45,581	110	0.2%	9,492
12/16	43,355	21	0.0%	9,607
12/15	29,359	305	1.0%	7,545
Annual Growth	11.6%	(15.7%)	—	4.5%

2019 Year-End Financials

Return on assets: 0.3%	Dividends
Return on equity: 3.5%	Yield: 1.7%
Long-term debt ($ mil.): —	Payout: 44,817.3%
No. of shares (mil.): —	Market value ($ mil.): —
Sales ($ mil): 2,512	

	STOCK PRICE ($) FY Close	P/E High/Low		PER SHARE ($) Earnings	Dividends	Book Value
12/19	8.61	63	34	0.00	0.15	0.01
12/18	13.60	45	36	0.00	0.09	0.01
12/17	13.44	120	87	0.00	0.00	0.01
12/16	12.44	414	328	0.00	0.56	0.01
12/15	11.70	25	19	0.00	1.95	0.01
Annual Growth	(7.4%)	—	—	(24.0%)	(47.4%)	14.0%

Itau Unibanco Holding S.A.

The Brazilian bank offers a variety of standard retail and commercial banking services as well as consumer credit financial management leasing foreign exchange and trade financing. The company is a leading bank in investments private banking and cards. It also provides investment banking securities brokerage and insurance services. Besides its network of more than 1000 physical branches and about 200 digital branches the firm boasts operations in Brazil Latin America and in about 20 countries. It leverages acquisitions such as its

2013 Credicard purchase to boost its presence. Banco Ita merged with Unibanco in 2009 to become Ita Unibanco. In 2019 the Acquisition of 51% equity stake in ZUP transpired.

Operations
The company has three business segments. These are Retail Banking (more than 45% of the total sales) Wholesale Banking (more than 30%) and Tradition and Institutional (more than 20%).

Retail Banking is its main business. It offers financial products including vehicle financing credit cards offered outside the branch network and payroll loans through the branches and banking correspondents. It offers exclusive services such as investment consulting exclusive ATMs a special hotline higher credit limits and a dedicated client relationship team.

Wholesale banking looks after customers with high financial net worth (private banking) through units in Latin America banking for middle-market and large companies and corporations.

Overall the company provides mortgage loans consortia brokerage private pension products and insurance just to name a few. It has partnerships with Itaucard Hipercard Credicard and Connect-Car.

Geographic Reach
Headquartered in S o Paulo Brazil it has its presence in Latin America's and with operations in 18 countries.

Sales and Marketing
Wholesale Banking looks after customers with high financial net worth (private banking) through units in Latin America banking for middle-market and large companies and corporations through the activities of Ita BBA the unit responsible for corporate clients and in its role as an investment bank. The company provides banking services to major corporations.

Retail Banking offers its services to account holders and non-account holders.

Financial Performance
Revenue for the year 2019 increased by R$21.5 billion to R$186.4 billion compared to $164.9 million in the prior year.

The company's net income attributable to the owners of the parent company increased by 9% amounting to R$27.1 billion in 2019 from $24.9 billion in 2018.

Strategy
The company's information security strategy was developed taking into consideration the global scenario the regulations and the best practices and market rules. It has a structure and governance that are resilient and appropriate to identify detect and react to threats as well as to establish recovery procedures for situations that require its action against cyber-attacks. Additionally the company invests in awareness campaigns for employees and clients so that they can continue to be prepared to identify and approach risks and threats.

These are direct results of the strategy adopted to expand microcredit as one of its main impacts on society. For this reason the company expanded its operations to six Brazilian states already available in the metropolitan areas of S o Paulo (State of S o Paulo) Rio de Janeiro (State of Rio de Janeiro) Montes Claros (State of Minas Gerais) Campina Grande (State of Para ba) Fortaleza (State of Cear) and Teresina (State of Piau). The company's 2020 target is to achieve R$80 million in microcredit and serve 40000 clients with this profile.

EXECUTIVES

EVP and Investor Relations, Alfredo Egydio Setubal, age 65
CEO, Candido Botelho Bracher, age 61

CFO and EVP, Caio Ibrahim David, age 51
EVP Wholesale Banking, Eduardo Vassimon
Head Retail Banking, Marcio Schettini
Chairman, Pedro Moreira Salles, age 61
Vice Chairman, Alfredo Egydio Arruda Villela Filho, age 50
Auditors: PricewaterhouseCoopers Auditores Independentes

LOCATIONS

HQ: Itau Unibanco Holding S.A.
  Praca Alfredo Egydio de Souza Aranha, n 100, Sao Paulo 04344-902
Phone: (55) 11 5019 1267
Web: www.itau.com.br

PRODUCTS/OPERATIONS

2015 Sales

	% of total
Interest and similar income	73
Banking service fees	15
Income related to insurance and private pension	11
Other income	1
Total	**100**

COMPETITORS

Banco Bradesco	Banco do Brasil
Banco Francés	Caixa Econ ´mica
Banco Santander	Federal

HISTORICAL FINANCIALS

Company Type: Public

Income Statement — FYE: December 31

	ASSETS ($ mil.)	NET INCOME ($ mil.)	INCOME AS % OF ASSETS	EMPLOYEES
12/19	981,409	16,249	1.7%	94,881
12/18	930,654	14,927	1.6%	100,300
12/17	860,035	14,326	1.7%	99,332
12/16	811,052	13,942	1.7%	94,779
12/15	765,007	15,427	2.0%	90,320
Annual Growth	**6.4%**	**1.3%**	**—**	**1.2%**

2019 Year-End Financials

Return on assets: 1.7%	Dividends
Return on equity: 19.8%	Yield: 7.0%
Long-term debt ($ mil.): —	Payout: 39.0%
No. of shares (mil.): —	Market value ($ mil.): —
Sales ($ mil): 125,515	

	STOCK PRICE ($) FY Close	P/E High/Low	Earnings	PER SHARE ($) Dividends	Book Value
12/19	9.15	4 3	1.66	0.64	16.55
12/18	9.14	7 3	1.53	0.55	16.53
12/17	13.00	6 4	1.46	0.26	16.30
12/16	10.28	5 2	1.41	0.22	14.61
12/15	6.51	5 2	1.71	0.24	14.72
Annual Growth	**8.9%**	**— —**	**(0.7%)**	**28.5%**	**3.0%**

ITOCHU Corp (Japan)

EXECUTIVES

President and CEO, Kenji Okada, age 69
Senior Managing Officer and Chief Compliance Officer, Masaaki Itoyama, age 70
Senior Managing Officer, Tatsunosuke Nagao, age 68

Senior Managing Officer, Masahiko Takasaka, age 63
CFO and CIO, Masayasu Tanaka, age 65
President Itochu Enex Home-Life Kanto, Masanori Toyoshima
Auditors: Deloitte Touche Tohmatsu LLC

LOCATIONS

HQ: ITOCHU Corp (Japan)
  3-1-3 Umeda, Kita-ku, Osaka 530-8448
Phone: (81) 6 7638 2121   **Fax:** 212 818-8293
Web: www.itochu.co.jp

PRODUCTS/OPERATIONS

2014 Sales

	% of total
Energy Trade	25
Car-Life	59
Total	13
Power and Utility	3
Other	-
Total	**100**

COMPETITORS

Marubeni	Showa Shell Sekiyu

HISTORICAL FINANCIALS

Company Type: Public

Income Statement — FYE: March 31

	REVENUE ($ mil.)	NET INCOME ($ mil.)	NET PROFIT MARGIN	EMPLOYEES
03/20	101,178	4,618	4.6%	174,713
03/19	104,750	4,519	4.3%	158,517
03/18	51,890	3,770	7.3%	132,062
03/17	43,275	3,150	7.3%	124,469
03/16	45,268	2,140	4.7%	135,026
Annual Growth	**22.3%**	**21.2%**		**6.7%**

2020 Year-End Financials

Debt ratio: 0.2%	No. of shares (mil.): 1,492
Return on equity: 16.8%	Dividends
Cash ($ mil.): 5,630	Yield: 3.9%
Current ratio: 1.21	Payout: 53.1%
Long-term debt ($ mil.): 20,198	Market value ($ mil.): 61,081

	STOCK PRICE ($) FY Close	P/E High/Low	Earnings	PER SHARE ($) Dividends	Book Value
03/20	40.92	0 0	3.09	1.63	18.49
03/19	36.14	0 0	2.93	1.35	17.40
03/18	39.19	0 0	2.43	1.13	16.19
03/17	28.41	0 0	2.00	0.97	13.69
03/16	24.56	0 0	1.35	0.78	12.35
Annual Growth	**13.6%**	**— —**	**22.9%**	**20.3%**	**10.6%**

Iyo Bank, Ltd. (Japan)

Auditors: KPMG AZSA LLC

LOCATIONS

HQ: Iyo Bank, Ltd. (Japan)
  1 Minami-Horibatacho, Matsuyama, Ehime 790-8514
Phone: (81) 89 941 1141
Web: www.iyobank.co.jp

Selected Branch Locations
  Head Offic
  Aichi
  Fukuoka

Hiroshima
Hyogo
Kagawa
Kochi
Oita
Okayama
Osaka
Tokushima
Tokyo
Yamaguchi

PRODUCTS/OPERATIONS

Selected Subsidiaries
Computer Services Inc. Iyogin
Iyogin Business Service Co. Ltd.
Iyogin Capital Co. Ltd.
Iyogin guarantee Ltd.
Iyogin Leasing Co. Ltd.
Iyogin Securities Co. Ltd.
Ltd. Iyo silver Regional Center for Economic Research
Ltd. Iyogin Dee Sea card

COMPETITORS

Aozora Bank	Shizuoka Bank
Miyazaki Bank	Toho Bank

HISTORICAL FINANCIALS

Company Type: Public

Income Statement — FYE: March 31

	ASSETS ($ mil.)	NET INCOME ($ mil.)	INCOME AS % OF ASSETS	EMPLOYEES
03/20	71,815	174	0.2%	4,485
03/19	64,704	167	0.3%	4,558
03/18	66,831	222	0.3%	4,589
03/17	61,260	194	0.3%	4,575
03/16	57,972	217	0.4%	4,511
Annual Growth	**5.5%**	**(5.4%)**	**—**	**(0.1%)**

2020 Year-End Financials

Return on assets: 0.2%	Dividends
Return on equity: 2.9%	Yield: —
Long-term debt ($ mil.): —	Payout: 23.4%
No. of shares (mil.): 316	Market value ($ mil.): —
Sales ($ mil): 1,165	

J Sainsbury PLC

J Sainsbury's trolley is filled with more than groceries. One of the UK's largest food retailer Sainsbury's operates some 610 supermarkets roughly 820 convenience stores throughout the UK and an e-commerce offering. In addition to groceries Sainsbury's sells apparel (under the Tu brand) homeware and cookware (Sainsbury's Home and Habitat) and consumer electronics. Its Argos brand sells consumer goods through standalone stores in Sainsbury's supermarkets and online. The company also offers consumer banking through Sainsbury's Bank which provides banking and insurance products to its more than two million customers. A mega-merger with Wal-Mart-owned Asda was blocked by UK regulators in 2019.

Operations

J Sainsbury operates more than 2300 supermarkets convenience stores and Argos stores in the UK and Ireland as well as its online business. The business are organized into three operating segments; Retail - Food; Retail - General Merchandising and Clothing; and Financial Services. The company's retailing business generates more than 95% of the company's total revenue while its financial services generates below 5% of the remaining sales. Financial services include Sainsbury's Bank plc and Argos Financial Services entities and provides its customers with affordable ways to manage its finances and reward them for their loyalty through Nectar. Argus operates in more than 880 stores nearly 610 Sainsbury's in supermarkets and approximately 820 Sainsbury's in convenient stores.

Geographic Reach

Based in London Sainsbury trades predominantly in the UK and the Republic of Ireland.

Sales and Marketing

Sainsbury has more than 28 million customer transactions per week across all its Sainsbury's and Argos channels - in stores online and on our mobile app. The company also has more than 18 million active Nectar card customers who benefit from the UK's leading loyalty programme. In the company's Financial Services business it has more than 2 million active Sainsbury's Bank customers and above 2 million Argos Financial Services customers.

Financial Performance

Note: Growth rates may differ after conversion to US Dollars.

Sainsbury's revenue has been growing strongly over the past five years but profits continued its decline for the same period.

In fiscal 2020 (ended March 3) the company's sales decreased by Å 14 million to Å 29 billion. Group and Retail sales both decreased by 0.1 per cent year-on-year. Retail sales decreased by 0.4 per cent driven by General Merchandise sales declines.

Net income fell 18% in 2020 to Å 152 million due to higher cost of sales and higher income tax credit.

Sainsbury's cash on hand fell Å 126 million during 2020 ending the year at Å 994 million. The company's operations generated Å 1.9 billion offset by Å 426 million used in investing activities and Å 1.1 billion used in financing. Sainsbury's main cash uses in 2020 were for capital expenditures borrowing repayments and dividends.

Strategy

To deliver Sainsbury's purpose and vision the company will focus on seven strategic priorities which are designed to ensure to continue to give its customers what they want in a rapidly changing retail marketplace while also delivering value for its shareholders.

Sainsbury is focused on offering customers quality products at affordable prices. It invests in its digital offer so that customers can shop easily and efficiently across its multi brand multi-channel business.

Sainsbury aims to deliver inflation covering cost savings as well as structurally reducing costs. This year the company have met its objective to make savings to cover the impact of cost inflation and are making good early progress with its target to structurally reduce its costs by approximately Å 500 million over five years by bringing Sainsbury's and Argos together.

Sainbury will create value for future generations by reducing the environmental impact of its business and by working with farmers growers and suppliers throughout its supply chain.

The company can serve more of its customers' needs by selling more distinctive and exclusive ranges. Because of its distinctive offer customers visit its stores to buy new and interesting products they cannot find elsewhere.

Great service and availability and faster ways to pay mean customers can save time as well as money by shopping with Sainsbury. The company are consistently improving its customer service scores driven by investment in more than 450 supermarkets and 362 convenience stores. It also

now have 306 Argos stores in Sainsbury's supermarkets.

EXECUTIVES

CFO, Kevin O'Byrne, age 55
CEO Sainsbury's Bank, Peter L. Griffiths, age 61
Property Director, John Rogers
CEO, Mike Coupe
Digital and Technology Director, Jon Rudoe
Chairman, David A. Tyler, age 67
Auditors: Ernst & Young LLP

LOCATIONS

HQ: J Sainsbury PLC
    33 Holborn, London EC1N 2HT
Phone: (44) 20 7921 6000
Web: www.about.sainsburys.co.uk

PRODUCTS/OPERATIONS

2019 sales

	% of total
Retailing	9
Financial services	2
Total	**100**

2019 Stores

	No.
Sainsbury's Supermarkets	608
Convenience stores	820
Argos	
Standalone	594
In Sainsbury's	281
In Homebase	8
Habitat	16
Total	**2,327**

PRODUCTS

Summer
Fruit & veg
Meat & fish
Dairy eggs & chilled
Bakery
Frozen
Food cupboard
Drinks
Health & beauty
Baby
Household
Pet
Home
Cook event
Electronics

COMPETITORS

ALDI	Musgrave Retail
ASDA	Partners
Co-operative Group	SNAX 24
Costcutter	SPAR (UK)
Supermarkets	Tesco
Iceland Foods	Waitrose
Lidl	Wm Morrison
METRO AG	Supermarkets
Marks & Spencer	

HISTORICAL FINANCIALS

Company Type: Public

Income Statement				FYE: March 7
	REVENUE ($ mil.)	**NET INCOME** ($ mil.)	**NET PROFIT MARGIN**	**EMPLOYEES**
03/20	37,734	197	0.5%	171,400
03/19	37,921	286	0.8%	179,900
03/18	39,329	427	1.1%	186,900
03/17	31,840	457	1.4%	181,900
03/16	33,615	673	2.0%	162,700
Annual Growth	2.9%	(26.4%)	—	1.3%

2020 Year-End Financials

Debt ratio: 6.0%	No. of shares (mil.): —
Return on equity: 1.8%	Dividends
Cash ($ mil.): 1,293	Yield: 0.0%
Current ratio: 0.63	Payout: 712.4%
Long-term debt ($ mil.): 1,624	Market value ($ mil.): —

	STOCK PRICE ($) FY Close	P/E High/Low		PER SHARE ($) Earnings	Dividends	Book Value
03/20	11.11	215	161	0.08	0.54	4.58
03/19	11.69	196	128	0.12	0.48	5.01
03/18	13.66	119	94	0.18	0.49	4.67
03/17	13.24	81	60	0.20	0.49	3.81
03/16	15.63	69	54	0.32	0.64	4.73
Annual Growth	(8.2%)	—	—	(30.4%)	(4.3%)	(0.8%)

Japan Airlines Co Ltd JAL

Auditors: KPMG AZSA LLC

LOCATIONS

HQ: Japan Airlines Co Ltd JAL
    Nomura Real Estate Bldg., 2-4-11 Higashi-Shinagawa,
    Shinagawa-ku, Tokyo 140-8637
Phone: (81) 3 5460 3121
Web: www.jal.com

HISTORICAL FINANCIALS

Company Type: Public

Income Statement				FYE: March 31
	REVENUE ($ mil.)	**NET INCOME** ($ mil.)	**NET PROFIT MARGIN**	**EMPLOYEES**
03/20	13,000	492	3.8%	36,797
03/19	13,429	1,361	10.1%	35,002
03/18	13,026	1,275	9.8%	34,006
03/17	11,528	1,468	12.7%	32,753
03/16	11,902	58	0.5%	31,986
Annual Growth	2.2%	70.7%	—	3.6%

2020 Year-End Financials

Debt ratio: 0.0%	No. of shares (mil.): 337
Return on equity: 4.7%	Dividends
Cash ($ mil.): 3,032	Yield: 5.5%
Current ratio: 1.47	Payout: —
Long-term debt ($ mil.): 1,610	Market value ($ mil.): 3,080

	STOCK PRICE ($) FY Close	P/E High/Low		PER SHARE ($) Earnings	Dividends	Book Value
03/20	9.14	0	0	1.43	0.51	29.93
03/19	17.58	0	0	3.90	0.51	30.16
03/18	20.37	0	0	3.61	0.70	28.43
03/17	15.86	0	0	4.08	0.57	24.59
03/16	18.39	0	0	4.29	0.42	20.71
Annual Growth	(16.0%)	—	—	(23.9%)	4.7%	9.6%

Japan Post Bank Co Ltd

Auditors: KPMG AZSA LLC

LOCATIONS

HQ: Japan Post Bank Co Ltd
2-3-1 Otemachi, Chiyoda-ku, Tokyo 100-8793
Phone: (81) 3 3477 0111
Web: www.jp-bank.japanpost.jp

HISTORICAL FINANCIALS

Company Type: Public

Income Statement				FYE: March 31
	REVENUE ($ mil.)	NET INCOME ($ mil.)	NET PROFIT MARGIN	EMPLOYEES
03/20	16,577	2,518	15.2%	16,383
03/19	16,663	2,403	14.4%	17,006
03/18	19,257	3,322	17.3%	17,635
03/17	16,111	2,792	17.3%	12,965
03/16	16,627	2,894	17.4%	12,905
Annual Growth	(0.1%)	(3.4%)	—	6.1%

2020 Year-End Financials

Debt ratio: —
Return on equity: 2.6%
Cash ($ mil.): 517,871
Current ratio: —
Long-term debt ($ mil.): —

No. of shares (mil.): —
Dividends
Yield: —
Payout: —
Market value ($ mil.): —

Japan Post Holdings Co Ltd

Auditors: KPMG AZSA LLC

LOCATIONS

HQ: Japan Post Holdings Co Ltd
2-3-1 Otemachi, Chiyoda-Ku, Tokyo 100-8791
Phone: (81) 03 3477 0111
Web: www.japanpost.jp

HISTORICAL FINANCIALS

Company Type: Public

Income Statement				FYE: March 31
	REVENUE ($ mil.)	NET INCOME ($ mil.)	NET PROFIT MARGIN	EMPLOYEES
03/20	110,089	4,456	4.0%	400,001
03/19	115,356	4,329	3.8%	407,488
03/18	121,675	4,337	3.6%	411,078
03/17	119,192	(259)	—	415,801
03/16	126,962	3,793	3.0%	424,827
Annual Growth	(3.5%)	4.1%	—	(1.5%)

2020 Year-End Financials

Debt ratio: —
Return on equity: 3.9%
Cash ($ mil.): 566,415
Current ratio: —
Long-term debt ($ mil.): —

No. of shares (mil.): —
Dividends
Yield: —
Payout: —
Market value ($ mil.): —

Japan Post Insurance Co Ltd

Auditors: KPMG AZSA LLC

LOCATIONS

HQ: Japan Post Insurance Co Ltd
3-1, Otemachi 2chome, Chiyoda-ku, Tokyo 100-8798
Phone: (81) 3 3477 2383
Web: www.jp-life.japanpost.jp

HISTORICAL FINANCIALS

Company Type: Public

Income Statement				FYE: March 31
	REVENUE ($ mil.)	NET INCOME ($ mil.)	NET PROFIT MARGIN	EMPLOYEES
03/20	65,291	1,388	2.1%	10,802
03/19	70,167	1,087	1.6%	10,983
03/18	73,896	983	1.3%	11,009
03/17	76,015	792	1.0%	11,036
03/16	85,452	756	0.9%	11,055
Annual Growth	(6.5%)	16.4%	—	(0.6%)

2020 Year-End Financials

Debt ratio: 0.0%
Return on equity: 7.4%
Cash ($ mil.): 41,145
Current ratio: —
Long-term debt ($ mil.): 921

No. of shares (mil.): 562
Dividends
Yield: —
Payout: —
Market value ($ mil.): —

Japan Tobacco Inc.

Japan Tobacco (JT) is the largest cigarette maker in Japan and among the largest in the world. The company controls around 60% of Japan's cigarette market — one of the largest in the world — driven by its MEVIUS brand followed by Winston and Seven Stars among others. Japan Tobacco International handles JT's business outside Japan where it has operations in more than 70 countries and sales in more than 130. Japan Tobacco owns or has international rights to such brands as Winston Camel MEVIUS and LD. The company also has holdings in the fast-growing pharmaceutical and processed food businesses. JT gets nearly two-thirds of its revenue from international markets.

Operations

Japan Tobacco's international business JT International generates around 60% of Japan Tobacco's revenue. It sells cigarettes under brands including Winston Camel and Natural American Spirit; loose tobacco for rolling; snus under the brand Nordic Snus; and vapes under the Logic and Ploom brands.

In Japan JT is the market leader in tobacco products with a 60% market share. Its primary brands are MEVIUS Winston and Seven Stars. Sales of tobacco products in Japan account for roughly 30% of JT's total sales.

Beyond tobacco the company is active in processed food and pharmaceuticals. TableMark Co. Ltd generates more than 5% of JT's sales and produces frozen and ambient processed food including frozen noodles frozen and cooked rice bread and seasoning. In the pharmaceutical business (another 5%) JT researches and develops treatments for metabolic diseases viral infections and autoimmune/inflammatory diseases. Subsidiary Torii Pharmaceutical Co handles its manufacturing sales and promotion in Japan.

Geographic Reach

Japan Tobacco's head office is in Tokyo. International subsidiary Japan Tobacco International (JTI) is headquartered in Geneva Switzerland. International markets include Europe Asia Africa Middle East and the Americas.

The company's cigarettes and other products are manufactured at more than 40 factories spanning all major continents including six in Japan. The International market generates nearly two-thirds of revenue and the remaining comes from Japan.

Sales and Marketing

Depending on the market JT sells its products through various channels such as supermarkets convenience stores street and train station kiosks and independent retailers.

The Megapolis Group in Russia is one of JTI's biggest customers representing more than 10% of its revenue in the international segment.

Financial Performance

Note: Growth rates may differ after conversion to US Dollars.

Revenue decreased Â 40.3 billion or 2% year-on-year to Â 2.2 trillion mainly due to lower revenue in the Japanese domestic tobacco business pharmaceutical business and processed food business. In the international tobacco business the solid performance driven by price/mix contribution was offset by currency headwinds.

Cash held by the company by the end of 2019 was Â 357.2 billion. Cash provided by operations was Â 540.4 billion while cash used for investing and financing activities were Â 123.6 billion and Â 333.8 billion respectively. Main use for cash was dividends paid to owners of the parent company.

Strategy

The tobacco business has been focusing on sustainable profit growth consistently playing a pivotal role in JT Group's profit growth. Its role continues to be of paramount importance for the achievement of mid to high single-digit adjusted operating profit growth at constant currency which is its main target. In light of the evolving operating environment the company has been enhancing its focus on the sustainability of the profit growth generated by the tobacco business. Additionally in order to strengthen and speed up the decision-making process Japan Tobacco has streamlined the management structure as demonstrated by its Group CEO Masamichi Terabatake directly heading the tobacco business.

Company Background

Japan Tobacco is the result of the liberalization of the Japanese tobacco market in the mid-1980s. The government department that held a monopoly on the sale of tobacco products in Japan from 1898 was converted into a joint stock company and foreign companies were allowed to compete in the Japanese marketplace. The company changed significantly in the late 90s with the acquisition of R. J. Reynolds' non-US tobacco business which included the brands Camel Winston and others. Around that time it also entered the pharmaceutical and processed foods business.

EXECUTIVES

President and CEO, Thomas A. (Tom) McCoy
Regional President The Americas, Michel Poirier
Regional President Asia Pacific, Stefan Fitz, age 54
EVP Business Development Corporate Affairs and Corporate Communications, Eddy Pirard, age 58

Regional President Middle East Near East Africa
 Turkey and Worldwide Duty Free, Fadoul Pekhazis
Deputy CEO; EVP Emerging Products and
 Corporate Strategy, Masamichi Terabatake
SVP Information Technology and CFO, Roland
 Kostantos
Regional President Central Europe, Jorge da Motta
SVP Global Leaf, Paul Neumann
Regional President CIS+, Kevin Tomlinson
Regional President Western Europe, Vassilis Vovos
Chairman, Yasutake Tango
Auditors: Deloitte Touche Tohmatsu LLC

LOCATIONS

HQ: Japan Tobacco Inc.
 2-2-1 Toranomon, Minato-ku, Tokyo 105-8422
Phone: (81) 3 3582 3111   Fax: (81) 3 5572 1441
Web: www.jti.co.jp

PRODUCTS/OPERATIONS

2018 Sales

	% of total
International tobacco	59
Japanese domestic tobacco	28
Processed food	7
Pharmaceutical	6
Total	**100**

COMPETITORS

Ajinomoto	Nippon Suisan Kaisha
Altadis	Nisshin Seifun Group
Altria	Philip Morris
British American	International
Tobacco	Reemtsma
Imperial Brands	Cigarettenfabriken
Nestlé	Vector Group

HISTORICAL FINANCIALS

Company Type: Public

Income Statement   FYE: December 31

	REVENUE ($ mil.)	NET INCOME ($ mil.)	NET PROFIT MARGIN	EMPLOYEES
12/19	20,039	3,207	16.0%	69,091
12/18	20,150	3,507	17.4%	70,586
12/17	19,016	3,487	18.3%	64,707
12/16	18,324	3,605	19.7%	52,571
12/15	18,714	4,034	21.6%	52,343
Annual Growth	**1.7%**	**(5.6%)**	—	**7.2%**

2019 Year-End Financials

Debt ratio: 0.1%
Return on equity: 13.1%
Cash ($ mil.): 3,289
Current ratio: 1.28
Long-term debt ($ mil.): 6,358

No. of shares (mil.): 1,773
Dividends
 Yield: 6.3%
 Payout: 39.3%
Market value ($ mil.): 19,725

	STOCK PRICE ($) FY Close	P/E High/Low		PER SHARE ($) Earnings	Dividends	Book Value
12/19	11.12	0	0	1.80	0.70	13.83
12/18	11.75	0	0	1.96	0.67	13.35
12/17	16.07	0	0	1.95	0.61	13.70
12/16	16.34	0	0	2.01	0.53	11.73
12/15	18.58	0	0	2.25	0.43	11.37
Annual Growth	**(12.0%)**	—	—	**(5.3%)**	**13.0%**	**5.0%**

Jardine Cycle & Carriage Ltd

EXECUTIVES

President Director PT Astra International Tbk
 (Indonesia), Prijono Sugiarto
Director Operations Cycle & Carriage Bintang
 Berhad (Malaysia), Ramasamy Devaraju
Group Managing Director, Alexander Newbigging
Group Finance Director, Adrian Teng
Managing Director Singapore Motor Operations,
 Eric Chan
President Director PT Tunas Ridean Tbk
 (Indonesia), Rico Setiawan
Chairman Truong Hai Auto Corporation
 (Vietnam), Tran Ba Duong
Chairman Refrigeration Electrical Engineering
 Corporation (Vietnam), Thi Mai Thanh Nguyen
Chairman Siam City Cement Public Company
 Limited (Thailand), Veraphan Teepsuwan
General Manager Myanmar Operations, Kee Min
 Chin
Auditors: PricewaterhouseCoopers LLP

LOCATIONS

HQ: Jardine Cycle & Carriage Ltd
 239 Alexandra Road, 159930
Phone: (65) 6473 3122   Fax: (65) 6475 7088
Web: www.jcclgroup.com

PRODUCTS/OPERATIONS

2015 Sales

	% of total
Sale of goods	72
Rendering of services	21
Financial services	7
Total	**100**

2015 Sales

	% of total
Indonesia	87
Others	13
Total	**100**

2015 Sales

	% of total
Astra	87
Direct motor interest	13
Total	**100**

Selected Operations

Astra International (50.1% Indonesia conglomerate with
 auto finance industrial agriculture infrastructure
 logistics and technology holdings)
Cycle & Carriage Automobile Myanmar (60% vehicle
 repair)
Cycle & Carriage Bintang (59% Malaysia vehicle retail
 and distribution)
Singapore Motors (retail and distribution)
Truong Hai Auto Corporation (32% Vietnam)
Tunas Ridean (44% Indonesia vehicle retailer)

COMPETITORS

Borneo Motors	Toyota Motor Thailand

HISTORICAL FINANCIALS

Company Type: Public

Income Statement   FYE: December 31

	REVENUE ($ mil.)	NET INCOME ($ mil.)	NET PROFIT MARGIN	EMPLOYEES
12/19	18,591	881	4.7%	250,000
12/18	18,991	419	2.2%	250,000
12/17	17,701	811	4.6%	250,000
12/16	15,764	701	4.5%	240,000
12/15	15,718	688	4.4%	250,000
Annual Growth	**4.3%**	**6.4%**	—	**0.0%**

2019 Year-End Financials

Debt ratio: 28.1%
Return on equity: 13.5%
Cash ($ mil.): 1,843
Current ratio: 1.12
Long-term debt ($ mil.): 3,620

No. of shares (mil.): 395
Dividends
 Yield: —
 Payout: 39.0%
Market value ($ mil.): —

Jardine Matheson Holdings Ltd.

Jardine Matheson Holdings (JMH) which gov-
erns the many interests of its affiliate Jardine
Strategic Holdings is a diversified Asian-based
group founded in China in 1832. Comprised with
a broad portfolio of market-leading businesses
which represent a combination of cash generating
activities and long-term property assets that are
closely aligned to the increasingly prosperous consumers of the region. JMH's subsidiaries include
Jardine Pacific and Jardine Motors Group Jardine
Cycle & Carriage Asian supermarket operator
Dairy Farm and Hongkong Land which owns
prime real estate in Hong Kong. Other businesses
include financial services hotels (Mandarin Oriental) construction mining and transport services.
Members of the Keswick family descendants of the
co-founder William Jardine control JMH and Jardine Strategic through a complex ownership structure.

Operations
Jardine Matheson operates it business into seven
reportable segment Astra Dairy Farm Jardine Motors Jardine Pacific Hongkong Land Mandarin Oriental and Jardine Cycle & Carriage.

Astra generates the higher revenue with more
than 40% of sales it offers automotive financial
services heavy equipment mining construction and
energy agribusiness infrastructure and logistics IT
and Property. With more than 230 subsidiaries
associated companies and other entities.

Dairy Farm segment accounts for nearly 30%
of sales operates under well-known brands across
five divisions being food (including Grocery Retail
and Convenience Stores) health and beauty home
furnishings restaurants and other retailing.

Jardine Motors with nearly 15% of sales is currently comprised of asian automotive businesses
including Zung Fu Motors Group in the Chinese
mainland Cycle & Carriage in Singapore Malaysia
and Myanmar and Tunas Ridean in Indonesia.

Jardine Pacific (engineering and construction
aviation and transport services restaurants and IT.)
and Hongkong Land (property investment management and development with offices in Hong
Kong Singapore Beijing Jakarta and other major
asian cities) both accounts for about 5% of sales.
Jardine Cycle & Carriage (Singapore-listed invest-

ment holding company) and Mandarin Oriental (hotel investment with about 35 hotels and seven residences in more than 20 countries and territories) accounts for the rest.

Geographic Reach

With its headquarters in Hongkong Jardine Matheson also operates in more than 20 countries such as Singapore Indonesia Cambodia Malaysia Vietnam Thailand Myanmar UK and London. They operate mainly in Greater China and Southeast Asia. Greater China and Southeast Asia generates more than 30% and nearly 60% of sales respectively. UK and other regions accounts for the rest.

Sales and Marketing

Jardine Matheson Holdings Limited provides a wide range of businesses including motor vehicles and related operations property investment and development food retailing health and beauty home furnishings engineering and construction transport services restaurants luxury hotels financial services heavy equipment mining energy and agribusiness. Jardine Matheson distributes its businesses by their subsidiaries and affiliate companies. For fiscal 2019 the company spend $4.6 billion in selling and marketing.

Strategy

The company is focused on growing its business in the fastest growing consumer market in the world Greater China and Southeast Asia. Their Hong Kong Land diversified its investment properties with acquisition of a large predominantly commercial mixed-use site in a prime waterside location in Shanghai. It also continues to consolidate its presence in the Chinese mainland in cities where it already has a presence with a total of five new residential development sites secured in 2019.

The company anticipates that a number of its businesses will face increasing changes both in technology and consumer behaviors. In order to ensure that all its businesses are well placed to benefit from these changes and deliver future growth they have made it a priority to invest in and promote innovation the development of talent and the adoption of sustainable business practices.

An important part of Jardine Matheson's strategy is to invest for growth and to build significant stakes in strong companies. The company aims to be the partner of choice for associates or joint ventures and to grow those businesses over time by developing strong relationships which add value through their role as a supportive shareholder to entrepreneurs and leading management teams.

Company Background

Jardine Matheson & Co (JM & Co) was founded in Canton in July 1832 by Scots William Jardine and James Matheson. Jardine Matheson sent its first private shipments of tea to England in 1834. Following years after that JM & Co completed the move of its main office to Hong Kong and opened its office in Shanghai. More offices were subsequently opened in Canton Amoy and Foochow.

In the 1860s JM & Co's trading activities were enhanced by the expansion of its shipping banking and insurance interests. They moved its main office from East Point to Central Hong Kong in 1864.

JM & Co constructed the first railway line in China from Shanghai to Woosung in 1876.

By the 1910s the heart of the business was in Shanghai and from 1912 onwards the city was regarded as the Firm's headquarters. The Firm began to expand into new products and services to meet the needs of the growing industrialization of China.

EXECUTIVES

Managing Director Jardine Matheson Holdings Limited and Chairman and Managing Director Jardine Matheson Limited, Ben Keswick

Chairman Matheson & Co. and Deputy Chairman Jardine Lloyd Thompson, Adam Keswick
Chairman Jardine Matheson (China) and Director, David Hsu
Deputy Managing Director Jardine Matheson Holdings Limited and Deputy Chairman and Deputy Managing Director Jardine Matheson Limited, Y.K. Pang
Group Finance Director, John Witt
Chairman, Henry Keswick
Auditors: PricewaterhouseCoopers LLP

LOCATIONS

HQ: Jardine Matheson Holdings Ltd.
    48th Floor, Jardine House, G.P.O. Box 70,
Phone: (852) 2843 8288   Fax: (441) 292 4072
Web: www.jardines.com

2016 sales

	$ mil.	% of total
Southeast Asia	21,612	58
Greater China	12,495	34
UK	2,665	7
Other regions	279	1
Total	**37,051**	**100**

PRODUCTS/OPERATIONS

2016 Revenues

	$ mil.	% of total
Astra (automotive financial services agribusiness heavy equipment & other)		
13,610	37	
Dairy Farm	11,201	30
Jardine Motors Group	5,197	14
Jardine Pacific	2,356	6
Jardine Cycle & Carriage	2,154	6
Hongkong Land	1,994	5
Mandarin Oriental	597	2
Adjustment	(58)	-
Total	**37,051**	**100**

2016 Revenues

	$ mil.	% of total
Motor vehicles	13,610	37
Retail and restaurants	11,201	30
Engineering construction and mining contracting	5,197	14
Property	1,989	5
Insurance broking and financial services	1,357	4
Hotels	596	2
Others	3,013	8
Total	**37,051**	**100**

Selected Major Subsidiaries and Affiliates

Astra International (automobile distribution and manufacturing financial and IT services heavy machinery)
Cycle & Carriage Ltd (69% motor trading Singapore)
Dairy Farm International Holdings Ltd (78%; supermarkets hypermarkets health and beauty and home furnishings stores convenience stores and restaurants)
Honkong Land Holdings Ltd (50% real estate)
Jardine Lloyd Thompson plc (32% insurance and brokerage UK)
Jardine Motors Group Holdings Ltd. (auto distribution sales and service; China Hong Kong Macao and the UK)
Jardine Pacific Holdings Ltd. (transport services engineering and construction restaurants and IT services)
Jardine Strategic Holdings Ltd. (81% holding company)
Mandarin Oriental International Ltd. (74% hotels)

COMPETITORS

Accor	Kumagai Gumi
CK Hutchison	Marriott
Carrefour	Marubeni
Chevalier	McDonald's
China Resources Beer	Samsung Group
Daiei	Seiyu
HSBC	Sime Darby
Hopewell Holdings	Swire Pacific
Hyatt	Tesco
ITOCHU	

HISTORICAL FINANCIALS

Company Type: Public

Income Statement   FYE: December 31

	REVENUE ($ mil.)	NET INCOME ($ mil.)	NET PROFIT MARGIN	EMPLOYEES
12/19	40,922	2,838	6.9%	464,000
12/18	42,527	1,732	4.1%	469,000
12/17	39,456	3,785	9.6%	443,700
12/16	37,051	2,503	6.8%	0
12/15	37,007	1,797	4.9%	440,000
Annual Growth	2.5%	12.1%	—	1.3%

2019 Year-End Financials

Debt ratio: 15.7%
Return on equity: 10.0%
Cash ($ mil.): 7,183
Current ratio: 1.21
Long-term debt ($ mil.): 8,673

No. of shares (mil.): 733
Dividends
    Yield: 2.9%
    Payout: 21.4%
Market value ($ mil.): 40,498

	STOCK PRICE ($) FY Close	P/E High/Low		PER SHARE ($) Earnings	Dividends	Book Value
12/19	55.25	9	7	7.56	1.62	41.41
12/18	69.05	15	12	4.59	1.52	35.74
12/17	60.74	7	6	10.04	1.42	83.07
12/16	55.47	9	7	6.68	1.35	70.78
12/15	48.28	14	9	4.81	1.35	65.19
Annual Growth (10.7%)	3.4%	—	—	12.0%	4.6%	

Jardine Strategic Holdings Ltd (Bermuda)

EXECUTIVES

Chairman and Managing Director, Ben Keswick
Deputy Chairman and Deputy Managing Director, Y. K. Pang
Group Finance Director, John R. Witt
Chairman, Henry Keswick
Auditors: PricewaterhouseCoopers LLP

LOCATIONS

HQ: Jardine Strategic Holdings Ltd (Bermuda)
    Jardine House, 33-35 Reid Street, Hamilton
Phone:
Web: www.jardines.com

PRODUCTS/OPERATIONS

2015 Sales

	% of total
Astra	47
Dairy Farm	38
Hong-Kong Land	6
Jardine Cycle & Carriage	7
Mandarin Oriental	2
Intersegment transaction	0
Total	**100**

2015 Sales

	% of total
Motor Vehicles	31
Retail	38
Mining	10
Property and hotels	9
Engineering and Construction	3
Agribusiness	3
Financial Services	4
Logistics and IT Services	2
Resturants	0
Total	**100**

2015 Sales

	% of total
Southeast Asia	72
Greater China	27
United Kingdom	0
Rest of World	1
Total	**100**

Subsidiaries

Astra International
Dairy Farm
Hongkong Land
Jardine Cycle & Carriage
Jardine Lloyd Thompson
Jardine Matheson
Jardine Motors
Jardine Pacific
Mandarin Oriental

COMPETITORS

Accor	Hopewell Holdings
Ahold Delhaize	Hyatt
China Resources Beer	ITOCHU
Continental Automotive	Marriott
Group	Marubeni
Daiei	McDonald's
HSBC	Swire Pacific

HISTORICAL FINANCIALS

Company Type: Public

Income Statement   FYE: December 31

	REVENUE ($ mil.)	NET INCOME ($ mil.)	NET PROFIT MARGIN	EMPLOYEES
12/19	32,665	2,178	6.7%	0
12/18	34,094	1,836	5.4%	0
12/17	31,556	4,119	13.1%	0
12/16	29,552	2,741	9.3%	0
12/15	29,391	1,953	6.6%	0
Annual Growth	**2.7%**	**2.8%**	**—**	**—**

2019 Year-End Financials

Debt ratio: 15.6%
Return on equity: 6.4%
Cash ($ mil.): 5,602
Current ratio: 1.16
Long-term debt ($ mil.): 8,673

No. of shares (mil.): 167
Dividends
Yield: 0.9%
Payout: 3.9%
Market value ($ mil.): 2,562

	STOCK PRICE ($) FY Close	P/E High/Low		Earnings	PER SHARE ($) Dividends	Book Value
12/19	15.34	5	4	3.86	0.15	214.11
12/18	18.48	6	5	3.23	0.14	181.16
12/17	19.63	3	2	7.11	0.13	170.66
12/16	16.80	4	3	4.67	0.13	143.64
12/15	13.61	6	4	3.25	0.12	126.95
Annual Growth	**3.0%**	**—**	**—**	**4.4%**	**5.8%**	**14.0%**

JBS SA

Auditors: Grant Thornton Auditores Independentes

LOCATIONS

HQ: JBS SA
Avenida Marginal Direita do Tiete, 500, Vila Jaguara,
Sao Paulo 05118-100
Phone: (55) 11 3144 4000   **Fax:** (55) 11 3144 4279
Web: www.jbs.com.br

HISTORICAL FINANCIALS

Company Type: Public

Income Statement   FYE: December 31

	REVENUE ($ mil.)	NET INCOME ($ mil.)	NET PROFIT MARGIN	EMPLOYEES
12/19	50,880	1,509	3.0%	242,000
12/18	46,811	6	0.0%	230,000
12/17	49,255	161	0.3%	235,000
12/16	52,349	115	0.2%	237,061
12/15	41,133	1,171	2.8%	230,000
Annual Growth	**5.5%**	**6.5%**	**—**	**1.3%**

2019 Year-End Financials

Debt ratio: 10.4%
Return on equity: 21.9%
Cash ($ mil.): 2,496
Current ratio: 1.47
Long-term debt ($ mil.): 12,674

No. of shares (mil.): —
Dividends
Yield: 0.0%
Payout: 0.1%
Market value ($ mil.): —

	STOCK PRICE ($) FY Close	P/E High/Low		Earnings	PER SHARE ($) Dividends	Book Value
12/19	12.93	7	3	0.57	0.00	2.70
12/18	5.93	636	423	0.00	0.02	2.48
12/17	5.91	40	19	0.06	0.02	2.57
12/16	7.00	58	37	0.04	0.24	2.56
12/15	6.20	6	3	0.40	0.10	2.45
Annual Growth	**20.2%**	**—**	**—**	**8.9%**	**(67.9%)**	**2.5%**

JD.com, Inc.

Auditors: Deloitte Touche Tohmatsu Certified Public Accountants LLP

LOCATIONS

HQ: JD.com, Inc.
20th Floor, Building A, No. 18 Kechuang 11 Street,
Daxing District, Beijing 101111
Phone: (86) 10 8911 8888
Web: www.jd.com

HISTORICAL FINANCIALS

Company Type: Public

Income Statement   FYE: December 31

	REVENUE ($ mil.)	NET INCOME ($ mil.)	NET PROFIT MARGIN	EMPLOYEES
12/19	82,907	1,751	2.1%	227,730
12/18	67,170	(362)	—	178,927
12/17	55,679	(23)	—	157,831
12/16	37,459	(548)	—	120,622
12/15	27,913	(1,443)	—	105,963
Annual Growth	**31.3%**	**—**	**—**	**21.1%**

2019 Year-End Financials

Debt ratio: 0.5%
Return on equity: 17.2%
Cash ($ mil.): 5,735
Current ratio: 0.99
Long-term debt ($ mil.): 1,444

No. of shares (mil.): —
Dividends
Yield: —
Payout: —
Market value ($ mil.): —

	STOCK PRICE ($) FY Close	P/E High/Low		Earnings	PER SHARE ($) Dividends	Book Value
12/19	35.23	9	5	0.59	0.00	4.02
12/18	20.93	—	—	(0.13)	0.00	3.00
12/17	41.42	—	—	(0.01)	0.00	2.80
12/16	25.44	—	—	(0.20)	0.00	1.72
12/15	32.27	—	—	(0.53)	0.00	1.72
Annual Growth	**2.2%**			**—**		**23.8%**

Jeronimo Martins S.G.P.S. SA

Jer "nimo Martins (JM) is a major Portuguese retailer with more than 4500 stores dispersed across Portugal Poland and Colombia. In Portugal its Pingo Doce chain is a leading supermarket with more than 455 stores while Recheio is a major player in the Cash & Carry sector. With more than 3000 stores Biedronka is Poland's biggest food retailer while in Colombia JM operates a network of more than 615 Ara-branded neighborhood stores. JM's specialized retail division consists of Hebe drugstores in Poland as well as Jeronymo coffee shops and Hussel confectioners in Portugal. JM generate about 70% of its sales from Poland.

Operations

The Biedronka business in Poland accounts for more than 65% of Jer "nimo Martins' total sales. Pingo Doce generates nearly 25% Recheio 5% and Ara business in Colombia generate the rest.

Geographic Reach

Jer "nimo Martins is headquartered in Portugal and its main operations are in Portugal Poland and Colombia. It supplies its store based from more than 15 distribution centers. JM generate about 70% of its revenue from Poland followed by Portugal which brings up more than 25% and the rest comes from Colombia.

Sales and Marketing

Jer "nimo Martins' serves more than five million customers while the Hebe drugstore has more than 3.7 million members.

The company's advertising costs for the years 2019 and 2018 were ?110 million and ?111 million respectively.

Financial Performance

Note: Growth rates may differ after conversion to US Dollars.

Jer "nimo Martins has achieved continuous revenue growth for the last five years with a recorded 36% increase from 2015 to 2019. Net income was fluctuating for the last five years recording its highest in 2016 and its lowest in 2015.

Revenue in 2019 was ?18.6 billion 8% less more than ?17.3 billion in the previous year. This resulted from an increase in revenue among all the company's segments.

Net income was ?390 million ?43 million less than in the previous year.

Cash and cash equivalents at the end of the year were ?929.3 million 70% higher compared to ?546 million the previous year. Cash provided by operating activities was ?1.5 billion. Investing activities used ?567 million primarily for acquisition of tangible and intangible assets while financing activities used ?549.5 million primarily for payment of leases and dividends.

Strategy

Jer "nimo Martins adopts continuous and sustainable value creation and growth.

The company's strategic vision is based on promoting profitable and sustainable growth through guiding principles of leadership responsibility and independence. Within this context when doing business the company has two core focuses: consumer whose characteristics needs and preferences require a progressive adjustment and reinforcement of the value proposition as well as a continuous and significant contribution towards the wellbeing of the communities surrounding the stores; and employee providing him or her with skills instruments and working conditions to be able to simultaneously be the agent for promoting profitable growth through satisfied consumers and also a decisive point of contact in the company for the surrounding communities.

EXECUTIVES

Chairman and CEO, Pedro Soares dos Santos

LOCATIONS

HQ: Jeronimo Martins S.G.P.S. SA
  Rua Actor Antonio Silva, n.o7, Lisboa 1649-033
Phone: (351) 21 753 20 00   **Fax:** (351) 21 752 61 74
Web: www.jeronimomartins.com

PRODUCTS/OPERATIONS

2017 Sales

	% of total
Poland Retail	68
Portugal Retail	25
Portugal Cash & Carry	6
Adjustments (2)	
Total	**100**

COMPETITORS

Auchan	METRO AG
Carrefour	REWE
E.Leclerc	Sonae
ITM Entreprises	Tesco
Lidl	

HISTORICAL FINANCIALS

Company Type: Public

Income Statement

FYE: December 31

	REVENUE ($ mil.)	NET INCOME ($ mil.)	NET PROFIT MARGIN	EMPLOYEES
12/19	20,926	437	2.1%	115,428
12/18	19,853	459	2.3%	108,560
12/17	19,511	461	2.4%	104,203
12/16	15,438	626	4.1%	96,233
12/15	14,952	363	2.4%	89,027
Annual Growth	**8.8%**	**4.8%**	—	**6.7%**

2019 Year-End Financials

Debt ratio: 8.4%
Return on equity: 20.7%
Cash ($ mil.): 1,043
Current ratio: 0.48
Long-term debt ($ mil.): 346

No. of shares (mil.): 628
Dividends
  Yield: 0.0%
  Payout: 104.7%
Market value ($ mil.): 20,837

	STOCK PRICE ($) FY Close	P/E High/Low	PER SHARE ($) Earnings	Dividends	Book Value
12/19	33.16	57 38	0.70	0.73	3.53
12/18	23.02	63 37	0.73	1.45	3.24
12/17	38.75	69 60	0.74	1.46	3.41
12/16	31.15	38 26	1.00	0.56	2.92
12/15	26.34	56 32	0.58	1.35	2.33
Annual Growth	**5.9%**	—	—	**4.8%(14.2%)**	**11.0%**

JFE Holdings Inc

JFE Holdings has an iron will unmatched in Japan and much of the rest of the world. The "J" in JFE stands for Japan; "F" is for Fe the chemical symbol for iron; and "E" stands for engineering. JFE Holdings' steel business unit JFE Steel accounts for more than 60% of total sales and manufactures steel products such as bars pipes steel frames tubes and stainless steel for the automotive construction and petroleum industries. JFE is among the world's largest steel companies ranking behind ArcelorMittal Japan's Nippon Steel & Sumitomo Metal and China's Hebei Iron and Steel and Baosteel.

Operations

JFE's engineering unit makes designs and builds facilities such as power generation & electricity water purification plants steelworks structures and bridges and steel structures used in the energy environmental and steel structural sectors. JFE's steel making unit engage in total steel-making process. JFE Holdings operates in three business Steel Business which generate for about 65% of company's revenue Engineering business (about 10%) and Trading business (about 25%).

Geographic Reach

While most of its steel production facilities are in Japan JFE's reach is global and it has offices in about 20 other countries. Its corporate headquarters Is located in Tokyo.

Financial Performance

The company's revenue after falling in 2016 and 2017 redeemed itself by rising in 2018 and 2019.

In 2019 the company's revenue grew 7% from Å 3.6 trillion to Å 3.9 trillion.

Net income increased 67% from Å 97.7 billion in 2018 to Å 163.5 billion in 2019.

The company's cash equivalent at the end of 2019 was at Å 75.1 billion. Operating activities generated Å 328.4 billion while investing and financing activities used Å 216.5 billion and Å 99.8 billion respectively.

Strategy

JFE Steel leverages world-class technologies and know-how to produce a wide range of products based on its "Only One Number One" strategy of focusing on unique and best-in-class products.

In order to respond to dramatic global changes with flexibility and speed JFE aims to be a dynamic company where employees can energetically take on new challenges. Technologies are being passed down to younger workers through the application of AI and IoT which is facilitating the transfer of on-site skills and expertise one of the sources of the company's strength in manufacturing.

As part of its focus in FY2019 the company will continue to develop manufacturing bases for steelworks and other works in Japan. Through measures to increase capabilities and optimize performance centering around West Japan Works the company will drastically strengthen its manufacturing capabilities.

Mergers and Acquisitions

In 2019 major Japanese steel-maker JFE Steel Corp. has acquired about 50 percent stake in a unit of China's top steel-maker China BiaoWu Steel Group Corp. and will start making high-grade specialty bar steel for Japanese automakers in China. JFE will inject about 690 million yuan into Baosteel Special Steel Shaoguan Co. a specialty bar steel-maker under BaoWu to help Japanese automakers with local procurement of high-grade specialty bar steel in the world's largest automotive market.

EXECUTIVES

President JFE Engineering, Sumiyuki Kishimoto
President and CEO, Eiji Hayashida
President and CEO JFE Shoji Trade Corporation, Tsutomu Yajima
EVP and CFO, Shinichi Okada
Auditors: Ernst & Young ShinNihon LLC

LOCATIONS

HQ: JFE Holdings Inc
  2-2-3 Uchisaiwai-cho, Chiyoda-ku, Tokyo 100-0011
Phone: (81) 3 3597 4321
Web: www.jfe-holdings.co.jp

PRODUCTS/OPERATIONS

2015 Sales

	% of total
Steel	53
Engineering	38
Trading	9
Adjustment	-
Total	**100**

Selected Products

Electrical Steel
Energy
Environment
Iron Powders
Pipes and Tubes
Plates
Shapes
Sheets
Slag
Stainless
Steel Bars and Wire Rods
Steel Structure
Titanium

COMPETITORS

ArcelorMittal
Baosteel
BlueScope Steel
Kobe Steel
Nippon Steel & Sumitomo Metal Corporation
Nippon Yakin
Nisshin Steel
Severstal
Shougang Corp.
United States Steel

HISTORICAL FINANCIALS

Company Type: Public

Income Statement

FYE: March 31

	REVENUE ($ mil.)	NET INCOME ($ mil.)	NET PROFIT MARGIN	EMPLOYEES
03/20	34,359	(1,821)		64,009
03/19	34,978	1,476	4.2%	62,083
03/18	34,642	1,362	3.9%	61,234
03/17	29,595	607	2.1%	60,439
03/16	30,559	299	1.0%	59,460
Annual Growth	**3.0%**	—	—	**1.9%**

2020 Year-End Financials

Debt ratio: 0.3%
Return on equity: (-11.1%)
Cash ($ mil.): 798
Current ratio: 1.47
Long-term debt ($ mil.): 13,245

No. of shares (mil.): 576
Dividends
  Yield: —
  Payout: —
Market value ($ mil.): —

Jiangxi Copper Co., Ltd.

EXECUTIVES

Chairman, Baomin Li
Auditors: Deloitte Touche Tohmatsu Certified Public
   Accountants LLP

LOCATIONS

HQ: Jiangxi Copper Co., Ltd.
   7666 Changdong Avenue, High and New Technology
   Development Zone, Nanchang, Jiangxi Province
   330096
Phone: (86) 791 82710117   **Fax:** (86) 791 82710114
Web: www.jxcc.com

Annual Sales

	$ mil.	% of total
China Mainland	24,686	81
Hong Kong	3,052	10
Other	2,592	8
Total	**30,331**	**100**

Exchange Rate CNY to USD: 6.760195

COMPETITORS

Mitsubishi Materials
Mitsui Mining and
   Smelting
Sumitomo Metal Mining
Tongling Nonferrous
   Metals

Yunnan Copper Industry
   (Group) Co. Ltd.
Zijin Mining

HISTORICAL FINANCIALS

Company Type: Public

Income Statement				FYE: December 31
	REVENUE ($ mil.)	NET INCOME ($ mil.)	NET PROFIT MARGIN	EMPLOYEES
12/19	34,543	354	1.0%	0
12/18	31,299	355	1.1%	0
12/17	31,509	246	0.8%	0
12/16	29,133	113	0.4%	0
12/15	28,520	106	0.4%	20,873
Annual Growth	**4.9%**	**35.2%**	—	—

2019 Year-End Financials

Debt ratio: 5.4%
Return on equity: 4.8%
Cash ($ mil.): 4,275
Current ratio: 1.23
Long-term debt ($ mil.): 827

No. of shares (mil.): —
Dividends
   Yield: 1.8%
   Payout: —
Market value ($ mil.): —

Johnson Controls International plc

Auditors: PricewaterhouseCoopers LLP

LOCATIONS

HQ: Johnson Controls International plc
   One Albert Quay, Cork T12 X8N6
Phone: (353) 21 423 5000
Web: www.johnsoncontrols.com

HISTORICAL FINANCIALS

Company Type: Public

Income Statement				FYE: September 30
	REVENUE ($ mil.)	NET INCOME ($ mil.)	NET PROFIT MARGIN	EMPLOYEES
09/20	22,317	631	2.8%	97,000
09/19	23,968	5,674	23.7%	104,000
09/18	31,400	2,162	6.9%	122,000
09/17	30,172	1,611	5.3%	121,000
09/16	37,674	(868)	—	209,000
Annual Growth	**(12.3%)**	—	—	**(17.5%)**

2020 Year-End Financials

Debt ratio: 19.1%
Return on equity: 3.3%
Cash ($ mil.): 1,951
Current ratio: 1.22
Long-term debt ($ mil.): 7,526

No. of shares (mil.): 726
Dividends
   Yield: 2.5%
   Payout: 92.0%
Market value ($ mil.): —

Johnson Matthey Plc (United Kingdom)

Johnson Matthey is truly a golden oldie. The company founded in 1817 is a leader in the refining and distribution of gold silver and platinum group metals. Johnson Matthey's Emission Control Technologies division produces emission control products and stationary emissions control fuel cells and process catalysts; and Process Technologies division is a global supplier of catalysts and licensing technologies. Its Chemicals processes makes base and precious metals catalysts. The Pharmaceutical products and services include active pharmaceutical ingredients (API) sold to pharmaceuticals manufacturers. Its largest geographic sales is in United Kingdom.

Operations

Johnson Matthey operates through different segments:

Clean air (more than 40%) is catalysts for cars other light duty vehicles trucks buses and non-road equipment.

Efficient Natural Resources generates around 55% is a specialty catalyst and additives process technology licenses.

Health generates less than 5 % of total revenue manufactures active pharmaceutical ingredients.

New Markets generates the remainder of the total revenue.

Geographic Reach

London-based Johnson Matthey operates in 30countries on six continents. Europe accounted more than 45% of its revenue in 2020 of which more than 20% was contributed by the UK. The Asia accounted for around 25% and US about 20%.

Sales and Marketing

The company is targeting industries such as environmental automotive chemical pharmaceutical/medical and recycling.

Financial Performance

The company's revenue has been fluctuating for the last five years with an overall growth of 36% between 2015 and 2019.

Revenue for the year was Â 14.6 billion a 36% increase from the previous year. All of the company's segments contributed to this growth except Health.

The company's profit for the year was Â 255 million a 38% decrease from the previous year. The decline was primarily due to a higher cost of sales for the year.

The company's cash for the year ended 2020 was Â 273 million a 28% decline from the previous year. Operating activities generated Â 598 million while investing activities used Â 331 million mainly for capital expenditures. Financing activities used Â 370 million mainly for payment of interests.

Strategy

The company uses its industry-leading capabilities across its sectors to create sustainable solutions. The company also invests in growth using equity from its shareholders debt finance and cash flow. It also sources raw materials and uses them as efficiently as possible.

HISTORY

Percival Johnson set up an assayer's shop in London in 1817. Using chemical and physical tests he determined the amount of gold in a given bar and guaranteed his results by offering to buy the bars he assayed. Johnson then set up a gold refinery in the early 1830s and developed a method for extracting platinum group metals. As part of that process he produced vitreous colors for pottery and glass refined nickel and silver nitrate for medical use and later for photographic uses.

George Matthey joined the company in 1838 and championed the platinum business securing a steady supply of platinum from Russia. The company thrived on business generated by gold rushes in California (1849) and Australia (1851). It built a silver refinery to melt down European coinage and extract component metals and in 1870 it bought a company that produced magnesium antimony vanadium and aluminum. In 1891 the company became Johnson Matthey & Co. Limited. Around the turn of the century it bought rolling mills and began forming metals into sheet tube and wire to better serve jewelers.

During WWI Johnson Matthey & Co. provided platinum catalysts and magnesium powder for explosives and in WWII the company was appointed the government's agent for controlling platinum stocks. Johnson Matthey & Co. expanded its international operations rapidly during the post-war boom adding holdings in Australia India North America and South Africa. It established subsidiaries in France and the Netherlands (1956) Italy (1959) Sweden (1960) Belgium (1961) and Austria (1962). The company also began conducting research on automotive catalytic converters to reduce pollution. It formed Johnson Matthey Bankers (JMB) to carry out its banking and trading activities.

A foray into the US jewelry business led to big losses in 1980 and the company pressed JMB to make higher-risk loans. JMB's contribution to profits went from less than 25% in 1981 (the year the company took its present name) to more than 60% in 1983. The bank ended up with so many bad loans that the Bank of England had to arrange a bailout in 1984. Gene Anderson who became CEO in 1985 cut 3000 jobs and reduced the number of divisions from 78 to 4. Profits rebounded but Anderson resigned in 1989 after failing to persuade the board to diversify away from platinum.

During the 1990s the company invested heavily in its electronics division which had been doing well since the 1989 acquisition of Cominco Electronic Materials (ultra-pure metals for microchips). By 1995 the division was responsible for about a third of Johnson Matthey's profits. In 1998 it bought Cookson Group's 50% share of its ceramics joint venture.

In 1998 Johnson Matthey shifted its focus to three core businesses: catalysts colors and coatings and precious metals. The next year it sold its electronic materials business Johnson Matthey Electronics to US-based AlliedSignal (now Honeywell International) and began looking for takeover opportunities in its core markets. In 2001 the company acquired pharmaceuticals manufacturers Meconic (now Macfarlan Smith; it's the UK's only maker of medical opiates — cocaine and heroin) and Pharm-Eco then used these acquisitions as the basis for a fourth division: Pharmaceutical Materials (now a part of its Fine Chemicals and Catalysts Division).

In 2002 the company acquired Cascade Biochem Limited to strengthen its Pharmaceutical Materials division and metal catalyst company Synetix. CEO Chris Clark retired in 2003. He was succeeded by Neil Carson former executive director of the precious metals and catalysts operations.

Following the sale of its Pigments & Dispersions unit to Rockwood Pigments in 2004 Johnson Matthey restructured its Colours and Coatings division by closing several of its manufacturing sites and transferring some operations to its Precious Metal Products division. The moves created what became the Ceramics division the 2007 sale of which was the last in the dismantling of the Colours and Coatings division.

At the beginning of 2008 the company acquired the Argillon Group which manufactured catalysts and advanced ceramic materials from Ceramics Luxembourg (owned by KKR). Later that year Johnson Matthey sold the acquired ceramic insulators alumina business for about $40 million.

In 2010 a Johnson Matthey subsidiary formed a joint venture with Aoxing Pharmaceutical to manufacture ingredients for narcotics and neurological drugs for the Chinese market. That same year Johnson Matthey acquired Intercat a supplier of fluid catalytic cracking services for the petroleum refining industry for $56 million. It became part of Johnson Matthey's Process Technologies division's Ammonia Methanol Oil and Gas unit.

EXECUTIVES

Executive Director Environmental Technologies Division and Director, Larry C. Pentz, age 65, $507,518 total compensation
Director Technology Centre, B. A. Murrer
Chief Executive, Robert MacLeod, age 56, $294,000 total compensation
Division Finance Director Catalysts Process Catalysts, G. P. Otterman
Division Director Precious Metals, W. F. (Bill) Sandford, $209,000 total compensation
President Pharmaceutical Materials and Services, J. B. Fowler
Managing Director Environmental Catalysts and Technologies Asia, J. F. Walker
General Manager Noble Metals Europe, C. C. Howlett
General Manager Noble Metals North America, J. D. Malanga
Managing Director Tracerco and Vertec, A. C. Hurst
President Global Research Chemicals, B. C. Singelais
President Davy Process Technology, D. J. Tomlinson
General Manager Gold North America, A. J. McCullough
Managing Director Emission Control Technologies Asia, J. V. Zubrickas
Managing Director Colour Technologies, R. L. P. J. van der Heijden
Managing Director Refineries and Gas Processing, J.K. Dunleavy
Managing Director Syngas and Gas to Products, A. Wright
Group Finance Director, Den Jones

Chairman, Tim E. P. Stevenson, age 71
Auditors: PricewaterhouseCoopers LLP

LOCATIONS

HQ: Johnson Matthey Plc (United Kingdom)
5th Floor, 25 Farringdon Street, London EC4A 4AB
Phone: (44) 20 7269 8400 **Fax:** (44) 20 7269 8433
Web: www.matthey.com

2015 Sales

	% of total
Europe	
UK	24
Germany	12
Rest of Europe	11
USA	25
Rest of North America	2
China (including Hong Kong)	11
Rest of Asia	10
Rest of World	5
Total	**100**

PRODUCTS/OPERATIONS

2015 Sales

	% of total
Precious Metals	56
Emission Control Technologies	33
Process Technologies	6
Fine Chemicals	4
New Businesses	1
Total	**100**

Businesses

Emission Control Technologies Division
Emission Control Technologies website
Stationary Emissions Control website
Process Technologies Division
Process Technologies website
Chemical Catalysts website
Johnson Matthey Formox website
Johnson Matthey Davy Technologies website
Tracerco website
Precious Metal Products Division
Services Businesses
Precious Metals Management
Global Precious Metal Refining website
Scavenging Technologies
PGM Database
Johnson Matthey & Brandenberger website
Manufacturing Businesses
Noble Metals website
Medical Device Components website
Metal Joining website
USA Jewellery Products
Advanced Glass Technologies website
Silver and Coating Technologies website
Chemical Products website
Piezoproducts website
Fine Chemicals Division
API Manufacturing
Johnnson Matthey Macfarlan Smith website
Johnson Matthey Pharmaceutical Materials - USA website
Johnson Matthey Pharma Services website

COMPETITORS

BASF Catalysts	Metalor USA Refining
GEA Group	Mitsui Mining and
Heraeus Holding	Smelting
Heraeus Precious	Showa Denko
Metals	Umicore
IBIDEN	Vectra
Impala Platinum	Vesuvius
Kyocera	

HISTORICAL FINANCIALS

Company Type: Public

Income Statement

FYE: March 31

	REVENUE ($ mil.)	NET INCOME ($ mil.)	NET PROFIT MARGIN	EMPLOYEES
03/20	18,008	315	1.7%	15,352
03/19	14,075	541	3.8%	14,795
03/18	19,844	418	2.1%	14,130
03/17	15,020	481	3.2%	12,306
03/16	15,421	479	3.1%	12,325
Annual Growth	4.0%	(10.0%)	—	5.6%

2020 Year-End Financials

Debt ratio: 22.6%
Return on equity: 9.3%
Cash ($ mil.): 375
Current ratio: 1.32
Long-term debt ($ mil.): 1,220

No. of shares (mil.): 193
Dividends
  Yield: 4.8%
  Payout: 124.8%
Market value ($ mil.): 8,459

	STOCK PRICE ($) FY Close	P/E High/Low		PER SHARE ($) Earnings	Dividends	Book Value
03/20	43.71	66	33	1.63	2.11	18.03
03/19	84.00	47	32	2.81	2.07	17.67
03/18	85.60	65	50	2.18	2.17	17.27
03/17	78.10	44	33	2.51	6.72	14.43
03/16	80.26	61	38	2.39	4.87	13.78
Annual Growth	(14.1%)	—	—	(9.1%)	(18.9%)	6.9%

JSC VTB Bank

Auditors: Ernst & Young LLC

LOCATIONS

HQ: JSC VTB Bank
29, Bolshaya Morskaya Street, St. Petersburg 190000
Phone: (7) 495 739 77 99 **Fax:** (7) 495 258 47 81
Web: www.vtb.ru

HISTORICAL FINANCIALS

Company Type: Public

Income Statement

FYE: December 31

	REVENUE ($ mil.)	NET INCOME ($ mil.)	NET PROFIT MARGIN	EMPLOYEES
12/19	22,305	3,245	14.6%	0
12/18	17,321	2,571	14.8%	0
12/17	21,724	2,080	9.6%	0
12/16	20,546	854	4.2%	94,966
12/15	16,439	144	0.9%	92,882
Annual Growth	7.9%	117.6%	—	—

2019 Year-End Financials

Debt ratio: —
Return on equity: 12.6%
Cash ($ mil.): 23,494
Current ratio: —
Long-term debt ($ mil.): —

No. of shares (mil.): —
Dividends
  Yield: —
  Payout: 15,010.9%
Market value ($ mil.): —

JTEKT Corp

Combine a "J" with the Greek word for technical skill "tekton" and voil you have JTEKT. The giant manufacturer of ball bearings and automotive steering devices has indeed got talent. Other automotive parts made by JTEKT include ABS sensors constant velocity (CV) joints oil seals steering gear systems and driveshafts. It also builds machine tools factory automation systems and heat technology products such as industrial furnaces and semiconductor manufacturing equipment. JTEKT caters primarily to the automotive needs of Toyota Motor (which owns about one-quarter of JTEKT) and to a lesser extent other Asian European and North American automakers.

Sales and Marketing
The company's products are primarily applied in the automobile bearing and machine tool industries.

Financial Performance
JTEKT's revenue increased from 2013 to 2014 primarily due to sizable increases from the North American and European markets.

Strategy
In 2014 the company invested $91 million to build a new manufacturing facility in San Luis Potosi Mexico which will provide the company with needed capacity to manufacture electric power steering systems for its growing customer base in the region.

Company Background
JTEKT was formed on January 1 2006 by a merger of Koyo Seiko Co. and Toyoda Machine Works.

EXECUTIVES

EVP, Takaaki Suzuki, age 72
President, Tetsuo Agata, age 67
EVP, Masakazu Isaka
EVP, Seiho Kawakami
Chairman, Atsushi (Art) Niimi, age 73
Vice Chairman, Shoji Ikawa, age 70
Auditors: PricewaterhouseCoopers Kyoto

LOCATIONS

HQ: JTEKT Corp
3-5-8 Minami-Semba, Chuo-ku, Osaka 542-8502
Phone: (81) 6 6245 0856   **Fax:** (81) 6 6245 3712
Web: www.jtekt.co.jp

2014 Sales

	% of total
Japan	44
North America	20
Asia Oceania and other	20
Europe	16
Total	**100**

PRODUCTS/OPERATIONS

2014 Sales

	% of total
Automotive components	59
Bearing	29
Machine tootls and mechatronics	12
Total	**100**

Selected Products
Bearings
  Automotive bearings & unit products
  Bearings for electric electronic products
  Bearings for extreme special environments
  Bearings for general industrial equipment
  General purpose bearings
  Machine tool bearings
  Steel mill bearings

Driveline components
  4WD couplings
  CVT oil pumps
  Damper pulleys
  Driveshafts
  Propeller shafts
  Proportionately controlled AT & CVT valves
  TORSENs
Machine tools
  Grinders line up
  Horizontal spindle machining centers line up
Mechatronics
  General operation board
  Motion controllers
  Toyopuc
Sensor systems
Steering systems
  Components
  Electric power steering
  Hydraulic power steering

COMPETITORS

Delphi Automotive Systems	NSK
FAG Kugelfischer	NTN
GKN	Nachi-Fujikoshi
MinebeaMitsumi	Timken
	Visteon

HISTORICAL FINANCIALS
Company Type: Public

Income Statement   FYE: March 31

	REVENUE ($ mil.)	NET INCOME ($ mil.)	NET PROFIT MARGIN	EMPLOYEES
03/20	13,071	(34)	—	56,639
03/19	13,733	222	1.6%	57,184
03/18	13,572	468	3.4%	55,450
03/17	11,790	425	3.6%	49,201
03/16	12,466	433	3.5%	49,120
Annual Growth	1.2%	—		3.6%

2020 Year-End Financials

Debt ratio: 0.2%
Return on equity: (-0.7%)
Cash ($ mil.): 1,242
Current ratio: 1.67
Long-term debt ($ mil.): 2,321
No. of shares (mil.): 343
Dividends
  Yield: 0.0%
  Payout: —
Market value ($ mil.): 7,251

	STOCK PRICE ($) FY Close	P/E High/Low		PER SHARE ($) Earnings	Dividends	Book Value
03/20	21.14	—	—	(0.10)	1.22	13.41
03/19	36.54	1	0	0.65	1.20	14.12
03/18	43.26	0	0	1.36	1.19	14.63
03/17	52.00	0	0	1.24	1.14	12.72
03/16	40.47	0	0	1.26	0.80	11.82
Annual Growth	(15.0%)	—	—	—	11.0%	3.2%

Juroku Bank, Ltd.

EXECUTIVES

President, YUKIO MURASE
Auditors: Deloitte Touche Tohmatsu LLC

LOCATIONS

HQ: Juroku Bank, Ltd.
8-26 Kanda-machi, Gifu 500-8516
Phone: (81) 58 265 2111
Web: www.juroku.co.jp

COMPETITORS

Mie Bank	Mizuho Financial
Mitsubishi UFJ Financial Group	Resona
	Sumitomo Mitsui

HISTORICAL FINANCIALS
Company Type: Public

Income Statement   FYE: March 31

	ASSETS ($ mil.)	NET INCOME ($ mil.)	INCOME AS % OF ASSETS	EMPLOYEES
03/20	59,626	118	0.2%	3,741
03/19	57,512	96	0.2%	3,911
03/18	57,413	93	0.2%	4,184
03/17	54,006	89	0.2%	4,319
03/16	55,297	119	0.2%	4,382
Annual Growth	1.9%	(0.1%)	—	(3.9%)

2020 Year-End Financials

Return on assets: 0.2%
Return on equity: 3.6%
Long-term debt ($ mil.): —
No. of shares (mil.): 37
Sales ($ mil): 984
Dividends
  Yield: —
  Payout: 23.2%
Market value ($ mil.): —

Jyske Bank A/S

EXECUTIVES

Board Member, Jens Aksel Borup
Board Member, Rina Asmussen
Board Member, Keld Norup
Board Member, Marianne Lillevang Jensen
Vice Chairman, Philip Baruch
Auditors: Deloitte Statsautoriseret Revisionsaktieseiskab

LOCATIONS

HQ: Jyske Bank A/S
Vestergade 8-16, Silkeborg DK-8600
Phone: (45) 89 89 89 89   **Fax:** (45) 89 89 19 99
Web: www.jyskebank.dk

COMPETITORS

Danske Bank	Sydbank
Nordea Bank	

HISTORICAL FINANCIALS
Company Type: Public

Income Statement   FYE: December 31

	ASSETS ($ mil.)	NET INCOME ($ mil.)	INCOME AS % OF ASSETS	EMPLOYEES
12/19	97,643	343	0.4%	3,593
12/18	92,009	363	0.4%	3,698
12/17	96,196	491	0.5%	3,932
12/16	83,329	439	0.5%	3,981
12/15	79,313	361	0.5%	4,021
Annual Growth	5.3%	(1.3%)	—	(2.8%)

2019 Year-End Financials

Return on assets: 0.3%
Return on equity: 6.5%
Long-term debt ($ mil.): —
No. of shares (mil.): 74
Sales ($ mil): 2,042
Dividends
  Yield: —
  Payout: —
Market value ($ mil.): —

Kajima Corp. (Japan)

As one of the world's leading construction firms Kajima was among the first skyscraper builders in Japan and continues to develop earthquake-resistant technologies. The group operates as a general contractor-developer providing a full array of engineering design development and construction services. It builds skyscrapers bridges highways and railways nuclear power plants and other commercial and civil projects. Projects have included the Suez Canal Bridge in Egypt and the Nukui Dam in Hiroshima. Kajima has a presence in more than 20 countries in Africa Asia Europe the Middle East and North America.

Operations
Kajima Corporation generated 45% of its total revenue from its building construction business in FY2015 (ended March 31) with its Civil Engineering business making up another 20%. Its domestic subsidiary and affiliate companies made up 17% of total revenues while its overseas subsidiaries and affiliates made up 15%. The remainder of revenues came from its real estate development business.

The company's Kajima USA subsidiary runs the North American arm of the business.

Geographic Reach
Kajima gets more than 80% of its revenues from its projects in Japan while another more than 15% of revenues are split between Asia and North America. Its offices in Japan are located in the cities of Hokkaido Tohoku Kanto Yokohama Hokuriku Chubu Kansai Shikoku Chugoku and Kyushu. Its international offices are in Taiwan Singapore Indonesia Vietnam Myanmar and Tanzania.

Financial Performance
Kajima Corporation's revenues have been slowly growing in recent years thanks to a strengthening Japanese construction market and the company's ability to secure more contract awards. Meanwhile Kajima's profits have struggled to consistently grow as it hasn't been able to control its operating expenses.

The builder's revenue grew by 11% to Å 1694 billion ($14.16 billion) in fiscal 2015 (ended March 31) with growth across its Civil Engineering Real Estate Development Domestic affiliates and overseas affiliates. A 7.5% decline in the company's building construction business offset some of this revenue growth however as its profits on certain construction projects deteriorated during the year.

Despite higher revenue in 2014 the builder's net income declined by 27% to Å 15.14 billion ($126.5 million) as its operating expenses nearly doubled during the year. Its operating cash climbed by nearly 80% to Å 59.21 billion ($494.9 million) despite lower earnings.

Mergers and Acquisitions
In March 2015 Kajima acquired a majority stake in the mid-tier builder Icon Co to expand its exposure to the Australian construction market. The deal came at a time when the country's biggest-ever housing boom was about to take off and when Icon had some $850 million worth of major contracts in the pipeline in Victoria NSW and Queensland.

Company Background
Founded in 1840 Kajima has had an illustrious and venerable history. It began earthquake remediation work in the early 1920s and built railroads and the first Western-style buildings in Japan.

EXECUTIVES

EVP, Naoki Atsumi

President, Mitsuyoshi Nakamura
EVP, Hiroshi Kaneko
EVP, Atsushi Hattori
EVP, Takashi Hinago
Managing Executive Officer, Tamiharu Tashiro
Auditors: Deloitte Touche Tohmatsu LLC

LOCATIONS

HQ: Kajima Corp. (Japan)
1-3-1 Motoakasaka, Minato-ku, Tokyo 107-8388
Phone: (81) 3 5544 1111
Web: www.kajima.co.jp

2013 Sales

	% of total
Asia	
Japan	85
Other countries	7
North America	6
Europe	1
Other regions	-
Total	**100**

PRODUCTS/OPERATIONS

2013 Sales

	% of total
Construction	88
Real Estate & others	12
Total	**100**

2013 Sales

	% of total
Building construction	50
Civil Engineering	18
Real estate development and others	4
Others	28
Total	**100**

Selected Subsidiaries
Act Technical Support Inc. (sales and services)
Azuma Kanko Kaihatsu Co. Ltd. (hotels and leisure)
Chung-Lu Construction Co. Ltd. (Taiwan)
East Real Estate Co. Ltd.
Green Materials Recycle Corporation (sales and services)
Hawaiian Dredging Construction Company Inc. (US)
Ilya Corporation (design and consulting)
Kajima Kress Co. Ltd. (procurement and construction)
Kajima Real Estate Investment Advisors Inc.
Kajima Tatemono Sogo Kanri Co. Ltd. (real estate development and management)
Public Relations Officer Corporation (sales and services)
Shinrinkohen Golf Club Co. Ltd.
Taiko Trading Co. Ltd. (procurement and construction)
Yaesu Book Center Co. Ltd. (culture)

COMPETITORS

Bechtel	Shimizu
CSCEC	Sumitomo Mitsui
Fluor	Construction
Hazama	TOA
Kumagai Gumi	Taisei
Mitsubishi Heavy	Takenaka
Industries	Tokyu Construction
Obayashi	

HISTORICAL FINANCIALS
Company Type: Public

Income Statement   FYE: March 31

	REVENUE ($ mil.)	NET INCOME ($ mil.)	NET PROFIT MARGIN	EMPLOYEES
03/20	18,523	951	5.1%	22,114
03/19	17,827	991	5.6%	21,616
03/18	17,239	1,193	6.9%	20,893
03/17	16,294	937	5.8%	19,561
03/16	15,518	644	4.2%	19,084
Annual Growth	4.5%	10.2%	—	3.8%

2020 Year-End Financials

Debt ratio: 0.1%
Return on equity: 13.3%
Cash ($ mil.): 2,422
Current ratio: 1.20
Long-term debt ($ mil.): 1,201

No. of shares (mil.): 513
Dividends
Yield: 4.3%
Payout: —
Market value ($ mil.): 5,526

	STOCK PRICE ($) FY Close	P/E High/Low		PER SHARE ($) Earnings	Dividends	Book Value
03/20	10.76	0	0	1.85	0.47	14.20
03/19	14.89	0	0	1.91	0.47	13.08
03/18	92.28	0	0	2.30	0.43	12.06
03/17	65.35	0	0	1.81	0.30	9.44
03/16	65.12	0	0	1.24	0.10	8.07
Annual Growth	(36.2%)	—	—	10.5%	48.5%	15.2%

Kansai Electric Power Co., Inc. (Kansai Denryoku K. K.) (Japan)

Japan's #2 electric utility (behind Tokyo Electric) the Kansai Electric Power Company (KEPCO) provides electricity to more than 13 million customers in Japan's Kansai region. The utility has a generating capacity of 33.1 MW produced at hydroelectric fire power and nuclear power plants. As deregulation takes effect KEPCO is moving into new business arenas including retail natural gas sales in Japan. Additionally Kansai Electric Power Company Inc is engaged in information technology telecommunications construction and engineering services environmental services home security real estate transportation leasing and other energy-related operations. It has about 85 main affiliated companies primarily in Japan.

Operations
Kansai Electric Power Company Inc.'s reportable segments consist of electrical power (about 80% of revenue) and other businesses (more than 20% of revenue).

The company's power plant portfolio includes more than 150 hydroelectric plants about a dozen fossil-fired plants and three nuclear plants. It has more than 132455 km of overhead distribution lines and nearly 18 825 km. of transmission lines.

Other businesses includes Information and telecommunication business Life/Business solution business.

Geographic Reach
Osaka-based Kansai Electric Power Company Inc's supply area includes all of Osaka Hyogo Kyoto and Wakayama prefectures.

Financial Performance
Note: Growth rates may differ after conversion to US Dollars.

The company's revenue decreased by 4% to 3.2 trillion yen in 2020 compared to 3.3 trillion yen in 2019 primarily due to the decrease on their electric operations.

Net income in 2020 increased by 11% to 130.0 billion yen compared to 115.1 billion yen in the prior year. The increase was due to not having loss on disasters and investment loss on subsidiaries and affiliates.

Strategy
Kansai Electric Power Company's Principles of International Business and Cooperation are: Increasing profits by developing overseas businesses;

Contributing to environmental issues of the host countries and global environmental issues by developing electricity infrastructure in the host country and mitigating global environmental load; and Enhancing competitiveness of our Group through overseas business activities.

In 2020 Kansai Electric Power Co Inc. has agreed to buy a minority stake in the firm holding the 211.4-MW Piiparinmaki wind project in central Finland. Kansai's subsidiary KPIC Netherlands BV has signed a deal to acquire from London-based fund manager Glennmont Partners a 15% stake in Glennmont Clean Energy Fund III Wind BV. The latter is the owner of Ilmatar Piiparinmaki Oy which is the special service vehicle of the wind project. This acquisition marks Kansai's fourth wind project in Europe and its first onshore wind investment in Finland. It increases the utility's net overseas generation capacity to about 2606 MW.

Company Background

The company was established in 1951.

KEPCO has a longstanding relationship with Australia's North West Shelf liquefied natural gas (LNG) joint venture. One of the venture's first customers in 1989 the company in 2009 signed a new deal guaranteeing the Japanese utility some 3.3 million metric tons a year in LNG supply.

EXECUTIVES

EVP, Masao Ikoma
EVP, Hideki Toyomatsu
EVP, Jiro Kagawa
President, Shigeki Iwane, age 67
Managing Director, Makoto Yagi, age 71
Auditors: Deloitte Touche Tohmatsu LLC

LOCATIONS

HQ: Kansai Electric Power Co., Inc. (Kansai Denryoku K. K.) (Japan)
3-6-16 Nakanoshima, Kita-ku, Osaka 530-8270
Phone: (81) 6 6441 8821
Web: www.kepco.co.jp

PRODUCTS/OPERATIONS

2016 Sales

	% of total
Electric power	86
IT/Communications	5
Other	9
Total	**100**

Selected Subsidiaries

Kanden Energy Solution Co. Inc
SAKAI LNG Corp
ECHIZEN ENELINE CO. INC
Osaka Bioenergy Co. Ltd
K-Opticom Corp
Kanden System Solutions Co. Inc
Kanden Realty & Development Co. Ltd.
Clearpass Co. Ltd
KANDEN AMENIX Corp
Kanden Community Co. Ltd
Kanden CS Forum Inc.
Kanden Oce Work Co. Inc
Kanden Power-Tech Corp
Kanden Business Support Corp.
San Roque Power Corporation
LNG EBISU Shipping Corporation
KPIC Netherlands B.V.

COMPETITORS

Chubu Electric Power
Chugoku Electric Power
Hokkaido Electric Power
Hokuriku Electric Power
Internet Initiative Japan
KDDI
Kobe Steel
Kyushu Electric Power

NTT
Nippon Steel & Sumitomo Metal Corporation
Osaka Gas
SOFTBANK MOBILE
Shikoku Electric
Tohoku Electric Power
Tokyo Electric
Tokyo Gas

HISTORICAL FINANCIALS

Company Type: Public

Income Statement — FYE: March 31

	REVENUE ($ mil.)	NET INCOME ($ mil.)	NET PROFIT MARGIN	EMPLOYEES
03/20	29,334	1,197	4.1%	44,251
03/19	29,867	1,039	3.5%	45,699
03/18	29,510	1,430	4.8%	45,916
03/17	26,933	1,259	4.7%	45,836
03/16	28,904	1,253	4.3%	45,647
Annual Growth	0.4%	(1.1%)	—	(0.8%)

2020 Year-End Financials

Debt ratio: 0.5%
Return on equity: 8.3%
Cash ($ mil.): 2,575
Current ratio: 0.55
Long-term debt ($ mil.): 28,819
No. of shares (mil.): 893
Dividends
  Yield: 4.2%
  Payout: —
Market value ($ mil.): 5,201

	STOCK PRICE ($) FY Close	P/E High/Low		PER SHARE ($) Earnings	Dividends	Book Value
03/20	5.82	0	0	1.34	0.46	16.50
03/19	7.58	0	0	1.16	0.20	15.30
03/18	6.33	0	0	1.60	0.19	15.32
03/17	6.18	0	0	1.41	0.00	13.24
03/16	4.31	0	0	1.40	0.00	11.76
Annual Growth	7.8%	—	—	(1.1%)	—	8.9%

Kao Corp

Kao (pronounced "cow") is one of Japan's leading makers of personal care laundry and cleaning products. Its brand names include Attack (a top laundry detergent in Japan) Bioré (skin care) Laurier (sanitary napkins) Merries (disposable diapers) and PureOra (toothpaste). The company also manufactures Healthya brand beverages (green tea and water) cooking oils and fatty chemicals printer and copier toner products and plastics used in products such as athletic shoe soles. Kao which generates nearly two-thirds of sales from Japan is well-diversified with all five of its business segments contributing more than 15% of revenue.

Financial Performance

Note: Growth rates may differ after conversion of USD.

Kao has seen its sales flat to slightly up over the past few years with overall revenue up about 2% since 2015. Net income has shown stronger growth up about 45% during that same time.

In 2018 the company reported revenue of 1.5 trillion yen (about $13.6 billion) up 1% from the prior year. The cosmetics skin and hair care and fabric and home care businesses grew that year offsetting flat sales in chemicals and a decline in human health care.

Net income jumped 5% that year to 153.7 billion yen as compared to 2017 boosted primarily by the slight revenue increase and lower income taxes.

Cash at the end of 2018 was 266 billion yen a decrease of 70.9 billion yen from the prior year.

Cash from operations contributed 195.6 billion yen to the coffers while investing activities used 157.9 billion yen mainly for capital expenditures and business combinations. Financing activities used another 108.6 billion yen for dividends to stockholders and purchase of treasury shares.

Strategy

Building a robust pipeline of innovative products and product enhancements is a key element of Kao's strategy. It invests some 4% of total sales in research & development to drive growth during a time when consumer attitudes and behaviors are rapidly changing. In late 2018 the company announced five new key technologies that will underpin new products in the coming years including fine fiber (a superfine membrane that will smooth the skin and improve the look of cosmetics) as well as RNA monitoring (non-invasive analytical method for monitoring RNA expression on the skin) Created Color (hair science) Bio IOS (a sustainable detergent base made from palm oil) and Package RecyCreation (eco-friendly upcycling).

Kao is also focused on brand building a key element of improving the cosmetics business (which has been struggling in recent years) among others. It has selected 11 global brands and 8 regional brands for investment.

In addition the company grows via acquisition and in mid-2018 strengthened its professional-use products business with the purchase of US-based Washing Systems LLC.

EXECUTIVES

President and CEO, Michitaka Sawada
Senior Managing Executive Officer, Toshiaki Takeuchi
Senior Managing Executive Officer, Katsuhiko Yoshida
Managing Executive Officer, Masumi Natsusaka
Executive Officer, Kazuyoshi Aoki
Managing Executive Officer, Yasushi Aoki
Managing Executive Officer, Motohiro Morimura
Managing Executive Officer, Hideko Aoki
Managing Executive Officer, Kozo Saito
Managing Executive Officer, Yoshihiro Hasebe
Auditors: Deloitte Touche Tohmatsu LLC

LOCATIONS

HQ: Kao Corp
1-14-10 Nihonbashi-Kayabacho, Chuo-ku, Tokyo 103-8210
Phone: (81) 3 3660 7111
Web: www.kao.com

PRODUCTS/OPERATIONS

2018 Sales

	% of total
Fabric & home care	23
Skin care & hair care	23
Chemical	18
Cosmetics	18
Human health care	18
Total	**100**

Selected Brand Names

Attack (laundry detergent)
Bioré; (skin care)
Bub (shower gel)
Curel (skin care)
Essential (hair care)
Jergens (skin care)
Laurier (sanitary napkins)
Magiclean (household cleaner)
Merries (disposable diapers)
Primavista (makeup)
PureOra (toothpaste)
Quickle Wiper (household wipers)

COMPETITORS

Alticor
Colgate-Palmolive
Johnson & Johnson
Kimberly-Clark
Kracie
Lion Corporation
Nestlé
Nisshin Oillio

Pfizer
Procter & Gamble
Republic of Tea
Revlon International
 Corporation
Shiseido
Snapple
Unicharm

HISTORICAL FINANCIALS

Company Type: Public

Income Statement				FYE: December 31
	REVENUE ($ mil.)	NET INCOME ($ mil.)	NET PROFIT MARGIN	EMPLOYEES
12/19	13,836	1,365	9.9%	45,796
12/18	13,713	1,397	10.2%	46,306
12/17	13,237	1,306	9.9%	46,898
12/16	12,462	1,082	8.7%	46,520
12/15	12,249	873	7.1%	45,595
Annual Growth	3.1%	11.8%	—	0.1%

2019 Year-End Financials

Debt ratio: 0.0%
Return on equity: 17.6%
Cash ($ mil.): 2,208
Current ratio: 1.70
Long-term debt ($ mil.): 936

No. of shares (mil.): 481
Dividends
 Yield: 1.3%
 Payout: 8.2%
Market value ($ mil.): 7,987

	STOCK PRICE ($) FY Close	P/E High/Low		PER SHARE ($) Earnings	Dividends	Book Value
12/19	16.58	0	0	2.82	0.23	16.40
12/18	14.90	0	0	2.86	0.11	15.34
Annual Growth	11.3%	—	—	(0.3%)	21.0%	1.7%

Kasikornbank Public Co Ltd

EXECUTIVES

Chairman and CEO, Banthoon Lamsam
EVP Systems Division, Teeranun Srihong
EVP Credit Management Division, Predee Daochai
Division Head Capital Markets Business Division, Thiti Tantikulanan
EVP Business Division, Pakorn Partanapat
President and Director, Kattiya Indaravijaya, age 55
Division Head Investment Banking Business Division, Panop Ansusinha
EVP SME Business Division, Patchara Samalapa
SEVP Corporate Secretariat Division, Adit Laixuthai
EVP Corporate Strategy Management Division, Ampol Polohakul
EVP Corporate Strategy Management Division, Prasopsuk Damrongchietanon
EVP Finance and Control Division, Chongrak Rattanapian
EVP Compliance and Audit Division, Surasak Dudsdeemaytha
EVP Corporate Strategy Management Division, Vasin Vanichvoranun
EVP SME Business Division, Vallop Vongjitvuttikrai
EVP Corporate Strategy Management Division, Thawee Teerasoontornwong
Head Private Banking Business, Jirawat Supornpaibul

SEVP WorldBusiness Division, Pipit Aneaknithi
EVP Customer and Enterprise Service Fulfillment Division, Pipatpong Poshyanonda
SEVP Enterprise Risk Management Division, Wirawat Panthawangkun
SEVP Human Resource Division, Krit Jitjang
EVP Corporate and SME Products Division, Srilawat Santivisat
EVP Retail Business Division, Noppawan Jermhansa
EVP Retail Business Division, Krisada Lamsam
Vice Chairperson, Khunying Suchada Kiranandana
Auditors: KPMG Phoomchai Audit Ltd.

LOCATIONS

HQ: Kasikornbank Public Co Ltd
 1 Soi Rat Burana 27/1, Rat Burana Road, Rat Burana Sub-District, Rat Burana District, Bangkok 10140
Phone: (66) 2 222 0000 **Fax:** (66) 2 470 1144
Web: www.kasikornbank.com

PRODUCTS/OPERATIONS

2013 Sales

	% of total
Interest income	53
Fees & service income	14
Other income	33
Total	**100**

Selected Companies

Kasikorn asset management co. ltd
Kasikorn factory & equipment co. ltd.
Kasikorn leasing co. ltd.
Kasikorn research center co. ltd.
Kasikorn securities pcl

COMPETITORS

Bangkok Bank
Bank of Ayudhya

Thanachart Capital
United Overseas Bank

HISTORICAL FINANCIALS

Company Type: Public

Income Statement				FYE: December 31
	ASSETS ($ mil.)	NET INCOME ($ mil.)	INCOME AS % OF ASSETS	EMPLOYEES
12/19	110,578	1,300	1.2%	0
12/18	97,531	1,188	1.2%	0
12/17	89,042	1,054	1.2%	0
12/16	79,504	1,122	1.4%	21,029
12/15	70,921	1,095	1.5%	0
Annual Growth	11.7%	4.4%	—	—

2019 Year-End Financials

Return on assets: 1.2%
Return on equity: 9.9%
Long-term debt ($ mil.): —
No. of shares (mil.): —
Sales ($ mil.): 9,482

Dividends
 Yield: 1.9%
 Payout: —
Market value ($ mil.): —

	STOCK PRICE ($) FY Close	P/E High/Low		PER SHARE ($) Earnings	Dividends	Book Value
12/19	20.05	2	1	0.54	0.40	5.70
12/18	22.69	2	1	0.50	0.40	4.86
12/17	29.58	2	2	0.44	0.39	4.47
12/16	19.70	1	1	0.47	0.36	3.76
12/15	16.43	2	1	0.46	0.37	3.31
Annual Growth	5.1%	—	—	4.4%	1.6%	14.5%

Kawasaki Heavy Industries Ltd (Japan)

Auditors: KPMG AZSA LLC

LOCATIONS

HQ: Kawasaki Heavy Industries Ltd (Japan)
 Kobe Crystal Tower, 1-1-3 Higashi-Kawasakicho, Chuo-ku, Kobe, Hyogo 650-8680
Phone: (81) 78 371 9551
Web: www.khi.co.jp

HISTORICAL FINANCIALS

Company Type: Public

Income Statement				FYE: March 31
	REVENUE ($ mil.)	NET INCOME ($ mil.)	NET PROFIT MARGIN	EMPLOYEES
03/20	15,120	171	1.1%	36,332
03/19	14,400	247	1.7%	35,691
03/18	14,825	272	1.8%	35,805
03/17	13,584	234	1.7%	35,127
03/16	13,723	410	3.0%	34,605
Annual Growth	2.5%	(19.5%)	—	1.2%

2020 Year-End Financials

Debt ratio: 0.2%
Return on equity: 3.9%
Cash ($ mil.): 977
Current ratio: 1.33
Long-term debt ($ mil.): 3,213

No. of shares (mil.): 167
Dividends
 Yield: 4.2%
 Payout: —
Market value ($ mil.): 1,002

	STOCK PRICE ($) FY Close	P/E High/Low		PER SHARE ($) Earnings	Dividends	Book Value
03/20	6.00	0	0	1.03	0.26	25.13
03/19	9.79	0	0	1.48	0.23	25.75
03/18	12.98	0	0	1.63	0.19	26.27
03/17	12.12	0	0	1.40	0.41	23.41
03/16	11.56	0	0	2.45	0.39	23.00
Annual Growth	(15.1%)	—	—	(19.5%)	(9.8%)	2.2%

KB Financial Group, Inc.

KB Financial GroupÂ holding company forÂ KookminÂ Bank provides commercial and consumerÂ banking servicesÂ in South Korea.Â It offers asset management and lifeÂ insurance through alliances with Netherlands-based ING Groep.Â The bank'sÂ lending activities mainly entail residential mortgages home equity loans consumer loans and corporate loans. Kookmin Bank has more than 1200 branches in its home country where it claims some 26 million customers orÂ about half of the population of South Korea. The bank provides corporate services such as foreign exchange and securities trading from offices at home and abroad in New York London Hong KongÂ Tokyo and Auckland New Zealand.

EXECUTIVES

Chairman and CEO, Jong Kyoo Yoon
Auditors: Samil PricewaterhouseCoopers

LOCATIONS

HQ: KB Financial Group, Inc.
 141, Uisadang-daero, Yeongdeungpo-gu, Seoul 07332
Phone: (82) 2 2073 7114   **Fax:** (82) 2 2073 2848
Web: www.kbfng.com

PRODUCTS/OPERATIONS

Selected Subsidiaries
KB Asset Management Co. Ltd. (80%)
KB Credit Information Co. Ltd. (99.7%)
KB Data Systems Co. Ltd. (99.99%)
KB Futures Co. Ltd. (99.98%)
KB Investment Co. Ltd. (99.99%)
KB Real Estate Trust Co. Ltd. (99.99%)
Kookmin Bank
Kookmin Bank Hong Kong Ltd.
Kookmin Bank International Ltd.

COMPETITORS

Busan Bank	Korea Exchange Bank
Citigroup	Samsung Life Insurance
Daegu Bank	Shinhan Financial
Hana Bank	Woori
Industrial Bank of Korea	

HISTORICAL FINANCIALS

Company Type: Public

Income Statement   FYE: December 31

	ASSETS ($ mil.)	NET INCOME ($ mil.)	INCOME AS % OF ASSETS	EMPLOYEES
12/19	449,100	2,868	0.6%	153
12/18	430,166	2,745	0.6%	185
12/17	409,700	3,106	0.8%	164
12/16	312,707	1,784	0.6%	159
12/15	279,689	1,443	0.5%	181
Annual Growth	12.6%	18.7%	—	(4.1%)

2019 Year-End Financials

Return on assets: 0.6%	Dividends
Return on equity: 8.9%	Yield: 4.0%
Long-term debt ($ mil.): —	Payout: 22.7%
No. of shares (mil.): 389	Market value ($ mil.): 16,119
Sales ($ mil): 27,278	

	STOCK PRICE ($) FY Close	P/E High/Low		PER SHARE ($) Earnings	Dividends	Book Value
12/19	41.37	0	0	7.27	1.68	85.65
12/18	41.98	0	0	6.88	1.79	80.93
12/17	58.51	0	0	7.74	1.17	79.95
12/16	35.29	0	0	4.63	0.81	64.76
12/15	27.87	0	0	3.72	0.71	63.10
Annual Growth	10.4%	—	—	18.2%	24.1%	7.9%

KBC Group NV

Auditors: PwC Bedrijfsrevisoren BV

LOCATIONS

HQ: KBC Group NV
 Havenlaan 2, Brussels 1080
Phone: (32) 2 429 49 16   **Fax:** (32) 2 429 44 16
Web: www.kbc.com

HISTORICAL FINANCIALS

Company Type: Public

Income Statement   FYE: December 31

	ASSETS ($ mil.)	NET INCOME ($ mil.)	INCOME AS % OF ASSETS	EMPLOYEES
12/19	326,427	2,794	0.9%	37,854
12/18	325,015	2,943	0.9%	38,368
12/17	350,446	3,086	0.9%	38,459
12/16	290,579	2,562	0.9%	36,315
12/15	274,868	2,874	1.0%	36,411
Annual Growth	4.4%	(0.7%)	—	1.0%

2019 Year-End Financials

Return on assets: 0.8%	Dividends
Return on equity: 12.4%	Yield: 3.3%
Long-term debt ($ mil.): —	Payout: 19.4%
No. of shares (mil.): 416	Market value ($ mil.): 15,634
Sales ($ mil): 12,381	

	STOCK PRICE ($) FY Close	P/E High/Low		PER SHARE ($) Earnings	Dividends	Book Value
12/19	37.55	7	5	6.57	1.27	54.91
12/18	31.96	8	5	6.85	1.13	54.03
12/17	42.76	7	6	7.23	1.07	53.85
12/16	30.99	6	4	6.00	0.33	43.81
12/15	31.15	9	6	4.14	0.79	41.19
Annual Growth	4.8%	—	—	12.2%	12.5%	7.5%

KDDI Corp

Auditors: PricewaterhouseCoopers Kyoto

LOCATIONS

HQ: KDDI Corp
 3-10-10 Iidabashi, Chiyoda-ku, Tokyo 102-8460
Phone: (81) 3 3347 0077
Web: www.kddi.com

HISTORICAL FINANCIALS

Company Type: Public

Income Statement   FYE: March 31

	REVENUE ($ mil.)	NET INCOME ($ mil.)	NET PROFIT MARGIN	EMPLOYEES
03/20	52,805	6,450	12.2%	83,308
03/19	51,224	6,227	12.2%	78,337
03/18	50,837	5,772	11.4%	73,508
03/17	47,875	5,511	11.5%	69,234
03/16	45,031	4,985	11.1%	65,972
Annual Growth	4.1%	6.7%	—	6.0%

2020 Year-End Financials

Debt ratio: 0.1%	No. of shares (mil.): —
Return on equity: 14.8%	Dividends
Cash ($ mil.): 3,722	Yield: 3.4%
Current ratio: 1.71	Payout: 18.3%
Long-term debt ($ mil.): 11,570	Market value ($ mil.): —

	STOCK PRICE ($) FY Close	P/E High/Low		PER SHARE ($) Earnings	Dividends	Book Value
03/20	14.60	0	0	2.78	0.51	19.19
03/19	10.72	0	0	2.61	0.42	17.91
03/18	12.81	0	0	2.37	0.40	15.81
03/17	13.16	0	0	2.23	0.34	14.57
03/16	13.34	0	0	1.99	0.26	13.39
Annual Growth	2.3%	—	—	8.7%	17.8%	9.4%

Keiyo Bank, Ltd. (The) (Japan)

EXECUTIVES

President, TOSHIYUKI KUMAGAI
Managing Director, Koshiro Iitaka
Managing Director, Kiyoshi Hashimoto
Auditors: Ernst & Young ShinNihon LLC

LOCATIONS

HQ: Keiyo Bank, Ltd. (The) (Japan)
 5-45 Chibaminato, Chuo-ku, Chiba 260-0026
Phone: (81) 43 306 2121
Web: www.keiyobank.co.jp

COMPETITORS

Chiba Bank	Chiba Kogyo Bank

HISTORICAL FINANCIALS

Company Type: Public

Income Statement   FYE: March 31

	ASSETS ($ mil.)	NET INCOME ($ mil.)	INCOME AS % OF ASSETS	EMPLOYEES
03/20	46,013	51	0.1%	3,071
03/19	44,204	95	0.2%	3,055
03/18	45,104	114	0.3%	3,108
03/17	41,128	104	0.3%	3,130
03/16	40,016	135	0.3%	3,111
Annual Growth	3.6%	(21.5%)	—	(0.3%)

2020 Year-End Financials

Return on assets: 0.1%	Dividends
Return on equity: 1.9%	Yield: —
Long-term debt ($ mil.): —	Payout: 47.1%
No. of shares (mil.): 130	Market value ($ mil.): —
Sales ($ mil): 629	

Kering SA

Kering (pronounced "caring") has transformed itself from a conglomerate to the world's third-largest luxury group (behind LVMH and Richemont). The Paris-based company's stable of global luxury brands includes Italian high end label Gucci as well as Alexander McQueen Balenciaga Bottega Veneta and Saint Laurent. Kering also owns German athletic shoemaker PUMA. More than a third of Kering's sales are generated from Asia-Pacific. Fran Şois Pinault founded the firm in 1963 as Pinault Group which eventually became Pinault-Printemps-Redoute (PPR) and later Kering.

Operations

Kering's top three brands by revenue include Gucci (more than 60% of the company's revenue) Saint Lauren (nearly 15%) and Bottega Veneta (more than 5%). Other houses account for the remainder.

In terms of product category leather goods account for about 60% of Kering's revenue. Other major categories include shoes (more than 15%) ready-to-wear (about 15%) and watches and jewelry (about 5%).

By distribution channel more than 60% of the company's sales are generated in wholesale sales and other revenue including royalties Retail channel account for the remaining 40%.

Geographic Reach

Paris-based Kering rings up about 35% of its sales in Asia-Pacific. Western Europe and North America are also important markets for the luxury goods maker representing more than 30% and about 20% of sales respectively. Japan accounts for about 10% of sales and the rest comes EMEA and South America.

Kering operates about 1400 direct operated stores of which more than 320 are in Western Europe 220 are in Japan and about 230 are in North America. More than 600 direct operated stores are located in emerging markets.

Sales and Marketing

ering's distribution channel is split into six sales formats: Mono brand stores specialty stores department stores outlets e-commerce and airport stores.

The company's retail channel operates a directly operated store network and its wholesale channel includes department stores independent high-end multi-brand stores and franchise stores.

Financial Performance

Note: Growth rates may differ after conversion to US Dollars.

In 2019 Kering reported revenue of ?15.9 billion up 16% from ?13.7 billion in 2018. The company attributes the increase to organic growth at Gucci where sales reached ?9.6 billion up 16% from the prior year and at Saint Laurent which increased its revenue by 18% to ?2 billion.

Net income from continuing operations rose to ?3.2 billion in 2018 up from ?2.8 billion in 2018 mainly due to higher revenue and a decrease in costs and expenses and a rise in income tax expense that year.

Cash at the end of 2019 was ?1.8 billion. Cash from operations was ?2.5 billion while investing activities used ?1.2 billion. Financing activities used ?1.5 billion. Kering's main cash uses in 2019 were purchases of property plant and equipment dividends paid to owners of the parent company and repayment of lease liabilities.

Strategy

Kering operates through a two-tiered strategy consisting of promoting organic growth and enhancing synergies through integration.

Its organic growth is centered on providing an improved in-store client experience which enables it to create and sustain lasting connections. With this in mind in 2019 Kering completed the roll-out of a dedicated application designed with Apple. It also internalized its Couture & Leather brands' e-commerce activities in 2020. With this move the group aims to oversee the whole value chain so as to provide clients with truly exceptional experience across all channels and touchpoints aligning the e-commerce side with the standards of excellence seen in its boutiques.

Kering strives to create value for its Houses and is geared to unlocking their creative potential. In order to enrich its brands' offerings the group draws on cross-business expertise. Kering is also constantly improving and adapting its operating model to ensure its structures are always more up-to-date and flexible. The group has launched an ambitious transformation project focusing on its information systems supply chain and logistics.

Company Background

Sixteen-year-old Fran Şois Pinault left school in 1952 to join the family timber business. He took over the firm when his father died in 1963; that year the company was renamed Pinault Group. Pinault diversified the company into wood importing and retailing eventually building a flourishing enterprise. In 1973 Pinault began to show his tal-

ent for the art of the deal. Sensing the demand for timber was peaking he sold 80% of the business buying it back two years later at an 85% discount.

Pinault began to diversify outside the timber industry in the 1990s. It acquired a series of companies including Au Printemps (owner of Printemps stores and 54% of catalog company Redoute) in 1992. The firm then became the Pinault-Printemps Group. In 1993 the group reorganized into four divisions: retail business-to-business financial services and international trade and eventually renamed itself Pinault-Printemps-Redoute (PPR).

In 2005 Fran Şois-Henri Pinault the son of the company's founder joined the company as its new CEO. During his 10 years at the helm Weinberg oversaw the transformation of the company from a business-to-business concern to a focused luxury retail group. To underscore the company's transformation begun in 2005 in 2013 PPR became Kering.

EXECUTIVES

CEO Bottega Veneta, Claus-Dietrich Lahrs
CEO Luxury Couture and Leather Goods
 Emerging Brands, Grita Loebsack
Chairman and CEO, Fran Şois-Henri Pinault, age 58
Group Managing Director, Jean Fran Şois Palus, age 57
CEO Brioni, Fabrizio Malverdi
CFO, Jean Marc Duplaix, age 49
CEO Kerin Luxury-Couture and Leather Goods;
 President Bottega Veneta, Marco Bizzarri, age 57
CEO Kering Luxury Watches and Jewelry
 Division, Albert Bensoussan
Chief Sustainability Officer and Head
 International Institutional Affairs, Marie Claire Daveu, age 46
CEO PUMA SE, Bj ¶rn Gulden
CEO Kering Eyewear, Roberto Vedovotto
COO, Jean-Philippe Bailly, age 52
CEO Alexander McQueen, Emmanuel Gintzburger, age 46
CEO Saint Laurent, Francesca Bellettini
CEO Christopher Kane, Nikolas Talonpoika, age 48
CEO Ulysse Nardin, Patrick Pruniaux, age 48
Vice Chair, Patricia Barbizet, age 65
Auditors: Deloitte & Associes

LOCATIONS

HQ: Kering SA
 40 Rue de Sevres, Paris 75007
Phone: (33) 1 45 64 61 00   **Fax:** (33) 1 45 64 60 00
Web: www.kering.com

2015 Sales

	% of total
Western Europe	31
Asia/Pacific	26
North America	23
Japan	10
Other countries	10
Total	**100**

PRODUCTS/OPERATIONS

2015 Sales

	% of total
Luxury	68
Sports & Lifestyle	32
Total	**100**

Selected Brands

Luxury
 Alexander McQueen
 Balenciaga
 Bottega Veneta
 Boucheron
 Brioni
 Christopher Kane
 Girard-Perregaux

Gucci
 JeanRichard
 Sergio Rossi
 Stella McCartney
 Yves Saint Laurent
Sport & lifestyle
 Electric
 Puma
 Volcom

Selected Operations

Luxury Goods
 Gucci Group N.V. (99.39% leather goods and apparel)
 PUMA (athletic footwear)
 Sowind Group (50.1% watches)
Retail
 Fnac (electronics books music; Belgium Brazil France Italy Monaco Portugal Spain Switzerland and Taiwan)
 Volcom Inc. (US young men's and women's apparel)

COMPETITORS

ASICS	NIKE
Abercrombie & Fitch	New Balance
Billabong	Patagonia Inc.
Burberry	Prada
Burton	Quiksilver
Chanel	Richemont
Christian Dior	Saucony
Columbia Sportswear	St ssy
Gianni Versace	Vans
K-Swiss	Vivarte
LVMH	adidas
Lost International	

HISTORICAL FINANCIALS

Company Type: Public

Income Statement

FYE: December 31

	REVENUE ($ mil.)	NET INCOME ($ mil.)	NET PROFIT MARGIN	EMPLOYEES
12/19	17,833	2,592	14.5%	38,068
12/18	15,649	4,254	27.2%	34,795
12/17	18,553	2,140	11.5%	44,055
12/16	13,077	858	6.6%	40,052
12/15	12,617	758	6.0%	38,801
Annual Growth	**9.0%**	**36.0%**	**—**	**(0.5%)**

2019 Year-End Financials

Debt ratio: 24.0%	No. of shares (mil.): 125
Return on equity: 22.8%	Dividends
Cash ($ mil.): 2,566	Yield: 8.9%
Current ratio: 0.93	Payout: 5.6%
Long-term debt ($ mil.): 3,505	Market value ($ mil.): 8,171

	STOCK PRICE ($) FY Close	P/E High/Low		PER SHARE ($) Earnings	Dividends	Book Value
12/19	65.36	4	2	20.66	5.84	92.31
12/18	46.76	2	1	33.77	5.38	90.14
12/17	47.07	3	2	16.99	0.55	113.42
12/16	22.35	4	2	6.82	0.42	94.23
12/15	17.25	4	3	6.01	0.38	94.45
Annual Growth	**39.5%**		**—**	**36.1%**	**98.0%**	**(0.6%)**

Kingfisher PLC

Kingfisher is an eye-catching home improvement company. The firm operates more than 1350 B&Q Screwfix Castorama and Brico Dép ´t stores in seven European countries plus Turkey and Russia. The UK is the company's home market and where the majority of the group's stores are located. Customers visit Kingfisher in-store and online to buy an array of home improvement products under the categories outdoor & garden home & bedroom building & hardware and kitchen & bathroom. Kingfisher operates the Ko Ştas joint venture in Turkey. It generates about 45% of sales in the UK and Ireland.

Operations

Kingfisher operates under retail banners including B&Q Castorama Brico Dép ́t Screwfix TradePoint and Ko Ştó. The company offers home improvement products and services to consumers and trade professionals.

In the UK Kingfisher's biggest market the company offers around 40000 home improvement and garden products at B&Q. Screwfix which has more than 11000 items in stock serves a professional customer base via mail-order and in store with trade tools plumbing electrical products and products for fixing and improving bathrooms and kitchens. In France and Poland Castorama-branded stores stock nearly 50000 products; and Brico Dép ́t addresses similar markets at a lower price.

Geographic Reach

Kingfisher operates more than 1350 stores in total. It has more than 980 in the UK and Ireland almost 220 in France some 80 in Poland approximately 35 in Romania about 30 in Spain roughly 20 in Russia and about five in Portugal.

Overall Kingfisher generates about 45% of revenue in the UK and Ireland more than 35% in France and about 15% in Poland.

Sales and Marketing

Kingfisher reaches customers via several different touchpoints. Its physical locations are its primary channel but it also offers online delivery and for professional customers mail-order. In the UK B&Q is aimed at DIYers while Screwfix serves wholesalers tradesmen and DIY experts.

Financial Performance

Note: Growth rates may differ after conversion to US Dollars.

Revenue for 2020 totaled Å 11.5 billion a 1% dip from the previous year.

The company had a profit of Å 8 million for the year ended 2020 a 96% decrease compared to the previous year.

The company's cash for the year ended 2020 was Å 195 million. Operating activities generated Å 897 million while investing activities used Å 138 million mainly for capital expenditures. Financing activities used another Å 757 million primarily for lease rental payments.

Strategy

Kingfisher's clear intent is to become a more digital and service orientated company using its strong store assets as a platform. The company will continue to develop its own exclusive brands as a differentiator cater for diverse local customer needs and each retail banner will have its own positioning and plan. The company will 'power' these banners as a group. This is Kingfisher's new strategic direction 'Powered by Kingfisher'. The company will rebalance local and group responsibilities with the overall aim of enabling its retail banners to have flexibility and agility to address specific needs in local markets. The company's key strategic priorities under 'Powered by Kingfisher' are as follows:

Focus and fix' in 2020 (including managing the impact of Covid-19 on the business); Move to a balanced simpler local-group operating model with an agile culture; Grow e-commerce sales; Build a mobile-first service orientated customer experience; Differentiate and grow through own exclusive brands (OEB); Test new store concepts and adapt its store footprint; Source and buy better reduce its costs and its inventory; and Lead the industry in Responsible Business practices.

Mergers and Acquisitions

In late 2020 Kingfisher plc has acquired NeedHelp one of Europe's leading home improvement services marketplaces for a total cash consideration of ?10 million. NeedHelp is an innovative B2B2C online platform that connects customers who need home improvement help either in-store or online with vetted professional tradespeople and other skilled experts. As part of the transaction Guillaume de Kergariou the founder of NeedHelp has reinvested proceeds from the sale in a 20% interest in the business resulting in Kingfisher owning 80%.

Company Background

Kingfisher traces its lineage back to the international expansion efforts of US retailer Woolworth which set up shop in Liverpool in 1909. The company grew quickly and went public in 1931 with Woolworth retaining a majority stake. Activity kicked up a notch in 1980 following which it acquired do-it-yourself chain B&Q was bought out by private equity acquired electronics retailer Comet renamed F.W. Woolworth stores as Woolworths acquired Superdrug and two further drugstore chains. At the end of the 1980s the company changed its name to Kingfisher. In the next few decades further acquisitions followed including several businesses (such as Castorama) in France as did spin-offs and divestitures such as Woolworth's and Superdrug in 2001.

EXECUTIVES

CEO Group Productivity and Development and Chairman Screwfix, Steve Willett
CFO and Director, Karen Witts
Group CEO, Véronique Laury
Chief Sales and Retail Operations Officer, Jean-Paul Constant
Chief Offer & Supply Chain Officer, Arja Taaveniku
Chairman, Daniel Bernard, age 74
Chairman Designate, Andy Cosslett
Auditors: Deloitte LLP

LOCATIONS

HQ: Kingfisher PLC
3 Sheldon Square, Paddington, London W2 6PX
Phone: (44) 20 7372 8008   **Fax:** (44) 20 7644 1001
Web: www.kingfisher.com

2019 Sales

	% of total
UK & Ireland	43
France	37
Poland	12
Others	8
Total	**100**

2019 Stores

	No.of Stores
UK & Ireland	923
France	224
Poland	76
Spain	29
Romania	38
Spain	28
Russia	20
Germany	19
Portugal	3
Total	**1,331**

COMPETITORS

Grafton Group
Grafton Merchanting
Homebase Limited
Leroy Merlin
METRO AG
MPS Builders and Merchants
Saint-Gobain Building Distribution
Tengelmann
Travis Perkins
Wolseley

HISTORICAL FINANCIALS

Company Type: Public

Income Statement

FYE: January 31

	REVENUE ($ mil.)	NET INCOME ($ mil.)	NET PROFIT MARGIN	EMPLOYEES
01/20	15,110	10	0.1%	78,000
01/19	15,345	286	1.9%	79,000
01/18	16,496	686	4.2%	78,000
01/17	13,983	759	5.4%	77,000
01/16	14,942	589	3.9%	76,000
Annual Growth	0.3%	(63.5%)	—	0.7%

2020 Year-End Financials

Debt ratio: 1.5%	No. of shares (mil.): 2,110
Return on equity: 0.1%	Dividends
Cash ($ mil.): 248	Yield: 4.5%
Current ratio: 1.12	Payout: 4,771.7%
Long-term debt ($ mil.): 122	Market value ($ mil.): 11,267

	STOCK PRICE ($) FY Close	P/E High/Low		PER SHARE ($)	
			Earnings	Dividends	Book Value
01/20	5.34	17531232	0.01	0.24	3.61
01/19	5.97	95 52	0.13	0.25	4.14
01/18	10.05	48 37	0.31	0.24	4.42
01/17	8.66	35 28	0.34	0.25	3.77
01/16	9.50	62 52	0.25	0.26	3.86
Annual Growth	(13.4%)	— —	(62.1%)	(1.5%)	(1.6%)

Kirin Holdings Co Ltd

You might say this company makes good-luck beer. Named for a unicorn which is a Japanese symbol of good fortune Kirin Holdings is a top beer maker in Japan through its Kirin Brewery Co. In addition to its domestic Kirin-branded beers the company owns brewers that serve overseas markets such as Australia's Lion and Philippines-based San Miguel Brewery. The beer brewer also makes soft drinks (coffee tea drinks and mineral water) the alcoholic fruit drink chu-hi and owns Japanese wine producer Mercian Corporation. Beyond beverages Kirin Holdings also has operations in health and dairy foods and pharmaceutical-manufacturing sectors. The company generates most of its sales in Japan.

Operations

The company has four segments: Japanese beer and spirits (about 35%) Japan non-alcoholic beverages (15%) Oceania integrated services (15%) and pharmaceuticals (15%).

For Japanese beer and spirits the company is called Kirin Brewery. In Japan non-alcoholic beverages it is known as Kirin Beverage Company it provides a number of famous brands and one of it is Kirin Gogo-no-Kocha. On the other hand Lion Pty Limited is carrying out an integrated beverage strategy in Oceania.

For pharmaceuticals the company has Kyowa Kirin Group. It is carrying out independent research from a unique perspective and development using advanced technology in the pharmaceuticals business and provides high-quality products globally.

In reference to others the company has Mercian Corporation (wine) Myanmar Brewery (beer) Coca-Cola Beverages (soft drinks) and Kyowa Hakko Bio (pharmaceuticals and infant foods). In addition manages share acquisition for investment in the Beer Business of San Miguel.

Geographic Reach

Tokyo Based Kirin Holdings has established local operations in Australia China the Philippines Myanmar Singapore the UK the US and Vietnam. In the US it owns soft-drink bottler Coca-Cola Bottling Company of Northern New England and bourbon maker Four Roses Distillery in Kentucky. The company generates more than 65% of total sales in its home country. Oceania accounts for around 15% and the remaining sales are from America and others.

Sales and Marketing

The company has retail stores suppliers and caters to pharmaceutical and industrial sectors. The company also integrates marketing activities spanning from advertising to in store campaigns.

Financial Performance

The company's revenue has been rising for the last few years after it dropped in 2016. In spite of the growth it still has an overall decline of 12% between 2015 and 2019.

Kirin Holdings' revenue rose 1% from Å 1.93 trillion in 2018 to Å 1.94 trillion in 2019. The increase was due to higher sales in America and Others.

In 2019 profit attributable to owners of the company decreased by 64% to Å 59.6 billion. This was mainly due to higher operating expenses for the year.

The company's cash at the end of 2019 was Å 173.1 billion a 4% decline from the previous year. Operating activities generated Å 178.8 billion while investing activities used Å 175.6 billion mainly for acquisition of equity-accounted investees and capital expenditures. Financing activities used another Å 1 billion primarily for repayments of long-term borrowings.

Strategy

In recent years consumers have expressed an increased awareness of health. Moreover according to a survey conducted by Kirin Brewery many respondents indicated concern about sugar carbohydrates and fat intake during meals. As a response Kirin Brewery and FANCL jointly developed a non-alcoholic beverage utilizing the unique strengths of FANCL's Calolimit which has sold more than 67 million units and Kirin Brewery's "Non-alcohol Chu-hi Zero Hi Hyo-Rei" (Hyo-Rei) with its refreshing taste that goes with meals.

Company Background

Kirin Brewery Co. Ltd. was established on February 23 1907 taking over the business of The Japan Brewery Co. Ltd. which had started marketing Kirin Beer in 1888.

Kirin Ichiban Shibori which first hit the market in 1990 went on to become one of the most popular beers in Japan. Kirin Brewery's soft-drink business division was spun off to become Kirin Beverage Co. Ltd. in 1991.

In 2007 celebrating its 100th anniversary Kirin Brewery changed its trade name to Kirin Holdings Co. Ltd. established as a pure holding company for the Kirin Group.

EXECUTIVES

Managing Director, Hirotake Kobayashi
President and CEO, Senji Miyake
Managing Director, Hajime Nakajima
CFO, Masahito Suzuki
Managing Director, Toru Suzuki
Chairman, Kazuyasu Kato, age 76
Auditors: KPMG AZSA LLC

LOCATIONS

HQ: Kirin Holdings Co Ltd
NAKANO CENTRAL PARK SOUTH, 4-10-2 Nakano,
Nakano-ku, Tokyo 164-0001
Phone: (81) 3 6837 7015
Web: www.kirinholdings.co.jp

2013 Sales

	% of total
Japan	65
Asia/Oceania	22
Others	13
Total	**100**

PRODUCTS/OPERATIONS

2013 sales

	% of total
Japan integrated beverages	45
Overseas integrated beverages	35
Pharmaceuticals and bio-chemicals	17
Others	3
Total	**100**

COMPETITORS

Anheuser-Busch InBev	Megmilk Snow Brand
Asahi Breweries	Mercian
Asia Pacific Breweries	Molson Coors
Carlsberg	Nippon Beet Sugar
Chugai	Novartis
Coca-Cola	Pabst
Diageo	PepsiCo
E. & J. Gallo	Red Bull
FEMSA	SABMiller
Fonterra	Sapporo
Heineken	Suntory Holdings
ITOCHU	Taiwan Tobacco & Wine
Kokubu	Takara
LVMH	Tsingtao

HISTORICAL FINANCIALS

Company Type: Public

Income Statement

FYE: December 31

	REVENUE ($ mil.)	NET INCOME ($ mil.)	NET PROFIT MARGIN	EMPLOYEES
12/19	17,880	549	3.1%	35,717
12/18	17,555	1,493	8.5%	36,376
12/17	16,563	2,151	13.0%	37,874
12/16	17,741	1,010	5.7%	46,439
12/15	18,249	(393)	—	46,613
Annual Growth	(0.5%)	—	—	(6.4%)

2019 Year-End Financials

Debt ratio: 0.1%
Return on equity: 6.5%
Cash ($ mil.): 1,525
Current ratio: 1.10
Long-term debt ($ mil.): 2,682

No. of shares (mil.): 868
Dividends
  Yield: 2.4%
  Payout: 86.5%
Market value ($ mil.): 18,956

	STOCK PRICE ($) FY Close	P/E High/Low		PER SHARE ($) Earnings	Dividends	Book Value
12/19	21.82	0	0	0.63	0.54	9.61
12/18	20.78	0	0	1.67	0.45	9.49
12/17	25.26	0	0	2.36	0.36	9.33
12/16	16.29	0	0	1.11	0.32	6.38
12/15	13.56	—	—	(0.43)	0.32	6.05
Annual Growth	12.6%	—	—	—	14.2%	12.3%

Kobe Steel Ltd (Japan)

One of Japan's top steel companies Kobe Steel (aka Kobelco) makes more than enough wire and rod to cage its markets. A diversified manufacturer Kobe Steel's portfolio includes aluminum copper titanium welding products and industrial machinery like compressors and rolling mill. The company also provides wholesale power supply operating two power plants in Kobe. Its real estate division rents manages and sells properties. A joint venture with US Steel? PRO-TEC Coating Company? produces hot-dipped galvanized steel sheet as well. The company was founded when major pre-war conglomerate Suzuki Shoten enters heavy industry field in 1905.

Operations

All operations at Kobe Steel are divide under iron & steel aluminium & copper welding construction machinery machinery engineering and electric Power.

Iron & Steel is the leading product of Kobe (about 40% revenue) while Aluminum and Copper business (more than 15%). Products range from steel castings and forgings to aluminum and copper sheets. Welding products and services adds nearly 5% more to the annual revenue.

Kobelco's Construction machinery segment alone makes up about 20% of annual sales by selling hydraulic excavators crawler and wheel cranes. 20% of combined revenue comes from each of Kobe's Machinery Engineering and Electric Power segments mostly catering to the energy and iron-making fields.

In addition the Kobe Steel Group engages in real estate and electronics materials businesses. These businesses account for less than 5% of the total revenue.

Geographic Reach

Japan-based Kobelco has more than 10 branch and sales offices (including head offices) four works facilities two R&D laboratories and six plants domestically. It has also operations overseas in China Germany Thailand and the US.

Sales and Marketing

Kobe Steel sells to automobile trains and shipbuilding industries as well as to energy industry and other industrial customers.

Financial Performance

Note: Growth rates may differ after conversion to US Dollars.

In the last five years Kobe Steel has seen fluctuating revenues. Revenues have risen and fallen over the years notably in recent years. The company's profits have also followed a similar fluctuating pattern as the company saw alternating years of loss and profit.

In fiscal 2019 (ended March 2020) revenue declined 5% to Å 1.9 trillion. All of the company's segments saw declines in sales especially its Iron & Steel Aluminum & Copper Engineering and Construction Machinery sales.

The company posted a loss of Å 68 billion in fiscal 2019 following a profit of Å 35.9 billion in fiscal 2018. Kobe Steel recognized a Å 50 billion loss on impairment and a Å 15.1 billion loss on valuation of investment securities which significantly affected its profits that year.

Cash and cash equivalents at the end of the year were Å 145.7 billion Å 52.3 billion less than the year prior. Operating activities generated Å 27 billion in fiscal 2019 while investing activities used Å 219 billion mainly for purchase of property plant and equipment. Financing activities provided Å 140.6 billion from issuance of long-term borrowings.

Strategy

Kobe Steel has been implementing a medium-term management plan focused on growth strategies for its three core business areas of materials machinery and electric power. Kobe Steel will continue to carry out this plan to reach its goals.

In mid-2020 Kobe Steel Ltd. together with its wholly-owned US subsidiary Midrex Technologies Inc. has reached a non-binding agreement with Vale S.A. the world's largest iron ore producer and Mitsui & Co. Ltd. a global trading and investment company with a diversified business portfolio to collaborate in providing low CO2 iron metallics and ironmaking solutions to the world's steel industry.

Kobe Steel has also obtained further subsidiaries. For example it turned its Chinese affiliate Wuxi Compressor Co. Ltd. into a subsidiary after acquiring additional shares in the company in early 2020. It also turned its Indian tire and rubber machinery joint venture L&T Kobelco Machinery Private Limited (or LTKM) into a wholly-owned subsidiary in early 2019.

As it operates new subsidiaries Kobe Steel has also decided to close select locations such as its closure of Kobe Steel Asia Pte. Ltd. in Singapore in early 2020. Kobe Steel moved KSA's business to Kobelco South East Asia Ltd. (KSEA) and integrate sales support for steel products and technical services at one location to make operations more efficient.

Furthermore Kobe Steel established Kobleco Europe GmbH (or KEU) in mid-2019 to serve as the European headquarters for the Kobe Steel Group. KEU plans to continue the business activities of KME while strengthening the management of Kobe Steel's operations in Europe starting with corporate governance and compliance. KEU aims to further promote coordination among the Kobe Steel Group companies in the region. Owing to good access KEU will also be responsible for the Group's locations in the Middle East.

Company Background

In 1905 general partnership trading company Suzuki Shoten acquired a steel business in Wakinohama Kobe called Kobayashi Seikosho operated by Seiichiro Kobayashi and changed its name to Kobe Seikosho. Then in 1911 Suzuki Shoten spun off the company to establish Kobe Steel Works Ltd. with a capital of ¥1.4 million of Wakinohama-cho Kobe. This was the beginning of the company that is today known as Kobelco.

EXECUTIVES

EVP; Manager Moka Plant, Tetsu Takahashi
**Officer Head Office and Technical Development
 Group,** Jun Tanaka
EVP, Hiroaki Fujiwara
EVP, Ikuhiro Yamaguchi
Senior Managing Director, Tsuyoshi Kasuya
President and CEO, Hiroya Kawasaki
Senior Managing Director, Kazuhide Naraki
Chairman, Hiroshi Sato, age 75
Auditors: KPMG AZSA LLC

LOCATIONS

HQ: Kobe Steel Ltd (Japan)
 2-2-4 Wakinohama-Kaigandori, Chuo-ku, Kobe, Hyogo
 651-8585
Phone: (81) 78 261 5185 **Fax:** (81) 78 261 4123
Web: www.kobelco.co.jp

PRODUCTS/OPERATIONS

2017 Sales

	% of total
Materials Businesses	
Iron & Steel	37
Aluminum & Copper	18
Welding	4
Machinery Business	
Construction Machinery	19
Machinery	8
Engineering	6
Electric Power Business	
Electric Power	4
Other Businesses	4
Total	**100**

Selected Products

Aluminum and Copper
  Aluminum plate
  Copper sheet and strip
Construction Machinery
  Crawler cranes
  Environmental Recycling Machinery
  Hydraulic excavators
  Mini hydraulic excavators
  Wheel cranes
Electric Power
  Kobe Power Plant
Engineering
  Advanced Urban Transit System
  Iron Unit Field
Iron and Steel
  Steel bars
  Steel castings and forgings
  Steel plates
  Steel powder
  Steel sheets
  Titanium
  Wire rod and bars
Machinery
  Standard compressors
  Rotating machinery
  Tire and rubber machinery
  Plastic processing machinery
  Advance Technology Equipment
  Rolling Mill
  Ultra High Pressure Equipment
  Energy & Chemical Field
Welding
  Electrodes
  Flux-cored wires
  Metallic flux-cored wire
  Solid wires
  Welding fluxes

COMPETITORS

AK Steel Holding Corporation
ArcelorMittal
Baosteel
JFE Holdings
Nippon Steel & Sumitomo Metal Corporation
Nisshin Steel
POSCO
ThyssenKrupp Steel
United States Steel
Yamato Kogyo

HISTORICAL FINANCIALS

Company Type: Public

Income Statement				FYE: March 31
	REVENUE ($ mil.)	NET INCOME ($ mil.)	NET PROFIT MARGIN	EMPLOYEES
03/20	17,225	(626)	—	47,807
03/19	17,805	324	1.8%	45,404
03/18	17,715	595	3.4%	44,083
03/17	15,167	(206)	—	43,513
03/16	16,232	(191)	—	42,635
Annual Growth	1.5%			2.9%

2020 Year-End Financials

Debt ratio: 0.3%	No. of shares (mil.): 364
Return on equity: (-9.7%)	Dividends
Cash ($ mil.): 1,345	Yield: —
Current ratio: 1.31	Payout: —
Long-term debt ($ mil.): 6,580	Market value ($ mil.): —

Koc Holdings AS

In Turkey Ko § (pronounced "coach") class equals first class. Led by its energy businesses Ko § Holding is Turkey's dominant industrial conglomerate. The company's Tofas unit an alliance with Fiat is Turkey's champion carmaker; Ko §'s joint venture with Ford Motor sells imported Ford models. Other businesses include consumer goods such as large household appliances (Ar §elik teaming up with LG Electronics) and energy (distribution of liquefied petroleum gas). Subsidiaries engage in food production construction international trading and hospitality and tourism. Ko § also operates banking securities brokerage and insurance businesses. The Ko § family one of the wealthiest in Turkey controls the company.

Operations

Ko § Holding is organized under five core business segments: Energy Automotive Consumer durables Finance and Other.

The Energy segment that generates more than 45% of total revenue offers petroleum products the Koc Group companies operating in the energy sector meet 55% of Turkey's demand for petroleum fuel products and provide more than half of nation's storage capacity. Ko § and Royal Dutch Shell together continue to drive about 50% stake in oil refiner T PRAS. T PRAS controls 40% ownership in the fuel distribution company Opet Petrolc l k.

Automotive generates about 25% of total revenue offers Automotive retailing and car rentals Commercial vehicles Buses Passenger cars and trucks.

Consumer durables generates about 15% of total revenue offers white goods appliances. The Koc Group is the leader in white goods sector in Turkey with above 50% market share.

The company's finance segment generates more than 10% of total revenue includes three main groups; banking insurance and consumer finance. Leasing factoring portfolio management custody and brokerage services are included in the banking sector.

Other business lines that generates roughly 5% of total revenue offers Tourism Food production I.T support and Marina Operations.

Geographic Reach

Koc Holding A.S. is headquartered in Nakkótepe Turkey. It operates in more than 150 countries with more than 60 production facilities worldwide some in Australia Egypt China Spain France and Russia. Roughly 70% of total revenues is generated domestically and the rest comes from sales Abroad.

Sales and Marketing

Ko § Holding serves more than 12 million customers for the year 2019 through its 11000 dealers and aftersales service points.

Financial Performance

In 2019 the company's consolidated revenues increased by 7% to TL 153.5 billion. Koc Holdings' combined international revenues stood at USD 19.3 billion supported notably with the contribution of the automotive and consumer durables sectors.

Net profit attributable to the equity holders of the parent stood at TL 4.4 billion. This was due to the increase on their expenses and tax expenses.

Cash held by the company at the end of 2019 increased by TL 12.7 billion to TL 36.0 billion compared to TL 23.2 billion in the prior year. Cash provided by operations TL 19.0 billion while cash used for investing and financing activities were TL 6.0 billion and TL 3.0 billion respectively.

Strategy

The Ko § Group innovation strategy includes: Building a culture of innovation and creating the right working environment to enhance their innovation capacity; Cultivating corporate entrepreneurship across the Group and supporting employees' entrepreneurial spirit and efforts; Extending innovative endeavors not only across product and service development activities but in all business units and operations; Increasing partnership with external stakeholders an important source of innovation and managing these collaborations more effectively; and Managing innovative operations via clear processes to ensure sustainability.

In order to implement its innovation strategy Ko § Holding has been conducting the Ko § Innovation Program since 2014. As part of this program innovation management infrastructures are built up at Ko § Group companies in line with the self-developed Ko § Innovation Management Model.

EXECUTIVES

President Tourism Food and Retailing Group, Tamer Hasimoglu
President Energy Group, Erol Memio °lu
CFO, Ahmet Ashabolu
President Defense Industry Other Automotive and IT Group, Kudret Onen
President Automotive Group, Cenk Cimen
President Banking and Insurance Group, Faik Acikalin
CEO, Levent akiroglu
Chairman, Mehmet O. Koc
Vice Chairman, Yildirim A. Koc
Auditors: PwC Bagimsiz Denetim ve Serbest Muhasebeci Mali Müsavirlik A.S.

LOCATIONS

HQ: Koc Holdings AS
Nakkastepe, Azizbey Sokak No. 1, Istanbul, Kuzguncuk 34674
Phone: (90) 216 531 0000   **Fax:** (90) 216 531 0099
Web: www.koc.com.tr

2016 Sales

	% of total
Domestic	74
Foreign	26
Total	**100**

PRODUCTS/OPERATIONS

2016 Sales

	% of total
Energy	42
Automotive	26
Finance	15
Consumer durables	11
Other	6
Total	**100**
Core Businesses	
Automotive	
Construction and mining	
Durable goods	
Food/Beverage/Tobacco	
Energy	
Financial services	
Information technology	
International trade	

Marinas
New business development
Tourism and services

COMPETITORS

Adam Opel	Renault
Caterpillar	Robert Bosch
Electrolux	Sabanci
Hellenic Petroleum	Siemens AG
Honda	Yazicilar
International Power	

HISTORICAL FINANCIALS
Company Type: Public

Income Statement
FYE: December 31

	REVENUE ($ mil.)	NET INCOME ($ mil.)	NET PROFIT MARGIN	EMPLOYEES
12/19	25,798	737	2.9%	92,990
12/18	27,074	1,046	3.9%	92,631
12/17	26,140	1,297	5.0%	94,111
12/16	20,103	980	4.9%	95,456
12/15	23,789	1,221	5.1%	91,304
Annual Growth	**2.0%**	**(11.8%)**	**—**	**0.5%**

2019 Year-End Financials
Debt ratio: 6.7%
Return on equity: 12.6%
Cash ($ mil.): 6,355
Current ratio: 1.39
Long-term debt ($ mil.): 6,555
No. of shares (mil.): —
Dividends
  Yield: 1.5%
  Payout: 84.3%
Market value ($ mil.): —

	STOCK PRICE ($) FY Close	P/E High/Low		PER SHARE ($) Earnings	Dividends	Book Value
12/19	17.05	10	7	0.29	0.26	0.02
12/18	13.20	8	5	0.41	0.32	0.02
12/17	24.43	13	9	0.51	0.32	0.03
12/16	19.42	16	11	0.39	0.31	0.03
12/15	18.84	17	13	0.48	0.28	0.03
Annual Growth	**(2.5%)**	**—**	**—**	**(11.8%)**	**(1.7%)**	**(6.3%)**

Komatsu Ltd

Auditors: KPMG AZSA LLC

LOCATIONS

HQ: Komatsu Ltd
2-3-6 Akasaka, Minato-ku, Tokyo 107-8414
Phone: (81) 3 5561 2604   **Fax:** 847 437-5814
Web: home.komatsu/en/

HISTORICAL FINANCIALS
Company Type: Public

Income Statement
FYE: March 31

	REVENUE ($ mil.)	NET INCOME ($ mil.)	NET PROFIT MARGIN	EMPLOYEES
03/20	24,651	1,551	6.3%	68,879
03/19	27,478	2,586	9.4%	68,674
03/18	25,218	1,980	7.9%	65,017
03/17	18,179	1,143	6.3%	50,614
03/16	18,703	1,385	7.4%	50,496
Annual Growth	**7.1%**	**2.9%**	**—**	**8.1%**

2020 Year-End Financials
Debt ratio: 0.2%
Return on equity: 8.5%
Cash ($ mil.): 2,517
Current ratio: 1.68
Long-term debt ($ mil.): 4,132
No. of shares (mil.): 945
Dividends
  Yield: 6.3%
  Payout: 63.7%
Market value ($ mil.): 15,509

	STOCK PRICE ($) FY Close	P/E High/Low		PER SHARE ($) Earnings	Dividends	Book Value
03/20	16.41	0	0	1.64	1.05	18.90
03/19	23.30	0	0	2.74	0.88	19.38
03/18	33.65	0	0	2.10	0.58	17.78
03/17	26.18	0	0	1.21	0.53	16.85
03/16	17.07	0	0	1.47	0.47	16.24
Annual Growth	**(1.0%)**	**—**	**—**	**2.8%**	**22.2%**	**3.9%**

Komercni Banka AS (Czech Republic)

Auditors: Deloitte Audit s.r.o.

LOCATIONS

HQ: Komercni Banka AS (Czech Republic)
Na Prikope 33/969, Prague 1 114 07
Phone: (420) 485 262 800   **Fax:** (420) 224 243 020
Web: www.kb.cz

HISTORICAL FINANCIALS
Company Type: Public

Income Statement
FYE: December 31

	ASSETS ($ mil.)	NET INCOME ($ mil.)	INCOME AS % OF ASSETS	EMPLOYEES
12/19	47,607	658	1.4%	8,351
12/18	47,183	660	1.4%	8,454
12/17	47,049	699	1.5%	8,696
12/16	36,059	534	1.5%	8,615
12/15	35,939	514	1.4%	8,575
Annual Growth	**7.3%**	**6.4%**	**—**	**(0.7%)**

2019 Year-End Financials
Return on assets: 1.3%
Return on equity: 14.5%
Long-term debt ($ mil.): —
No. of shares (mil.): 188
Sales ($ mil) 2,358
Dividends
  Yield: —
  Payout: —
Market value ($ mil.): —

Kommunalbanken A/S (Norway)

Auditors: Ernst & Young AS

LOCATIONS

HQ: Kommunalbanken A/S (Norway)
Haakon VIIs gate 5b, Oslo 0161
Phone: (47) 2150 2000
Web: www.kbn.org

HISTORICAL FINANCIALS
Company Type: Public

Income Statement				FYE: December 31
	ASSETS ($ mil.)	NET INCOME ($ mil.)	INCOME AS % OF ASSETS	EMPLOYEES
12/19	52,431	140	0.3%	85
12/18	52,730	166	0.3%	82
12/17	50,352	170	0.3%	80
12/16	48,620	77	0.2%	72
12/15	50,987	210	0.4%	72
Annual Growth	0.7%	(9.7%)	—	4.2%

2019 Year-End Financials

Return on assets: 0.2%
Return on equity: 7.7%
Long-term debt ($ mil.): —
No. of shares (mil.): 3
Sales ($ mil): 1,020
Dividends
Yield: —
Payout: —
Market value ($ mil.): —

KommuneKredit (Denmark)

LOCATIONS

HQ: KommuneKredit (Denmark)
Kultorvet 16, Copenhagen K DK-1175
Phone: (45) 33 11 15 12 **Fax:** (45) 33 91 15 21
Web: www.kommunekredit.dk

HISTORICAL FINANCIALS
Company Type: Public

Income Statement				FYE: December 31
	ASSETS ($ mil.)	NET INCOME ($ mil.)	INCOME AS % OF ASSETS	EMPLOYEES
12/19	35,606	67	0.2%	76
12/18	34,753	64	0.2%	70
12/17	35,836	78	0.2%	70
12/16	31,805	70	0.2%	66
12/15	31,118	15	0.0%	62
Annual Growth	3.4%	45.1%	—	5.2%

Kone OYJ

Auditors: PricewaterhouseCoopers Oy

LOCATIONS

HQ: Kone OYJ
Keilasatama 3, P.O. Box 7, Helsinki FIN-02150
Phone: (358) 9 204 751 **Fax:** (358) 9 204 75 4309
Web: www.kone.com

HISTORICAL FINANCIALS
Company Type: Public

Income Statement				FYE: December 31
	REVENUE ($ mil.)	NET INCOME ($ mil.)	NET PROFIT MARGIN	EMPLOYEES
12/19	15,707	1,465	9.3%	59,825
12/18	14,273	1,323	9.3%	57,359
12/17	14,071	1,523	10.8%	55,075
12/16	13,822	1,610	11.7%	52,104
12/15	13,607	1,624	11.9%	49,734
Annual Growth	3.7%	(2.5%)	—	4.7%

2019 Year-End Financials

Debt ratio: 9.7%
Return on equity: 29.8%
Cash ($ mil.): 1,042
Current ratio: 1.28
Long-term debt ($ mil.): 672
No. of shares (mil.): 517
Dividends
Yield: 2.8%
Payout: 32.7%
Market value ($ mil.): 16,895

	STOCK PRICE ($) FY Close	P/E High/Low		PER SHARE ($)		
				Earnings	Dividends	Book Value
12/19	32.63	18	13	2.83	0.93	9.64
12/18	23.88	18	14	2.56	1.02	9.34
12/17	26.78	15	11	2.96	0.82	8.85
12/16	22.35	13	10	3.13	0.77	8.53
12/15	21.01	12	9	3.15	0.66	7.75
Annual Growth	11.6%	—	—	(2.6%)	8.7%	5.6%

Koninklijke Ahold Delhaize NV

Koninklijke Ahold Delhaize is one of Europe's biggest retailers with nearly 7000 stores across its Benelux heartland as well as Europe the US and Indonesia. Formed in 2016 from the merger of Royal Ahold and Delhaize Group the company operates as Giant Food Stop & Shop Food Lion and other banners in the East Coast of the US. In Europe the company trades as Albert Heijn the market leader in the Netherlands Delhaize in Belgium and other retail chains across Central and Southeastern Europe. Other interests include meal kit delivery service Peapod in the US Gall & Gall liquor stores in the Netherlands and joint ventures in Portugal and Indonesia. All told Ahold Delhaize owns about 15 retail brands. Most of the company's sales were generated from the US accounting to around 60% of total sales.

Operations

Ahold Delhaize has four reporting segments based on geographic lines: The US The Netherlands Belgium and Central and Southeastern Europe.

In the US Ahold Delhaize's operates more than 2000 supermarkets and convenience stores under several brands. Food Lion accounts for about 1030 stores located in 10 Southeastern and Mid-Atlantic US states while it operates nearly 415 Stop & Shop convenience stores across Connecticut Massachusetts New Jersey New York and Rhode Island. Its other brands are Stop & Shop Food Lion Giant/Martin's Hannaford and Giant Food. Ahold Delhaize's US operation accounts for around 60% of its total sales.

In the Netherlands Ahold Delhaize has more than 2100 stores trading under the Albert Heijin (groceries/general) Etos (drugstores) and Gall & Gall (wine and liquor) banners; it also trades online at bol.com a Netherlands' online retailer. The Netherlands accounts for over 20% of sales.

Ahold Delhaize's Belgium business consists approximately 800 stores under the brands Delhaize and Albert Heijin as well as and bol.com. It accounts for about 10% of sales.

Ahold Delhaize's business in Central and Southeastern Europe comprises Albert the largest retail brand in the Czech Republic Alfa-Beta in Greece Mega Image in Romania and Tempo in Serbia. The segment which consists of 1700 store all told generates nearly 10% of sales.

Besides the above Ahold Delhaize holds a noncontrolling more than 50% stake in Super Indo a major supermarket chain in Indonesia and about 49% stake in JMR a supermarket chain in Portugal.

Overall the company's owned store sales generates some 85% of sales while franchise stores and online sales account for the rest.

Geographic Reach

Ahold Delhaize is headquartered in Zaandam the Netherlands. Its brands are active in Belgium the Czech Republic Greece Luxembourg the Netherlands Romania Serbia and the United States and we participate in joint ventures in Indonesia and Portugal. Ahold Delhaize local brands has nearly 7000 local grocery small format and specialty stores.

Sales and Marketing

Ahold Delhaize offers a number of reward schemes across its brands including Food Lion's Shop & Earn.

Financial Performance

Note: Growth rates may differ after conversion to US Dollars.

Net sales for the financial year ended December 29 2019 were ?66.3 billion an increase of ?3.5 billion or 6% compared to net sales of ?62.8 billion for the financial year ended December 30 2018. At constant exchange rates net sales were up by ?1.5 billion or 2%.

The company's net income decreased by ?14 million to ?1.77 billion in 2019 from ?1.78 billion.

Cash held by the company at the end of 2019 increased by ?591 million to ?3.7 billion from ?3.1 billion in the prior year. Cash provided by operations was ?5.5 billion while cash used for investing and financing activities were ?1.7 billion and ?3.2 billion respectively. Main cash uses in 2019 were for purchases of non-current assets dividends paid and payment of lease liabilities.

Strategy

The company's financial strategy and ambitions are intended to ensure it can achieve long-term value creation for its investors by delivering consistent and sustainable results with a focus on strong operational performance best-in-class cash generation and a disciplined and balanced approach to capital allocation.

Ahold Delhaize power digital and eCommerce strategies aimed at engaging consumers no matter when where or how it choose to shop and support Ahold Delhaize USA's great local brands to springboard growth through new eCommerce and digital capabilities.

Mergers and Acquisitions

In early 2019 Ahold Delhaize announces that Stop & Shop its largest brand in the United States has agreed to acquire King Kullen Grocery Co. as part of the brand's continued expansion on Long Island N.Y. The agreement includes King Kullen's 32 supermarkets five Wild by Nature stores and the use of its corporate offices located in Bethpage N.Y. The acquisition is currently expected to close during the first quarter of 2019 subject to customary closing conditions. Financial terms of the deal were not disclosed.

Company Background

Koninklijke Ahold Delhaize was formed in 2016 when supermarket giants Royal Ahold and Delhaize Group merged. The merger included bringing together Royal Ahold's 3200 stores and Delhaize Group's 3500 stores some of which competed in the same markets in the US and Europe. Delhaize's major pre-merger brands included the Food Lion supermarket chain as well as the Delhaize chain of stores in Europe and Super Indo in Indonesia while Royal Ahold's key brands comprised Giant Food Stop & Shop and Albert Heijn.

EXECUTIVES

CEO, A. Dick Boer, age 63, $895,750 total compensation
President and CEO Giant-Carlisle, Sander van der Laan, age 51
CFO, Jeff Carr, age 60
COO Ahold USA, James McCann, age 51
Vice Chairman, Tom de Swaan, age 75
Chairman, René Dahan, age 79
Auditors: PricewaterhouseCoopers Accountants N.V.

LOCATIONS

HQ: Koninklijke Ahold Delhaize NV
 Provincialeweg 11, Zaandam 1506 MA
Phone: (31) 88 659 5100
Web: www.aholddelhaize.com

2018 sales

	% of total
US	60
Netherlands	23
Belgium	8
Central and Southeastern Europe	9
Total	**100**

PRODUCTS/OPERATIONS

2018 sales

	% of total
Owned store sales	86
Franchise and affiliate store sales	9
Online sales	5
Wholesale sales	-
Other	-
Total	**100**

Selected Operations

Retail
 Europe
  Albert (supermarkets Czech Republic and Slovakia)
  Albert Heijn (supermarkets convenience stores)
  Alfa-Beta (supermarkets)
  Delhaize (supermarkets)
  Etos (drugstores online shopping)
  Gall & Gall (liquor stores)
  MAXI (supermarkets)
  Mega Image (supermarkets)
  Shop & Go (convenience stores)
 US
  Food Lion (supermarkets)
  Giant-Carlisle (supermarkets & superstores)
  Giant-Landover (supermarkets)
  Stop & Go (convenience stores)
  Stop & Shop (supermarkets)

COMPETITORS

A&P	METRO AG
ALDI	NorgesGruppen
BJ's Wholesale Club	Safeway
Big Y Foods	Shaw's
Carrefour	Target Corporation
Costco Wholesale	Tesco
Golub	Wal-Mart
Kooperativa F ¶rbundet	Wegmans
Kroger	Whole Foods
Lidl	

HISTORICAL FINANCIALS

Company Type: Public

Income Statement
FYE: December 29

	REVENUE ($ mil.)	NET INCOME ($ mil.)	NET PROFIT MARGIN	EMPLOYEES
12/19	73,853	1,968	2.7%	380,000
12/18	71,599	2,044	2.9%	372,000
12/17*	75,389	2,178	2.9%	369,000
01/17	52,472	876	1.7%	370,000
01/16	41,484	925	2.2%	236,000
Annual Growth	**15.5%**	**20.8%**	**—**	**12.6%**

*Fiscal year change

2019 Year-End Financials

Debt ratio: 18.7%
Return on equity: 12.2%
Cash ($ mil.): 4,142
Current ratio: 0.76
Long-term debt ($ mil.): 4,281
No. of shares (mil.): 1,087
Dividends
 Yield: 0.0%
 Payout: 51.4%
Market value ($ mil.): 27,525

	STOCK PRICE ($) FY Close	P/E High/Low	Earnings	PER SHARE ($) Dividends	Book Value
12/19	25.30	17 14	1.77	0.91	14.43
12/18	25.15	17 13	1.73	0.60	14.95
12/17*	22.01	17 12	1.71	0.57	14.81
01/17	20.99	29 24	0.86	0.00	13.51
01/16	21.14	20 14	1.18	0.60	7.93
Annual Growth	**4.6%**	**— —**	**10.8%**	**11.0%**	**16.2%**

*Fiscal year change

Koninklijke Philips NV

Auditors: Ernst & Young Accountants LLP

LOCATIONS

HQ: Koninklijke Philips NV
 Phillips Center, Amstelplein 2, Amsterdam 1096 BC
Phone: (31) 20 59 77 232
Web: www.philips.com

HISTORICAL FINANCIALS

Company Type: Public

Income Statement
FYE: December 31

	REVENUE ($ mil.)	NET INCOME ($ mil.)	NET PROFIT MARGIN	EMPLOYEES
12/19	30,656	1,836	6.0%	80,495
12/18	28,515	1,715	6.0%	77,400
12/17	27,978	2,607	9.3%	115,392
12/16	38,578	2,278	5.9%	113,678
12/15	38,150	1,014	2.7%	112,959
Annual Growth	**(5.3%)**	**16.0%**		**(8.1%)**

2019 Year-End Financials

Debt ratio: 31.7%
Return on equity: 9.4%
Cash ($ mil.): 2,242
Current ratio: 1.36
Long-term debt ($ mil.): 7,772
No. of shares (mil.): 890
Dividends
 Yield: 1.6%
 Payout: 40.5%
Market value ($ mil.): 43,480

	STOCK PRICE ($) FY Close	P/E High/Low	Earnings	PER SHARE ($) Dividends	Book Value
12/19	48.80	38 26	2.01	0.82	22.25
12/18	35.11	39 29	1.83	0.80	20.81
12/17	37.80	24 16	2.75	0.76	20.39
12/16	30.57	19 15	2.45	0.77	21.50
12/15	25.45	43 33	1.10	0.76	20.01
Annual Growth	**17.7%**	**— —**	**16.3%**	**1.9%**	**2.7%**

Korea Electric Power Corp

Auditors: KPMG Samjong Accounting Corp.

LOCATIONS

HQ: Korea Electric Power Corp
 55, Jeollyeok-ro, Naju-si, Jeollanam-do 58217
Phone: (82) 61 345 4299   **Fax:** (82) 2 3456 4298
Web: www.kepco.co.kr

HISTORICAL FINANCIALS

Company Type: Public

Income Statement
FYE: December 31

	REVENUE ($ mil.)	NET INCOME ($ mil.)	NET PROFIT MARGIN	EMPLOYEES
12/19	59,446	(2,380)	—	22,973
12/18	61,537	(1,334)	—	22,595
12/17	60,225	1,318	2.2%	22,196
12/16	61,093	7,154	11.7%	21,560
12/15	59,842	13,488	22.5%	20,603
Annual Growth	**(0.2%)**	**—**		**2.8%**

2019 Year-End Financials

Debt ratio: 0.0%
Return on equity: (-3.6%)
Cash ($ mil.): 1,837
Current ratio: 0.80
Long-term debt ($ mil.): 60,002
No. of shares (mil.): 641
Dividends
 Yield: —
 Payout: —
Market value ($ mil.): 7,594

	STOCK PRICE ($) FY Close	P/E High/Low	Earnings	PER SHARE ($) Dividends	Book Value
12/19	11.83	— —	(3.71)	0.00	106.72
12/18	14.75	— —	(2.08)	0.37	110.27
12/17	17.71	0 0	2.05	0.86	113.33
12/16	18.48	0 0	11.14	1.37	113.40
12/15	21.17	0 0	21.01	0.23	105.35
Annual Growth	**(13.5%)**	**— —**	**—**	**—**	**0.3%**

Krung Thai Bank Public Co. Ltd.

EXECUTIVES

Chairman of the Board, Prasong Poontaneat
Auditors: State Audit Office of the Kingdom of Thailand

LOCATIONS

HQ: Krung Thai Bank Public Co. Ltd.
 35 Sukhumvit Road, Klongtoey Nua, Wattana, Bangkok 10110
Phone: (66) 2 255 2222   **Fax:** (66) 2 255 9391
Web: www.ktb.co.th

COMPETITORS

Bangkok Bank	KASIKORNBANK
Bank of Ayudhya	Thanachart Capital

HISTORICAL FINANCIALS

Company Type: Public

Income Statement
FYE: December 31

	ASSETS ($ mil.)	NET INCOME ($ mil.)	INCOME AS % OF ASSETS	EMPLOYEES
12/19	101,122	983	1.0%	0
12/18	84,675	880	1.0%	0
12/17	87,610	688	0.8%	0
12/16	75,134	901	1.2%	0
12/15	78,138	790	1.0%	0
Annual Growth	6.7%	5.6%	—	—

2019 Year-End Financials

Return on assets: 1.0%	Dividends
Return on equity: 9.0%	Yield: —
Long-term debt ($ mil.): —	Payout: —
No. of shares (mil.): —	Market value ($ mil.): —
Sales ($ mil): 5,595	

KT Corp (Korea)

Auditors: Samil PricewaterhouseCoopers

LOCATIONS

HQ: KT Corp (Korea)
90, Buljeong-ro, Bundang-gu, Seongnam-si, Gyeonggi-do
Phone: (82) 31 727 0114   **Fax:** (82) 31 727 0949
Web: www.kt.co.kr

HISTORICAL FINANCIALS

Company Type: Public

Income Statement
FYE: December 31

	REVENUE ($ mil.)	NET INCOME ($ mil.)	NET PROFIT MARGIN	EMPLOYEES
12/19	21,564	562	2.6%	23,372
12/18	21,042	617	2.9%	23,835
12/17	21,937	447	2.0%	23,817
12/16	18,931	591	3.1%	23,575
12/15	18,937	469	2.5%	23,531
Annual Growth	3.3%	4.6%	—	(0.2%)

2019 Year-End Financials

Debt ratio: 0.0%	No. of shares (mil.): 245
Return on equity: 4.8%	Dividends
Cash ($ mil.): 1,997	Yield: 4.0%
Current ratio: 1.18	Payout: 20.9%
Long-term debt ($ mil.): 5,294	Market value ($ mil.): 2,845

	STOCK PRICE ($) FY Close	P/E High/Low		PER SHARE ($) Earnings	Dividends	Book Value
12/19	11.60	0	0	2.29	0.47	48.11
12/18	14.22	0	0	2.52	0.47	48.31
12/17	15.61	0	0	1.82	0.37	44.72
12/16	14.09	0	0	2.42	0.21	38.88
12/15	11.91	0	0	1.92	0.00	37.65
Annual Growth	(0.7%)	—	—	4.5%	—	6.3%

Kubota Corp. (Japan)

Kubota has been the hand that turns the earth's soil for over a century. The diversified enterprise is Japan's largest maker of tractors and farm equipment from rice transplanters to combine harvesters. It also leads in producing iron ductile pipe for water supply systems as well as PVC pipe and the engines for its agricultural and industrial movers. The company has also entered into building environmental control plants and pumps. International sales subsidiaries dot the globe. Kubota generates around half of its sales in Asia.

Operations

Kubota operates in the three segments: farm and industrial machinery water and environment and other.

Farm and industrial machinery segment accounts for more than 80% of the company's total sales. It includes production of agricultural machinery and agricultural-related products such as tractors and combine harvesters construction machinery inclusive of skid steer loaders and wheel loaders and engines.

The water and environment systems segment produces pipe systems water treatment facilities and plants for incinerating melting crushing and recycling wastes. It generates over 15% of total sales.

Geographic Reach

Kubota manufactures its products not only in Japan but also in overseas countries like the US China Thailand and Europe. It sells its products in Japan North America Europe Asia and other countries. Asia is the company's largest market generating around 50% of net sales. Other major markets include North America (approximately 35%) Europe (more than 10%) and other regions (about 5%).

Financial Performance

In 2019 the revenue of Kubota has increased by Å 69.7 billion [4%] from the prior year to Å 1.9 trillion. Domestic revenue increased by Å 48.0 billion [8%] from the prior year to Å 625.4 billion due to revenue in Water & Environment whose businesses are mainly related to public works projects increased mainly due to significantly increased sales of environment-related products and strong sales of ductile iron pipes.

Profit for the year increased by Å 8.9 billion [6.0%] from the prior year to Å 159.1 billion.

Strategy

Based on its corporate philosophy the company sets a long-term goal of building "Global Major Brand (GMB)" or in other terms a brand that can make the greatest social contribution as a result of being trusted by the largest number of customers. The company aims to establish the GMB Kubota make the greatest contribution to success of the Sustainable Development Goals (SDGs) promoted by the United Nations and achieve sustainable development over the long term. To these ends the company will team up and work together with various players across its business domains encompassing the areas of food water and the environment and provide society with total solutions created through those synergies.

Moreover to achieve the above objectives the company will engage in three initiatives — a more flexible and proactive task setting development of open and innovative technologies and business schemes creation and provision of total solutions through the promotion of DX by utilizing new IT. In addition the company will draw up its GMB 2030 long-term vision looking ten years ahead at the year 2030 and will also formulate its Mid-term Plan for making that vision a reality.

Company Background

Kubota Corporation was founded in 1890 as a casting manufacturer. The company developed the cultivator in 1947 and a tractor in 1960. It stated manufacturing mini-excavators in 1974. In 2011 it became the first company in the world to acquire the US CARB certificate. It established its manufacturing company in France in 2014 and water treatment facilities in Myanmar in 2015.

HISTORY

The son of a poor farmer and coppersmith Gonshiro Oode left home in 1885 at age 14 and moved to Osaka to find work. He began as an apprentice at the Kuro Casting Shop where he learned about metal casting. He saved his money and in 1890 opened Oode Casting.

Oode's shop grew rapidly thanks to the industrialization of the Japanese economy and the expansion of the iron and steel industries. One of Oode's customers Toshiro Kubota took a liking to the hardworking young man and in 1897 Kubota adopted him. Oode changed his own name to Kubota and also changed the name of his company to Kubota Iron Works.

Kubota made a number of technological breakthroughs in the early 1900s including a new method of producing cast-iron pipe (developed in 1900). The company became the first to make the pipe in Japan and it continued to grow as the country modernized its infrastructure.

Kubota began making steam engines machine tools and agricultural engines in 1917 and it also began exporting products to countries in Southeast Asia. In 1930 Kubota restructured and incorporated. It continued to add product lines including agricultural and industrial motors.

Although WWII brought massive destruction to Japan the peacetime that followed created plenty of work for Kubota's farm equipment and pipe operations as the country rebuilt. By 1960 the company was Japan's largest maker of farm equipment ductile iron pipe and cement roofing materials. That year Kubota introduced the first small agricultural tractor in Japan.

EXECUTIVES

Senior Managing Executive Officer, Shigeru Kimura
Executive Officer; President Siam Kubota, Hiroshi Kawakami
Director, Yasuo Masumoto, age 73
Senior Managing Executive Officer, Nobuyuki Toshikuni, age 70
EVP, Tetsuji (Mike) Tomita, age 70
Senior Managing Executive Officer, Masatoshi Kimata, age 69
Senior Managing Executive Officer, Satoru Sakamoto, age 68
Senior Managing Executive Officer, Toshihiro Kubo, age 67
Executive Office; President Kubota China Holdings, Takashi Uei
Executive Officer; President Kubota Manufacturing of America, Hironobu Kubota
Executive Officer; President Kubota Tractor, Masato Yoshikawa
Executive Officer; President Kubota Europe, Dai Watanabe
Auditors: Deloitte Touche Tohmatsu LLC

LOCATIONS

HQ: Kubota Corp. (Japan)
1-2-47 Shikitsuhigashi, Naniwa-Ku, Osaka 556-8601
Phone: (81) 6 6648 2115
Web: www.kubota.co.jp

2015 Sales

	% of total
Asia	
Japan	42
Other Asian countries	19
North America	24
Europe	12
Other regions	3
Total	**100**

PRODUCTS/OPERATIONS

2015 Sales

	% of total
Farm & industrial machinery	76
Water & environment systems	21
Other	3
Total	**100**

Selected Products

Farm & industrial machinery
Construction machinery (mini-excavators wheel loaders)
Engines (industrial applications)
Farm equipment (tractors combine harvesters rice transplanters power tillers reaper binders)
Other
Construction
Services & other businesses
Social infrastructure
Air conditioning equipment
Electronic-equipped machinery
Industrial castings
Steel pipes
Vending machines
Water & environment systems
Ductile iron pipes
Environmental control plants (water & sewage treatment plants submerged membrane systems biogas production systems pulverizing facilities irrigation systems)
Plastic pipes & fittings
Pumps
Valves

COMPETITORS

AGCO
Amerequip
Asahi/America
Caterpillar
Chang-on
Crane Co.
Deere
Fuji Electric
Gradall Industries
Hillco
Hitachi Construction Machinery
IHI Corp.
Iseki & Company
Isuzu
J C Bamford Excavators
Japan Steel Works
Komatsu
Marubeni-Komatsu
Mitsubishi Steel Mfg.
Nippon Steel & Sumitomo Metal Corporation
Sekisui House
Toro Company
Toyota

HISTORICAL FINANCIALS

Company Type: Public

Income Statement			FYE: December 31

	REVENUE ($ mil.)	NET INCOME ($ mil.)	NET PROFIT MARGIN	EMPLOYEES
12/19	17,684	1,372	7.8%	43,907
12/18	16,825	1,260	7.5%	43,206
12/17	15,566	1,212	7.8%	42,441
12/16	13,646	1,132	8.3%	41,571
12/15	10,340	914	8.8%	39,883
Annual Growth	**14.4%**	**10.7%**	—	**2.4%**

2019 Year-End Financials

Debt ratio: 0.2%	No. of shares (mil.): 1,220
Return on equity: 10.7%	Dividends
Cash ($ mil.): 1,431	Yield: 2.0%
Current ratio: 1.72	Payout: —
Long-term debt ($ mil.): 4,756	Market value ($ mil.): 96,401

	STOCK PRICE ($) FY Close	P/E High/Low		PER SHARE ($) Earnings	Dividends	Book Value
12/19	79.00	1	1	1.12	1.62	10.89
12/18	70.45	1	1	1.02	1.52	9.89
12/17	98.68	1	1	0.98	1.37	9.37
12/16	71.10	1	1	0.91	1.18	8.26
12/15	77.39	1	1	0.73	1.22	7.61
Annual Growth	**0.5%**	—	—	**11.1%**	**7.4%**	**9.4%**

Kuehne & Nagel International AG

EXECUTIVES

EVP Contract Logistics, Gianfranco Sgro, age 52
CIO, Martin Kolbe, age 59
CEO, Detlef Trefzger, age 57
EVP Overland, Stefan Paul
EVP Sea Logistics, Horst Joachim Schacht
EVP Air Logistics, Yngve Ruud, age 55
Chairman, Joerg W. Wolle, age 63
Vice Chairman, Karl Gernandt, age 59
Auditors: Ernst & Young Ltd

LOCATIONS

HQ: Kuehne & Nagel International AG
Kuehne & Nagel House, P.O. Box 67, Schindellegi CH-8834
Phone: (41) 44 786 95 11 **Fax:** (41) 44 786 95 95
Web: www.kuehne-nagel.com

COMPETITORS

APL Logistics
Agility Public Warehousing
Bollore
C.H. Robinson Worldwide
CEVA Logistics
DB Mobility Logistics
Damco
Expeditors
GEFCO
Geodis
Hellmann Worldwide Logistics
Nippon Express
Panalpina
Ryder System
Sinotrans
UPS Supply Chain Solutions
Wincanton

HISTORICAL FINANCIALS

Company Type: Public

Income Statement			FYE: December 31

	REVENUE ($ mil.)	NET INCOME ($ mil.)	NET PROFIT MARGIN	EMPLOYEES
12/19	21,820	825	3.8%	83,161
12/18	21,117	782	3.7%	81,900
12/17	19,051	755	4.0%	75,876
12/16	16,234	707	4.4%	70,038
12/15	16,847	680	4.0%	67,236
Annual Growth	**6.7%**	**4.9%**	—	**5.5%**

2019 Year-End Financials

Debt ratio: 4.3%	No. of shares (mil.): 119
Return on equity: 34.4%	Dividends
Cash ($ mil.): 941	Yield: 2.1%
Current ratio: 1.06	Payout: 11.0%
Long-term debt ($ mil.): 413	Market value ($ mil.): 4,066

	STOCK PRICE ($) FY Close	P/E High/Low		PER SHARE ($) Earnings	Dividends	Book Value
12/19	33.95	5	4	6.89	0.72	20.00
12/18	25.46	6	4	6.53	0.71	19.68
12/17	35.50	6	4	6.30	0.69	(0.00)
12/16	26.55	5	4	5.87	0.58	17.75
12/15	28.00	5	4	5.67	0.86	17.82
Annual Growth	**4.9%**	—	—	**5.0%**	**(4.1%)**	**2.9%**

Kunlun Energy Co., Ltd.

EXECUTIVES

CFO, Lau Hak Woon, age 68
CEO, Zhao Yongqi, age 60
President, Zhang Bowen, age 54
Assistant CEO, Xia Yu, age 57
Chairman, Huang Weihe
Auditors: KPMG

LOCATIONS

HQ: Kunlun Energy Co., Ltd.
39/F., 118 Connaught Road West,
Phone: (852) 2522 2282 **Fax:** (852) 2868 1741
Web: www.kunlun.com.hk

PRODUCTS/OPERATIONS

2016 Sales

	% of total
Natural Gas Distribution	
Natural Gas Sales	78
Natural Gas Pipeline	17
LNG Terminal	2
LNG Processing	1
Exploration & Production	2
Total	**100**

Selected Subsidiaries & Owned Oil Field Projects

Projects
Azerbaijan K&K Project (25% owned)Indonesia Bengara-II Project (70% owned)Kazakhstan Aktobe Project (15% owned)Liaohe Leng Jiapu Cooperation Project (70% owned)Oman Block 5 Project (25% owned)Peru Talara Project (50% owned)Thailand Sukhothai Project (96%
Subsidiaires
Binhai New Energy Co. Ltd.Cangzhou Gas Limited Company PetroChinaChina City Natural Gas Investment Group Co. Ltd.China Natural Gas Co. Ltd.CNPC Shennan Oil Technology Development Co. LtdGreen Ever Company LimitedHuagang Gas Group Company LimitedJilin Jig

COMPETITORS

Anadarko Petroleum	Eni
Apache	Exxon Mobil
BP	Royal Dutch Shell
CNOOC	Sinopec Corp.
Chevron	TOTAL

HISTORICAL FINANCIALS
Company Type: Public

Income Statement				FYE: December 31
	REVENUE ($ mil.)	NET INCOME ($ mil.)	NET PROFIT MARGIN	EMPLOYEES
12/19	16,284	797	4.9%	38,557
12/18	15,333	673	4.4%	42,278
12/17	13,631	731	5.4%	41,835
12/16	10,559	84	0.8%	37,281
12/15	5,372	17	0.3%	19,696
Annual Growth	31.9%	159.2%	—	18.3%

2019 Year-End Financials
Debt ratio: 3.3%
Return on equity: 11.9%
Cash ($ mil.): 2,678
Current ratio: 0.75
Long-term debt ($ mil.): 3,697

No. of shares (mil.): —
Dividends
  Yield: —
  Payout: 40.6%
Market value ($ mil.): —

Kweichow Moutai Co., Ltd.

Kweichow Moutai's liquor will really put some hair on your chest. The company makes Moutai (sometimes known as Maotai in the West) the national liquor of China. Moutai is a type of baijiu a 100 proof distilled spirit made of wheat and sorghum. Kweichow Moutai produces about 20000 tons of Moutai every year — the most expensive being an 80-year-old bottle that sells for hundreds of dollars. Moutai is exported to 100 countries including the US. The distillery is located in Moutai Town in Kweichow Province in southwestern China. Moutai has been made in China for thousands of years but the state-owned Kweichow Moutai company was formed in 1951.

Financial Performance
The company is targeting one billion yuan ($165 million) in sales in 2014 and has set the figure to 5 to 10 billion yuan ($826 million to $1.65 billion) in three to five years

Strategy
Kweichow Moutai is pursuing the high-end of the market with the formation in 2014 of Kweichow Moutai Custom-Made Marketing Limited which customizes maotai orders for individuals businesses celebrities and other groups. Bottles sell for as much as CNY100000 ($16500).

EXECUTIVES
President, Yaun Renguo, age 59
VP General Manager and Deputy Party Secretary Kweichow Moutai Winery, Liu Zili, age 65
Auditors: BDO China Shu Lun Pan Certified Public Accountants

LOCATIONS
HQ: Kweichow Moutai Co., Ltd.
  Maotai Town, Renhuai, Guizhou Province 564501
Phone: (86) 852 2386002   **Fax:** (86) 852 2386005
Web: www.moutaichina.com

PRODUCTS/OPERATIONS
Selected Products
Elite General
Great China

Kweichow Moutai liquor (Feitian)
Kweichow Moutai liquor (Five-Star)
Kweichow Moutai liquor (New Feitian)
Kweichow Moutai liquor (New Five-Star)
Moutai Prince
Moutai Ying Bin Chiew
Han jiang
Ren

COMPETITORS
Asahi Breweries	Kingway Brewery
Beam Suntory	Kirin Holdings Company
Beijing Shunxin Agriculture	Pernod Ricard
Diageo	Shaoxing Yellow Wine
Dynasty Fine Wines	Takara
	Tsingtao

HISTORICAL FINANCIALS
Company Type: Public

Income Statement				FYE: December 31
	REVENUE ($ mil.)	NET INCOME ($ mil.)	NET PROFIT MARGIN	EMPLOYEES
12/19	12,769	5,921	46.4%	0
12/18	11,223	5,118	45.6%	0
12/17	9,383	4,161	44.3%	0
12/16	5,782	2,407	41.6%	0
12/15	5,150	2,387	46.4%	0
Annual Growth	25.5%	25.5%		

2019 Year-End Financials
Debt ratio: —
Return on equity: 33.1%
Cash ($ mil.): 1,904
Current ratio: 3.87
Long-term debt ($ mil.): —

No. of shares (mil.): —
Dividends
  Yield: —
  Payout: —
Market value ($ mil.): —

Kyocera Corp

Auditors: PricewaterhouseCoopers Kyoto

LOCATIONS
HQ: Kyocera Corp
  6 Takeda Tobadono-cho, Fushimi-ku, Kyoto 612-8501
Phone: (81) 75 604 3500   **Fax:** (81) 75 604 3501
Web: www.kyocera.co.jp

HISTORICAL FINANCIALS
Company Type: Public

Income Statement				FYE: March 31
	REVENUE ($ mil.)	NET INCOME ($ mil.)	NET PROFIT MARGIN	EMPLOYEES
03/20	16,122	1,086	6.7%	75,505
03/19	16,371	1,040	6.4%	76,863
03/18	15,900	824	5.2%	75,940
03/17	14,345	1,047	7.3%	70,153
03/16	14,918	1,099	7.4%	69,229
Annual Growth	2.0%	(0.3%)	—	2.2%

2020 Year-End Financials
Debt ratio: 0.0%
Return on equity: 4.5%
Cash ($ mil.): 4,230
Current ratio: 3.03
Long-term debt ($ mil.): 453

No. of shares (mil.): 362
Dividends
  Yield: 2.5%
  Payout: 49.2%
Market value ($ mil.): 21,250

	STOCK PRICE ($)	P/E		PER SHARE ($)		
	FY Close	High/Low		Earnings	Dividends	Book Value
03/20	58.63	0	0	3.00	1.48	67.66
03/19	58.91	0	0	2.87	1.07	63.16
03/18	56.74	0	0	2.24	1.07	64.06
03/17	56.13	0	0	2.85	0.93	64.00
03/16	44.16	0	0	3.00	0.89	62.76
Annual Growth	7.3%	—	—	0.0%	13.5%	1.9%

Kyushu Electric Power Co Inc

Kyushu Electric Power generates transmits and distributes electricity on Japan's southernmost island. The company serves customers in the Kyushu region providing nuclear thermal and hydroelectric power generation. The company's other operations include telecommunications information system development business and data center business. It also sells wholesale electricity and has international power production and consulting operations primarily in Asia. Kyushu Electric was established in 1951. The power transmission and distribution business of Kyushu Electric Power was spun off as Kyushu Electric Power Transmission and Distribution Co. Inc. in 2020 to enhance the neutrality of the power transmission and distribution network.

Operations
Kyushu Electric's segments are Domestic Electric power (some 85% of sales) Other Energy Service (about 10%) Information and Communication Technology (ICT) Service (some 5%) and Other
The Domestic Electric Power segment is engaged in the business of power generation and retail electricity in Japan and electricity transmission and distribution in Kyushu region.
The Other Energy Service segment is engaged in the business that provides a stable supply of electric power such as construction and maintenance of electricity-related facilities selling gas and LNG a renewable energy business and overseas business.
The ICT Service segment is engaged in the data communication business optical broadband business construction and maintenance of telecommunications facilities information system development business and data center business.
Other segment is engaged in the real estate business nursing home business and other business.
Overall about 90% of sales were generated from electric operations.

Geographic Reach
Headquartered in Fukuoka Japan Kyushu Electric has around 55 offices across Japan.

Financial Performance
In terms of income as of March 31 for 2020 consolidated operating revenues decreased 0.2% from the previous fiscal year to Å 2.01 trillion despite an increase in sales in the ICT service business. Factors include a decrease in retail electricity sales and in electricity sales to other suppliers as well as an increase in renewable energy-related subsidies.
As a result of the foregoing factors net income attributable to owners of the parent declined by Å 31.3 billion over the previous fiscal year to Å 400 million.

Cash held by the company at the end of fiscal 2020 decreased to Â 205.5 billion compared to Â 245.3 billion in the prior. Cash provided by operation and financing activities were Â 226.9 billion and Â 158.0 billion respectively. Cash used for investing activities was Â 424.6 billion mainly for capital expenditures including nuclear fuel.

Strategy

In recent years there have been growing expectations toward efforts to bring about a sustainable society on a global scale. These include efforts to achieve the United Nations' sustainable development goals (SDGs) for the international community and ESG investment that evaluates companies' consideration of factors such as the environment. The company recognizes the importance of meeting these expectations.

That is why its group strategy and ESG initiatives are inseparable. To name an example its management vision includes a business performance target of contributing to the reduction of Kyushu's CO_2 emissions by 70%. This is consistent with Japan's plan to combat global warming (a 26% reduction from 2013 levels in 2030) under the Paris Agreement. We have set three strategies for achieving its vision: Strategy I tied to E (Environment) Strategy II tied to S (Society) and Strategy III tied to G (Governance). Its entire management vision is linked to ESG.

In Strategy I the company will contribute to a sustainable low-carbon society by improving our ratio of non-fossil fuel power sources Environment through the use of renewable and nuclear energy and by promoting electricity usage in many fields. Strategy II will contribute to the resolution of various issues affecting communities and wider society by creating markets through new businesses and services. Strategy III will strengthen the business foundations that support the growth of the Kyuden Group.

Mergers and Acquisitions

In 2019 Kyushu Electric Power Co. Inc. participates in the management of EGCO which is one of the largest Independent Power Producers in Thailand by acquiring indirect interest in the Electricity Generating Public Company Limited. With this participation its equity ownership in overseas electricity generation project is approximately 2300MW which approaches its target in its mid-term management policy to expand equity ownership of 5000MW by 2030. Terms were not disclosed.

EXECUTIVES

President, Michiaki Uriu
EVP, Tomoyuki Aramaki
EVP, Naofumi Satou
EVP, Kazuhiro Izaki
EVP, Yuuzou Sasaki
Senior Managing Executive Officer, Hideomi Yakushinji
Senior Managing Executive Officer, Yoshiro Watanabe
Senior Managing Executive Officer, Takashi Yamasaki
Senior Managing Executive Officer, Akira Nakamura
Senior Managing Executive Officer, Narumi Nagao
Chairman, Masayoshi Nuki
Auditors: Deloitte Touche Tohmatsu LLC

LOCATIONS

HQ: Kyushu Electric Power Co Inc
  2-1-82 Watanabe-dori, Chuo-ku, Fukuoka 810-8720
Phone: (81) 92 761 3031
Web: www.kyuden.co.jp

PRODUCTS/OPERATIONS

2016 Sales

	% of total
Electric power	92
IT and Telecommunication	4
Energy related Business	3
Others	1
Total	**100**

COMPETITORS

Chubu Electric Power	KEPCO
Chugoku Electric Power	Shikoku Electric
Hokkaido Electric Power	Tohoku Electric Power
Hokuriku Electric Power	Tokyo Electric
	Tokyo Gas

HISTORICAL FINANCIALS

Company Type: Public

Income Statement				FYE: March 31
	REVENUE ($ mil.)	NET INCOME ($ mil.)	NET PROFIT MARGIN	EMPLOYEES
03/20	18,544	(3)	—	21,180
03/19	18,214	279	1.5%	21,103
03/18	18,461	816	4.4%	20,968
03/17	16,345	708	4.3%	20,889
03/16	16,346	654	4.0%	20,929
Annual Growth	**3.2%**	**—**	**—**	**0.3%**

2020 Year-End Financials

Debt ratio: 0.6%	No. of shares (mil.): 473
Return on equity: (-0.0%)	Dividends
Cash ($ mil.): 1,879	Yield: —
Current ratio: 0.55	Payout: —
Long-term debt ($ mil.): 25,755	Market value ($ mil.): —

L'Air Liquide S.A. (France)

Auditors: ERNST & YOUNG et Autres

LOCATIONS

HQ: L'Air Liquide S.A. (France)
  75, quai d'Orsay, Paris, Cedex 07 75007
Phone: (33) 1 40 62 55 55
Web: www.airliquide.com

HISTORICAL FINANCIALS

Company Type: Public

Income Statement				FYE: December 31
	REVENUE ($ mil.)	NET INCOME ($ mil.)	NET PROFIT MARGIN	EMPLOYEES
12/19	24,836	2,516	10.1%	67,200
12/18	24,277	2,420	10.0%	66,000
12/17	24,659	2,636	10.7%	65,200
12/16	19,331	1,947	10.1%	66,700
12/15	18,051	1,913	10.6%	51,500
Annual Growth	**8.3%**	**7.1%**	**—**	**6.9%**

2019 Year-End Financials

Debt ratio: 37.8%	No. of shares (mil.): 471
Return on equity: 12.2%	Dividends
Cash ($ mil.): 1,151	Yield: 1.9%
Current ratio: 0.88	Payout: 10.1%
Long-term debt ($ mil.): 14,208	Market value ($ mil.): 13,225

	STOCK PRICE ($) FY Close	P/E High/Low		PER SHARE ($)		
				Earnings	Dividends	Book Value
12/19	28.05	6	5	5.31	0.54	44.94
12/18	24.67	6	5	5.13	0.56	43.26
12/17	25.16	6	5	5.60	0.53	41.67
12/16	22.24	5	4	4.45	0.88	37.68
12/15	22.43	7	5	4.59	0.47	32.56
Annual Growth	**5.7%**	**—**	**—**	**3.7%**	**3.5%**	**8.4%**

L'Oreal S.A. (France)

Auditors: Deloitte & Associés

LOCATIONS

HQ: L'Oreal S.A. (France)
  14, rue Royale, Paris 75008
Phone: (33) 1 47 56 70 00   **Fax:** (33) 1 47 56 86 42
Web: www.loreal.com

HISTORICAL FINANCIALS

Company Type: Public

Income Statement				FYE: December 31
	REVENUE ($ mil.)	NET INCOME ($ mil.)	NET PROFIT MARGIN	EMPLOYEES
12/19	33,541	4,210	12.6%	87,974
12/18	30,848	4,460	14.5%	85,000
12/17	31,196	4,293	13.8%	82,578
12/16	27,280	3,279	12.0%	89,331
12/15	27,510	3,591	13.1%	82,881
Annual Growth	**5.1%**	**4.1%**	**—**	**1.5%**

2019 Year-End Financials

Debt ratio: 2.1%	No. of shares (mil.): 558
Return on equity: 13.3%	Dividends
Cash ($ mil.): 5,934	Yield: 1.4%
Current ratio: 1.28	Payout: 11.5%
Long-term debt ($ mil.): 10	Market value ($ mil.): 32,856

	STOCK PRICE ($) FY Close	P/E High/Low		PER SHARE ($)		
				Earnings	Dividends	Book Value
12/19	58.87	9	7	7.48	0.86	59.18
12/18	45.66	7	6	7.92	0.86	55.11
12/17	44.28	7	6	7.62	0.79	53.15
12/16	36.41	7	6	5.81	0.67	46.19
12/15	33.75	7	5	6.36	0.60	45.93
Annual Growth	**14.9%**	**—**	**—**	**4.1%**	**9.3%**	**6.5%**

LafargeHolcim Ltd

Get set for some solid operations with Lafarge-Holcim the world's largest cement maker. Each year the Swiss company produces more than 500 million tonnes of building materials in the form of cement aggregates asphalt and ready-mix concrete products. It has a global presence managed through its offices scattered around approximately 80 countries The company's products are used by individuals and giant construction companies to build housing infrastructure oil & gas well and roadways. It also offers research import/export trading and management services for the construction industry. LafargeHolcim generates majority of its revenue from Europe.

Operations

LafargeHolcim operates four business segments: Cement Ready- Mix Concrete Aggregates and Solutions & Products.

The Cement segment generates some 60% of total sales and produces typical masonry products to high-performance offerings tailored for specialized uses. It sells more than 200 million tonnes of it to individuals buying bags of cement to businesses embarking on major construction projects.

The Ready-Mix segment delivers concrete in various forms all of them ready for individuals and businesses to deploy for its specific projects. The 50 million tonnes of it sold each year accounts for nearly 20% of sales.

The Aggregates segment (almost 15% of sales) provides the raw materials for concrete masonry and asphalt. It also produces base materials for roads buildings and landfills including recycled aggregates (such as crushed concrete and asphalt left over from deconstruction activities). LafargeHolcim delivers nearly 270 million tonnes of aggregates each year.

The fourth segment Solutions & Products works closely with customers to define and deliver solutions tailored to customers' requirements.

All told the company has around 2300 plants including more than 1400 ready-mix concrete almost 650 aggregates and nearly 265 cement and grinding plants.

Geographic Reach

Switzerland-headquartered LafargeHolcim has a large asset presence in around 80 countries and boasts a market presence in just about every developed region on the globe.

LafargeHolcim's sales are well-balanced across the world's major regions. The company generates almost 30% of its total sales from Europe; the Asia/Pacific regions accounts for nearly 25% North America brings in almost 25% of total sales; and Latin America Middle East and Africa together pull in the remaining more than 20% of Lafarge's total sales.

Sales and Marketing

LafargeHolcim's customers span major multinationals to small-scale businesses and individual customers. Its customers include manufacturers of prefabricated products concrete and asphalt producers construction and public work contractors.

Financial Performance

Note: Growth rates may differ after conversion to US Dollars.

LafargeHolcim's revenue has generally seen growth in the last five years despite its slight dip in 2019. Revenue grew 13% between 2015 and 2019 while its net income has struggled to maintain consistent growth in the same period. Net income has alternated between loss and profit in the years 2015 to 2018 only seeing consecutive profits in the later years.

In 2019 LafargeHolcim grew its sales 3% to CHF 26.7 billion. The growth was driven by good growth in Europe and North America and good price dynamics across all business segments and higher prices in most markets.

The company's net income increased CHF 794 million to CHF 2.5 billion in 2019 due to lower production cost distribution and selling expenses administration expenses and other financial expenses.

LafargeHolcim's cash position strengthened during 2019 ending the year CHF 2 billion higher at CHF 4 billion. The company's operations generated CHF 4.8 billion while investing activities used

CHF 219 million and financing activities used CHF 2.6 billion. Its primary cash uses in 2019 were capital expenditures dividend payouts and loan repayments.

Strategy

LafargeHolcim has a new strategy aptly named Strategy 2022 - "Building for Growth" which aims to drive profitable growth and simplify the business to deliver resilient returns and attractive value to stakeholders. It has four value drivers: Growth; Simplification & Performance; Financial Strength; and Vision & People.

In terms of the value driver Growth the group aims to capitalize on the underlying growth of the building materials market seeking to deliver above-market performance. The agile country-based growth strategies will target value-enhancing bolt-on acquisitions to leverage scale and margins.

The value driver Simplification & Performance will create a cost disciplined operating model and a corporate-light structure. There will be greater focus on countries with local markets empowered and fully profit and loss accountable. The simplification will allow LafargeHolcim to improve its cost efficiency considerably.

Financial Strength will ensure disciplined value creation through maintaining an investment grade credit rating and Vision & People further develops the values of trust and integrity the commitment to Health & Safety and the desire to be at the forefront of sustainable construction solutions and innovation.

Additionally LafargeHolcim is spearheading the transition towards low-carbon construction and is the leader in promoting a circular economy from alternative fuels to concrete recycling. Its four pillars of sustainability?Climate & Energy Circular Economy Environment and Communities?create value for its business and shareholders and underpin Strategy 2022.

Mergers and Acquisitions

In mid-2019 LafargeHolcim agreed to acquire Somaco. Somaco operates under ORESA is one of the leading precast concrete producer based in Romania. The transaction will allow the acquiring company to develop its position on the Romanian building materials market.

In early 2019 LafargeHolcim acquired Transit Mix Concrete Co. a leading supplier of building materials based in Colorado US. The acquisition will strengthen LafargeHolcim's position in the growing building materials market of the US.

In addition to the acquisition made in early 2019 the company also acquired the precast and ready-mix concrete businesses of Alfons Greten Betonwork based in Germany. Greten operates one ready-mix plant in the state of Lower Saxony. The transaction will expand LafargeHolcim's ready-mix concrete portfolio and will strengthen its solutions and products segment in the region.

EXECUTIVES

Group CFO, Ron H. Wirahadiraksa, age 60

Area Manager Central and South America, Oliver Osswald, age 49

Region Head Europe Australia/New Zealand and Trading, Roland K ¶hler, age 67

Area Manager North America and Mexico, Pascal Casanova, age 52

Head of Organization and Human Resources, Caroline Luscombe, age 61

CEO, Jan Jenisch, age 53

Area Manager Middle-East Africa, Sa d Sebbar

Area Manager India and South East Asia, Martin Kriegner, age 59

Co-Chairman, Bruno Lafont, age 64

Chairman, Beat W. Hess, age 71

Auditors: Deloitte AG

LOCATIONS

HQ: LafargeHolcim Ltd
Zurcherstrasse 156, Rapperswil-Jona CH-8645
Phone: (41) 58 858 58 58   **Fax:** (41) 58 858 87 19
Web: www.lafargeholcim.com

2018 sales

	% of total
Asia Pacific	27
Europe	28
Latin America	10
Middle East & Africa	11
North America	21
Corporate/Eliminations	2
Total	**100**

PRODUCTS/OPERATIONS

2018 sales

	% of total
Cement	60
Aggregates	14
Ready-mix concrete	18
Products and Solutions	8
Total	**100**

COMPETITORS

Boral	Martin Marietta
CEMEX	Materials
CRH	Sumitomo Osaka Cement
Dyckerhoff	Taiheiyo Cement
Franz Haniel	Tarmac
HeidelbergCement	Titan Cement
Italcementi	Vicat

HISTORICAL FINANCIALS

Company Type: Public

Income Statement   FYE: December 31

	REVENUE ($ mil.)	NET INCOME ($ mil.)	NET PROFIT MARGIN	EMPLOYEES
12/19	27,642	2,323	8.4%	72,452
12/18	27,920	1,526	5.5%	77,055
12/17	26,772	(1,716)	—	81,960
12/16	26,430	1,759	6.7%	90,903
12/15	23,747	(1,479)	—	100,956
Annual Growth	3.9%	—	—	(8.0%)

2019 Year-End Financials

Debt ratio: 22.5%	No. of shares (mil.): 613
Return on equity: 8.1%	Dividends
Cash ($ mil.): 4,290	Yield: 3.2%
Current ratio: 1.34	Payout: 9.9%
Long-term debt ($ mil.): 13,141	Market value ($ mil.): 6,787

	STOCK PRICE ($) FY Close	P/E High/Low		PER SHARE ($) Earnings	Dividends	Book Value
12/19	11.06	3	2	3.81	0.36	48.15
12/18	8.16	5	3	2.56	0.35	45.91
12/17	11.21	—	—	(2.85)	0.35	47.68
12/16	10.52	4	2	2.91	0.26	49.99
12/15	10.14	—	—	(3.13)	0.23	52.15
Annual Growth	2.2%	—	—	— 12.2%	(2.0%)	

Larsen & Toubro Ltd

Auditors: M/S Deloitte Haskins & Sells LLP

LOCATIONS

HQ: Larsen & Toubro Ltd
L&T House, Ballard Estate, Mumbai 400 001
Phone: (91) 22 6752 5656   **Fax:** (91) 22 6752 5893
Web: www.larsentoubro.com

HISTORICAL FINANCIALS

Company Type: Public

Income Statement				FYE: March 31
	REVENUE ($ mil.)	NET INCOME ($ mil.)	NET PROFIT MARGIN	EMPLOYEES
03/19	20,378	1,286	6.3%	44,761
03/18	18,423	1,132	6.1%	42,924
03/17	17,179	931	5.4%	41,466
03/16	15,698	769	4.9%	43,354
03/15	14,871	761	5.1%	44,081
Annual Growth	8.2%	14.0%	—	0.4%

2019 Year-End Financials

Debt ratio: 0.6%
Return on equity: 15.0%
Cash ($ mil.): 1,694
Current ratio: 1.24
Long-term debt ($ mil.): 10,711

No. of shares (mil.): 1,402
Dividends
Yield: —
Payout: 28.3%
Market value ($ mil.): —

Laurentian Bank of Canada

Laurentian Bank of Canada offers commercial and consumer banking services from some 155 branches located mostly in Quebec. Combined residential mortgages and personal loans account for 90% of the bank's loan portfolio. Other retail products include checking and savings accounts mutual funds and credit cards. The bank also has 38 commercial banking centers that cater to small to mid-sized businesses real estate developers and agricultural concerns. Subsidiary B2B Bank offers financial products to financial planners advisors and brokers. The fast-growing bank has roughly $43 billion in assets under administration.

Operations

Laurentian Bank operates through three main business segments: Personal & Commercial B2B Bank and Laurentian Bank Securities and Capital Markets.

The bank's Personal & Commercial segment generates nearly 70% of revenue and caters to the financial needs of business clients across Canada and retail clients in Quebec. The business offers retail clients savings accounts loans insurance and investment products and services and offers business clients a suite of financing options leasing solutions deposit accounts cash management and foreign exchange services. The segment gets the majority of its income in the form of interest from loans in which residential mortgages account for about 60% of the bank's loan portfolio while personal loans represent nearly 30%. Beyond loans the segment generates nearly a third of its income from lending fees investment commissions and insurance income.

Laurentian's B2B Bank (formerly B2B Trust) segment accounts for roughly 25% of revenue and provides banking products to brokers and financial advisors across Canada. While the segment makes most of its revenue from interest income from high-margin investment loans it also earns revenue from investment management fees and related service charges.

The makes the rest of its revenue from its Laurentian Bank Securities & Capital Markets segment which offers investors a variety of integrated brokerage services. The segment consists of Laurentian Bank Securities a full-service broker and the

bank's capital market activities which both mostly generate income from underwriting fees related to investment markets.

Geographic Reach

Montréal-based Laurentian Bank of Canada has more than 35 offices across Ontario Québec Alberta and British Columbia. A reported 100% of its retail service loan originate in Quebec while nearly 60% of its B2B Bank loans are based out of Ontario. The bank also generates a significant volume of B2B Bank loans from Western and Eastern Canada.

Sales and Marketing

The company provides its banking services to individuals and small and medium-sized enterprises real estate developers in Canada middle-class Quebec consumers Canadian independent advisors and Canadian small cap companies municipalities and bond issuers nationwide.

Financial Performance

Laurentian's revenue was fell by 8% to C$1.46 billion (about $1.3 billion) in fiscal 2014 as the bank earned less interest because of shrinking interest margins on loans and fewer high-margin investment loan originations and also because it collected less in prepayment penalties from mortgage loans. The bank did manage to grow its non-interest income however mostly thanks to higher lending fee collections from increased underwriting activity and loan prepayment penalties in the commercial loan portfolio.

Despite a dip in revenue net income rose by 5% to C$140.4 million (about $125.4 million) mostly as the bank cut its expenses through acquisition-related employee layoffs aggressive cost control measures on discretionary spending and decreased costs related to acquisitions as it wound down its integration processes in 2014.

Cash levels from were significantly healthier too with operations providing C$622.9 million (about $556.4 million) in 2014 (by comparison operations used C$1.15 billion in 2013). Most of the change was thanks to an influx of cash from deposits compared to an outflow of deposits in 2013 and because the bank used less cash to fund loans than the year before.

Strategy

Laurentian Bank has three main strategic priorities to grow: increase profitability by focusing on high-potential growth sectors improve efficiency of operations and cater to its local markets to ensure clientele loyalty.

Toward the first goal the bank plans to double both its B2B Bank's mortgage loan portfolio and its business loan portfolio to $8 billion and $10 billion respectively by 2018. The company has made great strides already toward growing its loan base through recent acquisitions (including AGF Trust) which increased its loans by more than 90% and its deposits by more than 30% over the last five years.

The bank has made several steps toward its efficiency goals including reducing its head count through strategic cuts in personnel from recently acquired companies (AGF Trust and MRS Companies) and through stringent cost control measures on discretionary spending — both of which helped the company achieve 5% profit growth in fiscal 2014. In 2016 the company responded to the industry trend of consumers banking online by announcing plans to shutter dozens of branch locations. To increase operating efficiencies further the company plans to utilize its partnerships more to offer services they specialize in. For example rather than be a mutual fund "manufacturer" itself the bank partnered with Mackenzie Financial to offer mutual fund products which enabled the bank to grow its mutual fund sale revenue by 30% in 2014.

Laurentian also intends to continue pleasing its niche market customers which include individuals and small and medium-sized enterprises real estate developers in Canada middle-class Quebec consumers Canadian independent advisors and Canadian small cap companies municipalities and bond issuers. The bank believes that its tailor-fit solutions to these target markets sets it apart from other banks and gives it a competitive advantage when it comes to fostering future business relationships from this local clientele across Canada.

Mergers and Acquisitions

In 2016 the company bought CIT Canada the Canadian equipment and corporate finance businesses of CIT Group. The transaction aligns with Laurentian's strategy of adding more products and services and serving a larger pool of customers. CIT Canada has more than $700 million in assets.

Company Background

Laurentian Bank traces its roots back to 1846 when it began as The Montreal City and District Savings Bank.

EXECUTIVES

EVP and CFO, Fran §ois Laurin
President and CEO Laurentian Bank Securities, Michel C. Trudeau
President and CEO, Fran §ois Desjardins, age 49, $209,769 total compensation
EVP Personal and Commercial Banking; President and CEO LBC Financial Services, Stephane Therrien
President and CEO B2B Bank; EVP Intermediary Banking and CIO Laurentian Bank, Deborah Rose
EVP Chief Risk Officer and Corporate Affairs, Susan Kudzman
Chairman, Isabelle Courville
Auditors: Ernst & Young LLP

LOCATIONS

HQ: Laurentian Bank of Canada
1360 Rene-Levesque Blvd West, Suite 600, Montreal, Quebec H3G 0E5
Phone:
Web: www.lbcfg.ca

2013 Loans

	% of total
Qué;bec	60
Ontario	29
Rest of Canada	11
Total	**100**

PRODUCTS/OPERATIONS

2016 Revenue

	% of total
Interest income:	
loans	71
securities	2
Other including derivatives	4
Other income:	
Fees and commissions on loans and deposits	10
Income from brokerage operations	5
Income from sales of mutual funds	3
Income from investment accounts	2
Insurance income net	1
Income from treasury and financial market operations	1
Other	1
Total	**100**

2016 Loans

	% of total
Residential mortgage	71
Personal	29
Total	**100**

Selected Subsidiaries

B2B Bank
Laurentian Bank Securities Inc.
Laurentian Trust of Canada Inc.

LBC Financial Services Inc.
LBC Investment Management Inc.
LBC Trust
V.R. Holding Insurance Holding Company Ltd.

COMPETITORS

BMO Financial Group	HSBC Bank Canada
CIBC	National Bank of
Caisse de dép´t et	Canada
placement du Québec	RBC Financial Group
Caisses centrale	Scotiabank
Desjardins	TD Bank

HISTORICAL FINANCIALS

Company Type: Public

Income Statement   FYE: October 31

	ASSETS ($ mil.)	NET INCOME ($ mil.)	INCOME AS % OF ASSETS	EMPLOYEES
10/20	44,724	115	0.3%	3,048
10/19	44,912	174	0.4%	3,256
10/18	46,473	227	0.5%	3,642
10/17	47,271	209	0.4%	3,732
10/16	43,548	153	0.4%	3,687
Annual Growth	0.7%	(6.9%)	—	(4.6%)

2020 Year-End Financials

Return on assets: 0.2%	Dividends
Return on equity: 4.3%	Yield: 0.0%
Long-term debt ($ mil.): —	Payout: 90.3%
No. of shares (mil.): 43	Market value ($ mil.): 857
Sales ($ mil): 1,732	

	STOCK PRICE ($) FY Close	P/E High/Low		PER SHARE ($) Earnings	Dividends	Book Value
10/20	19.82	15	8	2.40	2.17	61.15
10/19	34.32	9	7	3.82	2.65	61.00
10/18	31.86	9	6	5.16	2.57	60.07
10/17	46.83	9	7	5.47	2.49	60.56
10/16	36.40	9	7	4.61	2.39	59.09
Annual Growth	(14.1%)	—	—	(15.0%)	(2.4%)	0.9%

Legal & General Group PLC (United Kingdom)

Legal & General Group (L&G) is one of the UK's largest financial services companies. The London-based company operates in three primary business areas: investing and annuities (pensions) investment management and insurance. Holding about Å 95 billion in defined contribution pension scheme assets L&G's pensions business offers annuity contracts Longevity insurance contracts Lifetime mortgages and Life time care plan. The investment management business manages defined benefit pension funds and offers retail investment funds. L&G is also the UK's top life insurer. The firm operates in the US as Banner Life Insurance Company and William Penn Life Insurance Company of New York.

Operations

Legal & General (L&G) divides its operations into four business segments namely Legal & General Retirement (LGR) Legal & General Investment Management (LGIM) Legal & General Capital (LGC) and Legal & General Insurance (LGI).

LGR L&G's largest business accounting for 60% of operating profits serves institutional and retail

clients. It provides annuities defined benefit pension scheme buy-ins and buyouts lifetime mortgages and longevity (i.e. lifespan) insurance.

LGIM generates more than 15% of L&G's profits and offers a range of pooled index funds fixed income funds and defined benefit pension scheme de-risking.

LGC and LGI bring in more than 25% of profits combined. LGC makes capital investments in housing urban regeneration clean energy and SME finance (inc. venture capital). LGI offers life insurance in the UK and US.

All in L&G has more than Å 1.2 trillion in assets under management making it the largest investment manager in the UK.

Geographic Reach

Legal & General (L&G) is headquartered in London and has offices in Barnsley Birmingham Hove and Cardiff. L&G is dependent on the UK which accounts for the majority of its sales and customers (although it also serves customers in the US the Netherlands and Ireland).

About one-third of L&G's Å 1.2 trillion assets under management are held abroad.

Sales and Marketing

Legal & General serves more than 10 million individual customers It mainly distributes its insurance products in the UK and the US through direct distribution channels existing broker and agency channels.

Financial Performance

The company's revenue increased by Å 65.9 billion to Å 66.8 billion in 2019 from Å 894 million in the prior year. The increase was primarily due to a Å 53.0 billion of investment return.

L&G's net profit for 2019 maintained Å 1.8 billion same with the net profit of 2018. The small change was primarily due to the higher expenses offsetting the increase on their revenue.

Cash held by the company at the end of 2019 decreased by Å 3.8 billion to Å 18.0 billion from Å 13.9 billion in the prior year. Cash used for operations and financing activities were Å 3.3 billion and Å 692 million respectively. Cash provided by investing activities was Å 138 million primarily from net disposal of operations.

Strategy

The company's strategy is driven by long-term global trends which include ageing populations globalization of asset markets and climate change.

The drivers of the company's strategies includes: ageing demographics; welfare reforms; globalization of asset markets; Investing in the real economy; technological innovation; investing in the real economy; and addressing climate change.

L&G will increase its DC asset portfolio with total UK DC assets expected to more than double by 2028 to Å 955 billion. The company's investment in digital insurance solutions will improve efficiency and returns

Mergers and Acquisitions

n Mid-2019 Legal & General Retail Retirement acquired England-based MyFutureNow which specializes in pension pot tracing and consolidation for an undisclosed amount. MyFutureNow gives Legal & General an added benefit service for existing and potential customers across Legal & General's Retail Retirement and defined contribution pensions business.

EXECUTIVES

Managing Director Legal & General Insurance, Duncan Finch
CFO, Stephen Halliwell
CEO Legal & General Investment Management, Mark Zinkula
CEO Legal & General Investment Management America, Robert J. Moore

Interim President and CEO Legal & General America, Gene Gilbertson
Group CEO, Nigel Wilson
Managing Director Legal & General Retirement, Kerrigan Procter
CEO Legal & General Capital, Paul Stanworth
Managing Director Mature Savings, Jackie Noakes
CEO Modular Housing, Rosie Toogood
Chairman, John Kingman
Auditors: KPMG LLP

LOCATIONS

HQ: Legal & General Group PLC (United Kingdom)
One Coleman Street, London EC2R 5AA
Phone: (44) 20 3124 2000   **Fax:** (44) 20 3124 2500
Web: www.legalandgeneralgroup.com

PRODUCTS/OPERATIONS

2018 operating profit

	% of total
LGR (Retirement)	
LGR Retail	44
LGR Institutional	16
LGIM (Investment Management)	16
LGI (Insurance)	12
LGC (Capital)	12
Total	**100**

Selected Subsidiaries

Banner Life Insurance Company Inc - long-term business; US
First British American Reinsurance Company II - reinsurance; US
First British Bermudan Reinsurance Company II Limited - reinsurance; Bermuda
First British Vermont Reinsurance Company II - reinsurance; US
First British Vermont Reinsurance Company - reinsurance; US
Legal & General (France) SA - long-term business
Legal & General (Portfolio Management Services) Limited - institutional fund management
Legal & General (Unit Trust Managers) Limited - unit trust management
Legal & General Assurance (Pensions Management) Limited - long-term business
Legal & General Assurance Society Limited - long-term and general insurance
Legal & General Bank (France) SA - financial services
Legal & General Finance PLC1 - treasury operations
Legal & General Insurance Limited - general insurance
Legal & General International (Ireland) Limited - long-term business
Legal & General Investment Management America Inc - institutional fund management
Legal & General Investment Management Limited - institutional fund management
Legal & General Nederland Levensverzekering Maatschappij NV - long-term business; Netherlands
Legal & General Partnership Services Limited - provision of services
Legal & General Pensions Limited - reinsurance
Legal & General Property Limited - property management
Legal & General Resources Limited1 - provision of services
Legal & General Risques Divers (France) SA - insurance company
LGV Capital Limited - private equity
Nationwide Life Limited - long-term business
Suffolk Life Annuities Limited - long-term business
Suffolk Life Pensions Limited - long-term business
William Penn Life Insurance Company of New York Inc - long-term business; US

COMPETITORS

AEGON	Pension Insurance
AXA	Corporation
Allianz	Prudential
Aviva	Prudential plc
ING	Royal London Mutual
Lloyds Banking Group	Standard Life Aberdeen
MetLife	Zurich Insurance Group

HISTORICAL FINANCIALS
Company Type: Public

Income Statement   FYE: December 31

	ASSETS ($ mil.)	NET INCOME ($ mil.)	INCOME AS % OF ASSETS	EMPLOYEES
12/19	740,316	2,421	0.3%	8,542
12/18	628,826	2,332	0.4%	7,981
12/17	683,282	2,554	0.4%	7,629
12/16	575,526	1,547	0.3%	8,939
12/15	588,034	1,593	0.3%	10,148
Annual Growth	5.9%	11.0%	—	(4.2%)

2019 Year-End Financials

Return on assets: 0.3%	Dividends
Return on equity: 20.4%	Yield: 0.0%
Long-term debt ($ mil.): —	Payout: 255.3%
No. of shares (mil.): —	Market value ($ mil.): —
Sales ($ mil) 88,195	

	STOCK PRICE ($) FY Close	P/E High/Low	PER SHARE ($) Earnings	Dividends	Book Value
12/19	20.29	68 46	0.41	1.04	2.08
12/18	14.81	60 47	0.39	0.92	1.85
12/17	18.63	59 49	0.43	0.95	1.78
12/16	15.08	79 48	0.26	0.80	1.44
12/15	20.13	122 95	0.27	0.18	1.60
Annual Growth	0.2%	— —	11.0%	54.5%	6.8%

Lenovo Group Ltd

Lenovo Group tops the worldwide PC market ahead of HP Inc. and Dell Technologies and it operates competitive phone and server businesses. Through a series of acquisitions the Hong Kong-based company is focused on a bold vision to deliver smarter technology for all we are developing world-changing technologies that create a more inclusive trustworthy and sustainable digital society. Lenovo has resurrected the Motorola brand in smartphones. Besides ThinkPad-branded commercial PCs Lenovo turns out tablets and software. Its sales are evenly sourced from the major world markets of China Asia Pacific America and Europe-Middle East-Africa (EMEA).

Operations
Lenovo operates in two reportable segments: Intelligent Devices Group and Data Center Group.

Lenovo's Intelligent Devices Group includes the company's biggest business the PC and Smart Devices unit which accounts for about 80% of the company's revenue. It continues to lead the sector with record PC market share of nearly 25% continuing to extend its leadership as the #1 PC company in the world and with sustained industry-beating profitability. Intelligent Devices Group also includes the Mobile business which accounts for some 10% of revenue.

The Data Center Business Group about 10% of revenue offers servers storage networking software and services.

Geographic Reach
Lenovo's logistics teams work closely with logistics partners to ship products responsibly. Lighter and smaller products more compact and reusable packaging materials bulk shipping alternatives and regional distribution facilities allow for lighter loads load consolidation and full truckload shipments. The company sold less than 10% of its goods and services to its five largest customers. T

he company spent $796 million in 2020 and $708 million in 2019 on advertising and promotional expenses.

Financial Performance
After sales dipped in 2016 and 2017 it rebounded back the next two years. Profits also bounced back in 2019 and 2020 after a loss in 2018.

In 2020 (ended March) revenue fell by about 1% to $50.7 billion almost the same as the record revenue in 2019. The unprecedented outbreak of COVID-19 and the subsequent factory shutdowns had a material impact on the Group's revenue which dropped 9.7 percent year-on-year in the last quarter of the fiscal year.

Profit jumped by 22% to $804.5 million in fiscal 2020 brought about by lesser cost of sales.

Lenovo had $3.6 billion in cash and equivalents in 2020 compared to $2.7 billion from the year before. In 2020 operations generated $2.2 billion investing activities used $957 million and financing activities used another $238 million.

Strategy
Lenovo continues to execute its strategy to be the leader and enabler of Intelligent Transformation. The company has the vision of bringing smarter technology to all - through Smart Infrastructure Smart Verticals and Smart IoT. This "3S" strategy in parallel with its customer-centric positioning has led to a higher Software and Services attach rate. The Software and Services business is considered a strong long-term growth catalyst for profitable growth.

Smart infrastructure provides the computing storage and networking power to support smart devices. The company launched its next-generation data center solutions in SDI and expects it to remain a future growth catalyst. These new solutions which include collaboration with several partners based on the ThinkAgile platform have grown revenue at a double-digits rate during the fiscal year under review.

The company will continue to invest in Smart IoT consisting of a network of many touchpoints for the connected world we live in. Specifically the Lenovo's investments will accelerate in the area of edge computing cloud big data and AI in vertical industries to deepen its strategic transformation and further accentuate its core competencies. These investments aim to strengthen the company's capability as a competitive end-to-end solution provider in the era of Intelligent Transformation.

Company Background
Liu Chuanzhi an engineer at the Chinese Academy of Sciences who wrote industry research reports established Legend Group Holdings Co. in 1984 in Beijing. Backed by a modest investment from the academy Liu who went on to become something of an entrepreneurial hero in China and 10 other engineers were given a green light to form a retail business. They first bought and sold items ranging from TVs to roller skates but later focused on distributing computer products and eventually moved into manufacturing PCs for AST Research. Legend introduced its first proprietary product a Chinese character system for PCs in 1985.

In 1988 the company formed Legend Holdings Limited which was originally a Hong Kong-based PC distributor. The following year the parent company began designing and manufacturing motherboards and added systems integration services to its offerings. In 1990 China reduced import tariffs a move that opened the trade door for companies such as IBM and Compaq. That year Legend Group Holdings began making its own brand of PCs.

In the 2000s Lenovo bought computer and mobile phone operations from US companies and became the top PC maker.

EXECUTIVES
SVP and Chief Marketing Officer, David A. Roman
Vice Chairman President and CEO, Yang Yuanqing, age 57, $894,000 total compensation
SVP and Co-President Mobile Business Group China, Qiao Jian
SVP Global Services, Chen Xudong
President and COO and President PC and Smart Devices, Gianfranco Lanci, age 65
EVP and CFO, Wong Wai Ming, age 62
SVP Co-President Mobile Business Group and Chairman and President Motorola Mobility, Aymar de Lencquesaing
EVP and President Data Center Group, Kirk B. Skaugen
VP and President LATAM and EMEA, Luca Rossi
SVP Lenovo Capital and Incubator Group and Acting CTO, He (George) Zhiqiang
President EMEA, Francois Bornibus
SVP and CTO, Yong Rui
CIO, Arthur Hu
President Lenovo Brazil, Ricardo Bloj
Auditors: PricewaterhouseCoopers

LOCATIONS
HQ: Lenovo Group Ltd
23rd Floor, Lincoln House, Taikoo Place, 979 King's Road, Quarry Bay,
Phone: (852) 2590 0228   **Fax:** (852) 2516 5384
Web: www.lenovo.com

2018 Sales

	$ mil.	% of total
Americas (AG)	16,413	31
Europe Middle east & Africa (EMEA)	12,502	28
China	12,357	25
Asia Pacific (AP)	9,764	16
Total	**51,037**	**100**

PRODUCTS/OPERATIONS

2019 Sales

	% of total
Personal Computers & Smart Devices	75
Mobile Business	13
Data Center Group	12
Total	**100**

Product Categories
Laptops
Desktops & All-in-Ones
Smartphones
Tablet PCs
Network Storage
Workstations
Accessories & Upgrades

COMPETITORS

ASUSTeK	Hitachi
Acer	Huawei Technologies
Apple Inc.	LG Electronics
Dell	NEC
Founder Holdings	Nokia
Fujitsu	Samsung Electronics
HP	Sony
HTC Corporation	Toshiba
Hedy Holding	

Company Type: Public

Income Statement				FYE: March 31
	REVENUE ($ mil.)	NET INCOME ($ mil.)	NET PROFIT MARGIN	EMPLOYEES
03/20	50,716	665	1.3%	63,000
03/19	51,037	596	1.2%	57,000
03/18	45,349	(189)	—	54,000
03/17	43,034	535	1.2%	52,000
03/16	44,912	(128)		60,000
Annual Growth	3.1%	—	—	1.2%

2020 Year-End Financials

Debt ratio: 15.1%
Return on equity: 26.2%
Cash ($ mil.): 3,550
Current ratio: 0.81
Long-term debt ($ mil.): 1,564

No. of shares (mil.): —
Dividends
  Yield: 6.3%
  Payout: 1,249.9%
Market value ($ mil.): —

	STOCK PRICE ($) FY Close	P/E High/Low	PER SHARE ($) Earnings	Dividends	Book Value
03/20	10.71	341 171	0.05	0.68	0.20
03/19	17.99	370 182	0.05	0.64	0.22
03/18	10.25	— —	(0.02)	0.64	0.28
03/17	13.13	346 234	0.05	0.64	0.27
03/16	15.54	30 691344	0.01	0.64	0.25
Annual Growth	(8.9%)	— —	47.1%	1.3%	(5.2%)

Leonardo SpA

Italy's largest engineering and aerospace/defense group Leonardo (formerly Leonardo-Finmeccanica) makes helicopters military aircraft defense systems satellites and much more. The company's US-based DRS Technologies provides infrared technology persistent surveillance battle management satellite networks communications infrastructures and other technologies. Other operations make sensors defensive aids tracking targeting navigation simulation avionics logistics automation and other products. It works closely with the Italian British Polish and American militaries its biggest customers; the Italian government owns around 30% of Leonardo. About 85% of its revenue comes from outside of Italy.

Operations

Leonardo operates through Defense Electronics & Security (about 45%) Helicopters (some 30%) and Aeronautics (nearly 25%) Space and Other Activities (around 5%).

Defense Electronics & Security composed of two divisions: Electronics Division and Cyber Security Division. Electronic Division designs and develops airborne land and naval applications from advanced components to fully integrated ISRC4I ISTAR solutions; combat and mission management systems tactical unmanned systems radar communications electronic warfare optronics infrared search and track artillery underwater systems air and maritime traffic management automation systems and space payloads and equipment. Cyber Security Division designs develops and produces a competitive solutions and services for cybersecurity and homeland security critical infrastructure protection transportation.

Helicopters segment designs develops produces customer supports and markets an extensive range of helicopters from the 1.8 tons single-engine to the 16 tons three-engine.

Aeronautics designs develops produces logistics support for trainers combat and tactical transport aircraft multi-role and regional turboprop aircraft and unmanned systems.

Space designs and develops integrated satellite systems management of satellite communication networks and development of geo-information and Earth observation applications: Leonardo provides a full offer which includes sensors payloads advanced robotics systems solutions and services.

Leonardo participates in a number of joint ventures particularly with Thales (Telespazio Group and Thales Alenia Space Group) to develop satellite services and systems; and with Airbus (GIE ATP and MBDA Group) for the development of regional turboprop aircraft and missiles.

Geographic Reach

Based in Rome Leonardo has direct operations in Italy the UK Poland and the US. Outside those companies Leonardo operates through a network of subsidiaries joint ventures and strategic collaborations reaching customers in more than 150 countries.

Leonardo's most prominent sources of revenue are North America (nearly 30%) Italy (around 15%) the UK (about 10%) and Europe (excl. Italy and UK) nearly 25%. All other countries account for the remaining above 20%.

Sales and Marketing

Leonardo's main customers are national governments or public institutions.

Financial Performance

Note: Growth rates may differ after conversion to US Dollars.

In 2019 Leonardo's sales grew 13% to ?13.8 billion which was mainly attributable to an increase in sales from the Defence Electronics & Security and Aeronautics Divisions.

Net income climbed 61% to ?822 million due largely to higher revenue and lower non-recurring charges and restructuring costs.

Leonardo's cash on hand decreased by ?87 million during 2019 ending the year at ?2.0 billion. The company's operations generated ?645 million partially offset by ?466 million used in investing and ?262 million used in financing activities. Leonardo's main cash uses in 2019 were for investments in property plant and equipment and intangible assets and for bond redemption.

Strategy

The aim of the management of technological and product research in Leonardo is to ensure constant ongoing equilibrium between technological enhancement projects whose objectives are to develop technologies competencies and products with a medium- to long-term impact on one hand and to improve existing products on the other. In order to seize the best opportunities also on the basis of different TRLs (Technology Readiness Levels) Leonardo's technological strategy is to involve various other players in an Open Innovation scenario such as the major national and international universities and research centers and innovative start-ups and SMEs as well as to collaborate with other industrial players within the scope of financed projects.

In 2019 Leonardo invested about 11% of its revenues in R&D involving about 9000 highly qualified human resources (engineering graduates mostly in aeronautics aerospace electronics mechanics IT and telecommunications physics in addition to specialist technicians). These resources belong to its engineering departments and divisional facilities responsible for both technological and product innovation allocated to the following areas of competence: Technology Office Management Engineering Management System Engineering Aeronautic Engineering Mechanical Engineering Electronics Engineering Software Engineering and Verification and Validation Engineering.

The Group also takes part in regional domestic and European Research and Innovation projects and funding programs. The regional and domestic initiatives include the Italian Technology Clusters (Leonardo holds the chairmanship of the "National Aerospace Technology Cluster") and the Regional Technology Districts.

Mergers and Acquisitions

In 2020 Leonardo acquired Kopter Group AG (Kopter) from Lynwood (Schweiz). The purchase price on a cash and debt free basis consists of a $185 million fixed component plus an earn-out mechanism linked to certain milestones over the life of the programme starting from 2022. The acquisition of Kopter allows Leonardo to further strengthen its worldwide leadership and position in the rotorcraft sector in line with the Industrial Plan's objectives for the reinforcement of the core businesses.

EXECUTIVES

CEO, Alessandro Profumo, age 63
CFO, Gian Piero Cutillo
Head Security, Tommaso Profeta
Head Risk Management, Salvatore Lampone
Head Information and Communication Technology, Matteo Attrovio
Chairman, Giovanni De Gennaro, age 72
Auditors: KPMG S.p.A.

LOCATIONS

HQ: Leonardo SpA
Piazza Monte Grappa 4, Rome
Phone: (39) 06 324 731   **Fax:** (39) 06 320 8621
Web: www.leonardocompany.com

2018 Sales

	% of total
Europe	
Italy	15
UK	11
Rest of Europe	25
North America	8
Rest of the world	21
Total	**100**

PRODUCTS/OPERATIONS

2018 Sales

	% of total
Defense & Security Electronics	46
Helicopters	29
Aeronautics	22
Other activities	3
Space	-
Eliminations	-
Total	**100**

Selected Products

Defense electronics
  Air traffic management
  Avionics
  Command and control systems
  Communications equipment
  Electronic systems
  Radar
  Simulators
  Unmanned aerial vehicles
Helicopters
  A109 Light Utility Helicopter
  A109 Power
  A119 Koala
  A129
  AW139
  BA609
  EH 101
  Grand Light Utility Helicopter
  NH90
  Super Lynx 300
Aeronautics
  Control surfaces
  Fuselage components

Horizontal stabilizers
Mechanical parts
Winglet
Transportation
Chopper and inverter drives
Converters
DC AC and multi-voltage locomotives
DC and AC motors
Electric multiple units
High-speed trains
Light and heavy metropolitan railways
Trambuses
Trolley buses
Defense systems
Airborne and naval weaponry
Armored vehicles
Main battle tanks
Missile systems
Naval systems
Weapons systems
Energy
Boilers
Cogeneration plants
Combined cycle generators
Geothermal generators
Hydrogenerators
Nuclear power plants
Steam and gas turbines
Turbogas generators
Space
Modules
Satellites

Selected Operations

Alenia Aermacchi
Alenia Aeronautica (aerospace)
SELEX Sistemi Integrati SpA (formerly Alenia Marconi
    Systems)
Ansaldo Energia (energy)
AgustaWestland (helicopters)
DRS Technologies (military data systems)
MBDA (25% with EADS and BAE SYSTEMS)

COMPETITORS

ABB	General Dynamics
Airbus Helicopters	Kaman
Arianespace	Lockheed Martin
BAE SYSTEMS	Magellan Aerospace
Bell Helicopter	Northrop Grumman
Boeing	Raytheon
Bombardier	Robinson Helicopter
DIRECTV	Rockwell Automation
Daimler	Schneider Electric
Elbit Systems	Siemens AG
Embraer	Sikorsky
GE	

HISTORICAL FINANCIALS

Company Type: Public

Income Statement				FYE: December 31
	REVENUE ($ mil.)	NET INCOME ($ mil.)	NET PROFIT MARGIN	EMPLOYEES
12/19	21,690	1,291	6.0%	49,530
12/18	19,260	800	4.2%	46,462
12/17	18,138	428	2.4%	45,134
12/16	18,886	794	4.2%	45,631
12/15	20,448	766	3.7%	47,156
Annual Growth	1.5%	13.9%	—	1.2%

2019 Year-End Financials

Debt ratio: 29.2%	No. of shares (mil.): 578
Return on equity: 16.7%	Dividends
Cash ($ mil.): 3,087	Yield: 0.0%
Current ratio: 0.94	Payout: 2.2%
Long-term debt ($ mil.): 6,255	Market value ($ mil.): 3,353

	STOCK PRICE ($) FY Close	P/E High/Low		PER SHARE ($) Earnings	Dividends	Book Value
12/19	5.80	5	3	2.25	0.05	14.49
12/18	4.33	8	5	1.40	0.05	12.32
12/17	5.97	20	12	0.75	0.05	12.24
12/16	7.01	8	5	1.38	0.00	11.94
12/15	6.91	8	5	1.42	0.00	11.65
Annual Growth	(4.3%)	—	—	12.1%	—	5.6%

Lewis (John) Partnership Plc (United Kingdom)

Diversified retailer John Lewis Partnership (JLP) is Britain's greatest purveyor of the middle-class lifestyle. JLP operates two major upmarket retail businesses: John Lewis the department store chain that provides homeware clothing and electronics; and Waitrose one of the UK's largest supermarket chains. The company's department stores number is more than 40 while it runs 335 Waitrose branches. John Lewis operates an e-commerce site while Waitrose partners carry out home delivery. John Lewis Partnership is owned by its 80000 staff or partners.

Operations

The company's Waitrose business operates some 335 branches Waitrose also operates Waitrose farm which supplies its own shops with milk flour cox cider apple juice and sparkling wine among others. Sales from Waitrose constitute about 65% of total group revenue.

JLP's more than 40 department stores stock a wide range of home and garden products for essentially all conceivable purposes; clothing for men women and children including own-brand and designer goods; and electricals from personal items like tablets and wearable tech via television and audio to large electrical appliances like coffee machines fridges and washing machines. The company's department store activities account for more than 35% of revenue.

About 65% of sales were generated from groceries about 15% generated from EHT and over 10% came from home and fashion each.

Geographic Reach

London-based JLP operates mainly within the UK where it has more than 40 department stores and 335 Waitrose stores.

Sales and Marketing

The company follows a multichannel approach to selling its products; these include shops and online shops.

Financial Performance

Note: Growth rates may differ after conversion to US Dollars.

In fiscal 2020 revenue slid almost 2% coming in at Å 10.2 billion as sales from Waitrose and John Lewis fell.

The company increased its profits by 40% to Å 108.4 million. The increase in profit was due to lower cost of sale and an exceptional item of Å 107.4 million.

Net cash and cash equivalents at the end of the year was Å 598.3 million. Net cash generated from operating activities was Å 514.2 million while cash used in investing and financing activities were Å 209.8 million and Å 422.9 million respectively.

Main cash uses were for purchases of property plant and equipment intangible assets and payment of debts.

Strategy

In October 2020 the company unveiled its five-year self-funding Partnership Plan. It positions Waitrose and John Lewis as the go-to brands for customers who want quality value and sustainability and was the result of seven months' work where it listened to feedback from more than 10000 customers over 100 suppliers and local community groups and 12000 Partners who submitted more than 650 ideas.

The nature of the Partnership model allows it to invest with a longer-term perspective than a conventional business even in challenging times and amidst a very uncertain economic outlook. With this in mind its five-year plan is self-funding and takes into account uncertain trading. The Partnership Plan sees its business continuing to adapt rapidly to changing shopping habits getting closer to customers online and in-store. It will also expand in new areas where it believes its values can be a force for good.

The Plan aims to see the John Lewis Partnership reach Å 400m profit by year 5; Expansion of digital virtual and delivery services to get closer to customers; Inspirational new services and partnerships to rebalance business beyond retail; Pledge to recruit young people coming out of the care system; and Major commitments on cutting waste and net zero carbon.

Company Background

Founded in 1864 by John Lewis JLP became a partnership in 1929 when Lewis' son Spedan created a trust to own the company. All of the company's 85500 employees (called partners) are beneficiaries of the trust and as such receive unique perks as well as a share of the profits. A system of committees and councils made up of partners vote to determine the company's direction — and trustees. The Leckford Farm which supplies Waitrose supermarkets is also available for partners to use as a retreat.

EXECUTIVES

IT Director, Paul Coby
Managing Director, Andy Street
Vice Chairman and Managing Director Waitrose, Mark Price
Managing Director John Lewis Glasgow, Kim Lowe
Director Operations, Dino Rocos
Finance Director, Rachel Osborne
Retail Director, Andrew Murphy
Chairman, Charlie Mayfield
Auditors: KPMG LLP

LOCATIONS

HQ: Lewis (John) Partnership Plc (United Kingdom)
    171 Victoria Street, London SW1E 5NN
Phone: (44) 207 828 1000
Web: www.johnlewispartnership.co.uk

PRODUCTS/OPERATIONS

2013 Stores

	No.
Waitrose supermarkets	255
Waitrose convenience	35
John Lewis department stores	30
John Lewis at home	9
Total	**329**

2013 Sales

	% of total
Waitrose	64
John Lewis	36
Total	**100**

Selected Subsidiaries

Greenbee (travel leisure and financial services)
Herbert Parkinson Limited (weaving and making up)
JLP Holdings BV (investment holding company Holland)
JLP Insurance Limited (insurance Guernsey)
JPL Scottish Limited Partnership (investment holding undertaking)
JPL Scottish Partnership (investment holding undertaking)
JLP Victoria Limited (investment holding company)
John Lewis Properties plc (property holding company)
Waitrose Limited (food retailing)
Waitrose (Guernsey) Limited (food retailing Guernsey)
Waitrose (Jersey) Limited (food retailing Jersey)

COMPETITORS

ASDA	Iceland Foods
Arcadia	J Sainsbury
Argos	Marks & Spencer
Co-operative Group	Multiyork Furniture
Debenhams	NEXT plc
Fortnum & Mason	Selfridges
Harrods	Tesco
Harvey Nichols	Wm Morrison
House of Fraser	Supermarkets

HISTORICAL FINANCIALS

Company Type: Public

Income Statement				FYE: January 25
	REVENUE ($ mil.)	NET INCOME ($ mil.)	NET PROFIT MARGIN	EMPLOYEES
01/20	20,286	216	1.1%	80,800
01/19	20,616	154	0.7%	83,900
01/18	20,391	148	0.7%	85,500
01/17	20,036	706	3.5%	86,700
01/16	19,481	446	2.3%	91,500
Annual Growth	1.0%	(16.5%)	—	(3.1%)

2020 Year-End Financials

Debt ratio: 19.7%	No. of shares (mil.): 0
Return on equity: 4.2%	Dividends
Cash ($ mil.): 1,195	Yield: —
Current ratio: 1.00	Payout: —
Long-term debt ($ mil.): 1,437	Market value ($ mil.): —

Lewis (John) Plc (United Kingdom)

EXECUTIVES

Director, Loraine Woodhouse
Auditors: KPMG LLP

LOCATIONS

HQ: Lewis (John) Plc (United Kingdom)
171 Victoria Street, London SW1E 5NN
Phone:
Web: www.johnlewispartnership.co.uk

HISTORICAL FINANCIALS

Company Type: Public

Income Statement				FYE: January 25
	REVENUE ($ mil.)	NET INCOME ($ mil.)	NET PROFIT MARGIN	EMPLOYEES
01/20	20,286	215	1.1%	80,800
01/19	20,616	151	0.7%	83,900
01/18	20,391	143	0.7%	85,500
01/17	20,036	705	3.5%	86,700
01/16	19,481	444	2.3%	91,500
Annual Growth	1.0%	(16.6%)	—	(3.1%)

2020 Year-End Financials

Debt ratio: 72.4%	No. of shares (mil.): 6
Return on equity: 4.1%	Dividends
Cash ($ mil.): 1,195	Yield: —
Current ratio: 1.00	Payout: —
Long-term debt ($ mil.): 5,431	Market value ($ mil.): —

LG Display Co Ltd

The world is truly flat for LG Display — as in flat-panel displays. The company is one of the world's top producers of TFT-LCDs (thin-film transistor liquid-crystal displays) the lean screens that go into laptop and notebook computers desktop PC monitors TV sets and mobile phones. Other applications are in automotive navigation avionics consumer electronics instrumentation and medical equipment. LG Display is also a leader in the development and production of OLED panels which are even thinner than TFT-LCDs. LG Electronics is LG Display's biggest shareholder as well as one of its biggest customers. Most of LG Display's sales are made to China.

Operations

LG Display sells through five product categories. The company's biggest product televisions accounts for almost 35% of revenue. The mobile and other applications product category supplies more than a quarter of revenue and desktop monitors provide over 15% of revenue while notebook computers and tablet products account for about 10% each.

Geographic Reach

LG Display gets about two-thirds of revenue from sales to customers in China. Customers in other Asian countries comprise of approximately 10% of revenue and in Korea accounts for over 5% of revenue. The remaining revenues are from customers in the US (about 10%) Europe (more than 5%) and Poland (almost 5%).

All but one of the company's manufacturing sites are in Korea while the other is in China. It also operates assembly facilities in Korea China and Poland.

Sales and Marketing

LG Display sells through direct sales to end-brand customers and their system integrators and overseas subsidiaries. The company also sells through its affiliated trading company LG International and its subsidiaries.

Sales to LG Electronics account for about a quarter of revenue while LG Display's 10 biggest customers supply more than 80% of revenue.

Advertising expenses for the year ended in 2019 2018 and 2017 were ?193.4 billion ?112.4 billion and ?236.4 billion respectively.

Financial Performance

The company's revenue decreased by 4% from W24.3 trillion in 2018 to W23.5 trillion (US$20.3 billion) in 2019. The decrease in revenue resulted from a decrease in revenue derived from sales of panels for televisions and to a lesser extent decreases in revenue derived from sales of panels for notebook computers and desktop monitors which were in turn mainly due to decreases in the number of panels sold for televisions notebook computers and desktop monitors respectively offset in part by an increase in revenue derived from sales of panels for mobile and other applications and tablet computers.

The company's loss for the year increased significantly from W179 million in 2018 to W2.9 billion (US$2.5 billion) in 2019.

LG Display closed 2019 with W3.3 trillion in cash compared to W2.4 trillion in 2018. In 2019 cash from operations generated W2.7 trillion and financing activities provided W5 trillion while investing activities used W6.8 trillion.

Strategy

In connection with their strategy to further enhance the diversity and capacity of their display panel production the company anticipate that they will continue to incur significant capital expenditures for the construction of new production facilities and the maintenance and enhancement of existing production facilities particularly in connection with their continued investments in OLED technology. LG's significant recent and pending capital expenditures include: In response to and in anticipation of growing demand in the China market in July 2017 the company announced their plan to establish a joint venture with the government of Guangzhou to construct a new fabrication facility to manufacture next generation large-sized OLED panels which was established under the name of LG Display High-Tech (China) Co. Ltd. in July 2018. LG currently hold a 75% ownership interest in the joint venture and the government of Guangzhou holds the remaining 25% ownership interest. The company have invested approximately W5.0 trillion in capital expenditures for the joint venture and they plan to finalize their preparations for the commencement of operation at the new CO fabrication facility within the first half of 2020 while the expected timing for commencing mass production of large-sized OLED panels at such facility remains subject to the state of the ongoing global COVID-19 pandemic among other factors.

Company Background

LG Display was formed in 1999 when LG Electronics and Philips merged their LCD businesses. Philips no longer owns any part of LG Display.

EXECUTIVES

President and Chief Marketing Officer, Sang-Deog (Eddie) Yeo, age 65
Vice Chairman and CEO, Sang-Beom Han
SVP and CFO, Sang-Don Kim
EVP; Head TV Business Unit, Yong-Kee Hwang
EVP; Head Information Technology Business Unit, Kyong-Deuk Jeong
EVP; Head Mobile Business Unit, Hyung-Seok Choi
EVP and Chief Production Officer, Sang-Mun Shin
SVP and CTO, In-Byeong Kang
Chairman, Yu Sig Kang
Auditors: KPMG Samjong Accounting Corp.

LOCATIONS

HQ: LG Display Co Ltd
LG Twin Towers, 128 Yeoui-daero, Yeongdeungpo-gu, Seoul 07336
Phone: (82) 2 3777 1010   **Fax:** (82) 2 3777 0797
Web: www.lgdisplay.com

2017 Sales

	% of total
Asia/Pacific	
China	65
Other countries	8
Korea	7
Europe	9
Americas	10
Poland	1
Total	**100**

PRODUCTS/OPERATIONS

2017 Sales

	% of total
Televisions	42
Desktop monitors	16
Tablet products	9
Notebook computers	8
Mobile and others	25
Total	**100**

Products Selected
TV Display
Commercial Display
Monitor Display
Notebook Display
Mobile Display
Auto Display
IPS
AIT
Transparent flexible display
3D
OLED Light

COMPETITORS

AU Optronics	JDI
BOE Technology	Samsung Electronics
Chimei Innolux	Sharp Electronics
Chunghwa Picture Tubes	ViewSonic
HannStar Display	Wintek

HISTORICAL FINANCIALS
Company Type: Public

Income Statement				FYE: December 31
	REVENUE ($ mil.)	NET INCOME ($ mil.)	NET PROFIT MARGIN	EMPLOYEES
12/19	23,827	(2,872)	—	60,429
12/18	24,701	(210)	—	30,438
12/17	28,207	1,829	6.5%	33,335
12/16	26,901	920	3.4%	32,118
12/15	28,809	981	3.4%	32,603
Annual Growth	(4.6%)	—	—	16.7%

2019 Year-End Financials

Debt ratio: 0.0%
Return on equity: (-22.3%)
Cash ($ mil.): 3,465
Current ratio: 0.93
Long-term debt ($ mil.): 11,714

No. of shares (mil.): 357
Dividends
  Yield: —
  Payout: —
Market value ($ mil.): 2,483

	STOCK PRICE ($) FY Close	P/E High/Low		PER SHARE ($) Earnings	Dividends	Book Value
12/19	6.94	—	—	(8.03)	0.00	32.17
12/18	8.19	—	—	(0.59)	0.23	39.65
12/17	13.76	0	0	5.11	0.22	40.77
12/16	12.85	0	0	2.57	0.21	36.75
12/15	10.44	0	0	2.74	0.23	34.59
Annual Growth	(9.7%)	—	—	—	—	(1.8%)

LG Electronics Inc

LG Electronics is one the major consumer electronics and appliance companies making products found in the kitchen in the media room and on the go. A leader in consumer electronics mobile communications and home appliances LGE operates through almost 120 subsidiaries worldwide that design and make flat panel TVs audio and video products mobile handsets air conditioners washing machines refrigerators and more. About a third of LG Electronics is owned by South Korea's LG Corp.

Operations

The company operates in six operating segments: Home Appliance & Air Solutions Home entertainment Mobile communications Innotek Vehicle components solutions and Business solutions.

Home Appliances & Air Solutions with about a third of revenue manufactures and sells refrigerators washing machines vacuum cleaners and residential and commercial air conditioners. Home Entertainment segment which accounts for about a third of revenue manufactures and sells TVs monitors and digital media products.

Mobile Communication segment (about 10%) manufactures and sells mobile communications equipment. Vehicle Solutions segment (more than 10%) designs and manufactures automobile parts. Business Solutions segment (about 10%) manufactures and sells information display solar panels and others.

Innotek segment (more than 10%) operates LED optics solutions substrate materials and automotive components business.

Geographic Reach
LG Electronics is based in Seoul South Korea.
Financial Performance
LG Electronics has posted mixed revenue and net income in the past five with years.

In 2017 sales jumped 2% to 62.3 billion Korean Won from 61.3 billion Korean Won in 2018 each segment had higher sales in 2019 from 2018 except for a 24% and 1% sales dip in Mobile Communications and Home Entertainment segment respectively.

LG Electronics' net income fell to 179.9 million Korean Won in 2019 from 1.5 billion Korean Won in 2018 due to the 974.9 million Korean Won increase on their loss from equity valuation.

The company reported that its coffers held 799.6 million Korean Won in 2019 an increase of about 178.3 million Korean Won from 2018. Operations generated 769 million Korean Won in 2019 while investing activities used 354.3 million Korean Won and financing activities used 238.9 million Korean Won.

EXECUTIVES

President and CEO Home Entertainment Company, Bong-Suk Kwon
President Business to Business Sector, Lee Sangbong
President and CEO Vehicle Components, Lee Woo-Jong
Auditors: Samil Accounting Corporation (A Member Firm of PircewaterhouseCoopers)

LOCATIONS

HQ: LG Electronics Inc
LG Twin Towers, 128 Yeouido-dong, Yeongdeungpo-gu, Seoul 07336
Phone: (82) 2 3777 1114   **Fax:** (82) 2 3777 3428
Web: www.lge.com

2017 Sales

	% of total
Korea	33
North America	275
Asia	11
Europe	10
South America	7
Middle East & Africa	5
China	4
Other	3
Total	**100**

PRODUCTS/OPERATIONS

2017 Sales

	% of total
Home Appliance & Air Solution	31
Home Entertainment	30
Mobile communications	19
Innotek	11
Vehicle components	6
Other	3
Total	**100**

Selected Major Products & Services

Home Entertainment (LCD TVs plasma TVs audio video & optical storage)

Mobile Communication (mobile handsets mobile accessory)
Home Appliance & Air Solution (washing machines refrigerators cooking appliances vacuum cleaners built-in appliances air conditioners and air purifiers)
Business Solutions (monitors commercial displays car infotainment security business)
Vehicle Component Solutions (in-vehicle infotainment HVAC and Motor Vehicle Engineering)

COMPETITORS

Apple Inc.	Philips Electronics
BSH Home Appliances	SANYO
Electrolux	Samsung Electronics
GE Appliances & Lighting	Sony
Haier Group	Technicolor
Panasonic Corp	Toshiba
	Whirlpool

HISTORICAL FINANCIALS
Company Type: Public

Income Statement				FYE: December 31
	REVENUE ($ mil.)	NET INCOME ($ mil.)	NET PROFIT MARGIN	EMPLOYEES
12/19	53,962	27	0.1%	0
12/18	55,020	1,112	2.0%	37,698
12/17	57,589	1,618	2.8%	37,653
12/16	46,086	63	0.1%	37,909
12/15	48,029	105	0.2%	37,902
Annual Growth	3.0%	(28.8%)	—	—

2019 Year-End Financials

Debt ratio: 0.0%
Return on equity: 0.2%
Cash ($ mil.): 4,194
Current ratio: 1.12
Long-term debt ($ mil.): 7,659

No. of shares (mil.): 162
Dividends
  Yield: —
  Payout: 443.7%
Market value ($ mil.): —

Linde plc

Praxair Inc. a wholly-owned subsidiary of Linde plc since 2018 is a leading industrial gas company in North and South America and one of the largest worldwide. Praxair produces sells and distributes atmospheric process and specialty gases and high-performance surface coatings. Its products services and technologies are offered to a wide variety of industries including aerospace chemicals food and beverage electronics energy healthcare manufacturing primary metals and many others.

Operations
Praxair's business segments are gas supply and management; industrial services; oil and gas services; and surface coatings.

Gas supply and management offers cylinders and liquid containers; bulk and microbulk delivery; pipeline; on-site production; mobile nitrogen pumping service; and small on-site production.

Industrial services consists of refineries and chemical plants; pipeline services; terminals and pipeline leak location; dry ice blasting; CO2 services and applications; and specialty services.

Oil and gas provides services in enhanced oil recovery energized fluid fracking and well injection services. It is also a supplier of nitrogen and carbon dioxide.

Surface coatings' products prevent the effects of abrasion oxidation corrosion erosion wear and extreme heat.

Geographic Reach

Praxair does business in 50 countries around the world. It also has locations in around 30 countries in the Americas Europe Middle East and Asia.

Sales and Marketing

Praxair serves a wide range of industries which consists of additive manufacturing aerospace & aircraft automotive & transportation equipment chemicals electronics energy food & beverage healthcare metals & materials processing oil & gas as well as welding & metal fabrication among others.

Company Background

Praxair and Linde both go back to the origins of the industrial gas industry in the 19th century.

Karl von Linde a professor of mechanical engineering at the College of Technology in Munich Germany in the late 1800s created the cryogenic air liquefier. Von Linde built his first oxygen-production plant in 1902 and a nitrogen plant in 1904 and in the first decade of the 20th century he built a number of air-separation plants throughout Europe.

By 1907 von Linde founded Linde Air Products in Cleveland as the US subsidiary of his German company. Linde Air Products joined rival Union Carbide in 1911 in experimenting with the production of acetylene; it became a unit of Union Carbide in 1917 during World War I.

In the 1990s the gases business spun out of Union Carbide and became Praxair.

EXECUTIVES

Chairman President and CEO, Stephen F. (Steve) Angel, $1,318,750 total compensation

SVP; President White Martins Gases Industriais and Praxair South America, Domingos H. G. Bulus

EVP, Eduardo F. Menezes, $611,250 total compensation

President Praxair Europe, Daniel H. (Dan) Yankowski

VP and CIO, Earl Newsome

President Praxair Asia, John M. Panikar

President Praxair Europe, Eduardo Gil

SVP, Anne K. Roby, $471,250 total compensation

President US Industrial Gases, Kevin C. Foti

President Praxair Distribution Inc., Dick Marini

EVP, Scott E. Telesz, $615,000 total compensation

SVP and CFO, Matthew J. (Matt) White, $587,500 total compensation

CTO, Todd A. Skare

President Praxair Canada, Sean Durbin

President Praxair Mexico, Benjamin (Ben) Glazer

President Praxair Surface Technologies, Pierre L thi

Vice President Global Procurement and Materials Management, Luiz Oliveira

Vice President Global Communications and Public Relations, Lisa Esneault

Vice President Sales, Ed Haversang

Vice President Of Global Safety Of Health And Environment, Veerle Slenders

Vp Operations, Jeff Barnhard

Vice President Procurement, Joe Abdoo

Vice President And General Manager Us Praxair Distribution, Randall Brittingham

Vice President and Controller, Mathew White

Vice President and Chief Sustainability Officer, Riva Krut

Vice President and CHRO, David Strauss

Auditors: PricewaterhouseCoopers LLP

LOCATIONS

HQ: Linde plc
The Priestley Centre, 10 Priestley Road, Surrey Research Park, Guildford, Surrey 06810-6268
Phone: (44) 1483 242200
Web: www.linde.com

2016 Sales

	% of total
North America	53
Asia	15
South America	13
Europe	13
Surface technologies	6
Total	**100**

PRODUCTS/OPERATIONS

2016 Sales by End Market

	% of total
Manufacturing	21
Metals	16
Chemicals	14
Food & Beverage	12
Healthcare	11
Electronics	7
Energy	5
Aerospace	1
Other	13
Total	**100**

2016 Sales by Distribution Method

	% of total
Merchant(delivered liquids)	38
On-site (includes noncryogenics)	28
Packaged gases (cylinders)	31
Other	3
Total	**100**

COMPETITORS

Air Products	GKN Aerospace
Airgas	Chem-tronics
Balchem	L'Air Liquide
Chromalloy Gas Turbine	The Linde Group

HISTORICAL FINANCIALS

Company Type: Public

Income Statement				FYE: December 31
	REVENUE ($ mil.)	NET INCOME ($ mil.)	NET PROFIT MARGIN	EMPLOYEES
12/19	28,228	2,285	8.1%	79,886
12/18	14,900	4,381	29.4%	80,820
12/17	11,437	1,247	10.9%	26,461
12/16	10,534	1,500	14.2%	26,498
12/15	10,776	1,547	14.4%	26,657
Annual Growth	27.2%	10.2%	—	31.6%

2019 Year-End Financials

Debt ratio: 16.1%	No. of shares (mil.): 534
Return on equity: 4.5%	Dividends
Cash ($ mil.): 2,700	Yield: 1.6%
Current ratio: 0.85	Payout: 30.3%
Long-term debt ($ mil.): 10,693	Market value ($ mil.): —

LIXIL Corp

When opportunity knocks in Japan it's probably knocking on a LIXIL door. The company is a leading supplier of housing and building materials in Japan. Through more than 40 subsidiaries it provides such products as doors housing sashes storm shutters ceramic siding bathroom units and tile insulated panels and security systems. It also supplies storefronts for commercial buildings as well as skylights steel doors and customized store facades and shutters. LIXIL Group works with distributors and has sales offices throughout Japan. Other operations include a real estate brokerage franchise a chain of do-it-yourself stores and home services including inspections and warranties.

Operations

The Company's products and services are categorized in five business segments: Water Technology Housing Technology Building Technology Distribution & Retail Business and the Housing & Services Business.

The Water Technology business segment offers sanitaryware window sashes and bathtubs under global brands such as INAX GROHE and American Standard as well as Japan brands RICHELLE and SPAGE. This segment accounts for more than 40% of total revenue. Housing Technology (30% of total sales) offers products such as windows entrance doors exteriors wooden interior furnishing materials and interior fabrics under the brand names SUPERWALL LIXIL ASAHI TOSTEM EXSIOR INTERIO KAWASHIMA and SELKON. The Building Technology segment (more than 5%) offers curtain walls and building sashes with brand names LIXIL and PERMASTEELISA GROUP. It also provides project management services.

LIXIL's Distribution and Retail Business provides consumers with a unique array of housing and lifestyle-related products materials and services through its Super VIVA Home and VIVA Home stores in Japan. The company offers an extensive line-up of products including DIY merchandise for individuals who enjoy renovating their own homes as well as materials and equipment for industry professionals. This segment accounts for around 10% of total revenue.

LIXIL's Housing and Services Business accounts for less than 5% of total revenue. It offers comprehensive housing and lifestyle support to customers through all life stages. It comprises various operating companies providing dedicated services including home construction and renovation maintenance management home inspections real estate transactions real estate management and brokerage and housing-related financial services.

Geographic Reach

The company's head office is located in Tokyo Japan. LIXIL has almost 95 factories in some 15 countries. About half are in Japan more than 30 in Asia Pacific and about 10 in the Americas. The rest are in Europe and Africa. LIXIL also operates around 135 showrooms in over 20 countries with more than 100 of these in Japan. It strategically places its production and sales operations in areas adjacent to its target markets.

Sales and Marketing

The company sells directly to customers such as dealers sales agencies construction companies architectural firms developers wholesalers volume retailers and general consumers.

Financial Performance

Note: Growth rates may differ after conversion to US Dollars.

LIXIL's revenue has remained relatively flat over the past several years. Sales in 2018 were up slightly with a 2% increase to Å 1664.8 billion from the previous year. Growth factors included increased sales as a result of marketing activities specifically domestic and international sales of plumbing fixture products.

LIXIL's 2018 net profits were down 16% to Å 75.3 billion due to higher raw material and distribution costs and large increases in marketing and information technology expenses. New housing starts in Japan were also down during the fiscal year.

Cash at the end of 2018 was Å 138.8 billion up Å 17.2 billion from the prior year. Cash from operations contributed Å 116.4 billion to the coffers while investing activities used Å 52.6 billion mainly for purchases of property plant and equipment and acquisitions. Financing activities used another

Å 43.8 billion for dividends to stockholders and loan payments.

Strategy

In 2018 LIXIL Group initiated a new three-year strategic plan that includes streamlining and simplifying its organization. The company has eliminated layers of its organizational structure to accelerate decision-making divested certain subsidiaries and affiliates and sold off unused assets. LIXIL is also investing in areas including design marketing and digital to promote future growth.

In its most profitable water technology business (LWT) the company is aiming toward becoming a full bathroom solutions provider. The company has developed more differentiated LIXIL branded products with a design-oriented approach that addresses consumer challenges. As a result recent design awards have increased LIXIL's brand awareness in the market. LIXIL has also stepped up its marketing efforts with several promotions including a GROHE brand promotion in global airports and a direct-to-consumer campaign for American Standard walk-in tubs in the US. It has improved supply capacity by boosting manufacturing operations in key markets such as India the Dominican Republic Cypress and South Africa. And to expand its lineup of products it is investing in new showrooms and an R&D center in Asia.

LIXIL's housing technology business (LHT) is highly dependent on raw material costs and new housing starts especially in Japan. Part of its growth strategy in this business is to streamline operations differentiate its products in Japan and expand further in other parts of Asia. The company is consolidating aluminum extrusion factories increasing efficiency through a platform approach and accelerating launch cycles to respond more quickly to market trends.

Another key strategy to increase sales is shifting from mass marketing to data-driven targeted marketing programs.

Mergers and Acquisitions

The company has achieved revenue growth through the help of acquisitions. In 2017 LIXIL's major subsidiary LIXIL Corporations agreed to acquire its Johannesburg-based sanitaryware joint venture Grohe Dawn Watertech Holdings Propriety Limited (GDWT) from Distribution and Warehousing Network Limited (DAWN). LIXIL currently owns a controlling 51% stake in GDWT and will obtain the remaining 49% of shares from DAWN and GDWT will repay DAWN's shareholder loan for ZAR 324.5 million.

Company Background

LIXIL was founded in 2011 through the merger of five of Japan's most successful building materials and housing companies?TOSTEM INAX Shin Nikkei Sunwave and TOEX. From the early 20th Century the founding fathers of their legacy companies ushered in an era of innovation and laid down the principles that would make LIXIL one of the most respected names in the Japanese building and housing industry.

EXECUTIVES

Executive Officer and Senior Managing Director Technology, Ryo Nihei
President and CEO LIXIL Water Technology Americas, Steven P. Delarge, age 62
COO, Kinya Seto, age 60
EVP Finance Treasury M&A and CFO, Sachio Matsumoto
EVP Production Optimization, Ryuichi Kawamoto
Executive Officer and EVP Domestic Subsidiaries, Haruo Shirai

Executive Officer and Senior Managing Director Human Resources and General Affairs, Harumi Matsumura
Executive Officer and Senior Managing Director Marketing and Digital Chief Digital Officer (CDO), Yugo Kanazawa
Executive Officer and Senior Managing Director Legal Business and Chief Legal Officer (CLO), Laurence W. Bates
Chairman, Yoichiro Ushioda
Auditors: Deloitte Touche Tohmatsu LLC

LOCATIONS

HQ: LIXIL Corp
  2-1-1 Ojima, Koto-ku, Tokyo 136-8535
Phone: (81) 3 3638 8111
Web: www.lixil.com

2018 Sales

	% of total
Japan	76
EMEA	9
Americas	8
Asia/Pacific	7
Total	**100**

PRODUCTS/OPERATIONS

2018 Sales

	% of total
LIXIL Water Technology (LWT)	42
LIXIL Housing Technology (LHT)	32
Distribution & Retail Business (D&R)	10
LIXIL Kitchen Technology (LKT)	7
LIXIL Building Technology (LBT)	6
Housing & Services Business (H&S)	3
Total	**100**

Selected Subsidiaries

Kawashima Selkon Textiles (fabric manufacturer)
LIXIL Group Finance (financial services)
LIXIL Housing Research Institute (homebuilding franchise chain)
LIXIL Realty (real estate services)
LIXIL Viva (operates Viva Home and Super Viva Home retail chains)
LIXIL ENERGY Co. Ltd.
LIXIL Building Materials Manufacturing Corporation

Selected Brands

Global
  INAX
  GROHE
  American Standard
  TOSTEM
  LIXIL
Global Specialty
  Kawashima Selkon
  Cobra
  DXV
  Jaxson
  SATO
Japan
  RICHELLE
  SPAGE
  INTERIO
  EXSIOR
  SUPER WALL
  AHAHI TOTEM

COMPETITORS

CLEANUP CORPORATION	Panasonic Corp
KOHNAN SHOJI CO.LTD.	TAKARA STANDARD CO.
KOMERI CO.LTD.	LTD.
Kohler	TOTO
Masco	YKK

HISTORICAL FINANCIALS
Company Type: Public

Income Statement				FYE: March 31
	REVENUE ($ mil.)	NET INCOME ($ mil.)	NET PROFIT MARGIN	EMPLOYEES
03/20	15,609	115	0.7%	73,426
03/19	16,548	(471)	—	76,182
03/18	15,678	514	3.3%	74,895
03/17	15,978	380	2.4%	72,603
03/16	16,834	(228)	—	73,580
Annual Growth	(1.9%)	—	—	(0.1%)

2020 Year-End Financials

Debt ratio: 0.2%	No. of shares (mil.): 290
Return on equity: 2.4%	Dividends
Cash ($ mil.): 883	Yield: —
Current ratio: 0.92	Payout: 176.5%
Long-term debt ($ mil.): 3,347	Market value ($ mil.): —

Lloyds Bank plc

Auditors: PricewaterhouseCoopers LLP

LOCATIONS

HQ: Lloyds Bank plc
  25 Gresham Street, London EC2V 7HN
Phone:
Web: www.lloydsbankinggroup.com

HISTORICAL FINANCIALS
Company Type: Public

Income Statement				FYE: December 31
	REVENUE ($ mil.)	NET INCOME ($ mil.)	NET PROFIT MARGIN	EMPLOYEES
12/19	28,409	2,895	10.2%	70,083
12/18	27,659	6,014	21.7%	71,786
12/17	29,532	5,590	18.9%	73,438
12/16	25,709	1,355	5.3%	77,726
12/15	37,496	982	2.6%	85,703
Annual Growth	(6.7%)	31.0%	—	(4.9%)

2019 Year-End Financials

Debt ratio: —	No. of shares (mil.): 1,574
Return on equity: 5.5%	Dividends
Cash ($ mil.): 51,729	Yield: —
Current ratio: —	Payout: —
Long-term debt ($ mil.): —	Market value ($ mil.): —

Lloyds Banking Group Plc

Auditors: PricewaterhouseCoopers LLP

LOCATIONS

HQ: Lloyds Banking Group Plc
  25 Gresham Street, 5th Floor, London EC2V 7HN
Phone: (44) 20 7626 1500
Web: www.lloydsbankinggroup.com

HISTORICAL FINANCIALS
Company Type: Public

Income Statement
FYE: December 31

	ASSETS ($ mil.)	NET INCOME ($ mil.)	INCOME AS % OF ASSETS	EMPLOYEES
12/19	1,101,207	3,862	0.4%	63,069
12/18	1,018,342	5,492	0.5%	64,928
12/17	1,096,907	4,669	0.4%	67,905
12/16	1,006,000	2,537	0.3%	70,433
12/15	1,195,467	1,274	0.1%	75,306
Annual Growth	(2.0%)	31.9%	—	(4.3%)

2019 Year-End Financials
Return on assets: 0.3%
Return on equity: 6.0%
Long-term debt ($ mil.): —
No. of shares (mil.): —
Sales ($ mil): 66,539

Dividends
Yield: 4.9%
Payout: 378.2%
Market value ($ mil.): —

	STOCK PRICE ($) FY Close	P/E High/Low	Earnings	Dividends	Book Value
12/19	3.31	101 72	0.04	0.16	0.91
12/18	2.56	69 46	0.07	0.16	0.90
12/17	3.75	91 77	0.06	0.18	0.92
12/16	3.10	154 101	0.03	0.20	0.83
12/15	4.36	667 521	0.01	0.09	0.97
Annual Growth	(6.7%)	—	39.5%	15.5%	(1.5%)

Loblaw Companies Ltd

Auditors: KPMG LLP

LOCATIONS
HQ: Loblaw Companies Ltd
1 President's Choice Circle, Brampton, Ontario L6Y 5S5
Phone: 416 965-5209   **Fax:** 416 922-4394
Web: www.loblaw.ca

HISTORICAL FINANCIALS
Company Type: Public

Income Statement
FYE: December 28

	REVENUE ($ mil.)	NET INCOME ($ mil.)	NET PROFIT MARGIN	EMPLOYEES
12/19	36,687	825	2.3%	194,000
12/18	34,717	569	1.6%	197,000
12/17	37,253	1,198	3.2%	198,000
12/16*	34,419	734	2.1%	195,000
01/16	32,765	449	1.4%	196,000
Annual Growth	2.9%	16.4%	—	(0.3%)

*Fiscal year change

2019 Year-End Financials
Debt ratio: 19.4%
Return on equity: 9.2%
Cash ($ mil.): 865
Current ratio: 1.23
Long-term debt ($ mil.): 4,560

No. of shares (mil.): 360
Dividends
Yield: 0.0%
Payout: 42.7%
Market value ($ mil.): 18,363

	STOCK PRICE ($) FY Close	P/E High/Low	Earnings	Dividends	Book Value
12/19	51.00	20 16	2.21	0.95	23.83
12/18	44.75	26 19	1.48	0.86	24.24
12/17	54.34	16 14	2.99	0.85	26.87
12/16*	52.79	23 19	1.76	0.76	24.07
01/16	47.18	35 28	1.09	0.72	23.15
Annual Growth	2.0%	—	19.4%	7.2%	0.7%

*Fiscal year change

Longfor Group Holdings Ltd

EXECUTIVES
Chairman, Yajun Wu
Auditors: Deloitte Touche Tohmatsu

LOCATIONS
HQ: Longfor Group Holdings Ltd
18/F., CSC Fortune International Center, No. 5 An'ding Road, Chaoyang District, Beijing
Phone:
Web: www.longfor.com

HISTORICAL FINANCIALS
Company Type: Public

Income Statement
FYE: December 31

	REVENUE ($ mil.)	NET INCOME ($ mil.)	NET PROFIT MARGIN	EMPLOYEES
12/19	21,704	2,635	12.1%	26,316
12/18	16,835	2,360	14.0%	27,010
12/17	11,075	1,936	17.5%	19,903
12/16	7,891	1,318	16.7%	17,172
12/15	7,301	1,383	19.0%	15,633
Annual Growth	31.3%	17.5%	—	13.9%

2019 Year-End Financials
Debt ratio: 3.2%
Return on equity: 20.8%
Cash ($ mil.): 8,735
Current ratio: 1.48
Long-term debt ($ mil.): 18,980

No. of shares (mil.): —
Dividends
Yield: 2.9%
Payout: 407.3%
Market value ($ mil.): —

	STOCK PRICE ($) FY Close	P/E High/Low	Earnings	Dividends	Book Value
12/19	47.00	15 9	0.44	1.41	2.29
12/18	29.18	11 8	0.40	1.14	2.00
12/17	25.59	13 6	0.33	0.93	1.84
12/16	12.65	11 8	0.23	0.00	1.52
12/15	15.65	— —	0.24	0.00	1.45
Annual Growth	31.6%	—	17.0%	—	12.0%

LVMH Moet Hennessy Louis Vuitton

LVMH Mo «t Hennessy Louis Vuitton is the world's largest luxury goods company with brands that are bywords for the good life and everything showy. LVMH makes wines and spirits (Dom Pérignon Mo «t & Chandon Veuve Clicquot and Hennessy) perfumes (Christian Dior Guerlain and Givenchy) cosmetics (Make Up For Ever Fresh and Benefit) fashion and leather goods (Marc Jacobs Givenchy Kenzo and Louis Vuitton) and watches and jewelry (TAG Heuer Bulgari). LVMH's selective retail division includes Sephora cosmetics stores Le Bon Marché Paris department stores and DFS Group (duty-free shops). LVMH is owned by holding company Christian Dior and Bernard Arnault the richest man in France. In 2019 LVMH agreed to buy Tiffany for $16.2 billion.

Mergers and Acquisitions

LVMH agreed to pay $16.2 billion to buy the American jeweler Tiffany in 2019. The deal would add the well-known Tiffany name to LVMH's portfolio of luxury brands that include Dior Givenchy Fendi and Dom Pérignon as well as another jewelry company Bulgari. LVMH strengthens its presence in the jewelry business and in the US with the purchase. Overseas LVMH intends to increase Tiffany's presence in Europe and mainland China where Tiffany has lagged other jewelers. The deal is expected to close in mid-2020.

In 2018 LVMH's investment arm L Catterton acquired US HVAC company Airxcel. The company produces heating ventilation and related appliances for RVs classrooms and telecommunications enclosures under brands including Coleman-Mach MaxxAir Suburban Dicor and more.

HISTORY
Woodworker Louis Vuitton started his Paris career packing dresses for French Empress Eugenie. He later designed new types of luggage and in 1854 he opened a store to sell his designs. In 1896 Vuitton introduced the LV monogram fabric that the company still uses. By 1900 Louis Vuitton had stores in the US and England and by WWI Louis' son Georges had the world's largest retail store for travel goods.

Henry Racamier a former steel executive who had married into the Vuitton family took charge in 1977 repositioning the company's goods from esoteric status symbols to designer must-haves. Sales soared from $20 million to nearly $2.5 billion within a decade. Concerned about being a takeover target Racamier merged Louis Vuitton in 1987 with Mo «t Hennessy (which made wines spirits and fragrances) and adopted the name LVMH Mo «t Hennessy Louis Vuitton.

Mo «t Hennessy had been formed through the 1971 merger of Mo «t et Chandon (the world's #1 champagne maker) and the Hennessy Cognac company (founded by Irish mercenary Richard Hennessy in 1765). Mo «t Hennessy acquired rights to Christian Dior fragrances in 1971.

Racamier tried to reverse the merger when disagreements with chairman Alain Chevalier arose. Racamier invited outside investor Bernard Arnault to increase his interest in the company. Arnault gained control of 43% of LVMH and became chairman in 1989. Chevalier stepped down but Racamier fought for control for another 18 months and then set up Orcofi a partner of cosmetics rival L'Oréal.

LVMH increased its fashion holdings with the purchases of the Givenchy Couture Group (1988) Christian Lacroix (1993) and Kenzo (1993). The company also acquired 55% of French media firm Desfosses International (1993) Celine fashions (1996) the Ch teau d'Yquem winery (1996) and duty-free retailer DFS Group (1996). Next LVMH bought perfume chains Sephora (1997) and Marie-Jeanne Godard (1998). In 1998 LVMH integrated the Paris department store Le Bon Marché which was controlled by Arnault.

LVMH accumulated a 34% stake in Italian luxury goods maker Gucci in early 1999 and planned to buy all of it. Fellow French conglomerate Pinault-Printemps-Redoute (PPR) later thwarted LVMH by purchasing 42% of Gucci.

Through its LV Capital unit in 1999 LVMH began acquiring stakes in a host of luxury companies including a joint venture with fashion company Prada to buy 51% of design house Fendi (LVMH bought Prada's 25.5% stake for $265 million in November 2001). It has since upped its Fendi stake to about 70%. LVMH later added the Ebel Chaumet and TAG Heuer brands to its new watch division.

In early 2000 LVMH bought Miami Cruiseline Services which operates duty-free shops on cruise ships auction house L'Etude Tajan and 67% of Italian fashion house Emilio Pucci. The company later purchased 35% of French video game retailer Micromania and 51% of department store Samaritaine. In late 2000 LVMH acquired Gabrielle Studio which owns all Donna Karan licenses. In 2001 the company bought Donna Karan International.

LVMH bought in 2001 the Newton and MountAdam vineyards for about $45 million. It then began marketing De Beers diamond jewelry in a 50-50 joint venture with the diamond powerhouse. In March LVMH prompted the investigation of a Dutch court into the PPR-Gucci alliance. The company sold its stake in Gucci to PPR for $806.5 million in October.

In October 2002 LVMH ceased trading on the Brussels and Nasdaq exchanges to concentrate on its Euronext investors. In October 2003 the company sold Canard-Duchene to the Alain Thienot Group. LVMH shed several of the less productive of its 50 brands in 2003 including auction house Phillips de Pury & Luxemborg and fashion brand Michael Kors.

LVMH opened its biggest store — a four-story emporium on New York's Fifth Avenue — in February 2004. A few months later the company added whisky-maker Glenmorangie PLC to its subsidiary roster. LVMH also made its debut in the South African market in October 2004 opening its first sub-Saharan boutique in Johannesburg. Also during the year Bliss spas was sold off.

In early 2004 LVMH won a landmark lawsuit against Morgan Stanley alleging that the firm had used biased research in misstatements about the financial health of LVMH that caused damage to the company's image. The presiding Parisian court ordered Morgan Stanley to pay 100 million euros (about $38 million) in damages. Morgan Stanley appealed the ruling later that year.

In late 2005 LVMH opened its largest store to date on the Champs-Elysées in Paris and the De Beers brand was introduced in the US with stores in New York and Los Angeles. Also that year LVMH was the winning bidder for whisky maker Glenmorangie PLC for which it paid Â 300 million. On the sell side LVMH divested fashion design house Christian Lacroix SNC.

In May 2007 LVMH acquired a 55% stake in Chinese distillery Wenjun for an undisclosed amount. (Jiannanchun the distillery's previous owner retained a 45% stake in Wenjun.) In December 2007 the luxury goods firm acquired the French newspaper Les Echos from publisher Pearson. LVMH controls Les Echos' rival the financial daily La Tribune but has agreed to sell it. Group Les Echos deal includes the newspaper Web site business magazine Enjeux and other financial information services.

In late 2008 Sephora SA acquired a 45% stake in the Russian perfume and cosmetics chain Ile de Beauté. (The agreement which gave Sephora the option to become a majority shareholder allowed LVMH to up its share to 65% in mid-2011.) The firm acquired the luxury yacht-maker Royal Van Lent.

In August 2009 LVMH acquired 50% stakes in two French wine makers: privately-held Cheval Blanc; and La Tour du Pin owner of the Chateau Quinault l'Enclose estate.

In early 2010 LVMH acquired a 40% stake in Dondup an Italian apparel and denim brand for more than $43 million (or 30 million euros). Its plans are to expand Dondup's business internationally. Later in 2010 the company purchased a 70% stake in the Brazilian fragrance and cosmetics retailer Sack's. The acquisition estimated to be worth R$250 million is a move on LVMH's part to expand its Sephora beauty chain in Brazil one of the fastest-growing beauty markets in the world.

Adding to its vast portfolio of luxury brands in February 2011 LVMH acquired Ole Henriksen a leading luxury botanical skincare company founded and owned by its namesake. Later that same week LVMH bought a 70% stake in Nude Brands skin care as the company continues to acquire niche brands. The four-year-old line - described as "biocompatible luxury skin care" - was founded by Bryan Meehan and Ali Hewson wife of U2 front man Bono. In March LVMH fired Dior star designer John Galliano amid charges of anti-Semitism. In September LVMH completed its tender offer from Rome-based Bulgari acquiring about 98% of the shares.

EXECUTIVES

Chairman and CEO, Bernard Arnault, age 71
Group Managing Director, Antonio (Toni) Belloni, age 66
Director Strategy, Jean-Baptiste Voisin, age 53
Managing Director Groupe Arnault, Nicolas Bazire, age 63
Chairman and CEO Louis Vuitton, Michael Burke, age 63
Group EVP Human Resources and Synergies, Chantal Gaemperle
CFO, Jean-Jacques Guiony, age 59
CEO Sephora, Chris de Lapuente, age 55
CEO Moet Hennessy, Christophe Navarre
Chairman LVMH Investment Funds, Daniel Piette, age 75
Chairman and CEO LVMH Fashion Group, Pierre-Yves Roussel
Chairman and CEO DFS Group, Philippe Schaus, age 57
Vice Chairman, Pierre Gode, age 76
Auditors: ERNST & YOUNG Audit

LOCATIONS

HQ: LVMH Moet Hennessy Louis Vuitton
22 avenue Montaigne, Paris 75008
Phone: (33) 1 44 13 22 22   **Fax:** (33) 1 44 13 21 19
Web: www.lvmh.com

2018 Stores

	No.
Europe	
France	514
Other countries	1,153
Asia	
Japan	422
Other countries	1,289
US	783
Other regions	431
Total	**4,592**

2018 Sales

	% of total
Europe	
France	10
Other countries	19
Asia	
Japan	7
Other countries	29
US	24
Other regions	11
Total	**100**

PRODUCTS/OPERATIONS

2018 Sales

	% of total
Fashion & leather goods	39
Selective retailing	28
Wines & spirits	11
Perfumes & cosmetics	13
Watches & jewelry	9
Total	**100**

Selected Brands and Operations

Fashion and leather goods
  Berluti
  Celine
  Donna Karan
  Emilio Pucci
  Fendi
  Gabrielle Studio (Donna Karan label)
  Givenchy
  Kenzo
  Loewe
  Loro Piana
  Louis Vuitton
  Marc Jacobs
  Thomas Pink
Retailing
  DFS Group
  La Samaritaine
  Le Bon Marché;
  Miami Cruiseline Services (duty-free shops)
  Sephora
Fragrances and cosmetics
  Aqua di Parma
  BeneFit
  Bliss
  Fresh
  Guerlain
  Kenzo Parfums
  Make Up For Ever
  Marc Jacobs Fragrances
  Nude skin care
  Ole Henriksen
  Parfums Christian Dior
  Parfums Givenchy
Spirits and wines
  10 Cane
  Belvedere
  Canard-Duchêne
  Chandon Estates
  Château d'Yquem
  Dom Pé;rignon
  Hennessy
  Krug
  Mercier
  Moët & Chandon
  MountAdam
  Newton
  Ruinart
  Veuve Clicquot
Watches and jewelry
  Bulgari
  Chaumet
  De Beers
  Ebel
  Fred
  Omas
  TAG Heuer
  Zenith
Media (Desfosses International Group)
  Investir
  La Tribune
  Les Echos
  Radio Classique
Other
  Royal van Lent (luxury yachts)

COMPETITORS

Armani	Kering
Asprey	Kirin Holdings Company
Avon	L'Oréal
Bacardi	MacAndrews & Forbes
Brown-Forman	Oscar de la Renta
Calvin Klein	Patek Philippe
Chanel	Prada
Douglas Holding	Puig
E. & J. Gallo	Ralph Lauren
Escada	Richemont
Estée Lauder	Rolex
Galeries Lafayette	Rémy Cointreau
Gianni Versace	Shiseido
Harry Winston	Swatch
Herm"s	Taittinger
Hugo Boss	Tiffany & Co.
Inditex	Vera Wang

HISTORICAL FINANCIALS

Company Type: Public

Income Statement				FYE: December 31
	REVENUE ($ mil.)	NET INCOME ($ mil.)	NET PROFIT MARGIN	EMPLOYEES
12/19	84,499	11,284	13.4%	163,309
12/18	73,721	9,998	13.6%	156,088
12/17	67,087	8,071	12.0%	145,247
12/16	59,172	6,264	10.6%	134,476
12/15	56,100	5,622	10.0%	125,346
Annual Growth	10.8%	19.0%	—	6.8%

2019 Year-End Financials

Debt ratio: 20.7%	No. of shares (mil.): 503
Return on equity: 20.8%	Dividends
Cash ($ mil.): 8,927	Yield: 1.4%
Current ratio: 1.17	Payout: 6.1%
Long-term debt ($ mil.): 8,026	Market value ($ mil.): 46,976

	STOCK PRICE ($) FY Close	P/E High/Low		PER SHARE ($) Earnings	Dividends	Book Value
12/19	93.27	7	4	22.39	1.38	114.31
12/18	58.46	6	4	19.84	1.29	101.05
12/17	58.70	6	4	16.02	0.93	90.30
12/16	38.00	5	4	12.42	0.79	82.73
12/15	31.50	5	4	11.14	4.08	76.17
Annual Growth	31.2%	—	—	19.1%	(23.7%)	10.7%

LyondellBasell Industries NV

Auditors: PricewaterhouseCoopers LLP

LOCATIONS

HQ: LyondellBasell Industries NV
4th Floor, One Vine Street, London W1J0AH
Phone: (44) 207 220 2600
Web: www.lyb.com

HISTORICAL FINANCIALS

Company Type: Public

Income Statement				FYE: December 31
	REVENUE ($ mil.)	NET INCOME ($ mil.)	NET PROFIT MARGIN	EMPLOYEES
12/19	34,727	3,397	9.8%	19,100
12/18	39,004	4,690	12.0%	19,450
12/17	34,484	4,879	14.1%	13,400
12/16	29,183	3,836	13.1%	13,000
12/15	32,735	4,476	13.7%	13,000
Annual Growth	1.5%	(6.7%)		10.1%

2019 Year-End Financials

Debt ratio: 39.6%	No. of shares (mil.): 333
Return on equity: 36.6%	Dividends
Cash ($ mil.): 858	Yield: 4.3%
Current ratio: 1.83	Payout: 43.3%
Long-term debt ($ mil.): 11,614	Market value ($ mil.): —

M&G plc

Auditors: KPMG LLP

LOCATIONS

HQ: M&G plc
10 Fenchurch Avenue, London EC3M 5AG
Phone: (44) 207 626 4588
Web: www.mandgprudential.com

HISTORICAL FINANCIALS

Company Type: Public

Income Statement				FYE: December 31
	REVENUE ($ mil.)	NET INCOME ($ mil.)	NET PROFIT MARGIN	EMPLOYEES
12/19	42,428	1,479	3.5%	5,680
12/18	2,759	1,029	—	6,447
12/17	37,651	1,450	3.9%	6,823
12/16	40,084	1,394	3.5%	6,246
Annual Growth	1.9%	2.0%	—	(3.1%)

2019 Year-End Financials

Debt ratio: —	No. of shares (mil.): —
Return on equity: 16.0%	Dividends
Cash ($ mil.): 7,984	Yield: —
Current ratio: —	Payout: —
Long-term debt ($ mil.): —	Market value ($ mil.): —

	STOCK PRICE ($) FY Close	P/E High/Low	Earnings	PER SHARE ($) Dividends	Book Value
12/19	0.00	— —	0.57	0.00	2.62
Annual Growth		— —	—	—	—

Macquarie Group Ltd

One of the few domestically owned investment banks in Australia Macquarie Group does business at home and beyond. Boasting assets under management of around $A550 billion the holding company for Macquarie Bank and other subsidiaries operates an investment banking practice that provides asset management and finance banking advisory lending wealth management and risk and capital services across debt equity and commodities for institutional corporate government and retail clients. Founded in 1969 Macquarie Group has offices in about 25 countries. Domestic activities account for nearly 40% of the company's revenue.

Operations

Macquarie Group operates six divisions. This includes three "annuity style" businesses (that generated nearly 70% of overall profit in fiscal 2015 ended March): Macquarie Asset Management (35% of profit) or MAM which offers infrastructure and real asset management securities investment management and other fund and equity investment services; Corporate and Asset Finance (27% of profit) or CAF which provides specialty asset finance for corporations and and real estate credit lending; and Banking and Financial Services (7% of profit) or BFS which provides personal and business banking and wealth management services.

Macquarie Group operates five divisions. This includes three "annuity-style" businesses (that generate nearly 60% of net profit): Macquarie Asset Management (roughly 30% of net profit) or MAM which offers infrastructure and real asset management securities investment management and other fund and equity investment services; Corporate and Asset Finance (about 15%) or CAF which provides specialty asset finance and real estate and corporate principal financing; and Banking and Financial Services (some 10%) or BFS which provides personal and business banking and wealth management services.

The two "capital markets facing" business divisions include Commodities and Global Markets (CGM) and Macquarie Capital. CGM — which contributes roughly 30% to Macquarie's net profit — provides a platform for market access financing financial hedging research market analysis and physical execution across global markets including equities fixed income foreign exchange and commodities. Accounting for about 15% of the company's net profit Macquarie Capital offers advisory and capital raising services and invests Macquarie's balance sheet to develop and create assets platforms and businesses.

Fees and commission income makes up more than 45% of Macquarie's net operating income while roughly 40% is generated from net interest and trading income. The rest comes from net operating lease income and other operating income and charges (each less than 10%).

Geographic Reach

Sydney-based Macquarie Group generates nearly 40% of its total external customer revenue domestically in Australia. The Americas and the Europe Middle East and Africa (EMEA) regions each account for more than 25%. Less than 10% comes from the Asia Pacific region. Macquarie and its subsidiaries have offices in 25 countries in the Americas EMEA Asia Australia and New Zealand regions.

Sales and Marketing

Macquarie's customers include governmental institutional corporate retail and business clients as well as advisers and brokers.

Financial Performance

Note: Growth rates may differ after conversion to US dollars. This analysis uses financials from the company's annual report.

Macquarie Group has seen modest net operating income growth every year since its fiscal 2014 for overall five-year growth of 34% thanks to year-over-year gains in most of its segments. Macquarie's net income doubled in that time as it drew down roughly 15% of its cash and added about 15% to its long-term debt obligations.

The company's net operating income ticked up 5% to $A10.9 billion in 2018 thanks to improvements in commission income equity accounted income and reduced charges for provisions. Performance was driven by fee income that increased primarily due to the company's Macquarie European Infrastructure Fund III (MEIF3) and greater debt capital markets fee income from Macquarie Capital tied to greater market share and client activity in the US.

Net profits gained 15% to $A2.6 billion on the strength of Macquarie's net operating income expansion.

The holding company had cash of $A13 billion at the end of 2018 up $A1.3 billion from the previous year. Operations provided $4.5 billion; investments and financing activities used $A800 million (mostly on payments for acquisition of associates or capital contribution subsidiaries and businesses net of cash acquired) and $A2.4 billion (primarily for dividend payments) respectively.

Strategy

Macquarie Group is continuing to take measures to implement a medium-term strategy it outlined in 2015 including adopting a conservative risk management approach and balance sheet with diverse funding sources; diversifying its business mix across annuity-style and capital markets facing activities for institutional corporate government and retail clients; and expanding to adjacent geographies and product categories.

In January 2019 the company appointed a managing director to its Macquarie Capital business to lead the investing strategy of its digital infrastructure investments in Europe which will focus on private and governmental partners and emerging operating companies. In July 2018 the company closed its Macquarie Super Core Infrastructure Fund Series 1 at ?2.5 billion. The close complements Macquarie's existing European infrastructure funds.

The company acquired Luxembourg-based ValueInvest Asset Management in June 2018 expanding its investment management operations in Europe.

Green energy has been a focus for Macquarie: in June 2018 the company expanded its Green Investment Group (GIG) to North America In June 2018. The group focuses on asset creation in renewables and launched in its new region along with Candela Renewables which will develop US solar projects exclusive for GIG. That month Macquarie also closed project financing for Lal Lal Wind Farms which has two sites in Australia and made its first solar project debt investment in Spain.

Mergers and Acquisitions

Macquarie Group acquired Luxembourg-based ValueInvest Asset Management in June 2018 expanding its investment management operations in Europe. ValueInvest managed ?3.7 billion in assets.

That year Macquarie also purchased Munich-based real estate fund manager GLL Real Estate Partners. The company had about ?7 billion in assets under management and a portfolio of about 100 property investments and development projects across the office retail and industrial real estate sectors.

Company Background

Macquarie's predecessor organization Hill Samuel Australia launched in 1969 as a subsidiary of UK merchant bank Hill Samuel & Co. with three staff members. Macquarie Bank listed on the Australian Securities Exchange in 1996 and was established as non-operating holding company Macquarie Group in 2007.

HISTORY

Macquarie has made a slew of acquisitions in its past. It acquired several North America-based financial services companies including investment bank Fox-Pitt Kelton Cochran Caronia Waller. In 2010 Macquarie expanded upon its individual and institutional asset management business when it acquired US-based Delaware Investments. It also bought the Canadian investment dealing business of Blackmont Capital and rebranded it as Macquarie Private Wealth.

Two more US acquisitions were designed to enhance Macquarie Capital's advisory business. In 2010 Macquarie bought US-based specialist Presidio Partners which performs real estate advisory and capital raising advisory services. Macquarie also bought Los Angeles-based investment bank Regal Capital Advisors a specialist in strategic and financial advice for the gaming lodging and leisure industries.

Overseas Macquarie acquired the cash equities sales and research business of German private bank Sal. Oppenheim Jr. & Cie. in 2010. The acquisition broadened Macquarie's European business bolstering its presence in several key markets. Macquarie is looking to buy trading and investment banking businesses in Europe.

The company has also used acquisitions to bolster its position in the energy and other non-traditional banking markets.

In 2009 it acquired Canadian boutique investment bank Tristone Capital which served the oil and gas industry. Macquarie also acquired the downstream natural gas trading operations of Constellation Energy. The company then combined that business with its Macquarie Cook Energy business to form Macquarie Energy a larger North American wholesale gas company.

In 2010 Macquarie Energy acquired the wholesale electric marketing and trading portfolio of Integrys Energy Services in a deal that more than doubled Macquarie Energy's customer base and strengthened its position in key North American power markets. Also that year subsidiary Macquarie Aerospace agreed to purchase a portfolio of 53 aircraft from AIG unit International Lease Finance Corporation.

EXECUTIVES

Head Risk Management Group and Chief Risk Officer, Stephen Allen
Managing Director and CEO, Nicholas W. Moore, age 61, $358,522 total compensation
Head Commodities and Financial Markets, Andrew J. Downe, $479,234 total compensation
Deputy Managing Director and Head Banking and Financial Services Group, Greg C. Ward
Head Macquarie Asset Management, Shemara Wikramanayake
Head Macquarie Capital (USA), Tim Bishop
Co-Head Corporate and Asset Finance Group, Garry Farrell
Head Macquarie Securities Group, Stevan Vrcelj
Country Head USA, Michael McLaughlin
COO, Nicole Sorbara
Head Financial Management Group and CFO, Patrick Upfold
Co-Head Corporate and Asset Finance Group, Ben Brazil
Managing Director and CEO Macquarie Bank, Mary Reemst
CIO, Justin Raoul Moffitt
Chairman, Peter H. Warne, age 64
Auditors: PricewaterhouseCoopers

LOCATIONS

HQ: Macquarie Group Ltd
50 Martin Place, Sydney, New South Wales 2000
Phone: (61) 2 8232 3333   **Fax:** (61) 2 8237 1899
Web: www.macquarie.com

2018 Sales

	% of total
Australia	38
Europe Middle East and Africa	29
Americas	25
Asia/Pacific	8
Total	**100**

PRODUCTS/OPERATIONS

2018 Sales

	% of total
Lending	39
Financial markets	25
Asset & wealth management	18
Capital Markets	18
Total	**100**

2018 Sales

	% of total
Interest and similar income	38
Fee and commission income	36
Net trading income	15
Other operating income and charges	9
Others	2
Total	**100**

Selected Services

Bank Accounts
Transaction accounts
Savings account
Cash management accounts
Term deposits
Saving calculator
Credit Cards
Flexible Rewards
Qantas Rewards
Hilton Honors
Balance Transfer
Home Loans
Basic home loan
Offset home loan
Home loan calculators
Vehicle Loans
Car Loans
Motorcycle loans
Recreational vehicle loans
Investments
Online trading
Managed funds
Specialists investments
International Money Transfers
Macquarie Wrap
Private Bank
Financial Advice

COMPETITORS

Bank of America
Bank of China
Barclays
Citigroup
Credit Suisse
Deutsche Bank
Goldman Sachs
HSBC

JPMorgan Chase
Merrill Lynch
Mitsubishi UFJ
   Financial Group
Mizuho Financial
Morgan Stanley
UBS Investment Bank

HISTORICAL FINANCIALS

Company Type: Public

Income Statement

FYE: March 31

	ASSETS ($ mil.)	NET INCOME ($ mil.)	INCOME AS % OF ASSETS	EMPLOYEES
03/20	156,194	1,667	1.1%	15,849
03/19	144,076	2,114	1.5%	15,700
03/18	147,250	1,967	1.3%	14,469
03/17	139,887	1,695	1.2%	13,500
03/16	151,431	1,587	1.0%	14,372
Annual Growth	0.8%	1.2%	—	2.5%

2020 Year-End Financials

Return on assets: 1.1%
Return on equity: 14.0%
Long-term debt ($ mil.): —
No. of shares (mil.): 339
Sales ($ mil.): 10,173

Dividends
Yield: 7.9%
Payout: 79.3%
Market value ($ mil.): 18,002

	STOCK PRICE ($) FY Close	P/E High/Low		PER SHARE ($) Earnings	Dividends	Book Value
03/20	52.95	12	6	4.67	4.19	37.83
03/19	92.21	10	8	6.16	3.68	38.88
03/18	80.26	11	8	5.72	3.75	39.03
03/17	69.14	11	7	4.93	3.17	37.08
03/16	49.69	11	7	4.62	2.64	36.33
Annual Growth	1.6%	—	—	0.3%	12.3%	1.0%

Magna International Inc

Through its various subsidiaries and divisions Magna International makes just about everything needed to put together a motor vehicle. Besides being one of the world's largest automotive suppliers Magna also considers itself a technology company delivering mobility solutions. The company makes body exteriors and chassis powertrain active driver assistance electronics mechatronics seating systems roofing and lighting systems and mirrors. Operations in North America and Europe represent nearly 95% of total revenues.

Operations

The company based in Ontario Canada operates segments based on four global product-oriented operating segments: Body Exteriors & Structures (accounts for over 40% of the company's total sales) Power & Vision (nearly 30%) Complete Vehicles (more than 15%) and Seating Systems (around 15%).

The company's operating results are primarily dependent on the levels of North American European Chinese car and light truck production by the customers. While Magna International supply systems and components to every major original equipment manufacturer it do not supply systems and components for every vehicle nor is the value of the content consistent from one vehicle to the next.

Geographic Reach

Based on Ontario Canada Magna boasts over 345 manufacturing facilities and roughly 95 product development engineering and sales centers in more than 25 countries Its operations in North America generates about 50% of its total sales around 45% were produced in Europe Asia pacific

accounts for some 5% and the rest of the world for the remaining.

Sales and Marketing

A significant majority of Magna International's sales are to six customers: General Motors (generates around 15% of sales) BMW (around 15%) Ford (nearly 15%) Fiat Chrysler (roughly 15%) Daimler (more than 10%) and Volkswagen (some 10%). Other customer accounts for the remaining nearly 25% of its sales.

Financial Performance

Total sales decreased 3% to $39.4 billion in 2019 compared to $40.8 billion in 2018. The Company's sales in 2019 were negatively impacted by among other factors the weakening of a number of currencies against the U.S. dollar the divestiture of their Fluid Pressure & Controls ["FP&C"] business in the first quarter of 2019 and the impact of the labour strike at GM.

Net income attributable to Magna International Inc. decreased $531 million to $1.8 billion for 2019 compared to $2.3 billion for 2018 as a result of a decrease in income from operations before income taxes of $728 million partially offset by a loss attributable to non-controlling interests of $133 million in 2019 compared to income attributable to non-controlling interests of $36 million in 2018 and a decrease in income taxes of $28 million.

Cash held by the company at the end of 2019 increased by $590 million to $1.4 billion compared to $802 million in the prior year. Cash provided by operations was $4.0 billion while cash used for investing and financing activities were $434 million and $2.9 billion respectively

Strategy

Magna's capital strategy is to maintain a strong balance sheet ample liquidity and high investment-grade credit ratings. In December 31 2019 the company has over $4 billion of available liquidity between cash and credit lines. This strategy allows the company to invest prudently for growth through organic opportunities innovation spending and acquisitions that fit their strategy as well as to return capital to shareholders. It also leaves them well-positioned in times of economic downturn.

Aligned with Magna's customer product and geographic strategy their innovation approach focuses on three key trends:

Driver Assistance: Creating solutions that improve safety and provide a more comfortable driving experience. The company's technologies give drivers active guidance with a 360Â° view of their environment with the ability to detect various objects and predict their dynamic behavior around the vehicle and on its path.

Electrification: Developing powertrain innovations that are both modular and scalable - serving as building blocks to provide competitive solutions to automakers facing electric/hybrid powertrain proliferation.

Smart Mobility: Accommodating a variety of new mobility use cases like enhancing the occupant experience by making seats more flexible and reconfigurable.

Mergers and Acquisitions

In 2019 Magna has completed the acquisition of VIZA Geca SL a Spain-based supplier of seat structures and related systems. The transaction was made to further enhance Magna's capabilities in future-ready seating solutions that enable added functionality which starts with the streat structure itself. The terms of this acquisition were not disclosed.

Company Background

Magna International has historically expanded its product lines through acquisitions of other auto parts manufacturers. In early 2011 Magna Seating acquired Germany-based Vogelsitze GmbH which made seats for buses and passenger trains. In 2012 Magna obtained Verwaltungs GmbH a maker of

automotive vacuum engine and transmission pumps with two facilities in Germany and one in each of China and Bulgaria. Also in 2012 to strengthen its automotive pump operations Magna purchased the remaining 50% interest it didn't already own of STT Technologies which made transmission and engine related pumps for the North American market.

HISTORY

Magna International is rooted in a tool and die shop founded by Frank Stronach and friend Tony Czapka in Ontario Canada in 1957. Austrian-born Stronach immigrated to Canada in 1954. By the end of 1957 the business called Multimatic had 10 employees. Multimatic delved into car parts when it landed a contract in 1960 to make sun visor brackets for a General Motors division in Canada.

To go public Multimatic underwent a reverse merger in 1969 with Magna Electronics a publicly traded maker of components for aerospace defense and industrial markets. (Stronach retained control of the company.) Annual sales reached $10 million that year. The company expanded its automotive operations during the early 1970s by adding more stamped and electronic components. Magna was renamed Magna International in 1973.

With sales increasing steadily among its auto parts businesses Magna sold its aerospace and defense business (now part of Heroux-Devtek) in 1981. The new Magna consisted of five distinct automotive divisions that made seat tracks door latches electronic components and other auto parts. During the 1980s the company expanded by adding factories and product lines. It also capitalized on car makers' penchant for outsourcing labor and bypassing unions. By 1987 when sales reached $1 billion the company was producing systems for every area of the automobile. Stronach didn't spend all his time on cars however; he owned race horses and restaurants. He had opened restaurants tried various publishing ventures (which failed) and even made an unsuccessful run for a Canadian parliament seat in 1988.

Aggressive expansion during the 1980s eventually caught up with the company and in 1989 Magna began to restructure selling assets to pay off its debt. The company also was bailed out in part by two of its principal customers — General Motors and Chrysler. Having recovered somewhat Magna began acquiring small auto parts companies in Europe in 1992.

Magna expanded its European presence with the purchase of Austria-based Steyr-Daimler-Puch in 1998 adding about $1 billion in annual sales. The deal steered Magna into the auto assembly business. Stronach also added Santa Anita Park to his holdings that year. In late 1999 the company's racetrack interests were spun off as Magna Entertainment with Magna retaining a 78% stake. Stronach's horseRed Bullet won the 2000 Preakness. Later that year Magna sold its 50% stake in Webasto Sunroofs to privately-owned German auto parts maker Webasto.

Early in 2001 Stronach's daughter Belinda was named vice chairman and CEO. The company then prepared to spin off Magna Steyr and Intier (now Magna's interiors and seating divisions) as public companies; Intier was spun off later in 2001.

Magna acquired rival automotive mirror maker Donnelly in 2002 in a stock-and-debt deal worth $320 million. The company divested its stake in Magna Entertainment in 2003.

Belinda Stronach stepped down as president CEO and director in order to make a bid for the leadership of Canada's new Conservative Party. Her father assumed the role of interim president in early 2004. Ms. Stronach's bid for the leadership of the Conservative Party was not successful. Mr.

Stronach ran the company until 2005 when Magna adopted a co-CEO management structure with Donald Walker and Siegfried Wolf at the helm.

Magna and Daimler announced in 2004 that Magna would buy Daimler's drivetrain manufacturing subsidiary New Venture Gear for about $435 million. After approval by the European Commission New Venture Gear was acquired by a newly created joint venture called New Process Gear with Magna holding an 80% interest; Daimler held 20% until 2007 when Magna bought out its stake.

Russian conglomerate Basic Element led by Russian aluminum magnate Oleg Deripaska spent about $1.5 billion to purchase 20% of Magna in 2007. The transaction gave Magna entry to the Russian market but late in 2008 Deripaska's bank BNP Paribas made a margin call that forced the businessman to give up his shares. In 2008 Magna International acquired Technoplast a Russia-based manufacturer of plastic automotive interior and exterior parts which bolstered its capacity in Eastern Europe and Russia.

On the heels of the General Motors bankruptcy filing in 2009 the German government selected Magna International as a partner for Adam Opel and agreed to provide about ?1.5 billion (around $2 billion) in bridge loans while GM and Magna finalized the contract. A trusteeship for Opel was arranged to keep European operations separate from the Chapter 11 proceedings of GM.

Magna teamed up with Russian banking firm Sberbank to purchase a 55% interest in Opel and its UK-based Vauxhall unit. While GM initially agreed to the sale in September 2009 it backed out in November. The GM board decided to restructure Opel and its European operations instead because business conditions were improving and the Opel brand was important to its global strategy. In Europe the decision was met with demands by the German government that its ?1.5 billion in bridge loans be returned as well as protests and planned work stoppages by the German labor union.

The GM bankruptcy was brought on by the economic crisis of 2008 and 2009. Magna responded by implementing cost cutting measures which included reducing its headcount by approximately 11500 representing a 14% cutback between 2007 and 2009. It also sold off some of its non-core assets.

Founder and chairman Frank Stronach stepped down in 2010 citing the trend toward more regulatory limitations on company management as one of the reasons. He gave up his controlling share in the company and with it his voting control. The company purchased and cancelled all of its Class B shares held by the Stronach Group and issued Class A Common shares. This capital transaction ended the company's dual class stock structure. The former premier of Ontario Mike Harris took Stronach's place. Co-CEO Siegfried ("Sigi") Wolf also resigned which made co-CEO Donald Walker the sole CEO of Magna International as of mid-2011.

In early 2011 Magna Seating acquired Germany-based Vogelsitze GmbH which made seats for buses and passenger trains. In 2012 Magna obtained Verwaltungs GmbH a maker of automotive vacuum engine and transmission pumps with two facilities in Germany and one in each of China and Bulgaria.

EXECUTIVES

Chief Executive Officer; Director, Donald J. Walker, age 63

Executive Vice-President and Chief Financial Officer, Vincent J. Galifi, $110,500 total compensation
EVP Global Human Resources, Marc J. Neeb
COO, Tom Skudutis, $110,500 total compensation
EVP and Chief Strategy Officer, Herbert Demel, age 67
EVP, Alon Ossip
President Magna Europe, Guenther Apfalter
Chief Marketing Officer and President Magna Asia, James J. (Jim) Tobin
CTO, Burkhard Goeschel, age 73
Executive Vice-President Corporate Engineering & R&D, Seetarama Kotagiri
Chairman of the Board, William L. Young, age 64
Auditors: Deloitte LLP

LOCATIONS

HQ: Magna International Inc
  337 Magna Drive, Aurora, Ontario L4G 7K1
Phone: 905 726-2462   **Fax:** 905 726-7164
Web: www.magna.com

2017 Sales

	$ mil.	% of total
North America	20,905	53
Europe	15,177	39
Asia	2,791	7
Rest of World	584	1
Corporate & Other	(511)	-
Total	**38,946**	**100**

PRODUCTS/OPERATIONS

2017 Sales

	$ mil.	% of total
Body systems and chassis systems	9,744	25
Powertrain systems	6,773	17
Exterior systems	5,325	14
Seating systems	5,203	13
Tooling engineering & other	3,397	9
Complete vehicle assembly	2,944	8
Vision & electronic systems	2,891	7
Closure systems	2,669	7
Total	**38,946**	**100**

2017 Sales

	$ mil.	% of total
General Motors	6,854	18
Ford Motor Company	6,085	16
Fiat / Chrysler Group	5,502	14
Daimler AG	4,719	12
BMW	3,231	11
Volkswagen	4,025	10
Other	7,557	19
Total	**38,946**	**100**

Selected Operations Products and Services Body systems

  Chassis systems
  Seating
  Powertrain
  Electronics
  Mechatronics
  D-Optic headlights
  Clearview mirrors
  Vehicle engineering and manufacturing
  Hybrid dual clutch transmission
  Liteflex modular process
  48 volt edrive
  Driver monitoring systems
  MAX4 Autonomous Drive Platform

COMPETITORS

A.G. Simpson	Hella
Aisin Seiki	KUO
American Axle & Manufacturing	Lacks Enterprises
	Lear Corp
Benteler Automotive	Linamar Corp.
BorgWarner	Meritor
Calsonic Kansei	Plastic Omnium
Commercial Vehicle	Prodrive
DENSO	Robert Bosch

DURA Automotive	Tenneco
Dana	Textron
Delphi Automotive Systems	Torotrak
	Tower International
Faurecia	Toyota Auto Body
Ficosa	Valeo
GKN	Visteon
Gentex	ZF Friedrichshafen
Haldex	

HISTORICAL FINANCIALS
Company Type: Public

Income Statement

	REVENUE ($ mil.)	NET INCOME ($ mil.)	NET PROFIT MARGIN	EMPLOYEES
12/19	39,431	1,765	4.5%	0
12/18	40,827	2,296	5.6%	0
12/17	38,946	2,206	5.7%	0
12/16	36,445	2,031	5.6%	155,450
12/15	32,134	2,013	6.3%	129,000
Annual Growth	**5.2%**	**(3.2%)**	—	—

FYE: December 31

2019 Year-End Financials

Debt ratio: 12.2%
Return on equity: 16.3%
Cash ($ mil.): 1,276
Current ratio: 1.26
Long-term debt ($ mil.): 3,062

No. of shares (mil.): 303
Dividends
  Yield: 2.6%
  Payout: 26.1%
Market value ($ mil.): 16,630

	STOCK PRICE ($) FY Close	P/E High/Low		PER SHARE ($) Earnings	Dividends	Book Value
12/19	54.84	10	8	5.59	1.46	35.72
12/18	45.45	10	7	6.61	1.32	32.69
12/17	56.67	10	7	5.90	1.10	31.35
12/16	43.40	9	6	5.16	1.00	25.55
12/15	40.56	22	8	4.88	0.88	22.29
Annual Growth	**7.8%**	—	—	**3.5%**	**13.5%**	**12.5%**

Magnit PJSC

Auditors: Ernst & Young LLC

LOCATIONS

HQ: Magnit PJSC
  15/5, Solnechnaya Street, Krasnodar 350 072
Phone: (7) 861 210 98 10
Web: www.magnit-info.ru

HISTORICAL FINANCIALS
Company Type: Public

Income Statement

	REVENUE ($ mil.)	NET INCOME ($ mil.)	NET PROFIT MARGIN	EMPLOYEES
12/19	21,991	153	0.7%	0
12/18	17,748	485	2.7%	0
12/17	19,593	609	3.1%	0
12/16	16,033	811	5.1%	0
12/15	15,594	968	6.2%	0
Annual Growth	**9.0%**	**(36.9%)**	—	—

FYE: December 31

2019 Year-End Financials

Debt ratio: 0.3%
Return on equity: 4.3%
Cash ($ mil.): 143
Current ratio: 0.84
Long-term debt ($ mil.): 1,922

No. of shares (mil.): 97
Dividends
  Yield: —
  Payout: 150.2%
Market value ($ mil.): —

Mahindra & Mahindra Ltd

Auditors: B S R & Co. LLP

LOCATIONS

HQ: Mahindra & Mahindra Ltd
 Gateway Building, Apollo Bunder, Mumbai 400 001
Phone: (91) 22 22895500   **Fax:** (91) 22 22875485
Web: www.mahindra.com

HISTORICAL FINANCIALS

Company Type: Public

Income Statement				FYE: March 31
	REVENUE ($ mil.)	NET INCOME ($ mil.)	NET PROFIT MARGIN	EMPLOYEES
03/19	15,291	768	5.0%	42,875
03/18	14,432	1,154	8.0%	41,673
03/17	13,833	570	4.1%	20,366
03/16	11,878	485	4.1%	0
03/15	11,587	501	4.3%	0
Annual Growth	7.2%	11.2%	—	—

2019 Year-End Financials

Debt ratio: 0.4%	No. of shares (mil.): 1,087
Return on equity: 13.8%	Dividends
Cash ($ mil.): 1,262	Yield: —
Current ratio: 1.18	Payout: 17.4%
Long-term debt ($ mil.): 6,290	Market value ($ mil.): —

Malayan Banking Berhad

Malayan Banking Berhad (better known as Maybank) is Malaysia's largest financial services group. Boasting assets of RM640 billion ($145 billion) the firm and its subsidiaries provide deposit services mortgages credit cards and other loan products to businesses and individuals through some 400 branches in Malaysia nearly 430 branches in Indonesia over 20 branches in Singapore and 30-plus branches across Southeast Asia. The firm also offers investment banking asset management online banking brokerage insurance unit trusts and other investments and corporate finance services through 2400 offices in 20 countries. Amanah Raya a trust company controlled by the Malaysian government owns over 45% of Maybank.

Operations

Maybank also in 2014 ranked as South East Asia's fourth-largest bank the largest Islamic financing bank in Malaysia and the third-largest Islamic financing bank globally by assets. As Malaysia's largest bank it controlled an 18.4% market share of the loans advances and financing market in Malaysia as well as a 27.6% share of the savings deposit market and 21.1% share of the checking account market.

The bank categorizes its financial services under three key business pillars. Its Community Financial Services (which generated 35% of the company's net operating income or NOI in 2014) includes consumer banking SME and business banking services. The Global Banking pillar includes cor-porate banking (12% of NOI) investment banking (7%) global markets (8%) transaction banking and asset management. The Insurance & Takaful (8% of NOI) pillar offers insurance and Islamic services and also consists of Maybank's international business operations (28% NOI). Islamic financial services are also offered across all of its business units.Broadly speaking Maybank generates about half of its operating income from net interest income (mostly from loans and advances including from Islamic Banking Scheme operations). Around 20% of its operating income comes from net earned insurance premiums. The company had 46000 employees at the end of 2014.

Geographic Reach

Maybank's home markets are in Malaysia Singapore and Indonesia; which contributed nearly 89% of the group's profit before tax (PBT) in fiscal 2014. About 60% of its loans and 71% of its PBT were originated in Malaysia alone during the fiscal year. Singapore made up about 14% of its PBT. Outside of these markets Maybank operates in 20 countries (including 10 ASEAN countries) in major financial centers such as Hong Kong Shanghai London New York and Bahrain. It also has associates in Pakistan (MCB Bank's 1242 branches) and Vietnam (An Binh Bank's 145 branches).

Sales and Marketing

The firm serves more than 22 million individuals organizations and businesses (including those of Muslim faith).

Financial Performance

Note: Growth rates may differ after conversion to US dollars. This analysis uses financials from the company's annual report.

Maybank's revenues and profits have risen more than 30% since 2011 thanks largely to strong loan business growth.

The company's revenue rose by 7% to RM35.7 billion ($10.2 billion) in 2014 mostly thanks to higher interest income as its loan advances and financing assets grew by 13% driven by a 47.5% jump in international loan growth and buoyed by better-than-industry loan growth in Malaysia and Singapore. Its financial investment portfolio assets also grew 8% during the year which boosted interest income further.

Higher revenue in 2014 drove Maybank's net income up 3% to a record RM6.7 billion ($1.91 billion) for the year. The company's operating cash levels fell by 39% to RM5.27 billion ($1.5 billion) despite higher earnings due to unfavorable working capital changes mostly related to financial assets purchased under resale agreements and because it used more cash toward loans advances and financing.

Strategy

Maybank's strategic objectives over the past five years (2010 through 2015) have included: being Malaysia's no. 1 retail financial services provider in 2015; be the leading ASEAN Wholesale bank expanding into the Middle East China and India; be Malaysia's leading Insurance and Takaful provider and an emerging regional player in the field as well; become a "truly regional organization" with around 40% of pre-tax profit coming from international operations by 2015; and becoming a global leader in Islamic Finance.

Some of Maybank's fastest growing businesses include Islamic financing and Takaful (insurance) services that adhere to Islamic law which prohibits the collection of interest but allows profit-sharing and the sale and buy-back of homes (instead of the origination of mortgages). Serving Muslim individuals organizations and businesses the company is opening branches at home and abroad that offer such services. Indeed Islamic Financing grew by 25% during 2014 which increased its proportion of total Malaysia loans to 43.8% at the end of 2014 (from 38.9% at the end of 2013). The growth also solidified Maybank as the largest Islamic bank in Malaysia and the third-largest globally by assets.

Maybank also continues to expand its global reach beyond its home markets. During 2014 it opened its first branch in Myanmar and its third branch in Kunming China. That year it also launched its Etiqa Insurance and Private Wealth businesses in Singapore.

Company Background

Maybank has made several acquisitions in the past to boost its international presence. In 2011 the company acquired 100% of Singapore brokerage Kim Eng Holdings. The addition boosted Maybank's international profile and expanded its distribution capabilities.

In 2008 the bank completed its acquisition of the 250-branch Bank Internasional Indonesia (BII). The deal had stalled when banking regulator Bank Negara Malaysia prohibited the transaction but that decision was reversed and the acquisition was ultimately allowed. Also in 2008 the bank acquired minority stakes in Pakistan's MCB Bank and Vietnam's An Binh Bank (ABBank) as well as Kookmin Bank's minority stake in PT Bank Internasional Indonesia.

Auditors: Ernst & Young PLT

LOCATIONS

HQ: Malayan Banking Berhad
 14th Floor, Menara Maybank, 100, Jalan Tun Perak,
 Kuala Lumpur 50050
Phone: (60) 3 2070 8833   **Fax:** (60) 3 2031 0071
Web: www.maybank.com

PRODUCTS/OPERATIONS

2013 Sales

	% of total
Interest income	65
Income from islamic banking scheme operations	11
Non-interest income	24
Total	**100**

Selected Subsidiaries

BinaFikir Sdn. Bhd.
Etiqa Insurance Berhad
Etiqa Life International (L) Ltd.
Etiqa Takaful Berhad
Maybank (PNG) Limited2
Maybank Ageas Holding Berhad (formerly known as Maybank Fortis Holdings Berhad)
Maybank Allied Credit & Leasing Sdn. Bhd.
Maybank International (L) Ltd.
Maybank Investment Bank Berhad
Maybank Islamic Berhad
Maybank Philippines Incorporated1
Maysec Sdn. Bhd.
PT Bank Internasional Indonesia TBK1
PT Bank Maybank Syariah Indonesia1
PT BII Finance Centre1
PT Wahana Ottomitra Multiartha TBK1

COMPETITORS

AmBank Group	Malaysian Industrial
Bank Muamalat	Development Finance
Bank of China	OCBC Bank
Bank of East Asia	Public Bank
CIMB Group	RHB Capital
Hang Seng Bank	Standard Chartered
Hong Leong Bank	

HISTORICAL FINANCIALS

Company Type: Public

Income Statement				FYE: December 31
	ASSETS ($ mil.)	NET INCOME ($ mil.)	INCOME AS % OF ASSETS	EMPLOYEES
12/19	203,956	2,003	1.0%	43,000
12/18	195,251	1,963	1.0%	43,000
12/17	188,535	1,852	1.0%	43,000
12/16	164,056	1,503	0.9%	43,976
12/15	164,540	1,587	1.0%	45,000
Annual Growth	5.5%	6.0%	—	(1.1%)

2019 Year-End Financials

Return on assets: 1.0%	Dividends
Return on equity: 10.4%	Yield: —
Long-term debt ($ mil.): —	Payout: 87.0%
No. of shares (mil.): —	Market value ($ mil.): —
Sales ($ mil): 10,824	

Manulife Financial Corp

Manulife the holding company for The Manufacturers Life Insurance Company and John Hancock Financial Services is a leading international financial services group that helps people make their decisions easier and lives better. Manulife provides individual life insurance group life and health group pension products variable annuities wealth management and financial products in nearly 20 countries and territories worldwide. The US and Asia make up its largest operations. Manulife's reinsurance division provides life and property/casualty reinsurance. The company also provides investment management private banking estate solutions and securities lending services.

Operations

Manulife is Canada's largest insurer — it serves one in three of that country's residents — and is a top 10 global life insurer based on market capitalization. The company operates under the John Hancock brand in the US and as Manulife elsewhere. Altogether the company serves nearly 30 million customers and has almost C$1.2 trillion in assets under management and administration.

Its segments are composed of its geographic locations in Asia Canada and US. Other segments are: Global Wealth and Asset Management (more than 5%) which provides fee-based wealth solutions to retail retirement and institutional customers and Corporate & other which comprised of investment performance on assets backing capital net of amounts allocated to operating segments; financing costs; costs incurred by the corporate office related to shareholder activities; Property and Casualty Reinsurance business; and run-off reinsurance business lines.

Geographic Reach

Manulife operates in the Americas (Brazil Canada and the US) Europe (the UK) and the Asia region (Australia Cambodia China Hong Kong Indonesia Japan Macau Malaysia Philippines Singapore Taiwan Thailand and Vietnam.

The company's segment sales in Asia generates around 35% sales in the US bring in some 30% of Manulife's annual revenue and Canada accounts for the bulk of the rest.

Sales and Marketing

Manulife distributes its insurance products through agents brokers banks and financial planners. It also markets products directly to cus-

tomers. The group has over 98000 contracted agents in Asia.

The company's pension contracts mutual fund offerings annuities and banking products are distributed through affiliated insurance agents and brokers securities brokerage firms financial planners pension plan sponsors and consultants and banks.

Financial Performance

Note: Growth rates may differ after conversion to US Dollars.

Manulife's revenues have grown as the company has expanded its global operations over the past five years. Revenue grew 125% between 2015 and 2019 while net income increased by 156% in the same period.

In 2019 revenues increased C$40.6 billion to C$79.6 billion largely due to an increase in net investment income as well as higher net premium income (primarily in Asia). Lower interest rates and higher equity markets also contributed to the gain.

Net income which has been more volatile than revenue increased that year by 17% to C$5.6 billion from C$4.8 billion. The increase was due to growth in core earnings of C$400 million the non-recurrence of a 2018 restructuring charge and higher investment-related experience gains.

Cash at the end of 2019 was C$19.5 billion a C$4.6 billion increase from the year prior. Operations generated C$20.5 billion in 2019. Investing activities used C$13.8 billion mainly for purchases and mortgage advances. Financing activities used another C$2.1 billion mostly for redemption of capital instruments and share repurchases.

Strategy

Manulife has five strategic priorities it set out at the start of its transformation. These five strategic priorities being: Portfolio Optimization; Expense Efficiency; Accelerate Growth; Digital Customer Leader' and High Performing Team.

Its targets for 2022 include releasing a total $5 billion in capital from legacy businesses; achieve a 50% expense efficiency ratio; deliver $1 billion in expense efficiencies; generate two-thirds of core earnings from highest potential business' improve Net Promoter Score by 30 points as compared to a baseline of +1 in 2017; and achieve top quartile employee engagement compared to global financial services and insurance peers.

It has already made progress in 2019 through these five strategic priorities. Manulife achieved its medium-term target three years ahead of schedule and delivered $5.1 billion of cumulative capital benefits including $2.1 billion in 2019. It has also cumulative expense efficiencies of $700 million in pre-tax annual savings including $400 million in 2019.

Manulife also entered into a long-term strategic partnership with HaoDF.com in mainland China and agreed to enter into a joint venture with Mahindra Finance in India. It also expanded its behavioral insurance product base through the launch of ManulifeMOVE insurance program in Vietnam and Cambodia and the John Hancock Aspire program in the U.S.

Company Background

Manulife acquired US financial services giant John Hancock in a $10 billion deal in 2004 bringing Manulife into the top ranks of US and global life insurers. Manulife subsequently rebranded its US financial products with the more-recognizable John Hancock name and logo. Manulife also consolidated John Hancock's Canadian subsidiary Maritime Life Assurance Company into its flagship subsidiary The Manufacturers Life Insurance Company.

EXECUTIVES

SEVP and Chief Investment Officer; Chairman Manulife Asset Management, Warren A. Thomson
EVP and Global Head of Wealth and Asset Management; President and CEO Manulife Asset Management, Kai R. Sotorp
EVP and Chief Actuary, Steven A. (Steve) Finch
SEVP and General Manager Canadian Division; President and CEO Manulife Canada, Marianne Harrison
President and CEO John Hancock Financial Services, Craig R. Bromley
EVP General Account Investments, Scott S. Hartz
EVP Human Resources, Stephani E. Kingsmill
EVP and Chief Risk Officer, Rahim Hirji
SEVP and CFO, Stephen B. (Steve) Roder
EVP and CIO, Gregory A. (Greg) Framke
President CEO and Director, Roy Gori
EVP and Chief Innovation Officer, Timothy W. Ramza
SEVP and COO, Linda P. Mantia
EVP and General Counsel, James D. (Jim) Gallagher
EVP and Global Chief Marketing Officer, Gretchen H. Garrigues
Chairman, Richard B. DeWolfe
Auditors: Ernst & Young LLP

LOCATIONS

HQ: Manulife Financial Corp
  200 Bloor Street East, Toronto, Ontario M4W 1E5
Phone: 416 926-3000   **Fax:** 416 926-5454
Web: www.manulife.com

2017 Sales

	% of total
US	41
Asia	37
Canada	21
Other	1
Total	**100**

PRODUCTS/OPERATIONS

2017 Sales

	% of total
Premiums	
Life & health	44
Annuities & pensions	8
Net investment income	27
Other	21
Total	**100**

COMPETITORS

AEGON
AIG
Allianz
Canada Life
China Life Insurance
Dai-ichi Life
Fairfax Financial Holdings
ING
Industrial Alliance Insurance and Financial Servic
Liberty Mutual
Meiji Yasuda Life
MetLife
Nationwide
New York Life
Nippon Life Insurance
Power Financial
Principal Financial
Prudential
Sun Life
T&D Holdings
The Hartford
Tokio Marine

HISTORICAL FINANCIALS

Company Type: Public

Income Statement
FYE: December 31

	ASSETS ($ mil.)	NET INCOME ($ mil.)	INCOME AS % OF ASSETS	EMPLOYEES
12/19	819,328	5,672	0.7%	35,000
12/18	759,727	4,860	0.6%	34,000
12/17	738,728	2,130	0.3%	34,300
12/16	729,764	2,965	0.4%	3,500
12/15	713,524	2,218	0.3%	33,000
Annual Growth	3.5%	26.5%	—	1.5%

2019 Year-End Financials

Return on assets: 0.7%	Dividends
Return on equity: 11.8%	Yield: 3.7%
Long-term debt ($ mil.): —	Payout: 47.0%
No. of shares (mil.): 1,949	Market value ($ mil.): 39,545
Sales ($ mil): 80,572	

	STOCK PRICE ($) FY Close	P/E High/Low		PER SHARE ($) Earnings	Dividends	Book Value
12/19	20.29	7	5	2.80	0.75	25.40
12/18	14.19	9	6	2.36	0.71	23.66
12/17	20.86	22	17	0.99	0.83	21.07
12/16	17.82	13	8	1.43	0.75	21.57
12/15	14.98	18	14	1.06	0.52	21.23
Annual Growth	7.9%	—	—	27.4%	9.6%	4.6%

Mapfre SA

Auditors: KPMG Auditores S.L.

LOCATIONS

HQ: Mapfre SA
Carretera de Pozuelo 52, Madrid, Majadahonda
Phone: (34) 91 581 1100   **Fax:** (34) 91 581 1143
Web: www.mapfre.com

HISTORICAL FINANCIALS

Company Type: Public

Income Statement
FYE: December 31

	ASSETS ($ mil.)	NET INCOME ($ mil.)	INCOME AS % OF ASSETS	EMPLOYEES
12/19	81,411	684	0.8%	34,324
12/18	77,061	605	0.8%	35,390
12/17	80,999	839	1.0%	36,271
12/16	71,675	818	1.1%	37,020
12/15	69,153	772	1.1%	38,405
Annual Growth	4.2%	(3.0%)	—	(2.8%)

Marubeni Corp.

One of Japan's largest sogo shosha (general trading companies) Marubeni conducts a broad range of import/export activities across numerous sectors. These include lifestyle ICT & real estate business forest products food agri business chemicals power business energy metals & mineral resources plant aerospace & ship finance & leasing business construction auto & industrial machinery.

Its footprint spans around 135 branches in nearly 70 countries including twelve in Japan nearly 60 overseas branches and about 30 operated by overseas subsidiaries. Marubeni was founded in 1949.

Operations

Marubeni consists of six business group: Transportation & Industrial Machinery Financial Business Group (roughly 40% of sales); Food Agriculture and Chemical Group (about 30%); Consumer Product Group (nearly 25%); Power Business & Infrastructure Group (around 10%); Energy & Metals Group; and CDIO. Under these business groups it has about 15 business divisions.

The Transportation & Industrial Machinery Financial Business Group consists of Construction Industrial Machinery & Mobility Division (about 25% of sales) Aerospace and Ship Division (about 15%) and Finance & Leasing Business Division. The Construction Industrial Machinery & Mobility Division includes Sales services and financing of construction and mining equipment. The Aerospace & Ship Division is involved in aircraft & engine parts trading business and fund establishment and development investment. The Finance & Leasing Business Division includes Auto finance business aircraft and aircraft engine leasing business comprehensive leasing business leasing of various commercial vehicles and freight railcars private equity investment and asset management.

The Food Agriculture & Chemicals Group includes divisions such as Food (about 25%) Chemicals (some 5%) and Agri Business. The Food Division includes grain products such as corn soybeans wheat rapeseed etc; feed ingredients including soybean meal rapeseed meal fish meal etc; compound feed and fresh and processed meat among others. The Chemical Division includes basic petrochemical products and plastic derivatives salt and chlor-alkali products and life science-related products such as functional ingredients for foods functional feed additives oleochemicals and personal care ingredients. Its Agri Business Division crop protection products fertilizers seeds and proprietary products.

The Consumer Product Group makes up ICT & Real Estate Business Division (around 15%) Lifestyle Division (some 5%) and Forest Products Division (about 5%). The ICT & Real Estate Business Division provides a wide range of high-added-value services and solutions in operating domains related to consumers' everyday lives including ICT real estate logistics and insurance The Lifestyle Division is OEM/ODM manufacturing of products such as apparel and footwear. The Forest Products Division's products include wood chips and biomass fuel pulp and waste water paper paperboard and hygiene products as well as building & construction materials and wood products.

The Power Business & Infrastructure Group includes Power Business Division (around 10%) Infrastructure Project Division.

The Energy and Metals Group consists of Energy Division and Metals & Mineral Resources Division. The Energy Division is involved in exploration development and production of oil and gas. The Metals & Mineral Resources Division develops iron ore coal and copper mines smelting and refining of aluminum and magnesium trading of iron ore coal ferroalloy ferrous raw materials and cement-related materials.

The CDIO includes Next Generation Business Development which includes Chinese children education business inbound tourism business next-generation retail business and smart city and smart infrastructure business among others.

Geographic Reach

Headquartered in Tokyo Marubeni has more than 135 branches and offices spread across nearly 70 countries and regions. It has a dozen branches in Japan and nearly 60 overseas branches in addition to about 65 offices run by about 30 overseas corporate subsidiaries.

Financial Performance

The company's revenue has been fluctuating in the last five years with an overall decline of 6% between 2016 and 2020. The group's net income has been rising until in 2019 but dropped to a loss in 2020.

Revenue was down Â 573.6 billion (8%) from the fiscal year 2019 (ended March) to Â 6.8 trillion due mainly to a drop in grain trading volume for the Chinese market lower prices and production volumes in petrochemicals and weaker sales in the Gavilon grain business.

The Marubeni incurred a consolidated net loss of Â 197.5 billion in the fiscal year 2020 (ended March). This was a negative turnaround of Â 428.3 billion compared with the previous fiscal year.

The company's cash for the year ended 2020 was Â 522.5 million a 3% growth from the previous year. Operating activities generated Â 327 million while investing activities used Â 209.8 million mainly for purchases of investments in associates and joint ventures and other investments as well as capital expenditures. Financing activities used another Â 93.3 million mainly for repayments of long-term bonds and borrowings.

Strategy

In late 2020 Marubeni Corporation entered into a business alliance agreement with Tyrata Inc. a US.-based developer of autonomous tire tread wear measurement systems. The business alliance agreement will introduce Tyrata's automated tire tread wear measurement equipment and services to the Japanese market. Marubeni is currently making progress on demonstration tests for the domestic deployment of services related to the measurement equipment with a goal to offer subscription service within two years.

The company newly established "Clairvo Technologies Inc. is a company that will provide medical institutions with diagnostic support products that apply artificial intelligence (AI). Clairvo will form partnerships with domestic and overseas companies that develop diagnostic support products that apply AI and other technologies. By obtaining the needed licenses under the Pharma and Device Laws Clairvo will be able to apply for approval of relevant products to relevant authorities collaborate with opinion leaders in each specialized field and build a comprehensive distribution network for medical institutions.

In mid-2020 the company and Phase Four Inc. a company that makes radio frequency (RF) plasma engines for in-space propulsion entered into a capital and strategic partnership and concluded an exclusive representative agreement for the company's Maxwell line of satellite engines in Japan and other strategic markets around the world. Marubeni aims to provide various solutions that support satellite operators in launching and operating small satellites. In 2020 a satellite that is equipped with Phase Four's Maxwell thrusters is scheduled to launch and additional deliveries are scheduled for the future. Marubeni and Phase Four by provision of revolutionary RF engines to customers all over the world endeavor to promote new space missions including remote sensing high speed communications and space exploration and also strive to make a substantial contribution to the development of space industries worldwide.

Mergers and Acquisitions

In the latter part of 3rd quarter of 2020 Marubeni Corporation announces that the company acquired 25% of the shares of Mexico-based APP Coatzacoalcos Villahermosa S.A.P.I. De C.V. which is a concessionaire to execute a project for improvement and 7.5-year maintenance of 135km roads between Coatzacoalcos in Veracruz State and Villahermosa in Tabasco State located in southern Mexico under a Public Private Partnership from Hycsa group a local Mexican construction company. Marubeni considers PPP projects in the field of transport and infrastructure to be one of its core strategies and has been expanding its footprint in the market. Terms were not disclosed.

In mid-2020 Daio Paper Corporation and Marubeni Corporation agreed to jointly acquire indirectly all shares of Santher - F´brica de Papel Santa Therezinha S.A. through a joint investment company established in Brazil called H&PC BRAZIL PARTICIPA •ES S.A in which Daio and Marubeni hold 51.0% and 49.0% stake respectively. Marubeni seeks to enhance Santher's corporate value by integrating Marubeni's existing functions resources and networks as a general trading house and through Santher's business contribute to the realization of a hygienic environment and safe and comfortable lifestyles. Terms were not disclosed.

In early 2020 Marubeni Corporation has executed a Share Purchase Agreement with I Squared Capital to acquire Chenya Energy Co. Ltd a solar power developer and operator in Taiwan. Chenya will become a wholly owned subsidiary of Marubeni upon the conclusion of this transaction. By acquiring Chenya and Chenya's solar power generation assets including one of the world's largest floating solar power plants Marubeni will gain expertise in the floating solar power business and continue to enhance its renewable energy development capabilities. Terms were not disclosed.

In late 2019 Marubeni Corporation agreed to acquire shares of Alliance Magnesium Inc which will build a commercial plant to produce magnesium ingot in the province of Quebec Canada and signed a stock subscription agreement with AMI. The total project cost will be more than C$ 100 million and Marubeni's investment will be C$ 16.7 million. The project is to extract magnesium from tailings (mine waste) which were discharged and deposited at an abandoned mine site in Quebec and produce primary magnesium through the electrolysis process.

In 2019 Marubeni Corporation and Mizuho Leasing Co. Ltd. agreed to acquire aircraft lessor Connecticut-based Aircastle in a deal worth $7.4 billion. Marubeni will continue to provide support to Aircastle as a strategic partner to reinforce Aircastle's business platform further so as to take an advantage of anticipated strong market growth. Marubeni believes that the new ownership structure of Aircastle backed by two strategic partners Marubeni and Mizuho Leasing will enhance stability and credibility of the company supporting its future growth.

Also in 2019 Marubeni Corporation hereby announces that it has acquired the assets of Alabama-based Auto Electric & Carburetor Company LLC a distributor of quality automotive parts and Texas-based Poppe Automotive Warehouse Inc. a reliable supplier of automotive aftermarket parts for over 40 years. Marubeni aims to further expand its business scale by strengthening existing locations and expanding its sales network in the growing market of automotive parts sales mainly in the Sunbelt area of the United States where the number of registered automobiles is expected to increase due to population growth. Terms were not disclosed.

EXECUTIVES

President and CEO, Fumiya Kokubu
SEVP, Shigeru Yamazoe
SEVP, Mitsuru Akiyoshi
Managing Executive Officer, Nobuhiro Yabe
Managing Executive Officer, Hikaru Minami

Chairman, Teruo Asada
Auditors: Ernst & Young ShinNihon LLC

LOCATIONS

HQ: Marubeni Corp.
2-7-1 Nihonbashi, Chuo-ku, Tokyo 103-6060
Phone: (81) 3 3282 2111
Web: www.marubeni.co.jp

2016 Sales

	% of total
Japan	53
US	33
Singapore	4
Other countries	10
Total	**100**

PRODUCTS/OPERATIONS

2019 Sales

	% of total
Food	54
Chemical & Forest Products	22
Energy & Metals	11
Consumer Products	5
Transportation & Industrial Machinery	5
Power projects & Plant	3
Total	**100**

2019 Sales

	% of total
Goods	97
Commission on service & trading margins	3
Total	**100**

COMPETITORS

ITOCHU	Samsung Group
Jardine Matheson	Seika
Kanematsu	Showa Denko
LG Group	Sime Darby
Largo Vista	Sojitz
Mitsubishi Corp.	Sojitz Corporation of
Mitsubishi	America
International	Sumitomo
Mitsui	Sumitomo Heavy
Nissan Chemical	Industries
Rio Tinto plc	

HISTORICAL FINANCIALS

Company Type: Public

Income Statement				FYE: March 31
	REVENUE ($ mil.)	NET INCOME ($ mil.)	NET PROFIT MARGIN	EMPLOYEES
03/20	68,841	(1,990)	—	53,395
03/19	74,625	2,328	3.1%	50,540
03/18	76,027	2,130	2.8%	49,125
03/17	71,878	1,566	2.2%	47,938
03/16	73,607	627	0.9%	47,887
Annual Growth	**(1.7%)**	**—**	**—**	**2.8%**

2020 Year-End Financials

Debt ratio: 0.3%
Return on equity: (-11.2%)
Cash ($ mil.): 5,268
Current ratio: 1.22
Long-term debt ($ mil.): 17,763
No. of shares (mil.): 1,735
Dividends
Yield: 6.4%
Payout: —
Market value ($ mil.): —

Mashreqbank

Auditors: PricewaterhouseCoopers

LOCATIONS

HQ: Mashreqbank
P.O. Box 1250, Dubai
Phone: (971) 4 2223333   **Fax:** (971) 4 2226061
Web: www.mashreqbank.com

HISTORICAL FINANCIALS

Company Type: Public

Income Statement				FYE: December 31
	ASSETS ($ mil.)	NET INCOME ($ mil.)	INCOME AS % OF ASSETS	EMPLOYEES
12/19	43,412	562	1.3%	0
12/18	38,102	560	1.5%	0
12/17	34,088	558	1.6%	0
12/16	33,435	524	1.6%	0
12/15	31,352	654	2.1%	0
Annual Growth	**8.5%**	**(3.7%)**	**—**	**—**

2019 Year-End Financials

Return on assets: 1.3%
Return on equity: 9.9%
Long-term debt ($ mil.): —
No. of shares (mil.): 177
Sales ($ mil): 2,857
Dividends
Yield: —
Payout: —
Market value ($ mil.): —

Mazda Motor Corp. (Japan)

Mazda Zoom-Zooms along with the top automakers in Japan. Known for its "Zoom-Zoom" slogan Mazda sells about 1.5 million passenger cars and pickup trucks in about130 countries annually. The company has manufacturing operations in Japan China Thailand Mexico Vietnam Malaysia and Russia. Its lineup consists of the Mazda 2 3 6 and the MX-5 (passenger vehicles) the CX-3 -4 -5 -8 -30 -9 (crossover SUVs) and the BT-50 (pickup truck). The company produces the majority of its vehicles at home in Japan although North America is its largest market. Ford holds approximately 3.5% stake in the company. Mazda was founded in 1920.

Operations

Mazda has been introducing products featuring Skyactiv Technology and Kodo?Soul of Motion design which provide both driving pleasure and outstanding environmental and safety performance. The launch of the all-new Mazda3 in 2019 marked the roll-out of its first new-generation product. The company's major product line includes MAZDA CX-3 CX-30 CX-4 CX-5 CX-8 CX-9 MAZDA 2 MAZDA 3 MAZDA 6 MAZDA MX-5 and MAZDA BT-50.

Passenger vehicles account for some 50% of Mazda's sales and crossover vehicles the other about 50%.

Geographic Reach

Based in Hiroshima Japan North America is Mazda's biggest market at more than 25% of total sales. China accounts for over 15% Europe more than 15% and Japan under 15%. Australia the wider Asia/Pacific region and other markets account for the remaining revenue. Nearly 65% of Mazda's vehicles are produced in Japan.

Mazda has major production sites in Japan Mexico Thailand and China. The Company conducts sales in more than 130 countries and regions around the world.

Sales and Marketing

Mazda has around 220 sales companies in Japan and some 140 internationally.

Strategy

Mazda's long-term plan the catchily titled "Sustainable Zoom-Zoom 2030" is to produce cars that will develop a bond between driver and company. It will do this by increasing sustainability safety and driving pleasure. With fuel economy at or near the top of many consumers' priorities Mazda developed an engine technology that can reliably combust a leaner fuel/air mixture called SKYACTIV-X and runs 20% more efficiently in real-world driving conditions. To improve safety the company continues to tweak its driving positions and visibility and will roll out semi-autonomous driving technology by 2025. Lastly to provide an emotionally enriching driving experience the company will design its cars with the "horse and rider as one" philosophy in mind.

EXECUTIVES

EVP, Akira Marumoto

Senior Managing Executive Officer China Operations Domestic and Fleet Sales, Nobuhide Inamoto

Senior Managing Executive Officer and President and CEO Mazda Motor Europe GmbH, Jeffrey H. Guyton

President and CEO, Masamichi Kogai

Senior Managing Executive Officer; COO Europe Asia & Oceania Middle East Africa and New and Emerging Markets, Yuji Nakamine

Senior Managing Executive Officer, Yuji Harada

Senior Managing Executive Officer R&D and MDI, Kiyoshi Fujiwara

Senior Managing Executive Officer and President and CEO Mazda Motor of America Inc., Masahiro Moro

Senior Managing Executive Officer Corporate Planning Profit Control Global IT and MDI, Akira Koga

Managing Executive Officer Domestic Sales and Fleet Sales and President Mazda Chuhan Co. Ltd., Kazuyuki Fukuhara

Chairman, Seita Kanai

Auditors: KPMG AZSA LLC

LOCATIONS

HQ: Mazda Motor Corp. (Japan)
3-1 Shinchi, Fuchu-cho, Aki-gun, Hiroshima 730-8670
Phone: (81) 82 282 1111
Web: www.mazda.co.jp

2017 Sales

	% of total
Japan	18
North America	34
Europe	20
Other regions	28
Total	**100**

PRODUCTS/OPERATIONS

Selected Models
BT-50 (pickup)
CX-3 (crossover SUV)
CX-4 (crossover SUV)
CX-5 (crossover SUV)
CX-8 (crossover SUV)
CX-9 (crossover SUV)
Mazda 2 (Demio)
Mazda 3 (Axela hatchback sedan)
Mazda 6 (sport sedan)
Mazda 8 (MPV)
MX-5 (roadster)

Selected Subsidiaries and Affiliates

Mazda Australia Pty. Ltd.
Mazda Motor Logistics Europe NV (Belgium)
Mazda Motor of America Inc.

COMPETITORS

BMW	Kia Motors
Daimler	Nissan
FCA US	Peugeot
Fiat Chrysler	Renault
Ford Motor	Subaru
General Motors	Suzuki Motor
Honda	Toyota
Isuzu	Volkswagen

HISTORICAL FINANCIALS

Company Type: Public

Income Statement   FYE: March 31

	REVENUE ($ mil.)	NET INCOME ($ mil.)	NET PROFIT MARGIN	EMPLOYEES
03/20	34,586	122	0.4%	50,479
03/19	35,942	640	1.8%	49,998
03/18	35,027	1,129	3.2%	49,755
03/17	32,409	945	2.9%	42,849
03/16	34,348	1,355	3.9%	46,398
Annual Growth	**0.2%**	**(45.2%)**	**—**	**2.1%**

2020 Year-End Financials

Debt ratio: 0.2%	No. of shares (mil.): 629
Return on equity: 1.0%	Dividends
Cash ($ mil.): 5,262	Yield: 6.0%
Current ratio: 1.41	Payout: 83.0%
Long-term debt ($ mil.): 4,440	Market value ($ mil.): 1,677

	STOCK PRICE ($) FY Close	P/E High/Low		PER SHARE ($) Earnings	Dividends	Book Value
03/20	2.66	0	0	0.19	0.16	18.82
03/19	5.56	0	0	1.02	0.16	19.52
03/18	6.68	0	0	1.84	0.16	19.10
03/17	7.18	0	0	1.58	0.14	17.53
03/16	7.82	0	0	2.27	0.10	16.09
Annual Growth	**(23.6%)**	**—**	**—**	**(45.9%)**	**12.3%**	**4.0%**

mBank SA

Auditors: Ernst & Young Audyt Polska spolka z ograniczona odpowiedzialnoscia sp. k.

LOCATIONS

HQ: mBank SA
ul. Senatorska 18, Warsaw 00-950
Phone: (48) 22 829 00 00   **Fax:** (48) 22 829 00 33
Web: www.brebank.com.pl

HISTORICAL FINANCIALS

Company Type: Public

Income Statement   FYE: December 31

	ASSETS ($ mil.)	NET INCOME ($ mil.)	INCOME AS % OF ASSETS	EMPLOYEES
12/19	41,836	266	0.6%	9,352
12/18	38,830	350	0.9%	8,823
12/17	37,735	313	0.8%	8,556
12/16	31,974	291	0.9%	8,401
12/15	31,558	332	1.1%	8,587
Annual Growth	**7.3%**	**(5.4%)**	**—**	**2.2%**

2019 Year-End Financials

Return on assets: 0.6%	Dividends
Return on equity: 6.4%	Yield: —
Long-term debt ($ mil.): —	Payout: —
No. of shares (mil.): 42	Market value ($ mil.): —
Sales ($ mil): 1,992	

McKesson Europe AG

McKesson Europe(formerly Celesio) likes being a middleman when it comes to pharmaceuticals. The company is one of Europe's largest drug wholesalers holding market-leading positions in several of the countries it serves. Its largest wholesale markets are France Germany and the UK. In addition to more than 130 wholesale distribution branches serving 65000 pharmacies McKesson Europe owns retail chains consisting of 2200 pharmacies in Europe including Norway Italy and the UK. The company which was founded in 1835 and was acquired by North American pharmaceuticals distributor McKesson in 2014 has a presence in 14 countries.

Change in Company Type

McKesson purchased Celesio in 2014 in an $8.3 billion deal to expand its operations into Europe. Through an expanded global presence McKesson aims to increase globalization in a rapidly changing health care market; the combined entity is expected to benefit from increased purchasing power technology resources supply chain efficiencies and global sourcing capabilities.

Mergers and Acquisitions

In 2016 Celesio's LloydsPharmacy acquired UK grocer Sainsbury's pharmacy business for £125 million. The deal included 281 locations including 277 in-store pharmacies and four hospital pharmacies; they were all rebranded as LloydsPharmacy.

EXECUTIVES

President McKesson Specialty Health, Marc E. Owen, age 59

SVP and CFO McKesson U.S. Pharmaceutical, Alain Vachon

Chairman, John H. Hammergren, age 61

Deputy Chairman Supervisory Board, Ihno Goldenstein, age 47

Auditors: Deloitte GmbH

LOCATIONS

HQ: McKesson Europe AG
Stockholmer Platz 1, Stuttgart D-70137
Phone: (49) 711 5001 00   **Fax:** (49) 711 5001 1260
Web: www.mckesson.eu

2013 Sales

	% of total
France	30
UK	22
Germany	21
Brazil	9
Other	18
Total	**100**

PRODUCTS/OPERATIONS

2013 Sales

	% of total
Pharmacy solutions	84
Customer solutions	16
Total	**100**

Selected Subsidiaries

Pharmacy Solutions (wholesale distribution division)
AAH Pharmaceuticals Ltd. (UK)
AFM S.p.A. (Italy)
Cahill May Roberts Group Ltd (Ireland)
GEHE Pharma Handel GmbH (Germany)
GEHE Pharma Praha spol. S r.o. (Czech Republic)
Herba Chemosan Apotheker AG (Austria)
Kemofarmacija d.d. (Slovenia Romania and Croatia)
Laboratoria Flandria NV (Belgian)
Norsk Medisinaldepot AS (Norway)
OCP Repartition (France)
OCP Portugal Produtos Farmacêuticos SA (Portugal)
Panpharma Participacoes S.A. (54% Brazil)
Pharma Belgium SA
Rudolf Spiegel GmbH (Germany)
Tjellesen Max Jenne A/S (Denmark)
Patient and Consumer Solutions (retail pharmacies division)
Admenta Italia S.p.A.
Apotheke DocMorris (retail franchise)
Brocacef (45% Netherlands)
DocMorris Kooperationen GmbH (mail order)
Lé;ká;rny Lloyds s.r.o. (Czech Republic)
Lloyds Pharmacy Limited (UK)
Lloydspharma SA (Belgium)
Unicare Pharmacy Limited (Ireland)
Vitusapotek AS (Norway)

COMPETITORS

Cardinal Health	Sigma Pharmaceuticals
Co-operative Group	Superdrug
Mawdsleys	UDG Healthcare
PHOENIX Pharma	Walgreen
Profarma Distribuidora	Waymade

HISTORICAL FINANCIALS

Company Type: Public

Income Statement

FYE: March 31

	REVENUE ($ mil.)	NET INCOME ($ mil.)	NET PROFIT MARGIN	EMPLOYEES
03/19	23,782	(66)	—	32,946
03/18	25,998	(368)	—	34,338
03/17	22,055	(1,033)	—	35,716
03/16	24,388	447	1.8%	23,404
03/15	5,657	(239)	—	25,118
Annual Growth	43.2%	—	—	7.0%

2019 Year-End Financials

Debt ratio: 15.6%
Return on equity: (-3.0%)
Cash ($ mil.): 928
Current ratio: 1.45
Long-term debt ($ mil.): 1,102

No. of shares (mil.): 203
Dividends
Yield: 0.0%
Payout: —
Market value ($ mil.): 1,160

	STOCK PRICE ($) FY Close	P/E High/Low		PER SHARE ($) Earnings	Dividends	Book Value
03/19	5.71	—	—	(0.33)	0.12	10.94
03/18	6.37	—	—	(1.81)	0.13	11.51
03/17	5.52	—	—	(5.09)	0.12	9.85
03/16	5.65	3	3	2.20	0.16	15.32
03/15	5.80	—	—	(1.18)	0.04	13.31
Annual Growth	(0.4%)	—	—	—	32.2%	(4.8%)

Mediobanca Banca Di Credito Finanziario SpA

There's not much room for mediocrity at Mediobanca. A leading Italian investment bank the firm offers underwriting M&A support wholesale banking and financial advisory to corporate clients worldwide. It also offers retail banking private banking factoring credit management and leasing services. Despite being known as a top investment bank nearly 50% of Mediobanca's revenue comes from its Retail and Consumer Banking businesses which include Compass Futuro Compass RE Creditech and CheBanca! About 40% of its revenue comes from its Corporate and Investment Banking division. Mediobanca's international offices are in Frankfurt Istanbul London Madrid Mexico City New York and Paris.

Operations

Mediobanca operates four divisions. The bank's Retail and Consumer Banking (RCB) business (which made up 48% of its total revenue during fiscal 2015 ended June 30 2015) counts its consumer credit and retail banking business which includes Compass Futuro Compass RE Creditech and CheBanca!

Mediobanca's Corporate and Investment Banking (CIB) division (37% of revenue) consists of the Wholesale Banking (WSB) unit which includes lending structured finance and investment banking; as well as the Private Banking (PB) unit which counts Compagnie Monegasque de Banque Spafid and Prudentia and 50% of Banca Esperia pro rata. The Principal Investing (PI) division (12% of revenue) mostly counts the bank's 13% equity stake in Assicurazioni Generali. The Corporate division (3% of revenue) houses other businesses including the leasing business.

Broadly speaking about 75% of Mediobanca's revenue came from interest and similar income (about three-fourths of which came from retail loans) in FY2015 while about 15% came from fee and commission income. Around 47% of its ?30 billion loan book was tied to RCB loans while about 44% was tied to CIB loans.

Geographic Reach

Mediobanca generates most of its business in Italy though it also operates international branches and subsidiary offices in Frankfurt Istanbul London Madrid Mexico City New York and Paris. About 80% of its banking revenue came from Italy during FY2015 while 20% came from other parts of Europe. Around 55% of its wholesale banking revenue came from Italy that year while 24% came from the UK and another 16% was split between Germany France and Spain.

Sales and Marketing

About 48% of Mediobanca's revenue came from consumer finance and retail clients in FY2015 while 31% came from wholesale banking clients and 12% came from principal investing clients.

Financial Performance

Note: Growth rates may differ after conversion to US dollars. This analysis uses financials from the company's annual report.

Mediobanca's annual revenues and profits have been growing over the past few years with revenue growing more than 25% since fiscal 2013 (ended June). The bank's revenue jumped 12% to ?2.05 billion ($2.27 billion) during FY2015 while net profit rose 27% to ?590 million ($654.57 million).

Strategy

Mediobanca plans to continue building its capital-light fee-generating businesses to boost its overall profitability. Indeed during FY2015 the bank generated 47% of its before-tax profit from its Corporate and Investment Banking (CIB) division despite it making up 37% of its revenue. By comparison Mediobanca's interest-focused Retail and Consumer Banking (RCB) division generated nearly half of the group's revenue but only 17% of its profit.

Mergers and Acquisitions

In August 2015 Mediobanca agreed to buy a 51% majority interest in London-based credit asset manager and advisory firm Cairn Capital Group. The move would continue to build on Mediobanca's international Alternative Asset Management business which involves strategic partnerships with asset managers with strong track records "high quality" management teams and scalable platforms.

HISTORY

In 1946 the three Italian "banks of national interest" Banca Commerciale Italiana (Comit) Credito Italiano (now Unicredito Italiano) and Banco di Roma (now part of Banca di Roma) founded Mediobanca to offer medium-term credit a market they were barred from.

Enrico Cuccia was with Comit at the time Mediobanca was formed and moved over to head the new institution. In 1955 he created the shareholder structure that later caused a twin uproar in Italian banking and politics: Although the state owned well more than half of the bank's shares a group of wealthy shareholders who together owned less than 10% of the bank wielded the power.

Over the next several decades Cuccia and Mediobanca operated on the behalf of these powerful shareholders and their family businesses devising deals on terms that other companies could not get. Mediobanca also created a web of crossholdings in other banks which made money for the bank by selling its funds and other services.

In the 1960s and 1970s the bank was at the center of a number of deals not all of which were stellar successes. The bank engineered a merger between Pirelli and Dunlop which fizzled and also pushed the merger of chemical companies Montecatini and Edison into Montedison which took a beating in the marketplace.

In 1982 Cuccia ostensibly retired taking the title of honorary chairman. However his influence never waned and the 1980s brought a war for the soul of Italian business. In 1985 Romano Prodi head of IRI the state-run organization (liquidated in 2000) that owned nearly 60% of the bank planned to privatize the bank. Instead the noble wing came up with its own privatization plan: The private shareholders requested that the state bring its stake in Mediobanca to below 50% by selling some of its shares to the Mediobanca cabal. In 1988 privatization went through but as part of the pact it was stipulated that the new shareholders would share decision-making powers with the Ala Nobile.

If the 1980s were wild the 1990s were out of control. Italy's banking industry hampered by red tape and old alliances was left behind the rest of Europe. Many of Italy's banks became stock companies when banking laws changed and many merged to compete in the European Union. Many of those deals threatened Mediobanca's hegemony so it tried to block them. The bank nixed Unicredito's 1998 bid for Comit (which instead merged with Banca Intesa) as well as Sanpaolo IMI's 1999 offer for Banca di Roma.

In 2000 the bank still keeping a grip on the wheels of finance orchestrated investment firm Compart's buyout of Montedison (the merged entity took the Montedison name). That year the company launched an online private banking joint venture with Banca Mediolanum.

Also in 2000 its 46-year relationship with Lazard ended when the international investment banker announced plans to sell back to Mediobanca its 4% stake in the company along with its nearly 5% stake in Assicurazioni Generali.

After Cuccia's death in 2000 successor Vincenzo Maranghi battled such controlling shareholders as the Agnelli and Pirelli families and Deutsche Bank over the bank's future. These shareholders wanted to bring Mediobanca into the modern world by possibly merging it with another top Italian bank or even separating its investment management operations from its investment banking which generates a large majority of Mediobanca's profits.

However in a bid to stick to the old ways Maranghi arranged for backing (in exchange for a small stake in Mediobanca) from Swiss Life. Maranghi was blamed in part for the bank's decline: He forced out some of the investment banking division's top talent in the late 1990s and eventually resigned in 2003

Despite efforts to become more open some of the mystery surrounding Mediobanca remains. The shareholder dispute erupted after the death of Cuccia (whose body was subsequently robbed from its grave and later found).

Maranghi's replacement Gabriele Galateri di Genola had his work cut out for him repairing cracks in Mediobanca's image but he saw profits rise considerably. Under his watch the group has made its first foray into operations abroad opening an office in Paris. By 2004 the company posted improved financial results for a second consecutive year including a 20% increase in investment banking fees.

Galateri di Genola resigned from Mediobanca in 2007 after he lost the support of the supervisory board. He was succeeded by Alberto Nagel the company's general manager.

EXECUTIVES

General Manager, Alberto N. Nagel, age 55
General Manager Operations Division, Francesco Saverio Vinci, age 58
Deputy Chairman, Marco Tronchetti Provera, age 72
Deputy Chairman, Maurizia Angelo Comnenus, age 72
Chairman, Renato Pagliaro, age 63
Auditors: PricewaterhouseCoopers S.p.A.

LOCATIONS

HQ: Mediobanca Banca Di Credito Finanziario SpA
Piazzetta Enrico Cuccia 1, Milan 20121
Phone: (39) 02 8829 1   **Fax:** (39) 02 882 9367
Web: www.mediobanca.com

PRODUCTS/OPERATIONS

2015 Sales

	% of total
Retail and consumer banking	50
Corporate and private banking	32
Principal investing	15
Corporate center	3
Total	**100**

COMPETITORS

Banca Carige	Goldman Sachs
Banca Popolare di	Interbanca
Milano	Intesa Sanpaolo
Banco di Desio	Lazard
CREDEM	Morgan Stanley
Credit Suisse	UBS Investment Bank
Deutsche Bank	UniCredit
Gemina	Vontobel

HISTORICAL FINANCIALS

Company Type: Public

Income Statement

FYE: June 30

	ASSETS ($ mil.)	NET INCOME ($ mil.)	INCOME AS % OF ASSETS	EMPLOYEES
06/20	88,392	672	0.8%	4,746
06/19	74,989	439	0.6%	986
06/18	84,244	1,006	1.2%	4,717
06/17	80,338	855	1.1%	4,798
06/16	77,542	671	0.9%	4,036
Annual Growth	**3.3%**	**0.0%**	**—**	**4.1%**

2020 Year-End Financials

Return on assets: 0.8%	Dividends
Return on equity: 8.0%	Yield: 4.7%
Long-term debt ($ mil.): —	Payout: 44.4%
No. of shares (mil.): 769	Market value ($ mil.): 5,484
Sales ($ mil): 3,456	

	STOCK PRICE ($) FY Close	P/E High/Low		PER SHARE ($) Earnings	Dividends	Book Value
06/20	7.13	17	6	0.77	0.34	14.18
06/19	10.23	25	18	0.50	0.35	6.79
06/18	9.23	12	9	1.17	0.28	12.92
06/17	9.27	12	6	0.99	0.20	12.11
06/16	5.90	16	7	0.78	0.17	11.59
Annual Growth	**4.8%**	**—**	**—**	**(0.2%)**	**18.4%**	**5.2%**

Medipal Holdings Corp

In Japan Medipal Holdings keeps drug and household products retailers well-stocked. Its primary business is the wholesale distribution of prescription and OTC pharmaceuticals medical supplies cosmetics and personal sundries. In addition to supplying some 240000 Japanese pharmacies and retail stores Medipal distributes to hospitals and provides information technology support to its customers through its numerous subsidiaries and affiliates including Mediceo Everlth Atol and Paltac. Its MP Agro subsidiary distributes animal health products.

Operations
Medipal operates through three primary segments: Prescription Pharmaceutical Wholesale (accounting for more than 65% of net sales); Cosmetics Daily Necessities and OTC Pharmaceutical Wholesale (accounting for more than 30% of net sales); and Animal Health Products and Food Processing Raw Materials Wholesale (roughly 5% of net sales). The Prescription Pharmaceutical Wholesale business comprising about ten subsidiaries supplies hospitals clinics and pharmacies with pharmaceuticals medical equipment medical supplies and clinical diagnostics. Cosmetics Daily Necessities and OTC Pharmaceutical Wholesale operating through Paltac sells a range of products to drug stores supermarkets convenience stores and other retail establishments. Animal Health Products and Food Processing Raw Materials Wholesale business sells animal health products to animal hospitals and livestock and fishery businesses; through the newly established Medipal Foods Corporation (2016) it distributes raw materials for processing food to food manufacturers.

Geographic Reach
Medipal operates throughout Japan. Its corporate headquarters is located in Tokyo Japan.

Sales and Marketing
Medipal supplies to about 240000 customers in hospitals clinics pharmacies drugstores convenience stores animal hospitals livestock and fishery businesses and manufacturers of processed foods all across the nation coming from about 5000 suppliers.

Financial Performance
Consolidated net sales increased 1% year on year to Å 3.2 billion. In the Prescription Pharmaceutical Wholesale Business sales decreased 1% year on year but remained on par with the previous fiscal year in a flat market. In the Cosmetics Daily Necessities and OTC Pharmaceutical Wholesale Business sales increased 5% year on year. In the Animal Health Products and Food Processing Raw

Materials Wholesale Business sales increased 5%. Sales were firm in both businesses.

As of March 31 2019 cash and cash equivalents (cash) totaled Å 230.0 billion an increase of Å 9.4 billion from the end of the previous fiscal year. Cash provided by operations Å 63.7 billion while cash used for investing and financing activities were Å 23.5 billion and Å 30.8 billion respectively.

Strategy
The company's key strategies are: Establishing business partnerships to create new frameworks; Expansion of new businesses to strengthen the earnings foundation; and Innovation in existing businesses to resolve customer issues and increase productivity.

The MEDIPAL Group is steadily securing a foothold for overseas expansion. Since their investment in a Chinese pharmaceutical wholesaler in 2009 Medipal have accumulated overseas business experience know-how and cultivated human resources. They will use this know-how and these human resources to make inroads into ASEAN countries.

In the United States JCR USA Inc. their joint venture with JCR Pharmaceuticals Co. Ltd. is conducting clinical trials of new drugs using J-Brain Cargo a breakthrough technology for blood-brain barrier penetration. To enter the wholesale business in the United States and Europe the company think the most effective method will be to establish a standard business model for distribution of regenerative medicine products and cellular medicine products in Japan and then roll it out overseas.

Company Background
Medipal was formed when Mediceo Holdings took over household products distributor Paltac in 2005. Paltac brought with it a distribution network and logistical prowess which allowed the new firm to move further into the OTC and non-drugs business. Previously Mediceo Holdings become Japan's largest drug wholesaler in 2004 when it was formed through the merger of three smaller drug wholesalers (Kuraya Pharmaceuticals Sanseido and Tokyo Iyakuhin).

EXECUTIVES

President and CEO, Shuichi Watanabe
Managing Executive Officer; President SPLine, Hideaki Takemura
Senior Managing Executive Officer, Hiroshi Yarimizu
Senior Managing Director; CEO MEDICEO, Yasuhiro Choufuku
Director; CEO EVERLTH, Takuro Hasegawa
Director; CEO ATOL, Shinjiro Watanabe
Senior Managing Executive Officer, Tomohiko Kimura
Auditors: KPMG AZSA LLC

LOCATIONS

HQ: Medipal Holdings Corp
2-7-15 Yaesu, Chuo-ku, Tokyo 104-8461
Phone: (81) 3 3517 5800
Web: www.medipal.co.jp

PRODUCTS/OPERATIONS

2017 Net Sales

	% of total
Prescription Pharmaceutical Wholesale	68
Cosmetics Daily Necessities and OTC Pharmaceutical Wholesale	30
Animal Health Products Raw Materials Wholesale	2
Total	**100**

Selected Divisions and Brands
Atol Co. Ltd.
Everlth Co. Ltd.
Mediceo Corporation

M.I.C. (Medical Information College) Inc.
MM Corporation
MP Agro Co. Ltd.
Paltac Corporation
Trim Co. Ltd.

COMPETITORS

Alfresa   Toho Pharmaceutical
Suzuken

HISTORICAL FINANCIALS

Company Type: Public

Income Statement				FYE: March 31
	REVENUE ($ mil.)	NET INCOME ($ mil.)	NET PROFIT MARGIN	EMPLOYEES
03/20	29,968	349	1.2%	21,393
03/19	28,732	310	1.1%	21,731
03/18	29,630	327	1.1%	22,068
03/17	27,404	259	0.9%	20,984
03/16	26,966	274	1.0%	20,473
Annual Growth	2.7%	6.3%	—	1.1%

2020 Year-End Financials

Debt ratio: 0.0%   No. of shares (mil.): 209
Return on equity: 7.5%   Dividends
Cash ($ mil.): 1,911   Yield: 0.0%
Current ratio: 1.21   Payout: 24.2%
Long-term debt ($ mil.): 283   Market value ($ mil.): 4,159

	STOCK PRICE ($) FY Close	P/E High/Low		PER SHARE ($) Earnings	Dividends	Book Value
03/20	19.81	0	0	1.52	0.37	21.95
03/19	23.55	0	0	1.31	0.32	20.17
03/18	20.64	0	0	1.41	0.30	20.29
03/17	15.97	0	0	1.15	0.27	17.44
03/16	16.02	0	0	1.21	0.22	16.32
Annual Growth	5.5%	—	—	5.9%	14.0%	7.7%

Medtronic PLC

Auditors: PricewaterhouseCoopers LLP

LOCATIONS

HQ: Medtronic PLC
20 On Hatch, Lower Hatch Street, Dublin 2
Phone: (353) 1 438 1700
Web: www.medtronic.com

HISTORICAL FINANCIALS

Company Type: Public

Income Statement				FYE: April 24
	REVENUE ($ mil.)	NET INCOME ($ mil.)	NET PROFIT MARGIN	EMPLOYEES
04/20	28,913	4,789	16.6%	90,000
04/19	30,557	4,631	15.2%	90,000
04/18	29,953	3,104	10.4%	86,000
04/17	29,710	4,028	13.6%	91,000
04/16	28,833	3,538	12.3%	88,000
Annual Growth	0.1%	7.9%	—	0.6%

2020 Year-End Financials

Debt ratio: 27.3%   No. of shares (mil.): 1,341
Return on equity: 9.5%   Dividends
Cash ($ mil.): 4,140   Yield: 2.1%
Current ratio: 2.13   Payout: 54.8%
Long-term debt ($ mil.): 22,021   Market value ($ mil.): —

Meiji Yasuda Life Insurance Co.

Meiji Yasuda Life Insurance one of Japan's largest life insurers offers individual life and annuities group life and pensions and investment products. It also has some general insurance health care and investment and financial services operations. Meiji Yasuda provides its products to a range of customers including individuals small businesses and corporations. The company has about Å 116 trillion of life insurance policies in force and more than 6.4 million policy holders. While most of its operations are in Japan Meiji Yasuda also operates in Asia Europe and North America.

Operations

Meiji Yasuda's operating segments include Insurance businesses that provide accident insurance products for corporate customers; Asset management businesses that provide investment advisory services as well as building and real estate management; Outsourcing service businesses that provide policy maintenance and system development; and Health research and wellness promotion businesses including operation of nursing care facilities.

Geographic Reach

Meiji Yasuda is headquartered in Tokyo. It also has more than 95 regional offices more than 20 marketing centers and more than 1000 agency locations. The group has international affiliate locations in nine global cities: Beijing Frankfurt Hong Kong Honolulu London Los Angeles New York Shanghai and Warsaw.

Sales and Marketing

Meiji Yasuda sells its products through an internal sales force of nearly 32450 personnel. It makes some sales to banks and other financial institutions through general agents.

Financial Performance

Note: Growth rates may differ after conversion to US Dollars.

Meiji Yasuda's revenue increased only 2% to Å 4.2 trillion in fiscal 2019 (ended March) from Å 4.1 trillion the year prior as insurance premiums and investment and dividend income increased.

Net income that year was Å 230.9 billion a 13% decrease from Å 265.9 billion the year prior mainly due to an increase in expenses.

The company ended fiscal 2019 with Å 1.3 trillion in net cash Å 627.3 billion more than it had at the end of fiscal 2018. Operating activities provided Å 743.4 billion in cash and financing activities provided Å 101.8 billion while investment activities used Å 217.8 billion for purchase of securities and extended loans.

Strategy

Meiji Yasuda has been implementing the My Innovation 2020 a three-year program that encompasses a Medium-Term Business Plan and the Corporate Vision Realization Project. These two components are both designed to facilitate business innovation driving its transformative and creative initiatives aimed at realizing its corporate philosophy the "Meiji Yasuda Philosophy."

The company has also identified the Twelve Reforms that will drive its growth strategy and operating base reinforcement strategy effectively focusing its management resources and capital on these reforms. The Twelve Reforms encompass growth strategy initiatives to facilitate business innovation in the domestic life insurance business and the oversees insurance business as well as the domestic affiliate business along with its operating base

reinforcement strategy aimed at securing a more robust foundation for future growth.

For its Domestic Life Insurance Business Meiji Yasuda launched the "Wellness for All Project" on a full-scale in 2020. In conjunction with this move the company released "Best Style Health Cash Back" in 2019 aimed at providing customers with ongoing assistance to their health improvement efforts.

Meiji Yasuda has also expanded the lineup of paperless enrollment procedures duly named "Meister Mobile" in 2019. These procedures now also allow corporate customers to apply for enrollment in new policies. It has also upgraded the "MY Hoken Page" which is a website dedicated to policyholder services expanding the scope of procedures that can be performed via this website.

Company Background

Tracing its roots back to 1881 Meiji Yasuda in its current incarnation was formed through the merger of Meiji Life Insurance and Yasuda Mutual Life in 2004. Prior to their merger Meiji Life and Yasuda Mutual Life were part of the Mitsubishi Group and Mizuho Financial Group respectively.

In the US the company acquired StanCorp Financial Group (parent of Standard Insurance) for $5 billion in 2016. That company became Meiji Yasuda's primary US unit.

EXECUTIVES

President, Akio Negishi
Deputy President, Toshihiko Yamashita
Senior Managing Executive Officer; Chief Executive Individual Insurance Marketing, Takashi Ito
Senior Managing Executive Officer; Chief Executive General Agent Marketing, Tatsuo Ogoshi
Deputy President, Masahiro Ifuku
Senior Managing Executive Officer, Kikuo Asano
Senior Managing Executive Officer; Chief Executive Group Marketing, Akio Sakai
Senior Managing Executive Officer, Tadashi Onishi
Chairman, Nobuya Suzuki
Auditors: KPMG AZSA LLC

LOCATIONS

HQ: Meiji Yasuda Life Insurance Co.
2-1-1 Marunouchi, Chiyoda-ku, Tokyo 100-0005
Phone: (81) 3 3283 8293   **Fax:** (81) 3 3215 8123
Web: www.meijiyasuda.co.jp

PRODUCTS/OPERATIONS

Selected Subsidiaries

Meiji Yasuda America Incorporated
Meiji Yasuda Asia Limited
Meiji Yasuda Europe Limited
Pacific Guardian Life Insurance Company Limited (California)
Pacific Guardian Life Insurance Company Limited (Hawaii)
StanCorp Financial Group Inc

COMPETITORS

AXA Life Insurance	Mitsui Life
American Life Insurance	Nippon Life Insurance
Asahi Mutual Life	Prudential
Dai-ichi Life	Samsung Life Insurance
Daido Life	Sumitomo Life
Fukoku Mutual	Taiyo Life
Gibraltar Life Insurance	

HISTORICAL FINANCIALS

Company Type: Public

Income Statement				FYE: March 31
	REVENUE ($ mil.)	NET INCOME ($ mil.)	NET PROFIT MARGIN	EMPLOYEES
03/19	35,810	2,073	5.8%	42,950
03/18	36,930	2,495	6.8%	42,261
03/17	33,261	2,001	6.0%	41,872
03/16	38,082	1,906	5.0%	41,045
03/15	37,631	2,212	5.9%	40,793
Annual Growth	(1.2%)	(1.6%)	—	1.3%

2019 Year-End Financials

Debt ratio: 0.0%	No. of shares (mil.): —
Return on equity: 5.6%	Dividends
Cash ($ mil.): 13,739	Yield: —
Current ratio: 0.86	Payout: —
Long-term debt ($ mil.): —	Market value ($ mil.): —

Meituan

Auditors: PricewaterhouseCoopers

LOCATIONS

HQ: Meituan
Block B&C, Hengjiweiye Building, No.4 Wang Jing
East Road, Chaoyang District, Beijing 100102
Phone: (86) 10 5737 6600
Web: www.about.meituan.com

HISTORICAL FINANCIALS

Company Type: Public

Income Statement				FYE: December 31
	REVENUE ($ mil.)	NET INCOME ($ mil.)	NET PROFIT MARGIN	EMPLOYEES
12/19	14,016	321	2.3%	54,580
12/18	9,483	(16,788)	—	58,390
12/17	5,213	(2,906)	—	0
Annual Growth	64.0%	—	—	—

2019 Year-End Financials

Debt ratio: 0.4%	No. of shares (mil.): —
Return on equity: 2.5%	Dividends
Cash ($ mil.): 1,925	Yield: —
Current ratio: 2.24	Payout: —
Long-term debt ($ mil.): 67	Market value ($ mil.): —

	STOCK PRICE ($) FY Close	P/E High/Low	PER SHARE ($) Earnings	Dividends	Book Value
12/19	0.00	— —	0.05	0.00	2.28
12/18	0.00	— —	(6.16)	0.00	2.20
Annual Growth	—		—	—	1.9%

Melrose Industries Plc

Auditors: Deloitte LLP

LOCATIONS

HQ: Melrose Industries Plc
Leconfield House, Curzon Street, London W1J 5JA
Phone: (44) 20 7647 4500   **Fax:** (44) 20 7647 4501
Web: www.melroseplc.net

HISTORICAL FINANCIALS

Company Type: Public

Income Statement				FYE: December 31
	REVENUE ($ mil.)	NET INCOME ($ mil.)	NET PROFIT MARGIN	EMPLOYEES
12/19	14,482	(79)	—	56,092
12/18	10,986	(606)	—	62,350
12/17	2,825	(32)	—	11,960
12/16	1,093	(47)	—	13,114
12/15	386	2,085	538.9%	9,195
Annual Growth	147.3%	—	—	57.2%

2019 Year-End Financials

Debt ratio: 26.0%	No. of shares (mil.): —
Return on equity: (-0.7%)	Dividends
Cash ($ mil.): 418	Yield: —
Current ratio: 1.13	Payout: —
Long-term debt ($ mil.): 4,574	Market value ($ mil.): —

Merck KGaA (Germany)

Science and technology firm Merck KGaA develops manufactures and sells biotech pharmaceutical life science and specialty chemical products for global consumption. The company manufactures and sells prescription drugs including treatments for multiple sclerosis cancers growth disorders infertility and cardiovascular and metabolic diseases. It also produces laboratory research tools including chemicals antibodies and cells and bioprocessing systems. Merck's specialty chemicals include liquid crystals semiconductor materials and coatings. The company is known as EMD in the US and Canada. Merck KGaA is not affiliated with US pharmaceutical giant Merck & Co.

Operations

Merck operates through three divisions: Healthcare Life Science and Performance Materials.

The Healthcare segment accounting for about 40% of sales and is made up of two businesses Biopharma and Allergopharma. The Biopharma division makes and markets treatments for cancer multiple sclerosis growth disorders infertility and cardiovascular and metabolic diseases. Its top selling product is Rebif a MS treatment followed by cancer drug Erbitux diabetes treatment Glucophage and fertility medication Gonal-f. The Allergopharma unit makes immunotherapies for allergic rhinitis allergic asthma and other allergy-related conditions. The Healthcare segment operates as EMD Serono in the US and Canada.

Merck's Life Sciences segment also accounting for about 40% of revenue makes tools equipment and chemicals used in pharmaceutical biotech and academic laboratories. Its product portfolio numbers some 300000 and includes ultrapure reagents testing kits lab water systems antibodies and cells gene-editing technologies and bioprocessing systems. The division includes the Sigma-Aldrich subsidiary and operates as MilliporeSigma in the US and Canada.

The Performance Materials segment bringing in 20% of sales deals in high-tech chemicals for use in consumer electronics semiconductors automotive displays lighting pigments coatings and cosmetics. It includes the Display Solutions Semiconductor Solutions and Surface Solutions business units. The unit operates as EMD Performance Materials in the US and Canada.

Merck divested its Consumer Health unit which was part of the Healthcare segment and sold OTC wellness brands such as Floratil Neurobrion and Apaisyl in December 2018. It sold its Biosimilars unit which made generic biotech drugs and was also part of the Healthcare segment in 2017.

Geographic Reach

Merck is headquartered in Germany with operations spread across around 65 countries. The Asia-Pacific region is the company's single largest region accounting for about a third of sales closely followed by Europe (30% of revenue) and North America (25%). The remainder of sales comes from the Latin America (5%) and Middle East and Africa (5%) regions. The company operates as EMD in North America.

Financial Performance

Note: Growth rates may differ after conversion to US Dollars.

Merck has reported revenue growth over the past five years with an overall increase of 31% between 2014 and 2018 despite a decline in sales in 2017. Net income nearly tripled over the five-year period despite a slight dip in 2015.

Revenue increased 2% in 2018 to some ?14.8 billion fueled by organic growth in the Life Sciences and Healthcare business segments but offset by a decline in the Performance Materials segment due to negative exchange rate effects. Revenue increases were strongest in the Latin America and Asia/Pacific regions.

Net income rose about 30% to some ?3.4 billion in 2018 due to gains on the divestiture of the Consumer Health business in December.

The company ended 2018 with ?2.2 billion in cash up ?1.6 billion from 2017. Operating activities contributed ?2.2 billion while investing activities contributed ?2.2 billion (from asset disposals) and financing activities used ?2.8 billion via financial liability dividend and bond payments.

Strategy

Merck has transitioned itself from a classic pharmaceuticals and chemicals supplier into a science and technology company through a series of acquisitions and strategic moves over the past decade. The company continues to grow organically and through M&A activity in core business areas. It also is focused on expanding in high-growth markets in the Asia/Pacific and Latin America.

The Healthcare segment has ongoing drug research programs to expand its product offerings in core therapeutic fields. Its new MS drug Mavenclad has been launched in more than 40 countries and Merck has another MS drug in development stages. Through a collaboration with Pfizer Merck is developing new cancer drugs; carcinoma drug Bavencio was approved in several markets in 2017 and 2018.

The Life Sciences segment is introducing new technology-based lab equipment including digital lab ecosystems and end-to-end bioprocessing systems such as the BioContinuum platform for monoclonal antibodies launched in 2019. Merck is expanding the division's manufacturing capacity in India and China and invested ?40 million in an integrated cell culture facility in Korea in 2018. It also opened a ?13 million biologics testing lab in Singapore in 2018 and expanded its distribution facility in the UK in 2019.

The company launched a program to rejuvenate its Performance Materials unit in 2019 to offset a decline in its liquid crystals business. Merck hopes to return the unit to profitable growth by streamlining R&D projects and lowering costs in the Display Solutions unit while solidifying its position in electronics and focusing on growth in the Semiconductor Solutions segment.

In 2018 Merck sold its Consumer Health business (vitamins and supplements) to Procter & Gamble for ?3.4 billion to hone its focus on pharmaceuticals. Similarly the firm sold its Biosimilars (generic biotech drugs) unit in 2017.

Mergers and Acquisitions

In 2019 the company acquired US-based Versum Materials a maker of high-purity process chemicals gases and equipment used in the semiconductor manufacturing industry. The deal is expected to increase Merck's scale and product portfolio while strengthening its global supply chain. Later in 2019 Merck KGaA purchased electronic materials firm Intermolecular. Both acquisitions bolstered the company's Performance Materials segment.

Company Background

Merck KGaA was founded in 1668 as a pharmacy and is the oldest pharmaceuticals business in the world.

The German firm is ancestor to US drug giant Merck & Co. but the American firm broke away during WWI. Subsequently the company's current North American operations can't use the Merck name; they instead operate under the name EMD. Legal tussles over use of the name flare up sporadically as globalization brings the two into shared markets.

Merck launched an initiative in 2007 to transition from a classic pharmaceuticals and chemicals company to a science and technology company. The most significant move was the 2015 acquisition of Sigma-Aldrich a research equipment maker for $17 billion. Other major acquisitions include AZ Electronic Materials a supplier of high-tech materials for the electronics industry for $2.5 billion in 2014.

The firm sold its Biosimilars (generic biotech drugs) unit in 2017 to Fresenius for ?156 million plus ?497 in potential milestone payments.

EXECUTIVES

Chairman Executive Board and CEO, Stefan Oschmann, age 63
CEO Healthcare, Belén Garijo, age 60
CFO, Marcus Kuhnert, age 52
Chief Administration Officer, Kai Beckmann, age 55
CEO Life Science, Udit Batra, age 50
CEO Performance Materials, Walter Galinat, age 65
Vice Chairman, Michael Fletterich, age 62
Chairman Supervisory Board, Wolfgang B chele, age 61
Auditors: KPMG AG Wirtschaftsprüfungsgesellscha

LOCATIONS

HQ: Merck KGaA (Germany)
 Frankfurter Strasse 250, Darmstadt D-64293
Phone: (49) 6151 72 0   **Fax:** (49) 6151 72 5577
Web: www.merckgroup.com

2015 Sales

	% of total
Asia-Pacific	33
Europe	32
North America	21
Latin America	10
Middle East & Africa	4
Total	**100**

PRODUCTS/OPERATIONS

2015 Sales

	% of total
Healthcare	54
Life Sciences	26
Performance Materials	20
Total	**100**

Selected Pharmaceutical Products

Merck Serono
 Concor (antihypertensive)
 Erbitux (colorectal and neck cancer)
 Euthyrox (hypothyroid treatment)
 Glucophage (diabetes)
 Gonal-f (fertility)
 Pergoveris (fertility)
 Rebif (relapsing multiple sclerosis)
 Saizen (growth hormone deficiency)
 Serostim (HIV-associated wasting)
Consumer health care
 BION and MULTIBION (probiotic multivitamin)
 Cebion (vitamins and minerals)
 Fembion Metfolin (multivitamins for women)
 Flexagil Kytta and Seven Seas (natural joint pain remedies and supplements)
 Kidabion (children's vitamins)
 Nasivin (cold remedy)
 Seven seas (diet supplement)
 Sangobion (anemia remedy)

COMPETITORS

3M	Johnson & Johnson
Abbott Labs	Merck
Akzo Nobel	Merz
Amgen	Novartis
AstraZeneca	Pfizer
BASF SE	QIAGEN
Bayer AG	Roche Holding
Bio-Rad Labs	Sanofi
Bio-Techne	Sigma-Aldrich
Biogen	Teva
Boehringer Ingelheim	Thermo Fisher
Bristol-Myers Squibb	Scientific
Dow Chemical	UCB
Eli Lilly	Universal Display
GlaxoSmithKline	Viavi Solutions
Honeywell	
International	

HISTORICAL FINANCIALS

Company Type: Public

Income Statement				FYE: December 31
	REVENUE ($ mil.)	NET INCOME ($ mil.)	NET PROFIT MARGIN	EMPLOYEES
12/19	18,134	1,482	8.2%	57,071
12/18	16,990	3,863	22.7%	51,749
12/17	18,373	3,116	17.0%	52,880
12/16	15,863	1,720	10.8%	50,439
12/15	13,990	1,214	8.7%	49,613
Annual Growth	6.7%	5.1%	—	3.6%

2019 Year-End Financials

Debt ratio: 31.8%
Return on equity: 7.5%
Cash ($ mil.): 876
Current ratio: 0.76
Long-term debt ($ mil.): 9,752

No. of shares (mil.): 129
Dividends
 Yield: 0.7%
 Payout: 5.5%
Market value ($ mil.): 3,062

	STOCK PRICE ($) FY Close	P/E High/Low		PER SHARE ($) Earnings	Dividends	Book Value
12/19	23.70	8	6	3.41	0.19	155.20
12/18	20.76	3	2	8.89	0.20	152.41
12/17	21.50	8	4	7.17	1.50	129.89
Annual Growth	5.0%	—		(16.9%)	(40.6%)	4.6%

Metallurgical Corp China Ltd

EXECUTIVES

Chairman, Heting Shen
Auditors: PricewaterhouseCoopers Zhong Tian CPAs Limited Company

LOCATIONS

HQ: Metallurgical Corp China Ltd
 MCC Tower, 28 Shuguang Xili, Chaoyang District, Beijing 100028
Phone: (86) 10 59868666   **Fax:** (86) 10 59868999
Web: www.mccchina.com

HISTORICAL FINANCIALS

Company Type: Public

Income Statement				FYE: December 31
	REVENUE ($ mil.)	NET INCOME ($ mil.)	NET PROFIT MARGIN	EMPLOYEES
12/19	48,667	948	1.9%	0
12/18	42,093	926	2.2%	0
12/17	37,495	931	2.5%	0
12/16	31,618	774	2.4%	0
12/15	33,462	739	2.2%	0
Annual Growth	9.8%	6.4%	—	—

2019 Year-End Financials

Debt ratio: 2.6%
Return on equity: 7.2%
Cash ($ mil.): 6,277
Current ratio: 1.14
Long-term debt ($ mil.): 4,150

No. of shares (mil.): —
Dividends
 Yield: 0.0%
 Payout: —
Market value ($ mil.): —

	STOCK PRICE ($) FY Close	P/E High/Low		PER SHARE ($) Earnings	Dividends	Book Value
12/19	4.58	20	17	0.04	0.16	(0.00)
12/18	5.00	27	19	0.04	0.16	(0.00)
12/17	6.88	27	27	0.04	0.14	(0.00)
12/16	6.00	23	23	0.04	0.13	(0.00)
12/15	3.39	—	—	0.04	0.12	(0.00)
Annual Growth	7.8%	—	—	1.2%	6.5%	—

Metro AG (New)

Auditors: KPMG AG

LOCATIONS

HQ: Metro AG (New)
 Metro-Strase 1, Duesseldorf 40235
Phone: (49) 211 6886 0
Web: www.metroag.de/en

HISTORICAL FINANCIALS
Company Type: Public

Income Statement | | | | FYE: September 30

	REVENUE ($ mil.)	NET INCOME ($ mil.)	NET PROFIT MARGIN	EMPLOYEES
09/19	29,542	(137)	—	101,654
09/18	34,141	398	1.2%	152,426
09/17	35,329	383	1.1%	155,082
Annual Growth	(8.6%)	—	—	(19.0%)

2019 Year-End Financials

Debt ratio: —
Return on equity: (-4.3%)
Cash ($ mil.): 545
Current ratio: 0.93
Long-term debt ($ mil.): —

No. of shares (mil.): 360
Dividends
　Yield: 0.0%
　Payout: —
Market value ($ mil.): 2,859

	STOCK PRICE ($) FY Close	P/E High/Low		PER SHARE ($) Earnings	Dividends	Book Value
09/19	7.94	—	—	(0.38)	0.24	8.19
09/18	7.65	12	6	1.10	0.25	9.94
09/17	0.00	—	—	1.05	0.00	10.37
/0.00	—	—(0.00)		0.00	(0.00)	
Annual Growth	—	—	—	—	—	—

Metro Inc

EXECUTIVES

VP Produce and Baked Goods Metro Richelieu, Christian Bourbonnière
President CEO and Director, Eric Richer La Flèche, age 57, $267,400 total compensation
SVP and CFO, François Thibault
SVP and Metro Ontario Division Head, Carmen Fortino, age 62
VP Chief Marketing and Communications Officer, Marc Giroux
VP Information Systems, Frédéric Legault
Chairman, Réal Raymond, age 69
Auditors: Ernst & Young LLP

LOCATIONS

HQ: Metro Inc
　11011 Maurice-Duplessis Boulevard, Montreal, Quebec H1C 1V6
Phone: 514 643-1000　　**Fax:** 514 643-1215
Web: www.metro.ca

2015 Stores

	No.
Qué;bec	508
Ontario	336
Total	**844**

PRODUCTS/OPERATIONS

2015 Stores

	No.
Food	
Supermarkets	343
Discount stores	213
Partners	34
Drug	254
Total	**844**

Selected Retail Banners

Brunet (pharmacy)
Clini Plus (pharmacy)
Drug Basics (pharmacy)
Food Basics (discount supermarkets)
METRO (supermarkets)
METRO PLUS (supermarkets)
Super C (discount supermarkets)
The Pharmacy (pharmacy)

COMPETITORS

Costco Wholesale Canada	Loblaw
Couche-Tard	Shoppers Drug Mart
Jean Coutu	Sobeys
Katz Group	Uniprix
	Wal-Mart Canada

HISTORICAL FINANCIALS
Company Type: Public

Income Statement | | | | FYE: September 26

	REVENUE ($ mil.)	NET INCOME ($ mil.)	NET PROFIT MARGIN	EMPLOYEES
09/20	18,224	805	4.4%	90,000
09/19	16,978	720	4.2%	90,000
09/18	14,564	1,738	11.9%	90,000
09/17	13,341	599	4.5%	65,000
09/16	12,949	578	4.5%	65,000
Annual Growth	8.9%	8.6%	—	8.5%

2020 Year-End Financials

Debt ratio: 19.8%
Return on equity: 13.1%
Cash ($ mil.): 447
Current ratio: 1.34
Long-term debt ($ mil.): 2,644

No. of shares (mil.): 250
Dividends
　Yield: 0.0%
　Payout: 27.8%
Market value ($ mil.): 11,899

	STOCK PRICE ($) FY Close	P/E High/Low		PER SHARE ($) Earnings	Dividends	Book Value
09/20	47.55	15	12	3.18	0.89	24.85
09/19	43.52	16	11	2.82	0.79	23.75
09/18	31.26	5	4	7.25	0.71	22.35
09/17	33.06	13	11	2.60	0.64	12.98
09/16	33.08	15	11	2.42	0.54	11.61
Annual Growth	9.5%	—	—	7.1%	13.0%	21.0%

Metropolitan Bank & Trust Co. (Philippines)

EXECUTIVES

President & Chief Executive Officer, Fabian Dee
Senior Executive Vice President, Vicente Cuna Jr.
Chairman, Arthur Ty
Auditors: SyCip Gorres Velayo & Co.

LOCATIONS

HQ: Metropolitan Bank & Trust Co. (Philippines)
　Metrobank Plaza, Sen. Gil Puyat Avenue, Urdaneta Village, Makati City, Metro Manila 1200
Phone: (63) 2 898 8805
Web: www.metrobank.com.ph

COMPETITORS

Bank of the Philippine Islands	Maybank
DBS Group Holdings	Pag-IBIG Fund
	United Overseas Bank

HISTORICAL FINANCIALS
Company Type: Public

Income Statement | | | | FYE: December 31

	ASSETS ($ mil.)	NET INCOME ($ mil.)	INCOME AS % OF ASSETS	EMPLOYEES
12/19	48,400	554	1.1%	13,150
12/18	42,721	419	1.0%	12,851
12/17	41,760	365	0.9%	12,133
12/16	37,889	365	1.0%	0
12/15	37,581	397	1.1%	0
Annual Growth	6.5%	8.7%	—	—

2019 Year-End Financials

Return on assets: 1.2%
Return on equity: 9.4%
Long-term debt ($ mil.): —
No. of shares (mil.): —
Sales ($ mil): 2,885

Dividends
　Yield: —
　Payout: —
Market value ($ mil.): —

Mitsubishi Chemical Holdings Corp

Mitsubishi Chemical Holdings Corporation (MCHC) is among the largest chemical manufacturers in Japan. Its businesses are Mitsubishi Chemical which makes chemicals plastics and textiles; Mitsubishi Tanabe Pharma which makes pharmaceutical products for central nervous system diabetes and kidney; Life Sciences Institute which offers health and medical ICT solutions next generation healthcare and drug discovery; and Taiyo Nippon Sanso produces industrial gases. Headquartered in Tokyo MCHC generates about 70% of sales in Japan.

Operations

MCHC has four business segments: Chemicals Performance Products Industrial Gases and Health Care.

The Chemicals segment generates more than 30% of the revenue. It produces methyl methacrylate petrochemicals and carbon products.

The Performance Products segment generates around 30% of the company's revenue. It is further divided into two units: functional products which consists of ICT electronics & displays high performance films environment and living solutions and advanced moldings and composites; and performance chemicals which consists of advanced polymers high performance chemicals and new energy.

The Industrial Gases segment generates about 20% of the company's revenue. It consists of industrial gases and industrial gas-related equipment and facilities.

The Health Care segment which generates almost 15% of the company's sales consists of two divisions ethical pharmaceuticals and life science. Life science provides clinical testing diagnostic reagents capsules and pharmaceutical processing equipment and active pharmaceutical ingredients and intermediates.

Geographic Reach

Headquartered in Tokyo MCHC generates about 70% of its revenue from Japan while the rest come from other countries. It has about 750 subsidiaries and affiliates globally primarily in Japan (more than 300) the Asia/Pacific region (excluding Japan) and Europe.

Sales and Marketing

MCHC sells products globally to various industries including petrochemicals carbon products steels chemicals electronics and pharmaceuticals.

Financial Performance

Note: Growth rates may differ after conversion to US Dollars.

In fiscal 2020 (ended March 31) the company's sales decreased 7% to Å 3.6 trillion due to decreases in sales in the Performance Products Chemicals and Health Care segments partially offset by a increases in Industrial Gases segment.

Net income fell 60% to Å 86.6 billion due to higher selling general and administrative expenses and other operating expenses.

Mitsubishi Chemical Holdings' cash on hand fell Å 93.3 million during fiscal 2020 ending the year at Å 228.2 billion. The company's operations generated Å 452 billion while investing activities used Å 87.6 billion and financing used Å 450.5 billion. Mitsubishi Chemical Holdings' main cash uses in 2019 were for capital expenditures purchases and acquisitions.

Strategy

Key strategies being employed by the company are expanding high-performance higher value-added products and solutions business accelerating global development enhancing innovation through business integration and achieving profitability of new energy businesses at an early stage.

The company will accelerate the global expansion of higher value-added products by making full use of resources of overseas affiliates. It is constructing a new production facility in Thailand for multilayer co-extruded film DIAMIRON is widely used in food and medical packaging in order to expand business in the ASEAN where growing market demands are expected.

Going forward the company will continue to enhance its global supply chains through increased production capacity at overseas business bases and will meet its customers' needs for more sophisticated performance with its advanced technological capabilities.

Mergers and Acquisitions

In early 2019 the HyCO business of Linde Gas North America LLC in the United States and its related US business assets was acquired by Taiyo Nippon Sanso Corporation a subsidiary of MCHC for $413.7 million. The transaction provides large-scale supply of hydrogen and carbon monoxide for the acquiring company.

EXECUTIVES

Senior Managing Corporate Executive Officer, Noriyoshi Ohira

Senior Managing Corporate Executive Officer, Masanori Karatsu

President and CEO, Hitoshi Ochi

Senior Managing Corporate Executive Officer, Kenkichi Kosakai

Managing Corporate Executive Officer, Steve P. Yurich

Vice Chairman, Takumi Ubagai

Chairman, Yoshimitsu Kobayashi

Vice Chairman, Hiroaki Ishizuka

Auditors: Ernst & Young ShinNihon LLC

LOCATIONS

HQ: Mitsubishi Chemical Holdings Corp
1-1-1 Marunouchi, Chiyoda-ku, Tokyo 100-8251
Phone: (81) 3 6748 7115
Web: www.mitsubishichem-hd.co.jp

2018 Sales

	% of total
Japan	70
Other countries	30

Total	100

PRODUCTS/OPERATIONS

2018 Sales

	% of total
Performance Products	31
Chemicals	32
Industrial Gases	17
Health Care	15
Other	5
Total	**100**

COMPETITORS

Asahi Kasei	Mitsui Chemicals
Astellas	Nissan Chemical
BASF SE	Sinopec Group
Bayer AG	Sumitomo Chemical
Chugai	Sumitomo Dainippon
Daicel Chemical	Pharma
Daiichi Sankyo	Takeda Pharmaceutical
Evonik Degussa	Tokai Carbon
Hitachi Chemical	Tokuyama
Kyowa Hakko Kirin	

HISTORICAL FINANCIALS

Company Type: Public

Income Statement				FYE: March 31
	REVENUE ($ mil.)	NET INCOME ($ mil.)	NET PROFIT MARGIN	EMPLOYEES
03/19	35,428	1,530	4.3%	79,578
03/18	35,074	1,994	5.7%	76,658
03/17	30,195	1,397	4.6%	76,169
03/16	34,044	413	1.2%	75,955
03/15	30,474	507	1.7%	74,364
Annual Growth	3.8%	31.8%	—	1.7%

2019 Year-End Financials

Debt ratio: 0.3%	No. of shares (mil.): 1,423
Return on equity: 12.7%	Dividends
Cash ($ mil.): 2,903	Yield: —
Current ratio: 1.06	Payout: 36.3%
Long-term debt ($ mil.): 10,276	Market value ($ mil.): —

Mitsubishi Corp

In Japanese mitsubishi means "three diamonds" and Mitsubishi Corporation is one of Japan's crown jewels. It is one of the world's top integrated business enterprises with operations across many industries including retail and consumer products energy metals machinery and chemicals. Beyond its core businesses Mitsubishi also invests in diverse businesses like natural resources development new energy and technology-related businesses. With approximately 125 offices plus a network of more than 1700 group companies Mitsubishi is present in about 75 countries.

Operations

Mitsubishi has ten reporting segments that run the gamut from apparel to water infrastructure.

Mineral Resources generates about 40% of revenue. It engages in investing and developing mineral resources such as metallurgical coal copper iron ore and aluminium.

Natural Gases generates about 15% of revenue. It engages in natural gas/oil exploration production and development business and the liquefied natural gas (LNG) business.

Food Industry gives in roughly 10% of revenue. It engages in sales trading business development and other operations across a wide range of business areas related to food.

Other segments like Power Solution and Industrial Infrastructure gives in about 10% while Urban Development Industrial Materials Consumer Industry Automotive Mobility and Petroleum & Chemicals generate more than 20% of revenue combined.

Geographic Reach

Tokyo-based Mitsubishi has roughly 175 offices in Japan and in about 75 other countries. Its natural gases segment operates in North America South East Asia Australia Russia and other region.

Financial Performance

The company's revenue has been volatile in the past five years. Despite this revenues had a 113% growth between 2016 and 2020.

Revenues was Å 14.8 trillion a decrease of Å 1.3 billion or 8% year over year. This was mainly due to a decrease in transaction volumes in the Petrochemicals business.

Net income decreased to Å 535.4 billion in 2020 compared with Å 590.7 billion in 2019.

Cash and cash equivalents at the end of 2020 totaled Å 1.3 trillion. Operating activities provided Å 849.7 billion while investing activities used Å 500.7 billion. Financing activities used another Å 156.6 billion mainly for repayments of long-term debts.

Strategy

Mitsubishi Corporation has conceived its latest management plan entitled "Midterm Corporate Strategy 2021: Achieving Growth Through Business Management Model." It will take effect from fiscal year 2019.

The new strategy will lay the groundwork for MC's sustainable growth over the next three years recognizing how worldwide economic and geopolitical trends are putting pressure on enterprises to evolve its business models. Such trends include the US administration's America-First agenda China' One-Belt One-Road policy and the so-called "Fourth Industrial Revolution" the hallmarks of which are advancing digital technologies and the evolution of platform businesses.

Mergers and Acquisitions

In late 2019 Mitsubishi Corporation (MC) and Chubu Electric Power Co. Inc. (Chubu) were selected as the preferred buyers in a bid for the Netherland-based Energy Company Eneco an integrated energy company that is actively engaged in renewable power generation projects for 4.1 billion Euros. This acquisition will help Mitsubishi to accelerate its own renewable developments in Europe and around the world.

Company Background

Mitsubishi Corporation was founded and went public as Mitsubishi Shoji in 1954. In 1968 it took on the first large-scale international project in Brunei to develop LNG assets followed by iron-ore and metallurgical coal projects in Australia and Canada and salt field business in Mexico.

In 1971 the company made "Mitsubishi Corporation" its official English name. In 1989 it was listed on the London Stock Exchange.

EXECUTIVES

SEVP, Eiichi Tanabe

EVP; Group CEO Business Service Group, Toshimitsu Urabe

EVP; Regional CEO East Asia, Shunichi Matsui

President and CEO, Takehiko Kakiuchi

EVP; Group CEO Machinery Group, Kazushi Okawa

EVP Corporate Communications, Yasuhito Hirota

EVP; Group CEO Energy Business Group, Hajime Hirano
EVP; Group CEO Metals Group, Kanji Nishiura
EVP Regional Strategy, Kazuyuki Mori
EVP; Regional CEO North America, Hidemoto Mizuhara
EVP and CFO, Kazuyuki Masu
EVP; Group CEO Global Environmental and Infrastructure Business Group, Hiroshi Sakuma
EVP; Regional CEO Europe and Africa, Haruki Hayashi
EVP; Group CEO Chemicals Group, Takeshi Hagiwara
EVP; Group CEO Industrial Finance Logistics and Development Group, Shinya Yoshida
EVP; Group CEO Living Essentials Group, Yutaka Kyoya
SVP; Regional CEO Latin America and the Caribbean, Masaji Santo
SVP; Regional CEO Middle East and Central Asia, Katsuya Nakanishi
Chairman, Ken Kobayashi
Auditors: Deloitte Touche Tohmatsu LLC

LOCATIONS

HQ: Mitsubishi Corp
2-3-1 Marunouchi, Chiyoda-ku, Tokyo 100-8086
Phone: (81) 3 3210 2121
Web: www.mitsubishicorp.com

2018 Sales

	% of total
Japan	54
Singapore	13
US	12
Other countries	21
Total	**100**

PRODUCTS/OPERATIONS

2018 Sales

	% of total
Living Essentials	31
Energy	24
Metals	24
Chemicals	13
Machinery	7
Global Environmental & Infrastructure Business	1
Total	**100**

Selected Products and Services

Metals
  Bullion and metals futures
  Fabricated steel structures
  Metallurgical and thermal coal
  Nonferrous metal products
  Nonferrous metals
  Nuclear fuel and components
  Precious metals
  Raw materials for steel
  Semifinished products
  Steel materials
  Specialty steel
Living Essentials
  Apparel
  Canned foods
  Ceramic materials
  Cigarettes
  Coffee beans coffee and beverages
  Confections and snacks
  Contract food services
  Dairy foods and processed foods
  Fabrics
  Feedstuffs
  Fresh and frozen foods
  Grains and agricultural products
  Marine products
  Meat and livestock
  Mineral water
  Oils and fats
  Photosensitized materials
  Pulp paper and packaging materials
  Soft drinks
  Sweeteners

Textile raw materials
Textiles for industrial use
Tires
Wood wood products and construction materials
Machinery
  Automobiles
  Commercial aviation
  Defense systems and equipment
  Electronics products
  Industrial agricultural construction and other general machinery
  Plant and machinery for power generation electricity oil/gas/chemicals steel/cement and environmental protection
  Project development and construction
  Satellite communications
  Ships
  Space systems
  Transportation systems
Energy
  Carbon materials and products
  Crude oil
  LNG
  LPG
  Orimulsion
  Petroleum products
Chemicals
  Fertilizers
  Fine and specialty chemicals
  Inorganic chemicals
  Petrochemicals
  Plastics

COMPETITORS

ITOCHU	Mitsui
Marubeni	

HISTORICAL FINANCIALS

Company Type: Public

Income Statement

FYE: March 31

	REVENUE ($ mil.)	NET INCOME ($ mil.)	NET PROFIT MARGIN	EMPLOYEES
03/20	149,020	5,397	3.6%	110,006
03/19	162,370	5,956	3.7%	104,168
03/18	76,300	5,648	7.4%	98,146
03/17	64,789	4,439	6.9%	99,123
03/16	69,829	(1,506)	—	82,203
Annual Growth	**20.9%**	**—**	**—**	**7.6%**

2020 Year-End Financials

Debt ratio: 0.3%
Return on equity: 9.7%
Cash ($ mil.): 13,337
Current ratio: 1.30
Long-term debt ($ mil.): 43,228

No. of shares (mil.): 1,487
Dividends
  Yield: —
  Payout: 37.9%
Market value ($ mil.): —

Mitsubishi Electric Corp

Auditors: KPMG AZSA LLC

LOCATIONS

HQ: Mitsubishi Electric Corp
2-7-3 Marunouchi, Chiyoda-ku, Tokyo 100-8310
Phone: (81) 3 3218 2272
Web: www.mitsubishielectric.co.jp

HISTORICAL FINANCIALS

Company Type: Public

Income Statement

FYE: March 31

	REVENUE ($ mil.)	NET INCOME ($ mil.)	NET PROFIT MARGIN	EMPLOYEES
03/20	41,110	2,043	5.0%	146,518
03/19	40,814	2,046	5.0%	145,817
03/18	41,730	2,560	6.1%	142,340
03/17	37,910	1,882	5.0%	138,700
03/16	39,131	2,034	5.2%	135,160
Annual Growth	**1.2%**	**0.1%**	**—**	**2.0%**

2020 Year-End Financials

Debt ratio: 0.0%
Return on equity: 9.1%
Cash ($ mil.): 4,952
Current ratio: 1.87
Long-term debt ($ mil.): 1,231

No. of shares (mil.): 2,146
Dividends
  Yield: 2.9%
  Payout: 77.5%
Market value ($ mil.): 52,918

	STOCK PRICE ($) FY Close	P/E High/Low		PER SHARE ($) Earnings	Dividends	Book Value
03/20	24.65	0	0	0.95	0.74	10.43
03/19	25.73	0	0	0.95	0.72	10.09
03/18	32.41	0	0	1.19	0.60	9.91
03/17	28.81	0	0	0.88	0.49	8.50
03/16	20.93	0	0	0.95	0.43	7.64
Annual Growth	**4.2%**	**—**	**—**	**0.1%**	**14.2%**	**8.1%**

Mitsubishi Heavy Industries Ltd

A member of the Mitsubishi keiretsu (set of companies with intertwining relationships and shareholdings) Mitsubishi Heavy Industries (MHI) builds and supplies everything from nuclear power plants bridges and aircraft to engines ships and air conditioners and serves various industries and customers around the world. MHI operates through three main industry segments: Power Systems Industry & Infrastructure and Aircraft Defense & Space. The company's core market is Japan where it earns almost half its revenue but also does business in other parts of Asia the US Europe Central and South America Africa and the Middle East.

Operations

MHI operates through three reportable segments: Industry & Infrastructure (around 45% of total revenue); Power Systems (nearly 40%); and Aircraft Defense & Space (more than 15%).The Industry & Infrastructure segment manufactures products in such diverse fields such as material handling equipment metals machinery air-conditioning and refrigeration environmental systems and commercial ships to name a few.Power Systems has expertise in the energy-related fields of thermal power nuclear power and renewable energy supplying chemical plants and other industrial markets. Its product line consists of energy generation systems compressors and aero engines.

The Aircraft Defense & Space segment's core business has two divisions: Commercial Aircraft and Defense & Space equipment. The segment's products include Commercial aircraft Defense aircraft Missile systems Naval ships Special vehicles Maritime systems (torpedoes) and Space systems.

Geographic Reach

The company is based in Tokyo Japan and operates worldwide. Japan accounts for about 50%

of its total revenue and the US represents some 15%.

Financial Performance

Note: Growth rates may differ after conversion to US Dollars. MHI's revenues have been up and down in recent years but the company increased sales by 1% to Å 4 trillion in fiscal 2019. Sales were lower than expected partially due to deterioration in the industry and infrastructure segment.

Net income saw a decrease of 21% in fiscal 2019 to Å 87.1 billion from Å 110.3 billion due to increased expenses which resulted in an operating loss for the year as well as increased finance costs and an income tax expense of Å 139.9 billion.

Cash at the end of fiscal 2019 was Å 281.6 billion a decrease of Å 1.6 billion from the prior year. Cash from operations contributed Å 452.6 billion to the coffers while investing activities used Å 239.6 billion mainly for purchases of investment securities and property plant and equipment (buildings land and machinery and transportation equipment). Financing activities used another Å 204.5 billion for loan repayment and dividends to stockholders.

Strategy

To enhance its product performance reliability and price competitiveness MHI is working to maintain and strengthen the competitiveness of its products particularly through R&D and capital investment. MHI is also focusing efforts on incorporating external knowledge to propose new functions and solutions that anticipate market trends.

MHI's subsidiary Mitsubishi Power completed its renovation of the Otake Geothermal Power Station operated by Kyushu Electric Power Company. The facility is the first "double flash and dual pressure" method in Japan efficiently utilizing a mix of high and low pressure steam. Mitsubishi Power also broadened its digital and services business by expanding its Boiler Smart Inspection offering part of the company's suite of TOMONI digital solutions. The move is part of the company's drive to tap new customer categories as it works to become the world's leading energy solutions provider.

MHI's Mitsubishi Heavy Industries Machine Tool Co. Ltd developed new models of hobbing and gear shaping machines with highly accurate machining to manufacture precision reduction gears for robots. These new products are marketed as the "FR Series." MHI Machine Tools also launched a lineup of newly developed ultra-thin precision position detectors that perform machine positioning and feedback digitally marketed as the "MPFA Series."

Mergers and Acquisitions

In mid-2020 MHI acquired Canada-based Bombardier Inc.'s Canadair Regional Jet (CRJ) Program for a cash consideration of approximately $550 million. Bombardier's CRJ Program includes the maintenance support refurbishment marketing and sales activities for the CRJ Series aircraft along with the type certificates. MHI now owns CRJ's related services and support network mainly located in Mirabel Québec and Toronto Ontario in Canada Bridgeport West Virginia and Tucson Arizona in the United States.

EXECUTIVES

President and CEO, Shunichi Miyanaga, age 72
EVP, Masahiko Arihara, age 68
SEVP and President and CEO Commercial Aviation and Transportation Systems, Yoichi Kujirai, age 69
EVP and President and CEO Integrated Defense & Space Systems, Hisakazu Mizutani, age 69
EVP and Senior General Manager Nuclear Energy Systems Division Energy & Environment, Ei Kadokami

SEVP and President and CEO Energy and Environment, Kenji Ando
EVP, Koji Hasegawa
EVP Human Resources Labor Relations and Global Personnel, Mutsuo Hiroe
EVP and General Counsel, Takashi Funato, age 68
EVP and Head of Monozukuri Innovation Planning Dept of Technology & Innovation Headquarters, Yukio Kodama, age 66
EVP and President and CEO Machinery Equipment and Infrastructure, Kazuaki Kimura
EVP CFO and Head of Business Strategy Office, Masanori Koguchi
EVP CTO Head of Technology and Innovation Headquarters and Head of Global Business Planning & Operations Headquarters, Michisuke Nayama
EVP Assistant to President and CEO Commercial Aviation and Transportation Systems and President. Mitsubishi Aircraft Corporation, Hiromichi Morimoto
EVP and President Mitsubishi Heavy Industries America Inc., Kiyoshi Okazoe
Chairman, Hideaki Omiya, age 74
Auditors: KPMG AZSA LLC

LOCATIONS

HQ: Mitsubishi Heavy Industries Ltd
3-2-3 Marunouchi, Chiyoda-ku, Tokyo 100-8332
Phone: (81) 3 6275 6200
Web: www.mhi.co.jp

2018 Sales

	% of total
Asia	
Japan	46
Other countries	17
USA	15
Europe	11
Central and South America	4
Middle East	3
Africa	2
Other regions	2
Total	**100**

PRODUCTS/OPERATIONS

2018 Sales

	% of total
Industry & Infrastructure	45
Power Systems	35
Aircraft Defense & Space	17
Others	3
Total	**100**

Selected Products

Aerospace
 Aeroengines
 Civil aircraft
 Defense aircraft
 Guided weapon systems
 Laser radar surveillance system
 Launch vehicles
 Rocket engines
 Space stations
General Machinery & Special Vehicles
 Agricultural machinery
 Construction machinery
 Forklift trucks
 Medium- and small-sized engines
 Tractors
 Turbochargers
Machinery & Steel Structures
 Air brakes
 Automated people movers
 Chemical plants
 CO2 recovery plants
 Crane and material handling systems
 Flue gas desulphurization plants
 Injection molding machines
 Monorails
 Production robots
 Rail transit systems
 Sludge treatment systems

Testing equipment
Power Systems
 Boilers
 Desalination plants
 Fans and blowers
 Diesel engines
 Gas turbines
 Hydraulic equipment (actuators generators motors pumps and water pressure systems)
 Instrumentation and control systems
 Lithium-ion secondary batteries
 Solid oxide fuel cells
 Steam turbines
 Thin-film photovoltaic module
 Wind turbines
Shipbuilding & Ocean Development
 Cargo ships
 Floating facilities
 Marine engines
 Marine machinery
 Passenger ships
 Pure car carriers
 Special-purpose ships
 Tankers
Others
 Air conditioning and refrigeration systems
 Automotive thermal systems
 Centrifugal chillers
 Machine tools

COMPETITORS

ALSTOM
Aker Solutions
Baltija Shipbuilding
Bharat Heavy Electricals
DSME
Doosan Heavy Industries
Hanjin Heavy Industries & Construction
Hyundai Heavy Industries
IHI Corp.
Kajima
Kawasaki Heavy Industries
Marubeni
Obayashi
Subaru
Sumitomo Heavy Industries

HISTORICAL FINANCIALS

Company Type: Public

Income Statement

FYE: March 31

	REVENUE ($ mil.)	NET INCOME ($ mil.)	NET PROFIT MARGIN	EMPLOYEES
03/20	37,230	802	2.2%	93,075
03/19	36,826	915	2.5%	93,173
03/18	38,713	663	1.7%	95,927
03/17	35,007	784	2.2%	99,340
03/16	36,036	568	1.6%	100,784
Annual Growth	0.8%	9.0%	—	(2.0%)

2020 Year-End Financials

Debt ratio: 0.1%	No. of shares (mil.): 336
Return on equity: 6.5%	Dividends
Cash ($ mil.): 2,594	Yield: —
Current ratio: 1.01	Payout: 57.9%
Long-term debt ($ mil.): 5,543	Market value ($ mil.): —

Mitsubishi Materials Corp.

With operations in copper cement and aluminum Mitsubishi Materials makes a material difference with its end products. The Metals segment smelts copper and makes copper products (billets cake wire balls). Other divisions include Cement (cement concrete and other building materials) Aluminum (beverage cans and other aluminum products) Advanced Materials (sintered auto parts and cutting tools) and Electronic Materials (electronic components chemicals). Mitsubishi Materials is also involved in precious metals recycling-related products real estate fossil fuels and nuclear energy-related services. It is part of the Mitsubishi keiretsu (companies that share a common name and corporate culture).

Operations

Mitsubishi Materials operates through five segments: Metals (about 50% of total revenue) Cement Aluminum Advanced Materials & Tools and Electronic Materials & Components

Metals includes Copper smelting (copper gold and silver) and copper alloy products.

Cement includes cement and related products ready-mixed concrete and aggregate.

Aluminum consist of aluminum cans rolled aluminum products and processed aluminum products.

Advanced Materials & Tools includes cemented carbide products and high-performance alloy products.

Electronic Materials & Components includes advanced materials electronic components polycrystalline silicon and chemical products.

Geographic Reach

Mitsubishi Materials operates in 30 countries worldwide including in Europe (Germany the UK Spain and France) Asia (Indonesia South Korea Malaysia Singapore China Taiwan Hong Kong and Thailand) and in Australia Canada Brazil.

Japan accounts for about 65% of Mitsubishi Materials' total revenue.

Financial Performance

Note: Growth rates may differ after conversion to US Dollars.

The company reported a decline of 6.5% in revenue in fiscal 2016 (March year end) from Â 1517 billion to Â 1418 billion primarily due to a slowdown in key markets (including Japan and China) resulting in sluggish production. Copper and other metal prices fell and there was a drop of demand for cement in Japan. In addition equipment failure at a subsidiary plant resulted in an interruption in production.

Only Advance Materials & Tools saw significant revenue growth in fiscal 2016 (up about 18%) thanks to higher demand for cemented carbide products in Japan and globally.

Mitsubishi Materials' net income grew 9.2% to Â 61.3 billion in fiscal 2016 due in part to extraordinary income from the sale of some of its holding in SUMCO Corporation.

Net cash from operating activities grew by Â 10.6 billion to Â 118.6 billion due to higher income before income taxes and lower inventories.

Strategy

Against the backdrop of increased competition and volatile global commodity prices (copper) and weakening cement demand in Japan Mitsubishi Materials is focusing on upgrading its three core businesses.

In the Cement business the company plans to expand in the US (especially in Southern California) where there is a growing population and demand for infrastructure is increasing (in contrast to Japan where the lower birth rate and an aging population is resulting in cement demand trending down). To help achieve this goal Mitsubishi Materials has acquired a site Northwest of Los Angeles on which it plans to build a ready-mixed concrete plant.

In the Metals sector the company is boosting its recycling capacity for processing electronic devices from all over the world. In 2016 it built a second E-Scrap facility at the Naoshima Smelter & Refin-

ery. All told the company is the world's largest E-scrap business with the capacity to process 140000 tons a year.

The Advance Materials & Tools business is looking to achieve a global market share of more than 10% by the early 2020s. Specifically it is targeting growth markets (automotive aerospace and medical) and has set up technical centers in China Thailand the US and Europe to help it develop products based on feedback from local and regional markets.

Mergers and Acquisitions

To establish a global presence in the downstream copper industry in 2016 Mitsubishi Materials acquired the Special Products division of UK-based Luvata. This division has 14 plants and support offices in nine countries in the Americas Europe and Asia supplying products for automotive energy healthcare science and manufacturing customers.

EXECUTIVES

President, Akira Takeuchi
EVP; President Metal Company Aluminum Business and Corporate Production Engineering, Osamu Iida
EVP; President Cement Company Environment and CSR and Mineral Resource, Naoki Ono
Senior Managing Executive Officer, Nobuo Shibano
Senior Managing Executive Officer, Yasunobu Suzuki
Managing Executive Officer; President Mitsubishi Cement Corp; President MCC Development Corp; Chairman Robertson's Ready Mix Ltd., Kimball McCloud
Managing Executive Officer; President Mitsubishi Materials Shanghai, Chitoshi Mori
Managing Executive Officer, Yoshihiko Kimura
Managing Executive Officer, Hikaru Kimura
Managing Executive Officer, Fumio Tsurumaki
Managing Executive Officer, Soichi Fukui
Chairman, Hiroshi Yao
Auditors: KPMG AZSA LLC

LOCATIONS

HQ: Mitsubishi Materials Corp.
3-2-3 Marunouchi, Chiyoda-ku, Tokyo 100-8117
Phone: (81) 3 5252 5226
Web: www.mmc.co.jp

2016 Sales

	% of total
Asia	25
Japan	64
US	8
Europe	2
Others	1
Total	**100**

PRODUCTS/OPERATIONS

2016 Sales

	% of total
Metals	48
Cement	14
Aluminum	11
Advanced materials & tools	9
Electronic materials & components	4
Other	14
Total	**100**

COMPETITORS

ASARCO	Mitsui Mining and
Anglo American	Smelting
BHP Billiton	Rio Tinto Limited
Codelco	Sumitomo Metal Mining
Dowa Holdings	Toho Zinc
Furukawa	

HISTORICAL FINANCIALS

Company Type: Public

Income Statement				FYE: March 31
	REVENUE ($ mil.)	NET INCOME ($ mil.)	NET PROFIT MARGIN	EMPLOYEES
03/20	13,966	(671)	—	34,260
03/19	15,016	11	0.1%	34,079
03/18	15,063	325	2.2%	32,069
03/17	11,663	253	2.2%	29,811
03/16	12,626	546	4.3%	29,553
Annual Growth	2.6%	—		3.8%

2020 Year-End Financials

Debt ratio: 0.2%	No. of shares (mil.): 130
Return on equity: (-12.7%)	Dividends
Cash ($ mil.): 1,238	Yield: —
Current ratio: 1.20	Payout: —
Long-term debt ($ mil.): 2,824	Market value ($ mil.): —

Mitsubishi Motors Corp. (Japan)

Mitsubishi Motors is a small fish in the big pond of global car manufacturing. The company sells about a million cars per year (far below rival Toyota) worldwide. The 20 models of cars trucks minivans and SUVs are made at its plants in Asia Europe and the US. Mitsubishi products include the Lancer Pajero Triton Mirage and Outlander vehicles. It also offers an electric minicar under its i-MiEV model. Mitsubishi Corporation and Mitsubishi Heavy Industries together own about a 30% stake in Mitsubishi Motors which traces its roots to Heavy Industries' 1917 "Mitsubishi Model A" project. About 80% of sales come from outside of Japan. In 2016 Nissan bought 34% of Mitsubishi Motors for $2.2 billion.

Operations

Mitsubishi sees its future in electric vehicles which it has been developing since 1966. The company develops plug-in hybrids and other electric vehicles through its research and development facilities and through joint ventures with other auto makers. In 2014 it announced a partnership with Nissan and other car makers to develop and manufacture new electric minicars and promote a charging network.

Mitsubishi already has an electric minicar the i-MiEV on the market in Japan and Europe. (Minicars are a popular vehicle class in the Japanese and European markets and are gaining popularity in other parts of the world.) While it sells in Japan under its own brand the MiEV is sold in Europe through an agreement with French car maker Peugeot S.A. which buys and resells MiEV under a different brand.

Geographic Reach

Mitsubishi's largest market is Europe representing 24% of net sales. Other major markets include Japan (20%) Asia (19%) North America (13%) Oceania (10%) and other countries (14%). The company operates through seven facilities in four countries; six car manufacturing facilities in four countries; 12 car manufacturing facilities of affiliated companies and business partners in 11 countries and regions; and eight engine transmission and parts manufacturing facilities in five countries.

Financial Performance

In 2015 Mitsubishi's net sales increased by 4% in 2015 compared to 2014. The growth was driven by increased sales from both its automobile and automobile financing businesses. Stronger North American sales were driven by brisk sales of the Outlander Sport and Mirage as an economic recovery within the US grew stronger.

Mitsubishi's net income also climbed 13% from 2014 to 2015 due to increased sales decreased advertising and promotion expenses an absence of a share issuance cost and gains on a revision of its retirement benefit plan.

Strategy

As it has in years past the company also continues to turn to emerging markets to increase its sales and boost profits. It has been targeting its products to customers in emerging markets like China Russia the Ukraine and other countries in Asia and Eastern Europe. Other sales-boosting initiatives featured a new plant being launched in the Philippines in January 2015. The new plant is continuing with the production of the Adventure and L300 models and produces up to 50000 units per year exceeding the production capacity at a previous plant.

The company was hit by a major scandal in 2016 after it was revealed that it had cheated on fuel economy tests for several years.

In 2014 Mitsubishi acquired Asian Transmission Corporation (ATC) from Mitsubishi Motors Philippines Corporation (MMPC) and Sojitz Corporation (Sojitz) A production base for components ATC supplies transmissions and engines for automobiles and the deal will reinforce Mitsubishi 's production base in the ASEAN countries where the automobile market is expected to experience sustainable growth.

Company Background

Mitsubishi Motors Corporation was created in 1970 when Mitsubishi Heavy Industries spun off its motor vehicle division. Mitsubishi Heavy Industries was created in 1934 by the merger of Mitsubishi Aircraft and Mitsubishi Shipbuilding (which had been making cars since 1917).

EXECUTIVES

EVP Development and Quality, Mitsuhiko (Mike) Yamashita
Chairman and CEO, Osamu Masuko
EVP Overseas Operations and Global After Sales, Kozo Shiraji
COO, Trevor Mann
EVP Finance Controlling and Accounting and CFO, Koji Ikeya
Corporate VP and General Manager Global Marketing and Sales, Guillaume Cartier
Auditors: Ernst & Young ShinNihon LLC

LOCATIONS

HQ: Mitsubishi Motors Corp. (Japan)
3-1-21 Shibaura, Minato-ku, Tokyo 108-8410
Phone: (81) 3 3456 1111
Web: www.mitsubishi-motors.com

2015 Sales

	% of total
Europe	24
Japan	20
Asia	19
North America	13
Oceania	10
Other regions	14
Total	**100**

PRODUCTS/OPERATIONS

2015

	% of total
Automobiles	99
Financial services	1
Total	**100**

Selected Models

Challenger
Colt
Diamante
Eclipse
Eclipse Spyder
Endeavor
Galant
i MiEV
Lancer
Lancer Evolution
Mirage
Outlander
Raider

COMPETITORS

BMW	Kia Motors
Caterpillar	Mazda
Daihatsu	Nissan
Deere	Peugeot
FCA US	Renault
Fiat Chrysler	Subaru
Ford Motor	Suzuki Motor
General Motors	Toyota
Hino Motors	Volkswagen
Honda	Volvo
Isuzu	smart GmbH

HISTORICAL FINANCIALS

Company Type: Public

Income Statement				FYE: March 31
	REVENUE ($ mil.)	NET INCOME ($ mil.)	NET PROFIT MARGIN	EMPLOYEES
03/20	20,914	(237)	—	39,729
03/19	22,706	1,199	5.3%	39,996
03/18	20,646	1,013	4.9%	37,629
03/17	17,052	(1,775)	—	33,496
03/16	20,195	646	3.2%	34,070
Annual Growth	0.9%	—	—	3.9%

2020 Year-End Financials

Debt ratio: 0.1%
Return on equity: (-3.1%)
Cash ($ mil.): 3,681
Current ratio: 1.31
Long-term debt ($ mil.): 915
No. of shares (mil.): 1,488
Dividends
  Yield: —
  Payout: —
Market value ($ mil.): —

Mitsubishi Shokuhin Co., Ltd.

EXECUTIVES

President and CEO, Toru Moriyama
CFO, Daiichiro Suzuki
Division COO Information System Division, Michihiro Taniguchi
President and CEO Mitsubishi Shikoku, Yoichi Ichiura
Auditors: Deloitte Touche Tohmatsu LLC

LOCATIONS

HQ: Mitsubishi Shokuhin Co., Ltd.
1-1-1 Koishikawa, Bunkyo-ku, Tokyo 112-8778
Phone: (81) 3 4553 5111
Web: www.mitsubishi-shokuhin.com

PRODUCTS/OPERATIONS

2016 sales

	% of total
Frozen and chilled foods business	39
Processed food business	32
Alcoholic beverages business	18
Confectioneries business	11
Total	**100**

COMPETITORS

ITOCHU	Kokubu
Kato Sangyo	

HISTORICAL FINANCIALS

Company Type: Public

Income Statement				FYE: March 31
	REVENUE ($ mil.)	NET INCOME ($ mil.)	NET PROFIT MARGIN	EMPLOYEES
03/20	24,455	105	0.4%	6,429
03/19	23,661	108	0.5%	6,427
03/18	23,669	101	0.4%	6,474
03/17	21,568	110	0.5%	6,407
03/16	21,221	111	0.5%	6,616
Annual Growth	3.6%	(1.4%)	—	(0.7%)

2020 Year-End Financials

Debt ratio: 0.0%
Return on equity: 6.3%
Cash ($ mil.): 2
Current ratio: 1.13
Long-term debt ($ mil.): —
No. of shares (mil.): 57
Dividends
  Yield: —
  Payout: —
Market value ($ mil.): —

Mitsubishi UFJ Financial Group Inc

Mitsubishi UFJ Financial Group (MUFG) is a banking group in Japan with total assets of Å 331.75 trillion. The group is comprised of MUFG Bank Mitsubishi UFJ Trust and Banking Mitsubishi UFJ Morgan Stanley Securities (through Mitsubishi UFJ Securities Holdings) Mitsubishi UFJ NICOS and other subsidiaries and affiliates. The group provides commercial banking trust banking securities credit cards consumer finance asset management leasing and other fields of financial services. In Japan the company operates approximately 600 business locations and the group had the largest overseas network among Japanese banks consisting of approximately 2100 business locations in more than 50 countries including MUFG Union Bank in the United States Krungsri in Thailand and Bank Danamon in Indonesia. Other holdings include investment bank Mitsubishi UFJ Securities and California-based MUFG Union Bank. Domestic operations accounts for more than a third of total revenue.

Operations

Mitsubishi UFJ Financial Group (MUFG) operates an integrated business group system concentrated on six main business areas.

Retail & Commercial Banking (more than 35%) which integrates the Japanese retail and commercial banking businesses of MUFG Bank Mitsubishi UFJ Trust and Banking Mitsubishi UFJ Securities

Holdings and Mitsubishi UFJ NICOS. This business group offers retail and small and medium-sized enterprise customers in Japan an extensive array of commercial banking trust banking and securities products and services.

Global Commercial Banking (20%) which provides financial products and services including loans deposits fund transfers investments asset management services for local retail small and medium-sized enterprise and corporate customers globally through partner banks (including MUFG Union Bank in the US and among others).

Japanese Corporate & Investment Banking (almost 15%) covering the Japanese corporate businesses (including transaction banking investment banking trust banking and securities businesses) of MUFG Bank Mitsubishi UFJ Trust and Banking and Mitsubishi UFJ Securities Holdings. This business group offers large Japanese corporations advanced financial solutions.

Global Markets (approximately 15%) which covers customer business and treasury operations of MUFG Bank Mitsubishi UFJ Trust and Banking and Mitsubishi UFJ Securities Holdings. The customer business includes sales and trading in fixed income instruments currencies equities and other investment products.

Global Corporate & Investment Banking (about 10%) including the corporate investment and transaction banking businesses of MUFG Bank and Mitsubishi UFJ Securities Holdings.

Asset Management & Investor Services Business Group (more than 5%) covers the asset management and asset administration businesses of Mitsubishi UFJ Trust and Banking and MUFG Bank.

MUFG has a diversified revenue stream. Nearly 45% of its total revenue comes from loan interest (including fees); about 30% comes from fees and commissions. More than 15% comes from interest income on investments trading account assets and deposits in other banks. Investment security gains and equity earnings (if applicable) make up the remainder.

Geographic Reach
Mitsubishi UFJ Financial Group (MUFG) operates in the US Japan and more than 50 countries such as Europe and Asia/Oceania including MUFG Union Bank in the United States Krungsri in Thailand and Bank Danamon in Indonesia.

About 65% of its revenue came from Japan followed by the United States with approximately 30%.

Sales and Marketing
Mitsubishi UFJ Financial Group (MUFG) mainly markets its products through sales agents. The company also offers direct banking channels and internet banking services for corporate customers and to enhance productivity through migration to digital channels for the housing loan business and expanded use of robotics and artificial intelligence and primarily targets small- and medium-sized enterprise owners.

Financial Performance
Note: Growth rates may differ after conversion to US dollars.

Mitsubishi UFJ Financial Group (MUFG) revenues in the last five years fallen by 28% with its lowest at Â 1.9 trillion in 2017 before settling at Â 3.4 trillion in 2019. Net income followed a similar pattern as it has risen and fallen in the same period with Â 1.2 trillion in 2017 at its peak and Â 202.7 billion in 2017 at its lowest.

MUFG recognizes revenue from net interest income trust fees and commissions net trading profit and net other operating profit which together amounted to Â 4.1 trillion in 2020 up from Â 3.6 trillion.

The company's net income fell by 57% to Â 306 billion in 2020. General and administrative expenses for the year increased Â 154.7 billion to Â 2.8 trillion due to increase in expenses for overseas operations because of the expansion of business and expenses for regulatory compliance purposes.

The holding company added Â 3.9 trillion to its cash stores in 2020 to Â 78.6 trillion. Operations used Â 1.4 trillion mostly on reductions in trading account liabilities excluding foreign exchange contracts. The company used another Â 18.1 trillion for investments mostly for loans funds sold and receivables as well as the acquisition of Bank Danamon and FSI. Financing activities provided Â 23.8 trillion primarily from net increases in deposits call money funds purchased and payables under repurchase agreements and securities lending transactions.

Strategy
MUFG is implementing "Eleven Transformation Initiatives" - specific strategic initiatives designed to enable the company to cope with adverse changes in the domestic or overseas business environment and to achieve sustainable growth. Each initiative constitutes a pillar involving business operations that have large growth potential allows MUFG to expand its group capabilities to the fullest extent and is expected to grow as a core business or a foundation for such.

The company took strategic steps towards building a business platform in South East Asia through the expansion of Krungsri's business in Thailand and strategic investments in Security Bank in the Philippines and Bank Danamon in Indonesia. The Bank enhances the enterprise value of each of MUFG Union Bank in the United States and other major local commercial banking subsidiaries.

The bank will implement core strategies based on enhanced management policy due to the impact of the COVID-19 pandemic. These core strategies include digitalization of the domestic retail business restructuring of the global strategy implementation of further operational foundation and process reforms and creation of a work environment and operational infrastructure that reflect and support the diverse values of employees and work style reforms.

In relation with its implementation of these core strategies MUFG invested $706 million in Grab to jointly develop next generation bespoke financial services in Southeast Asia to boost financial inclusion in the region.

Mergers and Acquisitions
In August 2019 Mitsubishi UFJ Trust and Banking completed its acquisition of 100% of the shares in each of nine subsidiaries of Colonial First State Group Limited which collectively represent the global asset management business known as Colonial First State Global Asset Management or CFSGAM from Australian financial group Commonwealth Bank of Australia and its wholly-owned subsidiary Colonial First State Group Limited. As a result of the acquisition the nine subsidiaries became our consolidated subsidiaries. In September 2019 CFSGAM was rebranded as First Sentier Investors. The price was approximately AU$4.2 billion or Â 312 billion in cash.

In November 2019 MUFG Bank completed its acquisition from DVB Bank SE in Germany of DVB Bank's aviation finance lending portfolio employees and related operating infrastructure based on an agreement entered into among the two banks and BOT Lease Co. Ltd

Company Background
MUFG was formed in the 2005 merger of Mitsubishi Tokyo Financial Group and UFJ Holdings.

HISTORY
Mitsubishi Bank emerged from the exchange office of the original Mitsubishi zaibatsu (industrial group) in 1885. It evolved into a full-service bank by 1895 and became independent in 1919 though its primary customers were Mitsubishi group companies. The bank survived WWII but a US fiat dismantled the zaibatsu after the war. Mitsubishi Bank reopened as Chiyoda Bank in 1948. After reopening offices in London and New York the bank readopted the Mitsubishi name.

In the 1950s Mitsubishi Bank became the lead lender for the reconstituted Mitsubishi group (keiretsu). In the 1960s it followed its Mitsubishi partners overseas helping finance Japan's growing international trade. In 1972 it acquired the Bank of California and began doing more business outside the group.

Japan's overinflated real estate market of the 1980s devastated many of the country's banks including Nippon Trust Bank of which Mitsubishi owned 5%. Japan's Ministry of Finance (MoF) urged Mitsubishi to bail Nippon out; as a reward for raising its stake in Nippon to 69% and assuming a mountain of unrecoverable loans the MoF allowed Mitsubishi to begin issuing debt before other Japanese banks. In 1995 Mitsubishi Bank and Bank of Tokyo agreed to merge.

Bank of Tokyo (BOT) was established in 1880 as the Yokohama Specie Bank; the Iwasaki family founders of the Mitsubishi group served on its board. With links to the Imperial family the bank was heavily influenced by government policy. With Japan isolated after the Sino-Japanese War its international operations suffered greatly even before WWII. Completely dismantled after WWII the bank was re-established in 1946 as the Bank of Tokyo a commercial city bank bereft of its foreign exchange business. During the 1950s the government restored it as a foreign exchange specialist but regulations limited its domestic business.

BOT evolved into an investment bank in the 1970s; its reputation as the leading foreign exchange bank brought in international clients and successful derivatives trading and overseas banking. By the time BOT and Mitsubishi Bank agreed to merge BOT had 363 foreign offices (only 37 in Japan) with more foreign than Japanese employees.

The two banks merged in 1996 to form The Bank of Tokyo-Mitsubishi (BTM); Mitsubishi was the surviving entity. Their California banks merged to create Union Bank of California (UnionBanCal). The next year BTM reorganized its operations but had problems assimilating its disparate corporate cultures.

In 1998 Japanese banking regulators doled out nearly $240 billion to the industry to prop up failing banks and to strengthen healthier ones. Also that year BTM was fined for bribing MoF officials with entertainment gifts and posted a huge loss after writing off $8.4 billion in bad debt. Losses continued in 1999 and the bank responded by reorganizing operationally cutting jobs and offices and selling stock in UnionBanCal.

In 2000 BTM announced plans to form a financial group with Mitsubishi Trust Bank and Nippon Trust Bank. The following year the three banks unified and formed Mitsubishi Tokyo Financial Group. Before rolling into Mitsubishi Trust Financial Group BTM paid back the money showered upon it by the Japanese government in 1998.

In 2004 MTFG introduced a new organizational structure that focused on its three core markets — retail corporate and trust asset businesses. The company planned to unify business within each division and to improve decision-making companywide. The group also introduced a new executive officer system with the idea of separating company oversight and business execution. A mechanism for credit risk control was also added.

It was all to change in 2005 however. During this time Mitsubishi Tokyo Financial Group merged with UFJ Holdings emerging (at that time)

as the world's largest bank by assets. As a result of the merger the group was renamed Mitsubishi UFJ Financial Group (MUFG).

As with most of its peers MUFG was not immune to the global credit crisis that began in 2007. Its NICOS consumer lending subsidiary had a disappointing year due to the credit crunch. The unit sold its installment credit car loan and car leasing businesses to JACCS in 2008. In 2009 MUFG announced plans to close 50 branches and cut nearly 1000 jobs as a part of a long-term restructuring plan. In addition the bank shut down some 200 ATMs and relocated another 1000 employees.

In 2008 the group bought the rest of Union-BanCal and Mitsubishi UFJ NICOS it didn't already own and acquired a stake in bulge-bracket firm Morgan Stanley. MUFG also bought a 10% stake in UK-based Aberdeen Asset Management that year. (It later upped its interest to around 17%.)

EXECUTIVES

President and CEO Bank of Tokyo-Mitsubishi UFJ and Director, Takashi Oyamada, age 65
Senior Managing Executive Officer Group CSO and Group CHRO and Director, Tadashi Kuroda
President and Group CEO Mitsubishi UFJ Financial Group and Chairman Bank of Tokyo-Mitsubishi UFJ, Nobuyuki Hirano, age 69
Deputy Chairman President and CEO Mitsubishi UFJ Securities Holdings Company and President and CEO Mitsubishi UFJ Morgan Stanley Securities Company, Takashi Nagaoka
Managing Executive Officer Group Chief Risk Officer and Director, Masamichi (Mitch) Yasuda, age 59
Senior Managing Executive Officer Group CFO and Director, Muneaki Tokunari
Chairman Mitsubishi UFJ Trust and Banking Corporation and Director, Tatsuo Wakabayashi
Chief Executive and Managing Officer Europe Middle East and Africa (EMEA), Masahiro Kuwahara
Deputy Chairman, Mikio Ikegaya
Chairman, Kiyoshi Sono
Auditors: Deloitte Touche Tohmatsu LLC

LOCATIONS

HQ: Mitsubishi UFJ Financial Group Inc
7-1 Marunouchi 2-chome, Chiyoda-ku, Tokyo 100-8330
Phone: (81) 3 3240 8111   **Fax:** (81) 3 3240 7073
Web: www.mufg.jp

2018 Sales

	% of total
Japan	41
US	26
Europe	10
Asia/Oceania	15
Other regions	8
Total	**100**

PRODUCTS/OPERATIONS

2018 Sales

	% of total
Interest	
Loans including fees	44
Deposits in other banks	2
Investment securities	
Interest	4
Dividends	3
Trading account assets	8
Other	2
Noninterest	
Fees & commissions	28
Foreign exchange gains	-
Trading accounts profits	
Investment securities gains	6
Equity in earnings of equity method investees	4
Gains in sales of loans	

Other	1
Total	**100**

2018 Sales

	% of total
Retail & Commercial Banking Business Group	41
Japanese Corporate & Investment Banking Business Group	13
Global Corporate & Investment Banking Business Group	9
Global Commercial Banking Business Group	16
Asset Management & Investor Services Business Group	5
Global Markets Business Group	15
Total	**100**

COMPETITORS

Aozora Bank	ORIX
BNP Paribas Bangkok	Resona
Citigroup	Shinsei Bank
HSBC	Sony
Japan Post	Sumitomo Mitsui
Mizuho Financial	Sumitomo Mitsui Trust
Mizuho Trust & Banking	Holdings
Ltd	

HISTORICAL FINANCIALS

Company Type: Public

Income Statement
FYE: March 31

	ASSETS ($ mil.)	NET INCOME ($ mil.)	INCOME AS % OF ASSETS	EMPLOYEES
03/20	3,056,220	2,818	0.1%	168,400
03/19	2,756,168	6,489	0.2%	144,700
03/18	2,830,578	11,566	0.4%	144,000
03/17	2,658,025	1,812	0.1%	143,400
03/16	2,605,329	7,144	0.3%	139,900
Annual Growth	4.1%	(20.7%)	—	4.7%

2020 Year-End Financials

Return on assets: 0.1%	Dividends
Return on equity: 2.0%	Yield: 5.9%
Long-term debt ($ mil.): —	Payout: 100.7%
No. of shares (mil.): —	Market value ($ mil.): —
Sales ($ mil): 50,830	

	STOCK PRICE ($) FY Close	P/E High/Low		PER SHARE ($) Earnings	Dividends	Book Value
03/20	3.66	0	0	0.22	0.22	10.77
03/19	4.95	0	0	0.49	0.19	10.62
03/18	6.64	0	0	0.87	0.17	10.71
03/17	6.34	0	0	0.13	0.17	9.31
03/16	4.59	0	0	0.51	0.15	9.22
Annual Growth	(5.5%)	—	—	(19.4%)	10.4%	4.0%

Mitsui & Co., Ltd.

Auditors: Deloitte Touche Tohmatsu LLC

LOCATIONS

HQ: Mitsui & Co., Ltd.
1-2-1 Otemachi, Chiyoda-ku, Tokyo 100-8631
Phone: (81) 3 3285 1111   **Fax:** (81) 3 3285 9819
Web: www.mitsui.com

HISTORICAL FINANCIALS

Company Type: Public

Income Statement
FYE: March 31

	REVENUE ($ mil.)	NET INCOME ($ mil.)	NET PROFIT MARGIN	EMPLOYEES
03/20	69,420	3,947	5.7%	56,384
03/19	70,151	4,176	6.0%	54,347
03/18	49,326	4,219	8.6%	54,288
03/17	44,000	3,086	7.0%	52,304
03/16	47,990	(841)	—	54,395
Annual Growth	9.7%	—	—	0.9%

2020 Year-End Financials

Debt ratio: 0.3%	No. of shares (mil.): 1,707
Return on equity: 9.6%	Dividends
Cash ($ mil.): 10,674	Yield: 5.3%
Current ratio: 1.53	Payout: 648.8%
Long-term debt ($ mil.): 38,850	Market value ($ mil.): 468,439

	STOCK PRICE ($) FY Close	P/E High/Low		PER SHARE ($) Earnings	Dividends	Book Value
03/20	274.34	2	1	2.28	14.78	22.54
03/19	311.09	2	1	2.40	14.34	24.73
03/18	346.53	2	1	2.39	10.69	23.06
03/17	291.47	2	1	1.73	10.50	21.33
03/16	229.94	—	—	(0.47)	10.36	19.01
Annual Growth	4.5%	—	—	—	9.3%	4.4%

Mitsui Fudosan Co Ltd

EXECUTIVES

Chairman and CEO, Hiromichi Iwasa
EVP, Yoshiaki Iinuma
Senior Executive Managing Officer, Hitoshi Saito
President and CEO, Masanobu Komoda
Senior Executive Managing Officer, Yoshikazu Kitahara
Group Senior Officer Mitsui Fudosan Investment Advisors, Shogo Nakai
Group Senior Officer Mitsui Fudosan Reform, Masatoshi Ozaki
Group Officer Mitsui Fudosan Residential, Tooru Inoue
Senior Executive Managing Officer, Shoichiro Kawamoto
Executive Managing Officer, Kiyotaka Fujibayashi
Executive Managing Officer, Masatoshi Satou
Executive Managing Officer, Yasuo Onozawa
Executive Managing Officer, Hiroyuki Ishigami
Executive Managing Officer, Takashi Yamamoto
Executive Managing Officer, Akihiko Funaoka
Executive Managing Officer, Takashi Ueda
Auditors: KPMG AZSA LLC

LOCATIONS

HQ: Mitsui Fudosan Co Ltd
2-1-1 Nihonbashi-Muromachi, Chuo-ku, Tokyo 103-0022
Phone: (81) 3 3246 3055
Web: www.mitsuifudosan.co.jp

PRODUCTS/OPERATIONS

FY2016 Sales

	% of total
Leasing	31
Property Sales	29
Management	20
Mitsui Home	14
Other	6
Total	**100**

Selected Group Companies

Housing
  Daiichi Engei Co. Ltd.
  MITSUI Designtec Co. Ltd.
  Mitsui Fudosan Housing Lease Co. Ltd.
  Mitsui Fudosan Realty Co. Ltd.
  Mitsui Fudosan Reform Co. Ltd.
  Mitsui Fudosan Residential Co. Ltd.
  Mitsui Fudosan Residential Service Chugoku Co. Ltd.
  Mitsui Fudosan Residential Service Co. Ltd.
  Mitsui Fudosan Residential Service Hokkaido Co. Ltd.
  Mitsui Fudosan Residential Service Kansai Co. Ltd.
  Mitsui Fudosan Residential Service Kyusyu Co. Ltd.
  Mitsui Fudosan Residential Service Tohoku Co. Ltd.
  Mitsui Home Co. Ltd.
  Mitsui Home Estate Co. Ltd.
Office Buildings
  First Facilities West Co. Ltd.
  Mitsui Fudosan Building Management Co. Ltd.
  Mitsui Fudosan Facilities Co. Ltd.
  NBF Office Management Co. Ltd.
  Nippon Building Fund Management Ltd.
Retail Properties
  Frontier REIT SC Management Co. Ltd.
  Mitsui Fudosan Frontier REIT Management Inc.
  Mitsui Fudosan Retail Management Co.Ltd.
Accommodation
  Celestine Hotel Co. Ltd.
  Mitsui Fudosan Accommodations Fund Management.
  Mitsui Fudosan Hotel Management Co. Ltd.
  Mitsui Fudosan Housing Lease Co. Ltd.
Real Estate Solutions
  Mitsui Fudosan Investment Advisors Inc.
Resort
  Kyusin Kaihatsu Inc.
  LaLaport Agency Co. Ltd.

COMPETITORS

CBRE Group	Sumitomo Forestry
Daikyo	Sumitomo Realty
Heiwa Real Estate	Tokyu Corporation
Mitsubishi Estate	

HISTORICAL FINANCIALS

Company Type: Public

Income Statement

FYE: March 31

	REVENUE ($ mil.)	NET INCOME ($ mil.)	NET PROFIT MARGIN	EMPLOYEES
03/20	17,555	1,694	9.7%	34,555
03/19	16,806	1,522	9.1%	32,327
03/18	16,490	1,467	8.9%	31,612
03/17	15,244	1,178	7.7%	30,691
03/16	13,962	1,048	7.5%	30,379
Annual Growth	5.9%	12.8%	—	3.3%

2020 Year-End Financials

Debt ratio: 0.4%
Return on equity: 7.7%
Cash ($ mil.): 1,689
Current ratio: 2.30
Long-term debt ($ mil.): 28,016

No. of shares (mil.): 971
Dividends
  Yield: 2.7%
  Payout: 73.7%
Market value ($ mil.): 45,331

	STOCK PRICE ($) FY Close	P/E High/Low		PER SHARE ($) Earnings	Dividends	Book Value
03/20	46.68	0	0	1.73	1.28	22.86
03/19	75.63	0	0	1.55	1.14	21.55
03/18	63.00	0	0	1.48	1.02	21.02
03/17	53.85	—	—	1.19	0.88	17.97
03/16	53.85	—	—	1.06	0.75	17.33
Annual Growth	(3.5%)	—	—	13.1%	14.3%	7.2%

Miyazaki Bank, Ltd. (The)

Auditors: Deloitte Touche Tohmatsu LLC

LOCATIONS

HQ: Miyazaki Bank, Ltd. (The)
  4-3-5 Tachibanadori-Higashi, Miyazaki 880-0805
Phone: (81) 985 27 3131
Web: www.miyagin.co.jp

COMPETITORS

Aozora Bank	Mizuho Trust & Banking Ltd
Bank of Yokohama	
Iyo Bank	Norinchukin Bank
Michinoku Bank	Shizuoka Bank
Mitsubishi UFJ Financial Group	Towa Bank

HISTORICAL FINANCIALS

Company Type: Public

Income Statement

FYE: March 31

	ASSETS ($ mil.)	NET INCOME ($ mil.)	INCOME AS % OF ASSETS	EMPLOYEES
03/20	30,631	65	0.2%	1,942
03/19	28,007	87	0.3%	2,000
03/18	27,937	82	0.3%	2,027
03/17	26,640	82	0.3%	2,014
03/16	24,710	87	0.4%	2,023
Annual Growth	5.5%	(6.9%)	—	(1.0%)

2020 Year-End Financials

Return on assets: 0.2%
Return on equity: 4.7%
Long-term debt ($ mil.): —
No. of shares (mil.): 17
Sales ($ mil): 523

Dividends
  Yield: —
  Payout: 24.2%
Market value ($ mil.): —

Mizrahi Tefahot Bank Ltd

Auditors: Brightman Almagor Zohar & Co.

LOCATIONS

HQ: Mizrahi Tefahot Bank Ltd
  7 Jabotinsky Street, P.O. Box 3450, Ramat Gan 5252007
Phone: (972) 3 7559000   **Fax:** (972) 3 7559210
Web: www.mizrahi-tefahot.co.il

HISTORICAL FINANCIALS

Company Type: Public

Income Statement

FYE: December 31

	ASSETS ($ mil.)	NET INCOME ($ mil.)	INCOME AS % OF ASSETS	EMPLOYEES
12/19	79,083	533	0.7%	6,433
12/18	68,727	321	0.5%	6,355
12/17	69,014	388	0.6%	6,271
12/16	60,000	329	0.5%	6,141
12/15	53,474	289	0.5%	5,864
Annual Growth	10.3%	16.4%	—	2.3%

2019 Year-End Financials

Return on assets: 0.6%
Return on equity: 11.9%
Long-term debt ($ mil.): —
No. of shares (mil.): 234
Sales ($ mil): 2,800

Dividends
  Yield: —
  Payout: 30.5%
Market value ($ mil.): —

MMC Norilsk Nickel PJSC

Auditors: JSC KPMG

LOCATIONS

HQ: MMC Norilsk Nickel PJSC
  18 building 13, Stromynka Street, Moscow 107996
Phone: (7) 495 989 76 50   **Fax:** (7) 495 780 73 67
Web: www.nornik.ru

HISTORICAL FINANCIALS

Company Type: Public

Income Statement

FYE: December 31

	REVENUE ($ mil.)	NET INCOME ($ mil.)	NET PROFIT MARGIN	EMPLOYEES
12/19	13,563	5,782	42.6%	0
12/18	11,670	3,085	26.4%	75,901
12/17	9,146	2,129	23.3%	78,950
12/16	8,259	2,536	30.7%	82,006
12/15	8,542	1,734	20.3%	83,624
Annual Growth	12.3%	35.1%	—	—

2019 Year-End Financials

Debt ratio: 50.5%
Return on equity: 164.3%
Cash ($ mil.): 2,784
Current ratio: 1.21
Long-term debt ($ mil.): 8,713

No. of shares (mil.): 158
Dividends
  Yield: 11.7%
  Payout: 9.8%
Market value ($ mil.): 4,825

	STOCK PRICE ($) FY Close	P/E High/Low		PER SHARE ($) Earnings	Dividends	Book Value
12/19	30.49	1	1	36.50	3.58	24.10
12/18	18.84	1	1	19.50	2.13	20.37
12/17	18.91	2	1	13.50	1.11	27.34
12/16	16.92	1	1	16.10	1.11	24.15
12/15	12.70	2	1	11.00	2.06	14.26
Annual Growth	24.5%	—	—	35.0%	14.7%	14.0%

Morrison (Wm.) Supermarkets Plc

One of UK's largest grocery chain WM Morrison ("Morrisons") runs over 490 stores and some 330 adjoined petrol stations throughout England Scotland and Wales. The company stock the usual variety of groceries household goods and health and beauty products. It offers online delivery in partnership with Amazon and deferred entry into Ocado's Erith Customer fulfillment Centre until early 2021. It sells products wholesale to convenience store operator McColls under the Safeway brand. Founded by William Morrison in 1899 its purchase of the UK's Safeway chain transformed WM Morrison into a national brand with some 10% share of the UK grocery market.

Operations

Morrisons makes about 75% of its revenue from the sale of goods in store and online including its wholesale activities. Some 20% of its revenue comes from fuel sales and the remaining was generated from the other sales.

The shops are noted for their Market Street departments a collection of in-store specialty shops that ring the perimeter of the store. They include a bakery butcher shop and other highly skilled food specialist. Market Street departments also offer pies quiches pastries cheese and eggs as well as fruit and vegetables such as jackfruit pizza and vegan pasties. Outlets also have in-store cafes.

Morrisons also offers online delivery. The Morrisons have deferred its entry into Ocado's Erith Customer Fulfilment Centre (CFC) until early-2021 when there is an expected reduce start-up costs. In the meantime the company is now picking Morrisons.com orders from almost 40 stores and have extended coverage area to over 90% of British households. 'Morrisons at Amazon' where the Morrisons store on Prime Now the ultra-fast same day online grocery home delivery service has now extended to eight cities across the UK.

It operates about 20 manufacturing sites in the UK and manufactures around half of the fresh food it sells. Its distribution network consists of seven regional and one national distribution centers.

Geographic Reach

Morrisons boasts over 490 stores scattered across the UK along with some 50 Morrisons Daily convenience stores and around 335 petrol filling stations. There are over 115 stores located in the Northern parts of UK some 145 stores in Central and approximately 230 stores in the South.

Morrisons' headquarter is in Bradford UK.

Sales and Marketing

Morrison's reaches around 12 million customers each week. Customer service operations include contact center which receives emails and calls. The company's website www.morrisons.com allows the customer to shop online.

The company's More Card loyalty card scheme grants customers points on purchases.

Morrison has two principal wholesale customers. It supplies some 1100 McColls conveniences stores in the UK with products under the Safeway wholesale brand. It also supplies Amazon under a wholesale agreement where the Morrison stores on Prime Now our ultra-fast same day online grocery home delivery service has now extended to eight cities across the UK.

Financial Performance

Revenue of WM Morrison grew steadily since 2016 except in 2020 when it dipped slightly. In that span the revenue grew by 9%. Reported profit jumped 57% for the same period.

In fiscal 2020 WM Morrison's revenue decreased by 1% to Â 17.5 billion. Like-for-like sales (excluding fuel) were down 1% including negative contributions from supermarkets.

Net income increased 49% to Â 348 million in fiscal 2020 mainly due to an increase in operating profit.

WM Morrison's cash on hand increased in fiscal 2020 Â 41 million higher at Â 305 million compared to 2019. It generated Â 826 million from its operations while it used Â 467 million in its investing activities and Â 318 million in its financing activities. Morrison's main cash uses in 2020 were for property plant and equipment purchases debt repayments and dividends payments.

Strategy

WM Morrison employ the following strategies to ensure that its business is adequately prepared for the potential threats or opportunities these present: Strategic and operational horizon scanning across the business; Working with key strategic partners to share emerging consumer trends; and using third party experts to assist with the consideration of emerging risks and legislation.

A non-exhaustive list of emerging risks currently being monitored include: Consumer eating habits and trends; Sustainability and ethical trading; Environmental and climate change; and Continued innovation in technology.

Company Background

Wm Morrison was founded in 1899 by William Morrison in Bradford as an egg and butter wholesaler. It expanded into grocery retail in the 1920s and transitioned to the increasingly popular self-service format in the 1940s and 1950s. With William's son Ken at the helm from 1956 the company went public in the late 1960s but despite its growing size and store count did not stray much from its Northern England and Midlands base. This changed in 2004 when it acquired the much larger Safeway which owned nearly 500 stores across the South of England Wales and Scotland. Honorary president Ken Morrison passed away in 2017.

HISTORY

A former grocer's apprentice William Morrison founded his company in Bradford UK in 1899 as a wholesale seller of eggs and butter. Named William Morrison (Provisions) the business eventually expanded into retail by opening grocery stalls and by the 1920s was operating counter service shops as well.

Self-service stores became popular in the UK during the late 1940s and 1950s and the company began opening self-service outlets during that time. William's son Ken (born when William was 57 years of age) joined the company in 1950 and became chairman in 1956. The chain opened its first supermarket in Bradford in 1962 by converting an abandoned cinema. Wm Morrison Supermarkets went public five years later.

In 1979 Wm Morrison moved into Lancashire by purchasing the 10-store grocery chain Whelans Discount founded by Dave Whelan an ex-football star who also founded JJB Sports. Two years later it bought the Mainstop chain. The company's sales grew by a factor of 10 during the 1980s and 1990; it added about 50 stores in the 1990s. In 1993 Wm Morrison began opening stores on Sundays and in 1997 it teamed up with Midland Bank to offer in-store banking.

The company had operated mostly in northeastern England but a new distribution center that opened in 1996 in Cheshire allowed it to handle more distribution duties and gave it the base to expand west. Wm Morrison also turned south opening superstores in three southern regions (Oxford Essex and Kent) in 1998. The retailer also acquired two stores from Food Giant and three superstores (one near London) from Co-operative Retail Services that year. Wm Morrison expanded its Farmers Boy food processing operations by opening a new 180000-sq.-ft. facility in 1999. It opened four new stores in 2000 and bought three others.

The company's highly regarded Managing Director John Dowd resigned in March 2002 because of ill health. Soon after Marie Melnyk and Robert Stott were promoted to the positions of joint managing director. Morrison added six stores in fiscal year 2003 (ended January 2003).

On January 9 2003 Morrison made an offer of 1.32 Morrison shares for each share of Safeway plc. In March the company's bid for its rival lapsed after the Office of Fair Trading referred the bid to the Competition Commission.

Following clearance from Britain's High Court the company's acquisition of Safeway closed on March 8 2004. (Morrison shareholders own 60% of the enlarged company with Safeway shareholders left with 40%.)

In June 2006 the company named Marc Bolland formerly COO of brewer Heineken as CEO succeeding Bob Stott who retired. Stott became CEO in 2005.

Sir Kenneth Morrison retired as chairman in March 2008 after 55 years with the company. Morrison who was named honorary president was succeeded by former deputy chairman Sir Ian Gibson. The grocery chain opened eight new supermarkets in fiscal 2008.

In 2009 Morrisons acquired about 40 Co-operative Group and former Somerfield stores for about Â 220 million (about $330 million). In November Bolland resigned to join Marks and Spencer. He was succeeded by Dalton Philips who joined the business in March 2010.

In 2011 Morrisons acquired about 18 Netto UK stores from ASDA. In June it bought Flower World an importer and wholesaler of flowers in the UK in a bid to improve the flower offering at its supermarkets.

EXECUTIVES

CEO and Director, David T. Potts, age 63
CTO, Anna Barsby
CFO, Trevor Strain
Chairman, Andrew T. Higginson, age 62
Auditors: PricewaterhouseCoopers LLP

LOCATIONS

HQ: Morrison (Wm.) Supermarkets Plc
  Hilmore House, Gain Lane, Bradford BD3 7DL
Phone: (44) 845 611 5000
Web: www.morrisons.com

PRODUCTS/OPERATIONS

2018 Sales

	% of total
Food & general merchandise	75
Other sales	4
Fuel	21
Total	**100**

COMPETITORS

ALDI	Lidl
ASDA	Marks & Spencer
BP	Musgrave Retail
Co-operative Group	Partners
Exxon Mobil	Royal Dutch Shell
J Sainsbury	SPAR (UK)
John Lewis	Tesco

HISTORICAL FINANCIALS
Company Type: Public

Income Statement				FYE: February 2
	REVENUE ($ mil.)	NET INCOME ($ mil.)	NET PROFIT MARGIN	EMPLOYEES
02/20	23,015	456	2.0%	98,619
02/19	23,173	318	1.4%	103,630
02/18*	24,545	442	1.8%	105,487
01/17	20,452	382	1.9%	112,365
01/16	23,072	317	1.4%	120,913
Annual Growth	(0.1%)	9.5%	—	(5.0%)

*Fiscal year change

2020 Year-End Financials

Debt ratio: 16.1%	No. of shares (mil.): —
Return on equity: 7.6%	Dividends
Cash ($ mil.): 400	Yield: 0.0%
Current ratio: 0.39	Payout: 397.0%
Long-term debt ($ mil.): 1,454	Market value ($ mil.): —

	STOCK PRICE ($) FY Close	P/E High/Low	PER SHARE ($) Earnings	Dividends	Book Value
02/20	11.91	111 79	0.19	0.75	2.48
02/19	15.44	171 129	0.13	0.74	2.56
02/18*	15.61	135 110	0.19	0.33	2.74
01/17	15.00	117 82	0.16	0.26	2.18
01/16	12.62	157 104	0.14	0.75	2.30
Annual Growth	(1.4%)	— —	8.7%	0.2%	1.9%

*Fiscal year change

MS&AD Insurance Group Holdings

MS&AD Insurance Group has insurance in Japan covered. MS&AD Insurance Group is the holding company for several large Japanese insurance companies including Mitsui Sumitomo Insurance (MSI) Aioi Nissay Dowa Insurance (ADI) Mitsui Direct General MSI Aioi Life and MSI Primary Life. Together the insurance companies offer property/casualty (e.g. auto personal fire marine) and life insurance as well as asset management (mutual funds financial consulting) and risk management services. MS&AD Insurance's about 185 subsidiaries which serve individuals and businesses in Japan also offer products and services to customers in about 50 countries in Europe Asia and the Americas.

Operations
MS&AD has five primary operating divisions: domestic non-life (property/casualty) insurance domestic life insurance International business financial services and risk-related services. Each of its non-life firms underwrites policies in the fire and allied marine personal accident automobile and other arenas. The life insurers underwrite individual policies individual annuity insurance group insurance and other products.

Subsidiary MSI provides insurance and financial services around the world. In Japan it has a network of more than 250 branches about 1000 offices and more than 400 service centers.

Geographic Reach
MS&AD operates in about 50 nations in the Asia/Pacific region in Europe and in the Americas.

Sales and Marketing
MS&AD subsidiary MSI has about 1000 sales offices and more than 400 service centers in Japan. It also provides services in about 50 countries around the globe.

Mitsui Direct General sells automobile policies-supports safe driving by utilizing a dashboard camera. MSI Aioi Life markets its products through financial institutions life insurance agencies and a direct sales force.

Financial Performance
Revenue in 2019 was Â 5.5 trillion a Â 282.6 billion increase from the prior year. Thanks to increase in net premiums written income investment income and other ordinary income.

Net income in 2019 was Â 194.4 billion a Â 40.5 billion increase from the previous year. The increase was primarily due to a larger revenue in 2019.

Cash and cash equivalents at end of 2019 totaled Â 1.8 trillion. Operating activities generated Â 776.7 billion. Investing and financing activities used Â 252.4 billion and Â 33.3 billion respectively. Main cash uses in 2019 were for securities purchase and dividends paid.

Strategy
The MS&AD Insurance Group will enhance its competitiveness while responding to rapid changes in an uncertain environment by making the most of diversity as one of its strengths. Fiscal 2018 saw steady progress in product developments led by two domestic non-life insurance companies collaboration in the cyber security field utilizing the experience and capabilities of MS&AD InterRisk Research & Consulting and other similar initiatives. The company will continue to strengthen cooperation within the group to achieve a greater level of quality and administrative efficiency.

Given rapid advances in digital technology the company is now looking toward a period of transition in conventional lifestyles and business models. With the Chief Digitalization Officer (CDO) playing a central role the entire MS&AD Insurance Group is working to promote "digitalization*" and connecting it to a transformation of the company's business model. The MS&AD Insurance Group aims to enhance the value of experience for customers when they contact individual Group companies and improve the business productivity of the MS&AD Group at the same time.

Mergers and Acquisitions
In 2019 Ceylinco Insurance PLC acquired to become an equity affiliate by MSI.

In 2019 Sumitomo Mitsui Asset Management and Daiwa SB Investment merged to form Sumitomo Mitsui DS Asset Management.

Company Background
Formed in 2008 as a holding company for the Mitsui Sumitomo operations MS&AD Insurance became the parent of a larger group of insurance companies through a three-way merger between Mitsui Sumitomo Aioi Insurance and Nissay Dowa General Insurance in 2010.

EXECUTIVES
Chairman MSI, Toshiaki Egashira, age 72
President CEO and Representative Director, Yasuyoshi Karasawa, age 70
Executive Officer Marketing and Sales, Masaaki Nishikata
Executive Officer Administration and Information Systems, Tetsuya Yoshikawa
Chairman, Hisahito Suzuki, age 70
Auditors: KPMG AZSA LLC

LOCATIONS
HQ: MS&AD Insurance Group Holdings
2-27-2 Shinkawa, Chuo-ku, Tokyo 104-0033
Phone: (81) 3 5117 0270
Web: www.ms-ad-hd.com

PRODUCTS/OPERATIONS

2018 Sales

	% of total
Underwriting income	89
Investment income	11
Total	**100**

Selected Products
Compulsory Automobile Liability
Fire and Allied Insurance
Life
Marine
Personal Accident
Voluntary Automobile

COMPETITORS

Allianz	Prudential
Allstate	Prudential plc
Dai-ichi Life	Samsung Fire & Marine
Fuji Fire and Marine	Sompo Holdings
Hyundai Marine & Fire	Sumitomo Life
ING	Tokio Marine

HISTORICAL FINANCIALS
Company Type: Public

Income Statement				FYE: March 31
	REVENUE ($ mil.)	NET INCOME ($ mil.)	NET PROFIT MARGIN	EMPLOYEES
03/20	42,602	1,317	3.1%	50,633
03/19	48,721	1,740	3.6%	50,609
03/18	47,601	1,450	3.0%	51,040
03/17	47,225	1,882	4.0%	50,791
03/16	42,764	1,616	3.8%	50,790
Annual Growth	(0.1%)	(5.0%)	—	(0.1%)

2020 Year-End Financials

Debt ratio: —	No. of shares (mil.): 569
Return on equity: 5.4%	Dividends
Cash ($ mil.): 32,360	Yield: 4.8%
Current ratio: —	Payout: 29.5%
Long-term debt ($ mil.): —	Market value ($ mil.): 7,859

	STOCK PRICE ($) FY Close	P/E High/Low	PER SHARE ($) Earnings	Dividends	Book Value
03/20	13.81	0 0	2.29	0.67	39.71
03/19	15.24	0 0	2.97	0.61	42.56
03/18	15.61	0 0	2.45	0.64	46.76
03/17	15.92	0 0	3.14	0.48	40.90
03/16	13.87	0 0	2.66	0.29	39.80
Annual Growth	(0.1%)	— —	(3.7%)	23.6%	(0.1%)

Muenchener Rueckversicherungs-Gesellschaft AG (Germany)

Some companies live with risk... M nchener R ckversicherungs-Gesellschaft (Munich Re) on the other hand thrives on it. Reinsurance coverage (insurance for insurers) includes fire life motor and liability policies on both a facultative (individual risk) and treaty (categorized risk) basis. The company also provides direct insurance including life health and property coverage through Germany-based ERGO and other subsidiaries and it provides asset management services through MEAG MUNICH ERGO. Through Munich Re America Munich Re enjoys greater access to the US market. As one of the world's largest reinsurance and risk management firms the company's ERGO operates in more than 30 countries.

Operations

Munich Re divides its business into five segments: Life & Health Reinsurance and Property-Casualty Reinsurance which both operate globally; and ERGO Life & Health Germany (life and health and property-casualty insurance in Germany and global travel insurance) ERGO Property/Casualty Germany and ERGO International.

Life & health reinsurance generates almost 45% of total sales. It focuses on traditional reinsurance solutions that concentrate on the transfer of mortality risk. It is also active in the market of living benefits products such as occupational disability long-term care and critical illness. Property-casualty reinsurance produces nearly 25% of total sales.

Overall Reinsurance activities account for over 65% of total sales while ERGO generates the rest.

Munich Re also generates interest income on repurchase agreements on securities.

Geographic Reach

Headquartered in Munich Germany Europe is Munich Re's largest market accounting for almost 55% of the company's gross premiums written followed by North America that generates nearly 30% of gross premiums written. The remaining gross premiums written are from Asia & Australasia Africa Middle East and Latin America.

Sales and Marketing

Munich Re's ERGO does business with around 37 million private and corporate clients. As a reinsurer the company also writes its business in direct collaboration with primary insurers and also via brokers.

Financial Performance

Note: Growth rates may differ after conversion to US Dollars.

Munich Re's revenue has been declining by 1-2% per year over the last five years. Its revenue from gross written premiums has shown no signs of consistent growth while profits have also fluctuated in the same period. However figures for 2019 have shown improvement from the year prior.

In fiscal 2019 the company generated total revenue of ?51.5 billion from its gross written premiums a 5% increase from ?49.1 billion the prior year due to corresponding increases in its life and health and property/casualty segments partially offset by a decrease in ERGO.

In 2019 Munich Re posted a profit of ?2.7 billion an 18% increase from the year prior driven by the increase in gross premiums and other operating income despite an increase in overall expenses.

Munich Re ended 2019 with ?5 billion in the back a decrease of ?144 million. Cash from operations generated ?9.5 billion in 2019. Investing activities used ?6.9 billion mainly for acquisition sale and maturity of investments. Financing activities used another ?2.4 billion for dividends paid and other financing activities.

Strategy

Munich Re's strategies are built on the company's competitive advantage in its areas of expertise?a robust combination of financial strength risk know-how and solutions competence?and intimate knowledge of market processes. For its execution Munich Re has set three priorities: increase its earning power drive its digital transformation and reduce the complexity of its organization.

As part of Munich Re's initiatives to increase and stabilize value growth the company will seize business opportunities arising from the on-going demand for large and complex reinsurance programs. At the same time the reinsurance arm will leverage its underwriting competence to take on a wider range of risk in selected areas while rigorously adhering to the risk policies of Munich Re.

Munich Re is also focusing on streamlining and pruning its structures and processes as it has the potential to manage a growing business with fewer resources: the company can simplify or even do away with certain structures and processes without adversely affecting its business operations.

The company is also embracing digitalization and has set up divisions to capture structure and analyze data. Its units Munich Re New Ventures and Digital Partners are opening up new digital market access for Munich Re. Munich Re is also digitally enhancing its core competencies by investing in data analytics and artificial intelligence in order to support its clients in a targeted manner.

Another central pillar is its climate strategy. Munich Re has undertaken to make its investment portfolio climate-neutral by 2050 joining the Net-Zero Asset Owner Alliance under the leadership of the United Nations in which it is working with institutional investors with over $4 trillion in assets under management.

Company Background

Munich Re dates back to 1880 where it gained an upper hand on an already mature reinsurance industry by taking an international approach to reinsurance. The company's guiding principles remain true to this day namely independence from primary insurers a broad spread of risks an efficient system of treaty management working in partnership with clients and innovative insurance concepts.

EXECUTIVES

Management Board Member Reinsurance Corporate Underwriting and Information Technology, Torsten Jeworrek, $859,920 total compensation

Management Board Member Germany Asia Pacific and Africa Division, Ludger Arnoldussen, $573,280 total compensation

Management Board Member Special and Financial Risks Division, Thomas Blunck, $619,859 total compensation

Management Board Member Life Division, Joachim Oechslin

Management Board Member Europe and Latin America Division, Giuseppina Albo

Management Board Member Health Division, Doris H ¶pke

Senior Vice President Chief Financial Officer, Gary Gray

Chairman Management Board, jur. Nikolaus von Bomhard

Chairman Supervisory Board, Ing. Bernd Pischetsrieder

Deputy Chairman Supervisory Board, Marco N ¶renberg

Auditors: KPMG Bayerische Treuhandgesellschaft AG

LOCATIONS

HQ: Muenchener Rueckversicherungs-Gesellschaft AG (Germany)
Koeniginstrasse 107, Munich 80802
Phone: (49) 89 3891 8202   **Fax:** (49) 89 3891 3599
Web: www.munichre.com

2017 Premiums

	% of total
Europe	53
North America	32
Asia & Australasia	9
Latin America	3
Africa Near & Middle East	3
Total	**100**

PRODUCTS/OPERATIONS

2017 Sales

	% of total
Reinsurance	
Property/casualty	35
Life and health	29
ERGO	
Life and health Germany	19
Property/casualty Germany	7
International	10
Total	**100**

Selected Brands

ERGO (primary insurance)
  Deutscher Automobil Schutz (D.A.S. auto insurance)
  Deutsche Krankenversicherung (DKV)
  ERV
ERGO Direkt (commercial customer consulting)
DKV (domestic health insurance)
Munich Health (international health insurance domestic and international health reinsurance)
Munich Re
Munich Re America
  American Modern Insurance (specialty property/casualty insurance life insurance reinsurance)
  Hartford Steam Boiler (HSB specialty property/casualty insurance and reinsurance)

COMPETITORS

AEGON	Manulife Financial
AIG	MetLife
AXA	Nippon Life Insurance
Allianz	OdysseyRe
Allstate	PartnerRe
Berkshire Hathaway	Prudential plc
B loise-Holding	Reinsurance Group of
Chubb Limited	America
Everest Re	RenaissanceRe
General Re	Swiss Re
Hannover Re	Transatlantic Holdings
Helvetia Group	XL Group plc
ING	

HISTORICAL FINANCIALS

Company Type: Public

Income Statement				FYE: December 31
	ASSETS ($ mil.)	NET INCOME ($ mil.)	INCOME AS % OF ASSETS	EMPLOYEES
12/19	322,854	3,058	0.9%	39,662
12/18	309,395	2,645	0.9%	41,410
12/17	318,535	449	0.1%	42,410
12/16	282,770	2,724	1.0%	43,428
12/15	301,188	3,384	1.1%	43,554
Annual Growth	1.8%	(2.5%)	—	(2.3%)

2019 Year-End Financials

Return on assets: 0.9%
Return on equity: 9.5%
Long-term debt ($ mil.): —
No. of shares (mil.): 141
Sales ($ mil): 70,449

Dividends
Yield: 2.4%
Payout: —
Market value ($ mil.): 4,164

	STOCK PRICE ($) FY Close	P/E High/Low		Earnings	PER SHARE ($) Dividends	Book Value
12/19	29.44	2	1	21.30	0.71	241.76
12/18	21.85	1	1	17.78	0.71	207.11
12/17	21.64	10	8	2.92	0.70	222.01
12/16	18.83	1	1	17.03	0.60	212.09
12/15	19.99	1	1	20.40	0.57	205.21
Annual Growth	10.2%	—	—	1.1%	5.9%	4.2%

Murata Manufacturing Co Ltd

EXECUTIVES

President, Tsuneo Murata, age 69
Executive Deputy President, Yoshitaka Fujita
EVP, Yuichi Kojima
EVP, Toru Inoue
EVP, Norio Nakajima
EVP, Hiroshi Iwatsubo
SVP, Yoshito Takemura
VP; President Murata (China) Investment, Hideki Maruyama
EVP, Satoshi Sonoda
VP; President TOKO, Etsuo Hayakawa
Auditors: Deloitte Touche Tohmatsu LLC

LOCATIONS

HQ: Murata Manufacturing Co Ltd
1-10-1 Higashikotari, Nagaokakyo, Kyoto 617-8555
Phone: (81) 75 955 6525 **Fax:** (81) 75 955 6526
Web: www.murata.com

2018 Sales

	% of total
Greater China	50
Asia and Others	17
The Americas	15
Japan	9
Europe	9
Total	100

PRODUCTS/OPERATIONS

2018 Sales

	% of total
Components	70
Modules	30
Others	
Total	100

Selected Products

Ceramic Capacitors
  Disc
  High-frequency power
  High-voltage
  Monolithic
  Trimmer
Microwave Components
  Chip dielectric and multilayer antennas
  Chip multilayer hybrid couplers
  Dielectric resonators
  Field-effect transistors (FETs)
  High-frequency coaxial connectors
  High-frequency microchip and monolithic ceramic capacitors
  Isolators/circulators
  Oscillators
  Radio-frequency (RF) diode switches
Piezoelectric Components
  Buzzers
  Diaphragms
  Ringers
  Speakers
Power Devices
  DC/DC converters
  High-voltage and switching power supplies
Sensors
  Electric potential
  Magnetic pattern recognition
  Non-contact potentiometers
  Piezoelectric vibrating gyroscopes
  Pyroelectric infrared sensors and modules
  Rotary
  Shock
  Ultrasonic
Thermistors and Resistors
  High-voltage resistors
  Resistor networks
  Thermistors
  Trimmer potentiometers
Other
  Chip coils
  Delay lines
  Electromagnetic interference (EMI) suppression filters
  Filters
  Flyback transformers
  High-voltage multipliers
  Resonators
  TV/LCD tuners

COMPETITORS

AVX	ROHM
Anhui Tongfeng Electronics	Sanken Electric
	Sensata
CTS Corp.	Skyworks
Heico Ohmite	TDK-EPC
KEMET	TE Connectivity
Kyocera	Taiyo Yuden
Man Yue	Vishay Intertechnology

HISTORICAL FINANCIALS

Company Type: Public

Income Statement				FYE: March 31
	REVENUE ($ mil.)	NET INCOME ($ mil.)	NET PROFIT MARGIN	EMPLOYEES
03/20	15,467	1,845	11.9%	74,109
03/19	15,880	2,086	13.1%	77,571
03/18	13,831	1,472	10.6%	75,326
03/17	11,449	1,573	13.7%	59,985
03/16	12,208	2,054	16.8%	54,674
Annual Growth	6.1%	(2.7%)	—	7.9%

2020 Year-End Financials

Debt ratio: 0.0%
Return on equity: 11.0%
Cash ($ mil.): 2,416
Current ratio: 3.61
Long-term debt ($ mil.): 2

No. of shares (mil.): 639
Dividends
Yield: 3.4%
Payout: 14.9%
Market value ($ mil.): 8,036

	STOCK PRICE ($) FY Close	P/E High/Low		Earnings	PER SHARE ($) Dividends	Book Value
03/20	12.56	0	0	2.88	0.43	26.70
03/19	37.65	0	0	3.26	0.20	25.28
03/18	34.60	0	0	2.31	0.18	22.96
03/17	35.64	0	0	2.47	0.51	21.40
03/16	30.20	0	0	3.24	0.41	19.51
Annual Growth	(19.7%)	—	—	(2.8%)	1.6%	8.2%

Musashino Bank, Ltd.

Auditors: Ernst & Young ShinNihon LLC

LOCATIONS

HQ: Musashino Bank, Ltd.
1-10-8 Sakuragi-cho, Omiya-ku, Saitama 330-0854
Phone: (81) 48 641 6111
Web: www.musashinobank.co.jp

COMPETITORS

Hachijuni Bank	Toho Bank
Nanto Bank	

HISTORICAL FINANCIALS

Company Type: Public

Income Statement				FYE: March 31
	ASSETS ($ mil.)	NET INCOME ($ mil.)	INCOME AS % OF ASSETS	EMPLOYEES
03/20	43,058	74	0.2%	2,920
03/19	41,772	48	0.1%	3,003
03/18	42,949	102	0.2%	3,117
03/17	40,311	87	0.2%	3,206
03/16	38,548	111	0.3%	3,268
Annual Growth	2.8%	(9.7%)	—	(2.8%)

2020 Year-End Financials

Return on assets: 0.1%
Return on equity: 3.3%
Long-term debt ($ mil.): —
No. of shares (mil.): 33
Sales ($ mil): 625

Dividends
Yield: —
Payout: 33.2%
Market value ($ mil.): —

Nanto Bank, Ltd.

The Nanto Bank primarily serves the Nara region of Japan. The bank operates from about 135 offices branches and other facilities located in the Hyogo Kyoto Mie Nara Osaka Tokyo and Wakayama areas of the country. Nanto Bank provides a selection of financial services including consumer banking credit card services securities leasing and lending. The bank traces its historical roots back to 1934. Major subsidiaries include Nanto Credit Guarantee Co. Nanto Lease co. Nanto Estate Co. Nanto Staff Service Co. and Nanto Investment Management Co.

Strategy

The Nanto Bank aims to increase its balance of loans deposits and assets by expanding its branch net work mainly through the establishment of new branches. In Osaka Prefecture identified as an important strategic area two new branches — the

Eiwa branch and the Wakaeiwata branch — were built and opened in Higashiosaka City in September 2012. The company also opened in 2013 its Joto corporate business office and the Hokusetsu corporate business office with a plan to eventually developing these into branches.

EXECUTIVES

President, Takashi Hashimoto
Auditors: KPMG AZSA LLC

LOCATIONS

HQ: Nanto Bank, Ltd.
   16 Hashimoto-cho, Nara 630-8677
Phone: (81) 742 22 1131
Web: www.nantobank.co.jp

COMPETITORS

Aozora Bank
Kiyo Bank
Mitsubishi UFJ
   Financial Group
Shizuoka Bank
Towa Bank

HISTORICAL FINANCIALS

Company Type: Public

Income Statement				FYE: March 31
	ASSETS ($ mil.)	NET INCOME ($ mil.)	INCOME AS % OF ASSETS	EMPLOYEES
03/20	52,242	29	0.1%	3,677
03/19	52,362	100	0.2%	3,771
03/18	54,700	123	0.2%	3,830
03/17	52,010	111	0.2%	3,790
03/16	49,027	108	0.2%	3,771
Annual Growth	1.6%	(27.9%)	—	(0.6%)

2020 Year-End Financials

Return on assets: 0.0%
Return on equity: 1.1%
Long-term debt ($ mil.): —
No. of shares (mil.): 32
Sales ($ mil): 746

Dividends
   Yield: —
   Payout: 82.1%
Market value ($ mil.): —

National Australia Bank Ltd.

National Australia Bank (NAB) is one of Australia's Big Four banks (along with ANZ Westpac and Commonwealth Bank of Australia). It provides banking wealth management and investment banking services in Australia as well as in New Zealand through its Bank of New Zealand (BNZ) subsidiary. NAB also offers financial and debt capital markets specialized capital custody and alternative investments for institutional clients. The company has more than 30000 people serving 9 million customers at more than 900 locations in Australia New Zealand and around the world. NAB funds some of the most important infrastructure in its communities - including schools hospitals and roads.

Operations

NAB operates in five divisions: Business and Private Banking; Consumer Banking and Wealth; Corporate and Institutional Banking; New Zealand Banking; and Corporate Functions and Other. Business and

Private Banking focuses on serving the needs of three of NAB's priority customer segments: small businesses medium businesses and investors. Customers are served through an integrated banking model locally led by managing partners through business banking centers and through the small business customer hubs. The division accounts for about 40% of revenue.

Consumer Banking and Wealth provides customers with products and services through proprietary networks in NAB and UBank as well as third party and mortgage brokers. Customers are served through the Consumer Banking network to secure home loans or manage personal finances through deposit credit or personal loan facilities. The division accounts for about 30% of revenue.

Corporate and Institutional Banking provides a range of lending and transactional products and services related to financial and debt capital markets specialized capital custody and alternative investments. It includes Bank of New Zealand's Markets Trading operations. The division accounts for about 20% of revenue.

New Zealand Banking comprises the Consumer Banking Wealth Business Agribusiness Corporate and Insurance franchises and Markets Sales operations in New Zealand operating under the 'Bank of New Zealand' brand. The division accounts for around 15% of revenue.

Corporate Functions and Other includes functions that support all businesses including Treasury Technology and Operations Support Units and Eliminations.

Geographic Reach

The company operates in more than 900 locations in Australia New Zealand and around the world.

Sales and Marketing

NAB served more than 9 million customers during 2019. Business and Private Banking serves small to medium businesses and investors; and also high net worth customers through Private Bank and JBWere.

NAB spent A$200 million on advertising and marketing expenses in 2019 compared to A$226 million in 2018.

Financial Performance

The company's revenue fell by about A$1.2 billion million to A$17.9 billion from A$19.1 billion from the prior year. Net interest income increased by A$53 million including a decrease of A$133 million which was offset by movements in economic hedges in other operating income and customer-related remediation of A$72 million in the 2019 financial year. Other income decreased by A$1.2 billion or 22% including an increase of A$133 million which was offset by movements in economic hedges in net interest income and an increase of A$886 million in customer-related remediation.

Net profit attributable to owners of NAB (statutory net profit) decreased by $756 million or 14% primarily due to the decrease on their revenue.

The company's cash in 2019 increased for about A$9.1 billion to $47 billion from the prior year. Cash provided by operating activities and investing activities were A$10.4 billion and A$2.6 billion while cash used by financing activities was A$5.8 billion.

Strategy

The company's strategic focus supports its vision to be Australia's leading bank trusted by customers for exceptional service. Achieving this vision is underpinned currently by four key long term objectives: Net Promoter Score (NPS) positive and number 1 of major Australian banks in priority segments; cost to income ratio towards 35%; Number 1 ROE of major Australian banks; and Top quartile employee engagement.

The Group's capital management strategy is focused on adequacy efficiency and flexibility. The capital adequacy objective seeks to ensure sufficient capital is held in excess of internal risk-based required capital assessments and regulatory requirements and is within the Group's balance sheet risk appetite. This approach is consistent across the Group's subsidiaries.

HISTORY

Formed in 1858 in Melbourne National Bank of Australasia (NBA) just missed the peak of the Victoria gold rush. The bank expanded across the territory and was one of the first to lend to farmers and ranchers using land deeds as security. In the late 1870s drought imperiled Victoria. Seeking greener pastures NBA entered New South Wales in 1885 then headed into Western Australia. Economic instability continued; in 1893 the bank experienced its first panic and was shuttered for eight weeks. NBA reopened only to close a quarter of its branches between 1893 and 1896.

During the Australian commonwealth's early years Western Australia was the bank's salvation as the economies in Victoria and South Australia stagnated. NBA helped fund Australia's WWI efforts through public loans. A postwar consolidation wave in banking swept up NBA which made acquisitions in 1918 and 1922.

Overdue farm and ranch loans weakened the bank during the Depression. As WWII raged the Commonwealth Bank (established in 1912) took greater control of Australia's banks. With competition among banks primarily limited to branch growth NBA acquired Queensland National Bank in 1948 and Ballarat Banking Co. in 1955. The bank diversified into consumer finance through acquisition. In the 1960s Australia experienced an economic boom as immigration and industrialization grew. The boom went bust in the 1970s as the world sunk into recession. Still under the Commonwealth Bank's tight control the banks watched business that had once been theirs lost to building societies merchant banks and credit unions.

The 1980s brought banking deregulation. To vie with foreign banks entering Australia NBA in 1981 merged with Commercial Banking Co. of Sydney and became the National Commercial Banking Corp. of Australia in 1982. (It took its present name in 1984.) Throughout the 1980s the bank diversified and moved into the US and Japan. It invested in property and made loans to foreign countries. All too quickly though property values sank and countries defaulted on loans.

To fight recession NAB looked abroad for opportunities. In 1987 it bought Clydesdale Bank Northern Bank and National Irish Bank from Midland Bank Group (now part of HSBC Holdings). Three years later NAB bought Yorkshire Bank then turned the four banks around by linking them and tightening loan operations. In 1992 it bought the troubled Bank of New Zealand again tightening loan operations. Three years later NAB claimed Michigan National in the US.

After the mid-1990s economic recovery NAB bought HomeSide to try to adapt the US mortgage firm's efficient operations for all its banks.

NAB in 2000 bought Lend Lease's MLC fund management group. It also announced plans to launch a separate stock for its European businesses fueling speculation it might be on the prowl to buy or merge with a large UK bank. The Australian Competition and Consumer Commission (ACCC) that year accused NAB of credit card transaction price-fixing; the bank faced a possible fine of nearly $6 million but the ACCC dropped litigation against the group the following year.

Also in 2001 NAB sold US-based Michigan National Bank to ABN AMRO and sold mortgage lender HomeSide International to Washington Mutual the following year. In fiscal year 2002 the bank cut some 2000 jobs mostly in back-office operations.

During fiscal year 2003 the company booked pre-tax losses of some $360 million due to unauthorized trading in the company's foreign currency options department. By the end of March 2004 chairman Charles Allen chief executive Frank Cicutto and the heads of global markets and foreign exchange had resigned. Three more executives and at least five traders were fired. The fallout continued the next year as the company struggled to regroup.

NAB sold its Irish banks — National Irish Bank and Northern Bank– to Danske Bank in 2005. It retained its UK banks Yorkshire Bank (England) and Clydesdale Bank (Scotland).

In 2006 NAB sold its Custom Fleet vehicle leasing division to GE Capital as well as its Asian life insurance and wealth management operations. The downsizing was part of the company's move to streamline operations.

To establish a foothold in the US NAB acquired Great Western Bancorporation for $A836 million (nearly US$800 million) in 2008.

Also that year NAB took a 20% stake in Chinese property trust Union Trust and Investment. The deal made NAB the first foreign bank to buy into a Chinese trust firm.

EXECUTIVES

Managing Director and Group CEO, Andrew Thorburn
Group Chief Risk Officer, David Gall
Acting Chief Customer Officer Corporate and Institutional Banking, Cathryn Carver
Managing Director and CEO Bank of New Zealand, Anthony J. Healy
Chief Customer Officer Consumer Banking and Wealth Management, Andrew Hagger
COO and Group Executive Customer Products and Services, Antony Cahill
Group Executive Business Banking, Angela Mentis
CFO, Gary Lennon
Acting Chief Technology and Operations Officer, Bob Melrose
Chairman, Kenneth R. (Ken) Henry
Auditors: Ernst & Young

LOCATIONS

HQ: National Australia Bank Ltd.
Level 1, 800 Bourke Street, Docklands, Melbourne, Victoria 3008
Phone: (61) 3 8872 2461
Web: www.nabgroup.com

PRODUCTS/OPERATIONS

2015 Cash Earnings

	% of total
Australian banking	69
NZ banking	10
UK banking	10
NAB Wealth	8
Corporate function and others	3
Total	**100**

Selected Subsidiaries

Calibre Asset Management
Great Western Bancorporation
nabCapital (formerly Institutional Markets & Services)
National Australia Group Europe Limited
  Clydesdale Bank PLC
  Yorkshire Bank Home Loans Limited
  Yorkshire Bank Investments Limited
  National Australia Group Europe Services Limited
National HomeSia Group (NZ) Limited
  Bank of New Zealand
  BNZ International Funding Limited

National Australia Trustees Limited
National Wealth Management Holdings Limited
MLC Limited
  National Wealth Management International Holdings Limited

COMPETITORS

Australia and New Zealand Banking
Commonwealth Bank of Australia

Westpac Banking

HISTORICAL FINANCIALS

Company Type: Public

Income Statement

FYE: September 30

	ASSETS ($ mil.)	NET INCOME ($ mil.)	INCOME AS % OF ASSETS	EMPLOYEES
09/19	572,359	3,241	0.6%	33,950
09/18	581,681	4,005	0.7%	33,747
09/17	617,904	4,142	0.7%	33,746
09/16	592,435	268	0.0%	34,567
09/15	671,228	4,454	0.7%	41,849
Annual Growth	**(3.9%)**	**(7.6%)**	**—**	**(5.1%)**

2019 Year-End Financials

Return on assets: 0.5%
Return on equity: 8.8%
Long-term debt ($ mil.): —
No. of shares (mil.): —
Sales ($ mil): 22,685

Dividends
  Yield: 6.2%
  Payout: 53.4%
Market value ($ mil.): —

	STOCK PRICE ($) FY Close	P/E High/Low		PER SHARE ($) Earnings	Dividends	Book Value
09/19	10.07	6	4	1.11	0.63	13.06
09/18	10.08	6	5	1.40	0.68	13.94
09/17	12.40	7	5	1.48	0.76	15.03
09/16	10.68	142	103	0.12	1.02	14.76
09/15	10.52	6	4	1.72	0.89	15.22
Annual Growth	**(1.1%)**		**—**	**(10.4%)**	**(8.6%)**	**(3.7%)**

National Bank of Canada

Also known as National Bank Financial Group the National Bank of Canada offers personal commercial retail corporate and institutional banking services through about 450 branches in Canada primarily in Quebec. The bank's offerings include deposits mortgages loans and credit cards. Through subsidiaries it also provides insurance trust services wealth management online brokerage and private banking. The company's assets have grown to more than $230 billion. The bank operates in four segments: Personal and Commercial Wealth Management Financial Markets and its newest U.S. Specialty Finance and International.

EXECUTIVES

President and CEO, Louis Vachon, age 58, $656,080 total compensation
EVP Human Resources and Corporate Affairs, Lynn Jeanniot
EVP Finance and Treasury and CFO, Ghislain Parent

SVP; Co-President and Co-CEO National Bank Financial, Ricardo Pascoe, $246,030 total compensation
EVP Risk Management, William Bonnell
EVP Operations, Brigitte Hébert
EVP Personal and Commercial Banking, Diane Giard
EVP Corporate Development and Chief Marketing Officer, Karen Leggett
EVP Information Technology, Dominique Fagnoule
Co-President and Co-CEO National Bank Financial; EVP Wealth Management, Martin Gagnon
EVP Financial Markets, Denis Girouard
Chairman, Jean Houde
Auditors: Deloitte LLP

LOCATIONS

HQ: National Bank of Canada
600 De La Gauchetiere Street West, 4th Floor, Montreal, Quebec H3B 4L2
Phone: 514 394-5000   **Fax:** 514 394-8434
Web: www.nbc.ca

2016 sales

	% of total
Financial Markets	39
Personal and Commercial	38
Wealth Management	5
Other	18
Total	**100**

2016 sales

	% of total
Canada	89
United States	8
Other	3
Total	**100**

PRODUCTS/OPERATIONS

2016 Sales

	% of total
Interest	
Loans	50
Securities & other	8
Available-for-sale securities	4
Deposits with financial institutions	1
Noninterest	
Underwriting and advisory fees	5
Securities brokerage commissions	3
Mutual fund revenues	5
Trust service revenues	6
Credit fees	5
Card revenues	2
Deposit and payment service charges	3
Trading revenues (losses)	2
Gains (losses) on available-for-sale securities net	1
Insurance revenues net	1
Foreign exchange revenues other than trading	1
Other	3
Total	**100**

Selected Subsidiaries

Natbank (banking US)
NATCAN (75% portfolio management and investments)
National Bank Direct Brokerage (online brokerage)
National Bank Financial (investment banking)
National Bank General Insurance (home and auto coverage)
National Bank Insurance Firm (insurance brokerage)
National Bank Life Insurance Company
National Bank Securities (mutual funds)
National Bank Trust (trust services)

COMPETITORS

BMO Financial Group
CIBC
Caisses centrale
  Desjardins

Laurentian Bank
RBC Financial Group
Scotiabank
TD Bank

HISTORICAL FINANCIALS

Company Type: Public

Income Statement

FYE: October 31

	ASSETS ($ mil.)	NET INCOME ($ mil.)	INCOME AS % OF ASSETS	EMPLOYEES
10/20	335,804	1,947	0.6%	26,517
10/19	285,005	2,166	0.8%	25,487
10/18	265,779	2,065	0.8%	23,450
10/17	248,925	1,878	0.8%	21,635
10/16	235,132	1,131	0.5%	21,770
Annual Growth	9.3%	14.5%	—	5.1%

2020 Year-End Financials

Return on assets: 0.6%
Return on equity: 12.3%
Long-term debt ($ mil.): —
No. of shares (mil.): 336
Sales ($ mil): 11,391

Dividends
  Yield: 0.0%
  Payout: 49.8%
Market value ($ mil.): 16,004

	STOCK PRICE ($) FY Close	P/E High/Low		PER SHARE ($) Earnings	Dividends	Book Value
10/20	47.63	10	5	5.77	2.88	49.36
10/19	51.65	8	6	6.42	2.00	44.78
10/18	45.69	9	7	6.01	1.88	42.24
10/17	48.66	9	6	5.45	1.75	38.02
10/16	35.66	11	7	3.33	1.65	33.82
Annual Growth	7.5%	—	—	14.7%	14.9%	9.9%

National Bank Of Greece S A

Like the ancient ruins that dominate the landscape of Greece National Bank of Greece (NBG) dominates the banking landscape of the Mediterranean. In addition to holding the top position at home NBG has taken a leading position in the Balkans by acquiring controlling stakes in banks throughout the region. The bank offers such services as commercial and consumer banking asset management investment banking brokerage services financing and insurance. It has more than 500 domestic branches and another 1200 in nearly a dozen outside countries. NBG once served as the Greek central bank but the government sold its stake in the company in 2004.

Operations

Broadly speaking NBG generates 75% of its revenue in the form of interest income (mostly from loans) while the remainder comes from a mix of insurance income deposit account charges and other fees and commissions credit card fees and gains available-for-sale securities.NBG's Turkish Operations is the bank's largest segment generating more than 40% of the bank's total revenue. The unit offers a variety of commercial banking services through Finansbank and its subsidiaries in Turkey.

The Retail Banking division makes up another 20% of revenue and serves individual customers professionals small-medium and small sized companies (identified as businesses with revenues up to ?2.5 million or roughly $2.8 million) in Greece. Corporate & Investment Banking (20% of revenue) lends to large and medium-sized companies and also offers shipping finance and investment banking services.

The bank's International business (roughly 10% of revenue) offers commercial banking services including commercial and retail credit trade financing foreign exchange and traditional deposit banking to countries outside of Greece and Turkey. In addition to Finansbank in Turkey NBG's seven other non-Greek subsidiaries include: United Bulgarian Bank (UBB) Vojvodjanska Banka Banca Romaneasca Stopanska Banka the National Bank of Greece (Cyprus) Ltd. (NBG Cyprus) Banka NBG (NBG Albania) South African Bank of Athens (SABA) and NBG Bank (Malta) Ltd. (NBG Malta).

NBG also has an Insurance business (5% of revenue) as well as a Global Markets & Asset Management business. Other services include proprietary real estate management and hotel and warehousing services which make up less than 5% of revenue.

Geographic Reach

In addition to Greece NBG operates banks in Albania Bulgaria Cyprus Egypt Romania Serbia and FYROM South Africa and Turkey. While most of the bank's revenue comes from its home country about 40% of revenue comes from its operations in Turkey while another roughly 10% comes from countries outside of Greece and Turkey.

Sales and Marketing

NBG markets its products and services through agents and independent insurance brokers. It spent ?53 million ($64.4 million) on promotion and advertising in 2014 up from ?68 million ($82.65 million) in 2013.

Financial Performance

Note: Growth rates may differ after conversion to US dollars.

The bank has come a long way from its low point in 2011 caused by heavy trading losses and political turmoil in its home country. Still after two years of growth revenue in 2014 plunged by 27% to ?5.09 billion ($6.19 billion) mostly due to losses on its derivative investments but also because the bank collected less interest income from a rise in non-performing loans.

NBG returned to the red in 2014 reporting a net loss of ?2.5 billion ($3 billion) mostly due to a combination of lower revenue and higher loan loss provisions as the quality of its domestic loan portfolio worsened in the midst of intense political uncertainty and bad economic conditions in Greece. The bank's operations provided more cash in 2014 as most of its losses were related to non-cash loan loss provisions.

Strategy

Given the poor economic climate in Greece and heated political battles ensuing related to the country's debt levels NBG has been operating in a challenging business climate. To turn around its struggling loan portfolio which has been suffering from domestic property devaluations in troubled Greece and resulting loan asset impairments the bank has been focusing on strengthening its capital position in raising cash from share offerings and selling off riskier loan assets in favor of safer ones.

The bank has also been relying heavily on its Turkish Operations to generate loan business in Turkey where roughly 40% of its revenue came from in 2014.

Mergers and Acquisitions

In 2013 NGB made several acquisitions to expand its branch reach and loan business. In mid-2013 for example it purchased selected assets from the troubled banks Probank S.A. and First Business Bank S.A. (FBB) for a total of around ?1 billion ($1.3 billion) adding 19 FBB branches and 112 Probank branches to the NBG branch network.

HISTORY

The National Bank of Greece (NBG) can trace its banking heritage back to Pasion a metic (non-Greek) former slave living in Athens in the fourth century BC. To help his former master rebuild after one of Greece's many wars he obtained a small private bank that had been formed a few decades earlier and became one of Athens' greatest bankers.

The bank as it exists today though was established in 1841 and for most of its existence served as Greece's central bank. It listed on the Athens Stock Exchange in 1880. NBG survived WWI and Germany's occupation of Greece during WWII. It weathered the civil war in the late 1940s the military coup that overthrew the constitutional monarchy in the 1960s and democratic reformation in the 1970s.

As the 1980s dawned and Andreas Papandreou's socialist government came to power in Greece the bank launched a joint venture in Paris with Crédit Lyonnais and other investors. NBG caused plenty of problems for its privately owned competitors during the early part of the decade — as deposits declined profits shrank and labor costs rose the bank was able to undercut competitors thanks to its government backing.

A banking scandal involving NBG and Papandreou helped topple the socialist government in the late 1980s. The bank's US subsidiary Atlantic Bank of New York was one of two Greek banks charged with money laundering to the tune of $700 million. Rival political parties called for Papandreou already ailing to resign. (In 1992 the former leader was acquitted of corruption charges stemming from the scandal.)

Under the leadership of a different government in the early 1990s the bank looked to shake up its holdings to improve profits. It sold off a number of subsidiaries including a chain of luxury hotels an insurance unit and Traders Credit Bank a small commercial bank. These divestitures were just the beginning as the Greek government looked to privatize a number of its holdings. Turmoil in the Greek economy in the mid-1990s forced the bank to limit withdrawals hike interest rates and take other conservative measures as the government tried to prevent a devaluation of the native currency.

In the late 1990s Greece looked to join the Euro zone and its institutions began shaping up. Doing its part NBG took measures to clean up its balance sheet writing off a number of bad loans it had been pressured to make by the government. The bank focused on retail operations absorbed the National Mortgage Bank and transformed its ETEVA development banking subsidiary into a full-fledged investment bank. It began shoring up flagging overseas operations listed on the NYSE (1999) and looked to expand in the Balkans.

In 1997 the bank opened offices in Albania and three years later bought controlling interests in Macedonia's Skopanska Banka and United Bulgarian Bank. As the 20th century drew to a close NGB won more freedom from the Greek government when the finance ministry announced it would no longer appoint the bank's executive officers instead allowing NGB's board of directors and shareholders to make the decisions.

In 2000 the company launched subsidiary NBG Venture Capital which concentrates on Greece southeast Europe and the eastern Mediterranean. The government sold 10% of its stake in the bank in 2003 as part of its privatization program. Although the move dropped its holdings to 30% the government retained management control. The state divested its interest in the company in 2004.

EXECUTIVES

General Manager Treasury Global Markets and Private Banking, Petros Christodoulou, age 60, $420,769 total compensation

General Manager Risk Management, Michael Oratis, age 63, $454,123 total compensation

General Manager of Strategy & International Activities Chief Economist of the Group, Paul Mylonas, age 62, $410,515 total compensation

General Manager of Corporate Banking Chairman of the Board of Directors at Ethniki Insurance Co, Dimitrios G. Dimopoulos, age 74, $299,408 total compensation

General Manager of Retail Banking, Nelly Tzakou-Lambropoulou, age 59, $288,218 total compensation

General Manager Real Estate, Aristotelis Karytinos, age 65, $484,145 total compensation

CEO, Leonidas Fragkiadakis, age 55, $339,310 total compensation

Chief Financial Officer, Paula N. Hadjisotiriou, age 63

General Manager Group Retail Collections, Marianna Politopoulou

Chief of Operations, Damianos Charalampidis

Chief Credit Officer, Dimitris Frangetis

Group CIO, Nikos Christodoulou

Chair, Louka T. Katseli

Auditors: PricewaterhouseCoopers S.A.

LOCATIONS

HQ: National Bank Of Greece S A
86 Eolou St., Athens 10232
Phone: (30) 210 334 1000   **Fax:** (30) 210 334 2235
Web: www.nbg.gr

PRODUCTS/OPERATIONS

2014 Sales

	% of total
Turkish operation	41
Retail banking	19
International	12
Insurance	5
Corporate and investment banking	21
Others	2
Total	**100**

COMPETITORS

Alpha Bank	Emporiki Bank
Bank of Cyprus	HSBC
Citibank	Piraeus Bank S.A.
EFG Eurobank Ergasias	Royal Bank of Scotland

HISTORICAL FINANCIALS

Company Type: Public

Income Statement   FYE: December 31

	ASSETS ($ mil.)	NET INCOME ($ mil.)	INCOME AS % OF ASSETS	EMPLOYEES
12/13	147,091	50	0.0%	37,591
12/12	133,328	(3,344)	—	35,573
Annual Growth	10.3%	—	—	5.7%

2013 Year-End Financials

Return on assets: 0.0%	Dividends
Return on equity: —	Yield: —
Long-term debt ($ mil.): —	Payout: —
No. of shares (mil.): 15	Market value ($ mil.): —
Sales ($ mil): 9,707	

	STOCK PRICE ($) FY Close	P/E High/Low	Earnings	Dividends	Book Value
12/13	0.00	— —	6.20	0.00	200.53
12/12	0.00	—	(5,239.25)	0.00	
(12,621.44)					
/0.00	—	(0.00)	0.00	(0.00)	
Annual Growth	—	— —	—	—	—

National Grid plc

National Grid PLC keeps the home fires burning and the lights shining brightly in UK and the US. The company owns and operates England and Wales' electricity infrastructure and operates Scotland's (Scotland's infrastructure is owned separately) which together span over 7210 kilometers of overhead lines. It also operates the UK's gas transmission infrastructure including some 7630 kilometers of pipeline. National Grid PLC's UK customers are mainly electricity generation and gas shipping companies. In the US subsidiary National Grid USA manages electricity generation & transmission assets and gas distribution networks in the New England region of the US reaching 20 million people. National Grid PLC also conducts liquefied natural gas (LNG) business in the UK and US. Majority of the company's sales were generated in the US.

Operations

National Grid PLC operates three principal businesses: US Regulated (about 65% of sales) UK Electricity Transmission (around 25%) and UK Gas Transmission (around 5%). It also operates National Grid Ventures and Other (some 5%).

The US Regulated includes gas distribution networks electricity distribution networks and high-voltage electricity transmission networks in New York and New England and electricity generation facilities in New York.

The UK Electricity Transmission includes high-voltage electricity transmission networks in England and Wales and independent Great Britain system operator.

The UK Gas Transmission involves high-pressure gas transmission networks in Great Britain and system operator in Great Britain.

The National Grid Ventures comprises all commercial operations in metering LNG at the Isle of Grain in the UK electricity interconnectors and new investments in Geronimo Energy LLC (Geronimo) and Emerald Energy Venture LLC (Emerald).

Geographic Reach

The primary serviced areas for London-headquartered National Grid PLC are England Wales Scotland and the New England region of the US. The company's US operations are in New York Massachusetts and Rhode Island. Its US power generation facilities are on Long Island NY.

National Grid PLC owns and operate Grain LNG an importation terminal and storage facility at the Isle of Grain in Kent.

About two-thirds of National Grid's revenue comes from US operations and the rest comes from the UK.

Sales and Marketing

National Grid PLC is regulated by Ofgem in the UK. Its client base includes residential customers industrial companies and commercial enterprises.

Financial Performance

National Grid's 2020 revenue was Å 14.5 billion Å 393 million less than the previous year. This re-

sulted from a decrease in revenue of US Regulated and NGV and Other segments.

Net income fell 16% to Å 1.3 billion compared to the previous year which resulted from a decrease in earnings from continuing operations and negative earnings from discontinued operations.

Cash and cash equivalents at the end of the year were Å 73 million Å 179 million less than the previous year. Cash generated by operating activities was Å 4.7 billion. Investing activities used Å 3.2 billion primarily for purchases of property plant and equipment; financing activities used 1.6 billion primarily for repayment of loans.

Strategy

National Grid's strategy is to build own and operate large-scale long-life energy assets primarily in networks and renewables that deliver fair returns and high societal value. This strategy sets the bounds of National Grid's business and will ensure it is set up to play a leading role in the energy future. It will be delivered through four priorities: enable the energy transition for all deliver for customers efficiently grow organizational capability and empower colleagues for great performance.

For the company's digital transformation it is adopting a group-wide centralized hub model supported by regional delivery. The strategy for the transformation is formed centrally with regional autonomy. The company expanded a personalization platform to serve more than two million customers in Massachusetts and Rhode Island. Advanced data and analytics proactively identify eligible customers and present the next best offer to individuals increasing offer enrolment and reducing bad debt.

The company is supporting growth in distributed energy resources (DERs) in its US service territories where its US regulated business connected 314 MW of generation in the calendar year 2019. It also made investments in the grid to enable future growth including to increase distribution system capacity and to deploy advanced communications monitoring and control technologies essential to enhance DER integration.

Mergers and Acquisitions

In mid-2019 National Grid PLC completed the acquisition of Geronimo Energy a leading clean energy company based in Minneapolis MN for $100m. The acquisition is led by National Grid PLC's competitive business unit National Grid Ventures. Geronimo Energy has a strong track record of being farmer-friendly community-driven and customer focused which aligns with National Grid PLC's core value.

HISTORY

The National Grid Company was formed in 1990 as part of the privatization of the electricity industry in England and Wales. Until then the Central Electricity Generating Board (CEGB) a state monopoly responsible for power generation in England and Wales owned the national power grid (transmission system) and sold power to 12 area boards the regional authorities that distributed electricity to customers.

The Electricity Act of 1989 paved the way for competition; in 1990 the CEGB was split into The National Grid Company and three power-generating firms: National Power PowerGen and Nuclear Electric. The 12 area boards transferred their assets to 12 regional companies which jointly owned National Grid. The company keeping its monopoly status was charged to develop and operate an efficient coordinated and economical transmission system and to facilitate competition among power producers.

The company moved outside the UK when it invested in Citelec in 1993. An international consortium Citelec controlled Transener the surviving transmission system after Argentina privatized its electric utilities.

Also in 1993 National Grid set up Energis as a telecommunications firm to provide service to businesses. Piggybacking its fiber-optic lines on National Grid's transmission network Energis introduced national services in 1994 and by 1996 it had won several major customers including the BBC and Microsoft.

In 1995 National Grid went public as The National Grid Group. It also secured concessions to build transmission lines in Pakistan but in 1997 a new Pakistani government put the project on hold. That year it also upped its stake in Citelec from 15% to 41% which increased its control over the development of Argentina's transmission system. With partner CINergy Global it also acquired 80% of the Power Division of Zambia Consolidated Copper Mines in 1997 and it was chosen as a joint venture partner by India's Karnataka Electricity Board to build a transmission line in that state.

The company sold 26% of Energis in 1997; in 1998 it announced plans to sell the rest of Energis and launch a new company under the National Grid banner to set up telecom firms overseas. That year it laid plans to enter the US by agreeing to acquire New England Electric System (NEES). (The $3.2 billion purchase closed in 2000.)

In 1999 the company cut its stake in Energis to 46% and announced plans to shop for more US energy holdings. A deal was struck to purchase New York Utility Niagara Mohawk Holdings the following year. (The deal was completed in 2002.) Also in 2000 and 2001 the company continued to slim its stake in Energis (33%).

National Grid sold some noncore businesses in 2001 including UK metering company Datum Services and US energy marketer Allenergy and pulled out of the transmission project in India. It also agreed to manage the Alliance Regional Transmission Organization (RTO) in the US. In 2002 National Grid sold Niagara Mohawk's 50% interest in Canadian Niagara Power to Canadian utility Fortis.

The firm changed its name to National Grid Transco in 2002 upon completion of its acquisition of Lattice Group in a $21.5 billion deal.

In 2005 National Grid Transco sold four of its regional gas distribution networks; the North England network was acquired by a consortium that includes United Utilities and Cheung Kong Infrastructure; the South of England and Scotland networks were sold to Scottish and Southern Energy Borealis Infrastructure and Ontario Teachers' Pension Plan; and the Wales & West distribution network was purchased by a consortium managed by Macquarie Bank Limited. The company dropped Transco from its name in 2005.

National Grid dramatically boosted its North American assets in 2007 by acquiring gas distributor KeySpan for more than $7 billion. To comply with federal regulations connected to the KeySpan deal in 2008 National Grid sold its 2480-MW Ravenswood Generating Station in New York City to TransCanada for $2.9 billion.

In the second half of the decade to raise cash and narrow its operational focus the company jettisoned a number of noncore operations. National Grid sold its stakes in the alternative telecommunications network industry. The company also sold its telecom interests in Chile Argentina and Poland and wrote off its 33% stake in bankrupt UK telecommunications firm Energis which uses fiberoptic cable strung along National Grid's power lines. National Grid also sold former Lattice Group subsidiary 186k (fiber-optic networking) to Hutchison Whampoa and exited its telecom venture in Brazil. It also sold its electricity interconnector linking Australia to the island state of Tasmania.

In 2010 a National Grid and TenneT joint venture began laying the first section of a high-voltage cable that will link the power grids in the UK and the Netherlands bolstering power supply in both countries. The project will help the companies meet environmental goals by facilitating power flows from low-carbon generation plants.

With an eye on meeting ambitious European Union goals for carbon emission reductions in 2009 National Grid released a report that by 2020 half of the UK's heating needs could be provided by biogas (converted from sewage and injected into the national gas distribution system) compensating for a decline in North Sea gas supply. In 2010 the company had one renewable gas plant under development in the US and two in the UK.

The company reported a major jump in revenues and income in 2010 primarily driven by a rebounding economy (prompting increased demand for power and gas) and by improved rates in the US market. Revenues grew by 40% in 2011 and net income by 30% thanks to strong demand and higher prices in the UK and increased rates in the US.

In 2011 National Grid announced plans to save $200 million in a restructuring of its US operations including cutting 1200 jobs. Late in 2011 the company sold the Seneca-Upshur Petroleum subsidiary for approximately $152 million. The deal is a further move to return to core business operations in gas and electricity distribution. That year it also agreed to sell its non-regulated metering business in the UK (Onstream) to Macquarie Bank for about $440 million.

EXECUTIVES

Finance Director, Andrew R. J. Bonfield, age 57, $1,173,945 total compensation
President US, Dean S. Seavers, age 60
Executive Director UK, Nicola Shaw
CEO, John Pettigrew
CIO, Rich Adduci
CEO National Grid U.K. Pension Scheme, Chris Hogg
Chairman, Peter Gershon, age 73
Auditors: Deloitte LLP

LOCATIONS

HQ: National Grid plc
1-3 Strand, London WC2N 5EH
Phone: (44) 20 7004 3000   **Fax:** (44) 20 7004 3004
Web: www.nationalgrid.com

PRODUCTS/OPERATIONS

2018 sales

	%
US Regulated	66
UK Electricity Transmission	22
UK Gas Transmission	6
National Grid Ventures	6
Total	**100**

COMPETITORS

Con Edison	Northern Ireland
Enterprise Group	Electricity
Eversource Energy	Northern Powergrid
HomeServe	Scottish and Southern
IBERDROLA	Energy
Northern Electric	

HISTORICAL FINANCIALS

Company Type: Public

Income Statement

FYE: March 31

	REVENUE ($ mil.)	NET INCOME ($ mil.)	NET PROFIT MARGIN	EMPLOYEES
03/20	17,962	1,561	8.7%	23,069
03/19	19,561	1,979	10.1%	22,576
03/18	21,429	4,988	23.3%	23,023
03/17	18,770	9,731	51.8%	22,132
03/16	21,756	3,729	17.1%	25,068
Annual Growth	(4.7%)	(19.6%)	—	(2.1%)

2020 Year-End Financials

Debt ratio: 55.3%	No. of shares (mil.): —
Return on equity: 6.4%	Dividends
Cash ($ mil.): 90	Yield: 5.2%
Current ratio: 0.68	Payout: 663.5%
Long-term debt ($ mil.): 32,242	Market value ($ mil.): —

	STOCK PRICE ($) FY Close	P/E High/Low	PER SHARE ($) Earnings	Dividends	Book Value
03/20	58.27	180 131	0.45	3.06	6.89
03/19	55.84	131 108	0.58	3.08	6.87
03/18	56.43	75 51	1.43	3.12	7.27
03/17	63.48	34 27	2.57	0.55	6.78
03/16	71.42	105 85	0.99	0.62	5.21
Annual Growth	(5.0%)	—	— (17.9%)	48.9%	7.2%

National Westminster Bank Plc

One of the retail banking arms of The Royal Bank of Scotland (RBS) National Westminster Bank (NatWest) provides banking and financial services to individual and small business clients in the UK. The bank offers deposits mortgages credit cards and personal loans through a network of roughly 1300 bank branches. It also offers phone and app and browser-based internet banking as well as a network of cash machines. Subsidiary Ulster Bank conducts retail banking in Ireland. Other offerings include life insurance pensions private banking services carbon offsets and other more prosaic business services as well as investment and retirement management.

Operations
NatWest's four business divisions are UK Personal & Business Banking (which generates around 55% of revenue); Commercial Banking (around 30%); Private Banking (more than 5%); and Central Items & Other (less than 10%).

The bank generates around 60% of its net revenue from interest. The rest arises from fees and commissions.

Geographic Reach
Headquartered in London NatWest generates the vast majority of its revenue in the UK. Outside the UK the company has subsidiaries in Ireland (Ulster Bank Ireland DAC) and the US (RBS Holdings USA).

Sales and Marketing
NatWest has around 12 million customers.

Financial Performance
Note: Growth rates may differ after conversion to US Dollars.

In 2018 NatWest's revenue increased 17% to Â 9.5 billion due mostly to legal entity cost recharging and the effect of FX reserves recycling to revenue after the disposal of two foreign subsidiaries. There was also a 6% organic increase in interest income stemming from mortgage balance growth.

Net income jumped 32% to Â 2.7 billion thanks to the absence of loss on discontinued operations and a lower income tax expense partially offset by higher impairment losses.

NatWest's cash position reduced during 2018 ending the year Â 46.6 billion lower at Â 51.3 billion. Its operations recorded a cash outflow of Â 14.4 billion and investing activities absorbed Â 34.2 billion in cash. Financing activities produced a cash inflow of Â 1.8 billion. NatWest's main cash uses were investments in business interests and intangible assets and changes in customer deposits.

Strategy

NatWest will launch a personal finance app Mimo that will combine AI and data analytics to provide its customers with budgeting advice insight into their finances and the ability to switch between utilities and insurance providers. The app makes use of new regulatory framework that gives individuals more control over their personal data which they can share with third parties.

EXECUTIVES

CEO of NatWest Markets, Chris Marks
Auditors: Ernst & Young LLP

LOCATIONS

HQ: National Westminster Bank Plc
250 Bishopsgate, London EC2M 4AA
Phone: (44) 20 7085 5000
Web: www.natwest.com

PRODUCTS/OPERATIONS

2018 sales

	% of total
Interest income	61
Fees and commissions receivable	17
Other non-interest income	22
Total	**100**

2018 sales

	% of total
UK Personal & Business Banking	55
Commercial and Private Banking	33
Central Items & other	17
Total	**100**
Services	
Personal Banking	
Credit card	
Insurance	
Loans	
Mortgages	
Saving Account	
Private Banking	
Credit Cards	
Current Accounts	
Insurance	
Loans	
Mortgages	
Business Banking	
International business	
Startup business	

COMPETITORS

AIB	HSBC
Barclays	Lloyds Banking Group
Clydesdale Bank	Yorkshire Bank
Grupo Santander	

HISTORICAL FINANCIALS

Company Type: Public

Income Statement

FYE: December 31

	ASSETS ($ mil.)	NET INCOME ($ mil.)	INCOME AS % OF ASSETS	EMPLOYEES
12/19	420,589	942	0.2%	51,700
12/18	395,716	3,343	0.8%	55,400
12/17	460,373	2,789	0.6%	14,400
12/16	389,310	(1,066)	—	15,700
12/15	448,184	(1,785)	—	29,200
Annual Growth	**(1.6%)**	**—**		**15.4%**

2019 Year-End Financials

Return on assets: 0.2%	Dividends	
Return on equity: 3.6%	Yield: —	
Long-term debt ($ mil.): —	Payout: —	
No. of shares (mil.): 1,678	Market value ($ mil.): —	
Sales ($ mil): 14,816		

	STOCK PRICE ($) FY Close	P/E High/Low	PER SHARE ($) Earnings	Dividends	Book Value
12/19	0.00	— —	(0.00)	0.00	15.48
12/18	0.00	— —	(0.00)	0.00	15.11
Annual Growth					**0.6%**

Naturgy Energy Group SA

Auditors: Ernst & Young, S.L.

LOCATIONS

HQ: Naturgy Energy Group SA
Avenida San Luis 77, Madrid 28033
Phone: (34) 93 219 9199   **Fax:** (34) 93 402 5870
Web: www.naturgy.com

HISTORICAL FINANCIALS

Company Type: Public

Income Statement

FYE: December 31

	REVENUE ($ mil.)	NET INCOME ($ mil.)	NET PROFIT MARGIN	EMPLOYEES
12/19	25,862	1,573	6.1%	12,138
12/18	27,872	(3,231)	—	13,945
12/17	27,938	1,630	5.8%	15,374
12/16	24,479	1,422	5.8%	17,229
12/15	28,335	1,636	5.8%	19,939
Annual Growth	**(2.3%)**	**(1.0%)**	**—**	**(11.7%)**

2019 Year-End Financials

Debt ratio: 49.0%	No. of shares (mil.): 984	
Return on equity: 13.0%	Dividends	
Cash ($ mil.): 3,014	Yield: 4.2%	
Current ratio: 1.32	Payout: 13.3%	
Long-term debt ($ mil.): 17,628	Market value ($ mil.): 4,891	

	STOCK PRICE ($) FY Close	P/E High/Low	PER SHARE ($) Earnings	Dividends	Book Value
12/19	4.97	4 3	1.61	0.21	12.04
12/18	5.09	— —	(3.24)	0.23	12.53
12/17	4.57	4 3	1.63	0.17	17.65
12/16	3.74	3 2	1.43	0.20	16.06
12/15	4.09	3 2	1.71	0.15	15.64
Annual Growth	**5.0%**		**(1.6%)**	**10.0%**	**(6.3%)**

NatWest Group PLC

The Royal Bank of Scotland (RBS) is one of Europe's largest (and oldest) banking groups dating back to 1727. With total assets of nearly Â 700 million it offers retail banking under the brands RBS and NatWest and private banking through Coutts Child & Co. and Drummonds three of the oldest names in the banking world. RBS's 850 branches constitute the UK's second-largest branch network. Outside of Great Britain RBS operates as Ulster Bank in Ireland and Northern Ireland and has additional small operations in Europe the US and Asia. RBS was among the banks most badly hit by the 2008 financial crisis and was bailed out by the UK government which still retains a 60% stake.

Operations

RBS divides its operations into five operating segments. Personal & Business Bank is its largest segment accounting for more than 45% of annual revenue. It comprises the RBS NatWest and Ulster Bank brands and serves retail mass-affluent and small business (revenue 2 million) customers.

Commercial & Private Banking (CPB) comprises RBS's commercial banking (around 20% of sales) and private banking (5% of sales) activities. It provides trade and foreign exchange services to commercial and mid-corporate customers as well as high-net-worth individuals. It also services business owners and entrepreneurs with private banking.

The NatWest Markets is RBS's investment banking arm and accounts for more than 15% of sales. It provides global market access financing risk management and training solutions.

RBS International serves retail commercial corporate and financial institutions and brings in 5% of total sales. A fifth segment houses central corporate functions such as RBS Treasury finance risk management compliance legal and HR.

Geographic Reach

RBS is based in Edinburgh Scotland and besides the UK rings up sales in and Europe the Asia/Pacific region and the US. The UK is by far its largest market at around 90% of sales. A lack of geographic diversification disadvantages RBS's non-UK operations.

Sales and Marketing

RBS serves around 19 million customers including individuals high-net-worth individuals SMEs commercial enterprises corporates and financial institutions.

Financial Performance

Note: Growth rates may differ after conversion to US dollars.

The Royal Bank of Scotland (RBS) is growing its profits again having passed the long tail of the financial crisis although sales remain less than half its peak years.

In fiscal 2018 RBS grew its revenue 2% to Â 13.4 billion although the increase was more to do with fewer negative factors than a proliferation of positives. Its NatWest Markets business grew its total income due to a Â 630 million lower disposal loss from its toxic legacy assets; excluding the legacy business the unit's revenue would have fallen. Meanwhile RBS's main consumer and commercial banking divisions saw revenue dip due to lower net interest income a result of competitive pressure and lower commercial banking activity.

The bank recorded a second consecutive year of profitability in 2018 after years of net losses. Its net income of Â 2.1 billion was 47% higher than in the previous year. The improved result was mostly the result of a sharp decrease in operating expenses which included a Â 561 million reduction in what the company calls "strategic costs" namely the continuing efforts to reorient itself and leave issues relating to the financial crisis in the rear-view mirror. These include the ringfencing of the retail business winding down legacy businesses and reducing its property portfolio as well as investing in its core business infrastructure.

RBS's cash position weakened somewhat during 2018 ending the year £ 13.8 billion lower at £ 108.8 billion. It recorded a small cash outflow from operations and spent a net £ 7.1 billion on securities while cash used in financing activities was £ 6.3 billion.

Strategy

The Royal Bank of Scotland's recovery from the 2008 financial crisis has been a decade in the making but its repositioning as a smaller-scale UK-focused retail bank is now more or less complete. While much reduced in scope (it's 2019 revenue is roughly 40% of its 2007 revenue not adjusting for inflation) the bank posted consecutive years of profits in 2018 and 2019 and can turn its attention more fully to the future.

In the case of RBS — and indeed most major banks — it is leaning on digital to make up for reductions in branch counts and pull in younger generations. RBS has made severe cuts to its branch counts which have fallen from around 2000 in 2014 to less than 800 in 2018. Conversely the number of RBS's mobile customers increased 16% to 6.4 million regular users while three-quarters of personal and business banking customers are regular online users and digital channels now generate half of all product sales. The company's continual efforts to use technology have recently included the development of biometric credit and debt cards that use fingerprints as an extra layer of security allowing contactless purchases above the typical £ 30 limit.

The bank's goal is to reduce its cost-to-income ratio to less than 50% including a £ 300 million reduction in 2019.

Mergers and Acquisitions

In 2018 Royal Bank of Scotland acquired FreeAgent a cloud accounting services firm for small businesses for £ 53 million. The acquisition will help RBS a more integrated banking and accounting proposition for small businesses and start-ups.

Company Background

The group was crippled by both the global financial crisis and its ambitious international expansion primarily its disastrous 2007 investment in Dutch bank ABN AMRO. In late 2008 the UK took a 60% stake in RBS but the bank still ended up reporting an annual loss of some £ 28 billion ($41 billion) — the largest loss in British corporate history. The government stepped in at least twice more to help RBS manage its debt and interest payments intervening with the contingency that RBS make significant efforts to get back on solid ground. The UK government is progressively selling off its stake in RBS. Standing at around 62% in 2019 the government expects to sell its entire stake in the company by 2024.

HISTORY

Royal Bank of Scotland was founded in 1727 but its roots go back to the Darien Company a merchant expedition that was established to set up a Scottish trading colony in Panama. The Darien expedition ended disastrously in 1699. In 1707 England voted to compensate Scottish creditors for the colony's failure (in part because England had promised support then reneged contributing to the collapse) and a small industry sprang up around paying creditors and loaning them money. In 1727 the Equivalent Company the combined entity of these organizations was granted a

banking charter and became Royal Bank of Scotland.

In 1826 the Parliament voted to take away Scottish banks' right to issue banknotes for less than five pounds which would have required banks to use gold or silver. Few banks had such reserves and the move sparked an outcry. Novelist Sir Walter Scott's The Letters of Malachi Malagrowther which defended the Scottish one-pound note helped shoot down the proposal.

RBS expanded throughout Scotland over the next 50 years. It opened a London branch in 1874; it didn't establish a branch outside London until it bought Williams Deacon's Bank which had a branch network in North England. RBS continued to use the Williams Deacon's name as it did with Glyn Mills & Co. which it purchased in 1939.

In 1968 RBS took on its modern persona as a public company when it merged with National Commercial Bank. The company moved overseas during the 1970s establishing offices in Hong Kong and major US cities.

RBS spent the next 20 years trying to achieve another merger of the same scale as National Commercial. In 1981 the bank was wooed by Standard Chartered Bank and Hongkong and Shanghai Bank (now part of HSBC Holdings) but British regulators denied both suitors.

The bank moved into telephone operations in 1985 when it set up Direct Line for selling car insurance. In 1988 RBS bought New England bank Citizens Financial (but it plans to divest that business). In 1989 the company entered into an alliance with Banco Santander (now Santander Central Hispano) Spain's largest banking group. The alliance created a cross-pollination of ideas and strategies that boosted both banks' operations. The first fruit of the alliance came in 1991 with the launch of Interbank On-line Systems (IBOS) which connected several European banks and allowed for instantaneous money transfers.

In the 1990s RBS was linked with a variety of partners. It even made a bid for the much larger bank Barclays in a move regarded as cheeky but was rebuffed. In 1997 it announced a joint venture with Richard Branson's Virgin Group called Virgin Direct to offer personal banking. The company also bought Angel Trains Contract a rolling stock leasing company and established a transatlantic banking transfer system (similar to IBOS) with US bank CoreStates (now owned by First Union).

In 2000 RBS acquired NatWest after a prolonged takeover battle with rival Bank of Scotland (now part of HBOS plc). The bank sold Gartmore Investment Management its fund management unit to Nationwide Mutual Insurance Company. Royal Bank also sold the assets of NatWest's Equity Partners unit and launched NatWest Private Banking to target wealthy investors.

In 2004 RBS made several acquisitions to boost its US presence: It paid about $360 million for the credit card business of Connecticut-based People's Bank and bought payments processor Lynk Systems (now RBS Lynk) while Citizens Financial bought Cleveland-based bank Charter One Financial. Also that year Ulster Bank bought Ireland-based retail financial services provider First Active.

In 2007 RBS led the consortium that acquired the Dutch bank for ?71 billion in a deal that was called the largest ever in the banking industry. The buyers carved ABN AMRO into pieces; RBS took the global wholesale and international retail operations in Asia Eastern Europe and the Middle East. The ambitious takeover preceded the global economic crisis though and RBS was among the hardest hit financial groups.

The troubled company made several moves to try and raise capital. Early in 2008 the company announced a £ 12 billion rights issue. RBS also

tried but failed to find a buyer for its insurance arm. However other assets were divested that year. The company sold rolling stock leasing firm Angel Trains to Babcock & Brown and others and it sold its joint venture Tesco Personal Finance back to supermarket giant Tesco. The efforts proved inadequate though. The government took a controlling stake in the group in 2008 the same year that RBS reported the largest corporate loss in British history.

Also as part of the government rescue RBS went through a management shakeup. Fred Goodwin the architect of the bank's international expansion was removed as CEO. He was replaced by Stephen Hester formerly the CEO of British Land Company. Johnny Cameron chairman of the group's global banking and markets segment (which lost the group's most money in 2008) was also ousted and chairman Tom McKillop retired early.

RBS also shuffled its corporate structure in 2009. It split its UK retail and commercial banking division into three segments (retail commercial and wealth) and made Ulster Bank its own segment. The group folded its operations support division into other arms and established a segment to manage the selling and runoff of noncore operations. RBS retained the Global Banking & Markets Global Transaction Services US Retail & Commercial and RBS Insurance (including Churchill Insurance) segments although several of their components were transferred to the noncore segment.

RBS has scaled back on the international growth that weakened the group during the economic fallout with the ultimate goal of reducing non-UK operations to less than a quarter of its assets. In 2009 the group sold its 4% stake in Bank of China for some £ 1.6 billion ($2.4 billion); it also sold most of its operations in Southeast Asia to Australia and New Zealand Banking Group for about $550 million. RBS divested units in Argentina Colombia Chile the United Arab Emirates Kazakhstan and Pakistan — all assets gained as part of its ABN AMRO transaction.

With the government having to step in at least twice to bail out the bank by 2011 RBC was forced to cut costs and sell non-core operations to refocus on its core banking business. In 2010 it sold more than 300 branches and offices to Banco Santander for some £ 1.65 billion ($2.6 billion). RBS sold its factoring and invoice financing unit to GE Capital and its payment services unit Global Merchant Services to Advent International and Bain Capital. It also sold its interest in RBS Sempra Commodities. In 2012 the company sold the international private banking business of Coutts to Royal Bank of Canada. Other divisions have been simply wound down and closed. RBS was ordered by the Federal Reserve in 2011 to improve its US operations or risk losing permission to do business in America. In October 2012 RBS sold a 30% stake in Direct Line Group part of its insurance group in an IPO valued at £ 2.6 billion ($4.2 billion).

EXECUTIVES

Chief Executive RBS Citizens Financial Group, Bruce W. Van Saun, age 62, $530,335 total compensation

Global Head Global Restructuring Group, Derek S. Sach, age 65

Chief Executive Personal and Business Banking, Les Matheson

Finance Director, Nathan M. Bostock

Chief Executive Retail Direct, Chris Sullivan, age 62

Executive Chairman Corporate and Institutional Banking, Donald Workman

CEO Markets, Peter Nielsen

CEO RBS Insurance, Paul Geddes, age 50

Chief Executive, Ross McEwan
CEO UK Corporate and Institutional Banking,
 Mark Catton
Chief Executive Commercial and Private Banking,
 Alison Rose
Managing Director GTS Cash, Stuart Lawson
President Dmitry Medvedev, Igor Yurgens
Co-CEO CIB, Chris Marks
Co-CEO CIB, Mark Bailie
Chief Executive Williams & Glyn, Jim Brown
Chairman RBS Scotland, Malcolm Buchanan
Chairman, Howard J. Davies, age 70
Auditors: Ernst & Young LLP

LOCATIONS

HQ: NatWest Group PLC
 P.O. Box 1000, Gogarburn, Edinburgh EH12 1HQ
Phone: (44) 131 626 0000   **Fax:** (44) 131 626 3081
Web: www.rbs.com

2018 Sales

	% of total
Net interest income	65
Net fees and commissions	18
Income from trading activities	10
Other operating income	7
Total	**100**

2018 Sales

	% of total
UK	92
Other countries	8
Total	**100**

PRODUCTS/OPERATIONS

2018 Sales by Segment

	% of total
Personal & Business Banking	
UK Personal & Business Banking	43
Ulster Bank	4
Commercial and Private Banking	
Commercial Banking	22
Private Banking	4
RBS International	4
NatWest Markets	17
Central items & other	2
Total	**100**

Selected Subsidiaries

Citizens Financial Group Inc. (banking US)
Coutts & Co (private banking)
Direct Line Insurance Group plc
National Westminster Bank Plc
The Royal Bank of Scotland plc
Ulster Bank Limited (Northern Ireland)

COMPETITORS

AIB	JPMorgan Chase
Bank of America	Lloyds Banking Group
Bank of Ireland	PNC Financial
Barclays	Santander UK
Citigroup	Standard Chartered
HSBC	Standard Life Aberdeen
ING Direct UK	permanent tsb

HISTORICAL FINANCIALS

Company Type: Public

Income Statement   FYE: December 31

	ASSETS ($ mil.)	NET INCOME ($ mil.)	INCOME AS % OF ASSETS	EMPLOYEES
12/19	954,817	4,621	0.5%	62,900
12/18	886,372	2,438	0.3%	65,400
12/17	996,884	1,547	0.2%	69,700
12/16	982,459	(6,787)	—	79,099
12/15	1,208,390	(2,802)	—	90,158
Annual Growth	(5.7%)	—	—	(8.6%)

2019 Year-End Financials

Return on assets: 0.4%
Return on equity: 7.8%
Long-term debt ($ mil.): —
No. of shares (mil.): —
Sales ($ mil): 24,336

Dividends
 Yield: 0.0%
 Payout: 84.9%
 Market value ($ mil.): —

	STOCK PRICE ($) FY Close	P/E High/Low		PER SHARE ($) Earnings	Dividends	Book Value
12/19	6.44	28	18	0.34	0.29	4.76
12/18	5.59	59	38	0.17	0.00	4.85
12/17	7.64	123	94	0.09	0.00	5.46
12/16	5.53	—	—	(0.73)	0.00	5.06
12/15	8.87	—	—	(0.25)	0.00	6.81
Annual Growth	(7.7%)	—	—	—	—	(8.6%)

NEC Corp

Auditors: KPMG AZSA LLC

LOCATIONS

HQ: NEC Corp
 5-7-1 Shiba, Minato-ku, Tokyo 108-8001
Phone: (81) 3 3454 1111
Web: www.nec.co.jp

HISTORICAL FINANCIALS

Company Type: Public

Income Statement   FYE: March 31

	REVENUE ($ mil.)	NET INCOME ($ mil.)	NET PROFIT MARGIN	EMPLOYEES
03/20	28,514	920	3.2%	112,638
03/19	26,307	362	1.4%	110,595
03/18	26,787	431	1.6%	109,390
03/17	23,836	244	1.0%	107,729
03/16	25,122	612	2.4%	98,726
Annual Growth	3.2%	10.7%	—	3.4%

2020 Year-End Financials

Debt ratio: 0.1%
Return on equity: 11.2%
Cash ($ mil.): 3,309
Current ratio: 1.39
Long-term debt ($ mil.): 3,360

No. of shares (mil.): 259
Dividends
 Yield: —
 Payout: 18.1%
 Market value ($ mil.): —

Nedbank Group Ltd

Nedbank GroupÂ provides commercial and per-sonal financial services in South Africa and other parts of the continent. The company offers a range of wholesale and retail banking services through principal business clusters Nedbank Corporate Nedbank Retail Nedbank Wealth NedbankÂ Busi-ness BankingÂ and Nedbank Capital (investment banking and capital markets). Other services in-clude property finance private banking credit card processing insurance and foreign exchange and securities trading. UK-based insurer Old Mutual owns a controlling stake in Nedbank Group.

EXECUTIVES

CEO, Michael W. T. (Mike) Brown, age 53
Managing Executive Nedbank Capital, Brian
 Kennedy, age 59

Managing Executive Retail and Business Banking,
 Philip Wessels, age 61
Managing Executive Nedbank Corporate, Mfundo
 Nkuhlu, age 53
Managing Executive Business Banking, Sandile
 Shabalala, age 52
CIO, Fred Swanepoel, age 56
CFO, Raisibe K. Morathi, age 51
Chief Risk Officer, Trevor Adams
COO, Graham Wayne Dempster
Chairman, Vassi Naidoo
Auditors: Ernst & Young Inc.

LOCATIONS

HQ: Nedbank Group Ltd
 Nedbank 135 Rivonia Campus, 135 Rivonia Road,
 Sandown, Sandton, Johannesburg 2196
Phone: (27) 11 294 4444   **Fax:** (27) 11 294 6540
Web: www.nedbankgroup.co.za

COMPETITORS

Absa	Investec
Citigroup	Standard Chartered
FirstRand	

HISTORICAL FINANCIALS

Company Type: Public

Income Statement   FYE: December 31

	ASSETS ($ mil.)	NET INCOME ($ mil.)	INCOME AS % OF ASSETS	EMPLOYEES
12/19	81,411	854	1.0%	29,403
12/18	72,600	930	1.3%	30,877
12/17	79,872	943	1.2%	31,531
12/16	70,338	737	1.0%	32,401
12/15	59,366	687	1.2%	31,312
Annual Growth	8.2%	5.6%	—	(1.6%)

2019 Year-End Financials

Return on assets: 1.1%
Return on equity: 14.0%
Long-term debt ($ mil.): —
No. of shares (mil.): 481
Sales ($ mil): 7,819

Dividends
 Yield: 4.9%
 Payout: 44.3%
 Market value ($ mil.): 7,410

	STOCK PRICE ($) FY Close	P/E High/Low		PER SHARE ($) Earnings	Dividends	Book Value
12/19	15.40	1	1	1.75	0.76	12.96
12/18	19.32	1	1	1.89	0.77	12.21
12/17	20.68	1	1	1.93	0.77	13.80
12/16	17.20	1	1	1.51	0.61	11.53
12/15	12.25	1	0	1.42	0.65	10.06
Annual Growth	5.9%	—	—	5.4%	3.9%	6.5%

Neste Oyj

Neste Oyj or Neste Corporation in English (for-merly Neste Oil) is a Finnish oil refiner committed to a green energy strategy to lower carbon emis-sions. The state-controlled firm focuses on refining marketing and shipping oil products including gasoline biodiesel fuel and lubricants. Neste Oyj primarily sells its products domestically but also exports to customers in North America and Eu-rope. It operates about 850 gas stations in Finland and almost 320 outside the country (in Estonia Latvia Lithuania Poland and northwestern Russia). The company has a biodiesel plant and a diesel production line. It has a crude oil refining capacity of 15 million tons per year and renewable diesel production capacity of 2.4 million tons per year.

Operations

Neste Oyj operates through four segments: Oil Products Renewable Products Oil Retail and Other.

Oil Products markets and sells gasoline diesel fuel light and heavy fuel oil aviation fuel base oils liquefied petroleum gas and related oil products and services to wholesale markets.

Renewable Products markets and wholesales NEXBTL renewable diesel based on the company's proprietary technology.

Oil Retail segment markets and sells petroleum products and associated services directly to end-users of which the most important are private motorists industry transport companies farmers and heating oil customers. The company has a network of over 1000 service stations in the Baltic Sea region.

Other consists of group administration shared service functions research and technology Neste Jacobs and Nynas AB.

Geographic Reach

Neste Oyj markets and sales fuels and oil products in Finland the St. Petersburg region in Northwest Russia Estonia Latvia and Lithuania.

It also owns and operates a total of eight rail-connected terminals in Finland Tallinn in Estonia and Riga in Latvia.

Sales and Marketing

Neste Oyj serves a range of markets including aviation marine municipalities resellers and retail chains wholesalers and blenders and base oils companies.

Company Background

In 2008 Neste Oil announced plans to build a major renewable diesel plant in Rotterdam capable of producing 800000 metric tons a day. Construction on the facility began in 2009. Completed in 2011 the plant expanded the company's green diesel production capacity to 2 million tons per year.

To expand its base oil business the company completed a 400000 metric tons-per-year joint venture base oil plant in Bahrain in 2011.

At the end of 2010 Neste Oil merged its Oil Products and Renewable Fuels businesses to create Oil Products and Renewables to improve operational efficiency and create synergies between the two businesses. That year the company posted a jump in revenues and income as the global economy bounced make from a recession. The rebound triggered stronger demand for oil and gas and higher commodity prices.

The Finnish government owns 50.1% of the company which was founded shortly after WWII to ensure a steady oil supply for the country. Neste Oil was spun off by Fortum in 2005. In 2015 it changed its name to Neste Oyj (Neste Corporation).

EXECUTIVES

President and CEO, Matti Lievonen, age 63

SVP Communications and Brand Marketing, Osmo Kammonen, age 61

EVP Oil Retail, Sakari Toivola, age 68

CFO, Jyrki M ¤ki-Kala, age 59

EVP Oil Products, Matti Lehmus, age 47

SVP Technology, Lars P. Lindfors, age 57

EVP Oil Retail, Antti Tiitola, age 54

Vice Chairman, Maija-Liisa Friman, age 68

Chairman, Jorma Eloranta, age 70

Auditors: PricewaterhouseCoopers Oy

LOCATIONS

HQ: Neste Oyj
Keilaranta 21, P.O. Box 95, Espoo 00095
Phone: (358) 10 458 11   **Fax:** (358) 10 458 4442
Web: www.nesteoil.com

2013 Sales

	% of total
Europe	
Nordic countries	
Finland	46
Other	17
Baltic Rim	12
Other countries	25
North & South America	18
Other regions	2
Total	**100**

PRODUCTS/OPERATIONS

2013 Sales

	% of total
Oil products	65
Oil retail	22
Renewable fuels	12
Others	1
Total	**100**

COMPETITORS

BP	OMV
Biopetrol	Royal Dutch Shell
Chevron	Statoil
Exxon Mobil	TOTAL
LUKOIL	

HISTORICAL FINANCIALS

Company Type: Public

Income Statement				FYE: December 31
	REVENUE ($ mil.)	NET INCOME ($ mil.)	NET PROFIT MARGIN	EMPLOYEES
12/19	17,784	2,007	11.3%	4,413
12/18	17,084	890	5.2%	5,413
12/17	15,843	1,092	6.9%	5,339
12/16	12,342	991	8.0%	5,001
12/15	12,124	607	5.0%	4,856
Annual Growth	10.1%	34.8%	—	(2.4%)

2019 Year-End Financials

Debt ratio: 15.1%
Return on equity: 33.9%
Cash ($ mil.): 1,676
Current ratio: 2.31
Long-term debt ($ mil.): 1,212

No. of shares (mil.): 767
Dividends
Yield: 2.4%
Payout: 49.1%
Market value ($ mil.): 13,292

	STOCK PRICE ($) FY Close	P/E High/Low		PER SHARE ($) Earnings	Dividends	Book Value
12/19	17.32	30	7	2.60	0.42	8.66
12/18	38.20	28712024		0.02	0.98	0.10
12/17	31.93	27	16	1.42	0.78	6.78
12/16	19.04	17	11	1.29	0.53	5.14
12/15	15.00	20	15	0.79	0.35	4.38
Annual Growth	3.7%	—	—	34.7%	4.8%	18.6%

Nestle SA

With instant coffee baby food and bottled water in the mix Nestlé crunches more than just chocolate. Active in almost every country the world's one of the leading food and drinks company produces more than 2000 brands including the world's leading coffee brand Nescafé Haagen-Dazs ice cream Purina pet food DiGiorno pizza Kit-Kat chocolates and Perrier bottled water. Its brands produced at more than 400 factories globally include global regional and local favorites. The US is Nestlé's biggest market. It is also L'Oréal's second largest shareholder with a 23% stake in the leading beauty company.

Operations

Nestlé's more than 2000 brands are divided into seven product segments: Powdered & liquid beverages Nutrition & Health care Pet Care Milk Products & Ice Cream Prepared Dishes & cooking aids Confectionary and Water.

The Powdered and Liquid Beverages segment which includes Nescafe Nespresso and Nesquik generates about 25% of sales.

Nutrition and Health Science (more than 15% of sales) sells baby food infant nutrition and skin care products under brands including Gerber illuma and Cerelac.

Milk Products and Ice Cream covers brands including Haagen-Dazs Coffee Mate and Dreyer's and accounts for nearly 15% of sales.

PetCare makes pet food (around 15% of sales) under eight Purina sub-brands including Felix and Pro Plan. The Prepared Dishes and Cooking Aids segment also accounts for almost 15% of sales and includes DiGiorno pizza and Maggi.

The Water segment consists of San Pellegrino water and soft drinks Vittel Perrier Pure Life and Poland Spring. It generates nearly 10% of sales.

The Confectionery segment generated almost 10% of sales. The segment includes Kit-Kat.

Geographic Reach

Nestlé divides its geographical operations across the regions of Americas (accounting for over 45% of sales); Europe Middle East and North Africa (almost 30%); and Asia Oceanic and Africa (more than 25%). The Swiss-based food giant has operations in more than 185 countries worldwide and operates about 155 factories in Americas; over 140 in Europe Middle East and North Africa; and more than 100 in Asia Oceanic and Africa.

Sales and Marketing

Nestlé analyzes data to tailor messages and adapt contents to ensure it resonates with customers thus evolving the company's buying media and marketing to unknown audiences in connecting with customers in a relevant and personalized way.

Financial Performance

Note: Growth rates may differ after conversion to US dollars.

Nestlé has struggled to lift its revenue in recent years due to sluggish consumer spending in Europe and the US and changes in consumer tastes.

Total reported sales increased by 1.2% to CHF 92.6 billion (2018: CHF 91.4 billion). Net divestments had a negative impact of 0.8% and foreign exchange reduced sales by 1.5%. Net profit increased by 24.4% to CHF 12.6 billion in 2019. Net profit benefited from the sale of Nestlé Skin Health.

Strategy

2019 was a busy and successful year in terms of portfolio adjustment. Nestle delivered all that it announced at the start of the year and more. The company further sharpened its strategic focus on food beverages and nutritional health products. The most significant transaction was the divestment of Nestlé Skin Health for CHF 10.2 billion. This business was no longer core to the Nutrition Health and Wellness strategy as its future growth opportunities lie increasingly outside of Nestlé's strategic boundaries. Nestlé continued to shift its portfolio toward higher growth categories in a disciplined way to maximize the value of its assets. The company reached an agreement to sell its U.S. ice cream business to Froneri for USD 4 billion.

The company also agreed to sell a 60% stake of Herta and create a joint venture with Casa Tarradellas.

Nestlé also took the decision to migrate the globally-managed Nestlé Waters business to its three geographic Zones from the start of 2020. This represents a further step toward harmonizing and simplifying the company's organizational structure. The move is expected to increase responsiveness and competitiveness as Nestlé Waters generates around 60% of its sales through local brands. This structure change follows the successful migrations of Nestlé Nutrition and Nestlé Professional into the Zones.

Mergers and Acquisitions

In mid-2020 Nestlé acquired Zenpep and Viokace from Allergan through its subsidiary Nestlé Health Science (NHSc). Allergan is based in Dublin Ireland. Its Zenpep and Viokace products only available in Canada and the US are pancreatic medications. The acquisition expands Nestlé medical nutrition business.

Nestlé Health Science (NHSc) acquired Persona in late 2019. Persona is based in Washington and a leading personalized vitamin business founded in 2017. The transaction expands NHSc's personalized nutrition.

EXECUTIVES

Deputy EVP GLOBE Programme Information Systems Strategic Supply Chain eNestlé and Group Information Security, Chris Johnson, age 59
CEO and Director, Ulf M. (Mark) Schneider, age 54
EVP and Head of Zone EMENA (Europe Middle East and North Africa), Luis Cantarell, age 68
EVP Strategic Business Units Marketing Sales and Nespresso, Patrice Bula, age 65
EVP and Head Asia Oceania and Africa (AOA), Wan Ling Martello
EVP Head of Nestlé Waters, Marco Settembri, age 62
EVP and Head of Zone Americas (United States of America Canada Latin America Caribbean), Laurent Freixe, age 58
Deputy EVP and CEO Nestlé Professional, Martial C. Rolland
EVP and CFO, Fran Şois-Xavier Roger
Chairman and Managing Director South Africa, Ian Donald
EVP CTO and Head of Innovation Technology Research & Development, Stefan Catsicas
Deputy EVP Head of Human Resources and Centre Administration, Peter R. Vogt
EVP and Head of Operations, Magdi Batato
Deputy EVP and Head of Nestlé Nutrition, Heiko Schipper, age 51
CEO Tribe Mediterranean Foods, John McGuckin
CEO Nairobi, Cornel Krummenacher
Chairman, Paul Bulcke, age 66
Auditors: KPMG SA

LOCATIONS

HQ: Nestle SA
Avenue Nestle 55, Vevey, Vaud CH-1800
Phone: (41) 21 924 2111   **Fax:** (41) 21 924 4800
Web: www.nestle.com

2018 sales

	% of total
Americas	45
EMENA	29
Zone Asia Oceania and Africa	26
Total	**100**

2018 Factories

	No.
Americas	159
EMENA	146
Asia Oceania & Africa	108
Total	**413**

PRODUCTS/OPERATIONS

2018 Product Sales

	% of total
Powdered & liquid beverages	24
Nutrition & health care	18
Milk products & ice cream	14
Prepared dishes & cooking aids	14
Pet care	13
Confectionery	9
Water	8
Total	**100**

Selected Products and Brands

Bouillons soups seasonings pasta and sauces
  Buitoni
  Maggi
  Thomy
  Winiary
Chilled Nestlé:
  Chiquitin
  La Laitière
  La Lechera
  LC1
  Molico
  Ski
  Sveltesse
  Svelty
  Yoco
Chocolate confectionery and biscuits
  Kit Kat
Coffee
  Bonka
  Loumidis
  Nescafé:
  Nespresso
  Ricoré; Ricoffy
  Taster's Choice
  Zoé;gas
Foodservice and professional products
  Chef
  Davigel
  Minor's
  Santa Rica
Frozen foods (prepared dishes pizzas)
  Buitoni
  California Pizza Kitchen (licensed)
  Delissio (Canada only)
  Hot Pockets
  Jack's Pizza
  Lean Cuisine
  Maggi
  Stouffer's
  Tombstone
Healthcare and nutrition
  Clinutren
  Modulen
  Nutren
  Peptamen
Ice cream
  Antica Gelateria del Corso
  Chipwich
  Dreyer's
  Drumstick/Extrême
  Edy's
  Eskimo Pie
  Häagen-Dazs
  Maxibon/Tandem
  Mega
  Mövenpick
  Parar
  Sin Parar/Sem
Infant food and nutrition
  Beba
  Cé;ré;lac
  Gerber
  Good Start
  Guigoz
  Lactogen
  Nan
  Neslac
  Nestlé:
  Nestogen
  Nestum
Other beverages
  Carnation
  Caro
  Libby's
  Milo
  Nescau

Nesquik
Nestea
Performance nutrition
  PowerBar
  Pria
Pet care
  Alpo
  Beneful
  Cat Chow
  Dog Chow
  Fancy Feast
  Felix
  Gourmet
  Pro Plan
  Purina Friskies
  Purina ONE
  Tidy Cats
Refrigerated products (cold meat products dough pasta pizzas sauces)
  Buitoni
  Herta
  Nestlé:
  Toll House
Shelf-stable products
  Bear Brand
  Carnation
  Coffee-Mate
  Gloria
  Klim
  La Lechera
  Milkmaid
  Moça
  Molico
  Nestlé; Omega
  Nido
  Ninho
  Svelty
Water
  Acqua Panna
  Al Manhal
  Arrowhead
  Contrex
  Deer Park
  Hé;par
  Ice Mountain
  Levissima
  Nestlé; Aquarel
  Nestlé; Pure Life
  Nestlé; Vera
  Ozarka
  Perrier
  Poland Spring
  Qué;zac
  S.Pellegrino
  San Bernardo
  Vittel
  Zephyrhills

Selected Subsidiaries Joint Ventures and Affiliates

Beverage Partners Worldwide (50% with The Coca-Cola Company US)
Cereal Partners Worldwide (50% with General Mills US)
Galderma and Laboratoires inné;ov (29% with L'Oreal cosmetic and nutritional supplement products)
Gerber Products Company (infant nutrition US)
Jenny Craig Inc. (weight-loss centers and foods US)
Uncle Tobys (soups breakfast cereal snacks Australia)

COMPETITORS

Abbott Labs	Kerry Group
Associated British Foods	Lindt & Spr ngli
	Mars Incorporated
Atkins Nutritionals	Medifast
Bally Total Fitness	Mondelez International
Barilla	Nutrisystem
Beech-Nut	PepsiCo
Campbell Soup	Procter & Gamble
Coca-Cola	Revlon
ConAgra	Russell Stover
Danone	Slim-Fast
Danone Water	Smucker
Dean Foods	Starbucks
Dreyer's	Suntory Holdings
Fit America	Tata Global Beverages
GNC	United Biscuits
General Mills	Weight Watchers
Goya	International

HMG
Heinz
Hershey
Indofood
Kellogg
Kent Gida

Wimm-Bill-Dann
World's Finest
Chocolate
eDiets.com
maxingvest

HISTORICAL FINANCIALS
Company Type: Public

Income Statement				FYE: December 31
	REVENUE ($ mil.)	NET INCOME ($ mil.)	NET PROFIT MARGIN	EMPLOYEES
12/19	96,064	13,043	13.6%	291,000
12/18	93,269	10,302	11.0%	308,000
12/17	92,340	7,359	8.0%	323,000
12/16	88,206	8,380	9.5%	328,000
12/15	89,701	9,128	10.2%	335,000
Annual Growth	1.7%	9.3%	—	(3.5%)

2019 Year-End Financials
Debt ratio: 27.3%
Return on equity: 23.0%
Cash ($ mil.): 10,616
Current ratio: 0.86
Long-term debt ($ mil.): 20,437

No. of shares (mil.): —
Dividends
 Yield: 2.2%
 Payout: 56.5%
Market value ($ mil.): —

	STOCK PRICE ($) FY Close	P/E High/Low		PER SHARE ($)	
			Earnings	Dividends	Book Value
12/19	108.26	27 19	4.45	2.42	18.69
12/18	80.96	26 22	3.42	2.42	19.60
12/17	85.97	38 32	2.38	2.35	20.61
12/16	71.74	28 24	2.70	2.18	20.48
12/15	74.42	27 23	2.91	2.28	20.35
Annual Growth	9.8%	— —	11.2%	1.6%	(2.1%)

New China Life Insurance Co Ltd

Auditors: Ernst & Young Hua Ming LLP

LOCATIONS
HQ: New China Life Insurance Co Ltd
 NCI Tower, A12 Jianguomenwai Avenue, Chaoyang
 District, Beijing 100022
Phone: (86) 10 85213233   **Fax:** (86) 10 85213219
Web: www.newchinalife.com

HISTORICAL FINANCIALS
Company Type: Public

Income Statement				FYE: December 31
	REVENUE ($ mil.)	NET INCOME ($ mil.)	NET PROFIT MARGIN	EMPLOYEES
12/19	25,087	2,092	8.3%	0
12/18	22,413	1,151	5.1%	0
12/17	16,585	827	5.0%	0
12/15	24,242	1,324	5.5%	52,474
12/14	17,606	1,032	5.9%	0
Annual Growth	7.3%	15.2%	—	—

2019 Year-End Financials
Debt ratio: —
Return on equity: 19.4%
Cash ($ mil.): 1,691
Current ratio: 0.06
Long-term debt ($ mil.): —

No. of shares (mil.): —
Dividends
 Yield: —
 Payout: —
Market value ($ mil.): —

Nidec Corp

Nidec claims to be the #1 comprehensive motor manufacturer for everything that spins and moves from the smallest motors to some of the largest. Based in Japan the company holds the largest global market share for the tiny spindle motors that power hard-disk drives. It also makes midsize motors for home electronics and industrial equipment along with small precision fans power supplies and pivot assemblies. Nidec's brushless DC motors can be found in automobiles (power steering units) and home appliances (air conditioners and refrigerators). Japan and China are the company's largest markets each representing more than 20% of sales. Other major markets include the US Thailand and Germany. Nidec was founded in 1973 by Shigenobu Nagamori and three other engineers as Nippon Densan Corporation.

Financial Performance
Nidec's revenue has been increasing steadily over the past five years with an overall increase of 70% since 2014.

Sales in fiscal 2018 reached Â 1.5 trillion a 2% increase compared with 2017. The largest contributor to Nidec's bottom line was its Appliance Commercial and Industrial Product segment which showed a 4% increase as well as a 6% increase in operating profit.

Net income has also been trending upward except for a 15% drop in fiscal 2018 to Â 110.8 billion from Â 130.8 the previous year. This was mainly due to decreased operating profit in some of the company's larger business units including Small Precision Motors and Automotive Products.

Strategy
By leveraging the plentiful and cheap labor markets of East Asia and establishing relationships with blue-chip clients in the US that include 3M and IBM and Asian stalwarts such as Hitachi Nidec has nurtured what was a non-existent market in the 1970s into a critical supplier to the computer hardware and consumer electronics industries. Nidec plans to capitalize on the increased global demand for electronic data storage and accompanying high-capacity data center servers by stepping up production in its hard disk drive (HDD) motors business.

Going forward Nidec is focusing on its small precision motors business particularly in the appliance commercial and industrial markets to drive growth. As such in 2019 the company acquired Embraco the compressor business of Whirlpool Corporation. With stricter environmental regulations in Europe the Americas and China Nidec believes the acquisition will strengthen its compressor business for household and commercial refrigerators. It also plans to increase sales of its small electric motors such as its brushless DC motors fan motors and stepping motors for home appliances like room fans dryers blenders and cleaning robots.

To increase the efficiency of its management organization the company is creating five regional headquarters in Japan China Asia the Americas and Europe (including the Middle East and Africa).

EXECUTIVES
Chairman President and CEO, Shigenobu Nagamori, age 76
Vice Chairman and Chief Sales Officer (CSO), Hiroshi Kobe, age 71
Vice Chairman and CTO, Mikio Katayama, age 63
EVP, Akira Sato
EVP Fluid Dynamic Bearing Motor Business and General Application Motor & Solutions, Toshihiko Miyabe, age 62
First SVP and CFO, Masuo Yoshimatsu, age 62
Auditors: PricewaterhouseCoopers Kyoto

LOCATIONS
HQ: Nidec Corp
 338 Kuzetonoshiro-cho, Minami-ku, Kyoto 601-8205
Phone: (81) 75 922 1111   **Fax:** (81) 75 935 6101
Web: www.nidec.com

2018 Sales

	% of total
China	23
Japan	20
US	17
Thailand	9
Germany	9
Singapore	3
Other countries	19
Total	**100**

PRODUCTS/OPERATIONS

2018 Sales

	% of total
Nidec Motor	23
Nidec Motor & Actuators	16
Nidec Corporation	11
Nidec Sankyo	8
Nidec (H.K.)	7
Nidec Electronics (Thailand)	6
Nidec Techno Motor	5
Nidec Singapore	2
Nidec Copal	2
All Others	20
Total	**100**

2018 Sales

	% of total
Appliance commercial and industrial products	35
Small precision motors	29
Automotive products	19
Machinery	12
Electronic and optical components	5
Other	-
Total	**0**

Selected Products
Mid-size DC motors
Pivot assemblies
Power supplies
Small high-precision AC motors
Small high-precision DC motors
Small high-precision fans

COMPETITORS
AMETEK
Bodine Electric
Delta Electronics
Hitachi
 High-Technologies
Johnson Electric
LG Electronics
Mabuchi Motor

MinebeaMitsumi
Panasonic Corp
Panasonic Healthcare
SANYO
Samsung Electronics
Toshiba
Tsubaki Nakashima
WEG Electric

HISTORICAL FINANCIALS

Company Type: Public

Income Statement

FYE: March 31

	REVENUE ($ mil.)	NET INCOME ($ mil.)	NET PROFIT MARGIN	EMPLOYEES
03/20	15,475	605	3.9%	145,169
03/19	15,308	1,117	7.3%	137,791
03/18	15,004	1,325	8.8%	135,211
03/17	12,092	1,126	9.3%	132,766
03/16	11,880	925	7.8%	96,602
Annual Growth	6.8%	(10.1%)	—	10.7%

2020 Year-End Financials

Debt ratio: 0.2%
Return on equity: 6.1%
Cash ($ mil.): 2,086
Current ratio: 1.34
Long-term debt ($ mil.): 3,456

No. of shares (mil.): 585
Dividends
  Yield: 0.9%
  Payout: —
Market value ($ mil.): 15,433

	STOCK PRICE ($) FY Close	P/E High/Low		PER SHARE ($) Earnings	Dividends	Book Value
03/20	26.34	0	0	1.03	0.25	16.34
03/19	31.88	0	0	1.89	0.11	17.09
03/18	38.54	0	0	2.24	0.10	15.89
03/17	23.92	0	0	1.90	0.18	14.40
03/16	17.15	0	0	3.11	0.16	25.98
Annual Growth	11.3% (10.9%)	—	—	(24.1%)	11.8%	

Nintendo Co., Ltd.

Nintendo wants everyone — from apprentice Marios to alpha Donkey KongsÂ — to play preferably on one of its Nintendo DS handheld devices or its Wii home video game console. The market-leading game company achieved its status in part byÂ courting users that span generationsÂ and skill levels. Among the Big Three of the videogame console makers Nintendo's Wii (pronounced "we") is #1 battling with Microsoft'sÂ Xbox and Sony's PlayStation for the hearts and dollars ofÂ devoted gamers. Also leading in handheld consoles its DS device began in 2004Â the most recent incarnation its no-glasses 3-D version launched in 2011 the 3DS. Wii successor Wii U featuring aÂ controller with a touch screen is planned for 2012.

Auditors: PricewaterhouseCoopers Kyoto

LOCATIONS

HQ: Nintendo Co., Ltd.
  11-1 Kamitoba Hokotate-cho, Minami-ku, Kyoto 601-8501
Phone: (81) 75 662 9600
Web: www.nintendo.co.jp

2012 Sales

	% of total
The Americas	
US	33
Other Americas	6
Europe	33
Japan	23
Other	5
Total	**100**

PRODUCTS/OPERATIONS

2012 Sales

	% of total
Handheld Hardware	36
Handheld Software	20
Home Console Software	18
Home Console Hardware	18
Other	8
Total	**100**

Selected Consoles

3DS
3DS XL
DS
DS Lite
DSi
DSi XL
Wii
Wii U

Selected Games

Donkey Kong Country Returns
Kid Icarus: Uprising
Kirby Tilt 'n' Tumble
The Legend of Zelda
Mario & Sonic at the London 2012 Olympic Games
Mario Kart
Mario Party
Metroid Prime
Poké;mon
Punch-Out!!
Sin and Punishment: Star Successor
Spider-Man
Super Mario Galaxy
Super Smash Bros. Brawl
Wii Fit Plus
Wii Play
Wii Sports Resort
Xenoblade Chronicles
Yoshi

Selected Subsidiaries

Nintendo Australia Pty. Ltd.
Nintendo Benelux B.V. (The Netherlands)
Nintendo Espa Â Â a S.A. (Spain)
Nintendo France S.A.R.L.
Nintendo of America Inc. (US)
Nintendo of Canada Ltd.
Nintendo of Europe GmbH (Germany)

COMPETITORS

Activision Blizzard	NCsoft
Capcom	Namco Bandai
Editis	SEGA
Electronic Arts	Sony
Konami	Square Enix
LeapFrog	Take-Two
Lucasfilm	Ubisoft
Entertainment	Valve Corporation
Majesco Entertainment	ZeniMax Media
Microsoft	

HISTORICAL FINANCIALS

Company Type: Public

Income Statement

FYE: March 31

	REVENUE ($ mil.)	NET INCOME ($ mil.)	NET PROFIT MARGIN	EMPLOYEES
03/20	13,193	2,607	19.8%	6,200
03/19	12,104	1,956	16.2%	5,944
03/18	10,644	1,407	13.2%	6,030
03/17	4,931	1,034	21.0%	5,788
03/16	5,086	166	3.3%	5,697
Annual Growth	26.9%	99.0%	—	2.1%

2020 Year-End Financials

Debt ratio: —
Return on equity: 17.4%
Cash ($ mil.): 8,977
Current ratio: 4.22
Long-term debt ($ mil.): —

No. of shares (mil.): 119
Dividends
  Yield: 2.1%
  Payout: —
Market value ($ mil.): 5,751

	STOCK PRICE ($) FY Close	P/E High/Low		PER SHARE ($) Earnings	Dividends	Book Value
03/20	48.28	0	0	21.89	1.05	130.41
03/19	35.87	0	0	16.29	0.73	119.32
03/18	55.51	0	0	11.72	0.60	110.71
03/17	29.02	0	0	8.61	0.18	104.99
03/16	17.75	0	0	1.39	0.21	97.43
Annual Growth	28.4%	—	—	99.4%	49.0%	7.6%

Nippon Express Co Ltd

One of Japan's largest transportation companies Nippon Express moves all sorts of freight. The company's largest business motor transportation operates under brands including Arrow. Besides general freight transportation Nippon Express offers moving services and transportation of items such as cash and construction equipment. Nippon Express also provides warehousing services and air ocean and rail freight forwarding. The company operates from facilities throughout Japan which accounts for the vast majority of its sales and in more than 45 other countries around the world. Founded in 1937 Nippon Express also sells petroleum products and leases containers.

Operations

The company operates four segment reportable segments: Logistics Logistic Support Security Transportation and Heavy Haulage & Construction.

The Nippon Express' logistics segment has grown as transport modes have expanded from railways to automobiles ships and airplanes. It generates about 80% of total revenue.

Logistic Support segment generates some 20% of total revenue includes the sale e of distribution equipment wrapping and packaging materials vehicles petroleum liquefied petroleum (LP) gas etc. lease vehicle maintenance insurance agency mediation planning designing and management of real estate investigation and research logistics finance automobile driving instruction employee dispatching.

Security Transportation include security guard and motor cargo transportation.

Heavy Haulage & Construction includes heavy haulage and construction.

Geographic Reach

The company operates in Japan the Americas and Europe and stretching into the rapidly developing markets of East Asia South Asia and Oceania. It maintains a global presence with about 740 locations in nearly 320 cities spanning about 45 countries.

Financial Performance

Revenues decreased by Â 58.1 billion or 3% year on year to Â 2.1 trillion. The main factor in the decline on revenues was a drop of Â 4.2 billion due to the spread of COVID-19.

Cash held by the company at the end of 2019 decreased by Â 5.9 billion to Â 96.2 billion from Â 102.1 billion in the prior year. Cash provided by operation was Â 98.2 billion while cash used for financing activities was Â 11.7 million. Cash used for investing activities was Â 91.8 billion primarily for payment for purchase of property and equipment.

Strategy

The Nippon Express Group Business Plan 2023 ~"Dynamic Growth"~ which covers the period from fiscal 2019 to fiscal 2023 was formulated with the idea of answering the question of what the Nippon Express Group wanted to be as it approached the 100th anniversary of its founding in 2037. The plan also established the goal of being "a logistics company with a strong presence in the global market" as its long-term vision. The image for growth targets sales in fiscal 2037 of about Å 4.0 trillion and an overseas sales ratio of 50% equating to overseas sales of roughly Å 2.0 trillion. In working to achieve this long-term vision the company's framework is built on its efforts creating new value through innovation while cherishing its unchanging values and meeting the expectations of its stakeholders. The company believe "transformation" is key to achieving its long-term vision and are accordingly moving forward with changes to its business organization and corporate culture.

The Nippon Express Group Business Plan 2023 ~"Dynamic Growth"~ includes: Defines a three-dimensional (Customer (Industry) Business and Area) approach as a growth strategy for its core business; Defines a realization of the high profitability to build the base of the company's growth strategy as a strategy to enhance domestic businesses in Japan; Defines M&A as an inorganic growth strategy to reinforce and expand its global management base; and Establishes ESG-oriented business management to realize sustainable development (e.g. global governance) and improve corporate value.

EXECUTIVES

President and CEO, Kenji Watanabe, age 70
EVP, Jiro Nakamura, age 71
EVP, Keiji Hagio, age 72
Chairman, Masanori Kawai, age 77
Auditors: Ernst & Young ShinNihon LLC

LOCATIONS

HQ: Nippon Express Co Ltd
1-9-3 Higashi-Shimbashi, Minato-ku, Tokyo 105-8322
Phone: (81) 3 6251 1111   **Fax:** 212 758-2595
Web: www.nittsu.co.jp

PRODUCTS/OPERATIONS

2015 Sales

	% of total
Combined business	39
Goods sales	22
Air freight forwarding	11
Marine & harbor transportation	6
Others	22
Total	**100**

Selected Services
Air Freight
Fine Arts Transport
Heavy Haulage
Logistics Design & IT
Marine Transport
Moving Service

COMPETITORS

DHL	Mitsui-Soko
FedEx	NYK Line
Hub Group	Schenker
Janel World Trade	Seino Transportation
Japan Post	Co
Kintetsu	UPS
Mitsui O.S.K. Lines	Yamato Holdings

HISTORICAL FINANCIALS

Company Type: Public

Income Statement

FYE: March 31

	REVENUE ($ mil.)	NET INCOME ($ mil.)	NET PROFIT MARGIN	EMPLOYEES
03/20	19,164	160	0.8%	89,024
03/19	19,310	445	2.3%	88,835
03/18	18,790	61	0.3%	86,972
03/17	16,674	326	2.0%	87,765
03/16	17,000	317	1.9%	86,011
Annual Growth	3.0%	(15.7%)	—	0.9%

2020 Year-End Financials

Debt ratio: 0.2%
Return on equity: 3.2%
Cash ($ mil.): 1,301
Current ratio: 1.45
Long-term debt ($ mil.): 2,938

No. of shares (mil.): 93
Dividends
  Yield: —
  Payout: —
Market value ($ mil.): —

Nippon Life Insurance Co. (Japan)

Nippon Life Insurance also known as Nissay is a top life insurer in Japan. The company which has some 14 million policyholders uses a door-to-door sales corps and other representatives to peddle its traditional insurance products including individual and group life and annuity policies to Japanese consumers. In addition to its life insurance products the company administers pension plans and medical coverage plans and provides asset management services. Through its affiliates and subsidiaries the company also sells auto and other property/casualty insurance in Japan and it has some international life insurance operations as well as select real estate and financial service assets.

Operations
Nippon Life gets about 75% of its total revenue from its core insurance operations. In addition the group is involved in real estate investment mortgage lending and investment advisory among other financial services activities. Subsidiaries include NLI Commercial Mortgage Fund Nippon Insurance Service NLI Insurance Agency Nissay Asset Management and Nissay Capital.

Geographic Reach
Japan- based Nippon Life has more than 75 subsidiaries and affiliates and operates about 110 branch locations and more than 1500 sales offices. It operates in Australia China India Indonesia Japan Thailand the UK and the US.

Sales and Marketing
Nippon Life primarily sells policies through its dedicated field sales force as well as through retail store locations call centers and online. It also sells through select insurance brokerages and via partnerships with financial services firms including banks.

Financial Performance
Note: Growth rates may differ after conversion to US Dollars.

Nippon Life's revenue has steadily grown in the past couple of years. Revenue rose 11% between 2015 and 2019 having recovered from the slight dip in 2017. Net income however has struggled to return to its peak values despite rising in the past years. It fell 10% between 2015 and 2019.

Nippon Life's revenue increased 8% to Å 8.2 trillion in fiscal 2019 (ended March) as insurance and reinsurance investment and other income all rose.

Net income also increased by 14% to Å 278.7 billion that year. Death and other claims payouts increased as did surrender benefits annuity payments and reinsurance premiums. Those gains led to a 4% increase in expenses for Nippon Life.

The company ended fiscal 2019 with Å 2 trillion in net cash some Å 114.9 billion more than it had at the end of fiscal 2018. Operating activities provided Å 1.9 trillion in cash while investing activities used Å 1.9 trillion for purchases of securities purchase of tangible fixed assets and payments for acquisition of subsidiary's shares. Financing activities provided Å 148.3 billion mainly from debt borrowing proceeds.

Strategy
Nippon Life along with its competitors in Japan is faced with several market challenges including a declining population which brings a smaller customer pool and an aging population which brings more payouts on claims. Furthermore an ultra-low interest rate environment is prevailing under the Bank of Japan's negative interest rate policy as well as digitalization and advanced IT that spur rapid developments. To combat some of these problems Nippon Life has set goals to develop a business base for sustained growth so it can remain the dominant market leader. The goal incorporates two concepts: approach change in a positive way and build greater trust with customers and society in general. It has also formulated three specific strategies to achieve the new goal: strengthening profitability operational and business reform and the promotion of group management.

Nippon Life has also been growing through acquisitions. Its recent purchases include Grand Guardian Life Insurance Company Limited in Myanmar Reliance Nippon Life Asset Management Limited as well as a partial limited partnership investment in Resolution Life Group Holdings L.P. which is a global insurance company that assumes and manages portfolios of in-force policies worldwide.

Additionally earlier in 2020 Nippon Life established an open innovation hub named Nippon Life X to create new business for the Nippon Life Group and started activities under a unified brand from four global corners (Tokyo Silicon Valley in the US London and Beijing).

Mergers and Acquisitions
In mid-2019 Nippon Life reached an agreement to acquire 35% stake in Guardian Life Insurance Company Limited business in Myanmar equivalent to $21 million (Å 2.3 billion).

In mid-2019 Nippon Life reached a definitive agreement with India-based Reliance Capital Limited. Nippon Life acquired additional 32% stake for INR 45.2 billion (Å 72.8 billion) increasing its ownership to 75% in Reliance Nippon Life Asset Management.

Company Background
Nippon Life was founded as Nippon Life Assurance in 1889. Nippon Life was the first Japanese life insurer to offer profit dividends to its policyholders.

HISTORY

Nippon Life known as Nissay was a product of the modernization that began after US Commodore Matthew Perry opened Japan's ports to foreigners in 1854. Industry and trade were Japan's first focus but financial infrastructure soon followed. The country's first insurer (Meiji Mutual) opened in 1881. In 1889 Osaka banker Sukesaburo Hirose founded Nippon Life as a stock company. It grew and opened branches in Tokyo (1890) and Kyushu (1895).

In the 20th century the company developed a direct sales force and began lending directly to businesses. Lending remained the backbone of its asset strategy through most of the century. The insurance market in Japan grew quickly until the late 1920s but had already slowed by the eve of the Depression.

After WWII the company reorganized as a mutual and began mobilizing an army of women to build its sales of installment-premium basic life policies. In 1962 the company began automating its systems and established operations in the US (1972) and the UK (1981).

As interest rates rose in the wake of oil price hikes in the 1970s the company began offering term life and annuities and slowly moved to diversify its asset holdings from mostly government bonds (whose yields declined as rates rose) to stocks. This movement accelerated in the 1980s as the businesses that traditionally borrowed from Nippon Life turned directly to capital markets to raise money through debt issues. Seeking to replace its shrinking lending business the company began investing in US real estate and businesses whose values rose in the mid-1980s. The company reached its zenith in 1987; it owned about 3% of all the stocks on the Tokyo Exchange held more real estate than Mitsubishi's real estate units and had bought 13% of US brokerage Shearson Lehman from American Express.

By the end of the year thanks to the US stock market crash the value of the Shearson investment had fallen 40%. But the company felt confident enough of its importance as the world's largest insurance company (by assets) to crow its intentions to strong-arm Japan's Ministry of Finance into letting it diversify into trust and securities operations.

Then its bubble burst. In 1989 real estate crashed and the stock market lost more than half its value. Japan's economy failed to improve and Nippon Life was left struggling with nonperforming loans and assets whose value had declined. The company suffered further from policy cancellations and from the Ministry of Finance's focus on buoying banks. In 1997 the ministry asked Nippon Life to convert its subordinated debt from Nippon Credit Bank (now Aozora Bank) to stock. That year Nippon Life formed an alliance with Marsh & McLennan's Putnam Investments subsidiary to help manage its assets; the relationship deepened in 1998 when they began developing investment trust products.

The next year Nippon Life faced a shareholder lawsuit over its involvement in the collapse of Nippon Credit Bank; the company claims the Ministry of Finance tricked it into bailing out the bank even though it was beyond rescue. In 2001 the company merged its Nissay General subsidiary with Dowa Fire & Marine creating nonlife insurer Nissay Dowa.

EXECUTIVES

EVP, Kazuo Kobayashi, age 65
President, Yoshinobu Tsutsui, age 67
Senior Managing Executive Officer, Yoshinori Terajima, age 62
Senior Managing Executive Officer, Hiroshi Shimizu, age 60
Senior Managing Executive Officer, Takeshi Hayashi, age 62
Senior Managing Executive Officer, Keishi Kai, age 65
Chairman, Kunie Okamoto, age 76
Vice Chairman, Takeshi Furuichi, age 66
Auditors: Deloitte Touche Tohmatsu LLC

LOCATIONS

HQ: Nippon Life Insurance Co. (Japan)
3-5-12 Imabashi, Chuo-ku, Osaka 541-8501
Phone: (81) 6 6209 4500
Web: www.nissay.co.jp

PRODUCTS/OPERATIONS

2018 Sales

	% of total
Insurance & reinsurance	71
Investment income	26
Other	3
Total	**100**

Selected Products and Services

Products for Individuals
　Annuities
　Asset management
　Cancer Medical Insurance
　Dread Disease Insurance
　Endowment Insurance
　General Medical Insurance
　Limited Injury Insurance
　Non-life Insurance Products
　Nursing Care Insurance
　Physical Disability Insurance
　Products for Children
　Single-payment Products
　Term Life Insurance
　Term Life Insurance with Survival Benefits
　Whole Life Insurance
Products for Businesses
　Disability coverage
　Home buying preparation
　Medical coverage
　Retirement coverage
　Survivor coverage
　Various life plans

COMPETITORS

AXA Life Insurance	Gibraltar Life
American Life	Insurance
Insurance	Meiji Yasuda Life
Asahi Mutual Life	MetLife
Dai-ichi Life	Sumitomo Life
Daido Life	Taiyo Life
Fukoku Mutual	

HISTORICAL FINANCIALS

Company Type: Public

Income Statement				FYE: March 31
	ASSETS ($ mil.)	NET INCOME ($ mil.)	INCOME AS % OF ASSETS	EMPLOYEES
03/19	711,637	2,517	0.4%	0
03/18	700,581	2,297	0.3%	71,871
03/17	648,121	2,700	0.4%	70,651
03/16	628,761	3,592	0.6%	70,519
03/15	522,162	2,567	0.5%	70,783
Annual Growth	**8.0%**	**(0.5%)**	—	—

2019 Year-End Financials

Return on assets: 0.3%	Dividends
Return on equity: 4.1%	Yield: —
Long-term debt ($ mil.): —	Payout: —
No. of shares (mil.): —	Market value ($ mil.): —
Sales ($ mil): 74,446	

Nippon Steel Corp (New)

Nippon Steel (formerly Nippon Steel & Sumitomo Metal) the world's third-largest steelmaker after ArcelorMittal and China Baowu Group manufactures pig iron and ingots steel bars plates sheets pipes and tubes as well as specialty processed and fabricated steel products. Nippon Steel's annual crude steel output is around 47 million tons. The company's operations include steelmaking and fabrication engineering and construction chemicals and materials and system solutions. Though the company sells many products? from petrochemical to industrial machinery? the clear majority of its revenue comes from its steel products. The company was founded in 1950 and is based in Tokyo Japan. The company generates around 65% of sales in Japan.

Operations

Nippon Steel operates in four segments: Steelmaking and Steel Fabrication (more than 85% of total revenue) while Engineering and Construction Chemicals and Materials and System Solutions which accounts some 5% each.

Steelmaking and Steel Fabrication makes and markets steel products including pig iron and ingots steel bars plates sheets pipes and tubes and specialty processed and fabricated steel items.

Engineering and Construction make and markets industrial machinery and equipment and steel structures. It also offers construction work under contract waste processing and recycling services and supplies electricity civil engineering work pipe piling work building construction base-isolation vibration-control devices gas and heat.

Chemicals and new materials make and sell coal-based chemical products petrochemicals and electronic materials. In addition the company also makes materials and components for semiconductors and electronic parts carbon fiber and composite products and products that utilize technologies for metal processing are part of this segment. The System Solutions segment includes computer system engineering and consulting services; IT-enabled outsourcing and other services.

Geographic Reach

Nippon Steel has operations across the world. Its main operations are in Japan (headquarters) but it also has overseas branches in six countries including the US the U.K. China Singapore Thailand and Indonesia.

In Japan it has more than 10 steelworks three major research centers and laboratories in Futtsu Amagasaki and Hasaki

Sales and Marketing

Nippon Steel's customers include Fuji Xerox Panasonic and Navistar International Corp.

Financial Performance

Note: Growth rates may differ after conversion to US Dollars.

Sales decreased 4% from Â 6.2 trillion in 2018 to Â 5.9 trillion in 2019. Net income attributable to Nippon took a huge hit from a profit of Â 251.2 billion in 2018 to a loss of Â 431.5 billion in 2019.

Cash and cash equivalents at end of the year totaled Â 289.5 billion compared to Â 163.2 billion of the previous year. Operations generated Â 494.3 billion while investing and financing activities used Â 345.6 billion and Â 14.6 billion respectively.

Strategy

The Group utilizes derivatives including foreign exchange forward contracts interest rate swaps and currency swaps to hedge foreign currency risk and interest rate risk. These derivatives are initially recognized at fair value when the contract is entered into and are subsequently measured at fair value. Changes in fair value of derivatives are recognized in profit or loss. However the effective portion of cash flow hedges is recognized in other comprehensive income.

Mergers and Acquisitions

Nippon Steel acquired around 50% in Japan-based Sanyo Steel in 2019. The acquisition means that Nippon will also own Ovako AB the Swedish steel maker that Sanyo bought in June 2018. Sanyo manufactures special steel the market for which is set to grow in Asia. Terms were not disclosed. O

vako AB manufactures and sells special steel aimed mainly at the European Market. Through the acquisition Nippon Steel & Sumitomo Metal strengthened its technology product quality and product development capability for special steel.

ArcelorMittal and NIPPON STEEL CORPORATION completed the joint acquisition of Essar Steel India Limited in 2019 which was implemented by the joint venture of AM and Nippon Steel. ESIL will start anew as ArcelorMittal Nippon Steel India. Terms were not disclosed.

Company Background

As Japan prepared for war the government in 1934 merged Yawata Works the country's largest steel producer and other Japanese steelmakers into one giant company - Japan Iron & Steel.

As Japan lost the war Japan Iron & Steel was ordered to dissolve by the Allied forces. Two new companies? Yawata Iron & Steel and Fuji Iron & Steel?emerged from the dissolution.

With Western assistance the Japanese steel industry recovered from the war years in the 60s. Yawata and Fuji merged again in 1970 and became Nippon Steel the world's largest steelmaker.

The company diversified in the mid-1980s to wean itself from dependence on steel. It has remained a leading steel company since.

In 2012 Nippon acquired Sumitomo Metal Industries mating Japan's #1 and #3 steelmakers.

In 2019 the company shortened its name from Nippon Steel & Sumitomo Metal Corporation to Nippon Steel Corporation.

HISTORY

As Japan prepared for war the government in 1934 merged Yawata Works its largest steel producer and other Japanese steelmakers into one giant company — Japan Iron & Steel. During postwar occupation Japan Iron & Steel was ordered to dissolve. Yawata Iron & Steel and Fuji Iron & Steel emerged from the dissolution and with Western assistance the Japanese steel industry recovered from the war years. In the late 1960s Fuji Steel bought Tokai Iron & Steel (1967) and Yawata Steel took over Yawata Steel Tube Company (1968).

Yawata and Fuji merged in 1970 and became Nippon Steel the world's largest steelmaker. In the 1970s the Japanese steel industry was criticized in the US; American competitors complained that Japan was "dumping" low-cost exports. Meanwhile Nippon Steel aggressively courted China.

The company diversified in the mid-1980s to wean itself from dependence on steel. It created a New Materials unit in 1984 retraining "redundant" steelworkers to make silicon wafers and forming an Electronics Division in 1986. Nippon Steel began joint ventures with IBM Japan (small computers and software) Hitachi (office workstations) and C. Itoh (information systems for small and midsized companies) in 1988 as increased steel demand for construction and cars in Japan's "bubble economy" took the company to new heights.

In an atmosphere of economic optimism the company spent more than four times the expected expense to build an amusement park capable of competing with Tokyo Disneyland. The company plowed ahead spending some $230 million on the park. Space World amusement park opened on the island of Kyushu in 1990. The company's bubble burst that year. (The theme park declared bankruptcy in May 2005 and was sold to Kamori Kanko later that year.)

In response Nippon Steel cut costs and intensified its diversification efforts by targeting electronics information and telecommunications new materials and chemicals markets. Seeking to remake its steel operations the company began a drastic phased restructuring in 1993 that included a step most Japanese companies try to avoid — cutting personnel. A semiconductor division was organized that year as part of the company's diversification strategy.

Upgrading its steel operations Nippon Steel and partner Mitsubishi in 1996 introduced the world's first mass-production method for making hot-rolled steel sheet directly from smelted stainless steel. Profits were hurt that year by a loss-making project in the information and communications segment and by a steep decline in computer memory-chip prices.

The company began operation of a Chinese steelmaking joint venture Guangzhou Pacific Tinplate in 1997. The next year its Singapore-based joint venture with Hitachi Ltd. began mass-producing computer memory chips in hopes of stemming semiconductor losses. But falling prices convinced Nippon Steel to get out of the memory chip business and in 1999 it sold its semiconductor subsidiary to South Korea's United Microelectronics.

That year the US imposed antidumping duties on the company's steel products. The next year Nippon Steel agreed to form a strategic alliance with South Korea-based Pohang Iron and Steel (POSCO) at that time the world's #1 steel maker. The deal called for the exploration of joint ventures shared research and joint procurement as well as increased equity stakes in each other (at 2%-3%). Also in 2000 Nippon Steel agreed to provide Sumitomo Metal Industries and Nisshin Steel Co. with stainless steel products.

Early in 2001 Nippon Steel formed a cooperative alliance — focused on automotive sheet products — with French steel giant Usinor (now a part of ArcelorMittal). At the end of the year Nippon Steel decided to form an alliance with Kobe Steel to pare down costs and share in distribution and production facilities. In 2002 the company continued its series of comprehensive alliances by forming alliances with Japanese steelmaker Nippon Metal Industry to exchange its semi-finished stainless steel technologies and with POSCO to build environment-related businesses.

The company reported a loss of Å 51.69 billion ($430 million) for fiscal 2003 due to securities valuation losses and group restructuring charges. In 2004 Nippon Steel formed a joint venture with Baoshan Iron & Steel and Arcelor to manufacture high-grade automotive steel sheets.

Nippon Steel moved into the South American market in 2006 forming alliances with steelmaker Usiminas and iron miner CVRD. And the next year it created a JV with Baosteel and ArcelorMittal that produces automotive steel sheets.

The company joined up with Sumitomo Metal Industries in 2009 when the two companies agreed to form a joint venture that will combine their arc-welded stainless steel pipe and tube operations. Sumitomo will own 60% of the JV. The operations that make up the new company which will be called Sumikin & Nippon Steel Stainless Steel Pipe Co. achieved sales of more than $250 million in 2008.

EXECUTIVES

Representative Director and EVP, Kenji Takahashi
Chairman and CEO, Shoji Muneoka, age 74
Reprentative Director and President, Kosei Shindo
Representative Director and EVP, Soichiro Sakuma
Representative Director and EVP, Yasumitsu Saeki
Representative Director and EVP, Shinji Fujino
Representative Director and EVP, Eiji Hashmoto
Representative Director and EVP, Toshiharu Sakae
Auditors: KPMG AZSA LLC

LOCATIONS

HQ: Nippon Steel Corp (New)
2-6-1 Marunouchi, Chiyoda-ku, Tokyo 100-8071
Phone: (81) 3 6867 4111
Web: www.nipponsteel.com

2016 Sales

	% of total
Japan	66
Rest of Asia	22
Other	12
Total	**100**

PRODUCTS/OPERATIONS

2018 Sales

	% of total
Steelmaking & Steel Fabrication	88
Engineering & Construction	5
Chemicals	3
Systems Solutions	3
New Materials	1
Total	**100**

Selected Products and Services

Steelmaking and Steel Fabrication
  Fabricated and processed steels
  Pig iron and ingots
  Pipes and tubes
  Plates and sheets
  Sections
  Specialty sheets
Engineering and Construction
  Building construction
  Civil engineering
  Marine construction
  Plant and machinery
  Technical cooperation
Chemicals
  Aluminum products
  Ammonium sulfate
  Cement
  Ceramic products
  Coal tar
  Coke
  Ferrite
  Metallic foils
  Slag products
System Solutions
  Communications services
  Computers and equipment
  Data processing
  Systems development and integration
Urban Development
  Condominiums
  Theme parks
New Materials
  Semiconductor bonding wire
  Silicon wafers
  Titanium products
  Transformers
Other operations
  Services
  Energy services
  Financial services
  Insurance services
  Transportation
  Loading and unloading
  Marine and land transportation
  Warehousing

Selected Subsidiaries and Affiliates

Subsidiaries
  Nippon Steel & Sumikin Coated Sheet Corporation

Nippon Steel & Sumikin Metal Products Co. Ltd.
Nippon Steel & Sumikin Stainless Steel Corporation
Nippon Steel & Sumikin Welding Co. Ltd.
Nippon Steel Australia Pty. Limited
Nippon Steel Blast Furnace Slag Cement Co. Ltd.
Nippon Steel Drum Co. Ltd. 1654
Nippon Steel Logistics Co. Ltd.
Nippon Steel Shipping Co. Ltd.
Nippon Steel Transportation Co. Ltd.
Nippon Steel U.S.A. Inc.
Nittetsu Cement Co. Ltd.
Nittetsu Elex Co. Ltd.
Nittetsu Finance Co. Ltd.
Nittetsu Steel Pipe Co. Ltd. 4832
Nittetsu Tokai Steel Wire Co. Ltd.
NS Preferred Capital Limited
Osaka Steel Co. Ltd.
Siam Nippon Steel Pipe Co. Ltd.
The Siam United Steel (1995) Co. Ltd.
Affiliates
  Daiwa Can Company
  Geostr Corporation
  Godo Steel Ltd.
  Japan Casting & Forging Corporation
  Krosaki Harima Corporation
  Mitsui Mining Co. Ltd.
  Nichia Steel Works Ltd.
  Nippon Steel Trading Co. Ltd.
  Sanko Metal Industrial Co. Ltd.
  Sanyo Special Steel Co. Ltd.
  Sanyu Co. Ltd.
  Suzuki Metal Industry Co. Ltd.
  Taihei Kogyo Co. Ltd.
  Topy Industries Ltd.

COMPETITORS

ArcelorMittal	POSCO
BlueScope Steel	Tata Europe
JFE Holdings	ThyssenKrupp Steel
Kobe Steel	United States Steel
Marubeni	Vale
Mitsubishi Corp.	Yamato Kogyo

HISTORICAL FINANCIALS

Company Type: Public

Income Statement

FYE: March 31

	REVENUE ($ mil.)	NET INCOME ($ mil.)	NET PROFIT MARGIN	EMPLOYEES
03/20	54,551	(3,975)	—	126,324
03/19	55,785	2,268	4.1%	125,960
03/18	53,383	1,836	3.4%	109,918
03/17	41,436	1,171	2.8%	108,029
03/16	43,700	1,294	3.0%	100,170
Annual Growth	5.7%	—	—	6.0%

2020 Year-End Financials

Debt ratio: 0.3%
Return on equity: (-14.6%)
Cash ($ mil.): 2,666
Current ratio: 1.47
Long-term debt ($ mil.): 18,771
No. of shares (mil.): 922
Dividends
Yield: 0.0%
Payout: —
Market value ($ mil.): 7,929

	STOCK PRICE ($) FY Close	P/E High/Low		PER SHARE ($) Earnings	Dividends	Book Value
03/20	8.60	—	—	(4.32)	0.46	26.39
03/19	17.74	0	0	2.54	0.72	31.64
03/18	22.27	0	0	2.08	0.71	33.51
03/17	23.09	0	0	1.32	0.13	29.83
03/16	19.40	0	0	1.41	5.26	27.37
Annual Growth	(18.4%)	—	—	—	(45.6%)	(0.9%)

Nippon Steel Trading Corp

Nippon Steel & Sumikin Bussan is the steel-trading operation of Nippon Steel & Sumitomo Metal Japan's steelmaker. The company trades a range of products including steel bars hot- and cold-rolled coils and wire products in Asia Europe and North and Central America. Nippon Steel & Sumikin Bussan also imports steelmaking raw materials. Other materials the company trades include heavy machinery and non-ferrous metals. Steel products account for 85% of company sales. More than 70% of the company's total revenue comes from Japan. Nippon Steel & Sumikin Bussan was founded in 1941.

Operations

Nippon Steel & Sumikin Bussan operates in four segments: Steel (85% of total revenue); Foodstuffs (over 5%); Textiles (about 5%); and Industrial Supply and Infrastructure (less than 5%).

The Steel segment is engaged in a full range of steelmaking activities from buying raw materials to the delivery of steel products to customers.

Foodstuffs offers imported meats (including beef pork and chicken) fishery products agricultural products and Other foodstuffs and processed foods.

Centering on OEM production for apparel makers Textiles is engaged in everything from materials development to product planning production and distribution.

Industrial Supply and Infrastructure invests in new businesses with growth potential such as industrial machinery infrastructure businesses and materials.

Geographic Reach

Tokyo Japan-based Nippon Steel & Sumikin Bussan operates in about 20 countries in North and Central America Asia and Europe.

Japan accounts for more than 70% of total revenue and followed by Asia with over 20%.

Sales and Marketing

The company provide procurement fabrication and logistics systems to meet customer needs. Its steel segment focuses on infrastructure and automobile demand. Industrial supply & infrastructure focusing on the automotive parts business as well as the industrial park and power generation businesses.

Financial Performance

Note: Growth rates may differ after conversion to US Dollars.

Nippon Steel & Sumikin Bussan has generally grown its revenues in the last five years despite its decline in recent years. The company's profits have also followed a similar trend consistently rising in earlier years only to experience a slight drop in recent years.

The company's net sales dropped from Â 2.6 trillion in fiscal 2018 (ended March 2019) to Â 2.5 trillion in fiscal 2019 primarily due to a slump in steel sales and textiles.

Net income declined from Â 23.2 billion in fiscal 2018 to Â 20.7 billion in fiscal 2019 mainly due to the decline in revenue as the company's costs and expenses declined that year.

The company held Â 25.3 billion in cash and cash equivalents at the end of fiscal 2019 Â 1.3 billion more than the year prior. Operating activities generated Â 39.7 billion while investing activities used Â 5.7 billion mostly for purchase of property plant and equipment. Financing activities used another Â 32.7 billion mainly for long-term borrowings repayment and dividends paid.

Strategy

Nippon Steel & Sumikin Bussan is the uniting power of its four business division to become an excellent company which contributes to the success of clients and enrichment of society. The company is shifting power to growth strategies; providing services and solutions that address changes in society and industry; pursuing safety reliability and quality and ensuring legal compliance; and recruiting and training the next generation of employees responsible for its corporate future and ensuring pleasant workplaces and rewarding jobs.

In its Steel Business the company is looking to expand sales by strengthening its value chain procurement logistics and processing systems; by developing in new demand fields; and by synchronizing with Nippon Steel's Global Expanding Strategies. The company's new steel service center in Huston ramped up by early 2020 and the company has invested in QH-PLUS a major local distributor in Vietnam. It is also developing India MENA and US markets.

In its Industrial Supply & Infrastructure Business the company improved its profitability in the Automotive Parts Business by establishing Swastik Arai Tubular to produce headrest stays in a joint venture with Swastik AutoMech a manufacturer of automotive parts in India.

The company also improved the productivity of its Textiles Business and strengthened the supply by utilizing digital technologies partnering with Start-Up Companies and improving order entry operation.

The company's digital transformation is focused on reforming its trading companies' functions through digital technologies; remodeling its steel processing plant and sewing factory to Smart-Factory; and creating new valued solutions and services for upcoming "Society 5.0."

Company Background

In 2013 Nippon Steel Trading merged with Sumikin Bussan to form Nippon Steel & Sumikin Bussan Corporation.

EXECUTIVES

Senior Managing Executive Officer, Etsuo Shimotori
President, Kenji Hiwatari
EVP, Akio Tamagawa
EVP, Tsuneo Miyamoto
Senior Managing Executive Officer, Hiroshi Shono
Auditors: Deloitte Touche Tohmatsu LLC

LOCATIONS

HQ: Nippon Steel Trading Corp
8-5-27 Akasaka, Minato-ku, Tokyo, smc 107-8527
Phone: (81) 3 5412 5098   **Fax:** (81) 3 5412 5101
Web: www.nst.nipponsteel.com

2016 Sales

	% of total
Japan	74
Asia	22
others	4
Total	**100**

PRODUCTS/OPERATIONS

COMPETITORS

Hanwa	Mitsui
JFE Shoji Trade	Toyota Tsusho

HISTORICAL FINANCIALS

Company Type: Public

Income Statement

FYE: March 31

	REVENUE ($ mil.)	NET INCOME ($ mil.)	NET PROFIT MARGIN	EMPLOYEES
03/20	22,848	190	0.8%	7,971
03/19	23,031	209	0.9%	7,914
03/18	19,421	204	1.1%	7,785
03/17	16,469	163	1.0%	8,273
03/16	17,194	154	0.9%	8,179
Annual Growth	7.4%	5.4%	—	(0.6%)

2020 Year-End Financials

Debt ratio: 0.3%
Return on equity: 8.8%
Cash ($ mil.): 239
Current ratio: 1.61
Long-term debt ($ mil.): 1,347

No. of shares (mil.): 32
Dividends
  Yield: —
  Payout: —
Market value ($ mil.): —

Nippon Telegraph & Telephone Corp (Japan)

Auditors: KPMG AZSA LLC

LOCATIONS

HQ: Nippon Telegraph & Telephone Corp (Japan)
Otemachi First Square, East Tower, 1-5-1 Otemachi,
Chiyoda-ku, Tokyo 100-8116
Phone: (81) 3 6838 5481
Web: www.ntt.co.jp

HISTORICAL FINANCIALS

Company Type: Public

Income Statement

FYE: March 31

	REVENUE ($ mil.)	NET INCOME ($ mil.)	NET PROFIT MARGIN	EMPLOYEES
03/20	109,621	7,879	7.2%	370,826
03/19	107,273	7,716	7.2%	366,156
03/18	111,120	8,566	7.7%	363,014
03/17	101,881	7,156	7.0%	274,850
03/16	102,772	6,569	6.4%	241,450
Annual Growth	1.6%	4.7%	—	11.3%

2020 Year-End Financials

Debt ratio: 0.1%
Return on equity: 9.3%
Cash ($ mil.): 9,521
Current ratio: 1.01
Long-term debt ($ mil.): 19,951

No. of shares (mil.): —
Dividends
  Yield: 3.7%
  Payout: —
Market value ($ mil.): —

	STOCK PRICE ($) FY Close	P/E High	P/E Low	PER SHARE ($) Earnings	PER SHARE ($) Dividends	PER SHARE ($) Book Value
03/20	23.62	0	0	2.13	0.88	22.96
03/19	42.72	0	0	1.99	0.72	21.82
03/18	46.55	0	0	4.29	0.64	45.32
03/17	42.84	0	0	3.50	1.11	40.17
03/16	43.24	0	0	3.12	0.77	37.53
Annual Growth	(14.0%) (11.6%)	—	—	(9.1%)	3.2%	

Nippon Yusen Kabushiki Kaisha

Nippon Yusen Kabushiki Kaisha known as NYK Line is at home in ports around the globe. With a fleet of over 700 vessels the company is one of the world's largest marine transportation providers. The NYK Line fleet includes bulk carriers containerships tankers and a variety of specialized vessels including car carriers and liquefied natural gas (LNG) carriers; overall the fleet has a capacity of more than 65000k deadweight tons (DWT). The company operates in more than 45 countries.

Operations

NYK Line divides its operations into several segments. Global Logistics is its largest (and includes liner trade air cargo and logistics) contributing nearly 45% of the company's total sales in 2019. Bulk shipping generated more than 45% of the company's revenue. Its other operations accounted for the remainder of sales.

Geographic Reach

NYK Line has almost 610 logistics locations around the world. Around 200 logistics and warehouses are located in South Asia and Oceania nearly 125 in East Asia about 180 in Europe almost 125 in Japan and around 100 in the Americas.

NYK Line is headquartered in Tokyo Japan.

Financial Performance

The company had a revenue of Â 1.7 trillion in 2019 a 9% decrease from the previous year. Logistics and Bulk Shipping segments had lower sales volume for the year.

Profit for 2019 totaled Â 13.5 billion.

Operating activities generated Â 116.9 billion while investing activities used Â 54.9 billion. Financing activities used another Â 61.7 billion.

Strategy

The company is advancing a differentiation strategy in ESG management based on the "Digitalization and Green" theme in its medium-term management plan. From a "Green" standpoint the company is taking on the challenge of achieving zero emissions in ship operations by converting ship fuels and participating in the hydrogen and ammonia business. In order to increase the safety of ship operations the company intends to make advances in the "Digitalization" of technologies for ship operations and manned autonomous ships.

Mergers and Acquisitions

NYK Line (Vietnam) Co. Ltd. a subsidiary of NYK Line has acquired 15% of total issued shares of Thoresen Vinama Tug Co. Ltd. (TVT hereunder) and entered the tugboat business at Phu My and Cai Mep ports in Vietnam. TVT has two tugboats providing tugboat services at Phu My and Cai Mep ports located in the suburbs of Ho Chi Minh and the largest ports in the nation in terms of import/export cargo and inbound/outbound vessels.

EXECUTIVES

Senior Managing Corporate Officer; Chief Executive Technical, Naoya Tazawa
EVP and CIO, Tadaaki Naito
Corporate Officer, Fukashi Sakamoto
Senior Managing Corporate Officer and CFO, Kenji Mizushima
Senior Managing Corporate Officer; Chief Executive Energy Division, Hitoshi Nagasawa
Corporate Officer; President and CEO NYK Group Europe, Takuji Nakai
Managing Corporate Officer and CIO, Hidetoshi Maruyama
Senior Managing Corporate Officer; Chief Executive Automotive Transportation, Koichi Chikaraishi
Senior Managing Corporate Officer; Chief Executive Dry Bulk Division, Masahiro Samitsu
Managing Corporate Officer; Chief Executive General Affairs, Yoshiyuki Yoshida
Corporate Officer; Chairman and CEO NYK Ship Management, Tomoyuki Koyama
President, Yasumi Kudo
Auditors: Deloitte Touche Tohmatsu LLC

LOCATIONS

HQ: Nippon Yusen Kabushiki Kaisha
2-3-2 Marunouchi, Chiyoda-ku, Tokyo 100-0005
Phone: (81) 3 3284 5151
Web: www.nyk.com

2015 Sales

	% of total
Japan	75
Asia	9
North America	8
Europe	7
Other area	1
Total	**100**

PRODUCTS/OPERATIONS

2015 Sales

	% of total
Bulk shipping	42
Liner trade	28
Logistics	20
Air cargo transport	4
Cruise	2
Real estate	0
Other	4
Total	**100**

List of Items

Bulk Shipping Business
  Car Transport
  Dry Bulk Transport
  Offshore Business
  Tanker Transport (LNG Transport)
  Tanker Transport (Petroleum Chemical and LPG Transport)
Global Logistics
  Air Cargo Transportation Business
  Liner Trade Business
  Logistics Business
  Terminal and Harbor Transport Business
Real Estate Business
Others
Worldwide Service Network

COMPETITORS

A.P. M ller - M rsk
CMA CGM
COSCO Group
DHL
DP World
Dynagas LNG Partners
LP
Evergreen Marine
Expeditors
Hanjin Shipping
Hutchison Port Holdings
Kawasaki Kisen
Lufthansa Cargo
Mediterranean Shipping Company
Mitsui O.S.K. Lines
Mitsui-Soko
Neptune Orient
PSA International
Polar Air Cargo

HISTORICAL FINANCIALS

Company Type: Public

Income Statement   FYE: March 31

	REVENUE ($ mil.)	NET INCOME ($ mil.)	NET PROFIT MARGIN	EMPLOYEES
03/20	16,821	313	1.9%	44,508
03/19	18,444	(448)	—	45,401
03/18	22,012	203	0.9%	47,191
03/17	19,398	(2,679)	—	44,352
03/16	22,911	183	0.8%	40,059
Annual Growth	(7.4%)	14.3%	—	2.7%

2020 Year-End Financials

Debt ratio: 0.5%
Return on equity: 6.5%
Cash ($ mil.): 825
Current ratio: 0.93
Long-term debt ($ mil.): 7,544

No. of shares (mil.): 169
Dividends
  Yield: 2.4%
  Payout: —
Market value ($ mil.): 382

	STOCK PRICE ($) FY Close	P/E High/Low		PER SHARE ($) Earnings	Dividends	Book Value
03/20	2.25	0	0	1.86	0.06	27.51
03/19	2.96	—	—	(2.66)	0.07	28.98
03/18	3.83	0	0	1.21	0.30	32.81
03/17	4.32	—	—	(15.85)	0.04	31.06
03/16	3.82	0	0	1.08	0.15	46.00
Annual Growth (12.4%) (12.1%)		—	—	14.4%	(21.5%)	

Nissan Motor Co., Ltd.

Nissan Motor is one of Japan's leading automakers. The company's models include the Maxima Sentra and Altima sedans and the all-electric LEAF. Its lineup also includes SUVs and crossovers (Rogue Pathfinder Murano) trucks (Frontier and Titan) sports cars (370Z and GT-R) as well as the Infiniti brand of upscale sedans. Renault holds a 43% stake in Nissan Motor and Nissan has a 15% stake in Renault as well as a 34% stake in Mitsubishi Motors; these connections constitute the Renault Nissan Mitsubishi Alliance a leading global auto partnership. Nissan also holds a 50% stake in Dongfeng Motor Company a joint venture between Nissan and China's Dongfeng Group.

Operations

Nissan continues its quest to optimize product development and deliver highly innovative technology. INFINITI the premium brand from Nissan Motor Co. Ltd. is renowned internationally for its world-first technologies and award-winning designs. INFINITI promises a driving experience with unparalleled appeal. Datsun is the third global brand of Nissan Motor Co. Ltd. alongside Nissan and INFINITI. Datsun represents 80 years of accumulated Japanese car-making expertise and is an important part of the company's heritage. Today it offers personal mobility to customers in India Indonesia Russia and South Africa.

Geographic Reach

Nissan headquartered in Kanagawa Japan manufactures in more than 20 countries sells and offer services products worldwide. The company operates over 5 production facilities in Japan along with about 10 R&D facilities.

It also has facilities spread across North America Europe Asia Oceania the Caribbean and Africa (nearly 5 production facilities).

Sales and Marketing

Nissan's products are sold through a global network of independent dealers. The company's Infiniti brand is marketed in the US Canada Europe Russia the Middle East China South Korea and about 15 other countries. The Datsun brand is focused on emerging markets including India Indonesia Russia and South Africa.

The company's marketing efforts include media advertising (including print TV web and social) as well as participation is motorsports.

Strategy

In mid-2020 Nissan introduced the all-new Nissan Ariya an electric crossover SUV that lets customers travel farther while enjoying greater driving excitement confidence and comfort and connectivity.

With a 100% electric powertrain the Ariya promises powerful acceleration and smooth quiet operation. Drivers and passengers can relax and enjoy the ride thanks to autonomous driving technology concierge-level assistance seamless connectivity and a spacious lounge-like interior. With an estimated range of up to 610 kilometers the no-compromise Ariya is perfect for daily commutes and weekend road trips alike.

Earlier that year Nissan Motor Co. Ltd. unveiled a four-year plan to achieve sustainable growth financial stability and profitability by the end of fiscal-year 2023. The scalable plan involving cost-rationalization and business optimization will shift the company's strategy from its past focus on inflated expansion.

As part of the four-year plan Nissan will take decisive action to transform its business by streamlining unprofitable operations and surplus facilities alongside structural reforms. The company will also reduce fixed costs by rationalizing its production capacity global product range and expenses. Through disciplined management the company will prioritize and invest in business areas expected to deliver a solid recovery and sustainable growth.

Company Background

In 1911 US-trained Masujiro Hashimoto established Tokyo-based Kwaishinsha Motor Car Works to repair import and manufacture cars. Kwaishinsha made its first car sporting its DAT ("fast rabbit" in Japanese) logo in 1913. Renamed DAT Motors in 1925 the company consolidated with ailing Jitsuyo Motors in 1926. DAT introduced the son of DAT in 1931 — the Datsun minicar.

Tobata Casting (cast iron and auto parts) bought Datsun's production facilities in 1933. Tobata's Yoshisuke Aikawa believed there was a niche for small cars and the car operations were spun off as Nissan Motors that year.

During WWII the Japanese government limited Nissan's production to trucks and airplane engines; Nissan survived postwar occupation in part due to business with the US Army. The company went public in 1951 and signed a licensing agreement the next year with Austin Motor (UK) which put it back in the car business.

Nissan entered the US market in 1958 with the model 211 using the Datsun name; it established Nissan Motor Corporation in Los Angeles in 1960. In the 1970s Nissan expanded exports of fuel-efficient cars such as the Datsun B210.

The company's name change in the US from Datsun to Nissan during the 1980s confused customers and took six years to complete. It launched its high-end Infiniti line in the US in 1989.

HISTORY

In 1911 US-trained Masujiro Hashimoto established Tokyo-based Kwaishinsha Motor Car Works to repair import and manufacture cars. Kwaishinsha made its first car sporting its DAT ("fast rabbit" in Japanese) logo in 1913. Renamed DAT Motors

in 1925 and suffering from a strong domestic preference for American cars the company consolidated with ailing Jitsuyo Motors in 1926. DAT introduced the son of DAT in 1931 — the Datsun minicar ("son" means "damage or loss" in Japanese hence the spelling change).

Tobata Casting (cast iron and auto parts) bought Datsun's production facilities in 1933. Tobata's Yoshisuke Aikawa believed there was a niche for small cars and the car operations were spun off as Nissan Motors that year.

During WWII the Japanese government limited Nissan's production to trucks and airplane engines; Nissan survived postwar occupation in part due to business with the US Army. The company went public in 1951 and signed a licensing agreement the next year with Austin Motor (UK) which put it back in the car business. A 40% import tax allowed Nissan to compete in Japan even though it had higher costs than those of foreign carmakers.

Nissan entered the US market in 1958 with the model 211 using the Datsun name; it established Nissan Motor Corporation in Los Angeles in 1960. Exports rose as factory automation led to higher quality and lower costs. In the 1970s Nissan expanded exports of fuel-efficient cars such as the Datsun B210. The company became the leading US car importer in 1975.

The company's name change in the US from Datsun to Nissan during the 1980s confused customers and took six years to complete. In 1986 Nissan became the first major Japanese carmaker to build its products in Europe. It launched its high-end Infiniti line in the US in 1989.

EXECUTIVES

EVP and CFO, Joseph G. (Joe) Peter, age 57
EVP European Operations and Purchasing Board Member and Member of the Executive Committee, Hiroto Saikawa, age 67
EVP Total Customer Satisfaction and Chairman Japan Asia and Oceania, Kimiyasu Nakamura
EVP Alliance RNPO Global Purchasing, Yasuhiro Yamauchi
EVP, Jose Munoz
President Nissan Motor India, Ankush Arora
SVP; President Dongfend Motor, Jun Seki
SVP; President Infiniti, Roland Kr ger
EVP Global Marketing and Sales EV and Battery, Daniele Schillaci
President Nissan Korea Co., Huh Sung-joong
CEO Infiniti Korea Co., Kang Seung-won
Chairman Africa Middle East and India, Peyman Kargar, age 52
Regional VP Marketing and Sales Africa Middle East and India and President Nissan Middle East, Kalyana Sivagnanam
President Indian Operations, Thomas Kuehl
Corporate VP and CIO, Anthony (Tony) Thomas
Chairman, Carlos Ghosn, age 66
Vice Chairman, Toshiyuki Shiga
Auditors: Ernst & Young ShinNihon LLC

LOCATIONS

HQ: Nissan Motor Co., Ltd.
2 Takara-cho, Kanagawa-ku, Yokohama, Kanagawa 220-8623
Phone: (81) 45 523 5523
Web: www.nissan.co.jp

PRODUCTS/OPERATIONS

Selected Products
Forklifts
  Engine-powerd forklifts
  Electric-powered forklifts
  Warehouse products
  Order pickers

Pallet stackers
Pallet transporters
Reach trucks
Infiniti
  Infiniti Q50
  Infiniti Q60
  Infiniti Q70
  Infiniti Q70L
  Infiniti QX30
  Infiniti QX50
  Infiniti QX60
  Infiniti QX70
  Infiniti QX80
Nissan
  370Z
  370Z Roadster
  Altima
  Armada
  Frontier
  GT-R
  Juke
  Leaf EV
  Maxima
  Murano
  NV200 Cargo
  NV200 Taxi
  NV Passenger
  Pathfinder
  Rogue
  Rogue Sport
  Sentra
  Titan
  Titan XD
  Versa
  Versa Note

COMPETITORS

BMW	Hyundai Motor
CLARK Material	Isuzu
Handling	Kia Motors
Crown Equipment	Mazda
Daihatsu	NACCO Industries
Daimler	Peugeot
Deere	Subaru
FCA US	Suzuki Motor
Fiat Chrysler	Tata Motors
Ford Motor	Toyota
General Motors	Volkswagen
Honda	Volvo

HISTORICAL FINANCIALS

Company Type: Public

Income Statement				FYE: March 31
	REVENUE ($ mil.)	NET INCOME ($ mil.)	NET PROFIT MARGIN	EMPLOYEES
03/20	91,007	(6,183)	—	155,811
03/19	104,513	2,881	2.8%	160,183
03/18	112,548	7,033	6.2%	160,893
03/17	104,824	5,934	5.7%	158,633
03/16	108,547	4,664	4.3%	174,043
Annual Growth	(4.3%)	—		(2.7%)

2020 Year-End Financials

Debt ratio: 0.4%
Return on equity: (-14.2%)
Cash ($ mil.): 12,735
Current ratio: 1.32
Long-term debt ($ mil.): 28,940

No. of shares (mil.): —
Dividends
  Yield: 10.6%
  Payout: —
Market value ($ mil.): —

	STOCK PRICE ($) FY Close	P/E High/Low		PER SHARE ($) Earnings	Dividends	Book Value
03/20	6.70	—	—	(1.58)	0.71	8.93
03/19	16.42	0	0	0.74	0.99	11.42
03/18	20.68	0	0	1.80	0.96	12.10
03/17	19.26	0	0	1.48	0.82	10.38
03/16	18.51	0	0	1.11	0.61	9.42
Annual Growth	(22.4%)	—	—	—	4.0%	(1.3%)

NN Group NV (Netherlands)

Auditors: KPMG Accountants N.V.

LOCATIONS

HQ: NN Group NV (Netherlands)
  Schenkkade 65, The Hauge 2595 AS
Phone: (31) 70 513 03 03
Web: www.nn-group.com

HISTORICAL FINANCIALS

Company Type: Public

Income Statement				FYE: December 31
	ASSETS ($ mil.)	NET INCOME ($ mil.)	INCOME AS % OF ASSETS	EMPLOYEES
12/19	279,116	2,202	0.8%	15,194
12/18	256,805	1,279	0.5%	14,953
12/17	272,191	2,529	0.9%	14,971
12/16	177,921	1,255	0.7%	11,463
12/15	176,617	1,704	1.0%	11,561
Annual Growth	12.1%	6.6%	—	7.1%

2019 Year-End Financials

Return on assets: 0.8%
Return on equity: 6.8%
Long-term debt ($ mil.): —
No. of shares (mil.): 322
Sales ($ mil): 23,328

Dividends
  Yield: 4.5%
  Payout: 13.5%
Market value ($ mil.): 6,090

	STOCK PRICE ($) FY Close	P/E High/Low		PER SHARE ($) Earnings	Dividends	Book Value
12/19	18.91	4	3	6.46	0.87	113.41
12/18	19.59	7	6	3.61	0.76	84.27
12/17	21.63	4	3	7.43	0.71	87.83
Annual Growth	(6.5%)	—	—	(3.5%)	5.1%	6.6%

Nokia Corp

Nokia is one of the world's leading makers of the telecommunications infrastructure of mobile phone networks. Once a leading mobile phone handset manufacturer its current businesses are Networks which provides a wide range of professional services Nokia Software which offers the cloud core software portfolio and Nokia Technologies its research and development and intellectual property rights unit. First incorporated in the Finnish city it's named after Nokia has operations and customers in approximately 120 countries. Finland's largest company Nokia redoubled its commitment to telecom infrastructure with its acquisition of the telecom-equipment maker Alcatel-Lucent. Nokia generates some 30% of its revenue in North America.

Operations

Nokia has three reportable segments for financial reporting purposes: Networks Nokia Software and Nokia Technologies. Segment-level information for Group Common and Other is also presented.

Nokia's networks span the globe so it follows that the networks segment generates about 80% of the company's revenue. Networks segment comprises Mobile Networks Global Services Fixed Networks and IP/Optical Networks operations.

The Nokia Software operating segment generates more than 10% of revenue offers the cloud core software portfolio in addition to software applications spanning customer experience management.

The Nokia Technologies operating segment generates more than 5% of revenue focuses on building innovation and R&D technologies used in virtual mobile devices used today.

Group Common and Other includes Alcatel-Lucent Submarine Networks and Radio Frequency Systems which generates about 5% of revenue. Overall almost 85% of sales were generated from communication service providers and the rest came from enterprise licensees and others.

Geographic Reach

Finland-based Nokia generates roughly 30% of sales in North America Europe generates about 30% of sales Asia/Pacific region generates approximately 20% of sales while Middle East and Africa and Greater China both generates about 10% of sales and Latin America generates more than 5% of sales. It has key R&D and software development centers in many of the largest countries in those three regions as well including China the US Germany France India and the UK.

Sales and Marketing

Nokia's customers include communications service providers utility energy and transportation companies the public sector and other tech companies.

Financial Performance

Note: Growth rates may differ after conversion to US Dollars.

Nokia's revenue has fluctuated in the last five years failing to show consistent growth over the years. The acquisition of Alcatel-Lucent in 2016 added about ?11 billion to sales but the decline continued again in the years that followed before rebounding in 2019. Its profits have also seen a similar trend rising and falling in the last five years before recovering from a three-year consecutive net loss from the years 2016 to 2018.

Sales in 2019 were ?23.3 billion an increase of ?752 million or 3% compared to ?22.6 billion in 2018. The increase in sales was primarily due to an increase in Networks net sales and to a lesser extent Nokia Software net sales. This was partially offset by a decrease in Group Common and Other and Nokia Technologies net sales.

Profit in 2019 was ?14 million an increase of ?568 million compared to a loss of ?554 million in 2018. The change in profit attributable to equity holders of the parent was primarily due to the improvement in operating profit and to a lesser extent lower income tax expenses. This was partially offset by a net negative fluctuation in financial income and expenses.

Nokia's cash level decreased by ?351 million to ?5.9 billion. It generated ?390 million in cash from operations. Investing and financing activities used ?167 million and ?479 million respectively. Nokia's primary cash uses in 2019 were for purchase of property plant and equipment and repayment of long-term borrowings.

Strategy

Nokia's "Rebranding for growth" strategy sets the right direction for the company. Nokia has focused it to reflect the progress so far and to accelerate further execution. Nokia intends to become the leading trusted network equipment provider for end-to-end networks and the leader in customer intimacy. Over the long term it aims to differentiate with end-to-end solutions that allow it to offer its customers guaranteed mission-critical performance total cost of ownership savings time-to-market gains and higher reliability.

Nokia has various focus areas among which are implementing five end-to-end solutions such as 5G distributed cloud network slicing security and industrial automation. It is also investing in the architecture and 5G system-on-chip capabilities for its mobile radio network products and building technology leadership in its Optical Networks portfolio leveraging its PSE-3 chipset.

By the end of 2019 Nokia had won 62 commercial 5G deals and launched 18 commercial 5G networks with leading operators in particular in North America Korea Japan Australia and New Zealand Europe and Middle-East and Africa. It is also making progress with Mobile Networks radio design-to-cost reduction with significant annualized product cost and procurement savings.

Mergers and Acquisitions

In early 2020 Nokia acquired Elenion Technologies a U.S.-based company focusing on silicon photonics technology for an undisclosed amount. Elenion's technology expertise and unique design platform and services enable Nokia to expand its market footprint by addressing the critical and rapidly evolving optical connectivity requirements of 5G cloud and enterprise networking.

Company Background

Nokia has grown from its origins in 1865 as a papermill in Finland to one of the world's pre-eminent technology companies and whose fortunes have a tangible impact on the lives of the Finnish population. Nokia has found and nurtured success in several sectors over the years including cable paper products rubber boots and tires mobile devices and telecommunications infrastructure equipment. By 1998 Nokia was the world leader in mobile phones a position it enjoyed for more than a decade.

However its phones fell out of popularity in the smartphone era as the iOS and Android mobile operating systems vastly outperformed Nokia's Symbian software. A tie-up with Microsoft that saw Nokia's devices adopt Windows Phone 7 as their OS ultimately failed to save Nokia's device division as few people preferred Microsoft's OS either and Nokia sold the entire business to Microsoft.

The sale triggered a wholesale shift to telecoms equipment which Nokia took to the next level with the 2016 acquisition of Alcatel-Lucent.

HISTORY

Nokia got its start in 1865 when engineer Fredrik Idestam established a mill to manufacture pulp and paper on the Tammerkoski rapids of the Nokianvirta River in Finland. Although Nokia flourished within Finland the company was not well known to the rest of the world until it attempted to become a regional conglomerate in the early 1960s. French computer firm Machines Bull selected Nokia as its Finnish agent in 1962 and Nokia began researching radio transmission technology. In 1967 with the encouragement of Finland's government Nokia merged with Finnish Rubber Works (a maker of tires and rubber footwear formed in 1898) and Finnish Cable Works (a cable and electronics manufacturer formed in 1912) to form Nokia Corporation.

The company entered the phone business — after a series of deals that expanded its industrial holdings — when it acquired a 51% interest in the state-owned Finnish telecom company in 1981 and named it Telenokia.

Nokia caught the first wave of mobile phones riding the popularity of its handsets in the late 1990s and early 2000s. It however didn't move fast enough to compete against smartphones and it eventually sold the handset business to Microsoft.

EXECUTIVES

President Applications and Analytics, Bhaskar M. Gorti
President Mobile Networks, Marc Rouanne, age 58
President and CEO, Rajeev Suri, age 53
President IP and Optical Networks, Basil Alwan, age 59
President Nokia Technologies, Ramzi Haidamus, age 55
SVP and Corporate Controller, Kristian Pullola
President Fixed Networks, Federico Guillén, age 58
President Global Services, Igor Leprince
Group COO, Monika Maurer
President Nokia Bell Labs and CTO, Marcus Weldon
Chairman, Risto Siilasmaa, age 54
Vice Chairman, Olivier Piou, age 62
Auditors: PricewaterhouseCoopers Oy

LOCATIONS

HQ: Nokia Corp
Karakaari 7, Espoo FI-02610
Phone: (358) 1 0448 8000   **Fax:** (358) 1 0448 1002
Web: www.nokia.com

2017 Sales

	% of total
Europe	29
North America	28
Asia/Pacific	
Greater China	11
Other	18
Middle East & Africa	8
Latin America	6
Total	**100**

2017 Sales

	% of total
United States	26
China	9
Finland	8
India	6
France	6
United Kingdom	3
Japan	3
Germany	2
Italy	2
Saudi Arabia	2
Other	33
Total	**100**

PRODUCTS/OPERATIONS

2017 Sales

	% of total
Nokia Networks	
Ultra Broadband Networks	39
IP Networks and Applications	25
Global Services	25
Nokia Technologies	7
Group common and other	4
Total	**100**

Selected Products

Nokia Flexi Multiradio
 Telco Cloud
 NetAct
 IP routers
Switching systems
 · Radio contollers
 Base stations
 transmission systems
 mapping systems and software

COMPETITORS

Accenture	Microsoft
Amdocs	NEC
Cisco Systems	Oki Electric
Ericsson Inc.	Oracle
Fujitsu	Panasonic Mobile
Garmin	Communications
HP Enterprise Group	QUALCOMM
Huawei Technologies	SANYO
IBM	Sony Mobile
Kyocera	Tellabs
LG Group	ZTE

HISTORICAL FINANCIALS

Company Type: Public

Income Statement				FYE: December 31
	REVENUE ($ mil.)	NET INCOME ($ mil.)	NET PROFIT MARGIN	EMPLOYEES
12/19	26,177	7	0.0%	98,322
12/18	25,839	(389)	—	103,083
12/17	27,747	(1,790)	—	101,731
12/16	24,933	(808)	—	101,000
12/15	13,614	2,685	19.7%	55,718
Annual Growth	**17.8%**	**(76.7%)**		**15.3%**

2019 Year-End Financials

Debt ratio: 12.2%
Return on equity: 0.0%
Cash ($ mil.): 6,635
Current ratio: 1.39
Long-term debt ($ mil.): 4,474
No. of shares (mil.): —
Dividends
 Yield: 3.0%
 Payout: —
Market value ($ mil.): —

	STOCK PRICE ($) FY Close	P/E High/Low		PER SHARE ($) Earnings	Dividends	Book Value
12/19	3.71	—	—	(0.00)	0.11	3.07
12/18	5.82	—	—	(0.07)	0.22	3.13
12/17	4.66	—	—	(0.31)	0.20	3.47
12/16	4.81	—	—	(0.14)	0.27	3.71
12/15	7.02	13	8	0.69	0.66	2.90
Annual Growth	**(14.7%)**			**—**	**(35.8%)**	**1.4%**

Nomura Holdings Inc

Nomura Holdings is the parent company of Nomura Securities Japan's leading investment bank and brokerage house. The company performs trading equity and bond underwriting research and mergers and acquisitions (M&A) advisory services. It also makes private equity and venture capital investments and oversees some ¥ 110 trillion in retail client assets. Subsidiary Nomura Asset Management is Japan's largest asset management firm in terms of assets under management in investment trusts which it offers to retail investors and through institutional funds. Nomura Holdings has operations in more than 30 countries; Nomura Securities International is the company's US trading and investment banking unit.

Operations

Nomura operates through three business divisions. Wholesale which generated 50% of revenue in fiscal 2015 (ended March 31) includes the firm's global markets and investment banking operations and provides corporate and institutional products and services. Its Retail division (30% of revenue) provides investment products and offers investment consultation services to individuals and businesses from nearly 160 Nomura Securities locations across Japan.

Its Asset Management division (6% of revenue) which operates through Nomura Asset Management develops and manages investment trusts and provides investment advisory services. Additional units include Nomura Trust & Banking big-ticket financing firm Nomura Babcock & Brown and the Nomura Institute of Capital Markets Research.

The firm's revenue streams are fairly diversified. About 23% of its total revenue came from commissions in FY2015 with another 5% coming from its investment banking fees. The firm's interest and dividend income and asset management/portfolio service fees made up 23% and 11% of total revenue respectively. The remainder of its revenue came from non-recurring sources such as net gains on trading (28% of revenue) and gains on equity investments (1%).

Geographic Reach

Nearly 70% of the firm's revenue came from Japan in fiscal 2015 (ended March) while business in the Americas and Europe each made up 13% of revenue. The remaining 5% of revenue came from the Asia and Oceania region. Its operations are mostly in Japan but subsidiaries are also in the US the UK Singapore and Hong Kong Special Administrative Region.

Sales and Marketing

The firm offers its variety of financial services to individuals corporations financial institutions governments and governmental agencies.

Financial Performance

Note: Growth rates may differ after conversion to US dollars.

Nomura Holdings has struggled to grow its revenues in recent years though its profits have been steadily climbing as its managed to cut non-interest expenses and pay lower income tax rates with more deductible expenses related to foreign subsidiaries.

The firm's revenue climbed 6% to Å 1.9 trillion in fiscal 2015 (ended March 31) mostly thanks to a double-digit jump in net gains on trading. The firm's Wholesale business drove most of the recurring revenue growth with its income rising by 3% on weaker Yen an increase in overseas equity revenue and higher overseas M&A and fundraising activity. Its Asset Management business grew by 15% as its assets under management grew with inflows from its investment trust and investment advisory businesses and from new revenue from its recently acquired subsidiary in Taiwan. Nomura's retail business shrank by 7% on decreasing commissions from the distribution of investment trusts and brokerage services.

Higher revenue during FY2015 drove Nomura's net income higher by 5% to Å 224.8 million for the year. The firm's cash levels fell sharply with operations using Å 77 million during the year mostly as it purchased more securities under agreements to resell.

Strategy

Nomura is well-positioned to take advantage of expected growth in other Asian nations. The company expressed in 2015 that it expected Asia to account for half of global GDP by 2050 providing Nomura with Wholesale business opportunity as corporations continue to develop with higher demand for funding. It also expected that the region's growing middle class would increase demand for personal financial services over the next several decades creating another growth opportunity for its retail business.

Additionally the firm's wide variety of financial services gives its tremendous cross-selling opportunities that integrate both its Retail and Wholesale operations.

HISTORY

Tokushichi Nomura started a currency exchange Nomura Shoten in Osaka in 1872 and began trading stock. His son Tokushichi II took over and in 1910 formed Nomura's first syndicate to underwrite part of a government bond issue. It established the Osaka Nomura Bank in 1918. The bond department became independent in 1925 and became Nomura Securities. The company opened a New York office in 1927 entering stock brokerage in 1938.

The firm rebuilt and expanded retail operations after WWII. It encouraged stock market investing by promoting "million ryo savings chests" — small boxes in which people saved cash (ryo was an old form of currency). When savings reached 5000 yen savers could buy into investment trusts. Nomura distributed more than a million chests in 10 years.

Nomura followed clients overseas in the 1960s helped underwrite a US issue of Sony stock and opened a London office. It became Japan's leading securities firm after a 1965 stock market crash decimated rival Yamaichi Securities. The firm grew rapidly in the 1970s ushering investment capital in and out of Japan and competing with banks by issuing corporate debt securities.

As the Japanese economy soared in the 1980s the company opened Nomura Bank International in London (1986) and bought 20% of US mergers and acquisitions advisor Wasserstein Perella (1988 sold 2001).

Then the Japanese economic bubble burst. Nomura's stock toppled 70% from its 1987 peak and underwriting plummeted. In 1991 and 1992 amid revelations that Nomura and other brokerages had reimbursed favored clients' trading losses the firm was accused of manipulating stock in companies owned by Japanese racketeers. Nomura's chairman and president — both named Tabuchi — resigned admitting no wrongdoing.

The firm trimmed staff and offices and focused on its most efficient operations. From 1993 to 2000 it seesawed from red to black and back again.

Junichi Ujiie became president after the payoff scandal; he restructured operations to prepare for Japan's financial deregulation. Nomura invested in pub chain Inntrepreneur and William Hill a UK betting chain. It also created an entertainment lending unit to lend against future royalties or syndication fees and spun off a minority stake in its high-risk US real estate business which ceased lending altogether the next year.

In 1998 Nomura was dealt a double blow when Asian economies collapsed and Russia defaulted on its debts. Incurring substantial losses the firm refocused on its domestic market and reduced overseas operations. That year it teamed with Industrial Bank of Japan for derivatives sales in the UK and pension plan consulting in Japan.

In 1999 Nomura bailed out ailing property subsidiary Nomura Finance which had been crippled by the sinking Japanese real estate market. It also invested heavily in UK real estate and bought 40% of the Czech beer market with South African Breweries.

The next year the firm agreed to buy the business services arm of Welsh utilities firm Hyder; it also bought 114000 flats in Germany with local government authorities its first European deal outside the UK. Also in 2000 Nomura sold its assets in pachinko parlors and "love" hotels Japanese cultural traditions with less-than-sparkling reputations. British authorities that year fined Nomura traders in relation to charges of trying to rig Australia's stock market in 1996.

The company converted to a holding company structure in 2001 and months later made its debut on the NYSE. It made two big deals in the UK that year buying hotel chain Le Méridien and becoming the nation's largest pub owner via the purchase of some 1000 locations from Bass. The company also bought a stake in Thomas Weisel Partners to increase its participation in M&A action between US and Japanese firms. In 2002 the company decided to sell the network of more than 4100 pubs to a consortium of private investors for some $3 billion.

In 2007 Nomura acquired global agency brokerage Instinet. The deal allowed the company to begin offering electronic trading services.

In 2008 Japanese regulators chose a consortium led by Nomura to take control of troubled Ashikaga Bank from the government; Nomura's private equity arm took a stake of about 45% in Ashikaga. The deal marked Nomura's first foray into retail banking.

The global financial crisis heavily impacted Nomura which reported steep declines in 2008 and 2009. The company lost some Å 208 billion ($2 billion) in 2009 alone on trading and equity investments. The US subprime mortgage bust further hurt the group which lost money on mortgage-backed securities.

In response Nomura cut operating costs and fine-tuned its offerings. The following year the company boosted its global investment banking capabilities by acquiring parts of the fallen bulge-bracket firm Lehman Brothers including operations in Asia Europe and the Middle East as well as the India-based back office operations. (In its post-acquisition transition the company laid off some 11% of its UK workforce or about 1000 employees in its London office.) In an effort to boost its domestic asset management business Nomura bought NikkoCiti Trust and Banking from Citigroup in 2009. The company also exited the US residential mortgage-backed securities business entirely.

The Lehman Brothers acquisition helped boost Nomura's profile in European equities and fixed-income trading. Adding on to that purchase Nomura bought London-based Tricorn Partners — a move that further complements its UK corporate finance advisory business.

Nomura Asset Management also bought a 35% stake in LIC Mutual Fund Asset Management Company of India. The deal gave Nomura a larger foothold in the Indian market and strengthened its credentials as an international asset manager.

EXECUTIVES

Senior Managing Director, Paul Spanswick
COO, Tetsu Ozaki, age 63
Senior Managing Director, Yasuo Kashiwagi
Executive Managing Director, Shoichi Nagamatsu, age 69
Executive Managing Director Entity Structure, Yuji Nakata
Senior Management Director Asia Strategy, Toshihiro Iwasaki
CEO, Koji Nagai
Senior Managing Director Human Resources, Kenji Kimura
Senior Managing Director, Minoru Shinohara
Senior Managing Director, Toshiyasu Iiyama
Executive Managing Director Asset Management, Kunio Watanabe
Senior Managing Director, Kentaro Okuda, age 56
Senior Managing Director, Junko Nakagawa
Senior Managing Director Americas, David Findlay
Senior Managing Director Wholesale and Global Markets, Steven Ashley
Executive Managing Director; President Nomura Securities, Toshio Morita, age 58
Senior Managing Director and Chief Risk Officer, Lewis O'Donald
Senior Managing Director Banking, Chie Toriumi
Senior Managing Director, Yo Akatsuka
Senior Managing Director Europe Middle East and Africa, Jonathan Lewis
Senior Managing Director Americas, Tsutomu Takemura
Senior Managing Director, Takeo Aoki
Senior Managing Director Corporate Communications and Corporate Citizenship, Hajime Ikeda

Executive Managing Director and CFO, Takumi Kitamura

Senior Managing Director, Yutaka Nakajima

Senior Managing Director General Services, Rikiya Nonomura

Senior Managing Director and CIO, Kaoru Numata

Senior Managing Director and Chief Legal Officer, Yasushi Takayama

Senior Managing Director Group Compliance and Operations, Tomoyuki Teraguchi

Senior Managing Director Retail Division, Eiichiro Yamaguchi

Auditors: Ernst & Young ShinNihon LLC

LOCATIONS

HQ: Nomura Holdings Inc
13-1, Nihonbashi 1-chome, Chuo-Ku, Tokyo 103-8645
Phone: (81) 3 5255 1000
Web: www.nomuraholdings.com

2014 Sales

	% of total
Japan	69
Americas	13
Europe	13
Asia and Oceania	5
Total	**100**

PRODUCTS/OPERATIONS

2014 Sales

	% of total
Net gain on trading	28
Commissions	23
Interest and dividends	23
Asset management & portfolio service fees	11
Fees from investment banking	5
Gain on investments in equity securities	1
Other	9
Total	**100**

2014 Sales

	% of total
Wholesale	50
Retail	30
Asset Management	6
Others	14
Total	**100**

COMPETITORS

Bank of America	Goldman Sachs
Barclays	HSBC
Boom Securities	SMBC Nikko Securities
Daiwa Securities Group	UBS Investment Bank
Deutsche Bank	

HISTORICAL FINANCIALS

Company Type: Public

Income Statement   FYE: March 31

	ASSETS ($ mil.)	NET INCOME ($ mil.)	INCOME AS % OF ASSETS	EMPLOYEES
03/20	405,340	1,999	0.5%	26,629
03/19	369,947	(906)	—	27,864
03/18	382,263	2,065	0.5%	28,048
03/17	383,269	2,143	0.6%	28,186
03/16	365,906	1,171	0.3%	28,865
Annual Growth	**2.6%**	**14.3%**	**—**	**(2.0%)**

2020 Year-End Financials

Return on assets: 0.5%	Dividends
Return on equity: 8.1%	Yield: 3.8%
Long-term debt ($ mil.): —	Payout: 23.7%
No. of shares (mil.): —	Market value ($ mil.): —
Sales ($ mil): 10,467	

STOCK PRICE ($)		P/E		PER SHARE ($)		
	FY Close	High/Low		Earnings	Dividends	Book Value
03/20	4.27	0	0	0.61	0.16	8.04
03/19	3.59	—	—	(0.27)	0.13	7.18
03/18	5.85	0	0	0.58	0.19	7.63
03/17	6.27	0	0	0.59	0.11	7.07
03/16	4.44	0	0	0.32	0.19	6.66
Annual Growth	**(1.0%)**	**—**	**—**	**17.8%**	**(2.9%)**	**4.8%**

Nordea Bank ABp

Nordea Bank is one of the largest financial services groups in the Nordic and Baltic Sea regions. Sweden is its home but Nordea also has a major presence in Denmark Finland Norway and Russia. The bank splits its operations into three main divisions: retail banking wholesale banking and wealth management. The bank also provides life and pension products. Originally founded in the 1820s Nordea Bank now boasts a network of about 700 branches and serves some 11 million customers including about 1 million corporate clients — a key customer segment for Nordea. About 55% of its lending activity is to corporations.

Operations

The bank operates through three main segments. Retail Banking generates roughly 55% of the bank's overall income and offers a wide range of traditional deposit and loan products for both household customers and corporate clients mostly in the Nordic markets and the Baltic countries.

Wholesale Banking brings in another 25% of total revenue and provides banking and other financial services to large Nordic and global corporate institutional and public companies. This division also serves financial sector clients with funds and equity products as well as consulting services within asset allocation and fund sales. Nordea Bank Russia offers a full range of bank services to corporate and private customers in Russia. Capital Markets unallocated includes the result in Capital Markets which is not allocated to the main business areas.

Roughly 15% of revenue comes from the Wealth Management division which provides investment savings and risk management products. It also manages customers' assets and gives financial advice to affluent and high net worth individuals and institutional investors.

Additionally Nordea offers financing and other services to clients in the Shipping Offshore & Oil Services industries. The bank also has a Life & Pensions business and an Asset Management division that is responsible for all actively-managed investment products.

Geographic Reach

Nordea Bank has an international network of branches subsidiaries and representative offices in almost 20 countries around the world with most of its operations in Denmark Finland Norway and Sweden. More than 30% of revenue comes from Denmark while Sweden generates another nearly 25%. Finland and Norway markets contribute more than 15% each. Other large markets include the Baltic countries and Russia.

Sales and Marketing

The bank serves private customers (from general retail to the highly-affluent) corporations financial institutions and other global institutional customers.

Nordea's mobile banking activity has been growing. In 2014 transaction volume from its mobile bank channels grew by 90% with the number of active mobile banking users growing by 1000 per day.

Financial Performance

Note: Growth rates may differ after conversion to US dollars.

Nordea's annual revenues have remained mostly stable for the past few years while profits have steadily been rising. Revenue in 2014 grew by 3% to ?10.22 billion ($12.42 billion) mostly thanks to higher commission income from investment and lending services from the bank's growing Wealth Management and Retail Banking divisions.

Higher revenue in 2014 pushed profit higher for a third straight year with net income rising by 7% to ?3.33 billion ($4.05 billion). Also helping the bank's bottom line net loan loss provisions declined by 26% as its loan portfolio gained credit strength.

Cash levels fell despite higher earnings in 2014 with operations using ?10.82 billion ($13.15 billion) primarily as deposit funding from credit institutions and the broader public declined over the year.

Strategy

Nordea Bank has continued to focus more on its four key markets in the Nordic and Baltic regions (including Denmark Finland Norway and Sweden). In mid-2014 to better concentrate resources on these key markets Nordea exited its banking life and financing businesses in Poland through the sale of its Nordea Bank Polska S.A. to PKO Bank Polski SA for ?694 million ($927 million).

As the industry moves from brick-and-mortar branch banking to digital banking Nordea has also been expanding its electronic offerings via its mobile tablet Netbank and Facebook platforms. Indeed during 2014 the bank reported that the number of mobile transactions grew by 90% reflecting the change in consumer tastes in the banking industry. In late 2014 the company announced that it would increase its IT investments by 30-35% over the coming years building new core banking and payment platforms to keep up with the digital banking trend.

Company Background

Sampo owns more than 20% of Nordea. The Swedish government held a nearly 20% stake in the bank but reduced that to 13% in 2011 as part of its plan to raise capital. It plans to sell more and possibly all of its Nordea stake over time.

Growth in European markets has been a focus for Nordea. In 2009 the company purchased a 75% stake in Russian bank JSB Orgresbank rebranding it as OJSC Nordea Bank. Nordea also bought the Polish life insurance operations of Finnish banking group Sampo doubling Nordea's customer base in Poland. However Nordea put the breaks on aggressive growth and completely halted branch expansion in Russia and the Baltic countries in light of the global financial crisis.

HISTORY

Nordea traces its roots to 1974 when two Swedish government-owned banks Postbanken and Sveriges Kreditbank merged to form the country's largest bank Post-och Kreditbanken (PKbanken) in order to compete with S-E-Banken and Svenska Handelsbanken.

PKbanken didn't hold on to the top spot long. By the early 1980s a recession and languid profits sank the company to third. However the firm did expand teaming with Norway's Christiana Bank og Kreditkasse to open joint offices in Hong Kong Houston London S o Paolo and Singapore.

As regulatory restrictions in Sweden eased the government spun off 15% of its interest in the company on the Stockholm Stock Exchange in 1984.

PKbanken pulled out of its deal in London with Christiana Bank in 1986 but it bought a stake in London-based English Trust Group to expand its merchant banking services. In 1988 PKbanken acquired government-owned Carnegie Fondkommission Sweden's largest brokerage and in 1989 purchased the state-controlled Swedish Investment Bank a provider of funding to small and midsized businesses.

A year later PKbanken acquired regional Swedish bank Nordbanken and assumed the smaller firm's name. Soon after the government axed the combined firm's top officers and installed new management. The purging didn't help as another recession and a real estate market crash hammered the company's bottom line. In 1992 the Swedish government intervened again acquiring all of the outstanding shares of Nordbanken that it did not already own. The company rebounded quickly after selling bad loans to the state and cutting staff by a fifth.

In 1994 the Swedish government transferred its ownership of Gota Bank to Nordbanken. The company resumed trading on the Stockholm Stock Exchange the following year.

Across the border in Finland rivals Union Bank of Finland and Kansallis-Osake-Pankki merged in 1995 to create Merita Bank the country's largest.

In 1997 Nordbanken and Merita Bank combined to form MeritaNordbanken but their parents Nordbanken Holdings and Merita Ab remained separate. In 2000 the company bought Danish bank Unidanmark. MeritaNordbanken's holding companies united and assumed the name Nordic Baltic Holding. Later the company changed its name to Nordea an amalgamation of "Nordic" and "idea."

In 2001 Nordea bought Christiania Bank og Kreditkasse and later that year attached the Nordea Bank name to its banking subsidiaries in Denmark Finland Norway and Sweden.

By 2003 the company composed primarily of the four national banking groups — Nordea Bank Denmark Nordea Bank Finland Nordea Bank Norway and Nordea Bank Sweden — decided to change its complex legal structure and create one European company under the Nordea Bank banner.

Nordea acquired Denmark's Fionia Bank in 2009 including the bank's staff and its 29 branches but excluding some 2000 troubled corporate customers. The Denmark government had taken control of the failing bank earlier in the year.

EXECUTIVES

EVP Chief Risk Officer Head Group Risk Management Country Senior Executive Finland, Ari Kaperi, age 60
President and Group CEO, Casper von Koskull
EVP and Head of Retail Banking Country Senior Executive Sweden, Lennart Jacobsen, age 54
Deputy CEO and COO, Torsten Hagen J ,rgensen
Group CFO, Heikki Ilkka, age 50
EVP and Head of Wholesale Banking, Eric Ekman, age 51
EVP Deputy Head of Retail Banking and Country Senior Executive in Denmark, Mads G. Jakobsen, age 54
EVP Head of Wealth Management and Country Senior Executive in Norway, Snorre Storset, age 48
Chairman, Bj ¶rn Wahlroos, age 68
Vice Chairman, Marie Ehrling, age 65
Auditors: PricewaterhouseCoopers Oy

LOCATIONS

HQ: Nordea Bank ABp
 Smalandsgatan 17, Stockholm SE-105 71
Phone: (46) 8 614 78 00   **Fax:** (46) 8 614 87 70
Web: www.nordea.com

2014 Sales

	% of total
Denmark	31
Sweden	24
Finland	18
Norway	17
New European markets	4
Other	6
Total	**100**

PRODUCTS/OPERATIONS

2014 Sales

	% of total
Banking products	61
Capital markets products	19
Savings products and asset management	10
Life and pensions	5
Other	5
Total	**100**

2014 Sales

	% of total
Retail Banking	56
Wholesale Banking	24
Wealth Management	16
Group Corporate Centre	4
Total	**100**

2014 Sales

	% of total
Net Interest income	54
Net Fee abd commission income	28
Net results on items at fair value	14
Other Operating income	4
Total	**100**

COMPETITORS

BNP Paribas	KBC
Citigroup	SEB AB
Danske Bank	Schroders
Deutsche Bank	Skandia
HSBC	Svenska Handelsbanken
JPMorgan Asset Management	

HISTORICAL FINANCIALS

Company Type: Public

Income Statement

FYE: December 31

	ASSETS ($ mil.)	NET INCOME ($ mil.)	INCOME AS % OF ASSETS	EMPLOYEES
12/19	873,109	2,390	0.3%	29,300
12/18	867,695	4,830	0.6%	28,990
12/17	915,224	4,769	0.5%	30,399
12/16	968,801	5,926	0.6%	31,596
12/15	1,017,911	5,762	0.6%	29,826
Annual Growth	(3.8%)	(19.7%)	—	(0.4%)

2019 Year-End Financials

Return on assets: 0.2%	Dividends
Return on equity: 4.7%	Yield: 6.4%
Long-term debt ($ mil.): —	Payout: 87.6%
No. of shares (mil.): —	Market value ($ mil.): —
Sales ($ mil): 20,282	

	STOCK PRICE ($) FY Close	P/E High/Low		PER SHARE ($) Earnings	Dividends	Book Value
12/19	8.12	25	16	0.60	0.52	12.23
12/18	8.39	0	0	119.59	1.09	12.78
Annual Growth	(3.2%)			— — (73.4%)	(16.6%)	(1.1%)

Norsk Hydro ASA

Like the aluminum products it mines manufactures and sells Norwegian industrial giant Norsk Hydro is both enduring and flexible. The company delivered some 2.8 million metric tons of sourced alumina in 2019. Its global operations include casthouse products building systems extruded and rolled products and automotive and transport products distributed worldwide. Norsk Hydro ranks among the world's largest aluminum producers along with Canada's Rio Tinto Alcan Russia's RUSAL and the US's Alcoa. It also owns and operates over 15 hydroelectric power stations in Norway. Majority of the company's sale were generated from the Europe.

Operations

The fully integrated aluminum company has operations across all the major aspects of the aluminum value chain from bauxite and alumina mining through aluminum smelting and production to sales and marketing. It is a global energy player purchasing and consuming substantial quantities of energy for its smelters rolling mills and alumina refinery operations. Norsk Hydro is also the largest publicly owned power producer in Norway stakes in some 25 hydroelectric power plants (approximately 2000 MW of installed capacity in 2019).

Norsk Hydro has six operating segments: Extruded Solutions Metal Markets Rolled Products Bauxite & Alumina Primary Metal and Energy.

Extruded Solutions (more than 40% of sales) delivers products within extrusion profiles building systems and precision tubing and is present in about 40 countries.

Metal Markets (over 25%) includes all sales and distribution activities relating to products from its primary metal plants and operational responsibility for the company's stand-alone remelters. It also includes metal sourcing and trading activities which provides operational risk management through LME hedging activities.

Rolled Products (more than 15%) consists of five European rolling mills which include the company's some 50% interest in the AluNorf rolling mill in Germany (and the Rheinwerk primary aluminum smelter in Neuss Germany).

Bauxite and Alumina (nearly 10%) includes bauxite mining activities comprised of the Paragominas mine and some 5% in Mineracao Rio de Norte (both located in Brazil) as well as over 90% of Brazilian alumina refinery Alunorte.

Primary Metal (some 5%) consists of aluminum production remelting and casting activities at company smelters and at the company's partly owned companies.

Energy (less than 5%) manages Hydro Norsk's captive hydropower production and external power sourcing arrangements to the aluminum business.

Geographic Reach

Based in Norway Norsk Hydro has primary metal production facilities in Europe Canada Australia Brazil and Qatar and remelting plants in a range of countries in Europe and the US. It has employees in around 40 countries.

Worldwide consumption amounted to approximately 28 million tons in 2019. Europe and North America each accounted for some 20% of world consumption.

The five largest producers in Western Europe supply about 70% of the European market. China is the largest single market representing around 35% of global consumption.

Overall the Europe generates around 55% of the company's total sales.

Sales and Marketing

To ensure a strong market orientation Norsk Hydro's sales function is organized centrally along business lines. The company is supported by sales offices in Europe Brazil the US and Singapore where it optimizes market contact and sales potential. The customers can contact the company through online contact forms which can be used anonymously. The products from Extruded Solutions are delivered to such sectors as construction automotive and heating ventilation and air conditioning.

Financial Performance

Revenues of the company in 2019 decreased by 3.6 billion NOK to 149.8 billion NOK primarily due to lower revenues on every operation.

Cash held by the company at the end of 2019 increased by 6.3 billion NOK to 12.3 billion NOK compared to the prior year with 6.0 million NOK. Cash provided by operations and financing activities were 12.6 billion NOK and 2.9 billion NOK respectively. Cash used by investing activities was 9.2 billion NOK primarily for purchases of property plant and equipment.

Strategy

Norsk Hydro's new strategic agenda is based on cost-competitive assets operational excellence strong market positions innovation and differentiation on sustainable processes and products. A clear capital allocation framework is established based on different strategic modes for each business area. The company also introduced a new capital allocation framework with strategic growth modes for the different parts of its value chain designed to increase returns and ensure that capital is allocated according to the following strategic objectives: more stable earnings profile; increased exposure in areas with a competitive advantage; larger customer base downstream; and sustainable value chain with lower environmental footprint to reduce risk.

Mergers and Acquisitions

In early 2019 Hydro has completed the acquisition of German powder coating company Metallbeschichtung Gerstungen GmbH (MBG) and welcomes around 100 new employees to Hydro. The acquisition strengthens Hydro's position in the building systems segment. It also supports Hydro's strategy of further integrating and expanding the DACH (Germany Austria and Switzerland) region's logistics center. Terms were not disclosed.

Also in early 2019 Hydro acquired the remaining 50 percent of Technal Middle East a company based in Bahrain delivering tailor-made aluminium building solutions in the Middle East. The acquisition strengthens Hydro Building Systems in Asia where the market growth is amongst the highest in the world. Financial terms were not disclosed.

HISTORY

Norwegian entrepreneurs Sam Eyde and Kristian Birkeland began Norsk Hydro-Elektrisk Kvaelstofaktieselskap (Norwegian Hydro-Electric Nitrogen Corp.) in 1905. The company used electricity generated from waterfalls to extract nitrogen from the air to produce fertilizer.

After WWII the Norwegian government seized German holdings in Norsk Hydro and took a 48% stake in the company. It grew to be the largest chemical firm in Scandinavia. In 1965 when Norway granted licenses for offshore petroleum exploration the company formed partnerships with foreign companies. These included Phillips Petroleum which spurred the North Sea boom in 1969 when its drilling rig Ocean Viking struck oil in the giant Ekofisk field and Elf Aquitaine which oversaw the Frigg discovery in 1971. The Norwegian state increased its share of Norsk Hydro to 51% in 1972.

The company also branched out with hydroelectric-powered aluminum processing at its Karmoy Works (1967) and with a fish-farming subsidiary Mowi (1969). During much of the 1970s it focused on oil and gas development which added to the treasury and helped finance growth often through acquisitions.

Norsk Hydro pushed into the European fertilizer market by buying Dutch company NSM in 1979; during the 1980s it acquired interests in fertilizer operations in France Sweden and the UK. In petrochemicals it expanded by buying two British PVC makers. Norsk Hydro-controlled Hydro Aluminum merged with ASV another Norwegian aluminum company in 1986 and the company consolidated its aluminum holdings two years later.

Hydro served as operator in the Oseberg field which began production in 1988 and grew rapidly to become a major source of oil and gas. In 1990 it bought 330 Danish gasoline stations from UNO-X; in 1992 it purchased Mobil Oil's Norwegian marketing and distribution system. Two years later Norsk Hydro merged its oil and marketing operations in Norway and Denmark with Texaco's.

A weak world economy and increased competition limited its revenues in 1992 and 1993. The company countered slumping sales by selling noncore subsidiaries including pharmaceutical unit Hydro Pharma (1992) and chocolate maker Freia Marabou (1993).

Norsk Hydro expanded further during the early 1990s acquiring fertilizer plants in Germany the UK and the US as well as W. R. Grace's ammonia plants in Trinidad and Tobago. The firm acquired Fisons' NPK fertilizer business in 1994. The company agreed to an asset swap with Petro-Canada in 1996 becoming a partner in oil and gas fields off the east coast of Canada. That year Norsk Hydro bought UNO-X's Swedish gas station operations.

The Norwegian government's stake in Norsk Hydro was reduced from 51% to about 45% in 1999 when the company and state-owned Statoil made a deal to take over Saga Petroleum Norway's leading independent oil producer to keep it out of foreign hands.

In light of major losses in 1999 by Hydro Agri the company made plans in 2000 to close several European nitrogen fertilizer operations. However it agreed to modernize and expand its Hydro Aluminum Sunndal facility to make it the largest aluminum plant in Europe. That year the company also sold Saga UK (North Sea assets) to Conoco and its fish-farming unit to Dutch company Nutreco.

In 2001 the company acquired a stake in Soquimich an industrial minerals company in Chile and majority control of Slovakian aluminum producer Slovalco.

The new decade brought with it a new focus; the company began to make aluminum its primary business lines. Toward that end Norsk Hydro bought VAW Aluminum from E.On AG for $2.8 billion in a deal that enabled it to expand its product base in Europe and the US especially to key customers in the automobile industry. It then sold its flexible packaging unit to Alcan for about $545 million in 2003. Furthering the same goal the company announced in 2003 and then followed through on a spinoff of its agrochemical unit the following year. The resultant company was Yara International.

Norsk Hydro sold its chemicals business to Ineos for $900 million in 2008.

In 2009 Svein Richard Brandtz¦g took over as chief executive. He had been in charge of Hydro's Aluminum Products unit previously. Eivind Reiten resigned after eight years in charge of the company.

In 2011 Norsk Hydro acquired the Brazilian bauxite mining and alumina refining units of Vale SA for $5.7 billion making it a major bauxite and alumina miner.

The Vale purchase gave Norsk Hydro control of the world's third-largest bauxite mine and the world's biggest alumina refinery which have the capacity to supply the company with sufficient raw materials to operate without external suppliers for several decades. Norsk Hydro paid Vale about $1.1 billion in cash and a 22% stake in Norsk Hydro for the assets. The Norwegian government backed the deal and reduced its stake in Norsk Hydro by about 20%.

Although the Vale acquisition positioned Norsk Hydro for growth the aluminum markets have seen demand declining in 2011 and 30% of the aluminum producers losing money. Total demand growth declined to 7% in 2011 from a 19% increase in 2010. A drop in European demand has affected the market due primarily to uncertainty over eurozone debt. A weakening economy has Chinese producers starting to cut back on production and Hydro has stated that it would not restart its idled Sunndal smelter in Norway.

To raise cash in 2011 Norsk Hydro divested its 21% ownership stake in Norwegian power production company SKS Produksjon AS to Salten Kraftsamband AS for $187 million. The deal did not affect Hydro's other power grid holdings.

In 2012 it agreed to form an aluminum manufacturing joint venture with Orkla. The proposed joint venture which will retain the Sapa name (currently the aluminum products division of Orkla) will be equally owned by Norsk Hydro and Orkla and will combine their respective profiles building systems and tubing business to create the world's largest manufactured aluminum products provider.

EXECUTIVES

President Hydro Automotive Structures, Arvid Moss, age 62, $310,289 total compensation
EVP Primary Metal, Hilde M. Aasheim, age 62, $64,364 total compensation
EVP and CFO, Eivind Kallevik, age 53
President and CEO, Svein R. Brandtzaeg, age 63, $513,209 total compensation
EVP Metal Markets, Kjetil M. Ebbesberg, age 49
EVP Corporate Social Responsibility & General Counsel, Anne-Lene Midseim, age 52
EVP Communication & Public Affairs, Inger Sethov, age 50
EVP People and Health Safety and Environment, Hanne Simensen, age 53
EVP Bauxite and Alumina, Silvio Porto
Deputy Chairperson, Inge K. Hansen, age 75
Chairman, Dag Mejdell, age 64
Auditors: KPMG AS

LOCATIONS

HQ: Norsk Hydro ASA
Drammensveien 260, Oslo N-0240
Phone: (47) 22 53 81 00   **Fax:** (47) 22 53 85 53
Web: www.hydro.com

2016 sales

	% of total
European Union	49
Non-European Union	7
Norway	4
Outside Europe	40
Total	**100**

PRODUCTS/OPERATIONS

2016 sales

	% of total
Bauxite & Alumina	15
Primary metal	7
Metal market	48
Rolled Products	27
Energy	3
Other and eliminations	-
Total	**100**

Selected Operations

Aluminum products
  Hydro aluminum automotive
  Hydro aluminum extrusion
  Hydro aluminum rolled products and wire rod
Aluminum metal
Energy
  Hydroelectric power stations

COMPETITORS

Arconic	Kaiser Aluminum
BHP Billiton	RUSAL
CSR Limited	Rio Tinto Alcan
Chinalco	

HISTORICAL FINANCIALS

Company Type: Public

Income Statement   FYE: December 31

	REVENUE ($ mil.)	NET INCOME ($ mil.)	NET PROFIT MARGIN	EMPLOYEES
12/19	17,183	(206)	—	36,310
12/18	18,538	490	2.6%	36,236
12/17	13,866	1,071	7.7%	34,625
12/16	9,759	742	7.6%	12,911
12/15	10,060	229	2.3%	13,263
Annual Growth	**14.3%**	—	—	**28.6%**

2019 Year-End Financials

Debt ratio: 1.7%	No. of shares (mil.): 2,047
Return on equity: (-2.1%)	Dividends
Cash ($ mil.): 1,398	Yield: 3.8%
Current ratio: 1.81	Payout: —
Long-term debt ($ mil.): 2,145	Market value ($ mil.): 7,556

	STOCK PRICE ($) FY Close	P/E High/Low		Earnings	PER SHARE ($) Dividends	Book Value
12/19	3.69	—	—	(0.10)	0.14	4.44
12/18	4.54	3	2	0.24	0.22	4.83
12/17	7.60	2	1	0.52	0.15	5.19
12/16	4.72	2	1	0.36	0.11	4.66
12/15	3.77	5	3	0.11	0.14	4.12
Annual Growth	**(0.5%)**	—	—	—	**1.4%**	**1.9%**

North Pacific Bank Ltd

Auditors: KPMG AZSA LLC

LOCATIONS

HQ: North Pacific Bank Ltd
3-7 Odori-Nishi, Chuo-ku, Sapporo, Hokkaido 060-8661
Phone: (81) 11 261 1311
Web: www.hokuyobank.co.jp

COMPETITORS

Hokkoku Bank	Mizuho Financial
Hokuhoku Financial	Resona
Group	Sumitomo Mitsui

Hyakujushi Bank
Mitsubishi UFJ
  Financial Group

HISTORICAL FINANCIALS

Company Type: Public

Income Statement   FYE: March 31

	ASSETS ($ mil.)	NET INCOME ($ mil.)	INCOME AS % OF ASSETS	EMPLOYEES
03/20	92,013	69	0.1%	4,722
03/19	88,129	127	0.1%	4,955
03/18	89,469	128	0.1%	5,112
03/17	81,334	149	0.2%	5,271
03/16	75,376	160	0.2%	5,412
Annual Growth	**5.1%**	**(18.8%)**	—	**(3.4%)**

2020 Year-End Financials

Return on assets: 0.0%	Dividends
Return on equity: 1.8%	Yield: —
Long-term debt ($ mil.): —	Payout: 51.6%
No. of shares (mil.): 389	Market value ($ mil.): —
Sales ($ mil): 1,288	

Novartis AG Basel

Auditors: PricewaterhouseCoopers AG

LOCATIONS

HQ: Novartis AG Basel
Lichtstrasse 35, Basel CH-4056
Phone: (41) 61 324 1111   **Fax:** (41) 61 324 7826
Web: www.novartis.com

HISTORICAL FINANCIALS

Company Type: Public

Income Statement   FYE: December 31

	REVENUE ($ mil.)	NET INCOME ($ mil.)	NET PROFIT MARGIN	EMPLOYEES
12/20	49,898	8,072	16.2%	105,794
12/19	48,677	11,732	24.1%	103,914
12/18	53,166	12,611	23.7%	125,161
12/17	50,135	7,703	15.4%	121,597
12/16	49,436	6,712	13.6%	118,393
Annual Growth	**0.2%**	**4.7%**	—	**(2.8%)**

2020 Year-End Financials

Debt ratio: 27.2%	No. of shares (mil.): —
Return on equity: 14.3%	Dividends
Cash ($ mil.): 9,658	Yield: 2.1%
Current ratio: 0.90	Payout: 64.9%
Long-term debt ($ mil.): 26,259	Market value ($ mil.): —

	STOCK PRICE ($) FY Close	P/E High/Low		Earnings	PER SHARE ($) Dividends	Book Value
12/20	94.43	28	20	3.52	2.01	25.08
12/19	94.69	19	15	5.06	1.84	24.49
12/18	85.81	17	13	5.38	2.94	34.01
12/17	83.96	26	21	3.25	2.72	32.00
12/16	72.84	31	24	2.80	2.72	31.52
Annual Growth	**6.7%**	—	—	**5.9%**	**(7.3%)**	**(5.6%)**

Novatek Joint Stock Co

EXECUTIVES

Chairman Management Board and Director, Leonid
  V. Mikhelson, age 65
CFO and Director, Mark A. Gyetvay, age 63
Deputy Chairman Management Committee,
  Alexander M. Fridman
Deputy Chairman Management Committee and
  Director Legal, Tatyana S. Kuznetsova
Deputy Chairman Management Board for
  Economics and Finance, Viktor N. Belyakov
Deputy Chairman Management Board; Operations
  Director, Oleg V. Karpushin
Chairman, Alexander Y. Natalenko, age 74
Auditors: AO PricewaterhouseCoopers Audit

LOCATIONS

HQ: Novatek Joint Stock Co
22-A, Pobedy Street, Tarko-Sale, Yamal-Nenets
Autonomous Region 629850
Phone: (7) 495 730 60 00   **Fax:** (7) 495 721 22 53
Web: www.novatek.ru

PRODUCTS/OPERATIONS

2013 Sales

	% of total
Natural gas	69
Stable gas condensate	11
Naphtha	9
Liquefied petroleum gas	6
Crude oil	3
Other gas and gas condensate refined products	2
Total	**100**

COMPETITORS

EastSiberian	Sakhalin Energy
Gazprom	TNK-BP
Rosneft	Urals Energy

HISTORICAL FINANCIALS

Company Type: Public

Income Statement   FYE: December 31

	REVENUE ($ mil.)	NET INCOME ($ mil.)	NET PROFIT MARGIN	EMPLOYEES
12/19	13,863	13,906	100.3%	15,445
12/18	11,934	2,349	19.7%	13,694
12/17	10,087	2,705	26.8%	8,145
12/16	8,777	4,210	48.0%	7,515
12/15	6,436	1,007	15.7%	7,265
Annual Growth	**21.1%**	**92.8%**	—	**20.8%**

2019 Year-End Financials

Debt ratio: 0.1%	No. of shares (mil.): —
Return on equity: 68.8%	Dividends
Cash ($ mil.): 2,201	Yield: 2.3%
Current ratio: 4.24	Payout: 108.6%
Long-term debt ($ mil.): 2,367	Market value ($ mil.): —

	STOCK PRICE ($) FY Close	P/E High/Low		Earnings	PER SHARE ($) Dividends	Book Value
12/19	205.00	1	1	4.62	4.81	8.79
12/18	169.00	3	2	0.78	2.70	4.13
12/17	117.50	3	2	0.90	2.40	4.35
12/16	126.00	1	1	1.39	2.27	3.51
12/15	81.11	3	2	0.33	1.37	1.91
Annual Growth	**26.1%**	—	—	**92.9%**	**36.8%**	**46.4%**

Novo-Nordisk AS

Novo Nordisk is one of the world's leading producers of diabetes therapies including human insulin insulin analogues and injection devices. It makes modern insulin analogues Levemir and NovoLog (which mimic natural insulin regulation more closely than human insulin) Victoza for type 2 diabetes and Saxenda which treats obesity. The firm also has products in the areas of hemostasis management (blood clotting) human growth hormone and estrogen replacement therapy. The company has affiliates in some 80 countries and markets products in about 170 countries. The not-for-profit Novo Nordisk Foundation through its Novo A/S subsidiary controls the voting power in Novo Nordisk.

Operations

Novo Nordisk operates in two business segments: Diabetes and Obesity (which covers insulins oral anti-diabetic drugs and obesity therapies) and Biopharmaceuticals (which covers hemophilia care growth hormone therapy and hormone replacement therapy). Novo Nordisk is the world's leader in diabetes medicines with nearly half of the total insulin market in volume as well as nearly half of the market for modern and new-generation insulins.

The Diabetes and Obesity segment accounts for nearly 85% of annual revenue primarily from diabetes treatments. Top product offerings include Levemir and Tresiba (long-acting insulin) NovoMix/NovoLog Mix (premix insulin) Novo-Rapid/NovoLog (fast-acting insulin) Victoza (type 2 diabetes and weight management) and Saxenda (obesity).

The remainder of sales comes from the Biopharmaceuticals segment which includes the Novo-Seven (hemophilia) Norditropin (growth hormone deficiencies) and hormone replacement therapy offerings.

Geographic Reach

Novo Nordisk's primary production facilities are in Denmark; it also has plants in the US France China and Brazil.

Its primary markets are North America (about 50% of revenues) China Japan and major countries in Europe. The company's business in other markets including Algeria Argentina Australia Brazil India Russia and Turkey is also growing.

Financial Performance

Note: Growth rates may differ after conversion to US Dollars.

Novo Nordisk's revenue has been flat for the past three years following several years of growth. Overall revenue increased 26% between 2014 and 2018. Profits have increased in recent years with total net income growth of 46% over the five-year period.

Revenue was essentially flat in 2018 remaining at DKK 111.8 billion (up a slight tick from DKK 111.7 billion in 2017). The Diabetes and Obesity segment increased sales by 1% but the smaller Biopharmaceuticals segment declined 5%.

Net income grew 1% to DKK 38.6 billion in 2018 due to lower income tax expenses.

The company ended 2018 with DKK 15.6 billion in cash down DKK 1.5 billion from 2017. Operating activities contributed DKK 44.6 billion while investing activities used DKK 12.1 billion (mostly property plant equipment and intangible asset purchases) and financing activities used DKK 34.5 billion via dividends and treasury share purchases.

Strategy

Novo Nordisk has worked to keep its pipeline of products robust and productive especially as its core diabetes business sees competitive and pricing pressures. The company is looking towards treatments for other serious chronic diseases including expansion of obesity hemophilia and hormone disorder medicines. It is also working to develop treatments for non-alcoholic liver disease cardiovascular diseases heart failure and chronic kidney disease. Rybelsus a medication for improved glycemic control in type 2 diabetes patients was approved by the FDA in 2019.

The company spends about 13% of revenue on research and development costs. Novo Nordisk forms partnerships with other drug firms to further its R&D goals. It is also building digital health resources for patients with diabetes and other chronic diseases.

Novo Nordisk is building new production facilities to accommodate growing product demand. Plants in Clayton North Carolina (diabetes drug ingredients) and Kalundborg Denmark (hemophelia drugs) should be operational by 2020. Facilities in Hillerod Denmark (diabetes and obesity) and Malov Denmark (type 2 diabetes drugs) were completed in 2019.

The company announced some restructuring moves in 2018 including reorganizing its R&D operations by establishing four satellite research units (in the US UK and Denmark) and focusing on expanding and diversifying its pipeline.

Company Background

Novo Nordisk was formed by the 1989 merger of Danish insulin producers Novo and Nordisk. The company traces its roots to the founding of two Danish insulin companies Nordisk Insulinlaboratorium and Novo Terapeutisk Laboratorium in 1923 and 1925 respectively.

HISTORY

Novo Nordisk was formed by the 1989 merger of Danish insulin producers Novo and Nordisk.

Soon after Canadian researchers first extracted insulin from the pancreases of cattle Danish researcher August Krogh (winner of the 1920 Nobel Prize in physiology) and physician Marie Krogh his wife teamed up with H. C. Hagedorn also a physician to found Nordisk Insulinlaboratorium. One of their lab workers was an inventor named Harald Pedersen and in 1923 Nordisk hired Pedersen's brother Thorvald to analyze chemicals. The relationship was unsuccessful however and the brothers left the company.

The Pedersens decided to produce insulin themselves and set up operations in their basement in 1924. Harald also designed a syringe that patients could use for their own insulin injections. Within a decade their firm Novo Terapeutisk Laboratorium was selling its product in 40 countries.

Meanwhile Nordisk introduced a slow-acting insulin in 1936. NPH insulin launched in the US in 1950 soon became the leading longer-acting insulin. Nordisk later became a major maker of human growth hormone.

During WWII Novo produced its first enzyme trypsin used to soften leather. It began producing penicillin in 1947 and during the 1950s developed Heparin a trypsin-based drug used to treat blood clots. The company unveiled more industrial enzymes in the 1960s.

In 1981 Novo began selling its insulin in the US through a joint venture with E. R. Squibb (now part of Bristol-Myers Squibb). The next year Novo was the first to produce human insulin (actually a modified form of pig insulin) and in 1983 Nordisk introduced the Nordisk Infuser a pump that constantly released small quantities of insulin. Two years later Novo debuted the NovoPen a refillable injector that looked like a fountain pen.

Novo was the world's #2 insulin maker (and the world's largest maker of industrial enzymes) when it merged with #3 Nordisk in 1989. By combining their research and market share they were better able to compete globally with then-#1 Eli Lilly. After the merger Novo Nordisk introduced the NovoLet the world's first prefilled disposable insulin syringe.

Novo Nordisk introduced drugs for depression (Seroxat 1992) epilepsy (Gabitril 1995) and hemophilia (NovoSeven 1995). The company entered a joint marketing alliance with Johnson & Johnson subsidiary LifeScan the world's #1 maker of blood glucose monitors in 1995. It also began working with Rh ´ne-Poulenc Rorer on estrogen replacement therapies.

Eli Lilly raised a new challenge in 1996 with the FDA approval of Humalog (the US's first new insulin product in 14 years) which is absorbed faster giving users more flexibility in their injection schedule. (Novo Nordisk's own fast-acting insulin product NovoLog received FDA approval four years later.) A 1998 marketing pact with Schering-Plough signaled Novo Nordisk's desire to boost sales of its diabetes drugs in the US where Eli Lilly had historically dominated.

In 2000 Novo Nordisk split its health care and enzymes businesses; the split left Novo Nordisk with all the health care operations while a new company Novozymes was formed to carry out the enzyme business. It bought out the remaining shares in its Brazilian subsidiary Biobr´s in 2001. In 2002 the company spun off its US-based biotechnology firm ZymoGenetics. It retained a one-third of the company until selling its shares to Bristol-Myers Squibb in 2010.

Further boosting its portfolio of diabetes and obesity intellectual property the company acquired two US biopharmaceutical research firms (Calibrium and MB2) for undisclosed amounts in 2015.

EXECUTIVES

EVP and CFO, Jesper Brandgaard, age 57, $947,140 total compensation
EVP and Chief Science Officer, Mads Krogsgaard Thomsen, age 60, $947,140 total compensation
President and CEO, Lars Fruergaard J ̧rgensen, age 54, $718,520 total compensation
EVP North America Operations, Jakob Riis, age 54, $718,520 total compensation
EVP International Operations, Maziar Mike Doustdar, age 50
EVP Product Supply, Henrik Wulff, age 50
Vice Chairman, Jeppe Christiansen
Chairman, G ¶ran Ando
Auditors: PricewaterhouseCoopers Statsautoriseret Revisionsaktieselskab

LOCATIONS

HQ: Novo-Nordisk AS
Novo Alle, Bagsvaerd DK-2880
Phone: (45) 4444 8888   **Fax:** (45) 4449 0555
Web: www.novonordisk.com

PRODUCTS/OPERATIONS

2016 Sales

	% of total
Diabetes and obesity care	
NovoRapid/Novolog	18
Levemir	15
Victoza	18
NovoMix/NovologMix	10
Human insulin	10
Other diabetes and obesity care (including Saxenda)	5
New-generation insulin	4
Biopharmaceuticals	
Haemophilia	9
Norditropin	8
Other products	3
Total	**100**

2016 sales

	.	% of total
USA		51
Europe		19
Region China		9
Pacific		8
other countries		13
Total		**100**

Selected Products

Diabetes products
  Human insulins
    Actrapid
    Insulatard
    Mixtard 30
  Glucagon-like Peptide-1
    Victoza
  Modern insulins
    Levemir
    NovoMix
    NovoRapid
  Oral antidiabetic agents
    NovoNorm
    PrandiMet
Biopharmaceuticals
  NovoSeven (recombinant hemophilia therapy)
  Norditropin (human growth hormone)
  Hormone replacement therapy
    Activelle
    Estrofem
    Novofem
    Vagifem

COMPETITORS

Baxter International	Marina Biotech
Becton Dickinson	Medtronic
Biogen	Novartis
Eli Lilly	Pfizer
Genentech	Sanofi
GlaxoSmithKline	Wockhardt
MannKind	

HISTORICAL FINANCIALS

Company Type: Public

Income Statement   FYE: December 31

	REVENUE ($ mil.)	NET INCOME ($ mil.)	NET PROFIT MARGIN	EMPLOYEES
12/20	20,939	6,950	33.2%	45,323
12/19	18,337	5,853	31.9%	43,258
12/18	17,150	5,924	34.5%	43,202
12/17	17,984	6,139	34.1%	42,076
12/16	15,876	5,386	33.9%	41,971
Annual Growth	7.2%	6.6%	—	1.9%

2020 Year-End Financials

Debt ratio: 0.8%	No. of shares (mil.): —
Return on equity: 69.5%	Dividends
Cash ($ mil.): 2,104	Yield: 1.3%
Current ratio: 0.94	Payout: 34.0%
Long-term debt ($ mil.): —	Market value ($ mil.): —

	STOCK PRICE ($) FY Close	P/E High/Low		PER SHARE ($) Earnings	Dividends	Book Value
12/20	69.85	4	3	2.97	0.93	4.52
12/19	57.88	4	3	2.46	0.87	3.68
12/18	46.07	3	3	2.44	0.91	3.24
12/17	53.67	4	2	2.48	0.88	3.28
12/16	35.86	4	2	2.12	0.97	2.57
Annual Growth	18.1%			8.7%	(1.1%)	15.2%

NTT Data Corp

Auditors: KPMG AZSA LLC

LOCATIONS

HQ: NTT Data Corp
  3-3-3 Toyosu, Koto-ku, Tokyo 135-6033
Phone: (81) 3 5546 8119
Web: www.nttdata.com

HISTORICAL FINANCIALS

Company Type: Public

Income Statement   FYE: March 31

	REVENUE ($ mil.)	NET INCOME ($ mil.)	NET PROFIT MARGIN	EMPLOYEES
03/20	20,882	692	3.3%	136,464
03/19	19,537	845	4.3%	126,953
03/18	19,938	547	2.7%	121,020
03/17	15,495	587	3.8%	114,658
03/16	14,380	564	3.9%	83,990
Annual Growth	9.8%	5.2%	—	12.9%

2020 Year-End Financials

Debt ratio: 0.2%	No. of shares (mil.): 1,402
Return on equity: 8.0%	Dividends
Cash ($ mil.): 1,891	Yield: 0.0%
Current ratio: 1.09	Payout: —
Long-term debt ($ mil.): 4,061	Market value ($ mil.): 11,739

	STOCK PRICE ($) FY Close	P/E High/Low		PER SHARE ($) Earnings	Dividends	Book Value
03/20	8.37	0	0	0.49	0.16	6.17
03/19	10.64	0	0	0.60	0.14	5.96
03/18	10.20	1	0	0.39	0.15	5.60
03/17	23.69	1	0	0.42	0.13	5.09
03/16	25.52	1	1	0.40	0.11	4.70
Annual Growth	(24.3%)			5.2% 11.2%		7.0%

Nutrien Ltd

Auditors: KPMG LLP

LOCATIONS

HQ: Nutrien Ltd
  Suite 500, 122 - 1st Avenue South, Saskatoon,
  Saskatchewan S7K 7G3
Phone: 306 933-8523   **Fax:** 306 933-8877
Web: www.nutrien.com

HISTORICAL FINANCIALS

Company Type: Public

Income Statement   FYE: December 31

	REVENUE ($ mil.)	NET INCOME ($ mil.)	NET PROFIT MARGIN	EMPLOYEES
12/19	20,023	992	5.0%	22,300
12/18	19,636	3,573	18.2%	20,300
12/17	0	(0)	—	0
Annual Growth	—	—	—	—

2019 Year-End Financials

Debt ratio: 21.4%	No. of shares (mil.): 572
Return on equity: 4.2%	Dividends
Cash ($ mil.): 671	Yield: 3.6%
Current ratio: 1.17	Payout: 103.5%
Long-term debt ($ mil.): 8,553	Market value ($ mil.): 27,450

	STOCK PRICE ($) FY Close	P/E High/Low		PER SHARE ($) Earnings	Dividends	Book Value
12/19	47.91	33	27	1.70	1.76	39.91
12/18	47.00	10	8	5.72	1.63	40.14
12/17	0.00	—	—	(0.00)	0.00	
(2,294.67)						
/0.00	—		(0.00)	0.00	(0.00)	
Annual Growth	—			—	—	—

Obayashi Corp

Obayashi's buildings shake rattle and roll — but they don't fall. A leading global contractor and one of Japan's top four general contractors the company is a pioneer in the development of earthquake-resistant building techniques. Obayashi serves as architect consultant engineer and systems designer for buildings and large-scale civil engineering projects worldwide. Some of its projects have included the Dubai Urban Rail Transit System; the bobsled and luge runs used in the 1998 Winter Games in Nagano; the Ted Williams tunnel in Boston; and restoration of port facilities in Kobe Japan damaged by a 1995 earthquake.

Operations

Obayashi operates four core business segments. Its Domestic Building Construction business (which generated 54% of net sales in fiscal 2015 ended March) builds offices condos commercial facilities factories hospitals and schools and designs for customers concerned with environmental harm energy conservation seismic resistance and disaster readiness. Its Domestic Civil Engineering business (18% of net sales) builds various types of infrastructure as well as environmentally-friendly waste disposal facilities.

The company's Overseas Construction business (22% of net sales) builds infrastructure such as roads bridges and schools. Its Real Estate business (4% of net sales) works on redevelopment projects across Japan as a project partner or specified agent and sells properties for lease in favorable locations (mainly urban areas).

The company's Domestic Civil Engineering and Real Estate businesses boast the highest profit margins with each of these segments contributing 35% to Obayashi's overall operating income in FY2015 despite contributing a much smaller share of total revenue than the company's Domestic Building Construction Business. By comparison the Domestic Building Construction business and the Overseas Construction business contributed just 16% and 8% to overall operating income.

Geographic Reach

About 77% of Obayashi's net sales came from Japan in FY2015 while the rest came from North America (23% of sales) Asia (9%) and other regions (less than 1%). The Japan-based company's overseas offices are in London San Francisco Sydney Singapore Guam Taipei Hanoi Kuala Lampur Bangkok Yangon Dubai Auckland and Jakarta.

Financial Performance

Note: Growth rates may differ after conversion to US dollars. This analysis uses financials from the company's annual report.

Obayashi's net sales and profits have been rising over the past several years as its order volumes have increased with the strengthened economy in Japan and elsewhere and as its operation margins have remained stable.

The company's net sales rose 10% to a record Â 1773 billion ($14.8 billion) mostly thanks to firm orders from both public and private sectors in the domestic construction market.

Obayashi's profit jumped 10% to a record Â 28.7 billion ($240 million) thanks to increases in gross profit on completed construction contracts and the company's Real Estate Development business. Its operating cash doubled to Â 74.6 billion ($575 million) for the year thanks to higher cash earnings mostly from its domestic construction business.

Strategy
As part of of the company's Medium-Term Business Plan in 2015 and as Japan's aging and shrinking demographics continue to threaten its core domestic construction business Obayashi would continue to diversify its revenue stream and selectively expand overseas.

Indeed Obayashi's overseas building and civil construction businesses have been growing faster than its domestic businesses in recent years; its total overseas business accounted for 23% of its overall net sales in FY2015 up from 19% the year before. The company's overseas construction business is known for its work on national projects such as the Taiwan High Speed Rail and the Colorado River Bridge at the Hoover Dam which used "world-renowned technological capabilities like seismic resistance and shield tunneling."

After countering the downturn in Japan's construction industry Obayashi began venturing into environmental services including hazardous and radioactive waste containment. It has also committed itself to green building practices.

HISTORY

With the first wave of Japanese modernization in 1892 Yoshigoro Ohbayashi opened a small construction operation in Osaka. He won the bid for construction of the Abe Paper Mill. In 1898 he joined with partner Kamezo Shirasugi to lay the foundations for the Obayashi Corporation.

Obayashi's first big contract came in 1901 for the construction of buildings for Osaka's Fifth National Industry Fair. During the Russo-Japanese War the young corporation built 100 barracks in three weeks a feat that helped it win a contract to build Tokyo Station (completed 1914). Obayashi executives were invited to the US by the Fluor Company in the early 1920s to study advanced construction techniques. After a 1923 earthquake and firestorm leveled much of Tokyo Obayashi applied the technology it learned from Fluor to build quake-resistant fireproof buildings.

Like many Japanese companies Obayashi is quiet about its history in the years leading up to WWII and the rebuilding that followed. However the Korean War increased demand for company projects such as the Tokyo Station annex the Japan Broadcasting Corporation building and the first of 50 major dam projects.

In the 1960s Obayashi became the first Japanese construction firm to build an internal R&D facility. Its Technical Research Institute developed the OWS-Soletanche Diaphragm Wall Construction Method which it used on the New Osaka building in 1961 and has adapted to many other buildings since. In 1965 the company began its first major civil engineering project overseas doing its part in a 32-year-long excavation in Singapore that reclaimed about 3% of that country's land mass from the sea. Also that year Obayashi completed the first high-rise in Japan Yokohama's 21-story Hotel Empire.

Expo '70 in Osaka showcased Obayashi's air-membrane dome and roof lift-up method. During the 1970s the company played key roles in Japan's massive highway-building projects. In 1979 it was the first Japanese construction company to be awarded a public works contract in the US.

Obayashi completed thousands of projects during the 1980s. It helped build the Tsukuba Expo '85 and restored the Katsura Rikyu Detached Palace a national treasure.

In 1994 two former Obayashi executives were found guilty of giving a 10 million yen (about $100000) bribe to the mayor of Sendai two years earlier. The company was one of several major construction companies involved in the scandal.

In the 1990s Obayashi "mole" machines chewed through the earth to create the Tokyo Bay Aqualine tunnel. In 1996 the company developed anti-earthquake construction methods for structures built on soft ground (almost a fifth of buildings in Tokyo).

Obayashi was hard hit in 1998 and 1999 as financial crises created turmoil in Japan's construction industry. The company responded by reducing its workforce by about 5% taking advantage of economies of scale in materials purchasing and working with subcontractors to cut costs. Beefing up its project orders is another key strategy. New projects secured by Obayashi in 2000 included the Taiwan North-South High Speed Rail Project and a new head office for Japanese advertising giant Dentsu.

In 2002 the group completed the NHK Osaka Broadcasting Station and the renovation of Kobe Wing Stadium a site for part of the 2002 World Cup soccer finals. Obayashi and Kobe Steel won the contract to operate the stadium for 15 years.

Obayashi was caught in a building scandal in its home country in 2005 when it came to light that an outside architect had falsified documents regarding earthquake resistance for one of its projects a hotel. Obayashi said that the falsifications were too skillfully done to catch at the construction stage.

EXECUTIVES

President, Toru Shiraishi, age 73
EVP, Tadahiko Noguchi, age 73
EVP, Makoto Kanai, age 72
Senior Managing Executive Officer, Makoto Kishida, age 69
EVP, Shozo Harada, age 71
Senior Managing Executive Officer, Akihisa Miwa, age 68
Executive Managing Officer, Kenichi Shibata, age 71
Senior Managing Executive Officer, Nao Sugiyama, age 71
Chairman, Takeo Obayashi, age 66
Auditors: Ernst & Young ShinNihon LLC

LOCATIONS

HQ: Obayashi Corp
2-15-2 Konan, Minato-ku, Tokyo 108-8502
Phone: (81) 3 5769 1017   **Fax:** 650 589-8384
Web: www.obayashi.co.jp

2014 Sales

	% of total
Japan	81
Overseas	
North America	10
Asia	8
Others	1
Total	**100**

Obayashi has operations in Cambodia China Indonesia Japan Malaysia the Philippines Singapore Taiwan Thailand the UK the US and Vietnam.

PRODUCTS/OPERATIONS

2014 Sales

	% of total
Domestic Building Construction Business	56
Domestic Civil Engineering Business	20
Overseas Construction Business	18
Real Estate Business	3
Other Business	3
Total	**100**

Selected Subsidiaries and Affliates
Atelier G&B Co. Ltd.
E.W. Howell Co. Inc. (US)
James E. Roberts-Obayashi Corporation (50% housing projects US)
Mutsuzawa Green Co. Ltd. (golf club and restaurant operations)
Naigai Technos Corporation
Obayashi Real Estate Corporation
Obayashi Road Corporation
OC Finance Corporation
OC Real Estate Management LLC (US)
SOMA Environment Service Corporation
Taiwan Obayashi Corporation
Thai Obayashi Corporation Limited (49%)

COMPETITORS

ABB	Kumagai Gumi
Bechtel	Parsons Corporation
CSCEC	Penta-Ocean
Fluor	Construction
Hazama	Shimizu
Hyundai Engineering	TOA
and Construction	Taisei
ITOCHU	Takenaka
Kajima	

HISTORICAL FINANCIALS
Company Type: Public

Income Statement   FYE: March 31

	REVENUE ($ mil.)	NET INCOME ($ mil.)	NET PROFIT MARGIN	EMPLOYEES
03/20	19,097	1,041	5.5%	18,879
03/19	18,418	1,021	5.5%	18,832
03/18	17,899	872	4.9%	18,752
03/17	16,749	845	5.0%	18,525
03/16	15,831	564	3.6%	17,754
Annual Growth	4.8%	16.5%	—	1.5%

2020 Year-End Financials

Debt ratio: 0.1%	No. of shares (mil.): 718
Return on equity: 14.2%	Dividends
Cash ($ mil.): 2,902	Yield: —
Current ratio: 1.22	Payout: —
Long-term debt ($ mil.): 1,714	Market value ($ mil.): —

Oberbank AG (Austria)

Auditors: KPMG Austria GmbH

LOCATIONS

HQ: Oberbank AG (Austria)
Untere Donaulaende 28, Linz A-4020
Phone: (43) 732 78 02 0   **Fax:** (43) 732 78 58 10
Web: www.oberbank.com

COMPETITORS

BAWAG	Investkredit
Deutsche Bank	OTP Bank
Erste Bank	RZB Group

HISTORICAL FINANCIALS

Company Type: Public

		NET	INCOME	
	ASSETS ($ mil.)	INCOME ($ mil.)	AS % OF ASSETS	EMPLOYEES
12/19	35,923	338	0.9%	2,150
12/18	34,953	353	1.0%	2,101
12/17	32,779	314	1.0%	0
12/16	30,147	284	0.9%	2,049
12/15	28,707	261	0.9%	2,025
Annual Growth	5.8%	6.6%	—	1.5%

Income Statement   FYE: December 31

2019 Year-End Financials

Return on assets: 0.9%
Return on equity: 7.4%
Long-term debt ($ mil.): —
No. of shares (mil.): 32
Sales ($ mil): 1,128

Dividends
  Yield: —
  Payout: 18.7%
  Market value ($ mil.): —

Ogaki Kyoritsu Bank, Ltd.

Auditors: KPMG AZSA LLC

LOCATIONS

HQ: Ogaki Kyoritsu Bank, Ltd.
  3-98 Kuruwa-machi, Ogaki, Gifu 503-0887
Phone: (81) 584 74 2111
Web: www.okb.co.jp

COMPETITORS

Aozora Bank
Mitsubishi UFJ
  Financial Group
Shizuoka Bank

HISTORICAL FINANCIALS

Company Type: Public

Income Statement   FYE: March 31

		NET	INCOME	
	ASSETS ($ mil.)	INCOME ($ mil.)	AS % OF ASSETS	EMPLOYEES
03/20	55,118	50	0.1%	4,401
03/19	52,678	61	0.1%	4,484
03/18	54,190	91	0.2%	4,499
03/17	50,913	108	0.2%	4,457
03/16	47,992	126	0.3%	4,451
Annual Growth	3.5%	(20.5%)	—	(0.3%)

2020 Year-End Financials

Return on assets: 0.0%
Return on equity: 1.8%
Long-term debt ($ mil.): —
No. of shares (mil.): 41
Sales ($ mil): 1,062

Dividends
  Yield: —
  Payout: 53.2%
  Market value ($ mil.): —

Oita Bank Ltd (Japan)

Auditors: Deloitte Touche Tohmatsu LLC

LOCATIONS

HQ: Oita Bank Ltd (Japan)
  3-4-1 Funaimachi, Oita 870-0021
Phone: (81) 97 534 1111
Web: www.oitabank.co.jp

HISTORICAL FINANCIALS

Company Type: Public

Income Statement   FYE: March 31

		NET	INCOME	
	ASSETS ($ mil.)	INCOME ($ mil.)	AS % OF ASSETS	EMPLOYEES
03/20	31,257	46	0.1%	2,656
03/19	30,049	52	0.2%	2,711
03/18	30,325	56	0.2%	2,786
03/17	28,719	67	0.2%	2,866
03/16	28,158	86	0.3%	2,933
Annual Growth	2.6%	(14.3%)	—	(2.4%)

2020 Year-End Financials

Return on assets: 0.1%
Return on equity: 2.6%
Long-term debt ($ mil.): —
No. of shares (mil.): 15
Sales ($ mil): 561

Dividends
  Yield: —
  Payout: 27.6%
  Market value ($ mil.): —

Oji Holdings Corp

One of Japan's top paper makers along with Nippon Paper Industries Co. Oji Holdings produces pulp and paper and converted paper products through nearly 190 subsidiaries and affiliates worldwide. Its business segments include: Industrial Materials Household and Consumer Products Functional Materials Forest Resources and Environment Marketing Printing and Communications Media and other businesses which focus on real estate engineering trading business and logistic. Products include container board and corrugated containers boxboard and folding cartons among others. Japan is responsible for more 70% of the sales. Customers include overseas and domestic companies in the retail and energy sectors. The company was founded in 1873.

Operations

The company has four operating segments. These being: Household and Industrial Materials accounting for nearly 40% Functional Faterials generates some 15% Forest Resource and Environment Marketing brings in more than 15% and Printing and Communications Media gets less than 20%.

Industrial Materials segment focuses on containerboard and corrugated containers boxboard and folding cartons. Household and Consumer Products segment centers on tissue toilet tissue and wet wipes. Functional Materials segment provides specialty paper thermal paper and film. Forest Resources and Environment Marketing segment concentrates on pulp energyplantation service and lumber processing. Printing and Communications Media segment makes newsprint printing and publication and communications paper.

Geographic Reach

Headquartered in Tokyo Japan is Oji Holdings' largest market accounting for 70%. Other sales are made in Asia which accounts for nearly 20% Oceania Europe and the Americas each contributes some 5%.

Sales and Marketing

It serves various industries such as energy retail film packaging and newsprint among others.

Financial Performance

Oji Holdings' net sales has been in the Â 1.4 billion to Â 1.6 billion range for the past five years recording a 5% increase from 2015 to 2019. Meanwhile the company's net income has achieved year-over-year growth after its decline in 2017. Net income increased by 358% from 2015 to 2019.

Net sales decreased from Â 1.6 billion in 2018 to Â 1.5 billion in 2019. Household and Industrial Materials remains to have the top net sales per business segment comprising 38.8% of the company's 2019 revenue. This was followed by the Printing and Communications Media segment (16.5%) Other (16.4%) Forest Resources and Environment Marketing Business (16.1%) and Functional Materials (12.2%).

Cash and cash equivalents at the end of the year were Â 82.4 billion similar to the previous year. Cash provided by operations was Â 124.5 billion. Investing activities used Â 64.8 billion primarily for payment for acquisition of property plant equipment and intangible assets. Financing activities on the other hand used Â 58.1 billion primarily for repayment of long-term loans payable.

Strategy

Oji Holdings' new corrugated container plant in Funabashi City Chiba Prefecture has started commercial production in July 2020 to meet the growth in demand for corrugated containers in the Kanto region. The Industrial Materials Company will enhance its competitive strength in the corrugated container business in the Kanto region by aggressively capturing new demand for corrugated containers and expanding its supply volume. At the same time as part of its initiatives to restructure manufacturing in response to structural changes in domestic demand we will shut down the manufacturing facilities at the Oji Materia Nayoro Mill and transfer other facilities to Oji Paper Tomakomai Mill and production facilities for newsprint at the Tomakomai Mill are now in the midst of modification for containerboard and kraft paper. To further reinforce earnings bases through the integration of material and converting a range of investments will be made for the optimization of the domestic business structure.

The Industrial Materials Company conducts business at 45 sites in nine countries in Southeast Asia India and Oceania. It has been focusing mainly on expanding converting sites to respond to growing packaging demand and now it will install new containerboard production facilities in Malaysia which is scheduled to start commercial operation in 2021. Through these efforts the company will further progress the development of overseas businesses by integrating material and converting.

EXECUTIVES

President and Co-CEO, Susumu Yajima
Chairman and Co-CEO, Kiyotaka Shindo
EVP; President Oji Industrial Materials Management, Ryoji Watari
EVP; President Oji Functional Materials Progressing Center, Kazuo Fuchigami
Senior Executive Officer; President Oji Materia, Takashi Nozawa
Senior Executive Officer; President Oji Management Office, Gemmei Shimamura
Senior Executive Officer; President Oji Paper, Hidehiko Aoyama
Executive Officer; President Oji Engineering, Yoshiki Koseki
Executive Officer; President Oji F-Tex, Masatoshi Kaku
Executive Officer; President Oji Imaging Media, Ryuichi Kisaka
Executive Officer; President Forest Resources and Environment Marketing, Kazuhiko Kamada
Executive Officer; President Oji Green Resource, Shoji Fujiwara
Auditors: PricewaterhouseCoopers Aarata LLC

LOCATIONS

HQ: Oji Holdings Corp
4-7-5 Ginza, Chuo-ku, Tokyo 104-0061
Phone: (81) 3 3563 1111   **Fax:** (81) 3 3563 1135
Web: www.ojiholdings.co.jp

PRODUCTS/OPERATIONS

2016 Sales

	% of total
Household and industrial materials	42
Printing and communication media	21
Forest resource and environment marketing	19
Functional materials	15
Others	3
Total	**100**

COMPETITORS

Daio Paper	Nippon Paper
Georgia-Pacific	Nisshinbo
Hokuetsu Kishu Paper	Rengo Co.
International Paper	Stora Enso
Japan Pulp and Paper	Svenska Cellulosa
M-real	UPM-Kymmene
Mitsubishi Paper Mills	Weyerhaeuser

HISTORICAL FINANCIALS

Company Type: Public

Income Statement   FYE: March 31

	REVENUE ($ mil.)	NET INCOME ($ mil.)	NET PROFIT MARGIN	EMPLOYEES
03/20	13,888	535	3.9%	36,810
03/19	14,005	469	3.4%	36,309
03/18	13,993	341	2.4%	36,144
03/17	12,878	327	2.5%	38,389
03/16	12,766	135	1.1%	36,442
Annual Growth	2.1%	40.9%	—	0.3%

2020 Year-End Financials

Debt ratio: 0.2%
Return on equity: 8.4%
Cash ($ mil.): 681
Current ratio: 1.20
Long-term debt ($ mil.): 3,460

No. of shares (mil.): 992
Dividends
  Yield: 0.0%
  Payout: 102.0%
Market value ($ mil.): 55,992

	STOCK PRICE ($) FY Close	P/E High/Low		PER SHARE ($) Earnings	Dividends	Book Value
03/20	56.44	1	1	0.54	0.55	6.43
03/19	61.82	1	1	0.47	0.99	6.17
03/18	62.50	2	1	0.34	0.95	6.40
03/17	47.38	1	1	0.33	0.90	5.75
03/16	40.75	3	2	0.14	0.88	5.34
Annual Growth	8.5%	—	—	40.9%	(10.9%)	4.7%

Olam International Ltd.

Olam International is a leading global agribusiness serving more than 25000 customers across 60-plus countries. It farms processes and distributes food ingredients feed and fiber products and sources from a network of five million farmers. The company's top offering is food staples and packaged foods (rice sugar coffee cocoa and other packaged foods); its stable of products also includes confectionery and beverage ingredients (cocoa and coffee) Industrial raw materials Infrastructure and Logistics (cotton and wood items) and edible nuts spices and beans. Asia Middle East

and Australia is Olam's largest market accounting for approximately half of Olam's revenue.

Operations

Olam's has five business segments: Food Staples and Packaged Foods Confectionery and Beverage Ingredients Edible Nuts and Spices Industrial Raw Materials Infrastructure and Logistics and Commodity Financial Services.

Food Staples and Packaged Foods generate nearly 55% of revenue. Product includes of rice sugar and sweeteners grains and animal feed edible oils dairy and packaged foods. Confectionery and Beverage Ingredients gives in roughly 20% of revenue it offers cocoa and coffee based products.

Edible Nuts and Spices ring up about 15% of revenue product line includes cashew peanuts almonds hazelnuts pistachios walnuts. Olam is the leading supplier of edible nuts with 19500 hectares of plantation of almonds walnuts and pistachios.

Industrial Raw Materials Infrastructure and Logistics (accounts the remainder) offers cotton wood products rubber and fertilizer.

Commodity Financial Services offers risk management solutions market-making volatility and asset management and trade and structured finance.

Geographic Reach

Singapore-based Olam operates faciles comprising plants plantations warehouses and offices some are located in China India Indonesia Ethiopia Sudan Italy Georgia Germany Russia and South Africa. Asia Middle East and Australia generate roughly half of Olam's revenue followed by Europe which gives in roughly 20% Americas with more than 15% and Africa rings up about 15% of revenue.

Sales and Marketing

Olam serves more than 25000 customers. It includes food manufacturers retailers food service and e-commerce customers.

Financial Performance

Note: Growth rates may differ after conversion to US Dollar.

The company's revenue increased by 8% to S$33.0 billion in 2019 compared to the prior year with S$30.5 million. The increase was due to higher sales on the company's products in the food category.

Cash held by the company at the end of 2019 was S$3.0 billion compared to the previous year with S$2.4 billion. Cash provided by operations and financing activities were S$697.3 million and S$495.1 million respectively. Cash used for investing activities was S$562.7 million mainly for purchase of property plant and equipment.

Strategy

Capitalizing on key trends driven by consumers for healthier sustainable and natural products as well as ever advancing technologies for production and purchasing behavior the refreshed 2019 to 2024 Strategic Plan announced in early 2019 got off to a strong start. Deliverables are being met or even exceeded thanks to the focus and dedication of the Olam team.

The first strategic pathway of streamlining focusing and strengthening the portfolio saw the company reduce S$437.6 million of invested capital. S$1.1 billion was invested in strengthening the continuing businesses against the US$3.5 billion allocated for investment over the 6-year period.

The company's second pathway was to improve margins through capital and cost productivity. In this respect savings of some US$70 million were achieved and gearing is well within the net debt-to-equity target of 2.0 at 1.38 times. A significant element of these successes has been the focus on leveraging key enablers of operational excellence sustainability digitalization and leadership and talent. Innovative financing strategies demonstrate

just one way of how Olam is embedding these enablers into the strategy with a second sustainability-linked loan and a world-first digital loan.

Mergers and Acquisitions

In late 2019 Olam acquired California-based Hughson Nut Inc. an almond processor and ingredient manufacturer and associated real estate assets from APB Partners LLC for $54 million. The acquisition will enable Olam to offer a fully integrated solution across the almond value chain from the US.

In early 2019 Olam submits binding offer to acquire Dangote Flour Mills Plc in Nigeria for $361 million. The proposed acquisition supports the strategy of the Grain and Animal Feed business one of Olam's prioritized platforms for growth to expand its wheat milling capacity in high-growth markets.

In early 2019 Olam acquired 85% share of Indonesia-based YTS Holdings Pte Limited. The largest cocoa processor in Indonesia for $90 million. The acquisition will help Olam to capitalize on Asia's trajectory to become the largest global consumer of cocoa powder.

EXECUTIVES

Managing Director and Global Head Spices and Vegetable Ingredients and Country Head USA, Greg Estep
Group Managing Director and CEO, Sunny G. Verghese
SVP Wood Products, Ashok Hegde
Managing Director and Global Head Oil Palm Natural Rubber, Ranveer S. Chauhan
Senior Managing Director and regional Head Australia Asia and North South and Central America and Russia, Sridhar Krishnan
Managing Director & Global Head Cocoa Specialty Fats Sugar and Sweeteners, Gerard A. (Gerry) Manley
Managing Director Cotton, Jagdish Parihar
Managing Director and Global Head Coffee Dairy Products and CFS, Vivek Verma
Managing Director Cashew and Spices, Ashok Krishen
Managing Director Africa and Middle East, Venkataramani Srivathsan
Executive Director and Group COO, A. Shekar
Managing Director and Global Head Dairy and Sugar, Joe Kenny
Managing Director and Global Head Grains, K.C. Suresh
Chairman, Lim Ah Doo
Auditors: Ernst & Young LLP

LOCATIONS

HQ: Olam International Ltd.
7 Straits View, Marina One East Tower, #20-01, 018936
Phone: (65) 6339 4100   **Fax:** (65) 6339 9755
Web: www.olamgroup.com

2018 Sales

	% of total
Asia & the Middle East	43
Africa	15
Europe	25
Americas	17
Total	**100**

PRODUCTS/OPERATIONS

2018 Sales

	% of total
Food staples & packaged foods	48
Edible nuts spices & beans	14
Confectionery & beverage ingredients	23
Industrial raw materials	15
Total	**100**

COMPETITORS

ADM	ITOCHU
Adani Enterprises	Intraco
Amsterdam Commodities	MGP Ingredients
Barry Callebaut	McCormick & Company
Big Heart Pet Brands	Nestlé
Cargill	Plains Cotton
ConAgra	Sensient
Corbion	Sensient Dehydrated
Danisco A/S	Flavors
Dunavant Enterprises	Staplcotn
FFM	SunOpta
Fonterra	Syngenta Corporation
Food Corporation of	Tate & Lyle
India	Weil Brothers Cotton
Heinz	Wonderful Company
ITC	

HISTORICAL FINANCIALS

Company Type: Public

Income Statement   FYE: December 31

	REVENUE ($ mil.)	NET INCOME ($ mil.)	NET PROFIT MARGIN	EMPLOYEES
12/19	24,567	419	1.7%	87,600
12/18	22,447	255	1.1%	74,500
12/17	19,821	434	2.2%	72,100
12/16	14,280	243	1.7%	69,772
12/15	20,073	69	0.3%	62,500
Annual Growth	5.2%	56.5%	—	8.8%

2019 Year-End Financials

Debt ratio: 34.9%
Return on equity: 8.8%
Cash ($ mil.): 2,391
Current ratio: 1.27
Long-term debt ($ mil.): 4,016

No. of shares (mil.): —
Dividends
  Yield: 4.1%
  Payout: 858.3%
Market value ($ mil.): —

	STOCK PRICE ($) FY Close	P/E High/Low	Earnings	PER SHARE ($) Dividends	Book Value
12/19	26.45	186161	0.12	0.05	1.50
12/18	23.76	385259	0.07	1.00	1.46
12/17	30.44	197152	0.13	0.87	1.55
12/16	27.64	252186	0.08	0.79	1.37
12/15	25.81	986808	0.02	0.08	1.31
Annual Growth	0.6%	— —	55.6%	(7.9%)	3.5%

Old Mutual Ltd

Auditors: Deloitte & Touche

LOCATIONS

HQ: Old Mutual Ltd
Mutualpark, Jan Smuts Drive, Pinelands, Cape Town 7405
Phone:
Web: www.oldmutual.com

HISTORICAL FINANCIALS

Company Type: Public

Income Statement   FYE: December 31

	REVENUE ($ mil.)	NET INCOME ($ mil.)	NET PROFIT MARGIN	EMPLOYEES
12/19	12,540	668	5.3%	29,861
12/18	7,641	2,543	33.3%	30,365
12/17	14,290	1,167	8.2%	0
Annual Growth	(6.3%)	(24.3%)	—	—

2019 Year-End Financials

Debt ratio: —
Return on equity: 12.2%
Cash ($ mil.): 2,169
Current ratio: —
Long-term debt ($ mil.): —

No. of shares (mil.): —
Dividends
  Yield: —
  Payout: 58.4%
Market value ($ mil.): —

	STOCK PRICE ($) FY Close	P/E High/Low	Earnings	PER SHARE ($) Dividends	Book Value
12/19	0.00	— —	0.15	0.09	1.13
12/18	0.00	— —	0.54	0.15	1.10
Annual Growth	—	—	(48.0%)	(24.8%)	1.5%

OMV AG (Austria)

Oil and chemicals group OMV is Austria's largest industrial company. A leading oil and gas company in Central and Eastern Europe it explores for natural gas and crude oil; refines crude oil; and imports transports and stores gas. In 2014 OMV reported proved reserves of 1.1 billion barrels of oil equivalent; it produced about 309000 barrels of oil equivalent per day and sold 13 billion cu. ft. of gas. The bulk of OMV's sales come from refining and marketing with the company operating three refineries. OMV is focusing on growing its exploration and production assets.

Operations

The company operates in three major segments. OMV Exploration and Production's core countries in Romania and Austria OMV is focusing on reducing the natural decline and on enhancing the recovery rates from mature fields. It is looking to find new growth areas within the Caspian Middle East and Africa regions.

OMV Gas and Power ensures the supply of natural gas to its customers via a 2000 km gas pipeline in Austria. Its natural gas network serving about 90% of Austria's natural gas demand draws gas supplies from Russia Norway and Germany as well as from domestic reserves. Austria's gas market now dominated by OMV is slated for full competition and OMV is among state-controlled companies set for full privatization.

The company operates a gas pipeline network in Austria and owns gas storage facilities with a capacity of 2.7 bcm (30 TWh).

OMV Solutions is the integrated shared service center for all of the OMV Group companies. Its portfolio spans IT financial services and human resources administration.

Geographic Reach

OMV gets the bulk of its oil and gas from Austria and Romania but it also has assets in Africa Norway and the UK. The company operates refineries in Schwechat (Austria) Burghausen (Germany) and Petrobrazi (Romania).

Sales and Marketing

The company sells its product through industrial customers local distribution companies and wholesalers which focus on multi-country customers.

Financial Performance

OMV's revenues decreased by 15% in 2014 primarily due to decrease in gas and power sales due to the impairments of the Brazi power plant in Romania and the goodwill related to the Petrol Ofisi acquisition.

The company's net income declined by 69% in 2014 due to lower revenues and changes in interest expenses.

OMV's cash inflow decreased by 11% that year primarily due to lower net income and changes in

working capital as a result of changes in short-term provisions.

Strategy

To raise cash in 2017 OMV agreed to Petrol Ofisi (gas station network) to Vitol for $1.45 billion.

In 2016 OMV sold its 49% minority stake in Gas Connect Austria to Allianz and Snam for $627.26 million.

Reorganizing to be more operationally efficient in 2015 OMV integrated the Gas and Power and Refining and Marketing business segments. In 2014 the company sold its 45% stake in the German Bayernoil refinery network. The remaining OMV refineries were integrated into crude and/or petrochemicals with the associated competitive advantages in its core markets.

Exploration and production is the growth driver of OMV. As part of OMV's strategy to build up a new exploration business in the region of Sub-Saharan Africa in 2014 the company signed an agreement with Tullow Oil an exploration-led company successful in finding and developing new resources in Africa. The first steps were taken with entries into offshore Madagascar Gabon and Namibia.

In 2013 the company announced plans to direct more than two-thirds of future investments towards exploration and production of oil and gas. It also plans to grow its integrated natural gas assets and restructure its downstream business by selling non-core refining and marketing assets.

Mergers and Acquisitions

As part of OMV's strategy of focusing on exploration and production in politically stable markets in 2013 the company acquired assets in Norway and the UK (West of Shetland area) from Statoil. It bought 19% in the producing Gullfaks field and 24% in the Gudrun field; both offshore oil and gas fields on the Norwegian Continental Shelf. In addition OMV took over 30% in Rosebank and 5.88% in Schiehallion both located west of the Shetland Islands and assets where OMV already holds a stake in.

HISTORY

Oil exploration began in Austria in the 1920s largely as joint ventures with foreign firms such as Shell and Socony-Vacuum. Full-scale production did not get underway until 1938 when the Anschluss (the absorption of Austria by Germany) paved the way for Germany to exploit Austria's natural resources to fuel its growing war machine. In the division of spoils following WWII Russia gained control of Austria's oil reserves.

The Russian-administered oil assets were transferred to the new Austrian government in 1955 which authorized the company –sterreichische Mineral ¶lverwaltung (–MG) in 1956 to control state oil assets. –MG state-controlled by the Austrian Mineral Oil Administration set about building a major refinery in 1960 and acquiring marketing companies Martha and –ROP in 1965.

In 1968 –MG became the first Western company to sign a natural gas supply contract with Russia. In 1974 the company commissioned the Trans-Austria Gas Pipeline which enabled the supply of natural gas to Italy. That year –MG changed its name to –MV Aktiengesellschaft (–MV became OMV in 1995 for international markets).

During the 1970s OMV expanded its crude supply arrangements tapping supplies from Iran Iraq Libya and other Middle Eastern countries. It moved into oil and gas exploration in the mid-1980s forming OMV Libya (acquiring 25% of Occidental's Libyan production) and OMV UK.

With Austria moving toward increasing privatization in 1987 about 15% of OMV's shares were sold to the public. The government sold another

10% two years later. In 1989 OMV acquired PCD Polymere. With the aim of merging state-owned oil and chemical activities OMV acquired Chemie Linz in 1990. The company also opened its first OMV-branded service station that year. In 1994 OMV reorganized itself as an integrated oil and gas group based in Central Europe with international exploration and production activities and with other operations in the chemical and petrochemical sectors.

In 1995 OMV acquired TOTAL-AUSTRIA expanding its service stations by 59. The company introduced OMV lubricants to the Greek market in 1996. It also expanded its OMV service station network in Hungary to 66 stations after acquiring 31 Q8 (Kuwait) sites. In 1997 the Stroh Company's retail network in Austria was merged into OMV.

Expanding its retail network even farther OMV acquired BP's retail network in the Czech Republic Slovakia and Hungary in 1998. It also sold its stake in Chemie Linz and acquired a 25% stake in major European polyolefin producer Borealis which in turn acquired PCD Polymere. In 1999 the company pushed its retail network into Bulgaria and Romania. That year OMV also acquired Australian company Cultus Petroleum.

OMV and Shell agreed to develop North Sea fields together in 2000. That year OMV also formed a joint venture with Italy's Edison International to explore in Vietnam and acquired more than 9% of Hungarian rival MOL. It upped that stake to 10% in 2001.

In 2002 OMV opened its first gas station in Serbia and Montenegro. It also increased its German gas station count from 79 to 151 with the purchase of 32 units from Royal Dutch Shell and 40 stations from Martin GmbH & Co.

In 2003 the company acquired Preussag Energie's exploration and production assets for $320 million. That year the company moved into Bosnia-Herzegovina opening nine gas stations.

During 2004 the company bought up 51% of Romania's Petrom making it the top oil and gas producer in Central Europe. As part of the deal OMV chose to divest itself of its quarter-chunk of Rompetrol.

In 2006 Russian energy giant Gazprom signed long-term contracts for gas deliveries with OMV.

In a major consolidation move in 2006 OMV agreed to buy Austrian power firm Verbund for $17 billion but the move was rebuffed by government regulators. The next year the company announced plans to merge with Hungary's energy powerhouse MOL but those plans were called off as well due to European Commission regulatory concerns in 2008.

After plans to merge with Hungary's MOL went south OMV the next year sold its 21% stake in it to Russian oil company Surgutneftegas for ?1.4 billion ($1.85 billion). Also in 2009 in keeping with its focus on retail markets in the Danube region southeastern Europe and the Black Sea region OMV sold subsidiary OMV Italia; San Marco Petroli acquired the network of about 100 gas stations in the northern Italian region of Triveneto.

OMV has been disposing of some of its heating oil operations. In 2008 it unloaded Bayern GmbH and it plans to sell its OMV W□rme Vertriebs-gmbH by the end of 2010. At that point the sale of heating oil to private clients will be handled by partners but OMV will continue to service corporate customers.

Eyeing new areas of exploration that year OMV also acquired a 10% stake in Pearl Petroleum giving it access to gas-condensate fields in Iraq.

In 2010 the company boosted its share of Turkey-based oil products company Petrol Ofisi (renamed OMV Petrol Ofisi) from 42% to 96% by acquiring a 54% stake from Dogan Holding for

about $1.4 billion. The deal gave OMV access to not only Turkey but the Caspian region and the Middle East.

The acquisition of full control (in 2010) of Petrol Ofisi Turkey's leading filling station and retail business with the only nationwide filling station network in the country (approximately 2300 stations) built a strategic bridge in the growth market of Turkey.

In a further push to grow in the Middle East in 2011 the company acquired two Tunisia-based exploration and production units from Pioneer Natural Resources for $866 million. It also boosted its footprint in Pakistan acquiring Petronas Carigali (Pakistan) Ltd. in 2011.

In 2012 the company sold its gas station subsidiary in Croatia. That year it boosted it E&P assets entering Abu Dhabi and acquiring natural gas assets in Norway.

EXECUTIVES

Chairman and CEO, Rainer Seele, age 60
Executive Board Member Downstream (Refining Gas and Power and Marketing), Manfred Leitner
CFO, Reinhard Florey, age 56
Executive Board Member Upstream, Johann Pleininger, age 58
Deputy Chairman, Wolfgang C. Berndt, age 78
Auditors: Ernst & Young Wirtschaftsprufungsgesellschaft m.b.H.

LOCATIONS

HQ: OMV AG (Austria)
Trabrennstrasse 6-8, Vienna 1020
Phone: (43) 1 40440 0
Web: www.omv.com

2016 Sales

	% of total
Austria	25
Turkey	25
Romania	16
Germany	14
Rest of CEE	13
Rest of Europe	5
Rest of world	2
Total	**100**

PRODUCTS/OPERATIONS

2016 Sales

	% of total
D/S	95
U/S	5
Total	**100**

COMPETITORS

BP	MOL
Eni	PKN ORLEN
Exxon Mobil	Royal Dutch Shell
Hellenic Petroleum	Unipetrol

HISTORICAL FINANCIALS

Company Type: Public

Income Statement

FYE: December 31

	REVENUE ($ mil.)	NET INCOME ($ mil.)	NET PROFIT MARGIN	EMPLOYEES
12/19	36,918	2,640	7.2%	19,845
12/18	36,082	2,262	6.3%	20,231
12/17	31,821	684	2.2%	20,721
12/16	30,307	(634)	—	22,544
12/15	35,448	(1,730)	—	24,124
Annual Growth	**1.0%**	**—**		**(4.8%)**

2019 Year-End Financials

Debt ratio: 25.6%	No. of shares (mil.): 326
Return on equity: 13.4%	Dividends
Cash ($ mil.): 4,612	Yield: 2.5%
Current ratio: 1.20	Payout: 17.5%
Long-term debt ($ mil.): 9,255	Market value ($ mil.): 18,208

	STOCK PRICE ($) FY Close	P/E High/Low		PER SHARE ($) Earnings	Dividends	Book Value
12/19	55.70	12	9	8.07	1.42	62.64
12/18	44.32	16	10	6.92	1.27	57.34
12/17	63.37	49	26	2.09	0.98	54.06
12/16	35.46	—	—	(1.94)	0.81	52.61
12/15	28.74	—	—	(5.30)	1.02	56.27
Annual Growth	**18.0%**			**—**	**8.5%**	**2.7%**

Orange

For many in Europe and elsewhere the telecom landscape has an Orange glow. Orange is an operator of mobile and internet services in Europe and Africa and a global leader in corporate telecommunication services. The company serves more than 265 million customers in 25 countries. It is a leading European wireless operator and broadband service provider with about 210 million mobile customers and more than 20 million broadband subscribers. Orange's services for corporate clients are provided by its Orange Business Services unit which offers a wide range of managed business networking and data services.

Operations

The decisions regarding the allocation of resources and the performance assessment of the component parts of Orange (hereinafter referred to as "the Group") are made by the Chairman and Chief Executive Officer (main operational decision-maker) at operating segment level mainly consisting of the geographical establishments. The operating segments are: France (Enterprise excluded) with more than 40% of company's revenue; Spain with over 10% of revenue; Europe about 15% of revenue (Poland Belgium and Luxembourg and each Central European countries); Africa and Middle East with nearly 15% of revenue (in Senegal Orange Mali Orange Bissau Orange in Guinea and Orange in Sierra Leone) the C´te d'Ivoire subgroup (including Orange C´te d'Ivoire entities Orange in Burkina Faso and Orange in Liberia) and each of the other countries in Africa and Middle East); Enterprise with about 20% of revenue; International Carriers & Shared Services with nearly 5% (which contain certain resources mainly in the areas of networks information systems research and development and other shared Group activities as well as the Orange brand; and Orange Bank reportedly with no revenue.

Geographic Reach

Orange divides up its primary business — mobile and fixed-line telephony along with internet access services — by region with France comprising more than 40% of total operations. Spain Europe and Africa & the Middle East are its other two major regions with these services. The rest of the world makes up nearly a fifth of total revenues. The remaining business more than 15% of sales is largely the company's enterprise services operations.

Orange's retail network comprises more than 430 owned stores (including some 15 Megastores and over 120 Smart Stores) and over 200 exclusive partner stores (including nearly 25 G n rale de T 1 phone Smart Stores). Its retail operation accounts for more than 50% of sales.

Sales and Marketing

Orange serves over 265 million customers of which more than 210 million mobile customers and more than 20 million fixed broadband customers.

Advertising promotion sponsoring communication and brand marketing costs are recorded as expenses during the period in which they are incurred.

Financial Performance

Note: Growth rates may differ after conversion to US Dollars.

In fiscal 2019 the company grew its sales of two percent to ?42.2 billion from prior year despite the negative effects between the two periods of promotions on e-readers.

Consolidated net income rise up about 50% to ?3.2 billion in 2019 compared to ?2.2 billion from prior year. The increase was due to high sale in Telecom activities.

Orange's cash position up by ?847 million to ?6.5 billion at the end of 2019. Operating activities provided ?10.2 billion and financing activities also provided ?55 million while investing activities used ?9.4 billion.

Strategy

Orange's strategy is to accelerate its business in growth areas with a particular focus on mobile financial services (including Mobile Banking) B2B IT services and cyber security. Although building on the Group's strengths (digital expertise distribution strength capacity for innovation brand image and a strong presence in the MEA Region) the development of these new businesses requires substantial resources without any guarantee that the corresponding services will gain sufficient traction to generate a return on these investments.

The company has its new strategic plan named Engage 2025. With the Engage 2025 strategic plan Orange is staking its claim as an engaged and committed leader. The company's strength lies in reconciling business performance and a sustainable approach with customers employees stakeholders partners and society in general. With Engage 2025 Orange is capitalising on these strong choices and setting ambitious new targets for 2025 while making a responsible commitment to its employees customers and society at large. The company has 4 key ambitions for 2025: Reinvent its operator model; Accelerate in growth areas; Place data and AI at the heart of its innovation model; and Co-create a future-facing company.

In 2019 the company has two acquisitions. The SecureLink and SecureData for cyber security.

Mergers and Acquisitions

In early-2019 Orange acquired a 100% equity interest in SecureData a provider of cyber security solutions in the United Kingdom for 100 million euros. In mid-2019 the Group acquired 100% of SecureLink an independent cyber security operator in Europe for 377 million euros.

Company Background

Orange's history dates back to the foundation of the telegraph network in France. Much like BT Group in Britain which shares a similar timeline Orange in its present form is a result of the privatization of France's department for telecommunications. The department became an independent public entity in 1991 and was renamed France Télécom before being privatized six years later becoming a société anonyme (limited company) on 31 December 1996.

Over the next decade or so France Télécom grew organically and via acquisitions which included the purchase of Orange a British-founded mobile network sold by Vodafone as part of an anti-competition ruling. By the mid-00s France Télécom had become one of the world's largest telecoms companies and had built up significant operations outside France. It decided a new unifying brand identity was needed to replace the explicitly French "France Télecom" and with the use of mobile services on the sharp increase it settled on using Orange. Over the next decade the company brought its varied operations across the globe under the Orange brand and officially renamed itself Orange SA in 2013.

EXECUTIVES

Deputy CEO European Operations, Gervais Pellissier, age 61
Deputy CEO Operations Africa and the Middle East (MEA), Bruno Mettling, age 62
Chairman and CEO, Stéphane Richard, age 59
EVP Group General Secretary and France Carriers Division, Pierre Louette, age 58
EVP Africa the Middle-East and Asia, Marc Rennard, age 63
SEVP Communication and Brand, Béatrice Mandine
Deputy CEO Chief Finance and Strategy Officer, Ramon Fernandez, age 53
SEVP Corporate Social Responsibility Diversity Partnerships and Philanthropy, Christine Albanel, age 65
EVP Networks and Carriers and Research and Development, Thierry Bonhomme, age 64
CEO Orange Spain, Laurent Paillassot
SEVP Human Resources, Jér 'me Barré
SEVP Orange France, Fabienne Dulac
CEO Orange Healthcare, Elie Lobel
CEO Orange Egypt, Jean Marc Harion
SEVP Innovation Marketing and Technologies, Mari-No «lle Jégo-Laveissi ¨re, age 52
CEO Orange Belgium, Michael Trabbia
Auditors: KPMG Audit

LOCATIONS

HQ: Orange
 78 rue Olivier de Serres, Paris 75015
Phone: (33) 1 44 44 22 22
Web: www.orange.com

2017 sales

	% of total
France	42
Enterprise	17
Spain	13
Africa & Middle-East	12
Poland	6
Central European countries	4
International Carriers & Shared Services	4
Belgium & Luxembourg	2
Total	**100**

PRODUCTS/OPERATIONS

Selected Operations

Audience and advertising (Internet advertising business)
Content (partnerships with content providers and development of related technology platforms)
Enterprise communication services (communication services to companies)
Health (services to the health care industry)
Home communication services (residential communication services especially fixed-line broadband)
Personal communication services (communication services for individuals using mobile devices)

COMPETITORS

AT&T	Sky plc
BT	TalkTalk
Bouygues	Tele2
COLT Group	Telecom Italia
Cable & Wireless	Telef nica
Deutsche Telekom	Telef nica Europe

Equinix Group	Tiscali
HP Enterprise Services	Unisys
IBM Global Services	Virgin Mobile
KPN	Vivendi
Maroc Télécom	Vodafone
Proximus	

HISTORICAL FINANCIALS

Company Type: Public

Income Statement

	REVENUE ($ mil.)	NET INCOME ($ mil.)	NET PROFIT MARGIN	EMPLOYEES
12/19	47,432	3,375	7.1%	146,768
12/18	47,392	2,237	4.7%	150,711
12/17	49,271	2,284	4.6%	151,556
12/16	43,156	3,099	7.2%	141,257
12/15	43,784	2,888	6.6%	144,499
Annual Growth	2.0%	4.0%	—	0.4%

2019 Year-End Financials

Debt ratio: —	No. of shares (mil.): —
Return on equity: 9.6%	Dividends
Cash ($ mil.): 7,276	Yield: 5.3%
Current ratio: 0.90	Payout: 69.2%
Long-term debt ($ mil.): —	Market value ($ mil.): —

	STOCK PRICE ($) FY Close	P/E High/Low	PER SHARE ($) Earnings	PER SHARE ($) Dividends	PER SHARE ($) Book Value
12/19	14.59	16 14	1.15	0.78	13.44
12/18	16.19	28 24	0.71	0.81	13.24
12/17	17.40	30 26	0.74	0.78	13.74
12/16	15.14	17 13	1.10	0.64	12.18
12/15	16.63	20 15	1.00	0.67	12.71
Annual Growth	(3.2%)	— —	3.4%	3.9%	1.4%

Origin Energy Ltd

EXECUTIVES

CEO Integrated Gas, David A. Baldwin, $518,630 total compensation
Managing Director and CEO, Frank G. Calabria, $505,080 total compensation
Executive General Manager People and Culture, Carl McCamish
CFO, Lawrie Tremaine
Executive General Manager Origin Retail, Jon Briskin
Executive General Manager Future Energy and Business Development, Anthony (Tony) Lucas
Auditors: Ernst & Young

LOCATIONS

HQ: Origin Energy Ltd
 Level 32, Tower 1, 100 Barangaroo Avenue, Barangaroo, New South Wales 2000
Phone: (61) 2 8345 5000 **Fax:** (61) 2 9252 9244
Web: www.originenergy.com.au

2016 Sales

	% of total
Australia	98
New Zealand	1
Others	1
Total	**100**

PRODUCTS/OPERATIONS

2016 Sales

	% of total
Energy Markets	94
Integrated Gas	4
Contact Energy	2
Total	**100**

COMPETITORS

AGL Energy
International Power
Santos Ltd

HISTORICAL FINANCIALS

Company Type: Public

Income Statement				FYE: June 30
	REVENUE ($ mil.)	NET INCOME ($ mil.)	NET PROFIT MARGIN	EMPLOYEES
06/20	13,250	83	0.6%	5,200
06/19	14,796	1,214	8.2%	5,360
06/18	14,901	218	1.5%	5,565
06/17	13,874	(2,232)	—	5,894
06/16	11,991	(590)	—	5,811
Annual Growth	2.5%	—	—	(2.7%)

2020 Year-End Financials

Debt ratio: 25.6%
Return on equity: 0.6%
Cash ($ mil.): 1,243
Current ratio: 1.01
Long-term debt ($ mil.): 5,024

No. of shares (mil.): 1,758
Dividends
  Yield: 0.0%
  Payout: 326.5%
Market value ($ mil.): 7,647

	STOCK PRICE ($) FY Close	P/E High/Low		PER SHARE ($) Earnings	Dividends	Book Value
06/20	4.35	126	48	0.05	0.15	7.23
06/19	5.05	11	6	0.69	0.06	7.50
06/18	7.25	62	42	0.12	0.00	6.73
06/17	5.17	—	—	(1.27)	0.00	6.51
06/16	4.24	—	—	(0.37)	1.02	8.30
Annual Growth	0.6%	—	—	—	(37.6%)	(3.4%)

Orix Corp

An international financing leviathan ORIX is one of Japan's largest public financial services firms. The company finances everything from computers and measuring equipment to aircraft and ships; it rents out more than 32000 items and is adding more. ORIX also engages in consumer and corporate finance investment banking brokerage car rental and property development and management services in Japan and nearly 40 countries. The group owns nearly 900 consolidated companies and has investments in about 190 affiliates. Its retail offerings include banking life insurance credit cards and trust services. ORIX fields a professional baseball team the ORIX Buffaloes which splits time between Kobe and Osaka.

Operations
ORIX operates six main business segments:

Investment and Operation 49% of revenue invests in environmental and energy-related businesses principal investment and loan servicing (asset recovery).

Overseas Business about 15% provides leasing lending investment in bonds investment banking asset management and ship- and aircraft-related financing.

Retail about 15% offers life insurance banking and card loans.

Maintenance Leasing about 10% provides automobile leasing and rentals car sharing and test and measurement instruments as well as IT-related equipment rentals and leasing.

Real Estate about 5% focuses on development rental and financing facility operation REIT asset management and real estate investment advisory services

Corporate Financial Services about 5% is ORIX's lending leasing and fee business.

ORIX owns about 3 GW of renewable energy capacity and has 1.7 million vehicles and 200 airplanes under management. Its individual life insurance portfolio holds nearly 3.9 million policies. In total the company has approximately Å 9 trillion in assets under management.

ORIX generates about 40% of revenue from sales of goods and real estate although that amount fluctuates with the ups and downs of the real estate market. Services accounts for roughly 25% while life insurance premiums and operating lease income bring in a little less than 15% each. Finance revenue and gains on investment securities combine to generate some 10%.

Geographic Reach
Based in Japan ORIX has more than 1450 offices in the country and about 715 overseas. While ORIX has expanded internationally through acquisitions it relies on the Japanese market for about 85% of its revenue. The Americas region (mainly the US) supplies about 5% of revenue and other regions provide the rest.

Sales and Marketing
ORIX serves many global markets and industries including renewable energy electric power car rental facilities operations waste processing life insurance ocean-going vessels credit card health care corporate finance and aerospace.

Financial Performance
Note: Financial results are denoted in Japanese currency the Yen (Å). Growth rates may differ after conversion to US dollars.

ORIX's revenue and profit have risen in recent years thanks to its growing life insurance and services businesses coupled with expense management. Net income has moved higher nearly every year from a low of Å 20.6 billion in 2009 to a recent high of Å 313.1 billion in 2018 (ended March).

In 2018 revenue increased 7% to Å 2.86 trillion compared to Å 2.67 trillion in 2017 driven by more in-force life insurance policies and investment income which was boosted by assets under variable annuity and variable life insurance contracts. Further sales of goods and real estate were higher and services income increased on service expansion in asset management and environment and energy.

ORIX maintained a grip on costs in 2018 allowing net income to jump about 15% to Å 313.1 billion from 2017.

Cash on hand was Å 1.3 trillion in 2018 an increase of Å 281 billion from 2017. Cash flows provided by operating activities were Å 546 billion in 2018 while investing activities used Å 411.5 billion and financing activities provided Å 143.7 billion in 2018.

Strategy
Of its six operating segments ORIX is pushing its strongest growth strategy through Investment and Operation. It has invested in solar projects hydro-electric power and equity investments in businesses serving the health care funeral waterworks and solar power generation sectors. It also poured money into bonds and tangible assets such as aircraft and logistics centers. Looking forward the company sees great opportunity in environment and energy endeavors particularly in the US and Asia.

ORIX is rolling out its auto leasing and rental operations in overseas markets leveraging its experience in Japan where it has about 1.3 million vehicles under management. The company's auto rental business operates in Australia India and Southeast Asia. In another automotive push the company launched a product called EverDrive a driving monitoring service designed to reduce risk for families with elderly drivers. The product uses Orix's telematics technologies to track vehicles.

Mergers and Acquisitions
In 2018 ORIX invested $60 million in Wecash a Chinese financial technology company using artificial intelligence and big data to provide credit analysis services to more than 100 million users.

In 2017 ORIX USA acquired Lancaster Pollard Holdings a provider of investment banking mortgage banking and other credit services primarily to senior living and healthcare businesses.

EXECUTIVES

Deputy President, Tamio Umaki, age 73
EVP, Shintaro Agata, age 70
SVP; President ORIX USA, Hideto Nishitani, age 60
EVP; President ORIX Auto, Katsunobu Kamei, age 63
SVP and CIO, Satoru Katahira, age 61
EVP, Yuichi Nishigori, age 64
President and CEO, Makoto Inoue, age 68
Deputy President and CFO, Kazuo Kojima, age 64
EVP, Kiyoshi Fushitani, age 70
SVP; President ORIX Insurance Services, Kazunori Kataoka, age 65
Group Executive; President ORIX Credit, Hiroko Yamashina, age 57
Group Executive; President ORIX Real Estate, Toyonori Takahashi, age 55
Auditors: KPMG AZSA LLC

LOCATIONS

HQ: Orix Corp
  World Trade Center Building, 2-4-1 Hamamatsu-cho, Minato-ku, Tokyo 105-6135
Phone: (81) 3 3435 1274   **Fax:** (81) 3 3435 1276
Web: www.orix.co.jp

2018 Sales

	% of total
Japan	83
Americas	4
Others	13
Total	**100**

PRODUCTS/OPERATIONS

2018 Sales by Business Segment

	% of total
Corporate Financial Services	4
Maintenance Leasing	10
Real Estate	6
Investment and Operation	49
Retail	15
Overseas Business	16
Total	**100**

Selected Subsidiaries and Segments

ORIX Aircraft (aircraft leasing)
ORIX Asset Management & Loan Services Corporation (commercial mortgage servicing)
ORIX Auto (car rental and leasing)
ORIX Buffaloes Baseball Club (professional baseball team)
ORIX Life Insurance
ORIX Real Estate (real estate development and investment)
ORIX Real Estate Investment Advisors (asset management)
ORIX Rentec (rental operations)
ORIX Trust and Banking
ORIX USA
SUN Leasing Corporation (medical equipment leasing)

COMPETITORS

BlackRock	Mizuho Financial
CIT Group	Nomura Holdings
ILFC	Prudential
Mitsubishi UFJ	Rentokil Initial
Financial Group	Sumitomo

HISTORICAL FINANCIALS
Company Type: Public

Income Statement
FYE: March 31

	ASSETS ($ mil.)	NET INCOME ($ mil.)	INCOME AS % OF ASSETS	EMPLOYEES
03/20	120,382	2,788	2.3%	31,233
03/19	109,937	2,923	2.7%	32,411
03/18	107,602	2,948	2.7%	31,890
03/17	100,458	2,443	2.4%	34,835
03/16	97,927	2,316	2.4%	33,333
Annual Growth	5.3%	4.7%	—	(1.6%)

2020 Year-End Financials

Return on assets: 2.3%	Dividends
Return on equity: 10.2%	Yield: 6.3%
Long-term debt ($ mil.): —	Payout: 170.7%
No. of shares (mil.): 1,254	Market value ($ mil.): 74,139
Sales ($ mil): 20,869	

	STOCK PRICE ($) FY Close	P/E High/Low		PER SHARE ($) Earnings	Dividends	Book Value
03/20	59.10	0	0	2.18	3.73	21.98
03/19	71.87	0	0	2.28	3.12	20.44
03/18	89.86	0	0	2.30	2.66	19.74
03/17	74.33	0	0	1.87	2.09	17.22
03/16	71.39	0	0	1.77	2.33	15.71
Annual Growth	(4.6%)	—	—	5.4%	12.4%	8.8%

Osaka Gas Co Ltd (Japan)

Osaka Gas keeps Osaka Hyogo Kyoto Shiga and Wakayama cooking. A large Japanese gas supplier the utility serves more than 9 million customers in the Kansai region. The company imports a large amount of its gas and has production operations in Australia and Indonesia; it also owns liquefied natural gas (LNG) terminals and tankers. Osaka Gas has branched out into electricity: It generates and markets power to wholesale and large retail customers in Japan and abroad. It maintains a pipeline of approximately 62400 km and a power generation capacity of 2 megawatts in Japan. Other operations include gas appliance sales pipeline installation real estate management and leasing. Osaka Gas was established in 1897.

Operations
Osaka Gas operates through four reporting segments: Domestic Energy/Gas; Life & Business Solutions; Domestic Energy/Electricity; and International Energy.

Domestic Energy/Gas (more than 65% of revenues) manufactures supplies and sells city gas and gas appliances conducts gas pipelines installations and sells LNG LPG and industrial gas.

Life and Business Solutions includes real estate development and leasing IT services the marketing of fine materials and carbon material products. This segment represents 15% of the company's total sales.

Domestic Energy/Electricity produces and sell electricity and it accounts for about 15% of the revenue.

Comprised the remaining revenue International Energy Business includes overseas energy supply LNG vessel chartering business and petroleum and natural gas business development and investment.

Geographic Reach
The company's main natural gas reserves in Algeria Australia Brunei Canada China Egypt Indonesia Iran Iraq Kuwait Malaysia Nigeria Norway Oman Papua New Guinea Qatar Russia Saudi Arabia Turkmenistan the UAE the US and Venezuela.

Headquartered in Osaka Japan has also office in Tokyo and about 10 offices overseas located in the Australia Indonesia the Philippines Singapore Thailand UK and the US.

Sales and Marketing
Osaka Gas provides solutions that meets various needs of more than 9 million customers for household factories and offices.

The company also serves residential commercial and industrial customers.

Financial Performance
Osaka Gas has seen fluctuating revenue for the last five years recording a 4% increase from 2016 to 2020. The same trend as revenue was seen in the company's net income but with a recorded 50% decrease from 2016 to 2020.

Revenue was Â 1.4 trillion Â 3.2 billion less than in the previous year. Domestic Energy/Gas contributed the highest revenue per segment comprising 70% of the company's 2020 revenue. This was followed by Domestic Energy/Electricity (15%) and Life and Business Solutions (12%).

Net income increased from Â 33.6 billion in 2019 to Â 41.8 billion in 2020.

Cash and cash equivalents at the end of the year were Â 146.8 billion Â 31 billion more than in the previous year. Operating activities provided Â 182.9 billion to the coffers. Investing activities used Â 232.3 billion primarily for purchase of property plant and equipment while financing activities provided Â 79.3 billion mostly from proceeds from issuance of bonds.

Strategy
In 2020 Osaka Gas made significant progress in its International Energy Business especially in the US such as the commencement of commercial operations of the Freeport LNG Project and the Fairview natural gas-fired power plant as well as the acquisition of all shares in Sabine Oil and Gas Corporation a shale gas development company.

The company aims to maximize value for its customers and to reach the goals under the current Medium-term Management Plan as it develops strategies for future growth while preventing the spread of the coronavirus.

Mergers and Acquisitions
In late 2020 Osaka Gas has acquired issued shares of Palette Cloud (Japan based) which provides Palette Kanri the property management system provided by Palette Cloud for rental housing management companies. Palette Kanri is a cloud-based tenant management system designed exclusively for the real estate industry. The two companies aim to make the most of their respective strengths and produce a good synergy between them to contribute to greater convenience in rental collective housing and help continuous advancement in consumer and business life.

In late 2019 the company wholly-owned subsidiary Gas and Power Co Ltd has acquired all the equity help by JGC Holdings Corporation of the issued shares of JGC Mirai Solar Co Ltd a photovoltaic power generation business operator based in Oita City Oita Prefecture. As a result of the equity acquisition JGC Mirai will change its corporate name to Daigas Oita Mirai Solar Co Ltd as wholly-owned subsidiary of G& P.

In mid-2019 Osaka Gas entered into a definitive agreement with Texas based Sabine Oil & Gas Holding to acquire 100% of the outstanding shares of its subsidiary Oil & Gas Corporation (Sabine). Sabine holds acreage in East Texas located in Harrison Panola Rusk and Upshur counties among others totaling 175000 net acres which is producing shale gas in the amount of 210 mmcfed with approximately 1200 wells at present showing a significant drilling inventory on the Haynesville and Cotton Valley formation. Through this acquisitions Osaka Gas has also gained operatorship of the upstream business along with Sabine's excellent management and operations capabilities.

Company Background
Osaka Gas was established in 1897.

EXECUTIVES

President, Hiroshi Ozaki
EVP, Masato Kitamae
EVP, Takehiro Honjo
EVP, Hirofumi Kyutoku
Auditors: KPMG AZSA LLC

LOCATIONS

HQ: Osaka Gas Co Ltd (Japan)
4-1-2 Hiranomachi, Chuo-ku, Osaka 541-0046
Phone: (81) 6 6205 4537   **Fax:** 914 328-4430
Web: www.osakagas.co.jp

PRODUCTS/OPERATIONS

2015 Sales

	% of total
Gas	72
LPG Electricity and Other Energies	16
Life & Business Solutions	11
International Energies	1
Total	**100**

COMPETITORS

Apache	KEPCO
BHP Billiton	Kyushu Electric Power
Chubu Electric Power	Santos Ltd
Chugoku Electric Power	Shikoku Electric
Endesa S.A.	Tohoku Electric Power
Hokkaido Electric Power	Tokyo Electric
	Tokyo Gas
Hokuriku Electric Power	Woodside Petroleum

HISTORICAL FINANCIALS
Company Type: Public

Income Statement
FYE: March 31

	REVENUE ($ mil.)	NET INCOME ($ mil.)	NET PROFIT MARGIN	EMPLOYEES
03/20	12,608	384	3.1%	23,265
03/19	12,387	303	2.4%	23,044
03/18	12,207	355	2.9%	22,858
03/17	10,588	548	5.2%	23,701
03/16	11,772	750	6.4%	23,763
Annual Growth	1.7%	(15.4%)	—	(0.5%)

2020 Year-End Financials

Debt ratio: 0.3%	No. of shares (mil.): 415
Return on equity: 4.1%	Dividends
Cash ($ mil.): 1,356	Yield: —
Current ratio: 1.79	Payout: —
Long-term debt ($ mil.): 6,022	Market value ($ mil.): —

Otsuka Holdings Co., Ltd.

Auditors: Deloitte Touche Tohmatsu LLC

LOCATIONS

HQ: Otsuka Holdings Co., Ltd.
12F Shinagawa Grand Central Tower, 2-16-4 Konan,
Minato-ku, Tokyo 108-8241
Phone: (81) 3 6717 1410
Web: www.otsuka.com

HISTORICAL FINANCIALS

Company Type: Public

Income Statement   FYE: December 31

	REVENUE ($ mil.)	NET INCOME ($ mil.)	NET PROFIT MARGIN	EMPLOYEES
12/19	12,860	1,171	9.1%	37,837
12/18	11,748	750	6.4%	36,998
12/17	11,019	999	9.1%	37,184
12/16	10,221	791	7.7%	36,440
12/15	11,857	846	7.1%	36,523
Annual Growth	2.1%	8.4%	—	0.9%

2019 Year-End Financials

Debt ratio: 0.0%
Return on equity: 7.3%
Cash ($ mil.): 2,817
Current ratio: 2.24
Long-term debt ($ mil.): 1,257

No. of shares (mil.): 542
Dividends
 Yield: 2.0%
 Payout: 21.9%
Market value ($ mil.): 12,082

	STOCK PRICE ($) FY Close	P/E High/Low		Earnings	PER SHARE ($) Dividends	Book Value
12/19	22.28	0	0	2.13	0.46	30.00
12/18	20.22	0	0	1.38	0.46	28.61
12/17	21.92	0	0	1.84	0.44	29.41
12/16	21.92	0	0	1.46	0.42	26.99
12/15	17.80	0	0	1.56	0.38	26.04
Annual Growth	5.8%	—	—	8.0%	5.3%	3.6%

Oversea-Chinese Banking Corp. Ltd. (Singapore)

Singapore bank Oversea-Chinese Banking Corporation (OCBC Bank) operates more than 470 branches and offices in 15 countries including some 350 offices in Indonesia through its Bank OCBC NISP subsidiary. The company offers traditional banking services for individuals and businesses as well as financial services such as brokerage and asset management. Private banking for high-net-worth families is offered through the Bank of Singapore while Great Eastern Holdings which provides life and property/casualty insurance is the largest insurance company in Singapore and Malaysia. OCBC Bank was founded in 1912 to serve the Chinese business community of Singapore and other parts of Asia but now serves the general public.

Geographic Reach

The bank's main operations are in its home country of Singapore which accounts for 60% of business. Malaysia where it operates as OCBC Bank Malaysia and offers Islamic banking services through OCBC Al-Amin Bank accounts for about 20% of business. Indonesia and China each account for less than 10% of business.

In addition to its core markets OCBC also has a presence in Australia Brunei Dubai Hong Kong Japan The Philippines South Korea Taiwan Thailand the UK the US (in New York and Los Angeles) and Vietnam through branches and representative offices.

Strategy

With Singapore's population only 5 million people the bank has targeted China Indonesia and Malaysia as international growth markets. It plans to increase its Islamic banking and insurance operations in Malaysia home to almost 30 million people. In Indonesia (population 247 million) the bank consolidated its banking subsidiaries in order to grow the OCBC NISP brand there. And in China with 1.3 billion people the bank plans to cater to wealthy citizens by offering private banking services through the Bank of Singapore.

EXECUTIVES

SEVP Group Operations and Technology, Ching Wei Hong, age 60
Group CEO, Samuel N. (Sam) Tsien, age 65
SEVP and Head of Global Treasury and Investment Banking, Lam Kun Kin, age 57
Head Group Operations and Technology, Lim Khiang Tong, age 60
CFO, Darren S. P. Tan, age 49
Head of Global Commercial Banking, Linus T. L. Goh, age 57
CEO OCBC Bank China, Kng Hwee Tin
Group Risk Management, Vincent Choo, age 57
CEO Bank of Singapore, Bahren Shaari
CEO OCBC Wing Hang Bank, Na Wu Beng
President and CEO Bank OCBC NISP, Parwati Surjaudaja
Regional General Manager Northeast Asia, Tan Wing Ming
Group Legal and Regulatory Compliance, Loretta Yuen
Chairman, Ooi Sang Kuang, age 72
Auditors: KPMG LLP

LOCATIONS

HQ: Oversea-Chinese Banking Corp. Ltd. (Singapore)
63 Chulia Street, #10-00 OCBC Centre East, 049514
Phone: (65) 6363 3333   **Fax:** (65) 6534 3986
Web: www.ocbc.com

2012 Sales

	% of total
Singapore	63
Malaysia	20
Indonesia	7
China	7
Rest of Asia	2
Rest of world	1
Total	**100**

PRODUCTS/OPERATIONS

2012 Sales

	% of total
Interest	59
Noninterest	
Fees & commissions	12
Life insurance	7
General insurance	1
Rental income	1
Dividends	1
Other	19
Total	**100**

Selected Subsidiaries

Banking
 Bank of Singapore Limited
 OCBC Al-Amin Bank Berhad
 OCBC Bank (Malaysia) Berhad
 Singapore Island Bank Limited
Insurance
 Great Eastern Life Assurance (Malaysia) Berhad
 Overseas Assurance Corporation (Malaysia) Berhad
 The Great Eastern Life Assurance Company Limited
 The Overseas Assurance Corporation
Asset management
 Lion Global Investors Limited
 Great Eastern Holdings Limited
Stockbroker
 OCBC Securities Private Limited

COMPETITORS

ABN AMRO Group	Citigroup
AmBank Group	DBS Group Holdings
BNP Paribas	HSBC
Bank Central Asia	Hong Leong Finance
Bank Danamon Indonesia	Maybank
Bank Mandiri	Standard Chartered
Bank Rakyat	United Overseas Bank

HISTORICAL FINANCIALS

Company Type: Public

Income Statement   FYE: December 31

	ASSETS ($ mil.)	NET INCOME ($ mil.)	INCOME AS % OF ASSETS	EMPLOYEES
12/19	365,454	3,619	1.0%	30,492
12/18	343,351	3,298	1.0%	29,706
12/17	340,545	3,103	0.9%	29,174
12/16	283,660	2,403	0.8%	29,792
12/15	276,049	2,761	1.0%	29,847
Annual Growth	7.3%	7.0%	—	0.5%

2019 Year-End Financials

Return on assets: 1.0%
Return on equity: 10.9%
Long-term debt ($ mil.): —
No. of shares (mil.): —
Sales ($ mil): 25,494

Dividends
 Yield: 3.8%
 Payout: 75.7%
Market value ($ mil.): —

	STOCK PRICE ($) FY Close	P/E High/Low		Earnings	PER SHARE ($) Dividends	Book Value
12/19	16.20	16	14	0.83	0.62	7.96
12/18	16.62	19	14	0.78	0.50	7.28
12/17	18.65	19	14	0.73	0.47	6.97
12/16	12.27	16	12	0.57	0.44	6.12
12/15	12.54	15	13	0.67	0.81	5.94
Annual Growth	6.6%	—	—	5.4%	(6.7%)	7.6%

P.T. Astra International TBK

Auditors: Public Accountant Firm Tanudiredja, Wibisana, Rintis & Rekan (a member of the PricewaterhouseCoopers network of firms)

LOCATIONS

HQ: P.T. Astra International TBK
Menara Astra, Lantai 59, Jl. Jend. Sudirman Kav. 5-6, Jakarta 10220
Phone: (62) 21 5084 3888   **Fax:** (62) 21 6530 4957
Web: www.astra.co.id

HISTORICAL FINANCIALS

Company Type: Public

Income Statement
FYE: December 31

	REVENUE ($ mil.)	NET INCOME ($ mil.)	NET PROFIT MARGIN	EMPLOYEES
12/19	17,106	1,565	9.2%	226,105
12/18	16,627	1,506	9.1%	226,140
12/17	15,202	1,393	9.2%	218,463
12/16	13,472	1,127	8.4%	214,835
12/15	13,341	1,047	7.9%	221,046
Annual Growth	6.4%	10.6%	—	0.6%

2019 Year-End Financials

Debt ratio: 0.0%
Return on equity: 15.2%
Cash ($ mil.): 1,754
Current ratio: 1.29
Long-term debt ($ mil.): 3,646

No. of shares (mil.): —
Dividends
Yield: 0.0%
Payout: 552.7%
Market value ($ mil.): —

	STOCK PRICE ($) FY Close	P/E High/Low		PER SHARE ($) Earnings	Dividends	Book Value
12/19	9.89	0	0	0.04	0.21	0.26
12/18	11.28	0	0	0.04	0.18	0.24
12/17	12.35	0	0	0.03	0.17	0.23
12/16	12.20	0	0	0.03	0.17	0.21
12/15	8.53	0	0	0.03	0.22	0.18
Annual Growth	3.8%	—	—	10.6%	(1.2%)	9.6%

Pan Pacific International Holdings Corp

EXECUTIVES

Director & Chairman, Takao Yasuda
Auditors: UHY Tokyo & Co

LOCATIONS

HQ: Pan Pacific International Holdings Corp
2-19-10 Aobadai, Meguro-ku, Tokyo 153-0042
Phone: (81) 3 5725 7532   **Fax:** (81) 3 5725 7322
Web: www.ppi-hd.co.jp

HISTORICAL FINANCIALS

Company Type: Public

Income Statement
FYE: June 30

	REVENUE ($ mil.)	NET INCOME ($ mil.)	NET PROFIT MARGIN	EMPLOYEES
06/20	15,611	466	3.0%	47,709
06/19	12,338	448	3.6%	48,351
06/18	8,509	329	3.9%	28,392
06/17	7,400	295	4.0%	25,500
06/16	7,395	242	3.3%	24,423
Annual Growth	20.5%	17.8%	—	18.2%

2020 Year-End Financials

Debt ratio: 0.3%
Return on equity: 14.2%
Cash ($ mil.): 1,668
Current ratio: 1.59
Long-term debt ($ mil.): 4,666

No. of shares (mil.): 633
Dividends
Yield: 0.4%
Payout: 13.1%
Market value ($ mil.): 13,997

	STOCK PRICE ($) FY Close	P/E High/Low		PER SHARE ($) Earnings	Dividends	Book Value
06/20	22.08	0	0	0.73	0.10	5.47
06/19	15.89	0	0	0.71	0.09	4.84
06/18	11.94	0	0	0.52	0.06	4.15
06/17	9.51	0	0	0.47	0.05	3.66
06/16	9.20	10	0	0.38	0.04	3.56
Annual Growth	24.5%	—	—	17.6%	22.9%	11.3%

Panasonic Corp

Panasonic has been a prolific electronics manufacturers since 1919. Its offerings include automotive and industrial systems (including car infotainment products) and home appliances; the company also makes lighting products energy systems avionics systems and process automation machines and equipment. Panasonic sells its product to consumers (via retailers) as well as directly to original equipment manufacturers and other businesses. The company operates worldwide but generates nearly half its revenue from Japan.

Operations

Panasonic has five primary business segments: Appliances (around 30%) Life Solutions (more than 20%) Connected Solutions (over 10%) Automotive (more than 15%) and Industrial (around 15%).

Panasonic's appliances include air conditioners TVs cameras and devices. The company's life solutions offer office lighting fixtures LED floodlights for facilities home lighting fixtures energy system power-assisted bicycles and other products for elderly.

Connected Solutions handles aviation products for in-flight entertainment as well as factory process automation products logistics public services and entertainment technologies. The Automotive business manufactures and sales of in-vehicle infotainment in-vehicle electronics automotive mirrors and motorized systems such as BMC (Battery Management Controller).

The Industrial segment covers electronic devices such as sensors resistors motors compressors industrial batteries and other custom devices.

Geographic Reach

Panasonic sells its products and services in Asia the Americas India South Asia Middle East & Africa and Europe. The company is highly reliant on its home continent Japan which accounts for nearly half of total revenue.

Sales and Marketing

Panasonic's consumer products are mainly sold to distributors retailers mass-merchandisers through sales subsidiaries. Other products are sold through retail distributors logistics service providers public institutions and customers from the entertainment industry.

The company markets its products through print ads videos and TV commercials.

Financial Performance

Note: Growth rates may differ after conversion to US dollars.

Panasonic's revenue and net income has been fluctuating for the last five years.

Panasonic's consolidated group sales for fiscal 2020 decreased by 6% to Å 7.5 trillion from a year ago. Domestic sales decreased due to the deconsolidation of housing related businesses in addition to the impact of the spread of the novel coronavirus disease despite sales increases in PCs and Infotainment Systems such as IVI (In-Vehicle-Infotainment).

Net profit attributable to Panasonic Corporation stockholders decreased by 21% to Å 225.7 billion.

Cash at the end of fiscal 2020 was 1 trillion yen an increase of Å 244 billion from the prior year. Cash from operations contributed Å 430.3 billion to the coffers while investing activities used Å 206.1 billion primarily for purchases of property and equipment. Financing activities provided another Å 48.2 billion.

Strategy

Celebrating its centennial in 2018 Panasonic must show the flexibility and adaptability to grow amid a quickly changing business landscape driven by advanced technologies such as artificial intelligence (AI) and the internet of things (IoT). To accomplish this the company is embracing a "Champion and Challenger" strategy through which established divisions such as consumer electronics provide the funds needed for innovation and freedom.

The company's strategic plans are aimed at enhancing customer relationships developing new businesses through partnerships and introducing new solutions that help solve social issues. Through these approaches Panasonic targets sales of 100 billion yen in Southeast Asia in the fiscal year through March 2022.

Company Background

Grade school dropout Konosuke Matsushita took $50 in 1918 and went into business making electric plugs (with his brother-in-law Toshio Iue founder of SANYO). His mission to help people by making high-quality low-priced conveniences while providing his employees with good working conditions earned him the sobriquet "god of business management." The company grew across the decades expanding into new regions (it opened its first manufacturing facility outside Japan — in Thailand — in 1961) and new products (washing machines TVs and refrigerators were launched in the 1950s). In 2008 it took the name Panasonic Corporation and consolidated all its brands under the Panasonic name.

HISTORY

Grade school dropout Konosuke Matsushita took $50 in 1918 and went into business making electric plugs (with his brother-in-law Toshio Iue founder of SANYO). His mission to help people by making high-quality low-priced conveniences while providing his employees with good working conditions earned him the sobriquet "god of business management." Matsushita Electric Industrial grew by developing inexpensive lamps batteries radios and motors in the 1920s and 1930s.

During WWII the Japanese government ordered the firm to build wood-laminate products for the military. Postwar occupation forces prevented Matsushita from working at his firm for four years. Thanks to unions' efforts he rejoined his namesake company shortly before it entered a joint venture with Dutch manufacturer Philips in 1952. The following year it moved into consumer goods making televisions refrigerators and washing machines and later expanding into high-performance audio products. Matsushita bought a majority stake in Victor Company of Japan (JVC originally established by RCA Victor) in 1954. Its 1959 New York subsidiary opening began Matsushita's drive overseas.

Sold under the National Panasonic and Technics names the firm's products were usually not cutting-edge but were attractively priced. Under Masaharu Matsushita the founder's son-in-law who became president in 1961 the company became Japan's largest home appliance maker introducing air conditioners microwave ovens stereo components and VCRs in the 1960s and 1970s. JVC developed the VHS format for VCRs which beat out Sony's Betamax format.

Matsushita built much of its sales growth on new industrial and commercial customers in the 1980s. The company expanded its semiconductor office and factory automation auto electronics audio-visual housing and air-conditioning product offerings that decade. Konosuke died in 1989.

EXECUTIVES

EVP, Yasuo Katsura, age 73
Managing Director Industrial Sales and Board Member, Yoshihiko (Yoshi) Yamada, age 69
President, Kazuhiro Tsuga
Managing Executive Officer; President Panasonic Electronic Devices, Toshiaki Kobayashi
Managing Executive Officer and Director Corporate Management Division for Asia and Oceania; Managing Director Panasonic Asia Pacific Pte. Ltd., Ikuo Miyamoto
Managing Executive Officer and Head China and Northeast Asia, Hidetoshi Osawa
Executive Officer; Director Corporate Management Division for North America; Chairman and CEO North America, Joseph M. (Joe) Taylor
Managing Director; President AVC Networks Company, Yoshiyuki Miyabe
Managing Director and Board Member; President Home Appliances Company In Charge Of Lighting Company, Kazunori Takami, age 66
Managing Director Accounting and Finance, Hideaki Kawai
Executive Officer; President Panasonic France, Laurent Abadie
EVP and President Eco Solutions Company, Shusaku Nagae
Managing Executive Officer and Head Asia the Middle East and Africa, Yorihisa Shiokawa
Managing Director Technology Intellectual Property and Information Systems, Mamoru Yoshida
President Panasonic Healthcare Co. Ltd., Kenji Yamane
President CEO*, Patrick D. O'Brien
Chairman, Kunio Nakamura, age 81
Vice Chairman, Masayuki Matsushita, age 75
Managing Director; President AVC Company; Business Group Executive AVC Network Business Group, Fumio Ohtsubo, age 75
Auditors: KPMG AZSA LLC

LOCATIONS

HQ: Panasonic Corp
 1006 Oaza Kadoma, Kadoma, Osaka 571-8501
Phone: (81) 6 6908 1121
Web: www.panasonic.com/jp

2018 Sales

	% of total
Japan	47
Americas	17
China	12
Europe	10
Other Asia	14
Total	**100**

PRODUCTS/OPERATIONS

2018 Sales

	% of total
Automotive and industrial systems	32
Appliances	29
Eco solutions	18
Connected solutions	13
Other	8
Total	**100**

COMPETITORS

A123 Systems	Hitachi
BSH Bosch und Siemens Hausger ote	LG Electronics
BYD	Philips Electronics
Delphi Automotive PLC	Samsung Electronics
Electrolux	Sony
GE Appliances & Lighting	Technicolor
Haier Group	Toshiba
	Visteon
	Whirlpool

HISTORICAL FINANCIALS

Company Type: Public

Income Statement

FYE: March 31

	REVENUE ($ mil.)	NET INCOME ($ mil.)	NET PROFIT MARGIN	EMPLOYEES
03/20	69,005	2,079	3.0%	259,385
03/19	72,263	2,565	3.6%	271,869
03/18	75,170	2,222	3.0%	274,143
03/17	65,682	1,335	2.0%	257,533
03/16	67,265	1,720	2.6%	49,520
Annual Growth	**0.6%**	**4.8%**	**—**	**51.3%**

2020 Year-End Financials

Debt ratio: 0.1%
Return on equity: 11.5%
Cash ($ mil.): 9,364
Current ratio: 1.31
Long-term debt ($ mil.): 8,787

No. of shares (mil.): —
Dividends
 Yield: 3.6%
 Payout: 30.8%
Market value ($ mil.): —

	STOCK PRICE ($) FY Close	P/E High/Low		PER SHARE ($) Earnings	Dividends	Book Value
03/20	7.50	0	0	0.89	0.28	7.89
03/19	8.67	0	0	1.10	0.32	6.92
03/18	14.37	0	0	0.95	0.24	6.89
03/17	11.40	0	0	0.58	0.23	6.03
03/16	8.96	0	0	0.74	0.16	6.58
Annual Growth	**(4.3%)**	**—**	**—**	**4.7%**	**14.3%**	**4.6%**

Paragon Banking Group PLC

The Paragon Group of Companies offers various finance products specializing in mortgage loans for professional property investors (the buy-to-let market) in the UK through its Paragon Mortgages and Mortgage Trust brands. Paragon has Â 10 billion (about $15 billion) in buy-to-let loan assets under management and serves more than 480000 customer accounts. It also makes consumer and auto loans. Paragon's Idem Capital unit makes loan portfolio acquisitions while its Paragon Bank subsidiary is a retail-funded and regulated online lending bank. The company services its own loans and offers third-party loan servicing and collection services for banks private equity firms and specialist lenders.

Operations

About 68% of the group's total operating income came from its Paragon Mortgages segment in fiscal 2015 (ended September 30 2015) while Idem Capital contributed another 32% to operating income. Less than 1% of operating income came from its Paragon Bank which it established in early 2014.

Broadly speaking more than 95% of the group's income comes from interest on receivables.

Geographic Reach

The firm's head office is in West Midlands and most of its business is in the UK.

Financial Performance

Note: Growth rates may differ after conversion to US dollars. This analysis uses financials from the company's annual report.

The company's annual revenues have trended higher while its profits have nearly doubled since 2011 thanks to growing loan assets over the years.

Paragon's revenue grew 12% to Â 341 million ($517 million) during fiscal 2015 (ended September 30 2015) mostly thanks to a 7% rise in average loan book assets and buoyed by improving interest margins.

Strong revenue growth drove the group's profit up 10% to Â 107.1 million ($162.4 million) in FY2015. The group's operations used Â 25.9 million ($39.3 million) in cash during the year using significantly less than in FY2014 thanks to strong cash earnings growth.

Strategy

The Paragon Group of Companies continued in 2016 to grow its loan volume as well as establish a more sustainable and diversified funding base to decrease its overall risk. The group launched its Paragon Bank subsidiary in February 2014 to provide a reliable and cost-efficient funding source for new consumer product lines as well as to scale up the group's overall buy-to-let business over time.

Mergers and Acquisitions

In March 2015 subsidiary Paragon Bank purchased Five Arrows Leasing Group for Â 117 million expanding its service lines.

EXECUTIVES

CEO, Nigel S. Terrington, $730,418 total compensation
Director Mortgages, John A. Heron, $389,116 total compensation
Director Corporate Development, Richard Woodman, $389,116 total compensation
Chairman, Robert G. Dench
Auditors: KPMG LLP

LOCATIONS

HQ: Paragon Banking Group PLC
 51 Homer Road, Solihull, West Midlands B91 3QJ
Phone: (44) 121 712 2323   **Fax:** (44) 121 711 1330
Web: www.paragonbankinggroup.co.uk

PRODUCTS/OPERATIONS

2014

	% of total
Interest receivable	94
Other operating income	6
Total	**100**

COMPETITORS

Barclays Bank	Private & Commercial
HSBC	Finance Group
Lloyds Banking Group	Royal Bank of Scotland
Nationwide Building Society	

HISTORICAL FINANCIALS

Company Type: Public

Income Statement

FYE: September 30

	ASSETS ($ mil.)	NET INCOME ($ mil.)	INCOME AS % OF ASSETS	EMPLOYEES
09/20	30,986	182	0.6%	1,392
09/19	28,767	254	0.9%	1,368
09/18	29,006	291	1.0%	1,349
09/17	27,342	234	0.9%	1,317
09/16	27,015	231	0.9%	1,249
Annual Growth	3.5%	(5.8%)	—	2.7%

2020 Year-End Financials

Return on assets: 0.6%
Return on equity: 8.0%
Long-term debt ($ mil.): —
No. of shares (mil.): 261
Sales ($ mil): 1,013

Dividends
  Yield: —
  Payout: 40.4%
  Market value ($ mil.): —

Parkland Corp

Parkland Fuel is a Canadian fuel contractor and distributor supplying both retailers and wholesalers from distribution terminals in Alberta and British Columbia. The company also operates approximately 1855 gas stations in Canada under the Ultramar Esso Fas Gas Plus Chevron Pioneer and Race Trac retail fuel banners as well as the On the Run / Marché Express convenience store chain. Through its USA unit the company supplies and distributes petroleum across almost a dozen northern US states and owns and operates Farstad Oil Superpumper Rhinehart Oil and Hart's chain of gas stations. Other operations include the Burnaby Refinery in British Columbia. Parkland Fuel was formed in 2010. About 60% of company's total revenue comes from Canada.

Operations

Parkland Fuel has six operating segments: Canada Retail; International; Supply; Canada Commercial; USA; and Corporate.

Canada Retail (formerly Retail) generates more than a-quarter of the total sales. It operates and services a network of retail gas stations in Canada operating under many key retail brands including Ultramar Esso Fas Gas Plus Chevron Pioneer and Race Trac. In addition Parkland operates a convenience store brand On the Run / Marché Express as well as other convenience store brands.

International represents the contributions of the Sol business that was acquired in early 2019 which includes operations in some 25 countries predominantly located in the Caribbean and northern coast of South America. International operates and services a network of retail service stations under brands including Esso Shell and Sol. This segment accounts for beyond 25% of revenue.

Supply is responsible for managing Parkland's fuel supply contracts purchasing fuel from refiners refining and marketing fuel transporting and distributing fuel through ships rail and highway carriers and storing fuel in owned and leased facilities. This segment contributes for over 15% of revenue.

Canada Commercial (formerly Commercial; nearly 15% of revenue) delivers bulk fuel propane heating oil lubricants agricultural inputs oilfield fluids and other related products. Canada Commercial brands include Ultramar Bluewave Energy Pipeline Commercial Chevron Columbia Fuels and Sparlings Propane.

Representing the remaining revenue USA (formerly Parkland USA) operates and services a network of retail service stations and delivers gasoline distillates propane and lubricating oils in the US. Brands operated by USA include SPF Energy Farstad Oil Superpumper Rhinehart and Tropic.

Corporate includes centralized administrative services and expenses incurred to support operations. Due to the nature of these activities these costs are not specifically allocated to Parkland's operating segments.

Geographic Reach

Parkland Fuel is headquartered in Calgary Alberta with more than five regional offices located in Burnaby Dartmouth Minot Montreal and Victoria.

About 60% of company's total revenue comes from Canada and 20% contributes by the US.

Sales and Marketing

Parkland Fuel delivers a range of refined fuel and petroleum products to motorists businesses consumers resellers aviation and wholesale customers. Canada Retail and Canada Commercial segments contracts sell fuel and petroleum products to retail and commercial consumers. The company also sells branded and private label lubricants to commercial industrial and wholesale customers.

Financial Performance

Note: Growth rates may differ after conversion to US Dollars.

In the past five years Parkland Fuel's revenue has increased growing as much as 198% from 2015 to 2019.

In 2019 Parkland's revenue increased by 28% to C$18.5 billion. Fuel and petroleum product revenue increased by C$3.7 billion and Non-Fuel revenue increased by C$313 million.

Net earnings attributable to Parkland was CAD$382 million an increase of C$176 million from the year prior which was mainly attributable to higher revenue.

Cash at the end of the year increased C$217 million to C$257 million from C$40 million at the end of 2018. Cash from operations contributed C$897 million to the coffers while financing added C$879 million. Investing activities used C$1.5 billion primarily for expenditures on assets and from Sol Transaction.

Strategy

Parkland drives organic growth by selling petroleum and convenience products under highly valued brands while delivering great customer experiences. Parkland effectively deploys growth capital operates safely and efficiently and is a responsible steward of the environment. Its annual strategic organic growth target is 3-5%.

Parkland delivers a supply advantage by safely and reliably operating the Burnaby Refinery leveraging market inefficiencies and being a partner of choice for refiners. It sells its products through a variety of marketing channels including company retail gas stations commercial diesel card locks and commercial fuel propane and lubricant delivery branches. Parkland is a disciplined acquirer that actively seeks complementary scale and scope opportunities. It builds and leverages relationships with the objective of being the buyer of choice for vendors and effectively integrate acquisitions to drive operational efficiency create synergies and generate shareholder value.

People are at the core of its strategic imperatives. It is committed to enabling its teams to succeed by recruiting high caliber people fostering engagement building an industry-leading people culture and investing in technology. Its employees are its most important resource and by investing in its people it is directly contributing to the success of its organization.

Mergers and Acquisitions

In mid-2020 Parkland Fuel announced that through its wholly-owned US subsidiaries (collectively Parkland USA) it has completed the acquisition of ConoMart Super Stores. ConoMart Super Stores operates seven retail sites located in and around Billings Montana. This acquisition expands the company's Montana business and scales its existing Northern Tier Regional Operating Center.

In early 2020 through its wholly-owned US subsidiaries (Parkland USA) the company completed the acquisition of the entities and assets comprising Kellerstrass Oil Company (Kellerstrass). Based in Salt Lake City Kellerstrass is a regional retail dealer and commercial fuel business with branches in Utah Idaho and Wyoming. This acquisition will support the growth of the company's North America diesel platform create supply efficiencies and deliver logistical benefits.

In late 2019 through its US-based subsidiaries (Parkland USA) the company successfully completed the acquisition of all of the issued and outstanding equity interests of Tropic Oil Company Inc as well as equity interests and the assets of certain of its affiliates (Tropic Oil). Tropic Oil is headquartered in Miami Florida and transports distributes and markets a full range of fuels and lubricants across the central and south Florida region.

Company Background

Parkland Fuel was formed in 2010.

EXECUTIVES

President and CEO, Robert B. Espey
VP Administration and CIO, Donna Strating
CFO, Mike McMillan
Chairman, Jim Pantelidis
Auditors: PricewaterhouseCoopers LLP

LOCATIONS

HQ: Parkland Corp
  Suite 1800, 240 4 Ave SW, Calgary, Alberta T2P 4H4
Phone: 403 567-2500   **Fax:** 403 352-0042
Web: www.parkland.ca

2015 sales

	% of total
Canada	88
United States	12
Total	**100**

PRODUCTS/OPERATIONS

2015 sales

	% of total
Retail Fuels	34
Commercial Fuels	19
Parkland USA	12
Supply and Wholesale	35
Corporate	-
Total	**100**

COMPETITORS

Couche-Tard	Suncor
Imperial Oil	Superior Plus

HISTORICAL FINANCIALS

Company Type: Public

Income Statement

FYE: December 31

	REVENUE ($ mil.)	NET INCOME ($ mil.)	NET PROFIT MARGIN	EMPLOYEES
12/19	14,170	317	2.2%	4,635
12/18	10,605	151	1.4%	3,051
12/17	7,626	65	0.9%	4,363
12/16	4,649	35	0.8%	2,300
12/15	4,535	28	0.6%	0
Annual Growth	33.0%	82.9%	—	—

2019 Year-End Financials

Debt ratio: 32.5%
Return on equity: 22.0%
Cash ($ mil.): 187
Current ratio: 1.16
Long-term debt ($ mil.): 2,935

No. of shares (mil.): 148
Dividends
  Yield: 0.0%
  Payout: 46.6%
Market value ($ mil.): 5,434

	STOCK PRICE ($) FY Close	P/E High/Low	PER SHARE ($) Earnings	Dividends	Book Value
12/19	36.67	14 10	1.96	0.91	10.15
12/18	25.76	22 13	1.12	0.86	9.89
12/17	21.37	37 27	0.55	0.92	10.00
12/16	21.02	48 29	0.36	0.83	6.20
12/15	16.78	43 32	0.32	0.78	6.23
Annual Growth	21.6%	— —	56.8%	4.2%	12.9%

PetroChina Co Ltd

If you want petroleum in China or elsewhere then PetroChina is your company. A subsidiary of state-owned China National Petroleum Corporation (CNPC) PetroChina produces two-thirds of China's oil and gas. The company has proved reserves of 10.8 billion barrels of oil and 69.3 trillion cu. ft. of natural gas. In China it owns more than 53400 kilometers of natural gas and refined products pipeline and operates 29 refineries and 13 chemical plants. PetroChina was created in 2000 as a separate company to initially manage the domestic operations — and in recent years some key international assets — of CNPC.

Strategy

PetroChina is taking advantage of the growing consumption of natural gas in China by expanding its transmission infrastructure. It is also expanding its oil reserves and refining operations through the purchase of international oil fields and refineries including several assets from its parent.

In 2015 the company agreed to sell 50% of Central Asia Natural Gas Pipeline Co. to Mansong Holdings Ltd a subsidiary of China Reform Holdings Corp. Ltd. for 15 billion to 15.5 billion yuan.

EXECUTIVES

Vice Chairman and President, Wang Dongjin
VP and General Manager Exploration and Production, Zhao Zhengzhang, age 63
VP and General Manager PetroChina Natural Gas and Pipelines, Huang Weihe, age 62
Chief Engineer, Lin Aiguo, age 61
VP and General Manager PetroChina Refining and Chemical, Xu Fugui
VP and General Manager PetroChina International Company Limited (China National United Oil Corporation), Wang Lihua
VP and General Manager PetroChina International Exploration and Development and China National Exploration and Development, Lv Gongxun
VP and General Manager PetroChina Marketing Company, Tian Jinghui
CFO, Chai Shouping, age 59
Chairman, Wang Yilin, age 67
Vice Chairman, Zhang Jianhua, age 55
Auditors: KPMG Huazhen (Special General Partnership)

LOCATIONS

HQ: PetroChina Co Ltd
No. 9 Dongzhimen North Street, Dongcheng District, Beijing 100007
Phone: (86) 10 5998 6270   **Fax:** (86) 10 6209 9557
Web: www.petrochina.com.cn

2013 Sales

	% of total
Mainland China	67
Other countries	33
Total	**100**

PRODUCTS/OPERATIONS

2013 Sales

	% of total
Marketing	51
Refining & chemicals	23
Exploration & production	20
Natural gas & pipeline	6
Total	**100**

COMPETITORS

Bangchak Petroleum Public
CNOOC
Chevron
Exxon Mobil
Sinopec Shanghai Petrochemical

HISTORICAL FINANCIALS

Company Type: Public

Income Statement

FYE: December 31

	REVENUE ($ mil.)	NET INCOME ($ mil.)	NET PROFIT MARGIN	EMPLOYEES
12/19	358,162	6,500	1.8%	0
12/18	334,934	7,483	2.2%	0
12/17	286,877	3,243	1.1%	0
12/16	230,098	1,124	0.5%	0
12/15	245,542	5,054	2.1%	521,566
Annual Growth	9.9%	6.5%	—	—

2019 Year-End Financials

Debt ratio: 1.2%
Return on equity: 3.7%
Cash ($ mil.): 15,748
Current ratio: 0.71
Long-term debt ($ mil.): 24,820

No. of shares (mil.): —
Dividends
  Yield: 4.3%
  Payout: 6,089.4%
Market value ($ mil.): —

	STOCK PRICE ($) FY Close	P/E High/Low	PER SHARE ($) Earnings	Dividends	Book Value
12/19	50.33	274181	0.04	2.17	(0.00)
12/18	61.55	291207	0.04	2.02	(0.00)
12/17	69.94	678508	0.02	1.40	(0.00)
12/16	73.70	19041351	0.01	0.59	(0.00)
12/15	65.59	718336	0.03	2.25	0.92
Annual Growth	(6.4%)	— —	7.1%	(1.0%)	—

Petroleo Brasileiro SA

Petr leo Brasileiro (Petrobras) is one of Brazil's biggest companies. The vertically integrated oil and gas company explores for oil and gas and produces refines and transports oil and gas products. With extensive offshore assets Petrobras has proved oil and gas reserves of approximately 9.5 billion barrels of oil equivalent and its average daily production of more than 2 million barrels of oil equivalent. In Brazil it operates nearly 15 refineries and an extensive oil and gas pipeline network. Distribution arm Petrobras Distribuidora is Brazil's #1 retailer of oil products and fuel alcohol. Other units operate electricity (approximately 20 thermal power plants) petrochemicals and natural gas assets. Petrobras is controlled by the Brazilian government and generates majority of sales in its home country.

Operations

Petrobras operates through three business segments: Refining Transportation and Marketing Exploration and Production and Gas and Power.

The Refining Transporting and Marketing segment is Petrobras' most lucrative at over 50% of sales. Its refineries can be found is densely populated southeastern Brazil and have combined crude distillation capacity of 2.2 million barrels per day (mmbbl/d) and refining throughput of 1.7 mmbbl/d.

The Exploration and Production segment covers Petrobras' upstream activities including the exploration development and production of crude oil natural gas and natural gas liquids (NGLs) in Brazil and elsewhere. It owns approximately 5.9 billion barrels' worth of proved developed reserves and over 3.5 billion barrels of proved undeveloped reserves. The segment represents nearly 40% of total revenue.

Gas and Power accounting for almost 10% of sales covers Petrobras' natural gas and electricity logistics and trading electricity generation at thermoelectric plants and its interest in natural gas transport companies in Brazil and abroad. It also includes a fertilizer business.

The company also generates sales from corporate and other businesses. It include Petrobras' distribution and biofuels activities.

Geographic Reach

Rio de Janeiro-based Petrobras does most of its business in Brazil but also explores for and produces oil in Nigeria the UK the US and other Latin American countries. In addition to its explorations activities the company also has support activities such as trade and financial in London Rotterdam Houston and Singapore. Brazil represents nearly 75% of total sales. The remaining sales are generated from other countries. Most of Petrobras' oil fields are offshore.

Sales and Marketing

Petrobras serves industries such as Automotive Industrial Agriculture Rail Maritime and Aviation. It distributes its oil products through a company-owned retail network wholesale channels and by supplying other fuel wholesalers and retailers.

Crude oil is primarily sold through long-term contracts and also in the spot market. The company's overseas portfolio includes approximately 60 clients such as refiners that process or have processed Brazilian oils regularly. The company interacts with around 400 clients in Brazil in regards to liquid oil products seven of which account for over 65% of the total volume sold. The Natural gas is marketed to more than 20 clients most of which are distributors.

Financial Performance

Petrobras revenue has been decling in the last five years with the exception of 2018. It has an overall decline of 21% between 2015 and 2019.

Sales revenues were $76.6 billion in 2019 a 10% decrease ($8 billion) when compared to $84.6 billion in 2018 mainly due to the decrease in domestic revenues ($6.6 billion) mainly as a result of decrease in oil products revenues and lower electricity revenues.

Net income in 2019 was $10.2 billion compared to $7.2 billion in 2018. The growth was primarily due to lower expenses in 2019.

Petrobras' cash at the end of 2019 was $7.4 billion. Operating activities provided $25.6 billion while investing activities used $1.7 billion. Financing activities used another $32.1 billion mainly for repayments.

Strategy

Petrobras' 2020-2024 Strategic Plan (the "Strategic Plan" or "2020-2024 Strategic Plan") consists of the continuous evaluation of the business environment and the implementation of the plan allowing adjustments to be made in a more efficient way. The Plan is focused on oil and natural gas exploration and production notably in the Brazilian pre-salt area which is one of the company's greatest strengths and sources of value creation. Digital transformation has gained strength as an important instrument for adding value to its business in a competitive environment.

Mergers and Acquisitions

In late 2019 Petrobras acquired exploration and production rights of B zios and Itapu fields in Brazil. The fields are assets with significant reserves and low lifting cost that is resilient to a low oil price products. In addition B zios field is one of the largest discovered deepwater field in the world. The transaction is consistent with the company's strategy on focusing its investments to world class assets. Terms of the transaction were not disclosed.

HISTORY

"O petr leo é nosso!"

"The oil is ours!" proclaimed the Brazilian nationalists' slogan in 1953 and President Get lio Vargas approved a bill creating a state-run monopoly on petroleum discovery development refining and transport. The same year that PETR "LEO BRASILEIRO (PETROBRAS) was created a team led by American geologist Walter Link reported that the prospects of finding petroleum in Brazil were slim. The report outraged Brazilian nationalists who saw it as a ploy for foreign exploitation. PETROBRAS proved it could find oil but Brazil continued to import crude oil and petroleum products. By 1973 the company produced about 10% of the nation's needs.

When oil prices soared during the Arab embargo the government instead of encouraging exploration for domestic oil pushed PETROBRAS into a program to promote alcohol fuels. The company was forced to raise gasoline prices to make the more costly gasohol attractive to consumers. During the 1979 oil crunch the price of gasohol was fixed at 65% of gasoline. But during the oil glut of the mid-1980s PETROBRAS' cost of making gasohol was twice what it cost to buy gasoline — in other words PETROBRAS lost money.

PETROBRAS soon began overseas exploration. In 1980 it found an oil field in Iraq an important trading partner during the 1980s. The company also drilled in Angola and through a 1987 agreement with Texaco in the Gulf of Mexico.

In the mid-1980s PETROBRAS began production in the deepwater Campos basin off the coast of Rio de Janeiro state. Discoveries there in 1988 in the Marlim and Albacora fields more than tripled

its oil reserves. It plunged deep into the thick Amazon jungle in 1986 to explore for oil and by 1990 Amazon wells were making a significant contribution to total production. That year to ease dependence on imports PETROBRAS launched a five-year $16.9 billion plan to boost crude oil production. It also began selling its mining and trading assets.

Before the invasion of Kuwait Brazil relied heavily on Iraq trading weapons for oil. After the invasion spawned increases in crude prices PETROBRAS raised pump prices but yielding to the government's anti-inflation program still did not raise them enough to cover costs. It lost $13 million a day.

The company sold 26% of Petrobras Distribuidora to the public in 1993 and privatized several of its petrochemical and fertilizer subsidiaries. A 1994 presidential order bent on stabilizing Brazil's 40%-per-month inflation cut the prices of oil products. In 1995 the government loosened its grip on the oil and gas industry and allowed foreign companies to enter the Brazilian market. In the wake of this reform PETROBRAS teamed up with a Japanese consortium to build Brazil's largest oil refinery.

In 1997 PETROBRAS appealed a $4 billion judgment from a 1992 shareholder lawsuit; the suit alleged PETROBRAS had undervalued shares during the privatization of the loss-making Petroquisa affiliate. (The appeal was granted in 1999.)

As part of an effort to boost oil production PETROBRAS also began to raise money abroad in 1999. The next year PETROBRAS and Spanish oil giant Repsol YPF agreed to swap oil and gas assets in Argentina and Brazil in a deal worth more than $1 billion.

In 2000 the company announced plans to change its corporate name to PETROBRAX but fierce political and popular reaction forced the company to abort this plan in 2001. In an even greater public relations disaster that year one of PETROBRAS' giant rigs sank off of Brazil and 10 workers were killed. In 2001 PETROBRAS announced that it was going to spend as much as $3 billion to buy an oil company in order to increase its production in the Gulf of Mexico.

In 2002 the company expressed an interest in buying Argentina's major oil company (YPF) from Spanish/Argentine energy giant Repsol YPF. That year PETROBRAS bought control (59%) of Argentine energy company Perez Companc in a deal valued at $1 billion. PETROBRAS also reported its first oil find in Argentina in 2002.

In 2006 the company acquired a 50% stake in a deepwater block in Equatorial Guinea from a private group of companies for an undisclosed sum.

The company also restructured the Brazilian petrochemical industry to make it more efficient. Its actions included the purchase of the petrochemical assets of the Ipiranga Group in 2007 and Suzano Petroqu mica a leader in Latin American polypropylene resin production in 2008.

In 2007 PETROBRAS announced a major offshore oil discovery in the Tupi. In 2008 it reported it had discovered a major natural gas field near the Tupi find.

In 2011 it was operating more than 130 production platforms. PETROBRAS has made a number of major offshore oil discoveries in offshore Brazil since 2000 including the Tupi field (found in 2007) and which has the potential to boost Brazil's oil reserves by 40%. In 2010 PETROBRAS announced another major discovery a 3.7 to 15 billion-barrels-of-oil-reserves find (offshore of Rio de Janeiro) that could double Brazil's known reserves.

Streamlining its Petrobras Argentina operations in 2011 the company acquired that unit's Brazilian

petrochemicals business (Innova SA) for $332 million.

In 2012 it teamed up with GE Oil & Gas in a $1.1 billion deal through which the GE unit will supply 380 subsea wellhead systems to a number of PETROBRAS' oil and gas fields in offshore Brazil.

Brazil's government owns more than 55% of PETROBRAS.

EXECUTIVES

Chairman, Pedro Pullen Parente, age 67

CFO and Investor Relations Director, Ivan de Souza Monteiro, age 60

Exploration and Production Officer; Member of the Executive Board, Guilherme Estrella

CEO Transpetro, Ant ´nio Rubens Silva Silvino

President, Ivan de S˜ Pereira

Chairman, Luiz Nelson Guedes de Carvalho

Auditors: KPMG Auditores Independentes

LOCATIONS

HQ: Petroleo Brasileiro SA
Avenida Republica do Chile, 65, Rio de Janeiro 20031-912

Phone: (55) 21 3224 4477

Web: www.petrobras.com.br

2018 Sales

	% of total
Brazil	76
Other countries	24
Total	**100**

PRODUCTS/OPERATIONS

2018 Sales

	% of total
Refining transportation & marketing	44
Exploration & production	32
Distribution	17
Gas & Power	7
Biofuels	-
Total	**100**

Selected Subsidiaries

Downstream Participações S.A. (asset exchanges between Petrobras and Repsol-YPF)

Petrobras Argentina (59%; oil and gas Argentina)

Petrobras Comercializadora de Energia Ltda

Petrobras Distribuidora SA (BR; distribution and marketing of petroleum products fuel alcohol and natural gas)

Petrobras Gá;s SA (Gaspetro management of the Brazil-Bolivia pipeline and other natural gas assets)

Petrobras Internacional SA (Braspetro; overseas exploration and production marketing and services)

Petrobras International Finance Company - PIFCO (oil imports)

Petrobras Negócios Eletrônicos S.A.

Petrobras Quí;mica SA (Petroquisa petrochemicals)

Petrobras Transporte SA (Transpetro oil and gas transportation and storage)

COMPETITORS

Ashland	Marathon Oil
BHP Billiton	Norsk Hydro ASA
BP	Occidental Petroleum
Chevron	PEMEX
Devon Energy	Petr leos de
Eni	Venezuela
Exxon Mobil	Royal Dutch Shell
Imperial Oil	Sunoco
Koch Industries Inc.	TOTAL

Company Type: Public

Income Statement   FYE: December 31

	REVENUE ($ mil.)	NET INCOME ($ mil.)	NET PROFIT MARGIN	EMPLOYEES
12/19	76,589	10,151	13.3%	57,983
12/18	95,584	7,173	7.5%	63,361
12/17	88,827	(91)	—	0
12/16	81,405	(4,838)	—	68,829
12/15	97,314	(8,450)	—	78,470
Annual Growth	(5.8%)	—	—	(7.3%)

2019 Year-End Financials

Debt ratio: 37.9%	No. of shares (mil.): —
Return on equity: 14.0%	Dividends
Cash ($ mil.): 7,372	Yield: 1.3%
Current ratio: 0.97	Payout: 24.5%
Long-term debt ($ mil.): 76,915	Market value ($ mil.): —

	STOCK PRICE ($) FY Close	P/E High/Low	PER SHARE ($) Earnings	Dividends	Book Value
12/19	15.94	23 16	0.78	0.21	5.62
12/18	13.01	31 17	0.55	0.10	5.48
12/17	10.29	— —	(0.01)	0.00	6.12
12/16	10.11	— —	(0.37)	0.00	5.89
12/15	4.30	— —	(0.65)	0.00	5.00
Annual Growth	38.8%	— —	—	—	3.0%

Petroleos Mexicanos (Pemex) (Mexico)

Petr leos Mexicanos (PEMEX) not only fuels Mexico's automobile engines the state-owned oil company also fuels the nation's economy. The integrated company's operations spread throughout Mexico range from exploration and production to refining and petrochemicals. PEMEX's P.M.I. Comercio Internacional subsidiary manages the company's trading operations outside the country. PEMEX generates approximately 2.5 million barrels of oil daily and more than 5 million of cubic feet of natural gas. The company has over 5 refineries and petrochemical complexes and nearly 10 gas processing complexes. The company also has about 85 land and maritime terminals as well as oil and gas pipelines maritime vessels and varying fleets of ground transportation in order to supply over 10000 service stations throughout the country.

Operations

PEMEX operates through five major subsidiaries: PEMEX Exploraci n y Producci n (petroleum and natural gas exploration and production); PEMEX Gas y Petroqu mica B sica (natural gas liquids from natural gas and ethane processing); PEMEX Petroqu mica (petrochemical production); PEMEX Refinaci n (refining and marketing); and P.M.I. Comercio Internacional (international trading).

PEMEX's operations were conducted through eight business segments: Exploration and Production Industrial Transformation Drilling and Services Logistics Ethylene Fertilizers the Trading Companies and Corporate and Other Operating Subsidiary Companies.

Pemex Exploration and Production is in charge of exploration and extraction of crude oil and solid liquid or gaseous hydrocarbons in Mexico in the exclusive economic zone of Mexico and abroad as well as drilling services and repair and services of wells.

Pemex Industrial Transformation performs activities related to refining processing importing exporting trading and the sale of hydrocarbons as well as commercializes distributes and trades methane ethane and propylene directly or through others.

Pemex Logistics provide transportation storage and related services for crude oil petroleum products and petrochemicals to PEMEX and other companies through pipelines and maritime and terrestrial means and provide guard and management services. The company's Pemex Fertilizers produce distribute and commercialize ammonia fertilizers and its derivatives as well as provide related services.

Sales and Marketing

PEMEX's primary business is the exploration and production of crude oil and natural gas as well as the production processing marketing and distribution of petroleum and petrochemical products.

The exploration and production segment earns revenues from domestic sales of crude oil and natural gas and from exporting crude oil through certain of the Trading Companies. Export sales are made through PMI CIM to over 20 major customers in various foreign markets. Approximately half of PEMEX's crude oil is sold to Pemex Industrial Transformation.

Industrial transformation segment earns revenues from sales of refined petroleum products and derivatives mainly to third parties within the domestic market. They sell a significant portion of the fuel oil it produces to the Comisi n Federal de Electricidad (Federal Eletricity Commission or "CFE") and a significant portion of jet fuel produced to the Aeropuertos y Servicios Auxiliares.

The trading companies which consist of PMI CIM PMI NASA PMI Trading and MGAS (the "Trading Companies") earn revenues from trading crude oil natural gas and petroleum and petrochemical products in international markets.

Financial Performance

Note: Growth rates may differ after conversion to US Dollars.

PEMEX' net sales rose in 2018 but declined in 2019. The company suffered fluctuating net losses in the same period. PEMEX' sales declined 17% from MX$1.7 trillion in 2018 to MX$1.4 trillion in 2019.

The company's cash and cash equivalents at the end of 2019 totaled MX$60.6 billion. Operating and financing activities generated MX$85.2 billion and MX$5 billion respectively while investing activities used MX$111.3 billion.

Strategy

PEMEX enters into interest rate swaps occasionally for strategic reasons or in order to offset the expected inflows and outflows. Under its interest rate swap agreements PEMEX acquires the obligation to make payments based on a fixed interest rate and is entitled to receive floating interest rate payments based on LIBOR TIIE or a rate referenced to or calculated from TIIE.

As of December 31 2019 Petr leos Mexicanos was a party to four interest rate swap agreements denominated in U.S. dollars for an aggregate notional amount of U.S. $1178750 at a weighted average fixed interest rate of 2.35% and a weighted average term of 5.3 years.

HISTORY

Histories of precolonial Mexico recount the nation's first oil business: Natives along the Tampico coast gathered asphalt from naturally occurring deposits and traded with the Aztecs.

As the 20th century began Americans Edward Doheny and Charles Canfield struck oil near Tampico. Their success was eclipsed in 1910 by a nearby well drilled by British engineer Weetman Pearson leader of the firm that became Pearson PLC.

President Porfirio D az had welcomed foreign ownership of Mexican resources but revolution ousted D az and the 1917 Constitution proclaimed that natural resources belonged to the nation. Without enforcing legislation however foreign oil companies continued business as usual until a 1925 act limited their concessions. During a bitter labor dispute in 1938 President L zaro C rdenas expropriated foreign oil holdings — the first nationalization of oil holdings by a non-Communist state. Subsequent legislation created Petr leos Mexicanos (PEMEX).

Without foreign capital and expertise the new state-owned company struggled and Mexico had to import petroleum in the early 1970s. But for many Mexicans PEMEX remained a symbol of national identity and economic independence. That faith was rewarded in 1972 when a major oil discovery made PEMEX one of the world's top oil producers again. Ample domestic oil supplies and high world prices during the Iranian upheaval in the late 1970s fueled a boom and a government borrowing spree in Mexico. Between 1982 and 1985 PEMEX contributed more than 50% of government revenues.

When oil prices collapsed in 1985 Mexico cut investment in exploration and production dropped. To decrease its reliance on oil Mexico began lowering trade barriers and encouraging manufacturing even allowing some foreign ownership of petrochemical processing.

Elected in 1988 President Carlos Salinas de Gortari began to reform PEMEX. Labor's grip on the company was loosened in 1989 when a union leader was arrested and jailed after a gun battle. In 1992 after a PEMEX pipeline explosion killed more than 200 people in Guadalajara four of its executives and several local officials were sent to prison amid public cries for company reform.

President Ernesto Zedillo appointed Adri n Lajous Vargas head of PEMEX in 1994. Under the professorial Lajous PEMEX began to adopt modern business practices (such as trimming its bloated payroll) look for more reserves and improve its refining capability. Lajous tried to sell some petrochemical assets in 1995 but had to modify the scheme the next year after massive public protests by the country's nationalists. Still PEMEX began selling off natural gas production distribution and storage networks to private companies.

Though oil prices were dropping in 1998 Mexico finally upped PEMEX's investment budget and PEMEX dramatically increased exploration and production. In spite of 2000's looming national election (elections traditionally had caused bureaucrats to keep a low profile to protect their jobs) Lajous again fanned the flames of the opposition: In 1998 he signed a major deal to sell Mexican crude to Exxon's Texas refinery and in 1999 a four-year-old PEMEX/Shell joint venture announced it would expand its US refinery.

In 1999 Lajous resigned and was replaced by Rogelio Montemayor a former governor. The next year Vicente Fox was elected as Mexico's new president the country's first non-Institutional Revolutionary Party (PRI) leader in seven decades. He announced plans to replace PEMEX's politician-staffed board with professionals — Montemayor was among the casualties — and modernize the company but he ruled out privatizing PEMEX as politically unfeasible.

Fox appointed Ra l Muñoz formerly with Dupont Mexico in 2003 to lead PEMEX. Muñoz however was engulfed in a scandal involving the misuse of funds and forced to resign the following year. His replacement Luis Ram rez lasted until the next national election when incoming President Felipe Calder n appointed Jes s Reyes.

Reyes was replaced by Juan José Su rez Coppel in 2009.

In 2011 the company reported a major gas find in the Gulf of Mexico with estimated reserves of 400 to 600 billion cubic feet. The discovery is the tenth deepwater gas discovery PEMEX has made since 2004. However because of the persistence of low natural gas commodity prices the development of these fields is on hold while the company focuses on crude oil production (supported by high crude oil prices) mainly in southeast Mexico.

EXECUTIVES

CEO, Jose Antonio Gonzalez Anaya
President, Enrique Pena Nieto
Auditors: KPMG Cardenas Dosal, S.C.

LOCATIONS

HQ: Petroleos Mexicanos (Pemex) (Mexico)
Avenida Marina Nacional 329, Colonia Veronica Anzures, Mexico City 11300
Phone: (52) 55 1944 9700
Web: www.pemex.com

PRODUCTS/OPERATIONS

2016 Sales

	% of total
Domestic sales	62
Export sales:	
United States	21
Europe	6
Canada Central and South America	1
Other	9
Services income	1
Total	**0**

2016 Sales

	% of total
Trading Companies	35
Industrial Transformation	34
Exploration and Production	27
Logistics	3
Ethylene	1
Drilling and Service	-
Cogeneration and Services	-
Fertilizers	-
Corporate and other subsidiary companies	-
Total	**100**

Selected Subsidiaries

PEMEX Exploración y Producción (petroleum and natural gas exploration and production)
PEMEX Gas y Petroquí;mica Bá;sica (natural gas liquids from natural gas and ethane processing)
PEMEX Petroquí;mica (petrochemical production)
PEMEX Refinación (refining and marketing)
P.M.I. Comercio Internacional (international trading)

COMPETITORS

Ashland	Marathon Oil
BHP Billiton	Occidental Petroleum
BP	PETROBRAS
Chevron	Petr leos de
Devon Energy	Venezuela
Eni	Royal Dutch Shell
Exxon Mobil	Sunoco
Imperial Oil	TOTAL
Koch Industries Inc.	

HISTORICAL FINANCIALS

Company Type: Public

Income Statement

	REVENUE ($ mil.)	NET INCOME ($ mil.)	NET PROFIT MARGIN	EMPLOYEES
FYE: December 31				
12/19	74,101	(18,356)	—	122,646
12/18	85,491	(9,172)	—	124,818
12/17	70,914	(14,255)	—	124,660
12/16	52,173	(9,262)	—	126,940
12/15	67,138	(41,009)	—	138,397
Annual Growth	2.5%	—	—	(3.0%)

2019 Year-End Financials

Debt ratio: 5.4%
Return on equity: —
Cash ($ mil.): 3,204
Current ratio: 0.62
Long-term debt ($ mil.): 91,875
No. of shares (mil.): —
Dividends
  Yield: —
  Payout: —
Market value ($ mil.): —

Phoenix Group Holdings PLC

Apparently a Phoenix Group can hatch out of the right kind of Pearl. Formerly known as Pearl Group Phoenix Group operates through two primary companies: IGNIS Asset Management and Phoenix Life. Phoenix Life is made up of a handful of life insurance companies including Phoenix Life Ltd. London Life and NPI Ltd. However its companies don't sell new policies but instead maintain blocks of life insurance policies and pension products bought from other insurers (called closed life funds). It has more than 6 million such policies in force. Ignis Asset Management manages Â 67 billion of assets for customers within and outside of Phoenix Group.

Operations
Phoenix's operations include subsidiaries Phoenix Life Scottish Provident Scottish Mutual and Resolution Asset Management.

Mergers and Acquisitions
In 2018 Phoenix agreed to acquire Standard Life Aberdeen's insurance business for Â 3.2 billion. The deal is hoped to be mutually beneficial as Standard Life Aberdeen wants to be Phoenix's first-choice asset manager as Phoenix goes about accumulating insurance assets.

Company Background
In 2009 the company was acquired by Virgin Islands-based investment firm Liberty Acquisition Holdings. Following the acquisition — which valued Pearl Group at about Â 1.6 billion ($2.6 billion) — Liberty Acquisition a special purpose acquisition vehicle (or "blank check" company) changed its name to Pearl Group and began to inject up to Â 600 million ($987 million) into the new company with a focus on investing in additional financial service entities.

The company streamlined a bit in 2009 by merging its two asset management businesses Axial Investment management and Ignis into one company: Ignis Asset Management. It then began rebranding some products under the Phoenix Life name which paved the way for renaming the company Phoenix Group Holdings in 2010.

Internal mergers continued in 2011 when the company consolidated some of its life insurance businesses into Phoenix Life Ltd. Ultimately the company intends to have two primary life insurance companies under the Phoenix Life banner.

EXECUTIVES

Group Chief Executive, Clive C R Bannister, age 61
Group Finance Director, Jim McConville
Group Chief Risk Officer, Wayne Snow
Group Chief Actuary, Simon True
Chairman, Henry E. Staunton, age 71
Auditors: Ernst & Young LLP

LOCATIONS

HQ: Phoenix Group Holdings PLC
Juxon House, 100 St Paul's Churchyard, London EC4M 8BU
Phone:
Web: www.thephoenixgroup.com

PRODUCTS/OPERATIONS

2015 Sales

	% of total
Net investment income	91
Fees	8
Other	1
Total	**100**

COMPETITORS

AXA UK	Prudential plc
Aviva	Royal London Mutual
Legal & General Group	Standard Life Aberdeen
Liverpool Victoria	

HISTORICAL FINANCIALS

Company Type: Public

Income Statement

	ASSETS ($ mil.)	NET INCOME ($ mil.)	INCOME AS % OF ASSETS	EMPLOYEES
FYE: December 31				
12/19	320,470	112	0.0%	4,417
12/18	293,629	483	0.2%	4,088
12/17	112,705	(36)	—	1,249
12/16	105,790	(124)	—	1,301
12/15	95,606	297	0.3%	741
Annual Growth	35.3%	(21.7%)	—	56.3%

2019 Year-End Financials

Return on assets: 0.0%
Return on equity: 1.5%
Long-term debt ($ mil.): —
No. of shares (mil.): 721
Sales ($ mil): 38,512
Dividends
  Yield: —
  Payout: 544.1%
Market value ($ mil.): —

Ping An Insurance (Group) Co of China Ltd.

Ping An Insurance is one of China's largest insurance companies. It specializes in life and health coverage but offers a variety of other products including auto insurance corporate property and casualty insurance engineering insurance cargo insurance liability insurance guarantee insurance credit insurance home contents insurance accident and health insurance as well as international reinsurance business. The company also provides stock trading equity investment funds and bonds property leasing and asset management services through Ping An Trust; its Shenzhen Ping An Bank subsidiary offers retail banking and other consumer services such as credit card and mortgage lending. The group also includes Ping An Health Insurance. The company's name Ping An translates to "safe and well".

Operations

Ping An Insurance operates through these primary segments: Life and Health Insurance Property & Casualty Insurance Banking Trust Securities Other Asset Management and Technology.

The largest segment Life and Health Insurance brings in approximately 55% of the group's total revenue. It offers life and health coverage to individual and corporate customers. Offerings include term whole-life endowment annuity investment-linked universal life health insurance subsidiaries and medical insurance.

Property & Casualty Insurance provides automobile non-automobile accident and health insurance. The segment brings in some 20% of total revenue.

The Banking segment provides loan and intermediary business with corporate and retail business customers. It also provides wealth management and credit card services to individuals. It accounts for about 20% of revenue.

The Other Asset Management segment provides finance leasing investment management and other asset management services. It brings in about 5% of revenue.

The Technology provides various financial and daily-life services through internet platforms such as financial transaction information service platform health care service platform reflecting performance summary of the technology business subsidiaries associates and jointly controlled entities. Its operating units include Lufax Holding OneConnect and Ping An HealthKonnect. The segment brings in less than 5% of revenue.

The smallest segments are Trust which operates through Ping An Trust and Ping An Capital; and Securities which provides brokerage trading investment banking and asset management services.

Geographic Reach

Ping is based in Shenzhen China and it operates mainly in China.

Ping An Life provides customers with life insurance products through its nationwide service network of more than 40 branches (including seven telemarketing centers) and over 3300 business outlets.

Ping An Bank had more than 90 branches (including the Hong Kong branch) and about 1060 business outlets. Moreover Ping An Bank opened about 290 new retail stores.

OneConnect has also established a Japanese joint venture with SBI Neo Financial Services to serve local financial institutions with digital transformation. In Southeast Asia in addition to Singapore branches had also been opened in Jakarta Indonesia.

Sales and Marketing

Ping An Insurance distributes its offerings through a network of more than 40 branches and 2740 sub-branches sales service outlets and business outlets throughout China. It utilizes in-house sales representatives sales agents and insurance brokers as well as telemarketing online marketing and cross-selling.

The company has 200 million retail customers and more than 515 million internet users.

Financial Performance

Note: Growth rates may differ after conversion to US Dollars.

Ping An Insurance revenue has been growing steadily over the past five years helping the com-

pany surpass China Life Insurance as the nation's largest life insurer. Likewise net income has shown strong growth. In 2019 revenue increased 19% to RMB 1.1 trillion.

The net profit attributable to shareholders of the company gained 39% year on year to RMB 149.4 billion.

The company ended 2019 with RMB 303.5 billion in net cash some RMB 4.6 billion less than it had at the end of 2018. Operating activities provided RMB 249.4 billion and financing activities provided another RMB 125.1 billion while investing activities used RMB 380.2 billion.

Strategy

In terms of business strategies Ping An will focus on value creation and seek sustainable growth. It will upgrade the "1+N" product portfolio to provide more diverse and convenient one-stop integrated financial services. The company will continue to develop long-term protection products and long-term savings hybrid products that are customer-centric value-creating and sales-boosting to enhance its ability to serve the real economy. In asset allocation Ping An will maintain robust asset-liability management and prudent investment strategies supported by smart risk management and AI-enabled early warning. In this way the company can strike a balance between risks liabilities and investment to create value for shareholders. It will increase investment in technological innovations and prepare for the future. This fight against the COVID-19 outbreak highlights the importance of technology to the transformation of the country and industries.

In early 2019 OneConnect Smart Technology Co. Ltd. a member of Ping An Insurance Company of China Ltd. has recently entered into an agreement with SBI Neo Financial Services to set up a joint-venture company SBI OneConnect Japan in Japan.

Going forward SBI OneConnect Japan will foster the localization of OneConnect's fintech solutions in Japan starting with smartphone applications. SBI OneConnect Japan will fully leverage SBI Neo Financial Services and other SBI companies' networks and introduce OneConnect's fintech services to financial institutions and businesses across Japan.

Mergers and Acquisitions

Ping An Insurance (Group) Company of China Ltd. (hereafter "Ping An" or the "Group" is pleased to announce that agreements have been signed with Shionogi (Hong Kong) Company Ltd. ("Shionogi (Hong Kong)") a wholly owned subsidiary of Shionogi & Co. Ltd. ("Shionogi") to launch joint ventures in Shanghai and Hong Kong namely Ping An-Shionogi Co. Ltd. and Ping An-Shionogi (Hong Kong) Limited. The establishment of the joint ventures will enhance the level of health and medical care service in China in line with Ping An's healthcare ecosystem strategy.

Company Background

Ping An Insurance was founded in 1988 as China's first joint-stock insurance company. It ventured beyond insurance in 1995 by establishing Ping An Securities.

EXECUTIVES

Chairman and CEO, Ma Mingzhe
EVP, Sun A
Chief Investment Officer, Chen Dexian
Chief Actuary, Yao Bo
Auditors: PricewaterhouseCoopers Zhong Tian LLP

LOCATIONS

HQ: Ping An Insurance (Group) Co of China Ltd.
47th, 48th, 109th, 110th, 111th and 112th Floors,
Ping An Finance Center, No. 5033 Yitian Road, Futian
District, Shenzhen, Guangdong Province 518033
Phone: (86) 400 8866 338 **Fax:** (86) 755 8243 1029
Web: www.pingan.cn

PRODUCTS/OPERATIONS

2018 Sales by Segment

	% of total
Life and Health Insurance	51
Property & Casualty Insurance	21
Banking	19
Other Asset Management	4
Fintech & Healthtech	3
Trust	1
Securities	1
Total	**100**

2018 Sales

	% of total
Net earned premiums	62
Interest revenue from banking operations	15
Interest revenue from non-banking operations	8
Fees & commission revenue from non-insurance operations	4
Investment income	3
Share of profits & losses of associates & jointly controlled entities	2
Reinsurance commission revenue	1
Other revenue & other gains	5
Total	**0**

Selected Subsidiaries and Affiliates

China Ping An Insurance Overseas (Holdings) Limited
  China Ping An Insurance (Hong Kong) Company
  Limited (75%)
  Ping An of China Asset Management (Hong Kong)
  Company Limited
China Ping An Trust & Investment Co. Ltd.
  Ping An Securities Co. Ltd.
Ping An Annuity Insurance Company of China Ltd.
Ping An Health Insurance Company of China Ltd.
Ping An Life Insurance Company of China Ltd.
Ping An Property & Casualty Insurance Company of
  China Ltd.
Shenzhen Ping An Bank Co. Ltd.

COMPETITORS

CNinsure	China Pacific
China Insurance	Insurance
China Life Insurance	PICC Property

HISTORICAL FINANCIALS

Company Type: Public

Income Statement

FYE: December 31

	ASSETS ($ mil.)	NET INCOME ($ mil.)	INCOME AS % OF ASSETS	EMPLOYEES
12/19	1,170,190	21,261	1.8%	0
12/18	1,016,502	15,284	1.5%	376,900
12/17	924,018	12,677	1.4%	342,550
12/16	793,639	8,879	1.1%	318,588
12/15	678,121	7,713	1.1%	275,011
Annual Growth	14.6%	28.9%	—	—

2019 Year-End Financials

Return on assets: 1.9%	Dividends
Return on equity: 24.3%	Yield: 1.8%
Long-term debt ($ mil.): —	Payout: 37.5%
No. of shares (mil.): —	Market value ($ mil.): —
Sales ($ mil): 11,089	

STOCK PRICE ($) FY Close	P/E High/Low		PER SHARE ($) Earnings	Dividends	Book Value
12/19	23.80	3 2	1.19	0.45	(0.00)
12/18	17.39	4 3	0.86	0.48	4.33
12/17	20.89	4 2	0.71	0.25	3.68
12/16	9.96	3 2	0.50	0.13	2.99
12/15	11.04	11 3	0.42	0.17	2.60
Annual Growth 21.2%		—	—	29.5% 26.7%	—

Piraeus Financial Holdings SA

EXECUTIVES

chief executive, Christos John Megalou
Chairman, George Petros Hantzinikolaou
vice-chairman, Karel Gerard De Boeck
Auditors: Deloitte Certified Public Accountants S.A.

LOCATIONS

HQ: Piraeus Financial Holdings SA
  4 Amerikis str., Athens 105 64
Phone: (30) 210 333 5000   **Fax:** (30) 210 333 5080
Web: www.piraeusbankgroup.com

Branch Locations

	No.
Greece	1,037
Romanis	140
Bulgaria	83
Albania	53
Serbia	42
Egypt	41
Ukraine	37
Cyprus	14
London	1
Frankfurt	1
Total	**1,449**

PRODUCTS/OPERATIONS

Selected Subsidiaries
ATEbank
ETBA Industrial Areas S.A.
Marathon Bank of New York (USA)
OJSC Piraeus Bank ICB (Ukraine)
Picar S.A.
Piraeus Asset Management Mutual Funds S.A.
Piraeus Bank AD Beograd (Serbia)
Piraeus Bank Bulgaria AD
Piraeus Bank (Cyprus) Ltd
Piraeus Bank Egypt SAE
Piraeus Capital Management
Piraeus Card Services
Piraeus Direct Services S.A.
Piraeus Insurance and Reinsurance Brokerage S.A.
Piraeus Insurance Agency S.A.
Piraeus Factoring S.A.
Piraeus Leaases SA
Piraeus Leasing Bulgaria
Piraeus Bank Romania S.A.
Piraeus Leasing Romania
Piraeus Private Equity
Piraeus Real Estate S.A.
Piraeus Securities S.A.
Piraeus Wealth Management
Tirana Bank S.A. (Albania)
Tirana Leasing (Albania)

COMPETITORS

Alpha Bank	Emporiki Bank
Bank of Cyprus	National Bank of
EFG Eurobank Ergasias	Greece

HISTORICAL FINANCIALS

Company Type: Public

Income Statement   FYE: December 31

	ASSETS ($ mil.)	NET INCOME ($ mil.)	INCOME AS % OF ASSETS	EMPLOYEES
12/19	68,748	314	0.5%	12,613
12/18	70,864	(180)	—	15,000
12/17	80,815	(240)	—	18,581
12/16	86,055	(36)	—	18,995
12/15	95,336	(2,061)	—	20,719
Annual Growth	(7.8%)	—	—	(11.7%)

2019 Year-End Financials

Return on assets: 0.4%
Return on equity: 3.7%
Long-term debt ($ mil.): —
No. of shares (mil.): 436
Sales ($ mil): 3,028

Dividends
Yield: —
Payout: —
Market value ($ mil.): 2,837

STOCK PRICE ($) FY Close	P/E High/Low		PER SHARE ($) Earnings	Dividends	Book Value
12/19	6.50	11 2	0.37	0.00	19.70
12/18	1.80	— —	(0.22)	0.00	19.40
12/17	7.33	— —	(0.29)	0.00	25.87
12/16	0.44	— —	(0.08)	0.00	23.38
12/15	0.61	— —	(18.57)	0.00	24.72
Annual Growth 80.8%		— —	—	(5.5%)	

PJSC Gazprom

With prominent gas assets Gazprom Russia's largest company has proved and probable oil and gas reserves of 29 billion tons of coal equivalent and produces about 557 billion cu. meters of natural gas a year. With 16% of the world's gas reserves it is also the world's #1 gas producer. Majority-owned by the Russian government Gazprom is engaged in oil and gas exploration processing transport and marketing. It operates Russia's domestic gas pipeline network and delivers gas across Asia-Pacific Africa Central and South America Middle East and Europe. It also holds stakes in Russian financial institutions a polypropylene plant and a telecom network and produces 14% of Russia's electricity.

Operations
Gazprom operates one of the largest gas pipeline systems in the world and is responsible for the major part of gas production and high pressure gas transportation in the Russian Federation and is a major supplier of gas to European countries. It is engaged in oil production refining activities electric and heat energy generation.

Its reportable segments are: Gas production (roughly 50% of total revenue) Refining (more than 25% of total revenue) Crude oil & gas condensate (approximately 10% of total revenue) Electric & Heat generation (more than 5% of total revenue) and Gas transportation services (about 5% of total revenue).

The company owns the world's largest gas transmission network - the Unified Gas Supply System of Russia with the total length of approximately 175 thousand kilometers.

It also holds stakes in Russian financial institutions a polypropylene plant and its own telecom network and produces 14% of Russia's electric power.

Geographic Reach
Russian-based Gazprom operates in more than 20 countries and its products are supplied to more than 100 markets around the world. The company has offices in Algeria Bangladesh Bolivia Germany India Libya Nigeria Tajikistan Uzbekistan Venezuela Vietnam and The Netherlands.

Financial Performance
In 2019 Gazprom's net sales decreased by 7% to RUB 7.7 trillion primarily driven by lower net sales in gas.

Its net income dropped by RUB 253.4 billion (17%) compared to RUB 1.2 trillion in 2018.

In fiscal 2019 net cash provided by the operating activities decreased by 18% to RUB 696.1 billion primarily due to higher net debt.

Strategy
Strengthening its leadership among global energy companies by diversifying sales markets maintaining energy security and sustainability driving operational efficiencies and leveraging R&D capabilities are the strategic priorities of Gazprom.

In 2019 Gazprom launched the first-ever Russian pipeline gas supplies to China one of the world's most promising gas markets. Having been commissioned by the Company the Power of Siberia gas pipeline became the mainstay of a new powerful system of gas exports and gas supply to Russia's eastern regions.

Gazprom finished the construction of Turk-Stream a new high-tech pipeline for exporting gas to Europe with January 2020 seeing the launch of commercial gas supplies across the Black Sea. The Company also continued the construction of the Nord Stream 2 gas pipeline linking Russia and Germany via the Baltic Sea. Green energy supplies taking low carbon footprint routes are fully in line with the interests of its customers. In 2019 Gazprom's gas exports to Europe Turkey and China were 199.3 bcm - one of the best results in the Company's history. The Company continued to live up to its reputation as a responsible supplier by flexibly responding to market demand and offering a wide choice of contract terms to its customers. The extension of contracts for gas transportation across Belarus and Ukraine negotiated in 2019 was also an important factor in this context. In 2019 Gazprom Group produced over 500 bcm of gas the highest level for the last eight years starting from 2012.

HISTORY

Following the breakup of the Soviet Union in the early 1990s one of the first priorities of the Russian government was to move some state monopolies toward a free-market economic system. A presidential decree in 1992 moved the company toward privatization by calling for the formation of a Russian joint-stock company to explore for and produce gas gas condensates and oil; provide for gas processing; operate gas wells; and build gas pipelines and storage facilities.

By 1993 the government had converted its natural gas monopoly Gazprom into a joint-stock company; the company had dated back to the 1940s and the USSR Ministry of the Gas Industry had kept all of its assets when it became a corporation in 1989.

The new Gazprom was 15%-owned by Gazprom workers and 28% by people living in Russia's gas-producing regions. The state retained about a 40% share (boosted to 51% in 2003). The company inherited all of the former Soviet republics' export contracts to Western and Central Europe.

Thanks to the power of Viktor Chernomyrdin (Gazprom's former Soviet boss and gas industry minister who became Russia's prime minister in 1992) the company was able to enjoy large tax breaks and maintain its role as a monopoly — even as other industries were being more deeply privatized. However the privatization of Gazprom was later attacked as being manipulated to profit the company's top management including Chernomyrdin. Top managers were rumored to have each received 1%-5% of shares — holdings potentially worth $1.2 billion-$10 billion each.

Needing to raise cash in 1996 Gazprom offered 1% of its stock to foreigners the first sale of stock to foreign investors. In 1997 Gazprom and Royal Dutch/Shell formally became partners. That year Gazprom began building its Blue Stream pipeline across the Black Sea to Turkey. Italian group Eni helped back the project and became a partner by 1999.

In 1998 Gazprom acquired a stake in Promostroibank Russia's fourth-largest financial institution. German energy powerhouse Ruhrgas acquired a 3% stake in Gazprom in 1998 which it increased to nearly 4% the next year. Also in 1999 Gazprom started building its Yamal-Europe pipeline which was to stretch to Germany for exports to Europe.

The next year an attempt by Gazprom to muscle into Hungary's chemicals sector by offering cheaper raw materials was blocked by Hungary's TVK and Borsodchem and their allies. Also in 2000 Gazprom became embroiled in a politically controversial issue when it called for the country's leading private media holding group Media-MOST to sell shares to the gas giant in order to settle millions of dollars of debt. Because Media-MOST held NTV television a major critic of Russian President Vladimir Putin the deal was alleged to have been directed by the Kremlin. A government probe into the deal was later ordered. (By 2002 Gazprom owned a significant stake in NTV which it sold that year so it could focus on its core energy businesses.)

The alignment of Gazprom's board changed in 2000 after the annual shareholder's meeting. For the first time in Gazprom's history company managers did not have a majority of seats. A new chairman Dmitri Medvedev second in command to Putin was elected to replace Chernomyrdin. In 2001 the board fired CEO Rem Vyakhirev and replaced him with Deputy Energy Minister Alexei Miller a Putin ally.

Gazprom had announced plans in 2004 to acquire Rosneft (effectively giving the Russian government control of Gazprom) though the deal was complicated by Rosneft's acquisition of the Yugansk assets acquired from YUKOS. In 2005 Gazprom abandoned plans to merge with Rosneft and acquired Sibneft in an effort to add significant oil operations to its business. Millhouse Capital a holding company controlled by Russian oligarch Roman Abramovich sold its majority stake in what was then a major exploration and production company called Sibneft (now Gazprom Neft) to Gazprom for a reported $13 billion. At the time Sibneft was Russia's fifth-largest oil company.

In 2006 Gazprom signed long-term contracts for gas deliveries with Austrian energy giant OMV. That year Royal Dutch/Shell agreed to give control of the $22 billion Sakhalin-2 project (run by Sakhalin Energy Investment) in Russia's Far East to Gazprom.

Former Gazprom chairman Dmitri Medvedev was elected president of Russia in 2008.

The company became embroiled in a pricing dispute with neighbor Ukraine in 2009 resulting in the disruption of gas supplies to Ukraine and because of its transnational pipelines to dozens of other countries in Europe.

Wanting to expand its Russian and international assets and diversify its profile in 2009 Gazprom acquired Italian energy titan ENI's 20% share in oil producer Gazprom Neft raising the Russian giant's direct ownership to 79%. ENI had acquired

its stake in 2007 following the bankruptcy of YUKOS. Gazprom had the option to buy ENI's stake within two years and exercised that right in 2009 paying just more than $4 billion to ENI. Gazprom directly owns or indirectly controls through subsidiaries about 95% of Gazprom Neft.

In 2010 the company made its first entry into the US gas market when it began trading and marketing natural gas though Gazprom Marketing & Trading USA. It also signed a strategic partnership with Royal Dutch Shell to develop oil and gas assets in Russian Siberia and the Far East and process and market products in Russia and Europe.

To raise cash to pay down debt in 2010 the company sold its controlling stake in SeverEnergia (a natural gas project partly owned by ENI) to a joint venture owned by Gazprom Neft and OAO Novatek for $1.5 billion. To raise cash it sold 9% of its 19% stake in Novatek to Gazprombank for $2.8 billion.

In 2011 it installed 1.9 GW of combined heat and power generation units and deployed an offshore production platform at the Prirazlomnoye oil field in the Pechora Sea in the Arctic.

Expanding its energy footprint in 2011 Gazprom agreed to acquire power generation KES Holding (which owns four power companies) to create Russia's largest power company. KES Holding will hold 25% of the new joint venture.

To expand its gas supply in 2012 the company announced that it planned to spend 43 billion rubles (US $1.4 billion) that year to develop gas infrastructure projects (gas fields and pipelines) in the Sakhalin region of Eastern Russia. In 2011 Gazprom acquired TNK-BP's east Siberian Kovykta gas field for about $770 million. The purchase opens up the possibility of a major supply agreement with China.

EXECUTIVES

Deputy Chairman and CEO, Alexei B. Miller, age 59
Deputy Chairman Management Committee; Director General OOO Gazprom export, Alexander I. Medvedev, age 65
Member Management Committee; Head Marketing and Processing of Gas and Liquid Hydrocarbons Department; Director General OOO Mezhregiongaz, Kirill Gennadievich Seleznev, age 46
Member Management Committee; Head Legal Department, Nikolay N. Dubik, age 49
Member Management Committee; Director General OOO Gazprom komplektatsiya, Igor Y. Fyodorov, age 55
Head Information Policy Department, Alexander D. Bespalov, age 70
Member Management Committee and Head Department Gas Transportation Underground Storage and Utilization Department, Oleg E. Aksyutin
Member Management Committee; Head Gas Gas Condensate and Oil Production, Vsevolod Cherepanov, age 54
Deputy CFO, Alexander Ivannikov
Member of the Management Committee Department Head Gazprom, Sergey Prozorov, age 62
Head of Department 840, Natalia Borisenko, age 43
Chairman, Victor A. Zubkov, age 79
Auditors: FBK, LLC

LOCATIONS

HQ: PJSC Gazprom
Nametkina St., 16, V-420, GSP-7, Moscow 117997
Phone: (7) 812 609 4129   **Fax:** (7) 812 609 4334
Web: www.gazprom.com

PRODUCTS/OPERATIONS

2014 Sales

	% of total
Distribution	53
Refining	29
Electric and heat energy generation and sales	7
Production of crude oil and gas condensate	4
Transport	3
Gas storage	0
Production of gas	0
All other segments	4
Total	**100**

COMPETITORS

BP	Rosneft
Centrica	Sakhalin Energy
Gasunie	Surgutneftegas
LUKOIL	Tatneft
Qatar Petroleum	

HISTORICAL FINANCIALS

Company Type: Public

Income Statement

FYE: December 31

	REVENUE ($ mil.)	NET INCOME ($ mil.)	NET PROFIT MARGIN	EMPLOYEES
12/19	122,671	19,327	15.8%	473,800
12/18	118,259	20,894	17.7%	466,100
12/17	112,945	12,355	10.9%	469,600
12/16	99,856	15,541	15.6%	467,400
12/15	82,293	10,658	13.0%	462,400
Annual Growth	**10.5%**	**16.0%**	**—**	**0.6%**

2019 Year-End Financials

Debt ratio: 0.2%	No. of shares (mil.): —
Return on equity: 8.7%	Dividends
Cash ($ mil.): 11,184	Yield: 6.1%
Current ratio: 1.51	Payout: 355.2%
Long-term debt ($ mil.): 49,644	Market value ($ mil.): —

	STOCK PRICE ($) FY Close	P/E High/Low		PER SHARE ($) Earnings	Dividends	Book Value
12/19	8.22	0	0	0.86	0.50	9.58
12/18	4.42	0	0	0.95	0.24	8.62
12/17	4.41	0	0	0.56	1.64	9.09
12/16	5.09	0	0	0.69	1.51	8.19
12/15	3.67	0	0	0.46	0.23	6.24
Annual Growth	**22.3%**	**—**	**—**	**16.6%**	**22.3%**	**11.3%**

PJSC Lukoil

Russians look to LUKOIL for their energy needs. It is one of the largest publicly traded vertically integrated oil and gas companies in the world accounting for about 5% of the world's oil production and around 1% of the proved hydrocarbon reserves globally. Present across the entire value chain Lukoil has significant exploration & production refining and marketing operations concentrated in Russia but spreading out to Europe Central Asia and the Middle East. In addition it engages in power generation including some solar in Russia Romania and Bulgaria. Lukoil gas filling stations serve customers in around 30 countries. About 70% of Lukoil retail sales come from within Russia.

OperationsLukoil's makes money primarily from the sale of refined products (65% of annual sales) followed by crude oil (almost 30%). Its petrochemical products and Gas sales bring in 2% revenue each. Its proved hydrocarbon reserves include 12 billion barrels of crude oil and some 24000 billion cubic feet of gas. The company reports its activities under threecore business segments. Refining Marketing & Distribution is the core business of Lukoil. It includes refining petrochemical and gas processingmarketing and trading of crude oil natural gas and refined products generation transportation and sales of electricity plus heat and related services. Exploration & Production manages exploration development and production operations related to crude oil and gas. These activities are primarily located within Russia and internationally. Corporate and other includes finance activities.

Geographic Reach

Lukoil has significant operations in around 30 countries on four continents.

In Russia its major oil producing regions are Western Siberia Timan-Pechora Ural and Volga region. Internationally its upstream portfolio includes stakes in PSA's and other projects in Kazakhstan Azerbaijan Uzbekistan Romania Iraq Egypt Ghana Norway Cameroon Nigeria and Mexico.

Lukoil's refineries and petrochemical plants are concentrated in Russia with additional production in four European countries. Other than Russia power generation is concentrated in Romania and Bulgaria.

Lukoil gas filling stations are in around 30 countries worldwide.

Sales and Marketing

Lukoil has a hydrocarbon production rate about of 2.3 million boe per day plus 2.4 million barrels/day of refining throughput. Its products are sold through nearly 5300 retail networks globally.

Lukoil is a well-known brand around 30 countries worldwide thanks to its extensive network of filling stations selling around 15 million tons of refined products. In addition Lukoil has vessel bunkering infrastructure in four countries and aircraft refueling facilities in about 35 airports.

In 2019 the gross profit from non-fuel sales covered about 40% of the expenses of its Russian filling stations compared to some 35% in 2018 and around 30% in 2017.

Financial PerformanceLUKOIL'S sales for 2019 were RUB 7.8 trillion down by 2% year-on-year. The decline was driven by lower crude oil and petroleum products prices and lower petroleum product trading volumes. Profit increased to RUB 640 billion in 2019 from RUB 619 billion the year prior the net income increase was driven by better operating performance and cost reduction offsetting the effect of lower hydrocarbon prices. Free cash flow up by 26% year-on-year to RUB 702 billion driven by higher efficiency and cost reduction.

Strategy

LUKOIL's talent management strategy is aligned with its Strategic Development Program and the staffing demands of its business segments based on planning and budgeting processes that enable the workforce to be efficiently reallocated through insourcing as well as flexible recruitment professional training and developing talent.

As the Strategic Development Program of LUKOIL Group for 2018?2027 is aimed among other things at improving the company's operational efficiency its talent management strategy is focused on boosting labor productivity through business process digitization and automation as well as upgrading employee skills.

Mergers and Acquisitions

In 2019 company acquired a 5% interest in the Ghasha Concession in the United Arab Emirates from the Abu Dhabi National oil company for RUB 13.8 billion ($214 million).

Company Background

LUKOIL was formed from the combination of three major state-owned oil and gas exploration companies — Langepasneftegaz Uraineftegaz and Kogalymneftegaz — that traced their origins to the discovery of oil in western Siberia in 1964.

More than 25 years later after the Soviet Union broke up the oil and gas sector was one of the first industries marked for privatization.

In 1992 the government called for Langepasneftegaz Uraineftegaz and Kogalymneftegaz to merge and LUKOIL was created the next year. (The LUK of LUKOIL comes from the initials of the three companies.) Russian president Boris Yeltsin appointed Siberian oil veteran Vagit Alekperov as the company's first president. The Russian government also formed several other large integrated oil companies including Yukos Surgutneftegaz Sidanco and Sibneft.

LUKOIL went public on the fledgling Russian Trading System in 1994.

EXECUTIVES

First VP Economics and Finance, Sergei P. Kukura, age 67
Deputy Chairman and First EVP Exploration and Production, Ravil U. Maganov, age 66
President and Director, Vagit Y. Alekperov, age 70
SVP Finance, Alexander K. Matytsyn, age 59
VP; CEO of LUKOIL-West Siberia, Vladimir I. Nekrasov, age 63
SVP Oil and Gas Production, Azat Shamsuarov, age 57
VP Oil Sales and Supplies, Vadim Vorobyev
VP and General Counsel, Ivan Maslyaev, age 62
Chairman, Valery I. Grayfer, age 91
Auditors: JSC KPMG

LOCATIONS

HQ: PJSC Lukoil
    11 Sretensky Boulevard, Moscow 101000
Phone: (7) 495 627 4444   **Fax:** (7) 495 625 7016
Web: www.lukoil.com

2015 Sales

	% of total
Russia	30
Other countries	70
Total	**100**

PRODUCTS/OPERATIONS

2015 Sales

	% of total
Refining marketing and distribution	95
Exploration and production	4
Corporate and other	1
Total	**100**

2015 Sales

	% of total
Refined products	67
Crude oil	27
Gas & gas products	2
Petrochemicals	1
Sales of energy & related services	1
Other	2
Total	**100**

COMPETITORS

Ashland	PETROBRAS
BP	Petr leos de
Exxon Mobil	Venezuela
Gazprom Neft	Rosneft
Imperial Oil	Royal Dutch Shell
Norsk Hydro ASA	Surgutneftegas
Occidental Petroleum	TOTAL
PEMEX	Tatneft

HISTORICAL FINANCIALS

Company Type: Public

Income Statement

	REVENUE ($ mil.)	NET INCOME ($ mil.)	NET PROFIT MARGIN	EMPLOYEES
12/19	125,990	10,286	8.2%	101,400
12/18	115,299	8,883	7.7%	0
12/17	102,686	7,244	7.1%	0
12/16	85,364	3,377	4.0%	0
12/15	77,852	3,942	5.1%	0
Annual Growth	12.8%	27.1%	—	—

FYE: December 31

2019 Year-End Financials

Debt ratio: 0.1%
Return on equity: 15.9%
Cash ($ mil.): 8,291
Current ratio: 1.29
Long-term debt ($ mil.): 6,795

No. of shares (mil.): 652
Dividends
    Yield: 5.5%
    Payout: 37.5%
Market value ($ mil.): 64,446

	STOCK PRICE ($) FY Close	P/E High/Low		PER SHARE ($) Earnings	Dividends	Book Value
12/19	98.71	0	0	15.02	5.47	97.59
12/18	71.34	0	0	12.41	3.49	83.70
12/17	57.65	0	0	10.19	3.60	84.89
12/16	56.12	0	0	4.74	3.02	73.78
12/15	32.49	0	0	5.49	2.36	61.21
Annual Growth	32.0%		— —	28.6%	23.4%	12.4%

PJSC Rosseti

Auditors: RSM RUS LTD

LOCATIONS

HQ: PJSC Rosseti
    4 Belovezhskaya Street, Moscow 121353
Phone: (7) 495 363 2848   **Fax:** (7) 495 981 4121
Web: www.holding-mrsk.ru

HISTORICAL FINANCIALS

Company Type: Public

Income Statement

	REVENUE ($ mil.)	NET INCOME ($ mil.)	NET PROFIT MARGIN	EMPLOYEES
12/19	16,544	1,233	7.5%	0
12/18	14,658	1,305	8.9%	0
12/17	16,403	1,769	10.8%	0
12/16	14,763	1,218	8.3%	0
12/15	10,384	867	8.4%	0
Annual Growth	12.3%	9.2%	—	—

FYE: December 31

2019 Year-End Financials

Debt ratio: 0.3%
Return on equity: 6.6%
Cash ($ mil.): 1,269
Current ratio: 0.77
Long-term debt ($ mil.): 7,466

No. of shares (mil.): —
Dividends
    Yield: —
    Payout: 6.4%
Market value ($ mil.): —

Poly Real Estate Group Co., Ltd.

EXECUTIVES

Chairman, Guangju Song
Auditors: Daxin Certified Public Accountants

LOCATIONS

HQ: Poly Real Estate Group Co., Ltd.
29th - 33th Floor, South Tower, Poly International Building, No. 688, Yuejiang Zhonglu, Haizhu Distrct, Guangzhou, Guangdong Province 510308
Phone: (86) 20 89898833   **Fax:** (86) 20 89898666
Web: www.gzpoly.com

HISTORICAL FINANCIALS

Company Type: Public

Income Statement				FYE: December 31
	REVENUE ($ mil.)	NET INCOME ($ mil.)	NET PROFIT MARGIN	EMPLOYEES
12/19	33,913	4,018	11.8%	0
12/18	28,285	2,748	9.7%	0
12/17	22,488	2,401	10.7%	0
12/16	22,288	1,788	8.0%	0
12/15	19,005	1,901	10.0%	0
Annual Growth	15.6%	20.6%	—	—

2019 Year-End Financials

Debt ratio: 3.7%
Return on equity: 20.1%
Cash ($ mil.): 20,036
Current ratio: 1.56
Long-term debt ($ mil.): 29,258

No. of shares (mil.): —
Dividends
 Yield: —
 Payout: —
Market value ($ mil.): —

POSCO (South Korea)

POSCO posits itself firmly as global steel-maker selling more than 40 million tons of it annually. A steel producer in its home country to about 55 counties the company exports a wide range of steel products including hot rolled sheets plate wire rod cold rolled sheets galvanized sheets and stainless steel to 53 countries earning worldwide recognition for its superb technology and excellent quality. Beyond steel the company also engages in power generation materials trading and resource development activities. POSCO's Pohang and Gwangyang plants in Korea are the largest steel facilities in the world by production.

Operations

POSCO operates through four reportable operating segments - a steel segment a trading segment a construction segment and a segment that contains operations of all other entities.

The steel segment (nearly 50% of revenue) includes production of steel products and sale of such products.

The trading segment (about 40% revenue) consists primarily of global trading activities and natural resources development activities of POSCO International. POSCO International exports and imports a wide range of steel products that are both obtained from and supplied to POSCO as well as between other suppliers and purchasers in Korea and overseas.

The construction segment (more than 5% revenue) includes planning designing and construction of industrial plants civil engineering projects and commercial and residential buildings both in Korea and overseas.

The "others" segment (with over 5% revenue) includes power generation LNG logistics manufacturing of various industrial materials and network and system integration.

Geographic Reach

POSCO Steel is headquartered in Donghaeanro Nam-gu Pohang-si Gyeongsangbuk-do Republic of Korea. POSCO DAEWOO has some 85 local subsidiaries in South Korea and branches all around the world. Their principal properties are Pohang Works which is located at Youngil Bay on the southeastern coast of Korea and Gwangyang Works which is located in Gwangyang City in the southwestern region of Korea. It also maintain and operate production properties abroad including plants operated by Zhangjiagang Pohang Stainless Steel in China PT. Krakatau POSCO in Indonesia and POSCO SS VINA in Vietnam.

More than 35% of its revenue comes from Korea followed by China which accounts for almost 30%.

Financial Performance

Note: Growth rates may differ after conversion to US Dollars.

Both revenue and profit were volatile for the past five years.

In 2019 POSCO's revenue decreased by one percent to KRW 64.8 trillion from KRW 65.2 trillion the year prior. Almost all the segments slightly decrease its revenue except for Construction segment with 5% increase from prior year.

Net income was KRW 2.0 trillion for 2019 a 5% increase compared to KRW 1.9 trillion from 2018.

Cash flow increased slightly to KRW 3.5 trillion at the end of the year 2019. Operations provided KRW 5.6 trillion offset by KRW 3.8 trillion used in investments (primarily going towards acquisition of short-term financial instruments) and a further KRW 1.6 trillion used by financing activities.

Strategy

As part of POSCO's strategy to compete in this challenging landscape they will continue to invest in developing innovative products that offer the greatest potential returns and enhance the overall quality of their products as well as make additional investments in the development of new manufacturing technologies.

In part to prepare for the eventual maturation of the Korean steel market they have made investments in the past decade to secure new growth engines by diversifying into new businesses related to their steel operations that they believe will offer greater potential returns such as participation in EPC projects in the steel sector and natural resources development as well as entering into new businesses not related to their steel operations such as power generation and alternative energy solutions LNG and agricultural trading and production of anode and cathode materials for rechargeable batteries as well as other comprehensive materials such as lithium. From time to time they may selectively acquire or invest in companies to pursue such diversification strategy.

POSCO conducts international trading and construction operations abroad and their business relies on a global trading network comprised of overseas subsidiaries branches and representative offices. Although many of their subsidiaries and overseas branches are located in developed countries they also operate in numerous countries with developing economies. In addition they intend to continue to expand their steel production operations internationally by carefully seeking out promising investment opportunities particularly in China India Southeast Asia and Latin America in part to prepare for the eventual maturation of the Korean steel market. They may enter into additional joint ventures with foreign steel producers that would enable them to rely on these businesses to conduct their operations establish local networks and coordinate their sales and marketing efforts abroad. To the extent that they enter into these arrangements their success will depend in part on the willingness of their partner companies to dedicate sufficient resources to their partnership with them.

Company Background

POSCO traces its development very closely with that out its motherland South Korea. It was founded in April 1968 as the Pohang Iron and Steel Company. POSCO grew as South Korea grew hand-in-hand since the 1980s. In 1986 the CEO of POSCO also founded the Pohang University of Science & Technology (POSTECH University) the first research-oriented university in Korea. The company went private during the turn of the 21st Century. Today it is one of the world's most advanced integrated steel companies and one of the top five steelmakers by production.

EXECUTIVES

President, Hwang Eun-Yeon, age 62
CEO, Oh-Joon Kwon, age 69
President and Head Steel Production Division, Jin-Il Kim, age 67
SEVP and Head Corporate Infrastructure Division, Dong-Jun Yoon, age 61
SEVP and Head Finance and Investment Division, Young-Hoon Lee, age 60
SEVP and Head Steel Business Division, In-Hwan Oh, age 61
SEVP and Department Manager Legal Affairs, Se-Bin Song, age 57
SEVP and Head Technical Research Laboratories, Sung-Ho Park, age 63
SEVP and General Superintendent Gwangyang Works, Tong-Il An, age 60
SEVP and General Superintendent Pohang Works, Hag-Dong Kim, age 60
SEVP and Department Manager Value Management, Chung-Myong Cho, age 59
EVP and Department Manager Corporate Audit, Woo-Kyu Lee, age 62
EVP and General Manager Europe, Chang-Hee Yim
EVP and Department Manager Labor and Outside Services, Suk-Bum Ko, age 62
EVP and Project Manager Regional Head Office Establishment Team Indonesia, Jhi-Yong Kim, age 58
EVP and Department Manager New Business Development Department, Seong Yu, age 63
EVP and Department Manager Steel Solution Marketing, In-Hwa Chang, age 64
EVP and Department Manager External Relation, Dong-chang Jung, age 61
EVP and Project Manager Regional Head Office Establishment Team Vietnam, Sik Nam, age 63
EVP and President PT Krakatau POSCO Co. Ltd., Kyung-Zoon Min, age 61
EVP and Department Manager Energy and Shipbuilding Materials Marketing, Tak Jeong, age 60
EVP and Department Manager safety and Production Strategy, Tae-Ju Lee, age 61
EVP and Department Manager Steel Planning, Hong-Soo Kim, age 62
EVP and Department Manager Steel Business Strategy, Chang Hwan Son, age 59
Auditors: KPMG Samjong Accounting Corp.

LOCATIONS

HQ: POSCO (South Korea)
OSCO Center, 440 Teheran-ro, Seoul, Gangnam-gu 37859
Phone: (82) 2 3457 1386   **Fax:** (82) 2 3457 1997
Web: www.posco.co.kr

2017 Sales

	% of total
Domestic	65
China	11
Asia-other	13
Japan	4
North America	3
Others	4
Total	**100**

PRODUCTS/OPERATIONS

2017 Sales

	% of total
Steel	50
Trading	35
Construction	11
Others Segment	4
Total	**100**

COMPETITORS

Ansteel
ArcelorMittal
Baosteel
Hyundai Steel
JFE Holdings
Jiangsu Shagang
Nippon Steel & Sumitomo Metal Corporation
Shougang Concord Int'l Enterprises Co.
Tata Steel

HISTORICAL FINANCIALS

Company Type: Public

Income Statement   FYE: December 31

	REVENUE ($ mil.)	NET INCOME ($ mil.)	NET PROFIT MARGIN	EMPLOYEES
12/19	56,110	1,614	2.9%	35,261
12/18	58,281	1,516	2.6%	17,150
12/17	56,893	2,617	4.6%	17,055
12/16	44,186	1,134	2.6%	16,584
12/15	49,460	153	0.3%	17,045
Annual Growth	3.2%	80.1%	—	19.9%

2019 Year-End Financials

Debt ratio: 0.0%
Return on equity: 4.2%
Cash ($ mil.): 3,044
Current ratio: 2.12
Long-term debt ($ mil.): 10,300

No. of shares (mil.): 80
Dividends
  Yield: 4.6%
  Payout: 11.8%
Market value ($ mil.): 4,055

	STOCK PRICE ($) FY Close	P/E High/Low		PER SHARE ($) Earnings	Dividends	Book Value
12/19	50.62	0	0	20.08	2.35	480.58
12/18	54.94	0	0	18.76	1.94	486.27
12/17	78.13	0	0	32.33	2.39	512.77
12/16	52.55	0	0	13.84	1.71	440.90
12/15	35.36	0	0	1.57	1.78	438.12
Annual Growth	9.4%	—	—	89.2%	7.2%	2.3%

Poste Italiane SpA

Auditors: PricewaterhouseCoopers SpA

LOCATIONS

HQ: Poste Italiane SpA
Viale Europa 190, Rome 00144
Phone: (36) 06 59581   **Fax:** (36) 06 59589100
Web: www.poste.it

HISTORICAL FINANCIALS

Company Type: Public

Income Statement   FYE: December 31

	REVENUE ($ mil.)	NET INCOME ($ mil.)	NET PROFIT MARGIN	EMPLOYEES
12/19	12,683	1,506	11.9%	118,523
12/18	14,436	1,602	11.1%	122,665
12/17	13,313	825	6.2%	127,431
12/16	11,777	656	5.6%	132,502
Annual Growth	2.5%	31.9%	—	(3.6%)

2019 Year-End Financials

Debt ratio: —
Return on equity: 15.0%
Cash ($ mil.): 7,244
Current ratio: 0.49
Long-term debt ($ mil.): —

No. of shares (mil.): 1,300
Dividends
  Yield: —
  Payout: 44.8%
Market value ($ mil.): —

	STOCK PRICE ($) FY Close	P/E High/Low		PER SHARE ($) Earnings	Dividends	Book Value
12/19	0.00	—	—	1.16	0.52	8.37
Annual Growth	—	—	—	—	—	—

Power Corp. of Canada

Founded in the 1920s to develop hydroelectric power Power Corporation of Canada now generates cash not electricity. It is an international management and holding company that focuses on financial services in North America Europe and Asia. The company's core holdings are leading insurance retirement wealth management and investment businesses including a portfolio of alternative asset investment platforms. Through its majority stake in Power Financial the company controls one of Canada's leading mutual fund firms (IGM Financial) one of its largest life insurers (Great-West Lifeco) and other insurance firms. It owns Square Victoria Communication Group which publishes French-language media content and Pargesa Group which holds stakes in large European companies. Power generation is still in the mix as the company owns stakes in renewable energy companies. The Europe generates the largest sales with more than 50% of the company's total sales.

Operations

Power Corporation of Canada is a diversified holding company that holds interests in financial services renewable energy asset management media and other businesses in North America Europe and Asia.

Most of its operations occur within its Power Financial subsidiary which itself owns controlling interests in Great-West Lifeco and IGM Financial. Lifeco sells life insurance health insurance retire-

ment & investment services asset management and reinsurance through its wholly-owned business including Great-West Life Putnam Investments and Irish Life. Lifeco accounts for more than 90% of revenue and more than 75% of net earnings.

IGM (accounts for some 5%) is a wealth and asset management company supporting financial advisors the clients it serve in Canada and institutional investors throughout North America Europe and Asia. Through its operating companies IGM provides a broad range of financial and investment planning services to help Canadians meet their financial goals. IGM serves the financial needs of Canadians through multiple distinct businesses including IG Wealth Management Mackenzie Investments and Investment Planning Counsel.

Power Corporation shares ownership of Pargesa Holding SA with Belgium-based Fr"re family group. Through subsidiaries the partners invests large sums in well-known European companies such as LafargeHolcim (construction) Pernod Ricard (wines and spirits) and Adidas (sportswear).

The holding company also operates a Power Energy business through which it invests in companies that benefit from the global energy transition towards renewable sources. Power Corporation invests in companies that benefit from the global energy transformation and currently has invested in companies that develop own and operate solar and wind generating assets in North America.

Power Corporation of Canada also owns Square Victoria Communications a publisher of Canadian news and media content and Sagard Investment Funds.

Overall approximately 50% of the company's sales were accounted from premiums more than 25% were generated from investments and the fees generated around 20% of sales.

Geographic Reach

Power Corporation of Canada is headquartered in Montréal Québec Canada. Its subsidiaries and holdings operate throughout North America Europe and Asia. The Europe generates the largest sales with more than 50% of the company's total sales while the Canada accounts for the rest.

Sales and Marketing

In Canada through the Individual Customer and Group Customer business units Lifeco offers a broad portfolio of financial and benefit plan solutions for individuals families businesses and organizations including life disability and critical illness insurance products as well as wealth savings and income and other speciality products.

Financial Performance

Note: Financial results are denoted in the company's home currency the Canadian Dollar (CAD$)

In 2019 the company's revenue increased by CAD$743 million to CAD$48.8 billion from CAD$48.1 billion. The increase was primarily due to higher net investment income and fee income.

Power's net earnings decreased by CAD$424 million to CAD$3.0 billion in 2019 from CAD$3.5 billion in the prior year.

Cash on hand at the end of the year was CAD$564 million down some CAD$186 million from the previous year. Cash provided by operations and investment activities were CAD$689 million and CAD$1.2 billion respectively. Cash used for financing activities was $2.0 billion primarily for repurchase of subordinate voting shares under PCC SIB.

Strategy

Power's value creation strategy is focused upon three levers.

The first lever is the pursuit of clearly articulated organic growth strategies at each of the company's public operating companies. Across the businesses that make up Great-West Lifeco IGM Financial and

GBL the management teams are transforming its business models to meet the changing needs of its customers.

The second lever is the deployment of capital to add to growth inorganically such as via acquisition and the redeployment of capital from businesses not expected to meet its return aspirations. Power's public operating companies are continually reviewing opportunities to add to its competitive position and earnings potential through engaging in potential acquisition activity.

The third lever is the focus on actions it can take either at the Power level between Power and its operating companies or between its group companies. The recent collapse of Power's dual-holding-company structure the simultaneous share buybacks and the proposed simplification of Pargesa and GBL's structure all referred to above are examples of utilizing this third lever.

Mergers and Acquisitions

In 2019 The company acquired a 100% equity interest in Nautilus Solar Energy LLC a company headquartered in New Jersey US that acquires develops finances and manages distributed solar projects across community municipal/utility-scale commercial and industrial markets. Terms were not disclosed.

EXECUTIVES

SVP Power Corporation and Power Financial, Arnaud Vial, age 68, $407,265 total compensation

EVP, John A. Rae, $407,589 total compensation

Deputy Chairman President and Co-CEO, André R. Desmarais, age 64, $820,100 total compensation

Chairman and Co-CEO, Paul Desmarais, age 66, $820,100 total compensation

EVP and CFO, Gregory D. Tretiak

Vice Chairman Power Corporation and Power Financial, Henri-Paul Rousseau, age 71

Vice Chairman Power Corporation and of Power Financial, Michel Plessis-Bélair

Auditors: Deloitte LLP

LOCATIONS

HQ: Power Corp. of Canada
751 Victoria Square, Montreal, Quebec H2Y 2J3
Phone: 514 286-7400   **Fax:** 514 286-7484
Web: www.powercorporation.com

2017 sales by geographic location

	% of total
Canada	42
US	19
Europe	39
Total	**100**

PRODUCTS/OPERATIONS

2017 sales

	% of total
Premium incomenet	66
Net investment income	16
Fees income	16
Other revenue	2
Total	**100**

2017 sales

	% of total
Lifeco	91
IGM	6
Corporate	
Other	3
Total	**100**

Selected Investments

Communications
  Gesca Lté;e (newspaper publisher)
  Square Victoria Communications Group Inc.
  Square Victoria Digital Properties Inc.
Financial Services

Great-West Lifeco Inc. (68%)
  The Canada Life Assurance Company
  Great-West Life & Annuity Insurance Company
  The Great-West Life Assurance Company
  London Life Insurance Company
  Putnam Investments LLC
IGM Financial Inc. (57%)
  Investment Planning Counsel (91%)
  Investors Group
  Mackenzie Financial Corporation
Power Financial Corporation (66%)
  Victoria Square Ventures Inc.
Other
  Pergesa Holding S.A. (Switzerland)
  Eagle Creek Renewable Energy
  Lumenpulse Group
  Portage Ventures
  Wealthsimple
  Personal Capital

COMPETITORS

AGF Management	Dundee Corp.
Berkshire Hathaway	Loews
Brookfield Asset	Manulife Financial
Management	Onex
CI Financial	Ontario Teachers'
CPP Investment Board	Pension Plan
Caisse de dép ´t et	Street Capital
placement du Québec	

HISTORICAL FINANCIALS

Company Type: Public

Income Statement

	ASSETS ($ mil.)	NET INCOME ($ mil.)	INCOME AS % OF ASSETS	FYE: December 31 EMPLOYEES
12/19	366,498	39	0.0%	30,600
12/18	332,139	38	0.0%	0
12/17	355,386	41	0.0%	30,484
12/16	313,806	38	0.0%	30,259
12/15	304,453	37	0.0%	26,500
Annual Growth	4.7%	1.6%	—	3.7%

2019 Year-End Financials

Return on assets: 0.0%	Dividends
Return on equity: 0.3%	Yield: 0.0%
Long-term debt ($ mil.): —	Payout: 63.1%
No. of shares (mil.): 377	Market value ($ mil.): 9,710
Sales ($ mil): 37,669	

	STOCK PRICE ($) FY Close	P/E High/Low		PER SHARE ($) Earnings	Dividends	Book Value
12/19	25.71	10	7	1.94	1.23	28.83
12/18	17.96	9	6	2.03	1.10	26.62
12/17	25.55	10	8	2.20	1.13	28.06
12/16	22.40	10	9	1.72	0.98	24.82
12/15	20.87	6	5	2.76	0.88	24.37
Annual Growth	5.4%	—	—	(8.4%)	8.6%	4.3%

Prudential Plc

Prudential is a leading provider of insurance products in Asia with additional operations in the US and Africa. Its Prudential Corporation Asia division provides life and health insurance while the Eastspring division offers investment and asset management services in the region. In the US it mainly operates through its Jackson National Life Insurance subsidiary. Prudential plc was formed in 1848 to offer life insurance and loans to the professional people and is not affiliated with US insurance giant Prudential Financial.

Operations

About 15 million of Prudential's customers are in Asia. The US is Prudential's largest territory by revenue. Jackson National Life Insurance Company includes Jackson National Life Distributors Jackson National Asset Management LLC and Jackson National Life Insurance Company of New York.

Geographic Reach

Following the M&G demerger Prudential is focused on Asia the US and Africa. The company remains headquartered in London.

In Asia Prudential has operations in more than 10 markets including China India Vietnam Hong Kong Philippines Indonesia Singapore Malaysia and Cambodia. Prudential also operates in approximately five countries in Africa.

Sales and Marketing

In the US Prudential distributes products primarily through advice-based distribution channels. With a diverse customer base Prudential's five largest customers account for less than 30% of its annual sales.

Financial Performance

Note: Growth rates may differ after conversion to US Dollars.

Total revenue for 2019 jumped 162% to $93.7 million on the strength of increase in investment returns.

Net income fell 80% to $792 million due in large part to $1.2 billion loss from discontinued operations and higher tax charges.

In 2019 Prudential's cash in hand was $7 billion. Operations investing and financing activities all used $209 million $324 million and $2.5 billion respectively.

Strategy

Prudential's strategy is to capture the long-term structural opportunities for its markets and geographies while operating with discipline and seeking to enhance capabilities through innovation to deliver high-quality resilient outcomes for its customers.

The company aims to do this by: Serving the protection and investment needs of the growing middle class in Asia; Offering products to new customers in Africa one of the fastest-growing regions in the world; and Providing asset accumulation and retirement income products to US retirees.

Structural growth over the last 20 years has allowed its business to reach the scale where it can support its long-term goals through execution of its strategy and disciplined capital allocation. Prudential plc has a portfolio of businesses with access to the world's largest and fastest-growing markets.

Mergers and Acquisitions

In late 2019 Eastspring Investments the Asian asset management business of Prudential successfully completed its acquisition of 50.1% of Thanachart Fund Management Co. Ltd. ("TFUND") from Thanachart Bank Public Company Limited ("TBANK") and Government Savings Bank1 with TBANK holding the remaining 49.9% stake of TFUND. The acquisition complements Eastspring's purchase of 65% of TMB Asset Management now TMBAM Eastspring in September 2018. With the latest transaction Eastspring becomes Thailand's fourth largest asset manager with a market share of 12% and combined assets under management of THB 653 billion (USD 21.6 billion) through the two fund management firms.

Also in 2019 Prudential completed its acquisition of a majority stake in Group Beneficial a leading life insurer operating in West and Central Africa. Group Beneficial provides savings and protection products to over 300000 customers through more than 40 branches and more than 2000 agents. The acquisition enhances Prudential's growing scale in Africa by entering into Cameroon C ´te d'Ivoire and Togo which have a combined population of over 65 million. This demonstrates Prudential's continued commitment to Africa following the launch of businesses in Ghana Kenya Uganda Zambia and Nigeria in the last five years. Prudential now operates in markets in Africa with a total population of almost 400 million.

Company Background

Knock knock. Who's there? It's the Man from the Pru — one of Prudential plc's famous army of door-to-door salesmen and financial advisors. Or at least that was the story for around 150 years before the Pru went all modern in 2001. With the acquisition of Jackson National it entered the US in 1986 and (re)entered life insurance in Asia at the turn of the millennium. In 2019 Prudential de-merged its UK and Europe business M&G Prudential to focus on the US and Asia.

EXECUTIVES

Group CEO, Mike Wells
Chief Executive M&G and Executive Director, Anne Richards
Chairman and CEO Prudential North America, Barry L. Stowe, age 63, $1,028,819 total compensation
Chief Executive Prudential Corporation Asia, Nic Nicandrou, age 54
Chief Executive Prudential UK and Europe and Executive Director, John Foley
CFO, Mark T. FitzPatrick, age 52
Group Chief Risk Officer and Executive Director, Penny James
Chairman, Paul Manduca, age 68
Auditors: KPMG LLP

LOCATIONS

HQ: Prudential Plc
13th Floor, One International Finance Centre, 1 Harbour View Street, Central,
Phone: (44) 22 7220 7588
Web: www.prudential.co.uk

2017 Sales

	% of total
US	39
UK and Europe	33
Asia	28
Other	-
Total	**100**

COMPETITORS

AEGON	Lincoln Financial
AIA Group	Group
AIG	Lloyds Banking Group
AXA	Manulife Financial
Allianz	MetLife
Aviva	Mitsui Sumitomo
BlackRock	Insurance
Canada Life	Nationwide Financial
Cathay Life Insurance	New York Life
China Life Insurance	Nippon Life Insurance
China Pacific	Ping An Insurance
Insurance	Prudential
Citigroup	RSA Insurance
FMR	Samsung Life Insurance
Great Eastern Holdings	Schroders
HSBC	Standard Life Aberdeen
ING	State Farm
Invesco Perpetual	TIAA
Jupiter Fund	The Hartford
Management	Tokio Marine
Legal & General Group	Zurich Insurance Group

HISTORICAL FINANCIALS

Company Type: Public

Income Statement

FYE: December 31

	ASSETS ($ mil.)	NET INCOME ($ mil.)	INCOME AS % OF ASSETS	EMPLOYEES
12/19	599,817	1,034	0.2%	24,676
12/18	649,418	3,843	0.6%	28,206
12/17	667,161	3,226	0.5%	22,912
12/16	578,778	2,363	0.4%	22,498
12/15	573,490	3,821	0.7%	21,820
Annual Growth	1.1%	(27.9%)	—	3.1%

2019 Year-End Financials

Return on assets: 0.1%
Return on equity: 4.2%
Long-term debt ($ mil.): —
No. of shares (mil.): —
Sales ($ mil): 124,308

Dividends
Yield: 16.9%
Payout: 16.5%
Market value ($ mil.): —

	STOCK PRICE ($) FY Close	P/E High/Low		PER SHARE ($) Earnings	Dividends	Book Value
12/19	38.09	2	1	40.01	6.47	9.89
12/18	35.37	43	29	1.49	1.28	8.49
12/17	50.78	56	45	1.26	1.27	8.40
12/16	39.79	54	36	0.92	1.23	6.99
12/15	45.08	52	39	1.50	1.18	7.46
Annual Growth	(4.1%)	—	—	127.4%	53.0%	7.3%

Prysmian SpA

In the energy and telecom sectors Prysmian's got connections. The Milan-based company makes sub-marine and underground power cables needed to transmit high-voltage electricity and high-speed broadband. Prysmian operates through two main divisions: Energy Cables & Systems produces industrial cables needed for cars trains and underground mining while its Telecom Cables & Systems division makes optical fiber and copper cables for video data and voice transmission. The company sells its products worldwide to such customers as Verizon Siemens and Orange. Prysmian has over 50 plants in 21 countries subsidiaries in 38 countries and seven R&D centers in Europe and North and South America.

EXECUTIVES

CEO, Valerio Battista, age 64
CFO, Pier F. Facchini, age 57
Chief Strategy Officer, Fabio Romeo, age 65
Chairman, Massimo Tononi, age 56
Auditors: EY S.p.A.

LOCATIONS

HQ: Prysmian SpA
Via Chiese 6, Milan 20126
Phone: (39) 02 6449 1
Web: www.prysmiangroup.com

2016 Sales

	% of total
Europe Middle East & Africa:	
Italy	18
Other EMEA	49
North America	14
Asia/Pacific	13
Latin America	6
Total	**100**

PRODUCTS/OPERATIONS

2016 sales

	% of total
Energy Products:	
E& I	40
Industries & NWC	18
Others	1
Oil & Gas	4
Energy projects	22
Telecom	15
Total	**100**

Selected Products & Solutions:

POWER GRIDS
HV&Submarine Transmission
Distribution
Offshore Wind Farms
Power From Shore
Asset Monitoring Systems
OIL & GAS
Exploration & Production
Pipelines & LNG
Refineries & Petrochemical
Services
TELECOMS
Optical Fibre
Telecom Networks
Multimedia & Enterprise Networks
CONSTRUCTION & INFRASTRUCTURE
Power & Control
Multimedia
Railways
TRANSPORTATION & MOBILITY
Elevator
Aerospace
Automotive
Trains & Trams
Marine
INDUSTRIES
Military & Defense
Mining
Crane
Nuclear Plants
Solar & Photovoltaics
Wind Turbines
Other Plants

COMPETITORS

Alcatel-Lucent	Nexans
General Cable	Sumitomo Electric

HISTORICAL FINANCIALS

Company Type: Public

Income Statement

FYE: December 31

	REVENUE ($ mil.)	NET INCOME ($ mil.)	NET PROFIT MARGIN	EMPLOYEES
12/19	13,022	327	2.5%	28,714
12/18	11,694	148	1.3%	29,159
12/17	9,636	272	2.8%	21,050
12/16	8,018	259	3.2%	20,493
12/15	8,083	233	2.9%	19,316
Annual Growth	12.7%	8.9%	—	10.4%

2019 Year-End Financials

Debt ratio: 33.2%
Return on equity: 12.5%
Cash ($ mil.): 1,201
Current ratio: 1.22
Long-term debt ($ mil.): 3,252

No. of shares (mil.): 263
Dividends
Yield: 4.0%
Payout: 12.4%
Market value ($ mil.): 3,227

	STOCK PRICE ($) FY Close	P/E High/Low		PER SHARE ($) Earnings	Dividends	Book Value
12/19	12.26	11	8	1.25	0.49	10.30
12/18	9.75	32	16	0.61	0.50	9.83
12/17	16.44	17	13	1.26	0.17	8.45
12/16	13.03	11	8	1.15	0.14	7.14
12/15	10.75	11	8	1.09	0.15	6.50
Annual Growth	3.3%	—	—	3.4%	35.1%	12.2%

PT Bank Negara (Indonesia)

Auditors: Purwantono, Sungkoro & Surja

LOCATIONS

HQ: PT Bank Negara (Indonesia)
Gedung BNI, Jl. Jend. Sudirman Kav. 1, PO Box 1946,
Jakarta 10220
Phone: (62) 21 251 1946   **Fax:** (62) 21 251 1214
Web: www.bni.co.id

HISTORICAL FINANCIALS

Company Type: Public

Income Statement   FYE: December 31

	ASSETS ($ mil.)	NET INCOME ($ mil.)	INCOME AS % OF ASSETS	EMPLOYEES
12/19	60,993	1,109	1.8%	27,211
12/18	56,203	1,043	1.9%	27,224
12/17	52,334	1,004	1.9%	27,803
12/16	44,865	843	1.9%	28,390
12/15	36,837	656	1.8%	0
Annual Growth	13.4%	14.0%	—	—

2019 Year-End Financials

Return on assets: 1.8%
Return on equity: 13.6%
Long-term debt ($ mil.): —
No. of shares (mil.): —
Sales ($ mil): 5,324
Dividends
Yield: —
Payout: —
Market value ($ mil.): —

PT Global Chemical Public Co Ltd

Auditors: Deloitte Touche Tohmatsu Jaiyos Audit Co., Ltd.

LOCATIONS

HQ: PTT Global Chemical Public Co Ltd
555/1 Energy Complex, Building A, 14th - 18th Floor,
Vibhavadi Rangsit Road, Chatuchak, Bangkok 10900
Phone: (66) 2 265 8400   **Fax:** (66) 2 265 8500
Web: www.pttgcgroup.com

HISTORICAL FINANCIALS

Company Type: Public

Income Statement   FYE: December 31

	REVENUE ($ mil.)	NET INCOME ($ mil.)	NET PROFIT MARGIN	EMPLOYEES
12/19	13,858	392	2.8%	0
12/18	16,032	1,238	7.7%	6,427
12/17	13,503	1,279	9.5%	6,334
12/16	9,752	715	7.3%	0
12/15	11,197	571	5.1%	0
Annual Growth	5.5%	(9.0%)	—	—

2019 Year-End Financials

Debt ratio: 0.8%
Return on equity: 4.0%
Cash ($ mil.): 632
Current ratio: 1.97
Long-term debt ($ mil.): 3,253
No. of shares (mil.): —
Dividends
Yield: 0.0%
Payout: —
Market value ($ mil.): —

	STOCK PRICE ($) FY Close	P/E High/Low		PER SHARE ($) Earnings	Dividends	Book Value
12/19	9.04	4	3	0.09	0.51	2.14
12/18	9.39	2	1	0.27	0.57	2.03
12/17	12.61	1	1	0.27	0.48	1.87
12/16	8.33	1	1	0.16	0.30	1.54
12/15	6.32	2	1	0.13	0.30	1.44
Annual Growth	9.4%	—	—	(8.9%)	14.2%	10.4%

PTT Public Co Ltd

PTT is a fully integrated national petroleum and petrochemical company that operates through investment in subsidiaries joint ventures and associates (PTT Group) which are engaged in upstream and downstream petroleum coal electricity business and infrastructure business. Its PTT Oil Business operates over 1300 gas stations. PTT Gas Business covers supplying natural gas to both domestic and international industrial factories and petroleum service stations. PTT has a total refining capacity of about 355000 barrels per day or more than 25% of refining capacity in Thailand. PTT also has Petroleum Exploration and Production that focuses on exploration of natural gas condensate and crude oil. (in Thailand and elsewhere). They also produce petrochemicals and mine coal. PTT also undertakes full-function of international trading activities such as procurement import and export. The company is majority-owned by the Government of Thailand.

Operations

PTT's core businesses are Exploration & Production and Gas and Oil.

PTT invest in petroleum exploration and production business through subsidiary company such as PTT Exploration and Production Public Company Limited or PTTEP which provides exploration and production of petroleum such as natural gas condensate and crude oil in Thailand and other countries such as Vietnam Indonesia Myanmar Canada Australia Algeria Mozambique Kenya Oman and Brazil.

The Gas Business Group engages in natural gas supply procurement pipeline transmission separation distribution and natural gas-related value-added businesses through PTT subsidiaries.

The Oil Business Group operates oil distribution business covering petroleum products (fuel oil and LPG) lubricants and retail business (7-Eleven Jiffy and Café Amazon) in Thailand and overseas.

The International Trading Business Group covers procurement import-export and international trade in several products including: crude oil condensate LPG petroleum and petrochemical products chemical solvents crude palm oil refined palm oil palm kernel shells and other commodities.

On the investment side PTT invests in a wide range of its related businesses with an emphasis on petrochemical and oil refining businesses.

Geographic Reach

PTT's headquarter and main operation is located in Thailand. PTTEP also invested in nearly 40 projects in more than 10 countries around the globe including Canada Brazil Algeria Kenya Mozambique Oman and Australia.

Sales and Marketing

PTT engages in integrated natural gas business including natural gas supply procurement wholesale and distribution and natural gas-related value-added businesses through PTT subsidiaries. The natural gas is supplied by indigenous sources those imported from neighboring countries and LNG (Liquefied Natural Gas).

PTT's distribution pipeline system totals about 500 kilometers branching off from the transmission pipeline system to various industrial customers which today number more than 400.

PTT's gas transmission system consists of the onshore and the offshore systems combining for a total distance of approximately 4300 km connecting the Gulf gas fields LNG terminal and transmission pipelines from the Yadana Yetagun and Zawtika fields of Myanmar at the border with power generators GSPs and industrial customers.

Financial Performance

Note: Growth rates may differ after conversion to US Dollars.

PTT Group recorded revenue of THB 2.2 trillion in 2019 decreasing by THB 116.4 billion or 5% from 2018 mainly from Petrochemical and Refining businesses International Trading business and Oil business according to declined Petroleum and Petrochemical selling prices according to lower crude oil prices.

PTT Group reported net income of THB 93 billion in 2019 decreasing by THB 26696 million or 22% from 2018 driven by the decrease in operating income and increase in their selling general and administrative expenses.

PTT's cash in 2019 is THB 292.5 billion. It generated THB 265.1 billion from its operations while investing activities used THB 188.2 billion and its financing activities THB 70.2 billion mainly for the long-term loans.

Strategy

The company's goal for growth follow the 3D strategies that includes its "Do now Decide Now and Design Now" which focuses on energy security natural gas supply continual infrastructural construction and extension of past work for multiplication of successes. For "Do now" strategy PTT strives to enhance corporate caliber by raising business efficiency lowering production costs by applying innovations including a tool to predict potential equipment and machinery damage that leverages Big Data forecasting to plan preventive maintenance and the application of Artificial Intelligence (AI) & Robotics including drones and robots to survey gas transmission pipelines and inspect operation of assorted equipment.

PTT strives to apply innovation and technology to the corporation for long-term competitiveness by introducing Robotic Process Automation (RPA) to shorten the time for repetitive work such as the procurement process to bank transfer payment; related party transaction inspection process; a bank payment inspection process; and a process to issue invoices to gas customers _ which also encourage auditability to all procedures. Also the Chatbot has been harnessed in business support for key procedures including hiring and procurement.

For long-term growth PTT Group has recently driven investment including that in the petroleum exploration and production business by PTTEP Plc. and acquired the entire businesses of Murphy Oil Corporation in Malaysia as well as Partex Holding B.V. Another instance is investment growth in the power sector where Global Power Synergy Plc. (GPSC) acquired the business of Glow Energy Plc. Yet another PTT Oil and Retail Plc. (OR) has expanded retails in several countries specifically Café

Amazon coffee shops in new countries such as Singapore Malaysia and China.

Company Background

Thailand which created PTT to secure energy supplies during the oil crunch of the late 1970s sold a third of the company in a 2001 IPO.

In 2008 as part of PTT's energy diversification drive the company opened the world's largest NGV (natural gas vehicle) gas station in Thailand to respond to the growing number of NGV vehicles in the country.

EXECUTIVES

CFO, Wirat Uanarumit

President and CEO, Tevin Vongvanich, age 62

COO Infrastructure, Surong Bulakul, age 65

COO Upstream Petroleum and Gas, Nuttachat Charuchinda

COO Downstream Petroleum, Sarun Rungkasiri

SEVP Petrochemicals and Refining, Sarakorn Kulatham

SEVP Human Resources and Organization Excellence, Pitipan Tepartimargorn

SEVP Corporate Strategy, Chansin Treenuchagron

SEVP Gas, Charcrie Buranakanonda

SEVP Oil, Chavalit Punthong

SEVP International Trading, Boobpha Amornkiatkajorn

SEVP Sustainability Management and Project Engineering, Auttapol Rerkpibook

Chairman, Piyasvasti Amranand

Auditors: The State Audit Office of the Kingdom of Thailand

LOCATIONS

HQ: PTT Public Co Ltd
555 Vibhavadi-Rangsit Road, Chatuchak, Bangkok 10900
Phone: (66) 2 537 2000   **Fax:** (66) 2 537 3498 9
Web: www.pttplc.com

PRODUCTS/OPERATIONS

2011 Sales

	% of total
International trading	53
Oil	21
Natural gas	16
Exploration & production	6
Petrochemical	3
Coal	1
Other	-
Total	**100**

Selected Subsidiaries and Affiliates:

PetroAsia (Huizhou) Co. Ltd. (25%)
PTT Exploration and Production Public Co. Ltd. (66%)
PTT Mart Co. Ltd. (49%)
PTT Natural Gas Distribution Co. Ltd. (58%)
Star Petroleum Refining Co. Ltd. (36%)
Thai Lube Blending Co. Ltd. (49%)
Thai Oil Plc. (50%)

COMPETITORS

BP   Chevron

HISTORICAL FINANCIALS

Company Type: Public

Income Statement   FYE: December 31

	REVENUE ($ mil.)	NET INCOME ($ mil.)	NET PROFIT MARGIN	EMPLOYEES
12/19	74,518	3,120	4.2%	0
12/18	72,215	3,699	5.1%	0
12/17	61,259	4,149	6.8%	0
12/16	48,019	2,643	5.5%	0
12/15	56,256	553	1.0%	0
Annual Growth	**7.3%**	**54.1%**	**—**	

2019 Year-End Financials

Debt ratio: 0.8%
Return on equity: 10.6%
Cash ($ mil.): 9,820
Current ratio: 1.89
Long-term debt ($ mil.): 18,891

No. of shares (mil.): —
Dividends
  Yield: 0.0%
  Payout: —
Market value ($ mil.): —

	STOCK PRICE ($) FY Close	P/E High/Low		Earnings	PER SHARE ($) Dividends	Book Value
12/19	6.85	3	2	0.11	0.28	1.03
12/18	7.17	2	2	0.13	0.17	0.95
12/17	19.25	—		0.14	0.25	0.88
12/16	19.25	6	6	0.09	0.12	0.75
12/15	13.20	21	20	0.02	0.07	0.68
Annual Growth	**(15.1%)**	**—**	**—**	**54.9%**	**40.0%**	**11.1%**

Public Bank Berhad (Malaysia)

Auditors: Ernst & Young PLT

LOCATIONS

HQ: Public Bank Berhad (Malaysia)
Menara Public Bank, 146 Jalan Ampang, Kuala Lumpur 50450
Phone: (60) 3 2176 6000   **Fax:** (60) 3 2163 9917
Web: www.publicbankgroup.com

COMPETITORS

AmBank Group	Hong Leong Bank
Bank Muamalat	Lloyds Banking Group
Bank Pembangunan	Maybank
CIMB Group	RHB Capital
HSBC	

HISTORICAL FINANCIALS

Company Type: Public

Income Statement   FYE: December 31

	ASSETS ($ mil.)	NET INCOME ($ mil.)	INCOME AS % OF ASSETS	EMPLOYEES
12/19	105,797	1,347	1.3%	19,260
12/18	101,544	1,352	1.3%	18,721
12/17	97,377	1,347	1.4%	18,553
12/16	84,719	1,160	1.4%	18,651
12/15	84,496	1,175	1.4%	18,373
Annual Growth	**5.8%**	**3.5%**	**—**	**1.2%**

2019 Year-End Financials

Return on assets: 1.2%
Return on equity: 13.0%
Long-term debt ($ mil.): —
No. of shares (mil.): —
Sales ($ mil): 5,073

Dividends
  Yield: —
  Payout: 51.4%
Market value ($ mil.): —

Publicis Groupe S.A.

Publicis is one of the world's largest advertising and media firms. The European holding company provides a range of marketing services through four operating segments: Publicis Communications Publicis Sapient Publicis Media and Publicis Health. Well-known agency brands include Leo Burnett Digitas BBH Fallon and Saatchi & Saatchi. Its Starcom and Zenith units are among the world's largest media planning enterprises. The firm serves clients in over 100 countries. Marcel Bleustein-Blanchet founded Publicis in 1926 and named it after the French word for advertising combined with the French word for six his favorite number. North America generates majority of the company's sales.

Operations

Publicis is organized into four segments. Its Publicis Communications segment is the creative communications hub and includes Leo Burnett and Saatchi & Saatchi among several other creative agencies. Publicis Sapient is the company's digital and technology arm. Publicis Media operates media planning and buying services through agencies such as Zenith Digitas and Starcom. It creates value for clients through global media agency brands and scaled capabilities across investment strategy insights and analytics data and technology commerce performance marketing and content. Publicis Health's mission is to be the indispensable force for health and wellness business transformation through the alchemy of creativity and technology.

Geographic Reach

Publicis is headquartered in Paris and has operations in more than 100 countries. North America accounts for the largest share of the company's revenue at around 55% of total followed by Europe (more than 25%) Asia/Pacific (some 10%) and Latin America and Middle East/Africa (less than 5% each).

Sales and Marketing

Publicis serves clients in financial sector (brings in more than 15% of total sales) which is the largest among the sectors; automotive and TMT sectors (each account for about 15% of sales) non-food consumer products and food and beverages (both generates more than 10%) healthcare (some 10%) and leisure/ energy/ luxury and retail with nearly 10% each

Financial Performance

The company grew its revenue by 10% to Â 11 billion in 2019.

Net income attributable to the Groupe in 2019 totaled Â 841 million a 9% decrease from Â 919 million in 2018.

The company's cash at the end of 2019 was Â 3.4 million. Operating activities generated Â 2.3 million while investing activities used Â 4.3 million mainly for acquisitions. Financing activities generated another Â 2.1 million.

Strategy

In early 2019 Publicis Groupe and Alliance Data Systems have decided to forge a strategic partnership. This acquisition accelerates the implementation of Publicis Groupe's strategy of becoming the preferred partner of its customers in their transformation. The closing which took place on July 1 2019 was announced on July 2. At the end of 2019 the integration was largely completed. Epsilon was positioned as the Groupe core expertise in building enriching and activating first party data to irrigate all activities. Epsilon's advertising activities were folded into Leo Burnett while CJ Affiliate has been placed under strategic review to explore different ways to unlock value.

Additionally In January 2019 Publicis Groupe announced the definitive signing of the sale of Publicis Health Solutions (PHS)to Altamont Capital Partners (Altamont). PHS which belonged to the Publicis Health solution pole is an organization of medical and marketing representatives for pharmaceutical biotechnology medical device and diagnostic companies. Its brands including Touchpoint PDI Tardis Medical PHrequency and CustomPoint Recruiting offers a full range of services to customers.

Mergers and Acquisitions

In the third quarter of 2019 Publicis announced its acquisition of California-based Rauxa an independent full-service marketing agency. Rauxa has become part of Publicis Media the media solution hub of Publicis Groupe. Financial terms were not disclosed.

In addition Publicis acquired data-driven marketing firm Epsilon from Alliance Data Systems for about $4 billion. Epsilon creates personalized marketing campaigns using information its clients collect about its own customers so that companies can target ads more effectively. The business generates about $1.9 billion in revenue annually and Publicis is placing Epsilon at the center of its agency network. It made the purchase to gain a competitive advantage over direct rivals such as WPP and IPG as well as the smaller consulting firms that are encroaching on its territory.

The company acquired Proximedia group in 2019 for an undisclosed terms. Present in France Belgium Holland and Spain Proximedia provides digital services to VSEs SMEs traders and artisans for their presence on the Web and their promotion. The company also acquired over 80% of capital of Soft Computing French leader in Data Marketing at a price of 25 euros per share i.e. a total amount of approximately 43.4 million euros. The acquisition was carried out with the founding shareholders and their families and follows the lifting of all the suspensory conditions relating to the agreements signed in 2018.

Company Background

In 1926 Marcel Bleustein then 19 years old started France's first advertising agency which he called Publicis (a takeoff on "publicity" and "six"). The company has spent the subsequent decades expanding globally through partnerships and acquisitions.

A major purchase was Saatchi & Saatchi which it acquired in 2000 for about $1.9 billion. Along with the deal the company inherited Saatchi's 50% of media buying unit Zenith Media (jointly owned by Cordiant Communications). In 2001 it merged Optimedia and Zenith with Publicis owning 75% of the new business.

HISTORY

In 1926 Marcel Bleustein then 19 years old started France's first advertising agency which he called Publicis (a takeoff on "publicity" and "six"). He launched his own radio station Radio Cite after the French government banned all advertising on state-run stations and by 1939 he had expanded into film distribution and movie theaters. With the outbreak of WWII Bleustein fled to London to serve with the Free French Forces.

Having adopted the name Bleustein-Blanchet he returned to France following the liberation and revived his advertising business. In 1958 he bought the former Hotel Astoria on the Champs-Elys es and opened the first Le Drugstore. The original structure burned in a 1972 fire and legend has it that Bleustein-Blanchet tapped Maurice L vy to lead the company after he found L vy salvaging records amid the ruins.

To expand its business Publicis formed an alliance — Chicago-based Foote Cone & Belding

Communications (FCB) — in 1988. The partnership soured five years later however when Publicis acquired France's Groupe FCA. (FCB claimed the acquisition was a breach of contract and countered by establishing a new holding company for itself True North Communications.) Bleustein-Blanchet died in 1996 and his daughter Elisabeth Badinter was named chair of the supervisory board.

In 1997 Publicis and True North divided their joint network Publicis Communications with True North getting the European offices and Publicis getting Africa Asia and Argentina. Later that year Publicis attempted a $700 million hostile bid for the 81.5% of True North it didn't already own to stop True North's acquisition of Bozell Jacobs Kenyon & Eckhardt. The bid failed and Publicis' stake in True North was reduced to 11%. (True North was later acquired by Interpublic Group in 2001.)

The company gained new ground in the US through its acquisitions of Hal Riney & Partners and Evans Group in 1998. That year L vy helped soothe a bitter feud among the descendants of Marcel Bleustein: Elisabeth Badinter had battled with her sister Michele Bleustein-Blanchet over Bleustein-Blanchet's desire to sell her stake in Publicis' holding company. L vy's solution allowed Bleustein-Blanchet to sell her shares and left Badinter with control of the company.

Continuing its US expansion in 1999 Publicis bought a 49% stake in Burrell Communications Group (one of the largest African-American-owned ad agencies in the US).

In 2000 the company bought advertising outfit Fallon McElligott (now Fallon Worldwide) marketing firm Frankel & Co. and media buyer DeWitt Media (which was merged into Optimedia). Publicis capped off the year by acquiring Saatchi & Saatchi for about $1.9 billion. Along with the deal it inherited Saatchi's 50% of media buying unit Zenith Media (jointly owned by Cordiant Communications). In 2001 it merged Optimedia and Zenith with Publicis owning 75% of the new business.

2002 was a big year for Publicis and the ad industry in general; the decision to acquire Bcom3 catapulted the company into the really big leagues and created a distinct size difference between the top four advertising conglomerates and everyone else.

From 2002 to 2005 the company worked on integrating Bcom3 and Saatchi & Saatchi into its operational infrastructure as well as making small but selective acquisitions in order to maximize debt reduction.

In 2007 Publicis substantially beefed up its digital offerings when it bought US-based Digitas for $1.3 billion. A few months later Publicis acquired Business Interactif an interactive marketing agency based in France. The acquisition bolstered its French Digitas operations.

About that same time Publicis also snatched up Communication Central Group (CCG) one of the largest interactive marketing agencies in China. CCG was later rebranded as Digitas Greater China. In late 2008 Publicis acquired the search marketing business of DoubleClick's Performics operations. The deal gave Publicis 130 additional clients and 200 specialists in the Internet search marketing arena. Also in 2008 Leo Burnett's Asia/Pacific network got a boost when Publicis acquired W&K Communications an agency specializing in advertising promotion television production and media buying services and owning a presence in Beijing and Guangzhou China. W&K was later renamed Leo Burnett W&K Beijing Advertising Co.

EXECUTIVES

Chairman Publicis.Sapient, Alan J. Herrick, age 54

EVP and CFO, Jean-Michel Etienne, age 66
Chairman and CEO Leo Burnett Worldwide, Thomas (Tom) Bernardin
CEO Publicis Media, Steve King
CEO Publicis New York and Co-CSO Publicis Communications, Carla Serrano
Global Chairwoman and Global Chief Creative Officer Saatchi & Saatchi, Kate Stanners
CEO Leo Burnett Canada and Chief Creative Officer Leo Burnett North America, Judy John
CEO, Arthur Sadoun, age 50
CEO Publicis Communications GroupAustralia and New Zealand (ANZ) and Chairman and CEO Saatchi & Saatchi ANZ, Michael Rebelo
Managing Director Melbourne Australia, Melinda Geertz
Global CEO MSLGROUP, Guillaume Herbette
President Publicis Groupe France, Agathe Bousquet
CEO Publicis Communications North America, Andrew Bruce
Chairman Leo Burnett North America, Rich Stoddart
CEO Publicis Worldwide and Chairman Publicis Communications, Andrew Baxter
CEO Satchi & Saatchi Fallon London and Global President Saatchi & Saatchi, Magnus Djaba
CEO Publicis Conseil and Global President Publicis Worldwide, Valérie Henaff
CEO Publicis London and Global Co-lead Sapient Inside, Guy Wieynk
Vice Chairman, Sophie Dulac, age 63
Chairman, Maurice Lévy, age 77
Vice Chairman, Elisabeth Badinter, age 76
Auditors: ERNST & YOUNG et Autres

LOCATIONS

HQ: Publicis Groupe S.A.
133, avenue des Champs-Elysees, Paris 75008
Phone: (33) 1 44 43 77 88
Web: www.publicisgroupe.com

2016 Sales

	% of total
North America	54
Europe	28
Asia Pacific	11
Latin America	4
Middle East Africa	3
Total	**100**

COMPETITORS

Dentsu	Interpublic Group
Dentsu Aegis	Omnicom
Hakuhodo	WPP
Havas	

HISTORICAL FINANCIALS

Company Type: Public

Income Statement				FYE: December 31
	REVENUE ($ mil.)	NET INCOME ($ mil.)	NET PROFIT MARGIN	EMPLOYEES
12/19	17,311	1,323	7.6%	83,235
12/18	15,658	1,446	9.2%	75,588
12/17	15,248	1,356	8.9%	77,767
12/16	15,315	(829)	—	78,913
12/15	15,108	1,417	9.4%	77,574
Annual Growth	3.5%	(1.7%)	—	1.8%

2019 Year-End Financials

Debt ratio: 28.3%	No. of shares (mil.): 236
Return on equity: 11.8%	Dividends
Cash ($ mil.): 5,370	Yield: 5.2%
Current ratio: 0.88	Payout: 10.6%
Long-term debt ($ mil.): 6,744	Market value ($ mil.): 2,682

	STOCK PRICE ($) FY Close	P/E High/Low		PER SHARE ($) Earnings	Dividends	Book Value
12/19	11.32	4	3	5.59	0.59	49.15
12/18	14.16	5	3	6.17	0.59	46.63
12/17	16.99	5	4	5.89	0.52	41.42
12/16	17.20	—	—	(3.71)	0.35	42.28
12/15	16.73	5	4	6.28	0.33	46.61
Annual Growth	(9.3%)	—	—	(2.9%)	15.5%	1.3%

Qatar Islamic Bank

EXECUTIVES

Director & Chairman, Jassim bin Hamad Jassim bin Jabor Al- Thani
Auditors: KPMG

LOCATIONS

HQ: Qatar Islamic Bank
Grand Hamad Ave., P.O. Box 559, Doha
Phone: (974) 4409409 **Fax:** (974) 4412700
Web: www.qib.com.qa

HISTORICAL FINANCIALS
Company Type: Public

Income Statement   FYE: December 31

	ASSETS ($ mil.)	NET INCOME ($ mil.)	INCOME AS % OF ASSETS	EMPLOYEES
12/20	47,900	842	1.8%	0
12/19	44,938	839	1.9%	0
12/18	42,111	757	1.8%	0
12/17	41,326	661	1.6%	0
12/16	38,429	592	1.5%	0
Annual Growth	5.7%	9.2%	—	—

2020 Year-End Financials

Return on assets: 1.8%	Dividends
Return on equity: 2.5%	Yield: —
Long-term debt ($ mil.): —	Payout: 33.0%
No. of shares (mil.): —	Market value ($ mil.): —
Sales ($ mil) 1,666	

Qatar National Bank

Auditors: Global Balasubramaniam

LOCATIONS

HQ: Qatar National Bank
P.O. Box 1000, Doha
Phone: (974) 44425 444 **Fax:** (974) 4441 3753
Web: www.qnb.com.qa

HISTORICAL FINANCIALS
Company Type: Public

Income Statement   FYE: December 31

	ASSETS ($ mil.)	NET INCOME ($ mil.)	INCOME AS % OF ASSETS	EMPLOYEES
12/20	281,597	3,297	1.2%	0
12/19	259,621	3,943	1.5%	0
12/18	236,949	3,789	1.6%	0
12/17	222,900	3,607	1.6%	0
12/16	197,786	3,398	1.7%	0
Annual Growth	9.2%	(0.7%)	—	—

2020 Year-End Financials

Return on assets: 1.2%	Dividends
Return on equity: 12.6%	Yield: —
Long-term debt ($ mil.): —	Payout: 37.8%
No. of shares (mil.): —	Market value ($ mil.): —
Sales ($ mil): 13,526	

QBE Insurance Group Ltd.

QBE Insurance Group may be one of Australia's leading insurers but it also has a hefty global reach. The company offers a variety of insurance and reinsurance products through offices in about 30 countries. QBE provides general property/casualty policies as well as liability auto marine accident and health insurance workers' compensation and cybersecurity coverage. The company writes both individual and commercial insurance policies and also administers reinsurance coverage.

Operations

QBE operates through five primary divisions: North American Operations European Operations Australian & New Zealand Operations Asia Pacific Operations and Equator Re.

The largest division North American Operations generates more than 30% of revenue and offers commercial and individual property/casualty specialty and crop insurance. It also operates QBE Re part of its global reinsurance business.

The next-largest division is its European Operations (nearly 30% of revenue). It offers a similar portfolio of products; its largest lines of business include commercial and domestic property liability motor and motor casualty and marine energy (for oil and gas companies) and aviation coverage.

Next the Australian & New Zealand Operations division (about 25%) gets most of its premium income from its commercial and domestic property and motor and motor casualty businesses. Asia Pacific operations represents about 5% of sales and offers a range of property/casualty insurance products.

Equator Re (based in Bermuda) is QBE's captive reinsurance vehicle and accounts for about 10% of revenue.

For the 2019 fiscal year the group's entities in Asia will be combined with its European Operations to form a new International segment. Its Pacific entities will be combined with the Australian & New Zealand Operations segment to form a new Australia Pacific segment. Equator Re will no longer be a separate operating segment.

Geographic Reach

QBE is headquartered in Sydney Australia. It operates in nearly 30 countries in the Asia/Pacific region the Americas and Europe.

Sales and Marketing

QBE makes use of a distributed network of insurance agents and brokers for the sales and marketing of its insurance products. The company also markets and distributes insurance directly by phone and through the internet.

Financial Performance

After several years of decline QBE's revenue is finally showing signs of recovery however sales are down 35% since its peak performance in 2012.

Sales in 2018 reached $17.8 billion a 10% increase compared with $16.2 billion in 2017. The company saw growth in all its segments with improved underwriting and an increase in both gross written and net earned premiums.

Net income has been up and down. After plummeting to a $1.2 billion loss in 2017 the company returned to the black the following year. In 2018 QBE posted a profit of $567 million. The record loss in 2017 is largely attributed to several natural disasters globally such as catastrophic floods wildfires and earthquakes.

Cash at the end of fiscal 2018 was $863 million an increase of $291 million from the prior year. Cash from operations used $443 million primarily due to claims paid while investing activities provided $1.7 billion from the sale of interest-bearing financial assets. Financing activities used $915 million for loan payments dividends to stockholders and the company's stock repurchase program.

Strategy

QBE has been working to recover from a spate of troubling years with restructuring initiatives by divesting certain operations and remediating underperforming units. Going forward the company has a number of strategic initiatives in place in each of its segments to drive growth. QBE has been using more data analytics to improve its pricing and underwriting structure and is simplifying its operations by combining geographic segments.

In North American Operations QBE exited its underperforming retail personal lines business (Farmers Union) which will allow for sunsetting legacy systems and reducing its office footprint. Conversely it is strengthening the Crop business with improved data analytics for risk selection and commodity pricing. In its property and casualty and specialty programs businesses QBE in North America is using data to improve pricing structures and refine underwriting guidelines.

European Operations has established a fully-operational insurance and reinsurance company in Belgium in response to the instability around Brexit. It is leveraging its own team of data scientists to develop pricing and risk selection tools. With the goal of simplifying its operations in 2019 the group's Asia operations were incorporated with European Operations to form a new International division.

In the Australian & New Zealand Operations segment the group has implemented claims initiatives such as using data science and improved supply chain and vendor management to improve its claims ratio. In addition operations in the Pacific Islands and India have combined with Australia and New Zealand to form the Australia Pacific division.

Company Background

QBE was formed in 1973 with the merger of Australia's Queensland Insurance Bankers' and Traders' Insurance and Equitable Probate and General Insurance.

Queensland Insurance was founded in 1886 and by 1890 operated more than 36 agencies in London Hong Kong Singapore New Zealand and the Pacific Islands. In 1904 it opened its own offices in London and New York. Bankers' and Traders' started operations in 1921.

QBE is now one of the top 20 global insurance companies.

EXECUTIVES

CEO European Operations, Richard Pryce
CEO, John Neal, age 56
Group CEO, Patrick C. (Pat) Regan
CEO North American Operations, Russell (Russ) Johnston
CEO Emerging Markets, David Fried
Chief Risk Officer, Jason Brown
CFO, Michael Ford
Chairman, W. Marston (Marty) Becker
Deputy Chairman, John M. Green
Auditors: PricewaterhouseCoopers

LOCATIONS

HQ: QBE Insurance Group Ltd.
Level 27, 8 Chifley Square, Sydney, New South Wales 2000
Phone: (61) 2 9375 4444   **Fax:** (61) 2 9231 6104
Web: www.qbe.com

COMPETITORS

AEGON	GEICO
AIG	ING
AXA	Insurance Australia
Allianz	Nationwide
Allstate	RSA Insurance
Australia and New	Swiss Re
Zealand Banking	Travelers Companies
Aviva	UnitedHealth Group

HISTORICAL FINANCIALS

Company Type: Public

Income Statement   FYE: December 31

	ASSETS ($ mil.)	NET INCOME ($ mil.)	INCOME AS % OF ASSETS	EMPLOYEES
12/19	40,035	550	1.4%	11,704
12/18	39,582	390	1.0%	0
12/17	43,862	(1,249)	—	14,140
12/16	41,583	844	2.0%	14,226
12/15	42,176	687	1.6%	0
Annual Growth	(1.3%)	(5.4%)	—	—

2019 Year-End Financials

Return on assets: 1.3%	Dividends
Return on equity: 6.6%	Yield: 3.8%
Long-term debt ($ mil.): —	Payout: 84.1%
No. of shares (mil.): 1,305	Market value ($ mil.): 11,862
Sales ($ mil): 11,999	

	STOCK PRICE ($) FY Close	P/E High/Low	PER SHARE ($) Earnings	Dividends	Book Value
12/19	9.09	22 17	0.42	0.35	6.25
12/18	7.02	31 23	0.29	0.18	6.32
12/17	8.35	— —	(0.92)	0.40	6.52
12/16	8.96	15 11	0.61	0.37	7.51
12/15	9.10	23 16	0.50	0.29	7.67
Annual Growth	(0.0%)	— —	(4.5%)	4.6%	(5.0%)

Randstad NV

Randstad Holding has the supply to meet nearly any demand. The company is one of the largest temporary staffing and employment services agencies in the world (behind AEX). It operates primarily in Europe but also in Asia and North America under the Randstad brand and several others including Monster (US) Ausy GULP Twago Spherion Yacht (industrial staffing) and Tempo-Team (general staffing). Through nearly 4900 locations in some 30 countries Randstad supplies temporary workers for small assignments as well as large-scale deployments. It also offers permanent placement and HR project management and consultancy services. Randstad Holding was established in 1960.

Operations

Randstad's operations are divided across four business segments: staffing professionals in-house services and global businesses.

The largest segment bringing in more than half of all revenue is the staffing business. It targets blue- and white-collar job candidates seeking temporary or permanent placements as well as offering payrolling training and specialties.

The in-house services segment which brings in more than 20% of sales targets clients in the manufacturing and logistics industries.

The professionals segment also around 20% of sales recruits supervisors managers professionals specialists and consultants in a wide range of industries.

Global businesses which brings in around 5% of revenue provides range of services such as online talent acquisition managed services programs recruitment process outsourcing and outplacement.

Randstad makes more than 260700 permanent placements annually.

Geographic Reach

Randstad has nearly 4900 locations in around 30 nations. Its largest single market is North America which accounts for about 20% of total sales. France and Netherlands account for about 15% of sales each. Germany brings in nearly 10%.

Sales and Marketing

Randstad serves clients from multi-national blue-chip firms and government agencies to consulting firms and small- to midsized companies.

The company will connect with people beyond search selection staffing and recruitment. Through their smart solutions and online platforms they aim to be present at all stages in people's careers consistently improving their employability and providing training opportunities where this is appropriate. In today's fast changing world new technologies tools and solutions are redefining the way they interact with people. They combine this with the most important they have to offer: their human touch.

Marketing costs were 0.8% of revenue (2018: 0.8%).

Financial Performance

Note: Growth rates may differ after conversion to US Dollars.

Randstad's revenue and net income have been steadily climbing from 2015 to 2018 however slightly fell in 2019.

In 2019 revenue fell of some 1% to ?23.7 billion. Despite the increase to other three segments staffing segment decrease to about 5% compared from prior year.

With the decrease to revenue net income also fell at some 15% to ?606 million in 2019 from ?708 million in 2018.

The company ended 2019 with a cash of ?225 million a nearly 20% decrease compared to ?273 million at the end of 2018. Operating activities provided ?1.3 billion in net cash while investing activities used ?137 million. Financing activities used another ?1.2 billion primarily from reimbursement to financiers and dividend on ordinary and preference shares.

Strategy

The world of work is changing rapidly. At Randstad they combine the power of today's digital technology with their distinctive human approach supporting people and organizations in realizing their true potential. They aim to be the trusted advisor for talent in all steps of their working lives and the trusted HR partner for their clients in all their talent needs creating long-term value for all their stakeholders. Their strategy centers around three pillars that reinforce each other: digital operational excellence and accelerating growth.

The company strategy also consists of four building blocks: strong concepts best people excellent execution and superior brands. These are their responses to the external growth drivers and market trends in their industry. However these building blocks only work in unison. Strong concepts are of little value without the right people to make them work. Excellent execution is impossible without the right concepts and the best people. And once these blocks come together you can create the fourth building block: superior brands. Their strategic building blocks enable them to not only serve the interests of their stakeholders but to create lasting value for all of them - their clients their employees their candidates and society at large.

Mergers and Acquisitions

In 2019 the Group acquired 100% of the shares of the Aurec Group (Australia). In addition it acquired 100% of the shares of Optedis Sas (France) of which the Group already held 5% of the shares. These two acquisitions resulted in goodwill to the amount of - 13 million.

Company Background

Frits Goldschmeding founded Randstad Holding as Uitzendbureau Amstelveen near Amsterdam in 1960. Originally part of a student project the company turned a small profit its first year and was renamed Randstad Uitzendbureau in 1964. ("The Randstad" is the densely populated area including Amsterdam Rotterdam and the Hague.)

By 1970 Randstad had 32 branches in four countries including Germany and the UK. The company was recast as Randstad Holding in 1978. In 1985 Randstad celebrated its silver anniversary with 250 branches.

The company went public in 1990 listing its shares on the Amsterdam Stock Exchange. That year it moved its headquarters to the Amsterdam suburb of Diemen.

In 1993 Randstad entered the US market. By 1997 the company had more than 1000 branches in Europe and North America.

EXECUTIVES

CFO and Vice Chairman Executive Board, Robert-Jan van de Kraats, age 60, $809,758 total compensation
CEO and Chairman of the Executive Board, Jacques van den Broek, age 60, $712,300 total compensation
President Randstad North America, Linda Galipeau, age 57
Managing Director Randstad Netherlands, Chris Heutink, age 58
Group President Randstad US, Traci L. Fiatte
President and CEO Randstad Group France, Fran §ois Béharel, age 50
CEO Randstad Canada, Marc- tienne Julien
Chairman, Wout Dekker, age 64
Vice Chairman, Jaap Winter
Auditors: Deloitte Accountants B.V.

LOCATIONS

HQ: Randstad NV
Diemermere 25, Diemen 1112 TC
Phone: (31) 20 569 59 11   **Fax:** (31) 20 569 55 20
Web: www.randstad.com

2017 Sales

	% of total
Europe	
France	16
Netherlands	14
Germany	10
Italy	7
Belgium & Luxembourg	7
Iberia	6
Other	9
North America	18
Rest of world	8
Global businesses	5
Total	**100**

PRODUCTS/OPERATIONS

2017 Sales by Segment

	% of total
Staffing	53
In-house services	22
Professionals	20
Global businesses	5
Total	**100**

COMPETITORS

Adecco	Robert Half
Allegis Group	Technical Aid
CDI	Corporation
Kelly Services	Volt Information
ManpowerGroup	

HISTORICAL FINANCIALS

Company Type: Public

Income Statement — FYE: December 31

	REVENUE ($ mil.)	NET INCOME ($ mil.)	NET PROFIT MARGIN	EMPLOYEES
12/19	26,582	666	2.5%	687,280
12/18	27,269	791	2.9%	709,720
12/17	27,898	741	2.7%	706,730
12/16	21,839	607	2.8%	658,580
12/15	20,933	551	2.6%	627,150
Annual Growth	**6.2%**	**4.9%**	**—**	**2.3%**

2019 Year-End Financials

Debt ratio: 13.1%
Return on equity: 13.2%
Cash ($ mil.): 252
Current ratio: 1.01
Long-term debt ($ mil.): —

No. of shares (mil.): 182
Dividends
  Yield: 4.9%
  Payout: 41.8%
Market value ($ mil.): 5,547

	STOCK PRICE ($) FY Close	P/E High/Low		Earnings	PER SHARE ($) Dividends	Book Value
12/19	30.32	10	6	3.63	1.50	27.45
12/18	22.90	9	6	4.32	1.33	28.01
12/17	30.60	10	9	4.03	0.90	27.87
12/16	27.03	10	6	3.30	0.70	23.96
12/15	31.09	13	7	3.01	0.57	23.10
Annual Growth	**(0.6%)**	—	—	**4.8%**	**27.6%**	**4.4%**

RCI Banque S.A.

EXECUTIVES

Directeur General, Gianluca de Ficchy
Directeur des Territoires, Dominique Signora
Secretaire General et Directeur de la Gestion des Risques, Patrick Claude
Directeur Comptabilite et Contole de la Performance, Alice Altemaire

Directeur des Systemes d'Information, Umberto Marini
Directeur Commercial, Daniel Rebbi
Directeur Financements et Tresorerie, Jean-Marc Saugier
Directeur Clients et Operations, Jean-Philippe Vallee

LOCATIONS

HQ: RCI Banque S.A.
  15 rue d'Uzes, Paris 75002
Phone: (33) 1 49 32 80 00
Web: www.rcibs.com

PRODUCTS/OPERATIONS

2016 Sales

	% of total
Interest and similar income	63
Income of other activities	36
Fees and commission income	1
Total	**100**

COMPETITORS

BNP Paribas Personal Finance	Ford Motor Credit
Capital One Auto Finance	M&S Money
	Peugeot
Daimler Financial Services	Toyota Financial Services
	Volkswagen Bank

HISTORICAL FINANCIALS

Company Type: Public

Income Statement — FYE: December 31

	ASSETS ($ mil.)	NET INCOME ($ mil.)	INCOME AS % OF ASSETS	EMPLOYEES
12/19	65,210	1,013	1.6%	3,700
12/18	61,146	982	1.6%	3,481
12/16	45,740	635	1.4%	3,054
12/15	40,380	587	1.5%	2,913
12/14	38,919	511	1.3%	2,850
Annual Growth	**10.9%**	**14.7%**	**—**	**5.4%**

2019 Year-End Financials

Return on assets: 1.6%
Return on equity: 16.5%
Long-term debt ($ mil.): —
No. of shares (mil.): 1
Sales ($ mil): 4,345

Dividends
  Yield: —
  Payout: 22.1%
Market value ($ mil.): —

Reckitt Benckiser Group Plc

Auditors: KPMG LLP

LOCATIONS

HQ: Reckitt Benckiser Group Plc
  103 105 Bath Road, Slough, Berkshire SL1 3UH
Phone: (44) 1753 217800
Web: www.rb.com

HISTORICAL FINANCIALS

Company Type: Public

Income Statement — FYE: December 31

	REVENUE ($ mil.)	NET INCOME ($ mil.)	NET PROFIT MARGIN	EMPLOYEES
12/19	25,671	(7,360)	—	42,400
12/18	25,173	4,318	17.2%	42,400
12/17	23,005	12,334	53.6%	40,400
12/16	19,766	3,661	18.5%	34,700
12/15	17,733	3,483	19.6%	34,700
Annual Growth	**9.7%**	**—**	**—**	**5.1%**

2019 Year-End Financials

Debt ratio: 74.2%
Return on equity: (-30.5%)
Cash ($ mil.): 3,095
Current ratio: 0.56
Long-term debt ($ mil.): 16,570

No. of shares (mil.): 709
Dividends
  Yield: 2.4%
  Payout: —
Market value ($ mil.): 11,753

	STOCK PRICE ($) FY Close	P/E High/Low		Earnings	PER SHARE ($) Dividends	Book Value
12/19	16.56	—	—	(10.39)	0.41	26.36
12/18	15.13	7	5	6.09	0.42	41.64
12/17	19.01	2	2	17.34	0.40	38.43
12/16	16.80	8	6	5.13	0.39	22.85
12/15	18.74	8	6	4.81	0.37	18.73
Annual Growth	**(3.0%)**	—	—	**—**	**2.6%**	**8.9%**

Recruit Holdings Co Ltd

Auditors: Ernst & Young ShinNihon LLC

LOCATIONS

HQ: Recruit Holdings Co Ltd
  1-9-2 Marunouchi, Chiyoda-ku, Tokyo 100-6640
Phone: (81) 3 6835 1111
Web: www.recruit.co.jp

HISTORICAL FINANCIALS

Company Type: Public

Income Statement — FYE: March 31

	REVENUE ($ mil.)	NET INCOME ($ mil.)	NET PROFIT MARGIN	EMPLOYEES
03/20	22,104	1,657	7.5%	51,900
03/19	20,865	1,573	7.5%	48,305
03/18	20,467	1,428	7.0%	42,483
03/17	16,456	764	4.6%	47,966
03/16	14,146	574	4.1%	39,785
Annual Growth	**11.8%**	**30.3%**	**—**	**6.9%**

2020 Year-End Financials

Debt ratio: 0.0%
Return on equity: 18.3%
Cash ($ mil.): 3,880
Current ratio: 1.62
Long-term debt ($ mil.): 1,033

No. of shares (mil.): 1,649
Dividends
  Yield: 1.0%
  Payout: 5.4%
Market value ($ mil.): 8,514

	STOCK PRICE ($) FY Close	P/E High/Low		Earnings	PER SHARE ($) Dividends	Book Value
03/20	5.16	0	0	1.00	0.05	5.52
03/19	5.70	0	0	0.94	0.05	5.22
Annual Growth	**(9.5%)**	—	—	**1.4%**	**4.3%**	**1.4%**

Reliance Industries Ltd

Auditors: DTS & Associates

LOCATIONS

HQ: Reliance Industries Ltd
3rd Floor, Maker Chambers IV, 222, Nariman Point,
Mumbai 400 021
Phone: (91) 22 3555 50000   **Fax:** (91) 22 2204 2268
Web: www.ril.com

HISTORICAL FINANCIALS

Company Type: Public

Income Statement   FYE: March 31

	REVENUE ($ mil.)	NET INCOME ($ mil.)	NET PROFIT MARGIN	EMPLOYEES
03/19	85,216	5,721	6.7%	28,967
03/18	64,280	5,544	8.6%	29,533
03/17	52,369	4,610	8.8%	24,167
03/16	43,064	4,178	9.7%	24,121
03/15	61,404	3,767	6.1%	24,930
Annual Growth	8.5%	11.0%	—	3.8%

2019 Year-End Financials

Debt ratio: 0.3%	No. of shares (mil.): —
Return on equity: 11.6%	Dividends
Cash ($ mil.): 1,085	Yield: —
Current ratio: 0.72	Payout: 16.9%
Long-term debt ($ mil.): 29,988	Market value ($ mil.): —

Renault S.A. (France)

Auditors: Ernst & Young Audit

LOCATIONS

HQ: Renault S.A. (France)
13-15, quai Le Gallo, Boulogne-Billancourt, Cedex
92513
Phone: (33) 1 76 84 04 04
Web: www.groupe.renault.com

HISTORICAL FINANCIALS

Company Type: Public

Income Statement   FYE: December 31

	REVENUE ($ mil.)	NET INCOME ($ mil.)	NET PROFIT MARGIN	EMPLOYEES
12/19	62,355	(158)	—	179,565
12/18	65,755	3,781	5.8%	183,002
12/17	70,450	6,130	8.7%	181,344
12/16	54,106	3,610	6.7%	124,849
12/15	49,370	3,074	6.2%	120,136
Annual Growth	6.0%	—	—	10.6%

2019 Year-End Financials

Debt ratio: 52.5%	No. of shares (mil.): 291
Return on equity: (-0.4%)	Dividends
Cash ($ mil.): 16,821	Yield: 8.4%
Current ratio: 1.02	Payout: —
Long-term debt ($ mil.): 7,831	Market value ($ mil.): 2,743

	STOCK PRICE ($) FY Close	P/E High/Low		PER SHARE ($) Earnings	Dividends	Book Value
12/19	9.42	—	—	(0.58)	0.80	133.28
12/18	12.30	2	1	13.89	0.83	140.05
12/17	20.13	1	1	22.39	0.76	137.35
12/16	17.83	2	1	13.16	0.50	111.52
12/15	20.16	2	1	11.21	0.43	104.36
Annual Growth	(17.3%)	—	—	—	16.8%	6.3%

Repsol S.A.

Operating in some 35 countries Repsol is one the leading oil and gas companies of the world operating both upstream and downstream sectors. It provides refining transport of crude oil marketing and transport of natural gas and liquefied natural gas (LNG) as well as a range of petroleum derivative products sold to more than 90 countries from Italy to Peru. Gas makes up 65% of Repsol's upstream portfolio that is focused in North America Latin America and Southeast Asia regions. It has proven reserves of over 2 billion BOE. Based in Spain Repsol generates around half its sales in its home country.

Operations

Repsol has upstream (discovery and mining) and downstream (processing and distribution) oil and gas operations.

Downstream is its biggest business accounting for around 90% of sales. It engages in oil refining markets oil products and liquefied petroleum gas (LPG) and produces and markets petrochemical products. It also produces and markets lubricants asphalts and specialized products and carries out low emission power generation trades electricity and gas and develops renewable energy projects.

Repsol upstream's division is engaged in oil and natural gas exploration and production in the key regions of Latin America and North Africa. Strategic areas for short and medium-term growth include the US Gulf of Mexico and offshore fields in Brazil. The company has a capacity of about 715000 barrels per day with net proved reserves of about 2.4 billion BOE (roughly three-quarters being gas).

The company's LNG activities include the liquefaction transportation marketing and regasification of liquefied natural gas. It also carries out natural gas marketing in North America and electricity generation in Spain at the Bah a de Bizkaia Electricidad plant.

Geographic Reach

Repsol's upstream activities focus on Latin America (mainly Trinidad and Tobago Peru Venezuela Bolivia Colombia and Ecuador) and North Africa (Algeria and Libya). Strategic areas for short and medium-term growth include the US Gulf of Mexico and offshore fields in Brazil.

Sales and Marketing

Repsol serves a diverse client base ranging from large companies organizations and institutions to small and medium size companies and individual customers. Industries include energy construction agriculture marine and aviation.

Its products include fuels lubricants and specialized products liquefied petroleum gas (LPG) and other chemical.

The company sells fuel at some 4850 owned and licensed service stations located across Spain Portugal Peru Italy and Mexico. Through third par-

ties it sells derived products such as asphalts sulfurs oils paraffins and aviation fuels.

Financial Performance

Note: Growth rates may differ after conversion to US Dollars.

Repsol's revenue is tied closely to the oil price. In fiscal 2018 its revenue was flat at ?47 billion as a rise in oil prices balanced out the divestment of the 20% stake in Naturgy Energy Group and the associated lost revenue.

Net income grew 10% to ?2.3 billion as a strong rise in upstream earnings was partially offset by lower downstream earnings. Gains in the upstream business arose from higher oil prices and higher volumes sold particularly in Libya Trinidad & Tobago and the UK. Downstream was impacted by weakness in the international chemicals business.

Repsol's coffers grew slightly in 2018 ending the year ?185 million higher at ?4.8 billion. The company's operations generated ?4.6 billion while investing activities used ?14 billion and financing activities used ?3.0 billion.

Strategy

Despite a challenging oil market Repsol has maintained profitability and continues to be at the forefront of exploration and production activity with an impressively global span. However after averaging some $2 billion in CAPEX each year in the recent past as per the company's 2020 strategy Repsol will divest non-strategic assets and reduce investment levels going forward. The company also wants to free up cash to further reduce debt which the company has significantly lowered in the last 3 years.

Repsol recognizes the growing viability of renewable energy and will invest ?2.5 billion in developing its low emissions business in 2018-20. It acquired the Viesgo's low emission electricity production business in 2018 bringing nearly 3000MW of installed capacity serving 750000 customers. However Repsol remains committed to oil and gas investing a whopping ?12.5 billion in increasing oil and gas production in the same period. Continued falls in the cost of renewable energy particularly solar could reduce Repsol's return on investment.

In 2018 the company established a joint venture with Gazprom Neft that acquired a 100% interest in ASB Geo LLC which holds the exploration license for the Karabashsky 10 block. The partners will begin geological prospecting works using 2D seismic in 2019 marking a step further from its previously concluded Memorandum of Cooperation in investigating license blocks adjacent to Evrotek-Yugra assets.

Downstream the company has spent ?4 billion in upgrading refineries and products which has now made Repsol one of the highest integrated companies in the European market. At the same time it has sought to expand its market. For instance in 2017 Repsol entered the Mexican fuel market with an aim of capturing some 10% of the market by building 1200 service stations in the next 5 years. Including acquisitions it had nearly 200 station in Mexico at the end of 2018. It has also expanded in Peru bringing its fuel station total to more than 500.

In 2018 it entered into a 20-year one-million tons per anum deal to buy LNG from Venture Global LNG on a free on board (FOB) basis in Louisiana. It has also continuously launched new products like Neotech a new generation fuel to improve engine performance.

Mergers and Acquisitions

In late 2018 Repsol acquired Puma Energy's Peru filling station business adding 23 stations to Repsol's Peru portfolio.

Repsol acquired Valdesolar Hive in September 2018 for nearly $344 million. Valdesolar is a special purpose company that owns a 264 MW solar power project in Valdecaballeros in southern Spain. An ongoing solar facility project will construct a 400 KV transmission line costing more than $190 million.

Repsol acquired the unregulated low-emissions power generation operations including hydropower assets of fellow Spanish energy company Viesgo for EUR 750 million in June 2018. The transaction covers assets with a combined capacity of 2350 MW as well as almost 750000 retail customers. This will expand Repol's own installed capacity to 2950 MW. This helps Repsol reach its target 2.5 million retail natural gas and electricity customers in Spain by 2025.

In January 2018 Repsol acquired a 70% stake in Klikin a start-up that helps companies handle bookings payments and promotions digitally. The acquisition boosted Repsol's payment channel Waylet ending 2018 with more than 1 million registered users and 2400 linked shops.

EXECUTIVES

CFO, Miguel Mart nez San Mart n
Executive Managing Director Exploration and Production, Luis Cabra Dueñas, age 63
CEO; Executive Director; Member Executive Committee, Josu Jon Imaz San Miguel, age 56
Executive Managing Director Downstream, Maria Victoria Zingoni
Chairman, Antonio Brufau Niubo
First Vice Chairman, Gonzalo Gort zar Rotaeche
Second Vice Chairman, Manuel Manrique Cecilia
Auditors: PricewaterhouseCoopers Auditores, S.L.

LOCATIONS

HQ: Repsol S.A.
 Calle Mendez Alvaro 44, Madrid 28045
Phone: (34) 91 75 38 100   **Fax:** (34) 902 303 145
Web: www.repsol.com

2018 sales

	% of total
Spain	51
US	6
Peru	6
Portugal	5
Other	32
Total	**100**

PRODUCTS/OPERATIONS

2018 Sales

	% of total
Downstream	90
Upstream	10
Total	**100**

COMPETITORS

Anadarko Petroleum	Norsk Hydro ASA
BHP Billiton	Occidental Petroleum
BP	PEMEX
Devon Energy	PETROBRAS
Endesa S.A.	Petrobras Argentina
Eni	Petr leos de
Exxon Mobil	Venezuela
IBERDROLA	Pioneer Natural
Imperial Oil	Resources
Koch Industries Inc.	RasGas
Marathon Oil	Royal Dutch Shell
Murphy Oil	TOTAL
Noble Energy	

HISTORICAL FINANCIALS

Company Type: Public

Income Statement

	REVENUE ($ mil.)	NET INCOME ($ mil.)	NET PROFIT MARGIN	FYE: December 31 EMPLOYEES
12/19	55,396	(8,568)	—	24,634
12/18	57,263	2,680	4.7%	24,506
12/17	50,196	2,542	5.1%	24,226
12/16	36,763	1,833	5.0%	24,535
12/15	42,711	(1,336)	—	27,111
Annual Growth	**6.7%**	**—**		**(2.4%)**

2019 Year-End Financials

Debt ratio: 33.9%
Return on equity: (-27.4%)
Cash ($ mil.): 3,344
Current ratio: 1.09
Long-term debt ($ mil.): 12,284
No. of shares (mil.): 1,527
Dividends
 Yield: 5.2%
 Payout: —
Market value ($ mil.): 23,950

	STOCK PRICE ($) FY Close	P/E High/Low	PER SHARE ($) Earnings	Dividends	Book Value
12/19	15.68	— —	(2.78)	0.82	18.32
12/18	16.03	14 11	1.66	0.83	22.96
12/17	17.72	14 12	1.62	0.80	23.38
12/16	14.10	12 7	1.22	0.54	22.24
12/15	11.13	— —	(0.95)	0.92	22.14
Annual Growth	**8.9%**	**— —**	**—**	**(2.8%)**	**(4.6%)**

Resona Holdings Inc Osaka

Resona Holdings resonate in Japan's retail banking market. It's the holding company of Resona Bank and smaller regional banks Kinki Osaka Bank and Saitama Resona Bank which operate nearly 1450 branches across Japan mainly in the greater Tokyo area and the Kansai region. While it focuses on consumer and small business banking services Resona Bank also provides corporate pension management and real estate services corporate and personal trust services personal loans asset management and estate planning services. Altogether Resona Holdings boasts over Å 45 trillion ($375 billion) in total assets and Å 24 trillion ($20 billion) in trust assets.

Operations

Resona Holdings operates three core business segments: Consumer Banking which provides consumer loans asset management and asset succession services; Corporate Banking which provides corporate loans trust asset management real estate services corporate pension management and asset succession services; and Market Trading which provides short-term lending borrowing bond purchase and sale and derivatives trading in financial markets.

About 54% of its total revenue came from interest income in fiscal 2015 (ended March 31) while 23% came from non-trust fees and commissions and 3% came from trust fees. About 85% of its total loans and bills discounted were loans to small and medium-sized enterprises (SMEs). More than 60% of its deposits were from individuals.

Geographic Reach

Tokyo-based Resona Holdings has more than 1440 branches across Japan including more than 820 in the Kanto region and 579 in the Kansai region. Its Kinki Osaka Bank subsidiary has 128 manned branches mainly in the Kinki region. About 40% of its branches are manned while the majority are unmanned.

Financial Performance

Note: Growth rates may differ after conversion to US dollars.

Resona Holdings' revenues and profits have trended lower over the past several years mostly due to shrinking interest margins on loans amidst the low-interest environment.

The company had a breakout year in fiscal 2015 (ended March 31) however as its revenue rose by 4% to Å 861.4 billion ($7.2 billion) on higher fee and commission income from sales of its investment trust and insurance products. Its interest income continued to slide downward due to low interest margins.

Despite generating higher revenue in FY2015 the group's net income fell by 4% to Å 211.4 billion ($1.77 billion) mostly due to higher income taxes and a Å 23 billion charge related to the reversal of deferred tax assets in line with the reduction of the effective corporate tax rate. Resona's operating cash levels fell in half to Å 1103 billion ($9 billion) for the year mostly as it extended more of its cash toward loans and bills discounted.

Strategy

Resona Holdings in early 2015 launched its "New Mid-term Management Plan" for the next decade which set its sights on becoming the "No. 1 Retail Bank" through more proactive measures toward continued growth. Continuing to focus on its retail banking business and lending to SMEs the bank planned to "maximize customer value by maintaining its fundamental stance that 'Customers' joy and happiness are Resona's.'

The company also in 2015 outlined its three "ACL" initiatives which included: "All Resona" which aimed to offer collaboration of companies and services to provide SME customers with management consulting and other services as they grew; "Cross-selling promotion" which aimed to cross sell life insurance to the group's mortgage customers which numbered 560000 borrowers and grew by 40000 new borrowers annually; and "Low-cost operations" which rely on productivity-boosting initiatives such as installed communication terminals that allow tellers to serve customers more securely and efficiently.

Resona Holdings has significant market strength in its key markets in the greater Tokyo metro area and the Kansai region (the most populated and economically active parts of Japan). During 2015 it held 40% of the deposit market in the Saitama and Osaka Prefectures and nearly 20% of the loan market in the region as well.

EXECUTIVES

President and Representative Executive Officer, Kazuhiro Higashi, age 63
President Saitama Resona Bank, Masahito Kamijo
Representative Executive Officer, Toshiki Hara
Representative Executive Officer, Tetsuya Kan
President The Kinki Osaka Bank, Koji Nakamae
Auditors: Deloitte Touche Tohmatsu LLC

LOCATIONS

HQ: Resona Holdings Inc Osaka
 1-5-65 Kiba, Koto-ku, Tokyo 135-8582
Phone: (81) 3 6704 3111
Web: www.resona-gr.co.jp

PRODUCTS/OPERATIONS

2014 Sales

	% of total
Interest income	57
Fees and commissions	23
Other operating income	4
Trust fees	3
Other	13
Total	**100**

Selected Subsidiaries
Daiwa Guarantee Co. Ltd. (credit guarantee)
Resona Bank Ltd. (bank)
Resona Guarantee Co. Ltd. (credit guarantee)
Saitama Resona Bank Ltd. (bank)
Kinki Osaka Shinyo Hosho Co. Ltd. (credit guarantee)
The Kinki Osaka Bank Ltd. (bank)
P.T. Bank Resona Perdania (bank)
Resona Kessai Service Co. Ltd. (collections agency)
Resona Card Co. Ltd. (credit cards)
Resona Capital Co. Ltd. (private equity)
Resona Research Institute Co. Ltd. (consulting)
Resona Business Service Co. Ltd. (staffing)

COMPETITORS

Aozora Bank	Mitsubishi UFJ
Bank of Yokohama	Financial Group
Chiba Bank	Mizuho Financial
Chugoku Bank	Nishi-Nippon
Fukuoka Financial	Shinsei Bank
Group	Shizuoka Bank
Gunma Bank	Sumitomo Mitsui
Hachijuni Bank	Sumitomo Mitsui Trust
Hokuhoku Financial	Holdings
Group	Yamaguchi Financial
Iyo Bank	Group
Juroku Bank	

HISTORICAL FINANCIALS
Company Type: Public

Income Statement				FYE: March 31
	ASSETS ($ mil.)	NET INCOME ($ mil.)	INCOME AS % OF ASSETS	EMPLOYEES
03/20	557,460	1,404	0.3%	31,425
03/19	533,754	1,581	0.3%	32,924
03/18	473,163	2,224	0.5%	27,082
03/17	433,392	1,444	0.3%	27,704
03/16	437,469	1,637	0.4%	28,096
Annual Growth	6.2%	(3.8%)	—	2.8%

2020 Year-End Financials
Return on assets: 0.2%
Return on equity: 7.2%
Long-term debt ($ mil.): —
No. of shares (mil.): —
Sales ($ mil): 8,179

Dividends
  Yield: —
  Payout: 31.6%
Market value ($ mil.): —

Rexel S.A.

France-based Rexel distributes electrical parts and supplies that include wiring devices cabling systems lighting products electrical tools and climate control and security equipment. The company serves customers in the commercial sector (its largest market); industrial markets such as mining oil and gas and energy; and the residential market including new construction and upgrade projects. Subsidiaries include Conectis (voice and networking products) as well as North American units Rexel USA and Rexel Canada Electrical. The company has about 2000 branches and logistics centers in more than 25 countries around the world. It generates about 55% of its sales in Europe and about 35% in North America.

Financial Performance
Note: Growth rates may differ after conversion to US Dollars.

Rexel's revenue has inched up by single digits during the past five years with only a 4% increase since 2014.

Sales in 2018 reached ?13.4 billion about even with 2017. Currency translation negatively impacted sales particularly from the depreciation of the US dollar against the euro.

Rexel posted net income of ?151 million in 2018 a 43% jump from 2017 mainly due to losses in 2017 from the disposal of its Southeast Asia operations.

Cash at the end of fiscal 2018 was ?544.9 million a decrease of ?31.1 million from the prior year. Cash from operations contributed ?284.7 million to the coffers while investing activities used ?95.5 million mainly for acquisitions. Financing activities used another ?158.2 million primarily for dividends to stockholders.

Strategy
Rexel's strategic plan includes transitioning to a data-driven services company and using a more service-oriented customer approach. It also plans to add more SKUs to its product line and increase its customer base as well as its number of suppliers. The company is making investments in digital technologies to improve back-office functions such as invoicing credit and payment processes and human resources administration.

With a focus on its customers the company is working to segment its products and services by proximity (strengthened geographic presence and multi-channel distribution) projects (specific products for industrial or commercial customers) and specialty solutions (products and solutions for customers with specific needs).

Rexel's digital transformation includes using data analytics to improve efficiency. It is using customer experience data to improve service including a focus on personal data privacy issues. Another use case relates to a project to develop business intelligence around its suppliers allowing Rexel to provide vendors with information such as market position and digital conversion rate by product category.

Company Background
Rexel was founded in 1967 as Compagnie de Distribution de Matériel Electrique (CDME) and went public on the Paris bourse in 1983. It entered the US market in 1986. CDME was acquired by Pinault in 1990 and changed its name to Rexel in 1993. The company entered international markets in South America Asia Pacific and Eastern Europe in the late 1990s.

EXECUTIVES
CEO Rexel North America, Brian P. McNally
CEO, Patrick Berard, age 68
Deputy CEO and Group CFO, Catherine Guillouard, age 56
CEO Rexel France, Vincent Demange
President and CEO Platt Electric Supply and Rexel Commercial and Industrial, Jeff Baker
CEO Rexel Asia/Pacific, ric Gauthier
Chairman, Ian K. Meakins
Deputy Chairman, Fran çois Henrot
Auditors: KPMG Audit

LOCATIONS
HQ: Rexel S.A.
13 boulevard du Fort-de-Vaux, CS 60002, Paris, Cedex 17 75838
Phone: (33) 1 42 85 85 00   **Fax:** (33) 1 42 85 92 02
Web: www.rexel.com

2018 Sales

	% of total
Europe	55
North America	36
Asia/Pacific	9
Total	**100**

Rexel distributes electrical products in more than 30 countries around the world.

PRODUCTS/OPERATIONS

2018 Sales

	% of total
Commercial	45
Industrial	30
Residential	25
Total	**100**

Selected Solutions:
Smart Building
Lighting
Climate Control
Security
Datacom
Photovoltaics
Home Automation
Electric Vehicles
Industrial Solutions
Production Parts

COMPETITORS

Anixter International	Premier Farnell
Consolidated	Sonepar
Electrical	Steiner Electric
Electrocomponents	WESCO International
Graybar Electric	Wolseley

HISTORICAL FINANCIALS
Company Type: Public

Income Statement				FYE: December 31
	REVENUE ($ mil.)	NET INCOME ($ mil.)	NET PROFIT MARGIN	EMPLOYEES
12/19	15,429	229	1.5%	26,537
12/18	15,306	172	1.1%	27,015
12/17	15,955	126	0.8%	27,530
12/16	13,897	145	1.0%	27,550
12/15	14,745	18	0.1%	28,000
Annual Growth	1.1%	87.9%	—	(1.3%)

2019 Year-End Financials
Debt ratio: 35.5%
Return on equity: 4.8%
Cash ($ mil.): 577
Current ratio: 1.34
Long-term debt ($ mil.): 2,912

No. of shares (mil.): 302
Dividends
  Yield: —
  Payout: —
Market value ($ mil.): —

RHB Bank Berhad

Auditors: PricewaterhouseCoopers PLT

LOCATIONS
HQ: RHB Bank Berhad
Level 10, Tower One, RHB Centre, Jalan Tun Razak, Kuala Lumpur 50400
Phone: (60) 3 9287 8888   **Fax:** (60) 3 9281 9314
Web: www.rhbgroup.com

COMPETITORS

AmBank Group	Hang Seng Bank
Bank of China	Malaysian Industrial
Bank of East Asia	Development Finance
CIMB Group	Maybank

HISTORICAL FINANCIALS
Company Type: Public

Income Statement				FYE: December 31
	ASSETS ($ mil.)	NET INCOME ($ mil.)	INCOME AS % OF ASSETS	EMPLOYEES
12/19	62,963	606	1.0%	14,345
12/18	58,833	557	0.9%	14,425
12/17	56,713	480	0.8%	14,435
12/16	52,759	374	0.7%	14,790
12/15	53,593	351	0.7%	16,117
Annual Growth	4.1%	14.7%	—	(2.9%)

2019 Year-End Financials

Return on assets: 0.9%	Dividends
Return on equity: 10.1%	Yield: —
Long-term debt ($ mil.): —	Payout: 50.0%
No. of shares (mil.): —	Market value ($ mil.): —
Sales ($ mil): 2,832	

Ricoh Co Ltd

Ricoh is one of the world's leading manufacturers of printers copiers and supplies as well as fax machines video and web conferencing systems scanners and interactive whiteboards. Other products from the company which operates in about 200 countries include digital cameras servers software semiconductors printed circuit boards and optical equipment. Primarily serving its customers office needs Ricoh also has products for the healthcare education finance and manufacturing industries. Most of Japan-based Ricoh's revenue comes from international customers.

Operations
Ricoh operates through five segments: Office Printing some 50% of revenue Office Services about 30% of revenue Commercial Printing about 10% of revenue Thermal Media less than 5% of revenue Industrial Printing about 5% of revenue and Other about 10% of revenue.

Office Printing offers multifunctional printers imaging machines and related services.

Office Services provides teleconferencing products as well asPCs network support and user support services.

The Commercial Printing segment sells equipment such as cut sheet PP (production printer) continuous book PP related consumables services support software etc.

The Thermal Media segment manufactures and sells thermal paper used in point-of-sale labels for food products barcode labels and delivery labels as well as thermal transfer ribbon used to print clothing price tags brand tags and tickets.

Industrial Printing makes and sells industrial inkjet heads inkjet ink industrial printers and other items for printing on a range of surfaces that include furniture wallpaper automobile exteriors and furnishing fabric.

The Other segment encompasses optical equipment electrical equipment units semiconductors digital cameras industrial cameras 3D printing environment healthcare etc.

Geographic Reach
Sales in Ricoh's home country Japan account for about 45% of the company's revenue followed by the Americas over 25% Europe the Middle East and Africa over 20% and other (China South East Asia and Oceania) about 10%.

Financial Performance
Note: Growth rates may differ after currency conversion.

The company's revenue has been fluctuating in the last five years with an overall decline of 9% between 2016 and 2020.

Consolidated sales for the year ended 2020 declined 0.2% to Â 2 trillion reflecting the impact of what was by the fourth quarter a global pandemic.

The company's profit for 2020 was Â 39.5 billion a 20% decrease compared to the previous year. This was primarily due to the lower sales volume for the year coupled with a higher cost of sales.

The company's cash for the year ended 2020 was Â 263.7 billion. Operating activities generated Â 116.7 billion while investing activities used Â 164.6 billion primarily for capital expenditures. Financing activities provided another Â 75.8 billion.

Strategy
The company formulated growth strategies #0 #1 and #2 to leverage the company's strengths under RICOH Ignite. Growth Strategy #0 entails expanding customer value in core Office Printing business and streamlining operations to become more profitable.

The company created Growth Strategy #1 and #2 to draw on advanced combinations of these technologies with the company's printing technology and its base of 1.4 million corporate customers worldwide and cultivate fields that can become new earnings sources.

EXECUTIVES
President and CEO, Zenji Miura, age 71
Corporate EVP, Shiro Sasaki, age 71
Corporate EVP, Yohzoh Matsuura, age 64
Corporate EVP, Yoshinori Yamashita, age 63
Corporate EVP, Nobuo Inaba
Corporate EVP, Kunihiko Satoh
Chairman and CEO Ricoh Germany, Niculae Cantuniar
Chairman, Shiro Kondo
Auditors: Deloitte Touche Tohmatsu LLC

LOCATIONS
HQ: Ricoh Co Ltd
1-3-6 Nakamagome, Ota-ku, Tokyo 143-8555
Phone: (81) 3 3777 8111
Web: www.ricoh.co.jp

2019 Sales
	% of total
Japan	39
The Americas	28
Europe Middle East Africa	23
Other	10
Total	**100**

PRODUCTS/OPERATIONS

2019 Sales
	% of total
Office Printing	55
Office Services	22
Commercial Printing	9
Industrial Printing	1
Thermal Media	3
Other	10
Total	**100**

Selected Products
Imaging and Solutions
  Imaging Solutions
  Diazo copiers
  Digital duplicators
  Digital monochrome and color copiers
  Fax machines
  Imaging supplies and consumables
  Wide-format copiers
  Printing systems (laser multifunction)
  Scanners
  Network System Solutions
  Document management software
  Networking and applications software
  Network systems
  Personal computers
  Servers
  Services and support
Industrial
  Electronic components
  Measuring equipment
  Optical equipment
  Semiconductor devices
  Thermal media
Other
  Digital cameras and other photographic equipment
  Financing and logistics services
  Optical disks

COMPETITORS
Brother Industries	Kyocera Document
CASIO COMPUTER	Solutions
Canon	Lexmark
Dell	NEC
Eastman Kodak	Océ
FUJIFILM	Oki Electric
Fuji Xerox	Olympus
HP	Sharp Corp.
Hitachi	Toshiba
Konica Minolta	Xerox

HISTORICAL FINANCIALS
Company Type: Public

Income Statement				FYE: March 31
	REVENUE ($ mil.)	NET INCOME ($ mil.)	NET PROFIT MARGIN	EMPLOYEES
03/20	18,503	364	2.0%	90,141
03/19	18,179	447	2.5%	92,663
03/18	19,431	(1,274)	—	97,878
03/17	18,146	31	0.2%	105,613
03/16	19,671	560	2.9%	109,361
Annual Growth	(1.5%)	(10.2%)	—	(4.7%)

2020 Year-End Financials
Debt ratio: 0.0%	No. of shares (mil.): 724
Return on equity: 4.2%	Dividends
Cash ($ mil.): 2,421	Yield: 3.5%
Current ratio: 1.36	Payout: 47.6%
Long-term debt ($ mil.): 1,180	Market value ($ mil.): 4,958

	STOCK PRICE ($) FY Close	P/E High/Low		PER SHARE ($) Earnings	Dividends	Book Value
03/20	6.84	0	0	0.50	0.24	11.70
03/19	10.30	0	0	0.62	0.16	11.62
03/18	9.64	—	—	(1.76)	0.19	11.82
03/17	8.17	2	2	0.04	0.36	12.86
03/16	10.50	0	0	0.77	0.31	13.24
Annual Growth	(10.2%)	—	—	(10.2%)	(5.9%)	(3.1%)

Rio Tinto Ltd

Rio Tinto is on the lookout for pay dirt. Rio Tinto Limited one of the world's largest mining operations (along with BHP Billiton and Vale) is the Australian half of dual-listed sister companies with Rio Tinto plc taking up residence in London. Although each company trades separately the two Rio Tintos operate as one business. Rio Tinto explores for a variety of commodities: bauxite coal copper diamonds gold iron ore minerals (borates and titanium dioxide) nickel and potash. Iron ore makes up about 44% of the group's sales. It also produces aluminum through its Rio Tinto Alcan unit. Most of its businesses are in Australia and North America but it is expanding its operations in China and Mongolia.

Strategy

By focusing on a strategy of developing large-scale long-term mining operations and businesses Rio Tinto has tried to weather commodity prices that have dipped and risen over several years. The mining industry is affected by both oversupply and rising costs in raw materials. Like its rivals the company continues to seek acquisitions that will grow shareholder value as it cuts costs and improves productivity.

Company Background

Rio Tinto began life as the Zinc Corporation in 1905 to recover zinc from the tailings of the silver and lead mines around Australia's mineral-rich Broken Hill area. The company expanded steadily extending its operations into a wide range of mining and metallurgical activities primarily in Australia. By 1914 it had changed its name to Consolidated Zinc Corporation. The company discovered the world's largest deposit of bauxite (1955) and formed Hamersley Holdings with Kaiser Steel (1962) to mine iron ore.

Rio Tinto plc (UK) began with mining operations in Spain in 1873. It sold most of its Spanish holdings in 1954 and branched out to Australia Africa and Canada. In 1962 Rio Tinto and Australia's Consolidated Zinc merged to form RTZ. The companies merged their Australian interests as a partially owned subsidiary CRA (from Conzinc Riotinto of Australia).

In 1968 RTZ bought U.S. Borax which was built on one of the earth's few massive boron deposits. (The use of boron in cleansers was widespread in the late 19th century.) A 1927 discovery in the Mojave Desert led to development of a large boron mine. Until its Turkish mine was nationalized RTZ controlled the world's boron supply. It sold U.S. Borax's consumer products operations in 1988.

RTZ opened a large copper mine at Bougainville in Papua New Guinea in 1969. Subsidiary CRA discovered diamonds in Western Australia's Argyle region three years later. CRA then opened Australia's largest thermal-coal development at Blair Athol in 1984.

RTZ bought Kennecott Corporation in 1989 and expanded its copper operations. Kennecott had been formed by Stephen Birch and named for Robert Kennicott (a typo altered the spelling of the company's name); it had begun mining at Bingham Canyon Utah in 1904. Kennicott had died in Alaska while trying to establish an intercontinental telegraph line. Backed by J.P. Morgan and the Guggenheims Birch also built a railroad to haul the ore. Kennecott merged its railroad and mine operations in 1915. Kennecott consolidated its hold on Chile's Braden copper mine (1925) and on the Utah Copper Company (1936) and other US mines. When copper prices slumped British Petroleum's Standard Oil of Ohio subsidiary bought Kennecott (1981). In 1989 RTZ purchased British Petroleum's US mineral operations including Kennecott.

By the 1990s RTZ and CRA (by then 49%-owned by RTZ) were increasingly competing for mining rights to recently opened areas of Asia and Latin America. RTZ sold the last of its nonmining holdings (building products group) in 1993. In 1995 RTZ brought CRA into its operations. Through Kennecott RTZ purchased US coal mine operators Nerco Cordero Mining Company and Colowyo Coal Company. Also in 1995 the company acquired 13% of Freeport-McMoRan Copper & Gold (sold in 2004).

The RTZ and CRA company names were changed to Rio Tinto plc and Rio Tinto Limited respectively in 1997. Rio Tinto bought a Wyoming coal mine from Kerr-McGee for about $400 million in 1998. The next year Rio Tinto bought 80% of Kestrel (coal Australia) increased its ownership of Blair Athol from 57% to 71% and increased its stake in Comalco (aluminum) to 72%.

In 2000 CEO Leon Davis retired; his position passed to energy group executive Leigh Clifford. In a move that sparked an outcry from union officials Davis accepted a position as non-executive deputy chairman (he retired from the board in 2005). Later that year Rio Tinto acquired both North Limited and Ashton Mining. The company also bought Comalco's outstanding shares and the Peabody Group's Australian subsidiaries.

Rio Tinto sold its Norzink Zink Smelter to Outokumpu in 2001. It also increased its holdings in Queensland Alumina Coal & Allied Industries and Palabora Mining and it began developing the Hail Creek Coal Project in Australia which is based on one of the largest coking coal deposits in the world. In 2003 Rio Tinto sold its 25% stake in Minera Alumbrera (Argentina) and Peak Gold Mine (Australia) to Wheaton River Minerals for around $210 million.

Rio Tinto had owned 14% of Lihir Gold but divested its stake in the company. Prior to that decision the company had controlled Lihir and its management. In late 2005 though Rio Tinto reliquished its management rights and decided to sell its entire stake in Lihir.

Tom Albanese succeeded Clifford in 2007.

In 2007 Rio Tinto swooped in and made a successful $38 billion offer to buy Alcan then the world's #3 aluminum producer. That came not long after Alcoa #2 in the world had offered $33 billion. The deal combined Rio Tinto's own aluminum operations with Alcan's to form the new world leader Rio Tinto Alcan based in Canada. Rio Tinto's operations were located in Australia New Zealand and Africa as well as in Italy and the UK. Alcan's geographic strengths were in North America throughout Europe and in the Asia/Pacific region.

After that acquisition Rio Tinto announced a major divestment program saying it wanted to sell off $15 billion worth of assets. In early 2008 it began that program selling stakes in two North American properties to Hecla Mining and Barrick Gold. The properties had been a part of Kennecott Minerals and netted Rio Tinto about $2.5 billion. Later that year the company spun off most of its North American coal operations into a company called Cloud Peak Energy which it spun off through a public offering in 2009 using the almost $750 million it received to help recoup expenses from the purchase of Alcan. A major step in the divestment plan was taken in early 2009 when the company sold its undeveloped potash assets and a Brazilian iron ore mine to Vale for about $1.5 billion.

The company's most significant deals though have been the ones that didn't happen. In 2008 BHP Billiton approached Rio Tinto with an offer to buy its Anglo-Australian rival at a price that valued the company at nearly $150 billion. Rio Tinto's Board rejected the notion but BHP Billiton kept up its pursuit. The combination would have created the world's largest minerals company and one of the largest companies of any sort in terms of market cap. Months later though at the end of a year mired by the global economic meltdown BHP Billiton announced that the deal no longer provided value to its shareholders and called it off.

In an effort to obstruct BHP Billiton's takeover bid for Rio Tinto in 2008 Alcoa and Aluminum Corporation of China (Chinalco) had acquired 14% of Rio Tinto for $14 billion. Early the next year

Chinalco stepped in with an offer to assist Rio Tinto out of a portion of its debt which was considerable. The complicated arrangement would have given Rio Tinto $19.5 billion through investments in aluminum copper and iron ore joint ventures as well as through convertible bonds. Chinalco's stake in Rio Tinto would have been raised to 19% and the Chinese company would have had the right to name two members to Rio Tinto's Board.

However the transaction — never popular with domestic investors — fell through by mid-2009. Rio Tinto instead went with a rights issue hoping to raise $15 billion and an agreed-upon joint venture with BHP Billiton that would have combined the two companies' iron ore projects in Western Australia. However that deal fell through also after German authorities ruled in 2010 that it was anticompetitive.

In late 2010 Rio Tinto made a $3.5 billion tender offer for Australian coal producer Riversdale Mining Ltd. but ran into problems convincing two large institutional shareholders to sell their stakes. Rio Tinto upped the offer to about $4 billion in early 2011 but India's Tata Steel and Brazil's CSN — which together held about 47% of Riversdale — were still not willing to part with their shares. A couple of deadline extensions and price bumps later Rio Tinto acquired both the CSN and Tata stakes to control close to 100% of Riversdale's shares.

EXECUTIVES

Chairman, Jan P. du Plessis, age 65
Group executive Organisational Resources, Hugo Bague
Chief executive Rio Tinto Alcan, Alfredo (Alf) Barrios
CEO, Jean-Sebastien Jacques
CFO, Christopher Lynch
CEO Energy and Minerals, Bold Baatar
Group Executive Health Safety and Environment; Managing Director Australia, Joanne Farrell
Group Executive Growth and Innovation, Stephen McIntosh
Chief Executive Iron Ore, Chris Salisbury
Chief Executive Copper and Diamonds, Arnaud Soirat
Auditors: PricewaterhouseCoopers

LOCATIONS

HQ: Rio Tinto Ltd
  Level 7, 360 Collins Street, Melbourne, Victoria 3000
Phone: (61) 3 9283 3333   **Fax:** (61) 3 9283 3707
Web: www.riotinto.com

2015 Sales

	% of total
China	42
US	15
Other Asia	14
Japan	11
Europe (Excluding UK)	8
Canada	4
Australia	3
UK	1
Other	2
Total	**100**

PRODUCTS/OPERATIONS

2015 Sales

	% of total
Iron Ore	41
Aluminum	27
Copper	9
Coal	8
Industrial Minerals	6
Gold	3
Diamonds	2
Other	4
Total	**100**

Selected Holdings

Aluminum
  Bell Bay
  Boyne Island (59% smelting)
  Queensland Alumina Ltd. (80%)
  Tiwai Point (79% New Zealand)
  Weipa (Australia)
Iron Ore
  Hamersley Iron Pty. Ltd.
  Channar (60%)
  Marandoo mine (Pilbara Australia)
  Nammuldi
  Iron Ore Co. of Canada (59%)
  Robe River Iron Associates (53%)
Energy & Minerals
  Coal
  Bengalla (30% Australia)
  Blair Athol Coal (71%)
  Hail Creek Coal (82%)
  Hunter Valley Operations (76%)
  Kestrel (80%)
  Mt Thorley (61%)
  Warkworth (42%)
  Rio Tinto Diamonds & Minerals
  Rio Tinto Diamond (diamonds Australia Canada
  Zimbabwe)
  Rio Tinto Minerals (borates titanium dioxide
  Argentina/Australia/US)
Copper Products
  Escondida (30% Chile)
  Grasberg (40% Indonesia)
  Kennecott Utah Copper (US)
  Northparkes (80%)
  Palabora (58% South Africa)
Gold
  Barneys Canyon (US)
  Bingham Canyon (US)
  Escondida (30% Chile)
  Rawhide (51% US)

COMPETITORS

ALROSA	Glencore
ASARCO	Goldcorp
Anglo American	Grupo México
AngloGold Ashanti	ITOCHU
Arconic	Kaiser Aluminum
BHP Billiton	Marubeni
Barrick Gold	Newmont Mining
CONSOL Energy	Norsk Hydro ASA
Cliffs Natural	RUSAL
Resources	Recylex
Codelco	Southern Copper
Fortescue Metals	Teck
Freeport-McMoRan	Vale

HISTORICAL FINANCIALS

Company Type: Public

Income Statement

FYE: December 31

	REVENUE ($ mil.)	NET INCOME ($ mil.)	NET PROFIT MARGIN	EMPLOYEES
12/19	43,165	8,010	18.6%	46,007
12/18	40,522	13,638	33.7%	47,458
12/17	40,030	8,762	21.9%	46,807
12/16	33,781	4,617	13.7%	51,029
12/15	34,829	(866)	—	54,938
Annual Growth	5.5%	—	—	(4.3%)

2019 Year-End Financials

Debt ratio: 16.4%
Return on equity: 19.0%
Cash ($ mil.): 8,027
Current ratio: 1.56
Long-term debt ($ mil.): 13,093

No. of shares (mil.): 1,630
Dividends
  Yield: —
  Payout: 130.1%
Market value ($ mil.): —

Rio Tinto Plc

No you are not seeing double. Rio Tinto plc one of the world's largest mining operations (along with BHP Billiton and Vale) is the British half of a tandem of dual-listed companies. Rio Tinto plc's Australian counterpart is Rio Tinto Limited which has its headquarters in Melbourne. Rio Tinto explores for a variety of commodities: bauxite copper diamonds gold iron ore minerals (borates and titanium dioxide) and nickel. The company also produces aluminum through its Rio Tinto Alcan unit. Majority of the company's sales generates from China.

Operations

Rio Tinto consists of five business units based on their primary products: Iron Ore Aluminum Copper & Diamonds Energy & Minerals and Other Operations.

The Energy & Minerals product group includes businesses with products such as uranium borates and titanium dioxide feedstock together with Iron Ore Company of Canada and the Simandou iron ore project. The Copper & Diamonds product group also produces gold silver molybdenum and other by-products.

Sales of iron ore account for around 60% of the total aluminum nearly 25% industrial minerals nearly about 5% and coppers and diamonds more than 10%.

Geographic Reach

Based in London Rio Tinto has mining and corporate functions spanning the world but its areas of particular strength are Australia where it mines all the company's major ores and North America with significant additional other businesses in Asia Europe Africa and South America. China is Rio Tinto's largest geography by sales accounting for more than 50% of the total. Followed by the US with about 15% of total sales. The remaining sales are generated from: Asia excluding China and Japan (more than 10%); Japan (nearly 10%); Europe excluding the UK (over 5%); Canada Australia the UK and other countries (almost 10% combined).

Sales and Marketing

The Energy and Minerals portfolio includes titanium dioxide; rutile and zircon; borates; iron ore concentrate and pellets; and uranium. The company's products are used in everything from touch screens and hearing aids to high-strength steel and corrosion resistant coatings and in industries such as aerospace healthcare and low-carbon energy.

Copper and diamond businesses have rich expertise in underground mining processes and technology. As one of the world's largest producers of rough diamonds from its two mines the company supply a full range of sizes qualities and colours. The company's operations around the world are at various stages in the mining lifecycle from exploration to programme rehabilitation. Alongside copper the company also produce gold silver molybdenum and other materials such as rhenium. Rio Tinto supply customers in China Japan and the US.

Financial Performance

In the last five years Rio Tinto's revenue rose consistently except in 2016. It has an overall growth of 24%. In the same period its net income consistently grew but declined in 2019.

Rio Tinto's revenue rose 7% from $40.5 billion in 2018 to $43.2 billion in 2019. The increase was primarily due to the increase of sales in its iron ore business.

The company's net income declined 41% from $13.6 billion in 2018 to $8 billion in 2019.

Cash at the end of the year totaled $8 billion $2.9 billion decrease from the previous year. Cash from operations generated $14.9 billion. Investing and financing activities used $5.5 billion and $12.2 billion respectively.

Strategy

As the Rio Tinto ends the decade and begin another its focus will remain on delivering its value over volume strategy and striving to ensure that the company remains strong resilient and able to deliver superior returns to shareholders in the short medium and long term.

In 2019 the company did significant work on developing scenarios to help the company understand what it needs to do to thrive in this era of increasing complexity. Its focus on innovation operational and commercial excellence as well as high-value growth will be key.

HISTORY

Following a tough 2009 in which the global recession depressed commodity prices Rio Tinto rebounded strongly in 2010 posting a 35% increase in overall revenues due primarily to increased sales volumes and prices generated by the beginnings of an economic recovery. Leading the pack for Rio Tinto was its Iron Ore segment which saw an increase of 91% over the previous year followed by the Copper segment with a hike of 24% and the Energy unit with 15%. Profitability soared in 2010 as net income jumped more than 184% due to lower operating costs and significant reductions in debt.

Despite its failed effort the previous year to hike its 9% stake in Rio Tinto to 19% Aluminum Corporation of China (Chinalco) formed a joint venture with Rio Tinto in 2010 to operate an iron ore project in Guinea West Africa. A Chinalco subsidiary will hold 47% of Rio Tinto's Simandou project which is expected to begin producing up to 70 million tons of ore per year by 2015.

In 2011 Rio Tinto and Chinalco teamed up again on a new joint venture that will focus on mineral exploration in China. Chinalco is seeking to find and develop domestic sources of copper coal and potash to offset the cost of importing those raw materials. Chinalco will hold a 51% interest in the joint venture Chinalco Rio Tinto Exploration with Rio Tinto holding the remaining 49%.

One of the world's largest producers of copper Rio Tinto operates the Oyu Tolgoi project in Mongolia along with Canada's Ivanhoe Mines and the Mongolian government. Vancouver-based Ivanhoe controlled one of the world's largest untapped copper and gold deposits in Mongolia and Rio Tinto expects the mine to be one of the world's top 10 copper producers as well as one of the top gold producers by 2018. In 2012 Rio Tinto upped its holding in Ivanhoe from 49% to 51% to become the majority owner.

Also in early 2012 Rio Tinto completed its offer for Canada-based uranium producer Hathor Exploration valued at $578 million after rival Cameco Corp. made a takeover bid for the company in 2011. Hathor supplies about a fifth of the world's uranium.

In 2011 the company also started slimming its aluminum operations. It placed 13 assets on the chopping block allowing Rio Tinto Alcan to focus on its high-quality tier one assets (mostly in Canada) and improve performance. The company also planned to transfer its stakes in six Australian and New Zealand operations to a new business unit Pacific Aluminium. The new unit managed and reported separately from Rio Tinto Alcan would include the company's Gove bauxite mine and alumina refinery Boyne Smelters and Gladstone Power Station Tomago smelter and Bell Bay smelter in Australia. In New Zealand it would include the New Zealand Aluminium Smelters.

For at least a while longer the company is holding on to seven noncore assets managed by Rio Tinto Alcan including operations in France Germany the UK and the US. The company is in no hurry to sell and may wait until the economy improves before divesting certain operations. Rio Tinto has tried a similar divestment strategy before. It embarked on a divestment plan in the mid-2000s with the long-term goal of turning out $15 billion from its divestments. By 2010 the company had gained more than $10 billion from the divestment program.

Rio Tinto was formed in 1972.

EXECUTIVES

CFO, Christopher J. (Chris) Lynch, age 66
Group Executive Organisational Resources, Hugo Bague, age 59
Chief Executive Copper and Diamonds, Arnaud Soirat
Chief Executive Aluminium, Alfredo Barrios, age 54
Chief Executive, Jean-Sébastien Jacques, age 48
Chief Executive Iron Ore, Chris Salisbury
acting Technology & Innovation Group executive, Stephen McIntosh
Global Head of Health Safety Environment and Communities, Joanne Farrell
President and COO Diavik Diamond Mines, Patrick Boitumelo
Chief Executive Energy and Minerals, Bold Baatar
Human Resources Group Executive, Vera Kirikova
Chairman, Jan P. du Plessis, age 65
Auditors: PricewaterhouseCoopers LLP

LOCATIONS

HQ: Rio Tinto Plc
6 St. James's Square, London SW1Y 4AD
Phone: (44) 20 7781 2000   **Fax:** (44) 20 7781 1800
Web: www.riotinto.com

2017 Sales by Destination

	% of total
China	44
US	14
Asia (excl. China and Japan)	13
Japan	12
Europe (excl. UK)	7
Canada	3
Australia	2
UK	1
Other Countries	4
Total	**100**

PRODUCTS/OPERATIONS

2017 sales

	% of total
Iron ore	50
Aluminum	27
Copper	4
Coal	7
Industrial minerals	5
Gold	1
Diamonds	2
Other	4
Total	**100**

COMPETITORS

ALROSA	Glencore
ASARCO	Goldcorp
Anglo American	Grupo México
AngloGold Ashanti	ITOCHU
Arconic	Kaiser Aluminum
BHP Billiton	Marubeni
Barrick Gold	Newmont Mining
CONSOL Energy	Norsk Hydro ASA
Cliffs Natural	Phelps Dodge
Resources	Placer Dome
Codelco	RUSAL
DeBeers	Southern Copper
Falconbridge	Teck
Fortescue Metals	Vale
Freeport-McMoRan	WMC Resources

HISTORICAL FINANCIALS

Company Type: Public

Income Statement

FYE: December 31

	REVENUE ($ mil.)	NET INCOME ($ mil.)	NET PROFIT MARGIN	EMPLOYEES
12/19	43,165	(1,038)	—	46,007
12/18	40,522	287	0.7%	47,458
12/17	40,030	89	0.2%	46,807
12/16	33,781	159	0.5%	51,029
12/15	34,829	(853)	—	54,938
Annual Growth	**5.5%**	**—**	**—**	**(4.3%)**

2019 Year-End Financials

Debt ratio: 15.1%
Return on equity: (-2.4%)
Cash ($ mil.): 8,027
Current ratio: 1.56
Long-term debt ($ mil.): 13,341

No. of shares (mil.): 1,249
Dividends
  Yield: 10.7%
  Payout: 130.1%
Market value ($ mil.): 74,195

	STOCK PRICE ($) FY Close	P/E High/Low		PER SHARE ($) Earnings	Dividends	Book Value
12/19	59.36	13	9	4.88	6.35	32.43
12/18	48.48	8	6	7.88	3.08	34.18
12/17	52.93	11	8	4.87	2.37	33.32
12/16	38.46	16	9	2.55	1.51	28.58
12/15	29.12	—	—	(0.48)	2.21	27.18
Annual Growth	**19.5%**	**—**	**—**	**—**	**30.2%**	**4.5%**

Riyad Bank (Saudi Arabia)

EXECUTIVES

Vice President (Team Leader), Basim Sheikh
Director & Chairman, Abdullah Mohammed Ibrahim Al-Issa
Deputy Chairman, Jamal Abdulkarim Abdulkarim Al Abdulkarim Al-Rammah
Auditors: PricewaterhouseCoopers

LOCATIONS

HQ: Riyad Bank (Saudi Arabia)
Granada Oasis - A1 Tower, Riyadh - Al Shuhada District, Riyadh 11416
Phone: (966) 1 401 3030   **Fax:** (966) 1 404 2707
Web: www.riyadbank.com

COMPETITORS

Arab National Bank	Gulf International
Banque Saudi Fransi	Bank
Dallah Albaraka Group	

HISTORICAL FINANCIALS

Company Type: Public

Income Statement

FYE: December 31

	ASSETS ($ mil.)	NET INCOME ($ mil.)	INCOME AS % OF ASSETS	EMPLOYEES
12/19	70,877	1,493	2.1%	5,955
12/18	61,306	1,257	2.1%	5,973
12/17	57,675	1,052	1.8%	6,332
12/16	58,023	891	1.5%	6,337
12/15	59,483	1,078	1.8%	6,167
Annual Growth	**4.5%**	**8.5%**	**—**	**(0.9%)**

2019 Year-End Financials

Return on assets: 2.2%
Return on equity: 14.4%
Long-term debt ($ mil.): —
No. of shares (mil.): —
Sales ($ mil): 3,801

Dividends
  Yield: —
  Payout: 57.2%
Market value ($ mil.): —

Roche Holding Ltd

One of the world's largest pharmaceutical companies Roche sells its products in over 100 countries. Roche's prescription drugs include cancer therapies MabThera/Rituxan and Avastin Perjeta and Kadcyla for HER2-positive breast cancer idiopathic pulmonary fibrosis drug Esbriet macular degeneration therapy Lucentis and Tamiflu which is used for infectious diseases. The company markets many of its bestsellers through California-based subsidiary Genentech and Japanese affiliate Chugai Pharmaceutical. Roche's diagnostics arm offers clinical lab supplies genetic tests diabetes monitoring supplies and point-of-care diagnostics for health care providers. Roche records among the world's highest pharmaceutical R&D spend annually and generates majority of sales from North America.

Operations

Roche operates in two divisions: Pharmaceuticals and Diagnostics.

Its pharmaceuticals division accounts for nearly 80% of annual revenue with oncology drugs making the largest sales contribution (around 45%). It is also active in neuroscience infectious diseases immunology haemophilia A and ophthalmology.

The smaller yet faster-growing diagnostics segment which accounts for over 20% of annual revenue is a leading maker of in vitro (test tube) clinical diagnostic tests through its professional diagnostics segment; it is also an established provider of diabetes tests and glucose monitors.

Geographic Reach

Roche based in Basel Switzerland generates around 50% of its annual sales in North America and over 20 in Europe. Roche has three independent R&D teams in Switzerland California and Japan.

The largest geographic market for Roche's pharma segment is the US. The company also has a solid stance in the Japanese drug market through its 61.2% stake in Chugai Pharmaceutical and it is experiencing growth in Latin America and Asia.

In the Asia/Pacific region Roche's SPHERE (Scientific Partnership for HER2Testing Excellence) program helps to improve awareness and tests and treats breast and gastric cancers. It operates in a dozen markets: Bangladesh China Hong Kong India Indonesia Korea Malaysia Myanmar the Philippines Taiwan Thailand and Vietnam.

Sales and Marketing
Roche's product marketing efforts in the US are conducted through its main US subsidiary Genentech which is one of the world's largest biotech companies.

Financial Performance
Note: Growth rates may vary after conversion to US Dollars.

In 2019 Roche grew its sales 8% to CHF 61.5 billion due to the growth in both pharmaceuticals and diagnostics businesses.

Net income rose 29% from CHF 10.5 billion in 2018 to CHF 13.5 billion in 2019.

Roche's cash position decreased by CHF 606 million during 2019 ending the year at CHF 6.1 billion. It generated a healthy CHF 22.4 billion in cash from operations. Investing and financing activities used CHF 8.6 billion and CHF 14.2 billion respectively.

Strategy
Roche has entered into strategic alliances with various companies in order to gain access to potential new products or to utilize other companies to help develop the group's own potential new products. Potential future payments may become due to certain collaboration partners achieving certain milestones as defined in the collaboration agreements.

The group's risk management strategy is to hedge the transaction exposures arising through foreign currency flows or monetary positions held in foreign currencies as well as to generate an appropriate mix of fixed and floating rate exposures. The level of hedging depends on market conditions and business requirements of the group. The group designates a specific interest rate risk management objective to ensure that a predetermined level of its interest rate risk exposure is at a floating rate.

Mergers and Acquisitions
Acquisitions are also key elements in Roche's R&D growth strategy and have expanded its pharmaceutical segment in focused therapeutic areas.

In mid-2020 Roche acquired Stratos Genomics. Stratos Genomics is an early-stage sequencing technology company based in the US. The addition of the acquired company will provide Roche access to its unique chemistry Sequencing by Expansion (SBX) and is expected to provide the healthcare community an affordable result for multiple targeted clinical applications.

In late 2019 Roche completed the acquisition of Spark Therapeutics a gene therapy company based on Pennyslvania for about $4.3 billion. Spark makes an experimental and promising hemophilia treatment which Roche hopes will complement its existing haemophilia treatment Hemlibra.

Company Background
Roche can trace a direct line back to the foundation in 1896 of F.Hoffmann-La Roche & Co by entrepreneur Fritz Hoffman-La Roche. Pharmacist Carl Schaerges the first head of research together with chemist Emil C. Barell demonstrated the presence of iodine in thyroid extracts. This results in Roche's first patent and scientific publications. The company became the first to synthetic vitamin C on a mass scale in 1934 and in 1957 developed the benzodiazepines class of tranquilizers. Over the years Roche has expanded in Switzerland and abroad by making numerous acquisitions including Genentech in the US for a whopping $46.8 billion.

EXECUTIVES

Head of Genentech Research and Early
  Development (gRED), Michael D. Varney
Chairman and CEO Chugai, Osamu Nagayama, age 73

Chief Financial and IT Officer, Alan Hippe, age 53
CEO, Severin Schwan, age 53
COO Pharmaceuticals, Daniel O'Day, age 56
COO Diagnostics, Roland Diggelmann, age 53
Head of Roche Partnering, Sophie Kornowski-
  Bonnet, age 57
Head of Pharma Research and Early
  Development, John C. Reed, age 62
Chairman, Christoph Franz, age 60
Vice Chairman, André Hoffman, age 62
Auditors: KPMG AG

LOCATIONS

HQ: Roche Holding Ltd
  Grenzacherstrasse 124, Basel CH-4070
Phone: (41) 61 688 11 11   Fax: (41) 61 688 13 96
Web: www.roche.com

2017 Sales

	% of total
America	50
Europe	26
Asia	21
Africa Australia & Oceania	3
Total	**100**

PRODUCTS/OPERATIONS

2017 Sales

	% of total
Pharmaceuticals	
Oncology	48
Immunology	14
Neuroscience	3
Ophthalmology	3
Infectious disease	2
Other	7
Diagnostics	23
Total	**100**

Selected Products

Top Products (listed alphabetically)
  Actemra/RoActemra (rheumatoid arthritis)
  Activase/TNKase (cardiovascular)
  Alecensa
  Avastin (colorectal cancer non-small cell lung cancer breast cancer kidney cancer)
Bactrim (anti-infective)
Bondronat (bone disease in breast cancer patients)
Bonviva/Boniva (osteoporosis)
CellCept (transplantation)
Cotellic
Dilatrend
Dormicum (sedation)
Erivedge (basal cell carcinoma)
ESBRIET
FoundationOne
FoundationOne Heme
Fuzeon (HIV)
Gazyva/Gazyvaro
Harmony Prenatal test
Hemlibra
Herceptin (HER2-positive breast cancer)
Invirase (HIV)
Kadcyla
  Kytril (nausea and vomiting induced by chemotherapy or radiation therapy)
  Lariam
  Lucentis (wet age-related macular degeneration diabetic macular edema)
  MabThera SC/Rituxan Hycela
  MabThera/Rituxan (non-Hodgkin's lymphoma rheumatoid arthritis chronic lymphocytic leukemia)
  Madopar (Parkinson's disease restless leg syndrome)
  MIRCERA (predialysis)
  NeoRecormon (anemia oncology)
  Neupogen
  Ocrevus
  Pegasys (hepatitis B and C)
  Perjeta (breast cancer)
  Pulmozyme (cystic fibrosis)
  Roaccutane/Accutane (acne)
  Rocaltrol (osteoporosis)
  Rocephin (bacterial infections)
  Roferon-A (hepatitis C hairy cell leukemia AIDS-related Kaposi's sarcoma)

Tamiflu (treatment and prevention of influenza)
Tarceva (advanced non-small cell lung cancer advanced pancreatic cancer)
Tecentriq
Toradol (acute pain)
Valcyte (cytomegalovirus infection)
Valium (anxiety disorders)
Vesanoid (leukemia)
Viracept (HIV)
Xeloda
Xenical (weight loss weight control)
Xolair (asthma)
Zelboraf (metastatic melanoma)

COMPETITORS

Abbott Labs	Gilead Sciences
Allergan plc	GlaxoSmithKline
Amgen	Johnson & Johnson
Astellas	Merck
AstraZeneca	Merck KGaA
Bayer AG	Novartis
Becton Dickinson	Pfizer
Biogen	Sanofi
Bristol-Myers Squibb	Takeda Pharmaceutical
Eisai	Teva
Eli Lilly	

HISTORICAL FINANCIALS
Company Type: Public

Income Statement — FYE: December 31

	REVENUE ($ mil.)	NET INCOME ($ mil.)	NET PROFIT MARGIN	EMPLOYEES
12/19	65,947	13,961	21.2%	97,735
12/18	60,482	10,673	17.6%	94,442
12/17	57,118	8,845	15.5%	93,734
12/16	51,710	9,407	18.2%	94,052
12/15	50,753	8,924	17.6%	91,747
Annual Growth	6.8%	11.8%	—	1.6%

2019 Year-End Financials

Debt ratio: 17.8%
Return on equity: 44.7%
Cash ($ mil.): 6,284
Current ratio: 1.30
Long-term debt ($ mil.): 13,104

No. of shares (mil.): 862
Dividends
  Yield: 1.6%
  Payout: 4.3%
Market value ($ mil.): 35,072

	STOCK PRICE ($) FY Close	P/E High/Low		PER SHARE ($) Earnings	Dividends	Book Value
12/19	40.66	3	2	16.16	0.68	39.27
12/18	31.08	3	2	12.41	1.08	32.55
12/17	31.58	3	3	10.29	1.06	31.41
12/16	28.53	3	2	10.93	1.00	27.23
12/15	34.47	3	3	10.35	1.00	24.49
Annual Growth	4.2%	—	—	11.8%	(9.3%)	12.5%

Rogers Communications Inc

Rogers Communications is how much of Canada makes calls accesses the internet and watches TV. The company is Canada's #1 mobile phone outfit with about 10.8 million subscribers across the country. As the nation's #1 cable TV operator the company serves some 1.7 million subscribers through subsidiary Rogers Cable. Its cable unit also oversees the company's internet and nationwide landline and computer telephony services. Rogers Media is the company's broadcasting arm.

The company also owns a stake in Rogers Blue Jays Baseball Partnership which holds interests in the Toronto Blue Jays major league baseball team and Rogers Centre sports complex. The late founder Ted Rogers started the company with a single radio station.

Operations

Almost 60% of Rogers Communications' revenue is generated by its wireless unit which provides mobile broadband data services such as web access and streaming media in addition to standard voice and messaging services. The company's wireless brands are Rogers Fido and chatr. The company's cable business provides a bit more than 25% of revenue with the media business at about 15%.

Rogers also operates some 55 radio stations about 50 television stations seven digital services and five sports operations. Besides owning the Toronto Blue Jays Rogers own half of the Toronto Raptors in the NBA and manages NHL national broadcast rights in Canada.

Rogers owns 50% of Glentel Inc. which sells multicarrier wireless and wireline products and services through several hundred retail outlets in Canada.

Geographic Reach

Rogers provides services throughout Canada. The company's LTE reaches 96% of the Canadian population.

Sales and Marketing

Rogers' sales teams and third-party retailers sell services to the enterprise public sector and carrier wholesale markets. An extensive network of third-party channel distributors deals with IT integrators consultants local service providers and other indirect sales relationships.

Financial Performance

Note: Numbers are in Canadina dollars. Growth rates may differ after conversion to US dollars.

Rogers Communications has posted higher revenue two years in a row after two years of declining revenue. Net income also has risen for the past two years.

Sales rose 5% to $15.1 billion in 2018 a $727 million increase from 2017 with higher revenue in all its segments. Wireless service and equipment increased on higher demand for data and for higher-value devices. Higher internet revenue drove Cable sales up as customers moved to higher speed and usage tiers which was somewhat offset by Television subscriber losses. The Toronto Blue Jays pushed Media revenue a bit higher because of a financial distribution from Major League Baseball and higher network subscription revenue.

Rogers's net income rose 12% to $2.1 billion in 2018 from 2017 on the higher year-to-year sales.

The company had $313 million in cash and equivalents in 2018 compared to negative cash of $4.6 million in 2017. In 2018 operations generated $3.3 million while investing and financing activities used $2.2 million and $721 million respectively. In building out networks adding new technologies and creating Canadian-centric content Rogers's capital expenditures are on the rise. In 2018 its capex reached $2.8 billion a 15% increase from 2017 and it could reach $3.5 billion in 2019.

Strategy

With lagging results from its cable TV segment Rogers Communications pulled the plug on its in-house IPTV service. Instead Rogers struck a deal to license Comcast's X1 service. The company branded the service Ignite TV and began offering it to customers in 2018. Rogers looks for growth from the service which leverages its broadband service. It invested nearly $700 million to produce Canadian entertainment news and sports programming during the 2018 broadcast year.

In wireless Rogers moved to improve service adding cell sites expanding LTE coverage (it reaches 96% of Canadians) and deploying more 700 MHz spectrum. The company also sped up its move to 4.5G technology a stepping stone to 5G technology. In 2018 the company ramped up 5G trials and testing looking to offer 5G services for wireless broadband and the Internet of Things applications. It also partnered with Ericsson to provide 5G equipment and infrastructure.

Although Rogers is tops in wireless and cable in Canada the company faces intense competition. Its Canadian rivals such as BCE and Shaw are bolstering their offerings and streaming services such as Netflix Hulu and Amazon.com's Prime Video offer alternatives to cord-cutting customers. In addition changes to Canadian telecommunications regulations have made it easier for foreign companies to gain footholds in the country.

Company Background

Edward Rogers at age 21 transmitted Canada's first radio signal across the Atlantic in 1921. He invented the first alternating current (AC) radio tube in 1925 which revolutionized the home-receiver industry.

The son of a wealthy businessman Rogers founded Rogers Majestic in Toronto in the mid-1920s to make his radio tubes. He also established several radio stations including CFRB ("Canada's First Rogers Batteryless") which later commanded the country's largest audience.

In 1931 Rogers won the first experimental license to broadcast TV but his businesses were sold when he died in 1939. His son Ted Rogers Jr. was only five at the time but even as a youngster he showed business acumen buying up shares of Standard Broadcasting. In his twenties he bought CHFI a Toronto radio station that pioneered FM broadcasting.

Rogers moved into cable TV and in 1967 was awarded licenses for Toronto Brampton and Leamington. Rogers Cable TV expanded when it bought Canadian Cablevision (1979) and Premier Cablevision (1980). With the takeover of UA-Columbia Cablevision in 1981 Rogers became Canada's largest cable operator.

EXECUTIVES

Chairman and President and CEO Rogers Telecommunications Limited, Alan D. Horn, age 68
CTO, Robert F. (Bob) Berner
President Media Business Unit, Rick Brace
President and CEO, Joseph M. (Joe) Natale, age 55
Interim President Enterprise Business Unit, Terry A. Canning
EVP and CFO, Anthony (Tony) Staffieri
President Consumer Business Unit, Dirk Woessner
CIO, Jamie Williams
Vice Chairman, Philip B. (Phil) Lind, age 74
Auditors: KPMG LLP

LOCATIONS

HQ: Rogers Communications Inc
333 Bloor Street East, Toronto, Ontario M4W 1G9
Phone: 416 935-7777 **Fax:** 416 935-3548
Web: www.rogers.com

PRODUCTS/OPERATIONS

2018 Sales

	% of total
Wireless	60
Cable operations	26
Media	14
Corporate items and intercompany eliminations	-
Total	**100**

Selected Operations

Wireless Communications

Cellular service
Data service
Digital PCS
Cable and Telephone
  Cable television
  Broadband Internet access
  Dial-up Internet access
  Local access
  Long-distance
  Teleconferencing
Media
  Content
  e-Commerce
  Radio
  TV broadcasting
  Televised shopping
  Publishing
  Sports entertainment

COMPETITORS

Allstream	Netflix
Amazon.com	Quebecor
BCE	Shaw Communications
Bell Aliant	Sprint Communications
Bell Media	TELUS
CBC	Vonage
COGECO	YouTube
Hulu	

HISTORICAL FINANCIALS

Company Type: Public

Income Statement

FYE: December 31

	REVENUE ($ mil.)	NET INCOME ($ mil.)	NET PROFIT MARGIN	EMPLOYEES
12/19	15,262	2,068	13.6%	25,300
12/18	15,286	2,084	13.6%	26,100
12/17	14,321	1,732	12.1%	24,500
12/16	13,874	845	6.1%	25,200
12/15	13,583	1,398	10.3%	26,000
Annual Growth	**3.0%**	**10.3%**	**—**	**(0.7%)**

2019 Year-End Financials

Debt ratio: 49.8%
Return on equity: 23.2%
Cash ($ mil.): 500
Current ratio: 0.86
Long-term debt ($ mil.): 16,168
No. of shares (mil.): 504
Dividends
  Yield: 3.0%
  Payout: 50.3%
Market value ($ mil.): 25,080

	STOCK PRICE ($) FY Close	P/E High/Low	PER SHARE ($) Earnings	Dividends	Book Value
12/19	49.67	14 12	4.02	1.50	18.88
12/18	51.26	14 11	4.04	1.47	16.09
12/17	50.93	16 12	3.35	1.94	12.48
12/16	38.58	28 21	1.64	1.94	10.36
12/15	34.46	15 12	2.70	1.49	11.30
Annual Growth	**9.6%**	**— —**	**10.4%**	**0.3%**	**13.7%**

Rolls-Royce Holdings Plc

Rolls-Royce Holdings doesn't make cars so luxurious you'll cry (see Motor Cars) but it sure can make an aircraft engine whine. One of the world's largest aircraft engine makers Rolls-Royce through its Civil and Defense Aerospace businesses makes commercial and military engines for a broad customer base including airlines corporate and utility aircraft and helicopter operators and armed forces around the world. Beyond aviation its Energy unit supplies gas turbine power generation to the oil and gas industry while its Marine segment makes propulsion systems that power 70 navies worldwide. Rolls-Royce has operations in North America Europe and Asia with an emerging presence in the Middle East.

Operations

The company operates two divisions: Aerospace and Land & Sea.

The Aerospace division covers both civil and military aviation for which it develops manufactures markets and sells engines and power systems. The division's engines are found in the aircraft such as the Airbus A380 and on the defense side of things Rolls-Royce commands approximately one-quarter of the world's military engine manufacturing market share. Its portfolio covers all major sectors — combat helicopters unmanned and tactical aircraft training and transport. The Land & Sea division has three interests of power systems marine propulsion and nuclear power generation and propulsion. Its PWR2 nuclear propulsion system is found in the Royal Navy's Trident submarine fleet.

Geographic Reach

Headquartered in London Rolls-Royce has operations in over 50 countries and customers in over 150 worldwide. Europe is the company's biggest market at around 35% of sales followed by North America at 30% and Asia at 20%.

Strategy

Rolls-Royce is carrying out a streamlining process to enhance operational efficiency which included the axing of 600 management jobs since mid-2015 and the consolidation of its Civil Aerospace repair and overhaul activities allowing for the closure of sites in Brazil and the UK. It also sold its Michell Bearings business in November 2015 for Å 12.6 million and its L'Orange diesel parts maker to Woodward a US company for $859 million.

Rolls-Royce expects to see an uptick in its overseas business following the sharp fall in value of the Pound Sterling subsequent to the EU referendum in mid-2016.

Rolls-Royce is possibly weighing up an escalation of its nuclear activities after the UK government announced a Å 250 million competition to encourage development of small modular reactor (SMR) technologies which have potential uses as part of a 7 gigawatt network of SMRs.

Mergers and Acquisitions

In mid-2016 Rolls-Royce announced the purchase of the remaining 53% of shares in Industria de Turbo Propulsores (ITP) for ?720 million in order to strengthen its large engine growth program. ITP brings with it long-term aftermarket revenue including the high volume Trent 1000 and Trent XWB engines. The acquisition completed at the end of 2017.

In 2015 the company acquired R.O.V Technologies which makes products that allow for the remote inspection and cleaning of boiling/pressurized water reactors complementing Rolls-Royce's existing nuclear activities.

Auditors: PricewaterhouseCoopers LLP

LOCATIONS

HQ: Rolls-Royce Holdings Plc
Kings Place, 90 York Way, London N1 9FX
Phone: (44) 20 7222 9020
Web: www.rolls-royce.com

2015 Sales

	% of total
Europe	36
North America	30
Asia	21
Middle East	6
South America	3
Australasia	2
Africa	1
Other	1
Total	**100**

PRODUCTS/OPERATIONS

2015 Sales (by market)

	% of total
Civil Aerospace	52
Power Systems	18
Defence Aerospace	15
Marine	10
Nuclear	5
Total	**100**

Selected Products and Services

Aircraft engines
Automation and control equipment
Bearings and seals
Diesel and gas turbine engines
Electric propulsion systems
Engine support services
Helicopter engines
Fuel cells
Generators
Offshore drilling equipment
Overhaul and repair services
Ship designs
Technical publications
Training

Selected Subsidiaries

Civil aerospace
  Optimized Systems and Solutions Limited (OSyS) (advanced controls and predictive data management)
  Rolls-Royce Leasing Limited (engine leasing)
  Rolls-Royce Total Care Services Limited (aftermarket support services)
Corporate
  Rolls-Royce International Limited (international support and commercial information services)
  Rolls-Royce Power Engineering plc (power generation and marine systems)
Energy
  Rolls-Royce Fuel Cell Systems Limited (fuel cell system development)
  Rolls-Royce Power Development Limited (project development)
  Tidal Generation Limited (development of tidal generation systems)
Marine
  ODIM ASA (offshore drilling naval and power generation equipment)
  Rolls-Royce Marine Electrical Systems Limited (marine electrical systems)
  Rolls-Royce Power Development Limited (generation of electricity from independent power projects)
  Rolls-Royce Marine Power Operations Limited (nuclear submarine propulsion systems)
  Rolls-Royce Power Engineering plc (energy and marine systems)
p>#

COMPETITORS

Emerson Electric	McDermott
GE Aviation	Pratt & Whitney
GE Honda Aero Engines	SAFRAN
HEICO	Siemens AG
Honeywell Aerospace	Volvo
IHI Corp.	
Kawasaki Heavy Industries	

HISTORICAL FINANCIALS

Company Type: Public

Income Statement   FYE: December 31

	REVENUE ($ mil.)	NET INCOME ($ mil.)	NET PROFIT MARGIN	EMPLOYEES
12/19	21,904	(1,736)	—	51,700
12/18	20,082	(3,065)	—	54,500
12/17	22,025	5,682	25.8%	50,000
12/16	18,396	(4,959)	—	49,900
12/15	20,339	123	0.6%	50,500
Annual Growth	**1.9%**	**—**	**—**	**0.6%**

2019 Year-End Financials

Debt ratio: 23.2%
Return on equity: —
Cash ($ mil.): 5,867
Current ratio: 1.07
Long-term debt ($ mil.): 6,483

No. of shares (mil.): 1,931
Dividends
  Yield: —
  Payout: —
Market value ($ mil.): —

Rosneft Oil Co OJSC (Moscow)

Rosneft is one of the world's largest public energy companies accounting for about 5% of the world's oil (and 40% of Russia's) production. With assets in around 25 countries the Russian giant maintains one of the world's largest hydrocarbon reserves (some 140 billion BOE). Its wide range of activities include exploration and production of offshore hydrocarbon deposits gas extraction and processing as well as marketing of petrochemical products in Russia and neighboring countries. The company also has a dozen or so joint ventures in Europe and Asia. Though strongly Russian in its roots about 40% of Rosneft is owned by foreign shareholders primarily BP and QHG Oil Ventures.

Operations

Rosneft reports through three core business segments.

Refining and Distribution is its core business bringing in almost 65% of annual revenue. Activities include processing crude oil and other hydrocarbons to sell petroleum products across Russia and its neighbors.

Exploration and Production accounts for almost 35% of revenue and is engaged in field exploration and the production of crude oil and natural gas.

Forming a very small percentage of annual revenue Corporate and Other consists of activities like field development infrastructure maintenance and financial services.

Geographic Reach

Rosneft has a strong presence across 70 regions of Russia plus parts of Abkhazia Kyrgyzstan and Belarus. The company's assets however are highly dispersed in 25 countries across the world from Brazil and Canada to Egypt and Indonesia.

Sales and Marketing

The Rosneft trademark is one of the most recognizable in the oil products market of Russia. Operating the country's largest retail chain Rosneft has some 3000 oil filling stations. The company also serves stripped gas and jet fuels (30% of the market) plus some 1900 shops and about 1130 cafes.

Financial Performance

Note: Growth rates may differ after conversion to US Dollars.

Rosneft revenue jumped up 37% to RUB 8.2 trillion in 2018 from the RUB 6 trillion posted a year earlier. Favorable world prices of oil (41% spike in RUB terms) and bigger stakes in profits from several international projects (44% growth) strengthened its results.

Meanwhile net income in 2018 climbed 2.5 times from the previous year to RUB 549 million thanks to higher operating income growth and a 25% improvement in margins.

CAPEX reduced slightly to RUB 936 billion. The company posted RUB 1.1 trillion in free cash flow almost five times its 2017 results. Higher cash inflows from operations lower working capital expenses and a favorable price environment boosted its coffers. Debt burden dropped by $14 billion the company reported.

Strategy

Buoyed by margin improvements Rosneft registered robust growth in 2018. The company's current strategic plan wants to build on that momentum with a target to produce 250 mmtoe of hydrocarbons and about 100 bcm of gas annually by 2022.

To reach this ambitious goal Rosneft has made significant strides towards inorganic growth in its midstream (buying up shares in German and Indian refineries) and upstream (shares in Egypt's lucrative Zohr field) operations.

Organically Rosneft wants to expand its petrochemical product offerings like fuel station expansion of India's Nayara Energy in which Rosneft has a 49.13% ownership. The company also wants to fully develop a new gas chemical business.

But gas remains the pride of Rosneft? it wants to become a top-three gas producer in the world within the next five years. It is betting growth on two new projects in particular? the 2017 Laptev Sea field discovery (80 mmt of oil reserves) and the Erginsky pipeline project (260 mmt in reserves).

Besides investments Rosneft is taking a long-run approach to cost-savings measures. A majority of the company's 2019 CAPEX (RUB 1.2 trillion) is earmarked for technological upgrades in the upstream and refinery infrastructures that will reduce working capital. Rosneft already reaps benefits from strong operational efficiencies in the oilfield services?it has one of the lowest lifting costs per barrel among its peers.

Mergers and Acquisitions

In late 2017 Rosneft acquired a 30% stake in Egypt's Zohr field the largest gas field in the Mediterranean Sea from Italian company Eni S.p.A. The $1.1 billion acquisition gives Rosneft access to reserves exceeding 850 bcm that is sure to significantly boost the company's offshore production.

Earlier that year Rosneft also bought a 49.13% share of Essar Oil from Essar Energy Holdings and its affiliates. Essar has a vast retail network of over 3500 fuel stations across India. The acquisition came with a stake in Essar's Vadinar refinery as well which will help Rosneft create synergies with existing Indian assets.

HISTORY

Rosneft was formed in 1993.

In 2004 Rosneft acquired YUKOS' main oil unit — Yugansk — in a controversial $9.4 billion deal. The acquisition of Yugansk (also known as Yuganskneftegaz) has been more complicated than Rosneft may have wished as questions were raised about how the deal was handled and how the transaction was funded. In 2004 the company agreed to merge with Russian energy giant Gazprom. The Yugansk acquisition threw the merger with Gazprom into disarray with Rosneft claiming that terms of the deal should be renego-

tiated to account for the change in value of Rosneft's assets. In addition Group Menatep (majority owner of YUKOS) called for Rosneft to repay a loan estimated at about $900 million that is secured by Yugansk assets. In response Rosneft filed an $11 billion suit against YUKOS for unpaid taxes related to Yugansk.

In 2005 Rosneft approved the deal with Gazprom though the acquisition would exclude the Yugansk assets acquired from YUKOS. After months of conflicting reports state-controlled Gazprom abandoned the deal.

In 2006 Rosneft and BP teamed up to develop energy projects in Russia's Arctic. Rosneft raised $10.4 billion in a 2006 IPO (during which BP acquired a $1 billion stake).

In a move toward becoming a global oil company in 2011 Rosneft formed a strategic alliance with BP (involving a stock swap of 5% of BP's shares for 9.5% of Rosneft's) to help fund the exploration of three blocks on the Russian Arctic continental shelf. The blocks have a production capacity on a par with the UK North Sea. However rival Russian partners at TNK-BP (BP's established Russian joint venture) objected to the proposed deal saying that have the legal right to have first choice on BP expansion activities in Russia. An arbitration tribunal in the UK supported their position. BP subsequently agreed to pursue the Rosneft deal through TNK BP. This move was unsuccessful and in May 2011 the BP/Rosneft deal fell through.

It followed this by forming a joint venture with Exxon Mobil to explore oil and gas fields in the Arctic. (This plan was stymied by US sanctions imposed in 2014).

Growing its European refinery footprint in 2011 it also acquired a 50% stake in German refinery Ruhr Oel from PDVSA for about $1.6 billion. BP owns the other 50%.

Beefing up its Russian assets in 2012 also bought 51% of NGK ITERA LLC one of the largest independent producers and traders of natural gas in Russia for RUB 7 billion (US $227 million).

EXECUTIVES

President and Director, Eduard Khudainatov, age 60
VP Finance and Economics, Pavel Fyodorov
Auditors: Ernst & Young LLC

LOCATIONS

HQ: Rosneft Oil Co OJSC (Moscow)
26/1, Sofiyskaya Embankment, Moscow 117997
Phone: (7) 499 517 88 99   **Fax:** (7) 499 517 72 35
Web: www.rosneft.com

PRODUCTS/OPERATIONS

2016 Sales

	% of total
Oil gas Petroleum products & petrochemicals	98
Support services & other	2
Equity share in profits of associates & joint ventures	-
Total	**100**

2016 Sales

	% of total
Refining and distribution	66
Exploration and production	33
Other	1
Total	**100**

COMPETITORS

Exillon Energy	LUKOIL
Gazprom	Tatneft

HISTORICAL FINANCIALS

Company Type: Public

Income Statement

FYE: December 31

	REVENUE ($ mil.)	NET INCOME ($ mil.)	NET PROFIT MARGIN	EMPLOYEES
12/19	139,403	11,375	8.2%	334,600
12/18	118,199	7,877	6.7%	325,600
12/17	104,023	3,839	3.7%	318,000
12/16	81,460	2,955	3.6%	0
12/15	69,740	4,807	6.9%	261,500
Annual Growth	**18.9%**	**24.0%**	**—**	**6.4%**

2019 Year-End Financials

Debt ratio: 0.4%   No. of shares (mil.): —
Return on equity: 16.5%   Dividends
Cash ($ mil.): 3,663   Yield: 0.0%
Current ratio: 0.87   Payout: 40.1%
Long-term debt ($ mil.): 48,733   Market value ($ mil.): —

	STOCK PRICE ($) FY Close	P/E High/Low		PER SHARE ($) Earnings	Dividends	Book Value
12/19	7.33	0	0	1.07	0.43	6.85
12/18	6.10	0	0	0.74	0.31	5.49
12/17	5.05	0	0	0.36	0.17	5.91
12/16	6.43	0	0	0.28	0.20	5.10
12/15	3.41	0	0	0.45	0.11	3.69
Annual Growth	**21.1%**	**—**	**—**	**24.0%**	**41.7%**	**16.7%**

Royal Bank of Canada (Montreal, Quebec)

Royal Bank of Canada (RBC) is Canada's largest bank and one of the world's top 15 banks by assets and market capitalization. The bank provides a diversified set of personal and commercial banking wealth management insurance investor and treasury services and capital markets globally. It serves more than 15 million customers - businesses and group clients individual and institutional clients — through offices in Canada the US and about 35 other countries including the UK and other selected parts of Europe the Asia/Pacific region and the Caribbean. RBC which generates more than 60% of revenue from Canada has assets under management nearing C$756 billion.

Operations

RBC operates five business segments: Personal & Commercial Banking Capital Markets Wealth Management Insurance and Investor & Treasury Services.

Personal & Commercial Banking generates about 50% of total revenue. It provides a broad suite of financial products and services.

Capital Markets segment brings in around 20% of revenue and provides the technological and operational foundation required to effectively deliver products and services to its clients. The segment also includes finance human resources risk management internal audit and other functional groups as well as our Corporate Treasury function.

Wealth Management provides a comprehensive suite of investment trust banking credit and other wealth solutions to high net worth and ultra-high net worth clients. It also offers asset management services to institutional and individual clients. The segment accounts about 20% of revenue.

Around 5% of revenue comes from Insurance — life health home auto and other kinds of insurance. It includes insurance for individuals as well as reinsurance advice and solutions and business insurance services to business and group clients.

The Investor & Treasury Services accounts for the remaining sales. It is a provider of asset services a leader in Canadian cash management and transaction banking services and a provider of treasury services to institutional clients worldwide.

The company's noninterest income generates more than 55% of sales and its largest loan portfolio came from its retail loans accounting to over 65%.

Geographic Reach

Ontario-based RBC has more than 15 million clients in Canada the US and about three dozen other countries. The company's Personal & Commercial Banking segment provides products and services in Canada the Caribbean and the US.

Overall the company generates more than 60% of its revenue from Canada about 25% from the US and some 15% from other international sources.

Sales and Marketing

Royal Bank of Canada serves a wide range of customers including individuals institutional groups business clients high-net-worth and ultra-high-net-worth individuals and institutional clients.

Through its capital markets the company also serves the energy mining and infrastructure industrial consumer health care and technology markets and financial services.

The company's Capital Markets segment serves energy mining infrastructure industrial consumer healthcare technology and financial sectors.

Financial Performance

Note: Growth rates may differ after conversion to US dollars.

Total revenue increased $3.4 billion or 8% largely due to higher net interest income and an increase in insurance premiums investment and fee income (Insurance revenue). Higher investment management and custodial fees and other revenue also contributed to the increase. The impact of foreign exchange translation also increased total revenue by $339 million. These factors were partially offset by lower underwriting and other advisory fees.

RBC's net income for 2019 was CAD 12.9 billion a 4% increase from the previous year. The increase was due to higher sales.

Cash and due from banks at end of 2019 was CAD 26.3 billion. Operating activities generated CAD 14.3 billion while investing activities used CAD 11.1 billion. Financing activities used another CAD 7.5 billion. RBC's main cash uses in 2019 were primarily for purchases of investment securities and dividends paid.

Strategy

RBC will sustain its technological leadership by investing significantly in its digital and innovation strategies enabling RBC to deliver even more insights and advice that create meaningful value for clients. RBC's differentiated technology platform and strong data foundation are supporting business growth operational efficiencies and leading-edge capabilities. RBC's next-generation delivery platform including a multi-cloud strategy accelerates its ability to bring products and services to market quickly scale across businesses and leverage world-class artificial intelligence (AI) and analytics to deliver superior business outcomes.

Mergers and Acquisitions

In early 2020 RBC Ventures has acquired Dr. Bill a premium billing solution that simplifies and streamlines the billing and payment process for Canada's medical community. Currently available in Ontario British Columbia and Alberta Dr. Bill provides doctors with a user-friendly mobile billing platform as well as dedicated live agents to deliver

an industry-leading billing success rate. Terms were not disclosed.

In mid-2019 RBC announced the acquisition of Ontario-based WayPay a cloud-based payments firm from Burlington Ontario with an undisclosed terms. The deal expands RBC's portfolio of digitally-enabled capabilities.

Also in 2019 RBC acquires naming rights to the London Convention Centre located in the heart of downtown London. This announcement is yet another chapter in RBC's long-standing support of London and the surrounding communities and builds on the convention centre's established reputation as a leader in the meetings industry. Terms were not disclosed.

Company Background

Royal Bank of Canada (RBC) was created as Merchants Bank in 1864 and incorporated in 1869. It changed its name to The Royal Bank of Canada in 1901 and to Royal Bank of Canada in 1990.

EXECUTIVES

President and CEO, David I. (Dave) McKay, age 57, $476,450 total compensation
Group Chief Risk Officer, Mark Hughes
Chair and CEO RBC Capital Markets; Group Head Capital Markets and Investor and Treasury Services, A. Douglas McGregor
Group Head Personal and Commercial Banking, Jennifer Tory
Group Head Technology and Operations, Bruce Ross
CFO, Rod Bolger
Group Head RBC Wealth Management and RBC Insurance, Douglas A. Guzman
Chairman, Kathleen P. Taylor
Auditors: PricewaterhouseCoopers LLP

LOCATIONS

HQ: Royal Bank of Canada (Montreal, Quebec)
200 Bay Street, Toronto, Ontario M5J 2J5
Phone: 416 974-6715
Web: www.rbc.com

2018 Sales

	% of total
Canada	60
US	23
Other international	17
Total	**100**

PRODUCTS/OPERATIONS

2018 Sales

	% of total
Net interest income	43
Non-interest income	57
Total	**100**

2018 Sales

	% of total
Personal & commercial banking	39
Wealth management	25
Capital markets	20
Insurance	10
Investor & treasury services	6
Total	**100**

COMPETITORS

BMO Financial Group	HSBC Bank Canada
Bank of America	JPMorgan Chase
Barclays	Laurentian Bank
CIBC	National Bank of
Canadian Western Bank	Canada
Citigroup	Scotiabank
Deutsche Bank	TD Bank
Goldman Sachs	UBS

HISTORICAL FINANCIALS

Company Type: Public

Income Statement			FYE: October 31
	ASSETS ($ mil.)	NET INCOME ($ mil.)	INCOME AS % OF ASSETS	EMPLOYEES
10/20	1,221,243	8,593	0.7%	83,842
10/19	1,084,825	9,763	0.9%	82,801
10/18	1,016,511	9,443	0.9%	84,000
10/17	944,094	8,895	0.9%	78,210
10/16	882,207	7,777	0.9%	80,000
Annual Growth	8.5%	2.5%	—	1.2%

2020 Year-End Financials

Return on assets: 0.7%
Return on equity: 13.4%
Long-term debt ($ mil.): —
No. of shares (mil.): 1,422
Sales ($ mil): 46,028

Dividends
Yield: 0.0%
Payout: 54.8%
Market value ($ mil.): 99,559

	STOCK PRICE ($) FY Close	P/E High/Low		PER SHARE ($) Earnings	Dividends	Book Value
10/20	69.99	11	7	5.88	3.22	45.80
10/19	80.66	9	8	6.64	3.07	44.34
10/18	72.84	10	9	6.37	2.94	42.27
10/17	78.15	10	8	5.88	2.68	39.56
10/16	62.48	9	7	5.07	2.44	35.76
Annual Growth	2.9%	—	—	3.8%	7.3%	6.4%

Royal Dutch Shell Plc

The second-largest oil company and the third largest of any type globally Royal Dutch Shell (Shell) boasts worldwide proved reserves of 11.6 billion barrels of oil equivalent. Operating in over 70 countries the British-Dutch company pumps out 3.6 million barrels of crude oil liquefied natural gas (LNG) natural gas synthetic crude oil and bitumen. Among the company's many and varied operations it boasts the world's deepest oil and gas project in the Gulf of Mexico the world's largest offshore floating LNG production plant off the Australian coast and the world's largest retail fuel network at more than 44000 stations. Royal Dutch Shell also runs over 20 refineries transports natural gas trades gas and electricity and develops renewable energy.

Operations

Royal Dutch Shell divides its operations into three segments: Downstream Integrated Gas and Upstream.

Downstream turns crude oil and other raw materials into a range of products for domestic industrial and transport use. These include gasoline diesel heating oil aviation fuel marine fuel lubricants bitumen and sulfur. The segment also manages Royal Dutch Shell's North American Oil Sands operations which extracts bitumen from oil sands and converts it into synthetic crude oil. Downstream subsidiaries include Trading and Supply Shell Wholesale Commercial Fuels Shell Aviation Shell Bitumen Shell Sulphur and Shell Pipeline among others. Downstream activities generate more than 85% of sales.

Integrated Gas comprises the company's liquefied natural gas (LNG) operations including exploration extraction and transportation. Other activities include the marketing and trading of crude oil natural gas LNG electricity and carbon-emission rights and the sale of LNG as a fuel for heavy-duty vehicles and vessels. Shell's investments in renewable and other low-carbon energy forms its New Energies business are housed in this segment. Integrated Gas represents 10% of sales.

Shell's Upstream segment explores for and extracts crude oil natural gas and natural gas liquids. It also markets oil and gas and delivers them to market. The segment generates 5% of sales.

Royal Dutch Shell's Corporate segment manages the company's non-operating activities including Shell's holdings and treasury organization its headquarters and central functions as well as its self-insurance activities.

Geographic Reach

Listed in London but run out of The Hague in the Netherlands Royal Dutch Shell has enormous global reach producing oil and natural gas in more than 70 countries including Australia Brazil Brunei Canada China Denmark Germany Malaysia the Netherlands Nigeria Norway Oman Qatar Russia the UK and the US. It is active in onshore and offshore conventional plays as well as unconventional plays such as tight rock shale and coal. Some of its key interests are in the North Sea while the US (particularly the Permian Basin) accounts for two-thirds of the company's proved shale reserves.

Shell operates more than 44000 fuel stations across 75 countries. Royal Dutch Shell's lubricants business produces markets and sells products in over 100 countries and has four base oil manufacturing plants more than 30 lubricant blending plants nine grease plants and three gas-to-liquid base oil storage hubs.

Shell Aviation the jet fuel business is present in around 900 airports in more than 60. Shell Bitumen has 1600 customers across more than 35 countries.

It makes about 40% of revenue from its Asia/Oceania/Africa reporting region more than 30% from Europe and a quarter from the US. Other Americas (Brazil in particular) account for the remainder.

Financial Performance

The crash in the global oil price in the mid 2010s from nearly $100 per barrel (/b) to below $40/b had a predictably deleterious effect on Royal Dutch Shell's revenue. Revenue fell from $421.1 billion in fiscal 2014 to $265.0 billion the following year. With many companies suffering as a result policymakers in the industry took steps to normalize the oil price.

In fiscal 2018 Royal Dutch Shell's revenue surged 27% to $388.4 billion largely due to higher realized oil and gas prices. The average price for a barrel of Brent crude rose $17 dollars to $71.

Net income jumped 80% to $23.4 billion again thanks to higher realized prices in addition to gains on a series of divested assets. Upstream earnings benefited from lower impairment charges and the absence from the one-off tax impact from tax reform in the US. Downstream earnings declined however due to higher operating expenses and currency headwinds.

Royal Dutch Shell's cash balance grew $6.4 billion during 2018 to $26.7 billion. The company's operations generated $53.1 billion while investing activities used $13.7 billion and financing used $32.5 billion. The oil company's main cash uses in 2018 were capital expenditures dividends and share repurchases.

Strategy

The energy sector is changing and Royal Dutch Shell's directors have had to make some tough decisions. The oil price collapsed in the mid-2010s and while the industry was battling to stabilize the economic viability of renewable energy surged. The emergence of a new rival to oil-generated power increased the likelihood of a medium-term decline of the oil price which could have serious consequence for a company such as Shell. Shell settled on a conservative approach to managing the energy transition preparing for lower prices but not for a total collapse.

The company's first step has been to sell off assets with a high break-even point; these include its huge (and still-profitable) Canadian oil sands assets. Its targeted break even point is around $40 per barrel. In all Shell has divested assets worth some $30 billion spanning the North Sea Ireland Africa New Zealand and the Middle East. It will continue selling around $5 billion in assets each year until at least 2020.

Through its New Energies unit Shell is investing in renewable energy sources and electricity infrastructure such as transport fuels (biogas hydrogen and electric) and power (wind solar and natural gas). Recent green investments have included the Borssele III and IV offshore windfarms which will have an installed capacity of 731 MW; a joint venture wind farm off the US east coast; and a household energy storage system company. However investment in New Energies is just a fraction of its total annual capital investment budget of $25 billion.

Mergers and Acquisitions

Royal Dutch Shell has been acquiring all sorts of companies to boost its New Energies low-carbon generation and storage business. These include infrastructure/storage companies (Sonnen and Limejump) generation (various wind and solar farms) and liquefied natural gas platforms.

The company is also working to acquire Endeavor Energy for around $8 billion. Texas-based Endeavor holds drilling rights on 300000 acres in the US Permian Basin. The deal has been rumbling on since early 2018 with several competitors dropping out including Exxon Chevron and Conoco Phillips.

In 2018 Royal Dutch Shell through its African operation Vivo Energy was reported to be in an advanced talks to acquire all operations of Rwandan oil company Engen following a pattern of recent acquisitions in Africa where it distributes and markets Shell-branded fuels and lubricants. The deal brings 2100 gas stations across the continent for Vivo.

EXECUTIVES

CEO, Ben van Beurden, age 62
Director Downstream, John Abbott
Director Projects and Technology, Harry Brekelmans
Director Upstream, Andrew Brown
CFO, Jessica Uhl
Integrated Gas and New Energies Director, Maarten Wetselaar
Chairman, Charles O. (Chad) Holliday, age 72
Deputy Chairman, Hans Wijers, age 70
Auditors: Ernst & Young LLP

LOCATIONS

HQ: Royal Dutch Shell Plc
Carel van Bylandtlaan 30, The Hague 2596 HR
Phone: (31) 70 377 9111
Web: www.shell.com

2018 Sales

	% of total
Asia Oceania Africa	39
Europe	31
USA	23
Other Americas	7
Total	**100**

PRODUCTS/OPERATIONS

2018 Sales

	% of total
Downstream	86
Integrated Gas	11
Upstream	3
Total	**100**

COMPETITORS

7-Eleven	Koch Industries Inc.
Ashland	Marathon Oil
BHP Billiton	Norsk Hydro ASA
BP	Occidental Petroleum
Chevron	PEMEX
ConocoPhillips	PETROBRAS
Dow Chemical	PetroKazakhstan
Eastman Chemical	Petr leos de
Eni	Venezuela
Exxon Mobil	Repsol
FEC Resources	Sinopec Shanghai
Hess Corporation	Petrochemical
Huntsman International	Sunoco
Imperial Oil	TOTAL

HISTORICAL FINANCIALS

Company Type: Public

Income Statement				FYE: December 31
	REVENUE ($ mil.)	NET INCOME ($ mil.)	NET PROFIT MARGIN	EMPLOYEES
12/19	352,106	15,842	4.5%	83,000
12/18	396,556	23,352	5.9%	81,000
12/17	311,870	12,977	4.2%	84,000
12/16	240,033	4,575	1.9%	92,000
12/15	272,156	1,939	0.7%	93,000
Annual Growth	6.7%	69.1%	—	(2.8%)

2019 Year-End Financials

Debt ratio: 17.5%	No. of shares (mil.): —
Return on equity: 8.2%	Dividends
Cash ($ mil.): 18,055	Yield: 6.3%
Current ratio: 1.16	Payout: 192.8%
Long-term debt ($ mil.): 55,779	Market value ($ mil.): —

	STOCK PRICE ($) FY Close	P/E High/Low	PER SHARE ($) Earnings	Dividends	Book Value
12/19	58.98	34 28	1.95	3.76	23.73
12/18	58.27	26 20	2.80	3.76	24.17
12/17	66.71	42 32	1.56	3.76	23.38
12/16	54.38	96 64	0.58	3.76	22.91
12/15	45.79	216140	0.30	3.76	25.46
Annual Growth	6.5%	— —	59.7%	(0.0%)	(1.7%)

Royal Mail Plc

EXECUTIVES

Managing Director Corporate Affairs Regulation and Customer Experience, Shane O'Riordain
CEO, Moya M. Greene, age 66
Managing Director Consumer and Network Access, Stephen Agar
COO, Sue Whalley
CEO GLS, Rico Back
Managing Director Strategy Pricing and Growth, Jack Bertram
Group CTO, Phil Morris
CFO, Stuart Simpson
Chairman, Peter Long, age 68
Auditors: KPMG LLP

LOCATIONS

HQ: Royal Mail Plc
100 Victoria Embankment, London EC4Y 0HQ
Phone: (44) 020 7250 2888
Web: www.royalmailgroup.com

PRODUCTS/OPERATIONS

2019 Sales

	% of total
UK Parcels International & Letters	73
General Logistics Systems	27
Total	**100**

COMPETITORS

DX Group	Rentokil Initial
Deutsche Post	Royal TNT Post
FedEx	Swiss Post
La Poste	UK Mail
PostNL	UPS
Poste Italiane	

HISTORICAL FINANCIALS

Company Type: Public

Income Statement FYE: March 29

	REVENUE ($ mil.)	NET INCOME ($ mil.)	NET PROFIT MARGIN	EMPLOYEES
03/20	13,242	196	1.5%	160,772
03/19	13,860	229	1.7%	161,978
03/18	14,358	365	2.5%	159,117
03/17	12,216	339	2.8%	158,955
03/16	13,083	340	2.6%	156,535
Annual Growth	0.3%	(12.8%)	—	0.7%

2020 Year-End Financials

Debt ratio: 25.8%	No. of shares (mil.): 998
Return on equity: 3.1%	Dividends
Cash ($ mil.): 2,003	Yield: 0.1%
Current ratio: 0.96	Payout: 259.6%
Long-term debt ($ mil.): 1,997	Market value ($ mil.): 3,267

	STOCK PRICE ($) FY Close	P/E High/Low	Earnings	PER SHARE ($) Dividends	Book Value
03/20	3.27	41 20	0.20	0.51	6.87
03/19	6.21	95 35	0.23	0.55	6.05
03/18	14.86	63 40	0.36	0.58	6.26
03/17	10.63	50 37	0.34	0.48	6.30
03/16	13.38	62 49	0.34	0.52	6.31
Annual Growth	(29.7%)	—	(12.8%)	(0.3%)	2.2%

RWE AG

RWE doesn't stand for Runs With Electricity but it could. RWE has become an electricity generation from renewables as the result of an asset swap with E.ON. Through its subsidiaries RWE AG is a player in the field of renewable energy. Through innovation and investment the new RWE is creating the foundation for a carbon neutral future. It also owns major UK and Netherlands-based utilities and Germany-based electricity and gas supplier RWE Power. RWE owns oil and gas exploration and production unit RWE-DEA; other businesses include companies engaged in gas transportation and storage power generation energy trading information technology and coal mining. It generates almost 40% of its revenue in Germany.

Operations

In their 2019 financial report they divided the RWE Group into the following five segments: Lignite?&?Nuclear (about 10% of revenue) European Power (also about 10% of revenue) Supply?&?Trading innogy - continuing operations (over 70% of revenue) and Operations acquired from E.ON (nearly 5% of revenue).

Lignite?&?Nuclear encompasses their German electricity generation from lignite and nuclear power as well as their lignite production in the Rhineland. Operating responsibility for these activities lies with RWE Power. The segment also includes their investments in the Dutch nuclear power plant operator EPZ (30?%) and the German company URANIT (50?%) which holds a 33?% stake in Urenco a uranium enrichment specialist.

European Power is where the company reports on their electricity production from gas hard coal and biomass which focuses on Germany the United Kingdom and the Benelux region. The segment also includes their 70?% stake in the Turkish gas-fired power station Denizli some hydroelectric power plants in Germany and Luxembourg and RWE Technology International which specialises in project management and engineering services. All of these activities are overseen by RWE Generation.

Supply?&?Trading division encompasses the operations of RWE Supply?&?Trading the business activities of which are presented on pages 30 et seq. The company specializes in independent commodity trading acts as an intermediary for gas and supplies large industrial and corporate customers with energy. Furthermore it markets the electricity of their generation companies and optimizes the Group's power plant dispatch commercially; however earnings achieved through the latter activities are reported in the Lignite?&?Nuclear and European Power segments.

innogy - continuing operations the main element in this segment is innogy's renewable energy business. The company ranks among the leading producers of electricity from renewable sources with a strong focus on Europe - in particular Germany and the United Kingdom - and with footholds in North America and Australia. The focus in terms of energy sources rests on wind followed by hydro and solar. This segment also includes the German and Czech gas storage facilities as well as about 40% interest in the Austria-based energy utility Kelag.

Operations acquired from E.O is where they present the renewable energy operations they received from E.ON. Its geographical focus is on North America and Europe. By far its main source of energy is wind supplemented by smaller solar and energy storage activities. After their acquisition in September 2019 they pooled these operations in RWE Renewables GmbH which was founded in 2018.

Geographic Reach

RWE operates in Germany the Netherlands/Belgium the UK Asia and in Central Eastern and South Eastern Europe. Germany and UK accounted for about 40% of the company's revenue in 2019 each.

Sales and Marketing

Geographically the company will concentrate on markets in Europe the Americas and the Asia-Pacific region.

Financial Performance

RWE's revenue has been falling for the past five years.

Revenue fell 2% to ?13.1 billion in 2019 (excluding natural gas tax and electricity tax). The drop was primarily due to the 25?% decline in gas revenue to ?1156 million. Since mid-2019 gas sales by RWE Supply?&?Trading in the Czech Republic have been recognized as pure trading trans-actions and are therefore no longer considered in revenue.

RWE net income rose almost nine times of ?9.2 billion in 2019 compared to prior year. The reconciliation from adjusted EBIT to net income was greatly affected by the asset swap with E.ON. A ?8.3 billion book gain on the deconsolidation of innogy's grid and retail business and the stake in IGH came to bear in particular. It was the reason why they closed fiscal 2019 with unusually high net income.

RWE ended 2019 with ?3.2 billion in net cash about ?330 million less than it had at the end of 2018. Investing activities used in ?729 million and operating activities also used ?1.5 billion while financing activities provided ?224 million.

Strategy

RWE has been supplying Germany with electricity for more than a century and it has evolved to keep up with changes in the energy sector. Today it works with partners in renewable energy to provide secure dependable electricity: Wind and solar power often don't supply enough electricity because they rely on weather conditions.

The company has more reason to adapt to changes in the energy market. In early 2019 a German government coal commission advised that the nation should exit all coal mining for electricity by 2038. If implemented that plan would have significant consequences for RWE. The Dutch government has set even more ambitious goals to exit from coal by 2030 and the UK government aims to exit coal by 2035. With regard to Germany RWE has responded that 2038 is too soon a target date. It has begun shuttering certain lignite production facilities but planned to have them all shut down by the middle of the century.

Last year the company saw the launch of the new RWE: their asset swap with E.ON has turned them into one of the world's leading renewable energy companies. They are now an all-rounder in electricity generation and is leading the field in the creation of a sustainable energy system. For as long as necessary they will ensure security of supply with their flexible power plants. Sustainable power production must be carbon neutral. They intend to meet this ambition as early as 2040. To this end every year they will invest billions in wind and solar power as well as in energy storage. And they will play their part by exiting from coal-based electricity generation early in a socially acceptable manner.

RWE will be making huge investments in wind and solar energy as well as in storage technologies: The company plans net investments of approximately ?5 billion in Europe North America and Asia/Pacific in order to enlarge its existing renewable energy portfolio to over 13 gigawatts. ?1 billion of this sum is envisaged for projects in Germany. After all they want people to continue to take their electricity supply for granted and to know that this electricity is clean secure and affordable.

Mergers and Acquisitions

In mid to late-2019 the company acquired the 382 MW King's Lynn CCGT-plant in the UK from Centrica and a 49% stake in Slovak VSE Holding. The King's Lynn CCGT-plant's capacity is 382 megawatts. The power plant will receive reliable stable capacity payments until 2035 on the basis of a 15-years contract in the GB capacity market which starts in late-2020. V chodoslovensk energetika Holding a.s. (VSEH) a holding company based in Kosice whose subsidiaries are engaged primarily in the business of electricity supply and distribution in Slovakia.

RWE closes deal with E.ON. In the autumn of 2019 RWE acquired E.ON's renewable energy activities and now the last step is being taken by integrating innogy's operations.

Company Background

RWE traces its roots back to 1898 when Rheinisch-Westf ¤lisches Elektrizit ¤tswerk — or RWE for short — was established. In 1902 Hugo Stinnes an industrialist from M lheim acquired control of the company. He worked to build a large-scale efficient electricity supply.

EXECUTIVES

Chairman and CEO, Rolf Martin Schmitz, age 63
CFO and CEO RWE Supply and Trading, Markus Krebber
Deputy Chairman, Frank Bsirske
Auditors: PricewaterhouseCoopers GmbH

LOCATIONS

HQ: RWE AG
 Altenessener Strasse 35, Essen D-45141
Phone: (49) 201 5179 0   **Fax:** (49) 201 5179 5005
Web: www.rwe.com

2017 Sales

	% of total
European Union	
Germany	62
UK	17
Other	19
Rest of Europe	1
Other	1
Total	**100**

PRODUCTS/OPERATIONS

2017 Sales by Segment

	% of total
innogy	88
Supply & Trading	7
European Power	2
Lignite & Nuclear	3
Other	-
Total	**100**

COMPETITORS

BP	Exxon Mobil
Centrica	IBERDROLA
E.ON	Royal Dutch Shell
Enel	Vattenfall

HISTORICAL FINANCIALS

Company Type: Public

Income Statement   FYE: December 31

	REVENUE ($ mil.)	NET INCOME ($ mil.)	NET PROFIT MARGIN	EMPLOYEES
12/19	14,736	9,541	64.7%	38,082
12/18	15,331	383	2.5%	58,441
12/17	50,867	2,775	5.5%	59,333
12/16	46,025	(6,029)	—	59,073
12/15	50,492	(185)	—	59,350
Annual Growth	(26.5%)	—		(10.5%)

2019 Year-End Financials

Debt ratio: 10.0%	No. of shares (mil.): 614
Return on equity: 63.8%	Dividends
Cash ($ mil.): 3,583	Yield: 1.8%
Current ratio: 1.43	Payout: 3.6%
Long-term debt ($ mil.): 4,405	Market value ($ mil.): 18,848

	STOCK PRICE ($) FY Close	P/E High/Low		PER SHARE ($) Earnings	Dividends	Book Value
12/19	30.66	2	2	15.52	0.56	30.95
12/18	21.89	48	32	0.62	1.30	19.25
12/17	20.29	9	5	3.70	1.80	16.03
12/16	12.36	—	—	(9.81)	0.00	6.78
12/15	12.63	—	—	(0.30)	0.79	12.86
Annual Growth	24.8%		—	—	(8.2%)	24.6%

Ryanair Holdings Plc

A pioneer in European discount air travel Ryanair Holdings offers low-fare no-frills air transportation via its main subsidiary Ryanair. The carrier flies to about 200 destinations including around 30 in Ireland and the UK. Ryanair specializes in short-haul routes between secondary and regional airports. It operates from about 75 bases including airports in Belgium France Germany Italy Spain and Sweden as well as in Ireland and the UK. The carrier maintains a fleet of about 300 Boeing 737-800s. Ryanair generates majority of revenue outside its home country Ireland.

Operations

Ryanair operates a fleet of more than 400 Boeing 737 aircraft and over 25 Airbus A320 aircraft. It has placed additional orders for a further 210 new Boeing 737 aircraft as well as options for 100 more Boeing 737 MAX 200s. Ryanair plans for the purchases to enable it to lower fares and grow traffic. The company is comprised of four key separate airlines: Ryanair DAC which generates vast majority of revenue; Buzz Lauda and Malta Air.

Overall scheduled revenue accounts for more than 65% of total sales. The remaining is from ancillary.

Geographic Reach

Ryanair operates about 1000 daily flights.. Its flights connect to about 200 destinations in 30 countries. Ireland and the UK collectively account for about 30% of its overall sales.

Ryanair is headquartered in Ireland.

Sales and Marketing

The company flies about 150 million booked passengers annually.

Financial Performance

Ryanair's revenue jumped 10% to ?8.5 billion from ?7.7 billion in 2019 due to a 4% increase in traffic to approximately 149m a 2% increase in average fare and a 16% increase in ancillary spend per passenger.

Net income was ?649 million 27% lower compared to ?885 million in 2019.

Cash and cash equivalents at the end of the year were ?2.6 billion 53% more than the previous year. Cash provided by operating activities was ?1.9 billion. Cash used by investing activities and financing activities were ?918.1 million and ?287 million respectively. Main cash uses were capital expenditures and shareholder returns.

Strategy

Ryanair's objective is to establish itself as Europe's biggest scheduled passenger airline group through continued improvements and expanded offerings of its low-fares service. In the highly challenging current operating environment Ryanair seeks to offer low fares that generate increased passenger traffic while maintaining a continuous focus on cost-containment and operating efficiencies.

The company is continuously implementing new strategic initiatives that are expected to improve its customer service offering. In recent years the company introduced a series of customer-service related initiatives under the AGB (Always Getting Better) customer experience program including an easy-to-navigate website a mobile app reduced penalty fees allocated seating security fast track at selected airports and more customer-friendly baggage allowances and change flight policies.

The company's reservation system operates under a hosting agreement with Navitaire which currently extends to November 2025. As part of the implementation of the reservation system Navitaire developed an Internet booking facility. The Ryanair system allows Internet users to access its host reservation system and to make and pay for confirmed reservations in real time through the Ryanair.com website. The company also has a mobile app which makes it simpler and easier for customers to book Ryanair flights.

Safety is the primary priority of Ryanair. This commitment begins with the hiring and training of its pilots flight attendants and maintenance personnel and includes a policy of maintaining its aircraft in accordance with the highest European industry standards.

Mergers and Acquisitions

In mid-2019 Ryanair acquired Malta Air a Maltese start up airline into which Ryanair moves and grow its Malta based fleet of 6 B737 aircraft. The investment in Malta Air allows Ryanair to grow its already sizable presence in Malta and access non-EU markets (North Africa) from Malta.

Company Background

Tony Ryan and his sons Declan and Cathal founded Ryanair in 1985.

EXECUTIVES

CEO, Michael O'Leary, age 59
Director Personnel and In-flight, Edward (Eddie) Wilson, age 57
Group Director Operations, Michael Hickey, age 57
CFO, Neil Sorahan
Chairman, David Bonderman, age 77
Auditors: KPMG

LOCATIONS

HQ: Ryanair Holdings Plc
 Airside Business Park, Swords, County Dublin K67 NY94
Phone: (353) 1 812 1212   **Fax:** (353) 1 812 1213
Web: www.ryanair.com

COMPETITORS

Aer Lingus	Lufthansa
Air Berlin	SAS
Air France-KLM	Spanair
Alitalia	Virgin Atlantic
British Midland	Airways
Brussels Airlines	Vueling Airlines
IAG	easyJet

HISTORICAL FINANCIALS

Company Type: Public

Income Statement   FYE: March 31

	REVENUE ($ mil.)	NET INCOME ($ mil.)	NET PROFIT MARGIN	EMPLOYEES
03/20	13,367	1,020	7.6%	17,268
03/19	12,112	1,392	11.5%	16,840
03/18	11,252	2,282	20.3%	14,583
03/17	10,460	2,070	19.8%	13,026
03/16	10,284	2,453	23.9%	11,458
Annual Growth	6.8%	(19.7%)	—	10.8%

2020 Year-End Financials

Debt ratio: 42.3%
Return on equity: 12.7%
Cash ($ mil.): 4,038
Current ratio: 0.82
Long-term debt ($ mil.): 5,638

No. of shares (mil.): 1,089
Dividends
  Yield: 0.0%
  Payout: —
Market value ($ mil.): 57,825

	STOCK PRICE ($) FY Close	P/E High/Low		PER SHARE ($)		
			Earnings	Dividends	Book Value
03/20	53.09	165 82	0.91	0.00	7.10
03/19	74.94	160 85	1.21	0.00	7.24
03/18	122.85	104 68	1.90	0.00	6.00
03/17	82.98	83 63	1.65	0.00	5.71
03/16	85.82	75 55	1.82	0.46	4.39
Annual Growth	(11.3%)	—	(15.9%)	—	12.8%

Safran SA

Auditors: Mazars

LOCATIONS

HQ: Safran SA
2, boulevard du General Martial-Valin, Paris, Cedex 15 75724
Phone: (33) 1 40 60 80 80   **Fax:** (33) 1 40 60 81 02
Web: www.safran-group.com

HISTORICAL FINANCIALS

Company Type: Public

Income Statement   FYE: December 31

	REVENUE ($ mil.)	NET INCOME ($ mil.)	NET PROFIT MARGIN	EMPLOYEES
12/19	29,697	2,747	9.3%	95,443
12/18	25,177	1,469	5.8%	92,639
12/17	21,697	5,742	26.5%	58,324
12/16	18,771	2,014	10.7%	66,490
12/15	21,429	(461)	—	0
Annual Growth	8.5%	—	—	

2019 Year-End Financials

Debt ratio: 15.8%
Return on equity: 20.1%
Cash ($ mil.): 2,955
Current ratio: 0.88
Long-term debt ($ mil.): 2,818

No. of shares (mil.): 424
Dividends
  Yield: 1.3%
  Payout: 8.0%
Market value ($ mil.): 16,436

	STOCK PRICE ($) FY Close	P/E High/Low		PER SHARE ($)		
			Earnings	Dividends	Book Value
12/19	38.70	7 5	6.32	0.51	32.71
12/18	29.89	12 8	3.37	0.47	31.52
12/17	25.75	2 2	13.75	0.25	30.23
12/16	17.97	4 3	4.84	0.39	16.58
12/15	17.24	— —	(1.11)	0.34	14.72
Annual Growth	22.4%	— —	—	10.3%	22.1%

SAIC Motor Corp Ltd

SAIC Motor Corporation (SAIC Motor) is one of the largest automotive manufacturer listed on the A-Shares market in China. The company's subsidiary Shanghai Automotive Industry Corporation manufactures develops sells and invests on automobiles motorcycles and tractors. SAIC Motor's principal activities include research and development (R&D) and production and sale of spare parts (including engines transmissions powertrain chassis interior and exterior trim electronic appliances and intelligent products system). It is also engaged in auto service and trading business including logistics auto E-commerce mobility services energy-saving and recharging services; automobile-related finance insurance and investment businesses; overseas operations and international commerce; and trade business. Its operations include Shanghai Volkswagen SAIC-GM-Wuling SAIC-Iveco-Hongyan and Sunwin. It was founded in 1978 in Shanghai China.

Operations

SAIC Motor has two reportable segments: vehicles and parts (more than 95%) and financing (less than five percent). The reporting segments are determined based on the company's operating structure.

The vehicles and parts segment's products and services includes vehicles (about 75% of total sales) parts (around 20%) and trading and service which both account for some 5% of total sales. The company also offers loans and deposits to its customers.

Geographic Reach

SAIC Motor is based in Shanghai China. The country China also generates vast majority of its sales. The company's products are present in various countries including the UK the Netherlands Norway Hong Kong Thailand and Indonesia.

Sales and Marketing

SAIC Motor's major customers are from Automotive manufacturing industry which generates almost all of its sales. The company's advertising expenses were RMB 13.4 billion and RMB 13.5 billion in 2019 and 2018 respectively.

Financial Performance

The company's revenue increased 15% from RMB 730.6 billion in 2018 to RMB 843.3 billion 2019. The increase was due to the sales increase in all of its product segments.

Net profit attributable to shareholders of listed companies declined 29% from RMB 36 billion in 2018 to RMB 25.6 billion.

Cash at the end of 2019 was RMB 109.8 billion. Operating activities generated RMB 46.3 billion while investing activities used RMB 39.3 billion. Financing activities used another RMB 3.1 billion.

Strategy

The company will firmly grasp the major orientation of progress in science and technology the bigger picture of market evolution the general trend of changes in the industry make a deeper advancement of "new four modernizations?electrification intelligent networking sharing and internationalization" strategy insist in the philosophy of "innovation-leading a breakthrough at key points promotion with successful experiences in selected units and advancement in proper order" deeply layout and carry forward innovation chain construction while grasping market structured opportunity and promoting operational performance to spare no effort to seize vantage ground and commanding height and accelerate to push the business transformation and upgrading in the process of reconstitution of global automobile industry value chain striding forward globally competitive and influential comprehensive provider for traffic service and products.

To accelerate the innovation-driven development strategy SAIC Motor Corporation Limited made a non-public offering of shares on the domestic A-share market in 2017 and simultaneously implemented a core employee stock ownership plan.

Company Background

SAIC Motor Corporation was established in 1984 as Shanghai Volkswagen Automotive a 50-50 joint venture with Volkswagen.

EXECUTIVES

President, Chen Zhixin, age 61
VP; General Manager Passenger Vehicle Co.; Head Technology Center, Wang Xiaoqiu, age 56
VP; General Manager Shanghai General Motors Wuling, Shen Yang, age 59
VP; General Manager Commercial Vehicle and Shanghai Commercial Vehicle Co., Lan Qingsong, age 56
Acting CFO, Wei Yong, age 48
Chief Engineer, Cheng Jinglei, age 53
Chairman, Chen Hong, age 59
Auditors: Deloitte Touche Tohmatsu

LOCATIONS

HQ: SAIC Motor Corp Ltd
No. 489, Weihai Road, Jingan District, Shanghai 200041
Phone: (86) 21 22011138   **Fax:** (86) 21 22011199
Web: www.saicmotor.com

2015 Sales

	% of total
China	98
Others	2
Total	**100**

PRODUCTS/OPERATIONS

2015 Revenue by products

	% of total
Vehicles	75
Parts	19
Trading	1
Finance	1
Service and others	3
Total	**100**

2015 Revenue by Segment

	% of total
Vehicles and parts	99
Finance	1
Total	**100**

COMPETITORS

BMW	Honda
BYD	Hyundai Motor
Daimler	Kia Motors
Dongfeng Peugeot	Mazda
FCA US	Nissan
Fiat Chrysler	Peugeot
Ford Motor	Suzuki Motor
General Motors	Toyota

HISTORICAL FINANCIALS

Company Type: Public

Income Statement   FYE: December 31

	REVENUE ($ mil.)	NET INCOME ($ mil.)	NET PROFIT MARGIN	EMPLOYEES
12/19	121,198	3,679	3.0%	0
12/18	131,165	5,235	4.0%	0
12/17	133,791	5,287	4.0%	0
12/16	108,929	4,609	4.2%	0
12/15	103,232	4,587	4.4%	0
Annual Growth	4.1%	(5.4%)	—	—

2019 Year-End Financials

Debt ratio: 1.0%
Return on equity: 10.5%
Cash ($ mil.): 18,370
Current ratio: 1.10
Long-term debt ($ mil.): 5,072

No. of shares (mil.): —
Dividends
  Yield: —
  Payout: —
Market value ($ mil.): —

Samba Financial Group

EXECUTIVES

Chief Executive Officer, Raniya Mahmood
Abdulwahab Nashar
Auditors: Ernst & Young & Co.

LOCATIONS

HQ: Samba Financial Group
  King Abdul Aziz Road, P.O. Box 833, Riyadh 11421
Phone: (966) 1 477 4770   **Fax:** (966) 1 477 4770
Web: www.samba.com.sa

COMPETITORS

Al Rajhi Banking	Dallah Albaraka Group
Arab Banking Corp.	Qatar National Bank
Arab National Bank	Riyad Bank
Banque Saudi Fransi	Saudi British Bank

HISTORICAL FINANCIALS
Company Type: Public

Income Statement   FYE: December 31

	ASSETS ($ mil.)	NET INCOME ($ mil.)	INCOME AS % OF ASSETS	EMPLOYEES
12/19	68,161	1,062	1.6%	3,614
12/18	61,316	1,472	2.4%	3,497
12/17	60,696	1,338	2.2%	3,530
12/16	61,721	1,333	2.2%	3,560
12/15	62,659	1,388	2.2%	3,723
Annual Growth	2.1%	(6.5%)	—	(0.7%)

2019 Year-End Financials

Return on assets: 1.6%   Dividends
Return on equity: 9.1%   Yield: —
Long-term debt ($ mil.): —   Payout: 71.3%
No. of shares (mil.): 2,000   Market value ($ mil.): —
Sales ($ mil): 2,896

Sampo OYJ

Unlike the magic pillar of Finnish lore for which it's named Sampo can't pull treasure out of thin air. But it does what it can to help its clients. The holding company offers a variety of financial products primarily in Finland but also in Sweden Norway and Denmark and throughout the Baltic region. It provides property/casualty coverage through subsidiary If P&C which is one of the largest Nordic property/casualty insurers and the company's largest money maker. Sampo's Mandatum Life subsidiary provides life insurance pension and other long-term products in Nordic countries and the Baltics. Another unit the about 45%-owned Topdanmark is the second-largest property/casualty insurer in Denmark; it also offers life insurance. The company also owns about 20% of Nordea the region's largest bank. Most of its sales came from Denmark.

Operations

Sampo operates in four primary segments: If Topdanmark Mandatum Life and Holding (which includes its stake in Nordea).

If operates in four business areas. The Private division If's largest business insures more than 3.8 million household customers and accounts for nearly 60% of gross written premiums. The Commercial division serves companies with up to 500 employees; it has some 340000 customers. The Industrial division targets companies with about 500 employees; it serves some 1500 customers. The smallest business is its Baltic division which bring in some 5% of gross written premiums. Altogether If insures some 280000 million customers in the Nordic and Baltic countries.

Topdanmark is the #2 property/casualty insurer in Denmark with about 20% market share. The company also offers life insurance and pensions; it has distribution agreements with Sydbank and Danske Bank. It operates solely in Denmark.

Mandatum Life provides customer life insurance investment and wealth management services in Finland and the Baltic countries. Its offerings include pensions personal risk insurance and consultation services. It concentrates on unit-linked insurance such as group pension insurance and personnel funds. It sells its products through its own sales team and in partnership with Danske Bank. Mandatum has some 3000000 private customers and about 20000 corporate customers.

Nordea has some 11 million customers and is one of Europe's largest banks. It operates in four divisions: Personal Banking Commercial & Business Banking Wholesale Banking (corporate advisory services) and Wealth Management. The bank has some ?324 billion in assets under management.

About 60% of its gross premiums came from its private business area while commercial industrial and Baltic accounts for the rest. Among its business lines Motor accounts for the largest with some 40% of gross written premiums.

Geographic Reach

Finland based the company also has operations in Denmark (about 35%) Norway (more than 15%) Sweden (more than 15%) and Baltic (less than 5%). Norway in terms of gross premiums had some 35% which is the largest among all other countries.

Sales and Marketing

The company sales and marketing focuses on meeting the demands and needs of customers and providing customer with information necessary for a well-informed decision in their insurance coverage needs.

Financial Performance

Gross written premiums amounted to ?4.7 billion in 2019. With fixed currency rates premiums grew by 6% in January - December 2019. All businesses had growth.

Profits totaled ?1.1 billion a decrease of 33% from the previous year.

The company's cash at the end of 2019 was ?2.7 billion. Operating activities generated ?1.5 billion and investing activities generated ?530 million. Financing activities used ?1.7 billion mainly for dividends.

Strategy

In late 2020 Sampo announced the launch of an accelerated bookbuild offering to institutional investors of 162 million Nordea shares. The offering represents 4.0% of the outstanding shares in Nordea and would reduce Sampo's ownership in Nordea to 15.9%.

The planned disposal represents a step in steering Sampo towards the group's strategic focus area - its P&C insurance operations. Over time the group will explore options to continue this process with the aim of placing P&C insurance at the core of shareholder value creation. Sampo remains confident in Nordea's ability to deliver on its strategy and 2022 financial targets and continues to be the largest shareholder in the bank.

HISTORY

Industrialists from Turku Finland founded Keskin ¤inen Vakuutuslaitos Sampo in 1909 as a competitor for traditional insurance companies. Sampo started growing in the early 1970s when two non-life insurers merged with the company resulting in a name change to Sampo-Tarmo (Tarmo being one of the acquisitions). In the latter half of the 1970s Sampo expanded its services when it formed an alliance with Finland's oldest life insurer Kaleva Mutual. The 1980s saw Sampo form a pension insurance subsidiary (Sampo Pension Ltd) and in 1987 the group started trading on the Helsinki exchange.

In the mid 1990s Sampo Group acquired three life insurers (Industrial Insurance Otso Loss of Profits Insurance and Vahinko-Kansa). The latter half of the 1990s saw the company continue its acquisitive streak (Nova Life and Leonia Life); Sampo also formed its own life insurance subsidiary Sampo Life Insurance.

The foundation for Leonia was laid in 1887 with the opening of the government-owned Postis ¤ ¤st ¶pankki (Post and Savings Bank); operations included deposits made at post offices. Assets of Postis ¤ ¤st ¶pankki were initially invested in government bonds but after WWII banking activities expanded to include energy and industrial companies and housebuilding credit.

Postis ¤ ¤st ¶pankki changed its name to Postipankki in 1970. In 1988 the bank began operating as a full-service bank. At the end of the 1990s Postipankki merged with state-owned Finnish Export Credit Ltd forming the Leonia Group.

In 1999 Sampo and the Finnish government agreed on terms for the acquisition of the Leonia Group forming a full-service financial company. Leonia ended its century-old post office operations in 2000 as it increasingly emphasized internet and telephone transactions. The merger creating Sampo-Leonia was completed at the end of the year.

In 2001 the company bought Mandatum Bank a Finnish commercial bank and reverted to the Sampo name; Leonia Bank was renamed Sampo Bank.

EXECUTIVES

Chairman of the Executive Committee and Group President and CEO, Kari Stadigh, age 65
Group CFO, Peter Johansson, age 63
Managing Director and Head of Life Insurance, Petri Niemisvirta, age 50
Group EVP and Head of BA Commercial IF P&C, Ivar Martinsen, age 59
Deputy Managing Director If P&C Insurance Holding Ltd, Ricard Wennerklint, age 51
President CEO and Head IF P&C Insurance Holding, Torbj ¶rn Magnusson, age 57
Group EVP and Head of Business Area Private If P&C, Morten Thorsrud, age 49
Group EVP Managing Director If P&C Insurance Company (Finland) and Head of Business Area Baltic If P&C, Timo Vuorinen, age 56
Chairman, Bj ¶rn Wahlroos, age 68
Vice Chairperson, Eira Palin-Lehtinen, age 70
Auditors: Ernst & Young Oy

LOCATIONS

HQ: Sampo OYJ
  Fabianinkatu 27, Helsinki 00100
Phone: (358) 10 516 0100   **Fax:** (358) 10 516 0016
Web: www.sampo.com

COMPETITORS

HISTORICAL FINANCIALS

Company Type: Public

Income Statement

FYE: December 31

	REVENUE ($ mil.)	NET INCOME ($ mil.)	NET PROFIT MARGIN	EMPLOYEES
12/19	12,646	1,268	10.0%	9,813
12/18	8,935	1,931	21.6%	9,509
12/17	8,294	2,656	32.0%	9,364
12/16	6,548	1,742	26.6%	6,780
12/15	7,101	1,803	25.4%	6,755
Annual Growth	15.5%	(8.4%)	—	9.8%

2019 Year-End Financials

Debt ratio: —
Return on equity: 9.3%
Cash ($ mil.): 3,005
Current ratio: —
Long-term debt ($ mil.): —

No. of shares (mil.): 555
Dividends
  Yield: 8.2%
  Payout: 78.0%
Market value ($ mil.): 12,118

	STOCK PRICE ($) FY Close	P/E High/Low		PER SHARE ($) Earnings	Dividends	Book Value
12/19	21.82	12	10	2.29	1.79	24.07
12/18	22.15	9	7	3.48	1.55	25.54
12/17	27.48	7	6	4.75	1.37	27.73
12/16	22.39	8	6	3.11	1.15	22.50
12/15	25.30	9	7	3.22	1.06	22.19
Annual Growth	(3.6%)	—	—	(8.2%)	14.0%	2.1%

Samsung C&T Corp (New)

Auditors: Samil PricewaterhouseCoopers

LOCATIONS

HQ: Samsung C&T Corp (New)
  123, Olympic-ro 35-gil, Songpa-gu, Seoul 05510
Phone: (82) 2 759 0290
Web: www.samsungcnt.com

HISTORICAL FINANCIALS

Company Type: Public

Income Statement

FYE: December 31

	REVENUE ($ mil.)	NET INCOME ($ mil.)	NET PROFIT MARGIN	EMPLOYEES
12/19	26,642	909	3.4%	0
12/18	27,945	1,536	5.5%	9,374
12/17	27,463	600	2.2%	9,422
12/16	23,392	89	0.4%	10,252
12/15	11,342	2,334	20.6%	12,083
Annual Growth	23.8%	(21.0%)	—	—

2019 Year-End Financials

Debt ratio: 0.0%
Return on equity: 4.7%
Cash ($ mil.): 2,342
Current ratio: 1.08
Long-term debt ($ mil.): 610

No. of shares (mil.): 163
Dividends
  Yield: —
  Payout: —
Market value ($ mil.): —

Samsung Electronics Co Ltd

Auditors: Sami PircewaterhouseCoopers

LOCATIONS

HQ: Samsung Electronics Co Ltd
  129, Samsung-ro, Yeongtong-gu, Suwon-si, Gyeonggi-do 16677
Phone: (82) 31 200 1114   **Fax:** (82) 31 200 7538
Web: www.sec.co.kr

HISTORICAL FINANCIALS

Company Type: Public

Income Statement

FYE: December 31

	REVENUE ($ mil.)	NET INCOME ($ mil.)	NET PROFIT MARGIN	EMPLOYEES
12/19	199,547	18,625	9.3%	0
12/18	218,650	39,367	18.0%	0
12/17	224,719	38,780	17.3%	99,784
12/16	168,031	18,658	11.1%	93,200
12/15	170,545	15,889	9.3%	96,898
Annual Growth	4.0%	4.1%	—	—

2019 Year-End Financials

Debt ratio: 0.0%
Return on equity: 8.6%
Cash ($ mil.): 23,285
Current ratio: 2.84
Long-term debt ($ mil.): 2,747

No. of shares (mil.): —
Dividends
  Yield: —
  Payout: 1,122.6%
Market value ($ mil.): —

San Miguel Corp

A household name because of its brewery biz San Miguel Corporation (SMC) is one of the top food-to-power conglomerates in the Philippines. It operates more than 100 facilities in Southeast Asia Australia New Zealand and China. The company's flagship unit is San Miguel Brewery (beer and liquor) while its Pure Food unit manufactures a variety of staples including meats dairy products and coffee. SMC also has packaging operations. It owns a major stake in the country's biggest oil refiner Petron. SMC has other investments in energy and construction.

Operations

SMC has five operating segments: Petron accounts for approximately 50% of total sales Food & Beverage around 30% Power representing about 15% Packaging unit drove almost 5% and Infrastructure around 5%.

SMC owns about 70% of stake in Petron. One of the country's largest refiner of crude oil and marketer and distributor of refined petroleum products with about 2400 service stations.

Food & Beverage segment has San Miguel Food and Beverage Inc. which consists of three business groups: Beer and non-alcoholic beverages; spirits; and food. The company operates its beverage business through San Miguel Brewery Inc. and Ginebra San Miguel Inc. Food business has San Miguel Foods Inc. and subsidiaries which comprises manufacturers of national food brands such as Magnolia Monterey and Pure Foods among several. It is supported by partnerships with international companies such as Hormel Foods.

SMC's Power segment owns three power plants (coal-fired hydro-electric and one natural gas-fired) and a couple of greenfield power plant.

Packaging includes a handful of plants and facilities which make glass and polyethylene terephthalate (PET) plastic paper and metal containers for various customers.

The company's infrastructure segment includes road water treatment and distribution airports port and rail transit projects.

Geographic Reach

SMC is headquartered in the Philippines.

SMC's manufacturing operations extend beyond the Philippines to Hong Kong China Indonesia Vietnam Thailand and Malaysia. Its products are exported to major markets around the world

Sales and Marketing

SMC's packaging segment serves manufacturers of food pharmaceutical chemical beverages and personal care customers.

Financial PerformanceThe company's sales for 2019 totaled PHP1 trillion a minor decline from the previous year. Net Income attributable to equity holders of the parent company totaled PHP21.3 billion an 8% decline from the previous year. The company's consolidated cash balance increased by PHP43.3 billion ending at PHP286.5 billion as of December 31 2019.

Strategy

2019 was a significant year for San Miguel Corporation as it delivered on many of the key projects it outlined in previous years as being crucial to the company's future growth. Despite the year being a particularly challenging one for some of the company's major businesses its resolve to stay the course in terms of its overall strategy?continuing to build new capacities for the company's Food and Beverage business to address growing demand and accelerating development of growth-building infrastructure for the Philippines?again worked to the company's advantage.

EXECUTIVES

Vice Chairman President and COO, Ramon S. Ang
Chairman and CEO, Eduardo M. (Danding) Cojuangco
SVP and CFO, Ferdinand K. Constantino
SVP Senior Executive AssistantOffice of the President and COO, Aurora T. Calderon
Auditors: R.G. Manabat & Co.

LOCATIONS

HQ: San Miguel Corp
  No. 40 San Miguel Avenue, Mandaluyong City, Metro Manila 1550
Phone: (63) 2 632 3000   **Fax:** (63) 2 632 3099
Web: www.sanmiguel.com.ph

PRODUCTS/OPERATIONS

2016 Sales

	% of total
Fuel and Oil	48
Beverage	16
Food	15
Energy	11
Packaging	4
Infrastructure	3
Others	3
Total	**100**

COMPETITORS

Cargill
Coca-Cola
Dairy Farm
  International
Danone
Del Monte Pacific
Diageo

Metro Pacific
Nestlé
PepsiCo
SABMiller
Tsingtao
Tyson Foods

HISTORICAL FINANCIALS

Company Type: Public

Income Statement   FYE: December 31

	REVENUE ($ mil.)	NET INCOME ($ mil.)	NET PROFIT MARGIN	EMPLOYEES
12/19	20,153	421	2.1%	47,730
12/18	19,515	439	2.3%	28,598
12/17	16,583	566	3.4%	24,539
12/16	13,841	591	4.3%	22,396
12/15	14,384	265	1.8%	18,586
Annual Growth	8.8%	12.2%	—	26.6%

2019 Year-End Financials

Debt ratio: 1.0%
Return on equity: 6.3%
Cash ($ mil.): 5,657
Current ratio: 1.46
Long-term debt ($ mil.): 14,935

No. of shares (mil.): —
Dividends
  Yield: —
  Payout: —
Market value ($ mil.): —

San-In Godo Bank, Ltd. (The) (Japan)

EXECUTIVES

President, FUMIO ISHIMARU
Auditors: Ernst & Young ShinNihon LLC

LOCATIONS

HQ: San-In Godo Bank, Ltd. (The) (Japan)
  10 Uomachi, Matsue, Shimane 690-8686
Phone: (81) 852 55 1000
Web: www.gogin.co.jp

COMPETITORS

Aozora Bank
Mitsubishi UFJ
  Financial Group

Shizuoka Bank

HISTORICAL FINANCIALS

Company Type: Public

Income Statement   FYE: March 31

	ASSETS ($ mil.)	NET INCOME ($ mil.)	INCOME AS % OF ASSETS	EMPLOYEES
03/20	52,431	96	0.2%	3,337
03/19	50,563	119	0.2%	3,366
03/18	52,253	128	0.2%	3,263
03/17	48,400	119	0.2%	3,217
03/16	45,954	114	0.3%	3,185
Annual Growth	3.4%	(4.3%)	—	1.2%

2020 Year-End Financials

Return on assets: 0.1%
Return on equity: 2.8%
Long-term debt ($ mil.): —
No. of shares (mil.): 156
Sales ($ mil): 832

Dividends
  Yield: —
  Payout: 29.8%
Market value ($ mil.): —

Sandvik AB (Sweden)

Sandvik is a high-tech global manufacturer specializing in mining and rock excavation equipment for drilling crushing and loading applications. Its machining and tooling segment makes metal cutting tools and components for digital and additive manufacturing and the materials technology division develops stainless steels and powder-based and specialty alloys. Most of Sandvik's customers fall within the mining and engineering sectors but the company also sells to the automotive energy construction and aerospace markets. It operates in more than 160 countries worldwide. Europe represents close to 40% of annual revenue and North America and Asia each account for about 20%.

Financial Performance

Note: Growth rates may differ after conversion to US Dollars.

Sandvik's revenue has been increasing steadily over the past two years after a flat period during the previous three years (2014-2016).

Sales in 2018 reached 100.1 billion SEK ($11.5 billion) a 10% increase of over 2017 but net profit remained flat compared with the previous year. Revenue growth is attributed to sales from acquisitions. Its challenges are fierce competition from China and stiff import duties in the US.

Cash at the end of fiscal 2018 was 18.1 billion SEK an increase of 5.4 billion SEK from the prior year. Cash from operations contributed 14.9 billion SEK to the coffers while investing activities used 4.3 billion SEK mainly for acquisitions. Financing activities used another 5.2 billion SEK for loan payments and dividends to stockholders.

Strategy

In recent years Sandvik has moved toward a more decentralized operating structure resulting in greater product ownership and accountability and bringing decision-making closer to its customers. To drive growth the company continually makes strategic acquisitions and is focused on new product development.

It has streamlined operations with the divestitures of Sandvik Hyperion (super-hard and wear-resistant tools) and both its stainless wire and welding wire businesses in 2018. At the same time the company made several small acquisitions to round out its core business in the areas of metal cutting (Metrologic Group) directional drilling (Inrock) and industrial heating (Custom Electric Manufacturing). Sandvik added to its round tools portfolio with the addition of Dura-Mill and Kunshan Ousike Precision Tools.

Sandvik has launched many new products to capitalize on trends in digitalization and automation. Its Optimine data analytics product helps mining companies increase productivity using predictive analysis dashboards and 3D visualization of mine operations. Its new Leopard DI650i down-the-hole (DTH) drill reduces fuel consumption by 15%. Using a cloud-based monitoring system the company's Sentusys intelligent tube system allows industrial process customers to control things like vibration and temperature inside tubes within their operations.

In 2018

HISTORY

Sandvik's origins go back to 1862 when a steelworks called Hogbo Stal & Jernwerks was founded by Goran Fredrik Goransson in Sandviken Sweden. Its products in the 1860s included steam hammers and rock drills. Hogbo Stal & Jernwerks' primary financial backer Johan Holm had money

problems that left him and the company financially ruined; the company went bankrupt in 1866. Hogbo Stal & Jernwerks was reorganized and renamed Sandvikens Jernwerks AB and Anders Henrik Goransson the founder's son took over as the new manager.

By the 1890s the company's steel products included cold-rolled steel rod and strip and seamless tubing. It also made manufactured products such as saws boiler tubes for steamships and railway engines and wire for umbrellas. Sandvikens Jernwerks was listed on the Stockholm stock exchange in 1901.

EXECUTIVES

President and CEO, Olof Faxander, age 50
EVP and Head Human Resources, Anna Vikstr¶m Persson
President Sandvik Materials Technology, Jonas Gustavsson, age 54
President Sandvik Venture business area, Tomas Nordahl, age 53
EVP and Head R&D, Olle Wijk
EVP and CFO, Emil Nilsson
President Sandvik Materials Technology, Petra Einarsson
EVP Group Communications, Jessica Alm
EVP and CFO, Mats Backman, age 52
President Sandvik Construction business area, Dinggui Gao
President Sandvik Mining business area, Scot Smith
EVP and General Counsel, ...sa Thunman
EVP and Head Emerging Markets, ZZ Zhang
President of the Sandvik Venture business area, Jim Nixon
Chairman, Anders Nyren
Auditors: PricewaterhouseCoopers AB

LOCATIONS

HQ: Sandvik AB (Sweden)
  Storgatan 2, Sandviken SE-811 81
Phone: (46) 26 26 00 00   **Fax:** (46) 26 26 10 22
Web: www.sandvik.com

2018 Sales

	% of total
Europe	38
North America	21
Asia	20
Africa/Middle East	9
Australia	7
South America	5
Total	**100**

PRODUCTS/OPERATIONS

2018 Sales

	% of total
Sandvik Mining & Rock Technology	43
Sandvik Machining Solutions	40
Sandvik Materials Technology	15
Other Operations	2
Total	**100**

2018 Sales by Customer

	% of total
Mining industry	34
Engineering industry	23
Automotive industry	12
Energy industry	11
Construction industry	9
Aerospace industry	6
Other	5
Total	**100**

COMPETITORS

Aperam
Caterpillar
Furukawa
IMC Group
Kennametal
Komatsu
Metso Minerals
Mitsubishi Heavy Industries
Nippon Steel & Sumitomo Metal Corporation
Terex
Tubacex

HISTORICAL FINANCIALS

Company Type: Public

Income Statement				FYE: December 31
	REVENUE ($ mil.)	NET INCOME ($ mil.)	NET PROFIT MARGIN	EMPLOYEES
12/19	17,276	1,428	8.3%	40,246
12/18	16,746	2,127	12.7%	41,705
12/17	15,212	2,208	14.5%	43,024
12/16	13,647	921	6.8%	43,732
12/15	14,365	376	2.6%	45,809
Annual Growth	4.7%	39.6%	—	(3.2%)

2019 Year-End Financials

Debt ratio: 2.8%
Return on equity: 14.1%
Cash ($ mil.): 2,837
Current ratio: 2.21
Long-term debt ($ mil.): 2,948

No. of shares (mil.): 1,254
Dividends
  Yield: 2.2%
  Payout: 39.0%
Market value ($ mil.): 24,383

	STOCK PRICE ($) FY Close	P/E High/Low		PER SHARE ($) Earnings	Dividends	Book Value
12/19	19.44	3	2	1.14	0.44	8.25
12/18	14.41	2	1	1.70	0.40	7.80
12/17	17.50	2	1	1.76	0.31	6.50
12/16	12.26	3	2	0.73	0.31	5.23
12/15	8.64	7	4	0.30	0.29	4.53
Annual Growth	22.5%	—	—	39.6%	11.5%	16.2%

Sanofi

Auditors: PricewaterhouseCoopers Audit

LOCATIONS

HQ: Sanofi
  54, rue La Boetie, Paris 75008
Phone: (33) 1 53 77 40 00   **Fax:** (33) 1 53 77 43 03
Web: www.sanofi.com

HISTORICAL FINANCIALS

Company Type: Public

Income Statement				FYE: December 31
	REVENUE ($ mil.)	NET INCOME ($ mil.)	NET PROFIT MARGIN	EMPLOYEES
12/19	42,250	3,150	7.5%	100,409
12/18	40,857	4,931	12.1%	104,226
12/17	43,399	10,110	23.3%	106,566
12/16	36,647	4,972	13.6%	106,859
12/15	37,970	4,669	12.3%	115,631
Annual Growth	2.7%	(9.4%)	—	(3.5%)

2019 Year-End Financials

Debt ratio: 25.8%
Return on equity: 4.7%
Cash ($ mil.): 10,584
Current ratio: 1.40
Long-term debt ($ mil.): 23,710

No. of shares (mil.): 1,253
Dividends
  Yield: 3.4%
  Payout: 65.8%
Market value ($ mil.): 62,943

	STOCK PRICE ($) FY Close	P/E High/Low		PER SHARE ($) Earnings	Dividends	Book Value
12/19	50.20	23	18	2.50	1.72	52.77
12/18	43.41	13	11	3.93	1.79	54.14
12/17	43.00	8	6	7.98	5.36	55.54
12/16	40.44	11	10	3.83	4.63	47.78
12/15	42.65	17	12	3.54	1.61	48.57
Annual Growth	4.2%	—	—	(8.3%)	1.7%	2.1%

SAP SE

SAP SE's software forms a company's nerve center. Its enterprise resource planning software integrates back-office functions such as analytics accounting distribution and human resources and comes in on-premises and cloud-linked forms. While the sale and servicing of its legacy on-premises offering brings in the majority of the company's revenue SAP is going all-in on cloud computing and software-as-a-service with its flagship application suite S/4HANA as an alternative to its legacy SAP Business Suite. Besides enterprise software SAP Concur provides expenses management and SAP Fieldglass provides external workforce management. The company serves more than 440000 customers in upwards of 25 industries across more than180 countries. Germany is the largest single market accounts for about 15% of total revenue. In 2019 SAP acquired Qualtrics for $7.1 billion the second largest acquisition after Concur.

Operations

SAP has several revenue streams. The largest software licenses and support generates some 60% of sales and comprises SAP's legacy on-premise software and support services. SAP's Cloud subscriptions and support offerings which are growing as a proportion of the whole include S/4HANA and bring in roughly 25% of sales. Miscellaneous other services account for more than 15% of sales.

Broadly speaking SAP's products provide functionality such as analytics enterprise management supply chain management financial management and customer relationship management among other things. The products are scaled and tailored to fit companies of varying size and in a diversity of industries.

SAP Concur is a leading cloud-based expenses management platform SAP Fieldglass helps companies manage contingent workforces and SAP Ariba is a B2B supply chain management platform that connects vendors and suppliers.

Geographic Reach

Headquartered in Walldorf Germany SAP has customers in more than 180 countries. The EMEA region (Europe Middle East and Africa) is SAP's biggest region about 45% of sales of which Germany represents about 15%. The US accounts more than 40% of sales and the Asia/Pacific region contributes roughly 15% of sales.

Sales and Marketing

Most of SAP's sales are generated by the direct sales staffs within the organization although it also sells through partners.

SAP has customers in many industries including chemicals mining oil & gas banking agribusiness fashion retail aerospace & defense automotive industrial media telecoms higher education & research among others.

Financial Performance

Note: Growth rates may differ after conversion to US Dollars.

Total revenue increased from ?24.7 billion in 2018 to ?27.6 billion in 2019 representing an increase of ?2.8 billion or 12%. The growth in revenue resulted primarily from a ?1.9 billion increase in cloud revenue to ?6.9 billion. Cloud and software revenue represented 84% of total revenue in 2019 (2018: 83%). Service revenue increased 11% from ?4.1 billion in 2018 to ?4.5 billion in 2019 which was 16% of total revenue (2018: 17%).

The company's net income in 2019 decreased by ?762 million to ?3.3 billion from ?4.1 billion in 2018. The decrease was primarily due to the increase on operating expenses offsetting the increase of their revenue.

SAP's cash on hand fell ?3.3 billion during ending the year at ?5.3 billion. The company's operations generated ?3.5 billion and its financing activities generated ?102 million while investing activities used ?7.0 billion.

Strategy

SAP's strategy is to be the Experience Company powered by the Intelligent Enterprise. The company believes every digital interaction is an opportunity for a company to positively influence a customer. Through these interactions companies can measure "experiences" - such as customer satisfaction employee engagement partner collaboration and brand impact. These interactions are also opportunities for companies to understand how end users and customers perceive a vendor or a product. SAP want to help every SAP customer thrive in today's "experience economy" by equipping them with the technologies to become intelligent enterprises.

The company's vision for the intelligent enterprise an event-driven real-time business focuses on three key objectives: Create a new end-to-end customer experience through a platform for Experience Management that allows businesses to collect understand and act on feedback across their customers employees products and brands in real time. In particular the company enable other companies to enhance feedback with analytics so they not only can understand what is being said but also why. Achieve a step change in productivity through the next level of automation in business processes powered by artificial intelligence/machine learning (AI/ML) embedded in every part of the business process (across financials supply chain manufacturing procurement travel and human resources). AI is defined as algorithms that learn from data without being explicitly programmed thus empowering enterprises to scale by automating business processes. The key to doing so is improving the cycle time of business processes and injecting speed and increasing quality wherever possible. Help companies engage their workforces by delivering total workforce engagement across full-time and contingent labor.

Mergers and Acquisitions

SAP bought Qualtrics for about $7.1 billion in 2019. SAP intends to deploy Qualtrics technologies in its battle with Salesforce.com for customer relationship management customers. The deal is SAP's second biggest acquisition just behind the $8.3 billion it paid for Concur in 2014. For SAP the purchase adds Qualtrics' technologies for measuring customer experience and sentiment a fast-growing area to its software portfolio. For its part Qualtrics gets exposure to SAP's much larger number of customers.

Company Background

Founded in 1972 SAP's current phase kicked off with the launch of its HANA database technology in 2010 which revolutionized database infrastructure and provided serious competition to Oracle. HANA's competitive advantage is to store data in a huge amount of RAM storage (coupled with massive computational power) versus a disk storage approach as used by Oracle's enterprise database. A memory-based database is many times faster than a disk-based equivalent but the complexity of transferring to HANA has proved a big hurdle to customers slowing uptake. Longstanding CEO Bill McDermott stepped down in 2019.

EXECUTIVES

CEO, William R. (Bill) McDermott, age 58, $1,657,342 total compensation
President EMEA and Greater China Global Customer Operations, Adaire Fox-Martin
President Americas and Asia Pacific Japan Global Customer Operations, Jennifer Morgan
President Cloud Business Group, Robert (Rob) Enslin
EVP and Chief Business Officer Americas and Asia Pacific Japan (APJ), Stephen E. Shute
CIO, Thomas Saueressig, age 35
CFO, Luka Mucic
EMEA North Regional President, Brian Duffy
Member SAP Executive Board Digital Business Services, Michael Kleinemeier
Member SAP Executive Board Products & Innovation, Bernd Leukert
Chairman Supervisory Board, Hasso Plattner, age 76
Deputy Chairperson, Margret Klein-Magar
Auditors: KPMG AG Wirtschaftsprufungsgesellschaft

LOCATIONS

HQ: SAP SE
Dietmar-Hopp-Allee 16, Walldorf 69190
Phone: (49) 0 6227 7 47474 **Fax:** (49) 0 6227 7 57575
Web: www.sap.com

2018 Sales

	% of total
Europe Middle East & Africa	
Germany	15
Other countries	30
Americas	39
Asia/Pacific	16
Total	**100**

PRODUCTS/OPERATIONS

2018 Sales

	% of total
Software & Support	
Support	44
Licenses	19
Cloud Subscription & Support	20
Services	17
Total	**100**

Selected Customers

Aigo
City of Cape Town South Africa
Danone
Beaumont Health System
McLaren Group

Selected Software

SAP Business All-in-One
SAP Business ByDesign
SAP Business One
SAP Business Suite
SAP ERP
SAP HANA
SAP NetWeaver

Selected Services

Application hosting
Business consulting
Custom development
Financing
Implementation
Maintenance
Training

Selected Acquisitions

Concur (2014) Travel and expense management software for companiesHybris (2014) Real-time customer engagement and commerce platformSeeWhy (2014) Cloud-based behavioral target marketing softwareTicket-Web (2013) Ticketing software and Right Hemisphere (2012; enterprise visualization)
TechniData (2010; environmental health and safety)
Sybase (2010 business intelligence and database management)
Clear Standards (2009 environmental)
Highdeal (2009 billing)
Visiprise (2008 manufacturing process management)
Business Objects (2008 business intelligence)
OutlookSoft (2007 business performance management)
Pilot Software (2007 business performance management)

COMPETITORS

BMC Software	IBM
CA Inc.	MicroStrategy
CDC Software	Microsoft
Electronic Data	Oracle
Processing	Software AG
Epicor Software	Workday Inc.
HP	salesforce.com

HISTORICAL FINANCIALS

Company Type: Public

Income Statement

FYE: December 31

	REVENUE ($ mil.)	NET INCOME ($ mil.)	NET PROFIT MARGIN	EMPLOYEES
12/19	43,357	5,225	12.1%	10,330
12/18	38,880	6,425	16.5%	96,498
12/17	36,918	6,322	17.1%	88,543
12/16	34,716	5,737	16.5%	84,183
12/15	32,719	4,808	14.7%	76,986
Annual Growth	**7.3%**	**2.1%**	**—**	**(39.5%)**

2019 Year-End Financials

Debt ratio: 42.3%
Return on equity: 11.1%
Cash ($ mil.): 8,362
Current ratio: 1.05
Long-term debt ($ mil.): 20,335
No. of shares (mil.): 1,228
Dividends
Yield: 0.9%
Payout: 27.4%
Market value ($ mil.): 164,607

	STOCK PRICE ($) FY Close	P/E High/Low	Earnings	PER SHARE ($) Dividends	Book Value
12/19	133.99	50 34	4.37	1.20	39.38
12/18	99.55	37 28	5.38	1.19	38.01
12/17	112.36	35 26	5.27	0.98	33.63
12/16	86.43	30 24	4.78	0.93	34.63
12/15	79.10	32 25	4.03	0.88	30.56
Annual Growth	**14.1%**	**—**	**2.1%**	**8.1%**	**6.5%**

Saputo Inc

Saputo is the big cheese in Canada. The country's #1 dairy processor Saputo produces staple and specialty cheeses for retail foodservice and industrial customers mainly in Canada and the US. It is also the largest dairy processor in Australia as well as a leading dairy producer in Argentina. Armstrong Frigo Stella and Treasure Cave are some of its leading cheese brands. Saputo's other dairy products include Neilson and Dairyland fluid milk and yogurt and dairy ingredients. The company processes some 11 billion liters of milk annually. Originally a small mozzarella maker Saputo has grown through acquisitions.

Financial Performance

Growth rates may differ after conversion to US Dollar.

Saputo has seen solid revenue growth over the past five years with sales up 27% since fiscal 2015 (ended March). Net income has been a little more sporadic although it is generally up since 2015.

In fiscal 2019 the company reported revenue of C$13.5 billion up 17% from the prior year. The growth was powered primarily by acquisitions (Murray Goulburn in Australia) that boosted sales outside the Americas. Saputo saw growth across all three market segments with the Industrial segment leading the way.

Net income however fell 11% to C$755.3 million that year. Results were impacted most significantly by a more than doubling of income taxes.

Cash at the end of fiscal 2019 was C$112.7 million a decrease of nearly C$10 million from the prior year. Cash from operations contributed C$884.5 million to the coffers while investing activities used C$1.5 billion mainly for acquisitions. Financing activities added another C$606.1 million from proceeds from issuance of long-term debt.

Strategy

Growing through acquisitions is a key element of Saputo's long-term strategy. It has bought 30-plus companies since its 1997 IPO. The company rose to the top of the Australian dairy processing industry with the 2018 purchase of Murray Goulburn and the next year became the UK's largest maker of branded cheese with the acquisition of Dairy Crest. Other recent purchases have expanded Saputo's product portfolio.

Amid the acquisitions the company is also investing in facilities and systems. In fiscal 2019 and continuing through fiscal 2022 it is rolling out a new enterprise resource planning (ERP) system. In addition the dairy processor is building a new fluid milk manufacturing facility in British Columbia. The Canadian market is becoming increasingly competitive and Saputo saw no growth in the market in fiscal 2019.

Mergers and Acquisitions

Saputo has embarked on an acquisition spree in the last few years as it looks to expand its business.

In 2019 it reached an agreement with Dairy Crest to acquire the UK business for around Å 975 million in cash. Dairy Crest manufactures and markets cheese butters spreads and oils under brands including Cathedral City (cheddar) Clover (margarine) Country Life (butter) and Fry Light (cooking spray).

In late 2018 Saputo completed the acquisition of F&A Dairy Products which produces cheeses from facilities in New Mexico and Wisconsin. The deal expands Saputo's specialty cheese portfolio in the US as did the 2017 purchase of Wisconsin-based Betin (dba Montchevre).

Also in 2018 the company bought Australian dairy cooperative Murray Goulburn for about $1 billion. The deal adds to and enhances Saputo's dairy operations in the Australian market where it is already active through Warrnambool Cheese & Butter.

EXECUTIVES

CFO, Louis-Philippe Carri ̈re, $499,240 total compensation
Vice Chairman and CEO, Lino A. Saputo, $725,000 total compensation
President and COO Cheese Division USA, Terry Brockman
President and COO, Kai Bockmann
President and COO Dairy Foods Division (USA), Paul Corney
President and COO Dairy Division Canada, Carl Colizza
Chairman, Emanuele (Lino) Saputo
Auditors: Deloitte LLP

LOCATIONS

HQ: Saputo Inc
  6869 Metropolitain Blvd. East, Montreal, Quebec H1P 1X8
Phone: 514 328-6662
Web: www.saputo.com

2019 Sales

	% of total
US	48
Canada	30
Australia	17
Argentina	5
Total	**100**

PRODUCTS/OPERATIONS

2019 Sales

	% of total
Retail	47
Foodservice	35
Industrial	18
Total	**100**

COMPETITORS

Agropur cooperative
Associated British Foods
Bel Brands USA
BelGioioso Cheese
Cheesemakers Inc.
ConAgra
Crystal Farms Refrigerated Distribution Company
Dairy Farmers of America
Dean Foods
Flowers Foods
Foremost Farms
Fromageries Bel
General Mills
George Weston
Great Lakes Cheese
J & J Snack Foods
Kellogg U.S. Snacks
Lactalis
Land O'Lakes
Leprino Foods
Marathon Cheese
McKee Foods
Mondelez International
Nestle Canada
Original Herkimer County Cheese Company
Parmalat Canada
Ronald A. Chisholm Limited
Sargento
Sartori Foods
Schreiber Foods
Swiss Valley Farms
Tillamook County Creamery Association
Uplands Cheese Company Inc.

HISTORICAL FINANCIALS

Company Type: Public

Income Statement

FYE: March 31

	REVENUE ($ mil.)	NET INCOME ($ mil.)	NET PROFIT MARGIN	EMPLOYEES
03/20	15,131	590	3.9%	17,200
03/19	13,672	764	5.6%	16,800
03/18	11,687	863	7.4%	15,000
03/17	11,303	740	6.5%	12,800
03/16	11,130	608	5.5%	12,500
Annual Growth	8.0%	(0.8%)	—	8.3%

2020 Year-End Financials

Debt ratio: 29.8%
Return on equity: 9.7%
Cash ($ mil.): 323
Current ratio: 1.63
Long-term debt ($ mil.): 3,586
No. of shares (mil.): 408
Dividends
  Yield: 0.0%
  Payout: 46.5%
Market value ($ mil.): 9,818

	STOCK PRICE ($) FY Close	P/E High/Low	PER SHARE ($) Earnings	Dividends	Book Value
03/20	24.03	24 14	1.47	0.68	16.25
03/19	33.46	18 15	1.95	0.66	14.07
03/18	32.02	17 14	2.21	0.64	12.54
03/17	34.56	20 16	1.86	0.59	11.33
03/16	32.31	21 14	1.53	0.54	10.32
Annual Growth	(7.1%)	— —	(1.0%)	6.0%	12.0%

Saudi Basic Industries Corp - SABIC (Saudi Arabia)

EXECUTIVES

Vice Chairman and CEO, Mohamed H. Al-Mady
EVP Corporate Strategy and Planning, Yousef Al-Zamel
EVP Fertilizers, Khaled Al-Mana
EVP Corporate Human Resources, Fahad Al-Sheaibi
EVP Polymers, Mosaed Al-Ohali
EVP Innovative Plastics, Keith J. Smith
EVP Chemicals, Yousef A. Al-Benyan
EVP Metals, Abdulaziz S. Al-Humaid
EVP Performance Chemicals, Abdullah S. Al-Rabeeah
EVP Technology and Innovation, Ernesto Occhiello
EVP Shared Services, Omar A. Al-Amoudi
EVP Manufacturing, Awadh Al-Maker
Chairman, Saud bin Abdullah bin Thenayan Al-Saud
Auditors: Ernst & Young

LOCATIONS

HQ: Saudi Basic Industries Corp - SABIC (Saudi Arabia)
  Qurtubah District, Riyadh 11422
Phone: (966) 1 225 8000   **Fax:** (966) 1 225 9000
Web: www.sabic.com

2018 Sales

	% of total
Europe	23
Rest of Asia	22
China	17
Kingdom of Saudi Arabia	5
Americas	9
Others	14
Total	**100**

PRODUCTS/OPERATIONS

2018 Sales

	% of total
Petrochemicals & Specialties	89
Hadeed	6
Agri-Nutrients	5
Total	**100**

Selected Subsidiaries & Affiliates

Al-Jubail Petrochemical Co
Aluminum Bahrain
Arabian Industrial Fibers Co
Arabian Petrochemical Co
Eastern Petrochemical Co
Gulf Aluminum Rolling Mill Co
Gulf Petrochemical Industries Co
Jubail Fertilizer
Jubail United Petrochemical Co
Má;aden Phosphate Co.
National Chemical Carrier Company
National Chemical Fertilizer Co
National Industrial Gases Co
National Methanol Co
SABIC Innovative Plastics
Saudi Arabian Fertilizer Co
Saudi Iron & Steel Co
Saudi Kayan Petrochemical Co
Saudi Methanol Co
Saudi Organometallic Chemicals Co
Saudi Petrochemical Co
Saudi Specialty Chemicals Co
Saudi-Yanbu Petrochemical Co
Saudi-European Petrochemical Co
Sinopec SABIC Tianjin Petrochemical Co
Yanbu National Petrochemical

COMPETITORS

ArcelorMittal
BASF SE
Covestro
Dow Chemical
ExxonMobil Chemical
INEOS AG
Lucite
LyondellBasell
Nippon Steel & Sumitomo Metal Corporation
POSCO
Shell Chemicals
Sumitomo Chemical

HISTORICAL FINANCIALS

Company Type: Public

Income Statement

FYE: December 31

	REVENUE ($ mil.)	NET INCOME ($ mil.)	NET PROFIT MARGIN	EMPLOYEES
12/19	37,263	1,483	4.0%	0
12/18	45,100	5,738	12.7%	0
12/17	39,937	4,914	12.3%	34,000
12/16	35,415	4,756	13.4%	35,000
12/15	39,444	4,999	12.7%	40,000
Annual Growth	(1.4%)	(26.2%)	—	—

2019 Year-End Financials

Debt ratio: 3.6%
Return on equity: 3.2%
Cash ($ mil.): 10,216
Current ratio: 2.54
Long-term debt ($ mil.): 9,189
No. of shares (mil.): —
Dividends
  Yield: —
  Payout: 237.8%
Market value ($ mil.): —

Saudi British Bank (The)

Auditors: Ernst & Young & Co.

LOCATIONS

HQ: Saudi British Bank (The)
P.O. Box 9084, Riyadh 11413
Phone: (966) 1 405 0677 **Fax:** (966) 1 276 4809
Web: www.sabb.com

COMPETITORS

Ahli United Bank
Al Rajhi Banking
Arab Banking Corp.
Arab National Bank
British Arab
  Commercial Bank

Gulf International
  Bank
Samba Financial

HISTORICAL FINANCIALS

Company Type: Public

Income Statement   FYE: December 31

	ASSETS ($ mil.)	NET INCOME ($ mil.)	INCOME AS % OF ASSETS	EMPLOYEES
12/19	70,792	754	1.1%	4,537
12/18	46,550	1,315	2.8%	3,171
12/17	50,030	1,054	2.1%	3,263
12/16	49,607	1,038	2.1%	3,317
12/15	50,009	1,153	2.3%	3,451
Annual Growth	9.1%	(10.1%)	—	7.1%

2019 Year-End Financials

Return on assets: 1.2%
Return on equity: 6.4%
Long-term debt ($ mil.): —
No. of shares (mil.): 2,054
Sales ($ mil): 3,138

Dividends
 Yield: —
 Payout: 76.4%
Market value ($ mil.): —

Saudi Electricity Co

Auditors: KPMG Al Fozan & Partners

LOCATIONS

HQ: Saudi Electricity Co
P.O. Box 22955, Riyadh 11416
Phone: (966) 14053227 **Fax:** (966) 14032222
Web: www.se.com.sa

HISTORICAL FINANCIALS

Company Type: Public

Income Statement   FYE: December 31

	REVENUE ($ mil.)	NET INCOME ($ mil.)	NET PROFIT MARGIN	EMPLOYEES
12/19	17,344	370	2.1%	0
12/18	17,083	468	2.7%	34,599
12/17	13,497	1,842	13.6%	36,432
12/16	13,294	1,211	9.1%	38,329
12/15	11,064	411	3.7%	37,769
Annual Growth	11.9%	(2.6%)	—	—

2019 Year-End Financials

Debt ratio: 8.8%
Return on equity: 1.8%
Cash ($ mil.): 511
Current ratio: 0.33
Long-term debt ($ mil.): 37,189

No. of shares (mil.): —
Dividends
 Yield: —
 Payout: —
Market value ($ mil.): —

Saudi Telecom Co

Saudi Telecom Company (STC) is the leading provider of telecommunications services in the Kingdom of Saudi Arabia and it is among the largest operators in the Middle East. The company provides mobile and fixed telephone services along with Internet and other data services to residential and business customers. Operating the Jawal and Hatif networks STC also operates a submarine communications cable system connecting Saudi Arabia and Sudan in Africa through Arab Submarine Cables Company. The company generates majority of sales in its home country Kingdom of Saudi Arabia.

Operations

STC is engaged mainly in providing telecommunication services and related products. Majority of the company's revenues are from Saudi Telecom Company (stc) which accounts for more than 55% of total revenue; and stc Channels which produce approximately 25% of total.

Other operating segments (about 20% of total revenue) include: Kuwait Telecommunications Company (stc Kuwait) stc Bahrain Solutions by stc Specialized by stc Gulf Sapphire Aqalat Telecommunications Towers Company and Saudi Digital Payments Company

Geographic Reach

STC has a massive presence at home Kingdom of Saudi Arabia with more than 90% of total sales and it has expanded in the Middle East and nearby regions. It offers services in Turkey Kuwait Bahrain India Malaysia and South Africa.

Sales and Marketing

STC's customers primarily consist of local regional and international operators service providers and the regional business sector. The company's advertising and publicity expenses were SR 769.6 million in 2019 and SR 560.1 in 2018.

Financial Performance

Consolidated revenues increased by 5% in 2019 compared to the same period of the previous year to reach SAR 54.4 billion.

Cash held by the company at the end of 2019 decreased by SAR 124.1 million to SR 8.0 billion compared from the prior year with SAR 8.2 billion. Cash provided by operations was SAR 9.9 billion while cash used for investing and financing activities were SAR 2.0 billion and SAR 8.1 billion respectively. Main uses for cash were payments related to financial assets and movements in trade receivables and others.

Strategy

In 2019 the company culminated its strategy by launching STC's new brand in line with its leading position in the communications and information technology sector in the Kingdom. The new brand reflects the company's dynamism as a leading digital enabler locally regionally and globally. It also aligns with the company's progress in the field of digital transformation with digital payments media and entertainment in line with the digital data revolution and accelerating changes in the communications and information technology sector.

STC's vision is to be a leading digital services provider regionally thus enabling a diverse and digital economy in the Kingdom and the MENA region. STC's DARE strategy is a plan to achieve this vision by focusing on the following pillars: digitize STC; accelerate core asset performance; reinvent customer experience at world-class standards; and expand aggressively scale and scope.

Mergers and Acquisitions

In early 2020 STC entered in an agreement to acquire 55% stake in Vodafone Egypt for $2.4 billion. Vodafone Egypt is one of the leading player in the Egyptian mobile market and serves over 40 million customers. The potential acquisition of Vodafone Egypt is in line with STC expansion strategy in the MENA region. The company remains in discussions with Vodafone Group plc Vodafone Egypt's parent company to find a suitable agreement to enable the transaction to close.

EXECUTIVES

CEO, Khalid bin Hussain Al-Bayari
VP Wholesale, Homoud Mohammed Al Kusayer
VP Network, Abdullah Abdulrahman Al Alzmame
SVP Consumer Unit, Cenk Serdar
VP of Finance, Amin Fahad Al Shiddi
SVP Technology and Operations, Nasser Sulaiman Al Nasser
VP Information Technology, Omer Abdullah Al Nomany
VP Marketing, Markus Golder
SVP Enterprise Business Unit, Tariq Enaya
Chairman, Abdulaziz A. Alsugair
Vice Chairman, Mohamed A. Al Kharachi
Auditors: Ernst & Young & Co.

LOCATIONS

HQ: Saudi Telecom Co
King Abdulaziz Complex, Imam Mohammed Bin Saud Street, Al Mursalat Area, P.O. Box 87912, Riyadh 11652
Phone: (966) 1 452 5881 **Fax:** (966) 1 452 5869
Web: www.stc.com.sa

PRODUCTS/OPERATIONS

2014 Sales

	% of total
GSM	62
Landline	11
Data services	27
Total	**100**

2014 Sales

	% of total
Usage Charges	60
Subscription fees	38
Activation fee & others	2
Total	**100**

COMPETITORS

Etisalat
Ooredoo

Orascom Telecom
Saudi Binladin

HISTORICAL FINANCIALS

Company Type: Public

Income Statement   FYE: December 31

	REVENUE ($ mil.)	NET INCOME ($ mil.)	NET PROFIT MARGIN	EMPLOYEES
12/19	14,498	2,843	19.6%	0
12/18	13,856	2,874	20.7%	0
12/17	13,532	2,702	20.0%	0
12/16	14,044	2,372	16.9%	0
12/15	13,491	2,466	18.3%	0
Annual Growth	1.8%	3.6%	—	—

Debt ratio: 2.1%
Return on equity: 16.7%
Cash ($ mil.): 2,141
Current ratio: 1.35
Long-term debt ($ mil.): 2,379

No. of shares (mil.): 2,000
Dividends
  Yield: —
  Payout: 75.0%
Market value ($ mil.): —

Sberbank Of Russia

Whether you do your saving in Siberia or your asset management in Moscow the Savings Bank of the Russian Federation or Sberbank has a branch for you. With a history going back some 180 years Sberbank is one of the largest banking institutions in Russia boasting assets of about 31.2 trillion rubles and serving about 70% of nation's population. Its more than 14000 branches in Russia offers banking services ranging from savings to private and investment banking and a complete range of lending and credit services to corporate and retail customers. The Central Bank of the Russian Federation also known as The Bank of Russia controls Sberbank with more than 50% ownership stake.

Operations

In addition to its main retail banking services Sberbank also boasts a trade finance and an investment banking business. It also provides health life third-party liability and other insurance products for both retail and corporate clients.

Sberbank's online banking services are accessed by almost 55 million customers across the bank's app online portal and SMS service.

Sberbank is Russia's one of the leading credit card issuer with more than 15 million active credit cards in circulation. The bank's ATM network over 77000 terminals is among the world's largest.

Sberbank's Corporate and Investment Bank Sberbank CIB provides complex structured products to support major products in all sectors of the Russian economy.

Geographic Reach

Sberbank based in Moscow Russia has over 10 Regional Banks that operate more than 14000 branches in nearly all of Russia's 85 regions. Internationally Sberbank has subsidiaries branches and representative offices in more than 20 countries including Russia the UK US CIS and Central and Eastern Europe.

Some of its primary foreign subsidiary banks are: DB AO Sberbank (Kazakhstan) BPS-Sberbank (Belarus) AO Sberbank (Ukraine) and Sberbank Europe AG (Central and Eastern Europe).

Sales and Marketing

Sberbank serves individuals institutions and medium to large-sized businesses and corporations. All in Sberbank boast almost 100 million clients globally and holds some 45% of Russian retail deposits more than 40% of consumer loans almost 55% of mortgages and over 30% of the corporate lending market.

The bank spends roughly RUB 9.4 billion and RUB 8.4 on advertising and marketing for the years 2019 and 2018 respectively.

Financial Performance

Note: Growth rates may differ after conversion to US dollars. This analysis uses operating income (sum of net interest income fee and commission and insurance premiums) in place of revenue.

Sberbank's revenues and profits have been on the uptrend in recent years thanks to continued growth in its corporate and retail loan businesses. Total revenue grew from RUB 2.2 trillion in 2018 to RUB 2.3 trillion in 2019.

Net income grew 1% from RUB 832.9 billion in 2018 to RUB 844.9 billion in 2019.

Sberbank's coffers fell RUB 15.6 billion during 2019 to RUB 2.1 trillion. The bank generated RUB 532.8 billion from its operations while its investing activities used RUB 247.3 billion and its financing activities RUB 442.6 billion.

Strategy

As part of Sherbank's Strategy 2020 the bank has set a task to achieve a high level of efficiency in order to be able to compete with global technology companies while remaining a reliable and efficient bank for individuals and for businesses. Encouraging results have been achieved across all priority areas.

The key priorities of the company's Strategy 2020 consists of: best client experience and ecosystem; technological leadership; and people with new skills in effective teams.

2019 was a landmark year for Sberbank's transformation into a technological company: it launched its new digital platform. This is an important milestone on the path of implementing Strategy 2020 that aims to accomplish a seamless client experience in using the ecosystem services.

Mergers and Acquisitions

In mid-2020 Sberbank agreed to buy Yandex.Money for approximately RUB2.4 billion. Yandex.Money is based in Russia and one of the leading e-payment services in the country. The transaction will open up new opportunities in the development of e-commerce for the company.

In late 2019 Sberbank acquired Speech Technology Center (STC). STC is based in the US and an international leader in speech technology and multimodal biometrics. The acquisition completes and improves the products and services of the company's growing ecosystem.

Sberbank purchased Shiptor in mid-2020. Shiptor is based in the UK and its platform lets clients use delivery services at lower prices than directly organized delivery. Sberbank's acquisition is an important step in implementing its strategy for entering the logistics market.

In early 2019 Sberbank acquired Rambler Group. Rambler Gorup is one of the leaders of the Russian Media and entertainment industry based in Moscow Russia. The transaction is expected to boost the company's ecosystem and populate it with products where clients will engage on a daily basis and significantly increase its loyalty to the company.Sberbank entered the market of job search and recruitment services by acquiring Rabota.ru in early 2019. Rabota.ru is based in Moscow Russia and one of the leaders in the online recruitment market. The purchase will allow the bank to create ambitious player on the market and will deeply modernize the product and technological platform of the bank.

EXECUTIVES

Deputy Chairman, Stanislav K. Kuznetsov
Deputy Chairman, Alexander Torbakhov, age 48
Deputy Chairman, Bella Zlatkis
Deputy Chairman, Alexander Morozov
First Deputy Chairman, Lev Khasis, age 54
Chairman and CEO, Herman Gref, age 56
First Deputy Chairman, Maxim Poletaev
Chairman SberbankÀ's Severo-Zapadny Bank, Victor Ventimilla Alonso, age 57
Deputy Chairman, Yulia G. Chupina, age 60
Deputy Chairman, Oleg Ganeev
Auditors: AO PricewaterhouseCoopers Audit

LOCATIONS

HQ: Sberbank Of Russia
  19 Vavilova St., Moscow 117997
Phone: (7) 495 500 55 50   **Fax:** (7) 495 957 5731
Web: www.sberbank.com

PRODUCTS/OPERATIONS

Selected Subsidiary
DenizBank A.S.
Sberbank Europe AG
Sberbank Kazakhstan
BPS-Sberbank (Belarus)
Sberbank (Switzerland) AG

Selected Group companies
ActiveBusinessCollection LLC
Sberbank-Automated Trading System CJSC
Delovaya Sreda JSC
Sberbank Private Pension Funds JSC
Sberbank Leasing JSC
Sberbank-Services LLC
Sberbank Life Insurance LLC
Sberbank-Technology (Sbertech) JSC
Sovremennyye Tekhnologii LLC
Nonbanking Credit Institution Yandex.Money LLC

COMPETITORS

Alfa Group	Sistema
Deutsche Bank (Moscow)	VTB
MDM Bank	

HISTORICAL FINANCIALS

Company Type: Public

Income Statement   FYE: December 31

	REVENUE ($ mil.)	NET INCOME ($ mil.)	NET PROFIT MARGIN	EMPLOYEES
12/19	50,229	13,575	27.0%	281,300
12/18	39,817	11,950	30.0%	293,752
12/17	49,885	12,979	26.0%	310.277
12/16	45,941	8,827	19.2%	325,100
12/15	37,608	3,023	8.0%	330,700
Annual Growth	7.5%	45.6%	—	(4.0%)

2019 Year-End Financials

Debt ratio: —
Return on equity: 20.2%
Cash ($ mil.): 33,472
Current ratio: —
Long-term debt ($ mil.): —

No. of shares (mil.): —
Dividends
  Yield: 6.1%
  Payout: 169.1%
Market value ($ mil.): —

	STOCK PRICE ($) FY Close	P/E High/Low		Earnings	PER SHARE ($) Dividends	Book Value
12/19	16.40	0	0	0.62	1.01	3.35
12/18	10.96	0	0	0.55	0.76	2.57
12/17	17.03	1	0	0.60	0.39	2.76
12/16	11.58	0	0	0.41	0.13	2.14
12/15	5.79	1	0	0.14	0.03	1.49
Annual Growth	29.7%			45.0%	136.2%	22.5%

Schlumberger Ltd

Auditors: PricewaterhouseCoopers LLP

LOCATIONS

HQ: Schlumberger Ltd
  42 Rue Saint-Dominique, Paris 75007
Phone: 713 513-2000
Web: www.slb.com

Company Type: Public

Income Statement				FYE: December 31
	REVENUE ($ mil.)	NET INCOME ($ mil.)	NET PROFIT MARGIN	EMPLOYEES
12/20	23,868	(10,518)	—	86,000
12/19	33,250	(10,137)	—	105,000
12/18	33,179	2,138	6.4%	100,000
12/17	30,664	(1,505)	—	100,000
12/16	28,010	(1,687)	—	100,000
Annual Growth	(3.9%)	—	—	(3.7%)

2020 Year-End Financials

Debt ratio: 39.7%
Return on equity: (-58.5%)
Cash ($ mil.): 3,006
Current ratio: 1.23
Long-term debt ($ mil.): 16,036

No. of shares (mil.): 1,392
Dividends
Yield: 4.0%
Payout: —
Market value ($ mil.): 30,394

	STOCK PRICE ($) FY Close	P/E High/Low		PER SHARE ($)	
			Earnings	Dividends	Book Value
12/20	21.83	— —	(7.57)	0.88	8.67
12/19	40.20	— —	(7.32)	2.00	17.16
12/18	36.08	52 23	1.53	2.00	26.15
12/17	67.39	— —	(1.08)	2.00	26.62
12/16	83.95	— —	(1.24)	2.00	29.52
Annual Growth	(28.6%) (26.4%)	— —	—(18.7%)		

Schneider Electric SE

Schneider Electric is a leading global manufacturer of equipment for energy management and industrial automation - products like circuit breakers and switches switchgear and transformers motor starters and power grid automation and electric car charging systems. Its end markets span residential and commercial buildings utilities oil and gas infrastructures waste water plants machine manufacturers and data centers. Schneider Electric operates into two segment these are the energy management which provides a complete end-to-end technology offering enabled by EcoStruxure and industrial automation which includes industrial automation and industrial control activities across discrete process & hybrid industries. Majority of the company's sales come from outside Europe.

Operations

Schneider Electric's product groups are centered on two core offerings - energy management and industrial automation. Within those groups are its four operating segments. Energy management encompasses the Low Voltage Medium Voltage and Secure Power segments. Schneider's Industrial automation segment offers products and software for the automation and control of machines for manufacturing and industrial processes. Energy management segment generates nearly 80% of the company's revenue and industrial automation accounts for more than 20%.

The Low Voltage offers electrical distribution products for residential and commercial buildings and data centers span all industries and include several building automation products such as circuit breakers power monitoring (EcoStruxure is its IoT- enabled power management solution) and network connectivity.

The Industrial automation provides comprehensive product and software solutions for the au-

tomation and control of machinery used in manufacturing and other industrial plants. Smart automation solutions combine sensors motion systems and motor controllers with software for distributed control systems safety systems machine and process control and human-machine interface. The division also offers software for the design maintenance and operation of industrial processes.

Medium Voltage products include switchgear transformers electrical network protection and automation controls. This business also offers connected products and software for grid automation and infrastructure and pipeline management.

The Secure Power specializes in critical power products for data centers and networks and sells products like uninterruptable power supplies (UPS) IT rack systems power distribution units and security and cooling systems.

Geographic Reach

Headquartered in Rueil Malmaison France Schneider has operations in more than 100 countries. The Asia Pacific region and North America generate nearly 30% each of the revenue while Western Europe accounts for more than 25%. The rest of the world contributes more than 15%.

Sales and Marketing

Distributors account for more than 40% of Schneider Electric's total revenues through an extensive network of more than 190 countries all over the world. The company serves some 75 global customers including Apple BHP Billiton ExxonMobil Nestlé and Veolia Environment.

The company's main distributor includes electrical distributors (both global and regional players) such as Rexel Sonepar CED Edmunson Graybar Imelco Idee and Fegime buying groups with both online and offline presence Specialists in IT telecom and data center applications for critical infrastructures such as Tech Data and Ingram Micro DIY retailers such as Home Depot and Lowe's in the US Saint Gobain Distribution in France and Brazil and Adeo Group and Kingfisher in Europe and Russia Online marketplaces and e-tailers such as RS Components T-Mall and Grainger and specialist technical distributors for automation and industrial software solutions access control and security products.

Financial Performance

Note: Growth rates may differ after conversion to US Dollars.

Except for a dip in 2016 Schneider Electric's revenue has seen slow but steady growth the last five years rising about 2% between 2015 and 2019. The company's Energy Management segment has been the chief growth drivers since 2016.

Sales in 2019 increased about 6% to ?27.2 billion compared to ?25.7 billion in 2018. Growth in 2019 was due to consolidation of Aveva and disposal of Pelco and the US panels business and a positive exchange rate effect of +2% driven by the appreciation of the USD against the euro. Both businesses saw strong organic growth with Energy Management up 5% and with Industrial Automation at 1%.

Net income increased 4% to a record ?2.4 billion in 2019 compared to 2018 primarily due to lower net expenses to ?261 million driven by continued decrease in the cost of debt. The effective income tax rate was 22% down from 23% last year.

Cash at the end of 2019 was ?3.4 billion an increase of ?1.2 billion from the prior year. Cash from operations contributed ?4.3 billion to the coffers while investing activities used ?916 million mainly for long-term pension assets. Financing activities used ?2.2 billion primarily in the form of dividend payments.

Strategy

Schneider's strategy for growth hinges on four aspects?portfolio optimization open ecosystem innovation and culture. The company has already

made substantial progress towards these goals and is further outlining ways it can continue achieving these.

As part of its portfolio optimization Schneider has made the following developments in 2019: it had double digit growth in Software; a 50% growth in connected assets under management; the Pelco divestment closed and the disposal of US panels business in Q2; and the completion of sale of Energy Projects GmbH in December. Its priorities for 2020 is to further scale digital offers; grow Services by twice its average growth; and continue portfolio optimization by about ?1.5 to ?2 billion in 2021.

Schneider also aims to empower its unrivalled network of partners with digital innovation to seize new market values and champion open connected and interoperable solutions. In 2019 it launched Schneider Electric Exchange the world's first cross-industry open ecosystem that unleashes the power of collaboration in an open environment. It also plans on enhancing its EcoStruxure platform capabilities as a digital model across end-user applications.

Furthermore Schneider plans on increasing its investment in R&D and innovation digital sales force skills and marketing and communication. It also strives to be the most diverse inclusive and equitable company globally. To this end Schneider prioritizes boosting a high performance and innovation culture creating more development and career opportunities for all and building the next generation of leaders to achieve the company's growth ambitions.

Company Background

Schneider Electric's predecessor was founded in 1782 to make industrial equipment. After the upheavals of the French Revolution and the Napoleonic Wars the company came under the control of brothers Adolphe and Eugene Schneider in 1836. Within two years they had built the first French locomotive (the country's first rail line opened in 1832).

Schneider became one of France's most important heavy industry companies branching into a variety of machinery and steel operations.

The company rebuilt after WWII aided by the French government. It was restructured as a holding company and its operating units were split into three subsidiaries: civil and electrical engineering industrial manufacturing and construction.

In 1963 Schneider concluded an alliance with the Empain Group of Belgium and by 1969 three years after Schneider went public the two companies merged to become Empain-Schneider.

Schneider began reorganizing in 1980. The effort entered its final phase in 1993 with a major recapitalization that saw the merger of its former parent company Société Parisienne d'Entreprises et de Participations with Schneider SA and the issue of new stock to existing stockholders.

HISTORY

Schneider Electric's predecessor was founded in 1782 to make industrial equipment. After the upheavals of the French Revolution and the Napoleonic Wars the company came under the control of brothers Adolphe and Eugene Schneider in 1836. Within two years they had built the first French locomotive (the country's first rail line opened in 1832).

Schneider became one of France's most important heavy industry companies branching into a variety of machinery and steel operations. However the country's industrial development continued to trail that of Britain and Germany due to recurrent political strife including the revolution of 1848 and the Franco-Prussian War. France also possessed fewer coal and iron deposits.

During WWI Schneider was a key part of France's war effort. It entered the electrical contracting business in 1929 and fought off nationalization attempts in the mid-1930s. The blitzkrieg of 1939 brought much of France under Nazi occupation and the Schneider factories that were not destroyed were commandeered by the Germans.

The company rebuilt after the war aided by the French government. It was restructured as a holding company and its operating units were split into three subsidiaries: civil and electrical engineering industrial manufacturing and construction. Charles Schneider the last family member to lead the company died in 1950.

In 1963 Schneider concluded an alliance with the Empain Group of Belgium and by 1969 three years after Schneider went public the two companies merged to become Empain-Schneider. It was a period when the company made numerous non-core acquisitions entering such fields as ski equipment fashion publishing and travel.

Schneider began reorganizing in 1980. The effort entered its final phase in 1993 with a major recapitalization that saw the merger of its former parent company Société Parisienne d'Entreprises et de Participations with Schneider SA and the issue of new stock to existing stockholders.

EXECUTIVES

President and CEO North America Operations and Group Supply Chain Officer, Annette K. Clayton, age 57

Chairman and CEO, Jean-Pascal Tricoire, age 57

EVP Global Marketing and Chief Marketing Officer, Chris Leong

EVP Technology and CTO, Prith Banerjee, age 59

EVP Buildings and Partner, Philippe Delorme, age 49

EVP Europe Operations, Leonid Mukhamedov

EVP Information Systems and CIO, Hervé Coureil, age 50

EVP China Operations, Zhu Hai

EVP France Operations and President Schneider Electric France, Luc Rémont

EVP Infrastructure, Frédéric Abbal

EVP Global Human Resources, Olivier Blum

EVP Industry, Peter Herweck

President Middle East and Africa, Caspar Herzberg

EVP Strategy, Emmanuel Lagarrigue

EVP Global Solutions, Daniel Do mo

Country President Saudi Arabia and Yemen, Najib Abdulaziz Al-Naim

Auditors: ERNST & YOUNG et Autres

LOCATIONS

HQ: Schneider Electric SE
35, rue Joseph Monier, CS 30323, Rueil-Malmaison, Cedex 92506
Phone: (33) 1 41 29 70 00   **Fax:** (33) 1 41 29 71 00
Web: www.se.com

2017 Sales

	% of total
Asia/Pacific	28
Western Europe	27
North America	27
Rest of the world	18
Total	**100**

PRODUCTS/OPERATIONS

2017 Sales

	% of total
Low Voltage (Buildings)	44
Industrial Automation (Industry)	23
Medium Voltage (Infrastructure)	18
Secure Power (IT)	15
Total	**100**

Selected Products

Electrical Car Charging
Electrical Protection and Control
Home Automation and Security
Light Switches and Electrical Sockets
Surge Protection and Power Conditioning
Uninterruptible Power Supply (UPS)
Building Management
Emergency Lighting
Fire and Security
Network Infrastructure and Connectivity
Power Monitoring and Control
Variable Speed Drives and Soft Starters
Circuit Breakers and Switches
Contactors and Protection Relays
Electrical Car Charging
Electrical Protection and Control
Motor Starters and Protection Components
Surge Protection and Power Conditioning
Switchboards and Enclosures
Solar and Energy Storage
Grid Automation and SCADA Software
Switchgear Components and transformers
Protection Relays
Substation Automation
Critical Power Cooling and Racks
Data Center Software
IT Power Distribution
Prefabricated Data Center Modules
Security and Environmental Monitoring
Boxes Cabling and Interfaces
Human Machine Interfaces (HMI)
Measurement and Instrumentation
Motion Control and Robotics
Sensors and RFID System
Signaling Devices
Telemetry and Remote SCADA Systems

COMPETITORS

ABB	Larsen & Toubro
ALSTOM	Legrand
Alcatel-Lucent	Leonardo
Bechtel	Measurement
Beghelli	Specialties
Bharat Heavy	Mitsubishi Electric
Electricals	Nissin Electric
Checkpoint Systems	Rockwell Automation
Danaher	Roper Technologies
Delta Electronics	Sentry Technology
EMCOR	Siemens AG
Eaton	Technology Research
Electricité de France	Corp.
Emerson Electric	Transtector
Endress + Hauser	Vertiv
Fluor	Vicon Industries
GE	WEG Electric
Honeywell	Woodhead Industries
International	Yokogawa Electric
Itron	
Johnson Controls Power	
Solutions	

HISTORICAL FINANCIALS

Company Type: Public

Income Statement

FYE: December 31

	REVENUE ($ mil.)	NET INCOME ($ mil.)	NET PROFIT MARGIN	EMPLOYEES
12/19	30,492	2,709	8.9%	151,297
12/18	29,454	2,672	9.1%	155,286
12/17	29,660	2,577	8.7%	153,124
12/16	26,072	1,847	7.1%	143,901
12/15	29,016	1,532	5.3%	181,362
Annual Growth	1.2%	15.3%	—	(4.4%)

2019 Year-End Financials

Debt ratio: 18.3%
Return on equity: 11.4%
Cash ($ mil.): 4,032
Current ratio: 1.37
Long-term debt ($ mil.): 7,189
No. of shares (mil.): 551
Dividends
  Yield: 2.5%
  Payout: 10.8%
Market value ($ mil.): 11,241

	STOCK PRICE ($) FY Close	P/E High/Low		PER SHARE ($) Earnings	Dividends	Book Value
12/19	20.40	5	3	4.86	0.53	43.93
12/18	13.52	4	3	4.76	0.48	43.31
12/17	16.95	5	4	4.57	0.43	42.56
12/16	13.81	4	3	3.26	0.37	38.99
12/15	11.35	7	4	2.68	0.43	40.16
Annual Growth	15.8%	—	—	16.1%	5.3%	2.3%

SCOR S.E. (France)

This company knows the score in the global reinsurance market. SCOR provides treaty (groups of risks) and facultative (individual risks) reinsurance covering the risks of insurance underwriters around the globe. The company reinsures property/casualty life accident and health insurance lines. Most of SCOR's business comes from Europe and North America and is divided into two distinct business segments: Global Life (including long-term care and disability products) and Global P&C (including treaty corporate and specialty property/casualty lines). It serves customers in some 170 countries through offices that specialize in the needs of a specific industry or market.

Operations

The company's life insurance unit SCOR Global Life accounts for about 53% of revenue while SCOR Global P&C (property and casualty) brings in about 47%. Outside of its reinsurance operations the company has a third smaller business named SCOR Global Investments which provides asset and investment management services to the other operating SCOR facilities.

Geographic Reach

SCOR has about 40 offices in nearly 25 cities throughout in the Americas Europe and Asia. Europe contributed about 42% of revenue with France Germany Spain and Italy leading the charge. North America brings in about 40% and the rest comes from Asia and other countries (Australia and South Africa mainly).

Sales and Marketing

Reinsurance is written either through brokers or directly. SCOR employs both methods but breaks it down differently depending on the operating unit. Global Life is 90% direct and 10% broker while Global P&C is 63% broker and 37% direct.

Financial Performance

In 2013 the company reported a 7% increase in revenue as its Life unit performed well on the strength of an earlier acquisition of life insurance provider Generali US. Net income shot up 31% based on improved revenue gains made on the Generali purchase and increased investment returns. Cash flow however dropped due to cash used for acquisitions and investments.

Strategy

SCOR is focused on growing organically through new products and new markets and growing through acquisitions. It followed a large 2011 purchase with the acquisition of Generali US a life insurance provider. The company has also realigned its business portfolio to prioritize North America Asia and the rest of the world.

Mergers and Acquisitions

In mid-2017 SCOR agreed to acquire the 77% it doesn't already own in mutual reinsurer MutRé which has a strong presence in France's health reinsurance market. The deal will strengthen

SCOR's life and health reinsurance offerings. SCOR helped launch MutRé in 1998.

EXECUTIVES

Deputy CEO SCOR Global P&C SE, Benjamin Gentsch, age 60
Chairman and CEO, Denis Kessler, age 68, $682,000 total compensation
CEO SCOR Global P&C SE, Victor Peignet, age 63, $240,412 total compensation
CEO SCOR Global Life SE, Paolo De Martin, age 50
CEO SCOR Global Investments SE, Fran Sois De Varenne, age 54
CIO, Marc Philippe, age 52
CFO, Mark Kociancic, age 49
Chief Risk Officer, Frieder Kn pling, age 50
Deputy CEO SCOR Global Life SE, Simon Pearson, age 54
CFO Americas Hub, Paul Christoff, age 49
Managing Director Asia-Pacific Hub, Eric Pooi, age 52
Auditors: Mazars

LOCATIONS

HQ: SCOR S.E. (France)
5 avenue Kleber, Paris 75116
Phone: (33) 1 58 44 70 00   **Fax:** (33) 1 58 44 85 00
Web: www.scor.com

2013 Gross Written Premiums

	% of total
Europe	42
Americas	39
Asia-Pacific & other regions	19
Total	**100**

PRODUCTS/OPERATIONS

2013 Premiums

	% of total
Global P&C	53
Global Life	47
Total	**100**

COMPETITORS

AXIS Capital Holdings	RenaissanceRe
Everest Re	Scottish Re Group
General Re	Sompo International
Hannover Re	Swiss Re
Munich Re America	Transatlantic Holdings
Munich Re Group	XL Group plc
PartnerRe	
Reinsurance Group of America	

HISTORICAL FINANCIALS

Company Type: Public

Income Statement — FYE: December 31

	ASSETS ($ mil.)	NET INCOME ($ mil.)	INCOME AS % OF ASSETS	EMPLOYEES
12/19	52,633	473	0.9%	3,028
12/18	50,827	368	0.7%	2,887
12/17	51,826	342	0.7%	2,955
12/16	45,712	636	1.4%	2,802
12/15	45,316	699	1.5%	2,706
Annual Growth	**3.8%**	**(9.3%)**	**—**	**2.9%**

2019 Year-End Financials

Return on assets: 0.9%	Dividends
Return on equity: 6.9%	Yield: 4.5%
Long-term debt ($ mil.): —	Payout: 7.8%
No. of shares (mil.): 186	Market value ($ mil.): 797
Sales ($ mil): 18,657	

	STOCK PRICE ($) FY Close	P/E High/Low		PER SHARE ($) Earnings	Dividends	Book Value
12/19	4.28	2	2	2.53	0.20	38.24
12/18	4.41	3	2	1.95	0.20	36.11
12/17	4.06	3	2	1.81	0.20	39.58
12/16	3.50	1	1	3.38	0.16	38.05
12/15	3.80	1	1	3.68	0.16	37.07
Annual Growth	**3.0%**	**—**	**—**	**(9.0%)**	**5.5%**	**0.8%**

Sekisui House, Ltd. (Japan)

EXECUTIVES

Chairman and CEO, Isami Wada
EVP and CFO, Shiro Inagaki
President COO and Director, Toshinori Abe
Managing Officer and Director, Tetsuo Iku
Auditors: Ernst & Young ShinNihon LLC

LOCATIONS

HQ: Sekisui House, Ltd. (Japan)
1-1-88 Oyodonaka, Kita-ku, Osaka 531-0076
Phone: (81) 6 6440 3111   **Fax:** (81) 6 6440 3331
Web: www.sekisuihouse.co.jp

PRODUCTS/OPERATIONS

Selected Subsidiaries and Affiliates

Sekisui House Umeda Operation Co. Ltd.
Sekiwa Real Estate Chubu Ltd.
Sekiwa Real Estate Chugoku Ltd.
Sekiwa Real Estate Kansai Ltd.
Sekiwa Real Estate Kyushu Ltd.
Sekiwa Real Estate Sapporo Ltd.
Sekiwa Real Estate Tohoku Ltd.
SGM Operation Co. Ltd

COMPETITORS

Daikyo	Shimizu
Daiwa House Industry	Sumitomo Forestry
Minaean	Sumitomo Realty
Mitsubishi Estate	Taisei
Mitsui Fudosan	

HISTORICAL FINANCIALS

Company Type: Public

Income Statement — FYE: January 31

	REVENUE ($ mil.)	NET INCOME ($ mil.)	NET PROFIT MARGIN	EMPLOYEES
01/20	22,172	1,296	5.8%	27,397
01/19	19,886	1,183	6.0%	24,775
01/18	19,852	1,224	6.2%	24,391
01/17	17,843	1,072	6.0%	23,299
01/16	15,371	697	4.5%	23,089
Annual Growth	**9.6%**	**16.8%**	**—**	**4.4%**

2020 Year-End Financials

Debt ratio: 0.2%	No. of shares (mil.): 683
Return on equity: 11.5%	Dividends
Cash ($ mil.): 5,367	Yield: 3.3%
Current ratio: 2.21	Payout: 38.6%
Long-term debt ($ mil.): 3,478	Market value ($ mil.): 14,705

	STOCK PRICE ($) FY Close	P/E High/Low		PER SHARE ($) Earnings	Dividends	Book Value
01/20	21.51	0	0	1.89	0.73	17.01
01/19	15.09	0	0	1.71	0.71	15.83
01/18	18.44	0	0	1.77	0.62	15.93
01/17	16.13	0	0	1.54	0.56	14.08
01/16	15.73	0	0	0.99	0.43	12.48
Annual Growth	**8.1%**	**—**	**—**	**17.6%**	**14.0%**	**8.1%**

Seven & i Holdings Co. Ltd.

Japan's biggest retail conglomerate Seven & i Holdings has a store for almost every mood. It generates more than half its sales from convenience store operations both in Japan and elsewhere operating primarily under the 7-Eleven name. The company also has general merchandise superstores department stores and specialty stores (including Denny's restaurants) as well as a smaller division that provides financial services. All told Seven & I Holdings owns some 170 retail companies with more than 70000 stores worldwide; its major subsidiaries include Seven-Eleven Japan and 7-Eleven Inc. Ito-Yokado Co. Sogo & Seibu Seven & i Food Systems Tower Records Japan and Seven Bank. The company generates almost half of sales outside Japan.

Operations

Illustrating its name Seven & i Holdings operates through eight segments: domestic convenience stores overseas convenience stores superstores department stores specialty stores financial services corporate and other.

Domestic and overseas convenience stores together contribute about 55% to total revenue with overseas operations representing about two-thirds of that. The operations primarily include 7-Eleven convenience store locations in Japan and the US.

Superstores department stores and specialty stores located mostly in Japan together add another more than 40%. Superstores include general merchandise stores serving local communities (Ito-Yokado) and supermarkets such as York Mart and York Benimaru. Seven & i Holdings' leading department store is the Sogo & Seibu chain while its specialty stores include Seven & i Food Systems (operator of Denny's and other restaurants chains in Japan) The Loft (lifestyle merchandise) Francfranc (interior furniture and and accessories) and Tower Records Japan (music).

The financial services and other segments which bring in less than 5% of revenue provide a host of services to other Seven & I Holdings companies including supply of merchandise; lease of floor space property and equipment; and installation of ATMs (more than 25000 across Japan).

Geographic Reach

Seven & i Holdings is active in about 20 countries and regions in Europe Asia Australia and the Americas although it operates primarily in Japan (about 55% of revenue) and North America (more than 40%).

Sales and Marketing

Seven & i Holdings Co. Lyd. have developing stores that provide different kinds of value to meet the needs of society and customers. All deliveries from distribution centers to stores are made using environmentally-friendly delivery trucks (either hybrid vehicles or electric vehicles). Approximately 64 million customer visit the store everyday. Advertising expenses for the year 2019 and 2018 are 60.4 billion yen and 57.2 billion yen.

Financial Performance

Company's revenue in 2020 increased by 14.1 billion yen to 887.6 billion yen compared to 873.6 billion in the prior year.

Net income in 2020 increased by 15.2 billion to 218.2 billion yen compared to 203.0 billion yen in the prior year.

Cash held by the company at the end of 2020 increased by 44.1 billion yen to 1.4 trillion yen compared to 1.3 trillion yen in the prior year. Cash provided by operations was 576.7 billion yen while cash used for investing and financing activities were 318 billion yen and 213.2 billion yen respectively.

Strategy

Under its private brand Seven Premium the Group has developed products leveraging the methods for original product development cultivated by Seven-Eleven Japan and concentrating the infrastructure product development expertise and sales capabilities of its Group companies.

Product development staff in Seven & i Group companies are organized into 6 sections and 27 subcommittees to conduct joint product development with product manufacturers. As of February 29 2020 they supply 12 companies in total.

Around 50% of Seven Premium's higher-selling existing products are renewed each year. Through the Seven Premium Enhancement Committee a website community for product development that invites customers to participate the company researches customers' opinions create test products and conduct monitoring trials until they are satisfied. This process enables the company to develop products that offer high quality at an agreeable price.

Company Background

Seven & i Holdings was founded in late 2005 to provide infrastructure and business services to its group of operating companies. 7-Eleven Inc. became a wholly owned subsidiary shortly thereafter.

EXECUTIVES

President Seven-Eleven Japan, Kazuki Furuya
President, Ryuichi Isaka
Presiedent 7-Eleven, Joseph M. (Joe) DePinto, age 57
VP and Representative Director, Katsuhiro Goto
President York-Benimaru, Yukio Mafune
President Ito-Yokado, Atsushi Kamei
Executive Officer and CFO, Kunio Takahashi
President Sogo & Seibu, Ryu Matsumoto
President Seven & i Food Systems, Tsuneo Okubo
Managing Executive Officer, Tomihiro Saegusa
Managing Executive Officer, Takuji Hayashi
Auditors: KPMG AZSA LLC

LOCATIONS

HQ: Seven & i Holdings Co. Ltd.
8-8 Niban-cho, Chiyoda-ku, Tokyo 102-8452
Phone: (81) 3 6238 3000
Web: www.7andi.com

2018 Sales

	% of total
Japan	65
North America	33
Other regions	2
Total	**100**

PRODUCTS/OPERATIONS

2018 Sales

	% of total
Overseas convenience stores	33
Superstores	31
Domestic convenience stores	15
Department stores	11
Specialty stores	7
Financial services	3
Other	-
Total	**100**

Selected Subsidiaries and Affiliates

Convenience stores
  7-Eleven Inc.
  Seven-Eleven (Beijing) Co.
  Seven-Eleven China Co.
  Seven-Eleven Hawaii Inc.
  Seven-Eleven Japan Co.
Superstores
  Chengdu Ito-Yokado Co.
  Hua Tang Yokado Commercial Co.
  Ito-Yokado Co.
  KK. Sanei
  Marudai Co.
  SHELL GARDEN CO.
  York Mart Co.
  York-Benimaru Co.
Department stores
  Sogo & Seibu Co.
Specialty stores
  Barneys Japan
  Francfranc Corporation
  The Loft Co.
  Oshman's Japan Co.
  Seven & i Food Systems Co.
  Tower Records Japan
Financial services
  Seven Bank
  Seven Card Service Co.
  Seven Financial Service Co.

COMPETITORS

AEON	J. Front
Couche-Tard	Kirin Holdings Company
Daiei	Kokubu
FamilyMart UNY	LAWSON
Fast Retailing	Nisshin Seifun Group
Isetan Mitsukoshi	Seiyu
Izumi	Takashimaya

HISTORICAL FINANCIALS

Company Type: Public

Income Statement   FYE: February 29

	REVENUE ($ mil.)	NET INCOME ($ mil.)	NET PROFIT MARGIN	EMPLOYEES
02/20	66,993	2,199	3.3%	138,808
02/19	68,474	2,046	3.0%	144,628
02/18	60,877	1,826	3.0%	149,414
02/17	58,839	975	1.7%	140,938
02/16	60,957	1,622	2.7%	145,460
Annual Growth	**2.4%**	**7.9%**	**—**	**(1.2%)**

2020 Year-End Financials

Debt ratio: 0.1%	No. of shares (mil.): 884
Return on equity: 8.4%	Dividends
Cash ($ mil.): 13,689	Yield: 0.0%
Current ratio: 1.15	Payout: 17.4%
Long-term debt ($ mil.): 6,907	Market value ($ mil.): 14,906

	STOCK PRICE ($) FY Close	P/E High/Low		PER SHARE ($) Earnings	Dividends	Book Value
02/20	16.85	0	0	2.49	0.43	29.66
02/19	21.98	0	0	2.31	0.42	28.77
02/18	20.83	0	0	2.06	0.40	27.70
02/17	19.55	0	0	1.10	0.42	26.66
02/16	19.94	0	0	1.83	0.30	27.09
Annual Growth	**(4.1%)**	**—**	**—**	**7.9%**	**9.3%**	**2.3%**

Shanghai Construction Group Co., Ltd.

Auditors: PricewaterhouseCoopers Zhong Tian CPAs Limited Company

LOCATIONS

HQ: Shanghai Construction Group Co., Ltd.
No. 666, Dongdaming Road, Shanghai 200080
Phone: (86) 21 35100838   **Fax:** (86) 21 55886222
Web: www.shconstruction.cn

HISTORICAL FINANCIALS

Company Type: Public

Income Statement   FYE: December 31

	REVENUE ($ mil.)	NET INCOME ($ mil.)	NET PROFIT MARGIN	EMPLOYEES
12/19	29,532	564	1.9%	0
12/18	24,794	404	1.6%	0
12/17	21,833	397	1.8%	0
12/16	19,247	301	1.6%	0
12/15	19,313	288	1.5%	0
Annual Growth	**11.2%**	**18.3%**	**—**	**—**

2019 Year-End Financials

Debt ratio: 3.2%	No. of shares (mil.): —
Return on equity: 12.2%	Dividends
Cash ($ mil.): 9,498	Yield: —
Current ratio: 1.21	Payout: —
Long-term debt ($ mil.): 6,364	Market value ($ mil.): —

Shanghai Electric Group Co Ltd

Auditors: PricewaterhouseCoopers Zhong Tian LLP

LOCATIONS

HQ: Shanghai Electric Group Co Ltd
No. 212 Qinjiang Road, Shanghai 200233
Phone: (86) 21 33261888   **Fax:** (86) 21 34695780
Web: www.shanghai-electric.com

HISTORICAL FINANCIALS

Company Type: Public

Income Statement   FYE: December 31

	REVENUE ($ mil.)	NET INCOME ($ mil.)	NET PROFIT MARGIN	EMPLOYEES
12/19	18,324	503	2.7%	0
12/18	14,706	438	3.0%	0
12/17	12,223	408	3.3%	0
12/16	11,387	296	2.6%	0
12/15	12,011	320	2.7%	27,310
Annual Growth	**11.1%**	**11.9%**	**—**	**—**

2019 Year-End Financials

Debt ratio: 2.3%	No. of shares (mil.): —
Return on equity: 5.8%	Dividends
Cash ($ mil.): 3,084	Yield: —
Current ratio: 1.21	Payout: —
Long-term debt ($ mil.): 2,613	Market value ($ mil.): —

Shanghai Jinfeng Investment Co Ltd

Auditors: Ernst & Young Hua Ming Certified Public Accountants

LOCATIONS

HQ: Shanghai Jinfeng Investment Co Ltd
29th Floor, Tianan Center, No. 338, Nanjing West Road, Shanghai 200003
Phone: (86) 21 63592020   **Fax:** (86) 21 63586115
Web: www.ehousee.com

HISTORICAL FINANCIALS

Company Type: Public

Income Statement   FYE: December 31

	REVENUE ($ mil.)	NET INCOME ($ mil.)	NET PROFIT MARGIN	EMPLOYEES
12/19	61,521	2,118	3.4%	0
12/18	50,700	1,653	3.3%	0
12/17	44,628	1,388	3.1%	0
12/16	35,627	1,037	2.9%	0
12/15	31,955	1,060	3.3%	0
Annual Growth	17.8%	18.9%	—	—

2019 Year-End Financials

Debt ratio: 3.6%	No. of shares (mil.): —
Return on equity: 19.7%	Dividends
Cash ($ mil.): 12,776	Yield: —
Current ratio: 1.22	Payout: —
Long-term debt ($ mil.): 25,404	Market value ($ mil.): —

Shanghai Pharmaceuticals Holding Co Ltd

Auditors: PricewaterhouseCoopers Zhong Tian LLP

LOCATIONS

HQ: Shanghai Pharmaceuticals Holding Co Ltd
Shanghai Pharmaceutical Building, No. 200, Taicang Road, Shanghai 200020
Phone: (86) 21 63730908   **Fax:** (86) 21 63289333
Web: www.sphchina.com

HISTORICAL FINANCIALS

Company Type: Public

Income Statement   FYE: December 31

	REVENUE ($ mil.)	NET INCOME ($ mil.)	NET PROFIT MARGIN	EMPLOYEES
12/19	26,812	586	2.2%	0
12/18	23,128	564	2.4%	0
12/17	20,107	541	2.7%	0
12/16	17,391	460	2.6%	0
12/15	16,246	442	2.7%	41,173
Annual Growth	13.3%	7.3%	—	—

2019 Year-End Financials

Debt ratio: 3.0%	No. of shares (mil.): —
Return on equity: 10.1%	Dividends
Cash ($ mil.): 2,608	Yield: 2.4%
Current ratio: 1.31	Payout: —
Long-term debt ($ mil.): 881	Market value ($ mil.): —

Sharp Corp (Japan)

Best known for its consumer electronics Sharp is a recognized brand for electronic components and computer hardware and peripherals. The company's flagship products are LCDs and PCs. The company also produces solar cells laser diodes and optical sensors. Other Sharp offerings are printers and cell phones; consumer audio and video products such as Blu-ray disc players and LCD TVs; and a variety of appliances such as air purifiers and steam ovens. The company's largest geographical market is China. Sharp is owned by Hon Hai Precision Industry Co.

Operations

Sharp operates in three reportable segments: 8K Ecosystem (almost 50% of total sales) Smart Life (over 35%) and ICT (around 15%). 8K Ecosystem's products is comprised of automotive cameras commercial projectors POS systems and audio equipment among others. The Smart Life segment includes home appliances telephones storage batteries and water foundries while ICT's products are mobile phones and personal computers.

The company's largest revenue generating product LCD modules which accounts for about 30% of its total sales. Sensing devices accounts for some 15% of total sales and the remaining are from other products.

Geographic Reach

Sharp gets approximately 65% of sales from customers outside of Japan with China accounting for around 40% of sales. The company has operations in the Americas Europe the Middle-East and Africa Oceania and Asia.

Sharp is headquartered in Osaka Japan.

Sales and Marketing

Sharp's biggest customer accounting for about 25% of revenue is Apple which buys Sharp displays for its smartphones and other devices.

Financial Performance

Sharp's revenue has been uneven but trending lower over the past five years. The company has posted profits in the last three years after two years of losses.

In 2020 (ended March) Sharp reported Â 2.3 trillion in revenue down about Â 128.9 billion from the year before due to lower sales from overseas.

Sharp recorded net income of Â 21 billion in 2020 a decrease of Â 53.3 billion over 2019. The big fall in income was due to lower net sales higher selling general and administrative expenses and higher income tax.The company's coffers held about Â 170.3 billion in cash and equivalents in 2020 down Â 58.5 billion from the previous year. In 2020 operating activities produced Â 68.1 billion investing activities used Â 127.9 billion and financing activities used another Â 4.6 billion. Main cash uses for the year were for purchases of property plant and equipment and purchases of treasury shares.

Strategy

Sharp's basic strategy is focused on: Expansion of 8K+5G/AIoT devices through a full expansion of services/ solutions business creating new businesses (e.g. health/medical); Expansion of Japan/ASEAN-focused business by building global five-axis system (Japan ASEAN China Europe the Americas); and Execution of fundamental structural reform based on changes in world affairs and in society with & after COVID-19.

In a world first Sharp Corporation has developed an 8K real-time VVC decoder compatible with Versatile Video Coding (VVC) video coding standard. The 8K real-time VVC decoder developed by Sharp is the first software in the world able to decode VVC-encoded 8K video in real time. By combining the VVC decoder with video playback software and analytical devices users will additionally be able to display or analyze 8K content that has been compressed with VVC*3 even if their equipment does not have existing VVC video decoding capability. Sharp's proprietary high-speed decoding processes data in real time and realizes smooth playback of video with resolutions up to 8K.Towards realizing its 8K + 5G Ecosystem Sharp has been working on various fronts to provide solutions in areas such as equipment for video decoding codec assessment and analysis software sales and joint development with partners for bringing VVC to market.

Company Background

Tokuji Hayakawa established Hayakawa Electric Industry in 1912 to make a type of belt buckle he had designed. Three years later he invented the first mechanical pencil named the Ever-Sharp which was a commercial success. After an earthquake leveled much of Tokyo in 1923 including Hayakawa's business he moved to Osaka and sold the rights to his pencil to finance a new factory. He introduced Japan's first crystal radio sets in 1925 and four years later debuted a vacuum tube radio.

Following WWII Hayakawa Electric developed an experimental TV which it began mass-producing in 1953. The company was ready with color TVs when Japan initiated color broadcasts in 1960. Hayakawa Electric grew tremendously during the 1960s introducing microwave ovens (1962) solar cells (1963) the first electronic all-transistor-diode calculator (1964) and the first gallium arsenide LED (1969). The firm opened a US office in 1962. In 1970 the company began to make its own semiconductor devices and changed its name to Sharp Corp. a nod to the name of its first product.

EXECUTIVES

Senior Executive Managing Officer and President of Consumer Electronics Company, Yoshisuke Hasegawa, age 65

CEO Sharp Europe and Head of AIoT Business Strategy, Yoshihisa Ishida

EVP and Head of Accounting and Finance Group, Katsuaki Nomura

Executive Managing Officer and President of Display Device Company, Taimi Oketani

EVP Consumer Electronics Company Head of Global Sale and Marketing and Chairman Sharp Electronics (Malaysia) Sdn. Bhd., Akira Atarashi

Executive Managing Officer and President of Business Solutions Company and Chairman Sharp Business Solutions Corporation, Kazushi Mukai

Chairman and President Sharp Electronics Corporation, Toshiyuki Osawa

President, Tai Jeng-wu

Executive Managing Officer and President of Electronic Components and Devices Company, Kazuhiro Moritani

CEO Greater China Business Chairman and President Sharp (China) Investment Co.Ltd. and Chairman Sharp Electronics Sales (China) Co.Ltd., Akihiko Imaya

President Energy Solutions Company, Hiroshi Sasaoka

President Sharp Electronics Europe, Jun Ashida

President Sharp Information Systems Europe,
 Alex Hermann
Chairman, Shigeaki Mizushima, age 65
Auditors: PricewaterhouseCoopers Aarata LLC

LOCATIONS

HQ: Sharp Corp (Japan)
 1 Takumi-cho, Sakai-ku, Sakai, Osaka 590-8522
Phone: (81) 72 282 1221
Web: www.sharp.co.jp

PRODUCTS/OPERATIONS

2015 Sales

	% of total
Products business	54
Device business	46
Total	**100**

Selected Products

Consumer/information products
 Audiovisual and communication equipment
 Audio amplifiers
 Blu-ray disc players
 Digital cameras
 High-definition televisions
 Liquid crystal display DVD televisions
 Liquid crystal display televisions
 Liquid crystal display video projectors
 Mobile phones
 Video cameras
 Information equipment
 Calculators
 Digital copiers
 Fax machines
 Mobile business tools
 Personal computers
 Printers
 Home appliances
 Air cleaning systems
 Superheated steam ovens
Electronic components
 Flash memory
 Integrated circuits
 Laser diodes and other optoelectronic devices
 Radio-frequency components
 Satellite broadcasting components
 Solar cells and other photovoltaic devices

COMPETITORS

AU Optronics	NEC
Broadcom	Oki Electric
CASIO COMPUTER	Panasonic Corp
Canon	Philips Electronics
Electrolux	Pioneer Corporation
Epson	Ricoh Company
Ericsson	SANYO
First Solar	Samsung Electronics
Fujitsu	SolarWorld
HP	Sony
Hanwha Q Cells	SunPower
Hisense	Suntech Power
Hitachi	TCL
IBM	TPV Technology
Konica Minolta	Tatung
Kyocera	Toshiba
LG Electronics	Xerox
Lexmark	Yingli
Mitsubishi Electric	

HISTORICAL FINANCIALS

Company Type: Public

Income Statement

FYE: March 31

	REVENUE ($ mil.)	NET INCOME ($ mil.)	NET PROFIT MARGIN	EMPLOYEES
03/20	20,923	193	0.9%	52,876
03/19	21,672	670	3.1%	54,156
03/18	22,858	661	2.9%	47,171
03/17	18,340	(222)	—	41,898
03/16	21,920	(2,279)	—	43,511
Annual Growth	(1.2%)	—	—	5.0%

2020 Year-End Financials

Debt ratio: 0.3%
Return on equity: 6.6%
Cash ($ mil.): 2,073
Current ratio: 1.26
Long-term debt ($ mil.): 4,963

No. of shares (mil.): 532
Dividends
 Yield: 1.7%
 Payout: 15.1%
Market value ($ mil.): 1,379

	STOCK PRICE ($) FY Close	P/E High/Low		PER SHARE ($) Earnings	Dividends	Book Value
03/20	2.59	0	0	0.30	0.05	4.77
03/19	2.74	0	0	0.83	0.02	5.95
03/18	7.44	0	0	0.81	0.00	7.15
03/17	4.19	—	—	(0.61)	0.00	5.29
03/16	1.15	—	—	(13.77)	0.00	(2.27)
Annual Growth	22.5%	—	—	—	—	—

Shiga Bank, Ltd.

EXECUTIVES

President, SHOJIRO TAKAHASHI
Managing Director, Etsuo Mori
Managing Director, Yasuhiko Inoue
Managing Director, Hiroshi Nakagawa
Managing Director, Ikuo Yoshida
Managing Director, Yukio Nishizawa
Auditors: Deloitte Touche Tohmatsu LLC

LOCATIONS

HQ: Shiga Bank, Ltd.
 1-38 Hamamachi, Otsu, Shiga 520-8686
Phone: (81) 77 521 9530
Web: www.shigagin.com

COMPETITORS

Nanto Bank	Toho Bank
Oita Bank	

HISTORICAL FINANCIALS

Company Type: Public

Income Statement

FYE: March 31

	ASSETS ($ mil.)	NET INCOME ($ mil.)	INCOME AS % OF ASSETS	EMPLOYEES
03/20	57,899	114	0.2%	3,480
03/19	55,219	132	0.2%	3,487
03/18	55,327	130	0.2%	3,570
03/17	49,545	133	0.3%	3,627
03/16	44,751	138	0.3%	3,715
Annual Growth	6.7%	(4.6%)	—	(1.6%)

2020 Year-End Financials

Return on assets: 0.2%
Return on equity: 3.1%
Long-term debt ($ mil.): —
No. of shares (mil.): 50
Sales ($ mil.): 864

Dividends
 Yield: —
 Payout: 18.6%
Market value ($ mil.): —

Shimao Group Holdings Ltd

EXECUTIVES

Director, Sai Fei Liu
Auditors: PricewaterhouseCoopers

LOCATIONS

HQ: Shimao Group Holdings Ltd
 38th Floor, Tower One, Lippo Centre, 89 Queensway,
Phone: (852) 2511 9968   **Fax:** (852) 2511 0287
Web: www.shimaoproperty.com

HISTORICAL FINANCIALS

Company Type: Public

Income Statement

FYE: December 31

	REVENUE ($ mil.)	NET INCOME ($ mil.)	NET PROFIT MARGIN	EMPLOYEES
12/19	16,026	1,566	9.8%	10,854
12/18	12,432	1,284	10.3%	9,814
12/17	10,822	1,204	11.1%	8,394
12/16	8,537	744	8.7%	7,880
12/15	8,889	941	10.6%	7,223
Annual Growth	15.9%	13.6%	—	10.7%

2019 Year-End Financials

Debt ratio: 3.8%
Return on equity: 17.3%
Cash ($ mil.): 7,524
Current ratio: 1.38
Long-term debt ($ mil.): 12,901

No. of shares (mil.): —
Dividends
 Yield: 0.0%
 Payout: 365.6%
Market value ($ mil.): —

	STOCK PRICE ($) FY Close	P/E High/Low		PER SHARE ($) Earnings	Dividends	Book Value
12/19	32.17	10	7	0.48	1.74	2.89
12/18	25.99	11	9	0.38	1.39	2.62
12/17	21.80	10	7	0.36	1.11	2.63
12/16	13.58	10	8	0.22	0.00	2.24
12/15	18.78	12	10	0.27	0.00	2.23
Annual Growth	14.4%	—	—	15.0%	—	6.7%

Shimizu Corp.

Shimizu provides architectural engineering construction and development services for commercial industrial infrastructure and residential projects around the world. One of Japan's largest general contractors the company has worked on major projects including Tokyo's Metro subway Singapore's Changi Airport and the Malaysia-Singapore Bridge. Other areas of specialization range from offices and power stations to railroads and dams. Shimizu has increasingly focused on green building and urban renewal projects. Needless to say earthquake-resistant technologies and earthquake restoration projects are key to Shimizu's business. The company also provides facilities management. Shimizu was founded in 1804.

Operations

Shimizu generated about 71% of its total revenue from its construction contracts in fiscal 2014 (ended March) while its real estate development business contributed just over 1%. The company's real estate business develops rents and sells properties and is operates under the Investment and Development Division.

Geographic Reach

The company boasts nearly 75 offices mostly across Japan though it also operates in other parts of Asia the Middle East Europe Africa and North America. About 89% of Shimizu's revenue came from Japan in fiscal 2014 (ended March) while other countries in Asia contributed another 10% to revenues.

Sales and Marketing

Shimizu mostly serves the office medical and welfare educational and cultural production and research logistics and residential markets.

Financial Performance

Note: Growth rates may differ after conversion to US dollars.

Shimizu's revenues and profits have been growing for the past several years thanks to higher demand for construction and engineering services as the economies in Japan and other Asian countries have strengthened. (Note: In terms of US Dollars revenues have been in decline due to unfavorable foreign exchange rates.)

The company's revenue rose by 6% to Å 1497 billion ($14.5 billion) in fiscal 2014 (ended March) mostly thanks to 4% growth in its construction business as orders from both the public and private sectors increased. Shimizu also earned higher revenues from its other engineering businesses thanks to improved profitability of some of its subsidiaries including its domestic real estate company and overseas construction company.

Higher revenue in FY2014 also drove Shimizu's net income higher by 140% to Å 14 billion ($137.7 million). The firm's operating cash levels declined sharply for the year mostly as its notes and accounts receivable trade balances decreased.

Strategy

Shimizu in 2015 planned to grow through its long-term "Smart Vision 2010" plan positioning itself to capture business from the strengthening Japanese and other Asian markets and their increased demand for engineering and construction services. The company also expects strong demand for its with Tokyo being the chosen city to host the 2020 Summer Olympics and Paralympics events. It also stands ready for post-earthquake restoration services should they occur in the country in the future.

EXECUTIVES

EVP, Kozo Kobashi
Managing Officer, Susumu Hoshii
President, Yoichi Miyamoto
EVP, Kazuo Yoshida
Managing Officer, Seikichi Kurosawa
EVP, Tatsuo Kakiya
Chairman, Tetsuya Nomura
Auditors: Ernst & Young ShinNihon LLC

LOCATIONS

HQ: Shimizu Corp.
2-16-1 Kyobashi, Chuo-ku, Tokyo 104-8370
Phone: (81) 3 3561 1111
Web: www.shimz.co.jp

2014 Sales

	% of total
Japan	89
Asia	10
Other	1
Total	**100**

PRODUCTS/OPERATIONS

2014 Sales

	% of total
Construction contracts	90
Real estate development and other	10
Total	**100**

Selected Projects

Overseas Projects
Factory Toyota Industries Compressor Parts America Co. (TICA)HMSI 3rd FactoryKarawang Factory PT. SHARP ELECTRONICS INDONESIANipro Pharma Vietnam PlantUmiray BridgeUrban Suites
Domestic Project
Naoetsu LNG terminalOsaki Wiz CityShintakamatsu Data Center PowericoYomiuri Shimbun Tokyo Head OfficeSelected Subsidiaries
Daiichi Setsubi Engineering Corporation
Katayama Stratech Corp.
Milx Corporation
Shimizu Comprehensive Development Corporation
Super Regional Inc.
The Nippon Road Co. Ltd.
TTK Corporation

COMPETITORS

Bechtel	Kumagai Gumi
Bouygues	Nishimatsu
Chiyoda Corp.	Construction
Hazama	Obayashi
Hyundai Engineering	Taisei
and Construction	Takenaka
Kajima	Toda

HISTORICAL FINANCIALS

Company Type: Public

Income Statement FYE: March 31

	REVENUE ($ mil.)	NET INCOME ($ mil.)	NET PROFIT MARGIN	EMPLOYEES
03/20	15,645	911	5.8%	18,475
03/19	15,034	899	6.0%	18,499
03/18	14,309	800	5.6%	18,732
03/17	14,019	884	6.3%	18,917
03/16	14,826	528	3.6%	18,955
Annual Growth	1.4%	14.6%	—	(0.6%)

2020 Year-End Financials

Debt ratio: 0.2%
Return on equity: 13.5%
Cash ($ mil.): 3,240
Current ratio: 1.31
Long-term debt ($ mil.): 1,831
No. of shares (mil.): 764
Dividends
  Yield: 4.6%
  Payout: 127.9%
Market value ($ mil.): 24,850

	STOCK PRICE ($) FY Close	P/E High/Low		PER SHARE ($) Earnings	Dividends	Book Value
03/20	32.52	0	0	1.18	1.51	8.81
03/19	33.84	0	0	1.15	1.05	8.38
03/18	35.37	0	0	1.02	1.17	7.80
03/17	36.47	0	0	1.13	0.59	6.51
03/16	34.38	1	0	0.67	0.00	5.45
Annual Growth	(1.4%)	—	—	15.1%	—	12.8%

Shin-Etsu Chemical Co., Ltd.

In the high-tech and industrial materials kitchen Shin-Etsu Chemical Co. is a master chef. The company's organic and inorganic chemicals unit — which represents about half of the company's sales — makes polyvinyl chloride (PVC) and more than 4000 types of silicone while its electronics materials unit makes semiconductor silicon epoxy molding compounds and rare earth magnets. Shin-Etsu also produces synthetic quartz used for fiber-optic communications and in LCD panels. Shin-Etsu operates in the US as Shintech; it makes just about 30% of its sales at home in Japan. The rest of Asia including China also accounts for about 30%. The firm is benefiting from strong demand for PVC in the Asia-Pacific market.

EXECUTIVES

Senior Managing Director, Toshinobu Ishihara
President, Yasuhiko Saitoh, age 65
Vice Chairman, Fumio Akiya
President and Board Member, Chihiro Kanagawa, age 94
Auditors: Ernst & Young ShinNihon LLC

LOCATIONS

HQ: Shin-Etsu Chemical Co., Ltd.
2-6-1 Ohtemachi, Chiyoda-ku, Tokyo 100-0004
Phone: (81) 3 3246 5011
Web: www.shinetsu.co.jp

2015 Sales

	% of total
Japan	28
US	22
Asia/Oceania (excluding china)	19
Europe	12
China	10
Others	9
Total	**100**

PRODUCTS/OPERATIONS

2015 Sales

	% of total
PVC/Chlor-Alkali	36
Semiconductor Silicon	18
Electronics & Functional Materials	15
Silicones	14
Speciality Chemicals	9
Diversified	8
Total	**100**

Selected products

PVC Chlor-Alkali
Polyvinyl chloride
Caustic soda
Chloromethane
Specialty Chemicals
Cellulose derivatives
Silicon metal
Poval (Polyvinyl alcohol)
Synthetic pheromones
Silicones
Semiconductor Silicon
Electronics & Functional Materials
Rare earth magnets
Encapsulation materials
Photoresists
Photomask blanks
Synthetic quartz products
Epoxy molding compounds
Pellicles
Diversified Business
Processed plastics
Export of plant equipment

International trading
Engineering
Information processing
Wafer container

COMPETITORS

ADEKA
Asahi Glass
Asahi Kasei
Axiall
Denka
Dow Chemical
Dow Corning
INEOS ChlorVinyls
Kaneka
Mexichem
Mitsubishi Chemical
Mitsui Chemicals
Occidental Petroleum
Royal Group
Sekisui Chemical
Solvay Chemicals
Sumitomo Chemical
Tosoh
Xinjiang Zhongtai Chemical (Group) Co. Ltd.

HISTORICAL FINANCIALS

Company Type: Public

Income Statement   FYE: March 31

	REVENUE ($ mil.)	NET INCOME ($ mil.)	NET PROFIT MARGIN	EMPLOYEES
03/20	15,563	3,166	20.3%	25,697
03/19	16,072	3,116	19.4%	24,380
03/18	14,533	2,684	18.5%	22,667
03/17	12,476	1,773	14.2%	21,303
03/16	12,904	1,500	11.6%	20,393
Annual Growth	4.8%	20.5%	—	5.9%

2020 Year-End Financials

Debt ratio: 0.0%
Return on equity: 12.2%
Cash ($ mil.): 8,433
Current ratio: 4.83
Long-term debt ($ mil.): 152

No. of shares (mil.): 415
Dividends
Yield: 1.9%
Payout: 6.3%
Market value ($ mil.): 10,168

	STOCK PRICE ($) FY Close	P/E High/Low		PER SHARE ($) Earnings	Dividends	Book Value
03/20	24.45	0	0	7.61	0.49	64.35
03/19	21.03	0	0	7.32	0.39	59.67
03/18	25.98	0	0	6.29	0.28	55.59
03/17	21.71	0	0	4.16	0.27	50.44
03/16	12.88	0	0	3.52	0.21	48.01
Annual Growth	17.4%	—	—	21.2%	22.7%	7.6%

Shinhan Financial Group Co. Ltd.

Shinhan Financial Group one of South Korea's largest financial companies in terms of assets provides retail and corporate banking credit cards insurance asset management securities brokerage and credit reporting services to almost 30 million customers. Its primary subsidiary is Shinhan Bank which has one of the largest branch networks in the country with more than 900 locations. It also owns a stake in the 40-branch Jeju Bank. Shinhan Financial Group has international operations in about a half-dozen other countries including Shin-

han Bank America in New York. Other units include Shinhan Investment Corp. (about 100 offices) and Shinhan Life Insurance (about 200 offices).

Operations

Shinhan Financial which operates mainly through Shinhan Bank centers its business around three core segments: Retail Banking which provides traditional banking products and services to retail and affluent individuals and non-profit organizations; Corporate and Investment Banking services which makes loans to corporations and small to medium-sized businesses; International Banking which counts the business of Shinhan's overseas branch operations and other international businesses along with securities trading and administrative operations. Through its more than 30 direct and indirect subsidiaries the bank also provides insurance brokerage and asset management services as well as credit card products and services. Shinhan Financial generated roughly 75% its 2014 operating income from interest income one-third of which came from its retail loan business one-fifth coming from its credit card business and just over one-tenth coming from its corporate loan business. The majority of the remaining 25% of total revenue came from fee and commission income mostly from its retail banking and credit card businesses.

Geographic Reach

Shinhan Financial generated 96% of its operating income from South Korea in 2014. It had three-fourths of its 1250 locations in Korea with more than one-third of the its offices in the Seoul metropolitan market alone and about 20% of offices in the Kyunggi province. The rest of the Korean branches in the cities of Incheon Busan Kwangju Taegu Ulsan and Taejon. Shinhan Bank's international branches are in some 16 countries including Cambodia Canada China Germany Hong Kong India Japan Kazakhstan Myanmar Poland Singapore the UK the US and Vietnam. It has representative offices in Mexico and Uzbekistan.

Sales and Marketing

The company serves retail and affluent individuals small and mid-sized businesses non-profit organizations (such as hospitals airports and schools) and corporations. Its Shinhan Card business primarily sells through the banking and credit card branch network sales agents and business partnerships and affiliations with vendors.

Altogether the firm spent Wan$229.64 billion ($208.9 million) on advertising in 2014 up from W$211.3 billion ($192.2 million) and W$188.36 billion ($171.4 million) in 2013 and 2012 respectively.

Financial Performance

Note: Growth rates may differ after conversion to US dollars.

Shinhan Financial's revenues and profits have been trending lower in recent years due to shrinking interest margins on loans amidst the low-interest environment.

The firm's revenue dipped by 2% to W$16135 billion ($15.43 billion) in 2014 mostly as its interest income on loans dipped by 4% due to a continued decline in interest margins on both its retail loans and corporate loans. Shinhan's net fees and commission income however grew by 6% as its credit card fee income increased with higher consumer credit balances.

Despite lower revenues in 2014 Shinhan's net income jumped by 10% to W$2.08 billion ($1.89 million) mostly thanks to significant unrealized fair value gains of the firm's available-for-sale financial assets. The firm's cash levels fell sharply despite higher earnings during the year with operations using W$2.08 billion ($1.89 million) after adjusting Shinhan's earnings for non-cash interest expenses net insurance loss and net trading loss items.

Strategy

Shinhan Financial Group reiterated in 2015 that its long-term strategy (which it's followed since 2001) included: balanced growth among its banking and non-banking businesses; expansion of its service offerings to grow revenues and differentiate the bank from competitors; and strengthening of its management systems and core expertise in effort to become the market leader in Korea and a world-class financial holding company.To that end in 2015 the company planned to introduce more differentiated financial services; and continue its international expansion efforts by localizing its product offerings and operations and bolstering its local marketing expertise and distribution channels.Shinhan Financial is also moving toward digital banking channels that are quickly taking the industry by storm allowing the bank to slow the growth of its costly branch network and cut operating costs significantly. Indeed more than 8.6 million Shinhan customers — about one-third of its customer base — were enrolled in the firm's smart phone banking service in 2014; nearly double the size of its "Smart" customer base in 2012. Additionally about 59% of all Shinhan bank transactions were done over the bank's internet or mobile banking services while just 5% of transactions were at physical branch locations.

Mergers and Acquisitions

In June 2015 Shinhan Bank purchased a 75% stake in Centratama Nasional Bank along with its $81 million in assets and 41 offices in Indonesia. Similarly in April 2015 Shinhan obtained regulatory approval to acquired a 40% equity interest in Jakarta-based Bank Metro Express a small bank in Indonesia and expected to close the transaction in late 2015. The bank planned to merge the two Indonesian banks in 2016 to strengthen its operations in the Southeast Asia region.

EXECUTIVES

Chairman and CEO, Cho Yong-Byoung
Deputy President and Chief Strategic Officer, Kim Hyung-jin
Deputy President and CFO, Yim Bo-hyuk
EVP, Lee Chang-goo
EVP Corporate and Investment Banking Business, Woo Young-woong
Auditors: KPMG Samjong Accounting Corp.

LOCATIONS

HQ: Shinhan Financial Group Co. Ltd.
20 Sejong-daero 9-gil Jung-gu, Seoul 04513
Phone: (82) 2 6360 3129   **Fax:** (82) 2 6360 3098
Web: www.shinhangroup.com

PRODUCTS/OPERATIONS

2014 Sales

	% of total
Interest income	
Loans	57
Available for sale financia assets	3
Held to maturity financial assets	5
Trading assets	3
Cash and due from banks	1
Other interest income	2
Non Interest income	
Fee and commission income	21
Dividend income	1
Net trading income	2
Net gain on sale of available for sale financial assets	1
Net foreign currency transaction gain	4
Total	**100**

	% of total
Banking	67
Credit card	25
Securities	4
Life insurance	4
Other	
Total	**100**

Selected Subsidiaries

Jeju Bank (68.9%)
SHC Management
Shinhan AITAS (99.8%)
Shinhan Bank
Shinhan BNP Paribas Asset Management (65%)
Shinhan Capital
Shinhan Card
Shinhan Credit Information
Shinhan Data System
Shinhan Investment Corp.
Shinhan Life Insurance
Shinhan Private Equity Investment Management
Shinhan Savings Bank

COMPETITORS

Busan Bank
Daegu Bank
Hana Bank
Industrial Bank of Korea

KB Financial Group
Korea Exchange Bank
Samsung Life Insurance
Woori

HISTORICAL FINANCIALS

Company Type: Public

Income Statement

FYE: December 31

	ASSETS ($ mil.)	NET INCOME ($ mil.)	INCOME AS % OF ASSETS	EMPLOYEES
12/19	478,445	2,947	0.6%	22,204
12/18	412,238	2,831	0.7%	22,624
12/17	399,870	2,736	0.7%	143
12/16	329,360	2,309	0.7%	147
12/15	314,940	2,011	0.6%	147
Annual Growth	**11.0%**	**10.0%**	**—**	**250.6%**

2019 Year-End Financials

Return on assets: 0.6%	Dividends
Return on equity: 9.0%	Yield: 3.6%
Long-term debt ($ mil.): —	Payout: 22.5%
No. of shares (mil.): 474	Market value ($ mil.): 18,053
Sales ($ mil): 23,961	

	STOCK PRICE ($) FY Close	P/E High/Low	PER SHARE ($) Earnings	Dividends	Book Value
12/19	38.07	0 0	6.06	1.39	71.56
12/18	35.49	0 0	5.90	1.35	67.58
12/17	46.40	0 0	5.74	1.35	64.92
12/16	37.64	0 0	4.77	0.99	54.61
12/15	33.59	0 0	4.07	0.87	55.28
Annual Growth	**3.2%**	**— —**	**10.5%**	**12.5%**	**6.7%**

Shinsei Bank Ltd

Shinsei Bank provides retail and corporate banking and several other financial services from 35 branches throughout Japan. Shinsei used to focus on financing Japan's large industrial firms but has been cultivating its retail and small business banking operations. It offers retail banking services such as deposits mortgages and investments as well as higher-margin services such as wealth management market services and institutional asset management bond sales and under-writing trust services and specialty financing in the public and real estate sectors. Founded as the Long-Term Credit Bank of Japan in 1952 the company was reborn as Shinsei (Japanese for "new birth") Bank in 2000.

Operations

Shinsei Bank group operates three main business segments. The Individual Group segment (which generated 58% of Shinsei Bank's total revenue and 22% of its profit in fiscal 2015 ended March 31) provides retail banking personal loans credit cards mutual funds insurance housing loans and overseas remittance services. The Institutional Group (which contributed 32% to revenue and 65% to profit) provides public sector finance real estate finance specialty finance health care finance private equity and credit trading (through Shinsei PI Group) leasing and property management services (through Showa Leasing Co) and trust services (through Shinsei Trust). The Global Markets Group (7% of revenue 8% of profit) provides market wealth management and asset management services through subsidiaries such as Shinsei Investment Management and Shinsei Securities.

Broadly about 53% of the bank's revenue came from interest income (mostly from loans) in FY2015 while 16% came from fee and commission income. Around 4% of its revenue came from net trading income while the remaining 23% of its revenue came from (non-recurring) net gains on sales of certain non-trading assets.

While Shinsei Bank lends to a variety of different industries across Japan about 27% of its entire loan portfolio's value was tied to loans to customers in the finance and insurance and real estate industries. About 7% of its portfolio went to customers in the services industries while another 15% was lent to customers in the manufacturing electric power/gas/heat/water and transportation/postal service industries.

Geographic Reach

Shinsei Bank had 35 branch outlets across Japan in fiscal 2015 (ended March 31) with about one-third of them around Tokyo nine in the Kinki region seven in the Konto region (excluding Tokyo) and one each in the Chugoku Tohoku Tokai Shikoku Kyushi Hokkaido and Hokuriku/Koshinetsu regions of Japan. The bank also had over 43960 ATM locations in Japan with nearly 40% of them located in the Kanto/Tokyo region and another 15% in the Kinki region. Additionally it had ATMs in all the other regions where there were branches along with 434 ATM locations in Okinawa.

Financial Performance

Note: Growth rates may differ after conversion to US dollars. This analysis uses financials from the company's annual report.

In domestic currency terms Shinsei Bank's annual revenues and profits have been trending higher since fiscal 2013 (ended March 31 2013) thanks to loan business growth and non-interest growth from fees and commissions and sales of investment products.

The bank's total revenue (defined by the company as the total of net interest income and non-interest income) grew to Å 235.3 billion in FY2015 thanks to a combination of: higher net interest income as the bank decreased its funding costs and collected higher dividend income from securities investments in the Institutional Group; and non-interest income growth thanks to an improvement in market-related transaction revenues including ALM operations (the company's corporate internal trading division) as well as a rise in revenue from the installment sales finance business of the consumer finance business.

Higher revenue and a decline in loan loss provisions in FY2015 boosted Shinsei Bank's net income up 64% to Å 67.8 billion ($567 million) for the year. The bank's operating cash levels declined sharply despite higher earnings with operations using Å 509 billion or $4.25 billion (operations provided Å 524 billion in FY2014) as the bank's deposit levels fell and as its loan balances grew.

Company Background

During the late 2000s Shinsei had been battered by its exposure to toxic assets including loans to failed Lehman Brothers and structured asset-backed securities. It had also taken a hit in the domestic real estate market in which the company had been a significant lender. Record losses reported for 2008 sparked rumors that Shinsei would merge with Aozora Bank another struggling midsized bank that was nationalized in 2001. The two banks reached a merger agreement in 2009 but called those plans off due to strategic differences.

HISTORY

The Japanese government nationalized Shinsei Bank's debt-ridden Long-Term Credit Bank in 1998. It sold the bank to an international group led by US-based Ripplewood Holdings in 2000 making it one of the few major Japanese banks to come under foreign control. Ripplewood spun off the bank in 2004 placing it on the Tokyo Stock Exchange.

In 2007 Shinsei acquired a minority stake in global advisory firm Duff & Phelps.

In 2008 it acquired GE's consumer finance business in Japan consisting of credit card personal lending and mortgage operations. In 2010 Shinsei Bank sold Shinsei Asset Management its Mumbai-based asset management operation to Daiwa Bank. The company would use the proceeds to pay down its debt.

EXECUTIVES

President and CEO, Shigeki Toma, age 72
Senior Managing Executive Officer, Hitomi Sato, age 72
Senior Managing Executive Officer and Group CIO, Michiyuki Okano, age 60
Senior Managing Executive Officer, Sanjeev Gupta, age 60
Deputy President, Yukio Nakamura, age 66
Senior Managing Executive Officer and CFO, Shigeru Tsukamoto, age 70
Managing Executive Officer, Norio Funayama, age 63
Managing Executive Officer, Toru Myochin, age 55
Managing Executive Officer, Yoshiaki Kozano, age 58
Managing Executive Officer, Hironobu Satou, age 60
Managing Executive Officer, Shinichirou Seto, age 59
Managing Executive Officer, Masashi Yamashita, age 62
Auditors: Deloitte Touche Tohmatsu LLC

LOCATIONS

HQ: Shinsei Bank Ltd
2-4-3 Nihonbashi-Muromachi, Chuo-ku, Tokyo 103-8303
Phone: (81) 3 6880 7000
Web: www.shinseibank.com

PRODUCTS/OPERATIONS

2014 Sales

	% of total
Net interest income	54
Noninterest income	
Net fee and commission	12
Net trading income	7
Others	27
Total	**100**

COMPETITORS

Aozora Bank	Resona
Bank of Yokohama	Sumitomo Mitsui
Mitsubishi UFJ	Sumitomo Mitsui Trust
Financial Group	Holdings
Mizuho Financial	
Mizuho Trust & Banking	
Ltd	

HISTORICAL FINANCIALS

Company Type: Public

Income Statement — FYE: March 31

	ASSETS ($ mil.)	NET INCOME ($ mil.)	INCOME AS % OF ASSETS	EMPLOYEES
03/20	94,210	419	0.4%	6,738
03/19	86,426	472	0.5%	6,340
03/18	89,056	484	0.5%	6,413
03/17	82,806	453	0.5%	6,521
03/16	79,510	542	0.7%	6,668
Annual Growth	**4.3%**	**(6.2%)**	**—**	**0.3%**

2020 Year-End Financials

Return on assets: 0.4%
Return on equity: 5.0%
Long-term debt ($ mil.): —
No. of shares (mil.): 230
Sales ($ mil): 3,680

Dividends
Yield: 0.6%
Payout: 1.0%
Market value ($ mil.): 621

	STOCK PRICE ($) FY Close	P/E High/Low		PER SHARE ($) Earnings	Dividends	Book Value
03/20	2.69	0	0	1.76	0.02	36.06
03/19	2.82	0	0	1.91	0.02	32.84
03/18	3.16	0	0	1.87	0.02	31.81
03/17	3.69	0	0	1.74	0.02	28.32
03/16	2.69	0	0	2.04	0.02	26.23
Annual Growth	**(0.0%)**	**—**		**(3.7%)**	**3.2%**	**8.3%**

Shizuoka Bank Ltd (Japan)

Auditors: Deloitte Touche Tohmatsu LLC

LOCATIONS

HQ: Shizuoka Bank Ltd (Japan)
1-10 Gofuku-cho, Aoi-ku, Shizuoka 420-8761
Phone: (81) 54 261 3131
Web: www.shizuokabank.co.jp

HISTORICAL FINANCIALS

Company Type: Public

Income Statement — FYE: March 31

	ASSETS ($ mil.)	NET INCOME ($ mil.)	INCOME AS % OF ASSETS	EMPLOYEES
03/20	115,548	356	0.3%	6,328
03/19	107,046	423	0.4%	6,422
03/18	108,607	472	0.4%	6,469
03/17	98,874	261	0.3%	6,504
03/16	98,998	426	0.4%	6,622
Annual Growth	**3.9%**	**(4.4%)**	**—**	**(1.1%)**

2020 Year-End Financials

Return on assets: 0.3%
Return on equity: 3.8%
Long-term debt ($ mil.): —
No. of shares (mil.): 573
Sales ($ mil): 2,116

Dividends
Yield: —
Payout: 33.6%
Market value ($ mil.): —

Shoko Chukin Bank (The) (Japan)

Auditors: PricewaterhouseCoopers Aarata LLC

LOCATIONS

HQ: Shoko Chukin Bank (The) (Japan)
2-10-17 Yaesu, Chuo-ku, Tokyo 104-0028
Phone: (81) 3 3272 6111 **Fax:** (81) 3 3272 6169
Web: www.shokochukin.co.jp

HISTORICAL FINANCIALS

Company Type: Public

Income Statement — FYE: March 31

	ASSETS ($ mil.)	NET INCOME ($ mil.)	INCOME AS % OF ASSETS	EMPLOYEES
03/19	106,719	139	0.1%	5,149
03/18	112,606	351	0.3%	5,141
03/17	114,886	290	0.3%	5,127
03/16	111,939	110	0.1%	5,120
03/15	105,299	140	0.1%	4,140
Annual Growth	**0.3%**	**(0.2%)**	**—**	**5.6%**

2019 Year-End Financials

Return on assets: 0.1%
Return on equity: 1.6%
Long-term debt ($ mil.): —
No. of shares (mil.): —
Sales ($ mil): 1,642

Dividends
Yield: —
Payout: —
Market value ($ mil.): —

Siam Cement Public Co. Ltd.

EXECUTIVES

CEO, Kan Trakulhoon, age 64
SVP; President SCG Cement-Building Materials, Pichit Maipoom, age 63
VP Finance and Investment and CFO; President SCG Investments, Chaovalit Ekabut, age 62
SVP and President SCG Chemicals, Cholanat Yanaranop, age 60

President, Roongrote Rangsiyopash, age 56
President SCG Paper SCG Packaging, Tanawong Areeratchakul
VP Operations, Somchai Wangwattanapanich
Chairman, Chirayu Isarangkun Na Ayuthaya
Auditors: KPMG Phoomchai Audit Ltd.

LOCATIONS

HQ: Siam Cement Public Co. Ltd.
1 Siam Cement Road, Bangsue, Bangkok 10800
Phone: (66) 2 586 3333 **Fax:** (66) 2 586 2974
Web: www.scg.co.th

2014 Sales

	% of total
Thailand	61
China	7
Indonesia	6
Vietnam	6
Other	20
Total	**100**

PRODUCTS/OPERATIONS

2014 Sales

	% of total
Chemicals	50
Cement building materials	37
Paper	13
Other	-
Total	**100**

Selected Products

Chemicals
Olefins
Polyolefins
Paper & packaging
Corrugated boxes
Gypsum linerboard
Industrial paper
Printing paper
Writing paper
Cement
Dry mortar
Gray cement
Ready-mixed concrete
White cement
Building products
Ceramic tiles
Concrete paving blocks
Gypsum boards
Roof tiles
Sanitary fittings and wares

COMPETITORS

Exxon Mobil	PTT
Halliburton	Phoenix Pulp & Paper
Hanwa	Public Company
IRPC	SIAMP
Italcementi	Siam Syndicate Trading
Lafarge Malaysia	Ube
Michelin	

HISTORICAL FINANCIALS

Company Type: Public

Income Statement — FYE: December 31

	REVENUE ($ mil.)	NET INCOME ($ mil.)	NET PROFIT MARGIN	EMPLOYEES
12/19	14,703	1,074	7.3%	0
12/18	14,789	1,383	9.4%	0
12/17	13,841	1,689	12.2%	0
12/16	11,829	1,566	13.2%	0
12/15	12,201	1,260	10.3%	0
Annual Growth	**4.8%**	**(3.9%)**	**—**	**—**

2019 Year-End Financials

Debt ratio: 1.2%
Return on equity: 11.4%
Cash ($ mil.): 927
Current ratio: 1.25
Long-term debt ($ mil.): 5,215

No. of shares (mil.): 1,200
Dividends
  Yield: —
  Payout: —
Market value ($ mil.): —

Siam Commercial Bank Public Co Ltd (The)

EXECUTIVES

CFO, Kittiya Todhanakasem, age 62
SEVP and Head Special Business, Sarunthorn Chutima
SEVP and Head of Wealth Segment Wealth Products Retail Banking & sSME Solutions, Narong Srichukrin
President and CEO, Arthid Nanthawithaya
SEVP and Chief Legal and Control Officer, Wallaya Kaewrungruang
SEVP and Chief Risk Officer, Anucha Laokwansatit
SEVP and Chief Strategic Officer, Jens Lottner
SEVP and CTO, Colin R. Dinn
Head of Digital Ventures, Orapong Thien-Ngern
Head of Digital Ventures, Thana Thienachariya
SEVP and Chief People Officer, Phanporn Kongyingyong
SEVP and Head of Operations, Apiphan Charoenanusorn
SEVP and Chief Strategy Officer, Arak Sutivong
SEVP and Head of Multi-Corporate Segment and Corporate Segment, Wasin Saiyawan
SEVP and Head of SME Segment and Small SME Segment, Pikun Srimahunt
SEVP and Head of Commercial Banking Solutions, Pimolpa Suntichok
SEVP and Head of Retail Segment and Branch Network, Sarut Ruttanaporn
Chairman, Anand Panyarachun
Auditors: KPMG Phoomchai Audit Ltd.

LOCATIONS

HQ: Siam Commercial Bank Public Co Ltd (The)
9 Ratchadapisek Road, Jatujak, Bangkok 10900
Phone: (66) 2 544 1000   **Fax:** (66) 2 937 7721
Web: www.scb.co.th

PRODUCTS/OPERATIONS

2013 Sales

	% of total
Interest income	56
Net earned insurance premiums	23
Fees & service income	14
Net trading income	4
Dividend income	2
Net gain on investments	1
Total	**100**

Selected Group Companies

SCB Asset Management
SCB Life Assurance
SCB Securities
The Siam Commercial Bank

COMPETITORS

Bangkok Bank
Bank of Ayudhya
KASIKORNBANK

TMB Bank
Thanachart Capital

HISTORICAL FINANCIALS

Company Type: Public

Income Statement
FYE: December 31

	ASSETS ($ mil.)	NET INCOME ($ mil.)	INCOME AS % OF ASSETS	EMPLOYEES
12/19	99,495	1,357	1.4%	0
12/18	98,527	1,238	1.3%	0
12/17	92,823	1,324	1.4%	0
12/16	81,380	1,330	1.6%	0
12/15	76,999	1,309	1.7%	0
Annual Growth	**6.6%**	**0.9%**	**—**	**—**

2019 Year-End Financials

Return on assets: 1.3%
Return on equity: 10.3%
Long-term debt ($ mil.): —
No. of shares (mil.): —
Sales ($ mil): 8,275

Dividends
  Yield: 0.0%
  Payout: —
Market value ($ mil.): —

	STOCK PRICE ($) FY Close	P/E High/Low		PER SHARE ($) Earnings	Dividends	Book Value
12/19	16.23	2	1	0.40	0.59	3.96
12/18	16.16	2	1	0.36	0.54	3.46
12/17	18.27	2	1	0.39	0.53	3.29
12/16	16.45	1	1	0.39	0.49	2.75
12/15	12.95	1	1	0.39	0.53	2.51
Annual Growth	**5.8%**	**—**	**—**	**0.9%**	**2.7%**	**12.0%**

Sichuan Chang Hong Electric Co Ltd

EXECUTIVES

Chairman, Yong Zhao
Auditors: Shine Wing Certified Public Accountants

LOCATIONS

HQ: Sichuan Chang Hong Electric Co Ltd
No. 35, East Mianxing Road, High-Tech Park, Mianyang, Sichuan Province 621000
Phone: (86) 816 2418486   **Fax:** (86) 816 2418518
Web: www.changhong.com

HISTORICAL FINANCIALS

Company Type: Public

Income Statement
FYE: December 31

	REVENUE ($ mil.)	NET INCOME ($ mil.)	NET PROFIT MARGIN	EMPLOYEES
12/19	12,760	8	0.1%	0
12/18	12,122	46	0.4%	0
12/17	11,929	54	0.5%	0
12/16	9,673	79	0.8%	0
12/15	9,984	(304)		0
Annual Growth	**6.3%**	**—**	**—**	**—**

2019 Year-End Financials

Debt ratio: 3.5%
Return on equity: 0.4%
Cash ($ mil.): 2,800
Current ratio: 1.06
Long-term debt ($ mil.): 167

No. of shares (mil.): —
Dividends
  Yield: —
  Payout: —
Market value ($ mil.): —

Siemens AG (Germany)

It's probably easier to name the things this engineering titan doesn't do. Siemens is a global powerhouse focusing on the areas of electrification automation and digitalization. One of the largest electronics and industrial engineering companies in the world. The German conglomerate makes everything from healthcare and building technologies to factory automation and power distribution equipment. Siemens has facilities in most corners of the world and serves a global customer base of manufacturers and construction energy and healthcare businesses. Formed in 1847 as Siemens & Halske the company's technological innovations include the first long-distance telegraph system in Europe a high-efficiency dynamo for generating electricity and the SIMATIC industrial machine automation technology.

Operations

Siemens operates its business through eight reportable segments.

Publicly traded and separately managed company Siemens Healthineers generates more than 15% of total sales. The division develops manufactures and sells health imaging and diagnostic technology and clinical consulting services globally to healthcare providers.

The Digital Industries segment offers automation technology industrial software and services and a cloud-based industrial internet of things (IoT) operating system primarily for manufacturing. This segment generates nearly 20% of sales.

Gas and Power (some 20% of sales) offers products and solutions for generating electricity for production transport and downstream operations involving oil and gas and for installing and operating transmission grids. It offers services such as performance enhancements maintenance services customer training and professional consulting.

Smart Infrastructure (nearly 15% of sales) connects energy systems buildings and industries. The company do this from the macro to the micro level physical products components and systems to connected cloud-based digital offerings and services. From intelligent grid control and electrification to smart storage solutions from building automation and control systems to switches valves and sensors.

Siemens holds a 59% stake in SGRE a company formed through the incorporation of Siemens' wind power business into the publicly traded Gamesa Corporaci n Tecnol gica. The business sells onshore and offshore wind turbines and develops and sells wind farms.

Mobility segment combines all Siemens businesses in the area of passenger and freight transportation including rail vehicles rail automation systems rail electrification systems road traffic technology digital solutions and related services. It also provides its customers with consulting planning financing construction service and operation of turnkey mobility systems.

Other segments includes Financial Services and Portfolio Companies which accounts for more than 5% of sales combined.

Geographic Reach

Headquartered in Munich Germany Siemens has offices warehouses and R&D facilities in nearly every country across the globe and has diverse geographic revenue streams.

Siemens generates around half its revenue from the geographic region comprising Europe CIS Africa and the Middle East (of which Germany accounts for nearly 15%). The Americas accounts for over 25% of sales most of which comes from Siemens' largest single country the US. It derives more than 20% of sales from the Asia/Pacific region of which China accounts for roughly half.

Sales and Marketing

Siemens serves a range of customers including public and private power producers and transportation companies; engineering companies; building and infrastructure developers; original equipment discrete and process manufacturers; and pharmaceutical companies.

In its Smart Infrastructure segment it serves its customers through a broad variety of channels including its global product and systems sales organization distributors panel builders original equipment manufacturers (OEM) value added resellers and installers as well as by direct sales through the branch offices of its regional solutions and services units worldwide.

Financial Performance

Note: Growth rates may differ after conversion to US Dollars.

The company's revenue increased by 5% to ?16.1 billion in 2019 compared to ?15.6 billion in the prior year.

The company's net income decreased by 8% to ?5.6 billion in 2019 compared to 2018 with about ?6.1 billion. The fall was due to the increase on their Reconciliation to Consolidated Financial Statements.

Cash held by the company at the end of 2019 increased by ?1.3 billion to ?12.4 billion. Cash provided by operations was ?8.5 billion while cash used for investing and financing activities were ?5.0 billion and ?2.3 billion respectively.

Strategy

At the end of fiscal 2018 Siemens announced its "Vision 2020+" company strategy. The main aim of "Vision 2020+" is to give Siemens' individual businesses significantly more entrepreneurial freedom under the strong Siemens brand in order to sharpen their focus on their respective markets. As a result the company implemented a new organizational structure in fiscal 2019 consisting of the three Operating Companies Digital Industries Smart Infrastructure and Gas and Power and the three Strategic Companies Mobility Siemens Healthineers and Siemens Gamesa Renewable Energy. These six industrial businesses are reportable segments which together are reported as "Industrial Businesses". Financial Services (SFS) which supports the activities of our industrial businesses and also conducts its own business with external customers continues to be a reportable segment outside our Industrial Businesses. Furthermore Siemens report Portfolio Companies which comprises businesses that are managed separately to improve their performance.

Mergers and Acquisitions

Siemens is planning to acquire Process Systems Enterprise (PSE) in 2019 a technology- leading global supplier of software and services for advanced process modelling. This provides a wide range of state-of-the-art model-based solutions that strongly complement the Siemens portfolio in the process industry sector.

In 2019 Siemens acquired MultiMechanics Inc. a developer of MultiMech finite element software that helps companies virtually predict failure in advanced materials at an unprecedented level of speed and accuracy. The company plans to integrate MultiMechanics into Siemens Digital Industries Software which will add the ability for customers to create a digital twin of materials by closely integrating materials engineering with part design performance engineering and manufacturing through the unique TRUE Multiscale? technology for a broad range of material-driven applications.

Company Background

Electrical engineer Werner von Siemens and craftsman Johann Halske formed Siemens &

Halske in 1847. In 1874 the firm finished the first transatlantic telegraph cable which ran from Ireland to the US. The company also created Europe's first electric power transmission system (1876) the world's first electrified railway (1879) and one of the first elevators (1880).

HISTORY

In 1847 electrical engineer Werner von Siemens and craftsman Johann Halske formed Siemens & Halske. The firm's first major project linked Berlin and Frankfurt with the first long-distance telegraph system in Europe (1848). In 1870 it completed a 6600-mile telegraph line from London to Calcutta India and in 1874 it made the first transatlantic cable linking Ireland to the US.

The company's history of firsts includes Europe's first electric power transmission system (1876) the world's first electrified railway (1879) and one of the first elevators (1880). In 1896 it patented the world's first X-ray tube and completed the first European subway in Budapest Hungary.

By the next century it had formed light-bulb cartel OSRAM with German rivals AEG and Auer (1919) and created a venture with Furukawa Electric called Fuji Electric (1923). It developed radios and traffic lights in the 1920s and began producing electron microscopes in 1939.

Siemens & Halske played a critical role in Germany's war effort in WWII and suffered heavy losses. During the 1950s it recovered by developing data processing equipment silicates for semiconductors and the first implantable pacemaker. It moved into the nuclear industry in 1959 when its first reactor went into service at Munich-Garching. In 1966 the company reincorporated as Siemens AG.

EXECUTIVES

President and CEO, Joe Kaeser, age 63, $1,117,896 total compensation
CEO Financial Services, Roland W. Chalons-Browne, age 64
CEO Mobility, Jochen Eickholt, age 57
CTO, Roland Busch, age 56
CFO and Member of the Managing Board, Ralf P. Thomas, age 59
CEO Energy Management, Ralf Christian
Head Healthcare, Michael Sen, age 52
CEO Building Technologies Division, Matthias Rebellius
Member Managing Board Siemens AG, Klaus Helmrich, age 62
Chair and CEO Siemens Corporation USA; CEO Power and Gas Division the Wind Power and Renewables Division the Power Generation Services Division the Region North America and the Region South America, Lisa Davis, age 57
CEO Power and Gas Division, Willi Meixner, age 55
CEO Digital Factory, Jan Mrosik
CEO Wind Power and Renewables, Markus Tacke
CEO Healthcare, Bernd Montag
CEO Power Generation Services, Tim O. Holt, age 50
CEO Siemens Qatar, Adrian Wood, age 54
CEO Siemens Kuwait, Herbert Klausner, age 56
CEO Siemens Middle East and UAE, Dietmar Siersdorfer
Head Asia Australia Business and Energy Management Division, Cedrik Neike, age 47
Second Deputy Chairman, Werner Wenning, age 74
Chairman, Gerhard Cromme, age 78
First Deputy Chairwoman, Birgit Steinborn, age 60
Auditors: Ernst & Young GmbH

LOCATIONS

HQ: Siemens AG (Germany)
 Werner-von-Siemens-Str. 1, Munich D-80333
Phone: (49) 89 636 33443   **Fax:** (49) 89 636 30085
Web: www.siemens.com

2018 Sales

	% of total
Europe CIS Africa Middle East	51
Americas	27
Asia Australia	22
Total	**100**

PRODUCTS/OPERATIONS

2018 Sales

	% of total
Siemens Healthineers	16
Digital Factory	15
Power and Gas	15
Energy Management	14
Siemens Games Renewable Energy	11
Mobility	10
Process Industries and Drives	9
Building Technologies	8
Financial Services (SFS)	1
Total	**100**

Products & Services

Industrial Automation
Building Technologies
Drive Technology
Energy
Healthcare
Mobility
Financing
Consumer Products
Services
Solutions by Market
Aerospace
Automotive Manufacturing
Battery Manufacturing
Chemistry Industry
Cement
Cranes
Data Centers
Distributors
Electronics Industry
Fiber Industry
Food & Beverage
Glass Industry
Conveyor Technology
Machinery and Plant Construction
Marine
Mining Industry
Municipalities and DSOs
Oil & Gas
Panel Building
Pharmaceutical Industry
Power Utilities

COMPETITORS

ABB	Honeywell
ALSTOM	International
AREVA	Huawei Technologies
Abbott Labs	MAN
Alcatel-Lucent	McKesson
Avaya	Mitsubishi Electric
Beckman Coulter	Mitsubishi Heavy
Bharat Heavy	Industries
Electricals	Nichia
Bombardier	Nortel Networks
Capgemini	OSRAM Licht
Cerner	Philips Electronics
Computer Sciences	Philips Healthcare
Corp.	Roche Diagnostics
Danfoss Turbocor	Rockwell Automation
Danieli	Schneider Electric
Dassault	Senvion
Dresser-Rand	Sonova
Emerson Electric	Toshiba
FANUC	United Technologies
GE	Varian Medical Systems
GN ReSound	Veolia Environnement
Hitachi	Vestas Wind Systems
Hologic	

HISTORICAL FINANCIALS

Company Type: Public

Income Statement   FYE: September 30

	REVENUE ($ mil.)	NET INCOME ($ mil.)	NET PROFIT MARGIN	EMPLOYEES
09/20	66,901	4,718	7.1%	363,000
09/19	94,740	5,644	6.0%	385,000
09/18	96,187	6,726	7.0%	379,000
09/17	98,120	7,143	7.3%	363,000
09/16	88,907	6,083	6.8%	349,000
Annual Growth	(6.9%)	(6.2%)	—	1.0%

2020 Year-End Financials

Debt ratio: 40.0%
Return on equity: 9.5%
Cash ($ mil.): 16,439
Current ratio: 1.55
Long-term debt ($ mil.): 41,985

No. of shares (mil.): 799
Dividends
  Yield: 2.2%
  Payout: 21.5%
Market value ($ mil.): 55,672

	STOCK PRICE ($) FY Close	P/E High/Low		PER SHARE ($) Earnings	Dividends	Book Value
09/20	69.65	14	7	5.77	1.56	53.31
09/19	53.59	9	7	6.89	1.60	64.59
09/18	63.86	10	8	8.12	1.58	65.02
09/17	70.75	20	9	8.61	1.55	62.42
09/16	117.32	18	13	7.42	1.40	47.25
Annual Growth	(12.2%)	—	—	(6.1%)	2.7%	3.1%

Siemens Gamesa Renewable Energy SA

Wind farms have gotten a lot more pervasive thanks to Gamesa Corporaci n Tecnol gica. The company is one of the top manufacturers of wind turbines in the world having installed about 27000 MW of wind turbines in more than 40 countries around the globe. It manufactures nacelles towers blades root joints blade moulds generators and gearboxes. It also develops constructs and sells wind farms and has installed 6000 MW and has an 18000 MW capacity in Asia Europe and the US. In addition Gamesa provides engineering and maintenance services on its equipment. The company was founded in 1976.

Geographic Reach

The company has production centers in the wind markets of Brazil China India Spain and the US. Latin America is the company's biggest market accounting for 32% of sales. The US accounts for 20% while Europe and other countries contribute 27%.

Financial Performance

Gamesa saw its revenues fall 10% from $3.92 billion 2011 to $3.52 billion 2012. After years of profitability the company also suffered a net loss of $871 million during 2012.

Strategy

Fueled by the Global Wind Energy Council's (GWEC) forecast that wind energy and its installation rates increase significantly in the years ahead the company is making strategic acquisitions forging alliances expanding production facilities building its core capabilities and focusing on emerging markets. It has a particular eye on Latin America (Mexico and Brazil) as a region ripe for growth.

After suffering a net loss for 2012 the company is focused on trimming its workforce and reducing costs by closing facilities. In 2012 Gamesa discontinued its wind farm development operations in the US due to the high costs of gas prices and regulatory volatility.

EXECUTIVES

CEO Europe, Ricardo Chocarro
CEO India, Ramesh Kymal
CEO Latin America, José Antonio Miranda
Business CEO, Xabier Etxeberria
CEO USA, Borja Negro
CEO APAC, Alvaro Bilbao
CFO, Ignacio Art ̄zcoz
Chairman, Ignacio Martin
Deputy Chairman, Juan Luis Arregui
Auditors: Ernst & Young, S.L.

LOCATIONS

HQ: Siemens Gamesa Renewable Energy SA
  Parque Tecnologico de Bizkaia, Edificio 222, Vizcaya, Zamudio 48170
Phone: (34) 944 03 73 52
Web: www.siemensgamesa.com

2012 Sales

	% of total
Latin America	32
Europe & other	27
US	20
India	12
China	9
Total	**100**

COMPETITORS

ALSTOM	Mitsubishi Heavy
Acciona	Industries
American	Nordex
Superconductor	Senvion
EDP Renov veis	Siemens Energy
GE Energy	Vestas Wind Systems

HISTORICAL FINANCIALS

Company Type: Public

Income Statement   FYE: September 30

	REVENUE ($ mil.)	NET INCOME ($ mil.)	NET PROFIT MARGIN	EMPLOYEES
09/20	14,922	(1,444)	—	25,458
09/19	16,093	220	1.4%	23,882
09/18	14,354	110	0.8%	23,799
09/17*	10,288	(23)	—	22,432
12/16	7,452	474	6.4%	8,452
Annual Growth	19.0%	—	—	31.7%

*Fiscal year change

2020 Year-End Financials

Debt ratio: 11.3%
Return on equity: (-16.3%)
Cash ($ mil.): 2,552
Current ratio: 0.83
Long-term debt ($ mil.): 1,165

No. of shares (mil.): 679
Dividends
  Yield: 0.1%
  Payout: —
Market value ($ mil.): 3,703

	STOCK PRICE ($) FY Close	P/E High/Low		PER SHARE ($) Earnings	Dividends	Book Value
09/20	5.45	—	—	(2.12)	0.01	11.43
09/19	2.77	17	10	0.33	0.00	14.52
09/18	2.57	35	22	0.16	0.00	13.73
09/17*	2.59	—	—	(0.05)	0.61	14.93
12/16	4.00	4	3	1.71	0.02	9.94
Annual Growth	8.0%	—	—	(22.7%)	3.5%	

*Fiscal year change

Siemens Healthineers AG

Auditors: Ernst & Young GmbH

LOCATIONS

HQ: Siemens Healthineers AG
  HenkestraBe 127, Erlangen 91052
Phone: (49) 800 188 188 5
Web: www.siemens-healthineers.com

HISTORICAL FINANCIALS

Company Type: Public

Income Statement   FYE: September 30

	REVENUE ($ mil.)	NET INCOME ($ mil.)	NET PROFIT MARGIN	EMPLOYEES
09/19	15,837	1,709	10.8%	52,000
09/18	15,554	1,465	9.4%	50,000
09/17*	16,159	1,629	10.1%	48,000
10/16	0	0	—	0
Annual Growth	—	—	—	—

*Fiscal year change

2019 Year-End Financials

Debt ratio: 0.7%
Return on equity: 17.0%
Cash ($ mil.): 1,003
Current ratio: 1.39
Long-term debt ($ mil.): 67

No. of shares (mil.): 1,000
Dividends
  Yield: 1.3%
  Payout: 14.3%
Market value ($ mil.): 19,660

	STOCK PRICE ($) FY Close	P/E High/Low		PER SHARE ($) Earnings	Dividends	Book Value
09/19	19.66	14	11	1.71	0.26	10.66
09/18	22.25	18	16	1.46	0.00	10.02
09/17*	0.00	—	—	1.63	0.00	(0.00)
Annual Growth	—	—	—	1.7%	—	—

*Fiscal year change

Sinopec Shanghai Petrochemical Co., Ltd.

China's own entry into the world of giant petrochemical companies Sinopec Shanghai Petrochemical Company is one of that country's largest producers of ethylene a crucial ingredient in the manufacture of synthetic fibers and plastics. It also makes petroleum-based fuels and oils and other intermediate petrochemicals such as benzene. The company operates primarily within China; most of its revenues are from eastern China. Though it was founded as a maker of synthetic fibers that segment is Shanghai Petrochemical's smallest now; petroleum products account for almost half of sales. China Petroleum & Chemical (Sinopec) which is controlled by the Chinese government owns about 55% of Shanghai Petrochemical.

EXECUTIVES

Chairman and President, Wang Zhiqing, age 58
VP and CFO, Zhou Meiyun, age 50

Vice Chairman, Wu Haijun, age 55
Vice Chairman, Gao Jinping, age 54
Auditors: PricewaterhouseCoopers Zhong Tian LLP

LOCATIONS

HQ: Sinopec Shanghai Petrochemical Co., Ltd.
48 Jinyi Road, Jinshan District, Shanghai 200540
Phone: (86) 21 57943143   **Fax:** (86) 21 57940050
Web: www.spc.com.cn

PRODUCTS/OPERATIONS

2016 Sales

	% of total
Petroleum products	45
Trading of petrochemical products	27
Resins and plastics	13
Intermediate petrochemicals	12
Synthetic fibers	2
Others	1
Total	**100**

Selected Products

Petroleum Products
  Diesel
  Gasoline
  Jet oil
  Residual oil
Resins and Plastics
  LDPE film and pellets
  Polyester chips
  PP pellets
  PVA
Intermediate Petrochemicals
  Benzene
  Butadiene
  Ethylene
  Ethylene glycol
  Ethylene oxide
Synthetic Fibers
  Acrylic staple
  Acrylic top
  Polyester filament-POY
  Polyester staple
  PP fiber
  PVA fiber

COMPETITORS

BASF SE	Marubeni
CNOOC	PetroChina
ExxonMobil Chemical	Shell Chemicals
Formosa Plastics	

HISTORICAL FINANCIALS

Company Type: Public

Income Statement   FYE: December 31

	REVENUE ($ mil.)	NET INCOME ($ mil.)	NET PROFIT MARGIN	EMPLOYEES
12/19	14,421	318	2.2%	0
12/18	15,667	767	4.9%	0
12/17	14,139	943	6.7%	0
12/16	11,217	857	7.6%	0
12/15	10,322	504	4.9%	12,032
Annual Growth	**8.7%**	**(10.9%)**	**—**	**—**

2019 Year-End Financials

Debt ratio: 0.4%
Return on equity: 7.3%
Cash ($ mil.): 1,287
Current ratio: 1.44
Long-term debt ($ mil.): —

No. of shares (mil.): —
Dividends
  Yield: 10.5%
  Payout: 10,801.1%
Market value ($ mil.): —

	STOCK PRICE ($) FY Close	P/E High/Low	PER SHARE ($) Earnings	Dividends	Book Value
12/19	30.55	245 131	0.03	3.22	(0.00)
12/18	43.16	141 88	0.07	4.16	(0.00)
12/17	57.00	120 94	0.09	3.40	(0.00)
12/16	54.13	99 62	0.08	1.25	(0.00)
12/15	39.59	206 90	0.05	0.00	282.84
Annual Growth	**(6.3%)**	**— —**	**(10.9%)**	**—**	**—**

SK Telecom Co Ltd (South Korea)

SK Telecom (SKT) a member of the SK Group chaebol is the leading wireless communication services provider in South Korea. The company serves more than 30 million mobile customers (good for a better than 40% market share). In addition to cellular and wireless data services SKT provides broadband internet access through a controlling stake in the #2 South Korean alternative local-exchange carrier and ISP SK Broadband. It also operates internet portal NATE.com. SKT has international offices in China California and Japan but almost all revenue is from South Korea. SK Group owns 25% of SKT.

Operations
SKT operates in four segments: cellular services about 75% of revenue fixed-line telecommunications services about 15% of revenue e-commerce services about 5% of revenue and other businesses less than 5% of revenue.

SKT's cellular services offer wireless voice and data transmission and its sells wireless devices and provides Internet of Things technologies.

The company's fixed-line segment provides telephone broadband internet and Internet Protocol TV (IPTV) and business communications through subsidiaries SK Broadband and SK Telink.

The E-commerce services segment consists of marketplace business operated by the SK Planet subsidiary. The company's 11st service is an online marketplace that offers products through online and mobile devices.

The Others segment offers complementary products and services.

Geographic Reach
SKT gets 99% of its revenue from South Korea. It has offices in the US China Malaysia and Japan.

Financial Performance
SKT's revenue has bounced up and down in a narrow range for the past five years as it tries to find growth opportunities in South Korea's saturated mobile phone market.

The company's sales rose about 3% in 2017 to 17.5 trillion Korean won (KWN) compared to 17.1 trillion KWN in 2016. The increase came from a rise in broadband internet service revenue from more overall subscribers and more premium IPTV subscribers. Further device revenue rose from sales of higher-priced handset models released in 2017.

SKT's profit increased to 2.6 trillion KWN from 1.6 trillion KWN in 2016.

SKT had about 1.4 KWN trillion in cash and equivalents 2018 compared to 1.5 trillion KWN in 2017. Operating activities produced 3.8 trillion KWN in 2018 and investing activities provided 456 billion KWN while financing activities used 3.5 trillion KWN.

Strategy
SKT's path to growth is through 5G networks the new generation of wireless service that promises to provide faster service with lower response times. Advocates have said 5G will enable a range of capabilities such as vehicle-to-vehicle communications required for self-driving cars. The new network's technology is the leading element of SK's strategy to combined mobile communication media the Internet of Things and an artificial intelligence-based service platform.

South Korea was the first country to switch on 5G technology when SKT and competitors KT and LG Uplus started service for corporate customers in late 2018. SKT's 5G service branded 5GX was available in 13 areas in South Korea.

While SKT remains the biggest wireless provider in South Korea its market share has declined in recent years. It dropped to about 42% from about 44% in 2018. KT remained in second place with about 25% while fast-growing LG Uplus reached about 20%.

Company Background
SKT was founded in 1984 and offered carphone service and pager service in its first year. In subsequent years the company added pay-TV and wireless phone service. SKT has been the dominant telecommunications company in South Korea throughout its history.

EXECUTIVES

President and CEO, Park Jung-ho
Chairman, Chung Jay-Young
Auditors: KPMG Samjong Accounting Corp.

LOCATIONS

HQ: SK Telecom Co Ltd (South Korea)
65, Eulji-ro, Jung-gu, Seoul 04539
Phone: (82) 2 6100 2114   **Fax:** (82) 2 6100 7830
Web: www.sktelecom.com

PRODUCTS/OPERATIONS

2017 Sales

	% of total
Cellular services	76
Fixed-line telecommunication services	16
E-commerce Services	6
Other Businesses	2
Total	**100**

COMPETITORS

KT Corp.	NTT DoCoMo
LG Group	

HISTORICAL FINANCIALS

Company Type: Public

Income Statement   FYE: December 31

	REVENUE ($ mil.)	NET INCOME ($ mil.)	NET PROFIT MARGIN	EMPLOYEES
12/19	15,457	770	5.0%	40,543
12/18	15,199	2,805	18.5%	39,909
12/17	16,433	2,438	14.8%	4,498
12/16	14,227	1,395	9.8%	4,399
12/15	14,565	1,290	8.9%	4,046
Annual Growth	**1.5%**	**(12.1%)**	**—**	**77.9%**

2019 Year-End Financials

Debt ratio: 0.0%
Return on equity: 3.9%
Cash ($ mil.): 1,100
Current ratio: 1.04
Long-term debt ($ mil.): 7,990

No. of shares (mil.): 71
Dividends
  Yield: 4.1%
  Payout: 9.2%
Market value ($ mil.): 1,661

STOCK PRICE ($)	P/E		PER SHARE ($)		
FY Close	High/Low	Earnings	Dividends	Book Value
12/19	23.11	0	0	10.52	0.96 276.65
12/18	26.80	0	0	39.53	1.04 280.44
12/17	27.91	0	0	34.31	1.04 237.02
12/16	20.90	0	0	19.56	0.91 188.28
12/15	20.15	0	0	17.84	0.94 183.58
Annual Growth	3.5%	—	—(12.4%)	0.5% 10.8%

Skandinaviska Enskilda Banken

Snow banks are a common winter sight in Sweden; SEB banks are easy to spot year-round. Skandinaviska Enskilda Banken (SEB) provides merchant banking retail banking wealth management and life insurance in some 20 nations mostly in Northern Europe. Its merchant banking division provides lending debt capital markets trading finance and custody services to corporate clients and financial institutions. Its retail division provides business services including loans and card services. SEB Wealth Management offers asset management and private banking services to institutional and wealthy clients. Founded in 1856 the bank boasts nearly SK$3 trillion (around $350 billion) in assets.

Operations

The bank operates five main business segments: Merchant Banking which generated 38% of total revenue in 2014; Retail Banking (27% of revenue); Wealth Management (10% of revenue) which boasts around SK$1.8 billion ($208 million) in assets under management; Life (10% of revenue) which provides life insurance products; and Baltic (8% of revenue) which counts the bank's operations in the Baltic region.

More broadly SEB generated 48% of its total revenue from interest income in 2014 while 22% came from fee and commission income and 8% came from life insurance premium income. The remainder of the bank's revenue came from gains on the bank's investment securities.

Geographic Reach

SEB generated 60% of its operating income in Sweden in 2014. Its other top markets are in the Nordic countries of Denmark Finland Germany and Norway as well as in Baltic countries such as Estonia Latvia and Lithuania.

Sales and Marketing

Retail Banking served 1.7 million private customers and 200000 small and medium-sized businesses in 2014. Its Wealth Management division serves institutions life insurance companies and private individuals.

SEB's corporate customers come from a broad range of industries and sectors including manufacturing and service companies as well as investment and property companies.

Financial Performance

Note: Growth rates may differ after conversion to US dollars.

SEB's revenues and profits have been rising over the past several years mostly thanks to higher net interest income from its growing loan business and cheap borrowing rates as well as increasing fee and commission income from its growing corporate financing business. (Note: In terms of US Dollars the bank's revenue has struggled to grow due to unfavorable foreign exchange rates.)

The bank's revenue jumped by 15% to SK$98 billion ($12.4 billion) in 2014 thanks to a combination of higher fee and commission income from higher volumes of Merchant Banking transactions (such as mergers and acquisitions initial public offerings and new issues) and gains on the bank's investment securities and assets and liabilities held for trading. The bank's insurance business also grew thanks to higher fund values and higher premium volumes.

Higher revenue and strong staff cost controls in 2014 also pushed the bank's net income up by 30% to SK$19 billion ($2.46 billion). SEB's cash levels declined sharply with operations using SK$148 billion ($19 billion) during the year mostly due to a decrease in borrowing from credit institutions and a decline in short-term security issue funding compared to the prior year.

Strategy

SEB in 2015 continued to focus on growing its Merchant Banking and Retail divisions. Thanks to its heavy promotional investments in 2014 the bank landed 60 new large corporate and institutional customers 12700 new small and mid-sized enterprise (SME) customers and 27000 private customers.

In addition to growing on its own SEB also looks to acquire financial firms that complement its offerings and expand its geographic reach. In 2014 SEB acquisitions boosted its card business in two of its top Noridic markets: Finland and Norway.

With events in Russia and Ukraine causing political turmoil financial capitalization has also been an important priority for the bank. Fortunately for SEB the European Central Bank's 2014 stress test confirmed the bank's capital strength and asset quality passed muster.

Mergers and Acquisitions

In 2014 SEB bolstered its card businesses in Finland and Norway after acquiring Nets' Business Eurocard operations and DNB's corporate card portfolio respectively.

HISTORY

Skandinaviska Enskilda Banken (SEB) was incorporated in 1972 as a result of the merger between Stockholm's Enskilda Bank (founded in 1856 by the Wallenberg family) and Skandinaviska Banken (founded in 1864 and a pioneer in commercial lending in Scandinavia). By 1974 SEB had begun expanding its operations forming an investment management subsidiary. It then became one of the first Swedish banks to go international when it took a stake in the German Deutsch-Skandinavische Bank in 1976. By the end of the 1970s SEB had reached halfway around the world establishing a subsidiary in Singapore to handle Southeast Asian operations.

By the early 1980s SEB was leading the nation in industrial as well as private accounts largely due to deregulation and the introduction of new financial instruments including Swedish treasury bills a commercial paper market and market-rate state bonds. The bank continued to expand opening branches in the Cayman Islands Hamburg London and New York; it also began cross-border banking in Scandinavia through a regional alliance with Bergen Bank of Norway Privatbanken of Denmark and Union Bank of Finland.

In another step toward deregulation the Swedish government lifted the ban on foreign banking in 1985. Within a year a dozen international banks had established themselves in Sweden but SEB continued to expand; its investment banking subsidiary Enskilda Securities opened branches in Hong Kong London New York Paris and Singapore in the latter half of the 1980s.

In 1990 the bank acquired an option to buy about a third of Skandia Sweden's largest private insurance company. But facing strong resistance from Skandia's management SEB accepted defeat and sold most of its option to two Scandinavian insurance companies. Winds of change blew through Sweden in the early 1990s as the country suffered a severe economic recession. Deregulation in the mid-1980s followed by excessive lending to the property market led to inflated real estate prices and then a collapse of the market. Banks investing in property experienced huge losses; many banks (including SEB) had to turn to the government for help to strengthen their capital bases. The mid-1990s saw the bank still trying to recover selling several of its subsidiaries including a vehicle finance unit to GE Capital.

1997 saw SEB acquire Trygg-Hansa (now SEB Trygg Liv) one of Sweden's major insurers. The bank remained acquisitive in 1998 expanding aggressively into the Baltic by buying major stakes in banks in Estonia (Eesti hlspank) Latvia (Latvija Unibanken) and Lithuania (Vilnius Bankas).

In 1999 the bank further emphasized its Internet business making it a separate unit. Also that year SEB sold Trygg-Hansa's non-life business to Denmark's Codan Insurance in exchange for Codan's banking subsidiary and other assets. In 2000 the bank acquired Germany's almost 200-branch BfG Bank from Crédit Lyonnais; it then used BfG to create a cross-selling and Internet alliance with German insurer Gerling. Also in 2000 SEB upped its stake in Eesti hispank Vilniaus Bankas and Latvijas Unibanka.

The following year SEB announced plans to acquire fellow Swedish bank F ¶reningsSparbanken to create SEB SwedBank. EU regulators investigated the proposal and demanded significant concession. As a result the two banks dropped plans for the merger later in 2001.

SEB continued to boost its offerings and services — largely through acquisitions — during the early years of the 21st century. Purchases included Europay in Norway (2002) Danish life insurer Codan Pension (2004) Ukraine's Bank Agio (2005) and Russia's PetroEnergoBank (2006). In 2007 it acquired nearly all of Factorial Bank adding 65 branches in Eastern Ukraine. The following year it bought London-based hedge fund Key Asset Management.

EXECUTIVES

EVP and CFO, Jan Erik Back
President and CEO, Annika Falkengren
Deputy President and CEO, Magnus Carlsson
Country Manager SEB Germany, Fredrik Boheman
EVP and Head of Retail Banking, Mats Torstendahl
Country Manager SEB Denmark, Peter H Itermand
Head of Baltic Division, David Teare
Country Manager SEB Norway, William Paus
Country Manager and President SEB Latvia, Ieva Tetere
Country Manager and President SEB Estonia, Allan Parik
Co-Head Merchant Banking Division, Joachim Alpen
Head of Life Division, Peter Dahlgren
Head of Wealth Management, Christoffer Malmer
Co-Head of Merchant Banking Division, Johan Torgeby
Deputy Chairman, Urban Jansson
Vice Chairman, Jesper Ovesen
Chairman, Marcus Wallenberg
Auditors: Ernst & Young AB

LOCATIONS

HQ: Skandinaviska Enskilda Banken
Kungstradgardsgatan 8, Stockholm SE-106 40
Phone: (46) 771 62 10 00
Web: www.sebgroup.com

2014 Operating Income

	% of total
Scandinavia	
Sweden	60
Norway	8
Denmark	7
Finland	4
Baltics	
Lithuania	3
Estonia	3
Latvia	2
Germany	7
Other	6
Total	**100**

PRODUCTS/OPERATIONS

2014 Sales by Segment

	% of total
Merchant Banking	38
Retail Banking	27
Life	10
Wealth Management	10
Baltic	8
Other	7
Total	**100**

COMPETITORS

Citigroup Global Markets	Morgan Stanley
Danske Bank	Nordea Bank
Deutsche Bank	Skandia
DnB NOR	Storebrand ASA
Goldman Sachs	Svenska Handelsbanken
KBC	Swedbank AB
	UBS Investment Bank

HISTORICAL FINANCIALS

Company Type: Public

Income Statement   FYE: December 31

	ASSETS ($ mil.)	NET INCOME ($ mil.)	INCOME AS % OF ASSETS	EMPLOYEES
12/19	307,085	2,169	0.7%	15,819
12/18	286,832	2,584	0.9%	15,562
12/17	311,976	1,979	0.6%	15,804
12/16	289,111	1,171	0.4%	16,087
12/15	296,065	1,966	0.7%	16,599
Annual Growth	0.9%	2.5%	—	(1.2%)

2019 Year-End Financials

Return on assets: 0.7%   Dividends
Return on equity: 13.2%   Yield: 0.0%
Long-term debt ($ mil.): —   Payout: 69.3%
No. of shares (mil.): —   Market value ($ mil.): —
Sales ($ mil): 7,994

	STOCK PRICE ($) FY Close	P/E High/Low		PER SHARE ($) Earnings	Dividends	Book Value
12/19	9.49	1	1	1.00	0.69	7.74
12/18	9.70	1	1	1.19	0.63	7.68
12/17	11.75	2	2	0.91	0.65	8.10
12/16	10.46	2	2	0.54	0.58	7.17
12/15	10.80	2	1	0.89	0.55	7.72
Annual Growth	(3.2%)	—	—	2.8%	5.9%	0.1%

Skanska AB

Auditors: Ernst & Young AB

LOCATIONS

HQ: Skanska AB
Warfvinges vag 25, Stockholm SE-112 74
Phone: (46) 10 448 00 00   **Fax:** (46) 8 755 12 56
Web: www.group.skanska.com

HISTORICAL FINANCIALS

Company Type: Public

Income Statement   FYE: December 31

	REVENUE ($ mil.)	NET INCOME ($ mil.)	NET PROFIT MARGIN	EMPLOYEES
12/19	18,580	648	3.5%	34,756
12/18	19,184	510	2.7%	38,650
12/17	19,242	499	2.6%	40,759
12/16	16,036	631	3.9%	42,903
12/15	18,154	566	3.1%	48,470
Annual Growth	0.6%	3.4%		(8.0%)

2019 Year-End Financials

Debt ratio: 0.1%   No. of shares (mil.): 411
Return on equity: 19.4%   Dividends
Cash ($ mil.): 940   Yield: —
Current ratio: 1.35   Payout: 42.7%
Long-term debt ($ mil.): 200   Market value ($ mil.): —

Societe Generale

Auditors: ERNST & YOUNG et Autres

LOCATIONS

HQ: Societe Generale
29, Bd Haussman, Paris 75009
Phone: (33) 1 42 14 20 00
Web: www.societegenerale.com

HISTORICAL FINANCIALS

Company Type: Public

Income Statement   FYE: December 31

	ASSETS ($ mil.)	NET INCOME ($ mil.)	INCOME AS % OF ASSETS	EMPLOYEES
12/19	1,522,810	3,646	0.2%	138,240
12/18	1,499,550	4,425	0.3%	149,022
12/17	1,528,565	3,363	0.2%	147,125
12/16	1,459,485	4,090	0.3%	145,672
12/15	1,453,433	4,357	0.3%	145,703
Annual Growth	1.2%	(4.4%)	—	(1.3%)

2019 Year-End Financials

Return on assets: 0.2%   Dividends
Return on equity: 5.2%   Yield: 7.0%
Long-term debt ($ mil.): —   Payout: 14.5%
No. of shares (mil.): 845   Market value ($ mil.): 5,904
Sales ($ mil): 56,517

	STOCK PRICE ($) FY Close	P/E High/Low		PER SHARE ($) Earnings	Dividends	Book Value
12/19	6.99	2	2	3.42	0.49	84.40
12/18	6.29	3	1	4.86	0.51	88.59
12/17	10.36	4	3	3.50	0.53	89.45
12/16	9.82	2	1	4.50	0.42	81.82
12/15	9.22	2	2	4.89	0.26	80.71
Annual Growth	(6.7%)	—	—	(8.5%)	17.2%	1.1%

Sodexo

This foodservice provider has its fingers in many pies besides. Sodexo is a contract foodservice provider (after Compass Group) but also offers an array of services for corporations and institutions in fields as diverse as Soft Facilities Management Services Hard Facilities Management Services Benefits & Rewards Services and Personal & Home Services. Founded in 1966 by Pierre Bellon Sodexo is the global leader in Quality of Life services. Sodexo's services contribute to the performance of their clients the satisfaction of the company's consumers the fulfillment of their teams and the economic social and environmental development of their local communities.

Operations

Sodex operates through two business segments: On-Site Services which accounts for 95% of group sales and provides foodservice and facilities management; and Benefits and Rewards Services and Personal & Home Services.

On-Site Services is further sub-divided into three units Business & Administrations Health Care & Seniors and Education. Services are diverse and include catering cleaning and waste services workplace design reception services and medical equipment sterilization among plenty more.

The Benefits & Rewards segment provides rewards and benefits for companies' employees and travel and expense management. It generates around 5% of sales.

The Personal & Home Services segment provides childcare concierge and home care services.

Geographic Reach

Sodexo generates around 45% of its revenue in the US nearly 40% in Europe and more than 15% in Africa Asia Latin America and the Middle East.

Sodexo Group headquartered in 255 Quai de la Bataille de Stalingrad - 92130 Issy les Moulineaux France.

Sales and Marketing

Sodexo's customers are diverse but include government departments (such as military and health) onshore and offshore oil and gas companies sporting event organizers and companies with significant facilities and catering needs. Sodexo has around 100 million customers in total.

Financial PerformanceNote: Growth rates may differ after conversion to US Dollars.

From 2015 to 2017 the company's revenue and profit were steadily increasing but slightly fell in 2018 and recovered of 5% in 2019.

Sodexo's revenue has increase of nearly 10% to ?22.0 billion in 2019 compared to ?20.4 billion in 2018. The increase was due to the growth of all segments.

Net income in fiscal year 2019 increased nearly 25% to ?597 million from ?481 million of prior year.

Sodexo's cash balance up ?108 million during 2019 ending the year at ?1.7 billion. The company's operations produced ?1.3 billion while investing activities used ?809 million and financing activities used ?408 million. Sodexo's main cash uses during 2019 were capital expenditures acquistions borrowing repayments and dividend.

Strategy

During the year the Group also acquired minority stakes in the digital/tech companies Meican in China and Zeta in India which were already providing On-site and Benefits & Rewards operations with technology platforms in their home countries. The strategy is to deploy these platforms in other countries around the world.

The Focus on Growth strategic agenda has delivered growth of more than 3% this year. There are many action plans around the group with initiatives to enhance quality of new and renewed contracts operational efficiency and growth.

The Group's strategic agenda Focus on Growth has oriented the actions to generate productivity by enhancing operational efficiency to free up the means to continue to invest in growth by being more client and consumer centric. In line with the strategic agenda productivity gains are being achieved. On-site clear signs of better control of food costs and labor management are coming through although some of this has been offset by continued wage inflation particularly in North America. Off-site the results of the Fit for the Future program to streamline standardize and mutualize SG&A costs are also helping to reduce costs.

Mergers and Acquisitions

Acquisitions net of disposals amounted to 301 million euro for the year including: In On-site food services Novae and Alliance in Partnership strengthening the Group's presence in high end Corporate Services in Switzerland and public-sector Education in the United Kingdom; In Homecare several companies strengthening the Group's positions in North America France and the United Kingdom and entering the Brazilian market and Asia; In Childcare with the acquisition of Crèche de France doubling our presence in the French market and entering the German market with Elly & Stoffl; and During the year the Group also acquired minority stakes in the digital/tech companies Meican in China and Zeta in India which were already providing On-site and Benefits & Rewards operations with technology platforms in their home countries. The strategy is to deploy these platforms in other countries around the world.

EXECUTIVES

CEO Corporate Services Worldwide, Sylvia Metayer
CEO Energy and Resources Worldwide, Nicholas Japy, age 64
CEO Schools and Universities Worldwide, Patrick E. (Pat) Connolly
Group Chief Strategy Organization Research and Development and Innovation Officer, Damien Verdier, age 63
Group Comex EVP CEO Sports and Leisure Worldwide and Chairman of Benefits and Reward Services, Pierre Henry, age 69
CEO Justice Defense and Government Agencies Worldwide, Tony Leech
CEO Geographic Régions and Region Chair for North America, Lorna C. Donatone
CEO, Denis Machuel
CEO Service Operations Worldwide, Satya-Christophe Menard
Group CFO, Marc Rolland
CEO Seniors Worldwide, Marc Plumart
CEO Sodexo Benefits and Rewards Romania, Sven Marinus
Chair Asia Pacific Region, Johnpaul Dimech
CEO Mining Worldwide, Paul Bean
Vice Chairman, Sophie Bellon
Auditors: PricewaterhouseCoopers Audit

LOCATIONS

HQ: Sodexo
255, quai de la Bataille de Stalingrad, Issy-les-Moulineaux, Cedex 9 92866
Phone: (33) 1 30 85 75 00
Web: www.sodexo.com

2018 Sales

	% of total
North America	45
Europe	39
Africa Asia Australia LatAm Middle East	16
Total	**100**

PRODUCTS/OPERATIONS

2018 Sales

	% of total
On-site Services	
Business & Administrations	54
Health Care and Seniors	23
Educations	10
Benefits & Services	4
Total	**100**

2018 sales

By type of service	% of total
On-site Services revenues	
Foodservices	65
Facilities management services	31
Benefits and Rewards Services	4
Total	**100**

COMPETITORS

ARAMARK	Elior
Accor	Healthcare Services
Autogrill	ISS A/S
Berendsen	SSP
Cintas	SSP America
Compass Group	UniFirst
Delaware North	

HISTORICAL FINANCIALS

Company Type: Public

Income Statement   FYE: August 31

	REVENUE ($ mil.)	NET INCOME ($ mil.)	NET PROFIT MARGIN	EMPLOYEES
08/19	24,235	734	3.0%	470,237
08/18	23,771	758	3.2%	460,663
08/17	24,504	855	3.5%	427,268
08/16	22,542	709	3.1%	425,594
08/15	22,211	784	3.5%	422,844
Annual Growth	**2.2%**	**(1.7%)**	**—**	**2.7%**

2019 Year-End Financials

Debt ratio: 26.0%
Return on equity: 17.1%
Cash ($ mil.): 1,966
Current ratio: 0.97
Long-term debt ($ mil.): 4,307

No. of shares (mil.): 146
Dividends
  Yield: 0.0%
  Payout: 12.2%
Market value ($ mil.): 3,301

	STOCK PRICE ($) FY Close	P/E High/Low		PER SHARE ($) Earnings	Dividends	Book Value
08/19	22.61	5	4	4.97	0.61	33.69
08/18	20.71	6	4	5.06	0.68	26.27
08/17	23.35	6	5	5.67	0.51	28.17
08/16	23.16	6	4	4.62	0.49	27.11
08/15	17.59	23	4	5.09	0.41	27.31
Annual Growth	**6.5%**	**—**	**—**	**(0.6%)**	**10.6%**	**5.4%**

SoftBank Corp (New)

Auditors: Deloitte Touche Tohmatsu LLC

LOCATIONS

HQ: SoftBank Corp (New)
1-9-1 Higashi-shimbashi, Minato-ku, Tokyo 105-7317
Phone: (81) 3 2889 2000
Web: www.softbank.jp

HISTORICAL FINANCIALS

Company Type: Public

Income Statement   FYE: March 31

	REVENUE ($ mil.)	NET INCOME ($ mil.)	NET PROFIT MARGIN	EMPLOYEES
03/20	44,783	4,358	9.7%	50,950
03/19	33,828	3,889	11.5%	29,609
03/18	33,738	3,774	11.2%	25,889
Annual Growth	**15.2%**	**7.5%**	**—**	**40.3%**

2020 Year-End Financials

Debt ratio: 0.4%
Return on equity: 41.9%
Cash ($ mil.): 10,537
Current ratio: 0.75
Long-term debt ($ mil.): 30,133

No. of shares (mil.): —
Dividends
  Yield: 3.0%
  Payout: 43.6%
Market value ($ mil.): —

	STOCK PRICE ($) FY Close	P/E High/Low		PER SHARE ($) Earnings	Dividends	Book Value
03/20	12.90	0	0	0.90	0.39	1.94
03/19	11.50	0	0	0.81	0.34	2.35
03/18	0.00	—	—	0.92	1.71	(0.00)
/0.00	—	—	(0.00)	0.00	(0.00)	
Annual Growth						

Sojitz Corp

Sojitz Corporation is one of Japan's largest trading houses. With five domestic branches and about 85 overseas the company's approximately 400 subsidiaries trades in commodities from the chemicals metals retail transportation energy and foods & agriculture industries. Its North American unit Sojitz Corporation of America is one of Sojitz's leading overseas businesses though operations are spread across Europe Africa and the Middle East and Oceania. About half of the company's total sales comes from Japan. It was created by the coming together of its predecessor trading houses Nichimen Corporation and Nissho Iwai.

Operations

Sojitz reports ten business divisions.

Its leading segment is Chemicals (30% sales) which trades liquid chemicals petrochemical and mineral-related products.

Metals & Coal (20%) includes coal steel and base metals trading and investment in rare metals such as niobium and steel-related businesses such as alumina refining.

Retail & Lifestyle trading (about 15%) is focused on clothing and shelter plus lumber and textile businesses.

Automotive (about 10%) includes vehicle export dealership and component businesses.

Foods & Agriculture (another 10%) sells fertilizer grain and feed fish farming and other agricultural products.

Some 5% revenue comes from each of Sojitz's Infrastructure & Environment Business (machinery and solar plants) and Aerospace & IT segments (aircraft and marine equipment sales rep).

Industrial Infrastructure & Urban Development (less than 5%) includes the J-REIT business and the overseas industrial park business real-estate business and overseas urban infrastructure development business.

Energy (about 5%) has interests in the US the UK North Sea the Middle East and Africa; It also the LNG business in Indonesia and the nuclear power business.

Other (less than 5%) business includes domestic branches logistics and insurance services.

Geographic Reach

The company has operations in Japan (roughly half of total revenue) Africa China Europe the Middle East Asia and Oceania and the Americas.

Financial Performance

Note: Growth rates may differ after conversion to US Dollars.

Sojitz's sale hiked almost 17% YOY to JPY 1.8 trillion in 2018 (ended March 31) though growth has been anemic in the last five years. Most of this year's growth came from the extra revenue added by the new acquisition of a European chemical distributor. Higher plastic resin sale volumes and higher prices of coal also added to the revenue increase.

Profit increased by JPY 16 billion to JPY 56.8 billion thanks to higher automobile sales volumes overseas (largely in emerging economies) higher overseas coal prices as well as bigger margins in the infrastructure-related businesses. Unlike revenue the company's profit has seen an upward trajectory since 2013 growing four-fold in the last five years.

Operating activities provided net cash flow of JPY 98 billion offset by investing activities using net cash of JPY 86 billion and financing activities using net cash of JPY 13 billion. Sojitz ended the year with cash and cash equivalents of JPY 305 billion.

Strategy

After encountering some serious economic headwinds in recent years that forced the company to shed assets and restructure its operations Sojitz is planning to invest in non-resource assets compared to a market-volatile portfolio it held earlier. Another part of its strategy is to create new business divisions (nine were created in 2015 to maximize profitability) that can yield JPY 10 billion or more in profits every year.

In 2017 Sojitz raised JPY 315 billion to invest in non-resource assets. A solid 2017-18 business performance should help towards that aim. In 2016 only Sojitz's chemicals division proved profitable. At the end of March 2018 the company added four more segments to the profitable list: automotive infrastructure metals and retail. The company hopes to cross JPY 75 billion in profits by 2020. Beyond its prime business divisions Sojitz is putting emphasis on development in Asia like chemicals foods and agriculture and retail businesses.

Sojitz may also invest in high potential markets in Asia. In 2018 the company announced plans to buy 15 million shares of Vietnamese agricultural firm that provide landscaping services PAN Group JSC for VND 817 billion.

Mergers and Acquisitions

In 2018 Sojitz acquired Saigon Paper one of Vietnam's largest paper manufacturers. This acquisition marks Sojitz's entrance into Vietnam's household paper and container board manufacturing business. Sojitz spent $91 million acquiring 95% stake of Saigon.

Company Background

In April 2003 Nichimen Corporation and Nissho Iwai Corporation established a joint holding company integrating their businesses the following year to become the Sojitz Group. Both companies trace their history back to three trading company titans (Japan Cotton Trading Co. Ltd. Iwai & Co. Ltd. and Suzuki & Co. Ltd.) who played an instrumental role in the development of modern Japan.

HISTORY

The Nissho and Iwai companies got their acts together as Nissho Iwai in 1968 but each company dates back to the middle of the 19th century. In 1863 Bunsuke Iwai opened a shop in Osaka to sell imported goods such as glass oil products silk and wine. The Meiji government which came to power in 1868 encouraged modernization and industrialization a climate in which Iwai's business flourished. In 1877 Iwajiro Suzuki established a similar trading concern Suzuki & Co. that eventually became Nissho.

After cotton spinning machines were introduced in Japan in the 1890s both Iwai and Suzuki imported cotton. Iwai began to trade directly with British trader William Duff & Son (an innovation in Japan where the middleman or shokan played the paramount role in international trade). Iwai became the primary agent for Yawata Steel Works in 1901 and was incorporated in 1912. Meanwhile Suzuki solely engaged in the import trade emerged as one of the top sugar brokers in the world and established an office in London.

To protect itself from foreign competition Iwai established a number of companies to produce goods in Japan including Nippon Steel Plate (1914) and Tokuyama Soda (1918). Stagnation after WWI forced Suzuki to restructure. In 1928 the company sold many of its assets to trading giant Mitsui and reorganized the rest under a new name Nissho Co.

Both Iwai and Nissho subsequently grew as they helped fuel Japan's military expansion in Asia in the 1930s. But Japan's defeat in WWII devastated the companies. When the occupation forces broke up Mitsui and other larger trading conglomerates both companies took advantage of the situation to move into new business areas. In 1949 Nissho established Nissho Chemical Industry Nissho Fuel and Nijko Shoji (a trading concern). It also opened its US operations Nissho American Corp. in 1952.

Poor management by the Iwai family led the company into financial trouble in the 1960s and prompted the Japanese government to instruct the profitable Nissho to merge with Iwai in 1968.

In 1979 Nissho Iwai was accused of funneling kickbacks from US aircraft makers to Japanese politicians. The scandal led to arrests the resignation of the company's chairman and the suicide of another executive. Nissho Iwai exited the aircraft marketing business in 1980.

Despite Japan's recession in the 1990s Nissho Iwai managed to make some significant investments. In 1991 the company teamed up with the Russian government to develop a Siberian oil refinery. A year later Nissho acquired a stake in courier DHL International and in 1995 it set up a unit to process steel plates in Vietnam.

However in the late 1990s rough economic conditions caught up with the firm. It dissolved its NI Finance unit (domestic financing) in 1998 after its disastrous performance. The large trading firm or sogo shosha also began a major restructuring effort to get back on track.

In 1999 Nissho Iwai sold its headquarters its 5% stake in DHL International and its stake in a Japanese ISP Nifty. CEO Masatake Kusamichi resigned. He was replaced by Shiro Yasutake who took charge of the firm's restructuring. In 2000 the company's ITX Corp. acquired five IT-related affiliates of Nichimen Corp.

As part of the group's streamlining efforts in 2001 Nissho Iwai spun off its nonferrous marketing unit (Alconix) and agreed to merge the group's LNG operations with Sumitomo's LNG business. The next year Hidetoshi Nishimura replaced Yasutake as CEO.

In 2003 Nissho Iwai merged with the smaller Nichimen Corp. to form Nissho Iwai-Nichimen

Holdings. Hidetoshi Nishimura president and CEO of Nissho Iwai and Toru Hambayashi president of Nichimen became co-CEOs of the new holding company. Former board member Akio Dobashi took over the reins as president and sole CEO early in 2004; in April he moved over to the chairman's seat and Yutaka Kase assumed the president and CEO titles. In June the company changed its name from Nissho Iwai-Nichimen Holdings to Sojitz Holdings Corporation.

As part of its ongoing reorganization in 2005 the company renamed itself again when it merged the holding company into Sojitz Corporation.

The company formed a subsidiary in China in 2009 to enter key businesses such as the automotive ball bearing textiles and plastics industries. That year it transferred its domestic foodstuffs business to a wholly owned subsidiary called Sojitz Foods Corporation.

Sojitz also began searching in 2010 for sources other than China for rare earth metals. It signed a contract in mid-year with Lynas Corporation in Australia to purchase about 8500 tons a year some 30% of Japan's annual demand. It also entered a joint venture with Toyota Tusho to import another 3000 tons from Vietnam. Shipments from China which mines and sells most of the world's rare earth metals were delayed in 2010 in a move Japan said was a de facto blockade. Rare earth metals such as palladium are a key element in the production of electronic components and lithium-ion batteries.

EXECUTIVES

Senior Managing Executive Officer; President Sojitz Research Institute, Hiroshi Matsumura
EVP, Shinichi Taniguchi
President and CEO, Yoji Sato
EVP, Yoshio Mogi
EVP, Satoshi Mizui
Managing Executive Officer; President and CEO China, Masao Goto
Senior Managing Executive Officer, Masato Takei
Managing Executive Officer; President and CEO Middle East and Africa, Masashi Shinohara
Managing Executive Officer; President and CEO Asia and Oceania, Hideaki Kato
Senior Managing Executive Officer, Toshiharu Yoshimura
Senior Managing Executive Officer, Shigeru Nishihara
Senior Managing Executive Officer, Masayoshi Fujimoto
Managing Executive Officer, Seiichi Tanaka
Executive Officer, Satoru Takahama
Executive Officer; President Sojitz Logistics, Masaatsu Hirakawa
Executive Officer; President and CEO The Americas, Koji Izutani
Executive Officer; President and CEO Europe, Shigeya Kusano
Chairman, Yutaka Kase
Vice Chairman, Shigeki Dantani
Vice Chairman, Takashi Hara
Auditors: KPMG AZSA LLC

LOCATIONS

HQ: Sojitz Corp
2-1-1 Uchisaiwai-cho, Chiyoda-ku, Tokyo 100-8691
Phone: (81) 3 6871 5000   Fax: (81) 3 6871 2430
Web: www.sojitz.com

2018 Sales

	% of total
Japan	47
Asia and Oceania	35
The Americas	8
Europe	8
Others	2
Total	100

PRODUCTS/OPERATIONS

2018 Sales

	% of total
Chemicals	28
Metals & Coal	18
Foods & Agriculture Business	8
Retail & Lifestyle	16
Automotive	11
Industrial Infrastructure & Urban Development	3
Aerospace & IT Business	4
Infrastructure & Environment Business	7
Energy	3
Others	2
Total	**100**

COMPETITORS

Chori	Mitsui
ITOCHU	Sekisui House
International Paper	Sumitomo
Kanematsu	Sumitomo Forestry
Marubeni	Svenska Cellulosa
Mitsubishi Corp.	Toyota Tsusho

HISTORICAL FINANCIALS

Company Type: Public

Income Statement				FYE: March 31
	REVENUE ($ mil.)	NET INCOME ($ mil.)	NET PROFIT MARGIN	EMPLOYEES
03/20	16,166	560	3.5%	22,330
03/19	16,761	635	3.8%	21,909
03/18	17,106	535	3.1%	22,778
03/17	13,911	364	2.6%	17,311
03/16	14,765	325	2.2%	17,524
Annual Growth	2.3%	14.6%		6.2%

2020 Year-End Financials

Debt ratio: 0.3%	No. of shares (mil.): 1,220
Return on equity: 10.1%	Dividends
Cash ($ mil.): 2,511	Yield: —
Current ratio: 1.61	Payout: 34.7%
Long-term debt ($ mil.): 6,508	Market value ($ mil.): —

Solvay SA

Solvay produces and sells chemicals advanced plastics and lightweight materials. End markets for its products are diverse and include automotive aerospace consumer goods electronics energy and the environment. Solvay operates some 145 plants in 53 countries and has major operations in Europe North America and the Asia-Pacific region as well as a smaller operation in Latin America. The Solvay process a method of producing sodium carbonate or soda ash is named after company founder Ernest Solvay who invented it in the 1860s. The compound remains a core product and still brings in ?1.5 billion a year.

Operations

The company operates four main segments: Advanced Materials Advanced Formulations Performance Chemicals and Functional Polymers. Materials and Chemicals bring in around 30% of revenue each with Formulations at 25% and Polymers 15%.

Metal-replacement high-performance polymers is the Advanced Materials segment's biggest product in which it ranks first globally. Customers include Boeing and Solvay's products were used in the experimental solar-powered Solar Impulse aircraft which made headlines in 2016 after it cir-

cumnavigated the world on solar power alone. Performance Chemicals is the world's largest producer of soda ash (sodium carbonate) and hydrogen peroxide and also deals in cellulose acetate tow which is used in cigarette filters. Formulations' outputs include surfactants phenol and vanillin for agriculture consumer goods and food market segments. Functional Polymers makes polyamides.

US lightweight materials company Cytec acquired in 2015 as part of a major strategic shift towards lightweight materials has been divided into two global business units Composite Materials part of the Advanced Materials segment and Technology Solutions part of Advanced Formulations.

Geographic Reach

The company operates 145 industrial sites across the world with the greatest concentration in Europe. The Asia-Pacific region is the largest by revenue (and also the fastest growing) at 35% of total followed by the Europe at 32% and North America at 23%.

Financial Performance

Note: Growth rates may differ after conversion to US Dollars.

Sales grew in 2015 by 4% to ?10.6 billion mostly due to favorable exchange rate effects. Weakness in the Advanced Formulations segment was due to the significant downturn in the US unconventional oil and gas markets with the Novecare business hurting in particular. Advanced Materials grew strongly however and ended the year as Solvay's biggest segment by revenue overtaking both Formulations and Chemicals. Its specialty polymers business was aided by strong demand from the smart device industry. Overall Performance Chemicals was up but strength in Soda Ash was counterbalanced to an extent by weakness in the cigarette market on which acetate tow sales (down 16%) depend.

Net income of ?454 million was ?441 million higher than 2014 due to an increase in sales.

Cash flow from operating activities fell to ?1.4 billion due to lower depreciation amortization and impairments.

Strategy

Solvay is undertaking a strategic shift towards advanced and lightweight materials. The company expects the sector to expand as lightweighting becomes key to increased energy efficiency and feeds into the global push towards energy reduction. Automotive is expected to be a major part of this increase in demand as the technology makes its way from high-tech F1 and luxury cars into the consumer segment. In 2015 Solvay acquired lightweight materials company Cytec. The acquisition made the company the world's second largest player in aerospace composite materials and is hoped to achieve ?100 million in combined synergies a year. In addition the Cytec acquisition is part of a geographic repositioning towards the US in search of growth opportunities and has increased its talent pool in the region. Indeed the company focused the majority of its capital investment for 2015 into its Advanced Formulations and Materials segments.

The strategy is also a shift away from the volatile world of commodities: Solvay is vulnerable to downturns in oil and gas as seen in recent years. To raise cash in 2016 the company agreed to sell its 58.77% stake in Thai-based plastics maker Vinythai to Asahi Glass for 33.5 billion yen ($291 million).

That year it also sold its 70.59% stake in Solvay Indupa to Brazilian chemical group Unipar Carbocloro.

Mergers and Acquisitions

The company acquired Cytec a US lightweight materials company for ?4.9 billion as part of a major shift in strategy towards advanced and lightweight materials.

In 2014 Solvay acquired Chevron's Ryton business for $220 million enhancing its polymers offering and acquired automotive heat exchange manufacturer Flux to expand its aluminium brazing capabilities.

Solvay divested its 50% stake in its Inovyn joint venture with INEOS two years ahead of schedule for ?335 million.

EXECUTIVES

Chairman of the Executive Committee and CEO, Jean-Pierre Clamadieu, age 62

Member Executive Committee and Head of Aroma Performance Coatis Emerging Biochemicals Novecare Technology Solutions, Vincent De Cuyper, age 60

Member Executive Committee and Head of Composite Materials Silica Special Chem Specialty Polymers, Roger Kearns, age 58

CFO, Karim Hajjar

President Composite Materials Global Business Unit, Carmelo Lo Faro

Chairman, Nicolas Bo «I, age 58

Auditors: Deloitte Bedrijfsrevisoren / Reviseurs d'Entreprises CVBA/SCRL

LOCATIONS

HQ: Solvay SA
Rue de Ransbeek, 310, Brussels 1120
Phone: (32) 2 264 2111 **Fax:** (32) 2 264 3061
Web: www.solvay.com

2015 Sales

	% of total
Asia and Rest of the World	35
Europe	30
Other Europe	2
North America	23
Latin America	10
Total	**100**

PRODUCTS/OPERATIONS

2015 Sales

	% of total
Advanced Materials	32
Performance Chemicals	29
Advanced Formulations	25
Functional Polymers	14
Others	-
Total	**100**

COMPETITORS

Akzo Nobel	INEOS ChlorVinyls
Arkema	Occidental Chemical
Celanese	PolyOne
FMC	

HISTORICAL FINANCIALS

Company Type: Public

Income Statement				FYE: December 31
	REVENUE ($ mil.)	NET INCOME ($ mil.)	NET PROFIT MARGIN	EMPLOYEES
12/19	12,605	132	1.1%	24,100
12/18	12,939	982	7.6%	24,500
12/17	13,055	1,271	9.7%	24,500
12/16	12,040	655	5.4%	27,000
12/15	12,032	442	3.7%	30,900
Annual Growth	1.2%	(26.0%)	—	(6.0%)

2019 Year-End Financials

Debt ratio: 21.8%	No. of shares (mil.): 103
Return on equity: 1.1%	Dividends
Cash ($ mil.): 908	Yield: 2.3%
Current ratio: 1.53	Payout: 20.4%
Long-term debt ($ mil.): 3,385	Market value ($ mil.): 1,188

	STOCK PRICE ($)	P/E		PER SHARE ($)		
	FY Close	High/Low	Earnings	Dividends	Book Value
12/19	11.49	11 8	1.29	0.27	103.30
12/18	10.03	2 1	9.47	0.27	116.65
12/17	13.77	2 1	12.22	0.26	111.84
12/16	11.93	2 2	6.32	0.00	99.28
Annual Growth	(1.2%)	—	—(32.8%)	—	1.0%

Sompo Holdings Inc

Sompo Holdings (formerly Sompo Japan Nipponkoa Holdings) owns several companies that are primarily engaged in the insurance sector. Its subsidiaries include property/casualty units Sompo Japan Nipponkoa Saison Automobile & Fire and Sonpo 24 and a handful of overseas insurance companies. Domestic property/casualty insurance brings in about 65% of the group's total earnings. Other operations include asset and risk management services pension plans and some supplemental health insurance products. The company also owns SOMPO Care which provides nursing care services. Vast majority of the company's total sales come from Japan.

Operations

Sompo operates through four segments: Domestic P&C Insurance (which accounts for about 60% of total sales) Overseas Insurance Domestic Life Insurance and Nursing Care & Healthcare.

The Overseas Insurance segment which brings in nearly 15% of sales includes such units as Sompo International Holdings Sompo America Sompo Japan and Sompo Seguros. The Domestic Life Insurance segment brings in some 10% of sales and includes Sompo Japan Nipponkoa Himarai Life Insurance. Nursing Care & Healthcare businesses bring in about 5% of sales include Sompo Care and Sompo Risk Management & Health Care.

Sompo consists of about 95 subsidiaries and around 20 affiliates.

Geographic Reach

Headquartered in Japan Sompo has operations in around 220 cities in approximately 30 countries in Africa the Americas Asia Europe and the Middle East. It earns most of its revenues in the Japanese market.

Sales and Marketing

Sompo markets its products through insurance agencies while Sonpo 24 and Saison Automobile and Fire sells directly to customers.

Financial Performance

Sompo's revenue ranged from Å 3.2 trillion to Å 3.8 trillion for the last five years.

Revenue in 2019 jumped 32% to Å 3.8 trillion compared to Å 3.6 trillion in 2018. Thanks to higher sales in Domestic P&C insurance business partially offset by the three other segments.

Net income showed a 16% decrease to Å 122.5 billion in 2019 from Å 146.6 billion in 2018.

The company's cash and equivalents stood at $967.8 million at the end of 2019 (March) compared to $3.0 billion the year before. Cash from operations contributed $356 million while investing activities used $140.1 billion mainly for acquisitions. Financing activities provided $230.6 million primarily received from dividends paid and repayments of borrowings.

Strategy

Reflecting a sense of crisis in relation to the possibility of becoming unsustainable Sompo is building new business models that leverage digital technologies to provide security health and wellbeing. As part of these efforts the Group has tasked SOMPO Digital Labs with the digitalization of existing businesses and the creation of new businesses and services. Accordingly the labs are referring to and analyzing progressive examples from overseas as they conduct R&D on increasing work efficiency adapting to changes in customer experiences developing marketing approaches for digital natives (how to create points of contact with customers whom it could not reach before) and creating new business models. Specifically the labs are incorporating AI into underwriting and claims services developing IoT-enabled insurance and services unbundling insurance functions to facilitate open innovation with partners and using Palantir's technologies to develop co-creation businesses with other companies.

From the establishment of the Digital Strategy Planning Department in fiscal 2016 through the end of fiscal 2019 it conducted 253 proof-of-concept (PoC) tests. These PoC tests have resulted in the commercialization of 37 projects including those slated for commercialization.

The group will further strengthen its AI big data CX agile development and design approaches; prepare and forge ahead with digital strategies; and create and advance new businesses enabled by digital technologies. As well as contributing to profits and continuing to drive the group's digital transformation the aforementioned measures will embed digital technologies into society thereby helping address some of the issues that companies and society face.

Company Background

Sompo Holdings was created to hold two insurance companies: Sompo Japan and Nipponkoa Insurance. While already strong players in Japan's property/casualty and life insurance markets when merger mania hit the industry they didn't want to be left out and formed the joint holding company in 2010. The two companies merged into one entity Sompo Japan Nipponkoa Insurance in 2014.

Why merge in the first place? Sompo cited pressures on its industry from several sources including the country's declining birthrate its rapidly aging population and the effects of climate change. While those are real challenges to the industry the Sompo/Nipponkoa merger also took place at the same time as several other large mergers among Japanese insurance companies.

EXECUTIVES

President and Executive Officer (Group CEO) and Representative Director, Kengo Sakurada
Deputy President and Senior Managing Executive Officer (Group CIO) and Director, Keiji Nishizawa
Deputy President Senior Managing Executive Officer and Director, Shinji Tsuji
Managing Executive Officer and General Manager The Americas Regional Headquarters, Masato Fujikura
Executive Officer General Manager Global Business Planning Department and General Manager China & East Asia Regional Headquarters, Junichi Tanaka
Executive Officer and General Manager South Asia and Pacific Regional Headquarters, Nobuhiro Kojima
Executive Officer and General Manager Europe Regional Headquarters, Takashi Yoshino
Chairman, Masaya Futamiya
Auditors: Ernst & Young ShinNihon LLC

LOCATIONS

HQ: Sompo Holdings Inc
1-26-1 Nishi-Shinjuku, Shinjuku-ku, Tokyo 160-8338
Phone: (81) 3 3349 3000
Web: www.sompo-hd.com

2018 Sales by Segment

	% of total
Domestic P&C Insurance	59
Overseas Insurance	17
Domestic Life Insurance	9
Nursing Care & Healthcare	3
Other	1
Adjustments	11
Total	**100**

2018 Sales

	% of total
Japan	79
US	10
Other	11
Total	**100**

Selected Locations

Belgium
Bermuda
France
Germany
Italy
Mexico
Singapore
Spain
Switzerland
UK
US

COMPETITORS

Aspen Insurance	GeoVera
CNA Surety	MS&AD Holdings
Capitol Indemnity	Tokio Marine
Fuji Fire and Marine	Zurich Insurance Group

HISTORICAL FINANCIALS

Company Type: Public

Income Statement FYE: March 31

	REVENUE ($ mil.)	NET INCOME ($ mil.)	NET PROFIT MARGIN	EMPLOYEES
03/20	34,115	1,128	3.3%	79,441
03/19	32,567	1,324	4.1%	81,115
03/18	35,228	1,316	3.7%	80,938
03/17	30,215	1,488	4.9%	80,667
03/16	28,745	1,421	4.9%	80,668
Annual Growth	**4.4%**	**(5.6%)**	**—**	**(0.4%)**

2020 Year-End Financials

Debt ratio: —	No. of shares (mil.): 365
Return on equity: 7.2%	Dividends
Cash ($ mil.): 8,825	Yield: —
Current ratio: —	Payout: 44.9%
Long-term debt ($ mil.): —	Market value ($ mil.): —

Sony Corp

Sony is synonymous with consumer electronics particularly in gaming consoles (such as the PlayStation) and televisions. Officially named Sony Kabushiki Kaisha in 1958 the company designs makes and sells a host of electronic equipment instruments and devices for consumer professional and industrial markets. Other products include video cameras mobile phones audio equipment and semiconductors Sony is also engaged in the production of motion pictures in the areas of music

TV and film and digital networks. In addition Sony has several financial services businesses (insurance and banking). Japan and the US are the company's largest single markets together accounting for more than half of sales.

Operations

Sony reports revenue through nine business segments. Its largest accounting for just more than 20% of sales is Game & Network Services primarily hardware software content and services for and related to the PlayStation gaming console. Financial Services (insurance and banking operations in Japan) and Home Entertainment & Sound (primarily televisions) each contribute about 15% of revenue.

Other Sony business segments include Pictures (motion pictures television production and media networks) with more than 10% of sales Semiconductors which accounts for about 10% of sales — as well as Mobile Communications (mobile phones and tablets) Imaging Products & Solutions (digital and video cameras and related products) Music (recorded music music publishing visual media and platform) and other operating activities that accounts for nearly 5% of sales such as recording media and storage media businesses.

Geographic Reach

Sony has facilities throughout the world although its primary manufacturing plants are located in Japan. Other plant locations include China Malaysia Thailand Europe and the US.

The company's corporate headquarters is located at Tokyo Japan.

Japan is also the company's single largest market by sales (about a third) with the US and Europe accounting for more than 20% each.

Sales and Marketing

Sony's products are marketed worldwide by sales subsidiaries and unaffiliated distributors as well as direct online sales. The company's electronics products and services are marketed under the trademark "Sony" which has been registered in approximately 200 countries and territories.

Along with its global corporate functions in Japan Sony Mobile also has sales and marketing operations in many major regions of the world as well as manufacturing sites in China and product development sites in Japan and Sweden.

Sony's advertising cost spending is 300-400 million yen annually.

Financial Performance

After several years of flat or declining revenue (as a result of foreign exchange rates as well as a slowdown in smartphones) Sony saw a significant rebound in fiscal 2018. It has been continuously increasing since then. Net income has followed a similar trajectory during that time.

In fiscal 2019 (ended March) Sony reported revenue of 8666 billion yen an increase of 122 billion yen or 1% from the prior year. The results were powered by its Game & Network Services segment (PlayStation 4 software) as well as strong results from Music and Financial Services. The Mobile Communications segment continued to shrink as smartphone sales fell. Sony saw improvements across all geographic regions.

The company's 2019 net income exploded jumping to 916 billion yen from 491 billion yen in fiscal 2018. Sony kept a tight rein on expenses (selling general and administrative expenses by only rose 5%) and reduced other operating expenses from 149 billion yen to 4 billion yen.

Strategy

Sony invests heavily in production facilities and equipment in its electronics businesses including fabrication facilities used to make image sensors for smartphones and other products. In 2019 Sony invested 129 billion yen of capital mainly for the purpose of increasing image sensor production capacity.

Sony is pursuing to make its PlayStation "The Best Place to Pay" by leveraging the latest computing streaming cloud 5G technologies and content. Its PlayStation streaming Remote Play and PlayStation Now turns PS4 into a streaming game server providing streaming content at the closest point to users. This newly developed streaming is expected to reach 100 million units in cumulative sales.

To strengthen the competitiveness of its products and services Sony will continue to invest in research and development particularly in growth areas such as image sensors and its Game & Network Services segment as the company believes that integrating its hardware software entertainment content and network services and investing in R&D is essential in generating revenue growth. Sony also actively engages in acquisitions joint ventures capital expenditures and other strategic investments to acquire new technologies develop new businesses and enhance their business competitiveness.

Cash at the end of fiscal 2019 was 1470 billion yen a decrease of 116 billion yen from the prior year. Cash from operations contributed 1259 billion yen to the coffers while investing activities used 1307 billion yen mainly on payments for investments and advances. Financing activities added another 123 billion yen due to increases in short-term borrowings and in deposits from customers.

Company Background

Tokyo Telecommunications Engineering Corporation the predecessor of Sony was established in 1946 with about 20 employees. It listed on the over-the-counter market of the Toyko Stock Exchange (TSE) in 1955 and three years later changed its name to Sony Corporation. The company also listed on the TSE that year.

EXECUTIVES

President and CEO, Kazuo (Kaz) Hirai, age 60
Executive Deputy President, Tomoyuki Suzuki
EVP; Global CEO Sony Interactive Entertainment, Andrew House
EVP; President Professional Solutions and Services, Shigeki Ishizuka
EVP, Masashi Imamura
EVP, Shiro Kambe
Executive Deputy President and CFO, Kenichiro Yoshida
EVP; CEO Sony Mobile Communications, Hiroki Totoki
EVP; President Sony Visual Products, Ichiro Takagi
EVP, Kazushi Ambe
Auditors: PricewaterhouseCoopers Aarata LLC

LOCATIONS

HQ: Sony Corp
7-1, Konan 1-chome, Minato-ku, Tokyo 108-0075
Phone: (81) 3 6748 2111   **Fax:** 212 833-6849
Web: www.sony.co.jp

2018 Sales

	% of total
Japan	31
Europe	22
US	21
Asia/Pacific (except Japan and China)	12
China	8
Other	6
Total	**100**

PRODUCTS/OPERATIONS

2018 Sales

	% of total
Game & Network services	22
Home entertainment & sound	14
Mobile communications	8
Financial services	14
Semiconductors	10
Pictures	11
Imaging products & solutions	7
Music	9
Other	5
Total	**100**

COMPETITORS

21st Century Fox	Nintendo
Apple Inc.	Panasonic Corp
Disney	Philips Electronics
Fujitsu	Pioneer Corporation
Hitachi	Samsung Group
Intel	Time Warner
LG Electronics	Toshiba
Microsoft	

HISTORICAL FINANCIALS

Company Type: Public

Income Statement				FYE: March 31
	REVENUE ($ mil.)	NET INCOME ($ mil.)	NET PROFIT MARGIN	EMPLOYEES
03/20	76,092	5,363	7.0%	111,700
03/19	78,249	8,273	10.6%	114,400
03/18	80,461	4,621	5.7%	117,300
03/17	68,003	655	1.0%	128,400
03/16	72,181	1,316	1.8%	125,300
Annual Growth	1.3%	42.1%	—	(2.8%)

2020 Year-End Financials

Debt ratio: 0.0%	No. of shares (mil.): 1,220
Return on equity: 14.7%	Dividends
Cash ($ mil.): 13,932	Yield: 0.6%
Current ratio: 0.92	Payout: 7.6%
Long-term debt ($ mil.): 5,849	Market value ($ mil.): 72,209

	STOCK PRICE ($) FY Close	P/E High/Low		PER SHARE ($)		
				Earnings	Dividends	Book Value
03/20	59.18	0	0	4.25	0.37	31.15
03/19	42.24	0	0	6.39	0.27	27.05
03/18	48.34	0	0	3.58	0.21	22.08
03/17	33.73	1	0	0.51	0.18	17.69
03/16	25.72	0	0	1.05	0.08	17.39
Annual Growth	23.2%	—	—	42.0%	45.9%	15.7%

Standard Bank Group Ltd

Standard Bank Group sets the standard for sub-Saharan banking. Standard Bank South Africa's largest bank offers a variety of retail and commercial banking corporate andÂ investment banking investment management and lifeÂ insurance services through aboutÂ 700 locations in its home country. The group alsoÂ includesÂ 500-plus additional branches more than 15 otherÂ African nations where it operates as Stanbic Bank. Beyond AfricaÂ the bank hasÂ offices in Asia Europe and the Americas including many emerging markets.Â It serves individuals and business and corporate customers. Standard Bank holds a controlling stake in South African insuranceÂ firm LibertyÂ Holdings.

Operations

In addition to personal commercial and corporate banking services SBG'sÂ Â insurance arm 53%-owned Liberty offers life insurance andÂ investment and wealth management services to individuals and corporations in select African markets.

Geographic Reach

Contributing almost 85% of Standard Bank Group's revenue South Africa isÂ its largest market by far. SBG also operates in 17 other African nations (from Angola to Zambia) as well as the UK and the US. Emerging markets include Argentina Brazil China Turkey and Russia.

Financial Performance

Standard Bank Group struggled during the prolonged global recession. Low interest ratesÂ weak demand for credit and other financial factors impacted the company's revenues in 2009 and 2010. In 2011 the bank's revenue was essentially flat (up less than 1%) vs. the prior year while net income rose 23% over the same period. The modest uptick in revenue was credited to increase in banking activities partially offset by decreasing revenues at Liberty.

The personal and business banking division (up 8% in 2011 vs. 2010)Â outperformed the bank's other units. Revenue in South Africa the bank's largest market declined 1% while revenue from the rest of Africa was up 15% year over year. Revenue from outside of Africa fell 6%.

Strategy

Standard Bank Group is one of four full-service South African banks and claims to be the largest by assets and earnings. SBG aspires to be Africa's leading corporate and investment bank with a deep specialization in natural resources. To that end the bankÂ is strengthening its focus on itsÂ core market and is looking to expand in Nigeria and Namibia. The company intends to grow its commercial banking operations there by building new branches. It opened more than 70Â branches in Nigeria in 2010 alone.

Despite its Afro-centric focus SBG is also active in emerging markets worldwide including Russia. Indeed Standard Bank acquiredÂ about a third of Russian investment bank Troika Dialog in 2009. The partnership helped the group establish a presence in Russia where there is an opportunity to create a substantial domestic andÂ cross-border franchise. However in early 2012 the company sold its stake in Troika DialogÂ to Russia's Sberbank for $372 million plus additional funds if Troika performs well. Standard Bank hopes to utilize its relationship with Troika to establish partnerships with Sberbank in the future. Other key emerging markets for the bank are Argentina BrazilÂ and Turkey.

EXECUTIVES

Joint Group CEO, Simpiwe (Sim) Tshabalala, age 52
Joint Group CEO, Ben Kruger, age 60
CEO PBB Group, Peter Schlebusch, age 53
Chief Executive Standard Bank Wealth, Margaret Nienaber
CEO Corporate Investment Banking, Kenny Fihla
Group Financial Director, Arno Daehnke
Chief Executive Africa Regions, Sola David-Borha
Chief Executive PBB South Africa, Funeka Montjane
Group CIO, Brenda Niehaus
Chairman, Thulani Gcabashe, age 62
Auditors: KPMG Inc.

LOCATIONS

HQ: Standard Bank Group Ltd
9th Floor, Standard Bank Centre, 5 Simmonds Street, Johannesburg 2001
Phone: (27) 11 636 9111   **Fax:** (27) 11 636 4207
Web: www.standardbank.com

2011 Total Income

	% of total
South Africa	84
Rest of Africa	10
Outside of Africa	5
Central and other	1
Total	**100**

Selected Markets

Africa
  Angola
  Botswana
  DRC
  Ghana
  Kenya
  Lesotho
  Malawi
  Mauritius
  Mozambique
  Namibia
  Nigeria
  South Africa
  Swaziland
  Tanzania
  Uganda
  Zambia
Americas
  Argentina
  Brazil
  US
Europe/Asia Pacific
  China
  Hong Kong
  Isle of Man
  Japan
  Jersey
  Russia
  Singapore
  Taiwan
  Turkey
  United Arab Emirates
  United Kingdom

PRODUCTS/OPERATIONS

2011 Revenue

	% of total
Liberty	45
Personal & business banking	34
Corporate & investment banking	21
Central & other	—
Total	**100**

COMPETITORS

Absa	Old Mutual
Citigroup	Sanlam
Commerzbank	Scotiabank
FirstRand	Standard Chartered
Nedcor	

HISTORICAL FINANCIALS

Company Type: Public

Income Statement   FYE: December 31

	ASSETS ($ mil.)	NET INCOME ($ mil.)	INCOME AS % OF ASSETS	EMPLOYEES
12/19	162,031	1,811	1.1%	50,691
12/18	147,921	1,909	1.3%	53,178
12/17	164,724	2,131	1.3%	54,558
12/16	142,297	1,616	1.1%	54,767
12/15	126,935	1,523	1.2%	54,361
Annual Growth	6.3%	4.4%	—	(1.7%)

2019 Year-End Financials

Return on assets: 1.1%	Dividends
Return on equity: 14.2%	Yield: 4.3%
Long-term debt ($ mil.): —	Payout: 46.3%
No. of shares (mil.): 1,594	Market value ($ mil.): 18,938
Sales ($ mil): 16,541	

	STOCK PRICE ($) FY Close	P/E High/Low		PER SHARE ($) Earnings	Dividends	Book Value
12/19	11.88	1	1	1.13	0.52	8.14
12/18	12.73	1	1	1.19	0.53	7.60
12/17	15.86	1	1	1.31	0.49	8.41
12/16	11.05	1	1	1.00	0.39	7.10
12/15	7.25	1	0	0.95	0.38	6.25
Annual Growth	13.1%	—	—	4.5%	8.1%	6.8%

Standard Chartered Plc

While the British Empire isn't as global as it used to be that hasn't stopped Standard Chartered. The UK-based banking group known as Stanchart primarily operates in its target markets of Asia the Middle East and Africa home to many of the world's fastest-growing economies. It also operates in Europe and the Americas. In all Stanchart has more than 1000 branches in 60 countries and serves customers in roughly 150. The company's activities center on retail banking (deposit accounts loans cards and investment products) and corporate and institutional banking (capital markets cash management international trade custody and clearing services); it also has commercial banking and private banking functions. Stanchart traces its roots back more than 160 years.

Operations

Because the bank's strategy is centered around client relationships Stanchart organizes its business around four client segment groups.

Corporate and Institutional Banking generates around 45% of Stanchart's annual sales providing transaction services corporate finance financial markets and borrowing. Retail banking which encompasses typical services such as current accounts loans cards and investment products pulls in some 35% of sales.

Stanchart's Commercial Banking (10%) unit provides international banking services to its client base of 45000 SMEs and local corporations who depend on Stanchart as their main international bank. The Private Banking segment which generates 5% of sales offers investment credit wealth planning and private wealth services to its 8000 clients.

Geographic Reach

UK-based Standard Chartered (Stanchart) does business from more than 1000 branches in around 60 markets mostly in Asia Africa and the Middle East but also in Europe and the Americas. Stanchart's biggest territories are Greater China and North Asia (40% of sales) Southeast and South Asia (more than 25%) and Africa and the Middle East (20%). Stanchart's Private and International Banking activities are carried out mainly through its London office.

Stanchart divides its four business segments into two groups Global and Local. Global (Corporate & Institutional Banking and Private Banking) serves customers through relationship managers with a global remit while the Local business (Retail and Commercial Banking) deploys country-level relationship managers.

Sales and Marketing

The Corporate & Institutional business serves financial institutions and global and local corporate clients; while the Retail group serves individuals and small businesses. Private Banking clients include high-net-worth individuals and Commercial Clients include mid-sized companies. The bank serves clients from a variety of sectors: including energy manufacturing commercial real estate consumer durables and construction.

Since 2010 Stanchart has been the lead sponsor of Liverpool Football Club one of Europe's leading soccer teams and which has multitudes of fans in the company's target markets. The current deal runs until the end of the 2022/23 season.

Financial Performance

Standard Chartered has struggled to achieve sustained revenue growth in its recent past. In fiscal 2018 the company's revenue grew 3% to $14.8 billion due to strong increases in net interest income and net trading income partially offset by a reduction in miscellaneous operating income particularly the absence from the books of a $235 million gain on available-for-sale investments recorded in 2017.

Net income declined 13% to $1.1 billion as Stanchart's operating profits were impacted by the decision to put aside $900 million for fines that could arise from FX trading investigations and sanction breaches in the US and UK. Partially offsetting that item was a sharp reduction in impairment expenses.

Stanchart's cash balance strengthened during 2018 ending the year $11.8 billion higher at $97.5 billion. It generated $25.3 billion in cash from its operations while its investing activities absorbed $12.4 billion and its financing activities used $1.0 billion. The bank's primary cash uses were net purchases of investment securities debt repayments and dividend payouts.

Strategy

As major part of Standard Chartered's (Stanchart) investment program is in digital with the goal to accelerate internal transformation and develop new revenue channels. Company-wide investment reached $1.6 billion in 2018 up on $1.5 billion and $1.4 billion in the two preceding years. It is launching digital retail banking in Africa with an initial roll-out in Cote d'Ivoire followed up by Uganda Tanzania and Ghana in 2018 and Kenya and Stanchart's other African nations in 2019. Additionally more than 50 banking services are available on Stanchart's banking app in India while it established a challenger bank in Hong Kong in partnership with e-commerce giant Alibaba.

Stanchart sees great potential in developing its trade finance business by capitalizing on its virtually unrivaled position in emerging markets particularly Africa and Asia. The company has seen large multinationals in increasing numbers ask it to handle their trade finance requirements across multiple borders; some two-thirds of revenue in the Corporate and Institutional Banking segment now arises from its trade finance network. Going forward Stanchart will look to deepen its position in India South Korea the UAE and Indonesia.

Mergers and Acquisitions

Helping to position Stanchart as a top South African custodian the company in 2013 acquired the South African custody and trustee business of Absa Bank which had developed a profitable custody model across more than 20 sub-Saharan African countries.

Company Background

Asia Africa and the Middle East have been among Stanchart's targeted areas for growth. It owns First Africa Group which provides mergers and acquisitions advisory services to companies wanting to invest in Africa. Stanchart bought Barclays Bank's custody business in 2010 adding operations in eight African nations. In late 2011 the company bought the performing segment of Barclays' credit card business in India at a discount. In 2012 to expand its wholesale banking business in Turkey Stanchart purchased Credit Agricole Yatirim Bankasi Turk A.S. (CAYBT) a fully-owned subsidiary of Credit Agricole Corporate and Investment Bank. It exited the equity capital markets in 2015. The company's trans-border nature means it sometimes falls foul of sanction regimes; it faces $900 million in fines from the US Government for violating sanctions against Iran and other countries.

HISTORY

Standard Chartered began in 1853 as the Chartered Bank of India Australia and China to finance trade between the UK and its Asian colonies. It began establishing offices in 1858. Over the next 40 years The Chartered Bank expanded throughout Asia. In the 20th century the bank opened branches in Germany and the US. In 1957 Chartered entered the Middle East by acquiring Eastern Bank. In 1969 it agreed to merge with Standard Bank.

In 1862 schoolmaster John Paterson established the Standard Bank of British South Africa Ltd. to fund trade with mining businesses. Within two years the bank had 15 branches. Like Chartered Standard had moved into Germany and the US by 1905 and operated in central and southern Africa by 1912.

In 1962 the bank was renamed The Standard Bank Ltd. Three years later it expanded into Gambia Ghana Nigeria and Sierra Leone but the end of colonialism meant instability; business was threatened and ruling parties often nationalized Standard's banks. In 1969 the bank agreed to merge with Chartered Bank.

Asian and Middle Eastern business flourished in the early 1970s while South African branches struggled under growing international pressure on the country's apartheid regime. In response the company diversified into metals trading and consumer finance. It also expanded in the US market with the purchase of Union Bancorp of California.

Standard Chartered failed in a 1981 attempt to gain entry to the UK market through purchasing Royal Bank of Scotland. Four years later that bank went public.

In 1986 Lloyds Bank tried to take over Standard Chartered but investors Robert Holmes a Court Yue-Kong Pao and Khoo Teck Puat acquired enough of the company to block the play. Meanwhile overseas financial deregulation brought more competition and Hong Kong Singapore and Malaysia sank into recession.

Hit by trade sanctions against South Africa the bank in 1987 sold its operations there. As the world tumbled deeper into recession Standard Chartered's loan losses climbed. But the bank began to recover the next year as it trimmed its US bank holdings.

Scandal hit the bank in the 1990s. In 1992 Standard Chartered paid $515 million in restitution after a broker in its Mumbai India office embezzled some $1.2 billion from Indian banks. In 1994 executives with Mocatta were convicted of bribery and the Hong Kong government banned Standard Chartered Securities (sold in 1996) from underwriting stock offerings for nine months after it falsified six IPOs.

In 1997 Standard Chartered refocused on retail banking with its 1998 purchase of what is now Banco Standard Chartered in Latin America and its bank/insurance tie-ups with CGU (now CGNU) and Prudential plc. The promotion of Rana Talwar to CEO brought a strategic focus on emerging markets from which other banks were withdrawing.

Standard Chartered in 1999 bought Thailand's Nakornthon Bank and the non-Swiss trade financing operations of UBS AG and expanded into China through a pact with the Bank of China. In 2000 the company bought Australia and New Zealand Banking Group's Grindlays operations in South Asia and the Middle East. The following year Stanchart began cutting 20% of its workforce. It also folded Grindlay's operations into its own while retaining the brand's name.

In 2004 Stanchart bought the majority of Australia and New Zealand Banking Group's project finance business which is headquartered in London. The business which cost Stanchart about $1.5 billion operates in four regions: the UK the US the Middle East and South Asia (especially India).

In 2005 the bank acquired Korea First Bank (now SC First Bank); the deal was the biggest foreign investment ever for South Korea's financial sector. The following year Stanchart paid about $1.2 billion for Taiwan's Hsinchu Bank making it the first foreign bank owner in that country. Also in 2006 the bank acquired 20% of China Bohai Bank.

In 2008 the UK government responded to the global financial crisis by investing Å 50 billion ($87.9 billion) in the nation's top banks including Stanchart. It agreed to guarantee another Å 250 billion ($438 billion) in bonds and provide additional liquidity of at least Å 200 billion ($350 billion) to the banks. The bailout plan was initiated to provide capital directly to the banks in order to revitalize lending activities.

Also in 2008 the company made some acquisitions for further international expansion. It bought Asia Trust and Investment Corporation which added some 10 branches in the lucrative Taipei market. Stanchart also bought some of the Brazil operations of Lehman Brothers after that company filed for bankruptcy protection.

EXECUTIVES

Group CEO, William T. (Bill) Winters, age 59
Chief Executive India Operations, Zarin Daruwala
Regional CEO ASEAN and South Asia, Ajay Kanwal
Regional CEO India and South Asia, Sunil Kaushal
CEO Corporate and Institutional Banking, Simon Cooper
Group CIO, Michael Gorriz, age 60
Group Finance Director, Andy Halford
CEO Iraq, Andreas Meletiou
CEO Singapore, Judy Hsu
Director Compliance People and Communications and Regional CEO Europe and Americas, Tracy Clarke
CEO Retail Banking, Karen Fawcett
Group COO, Doris Honold
Regional CEO Greater China and North Asia, Benjamin P. C. (Ben) Hung
Group Chief Risk Officer, Mark Smith
Chairman, José Viñals
Auditors: KMPG LLP

LOCATIONS

HQ: Standard Chartered Plc
32nd Floor, 4-4A Des Voeux Road, Central,
Phone: (44) 20 7885 8888   **Fax:** (44) 20 7885 9999
Web: www.sc.com

2018 Sales

	% of total
Greater China & North Asia	42
ASEAN & South Asia	27
Africa & the Middle East	18
Europe & Americas	11
Central and other	2
Total	**100**

PRODUCTS/OPERATIONS

2018 Sales

	% of total
Net Interest Income	59
Net Fee and Commission Income	24
Net Trading Income	11
Other Operating Income	6
Total	**100**

2018 Sales

	$mil	%
Corporate & Institutional Banking	6,606	45
Retail Banking	5,041	34
Commercial Banking	1,390	9
Private Banking	518	4
Central & Other Items	1,234	8
Total	**14,789**	**100**

COMPETITORS

Bank of America	Hang Seng Bank
Bank of China	Lloyds Banking Group
Bank of East Asia	Maybank
Barclays	OCBC Bank
Citigroup	Royal Bank of Scotland
DBS Group Holdings	Standard Bank Group
Deutsche Bank	State Bank of India
Grupo Santander	United Overseas Bank
HSBC	Woori

HISTORICAL FINANCIALS

Company Type: Public

Income Statement				FYE: December 31
	ASSETS ($ mil.)	NET INCOME ($ mil.)	INCOME AS % OF ASSETS	EMPLOYEES
12/19	720,398	2,303	0.3%	84,398
12/18	688,762	1,054	0.2%	85,402
12/17	663,501	1,219	0.2%	86,021
12/16	646,692	(247)	—	86,693
12/15	640,483	(2,194)	—	84,076
Annual Growth	3.0%	—		0.1%

2019 Year-End Financials

Return on assets: 0.3%
Return on equity: 4.5%
Long-term debt ($ mil.): —
No. of shares (mil.): —
Sales ($ mil): 25,188

Dividends
  Yield: 0.0%
  Payout: 39.0%
Market value ($ mil.): —

	STOCK PRICE ($) FY Close	P/E High/Low		PER SHARE ($) Earnings	Dividends	Book Value
12/19	19.15	34	27	0.56	0.22	15.78
Annual Growth	—	—	—	—	—	—

State Bank of India

Auditors: J.C.Bhalla & Co

LOCATIONS

HQ: State Bank of India
  Central Office, Madam Cama Road, Nariman Point,
  Mumbai 400 021
Phone: (91) 22 2283 0535   **Fax:** (91) 22 2285 5348
Web: www.sbi.co.in

HISTORICAL FINANCIALS

Company Type: Public

Income Statement				FYE: March 31
	ASSETS ($ mil.)	NET INCOME ($ mil.)	INCOME AS % OF ASSETS	EMPLOYEES
03/20	555,704	2,617	0.5%	249,448
03/19	561,960	332	0.1%	257,252
03/18	555,855	(700)	—	264,041
03/17	531,232	37	0.0%	209,567
03/16	449,244	1,848	0.4%	222,809
Annual Growth	5.5%	9.1%	—	2.9%

2020 Year-End Financials

Return on assets: 0.4%
Return on equity: 8.1%
Long-term debt ($ mil.): —
No. of shares (mil.): —
Sales ($ mil): 49,113

Dividends
  Yield: —
  Payout: —
Market value ($ mil.): —

	STOCK PRICE ($) FY Close	P/E High/Low		PER SHARE ($) Earnings	Dividends	Book Value
03/20	25.60	2	1	0.29	0.00	3.72
03/19	43.95	17	13	0.04	0.00	3.80
03/18	40.11	—	—	(0.08)	0.38	3.97
03/17	43.17	140	84	0.00	0.38	4.20
03/16	30.40	3	1	0.24	0.53	3.52
Annual Growth	(4.2%)	—	—	5.0%	—	1.4%

Steinhoff International Holdings NV

LOCATIONS

HQ: Steinhoff International Holdings NV
  Building B2, Vineyard Office Park, Cnr Adam Tas &
  Devon Valley Road, Stellenbosch 7600
Phone: (27) 21 8080700   **Fax:** (27) 21 8080800
Web: www.steinhoffinternational.com

HISTORICAL FINANCIALS

Company Type: Public

Income Statement				FYE: September 30
	REVENUE ($ mil.)	NET INCOME ($ mil.)	NET PROFIT MARGIN	EMPLOYEES
09/19	13,081	(1,769)	—	108,361
09/18	14,857	(1,444)	—	123,054
09/17	22,233	(4,768)	—	125,501
09/16*	18,351	1,604	8.7%	105,866
06/15	10,969	1,090	9.9%	91,114
Annual Growth	4.5%	—	—	4.4%

*Fiscal year change

2019 Year-End Financials

Debt ratio: 84.9%
Return on equity: —
Cash ($ mil.): 1,958
Current ratio: 1.42
Long-term debt ($ mil.): 11,313

No. of shares (mil.): —
Dividends
  Yield: —
  Payout: —
Market value ($ mil.): —

Stellantis NV

Auditors: EY S.p.A

LOCATIONS

HQ: Stellantis NV
  25 St. James's Street, London SW1A 1HA
Phone: (44) 20 7766 0311
Web: www.fcagroup.com

HISTORICAL FINANCIALS

Company Type: Public

Income Statement				FYE: December 31
	REVENUE ($ mil.)	NET INCOME ($ mil.)	NET PROFIT MARGIN	EMPLOYEES
12/19	121,468	7,434	6.1%	191,752
12/18	126,443	4,131	3.3%	198,545
12/17	132,982	4,184	3.1%	235,915
12/16	117,222	1,903	1.6%	231,019
12/15	120,461	363	0.3%	234,621
Annual Growth	0.2%	112.6%	—	(4.9%)

2019 Year-End Financials

Debt ratio: 14.7%
Return on equity: 24.8%
Cash ($ mil.): 16,857
Current ratio: 0.81
Long-term debt ($ mil.): 9,010

No. of shares (mil.): 1,567
Dividends
  Yield: 20.8%
  Payout: 41.1%
Market value ($ mil.): —

Stora Enso Oyj

    Stora Enso's roots reach back more than 700 years. The forest products company is a global leader in fiber-based renewable products and is the #2 paper manufacturer in Europe (behind UPM) providing a range of recycled and virgin fiber papers for print and office use. The company also makes commercial and consumer packaging products (carton and corrugated cardboard) bio-materials (pulp and byproducts such as tall oil and turpentine) and wood products for construction as well as wood pellets for heating. Stora Enso is based in Helsinki Finland. Close to 75% of its sales are generated in Europe but the company operates in more than 30 countries.

Financial Performance

    Note: Growth rates may differ after conversion to US Dollars.

    Stora Enso's sales have remained relatively flat over the last several years up only 3% since 2014. Revenue in 2018 reached ?10.5 billion up by 4% compared with 2017. The increase was primarily due to higher sales and a favorable product mix in all its segments.

    Profits climbed 62% to ?1.0 billion in 2018 after posting ?625 million in profits the previous year.

    Cash at the end of fiscal 2018 was ?1.1 billion an increase of ?521 million from the prior year. Cash from operations contributed ?1.1 billion to the coffers while investing activities used ?497 million mainly for capital expenditures. Financing activities used another ?73 million for loan payments and dividends to stockholders.

Strategy

    As consumers increasingly turn to more eco-friendly products Stora Enso is focused on replacing fossil fuel-based products with renewable products derived from trees. Some of its recent R&D activities include the development of biodegradable straws renewable caps and closures for liquid packages and new paper-based RFID tags for digital package tracking and management (the company recently established a new intelligent packaging unit).

The company sources most of its wood from private forest owners and in Europe from its partners Bergvik Skog and Tornator. In Latin America it owns 50% of the Veracel Celulose pulp mill an important source of low-cost pulp from tree plantations. Stora Enso also operates the Montes del Plata pulp mill in Uruguay a joint operation between Stora Enso and Arauco.

To meet the growing demand for its products in China the company has increased production at its consumer board mill in Beihai in the Guangxi region.

HISTORY

Stora Enso's corporate ancestors were mining Kopparberg Mountain in Sweden as long ago as 1288. The mountain housed a copper mine that Swedish nobles and German merchants managed as a cooperative. By the 17th century King Karl IX instituted German mining methods to increase production. Copper became Sweden's largest export at one point accounting for 60% of the country's gross national product.

Copper production slowed after two cave-ins in 1655 and 1687 and exploitation of the region's timber and iron ore resources began. By the early 1800s the company was producing pig and bar iron. In 1862 all of the company's activities were combined to form Stora Kopparbergs Bergslag. The role of copper became less important as the company consolidated its iron works and ventured into forest products. The firm reorganized as a limited liability company in 1888.

By 1915 Stora Kopparbergs had firmly established pulp and paper mills as well as iron and steel works concentrated along the Dalalven River Basin. The company's activities revolved around these facilities for the next 60 years.

EXECUTIVES

CEO, Karl-Henrik Sundstr ¶m, age 60
EVP Sustainability, Noel Morrin, age 62
EVP Division Biomaterials, Juan Carlos Bueno, age 52
CFO Deputy CEO and Country Senior Executive Finland, Seppo Parvi, age 56
EVP Sourcing, Johanna Hagelberg, age 48
EVP Division Paper, Kati ter Horst, age 52
EVP Global Communications, Ulrika Lilja, age 45
EVP Legal General Counsel and Country Manager Sweden, Per Lyrvall, age 61
SVP and Head Building and Living Division, Jari Suominen, age 51
EVP Division Packaging Solutions, Gilles Van Nieuwenhuyzen, age 61
CTO, Markus Mannstr ¶m, age 57
EVP Consumer Board Division, Annica Bresky
EVP Human Resources, Malin Bendz, age 44
Chairman, Gunnar Brock, age 71
Vice Chairman, Jorma Eloranta, age 70
Auditors: PricewaterhouseCoopers Oy

LOCATIONS

HQ: Stora Enso Oyj
Kanavaranta 1, Helsinki FIN-00160
Phone: (358) 2046 21242   **Fax:** (358) 2046 21206
Web: www.storaenso.com

2018 Sales by Destination

	% of total
Europe	73
Asia Pacific	18
North America	4
South America	2
Other	3
Total	**100**

PRODUCTS/OPERATIONS

2018 Sales

	% of total
Paper	22
Consumer Board	19
Wood Products	12
Biomaterials	12
Packaging Solutions	10
Other	25
Eliminations	-
Total	**100**

Selected Products

Book paper
Business forms
Cartonboards
Coreboards and tubes
Corrugated boxes
Digital papers
Directory paper
Document papers
Envelope papers
Fluff pulp
Foodservice boards
Graphic board
Graphic paper
Kraft papers
Laminated papers
Liquid packaging boards
Magazine paper
Newsprint
Paper-grade pulp
Sawn boards
Scholastic paper

COMPETITORS

DS Smith	OfficeMax
Georgia-Pacific	Sappi
Holmen AB	Smurfit Kappa
International Paper	Svenska Cellulosa
M-real	UPM-Kymmene
Mets ᴑliitto	Wausau Paper
Mondi	Weyerhaeuser
Norske Skog	

HISTORICAL FINANCIALS

Company Type: Public

Income Statement				FYE: December 31
	REVENUE ($ mil.)	NET INCOME ($ mil.)	NET PROFIT MARGIN	EMPLOYEES
12/19	15,822	1,384	8.8%	24,390
12/18	16,500	1,594	9.7%	26,129
12/17	15,806	983	6.2%	25,700
12/16	15,424	728	4.7%	25,447
12/15	15,798	1,269	8.0%	25,680
Annual Growth	0.0%	2.2%	—	(1.3%)

2019 Year-End Financials

Debt ratio: 43.8%
Return on equity: 12.4%
Cash ($ mil.): 1,378
Current ratio: 1.23
Long-term debt ($ mil.): 5,085

No. of shares (mil.): 788
Dividends
 Yield: 3.8%
 Payout: 32.0%
Market value ($ mil.): 11,451

	STOCK PRICE ($) FY Close	P/E High/Low		PER SHARE ($) Earnings	Dividends	Book Value
12/19	14.52	13	9	1.76	0.57	14.83
12/18	11.61	17	9	2.01	0.91	13.40
12/17	15.78	20	13	1.24	0.40	11.99
12/16	10.65	18	13	0.93	0.37	11.59
12/15	9.10	11	7	1.61	0.34	10.75
Annual Growth	12.4%	—	—	2.4%	13.6%	8.4%

Storebrand ASA

EXECUTIVES

Chairman Of The Board, Odd Arild Grefstad
Auditors: PricewaterhouseCoopers AS

LOCATIONS

HQ: Storebrand ASA
Professor Kohts vei 9, Lysaker NO-1327
Phone: (47) 915 31 50 50   **Fax:** (47) 22 48 98 90
Web: www.storebrand.no

HISTORICAL FINANCIALS

Company Type: Public

Income Statement				FYE: December 31
	ASSETS ($ mil.)	NET INCOME ($ mil.)	INCOME AS % OF ASSETS	EMPLOYEES
12/19	72,048	235	0.3%	1,759
12/18	66,529	424	0.6%	1,789
12/17	69,389	289	0.4%	1,795
12/16	60,401	246	0.4%	1,745
12/15	59,153	133	0.2%	2,298
Annual Growth	5.1%	15.2%	—	(6.5%)

2019 Year-End Financials

Return on assets: 0.3%
Return on equity: 6.2%
Long-term debt ($ mil.): —
No. of shares (mil.): 467
Sales ($ mil): 9,947

Dividends
 Yield: —
 Payout: —
Market value ($ mil.): —

Strabag SE-BR

Auditors: KPMG Austria GmbH Wirtschaftsprufungs- und Steuerberatungsgesellschaft

LOCATIONS

HQ: Strabag SE-BR
Triglavstrasse 9, Villach 9500
Phone: (43) 800 880 890
Web: www.strabag.com

HISTORICAL FINANCIALS
Company Type: Public

Income Statement				FYE: December 31
	REVENUE ($ mil.)	NET INCOME ($ mil.)	NET PROFIT MARGIN	EMPLOYEES
12/19	17,627	417	2.4%	76,919
12/18	17,394	404	2.3%	75,460
12/17	16,136	334	2.1%	72,904
12/16	13,152	293	2.2%	71,839
12/15	14,271	170	1.2%	73,315
Annual Growth	5.4%	25.1%	—	1.2%

2019 Year-End Financials

Debt ratio: —	No. of shares (mil.): 102
Return on equity: 9.9%	Dividends
Cash ($ mil.): 2,762	Yield: —
Current ratio: 1.16	Payout: 24.8%
Long-term debt ($ mil.): —	Market value ($ mil.): —

Subaru Corporation

Subaru Corporation (formerly Fuji Heavy Industries) is the parent of Subaru of America the automotive company known for its all-wheel-drive (AWD) technology found in crossover vehicles (a sedan drive with SUV looks) such as the Forester and Outback and in the Impreza Legacy and Tribeca models. In addition to Subaru of America based in the US the company operates through more than 75 subsidiaries in Japan China and Taiwan and 10 equity-method affiliated companies. The company also makes aircraft and structural components within its Aerospace Company. Its core business however is Subaru automobiles representing almost 90% of sales.

Operations

The company operates in three business units: the Automotive Business Unit the Aerospace Company and Other Businesses.

The Automotive Business Unit manufactures cars equipped with outstanding safety and driving performance in a variety of driving conditions. This is reflected in the vehicles the company makes which has the Symmetrical All-Wheel Drive (AWD) System which features a symmetrically-laid-out drivetrain and the horizontally-opposed engine. The automotive business unit accounts for roughly 90% of the company's total revenue.

The Aerospace Company develops and produces a wide variety of aircraft in various programs. It provides maintenance and repair for products such as the UH-1J utility helicopter used by the Japan Ground Self-Defense Force as well as the T-5 Maritime Self-Defense Force trainer unmanned aerial vehicles and flight simulators. It also participates in development projects for Boeing aircrafts such as its Center Wing and integration with main landing gear wheel wells and doors. This business unit accounts for about 10% of total revenue.

Geographic Reach

The head office of Subaru Corporation is located in Tokyo Japan. The company's Automotive Business Unit operates from three plants: Gunma Main Plant Yajima Plant and Oizumi Plant. The Aerospace Company has three manufacturing plants located across Japan: Handa Plant Handa West Plant and Utsunomiya Plant.

The company generates the majority of its revenue from North America which represents 70% of the company's sales followed by Japan which represents 20%.

Financial Performance

Note: Growth rates may differ after conversion to US Dollars.

Subaru Corporation has seen modest growth in sales over the past five years. Revenue in fiscal 2019 decreased 2% to Å 3.1 trillion compared with Å 3.2 trillion in 2018 mainly due to the fall in automobile unit sales as well as in the increase of quality-related expenses triggered by the recall of engine parts.

Net income declined significantly falling 40% in fiscal 2019 to Å 147.8 billion. This loss is mainly due to selling expenses as well as plant shutdown costs which amounted to Å 405.7 billion.

Cash at the end of fiscal 2019 was Å 702.3 billion an increase of Å 63 billion from the prior year. Cash from operations contributed Å 174 billion to the coffers while investing activities used Å 158.3 billion mainly for purchases of securities and noncurrent assets. Financing activities used another Å 96.6 billion for loan payments and dividends.

Strategy

Subaru recognizes that the automotive industry is in a period of transition to a new era and social demands for new technologies are increasing. The company is keen on determining business sectors in which it can leverage its strengths and intensively invest in necessary resources to the improvement of medium and long-term corporate value and sustained growth.

The company's engineering and product development divisions have studied and begun implementing fundamental quality reforms starting from the development planning and design stages. These reforms include a review of development schedules and supplier selection and collaboration to enable reliable confirmation of quality sharing of parts across models updating of durability testing facilities and increasing personnel.

The company also announced a target of unit sales of 1.3 million vehicles worldwide in 2025 as well as increasing its dealer network to about 650 dealers. To achieve this the company is securing dealer income through increasing unit sales per dealer. Since the US is its key market the company will continue to advance on its potential; the company has planned for a consolidated unit sales of more than 1 million vehicles particularly the Ascent Forester and Crosstrek.

Additionally the company aims to utilize its all-new Forester and Subaru XV models equipped with its e-BOXER system to support sales in the Chinese and European markets.

EXECUTIVES

Deputy President, Jun Kondo
EVP, Naoto Muto
President and CEO, Yasuyuki Yoshinaga, age 44
EVP, Takeshi Tachimori
EVP, Hisashi Nagano
EVP and CFO, Mitsuru Takahashi
EVP, Masahiro Kasai
EVP, Tomomi Nakamura
EVP, Kazuo Hosoya
EVP, Nobuhiko Murakami, age 61
EVP, Masaki Okawara
Auditors: KPMG AZSA LLC

LOCATIONS

HQ: Subaru Corporation
1-20-8 Ebisu, Shibuya-ku, Tokyo 150-8554
Phone: (81) 3 6447 8825   **Fax:** (81) 3 6447 8184
Web: www.subaru.co.jp

2018 Sales

	% of total
North America	68
Japan	20
Asia	4
Europe	3
Others	5
Total	**100**

PRODUCTS/OPERATIONS

2018 Sales

	% of total
Automobiles	94
Aerospace	4
Other	2
Total	**100**

Selected Products and Divisions

Aerospace
  AH-64D combat helicopter
  Center-wing section (Boeing B-777)
  Design and training simulators
  Fixed-wing aircraft
  T-1 Trainer
  Unmanned aircraft
Automobiles
  Dex
  Dias Wagon
  Exiga
  Forester
  Impreza (wagon sedan)
  Legacy (touring B4 Outback)
  Outback (sport wagon sedan)
  Sambar (van truck wagon)
  Stella (R1 R2 Pleo)
  Tribeca
Eco Technologies
  Clean Robot floor-cleaning system
  Intermediate refuse collection systems
  Maintenance and sanitation vehicles
  Refuse management systems
  Special purpose vehicles
  Sweepers and scrubbers
  Wind-power systems

Selected Subsidiaries:

Fuji Heavy Industries U.S.A. Inc.
Fuji Machinery Co. Ltd. (Japan)
Subaru Canada Inc.
Subaru of China Ltd.
Subaru Europe N.V./S.A. (Belgium)
Subaru of America Inc. (US)
Subaru of Indiana Automotive Inc.

COMPETITORS

Daimler	Mitsubishi Heavy
FCA US	Industries
Ford Motor	Mitsubishi Motors
General Motors	Nissan
Honda	Sumitomo Heavy
Kawasaki Heavy	Industries
Industries	Suzuki Motor
Mazda	Toyota

HISTORICAL FINANCIALS
Company Type: Public

Income Statement				FYE: March 31
	REVENUE ($ mil.)	NET INCOME ($ mil.)	NET PROFIT MARGIN	EMPLOYEES
03/20	30,807	1,405	4.6%	44,747
03/19	28,538	1,334	4.7%	43,057
03/18	32,068	2,075	6.5%	41,998
03/17	29,747	2,525	8.5%	40,737
03/16	28,783	3,888	13.5%	38,319
Annual Growth	1.7%	(22.5%)	—	4.0%

2020 Year-End Financials

Debt ratio: 0.0% No. of shares (mil.): 767
Return on equity: 9.1% Dividends
Cash ($ mil.): 7,860 Yield: 7.0%
Current ratio: 2.01 Payout: —
Long-term debt ($ mil.): 2,091 Market value ($ mil.): 7,212

	STOCK PRICE ($) FY Close	P/E High/Low		PER SHARE ($) Earnings	Dividends	Book Value
03/20	9.40	0	0	1.83	0.67	20.57
03/19	11.35	0	0	1.74	0.65	18.90
03/18	16.57	0	0	2.71	0.69	19.06
03/17	18.37	0	0	3.27	0.66	17.01
03/16	70.60	0	0	4.98	0.44	15.33
Annual Growth	(39.6%)	—	—	(22.1%)	10.9%	7.6%

SUEZ SA

SUEZ Environnement conducts a variety of activities including the treatment production and distribution of drinking water; the collection recovery and treatment of wastewater; and the collection and processing of nonhazardous and hazardous waste recycling of waste and street cleaning. Supplying some 92 million people with drinking water the firm manages about 1200 drinking water production plants and 150000 kms (95000 miles) of sewage lines. It operates through subsidiaries such as Ondeo (drinking water and sanitation services) Degrémont (water treatment services) and SITA (waste management services).It acquired GE Water in 2017 for around $3.4 billion.

EXECUTIVES

EVP Innovation and Business Performance, Thierry M. Mallet, age 60
Waste Europe Activities; Chairman and CEO SITA France, Christophe Cros, age 61
EVP Human Resources, Denys Neymon, age 60
CEO, Jean-Louis Chaussade, age 69
SEVP International Activity, Marie-Ange Debon, age 55
SEVP Finance, Jean-Marc Boursier, age 53
EVP; Director Sustainable Development and Communications, Frédérique Raoult, age 54
SEVP Water Activity Europe, Angel Simon, age 63
CEO Australia, Mark Venhoek
CEO Water and Treatment Solutions, David Lamy
CEO SUEZ environnement South-East Asia, Roch Cheroux
CEO SUEZ environnement North America, Eric Gernath
Chairman, Gérard Mestrallet, age 71
Auditors: Mazars

LOCATIONS

HQ: SUEZ SA
Tour CB21 - 16 place de l'Iris, Paris La Defense, Cedex 92040
Phone: (33) 1 58 81 20 00 **Fax:** (33) 1 58 81 25 00
Web: www.suez.com

2013 Sales

	% of total
Europe	69
Oceania	8
North America	6
South America	6
Africa & Middle East	6
Asia	5
Total	100

PRODUCTS/OPERATIONS

Selected Subsidiaries

Chine
Degré;mont
Lyonnaise des Eaux
Ondeo IS
Ondeo Systems
Safege
SITA.France
SITA Trashco
SITA UK
United Water

COMPETITORS

Biffa
Bouygues
Safety-Kleen
Severn Trent
Shanks
Smurfit Kappa
Séché Environnement
United Utilities
Veolia Environnement

HISTORICAL FINANCIALS

Company Type: Public

Income Statement

FYE: December 31

	REVENUE ($ mil.)	NET INCOME ($ mil.)	NET PROFIT MARGIN	EMPLOYEES
12/19	28,348	553	2.0%	0
12/18	27,272	527	1.9%	88,775
12/17	24,975	474	1.9%	88,576
12/16	24,110	661	2.7%	83,921
12/15	23,815	641	2.7%	82,536
Annual Growth	4.5%	(3.6%)	—	—

2019 Year-End Financials

Debt ratio: 55.3% No. of shares (mil.): 618
Return on equity: 5.4% Dividends
Cash ($ mil.): 5,827 Yield: —
Current ratio: 0.95 Payout: 135.4%
Long-term debt ($ mil.): 15,600 Market value ($ mil.): —

Sumitomo Chemical Co., Ltd.

Auditors: KPMG AZSA LLC

LOCATIONS

HQ: Sumitomo Chemical Co., Ltd.
2-27-1 Shinkawa, Chuo-ku, Tokyo 104-8260
Phone: (81) 3 5543 5160 **Fax:** (81) 3 5543 5901
Web: www.sumitomo-chem.co.jp

HISTORICAL FINANCIALS

Company Type: Public

Income Statement

FYE: March 31

	REVENUE ($ mil.)	NET INCOME ($ mil.)	NET PROFIT MARGIN	EMPLOYEES
03/20	22,442	311	1.4%	37,453
03/19	23,377	1,189	5.1%	36,384
03/18	22,086	1,348	6.1%	35,829
03/17	19,704	861	4.4%	35,590
03/16	21,191	821	3.9%	34,139
Annual Growth	1.4%	(21.5%)	—	2.3%

2020 Year-End Financials

Debt ratio: 0.3% No. of shares (mil.): 1,635
Return on equity: 3.2% Dividends
Cash ($ mil.): 1,821 Yield: 6.9%
Current ratio: 1.13 Payout: —
Long-term debt ($ mil.): 8,450 Market value ($ mil.): 23,833

	STOCK PRICE ($) FY Close	P/E High/Low		PER SHARE ($) Earnings	Dividends	Book Value
03/20	14.58	1	1	0.19	1.01	5.69
03/19	23.36	0	0	0.73	1.03	6.16
03/18	29.07	0	0	0.82	0.76	5.72
03/17	28.03	1	0	0.53	0.58	5.06
03/16	22.70	1	0	0.50	0.44	4.73
Annual Growth	(10.5%)	—	—	(21.5%)	22.9%	4.7%

Sumitomo Corp. (Japan)

Auditors: KPMG AZSA LLC

LOCATIONS

HQ: Sumitomo Corp. (Japan)
2-3-2 Otemachi, Chiyoda-ku, Tokyo 100-8601
Phone: (81) 3 6285 5000 **Fax:** 212 207-0456
Web: www.sumitomocorp.co.jp

HISTORICAL FINANCIALS

Company Type: Public

Income Statement

FYE: March 31

	REVENUE ($ mil.)	NET INCOME ($ mil.)	NET PROFIT MARGIN	EMPLOYEES
03/20	48,823	1,578	3.2%	100,246
03/19	48,212	2,894	6.0%	91,362
03/18	45,460	2,905	6.4%	98,635
03/17	35,748	1,528	4.3%	91,365
03/16	35,716	663	1.9%	87,173
Annual Growth	8.1%	24.2%	—	3.6%

2020 Year-End Financials

Debt ratio: 0.3% No. of shares (mil.): 1,249
Return on equity: 6.4% Dividends
Cash ($ mil.): 6,544 Yield: 6.7%
Current ratio: 1.54 Payout: 60.5%
Long-term debt ($ mil.): 22,429 Market value ($ mil.): 14,083

	STOCK PRICE ($) FY Close	P/E High/Low		PER SHARE ($) Earnings	Dividends	Book Value
03/20	11.27	0	0	1.26	0.77	18.76
03/19	13.84	0	0	2.32	0.64	20.04
03/18	16.88	0	0	2.33	0.50	19.30
03/17	13.54	0	0	1.22	0.46	16.96
03/16	9.90	0	0	0.53	0.40	16.06
Annual Growth	3.3%	—	—	24.1%	17.3%	4.0%

Sumitomo Electric Industries, Ltd. (Japan)

Sumitomo Electric Industries (SEI) is Japan's largest producer of wire and cable and makes several other products including wiring harnesses for cars flexible printed circuits and optical fiber for telecommunications. The company has around 390 subsidiaries and affiliates around the globe. It sells more than 50% of its products to companies in the automotive industry; SEI also serves customers in the electronics telecommunications and environmental and energy industries. The company generates almost half its business in Japan.

Operations

SEI operates five business segments categorized according to the products offered: Automotive Environment and Energy Industrial Materials Electronics and Infocommunications (information and communications).

The Automotive business offers wiring harnesses and electrical components and steel cords for tire reinforcement. This business segment accounts for about 55% of the company?s net sales.

Environment and Energy offers magnet wires wind profiler radar aluminum materials industrial electric wires and cables photovoltaic systems temperature sensors and wire rods. The segment accounts for more than 20% of sales.

Industrial Materials (10% of sales) includes products for electronic devices laser optics tool-related products steel wires for springs sintered parts plastic working tools and wear-resistant parts. Electronics (more than 5%) includes wiring materials plated wires and alloy wires for electronic parts home products optical lenses and compound semiconductors. Infocommunications (about 5%) comprises optical fiber cables and transceiver modules and optical and wireless devices.

Geographic Reach

SEI operates in around 285 business locations located in 40 countries. The company?s primary operating facilities in Japan are located in Osaka Tokyo Itami Yokohama and Ibaraki. The company also owns several branch and sales offices throughout the country. The company's largest market is Japan with approximately 50% of revenue followed by Asia (excluding Japan) with around 30% of sales and the Americas with about 15%.

Financial Performance

Note: Growth rates may differ after conversion to US Dollars.

SEI's revenue has been on a generally upward trend over the past several years with an overall increase of 35% since 2012.

Sales in 2018 reached Å 3.18 trillion a 3% increase of over Å 3.08 trillion in 2017. Growth was driven by higher revenue in both its Japan and Americas regions.

The company profits however slipped back 2% in 2018 after two consecutive years of double-digit profit growth primarily due to higher tax expenses.

Cash at the end of fiscal 2018 was Å 168.9 billion a decrease of Å 11.9 billion from the prior year. Cash from operations contributed Å 177.9 billion to the coffers while investing activities used Å 184.6 billion mainly for purchases of property plant and equipment. Financing activities used another Å 4.3 billion for loan payments and dividends to stockholders.

Strategy

SEI's growth strategy includes a focus on trends in the mobility renewable energy and communications fields. The company aims to anticipate changes in these areas and develop new technologies products and services using innovative technologies like data analytics and artificial intelligence.

The company also plans to increase its global presence. In 2019 it expanded its European operations with the acquisition of the powder metallurgy businesses of the Sinterwerke Group.

Mergers and Acquisitions

In 2019 Sumitomo Electric Industries acquired the powder metallurgy businesses of both Sinterwerke Herne GmbH (Germany) and Sinterwerke Grenchen AG (Switzerland). Together the two Sinterwerke businesses produce a wide range of powder metallurgy components primarily for the automotive and power tool markets. The acquisition adds automotive tier1 suppliers and OEM customers and will help SEI expand its powder metallurgy products business in Europe.

Company Background

Sumitomo Electric Industries as a part of the Sumitomo group business began nearly 400 years ago with the paired talents of spiritual founder Masatomo Sumitomo (who had received training as a Buddhist priest) and his disciple and brother-in-law Riemon Soga. Sumitomo wrote treatises on the conduct of commercial activity and Soga applied his technological skill in extracting silver from copper ore improving upon traditional Western methods and opened a copper business in Kyoto in 1590 that soon transformed the copper refining industry in Japan.

The company later diversified its business to include flexible printed circuits (1960s) fiber optic cables for telecommunications (1970s) and wiring harnesses for automobiles made with its newly-developed aluminum alloy wires (2010s).

EXECUTIVES

President and CEO, Masayoshi Matsumoto
EVP, Fumikiyo Uchioke
Senior Managing Director, Mitsuo Nishida
Executive Officer, Fumiyoshi Kawai
Auditors: KPMG AZSA LLC

LOCATIONS

HQ: Sumitomo Electric Industries, Ltd. (Japan)
Sumitomo Bldg., 4-5-33 Kitahama, Chuo-ku, Osaka 541-0041
Phone: (81) 6 6220 4141
Web: www.sei.co.jp

2018 sales

	% of total
Japan	48
Asia	30
Americas	14
Europe and Others	8
Total	**100**

PRODUCTS/OPERATIONS

2018 sales

	% of total
Automotive	54
Environment and Energy	22
Industrial materials & other	11
Electronics	7
Information & communications	6
Total	**100**

Products

Automotive
Information and Communication System
Electronics / Consumer Electronics
Semiconduc
Energy
Environment
Infrastructure
Industrial
Bankruptcy

Wiring harnesses
Vibration-proof rubber
Automotive hoses
Car electrical equipment
Electronic wire products
Compound semiconductors
Metallic material for electronic parts
Electric-beam irradiation products
Flexible printed circuits
Fluorine resin products
Electric conductors
Power transmission wires/ cables/equipment
Magnet wires
Air cushions for railroad vehicles
Power systems
Equipment such as substation equipment/control systems
Charged beam equipment and processing
Electrical/power supply work and engineering porous metals

COMPETITORS

Alcatel-Lucent	Furukawa Electric
American Superconductor	General Cable
Amphenol	Hitachi Cable
Asia Pacific Wire & Cable	LEONI
Delphi Automotive Systems	Magna International
Fujikura Ltd.	Mitsubishi Electric
	OFS BrightWave
	Southwire
	Valeo

HISTORICAL FINANCIALS

Company Type: Public

Income Statement

FYE: March 31

	REVENUE ($ mil.)	NET INCOME ($ mil.)	NET PROFIT MARGIN	EMPLOYEES
03/20	28,622	669	2.3%	320,975
03/19	28,696	1,066	3.7%	312,930
03/18	29,026	1,133	3.9%	293,269
03/17	25,172	962	3.8%	286,498
03/16	26,119	810	3.1%	279,989
Annual Growth	2.3%	(4.6%)	—	3.5%

2020 Year-End Financials

Debt ratio: 0.1%	No. of shares (mil.): 780
Return on equity: 4.7%	Dividends
Cash ($ mil.): 2,308	Yield: 0.0%
Current ratio: 1.73	Payout: —
Long-term debt ($ mil.): 2,564	Market value ($ mil.): 8,002

	STOCK PRICE ($) FY Close	P/E High/Low		PER SHARE ($) Earnings	Dividends	Book Value
03/20	10.26	0	0	0.86	0.45	17.93
03/19	13.37	0	0	1.37	0.44	17.95
03/18	15.03	0	0	1.44	0.41	18.58
03/17	16.73	0	0	1.23	0.32	16.23
03/16	12.03	0	0	1.02	0.31	15.27
Annual Growth	(3.9%)	—	—	(4.2%)	9.8%	4.1%

Sumitomo Life Insurance Co. (Japan)

Sumitomo Life is a life insurance company. The firm sells individual group life and specialized health policies through more than 85 branch offices and more than 1400 district offices. In addition the company includes quick and simple processing of insurance claims benefits and policyholder loans extension of the grace period on premium payments and interest rate reduction or exemption on policyholder loans. Along with its sales force Sumitomo Life sells its products through a network of financial institutions and affiliates. It also administers pension and employee benefit plans and offers brokerage and consulting. The company has a total of approximately $25 billion policies in force. Sumitomo Life has operations in other Asian and North American countries. Sumitomo Life was established in May 1907 under the name of Hinode Life Insurance Co. Ltd.

Operations

Sumitomo Life's insurance premiums & other generate more than 70% of total sales. The company's investment income accounts for almost 25%. The remaining sales are from other ordinary income.

In terms of the core business profit it decreased by less than five percent to $3.6 billion.

Furthermore in January 2019 the company digitalized the application for new life insurance policies through the Sumisei Lief.

In March 2020 the company introduced "Dementia PLUS" a new rider designed to offer coverage early on and provide financial support for dementia.

The company also launched "Sumisei Family Assist Plus" in March 2020. The service is intended to enhance support for policy maintenance after a policyholder or an insured person progresses dementia or other cognitive issues and it enables family members of the policyholder or insured person to check the policy contents and initiate procedures on behalf of that person.

Geographic Reach

The company is based in Osaka Japan. It has operations in China Vietnam Indonesia and the US. In addition the company invested in Singlife in Singapore in mid-2019.

The company has representative offices in New York London Beijing and Hanoi.

Sales and Marketing

Sumitomo Life's principal selling channels are its sales force of more than 32000 representatives.

The company focused on promoting insurance sales through channels such as "bancassurance" and "insurance outlets". The bancassurance network is highly effective and ranks as one of the industry's largest with over 300 participating banks and financial institutions.

Furthermore in early 2019 the company digitalized the application for new life insurance policies through the Sumisei Lief.

In early 2020 the company introduced "Dementia PLUS" a new rider designed to offer coverage early on and provide financial support for dementia.

In addition the company also launched "Sumisei Family Assist Plus". The service is intended to enhance support for policy maintenance after a policyholder or an insured person progresses dementia or other cognitive issues and it enables family members of the policyholder or insured person to check the policy contents and initiate procedures on behalf of that person.

Financial Performance

Sumitomo Life's revenue decreased by Å 224 million to Å 3.6 trillion in fiscal 2020 (ended March). Insurance premium income fell by Å 158.9 billion that year which primarily drove that decline.

The continuous fall of revenue of the company net income fell by Å 43.1 billion to Å 5.2 billion in 2019.

The company ended fiscal 2020 with Å 584.2 billion in net cash Å 149.1 billion more than it had at the end of fiscal 2019. Operating activities provided Å 849 billion in net cash and financing ac-

tivities provided another Å 98.8 billion while investing activities used Å 798.3 billion.

Strategy

To achieve sustainable growth in addition to the traditional mortality products the company is actively developing growth areas such as nursing care (including work disability) medical insurance and retirement planning which are expected to grow along with the advent of a highly graying society and changes in lifestyle. Moreover focusing on the increase in awareness of health they launched SUMITOMO LIFE Vitality Shared-Value Insurance in July 2018.

Sumitomo Life is marketing products in these growth areas through its sales representatives as well as through its bancassurance network including banks and financial institutions. In addition the company's subsidiary Medicare Life Insurance Co. Ltd. mainly provides affordable medical insurance that offers total support covering cancer medical treatments and others through insurance outlets the Internet and bancassurance. AIARU Small Amount & Short Term Insurance Co. LTD. is contributing to the Sumitomo Life's marketing strategy by leveraging its flexibility as a small-amount and short-term insurance company to launch new products and develop niche markets.

Mergers and Acquisitions

The company acquired AIARU Small Amount & Short Term Insurance Co. LTD. or AIRU as a subsidiary in mid-2019. AIRU offers small-amount and short-term insurances based in Tokyo. The acquisition was aimed at capitalizing on the subsidiary's ability to launch new products and develop niche markets with the flexibility as a small-amount and short-term insurance company.

In addition to mid-2019 transaction Sumimoto Life acquired about 25% of Singapore Life Pte. for $90 million. Singapore Life offers term insurance universal life critical illness and endowment plans based in Singapore. Sumitomo Life aims to utilize the acquired company's digital technology to bring synergies to its own sales in Japan and abroad.

Company Background

Predecessor Hinode Life Insurance was founded in 1907. It changed its name to Sumitomo Life Insurance after it was acquired by Sumitomo Goshi Company in 1925.

The company established its New York representative office in 1972.

EXECUTIVES

President and CEO, Masahiro Hashimoto
Senior Managing Executive Officer, Yukio Noro
Senior Managing Executive Officer, Masaya Honjo
Senior Managing Executive Officer, Hidenori Shinohara
Chairman, Yoshio Sato
Auditors: KPMG AZSA LLC

LOCATIONS

HQ: Sumitomo Life Insurance Co. (Japan)
1-4-35 Shiromi, Chuo-ku, Osaka 540-8512
Phone: (81) 6 6937 1435
Web: www.sumitomolife.co.jp

PRODUCTS/OPERATIONS

2018 Sales

	% of total
Insurance premiums & other	72
Investment income	24
Other ordinary income	4
Total	**100**

COMPETITORS

AXA Life Insurance	Gibraltar Life
American Life	Insurance
Insurance	Meiji Yasuda Life
Asahi Mutual Life	Mitsui Life
Dai-ichi Life	Nippon Life Insurance
Daido Life	Taiyo Life
Fukoku Mutual	

HISTORICAL FINANCIALS

Company Type: Public

Incóme Statement · FYE: March 31

	ASSETS ($ mil.)	NET INCOME ($ mil.)	INCOME AS % OF ASSETS	EMPLOYEES
03/19	341,431	435	0.1%	42,954
03/18	339,368	657	0.2%	42,848
03/17	307,252	501	0.2%	42,835
03/16	283,151	588	0.2%	42,245
03/15	229,128	1,044	0.5%	42,115
Annual Growth	10.5%	(19.6%)	—	0.5%

2019 Year-End Financials

Return on assets: 0.1%
Return on equity: 2.9%
Long-term debt ($ mil.): —
No. of shares (mil.): —
Sales ($ mil): 30,216

Dividends
Yield: —
Payout: —
Market value ($ mil.): —

Sumitomo Mitsui Financial Group Inc Tokyo

Sumitomo Mitsui Financial Group (SMFG) is the holding company for Sumitomo Mitsui Banking which boasts some 440 domestic branches (mostly in the Tokyo and Osaka regions of Japan) and another nearly 40 locations abroad. As one of Japan's largest banks SMFG provides retail corporate and investment banking; asset management; securities trading; and lending. Other units of SMFG include credit card firm Sumitomo Mitsui Card brokerage SMBC Friend Securities management consulting firm Japan Research Institute and Sumitomo Mitsui Finance and Leasing. SMFG also operates the California-based Manufacturers Bank.

Operations

Sumitomo Mitsui Financial Group operates four principal business segments: Wholesale Retail International and Global Markets.

Wholesale provides financing investment management risk hedging and settlement services to large and mid-sized corporate clients in Japan. It consists of the wholesale businesses of SMBC (Sumitomo Mitsui Banking Corporation) SMBC Nikko Securities SMBC Trust Bank and SMFL (Finance and Leasing). It generates around 25% of Sumitomo Mitsui's gross profit.

Retail provides retail banking services such as wealth management settlement services consumer finance foreign currency deposits and more to Japanese consumers and corporations. It primarily consists of the retail banking units of SMBC SMBC Nikko Securities and SMBC Trust Bank as well as three consumer finance companies Sumitomo Mutsui Card Cedyna and SMBC Consumer Finance. Retail generates more than 40% of gross profit.

The International business is active outside of Japan and supports Japanese companies operating overseas foreign companies financial institutions and government agencies and public bodies in various countries. It has a network of some 130 offices in 40 countries and regions. The segment accounts for some 20% of gross profit.

Global Markets offers foreign exchange services derivatives bonds stocks and other financial products. It brings in the remaining 10% of gross profit.

Geographic Reach

About 70% of Sumitomo Mitsui Financial Group's operating income comes from its domestic business in Japan. The rest came from customers in the Europe and Middle East region (13% of operating income) the Asia and Oceania region (less than 10%) and the Americas (less than 10%).

Financial Performance

Note: Growth rates may differ after conversion to US dollars.

Sumitomo Mitsui's revenue has grown steadily in recent years in line with its expanding asset base. In fiscal 2018 (ended March 31) the bank's revenuegrew 14% to Å 3.8 trillion (around $33.8 billion). The growth drivers were net investment income which grew thanks to gains on the disposal of equity instruments and other income which surged on higher income related to the disposal of assets leased.

Net income grew 20% to Å 889.6 billion due to higher operating revenue and a reduction in impairment charges.

Operating cash flow strengthened 30% to Å 11.2 trillion due to changes in loans and advances.

Strategy

Sumitomo Mitsui's strategy is straightforwards and rests on conducting its regularly activities as efficiently and sustainably as possible. It allocates resources to strengthen control of its risk-based assets including reducing low-margin assets while deepening investment in its more profitable and asset-efficient units. The bank is also digitizing its products and back-end systems with a view to enhance customer experience generate new business and improve productivity. Business opportunities include creating new platforms such as a biometric authentication business.

Mergers and Acquisitions

In mid 2017 Sumitomo Mitsui acquired American Railcar Leasing a US railcar leasing company for around $2.8 billion. Sumitomo will invest in the company by enhancing its fleet.

In 2016 the company acquired General Electric's leasing business in Japan adding some ¥500 billion in assets and 1000 new employees to SMFG subsidiary Sumitomo Mitsui Finance and Leasing boosting the subsidiary's assets by more than 10% and making it Japan's second-largest leasing company ahead of Mitsubishi UFJ Lease & Finance.

EXECUTIVES

Director; President Sumitomo Mitsui Banking, Takeshi Kunibe
President, Koichi Miyata
Director, Ken Kubo
Director, Yujiro Ito
Managing Director, Jun Ohta
Managing Director, Yasuyuki Kawasaki
Managing Director, Fumiaki Kurahara
Deputy President Head of Corporate Banking and Head of International Banking Sumitomo Mitsui Banking, Masayuki Oku, age 76
Auditors: KPMG AZSA LLC

LOCATIONS

HQ: Sumitomo Mitsui Financial Group Inc Tokyo
1-2 Marunouchi, 1-chome, Chiyoda-ku, Tokyo 100-0005
Phone: (81) 3 3282 8111
Web: www.smfg.co.jp

PRODUCTS/OPERATIONS

2013 Sales

	% of total
Interest	
Loans & advances	43
Investment securities	2
Other	1
Noninterest	
Fees & commissions	27
investment income	9
Trading profits	4
Other	14
Total	**100**

COMPETITORS

Bank of Yokohama	Norinchukin Bank
Credit Saison	Resona
Mitsubishi UFJ	Shinsei Bank
Financial Group	Sumitomo Mitsui Trust
Mizuho Financial	Holdings

HISTORICAL FINANCIALS

Company Type: Public

Income Statement

FYE: March 31

	ASSETS ($ mil.)	NET INCOME ($ mil.)	INCOME AS % OF ASSETS	EMPLOYEES
03/20	2,139,144	2,017	0.1%	98,300
03/19	1,971,218	5,464	0.3%	99,800
03/18	1,937,662	7,662	0.4%	88,100
03/17	1,927,331	6,330	0.3%	93,200
03/16	1,816,639	8,509	0.5%	90,000
Annual Growth	**4.2%**	**(30.2%)**	**—**	**2.2%**

2020 Year-End Financials

Return on assets: 0.1%
Return on equity: 1.8%
Long-term debt ($ mil.): —
No. of shares ($ mil.): 1,373
Sales ($ mil): 40,557

Dividends
Yield: 7.1%
Payout: 23.3%
Market value ($ mil.): 6,577

	STOCK PRICE ($) FY Close	P/E High/Low		Earnings	PER SHARE ($) Dividends	Book Value
03/20	4.79	0	0	1.47	0.34	79.85
03/19	7.03	0	0	3.91	0.31	81.49
03/18	8.50	0	0	5.43	0.28	80.51
03/17	7.25	0	0	4.62	0.28	74.24
03/16	6.01	0	0	6.22	0.25	70.09
Annual Growth	**(5.5%)**	**—**	**—**	**(30.3%)**	**7.9%**	**3.3%**

Sumitomo Mitsui Trust Holdings Inc

Auditors: KPMG AZSA LLC

LOCATIONS

HQ: Sumitomo Mitsui Trust Holdings Inc
1-4-1 Marunouchi, Chiyoda-ku, Tokyo 100-8233
Phone: (81) 3 6256 6000
Web: www.smth.jp

HISTORICAL FINANCIALS

Company Type: Public

Income Statement

FYE: March 31

	ASSETS ($ mil.)	NET INCOME ($ mil.)	INCOME AS % OF ASSETS	EMPLOYEES
03/20	569,682	1,643	0.3%	23,807
03/19	575,011	1,753	0.3%	23,639
03/18	689,225	1,552	0.2%	24,898
03/17	659,954	1,224	0.2%	24,816
03/16	587,119	1,682	0.3%	24,546
Annual Growth	**(0.8%)**	**(0.6%)**	**—**	**(0.8%)**

2020 Year-End Financials

Return on assets: 0.2%
Return on equity: 6.2%
Long-term debt ($ mil.): —
No. of shares (mil.): 374
Sales ($ mil): 15,512

Dividends
Yield: 4.7%
Payout: 3.1%
Market value ($ mil.): 1,080

	STOCK PRICE ($) FY Close	P/E High/Low		Earnings	PER SHARE ($) Dividends	Book Value
03/20	2.88	0	0	4.38	0.14	68.74
03/19	3.60	0	0	4.62	0.12	70.70
03/18	4.13	0	0	4.07	0.12	69.57
03/17	3.45	0	0	3.20	0.12	64.92
03/16	2.94	0	0	4.37	0.11	62.33
Annual Growth	**(0.5%)**	**—**	**—**	**0.0%**	**7.0%**	**2.5%**

Sun Life Financial Inc

Sun Life Financial offers insurance wealth and asset management products to individuals and business entities in Canada the US and Asia as well as Europe. Sun Life's products include individual and group life and health insurance individual and group annuities group pensions mutual funds and asset management services. The US subsidiaries include Massachusetts Financial Services Company Ryan Labs Asset Management and Prime Advisors. Sun Life's products and services are distributed through direct and independent sales agents and advisors as well as banks and consultants. With almost 126000 advisors Sun Life has about $1.1 trillion assets under management.

Operations

Sun Life Financial operates through five business segment: Sun Life Financial Canada (about 50% of total revenue) Sun Life Financial U.S. (around 20%) Sun Life Financial Asia (some 15%) Sun Life Financial Asset Management (more than 10% of total revenue) and Corporate (less than 5%).

Sun Life Financial's Canada segment (SLF Canada) operates through three business units: Individual Insurance & Wealth Group Retirement Services and Group Benefits. The Individual Insurance & Wealth unit provides insurance and investment products to individuals and families. Group Retirement Services provides pension plans and defined benefit solutions to employers while Group Benefits offers life dental extended health care disability and critical illness and other insurance products to employers.

The Sun Life Financial's U.S. operates through Group Benefits and In-force Management. The Group Benefits unit offers life disability absence management medical stop-loss dental vision and voluntary insurance products. In-force Management provides more than 100000 individual life insurance policies.

Sun Life Financial's Asset Management operates through MFS Investment Management and SLC Management. MFS Investment Management manages assets for institutional and retail investors; it has more than $527 million in assets under management. SLC Management delivers LDI alternative fixed income and real estate products in the US and Canada.

Sun Life Financial's Asia operates through two business units: Insurance and Wealth and International. The Insurance and Wealth unit offers a variety of financial planning products in seven Asian markets. International serves wealthy individuals outside of the US and Canada.

The Corporate segment includes the UK business (a run-off block of life and pension policies) and Corporate Support.

Geographic Reach

Sun Life has operations in a number of markets worldwide including Canada (its home market) the United States the United Kingdom Ireland Hong Kong the Philippines Japan Indonesia India China Australia Singapore Vietnam Malaysia and Bermuda.

Sales and Marketing

Sun Life Financial distributes its products through its own career sales force and through independent brokers sales representatives independent advisors and benefits consultants among others.

Financial Performance

Note: Growth rates may differ after conversion to US Dollars.

Sun Life Financial's revenue increased 47% in 2019 to $39.7 billion compared to 2018 primarily driven by increases in the fair value in FVTPL assets predominantly due to the impact of interest rates as well as equity market movements and increased net premium revenue in Canada Asia and the US. The impacts of foreign exchange translation increased revenue by $422 million.

Net income increased 4% in 2019 to $2.6 billion driven by less unfavorable assumption changes and management actions impacts partially offset by higher fair value adjustments on MFS's share-based payment awards and unfavorable market-related impacts.

Cash and equivalents at the end of the year were $9.5 billion a $143 million higher from the year prior. Operating activities generated $2.5 billion while investing and financing activities used $430 million and $2.4 billion respectively. Sun Life's main cash uses in 2019 were acquisitions dividends paid and redemption of senior debentures and subordinated debt.

Strategy

Sun Life Financial to provide outstanding value to its clients. The company's strategy places the client at the center of everything it does. Sun Life's four pillar approach defines the businesses and markets in which it competes. Currently in its four pillars Sun Life is a leader in insurance and wealth solutions in its Canadian Home Market; a leader in US group benefits; a leader in Global Asset Management; and a leader in Asia through distribution excellence in higher growth markets.

Sun Life's client-centric strategy has five key areas of focus that the company is pursuing across each of its four pillars. These areas of focus define how the company competes in its markets extends its competitive advantages fulfills its purpose and support its ambition to be one of the best insurance and asset management companies in the world.

One of Sun Life's key areas is its clients. The company is focused on building lasting and trusted client relationships by providing quality products and services that deliver on its purpose. The company achieves this by making it easier to do busi-

ness with the company; being more proactive in contracting and engaging with its clients; and delivering consistently superior client service.

Another pillar is Distribution Excellence: Sun Life continues to invest in its distribution capabilities through digital channels and by enabling its advisors agents partners and brokers to deliver great client experiences and focus on meeting client needs.

For its Digital Data & Analytics Sun Life is investing in new capabilities across its businesses to reach its clients more effectively drive efficiencies and explore new business opportunities. Its focus in these areas is to digitize current processes and interactions; be more proactive predictive and personalized with its clients; and build and deploy new digital business models.

For its Financial Discipline Sun Life is focusing on delivering strong earnings growth and disciplined expense management to support the enterprise's medium-term objectives; and create a culture of accountability purpose and passion for long-term client and business value embodied by all employees including a strong focus on efficient use of resources to drive top and bottom line growth.

Lastly for its Talent and Culture Sun Life maintains its focus on attracting retaining and developing the best talent while also continuing to evolve its talent and culture to manage the increasing pace of change. Its talent goals are to continue to attract a disproportionate share of top talent across its geographies wrapped in an empowering culture; build on its high performance culture and support and reward its diverse talented workforce; ensure that its focus on its clients becomes deeply embedded in its unique and inclusive culture; and remain committed to the highest standards of business ethics and good governance.

Mergers and Acquisitions

In 2021 Sun Life Financial acquires 51% majority stake of US- based Crescent Capital Group a global alternative credit investment manager for up to US$338 million (approximately C$450 million). Crescent will form part of SLC Management Sun Life's alternatives asset management business. The acquisition will extend SLC Management's solutions in alternative credit which will benefit existing and prospective clients.

In 2020 Sun Life Financial completed the acquisition of majority stake of UK- based InfraRed a global infrastructure and real estate manager for cash consideration of À 300 million (approximately US$390 million C$515 million). InfraRed advises institutional and pooled fund Clients on approximately US$12 billion (C$17 billion) in assets under management. InfraRed will be part of SLC Management Sun Life's alternatives asset management business. The acquisition will broaden SLC Management's investment solutions for institutional Clients to include infrastructure equity and advance sustainable investment options.

In 2019 Sun Life Financial completed the acquisition of majority stake BentallGreenOak. The acquisition adds organizational depth and a full spectrum of solutions including equity and debt real estate strategies while adding to the capabilities of its alternatives manager SLC Management.

Company Background

Sun Life was founded in 1865. It demutualized in 2000 and the money it raised as a publicly traded company helped finance growth. During the first 10 years of its public status it grew through a steady pace of acquisitions beginning with its buy of Clarica Life in 2002. Clarica's products were later rebranded with the Sun Life name. International acquisitions have included Assurant Employee Benefits (2016) Genworth's US employee benefits group (2007) and insurance and

pension operations in Hong Kong from Commonwealth Bank of Australia (2005).

EXECUTIVES

CEO Sun Life Vietnam, Larry R. Madge
CEO Bentall Kennedy, Gary Whitelaw
Chief Investment Officer Sun Life Financial, Randolph B. (Randy) Brown
President Sun Life Financial Canada, Kevin P. Dougherty, $428,700 total compensation
Chairman and CEO MFS Investment Management, Robert J. (Rob) Manning
EVP and Chief Risk Officer, Colm J. Freyne, $318,598 total compensation
President Sun Life Financial Asia, Claude A. Accum
Chief Investment Officer and President Sun Life Investment Management, Stephen C. Peacher, $113,006 total compensation
President and CEO, Dean A. Connor, $513,100 total compensation
President Sun Life Financial U.S., Daniel R. Fishbein
President Sun Life Investment Management Inc., Carl S. Bang
EVP and CFO, Kevin D. Strain
President and CEO Sun Life Canada (Philippines) Inc., Rizalina G. Mantaring
EVP and CIO, Mark S. Saunders
SVP Enterprise Infrastructure and CTO, Stevan Lewis
Executive Chair Sun Life Financial Quebec, Isabelle Hudon
CEO Sun Life Financial U.K., Katherine Garner
VP and Country Head India Sun Life Financial Asia, Sandeep Asthana
EVP Human Resources, Carrie Blair
EVP and Chief Legal and Public Affairs Officer, Melissa J. Kennedy
CEO Sun Life Malaysia, Ooi Say Teng
President and CEO MFS Investment Management, Michael W. Roberge
CEO MFS Investment Management Canada Limited, Peter Kotsopoulos
SVP and Chief Marketing Officer, Lisa Ritchie
President Director Sun Life Financial Indonesia, Elin Waty
President and CEO Prime Advisors Inc., Don McDonald
President Ryan Labs Asset Management Inc., Sean F. McShea
Chairman, William D. (Bill) Anderson, age 71
Auditors: Deloitte LLP

LOCATIONS

HQ: Sun Life Financial Inc
1 York Street, Toronto, Ontario M5J 0B6
Phone: 416 979-9966   **Fax:** 416 979-3209
Web: www.sunlife.com

PRODUCTS/OPERATIONS

2018 Sales by Segment

	% of total
SLF Canada	56
SLF U.S.	19
SLF Asset Management	15
SLF Asia	9
Corporate	1
Total	**100**

COMPETITORS

AGF Management
AIA Group
Aviva
Canada Life
China Life Insurance
Fairfax Financial Holdings

Great-West Life Assurance
Great-West Lifeco
Industrial Alliance Insurance and Financial Servic
Manulife Financial
MetLife
Prudential
Standard Life Aberdeen
The Hartford

HISTORICAL FINANCIALS
Company Type: Public

Income Statement				FYE: December 31
	ASSETS ($ mil.)	NET INCOME ($ mil.)	INCOME AS % OF ASSETS	EMPLOYEES
12/19	228,232	2,083	0.9%	40,600
12/18	199,610	1,921	1.0%	22,318
12/17	214,666	1,788	0.8%	21,495
12/16	191,620	1,915	1.0%	20,980
12/15	177,731	1,645	0.9%	18,330
Annual Growth	6.5%	6.1%	—	22.0%

2019 Year-End Financials
Return on assets: 0.9%
Return on equity: 11.0%
Long-term debt ($ mil.): —
No. of shares (mil.): 587
Sales ($ mil): 30,471

Dividends
Yield: 3.4%
Payout: 62.1%
Market value ($ mil.): 26,786

	STOCK PRICE ($) FY Close	P/E High/Low		PER SHARE ($) Earnings	Dividends	Book Value
12/19	45.57	11	8	3.38	1.58	31.99
12/18	33.19	10	8	3.04	1.47	30.15
12/17	41.26	12	10	2.78	1.39	30.01
12/16	38.41	10	7	2.99	1.20	27.05
12/15	31.20	9	7	2.56	1.18	25.18
Annual Growth	9.9%	—	—	7.2%	7.7%	6.2%

Sunac China Holdings Ltd

Auditors: PricewaterhouseCoopers

LOCATIONS
HQ: Sunac China Holdings Ltd
10/F, Building C7, Magnetic Plaza, Binshuixi Road, Nankai District, Tianjin 300381
Phone:
Web: www.sunac.com.cn

HISTORICAL FINANCIALS
Company Type: Public

Income Statement				FYE: December 31
	REVENUE ($ mil.)	NET INCOME ($ mil.)	NET PROFIT MARGIN	EMPLOYEES
12/19	24,333	3,740	15.4%	50,834
12/18	18,136	2,408	13.3%	38,040
12/17	10,122	1,690	16.7%	19,271
12/16	5,089	356	7.0%	13,294
12/15	3,543	507	14.3%	8,271
Annual Growth	61.9%	64.7%	—	57.5%

2019 Year-End Financials
Debt ratio: 4.8%
Return on equity: 35.1%
Cash ($ mil.): 11,201
Current ratio: 1.17
Long-term debt ($ mil.): 26,808

No. of shares (mil.): —
Dividends
Yield: —
Payout: 20.8%
Market value ($ mil.): —

Suncor Energy Inc

Suncor Energy takes a shine to the cold of Canada. That country's largest energy firm explores for processes and markets oil and natural gas. In 2015 it reported gross proved and probable reserves of 7.6 billion barrels of oil equivalent. Suncor Energy was first company to produce commercial crude oil from Canada's Athabasca oil sands. Its Sunoco unit refines crude oil and processes and distributes fuels petrochemicals and heating oils invests in renewable energy and operates a network of gas stations. In 2016 Suncor Energy acquired rival Canadian Oil Sands. Already a stakeholder that year it also agreed to buy a majority stake in Canada's primary oil sands project Syncrude.

Operations
Suncor Energy is one of Canada's largest oil sands producers. It oil sands assets include a 36% interest in the Joslyn North mine 41% in the Fort Hills mine and 51% of the Voyageur upgrader project as well as a 12% stake in the Syncrude oil sands mining venture.

The company also has conventional natural gas assets as well as international and offshore oil exploration and production holdings. In addition to its production refining and marketing operations across Canada (and in Colorado) the company has exploration assets in Libya Norway Syria and the UK.

The company has four refineries (in Alberta Ontario Quebec and Colorado — 460000 barrels of combined capacity per day) and a network of 1460 Petro-Canada retail gas stations.

Its Renewable Energy interests include seven wind facilities across Canada including Adelaide which is the most recent addition to the portfolio and the St. Clair ethanol plant in Ontario. An eighth wind farm Cedar Point is planned to commence commercial operations later in 2015.

Suncor's Energy Trading activities primarily involve the marketing supply and trading of crude oil natural gas power and byproducts and the use of midstream infrastructure and financial derivatives to optimize related trading strategies.

Geographic Reach
The company has operations in Canada Germany Libya the Netherlands Norway Syria the UK and the US. In 2012 Canada accounted for 79% of Suncor Energy's revenues.

Sales and Marketing
The company's primary markets for synthetic oil and bitumen production from Suncor's Oil Sands segment which is sold to and subsequently marketed by Suncor's Energy Trading business include refining operations in Alberta Ontario the US Midwest and the U.S. Rocky Mountain regions and markets in the US Gulf Coast. Diesel production from upgrading operations is sold primarily in Western Canada marketed by Suncor's Refining and Marketing business.

Oil and gas production from East Coast Canada the North Sea and from North America Onshore is either marketed by the company's Energy Trading business acting as a marketing agent or sold to its Energy Trading business which then markets the products to customers under direct sales arrangements.

Suncor's retail service station network operates nationally in Canada primarily under the Petro-Canada brand. This network consists of 1465 outlets across Canada excluding Pioneer retail locations. In addition refined products are marketed through independent dealers and joint arrangements. Suncor's Canadian retail network had annual sales of gasoline motor fuels averaging approximately 4.8 million liters per site in 2014 and holds a 17.3% share (2013 - 17.7%) of the national retail urban market.

Financial Performance
In 2014 the company's revenue increased by 1%due to increase revenue from the oil sands business. Oil Sands operations increased production by 8% in 2014 compared to 2013 driven primarily by increased Firebag production.

Suncor's net income decreased by 31% in 2014 due to higher operating expenses as a result of higher depreciation and exploration costs.

The company's operating cash inflow decreased by 12% in 2014 primarily due to a decline in net income and a change in working capital items.

Strategy
Oil sands which hold deposits of heavy bitumen make up nearly a third of Canada's oil production and Suncor's long term business focus is developing synthetic oil from its oil sands holdings in Alberta. Suncor plans to produce 1 million barrels per day of oil equivalent from its oil sands holdings by 2020.

To raise cash in 2017 Suncor sold its Petro-Canada Lubricants business to HollyFrontier for about C$1.1 billion.

In 2014 Suncor signed a farm-in agreement with Shell Canada to acquire a 20% interest in a deepwater exploration opportunity in the Shelburne Basin offshore Nova Scotia. In December 2014 Suncor acquired a 30% interest in an exploration licence in the Flemish Pass off the coast of Newfoundland and Labrador and a 50% interest in another exploration licence in the Carson Basin near the Flemish Pass.

On the product shipment front that year the rail offloading facilities at Tracy Quebec were used to move crude to new and existing markets. Suncor also started transporting heavy crude on TransCanada's Gulf Coast Pipeline which provided increased access to global-based pricing.

In 2014 the Libya National Oil Company declared force majeure on oil exports from two terminals resulting in the shut in of substantially all of the Suncor's production in that country. Consequently Suncor also declared force majeure for all exploration commitments in Libya.

In 2014 the company agreed to sell the assets of Pioneer Energy to Parkland Fuel Corporation for $378 million.

It also agreed to sell its Wilson Creek assets located near Rimbey Alberta to Tamarack Acquisition Corp for $168.5 million.

Mergers and Acquisitions
In 2015 the company agreed to purchase an additional 10% working interest in the Fort Hills oil sands project from Total E&P Canada Ltd. for $310 million. As part of the transaction Suncor acquires a further proportionate interest in Fort Hills related logistics including pipelines storage terminals and third-party pipeline capacity agreements. The acquisition of the additional working interest also presents an opportunity for Suncor to lower its capital cost per barrel and enhance its projected return on the Fort Hills project

Company Background
To focus on its growth markets and to pay down debt in 2013 the company agreed to sell its conventional natural gas business in Western Canada

to a Centrica and Qatar Petroleum partnership for $1 billion.

To further develop its oil sands assets in 2010 the company formed a strategic alliance with TOTAL. As part of the deal France-based TOTAL paid Suncor Energy about $1.7 billion to acquire 19% of Suncor Energy's 60% interest in the Fort Hills mining project and a 49% stake in the Voyageur Upgrader project near Fort McMurray. Suncor Energy acquired about 37% of TOTAL's stake in the Joslyn project.

Boosting its profile as an integrated energy company in 2009 the company acquired Petro-Canada in a $15 billion deal. The acquisition created an energy behemoth with extensive holdings in oil sands solid conventional exploration and production assets and a major refining and retailing network. Following the Petro-Canada deal the company divested about $1.5 billion of non-core assets in Western Canada the US Trinidad and Tobago and the North Sea. In 2010 Suncor Energy sold its North Sea exploration assets (of Petro Canada Netherlands) to Dana Petroleum for $393 million. Later that year it sold a pair of natural gas properties in Alberta to a subsidiary of Abu Dhabi National Energy Company for $285 million. It also sold its Wildcat Hills assets which produce some 80 million cu. ft. of natural gas per day to Direct Energy for about $360 million.

EXECUTIVES

President, Mark Little
Executive Vice President, Eric Axford
Executive Vice President, Alister Cowan
Senior Vice President Human Resources, Paul Gardner
Executive Vice President, Mike MacSween
Executive Vice President, Steve Reynish
Executive Vice President, Kris Smith
Senior Vice President, Arlene Strom
Chairman of the Board, Michael Wilson
Auditors: KPMG LLP

LOCATIONS

HQ: Suncor Energy Inc
150 - 6th Avenue S.W., Calgary, Alberta T2P 3E3
Phone: 403 296-8000 **Fax:** 403 296-3030
Web: www.suncor.com

COMPETITORS

Anadarko Petroleum	Husky Energy
BP NGL	Imperial Oil
Canadian Natural	Murphy Oil
Devon Energy	Nordex
Dominion Energy	Repsol Oil & Gas
Encana	Shell Canada

HISTORICAL FINANCIALS

Company Type: Public

Income Statement   FYE: December 31

	REVENUE ($ mil.)	NET INCOME ($ mil.)	NET PROFIT MARGIN	EMPLOYEES
12/19	39,480	2,935	7.4%	12,889
12/18	39,477	3,334	8.4%	12,480
12/17	32,581	4,514	13.9%	12,381
12/16	27,307	450	1.7%	12,837
12/15	30,054	(2,020)	—	13,190
Annual Growth	7.1%	—		(0.6%)

2019 Year-End Financials

Debt ratio: 23.3%	No. of shares (mil.): 1,531
Return on equity: 6.7%	Dividends
Cash ($ mil.): 1,984	Yield: 3.8%
Current ratio: 0.94	Payout: 117.6%
Long-term debt ($ mil.): 18,354	Market value ($ mil.): 50,245

	STOCK PRICE ($) FY Close	P/E High/Low	Earnings	Dividends	Book Value
12/19	32.80	19 15	1.88	1.26	26.06
12/18	27.97	21 13	2.05	1.10	28.12
12/17	36.72	14 11	2.71	1.30	28.00
12/16	32.69	119 70	0.28	1.17	27.10
12/15	25.80	— —	(1.40)	0.88	27.34
Annual Growth	6.2%	— —	—	9.3%	(1.2%)

Suncorp Group Ltd.

EXECUTIVES

Managing Director and Group CEO, Michael A. Cameron
CEO Suncorp Bank, John Nesbitt
Chief Risk Officer, Clayton Herbert
CFO, Steve Johnston
CEO Commercial Insurance, Anthony Day
CEO Personal Insurance, Gary Dransfield
CEO Suncorp Business Services, Matt Pancino
Acting CEO Suncorp Life, Jeremy Robson
CEO Vero New Zealand, Paul Smeaton
Chairman, Zygmunt Switkowski
Auditors: KPMG

LOCATIONS

HQ: Suncorp Group Ltd.
Level 28, Brisbane Square, 266 George Street, Brisbane, Queensland 4000
Phone: (61) 7 3362 1222 **Fax:** (61) 7 3135 2940
Web: www.suncorpgroup.com.au

PRODUCTS/OPERATIONS

2013 Sales

	% of total
General Insurance	
Personal	35
Commercial	23
Banking	19
Life and Wealth Management	13
New Zealand General Insurance	10
Total	**100**

Selected Subsidiaries

Asteron Group Ltd. (life insurance)
GIO General Ltd (general insurance products)
Suncorp Life & Superannuation Limited life (insurance products)
Suncorp Metway Insurance Ltd (general insurance products)
Suncorp Metway Investment Management Limited (investment schemes and provides investment management services)
Vero Insurance Ltd. (New Zealand general insurance)

COMPETITORS

AMP Limited	Insurance Australia
AXA Asia Pacific	Macquarie Group
Australia and New Zealand Banking	National Australia Bank
Commonwealth Bank of Australia	Westpac Banking

HISTORICAL FINANCIALS

Company Type: Public

Income Statement   FYE: June 30

	ASSETS ($ mil.)	NET INCOME ($ mil.)	INCOME AS % OF ASSETS	EMPLOYEES
06/20	65,611	625	1.0%	13,500
06/19	67,425	122	0.2%	0
06/18	73,346	781	1.1%	0
06/17	74,613	825	1.1%	0
06/16	71,238	772	1.1%	0
Annual Growth	(2.0%)	(5.1%)		

2020 Year-End Financials

Return on assets: 0.9%	Dividends
Return on equity: 7.0%	Yield: 0.0%
Long-term debt ($ mil.): —	Payout: 30.8%
No. of shares (mil.): 1,279	Market value ($ mil.): 8,215
Sales ($ mil): 10,121	

	STOCK PRICE ($) FY Close	P/E High/Low	Earnings	Dividends	Book Value
06/20	6.42	13 7	0.47	0.14	6.83
06/19	9.51	81 61	0.09	0.55	7.08
06/18	10.91	13 11	0.59	0.60	7.97
06/17	11.29	14 11	0.63	0.00	8.19
06/16	8.92	13 10	0.59	0.58	7.84
Annual Growth (3.4%)	(7.9%)	— —	(5.9%)	(29.5%)	

Suning.com Co Ltd

EXECUTIVES

Legal Representative, Yang Bo
Auditors: PricewaterhouseCoopers

LOCATIONS

HQ: Suning.com Co Ltd
No. 68, Huaihai Road, Nanjing, Jiangsu Province 210005
Phone: (86) 25 84418888 **Fax:** (86) 25 84467008
Web: www.cnsuning.com

HISTORICAL FINANCIALS

Company Type: Public

Income Statement   FYE: December 31

	REVENUE ($ mil.)	NET INCOME ($ mil.)	NET PROFIT MARGIN	EMPLOYEES
12/19	38,692	1,414	3.7%	0
12/18	35,613	1,937	5.4%	0
12/17	28,878	647	2.2%	0
12/16	21,397	101	0.5%	0
12/15	20,871	134	0.6%	0
Annual Growth	16.7%	80.1%		

2019 Year-End Financials

Debt ratio: 2.1%	No. of shares (mil.): —
Return on equity: 11.6%	Dividends
Cash ($ mil.): 4,872	Yield: —
Current ratio: 1.00	Payout: —
Long-term debt ($ mil.): 2,329	Market value ($ mil.): —

Surgutneftegas PJSC

Based in the Siberian provincial city of Surgut Surgutneftegas is one of Russia's top-five integrated oil and natural gas companies accounting for more than 10% of the country's oil production. Surgutneftegas assets include pipelines refineries oil storage tanks and about 300 gas stations. The company also constructs power transmission lines and builds roads as part of its business operations. Operations are concentrated on the Russian regions of Western Siberia Eastern Siberia and Timano-Pechora. More than 70% of the company's sales comes from the domestic Russian market.

Operations

Surgutneftegas reports four core operations: Hydrocarbon Exploration and Production Manufacturing and Marketing of Oil Products Production of Petrochemicals and Gas Processing and Power Generation. The company reports its revenue under two broad segments: Exploration and Production accounts for almost 60% of total sales with the rest listed under Refining and Sale activities.

Its leading segment Exploration and Production engages in prospecting exploration and operation of oil and gas fields. Manufacturing and Marketing manages crude oil refining production of oil products and wholesale and retail trade in oil products. Hydrocarbons are converted into raw materials for chemicals under the Production of Petrochemicals segment. Lastly the segment Gas Processing and Power Generation includes processing of petroleum gas sale of commercial gas and liquid hydrocarbons and construction and operation of gas turbine power plants.

Geographic Reach

Surgutneftegas has substantial assets in three of the largest Russian oil and gas provinces? Western Siberia Eastern Siberia and Timano-Pechora. The key areas of hydrocarbon production are Khanty-Manyisky Yamalo-Nenetsky Tyumenskaya Oblast in Western Siberia and the Republic of Sakha in Eastern Siberia. Refining facilities are located in two regions? the oil refinery in the city of Kirishi Leningradskaya Oblast and the gas processing plant in Surgutsky District.

The company's oil products are sold in both wholesale and retail outlets in Saint Petersburg Leningrandskaya Tverskaya Novgorodskaya Pskovskaya and Kaliningradskaya Oblasts. Some 30% of the company's sales comes from outside its Russian domestic market.

Sales and Marketing

Surgutneftegas is accreted at two of the biggest Russian exchange platforms: Saint-Petersburg International Mercantile Exchange and Exchange Saint-Petersburg. Wholesale contracts are often long-term. In addition the company has about 300 gas stations across Russia offering retail products.

Financial Performance

Note: Growth rates may differ after conversion to US Dollars.

Revenue for Surgutneftegas in 2017 improved some 15% to RUB 1.17 trillion climbing from RUB 1.02 trillion a year earlier.

In the 2015-17 period the company's operating profit has remained stable despite low oil prices and restricted production requirements by the OPEC. Net income jumped from a loss of RUB 62 billion posted in 2016 to a profit of RUB 194 billion a year later. The improved result was almost entirely due to a RUB 320 million reduction in net exchange rate differences for 2017.

The company's cash and cash equivalents surged by RUB 110 billion ending 2017 with $217 billion on hand. Cash from operations generated $356 billion while cash from investing used $290 billion ($160 billion on CAPEX). Financing activities saw a positive cash inflow of $43 million.

Strategy

As one of Russia's top five oil companies Surgutneftegas aims to maintain its upstream portfolio through new property leasing expand its midstream production output and stimulate growth that's led by R&D.

To replenish its production resource base Surgutneftegas secures new licenses for exploration or geological studies especially in the Western and Eastern Siberia. But a declining trend in the production rate of the company's mature oil fields in Western Siberia is a concern for the company.

The company also invests heavily on its refineries especially the KINEF facility. It completed the construction of a large high-octane gasoline plant there. These growth projects allow Surgutneftegas to remain a major producer of oil products in Saint Petersburg and neighboring states.

Organically the company grows through in-house research spending (96 projects carried out in 2017 in fields like oil recovery and field development) and cost reduction programs (RUB 5.3 billion in 2017).

Despite stringent growth efforts adverse external factors negatively affected the company. In 2017 it produced 60.5 mt of refined products (61.8 mt in 2016) due to OPEC constraints. Surgutneftgas like all Russian oil companies is also heavily dependent on government tax breaks for posting profits?more than half of the company's net income in 2017 came from it?that makes it vulnerable to changes in politics.

Company Background

Surgutneftegas traces its roots back to the 1970s when petroleum production associations were established in Surgut Nizhnevartovsk and Nefteyugansk. A 1992 reorganization led to the merger of Surgutneftegas with Kirishi oil refinery and petroleum product suppliers in Northwest Russia. The very next year it became a joint stock company as part of the privatization effort of Russia's oil industry.

The company takes pride in transforming some of the remotest parts of Russia into profitable oil and gas fields.

EXECUTIVES

General Director, Vladimir L. Bogdanov, age 69
Head Oil and Gas Production Division Fyodorovskneft and Director, Sergei A. Ananyev, age 60
Head Oil and Gas Production Division Surgutneft and Director, Alexander N. Bulanov, age 60
Head Oil and Gas Production Division Bystrinskneft, Igor N. Gorbunov, age 52
Deputy Director General Capital Construction, Alexander F. Resyapov, age 67
Financial Division Head, Taisiya Klinovskaya, age 74
Chairman, Vladimir P. Erokhin
Auditors: Crowe Expertiza LLC

LOCATIONS

HQ: Surgutneftegas PJSC
ul.Grigoriya Kukuyevitskogo 1, bld. 1, Surgut, Khanty-Mansiysky Autonomous Okrug-Yugra, Tyumenskaya Oblast 628415
Phone: (7) 3462 42 60 28
Web: www.surgutneftegas.ru

2017 Sales

	% of total
Domestic market	72
Export	28
Total	**100**

PRODUCTS/OPERATIONS

2017 Sales

	% of total
Exploration and Production	61
Refining and Sale	39
Total	**100**

COMPETITORS

Bashneft JOSC	LUKOIL
Gazprom	Rosneft
Gazprom Neft	Tatneft

HISTORICAL FINANCIALS

Company Type: Public

Income Statement				FYE: December 31
	REVENUE ($ mil.)	NET INCOME ($ mil.)	NET PROFIT MARGIN	EMPLOYEES
12/19	66,704	4,508	6.8%	0
12/18	66,071	36,108	54.7%	115,000
12/17	49,895	8,265	16.6%	116,000
12/16	43,348	(2,636)	—	114,275
12/15	42,574	32,338	76.0%	118,000
Annual Growth	11.9%	(38.9%)	—	—

2019 Year-End Financials

Debt ratio: —	No. of shares (mil.): —
Return on equity: 2.3%	Dividends
Cash ($ mil.): 51,668	Yield: 18.7%
Current ratio: 3.68	Payout: 990.8%
Long-term debt ($ mil.): —	Market value ($ mil.): —

	STOCK PRICE ($) FY Close	P/E High/Low		PER SHARE ($) Earnings	Dividends	Book Value
12/19	6.21	2	2	0.12	1.16	5.29
12/18	5.49	0	0	0.94	0.21	5.36
12/17	4.91	1	1	0.22	0.10	4.29
12/16	5.13	—	—	(0.07)	1.06	4.09
12/15	5.95	0	0	0.84	1.28	4.26
Annual Growth	1.1%	—	—	(38.9%)	(2.4%)	5.6%

Suruga Bank, Ltd.

EXECUTIVES

President, KOSUKE SAGA
Executive Vice President, KOSUKE KATO
Managing Director, TOMOAKI TSUTSUMI
Auditors: Ernst & Young ShinNihon LLC

LOCATIONS

HQ: Suruga Bank, Ltd.
23 Toriyoko-cho, Numazu, Shizuoka 410-8689
Phone: (81) 55 962 0080
Web: www.surugabank.co.jp

COMPETITORS

Aozora Bank	Norinchukin Bank
Bank of Kyoto	Shimizu Bank
Bank of Yokohama	Shinsei Bank
Mitsubishi UFJ Financial Group	Shizuoka Bank

HISTORICAL FINANCIALS

Company Type: Public

Income Statement

FYE: March 31

	ASSETS ($ mil.)	NET INCOME ($ mil.)	INCOME AS % OF ASSETS	EMPLOYEES
03/20	32,073	233	0.7%	2,514
03/19	30,957	(877)	—	2,645
03/18	42,016	65	0.2%	2,661
03/17	39,995	381	1.0%	2,743
03/16	39,094	326	0.8%	2,771
Annual Growth	(4.8%)	(8.1%)	—	(2.4%)

2020 Year-End Financials

Return on assets: 0.7%
Return on equity: 10.1%
Long-term debt ($ mil.): —
No. of shares (mil.): 231
Sales ($ mil): 1,087

Dividends
Yield: —
Payout: —
Market value ($ mil.): —

Suzano SA

LOCATIONS

HQ: Suzano SA
Avenida Professor Magalhaes Neto 1752, 10th Floor,
Rooms 1010 and 1011, Salvador 41810-012
Phone: (55) 11 3503 9000
Web: www.suzano.com.br

PRODUCTS/OPERATIONS

Selected Products

Coated woodfree printing and writing paper
Cut-size printing and writing paper
Eucalyptus pulp (bleached eucalyptus kraft pulp)
Paperboard
Uncoated woodfree (100% eucalyptus fiber) printing and
writing paper

COMPETITORS

Bio Pappel	Fibria
CMPC	International Paper
Cartiere Burgo	Klabin
Clearwater Paper	Powerflute

HISTORICAL FINANCIALS

Company Type: Public

Income Statement

FYE: December 31

	REVENUE ($ mil.)	NET INCOME ($ mil.)	NET PROFIT MARGIN	EMPLOYEES
12/19	15,590	(1,688)	—	14,534
12/18	8,057	191	2.4%	9,385
12/17	6,305	1,083	17.2%	7,830
12/16	5,922	1,014	17.1%	7,483
12/15	6,127	(554)	—	7,605
Annual Growth	26.3%	—	—	17.6%

2019 Year-End Financials

Debt ratio: 38.9%
Return on equity: (-18.7%)
Cash ($ mil.): 1,947
Current ratio: 1.65
Long-term debt ($ mil.): 34,435

No. of shares (mil.): 1,349
Dividends
Yield: 1.0%
Payout: —
Market value ($ mil.): 13,276

STOCK PRICE ($) / P/E / PER SHARE ($)

	FY Close	High/Low	Earnings	Dividends	Book Value
12/19	9.84	— —	(1.25)	0.10	7.98
12/18	19.80	94 41	0.18	0.18	6.58
12/17	12.00	8 5	0.99	0.14	6.38
12/16	8.58	6 4	0.87	0.07	16.69
12/15	9.30	— —	(0.48)	0.07	15.12
Annual Growth (14.8%)	1.4%		—	10.8%	

Suzuken Co Ltd

Auditors: Deloitte Touche Tohmatsu LLC

LOCATIONS

HQ: Suzuken Co Ltd
8 Higashi-Katahamachi, Higashi-ku, Nagoya, Aichi
461-8701
Phone: (81) 52 961 2331
Web: www.suzuken.co.jp

HISTORICAL FINANCIALS

Company Type: Public

Income Statement

FYE: March 31

	REVENUE ($ mil.)	NET INCOME ($ mil.)	NET PROFIT MARGIN	EMPLOYEES
03/20	20,391	259	1.3%	18,998
03/19	19,254	272	1.4%	19,122
03/18	20,002	177	0.9%	19,459
03/17	19,024	190	1.0%	20,163
03/16	19,842	257	1.3%	19,833
Annual Growth	0.7%	0.2%	—	(1.1%)

2020 Year-End Financials

Debt ratio: —
Return on equity: 6.9%
Cash ($ mil.): 1,543
Current ratio: 1.28
Long-term debt ($ mil.): —

No. of shares (mil.): 89
Dividends
Yield: —
Payout: —
Market value ($ mil.): —

Suzuki Motor Corp. (Japan)

Suzuki Motor Corporation is one of the leading Japanese carmakers and a global motorcycle manufacturer. Suzuki's passenger car models include the Alto Grand Vitara Swift and SX4. Its motorcycle products include cruiser motocross off-road scooter street and touring models as well as ATVs. Suzuki Motor's non-vehicle products include outboard motors for boats and motorized wheelchairs. It builds its lineup on its own and through numerous subsidiaries and joint ventures overseas. Japan accounts for nearly 35% of sales. Suzuki entered the US car market in 1985 with the Samurai the country's first compact SUV.

Operations

Suzuki divides its operations into three reportable segments: automobile (some 90%) motorcycles (more than 5%) and marine and other.

The group's automobile segment's main products are mini vehicles sub-compact vehicles standard-sized vehicles while its motorcycle products are all-terrain vehicles and motorcycles. The marine and other segment accounts for the remaining revenue and includes outboard motors and houses.

Geographic Reach

Suzuki's products are manufactured in more than 25 companies in about 20 overseas countries and serves more than 210 countries. Outside of Japan (around 35% of its total sales; headquarters) Asian consumers including India represent nearly 45% of its sales whereas North American and European purchases combined account for approximately 15%. Suzuki subsidiary Maruti Suzuki India is one of India's largest passenger car company.

Suzuki is headquartered in Hamamatsu-shi Japan.

Sales and Marketing

Suzuki distributes its products around the world through its dealers distributors and other partners. Some of the group's distributors are Derco Peru Apex Car Rental Uttara Motors Mirkat Lusolanda and Mayfairs W'Sale.

Financial Performance

The group's net sales at the end of 2019 decreased by 10% to 3.5 trillion yen. Sales in Asia decreased by 2% owing to the impact of COVID-19 despite an increase in India

Net income for the year 2019 decreased by 25% to 1342 billion yen compared to the prior year with 178.8 billion yen.

Cash held by the group at the end of 2019 decreased by 127.7 billion yen to 473.1 million. Cash provided by operations was 383.4 billion while cash used for investing and financing activities were 250.8 billion and 256.1 billion yen. Main uses for cash were purchase of short-term investment securities and purchase of convertible bond with stock acquisition rights.

Strategy

The group has established the New Mid-Term Management Plan SUZUKI NEXT 100 - Strengthening of management base toward the 100th anniversary of foundation and the next 100 years a five-year plan from 2015.

The group will be celebrating its 100th anniversary of foundation in 2020. In order for the group to continuously grow for the next 100 years the group will put efforts into strengthening of management base by positioning the next five years as the period to stabilize the foundation of management. The group will tackle as Team Suzuki to globally develop manufacturing base and overhaul working procedure.

EXECUTIVES

EVP, Toshihiro Suzuki
Senior Technical Executive, Osamu Honda
Executive General Manager Global Business Administration and Planning, Takashi Iwatsuki
Executive Genaral Manager Manufacturing Engineering, Hiroaki Matsuura
Executive General Manager Corporate Planning, Masahiko Nagao
Chairman and CEO, Osamu Suzuki
Vice Chairman, Yasuhito Harayama
Auditors: Seimei Audit Corp.

LOCATIONS

HQ: Suzuki Motor Corp. (Japan)
300 Takatsuka-cho, Minami-ku, Hamamatsu, Shizuoka 432-8611
Phone: (81) 53 440 2030
Web: www.suzuki.co.jp

2016 Sales

	% of total
Asia	44
Japan	41
Europe	10
Other regions	5
Total	**100**

PRODUCTS/OPERATIONS

2016 Salles

	% of total
Automobiles	91
Motorcycles	7
Marine and power products	2
Total	**100**

List of Items

Automobiles
 Alto/CELERIO
 APV
 Grand Vitara SUV
 Jimny
 Kizashi sport sedan
 Splash
 Swift
 SX4 Crossover Sport SportBack
Motorcycles/ATV
 Cruiser
 Dual purpose
 Motocross
 Offroad
 Scooter
 Sport Enduro Tourer
 Street
 Supersport
Outboard motors
 Carburetor
 Electronic
 Kerosene O

COMPETITORS

BMW	Mahindra
Bajaj Auto	Mazda
Brunswick Corp.	Nissan
Daimler	Piaggio & Co.
Ducati	Polaris Industries
FCA US	Renault
Ford Motor	Tata Motors
General Motors	Toyota
Harley-Davidson	Triumph Motorcycles
Honda	Volkswagen
Hyundai Motor	Yamaha Motor
Kawasaki Heavy	
Industries	

HISTORICAL FINANCIALS

Company Type: Public

Income Statement   FYE: March 31

	REVENUE ($ mil.)	NET INCOME ($ mil.)	NET PROFIT MARGIN	EMPLOYEES
03/20	32,136	1,236	3.8%	102,572
03/19	34,958	1,614	4.6%	101,523
03/18	35,383	2,031	5.7%	93,065
03/17	28,348	1,430	5.0%	86,969
03/16	28,323	1,038	3.7%	81,895
Annual Growth	**3.2%**	**4.5%**	**—**	**5.8%**

2020 Year-End Financials

Debt ratio: 0.1%	No. of shares (mil.): 485
Return on equity: 9.2%	Dividends
Cash ($ mil.): 4,475	Yield: 2.8%
Current ratio: 1.26	Payout: 103.4%
Long-term debt ($ mil.): 1,894	Market value ($ mil.): 45,993

	STOCK PRICE ($) FY Close	P/E High/Low		PER SHARE ($) Earnings	Dividends	Book Value
03/20	94.75	1	0	2.64	2.73	28.23
03/19	177.25	1	0	3.57	2.95	27.25
03/18	217.61	1	0	4.46	2.15	27.66
03/17	168.75	0	0	3.24	1.24	20.40
03/16	103.42	1	0	2.09	0.53	19.34
Annual Growth	**(2.2%)**	**—**	**—**	**6.0%**	**50.9%**	**9.9%**

Svenska Handelsbanken

Svenska Handelsbanken is Swedish for universal banking. The group provides corporate and individual clients with deposit products loans credit cards and other banking services. Subsidiaries operate in several related areas including life insurance mortgages pensions fund management and Internet banking. The bank boasts more than 830 branches in 25 countries with most in Sweden the UK Denmark Finland Norway and the Netherlands. Subsidiaries include corporate financing unit Handelsbanken Finans Handelsbanken Asset Management and Handelsbanken Liv. Founded in 1871 the bank's assets now exceed $360 billion.

Operations

The bank operates in seven business segments mostly based on geography. These include branch operation segments in Sweden the UK Denmark Finland Norway and the Netherlands as well as a Capital Markets segment.

The bank made more than 80% of its total revenue in 2014 from interest income mostly from corporate loans and mortgage loans but also from consumer loans. The majority of the remaining revenues came from fee and commission income from its investment banking and other corporate finance services with a small portion (3% of revenues) coming from its insurance and pensions operations.

Geographic Reach

Svenska Handelsbanken generates more than 60% of its revenue in Sweden while its operations in Norway and the UK each bring in 10% of total revenue. The banks other top markets include Denmark Finland and the Netherlands. It also has a presence in countries including Austria China Hong Kong Russia and the US.

Financial Performance

The bank's net revenues and profits have been on the rise in recent years thanks to a combination of low borrowing rates on deposits growing investment banking and loan business from aggressive branch expansion rising investment gains and strong controls on staffing costs.

Svenska's revenue dipped by 5% to SK$63.5 billion ($8.14 billion) in 2014 despite higher loan volumes mostly as interest margins on loans and securities shrank amidst the low-interest environment. Despite lower revenues the bank's net income rose by 6% to SK$15 billion ($1.9 billion) thanks to a decline in interest expenses on deposits and a slower rise in staff costs.

The bank's operating cash fell by more than 50% to SK$52.8 billion ($6.76 billion) despite higher earnings in 2014 mostly as it used more cash toward loans to the public and other credit institutions.

Strategy

With its focus on being as local to its customer as possible Svenska Handelsbanken continues to grow its digital banking and its physical branch network in new markets around the world. During 2014 the bank opened 24 new branches across several countries including 17 in the UK two in each Norway and the Netherlands and one branch in each of Denmark and Finland.

HISTORY

Svenska Handelsbanken (roughly translated as The Swedish Commercial Bank) was founded as Stockholms Handelsbank in 1871 by former directors of Stockholms Enskilda Bank who lost an internal power struggle. Industrialization in the latter stages of the 19th century saw Stockholms Handelsbank expand nationwide with the bank pursuing an aggressive lending policy. Larger companies required larger financing resulting in smaller local banks running into trouble and forcing them to merge with bigger ones. Through a series of mergers of this kind Stockholms Handelsbank exploded in size and branches increased from seven (all Stockholm-based) to 250 nationwide by 1919. To reflect this growth the company changed its name to Svenska Handelsbanken the same year.

Sweden remained neutral during WWI allowing business to prosper but the depression hit hard. The bank had to write off millions in bad loans and additions to its reserves. During the 1930s Handelsbanken regained stability largely thanks to its geographical diversity; operations in areas with high economic activity made up for struggling regions.

Sweden once again remained neutral during WWII but political uncertainty kept deposits high and it became difficult to maintain profitable loan volumes. In the 1940s Svenska Handelsbanken divested many of its industrial holdings and began to rededicate itself to small- and medium-scale lending.

Through a string of purchases in the 1950s and 1960s the bank became the largest bank in Scandinavia and began looking to expand internationally. Joint ventures and acquisitions saw the company move into other parts of Europe and the US in the 1970s. Nordic American Banking a US subsidiary was set up to handle import and export financing for North and South American clients doing business with Scandinavian countries. The 1980s saw the company establish a merchant-banking subsidiary in London and enter the Asian market forming Svenska Handelsbanken Asia (based in Singapore).

The bank remained acquisitive during the first half of the 1990s including a purchase of life insurance company RKA (later renamed Handelsbanken Liv) and parts of the Finnish Skopbank. In 1996 Handelsbanken acquired Swedish mortgage company Stadshypotek.

During the latter half of the 1990s it ventured into e-business and increased its presence in the Nordic countries and the UK. In 1999 the company acquired the Norwegian Bergensbanken after having been beaten by MeritaNordbanken in the chase for Christiania Bank (which was Norway's second-largest at the time). The next year Handelsbanken acquired Spartacus a Danish consumer finance company. In 2001 it made another Danish purchase Midtbank making it one of Denmark's largest bankers. That year it also acquired Swedish life insurance company SPP.

In 2004 Handelsbanken bought Swedish fund manager XACT Fonder from OMHEX (now OMX).

The company bought Lokallbanken in Denmark in 2008. The deal added about 15 branches to Handelsbanken's network.

EXECUTIVES

President and Group Chief Executive, Anders Bouvin, age 63
EVP and Head Capital Markets, Per Beckman, age 59
CEO Handelsbanken Norway, Dag Tjernsmo
Chairman Stadshypotek Bank, Yonnie Bergqvist, age 59
Deputy Group CEO Group Management and Head Handelsbanken Stockholm, Carina ...kerstr ¶m
Chief Risk Officer Group Risk Control, Maria Hedin
CEO Handelsbanken Finland, Nina Arkilahti
Head Markets and Asset Management, Per Elcar
Head Handelsbanken Northern Sweden, Magnus Ericson
Head Handelsbanken Southern UK, John Hodson
Head Handelsbanken Western Sweden, Katarina Ljungqvist
Head Handelsbanken Yorkshire and North East UK, Simon Lodge
Head Handelsbanken Central UK, Nick Lowe
CEO Handelsbanken Denmark, Lars Moesgaard
Chairman Swedish Subsidiary Boards and International Regional Bank Boards, Stefan Nilsson
Head Handelsbanken Northern UK, John Parker
Head Handelsbanken South East Sweden, G ¶ran Stille
CEO Stadshypotek, Ulrika Stolt Kirkegaard
Head Handelsbanken Central Sweden, Pontus ... hlund
CEO Handelsbanken UK, Mikael S ,rensen
CEO Handelsbanken The Netherlands, Jens Wiklund
Acting CEO Handelsbanken UK, Andrew Copsey
CEO Handelsbanken Liv Pension and Life, Louise Sander
Head Handelsbanken South West UK, Chris Teasdale
CIO Group IT, Agneta Lilja
Acting CFO, Rolf Marquardt
Vice Chairman, Fredrik Lundberg, age 70
Chairman, P ☐r Boman
Auditors: Ernst & Young AB

LOCATIONS

HQ: Svenska Handelsbanken
Kungstradgardsgatan 2, Stockholm SE-106 70
Phone: (46) 8 701 10 00
Web: www.handelsbanken.se

2014 Sales

	% of total
Sweden	63
Norway	10
UK	10
Denmark	6
Finland	6
Netherlands	4
Other countries	1
Total	**100**

PRODUCTS/OPERATIONS

2014 Sales by Segment

	% of total
Branch operations	
Sweden	52
Other countries	33
Capital markets	15
Total	**100**

COMPETITORS

BNP Paribas	Deutsche Bank
Citigroup	Nordea Bank
Crédit Agricole	SEB AB
Danske Bank	Société Générale

HISTORICAL FINANCIALS

Company Type: Public

Income Statement

FYE: December 31

	ASSETS ($ mil.)	NET INCOME ($ mil.)	INCOME AS % OF ASSETS	EMPLOYEES
12/19	329,984	1,819	0.6%	12,548
12/18	332,708	1,938	0.6%	12,307
12/17	337,253	1,962	0.6%	11,832
12/16	289,876	1,792	0.6%	11,759
12/15	299,169	1,938	0.6%	11,819
Annual Growth	**2.5%**	**(1.6%)**	**—**	**1.5%**

2019 Year-End Financials

Return on assets: 0.5%
Return on equity: 11.2%
Long-term debt ($ mil.): —
No. of shares (mil.): 1,980
Sales ($ mil): 7,407

Dividends
Yield: 5.5%
Payout: 32.1%
Market value ($ mil.): 10,508

	STOCK PRICE ($) FY Close	P/E High/Low		PER SHARE ($) Earnings	Dividends	Book Value
12/19	5.31	1	1	0.92	0.30	8.68
12/18	5.55	1	1	0.99	0.45	8.17
12/17	6.78	1	1	1.00	0.30	8.88
12/16	6.91	1	1	0.92	0.33	7.74
12/15	6.60	3	1	1.00	0.34	7.98
Annual Growth	**(5.3%)**	**—**	**—**	**(1.9%)**	**(3.2%)**	**2.1%**

Swedbank AB

Auditors: PricewaterhouseCoopers AB

LOCATIONS

HQ: Swedbank AB
Landsvaegen 40, Sundbyberg SE-172 63
Phone: (46) 8 585 900 00   **Fax:** (46) 8 796 80 92
Web: www.swedbank.com

HISTORICAL FINANCIALS

Company Type: Public

Income Statement

FYE: December 31

	ASSETS ($ mil.)	NET INCOME ($ mil.)	INCOME AS % OF ASSETS	EMPLOYEES
12/19	403,006	3,296	0.8%	16,327
12/18	375,873	3,541	0.9%	15,879
12/17	370,274	3,238	0.9%	14,588
12/16	360,496	3,269	0.9%	14,061
12/15	359,601	2,631	0.7%	13,893
Annual Growth	**2.9%**	**5.8%**	**—**	**4.1%**

2019 Year-End Financials

Return on assets: 0.8%
Return on equity: 14.2%
Long-term debt ($ mil.): —
No. of shares (mil.): 1,118
Sales ($ mil): 10,346

Dividends
Yield: 10.2%
Payout: 52.0%
Market value ($ mil.): 16,640

	STOCK PRICE ($) FY Close	P/E High/Low		PER SHARE ($) Earnings	Dividends	Book Value
12/19	14.88	1	1	2.94	1.53	20.74
12/18	22.39	1	1	3.16	1.55	20.59
12/17	24.05	2	1	2.90	1.46	20.04
12/16	24.15	1	1	2.93	1.32	19.51
12/15	22.00	2	1	2.36	1.31	18.65
Annual Growth	**(9.3%)**	**—**	**—**	**5.6%**	**3.9%**	**2.7%**

Swire (John) & Sons Ltd. (United Kingdom)

LOCATIONS

HQ: Swire (John) & Sons Ltd. (United Kingdom)
Swire House, 59 Buckingham Gate, London SW1E 6AJ
Phone:

HISTORICAL FINANCIALS

Company Type: Public

Income Statement

FYE: December 31

	REVENUE ($ mil.)	NET INCOME ($ mil.)	NET PROFIT MARGIN	EMPLOYEES
12/19	22,781	1,035	4.5%	91,022
12/18	21,142	801	3.8%	92,256
12/17	20,891	841	4.0%	94,235
12/16	15,909	49	0.3%	80,820
12/15	13,860	231	1.7%	0
Annual Growth	**13.2%**	**45.4%**	**—**	**—**

2019 Year-End Financials

Debt ratio: 38.9%
Return on equity: 3.8%
Cash ($ mil.): 4,740
Current ratio: 1.10
Long-term debt ($ mil.): 11,870

No. of shares (mil.): 100
Dividends
Yield: —
Payout: —
Market value ($ mil.): —

Swiss Life Holding AG

Auditors: PricewaterhouseCoopers AG

LOCATIONS

HQ: Swiss Life Holding AG
General-Guisan-Quai 40, P.O. Box 2831, Zurich CH-8022
Phone: (41) 43 284 33 11   **Fax:** (41) 43 284 63 11
Web: www.swisslife.com; www.swisslife.com

HISTORICAL FINANCIALS

Company Type: Public

Income Statement

FYE: December 31

	REVENUE ($ mil.)	NET INCOME ($ mil.)	NET PROFIT MARGIN	EMPLOYEES
12/19	25,157	1,240	4.9%	9,330
12/18	20,394	1,093	5.4%	8,624
12/17	19,231	1,031	5.4%	7,979
12/16	19,360	905	4.7%	7,801
12/15	20,697	878	4.2%	7,595
Annual Growth	**5.0%**	**9.0%**	**—**	**5.3%**

2019 Year-End Financials

Debt ratio: —
Return on equity: 7.6%
Cash ($ mil.): 8,531
Current ratio: —
Long-term debt ($ mil.): —

No. of shares (mil.): 31
Dividends
Yield: 0.0%
Payout: 1.4%
Market value ($ mil.): 808

	STOCK PRICE ($) FY Close	P/E High/Low		PER SHARE ($) Earnings	Dividends	Book Value
12/19	25.34	1	1	37.74	0.53	530.51
12/18	18.70	1	1	32.01	0.63	449.48
12/17	16.94	1	0	30.36	0.51	465.67
12/16	13.88	0	0	26.79	0.38	420.70
12/15	13.53	0	0	26.03	0.29	385.26
Annual Growth	17.0%	—	—	9.7%	15.9%	8.3%

Swiss Re Ltd

Auditors: PricewaterhouseCoopers Ltd.

LOCATIONS

HQ: Swiss Re Ltd
Mythenquai 50/60, Zurich 8022
Phone: (41) 43 285 2121   **Fax:** (41) 43 285 2999
Web: www.swissre.com

HISTORICAL FINANCIALS

Company Type: Public

Income Statement — FYE: December 31

	ASSETS ($ mil.)	NET INCOME ($ mil.)	INCOME AS % OF ASSETS	EMPLOYEES
12/19	238,567	727	0.3%	15,401
12/18	207,570	462	0.2%	14,943
12/17	222,526	398	0.2%	14,485
12/16	215,065	3,626	1.7%	14,053
12/15	196,135	4,665	2.4%	12,767
Annual Growth	5.0%	(37.2%)	—	4.8%

2019 Year-End Financials

Return on assets: 0.3%
Return on equity: 2.5%
Long-term debt ($ mil.): —
No. of shares (mil.): 327
Sales ($ mil): 49,314

Dividends
Yield: 4.9%
Payout: 36.0%
Market value ($ mil.): 9,207

	STOCK PRICE ($) FY Close	P/E High/Low		PER SHARE ($) Earnings	Dividends	Book Value
12/19	28.12	11	9	2.39	1.40	89.34
12/18	22.91	19	16	1.37	1.27	82.48
12/17	23.38	24	21	1.03	1.22	97.65
12/16	23.76	2	2	9.82	0.97	109.31
12/15	24.52	7	2	12.28	7.59	99.24
Annual Growth	3.5%	—	—	(33.6%)	(34.4%)	(2.6%)

T&D Holdings Inc

No mystery in a name here: T&D Holdings serves as the holding company for Japanese insurance companies Taiyo Life and Daido Life. Combined the companies constitute one of Japan's top life insurers. Taiyo Life gears its products to individuals while Daido Life's products are targeted toward small businesses. Another subsidiary T&D Financial Life sells whole life policies through financial institutions the likes of banks securities firms and insurance shop agents. Other businesses under the T&D umbrella include T&D Asset Man-agement T&D Customer Services (administrative services) and Pet & Family (pet insurance) and T&D Information Systems (computer processing).

Operations

T&D Holdings' Taiyo Life division which accounts for 40% of the holding company's annual revenues serves households with comprehensive life products including death benefits and medical or nursing care coverage. Meanwhile the Daido Life unit (another 40% of sales) focuses on the sale of term life insurance and illness policies through business accounts. The third-largest business unit T&D Financial Life sells whole life policies.

Geographic Reach

The company operates in Japan.

Sales and Marketing

The operating units of T&D Holdings use targeted sales techniques. With a focus on selling to housewives and middle-aged women Taiyo Life employs a sales force made up of some 8600 women (similar in age to their target market base) who visit homes to present tailor-made coverage options. Daido Life gears its marketing efforts towards small and midsized businesses by partnering with enterprise associations (such as the National Federation of Corporate Taxpayers Association); it has some 3800 in-house sales representatives. The company's T&D Financial Life unit markets through a network of some 120 agencies including financial institutions.

Financial Performance

In fiscal 2014 (ended March) revenue decreased 14% to Â 2085 billion as new policy sales in the Taiyo Life and Daido Life units declined. The decline in new policies primarily reflected the impact of an increase in insurance premiums in 2013. It was partially offset by an increase in revenue from T&D Financial Life.

Net income rose 24% to Â 78.9 billion in fiscal 2014 as provisions for policy and other reserves declined and operating expenses decreased. Cash flow from operations fell 75% to Â 159 billion.

Strategy

T&D Holdings is seeking to grow by branching out beyond its traditional market segments. Its Taiyo Life unit is working to expand policy sales by marketing policies geared at men and children. Daido Life is adding products for business owners such as living protection coverage while T&D Financial Life is introducing new products for bereaved families and retirees. The group is also seeking to expand its international operations.

T&D Holdings is also growing its operations into the provision of short-term small-amount policies for pet shops. The company seeks to expand in new and existing business fields through alliances and acquisitions as well.

In 2014 Daido Life launched a new whole life product Life Gift which meets the growing demand for inheritance planning as Japan's population ages.

Company Background

T&D Holdings was formed through the merger of Taiyo Life and Daido Life in 2004. The companies first began working together through an alliance formed in 1999.

EXECUTIVES

President and Representative Director, Kenji Nakagome, age 67
Senior Executive Officer and Director Finance and Accounting Department, Tamiji Matsumoto, age 66
EVP and Representative Director Group Planning Department, Sonosuke Usui
Senior Executive Officer and Director, Terunori Yokoyama, age 67
Senior Managing Executive Officer and Director Daido Life, Masahiro Ueda
Managing Executive Officer and Director Taiyo Life, Kouichi Seike
Auditors: Ernst & Young ShinNihon LLC

LOCATIONS

HQ: T&D Holdings Inc
2-7-1 Nihonbashi, Chuo-ku, Tokyo 103-6031
Phone: (81) 3 3272 6104   **Fax:** (81) 3 3272 6552
Web: www.td-holdings.co.jp

PRODUCTS/OPERATIONS

2014 Sales

	% of total
Daido Life	40
Taiyo Life	37
T&D Financial Life	20
Other	3
Total	**100**

Selected Subsidiaries and Affiliates

AIC Private Equity Fund General Partner Ltd
Alternative Investment Capital Ltd.
Daido Life Insurance Company
Daido Management Service Co. Ltd.
Nihon System Shuno Inc.
Pet & Family Small-amount Short-term Insurance Company
T&D Asset Management Cayman Inc.
T&D Asset Management Co. Ltd.
T&D Confirm Ltd.
T&D Customer Services Co. Ltd.
T&D Financial Life Insurance Company
T&D Information System Ltd.
T&D Lease Co. Ltd.
Taiyo Credit Guarantee Co. Ltd.
Taiyo Life Insurance Company
Toyo Insurance Agency Co. Ltd.
Zenkoku Business Center Co. Ltd.

COMPETITORS

Aflac	Gibraltar Life
American Life Insurance	Insurance
	Meiji Yasuda Life
Asahi Mutual Life	Mitsui Life
Dai-ichi Life	Nippon Life Insurance
Fukoku Mutual	Sumitomo Life

HISTORICAL FINANCIALS

Company Type: Public

Income Statement — FYE: March 31

	ASSETS ($ mil.)	NET INCOME ($ mil.)	INCOME AS % OF ASSETS	EMPLOYEES
03/20	152,188	618	0.4%	20,106
03/19	142,623	657	0.5%	20,576
03/18	143,731	730	0.5%	20,960
03/17	133,186	672	0.5%	21,109
03/16	130,673	646	0.5%	21,121
Annual Growth	3.9%	(1.1%)	—	(1.2%)

2020 Year-End Financials

Return on assets: 0.4%
Return on equity: 5.8%
Long-term debt ($ mil.): —
No. of shares (mil.): 601
Sales ($ mil): 18,985

Dividends
Yield: 5.1%
Payout: 20.2%
Market value ($ mil.): 2,376

	STOCK PRICE ($) FY Close	P/E High/Low		PER SHARE ($) Earnings	Dividends	Book Value
03/20	3.95	0	0	1.00	0.20	17.11
03/19	5.24	0	0	1.05	0.18	17.01
03/18	8.00	0	0	1.15	0.17	17.39
03/17	7.27	0	0	1.03	0.21	15.47
03/16	4.64	0	0	0.97	0.10	16.63
Annual Growth	(3.9%)	—	—	0.8%	19.1%	0.7%

Taisei Corp

Auditors: KPMG AZSA LLC

LOCATIONS

HQ: Taisei Corp
1-25-1 Nishi-Shinjuku, Shinjuku-ku, Tokyo 163-0606
Phone: (81) 3 3348 1111
Web: www.taisei.co.jp

HISTORICAL FINANCIALS

Company Type: Public

Income Statement				FYE: March 31
	REVENUE ($ mil.)	NET INCOME ($ mil.)	NET PROFIT MARGIN	EMPLOYEES
03/19	14,907	1,016	6.8%	18,082
03/18	14,931	1,194	8.0%	17,672
03/17	13,302	810	6.1%	17,933
03/16	13,766	686	5.0%	17,759
03/15	13,112	318	2.4%	17,634
Annual Growth	3.3%	33.7%	—	0.6%

2019 Year-End Financials

Debt ratio: 0.1%
Return on equity: 16.2%
Cash ($ mil.): 4,223
Current ratio: 1.30
Long-term debt ($ mil.): 1,142

No. of shares (mil.): 218
Dividends
Yield: 0.0%
Payout: —
Market value ($ mil.): 2,617

	STOCK PRICE ($) FY Close	P/E High/Low		PER SHARE ($) Earnings	Dividends	Book Value
03/19	12.00	0	0	4.62	0.31	29.82
03/18	13.00	0	0	5.29	0.26	28.02
03/17	6.92	0	0	3.51	0.22	22.21
03/16	5.95			2.93	0.11	19.71
03/15	5.95	0	—	1.40	0.07	17.45
Annual Growth	19.2%	—	—	34.9%	46.1%	14.3%

Taiwan Semiconductor Manufacturing Co., Ltd.

Taiwan Semiconductor Manufacturing Co. (TSMC) is the largest dedicated contract semiconductor manufacturer in the world with roughly 50% market share. The company handles manufacturing for semiconductor and integrated device companies that don't have their own manufacturing facilities. Overall it makes which make more than 10760 products using more than 270 technologies for about 500 customers. Taiwan Semiconductor Manufacturing Co's fabless customers include AMD Broadcom NVIDIA and QUALCOMM and among its integrated device manufacturer customers are Broadcom Limited Hisilicon Technologies Co. Ltd. and Intel Corporation. Geographically TSMC has factories in Taiwan China and the US and US customers account for about 60% of revenue.

Operations

Wafer manufacturing makes up more than 85% of sales and Taiwan Semiconductor Manufacturing Co. also makes fabricating masks and provides services such as design probing and testing and assembly. Constituting its largest-selling product logic semiconductors are standard logic devices such as microprocessors microcontrollers digital signal processors graphic chips and chip sets.

About 50% of revenue comes from Smartphone Roughly 30% is from High performance computing Internet of Things generates nearly 10% of revenue and Digital consumer electronics Automotive and Others generates about 5% of revenue each.

Geographic Reach

Taiwan Semiconductor Manufacturing Co. headquartered in Hsinchu City Taiwan has offices around the world. Customers in the US account for about 60% of the company's revenue followed by China with approximately 20% of company's revenue and Taiwan with about 10% of company's revenue.

Most of Taiwan Semiconductor Manufacturing Co.'s production capacity is in Taiwan but it also has facilities in the US Shanghai and Nanjing China.

Sales and Marketing

Taiwan Semiconductor Manufacturing Co.'s revenue is tied to its 10 largest customers who accounts for more than 70% of company's net revenue. The company's largest customer supplies about 25% of revenue. Taiwan Semiconductor Manufacturing Co. Is also a major supplier of chips used in Apple's iPhones and a slowdown in iPhone sales could have an impact of the company. Taiwan Semiconductor Manufacturing Co. spent NT$6 million NT$6 million and NT$6.3 million for marketing expense for fiscal year 2017 2018 and 2019 respectively

Financial Performance

Note: Growth rates may differ after conversion to US Dollars.

The company's revenue increased by 4% compared to 2018 mainly attributed to the growing demand for 7-nanometer products and the depreciation of NT dollar against the US dollar on a weighted average basis from 2018 to 2019 partially offset by the decline in demand for most mature technology products.

Net income decreased about 3%.

Taiwan Semiconductor Manufacturing Co.'s cash and equivalents declined 21% in 2019 from 2018. In 2019 cash from operations increased 5% and the company used 46% more cash for investing activities and 10% more cash for financing activities than in 2019.

Strategy

Taiwan Semiconductor Manufacturing Co. manages its overall capacity and technology upgrade plans based on long term market demand forecasts for its products and services. According to its current market demand forecasts the company intends to maintain the strategy of expanding manufacturing capacity and upgrading manufacturing technologies to meet both the fabrication and the technology needs of customers.

Taiwan Semiconductor Manufacturing Co.'s capital expenditures in 2017 2018 and 2019 were NT$330.6 billion NT$315.6 billion and NT$460.4 billion (US$14.9 billion translated from a weighted average exchange rate of NT$30.90 to US$1.00) respectively. Its capital expenditures in 2020 are expected to be between US$15 billion to US$16 billion which depending on market conditions may be adjusted later. The company's capital expenditures for 2020 are expected to be funded primarily by its operating cash flow and partially by the issuance of corporate bonds. In 2020 Taiwan Semiconductor Manufacturing Co. anticipates its capital expenditures to focus primarily on the following: installing and expanding capacity mainly for 5-nanometer and 3-nanometer nodes; expanding capacity for advanced packaging and mask operations; expanding buildings/facilities for Fab 18 in Southern Taiwan Science Park; and investing in research and development projects for new process technologies.

Company Background

Morris Chang learned early to adapt to rapid change. The future founder and chairman of Taiwan Semiconductor Manufacturing Company (TSMC) lived in six cities before age 18 as his family fled the ravages of the Sino-Japanese War and WWII in China. Chang immigrated to the US to attend MIT and Stanford where he ultimately earned a Ph.D. in electrical engineering.

In 1987 Chang founded TSMC as the world's first dedicated contract semiconductor manufacturer — the first silicon foundry. Chang's pioneering role in the foundry industry has earned him many accolades including the first-ever Robert N. Noyce Medal of the Institute of Electrical and Electronics Engineers and the first-ever Exemplary Leadership award (subsequently named in his honor) of the Fabless Semiconductor Association (now the Global Semiconductor Alliance). Known for his analytical mind Chang was once ranked among the top 1000 players of contract bridge in the world.

TSMC became profitable within 15 months of its founding. Throughout the 1990s it continued to be among industry leaders both in production capacity and in deployment of cutting-edge technology.

EXECUTIVES

President TSMC Japan, Makoto Onodera
VP Fab 8 and Fab 12, Mark Liu
SVP and CIO, Stephen T. (Steve) Tso
SVP and CFO, Lora Ho
President TSMC Europe, Maria Marced
President TSMC China, L.C. Tu
SVP and President TSMC North America, Rick Cassidy, age 69
VP Research and Development; CTO, Jack Sun
President and Co-CEO, C.C. Wei
VP Operations Mainstream Fabs, J.K. Lin
VP Operations 300mm Fabs, J.K. Wang
Vice Chairman, F. C. Tseng
Chairman, Morris Chang, age 89
Auditors: Deloitte & Touche

LOCATIONS

HQ: Taiwan Semiconductor Manufacturing Co., Ltd.
No. 8, Li-Hsin Road 6, Hsinchu Science Park, Hsinchu 300
Phone: (886) 3 563 6688   **Fax:** (886) 3 563 7000
Web: www.tsmc.com

2017 Sales by Geography

	% of total
United States	64
Asia	20
Taiwan	9
Europe the Middle East and Africa	7
Total	**100**

2017 Sales by Region

	% of total
North America	64
China	12
Asia/Pacific	11
Europe Middle East and Africa	7
Japan	6
Total	**100**

PRODUCTS/OPERATIONS

2017 Sales

	% of total
Wafer	89
Others	11
Total	**100**

2017 Sales

	% of total
Fabless semiconductor companies/systems companies	80
Integrated device manufacturers	20
Total	**100**

2017 Sales

	% of total
Communication	59
Industrial/Standard	23
Computer	10
Consumer	8
Total	**100**

COMPETITORS

Advanced Semiconductor Engineering	SK Hynix
	SMIC
Advanced Semiconductor Manufacturing	Samsung Electronics
	Shanghai Hua Hong NEC
ChipMOS	Toppan Photomasks
Dai Nippon Printing	Tower Semiconductor
Dongbu HiTek	UMC
GLOBALFOUNDRIES	Winbond Electronics
Grace Semiconductor	X-FAB Silicon
MagnaChip	Foundries

HISTORICAL FINANCIALS

Company Type: Public

Income Statement — FYE: December 31

	REVENUE ($ mil.)	NET INCOME ($ mil.)	NET PROFIT MARGIN	EMPLOYEES
12/19	35,739	11,822	33.1%	51,297
12/18	33,721	11,480	34.0%	48,752
12/17	32,963	11,571	35.1%	48,602
12/16	29,299	10,331	35.3%	0
12/15	25,669	9,216	35.9%	40,483
Annual Growth	8.6%	6.4%	—	6.1%

2019 Year-End Financials

Debt ratio: 0.2%	No. of shares (mil.): —
Return on equity: 21.5%	Dividends
Cash ($ mil.): 15,211	Yield: 2.7%
Current ratio: 1.37	Payout: 362.5%
Long-term debt ($ mil.): 838	Market value ($ mil.): —

	STOCK PRICE ($) FY Close	P/E High/Low		PER SHARE ($) Earnings	Dividends	Book Value
12/19	58.10	4	3	0.46	1.60	2.08
12/18	36.91	3	3	0.44	1.04	2.11
12/17	39.65	3	2	0.45	0.94	1.98
12/16	28.75	2	2	0.40	0.76	1.66
12/15	22.75	2	2	0.36	0.58	1.40
Annual Growth	26.4%		—	6.4%	29.0%	10.4%

Takeda Pharmaceutical Co Ltd

The work of Takeda Pharmaceutical Company started way back in 1781 when its predecessor began selling traditional Japanese and Chinese remedies. These days Takeda is one of the world's largest pharmaceutical companies making branded prescription drugs that it sells in some 100 countries worldwide. Top-selling products include ulcerative colitis drug Entyvio anti-cancer agent Adcetris and antidepressant Trintellix. The company is also a leading maker of over-the-counter medications such as cold remedies and vitamins. Its largest market is the US which brings in about 35% of revenue. In early 2019 Takeda nearly doubled its size with the $62 billion acquisition of UK-based biopharmaceutical Shire.

Operations

Product sales contribute more than 95% of Takeda's total revenue. The company also makes money on royalties and services provided.

Prior to the acquisition of Shire Takeda focused on three core areas: gastroenterology (GI) oncology and neuroscience. Its best-selling product was GI treatment Entyvio for severe ulcerative colitis and Crohn's disease. Other major GI products treat gastroesophageal reflux disease acid-related diseases and constipation. Oncology products Velcade and Leuprorelin are two of the company's top sellers. Takeda's primary neuroscience product is Trintellix.

After the acquisition of Shire which greatly expanded the company's rare disease operations Takeda is focused on five core areas: oncology gastrointestinal conditions neuroscience rare diseases and plasma-derived therapies.

Geographic Reach

Takeda's head offices are located in Tokyo and Osaka Japan but the company plans to sell its original Osaka headquarters. It has major regional locations in Japan Singapore Switzerland and the US.

Prior to the Shire acquisition the company's network spanned more than 70 countries and regions in the Asia/Pacific the Americas Europe the Middle East and Africa. The US is Takeda's largest market bringing in some 35% of revenue followed by Japan with more than 30% of revenue. Europe and Canada combined bring in more than 15% of total revenue.

Sales and Marketing

Takeda sells its products to major pharmaceutical wholesalers and distributors and retail pharmacy chains. Prior to the Shire acquisition the company's largest customer was Medipal Holdings which brought in more than 10% of total sales.

Financial Performance

Takeda's revenue has hovered between Å 1.7 trillion and Å 1.8 trillion for the past five years. After fiscal 2015 when a huge income tax provision led the company to post a net loss of Å 145.8 billion Takeda has seen its profits rise significantly.

In fiscal 2018 (ended March) revenue increased 2% to Å 1.8 trillion due largely to a 41% increase in sales of Entyvio the company's largest earner. Another GI product Takecab also had higher sales that year. In oncology Ninlaro sales increased 58% while the newly acquired drugs Iclusig and Alunbrig contributed to growth. Antidepressant Trintellix sales rose 52%. Those gains were partially offset by lower sales of Velcade which lost patent exclusivity in the US that year.

Net income rose 63% to Å 186.9 billion in fiscal 2018 as the company kept its operating expenses in check and lowered its cost of revenue. Interest income also boosted the bottom line.

The company ended fiscal 2018 with Å 294.5 billion in net cash about Å 50 billion less than it had at the end of fiscal 2017. Operating activities provided Å 377.9 billion in cash while financing activities used Å 326.2 billion and investing activities used another Å 93.3 billion.

Strategy

Takeda's key priorities for mid-term growth include expanding its portfolio strengthening its candidate pipeline and boosting profitability. Recently the company has significantly realigned its drug portfolio steering away from such areas as cardiovascular and metabolic disease for example. In 2019 it acquired the larger UK biopharmaceutical Shire for $62 billion. (It was the largest deal in Japan's history.) With that purchase Takeda strengthened its rare disease operations and expanded its global presence particularly in the US. Shire's marketed products include immunology drug Hyqvia hematology drug Vonvendi and neuroscience drug Adderall XR.

However the Shire acquisition added to the company's already steep debt levels which neared Å 1 trillion at the end of fiscal 2018 (ended March). With that amount of debt the company is somewhat hamstrung in terms of making strategic moves. Takeda is working to cut its leverage through such measures as selling non-core assets. In fiscal 2019 its sold Brazilian arm Multilab to Novamed Fabri § o de Produtos Farmac uticos for an undisclosed price. Brazil was previously a target market for growth for Takeda. It sold its stake in Guangdong Techpool Bio-Pharma in mid-2018. The company is now exploring the sale of some non-core emerging-market drugs and other overseas assets.

Like other pharmaceuticals Takeda faces pricing pressure in the US its largest market. The same pressure is being felt in Europe as well. And though international sales have been rising the company's domestic sales have languished in part due to price reductions imposed by Japan's National Health Insurance agency.

In terms of specific products Takeda is counting on the ongoing growth of Entyvio its highest seller as well as Ninlaro Takecab Trintellix and the recently acquired Iclusig and Alunbrig. Keeping its pipeline robust is key to offset sales declines of products that lose their exclusivity such as cancer drug Velcade.

The company often enters collaborations with other pharmaceuticals or biotech firms to develop and/or commercialize new products. In fiscal 2018 alone it entered into more than 50 collaborations with third parties. While these partnerships provide Takeda with access to a greater number of drug candidates it also leaves the company vulnerable to threats beyond its control such as a collaborator dropping a development program.

Mergers and Acquisitions

In 2019 Takeda bought UK-based biopharmaceutical Shire for $62 billion. With the acquisition Takeda became the 10th largest drug maker in the world. It expanded its US operations as well as its rare disease portfolio.

In 2018 Takeda bought biopharmaceutical firm TiGenix for $627 million. TiGenix is expected to soon receive European approval of stem cell therapy Cx601 for the treatment of Crohn's disease.

In early 2017 Takeda acquired US-based cancer drug developer Ariad Pharmaceuticals for $5.2 billion. That deal helped the company expand in oncology another priority therapeutic area.

Company Background

In 1787 Chobei Takeda I started a business selling tradition Japanese and Chinese herbal medicines in Osaka Japan. In the 1860s with his great-grandson at the helm the business started importing western medicines. The company entered the manufacturing business in 1895 and in 1914 it established a research division so that it could develop its own products.

The company was incorporated as Chobei Takeda & Co. in 1925 transitioning from an individually owned business to a corporate organization. Chobei Takeda was renamed Takeda Pharmaceutical in 1943. It went public in 1949. In the 1960s Takeda began operating in other Asian markets. It entered the US and European markets in the 1990s.

EXECUTIVES

President Global Oncology, Christophe M. Bianchi, age 57
President Europe and Canada, Marc Princen
President Global Vaccine, Rajeev Venkayya
President Takeda Pharmaceuticals International, Shinji Honda
President Japan Pharma, Masato Iwasaki
President and CEO, Christophe Weber
CFO, James Kehoe, age 58
President US, Ramona Sequeira
Chief Medical and Scientific Officer, Andrew S. Plump
President Emerging Markets, Giles Platford
Chairman, Yasuchika Hasegawa
Auditors: KPMG AZSA LLC

LOCATIONS

HQ: Takeda Pharmaceutical Co Ltd
2-1-1 Nihonbashi-Honcho, Chuo-ku, Tokyo 103-8668
Phone: (81) 3 3278 2111   **Fax:** (81) 3 3278 2000
Web: www.takeda.co.jp

2018 Sales

	% of total
US	34
Japan	33
Europe & Canada	18
Latin America	6
Russia/CIS	4
Asia (excluding Japan) & other	4
Other	2
Total	**100**

PRODUCTS/OPERATIONS

Selected Products
Prescription drugs
Actos (type 2 diabetes)
Adecut (high blood pressure)
Amasulin (anti-infective)
Blopress (high blood pressure)
Bronica (asthma)
Ceuleuk (angiosarcoma)
Dexilant (acid reflux)
Eurodin (central nervous system)
Lupron Depot (prostate cancer endometriosis)
Osten (osteoporosis)
Pansporin (anti-infective)
Prevacid (peptic ulcers)
Rozerem (insomnia)
Takesulin (anti-infective)
Uloric (gout)
Velcade (multiple myeloma)
Consumer health care
Alinamin (vitamins)
Benza (cold remedy)
Scorba (athlete's foot)

Selected Subsidiaries
Amato Pharmaceutical Products Ltd. (30%)
Millennium Pharmaceuticals Inc. (US)
Nihon Pharmaceutical Co. Ltd. (88%)
Laboratoires Takeda (France)
Takeda America Holdings Inc. (US)
Takeda Europe Holdings B.V. (Netherlands)
Takeda Cambridge Limited (UK)
Takeda Healthcare Products Co. Ltd.
Takeda Italia Farmacetici S.p.A. (77%)
Takeda Pharma AG (Switzerland)
Takeda Pharma GmbH (Germany)
Takeda Pharma Ireland Limited
Takeda Pharmaceuticals Europe Limited (UK)
Takeda Pharmaceuticals North America Inc. (US)
Takeda Research Investment Inc. (US)
Takeda San Diego Inc. (US)
Takeda San Francisco Inc. (US)
Takeda Singapore Pte Limited
Takeda (Thailand) Ltd. (48%)
Tianjin Takeda Pharmaceuticals Co. Ltd. (75% China)

COMPETITORS

AbbVie	Daiichi Sankyo
Allergan plc	Janssen Biotech
Amgen	Merck
AstraZeneca	Novartis
Bayer HealthCare	Pfizer
Pharmaceuticals	Roche Holding
Bristol-Myers Squibb	Shionogi & Co.
Celgene	UCB

HISTORICAL FINANCIALS
Company Type: Public

Income Statement
FYE: March 31

	REVENUE ($ mil.)	NET INCOME ($ mil.)	NET PROFIT MARGIN	EMPLOYEES
03/20	30,319	407	1.3%	47,495
03/19	18,937	985	5.2%	49,578
03/18	16,673	1,759	10.6%	27,230
03/17	15,491	1,028	6.6%	29,900
03/16	16,094	713	4.4%	31,168
Annual Growth	17.2%	(13.1%)	—	11.1%

2020 Year-End Financials

Debt ratio: 0.3%
Return on equity: 0.8%
Cash ($ mil.): 1,737
Current ratio: 1.13
Long-term debt ($ mil.): 41,515

No. of shares (mil.): 1,576
Dividends
Yield: 5.4%
Payout: 318.9%
Market value ($ mil.): 23,927

	STOCK PRICE ($) FY Close	P/E High/Low		PER SHARE ($) Earnings	Dividends	Book Value
03/20	15.18	1	0	0.26	0.83	27.61
03/19	20.37	0	0	1.02	0.81	29.77
03/18	24.41	0	0	2.24	0.86	23.68
03/17	23.64	0	0	1.31	0.83	21.44
03/16	22.82	0	0	0.91	0.73	21.97
Annual Growth	(9.7%)	—	—	(26.8%)	3.2%	5.9%

Talanx AG

Talanx Group offers its customers an army of protection. The Germany-based company is the third-largest insurance group in the country. Also known as Talanx it operates in property/casualty insurance life insurance and financial services as well as reinsurance in both the property/casualty and life categories. Brands include HDI which provides insurance policies to both private and industrial customers; Hannover Re one of the world's largest reinsurers; and asset manager Ampega among others. Talanx has operations in more than 150 countries worldwide. The group is controlled by HDI Haftpflichtverband der Deutschen Industrie. Europe is its largest market giving more than half of its gross written premiums.

Operations
Talanx reports its business in six insurance segments: Industrial Lines Retail Germany Property Casualty Retail Germany Life Retail International Property/Casualty Reinsurance and Life/Health Reinsurance. The group also has a Corporate Operations segment. The group's primary brands include HDI Hannover Re Targo Versicherungen PB Versicherungen Neue Leben Warta and Ampega.

Property/Casualty Reinsurance leads the pack with nearly 35% of total gross written premiums. Life/Health Reinsurance (about 20%) and Industrial lines (more than 15%) follow.

Property/Casualty Reinsurance is primarily handled by subsidiary Hannover R ck. Its target markets are North America and Continenal Europe.

Retail Germany (Talanx Deutschland) serves retail clients and small to midsized companies in Germany.

Retail International focuses on target growth markets of Central and Eastern Europe and Latin America.

The Industrial Lines segment offers coverage around the world. It is a major player in Europe and is working to grow its operations beyond the continent — again with a focus on Central and Eastern Europe and Latin America.

Geographic Reach
Europe accounts for more almost 55% of Talanx's gross premiums written with Germany bringing in more than 20% on its own. The US is the company's largest non-European region with approximately 20% of total gross written premiums.

The company also does business in the rest of the Americas Africa and the Asia/Pacific region.

Talanx prefers to operate semi-independent businesses in local markets and expand by acquiring or opening divisions in new territories. It operates in more than 150 countries.

Sales and Marketing
TTalanx AG sells its products by its own field organisation independent brokers and multiple agents via partnerships online and direct channels.

Financial Performance
Note: Growth rates may differ after conversion to US Dollars.

Talanx's revenue has been rising since 2016. It has an overall growth of 24% between 2015 and 2019.

The company's revenue grew from ?33.8 billion in 2018 to ?37.8 billion in 2019.

Net income attributable to shareholders of the company totalled ?923 million a 31% growth from the previous year.

Talanx's cash at the end of 2019 totaled ?3.5 billion. Operating activities provided ?7 billion while investing and financing activities used ?6.7 billion and ?203 million respectively.

Strategy
The Talanx Group is active in primary insurance and reinsurance around the world in both the property/casualty and life insurance businesses. The company attaches particular importance to close collaboration between itself and its industrial partners and retail clients many of whom have worked with the group for many years in order to provide it with the best possible service. The Talanx Group optimizes the relationship between insurance and reinsurance as an integral component of its business model with the aim of consistently enhancing its opportunity/risk profile and improving capital efficiency. The composition of the Group's portfolio ensures that it has sufficient independent risk capacities in all market phases to support its clients reliably and over the long term and to tap into promising markets. This diversification approach bolsters its independence minimizes its exposure to risk and enables us to sustainably grow the Group's success to the benefit of clients investors and employees.

Mergers and Acquisitions
In mid-2019 Talanx acquired the property/casualty insurer ERGO Sigorta A.S. from Munich Re for an undisclosed amount. ERGO Sigorta A.S. is based in Turkey. The deal is in line with the company's business strategy for its five core retail international markets in that moves the company closer to its goal of ranking among the top five insurers in Turkey.

Company Background
The company traces its roots back over a century but began operating as a holding company under the name HDI Beteilgung AG in 1996. In 1998 it was renamed Talanx which is a blend of

the words "talent" and "phalanx" (a Greek word referring to a battle formation).

In 2012 the company completed its IPO and began trading on Germany's Frankfurt Stock Exchange. The company raised about €817 million which it used to grow its business. Post-IPO HDI Haftpflichtverband der Deutschen Industrie maintained a majority stake in Talanx.

EXECUTIVES

Chairman Management Board, Herbert K. Haas, age 66

Member Management Board, Immo Querner

Member Management Board Reinsurance, Ulrich Wallin, age 59

Member Management Board, Thomas Noth

Member Management Group Retail Germany, Heinz-Peter Ro

Chairman Supervisory Board, Wolf-Dieter Baumgartl, age 77

Deputy Chairman Supervisory Board, Eckhard Rohkamm

Deputy Chairman Supervisory Board, Ralf Rieger

Auditors: PricewaterhouseCoopers GmbH

LOCATIONS

HQ: Talanx AG
   HDI-Platz 1, Hannover D-30659
Phone: (49) 511 3747 0   **Fax:** (49) 511 3747 2525
Web: www.talanx.com

2017 Gross Written Premiums

	% of total
Germany	26
Central & Eastern Europe including Turkey	9
UK	8
Rest of Europe	15
US	18
Rest of North America	2
Asia & Australia	12
Latin America	8
Africa	2
Total	**100**

PRODUCTS/OPERATIONS

2017 Gross Written Premiums by Segment

	% of total
Property/Casualty Reinsurance	31
Life/Health Reinsurance	21
Retail International	16
Retail Germany — Life Insurance	14
Industrial Lines	13
Retail Germany — Property/Casualty Insurance	5
Total	**100**

COMPETITORS

AEGON	Generali
AXA	Munich Re Group
Allianz	Swiss Re
General Re	Zurich Insurance Group

HISTORICAL FINANCIALS

Company Type: Public

Income Statement   FYE: December 31

	REVENUE ($ mil.)	NET INCOME ($ mil.)	NET PROFIT MARGIN	EMPLOYEES
12/19	42,032	1,036	2.5%	21,516
12/18	38,257	805	2.1%	20,780
12/17	38,386	805	2.1%	22,059
12/16	32,815	957	2.9%	21,649
12/15	33,888	799	2.4%	21,965
Annual Growth	5.5%	6.7%	—	(0.5%)

2019 Year-End Financials

Debt ratio: —	No. of shares (mil.): 252
Return on equity: 9.7%	Dividends
Cash ($ mil.): 3,949	Yield: —
Current ratio: —	Payout: —
Long-term debt ($ mil.): —	Market value ($ mil.): —

Tata Motors Ltd

Tata Motors is an automobile maker. The company produces passenger cars including popular models such as Jaguar Land Rover Safari and Sumo and commercial vehicles such as buses trucks tractor-trailers light commercial vehicles and defense and construction equipment. Furthermore Tata Motors has OEMs offering an extensive range of integrated smart and e-mobility solutions. Tata Motors sells its vehicles through an extensive dealer network in India and exports vehicles to countries in Africa Asia Europe the Middle East and South America. In addition the company distributes Fiat-brand cars in India through its joint venture with Fiat. Tata Motors rolled out its first commercial truck in 1945. Its vehicles can now be found on the roads in more than 125 countries. The company generates majority of sales from international markets.

Operations

Tata Motors' business segments are primarily divided by its automotive operations and other all other operations.

Automotive operations represent the company's primary segment which includes Tata Commercial Vehicles Tata Passenger Vehicles Jaguar Land Rover and Vehicle financing. Jaguar and Land Rover brands account for around 80% of total revenue with Tata and other brand vehicles including vehicle financing bringing in the rest. Vehicles are categorized as car and sport utility vehicles (SUVs) trucks and buses and defense vehicles and equipment.

Car models include the Tigor Tiago Bolt and the smaller GenX Nano; SUVs are the Harrier Nexon Hexa Safari Storme and Sumo Gold.

Tata Motors' trucks include its Prima Ace Mega ICV truck Super Ace Mint Ultra and Zip Gold trucks which are used for various applications such as refuse trucks road sweepers and suction machine trucks. Part of its truck business operates through subsidiary Tata Daewoo Commercial Vehicle Company (TDCV) which is South Korea's second largest manufacturer of medium- and heavy-duty trucks exporting vehicles to more than 60 countries. Tata Motors also makes buses including city buses school buses coaches and what it calls its "Smart City" STARBUS electric and hybrid buses.

Its defense vehicles include troop carriers water tankers tippers load carriers prison vans and fire tenders.

Other operations include information technology services machine tools and factory automation services.

Geographic Reach

Through subsidiaries and affiliated companies Tata Motors has operations in India the UK South Korea Thailand Spain and South Africa. The US is its largest market representing around 20% of its total sales. It is followed by India for almost 20%. The UK generates more than 15% of total sales and China for more than 10%. Other European countries also account for over 15% of total sales while the rest of the world contributes the remaining revenue.

Tata Motors has manufacturing facilities across India; Jaguar Land Rover has manufacturing facilities in the UK as well as in Austria Brazil China Slovakia and India; Daewoo manufacturing facilities are located in South Korea. In addition the company operates R&D and design facilities across Asia and Europe. Tata Motors is headquartered in Mumbai India.

Sales and Marketing

Tata Motors' vehicles are sold through a network of authorized dealers and service centers across the Indian market and a network of distributors and local dealers in international markets. All told the company has more than 6500 sales and service points worldwide.

Moreover digital channels such as online sales and remote servicing via SOTA are helping improve customer service.

Financial Performance

Note: Growth rates may differ after conversion to US Dollars.

Tata Motors has seen significant growth in the past years despite it falling considerably in fiscal 2020. Revenue fell by 11% between fiscal 2018 and fiscal 2020 with ?3.01 trillion in fiscal 2019. A steep volume decline a general economic slowdown the impact of the COVID-19 pandemic towards the year-end and the resulting negative operating leverage of the company impacted profitability and cash flows.

Revenue fell by 14% in fiscal 2020 to ?2.6 trillion compared to ?3.01 the prior year due to a decrease in wholesale volumes in both Tata and Jaguar Land Rover brands.

Tata Motors did not fare better in terms of profits either. The company experienced consecutive net loss of ?12.1 trillion in fiscal 2020 following the loss of ?28.8 trillion the year prior. The COVID-19 pandemic has severely affected the company's performance as well as lower demand thus disrupting its steady delivery of profit in the past years.

Cash at the end of the period was ?184.7 trillion. Cash from operations generated ?266.3 billion and financing activities added another ?33.9 billion from proceeds from issue of shares and long-term borrowings. Investing activities used ?341.7 billion mainly for payments for assets and purchase of investments.

Strategy

Tata Motors continues its Turnaround 2.0 strategy which was launched in FY19 by emphasizing operational efficiency using common platforms initiating cost reduction and capex rationalization programmes leveraging on developments in EV markets and launching a new BSVI portfolio that offers exciting features and delivers an enhanced value proposition. Key priorities include enhancing retail sales efficiently managing dealer network inventories and improving dealer performance profitability and network expansion.

Tata Motors introduced 'Click to drive' an end-to-end online sales experience enabling customers to buy the car of their choice with a click of a button from the comfort of their homes as a response to customer uncertainty due to the pending transition from BSIV to BSVI the liquidity crisis and the rising cost of vehicle ownership among other reasons.

In terms of electric vehicles Tata Motors launched the Nexon EV in January 2020 which is powered by the state-of-the-art EV technology 'ZIPTRON' a high voltage high performance technology designed specifically for Indian conditions. It also launched the Tigor EV+ with 213 km range which has received a strong market response and is the highest selling EV in India.

Company Background

Tata Motors is part of the Tata Group which was founded in 1868 by Jamsetji Tata. Tata Motors began manufacturing locomotives and other engineering products in 1945 and rolled out its first commercial truck?the TMB 312?in 1954. Tata Motors' 1210 series of vehicles began production in 1964 and in 1975 the company began producing the Tata 1210 semi-forward model.

In 1983 the company started making heavy commercial vehicles and in 2005 it launched its first fully built buses and coaches called GLOBUS and STARBUS brands. The popular Tata Nano mini car and Jaguar Land Rover were both introduced in 2009. In 2014 the company started making defense vehicles the first being the Armoured Personnel Carrier (APC). Its first electric vehicle the Tata Tigor was launched in 2017.

EXECUTIVES

CEO and Managing Director Jaguar Land Rover, Ralf Speth, age 65
COO, Satish B. Borwankar
Group CFO, P. B. Balaji, age 50
President Passenger Vehicle Business Unit, Mayank Pareek
CEO and Managing Director, Guenter Butschek, age 60
Chairman, Natarajan (Chandra) Chandrasekaran, age 57
Auditors: KPMG Assurance and Consulting Services LLP

LOCATIONS

HQ: Tata Motors Ltd
Bombay House, 24, Homi Mody Street, Mumbai, Maharashtra 400 001
Phone: (91) 22 6665 8282   **Fax:** (91) 22 6665 7799
Web: www.tatamotors.com

2018 Sales

	% of total
India	20
UK	17
Rest of Europe	16
United States	15
China	15
Rest of the World	17
Total	**100**

PRODUCTS/OPERATIONS

2018 Sales

	% of total
Jaguar Land Rover Vehicles	76
Tata and Flat Vehicles	20
Tata Daewoo Commercial Vehicles	2
Financial Revenues	1
Others	1
Total	**100**

Selected Products and Services

Cars and Sport Utility Vehicles
  Hatchbacks
  Sedans
  Sport Utility Vehicles
Defence
  Logistic
  Troop Carriers
  Water Tankers
  Tippers
  Load Carriers
  Prison Vans
  Fire tenders
  Aid & Development Vehicles
  Ambulances
  Buses
  Recovery Trucks
  Refrigerated Trucks
  Utility Trucks/Troop Carriers
  Armored Trucks
  Combat Vehicles
  Combat Support Vehicles
Trucks and Buses
  Trucks and Buses
  Municipal Solutions

Selected Subsidiaries

Concorde Motors (India) Limited
Jaguar Land Rover PLC-UK
PT Tata Indonesia
Sheba Properties Ltd-India
TAL Manufacturing Solutions Ltd-India
Tata Daewoo Commercial Vehicle Co Ltd- South Korea
Tata Hispano Motors Carrocera SA- Spain
Tata Marcopolo Motors Ltd-India.
Tata Motors (SA) Proprietary Ltd -South Africa.
Tata Motors European Technical center PLC -UK
Tata Motors Finance Ltd -India
Tata Motors Insurance Broking and Advisory Services Ltd-India
Tata Motors(Thailand) Ltd
Tata Precision Industries Pts Ltd-Singapore
Tata Technologies Ltd-India
TML Distribution Company Ltd-India
TML Drivelines Ltd-India
TML Holdings Pte Ltd- Singapore

COMPETITORS

BMW	Kia Motors
Bajaj Auto	Komatsu
Caterpillar	Mahindra
Daimler	Mazda
FCA US	Nissan
Fiat Chrysler	Renault
Ford Motor	Subaru
General Motors	Suzuki Motor
Hindustan Motors	Toyota
Honda	Volkswagen
Hyundai Motor	Volvo
Isuzu	

HISTORICAL FINANCIALS

Company Type: Public

Income Statement

FYE: March 31

	REVENUE ($ mil.)	NET INCOME ($ mil.)	NET PROFIT MARGIN	EMPLOYEES
03/20	64,622	(2,838)	—	78,906
03/19	74,571	(7,302)	—	82,797
03/18	71,813	1,660	2.3%	81,090
03/17	66,172	1,524	2.3%	79,558
03/16	67,191	2,388	3.6%	76,598
Annual Growth	(1.0%)	—	—	0.7%

2020 Year-End Financials

Debt ratio: 0.9%
Return on equity: (-19.8%)
Cash ($ mil.): 8,294
Current ratio: 0.86
Long-term debt ($ mil.): 20,750

No. of shares (mil.): —
Dividends
  Yield: —
  Payout: —
Market value ($ mil.): —

	STOCK PRICE ($) FY Close	P/E High/Low		PER SHARE ($) Earnings	Dividends	Book Value
03/20	4.72	—	—	(0.82)	0.00	4.08
03/19	12.56	—	—	(2.15)	0.00	4.05
03/18	25.70	2	1	0.49	0.00	6.66
03/17	35.65	2	2	0.45	0.01	3.92
03/16	29.05	2	1	0.71	0.00	5.60
Annual Growth	(36.5%)	—	—	—	—	(7.6%)

Tata Steel Ltd

Tata Steel is India's private sector steel company. The company's steel-making and finishing facilities have the capacity to produce nearly 20.6 million tons of crude steel a year. Tata Steel's products include hot and cold rolled coils and sheets tubes wire rods rings and bearings. Its domestic facilities are located in Jamshedpur in eastern India and

Tata Steel's international operations include UK-based subsidiary Tata Steel Europe Singapore's NatSteel and Tata Steel Thailand. The company also owns interests in coal and iron projects that supply the steel maker with raw materials. More than half of the company's total revenue comes from domestic operations. Tata Steel was established in in 1907.

Operations

The company is primarily engaged in the business of manufacture and distribution of steel products across the globe. Operating segments are based on the different geographical areas: Tata Steel India (more than a-third of revenue); Tata Steel Europe (over 30%); Bamnipal steel (10% of revenue; including Tata Steel BSL); Tata Steel long products (less than 5%); other Indian operations (5%); other trade related operations (about 20%); and rest of the world.

Overall approximately 90% of the Tata Steel's revenue comes from Steel products.

Geographic Reach

India-based Tata Steels operates in over 25 countries and has a commercial presence in over 50 countries across five continents. More than half of the total revenue comes from India. Its global offices are located in London Singapore and Thailand.

Sales and Marketing

Tata Steel has diversified offerings across market segments: agriculture; automotive; construction; and industrial and general engineering. Its online and channel sales enabled through digital platforms such as Aashiyana COMPASS DigEca enabled digital sales of products and services.

Financial Performance

Note: Growth rates may differ after conversion to US Dollars.

Tata Steel's revenues declined 11% to ?1.4 trillion in 2020 compared to ?1.6 trillion in 2019. The decrease was primarily due to a decline in realizations across geographies along with lower deliveries. Tata Steel Europe reported a decrease mainly on account of a decrease in average revenue per ton lower deliveries by 4% along with adverse forex impact on translation. Tata Steel BSL Limited also decreases due to lower realization partially offset by higher volumes.

Net income also declined falling 85% to ?15.6 billion in 2020 from ?102.2 billion the year prior. The decline was mainly due to the decrease in revenue as well as recorded losses from discontinued operations.

Cash and cash equivalents at the end of the year were ?77.3 billion in 2020 a ?39.4 billion increase from the year prior. Operating activities generated ?201.7 billion in 2020 while investing activities used ?145.3 billion mainly for purchase of capital assets and acquisition of subsidiaries. Financing activities used ?16.9 billion mostly for long-term borrowings repayment.

Strategy

Tata Steel has gone through a massive restructuring phase in the last several years. In 2019 Tata agreed to sell 70% of its stake in Tata Steel Thailand to Dubai-based Synergy Metals and Mining Fund. Tata Steel also planned to sell its South-East Asian subsidiaries including Singapore-based NatSteel and Tata Steel Thailand to HBIS Group Co. Ltd.

Tata Steel has recently made strategic acquisitions to aid in its production capabilities. The steel business Usha Martin Limited was acquired by Tata Steel Long Products Limited in 2019 increasing the total deliveries of the group. Tata Steel BSL Limited also completed the acquisition of Bhushan Energy Limited in 2019.

Tata Steel is also developing cutting-edge technologies and designing solutions that help transform processes improve efficiencies and enhance the customer experience. It has embarked on a long-term digital technology-led business transformation program to drive value creation. The company aims to become the industry leader in steel; to consolidate its position as a global cost leader; to insulate revenues from steel cyclicality; and to become an industry leader in CSR and SHE. Tata Steel also continues to minimize its environmental footprint despite being part of a 'hard to abate' industry through its various inclusive programs and organizational partnerships.

Mergers and Acquisitions

In early 2019 Tata Sponge Iron Limited a subsidiary of Tata Steel has acquired the India-based steel business of Usha Martin Limited (UML). The acquisition includes captive power plants pursuant to a cash consideration (after adjustment for negative working capital and debt like items) payable to UML of Rs. 4094 crore which is subject to further hold backs of Rs.640 crore pending transfer of some of the assets including mines and certain land parcels. The acquisition also involves UML's 1.0 MnTPA specialty steel plant in Jamshedpur that makes alloy based long products a functional iron ore mine and a coal mine under development and captive power plants.

Company Background

Tata Steel was founded in 1907 as Asia's first private sector integrated steel company.

EXECUTIVES

Group CFO, Koushik Chatterjee, age 53
Managing Director Tata Steel India and South East Asia, T. V. Narendran, age 55
Chairman, Natarajan (Chandra) Chandrasekaran, age 57
Auditors: Price Waterhouse & Co Chartered Accountants LLP

LOCATIONS

HQ: Tata Steel Ltd
Bombay House, 24 Homi Mody Street, Mumbai 400 001
Phone: (91) 22 6665 8282   **Fax:** (91) 22 6665 7724
Web: www.tatasteel.com

2016 Sales

	% of total
Outside India	68
Within India	32
Total	**100**

PRODUCTS/OPERATIONS

2016 Sales

	% of total
Steel	91
Others	9
Total	**100**

Selected Operations

Steel
Ferroalloys & Minerals (chrome mines & manufacturing ferro chrome & ferro manganese)
Bearings (ball bearings clutch release bearings & double row self-aligning bearings)
Tubes
Wire

COMPETITORS

ArcelorMittal
Baosteel
Essar Group
JFE Holdings
Kobe Steel
Mitsubishi Materials
Nippon Steel & Sumitomo Metal Corporation
POSCO
Steel Authority of India
United States Steel

HISTORICAL FINANCIALS

Company Type: Public

Income Statement

FYE: March 31

	REVENUE ($ mil.)	NET INCOME ($ mil.)	NET PROFIT MARGIN	EMPLOYEES
03/20	18,510	206	1.1%	70,212
03/19	22,786	1,476	6.5%	75,294
03/18	20,444	2,064	10.1%	65,144
03/17	18,187	(653)	—	67,902
03/16	18,308	(461)	—	76,952
Annual Growth	**0.3%**	**—**	**—**	**(2.3%)**

2020 Year-End Financials

Debt ratio: 0.5%
Return on equity: 2.1%
Cash ($ mil.): 1,066
Current ratio: 0.93
Long-term debt ($ mil.): 11,677
No. of shares (mil.): 1,202
Dividends
  Yield: —
  Payout: 97.7%
Market value ($ mil.): —

	STOCK PRICE ($) FY Close	P/E High/Low	PER SHARE ($) Earnings	Dividends	Book Value
03/20	0.00	— —	0.16	0.15	8.10
03/19	15.00	— —	1.27	0.12	8.28
03/18	15.00	— —	1.97	0.35	7.78
03/17	15.00	— —	(0.69)	0.10	6.01
Annual Growth	**—**	**— —**	**—**	**10.4%**	**7.7%**

Tatneft PJSC

Auditors: AO PricewaterhouseCoopers Audit

LOCATIONS

HQ: Tatneft PJSC
Lenina St. 75, Almetyevsk, Tatarstan 423450
Phone: (7) 8553 371 111   **Fax:** (7) 8553 376 151
Web: www.tatneft.ru

HISTORICAL FINANCIALS

Company Type: Public

Income Statement

FYE: December 31

	REVENUE ($ mil.)	NET INCOME ($ mil.)	NET PROFIT MARGIN	EMPLOYEES
12/19	15,342	3,089	20.1%	0
12/18	13,398	3,039	22.7%	0
12/17	12,317	2,129	17.3%	0
12/16	9,604	1,753	18.3%	0
12/15	7,484	1,339	17.9%	0
Annual Growth	**19.7%**	**23.2%**	**—**	**—**

2019 Year-End Financials

Debt ratio: 0.0%
Return on equity: 25.3%
Cash ($ mil.): 404
Current ratio: 0.71
Long-term debt ($ mil.): 347
No. of shares (mil.): 2,103
Dividends
  Yield: —
  Payout: 99.3%
Market value ($ mil.): —

TC Energy Corp

TC Energy Corporation (formerly TransCanada) is a provider of gas transmission and power generation. It owns 57900 miles of natural gas pipeline; connects growing supply in the most prolific basins on the continent to key markets. The company also owns a major oil pipeline (Keystone) and stakes in several other gas pipelines. TC Energy has nearly 655 billion cu. ft. of natural gas storage assets. On the power side of its business portfolio it owns operates or controls about 10 power plants in Canada and the US with approximately 6000 MW of power generation capacity. The company changed its name from TransCanada to TC Energy to better reflect its position as an energy infrastructure company in all of North America.

Operations

TC Energy operate in three core businesses: Natural Gas Pipelines (accounts for more than 70% of the total revenue); Liquids Pipelines (over 20%); and Power and Storage accounts the remainder.

Natural gas pipeline has 93300-kilometre (57900-mile) network that supplies more than 25% of the clean-burning natural gas consumed daily across North America. This pipeline network strategically connects growing supply in the most prolific basins on the continent to key markets across Canada the US and Mexico. It also operate one of the continent's largest natural gas storage businesses with about 655 billion cubic feet of regulated and non-regulated storage capacity.

The company's 4900-kilometre (3000-mile) liquids pipeline system connects growing continental oil supplies to key markets and refineries. The Keystone Pipeline System delivers approximately 20% of western Canadian exports to the U.S. Midwest and Gulf Coast where it is converted into fuel and other useful petroleum products.

The previously described Energy segment has been renamed the Power and Storage segment. This business consists of power generation and non-regulated natural gas storage assets. Its power business includes approximately 6000 MW of generation capacity that currently own or developing.

Geographic Reach

Headquartered in Canada TC Energy's operations in the US is the largest markets in terms of revenue which accounts for more than 55% followed by Canada that contributes around 40% and the remaining 5% revenue comes from Mexico.

The company has four natural gas-fired cogeneration facilities in Alberta and 10 power generation facilities - enough to power more than 5 million homes.

Sales and Marketing

TC Energy's liquids business provides customers with a variety of crude oil marketing services including transportation storage and crude oil management primarily through the purchase and sale of physical crude oil. Its natural gas pipeline network transports natural gas from supply basins to local distribution companies power generation plants industrial facilities interconnecting pipelines LNG export terminals and other businesses.

Financial Performance

The company's revenue has been rising in the last five years with the exception of 2019. Still it has an overall growth of 17% between 2015 and 2019.

The company's revenue totaled C$13.3 million a 3% decline from the previous year. The decline was primarily due to lower sales in Power and Storage segment.

Net income for 2019 totaled C$4.1 billion a 12% increase from the previous year.

The company's cash at the end of the year was C$1.3 billion. Operating activities generated C$7.1 billion while investing activities used C$6.9 billion mainly for capital expenditures. Financing activities generated C$ 693 million.

Strategy

Key components of TransCanada's strategy:
Maximizing the full-life value of its infrastructure assets and commercial positions - The company's

power and non-regulated storage assets are primarily under long-term contracts that provide stable cash flows and earnings.

Commercially developing and building new asset investment programs - The company is developing high quality long-life assets under its current capital program comprised of $30 billion in secured projects and $21 billion in largely commercially-supported projects under development. These investments will contribute incremental earnings and cash flows as they are placed in service.

Cultivating a focused portfolio of high-quality development and investment options - The company assess opportunities to develop and acquire energy infrastructure that complements its existing portfolio considers future resilience and diversifies access to attractive supply and market regions within its risk tolerance profile. Refer to the Enterprise risk management section for additional information.

Maximizing its competitive strengths - The company is continually refining core competencies in key sustainability and ESG areas such as safety operational excellence supply chain management project execution and stakeholder relations to ensure it deliver maximum shareholder value over the short medium and long terms.

Mergers and Acquisitions

In late 2020 TC Energy has made a non-binding offer to acquire all the outstanding common units of the master limited partnership Texas-based TC PipeLines LP (TCP) not beneficially owned by TC Energy or its affiliates in exchange for TC Energy common shares. The transaction is subject to the review and favorable recommendation by the Conflicts Committee of the TCP Board and approvals by the TCP Board the Board of Directors of TC Energy and the holders of a majority of the outstanding common units of TCP. The proposed exchange ratio reflects a value for all the publicly held common units of TCP of approximately US$1.48 billion or 35.2 million TC Energy common shares if completed on the terms offered based on the closing price of TC Energy's common shares.

In early 2020 the company announced that its wholly owned subsidiary NOVA Gas Transmission Ltd. (NGTL) has executed an exclusive letter of intent with Tidewater Midstream and Infrastructure Inc and TransAlta Corporation to purchase the Pioneer Pipeline for $255 million. The Pioneer Pipeline consists of 131 km of operating pipeline that upon closing of the transaction will be integrated into the NGTL System. The pipeline is located within Alberta and runs from west of Drayton Valley to west of Edmonton. The acquisition will to connect Western Canadian Sedimentary Basin (WCSB) supply to Alberta power generation demand which supports coal-to-gas conversion and lowers carbon emissions.

HISTORY

TransCanada had become financially overextended by branching into a range of energy businesses. It sold its gas marketing business to US energy marketer Mirant (now GenOn Energy) and divested its operations in Latin America. In the past few years the company has been growing its power business. In 2003 it acquired 33% of nuclear plant operator Bruce Power for C$376 million. It also has been building a 550 MW natural gas-fired cogeneration plant in Quebec. However the group sold a power generation subsidiary TransCanada Power to EPCOR Utilities in 2005. The subsidiary operated 11 power generation plants in Canada and the US. That sale enabled TransCanada to focus on its larger directly owned power businesses in Canada and the US.

Also sold was the company's general partner interest in ONEOK Partners a subsidiary of ONEOK.

The company expanded its transportation and generation operations by acquiring Gas Transmission Northwest from bankrupt National Energy & Gas Transmission (NEGT) for $1.7 billion in 2004. It also acquired the hydroelectric generation assets of USGen New England a NEGT subsidiary in 2005.

The company became the operator of Northern Border Pipeline in early 2007. Northern Border Pipeline owns a 1249-mile interstate pipeline system that transports gas from the Montana-Saskatchewan border to the upper Midwest region of the US. In a major move that expanded its US operations in 2007 it acquired ANR Pipeline its storage assets in Michigan and control of Great Lakes Gas Transmission from El Paso Corporation for just over $4 billion (including assumed debt).

In 2008 the company was selected as the lead bidder for the proposed $26 billion Alaska Pipeline Project which will link North Slope gas fields to end users across Canada and in the lower 48 states. In 2009 the company signed up Exxon Mobil to work with it in developing the project.

Pursuing an expansion strategy on the power side of the ledger in 2008 TransCanada acquired the 2480 MW Ravenswood Generating Station in New York City from National Grid for $2.9 billion. In 2009 the company announced plans to build a $1.2 billion power plant in Southern Ontario due to begin producing power by the end of 2013. This segment is also developing wind farms as a green energy option.

To raise cash to pay down debt in 2011 the company sold 25% of Gas Transmission Northwest and Bison Pipeline to subsidiary TC Pipelines for $605 million.

Expanding its pipeline business in 2012 the company signed a deal with Phoenix Energy Holdings Limited to develop the $3 billion Grand Rapids (oil) Pipeline project in Northern Alberta. It also agreed to acquire BP's 40% stake in the Crossfield Gas Storage facility and BP's interest in CrossAlta Gas Storage & Services Ltd. a marketing joint venture between the two companies. This deal was valued of $210 million.

In 2019 the company changed its name from TransCanada to TC Energy (TC nergie in French and TC Energ a in Spanish) to better reflect its position as an energy infrastructure company in all of North America.

EXECUTIVES

President and CEO, Russell K. (Russ) Girling, age 57, $394,523 total compensation
Director Planning Evaluation and Rates; VP TC PipeLines, Wendy Hanrahan, age 59
EVP; President US Natural Gas Pipelines, Stanley G. (Stan) Chapman
VP Finance and Treasurer, Donald R. (Don) Marchand
EVP; President Canada and Mexico Natural Gas Pipelines and Energy, Karl Johannson
EVP; President Liquids Pipelines, Paul Miller
EVP Stakeholder and Technical Services and General Counsel, Kristine L. Delkus
EVP Strategy and Corporate Development, Fran ̧Sois Poirier
Chairman, Siim A. Vanaselja
Auditors: KPMG LLP

LOCATIONS

HQ: TC Energy Corp
450 - 1st Street S.W., Calgary, Alberta T2P 5H1
Phone: 403 920-6411   **Fax:** 403 920-2467
Web: www.tcenergy.com

2014 Sales

	% of total
Canada	52
US	46
Mexico	2
Total	**100**

PRODUCTS/OPERATIONS

2014 Sales

	% of total
Natural gas pipeline	48
Energy	37
Liquids pipelines	15
Total	**100**

Selected Pipelines

Alberta System
Canadian Mainline
Foothills System
Keystone (under construction)
Great Lakes Gas Transmission Company (69%)
Gas Transmission Northwest (83%)
Iroquois Gas Transmission System (45%)
Northern Border Pipeline (17%)
Portland Natural Gas Transmission System (62%)
Tamazunchale Pipeline
Trans Qué;bec & Maritimes (50%)
Tuscarora Gas Transmission (33%)

Selected Power Plants

Bear Creek (Alberta)
Bé;cancour (Qué;bec)
Cancarb (Alberta)
Carseland (Alberta)
Coolidge (Arizona)
Deerfield River System
Grandview (New Brunswick)
Halton Hills (Ontario)
Kirby Wind Power
MacKay River (Alberta)
Ocean State (Rhode Island)
Ravenswood (New York)
Redwater (Alberta)

COMPETITORS

Berkshire Hathaway Energy	Marathon Oil
Buckeye Partners	Ontario Power Generation
Enbridge	TransAlta
Enron	U.S. Transmission
Fortis Inc.	Williams Companies
Imperial Oil	

HISTORICAL FINANCIALS

Company Type: Public

Income Statement   FYE: December 31

	REVENUE ($ mil.)	NET INCOME ($ mil.)	NET PROFIT MARGIN	EMPLOYEES
12/19	13,422	4,192	31.2%	7,305
12/18	13,851	3,748	27.1%	7,081
12/17	13,618	3,196	23.5%	6,779
12/16	12,662	235	1.9%	7,165
12/15	11,442	(1,160)	—	5,512
Annual Growth	4.1%	—	—	7.3%

2019 Year-End Financials

Debt ratio: 46.5%	No. of shares (mil.): 938
Return on equity: 13.7%	Dividends
Cash ($ mil.): 1,359	Yield: 4.2%
Current ratio: 0.59	Payout: 91.4%
Long-term debt ($ mil.): 43,434	Market value ($ mil.): 50,026

	STOCK PRICE ($) FY Close	P/E High/Low		PER SHARE ($) Earnings	Dividends	Book Value
12/19	53.31	13	9	4.32	2.27	33.20
12/18	35.70	13	9	3.97	2.10	32.36
12/17	48.64	15	13	3.47	2.53	28.77
12/16	45.15	302	184	0.16	2.29	29.82
12/15	32.59	—	—	(1.77)	1.60	23.69
Annual Growth	13.1%	—	—	—	9.1%	8.8%

TDK Corp

TDK puts materials to work to transfer and store energy as well as store digital information. The company branched out from its original focus in the 1930s of commercializing ferrite a magnetic material. TDK is a leading maker of capacitors transformers inductors and other products that are key parts of modern electronics. It also makes rechargeable batteries for smartphones and other mobile devices as well as hard disk drives and components. TDK targets the communications automobile industrial equipment energy and information appliances markets. With operations around the world Japan-based TDK generates about 90% of its sales outside of its home country.

Financial Performance

TDK's revenue has trended higher over the past five years rising an average of 5% a year.

In 2019 (ended March) revenue rose about 9% to Å 1.4 trillion. The company's Energy Applications segment drove the increase posting a 21% sales jump on a stronger performance by rechargeable batteries for smartphones tablets and laptops. Higher capacitor sales boosted the Passive Components segment's sales about 4%. Sales in the Magnetic Applications and Sensor Applications segments fell about 4% and 1% year-over-year respectively.

TDK posted net income of more than Å 82 billion in 2019 an 18% increase from 2018 pushed by stronger sales in 2019 compared to 2018. The Magnetic Applications segment contributed to higher profit by shipping more high-value HDD products for use in data centers.

The company had Å 2.6 trillion in cash in 2019 compared to Å 1.2 trillion in 2018. Operating activities produced Å 1.2 trillion while investing activities used Å 1.2 trillion and financing activities provided Å 85 billion.

Strategy

TDK expects that near-term growth might be stifled by international trade issues like the US-China trade battle and the UK's exit from the European Union. With that in mind the company is focusing on developing plans for mid-term and long-term growth.

TDK invests in its capacitors to build on their strong position in the automotive market and its rechargeable batteries business to leverage its strength in smartphones to develop other markets.

An element of the US-China trade dispute that could affect TDK is Huawei the Chinese manufacturer of telecommunications equipment. It accounts for an estimated 10% of TDK's sales. The US government has threatened to ban Huawei doing business with American companies because of security concerns. TDK could have to choose between doing business with US firms who might be barred from using Huawei equipment or doing business with Huawei.

EXECUTIVES

Senior Managing Executive Officer; President and CEO TDK-EPC, Hiroyuki Uemura, age 65
Senior Managing Executive Officer, Atsuo Kobayashi, age 61
President and CEO, Shigenao Ishiguro
SVP and CFO, Joachim Zichlarz
Chairman, Takehiro Kamigama, age 63
Auditors: KPMG AZSA LLC

LOCATIONS

HQ: TDK Corp
2-5-1 Nihonbashi, Chuo-ku, Tokyo 103-6128
Phone: (81) 3 6778 1060   **Fax:** 516 294-8318
Web: www.jp.tdk.com

PRODUCTS/OPERATIONS

2019 Sales

	% of total
Energy Application Products	39
Passive Application Products	31
Magnetic Application Products	20
Sensor Application Products	6
Other	4
Total	**100**

2019 Sales

	% of total
Asia and others	72
Europe	12
Americas	8
Japan	8
Total	**100**

Selected Products

Data Storage
  Magnetic heads (hard disk drives)
  Thermal-assist magnetic heads (scheduled to begin production in March 2013)
Electronic Components
  Anechoic chambers
  Capacitors
  Converters
  Cores and magnets
  Ferrite
  Metal
  Inductors
  Power supplies
  Sensors
  Transformers
  Varistors
Other
  Factory automation equipment
  Organic EL displays

COMPETITORS

ALPS Holdings	Murata Manufacturing
Bosch Corp.	Panasonic Corp
Delta Electronics	STMicroelectronics
FUJIFILM	Samsung Group
Hitachi Metals	Seagate Technology
Infineon Technologies	Taiyo Yuden
Kyocera	Western Digital

HISTORICAL FINANCIALS

Company Type: Public

Income Statement

FYE: March 31

	REVENUE ($ mil.)	NET INCOME ($ mil.)	NET PROFIT MARGIN	EMPLOYEES
03/20	13,743	582	4.2%	107,138
03/19	13,932	828	5.9%	104,781
03/18	12,822	639	5.0%	102,883
03/17	11,880	1,463	12.3%	99,693
03/16	11,617	653	5.6%	91,648
Annual Growth	**4.3%**	**(2.8%)**	**—**	**4.0%**

2020 Year-End Financials

Debt ratio: 0.2%
Return on equity: 6.7%
Cash ($ mil.): 3,354
Current ratio: 1.34
Long-term debt ($ mil.): 1,412
No. of shares (mil.): 126
Dividends
  Yield: 2.0%
  Payout: 34.1%
Market value ($ mil.): 9,663

	STOCK PRICE ($) FY Close	P/E High/Low		PER SHARE ($) Earnings	Dividends	Book Value
03/20	76.50	0	0	4.60	1.57	67.36
03/19	78.50	0	0	6.55	1.34	70.04
03/18	89.47	0	0	5.06	1.06	65.86
03/17	63.58	0	0	11.57	1.11	63.41
03/16	55.65	0	0	5.09	0.89	53.99
Annual Growth	**8.3%**	**—**	**—**	**(2.5%)**	**15.2%**	**5.7%**

TechnipFMC plc

Auditors: PricewaterhouseCoopers LLP

LOCATIONS

HQ: TechnipFMC plc
One St. Paul's Churchyard, London EC4M 8AP
Phone: (44) 203 429 3950
Web: www.technipfmc.com/

HISTORICAL FINANCIALS

Company Type: Public

Income Statement

FYE: December 31

	REVENUE ($ mil.)	NET INCOME ($ mil.)	NET PROFIT MARGIN	EMPLOYEES
12/19	13,409	(2,415)	—	37,000
12/18	12,552	(1,921)	—	37,000
12/17	15,056	113	0.8%	37,000
12/16	0	(0)	—	0
12/15	0	0	—	0
Annual Growth	**—**			

2019 Year-End Financials

Debt ratio: 19.0%
Return on equity: (-26.7%)
Cash ($ mil.): 5,239
Current ratio: 1.17
Long-term debt ($ mil.): 3,980
No. of shares (mil.): 447
Dividends
  Yield: 2.4%
  Payout: —
Market value ($ mil.): —

Telecom Argentina SA

EXECUTIVES

President, Carlos Alberto Moltini
Vice President, Mariano Marcelo Ibañez
Auditors: Price Waterhouse & Co. S.R.L.

LOCATIONS

HQ: Telecom Argentina SA
Avenida Alicia Moreau de Justo 50, Buenos Aires C1107AAB
Phone: (54) 11 4968 3628   **Fax:** (54) 11 4312 7055
Web: www.telecom.com.ar

PRODUCTS/OPERATIONS

2014 Sales

	% of total
Voice	39
Data	31
Internet	18
Equipment	12
Total	**100**

2014 Sales

	% of total
Personal Mobile Services	70
Fixed Services	26
Nucleo Mobile Services	4
Total	**100**

Selected Products & Services

Voice
Internet
Hardware
Data
IT Solutions
Public Telephones

COMPETITORS

América M vil	Telef nica de
NII Holdings	Argentina
TGS	

HISTORICAL FINANCIALS

Company Type: Public

Income Statement

FYE: December 31

	REVENUE ($ mil.)	NET INCOME ($ mil.)	NET PROFIT MARGIN	EMPLOYEES
12/19	74,958	(1,390)	—	23,728
12/18	53,144	1,674	3.2%	25,343
12/17	20,657	2,412	11.7%	15,396
12/16	16,863	1,257	7.5%	15,970
12/15	12,820	1,076	8.4%	16,224
Annual Growth	**55.5%**	—	—	**10.0%**

2019 Year-End Financials

Debt ratio: 6.3%	No. of shares (mil.): —
Return on equity: (-1.6%)	Dividends
Cash ($ mil.): 8,090	Yield: 10.9%
Current ratio: 0.59	Payout: —
Long-term debt ($ mil.): 36,911	Market value ($ mil.): —

	STOCK PRICE ($) FY Close	P/E High/Low		PER SHARE ($) Earnings	Dividends	Book Value
12/19	11.35	—	*	(0.65)	1.24	44.80
12/18	15.56	16	6	0.78	3.43	33.14
12/17	36.63	5	2	2.49	1.14	7.53
12/16	18.17	5	4	1.30	0.65	6.31
12/15	16.07	7	4	1.11	1.02	5.61
Annual Growth	**(8.3%)**	—	—	—	**5.1%**	**68.1%**

Telecom Italia SpA

Telecom Italia SpA (TIM) is Italy's #1 telephone operator with more than 17100 fixed retail and wholesale access lines and more than 30800 mobile lines for retail and wholesale customers. The company has the largest customer base in Italy. It also operates in Brazil where it boasts about 55000 subscribers to its mobile services. Subsidiary Inwit is responsible for the management and operations of telecom towers used by TIM and other operators. Besides telecommunications TIM's Olivetti

brand makes IT products such as printers calculators cash registers and digital school equipment for businesses and other organizations. TIM generates more than 75% of its sales in Italy.

Operations

TIM operates in three reportable segments: Domestic Brazil and Other Operations.

TIM's domestic segment generates about 80% of revenue. The segment also includes Olivetti (products and services for IT) INWIT (electronic communications) and Telecom Italia Sparkle Group (fiber-optic networks for wholesale).

The Brazil business unit generates about 20% of TIM's revenue. It provides mobile telephone service using UMTS GSM and LTE Technologies.

Other operations segment includes the financial companies (Telecom Italia Capital S.A. and Telecom Italia Finance S.A.) and other minor companies not strictly related to the TIM Group's core business.

Overall The company's services account for about 90% of total revenue while equipment sales and construction contracts account for the remaining.

Geographic Reach

Based in Rome TIM's main geographies are Italy (80% of sales) and Brazil (20%). Through subsidiary Sparkle the company operates in Europe the Mediterranean South America.

Sales and Marketing

TIM divides its sales organizations for consumers business wholesale and other.

The consumer unit is made up of fixed and mobile voice and internet services and products for individuals families and public telephony. The segment includes TIM Retail.

The business unit consists of voice data and internet services and products as well as ICT technologies for small and medium businesses home offices public sector large. accounts and enterprises in the fixed and mobile telecoms markets. The segment includes Olivetti TI Trust Technologies and Tesly.

Wholesale manages and develops of the portfolio of the regulated and unregulated whole services for fixed-line and mobile telecommunications operators in the domestic market and open access operations. The segment includes TN Fiber TI San Marino and Telefonia Mobile Sammarinese.

Financial Performance

Note: Growth rates may differ after conversion to US Dollars.

Total TIM Group revenues decreased 5% to 17974 million euros for 2019 compared with the previous year. This was primarily due to lower sales in the company's services segment.

2019 Net profit for the year attributable to owners of the parent amounted to 916 million euros (while a net loss of 1.4 billion euros was posted in 2018).

Cash at the end of 2019 was 3.2 billion euros. Operating activities generated 5.9 billion euros while investing activities used 3.2 billion euros mainly for purchases of intangible tangible and rights of use assets on a cash basis. Financing activities used another 1.1 billion euros primarily for repayments of non-current financial liabilities.

Strategy

TIM has four strategic initiatives consist of:

Network-sharing partnership with INWIT and Vodafone Italia: following the green light from the European antitrust authority the creation of the new INWIT and the implementation of the planned programs for the sharing of passive mobile network infrastructure with Vodafone will be monitored with benefits in terms of lower capital invested and shorter development times for 5G networks.

Fiber networks: a period of exclusivity has been granted to the KKR Infrastructure fund as a finan-

cial partner for the development of the fiber network in Italy following the submission of a non-binding offer for the purchase of approximately 40% of TIM's secondary fiber/copper network and given the desired integration with Open Fiber.

Partnership for Cloud Services: signed the final agreements with Google Cloud which start a technological collaboration to create cloud services and enrich TIM's technological services offering which will lead to the development of business of about 1 billion euros in revenues and 400 million euros in EBITDA up to 2024.

Exclusive deal with Disney: the big world player in the content industry has chosen TIM Vision for the exclusive distribution of Disney+ in Italy confirming TIM Vision as the reference operator in the aggregation of premium content in Italy a position achieved in just one year.

Company Background

Telecom Italia S.p.A. is a leader in fixed-line and wireless telecommunication services in Italy. As a holding company with majority ownership in numerous subsidiaries it provides domestic and international fixed-line and wireless telecommunication operations as well as Internet information technology and satellite communication services. Its international operations include fixed-line and wireless communications in Latin America and the Mediterranean region. It is the majority owner of Telecom Italia Mobile (TIM) Italy's leading provider of wireless communications. Telecom Italia is the former government telephone monopoly which was privatized in 1997 and controlled by Olivetti in 1999 in a hostile takeover. Telecom Italia faces increasing competition in both domestic and international markets.

EXECUTIVES

CEO, Flavio Cattaneo, age 57
Head of Technology, Giuseppe R. Opilio, age 62
CFO, Piergiorgio Peluso, age 52
CEO TIM Participa § ões S.A., Rodrigo Modesto Abreu
Chairman, Arnaud Roy de Puyfontaine, age 56
Deputy Chairman, Giuseppe Recchi, age 56
Auditors: EY S.p.A.

LOCATIONS

HQ: Telecom Italia SpA
Via Gaetano Negri 1, Milan 20123
Phone: (39) 06 36 88 1
Web: www.telecomitalia.com

2018 Sales

	% of total
Italy	79
Other regions	21
Total	**100**

PRODUCTS/OPERATIONS

2018 Sales

	% of total
Services	92
Equipment sales	8
Total	**100**

2017 Sales

	% of total
Domestic	79
Brazil	21
Total	**100**

COMPETITORS

América M vil	Orange
BT	Tele2
Cable & Wireless	Telef nica
Deutsche Telekom	Tiscali

FastWeb Vivo Participa § μes
Iliad S.A. Vodafone Omnitel
Millicom Wind Telecomunicazioni

HISTORICAL FINANCIALS
Company Type: Public

Income Statement				FYE: December 31
	REVENUE ($ mil.)	NET INCOME ($ mil.)	NET PROFIT MARGIN	EMPLOYEES
12/19	21,831	1,028	4.7%	55,198
12/18	22,733	(1,615)	—	57,901
12/17	25,146	1,343	5.3%	59,429
12/16	21,091	1,909	9.1%	61,229
12/15	22,504	(78)	—	65,867
Annual Growth	(0.8%)	—	—	(4.3%)

2019 Year-End Financials
Debt ratio: 38.3%
Return on equity: 4.6%
Cash ($ mil.): 3,523
Current ratio: 1.18
Long-term debt ($ mil.): 26,884
No. of shares (mil.): —
Dividends
Yield: 0.0%
Payout: 25.0%
Market value ($ mil.): —

	STOCK PRICE ($) FY Close	P/E High/Low	PER SHARE ($) Earnings	Dividends	Book Value
12/19	6.18	162 121	0.04	0.01	1.51
12/18	5.55	— —	(0.08)	0.00	1.49
12/17	8.63	221 160	0.06	0.00	1.72
12/16	8.89	151 83	0.08	0.00	1.49
12/15	12.65	— —	(0.00)	0.00	1.44
Annual Growth	(16.4%)	— —	—	—	1.3%

Telefonica SA

Auditors: PricewaterhouseCoopers Auditores, S.L.

LOCATIONS

HQ: Telefonica SA
Distrito Telefonica, Ronda de la Comunicacion, s/n,
Madrid 28050
Phone: (34) 91 482 8700 **Fax:** (34) 91 482 8600
Web: www.telefonica.com

HISTORICAL FINANCIALS
Company Type: Public

Income Statement				FYE: December 31
	REVENUE ($ mil.)	NET INCOME ($ mil.)	NET PROFIT MARGIN	EMPLOYEES
12/19	54,366	1,282	2.4%	113,819
12/18	55,762	3,814	6.8%	120,138
12/17	62,344	3,754	6.0%	122,718
12/16	54,943	2,501	4.6%	127,323
12/15	51,431	2,989	5.8%	129,890
Annual Growth	1.4%	(19.1%)	—	(3.2%)

2019 Year-End Financials
Debt ratio: 49.4%
Return on equity: 6.5%
Cash ($ mil.): 6,783
Current ratio: 0.81
Long-term debt ($ mil.): 48,602
No. of shares (mil.): —
Dividends
Yield: 6.4%
Payout: 62.2%
Market value ($ mil.): —

	STOCK PRICE ($) FY Close	P/E High/Low	PER SHARE ($) Earnings	Dividends	Book Value
12/19	6.97	52 39	0.19	0.45	3.76
12/18	8.46	17 13	0.65	0.46	4.01
12/17	9.68	23 17	0.67	0.48	3.96
12/16	9.20	26 19	0.44	0.77	3.92
12/15	11.06	30 22	0.56	0.98	4.03
Annual Growth	(10.9%) (1.7%)	— —	(23.4%)	(17.8%)	

Telenor ASA

Telenor is a leading Scandinavian telecommunications provider offering mobile broadband and TV services. The Norway-based company's mobile business has about 174 million subscribers in its home country Sweden and Denmark and across the world in Pakistan Bangladesh Thailand Malaysia and Myanmar. Telenor entered Finland's telecom market in 2019 by taking a controlling stake in DNA the country's third-largest mobile firm. Norway is Telenor's biggest market accounting for about a quarter of revenue while Southeast Asian operations combine to provide more than 50% of revenue.

Financial Performance
Telenor's annual revenue peaked at more than $128 billion Norwegian krone (NOK) in 2015 and has declined since as its number of landline customers has shrunk. Paring cost helped strengthen the company's profits in 2017 and 2018.

Revenue in 2018 dipped to NOK 110.4 billion down 1.5% dip from 2017 due to lower handset sales a diminished customer base for legacy products and interconnect revenue. The company reported growth in mobile subscriptions and traffic revenue as well as in the number of high-speed internet customers.

Net income rose to NOK 14.7 billion in 2018 up NOK 2.7 billion from 2017 boosted by the partial sale of ownership of Telenor Microfinance Bank and the disposal of assets in Central and Eastern Europe.

In 2018 Telenor's cash coffers had NOK 18.3 billion compared to NOK 22.3 billion the year before. In 2018 operating activities generated NOL 36.4 billion while investing and financing activities used NOK 613 million and NOK 39.5 billion.

Strategy
Telenor's far-flung operations are governed by three strategic watchwords: Growth efficiency and simplification. Seeking efficiency the company continues to cut expenses reducing its operational costs 3% in 2018. Telenor has saved some money by outsourcing network and IT operations and sharing infrastructure in some Asian markets.

In simplifying Telenor divested its operations in India sharply reduced its stake in VEON (a telecom firm with businesses in Asia Africa and Europe) and sold its operations in Central and Eastern Europe including the merger of its 701Search business with Carousell a fast-growing Asian classifieds marketplace.

Those actions free Telenor to concentrate on its businesses in Scandinavia and Southeast Asia. By claiming a controlling interest in DNA the third-ranking telecom in Finland Telenor now has operations throughout the region. In Scandinavia Telenor is upgrading networks adding base stations and offering new subscription plans designed to keep customers and attract new ones.

In Southeast Asia Telenor is upgrading networks and offering more services. In Pakistan where the company has built a 2.3 gHz network it is developing mobile financial services through a joint venture with Ant Financials.

Further Telenor invests in developing capabilities in artificial intelligence robotics and security.

Telenor faces competition from Telia Co. its Sweden-based rival for Nordic domination. Telia divested holdings in Central and Eastern Europe to focus on the Nordic countries. Telia last year widened its presence in Norway in 2018 by buying TDC A/S's Norwegian business. And Telia bolstered its TV holdings in buying Bonnier AB's TV operations in Sweden and Finland.

EXECUTIVES

EVP and CTO, Berit Svendsen, age 57
EVP and Chief Corporate Affairs Officer, Wenche Agerup, age 56
Acting EVP; CEO Grameenphone Bangladesh, Petter-Borre Furberg
EVP; CEO Telenor Hungary, Alexandra Reich, age 57
EVP and CFO, J rgen C. Arentz Rostrup, age 54
EVP and Head Asia Operations, Sigve Brekke, age 61
EVP and Chief People Officer, Jon E. Haug, age 59
Acting CEO Sweden, Lars- ...ke Norling, age 53
EVP and Chief Marketing Officer, Vivek Sood, age 57
EVP and CEO Grameenphone (Bangladesh), Michael Foley, age 59
EVP; CEO Telenor India, Sharad Mehrotra, age 54
EVP and CTO, Ruza Sabanovic, age 50
EVP and Chief Digital Officer, Jon Gravr k, age 43
EVP; CEO Telenor Myanmar, Lars E. Tellmann
EVP; CEO Telenor Sweden, Patrik Hofbauer, age 53
EVP; CEO Telenor Denmark, Jesper Hansen, age 56
EVP; CEO Telenor Montenegro and Serbia, Ingeborg fsthus, age 53
EVP and CEO Digi Malaysia, Albern Murty, age 49
EVP and Chief Transformation Officer, Morten K. S rby, age 61
EVP; CEO Telenor Pakistan, Irfan W. Khan
Chief Corporate Development Officer Telenor Hungary, Ole Bj rn Sjulstad
President and CEO Telenor Microfinance Bank, Shahid Mustafa
Chairman, Gunn W rsted, age 65
Auditors: Ernst & Young AS

LOCATIONS

HQ: Telenor ASA
Snaroyveien 30, Fornebu N-1360
Phone: (47) 678 90 000
Web: www.telenor.com

2018 Sales

	% of total
Norway	26
Sweden	13
Other Nordic	5
Thailand	17
Malaysia	12
Bangladesh	12
Other Asia	13
Other Countires	2
Total	**100**

PRODUCTS/OPERATIONS

2018 Sales

	% of total
Mobile Subscription and Traffic	63
Fixed Internet/TV	8
Canal Digital DTH	4
Fixed Telephony	1
Fixed Data Services	1
Other Revenue	23
Total	**100**

COMPETITORS

BT	Modern Times Group AB
CELCOM	Orange
Deutsche Telekom	Pakistan Telecom
Hutchison	Tele2
Telecommunications	TeliaSonera
Maxis	Tieto

HISTORICAL FINANCIALS

Company Type: Public

Income Statement
FYE: December 31

	REVENUE ($ mil.)	NET INCOME ($ mil.)	NET PROFIT MARGIN	EMPLOYEES
12/19	22,168	1,515	6.8%	20,000
12/18	21,523	2,872	13.3%	21,000
12/17	24,331	2,337	9.6%	31,000
12/16	25,632	552	2.2%	36,000
12/15	24,997	665	2.7%	35,000
Annual Growth	(3.0%)	22.8%	—	(13.1%)

2019 Year-End Financials

Debt ratio: 8.0%	No. of shares (mil.): 1,422
Return on equity: 17.7%	Dividends
Cash ($ mil.): 2,704	Yield: 5.2%
Current ratio: 0.64	Payout: 89.1%
Long-term debt ($ mil.): 16,682	Market value ($ mil.): 25,476

	STOCK PRICE ($) FY Close	P/E High/Low	PER SHARE ($) Earnings	Dividends	Book Value
12/19	17.91	4 3	1.05	0.94	5.22
12/18	19.37	2 2	1.95	1.52	6.61
12/17	21.39	3 2	1.56	0.94	7.47
12/16	14.92	26 8	0.37	0.90	6.61
12/15	49.78	32 21	0.44	2.67	7.59
Annual Growth	(22.6%)	—	24.2%	(23.0%)	(9.0%)

Telstra Corp., Ltd.

Telstra is Australia's #1 telecommunications carrier serving more than 18.3 million retail mobile phone customers 3.7 million fixed-line bundle and standalone data subscribers and about 1.4 million standalone voice subscribers. It is also a leading ISP with more than 7.3 million fixed line broadband subscribers. Telstra's largest market is consumer and residential customers. The company also provides wholesale network services to other communications companies. Telstra has installed fifth generation (5G) network services in 10 Australian cities preparing for the broader roll out of the technology in the coming years. Telstra has the Asia/Pacific region's largest subsea cable network measuring about 400000 kilometers.

Operations

Telstra operates through four segments: Telstra Consumer and Small Business (TC&SB) Telstra Enterprise (TE) Telstra InfraCo and Networks and IT (N&IT).

The TC&SB segment 55% of revenue provides telecommunications products and mobile services fixed and mobile broadband telephone and Pay TV/IPTV and digital content.

The TE segment about a third of sales manages Telstrós business with larger companies. It manages data and internet protocol (IP) networks mobility services and network applications and services products such as managed network unified communications cloud and integrated services

The Telstra InfraCo segment about 10% of revenue provides telecommunication products and services delivered over Telstra's network to other carries carriage services providers and inter-service providers.

The N&IT segment builds and manages the shared platforms infrastructure cloud services software and technologies for internal functions.

Geographic Reach

Australia accounts for 95% of Telstra's revenue. The company's international operations headquartered in Hong Kong provide services to customers across the Asia/Pacific region Europe the Americas the Middle East and Africa.

Financial Performance

Australian dollars are used in this financial report.

Telstra's revenue has been stagnant in the past five years as it has coped with increased competition in the Australian communications market.

In 2019 (ended June) revenue dropped to $27.8 billion down about $1 billion from 2018. The company blamed the decrease on the National Broadband Network (nbn) a national wholesaler of broadband service that Telstra and other carriers buy service from. The company reported growth in its mobile wholesale and fixed-line businesses.

Telstra's profit also decreased dropping to $2.1 billion in 2019 about 40% lower than the previous year despite cost reductions made in 2019.

The company's coffers held $604 million in cash and equivalents at the end of 2019 compared to $620 million at the close of 2018. In 2019 operations generated $6.7 billion while investing activities used $3.6 billion and financing activities used about $3 billion.

Strategy

The launch of a national broadband network known as nbn has meant headaches for Telstra. In 2019 (ended June) the network cost the company about $600 million in revenue. As the top telecom provider in Australia Telstra had been the de facto broadband provider in the country. But that role will go to nbn when the transition is complete. Telstra created its InfraCo segment in response to nbn and it positions the unit as an alternative infrastructure provider.

In the meantime Telstra aims to improve its overall business through a plan of simplification. It is simplifying its business structure cutting about $456 million in costs in 2019. It has made its offerings to consumers and businesses less complex reducing the number of plans available to 20 from some 1800.

Telstra is rolling out 5G service to more Australian cities and has begun selling 5G handsets. The emergence of the faster network could leapfrog the technologies sold by nbn and feed Telstra's revenue in the coming years.

Auditors: Ernst & Young

LOCATIONS

HQ: Telstra Corp., Ltd.
Level 41, 242 Exhibition Street, Melbourne, Victoria 3000
Phone: (61) 3 8647 4838   **Fax:** (61) 3 8600 9800
Web: www.telstra.com.au

2019 Sales

	% of total
Australia	94
Other countries	6
Total	**100**

PRODUCTS/OPERATIONS

2019 Sales

	% of total
Fixed	21
Mobile	42
Data & IP	9
Network applications & services	14
Media	3
Global connectivity	7
Other	4
Total	**100**

2015 Sales

	% of total
TC&SB	56
TE	33
Telstra InfraCo	11
N&IT	-
Other	-
Total	**100**

Selected Services

Advertising and directory services
Audio video and Internet conferencing
Broadband ISP
Cable TV
Data transmission
E-mail
Enhanced fax products and services
Freecall (toll-free 1-800 phone service)
Information technology (IT) services
Internet access
Mobile phone service
Prepaid telephony
Satellite transmission

COMPETITORS

Hutchison Telecommunications Australia
Optus
PowerTel
Spark New Zealand
Vodafone

HISTORICAL FINANCIALS

Company Type: Public

Income Statement
FYE: June 30

	REVENUE ($ mil.)	NET INCOME ($ mil.)	NET PROFIT MARGIN	EMPLOYEES
06/20	16,248	1,246	7.7%	28,959
06/19	17,697	1,509	8.5%	29,769
06/18	19,206	2,630	13.7%	32,293
06/17	19,986	2,989	15.0%	32,293
06/16	19,278	4,300	22.3%	33,482
Annual Growth	(4.2%)	(26.6%)	—	(3.6%)

2020 Year-End Financials

Debt ratio: 24.4%	No. of shares (mil.): —
Return on equity: 12.5%	Dividends
Cash ($ mil.): 341	Yield: 4.5%
Current ratio: 0.65	Payout: 482.8%
Long-term debt ($ mil.): 8,953	Market value ($ mil.): —

	STOCK PRICE ($) FY Close	P/E High/Low	PER SHARE ($) Earnings	Dividends	Book Value
06/20	10.80	90 66	0.10	0.49	0.83
06/19	13.44	75 51	0.13	0.64	0.86
06/18	9.74	54 32	0.22	0.92	0.93
06/17	16.52	69 47	0.25	1.14	0.94
06/16	20.80	51 40	0.35	1.09	0.97
Annual Growth	(15.1%) (3.6%)	—	— (26.1%)	(18.0%)	

Tencent Holdings Ltd.

Auditors: PricewaterhouseCoopers Certified Public Accountants

LOCATIONS

HQ: Tencent Holdings Ltd.
Tencent Binhai Towers, No. 33 Haitian 2nd Road, Nanshan District, Shenzhen, Guangdong Province 518054
Phone: (86) 755 86013388   **Fax:** (86) 755 86013399
Web: www.tencent.com

HISTORICAL FINANCIALS
Company Type: Public

Income Statement   FYE: December 31

	REVENUE ($ mil.)	NET INCOME ($ mil.)	NET PROFIT MARGIN	EMPLOYEES
12/19	54,221	13,410	24.7%	62,885
12/18	45,461	11,444	25.2%	54,309
12/17	36,536	10,988	30.1%	44,796
12/16	21,880	5,918	27.0%	38,775
12/15	15,838	4,435	28.0%	30,641
Annual Growth	36.0%	31.9%	—	19.7%

2019 Year-End Financials

Debt ratio: 3.3%
Return on equity: 24.6%
Cash ($ mil.): 19,112
Current ratio: 1.06
Long-term debt ($ mil.): 26,958
No. of shares (mil.): —
Dividends
Yield: 0.2%
Payout: 8.0%
Market value ($ mil.): —

	STOCK PRICE ($) FY Close	P/E High/Low		PER SHARE ($) Earnings	Dividends	Book Value
12/19	48.01	5	4	1.39	0.12	6.56
12/18	39.47	7	4	1.20	0.10	4.97
12/17	51.92	8	3	1.15	0.07	4.14
12/16	24.22	6	4	0.62	0.05	2.65
12/15	19.62	7	4	0.47	0.04	1.97
Annual Growth	25.1%	—	—	31.0%	29.6%	35.2%

Tesco PLC (United Kingdom)

Auditors: Deloitte LLP

LOCATIONS

HQ: Tesco PLC (United Kingdom)
Tesco House, Shire Park, Kestrel Way, Welwyn Garden City AL7 1GA
Phone: (44) 1992 632222   **Fax:** (44) 1992 630794
Web: www.tescoplc.com

HISTORICAL FINANCIALS
Company Type: Public

Income Statement   FYE: February 29

	REVENUE ($ mil.)	NET INCOME ($ mil.)	NET PROFIT MARGIN	EMPLOYEES
02/20	83,354	1,249	1.5%	423,092
02/19	83,156	1,720	2.1%	464,505
02/18	80,368	1,685	2.1%	448,988
02/17	70,173	(50)	—	464,520
02/16	75,950	192	0.3%	482,152
Annual Growth	2.4%	59.6%	—	(3.2%)

2020 Year-End Financials

Debt ratio: 18.4%
Return on equity: 6.7%
Cash ($ mil.): 4,386
Current ratio: 0.73
Long-term debt ($ mil.): 7,729
No. of shares (mil.): —
Dividends
Yield: 0.0%
Payout: 206.6%
Market value ($ mil.): —

	STOCK PRICE ($) FY Close	P/E High/Low		PER SHARE ($) Earnings	Dividends	Book Value
02/20	8.77	100	82	0.13	0.26	1.74
02/19	8.71	76	54	0.18	0.14	1.97
02/18	8.64	61	48	0.21	0.04	1.79
02/17	7.10	—	—	(0.01)	0.00	0.99
02/16	7.72	617	344	0.02	0.00	1.48
Annual Growth	3.3%	—	—	52.6%	—	4.2%

Teva Pharmaceutical Industries Ltd

Teva Pharmaceutical Industries is part of the no-name world of generic pharmaceuticals. The company makes affordable medicines and benefit from innovations to improve their health including generics specialty medicines and biopharmaceuticals improving the lives of patients. Headquartered in Israel Teva is a generic medicines maker using its portfolio of more than 1800 molecules to produce generics in nearly every therapeutic area. In specialty medicines Teva is making innovative treatments for disorders of the central nervous system (CNS) as well as respiratory products. The company operates in three segments: North America Europe and International Markets. Around half of the company's total sales were generated from the North America.

Operations

Teva operates its business through three segments: North America (accounts more than 50% of company's revenue) Europe (about 30% of revenue) and International Markets (nearly 15% of revenue).

The North America segment includes the United States and Canada. Its specialty portfolio has an established presence in central nervous system (CNS) medicines.

Europe segment includes the European Union and certain other European countries. Its specialty portfolio focuses on three main areas: CNS and pain respiratory and oncology.

The International Markets segment includes all countries in which the company operate other than those in its North America and Europe segments. These markets comprise more than 35 countries covering a substantial portion of the global pharmaceutical market. Its specialty portfolio in International Markets focuses on three main areas: CNS and pain respiratory and oncology.

Generic medicines produced by Teva include chemical and therapeutic versions of tablets capsules injectables inhalants liquids ointments and creams. Specialty medicines include Copaxone Ajovy Austedo Bendeka and Treanda ProAir (ProAir HFA ProAir Digihaler and ProAir RespiClick) QVAR (QVAR and QVAR RediHaler) Cinqair/Cinqaero AirDuo RespiClick/ArmonAir RespiClick/AirDuo Digihaler and Braltus. In addition to focusing on therapeutic areas of CNS and respiratory medicines Teva provides specialty medicines in oncology and selected other areas.

The company also supplies active pharmaceutical ingredients (APIs) the essential raw materials used in drug manufacturing.

The company has a collaboration with Takeda Pharmaceutical through which Takeda can commercialize Teva's treatments for Parkinson's disease (Copaxone) and multiple sclerosis (Azilect) in Japan.

Teva holds a portfolio of more than 1800 molecules; it produces some 85 billion tablets and capsules annually at its 90 manufacturing facilities.

Geographic Reach

Teva has 90 manufacturing and R&D facilities in more than 60 countries. The company is structured into three geographic segments — North America (which accounts for more than half of total sales) Europe (less than 30% of sales) and International Markets (about 15% of sales).

Its primary manufacturing technologies solid dosage forms injectables and blow-fill-seal are available in North America Europe Latin America and Israel. The manufacturing sites located in Israel Germany Hungary Croatia Bulgaria India Spain Poland and the Czech Republic make up the majority of its production capacity.

Sales and Marketing

Teva's generic sales in the United States are made to directly to retail drug chains mail order distributors and wholesaler.

In North America the group participates in pharmaceutical conferences and advertises in professional journals and on pharmacy websites.

The company's advertising costs for the years 2019 2018 and 2017 were $213 million $256 million and $318 million respectively.

Financial Performance

Teva's revenue has been declining since 2017. Its net income suffered consecutive net losses since 2017.

Teva's revenues in 2019 were $16.9 million a decrease of 8% in US dollar or 5% in local currency terms compared to 2018 mainly due to generic competition to COPAXONE a decline in revenues from its US generics business BENDEKA/TREANDA and Japan partially offset by higher revenues from AUSTEDO AJOVY and QVAR in the United States.

Net loss attributable to Teva was $999 million in 2019 compared to a net loss of $2.2 million in 2018.

Teva ended 2018 with $2 billion in net cash 11% more than what it had at the end of 2018. Operating activities provided $748 million and investing activities provided another $1.4 billion while financing activities (primarily the repayment of liabilities) used $1.9 billion.

Strategy

In December 2017 Teva announced a comprehensive two-year restructuring plan intended to reduce its cost base by $3 billion unify and simplify its organization and improve business performance profitability cash flow generation and productivity. This plan achieved its goals including a total cost base reduction of $3 billion by the end of 2019. The company is continuing to evaluate opportunities to further optimize its manufacturing and supply network to achieve additional operational efficiencies.

All of the company's R&D activities are concentrated under one global group with overall responsibility for generics specialty and biologics enabling better focus and efficiency.

A strong focus for Teva is the development of new generic medicines. Teva develops generic products for the United States Europe and its International Markets segment. The company's focus is on developing complex formulations with complex technologies which have higher barriers to entry. Generic R&D activities which are carried out in development centers located around the world include product formulation analytical method development stability testing management of bioequivalence bio-analytical studies other clinical studies and registration of generic drugs in all of the markets where Teva operates.

HISTORY

Teva traces its origins to Salomon Levin and Elstein Ltd. a drug distribution firm based in Jerusalem which at the time was a Jewish section of British-controlled Palestine.

Ironically in the 1930s the company benefited from the emigration of Jewish people many of whom were scientists seeking to escape the Nazi regime in Germany which at the time was the global leader in drug development. The company went public in 1951.

In 1968 Eli Hurvitz was appointed to Teva's board of directors and scripted much of the company's growth. In 1970 Teva merged with Assia Chemical Laboratories (Hurvitz's old employer) and another company to form Teva Pharmaceutical Industries.

Ten years later Teva sold a 20% stake of itself to Koor Industries in exchange for Koor subsidiary Ikapharm Teva's closest competitor. (Koor later launched a takeover bid but the Founders Group Teva's controlling shareholders foiled the attempt.)

In 1985 Teva moved into the US. It formed a joint venture with W. R. Grace called TAG Pharmaceuticals (Teva bought out W. R. Grace's portion in 1991). In 1985 TAG bought Lemmon Co. famous — or infamous — for its tranquilizer Quaalude which had gained notoriety as the recreational drug of choice for many young people. Lemmon which ceased production of Quaalude prior to Teva's purchase became the acquirer's generic manufacturing division.

Teva bought Abic Israel's #2 drugmaker in a complex 1988 transaction that gave Canadian investor and Seagram's heir Charles Bronfman a stake in the company. British publisher Robert Maxwell also bought a substantial stake in Teva. (Following Maxwell's mysterious death in 1993 his estate sold his stake.)

In the 1990s Teva turned its attention to Europe buying companies in France Hungary Italy and the UK. In 1996 the company bought US firm Biocraft Laboratories merging it with Lemmon and forming Teva Pharmaceuticals USA.

In 1998 the company reorganized after officials realized that it had to evolve from being a collection of disparate operating entities to a more centralized operation. It also divested several operations — including its Russian joint venture its yeast and alcohol fermentation business and some of its German operations — in order to concentrate on pharmaceuticals.

EXECUTIVES

President and CEO, K re Schultz, age 59
EVP Business Development Strategy and Commercial Innovation, Timothy R. Wright, age 63

President and CEO Global Operations, Carlo de Notaristefani, age 62
President and CEO Global Generic Medicines Group, Sigurdur O. (Siggi) Olafsson, age 51
President of Global R&D and Chief Scientific Officer, Michael Hayden
President and CEO Specialty Medicines, Robert Koremans
Group EVP Corporate Marketing and Communications, Iris Beck-Codner
EVP Human Resources, Mark Sabag
General Manager UK and Ireland, Kim Innes
EVP and Chief Internal Auditor, Nir Baron
Chairman, Sol J. Barer, age 73
Auditors: Kesselman & Kesselman

LOCATIONS

HQ: Teva Pharmaceutical Industries Ltd
 5 Basel Street, Petach Tikva 4951033
Phone: (972) 3 914 8171
Web: www.tevapharm.com

2018 Sales

	$ mil.	% of total
North America	927	49
Europe	5,187	28
International Markets	3,005	16
Other activities	1,366	7
Total	**18,854**	**100**

PRODUCTS/OPERATIONS

2018 Sales

	$ mil.	% of total
Sales of goods	15,881	84
Distribution	1,956	10
Licensing arrangements	165	1
Other	852	5
Total	**18,854**	**100**

Selected Products

Branded products
 Central nervous system
  Azilect (Parkinson's)
  Copaxone (multiple sclerosis)
  Provigil (narcolepsy)
 Specialty respiratory
  ProAir (bronchial spasms)
  Qvar (chronic asthma)
Biosimilars
 Eporatio (erythopoietin treatment for chemotherapy-induced anemia)
 Granulocyte Colony Stimulating Factor (anti-infective for oncology patients)
 Tev-Tropin (human growth hormone)
Generic products
 Amoxicillin (Amoxil)
 Atorvastatin (Lipitor)
 Bromatapp (Dimetapp)
 Candesartan (Atacand)
 Cimetidine (Tagamet)
 Ciprofloxacin (Cipro)
 Clemastine fumarate (Tavist)
 Clotrimazole (Lotrimin)
 Diclofenac extended release (Voltaren XR)
 Diltiazem HCl (Cardizem)
 Donepezil (Aricept)
 Fluconazole Injection (Diflucan)
 Fluoxetine (Prozac)
 Galantamine (Reminyl)
 Ketoconazole cream (Nizoral Cream)
 Lamivudine (Epivir)
 Lovastatin (Mevacor)
 Metronidazole (Flagyl)
 Quetiapine (Seroquel)
 Sotalol hydrochloride (Betapace)
 Sulfamethoxazole and Trimethoprim (Bactrim)
 Tizanidine (Zanaflex)
 Tramadol hydrochloride (Ultram/Ultracet)

COMPETITORS

Abbott Labs	Merck
Allergan plc	Mylan
AstraZeneca	Novartis
Bayer HealthCare Pharmaceuticals Inc.	Sandoz International GmbH
Biogen	Sanofi
Boehringer Ingelheim	Taro
Dr. Reddy's	

HISTORICAL FINANCIALS

Company Type: Public

Income Statement

FYE: December 31

	REVENUE ($ mil.)	NET INCOME ($ mil.)	NET PROFIT MARGIN	EMPLOYEES
12/19	16,887	(999)	—	40,039
12/18	18,854	(2,150)	—	42,535
12/17	22,385	(16,265)	—	51,792
12/16	21,903	329	1.5%	56,960
12/15	19,652	1,588	8.1%	42,888
Annual Growth	(3.7%)	—		(1.7%)

2019 Year-End Financials

Debt ratio: 46.8%
Return on equity: (-6.9%)
Cash ($ mil.): 1,975
Current ratio: 0.98
Long-term debt ($ mil.): 24,562

No. of shares (mil.): 1,092
Dividends
 Yield: —
 Payout: —
Market value ($ mil.): 10,702

	STOCK PRICE ($) FY Close	P/E High/Low	PER SHARE ($) Earnings	Dividends	Book Value
12/19	9.80	— —	(0.91)	0.00	12.79
12/18	15.42	— —	(2.35)	0.00	13.49
12/17	18.95	— —	(16.26)	0.72	17.07
12/16	36.25	941500	0.07	1.16	32.84
12/15	65.64	39 30	1.82	1.16	32.80
Annual Growth	(37.8%)	— —			
(21.0%)					

Thales

Thales develops and manufactures weapons munitions and equipment for waging war across all defensible spheres: land air water space and digital. Thales' primary customers are national defense forces across the globe with a particular focus on Europe which accounts for nearly 55% of sales. Besides defense and security products Thales' aerospace division outfits commercial planes with in-flight entertainment and connectivity equipment and provides flight simulator-based pilot training while a transport division provides rail signaling monitoring and ticketing for rail networks. Thales signaled its intent to grow in cybersecurity with the 2019 acquisition of Gemalto. The French government owns about 25% of Thales and aerospace company Dassault holds nearly 25%.

Operations

Thales is divided into four reportable segments.

The largest Defense & Security accounts for about 45% of sales. It provides air land and naval defense capabilities for a wide range of scenarios. These include guns ammunition missiles mortars and information and communication systems on land; short- and medium-range missiles missile electronic sub-systems rockets jet and helicopter optronics and support and repair services for air forces; and above water and underwater warfare such as radar sonar communications at sea.

The Aerospace segment generates around a third of sales. It's divided in two: Aeronautics makes in-flight entertainment connectivity equipment and civil and military flight simulators; and Space a joint-venture with Italy's Leonardo makes orbital infrastructure satellite systems and navigation and earth observation systems.

The Transport segment (about 10% of sales) provides urban transport systems (subways and trams) and mainline networks with signaling monitoring control and ticketing.

The Digital Identity and Security (about 15%) segment includes certification of physical and digital identities various authentication methods (including biometrics) IoT connectivity and data encryption.

Geographic Reach

Based in Paris France Thales' customers in Europe represent nearly 55% of sales. The Asia/Pacific region generates nearly 15% of sales while North America accounts for more than 10% of sales and Middle East some 10%. Australia/New Zealand and all other countries generates around 5% each.

The company has operations in nearly 70 countries including Europe in France Germany the Netherlands Spain and the UK as well as in Australia and the US. The company extends its global presence through joint ventures and partnerships.

Sales and Marketing

Customers include some of the world's largest corporations as well as government. Almost 60% of Thales' revenues comes from government customers and more than 40% of its revenue comes from non-government customers (private operators of critical infrastructure aircraft manufactures etc.).

Financial Performance

Note: Growth rates may differ after conversion to US Dollars.

2019 sales amounted to ?18.4 billion compared to ?15.9 billion in 2018 an increase of 16% after the consolidation of Gemalto.

The company had a consolidated net income of ?1.1 billion a 14% increase from the previous year.

The company's cash for the year ended 2019 totaled ?2.9 billion. Operating activities generated ?1.8 billion while investing activities used ?4.6 billion mainly for investments in subsidiaries and affiliates. Financing activities generated ?128.3 million.

Strategy

The company's strategic priorities for the year consists of:

Accelerating the sales transformation project; Streamlining the organization of international development; Implementing a new management for key accounts; and Paying increased attention to opportunities in the support and maintenance of installed bases.

Thales Alenia Space continued to develop a strategic partnership to meet the new needs of the market particularly with the signing of a partnership agreement with Héméria to target the nanosatellite market. In 2019 LeoStella a joint venture between Thales Alenia Space and SpaceFlight Industries opened its new small satellite production facility in Seattle in the United States where it began the integration of the BlackSky constellation for low - orbit Earth observation with a high revisit rate. Thales Alenia Space also opened its new automated production site for assembling photovoltaic cells on satellite solar panels in Hasselt Belgium.

Mergers and Acquisitions

In 2019 Thales acquired Franco-Dutch digital security company Gemalto for around $4.6 billion. The deal which will see Gemalto combined with Thales' digital security business and will add around $19 billion to sales.

Also in 2019 Thales acquired Psibernetix (Ohio-based) a company known for its aerial combat AI; Ercom a communication and device security expert; and Suneris a provider of solutions for supervision and control of telecommunication network traffic.

EXECUTIVES

SEVP Human Resources, David Tournadre, age 51
EVP International Development, Pascale Sourisse
CEO, Victor Chavez
EVP Secure Communications and Information Systems, Marc Darmon, age 54
SEVP COO and Chief Performance Officer, Pierre-Eric Pommellet, age 55
EVP Air Operations; EVP Land Defence, Alex Cresswell, age 55
EVP Defence Mission Systems, Philippe Duhamel
EVP Strategy Research and Technology, Hervé Multon
EVP Space, Jean-Lo c Galle, age 60
EVP Transportation Systems, Jean-Pierre Forestier, age 72
SEVP; CFO, Pascal Bouchiat
Chairman and CEO, Patrice Caine
CEO Germany, Christoph Hoppe
Auditors: Mazars

LOCATIONS

HQ: Thales
Tour Carpe Diem, Place des Corolles Esplanade Nord, Courbevoie 92400
Phone: (33) 1 57 77 80 00
Web: www.thalesgroup.com

2018 Sales

	% of total
Europe	55
Asia	14
Middle East	10
North America	9
Australia & New Zealand	5
Rest of the World	6
Total	**100**

PRODUCTS/OPERATIONS

2018 Sales

	% of total
Defense & Security	51
Aerospace	36
Transport	13
Total	**100**

Selected Divisions

Air operations
Avionics
Defense & security C4I systems
Defense mission systems
Land defense
Space
Transportation systems

Selected Subsidiaries

TDA Armements
Thales Air Systems
Thales Alenia Space
Thales Avionics
Thales Communications
Thales Electron Devices (TED)
Thales Optronique
Thales Raytheon Systems
Thales Security Solutions & Services SAS
Thales Services
Thales Systèmes Aé;roporté;s
Thales Underwater Systems

COMPETITORS

AT&T	Harris Corp.
Aero Simulation	Honeywell
Airbus Group	International
Ansaldo STS	IBM
Argon ST	ITT Corp.
BAE SYSTEMS	Indra
Ball Aerospace	Innovative Solutions
Boeing	Lockheed Martin
CAE USA	MBDA
Chemring	Meggitt-USA
Cubic Corp.	Motorola Solutions

Cubic Simulation Systems	Nokia
	Nortel Networks
Diebold	Northrop Grumman
Ducommun LaBarge Technologies	RUAG Holding
	Saab AB
FLIR Systems	Siemens AG
GE	Ultra Electronics
General Dynamics	

HISTORICAL FINANCIALS

Company Type: Public

Income Statement				FYE: December 31
	REVENUE ($ mil.)	NET INCOME ($ mil.)	NET PROFIT MARGIN	EMPLOYEES
12/19	20,660	1,259	6.1%	82,605
12/18	18,156	1,124	6.2%	66,135
12/17	18,934	985	5.2%	64,860
12/16	15,716	999	6.4%	63,783
12/15	15,317	833	5.4%	61,848
Annual Growth	7.8%	10.9%	—	7.5%

2019 Year-End Financials

Debt ratio: 22.5%
Return on equity: 20.1%
Cash ($ mil.): 3,291
Current ratio: 0.91
Long-term debt ($ mil.): 4,835

No. of shares (mil.): 212
Dividends
  Yield: 2.3%
  Payout: 826.7%
Market value ($ mil.): 4,483

	STOCK PRICE ($) FY Close	P/E High/Low		PER SHARE ($)	
			Earnings	Dividends	Book Value
12/19	21.07	23 14361	0.06	0.48	28.76
12/18	118.00	28 26	5.27	0.52	30.72
Annual Growth	(82.1%)	—	(67.5%)	(1.5%)	(1.6%)

ThyssenKrupp AG

Thyssenkrupp (pronounced TISS-in kroop) is an industrial giant and a leading European supplier of flat steel. The German company's operations span around 90 sites and numerous sectors and fields including components technology elevator technology industrial solutions marine systems material services and steel manufacture. Thyssenkrupp is active in nearly 80 countries worldwide but gets about 70% of total sales outside Germany. The company was formed in 1999 via the merger of German industrial companies Thyssen and Krupp. Thyssenkrupp is trying to spin off its steel division but the EU Commission put the kibosh on a planned joint venture with Tata Steel's European operation.

Operations

The truly vast operations of Thyssenkrupp are organized into six segments - Materials Services Steel Europe Elevator Technology Components Technology Industrial Solutions and Marine Systems.

The Materials Services segment Thyssenkrupp's biggest earner at around 30% of annual sales is responsible for the global materials distribution and stainless steel production. It offers services such as quality management logistics services and supply chain solutions. It also offers warehousing and inventory management.

Steel Europe (nearly 20% of sales) manufactures high-quality flat- rolled carbon steel products custom-made for the auto industry and other steel-using industries.

The Elevators Technology segment pulls in roughly 20% of sales and develops and manufactures passenger and freight elevators escalators and moving walks passenger boarding bridges stair and platform lifts and related services through 1000 locations.

Thyssenkrupp's Components Technology segment (about 15% of sales) serves the automotive and machinery sectors. Products include steering and damping systems springs and stabilizers camshafts construction equipment and wind turbines.

Industrial Solutions accounts for some 10% of sales. It constructs ions and other types of plant for customers in the chemical cement mining and mineral industries. It also develops automated production systems for the auto industry.

Marine Systems accounts for less than 5% of sales. It supplies system for submarines and surface vessels and for maritime electronics and security technology

Geographic Reach

Thyssenkrupp is headquartered in Essen Germany and has regional HQs in North and South America Greater China India the Asia/Pacific region and the Middle East & Africa region as well as the regional offices and Group representative offices. It operates from 1800 locations in some 80 countries. The company's geographic sales mix is diversified drawing some 30% of sales from German-speaking Europe (Germany Austria and Switzerland) nearly 20% from North America and roughly 20% from Western Europe.

Sales and Marketing

Thyssenkrupp sells its products to industries including the automotive sector (about 25% of annual sales) steel & processing (around 10%) and trading (nearly 15%) as well as construction engineering energy & utility packaging and the public sector.

Financial Performance

In fiscal 2019 (ended September 30) Thyssenkrupp's revenue rose 1% to ?42 billion. The components and elevator businesses as well as the plant construction activities contributed to the rise; and was partly offset by declines at the materials businesses. Cost of sales increased at a higher rate than net sales mainly due to higher personnel and materials expenses.

The Company has been struggling for profitability of late. In 2019 its losses grew ?242 million.

Thyssenkrupp's cash and cash equivalents strengthened during 2019 ending the fiscal year ?700 million higher at ?3.7 billion. The company generated cash of ?1.2 billion from its operations. It used ?2.1 billion for its financing activities while investing activities used cash of ?1.3 billion. Thyssenkrupp's main cash uses in 2019 were capital expenditures and repayments of bonds.

Strategy

Thyssenkrupp is trying to spin off its Steel Europe business although a merger with Tata Steel's European business was denied by EU regulators (it will explore other options). The steel industry is going through a tough spell amid oversupply from China and US import tariffs. Thyssenkrupp views consolidation as a sound defensive strategy while ridding a loss-making division from its books.

In connection with its new strategy "newtk" among other things the business area level will be largely dissolved. The businesses under the umbrella of Components Technology will be managed by a lean office in the future. From fiscal year 2019/2020 it will focus on managing the operating and financial performance of the businesses and on evaluating partnerships as part of the flexible portfolio initiative. The unit will also be given a new name - Components Technology will become Automotive Technology and from fiscal 2019/2020 will also include System Engineering. The bearings and forged technologies businesses were removed from the business area as of Octo-

ber 1 2019 and since then have been managed directly by thyssenkrupp AG. In the future the two units will report under the name Industrial Components.

Mergers and Acquisitions

In 2019 Thyssenkrupp Elevator has acquired the Elevator division of US- based Nashville Machine Company. Formerly the exclusive distributor in the Middle Tennessee area for thyssenkrupp Elevator Nashville Machine Elevator (NME) has 130 employees all of which will be given the opportunity to join thyssenkrupp. The office will be integrated into thyssenkrupp as one of its branches in the Southeast joining sister locations in Knoxville Chattanooga and Memphis Tennessee. Terms were not disclosed.

EXECUTIVES

Chairman Executive Board, Heinrich Hiesinger, age 60
CEO ThyssenKrupp Materials Services, Joachim Limberg, age 66
CEO Components Technology Business, Karsten Kroos, age 61
CEO ThyssenKrupp Steel Europe, Andreas J. Goss, age 56
CEO ThyssenKrupp Elevator, Andreas Schierenbeck
CFO, Guido Kerkhoff, age 53
CEO ThyssenKrupp North America, Patrick Bass
CIO, Martin H ¶lz
CEO Industrial Solutions, Stefan Gesing, age 42
CEO Thyssenkrupp Industrial Solutions, Peter Feldhaus, age 53
CEO thyssenkrupp Marine Systems, Rolf Wirtz
Chairman Supervisory Board, Ulrich Lehner, age 74
Auditors: PricewaterhouseCoopers GmbH Wirtschaftsprüfungsgesellschaft

LOCATIONS

HQ: ThyssenKrupp AG
ThyssenKrupp Allee 1, Essen D-45143
Phone: (49) 201 844 0 **Fax:** (49) 201 844 53600
Web: www.thyssenkrupp.com

Sales 2018

	% of total
Germany	29
USA	16
China	7
Other	48
Total	**100**

PRODUCTS/OPERATIONS

Sales 2018

	% of total
Components Technology	17
Elevator Technology	17
Industrial Solutions	11
Materials Services	33
Steel Europe	21
Corporate	1
Total	**100**

COMPETITORS

Acerinox
ArcelorMittal
Bechtel
Descours & Cabaud
GEA Group
ITOCHU
Ingersoll-Rand
JFE Holdings
Kobe Steel
MAN
Magna International
Marubeni
Nippon Steel & Sumitomo Metal Corporation
POSCO

Qingdao Iron and Steel
Schindler Holding
Tata Europe
United States Steel
United Technologies

HISTORICAL FINANCIALS

Company Type: Public

Income Statement

FYE: September 30

	REVENUE ($ mil.)	NET INCOME ($ mil.)	NET PROFIT MARGIN	EMPLOYEES
09/19	45,811	(331)	—	162,372
09/18	40,281	9	0.0%	161,096
09/17	48,968	(766)	—	158,739
09/16	43,829	330	0.8%	156,487
09/15	47,960	346	0.7%	154,906
Annual Growth	(1.1%)	—		1.2%

2019 Year-End Financials

Debt ratio: 22.1% No. of shares (mil.): 622
Return on equity: (-13.3%) Dividends
Cash ($ mil.): 4,042   Yield: 0.7%
Current ratio: 1.19   Payout: —
Long-term debt ($ mil.): 7,122 Market value ($ mil.): 8,700

	STOCK PRICE ($) FY Close	P/E High/Low		Earnings	PER SHARE ($) Dividends	Book Value
09/19	13.98	—	—	(0.53)	0.11	3.07
09/18	25.24	3065	2176	0.01	0.11	5.22
09/17	29.44	—	—	(1.36)	0.11	5.48
09/16	24.89	—	—	0.58	0.00	4.15
09/15	17.05	54	31	0.62	0.00	6.30
Annual Growth	(4.9%)	—	—	—	—	(16.5%)

Tianjin Tianhai Investment Co Ltd

EXECUTIVES

Chairman, Weijian Li
Auditors: Zhong He Zheng Xin CPAs Co., Ltd.

LOCATIONS

HQ: Tianjin Tianhai Investment Co Ltd
No. 207, Machang Road, Hexi District, Tianjin 300204
Phone: (86) 22 23281780 **Fax:** (86) 22 23286115

HISTORICAL FINANCIALS

Company Type: Public

Income Statement

FYE: December 31

	REVENUE ($ mil.)	NET INCOME ($ mil.)	NET PROFIT MARGIN	EMPLOYEES
12/19	47,016	75	0.2%	0
12/18	48,917	8	0.0%	0
12/17	48,476	126	0.3%	0
12/16	5,409	46	0.9%	0
12/15	110	37	34.3%	0
Annual Growth	353.8%	18.5%	—	—

Debt ratio: 4.8%	No. of shares (mil.): —
Return on equity: 3.8%	Dividends
Cash ($ mil.): 906	Yield: —
Current ratio: 1.09	Payout: —
Long-term debt ($ mil.): 2,134	Market value ($ mil.): —

TMB Bank Public Co Ltd

EXECUTIVES

Chief Executive Officer, Piti Tantakasem
Auditors: KPMG Phoomchai Audit Ltd.

LOCATIONS

HQ: TMB Bank Public Co Ltd
3000 Phaholyothin Road, Chomphon, Chatuchak,
Bangkok 10900
Phone: (66) 2 299 1111 **Fax:** (66) 2 299 1211
Web: www.tmbbank.com

COMPETITORS

Bangkok Bank	Siam Commercial
DBS Group Holdings	Thanachart Capital
KASIKORNBANK	United Overseas Bank

HISTORICAL FINANCIALS

Company Type: Public

Income Statement   FYE: December 31

	ASSETS ($ mil.)	NET INCOME ($ mil.)	INCOME AS % OF ASSETS	EMPLOYEES
12/19	62,381	242	0.4%	0
12/18	27,564	358	1.3%	0
12/17	25,902	266	1.0%	0
12/16	22,936	229	1.0%	0
12/15	23,284	259	1.1%	0
Annual Growth	27.9%	(1.6%)	—	—

2019 Year-End Financials

Return on assets: 0.5%	Dividends
Return on equity: 4.9%	Yield: 0.0%
Long-term debt ($ mil.): —	Payout: 16,149.5%
No. of shares (mil.): —	Market value ($ mil.): —
Sales ($ mil): 1,881	

	STOCK PRICE ($) FY Close	P/E High/Low	PER SHARE ($) Earnings	Dividends	Book Value
12/19	12.55	89 84	0.00	0.81	0.07
12/18	23.32	86 86	0.01	0.36	0.07
12/17	22.44	113 113	0.01	0.00	0.06
Annual Growth	(25.2%)	— —	(4.8%)	357.2%	1.9%

Toho Bank, Ltd. (The)

EXECUTIVES

President, MINORU SATO
Managing Director, Michio Sakai
Managing Director, Hideho Suto
Auditors: Ernst & Young ShinNihon LLC

LOCATIONS

HQ: Toho Bank, Ltd. (The)
3-25 Ohmachi, Fukushima 960-8633
Phone: (81) 24 523 3131
Web: www.tohobank.co.jp

COMPETITORS

Aozora Bank	Miyazaki Bank
Iyo Bank	Shizuoka Bank
Mitsubishi UFJ Financial Group	Towa Bank

HISTORICAL FINANCIALS

Company Type: Public

Income Statement   FYE: March 31

	ASSETS ($ mil.)	NET INCOME ($ mil.)	INCOME AS % OF ASSETS	EMPLOYEES
03/20	55,465	25	0.0%	2,725
03/19	53,367	32	0.1%	2,821
03/18	56,759	69	0.1%	2,927
03/17	53,872	63	0.1%	2,951
03/16	52,224	162	0.3%	2,866
Annual Growth	1.5%	(37.3%)	—	(1.3%)

2020 Year-End Financials

Return on assets: 0.0%	Dividends
Return on equity: 1.4%	Yield: —
Long-term debt ($ mil.): —	Payout: —
No. of shares (mil.): 252	Market value ($ mil.): —
Sales ($ mil): 586	

Tohoku Electric Power Co., Inc. (Japan)

EXECUTIVES

President, Hiroya Harada, age 64
EVP, Mitsuhiro Sakamoto
EVP, Takao Watanabe
EVP, Shinichi Okanobu
EVP, Toshiro Sasagawa
Chairman, Makoto Kaiwa, age 70
Auditors: Ernst & Young ShinNihon LLC

LOCATIONS

HQ: Tohoku Electric Power Co., Inc. (Japan)
1-7-1 Honcho, Aoba-ku, Sendai, Miyagi 980-8550
Phone: (81) 22 225 2111
Web: www.tohoku-epco.co.jp

**Tohoku Electric Power distributes electricity in the
seven prefectures of the Tohoku region of
Japan.FY2016 Sales**

	% of total
Electric Power Business	77
Construction Business	13
Other	10
Total	**100**

COMPETITORS

Chubu Electric Power	KEPCO
Chugoku Electric Power	Kyushu Electric Power
Hokkaido Electric Power	Osaka Gas
Hokuriku Electric Power	Shikoku Electric
	Tokyo Electric

HISTORICAL FINANCIALS

Company Type: Public

Income Statement   FYE: March 31

	REVENUE ($ mil.)	NET INCOME ($ mil.)	NET PROFIT MARGIN	EMPLOYEES
03/20	20,694	581	2.8%	24,870
03/19	20,265	419	2.1%	25,032
03/18	19,506	444	2.3%	25,058
03/17	17,437	625	3.6%	24,771
03/16	18,661	866	4.6%	24,285
Annual Growth	2.6%	(9.5%)	—	0.6%

2020 Year-End Financials

Debt ratio: 0.5%	No. of shares (mil.): 499
Return on equity: 8.0%	Dividends
Cash ($ mil.): 2,247	Yield: —
Current ratio: 0.64	Payout: 34.0%
Long-term debt ($ mil.): 18,934	Market value ($ mil.): —

Tokio Marine Holdings Inc

Japan's oldest property/casualty insurance company Tokio Marine Holdings has one of the largest insurance sales networks in the country. The company also serves customers in about 45 additional countries in Asia Oceania Europe Africa the Middle East and the Americas. Through Tokio Marine & Nichido Fire (TMNF) and other subsidiaries Tokio Marine provides property/casualty policies including specialty marine personal accident fire and auto coverage. It also offers life insurance and financial services such as asset management investment consulting and staffing.

Operations

Tokio Marine operates in four segments: Domestic Non-Life Insurance Domestic Life Insurance International Insurance and Financial and Other.

The Domestic Non-Life Insurance segment accounting for about half of sales provides property/casualty insurance policies including fire marine accident and voluntary and compulsory auto coverage. Subsidiaries include core unit Tokio Marine & Nichido Fire Nishin Fire E.design Tokio Marine Millea and Tokio Marine West.

The International Insurance segment (about 35% of sales) provides property/casualty coverage in about 45 countries worldwide. Its subsidiaries include Philadelphia Insurance (US) Delphi Financial (US) Tokio Marine HCC (US) Tokio Marine Kiln (UK) Tokio Marine Asia (Singapore) and Tokio Marine Seguradora (Brazil).

The Domestic Life Insurance segment (15% of sales) provides life policies and annuities to individuals and groups in Japan. Tokio Marine's core life unit is Tokio Marine & Nichido Life (established in 1996). The Financial and Other segment provides asset management consulting and human resource services.

Geographic Reach

Tokio Marine has insurance operations in about 45 countries throughout Asia Oceania Europe Africa the Middle East and the Americas. The majority of Tokio Marine's revenue comes from Japan (more than 60%) followed by the US (25%).

Sales and Marketing

Tokio Marine markets its products through a network of about 50000 domestic agents. The company provides products and services to businesses and individuals.

Financial Performance

Tokio Marine's revenue has been trending upward during recent years increasing more than 25% between 2014 and 2018. Net income increased each year except 2018 for total growth of more than 10% over the five-year period.

In fiscal 2018 (ended March 2019) revenue increased more than 1% to Å 5.5 trillion due to rising underwriting income offset by a decline in investment income. Growth came from the Domestic Non-Life International Insurance and Financial and Other segments while the Domestic Life segment experienced declining sales.

Net income declined 3% to Å 274.6 billion in 2018 due to higher income tax expenses.

The company ended 2018 with Å 1 trillion in cash down Å 5.4 billion from 2017. Operating activities contributed Å 945.4 billion while investing activities used Å 566.8 billion (mostly purchases of assets and subsidiary shares) and financing activities used Å 379.1 billion via dividends and stock purchases.

Strategy

Historically a property/casualty-focused group Tokio Marine has been building up its life insurance and international operations to reduce its dependence on the saturated and disaster-prone Japanese market.

The company sees growth opportunities in its life and annuity businesses in Japan as the country's population ages. It hopes to meet new needs such as growing demand for nursing care home care and inability-to-work coverage.

Internationally Tokio Marine is working to become a top specialty insurer in the US market; it is also focusing on growth in emerging markets. It purchased insurers in Thailand and Indonesia in 2018 and in 2019 it agreed to purchase a US insurance firm. Also in 2018 Tokio Marine established an insurance company in Luxembourg which will allow it to continue operating in Europe post-Brexit.

Within Japan the company has expanded by offering new products such as Super Insurance which includes both property/casualty and life coverage within a single policy. In 2018 it introduced accident coverage for certified drone pilots. The company is also adopting digital technologies to improve processes.

However like most property/casualty insurers Tokio Marine has been hit hard by weather events and natural disasters in recent years. To help prepare against larger-than-usual claims volumes insurers must make sure they set aside sufficient reserves and carefully analyze rate increase needs.

In 2019 the company sold its Tokio Millennium Re unit to RenaissanceRe for Å 168.5 billion ($1.5 billion) exiting the reinsurance business to focus on its core insurance offerings.

Mergers and Acquisitions

In 2018 Tokio Marine purchased the Thai and Indonesian property/casualty insurance units of Insurance Australia Group for Å 40 billion. It also acquired a 23% stake in South African insurer Hollard Holdings.

The following year the company acquired the remaining 51% ownership interest in US-based NAS Insurance Services a managing agency for cyber and professional liability coverage through its HCC division.

It also agreed to acquire Privlege Underwriters (operating as Pure Group) a US provider of high-net-worth policies for some Å 325.5 billion ($3.1 billion).

Company Background

Japan's first insurance company Tokio Marine and Fire Insurance was founded in 1879 to provide marine insurance in Japan. The firm expanded overseas rapidly establishing offices in London Paris and New York. It later added fire personal accident theft and auto coverage.

In 1944 Tokio merged with Mitsubishi Marine Insurance and Meiji Fire Insurance. After the war Tokio slowly recovered and resumed overseas operations. During the 1950s and 1960s the company grew its personal lines adding homeowners coverage. Domestic business slowed during the 1970s and 1980s and Tokio boosted operations overseas.

Millea Holdings was created in 2002 as the holding company for the merger between Tokio Marine and Fire and Nichido Fire and Marine. The two companies combined to become main operating subsidiary Tokio Marine & Nichido Fire Insurance in 2004. In 2008 Millea Holdings changed its name to Tokio Marine Holdings to reflect positive brand recognition associated with the Tokio Marine name.

Later acquisitions included Real Seguros (Brazil 2005) Nisshin Fire and Marine (Japan 2006) Asia General (Singapore 2007) Nihon Kousei (Japan 2007) Kiln (UK 2008) Philadelphia Consolidated (US 2008) Delphi Financial (US 2012) and HCC (US 2015).

HISTORY

After the US forced Japan to open to trade in 1854 Western marine insurers began operating there. In 1878 Japan's government organized backers for a Japanese marine insurance firm. Tokio Marine and Fire Insurance was founded the next year.

Tokio grew quickly insuring trading companies like Mitsubishi and Mitsui; it soon had offices in London Paris and New York. Increased competition in the 1890s forced it to curtail its foreign operations and begin using brokers in most other countries.

Victory in the Russo-Japanese War of 1904-05 buoyed the country but the economy slowed as it demobilized. Businesses responded by forming cooperative groups known as zaibatsu. Tokio Marine and Fire was allied with the Mitsubishi group.

Before WWI Tokio expanded by adding fire personal accident theft and auto insurance and it continued to buy foreign sales brokers. Japan's insurance industry consolidated in the 1920s and the company bought up smaller competitors. The 1923 Tokyo earthquake hit the industry hard but Tokio's new fire insurance operations had little exposure.

Most of Tokio's foreign operations were seized during WWII. In 1944 Tokio merged with Mitsubishi Marine Insurance and Meiji Fire Insurance. Business grew in WWII but wartime destruction left Tokio with nothing to insure and no money to pay claims.

After the war Tokio slowly recovered and resumed overseas operations. Although the US had dismantled the zaibatsu during occupation Tokio allied once again with Mitsubishi when Japan's government rebuilt most of the old groups as keiretsu.

During the 1950s and 1960s the company grew its personal lines adding homeowners coverage. Domestic business slowed during the 1970s and 1980s and Tokio boosted operations overseas. It added commercial property/casualty insurer Houston General Insurance (a US company sold in 1997) Tokio Reinsurance and interests in insurance and investment management firms.

In the 1980s the firm invested heavily in real estate through jusen (mortgage companies). Japan's overheated real estate market collapsed in the early 1990s dumping masses of nonperforming assets on jusen and their investors (the country's major banks and insurers including Tokio).

Deregulation began in 1996 and economic recession soon followed. In 1998 Tokio joined other members of the Mitsubishi group including Bank of Tokyo-Mitsubishi and Meiji Life Insurance to form investment banking pension and trust joint ventures. The firm also formed its own investment trust and allied with such foreign financial companies as BANK ONE and United Asset Management to develop new investment products. Brokerage firm Charles Schwab Tokio Marine Securities a joint venture was launched in 1999. That year Tokio consolidated its foreign reinsurance operations into Tokio Marine Global Re in Dublin Ireland and kicked off a business push that included reorganizing its agent force and planning for online sales.

Millea Holdings was created in 2002 as the holding company for the merger between Tokio Marine and Fire and Nichido Fire and Marine. The two were combined and renamed Tokio Marine & Nichido Fire Insurance a subsidiary of Millea Holdings.

The company's 2005 acquisition of Real Seguros allowed the company to bring its life insurance products to Brazil (renamed Tokio Marine Seguradora). In 2006 Millea acquired Nisshin Fire and Marine Insurance Company as a separately operated subsidiary. In 2007 the firm purchased Asia General Holdings and its life insurance subsidiaries which operated in Singapore and Malaysia. It also purchased Japanese fire insurance provider Nihon Kousei Kyousaikai.

In 2008 Millea Holdings changed its name to Tokio Marine Holdings to reflect the positive brand recognition associated with the Tokio Marine name.

The company made several key acquisitions to further expand its international operations including purchases of Kiln (UK 2008) Philadelphia Consolidated (US 2008) Delphi Financial (US 2012) and HCC (US 2015).

In late 2017 Tokio Marine subsidiary HCC acquired the medical stop-loss insurance operations of US giant AIG. The acquired business included some Å 40.8 billion in gross written premiums.

EXECUTIVES

EVP, Takaaki Tamai, age 70
President and CEO, Tsuyoshi Nagano
Managing Executive Officer, Masashi Oba
President Tokio Marine & Nichido Life, Toshifumi Kitazawa
EVP, Kazuo Kouduki
Chairman, Shuzo Sumi
Auditors: PricewaterhouseCoopers Aarata LLC

LOCATIONS

HQ: Tokio Marine Holdings Inc
  1-2-1 Marunouchi, Chiyoda-ku, Tokyo 100-0005
Phone: (81) 3 6212 3333
Web: www.tokiomarinehd.com

PRODUCTS/OPERATIONS

COMPETITORS

AIG	ING
Allianz	MS&AD Holdings
Aviva	Markel
Brit Insurance	Nippon Life Insurance
Dai-ichi Life	Prudential plc
Daido Life	Sompo Holdings
Equity Insurance	Sumitomo Life
Fuji Fire and Marine	Travelers Companies
Hiscox	Zurich Insurance Group

HISTORICAL FINANCIALS

Company Type: Public

Income Statement
FYE: March 31

	ASSETS ($ mil.)	NET INCOME ($ mil.)	INCOME AS % OF ASSETS	EMPLOYEES
03/20	232,647	2,393	1.0%	41,101
03/19	203,454	2,479	1.2%	40,848
03/18	215,939	2,676	1.2%	39,191
03/17	202,202	2,449	1.2%	36,842
03/16	194,621	2,266	1.2%	36,902
Annual Growth	4.6%	1.4%	—	2.7%

2020 Year-End Financials

Return on assets: 1.0%	Dividends
Return on equity: 7.4%	Yield: 4.4%
Long-term debt ($ mil.): —	Payout: 60.0%
No. of shares (mil.): 697	Market value ($ mil.): 31,753
Sales ($ mil): 49,633	

	STOCK PRICE ($) FY Close	P/E High/Low		PER SHARE ($) Earnings	Dividends	Book Value
03/20	45.50	0	0	3.40	2.03	44.55
03/19	48.50	0	0	3.46	2.16	45.71
03/18	45.68	0	0	3.60	1.45	49.43
03/17	42.35	0	0	3.25	1.15	42.26
03/16	33.89	0	0	3.00	0.87	41.15
Annual Growth	7.6%	—	—	3.2%	23.6%	2.0%

Tokyo Electric Power Company Holdings Inc

Japan would grind to a halt without Tokyo Electric Power Company (TEPCO) which supplies power to over 29 million customers in Tokyo Yokohama and the rest of the Kanto region. As one of the world's largest electric utilities TEPCO generates more than 5 billion kWh of solar power/wind power purchase amount. TEPCO is still committed to carrying out the complex multilayer and large-scale decommissioning project followed by the major crisis in 2011 when its Fukushima Dai-ichi nuclear plant complex experienced a partial meltdown at three reactors and radioactive material was released in the wake of a major earthquake and tsunami which will take 30 to 40 years.

Operations

TEPCO holds three independent business entities which also generates the company's revenues: TEPCO Energy Partner (almost 70% of total revenues) TEPCO Power Grid (over 20%) TEPCO Fuel & Power and TEPCO Holdings segment (around 10%).

TEPCO Energy Partner's major businesses are electricity retailing and gas business while TEPCO Power Grid's major activities are general power transmission and distribution real estate rental and power generation on remote islands.

Geographic Reach

TEPCO is headquartered in Tokyo Japan and has offices in Washington DC and London.

Financial Performance

Revenue for the year ended 2019 was Å 6.2 trillion a 2% decrease from the previous year due to decreases in electricity sales volume.

Net Income attributable to owners of parent totaled Å 50.7 billion a 78% decrease compared to the previous year. This was due to operational ex-

penses for fuel debris retrieval as extraordinary loss on disaster.

The company's cash for the year ended 2019 was Å 812.1 billion. Operating activities generated Å 323.4 billion while investing activities used Å 508.2 billion primarily for capital expenditures. Financing activities generated another Å 13.5 billion.

HISTORY

The Tokyo Electric Power Company (TEPCO) descended from Tokyo Electric Light which was formed in 1883. In 1887 the company switched on Japan's first power plant a 25-KW fossil fuel generator. Fossil fuels were the main source of electricity in Japan until 1912 when long-distance transmission techniques became more efficient making hydroelectric power cheaper.

In 1938 Japan nationalized electric utilities despite strong objections from Yasuzaemon Matsunaga a leader in Japan's utility industry and former president of the Japan Electric Association. After WWII Matsunaga championed public ownership of Japan's power companies which helped in 1951 to establish the current system of 10 regional companies each with a service monopoly. Tokyo Electric Power was the largest. That year it was listed on the Tokyo Stock Exchange and was regulated by the Ministry of International Trade and Industry. (The ministry has regulated electric utilities since 1965.)

Fossil fuel plants made a comeback in Japan in the postwar era because they could be built more economically than hydroelectric plants. When the OPEC oil embargo of the 1970s demonstrated Japan's dependence on foreign oil TEPCO increased its use of liquefied natural gas (LNG) and nuclear energy sources. (It brought its first nuke online in 1971.) In 1977 it formed the Energy Conservation Center to promote conservation and related legislation.

To further reduce its oil dependence TEPCO joined other US and Japanese firms in building a coal gasification plant in California's Mojave Desert in 1982. Two years later TEPCO announced it would begin building its first coal-burning generator since the oil crisis. It established Tokyo Telecommunication Network (TTNet) a partnership to provide telecommunications services in 1986 and TEPCO Cable TV in 1989.

As part of its interest in alternative energy systems TEPCO established a global environment department in 1990 to conduct R&D on energy and the environment. Its environmental program has included reforestation and fuel cell research.

Liberalization in 1995 allowed Japan's electric utilities to buy power from independent power producers; TEPCO quickly lined up 10 suppliers. The company proceeded with energy experimentation in 1996 trying a 6000-KW sodium-sulfur battery at a Yokohama transformer station. The next year the company announced that it would become the first electric utility to sell liquefied natural gas as part of its energy mix and finished building the world's largest nuclear plant.

To gain experience in deregulating markets TEPCO invested in US power generating company Orion Power in 1999. (It agreed to sell its 5% stake to Reliant Energy in 2001.) At home the firm joined Microsoft and SOFTBANK to form SpeedNet which provides Internet access over TTNet's network. In 2000 TEPCO got its first taste of deregulation when large customers (accounting for about a third of the market) began choosing their electricity suppliers. Also in 2000 TEPCO joined a group of nine Japanese electric companies to create POWEREDCOM. (In 2005 TEPCO sold its stake in POWEREDCOM to KDDI in order to focus on its core power business).

In 2001 TEPCO joined up with Sumitomo and Electricité de France to build Vietnam's first independent power plant.

To raise cash in 2006 Mirant (now GenOn Energy) sold its power plants in the Philippines to TEPCO and Marubeni for $3.4 billion.

Public confidence was shaken by a rash of accidents within Japan's nuclear industry. The company had struggled to restore its credibility after the Japanese government shut down TEPCO's 17 nuclear reactors due to safety concerns prompted by the company's admittance of falsifying safety data to cover up faults at several of its nuclear facilities in 2002. In 2009 it reopened the Kashiwazaki-Kariwa Nuclear Power Station which was closed in 2007 due to a major earthquake in the region.

Through affiliates TEPCO also offers cable TV and Internet services international consulting and investing in non-Japan-based independent power producers. Other businesses include construction real estate and transportation companies.

The company is developing new green energy sources such as wind and solar in order to meet carbon emission reduction targets. In 2009 the company agreed to build a major solar project in Kawasaki Kanagawa to serve about 5900 households. In 2010 it teamed up with Toyota Tsusho to fund wind power company Eurus Energy Holdings which acquired solar power company Jindosun Park in 2011. Jindosun oversees the generation of 2974 KW of electricity mostly in South Korea and activated a 45000 KW plant in the US in mid-2011.

Broadening its international power assets in 2011 the company agreed to buy 12% of Thailand-based independent power producer Electricity Generating PCL for about $274 million. However the daunting financial impact of the Fukushima disaster has cast a pall over the company's international expansion plans.

In 2012 it agreed to sell its 67.5% stake in Australian power station Loy Yang A to the plant's minority owner AGL Resources for $1.6 billion.

EXECUTIVES

EVP, Hiroshi Yamaguchi
EVP, Zengo Aizawa
EVP, Yoshiyuki Ishizaki
President, Tomoaki Kobayakawa
Chairman, Takashi Kawamura, age 81
Vice Chairman, Naomi Hirose
Auditors: Ernst & Young ShinNihon LLC

LOCATIONS

HQ: Tokyo Electric Power Company Holdings Inc
1-1-3 Uchisaiwai-cho, Chiyoda-Ku, Tokyo 100-8560
Phone: (81) 3 6373 1111
Web: www.tepco.co.jp

PRODUCTS/OPERATIONS

Selected Subsidiaries

TEPCO CABLE TELEVISION Inc. (85% cable television)
TEPCO SYSTEMS CORPORATION (information software and services)
Toden Kogyo Co. Ltd. (facilities construction and maintenance)
Toden Real Estate Co. Inc. (property management)
Tokyo Densetsu Service Co. Ltd. (facilities construction and maintenance)
Tokyo Electric Power Environmental Engineering Company Incorporated (facilities construction and maintenance)
Tokyo Electric Power Services Company Limited (facilities construction and maintenance)

HISTORICAL FINANCIALS

Company Type: Public

Income Statement   FYE: March 31

	REVENUE ($ mil.)	NET INCOME ($ mil.)	NET PROFIT MARGIN	EMPLOYEES
03/20	57,498	467	0.8%	40,734
03/19	57,235	2,098	3.7%	44,042
03/18	55,100	2,995	5.4%	44,610
03/17	47,919	1,187	2.5%	45,217
03/16	54,052	1,253	2.3%	45,710
Annual Growth	1.6%	(21.9%)	—	(2.8%)

2020 Year-End Financials

Debt ratio: 0.3%	No. of shares (mil.): 1,603
Return on equity: 1.7%	Dividends
Cash ($ mil.): 7,492	Yield: —
Current ratio: 0.43	Payout: —
Long-term debt ($ mil.): 18,179	Market value ($ mil.): 5,341

	STOCK PRICE ($) FY Close	P/E High/Low		PER SHARE ($) Earnings	Dividends	Book Value
03/20	3.33	0	0	0.09	0.00	16.66
03/19	6.34	0	0	0.42	0.00	16.27
03/18	3.80	0	0	0.61	0.00	15.57
03/17	3.79	0	0	0.24	0.00	13.07
03/16	5.42	0	0	0.23	0.00	12.19
Annual Growth	(11.5%)	—	—	(20.0%)	—	8.1%

Tokyo Gas Co Ltd

Auditors: KPMG AZSA LLC

LOCATIONS

HQ: Tokyo Gas Co Ltd
  1-5-20 Kaigan, Minato-ku, Tokyo 105-8527
Phone: (81) 3 5400 7736   **Fax:** 646 865-0592
Web: www.tokyo-gas.co.jp

HISTORICAL FINANCIALS

Company Type: Public

Income Statement   FYE: March 31

	REVENUE ($ mil.)	NET INCOME ($ mil.)	NET PROFIT MARGIN	EMPLOYEES
03/20	19,411	437	2.3%	16,591
03/19	19,785	852	4.3%	16,708
03/18	17,920	756	4.2%	17,138
03/17	16,002	535	3.3%	16,823
03/16	19,002	1,128	5.9%	16,998
Annual Growth	0.5%	(21.1%)	—	(0.6%)

2020 Year-End Financials

Debt ratio: 0.3%	No. of shares (mil.): 441
Return on equity: 3.7%	Dividends
Cash ($ mil.): 1,525	Yield: 2.5%
Current ratio: 1.52	Payout: —
Long-term debt ($ mil.): 8,414	Market value ($ mil.): —

Tongling Nonferrous Metal Group Co Ltd

They may not make copper pennies in China but the metal has still been lucky for Tongling Nonferrous Metals. The company ranks among China's largest copper producers. Its products include alloy powder tubes coils and cathodes; other non-ferrous items include brass wires and tubes gold and silver ingots palladium platinum silver nitrate and sulfuric acid. Tongling distributes its copper and other products in the provinces of eastern China. It is owned by the Anhui provincial government. The company joined with China Railway Construction Corp. in 2009 to buy Canadian copper company Corriente Resources for C$680 million (US$650 million).

Operations

Tongling is engaged in geological exploration mining mineral processing copper lead and zinc smelting and refining copper gold silver and alloy products processing.

Geographic Reach

The company is based in Tongling Anhui in China and exports its products to more than 10 countries including Japan Germany the US and Singapore.

Sales and Marketing

The company serves industries such as construction and installation shaft and drift construction scientific research and design transportation and real estate development.

EXECUTIVES

General Manager, Jianghong Wei, age 58
Chief Accountant, Libao Wang, age 64
Auditors: Huapu Tianjian Certified Public Accountants (Beijing) Co., Ltd.

LOCATIONS

HQ: Tongling Nonferrous Metal Group Co Ltd
  Colored West Yard Building, Changjiang West Road, Tongling, Anhui Province 244000
Phone: (86) 562 5860159   **Fax:** (86) 562 2825082
Web: www.tlys.cn

COMPETITORS

China Gold	Zijin Mining
Jiangxi Copper	

HISTORICAL FINANCIALS

Company Type: Public

Income Statement   FYE: December 31

	REVENUE ($ mil.)	NET INCOME ($ mil.)	NET PROFIT MARGIN	EMPLOYEES
12/19	13,358	122	0.9%	0
12/18	12,297	103	0.8%	0
12/17	12,667	84	0.7%	0
12/16	12,481	25	0.2%	0
12/15	13,379	(102)	—	0
Annual Growth	(0.0%)	—	—	—

2019 Year-End Financials

Debt ratio: 4.8%	No. of shares (mil.): —
Return on equity: 4.7%	Dividends
Cash ($ mil.): 741	Yield: —
Current ratio: 1.09	Payout: —
Long-term debt ($ mil.): 561	Market value ($ mil.): —

Toppan Printing Co Ltd

Toppan Printing operates in three business segments: Information & Communication (marketing materials business forms magazines and books) Living & Industry (packaging and labels) and Electronics (materials for digital displays and semiconductors). Toppan boasts about 190 group companies across the Asia/Pacific region as well as in Europe and North America. Japan accounts for more than 80% of sales and the company is working to grow its business outside the country. The company was founded in 1900 by engineers from the printing bureau of Japan's Ministry of Finance. "Toppan" is the Japanese word for "relief printing."

Financial Performance

Toppan experienced slow revenue growth between 2015 and 2019 with total revenue at the end of the five-year-period slightly below the Å 1.52 revenue reported in 2015. The company cites a tough operating environment for the printing industry reflecting declining demand for paper media. Net income jumped from Å 22.86 million in 2015 to Å 41.06 million in 2019 as the company has worked to reduce costs and strengthen its technology development.

Revenues reached Å 1.46 billion in 2019 up less than 1% from Å 1.45 billion in 2018. Revenues from the Information & Communication segment decreased by 0.7% the Living & Industry segment increased by 1.5% and Electronics segment decreased by 1.6%.

Net income dropped 2.9% from Å 42.27 billion in 2018 to Å 41.06 billion in 2019. Selling general and administrative expenses including salaries and travel costs increased that year.

The company had Å 272.99 million cash on hand at the end of 2016. Cash flows from operating activities were Å 76.76 million while investing activities used Å 73.87 million and financing activities used Å 1.26 million.

Strategy

Information & Communication accounts for 59% of sales while Living & Industry accounts for 27%. The remaining 14% comes from Electronics.

Toppan has identified four business fields for growth for its TOPPAN VISION 21 which sets out its corporate strategy for the 21st century. These areas include Healthcare & Life Sciences Education & Cultural Exchange Urban Space & Mobility and Energy & Food Resources.

The company is committed to expanding its overseas sales from about 20% to 30%. As part of this strategy it recently announced plans to acquire INTERPRINT. Headquartered in Germany INTERPRINT is a décor printer with 8 production sites in Germany the US Poland Malaysia China Russia and Brazil. INTERPRINT will serve as an "umbrella" for the company's decor printing activities outside Japan and serve as the foundation for Toppan's global expansion.

Mergers and Acquisitions

In late 2019 Toppan acquired Interprint from Wrede Industrieholding GmbH & Co. KG. The deal expands Toppan's decor printing capabilities and furthers its stated goal of generating 30% of sales from outside Japan.

EXECUTIVES

EVP, Jitsumei Takamiyagi
President, Shingo Kaneko
EVP, Yoshihiro Furuya
Managing Director Higashinihon Division, Atsushi Ito

Managing Director Finance and Accounting Division, Hidetaka Kakiya
EVP and Head Nishinihon Division, Yoshiyuki Nagayama
Senior Managing Director Sales Business Development and Public Relations, Yukio Maeda
Senior Managing Director Living and Industry, Naoyuki Matsuda
Senior Executive Officer Toppan Idea Center and Media Business Division, Mitsuhiro Nakao
Senior Executive Officer Information and Communication Technology Management and ICT Strategy Center, Yuji Sato
Senior Executive Officer Chubu Division, Kazunori Sakai
Senior Executive Officer Packaging Solutions Living and Industry Division, Haruhiko Noguchi
Senior Executive Officer Kansai Information and Communication Subdivision and Nishinihon Division, Masanori Saito
Managing Director Toppan U.K. and Toppan Europe, Hideo Yoshikawa
President Indonesian Toppan Printing, Takao Ikeda
Chairman, Naoki Adachi
Auditors: KPMG AZSA LLC

LOCATIONS

HQ: Toppan Printing Co Ltd
 1 Kanda-Izumicho, Chiyoda-ku, Tokyo 101-0024
Phone: (81) 3 3835 5660
Web: www.toppan.co.jp

2016 Sales

	% of total
Japan	85
Asia	11
Other	4
Total	**100**

PRODUCTS/OPERATIONS

Selected Offerings
Information & Networks
 Publications Printing
 Magazines
 Books
 Electronic publications
 Publication planning & editing
 Advertising
 Commercial Printing
 Posters
 Catalogs
 Brochures
 Flyers
 Direct mail
 Calendars
 Corporate communications materials
 Business Forms
 Cards
 Envelopes
 Continuous forms
Living Environment
 Packaging & industrial materials
 Interior decor materials
Electronics
 Displays
 Semiconductors

COMPETITORS

Corning Japan	Nippon Carbide
Dai Nippon Printing	Photronics
Hoya Corp.	Quad/Graphics
Kodansha	R.R. Donnelley
Metro Packaging and Imaging	Times Publishing Limited

HISTORICAL FINANCIALS

Company Type: Public

Income Statement   FYE: March 31

	REVENUE ($ mil.)	NET INCOME ($ mil.)	NET PROFIT MARGIN	EMPLOYEES
03/20	13,689	801	5.9%	58,102
03/19	13,226	370	2.8%	57,147
03/18	13,681	398	2.9%	57,878
03/17	12,804	290	2.3%	57,017
03/16	13,132	313	2.4%	53,072
Annual Growth	1.0%	26.4%	—	2.3%

2020 Year-End Financials

Debt ratio: 0.1%
Return on equity: 7.3%
Cash ($ mil.): 2,645
Current ratio: 1.84
Long-term debt ($ mil.): 1,687
No. of shares (mil.): 348
Dividends
 Yield: —
 Payout: —
Market value ($ mil.): —

Toray Industries, Inc.

Auditors: Ernst & Young ShinNihon LLC

LOCATIONS

HQ: Toray Industries, Inc.
 2-1-1 Nihonbashi-Muromachi, Chuo-ku, Tokyo 103-8666
Phone: (81) 3 3245 5201   **Fax:** (81) 3 3245 5054
Web: www.toray.co.jp

HISTORICAL FINANCIALS

Company Type: Public

Income Statement   FYE: March 31

	REVENUE ($ mil.)	NET INCOME ($ mil.)	NET PROFIT MARGIN	EMPLOYEES
03/20	20,401	513	2.5%	48,031
03/19	21,570	716	3.3%	48,320
03/18	20,763	903	4.4%	45,762
03/17	18,124	889	4.9%	46,248
03/16	18,739	802	4.3%	45,839
Annual Growth	2.1%	(10.6%)	—	1.2%

2020 Year-End Financials

Debt ratio: 0.3%
Return on equity: 4.9%
Cash ($ mil.): 1,600
Current ratio: 1.79
Long-term debt ($ mil.): 6,200
No. of shares (mil.): 1,600
Dividends
 Yield: 3.4%
 Payout: 92.7%
Market value ($ mil.): 13,639

	STOCK PRICE ($) FY Close	P/E High/Low		PER SHARE ($) Earnings	Dividends	Book Value
03/20	8.52	0	0	0.32	0.29	6.30
03/19	12.72	0	0	0.45	0.29	6.39
03/18	19.03	0	0	0.56	0.26	6.43
03/17	17.75	0	0	0.56	0.26	5.72
03/16	16.93	2	0	0.50	0.19	5.27
Annual Growth	(15.8%)	—	—	(10.7%)	11.1%	4.6%

Toronto Dominion Bank

The Toronto-Dominion Bank wants to score financial TDs at home and abroad. Also known as TD Bank Group (or just plain "TD" for short) it is the fifth largest bank in North America by number of branches. The bank serves more than 25 million customers through three business segments: Canadian Retail which includes Canadian personal and commercial banking wealth and insurance businesses; US Retail which includes US personal and business banking operations wealth management services and TD Ameritrade; and Wholesale Banking (operating as TD Securities). TD also provides financial services to online and mobile customers. The bank had some $1.4 trillion in assets in fiscal 2019.

Operations

The company has three key business segments: Canadian Retail U.S. Retail and Wholesale Banking.

TD Bank generates about 60% of revenue from Canadian Retail which offers a full range of financial products and services to over 15 million customers in the Canadian personal and commercial banking wealth and insurance businesses. The credit cards business provides a comprehensive line-up of credit cards including proprietary co-branded and affinity credit card programs. Additionally under the TD Canada Trust brand this business unit offers personal and small business banking products and services to customers through its network of some 1100 branches and some 3500 ATMs.

US Retail which brings in roughly 30% of revenue operates under the brand TD Bank and comprises the T-D Bank's US-based retail commercial and wealth management services. Retail provides a full suite of financial products and services through its network of over 1200 branches located along the east coast of the from Maine to Florida. The unit refers affluent clients to affiliate TD Ameritrade for advice and investment services.

Wholesale Banking operating under the brand name TD Securities contributes less than 10% of TD Bank's revenue. The unit provides a variety of capital market investment banking and corporate banking products and services. TD Securities also offers underwriting and distribution of new debt and equity issues advice on strategic acquisitions and divestitures and various assistance with trading and investment activities.

Geographic Reach

Calling its namesake Canadian city home the Toronto-base Toronto-Dominion Bank operates across the entire country of Canada. It also operates within the US (particularly up and down the East Coast) and has offices in Ireland Japan Netherlands Singapore and the UK.

The Canada accounts for over 55% of company's sales and U.S. for nearly 40% while other countries account for the remaining.

Sales and Marketing

Canadian Retail serves over 15 million customers in the Canadian personal and commercial banking wealth and insurance businesses. Personal Banking provides a full range of financial products and services through its network of nearly 1200 branches more than 3500 automated teller machines (ATMs) telephone internet and mobile banking.

US Retail provides products and services to nearly 10 million retail customers through multiple delivery channels including a network of nearly over 1200 stores located along the east coast from Maine to Florida mobile and internet banking ATM and telephone.

Wholesale Banking clients include companies governments and institutions in key financial markets around the world.

Financial Performance

TD Bank's revenue and net income have grown steadily year-to-year over the past five years.

TD Bank's revenue has been consistently growing in the last five years with an overall growth of 31%. Net income follows a similar pattern with an overall growth of 46% in the same period.

Reported revenue was C$41.1 billion an increase of C$2.2 billion or 6% compared with last year. Adjusted revenue was C$41.1 billion an increase of C$2.1 billion or 5% compared with last year.

Reported net income for 2019 was C$11.7 billion an increase of C$352 million or 3% compared with last year. The increase reflects higher revenue a higher contribution from TD Ameritrade and the impact from U.S. tax reform in the prior year partially offset by higher non-interest expenses including charges related to the agreement with Air Canada higher provisions for credit losses (PCL) and higher insurance claims.

Cash on hand at the end of 2019 was C$4.9 billion. Cash from operations was C$271 million while investing activities provided $5.7 billion. Financing activities used C$5.7 billion.

Strategy

TD Bank continues to invest in personalized customer service while strengthening its omnichannel strategy to allow customers to move seamlessly across channels.

In the U.S. the company's customer-centric "Unexpectedly Human" approach showcases its commitment to making an impact in local communities and demonstrates focus on how TD Bank does things differently. From the extra conveniences it offers customers to the ways it engages with them or the improvements to the company's distribution networks and platforms. Each of these investments is making banking faster and simpler for customers across every channel.

Focusing on what matters the company invests in its branch colleagues and their training coaching and accreditation. TD Bank also hires more frontline colleagues and has created new specialized roles like senior financial advisors.

Company Background

The Bank of Toronto was established in 1855 by flour traders who wanted their own banking facilities. Its growth encouraged another group of businessmen to found the Dominion Bank in 1869. Dominion emphasized commercial banking and invested heavily in railways and construction.

As the new nation expanded westward both banks established branch networks. They helped fund Canada's primary industries — dairy mining oil pulp and textiles. After growing during and after WWII The Bank of Toronto and Dominion Bank decided to increase their capital base merging into a 450-branch bank in 1955.

HISTORY

The Bank of Toronto was established in 1855 by flour traders who wanted their own banking facilities. Its growth encouraged another group of businessmen to found the Dominion Bank in 1869. Dominion emphasized commercial banking and invested heavily in railways and construction.

As the new nation expanded westward both banks established branch networks. They helped fund Canada's primary industries — dairy mining oil pulp and textiles. True to its pioneering spirit a Bank of Toronto official claimed to be the first to have set up a branch office with the help of aviation (in Manitoba in the 1920s).

The demand for agricultural products and commodities dropped after WWI but production continued full throttle creating a world grain glut that

helped trigger the stock market crash of 1929. Both the Bank of Toronto and Dominion Bank contracted during the 1930s. After growing during and subsequent to WWII The Bank of Toronto and Dominion Bank decided to increase their capital base merging into a 450-branch bank in 1955.

In the 1970s TD Bank opened offices in Bangkok Beirut and Frankfurt among other cities abroad. During the 1980s it was active in making loans to less-developed countries. After the deregulation of the Canadian securities industry in 1987 then-CEO Richard Thomson reduced international lending and began focusing on brokerage activities. The strategy paid off when several Latin American countries fell behind on their loans in the late 1980s.

As the North American economy slowed in the early 1990s TD Bank's nonperforming loans increased and with it its loan loss reserves. The bank still made acquisitions including Central Guaranty Trust (1993) and Lancaster Financial Holdings (1995 investment banking). It worked to build its financial services expanding its range of service offerings and geographic coverage and buying New York-based Waterhouse Investor Services (1996); 97% of Australia-based Pont Securities (1997); and California-based Kennedy Cabot & Co. (1997). In 1998 the bank sold its payroll services to Ceridian and its Waterhouse Securities unit bought US discount brokerage Jack White & Co.

That year the government nixed TD Bank's merger with Canadian Imperial on the same day it voided the Royal Bank of Canada/ Bank of Montreal deal. The banks believed the consolidation was necessary to stave off foreign banks' encroachment into Canada but the government had domestic antitrust concerns: Though Canada has one-tenth the population of the US its five top banks all ranked in the top 15 in North America.

In 1999 TD Bank bought Trimark Financial's retail trust banking business and spun off part of Waterhouse Investor Services which would become part of TD Waterhouse Group. That year the bank ramped up its focus on Internet banking.

Not giving up on acquisition-fueled growth in 2000 the company bought CT Financial Services (now TD Canada Trust) from British American Tobacco. As a condition for government approval TD Bank had to sell its MasterCard credit portfolio (sold to Citibank Canada) and a dozen southern Ontario branches (to Bank of Montreal).

The company's plans to hitch a ride on the Wal-Mart gravy train derailed in 2001. Arrangements to open bank branches in some US-based Wal-Mart stores were squelched by regulators enforcing the banking and commerce barrier. TD Bank later closed all of its existing branches (more than 100 in all) inside Canadian Wal-Marts as part of a broader restructuring.

TD Bank suffered its first-ever annual loss during fiscal year 2002. Write-downs on loans to telecommunications technology and energy firms contributed mightily to the dismal results.

Frustrated by limited growth opportunities at home in 2005 TD Bank ventured south of the border with its purchase of a stake in Banknorth. TD Bank paid about $4.8 billion in cash and stock for its original 51% stake (it bought the rest in 2007). Additionally in 2006 the company assumed about a 40% ownership in TD AMERITRADE as part of the sale of TD Waterhouse.

In 2008 the company acquired New Jersey-based Commerce Bancorp. The $8.5 billion acquisition deal added some 450 branches along the eastern seaboard to TD Bank's US network and exemplified the company's plans to expand abroad. TD merged Commerce with its TD Banknorth unit to create TD Bank.

EXECUTIVES

SVP Corporate Development, Riaz E. Ahmed
Group Head Wholesale Banking and Chairman President and CEO TD Securities, Robert E. (Bob) Dorrance, age 64, $476,450 total compensation
EVP Insurance and President and CEO TD Insurance, Kenn W. Lalonde
President and CEO, Bharat B. Masrani, age 64, $557,113 total compensation
Group Head Risk Management and Chief Risk Officer, Mark R. Chauvin
EVP Canadian Business Banking, Paul C. Douglas
Group Head Direct Channels Technology Marketing and Corporate & Public Affairs, Colleen M. Johnston, $467,182 total compensation
Group Head Canadian Personal Banking, Theresa L. (Teri) Currie
Group Head Legal Compliance and Anti-Money Laundering Financial Crimes and Fraud Management Enterprise Projects and General Counsel, Norie C. Campbell
CEO TD Bank USA, Greg Braca
EVP Human Resources, Sue Cummings
President Suburban New York, Anthony Esernio
Chairman, Brian M. Levitt, age 73
Deputy Chair, Frank J. McKenna, age 72
Auditors: Ernst & Young LLP

LOCATIONS

HQ: Toronto Dominion Bank
66 Wellington Street West, Toronto, Ontario M5K 1A2
Phone: 416 944-6367   **Fax:** 416 982-6166
Web: www.td.com

PRODUCTS/OPERATIONS

FY2017 Revenue

	% of total
Interest	
Loans	53
Securities:	
Interest	9
Dividends	2
Deposits with banks	1
Non interest	
Investment and securities services	10
Insurance revenue	9
Service charges	6
Card services	6
Credit fees	3
Trading income	1
Total	**100**

FY2017 Revenue by Segment

	% of total
Canadian Retail	59
US Retail	28
Wholesale Banking	9
Corporate	4
Total	**100**

FY2017 Revenue by Country

	% of total
Canada	59
US	36
Other	5
Total	**100**

Selected Canadian Subsidiaries

CT Financial Assurance Company (99.9%)
Meloche Monnex Inc.
   Security National Insurance Company
   Primmum Insurance Company
   TD Direct Insurance Inc.
   TD General Insurance Company
     TD Home and Auto Insurance Company
TD Asset Finance Corp.
TD Asset Management Inc.
   TD Waterhouse Private Investment Counsel Inc.
TD Investment Services Inc.
TD Life Insurance Company
TD Mortgage Corporation
   The Canada Trust Company

TD Pacific Mortgage Corporation
TD Mortgage Investment Corporation
TD Nordique Investments Limited
TD Parellel Private Equity Investors Ltd.
TD Securities Inc.
TD Timberlane Investments Limited
  TD McMurray Investments Limited
  TD Redpath Investments Limited
  TD Riverside Investments Limited
TD Vermillion Holdings ULC
  TD Financial International Ltd. (Bermuda)
  Canada Trustco International Limited (Barbados)
  TD Reinsurance (Barbados) Inc.
  Toronto Dominion International Inc. (Barbados)
TD Waterhouse Canada Inc.
  thinkorswim Canada
Truscan Property Corporation

Selected US Subsidiaries

TDAM USA Inc.
TD Prime Services
Toronto Dominion Holdings (U.S.A.) Inc.
  TD Holdings II Inc.
  TD Securities (USA) LLC
  Toronto Dominion (Texas) LLC
  Toronto Dominion Capital (U.S.A.) Inc.
  Toronto Dominion Investments Inc.

Selected Other International Subsidiaries

Internaxx Bank S.A. (Luxembourg)
NatWest Personal Financial Management Limited (50% UK)
  NatWest Stockbrokers Limited
TD Ireland
  TD Global Finance
TD Waterhouse Bank N.V. (The Netherlands)
TD Waterhouse Investor Services (UK) Limited
  TD Waterhouse Investor Services (Europe) Limited (UK)
Toronto Dominion (South East Asia) Limited (Singapore)

COMPETITORS

BMO Financial Group	Edward Jones
Bank of America	FMR
Berkshire Hills Bancorp	KeyCorp
CI Financial	Laurentian Bank
CIBC	Morgan Stanley
Caisses centrale Desjardins	National Bank of Canada
Charles Schwab	RBC Financial Group
E*TRADE Financial	Scotiabank
	Sovereign Bank

HISTORICAL FINANCIALS

Company Type: Public

Income Statement				FYE: October 31
	ASSETS ($ mil.)	NET INCOME ($ mil.)	INCOME AS % OF ASSETS	EMPLOYEES
10/20	1,289,890	8,741	0.7%	89,598
10/19	1,074,466	8,666	0.8%	89,031
10/18	1,016,639	8,413	0.8%	84,383
10/17	995,579	7,942	0.8%	83,160
10/16	879,748	6,488	0.7%	81,233
Annual Growth	10.0%	7.7%	—	2.5%

2020 Year-End Financials

Return on assets: 0.7%
Return on equity: 12.6%
Long-term debt ($ mil.): —
No. of shares (mil.): 1,815
Sales ($ mil): 41,206

Dividends
  Yield: 0.0%
  Payout: 48.3%
Market value ($ mil.): 80,304

	STOCK PRICE ($) FY Close	P/E High/Low		PER SHARE ($) Earnings	Dividends	Book Value
10/20	44.23	9	6	4.83	2.34	39.54
10/19	57.07	9	8	4.74	2.17	36.75
10/18	55.46	10	9	4.58	2.03	32.93
10/17	56.85	10	8	4.28	1.81	31.40
10/16	45.38	10	8	3.49	1.62	29.20
Annual Growth	(0.6%)	—	—	8.5%	9.6%	7.9%

Toshiba Corp

Auditors: PricewaterhouseCoopers Aarata LLC

LOCATIONS

HQ: Toshiba Corp
1-1-1 Shibaura, Minato-ku, Tokyo 105-8001
Phone: (81) 3 3457 4511   **Fax:** (81) 3 3456 1631
Web: www.toshiba.co.jp

HISTORICAL FINANCIALS

Company Type: Public

Income Statement				FYE: March 31
	REVENUE ($ mil.)	NET INCOME ($ mil.)	NET PROFIT MARGIN	EMPLOYEES
03/20	31,541	(1,056)	—	125,648
03/19	33,971	9,149	26.9%	128,697
03/18	39,084	7,571	19.4%	141,256
03/17	44,354	(8,636)	—	153,492
03/16	52,569	(4,096)	—	187,809
Annual Growth	(12.0%)	—	—	(9.6%)

2020 Year-End Financials

Debt ratio: 0.0%
Return on equity: (-9.5%)
Cash ($ mil.): 3,472
Current ratio: 1.46
Long-term debt ($ mil.): 1,600

No. of shares (mil.): 453
Dividends
  Yield: 1.6%
  Payout: —
Market value ($ mil.): 4,917

	STOCK PRICE ($) FY Close	P/E High/Low		PER SHARE ($) Earnings	Dividends	Book Value
03/20	10.84	—	—	(2.18)	0.18	19.09
03/19	15.86	0	0	14.83	0.09	24.30
03/18	17.24	0	0	15.34	0.00	11.32
03/17	12.79	—	—	(20.40)	0.00	(11.68)
03/16	11.65	—	—	(9.67)	0.00	6.92
Annual Growth	(1.8%)			—	—	28.9%

Total SE

TOTAL S.E. is an oil and gas company and provides natural gas and low-carbon energy. Covering the entire energy value chain this century-old French company produces and refines oil & gas sells petrochemical products and transports metric tons of crude oil and refined products. With presence in more than 130 countries TOTAL has more than 12000 Bboe of proven liquids and gas reserves and produces 3 million barrels of oil equivalent daily. SunPower and TOTAL Solar ensure that the multinational is also a major player in the solar energy scene. Its global chain of 15000 gas service stations serves 8 million customers daily. In 2019 TOTAL acquired stake in India's Adani Gas for $600 million In terms of sales Europe accumulated more than 70% of the total revenue.

Operations

TOTAL's has four business segments: Refining & Chemicals Marketing and Services Gas Renewables & Power and Exploration & Production.

TOTAL's biggest business is its Refining & Chemicals segment collecting almost 45% of annual sales. Operations in this segment involves transforming crude oil and natural gas into finished products or intermediates including for further use in manufacturing chemicals. TOTAL also sells polymers (polyethylene polypropylene polystyrene and hydrocarbon resins) and specialty chemicals like elastomers. This segment also includes trading and shipping.

The Marketing and Services segments accounts for nearly 45%. It comprises TOTAL's distribution and related services worldwide including the operation of TOTAL's global service station network of 15600 locations (25% in France). It also produces lubricants (4th worldwide distributor) supplying customers worldwide and provides bulk fuels aviation fuel special fluids LPG bitumens heavy fuels and marine bunkers to commercial clients.

The Gas Renewables & Power segment provides low-carbon energy from LNG and solar sources. SunPower manufactures solar panels while Saft Groupe is active in electricity storage. The segment accounts for around 10% of total revenue. In addition the company plans to produce one million batteries by building a pilot plant facility in Nersac France.

The Exploration & Production segment brings in some 5% of revenue. It boasts proved reserves of more than 12000 Mboe (million barrels of oil equivalent) diversified across the world's major regions (Europe and Central Asia Middle East and North Africa Americas Africa and Asia/Pacific). Daily production runs at 2.5million boe/d liquids representing roughly 55% of that and natural gas 45%. Moreover this segment aims to discover and develop oil and gas fields to meet the energy demand.

Geographic Reach

France -based TOTAL has presence in more than 130 countries across five continents. However Europe the Middle East and Africa remain the core of TOTAL's focus. Europe is its decision-making hub while it forms major partnerships with all the Middle Eastern national oil companies and has the largest African production volume and branded service presence among all the oil majors.

The company is currently working on industrial projects in Russia. Largest sales are evident in Europe for more than 70% of the total revenue.

Sales and Marketing

TOTAL has an extensive global network of customers and suppliers including companies active in the automotive metal wood sectors and multinational industrial groups. TOTAL serves local customers through services stores and car washes brands such as TOTAL WASH. Its global chain of gas service stations serves 8 million retail customers daily.

Marketing and Service segment promotes the brand awareness through advertising campaigns.

Financial Performance

The company's revenue decreased by $7.9 billion in 2019 to $176.2 billion from $184.1 billion in the prior year. The fall was due to the decrease on their sales.

The company's net income in 2019 decreased by $112 million to $11.4 billion compared to $11.6 billion in 2018.

Cash held by the company at the end of 2019 decreased by $555 million to $27.4 billion compared to $27.9 billion in the prior year. Cash provided by operations was $24.7 billion while cash used for investing activities and financing activities were $17.2 billion and $7.7 billion respectively.

Strategy

The Group's strategy takes into account the evolution of energy markets to respond to the challenges of climate change notably relying on scenarios of the International Energy Agency. Consequently the Group's strategy relies on four pillars: expanding along the natural gas value chain; developing profitable low-carbon electricity businesses; focusing on oil assets at a low breakeven points; and investing in technologies and businesses that contribute to carbon neutrality.

Mergers and Acquisitions

TOTAL has a busy acquisition schedule comprising major acquisitions and an array of bolt-ons.

In 2019 it acquired a 37% stake in Adani Gas an Indian fuel distributor developing import terminals and gas stations across the country for $600 million. The deal gives Total a foothold in a fast growing natural gas market.

HISTORY

A French consortium formed the Compagnie Fran Şaise des Pétroles (CFP) in 1924 to develop an oil industry for the country. Lacking reserves within its borders France had a 24% stake in the Turkish Petroleum Company (TPC) acquired from Germany in 1920 as part of the spoils from WWI. When oil was discovered in Iraq in 1927 the TPC partners (CFP; Anglo-Persian Oil later BP; Royal Dutch Shell; and a consortium of five US oil companies) became major players in the oil game.

After WWII CFP diversified its sources for crude opening a supply in 1947 from the Venezuelan company Pantepec and making several major discoveries in colonial Algeria in 1956. It also began supplying crude to Japan South Korea and Taiwan in the 1950s. To market its products in North Africa and France and other European areas it introduced the brand name TOTAL in 1954. It began making petrochemicals in 1956. Decades later in 1985 the company adopted its brand name as part of its new name TOTAL Compagnie Fran Şaise des Pétroles shortened in 1991 to TOTAL.

EXECUTIVES

SVP Human Resources and Corporate Communications, Jean-Jacques Guilbaud, age 68
President Exploration and Production, Yves-Louis Darricarrére, age 69
President Marketing and Services and New Energies, Philippe Boisseau, age 58
President Exploration and Production, Arnaud Breuillac
CEO Total E&P Nigeria, Elisabeth Proust
CFO, Patrick de La Chevardi¨re
Chairman and CEO, Patrick Pouyanné, age 57
CEO Total E&P Canada, Laurent Maurel
President Refining and Chemicals, Philippe Sauquet
CIO, Patrick Hereng
President Gas Division, Laurent Vivier
President of the Executive Committee, Patrick PouyannÅ
Auditors: Ernst & Young Audit

LOCATIONS

HQ: Total SE
2 place Jean Millier, Courbevoie, La Defense 92400
Phone: (33) 1 47 44 45 46   **Fax:** (33) 1 47 44 49 44
Web: www.total.com

2018 Sales

	% of total
Europe	
France	23
Other countries	48
Africa	11
North America	11
Other regions	8
Total	**100**

PRODUCTS/OPERATIONS

2018 Sales

	% of total
Refining & Chemicals	49
Marketing & Services	27
Exploration & Production	17
Gas Renewables & Power	7
Total	**100**

COMPETITORS

Akzo Nobel	Norsk Hydro ASA
Ashland	Occidental Petroleum
BASF SE	PEMEX
BHP Billiton	PETROBRAS
BP	Pakistan State Oil
Chevron	Petr leos de
ConocoPhillips	Venezuela
Eni	Royal Dutch Shell
Exxon Mobil	Statoil
Imperial Oil	ZaZa Energy
MOL	

HISTORICAL FINANCIALS

Company Type: Public

Income Statement   FYE: December 31

	REVENUE ($ mil.)	NET INCOME ($ mil.)	NET PROFIT MARGIN	EMPLOYEES
12/19	176,249	11,267	6.4%	107,776
12/18	184,106	11,446	6.2%	104,460
12/17	149,099	8,631	5.8%	98,277
12/16	127,925	6,196	4.8%	102,168
12/15	143,421	5,087	3.5%	96,019
Annual Growth	**5.3%**	**22.0%**	**—**	**2.9%**

2019 Year-End Financials

Debt ratio: 20.6%
Return on equity: 9.7%
Cash ($ mil.): 27,352
Current ratio: 1.21
Long-term debt ($ mil.): 41,510

No. of shares (mil.): —
Dividends
Yield: 5.2%
Payout: 103.7%
Market value ($ mil.): —

	STOCK PRICE ($) FY Close	P/E High/Low	PER SHARE ($) Earnings	Dividends	Book Value
12/19	55.30	14 11	4.17	2.89	45.15
12/18	52.18	15 12	4.24	2.95	44.34
12/17	55.28	17 14	3.34	5.64	44.26
12/16	50.97	20 16	2.52	5.40	40.78
12/15	44.95	26 20	2.16	2.70	39.76
Annual Growth	**5.3%**	**—**	**17.9%**	**1.8%**	**3.2%**

Toyota Boshoku Corp

Toyota Boshoku wants to make your car ride more comfortable. The company develops auto interior components including seats fabric goods air bags and seat belt webbing. Toyota Boshoku also makes air oil and gas filters powertrain components door trims package trays and bumpers and fender liners. The company uses recycled materials in its products to reduce the impact on the environment. Founded in 1918 by Sakichi Toyoda the company makes seats for Toyota Yaris model. Toyota Boshoku has about 100 companies around the globe. The company generates more than half of total sales from its home country Japan.

Operations

Toyota Boshoku is a manufacturing company producing interior components filtration textiles and exterior components.

The company's Seat business (around 70% of total sales) develops seats that elicit the maximum potential of each car seats that make the vehicle easier to drive and that ensure the ultimate in comfort and pleasure. Its products include sports seats and seat frames.

Interior & Exterior business (some 20%) strives to deliver automobile interior spaces in which people from every country and region of the world. Products include interior systems fender liners and headliners.

The remaining sales are from: Unit Components business which manufactures filters air induction systems electric powertrain and fuel cell products; and others including seat fabrics webbings and curtain-shield airbags.

Geographic Reach

Toyota Boshoku has its head office in Kariyashi Aichi. The company has business development facilities in more than 25 countries and regions and operates nearly 100 companies in the Americas Asia and Oceania China Europe and Africa and in Japan.

Toyota Boshoku generates about 55% of total sales in Japan nearly 25% from Asia and Oceania almost 20% from North Central and South America and the remainder from Europe and Africa.

Financial Performance

Revenue for the year ended 2020 dipped 3% to Å 1.4 trillion compared to the previous year.

Net income totaled Å 24.8 billion a 10% decline from the previous year.

The company's cash for the year ended 2020 was Å 163.4 billion. Operating activities generated Å 79.7 billion while investing activities used Å 54.2 billion mainly for capital expenditures. Financing activities used another Å 14 billion primarily for dividends.

Strategy

Toyota Boshoku instituted its long-term management vision "2020 Vision" and "Mid-term Management Plan until 2015" with the aim to achieving its major goals by 2020.It continues to expand its business around the world.

Company Background

The company ramped up its interior operation in mid-2011 with the acquisition of Austria-based POLYTEC Holding's interior business. The deal will give Toyota Boshoku manufacturing and research facilities in Germany Poland and South Africa. Toyota Boshoku agreed in 2009 to merge its automotive fabric business with Kawashima Selkon Textiles and Toyota Tsusho Corporation. The new company which is named TB Kawashima will produce fabrics for seats and doors headliners as well as other interior fabrics for automobiles trains and aircraft. Toyota Boshoku holds a 35% stake in the joint venture. The company is also partnered with Japan-based automotive parts maker Aisin Seiki to produce car interior parts in Poland. The joint venture which is 70% controlled by Toyota Boshoku is called TBAI Poland. Production scheduled to begin in 2011 will supply the company's seat plants in Russia and Turkey.

EXECUTIVES

EVP, Shuhei Toyoda
EVP, Mitsuyuki Noguchi
EVP, Hiroyoshi Ono
EVP, Ritsuo Torii
Chairman CEO, Shigetoshi Miyoshi
Auditors: PricewaterhouseCoopers Aarata LLC

LOCATIONS

HQ: Toyota Boshoku Corp
1-1 Toyoda-cho, Kariya, Aichi 448-8651
Phone: (81) 566 23 6611
Web: www.toyota-boshoku.com

PRODUCTS/OPERATIONS

Selected Products
Air cleaners
Door trims
Electric sunshade system
Filters (oil air cabin automatic transmission fluid
   hydrocarbon absorption)
Floor carpets
Headliner lightings
Molded headliners
Package trays
Seats
Silencers
Textiles (seat fabrics airbags seatbelt webbing uniforms
   bumpers fenders partition net)

COMPETITORS

Autoliv	Key Safety Systems
Delphi Automotive	Nihon Plast
Systems	

HISTORICAL FINANCIALS

Company Type: Public

Income Statement				FYE: March 30
	REVENUE ($ mil.)	NET INCOME ($ mil.)	NET PROFIT MARGIN	EMPLOYEES
03/20	12,708	229	1.8%	52,392
03/19	12,798	247	1.9%	51,991
03/18	13,179	402	3.1%	50,119
03/17	12,145	405	3.3%	51,023
03/16	12,607	34	0.3%	50,188
Annual Growth	0.2%	60.3%	—	1.1%

2020 Year-End Financials

Debt ratio: 0.1%
Return on equity: 8.5%
Cash ($ mil.): 1,512
Current ratio: 1.46
Long-term debt ($ mil.): 687
No. of shares (mil.): 186
Dividends
   Yield: —
   Payout: —
Market value ($ mil.): —

Toyota Industries Corporation (Japan)

If you're in the market for a forklift call Toyota Industries. Those on the hunt for a Corolla should call Toyota Motor. Toyota Industries builds forklifts and other lift trucks automotive parts (engines air-conditioning compressors and electronics) and textile machinery (which established the company in 1926). It also offers logistics services. The company does make one Toyota-brand passenger vehicle — the RAV4. Toyota Industries has more than 30 production plants in Asia Europe North America and Oceania. Its largest shareholders are Toyota Motor which owns nearly 25% of the company and DENSO which has a 9% stake.

Financial Performance

In fiscal 2019 Toyota Industries' revenues increased by 11% compared to the prior year. Sales for the company's material handling segment grew 14% driven by strong demand in Europe and China and the introduction of new products. Rev-

enues for Toyota Industries' automobile division rose 3% in 2019. The vehicle business saw sales rise 14% due mainly to production of the updated RAV4. Sales for the engines business grew 10% amid new engine launches. Sales in the air conditioning compressor business fell 1% on slower sales in Europe and Japan. Electronics parts sales grew 1%. Sales for Toyota Industries' textile machinery segment grew 17% primarily due to higher weaving machinery demand in China.

Toyota Industries' profits fell about 8% in fiscal 2019 primarily due to higher raw materials costs and despite cost reduction efforts.

Strategy

Pursuing business expansion is the cornerstone of Toyota Industries' strategy for promoting its portfolio of products and services. Hybrid and electric powered technologies which are lighter weight and more energy efficient than the industries' current offerings figure prominently on the company's workbench.

Toyota Industries is integrating a slew of such green technologies into its automotive and materials handling products specifically in hopes of appealing to customers in North America and China. Toyota Industries is taking every opportunity to target developing economies such as Eastern Europe China India and Latin America that promise strong demand by expanding its sales network.

EXECUTIVES

Managing Officer, Kazue Sasaki
President, Akira Onishi, age 62
EVP, Shinya Furukawa, age 67
EVP and Director, Masaharu Suzuki
**President and CEO Toyota Advanced Logistics
 Systems (TALS),** Michael B. Romano
Chairman, Tetsuro Toyoda
Auditors: PricewaterhouseCoopers Aarata LLC

LOCATIONS

HQ: Toyota Industries Corporation (Japan)
2-1 Toyoda-cho, Kariya, Aichi 448-8671
Phone: (81) 566 22 2511   **Fax:** (81) 566 27 5650
Web: www.toyota-shokki.co.jp

PRODUCTS/OPERATIONS

Selected Products
Automobile
   Car air-conditioning compressors
   Diesel and gasoline engines
   Electronics components
   Foundry parts
   Passenger vehicles
Materials Handling Equipment
   Aerial work platforms
   Automated storage and retrieval systems
   Automatic guided vehicles
   Counterbalanced lift trucks
   Warehouse trucks
Logistics
   Collection and delivery of cash and management of
   sales proceeds
   Logistics planning
   Management collection and delivery of corporate
   documents
   Operation of distribution centers
   Secure storage
   Transportation services
Textile Machinery
   Air-jet looms
   High-speed ring spinning frames
   High-speed roving frames
Other
   Semiconductor package substrates

COMPETITORS

Aisin Seiki	Linde Lift Truck
Atlas Copco	NACCO Materials

CLARK Material Handling	Handling
Handling	Picanol
Cummins	Rieter Holding
Daifuku	Shiloh Industries
Detroit Diesel	Standard Motor
Hino Motors	Products
Jungheinrich	UniCarriers Americas
Komatsu	Valeo

HISTORICAL FINANCIALS

Company Type: Public

Income Statement				FYE: March 31
	REVENUE ($ mil.)	NET INCOME ($ mil.)	NET PROFIT MARGIN	EMPLOYEES
03/20	20,003	1,343	6.7%	79,266
03/19	20,000	1,379	6.9%	77,266
03/18	18,872	1,583	8.4%	72,857
03/17	14,982	1,175	7.8%	63,618
03/16	19,848	1,629	8.2%	61,329
Annual Growth	0.2%	(4.7%)	—	6.6%

2020 Year-End Financials

Debt ratio: 0.2%
Return on equity: 5.9%
Cash ($ mil.): 4,913
Current ratio: 1.79
Long-term debt ($ mil.): 9,310
No. of shares (mil.): 310
Dividends
   Yield: 3.1%
   Payout: —
Market value ($ mil.): —

Toyota Motor Corp

Toyota Motor also known as Toyota is among the world's largest automotive manufacturers. The company designs and manufactures a diverse product line-up that ranges from subcompacts to luxury and sports vehicles to SUVs trucks minivans and buses. Its vehicles are produced either with combustion engines or hybrid-electric propulsion systems as with the iconic Prius. Popular models include the Camry Corolla Land Cruiser and luxury Lexus line as well as the Tundra truck. Toyota's subsidiaries also manufacture vehicles: Daihatsu Motor produces mini-vehicles while Hino Motors produces trucks and buses. Additionally Toyota makes automotive parts for its own use and for sale to others. The company's domestic sales account for nearly 45% of the company's revenue.

Operations

Major Toyota subsidiaries include Toyota Auto Body Co. Ltd. Toyota Motor Sales U.S.A. Toyota Motor North America Toyota Motor Engineering & Manufacturing North America Toyota Financial Services Corporation and Toyota Motor Credit Corporation.

Toyota divides its operations into the three segments of automotive (about 90% of total sales) financial services (more than 5%) and all other (nearly 5%). Automotive is obviously Toyota's bread and butter; the segment makes passenger and commercial vehicles minivans trucks and related parts and accessories. It's less known financial services segment provides financing to dealers and their customers for the lease or purchase of Toyota vehicles. The financial services business also provides retail installment credit and leasing through loans and contracts originated by Toyota dealers. Toyota's all other operations include the design and manufacture of prefabricated housing and information technology-related businesses such as GAZOO.com which offers a web portal for general automobile information and car racing.

Overall its sales of production accounts nearly 95% of total sales while financing operation accounts the remainder.

Geographic Reach

Toyota maintains a vast geographic reach selling to approximately 200 countries and regions through nearly 530 consolidated subsidiaries and some 200 affiliated companies. More than 55% of its sales come from Asia (Japan counts for nearly 45%) while North America generates nearly 30% of sales. Countries in Europe Africa the Middle East Oceania Central and South America account for the remainder.

Toyota and affiliated companies produce automobiles and related parts and components through more than 50 overseas manufacturing companies in more than 25 countries and regions besides Japan. Toyota's major manufacturing facilities include plants in Japan the US Canada the UK France Turkey Thailand China Taiwan India Indonesia South Africa and Argentina.

Daihatsu brand vehicles are produced in nearly five factories in Japan and two in Indonesia and Malaysia. Hino brand vehicles are produced at four factories in Japan and at about a dozen facilities in more than ten countries including Indonesia and Thailand.

Sales and Marketing

Toyota sells its products mainly through dealers and distributors as well as certain of Toyota's third-party suppliers and business partners. The company spent Å 470.8 billion Å 490.1 billion and Å 509.7 billion in advertising for the years ended in 2020 2019 and 2018 respectively.

Financial Performance

Toyota had net revenues for fiscal 2020 of Å 29.9 trillion a decrease of Å 295.6 billion or 1.0% compared to the prior fiscal year. The decrease resulted mainly from the Å 880.0 billion unfavorable impact of changes in exchange rates partially offset by the Å 440.0 billion impact of changes in vehicle unit sales and sales mix.

Net income attributable to the shareholders of Toyota Motor Corporation increased by Å 193.3 billion or 10% to Å 2.1 trillion during fiscal 2020 compared to the prior fiscal year.

Cash held by the company at the end of 2020 increased to Å 4.4 trillion compared to Å 3.7 trillion in the prior year. Cash provided by operations and financing activities were Å 3.6 trillion and Å 397.1 billion respectively. Cash used for investing activities Å 3.2 trillion mainly for additions to finance receivables.

Strategy

In promoting a sustainable growth strategy establishing a system capable of providing optimal supply of products in the global market is integral to Toyota's strategy.

In line with its basic policy of manufacturing in countries or regions where there is demand and where Toyota is truly competitive Toyota will make efficient use of and maximize capacity utilization at its existing plants to respond to the expanding market and will continue to focus on making efficient capital investments as necessary. Furthermore Toyota will continue to place top priority on safety and quality in strengthening true competitiveness with the aim of achieving sustainable growth.

Company Background

Toyota was founded in 1937. During World War II the company made military trucks and in the 1950s it launched the four-wheel-drive Land Cruiser full-sized Crown and the small Corona. Toyota Motor Sales U.S.A. debuted the Toyota Corolla which became the best-selling car of all time in 1968. By 1970 Toyota was the world's fourth-largest automaker.

Toyota expanded rapidly in the US. During the 1970s the oil crisis caused demand for fuel-efficient cars and Toyota was there to grab market share from US makers. In 1975 Toyota displaced Volkswagen as the US's #1 auto importer. Toyota began auto production in the US in 1984 through NUMMI its joint venture with General Motors. The Lexus line was launched in the US in 1989.

Because of European restrictions on Japanese auto imports until 2000 Toyota's European expansion slowed. Toyota responded in 1992 by agreeing to distribute cars in Japan for Volkswagen and also by establishing an engine plant (later moved to full auto production) in the UK.

The SUV mania of the 1990s spurred Toyota's introduction of luxury minivans and light trucks. In 1997 Toyota introduced the Prius a hybrid electric- and gas-powered car. That was the beginning of Toyota's push to provide an electrified version of all its models by 2025.

HISTORY

In 1926 Sakichi Toyoda founded Toyoda Automatic Loom Works. In 1930 he sold the rights to the loom he invented and gave the proceeds to his son Kiichiro Toyoda to begin an automotive business. Kiichiro opened an auto shop within the loom works in 1933. When protectionist legislation (1936) improved prospects for Japanese automakers Kiichiro split off the car department took it public (1937) and changed its name to Toyota.

During WWII the company made military trucks but financial problems after the war caused Toyota to reorganize in 1950. Its postwar commitment to R&D paid off with the launch of the four-wheel-drive Land Cruiser (1951); full-sized Crown (1955); and the small Corona (1957).

Toyota Motor Sales U.S.A. debuted the Toyopet Crown in the US in 1957 but it proved underpowered for the US market. Toyota had better luck with the Corona in 1965 and with the Corolla (which became the best-selling car of all time) in 1968. By 1970 Toyota was the world's fourth largest carmaker.

Toyota expanded rapidly in the US. During the 1970s the oil crisis caused demand for fuel-efficient cars and Toyota was there to grab market share from US makers. In 1975 Toyota displaced Volkswagen as the US's #1 auto importer. Toyota began auto production in the US in 1984 through NUMMI its joint venture with General Motors. The Lexus line was launched in the US in 1989.

Because of European restrictions on Japanese auto imports until 2000 Toyota's European expansion slowed. Toyota responded in 1992 by agreeing to distribute cars in Japan for Volkswagen and also by establishing an engine plant (later moved to full auto production) in the UK.

The SUV mania of the 1990s spurred Toyota's introduction of luxury minivans and light trucks. Hiroshi Okuda a 40-year veteran with Toyota and the first person from outside the Toyoda family to run the firm succeeded Tatsuro Toyoda as president in 1995. The next year Toyota consolidated its North American production units into Cincinnati-based Toyota Motor Manufacturing North America.

In 1997 Toyota introduced the Prius a hybrid electric- and gas-powered car. The next year Toyota boosted its stake in affiliate Daihatsu Motor (mini-vehicles) to about 51% and started Toyota Mapmaster (51% owned) to make map databases for car navigation systems. Okuda became chairman in 1999 replacing Shoichiro Toyoda and Fujio Cho became president (later chairman). Also that year Toyota agreed to form a joint venture with Isuzu Motors to manufacture buses.

In 2000 Toyota launched the WiLL Vi a sedan aimed at young people. It announced that it was building an online replacement parts marketplace with i2 Technologies and formed a financial serv-ices company (Toyota Financial Service) and a brokerage firm (Toyota Financial Services Securities Corp.). Toyota also bought a 5% stake in Yamaha Motor (the world's #2 motorcycle maker) and raised its stake in truck maker Hino Motors from about 20% to around 34%.

International developments included Toyota's agreement with the Chinese government to produce passenger cars for sale in China built by Tianjin Toyota Motor Corp. a joint venture between Chinese carmaker Tianjin Automobile Xiali and Toyota. In 2001 Toyota opened a plant in France. Later that year Toyota also increased its stake in Hino Motors to 50%. With partners Toyoda Gosei and Horie Metal Co. Ltd. Toyota formed a joint venture in 2002 to manufacture resin fuel tank systems. In 2004 Toyota forged a joint venture agreement with Guangzhou Automobile Group to build engines in China. The following year Toyota established 14 Lexus dealerships in China. The company began joint car production in Europe with Peugeot S.A. in 2005. Also in 2005 Toyota bought just under 9% of Fuji Heavy Industries — the Japanese maker of Subaru passenger vehicles. The two companies began production of Toyota Camrys at Fuji Heavy Industries' underutilized Subaru of Indiana plant in 2007.

After suffering through the Great Recession from 2008 to 2010 Toyota faced another unforeseen crisis. In March 2011 its business suffered unexpectedly from the Great East Japan Earthquake which triggered a deadly tsunami and subsequent nuclear crisis that forced Tokyo Electric Power (Tepco) to shut down reactors at two nuclear power plants and five other conventional power plants. The events forced manufacturers to reduce their output or move production to other regions. Toyota along with its rivals (Nissan Honda and Mazda) were forced to close their factories days after the devastation.

EXECUTIVES

President, Akio Toyoda, age 64
EVP and Chief Risk Officer, Shigeki Terashi, age 65
Executive General Manager Toyota Motor Corporation (TMC) and EVP and Chief Quality Officer Product Support Toyota Motor North America (TMNA), Chris Nielsen
EVP Safety and Health Promotion, Mitsuru Kawai, age 73
EVP and Chief Competitive Officer, Didier Leroy, age 63
Managing Officer General Counsel and Deputy Chief Officer General Administration and Human Resources and Chief Diversity Officer Toyota Motor North America (TMNA), Christopher P. (Chris) Reynolds
EVP and CFO, Osamu (Simon) Nagata, age 63
Managing Officer Toyota Motor Corporation (TMC) Vice Chairman and President Toyota Motor Engineering & Manufacturing China Co. Ltd. and EVP Toyota Motor China Investment Co. Ltd., Seiya Nakao
Executive General Manager and EVP Toyota Motor Engineering & Manufacturing North America Inc. (TEMA), Osamu Ushio
Managing Officer, Tetsuo Ogawa
Executive General Manager Toyota Motor Corporation (TMC) and EVP Manufacturing Toyota Motor North America (TMNA), Tadahisa Isono
EVP Research and Development; President Toyota Motor Engineering & Manufacturing North America, Shinichi Yasui
Executive General Manager Toyota Motor Corporation (TMC) EVP Sales Toyota Motor North America (TMNA) and President Toyota Motor Sales U.S.A. Inc. (TMS), Bob Carter

Chief Communications Officer, Nobuhiko Murakami, age 61
Chief Branding Officer, Tokuo Fukuichi, age 69
Chief Safety Technology Officer, Kiyotaka Ise, age 65
Global Chief Quality Officer, Kazuhiro Sato, age 64
President Lexus International, Yoshihiro Sawa, age 63
Chairman, Takeshi Uchiyamada, age 74
Vice Chairman, Shigeru Hayakawa, age 67
Auditors: PricewaterhouseCoopers Aarata LLC

LOCATIONS

HQ: Toyota Motor Corp
1 Toyota-cho, Toyota, Aichi 471-8571
Phone: (81) 565 28 2121
Web: www.toyota.co.jp

2018 Sales

	% of total
Japan	43
North America	28
Asia	14
Europe	9
Other	6
Total	**100**

PRODUCTS/OPERATIONS

2018 Sales

	% of total
Automotive	88
Financial services	7
Other	5
Total	**100**

2018 Sales

	% of total
Sales of products	93
Financing operations	7
Total	**100**

Selected Products

Vehicles
 4Runner
 Allion (sold in Japan)
 Alphard (minivan sold in Japan)
 Aurus (hybrid)
 Avalon
 Camry (also hybrid)
 Corolla
 Corolla Rumion
 Crown
 FJ Cruiser
 Highlander (also hybrid)
 Land Cruiser
 Lexus
 GX
 LS600h (hybrid)
 LX (SUV)
 RX
 SC
 Mark X (sold in Japan)
 Matrix
 Premio (sold in Japan)
 Prius (hybrid)
 RAV4
 Scion
 Sequoia
 Sienna (minivan)
 Tacoma (truck)
 Tundra (truck)
 Vanguard
 Vellfire (minivan)
 Venza
 Wish (minivan sold in Japan)
 Yaris (marketed in Japan as the Vitz)
Other products
 Factory automation equipment
 Forklifts and other industrial vehicles
 Housing products

COMPETITORS

BMW	Kia Motors
Caterpillar	Mitsubishi Motors
Daimler	Nissan
Fiat Chrysler	Subaru
Ford Motor	Suzuki Motor
General Motors	Volkswagen
Honda	Volvo
Hyundai Motor	

HISTORICAL FINANCIALS

Company Type: Public

Income Statement — FYE: March 31

	REVENUE ($ mil.)	NET INCOME ($ mil.)	NET PROFIT MARGIN	EMPLOYEES
03/20	275,724	19,126	6.9%	359,542
03/19	272,933	17,002	6.2%	370,870
03/18	276,677	23,486	8.5%	369,124
03/17	246,829	16,377	6.6%	364,445
03/16	252,928	20,594	8.1%	348,877
Annual Growth	2.2%	(1.8%)	—	0.8%

2020 Year-End Financials

Debt ratio: 0.3%
Return on equity: 10.2%
Cash ($ mil.): 52,486
Current ratio: 1.04
Long-term debt ($ mil.): 98,506
No. of shares (mil.): —
Dividends
 Yield: 3.3%
 Payout: 50.4%
Market value ($ mil.): —

	STOCK PRICE ($) FY Close	P/E High/Low		PER SHARE ($) Earnings	Dividends	Book Value
03/20	119.95	0	0	6.72	4.02	68.49
03/19	118.02	0	0	5.83	3.95	63.27
03/18	130.37	0	0	7.84	3.96	62.23
03/17	108.62	0	0	5.36	3.79	54.12
03/16	106.32	0	0	6.55	3.64	50.50
Annual Growth	3.1%	—	—	0.7%	2.5%	7.9%

Toyota Tsusho Corp

Auditors: PricewaterhouseCoopers Aarata LLC

LOCATIONS

HQ: Toyota Tsusho Corp
 Century Toyota Bldg., 4-9-8 Meieki, Nakamura-ku, Nagoya, Aichi 450-8575
Phone: (81) 52 584 5482   **Fax:** (81) 52 584 5659
Web: www.toyota-tsusho.com

HISTORICAL FINANCIALS

Company Type: Public

Income Statement — FYE: March 31

	REVENUE ($ mil.)	NET INCOME ($ mil.)	NET PROFIT MARGIN	EMPLOYEES
03/20	61,667	1,248	2.0%	71,033
03/19	61,066	1,197	2.0%	63,728
03/18	61,128	1,226	2.0%	62,269
03/17	51,851	965	1.9%	61,472
03/16	72,755	(389)	—	61,707
Annual Growth	(4.0%)	—	—	3.6%

2020 Year-End Financials

Debt ratio: 0.3%
Return on equity: 11.3%
Cash ($ mil.): 4,572
Current ratio: 1.50
Long-term debt ($ mil.): 9,399
No. of shares (mil.): 352
Dividends
 Yield: —
 Payout: —
Market value ($ mil.): —

Trane Technologies plc

Auditors: PricewaterhouseCoopers LLP

LOCATIONS

HQ: Trane Technologies plc
 170/175 Lakeview Dr., Airside Business Park, Swords, Co. Dublin
Phone: (353) 0 18707400
Web: www.ingersollrand.com

HISTORICAL FINANCIALS

Company Type: Public

Income Statement — FYE: December 31

	REVENUE ($ mil.)	NET INCOME ($ mil.)	NET PROFIT MARGIN	EMPLOYEES
12/19	16,598	1,410	8.5%	50,000
12/18	15,668	1,337	8.5%	49,000
12/17	14,197	1,302	9.2%	46,000
12/16	13,508	1,476	10.9%	45,000
12/15	13,300	664	5.0%	45,000
Annual Growth	5.7%	20.7%	—	2.7%

2019 Year-End Financials

Debt ratio: 27.2%
Return on equity: 19.7%
Cash ($ mil.): 1,303
Current ratio: 1.28
Long-term debt ($ mil.): 4,922
No. of shares (mil.): 238
Dividends
 Yield: 1.5%
 Payout: 36.7%
Market value ($ mil.): —

Transneft

EXECUTIVES

General Director Transsibneft, Oleg Chepurnoy
Head Administrative Board and President of OJSC Transneft, Nikolai P. Tokarev, age 71
Head Dispatching OJSC AK Transneft, Juriy L. Kritskij, age 56
Auditors: JSC KPMG (member of KPMG International)

LOCATIONS

HQ: Transneft
 4 bldg. 2, Presnenskaya Embankment, Moscow 123112
Phone: (7) 495 9508178   **Fax:** (7) 495 9508900
Web: www.transneft.ru

2015 Sales

	% in total
Russian Federation	80
China	17
Other Countries	3
Total	**100**

PRODUCTS/OPERATIONS

2015 Sales

	% of total
Oil transportation services	71
Oil products transportation services	8
Trading operations for sale of oil and oil products	21
Total	**100**

Selected Subsidiaries

Baltnefteprovod Ltd
CJSC Transneft
JSC Center for metrology maintenance
OJSC Chernomortransneft (CHMT)
OJSC Diascan Center for Technical Diagnosis

OJSC Druzhba MN
ОJSC Giprotruboprovod
OJSC Privolzhsknefteprovod
OJSC Severny MN
OJSC Severo-Zapadny MN
OJSC Sibnefteprovod
OJSC Svyaztransneft
OJSC Transsibneft
OJSC Tsentrsibnefteprovod (CSN)
OJSC Uralsibnefteprovod
OJSC Verkhnevolzhsknefteprovod
OJSC Volzhsky podvodnik
Strojneft TSUP Ltd.
Transneft Trade House Ltd.
Transneft UK Limited
Transpress Ltd.

COMPETITORS

Gazprom   LUKOIL
Gazprom Neft

HISTORICAL FINANCIALS

Company Type: Public

Income Statement   FYE: December 31

	REVENUE ($ mil.)	NET INCOME ($ mil.)	NET PROFIT MARGIN	EMPLOYEES
12/19	17,093	2,882	16.9%	0
12/18	14,060	3,218	22.9%	1,322
12/17	15,296	3,320	21.7%	0
12/16	13,851	3,802	27.5%	0
12/15	11,045	1,941	17.6%	0
Annual Growth	11.5%	10.4%	—	—

2019 Year-End Financials

Debt ratio: 0.3%   No. of shares (mil.): 5
Return on equity: 8.6%   Dividends
Cash ($ mil.): 1,343   Yield: —
Current ratio: 1.56   Payout: —
Long-term debt ($ mil.): 8,927   Market value ($ mil.): —

TSB Banking Group Plc

Auditors: PricewaterhouseCoopers LLP

LOCATIONS

HQ: TSB Banking Group Plc
  20 Gresham Street, London EC2V 7JE
Phone: (44) 20 7003 9000
Web: www.tsb.co.uk

HISTORICAL FINANCIALS

Company Type: Public

Income Statement   FYE: December 31

	ASSETS ($ mil.)	NET INCOME ($ mil.)	INCOME AS % OF ASSETS	EMPLOYEES
12/19	52,189	34	0.1%	8,198
12/18	52,505	(80)	—	8,439
12/17	57,438	160	0.3%	8,583
12/16	45,755	157	0.3%	8,296
12/15	46,856	131	0.3%	8,620
Annual Growth	2.7%	(28.3%)	—	(1.2%)

2019 Year-End Financials

Return on assets: 0.0%   Dividends
Return on equity: 1.4%   Yield: —
Long-term debt ($ mil.): —   Payout: —
No. of shares (mil.): 500   Market value ($ mil.): —
Sales ($ mil): 1,628

TUI AG

European sunseekers flock to TUI. The world's largest integrated tourism company TUI sells end-to-end leisure travel packages and other travel services via a network of approximately 1600 travel agencies mostly in Germany the UK and France. It has a nearly 355-strong owned hotel portfolio in several dozen destinations across the Caribbean Mediterranean and North Africa under brands such as Riu Robinson and Blue Diamond. Its fleet of approximately 150 aircraft makes TUI a major regional airline in its own right. It also offers cruises on more than 15 cruise liners under the brands Hapag-Lloyd Marella Cruises and TUI Cruises.

Operations

TUI operates through two principal businesses: Markets & Airlines and Holiday Experiences.

Markets & Airlines accounts for approximately 85% of sales and consists of TUI's approximately 1600 group-owned joint venture and third-party travel agencies. It also has around 150-strong aircraft fleet that flies under the banners TUI Airways TUI fly TUI fly Belgium/Netherlands/Nordic and Corsair which together serve approximately115 destinations worldwide. The segment is divided into North (Nordics UK and Ireland Sunwing in Canada and TUI Russia) Central (Germany Austria Switzerland and Poland) and Western (Belgium the Netherlands and France). The segment serves around 20 million customers annually.

The Holiday Experiences segment generates approximately 15% of sales and comprises TUI's hotels and cruises businesses. Its roughly 355 hotels are diversified across resort destinations of the Caribbean Eastern and Western Mediterranean and North Africa and Egypt. Riu is the largest brand and its premium and comfort segment hotels are mostly in Spain Mexico and the Caribbean. Other hotel brands are Robinson and Blue Diamond. In addition it owns about 55 concept hotels operated by third parties under the TUI Sensatori TUI Sensimar and TUI Family Life brands. The cruise business consists of more than 15 cruise ships held by Hapag-Lloyd Cruises the joint venture TUI Cruises and Marella Cruises.

Geographic Reach

Germany-based TUI has headquarters in Hanover and Berlin. It whisks primarily European tourists to 180 countries with a focus on sunnier climes particularly in the Mediterranean Egypt the Caribbean and the Americas. Outside of its focus on mature markets in Europe TUI also runs a strategic Canada venture Sunwing and has a Russian joint venture TUI Russia.

Germany and the UK are TUI's biggest markets both accounting for around 30% of sales.

Sales and Marketing

TUI serves around 30 million customers annually. In the cruises business the Hapag-Lloyd and TUI Cruises brands serve the German market and Marella Cruises serves the UK. TUI holds strong positions in the third fourth and fifth largest source markets in the world (Germany the UK and France).

Financial Performance

Note: Growth rates may differ after conversion to US Dollars.

The company's revenue declined by 249.5 million euros to 893.3 million euros due to particular by external challenges in Markets & Airlines such as the grounding of Boeing 737 Max jets overcapacities for flights to Spain and the ongoing uncertainty surrounding Brexit.

Net profit for the year 2019 decreased by 863.4 million euros due to the decrease on the company's net income from investments.

Cash held by the company at the end of 2019 decreased by 790.3 million euros to 1.7 billion euros from 2.5 billion euros from the prior year. Cash provided by operations was 1.1 billion euros while cash used for investing and financing activities were 1.1 billion euros and 790.3 million euros respectively.

Strategy

The company's group strategy is driven by four specific strategic initiatives: first Markets & Airlines: protect and where possible extend strong positions; second Hotels and Cruises: expansion at scale driving returns by benefitting from vertical integrations; GDN-OTA Platform: building scale on competitive pricing to attract customer to join the TUI Ecosystem; and Destination experiences platform: building scale in the 'the things to do'-market and attracting customers to join the TUI ecosystem.

TUI has launched a new online travel agency platform in six markets complementary to its existing Markets & Airline businesses currently focusing in particular on the accommodation only market metasearch business and flight combined offerings based on Airline partnerships.

Mergers and Acquisitions

In mid-2019 TUI acquired Renco (Zanzibar) Limited an accommodation service company located in Tanzania for - 50.4 million.

Also in mid-2019 the company acquired Papir s Otelcilik Yatirim Tuizm Seyahat Insaat Ticaret a Turkey-based company. It is also an accommodation service company acquired at a consideration price of ?56.6 million. This serves to secure accommodation capacity in Turkey as a destination and to increase the earnings potential of Club Magic Life Masmavi.

In early 2019 it acquired Evre Grup Turizm Yatirim Anonim Sikreti Ankara and is based in Turkey. The goal of the transaction is to increase TUI's earnings potential acquired at a consideration price of ?71.8 million. The business activities of the company are accommodation service.

EXECUTIVES

Chief HR and Legal Affairs, Peter Engelen, age 64
Chief Tourism; CEO First Choice Holidays and TUI Travel, Peter Long, age 68
CFO, Mikhail Noskov
Chairman, Michael Frenzel, age 73
Deputy Chairman, Petra Gerstenkorn, age 66
Auditors: Deloitte GmbH
  Wirtschaftspruefungsgesellschaft

LOCATIONS

HQ: TUI AG
  Karl-Wiechert-Allee 4, Hanover D-30625
Phone: (49) 511 566 00   **Fax:** (49) 511 56 1901
Web: www.tuigroup.com

2018 sales

	% of total
UK	31
Germany	28
Spain	1
Other Europe	36
North and South America	4
Rest of the World	1
Total	**100**

PRODUCTS/OPERATIONS

2018 sales

Markets & Airlines	% of total
Northern Region	35
Central Region	34
Western Region	18
Holiday Experiences	
Hotels & Resorts	3
Cruise	5
Destination Experiences	1
All other segments	4
Total	**100**

COMPETITORS

Accor	REWE
American Express	Royal Caribbean
Carlson Wagonlit	Cruises
Carnival Corporation	Thomas Cook
Club Med	Travelport

HISTORICAL FINANCIALS

Company Type: Public

Income Statement				FYE: September 30
	REVENUE ($ mil.)	NET INCOME ($ mil.)	NET PROFIT MARGIN	EMPLOYEES
09/20	12,500	(4,954)	—	48,330
09/19	29,785	654	2.2%	71,473
09/18	30,722	1,152	3.8%	69,546
09/17	29,166	1,014	3.5%	62,002
09/16	27,041	1,632	6.0%	69,218
Annual Growth	**(17.5%)**	—	—	**(8.6%)**

2020 Year-End Financials

Debt ratio: 43.7%	No. of shares (mil.): 590
Return on equity: (-208.9%)	Dividends
Cash ($ mil.): 1,940	Yield: 10.1%
Current ratio: 0.43	Payout: —
Long-term debt ($ mil.): 5,809	Market value ($ mil.): 1,098

	STOCK PRICE ($) FY Close	P/E High/Low		PER SHARE ($) Earnings	Dividends	Book Value
09/20	1.86	—		(8.40)	0.19	(1.20)
09/19	5.79	14	6	1.12	0.26	9.23
09/18	9.50	10	7	1.97	0.26	9.90
09/17	8.55	8	6	1.73	0.22	7.88
09/16	7.09	5	3	2.79	0.20	7.17
Annual Growth	**(28.4%)**	—	—	—		**(1.8%)**

Turkiye Petrol Rafinerileri AS

T rkiye Petrol Rafinerileri (Turkish Petroleum Refineries) also known as T PRAS makes petroleum products including naphtha gasoline and lubricants for civilian and military customers and operates four crude oil refineries in Turkey. T PRAS which has a processing capacity of about 28.1 million tons of crude oil a year obtains its supply primarily from sources in Algeria Iran Iraq Libya Russia Saudi Arabia and Syria. The company also owns 80% of petroleum shipping company D?Tó and 40% of Opet Petrolc l k which operates more than 1390 gas stations in Turkey and holds a market share of 14%. A consortium

led by Turkish conglomerate Ko § Holding controls 51% of the company.

Operations

T PRAS is engaged in providing and refining crude oil importing and exporting petroleum products operating domestic and foreign refineries. T PRAS supplies Turkey with about 70% of its fuel and controls about 60% of Turkey's total petroleum storage capacity. It also has a petrochemical plant that produces emulsion styrene butadiene rubber polystyrene and carbon black.

In 2014 K?r?kkale Refinery processed 3.1 million tons of crude oil - a total of 3.3 million tons of material including semi-finished products; the refinery's capacity utilization rate stood at 66.5%.

That year a total of 8.3 million tons of material including semi-finished products was processed at Izmir Refinery; the refinery's capacity utilization rate stood at 75.1%.

Batman Refinery has a capacity utilization rate 37.2% and a storage capacity of 253 million.

In 2014 T PRAS produced 20.1 million tons of products.

Serving customers through nearly 1400 Opet and Sunpet dealers Opet is engaged in retail commercial and industrial sales storage operations and international trade of petroleum products. The company manufactures and sells lubricating oil through Opet-Fuchs its 50/50 joint venture company with Fuchs the German lubricant manufacturer.

The company also engages in jet fuel supply and sales through THY-Opet a 50/50 partnership between Opet and Turkish Airlines.THY-Opet provides service to domestic and international airline companies at 51 airports in Turkey.

In 2014 D?Tó transported 4.8 million tons of crude oil and 3.5 million tons of petroleum products 8.3 million tons in total.

Geographic Reach

The company has offices across Turkey and a presence elsewhere in Europe and in the US.

Financial Performance

The slump in crude oil prices and lower volumes led to T PRAS' net sales falling by 3% in 2014.

Net income increased by 21% due to lower cost of sales (marketing selling and distribution expenses and research and development costs).

T PRAS' cash from operating activities increased by 6% in 2014 due to changes in inventories and trade receivables.

Strategy

The company is focused on upgrading its aging refineries and streamlining other operations to better compete with its peers across Europe. The Residuum Upgrading Facility is the largest single industrial investment ever made in Turkey with a total capital investment of $ 3 billion including pier railroad links and financing costs.

This completed project at Izmit Refinery allows T PRAS to process about 4.2 million tons of high-sulfur fuel oil and related heavy products consumption of which has been falling rapidly in recent years. This will yield 2.9 million tons of diesel/jet fuel 522000 tons of gasoline and 69000 tons of LPG for a total of 3.5 million tons of valuable white products at Euro-V standards as well as 690000 tons of petroleum coke and 86000 tons of sulfur.

As part of its R&D efforts in 2014 the company continued to work on 12 major projects.

T PRAS aims to increase its competitive power in Turkey through its existing infrastructure and customer relations while it aims to increase market share in the imported products alongside production. It also plans to make use of the growing international market prospects.

Company Background

In 2006 a private consortium of Turkish companies acquired the Turkish government's controlling stake in T PRAS for more than $4.1 billion.

EXECUTIVES

Assistant General Manager, Hasan Tan
General Manager, Ibrahim Yelmenoglu
Assistant General Manager, M. Mesut lter
Assistant General Manager, Dogan Korkmaz
Vice Chairman, Ali Y. Ko §
Chairman, –mer M. Ko §

LOCATIONS

HQ: Turkiye Petrol Rafinerileri AS
 Petrol Caddesi No. 25, Korfez, Kocaeli 41790
Phone: (90) 262 316 30 00   **Fax:** (90) 262 316 30 10
Web: www.tupras.com.tr

COMPETITORS

NIOC	Rosneft
NOC	

HISTORICAL FINANCIALS

Company Type: Public

Income Statement				FYE: December 31
	REVENUE ($ mil.)	NET INCOME ($ mil.)	NET PROFIT MARGIN	EMPLOYEES
12/19	15,057	88	0.6%	6,098
12/18	16,736	701	4.2%	5,952
12/17	14,263	1,007	7.1%	5,499
12/16	9,878	508	5.1%	5,296
12/15	12,629	873	6.9%	5,131
Annual Growth	**4.5%**	**(43.6%)**	—	**4.4%**

2019 Year-End Financials

Debt ratio: 5.7%	No. of shares (mil.): —
Return on equity: 4.6%	Dividends
Cash ($ mil.): 1,790	Yield: —
Current ratio: 0.99	Payout: —
Long-term debt ($ mil.): 2,335	Market value ($ mil.): —

UBS Group AG

Auditors: Ernst & Young Ltd.

LOCATIONS

HQ: UBS Group AG
 Bahnhofstrasse 45, Zurich CH-8001
Phone: (41) 44 234 11 11
Web: www.ubs.com

HISTORICAL FINANCIALS

Company Type: Public

Income Statement				FYE: December 31
	REVENUE ($ mil.)	NET INCOME ($ mil.)	NET PROFIT MARGIN	EMPLOYEES
12/19	41,562	4,304	10.4%	68,601
12/18	43,077	4,516	10.5%	66,888
12/17	19,729	1,055	5.4%	61,253
12/16	19,388	3,213	16.6%	59,387
12/15	20,082	6,220	31.0%	60,099
Annual Growth	**19.9%**	**(8.8%)**	—	**3.4%**

2019 Year-End Financials

Debt ratio: —	No. of shares (mil.): —
Return on equity: 8.0%	Dividends
Cash ($ mil.): 107,068	Yield: 5.4%
Current ratio: —	Payout: —
Long-term debt ($ mil.): —	Market value ($ mil.): —

Ultrapar Participacoes SA

Brazil-based Ultrapar Participa § μes is a holding company for a number of midstream and downstream liquefied petroleum gas (LPG) companies. Ultragaz distributes LPG to residential commercial and industrial customers; Ipiranga distributes gasoline ethanol disel fuel oil kerosene natural gas for vehicles and lubricants from 7090 service stations in Brazil and directly to large customers; Oxiteno manufactures ethylene oxide (plus derivatives) and specialty chemicals including surfactants; and Ultracargo provides liquid storage via six terminals. Ultrapar also operates a chain of more than 415 drugstores under the Extrafarma banner. Ultra S.A holds a 20% stake in Ultrapar.

Operations

Ultrapar operates five main business segments: gas distribution fuel distribution chemicals storage and drugstores.

The fuel distribution segment (Ipiranga) operates the distribution and marketing of gasoline ethanol diesel fuel oil kerosene natural gas for vehicles and lubricants and related activities throughout all the Brazilian territory. Ipiranga sells fuel at 7090 service stations and accounts for 85% of total sales.

The gas distribution segment (Ultragaz) distributes LPG to residential commercial and industrial consumers especially in the South Southeast and Northeast regions of Brazil. Ultragaz has a roughly 25% share of the Brazilian market and generates about 10% of sales.

The chemicals segment (Oxiteno) produces ethylene oxide and its main derivatives and fatty alcohols which are raw materials used in cosmetics detergents crop protection chemicals packaging textiles and coatings. Oxiteno generates 5% of sales.

Extrafarma the drugstore segment retails pharmaceutical hygiene and beauty products through 415-plus drugstores in the states of Par ¯ Amap ¯ Maranh o Tocantins Pernambuco Cear ¯ Bahia Rio Grande do Norte Para ba Sergipe and S o Paulo. Extrafarma operates three distribution centers.

The storage segment (Ultracargo) operates liquid bulk terminals especially in the Southeast and Northeast regions of Brazil. Accounting for one percent of sales.

The company also manufactures approximately 1000 products used in various industrial sectors such as cosmetics detergents crop protection chemicals packaging textiles and coatings.

Geographic Reach

Ultrapar is headquartered in Sao Paulo and generates virtually all its revenue within Brazil. Subsidiary Ultragaz operates in all regions of Brazil through a distribution network comprising about 20 filling plants. Ipiranga's 7090 service stations are spread across the country. Extrafarma operates in more than 10 states in Brazil and has three distribution centers in Benevides Aquiraz and Guarulhos.

Subsidiary Oxiteno operates three plants in Mexico. Oxiteno's more than 10 international plants produce specialty chemicals. It also has commercial offices in Argentina Belgium China and Colombia.

Sales and Marketing

Ultragaz distributes LPG to residential commercial and industrial market segments. Ipiranga distributes gasoline ethanol diesel NGV fuel oil kerosene and lubricants through a network of 7090 service stations and directly to large cus-

tomers. It delivers LPG to 11 million households and 55000 business customers.

Financial Performance

Note: Growth rates may differ after conversion to US Dollars.

Ultrapar's fortunes are tied to commodity prices fluctuations in the local currency (the reais) and the health of the Brazilian economy. Its revenues have steadily grown in the past years despite a slight drop in 2019. Overall revenue grew 18% between 2015 and 2019. Net income has also declined in 2019 following four years of profits averaging R$1.5 billion; net income fell 73% in the last five years.

Ultrapar's net revenue from sales and services decreased 2% from R$90.7 billion in 2018 to R$89.3 billion in 2019. This was due to decreases in revenues from Ipiranga and Oxiteno offset by minimal increases in revenues from Utragaz Ultracargo and Extrafarma.

Net income in 2019 was R$402.9 million a 64% decrease from R$1.1 billion in 2018 mainly due to the decline in operating income and share of profit of joint-ventures and associates between the periods and higher net financial expenses.

Ultrapar's cash on hand fell by R$1.8 billion during 2019 ending the year at $2.1 billion. The company's operations generated R$2.9 billion while its investing activities used R$1.8 billion and its financing used R$2.9 billion. Ultrapar's main cash uses in 2019 were capital increase in joint ventures paid interests lease payments and redemption of non-controlling shares of Oxiteno Nordeste.

Strategy

Ultrapar has a multi-faceted strategy each focusing on the company's key aspects for growth and development. The company intends to reinforce its high brand recognition associated with quality safety and efficiency by continuing to supply high-quality products and services and to introduce new services and distribution channels.

The company also aims to maintain strong relationships with its resellers in the LPG and fuel distribution business. It plans to continue to invest in training its dealers in order to maximize efficiency to further strengthen its relationship and to promote the high standards for its distribution network. In parallel it plans to continue to increase its operational efficiency and productivity at Ultragaz and Ipiranga.

Its sales strategy is to increase Ipiranga's market by improving the performance of the existing resale and expanding its network of service stations with high profitability and lower market share. Ipiranga's strategy also includes expanding its logistics infrastructure to support the growing demand for fuels in Brazil and initiatives aiming at differentiating its products and services.

It also aims to enhance its retail network. In 2019 Ipiranga launched Km de Vanatgens (KVM) a loyalty program through which customers and resellers may redeem rewards and benefits in areas of entertainment tourism magazines airline tickets car rental and others. With over 32 million participants in 2019 KMV has served as an important platform strengthening relationships with Ipiranga's customers and resellers.

Company Background

In 2008 Ultrapar acquired Chevron's Texaco-branded fuel distribution business (2000 gas stations) in Brazil for $720 million.

In 2010 it bought fuel distributor Distribuidora Nacional de Petroleo (DNP) for about $50 million. DNP has a network of 110 gas stations in the northern Brazilian states of Acre Amazonas Mato Grosso Para Rondonia and Roraima.

EXECUTIVES

CEO, Thilo Mannhardt, age 65
CEO Ultragaz, Pedro Jorge Filho, age 67
CEO Oxiteno, Jo o Benjamin Parolin, age 61
CEO Extrafarma, André Covre, age 49
CEO Ipiranga, Leocadio Antunes de Almeida Filho, age 69
CEO Ultracargo, Ricardo Isaac Catran, age 65
Chief Financial and Investor Relations Officer, André Pires de Oliveira Dias, age 53
Vice Chairman, Lucio de Castro Andrade Filho, age 76
Chairman and CEO; CEO Oxiteno Ultragaz and Ultracargo, Paulo Guliherme Aguiar Cunha, age 81
Auditors: KPMG Auditores Independentes

LOCATIONS

HQ: Ultrapar Participacoes SA
Avenida Brigadeiro Luis Antonio 1343, 9 Andar, Sao Paulo 01317-910
Phone: (55) 11 3177 6695   **Fax:** (55) 11 3177 6107
Web: www.ultra.com.br

PRODUCTS/OPERATIONS

2018 Sales

	% of total
Ipiranga	84
Ultragaz	8
Oxiteno	5
Extrafarma	2
Ultracargo	1
Total	**100**

Selected Subsidiaries

Ipiranga (fuels & lubricants)
Oxiteno (petrochemicals)
Ultracargo (transportation logistics)
Ultragaz (LPG distribution)

COMPETITORS

Eni

HISTORICAL FINANCIALS

Company Type: Public

Income Statement

FYE: December 31

	REVENUE ($ mil.)	NET INCOME ($ mil.)	NET PROFIT MARGIN	EMPLOYEES
12/19	22,215	92	0.4%	16,024
12/18	23,369	296	1.3%	17,034
12/17	24,151	475	2.0%	16,448
12/16	23,766	479	2.0%	15,173
12/15	19,101	379	2.0%	14,597
Annual Growth	3.8%	(29.7%)	—	2.4%

2019 Year-End Financials

Debt ratio: 11.4%
Return on equity: 3.9%
Cash ($ mil.): 526
Current ratio: 2.90
Long-term debt ($ mil.): 3,302

No. of shares (mil.): 1,086
Dividends
  Yield: 2.0%
  Payout: 144.7%
Market value ($ mil.): 6,799

	STOCK PRICE ($) FY Close	P/E High/Low		PER SHARE ($) Earnings	Dividends	Book Value
12/19	6.26	42	11	0.09	0.13	2.17
12/18	13.54	20	9	0.27	0.40	2.24
12/17	22.73	17	13	0.44	0.26	2.61
12/16	20.74	17	12	0.44	0.25	2.41
12/15	15.25	13	9	0.35	0.45	1.85
Annual Growth	(20.0%)	—	—	(29.6%)	(26.8%)	4.1%

Umicore SA

Umicore aims to do more. Uniquely positioned in all aspects of clean mobility materials and in recycling Umicore provides clean-mobility solutions for all platform types and recycles these materials when they reach the end of their useful life. It also provides automotive catalysts for lightduty and heavy-duty vehicles of all fuel types and the rechargeable battery materials and automotive catalysts that are required to power. Operates one of the world's most sophisticated precious metals recycling facilities and across its activities Umicore can recover about 30 precious and non-ferrous metals from industrial residues used electronic scrap batteries automotive and industrial catalysts fuel cells and more. The company owns around 40% of Element Six Abrasives a joint venture with industrial diamond producer Element Six. Another joint venture with Zinifex combines the two companies' zinc businesses into the world's largest zinc producer called Nyrstar. Majority of its sales come from Europe.

Operations

Its diversified business includes segments including: Recycling (some 60% of sales) Catalysis (about 25%) and Energy & Surface Technologies (nearly 15%).

The Recycling segment treats complex waste streams containing precious and other specialty metals. The operations can recover some 20 of these metals from a wide range of input materials ranging from industrial residues to end-of-life materials. Other activities include production of precious metals-based materials that are essential for applications as diverse as high-tech glass production electrics and electronics.

The Catalysis segment provides automotive catalysts to clean the exhaust gases from internal combustion engines for gasoline and diesel light- and heavy-duty diesel applications including on-road and non-road vehicles. The business group also offers stationary catalysis for industrial emissions control and produces precious metals-based compounds and catalysts for use in the pharmaceutical and fine chemicals industries.

The Energy & Surface Technologies segment is focused on products that are found in applications used in the production and storage of clean energy and in a range of applications for surface technologies that bring specific properties and functionalities to end products. All the activities offer a closed loop service for the customers.

Geographic Reach

The Brussels Belgium-based company has regional management platforms in China North America Japan and South America. Its business is global in nature with some 50 production sites in about 35 countries.

Around 45% of sales were generated in Europe about 30% in Asia Pacific and over 20% in North America while South America and Africa accounts for less than 5% combined.

Financial Performance

Revenues for the full year grew by 3% to - 3.4 billion in 2019 compared to ?3.3 million in 2018.

Cash held by the company at the end of 2019 increased to ?257.1 million while cash held in 2018 was ?239.2 million. Cash provided by operations and financing activities were ?91.8 million and ?706.1 million respectively. Cash used by investing activities was ?577.0 million mainly for acquisitions.

Strategy

The 3 megatrends that Umicore identified in its Horizon 2020 strategy remain its drivers for long-term structural growth.

The long-term prospects for electrified vehicles are stronger than ever as the authorities in several regions are pushing for an accelerated transition to decarbonized mobility. In 2019 it continued to position Umicore to benefit from this trend and capture significant future growth. The company signed multiyear agreements with leading EV battery producers LG Chem and Samsung SDI for deliveries from its plants in Korea China and Europe.

The accelerated trend to cleaner mobility was also confirmed in 2019 by the early introduction of China 6 emission norms in some cities. More stringent norms in Europe and India will provide continued value growth in automotive catalysts especially given Umicore's leading position in particulate filters for gasoline engines and the emerging fuel cell business served by its newly extended plant in Korea.

The geo-political environment was a major driver in 2019 and many of the sources of the turbulence in 2019 - such as trade tensions political change in Europe and an evolving automobile industry - remain unresolved and limit visibility. The company remains committed to its strategic goals and are convinced that the major steps taken in 2019 have prepared Umicore well to capture future growth while it will continue to remain agile in the face of evolving market needs.

Mergers and Acquisitions

In late 2019 Umicore has completed the acquisition of the cobalt refining and cathode precursor activities in Kokkola Finland from Freeport Cobalt for an amount of $ 203 million on a debt and cash free basis. The acquisition of the Kokkola refinery and cathode precursor production marks an important step in expanding Umicore's battery materials value chain. With R&D refining precursor production cathode materials production and battery recycling operations located in Europe Umicore will be ideally placed to serve the European operations of its battery cell and automotive customers with a fully integrated sustainable and local battery materials supply chain.

EXECUTIVES

EVP Recycling, Hugo Morel, age 70
EVP Energy Materials, Marc van Sande, age 68
CEO, Marc Grynberg, age 55
EVP Performance Materials, Stephan Csoma, age 55
EVP Catalysis, Pascal Reymondet, age 61
CTO, Denis Goffaux, age 52
CFO, Filip Platteeuw, age 47
Chairman, Thomas Leysen, age 60
Auditors: PricewaterhouseCoopers Bedrijfsrevisoren/Réviseurs d'Entreprises

LOCATIONS

HQ: Umicore SA
 Rue du Marais 31 Broekstraat, Brussels B-1000
Phone: (32) 2 227 71 11   **Fax:** (32) 2 227 79 00
Web: www.umicore.com

2015 Sales

	% of total
Europe	65
Asia pacific	17
North America	13
South America	3
Africa	2
Total	**100**

PRODUCTS/OPERATIONS

2015 Sales

	% of total
Recycling	60
Catalysis	26

Energy & Surface Technologies	14
Total	**100**

Selected Business Units

Catalysis
Automotive Catalysts
Precious Metals Chemistry
Energy & Surface Technologies
Cobalt & Specialty Materials
Electro-Optic Materials
Electroplating
Rechargeable Battery Materials
Thin Film Products
Recycling
Battery Recycling
Jewellery & Industrial Metals
Platinum Engineered Materials
Precious Metals Management
Precious Metals Refining
Technical Materials
Other
Zinc Chemicals
Building Products - VMZINC

COMPETITORS

BASF Catalysts	Recylex
Johnson Matthey	Sumitomo Metal Mining
Mitsubishi Materials	Teck
Mitsui Mining and Smelting	Vectra

HISTORICAL FINANCIALS

Company Type: Public

Income Statement   FYE: December 31

	REVENUE ($ mil.)	NET INCOME ($ mil.)	NET PROFIT MARGIN	EMPLOYEES
12/19	19,767	323	1.6%	11,152
12/18	15,824	363	2.3%	13,600
12/17	14,408	254	1.8%	13,129
12/16	11,090	138	1.2%	13,117
12/15	10,626	184	1.7%	13,730
Annual Growth	16.8%	15.1%	—	(5.1%)

2019 Year-End Financials

Debt ratio: 27.4%	No. of shares (mil.): 240
Return on equity: 11.0%	Dividends
Cash ($ mil.): 305	Yield: 1.0%
Current ratio: 1.57	Payout: 10.0%
Long-term debt ($ mil.): 1,292	Market value ($ mil.): 2,925

	STOCK PRICE ($) FY Close	P/E High/Low		PER SHARE ($) Earnings	Dividends	Book Value
12/19	12.15	10	6	1.34	0.13	12.09
12/18	9.86	11	7	1.50	0.13	12.40
12/17	11.94	50	12	1.16	0.13	9.85
12/16	27.53	52	29	0.63	0.11	8.64
12/15	21.05	32	22	0.84	0.09	8.73
Annual Growth	(12.8%)	—	—	12.2%	10.6%	8.5%

Unicredito SpA

UniCredit is one of Italy's two largest banks along with Intesa Sanpaolo and among the biggest in Europe. The financial services group operates in some 15 core European countries plus nearly 20 more international markets. Germany and Austria operates as UniCredit Bank and UniCredit Bank Austria. UniCredit's structure is based on four geographic-focused retail banking divisions plus a corporate and investment bank and others. The bank has assets of approximately ?855 billion and generates majority of sales in Italy. UniCredit is the result of the merger of several Italian banks in the late 1990s.

Operations

UniCredit operates through seven divisions: Commercial Banking (CB) Italy CB Germany CB Austria a Central and Eastern Europe division a Corporate & Investment Bank Group Corporate Centre and Non Core.

CB Italy Germany and Austria carry out comparable activities in their respective territories including commercial banking via a branch network and online private banking and other functions typical of a large bank. CB Italy generates more than 35% of UniCredit's revenue CB Germany roughly 15% and CB Austria nearly 10%.

The Central and Eastern Europe segment offers products and services to retail corporate and institutional clients in 12 countries in the region: Azerbaijan Bosnia and Herzegovina Bulgaria Croatia Czech Republic Hungary Romania Russia Serbia Slovakia Slovenia and Turkey. The segment accounts for more than 20% of total revenue.

The Corporate & Investment Bank serves multinational and large corporations with structured financing hedging and treasury solutions for corporate and investment products. It accounts for around 20% of sales.

Net interest income accounts for over 60% of sales while fees and commissions generate about 25%.

Geographic Reach

From its Milan base UniCredit's international branch network numbers around 3800 across its 14 core markets (nearly 2500 being in Italy). UniCredit reaches customers in another nearly 20 countries via a network of international representative offices and branches. Italy accounts for more than 45% of UniCredit's sales followed by Germany for over 20%. The remaining sales are from Other European countries (exceeding 20%) Austria (nearly 10%) and America.

Sales and Marketing

UniCredit boasts more than 15 million clients.

Financial Performance

Note: Growth rates may differ after conversion to US dollars.

UniCredit's net revenue has been on a downward trajectory. In 2019 the bank's revenue declined again down 1% to ?19.3 billion.

Net income fell 19% to ?3.2 billion in 2019 from ?4 billion in 2018.

UniCredit's cash balance fell ?13.7 billion from ?31 billion in 2018 to ?17.3 billion in 2019. Operating activities used ?16.2 billion. Investment activities generated ?2.8 billion while funding activities used another ?315 million.

Strategy

UniCredit has a new plan called Team 23 in recognition of the outstanding work done together for Transform 2019. Team 23 is based on four strategic pillars: Grow and strengthen client franchise; Transform and maximise productivity; Disciplined risk management & controls; Capital and balance sheet management.

The company successfully concluded its three year strategic plan Transform 2019 launched in 2016 exceeding many of its initial targets. This success is thanks to the drive and unwavering commitment from all of the company's team members and the support of its shareholders have shown throughout the plan.

HISTORY

UniCredito Italiano's ancestor Banca di Genova was formed in 1870 just after Italy unified. Within a year the bank was in a South American banking venture Banco de Italia y Rio de la Plata. A banking crisis beginning in the late 1880s threatened the company which was saved and reorganized with the aid of German banking interests. The changes gave the bank — which was renamed Credito Italiano — an advantage over home-grown rivals and pointed it in the direction of German-style universal banking including making direct investments in Italy's late-blooming industrial sector.

In the early 20th century Credito Italiano joined other banks in foreign ventures in Albania Brazil and China and opened offices in London and New York.

After the 1929 crash Credito Italiano acquired several failed banks. But Credito Italiano itself was none too healthy: Government attempts in the 1920s to peg the lira to the pound led to industrial stagnation leaving the bank holding highly illiquid industrial investments and by the early 1930s it was essentially an industrial holding company.

Credito Italiano's existence was threatened when the Depression hit in earnest. To save the bank and its peers Mussolini established the Istituto per la Ricostruzione Industriale (IRI) in 1933 as a "temporary" Resolution Trust-style holding company (IRI was finally liquidated in 2000) to take over the industrial assets of Credito Italiano and several other banks. IRI was instantly a major shareholder in Credito Italiano. IRI-held banks were designated "banks of national interest" three years later and were allowed to provide only short-term commercial banking services a limit that remained in effect for more than 50 years.

In 1946 to fill the need for long-term industrial credit to rebuild war-torn Italy Credito Italiano joined with Banca Commerciale Italiana (now part of IntesaBci) and Banco di Roma to form Mediobanca.

Credito Italiano went public in 1969 (IRI sold its interest in the bank in 1993). As a bank of national interest Credito Italiano was called upon to help bail out several of the country's industrial groups in 1979 (it did so reluctantly).

Changing laws allowed the company to expand its branch network in 1980 and in 1982 IRI allowed Credito Italiano to raise capital (although it was still obliged to prop up struggling state industries). But the 1987 US stock market crash caused Credito Italiano's earnings to plunge 33%. Two years later it bought a stake in Banca Nazionale dell'Agricoltura then Italy's largest private bank.

In 1995 the company joined forces with Rolo Banca 1473 (named for the year its progenitor was founded) to form Credito Italiano Group. Two years later Alessandro Profumo became CEO. He would usher in more than a decade of rapid and agressive expansion.

Credito Italiano merged in 1998 with UniCredito a collection of several northern Italian banks. One Cassa di Risparmio di Verona Vicenza Belluno e Ancona (Cariverona) began in 1501 as a pawnshop operated by monks.

Foreshadowing the bank's shift to an Internet growth strategy (announced after talks with Spain's Banco Bilbao Vizcaya Argentaria fell through) UniCredito in 1999 announced plans for an electronic stock market to include after-hours trading. It also continued to boost holdings in Eastern European banks. In 2000 the company entered into securities brokerage and mutual fund administration with its purchase of US-based Pioneer Investment Management.

In 2001 UniCredito bought 10% of the Pirelli/Benetton-owned holding company formed to control Italian telecommunications company Olivetti. The following year the company partnered with Ko § Holding to take a majority stake in Yapi Kredi.

The bank acquired HVB and Bank Austria in 2005 in an $18 billion cross-border deal one of the largest such deals ever seen in Europe. The bank strengthened its hold at home in 2007 with the nearly $30 billion purchase of Italian bank Capitalia. Antitrust authorities ordered UniCredit to sell its stake in Assicurazioni Generali following the Capitalia transaction.

EXECUTIVES

CEO, Jean-Pierre Mustier, age 59
Deputy General Manager and COO, Paolo Fiorentino, age 65
Deputy General Manager and Head of Strategy and Finance, Marina Natale, age 58
Country Chairman Italy, Gabriele Piccini, age 64
Country Chairman Austria, Robert Zadrazil
Country Chairman Germany, Theodor Weimer, age 61
Country Chairman Poland, Luigi Lovaglio, age 65
Deputy General Manager and Head CIB Division, Gianni Franco Papa, age 64
Head Asset Gathering and CEO and General Manager FinecoBank, Alessandro Foti, age 60
Head Central and Eastern Europe Division, Carlo Vivaldi, age 55
Chief Risk Officer, Massimiliano Fossati, age 53
Vice Chairman, Fabrizio Palenzona, age 67
Chairman, Giuseppe Vita, age 85
Deputy Vice Chairman, Vincenzo Calandra Buonaura, age 74
Vice Chairman, Luca Cordero di Montezemolo, age 73
Auditors: Deloitte & Touche S.p.A.

LOCATIONS

HQ: Unicredito SpA
  Piazza Gae Aulenti 3 - Tower A, Milano 20154
Phone: (39) 2 88 621   **Fax:** (39) 2 8862 3463
Web: www.unicreditgroup.eu

2014 Sales

	% of total
Italy	48
Germany	20
Austria	9
Poland	7
Other countries	16
Total	**100**

PRODUCTS/OPERATIONS

2017 Sales

	% of total
Commercial banking Italy	36
Corporate & investment banking	20
Central & Eastern Europe	20
Commercial Banking Germany	13
Commercial Banking Austria	8
Asset gathering	3
Total	**100**

COMPETITORS

ABN AMRO Group	Banco Popolare
Antonveneta	Credit Suisse
BNL bc	Deutsche Bank
BNP Paribas	Intesa Sanpaolo
Banca Popolare di Milano	UBS

HISTORICAL FINANCIALS

Company Type: Public

Income Statement				FYE: December 31
	ASSETS ($ mil.)	NET INCOME ($ mil.)	INCOME AS % OF ASSETS	EMPLOYEES
12/19	960,691	3,787	0.4%	94,514
12/18	952,193	4,457	0.5%	97,775
12/17	1,003,105	6,560	0.7%	103,771
12/16	907,566	(12,448)	—	130,931
12/15	937,193	1,845	0.2%	139,469
Annual Growth	0.6%	19.7%	—	(9.3%)

2019 Year-End Financials

Return on assets: 0.4%
Return on equity: 5.7%
Long-term debt ($ mil.): —
No. of shares (mil.): —
Sales ($ mil): 28,253

Dividends
Yield: 1.3%
Payout: 6.0%
Market value ($ mil.): —

	STOCK PRICE ($) FY Close	P/E High/Low		PER SHARE ($) Earnings	Dividends	Book Value
12/19	7.25	5	3	1.63	0.10	30.88
12/18	5.62	6	3	1.95	0.12	28.67
12/17	9.60	4	3	3.33	0.00	31.96
Annual Growth	(13.1%)	—	—	(16.3%)	—	(0.9%)

Unilever Plc (United Kingdom)

Unilever PLC along with its Dutch counterpart Unilever N.V. constitute a global food personal care and household products powerhouse. The group's vast portfolio of consumer products includes more than a dozen global brands — including Hellmann's (mayonnaise) Knorr (soups) Lipton (tea) Axe (deodorant) and Dove (soaps) — that each brings up more than ?1 billion in sales. Unilever's consumer goods are sold in more than 190 countries and its largest market is in the US. Based in the UK Unilever PLC trades on the London and New York stock exchanges.

Operations

Unilever's 400 brands are divided into three groups.

The Beauty & Personal Care product category sells skin cleansing (soap shower) skin care (face hand and body moisturisers) hair care (shampoo conditioner styling) and deodorants ?Brands include Axe Dove Lux Rexona and Sunsilk — as well as other household names such as TRE-Semmé Signal Lifebuoy and Vaseline. It generates more than 40% of Unilever's total sales.

The Home Care segment produces cleaning products of various kinds led by the billion-euro Dirt is Good (Persil and Omo) and Surf brands alongside Seventh Generation Domestos Sunlight Cif and more. It brings in more than 20% of overall sales.

The Food & Refreshment primarily sells ice cream savoury (soups bouillons seasoning) dressing (mayonnaise ketchup) and tea. It comprises of brands Knorr stocks Hellmann's mayonnaise Heartbrand Lipton Magnum Pukka and more. The segment accounts for more than 35% of sales.

Geographic Reach

Based in London UK Unilever has operations in more than 190 countries and its products are sold in virtually every country in the world. It has 300 factories in nearly 70 countries and a global network of more than 400 warehouses.

Geographically Unilever's revenue is highly diversified. The US is its single largest market that generates more than 15% of sales while the UK and Netherlands (its home markets) generate slightly more than 5% combined. Emerging markets are growing as a percentage of sales and generate more than 75% of the total.

Sales and Marketing

Unilever's customer base consists of ten different channels: super and hypermarkets drug stores e-commerce retailers small stores discounters Food Solutions out-of-home Unilever International prestige and global retail. Its products end up in around 25 million stores globally.

Unilever racks up the world's second-largest advertising spend.

Financial Performance

Note: Growth rates may differ after conversion to US dollars.

Unilever's revenue growth has fluctuated in the past few years with an overall decline of 2%. Its net income has been rising consecutively but dropped in 2019.

Revenue in 2019 totalled ?52 billion a 2% increase compared to ?51 billion 2018. The increase was primarily due to the ?1.2 billion increase in beauty and personal care products sales.

Net income declined 40% to ?5.6 billion.

Cash and cash equivalents at the end of the year totalled ?4.1 billion. Operating activities generated ?8.1 billion while investing and financing activities used ?2.2 billion and ?4.7 billion respectively.

Strategy

Unilever's business model describes how the company operates to create sustained value for its stakeholders which is to focus on consumer insights innovation sourcing and marketing.

Consumer insights. Unilever tracks changing customer sentiment through its 30 People Data Centres around the world combining social listening with traditional consumer research.

Innovation. Its marketing and R&D teams use these insights plus the best ideas and thinking from specialists outside Unilever to develop its brands and products. The company spent ?840 million on R&D in 2019.

Sourcing. Each year the company buys raw material and packaging materials worth ?21 billion to make its products and services worth ?14 billion to help its business run.

Marketing. Unilever creates an increasing amount of tailored digital content to connect with consumers and make it easy to choose a Unilever brand.

Mergers and Acquisitions

In early 2020 Hindustan Unilever Limited (HUL) India's largest fast-moving consumer goods company and Unilever's listed subsidiary in India has successfully completed the merger of Singapore-based GlaxoSmithKline Consumer Healthcare Limited (GSKCH) with HUL. Unilever has also completed the related acquisition of Horlicks brands rights and other Consumer Healthcare nutrition assets from GSK in other predominantly Asian markets.

In mid-2019 Unilever acquired San Francisco-based Tatcha a modern skincare brand rooted in classical Kyoto rituals for $500 million. Vasiliki Petrou Unilever EVP and CEO Prestige said: "We are delighted to have Tatcha joining our portfolio of Prestige brands. Inspired by Japanese pure beauty rituals Tatcha is one of the best performing beauty brands in North America famous for its exceptional product experience and unique combination of natural ingredients and high product efficacy.

In 2019 Unilever acquired San Francisco-based OLLY Nutrition a wellbeing business in the vitamins minerals and supplements (VMS) category for an undisclosed amount. The acquisition accelerates Unilever's presence and competitiveness in the wellness market.

Also in 2019 Unilever acquired Garancia a French derma-cosmetic brand for an undisclosed amount. The acquisition strengthens Unilever's prestige portfolio in the pharmacy channel.

In 2019. Unilever acquired London-based Graze the UK's leading healthy snacking brand for Â 150 million. With a broad portfolio of healthy snack products Graze accelerates Unilever's presence in the fast-growing healthy snacking and out of home markets.

Company Background

Unilever traced its roots 1890's Although Unilever wasn't formed until 1930 the companies that joined forces to create the business we know today were already well established before the start of the 20th century. In 1929 With businesses expanding fast companies set up negotiations intending to stop others producing the same types of products. But instead they agree to merge and so Unilever is created.

EXECUTIVES

CFO, Graeme Pitkethly
President Refreshment, Kevin Havelock, age 63
CEO, Paul Polman, age 63
Chief Research and Development Officer, David Blanchard
President Home Care, Nitin Paranjpe, age 56
President Foods, Amanda Sourry
President Europe, Jan Zijderveld
President Personal Care, Alan Jope
President North America, Kees Kruythoff
Chief Supply Chain Officer, Marc Engel
Chairman, Marijn Dekkers
Auditors: KPMG LLP

LOCATIONS

HQ: Unilever Plc (United Kingdom)
100 Victoria Embankment, London EC4Y 0DY
Phone: (44) 20 7822 5252 **Fax:** (44) 20 7822 5464
Web: www.unilever.com

2016 Sales

	% of total
US	16
Netherlands / UK	7
Others	77
Total	**100**

PRODUCTS/OPERATIONS

2017 Sales

	% of total
Personal Care	39
Foods	23
Refreshment	18
Home Care	20
Total	**100**

Selected Global Brands

Axe
Dirt is Good (OMO)
Dollar Shave Club
Dove
Family Goodness (Rama)
Hellmann's
Knorr
Lipton
Lux
Magnum
Rexona
Sunsilk
Surf

COMPETITORS

Church & Dwight Canada
Henkel
Kraft Heinz
Mondelez International
Nestlé
Premier Foods
Procter & Gamble
R&R Ice Cream
Reckitt Benckiser

HISTORICAL FINANCIALS

Company Type: Public

Income Statement   FYE: December 31

	REVENUE ($ mil.)	NET INCOME ($ mil.)	NET PROFIT MARGIN	EMPLOYEES
12/19	58,361	6,315	10.8%	153,000
12/18	58,384	10,752	18.4%	155,000
12/17	64,391	7,256	11.3%	165,000
12/16	55,658	5,473	9.8%	168,832
12/15	58,024	5,346	9.2%	168,921
Annual Growth	0.1%	4.3%	—	(2.4%)

2019 Year-End Financials

Debt ratio: 44.8%
Return on equity: 45.4%
Cash ($ mil.): 4,698
Current ratio: 0.78
Long-term debt ($ mil.): 24,496

No. of shares (mil.): —
Dividends
  Yield: 3.1%
  Payout: 74.9%
Market value ($ mil.): —

	STOCK PRICE ($) FY Close	P/E High/Low		PER SHARE ($) Earnings	Dividends	Book Value
12/19	57.17	31	24	2.40	1.80	5.66
12/18	52.25	16	14	3.99	1.81	5.07
12/17	55.34	28	21	2.58	1.65	5.97
12/16	40.70	25	21	1.92	1.33	6.04
12/15	43.12	27	21	1.87	1.30	5.89
Annual Growth	7.3%	—	—	6.4%	8.4%	(1.0%)

Union Bank Of India

LOCATIONS

HQ: Union Bank Of India
  Union Bank Bhavan, 239, Vidhan Bhavan Marg,
  Nariman Point, Mumbai 400 021
Phone: 1800 208 2244
Web: www.unionbankofindia.co.in

HISTORICAL FINANCIALS

Company Type: Public

Income Statement   FYE: March 31

	ASSETS ($ mil.)	NET INCOME ($ mil.)	INCOME AS % OF ASSETS	EMPLOYEES
03/20	73,543	(413)	—	37,318
03/19	72,054	(422)	—	37,262
03/18	75,490	(801)	—	37,587
03/17	70,263	88	0.1%	36,877
03/16	61,599	205	0.3%	35,473
Annual Growth	4.5%	—	—	1.3%

2020 Year-End Financials

Return on assets: (-0.5%)
Return on equity: (-10.2%)
Long-term debt ($ mil.): —
No. of shares (mil.): —
Sales ($ mil): 5,717

Dividends
  Yield: —
  Payout: —
Market value ($ mil.): —

Unipol Gruppo SpA

Unipol Gruppo is an Italian firm with dozens of subsidiaries in the insurance real estate banking and other industries. It primarily operates through subsidiary UnipolSai Assicurazioni. That unit provides property/casualty and life insurance and reinsurance as well as financial investment services. Banking unit Unipol Banca provides retail and commercial services both online and through a network of branches. Other businesses include agriculture and hospitality. Until late 2017 holding company Holmo controlled Unipol through Finsoe but that unit was shuttered and its stakes in Unipol were transferred to a group of 18 newly created Italian firms.

Financial Performance

In 2017 Unipol had net profit of €213.4 million a 33% increase over the prior year. Factors contributing to that gain included capital gains received from asset sales and dividends received from the group's subsidiaries. UnipolSai Assicurazioni's profit increased 26% to €577.2 million. In general though property/casualty insurance premiums remained flat that year and the company had an increase in claims from atmospheric events. Life insurance didn't fare much better. Bank subsidiary Unipol Banca had a €751.7 million loss as a result of the group's reorganization activities which led to write-downs of bad and doubtful loans.

Strategy

Unipol has been working to consolidate its operations its customer relationships and its distribution network. As part of its reorganization activities the company hopes to develop an integrated multi-channel model while preserving the identities of its various operating un units.

The group has also been focused on product innovation especially around the use of telematics.

To increase the value of its real estate portfolio and generate additional income Unipol is also renovating certain properties especially properties located in Milan.

EXECUTIVES

CEO and Managing Director, Carlo Cimbri
President, Pierluigi Stefanini
Vice Chairman, Giovanni Antonelli
Auditors: PricewaterhouseCoopers S.p.A.

LOCATIONS

HQ: Unipol Gruppo SpA
  Via Stalingrado, 45, Bologna 40128
Phone: (39) 051 5076111   **Fax:** (39) 051 5076666
Web: www.unipol.it

PRODUCTS/OPERATIONS

Selected Subsidiaries

Atahotels (hotels)
DDOR Novi Sad (Serbia insurance)
Linear Assicurazioni (direct insurance)
Marina di Loano (port management)
Tenute de Cerro (agriculture)
UNA Hotels & Resorts (hotels)
Unipol Banca (banking)
UnipolSai Assicurazioni S.p.A. (insurance holding company)UniSalute (health care insurance)

COMPETITORS

Allianz S.p.A.	Intesa Sanpaolo
BNL bc	Milano Assicurazioni
Banco Popolare	Monte dei Paschi di
Cattolica	Siena

Assicurazioni	UniCredit
ERGO Previdenza	Vittoria Assicurazioni
Generali	

HISTORICAL FINANCIALS

Company Type: Public

Income Statement   FYE: December 31

	REVENUE ($ mil.)	NET INCOME ($ mil.)	NET PROFIT MARGIN	EMPLOYEES
12/19	18,638	1,013	5.4%	12,337
12/18	16,282	459	2.8%	14,241
12/17	15,787	(414)	—	14,188
12/16	17,565	348	2.0%	0
12/15	20,241	296	1.5%	13,864
Annual Growth	(2.0%)	36.0%	—	(2.9%)

2019 Year-End Financials

Debt ratio: —
Return on equity: 15.4%
Cash ($ mil.): 1,130
Current ratio: —
Long-term debt ($ mil.): —

No. of shares (mil.): 716
Dividends
  Yield: —
  Payout: 22.2%
Market value ($ mil.): —

UnipolSai Assicurazioni SpA

Auditors: PricewaterhouseCoopers SpA

LOCATIONS

HQ: UnipolSai Assicurazioni SpA
  Via Stalingrado 45, Bologna 40128
Phone: (39) 051 5077111   **Fax:** (39) 051 7096584
Web: www.unipolsai.com

HISTORICAL FINANCIALS

Company Type: Public

Income Statement   FYE: December 31

	REVENUE ($ mil.)	NET INCOME ($ mil.)	NET PROFIT MARGIN	EMPLOYEES
12/19	17,988	704	3.9%	12,274
12/18	15,591	1,036	6.6%	11,935
12/17	15,502	604	3.9%	11,529
12/16	14,625	525	3.6%	10,280
12/15	17,394	774	4.5%	9,951
Annual Growth	0.8%	(2.3%)	—	5.4%

2019 Year-End Financials

Debt ratio: —
Return on equity: 10.1%
Cash ($ mil.): 838
Current ratio: —
Long-term debt ($ mil.): —

No. of shares (mil.): —
Dividends
  Yield: —
  Payout: —
Market value ($ mil.): —

UNIQA Insurance Group AG

Auditors: PwC Wirtschaftsprufung GmbH

LOCATIONS

HQ: UNIQA Insurance Group AG
Untere Donaustrasse 21, Vienna 1029
Phone: (43) 1 211 75 3773   **Fax:** (43) 1 211 75 793773
Web: www.uniqagroup.com

HISTORICAL FINANCIALS

Company Type: Public

Income Statement   FYE: December 31

	ASSETS ($ mil.)	NET INCOME ($ mil.)	INCOME AS % OF ASSETS	EMPLOYEES
12/19	32,255	260	0.8%	13,038
12/18	32,642	278	0.9%	12,818
12/17	34,456	193	0.6%	12,839
12/16	35,519	156	0.4%	12,855
12/15	36,029	360	1.0%	14,113
Annual Growth	(2.7%)	(7.8%)	—	(2.0%)

2019 Year-End Financials

Return on assets: 0.8%
Return on equity: 7.2%
Long-term debt ($ mil.): —
No. of shares (mil.): 306
Sales ($ mil): 5,946

Dividends
Yield: —
Payout: 71.0%
Market value ($ mil.): —

United Overseas Bank Ltd. (Singapore)

One of Singapore's top financial institutions United Overseas Bank (UOB) provides a range of commercial banking and personal financial services. The bank's offerings include asset management private equity fund management and insurance services. It is also one of the largest capital market issuers in the Asia-Pacific region. Altogether the bank has more than 500 branches and 1.3 million ATMs in almost 20 countries. Most of UOB's revenue comes from Singapore.

Operations

UOB is organized into three businesses - Retail Wholesale and Global Markets and Investment Management. Its retail business covers personal accounts private banking and small businesses. It accounts for about 45% of revenue. The wholesale division serves large corporations and financial institutions; it accounts for more than 40% of revenue. Global markets and investment management which provides asset management foreign exchange money market funds derivatives and other capital market activities accounts for more than 5% of revenue and the rest comes from other activities.

Overall UOB generates roughly 65% of its revenue from interest income and the rest comes from non-interest income.

Geographic Reach

Altogether the bank has operations in about 20 Asian countries. While its headquarters is located in Singapore UOB operates more than 500 branches and offices in Asia Pacific Europe and North America. It generates revenue from China (almost 10% of total revenue) Indonesia (some 5%) Malaysia (over 10%) and Thailand (around 10%) among others.

Financial Performance

The company's revenue increased to $10.0 billion in 2019 compared to $9.1 billion in the previous year. The increase was due to higher net interest income and net fee and commission income.

Net income increased by 8% to $4.3 billion compared to $4.0 million in the previous year.

Cash held by the company at the end of 2019 was $20.2 billion. Cash provided by operations was $8.3 billion while cash used for investing and financing activities were $500.1 million and $7.6 billion respectively. Main uses of cash were purchase of properties and other fixed assets and redemption of debts issued.

Strategy

UOB with its established Asian heritage and franchise is well positioned. The company connects its corporate clients to regional opportunities and provide financial solutions to our retail customers as their needs evolve with rising affluence.

UOB fulfill its purpose by pursuing a strategy based on the following pillars: deepening its regional connectivity through its network sector solutions and cross-border advisory capabilities; offering the complete customer experience with best-in-class products and services through its holistic omni-channel approach and Digital Bank; investing in people and technology for the long term; and being disciplined in risk and balance sheet management to navigate through economic cycles.

Company Background

UOB was founded in 1935 as the United Chinese Bank and catered mainly to the Fujian community in Singapore. The bank changed its name to United Overseas Bank in 1965.

EXECUTIVES

Head Group Retail, Francis C. Y. Lee
Head Global Markets and Investment Management, Terence S. E. Ong
Chief Risk Officer, Chan Seong
CFO, Lee Wai Fai
Deputy Chairman and CEO, Wee Ee Cheong, age 66
Head Group Wholesale Banking, Frederick V. F. Chin
Head Group Technology and Operations, Susan W. C. Hwee
President and Director PT Bank UOB Indonesia, Armand B. Arief
President and CEO United Overseas Bank (Thai) Public Company Limited, Peter M. T. Foo
President and CEO United Overseas Bank (China) Limited, Eric V. F. Lian
CEO United Overseas Bank (Malaysia) Bhd, Wong Kim Choong
Chairman, Hsieh Fu Hua, age 68
Auditors: Ernst & Young LLP

LOCATIONS

HQ: United Overseas Bank Ltd. (Singapore)
80 Raffles Place, UOB Plaza, 048624
Phone: (65) 6222 2121   **Fax:** (65) 6534 2334
Web: www.uobgroup.com

2012 Sales

	% of total
Singapore	58
Malaysia	15
Thailand	8
Indonesia	7
China	6
Other	6
Total	**100**

Selected Subsidiaries

Far Eastern Bank Limited (Singapore)
PT Bank UOB Indonesia
United Overseas Bank (China)
United Overseas Bank (Malaysia)
United Overseas Bank (Philippines)
United Overseas Bank (Thailand)
United Overseas Insurance Limited Singapore
UOB Australia Limited
UOB Capital Investments Pte Ltd Singapore
UOB Capital Management Pte Ltd Singapore
UOB Holdings Private Limited Singapore
UOB Insurance (H.K.) Limited Hong Kong
UOB International Investment Private Limited

PRODUCTS/OPERATIONS

2012 Sales

	% of total
Interest income	61
Fees & commission	23
Other non-interest income	16
Total	**100**

2012 Sales

	% of total
Retail	36
Wholesale	36
Global markets & investment mgmt.	19
Other	9
Total	**100**

COMPETITORS

Astra International	Edaran Otomobil
Bangkok Bank	HSBC
Bank Central Asia	Hang Seng Bank
Bank Danamon Indonesia	Hong Leong Finance
Bank Mandiri	Maybank
Bank Rakyat	OCBC Bank
Bank of China	Standard Chartered
DBS Group Holdings	

HISTORICAL FINANCIALS

Company Type: Public

Income Statement   FYE: December 31

	ASSETS ($ mil.)	NET INCOME ($ mil.)	INCOME AS % OF ASSETS	EMPLOYEES
12/19	300,580	3,228	1.1%	26,872
12/18	285,005	2,943	1.0%	0
12/17	268,425	2,537	0.9%	0
12/16	235,316	2,142	0.9%	0
12/15	223,570	2,270	1.0%	0
Annual Growth	7.7%	9.2%	—	—

2019 Year-End Financials

Return on assets: 1.1%
Return on equity: 11.2%
Long-term debt ($ mil.): —
No. of shares (mil.): 1,668
Sales ($ mil): 11,948

Dividends
Yield: 4.6%
Payout: 98.1%
Market value ($ mil.): 65,591

	STOCK PRICE ($)	P/E	PER SHARE ($)		
	FY Close	High/Low	Earnings	Dividends	Book Value
12/19	39.32	16 14	1.89	1.81	17.66
12/18	36.12	19 15	1.71	1.71	16.59
12/17	39.64	20 15	1.48	1.05	16.59
12/16	28.14	16 13	1.28	0.96	13.91
12/15	27.55	18 13	1.37	1.60	13.59
Annual Growth	9.3%	— —	8.4%	3.1%	6.8%

UPM - Kymmene Corp. (Finland)

Auditors: PricewaterhouseCoopers Oy

LOCATIONS

HQ: UPM - Kymmene Corp. (Finland)
 Alvar Aallon katu 1, P.O. Box 380, Helsinki FIN-00101
Phone: (358) 204 15 111   **Fax:** (358) 204 15 110
Web: www.upm.com

HISTORICAL FINANCIALS

Company Type: Public

Income Statement   FYE: December 31

	REVENUE ($ mil.)	NET INCOME ($ mil.)	NET PROFIT MARGIN	EMPLOYEES
12/19	16,110	1,669	10.4%	18,742
12/18	16,496	2,352	14.3%	18,978
12/17	15,751	1,531	9.7%	19,111
12/16	15,440	1,383	9.0%	19,390
12/15	15,953	1,441	9.0%	19,578
Annual Growth	0.2%	3.7%	—	(1.1%)

2019 Year-End Financials

Debt ratio: 13.8%
Return on equity: 10.6%
Cash ($ mil.): 2,417
Current ratio: 2.51
Long-term debt ($ mil.): 1,880

No. of shares (mil.): 533
Dividends
 Yield: 0.0%
 Payout: 65.3%
Market value ($ mil.): 18,440

	STOCK PRICE ($)	P/E	PER SHARE ($)		
	FY Close	High/Low	Earnings	Dividends	Book Value
12/19	34.58	17 13	3.13	2.05	29.69
Annual Growth	—	— —	—	—	—

Vale SA

Brazilian mining company Vale is the world's top producer of metals such as iron ore iron ore pellets and nickel the key raw materials for steelmaking and stainless steel. Its Cajar´s mine in Northern Brazil boasts the highest grade iron ore anywhere in the world. With greenfield mineral exploration in five countries Rio de Janeiro-based Vale maintains a network integrating its mines with railroads ports and ships. Additionally it has a sustainable energy project in Brazil hydroelectric plants in Brazil Canada and Indonesia and pursues investments in energy and steel businesses through affiliates and joint ventures. About half of its revenue comes from China.

OperationsVale reports four segments based on its products and operations — ferrous minerals; base metals; coal; and logistics infrastructure (others). Ferrous minerals account for around 80% of annual sales the two leading products being iron ore and iron ore pellets. Vales operates four systems in Brazil for producing and distributing iron ore plus eleven pellet plants in Brazil and two in Oman. In addition it has a 50% stake in Samarco and 25% stakes in two pellet companies in China. Vale also has ferroalloy and manganese mining operations through several subsidiaries. Base Metal (about 15% of revenue) manages nickel mine production and processing as well as refining. The company also produces copper cobalt PGMs (platinum group metals) and other precious metals. The company's coal operations (nearly 5%) are focused on metallurgical and thermal coal operations. Vales logistics infrastructure is top-notch with railroads maritime terminals distribution centers and ports. The company owns and charters dry bulk vessels to transport its own products.

Geographic Reach

Based in Rio de Janeiro Brazil Vale has operation that cover approximately 30 countries. It produces ferrous metals copper and manganese in Brazil; nickel cobalt and platinum group metals in Canada; and coal in Mozambique.

In Brazil Vale divides its iron ore operations into four regional systems. The Northern and Southeastern regions are fully integrated containing mines railroads marine terminals and a port. The Southern system comprises three mines and two terminals. The company owns two railroads that connect production regions with export terminals the Vit ria-Mians and Caraj´s railroads. Vale has about eleven pellet plants in Brazil (plus two in Oman).

Most of Vale's nickel production is in Canada but it has additional mining operations in Indonesia and Brazil and refineries in the UK Japan and China.

Its products are sold across the world with China the leading market (about half of its annual sales) and followed by Europe (except Germany) Brazil and Asia (except Japan and China) each accounts nearly 10% of sales. Japan Germany the US and some other countries accounts the remainder.

Sales and Marketing

The company sales copper concentrates from Sossego and Salobo under medium and long-term contracts to copper smelters in Europe India and Asia. It have medium-term copper supply agreements with domestic customer for part of the copper concentrates and copper matte produced in Sudbury which are also sold under long-term contracts in Europe and Asia. The sale of copper concentrates from Voisey's Bay under medium and long-term contracts to customers in Europe and electrowon copper cathodes from Sudbury and Long Harbour in North America under short-term sales agreements.

Financial Performance

Despite the tendency of industrial production to be the most cyclical and volatile component of global economic activity Vale's financial performance has improved over the years. Revenue grew 61% between 2015 and 2019. However Vale's net income has not fared better in the last five years with losses in 2015 and 2019 and figures not exceeding $6 million in the years between.

In 2019 Vale's revenue grew 3% to $37.6 billion thanks mainly to higher realized prices of iron ore and iron ore pellet sales prices partially offset by lower iron ore and iron ore pellets sales volumes as well as lower sales volumes from its base metals business.

Vale recorded a loss of $1.2 billion in 2019 compared to a net income of $6.9 billion in 2018. This loss was mainly driven by provisions of $7.4 billion for emergency actions reparation and remediation measures associated with the rupture of Dam I impairment charges of $4.2 billion on its nickel and coal mine assets and additional provisions for the Renova Foundation and the decharacterization of Samarco's Germano dam of $758 million.

Vale's cash balance grew by $1.6 billion to $7.4 billion during 2019. Operating activities generated $12.1 billion investing used $7 billion and financing used $3.5 billion. Vale's main cash uses were loan repayments capital expenditures and judicial deposits.

Strategy

As 2019 was a challenging year for Vale it is dedicated in going beyond its commitment to restore Brumadinho and to better itself based on the following main pillars: safety and operational excellence; new pact with society; maximize flight-to-quality in iron ore; base metals transformation; and discipline in capital allocation.

In 2019 Vale created a new position in its Board of Executive Officers for an executive officer for Satefy and Operational Excellence. It also revised and relaunched its management system (Vale Production System) in 2019 with more than 60000 people trained as a means to support the ongoing safety cultural transformation within Vale.

Vale also revised its sustainability goals in line with the Sustainable Development Goals of the UN 2030 Agenda. Vale's 2030 Commitments include: Energy; Forest Protection; Climate Change; and Environmental Social and Governance Gaps.

With the continuous increase of the share of dry processing production aimed at 70% by 2023 Vale announced an estimated investment of $1.8 billion between 2020 and 2024 in some of its sites including Cau Concei § o and Brucutu Mines. Vale also acquired New Steel in 2019 bringing in innovative technologies for the dry beneficiation of iron ore. It also announced its investment of $100 million in the world's first industrial-scale dry magnetic fines concentration to produce 1.5Mt starting in 2022. It also launched the GF88 a new product to supply the growing market of pellet production in China.

Mergers and Acquisitions

In late 2019 Vale acquired New Steel Global from Hankoe FIP for $500 million. New Steel Global develops iron ore technologies in Brazil. The acquisition supports the development of Vale's high-grade pellet feed initiatives.

In mid-2019 Vale acquired Ferrous Resources an owner and operator of iron ore mines proximal to Vale's existing locations in the Brazilian state Minas Gerais for $550 million. The acquisition is in line to the company's strategy of maximizing the flight to quality in the Iron Ore business.

EXECUTIVES

CFO, Luciano Siani Pires, age 50
Executive Director Fertilizers and Coal, Roger Downey
Executive Director Logistics and Mineral Research, Humberto Freitas
Executive Director Ferrous Minerals, Peter Poppinga
Executive Director Base Metals; CEO Vale Canada, Jennifer Maki
CEO, Fabio Schvartsman
President Board of Directors, Gueitiro Matsuo Genso
Vice President Board of Directors, Fernando Jorge Buso Gomes
Auditors: KPMG Auditores Independentes

LOCATIONS

HQ: Vale SA
   Praia de Botafogo, 186, Rio de Janeiro 22250-145
Phone: (55) 21 3814 4477   **Fax:** (55) 21 3814 9935
Web: www.vale.com

2018 Sales

	$ mil.	% of total
China	15,242	42
Europe (excl. Germany)	4,454	12
Brazil	3,248	9
Japan	2,743	7
Germany	1,653	5
Asia except Japan and China	3,666	10
Americas (excl. US and Brazil)	1,476	4
Middle East/Africa/Oceania	2,738	7
US	1,353	4
Total	**36,575**	**100**

PRODUCTS/OPERATIONS

2018 sales

	$ mil.	% of total
Ferrous minerals	27,933	76
Coal	1,643	5
Base metals	6,703	18
Others	296	1
Total	**36,575**	**100**

COMPETITORS

AHMSA	Exxaro
Anglo American	Freeport-McMoRan
Arconic	Kumba Iron Ore
BHP Billiton	Norilsk Nickel
Cliffs Natural Resources	Rio Tinto Limited
	Teck

HISTORICAL FINANCIALS

Company Type: Public

Income Statement
FYE: December 31

	REVENUE ($ mil.)	NET INCOME ($ mil.)	NET PROFIT MARGIN	EMPLOYEES
12/19	37,570	(1,683)	—	71,149
12/18	36,575	6,860	18.8%	70,270
12/17	33,967	5,507	16.2%	73,596
12/16	27,488	3,982	14.5%	73,062
12/15	25,609	(12,129)	—	74,098
Annual Growth	**10.1%**	**—**	**—**	**(1.0%)**

2019 Year-End Financials

Debt ratio: 14.2%
Return on equity: (-4.0%)
Cash ($ mil.): 7,350
Current ratio: 1.23
Long-term debt ($ mil.): 11,842

No. of shares (mil.): —
Dividends
   Yield: 2.2%
   Payout: —
Market value ($ mil.): —

	STOCK PRICE ($) FY Close	P/E High/Low		PER SHARE ($) Earnings	Dividends	Book Value
12/19	13.20	—	—	(0.33)	0.30	7.81
12/18	13.19	12	9	1.32	0.53	8.58
12/17	12.23	12	7	1.05	0.34	8.36
12/16	7.62	12	3	0.77	0.04	12.26
12/15	3.29	—	—	(2.35)	0.25	10.54
Annual Growth	**41.5%**			**—**	**4.6%**	**(7.2%)**

Valeo SA

Auditors: Mazars

LOCATIONS

HQ: Valeo SA
   43, rue Bayen, Paris, Cedex 17 75848
Phone: (33) 1 40 55 20 20   **Fax:** (33) 1 40 55 21 71
Web: www.valeo.com

HISTORICAL FINANCIALS

Company Type: Public

Income Statement
FYE: December 31

	REVENUE ($ mil.)	NET INCOME ($ mil.)	NET PROFIT MARGIN	EMPLOYEES
12/19	21,602	351	1.6%	114,700
12/18	21,773	625	2.9%	113,600
12/17	22,263	1,062	4.8%	111,600
12/16	17,506	976	5.6%	91,800
12/15	15,902	794	5.0%	82,800
Annual Growth	**8.0%**	**(18.4%)**	**—**	**8.5%**

2019 Year-End Financials

Debt ratio: 28.9%
Return on equity: 6.8%
Cash ($ mil.): 1,990
Current ratio: 0.96
Long-term debt ($ mil.): 4,959

No. of shares (mil.): 239
Dividends
   Yield: 3.9%
   Payout: 47.6%
Market value ($ mil.): 4,191

	STOCK PRICE ($) FY Close	P/E High/Low		PER SHARE ($) Earnings	Dividends	Book Value
12/19	17.54	16	10	1.47	0.70	21.74
12/18	14.58	17	6	2.61	0.73	22.06
12/17	37.34	11	9	4.41	0.75	22.24
12/16	28.60	19	5	4.08	0.53	18.27
12/15	77.42	27	18	3.32	1.20	16.07
Annual Growth	**(31.0%)**			**—**	**(18.4%)** **(12.6%)**	**7.8%**

Valiant Holding Bern (Switzerland)

EXECUTIVES

Chairman Of The Board, Markus Gygax
Vice Chairman Of The Board, Christoph B hler
Board Member, Barbara Artmann
Board Member, Jean-Baptiste Beuret
Board Member, Maya Bundt Aeby
Board Member, Nicole Pauli
Board Member, Othmar St ¶ckli
Board Member, Ronald Tr ¤chsel
Board Member, Franziska von Weissenfluh
Auditors: PricewaterhouseCoopers AG

LOCATIONS

HQ: Valiant Holding Bern (Switzerland)
   Pilatusstrasse 39, Lucerne 6003
Phone: (41) 31 310 71 11   **Fax:** (41) 31 310 71 12
Web: www.valiant.ch

COMPETITORS

Bank Sarasin	Lombard Odier Darier
Citigroup	Hentsch
Credit Suisse	UBS

Deutsche Bank	Vontobel
Julius Baer	

HISTORICAL FINANCIALS

Company Type: Public

Income Statement
FYE: December 31

	ASSETS ($ mil.)	NET INCOME ($ mil.)	INCOME AS % OF ASSETS	EMPLOYEES
12/19	30,936	125	0.4%	1,045
12/18	27,836	122	0.4%	1,013
12/17	28,242	122	0.4%	1,000
12/16	25,635	115	0.5%	957
12/15	25,625	115	0.4%	926
Annual Growth	**4.8%**	**2.1%**	**—**	**3.1%**

2019 Year-End Financials

Return on assets: 0.4%
Return on equity: 5.2%
Long-term debt ($ mil.): —
No. of shares (mil.): 15
Sales ($ mil): 499

Dividends
   Yield: —
   Payout: 65.1%
Market value ($ mil.): —

Veolia Environnement

Auditors: KPMG Audit

LOCATIONS

HQ: Veolia Environnement
   21 rue La Boetie, Paris 75008
Phone: (33) 1 71 75 00 00
Web: www.veolia.com

HISTORICAL FINANCIALS

Company Type: Public

Income Statement
FYE: December 31

	REVENUE ($ mil.)	NET INCOME ($ mil.)	NET PROFIT MARGIN	EMPLOYEES
12/19	42,784	983	2.3%	178,021
12/18	40,773	691	1.7%	171,495
12/17	39,536	631	1.6%	168,800
12/16	38,380	602	1.6%	163,226
12/15	39,284	708	1.8%	173,959
Annual Growth	**2.2%**	**8.5%**	**—**	**0.6%**

2019 Year-End Financials

Debt ratio: 57.9%
Return on equity: 10.4%
Cash ($ mil.): 9,195
Current ratio: 0.90
Long-term debt ($ mil.): 14,739

No. of shares (mil.): 554
Dividends
   Yield: 3.8%
   Payout: 58.3%
Market value ($ mil.): 14,746

	STOCK PRICE ($) FY Close	P/E High/Low		PER SHARE ($) Earnings	Dividends	Book Value
12/19	26.58	25	19	1.76	1.03	16.83
12/18	20.41	39	28	1.02	0.99	17.03
12/17	25.50	43	27	0.91	0.87	21.48
12/16	16.95	45	30	0.90	0.84	22.24
12/15	23.59	35	24	1.09	0.79	23.88
Annual Growth	**3.0%**			**12.9%**	**6.9%**	**(8.4%)**

Vestas Wind Systems A/S

Vestas Wind Systems and its subsidiaries manufacture and sell land-based wind turbines used to produce electricity. In all Vestas has installed about 59000 wind turbines in more than 70 countries. Besides installation Vestas is the world's largest servicer of wind turbines and maintains more than 42000 turbines with a combined capacity of 87000 GW. Offshore turbines are offered through MHI Vestas Offshore Wind - a 50:50 joint venture with Mitsubishi Heavy Industries. The company's data analytics offerings help customers improve predictability and efficiency and better integrate with energy grids. Vestas generates about 45% of its sales in the Americas.

Financial Performance

Note: Growth rates may differ after conversion to US Dollars.

Except for a slight dip in 2017 Vestas' revenue has grown steadily the last five years rising more than 46% between 2014 and 2018. Strong demand for wind power globally and a healthy backlog have driven the company's growth.

Sales in 2018 increased nearly 2% to ?10.1 billion compared to ?9.9 billion in 2017. Growth in 2018 was fueled by Vestas' onshore service business which saw sales increase 10% over 2017 as the company's growing fleet of installed wind turbines generated more revenue. Wind turbine sales in 2018 improved slightly over 2017 levels. Stronger turbine sales were offset somewhat by downward pressure on pricing.

Profit for 2018 fell 23% to ?684 million in 2018 compared to 2017 primarily due to lower margins on turbine sales that were driven by increased competition and lower prices as well as ramp-up costs associated with new products. These effects were partially offset by improved profits in the service segment.

Cash at the end of 2018 was ?2.9 billion a decrease of ?735 million from the prior year. Cash from operations contributed ?1 billion to the coffers while investing activities used ?603 million mainly for capital expenditures. Financing activities used ?639 million primarily for the purchase of treasury shares and dividend payments.

Strategy

The combined pressures of climate change rising global population and increasing energy consumption add up to opportunity for Vestas Wind Systems. The company is the global leader for its number of onshore turbines and onshore service and is the number two player in offshore turbines through its 50% stake in MHI Vestas Offshore Wind.

Vestas plans to maintain its leading positions by growing faster than the overall market while keeping margins up and offering customers more efficient products and services that keep energy production costs down. The company hopes to capitalize as mature energy markets decarbonize and electricity demand in emerging markets rises sharply.

Vestas wants to increase its onshore systems' market share and global presence in the fastest-growing emerging markets. The company is also focused on more integrated onshore offerings including engineering procurement and construction contracts to capture more revenue in the renewable energy value chain.

In its onshore service business Vestas plans to better leverage its installed base of onshore turbines through artificial intelligence and automation to deliver insights that help customers improve predictability and efficiency and better integrate with energy grids.

Offshore the company is targeting countries including Taiwan Japan and the US for growing its number of installed turbines while maintaining its strong position in the North Sea region. Key to this strategy is MHI Vestas' V164 offshore turbine (including the V164 -10MW - the industry's largest turbine) that the company believes will help it win more business in established and emerging markets.

EXECUTIVES

EVP and Chief Sales Officer, Juan Araluce, age 58
EVP and CTO, Anders Vedel, age 63
EVP and CFO, Marika Fredriksson, age 57
EVP and COO, Jean-Marc Lech ne, age 62
President and CEO, Anders Runevad, age 60
Group SVP and President Vetas Central Europe, Nils de Baar
General Manager Brazil, Rogerlo Zampronha
Chairman, Bert Nordberg
Deputy Chairman, Lars Josefsson
Auditors: PricewaterhouseCoopers Statsautoriseret Revisionspartnerselskab

LOCATIONS

HQ: Vestas Wind Systems A/S
 Hedeager 42, Aarhus N. 8200
Phone: (45) 97 30 00 00 **Fax:** (45) 97 30 00 01
Web: www.vestas.com

2018 sales

	% of total
Americas	44
Europe Middle East and Africa	42
Asia/Pacific	14
Total	**100**

PRODUCTS/OPERATIONS

2018 sales

	% of total
Power Solutions	84
Service	16
Total	**100**

2018 sales

	% of total
Supply-and-install	43
Supply only	33
Service	16
Turnkey	8
Total	**100**

COMPETITORS

Acciona	Nordex
American Superconductor	Norwin
	Senvion
Clipper Windpower	Sinovel
Enercon	Statoil
GE Energy	YTO Group
Gamesa	
Mitsubishi Power Systems	

HISTORICAL FINANCIALS

Company Type: Public

Income Statement

FYE: December 31

	REVENUE ($ mil.)	NET INCOME ($ mil.)	NET PROFIT MARGIN	EMPLOYEES
12/19	13,638	790	5.8%	25,541
12/18	11,605	783	6.7%	24,648
12/17	11,931	1,071	9.0%	23,303
12/16	10,809	1,018	9.4%	21,824
12/15	9,174	746	8.1%	20,507
Annual Growth	10.4%	1.5%	—	5.6%

2019 Year-End Financials

Debt ratio: 4.8%	No. of shares (mil.): 195
Return on equity: 22.0%	Dividends
Cash ($ mil.): 3,242	Yield: 0.6%
Current ratio: 1.12	Payout: 5.8%
Long-term debt ($ mil.): 519	Market value ($ mil.): 6,577

	STOCK PRICE ($) FY Close	P/E High/Low		PER SHARE ($) Earnings	Dividends	Book Value
12/19	33.67	10	7	3.99	0.23	18.93
12/18	25.18	8	6	3.88	0.32	17.95
12/17	23.08	8	5	5.03	0.32	18.32
12/16	21.72	6	4	4.64	0.20	15.76
12/15	23.47	8	3	3.34	0.13	14.42
Annual Growth	9.4%	—	—	4.5%	16.5%	7.0%

Vinci SA

The world's largest construction company by revenue France's Vinci operates two semi-connected businesses: Contracting which builds roads buildings and infrastructure; and Concessions which operates and maintains toll roads railways airports and more. Vinci seeks synergistic projects that allow its Construction arm to hand over completed projects for operation by its Concessions arm. Vinci is active in more than100 countries but does more than half its total business in France. Its primary businesses are Vinci Construction Eurovia (roads) Vinci Energies Vinci Autoroutes and Vinci Airports. It also has a property development business Vinci Immobilier. Vinci was founded in 1899 and is run by CEO and Chairman Xavier Huillard. About 55% of its revenue comes from France.

Operations

Vinci divides its business into two segments: Contracting and Concessions.

The Contracting business generates some 80% of Vinci's total sales and consists of three multibillion euro businesses: Vinci Construction Vinci Energies and Eurovia.

Vinci Construction is the leading French building and civil engineering group. Its three units build major projects such as large bridges and tunnels and provide geotechnical engineering nuclear digital services for construction and green energy. It also has a local network of small-scale constructors in France. Vinci Construction generates more than 30% of Vinci's total revenue.

Vinci Energies is a leading electrical engineering and construction company consisting of 1800 companies in more than 55 countries. It is active in infrastructure industry the service sector and ICT. Vinci Energies has a presence in North America via PrimeLine Utility Services. The unit generates around 30% of Vinci's total revenue.

Vinci's road-building unit Eurovia builds and refurbishes roads motorways railways urban transport lines and hard surfaces for airports and industrial and commercial facilities. It operates in more than 10 countries. Eurovia also manages 60000km of roads and railways. It generates more than 20% of Vinci's revenue.

The Concessions segment consists of the management and operations of roads airports and stadia primarily in France. It generates more than 15% of total revenue.

Vinci Immobilier the group's real estate unit accounts for about 5% of sales.

Geographic Reach

Across its many subsidiaries Vinci does business in almost all corners of the globe. Its home market of France generates some 55% of total sales. Other important markets for the firm include Germany and the UK. Beyond Western Europe the group is active in Central and Eastern Europe the Asia/Pacific region Africa the Americas and the Middle East.

Headquartered in France Vinci Construction operates in more than 100 countries in five continents. Vinci Energies ranks among the top players in Germany Switzerland Belgium Netherlands Portugal Romania Scandinavia and Morocco. Vinci Airports is active in seven countries: Portugal France Cambodia the Dominican Republic Chile Costa Rica Serbia Japan and Brazil.

Sales and Marketing

The Group has strong local roots in the countries where it operates because of its direct activities as well as its purchases. The company market its business by using local suppliers and subcontractors across its regions.

Financial Performance

Note: Growth rates may differ after conversion to US Dollars.

Vinci's revenue has been growing strongly over the last few years.

In 2019 the company's sales grew 10% to ?48.8 billion. Organic growth was 5% while changes in scope boosted revenue by 5% and currency movements by 1% since several currencies particularly the US dollar rose against the euro during the year. Concessions revenue totaled ?8.5 billion and Contracting revenue totaled ?38.9 billion up by 9% from 2018.

Net income grew % to ?3.3 billion as profits grew in line with revenue growth.

Cash provided by operating activities was ?7.1 billion in 2019 while investing activities used ?6 billion. Financing activities provided another ?656 million. The company ended fiscal 2019 with ?7.3 billion in cash and cash equivalents.

Strategy

VINCI is committed on developing solutions by 2030 that will contribute to improving the living environment and mobility while managing and reducing the direct impact of its businesses. This goal covers three areas: climate change the circular economy and the natural environment. VINCI is committed on taking concrete action to reduce its greenhouse gas emissions (Scopes 1 and 2) in line with the 2Â°C scenario established in the Paris Climate Agreement. As a consequence the Group aims to reduce its direct emissions by 40% by 2030 (against its historic scope as at 2018).

As part of its long-term strategy VINCI Airports is also studying the possibility of increasing Gatwick's capacity by converting part of the aircraft taxiways into a second runway. Following the 2018 acquisition of Airports Worldwide (AWW) VINCI Airports became freehold owner and operator of Belfast International Airport in Northern Ireland. Traffic at this airport was stable over the year at 6.3 million passengers. In 2019 VINCI Airports extended its Lisbon's airport capacity. It provides for upgrading the existing Humberto Del-

gado Airport and building a new civil airport on the Montijo Air base opposite the city at the eastern end of the Tagus estuary. VINCI Airports will invest ?1.15 billion over the next 10 years in this two-pronged project. Chosen as a centre of innovation excellence for the VINCI Airports network along with Gatwick and Lyon - Saint Exupéry the Lisbon airport will be equipped over the next few years with cuttingedge technologies in the field of passenger flow management. The innovations that emerge will later be rolled out to other airports in the network.

The company is continuously pursuing its strategy of using innovation to drive performance by developing new digital tools for processing track geometry data (SEA Cloud) real-time monitoring of incidents and management of technician and machinery movements (TIME application). In its environmental management of the line LISEA continues to implement compensatory mitigation measures in partnership with government services environmental non-profits scientific experts and farming sector stakeholders.

Mergers and Acquisitions

Vinci makes numerous acquisitions each year.

In 2019 following on from the agreement signed in 2018 VINCI Airports finalized its bid to take control of London Gatwick Airport by acquiring a 50% shareholding. Acquisition of this freehold property asset dovetails with the Group's strategy of long-term investment in concessions. VINCI Airports is now the owner and operator of the UK's second-largest airport in a London aviation market that is itself the largest in the world.

In 2019 VINCI Energies acquires Koning & Hartman a company specialised in communication networks in the Netherlands. This acquisition strengthens the company's portfolio in the ICT (Information and Communication Technologies) and industry sectors.

HISTORY

VINCI's origins lie with French conglomerate Vivendi (now Vivendi Universal) which was founded in 1853 as Compagnie G n rale des Eaux. Its mission was to irrigate French farmland and supply water to towns. The company won contracts to serve Lyons (1853) Nantes (1854) Paris (1860) and Venice (1880). G n rale des Eaux moved into construction in 1972 building an office tower (and later hotels and houses) in Paris. The company also entered communications in the 1980s.

In 1988 G n rale des Eaux acquired control of construction and civil engineering giant Soci t G n rale d'Entreprises. SGE subsidiaries included Campenon Bernard SGE (part of G n rale des Eaux since 1981) Sogea Freyssinet Cochery Bourdin Chauss Saunier Duval Tunzini Lefort Francheteau and Wanner. SGE traces its construction roots to 1910. It became a subsidiary of G n rale d'Electricit in 1966. Glassmaker Saint-Gobain acquired control of SGE in 1984. Under G n rale des Eaux SGE enhanced its European profile through acquisitions including British builder Norwest Holst (1989) German road builder VBU (1991) and German pipe and duct maker MLTU (1992).

G n rale des Eaux acquired publisher Havas in 1998 and took the name Vivendi — representing vivacity and mobility. Its purchase of USFilter in 1999 made Vivendi the world's largest water company. Vivendi's SGE unit (renamed VINCI) agreed to acquire the construction arm of rival conglomerate Suez's GTM unit in 2000.

Groupe GTM traces its roots to Soci t Lyonnaise des Eaux et de L'Eclairage a leading French water utility. Formed in 1880 Lyonnaise des Eaux built up its French and international operations to

include water distribution as well as gas and electricity production and distribution. A century later the company had diversified into such businesses as heating (Cofreth) waste management (Sita) and communications acquiring a stake in Lyonnaise Communications (now Lyonnaise C ,ble) in 1986.

In 1990 Lyonnaise des Eaux acquired construction firm Dumez whose subsidiary GTM-Entrepose was France's largest car park manager. Four years later Dumez-GTM was formed to consolidate the construction and civil engineering businesses of Dumez and GTM-Entrepose. In 1997 Lyonnaise des Eaux and Compagnie de Suez merged to create a leading provider of private infrastructure services Suez Lyonnaise des Eaux (which shortened its name to SUEZ in 2001). Compagnie Universal du Canal Maritime de Suez the builder of the Suez Canal was founded in 1858 and became Financi re de Suez in 1958. In 1967 Financi re de Suez acquired control of Lyonnaise des Eaux.

SGE changed its name to VINCI in 2000. That year as part of their strategy to rationalize operations and focus on core businesses Vivendi and SUEZ agreed to a friendly takeover of GTM by VINCI. SUEZ emerged as the combined company's largest shareholder but by the following year both SUEZ and Vivendi Universal had exited most of VINCI's capital leaving no core stockholder.

To better control its car park management operations the company in 2001 created VINCI Park to operate as an umbrella of its VINCI Concessions unit. It expanded its concessions holdings even more in 2002 by hooking up with construction group Eiffage to grab a 17% stake in Europe's second-largest toll road operator ASF which was floated that year by the French government.

In 2003 the group won the contract to manage the restoration of the historic Hall of Mirrors. It also won the concession contract to operate along with joint venture partner Keolis the International Airport of Grenoble.

VINCI completed its acquisition of ASF in 2005. The deal was part of a government program to privatize motorway companies.

The company has had volatile internal struggles. There was unrest in the board room during 2006 as chairman Antoine Zacharias reportedly wanted to oust CEO Xavier Vuillard in favor of Nexity CEO Alain Dinin. Zacharias was the one who ended up resigning and at the end of 2006 Dinin resigned from VINCI's board.

In 2007 VINCI's top French construction businesses Sogea Construction and GTM Construction merged to create VINCI Construction France its domestic construction giant.

The company strengthened its position in the UK in 2008 when it bought British construction and facilities management firm Taylor Woodrow from Taylor Wimpey. The deal consolidated VINCI's position in UK facilities management and public-private partnership projects such as rail airports and energy infrastructure. In 2009 VINCI Construction acquired the troubled UK builder Haymills Group as that company teetered on the brink of collapse.

In 2008 Eurovia branched out from the road to the rails when it acquired rail infrastructure firm Vossloh Infrastructure Services (now ETF-Eurovia Travaux Ferroviaires) from Vossloh. The division specializes in rail track maintenance and installation.

EXECUTIVES

COO Energy Business Line, Yves Meignié, age 64
VP Corporate Communications Human Resources and Synergies, Pierre Coppey, age 57
Executive Vice-President and Chief Financial Officer, Christian Labeyrie, age 64

Chairman and Chief Executive Officer, Xavier Huillard, age 66
Chairman VINCI Construction, Jean Rossi, age 71
Executive Vice-President Contracting, Richard Francioli, age 61
Chairman and Chief Executive Officer Eurovia, Jacques Tavernier, age 70
CEO VINCI Concessions, Louis-Roch Burgard, age 52
Auditors: Deloitte & Associés

LOCATIONS

HQ: Vinci SA
1, cours Ferdinand-de-Lesseps, Rueil-Malmaison, Cedex 92851
Phone: (33) 1 47 16 35 00   **Fax:** (33) 1 47 16 33 60
Web: www.vinci.com

2018 Sales

	% of total
France	57
Germany	7
United Kingdom	5
Central and Eastern Europe	4
Benelux	3
Other European countries	7
North Americas	4
Central and South America	3
Africa	3
Russia Asia Pacific and Middle East	3
Oceania	3
Total	**100**

PRODUCTS/OPERATIONS

2018 Sales

	% of total
Contracting	
VINCI Construction	32
VINCI Energies	28
Eurovia	20
Concessions	
VINCI Autoroutes	12
VINCI Airports	4
Other Concessions	1
VINCI Immobilier	3
Total	**100**

Selected Subsidiaries

VINCI Construction
  CFE (12.11%; Benelux)
  VINCI Construction France
  VINCI PLC (UK)
  VINCI Construction Filiales Internationales (Germany Central Europe overseas France Africa)
  VINCI Construction Grands Projets
  Freyssinet (specialized civil engineering)
VINCI Concessions
VINCI Park
Eurovia
VINCI Energies
  Actemium (industry solutions)
  Axians (voice-data-image communication)
  Cité;os (urban lighting)
  Graniou (telecommunications infrastructure)
  Omexom (high-voltage power transmission)
  Opteor (maintenance)

COMPETITORS

Atlantia	Groupe SNEF
Bechtel	HOCHTIEF
Bilfinger	Louis Berger
Bouygues	Parsons Corporation
CRH	SPIE
Colas	Schneider Electric
EIFFAGE	Skanska
Engie	WS Atkins
FCC Barcelona	Walsh Group

HISTORICAL FINANCIALS

Company Type: Public

Income Statement

FYE: December 31

	REVENUE ($ mil.)	NET INCOME ($ mil.)	NET PROFIT MARGIN	EMPLOYEES
12/19	55,197	3,660	6.6%	222,397
12/18	50,894	3,416	6.7%	211,233
12/17	49,416	3,292	6.7%	194,428
12/16	40,912	2,644	6.5%	183,487
12/15	42,925	2,228	5.2%	185,452
Annual Growth	**6.5%**	**13.2%**	**—**	**4.6%**

2019 Year-End Financials

Debt ratio: 37.7%
Return on equity: 16.4%
Cash ($ mil.): 9,270
Current ratio: 0.90
Long-term debt ($ mil.): 29,612

No. of shares (mil.): 554
Dividends
  Yield: 2.7%
  Payout: 11.5%
Market value ($ mil.): 15,328

	STOCK PRICE ($) FY Close	P/E High/Low		PER SHARE ($) Earnings	Dividends	Book Value
12/19	27.63	5	3	6.53	0.75	41.37
12/18	20.51	5	4	6.09	0.75	39.60
12/17	25.50	5	4	5.89	0.65	38.48
12/16	16.97	4	3	4.73	0.50	31.35
12/15	16.05	5	3	4.02	0.49	29.71
Annual Growth	**14.6%**	**—**		**12.9%**	**11.4%**	**8.6%**

Vipshop Holdings Ltd

Auditors: Deloitte Touche Tohmatsu

LOCATIONS

HQ: Vipshop Holdings Ltd
128 Dingxin Road, Guangzhou 510220
Phone: (86) 20 2233 0000   **Fax:** (86) 20 2233 0111
Web: www.vip.com

HISTORICAL FINANCIALS

Company Type: Public

Income Statement

FYE: December 31

	REVENUE ($ mil.)	NET INCOME ($ mil.)	NET PROFIT MARGIN	EMPLOYEES
12/19	13,364	577	4.3%	20,442
12/18	12,288	309	2.5%	57,638
12/17	11,204	299	2.7%	58,702
12/16	8,149	293	3.6%	45,302
12/15	6,190	244	4.0%	29,720
Annual Growth	**21.2%**	**23.9%**	**—**	**(8.9%)**

2019 Year-End Financials

Debt ratio: 0.3%
Return on equity: 20.5%
Cash ($ mil.): 944
Current ratio: 0.96
Long-term debt ($ mil.): 9

No. of shares (mil.): 134
Dividends
  Yield: —
  Payout: —
Market value ($ mil.): 1,900

	STOCK PRICE ($) FY Close	P/E High/Low		PER SHARE ($) Earnings	Dividends	Book Value
12/19	14.17	0	0	4.25	0.00	23.39
12/18	5.46	1	0	2.27	0.00	18.88
12/17	11.72	1	0	2.45	0.00	16.74
12/16	11.01	1	1	2.43	0.00	7.08
12/15	15.27	2	1	2.04	0.00	4.74
Annual Growth	**(1.9%)**	**—**		**20.2%**	**—**	**49.1%**

Vivendi

Vivendi is one of the world's biggest media companies offering music movies and TV games and more. Its Universal Music Group (UMG) is the world's biggest recorded music company featuring artists such as Ariana Grande Post Malone Taylor Swift and the Rolling Stones. Canal+ Group is a pay-TV provider in France Africa Europe and Asia. It also is a major producer and distributor of motion pictures. The Vivendi property Havas is a global advertising and public relations agency. The Gameloft unit develops and produces video games with an emphasis on mobile games such as Asphalt Minion Rush and Dragon Mania. France Vivendi's home country accounts for about 30% of revenue.

Operations

UMG (generates around 45% of total revenue) communicates regularly with a wide range of outside stakeholders including but not limited to: artists and their managers; songwriters; retailers and digital music services; performers rights organizations (such as Broadcast Music Inc. ASCAP and SESAC); local provincial and national officials in countries in which the company operates (as well as others such as European authorities); trade associations; and ad hoc working groups or coalitions (such as the Digital Creators Coalition and the US Alliance for Music) among many others.

Canal+ Group (around 35% of revenue) is a collective of private and public institutional organizations from the audiovisual industry.

The Havas Group's (around 15%) agencies belong to numerous professional associations and bodies providing a forum for consultations with industry stakeholders including peers customers suppliers regulators and consumers

Editis (around 5% of revenue) is France's second-largest publishing group and a major player in the European book market. A leading operator among publishers authors bookstores and all sale outlets it offers stellar support and service on both paper and digital formats.

Gameloft (less than 5%) is one of the french video game publisher flagships Gameloft enjoys world-renowned expertise with around 190 smartphone games developed in its over 15 studios.

Geographic Reach

Paris-based Vivendi has operations located in France (generates around 30% of total revenue) Americas (more than 31%) Rest of Europe (around 25% of revenue) Asia and Oceania (around 10% of revenue) and Africa (around 5%).

Sales and Marketing

With 8.4 million subscribers in mainland France as of December 31 2019 Canal+ Group boasts the largest portfolio of pay-TV customers. This figure includes 3 million customers from partnerships with telecom operators.

Interforum has been a key link in the publishing chain for more than forty years connecting publishers to sales outlets Broad and qualitative marketing is a means for Interforum to offer its partner publishers access to all sales outlets from bookstores to large cultural retailers hypermarkets supermarkets online sales specialized bookstores and export companies. Interforum has a total of over 15000 customers. Games are delivered through smartphone and tablet app stores such as the Apple App Store Google Play the Windows Store and Amazon Appstore.

Advertising costs amounted to ?416 million in 2019 (compared to ?371 million in 2018).

Financial Performance

UMG enjoyed a record year in 2019 with revenues of ?7.2 billion a 14% increase on a constant basis compared to 2018. This strong growth continues to be primarily driven by streaming an activity that is steadily growing spearheaded by several successful UMG artists.

The company's net income in 2019 increased to ?1.7 million compared to ?1.2 million in the prior year.

Cash held by the company at the end of 2019 decreased to ?2.1 million. Cash provided by operations was ?1.3 million while cash used for investing and financing activities were ?1.6 million and ?1.3 million respectively. Main uses of cash were for investments and transactions with shareowners.

Strategy

In 2019 Vivendi carried out a number of strategic transactions including the acquisition of Editis the announcement of the partial sale of Universal Music Group's (UMG) share capital the acquisition of M7 and the completion of agreements with Netflix and Disney. All these transactions contributed to its strategic roadmap and clear and unwavering pursuit since 2014 to become a world leader in the culture at the crossroads of entertainment media and communications.

The company's decision in 2014 to refocus on content and media has more than paid off with each new investment and each new project embodying this strategy and uniting the group around its core DNA: entertainment. Currently at least 83% of the population considers entertainment to be a vital need. It is ever present and will be even more so for generations to come. Vivendi's results for 2019 clearly indicate that it is fully equipped to create and assist brands in delivering original quality and diverse content

Mergers and Acquisitions

In early 2020 Vivendi announced he acquisition of 10.6% of the Lagard¨re share capital. This acquisition is a long-term financial investment reflecting Vivendi's confidence in the future prospects of the French group which enjoys international leadership positions in its businesses and which like many others is experiencing difficult times at the moment. Terms were not disclosed.

In 2019 Vivendi acquired Editis the second-largest French-language publishing group for ?900 million. The deal adds another market leading media company to Vivendi's portfolio.

HISTORY

Authorized by an imperial decree Compagnie Générale des Eaux was founded in 1853 by investors such as the Rothschild family and Napoleon III's half-brother to irrigate French farmland and supply water to towns. It won contracts to serve Lyons (1853) Nantes (1854) Paris (1860) and Venice (1880).

A supplier of water and other basic services for most of its history the company that became Vivendi didn't move strongly into other areas until the 1980s when it made investments and acquisitions into telecommunications and then media and entertainment in the 1990s.

EXECUTIVES

CEO, Arnaud Roy de Puyfontaine, age 56
SEVP Communications and Chairman Vivendi Village, Simon Gillham, age 64
CFO, Hervé Philippe, age 62
COO, Stéphane Roussel, age 59
SEVP and Group General Counsel, Frédéric R. Crépin, age 50
Chairman Supervisory Board, Vincent Bolloré, age 68

Vice Chairman Supervisory Board, Philippe Bénacin, age 62
Auditors: Deloitte & Associes

LOCATIONS

HQ: Vivendi
42, avenue de Friedland, Paris, Cedex 08 75380
Phone: (33) 1 71 71 10 00   **Fax:** (33) 1 71 71 10 01
Web: www.vivendi.com

PRODUCTS/OPERATIONS

2018 Sales

	% of total
Universal Music Group	43
Canal+ Group	37
Havas	17
Gameloft	2
Vivendi Village	1
New Initiatives	-
Elimination	-

2018 Sales

	% of total
Intellectual Property Licensing	47
Subscription Services	32
Advertising Merchandising and Other	21
Total	**100**

COMPETITORS

BMG Rights Management	Microsoft Game Studios
Bouygues	NCsoft
Chrysalis	Nintendo
Electronic Arts	Orange
ITV	Sony
Konami	Take-Two
Lucasfilm	Warner Music
Entertainment	

HISTORICAL FINANCIALS

Company Type: Public

Income Statement   FYE: December 31

	REVENUE ($ mil.)	NET INCOME ($ mil.)	NET PROFIT MARGIN	EMPLOYEES
12/19	17,854	1,777	10.0%	44,641
12/18	15,962	145	0.9%	41,600
12/17	15,092	1,472	9.8%	33,200
12/16	11,423	1,326	11.6%	22,603
12/15	11,722	2,104	18.0%	16,395
Annual Growth	11.1%	(4.1%)	—	28.5%

2019 Year-End Financials

Debt ratio: 20.8%
Return on equity: 9.6%
Cash ($ mil.): 2,391
Current ratio: 0.78
Long-term debt ($ mil.): 5,787

No. of shares (mil.): 1,170
Dividends
Yield: 1.9%
Payout: 38.9%
Market value ($ mil.): 33,888

	STOCK PRICE ($) FY Close	P/E High/Low	Earnings	Dividends	Book Value
12/19	28.95	23 18	1.44	0.56	14.73
12/18	24.15	284233	0.11	0.55	15.64
12/17	26.82	29 20	1.14	0.48	16.84
12/16	18.95	— —	1.00	0.00	16.25
12/15	21.35	19 14	1.54	2.19	16.92
Annual Growth 7.9% (3.4%)		— —	(1.6%)	(28.8%)	

Vodafone Group Plc

Vodafone is one of the world's top wireless phone carriers with its more than half a billion subscribers (across some 25 countries) behind only China Mobile. A network of partnerships with other mobile networks extends its reach into another 45 countries. As well as telephony it has 27 million fixed broadband customers and more than 20 million TV customers. The company generates the majority of its business in Europe where it is a leader in the wireless markets in the UK and Germany. Vodafone increasingly serves callers in Africa the Middle East and Asia through subsidiaries and joint ventures. It holds a 45% stake in Vodafone Idea Limited the company formed by the merger of Vodafone India and local carrier Idea.

Operations

Vodafone's Consumer segment generates two-thirds of the company's revenue and provides the standard range of mobile services and fixed line services such as broadband TV and voice as well as other value-added services. Vodafone's Enterprise segment (almost 30% of sales) offers telephony services for corporations as well as cloud and hosting and Internet of Things services. Vodafone generates almost 10% of sales from renting capacity to mobile virtual operators.

Geographic Reach

Vodafone's geographic footprint is well-diversified and it holds #1 or #2 market positions in most of the markets in which it directly operates. The UK-based company operates in 22 countries and two geographic regions - Europe and Rest of the world.

Europe is Vodafone's biggest market representing more than 75% of sales. Germany is its most lucrative country followed by Italy then its home territory of the UK Spain and others. It has almost 65 million mobile customers 25 million broadband customers 14 million TV customers and more than 7 million "converged" customers — those high-value customers that subscribe to all three product types.

Vodacom is Vodafone's African business which counts more than 100 million customers in South Africa Tanzania the DRC Mozambique Lesotho and Kenya. It brings in some 15% of sale.

Vodafone is also active in the Asia/Pacific region including India and the Middle East; the region also accounts for almost 10% of sales.

Sales and Marketing

Vodafone uses data analytics to support personalization and increase revenue per customer. Digital is increasingly becoming Vodafone's primary customer acquisition channel as well as its main customer support method. Chat bots and digital agents enhanced with AI will become Vodafone's primary customer interface.

Financial Performance

Note: Growth rates may differ after conversion to US Dollars.

Vodafone's revenue has fallen for consecutive financial years but grew in 2019.

In fiscal 2019 the company's sales rose 3% to Å 45 billion primarily due to the 6% growth in European Service Revenue. In 2019 the company significantly reduced their losses from Å 8 billion on 2018 tp Å 920 million.

Vodafone had Å 13.3 billion of cash and cash equivalents in its coffers. It had an inflow of Å 17.4 billion from operations. Vodafone had outflows of Å 8 billion and Å 9.4 billion from investing and financing activities respectively.

Strategy

Vodafone's strategy is focused on two scaled and differentiated regional platforms?Europe and Africa

Its priorities consists of: Deepening customer engagement; Accelerating digital transformation; Improving asset utilization; and Optimizing the portfolio.

Vodafone completed its sale of its New Zealand business for about $2.2 billion to New Zealand-based infrastructure investor Infratil and Canadian alternative asset management firm Brookfield Asset Management in an effort to reduce its debt.

Mergers and Acquisitions

Vodafone announces in mid-2020 that Vodafone Hutchison Australia Pty Limited (VHA) and TPG Telecom Limited (TPG) have completed their merger to establish a fully integrated telecommunications operator in Australia. The merged entity has been admitted to the Australian Securities Exchange (ASX) and will trade under the name TPG Telecom Limited. The new TPG Telecom will trade using a range of brands including Vodafone and TPG.

Vodafone Telecom Italia Group ("TIM") and INWIT completed the merger of Vodafone Italy's towers into INWIT in early 2020. INWIT is now Italy's largest tower operator and will focus on maximizing tower utilization which also supporting the deployment of TIM and Vodafone Italy's respective 5G networks. Vodafone and TIM intend to retain joint control but over time will consider jointly reducing their respective ownership levels to a minimum of 25.0%. On 31 March Vodafone will receive 360200000 ordinary INWIT shares and cash proceeds of ?2140 million which will be used to reduce net debt.

In mid-2019 Vodafone acquired German and Eastern European assets including Unitymedia from Liberty Global in a $18.4 billion deal. Vodafone Group CEO Nick Read said: "With the acquisition of Liberty's assets in Germany and CEE we have completed our transformation into Europe's leading converged operator. Not only have we reshaped our business becoming the owner of the largest gigabit-capable next generation network infrastructure in the region we are now able to play our part in realizing the digital society for millions of customers."

Company Background

Vodafone was formed in 1983 as a joint venture between Racal Electronics (a UK electronics firm) and Millicom (a US telecom company) and was granted one of two mobile phone licenses in the UK (the other was held by Cellnet). Its service launched in 1985. In 1988 Racal offered 20% of Vodafone to the public; three years later the rest of the firm was spun off to become Vodafone Group. It made a landmark acquisition of Mannesmann in Germany making it one of the country's largest carriers and began its partner networks business model in 2011. Vodafone sold its 45% stake in Verizon Wireless for $130 billion in 2013 one of the biggest ever corporate deals.

EXECUTIVES

CEO, Vittorio A. Colao, age 57, $1,724,052 total compensation
CEO India, Marten Pieters, age 67
CFO, Nicholas J. (Nick) Read, age 54
Group Chief Commercial and Operations Officer, Paolo Bertoluzzo, age 54
CEO UK Business, Jeroen Hoencamp
CEO Ghana, Haris Broumidis
CEO Australia, Iñaki Berroeta
CEO New Zealand, Russell Stanners
CEO Egypt, Hatem Dowidar
CEO Africa Middle East and Asia-Pacific, Vivek Badrinath, age 50
CEO Germany, Jens Schulte-Bockum
Regional CEO Europe, Philipp Humm, age 61
EVP Managed Network and Services, Nick Lambert
CEO Vodafone Fiji, Pradeep Lal
CEO Vodafone Uganda, John Ndego
Vice Chairman Vodafone Turkey Corporate Business, Meltem Sahin
Chairman, Gerard J. Kleisterlee, age 72
Auditors: Ernst & Young

LOCATIONS

HQ: Vodafone Group Plc
Vodafone House, The Connection, Newbury, Berkshire RG14 2FN
Phone: (44) 1635 33251
Web: www.vodafone.com

2018 Sales

	% of total
Europe	
Germany	23
UK	15
Italy	13
Spain	11
Other Europe	11
Africa Middle East and Asia Pacific (AMAP)	
Vodacom	12
Other AMAP	12
Common Functions	3
Total	**100**

PRODUCTS/OPERATIONS

2018 Sales

	% of total
Service revenue	88
Other revenue	12
Total	**100**

Countries of Operation (controlled interests)

Africa/the Middle East/Asia-Pacific
Australia
Democratic Republic of Congo
Egypt
Ghana
India
Lesotho
Mozambique
New Zealand
Qatar
South Africa
Tanzania
Europe
Albania
Czech Republic
Germany
Greece
Hungary
Ireland
Italy
Malta
Portugal
Romania
Spain
The Netherlands
Turkey
UK

COMPETITORS

AT&T Mobility	Orange
BT	Proximus
China Mobile	Swisscom
Deutsche Telekom	Telef nica Europe
KPN	Telekom Austria
M1	Telstra
NTT DoCoMo	Virgin Mobile Telecoms

HISTORICAL FINANCIALS

Company Type: Public

Income Statement

				FYE: March 31
	REVENUE ($ mil.)	NET INCOME ($ mil.)	NET PROFIT MARGIN	EMPLOYEES
03/20	49,269	(1,007)	—	95,219
03/19	49,038	(9,006)	—	98,996
03/18	57,410	3,006	5.2%	106,135
03/17	50,888	(6,727)	—	111,556
03/16	58,977	(5,792)	—	111,684
Annual Growth	**(4.4%)**	**—**	**—**	**(3.9%)**

2020 Year-End Financials

Debt ratio: 48.6%
Return on equity: (-1.4%)
Cash ($ mil.): 14,552
Current ratio: 1.01
Long-term debt ($ mil.): 68,899
No. of shares (mil.): —
Dividends
  Yield: 6.8%
  Payout: —
Market value ($ mil.): —

	STOCK PRICE ($) FY Close	P/E High/Low	PER SHARE ($) Earnings	Dividends	Book Value
03/20	13.77	— —	(0.03)	0.94	2.51
03/19	18.18	— —	(0.33)	1.64	2.57
03/18	27.82	384312	0.11	1.88	3.13
03/17	26.43	— —	(0.24)	1.50	2.90
03/16	32.05	— —	(0.22)	1.68	3.57
Annual Growth	**(19.0%)**	**— —**		**(13.5%)**	**(8.4%)**

voestalpine AG

EXECUTIVES

CEO, Wolfgang Eder, age 69
Deputy Manager Motion Division, Robert Ottel, age 54
Head Metal Engineering Division, Franz Kainersdorfer, age 54
Head Special Steel Division, Franz Rotter, age 64
Head Steel Division, Herbert Eibensteiner, age 58
Head Metal Forming Division, Peter Schwab, age 57
Chairman Supervisory Board, Joachim Lemppenau
Deputy Chairman, Heinrich Schaller
Auditors: Deloitte Audit Wirtschaftsprufungs GmbH

LOCATIONS

HQ: voestalpine AG
Voestalpine Strasse 1, Linz 4020
Phone: (43) 70 50304 15 2090 **Fax:** (43) 70 50304 55 8981
Web: www.voestalpine.com

PRODUCTS/OPERATIONS

2016 Sales

	% of total
Steel	30
Metal Engineering Division	23
Special Steel Division	21
Metal Forming Division	18
Others	8
Total	**100**

COMPETITORS

ArcelorMittal
Eramet
Metal rgica Gerdau
Nippon Steel & Sumitomo Metal Corporation
Severstal

Tata Europe
ThyssenKrupp Steel
United States Steel

HISTORICAL FINANCIALS

Company Type: Public

Income Statement				FYE: March 31
	REVENUE ($ mil.)	NET INCOME ($ mil.)	NET PROFIT MARGIN	EMPLOYEES
03/20	13,931	(243)		49,005
03/19	15,229	458	3.0%	50,102
03/18	15,899	955	6.0%	48,904
03/17	12,067	530	4.4%	47,186
03/16	12,606	666	5.3%	46,423
Annual Growth	2.5%	—	—	1.4%

2020 Year-End Financials

Debt ratio: 33.9%	No. of shares (mil.): 178
Return on equity: (-3.6%)	Dividends
Cash ($ mil.): 870	Yield: —
Current ratio: 1.52	Payout: —
Long-term debt ($ mil.): 4,261	Market value ($ mil.): —

Volkswagen AG

Bolting together nearly 11 million vehicles each year Volkswagen AG (VW) tussles with Toyota for position as the world's most prolific auto manufacturer. The company produces cars motorbikes and commercial vehicles of all sizes under more than 10 independently operating brands including VW Audi SKODA SEAT Porsche Lamborghini and Scania. VW's extensive manufacturing footprint spans over 120 plants in more than 30 countries (two-thirds being European) and it has customers in virtually all the world's markets. VW also offers leasing financing and fleet solutions for its corporate customers. In response to shifts in the nature of car ownership and the growth in demand for electric vehicles VW is investing in its mobility solutions business and introducing electric vehicles across its entire range.

Operations

Volkswagen Group is divided into two business — Automotive and Financial Services.

The Automotive division generates some 85% of sales and comprises VW's passenger and commercial vehicle business as well as its Power Engineering unit. Its more than 10 independently operating brands are VW Audi SKODA SEAT (mass-market vehicles); Bentley Bugatti Lamborghini Porsche (luxury cars); Ducati (motorbikes); Volkswagen Commercial Vehicles Scania and MAN (commercial vehicles). By brand VW generates roughly a third of total group sales followed by Audi (about 20%) and Porsche (around 10%). Audi is its most profitable brand. All told Volkswagen produces some 365 different models.

Power Engineering manufactures large-bore diesel engines turbomachinery special gear units propulsion components and testing systems.

The Financial Services segment (about 15% of sales) provides dealer and customer financing leasing banking and insurance activities fleet management and mobility offerings.

Geographic Reach

Volkswagen is based in Wolfsburg Germany a city that could reasonably be described as Volkswagen-ville and which grew upon the wealth generated by the auto manufacturer and its legions of employees. The city is home to the world's largest car manufacturing plant.

Outside Wolfsburg VW has more than 120 production sites in about 20 European countries and a dozen more in some 10 countries in the Americas the Asia/Pacific region and Africa. Europe accounts for more than 60% of the company's total sales while the Americas and Asia each generate around 20% each. Key markets include Western Europe China the US Brazil Russia Poland and Mexico.

Sales and Marketing

Volkswagen holds a global market share of more than 10%. With cars becoming increasingly sophisticated from a technology standpoint VW has partnerships with major technology companies such as Microsoft Infineon Cree/Wolfspeed and AVL List.

The emissions scandal that broke in 2015 where VW was caught cheating CO2 testing has cost the company around ?30 billion in accumulated fines recalls and other associated costs and has damaged VW's reputation worldwide. Its reputation in the US was particularly badly affected and sales have continued to fall in the country.

Financial Performance

Note: Growth rates may differ after conversion to US Dollars.

Sales revenue rose by 7% to ?252.6 billion primarily to 4.9 million vehicles unit sales in the Europe/Other market region were up 3% compared with the previous year and in North America the company increased unit sales by 3% to 1.0 million vehicles.

The company's net income increased by ?338 million to ?5.0 billion in 2019 primarily due to higher sales for the year.

Cash held by the company at the end of 2019 decreased ?3.8 billion to ?24.3 billion compared to ?28.1 billion in the prior year. Cash provided by operations was ?18 billion while cash used for investing and financing activities were ?21.1 billion and ?865 million respectively.

Strategy

The company's enhanced TOGETHER 2025+ Group strategy comprises consistent strategic decisions and specific modules aimed at safeguarding the long-term future of the Group and generating profitable growth. These modules are namely Best Governance Best Performance Best Brand Equity Software-enabled Car Company and Excellent Leadership.

The aim of the best performance module is to achieve a sustainable increase in our enterprise value by increasing efficiency productivity and profitability.

In the best brand equity module the focus is in realigning the brand portfolio making a significant increase in the value of brands by 2025.

In the Software-enabled Car Company module the company are working to make software development one of the Volkswagen Group's core competencies. To achieve this the company pooling existing expertise substantially strengthening their resources and establishing a dedicated organizational unit. By 2025 all new vehicle across the Group will be based on their own cross-brand software platform. This approach will enable us to leverage synergies between the individual brands and vehicle projects.

The excellent leadership module will accelerate the transformation to a more open more partnership-based and more value-based leadership.

HISTORY

Since the early 1920s auto engineer Ferdinand Porsche (whose son later founded the Porsche car company) had wanted to make a small car for the masses. He found no backers until he met Adolf Hitler in 1934. Hitler formed the Gesellschaft zur Vorbereitung des deutschen Volkswagen (Company for the Development of the German People's Car) in 1937 and built a factory in Wolfsburg Germany. No cars were delivered during WWII as the company produced military vehicles using the slave labor of Jews and Russian prisoners of war.

Following WWII British occupation forces oversaw the rebuilding of the bomb-damaged plant and initial production of the odd-looking "people's car" (1945). The British appointed Heinz Nordhoff to manage Volkswagen (1948) and then turned the company over to the German government (1949).

In the 1950s VW launched the Microbus and built foreign plants. Although US sales began slowly by the end of the decade acceptance of the little car had increased. Advertising that coined the name "Beetle" helped carve VW's niche in the US.

VW sold stock to the German public in 1960. In 1966 it purchased Auto Union (AUDI) from Daimler-Benz. The Beetle became a counterculture symbol in the 1960s and US sales took off. By the time of Nordhoff's death in 1968 the Beetle had become the best-selling car in history.

EXECUTIVES

Member Management Board China, Jochem Heizmann, age 69
Member Management Board and Chairman Board of Management Audi AG, Rupert Stadler, age 57
Member Management Board Finance and Contrilling, Frank Witter, age 61
Member Board of Management Commercial Vehicles, Andreas Renschler, age 62
Chairman, Hans D. P ¶tsch, age 69
Member Management Board Procurement, Francisco J. Garc a Sanz, age 64
Chairman Voksagen Passenger Cars, Herbert Diess, age 62
CEO, Matthias M ller, age 67
CEO Moia, Ole Harms
Auditors: PricewaterhouseCoopers GmbH Wirtschaftspruefungsgesellschaft

LOCATIONS

HQ: Volkswagen AG
Letterbox 1848-2, Wolfsburg D-38436
Phone: (49) 5361 9 0 **Fax:** (49) 5361 928282
Web: www.volkswagen.com

2018 sales

	% of total
Europe/Other Markets	61
Asia/Pacific	18
North America	16
South America	4
Unallocated	1
Total	**100**

PRODUCTS/OPERATIONS

2018 sales

	% of total
Automotive	
Passenger Cars	68
Commercial Vehicles	16
Power Engineering	1
Financial Services	15
Total	**100**

2018 sales

	% of total
Vehicles	62
Leasing business	11
Genuine parts	7
Used vehicles and third-party products	5
Engines powertrains and parts deliveries	5
Other sales revenue	4
Interest and similar income	3
Power Engineering	2
Hedges sales revenue	1
Motorcycles	—
Total	**100**

Selected Brands

Audi
Bentley
Bugatti
Ducati
Lamborghini
MAN Commercial Vehicles
MAN Power Engineering
Porsche
Scania
SEAT
ŠKODA
Volkswagen
Volkswagen Commercial Vehicles

COMPETITORS

BMW	Mazda
Daimler	Nissan
FCA US	Peugeot
Fiat Chrysler	Renault
Ford Motor	Subaru
General Motors	Suzuki Motor
Honda	Tesla Motors
Hyundai Motor	Toyota
Isuzu	

HISTORICAL FINANCIALS

Company Type: Public

Income Statement

FYE: December 31

	REVENUE ($ mil.)	NET INCOME ($ mil.)	NET PROFIT MARGIN	EMPLOYEES
12/19	283,646	14,984	5.3%	671,200
12/18	270,093	13,544	5.0%	664,496
12/17	276,531	13,610	4.9%	642,292
12/16	229,408	5,431	2.4%	626,715
12/15	232,319	(1,723)	—	610,076
Annual Growth	**5.1%**	**—**	**—**	**2.4%**

2019 Year-End Financials

Debt ratio: 46.3%
Return on equity: 11.1%
Cash ($ mil.): 29,105
Current ratio: 1.12
Long-term debt ($ mil.): 127,495

No. of shares (mil.): 295
Dividends
Yield: 1.7%
Payout: 1.1%
Market value ($ mil.): 5,692

	STOCK PRICE ($) FY Close	P/E High/Low		PER SHARE ($) Earnings	Dividends	Book Value
12/19	19.29	1	1	29.87	0.34	463.35
12/18	15.60	1	1	26.99	5.50	454.51
Annual Growth	**23.7%**	**—**	**—**	**2.6%**	**(50.0%)**	**0.5%**

Volvo AB

AB Volvo is one of the world's largest makers of trucks buses construction equipment and marine and industrial engines with about 55 production facilities in almost 20 countries. It makes trucks under the ten brands including Volvo UD Trucks Prevost Renault Trucks and Mack. The company also provides financing services though Volvo Financial Services and it generates majority of sales from Europe. AB Volvo is not to be confused with Volvo Cars an automobile division of Chinese auto group Geeley.

Operations

The Volvo Group organizes itself into six main business segments: Trucks Construction Equipment Buses Volvo Penta Financial Services and Group functions & other.

The Trucks segment is the largest with nearly 65% of net sales and produces light- and heavy-duty trucks and provides maintenance and repair services performed at its dealerships through customer service contracts.

Construction Equipment (more than 20% of sales) makes products for the construction extraction waste processing forestry and materials handling sectors and markets its vehicles under the Volvo SDLG and Terex Truck brands.

Other smaller units include Volvo Buses (more than 5% of sales) one of the world's largest manufacturers of buses coaches and bus chassis. Volvo Penta (less than 5%) which makes engines and power systems for marine and industrial applications. The Financial Services segment provides financing services in almost 50 countries and represents almost 5% of net sales and Group functions & other (less than 5%) that includes Arquus brand.

Overall the company generates more than 75% of sales from vehicles and almost 25% from services.

Geographic Reach

Volvo headquartered in Gothenburg Sweden has production facilities in nearly 20 countries and sells its products and services in more than 190 markets worldwide. Europe accounts for almost 40% of sales. Other major markets include North America (about 30 %) Asia (nearly 20%) South America (more than 5%) and Africa and Oceania (over 5%).

The company's wide range of truck types supply the needs of its diverse geographies. For instance in France distribution trucks dominate AB Volvo's sales profile while in Indonesia sales are led by mining-related vehicles.

Sales and Marketing

The Volvo Group's products are sold and distributed to business customers through wholly-owned and independent dealerships.

The company partners in alliances and joint ventures with SDLG Eicher and Dongfeng.

Financial Performance

Note: Growth rates may differ after conversion to US Dollars.

During 2019 net sales increased by 11% to SEK 432 billion. Adjusted for currency movements and acquired and divested operations the increase was 5%. As a result of higher sales net income rose 22% to SEK25.4 billion (roughly $2.6 billion) AB Volvo's best ever result.

AB Volvo's cash position strengthened during 2019 ending the year SEK 14.5 billion higher at SEK 61.5 billion. The company generated cash of SEK 39.0 billion from its operations while its investing activities used SEK 14.6 billion and its financing activities used SEK 11.0 billion

Strategy

The company's seven strategic priorities consist of areas with large benefits for both our customers and us in the Volvo Group. The strategy guides the company's decision making and result in actions but should not be seen as detailed action plans fixed to a specific time frame. The seven strategic priorities includes: reinforce Volvo; capture growth in Asia; create the desirable heavy duty product and service; secure robust profitability; have brand specific sales operation; leverage group assets; and revitalize the Volvo group culture.

During 2019 the work within each area continued. Volvo's customer offering was strengthened with new products and their regional advantages were further utilized through strong collaboration and by the offer of tailor-made solutions to the company's customers. The work to drive continuous improvement in product development production sales and administration together with an expanded brand responsibility sets the right focus. By leveraging Group assets for trucks and other business areas Volvo generate additional profits through synergies. By utilizing the Group's centers of excellence in new technology they strive to reach technology leadership.

Company Background

Swedish ball bearing maker SKF formed Volvo (Latin for "I roll") as a subsidiary in 1915. Volvo began building cars in 1926 trucks in 1928 and bus chassis in 1932 in Gothenburg. Sweden's winters and icy roads made the company keenly attentive to engineering and safety. The Volvo Group sold its Volvo Cars division to Ford Motor Company in 1999; Volvo Cars was subsequently acquired by Chinese Zhejiang Geely Holding Group Co. Ltd in 2010.

EXECUTIVES

CFO, Jan Gurander
EVP Corporate Strategy, Karin Falk
President Volvo 3P, Torbj ¶rn Holmstr ¶m
EVP Group Trucks Sales and Marketing EMEA, Peter Karlsten
EVP Group Trucks Sales and Marketing Americas, Dennis R. (Denny) Slagle
Head Volvo Group Media Relations, M rten Wikforss
EVP Business Areas, H kan Karlsson
President and CEO, Olof Persson
EVP Group Trucks Operations, Mikael Bratt
EVP Corporate Human Resources, Kerstin Renard
EVP Corporate Process IT and CIO, Magnus Carlander
EVP Group Truck Sales and Marketing and JVs APAC, Joachim Rosenberg
EVP Volvo Construction Equipment, Martin Weissburg
EVP Corporate Legal and Compliance and General Counsel, Sofia Fr ¤ndberg
EVP Corporate Sustainability and Public Affairs, Niklas Gustavsson
EVP Volvo Financial Services, Scott Rafkin
Chairman, Carl-Henric Svanberg
Auditors: Deloitte AB

LOCATIONS

HQ: Volvo AB
Volvo Bergegaards v., Goeteborg SE-405 08
Phone: (46) 31 66 00 00   **Fax:** (46) 31 53 72 96
Web: www.volvogroup.com

2018 Sales

	% of total
Europe	41
North America	27
Asia	20
South America	5
Africa & Oceania	7
Total	**100**

PRODUCTS/OPERATIONS

2018 Sales

	% of total
Trucks	63
Construction Equipment	21
Buses	7
Volvo Penta	4
Group Functions & Other	2
Financial Services	3
Total	**100**

Selected Products & Brands

Volvo
Volvo Trucks
Volvo Buses
Volvo Construction Equipment
Volvo Penta
Volvo Penta Marine Leisure
Volvo Penta Marine Commercial
Volvo Penta Industrial
Terex Trucks
Renault Trucks
Prevost
Nova Bus Global
Mack Trucks
Arquus
Arrow Truck

COMPETITORS

Cummins Westport	Navistar
Daimler	Navistar International
Daimler Trucks North	Nissan
America	Oshkosh Truck
Deere	PACCAR
Fiat Chrysler	Penske
General Motors	Scania
Hino Motors	Subaru
Honda	Suzuki Motor
Isuzu	Toyota
MAN	Volkswagen
Mitsubishi Motors	

HISTORICAL FINANCIALS

Company Type: Public

Income Statement				FYE: December 31
	REVENUE ($ mil.)	NET INCOME ($ mil.)	NET PROFIT MARGIN	EMPLOYEES
12/19	46,437	3,855	8.3%	103,985
12/18	43,662	2,781	6.4%	105,175
12/17	40,800	2,557	6.3%	99,488
12/16	33,307	1,450	4.4%	94,914
12/15	37,069	1,786	4.8%	99,501
Annual Growth	5.8%	21.2%	—	1.1%

2019 Year-End Financials

Debt ratio: 3.2%	No. of shares (mil.): 2,033
Return on equity: 27.3%	Dividends
Cash ($ mil.): 6,606	Yield: 6.4%
Current ratio: 1.45	Payout: 56.6%
Long-term debt ($ mil.): 10,923	Market value ($ mil.): 33,776

	STOCK PRICE ($) FY Close	P/E High/Low		PER SHARE ($) Earnings	Dividends	Book Value
12/19	16.61	1	1	1.90	1.08	7.33
12/18	13.03	2	1	1.37	0.50	6.78
12/17	18.49	2	1	1.26	0.39	6.42
12/16	11.60	2	1	0.71	0.33	5.22
Annual Growth	12.7%		—	27.7%	34.2%	8.9%

Wal-Mart de Mexico S.A.B. de C.V.

Wal-Mart de México (operating as Wal-Mart de México y Centroamérica) is the numero uno retailer in Mexico Costa Rica El Salvador Guatemala Honduras and Nicaragua with about 3000 stores. These include Bodega food and general merchandise stores and Superama supermarkets as well about 10 Medimart Farmacia de Walmart. It also runs Wal-Mart Supercenters SAM'S CLUB and ClubCo warehouse stores. Its stores are located in more than 500 cities throughout the region. Wal-Mart Stores formed a joint venture with Mexico's Cifra in 1991 and in 2000 acquired it and renamed it Wal-Mart de México. Wal-Mex then added Wal-Mart's operations in Central America and became Wal-Mart de México y Centroamérica in 2010.

Operations

In Mexico alone the company has 1719 Bodega Aurrera discount stores 256 Walmart hypermarkets 160 Sam's Club membership self-service wholesale stores 95 Superama supermarkets 10 Medimart pharmacies and 114 Suburbia apparel and accessories stores in Mexico. In addition it imports and sells goods; develops properties; and manages real estate companies.

In Costa Rica Guatemala Honduras Nicaragua and El Salvador Wal-Mart de México y Centroamérica operates through 484 discount stores 99 supermarkets 102 discount warehouse stores 24 Walmart hypermarkets and 1 ClubCo membership self-service wholesale store.

Geographic Reach

Wal-Mart de México y Centroamérica owns and operates self-service retail stores in Mexico and Central America.

It operates in Costa Rica (230 stores) El Salvador (88) Guatemala (217) Honduras (82) Mexico (2363) and Nicaragua (92).

Strategy

The company is focusing on growth it of its core assets by selling of some of its businesses. It has refocused on its stores after selling restaurants and a bank.

In 2016 it planned to invest 14.7 billion pesos ($822.6 million). Some 39% of the total would be earmarked to opening new stores 31% to remodeling and maintaining existing ones 24% to technology and e-commerce and the remaining 6% to logistical improvements.

In 2016 Wal-Mart de México y Centroamérica agreed to sell its Suburbia clothing chain to El Puerto de Liverpool SAB Mexico's biggest department store chain operator in a deal valued at 19 billion pesos ($1.03 billion).

Banco Wal-Mart (launched in 2007) operates more than 260 branches located inside Bodega Aurrer Wal-Mart and SAM'S CLUB stores in some 30 cities and cater to a clientele that for the most part is new to banking. The bank has been losing money for its parent though. To cut its losses in late 2014 Wal-Mart de México y Centroamérica sold the banking unit to a group of buyers that includes Grupo Financiero Inbursa the financial services operations of billionaire Carlos Slim Hel . The deal was valued at MXN 3.6 billion ($247 million).

HISTORY

Spanish-born Jer nimo Arango Arias studied art and literature at several American universities without graduating. In his twenties he wandered around Spain Mexico and the US. He struck upon an idea after seeing a crowd waiting in line at the E. J. Korvette discount department store in New York City. Jer nimo called his two brothers Pl - cido and Manuel and convinced them to join him in a new business venture.

Borrowing about $250000 from their father a Spanish immigrant to Mexico successful in textiles the three brothers opened their first Aurrer Bolivar discount store in downtown Mexico City in 1958. Offering goods and clothing well below manufacturers' list prices the store was an immediate hit with consumers but encountered hostility from competing Mexico City retailers. When local retailers threatened to boycott the Arangos' suppliers the company turned to suppliers in Guadalajara and Monterrey.

In 1965 the Arango brothers formed a joint venture with Jewel Cos. of Chicago to open new Aurrer stores. Jewel bought a 49% interest in the business a year later. Pl cido and Manuel left the business with their portion of the money but Jer nimo stayed as head of the company taking it public in 1976.

By 1981 almost a third of Jewel's earnings came from its operations in Mexico. But the next year the peso crashed obliterating its earnings there. American Stores took over Jewel in 1984 and Jer nimo bought back Jewel's stake in the company (which was renamed Cifra that year).

With the Mexican economy staggering from the peso devaluation weak oil markets and a huge debt crisis Jer nimo was taking a major risk. Although no new stores were opened none were closed. Employees were expected to work longer and those who left were not replaced. With Mexico's middle class hit hard Jer nimo emphasized the Bodega Aurrer no-frills warehouses which discounted all kinds of nonperishable merchandise from canned chili to VCRs.

Cifra and Wal-Mart Stores formed a joint venture in 1991 to open Club Aurrer membership clubs similar to Sam's Club outlets. The two companies expanded the venture the next year to include the development of Sam's Club and Wal-Mart Supercenters in Mexico. Remodeling began on Cifra's stores in 1992. The work was completed two years later and the company was poised to take advantage of Mexico's much-improved economy.

However devaluation struck again late in 1994. The resulting contraction of credit and rise in prices hit Mexican consumers hard and Cifra's 1995 sales declined 15%. But again it kept on as many employees as possible transferring them to new stores that had been in development. Despite the hard times Cifra opened 27 new stores (including 15 restaurants). The company was able to withstand the difficulties in part because it stayed debt-free.

Wal-Mart consolidated its joint venture into Cifra in 1997 in exchange for about 34% of that company; Wal-Mart later raised its stake to 51%. The cost-conscious companies combined the joint venture stores and Cifra's separate stores under one umbrella. Cifra opened 11 stores and eight restaurants that year.

Cifra opened nine stores and 17 restaurants in 1998; the next year it opened about 20 stores and nearly 25 restaurants. In early 2000 Cifra was renamed Wal-Mart de México. Shortly thereafter Wal-Mart upped its stake in Wal-Mart de México to about 61%.

In 2001 all the Aurrer stores were converted to either Wal-Mart Supercenters or Bodega stores.

Eduardo Castro-Wright was promoted in 2002 from COO to CEO of Wal-Mart de México succeeding Cesareo Fernandez who retained the chairman's title. The retailer opened 50 new outlets that year.

In March 2003 Mexico's Federal Competition Commission closed an investigation of Wal-Mex's purchasing practices citing a lack of evidence that the retailer violated competition laws. Overall that year Wal-Mex entered nine new cities in Mexico and added 46 new outlets. In 2004 Mexico's largest retailer grew bigger adding 17 restaurants 23 Aurrer stores eight SAM'S CLUBS six supercenters and four Superama stores.

In January 2005 Fernandez stepped down as chairman and was succeeded by Ernesto Vega. A month later Castro-Wright left Wal-Mex to become EVP and COO of the Wal-Mart Stores Division in the US. He was succeeded by Eduardo Solorzano formerly COO of Wal-Mex. Also that year Wal-

Mex acquired the Mexican assets of French retailer Carrefour. Carrefour which operated 29 hypermarkets in Mexico restructured its operations and left the Mexican market.

In November 2006 Wal-Mex received a license from Mexico's Finance Ministry to organize and operate a bank there. Overall in 2006 the retailer opened 120 new locations including stores in Monterrey the country's most affluent city and throughout northern Mexico where its Texas rival H. E. Butt Grocery is well established. In November 2007 Wal-Mart Bank began operations with 16 branches in five Mexican states.

Wal-Mex inked a deal with Tobacco One in August 2008 to distribute the tobacco firm's Rojo cigarette line in about 140 supercenters and some 60 Superarma stores throughout Mexico.

In December 2009 Wal-Mex announced the acquisition of Walmart's operations in Central America from Walmart Stores and two minority partners. The transaction was completed in early 2010 and Wal-Mex became Walmart México and Central America.

The company discontinued its Vips restaurant business in early 2014 with an agreement to sell the 360 restaurants to Alsea S.A.B. de C.V. for about $625 million.

EXECUTIVES

CFO, Pedro Farah
CEO, Guilherme Loureiro
COO, Todd Harbaugh
Chairman, Enrique Ostalé
Auditors: Mancera, S.C. (member of Ernst & Young Global)

LOCATIONS

HQ: Wal-Mart de Mexico S.A.B. de C.V.
Blvd. Manuel Avila Camacho 647, Colonia Periodista, Alcaldia Miguel Hidalgo, Mexico City 11220
Phone: (52) 55 5283 0100   **Fax:** (52) 55 5328 3557
Web: www.walmex.mx

2015 Stores

	No.
Mexico	2,363
Costa Rica	230
Guatemala	217
El Salvador	88
Nicaragua	92
Honduras	82
Total	**3,072**

PRODUCTS/OPERATIONS

2015 Mexico Stores

	% of total
Bodega Aurrera Express	924
Bodega Aurrera	475
Mi Bodega Aurrera	324
Walmart Supercenter	256
Sam's Club	160
Suburbia	114
Superama	95
Medimart Farmacia de Walmart	10
Zona Suburbia	5
Total	**2,363**

Selected Operations

Bodegas & discount stores
  Bodega Aurrera
  Dispensa Familiar
  MAXI Bodega
  PALI
Hypermarkets
  Hiper Paiz
  Hiper Mas
  Walmart
Warehouse clubs
  Sam's Club
  ClubCo

Supermarkets
  La Union
  Mas por Menos
  Paiz
  Superama
Apparel Stores
  Suburbia
Restaurants
  El Porton
  VIPS

COMPETITORS

Comerci	H-E-B
Costco Wholesale	Safeway
El Puerto de Liverpool	Sanborns
Gigante	Soriana
Grupo Carso	

HISTORICAL FINANCIALS

Company Type: Public

Income Statement   FYE: December 31

	REVENUE ($ mil.)	NET INCOME ($ mil.)	NET PROFIT MARGIN	EMPLOYEES
12/19	34,189	2,003	5.9%	238,972
12/18	31,372	1,869	6.0%	234,431
12/17	29,099	2,023	7.0%	237,055
12/16	25,729	1,611	6.3%	228,854
12/15	28,169	1,518	5.4%	231,996
Annual Growth	**5.0%**	**7.2%**	**—**	**0.7%**

2019 Year-End Financials

Debt ratio: —
Return on equity: 22.7%
Cash ($ mil.): 1,630
Current ratio: 1.00
Long-term debt ($ mil.): —
No. of shares (mil.): —
Dividends
  Yield: 3.3%
  Payout: —
Market value ($ mil.): —

	STOCK PRICE ($) FY Close	P/E High/Low		PER SHARE ($) Earnings	Dividends	Book Value
12/19	28.59	14	12	0.11	0.96	0.51
12/18	25.45	14	11	0.11	0.68	0.48
12/17	24.42	11	8	0.12	1.13	0.46
12/16	17.87	12	9	0.09	0.78	0.46
12/15	25.15	18	11	0.09	1.14	0.50
Annual Growth	**3.3%**		**—**	**7.2%**	**(4.2%)**	**0.4%**

Weichai Power Co Ltd

Auditors: Ernst & Young Hua Ming LLP

LOCATIONS

HQ: Weichai Power Co Ltd
197, Section A, Fu Shou East Street, High Technology Industrial Development Zone, Weifang, Shandong Province 261061
Phone: (86) 536 819 7069   **Fax:** (86) 536 819 7073
Web: www.weichaipower.com

HISTORICAL FINANCIALS

Company Type: Public

Income Statement   FYE: December 31

	REVENUE ($ mil.)	NET INCOME ($ mil.)	NET PROFIT MARGIN	EMPLOYEES
12/19	25,058	1,308	5.2%	0
12/18	23,153	1,258	5.4%	0
12/17	23,291	1,046	4.5%	0
12/16	13,419	351	2.6%	0
12/15	11,351	214	1.9%	66,000
Annual Growth	**21.9%**	**57.2%**	**—**	**—**

2019 Year-End Financials

Debt ratio: 2.2%
Return on equity: 21.5%
Cash ($ mil.): 7,015
Current ratio: 1.19
Long-term debt ($ mil.): 3,114
No. of shares (mil.): —
Dividends
  Yield: 2.2%
  Payout: 226.3%
Market value ($ mil.): —

	STOCK PRICE ($) FY Close	P/E High/Low		PER SHARE ($) Earnings	Dividends	Book Value
12/19	16.87	14	7	0.17	0.37	(0.00)
12/18	9.02	10	7	0.16	0.40	(0.00)
12/17	8.75	31	9	0.13	0.21	(0.00)
12/16	12.26	22	11	0.09	0.09	(0.00)
12/15	8.70	50	20	0.05	0.06	1.22
Annual Growth	**18.0%**		**—**	**32.3%**	**59.5%**	**—**

Wesfarmers Ltd.

Auditors: Ernst & Young

LOCATIONS

HQ: Wesfarmers Ltd.
Level 14, Brookfield Place Tower 2, 123 St Georges Terrace, Perth, Western Australia 6000
Phone: (61) 8 9327 4211   **Fax:** (61) 8 9327 4216
Web: www.wesfarmers.com.au

HISTORICAL FINANCIALS

Company Type: Public

Income Statement   FYE: June 30

	REVENUE ($ mil.)	NET INCOME ($ mil.)	NET PROFIT MARGIN	EMPLOYEES
06/20	21,138	1,162	5.5%	107,000
06/19	19,561	3,860	19.7%	105,000
06/18	49,386	883	1.8%	217,000
06/17	52,588	2,207	4.2%	223,000
06/16	49,091	302	0.6%	220,000
Annual Growth	**(19.0%)**	**40.0%**	**—**	**(16.5%)**

2020 Year-End Financials

Debt ratio: 7.1%
Return on equity: 17.5%
Cash ($ mil.): 1,996
Current ratio: 1.11
Long-term debt ($ mil.): 1,475
No. of shares (mil.): 1,133
Dividends
  Yield: 2.7%
  Payout: 43.2%
Market value ($ mil.): 17,654

	STOCK PRICE ($) FY Close	P/E High/Low		PER SHARE ($) Earnings	Dividends	Book Value
06/20	15.57	11	7	1.03	0.43	5.65
06/19	12.61	4	2	3.41	5.44	6.16
06/18	18.26	17	14	0.78	0.72	14.82
06/17	15.38	7	6	1.95	0.66	16.22
06/16	14.98	46	38	0.27	0.64	15.16
Annual Growth (21.9%)	1.0%			—	39.7%	(9.5%)

West Japan Railway Co

EXECUTIVES

VP and Executive Officer, Tatsuo Kijima
Auditors: Ernst & Young ShinNihon LLC

LOCATIONS

HQ: West Japan Railway Co
2-4-24 Shibata, Kita-ku, Osaka 530-8341
Phone: (81) 6 6376 6060
Web: www.westjr.co.jp

PRODUCTS/OPERATIONS

2016 sales

	% of total
Transportation	64
Sales of goods & food services	16
Real estate business	8
Other business	12
Total	**100**

COMPETITORS

Keihin Electric Express Railway	Nagoya Railroad
Keio Corporation	Odakyu Electric Railway
Keisei Electric Railway	Tobu Railway

HISTORICAL FINANCIALS

Company Type: Public

Income Statement   FYE: March 31

	REVENUE ($ mil.)	NET INCOME ($ mil.)	NET PROFIT MARGIN	EMPLOYEES
03/20	13,894	823	5.9%	60,940
03/19	13,809	927	6.7%	60,120
03/18	14,130	1,040	7.4%	59,833
03/17	12,891	816	6.3%	59,861
03/16	12,923	764	5.9%	59,768
Annual Growth	1.8%	1.9%	—	0.5%

2020 Year-End Financials

Debt ratio: 0.2%	No. of shares (mil.): 191
Return on equity: 8.1%	Dividends
Cash ($ mil.): 723	Yield: 2.5%
Current ratio: 0.62	Payout: —
Long-term debt ($ mil.): 7,782	Market value ($ mil.): 12,772

	STOCK PRICE ($) FY Close	P/E High/Low		PER SHARE ($) Earnings	Dividends	Book Value
03/20	66.75	0	0	4.30	1.69	53.83
03/19	75.51	0	0	4.82	1.51	50.65
03/18	71.00	0	0	5.37	1.43	49.63
03/17	65.37	0	0	4.22	1.27	43.42
03/16	61.67	0	0	3.95	1.05	40.35
Annual Growth	2.0%			—	2.2% 12.5%	7.5%

Weston (George) Ltd

George Weston Limited fuels Canadians through those long winters. More than 90% of the company's sales come from its majority-owned Loblaw Companies Limited Canada's largest retailer with more than 2400 grocery stores markets and drug stores across the country. Its locations (both corporate-owned and franchised) operate under such banners as Loblaws Joe Fresh Shoppers Drug Mart and President's Choice Bank. Loblaw Companies also provides banking and other financial services through PC Financial. In addition George Weston owns Weston Foods with operations in Canada and the US which makes freshly baked goods frozen dough biscuits and other bakery products. (Its Interbake Foods division is a major supplier of Girl Scout cookies in the US.)

Operations

George Weston operates through three operating segments: Loblaw Choice Properties and Weston Foods.

The Loblaw operating segment accounts for more than 90% of company revenue and includes grocery and drug store chains as well as financial services through PC Financial. Its banners include Loblaws Joe Fresh President's Choice Bank and Shoppers Drug Mart.

Weston Foods is a leading food manufacturer in North America known for fresh and frozen bakery items (breads rolls pies cakes cookies crackers). Some of Weston foods brands include Wonder Ace Bakery Country Harvest and D' Italiano. This segment accounts for around 5% of George Weston's revenue.

Choice properties which accounts for about 5% of George Weston's revenue is a large diversified owner manager and developer of real estate properties. It is comprised of retail properties predominantly leased to necessity?based tenants industrial office and residential assets concentrated in attractive markets and offers an impressive and substantial development pipeline.

Geographic Reach

Based in Toronto George Weston operates across Canada and generates more than 95% of its revenue there. It has limited operations in the US through Weston Foods.

Sales and Marketing

George Weston serves retail customers through some 2400 grocery stores markets and drug stores across Canada. Its Weston Foods segment serves retail and wholesale customers.

Financial Performance

For a five-year period starting in 2015 the company registered steady growth. The revenue grew 7% in that span. In that same period net income grew on its first 3 years but declined the last two years.

In 2019 the company reported revenue of $50.1 billion up by 3% compared to 2018. The growth was powered completely by increase in retail sales in all its operating segments.

Net income that year was $242 million down by 58% from $574 million in 2018.

Cash at the end of fiscal 2019 was $1.8 billion an increase of $313 million from the prior year. Cash from operations contributed $4.6 billion to the coffers while investing activities used $1.1 billion primarily due to acquisition of CREIT. Financing activities used another $2.8 billion for higher net repayments of long term debt and short term debt partially offset by proceeds received from Choice Properties' portfolio transaction issuances of Choice Properties units and lower repurchases of Loblaw's common shares.

Strategy

George Weston's three operating segments has its own strategy.

Loblaw's strategy is committed to delivering industry leading financial performance by leveraging data-driven insights and by delivering process and efficiency excellence. This model ultimately fuels truly customer-centric investments in Everyday Digital Retail Payments and Rewards and Connected Healthcare.

For Choice Properties its goal is to provide net asset value appreciation stable net operating income ("NOI") growth and capital preservation with a long term focus.

Weston Foods is committed to offering superior products and services to its consumers and customers in an increasingly competitive environment.

Company Background

A baker's apprentice George Weston began delivering bread in Toronto with a single horse in 1882. He added the Model Bakery in 1896 and began making cookies and biscuits in 1908.

Upon George's death in 1924 his son Garfield gained control of the company and took it public as George Weston Limited in 1928.

During the 1940s the company made a number of acquisitions including papermaker E.B. Eddy (1943; sold 1998 to papermaker Domtar giving it a 20% stake in Domtar) Southern Biscuit (1944) Western Grocers (1944 its first distribution company) and William Neilson (1948 chocolate and dairy products).

In 1953 it acquired a controlling interest in Loblaw Groceterias Canada's largest grocery chain. George Weston continued its acquisitions during the 1950s and 1960s adding grocer National Tea and diversifying into packaging (Somerville Industries 1957) and fisheries (British Columbia Packers 1962; Conners Bros. 1967).

EXECUTIVES

Chairman and CEO George Weston Limited and Loblaw Companies Ltd., Galen G. Weston, age 47
President and CFO, Richard Dufresne
President Weston Foods, Luc Mongeau
EVP and Chief Legal Officer, Gordon A.M. Currie
Chief Administrative Officer Loblaw Companies Ltd., Sarah R. Davis
EVP and Chief Talent Officer, Rashid Wasti
Deputy Chairman, Alannah Weston
Auditors: KPMG LLP

LOCATIONS

HQ: Weston (George) Ltd
22 St. Clair Avenue East, Toronto, Ontario M4T 2S5
Phone: 416 922-2500
Web: www.weston.ca

2017 Sales

	% of total
Canada	97
US	3
Total	**100**

PRODUCTS/OPERATIONS

2017 Sales

	% of total
Loblaw	95
Weston Foods	5
Total	**100**

Selected Operations

Loblaw Companies Limited
Shoppers Drug Mart
Choice Properties REIT
President's Choice Financial
Weston Foods

COMPETITORS

Costco Wholesale Canada	Maple Leaf Foods
Jean Coutu	North West
Jim Pattison Group	Shoppers Drug Mart
Katz Group	Sobeys
METRO	Wal-Mart Canada

HISTORICAL FINANCIALS

Company Type: Public

Income Statement				FYE: December 31
	REVENUE ($ mil.)	NET INCOME ($ mil.)	NET PROFIT MARGIN	EMPLOYEES
12/19	50,740	245	0.5%	194,000
12/18	49,180	581	1.2%	197,000
12/17	48,900	768	1.6%	198,000
12/16	48,603	556	1.1%	6,500
12/15	47,485	533	1.1%	0
Annual Growth	1.7%	(17.7%)	—	—

2019 Year-End Financials

Debt ratio: 35.8%	No. of shares (mil.): 153
Return on equity: 3.0%	Dividends
Cash ($ mil.): 1,857	Yield: 0.0%
Current ratio: 1.18	Payout: 165.8%
Long-term debt ($ mil.): 12,872	Market value ($ mil.): 12,185

	STOCK PRICE ($) FY Close	P/E High/Low	PER SHARE ($) Earnings	Dividends	Book Value
12/19	79.29	66 52	1.28	2.12	50.14
12/18	65.55	22 16	4.04	1.97	53.08
12/17	86.74	16 15	5.60	1.83	62.50
12/16	83.72	23 17	3.95	1.77	61.47
12/15	77.03	23 20	3.79	1.72	60.95
Annual Growth	0.7%	—	— (23.8%)	5.4%	(4.8%)

Westpac Banking Corp

Founded in 1817 Westpac Banking is a stalwart financial institution serving clients in Australia New Zealand and neighboring Pacific Islands. The company attends to approximately 14.2 million customers through about 1150 branches and more than 2800 ATMs. Westpac is one of the largest banks in Australia with a loan portfolio of around $718 million. Across its operating segments the group is recognized for several of its bank brands: Westpac Bank of Melbourne St. George Bank SA RAMS and BT Brands. More than 85% of its revenue come from domestic operations.

Operations

Westpac Banking operates five reporting segments: Consumer Bank Business Bank Westpac Institutional Bank Westpac New Zealand and Group Businesses.

The Consumer Bank contributes nearly 45% of revenue and serves consumer customers in Australia. It provides its services via several branded banks including its namesake Westpac Bank of Melbourne St George Bank SA and RAMS.

The Business Bank segment generates more than 30% of revenue by tending to the financial needs of its commercial small-to-medium enterprise and agribusiness customers. The Business Bank offers financial facilities up to $150 million. The segment provides services though all the same bank brands as its affiliate Consumer segment except RAMS.

The Westpac Institutional Bank provides services to commercial corporate institutional and government clients in Australia New Zealand the US UK and Asia. It is also responsible for Westpac Pacific a bank in Fiji and Papua New Guinea. The segment provides roughly 15% of total revenue.

The Westpac New Zealand segment addresses all customer types (including consumer business institutional etc.) across New Zealand. Westpac New Zealand account for about 10% of total revenue.

Less than 5% of Westpac's revenue is derived from its Group Businesses segment. It houses its Treasury (which manages the company's balance sheet) technology strategy and architecture arm Group Technology and operational division Core Support.

Net interest income generates over 80% of Westpac's sales.

Geographic Reach

Australia accounts for more than 85% of New South Wales-headquartered Westpac Banking's revenue. New Zealand provides more than 10%; less than 5% comes from overseas territories including the Pacific Islands Asia the Americas and Europe. In addition to about 1150 branches it has foreign offices in Shanghai Beijing Jakarta Mumbai London New York City Hong Kong and Singapore.

Sales and Marketing

Westpac Banking's retail services are promoted through its retail banking locations as well as through relationship managers wealth specialists business banking centers customer service channels and online. The institutional segment conducts sales through dedicated industry relationship and specialist product teams. Westpac's advertising expenses for 2019 2018 and 2017 were A$245 million A$173 million and A$155 million respectively.

Financial Performance

(Note: Growth rates may differ after conversion to US dollars.)

After rising for the last few years Westpac Banking's 2019 revenue dropped 6% to an amount that is basically the same as 2015's.

Its net income fluctuated with a major drop in 2019. Reported net profit in Full Year 2019 was $6784 million down from $8095 million in 2018.

Cash and balances with central banks as at the end of 2019 totalled $20.1 billion $6.7 billion lower than the previous year. Operating activities generated $7.1 billion. Investing and financing activities used $10.8 billion and $3.6 billion respectively.

Strategy

Westpac Banking has three strategic priorities for the year ahead:

Deal with outstanding issues. In recent years a number of issues have emerged relating to past business practices operational errors gaps in compliance or changes in regulation. These were identified through the Royal Commission the company's CGA self-assessment ongoing product reviews and various regulatory actions. The faster Westpac Banking resolves these issues the sooner it can refocus investment and management attention on delivering more for customers thereby increasing the value of its franchise.

Maintaining momentum in its customer franchise. The long-term success of the company's business depends on the strength and depth of its customer relationships. In 2019 the company continued to improve its service offering and the technology needed to deliver better service in the future.

Increasing structural productivity. Using technology to drive down costs is an important part of the company's strategy to remain competitive and deliver good returns over time. This is increasingly important in a low-rate slow-growth environment where margins are under pressure and regulatory and compliance costs are rising. At the same time emerging competitors have no physical networks to support and have a cost advantage in delivering some products.

Company Background

Westpac Banking launched in 1817 as the Bank of New South Wales—the first bank established in the country. It changed its name to Westpac Banking Corporation in 1982 after it acquired the Commercial Bank of Australia. In 2011 it merged with St.George which then launched the Bank of Melbourne.

HISTORY

Westpac proudly calls itself Australia's "First Bank." But when predecessor Bank of New South Wales was founded in 1817 some 90% of the eponymous colony's inhabitants were convicts or their relatives. (The penal colony was established just 30 years before the bank.) The British challenged the bank's charter forcing it to become a joint-stock company.

New South Wales' parliament rechartered the company as a bank in 1850 amidst the country's first gold rushes. (Some bank branches consisted of tents in mining camps.) Heavy British investment and an influx of colonists kept the country growing. The bank's future partner Commercial Bank of Australia was founded in 1866 in Melbourne in the neighboring colony of Victoria. More than half of the country's banks disappeared in a panic at the end of the century when land speculation and a collapse in wool prices caused a depression.

Australia became a country with the onset of the 20th century and its government formed Commonwealth Bank a central bank. The Bank of New South Wales now known as "The Wales" helped finance Australia's WWI efforts. Along with the rest of the world the country and the bank rode up the Roaring '20s and down the Great Depression.

About 65% of the bank's male staff enlisted during WWII. Its New Guinea branches closed; others were hit by air raids. In 1947 the government moved to nationalize the prospering country's banks within the Commonwealth Bank but the courts helped the banks fend off the attack on their independence.

The Bank of New South Wales moved into the newly opened savings banking market in 1956. The next year it bought into Australian Guarantee Corporation (it bought the rest in 1988).

The bank expanded abroad and diversified operations in the 1970s. Battered by a lagging protectionist economy Australia moved to deregulate banking in the 1980s. As foreign banks hustled in Bank of New South Wales and Commercial Bank of Australia in 1982 made what was then the largest merger in Australia's history.

The new bank known as Westpac (for its Western Pacific market area) began building its non-teller-based banking networks in the early 1980s. The company developed an extensive ATM network and established telephone and computerized banking. Later that decade it bought a stake in London gold dealer Johnson Matthey (1986) and all of William E. Pollock Government Securities (1987).

In 1992 Australia's wealthiest man Kerry Packer took a 10% share in troubled Westpac gaining board seats for himself and friend "Chainsaw" Al Dunlap. Packer's power grab failed and he sold the stake in 1993.

After buying itself into the equities market in the mid-1980s Westpac sold its Ord Minnett brokerage division in 1993. The bank withdrew from Asia and expanded closer to home in the mid

1990s buying Western Australia's Challenge Bank in 1995 Trust Bank of New Zealand in 1996 and Victoria's Bank of Melbourne in 1997.

In 1998 the bank agreed to merge its back-office operations with those of ANZ Banking Group providing economies of scale while avoiding antitrust issues. The next year Westpac announced 3000 job cuts mainly through attrition to ready itself for increased competition from changes in Australian law. Pacific operations caused waves in 2000: Westpac said it would pull out of Kiribati in response to government action and a coup in Fiji prompted the bank to reduce employees' hours (a move that was criticized by the Fiji government). The next year however Westpac was strengthening ties to the Pacific market. It doubled its holdings in the Bank of Tonga (on the island of Tonga) and its share of Pacific Commercial Bank (on the island of Samoa).

In 2007 subsidiary Westpac Essential Services Trust formed a joint venture with another Australian firm to operate the Airport Link Company a rail-to-airport passenger service in Sydney. The trust was established so investors could invest in public-private partnership (PPP) assets.

Westpac's acquisition of St.George Bank in 2008 catapulted Westpac from fourth to second among Australia's leading banks. The combination set Westpac and its St.George subsidiary behind only the National Australia Bank in terms of assets.

EXECUTIVES

CEO, Brian C. Hartzer, age 53
COO, John Arthur
Deputy CEO, Philip (Phil) Coffey, age 61, $660,755 total compensation
CEO St.George Banking Group, George Frazis, age 56
Group Executive Westpac Institutional Bank, Rob Whitfield, age 53, $320,564 total compensation
CEO BT Financial Group, Brad Cooper, age 57, $354,583 total compensation
Group Executive Westpac Retail and Business Banking, Jason Yetton
CIO, David Curran
Chief Risk Officer, Alexandra Holcomb
CFO, Peter King
Acting CEO Westpac New Zealand Limited, David McLean
Chairman, Lindsay P. Maxsted
Auditors: PricewaterhouseCoopers

LOCATIONS

HQ: Westpac Banking Corp
275 Kent Street, Sydney, New South Wales 2000
Phone: (61) 2 9374 7113   **Fax:** (61) 2 8253 4128
Web: www.westpac.com.au

2018 Sales

	% of total
Australia	86
New Zealand	11
Other countries	3
Total	**100**

PRODUCTS/OPERATIONS

2018 Sales by Segment

	% of total
Consumer Bank	39
Business Bank	24
BT Financial Group Australia	10
Westpac Institutional Bank	13
Westpac New Zealand	10
Group Businesses	4
Total	**100**

2018 Sales

	% of total
Net interest income	74
Non-interest income	26
Total	**100**

Selected Products and Services

Bank accounts
Home loans
Credit cards
Personal loans
Travel money card
Share trading
Insurance
Savings accounts
Credit cards
Business loans
Merchant services

COMPETITORS

AMP Limited	Commonwealth Bank of
Australia and New	Australia
Zealand Banking	HBOS Australia
BANK OF QUEENSLAND	HSBC
LIMITED	Macquarie Group
BENDIGO AND ADELAIDE	National Australia
BANK LIMITED	Bank

HISTORICAL FINANCIALS

Company Type: Public

Income Statement   FYE: September 30

	ASSETS ($ mil.)	NET INCOME ($ mil.)	INCOME AS % OF ASSETS	EMPLOYEES
09/20	914,653	2,296	0.3%	36,849
09/19	909,317	6,804	0.7%	33,288
09/18	882,203	8,119	0.9%	35,029
09/17	854,403	8,013	0.9%	35,096
09/16	841,693	7,467	0.9%	35,280
Annual Growth	2.1%	(25.5%)	—	1.1%

2020 Year-End Financials

Return on assets: 0.2%	Dividends
Return on equity: 3.4%	Yield: 9.9%
Long-term debt ($ mil.): —	Payout: 85.4%
No. of shares (mil.): —	Market value ($ mil.): —
Sales ($ mil): 32,620	

	STOCK PRICE ($) FY Close	P/E High/Low		Earnings	PER SHARE ($) Dividends	Book Value
09/20	12.04	31	13	0.64	1.19	18.89
09/19	19.99	10	8	1.90	1.31	18.81
09/18	20.01	11	8	2.31	1.41	18.84
09/17	25.22	11	9	2.30	1.38	18.12
09/16	22.74	11	9	2.18	1.50	17.44
Annual Growth	(14.7%)	—	—	(26.5%)	(5.5%)	2.0%

WH Group Ltd

Auditors: Ernst & Young

LOCATIONS

HQ: WH Group Ltd
Unit 7602B-7604A, Level 76, International Commerce Centre, 1 Austin Road West, Kowloon,
Phone:
Web: www.wh-group.com

HISTORICAL FINANCIALS

Company Type: Public

Income Statement   FYE: December 31

	REVENUE ($ mil.)	NET INCOME ($ mil.)	NET PROFIT MARGIN	EMPLOYEES
12/19	24,103	1,465	6.1%	101,000
12/18	22,605	943	4.2%	112,000
12/17	22,379	1,133	5.1%	110,000
12/16	21,534	1,036	4.8%	104,000
12/15	21,209	786	3.7%	0
Annual Growth	3.2%	16.8%	—	—

2019 Year-End Financials

Debt ratio: 17.8%	No. of shares (mil.): —
Return on equity: 17.8%	Dividends
Cash ($ mil.): 552	Yield: 2.5%
Current ratio: 1.73	Payout: 480.8%
Long-term debt ($ mil.): 2,187	Market value ($ mil.): —

	STOCK PRICE ($) FY Close	P/E High/Low	PER SHARE ($) Earnings	Dividends	Book Value
12/19	20.60	246147	0.10	0.03	0.59
12/18	15.36	389214	0.06	0.65	0.53
12/17	22.60	294187	0.08	0.63	0.51
Annual Growth	(4.5%)	— —	6.3%	(55.1%)	3.8%

Wilmar International Ltd

EXECUTIVES

Chairman and CEO, Kuok Khoon Hong
Country Head Indonesia, Hendri Saksti
Country Head Malaysia, Yee Chek Toong
Head Technical Division, Matthew J. Morgenroth
Head Plantations Division, Goh Ing Sing
Vice Chairman China, Mu Yankui
Chief Scientific Advisor, Chua Nam-Hai
Head Oleochemicals and Biofuels, Rahul Kale
Head Sugar Division, Bohbot Jean-Luc
Head Shipping Division, Kenny B. H. Chwee
CFO, Ho Kiam Kong
COO, Pua Seck Guan
Executive Deputy Chairman, Martua Sitorus
Auditors: Ernst & Young LLP

LOCATIONS

HQ: Wilmar International Ltd
56 Neil Road, 088830
Phone: (65) 6216 0244   **Fax:** (65) 6536 2192
Web: www.wilmar-international.com

2017 Sales

	% of total
China	51
Southeast Asia	20
Europe	6
Africa	6
India	4
Australia/New Zealand	2
Other	11
Total	**100**

PRODUCTS/OPERATIONS

2017 Sales

	% of total
Oilseeds & grains	44
Tropical oils	40
Sugar	11
Other	5
Total	**100**

Selected Operations

Palm oil cultivation
Oilseed crushing
Edible oil refining
Sugar milling & refining
Grain processing
Fertilizer manufacturing

COMPETITORS

Anglo-Eastern Plantations	IOI Corporation
Asia Food & Properties	Kuala Lumpur Kepong
Bunge Limited	Narborough Plantations
Golden Agri-Resources	New Britain Palm

HISTORICAL FINANCIALS

Company Type: Public

Income Statement

FYE: December 31

	REVENUE ($ mil.)	NET INCOME ($ mil.)	NET PROFIT MARGIN	EMPLOYEES
12/19	42,640	1,293	3.0%	90,000
12/18	44,497	1,128	2.5%	90,000
12/17	43,846	1,219	2.8%	0
12/16	41,401	972	2.3%	90,000
12/15	38,776	1,056	2.7%	92,000
Annual Growth	**2.4%**	**5.2%**	**—**	**(0.5%)**

2019 Year-End Financials

Debt ratio: 50.3%	No. of shares (mil.): —
Return on equity: 7.8%	Dividends
Cash ($ mil.): 2,113	Yield: 0.0%
Current ratio: 1.11	Payout: 317.6%
Long-term debt ($ mil.): 5,419	Market value ($ mil.): —

	STOCK PRICE ($) FY Close	P/E High/Low	PER SHARE ($) Earnings	Dividends	Book Value
12/19	30.10	155108	0.20	0.65	2.64
12/18	23.42	139121	0.18	0.70	2.54
12/17	22.99	145117	0.19	0.45	2.52
12/16	24.61	179119	0.15	0.51	2.29
12/15	20.50	153106	0.17	0.52	2.39
Annual Growth	**10.1%**	**—**	**5.3%**	**5.6%**	**2.5%**

Wipro Ltd

When companies outsource work Wipro is often on the insourcing end. The company provides systems integration software application development and maintenance research and development for hardware and software design and outsourcing services for customers around the world. Operating in more than 50 countries the company generates more than half of its revenue from the Americas (largely the US). Wipro offers services to companies in a wide range of industries including aerospace and defense automotive banking communications electronics construction healthcare pharmaceuticals retail and oil and gas.

Operations

Wipro operates in three segments: IT Services IT Products and India State Run Enterprise (ISRE).

The company depends on its IT Services segment for a whopping 95% of its revenue. The segment provides digital strategy design technology consulting custom application design development re-engineering and maintenance and systems integration and implementation as well as cloud infrastructure services analytics services business process services research and development and hardware and software design.

The IT Products business less than 5% of revenue helps implement the IT Services segment's offerings with hardware and software products and integration services.

ISRE about 1% of revenue provides services to agencies of the Indian government as well as corporate entities that are at least 51% controlled by the Indian government.

Geographic Reach

Wipro is based in India and has operations around the world. About 55% of its revenue originates from customers in the Americas followed by Europe with about a quarter of revenue and the rest of the world about 20%.

Sales and Marketing

Wipro's direct sales force gets the company's service offerings in front of a wide variety of customers. Customers include government agencies including defense telecommunications manufacturing utility education and financial services companies.

Financial Performance

Note: Growth rates may differ after currency conversion.

Wipro's revenue has fluctuated over the past five years.

In 2019 (ended March) the company's revenue rose to $8.5 billion from $8.4 billion in 2018. Two of the company's largest industry verticals Banking Financial Services and Insurance and Consumer Business contributed to the higher revenue as did the depreciation of the Indian Rupee against foreign currencies.

Wipro's profit advanced to $1.3 billion in 2019 from $1.2 billion in 2018 boosted by the increase in revenue.

Wipro's cash holdings were $1.45 billion in 2019 compared to $690 million in 2018.

Strategy

Wipro has identified four technologies that are key to its future: digital cloud engineering services and cyber security. Wipro has ramped up investments in those areas which the company call its "big bets." Some of the investment might be paying dividends. Wipro's digital revenue jumped more than 30% in 2019 from 2018 and included its largest customer deal worth $1.5 billion. In cyber security Wipro is building up its Cyber Defense Assurance Platform and working with security partners and governing bodies to sharpen its capabilities. The company's cyber security-as-a-service offering grew 16% year-over-year.

As Wipro moves into new technologies it wants to bring its current employees with it. To do so the company has invested in training its employees in new skills. As part of the training process the company uses its social learning and crowdsourcing platform TopGear.

Wipro got out of the data center business in 2018 selling its operations to Ensono Holdings which improved Wipro's return on capital employed. In another divestment Wipro sold its Workday and CornerstoneOnDemand practices to Alight for about $110 million in 2019.

Part of Wipro's advantage has been that it hires lower-cost workers in emerging markets which has helped keep its costs down. Wages in many of those markets are rising and that might diminish the company's financial edge.

EXECUTIVES

President Wipro Consumer Care and Lighting, Vineet Agrawal, age 58, $198,735 total compensation
President Wipro Infrastructure Engineering, Pratik Kumar, age 54, $184,194 total compensation
President and CEO Global Infrastructure Services (GIS), G. K. Prasanna, age 61
CTO Global IT Business, K. R. Sanjiv, age 54
CEO and Director, Abidali Z. Neemuchwala, age 53
Head of Wipro Digital, Rajan Kohli
CEO Manufacturing and Hi-Tech, N. S. Bala
CFO, Jatin Dalal
President India and Middle East, Soumitro Ghosh
President and CEO BFSi, Shaji Farooq
President; CEO Energy Natural Resources and Utilities, Anand Padmanabhan
SVP and Head Global Communication Service Provider, Anil K. Jain
CEO Products and Solutions, Balasubramanian (Ganesh) Ganesh
CEO Application Services and Strategic Alliances, B.M. Bhanumurthy
SVP and Global Head Human Resources, Saurabh Govil
President Consumer Vertical, Srini Pallia
SVP Continental Europe and Africa, Ulrich Meister
SVP and Global Head Advanced Technologies and Solutions (ATS), Jeff Heenan-Jalil
Global Head Business Process Outsourcing Services, Nagendra P. Bandaru
Global Head Strategic Engagements and Go-to-Market Transformation, A. (Amar) Amarnath
Chairman, Azim H. Premji, age 74
Auditors: Deloitte Haskins & Sells LLP

LOCATIONS

HQ: Wipro Ltd
Doddakannelli, Sarjapur Road, Bengaluru, Karnataka 560035
Phone: (91) 80 2844 0011   **Fax:** (91) 80 2844 0051
Web: www.wipro.com

2019 Sales

	% of total
Americas	55
Europe	25
India	5
Other countries	15
Total	**100**

PRODUCTS/OPERATIONS

2019 Sales

	% of total
IT services	96
IT products	3
Reconciling items	1
Total	**100**

Selected Acquisitions

Citi Technology Services (2009 IT infrastructure services operations)
Gallagher Financial Systems (2008 loan origination software and services)
OKI Techno Centre Singapore (2007 wireless digital communication services)
Infocrossing (2007 networking infrastructure outsourcing services)
Unza Holdings (2007 cosmetics and toiletries manufacturing)
Quantech Global Services (2006 engineering design services)
Hydrauto Group (2006 hydraulic components)
Saraware (2006 software engineering services)
Enabler (2006 retail consulting and integration services)
cMango (2006 business service management)

COMPETITORS

Accenture	Hindustan Unilever
BearingPoint	Hitachi
Capgemini	IBM
Cognizant Tech	Infosys
Solutions	Komatsu
Computer Sciences	Lenovo
Corp.	Redington Group
Convergys	Tata Consultancy
HCL Technologies	Tech Mahindra

HISTORICAL FINANCIALS

Company Type: Public

Income Statement — FYE: March 31

	REVENUE ($ mil.)	NET INCOME ($ mil.)	NET PROFIT MARGIN	EMPLOYEES
03/20	15,200	2,421	15.9%	175,000
03/19	14,593	2,242	15.4%	170,000
03/18	13,572	1,994	14.7%	160,000
03/17	13,710	2,114	15.4%	160,000
03/16	12,764	2,215	17.4%	150,000
Annual Growth	4.5%	2.3%	—	3.9%

2020 Year-End Financials

Debt ratio: 0.2%	No. of shares (mil.): —
Return on equity: 17.2%	Dividends
Cash ($ mil.): 3,599	Yield: 0.4%
Current ratio: 2.40	Payout: 3.3%
Long-term debt ($ mil.): 120	Market value ($ mil.): —

	STOCK PRICE ($) FY Close	P/E High/Low		PER SHARE ($) Earnings	Dividends	Book Value
03/20	3.10	0	0	0.41	0.01	2.44
03/19	3.98	0	0	0.37	0.01	2.36
03/18	5.16	1	0	0.31	0.01	2.00
03/17	10.23	1	1	0.33	0.02	2.01
03/16	12.58	1	1	0.34	0.09	1.77
Annual Growth	(29.5%)	—	—	5.2%	(37.4%)	8.4%

Wistron Corp

EXECUTIVES

President and CEO, Robert P. T. Hwang, age 63
CFO, Henry Lin, age 64
CTO; President Enterprise Business Group,
Donald Hwang, age 62
President Consumer and Smart Product Business Group and Smart Devices Business Group, David Shen, age 53
Chairman, Simon H. M. Lin, age 67
Auditors: KPMG

LOCATIONS

HQ: Wistron Corp
5, Hsin An Road, Hsinchu Science Park, Hsinchu 30076
Phone: (886) 3 577 0707
Web: www.wistron.com

2013 Sales

	% of total
Asia/Pacific	
Taiwan	65
Other countries	17
Other regions	18
Total	**100**

PRODUCTS/OPERATIONS

Selected Products

Application PC
Desktop computers
Information appliance
Interface cards
LCD TVs
Mobile television
Monitors
Motherboards
Netbook computers
Network storage system
Notebook computers
Portable navigation devices
Printed circuit boards (PCBs)
Rugged mobile computers
Set-top boxes
Servers
Smartphone
Spare parts
Storage products
Tablet PC
Voice over Internet Protocol (VoIP) phones
Wireless data products
Workstations

Selected Services

Design and product development
Logistics
Outsourcing management
Prototyping
Repair
Safety and compliance testing
Supply chain management
Usability and reliability testing

COMPETITORS

ASUSTeK	MiTAC
Compal Electronics	Orient Semiconductor
First International	Pegatron
Computer	Quanta Computer
Flextronics	SYNNEX
Hon Hai	Sanmina
Inventec	Super Micro Computer
Lenovo	Universal Scientific

HISTORICAL FINANCIALS

Company Type: Public

Income Statement — FYE: December 31

	REVENUE ($ mil.)	NET INCOME ($ mil.)	NET PROFIT MARGIN	EMPLOYEES
12/19	29,335	227	0.8%	0
12/18	29,084	160	0.6%	0
12/17	28,196	131	0.5%	0
12/16	20,397	91	0.4%	0
12/15	18,967	40	0.2%	0
Annual Growth	11.5%	53.8%	—	—

2019 Year-End Financials

Debt ratio: 0.7%	No. of shares (mil.): —
Return on equity: 9.5%	Dividends
Cash ($ mil.): 1,583	Yield: —
Current ratio: 1.17	Payout: —
Long-term debt ($ mil.): 526	Market value ($ mil.): —

Woolworths Group Ltd

Woolworths Group (Woolworths) is a diversified retailer with more than 3350 stores in Australia and New Zealand including more than 985 supermarkets under the Woolworths and Countdown banners. It also operates BWS and Dan Murphy's liquor stores. In addition Woolworths sells gasoline directly and in association with Caltex to which it also supplies groceries wholesale. Woolworths' 180-odd general merchandise discount stores operate under the Big W name. Woolworths also operates upwards more than 330 hotels. The company was founded in 1924 in Sydney. It generates almost 90% of sales in its home country.

Operations

Woolworths is consists of five main divisions: Australian Food New Zealand Food Endeavour Drinks BIG W and Hotels.

Australian Food generates more than 65% of Woolworths' revenue. It consists of around 1050 supermarkets in Australia that sells fruit and vegetables meat and seafood bakery and dairy products frozen food drinks liquor petcare health and beauty and household products. The segment also includes Woolworths' co-branded fuel operation with Caltex a discount program a small convenience store operation (Pitt Street Metro) and a financial services arm that offers credit cards gift cards and insurance.

New Zealand Food (more than 10%) consists of more than 180 stores in New Zealand under the Countdown banner that serve up a similar range as Woolworths in Australia.

Woolworths' Endeavour Drinks business brings in about 15% of annual sales through the sale of alcoholic drinks under four banners: Dan Murphy's and BWS (liquor stores) Cellarmasters (wine home delivery) and Langton's (wine auction).

The BIG W general merchandise chain generates more than 5% of Woolworths' revenue across more than 170 stores. The Hotels business ALH Hotels (less than five percent of sales) operates more than 330 hotels including bars dining gaming accommodation and venue hire operations. The company's revenue mainly comprises the sale of goods in?store (more than 90% of total sales) and online (around 5%) and leisure and hospitality services.

Geographic Reach

Australia accounts for nearly 90% of Sydney-based Woolworths' revenue; New Zealand generates the rest. With operations in just two countries Woolworths is exposed to the fortunes of Oceania.

Sales and Marketing

Woolworths racks up around 29 million customer visits each week — an impressive figure given the combined population of Australia and New Zealand is only around 29 million.

Financial Performance

Woolworth's sales increased 6% from $60 billion in 2019 to $63.7 million. All businesses excluding Hotels reported strong sales growth on the prior year.

The company's profits in 2020 was $1.2 billion compared to $2.7 billion in 2019.

Cash at the end of 2020 was $2.1 billion. Operating activities provided $4.6 billion while investing activities used $1.9 billion. Financing activities used another $1.6 billion primarily for dividends and repayment of lease liabilities.

Strategy

Woolworths is trialing a new voluntary contact tracing solution for customers with smartphones to better assist health authorities with rapid contact tracing efforts. The QR Code Contact Tracing initiative is being trialed across 11 Woolworths Supermarkets in Victoria and one Woolworths Metro in NSW. Customers in trial stores can use a QR code at the entrance to check - in and register their contact details.

Woolworths customers nationwide will have the option of purchasing paper shopping bags to carry their shopping home in. The new carry bags which were trialed successfully at several Woolworths stores last year have been introduced to meet growing customer demand for alternatives that can be easily recycled in the household curbside collection. Made from 70 percent recycled paper the bags will be sold at cost for 20 cents in addition to the supermarket's existing reusable plastic bags and Bag for Good options. All paper used has been sourced responsibly as certified by the Forest Stewardship Council with the non-recycled paper used in conjunction with recycled paper to provide a stronger structure. The bags have been tested to carry up to 6kg worth of groceries.

Company Background

Woolworths was founded in 1924 by Percy Christmas as Woolworths Stupendous Bargain Basement touting its wide range of goods offered at cheap prices. It took its name from a US chain F.W. Woolworth which did not hold the copyright to the Woolworth name in Australia at the time. It entered New Zealand shortly after in 1929 and the next near-century was marked by steady organic and inorganic expansion and brand diversification. It began selling petrol in 1996 and liquor in 1998.

EXECUTIVES

Managing Director CEO and Managing Director Food Group, Bradford (Brad) Banducci
CFO, David Marr
CEO BIG W, Sally Macdonald
Managing Director Woolworths Liquor Group, Martin Smith
Chairman, Gordon M. Cairns, age 63
Auditors: Deloitte Touche Tohmatsu

LOCATIONS

HQ: Woolworths Group Ltd
 1 Woolworths Way, Bella Vista, Sydney, New South Wales 2153
Phone: (61) 2 8885 0000
Web: www.woolworthsgroup.com.au

2016 Sales

	% of total
Australia	90
New Zealand	10
Total	**0**

PRODUCTS/OPERATIONS

2018 Sales

	% of total
Australian Food	66
New Zealand Food	10
Endeavour Drinks	14
BIG W	6
Hotels	3
Unallocated	1
Total	**100**

Selected Brands

Australian Food
Woolworths Supermarkets Caltex Woolworths
 Woolworths Rewards Financial Services & Insurance
New Zealand Food
Countdown
Endeavor Drinks
Dan Murphy's BWS Cellarmasters Langton's
Portfolio
BIG W ALH Group

COMPETITORS

ALDI	Metcash
BP	Wesfarmers
Harvey Norman Holdings	

HISTORICAL FINANCIALS

Company Type: Public

Income Statement

FYE: June 28

	REVENUE ($ mil.)	NET INCOME ($ mil.)	NET PROFIT MARGIN	EMPLOYEES
06/20	43,768	800	1.8%	215,000
06/19	42,026	1,886	4.5%	196,000
06/18	42,307	1,280	3.0%	202,000
06/17	42,134	1,160	2.8%	202,000
06/16	43,244	(916)	—	205,000
Annual Growth	**0.3%**	**—**	**—**	**1.2%**

2020 Year-End Financials

Debt ratio: 7.0%
Return on equity: 12.2%
Cash ($ mil.): 1,421
Current ratio: 0.62
Long-term debt ($ mil.): 1,308
No. of shares (mil.): 1,258
Dividends
 Yield: —
 Payout: 101.9%
Market value ($ mil.): —

Woori Financial Group Inc

EXECUTIVES

President, Gwang Goo Lee
Auditors: Deloitte Anjin LLC

LOCATIONS

HQ: Woori Financial Group Inc
 51, Sogong-ro, Jung-gu, Seoul 04632
Phone: (82) 2 2125 2050   **Fax:** (82) 2 0505001 0451
Web: www.wooribank.com

HISTORICAL FINANCIALS

Company Type: Public

Income Statement

FYE: December 31

	ASSETS ($ mil.)	NET INCOME ($ mil.)	INCOME AS % OF ASSETS	EMPLOYEES
12/19	367,410	1,900	0.5%	15,529
12/18	345,553	2,063	0.6%	15,085
12/17	321,039	1,534	0.5%	14,458
12/16	315,342	1,280	0.4%	15,534
12/15	296,236	1,075	0.4%	15,850
Annual Growth	**5.5%**	**15.3%**	**—**	**(0.5%)**

2019 Year-End Financials

Return on assets: 0.5%
Return on equity: 8.6%
Long-term debt ($ mil.): —
No. of shares (mil.): 722
Sales ($ mil): 12,805
Dividends
 Yield: 0.0%
 Payout: 25.6%
Market value ($ mil.): 21,856

	STOCK PRICE ($) FY Close	P/E High/Low		PER SHARE ($) Earnings	Dividends	Book Value
12/19	30.26	0	0	2.77	0.71	30.23
Annual Growth	**—**			**—**	**—**	**—**

WPP Plc (New)

Once upon a time WPP sold wiring and plastics products but now it's the world's largest marketing and advertising agency. The company operates through more than 3000 offices in upwards of 112 countries and works with some 350 of the Fortune 500 Global Companies among others. Its advertising agency networks including Grey Worldwide JWT Ogilvy & Mather and Young & Rubicam offer creative campaign development and brand management services. WPP's holdings also include public relations firms media buying and planning agencies and many specialized marketing and communications units. In addition its Kantar Group division is one of the world's leading market research organizations.

Operations

WPP operates four business segments: Advertising and Media Investment Management (45% of total revenue); Data Investment Management (20%); Public Relations & Public Affairs (8%); and Branding Identity Healthcare and Specialist Communications (27%).

The Advertising segment produces advertising content across essentially all sectors such as television internet radio magazines and newspapers. The segment also includes GroupM which is WPP's media investment management operation and is the largest global player in its field; GroupM boasts that it serves one in three adverts globally. In 2019 the WPP agreed to sell a 60% stake in marketing data consultancy Kantar to Bain Capital for proceeds of about $3.1 billion.

WPP's Data Investment Management segment is organized under the Kantar Group umbrella which comprises 12 specialized operating brands that together aim to offer a complete view of consumers. Public Relations offers advice to clients looking to communicate to customers governmental bodies and other businesses. Lastly the Branding & Identity segment offers branding and design services; marketing solutions for healthcare firms; and a range of specialist and customer services including for sports youth and entertainment marketing.

The company's nine 'billion-dollar brands' include Ogilvy J. Walter Thompson Mindshare MEC MediaCom Y&R MillwardBrown TNS and Wunderman.

Geographic Reach

WPP has a worldwide reach and operates out of upwards of 3000 offices in 112 countries. North America (mostly the US) is the company's most valuable region by revenue at around 37% of total; the UK and Western Continental Europe pull in approximately 34%. The Asia-Pacific region Latin America the Middle East and North Africa and Eastern Europe make up the rest.

The company generated revenue of more than $1 billion in five markets: the US the UK Germany Australia/New Zealand and Greater China.

Financial Performance

Note: Growth rates may differ after conversion to US Dollars.

Total revenue in 2015 was up on prior year by 6% to Å 12.2 billion after taking into account headwinds from foreign currency movements - the strength of the pound against the euro detracted from revenue by 1.4%. This was the fifth consecutive year of record sales. The strongest growth was in the Advertising and Media Investment Management segment which grew by Å 400 million. The second-largest segment Branding & Identity brought in Å 3.3 billion. Factors behind the year's strong results include an industry-leading performance in winning new business and customer retention as well as greater focus on emerging markets.

By region North America generated sales of Å 4.5 billion - representing growth of around 15%. Western Continental Europe was the only region to see sales fall in 2015 down nearly 6% on prior year to Å 2.4 billion - this was due to a poor macroeconomic climate and unfavorable currency movements.

Net income was up to Å 1245 for the year. Factors in this include exceptional gains of Å 296 million in 2015 which came from the sale of Kantar's internet measurement business and WPP's stakes in e-Rewards and Chime Communications. On the other hand WPP incurred Å 106 million in restructuring costs almost half of which was severance-related from the Data Investment Management business in Western Continental Europe.

The company's cash flow from operating activities fell from Å 1703 million in 2014 to a still-considerable Å 1360 million.

Strategy

WPP strategy comprises four key tenets: 'horizontality' which means closer links between the various WPP businesses via global client leaders and regional sub-regional and country managers (there are 45 cross-group client teams today up from 10 in 2010); a concerted effort to increase emerging market revenue to 40-45% of total sales (currently at 19% up a point since 2010); a focus on expanding new media to 40-45% of revenue (currently at 38% up 9 points since 2010); and hold firm in the more measureable marketing services such as Data Investment Management at 50% of revenue.

WPP aims to increase flexibility in cost structure particularly in staffing costs in order to mitigate against WWP's vulnerability and overreliance on large clients (the company's 10 largest customers account for 16% of revenue in 2015) which can scale back marketing budgets at short notice.

Acquisitions are a big part of WPP strategy particularly as a means to access new markets. Of the 52 new acquisitions in 2015 18 were in new markets and 37 in quantitative and digital. This was in line with the company's drive to expand the share of revenue in the Asia-Pacific region Latin America Eastern Europe and the Middle East and Africa to 40-45% and in new media to 40-45% also.

Mergers and Acquisitions

WPP has long been exceptionally active on the acquisition front and 2015 was no exception - indeed it was among the industry's most prolific acquirer for the year. The group made 40 acquisitions to a sum of Å 693.1 million up 40% on 2014's Å 495 million (although down in number from 52). The most notable acquisition includes GroupM's purchase of a majority stake of Essence the world's largest independent buyer of digital media alongside a number of bolt-ons such as ABS Creative (?2.8 million revenue in 2015) Webling Interactive (A$4.4 million) and WANDA Digital ($3.4 million). Emerging market acquisitions include nudeJEH in Thailand and Ideal Group and J ssi Intention Marketing in Brazil.

HISTORY

WPP Group began as Wire and Plastic Products a maker of grocery baskets and other goods founded in 1958 by Gordon Sampson (who retired from the company in 2000). Investors led by former Saatchi & Saatchi advertising executive (and current WPP CEO) Martin Sorrell bought the company in 1985 and began acquiring marketing firms under the shortened name of WPP. In 1987 Sorrell used revenue from these businesses (and a sizable loan) to buy US advertising warhorse J. Walter Thompson (now JWT).

JWT was founded by William James Carlton as the Carlton & Smith agency in 1864. The New York City-based firm was bought by James Walter Thompson in 1877 and was later responsible for Prudential Insurance's Rock of Gibraltar symbol (1896). It began working for Ford (which is still a client) in 1943. JWT went public in 1969.

Following its acquisition of JWT WPP formed European agency Conquest in 1988. The company (and its debt) grew the next year when it bought the Ogilvy Group (founded by David Ogilvy in 1948) for $860 million making WPP the world's largest advertising company. But its acquisition frenzy also positioned the company for a fall in 1991 when depressed economies in the US and the UK slowed advertising spending. Saddled with debt WPP nearly went into receivership before recovering the next year.

WPP began a period of controlled growth with no major acquisitions in 1993. It expanded internationally in 1994 opening new offices in South America Europe the Middle East and Asia. Winning IBM's$500 million international advertising contract that year also aided WPP's financial recovery. However this led to the loss of business from IBM's rivals including AT&T Compaq's European division (Compaq was purchased by Hewlett-Packard in 2002) and Microsoft.

By 1997 the company was again ready to flex its acquisition muscle. The firm bought 21 companies that year including a stake in IBOPE (a market research firm in Latin America) and a share of Batey Holdings (the majority owner of Batey Ads a prominent ad agency in the Asia/Pacific region). That year WPP also created its media planning unit Mindshare.

More acquisitions followed in 1998 including a 20% stake in Asatsu (the #3 advertising agency in Japan). The next year the company bought Texas-based market research firm IntelliQuest Information Group which was merged with WPP's Millward Brown unit. Along with its acquisitions WPP snagged some significant new accounts in 1998 and 1999 lining up business with Kimberly-Clark Merrill Lynch and the embattled International Olympic Committee.

In 2000 the company bought US-based rival Young & Rubicam for about $4.7 billion — one of the largest advertising mergers ever. The move catapulted WPP to the top spot among the world's advertising firms. As if that wasn't enough its Mindshare unit later snagged the $700 million media planning account of consumer products giant Unilever. WPP also took a 49% stake in Uni-World Group the largest African-American-owned ad agency in the US.

Hamish Maxwell chairman since 1996 retired in 2001 and was replaced by Philip Lader the former US ambassador to the UK. That year however WPP's top ranking was stolen away by Interpublic Group following its acquisition of True North Communications. It later sparked a bidding war with Havas Advertising when it offered $630 million to buy UK media services firm Tempus Group. WPP grudgingly completed its acquisition of Tempus in 2002. The following year the company acquired Cordiant Communications.

WPP positioned itself for both short- and long-term growth in 2005 when it completed a $1.75 billion acquisition of US-based rival Grey Group beating out bids from private equity players (including Kohlberg Kravis Roberts & Co.) and rival advertising firm Havas.

WPP in 2007 expanded its digital marketing and advertising services by acquiring 24/7 Real Media. The company snatched up Blast Radius an interactive marketing agency a few months later and aligned Blast Radius with Wunderman a marketing communications unit of WPP's Young & Rubicam Brands division.

During the same year WPP signed a lucrative $4.5 billion three-year deal for providing advertising and marketing services to Dell. In an unconventional move WPP created a new agency Enfatico to cater to the computer giant during the three-year contract.

Throughout 2008 market research rival TNS rejected several unsolicited takeover bids from WPP (including a $2.1 billion offer in July). However TNS eventually acquiesced to the proposal when more than 60% of its shareholders accepted WPP's offer in October. The deal greatly enhanced WPP's Kantar operations and created a global market research juggernaut. In late 2008 WPP also shortened its legal name from WPP Group plc to WPP plc.

The next year WPP worked to streamline its operating structure when it integrated TNS Custom with its Research International subsidiary to create the world's largest custom research group. Throughout 2010 WPP focused on acquisitions and investments in the digital arena deriving from China Brazil Singapore the UK and the US.

EXECUTIVES

Chief Executive Officer, Martin Sorrell
Chairman, Philip Lader
Auditors: Deloitte LLP

LOCATIONS

HQ: WPP Plc (New)
Sea Containers, 18 Upper Ground, London SE1 9GL
Phone: (44) 20 7282 4600
Web: www.wpp.com

22015 Sales

	% of total
North America	37
Asia-Pacific Latin America Africa & Middle East and Central & Eastern Europe	29
Western Continental Europe	20
United Kingdom	14
Total	**100**

PRODUCTS/OPERATIONS

2015 Sales

	% of total
Advertising and Media Investment Management	45
Branding Identity Healthcare and Specialist Communications	27
Data Investment Management	20
Public Relations & Public Affairs	8
Total	**100**

Selected Operations

Advertising
  Asatsu-DK (21% Japan)
  Bates Asia (China)
  Diamond Ogilvy
  Direct.com (US)
  Gallagher Group (US)
  Grey Worldwide (US)
  JWT (US)
  Kinetic Worldwide
  Malone Advertising (US)
  Ogilvy & Mather Worldwide (US)
  Red Cell (US)
  Soho Square (US)
  Studio.com (US)
  Tarantula
  The Weinstein Company (US)
  The Voluntarily United Group of Creative Agencies
  Y&R (US)
  Rainey Kelly Campbell Roalfe / Y&R (UK)
  SicolaMartin (US)
Media services
  GroupM
  MAXUS
  MediaCom Worldwide (US)
  Mediaedge:cia
  The Digital Edge
  Outrider
  Wunderman Media (US)

Mindshare
Performance
Portland Outdoor
Research information and consulting
  The Kantar Group (US)
  Added Value Group
  Cheskin Added Value
  ASI/Kantar Research
  BPRI
  Cannondale Associates (US)
  Center Partners (US)
  Everystone
  Fusion 5 (US)
  The Futures Company
  Glendinning Management Consultants
  IMRB International (India)
  KMR
  AGBNielsen Media Research (50%)
  BMRB International
  Mediafax (Puerto Rico)
  Lightspeed Research (US)
  MVI
  Mattson Jack Group (US)
  Millward Brown (US)
  Research International
  RMS Instore
  TNS
  Ziment (US)
  ohal
Public relations and public affairs
  ABC Public Relations (Denmark)
  BKSH (US)
  Blanc & Otus
  Buchanan Communications
  Bulletin International
  Burson-Marsteller (US)
  Chime Communications (21%)
  Clarion Communications
  Cohn & Wolfe (US)
  Federalist Group (US)
  Finsbury
  Hill & Knowlton (US)
  Blanc & Otus (US)
  Wexler & Walker Public Policy Associates (US)
  Impact Employee Communications (Australia)
  IPR Asia Holdings (China)
  Ogilvy Public Relations Worldwide (US)
  Penn Schoen & Berland (US)
  Quinn Gillespie (US)
  Robinson Lerer & Montgomery (US)
  Timmons & Company (US)
  Wexler & Walker Public Policy Associates
Branding and corporate identity services
  Addison Corporate Marketing
  BDGMcColl
  BDGworkfutures
  The Brand Union
  Coley Porter Bell
  Dovetail
  Fitch (US)
  G2 Worldwide
  Lambie-Nairn
  Landor Associates (US)
  The Partners
  MJM Creative Services (US)
  WalkerGroup (US)
  Warwicks
Direct marketing promotions and relationship
  marketing
  A. Eicoff & Company (US)
  Bridge Worldwide
  Dialog Marketing
  Einson Freeman (US)
  EWA
  Good Technology
  G2
  G2 Branding & Design (US)
  G2 Direct & Digital (US)
  G2 Interactive (US)
  G2 Promotional Marketing (US)
  Headcount Worldwide Field Marketing
  High Co. (34% France)
  Imaginet (US)
  Mando Brand Assurance
  Maxx Marketing (China)
  OgilvyAction (formerly 141 Worldwide)
  OgilvyOne Worldwide (US)
  rmg:connect
  RTC Relationship Marketing (US)
  VML (US)
  Wunderman

KBM Group (US)
Health care communications
  Grey Healthcare Group (US)
  Feinstein Kean Healthcare (US)
  Geoff Howe Marketing Communications (US)
  Ogilvy CommonHealth Worldwide (US)
  Sudler & Hennessey (US)
Specialized communications
  Alliance Agency (US)
  Banner Corporation
  The Bravo Group (US)
  The Farm Group
  The Food Group (US)
  Forward
  G WHIZ (US)
  The Geppetto Group (US)
  Global Sportnet (Germany)
  JWT Specialized Communications (US)
  Kang & Lee (US)
  MosaicaMD (US)
  Metro Group
  Ogilvy Primary Contact
  PACE (US)
  PCI Fitch
  Première Group
  PRISM Group
  Spafax
  UniWorld Group (49% US)
  WING Latino (US)

COMPETITORS

Dentsu	Ipsos
Dentsu Aegis	Nielsen
GfK	Nielsen Audio
GfK NOP	Omnicom
Havas	Publicis Groupe
Interpublic Group	

HISTORICAL FINANCIALS
Company Type: Public

Income Statement				FYE: December 31
	REVENUE ($ mil.)	NET INCOME ($ mil.)	NET PROFIT MARGIN	EMPLOYEES
12/19	17,476	824	4.7%	106,786
12/18	19,920	1,357	6.8%	134,281
12/17	20,618	2,453	11.9%	134,413
12/16	17,700	1,722	9.7%	134,341
12/15	18,131	1,719	9.5%	128,123
Annual Growth	(0.9%)	(16.8%)	—	(4.5%)

2019 Year-End Financials

Debt ratio: 19.0%	No. of shares (mil.): 1,257
Return on equity: 7.1%	Dividends
Cash ($ mil.): 3,920	Yield: 5.3%
Current ratio: 0.99	Payout: 604.0%
Long-term debt ($ mil.): 5,344	Market value ($ mil.): 88,381

	STOCK PRICE ($) FY Close	P/E High/Low	PER SHARE ($) Earnings	Dividends	Book Value
12/19	70.29	142 105	0.65	3.75	8.48
12/18	54.80	109 61	1.08	3.97	9.49
12/17	90.56	90 59	1.92	4.06	10.10
12/16	110.66	104 76	1.33	2.94	8.96
12/15	114.74	133 107	1.31	3.28	8.74
Annual Growth	(11.5%)	— —	(16.0%)	3.4%	(0.8%)

X5 Retail Group NV

EXECUTIVES

Commissioner, Dmitry Dorofeev
Auditors: Ernst & Young Accountants LLP

LOCATIONS

HQ: X5 Retail Group NV
  Prins Bernhardplein 200, Amsterdam 1097 JB
Phone:
Web: www.x5.ru

HISTORICAL FINANCIALS
Company Type: Public

Income Statement				FYE: December 31
	REVENUE ($ mil.)	NET INCOME ($ mil.)	NET PROFIT MARGIN	EMPLOYEES
12/19	27,866	313	1.1%	307,444
12/18	21,989	410	1.9%	278,399
12/17	22,399	543	2.4%	250,874
12/16	16,881	364	2.2%	196,128
12/15	10,952	191	1.8%	147,498
Annual Growth	26.3%	13.0%	—	20.2%

2019 Year-End Financials

Debt ratio: 0.3%	No. of shares (mil.): 67
Return on equity: 13.8%	Dividends
Cash ($ mil.): 298	Yield: —
Current ratio: 0.49	Payout: 26.4%
Long-term debt ($ mil.): 2,461	Market value ($ mil.): —

Xiamen C & D Inc

EXECUTIVES

General Manager and Director, Wen Zhou Huang
Auditors: Ascenda Certified Public Accountants Co., Ltd.

LOCATIONS

HQ: Xiamen C & D Inc
  7/F., Seaside Building, No. 52, Lujiang Road, Xiamen, Fujian Province 361001
Phone: (86) 592 2132319   **Fax:** (86) 592 2112185
Web: www.chinacnd.com

COMPETITORS

Anhui Technology	Sinochem
COFCO	Sinotrans
COSCO Group	

HISTORICAL FINANCIALS
Company Type: Public

Income Statement				FYE: December 31
	REVENUE ($ mil.)	NET INCOME ($ mil.)	NET PROFIT MARGIN	EMPLOYEES
12/19	48,466	671	1.4%	0
12/18	40,763	679	1.7%	0
12/17	33,592	511	1.5%	0
12/15	19,722	406	2.1%	0
12/14	19,483	403	2.1%	0
Annual Growth	20.0%	10.7%	—	—

2019 Year-End Financials

Debt ratio: 3.7%	No. of shares (mil.): —
Return on equity: 16.0%	Dividends
Cash ($ mil.): 5,080	Yield: —
Current ratio: 1.61	Payout: —
Long-term debt ($ mil.): 8,200	Market value ($ mil.): —

Xiamen International Trade Group Corp Ltd

Auditors: Ascenda Certified Public Accountants

LOCATIONS

HQ: Xiamen International Trade Group Corp Ltd
Level 16 - 18, International Trade Building, Hubin
South Road, Xiamen, Fujian Province 361004
Phone: (86) 592 5161888   **Fax:** (86) 592 5160280
Web: www.itg.com.cn

HISTORICAL FINANCIALS

Company Type: Public

Income Statement   FYE: December 31

	REVENUE ($ mil.)	NET INCOME ($ mil.)	NET PROFIT MARGIN	EMPLOYEES
12/19	31,336	331	1.1%	0
12/18	30,036	318	1.1%	0
12/17	25,301	293	1.2%	0
12/16	14,123	150	1.1%	0
12/15	9,888	100	1.0%	0
Annual Growth	33.4%	34.9%	—	—

2019 Year-End Financials

Debt ratio: 3.0%
Return on equity: 9.5%
Cash ($ mil.): 963
Current ratio: 1.33
Long-term debt ($ mil.): 1,046

No. of shares (mil.): —
Dividends
  Yield: —
  Payout: —
Market value ($ mil.): —

Xiamen Xiangyu Co Ltd

Auditors: Grant Thornton LLP

LOCATIONS

HQ: Xiamen Xiangyu Co Ltd
2F, Yinsheng Mansion, Xiangyu Bonded Area, Xiamen,
Fujian Province 361006
Phone: (86) 592 6516003   **Fax:** (86) 592 5051631
Web: www.xiangyu.cn

HISTORICAL FINANCIALS

Company Type: Public

Income Statement   FYE: December 31

	REVENUE ($ mil.)	NET INCOME ($ mil.)	NET PROFIT MARGIN	EMPLOYEES
12/19	39,149	158	0.4%	0
12/18	34,021	145	0.4%	0
12/17	31,239	109	0.4%	0
12/16	17,146	61	0.4%	0
12/15	9,226	44	0.5%	0
Annual Growth	43.5%	37.5%	—	—

2019 Year-End Financials

Debt ratio: 3.2%
Return on equity: 8.6%
Cash ($ mil.): 1,036
Current ratio: 1.35
Long-term debt ($ mil.): 801

No. of shares (mil.): —
Dividends
  Yield: —
  Payout: —
Market value ($ mil.): —

Xiaomi Corp

Auditors: PricewaterhouseCoopers

LOCATIONS

HQ: Xiaomi Corp
Xiaomi Campus, Anningzhuang Road, Beijing, Haidian
District
Phone:
Web: www.mi.com

HISTORICAL FINANCIALS

Company Type: Public

Income Statement   FYE: December 31

	REVENUE ($ mil.)	NET INCOME ($ mil.)	NET PROFIT MARGIN	EMPLOYEES
12/19	29,582	1,443	4.9%	18,170
12/18	25,430	1,970	7.7%	16,683
12/17	17,614	(6,734)	—	0
12/16	9,855	79	0.8%	0
12/15	10,287	(1,167)	—	0
Annual Growth	30.2%	—	—	—

2019 Year-End Financials

Debt ratio: 1.3%
Return on equity: 13.1%
Cash ($ mil.): 3,725
Current ratio: 1.49
Long-term debt ($ mil.): 687

No. of shares (mil.): —
Dividends
  Yield: —
  Payout: —
Market value ($ mil.): —

Yamada Holdings Co Ltd

EXECUTIVES

Vice Chairman and CEO, Tadao Ichimiya, age 65
COO, Mitsumasa Kuwano, age 66
President CEO and Director, Noboru Yamada, age 77
Auditors: KPMG AZSA LLC

LOCATIONS

HQ: Yamada Holdings Co Ltd
1-1 Sakae-cho, Takasaki, Gunma 370-0841
Phone: (81) 570 078 181
Web: www.yamada-denki.jp

PRODUCTS/OPERATIONS

2014

	% of total
Home electrical	59
Home Information	29
Other products	12
Total	**100**

COMPETITORS

AEON	Edion
Costco Wholesale	Seven & i

HISTORICAL FINANCIALS

Company Type: Public

Income Statement   FYE: March 31

	REVENUE ($ mil.)	NET INCOME ($ mil.)	NET PROFIT MARGIN	EMPLOYEES
03/20	14,846	226	1.5%	29,481
03/19	14,453	132	0.9%	28,373
03/18	14,821	280	1.9%	29,329
03/17	13,979	308	2.2%	28,908
03/16	14,361	270	1.9%	29,402
Annual Growth	0.8%	(4.3%)	—	0.1%

2020 Year-End Financials

Debt ratio: 0.2%
Return on equity: 4.0%
Cash ($ mil.): 450
Current ratio: 1.83
Long-term debt ($ mil.): 1,250

No. of shares (mil.): 880
Dividends
  Yield: —
  Payout: 37.0%
Market value ($ mil.): —

Yamaha Motor Co Ltd

Best known for its extensive line of motorcycles Yamaha Motor also makes scooters electric-hybrid bicycles four-wheel ATVs leisure and fishing boats racing and golf carts and snowmobiles. Other products include engines swimming pools electric wheelchairs robots and helicopter drones used to spray agricultural crops. Motorcycles which make up about 60% of the company's sales have about a 20% market share in North America. Overseas markets account for about 90% of sales. Founded in 1955 Yamaha Motor and its more than 140 subsidiaries and affiliates operate sales and manufacturing plants throughout the world. Musical instrument manufacturer Yamaha Corporation owns about 10% of the company.

Financial Performance

Note: Growth rates may differ after conversion to US Dollars.

Except for a dip in 2016 Yamaha Motors' revenue has seen slow but steady growth the last five years rising 10% between 2014 and 2018. During this period growth has been driven primarily by motorcycles and marine products.

Sales in 2018 were flat rising only 0.2% compared to Â 1.7 trillion the prior year. The company's marine products segment saw the strongest growth in 2018 increasing 6.4%. Demand for industrial machines and robots grew 3.4%. Motorcycle revenue dropped 2.2% in 2018.

Net income fell 8.1% to Â 93.4 billion in 2018 compared to 2017 primarily due to reduced motorcycle sales.

Cash at the end of 2018 was Â 138 billion a decrease of Â 18 billion from the prior year. Cash from operations contributed Â 59 million to the coffers while investing activities used Â 48.3 billion mainly for capital expenditures. Financing activities used Â 26.4 billion primarily for dividend payments and loan repayment.

EXECUTIVES

President, Hiroyuki Yanagi
Senior Executive Officer Automobile Engine Operations, Takaaki Kimura
Senior Executive Officer; President Yamaha Motor Corporation U.S.A., Toshizumi Kato
Managing Executive Officer Business Development, Masahiro Takizawa

Managing Executive Officer Procurement, Nobuya Hideshima
Senior Executive Officer; President Yamaha Indonesia Motor Manufacturing, Yoichiro Kojima
Managing Executive Officer Corporate Planning and Finance, Kozo Shinozaki
Auditors: Ernst & Young ShinNihon LLC

LOCATIONS

HQ: Yamaha Motor Co Ltd
2500 Shingai, Iwata, Shizuoka 438-8501
Phone: (81) 538 32 1144
Web: www.yamaha-motor.co.jp

2015 Sales

	% of total
Asia	
Japan	10
Other countries	42
North America	22
Europe	13
Others	13
Total	**100**

PRODUCTS/OPERATIONS

2015 Sales

	% of total
Motorcycles	63
Marine products	19
Power products	10
Industrial machinery & robots	3
Other products	5
Total	**100**

Selected Products

Marine products
  Boats (power sail & utility)
  Diesel engines
  Outboard motors
  Personal watercraft
  Swimming pools
Motorcycles
  Motocrossers
  Road racers
  Scooters
  Sports bikes
  Trail bikes
Power products
  All-terrain vehicles (ATVs)
  Generators
  Golf carts
  Multi-purpose engines
  Racing kart engines
  Side-by-side vehicles
  Snowmobiles
  Snow throwers
Other products
  Automotive components
  Automotive engines
  Electric wheelchairs
  Electro-hybrid bicycles (PAS)
  Industrial robots
  Surface mounters
  Unmanned helicopters

COMPETITORS

Arctic Cat	Lion Group
BMW	Marine Products Corp.
Bajaj Auto	Mercury Marine
Brunswick Corp.	Piaggio & Co.
Bénéteau	Piscines Desjoyaux
Cigarette Racing Team	Polaris Industries
Ducati	Suzuki Motor
Fountain Powerboat	Triumph Motorcycles
Harley-Davidson	Ultra Motorcycle
Honda	Viper Motorcycle
Kawasaki Heavy Industries	Westerbeke Corp.

HISTORICAL FINANCIALS

Company Type: Public

Income Statement

FYE: December 31

	REVENUE ($ mil.)	NET INCOME ($ mil.)	NET PROFIT MARGIN	EMPLOYEES
12/19	15,333	697	4.5%	68,164
12/18	15,214	849	5.6%	67,071
12/17	14,842	902	6.1%	64,180
12/16	12,849	539	4.2%	62,322
12/15	13,550	498	3.7%	64,412
Annual Growth	**3.1%**	**8.8%**	**—**	**1.4%**

2019 Year-End Financials

Debt ratio: 0.2%
Return on equity: 11.1%
Cash ($ mil.): 1,147
Current ratio: 1.76
Long-term debt ($ mil.): 1,648
No. of shares (mil.): 349
Dividends
  Yield: —
  Payout: —
Market value ($ mil.): —

Yamanashi Chuo Bank, Ltd. (Japan)

EXECUTIVES

President, MITSUYOSHI SEKI
Managing Director, Yukio Osada
Managing Director, Norihiko Tanaka
Managing Director, Yutaka Fujita
Managing Director, Yoshiaki Furuya
Auditors: Deloitte Touche Tohmatsu LLC

LOCATIONS

HQ: Yamanashi Chuo Bank, Ltd. (Japan)
1-20-8 Marunouchi, Kofu, Yamanashi 400-8601
Phone: (81) 55 233 2111
Web: www.yamanashibank.co.jp

COMPETITORS

Miyazaki Bank	Towa Bank

HISTORICAL FINANCIALS

Company Type: Public

Income Statement

FYE: March 31

	ASSETS ($ mil.)	NET INCOME ($ mil.)	INCOME AS % OF ASSETS	EMPLOYEES
03/20	32,348	34	0.1%	2,342
03/19	31,431	44	0.1%	2,394
03/18	31,138	46	0.1%	2,428
03/17	29,384	65	0.2%	2,353
03/16	28,844	84	0.3%	2,322
Annual Growth	**2.9%**	**(19.9%)**	**—**	**0.2%**

2020 Year-End Financials

Return on assets: 0.1%
Return on equity: 1.8%
Long-term debt ($ mil.): —
No. of shares (mil.): 31
Sales ($ mil): 438
Dividends
  Yield: —
  Payout: 30.1%
Market value ($ mil.): —

Yamato Holdings Co., Ltd.

The well-known black cat logo of express delivery giant Yamato Holdings crosses paths throughout Japan. The holding company's flagship unit Yamato Transport delivers millions of parcels and pieces of mail yearly from a network of thousands of delivery centers throughout Japan. Besides Yamato Transport and its signature next-day TA-Q-BIN (door-to-door parcel delivery) and Kuroneko Mail (document delivery) businesses Yamato Holdings' operations include B2B logistics information system development financial transaction processing fleet maintenance and household moving services. Yamato Transport accounts for the bulk of the holding company's annual revenue.

Operations

Yamato Holdings operates through 45 subsidiaries and seven affiliates. Its businesses are divided into six primary operating segments: Delivery business logistics home convenience e-business financial and truck maintenance. The delivery business provides international transport services in addition to the main domestic operations.

Strategy

The company expands by refining its distribution network creating an innovative logistics system and creating new services that improve customer convenience. Yamato Holdings often expands its operations through joint ventures and partnerships with other mail and logistics entities.

Company Background

Yamato Holdings adopted its current corporate structure in 2005 when the former Yamato Transport reorganized itself into a holding company with about 40 subsidiaries. The company's core delivery business was transferred to a subsidiary which inherited the Yamato Transport name.

EXECUTIVES

Senior Managing Executive Officer, Kenji Minaki
President, Masaki Yamauchi
Senior Managing Executive Officer, Kenichi Shibasaki
Executive Officer; President Yamato Financial, Toshizo Kurisu
VP and Executive Officer, Haruo Kanda
Executive Officer; President Yamato Home Convenience, Atsushi Ichino
Senior Managing Executive Officer, Hitoshi Kanamori
Managing Executive Officer, Hideo Tanzawa
Executive Officer; President Yamato System Development, Yoshihiko Hoshino
Executive Officer; President Yamato Transport, Yutaka Nagao
Executive Officer; President Yamato Logistics, Koji Homma
Executive Officer; President Yamato Autoworks, Tetsuya Egashira
Chairman, Makoto Kigawa
Auditors: Deloitte Touche Tohmatsu LLC

LOCATIONS

HQ: Yamato Holdings Co., Ltd.
2-16-10 Ginza, Chuo-ku, Tokyo 104-8125
Phone: (81) 3 3541 4141
Web: www.yamato-hd.co.jp

2016 Sales

	% of total
Japan	98
North America	1
Other	1
Total	**100**

PRODUCTS/OPERATIONS

2016 Sales

	% of total
Delivery	78
BIZ-Logistics	8
Financial	5
Home Convenience	3
e-Business	3
Autoworks	2
Other	1
Total	**100**

2016 Sales

	% of total
TA-Q-BIN	66
Kuroneko DM-Bin	6
Other	28
Total	**100**

COMPETITORS

Expeditors	Kintetsu World Express
FedEx	Nippon Express
Japan Post	TNT Express

HISTORICAL FINANCIALS

Company Type: Public

Income Statement · FYE: March 31

	REVENUE ($ mil.)	NET INCOME ($ mil.)	NET PROFIT MARGIN	EMPLOYEES
03/20	15,017	205	1.4%	224,945
03/19	14,676	231	1.6%	225,125
03/18	14,491	171	1.2%	213,096
03/17	13,119	161	1.2%	201,784
03/16	12,613	351	2.8%	196,582
Annual Growth	**4.5%**	**(12.5%)**	**—**	**3.4%**

2020 Year-End Financials

Debt ratio: 0.0%
Return on equity: 3.9%
Cash ($ mil.): 1,816
Current ratio: 1.33
Long-term debt ($ mil.): 128

No. of shares (mil.): 385
Dividends
  Yield: 0.0%
  Payout: —
Market value ($ mil.): 5,759

	STOCK PRICE ($) FY Close	P/E High/Low		PER SHARE ($) Earnings	Dividends	Book Value
03/20	14.95	0	0	0.52	0.27	13.28
03/19	25.01	0	0	0.59	0.25	12.96
03/18	25.08	1	0	0.44	0.25	13.14
03/17	21.48	1	0	0.41	0.25	12.23
03/16	20.49	0	0	0.85	0.23	12.02
Annual Growth	**(7.6%)**	**—**		**(11.5%)**	**3.9%**	**2.5%**

Yanzhou Coal Mining Co Ltd

EXECUTIVES

Chairman, Li Xiyong
CFO, Qingchun Zhao
Deputy General Manager, Chengzhong Shi
Deputy General Manager, Chun Liu
Deputy General Manager, Guangmu Ding
Deputy General Manager, Honggang Zhao
Chairman Supervisory Committee, Zhang Shengdong, age 63
Vice Chairman Supervisory Committee, Gu Shisheng
Auditors: SHINEWING (HK) CPA Limited

LOCATIONS

HQ: Yanzhou Coal Mining Co Ltd
298 Fushan South Road, Zoucheng, Shandong Province 273500
Phone: (86) 537 5382319   **Fax:** (86) 537 5383311
Web: www.yanzhoucoal.com.cn

PRODUCTS/OPERATIONS

2013 sales

	% of total
Coal mining revenue	97
Methanol electricity and heat supply revenue	3
Railway transportation revenue	1
Unallocated and eliminations (1)	
Total	**100**

COMPETITORS

BHP Billiton	U.S. China Mining
China Shenhua Energy	Group
Nippon Coke & Engineering	

HISTORICAL FINANCIALS

Company Type: Public

Income Statement · FYE: December 31

	REVENUE ($ mil.)	NET INCOME ($ mil.)	NET PROFIT MARGIN	EMPLOYEES
12/19	28,835	1,245	4.3%	0
12/18	23,698	1,149	4.9%	0
12/17	23,239	1,040	4.5%	0
12/16	4,791	237	5.0%	68,550
12/15	5,605	25	0.5%	65,894
Annual Growth	**50.6%**	**164.8%**	**—**	**—**

2019 Year-End Financials

Debt ratio: 4.2%
Return on equity: 13.9%
Cash ($ mil.): 3,919
Current ratio: 0.87
Long-term debt ($ mil.): 5,849

No. of shares (mil.): —
Dividends
  Yield: 21.2%
  Payout: 754.5%
Market value ($ mil.): —

	STOCK PRICE ($) FY Close	P/E High/Low		PER SHARE ($) Earnings	Dividends	Book Value
12/19	9.00	6	4	0.25	1.92	(0.00)
12/18	7.94	11	5	0.23	0.80	(0.00)
12/17	11.70	9	5	0.21	0.15	(0.00)
12/16	6.68	23	10	0.05	0.01	1.28
12/15	4.58	390	140	0.00	0.03	1.32
Annual Growth	**18.4%**	**—**		**—**	**172.2%**	**194.3%**

Yapi Ve Kredi Bankasi AS

Yapi ve Kredi Bankasi (Yapi Kredi for short) boasts over $80 billion in assets making it Turkey's fourth-largest private bank. Yapi Kredi provides financial services — including retail corporate and private banking services — in Turkey through more than 1000 branches and about 4025 ATMs. It also operates in Bahrain and has subsidiary banks in Azerbaijan Germany the Netherlands and Russia. Yapi Kredi which launched Turkey's first credit card in 1988 now has 6 million cardholders. The bank also provides leasing factoring mutual funds insurance investment banking and brokerage services. Ko § Financial Services (KFS) jointly owned by UniCredit and Ko § Holding owns 82% of Yapi Kredi.

Operations

Yapi Kredi's operates three major business segments. Its Retail Banking segment serves individuals and small- to medium- enterprises (SMEs) with consumer loans (auto mortgage and general purpose) and commercial installment loans respectively. About 59% of its loans were corporate and commercial loans in 2014 while retail loans and credit card receivables made up 27% and 14% of its total portfolio. The Retail Banking segment also provides card payment systems investment accounts insurance products and payroll services.

Its Corporate & Commercial Banking segment has three subgroups: Corporate Banking for large-scale companies Commercial Banking for medium-sized companies and Multinational Companies Banking. Yapi Kredi's Private Banking and Wealth Management segment provides investment products to high net worth customers.

About 80% of Yapi Kredi's total revenue came from interest income (mostly from loans) in 2014 while another 14% came from fees and commissions income. The rest of its revenue came from trading gains (2%) and other miscellaneous income sources (4%).

Geographic Reach

Beyond its 1000 branches in Turkey Yapi Kredi has subsidiary-owned branches in Amsterdam Moscow Baku (in Azerbaijan) and an offshore branch in Bahrain.

Sales and Marketing

Yapi Kredi's retail banking arm serves individuals with up to T$500000 (roughly $170000) in financial assets and SMEs with annual turnovers of less than $10 million. Its commercial banking customers typically have annual turnover of more than $10 million while its corporate banking customers are businesses with turnover of more than $100 million. The bank served more than 10 million customers in 2014.

Financial Performance

Note: Growth rates may differ after conversion to US dollars. This analysis uses financials from the company's annual report.

Yapi Kredi's revenue jumped 21% to T$15.9 billion ($6.8 billion) in 2014 mostly from higher interest income as its loan assets swelled by 26% (compared to sector growth of 18%) with growth in TL company general purpose and SME loans during the year. Its fee and commission income grew by 10% despite new regulations while deposits rose by 22%.

Even with revenue growth the bank's net income fell 44% to T$2.06 billion ($887 million) mostly as its discontinued operations had generated some T$1.6 billion in 2013 but also because the bank incurred higher provisions for loan and other receivable impairments.

Yapi Kredi's operating cash levels jumped 72% with operations using T$1.13 billion ($486 million) — compared to T$3.97 billion ($1.86 billion) in 2013 — mostly thanks to favorable working capital changes and higher cash earnings.

Strategy

Yapi Kredi has been moving toward digital banking channels that are quickly taking the industry by storm allowing the bank to slow expensive branch-expansion plans and cut operating costs significantly while giving customers faster access to banking services.

To this end the bank in 2015 planned to continue boosting its mobile and internet banking customer base (which reached 1.2 million and 4.2 million users at the end of 2014 respectively). It also would continue to expand its ATM network and self-service banking corners implement video channel for digital banking customers increase IVR self service usage for its call center and divert more of its calls away from branches into a central location. Though its brick-and-mortar expansion plans have slowed compared to prior years Yapi Kredi still added 54 physical branches to its network in 2014 to grow its business.

Yapi Kredi's aggressive expansion over the years has been effective at growing its customer base and overall business. Indeed during 2014 the bank added 600000 new customers to its business growing its base about 2.7 times faster than in previous years and bringing its total customer count to 10.6 million.

The bank has been the market leader in credit card market share since 1988 and controlled nearly a 22% market share of the outstanding volume nearly 20% of the issuing volume and an 18% market share on the number of credit cards outstanding during 2014. Yapi Kredi was also the market leader in leasing and factoring and was number two in mutual funds and brokerage categories.

Company Background

Yapi Kredi was previously controlled by ukurova one of Turkey's largest business congomerates. ukurova fell to near-collapse in the aftermath of Turkey's economic crisis in 2001 and the group sold Yapi Kredi to Ko Şbank owner Ko § Financial Services (KFS) in 2005. The following year KFS merged Yapi Kredi and Ko Şbank in what was the largest bank merger Turkey had seen. The combined group took the Yapi Kredi name.

Ko § Financial Services (KFS) which is jointly owned by UniCredit and Ko § Holding owns 82% of Yapi Kredi which was founded in 1944.

EXECUTIVES

chairman, Yildirim Ali Koc
vice-chairman, Levent Cakiroglu
Auditors: PwC Bagimsiz Denetim ve Serbest Muhasebeci Mali Musavirlik A.S.

LOCATIONS

HQ: Yapi Ve Kredi Bankasi AS
  Yapi Kredi Plaza D Blok, Istanbul, Levent 34330
Phone: (90) 212 339 70 00   **Fax:** (90) 212 339 60 00
Web: www.yapikredi.com.tr

COMPETITORS

Akbank	GarantiBank
Citigroup	HSBC
Deutsche Bank	Isbank
Finansbank	T rk Ekonomi Bankasi

HISTORICAL FINANCIALS

Company Type: Public

Income Statement   FYE: December 31

	ASSETS ($ mil.)	NET INCOME ($ mil.)	INCOME AS % OF ASSETS	EMPLOYEES
12/19	69,101	604	0.9%	17,446
12/18	70,569	882	1.3%	18,448
12/17	84,625	955	1.1%	18,839
12/16	76,846	831	1.1%	19,419
12/15	80,540	653	0.8%	19,345
Annual Growth	(3.8%)	(1.9%)	—	(2.6%)

2019 Year-End Financials

Return on assets: 0.9%
Return on equity: 8.9%
Long-term debt ($ mil.): —
No. of shares (mil.): —
Sales ($ mil): 7,627

Dividends
  Yield: —
  Payout: —
Market value ($ mil.): —

Yara International ASA

Yara International has its feet firmly planted in fertilizer. The global chemical company converts energy natural minerals and nitrogen into fertilizers for farmers and other products for industrial and environmental use. With sales in about 160 countries Yara's largest market is Europe. It is one of the largest producer of ammonia in the world. Yara also provides local customer service and agronomical support helping farmers improve crop yields and quality.

Operations

Yara's business activities are carried out within three operational segments: Sales & Marketing New Business and Production

Yara's Sales and Marketing segment markets and distributes a complete range of crop nutrition products and programs globally. By combining agronomic knowledge with range of premium products and digital tools the segment helps farmers across the globe improve profitability while at the same time reducing the carbon footprint to its production. The segment generates almost 85% of the company's total sales.

New Business segment which accounts for around 10% of total sales develops and markets environmental solutions and essential products for industrial applications. It offers a growing portfolio of emission abatement for the transportation and maritime sectors as well as water treatment products. New Business also provides essential products to modern cement and mining companies.

The company's Production segment is one of the world's leading producer of ammonia nitrates and NPKs providing the foundation for crop nutrition and industrial solutions. It brings in more than 5% of total sales.

In terms of Yara's products grouped by nature its fertilizer and chemical generates more than 90% of the company's total revenue. The remaining are produced by freight/insurance services and others.

Yara's major revenue generating product is compound fertilizer (NPK) which accounts for more than 30% of total revenue. It is followed by Urea for over 20% and Nitrate for around 15% of total. The remaining are from Ammonia Calcium Nitrates (CN) Urea Ammonium Nitrate (UAN) and others.

Geographic Reach

The company has production facilities on six continents operations in more than 60 countries and it sells its products in some 160 countries.

Norway-based company Yara generates almost 35% of its revenue from Europe almost 30% from Brazil more than 10% in Asia and around 5% each in Latin America and Africa. The company also has approximately 10800 Yara-branded retail outlets around the world.

Sales and Marketing

Yara's global distribution and marketing network includes more than 200 terminals warehouses blending plants and bagging facilities located in more than 60 countries.

Financial Performance

Despite its fluctuation in the last five years Yara's revenue has an overall growth of 5% between 2015 and 2019.

Total revenue dipped 1% to $12.8 million. The decline was primarily due to lower sales in the company's sales and marketing segment.

The company's net income almost quadrupled from $159 million in 2018 to $599 million in 2019.

The company's cash at the end of 2019 was $301 million. Operating activities provided $1.9 billion while investing activities used $1 billion mainly for capital expenditures. Financing activities used another $758 million mainly for principal payments.

Strategy

Yara's strategy is designed to unlock the value potential of our business model and to help us reach its ambition of becoming the Crop Nutrition Company for the Future. Its strategy focuses on increasing deliveries of premium products notably nitrate-based products and reaching higher margins.

The company's strategic priorities include: Advancing Operational Excellence; Driving innovative growth; and creating scalable growths.

Yara has strategic partnerships with Pepsico IBM and Lantmannen.

As part of Yara's crop nutrition focused strategy Yara has simplified its operating model and changed its operating segments effective from 1 January 2019.

Company Background

Yara was spun off in 2004 by Norwegian aluminum giant Norsk Hydro which produced the world's first chemical nitrogen fertilizer.

EXECUTIVES

CFO, Torgeir Kvidal, age 56
SVP and Head of Industrial, Yves Bonte, age 60
SVP and Head of Partner Operations, Alvin Rosvoll, age 64
President and CEO, Svein Tore Holsether
SVP and Head of Crop Nutrition, Terje Knutsen, age 58
SVP and Head of Supply Chain, Tove Andersen, age 50
SVP and Head of Production, Petter stb ,, age 41
SVP and Head of Yara Brazil, Lair Hanzen, age 53
CTO, Pierre Herben, age 57
Chairman, Leif Teksum, age 68
Vice Chair, Maria Moraeus Hanssen, age 55
Auditors: Deloitte AS

LOCATIONS

HQ: Yara International ASA
  Drammensveien 131, Oslo NO0277
Phone: (47) 24 15 70 00   **Fax:** (47) 24 15 70 01
Web: www.yara.com

2014 Sales

	% of total
Europe	
EU	36
Norway and other countries	3
Brazil	25
North America	13
Asia	10
South & Central America	6
Africa	5
Australia & New Zealand	2
Total	**100**

PRODUCTS/OPERATIONS

2014 Sales

	% of total
Downstream operations	75
Industrial operations	16
Upstream operations	9
Others	-
Total	**100**

Selected Products

Analytical services
Animal Nutrition
Fertilizers
Industrial Solutions
Logistics and distribution
Safety data sheets

COMPETITORS

Air Products	Orica
BASF SE	Potash Corp
Dow Chemical	Syngenta
K+S	

HISTORICAL FINANCIALS

Company Type: Public

Income Statement				FYE: December 31
	REVENUE ($ mil.)	NET INCOME ($ mil.)	NET PROFIT MARGIN	EMPLOYEES
12/19	12,936	599	4.6%	599
12/18	13,054	159	1.2%	16,757
12/17	11,441	481	4.2%	15,527
12/16	11,293	739	6.5%	14,736
12/15	12,696	917	7.2%	12,883
Annual Growth	**0.5%**	**(10.1%)**	**—**	**(53.6%)**

2019 Year-End Financials

Debt ratio: 21.4%	No. of shares (mil.): 271
Return on equity: 6.8%	Dividends
Cash ($ mil.): 300	Yield: 1.7%
Current ratio: 1.44	Payout: —
Long-term debt ($ mil.): 2,698	Market value ($ mil.): 5,627

	STOCK PRICE ($) FY Close	P/E High/Low		PER SHARE ($) Earnings	Dividends	Book Value
12/19	20.76	11	8	2.20	0.37	32.58
12/18	19.28	86	32	0.58	0.40	31.84
12/17	45.84	3	3	1.76	1.02	33.72
12/16	39.28	2	1	2.70	0.86	31.67
12/15	42.88	2	1	3.33	1.72	30.58
Annual Growth	**(16.6%)**	**—**	**—**	**(9.9%)**	**(31.8%)**	**1.6%**

Yorkshire Building Society

Yorkshire Building Society (YBS) provides mortgages savings personal loans and brokerage services. One of the UK's largest mutually owned financial institutions the group also offers insurance coverage including mortgage-payment policies and home and auto insurance. YBS's brands include the Chelsea Building Society the Norwich & Peterborough Building Society YBS Share Plans and other subsidiaries including Accord Mortgages. All together YBS operates more than 200 branches and agency offices in the UK and Northern Ireland. It has 3.1 million members and assets of more than Â 39 billion.

Operations

YBS is one of the largest building societies in the UK and as a mutual organization is owned by and run for the benefit of members. It has no external shareholders. Its YBS Share Plans unit has been administering share plans for more than 30 years.

Geographic Reach

YBS is based in Bradford in the North of England.

Financial Performance

Note: Growth rates may differ after conversion to US Dollars.

In fiscal 2015 interest income fell 4% to Â 1.3 billion. A few factors were behind the fall: a reduction in mortgage rates due to high industry competition and the continued availability of low-cost retail funding. Net interest income (interest income less interest payable) was also down by 3% to Â 534 million. Similarly profit was down 6% to Â 144.6 million.

Strategy

YBS decided in 2015 to reduce its target lending volumes to avoid competing in over-heated parts of the market.

In 2016 the company re-jigged its brand portfolio retiring its Barnsley Building Society brand in 2016 and making Chelsea Building Society online and telephone only. Branches under the two brands were rebranded as Yorkshire Building Society. The change will allow customers of both brands access the wider YBS network of more than 250 branches and agencies across the UK. YBS also enacted a consolidation process whereby if it operated two or more brands in any given area the number of branches would be reduced to one.

Company Background

The society merged with Chelsea Building Society in 2010 and with Norwich & Peterborough Building Society the following year; the two institutions continue to operate under their own brands.

The company was established in 1864 as the Huddersfield Equitable Permanent Benefit Building Society.

EXECUTIVES

Finance Director, Robin Churchouse
COO, Stephen White
Chief Executive, Mike Regnier
Vice Chairman, Mark A. Pain
Chairman, John Heaps
Auditors: PricewaterhouseCoopers LLP

LOCATIONS

HQ: Yorkshire Building Society
  Yorkshire House, Yorkshire Drive, Bradford BD5 8LJ
Phone:
Web: www.ybs.co.uk

PRODUCTS/OPERATIONS

2015 Sales

	% of total
Interest receivable and similar income	96
Fees and commissions receivable	3
Other operating income	1
Total	**100**

COMPETITORS

The Newcastle	West Bromwich Building
The Principality	Society

HISTORICAL FINANCIALS

Company Type: Public

Income Statement				FYE: December 31
	ASSETS ($ mil.)	NET INCOME ($ mil.)	INCOME AS % OF ASSETS	EMPLOYEES
12/19	58,471	170	0.3%	3,536
12/18	54,970	191	0.3%	3,906
12/17	56,792	168	0.3%	4,220
12/16	48,708	140	0.3%	4,542
12/15	56,637	205	0.4%	4,576
Annual Growth	**0.8%**	**(4.6%)**	**—**	**(6.2%)**

2019 Year-End Financials

Return on assets: 0.3%	Dividends
Return on equity: 0.3%	Yield: —
Long-term debt ($ mil.): —	Payout: —
No. of shares (mil.): —	Market value ($ mil.): —
Sales ($ mil): 1,339	

Zhejiang Material Industrial Zhongda Yuantong Group Co., Ltd.

EXECUTIVES

Chairman, Jida Chen
Auditors: Pan-China Certified Public Accountants Co., Ltd.

LOCATIONS

HQ: Zhejiang Material Industrial Zhongda Yuantong
  Group Co., Ltd.
  Tower A, Zhongda Plaza, Hangzhou, Zhejiang Province 310003
Phone: (86) 571 85777029   **Fax:** (86) 571 85778008
Web: www.zhongda.com

HISTORICAL FINANCIALS
Company Type: Public

Income Statement
FYE: December 31

	REVENUE ($ mil.)	NET INCOME ($ mil.)	NET PROFIT MARGIN	EMPLOYEES
12/19	51,582	392	0.8%	0
12/18	43,693	348	0.8%	0
12/17	42,508	343	0.8%	0
12/16	29,834	310	1.0%	0
12/15	28,111	213	0.8%	0
Annual Growth	16.4%	16.5%	—	—

2019 Year-End Financials
Debt ratio: 2.4%
Return on equity: 11.1%
Cash ($ mil.): 2,221
Current ratio: 1.14
Long-term debt ($ mil.): 1,094

No. of shares (mil.): —
Dividends
  Yield: —
  Payout: —
Market value ($ mil.): —

Zhongsheng Group Holdings Ltd.

Auditors: Ernst & Young

LOCATIONS
HQ: Zhongsheng Group Holdings Ltd.
  No. 20 Hequ Street, Shahekou District, Dalian
Phone: Fax: (852) 2803 5676
Web: www.zs-group.com.cn

HISTORICAL FINANCIALS
Company Type: Public

Income Statement
FYE: December 31

	REVENUE ($ mil.)	NET INCOME ($ mil.)	NET PROFIT MARGIN	EMPLOYEES
12/19	17,826	646	3.6%	29,293
12/18	15,663	528	3.4%	26,969
12/17	13,260	514	3.9%	25,577
12/16	10,310	267	2.6%	19,878
12/15	9,106	70	0.8%	16,650
Annual Growth	18.3%	73.8%	—	15.2%

2019 Year-End Financials
Debt ratio: 5.7%
Return on equity: 22.5%
Cash ($ mil.): 914
Current ratio: 1.17
Long-term debt ($ mil.): 1,181

No. of shares (mil.): —
Dividends
  Yield: 0.0%
  Payout: 152.5%
Market value ($ mil.): —

	STOCK PRICE ($) FY Close	P/E High/Low	PER SHARE ($) Earnings	Dividends	Book Value
12/19	30.55	16 13	0.28	0.42	1.38
12/18	34.00	20 13	0.23	0.38	1.17
12/17	17.30	12 12	0.23	0.35	1.08
12/16	10.18	11 6	0.12	0.05	0.82
12/15	3.73	32 17	0.03	0.10	0.81
Annual Growth	69.2%	— —	70.9%	44.1%	14.2%

Zijin Mining Group Co Ltd

Auditors: Ernst & Young Hua Ming LLP

LOCATIONS
HQ: Zijin Mining Group Co Ltd
  1 Zijin Road, Shanghang County, Longyan, Fujian Province 364200
Phone: (86) 592 2933662   **Fax:** (86) 592 2933580
Web: www.zjky.cn

HISTORICAL FINANCIALS
Company Type: Public

Income Statement
FYE: December 31

	REVENUE ($ mil.)	NET INCOME ($ mil.)	NET PROFIT MARGIN	EMPLOYEES
12/19	19,559	615	3.1%	0
12/18	15,409	595	3.9%	0
12/17	14,529	539	3.7%	0
12/16	11,355	264	2.3%	0
12/15	11,440	254	2.2%	19,011
Annual Growth	14.3%	24.7%	—	—

2019 Year-End Financials
Debt ratio: 4.6%
Return on equity: 9.3%
Cash ($ mil.): 894
Current ratio: 0.86
Long-term debt ($ mil.): 3,706

No. of shares (mil.): —
Dividends
  Yield: 2.8%
  Payout: 437.7%
Market value ($ mil.): —

Zte Corp.

ZTE Corporation is one of China's largest telecommunications manufacturers. The company offers a variety of telecom hardware including base stations phones and systems for switching optical transport videoconferencing power supply and monitoring. The company is a leading holder of intellectual property (patents) and one of the largest telecommunications equipment exporters in China. ZTE sells to more than 500 telecom carriers worldwide with customers that include AT&T China Mobile China Unicom and China Telecom. ZTE was founded in 1985 as Zhongxing Semiconductor Co. Ltd.

Operations
ZTE gets 57% of its revenue from carriers and another 32% from its consumer business. Sales to government and corporate customers accounts for the remainder. About 19% of revenue comes from one customer and ZTE's five biggest customers account for 43% of the company's revenue.

The company does its own manufacturing from major production facilities in Brazil China Sweden France Japan Canada and the US.

Geographic Reach
ZTE has been focusing on globalization introducing more of its products and services to international markets. Some 47%of sales come from customers outside of China. ZTE offers its products and services in 160 countries with customers in every region including Asia/Pacific South Asia Europe North America Latin America and Africa.

Financial Performance
ZTE rang up higher sales profit and cash flow in 2015 from 2014.

Revenue rose 16.6% to $15.5 billion in 2015 from 2014. It posted gains in all business and geographic segments emphasized by higher increases in its biggest business and market.

Profit followed revenue rising 11.5% in 2015 to $494 million from $428 million.

Cash poured in to the tune of $869 million in 2015 compared to $179 million in 2014.

Strategy
ZTE sees an opportunity for growth in the construction of mobile and wireline broadband networks where growth is being spurred by the mobile Internet and cloud computing. The company is looking to shift its focus from supply of products to integrated product offerings for the government enterprise and service market segments while continuing to offer more in-depth products to the traditional carrier segment.

EXECUTIVES
EVP, Tian Wenguo, age 52
EVP and CFO, Wei Zaisheng, age 59
Executive Director, He Shiyou, age 54
EVP Logistics and Administration Affairs, Qiu Weizhao, age 58
President, Zhao Xianming, age 55
EVP, Fan Qingfeng, age 52
EVP Terminals Division, Zeng Xuezhong, age 48
CEO India, Liu Peng
Chairman, Yin Yimin, age 58
Vice Chairman, Xie Weiliang, age 65
Vice Chairman, Zhang Jianheng, age 60
Auditors: Ernst & Young Hua Ming LLP

LOCATIONS
HQ: Zte Corp.
  ZTE Plaza, Keji Road South, Hi-Tech Industrial Park, Nanshan District, Shenzhen, Guangdong Province 518057
Phone: (86) 755 26770282   **Fax:** (86) 755 26770286
Web: www.zte.com.cn

PRODUCTS/OPERATIONS

2015 Sales
	% of total
Carriers' networks	57
Consumer business	32
Government and corporate business	11
Total	**100**

2015 Sales
	% of total
Asia	
PRC (People's Republic of China)	53
Other countries	15
Europe the Americas and Oceania	25
Africa	7
Total	**100**

COMPETITORS
Alcatel-Lucent
CHINA PUTIAN
Cisco Systems
Datang Telecom Technology
Ericsson
Huawei Technologies

Motorola Mobility
NEC
Nokia
Qiao Xing
Samsung Electronics
UTStarcom

HISTORICAL FINANCIALS

Company Type: Public

Income Statement

FYE: December 31

	REVENUE ($ mil.)	NET INCOME ($ mil.)	NET PROFIT MARGIN	EMPLOYEES
12/19	13,040	739	5.7%	0
12/18	12,432	(1,015)	—	0
12/17	16,721	701	4.2%	0
12/16	14,578	(339)	—	0
12/15	15,426	493	3.2%	84,622
Annual Growth	(4.1%)	10.6%	—	—

2019 Year-End Financials

Debt ratio: 3.8%	No. of shares (mil.): —
Return on equity: 16.0%	Dividends
Cash ($ mil.): 4,787	Yield: —
Current ratio: 1.19	Payout: —
Long-term debt ($ mil.): 1,443	Market value ($ mil.): —

	STOCK PRICE ($) FY Close	P/E High/Low		PER SHARE ($) Earnings	Dividends	Book Value
12/19	6.04	5	3	0.18	0.00	(0.00)
12/18	3.69	—	—	(0.24)	0.00	(0.00)
12/17	7.50	8	3	0.17	0.00	(0.00)
12/16	3.35	—	—	(0.08)	0.06	(0.00)
12/15	4.40	9	4	0.12	0.04	1.45
Annual Growth	8.2%	—	—	10.3%	—	—

Zurich Insurance Group AG

Active in nearly every country globally Zurich Insurance Group is a major global provider of property & casualty and life insurance. Focused on markets in Europe and North America the company's property and casualty arm offers car home and commercial insurance. Its life insurance division offers life and health insurance annuities endowments and other investment products. Zurich's Farmers Group business includes all reinsurance assumed from the Farmers Exchanges by the Group. The company was founded in 1872.

Operations

Zurich operates through five segments: Property & Casualty Life Farmers Group Functions and Operations and Non-Core Businesses.

The Farmers provides through Farmers Group Inc. (FGI) and its subsidiaries certain non-claims services and ancillary services to the Farmers Exchanges as attorney-in-fact. FGI receives fee income for providing services to the Farmers Exchanges which are owned by their policyholders and managed by Farmers Group Inc. a wholly owned subsidiary of the Group. This segment also includes all reinsurance assumed from the Farmers Exchanges by the Group. Farmers Exchanges are prominent writers of personal and small commercial lines of business in the US. In addition this segment includes the activities of Farmers Life a writer of individual life insurance business in the US.

Property & Casualty offers insurance and reinsurance in Europe Africa North America Latin America and the Asia Pacific region. It offers car home and commercial insurance and services to individuals and small to large businesses. The Life segment also operates globally offering comprehensive range of life and health insurance products for individuals and groups including annuities endowment and term insurance unit-linked and investment-oriented products as well as full private health supplemental health and long-term care insurance.

Group Functions and Operations comprise the Group's Holding and financing. Certain alternative investment positions not allocated to business operating segments are included within Holding and Financing. In addition Group Functions and Operations includes operational technical governance activities relating to technology underwriting claims actuarial and pricing.

Non-Core Businesses include insurance and reinsurance businesses that the Group does not consider core to its operations and that are therefore mostly managed to achieve a beneficial run-off. Non-Core Businesses are mainly situated in the US Bermuda and the UK.

Geographic Reach

Headquartered in Zurich Switzerland Zurich's general insurance division's core markets include Germany Italy Spain Switzerland the UK and the US in addition to the domestic Swiss market. Other international business units are focused in Latin America the Asia/Pacific region and other emerging markets. The company provides a wide range of property and casualty and life insurance products and services in more than 215 countries and territories.

Sales and Marketing

All of Zurich's operating segments use a mixture of distribution channels to promote their products. The company has affiliated agents and it also uses independent brokers employee benefits consultants financial advisors bank representatives travel providers and car dealerships to promote its policies. Zurich markets its products to individual small businesses commercial and corporate customers.

Financial Performance

Zurich's revenue has been rising and falling over the past few years with a high of $72.6 billion in 2014. Revenue fell for a second-consecutive year in 2018 down 26% to $47.2 billion due more or less entirely to a $17 billion decrease in net investment income. Earned premiums were stable across 2017 and 2018.

In 2019 Zurich's net income grew about 12% to $4.1 billion compared to $3.7 billion in 2018.

Zurich's cash on hand fell $583 million during 2019 ending the year at $8.5 billion. The company's operations generated $4.9 billion while its investing activities used $2.2 billion and its financing used $3.3 billion. Zurich's main cash uses were acquisitions of companies dividends paid and repayment of debts.

Strategy

Zurich's strategy for growth is centered around simplifying (e.g. its business structure) and innovating despite its extensive global presence and product mix. In 2019 to improve customer satisfaction and to drive profitable growth the company established a Customer Office. The company expanded its net promoter score (NPS) program to more countries and customer responses increased to about one million. Besides growing organically and through targeted acquisitions the company has signed new distribution agreements giving access to over 80 million potential new distribution customers from 2016 through 2019. The company ensures an increased focus on customers across the organization the company announced two customer key performance indicators (KPIs) to complement our financial targets.

The company simplified its products and services which included significantly reducing the number of products in some markets. After focusing on infrastructure and applications the company is shifting its focus to simplifying products and processes directly related to customers. The company had tested and launched many propositions to offer customers holistic solutions around mobility wellcare property and travel and introduced products and services to support these and further developed Zurich Customer Active Management a unit which allows the company to understand the customer needs.

Additionally Zurich is embracing advances in technology to better serve its customers. In Italy the company is developing smart home products to monitor home security remotely while Farmers launched Toggle an insurance brand aimed at digital natives in Illinois and Wisconsin.

Mergers and Acquisitions

In 2019 Zurich acquired OnePath ANZ's life insurance business. The acquisition expands Zurich's bank distribution footprint in Australia adding up to 6 million new customers. Subsequent to the acquisition Zurich's market shares will grow to around 20 percent in retail life and six percent in the local group life market.

In 2018 Zurich struck a deal to acquire the Latin American operations of QBE Insurance for $409 million. That transaction will make Zurich Argentina's largest insurer and will boost its operations in Brazil Colombia Mexico and Ecuador.

Later in 2018 the company agreed to buy 80% of Adira Insurance an Indonesian property/casualty insurer for some $411 million. Bank Danamon Indonesia will hold the remaining 20% of Adira.

Also in 2018 Zurich acquired Travel Ace and Universal Assistance the leading providers of travel assistance in Latin America for $82 million. It also acquired EuroAmerica in Chile for $145 million.

HISTORY

The roots of Zurich Financial Services stretch back to the 1872 founding of a reinsurer for Switzerland Transport Insurance. The company soon branched out into accident travel and workers' compensation insurance and in 1875 it changed its name to Transport and Accident Insurance plc Zurich to reflect the changes. It then expanded into Berlin (the jumping-off point for its expansion into Scandinavia and Russia) and Stuttgart Germany. The company exited marine lines in 1880; it later left the reinsurance business and expanded into liability insurance; in 1894 it changed its name to Zurich General Accident and Liability Insurance.

In 1912 Zurich crossed the Atlantic expanding operations into the US. It agreed in 1925 to provide insurance for Ford cars at favorable terms. Zurich's business was hard hit during the war years of the late 1930s and 1940s. In 1955 the company changed its name to Zurich Insurance.

Starting in the 1960s Zurich began buying other insurers including Alpina (1965 Switzerland) Agrippina (1969 Germany) and Maryland Casualty Group (1989 US). It also bought the property liability operations of American General.

The company shifted its strategy in the early 1990s expanding into what it deemed underrepresented markets in the UK and the US. Being big wasn't enough; Zurich needed to find a focus. It also jettisoned such marginal or unprofitable business lines as commercial fire insurance in Germany.

In 1995 Zurich bought struggling Chicago-based asset manager Kemper and in 1997 bought lackluster mutual fund manager Scudder Stevens & Clark forming Scudder Kemper. That year it also bought failed Hong Kong investment bank Peregrine Investment Holdings.

Zurich merged in 1998 with the financial services businesses of B.A.T Industries formerly known as the British-American Tobacco Co. created in 1902 as a joint venture between UK-based Imperial

Tobacco and American Tobacco. As public disapproval of smoking grew in the 1970s British-American Tobacco began diversifying; it changed its name to B.A.T Industries in 1976 and moved into insurance. In 1984 it rescued UK insurer Eagle Star from a hostile offer by German insurance giant Allianz. The next year it bought Hambro Life Assurance renaming it Allied Dunbar. Moving into the large US market in 1988 B.A.T bought Farmers Insurance Group.

While B.A.T battled the antismoking army of the 1990s the insurance industry struggled with stagnant growth. In 1997 Europe's largest insurance firms were named as defendants in class action lawsuits that sought recovery for unpaid claims on Holocaust-era insurance policies. In 1998 Zurich became a founding member of the International Commission on Holocaust Era Insurance Claims (ICHEIC).

Also in 1998 Zurich and B.A.T's insurance units merged to create Zurich Financial Services. The firm reshuffled some of its holdings and sold Eagle Star Reinsurance. In 1999 Zurich spun off its real estate holdings into PSP Swiss Property and at the turn of the century it focused on expansion buying the new business of insurer Abbey Life which it merged into Allied Dunbar. In 2000 the holding companies formed to own Zurich (Zurich Allied and Allied Zurich) were merged into the firm.

EXECUTIVES

Group CEO, Mario Greco, age 61
COO and CTO, Robert Dickie, age 60
CEO Farmer's Group, Jeffrey J. (Jeff) Dailey, age 63
CEO North American Commercial; Regional Chairman North America, Mike Foley, age 59
CEO General Insurance, Kristof Terryn, age 54
CFO and Regional Chairman EMEA, George Quinn
Chief Risk Officer and Regional Chairman Asia Pacific, Cecilia Reyes, age 62
Chief Investment Officer, Urban Angehrn, age 56
CEO UK, Tulsi R. Naidu
CEO-Designate Zurich North America, Kathleen Savio
Chief Human Resources Officer; Regional Chairman Latin America, Isabelle Welton, age 57
CEO UK Life and Interim CEO Global Life Europe the Middle East and Asia (EMEA), Gary Shaughnessy, age 54
Chairman, Tom de Swaan, age 75
Vice Chairman, Fred Kindle, age 61
Auditors: PricewaterhouseCoopers AG

LOCATIONS

HQ: Zurich Insurance Group AG
 Mythenquai 2, Zurich 8002
Phone: (41) 0 625 25 25   **Fax:** (41) 0 625 35 55
Web: www.zurich.com

PRODUCTS/OPERATIONS

Selected Subsidiaries
Farmers Group Inc. (property/casualty US)
 21st Century Insurance Company (property/casualty US)
 Farmers New World Life Insurance Company (life insurance US)
 Foremost Insurance Company (specialty insurance US)
 Bristol West Holdings Inc. (specialty insurance US)
 Zurich American Insurance Company (general insurance US)
Zurich Insurance plc (general insurance UK)
Zurich International Life Limited (life insurance UK)

COMPETITORS

AEGON	MetLife
AIG	Mitsui Sumitomo
AXA	Insurance
Allianz	Prudential
Aviva	Prudential plc
CNA Financial	State Farm
GEICO	The Hartford
Generali	Travelers Companies
ING	

HISTORICAL FINANCIALS

Company Type: Public

Income Statement   FYE: December 31

	ASSETS ($ mil.)	NET INCOME ($ mil.)	INCOME AS % OF ASSETS	EMPLOYEES
12/19	404,688	4,147	1.0%	55,369
12/18	395,342	3,716	0.9%	53,535
12/17	422,065	3,004	0.7%	53,146
12/16	382,679	3,211	0.8%	53,894
12/15	381,972	1,842	0.5%	54,335
Annual Growth	1.5%	22.5%	—	0.5%

2019 Year-End Financials

Return on assets: 1.0%	Dividends
Return on equity: 12.7%	Yield: 4.6%
Long-term debt ($ mil.): —	Payout: 6.8%
No. of shares (mil.): 148	Market value ($ mil.): 6,070
Sales ($ mil): 71,792	

	STOCK PRICE ($) FY Close	P/E High/Low		PER SHARE ($) Earnings	Dividends	Book Value
12/19	41.00	1	1	27.69	1.90	236.42
12/18	29.81	1	1	24.83	1.86	205.00
12/17	30.41	2	1	19.90	1.68	220.14
12/16	27.57	1	1	21.36	1.75	205.22
12/15	25.63	3	2	12.33	1.72	209.02
Annual Growth	12.5%	—	—	22.4%	2.5%	3.1%

Hoover's Handbook of

World
Business

Executive index

Index of Executives

Q

R

This Page left intentionally blank